Hoover's Handbook of

Private Companies
2013

HOOVERS™

A D&B COMPANY

Austin, Texas

DISCARD

Hoover's Handbook of American Business 2013 is intended to provide readers with accurate and authoritative information about the enterprises covered in it. Hoover's researched all companies and organizations profiled, and in many cases contacted them directly so that companies represented could provide information. The information contained herein is as accurate as we could reasonably make it. In many cases we have relied on third-party material that we believe to be trustworthy, but were unable to independently verify. We do not warrant that the book is absolutely accurate or without error. Readers should not rely on any information contained herein in instances where such reliance might cause financial loss. The publisher, the editors, and their data suppliers specifically disclaim all warranties, including the implied warranties of merchantability and fitness for a specific purpose. This book is sold with the understanding that neither the publisher, the editors, nor any content contributors are engaged in providing investment, financial, accounting, legal, or other professional advice.

The financial data (Historical Financials sections) in this book are from a variety of sources. Mergent, Inc., provided selected data for the Historical Financials sections of publicly traded companies. For private companies and for historical information on public companies prior to their becoming public, we obtained information directly from the companies or from trade sources deemed to be reliable. Hoover's, Inc., is solely responsible for the presentation of all data.

Many of the names of products and services mentioned in this book are the trademarks or service marks of the companies manufacturing or selling them and are subject to protection under US law. Space has not permitted us to indicate which names are subject to such protection, and readers are advised to consult with the owners of such marks regarding their use. Hoover's is a trademark of Hoover's, Inc.

A D&B COMPANY

10 9 8 7 6 5 4 3 2 1

Publishers Cataloging-in-Publication Data

Hoover's Handbook of American Business 2013

    Includes indexes.

    ISBN: 978-1-59274-647-7

    ISSN 1073-6433

    1. Business enterprises — Directories. 2. Corporations — Directories.

HF3010 338.7

    Hoover's Company Information is also available on the Internet at Hoover's Online (www.mergent/hoovers.com).

U.S. AND WORLD BOOK SALES

Mergent Inc.

580 Kingsley Park Drive
Fort Mill, SC
29715
Phone: 800-342-5647
e-mail: orders@mergent.com
Web: www.mergent.com

Mergent Inc.

CEO: Jonathan Worrall

Executive Managing Director: John Pedernales

Executive Vice President of Sales: Fred Jenkins

Managing Director of Relationship Management: Chris Henry

Managing Director of Print Products: Thomas Wecera

Production Research Assistant: Erin Keane

MERGENT CUSTOMER SERVICE

Support and Fulfillment Manager: Melanie Horvat

ABOUT MERGENT INC.

Mergent, Inc. is a leading provider of business and financial data on global publicly listed companies. Based in the U.S, the company maintains a strong global presence, with offices in New York, Charlotte, San Diego, London, Tokyo and Melbourne.

Founded in 1900, Mergent operates one of the longest continuously collected databases of: descriptive and fundamental information on domestic and international companies; pricing and terms and conditions data on fixed income and equity securities; and corporate action data. In addition, Mergent's Indxis subsidiary develops and licenses equity and fixed income investment products based on its proprietary investment methodologies. Our licensed products have over $9 billion in assets under management and are offered by major investment management firms. The Indxis calculation platform is the chosen technology for some of the world's largest index companies. Its index calculation and pricing distribution protocols are used to administer index rules and distribute real-time pricing data .

Abbreviations

AFL-CIO – American Federation of Labor and Congress of Industrial Organizations
AMA – American Medical Association
AMEX – American Stock Exchange
ARM – adjustable-rate mortgage
ASP – application services provider
ATM – asynchronous transfer mode
ATM – automated teller machine
CAD/CAM – computer-aided design/computer-aided manufacturing
CD-ROM – compact disc – read-only memory
CD-R – CD-recordable
CEO – chief executive officer
CFO – chief financial officer
CMOS – complementary metal oxide silicon
COO – chief operating officer
DAT – digital audiotape
DOD – Department of Defense
DOE – Department of Energy
DOS – disk operating system
DOT – Department of Transportation
DRAM – dynamic random-access memory
DSL – digital subscriber line
DVD – digital versatile disc/digital video disc
DVD-R – DVD-recordable
EPA – Environmental Protection Agency
EPS – earnings per share
ESOP – employee stock ownership plan
EU – European Union
EVP – executive vice president
FCC – Federal Communications Commission
FDA – Food and Drug Administration
FDIC – Federal Deposit Insurance Corporation
FTC – Federal Trade Commission
GATT – General Agreement on Tariffs and Trade

GDP – gross domestic product
HMO – health maintenance organization
HR – human resources
HTML – hypertext markup language
ICC – Interstate Commerce Commission
IPO – initial public offering
IRS – Internal Revenue Service
ISP – Internet service provider
kWh – kilowatt-hour
LAN – local-area network
LBO – leveraged buyout
LCD – liquid crystal display
LNG – liquefied natural gas
LP – limited partnership
Ltd. – limited
mips – millions of instructions per second
MW – megawatt
NAFTA – North American Free Trade Agreement
NASA – National Aeronautics and Space Administration
NASDAQ – National Association of Securities Dealers Automated Quotations
NATO – North Atlantic Treaty Organization
NYSE – New York Stock Exchange
OCR – optical character recognition
OECD – Organization for Economic Cooperation and Development
OEM – original equipment manufacturer
OPEC – Organization of Petroleum Exporting Countries
OS – operating system
OSHA – Occupational Safety and Health Administration
OTC – over-the-counter
PBX – private branch exchange
PCMCIA – Personal Computer Memory Card International Association
P/E – price to earnings ratio
RAID – redundant array of independent disks

RAM – random-access memory
R&D – research and development
RBOC – regional Bell operating company
RISC – reduced instruction set computer
REIT – real estate investment trust
ROA – return on assets
ROE – return on equity
ROI – return on investment
ROM – read-only memory
S&L – savings and loan
SEC – Securities and Exchange Commission
SEVP – senior executive vice president
SIC – Standard Industrial Classification
SOC – system on a chip
SVP – senior vice president
USB – universal serial bus
VAR – value-added reseller
VAT – value-added tax
VC – venture capitalist
VoIP – Voice over Internet Protocol
VP – vice president
WAN – wide-area network

Contents

Companies Profiled

Companies Profiled (continued)

Companies Profiled (continued)

Companies Profiled (continued)

Companies Profiled (continued)

Companies Profiled (continued)

Companies Profiled (continued)

Companies Profiled (continued)

Companies Profiled (continued)

Companies Profiled (continued)

Companies Profiled (continued)

Companies Profiled (continued)

About Hoover's Handbook of Private Companies 2013

Finding current relevant information about non-public companies can be a challenge, as many of these organizations see secrecy as a competitive strategy. In this edition of *Hoover's Handbook of Private Companies*, we have done for you the tough work of compiling these hard-to-find facts.

We consider this volume to be one of the premier sources of business information on privately held enterprises in the US. It features the facts on 900 of the largest and most influencial of those enterprises. Entries feature overviews of company operations, up to five years of financial information, product information, and lists of company executives as found in Hoover's huge database of company information. Some larger and more visable companies will feature an additional History section.

MERGENT INTELLECT ONLINE FOR BUSINESS NEEDS

In addition to Hoover's widely used MasterList and Handbooks series, comprehensive coverage of more than 40,000 business enterprises is available in electronic format on our website at www.hoovers.com. Our goal is to provide our customers with the fastest path to business with insight and actionable information about companies, industries, and key decision makers, along with the powerful tools to find and connect to the right people to get business done. Hoover's has partnered with other presigious business information and service providers to bring you all the right business information, services, and links in one place.

We welcome the recognition we have received as a provider of high-quality company information — online, electronically, and in print — and continue to look for ways to make our products more available and more useful to you.

Hoover's Handbook of Private Companies is one of our four-title series of handbooks that covers, literally, the world of business. The series is available as an indexed set, and also includes *Hoover's Handbook of American Business, Hoover's Handbook of World Business,* and *Hoover's Handbook of Emerging Companies.* This series brings you information on the biggest, fast-growing, and most influential enterprises in the world.

We believe that anyone who buys from, sells to, invests in, lends to, competes with, interviews with, or works for a company should know all there is to know about that enterprise. Taken together, this book and the other Hoover's products and resources represent the most complete source of basic corporate information readily available to the general public.

HOW TO USE THIS BOOK

This book has four sections:

1. "Using Hoover's Handbooks" describes the contents of our profiles and explains the ways in which we gather and compile our data.

2. "A List-Lover's Compendium" contains lists of the largest and fastest-growing private companies. The lists are based on the information in our profiles, or compiled from well-known sources.

3. The company profiles section makes up the largest and most important part of the book — 900 profiles of major private enterprises, arranged alphabetically.

4. Three indexes complete the book. The first sorts companies by industry groups, the second by headquarters location. The third index is a list of all the executives found in the Executives section of each company profile.

Using Hoover's Handbooks

SELECTION OF THE COMPANIES PROFILED

The 900 enterprises profiled in this book include the largest and most influential companies in America. Among them are:

- private companies, from the giants (Cargill and Koch) to the colorful and prominent (Bad Boy Entertainment and L.L. Bean)
- mutuals and cooperative organizations owned by their customers (State Farm Insurance, Ace Hardware, Ocean Spray Cranberries)
- not-for-profits (Red Cross, Kaiser Permanente, Smithsonian Institution)
- joint ventures (Motiva Enterprises, Dow Corning)
- partnerships (PricewaterhouseCoopers, Baker & McKenzie)
- universities (Columbia, Harvard, University of California)
- government-owned corporations (US Postal Service and New York City's Metropolitan Transportation Authority)
- and a selection of other enterprises (National Basketball Association, AFL-CIO, Texas Lottery Commission).

ORGANIZATION

The profiles are presented in alphabetical order. You will find the commonly used name of the enterprise at the beginning of the profile; the full, legal name is found in the Locations section. If a company name is also a person's name, such as Henry Ford Health System or Mary Kay, it will be alphabetized under the first name; if the company name starts with initials, for example, L.L. Bean or S.C. Johnson, look for it under the combined initials (in the above examples, LL and SC, respectively).

Basic financial data are listed under the heading Historical Financials. The annual financial information contained in the profiles is current through fiscal year-ends occuring as late as October 2010. We have included certain nonfinancial developments , such as officer changes, through December 2010.

OVERVIEW

In the first section of the profile, we have tried to give a thumbnail description of the company and what it does. The description will usually include information on the company's strategy, reputation, and ownership. We recommend that you read this section first.

HISTORY

This extended section, which is available for some of the larger and more well-known companies, reflects our belief that every enterprise is the sum of its history and that you have to know where you came from in order to know where you are going. While some companies have limited historical awareness, we think the vast majority of the enterprises in this book have colorful backgrounds. We have tried to focus on the people who made the enterprises what they are today. We have found these histories to be full of twists and ironies; they make fascinating reading.

EXECUTIVES

Here we list the names of the people who run the company, insofar as space allows. In the few cases where available, we have shown the ages and pay of key officers. In some instances the published data is for the previous year, although the company has announced promotions or retirements since year-end. The pay represents cash compensation, including bonuses, but excludes stock option programs.

Although companies are free to structure their management titles any way they please, most modern corporations follow standard practices. The ultimate power in any corporation lies with the shareholders, who elect a board of directors, usually including officers or "insiders" as well as individuals from outside the company. The chief officer, the person on whose desk the buck stops, is usually called the chief executive officer (CEO). Often, he or she is also the chairman of the board.

As corporate management has become more complex, it is common for the CEO to have a "right-hand person" who oversees the day-to-day operations of the company, allowing the CEO plenty of time to focus on strategy and long-term issues. This right-hand person is usually designated the chief operating officer (COO) and is often the president of the company. In other cases one person is both chairman and president.

A multitude of other titles exists, including chief financial officer (CFO), chief administrative officer, and vice chairman. We have always tried to include the CFO, the chief legal officer, and the chief human resources or personnel officer.

The people named in the Executives section are indexed at the back of the book.

The Executives section also includes the name of the company's auditing (accounting) firm, where available.

LOCATIONS

Here we include the company's full legal name and its headquarters, street address, telephone and fax numbers, and Web site, as available. The back of the book includes an index of companies by headquarters locations.

In some cases we have also included information on the geographic distribution of the company's business, including sales and profit data. Note that these profit numbers, like those in the Products/Operations section below, are usually operating or pretax profits rather than net profits. Operating profits are generally those before financing costs (interest income and payments) and before taxes, which are considered costs attributable to the whole company rather than to one division or part of the world. For this reason the net income figures (in the Historical Financials section) are usually much lower, since they are after interest and taxes. Pretax profits are after interest but before taxes.

Headquarters for companies that are incorporated in Bermuda, but whose operational headquarters are in the US, are listed under their US address.

PRODUCTS/OPERATIONS

This section contains selected lists of products, services, brand names, divisions, subsidiaries, and joint ventures. We have tried to include a company's major lines and most familiar brand names.

The nature of this section varies by company and the amount of information contained in Hoover's storehouse of business information. If the company publishes sales and profit information by type of business, we have included it.

COMPETITORS

In this section we have listed companies that compete with the profiled company. This feature is included as a quick way to locate similar companies and compare them. The universe of competitors includes all public companies and all private companies with sales in excess of $500 million. In a few instances we have identified smaller private companies as key competitors.

HISTORICAL FINANCIALS

Here we have tried to present as much data about each enterprise's financial performance as we could compile in the allocated space. The information varies somewhat from industry to industry and is less complete in the case of private companies that do not release data. (We have always tried to provide annual sales and employment, although in some instances those numbers are simply not available). There are a few industries, venture capital and investment banking, for example, for which revenue numbers are not reported as a rule. In the case of private companies that do not publicly dis-close financial information, we have statistics when reliable sources are available.

The following information is generally present.

A five-year table, with relevant annualized compound growth rates, covers:

- Sales — fiscal year sales (year-end assets for most financial companies)
- Net income — fiscal year net income (before accounting changes)
- Net profit margin — fiscal year net income as a percent of sales (as a percent of assets for most financial firms)
- Employees — fiscal year-end or average number of employees

The information on the number of employees is intended to aid the reader interested in knowing whether a company has a long-term trend of increasing or decreasing employment. As far as we know, we are the only company that publishes this information in print format.

The numbers on the left in each row of the Historical Financials section give the month and the year in which the company's fiscal year actually ends. Thus, a company with a March 31, 2010, year-end is shown as 3/10. The last item in the Financials section is a graph, which for private companies shows net income, or, if that is unavailable, sales.

Key year-end statistics are included in this section for insurance companies and companies required to file reports with the SEC. They generally show the financial strength of the enterprise, including:

- Debt ratio (long-term debt as a percent of shareholders' equity)
- Return on equity (net income divided by the average of beginning and ending common shareholders' equity)
- Cash and cash equivalents
- Current ratio (ratio of current assets to current liabilities)
- Total long-term debt (including capital lease obligations)
- Fiscal year sales for financial institutions

Hoover's Handbook of

Private Companies

A List-Lover's
Compendium

The 300 Largest Companies by Sales in Hoover's Handbook of Private Companies 2013

Rank	Company	Sales ($ thous.)
1	St. Vin Randolph Hos.	$33,770,183
2	Transammonia Inc.	$11,303,397
3	Wakefern Food Corp.	$10,325,967
4	Olam Americas Inc	$9,870,093
5	Allegis Group Inc.	$8,275,453
6	Assoc Wholesale Grocers	$7,766,807
7	Hy-Vee Inc.	$7,681,997
8	Sutter Health	$7,179,000
9	Zen-Noh Grain Corp.	$6,217,159
10	Univ Of Pennsylvania	$6,036,032
11	U.S. Venture Inc.	$5,906,874
12	Battelle Mem Inst Inc	$5,499,016
13	Trustees of The Univ of PA	$5,330,197
14	Placid Refining Co Llc	$4,699,597
15	Aerotek Inc.	$4,481,292
16	St. Joseph Hlth System	$4,223,055
17	Intermtn Hlth Care Inc	$4,049,200
18	Lexa Intl Corporation	$3,954,446
19	Axel Johnson Inc.	$3,954,424
20	Sentara Healthcare	$3,930,418
21	Whiting-Turner Cont.	$3,897,399
22	Biourja Trading Llc	$3,842,414
23	Unified Grocers Inc.	$3,796,272
24	Christus Health	$3,780,953
25	Shi International Corp.	$3,757,637
26	Raley's	$3,162,266
27	LA Dept Of Water & Power	$3,125,957
28	Truman Arnold Comps	$3,023,104
29	Wilbur-Ellis Company	$2,812,045
30	Petroleum Trders Corp	$2,796,246
31	Cedars-Sinai Med Cntr	$2,658,119
32	NY Power Authority	$2,655,000
33	Flwrs Fds Spec Grp LLC	$2,573,769
34	Black & Veatch Hldg Co	$2,559,996
35	Iowa Health System	$2,380,167
36	Ohiohealth Corp	$2,328,429
37	The Washington Univ	$2,307,907
38	The Methodist Hospital	$2,284,690
39	M. A. Mortenson Co.	$2,257,968
40	Temple U-Cmmonwealth	$2,254,811
41	A-1 Spec Svcs & Supp Inc.	$2,214,696
42	Dpr Construction	$2,111,582
43	City Pub Svcs Of San Ant	$2,068,686
44	Knights Of Columbus	$2,059,330
45	OR Health & Science U	$1,975,605
46	J.E. Dunn Const Co	$1,937,487
47	School Bd Of Orange Cty Fl	$1,895,582
48	True Value Company	$1,864,846
49	Nysarc Inc.	$1,788,880
50	Mem Health Svcs Corp	$1,788,375
51	Estes Express Lines Inc.	$1,738,192
52	Wheaton Francis Svcs	$1,723,542
53	Walsh Const Company	$1,697,948
54	Children's Hos Med Ctr	$1,693,408
55	Pcl Const Enterprises	$1,689,102
56	Umass Mem Hlth Cre Inc	$1,671,033
57	Lehigh Vlly Hlth Ntwrk	$1,620,530
58	Sutter W Bay Hospitals	$1,616,000
59	Coc Properties Inc.	$1,607,670
60	Prairie Farms Dairy Inc.	$1,607,157
61	D/L Cooperative Inc.	$1,584,836
62	Expert Glob Sltns Inc.	$1,541,709
63	Ferr Prcssng Trdng	$1,506,483
64	Yale-New Haven Hosp	$1,488,697
65	Aff Foods Mw Coop. Inc.	$1,486,310
66	Api Group Inc.	$1,484,918
67	Baltimore Pub School Syst	$1,480,466
68	Ngl Energy Partners Lp	$1,461,946
69	Scott And White Mem Hosp	$1,446,494
70	Rush Univ Medical Center	$1,441,221
71	Palo Alto Med Foundation	$1,434,000
72	T. Jefferson Univ Hosp	$1,431,448
73	Atlantic Diving Supply Inc.	$1,409,946
74	Main Line Health Inc.	$1,405,174
75	The Mitre Corporation	$1,389,458
76	Umass Mem Med Center	$1,366,937
77	Md And Va Milk Prod Assn	$1,362,495
78	Maxim Healthcare Services	$1,341,647
79	C.R. England Inc.	$1,315,271
80	Univ Hlth Syst Of E Carolina	$1,304,298
81	Milwaukee Public Schools	$1,292,859
82	Barry-Wehmiller Group Inc.	$1,240,957
83	Fresno Comm Hosp & Med	$1,207,947
84	Coborn's Incorporated	$1,191,778
85	Duval County Public Schools	$1,187,203
86	Boe-Memphis City Schools	$1,173,382
87	Petrocard Inc.	$1,173,249
88	Barton Malow Enterprises	$1,164,078
89	Coastal Pac Food Distr.	$1,162,669
90	Big River Resources Llc.	$1,162,307
91	Task Force For Global Hlth	$1,160,227
92	Riceland Foods Inc.	$1,159,154
93	Anne Arundel County Boe	$1,144,724
94	Nypro Inc.	$1,144,189
95	Chenega Corporation	$1,108,717
96	Dekalb County Boe	$1,106,727
97	Doctor's Associates Inc.	$1,102,749
98	Moses H Cone Mem Hosp	$1,096,381
99	Associated Elect Coop Inc.	$1,083,734
100	Petroleum Marketers Inc.	$1,081,357
101	Swinerton Incorporated	$1,080,182
102	Spf Energy Inc.	$1,078,835
103	Carnegie Mellon University	$1,061,927
104	The Wills Group Inc	$1,052,865
105	Nch Corporation	$1,045,097
106	Stemcor Usa Inc.	$1,019,898
107	University Of South Florida	$1,013,606
108	Strack And Van Til Sup Mkt	$1,009,074
109	Dana-Farber Cancer Inst	$1,002,464
110	Temple U Health System Inc.	$994,189
111	Ak Permanent Fund Corp	$988,402
112	Methodist Hospitals Of Dallas	$985,568
113	Sargento Foods Inc.	$980,979
114	Froedtert Mem Luth Hosp	$980,429
115	Blue Tee Corp.	$964,332
116	American Cancer Soc Ca Div	$953,576
117	Riverside Healthcare Assn	$952,444
118	Swinerton Builders	$948,136
119	Lucile Salter Packard Hosp.	$942,209
120	New Prime Inc.	$941,392
121	Loyola U Medical Center	$938,648
122	The Medical College Of WI	$936,188
123	Texas Aromatics Lp	$928,328
124	Averitt Express Inc.	$917,175
125	U.R.M. Stores Inc.	$913,858
126	U Of KY Hospital Aux Inc.	$912,826
127	Pepper Construction Grp LLC	$911,753
128	Hawaii Pacific Health	$901,640
129	Drexel University	$896,956
130	St. John Health System Inc.	$895,465
131	The Amalgamated Sugar Co.	$886,061
132	Unipro Foodservice Inc	$881,207
133	Mercy Hospital Springfield	$880,697
134	Fin Industry Reg Auth Inc.	$880,100
135	Snake River Sugar Company	$876,134
136	LA County Office Of Educ.	$863,484
137	Redner's Markets Inc.	$858,008
138	Lancaster Gen Hospital Inc	$852,016
139	Howard University Inc.	$851,324
140	The BOE Of Howard County	$850,371
141	South Baptist Hosp Of FL Inc.	$847,766
142	Pan Amer Hlth Org Inc	$838,474
143	Our Lady Of The Lake Hosp	$826,528
144	Trinity Health Corporation	$814,477
145	Temple Univ Hospital Inc.	$813,587
146	York Hospital	$807,885
147	Willis-Knighton Med Center	$807,345
148	Ind Pharm Cooperative	$806,342
149	Jaco Oil Company	$794,663
150	Plains Cotton Coop Assn	$793,653
151	Fed Home Loan Bnk-San Fran	$792,000
152	VA Beach Pub School System	$788,915
153	Loudoun Cty Pub School Dist	$783,715
154	H. Lee Moffitt Cancer Center .	$771,561
155	Rady Chldrn's Hosp San Dieg	$756,646
156	Albert Einstein Med Center	$744,499
157	Steel And Pipe Supp Co Inc.	$744,391
158	Rouse's Enterprises L.L.C.	$739,408
159	Chi-Iowa Corp	$738,840
160	Piggly Wiggly AL Dist Co. Inc.	$733,606
161	Mountain States Hlth Alliance	$729,356
162	Rex Healthcare Inc.	$719,912
163	TX Cty & Dist Retiremnt Syst	$718,976
164	Fed Home Loan Bnk Of NY	$712,705
165	College Entrance Exam Board	$705,149
166	Sutter Medical Foundation	$705,000
167	Abington Mem Hospital Inc	$702,609
168	Sutter Cent Valley Hospitals	$701,000
169	Christus Spohn Hlth Syst Corp	$698,687
170	Guilford Cty School System	$692,647
171	Sinai Hosp Of Baltimore Inc	$691,619
172	University Of Georgia	$691,453
173	Mgmt & Training Corporation	$687,086
174	Rochester City School District	$681,675
175	Orna Kokosing Constr Co	$676,769
176	St Francis Hosp And Med Ctr	$674,542
177	Trin Mother Frances Hlth Syst	$674,180
178	Wellmont Health System	$673,345
179	Americares Foundation Inc.	$671,618
180	Carter-Jones Companies Inc	$671,419

SOURCE: MERGENT, INC., DATABASE, DECEMBER 2012

The 300 Largest Companies by Sales in
Hoover's Handbook of Private Companies 2013 (continued)

Rank	Company	Sales ($ thous.)	Rank	Company	Sales ($ thous.)	Rank	Company	Sales ($ thous.)
181	National Christian Charitable	$665,608	241	Covenant Medical Center Inc	$530,620			
182	Nova Southeastern Univ Inc.	$661,629	242	Aspirus Inc.	$529,752			
183	St. Joseph Hosp Of Orange	$661,270	243	Winston-Salem/Forsyth Sch	$528,817			
184	River City Petroleum Inc.	$656,968	244	Sch Dist Multnomah Cty OR	$527,922			
185	Trustees Of Boston College	$653,663	245	Estate of Bernice Pauahi Bish	$524,042			
186	Krueger International Inc.	$649,735	246	PA Hosp of The Univ Of PA	$521,624			
187	Hoosier Energy Rural Electric	$649,608	247	Stephen Gould Corporation	$519,064			
188	Welch Foods Inc	$649,536	248	Fordham University	$518,137			
189	Natl Grape Co-Operative Assn	$649,536	249	Prtnrshp for Supp Chn Mgmt	$517,119			
190	Dialysis Clinic Inc.	$642,945	250	The Charles Stark Draper Lab	$514,059			
191	Euramax Holdings Inc.	$641,648	251	Clayco Inc.	$511,324			
192	Powersouth Enrgy Coop.	$640,183	252	Don Ford Sanderson Inc	$510,656			
193	Christus Santa Rosa Hlth Care	$633,018	253	Middle TN Electr Mbrshp Corp	$510,489			
194	Lodging Rlj Trust L P	$631,667	254	St Alphonsus Reg Med Cntr	$509,783			
195	North Dakota Univ System	$626,469	255	Jfk Health System Inc.	$509,585			
196	R. Wood Johnson Univ Hosp	$622,546	256	Conemaugh Hlth System Inc.	$509,554			
197	Farmers Grain Terminal Inc.	$615,495	257	Liberty Prop Ltd Prtnrship	$509,326			
198	N. MS Medical Center Inc.	$614,218	258	Silver Towne L.P.	$509,166			
199	Abington Reldan Metals Llc	$613,913	259	Arkansas Children's Hospital	$509,166			
200	Rusal America Corp.	$611,628	260	Steel Resources Llc	$504,209			
201	Maricopa Health Foundation	$607,693	261	Sam Kane Beef Processors	$502,721			
202	R. E. Michel Company Inc.	$606,962	262	St. Jude Hospital	$496,563			
203	Univ of WI Med Fndn Inc.	$604,826	263	Rockefeller University	$495,067			
204	Mcnaughton-Mckay Elec. Co.	$603,373	264	Saint Thomas Hospital	$493,954			
205	New Hanover Reg Med Cntr	$602,985	265	Edward Hospital	$493,681			
206	Gwinnett Health System Inc.	$599,310	266	Bayhealth Medical Center Inc.	$490,338			
207	Watonwan Farm Service Inc	$592,458	267	Agmark Llc	$489,379			
208	Coop. For Assist & Relief	$589,665	268	Wheeling-Nisshin Inc.	$489,271			
209	Baptist Health System Inc.	$587,748	269	Nibco Inc.	$487,841			
210	Heartland Health	$584,839	270	Saint Agnes Medical Center	$487,591			
211	R. M. Parks Inc.	$583,451	271	OH State Univ Research Fndn	$485,560			
212	Southwest Research Inst Inc	$581,385	272	Altoona Reg Health System	$485,233			
213	Key Food Stores Co-Oper Inc.	$578,574	273	Federal Home Loan Bnk of IN	$483,458			
214	Mills-Peninsula Hlth Services	$572,000	274	Nch Healthcare System Inc.	$483,133			
215	Legacy Emanuel Hosp & Hlth	$571,284	275	Transunion Corp.	$482,600			
216	Henry Modell & Company Inc.	$570,335	276	U.S. Commodities Llc	$481,694			
217	Mainline Info Systems Inc.	$567,357	277	Five Star Cooperative	$479,091			
218	Stevens Transport Inc.	$566,898	278	Producers Rice Mill Inc.	$478,562			
219	Alberici Group Inc.	$565,898	279	The First District Association	$476,602			
220	Heartland Regional Med Cntr	$564,256	280	South MN Beet Sugar Coop.	$474,593			
221	The Ford Foundation	$559,085	281	Centimark Corporation	$474,251			
222	Soka Univ Of America Inc	$557,421	282	Warren Distribution Inc.	$470,203			
223	Alsco Inc.	$556,192	283	Long Island University	$468,611			
224	Big-D Construction Corp.	$554,753	284	St. Francis Hospital Inc.	$468,442			
225	Common Fund Non-Profit Org	$552,311	285	St. Anthony's Medical Center	$467,160			
226	Compassion International Inc	$551,964	286	Riverside Hospital Inc.	$466,140			
227	Bethco Corporation	$551,472	287	Dcr Workforce Inc.	$464,827			
228	William Marsh Rice Univ Inc	$551,001	288	Citizens Energy Group	$463,605			
229	De Paul University	$546,424	289	West Farmers Electric Coop.	$462,895			
230	American Infrastructure Inc.	$545,615	290	Pressure Vessel Service Inc.	$461,105			
231	BOE Of Frederick Cty MD	$543,580	291	Cedarwood-Young Company	$456,244			
232	Alberici Constructors Inc.	$543,369	292	United Hlth Svcs Hospital Inc.	$455,941			
233	M. M. Fowler Inc.	$542,967	293	W.S. Badcock Corporation	$455,914			
234	Njvc Llc	$542,243	294	Eisenhower Medical Center	$455,514			
235	Paterson Pub School District	$541,235	295	Jwm Ventures Llc	$455,380			
236	Harford County BOE	$536,454	296	Heritage Valley Hlth Syst Inc.	$453,390			
237	Billings Clinic	$533,341	297	Medstar Franklin Sq Med Ctr	$452,920			
238	Mother Frances Hosp Region	$533,260	298	Src Tec Inc.	$452,903			
239	Creative Management Inc	$532,493	299	Bogopa Enterprises Inc.	$452,793			
240	Perez Trading Company Inc.	$532,009	300	Turtle & Hughes Inc	$452,278			

The 300 Largest Employers in
Hoover's Handbook of Private Companies 2013

Rank	Company	Employees	Rank	Company	Employees	Rank	Company	Employees
1	Allegis Group Inc.	85000	61	Lehigh Valley Health Network Inc.	7000	121	Barry-Wehmiller Group Inc.	4500
2	Hy-Vee Inc.	58000	62	The Mitre Corporation	7000	122	Chenega Corporation	4500
3	Trinity Health Corporation	51100	63	The Moses H Cone Memo Hosp	7000	123	Christus Spohn Hlth System Corp	4500
4	Sutter Health	44000	64	The Children's Hosp Of Phila Fndn	7000	124	The University Of Dayton	4500
5	Maxim Healthcare Services Inc.	35000	65	Lincoln Public Schools Inc	6950	125	Durham Pub Sch Schlrshp Fndn	4500
6	Heartland Health	32000	66	Winston-Salem/Forsyth Cty Sch	6841	126	Calcasieu Parish School Board	4500
7	Nysarc Inc.	28000	67	East Baton Rouge Parish Sch Dist	6800	127	Webster University	4500
8	Expert Global Solutions Inc.	26900	68	The Reading Hospital	6800	128	Yng Men's Christian Assn-Grtr NY	4500
9	Christus Health	25000	69	Jfk Health System Inc.	6735	129	New York Power Authority	4450
10	School Board Of Orange Cty FL	25000	70	Coborn's Incorporated	6695	130	Mercy Hospital Springfield	4400
11	Intermountain Health Care Inc	23000	71	Temple Univ Health System Inc.	6500	131	St Tammany Parish School Board	4400
12	Sentara Healthcare	22000	72	Intl Rescue Committee Inc.	6500	132	Inter American Univ Of PR Inc	4306
13	St. Joseph Health System	21500	73	Midmichigan Health	6500	133	Baptist Health System Inc.	4300
14	Trustees Of The Univ Of PA	20433	74	Cumberland County Schools	6210	134	Pride Industries	4300
15	Iowa Health System	18923	75	York Hospital	6200	135	Heritage Valley Hlth System Inc.	4291
16	Wheaton Franciscan Svcs Inc.	18000	76	Contrack International Inc.	6200	136	Api Group Inc.	4237
17	University Of Georgia	17800	77	Independent Sch Dist 1-Tulsa Cty	6115	137	St. Mary's Medical Center	4209
18	University Of South Florida	16165	78	Wellmont Health System	6114	138	Aerotek Inc.	4200
19	Nypro Inc.	16000	79	Chi-Iowa Corp	6100	139	Redner's Markets Inc.	4200
20	Dekalb County BOE	16000	80	Yale-New Haven Hospital Inc.	6000	140	Rapid City Regional Hospital Inc.	4200
21	Ohiohealth Corporation	15000	81	North Mississippi Med Center Inc.	6000	141	Automation Personnel Svcs Inc.	4200
22	Milwaukee Public Schools	14154	82	Devereux Foundation	6000	142	Fordham University	4070
23	Raley's	14000	83	Mountain States Health Alliance	5978	143	Abington Memorial Hospital Inc	4018
24	The Methodist Hospital	14000	84	Main Line Health Inc.	5840	144	St. John Health System Inc.	4011
25	Hospital Sisters Health System	14000	85	Howard University Inc.	5600	145	LA County Office Of Education	4000
26	Alsco Inc.	13585	86	Associated Wholesale Grocers Inc.	5500	146	Southern Baptist Hospital Of FL	4000
27	Estes Express Lines Inc.	13000	87	Rex Healthcare Inc.	5500	147	Washington Healthcare Mary	4000
28	Duval County Public Schools	13000	88	Special Sch Dist-St Louis Cty MO	5500	148	Des Moines Independent Sch Dist	4000
29	Boddie-Noell Enterprises Inc.	13000	89	Salo Incorporated	5500	149	Archdiocese Of St. Louis	4000
30	Uc Health	13000	90	Rochester City School District	5470	150	Wildlife Conservation Society	4000
31	Oregon Health & Science Univ	12600	91	The BOE Of Howard County	5456	151	Sunrise Community Inc.	4000
32	BOE-Memphis City Schools	12015	92	Henry Modell & Company Inc.	5430	152	Transunion Corp.	3908
33	Baltimore City Pub Sch Systems	12000	93	Hawaii Pacific Health	5400	153	Covenant Medical Center Inc	3900
34	Prog For Appr Tech In Health	12000	94	Harford County BOE	5400	154	Aspirus Inc.	3900
35	VA Beach Public School System	10576	95	Sistema Univ Ana G. Mendez	5387	155	St. Anthony's Medical Center	3900
36	Umass Memorial Health Care Inc	10000	96	Sch Dist-Multnomah County OR	5244	156	Firsthealth Of The Carolinas Inc.	3897
37	Coop For Assist And Relief Inc.	10000	97	Rouse's Enterprises L.L.C.	5200	157	De Paul University	3895
38	Pds Tech Inc.	10000	98	Kogap Enterprises Inc.	5075	158	Medical Information Tech Inc.	3845
39	Umass Memorial Hospitals Inc.	10000	99	Fresno Comm Hosp & Med Ctr	5045	159	Gaston County School District	3824
40	The Washington University	9600	100	Coastal International Security Inc.	5003	160	Mainegeneral Health	3800
41	Temple Univ-Commonwealth Syst	9061	101	Lancaster General Hospital Inc	5000	161	Bibb County Board Of Education	3800
42	Air Serv Corporation	9000	102	Dialysis Clinic Inc.	5000	162	City Public Svcs Of San Antonio	3743
43	Creighton Alegent Health	8600	103	United Health Services Hosp Inc.	5000	163	H. Lee Moffitt Cancer Center	3700
44	Nch Corporation	8500	104	Genesis Health System	5000	164	Christus Santa Rosa Hlth Care	3700
45	Univ Health Syst Of East Carolina	8373	105	Creighton University	5000	165	Arkansas Children's Hospital	3700
46	Averitt Express Inc.	8208	106	Aurora Public Schools	5000	166	Memorial Hosp Of South Bend Inc	3700
47	LA Dept Of Water And Power	8000	107	Young Adult Institute Inc.	5000	167	Centegra Health System	3700
48	Cedars-Sinai Medical Center	8000	108	Columbia St. Mary's Inc.	5000	168	New Hanover Regional Med Ctr	3692
49	Scott And White Mem Hosp	8000	109	Abacus Corporation	5000	169	Legacy Emanuel Hosp & Hlth Ctr	3619
50	Rush University Medical Center	8000	110	Saint Clare's Hospital Inc.	4916	170	Montgomery College Fndn Inc.	3600
51	Loudoun County Public Sch Dist	8000	111	Carnegie Mellon University	4913	171	The H T Hackney Co	3600
52	Guilford County School System	8000	112	Methodist Hospitals Of Dallas Inc	4804	172	Sutter West Bay Hospitals	3597
53	Catholic Diocese Of Erie	8000	113	Presbyterian Homes And Services	4750	173	Trin Mother Frances Hlth Syst	3551
54	Management & Training Corp	7800	114	Embry-Riddle Aeronautical Univ	4719	174	Wakefern Food Corp.	3500
55	Children's Hospital Medical Center	7700	115	T. Jefferson Univ Hospitals Inc.	4701	175	BOE Of Frederick County Md (Inc)	3500
56	Battelle Memorial Institute Inc	7457	116	The Medical College Of WI Inc	4700	176	Saint Alphonsus Reg Med Ctr Inc.	3500
57	Anne Arundel County BOE	7200	117	R. Wood Johnson Univ Hospital	4674	177	Conemaugh Health System Inc.	3500
58	Crozer-Keystone Health System	7100	118	New Prime Inc.	4600	178	Nch Healthcare System Inc.	3500
59	Riverside Healthcare Assn Inc.	7050	119	Touro College	4600	179	Riverside Hospital Inc.	3500
60	Black & Veatch Holding Company	7017	120	C.R. England Inc.	4500	180	Guest Services Inc.	3500

SOURCE: MERGENT, INC., DATABASE, DECEMBER 2012

Rank	Company	Employees	Rank	Company	Employees	Rank	Company	Employees
181	Dayton Board Of Education	3500	243	Bayhealth Medical Center Inc.	2790			
182	Parks Xanterra & Resorts Inc	3500	244	Colorado Seminary	2770			
183	Belcan Svcs Group Ltd Prtnrshp	3500	245	University Of North Dakota	2756			
184	Fayette County BOE	3500	246	Terracon Consultants Inc.	2753			
185	New Hanover County Schools	3500	247	Wright State University	2748			
186	Mosaic	3500	248	Mother Frances Hosp Regl Hlth	2747			
187	The Budd Group Inc	3500	249	Dekalb Medical Center Inc.	2700			
188	Lvi Services Inc.	3500	250	Hardin County Board Of Education	2700			
189	Rom Catholic Bishop Of Louisville	3500	251	Commonwealth Hlth Corp Inc	2700			
190	Froedtert Mem Lutheran Hosp Inc	3459	252	Holy Spirit Hosp-Sisters Of Chris.	2698			
191	Lafayette Parish School Board	3400	253	Heartland Regional Medical Center	2600			
192	Rapides Parish School District	3400	254	William Marsh Rice University Inc	2600			
193	St. James Security Services Inc.	3400	255	St. Jude Hospital	2600			
194	Unique Staff Leasing I Ltd.	3400	256	Holy Cross Hosp of Slvr Sprng Inc	2600			
195	Bradford Holding Company Inc	3400	257	Sumter School District	2600			
196	Southwest Research Institute Inc	3352	258	Hss Inc.	2600			
197	Pcl Construction Enterprises Inc	3300	259	Guthrie Healthcare System	2575			
198	Financial Industry Reg Auth Inc.	3300	260	Cedar Rapids Comm Sch Dist Fnd	2540			
199	St. Joseph Hospital Of Orange	3300	261	St. Claire Medical Center Inc.	2527			
200	Billings Clinic	3300	262	Providence Hospital	2517			
201	Long Island University	3300	263	Snake River Sugar Company	2500			
202	Chapman University	3300	264	Nova Southeastern University Inc.	2500			
203	Ascension Parish School Board	3300	265	Edward Hospital	2500			
204	Iredell-Statesville Schools	3300	266	The Union Memorial Hospital	2500			
205	Community Dev Inst Head Start	3272	267	University Of Rhode Island	2500			
206	St Francis Hospital And Med Ctr	3270	268	BOE Of Carroll County	2500			
207	Carter-Jones Companies Inc	3225	269	Sec Finance Corp Of Spartanburg	2500			
208	Wilbur-Ellis Company	3200	270	Mmr Group Inc.	2500			
209	Univ Of WI Medical Fndn Inc.	3200	271	Millard Public Schools	2500			
210	IN Univ Health Bloomington Inc	3200	272	Mmr Constructors Inc.	2500			
211	Excelitas Technologies Corp.	3200	273	Alexandria City School District	2500			
212	Douglas County BOE	3200	274	Foxworth Galbraith Lumber Co	2500			
213	Salt Lake Community College	3200	275	Amer Baptist Homes Of The West	2500			
214	Comm College Of Allegheny Cty	3200	276	Medicalodges Inc.	2500			
215	Bethesda Lutheran Comm Inc.	3106	277	Park University	2500			
216	North Kansas City Hospital	3100	278	Think Together	2500			
217	Orange Unified School Dist (Inc)	3100	279	Lansing Community College	2500			
218	Young Life Inc.	3100	280	National Convention Services Llc	2500			
219	Willis-Knighton Medical Center	3089	281	El Paso Cty Comm College District	2499			
220	Paterson Public School District	3055	282	Altoona Regional Health System	2494			
221	Medstar Franklin Sq Med Ctr Inc	3019	283	Western Maryland Health System	2460			
222	True Value Company	3000	284	Overlake Hospital Medical Center	2450			
223	Walsh Construction Company	3000	285	Davenport Community Sch Dist	2450			
224	Dana-Farber Cancer Institute Inc.	3000	286	Avera Health	2450			
225	Trustees Of Boston College	3000	287	Nibco Inc.	2420			
226	Saint Vincent Health Center Inc	3000	288	Childrens Mem Medical Center Inc	2420			
227	Beth Abraham Health Services	3000	289	Saint Agnes Medical Center	2400			
228	Edward W. Sparrow Hospital Assn	3000	290	St. Mary Medical Center	2400			
229	Thompson Hospitality	3000	291	South Nassau Communities Hosp	2400			
230	Portland Community College	3000	292	Harrison Medical Center	2400			
231	Carondelet Health	3000	293	Floyd Healthcare Mgmt Inc.	2400			
232	Rom Catholic Diocese Of Syracuse	3000	294	Central Michigan University	2388			
233	Unified Grocers Inc.	2950	295	Acadian Ambulance Service Inc.	2385			
234	Mobile Infirmary Association	2938	296	St. Vincent Hosp -Sisters 3rd Ordr	2360			
235	Stephen F Austin State University	2914	297	John Carroll University (Inc)	2343			
236	University Of Kentucky Hosp Aux	2879	298	High Point Regional Hlth System	2338			
237	Drexel University	2868	299	Southern Reg Hlth System Inc.	2315			
238	Central Texas College	2853	300	Rady Children's Hosp-San Diego	2313			
239	Duquesne Univ Of The Holy Spirit	2836						
240	Rialto Unified School District	2833						
241	Ouachita Parish School District	2804						
242	Boy Scouts Of America	2800						

The Top 100 Companies by Total Assets in
Hoover's Handbook of Private Companies 2013

Rank	Company	Sales ($ thous.)	Rank	Company	Sales ($ thous.)	Rank	Company	Sales ($thous.)
1	Fed Home Loan Bnk-NY	$107,130,077	61	Christian Bros Inv Svc Inc	$2,079,382			
2	Fed Home Loan Bnk-SF	$102,662,000	62	Amer Cancer Soc CA Div	$2,039,204			
3	AK Permanent Fund Corp	$45,043,005	63	Allegis Group Inc.	$2,031,298			
4	Fed Home Loan Bank-IN	$41,231,339	64	Ngl Energy Partners Lp	$2,029,419			
5	Knights Of Columbus	$18,026,582	65	The Ucla Foundation	$2,022,720			
6	TX Cty Dist Rtrmnt Sys	$17,828,923	66	Hines Global Reit Inc.	$2,005,465			
7	Univ Of Pennsylvania	$13,867,485	67	Yale-New Haven Hosp Inc	$1,997,566			
8	Trust of The Univ of PA	$12,912,074	68	Scott-White Mem Hosp	$1,997,453			
9	LA Dept Of Wtr And Pwr	$12,520,138	69	Lehigh Vlly Hlth Ntwrk	$1,969,291			
10	Sutter Health	$12,440,000	70	Umass Meml Hlth Care	$1,940,983			
11	The Ford Foundation	$10,344,932	71	University Of Georgia	$1,919,435			
12	City Pub Svcs Of San Ant	$9,735,453	72	NY Comm Trust & Funds	$1,908,884			
13	The Washington Univ	$9,158,653	73	Swarthmore College	$1,905,688			
14	Trinity Health Corp	$9,158,410	74	Powersouth Enrgy Coop	$1,836,924			
15	NY Power Authority	$9,035,000	75	Intl Bhd of Elect Wrkrs	$1,813,282			
16	NW Farm Credit Svcs Aca	$8,696,747	76	Mercy Housing Inc.	$1,803,283			
17	Olam Americas Inc	$8,030,960	77	Whiting-Turner Cont Co	$1,793,254			
18	Comm Fund Non-Prof Org	$7,362,300	78	City Utili-Springfield MO	$1,776,280			
19	Est Of Bernice Pauahi Bish	$7,277,105	79	Transammonia Inc.	$1,775,846			
20	William Marsh Rice Univ	$6,235,521	80	Moses H Cone Mem Hosp	$1,741,031			
21	Intermountain Hlth Care	$5,758,100	81	Univ Of FL Fndn Inc	$1,711,205			
22	The Methodist Hospital	$5,558,443	82	Trustees Of Grinnell Coll	$1,699,622			
23	St. Joseph Health System	$5,027,453	83	Yosemite Farm Credit Aca	$1,676,164			
24	Liberty Prop Ltd Prtnrshp	$4,956,365	84	Dekalb County BOE	$1,672,026			
25	Sentara Healthcare	$4,845,256	85	Utah Housing Corp	$1,668,445			
26	American Agcredit Aca	$4,718,723	86	Fordham University	$1,655,681			
27	School Bd-Orange Cty FL	$4,684,735	87	Drexel University	$1,638,787			
28	Christus Health	$4,671,112	88	Georgia Tech Fndn Inc.	$1,631,650			
29	Transunion Corp.	$4,243,800	89	Lucile Salter Packard CH	$1,584,356			
30	Cedars-Sinai Med Center	$3,688,621	90	Mtn States Hlth Alliance	$1,573,869			
31	Temple U-Syst Higher Ed	$3,605,383	91	Sutter West Bay Hosps	$1,572,000			
32	Trustees Of Boston Coll	$3,394,746	92	U Hlth Syst-East Carolina	$1,570,917			
33	Lodging Rlj Trust L P	$3,345,237	93	Hoosier Enrgy Rural Coop	$1,559,431			
34	Cole Credit Prop Trust	$3,337,819	94	Apple Reit Nine Inc.	$1,553,916			
35	University Of Richmond	$3,331,787	95	Coachella Valley Wtr Dist	$1,544,336			
36	Citizens Energy Group	$3,321,877	96	Loudoun Cty Pub Sch Dis	$1,543,021			
37	Ohiohealth Corporation	$3,307,423	97	Duval Cty Public Schools	$1,529,929			
38	Iowa Health System	$3,298,436	98	Wakefern Food Corp.	$1,498,548			
39	OR Hlth & Science Univ	$3,138,330	99	Cap Improvement BOM	$1,493,731			
40	Options Clearing Corp	$3,062,209	100	Dana-Farber Cancer Inst.	$1,487,621			
41	Cnl Lifestyle Prop Inc.	$2,983,577						
42	Rockefeller U Fac&Stdnts	$2,980,030						
43	Rockefeller University	$2,978,431						
44	Assoc Electric Coop Inc.	$2,971,028						
45	Prospect Capital Corp	$2,912,597						
46	Farm Credit Svcs IL Aca	$2,843,616						
47	University Of South FL	$2,763,976						
48	Rush Univ Medical Ctr	$2,583,548						
49	Children's Hosp Med Ctr	$2,468,440						
50	Main Line Health Inc.	$2,400,858						
51	Santa Clara Vlly Wtr Dist	$2,383,160						
52	Carnegie Mellon Univ	$2,374,418						
53	Pomona College	$2,368,878						
54	Pres & Trust-Williams Coll	$2,361,903						
55	Wheaton Franc Svcs Inc.	$2,310,333						
56	Acapita Educ Fin Corp	$2,297,668						
57	J.S. & J.L. Knight Fndn	$2,192,836						
58	Fin Indus Reg Auth Inc.	$2,173,300						
59	Mem Hlth Svcs Corp	$2,170,152						
60	Hy-Vee Inc.	$2,091,798						

SOURCE: MERGENT, INC. NOVEMBER 2012

Hoover's Handbook of

Private Companies

The Companies

2CHECKOUT.COM INC

LOCATIONS

HQ: 2CHECKOUT.COM INC
  1785 OBRIEN RD, COLUMBUS, OH 43228-3895
Phone: 614-921-2524
Web: www.2checkout.com

HISTORICAL FINANCIALS

Company Type: Private

Income Statement

FYE: December 31

	REVENUE ($ mil.)	NET INCOME ($ mil.)	NET PROFIT MARGIN	EMPLOYEES
12/11	269	4	1.6%	114
12/10	218	1	0.7%	0
12/09	207	2	1.4%	0
12/08	214	2	1.1%	0
Annual Growth	8.0%	24.6%	—	—

2011 Year-End Financials

Debt ratio: —
Return on equity: 1.60%
Cash ($ mil.): 11
Current ratio: 1.20
Long-term debt ($ mil.): —

Dividends
  Yield: —
  Payout: —
  Market value ($ mil.): —

---

3 I INFOTECH INC.

LOCATIONS

HQ: 3 I INFOTECH INC.
  450 RRITAN CTR PKWY STE B, EDISON, NJ 08837
Phone: 732-710-4444
Web: www.3i-infotech.com/

HISTORICAL FINANCIALS

Company Type: Private

Income Statement

FYE: March 31

	REVENUE ($ mil.)	NET INCOME ($ mil.)	NET PROFIT MARGIN	EMPLOYEES
03/11	84	0	0.4%	350
03/09	27	2	9.2%	0
Annual Growth	204.2%	(87.3%)	—	—

2011 Year-End Financials

Debt ratio: ——
Return on equity: 0.40%
Cash ($ mil.): 2
Current ratio: —
Long-term debt ($ mil.): —

Dividends
  Yield: —
  Payout: —
  Market value ($ mil.): —

4- COUNTY ELECTRIC POWER ASSOCIATION

LOCATIONS

HQ: 4- COUNTY ELECTRIC POWER ASSOCIATION
  5265 S FRONTAGE RD, COLUMBUS, MS 39701-8562
Phone: 662-327-8900
Web: www.4county.net

HISTORICAL FINANCIALS

Company Type: Private

Income Statement

FYE: June 30

	REVENUE ($ mil.)	NET INCOME ($ mil.)	NET PROFIT MARGIN	EMPLOYEES
06/12	106	3	3.6%	161
06/11	112	4	4.2%	0
06/10	100	5	5.2%	0
06/09	104	3	3.1%	0
Annual Growth	0.6%	5.3%	—	—

2012 Year-End Financials

Debt ratio: ——
Return on equity: 3.60%
Cash ($ mil.): 1
Current ratio: 0.50
Long-term debt ($ mil.): —

Dividends
  Yield: —
  Payout: —
  Market value ($ mil.): —

A & A MANUFACTURING COMPANY INC.

LOCATIONS

HQ: A & A MANUFACTURING COMPANY INC.
  1675 SAMPSON AVE, CORONA, CA 92879-1889
Phone: 951-371-8090

HISTORICAL FINANCIALS

Company Type: Private

Income Statement

FYE: September 30

	REVENUE ($ mil.)	NET INCOME ($ mil.)	NET PROFIT MARGIN	EMPLOYEES
09/11	152	2	1.9%	2
Annual Growth	—	—	—	—

2011 Year-End Financials

Debt ratio: ——
Return on equity: 1.90%
Cash ($ mil.): 2
Current ratio: 0.70
Long-term debt ($ mil.): —

Dividends
  Yield: —
  Payout: —
  Market value ($ mil.): —

A C & T CO INC

LOCATIONS

HQ: A C & T CO INC
  11535 HOPEWELL RD, HAGERSTOWN, MD 21740-2178
Phone: 301-582-2700
Web: www.acandt.com

HISTORICAL FINANCIALS

Company Type: Private

Income Statement

FYE: June 30

	REVENUE ($ mil.)	NET INCOME ($ mil.)	NET PROFIT MARGIN	EMPLOYEES
06/12	343	4	1.3%	300
06/11	310	2	0.9%	0
06/10	244	6	2.5%	0
Annual Growth	18.4%	(15.5%)	—	—

2012 Year-End Financials

Debt ratio: —
Return on equity: 1.30%
Cash ($ mil.): 5
Current ratio: 1.40
Long-term debt ($ mil.): —

Dividends
  Yield: —
  Payout: —
  Market value ($ mil.): —

A-1 SPECIALIZED SERVICES & SUPPLIES INC.

LOCATIONS

HQ: A-1 SPECIALIZED SERVICES & SUPPLIES INC.
  2707 STATE RD, CROYDON, PA 19021-6969
Phone: 215-788-9200
Web: www.a-1specialized.com

HISTORICAL FINANCIALS

Company Type: Private

Income Statement

FYE: December 31

	REVENUE ($ mil.)	NET INCOME ($ mil.)	NET PROFIT MARGIN	EMPLOYEES
12/11	2,214	1	0.1%	100
12/10	1,359	7	0.6%	0
12/09	1,205	2	0.2%	0
12/08	2,637	15	0.6%	0
Annual Growth	(5.7%)	(53.8%)	—	—

2011 Year-End Financials

Debt ratio: —
Return on equity: 0.10%
Cash ($ mil.): 4
Current ratio: 0.30
Long-term debt ($ mil.): —

Dividends
  Yield: —
  Payout: —
  Market value ($ mil.): —

A. T. STILL UNIVERSITY OF HEALTH SCIENCES

LOCATIONS

HQ: A. T. STILL UNIVERSITY OF HEALTH SCIENCES
800 W JEFFERSON ST, KIRKSVILLE, MO 63501-1443
Phone: 660-626-2325

HISTORICAL FINANCIALS
Company Type: Private

Income Statement
FYE: June 30

	REVENUE ($ mil.)	NET INCOME ($ mil.)	NET PROFIT MARGIN	EMPLOYEES
06/12	111	3	3.3%	450
06/11	122	21	17.3%	0
06/10	104	12	12.4%	0
06/09	80	(3)	—	0
Annual Growth	11.3%	—	—	—

2012 Year-End Financials

Debt ratio: ——
Return on equity: 3.30%
Cash ($ mil.): 17
Current ratio: —
Long-term debt ($ mil.): —

Dividends
  Yield: —
  Payout: —
  Market value ($ mil.): —

A.G.ROYCE METAL MARKETING. LLC

LOCATIONS

HQ: A.G.ROYCE METAL MARKETING. LLC
1381 SAWGRS CORP PKWY, SUNRISE, FL 33323-2889
Phone: 954-561-3607
Web: www.crpsteel.com

HISTORICAL FINANCIALS
Company Type: Private

Income Statement
FYE: December 31

	REVENUE ($ mil.)	NET INCOME ($ mil.)	NET PROFIT MARGIN	EMPLOYEES
12/11	142	4	2.9%	18
12/10	100	3	3.5%	0
12/09	80	0	0.6%	0
12/08	249	7	3.0%	0
Annual Growth	(17.1%)	(17.2%)	—	—

2011 Year-End Financials

Debt ratio: ——
Return on equity: 2.90%
Cash ($ mil.): 0
Current ratio: 1.90
Long-term debt ($ mil.): —

Dividends
  Yield: —
  Payout: —
  Market value ($ mil.): —

AARON AND COMPANY INC

Aaron & Company knows a thing or two about staying cool. Catering primarily to contractors in New Jersey and eastern Pennsylvania the wholesaler offers plumbing and HVAC supplies through more than five locations in the Garden State. Three of these outlets house Aaron Kitchen & Bath Design Galleries which feature complete kitchen and bathroom set-ups to help customers with building and remodeling plans. Aaron & Company is served by a single 120000-sq.-ft. distribution center that is stocked with more than 15000 items.

One of the top 100 distributors or plumbing and HVAC products in the US the firm has expanded its footprint in New Jersey over the years through acquisitions. In late 2010 the company acquired the operations of regional wholesaler S. Franklin & Son whose branch in Fairfield New Jersey became Aaron & Company's seventh location.

The company was founded in the early 1900s by plumber Isadore Aaron. The Portnoy and Laudino families bought into the business in 1979. All three families ran the company until Jeffrey Aaron the founder's grandson retired in 2002 leaving the firm without an Aaron for the first time. The second-generation Portnoys and Laudinos control the firm today.

EXECUTIVES

President, Barry Portnoy
VP MIS, Frank Laudino Jr.
VP and Treasurer, Richard Laudino
Operations Manager, Anthony Panko
Controller, Victor DeRosa
Human Resources, Margie Mish
Director Business Development, Kevin Manning
HVAC Division Manager, John Provenzano
Manager, Alan Mandel
Training Manager Piscataway Sales, Allen Rice
Purchasing Manager, Steve Rush
Division Manager, Bruce Sax
Marketing Coordinator, Suzanne Lynch
Branch Manager, Keith Jaeger
Executive Assistant, Jackie Piano

LOCATIONS

HQ: AARON AND COMPANY INC
30 TURNER PL, PISCATAWAY, NJ 08854-3839
Phone: 732-752-8200
Web: www.aaronandco.com

COMPETITORS

Ace Hardware	True Value
Hajoca Corporation	Wal-Mart
HD Supply	Watsco
Lowe's	WinWholesale
Sears	Wolseley

HISTORICAL FINANCIALS
Company Type: Private

Income Statement
FYE: December 31

	REVENUE ($ mil.)	NET INCOME ($ mil.)	NET PROFIT MARGIN	EMPLOYEES
12/11	68	0	1.2%	0
12/09	54	0	1.2%	0
12/08	63	0	1.3%	0
12/07	66	1	1.8%	0
Annual Growth	0.9%	(10.8%)	—	—

2011 Year-End Financials

Debt ratio: ——
Return on equity: 1.20%
Cash ($ mil.): 0
Current ratio: 0.60
Long-term debt ($ mil.): —

Dividends
  Yield: —
  Payout: —
  Market value ($ mil.): —

ABACUS CORPORATION

LOCATIONS

HQ: ABACUS CORPORATION
610 GUSRYAN ST, BALTIMORE, MD 21224-2933
Phone: 410-633-1900
Web: www.abacuscorporation.com

HISTORICAL FINANCIALS
Company Type: Private

Income Statement
FYE: December 31

	REVENUE ($ mil.)	NET INCOME ($ mil.)	NET PROFIT MARGIN	EMPLOYEES
12/11	102	0	0.4%	5,000
12/10	89	(0)	—	0
12/09	71	(0)	—	0
12/07	60	0	0.3%	0
Annual Growth	19.2%	29.1%	—	—

2011 Year-End Financials

Debt ratio: ——
Return on equity: 0.40%
Cash ($ mil.): 0
Current ratio: 0.80
Long-term debt ($ mil.): —

Dividends
  Yield: —
  Payout: —
  Market value ($ mil.): —

ABINGTON MEMORIAL HOSPITAL INC

Abington Memorial Hospital brings health care to residents of southeastern Pennsylvania. Serving Montgomery Bucks and Philadelphia counties the not-for-profit community hospital has some 670 beds. In addition to general medical and surgical care the hospital offers specialized care centers for cancer and cardiovascular conditions operates high-tech orthopedic and neurological surgery units and serves as a regional trauma care facility. It also runs an inpatient pediatric unit in affiliation with The Children's Hospital of Philadelphia.

Abington Memorial also known as Abington Health operates the neighboring 125-bed Lansdale Hospital and several area outpatient facilities.

Geographic Reach

Abington Memorial provides care to residents of southeastern Pennsylvania. The hospital serves Montgomery Bucks and Philadelphia counties

Operations

The not-for-profit community hospital has some 670 beds. Abington Memorial is affiliated with several medical schools including the Temple University School of Medicine and offers residency programs and postgraduate medical education.

In addition to its hospitals Abington Memorial operates an extensive outpatient care facility named Abington Health Center-Warminster. The Warminster facility added an inpatient hospice center in 2009. Other outpatient facilities include Abington Health Center-Schilling and Abington Physicians at Montgomeryville.

Additionally Abington Memorial operates a nursing school and a clinical research center.

Strategy

Abington Memorial began using the Abington Health moniker to reflect its larger network of facilities after it acquired Lansdale Hospital which was previously known as Central Montgomery Medical Center from Universal Health Services in 2008. Abington Memorial has since invested in a number of improvements at the acquired hospital including expanded inpatient outpatient and surgery services. It opened a new orthopedic institute at the hospital in early 2011. The hospital's obstetrics operations were transferred to Abington's main campus due to low patient volume.

Company Background

Abington Memorial first opened its doors in 1914.

Laurence Merlis was appointed as president and CEO of Abington Health and Abington Memorial Hospital in early 2010. He replaced Richard Jones who chose to retire.

EXECUTIVES

VP Marketing and Communications, Mary Thomson
EVP and COO, Margaret M. (Meg) McGoldrick
CIO, Alison L. Ferren
Chief of Internal Medicine and Medical Director Physician Network, Keith Sweigard
Chief Patient Safety Officer, John J. Kelly
SVP Professional Services and Quality Assurance, Gary R. Candia
SVP Finance and CFO, Michael Walsh
SVP Patient Services and Chief Nursing Officer, Barbara Wadsworth
Public Relations Manager, Barbara Vasco
VP Personnel, Meghan Patton
Chairman, John Durham
President and CEO Abington Health and Abington Memorial Hospital, Laurence M. Merlis
Auditors: PricewaterhouseCoopersLLP

LOCATIONS

HQ: Abington Memorial Hospital
1200 Old York Rd., Abington PA 19001
Phone: 215-481-2000   **Fax:** 215-481-3619
Web: www.amh.org

PRODUCTS/OPERATIONS

Selected Facilities

Abington Memorial Health Center Schilling Campus (Willow Grove PA)
Abington Memorial Health Center Warminster Campus (Warminster PA)

Abington Memorial Hospital (Abington PA)
Abington Physicians at Montgomeryville (North Wales PA)
Lansdale Hospital (Lansdale PA)

COMPETITORS

Albert Einstein Healthcare Network
Aria Health
Crozer-Keystone Health System
Doylestown Hospital
Grand View
Jefferson Health System
Memorial Hospital (PA)
Mercy Health System
Moses Taylor Hospital
North Philadelphia Health System
Tenet Healthcare
TUHS
University of Pennsylvania Health System
Virtua Memorial

HISTORICAL FINANCIALS

Company Type: Private - Not-for-Profit

Income Statement

FYE: June 30

	REVENUE ($ mil.)	NET INCOME ($ mil.)	NET PROFIT MARGIN	EMPLOYEES
06/11	702	21	3.1%	4,018
06/10	783	16	2.1%	0
06/09	704	(36)	—	0
06/08	28	25	87.1%	0
Annual Growth	189.7%	(4.7%)	—	—

2011 Year-End Financials

Debt ratio: ——
Return on equity: 3.10%
Cash ($ mil.): 48
Current ratio: 1.80
Long-term debt ($ mil.): —

Dividends
Yield: —
Payout: —
Market value ($ mil.): —

ABINGTON RELDAN METALS LLC

LOCATIONS

HQ: ABINGTON RELDAN METALS LLC
550 OLD BORDENTOWN RD, FAIRLESS HILLS, PA 19030-4510
Phone: 215-335-3200

HISTORICAL FINANCIALS

Company Type: Private

Income Statement

FYE: December 31

	REVENUE ($ mil.)	NET INCOME ($ mil.)	NET PROFIT MARGIN	EMPLOYEES
12/11	613	31	5.2%	52
12/10	380	17	4.5%	0
12/09	354	15	4.3%	0
12/08	440	5	1.3%	0
Annual Growth	11.7%	77.4%	—	—

2011 Year-End Financials

Debt ratio: ——
Return on equity: 5.20%
Cash ($ mil.): 1
Current ratio: 0.80
Long-term debt ($ mil.): —

Dividends
Yield: —
Payout: —
Market value ($ mil.): —

ACADIA HOSPITAL

LOCATIONS

HQ: ACADIA HOSPITAL
43 WHITING HILL RD, BREWER, ME 04412-1005
Phone: 207-973-7064

HISTORICAL FINANCIALS

Company Type: Private

Income Statement

FYE: September 24

	REVENUE ($ mil.)	NET INCOME ($ mil.)	NET PROFIT MARGIN	EMPLOYEES
09/11	88	2	3.1%	0
09/10	86	1	1.9%	0
09/09	81	2	2.6%	0
Annual Growth	4.5%	13.2%	—	—

2011 Year-End Financials

Debt ratio: ——
Return on equity: 3.10%
Cash ($ mil.): 4
Current ratio: 0.70
Long-term debt ($ mil.): —

Dividends
Yield: —
Payout: —
Market value ($ mil.): —

ACADIAN AMBULANCE SERVICE INC.

From ground to air and back again Acadian Ambulance Service is all about getting Southerners to the hospital safe and sound. The company provides ground and air medical transportation service to millions of residents in Louisiana Mississippi and Texas. Along with its ground ambulances the company operates a handful of helicopter ambulances through affiliate Metro Aviation. Its many subsidiaries provide a broad array of additional services including telemedicine (remote patient monitoring) paramedic training services chartered transportation and emergency medical services to offshore oil projects. Established in 1971 Acadian Ambulance Service is owned by its employees through a private stock option plan.

Operations

Acadian's fleet includes more than 400 ground ambulances helicopters and fixed-wing aircraft.

Strategy

The company has expanded its operations through the years through occasional acquisitions. Building its business in Texas in late 2012 Acadian acquired StarPlus EMS in McKinney. The purchase expanded the firm's presence in North Texas and added 50 employees eight ambulances and three wheelchair vans to Acadian's Texas fleet. In 2011 it purchased Central Texas EMS an emergency and non-emergency transport services provider in three counties as well as Humble-based NorthStar EMS which extended operations in Harris and Montgomery counties.

EXECUTIVES

Chairman and CEO, Richard Zuschlag
President and COO, David A. Pierce
EVP and CFO, David L. Kelly
EVP and Chief Medical Officer, Ross D. Judice
VP Public Relations and Marketing, W. Keith Simon

LOCATIONS

HQ: ACADIAN AMBULANCE SERVICE INC.
130 E KALISTE SALOOM RD, LAFAYETTE, LA 70508-8308
Phone: 337-291-3333
Web: www.acadianonwatch.com

PRODUCTS/OPERATIONS

Selected Subsidiaries
Acadian Ambulance Service
Acadian Monitoring Services
Air Med Services LLC
Executive Aircraft Charter Service
National EMS Academy
Safety Management Systems LLC

COMPETITORS

Air Methods	LogistiCare
CHC Helicopter	Rural/Metro
Emergency Medical Services	Safe Ride Services
	Wackenhut Services

HISTORICAL FINANCIALS

Company Type: Private

Income Statement
FYE: December 31

	REVENUE ($ mil.)	NET INCOME ($ mil.)	NET PROFIT MARGIN	EMPLOYEES
12/11	380	9	2.4%	2,385
12/10	358	7	2.0%	0
12/09	290	4	1.6%	0
12/08	274	10	3.8%	0
Annual Growth	11.5%	(3.6%)	—	—

2011 Year-End Financials

Debt ratio: ——
Return on equity: 2.40%
Cash ($ mil.): 5
Current ratio: 0.90
Long-term debt ($ mil.): —
Dividends
Yield: —
Payout: —
Market value ($ mil.): —

ACAPITA EDUCATION FINANCE CORP

LOCATIONS

HQ: ACAPITA EDUCATION FINANCE CORP
2600 WASHINGTON AVE, WACO, TX 76710-7449
Phone: 254-753-0915

HISTORICAL FINANCIALS

Company Type: Private

Income Statement
FYE: June 30

	ASSETS ($ mil.)	NET INCOME ($ mil.)	INCOME AS % OF ASSETS	EMPLOYEES
06/12	2,297	(122)	—	1
06/11	2,563	(153)	—	0
06/10	2,828	97	3.5%	0
Annual Growth	(9.9%)	—	—	—

2012 Year-End Financials

Debt ratio: ——
Return on equity: (-271.00)%
Cash ($ mil.): 46
Current ratio: ——
Long-term debt ($ mil.): —
Dividends
Yield: —
Payout: —
Market value ($ mil.): —

ACCESS COMMUNITY HEALTH NETWORK

LOCATIONS

HQ: ACCESS COMMUNITY HEALTH NETWORK
222 N CANAL ST, CHICAGO, IL 60606-1206
Phone: 312-526-2200
Web: www.accesscommunityhealth.net

HISTORICAL FINANCIALS

Company Type: Private

Income Statement
FYE: June 30

	REVENUE ($ mil.)	NET INCOME ($ mil.)	NET PROFIT MARGIN	EMPLOYEES
06/11	133	(6)	—	650
06/10	132	2	1.9%	0
06/09	119	3	2.6%	0
06/08	113	4	3.6%	0
Annual Growth	5.3%	—	—	—

2011 Year-End Financials

Debt ratio: ——
Return on equity: (-4.60)%
Cash ($ mil.): 4
Current ratio: 0.50
Long-term debt ($ mil.): —
Dividends
Yield: —
Payout: —
Market value ($ mil.): —

ACCRETIVE TECHNOLOGY GROUP INC.

LOCATIONS

HQ: ACCRETIVE TECHNOLOGY GROUP INC.
2019 3RD AVE STE 200, SEATTLE, WA 98121-2430
Phone: 206-443-0751
Web: www.cbrowser.com

HISTORICAL FINANCIALS

Company Type: Private

Income Statement
FYE: June 30

	REVENUE ($ mil.)	NET INCOME ($ mil.)	NET PROFIT MARGIN	EMPLOYEES
06/12	299	3	1.2%	80
06/11	205	7	3.7%	0
06/10	99	1	2.0%	0
06/09	74	2	3.5%	0
Annual Growth	59.3%	11.6%	—	—

2012 Year-End Financials

Debt ratio: ——
Return on equity: 1.20%
Cash ($ mil.): 16
Current ratio: 0.80
Long-term debt ($ mil.): —
Dividends
Yield: —
Payout: —
Market value ($ mil.): —

ACDI/VOCA

LOCATIONS

HQ: ACDI/VOCA
50 F ST NW STE 1075, WASHINGTON, DC 20001-1532
Phone: 202-469-6000
Web: www.acdivocabolivia.org

HISTORICAL FINANCIALS

Company Type: Private

Income Statement
FYE: December 31

	REVENUE ($ mil.)	NET INCOME ($ mil.)	NET PROFIT MARGIN	EMPLOYEES
12/11	168	0	0.5%	1,085
12/10	142	2	1.8%	0
12/09	145	8	6.1%	0
12/08	115	4	4.2%	0
Annual Growth	13.3%	(43.4%)	—	—

2011 Year-End Financials

Debt ratio: ——
Return on equity: 0.50%
Cash ($ mil.): 24
Current ratio: ——
Long-term debt ($ mil.): —
Dividends
Yield: —
Payout: —
Market value ($ mil.): —

ACME PAPER & SUPPLY CO. INC.

LOCATIONS

HQ: ACME PAPER & SUPPLY CO. INC.
8229 SANDY CT, SAVAGE, MD 20763
Phone: 410-792-2333
Web: www.acmepaper.com

HISTORICAL FINANCIALS

Company Type: Private

Income Statement				FYE: May 31
	REVENUE ($ mil.)	NET INCOME ($ mil.)	NET PROFIT MARGIN	EMPLOYEES
05/11	90	1	1.5%	190
05/10	0	0	—	0
05/09	93	0	1.0%	0
Annual Growth	(1.4%)	21.7%	—	—

ACME TRUCK LINE INC.

LOCATIONS

HQ: ACME TRUCK LINE INC.
200 WESTBANK EXPY, GRETNA, LA 70053-5615
Phone: 504-365-3400
Web: www.acmetruck.com

HISTORICAL FINANCIALS

Company Type: Private

Income Statement				FYE: December 31
	REVENUE ($ mil.)	NET INCOME ($ mil.)	NET PROFIT MARGIN	EMPLOYEES
12/11	302	18	6.2%	2,100
12/10	199	13	6.5%	0
12/09	136	(0)	—	0
12/08	202	11	5.7%	0
Annual Growth	14.3%	17.4%	—	—

2011 Year-End Financials

Debt ratio: ——
Return on equity: 6.20%
Cash ($ mil.): 4
Current ratio: 1.70
Long-term debt ($ mil.): —
Dividends
  Yield: —
  Payout: —
Market value ($ mil.): —

ACTION FOR BOSTON COMMUNITY DEVELOPMENT INC.

Action For Boston Community Development (ABCD) strives to make helping others as easy as 1-2-3. The not-for-profit serves more than 100000 low-income people in New England in areas such as advocacy child care consumer services education health and housing. The group operates through a decentralized model that utilizes a city-wide network of Area Planning Action Councils Neighborhood Service Centers and Head Start and Child Care Centers. It partners with more than a dozen programs like SUMMERWORKS (work experience for low-income teens) Foster Grandparents Urban College of Boston and another 10 or so government agencies. ABCD was established in 1962 as one of several national programs to combat poverty.

One initiative of the ABCD group is ensuring that people have heating assistance during the cold winter months. It supplements the funds provided by the federal fuel assistance funds.

EXECUTIVES

Vice Chairman, Thelma D. Burns
Vice Chairman, Kathleen Flynn
VP Administration and Human Resources, Harold Mezoff
President and CEO, John J. Drew
General Counsel, Anita Lichtblau
VP Workforce Development and Technology Services, Mark Isenburg
Vice Chairman, James A. Owens Jr.
Treasurer, Jean Babcock
Chairperson, Juliette Mayers
Vice Chairperson, Johnnett West-Netter
EVP, Sharon Scott-Chandler
VP Field Operations, Michael Vance
VP Real Estate and Energy Serives, John Wells
Finance, Marjorie Lombard
CTO, Ken Grout
Public Information, Susan Kooperstein
Vice Chairman, Ruth Ann Moriarty
Vice Chairman, Thelma D. Burns
Vice Chairman, Kathleen Flynn
Vice Chairman, James A. Owens Jr.
Vice Chairperson, Johnnett West-Netter
Vice Chairman, Ruth Ann Moriarty
Auditors: KPMGLLP

LOCATIONS

HQ: Action For Boston Community Development Inc.
178 Tremont St., Boston MA 02111
Phone: 617-357-6000   **Fax:** 617-357-6041
Web: www.bostonabcd.org

HISTORICAL FINANCIALS

Company Type: Private - Not-for-Profit

Income Statement				FYE: August 31
	REVENUE ($ mil.)	NET INCOME ($ mil.)	NET PROFIT MARGIN	EMPLOYEES
08/11	150	(0)	—	1,000
08/10	151	(0)	—	0
08/09	143	0	0.2%	0
Annual Growth	2.4%	—	—	—

2011 Year-End Financials

Debt ratio: —
Return on equity: (-0.20)%
Cash ($ mil.): 8
Current ratio: 1.90
Long-term debt ($ mil.): —
Dividends
  Yield: —
  Payout: —
Market value ($ mil.): —

ACTIONTEC ELECTRONICS INC.

Actiontec Electronics aims to broaden your approach to networking. The company makes gateways routers modems and other broadband connection equipment used to create wireless home networks. Its fiber optic routers allow broadband television and other content to be distributed to multiple devices throughout the home over coaxial cables. The company sells its equipment through partnerships with broadband service providers and equipment makers such as Qwest Verizon Cisco and Entropic. It also sells directly through retailers including Amazon.com Best Buy and Wal-Mart. Founded in 1993 Actiontec has offices in the US China and Taiwan.

The company has strategically positioned itself to capitalize on the proliferation of wireless home networks and entertainment devices offering a product portfolio that encompasses IP-based video services DSL modems wireless networking devices and network adapters. Actiontec's zControl home automation controller lets the user manage electronics such as lights thermostats and garage door openers from an Internet-enabled computer mobile phone or TV.

Actiontec has announced a new product called MyWirelessTV a Wi-Fi HDMI transmitter and receiver that will be available in the second half of 2011. Targeted towards the growing number of consumers who stream Internet content on multiple home displays MyWirelessTV will support wireless 3-D HD video streaming from an HDMI-enabled device to any display in the home. It was developed using video processors and technology from Cavium Networks.

EXECUTIVES

Chief Business Development Officer, Brian Henrichs
President and CEO, Dean Chang
Director Marketing, Lesley Kirchman
CFO, Brian Paul
VP Operations, Minsiu Huang
VP Engineering, Chuang Li
VP North America Channel Sales, Mike Ehlenberger
VP Software Engineering and Quality Assurance, David Lin

LOCATIONS

HQ: Actiontec Electronics Inc.
760 N. Mary Ave., Sunnyvale CA 94085
Phone: 408-752-7700   **Fax:** 408-541-9003
Web: www.actiontec.com

COMPETITORS

Belkin
Buffalo Technology
D-Link
NETGEAR
SMC Networks
ZyXEL Communications

HISTORICAL FINANCIALS
Company Type: Private

Income Statement
FYE: December 31

	REVENUE ($ mil.)	NET INCOME ($ mil.)	NET PROFIT MARGIN	EMPLOYEES
12/11	201	5	2.8%	440
12/10	162	1	1.1%	0
12/07	183	0	—	0
12/06	145	0	—	0
Annual Growth	**11.4%**	—	—	—

2011 Year-End Financials
Debt ratio: ——
Return on equity: 2.80%
Cash ($ mil.): 34
Current ratio: 0.50
Long-term debt ($ mil.): —

Dividends
Yield: —
Payout: —
Market value ($ mil.): —

ADAMS FAIRACRE FARMS INC.

From seeds to seafood and fertilizer to fencing Adams Fairacre Farms has a few things covered. The company's four locations in New York's Hudson River Valley offer groceries including fresh produce power equipment (John Deere tractors and mowers chippers chain saws) fencing supplies landscaping materials and gifts and gardening supplies (plants seeds soil pest control). Adams Fairacre Farms was founded in 1919 by Ralph Adams Sr. as a roadside produce stand where the Adams family sold the excess from its 50-acre farm. The company added other items as customers requested them. Descendants of Adams including some third-generation members own and run the family business.

The company opened its fourth location in Wappinger New York in November 2011. The Wappinger store sells prepared foods flowers and gifts housewares and provides several self-serve hot foods islands and seating stations.

EXECUTIVES
VP and Owner, Donald Adams
President and Owner, Ralph Adams
Kingston Store Manager and Owner, Steve Adams
General Manager Kingston Garden Center, Phil Burley
General Manager Adams Power Equipment, Joseph (Joe) Conte
General Manager Poughkeepsie Garden Center, Greg Draiss
Newburgh Store Manager, Barbara Johnson
Director Marketing, William (Bill) Lessner
Controller, Joseph N. Proto
Manager Human Resources, Gaye Mallet
General Manager Newburgh Garden Center, Eric Foose
IT Manager, Tom Privitera
Adams Cafe Manager and Executive Chef, Joseph (Joe) DeMichiel
General Manager Adams Fences, Ken Fredericks
Manager Poughkeepsie Seafood, Frank LaManna
General Manager and Owner, Patrick Adams
Manager Newburgh Meat Department, Bob DeWitt

LOCATIONS
HQ: Adams Fairacre Farms Inc.
765 Dutchess Turnpike, Poughkeepsie NY 12603
Phone: 845-454-4330   **Fax:** 845-454-4337
Web: www.adamsfarms.com

COMPETITORS
Cumberland Farms
Golub
Harry and David
Home Depot
Lowe's
Sears

Stop & Shop
Target Corporation
TOPS Markets
Wal-Mart
Wegmans

HISTORICAL FINANCIALS
Company Type: Private

Income Statement
FYE: January 31

	REVENUE ($ mil.)	NET INCOME ($ mil.)	NET PROFIT MARGIN	EMPLOYEES
01/12	122	0	0.7%	550
01/11	115	1	1.3%	0
01/09	113	1	1.6%	0
01/08	109	2	2.6%	0
Annual Growth	**3.7%**	**(34.0%)**	—	—

2012 Year-End Financials
Debt ratio: ——
Return on equity: 0.70%
Cash ($ mil.): 3
Current ratio: 0.60
Long-term debt ($ mil.): —

Dividends
Yield: —
Payout: —
Market value ($ mil.): —

ADLAI E STEVENSON HIGH SCHOOL DISTRICT 125

LOCATIONS
HQ: ADLAI E STEVENSON HIGH SCHOOL DISTRICT 125
2 STEVENSON DR, LINCOLNSHIRE, IL 60069-2824
Phone: 847-415-4000
Web: www.d125.org

HISTORICAL FINANCIALS
Company Type: Private

Income Statement
FYE: June 30

	REVENUE ($ mil.)	NET INCOME ($ mil.)	NET PROFIT MARGIN	EMPLOYEES
06/12	104	7	7.5%	550
06/11	105	6	6.6%	0
06/10	104	13	12.8%	0
06/09	98	6	6.2%	0
Annual Growth	**2.0%**	**8.8%**	—	—

2012 Year-End Financials
Debt ratio: ——
Return on equity: 7.50%
Cash ($ mil.): 85
Current ratio: —
Long-term debt ($ mil.): —

Dividends
Yield: —
Payout: —
Market value ($ mil.): —

ADVANCED BIOENERGY LLC

LOCATIONS
HQ: ADVANCED BIOENERGY LLC
8000 NORMAN CENTER DR # 610, BLOOMINGTON, MN 55437-1178
Phone: 763-226-2701
Web: www.advancedbioenergy.com

HISTORICAL FINANCIALS
Company Type: Private

Income Statement
FYE: June 30

	REVENUE ($ mil.)	NET INCOME ($ mil.)	NET PROFIT MARGIN	EMPLOYEES
06/12*	440	0	0.0%	129
09/11	571	1	0.3%	0
09/09	355	(54)	—	0
09/08	394	(57)	—	0
Annual Growth	**3.8%**	—	—	—

*Fiscal year change

2012 Year-End Financials
Debt ratio: ——
Return on equity: —
Cash ($ mil.): 19
Current ratio: 1.00
Long-term debt ($ mil.): —

Dividends
Yield: —
Payout: —
Market value ($ mil.): —

ADVANCED HOME CARE INC.

LOCATIONS
HQ: ADVANCED HOME CARE INC.
4001 PIEDMONT PKWY, HIGH POINT, NC 27265-9402
Phone: 336-878-8822
Web: www.advhomecare.org

HISTORICAL FINANCIALS
Company Type: Private

Income Statement
FYE: September 30

	REVENUE ($ mil.)	NET INCOME ($ mil.)	NET PROFIT MARGIN	EMPLOYEES
09/11	147	9	6.2%	1,500
09/10	143	16	11.2%	0
09/09	131	14	11.3%	0
09/07	61	8	13.8%	0
Annual Growth	**33.8%**	**2.4%**	—	—

2011 Year-End Financials
Debt ratio: ——
Return on equity: 6.20%
Cash ($ mil.): 20
Current ratio: 2.20
Long-term debt ($ mil.): —

Dividends
Yield: —
Payout: —
Market value ($ mil.): —

ADVANCED MP TECHNOLOGY INC.

Advanced MP Technology advances the cause of global electronic components distribution services for high-tech manufacturers. The company distributes linear and digital integrated circuits such as logic devices; DRAMs static random-access memories (SRAMs) and flash memories; and microprocessors. It also distributes passive components such as capacitors. The company which was founded by CEO Jeff Yassai in 1978 offers inventory management services including inventory reduction programs designed to keep customers from getting stuck with excess inventory during industry downturns. Yassai owns half of the company while president Homey Shorooghi owns the other half.

Advanced MP Technology is growing internationally by focusing on regions with greater customer growth potential particularly China. In 2008 the company expanded its facilities in Hong Kong Germany and Hungary. It also has locations in China Sweden the UK and the US.

The company was created in the 1994 merger of Advanced Silicon Technology and MP Systems.

EXECUTIVES

CEO, Jafar (Jeff) Yassai
President, Homayoun (Homey) Shorooghi
SVP Marketing, Kamran Malek
Global VP Sales, Jens Gamperl
OEM Sales America, Sam Tombs
Senior Product Manager, John Gulling
Manager Global Purchasing, Jennifer Strawn
OEM Sales Europe, Yashar Shahabi
OEM Sales Asia, Kevin Wang
OEM Sales America, Eric Bettencourt
Global Marketing Coordinator, Christy Rumbaugh

LOCATIONS

HQ: Advanced MP Technology Inc.
1010 Calle Sombra, San Clemente CA 92673-6480
Phone: 949-492-3113   **Fax:** 949-492-9589
Web: www.advancedmp.com

COMPETITORS

All American	Future Electronics
Semiconductor	N.F. Smith
America II Electronics	Premier Farnell
Arrow Electronics	Richardson Electronics
Avnet	TTI Inc.

HISTORICAL FINANCIALS
Company Type: Private

Income Statement

FYE: December 31

	REVENUE ($ mil.)	NET INCOME ($ mil.)	NET PROFIT MARGIN	EMPLOYEES
12/11	115	2	2.4%	274
12/01	227	31	13.7%	0
12/00	455	147	32.3%	0
12/99	167	21	13.0%	0
Annual Growth	(11.5%)	(49.3%)	—	—

2011 Year-End Financials

Debt ratio: ——
Return on equity: 2.40%
Cash ($ mil.): 2
Current ratio: 0.60
Long-term debt ($ mil.): —
Dividends
Yield: —
Payout: —
Market value ($ mil.): —

AEROTEK INC.

Aerotek a unit of staffing powerhouse Allegis Group offers commercial and technical staffing services throughout North America. Through several divisions Aerotek staffs workers such as engineers mechanics scientists and technical professionals as well as administrative staff members general laborers and tradespeople. It also provides training and support services. Along with aerospace auto and engineering companies Aerotek's clients include companies from the construction energy manufacturing health care and finance industries. Established as a small staffing firm in 1983 Aerotek now operates from more than 200 non-franchised offices in the US and Canada as well as parts of Europe.

Operations

Aerotek has expanded its operations over the years through organic growth and acquisitions especially in niche markets such as the biotechnology health care clinical research chemical and plastics sectors. Despite the economic downturn demand within these industries has been consistent along with engineering giving Aerotek some continuity during the recession. Aerotek has also widened its client focus to include the niche market of minority and woman-owned companies.

EXECUTIVES

President and CEO, Thomas M. (Tom) Thornton
VP Marketing and Communications, Todd Gardner
President, Todd M. Mohr
CFO, Thomas B. (Tom) Kelly
Director Communications, Erin Mulgrew
SVP Strategic Sales & Operations, Chad Koele
SVP Recruiting Operations, John Flanigan
VP HR, Rodney H. Scaife

LOCATIONS

HQ: Aerotek Inc.
7301 Parkway Dr., Hanover MD 21076
Phone: 410-694-5100   **Fax:** 410-540-7055
Web: www.aerotek.com

PRODUCTS/OPERATIONS

Selected Industries

Accounting and Finance
Administrative
Aerospace & Defense
Architecture
Automotive
Aviation
Call Center
Clinical Research
Construction
Energy
Engineering
Environmental
Labor
Manufacturing
Mortgage
Scientific

COMPETITORS

Adecco	Medical Staffing
AMN Healthcare	Network
Bryant Bureau	MSX International
CDI	On Assignment
COMFORCE	Pinnacle Staffing
Kelly Services	Randstad Holding
Kforce	Robert Half
ManpowerGroup	

HISTORICAL FINANCIALS
Company Type: Subsidiary

Income Statement

FYE: December 31

	REVENUE ($ mil.)	NET INCOME ($ mil.)	NET PROFIT MARGIN	EMPLOYEES
12/11	4,481	226	5.0%	4,200
12/10	3,446	193	5.6%	0
12/09	2,372	87	3.7%	0
12/08	2,838	167	5.9%	0
Annual Growth	16.4%	10.5%	—	—

2011 Year-End Financials

Debt ratio: ——
Return on equity: 5.00%
Cash ($ mil.): 6
Current ratio: 3.30
Long-term debt ($ mil.): —
Dividends
Yield: —
Payout: —
Market value ($ mil.): —

AFFILIATED FOODS MIDWEST COOPERATIVE INC.

Affiliated Foods Midwest Cooperative is a wholesale food distribution cooperative that supplies more than 800 independent grocers in some 15 Midwestern states. From its handful of distribution centers in Kansas Nebraska and Wisconsin the co-op distributes fresh produce meats deli items baked goods dairy products and frozen foods as well as general merchandise and equipment. It distributes goods under the Shurfine brand (from Topco Associates) and IGA labels. Additionally Affiliated Foods Midwest provides marketing merchandising and warehousing support services for its members. The cooperative was formed in 1931 to make wholesale purchases for a group of retailers in Nebraska.

EXECUTIVES

CFO, Dwayne Severson
President, Martin W. (Marty) Arter
Retail Supervisor Nebraska, Brad Brooks
Director Retail Development, Bob Frady
General Manager Elwood, Ron Kuhn
Retail Supervisor Nebraska, Duane Schwartz
Manager Human Resources, Audry Cravatt
Manager Human Resources Elwood, Mike Murphy
Retail Supervisor Elwood, Rich York
Director Business Development, Wayne Hall
Director, Marc King
Director, William Sanger
Director, Carmen Diehl
Director, John Clarke
Director, Doug Fallgatter

Director, Larry Hilty
Director, Stu Wilsman

LOCATIONS

HQ: Affiliated Foods Midwest Cooperative Inc.
1301 Omaha Ave., Norfolk NE 68702
Phone: 402-371-0555   **Fax:** 402-371-6045
Web: afmidwest.com

COMPETITORS

Associated Wholesale	Kroger
Grocers	McLane
C&S Wholesale	Nash-Finch
Central Grocers	SUPERVALU
Certco	Wal-Mart
Dearborn Wholesale	
Grocers	

HISTORICAL FINANCIALS
Company Type: Private - Cooperative

Income Statement
FYE: June 30

	REVENUE ($ mil.)	NET INCOME ($ mil.)	NET PROFIT MARGIN	EMPLOYEES
06/12	1,486	2	0.2%	850
06/11	1,356	2	0.2%	0
06/10	1,241	4	0.4%	0
06/09	1,223	2	0.2%	0
Annual Growth	6.7%	2.9%	—	—

2012 Year-End Financials

Debt ratio: ——
Return on equity: 0.20%
Cash ($ mil.): 14
Current ratio: 0.10
Long-term debt ($ mil.): —

Dividends
Yield: —
Payout: —
Market value ($ mil.): —

AFRICARE

Africare helps Africans help themselves. The not-for-profit organization provides support to communities in Africa in areas such as health care and HIV/AIDS prevention food security agriculture education environmental management and water resource development. It also works to help people create small businesses such as growing sunflowers and pressing the seeds into cooking oil and to provide emergency humanitarian aid when needed. Africare has given more than $800 million in aid to some 35 countries in Africa funding more than 2500 projects. William and Barbara Kirker founded the organization in 1970.

Microenterprise is one of the biggest trends in international aid. It involves helping a small group of people usually women set up a business that provides food for their families and gives them a way to earn money. For example Africare's "edible oil" program teaches how to produce sunflower seed cooking oil for sustenance and also for sale; it has become a self-sustaining program and continues to grow.

EXECUTIVES

Chairman, W. Frank Fountain Jr., age 67
SVP, Jeannine B. Scott
Director Human Resources, Carolyn W. Gullatt
VP Finance and Management, Jack Campbell

Director Office of Health and HIV/AIDS, Clarence S. Hall
Director Francophone West and Central Africa Region, William P. Noble
Director Management Information Systems, Jean Denis
Vice Chair, Larry D. Bailey
Secretary and Director, Joseph C. Kennedy
Treasurer, Barbara A. McKinzie
Director Southern Africa Region, Peter M. Persell
Director East and Anglophone West Africa Region, Ruth Mufute
Country Representative Tanzania, Sekai Chikowero
President, Darius Mans
Director Office of Food for Development, Harold V. Tarver
Deputy Director Office of Food for Development, Ange Tingbo
Director Management Services, J. Margaret Burke
Director Development, Cynthia Jacobs Carter
Director Communications and Marketing, Trudi Rishikof
Executive Director Africare-Canada, Brian Harrigan
Controller, Ukeme Falade
Country Representative Angola, Charles Christian Isely
Country Representative Benin and Cote d?Ivoire, Josette Vignon
Country Representative Burkina Faso, Ahmed Moussa N?Game
Country Representative Chad, Abraham Usman
Country Representative Democratic Republic of Congo, Francis Hammond
Country Representative Ghana, Kwasi Ampofo
Country Representative Liberia, Chris Seubert
Country Representative Malawi, Joshua Karuma
Country Representative Mali, Edward Baxter
Country Representative Mozambique, Collin A. Elias
Country Representative Niger, Anthony Angosi
Country Representative Nigeria, Maisha Strozier
Country Representative Rwanda, Willis E. Obura
Senior Country Representative Senegal, Al-Hassana Outman
Country Representative Sierra Leone, Vicki Johnson
Chief of Party South Africa, Joan Littlefield
Country Representative Uganda, Hyghten Mungoni
Country Representative Zambia, Gordon K. Brown
Officer-in-Charge Zimbabwe, Paul P. Chimedza
Country Representative Burundi, James Bariyanga
Honorary Chairman, Nelson R. Mandela
Honorary Vice Chair, Maria Walker
Director, Alexander B. (Alex) Cummings Jr., age 55
Director, Louis W. Sullivan, age 77
Chairman, W. Frank Fountain Jr., age 67
Director, Rodney E. Slater, age 57
Director, Howard F. Jeter, age 64
Director, Curtin Winsor Jr., age 72
Vice Chair, Larry D. Bailey
Secretary and Director, Joseph C. Kennedy
Director, Lauretta J. Bruno
Director, Stephen D. Cashin
Director, Alice M. Dear
Director, George W. Haley
Director, William O. Kirker
Director, Zouera G. Youssoufou
Director, William H. (Bill) Frist, age 60
Honorary Vice Chair, Maria Walker
Director, Alan Detheridge
Director, Mosina H. Jordan
Director, C. Payne Lucas Sr.
Director, F. Euclid Walker

LOCATIONS

HQ: Africare
440 R St. NW, Washington DC 20001-1935
Phone: 202-462-3614   **Fax:** 202-387-1034
Web: www.africare.org

HISTORICAL FINANCIALS
Company Type: Private - Not-for-Profit

Income Statement
FYE: June 30

	REVENUE ($ mil.)	NET INCOME ($ mil.)	NET PROFIT MARGIN	EMPLOYEES
06/11	76	0	1.1%	1,000
06/10	54	(1)	—	0
06/08	46	(1)	—	0
06/06	59	10	17.5%	0
Annual Growth	8.9%	(57.0%)	—	—

2011 Year-End Financials

Debt ratio: ——
Return on equity: 1.10%
Cash ($ mil.): 32
Current ratio: —
Long-term debt ($ mil.): —

Dividends
Yield: —
Payout: —
Market value ($ mil.): —

AGILEX TECHNOLOGIES INC.

LOCATIONS

HQ: AGILEX TECHNOLOGIES INC.
5155 PARKSTONE DR, CHANTILLY, VA 20151-3812
Phone: 888-324-4539
Web: www.customerchemistry.com

HISTORICAL FINANCIALS
Company Type: Private

Income Statement
FYE: December 31

	REVENUE ($ mil.)	NET INCOME ($ mil.)	NET PROFIT MARGIN	EMPLOYEES
12/11	85	5	7.0%	475
12/10	63	4	7.6%	0
12/09	37	0	1.5%	0
12/08	20	(4)	—	0
Annual Growth	60.7%	—	—	—

AGMARK LLC

LOCATIONS

HQ: AGMARK LLC
204 E COURT ST, BELOIT, KS 67420-3242
Phone: 785-738-9641
Web: www.agmarkllc.com

HISTORICAL FINANCIALS

Company Type: Private

Income Statement

FYE: January 31

	REVENUE ($ mil.)	NET INCOME ($ mil.)	NET PROFIT MARGIN	EMPLOYEES
01/12	489	25	5.2%	25
01/10	329	10	3.2%	0
Annual Growth	48.5%	142.9%	—	—

2012 Year-End Financials

Debt ratio: ——
Return on equity: 5.20%
Cash ($ mil.): 1
Current ratio: ——
Long-term debt ($ mil.): —

Dividends
Yield: —
Payout: —
Market value ($ mil.): —

AGNES SCOTT COLLEGE INC.

Great Scott Agnes it's a liberal arts college for women! Agnes Scott College (ASC) offers bachelor of arts degrees in 33 majors and 27 minors with pre-law and pre-medicine programs and dual degree programs in architecture engineering and nursing as well as post-baccalaureate programs. The school also grants master of arts in teaching degrees in English biology chemistry physics and mathematics. Enrollment in 2008 was about 850 students. Founded in 1889 ASC is affiliated with the Presbyterian Church and has an endowment of about $300 million. Tuition fees room and board cost $39000 per year. The 100-acre campus rated one of the most beautiful in the country is in Decatur Georgia.

ACS President Elizabeth Kiss (pronounced "quiche") was appointed in 2006. Prominent alumnae include Pulitzer Prize-winning playwright Marsha Norman; Katherine Krill CEO of Ann Taylor Stores; and Grammy Award winning musician Jennifer Nettles.

EXECUTIVES

Chair, Harriet M. King
VP Academic Affairs and Dean College, Rosemary Levy Zumwalt
VP Business and Finance, John P. Hegman
Director Information Technology, LaNeta Counts
Registrar, Nancy C. Albert
Director Assessment, Laura Palucki Blake
Director International Education, Jennifer A. Lund
Director Athletics, Joeleen Akin
Controller, Lai Chan
Director Human Resources, Karen Gilbert
VP Student Life and Dean of Students, Donna A. Lee
President, Elizabeth Kiss
Secretary and Trustee, Lea Ann Grimes Hudson
Director Public Safety, Henry Hope
Dean Admission and Associate VP Enrollment Management, Stephanie S. Balmer
Interim Director Communications, Jennifer Bryon Owen
Director Alumnae Relations, Kimberly A. Vickers
Interim VP Institutional Advancement and Director Development, Amy F. Nash
Director Library Services, Elizabeth Bagley

Trustee, Dennis P. Lockhart, age 63
Trustee, Clyde C. Tuggle, age 49
Trustee, Gay O. Abbott
Trustee, Lawrence L. (Larry) Gellerstedt III, age 56
Trustee, Kathy Blee Ashe
Trustee, Mary G. Bankston
Trustee, David D. Weitnauer
Trustee, Linda Kay McGowan
Trustee, Elizabeth D. Holder
Secretary and Trustee, Lea Ann Grimes Hudson
Trustee, Pamela J. Bevier
Trustee, Robert L. Brown Jr.
Trustee, Mary T. Carr
Trustee, John W. Drake
Trustee, Suzanne C. Feese
Trustee, Barbara B. Gaines
Trustee, Audrey L. Grant
Trustee, Sandra Thome Johnson
Trustee, Elizabeth Rhett Jones
Trustee, Nancy Moore Kuykendall
Trustee, Jeanne Kaufmann Manning
Trustee, Phil Noble Jr.
Trustee, Marsha Norman
Trustee, Mildred Love Petty
Trustee, B. Clayton Rolader
Trustee, Susan E. Gamble Smathers
Trustee, Bolling P. Spalding
Trustee, O. Benjamin Sparks
Trustee, David L. Warren
Trustee, Robert C. Williams

LOCATIONS

HQ: Agnes Scott College
141 E. College Ave., Decatur GA 30030
Phone: 404-471-6000   **Fax:** 404-471-6414
Web: www.agnesscott.edu

HISTORICAL FINANCIALS

Company Type: School

Income Statement

FYE: June 30

	REVENUE ($ mil.)	NET INCOME ($ mil.)	NET PROFIT MARGIN	EMPLOYEES
06/11	62	(3)	—	350
06/10	51	5	9.8%	0
06/09	0	0	—	0
06/08	18	(25)	—	0
Annual Growth	49.9%	—	—	—

2011 Year-End Financials

Debt ratio: ——
Return on equity: (-5.80)%
Cash ($ mil.): 12
Current ratio: ——
Long-term debt ($ mil.): —

Dividends
Yield: —
Payout: —
Market value ($ mil.): —

AGNESIAN HEALTHCARE INC.

LOCATIONS

HQ: AGNESIAN HEALTHCARE INC.
430 E DIVISION ST, FOND DU LAC, WI 54935-4560
Phone: 920-929-2300
Web: www.agnesian.com

HISTORICAL FINANCIALS

Company Type: Private

Income Statement

FYE: June 30

	REVENUE ($ mil.)	NET INCOME ($ mil.)	NET PROFIT MARGIN	EMPLOYEES
06/11	311	23	7.7%	6
06/10	281	11	4.0%	0
06/09	276	0	—	0
06/08	265	6	2.6%	0
Annual Growth	5.5%	51.7%	—	—

2011 Year-End Financials

Debt ratio: ——
Return on equity: 7.70%
Cash ($ mil.): 31
Current ratio: 0.40
Long-term debt ($ mil.): —

Dividends
Yield: —
Payout: —
Market value ($ mil.): —

AGRI SERVICES OF BRUNSWICK LLC

LOCATIONS

HQ: AGRI SERVICES OF BRUNSWICK LLC
HWY 24 W, BRUNSWICK, MO 65236
Phone: 660-549-3351
Web: www.agriservices.com

HISTORICAL FINANCIALS

Company Type: Private

Income Statement

FYE: August 31

	REVENUE ($ mil.)	NET INCOME ($ mil.)	NET PROFIT MARGIN	EMPLOYEES
08/12	196	3	1.6%	50
08/11	170	5	3.2%	0
08/10	121	1	1.1%	0
08/09	101	(23)	—	0
Annual Growth	24.7%	—	—	—

2012 Year-End Financials

Debt ratio: ——
Return on equity: 1.60%
Cash ($ mil.): 1
Current ratio: 0.50
Long-term debt ($ mil.): —

Dividends
Yield: —
Payout: —
Market value ($ mil.): —

AGRI-AFC LLC

LOCATIONS

HQ: AGRI-AFC LLC
121 SOMERVILLE RD NE B, DECATUR, AL 35601-2659
Phone: 256-560-2848
Web: www.agri-afc.com

HISTORICAL FINANCIALS
Company Type: Private

Income Statement
FYE: July 31

	REVENUE ($ mil.)	NET INCOME ($ mil.)	NET PROFIT MARGIN	EMPLOYEES
07/12	312	6	2.0%	165
07/11	281	8	2.9%	0
07/10	224	6	2.7%	0
07/08	193	10	5.2%	0
Annual Growth	17.3%	(15.3%)	—	—

2012 Year-End Financials

Debt ratio: ——
Return on equity: 2.00%
Cash ($ mil.): 2
Current ratio: 0.70
Long-term debt ($ mil.): —

Dividends
Yield: —
Payout: —
Market value ($ mil.): —

AIKEN ELECTRIC COOPERATIVE INC.

LOCATIONS

HQ: AIKEN ELECTRIC COOPERATIVE INC.
2790 WAGENER RD, AIKEN, SC 29801-8126
Phone: 803-649-6245
Web: www.aikenco-op.org

HISTORICAL FINANCIALS
Company Type: Private

Income Statement
FYE: May 31

	REVENUE ($ mil.)	NET INCOME ($ mil.)	NET PROFIT MARGIN	EMPLOYEES
05/12	102	0	0.9%	140
05/11	105	0	0.6%	0
05/10*	102	4	4.7%	0
12/09	98	1	2.0%	0
Annual Growth	1.6%	(22.2%)	—	—

*Fiscal year change

2012 Year-End Financials

Debt ratio: ——
Return on equity: 0.90%
Cash ($ mil.): 8
Current ratio: 0.60
Long-term debt ($ mil.): —

Dividends
Yield: —
Payout: —
Market value ($ mil.): —

AIR SERV CORPORATION

Airlines hire Air Serv to provide the ground-based services that help passengers and cargo take to the skies. Its offerings include cargo handling ground transportation passenger services (such as baggage handling ticket verification and electric cart drivers) and ramp services. Air Serv operates at more than two dozen airports throughout the US; the company also does business in the UK. Customers have included Delta Air Lines FedEx and United Continental's United Airlines. The com-

pany's Texas-based International RAM Associates (IRAM) unit performs aviation security at about 50 airports since 2009.

In 2010 IRAM along with ARINC Cogent and Flo Corporation developed iQueue a program to pre-approve travelers at airport security check-points around the country.

Chairman Frank Argenbright founder of Argenbright Security started Air Serv in 2002.

EXECUTIVES

CEO and Director, Thomas J. (Tom) Marano
Founder and Chairman, Frank A. Argenbright Jr.
SVP Operations, Douglas Kreuzkamp
Senior Vice President Environment Safety, John Montgomery
Director Finance and Business Planning, Toan Nguyen
SVP, Don Ridgway
VP Transportation, Edwin Smith
Regional Manager Atlanta, Leon Scott
Regional Manager Lexington, Paul DeBellevue
Regional Manager Dallas, John Gonzales
Regional Manager Washington D.C. and Dulles, Steve Wragg
EVP Operations Planning and Performance, Michael B. (Mike) Lewis
Regional Manager Boston, Derrick Small
Regional Manager Los Angeles, Heidi Harper
Regional Manager Memphis, Gregory Weathers
Regional Manager Bozeman, Nick Vitali
Regional Manager Manchester England, Mohammed Khan
Regional Manager Cincinnati, Mike Ostendorf
VP Passenger Service, Mike Hough
Director People Development, Teddy Gil
Chief Compliance Officer and General Counsel, Megan Jones
CFO and Director, David L. Gamsey
Managing Director UK, Ian Thornley
President, Shannon Conklin
Director of Human Resources, Suzanne Fountain
Director, Donald J. (Don) Carty Jr., age 65
CEO and Director, Thomas J. (Tom) Marano
Director, Daniel K. Doyle
Director, William L. McMahon
CFO and Director, David L. Gamsey

LOCATIONS

HQ: Air Serv Corporation
3399 Peachtree Rd. NE Ste. 1800, Atlanta GA 30326
Phone: 404-926-4200   **Fax:** 404-267-2230
Web: www.airservcorp.com

Selected Locations
US
  Los Angeles CA
  Oakland CA
  San Francisco CA
  Denver CO
  Washington DC
  Orlando FL
  Tampa FL
  Atlanta GA
  Cedar Rapids IA
  Chicago IL
  Moline IL
  Lexington KY
  Louisville KY
  Boston MA
  Bozeman MT
  Newark NJ
  Cincinnati OH
  Reno NV
  Dallas TX
  Memphis TN
  Salt Lake City UT
  Seattle WA
UK

Manchester England

PRODUCTS/OPERATIONS

Selected Services
Cargo handling
  Cargo transfer
  Document control
Cleaning
  Aviation janitorial services
  Commercial janitoral services
  LAV/Water services (service aircraft lavatories)
Ground transportation
  Airport shuttle
  Employee shuttle
  Crew transport
  Fixed route
  Paratransit
Passenger services
  Skycap
  Baggage handling
  Ticket verification
  Wheelchair service
  Lobby management
  Customer service
  Unaccompanied minor
  TWOV service
  Electric cart drivers
  Door guarding
Ramp services
  Cabin cleaning
  LAV/water service
  GSE maintenance
  Ground handling
  Ramp screening
Security
  Avation security (screen employees for prohibited items prior to entering an aircraft and aircraft for potentially threatening items)
  Commercial security (for commercial and residential high rises warehouses industrial areas)
  Pre-departure screening
  Cargo screening

COMPETITORS

ASIG
AvStar Aviation
Evergreen Aviation Ground Logistics Enterprise
ICTS International
Menzies Aviation
Mercury Air Group
PrimeFlight
Servisair
Swissport
Swissport USA Inc.
WFS

HISTORICAL FINANCIALS
Company Type: Private

Income Statement
FYE: June 30

	REVENUE ($ mil.)	NET INCOME ($ mil.)	NET PROFIT MARGIN	EMPLOYEES
06/12	298	1	0.6%	9,000
Annual Growth	—	—	—	—

2012 Year-End Financials

Debt ratio: ——
Return on equity: 0.60%
Cash ($ mil.): 1
Current ratio: 1.00
Long-term debt ($ mil.): —

Dividends
Yield: —
Payout: —
Market value ($ mil.): —

AIREKO CONSTRUCTION CORP

LOCATIONS

HQ: AIREKO CONSTRUCTION CORP
LAS CASAS 20 VILLA BLANCA ST LAS CAS, CAGUAS,
PR 00725
Phone: 787-653-6300
Web: www.aireko.com

HISTORICAL FINANCIALS

Company Type: Private

Income Statement

	REVENUE ($ mil.)	NET INCOME ($ mil.)	NET PROFIT MARGIN	EMPLOYEES
03/12	96	4	4.6%	450
03/06	0	0	—	0
03/03	87	4	4.7%	0
03/02	926	0	—	0
Annual Growth	(52.9%)	8120.7%		

FYE: March 31

2012 Year-End Financials

Debt ratio: ——
Return on equity: 4.60%
Cash ($ mil.): 10
Current ratio: 0.40
Long-term debt ($ mil.): —

Dividends
Yield: —
Payout: —
Market value ($ mil.): —

AKRON SERVICES INC.

LOCATIONS

HQ: AKRON SERVICES INC.
17705 N ELEVATOR RD, EDELSTEIN, IL 61526-9716
Phone: 309-249-2700
Web: www.akronservices.com

HISTORICAL FINANCIALS

Company Type: Private

Income Statement

	REVENUE ($ mil.)	NET INCOME ($ mil.)	NET PROFIT MARGIN	EMPLOYEES
07/12	160	0	0.3%	30
07/11	121	0	0.2%	0
07/10	84	0	0.3%	0
07/09	104	0	0.4%	0
Annual Growth	15.3%	10.3%	—	—

FYE: July 31

2012 Year-End Financials

Debt ratio: ——
Return on equity: 0.30%
Cash ($ mil.): 1
Current ratio: 0.20
Long-term debt ($ mil.): —

Dividends
Yield: —
Payout: —
Market value ($ mil.): —

ALACARE HOME HEALTH SERVICES INC.

LOCATIONS

HQ: ALACARE HOME HEALTH SERVICES INC.
2400 JOHN HAWKINS PKWY, HOOVER, AL
35244-3500
Phone: 205-981-8000

HISTORICAL FINANCIALS

Company Type: Private

Income Statement

	REVENUE ($ mil.)	NET INCOME ($ mil.)	NET PROFIT MARGIN	EMPLOYEES
12/11	95	11	12.1%	935
12/10	96	14	14.8%	0
12/09	89	13	15.4%	0
12/08	82	9	11.6%	0
Annual Growth	4.8%	6.5%	—	—

FYE: December 31

2011 Year-End Financials

Debt ratio: ——
Return on equity: 12.10%
Cash ($ mil.): 5
Current ratio: 1.10
Long-term debt ($ mil.): —

Dividends
Yield: —
Payout: —
Market value ($ mil.): —

ALASKA NATIVE TRIBAL HEALTH CONSORTIUM

The Alaska Native Tribal Health Consortium (ANTHC) is a not-for-profit statewide health care organization of Alaska Native tribal governments and regional health organizations (also known as RHIOs) that connect disparate health providers. The 2000-strong organization provides a range of health programs and services including public health advocacy and education initiatives health research (including water and sanitation) community health care and medical supply distribution. The Alaska Native Medical Center a native-owned hospital is jointly managed by ANTHC and Southcentral Foundation a regional health corporation based in the Cook Inlet region.

ANTHC provides administrative support to Alaska's Tribal health groups and it supports state legislative efforts such as the reauthorization of the Indian Health Care Improvement Act. The consortium formed in 1997 also works to improve the Alaskan health system by participating in strategic summit meetings and sponsoring electronic health record initiatives. The ANTHC's primary goal is to create a continuum of care for its members so they can move smoothly through the health care process from their first visit to any specialist referrals and follow-ups after discharge. The hospital is the regional hub of that health care continuum offering treatment for most ailments and many specialists even way up in Alaska.

The medical center's services are reserved primarily for Alaska Native Tribal groups with the exception of its Urgent Care centers and Emergency Room. (Emergency rooms throughout the US are compelled to take patients of all types under a rule called EMTALA meant to keep health care fair especially in the case of those who are uninsured.)

In 2010 the medical center opened the only Level II trauma center in Alaska meaning it is certified to treat major traumas and can serve as a referral hospital for such injuries. Also have a such a trauma center can reduce trauma deaths by 25%-30%. The group also launched a website to help teens make healthy lifestyle choices (such as smoking cessation programs which have led to a 30% drop in teen smoking over the past decade or so) and published a paper on the near-eradication of hepatitis A in Alaska - which may not sound like huge news until you hear that Alaska Natives' rates of the disease went from the worst in the US to the best in 2010.

The consortium also grew its Behavioral Health sector - especially with regard to addressing the growing problem of methamphetamine use among area residents and the increasing occurrence of suicides (ANTHC helped more than 560 suicidal patients in 2010 alone).

ANTHC also has one of the largest telemedicine networks in the world - about 20000 telehealth cases were created in 2010 a 25% increase compared to the previous year. Among the growing number of systems worldwide AFHCAN equipped three major Indian Health Service medical centers with telehealth systems that allow providers to care for and consult with patients in outlying areas. Telemedicine is becoming an increasingly popular way for specialists to see patients without the expense related to luring them outlying areas that may not have the most advanced technologies or that many procedures for them to perform (both huge factors in physician satisfaction rates).

EXECUTIVES

CEO and Director, Don Kashevaroff
Administrator, Daniel E. (Dan) Jessop
Vice Chair, Lincoln A. Bean Sr.
Director Public Relations and Communications, Joaqlin Estus
Chairman and President, Ray Alstrom
Director Operations, Vivian Echavarria
COO, Susan Childers
CEO and Director, Don Kashevaroff
Director, Robert J. Henrichs
Director, Andrew (Andy) Jimmie, age 76
Director, Evelyn Beeter
Director, Mike Zacharof
Director, H. Sally Smith
Director, Linda Clement
Director, Emily Hughes
Director, Katherine Gottlieb
Vice Chair, Lincoln A. Bean Sr.
Director, Frederica Schaeffer
Director, Bernice Kaigelak
Director, Charlene Nollner
Director, Andrew (Andy) Teuber

LOCATIONS

HQ: Alaska Native Tribal Health Consortium
4000 Ambassador Dr., Anchorage AK 99508
Phone: 907-729-1900   **Fax:** 907-729-1901
Web: www.anthc.org

COMPETITORS

HCA
Immediate Care
PeaceHealth
Providence Health
& Services

South Peninsula
Hospital
Tenet Healthcare

HISTORICAL FINANCIALS
Company Type: Private - Not-for-Profit

Income Statement
FYE: September 30

	REVENUE ($ mil.)	NET INCOME ($ mil.)	NET PROFIT MARGIN	EMPLOYEES
09/11	427	24	5.8%	1,850
09/10	414	28	6.8%	0
09/09	348	14	4.2%	0
09/08	342	10	3.0%	0
Annual Growth	7.7%	33.2%	—	—

2011 Year-End Financials
Debt ratio: —
Return on equity: 5.80%
Cash ($ mil.): 172
Current ratio: 3.20
Long-term debt ($ mil.): —
Dividends
Yield: —
Payout: —
Market value ($ mil.): —

ALASKA PERMANENT FUND CORPORATION

LOCATIONS
HQ: ALASKA PERMANENT FUND CORPORATION
801 W 10TH ST STE 302, JUNEAU, AK 99801-1878
Phone: 907-796-1500
Web: www.apfc.org

HISTORICAL FINANCIALS
Company Type: Private

Income Statement
FYE: June 30

	ASSETS ($ mil.)	NET INCOME ($ mil.)	INCOME AS % OF ASSETS	EMPLOYEES
06/12	45,043	192	0.4%	36
06/11	45,240	6,885	15.2%	0
06/10	37,052	3,338	9.0%	0
06/09	34,433	0	—	0
Annual Growth	9.4%	—	—	—

2012 Year-End Financials
Debt ratio: —
Return on equity: 19.50%
Cash ($ mil.): 1,995
Current ratio: —
Long-term debt ($ mil.): —
Dividends
Yield: —
Payout: —
Market value ($ mil.): —

ALBANY COLLEGE OF PHARMACY AND HEALTH SCIENCES

Students with a prescription for medical and pharmaceutical training get their fill at Albany College of Pharmacy and Health Sciences (ACPHS). The college offers health care degree programs including pharmacy pre-med clinical laboratory sciences cytotechnology and biomedical technology. The school also is home to the Pharmaceutical Research Institute and Center for NanoPhamaceuticals which focuses on drug discovery and development. A satellite campus in Vermont offers doctor of pharmacy degrees. ACPHS enrolls more than 1500 students and was founded in 1881. The school changed its name to include "Health Sciences" in 2008. The change was made to better reflect the school's range of offerings.

EXECUTIVES
President, James J. Gozzo
Director Library Services, Susan (Sue) Iwanowicz
EVP and Chairman Pharmaceutical Research Institute, Shaker A. Mousa
VP Finance and Administrative Operations, Robert J. Gould
VP Institutional Advancement, Vicki A. DiLorenzo
Director of College Publications, Christine Shields
Dean, Mehdi Boroujerdi
Director Cytotechnology Program, Indra Balachandran
Director Experiential Education, Laurie L. Briceland
Director Annual Programs, Shelly A. Calabrese
Director Admissions, Carly T. Connors
Director Physical Plant, Thomas Della Rocca
General Counsel, Gerald H. Katzman
VP Enrollment Management, Tiffany M. Gutierrez
Human Resources Manager, Heather Landry
Director Information Systems, Mark Mafilios
Director Technology, Scott Rogler
Registrar, Judith A. Schmonsky
Comptroller, Michele Vien
Assistant VP Institutional Advancement, David Zdunczyk
Executive Director Marketing and Communications, Gil Chorbajian

LOCATIONS
HQ: Albany College of Pharmacy and Health Sciences
106 New Scotland Ave., Albany NY 12208-3492
Phone: 518-445-7200   **Fax:** 518-445-7202
Web: www.acphs.edu

HISTORICAL FINANCIALS
Company Type: School

Income Statement
FYE: June 30

	REVENUE ($ mil.)	NET INCOME ($ mil.)	NET PROFIT MARGIN	EMPLOYEES
06/11	53	5	11.3%	110
06/10	50	9	18.8%	0
06/09	43	0	—	0
06/08	40	8	20.7%	0
Annual Growth	9.7%	(10.4%)	—	—

2011 Year-End Financials
Debt ratio: —
Return on equity: 11.30%
Cash ($ mil.): 20
Current ratio: —
Long-term debt ($ mil.): —
Dividends
Yield: —
Payout: —
Market value ($ mil.): —

ALBANY INDUSTRIES INC.

LOCATIONS
HQ: ALBANY INDUSTRIES INC.
504 N GLENFIELD RD, NEW ALBANY, MS 38652-2214
Phone: 662-534-9800
Web: www.albanyindustries.com

HISTORICAL FINANCIALS
Company Type: Private

Income Statement
FYE: December 31

	REVENUE ($ mil.)	NET INCOME ($ mil.)	NET PROFIT MARGIN	EMPLOYEES
12/11	96	5	5.4%	485
12/10	81	4	5.2%	0
12/09	90	10	11.3%	0
12/08	106	8	7.6%	0
Annual Growth	(3.4%)	(13.7%)	—	—

2011 Year-End Financials
Debt ratio: —
Return on equity: 5.40%
Cash ($ mil.): 0
Current ratio: 0.80
Long-term debt ($ mil.): —
Dividends
Yield: —
Payout: —
Market value ($ mil.): —

ALBERICI CONSTRUCTORS INC.

LOCATIONS
HQ: ALBERICI CONSTRUCTORS INC.
8800 PAGE AVE, SAINT LOUIS, MO 63114-6106
Phone: 314-733-2000
Web: www.alberici.com

HISTORICAL FINANCIALS
Company Type: Private

Income Statement
FYE: December 31

	REVENUE ($ mil.)	NET INCOME ($ mil.)	NET PROFIT MARGIN	EMPLOYEES
12/11	543	0	—	2,000
12/10	551	0	—	0
12/09	619	0	—	0
12/08	0	0	—	0
Annual Growth	—	—	—	—

2011 Year-End Financials
Debt ratio: —
Return on equity: —
Cash ($ mil.): 84
Current ratio: 0.90
Long-term debt ($ mil.): —
Dividends
Yield: —
Payout: —
Market value ($ mil.): —

ALBERICI GROUP INC.

LOCATIONS

HQ: ALBERICI GROUP INC.
8800 PAGE AVE, SAINT LOUIS, MO 63114-6106
Phone: 314-733-2000
Web: www.albericigroup.com

HISTORICAL FINANCIALS

Company Type: Private

Income Statement
FYE: December 31

	REVENUE ($ mil.)	NET INCOME ($ mil.)	NET PROFIT MARGIN	EMPLOYEES
12/11	565	0	—	2,000
12/10	565	0	—	0
12/09	0	0	—	0
12/08	0	0	—	0
Annual Growth	—	—	—	—

2011 Year-End Financials

Debt ratio: —
Return on equity: —
Cash ($ mil.): 99
Current ratio: 1.00
Long-term debt ($ mil.): —

Dividends
Yield: —
Payout: —
Market value ($ mil.): —

ALBERT C. KOBAYASHI INC.

LOCATIONS

HQ: ALBERT C. KOBAYASHI INC.
94-535 UKEE ST STE 101, WAIPAHU, HI 96797-4275
Phone: 808-671-6460
Web: www.ack-inc.com

HISTORICAL FINANCIALS

Company Type: Private

Income Statement
FYE: July 31

	REVENUE ($ mil.)	NET INCOME ($ mil.)	NET PROFIT MARGIN	EMPLOYEES
07/12	195	3	1.8%	115
07/11	122	3	3.2%	0
07/10	64	1	2.5%	0
07/09	213	3	1.5%	0
Annual Growth	(2.9%)	5.2%	—	—

2012 Year-End Financials

Debt ratio: ——
Return on equity: 1.80%
Cash ($ mil.): 47
Current ratio: 0.70
Long-term debt ($ mil.): —

Dividends
Yield: —
Payout: —
Market value ($ mil.): —

ALBERT EINSTEIN MEDICAL CENTER

LOCATIONS

HQ: ALBERT EINSTEIN MEDICAL CENTER
5501 OLD YORK RD STE 1, PHILADELPHIA, PA 19141-3098
Phone: 215-456-8710
Web: www.alberteinsteinmedicalcenter.com

HISTORICAL FINANCIALS

Company Type: Private

Income Statement
FYE: June 30

	REVENUE ($ mil.)	NET INCOME ($ mil.)	NET PROFIT MARGIN	EMPLOYEES
06/11	744	52	7.1%	0
06/10	713	(38)	—	0
06/09	635	23	3.7%	0
06/01	345	14	4.2%	0
Annual Growth	29.2%	54.1%		—

2011 Year-End Financials

Debt ratio: ——
Return on equity: 7.10%
Cash ($ mil.): 13
Current ratio: 0.30
Long-term debt ($ mil.): —

Dividends
Yield: —
Payout: —
Market value ($ mil.): —

ALBERT S. SMYTH CO. INC.

LOCATIONS

HQ: ALBERT S. SMYTH CO. INC.
2020 YORK RD, LUTHERVILLE TIMONIUM, MD 21093-4244
Phone: 410-252-6666
Web: www.smythjewelers.com

HISTORICAL FINANCIALS

Company Type: Private

Income Statement
FYE: December 31

	REVENUE ($ mil.)	NET INCOME ($ mil.)	NET PROFIT MARGIN	EMPLOYEES
12/11	93	3	4.1%	189
12/09	46	0	1.7%	0
12/08	43	0	0.8%	0
12/07	46	0	1.4%	0
Annual Growth	26.4%	82.5%	—	—

2011 Year-End Financials

Debt ratio: ——
Return on equity: 4.10%
Cash ($ mil.): 0
Current ratio: —
Long-term debt ($ mil.): —

Dividends
Yield: —
Payout: —
Market value ($ mil.): —

ALBION COLLEGE

Albion College is a private co-educational liberal arts college in Michigan associated with the Methodist church. The college offers Bachelor of Arts in about 30 subjects and Bachelor of Fine Arts degrees in art and art history. It employs some 130 full-time faculty members and has an enrollment of almost 2000. Albion can trace its roots to 1835 when early Methodist settlers of the Michigan Territory worked to get the college a charter from the Michigan Territorial Legislature. Notable alumni include chairman and editor-in-chief of Newsweek magazine Richard Smith and Broadway producer Michael David founder of Dodger Theatricals.

EXECUTIVES

Associate VP Communications, Sarah F. Briggs
VP Student Affairs and Dean Students, Sally J. Walker
EVP, Troy D. VanAken
President, Donna M. Randall
Director Media Relations, Morris J. Arvoy
Manager Accounting, Thomas W. Pitt
Assistant Dean Community Standards and Director Campus Safety, Kenneth E. Snyder
Associate VP Facilities Operations, Kenneth E. Kolmodin
VP Academic Affairs and Dean Faculty, Royal A. Ward
Director Corporate and Foundation Relations, Barbara L. Rafaill
Associate VP Information Services and CIO, Scott W. Stephen
Interim VP Enrollment, M. Doug Kellar
Director Human Resources, Lisa A. Locke
Manager Purchasing, Susan L. Clark
Controller, Mark S. Holbrook
Associate Dean Academic Affairs and Registrar, Andrew M. Dunham
Associate Director Admission and Financial Aid, Amanda M. Dubiel
Associate Director Alumni and Parent Relations, Stacey L. Markin

LOCATIONS

HQ: Albion College
611 E. Porter St., Albion MI 49224
Phone: 517-629-1000   **Fax:** 517-629-0214
Web: www.albion.edu

COMPETITORS

Alma College
Michigan State

University of Detroit Mercy

HISTORICAL FINANCIALS

Company Type: School

Income Statement
FYE: June 30

	REVENUE ($ mil.)	NET INCOME ($ mil.)	NET PROFIT MARGIN	EMPLOYEES
06/12	49	(15)	—	600
06/11	50	32	63.5%	0
06/10	45	(7)	—	0
06/09	52	(58)	—	0
Annual Growth	(1.6%)	—	—	—

2012 Year-End Financials

Debt ratio: ——
Return on equity: (-30.10)%
Cash ($ mil.): 5
Current ratio: ——
Long-term debt ($ mil.): ——

Dividends
  Yield: ——
  Payout: ——
  Market value ($ mil.): ——

ALDRIDGE ELECTRIC INC

Aldridge Electric powers up the Windy City and other parts of the Midwest. The electrical contractor divides its business into six main areas: airport industrial power drilling highway and transit. It works on projects ranging from Chicago's subway system to its airport runways. Additional activities include services for street lighting traffic signals high-voltage cabling and splicing and foundation drilling. Aldridge Electric has worked for clients such as Commonwealth Edison Company and Exelon Corporation. The company is owned by CEO Ken Aldridge grandson of company founder Leonard "Len" Aldridge who started the business in the 1930s and incorporated it in 1952.

Aldridge Electric was the general contractor and subcontractor of choice for the multi-million dollar O'Hare Modernization Program (OMP) intended to reduce delays and improve efficiency at the Chicago international airport. Aldridge completed several OMP contracts involving the construction extension and relocation of several runways in addition to the installation of taxiway lights and navigational equipment.

Aldridge's drilling division has enjoyed a robust backlog due to the growing demand in the wind energy market. The division has worked to drill foundations for wind turbines and transmission lines that criss cross the US.

EXECUTIVES

CEO, Kenneth W. (Ken) Aldridge
President, Stephen E. (Steve) Rivi
VP Business Development, Tom McLinden
EVP Transit, Warren Aldridge
EVP and Division Manager Drilling Highway and Telecom, Ed Kutschke
Division Manager National Power, Wayne Gearig

LOCATIONS

HQ: Aldridge Electric Inc.
844 E. Rockland Rd., Libertyville IL 60048
Phone: 847-680-5200 **Fax:** 847-680-5298
Web: www.aldridge-electric.com

PRODUCTS/OPERATIONS

Selected Divisions and Services
Airport
  Approach lighting systems
  Control system
  Electrical vaults
  Hangar facility electrical
  High-voltage cable pulling splicing and terminating
  Hold pad perimeter lighting and limit lighting
  Parking lot lighting
  Parking structure rehabilitation
  Runway and taxiway lighting
  Site utility work
  Terminal rehabilitation work
  Traffic management and control
Drilling
  Bridge foundations
  Building structure foundations

  Communication tower foundations
  Drilled shafts for sewer lift stations
  Drilling for earth-retention systems
  High-mast lighting tower foundations
  Sign foundations
  Transmission line foundations
Highway
  Closed-loop detection
  High-mast lighting
  Highway lighting
  Intelligent transportation systems
  Lighting systems design/build
  Municipal street lighting
  RTMS detection systems
  Subdivision street lighting
  Surveillance camera systems
  Surveillance systems
  Traffic interconnect systems
  Traffic signal systems
  Variable message signs
Industrial
  Design/build capabilities
  Electrical maintenance and renovations
  Electrical power distribution and lighting for new construction and existing facilities
  Energy conservation upgrades and retrofits
  Fire alarm and security
  Movable bridge power lighting and control systems
  Process control systems
  Supervisory control and data acquisition systems
  Tenant build-out
  Voice data communication systems and CCTV
Power
  Design/build
  Fiber optic cabling
  Interconnect yard construction
  Project management
  Overhead elecrical construction
  Substation construction
  Solar panal installation
  Turbine wiring
  Underground electrical construction
Transit
  Catenary systems
  Communications systems
  Traction power 3rd rail systems
  Train control

COMPETITORS

Bayview Electric Company	Integrated Electrical Services
EEI	Kelso-Burnett
EMCOR	Mass Electric
Faith Technologies	Motor City Electric

HISTORICAL FINANCIALS
Company Type: Private

Income Statement
FYE: March 31

	REVENUE ($ mil.)	NET INCOME ($ mil.)	NET PROFIT MARGIN	EMPLOYEES
03/11	208	2	1.0%	500
03/10	272	10	3.8%	0
Annual Growth	(23.2%)	(79.8%)	—	—

2011 Year-End Financials

Debt ratio: ——
Return on equity: 1.00%
Cash ($ mil.): 12
Current ratio: 1.50
Long-term debt ($ mil.): ——

Dividends
  Yield: ——
  Payout: ——
  Market value ($ mil.): ——

ALEGENT HEALTH - IMMANUEL MEDICAL CENTER

LOCATIONS

HQ: ALEGENT HEALTH - IMMANUEL MEDICAL CENTER
6901 N 72ND ST, OMAHA, NE 68122-1709
Phone: 402-572-2121
Web: www.alegent.com

HISTORICAL FINANCIALS
Company Type: Private

Income Statement
FYE: June 30

	REVENUE ($ mil.)	NET INCOME ($ mil.)	NET PROFIT MARGIN	EMPLOYEES
06/11	288	39	13.8%	2,313
06/10	279	9	3.5%	0
06/09	272	16	5.9%	0
06/08	281	44	15.9%	0
Annual Growth	0.9%	(3.7%)	—	—

2011 Year-End Financials

Debt ratio: ——
Return on equity: 13.80%
Cash ($ mil.): 50
Current ratio: 0.50
Long-term debt ($ mil.): ——

Dividends
  Yield: ——
  Payout: ——
  Market value ($ mil.): ——

ALEUT MANAGEMENT SERVICES LLC

LOCATIONS

HQ: ALEUT MANAGEMENT SERVICES LLC
5520 TECH CENTER DR # 200, COLORADO SPRINGS, CO 80919-2352
Phone: 719-531-9090
Web: www.aleutmgt.com

HISTORICAL FINANCIALS
Company Type: Private

Income Statement
FYE: March 31

	REVENUE ($ mil.)	NET INCOME ($ mil.)	NET PROFIT MARGIN	EMPLOYEES
03/11	110	4	3.8%	415
03/10	127	8	6.4%	0
03/05	67	3	5.8%	0
Annual Growth	28.0%	3.9%	—	—

2011 Year-End Financials

Debt ratio: ——
Return on equity: 3.80%
Cash ($ mil.): 2
Current ratio: 1.70
Long-term debt ($ mil.): ——

Dividends
  Yield: ——
  Payout: ——
  Market value ($ mil.): ——

ALEXANDRIA CITY SCHOOL DISTRICT

LOCATIONS

HQ: ALEXANDRIA CITY SCHOOL DISTRICT
2000 N BEAUREGARD ST # 103, ALEXANDRIA, VA
22311-1749
Phone: 703-824-6646

HISTORICAL FINANCIALS
Company Type: Private

Income Statement				FYE: June 30
	REVENUE ($ mil.)	NET INCOME ($ mil.)	NET PROFIT MARGIN	EMPLOYEES
06/11	222	1	0.9%	2,500
06/06	178	(5)	—	0
06/04	161	1	1.1%	0
06/03	154	4	2.6%	0
Annual Growth	13.1%	(21.5%)	—	—

ALFRED UNIVERSITY

Alfred University was a progressive bastion of learning from the start. A private university in Western New York the small non-sectarian school serves about 2400 students. Its academic programs range from the liberal arts and sciences to engineering business and art and design with degrees from a bachelor's to a Ph.D. The school also houses the New York State College of Ceramics. The student-faculty ratio is 12-to-1. The university was founded as the Select School in 1836 providing a coeducational environment from the school's beginnings. Alfred University (and the village it's in) is named for Alfred the Great ninth-century ruler of southern England. Its mascot is of course the Saxons.

EXECUTIVES

President, Charles M. (Charley) Edmondson
Controller, Tammy Raub
Director Office Services, Susan M. (Sue) Peck
Director Human Resources, Mary L. Kelly
Director Communications, Susan (Sue) Goetschius
VP Student Affairs and Director Career Development Center, Kathleen H. (Kathy) Woughter
VP Enrollment Management, Wendy C. Beckemeyer
Director Financial Aid, Earl E. Pierce
Executive Director Annual Giving and Alumni Relations, Mark S. Shardlow
Provost and VP Academic Affairs, Suzanne C. Buckley
Director Information Technology Services, Gary Roberts
Acting VP Business and Finance, Giovina M. Lloyd
VP University Relations, Stanley A. Colla Jr.
Chief of Public Safety, John M. Dougherty
Registrar, Larry Casey
Director Graduate Extension Programs, Jay Cerio

LOCATIONS

HQ: Alfred University
1 Saxon Dr., Alfred NY 14802
Phone: 607-871-2111   **Fax:** 607-871-2198
Web: www.alfred.edu

PRODUCTS/OPERATIONS

Schools and colleges
College of Business
College of Liberal Arts and Sciences
New York State College of Ceramics
School of Art and Design
Kazuo Inamori School of Engineerin .
The Graduate School

HISTORICAL FINANCIALS
Company Type: School

Income Statement				FYE: June 30
	REVENUE ($ mil.)	NET INCOME ($ mil.)	NET PROFIT MARGIN	EMPLOYEES
06/12	64	2	4.2%	530
06/11	68	18	26.7%	0
06/10	63	11	18.2%	0
06/09	65	(33)	—	0
Annual Growth	(0.5%)	—	—	—

2012 Year-End Financials

Debt ratio: ——
Return on equity: 4.20%
Cash ($ mil.): 1
Current ratio: —
Long-term debt ($ mil.): —
Dividends
Yield: —
Payout: —
Market value ($ mil.): —

ALL ACCESS APPAREL INC.

LOCATIONS

HQ: ALL ACCESS APPAREL INC.
1515 GAGE RD, MONTEBELLO, CA 90640-6613
Phone: 323-889-4300
Web: www.selfesteemclothing.com

HISTORICAL FINANCIALS
Company Type: Private

Income Statement				FYE: December 31
	REVENUE ($ mil.)	NET INCOME ($ mil.)	NET PROFIT MARGIN	EMPLOYEES
12/11	90	0	0.5%	134
12/07*	125	9	7.9%	0
06/06	0	0	—	0
06/05	61	3	6.2%	0
Annual Growth	13.7%	(52.3%)	—	—
*Fiscal year change

2011 Year-End Financials

Debt ratio: ——
Return on equity: 0.50%
Cash ($ mil.): 0
Current ratio: 0.10
Long-term debt ($ mil.): —
Dividends
Yield: —
Payout: —
Market value ($ mil.): —

ALL-STATE INDUSTRIES INC.

LOCATIONS

HQ: ALL-STATE INDUSTRIES INC.
520 S 18TH ST, WEST DES MOINES, IA 50265-6449
Phone: 515-223-5843
Web: www.all-stateind.com

HISTORICAL FINANCIALS
Company Type: Private

Income Statement				FYE: December 31
	REVENUE ($ mil.)	NET INCOME ($ mil.)	NET PROFIT MARGIN	EMPLOYEES
12/11	95	7	8.2%	270
12/10	73	7	9.6%	0
12/09	59	4	7.1%	0
12/08	72	3	5.2%	0
Annual Growth	9.8%	27.7%	—	—

2011 Year-End Financials

Debt ratio: ——
Return on equity: 8.20%
Cash ($ mil.): 0
Current ratio: 1.00
Long-term debt ($ mil.): —
Dividends
Yield: —
Payout: —
Market value ($ mil.): —

ALLEGHENY COLLEGE

Allegheny College ranks among the oldest colleges and universities in the US. The private co-educational liberal arts school was founded in 1815 with a class of just four students. Today approximately 2100 enrolled students can pursue Bachelor of Arts and Bachelor of Science degrees in more than 50 academic programs; the college requires students to declare both a major and minor. Departments with the most graduates include biology chemistry neuroscience English political science and psychology. About half of Allegheny's students go on to pursue graduate degrees. Though the college is non-sectarian it maintains a historic affiliation with the United Methodist Church.

EXECUTIVES

Dean College, Linda C. DeMeritt
Director Human Resources and Payroll, Patricia A. Ferrey
Controller, Martin D. Ahl
VP Enrollment Management and Communications, W. Scott Friedhoff
Director Alumni Affairs, Philip Foxman
Director Financial Services, Linda S. Wetsell
Director Career Services, Michaeline Shuman
Executive Director Learning and Information and Technology Services, Richard Holmgren
Dean Students, Joe DiChristina
Director Foundation and Corporate Relations, Ann Areson
VP Development and Alumni Affairs, Marjorie Klein
Executive Vice President Treasurer, David McInally

Registrar and Associate Dean College, Benjamin D. (Ben) Haytock
Director Campus Security, Ken Kensill
Director Admissions, Jennifer D. Winge
Director Financial Aid, Sheryle Proper
Purchasing and Student Service Coordinator, Kathleen Conaway
President, James H. (Jim) Mullen Jr.

LOCATIONS

HQ: Allegheny College
520 N. Main St., Meadville PA 16335
Phone: 814-332-3100   **Fax:** 309-794-3461
Web: www.augustana.edu

HISTORICAL FINANCIALS

Company Type: School

Income Statement

	REVENUE ($ mil.)	NET INCOME ($ mil.)	NET PROFIT MARGIN	EMPLOYEES
06/12	78	(9)	—	479
06/11	130	23	17.9%	0
06/10	111	11	10.1%	0
06/09	95	0	0.6%	0
Annual Growth	(6.3%)	—	—	—

FYE: June 30

2012 Year-End Financials

Debt ratio: ——
Return on equity: (-12.40)%
Cash ($ mil.): 7
Current ratio: ——
Long-term debt ($ mil.): ——
Dividends
 Yield: —
 Payout: —
Market value ($ mil.): —

ALLEGHENY COUNTY SANITARY AUTHORITY

LOCATIONS

HQ: ALLEGHENY COUNTY SANITARY AUTHORITY
3300 PREBLE AVE, PITTSBURGH, PA 15233-1092
Phone: 412-766-4810
Web: www.alcosan.org

HISTORICAL FINANCIALS

Company Type: Private

Income Statement

	REVENUE ($ mil.)	NET INCOME ($ mil.)	NET PROFIT MARGIN	EMPLOYEES
12/11	106	(0)	—	350
12/10	109	4	4.4%	0
12/09	101	1	1.1%	0
12/08	91	(5)	—	0
Annual Growth	5.3%	—	—	—

FYE: December 31

2011 Year-End Financials

Debt ratio: ——
Return on equity: (-0.60)%
Cash ($ mil.): 46
Current ratio: 2.40
Long-term debt ($ mil.): ——
Dividends
 Yield: —
 Payout: —
Market value ($ mil.): —

ALLEGIS GROUP INC.

Clients in need of highly skilled technical and other personnel might want to take the pledge of Allegis. One of the world's largest staffing and recruitment firms Allegis Group has more than 300 offices in North America and Europe. Among its companies are Aerotek (engineering automotive and scientific professionals) Stephen James Associates (recruitment for accounting financial and cash management positions) and TEKsystems (information technology staffing and consulting). Other Allegis units include sales support outsourcer MarketSource. Chairman Jim Davis helped found the company (originally known as Aerotek) in 1983 to provide contract engineering personnel to two clients in the aerospace industry.

Allegis has expanded its geographical footprint and improved its position in specialist staffing markets through the use of acquisitions. In 2011 it obtained Aston Carter a London-based information technology recruitment firm with expertise in serving the banking and financial services sectors. The deal extended Allegis' international presence as Aston has more than half a dozen offices sprinkled throughout Europe and Asia.

In 2009 the company's Stephen James Associates beefed up its presence on the East Coast with the acquisition of professional recruiting firm Stafford Paige. The recession forced to apply the brakes on its acquisition strategy somewhat and the company cut 10% of its workforce in 2009.

EXECUTIVES

EVP Human Resources, Neil Mann
CIO, Kevin Apperson
General Counsel, Randall (Randy) Sones
President and CEO Aerotek, Thomas M. (Tom) Thornton
CEO, Michael (Mike) Salandra
Chairman, James C. (Jim) Davis
CFO, Paul Bowie

LOCATIONS

HQ: ALLEGIS GROUP INC.
7301 PARKWAY DR, HANOVER, MD 21076-1159
Phone: 410-579-3000
Web: www.allegisgroup.com

PRODUCTS/OPERATIONS

Selected Subsidiaries
Aerotek
 Aerotek Automotive
 Aerotek Aviation LLC
 Aerotek Canada
 Aerotek CE
 Aerotek Commercial Staffing
 Aerotek E&E
 Aerotek Energy Services
 Aerotek Germany
 Aerotek Netherlands
 Aerotek Professional Services
 Aerotek Scientific LLC
 Aerotek United Kingdom
Allegis Group Canada
Allegis Group Europe
Allegis Group India
Allegis Group Services
InSearch Worldwide
Major Lindsey & Africa
MarketSource Inc
Stephen James Associates
TEKsystems
 TEKsystems Canada
 TEKsystems Germany

TEKsystems Netherlands
TEKsystems United Kingdom

COMPETITORS

Adecco	Kelly Services
ASG Renaissance	Korn/Ferry
CDI	ManpowerGroup
Curran Partners	Randstad Holding
ExecuNet	RDL Corporation
Heidrick &	Robert Half
Struggles	Snelling Staffing
Horton International	Volt Information
Innovative Management	
Solutions Group	

HISTORICAL FINANCIALS

Company Type: Private

Income Statement

	REVENUE ($ mil.)	NET INCOME ($ mil.)	NET PROFIT MARGIN	EMPLOYEES
12/11	8,275	438	5.3%	85,000
12/10	6,405	406	6.3%	0
12/09	4,880	316	6.5%	0
12/08	5,737	378	6.6%	0
Annual Growth	13.0%	5.0%	—	—

FYE: December 31

2011 Year-End Financials

Debt ratio: ——
Return on equity: 5.30%
Cash ($ mil.): 190
Current ratio: 2.80
Long-term debt ($ mil.): ——
Dividends
 Yield: —
 Payout: —
Market value ($ mil.): —

ALLIANCE OF PROFESSIONALS & CONSULTANTS INC.

Alliance of Professionals & Consultants (APC) provides information technology and other technical staffing services for clients in the telecommunications financial manufacturing e-commerce pharmaceutical and health care industries. The company offers temp-to-hire and permanent placement —as well as total outsourcing arrangements —in such areas as application development quality assurance and testing network engineering and security and project management. It also operates staffing and consulting practices in engineering and business services. APC which was founded in 1993 uses subcontractors to supply its clients with personnel for some projects.

EXECUTIVES

President and CEO, Roy Roberts
COO, Troy Roberts

LOCATIONS

HQ: ALLIANCE OF PROFESSIONALS & CONSULTANTS INC.
8200 BROWNLEIGH DR, RALEIGH, NC 27617-7411
Phone: 919-510-9696
Web: www.apc-services.com

HISTORICAL FINANCIALS

Company Type: Private

Income Statement
FYE: December 31

	REVENUE ($ mil.)	NET INCOME ($ mil.)	NET PROFIT MARGIN	EMPLOYEES
12/11	60	1	3.2%	735
12/10	40	0	0.8%	0
12/09	40	0	1.1%	0
12/08	52	1	2.4%	0
Annual Growth	4.7%	15.4%	—	—

2011 Year-End Financials

Debt ratio: ——
Return on equity: 3.20%
Cash ($ mil.): 1
Current ratio: 1.60
Long-term debt ($ mil.): —

Dividends
Yield: —
Payout: —
Market value ($ mil.): —

ALLIED BUILDING STORES INC.

LOCATIONS

HQ: ALLIED BUILDING STORES INC.
850 KANSAS LN, MONROE, LA 71203-4776
Phone: 318-699-9100
Web: www.absweb.biz

HISTORICAL FINANCIALS

Company Type: Private

Income Statement
FYE: August 31

	REVENUE ($ mil.)	NET INCOME ($ mil.)	NET PROFIT MARGIN	EMPLOYEES
08/11	440	0	0.0%	125
08/10	428	0	0.0%	0
08/09	453	0	0.0%	0
08/08	479	0	0.0%	0
Annual Growth	(2.8%)	76.7%	—	—

2011 Year-End Financials

Debt ratio: ——
Return on equity: —
Cash ($ mil.): 3
Current ratio: 0.90
Long-term debt ($ mil.): —

Dividends
Yield: —
Payout: —
Market value ($ mil.): —

ALLIED OIL & TIRE COMPANY

LOCATIONS

HQ: ALLIED OIL & TIRE COMPANY
2209 S 24TH ST, OMAHA, NE 68108-3815
Phone: 402-344-4343
Web: www.alliedoil.com

HISTORICAL FINANCIALS

Company Type: Private

Income Statement
FYE: December 31

	REVENUE ($ mil.)	NET INCOME ($ mil.)	NET PROFIT MARGIN	EMPLOYEES
12/11	112	0	0.3%	260
12/10	99	0	0.2%	0
12/09	91	1	1.9%	0
12/08	106	0	0.7%	0
Annual Growth	1.8%	(24.0%)	—	—

2011 Year-End Financials

Debt ratio: ——
Return on equity: 0.30%
Cash ($ mil.): 0
Current ratio: 0.40
Long-term debt ($ mil.): —

Dividends
Yield: —
Payout: —
Market value ($ mil.): —

ALLPLUS COMPUTER SYSTEMS CORP.

LOCATIONS

HQ: ALLPLUS COMPUTER SYSTEMS CORP.
3075 NW 107TH AVE, DORAL, FL 33172-2134
Phone: 305-436-3993
Web: www.allpluscomputer.com

HISTORICAL FINANCIALS

Company Type: Private

Income Statement
FYE: September 30

	REVENUE ($ mil.)	NET INCOME ($ mil.)	NET PROFIT MARGIN	EMPLOYEES
09/11*	243	2	1.1%	35
03/11	87	1	1.9%	0
12/09	257	1	0.4%	0
12/07	243	3	1.4%	0
Annual Growth	0.0%	(7.0%)	—	—

*Fiscal year change

2011 Year-End Financials

Debt ratio: ——
Return on equity: 1.10%
Cash ($ mil.): 5
Current ratio: 1.10
Long-term debt ($ mil.): —

Dividends
Yield: —
Payout: —
Market value ($ mil.): —

ALSCO INC.

Alsco has built a big business outfitting its customers in uniforms linens and related products. Operating from some 130 branches in 10 countries worldwide the company (whose name stands for American linen supply company) rents and sells uniforms linens towels and clean room garments to more than 140000 customers in North America. It also manages janitorial services provides washroom supplies and launders and sterilizes garments. Alsco serves the automotive food processing restaurant medical and IT industries as well as the federal government. Founded in 1889 by George Steiner the company is owned and operated by the Steiner family.

Operations

Alsco heavily promotes its green cleaning solutions and the company has focused on international expansion in recent years. It has operations in Australia Brazil Canada China Germany Italy New Zealand Singapore Switzerland and Thailand.

Company Ownership

Alsco is owned and operated by the founding George Steiner family.

EXECUTIVES

Co-President, Kevin Steiner
Manager National Sales, Russ Meredith
CFO, Jim Kearns
Director Human Resources, Tim Weiler
Co-President, Robert Steiner
Director Information Systems, Larry Tomsic
Director Sales and Marketing, Jim Divers
VP Operations Alsco North America, Steve Larson

LOCATIONS

HQ: Alsco Inc.
505 E. South Temple, Salt Lake City UT 84102
Phone: 801-328-8831 **Fax:** 801-363-5680
Web: www.alsco.com

PRODUCTS/OPERATIONS

Selected Products and Services
Clean room garments
Gown room management
Hospitality/restaurant apparel
Laundry services
Linens
Mats
Mops
Napkins
Restroom service
Towels
Uniform rental and sales
Vacuum filters
Washroom supplies

COMPETITORS

Angelica Corporation	ISS A/S
ARAMARK	Rentokil Initial
Berendsen	ServiceMaster
Cintas	Sodexo USA
Crothall Healthcare	Superior Uniform Group
Diversey	Swisher Hygiene
Ecolab	Tranzonic
G&K Services	UniFirst
Healthcare Services	

HISTORICAL FINANCIALS

Company Type: Private

Income Statement

FYE: December 31

	REVENUE ($ mil.)	NET INCOME ($ mil.)	NET PROFIT MARGIN	EMPLOYEES
12/11	556	43	7.8%	13,585
12/10	544	53	9.8%	0
12/09	551	54	9.9%	0
12/08	596	59	9.9%	0
Annual Growth	(2.3%)	(9.7%)	—	—

2011 Year-End Financials

Debt ratio: —
Return on equity: 7.80%
Cash ($ mil.): 48
Current ratio: 1.70
Long-term debt ($ mil.): —

Dividends
Yield: —
Payout: —
Market value ($ mil.): —

ALTARUM INSTITUTE

The Altarum Institute is a not-for-profit organization that provides health care research and consulting services primarily to government agencies. Altarum's services include policy analysis program development and management business operations planning and finance clinical research support strategic communications and event design and management. Key customers include the US Department of Health and Human Services the US Department of Defense Military Health System and the US Department of Veterans Affairs. Altarum operates in California Georgia Maine Michigan Texas and the Washington DC area.

Altarum has grown its health care practice through acquisitions. In 2011 Altarum acquired Maryland-based Palladian Partners which focuses on communications planning publication website design and other services for clients in science and health care on a for-profit basis. In 2009 Altarum bought KAI Research adding clinical research services to its portfolio. Through KAI Altarum is the clinical trials coordinating center for the development of an anthrax vaccine.

In 2008 the organization launched a self-funded Mission Projects initiative which seeks to improve human health using systems methodology. Altarum launched the second phase of the research initiative late in 2010 when it created four research centers: Center for Consumer Choice in Health Care Center for Elder Care and Advanced Illness Center for Healthy Child and Youth Development and Center for Sustainable Health Spending. Altarum has initially funded each research center with $1 million which it plans to supplement with additional funding from foundations government grants and other public and private sector sources.

Altarum traces its lineage to the Michigan Aeronautical Research Laboratory established during the Cold War at the University of Michigan to perform research for the Department of Defense. In 2006 the company bought HSR and changed its focus to health and heath care consulting.

EXECUTIVES

Chairman, Robert P. (Bob) Kelch
President CEO and Trustee, Lincoln T. (Linc) Smith
SVP and Chief Development Officer, Jeffrey G. (Jeff) Moore

SVP and Corporate Officer Human Resources Information Technology and Facilities, Patricia H. Ferguson
VP and Director Community Health Systems, Jesse Milan Jr.
SVP CFO and Trustee, Mark A. Kielb
SVP Operations and Acting Director Medical Care Systems, Michael N. Potter
VP Integrated Strategic Business Development, James A. Lee
VP and Director Health Financial Systems, Glen Greenlee
VP and Director Information and Technology Strategies, Daniel Armijo
Director Altarum Center for Elder Care and Advanced Illness, Joanne Lynn
Research Director Innovative Care Delivery Co-Director Altarum Center for Consumer Choice in Health Care, Brad Smith
VP and Corporate Controller, Douglas R. Gilbert
VP and Director Health Care Operations, Ryan Lay
VP Corporate Information Security and Technology, Steven J. Towell
Director Medical Research and Health Communications, Beth Maloney
Trustee, Ronald J. Gardhouse, age 63
Trustee, Larry G. Garberding, age 73
Trustee, Douglas E. Van Houweling, age 68
President CEO and Trustee, Lincoln T. (Linc) Smith
Trustee, Alonzo Plough
Trustee, L.J. Evans Jr.
Trustee, David J. Brophy, age 75
SVP CFO and Trustee, Mark A. Kielb
Trustee, Marvin H. McKinney
Trustee, Maxine Hayes
Trustee, Mary K. Ousley
Trustee, John J.H. (Joe) Schwarz
Trustee, Ed Martin
Trustee, Karen Aldridge-Eason
Auditors: Ernst&YoungLLP

LOCATIONS

HQ: Altarum Institute
3520 Green Ct. Ste. 300, Ann Arbor MI 48105
Phone: 734-302-4600   **Fax:** 734-302-4991
Web: www.altarum.org

COMPETITORS

Battelle Memorial	MITRE
Charles River	Quintiles
Laboratories	Transnational
Covance	SwRI

HISTORICAL FINANCIALS

Company Type: Private - Not-for-Profit

Income Statement

FYE: December 31

	REVENUE ($ mil.)	NET INCOME ($ mil.)	NET PROFIT MARGIN	EMPLOYEES
12/11	84	(4)	—	455
12/10	73	(6)	—	0
12/09	57	(7)	—	0
12/08	60	(14)	—	0
Annual Growth	11.6%	—	—	—

2011 Year-End Financials

Debt ratio: —
Return on equity: (-5.40)%
Cash ($ mil.): 6
Current ratio: 0.50
Long-term debt ($ mil.): —

Dividends
Yield: —
Payout: —
Market value ($ mil.): —

ALTHEA TECHNOLOGIES INC.

Althea Technologies helps biopharmaceutical developers take a drug from discovery and testing all the way to market. The company provides biotech contract development and manufacturing services brewing up cell lines and specialty biologic compounds and then helping clients formulate them into a product. It offers preclinical services including biologic validation fermentation purification and stabilization. When a product is ready for testing Althea's large scale commercial facility can produce the prefilled syringes or vials used in clinical trials. The company also offers regulatory support and contract manufacturing of finished products. Althea agreed to be acquired by Ajinomoto in 2013.

Geographic Reach

All of Althea Technologies research consulting development and manufacturing services are located at its San Diego California headquarters location.

Operations

Althea Technologies offers specialized formulation services for large molecule (biotech) drugs using its Crystalomics technology which allows for the delivery of high-concentration or sustained-release biologic drug compounds. It also provides lyophilization which stabilizes biotech compounds through freeze-drying.

Strategy

Signing on new pharmaceutical customers for its research and contract manufacturing services is core to Althea Technologies' growth efforts. For instance in 2011 the company entered a commercial supply agreement with Biotest Pharmaceuticals to fill commercial products sold by Biotest in the US.

In addition Althea Technologies expands its service offerings through acquisitions partnerships and organic growth measures. It added drug and biologic storage labeling packaging and distribution services by forming a co-marketing agreement with Sherpa Clinical Packaging in 2011. Sherpa was founded in 2011 and is located next door to the Althea manufacturing facilities.

Mergers and Acquisitions

Althea Technologies grew its portfolio with the addition of a protein crystal technology and a controlled-release injectable technology in 2010 when it acquired the assets of bankrupted Altus Pharmaceuticals. The purchase also added several drug candidates in clinical trial stages which Althea is looking to license out to third parties.

Ownership

In 2013 Althea Technologies agreed to be acquired by Japanese manufacturing firm Ajinomoto which is looking to expand its biopharmaceuticals manufacturing business in the US.

Company Background

Francois Ferre and Magda Marquet —who hold Ph.Ds in molecular oncology and biochemical engineering —founded the company in 1998. Late in 2008 Ferre and Marquet stepped down as co-CEOs and became co-chairs of the board. The company spun off its diagnostics division into a new entity Althea Diagnostics in early 2008.

EXECUTIVES

Co-Chairman, J. Matthew (Matt) Mackowski, age 52
Co-Chairman, Magda Marquet

EVP and Chief Business Officer, Alan Moore
President, Rick Hancock
VP and Chief Scientific Officer, Joe Monforte
VP Operations, Christopher (Chris) Duffy
CFO, R. Gary Gilmore
VP Quality and Regulatory, E. J. Brandreth
President Bio-Services Division, Karen Daniels
Director, Deval A. Lashkari
Director, James B. Glavin, age 77
Co-Chairman, J. Matthew (Matt) Mackowski, age 52
Director, Timothy J. Wollaeger, age 67
Director, Francois Ferre
Co-Chairman, Magda Marquet
Director, Richard T. L. Chan, age 58

LOCATIONS

HQ: Althea Technologies Inc.
  11040 Roselle St., San Diego CA 92121-1205
Phone: 858-882-0123   **Fax:** 858-882-0133
Web: www.altheatech.com/home.html

PRODUCTS/OPERATIONS

Selected Services

Analytical Method Development
Biologics Manufacturing
Biologics Process Development (including fermentation
  product recovery and purification)
Cell Line Development
cGMP Protein & DNA Plasmid Production
Lyophilization Cycle Development
Microbial and Yeast Expression Systems
Process Development
Protein Analytics Stability (including validation and
  testing)
Sterile Syringe Filling
Sterile Vial Filling

Selected Products

Adjuvants
Conjugates
Liposomes
Nanoparticlees
Plasmid DNA
Recombinant Protein
Vaccines

COMPETITORS

Akorn	Hospira
Albany Molecular	NextGen Group
Research	NextPharma
Ben Venue	Odyssey Thera
CBL	Patheon
Covance	Pharmaceutical Product
CXR Biosciences	Development
DPT Labs	Quintiles
Furiex	Transnational

HISTORICAL FINANCIALS

Company Type: Private

Income Statement

	REVENUE ($ mil.)	NET INCOME ($ mil.)	NET PROFIT MARGIN	EMPLOYEES
12/11	38	(3)	—	164
12/10	43	3	7.9%	0
12/07	28	2	8.1%	0
12/04	10	0	3.0%	0
Annual Growth	**52.0%**	—	—	—

FYE: December 31

2011 Year-End Financials

Debt ratio: —
Return on equity: (-9.20)%
Cash ($ mil.): 9
Current ratio: 1.00
Long-term debt ($ mil.): —
Dividends
  Yield: —
  Payout: —
Market value ($ mil.): —

ALTOONA REGIONAL HEALTH SYSTEM

Altoona Regional Health System moves patients upstream towards better health. Operating in Altoona and surrounding areas in central Pennsylvania the health system's facilities include Altoona Hospital an acute care center with 380 licensed beds that provides specialized care in areas including cardiovascular ailments cancer behavioral health and neurology as well as general emergency trauma birthing and surgery services. Altoona Regional Health System also offers a variety of outpatient care facilities and programs including home health care a primary care physicians' group and laboratory services. The not-for-profit system is governed by a board of community representatives.

Geographic Reach

Altoona Regional Health System provides services to residents of about 20 counties in central Pennsylvania.

Operations

Altoona Regional Health System was a two-hospital system until March 2012 when it closed the Bon Secours-Holy Family Hospital. At that time one of Altoona Regional Health System's sponsors Catholic hospital operator Bon Secours Health System withdrew from the partnership.

While it worked towards closing one campus the company conducted numerous expansion and upgrade projects at its Altoona Hospital campus to prepare for the resulting increase in patients and to provide a consolidated efficient and modern regional care center. It also moved a number of ambulatory care services to the outpatient facility Station Medical Center.

Company Background

In 2004 Altoona Hospital's parent Central Pennsylvania Health Services Corporation and Bon Secours-Holy Family Hospital's parent Bon Secours Health System merged the two campuses and affiliated companies to form Altoona Regional Health System.

EXECUTIVES

SVP Human Resources, Gary R. Naugle
SVP and CFO, Charles R. (Charlie) Zorger
VP and Assistant to CEO, Dee A. Shellenberger
COO, Ronald J. (Ron) McConnell
Marketing and Communications Specialist, Patt Frank
SVP Quality and Medical Affairs and Chief Medical Officer, David L. Cowger
SVP and Chief Nursing Officer, Chris Rickens
VP Supply Chain, Gary W. Zuckerman
President and CEO, Gerald E. (Jerry) Murray

LOCATIONS

HQ: Altoona Regional Health System
  620 Howard Ave., Altoona PA 16601-4899
Phone: 814-889-2011   **Fax:** 814-946-7808
Web: www.altoonaregional.org/

PRODUCTS/OPERATIONS

Selected Services

Behavioral Health
Birth & Growth
Cancer Care
Cardiac Care
Center for Weight Loss and Bariatric Surgery

Central Pennsylvania Cardiovascular Associates
Emergency Medicine and Trauma
HealthForce (Occupational Medicine)
Imaging Services
Institute for Sleep Medicine
Neurosurgery
Orthopedics
Physical Medicine and Rehabilitation
Primary Stroke Center
Surgical Services
Wound Care and Ostomy Program

COMPETITORS

Clearfield Area Health	J. C. Blair Memorial
Services	Hospital
Conemaugh Health	
System	

HISTORICAL FINANCIALS

Company Type: Private - Not-for-Profit

Income Statement

	REVENUE ($ mil.)	NET INCOME ($ mil.)	NET PROFIT MARGIN	EMPLOYEES
06/12	485	36	7.5%	2,494
06/10*	321	5	1.6%	0
12/09	0	0	3.2%	0
06/09	436	(33)	—	0
Annual Growth	**3.6%**	—	—	—

FYE: June 30
*Fiscal year change

2012 Year-End Financials

Debt ratio: —
Return on equity: 7.50%
Cash ($ mil.): 30
Current ratio: 1.50
Long-term debt ($ mil.): —
Dividends
  Yield: —
  Payout: —
Market value ($ mil.): —

ALVERNIA UNIVERSITY

Alvernia University (formerly Alvernia College) is a private Catholic Franciscan liberal arts college. It offers about 40 undergraduate majors and about 20 undergraduate minors as well as associate of science degrees in business and computer information systems six master's degrees programs and a doctor of philosophy program. Its main campus is located in Reading Pennsylvania with additional courses taught in Pottsville and Philadelphia. The university has a total enrollment of some 3000 students. Alvernia was founded in 1958 by the Bernardine Franciscan Sisters. The institution gained university status in 2008.

EXECUTIVES

Registrar, Beki Stein
President, Thomas F. Flynn
VP Finance and Administration, Douglas F. Smith
VP Mission and Ministry, Sister Rosemary Stets
Director Alumni Relations, Darlene A. Berk
Director Information Services, John H. Kissinger
Provost, Shirley J. Williams
VP Advancement, J. Michael Pressimone
VP College Life and Student Learning Services, Sister Margaret Anne Dougherty
VP Enrollment Management, John McCloskey Jr.
Coordinator Career Services, Jennifer Gittings-Dalton

LOCATIONS

HQ: Alvernia University
400 St. Bernardine St., Reading PA 19607
Phone: 610-796-8200   **Fax:** 610-796-8324
Web: www.alvernia.edu

HISTORICAL FINANCIALS

Company Type: School

Income Statement

	REVENUE ($ mil.)	NET INCOME ($ mil.)	NET PROFIT MARGIN	EMPLOYEES
06/11	63	5	8.9%	293
06/10	55	4	7.4%	0
06/09	53	0	—	0
06/08	52	5	10.8%	0
Annual Growth	6.7%	(0.1%)	—	—

2011 Year-End Financials

Debt ratio: ——
Return on equity: 8.90%
Cash ($ mil.): 3
Current ratio: —
Long-term debt ($ mil.): —

Dividends
Yield: —
Payout: —
Market value ($ mil.): —

ALVERNO COLLEGE

Alverno College is an independent liberal arts institution with an enrollment of more than 2300 undergraduates and about 350 graduate students. It confers associate's bachelor's and master's degrees in more than 60 areas of study at four schools: Arts and Sciences Business Education and Nursing. Matriculating only women in its undergraduate programs Alverno accepts men as graduate students. Alverno takes its name from a mountain in Italy (La Verna) that was given to St. Francis as a gift and used by his followers as a place of reflection. The school was founded by the School Sisters of St. Francis in 1887.

EXECUTIVES

President, Mary J. Meehan
Director Academic Advising, Katherine (Kathy) Bundalo
Director Career Education Center, Debra Chomicka
Registrar, Patricia (Pat) Hartmann
Executive Director Technology Services, Anita Eikens
SVP Academic Affairs, Kathleen O'Brien
SVP Finance and Management Services, James K. Oppermann
VP College Advancement, Joanne MacInnes
VP Enrollment Planning and Management, Susan M. Smith
Director Alumnae Relations, Mary M. Frieseke
Director Financial Aid Office, Dan Goyette
Assistant VP Marketing Communications, Michael Harryman
Associate VP Student Services and Dean Students, Virginia Wagner

LOCATIONS

HQ: Alverno College
3400 S. 43rd St., Milwaukee WI 53219-4844
Phone: 414-382-6000   **Fax:** 414-382-6354
Web: www.alverno.edu

HISTORICAL FINANCIALS

Company Type: School

Income Statement

	REVENUE ($ mil.)	NET INCOME ($ mil.)	NET PROFIT MARGIN	EMPLOYEES
06/11	45	4	9.7%	1,000
06/10	53	0	0.9%	0
06/09	46	0	—	0
06/08	52	7	13.3%	0
Annual Growth	(5.0%)	(14.6%)	—	—

2011 Year-End Financials

Debt ratio: ——
Return on equity: 9.70%
Cash ($ mil.): 0
Current ratio: —
Long-term debt ($ mil.): —

Dividends
Yield: —
Payout: —
Market value ($ mil.): —

ALY MCCANN SCHOLARSHIP

LOCATIONS

HQ: ALY MCCANN SCHOLARSHIP
4201 S WASHINGTON ST, MARION, IN 46953-4974
Phone: 765-674-6901

HISTORICAL FINANCIALS

Company Type: Private

Income Statement

	REVENUE ($ mil.)	NET INCOME ($ mil.)	NET PROFIT MARGIN	EMPLOYEES
06/11	203	32	15.7%	1,729
06/09	159	12	7.6%	0
06/08	151	15	9.9%	0
06/07	0	0	—	0
Annual Growth	—	11802.6%	—	—

2011 Year-End Financials

Debt ratio: ——
Return on equity: 15.70%
Cash ($ mil.): 21
Current ratio: —
Long-term debt ($ mil.): —

Dividends
Yield: —
Payout: —
Market value ($ mil.): —

ALZHEIMER'S DISEASE AND RELATED DISORDERS ASSOCIATION INC.

Alzheimer's Association wants you to "maintain your brain". The charitable organization is working to prevent treat and hopefully cure Alzheimer's a progressive brain disorder that destroys memory and the ability to learn reason and do other daily activities. The group has more than 75 local chapters throughout the US and numerous service programs including a 24-hour helpline support groups information libraries public advocacy an online community and a registration program so wandering Alzheimer patients can be returned home safely. Alzheimer's Association also funds research and hosts national and international conferences for scientists and caregivers. Its annual fund raiser is the Walk to End Alzheimer's.

There are currently more than 5 million people with Alzheimer's disease in the US. Projections have the number increasing to 16 million in the US by mid-century.

To help battle against the disease the Alzheimer's Association has set a strategic goal for contribution growth rate at 6% annually thereby reaching a targeted 2014 revenue goal of approximately $240 million.

EXECUTIVES

Chief Medical and Scientific Officer, William Thies
President and CEO, Harry Johns
Chair Elect, Paul Attea
Vice Chair, Samuel E. Gandy
Chief Strategy Officer, Angela Geiger
COO and CFO, Richard Hovland
VP Relationship Development, Heather Hutchison
Chair, Evan Thompson
Secretary, Laurel Coleman
Treasurer, Michael Urbut
Chair Elect, Paul Attea
Vice Chair, Samuel E. Gandy
Director, Michael Arthur
Director, Lane Bowen
Director, Alan Silverglat
Director, William Bridgwater
Director, Meryl Comer
Director, John Sabl
Director, Darlene Shiley
Director, Joanne Vidinsky
Director, Shelley Fabares
Director, Marshall Gelfand
Director, Colleen Goldhammer
Director, Dennis Revell
Director, Rita Hortenstine
Director, Larry Jodsaas
Director, David Moscow
Director, Thomas J. Winkel
Director, Deborah Jones
Director, Stewart Putnam
Director, Jim Prugh
Director, Marilyn Albert
Director, Linda Mendelson
Director, Cathy L. Edge
Director, R. Thomas Bodkin
Director, Robert K. Burke
Director, Bonnie H. Marcus
Director, Deborah A. Randall
Director, Suzanne B. Swift
Director, Carl E. Tuerk Jr.
Director, Thomas Yoshikawa
Director, Ronald Schilling
Director, John E. Maggio
Director, Steven DeKosky
Director, Richard Della Penna
Director, Karen Kauffman
Director, Peggye Dilworth-Anderson
Auditors: GrantThorntonLLP

LOCATIONS

HQ: Alzheimer' s Disease and Related Disorders
Association Inc.
225 N. Michigan Ave. Fl. 17, Chicago IL 60601-7633
Phone: 312-335-8700 **Fax:** 866-699-1246
Web: www.alz.org

HISTORICAL FINANCIALS

Company Type: Private - Not-for-Profit

Income Statement

FYE: June 30

	REVENUE ($ mil.)	NET INCOME ($ mil.)	NET PROFIT MARGIN	EMPLOYEES
06/12	110	2	2.5%	200
06/11	98	10	11.0%	0
06/10	87	1	1.8%	0
06/09	80	0	—	0
Annual Growth	10.9%	—	—	—

2012 Year-End Financials

Debt ratio: ——
Return on equity: 2.50%
Cash ($ mil.): 12
Current ratio: 0.30
Long-term debt ($ mil.): —

Dividends
Yield: —
Payout: —
Market value ($ mil.): —

AMERICA'S HOME PLACE INC.

America's Home Place builds custom homes on its customers' land. The company builds single-family detached houses with more than 100 custom floor plans and designs. Its two- to five-bedroom cabin chalet ranch two-story and split-level houses range in price from about $80000 to more than $300000. Sizes start at about 900 sq. ft. and go up to to 4000 sq. ft. America's Home Place operates nearly 40 home building and model centers in the southeastern US. Buyers typically already own their land from a single lot to many acres. The company also assists buyers who are not landowners in locating available property. President Barry Conner owns the company he founded in 1972.

Customizable home options include choice of flooring lighting roofing siding cabinets and countertops. The company uses products with such brand names as Armstrong (flooring) CertainTeed (roofing and siding) Sherwin-Williams (paint) and Whirlpool (appliances).

America's Home Place traditionally services its customers at retail outlets where buyers select their design carpet paint tile and window options. However the company added to its marketing strategy to begin providing model centers which feature full-sized model homes plus product and sales centers. The company builds its homes in Florida Georgia Louisiana Mississippi North Carolina South Carolina and Tennessee.

America's Home Place does not offer financing. However it does have relationships with several preferred lenders that are recommended to home-buyers.

EXECUTIVES

President, Barry G. Conner
Manager Finance, Sonya Brown
Director Marketing, Greg Griffith

IT Manager, Alan Cooper
VP, Van Conner
General Manager Albany GA, Troy Rollins
General Manager Anderson SC, Kirk Doss
General Manager Asheville NC, Russell Miskin
General Manager Athens GA, Jennifer Bombardo
General Manager Augusta GA, Bob Helms
General Manager Baton Rouge LA, Austin Round
General Manager Blairsville GA, Glenn Wagoner
General Manager Calhoun GA, Dan Poole
General Manager Cashiers NC, K. Stacy Buchanan
General Manager North Charleston SC, Shannon Dwinnell
CFO, Wayne O. Norris

LOCATIONS

HQ: America' s Home Place Inc.
2144 Hilton Dr., Gainesville GA 30501
Phone: 770-532-1128 **Fax:** 320-255-5714
Web: www.centracare.com

COMPETITORS

Beazer Homes
D.R. Horton
David Weekley Homes
KB Home
Lennar

M.D.C.
NVR
PulteGroup
Standard Pacific
The Ryland Group

HISTORICAL FINANCIALS

Company Type: Private

Income Statement

FYE: December 31

	REVENUE ($ mil.)	NET INCOME ($ mil.)	NET PROFIT MARGIN	EMPLOYEES
12/11	125	4	3.7%	275
12/07	173	8	4.9%	0
12/06	184	11	6.3%	0
12/05	1,667	0	—	0
Annual Growth	—	1641.0%	—	—

2011 Year-End Financials

Debt ratio: ——
Return on equity: 3.70%
Cash ($ mil.): 2
Current ratio: 1.50
Long-term debt ($ mil.): —

Dividends
Yield: —
Payout: —
Market value ($ mil.): —

AMERICAN ACADEMY OF PEDIATRICS

The American Academy of Pediatrics (AAP) is a membership group of some 60000 pediatricians pediatric specialists and pediatric surgeons dedicated to improving the health and well-being of infants children teenagers and young adults. The not-for-profit organization executes research on a number of topics including school health common childhood illnesses and immunizations and acts as an advocate on behalf of children's health needs. It also provides continuing education for its members through courses scientific meetings and publications such as Pediatrics and Pediatrics in Review. The organization is funded by membership dues grants gifts and its own activities. AAP was founded in 1930.

Other areas that AAP concerns itself with include behavioral and mental health family health

healthy development and children with unique health care needs.

Both membership dues and subscriptions accounted for some 40% of revenues in 2011; while manuals and publications and contracts and grants accounted for around 25% of revenues that same year.

EXECUTIVES

Executive Director/CEO, Errol R. Alden
President-Elect, David T. Tayloe Jr.
President, Judith S. (Judy) Palfrey
President, Robert W. Block
President-Elect, Thomas K. McInerny
Director, Edward N. Bailey
Director, Henry Schaeffer
Director, Sandra Gibson Hassink
Director, Michael V. Severson
Director, Mary Brown
Director, Myles B. Abbott
Director, John Curran
Director, Francis E. Rushton Jr.
Director, Kenneth E. Mathews
President, Judith S. (Judy) Palfrey
Director, Marilyn J. Bull
Auditors: BlackmanKallickBartelsteinLLP

LOCATIONS

HQ: American Academy Of Pediatrics
141 NW Point Blvd., Elk Grove Village IL 60007-1098
Phone: 847-434-4000 **Fax:** 847-434-8000
Web: www.aap.org

PRODUCTS/OPERATIONS

2011 Revenues

% of total	
Membership	23
Subscriptions	17
Manuals &	16
Contracts &	11
Contributions	9
Advertising	5
NCE &	5
Continuing	5
Royalties	5
Net investment	2
Other	2
Total	**100**

HISTORICAL FINANCIALS

Company Type: Private - Not-for-Profit

Income Statement

FYE: June 30

	REVENUE ($ mil.)	NET INCOME ($ mil.)	NET PROFIT MARGIN	EMPLOYEES
06/12	104	1	1.8%	400
06/11	93	7	7.8%	0
06/10	87	2	2.6%	0
06/09	81	(1)	—	0
Annual Growth	8.7%	—	—	—

2012 Year-End Financials

Debt ratio: ——
Return on equity: 1.80%
Cash ($ mil.): 6
Current ratio: 0.60
Long-term debt ($ mil.): —

Dividends
Yield: —
Payout: —
Market value ($ mil.): —

AMERICAN ACRYL NA LLC

LOCATIONS

HQ: AMERICAN ACRYL NA LLC
4631 OLD HIGHWAY 146, PASADENA, TX 77507-1849
Phone: 281-909-2600

HISTORICAL FINANCIALS

Company Type: Private

Income Statement

FYE: December 31

	REVENUE ($ mil.)	NET INCOME ($ mil.)	NET PROFIT MARGIN	EMPLOYEES
12/11	188	0	—	52
12/10	62	0	—	0
12/09	106	0	—	0
12/08	179	0	—	0
Annual Growth	1.6%	—	—	—

2011 Year-End Financials

Debt ratio: ——
Return on equity: —
Cash ($ mil.): 11
Current ratio: 1.00
Long-term debt ($ mil.): —

Dividends
Yield: —
Payout: —
Market value ($ mil.): —

AMERICAN AGCREDIT ACA

LOCATIONS

HQ: AMERICAN AGCREDIT ACA
200 CONCOURSE BLVD, SANTA ROSA, CA
95403-8210
Phone: 707-545-1200
Web: www.agloan.com

HISTORICAL FINANCIALS

Company Type: Private

Income Statement

FYE: December 31

	ASSETS ($ mil.)	NET INCOME ($ mil.)	INCOME AS % OF ASSETS	EMPLOYEES
12/11*	4,718	180	3.8%	221
03/10	4,839	26	0.5%	0
12/06	2,990	163	5.5%	0
12/05	2,850	52	1.8%	0
Annual Growth	18.3%	51.3%	—	—

*Fiscal year change

2011 Year-End Financials

Debt ratio: ——
Return on equity: 52.80%
Cash ($ mil.): 18
Current ratio: —
Long-term debt ($ mil.): —

Dividends
Yield: —
Payout: —
Market value ($ mil.): —

AMERICAN ALLOY STEEL INC.

LOCATIONS

HQ: AMERICAN ALLOY STEEL INC.
6230 N HOUSTON ROSSLYN RD, HOUSTON, TX
77091-3410
Phone: 713-462-8081
Web: www.aasteel.com

HISTORICAL FINANCIALS

Company Type: Private

Income Statement

FYE: December 31

	REVENUE ($ mil.)	NET INCOME ($ mil.)	NET PROFIT MARGIN	EMPLOYEES
12/11	252	14	5.9%	200
12/10	163	11	7.1%	0
12/08	339	23	6.8%	0
12/07	241	15	6.3%	0
Annual Growth	1.5%	(0.5%)	—	—

2011 Year-End Financials

Debt ratio: ——
Return on equity: 5.90%
Cash ($ mil.): 17
Current ratio: 2.40
Long-term debt ($ mil.): —

Dividends
Yield: —
Payout: —
Market value ($ mil.): —

AMERICAN ASSOCIATED PHARMACIES

LOCATIONS

HQ: AMERICAN ASSOCIATED PHARMACIES
211 LNNIE E CRAWFORD BLVD, SCOTTSBORO, AL
35769-7408
Phone: 256-574-6819

HISTORICAL FINANCIALS

Company Type: Private

Income Statement

FYE: December 31

	REVENUE ($ mil.)	NET INCOME ($ mil.)	NET PROFIT MARGIN	EMPLOYEES
12/11	439	1	0.3%	75
12/10	375	0	0.2%	0
12/09	124	0	0.2%	0
Annual Growth	87.6%	139.4%	—	—

2011 Year-End Financials

Debt ratio: ——
Return on equity: 0.30%
Cash ($ mil.): 25
Current ratio: 0.70
Long-term debt ($ mil.): —

Dividends
Yield: —
Payout: —
Market value ($ mil.): —

AMERICAN BANKERS ASSOCIATION INC

The American Bankers Association (ABA) brings together banks of various types and sizes. Its members include bank holding companies; community regional and money center banks; savings associations; savings banks; and trust companies. The ABA serves as an advocate for its members in legislative and regulatory arenas; it also engages in consumer education research and training efforts. The ABA's BankPac the banking industry's largest political action committee provides financial support to candidates for the US Senate and House of Representatives. The ABA was founded in 1875 and claims to represent more than 95% of banking assets. The group merged with the America's Community Bankers association in 2007.

EXECUTIVES

Chairman, Stephen P. Wilson, age 61
President and CEO, Edward L. (Ed) Yingling
Treasurer and Director, Warren K. K. Luke
Chairman-Elect, Albert C. (Kell) Kelly Jr.
SEVP and COO, Diane M. Casey-Landry
Director, Thomas L. Hoy, age 63
Director, Richard E. Anthony, age 66
Director, William J. (Bill) Small, age 61
Director, Stephen J. (Steve) Gurgovits, age 68
Director, Craig G. Blunden, age 64
Director, Richard K. Davis, age 54
Director, Robert Harmon
Director, Lisa B. Binder, age 55
Chairman, Stephen P. Wilson, age 61
Director, Barrie G. Christman
Director, Ronald A. Wilbur
Treasurer and Director, Warren K. K. Luke
Director, Robert L. (Bob) Fenstermacher
Director, Arthur C. Johnson
Director, Dirk L. Gasterland
Director, Michael D. Hensley
Director, Scott Smith Jr.
Director, Guy T. Williams
Director, Gary D. Hemmer
Director, Patrick D. Redmond
Director, Kent A. Steinwert
Director, Peter Y. Waller
Director, Austin L. Roberts
Director, L. Wesley Smith
Director, Michael C. Miller
Director, Michael M. Buskirk
Director, Raymond G Hallock
Director, Kenneth J. Redding
Director, William R. White
Director, Kathleen E. Marinangel
Director, James F. McKenna
Director, Steven J. Swinotek

LOCATIONS

HQ: American Bankers Association
1120 Connecticut Ave. NW, Washington DC 20036
Phone: 202-663-5000   **Fax:** 202-828-4548
Web: www.aba.com

HISTORICAL FINANCIALS

Company Type: Private - Association

Income Statement

	REVENUE ($ mil.)	NET INCOME ($ mil.)	NET PROFIT MARGIN	EMPLOYEES
08/11	85	4	5.1%	354
08/10	80	0	1.0%	0
08/09	64	(22)	—	0
08/08	83	(2)	—	0
Annual Growth	0.5%	—	—	—

FYE: August 31

2011 Year-End Financials

Debt ratio: ——
Return on equity: 5.10%
Cash ($ mil.): 12
Current ratio: —
Long-term debt ($ mil.): —

Dividends
 Yield: —
 Payout: —
 Market value ($ mil.): —

AMERICAN BAPTIST HOMES OF THE WEST

American Baptist Homes of the West (ABHOW) preaches the gospel of the active senior lifestyle operating more than 40 senior living facilities in four western states. Nearly three-fourths of ABHOW's communities are government-subsidized apartments for low-income seniors. About a dozen of its residences however are continuing care retirement communities which offer a continuum of care –residential living assisted living or skilled nursing –depending on residents' needs. The communities also schedule social activities and offer wellness programs and transportation services. Parent company Cornerstone Affiliates acquires and develops communities with ABHOW.

Operations ABHOW established its first retirement community serving retired ministers and missionaries of the American Baptist denomination in 1949. Today it takes all comers regardless of religious affiliation. All in all the company houses some 5000 seniors throughout California as well as in Arizona Nevada and Washington. The company's Seniority subsidiary provides consulting and management services to other not-for-profit retirement communities. Clients include Christian Living Communities in Colorado and Nikkei Senior Gardens and Cottonwood Court in California.

Strategy The company works to grow its customer base by tailoring the services it offers to meet customer needs such as offering flexible contracts larger living areas and wellness programs. Part of its sales strategy its "hook" if you will is that it has the capability to offer residents increasing levels of care depending on their specific needs as they age. The company believes that is a feature that keeps its residents from having to move as their health needs become more complicated.

EXECUTIVES

SVP Human Resources, Terese Farkas
President and CEO, David B. Ferguson
SVP Finance and CFO, Pamela S. Claassen
President ABHOW Foundation, Joseph (Joe) Anderson
SVP and General Counsel, David A. Grant
SVP Strategic Planning, Kay Kallander

SVP Affordable Housing, Ancel Romero
Secretary and Director, Leon L. Gean
Vice Chair, Bruce Laycook
Chief Governance Officer, Randall L. Stamper
SVP Sales and Marketing; President Seniority, Sloan Bentley
SVP and Chief Operations Manager, Jeff Glaze
Secretary and Director, Leon L. Gean
Director, Hector M. Gonzalez
Director, James Ella James
Director, Donald N. Jones
Vice Chair, Bruce Laycook
Director, Gloria P. Marshall
Director, Phyllis J. Stuewig
Director, Rev Marcia J. Patton
Director, Joel P. Martin
Director, Stephen A. Elliott
Director, Rev Samuel S. Chetti
Director, Douglas W. Holmes
Director, Rev Lloyd E. Howard
Director, Julie B. Michaels
Auditors: MossAdamsLLP

LOCATIONS

HQ: American Baptist Homes of the West
 6120 Stoneridge Mall Rd. 3rd Fl., Pleasanton CA 94588
Phone: 925-924-7100   **Fax:** 925-924-7101
Web: www.abhow.com

COMPETITORS

ACTS Retirement-Life Communities
Amedisys
Assisted Living Concepts
BPM Senior Living
Brookdale Senior Living
Capital Senior Living

Emeritus Corporation
Ensign Group
Five Star Quality Care
Golden Horizons
HCR ManorCare
Life Care Centers
SavaSeniorCare
Sunrise Senior Living

HISTORICAL FINANCIALS

Company Type: Private - Not-for-Profit

Income Statement

	REVENUE ($ mil.)	NET INCOME ($ mil.)	NET PROFIT MARGIN	EMPLOYEES
09/11	158	(0)	—	2,500
09/10	149	12	8.1%	0
09/09	145	0	0.5%	0
09/08	135	(16)	—	0
Annual Growth	5.2%	—	—	—

FYE: September 30

2011 Year-End Financials

Debt ratio: ——
Return on equity: (-0.20)%
Cash ($ mil.): 13
Current ratio: 0.20
Long-term debt ($ mil.): —

Dividends
 Yield: —
 Payout: —
 Market value ($ mil.): —

AMERICAN BAR ASSOCIATION

The world's largest voluntary professional organization American Bar Association (ABA) promotes improvements in the American justice system and develops guidelines for the advancement of the legal profession and education. The association provides law school accreditation continuing education legal information and other services to assist legal professionals. The ABA's roster of about 400000 members includes lawyers judges court administrators law librarians and law school professors and students. The organization cannot discipline lawyers nor enforce its rules; it can only develop guidelines. The ABA was founded in 1878.

Operations

The ABA releases books magazines journals and newsletters in various formats through its ABA Publishing division. Popular materials run the gamut of topics including administrative practices for lobbyists immigration law guides for criminal lawyers and leadership and empowerment for women lawyers. Publications are sold through the ABA's online store.

Financial Analysis

The ABA's fiscal 2011 (ends August) revenue was essentially unchanged vs. the prior year while net income popped 979% over the same period. Revenue from membership dues (the ABA's largest source of funds) dropped by 4%. Grants and gifts increased 16% in fiscal 2011. Indeed the ABA's revenue trend has been flat since fiscal 2007.

HISTORY

One hundred lawyers from 21 states met in Saratoga New York in 1878 and drafted the constitution for the American Bar Association. As the ABA grew over the next hundred years it came to influence the direction of legal education and the nomination and confirmation of judicial candidates. This brought the ABA into the political arena where its stance on controversial issues politicized the group and opened it to charges of partisan bias.

Its activities also have led to lawsuits (imagine that) including a 1993 suit by the Massachusetts School of Law claiming that the ABA's law school accreditation practices impinged on the university's right to set school policy. The Justice Department agreed saying the ABA's requirements raised costs without improving educational quality so in 1995 the association changed its accreditation process.

Its influence over judicial nominations took a beating in 1997 when the Senate Judiciary Committee announced that it would no longer await ABA pronouncements before acting on a nomination. The ABA's accreditation process came under fire again in 1998 when the government agency that oversees educational accreditation agencies threatened to penalize or terminate the ABA unless its accreditation policies complied with federal law. Supreme Court Justice Clarence Thomas levied his own attack in 1999 by charging that the ABA's political platforms compromised its objectivity in reviewing judicial nominations.

The ABA joined with the Federal Bar Association in 2001 to support a pay increase for federal judges. In 2002 the ABA voted to recommend that alleged terrorists tried before military tribunals should be guaranteed the same legal protections as criminal defendants in US courts.

EXECUTIVES

President, Stephen N. Zack, age 63
President, William T. (Bill) Robinson III
Executive Director and COO, Henry F. White Jr.
President-Elect, Laurel G. Bellows
Chair House of Delegates, William (Bill) Hubbard
Chair ABA House of Delegates, Linda A. Klein
Treasurer, Alice E. Richmond
Secretary, Bernice Donald

Executive Director, Jack L. Rives
Secretary, Cara Lee Neville
Treasurer, Lucian Pera
Auditors: GrantThorntonLLP

LOCATIONS

HQ: American Bar Association
321 N. Clark St., Chicago IL 60654-7598
Phone: 312-988-5000   **Fax:** 312-988-5177
Web: www.americanbar.org

PRODUCTS/OPERATIONS

2011 Revenues

	$ mil.	% of total
Membership dues	75	37
Gifts and grants	59	29
Meeting fees	27	13
Publications	12	6
Royalties	7	3
Investment income	6	3
Advertising	3	2
Designated reserve for operations	3	2
Rental income	3	2
Accreditation fees	1	1
Net assets released from restrictions	1	1
Other	2	1
Total	**205**	**100**

Selected Committees Forums and Other Groups

Coalition for Justice
Commission on Domestic Violence
Commission on Mental and Physical Disability Law
Commission on Racial and Ethnic Diversity in the
    Profession
Death Penalty Moratorium Project
Division for Public Services
Forum Committee on Affordable Housing
Forum Committee on Entertainment and Sports
    Industries
Law Student Division
Lawyers' Professional Liability
Office of the President
Pro Bono and Public Service
Section of Administrative Law and Regulatory Practice
Section of Business Law
Senior Lawyers Division
Special Committee on Gun Violence
Standing Committee on Election Law
Standing Committee on Judicial Independence
Young Lawyers Division

HISTORICAL FINANCIALS

Company Type: Private - Association

Income Statement

FYE: August 31

	REVENUE ($ mil.)	NET INCOME ($ mil.)	NET PROFIT MARGIN	EMPLOYEES
08/11	140	10	7.7%	900
08/10	140	4	2.9%	0
08/09	148	10	6.9%	0
Annual Growth	**(2.7%)**	**2.9%**	**—**	**—**

2011 Year-End Financials

Debt ratio: —
Return on equity: 7.70%
Cash ($ mil.): 25
Current ratio: 0.40
Long-term debt ($ mil.): —
Dividends
    Yield: —
    Payout: —
    Market value ($ mil.): —

AMERICAN CANCER SOCIETY CALIFORNIA DIVISION INC

LOCATIONS

HQ: AMERICAN CANCER SOCIETY CALIFORNIA
DIVISION INC
1710 WEBSTER ST, OAKLAND, CA 94612-3412
Phone: 510-893-7900

HISTORICAL FINANCIALS

Company Type: Private

Income Statement

FYE: August 31

	REVENUE ($ mil.)	NET INCOME ($ mil.)	NET PROFIT MARGIN	EMPLOYEES
08/11	953	66	7.0%	530
08/10	89	(1)	—	0
08/09	78	(11)	—	0
08/06	101	0	0.1%	0
Annual Growth	**110.9%**	**769.2%**	**—**	**—**

2011 Year-End Financials

Debt ratio: —
Return on equity: 7.00%
Cash ($ mil.): 129
Current ratio: —
Long-term debt ($ mil.): —
Dividends
    Yield: —
    Payout: —
    Market value ($ mil.): —

AMERICAN CANCER SOCIETY EAST CENTRAL DIVISION INC.

LOCATIONS

HQ: AMERICAN CANCER SOCIETY EAST CENTRAL
DIVISION INC.
SIPE AVE RR 422, HERSHEY, PA 17033
Phone: 717-533-6144

HISTORICAL FINANCIALS

Company Type: Private

Income Statement

FYE: August 31

	REVENUE ($ mil.)	NET INCOME ($ mil.)	NET PROFIT MARGIN	EMPLOYEES
08/11	91	4	5.0%	560
08/08	58	1	3.4%	0
08/07	65	8	13.1%	0
08/06	1,073	0	—	0
Annual Growth	**—**	**3007.1%**	**—**	**—**

2011 Year-End Financials

Debt ratio: —
Return on equity: 5.00%
Cash ($ mil.): 54
Current ratio: 1.40
Long-term debt ($ mil.): —
Dividends
    Yield: —
    Payout: —
    Market value ($ mil.): —

AMERICAN CANCER SOCIETY SOUTH ATLANTIC DIVISION INC.

LOCATIONS

HQ: AMERICAN CANCER SOCIETY SOUTH ATLANTIC
DIVISION INC.
250 WILLIAMS ST NW # 6000, ATLANTA, GA
30303-1032
Phone: 404-816-7800

HISTORICAL FINANCIALS

Company Type: Private

Income Statement

FYE: August 31

	REVENUE ($ mil.)	NET INCOME ($ mil.)	NET PROFIT MARGIN	EMPLOYEES
08/11	112	5	5.3%	661
08/10	113	7	6.8%	0
08/07	139	16	12.0%	0
08/03	60	0	0.9%	0
Annual Growth	**22.8%**	**121.2%**	**—**	**—**

2011 Year-End Financials

Debt ratio: —
Return on equity: 5.30%
Cash ($ mil.): 1
Current ratio: 0.10
Long-term debt ($ mil.): —
Dividends
    Yield: —
    Payout: —
    Market value ($ mil.): —

AMERICAN CHEMET CORPORATION

LOCATIONS

HQ: AMERICAN CHEMET CORPORATION
740 WAUKEGAN RD STE 202, DEERFIELD, IL
60015-4400
Phone: 847-948-0800
Web: www.chemet.com

HISTORICAL FINANCIALS

Company Type: Private

Income Statement
FYE: June 30

	REVENUE ($ mil.)	NET INCOME ($ mil.)	NET PROFIT MARGIN	EMPLOYEES
06/12	246	6	2.6%	140
06/11	254	9	3.8%	0
06/10	187	2	1.5%	0
06/09	194	4	2.4%	0
Annual Growth	8.1%	9.9%	—	—

2012 Year-End Financials

Debt ratio: ——
Return on equity: 2.60%
Cash ($ mil.): 1
Current ratio: 1.00
Long-term debt ($ mil.): —

Dividends
Yield: —
Payout: —
Market value ($ mil.): —

AMERICAN COLLEGE OF RADIOLOGY INC

LOCATIONS

HQ: AMERICAN COLLEGE OF RADIOLOGY INC
1891 PRESTON WHITE DR 1, RESTON, VA
20191-4397
Phone: 703-648-8900
Web: www.acr.org

HISTORICAL FINANCIALS

Company Type: Private

Income Statement
FYE: June 30

	REVENUE ($ mil.)	NET INCOME ($ mil.)	NET PROFIT MARGIN	EMPLOYEES
06/11	95	6	7.2%	350
06/10	80	4	5.6%	0
06/08	0	0	78.0%	0
06/06	73	4	5.8%	0
Annual Growth	9.0%	17.3%	—	—

2011 Year-End Financials

Debt ratio: ——
Return on equity: 7.20%
Cash ($ mil.): 4
Current ratio: 0.70
Long-term debt ($ mil.): —

Dividends
Yield: —
Payout: —
Market value ($ mil.): —

AMERICAN COLLEGE OF SURGEONS INC

LOCATIONS

HQ: AMERICAN COLLEGE OF SURGEONS INC
633 N SAINT CLAIR ST # 2600, CHICAGO, IL
60611-5927
Phone: 312-202-5000
Web: www.facs.org

HISTORICAL FINANCIALS

Company Type: Private

Income Statement
FYE: June 30

	REVENUE ($ mil.)	NET INCOME ($ mil.)	NET PROFIT MARGIN	EMPLOYEES
06/11	81	20	25.8%	257
06/09*	14	0	—	0
12/08	1	0	—	0
06/08	1,037	0	—	0
Annual Growth	—	986.1%	—	—

*Fiscal year change

2011 Year-End Financials

Debt ratio: ——
Return on equity: 25.80%
Cash ($ mil.): 1
Current ratio: 0.10
Long-term debt ($ mil.): —

Dividends
Yield: —
Payout: —
Market value ($ mil.): —

AMERICAN ENVIRONMENTAL GROUP LTD.

LOCATIONS

HQ: AMERICAN ENVIRONMENTAL GROUP LTD.
3600 BRECKSVILLE RD # 100, RICHFIELD, OH
44286-9668
Phone: 330-659-5930
Web: www.aegl.net

HISTORICAL FINANCIALS

Company Type: Private

Income Statement
FYE: December 31

	REVENUE ($ mil.)	NET INCOME ($ mil.)	NET PROFIT MARGIN	EMPLOYEES
12/11	82	7	9.4%	450
12/10	66	5	8.5%	0
12/09	47	4	9.3%	0
12/08	0	0	—	0
Annual Growth	—	—	—	—

2011 Year-End Financials

Debt ratio: ——
Return on equity: 9.40%
Cash ($ mil.): 1
Current ratio: 1.70
Long-term debt ($ mil.): —

Dividends
Yield: —
Payout: —
Market value ($ mil.): —

AMERICAN FEDERATION OF LABOR & CONGRESS OF INDUSTRIAL ORGANZATIO

LOCATIONS

HQ: AMERICAN FEDERATION OF LABOR &
CONGRESS OF INDUSTRIAL ORGANZATIO
815 16TH ST NW, WASHINGTON, DC 20006-4101
Phone: 202-637-5000
Web: www.aflcio.org

HISTORICAL FINANCIALS

Company Type: Private

Income Statement
FYE: June 30

	REVENUE ($ mil.)	NET INCOME ($ mil.)	NET PROFIT MARGIN	EMPLOYEES
06/11*	168	6	3.8%	380
08/09	0	0	—	0
06/08	150	(2)	—	0
06/07	0	0	—	0
Annual Growth	—	122.4%	—	—

*Fiscal year change

2011 Year-End Financials

Debt ratio: ——
Return on equity: 3.80%
Cash ($ mil.): 18
Current ratio: 0.30
Long-term debt ($ mil.): —

Dividends
Yield: —
Payout: —
Market value ($ mil.): —

AMERICAN FURNITURE WAREHOUSE CO INC

Tony the Tiger hawking home furnishings might give some marketers pause but the combination seems to work for American Furniture Warehouse. American Furniture's television commercials often spotlight white-haired president and CEO Jake Jabs (who has become a well-known personality in the state as well as in the home furnishings industry) accompanied by baby exotic animals mostly tigers. The company sells furniture and electronics at discounted prices through about a dozen retail locations in Colorado and via its website which also features bridal and gift registries. The company has built a reputation as a home-spun local furniture retailer. Jabs bought the company in 1975.

While privately-owned American Furniture Warehouse doesn't report financial results the company reported an estimated $328 million in sales in 2011 up more than 9% in 2010.

As the US economy has rebounded the company in 2011 opened a 100000-sq.-ft. showroom which includes a 50000-sq.-ft. warehouse in Grand Junction Colorado.

EXECUTIVES

President and CEO, Jacob (Jake) Jabs
CFO, Bob Schwartz
VP Purchasing, Tony Mitchell
Director Advertising, Dave Duncomb

LOCATIONS

HQ: American Furniture Warehouse Co. Inc.
8820 American Way, Englewood CO 80112
Phone: 303-799-9044   **Fax:** 720-873-8600
Web: www.afwonline.com

PRODUCTS/OPERATIONS

Selected Products

Decorative accessories (fountains wall art)
Electronics (AV equipment TV)
Furniture (bedroom dining room entertainment
  outdoor)
Lighting
Mattresses
Rugs

COMPETITORS

Ashley Furniture	Pier 1 Imports
Big Lots	Rooms To Go
Costco Wholesale	Sears
J. C. Penney	Target Corporation
Kmart	Wal-Mart

HISTORICAL FINANCIALS

Company Type: Private

Income Statement

FYE: March 31

	REVENUE ($ mil.)	NET INCOME ($ mil.)	NET PROFIT MARGIN	EMPLOYEES
03/11	306	11	3.8%	1,550
03/10	295	15	5.2%	0
03/09	298	8	3.0%	0
03/08	330	11	3.5%	0
Annual Growth	(2.5%)	0.7%	—	—

2011 Year-End Financials

Debt ratio: ——
Return on equity: 3.80%
Cash ($ mil.): 1
Current ratio: 0.10
Long-term debt ($ mil.): —

Dividends
  Yield: —
  Payout: —
Market value ($ mil.): —

AMERICAN INFRASTRUCTURE INC.

American Infrastructure provides heavy civil construction services for projects in the Mid-Atlantic. Operating as Allan A. Myers in Pennsylvania and Delaware and as American Infrastructure in Maryland and Virginia the company builds and reconstructs highways water treatment plants medical facilities and shopping centers and offers site development for homebuilders. Its quarries and asphalt plants operate under the Independence Construction Materials (ICM) subsidiary which supplies aggregates asphalt and ready-mixed concrete to its construction companies. The family-run business was established in 1939 as Allan A. Myers

and Son a local hauling company in the suburbs of Philadelphia.

Geographic Reach

The company and its subsidiaries operate in the Mid-Atlantic region through about 20 locations (including quarries and plants) in Pennsylvania Maryland Virginia and Delaware.

Operations

As a land developer interested in conservation American Infrastructure offers a unique all-terrain tree spade vehicle that is designed to carry large mature trees harvested from heavily wooded sites intended to be replanted on developed sites. The process allows mature trees to be saved and relocated on a developed site.

Sales and Marketing

American Infrastructure counts several companies and organizations among its current and former clients such as Hunt Building Company the City of Wilmington and Maryland State Highway Administration. Some past projects include Eagle Heights at Dover Air Force Base ($13.3 million) Cool Springs Reservoir ($18.6 million) and MD 43 ($46.7 million) located in Baltimore County Maryland.

EXECUTIVES

Chairman and CEO, A. Ross Myers, age 62
EVP CFO and Treasurer, William Murdock III
Manager of Business Development American Infrastructure-Maryland, Barrett Tucker
VP Business Development, Joseph D. (Joe) Prego
VP and Equipment Fleet Manager, Dave Markey
Secretary, Teresa S. Hasson
Controller, Carolann Buchler
Manager of Business Development Allan A. Myers, David Bates
VP Purchasing, Bob Semion

LOCATIONS

HQ: American Infrastructure Inc.
1805 Berks Rd., Worcester PA 19490
Phone: 610-222-8800   **Fax:** 610-222-3300
Web: www.americaninfrastructure.com

PRODUCTS/OPERATIONS

Selected Services

Site Development
  Concrete flatwork
  Excavation and grading
  Hauling
  Large-diameter tree relocation
  Milling and paving
  Rock drilling and blasting
  Soft dig capabilities
  Stone and curb
  Stormwater management
  Survey and stakeout
  Underground utilities
Transportation
  Asphalt paving
  Box culverts
  Bridges and structures
  Concrete paving
  Maintenance of traffic
Water Resources
  New water/wastewater treatment plants
  Reservoirs and dams
  Underground reservoirs
  Water and sewer transmission lines
  Wetland mitigation and reconstruction

Selected Subsidiaries

Allan A. Myers Inc.
American Infrastructure-Maryland
American Infrastructure-Virginia
Independence Construction Materials

COMPETITORS

Angelo Iafrate	English Construction
Balfour Beatty	Company
Infrastructure	Lane Construction
Barnhill Contracting	Peter Kiewit Sons'
Branch Group	Skanska USA Civil
Cherry Hill	Traylor Bros.
Construction	Vecellio & Grogan

HISTORICAL FINANCIALS

Company Type: Private

Income Statement

FYE: December 31

	REVENUE ($ mil.)	NET INCOME ($ mil.)	NET PROFIT MARGIN	EMPLOYEES
12/11	545	(0)		2,045
12/10	476	20	4.2%	0
12/08	484	5	1.1%	0
12/07	463	9	2.1%	0
Annual Growth	5.6%	—	—	—

2011 Year-End Financials

Debt ratio: ——
Return on equity: (-0.10)%
Cash ($ mil.): 4
Current ratio: 0.90
Long-term debt ($ mil.): —

Dividends
  Yield: —
  Payout: —
Market value ($ mil.): —

AMERICAN INSTITUTE OF PHYSICS INCORPORATED

Who says scientists don't know how to get physical? The American Institute of Physics (AIP) publishes magazines (Physics Today) journals (Journal of Applied Physics) conference proceedings online products and other publications in the sciences of physics and astronomy. The company provides publishing services for its own publications as well as for its member societies and other publishers. Scitation AIP's online publishing platform hosts 1.6 million articles from 190 sources. AIP was founded in New York in 1931 by a group of American physical science societies. It was chartered as a membership corporation to advance and diffuse knowledge of the science of physics and its applications to human welfare.

In 2011 the company re-shifted its focus to providing publishing services for its Member Societies and the at-large physical sciences community rather than the global scientific community. It made the strategic move in order to more effectively allocate its resources. AIP's 10 physical science societies include The American Physical Society and the American Geophysical Union and represent more than 135000 scientists engineers and educators. AIP publishes a total of 13 journals and two magazines.

In addition to journals and magazines the publishes findings presented at scientific meetings around the world through its AIP Conference Proceedings series. The API also operates UniPHY a social and professional networking site for the physical sciences community. Other holdings include the Physics Today Career Network Gradschoolshopper.com and Online History Exhibits.

As part of a global expansion strategy in 2010 AIP opened its first international office in Beijing. The Chinese location joined the organization's existing US offices in College Park Maryland and Melville New York.

EXECUTIVES

CFO and Treasurer, Richard Baccante
Director Publication Sales and Market Development, Douglas LaFrenier
SVP Publishing, Darlene Walters
Director Strategic Initiatives and Publisher Relations, Tim Ingoldsby
Senior Director Publishing Services, James Donohue
VP Human Resources, Theresa C. Braun
Director Editorial Operations, Doreene Berger
Director Publishing Services Sales, Richard Kobel
Manager Strategic Planning and Corporate Communications, Eva Adams
Editor Magazines and Physics Today, Stephen Benka
Copyright and Permissions and Intellectual Property Rights, Susann Brailey
Director Fulfillment and Marketing Services, Lori Carlin
Publisher Journals and Technical Publications, Mark Cassar
Manager Facility Services, Thea Cohen
Manager Office Services, Debra Dillon
Director Publishing Technology, William Filaski
Director Journal Advertising and Exhibits, Robert Finnegan
Director Production Operations and Customer Services, Carol Fleming
Director Special Publications and Proceedings, Maya Flikop
Director Compensation and Benefits, Jonathan Goodwin
Manager Melville Human Resources, Margaret Griesmer
Director Education, Jack Hehn
Director Business Analysis Publishing, Patricia Hoeffner
Director Business Systems and Operations, Wendy Marriott
Director Production Operations Support Services, Chris McMahon
Publisher Magazines and Physics Today, Randolph Nanna
Corporate Secretary, Benjamin Snavely
VP Physics Resources Center, James Stith
Controller and Assistant Treasurer, Gigi Swartz
Director Society of Physics Students and Assistant Director Education, Gary White
Director Emerging Technology, James Wonder
Director Web Strategy and Management, Jenny Krivanek
Director Industrial Outreach and Corporate Associates, Jerry R. Hobbs
Executive Director and CEO, H. Frederick Dylla
VP Publishing, John S. Haynes
Chief Information Officer, Evan Owens
Director Publishing Operations, Lisa McLaughlin

LOCATIONS

HQ: American Institute Of Physics Incorporated
1 Physics Ellipse, College Park MD 20740-3843
Phone: 301-209-3100   **Fax:** 604-6848092
Web: www.atlatsaresources.co.za

PRODUCTS/OPERATIONS

Selected Publications
Applied Physics Letters
Computing in Science & Engineering
Journal of Applied Physics
The Journal of Chemical Physics
Journal of Mathematical Physics
Low Temperature Physics
Physics of Plasmas
Physics Today

Selected Member Societies
Acoustical Society of America (ASA)
American Association of Physicists in Medicine (AAPM)
American Association of Physics Teachers (AAPT)
American Astronomical Society (AAS)
American Crystallographic Association (ACA)
American Geophysical Union
American Physical Society (APS)
AVS The Science and Technology Society (AVS)
Optical Society of America (OSA)
The Society of Rheology (SoR)

COMPETITORS

Axel Springer	MIT
Discovery	NASA
Communications	National Geographic
Harvard University	Reed Elsevier Group
Press	University of
Los Alamos National	Cambridge
Lab	University of Texas
McGraw-Hill	Wolters Kluwer

HISTORICAL FINANCIALS

Company Type: Private - Association

Income Statement
FYE: December 31

	REVENUE ($ mil.)	NET INCOME ($ mil.)	NET PROFIT MARGIN	EMPLOYEES
12/11	73	(8)	—	273
12/10	75	8	11.4%	0
12/09	77	23	29.7%	0
12/08	76	(39)	—	0
Annual Growth	(1.3%)	—	—	—

2011 Year-End Financials

Debt ratio: —
Return on equity: (-11.30)%
Cash ($ mil.): 24
Current ratio: 1.20
Long-term debt ($ mil.): —

Dividends
Yield: —
Payout: —
Market value ($ mil.): —

AMERICAN INSTITUTES FOR RESEARCH IN THE BEHAVIORAL SCIENCES

The American Institutes for Research (AIR) lives and breathes to enhance human performance. The not-for-profit organization conducts behavioral and social science research on topics related to education and educational assessment health international development and work and training. Clients including several federal agencies use AIR's research to help develop policies. The organization has an ongoing major initiative to provide tools to improve education both in the US and internationally particularly in disadvantaged areas. John Flanagan who developed the Critical Incident Technique personnel-selection tool to identify human success indicators in the workplace founded the organization in 1946.

Broadly the organization's programs consist of assessment; international human and social development; health; and federal statistics. AIR's assessment program focuses on score reports and online reporting tools to translate large-scale testing data on student achievement into a benchmark for school performance. International human and social development programs aim to improve the quality of life and education in developing areas through teacher and school administrator training curriculum development and teaching materials coupled with mobilizing health communications HIV/AIDS education and raising awareness about such issues as child labor exploitation. Working with governments and private health care providers and the general public AIR's health programs design implement and evaluate the impact of health care policies. The organization's successes include campaigns that address public health emergencies such as the flu and H1N1 and the prevention of HIV/AIDS heart disease and birth defects. The National Center for Education Statistics a key source for statistical data about education and AIR team up to develop large-scale databases for policymaking. Among various efforts AIR designs surveys and assessments develops questionnaires and tests items as well as informational materials. It also helps in producing The Condition of Education the agency's chief report.

AIR started as a small research group tied to the University of Pittsburgh and now spans more than 30 offices in more than a dozen countries worldwide. Reflecting its growth AIR has posted year-over increases in revenue since 2001. In fiscal 2010 (ends December) revenues from contracts and grants jumped approximately 5% over 2007. More than 95% of the organization's revenues go toward its projects.

Adding to its educational research capabilities AIR has pursued a number of strategic alliances and acquisitions. In mid 2011 the National Center for Analysis of Longitudinal Data in Educational Research (CALDER) began operating as a joint project of AIR. CALDER examines how public policies and community conditions impact teacher-student results. A year earlier AIR acquired Learning Point Associates a Chicago-based firm that delivers research in the educational sector. Its clients include state education agencies single-school districts private foundations and for-profit organizations.

EXECUTIVES

SVP and CFO, Marijo L. Ahlgrimm, age 51
General Counsel Ethics Officer and Secretary, Dona Kilpatrick
EVP and Chief Strategy Officer, Michael B. Kane
SVP Human Resources and Administration, Mark S. Fanning
SVP and Deputy Director Education Human Development and the Workforce, Mark Kutner
SVP and Director Health, Marilyn Moon
EVP and Director Assessment, Jon Cohen
SVP and Director Federal Statistics, Laura Salganik
Managing Director Education Group, Larry Condelli
VP Human and Social Development, David Osher
VP Education Human Development and the Workforce, Deborah Parrish
Director of SEEP, Jay G. Chambers
Director of CSEF, Thomas (Tom) Parrish
Deputy Director of CSEF/SEEP, Jenifer J. Harr

VP Education Human Development and the Workforce, Michael S. (Mike) Garet

Managing Research Scientist, Jennifer O'Day

Co-Director Communication & Social Marketing Group, Julia Hunter Galdo

Managing Director Health Financing and Cost Containment, Steven A. Garfinkel

Vice President Assessment, Gary Phillips

VP and Director International Development, Jane Benbow

Principal Research Scientist, Nancy Matheson

VP Education Human Development and the Workforce, Dwayne Norris

Director Communications, Larry McQuillan

President CEO and Director, David Myers

Co-Director Communication & Social Marketing Group, Don L. Mullins Jr.

Managing Director, Matt Mangan

Chairman, Patricia B. Gurin

Vice Chairman, Lawrence D. Bobo

VP Education Human Development and the Workforce, Mark S. Schneider

EVP and Director Education Human Development and the Workforce, Gina Burkhardt

VP and Executive Director, Steve Kromer

VP Education Human Development and the Workforce, Hans Bos

VP Education Human Development and the Workforce, Sabrina Laine

SVP and Director Human and Social Development, Cheryl Vince Whitman

Executive Director Communications and Public Affairs, Patrick R. Riccards

VP Information Technology, Robert Holstein

Director, Edward L. Hamburg, age 60

Director, Delano E. Lewis, age 73

Director, Sol H. Pelavin

President CEO and Director, David Myers

Vice Chairman, Lawrence D. Bobo

Director, Greg Baroni

Director, Robert F. Boruch

Director, Nancy E. Cantor

Director, Sara Kiesler

Director, Kathy McKinless

Director, Richard A. Smith

Director, Andrew Liakopoulos

LOCATIONS

HQ: American Institutes for Research in the Behavioral Sciences
1000 Thomas Jefferson St. NW, Washington DC 20007-3835
Phone: 202-403-5000 **Fax:** 202-403-5001
Web: www.air.org

PRODUCTS/OPERATIONS

Selected Program Areas
Education
Education assessment
Health
International development
Work and training

HISTORICAL FINANCIALS

Company Type: Private - Not-for-Profit

Income Statement FYE: December 31

	REVENUE ($ mil.)	NET INCOME ($ mil.)	NET PROFIT MARGIN	EMPLOYEES
12/11	300	13	4.3%	1,175
12/10	285	21	7.5%	0
12/09	299	18	6.0%	0
12/08	301	15	5.3%	0
Annual Growth	(0.2%)	(6.6%)	—	—

2011 Year-End Financials
Debt ratio: ——
Return on equity: 4.30%
Cash ($ mil.): 15
Current ratio: 1.30
Long-term debt ($ mil.): —
Dividends
Yield: —
Payout: —
Market value ($ mil.): —

AMERICAN MANAGEMENT ASSOCIATION INTERNATIONAL

American Management Association (AMA) is a not-for-profit membership association that provides a variety of educational and management development services to businesses government agencies and individuals. AMA offers more than 140 training seminars in about 25 subject areas of business management and workforce development. It also sponsors conferences and workshops and provides webcasts podcasts and books in such areas as communication leadership project management sales and marketing human resources and finance and accounting. AMA was founded in 1913 as the National Association of Corporation Schools; it adopted the name American Management Association in 1923.

Many FORTUNE 500 companies utilize AMA's professional development services to enhance the skills abilities and knowledge of their employees.

The company and its global network have Executive Conference Centers in Atlanta Chicago New York San Francisco and Arlington Virginia and in Brussels Toronto Mexico City Tokyo Shanghai Beijing and Istanbul. In 2012 AMA completed a $1 million renovation of its 23000-sq.-ft. Executive Conference Center in Atlanta. The work included technology upgrades and enhancements to its meeting rooms business center bookstore lounges and other common areas. In 2011 the center accommodated AMA's 200-plus public seminars with more than 2100 attendees from the US and 20 other countries.

To attract more clients and expand its distance learning capabilities AMA formed a strategic partnership in 2012 with European distance learning solutions leader CrossKnowledge to offer that company's on-demand e-learning solutions to customers in the US. AMA will have access to CrossKnowledge's library of more than 15000 learning contents for management leadership and soft skills which are offered in 15 languages.

EXECUTIVES

President CEO and Trustee, Edward T. Reilly, age 64

EVP CFO and Treasurer, Vivianna Guzman

EVP US Management Education, Patricia (Pat) Leonard

SVP General Counsel and Secretary, Arthur J. Levy

SVP Sales, Keith S. Dalton

Vice Chairman, Sir Paul Judge, age 62

VP Internal Audit, Robert G. Morales

SVP Global Human Resources, Manny Avramidis

SVP USME Instruction and Development, Diane Laurenzo

SVP Marketing and Membership, Robert G. Smith

VP Seminar Marketing, Tricia Beltrano

VP Event Management, Joan Castonguay

VP Finance, Cathy Liberty

VP National Account Development USME, Sam Davis

VP Strategic Sourcing and Facilities, Martin Delahay

VP Councils, Virginia O'Connor

Managing Director Europe Middle East and Africa, Francis van den Bosch

Public Relations Manager, Roger Kelleher

SVP and CIO, Richard J. Barton

President and Publisher AMACOM, Hank Kennedy

Managing Director Japan, Toshio Fukuda

Managing Director Mexico, Jorge Perez Rubio

Chair, Charles R. Craig

VP Sales and Marketing AMACOM, Rosemary Carlough

VP Design and Development, Daniel Tobin

President and Managing Director Canada, Greg Breen

Trustee, Edward D. (Ed) Horowitz, age 64

Trustee, Peter W. Bruce, age 66

President CEO and Trustee, Edward T. Reilly, age 64

Trustee, Douglas W. (Doug) McCormick, age 62

Trustee, Barry L. Williams, age 67

Trustee, James H. (Jim) Wall

Vice Chairman, Sir Paul Judge, age 62

Trustee, Tony Le Dinh

Trustee, Diane C. Yu

Trustee, Lew W. Cramer

Trustee, Pamela Grunder Sheiffer

Auditors: KPMGLLP

LOCATIONS

HQ: American Management Association International
1601 Broadway, New York NY 10019-7406
Phone: 212-586-8100 **Fax:** 212-903-8168
Web: www.amanet.org

PRODUCTS/OPERATIONS

Selected Subject Areas
Business analysis
Business enhancement skills
Business writing
Communication skills
Customer service
Finance and accounting
Human resource management
Information technology management
Interpersonal skills
ITIL (IT service management)
Leadership
Management and supervisory skills
Marketing
Office and administrative support
Presentation skills
Project management
Purchasing and supply management
Sales
Strategic alliance management
Strategic planning
Thinking and innovation
Time management
Training and development

Selected AMA Certificate Programs
Administrative Excellence
Business Communication
Business Management for IT and Technical Professionals
Finance
Human Resources and Training
Leadership
Management Excellence
Marketing

Sales
Supervisory Skills
Project Management

COMPETITORS

2logical	Management Forum
Afterburner	Nightingale-Conant
American Management	Root Learning
Development Group	Shapiro Negotiations
BlessingWhite	Institute
Dale Carnegie	SkillSoft
Franklin Covey	

HISTORICAL FINANCIALS

Company Type: Private - Not-for-Profit

Income Statement

FYE: March 31

	REVENUE ($ mil.)	NET INCOME ($ mil.)	NET PROFIT MARGIN	EMPLOYEES
03/11	87	(3)	—	500
03/10	83	(2)	—	0
03/09*	136	0	—	0
12/04	138	16	11.6%	0
Annual Growth	(14.1%)	—	—	—

*Fiscal year change

2011 Year-End Financials

Debt ratio: ——
Return on equity: (-4.20)%
Cash ($ mil.): 5
Current ratio: 0.20
Long-term debt ($ mil.): —

Dividends
  Yield: —
  Payout: —
Market value ($ mil.): —

AMERICAN PETROLEUM CO INC

LOCATIONS

HQ: AMERICAN PETROLEUM CO INC
  KM 0 HM 2 CAM RR 865, TOA BAJA, PR 00949
Phone: 787-794-1985
Web: www.americanpetroleumpr.com

HISTORICAL FINANCIALS

Company Type: Private

Income Statement

FYE: December 31

	REVENUE ($ mil.)	NET INCOME ($ mil.)	NET PROFIT MARGIN	EMPLOYEES
12/11	144	0	0.1%	80
12/10	115	0	0.8%	0
12/09	117	(0)	—	0
12/08	147	0	0.0%	0
Annual Growth	(0.7%)	29.6%	—	—

2011 Year-End Financials

Debt ratio: ——
Return on equity: 0.10%
Cash ($ mil.): 0
Current ratio: 1.20
Long-term debt ($ mil.): —

Dividends
  Yield: —
  Payout: —
Market value ($ mil.): —

AMERICAN PLANT FOOD CORPORATION

LOCATIONS

HQ: AMERICAN PLANT FOOD CORPORATION
  903 MAYO SHELL RD, GALENA PARK, TX 77547-3291
Phone: 713-675-2231
Web: www.apfcorp.net

HISTORICAL FINANCIALS

Company Type: Private

Income Statement

FYE: October 31

	REVENUE ($ mil.)	NET INCOME ($ mil.)	NET PROFIT MARGIN	EMPLOYEES
10/11	225	13	5.9%	110
10/10	167	7	4.4%	0
10/09	139	9	6.6%	0
10/08	211	11	5.3%	0
Annual Growth	2.3%	5.8%	—	—

2011 Year-End Financials

Debt ratio: ——
Return on equity: 5.90%
Cash ($ mil.): 11
Current ratio: 1.20
Long-term debt ($ mil.): —

Dividends
  Yield: —
  Payout: —
Market value ($ mil.): —

AMERICAN PLASTIC TOYS INC.

If your child spends hours applying pretend makeup at her Enchanted Beauty Salon or hammering away at his Build & Play Tool Bench or digging in the sand with her Castle Pail of Toys you can thank American Plastic Toys for the much-needed break. The company manufactures plastic toys including doll accessories (strollers nurseries) children's furniture role-playing items (kitchen sets tool benches) riding toys (trikes wagons) seasonal toys (pail and shovel sets) and vehicles (dump trucks airplanes). Products are sold by such retailers as Wal-Mart Kmart and Toys "R" Us across the US as well as in Canada the Caribbean Central and South America and Mexico. The company was founded in 1962.

EXECUTIVES

Chairman, David B. Littleton
President, John Gessert
Head International Sales, Dan Volz
Human Resources Manager, Patricia Worden
Treasurer, James Grau

LOCATIONS

HQ: American Plastic Toys Inc.
  799 Ladd Rd., Walled Lake MI 48390-0100
Phone: 248-624-4881   **Fax:** 248-624-4918
Web: www.aptoys.net

COMPETITORS

Little Tikes	Smoby
Mattel	Step2

HISTORICAL FINANCIALS

Company Type: Private

Income Statement

FYE: December 31

	REVENUE ($ mil.)	NET INCOME ($ mil.)	NET PROFIT MARGIN	EMPLOYEES
12/11	45	(1)	—	300
12/10	51	4	7.8%	0
12/09	48	7	16.5%	0
12/08	0	0	—	0
Annual Growth	—	—	—	—

2011 Year-End Financials

Debt ratio: ——
Return on equity: (-3.20)%
Cash ($ mil.): 2
Current ratio: 6.30
Long-term debt ($ mil.): —

Dividends
  Yield: —
  Payout: —
Market value ($ mil.): —

AMERICAN PSYCHOLOGICAL ASSOCIATION INC.

The American Psychological Association (APA) works to advance mental health: yours and that of its members. The APA is the largest scientific and professional organization representing psychology in the US as well as the world's largest association of psychologists. The association seeks to advance the study and practice of psychology in the US. It is also vocal about the role of psychological services in health care reform. It offers members career resources insurance and financial and other services. The APA has more than 137000 members including researchers educators clinicians consultants and students as well some 55 professional divisions.

EXECUTIVES

CEO EVP and Director, Norman B. Anderson
Recording Secretary and Director, Barry S. Anton
Staff Liaison, Judy A. Strassburger
COO Deputy CEO Executive Director Central Programs, L. Michael Honaker
General Counsel, Nathalie Gilfoyle
Executive Director Public and Member Communications, Rhea K. Farberman
CIO, Tony Habash
President, Alan E. E. Kazdin
President-Elect, James H. Bray
CFO, Archie Turner
CEO EVP and Director, Norman B. Anderson
Recording Secretary and Director, Barry S. Anton
Director, Lisa Grossman
Director, Douglas C. Haldeman
Director, Armand R. Cerbone
Director, Melba J. T. Vasquez
Director, Michael Wertheimer

LOCATIONS

HQ: American Psychological Association
750 1st St. NE, Washington DC 20002-4242
Phone: 202-336-5500   **Fax:** 703-995-4398
Web: www.plp.com

HISTORICAL FINANCIALS

Company Type: Private - Association

Income Statement

FYE: December 31

	REVENUE ($ mil.)	NET INCOME ($ mil.)	NET PROFIT MARGIN	EMPLOYEES
12/11	130	(7)	—	550
12/06	5	0	5.0%	0
12/05	0	0	—	0
12/03	1,452	0	0.0%	0
Annual Growth	(55.3%)	—	—	—

2011 Year-End Financials

Debt ratio: —
Return on equity: (-5.50)%
Cash ($ mil.): 45
Current ratio: 0.90
Long-term debt ($ mil.): —

Dividends
Yield: —
Payout: —
Market value ($ mil.): —

AMERICAN SOCIETY FOR TESTING AND MATERIALS

The American Society for Testing and Materials —which does business as ASTM International —is a not-for-profit standards organization focused on developing voluntary codes and regulations for technical materials products systems and services. Established in 1898 to set standards for railroad steel the organization also works in such areas as petroleum medical devices consumer products and environmental assessment. ASTM International publishes its technical specifications in the Annual Book of ASTM Standards a more than 70-volume set. Its income is derived from selling its publications and through annual administrative fees. The organization has more than 30000 members in over 120 countries.

EXECUTIVES

President, James A. (Jim) Thomas
SVP Operations, Kenneth Pearson
Manager Customer Relations and Sales, Derek Franco
VP Information Technology Development and Application, Philip Lively
VP Global Cooperation, Teresa Cendrowska
VP Publications and Marketing, John Pace
Director Corporate Communications, Barbara Schindler
Director Information Processing Services, William Yonker
Director New Activities Technical Committee Support, Pat Picariello
Director International Sales Canada Europe and Middle East, Jim S. Thomas
VP Global Policy and Industry Affairs, Jeff Grove
Executive Director Consortium on Standards and Conformity Assessment, Chris Lanzit

VP Technical Committee Operations, Kathie Morgan
Director External Relations Global Cooperation, Jim Olshefsky
Director Meetings Technical Committee Support, Betty Schultz
Manager Contract and Project Management Services, Anne McKlindon
Director Educational Services, Scott Murphy
Manager Symposia Educational Services, Dorothy Fitzpatrick
Manager Sales, George Zajdel
Manager Member Promotion and Academic Outreach, Ileane B. Smith
Assistant VP Publishing Services, Robert Dreyfuss
Director Web Site Development, Joyce Barton
Director International Sales Asia/Pacific India and South America, Marty Farrell
Editor-in-Chief Standardization News, Maryann Gorman
Chairman, Roger E. Stoller
Vice Chair, Catherine H. (Kitty) Pilarz
Director Public Policy and International Trade, Anthony Quinn
Director Interlaboratory Study Program Technical Committee Support, Phillip Godorov
Director Committee Services Technical Committee Support, Dan Schultz
Finance Accounting Treasurer and Secretary, Margaret M. (Marge) Cassidy
Director Product Development and Promotion, David von Glahn
Director Human Resources, Eileen Mullen
Vice Chair, Kenneth F. Yarosh
VP and General Counsel, Tom O'Brien
Director, Warren O. Haggard, age 55
Director, Paul K. Whitcraft
Director, Mary H. Saunders
Vice Chair, Catherine H. (Kitty) Pilarz
Director, Torsten Bahke
Director, Eric R. Boes
Director, Benedict R. Bonazza
Director, Carroll D. Davis
Director, Ricardo Rodrigues Fragoso
Director, Daniel M. Harrington
Director, Mary C. McKiel
Director, Toy S. Poole
Director, Paul H. Shipp
Director, Masami Tanaka
Director, Michael R. Withers
Director, Peter M. Woyciesjes
Vice Chair, Kenneth F. Yarosh
Director, Marilyn L. Baker
Director, Ronald J. Ebelhar
Director, Randy F. Jennings
Director, Ricky W. Magee
Director, Robert D. Thomas
Auditors: Ernst&YoungLLP

LOCATIONS

HQ: American Society for Testing and Materials
100 Barr Harbor Dr., West Conshohocken PA 19428-2959
Phone: 610-832-9500   **Fax:** 610-832-9555
Web: www.astm.org

HISTORICAL FINANCIALS

Company Type: Private - Not-for-Profit

Income Statement

FYE: December 31

	REVENUE ($ mil.)	NET INCOME ($ mil.)	NET PROFIT MARGIN	EMPLOYEES
12/11	55	(9)	—	185
12/10	53	21	40.6%	0
12/09	48	35	74.5%	0
12/02	35	(1)	—	0
Annual Growth	15.5%	—	—	—

2011 Year-End Financials

Debt ratio: —
Return on equity: (-17.20)%
Cash ($ mil.): 3
Current ratio: 0.80
Long-term debt ($ mil.): —

Dividends
Yield: —
Payout: —
Market value ($ mil.): —

AMERICAN SYSTEMS CORPORATION

American Systems provides government and commercial clients with IT management and consulting services including custom engineering and application development. Its consulting division advises clients on such issues as network access and identity management data security and process optimization. The company also provides managed technical support and staffing. American Systems works with government customers to develop systems related to command and control logistics and national security functions. Its commercial-focused operations serve the energy financial services retail and telecom industries among others.

Geographic Reach

The company has 16 offices along the Eastern Seaboard and in Arizona and California.

Operations

American Systems' government unit serves every branch of the US military as well as government agencies ranging from the Federal Aviation Administration to the Department of Agriculture. Its commercial unit on the other hand has served such companies as AT&T The Coca-Cola Company and The Home Depot.

Mergers and Acquisitions

In 2012 company completed the acquisition of Science Applications International Corporation's (SAIC's) Test & Evaluation (T&E) business unit. The acquisition strengthened American Systems' T&E capabilities and expanded the company's offerings to include testing scientific engineering logistic administrative and ancillary support.

Company Background

The employee-owned company was established in 1975 as American Communications Corporation.

EXECUTIVES

Director, L. Kenneth (Ken) Johnson, age 64
COO, Peter Smith
VP Human Relations, Chris Braccio
President and CEO, William C. Hoover, age 61
CFO, Mark Danisewicz, age 58
VP Professional Technical and IT Services, Michael (Mike) Innella

EVP and General Manager Business Development,
Finley B. Foster
CIO and CTO, Brian Neely
VP Contracts and Administration, Joe Kopfman
Chairman, Donald R. Burklew
VP Operational Services Directorate, Earle (Chip) Engle
VP Civilian Federal Market; Professional Technical and IT Services, Shawn O'Rourke
VP Identity Management and Information Assurance, Raymond (Ray) Rafaels
VP Custom Business Applications, Peter Pflugrath
Director, L. Kenneth (Ken) Johnson, age 64
Director, Patrick C. FitzPatrick, age 71
Auditors: Deloitte&ToucheLLP

LOCATIONS

HQ: American Systems Corporation
14151 Park Meadow Dr. Ste. 500, Chantilly VA 20151
Phone: 703-968-6300 **Fax:** 703-968-5151
Web: www.2asc.com

PRODUCTS/OPERATIONS

Selected Mergers and Acquisitions

FY2012
Science Applications International Corporation's (SAIC's) Test & Evaluation (T&E) business unit (undisclosed price; Raleigh NC; testing and evaluation services)

COMPETITORS

Affiliated Computer Services
Alion
Allen Corporation of America
Booz Allen
CACI International
Computer Sciences Corp.
General Dynamics Information Technology
HP Enterprise Services
IBM Global Services
Jacobs Engineering
Kratos Defense & Security Solutions
Lockheed Martin Information Systems
ManTech
Northrop Grumman Info Systems
Raytheon IIS
SAIC
SRA International
Unisys
Ventera

HISTORICAL FINANCIALS

Company Type: Private

Income Statement

	REVENUE ($ mil.)	NET INCOME ($ mil.)	NET PROFIT MARGIN	EMPLOYEES
12/11	250	16	6.7%	1,150
12/10	273	10	3.7%	0
12/09	230	6	3.0%	0
12/08	205	1	0.6%	0
Annual Growth	6.8%	143.4%	—	—

2011 Year-End Financials

Debt ratio: ——
Return on equity: 6.70%
Cash ($ mil.): 31
Current ratio: 2.80
Long-term debt ($ mil.): —

Dividends
Yield: —
Payout: —
Market value ($ mil.): —

AMERICAN TECHNOLOGIES INC.

LOCATIONS

HQ: AMERICAN TECHNOLOGIES INC.
210 W BAYWOOD AVE, ORANGE, CA 92865-2603
Phone: 714-283-9990
Web: www.amer-tech.com

HISTORICAL FINANCIALS

Company Type: Private

Income Statement   FYE: December 31

	REVENUE ($ mil.)	NET INCOME ($ mil.)	NET PROFIT MARGIN	EMPLOYEES
12/11	111	5	5.4%	500
12/10	98	4	4.4%	0
12/09	77	1	2.3%	0
12/08	88	3	3.7%	0
Annual Growth	8.1%	23.1%	—	—

2011 Year-End Financials

Debt ratio: ——
Return on equity: 5.40%
Cash ($ mil.): 2
Current ratio: 1.70
Long-term debt ($ mil.): —

Dividends
Yield: —
Payout: —
Market value ($ mil.): —

AMERICARES FOUNDATION INC.

AmeriCares Foundation provides emergency medical aid around the world. The not-for-profit charitable organization helps victims of natural disasters and supports long-term humanitarian programs by collecting medical supplies in the US and overseas and delivering them to places where they are needed. AmeriCares has provided aid in more than 135 countries worldwide. In the US the organization offers medical assistance runs a camp for kids with HIV/AIDS and conducts HomeFront a program that renovates housing for the needy in parts of Connecticut and New York. Robert C. Macauley founded AmeriCares in 1982.

In 2007 more than 98% of AmeriCare's expenses were allocated toward program services. About 1% was spent on fundraising with the balance of its funding going toward management and general expenses.

EXECUTIVES

President and CEO, Curtis R. (Curt) Welling, age 62
Chairman and Founder, Robert C. (Bob) McCauley
Vice-Chairman and Co-Founder, Alma Jane (Leila) McCauley
Chief of Staff and SVP Community Programs, Carol Shattuck
SVP Development and Communications, Carolyn O'Brien
VP Operations, Dennis Brown
VP Emergency Response, Chrisoph Gorder
Director Corporate Relations, Geoff Kneisel

Director Logistics, Peter Tokarczyk
SVP Human Resources, Kevin R. Gilrain
Medical Director, Frank Bia
VP; Managing Director AmeriCares India, Purvish M. Parikh
Director Communications, Peggy Atherlay
SVP Finance and Technology, Katherine A. Sears

LOCATIONS

HQ: AmeriCares Foundation Inc.
88 Hamilton Ave., Stamford CT 06902
Phone: 203-658-9500 **Fax:** 203-966-6028
Web: www.americares.org

HISTORICAL FINANCIALS

Company Type: Private - Foundation

Income Statement   FYE: June 30

	REVENUE ($ mil.)	NET INCOME ($ mil.)	NET PROFIT MARGIN	EMPLOYEES
06/11	671	(0)	—	125
06/10	795	(59)	—	0
06/09	1,197	35	3.0%	0
06/08	1,013	(46)	—	0
Annual Growth	(12.8%)	—	—	—

2011 Year-End Financials

Debt ratio: ——
Return on equity: (-0.10)%
Cash ($ mil.): 11
Current ratio: 1.90
Long-term debt ($ mil.): —

Dividends
Yield: —
Payout: —
Market value ($ mil.): —

AMERICON CONSTRUCTION INC.

LOCATIONS

HQ: AMERICON CONSTRUCTION INC.
44 W 18TH ST FL 6, NEW YORK, NY 10011-4643
Phone: 212-274-0190
Web: www.americoninc.com

HISTORICAL FINANCIALS

Company Type: Private

Income Statement   FYE: September 30

	REVENUE ($ mil.)	NET INCOME ($ mil.)	NET PROFIT MARGIN	EMPLOYEES
09/11	95	1	1.1%	72
Annual Growth	—	—	—	—

2011 Year-End Financials

Debt ratio: ——
Return on equity: 1.10%
Cash ($ mil.): 3
Current ratio: 1.00
Long-term debt ($ mil.): —

Dividends
Yield: —
Payout: —
Market value ($ mil.): —

AMERIGREEN ENERGY INC.

LOCATIONS

HQ: AMERIGREEN ENERGY INC.
1862 CHARTER LN STE 101, LANCASTER, PA
17601-6764
Phone: 717-945-1392
Web: www.amerigreen.com

HISTORICAL FINANCIALS

Company Type: Private

Income Statement

	REVENUE ($ mil.)	NET INCOME ($ mil.)	NET PROFIT MARGIN	EMPLOYEES
				FYE: September 30
09/11	95	0	1.0%	15
Annual Growth	—	—	—	—

2011 Year-End Financials

Debt ratio: —
Return on equity: 1.00%
Cash ($ mil.): 0
Current ratio: 0.40
Long-term debt ($ mil.): —

Dividends
Yield: —
Payout: —
Market value ($ mil.): —

AMERY REGIONAL MEDICAL CENTER INC.

If your arteries have become a bit clogged from too much cheese eating Amery Regional Medical Center in Amery Wisconsin is here to help. The not-for-profit community-owned hospital provides a range of medical services including emergency medicine obstetrics home and hospice care physical therapy surgery and pain management. Amery Regional Medical Center also provides community services such as wellness classes nutritional counseling and support groups. Its affiliates include Clear Lake Clinic Regions Hospital and Luck Medical Clinic.

EXECUTIVES

CEO, Michael Karuschak Jr.
Administrator Patient Care Services, Joyce Schaefer
Administrator Financial and General Services, Scott Edin
Administrator Human Resources and Community Relations, Joanne Jackson
Administrator Clinical Services and Quality Improvement, Sandi Reed
Chief Medical Officer, James Quenan

LOCATIONS

HQ: Amery Regional Medical Center
265 Griffin St. East, Amery WI 54001
Phone: 715-268-8000   **Fax:** 715-268-1376
Web: www.amerymedicalcenter.org

COMPETITORS

Bethesda Hospital
Fairview Health
HealthEast Care System
Regina Medical
Regions Hospital
St. John' s Hospital (Minnesota)
University of Minnesota Medical Center

HISTORICAL FINANCIALS

Company Type: Private - Not-for-Profit

Income Statement

	REVENUE ($ mil.)	NET INCOME ($ mil.)	NET PROFIT MARGIN	EMPLOYEES
				FYE: April 30
04/12	50	1	3.1%	480
04/11	50	0	1.4%	0
04/10*	48	0	1.4%	0
12/08	44	(1)	—	0
Annual Growth	4.3%	—	—	—

*Fiscal year change

2012 Year-End Financials

Debt ratio: —
Return on equity: 3.10%
Cash ($ mil.): 3
Current ratio: 1.90
Long-term debt ($ mil.): —

Dividends
Yield: —
Payout: —
Market value ($ mil.): —

AMNEAL PHARMACEUTICALS LLC

LOCATIONS

HQ: AMNEAL PHARMACEUTICALS LLC
440 US HIGHWAY 22 STE 104, BRIDGEWATER, NJ
08807-2477
Phone: 631-952-0214
Web: www.amneal.com

HISTORICAL FINANCIALS

Company Type: Private

Income Statement

	REVENUE ($ mil.)	NET INCOME ($ mil.)	NET PROFIT MARGIN	EMPLOYEES
				FYE: June 30
06/12*	165	52	31.8%	245
12/11	323	42	13.2%	0
Annual Growth	(48.8%)	23.2%	—	—

*Fiscal year change

2012 Year-End Financials

Debt ratio: —
Return on equity: 31.80%
Cash ($ mil.): 10
Current ratio: 1.30
Long-term debt ($ mil.): —

Dividends
Yield: —
Payout: —
Market value ($ mil.): —

AMNEAL PHARMACEUTICALS OF NEW YORK LLC

LOCATIONS

HQ: AMNEAL PHARMACEUTICALS OF NEW YORK LLC
85 ADAMS AVE, HAUPPAUGE, NY 11788-3629
Phone: 908-231-1911
Web: www.amneal.com

HISTORICAL FINANCIALS

Company Type: Private

Income Statement

	REVENUE ($ mil.)	NET INCOME ($ mil.)	NET PROFIT MARGIN	EMPLOYEES
				FYE: June 30
06/11*	153	22	14.6%	245
12/09	163	6	4.2%	0
Annual Growth	(5.8%)	224.6%	—	—

*Fiscal year change

2011 Year-End Financials

Debt ratio: —
Return on equity: 14.60%
Cash ($ mil.): 13
Current ratio: 2.50
Long-term debt ($ mil.): —

Dividends
Yield: —
Payout: —
Market value ($ mil.): —

ANALYSIS & DESIGN APPLICATION CO. LTD.

LOCATIONS

HQ: ANALYSIS & DESIGN APPLICATION CO. LTD.
60 BROADHOLLOW RD, MELVILLE, NY 11747-2504
Phone: 631-549-2300
Web: www.adapco.com

HISTORICAL FINANCIALS

Company Type: Private

Income Statement

	REVENUE ($ mil.)	NET INCOME ($ mil.)	NET PROFIT MARGIN	EMPLOYEES
				FYE: September 30
09/11	122	3	3.2%	165
09/10	37	2	8.0%	0
09/04	46	0	0.6%	0
09/03	38	(2)	—	0
Annual Growth	46.6%	—	—	—

2011 Year-End Financials

Debt ratio: —
Return on equity: 3.20%
Cash ($ mil.): 31
Current ratio: 1.10
Long-term debt ($ mil.): —

Dividends
Yield: —
Payout: —
Market value ($ mil.): —

ANDERSON AND DUBOSE INC.

You might say this company keeps the Big Mac big and the Happy Meals happy. Anderson-DuBose Pittsburgh is a leading wholesale distributor that supplies food and non-food items to McDonald's and Chipotle fast-food restaurants in Ohio Pennsylvania New York and West Virginia. It serves about 500 Golden Arches locations with frozen meat and fish dairy products and paper goods and packaging as well as toys for Happy Meals. One of the largest black-owned companies in the US Anderson-DuBose was started in 1991 by Warren Anderson and Stephen DuBose who purchased control of a McDonald's distributorship from Martin-Brower. Anderson became sole owner in 1993 when he bought out his partner's stake in the business.

EXECUTIVES

CFO, Tony Wiglusz
President and CEO, Warren E. Anderson, age 59
VP Technology, Mike Campbell
Manager Human Resources, Allie Krsak
Manager Purchasing, Marty Stroh

LOCATIONS

HQ: Anderson-DuBose Pittsburgh LLC
6575 Davis Industrial Pkwy., Solon OH 44139-3549
Phone: 440-248-8800   **Fax:** 440-248-6208

COMPETITORS

Golden State Foods	Performance Food
Gordon Food Service	Reinhart FoodService
Keystone Foods	Sysco
MAINES	US Foods
Martin-Brower	
Meadowbrook Meat	
Company	

HISTORICAL FINANCIALS

Company Type: Private

Income Statement
FYE: December 30

	REVENUE ($ mil.)	NET INCOME ($ mil.)	NET PROFIT MARGIN	EMPLOYEES
12/11	372	1	0.3%	100
12/10	341	1	0.5%	0
12/09	329	1	0.5%	0
12/08	323	1	0.5%	0
Annual Growth	4.8%	(6.7%)	—	—

ANIMAL HUMANE SOCIETY

LOCATIONS

HQ: ANIMAL HUMANE SOCIETY
845 MEADOW LN N, GOLDEN VALLEY, MN 55422-4831
Phone: 763-522-4325
Web: www.animalhumanesociety.org

HISTORICAL FINANCIALS

Company Type: Private

Income Statement
FYE: December 31

	REVENUE ($ mil.)	NET INCOME ($ mil.)	NET PROFIT MARGIN	EMPLOYEES
12/11*	167	(4)	—	200
06/11	13	0	7.3%	0
06/10	5	(0)	—	0
12/09	11	(0)	—	0
Annual Growth	146.1%	—	—	—

*Fiscal year change

2011 Year-End Financials

Debt ratio: ——
Return on equity: (-2.80)%
Cash ($ mil.): 25
Current ratio: ——
Long-term debt ($ mil.): ——

Dividends
Yield: —
Payout: —
Market value ($ mil.): —

ANKENY COMMUNITY SCHOOLS INC

LOCATIONS

HQ: ANKENY COMMUNITY SCHOOLS INC
306 SW SCHOOL ST, ANKENY, IA 50023-3063
Phone: 515-965-9607
Web: www.ankenyschools.org

HISTORICAL FINANCIALS

Company Type: Private

Income Statement
FYE: June 30

	REVENUE ($ mil.)	NET INCOME ($ mil.)	NET PROFIT MARGIN	EMPLOYEES
06/11*	104	29	27.9%	850
03/05	0	0	13.3%	0
06/02	48	(6)	—	0
06/01	610	0	—	0
Annual Growth	—	4628.2%		

*Fiscal year change

2011 Year-End Financials

Debt ratio: ——
Return on equity: 27.90%
Cash ($ mil.): 85
Current ratio: 1.90
Long-term debt ($ mil.): ——

Dividends
Yield: —
Payout: —
Market value ($ mil.): —

ANNA JAQUES HOSPITAL

LOCATIONS

HQ: ANNA JAQUES HOSPITAL
25 HIGHLAND AVE, NEWBURYPORT, MA 01950-3894
Phone: 978-463-1000
Web: www.ajh.org

HISTORICAL FINANCIALS

Company Type: Private

Income Statement
FYE: September 30

	REVENUE ($ mil.)	NET INCOME ($ mil.)	NET PROFIT MARGIN	EMPLOYEES
09/11	108	1	0.9%	1,150
Annual Growth	—	—	—	—

2011 Year-End Financials

Debt ratio: ——
Return on equity: 0.90%
Cash ($ mil.): 11
Current ratio: 2.00
Long-term debt ($ mil.): ——

Dividends
Yield: —
Payout: —
Market value ($ mil.): —

ANNE ARUNDEL COUNTY BOARD OF EDUCATION

LOCATIONS

HQ: ANNE ARUNDEL COUNTY BOARD OF EDUCATION
2644 RIVA RD, ANNAPOLIS, MD 21401-7427
Phone: 410-222-5000
Web: www.aahealth.org

HISTORICAL FINANCIALS

Company Type: Private

Income Statement
FYE: June 30

	REVENUE ($ mil.)	NET INCOME ($ mil.)	NET PROFIT MARGIN	EMPLOYEES
06/11	1,144	10	0.9%	7,200
06/04	712	0	0.1%	0
06/03	701	50	7.1%	0
06/02	701	50	7.1%	0
Annual Growth	17.8%	(40.7%)	—	—

2011 Year-End Financials

Debt ratio: ——
Return on equity: 0.90%
Cash ($ mil.): 138
Current ratio: ——
Long-term debt ($ mil.): ——

Dividends
Yield: —
Payout: —
Market value ($ mil.): —

ANNE ARUNDEL MEDICAL CENTER INC.

The ill and infirm get the royal treatment at Anne Arundel Medical Center. The full-service acute-care hospital serves the residents of Anne Arundel Calvert Prince George's Queen Anne and Talbot counties in Maryland. With about 325 beds the hospital administers care for women's health oncology pediatrics neurology orthopedics and pain management. The medical center also has cancer sleep disorder and vascular centers. Anne Arundel which opened its doors in 1902 and is part of the Anne Arundel Health System has expanded its service offerings through various affiliations with regional specialty and primary care clinics. It also has a partnership with Johns Hopkins Medicine.

Johns Hopkins and the not-for-profit Anne Arundel share some services faculty and patients through their collaboration. They also operate a joint outpatient urgent-care facility. Additionally the two organizations work together to perform on clinical research and on the development of physician graduate medical education programs.

Anne Arundel in in the midst of a construction project designed to double the size of the medical center (expected to be complete in 2011) through phases of expansion projects totaling $424 million including a new patient tower and expanded emergency operating pediatric and outpatient facilities. The project is meant to help Anne Arundel keep up with a continued growth in demand for health care services throughout its service area.

EXECUTIVES

President and CEO, Martin L. Doordan
SVP and Chief Development Officer, Lisa Hillman
CFO, William L. Hughes
VP Medical Affairs, Joseph D. (Joe) Moser
COO, Victoria Bayless
CIO, Douglas A. Abel
SVP Corporate Services; President Diagnostics Imaging, Carolyn W. Core
VP Quality and Patient Safety; Corporate Compliance Officer; President Pathways, Shirley J. Knelly
VP Strategic Planning and Business Development, Vanessa Aburn
Media Relations, Justin D. Paquette
Director Geaton and JoAnn DeCesaris Cancer Institute, Barry R. Meisenberg
VP Human Resources, Nancy Luttrell
Interim Director Marketing and Public Relations, Annamarie DeCarlo
Chief Medical Officer; President Physician Enterprise, Mitchell (Mitch) Schwartz
Auditors: Ernst&YoungLLP

LOCATIONS

HQ: Anne Arundel Medical Center Inc.
2001 Medical Pkwy., Annapolis MD 21401
Phone: 443-481-1000   **Fax:** 443-481-1951
Web: www.aahs.org

COMPETITORS

Ascension Health	Johns Hopkins Medicine
Bon Secours Health	LifeBridge Health
Catholic Health East	MedStar Health
Dimensions Healthcare	Sinai Hospital of
Franklin Square	Baltimore
Hospital Center	St. Agnes HealthCare
GBMC	Sun Healthcare
Harbor Hospital	University of Maryland
Johns Hopkins Health	Medical System
System	

HISTORICAL FINANCIALS

Company Type: Private - Not-for-Profit

Income Statement

FYE: June 30

	REVENUE ($ mil.)	NET INCOME ($ mil.)	NET PROFIT MARGIN	EMPLOYEES
06/11	445	24	5.4%	1,890
06/10	413	20	4.9%	0
06/09	398	0	—	0
06/08	7	4	54.2%	0
Annual Growth	284.9%	78.6%	—	—

2011 Year-End Financials

Debt ratio: ——
Return on equity: 5.40%
Cash ($ mil.): 4
Current ratio: 0.70
Long-term debt ($ mil.): —
Dividends
Yield: —
Payout: —
Market value ($ mil.): —

ANNESE & ASSOCIATES INC.

Annese & Associates has been distributing implementing and servicing communications networking systems in upstate New York since it was founded in 1970 by chairman Frank Annese. The company provides network planning and design management and support from six offices in the state. It specializes in systems for computer telephony audio- and videoconferencing unified messaging and call centers. Annese & Associates serves state and local government agencies as well as commercial clients in such industries as education finance and retail. While it has partnerships with several hardware and software makers including Juniper and Tandberg the company deals heavily in products from Cisco Systems.

Annese & Associates has said that its plan for growth includes ongoing investment in its sales efforts. To that end the company in 2009 expanded its regional sales and engineering services staff.

The previous year founder and chairman Frank Annese stepped down as CEO. He was replaced by veteran Annese & Associates salesman Raymond Apy. Other changes to the executive lineup were also made at that time.

EXECUTIVES

Chairman, Frank J. Annese, age 73
Manager East Regional Sales, Anthony J. Annese Jr.
President and CEO, Raymond H. (Ray) Apy
Director of IT/Operations, Jamie Aiello
VP Human Resources, Francine Annese Apy
Manager Financial Services, Cindy Brown
Contract Support Supervisor, Heather Golden
CTO, Rus Healy
CFO, Joe LoRe
VP Corporate Projects, Yvonne A. LoRe
VP Annese Services, Robert (Rob) Scott
Manager Human Resources, Rosemary Smith
Manager Western Regional Sales, Rob North
Manager Marketing, Kara Chase

ARMS Coordinator, Bill Leinauer
Manager Regional Engineering Western New York, Julia MacMurray
Manager Metro Regional Sales, Mike Stepkoski

LOCATIONS

HQ: Annese & Associates Inc.
4781 State Rte. 5 West, Herkimer NY 13350
Phone: 315-866-2213   **Fax:** 315-866-2207
Web: www.annese.com

COMPETITORS

Comm-Works	IBM
HP Enterprise Services	NetVersant

HISTORICAL FINANCIALS

Company Type: Private

Income Statement

FYE: December 31

	REVENUE ($ mil.)	NET INCOME ($ mil.)	NET PROFIT MARGIN	EMPLOYEES
12/11	62	2	4.3%	110
Annual Growth	—	—	—	—

2011 Year-End Financials

Debt ratio: ——
Return on equity: 4.30%
Cash ($ mil.): 3
Current ratio: 1.40
Long-term debt ($ mil.): —
Dividends
Yield: —
Payout: —
Market value ($ mil.): —

ANTHONY VINEYARDS INC

LOCATIONS

HQ: ANTHONY VINEYARDS INC
5512 VALPREDO AVE, BAKERSFIELD, CA 93307-9178
Phone: 661-858-6211
Web: www.anthonyvineyards.com

HISTORICAL FINANCIALS

Company Type: Private

Income Statement

FYE: December 31

	REVENUE ($ mil.)	NET INCOME ($ mil.)	NET PROFIT MARGIN	EMPLOYEES
12/11	94	21	22.3%	150
12/10	24	15	62.3%	0
12/09	19	11	57.9%	0
12/08	22	13	62.1%	0
Annual Growth	62.6%	15.6%	—	—

2011 Year-End Financials

Debt ratio: ——
Return on equity: 22.30%
Cash ($ mil.): 20
Current ratio: 4.90
Long-term debt ($ mil.): —
Dividends
Yield: —
Payout: —
Market value ($ mil.): —

API GROUP INC.

Holding company APi Group has a piece of the action in two main sectors: industrial and specialty construction services and fire protection systems. APi has more than three dozen subsidiaries which operate as independent companies across the US (nearly half of them in Minnesota) the UK and Canada. Services provided by the company's construction subsidiaries include HVAC and plumbing system installation; electrical industrial and mechanical contracting; industrial insulation; and garage door installation. Safety-focused units install a host of fire sprinkler detection security and alarm systems. The family-owned company was founded in 1926 by Reuben Anderson father of chairman Lee Anderson.

Strategy Although APi Group companies are independent they often pool resources and work together to service clients.

Mergers and Acquisitions The highly acquisitive APi Group is constantly on the lookout for new companies to add to its growing group. In 2012 it welcomed Canada-based Fire Stop Enterprises which offers fire protection systems in Nova Scotia and Cape Breton Island; Ohio-based 3S another fire protection firm that operates across North America; and Kansas-based mainline pipeline contractor Jomax Construction. Historical acquisitions include Island Fire Sprinkler Reliance Fire Protection and Northern Fire and Communication on the fire protection side and United Piping J. Koski Co. and Metropolitan Mechanical Contractors on the construction side.

EXECUTIVES

CFO and Treasurer, Gregory J. Keup, age 53
Chairman, Lee R. Anderson Sr.
President and CEO, Russell (Russ) Becker
CIO, Julius J. Chepey
President and CEO Jamar, Michael P. (Mike) McParlan
President and CEO Western States Fire Protection, Gene Postma
VP APi Construction Company, Jerald P. (Jerry) Pederson
COO, Paul Grunau
VP Acquisitions, Scott Hatfield
President VFP Fire Systems Inc., Andy McCleery
President Doody Mechanical and LeJeune Steel, Jim Torborg
VP APi Construction Company, Mark Udager
VP Distribution, John deGrood
President APi Electric, Brad Boos
VP Api Electric, Jeff Tyllia
General Manager APi Electric, Shane Shipman
VP Industrial APi Electric, Todd Lyden
VP Operations APi Electric, Floyd Cochran
CEO Classic Industrial Services, Bernie Vining
President Classic Industrial Services, Mark Beuerle
CEO Garage Door Store, Tom Prody
President Grunau Company, Lawrence (Larry) Loomis
President and CEO Industrial Contractors, E. Lloyd Bushong
Plant Manager Industrial Fabricators, Peter Kaz
President NYCO, Curt Mages
VP NYCO, Richard (Rick) Hansen
President Tessier's, Mark Buche
VP Tessier's, Gopal Vyas
President Twin City Garage Door, Lisa Donabauer
President Alliance Fire Protection, Fred L. Kroll
President APi National Service Group, Rock Marcone

President and CEO Davis-Ulmer Sprinkler, R. Steve Ulmer
President Delta Fire Systems, Danny Schindler
President International Fire Protection, Kamran Malek
VP International Fire Protection, Ronnie Davidson
President and CEO Security Fire Protection, David Dixon
President Rich Fire Protection, Frank Rich Jr.
CEO United States Fire Protection, Gregg Huennekens
President United States Fire Protection, Chad Huennekens
President and CEO VFP Fire Systems and Viking Automatic Sprinkler, Ryan Johnston
VP Vipond Fire Protection, Grant R. Neal
VP Operations Vipond Fire Protection, Bernie M. Beliveau
Managing Director Vipond Fire Protection, John McCann
VP Vipond Systems Group, Michael (Mike) Godara
President APi Systems Integrators, Tim Pietrzak
President APi CAD Services, Brad Moore
CEO and President United Piping, R. J. (Bob) Schoneberger
VP and General Superintendent United Piping, Dave Rickard
President Island Fire Sprinkler, Brian McMahon
President Reliance Fire Protection, Dave Shilling
VP Vipond Systems, Bruce Tait
VP and Controller, Mark Polovitz

LOCATIONS

HQ: APi Group Inc.
1100 Old Hwy. 8 NW, New Brighton MN 55112
Phone: 651-636-4320   **Fax:** 651-636-0312
Web: www.apigroupinc.com

PRODUCTS/OPERATIONS

Selected Subsidiaries
Fire Protection Systems
  Alliance Fire Protection Inc.
  API National Service Group
  Davis-Ulmer Sprinkler Company
  Delta Fire Systems Inc.
  Grunau Company
  Halon Banking Systems
  International Fire Protection Inc.
  Island Fire Sprinkler Inc.
  Reliance Fire Protection
  Rich Fire Protection Co Inc.
  Security Fire Protection Company
  United States Fire Protection Company
  VFP Fire Systems Inc.
  Viking Automatic Sprinkler Company
  Vipond Fire Protection Inc. (Canada)
  Vipond Fire Protection Ltd. (UK)
  Western States Fire Protection Inc.
Industrial and Specialty Construction Services
  3S Incorporated
  Anco Products Inc.
  APi CAD Services
  APi Construction Company (industrial insulation)
  APi Distribution Inc.
  APi Electric (electrical contracting)
  APi Supply Inc. (rental sales service of aerial work platforms)
  Classic Industrial Services Inc.
  Doody Mechanical Inc. (mechanical contracting including heating ventilation and air-conditioning)
  Garage Door Store (residential and commercial garage and specialty doors)
  Grunau Company Inc. (mechanical and fire protection systems)
  Industrial Contractors Inc. (energy industry contracting)
  Industrial Fabricators Inc. (industrial silencers)
  Jamar Company (mechanical and specialty contracting)
  Jomax Construction Co.

  LeJeune Steel Company (structural steel)
  NYCO Inc. (mechanical insulation)
  Tessier's Inc. (heating ventilating air conditioning installation)
  Twin City Garage Door Company (installation and servicing of overhead doors)
Low Voltage
  APi Systems Group Inc. (fire gas detection and alarm security)
  APi Systems Integrators (life safety)
  Vipond Systems Group

COMPETITORS

Comfort Systems USA	TDIndustries
EMCOR	Team
Integrated Electrical Services	Turner Industries
Irex	Tyco Fire & Security
John E. Green	

HISTORICAL FINANCIALS
Company Type: Private

Income Statement   FYE: December 31

	REVENUE ($ mil.)	NET INCOME ($ mil.)	NET PROFIT MARGIN	EMPLOYEES
12/11	1,484	52	3.6%	4,237
12/10	1,238	63	5.1%	0
12/09	1,358	63	4.7%	0
12/08	1,604	105	6.6%	0
Annual Growth	(2.6%)	(20.6%)	—	—

2011 Year-End Financials

Debt ratio: —
Return on equity: 3.60%
Cash ($ mil.): 35
Current ratio: 1.20
Long-term debt ($ mil.): —
Dividends
 Yield: —
 Payout: —
Market value ($ mil.): —

APPALACHIAN ELECTRIC COOPERATIVE

LOCATIONS

HQ: APPALACHIAN ELECTRIC COOPERATIVE
1109 HILL DR, NEW MARKET, TN 37820-3832
Phone: 865-475-2032
Web: www.appalachianelectric.coop

HISTORICAL FINANCIALS
Company Type: Private

Income Statement   FYE: June 30

	REVENUE ($ mil.)	NET INCOME ($ mil.)	NET PROFIT MARGIN	EMPLOYEES
06/12	95	3	3.8%	90
06/11	99	2	2.8%	0
06/10	86	3	3.6%	0
06/09	92	2	2.4%	0
Annual Growth	1.1%	18.4%	—	—

2012 Year-End Financials

Debt ratio: —
Return on equity: 3.80%
Cash ($ mil.): 8
Current ratio: 1.10
Long-term debt ($ mil.): —
Dividends
 Yield: —
 Payout: —
Market value ($ mil.): —

APPALACHIAN REGIONAL HEALTHCARE SYSTEM

LOCATIONS

HQ: APPALACHIAN REGIONAL HEALTHCARE SYSTEM
336 DEERFIELD RD, BOONE, NC 28607-5008
Phone: 828-262-4100

HISTORICAL FINANCIALS
Company Type: Private

Income Statement

FYE: September 30

	REVENUE ($ mil.)	NET INCOME ($ mil.)	NET PROFIT MARGIN	EMPLOYEES
09/11	146	10	7.1%	1,400
09/10	23	0	—	0
09/09	18	0	—	0
Annual Growth	182.9%	—	—	—

2011 Year-End Financials

Debt ratio: ——
Return on equity: 7.10%
Cash ($ mil.): 39
Current ratio: 2.30
Long-term debt ($ mil.): —

Dividends
Yield: —
Payout: —
Market value ($ mil.): —

APPLE REIT EIGHT INC.

LOCATIONS

HQ: APPLE REIT EIGHT INC.
814 E MAIN ST, RICHMOND, VA 23219-3306
Phone: 804-344-8121
Web: www.applereiteight.com

HISTORICAL FINANCIALS
Company Type: Private

Income Statement

FYE: September 30

	ASSETS ($ mil.)	NET INCOME ($ mil.)	INCOME AS % OF ASSETS	EMPLOYEES
09/12*	925	7	0.8%	6
12/11	935	9	1.0%	0
12/10	962	10	1.1%	0
12/09	998	5	0.6%	0
Annual Growth	(2.5%)	11.5%	—	—

*Fiscal year change

APPLE REIT NINE INC.

LOCATIONS

HQ: APPLE REIT NINE INC.
814 E MAIN ST, RICHMOND, VA 23219-3306
Phone: 804-344-8121
Web: www.applereitnine.com

HISTORICAL FINANCIALS
Company Type: Private

Income Statement

FYE: September 30

	ASSETS ($ mil.)	NET INCOME ($ mil.)	INCOME AS % OF ASSETS	EMPLOYEES
09/12*	1,553	62	4.0%	6
12/11	1,700	69	4.1%	0
12/10	1,745	16	0.9%	0
Annual Growth	(5.7%)	95.8%	—	—

*Fiscal year change

2012 Year-End Financials

Debt ratio: ——
Return on equity: 22.40%
Cash ($ mil.): 19
Current ratio: —
Long-term debt ($ mil.): —

Dividends
Yield: —
Payout: —
Market value ($ mil.): —

APPLE REIT SEVEN INC.

LOCATIONS

HQ: APPLE REIT SEVEN INC.
814 E MAIN ST, RICHMOND, VA 23219-3306
Phone: 804-344-8121
Web: www.applereitcompanies.net

HISTORICAL FINANCIALS
Company Type: Private

Income Statement

FYE: September 30

	ASSETS ($ mil.)	NET INCOME ($ mil.)	INCOME AS % OF ASSETS	EMPLOYEES
09/12*	851	20	2.5%	6
12/11	865	25	2.9%	0
12/10	891	28	3.2%	0
12/09	923	20	2.2%	0
Annual Growth	(2.7%)	0.4%	—	—

*Fiscal year change

APPLE REIT SIX INC.

LOCATIONS

HQ: APPLE REIT SIX INC.
814 E MAIN ST, RICHMOND, VA 23219-3306
Phone: 804-344-8121
Web: www.applereitsix.com

HISTORICAL FINANCIALS
Company Type: Private

Income Statement

FYE: September 30

	ASSETS ($ mil.)	NET INCOME ($ mil.)	INCOME AS % OF ASSETS	EMPLOYEES
09/12*	747	43	5.8%	50
12/11	759	45	5.9%	0
12/10	788	34	4.4%	0
12/09	815	33	4.1%	0
Annual Growth	(2.9%)	8.9%	—	—

*Fiscal year change

APPLE REIT TEN INC.

LOCATIONS

HQ: APPLE REIT TEN INC.
814 E MAIN ST, RICHMOND, VA 23219-3306
Phone: 804-344-8121
Web: www.applereitten.com

HISTORICAL FINANCIALS
Company Type: Private

Income Statement

FYE: September 30

	REVENUE ($ mil.)	NET INCOME ($ mil.)	NET PROFIT MARGIN	EMPLOYEES
09/12*	88	13	15.1%	0
12/11	42	(5)	—	0
Annual Growth	110.1%	—	—	—

*Fiscal year change

2012 Year-End Financials

Debt ratio: ——
Return on equity: 15.10%
Cash ($ mil.): 125
Current ratio: —
Long-term debt ($ mil.): —

Dividends
Yield: —
Payout: —
Market value ($ mil.): —

AQUATECH INTERNATIONAL CORPORATION

LOCATIONS

HQ: AQUATECH INTERNATIONAL CORPORATION
1 FOUR COINS DR, CANONSBURG, PA 15317-1776
Phone: 724-746-5300
Web: www.aquatech.com

HISTORICAL FINANCIALS
Company Type: Private

Income Statement
FYE: December 31

	REVENUE ($ mil.)	NET INCOME ($ mil.)	NET PROFIT MARGIN	EMPLOYEES
12/11	132	9	6.8%	500
12/10	101	6	6.2%	0
12/09	83	1	2.3%	0
12/08	126	4	3.5%	0
Annual Growth	1.6%	26.5%	—	—

2011 Year-End Financials
Debt ratio: ——
Return on equity: 6.80%
Cash ($ mil.): 17
Current ratio: 0.80
Long-term debt ($ mil.): —

Dividends
Yield: —
Payout: —
Market value ($ mil.): —

HISTORICAL FINANCIALS
Company Type: Private

Income Statement
FYE: June 30

	REVENUE ($ mil.)	NET INCOME ($ mil.)	NET PROFIT MARGIN	EMPLOYEES
06/11	278	41	14.8%	4,000
06/06	219	21	9.6%	0
06/05	219	21	9.6%	0
06/03	197	(26)	—	0
Annual Growth	12.2%	—	—	—

2011 Year-End Financials
Debt ratio: ——
Return on equity: 14.80%
Cash ($ mil.): 15
Current ratio: 0.10
Long-term debt ($ mil.): —

Dividends
Yield: —
Payout: —
Market value ($ mil.): —

HISTORICAL FINANCIALS
Company Type: Private

Income Statement
FYE: June 30

	REVENUE ($ mil.)	NET INCOME ($ mil.)	NET PROFIT MARGIN	EMPLOYEES
06/12	86	26	30.1%	200
06/11	71	21	30.4%	0
06/10	49	6	12.7%	0
06/09	47	13	29.3%	0
Annual Growth	22.1%	23.3%	—	—

2012 Year-End Financials
Debt ratio: ——
Return on equity: 30.10%
Cash ($ mil.): 81
Current ratio: 1.30
Long-term debt ($ mil.): —

Dividends
Yield: —
Payout: —
Market value ($ mil.): —

ARCATA ASSOCIATES INC.

LOCATIONS
HQ: ARCATA ASSOCIATES INC.
2588 FIRE MESA ST STE 110, LAS VEGAS, NV 89128-9022
Phone: 702-642-9500
Web: www.arcataassoc.com

HISTORICAL FINANCIALS
Company Type: Private

Income Statement
FYE: December 31

	REVENUE ($ mil.)	NET INCOME ($ mil.)	NET PROFIT MARGIN	EMPLOYEES
12/11	92	3	3.4%	425
12/10	103	2	2.8%	0
12/09	120	2	2.2%	0
Annual Growth	(12.4%)	8.9%	—	—

2011 Year-End Financials
Debt ratio: ——
Return on equity: 3.40%
Cash ($ mil.): 9
Current ratio: 3.80
Long-term debt ($ mil.): —

Dividends
Yield: —
Payout: —
Market value ($ mil.): —

ARCHDIOCESE OF ST. LOUIS

LOCATIONS
HQ: ARCHDIOCESE OF ST. LOUIS
20 ARCHBISHOP MAY DR, SAINT LOUIS, MO 63119-5738
Phone: 314-633-2222
Web: www.holyr.org

ARETT SALES CORP

LOCATIONS
HQ: ARETT SALES CORP
9285 COMMERCE HWY, PENNSAUKEN, NJ 08110-1201
Phone: 856-751-1224
Web: www.goodprod.com

HISTORICAL FINANCIALS
Company Type: Private

Income Statement
FYE: December 31

	REVENUE ($ mil.)	NET INCOME ($ mil.)	NET PROFIT MARGIN	EMPLOYEES
12/11	120	3	2.5%	150
12/10	143	5	3.7%	0
12/09	128	4	3.5%	0
12/08	124	3	2.4%	0
Annual Growth	(1.1%)	0.0%	—	—

2011 Year-End Financials
Debt ratio: ——
Return on equity: 2.50%
Cash ($ mil.): 3
Current ratio: 1.00
Long-term debt ($ mil.): —

Dividends
Yield: —
Payout: —
Market value ($ mil.): —

ARGO DATA RESOURCE CORPORATION

LOCATIONS
HQ: ARGO DATA RESOURCE CORPORATION
1500 N GREENVILLE AVE # 500, RICHARDSON, TX 75081-2265
Phone: 972-866-3300
Web: www.argodata.com

ARIZONA STATE UNIVERSITY FOUNDATION FOR A NEW AMERICAN UNIVE

LOCATIONS
HQ: ARIZONA STATE UNIVERSITY FOUNDATION FOR A NEW AMERICAN UNIVE
300 E UNIVERSITY DR, TEMPE, AZ 85281-2061
Phone: 480-965-3759
Web: www.asufoundation.org

HISTORICAL FINANCIALS
Company Type: Private

Income Statement
FYE: June 30

	REVENUE ($ mil.)	NET INCOME ($ mil.)	NET PROFIT MARGIN	EMPLOYEES
06/11	161	73	45.2%	170
06/10	104	19	18.7%	0
06/08	122	43	35.2%	0
06/05	89	32	36.7%	0
Annual Growth	21.8%	30.6%	—	—

2011 Year-End Financials
Debt ratio: ——
Return on equity: 45.20%
Cash ($ mil.): 13
Current ratio: —
Long-term debt ($ mil.): —

Dividends
Yield: —
Payout: —
Market value ($ mil.): —

ARKANSAS CHILDREN'S HOSPITAL

As the only pediatric medical center in the state Arkansas Children's Hospital (ACH) serves the youngest Razorbacks from birth to age 21. The not-for-profit hospital has some 370 beds.When it comes to children's health there's not much this hospital doesn't do. Specialties include childhood cancer pediatric orthopedics and neonatology. In addition to its acute care services it operates many specialty clinics and outpatient centers. ACH is one of the largest pediatric hospitals in the US and is also engaged in teaching and medical research through its affiliation with the University of Arkansas for Medical Sciences the academic medical center of the University of Arkansas System.

The hospital opened a new $121 million south wing in 2012 that added more than 50 inpatient beds to the hospital's capacity. The nearly 260000-square foot four story building features telemedicine technology (for remote patient care) new trauma rooms a dedicated orthopedics suite and a decontamination unit.

ACH's Circle of Friends clinic treats more than 20000 patients annually. The clinic which opened in 2008 provides primary care as well as a broad range of specialty care services related to endocrinology dermatological conditions hemophilia and tuberculosis.

The hospital also offers community outreach services that include help for children of domestic abuse and wellness programs as well as a number of clinics to support those with eating disorders and diabetes.

In 2010 ACH became the state's only pediatric Level I trauma center after receiving a four-year designation from the Arkansas Department of Health. The designation means that the hospital is equipped for and capable of taking care of children with the most severe of traumas. Level I trauma centers serve as referral locations for hospitals that are unable to provide the same level of care.

EXECUTIVES

Secretary and Director, J. French Hill, age 55
President CEO and Director, Jonathan R. (Jon) Bates
VP Human Resources, Andre Trosclair
EVP, Scott R. Gordon
Director; President Arkansas Children's Hospital Research Institute, Richard F. Jacobs
SVP and Medical Director, Bonnie J. Taylor
President Arkansas Children's Hospital Foundation, John E. Bel
SVP and CIO, Darrell T. Leonhardt
SVP and CFO, Gena G. Wingfield
SVP Medical Services and Chief Business Development Officer, Carole J. Zylman
SVP and COO, David T. Berry
Chairman, Dorsey Jackson
Vice Chairman, Tom Baxter
Treasurer and Director, Paul Hart
Chief of Staff and Director, Charles M. Bower
SVP Public Affairs, Tom W. Bonner
SVP and Chief Nursing Officer, Lori J. Brown
Director Communications, Dan McFadden
Manager Advertising and Marketing, Melissa Wilcoxson
Secretary and Director, J. French Hill, age 55
President CEO and Director, Jonathan R. (Jon) Bates

Director; President Arkansas Children's Hospital Research Institute, Richard F. Jacobs
Director, Harry C. Erwin III
Director, Marion Humphrey
Vice Chairman, Tom Baxter
Treasurer and Director, Paul Hart
Chief of Staff and Director, Charles M. Bower
Director, John Bale Jr.
Director, Patrick H. Casey
Director, Ron Clark
Director, Haskell Dickinson
Director, Edward Drilling
Director, Rhonda Forrester
Director, Lisa Kirkpatrick
Director, Diane Mackey
Director, Holly Marr
Director, Mark McCaslin
Director, Barbara Moore
Director, Beverly A. Morrow
Director, Jeffery Nolan
Director, Daniel W. Rahn
Director, Katie Ransdell
Director, Skip Rutherford
Director, Mark Saviers
Director, Philip W. Schmidt
Director, Robert Shults
Director, Bonnie J. Taylor
Director, Everett Tucker III
Director, Charles B. Whiteside III

LOCATIONS

HQ: Arkansas Children's Hospital
1 Children's Way, Little Rock AR 72202-3591
Phone: 501-364-1100 **Fax:** 501-364-7219
Web: www.archildrens.org

COMPETITORS

Arkansas Heart Hospital
Baptist Health (Arkansas)
Children's Healthcare of Atlanta
Children's Medical Center of Dallas
Children's Mercy Hospital
Children's National Medical Center
Cook Children's Health Care System
Dell Children's Medical Center
East Tennessee Children's Hospital
Jefferson Regional Medical Center of Arkansas
Methodist Healthcare
Shriners Hospitals For Children
St. Joseph's Mercy Health Center
St. Jude Children's Research Hospital
St. Vincent Health System
Texas Children's Hospital
Universal Health Services
White County Medical Center

HISTORICAL FINANCIALS

Company Type: Private - Not-for-Profit

Income Statement

FYE: June 30

	REVENUE ($ mil.)	NET INCOME ($ mil.)	NET PROFIT MARGIN	EMPLOYEES
06/11	509	48	9.5%	3,700
06/10	513	42	8.4%	0
06/08	1	(0)	—	0
06/06	0	0	—	0
Annual Growth	—	—	—	—

2011 Year-End Financials

Debt ratio: ——
Return on equity: 9.50%
Cash ($ mil.): 66
Current ratio: 2.30
Long-term debt ($ mil.): —
Dividends
  Yield: —
  Payout: —
Market value ($ mil.): —

ARKANSAS ELECTRIC COOPERATIVES INC.

LOCATIONS

HQ: ARKANSAS ELECTRIC COOPERATIVES INC.
1 COOPERATIVE WAY, LITTLE ROCK, AR 72209-5493
Phone: 501-570-2200
Web: www.aeci.com

HISTORICAL FINANCIALS

Company Type: Private

Income Statement

FYE: December 31

	REVENUE ($ mil.)	NET INCOME ($ mil.)	NET PROFIT MARGIN	EMPLOYEES
12/11	357	18	5.1%	840
12/10	313	13	4.2%	0
12/09	311	20	6.7%	0
12/08	440	55	12.6%	0
Annual Growth	(6.7%)	(31.1%)	—	—

2011 Year-End Financials

Debt ratio: ——
Return on equity: 5.10%
Cash ($ mil.): 73
Current ratio: 3.10
Long-term debt ($ mil.): —
Dividends
  Yield: —
  Payout: —
Market value ($ mil.): —

ARKANSAS TECH UNIVERSITY

These days you can pick up more than a high school diploma at Arkansas Tech University.Arkansas Tech was originally founded in 1909 as the Second District Agricultural School which offered classes that led to a high school degree. These days the state-supported institution of higher education offers undergraduate and graduate degrees in a variety of disciplines to more than 8800 students. Based in Russellville Arkansas the school employs more than 400 faculty members and also operates a small satellite campus in the town of Ozark. The school's purpose and name were changed in 1925 when it became Arkansas Polytechnic College; it was renamed Arkansas Tech University in 1976.

EXECUTIVES

Associate VP Administration and Finance, Carol Trusty
Associate VP Academic Affairs, David G. Underwood
President, Robert C. Brown
VP Development, Jayne W. Jones
VP Administration and Finance, David C. Moseley
VP Academic Affairs, Jack R. Hamm
VP Student Services, Gary M. Biller
Director Administrative Services, Fred W. Clayton
Controller, Gary H. Hodges
Director Student Aid, Shirley M. Goines
Purchasing Agent, Beth Foster
Associate Dean Students and Director Public Safety, Steve Lawrence

Director Corporate and Athletic Relations, Kelly Davis
Assistant Director Computer Services Networked Systems, Kenneth D. Wester
VP Governmental Relations, Phil Jacobs
Director Career Services, David Boop
Dean Students, Jerry Forbes
Assistant VP Enrollment Management, Shauna Donnell
Registrar, Tammy Rhodes

LOCATIONS

HQ: Arkansas Tech University
  1509 N. Boulder Ave., Russellville AR 72801
Phone: 479-968-0389   Fax: 479-968-0227
Web: www.atu.edu

HISTORICAL FINANCIALS
Company Type: School

Income Statement			FYE: June 30
	REVENUE ($ mil.)	NET INCOME ($ mil.)	NET PROFIT MARGIN	EMPLOYEES
06/12	66	9	14.7%	1,039
06/11	59	11	19.2%	0
06/10	48	3	7.1%	0
06/09	46	8	19.3%	0
Annual Growth	13.0%	3.3%	—	—

2012 Year-End Financials
Debt ratio: ——
Return on equity: 14.70%
Cash ($ mil.): 27
Current ratio: 4.10
Long-term debt ($ mil.): —
Dividends
  Yield: —
  Payout: —
  Market value ($ mil.): —

ARLINGTON INDUSTRIES INC

Thank goodness for zinc's abundance; the element has enabled Arlington Industry's dominance in manufacturing individual zinc die-cast line items. Arlington manufactures and distributes a slew of metallic and non-metallic fittings and connectors. Its lineup includes bushings cable connectors concrete pipe sleeves conduit bodies gaskets and screw couplings used in the electrical and construction markets. The company operates a sole plant in Scranton Pennsylvania. It sells its products through stocking sales reps who supply distributors' inventories. Arlington began in 1949 as a regional supplier of zinc fittings to the electrical industry. Since 2003 it has introduced more than 400 new products.

Arlington attributes its ability to ride the economic downturn to product development. Such developments focus on labor-saving devices offered a competitive prices for electrical contractors. The company reports that more than 50% of its revenues are from its new patent-pending offerings enabling it to resist pricing pressures as well as motivate sales representatives with better commissions. Moreover its investment in R&D has helped to expand its customer base. Arlington in 2009 began catering to audio/visual applications with a line of TV boxes and scoops and low-voltage mounting brackets. Many of the innovations are driven by company president Thomas Stark and general manager Thomas Gretz.

EXECUTIVES
President, Thomas Stark
VP Human Resources, Elizabeth B. D'arienzo
VP Marketing and Sales, Ray Kennedy
Manager Customer Service, James Cortese
VP, Joseph Sullivan

LOCATIONS

HQ: Arlington Industries Inc.
  1 Stauffer Industrial Park, Scranton PA 18517
Phone: 570-562-0270   Fax: 570-562-0646
Web: www.aifittings.com

PRODUCTS/OPERATIONS

Selected Products
Cord grip fittings
EMT (electrical metallic tubing) fittings
Fan/specialty boxes
Flex/AC/MC fittings
Grounding
Home theater security communications
NM (non-metallic) cable fittings & supports
Liquid-tight fittings
Mast parts
Rigid/IMC (intermediate metal conduit) fittings
Siding mounting blocks
Weatherproof products

COMPETITORS

Chicago Rivet   Leviton
Federal Screw Works   Woodhead Industries
Koch Enterprises

HISTORICAL FINANCIALS
Company Type: Private

Income Statement			FYE: December 31
	REVENUE ($ mil.)	NET INCOME ($ mil.)	NET PROFIT MARGIN	EMPLOYEES
12/11	99	0	—	320
12/09	89	0	—	0
12/08	125	0	—	0
12/07	138	0	—	0
Annual Growth	(10.6%)	—	—	—

2011 Year-End Financials
Debt ratio: ——
Return on equity: —
Cash ($ mil.): 8
Current ratio: 1.70
Long-term debt ($ mil.): —
Dividends
  Yield: —
  Payout: —
  Market value ($ mil.): —

ARMSTRONG COUNTY MEMORIAL HOSPITAL

LOCATIONS

HQ: ARMSTRONG COUNTY MEMORIAL HOSPITAL
  1 NOLTE DR, KITTANNING, PA 16201-7111
Phone: 724-543-8500
Web: www.acmh.org

HISTORICAL FINANCIALS
Company Type: Private

Income Statement			FYE: June 30
	REVENUE ($ mil.)	NET INCOME ($ mil.)	NET PROFIT MARGIN	EMPLOYEES
06/11	95	4	4.7%	990
06/10	96	4	4.9%	0
06/09	85	(1)	—	0
06/08	84	1	2.0%	0
Annual Growth	4.1%	38.3%	—	—

2011 Year-End Financials
Debt ratio: ——
Return on equity: 4.70%
Cash ($ mil.): 14
Current ratio: 2.60
Long-term debt ($ mil.): —
Dividends
  Yield: —
  Payout: —
  Market value ($ mil.): —

ARNOLD MACHINERY COMPANY

Arnold Machinery helps keep construction on the move. Through its four divisions the company distributes construction mining industrial and material handling equipment as well as farm machinery throughout the US. Arnold Machinery also offers used equipment and provides repair and maintenance rebuild exchange and rental services. OEM equipment suppliers include Volvo and Hitachi (construction and mining equipment); Hyster (a NACCO brand) and Unarco (forklifts warehouse equipment and other material handling equipment); and Buhler and McFarlane (farm equipment). Chairman Alvin Richer has the controlling interest in the company.

The company's divisions include General Implement Distributors Mining Equipment Construction Equipment and Material Handling. Arnold Machinery operates about 20 branch facilities covering some 15 states in the Western US.

Since its founding the company has expanded geographically and built its product offerings by acquiring complementary businesses. Arnold Machinery continues to acquire other distributors in its territory and to expand its facilities in many markets.

L. E. "Doc" Arnold and Floyd Stannard founded predecessor company Stannard-Arnold Machinery Company in 1929. The company's name was changed to Arnold Machinery Company upon the resignation of Stannard later that year.

EXECUTIVES
Chairman, Alvin Richer
President and CEO, Russ Fleming
CFO, Kayden Bell
Division VP and Director Financial Services, Gary Bryden
Director Information Systems, Gene Garcia
President Mining Equipment Division, Tom Younger
VP Sales and Marketing, Charlie Fricks
President Material Handling Division, Rex Mecham
Sales Manager Material Handling Division, Don Quinn
Co-President MH Division, Kirk Reese

Corporate VP; President GID Division, Wendell Nelson
VP and Operations Manager General Implement Distributors, Frank Loeffler
Director Human Resources, Rohana Parker
President Construction Equipmment Division, Tom O'Byrne
Corporate VP; President Mining Division, John Ragsdale

LOCATIONS

HQ: Arnold Machinery Company
  2975 W. 2100 South, Salt Lake City UT 84119
Phone: 801-972-4000   **Fax:** -9735
Web: www.mapperlithography.com

COMPETITORS

Cashman Equipment	RSC Equipment Rental
Empire Southwest	Sunbelt Rentals
NES Rentals	United Rentals

HISTORICAL FINANCIALS
Company Type: Private

Income Statement
FYE: September 30

	REVENUE ($ mil.)	NET INCOME ($ mil.)	NET PROFIT MARGIN	EMPLOYEES
09/11	235	11	4.8%	450
09/10	191	5	2.8%	0
09/09	203	6	3.0%	0
09/08	229	7	3.2%	0
Annual Growth	0.9%	15.1%	—	—

2011 Year-End Financials

Debt ratio: ——
Return on equity: 4.80%
Cash ($ mil.): 3
Current ratio: 0.70
Long-term debt ($ mil.): ——
Dividends
  Yield: —
  Payout: —
  Market value ($ mil.): —

ARPIN GROUP INC.

LOCATIONS

HQ: ARPIN GROUP INC.
  99 JAMES P MURPHY IND HWY, WEST WARWICK, RI 02893-2382
Phone: 401-828-8111

HISTORICAL FINANCIALS
Company Type: Private

Income Statement
FYE: December 31

	REVENUE ($ mil.)	NET INCOME ($ mil.)	NET PROFIT MARGIN	EMPLOYEES
12/11	179	0	0.3%	555
12/07	177	2	1.7%	0
12/06	175	0	0.5%	0
Annual Growth	1.2%	(19.2%)	—	—

2011 Year-End Financials

Debt ratio: ——
Return on equity: 0.30%
Cash ($ mil.): 4
Current ratio: 0.20
Long-term debt ($ mil.): ——
Dividends
  Yield: —
  Payout: —
  Market value ($ mil.): —

ART CENTER COLLEGE OF DESIGN INC

Art Center College of Design (ACCD) is designing a future of creativity for its students. The college offers undergraduate and graduate degrees in such fields as advertising film fine art media graphic design illustration photography product design and transportation design. The college has about 1500 students enrolled and a low student-teacher ratio of 9:1. ACCD was founded in downtown Los Angeles in 1930 by advertising man Edward A. "Tink" Adams. Photographer Ansel Adams taught there and notable alumni include film director Michael Bay. In 1976 the school's campus moved from LA to Pasadena California. It operates a two locations in Pasadena.

ACCD offers its students more than 700 different course sections. Part of its 1500 student enrollment is roughly 84 graduate students. The school's most popular majors are illustration (435 students) graphic design (254 students) transportation (176 students) product design (142) photography (135) environmental design (87 students) entertainment design (85 students) film (84 students) advertising (80 students) and fine art (72 students).

The school is undergoing a five-year strategic plan to "help bring the school into the 21st century." ACCD intends to create a "conservatory" experience which is typically associated with performing arts schools. What that means for this school is that it plans to create a curriculum of project-based learning with a focus on social and environmental challenges to provide a depth of purpose to its educational offerings. It also plans to create new learning spaces and focus on diversity.

EXECUTIVES

President and Trustee, Richard Koshalek
SVP Real Estate and Operations, George E. Falardeau
SVP Educational Planning and Architecture, Patricia Belton Oliver
SVP International Initiatives, Erica Clark
SVP and Chief Human Resources Officer, Jean L. Ford
SVP Marketing and Communications, Iris Gelt
VP and Library Director, Elizabeth Galloway
Director Williamson Gallery, Stephen L. Nowlin
SVP and CTO, A. Michael Berman
Dean Humanities and Design Sciences, Mark Breitenberg
VP International Initiatives and Director Designmatters, Mariana Amatullo
Director Application Services, Hans Ghekiere
Director Internal Communications and Community Relations, Jered Gold
SVP and CFO, Richard Haluschak
Director External Communications and Media Relations, Christine Hanson
Director Photographic Services, Steven A. Heller
Director Architectural Documentation and Special Projects, Dana Hutt
Director Special Programs, Leslie Marcus
Director Facilities, Neal McCarthy
Director Financial Aid, Clema McKenzie
Director Foundation Giving, Kimberly Miller
Director Career Development, Jean Mitsunaga
VP Educational Initiatives, Dave Muyres
Registrar, Jeff Roames
Director Support Services, Annie Rothschild
Director Safety, William Sparling
Director Special Events, JoJo Tardino
VP Information Technology, Theresa Zix
Chairman Emeritus, Cleon T. (Bud) Knapp
Chairman, John Puerner
Director Alumni Relations, Kristine Bowne
Dean Academic Affairs, Fred Fehlau
Dean Communication Design, Nik Hafermaas
Senior Director Development, C. Wayne Herron
Associate Dean Students and Director Student Life, Jeff Hoffman
Director Color Materials and Trends Exploration Lab, Karen Hofmann
Director Copy Services, Sallie Horn
Director Corporate Giving, Molly Ann Mroczynski
Dean Industrial Design, Andy Ogden
VP Student Affairs and Dean Students, Tracy Poon Tambascia
Director Annual Giving, Amy Swain
Managing Director Public Programs and Director Art Center at Night, Dana Walker
Controller, Diane Wittenberg
President and Trustee, Richard Koshalek
Trustee, Robert C. (Bob) Davidson Jr., age 66
Trustee, Judy C. Webb
Trustee, William T. Gross
Trustee, Raymond Hemann
Trustee, Kit Hinrichs
Trustee, Timothy Kobe
Trustee, Samuel Mann
Trustee, Fred Nicholas
Chairman, John Puerner
Trustee, Michael Reese
Trustee, Paul A. Violich
Trustee, Alyce de Roulet Williamson

LOCATIONS

HQ: Art Center College of Design
  1700 Lida St., Pasadena CA 91103-1999
Phone: 626-396-2200   **Fax:** 626-405-9104
Web: www.artcenter.edu

HISTORICAL FINANCIALS
Company Type: School

Income Statement
FYE: June 30

	REVENUE ($ mil.)	NET INCOME ($ mil.)	NET PROFIT MARGIN	EMPLOYEES
06/11	107	5	5.2%	400
06/10*	41	0	0.6%	0
12/04	56	4	7.5%	0
12/03	52	8	15.8%	0
Annual Growth	26.5%	(12.5%)	—	—

*Fiscal year change

2011 Year-End Financials

Debt ratio: ——
Return on equity: 5.20%
Cash ($ mil.): 18
Current ratio: ——
Long-term debt ($ mil.): ——
Dividends
  Yield: —
  Payout: —
  Market value ($ mil.): —

ASCENSION PARISH SCHOOL BOARD

LOCATIONS

HQ: ASCENSION PARISH SCHOOL BOARD
1100 WEBSTER ST, DONALDSONVILLE, LA
70346-2754
Phone: 225-257-2000

HISTORICAL FINANCIALS
Company Type: Private

Income Statement
FYE: June 30

	REVENUE ($ mil.)	NET INCOME ($ mil.)	NET PROFIT MARGIN	EMPLOYEES
06/11	215	22	10.6%	3,300
06/10	0	0	—	0
Annual Growth	—	—	—	—

2011 Year-End Financials

Debt ratio: ——
Return on equity: 10.60%
Cash ($ mil.): 20
Current ratio: ——
Long-term debt ($ mil.): —

Dividends
Yield: —
Payout: —
Market value ($ mil.): —

ASHLAND UNIVERSITY

LOCATIONS

HQ: ASHLAND UNIVERSITY
401 COLLEGE AVE, ASHLAND, OH 44805-3799
Phone: 419-289-4142
Web: www.wediducan.com

HISTORICAL FINANCIALS
Company Type: Private

Income Statement
FYE: June 30

	REVENUE ($ mil.)	NET INCOME ($ mil.)	NET PROFIT MARGIN	EMPLOYEES
06/11	135	4	3.6%	620
06/10	127	8	6.3%	0
06/09	114	0	—	0
06/08	100	4	4.4%	0
Annual Growth	10.4%	3.0%	—	—

2011 Year-End Financials

Debt ratio: ——
Return on equity: 3.60%
Cash ($ mil.): 10
Current ratio: ——
Long-term debt ($ mil.): —

Dividends
Yield: —
Payout: —
Market value ($ mil.): —

ASPIRE PUBLIC SCHOOLS

LOCATIONS

HQ: ASPIRE PUBLIC SCHOOLS
1001 22ND AVE STE 100, OAKLAND, CA 94606-5232
Phone: 510-434-5000
Web: www.aspirepublicschools.org

HISTORICAL FINANCIALS
Company Type: Private

Income Statement
FYE: June 30

	REVENUE ($ mil.)	NET INCOME ($ mil.)	NET PROFIT MARGIN	EMPLOYEES
06/12	117	16	14.4%	1,400
06/11	102	7	7.0%	0
06/10	84	4	4.8%	0
06/09	68	0	—	0
Annual Growth	19.6%	—	—	—

2012 Year-End Financials

Debt ratio: ——
Return on equity: 14.40%
Cash ($ mil.): 12
Current ratio: 1.60
Long-term debt ($ mil.): —

Dividends
Yield: —
Payout: —
Market value ($ mil.): —

ASEA AFSCME LOCAL 52 HEALTH BENEFITS TRUST

LOCATIONS

HQ: ASEA AFSCME LOCAL 52 HEALTH BENEFITS
TRUST
111 W CATALDO AVE, SPOKANE, WA 99201-3201
Phone: 509-328-0300

HISTORICAL FINANCIALS
Company Type: Private

Income Statement
FYE: June 30

	REVENUE ($ mil.)	NET INCOME ($ mil.)	NET PROFIT MARGIN	EMPLOYEES
06/11	130	15	12.0%	3
06/10	108	4	4.1%	0
Annual Growth	20.3%	254.6%	—	—

2011 Year-End Financials

Debt ratio: ——
Return on equity: 12.00%
Cash ($ mil.): 0
Current ratio: 0.10
Long-term debt ($ mil.): —

Dividends
Yield: —
Payout: —
Market value ($ mil.): —

ASPEN CONTRACTING INC.

LOCATIONS

HQ: ASPEN CONTRACTING INC.
4141 NE LKWD WAY 200, LEES SUMMIT, MO 64064
Phone: 877-784-7663
Web: www.roofsbyaspen.com

HISTORICAL FINANCIALS
Company Type: Private

Income Statement
FYE: December 31

	REVENUE ($ mil.)	NET INCOME ($ mil.)	NET PROFIT MARGIN	EMPLOYEES
12/11	90	1	1.8%	284
12/09	63	4	7.2%	0
12/08	48	5	11.1%	0
12/07	26	0	2.2%	0
Annual Growth	49.8%	40.5%	—	—

2011 Year-End Financials

Debt ratio: ——
Return on equity: 1.80%
Cash ($ mil.): 0
Current ratio: 0.80
Long-term debt ($ mil.): —

Dividends
Yield: —
Payout: —
Market value ($ mil.): —

ASPIRUS INC.

Aspirus provides a comprehensive range of health and medical services to residents in a 14-county region of central and northern Wisconsin as well as Michigan's Upper Peninsula. The health system operates the Aspirus Wausau Hospital a 320-bed multi-specialty regional health center and five smaller community hospitals. It also owns and operates the Aspirus Wausau Family Medicine residency program sponsored by the University of Wisconsin School of Medicine and Public Health. Its hospitals and network of community clinics provide specialized primary and emergency care. Aspirus also operates imaging centers hospice services home health care long-term care facilities and an outpatient dialysis center.

In 2012 Aspirus acquired the Wausau Family Medicine Residency Clinic from the University of Wisconsin School of Medicine and Publich Health and renamed it Aspirus Wausau Family Medicine the assumed operational accountability for the clinical practice. The residency program is accredited to train both osteopathic and allopathic (DO and MD) physicians and is sponsored by UW SMPH which also provides educational oversight.

EXECUTIVES

President and CEO, Duane L. Erwin, age 60
VP Information Technology, Jerry Mourey
SVP Finance and CFO, Sidney Sczygelski
VP Human Resources, Roger Lucas
VP and COO Aspirus Clinics, Dean Danner
Regional COO, Robert J. (Bob) Erickson
VP Corporate Quality Services and Patient Safety Officer Aspirus Wausau Hospital, Jeanne Scinto

LOCATIONS

HQ: Aspirus
425 Pine Ridge Blvd., Wausau WI 54401
Phone: 715-847-2118   **Fax:** 715-847-2133
Web: www.aspirus.org

PRODUCTS/OPERATIONS

Selected Facilities

Aspirus Grand View (Ironwood MI)
Aspirus Keweenaw (Laurium MI)
Aspirus Ontonagon (Ontonagon MI)
Aspirus Wausau Hospital (Wausau WI)
Langlade Hospital (Antigo WI)
Memorial Health Center (Medford WI)

COMPETITORS

Dean Health Systems Inc.
Howard Young Health Care
Luther Midelfort
ThedaCare Inc.
University of Wisconsin Hospital and Clinics

HISTORICAL FINANCIALS

Company Type: Private - Not-for-Profit

Income Statement

FYE: June 30

	REVENUE ($ mil.)	NET INCOME ($ mil.)	NET PROFIT MARGIN	EMPLOYEES
06/12	529	26	4.9%	3,900
06/11	503	86	17.2%	0
06/10	0	0	—	0
06/09	433	(12)	—	0
Annual Growth	6.9%	—	—	—

2012 Year-End Financials

Debt ratio: ——
Return on equity: 4.90%
Cash ($ mil.): 75
Current ratio: 2.60
Long-term debt ($ mil.): —

Dividends
Yield: —
Payout: —
Market value ($ mil.): —

ASSOCIATED ELECTRIC COOPERATIVE INC.

Associated Electric Cooperative makes the connection between power and cooperatives. The utility provides transmission and generation services to its six member/owner companies which in turn provide power supply services to 51 distribution cooperatives in three Midwest states. (The distribution cooperatives have a combined customer count of more than 875000 people.) Associated Electric operates 9645 miles of power transmission lines and has about 5895 MW of generating capacity from interests in primarily coal- and gas-fired power plants and from wholesale energy transactions with other regional utilities.

The cooperative is engaged in the wholesale transmission business with more than 70 investor-owned and municipal utilities electric cooperatives power marketing firms and regional transmission organizations. Associated Electric supplies wholesale power to 39 distribution cooperatives in Missouri three in southeast Iowa and nine in northeast Oklahoma.

An increase in rates and a jump in demand (as the economy bounced back for the recession) helped the company to post stronger revenues in 2010. In 2011 Associated Electric reported a further rise in sales despite lower member demand (due to mild winter temperatures) largely because of higher prices (a lower rate discount) and stronger sales to non-members. The overall jump in revenues also allowed the company to report a rise in net income for the year.

In 2011 Associated Electric got 78% of its owned power production from coal-based plants and 22% from natural gas facilities. To meet growing demand the company is boosting its fossil-fueled power assets. In 2011 it completed a 540 MW combined-cycle natural gas plant adjacent to its existing Chouteau Power Plant in Pryor Oklahoma boosting that location's overall capacity to 1062 MW.

The company is also looking to increase power generated from renewable sources in order to meet tightening emission regulations. It has contracted hydropower sources and it also gets wind energy from Missouri's first utility-scale wind farms the fourth of which the 150 MW Lost Creek Wind Farm was opened in 2010. In 2012 Associated Electric signed a long-term power purchase agreement for 314 MW of power from BP Wind Energy's proposed Flat Ridge 2 Wind farm in Kansas.

The six generation and transmission cooperatives/owners formed Associated Electric in 1961 to provide them with a wholesale power supply.

EXECUTIVES

Special Assistant to the CEO and General Manager, Keith E. Hartner
Director Human Resources, David P. Stump
Special Assistant to the CEO and General Manager, Michael M. (Mike) Miller
CEO and General Manager, James J. Jura
President Board of Directors, O. B. Clark
Director Power Production, Duane D. Highley
Secretary, R. Layne Morrill
Treasurer, Charles C. Baile
VP Board of Directors, Emery O. Geisendorfer Jr.
CIO, Ronald H. Murphy
Manager Internal Audit, Michael E. (Mike) King
General Counsel, Patrick A. Baumhoer
CFO, David W. McNabb
Director Engineering and Operations, Roger S. Clark
Director Member Services and Corporate Communications, Joseph E. Wilkinson
Director, Harold E. Jordan
Director, Donald W. Shaw
Director, J. Chris Cariker
Director, John C. Farris
Director, Douglas H. Aeilts
VP Board of Directors, Emery O. Geisendorfer Jr.
Director, Don R. McQuitty
Director, Jerry W. Divin
Auditors: KPMGLLP

LOCATIONS

HQ: ASSOCIATED ELECTRIC COOPERATIVE INC.
2814 S GOLDEN AVE, SPRINGFIELD, MO 65807-3213
Phone: 417-881-1204
Web: www.aeci.org

PRODUCTS/OPERATIONS

2011 Sales

	$ mil.	% of total
Members	883	82
Nonmembers	199	18
Total	**1,083**	**100**

Member Transmission and Distribution Cooperativ
Central Electric Power Cooperativ
KAMO Power
M&A Electric Power Cooperativ
Northeast Missouri Electric Power Cooperativ
NW Electric Power Cooperative Inc.
Sho-Me Power Electric Cooperativ

COMPETITORS

Ameren
Empire District Electric
GenOnEnergy

Great Plains Energy
Southern Union
Westar Energy
Xcel Energy

HISTORICAL FINANCIALS

Company Type: Private - Cooperative

Income Statement

FYE: December 31

	REVENUE ($ mil.)	NET INCOME ($ mil.)	NET PROFIT MARGIN	EMPLOYEES
12/11	1,083	46	4.3%	600
12/10	1,055	45	4.3%	0
12/09	988	37	3.8%	0
12/08	1,084	57	5.3%	0
Annual Growth	(0.0%)	(6.7%)	—	—

2011 Year-End Financials

Debt ratio: ——
Return on equity: 4.30%
Cash ($ mil.): 86
Current ratio: 0.60
Long-term debt ($ mil.): —

Dividends
Yield: —
Payout: —
Market value ($ mil.): —

ASSOCIATED GROCERS OF NEW ENGLAND INC.

AGNE gets the products you want on to grocers' shelves. Associated Grocers of New England (AGNE) is a leading wholesale grocery distributor. The organization serves more than 600 independent grocers and convenience stores in six New England states and the Upstate New York and Albany area. AGNE supplies customers with baked goods fresh produce and meat as well as general grocery items and other merchandise. The grocery distributor also offers such retail support services as advertising marketing and merchandising. AGNE's retail arm operates about a half a dozen supermarkets under the Harvest Market and Vista Foods banners. The retailer-owned cooperative was formed in 1946.

The 2011 liquidation of rival Associated Grocers of Maine which distributed products to hundreds of small independent grocery stores in Maine should boost AGNE's business in the state.

AGNE's acquisition of New Hampshire-based Manchester Wholesale Distributors (in 2009) helped boost sales during the economic downturn as did improved performance at its Associated Convenience Grocers division. Manchester Wholesale Distributors supplied convenience stores and foodservice operators throughout New Hampshire.

EXECUTIVES

SVP Treasurer and CFO, Steven N. (Steve) Murphy
President and CEO, Michael C. (Mike) Bourgoine

Manager Warehousing, James (Jim) Johnson
VP Wholesale Merchandising and Procurement, Richard K. (Rick) Wheeler
Chairman, Thomas E. Bradbury
SVP Warehousing and Transportation, Stephen M. (Steve) Creed
Manager Environmental Safety and Health, Jeffrey (Jeff) Sawyer
Director Business Development, Joseph B. (Joe) Powers
Manager Center Store Purchasing, Karen St. Louis
Director Procurement Strategy, Clement (Clem) Deschenes
Director Procurement Meat and Seafood, Robin Plamondon
General Manager Convenience Store Division, Stephen Felton
Director Transportation, Kevin P. Murray
Manager Human Resources, Hope Kelly
SVP Sales and Retail Development, Michael J. (Mike) Violette
Director Retail Programs, Curt O'Hara
Director Information Technology, Kenneth (Ken) Peperissa
Manager Information Systems and Computer Operations, Sheri Pendexter
Manager Information Systems Programs, Jodi Pike
Manager Retail Bookkeeping, William (Bill) Loscocco
Manager Loss Prevention, Alan Cote
General Manager AG Supermarkets, Tim Merrill
Manager Inventory Control, Joseph (Joe) Donahue
Buyer and Merchandiser, Stephen (Steve) Gorski
Manager Sales and Purchasing Bakery and Deli, William Carter
Manager Retail Accounts, Paul Greenan
Senior Manager Advertising and Marketing, Susan (Sue) Johnson
Manager Store Merchandising and Design, Steve Picarillo
Secretary, Benjamin F. Gayman
Manager Customer Service, Cynthia Smith
Controller, Cynthia (Cindy) Caldwell
Assistant Controller, Christine Lyle
Store Manager Laconia NH, Leroy Burke
Store Manager Bedford NH, Janice Morin
Store Manager Hollis NH, Edward Murphy
Store Manager Wolfeboro NH, Eric Tinker
Manager Credit, Mitchell Merson
Manager Sales and Purchasing Produce, Lenny Miner
Store Co-Manager Newport VT, Linda Rhodes
Manager Advertising and Marketing, Kathleen McCarthy
Store Co-Manager Newport VT, Heath Geoffrey
VP Non-Member Business Development, Raymond R. (Ray) Tetu
Director, Norman J. (Norm) Turcotte
Director, John T. deBettencourt
Director, Stanley S. Plifka Jr.
Director, Donald R. Tranten
Director, Thomas D. (Tom) Rath
Director, Terry P. Appleby
Director, Alan M. Couturier
Director, James G. (Jim) Crosby
Director, Richard D. Delay Sr.
Director, Peter A. Dole
Director, Robert J. George
Director, Peter M. Davenport

LOCATIONS

HQ: Associated Grocers of New England Inc.
11 Cooperative Way, Pembroke NH 03275
Phone: 603-223-6710   **Fax:** -4488
Web: www.elephanttalk.com

COMPETITORS

Associated Wholesalers	McLane
Bozzuto's	Nash-Finch
C&S Wholesale	Pine State Trading
Dole & Bailey Inc.	SUPERVALU

HISTORICAL FINANCIALS
Company Type: Private - Cooperative

Income Statement
FYE: April 2

	REVENUE ($ mil.)	NET INCOME ($ mil.)	NET PROFIT MARGIN	EMPLOYEES
04/11*	381	0	0.1%	625
03/09	340	0	0.2%	0
03/08	315	0	0.1%	0
03/07	280	0	0.0%	0
Annual Growth	10.9%	60.1%	—	—

*Fiscal year change

2011 Year-End Financials

Debt ratio: —
Return on equity: 0.10%
Cash ($ mil.): 0
Current ratio: 0.30
Long-term debt ($ mil.): —

Dividends
Yield: —
Payout: —
Market value ($ mil.): —

ASSOCIATED WHOLESALE GROCERS INC.

Associated Wholesale Grocers (AWG) knows its customers can't live on bread and milk alone. The second-largest retailer-owned cooperative in the US (behind Wakefern Food Corporation) AWG supplies more than 2800 retail outlets in some two dozen states from eight distribution centers. In addition to its wholesale grocery operation AWG offers a variety of business services to its members including marketing and merchandising programs shelf management insurance and store design. The firm sold its company-owned retail stores which operated under the Homeland and other banners in 2011 to focus on its wholesale business. AWG was founded by a group of independent grocers in 1924.

Geographic Reach

AWG's trade area encompasses 24 US states including: Alabama Arkansas Florida Georgia Illinois Indiana Iowa Kansas Kentucky Louisiana Michigan Mississippi Missouri Nebraska New Mexico North Carolina Oklahoma Ohio South Carolina Tennessee Texas Virginia West Virginia and Wisconsin.

Financial Analysis

AWG's 2011 sales increased by 7% vs. 2010 to a record $7.7 billion. Net income rose more than 3% to $169.5 million over the same period. The grocery wholesale is working to control costs. Indeed in 2011 its general and administrative expenses were 3.45% of sales a decline of 13 basis points from 2010 a record low as a percentage for the company.

Strategy

A decade after acquiring the Homeland chain of grocery stores in Oklahoma out of bankruptcy AWG sold its supermarket business known as Associated Retail Grocers (ARG) to a group of employees in a transaction valued at $145 million. (AWG paid $47 million for the 44 stores in 2001 and over the years grew ARG to 76 stores through subsequent acquisitions.) The sale frees AWG to focus on its growing wholesale business and supply chain. To that end in 2012 AWG completed construction of a new warehouse in Pearl River Louisiana that will better serve retailers from Texas to Florida. In late 2012 AWG completed an addition to its headquaters in Kansas City bringing all its corporate resources under one roof for the first time in 20 years making for a more efficient operation.

AWG continues to build sales of its billion-dollar private-label products line which includes the Best Choice IGA and Always Save brands. In addition to marketing the products as lower-cost alternatives to brand-name products the co-op has been investing in efforts to make sure the quality of its private-label items matches competing national brands. The company also owns and operates the Value Merchandisers Company (VMC) which offers some 22000 nonfood items to its members including health and beauty care general merchandise and seasonal and promotional products.

Operating in a fragmented business AWG competes with a large number of local and regional suppliers as well as distributors of specialty items. The food wholesale business also has its share of national giants including C & S Wholesale Nash-Finch and wholesale grocery and retail company SUPERVALU.

HISTORY

About 20 Kansas City Kansas-area grocers met in a local grocery in 1924 and organized the Associated Grocers Company to get better deals on purchases and advertising. They elected J. C. Harline president and each chipped in a few hundred dollars to make their first purchases. It took a while to find a manufacturer who would sell directly to them; a local soap maker was finally convinced and others gradually followed.

In 1926 the group was incorporated as Associated Wholesale Grocers (AWG). It outgrew two warehouses in four years finally moving to a 16000-sq.-ft. facility big enough to add new lines and more products. Membership doubled between 1930 and 1932 as grocers moved from ordering products a year ahead to the new wholesale concept and members took seriously the slogan: "Buy Sell Buy Some More." They met every week to plan how to sell their products and buyer and advertising manager Harry Small gave sales presentations and advertising ideas (his trade-in plan for old brooms sold more than two train-carloads of brooms in two weeks). Heavy newspaper advertising also paid off; AWG topped $1 million in sales in 1933.

The cooperative made its first acquisition in 1936 buying Progressive Grocers a warehouse in Joplin Missouri; a second warehouse named Associated Grocers was acquired the next year in Springfield Missouri. AWG continued building and expanding warehouses and annual sales were at $11 million by 1951.

Louis Fox became CEO in 1956. Fox maximized year-end rebates for members led several acquisitions and formed a new subsidiary for financing stores and small shopping centers where AWG members had a presence (Supermarket Developers). Sales increased nearly 15-fold to over $200 million in his first 15 years.

James Basha who succeeded Fox when he retired in 1984 saw sales reach $2.4 billion by the time of his own retirement in 1992.

Basha was followed by former COO Mike De-Fabis once a deputy mayor of Indianapolis. De-Fabis orchestrated several acquisitions including 41 Kansas City-area stores –most of which were quickly bought by members –from bankrupt Food Barn Stores in 1994 and 29 Oklahoma stores and a warehouse from Safeway spinoff Homeland Stores in 1995 (members bought all the stores).

AWG's non-food subsidiary Valu Merchandisers was established in 1995; its new Kansas warehouse began shipping health and beauty aids and housewares the following year to help members battle big discounters. Members narrowly defeated a proposal in late 1996 to convert the cooperative into a public company. Proponents promptly petitioned for a second vote which was defeated early the next year.

AWG veteran Doug Carolan succeeded DeFabis in 1998 becoming only the fifth CEO in the cooperative's history. The company bought five Falley's and 33 Food 4 Less stores in Kansas and Missouri from Fred Meyer in 1998 for $300 million. In a break with tradition AWG began operating the stores rather than selling them to members.

In 2000 after a months-long labor dispute with the Teamsters was resolved Carolan left AWG. The company's CFO Gary Phillips was named president and CEO later that year. In 2001 the company debuted a new format ALPS (Always Low Price Stores) –small stores that carry a limited selection of grocery top-sellers. Also that year AWG's Kansas City division began distributing to more than 10 new stores that had formerly been served by Fleming at the time the #1 US wholesale food distributor.

In 2002 supermarket operator Homeland Stores which operates stores in Oklahoma emerged from bankruptcy as a fully owned subsidiary of AWG. AWG formed a new subsidiary Associated Retail Grocers to oversee Homeland and its Falley's chain.

As a result of the 2003 sale of Fleming Companies' wholesale distribution business AWG picked up food distribution centers in Nebraska (two) Oklahoma (one) and Tennessee (two) and general-merchandise distribution centers in Tennessee and Kansas.

Introducing a "dollar" section in its stores in 2004 proved successful leading AWG to expand the category to more than 1000 food and non-food items. The following year it merged the corporate offices of its Homeland and Food 4 Less chains.

AWG took steps to expand its capacity and its territory in 2007 when it acquired a distribution center in Fort Worth from Albertsons. The cooperative also took on supply operations for Albertsons locations in Arkansas Louisiana and Texas.

In 2009 AWG acquired the assets of Little Rock Arkansas-based Affiliated Foods Southwest in 2009 adding about a dozen new stores.

During 2010 the firm introduced a paperless coupon program.

In December 2011 AWG sold its corporate supermarkets to a group of employees. The corporate stores included 76 retail locations operating under the Homeland United of Oklahoma and Country mart banners in Oklahoma and the Super Saver banner in northern Texas.

In late 2012 AWG completed a 35000-square-foot addition to its corporate headquarters in Kansas City. The location is also home to AWG's Kansas City distribution centers and its Valu Merchandisers division.

EXECUTIVES

SVP Grocery Products, Dennis Kinser, age 67
SVP General Counsel and Corporate Secretary, Frances Pellegrino Puhl, age 62
VP Corporate Sales, Bill Lancaster, age 72
President and CEO, Jerry Garland, age 61
EVP and CFO, Robert C. (Bob) Walker
SVP Real Estate and Store Engineering, Scott Wilmoski, age 59
COO, Michael (Mike) Rand
VP Corporate Sales Development, Stephen G. (Steve) Dillard
SVP Perishables, Lucky Hicks
SVP and Division Manager Kansas City, William A. (Bill) Quade
SVP and Division Manager Kansas City, Gary Jennings
SVP and Division Manager Nashville, Milton Milam
VP and CIO, Keith Martin
VP Distribution, John F. Lane
Corporate Executive Director Risk Management and Loss Prevention, Chuck Dillion
VP Sales Valu Merchandisers, Joe Busch
Assistant Electronic Data Interchange, Cari Carpenter
Chairman, Bob Hufford
Director of Training and Development, Pat Carr
Auditors: GrantThorntonLLP

LOCATIONS

HQ: Associated Wholesale Grocers Inc.
5000 Kansas Ave., Kansas City KS 66106
Phone: 913-288-1000   **Fax:** 913-288-1587
Web: www.awginc.com

Selected States Served

Alabama
Arkansas
Florida
Georgia
Illinois
Indiana
Iowa
Kansas
Kentucky
Louisiana
Michigan
Mississippi
Missouri
Nebraska
New Mexico
North Carolina
Oklahoma
Ohio
South Carolina
Tennessee
Texas
Virginia
West Virginia
Wisconsin

COMPETITORS

Affiliated Foods	GSC Enterprises
Affiliated Foods Midwest	H. T. Hackney
Alex Lee	Kroger
Associated Grocers Inc.	McLane
C&S Wholesale	Nash-Finch
Central Grocers	Spartan Stores
Dearborn Wholesale Grocers	SUPERVALU
	Wakefern Food
	Wal-Mart

HISTORICAL FINANCIALS

Company Type: Private - Cooperative

Income Statement

	REVENUE ($ mil.)	NET INCOME ($ mil.)	NET PROFIT MARGIN	EMPLOYEES
12/11	7,766	169	2.2%	5,500
12/10	7,251	164	2.3%	0
12/09	7,057	147	2.1%	0
12/08	6,853	134	2.0%	0
Annual Growth	4.3%	8.0%	—	—

FYE: December 31

2011 Year-End Financials

Debt ratio: ——
Return on equity: 2.20%
Cash ($ mil.): 82
Current ratio: 0.50
Long-term debt ($ mil.): —

Dividends
Yield: —
Payout: —
Market value ($ mil.): —

ATLANTA CLARK UNIVERSITY INC

Clark Atlanta University (CAU) is a historically African-American liberal arts college that enrolls about 4000 students. The school which is affiliated with the United Methodist Church offers undergraduate and graduate degrees through its four schools: Arts and Sciences Business Administration Education Social Work. CAU is a member of the Atlanta University Center a consortium of educational institutions that includes Spelman College and Morehouse College. Clark Atlanta University was formed by the 1988 merger of two colleges founded in the 1860s –Clark College and Atlanta University.

In 2009 Clark Atlanta cut some 100 jobs from its faculty and staff blaming a reduction in enrollment. About 98% of the university's student qualify for financial aid. The economic recession proved to be too much for some students who no longer could afford to attend the private college.

EXECUTIVES

VP Management, Michael Lacour
Chair, Juanita Powell Baranco, age 63
General Counsel, Lance Dunnings
Dean School of Arts and Sciences, Shirley Williams-Kirksey
Associate Dean School of Business, Juanita F. Carter
Director Administrative Support Service Center, Anita O'Neal
Dean Office of Graduate Studies, William Boone
Dean Office of Undergraduate Studies, Alexa B. Henderson
Associate Dean Undergraduate Academic Services, Isabella T. Jenkins
Assistant VP Financial Planning and Evaluation, Janet Scott
Associate VP IT and CIO, Johann R. Lawton
Vice Chair, Elridge W. McMillan
Board Secretary, Delores P. Aldridge
Director Human Resources, Valerie Vinson
Interim Senior Director Marketing and Communications, Jennifer Jiles
Senior Media Relations Manager Marketing and Communications, Larry Calhoun
President and Trustee, Carlton E. Brown

LOCATIONS

HQ: Clark Atlanta University
223 James P. Brawley Dr. SW, Atlanta GA 30314
Phone: 404-880-8000   **Fax:** 404-880-6115
Web: www.cau.edu

PRODUCTS/OPERATIONS

Selected Schools

The School Of Arts And Sciences
  The Division of the Humanities
  The Division of Communication Arts
  The Division of Natural Sciences and Mathematics
  The Division of Social Sciences
The School Of Business Administration
The School Of Education
The School Of Social Work

HISTORICAL FINANCIALS
Company Type: School

Income Statement

FYE: June 30

	REVENUE ($ mil.)	NET INCOME ($ mil.)	NET PROFIT MARGIN	EMPLOYEES
06/11	99	9	10.0%	1,150
06/10	94	5	6.1%	0
06/09	85	(7)	—	0
06/08	91	1	1.3%	0
Annual Growth	3.0%	103.2%	—	—

2011 Year-End Financials

Debt ratio: ——
Return on equity: 10.00%
Cash ($ mil.): 17
Current ratio: —
Long-term debt ($ mil.): —

Dividends
  Yield: —
  Payout: —
  Market value ($ mil.): —

ATLANTIC BROADBAND FINANCE LLC

LOCATIONS

HQ: ATLANTIC BROADBAND FINANCE LLC
1 BATTERYMARCH PARK # 405, QUINCY, MA
02169-7454
Phone: 617-786-8800

HISTORICAL FINANCIALS
Company Type: Private

Income Statement

FYE: December 31

	REVENUE ($ mil.)	NET INCOME ($ mil.)	NET PROFIT MARGIN	EMPLOYEES
12/11	329	59	18.2%	662
12/10	316	46	14.6%	0
12/09	301	39	13.0%	0
Annual Growth	4.4%	23.2%	—	—

2011 Year-End Financials

Debt ratio: ——
Return on equity: 18.20%
Cash ($ mil.): 6
Current ratio: 0.30
Long-term debt ($ mil.): —

Dividends
  Yield: —
  Payout: —
  Market value ($ mil.): —

ATLANTIC COAST CONFERENCE

LOCATIONS

HQ: ATLANTIC COAST CONFERENCE
4512 WEYBRIDGE LN, GREENSBORO, NC
27407-7876
Phone: 336-854-8787
Web: www.theacc.com

HISTORICAL FINANCIALS
Company Type: Private

Income Statement

FYE: June 30

	REVENUE ($ mil.)	NET INCOME ($ mil.)	NET PROFIT MARGIN	EMPLOYEES
06/11	167	1	0.7%	26
06/10	158	(0)	—	0
06/08	162	4	2.5%	0
06/00	82	0	0.9%	0
Annual Growth	26.8%	16.0%	—	—

2011 Year-End Financials

Debt ratio: ——
Return on equity: 0.70%
Cash ($ mil.): 17
Current ratio: 2.10
Long-term debt ($ mil.): —

Dividends
  Yield: —
  Payout: —
  Market value ($ mil.): —

ATLANTIC DIVING SUPPLY INC.

Atlantic Diving Supply (doing business as ADS Tactical) is geared toward gearing up the military. Serving agencies in the Department of Defense the company specializes in helping customers procure tactical and operational military equipment. Like a retailer it sells 160000 products manufactured by some 1500 vendors including Camelbak FLIR L-3 Communications and Oakley but its niche offering is its supply management services. These services which are tailored to military customers include kitting (packaging related products in groups) assembly training custom sourcing product research and development and quality assurance. ADS Tactical filed an IPO in early 2011 but withdrew it six months later.

IPO

ADS Tactical in July 2011 called off its IPO just days before the company was to begin selling stock. (In August it formally withdrew its IPO filing.) The company cited "adverse market conditions" for the withdrawal. ADS sought up to $200 million in its IPO but wouldn't have received any of the proceeds which were earmarked to go to company owners and selling stockholders.

Sales and Marketing

While most of ADS Tactical's customers are within the Department of Defense and the Department of Homeland Security other customers include federal agencies defense contractors law enforcement and public safety organizations including fire departments and EMS. The company claims to employ many retired US military and law enforcement personnel.

Strategy

ADS Tactical's sales soared during the 2000s when it became a kind of middle-man for the Pentagon as the wars in Iraq and Afghanistan unfolded following the 9/11 attacks. Indeed the company enjoyed a steady rise in profits due in large part to year-over-year increases in its sales revenue and relatively low selling and administrative costs and other expenses. ADS intends to continue driving growth through a handful of long-term strategic efforts including continuing the expansion of its sales force broadening its product offerings to keep pace with the evolving technological needs of the military and attracting new customers from other defense-oriented government agencies and private security services organizations. However with the DOD and Homeland Security making up most of its business the company is vulnerable to cuts in the defense budget.

Ownership

CEO Luke Hillier owns a 58% stake in ADS while R. Scott LaRose holds a 25% stake and Daniel Clarkson a 17% stake.

EXECUTIVES

EVP, Bruce Dressel, age 47
Director, William A. (Bill) Roper Jr., age 66
Chairman and CEO, Luke Hillier, age 40
President, Daniel Clarkson, age 41
CFO, Patricia Bohlen, age 52
COO, Jason S. Wallace, age 41
EVP, Donald L. Sayre
VP Marketing, Chris Philbrick
VP Operations, Thomas Hazelbaker
VP Programs and Business Development, Lushana Offutt
VP Integration Programs, Amy S. Coyne
VP Product Management, Kevin Hickey
VP Human Resources, Jennifer Edwards
Contracts Director, Brad Anderson
VP Corporate Development, Nick Horbaczewski
VP Sales, Brant Feldman
Director, William A. (Bill) Roper Jr., age 66
VP COO Secretary Treasurer and Director, Daniel Clarkson, age 41
Director, R. Scott LaRose, age 43
Auditors: KPMGLLP

LOCATIONS

HQ: ATLANTIC DIVING SUPPLY INC.
621 LYNNHVEN PKWY STE 400, VIRGINIA BEACH, VA 23452
Phone: 757-481-7758

PRODUCTS/OPERATIONS

Selected Products

Apparel
Bags packs and cases
Eyewear
Footwear
Hydration systems
Knives
Lighting
Medical
Tools
Training aids

COMPETITORS

Army and Air Force Exchange
Navy Exchange
Target Corporation
Tyco Safety Products
Wal-Mart

HISTORICAL FINANCIALS

Company Type: Private

Income Statement

FYE: December 31

	REVENUE ($ mil.)	NET INCOME ($ mil.)	NET PROFIT MARGIN	EMPLOYEES
12/11	1,409	50	3.6%	400
12/10	1,327	77	5.8%	0
12/09	938	54	5.8%	0
12/08	650	40	6.2%	0
Annual Growth	29.4%	7.8%	—	—

2011 Year-End Financials

Debt ratio: —
Return on equity: 3.60%
Cash ($ mil.): 1
Current ratio: 1.00
Long-term debt ($ mil.): —
Dividends
Yield: —
Payout: —
Market value ($ mil.): —

ATLANTIC METHANOL PRODUCTION COMPANY LLC

Atlantic Methanol Production Company (AMPCO) must have adopted "Waste not want not" as its motto. It tries not to waste the natural gas that is a by-product of its parent companies' production processes. Atlantic Methanol was founded in 1997 to make use of natural gas being expent off the coast of Equitorial Guinea. It began production four years later. Operating one of the largest methanol plants in the world it produces about 1 million tons of methanol annually –2% of the global market. It also distributes using three vessels and five terminals in Europe and US where it sells most of its production. Noble Energy and Marathon Oil each own 45% with the state-controlled SONAGAS owning the remaining 10%.

AMPCO's plant located on Bioko Island in Equatorial Guinea has the capacity to produce 3000 metric tons per day of methanol. The global demand for methanol is about 50 million tons per year of which Equitorial Guinea supplies 2% from its single plant. Methanol is used as an intermediate in the manufacture of several everyday products including adhesive resins for plywood and pressboard polyester fibers and packaging paints and coatings plastics and fuels and fuel additives. Some of methanol's fastest growth areas are in the acetic acid and fuels areas including biodiesel. Other applications include using methanol for fuel cells.

The company manages its marketing and sales from its US-based headquarters in Houston. It markets in Europe through an agent solvadis methanol in Frankfurt Germany. It expects demand to increase for methanol in the oilfield services sector along the Western Africa coast and it expects to equip the plant site there.

Feedstock for AMPCO's plant is supplied from natural gas production from the Alba field in Equatorial Guinea (operated by Marathon Oil and Noble Energy) under a contract that runs through 2026. In 2011 the plant was supplied a gross 127 million cu. ft. per day of dry natural gas for use in production and was able to sell 1.04 million metric tons of methanol in 2011 to customers in Europe and the US. Noble Energy's share of AMPCO's sales was $68 million in fiscal 2011 compared to $29 million in 2010. The company's net income from AMPCO increased because of higher average realized methanol prices following a rebound in global economic conditions as well as an increase in methanol sales volumes that year (compared to a halt in production in 2010 for a major turnaround) at the plant.

Although AMPCO delivers 2% of the world's total demand global demand for methanol is limited which has an impact on AMPCO's earnings.

EXECUTIVES

VP Commercial Operations, Roger Dickson
Marketing Manager, Hank Williams
Vice Chairman President and General Manager, Paul Moschell
Customer Support Representative, Christina Peguero
VP Operations and Resident Manager, Philip (Phil) Sharp
Office Administrator and Insurance, Sharon Tibbs
Manager Human Resources and Administration, Arthur (Budd) Buschmann
Senior Buyer, Molly Thompson
Human Resources Administrative Assistant, Doris Anderson
Chairman, W. Ken Keag
Vice Chairman, Juan A. Ndong
Procurement Manager, Edson Jones
Secretary, Darla McBryde
Manager Finance and Administration, Jim O'Casek
Vice Chairman President and General Manager, Paul Moschell
Vice Chairman, Juan A. Ndong

LOCATIONS

HQ: ATLANTIC METHANOL PRODUCTION COMPANY LLC
12600 NORTHBOROUGH DR # 150, HOUSTON, TX 77067-3200
Phone: 281-872-8324
Web: www.atlanticmethanol.com

COMPETITORS

Celanese
Eastman Chemical
LyondellBasell
Methanex

HISTORICAL FINANCIALS

Company Type: Joint Venture

Income Statement

FYE: December 31

	REVENUE ($ mil.)	NET INCOME ($ mil.)	NET PROFIT MARGIN	EMPLOYEES
12/11	368	143	39.1%	342
12/10	254	65	25.8%	0
12/08	341	122	35.8%	0
12/07	389	178	45.8%	0
Annual Growth	(1.9%)	(7.0%)	—	—

2011 Year-End Financials

Debt ratio: —
Return on equity: 39.10%
Cash ($ mil.): 5
Current ratio: 0.30
Long-term debt ($ mil.): —
Dividends
Yield: —
Payout: —
Market value ($ mil.): —

ATTRONICA COMPUTERS INC.

Attronica hopes to offer an alternative to chunking your old outdated computers out the window. The company provides a variety of information technology (IT) services including network and systems integration product consulting and hardware procurement to middle-market businesses in the mid-Atlantic states. Attronica also offers such services as network security support inventory management and training. The company's customers come from a wide range of industries including financial services health care manufacturing retail consumer goods and transportation. It operates from four offices in Maryland and Virginia. Attronica was co-founded by CEO Atul Tucker in 1983.

EXECUTIVES

President and CEO, Atul Tucker (Thakkar)
SVP and Director, Carol P. Cornwell
SVP Sales and Director, Niel Tucker (Thakkar)
VP Engineering Services, Ali Tajdar
VP Management Information Services, Esmail Sadeghi
COO, Vivek Karkhanis

LOCATIONS

HQ: Attronica Computers Inc.
  15867 Gaither Dr., Gaithersburg MD 20877
Phone: 301-417-0070   **Fax:** 240-454-6494
Web: www.attronica.com

COMPETITORS

A&T Systems	HP Enterprise Services
Affiliated Computer Services	IBM Global Services
	Ingram Micro
Computer Sciences Corp.	SAIC
	Tech Data
Daly Computers	Unisys
Dataprise	

HISTORICAL FINANCIALS
Company Type: Private

Income Statement
FYE: December 31

	REVENUE ($ mil.)	NET INCOME ($ mil.)	NET PROFIT MARGIN	EMPLOYEES
12/11	57	0	0.7%	61
12/10	55	0	0.4%	0
12/09	43	0	0.7%	0
12/08	39	(0)	—	0
Annual Growth	13.3%			

2011 Year-End Financials

Debt ratio: ——
Return on equity: 0.70%
Cash ($ mil.): 0   Dividends
Current ratio: 0.70   Yield: —
Long-term debt ($ mil.): —   Payout: —
          Market value ($ mil.): —

AUGUSTA FIBERGLASS COATINGS INC.

LOCATIONS

HQ: AUGUSTA FIBERGLASS COATINGS INC.
  86 LAKE CYNTHIA DR, BLACKVILLE, SC 29817-4126
Phone: 803-284-2246
Web: www.augustafiberglass.com

HISTORICAL FINANCIALS
Company Type: Private

Income Statement
FYE: September 30

	REVENUE ($ mil.)	NET INCOME ($ mil.)	NET PROFIT MARGIN	EMPLOYEES
09/11	95	0	—	300
09/10	95	0	—	0
09/09	95	0	—	0
09/08	0	0	—	0
Annual Growth	—	—	—	—

2011 Year-End Financials

Debt ratio: ——
Return on equity: —
Cash ($ mil.): 1   Dividends
Current ratio: 6.20   Yield: —
Long-term debt ($ mil.): —   Payout: —
          Market value ($ mil.): —

AUGUSTANA CARE

LOCATIONS

HQ: AUGUSTANA CARE
  1007 E 14TH ST, MINNEAPOLIS, MN 55404-1314
Phone: 612-238-5101
Web: www.augustanacare.org

HISTORICAL FINANCIALS
Company Type: Private

Income Statement
FYE: September 30

	ASSETS ($ mil.)	NET INCOME ($ mil.)	INCOME AS % OF ASSETS	EMPLOYEES
09/11	169	3	2.0%	2,000
09/10	39	5	13.5%	0
09/08	5	(0)	—	0
09/05	70	(0)	—	0
Annual Growth	34.0%	—	—	—

2011 Year-End Financials

Debt ratio: ——
Return on equity: 3.20%
Cash ($ mil.): 8   Dividends
Current ratio: 1.20   Yield: —
Long-term debt ($ mil.): —   Payout: —
          Market value ($ mil.): —

AUGUSTANA COLLEGE

Augustana College is a private liberal arts college located near the Mississippi River in northwestern Illinois. The school offers undergraduate degrees in some 50 areas of study plus pre-professional programs in fields including dentistry law medicine and veterinary medicine. It enrolls approximately 2500 students. The Swenson Center a national archive dedicated to the study of Swedish immigration to the US is housed on the Augustana campus. Augustana College was founded in 1860 by Swedish settlers and is associated with the Evangelical Lutheran Church.

EXECUTIVES

President, Steven C. Bahls
Director Library, Carla Tracy
Chief Business and Financial Officer, Paul Pearson
Controller, Mary Doonan
Director Human Resources, Kenneth H. (Ken) Johnson
Dean of the College, Jeff Abernathy
Director Advising, Bill Coker
Director Career Center, Kristi Gimmel Becker
Dean of Enrollment, Kent Barnds
Director Fiscal Operations, Darlene Link
Purchasing Coordinator, Tom Schaubroeck
Network Manager, Scott Dean
Director Information Technology Services Development, Chris Vaughan

LOCATIONS

HQ: AUGUSTANA COLLEGE
  639 38TH ST, ROCK ISLAND, IL 61201-2296
Phone: 309-794-7000
Web: www.wvik.org

HISTORICAL FINANCIALS
Company Type: School

Income Statement
FYE: June 30

	REVENUE ($ mil.)	NET INCOME ($ mil.)	NET PROFIT MARGIN	EMPLOYEES
06/12	78	8	11.2%	650
06/11	106	38	36.6%	0
06/10	104	7	6.8%	0
06/09	93	(10)	—	0
Annual Growth	(5.9%)	—	—	—

2012 Year-End Financials

Debt ratio: ——
Return on equity: 11.20%
Cash ($ mil.): 9   Dividends
Current ratio: —   Yield: —
Long-term debt ($ mil.): —   Payout: —
          Market value ($ mil.): —

AURORA FLIGHT SCIENCES CORP

Pilots? For most of its products Aurora Flight Sciences doesn't need pilots (at least not ones who sit in a cockpit of a plane). The company makes unmanned aerial vehicles (UAVs aka drones) and composite structures for aircraft with both military and scientific applications. It also provides flight operations and testing services for a variety of aircraft. Customers include major aerospace contractors such as Raytheon and US government agencies. Aurora Flight Sciences along with Georgia Institute of Technology is developing next-generation distributed controllers for turbine engines for the Air Force Research Laboratory.

Geographic Reach
Aurora Flight Sciences operates from facilities in Massachusetts Mississippi Virginia and West Virginia.

Strategy
Although defense spending is expected to decline in the near future Aurora Flight Sciences is poised to benefit from an increased interest in unmanned combat aerial vehicles (UCAV). According

to published reports the US Department of Defense will spend as much as $3 billion per year on UCAVs between 2010 and 2019.

Orion is in development for the US Air Force to provide an affordable 5-day endurance Multi-Intelligence Surveillance Reconnaissance platform for the changing global security environment. Orion will be capable of flying with 1000 lbs of payload at 20000 ft. for 120 hrs.

It is also developing the Skate? Small Unmanned Aerial System (SUAS) —a lightweight easily transported system capable of autonomous operation while delivering long endurance on quiet electric power.

Aurora is also combining its unmanned expertise with more traditional aircraft navigation. The company has been testing its Centaur Optionally Piloted Aircraft (OPA). The OPA can be flown by a pilot or as an unmanned aircraft.

To keep up with demand in 2013 Aurora completed the construction of a 30000-sq.-ft. $17 million plant at the Golden Triangle Regional Airport in Columbus Mississippi. The new facility will allow the company to increase its commercial composites manufacturing operations creating 250 new jobs.

Company Background

Company president John Langford founded Aurora Flight Sciences in 1989.

EXECUTIVES

Principal Engineer for Propulsion, Jack L. Kerrebrock, age 78
Director Development, Greg Stewart
Program Manager GoldenEye, Carl Schaefer
Chairman and CEO, John S. Langford
VP Business Operations, Kristine T. Miller
VP Strategic Partnerships, A. Morag
Chief Technical Officer and VP of Development Programs, Tom Clancy
VP and CFO, Ralph Koch
VP Science Applications, John Appleby
VP Business Development, John Tylko
VP Tactical Systems, Matt Hutchinson
VP Research and Development Cambridge, Thomas Vaneck
VP Production Programs, Dan Brady
Chief Scientist, Javier de Luis
General Manager Virginia Operations, Joe Granata
General Manager Cabridge R&D Center, Tim Dawson-Townsend
General Manager Aurora West Virginia, Ronald C. (Ron) Richman
General Manager Mississippi Manufacturing Operations, Rob Penrod
VP Manufacturing and Quality, Jeff A. Tillery
Director Public Relations, Patti Woodside
President and COO, Mark C. Cherry

LOCATIONS

HQ: Aurora Flight Sciences Corporation
9950 Wakeman Dr., Manassas VA 20110
Phone: 703-369-3633   **Fax:** 703-369-4223
Web: www.aurora.aero

PRODUCTS/OPERATIONS

Selected Products
Aerostructures
  Advanced Composite Cargo Aircraft (ACCA)
  Sikorsky EWR (Engineering Work Request)
  Sonobuoy (launcher for the MH-60R helicopter)
Under Development
  Centaur (Optionally Piloted Aircraft)
  Orion (Multi-Intelligence Surveillance Reconnaissance Platform)

Skate (Small Unmanned Aerial System)

COMPETITORS

AAI Corporation	L-3 Communications
AeroVironment	Meggitt-USA
Elbit Systems	Northrop Grumman
Insitu	Williams International

HISTORICAL FINANCIALS
Company Type: Private

Income Statement
FYE: September 30

	REVENUE ($ mil.)	NET INCOME ($ mil.)	NET PROFIT MARGIN	EMPLOYEES
09/11	72	0	0.1%	292
09/10	62	0	0.2%	0
09/09	65	(1)	—	0
09/08	51	(7)	—	0
Annual Growth	**12.1%**	—	—	—

2011 Year-End Financials
Debt ratio: —
Return on equity: 0.10%
Cash ($ mil.): 4
Current ratio: 0.10
Long-term debt ($ mil.): —
Dividends
  Yield: —
  Payout: —
Market value ($ mil.): —

AURORA PUBLIC SCHOOLS

LOCATIONS

HQ: AURORA PUBLIC SCHOOLS
   15701 E 1ST AVE STE 106, AURORA, CO 80011-9037
Phone: 303-365-5813
Web: www.murphycreek.aurorak12.org

HISTORICAL FINANCIALS
Company Type: Private

Income Statement
FYE: June 30

	REVENUE ($ mil.)	NET INCOME ($ mil.)	NET PROFIT MARGIN	EMPLOYEES
06/12	333	(32)	—	5,000
06/11	341	27	7.9%	0
06/10	341	(45)	—	0
06/09	319	124	39.0%	0
Annual Growth	**1.4%**	—	—	—

2012 Year-End Financials
Debt ratio: —
Return on equity: (-9.80)%
Cash ($ mil.): 61
Current ratio: 1.10
Long-term debt ($ mil.): —
Dividends
  Yield: —
  Payout: —
Market value ($ mil.): —

AUSTIN COLLEGE

Located in the North Texas city of Sherman rather than in Austin Austin College is a small private liberal arts college. The educational institution sits on an 85-acre campus and draws an enrollment of about 1350 full-time undergraduate students including graduate students working on a Master of Arts in Teaching. It's nationally known for its focus on international education pre-professional training and leadership studies. Tuition and fees at Austin College run about $26500 and housing costs are typically $8600 per year. Affiliated with the Presbyterian Church Austin College was founded in 1849 by missionary Daniel Baker. It plans to open its new IDEA Center in fall 2013.

Strategy

In mid-2011 Austin College broke ground on a $38 million IDEA Center to house its departments of biology chemistry computer science environmental studies mathematics and physics. The science building will help facilitate interactive learning and interdisciplinary studies. The IDEA Center serves the liberal arts college's strategy to integrate science and technology into its curriculum and maintain a competitive program.

Operations

Austin College is the oldest institution of higher education in Texas operating under original charter and name. It's spotlighted in the book Colleges that Change Lives authored by Loren Pope among the 40 schools profiled in the publication.

The college boasts more than 90 full-time faculty members of which 93% are tenured or tenure-track faculty who have a Ph.D. or equivalent terminal degree. Austin College has a student-faculty ratio of 13:1.

Company Background

General Sam Houston and Anson Jones both presidents of the Republic of Texas sat on the original Board of Trustees.

EXECUTIVES

Director Finance, Sheryl Bradshaw
VP Institutional Enrollment, Nan M. Davis
VP Academic Affairs and Dean Faculty, Michael A. Imhoff
VP Student Affairs and Athletics, Timothy P. (Tim) Millerick
Director Admission, Stephanie Bierman
Chief of Campus Police, Larry Caylor
Executive Director Information Technology, Bill Edgette
Assistant Director Financial Aid, Tanya McKee
Director Career Services, Margie Norman
Registrar, Phyllis Rieser
VP Business Affairs, Heidi B. Ellis
VP Institutional Advancement, Jerry Holbert
Director Human Resources, Keith Larey
Director Alumni and Parent Relations, Victoria Martinsen
Executive Director College Relations, Michael Strysick
President, Marjorie Hass

LOCATIONS

HQ: Austin College
   900 N. Grand Ave., Sherman TX 75090
Phone: 903-813-2000   **Fax:** 312-419-8419
Web: www.bgglobal.com

PRODUCTS/OPERATIONS

Selected Centers
Center for Environmental Studies
Center for Global Learning
Center for Southwestern and Mexican Studies
Robert & Joyce Johnson Center for Faculty Development and Excellence in Teaching

Posey Leadership Institute

HISTORICAL FINANCIALS
Company Type: School

Income Statement
FYE: June 30

	REVENUE ($ mil.)	NET INCOME ($ mil.)	NET PROFIT MARGIN	EMPLOYEES
06/11	40	0	1.7%	325
06/10	41	3	9.3%	0
06/09	37	(29)	—	0
06/08	41	3	8.9%	0
Annual Growth	(1.0%)	(42.9%)	—	—

2011 Year-End Financials

Debt ratio: ——
Return on equity: 1.70%
Cash ($ mil.): 4
Current ratio: —
Long-term debt ($ mil.): —

Dividends
Yield: —
Payout: —
Market value ($ mil.): —

AUTOMATION PERSONNEL SERVICES INC.

LOCATIONS

HQ: AUTOMATION PERSONNEL SERVICES INC.
401 SOUTHGATE DR, PELHAM, AL 35124-1186
Phone: 205-733-3700
Web: www.apstemps.com

HISTORICAL FINANCIALS
Company Type: Private

Income Statement
FYE: December 31

	REVENUE ($ mil.)	NET INCOME ($ mil.)	NET PROFIT MARGIN	EMPLOYEES
12/11	117	1	1.2%	4,200
12/10	94	1	1.2%	0
12/09	68	0	0.0%	0
12/08	84	1	2.0%	0
Annual Growth	11.8%	(6.1%)	—	—

2011 Year-End Financials

Debt ratio: ——
Return on equity: 1.20%
Cash ($ mil.): 0
Current ratio: 1.10
Long-term debt ($ mil.): —

Dividends
Yield: —
Payout: —
Market value ($ mil.): —

AVE MARIA UNIVERSITY INC.

Ave Maria University offers four-year bachelor's degrees with majors and minors in biology and chemistry classics and early Christian literature economics history literature mathematics and physics philosophy politics sacred music and theology. The university also offers a Masters of Arts degree in Theology. In addition to its main campus has a branch campus in San Marcos Nicaragua. Ave Maria University which opened in 2003 was the first new Catholic institution of higher learning to open in the US in 40 years. Ave Maria is Latin for Hail Mary.

EXECUTIVES

VP University Relations, Carole Carpenter
CFO and Trustee, Paul Roney
VP Student Affairs, Dan Dentino
President COO and Trustee, Nicholas J. (Nick) Healy Jr.
Chancellor and Trustee, Thomas S. Monaghan
Dean Faculty and Associate Professor of Theology, Michael A. Dauphinais
Controller, Tony Beata
Manager Operations, Wally Hedman
VP Technology Systems Engineering, Bryan Mehaffey
Director Physical Plant and Campus Security, Thomas Minick
SVP Administration, John E. (Jack) Sites
Director Marketing, Forrest Wallace
Managing Financial Aid Director, Anne Hart
Bursar, Pat Knight
Trustee, Michael D. (Mike) Soignet, age 52
Trustee, John F. Donahue, age 88
Trustee, Richard M. (Dick) Gabrys, age 70
CFO and Trustee, Paul Roney
President COO and Trustee, Nicholas J. (Nick) Healy Jr.
Chancellor and Trustee, Thomas S. Monaghan
Trustee, Patricia D. Dolan
Trustee, Edward W. Easton
Trustee, Father Benedict J. Groeschel
Trustee, Barbara B. Henkels
Trustee, Laurence E. Higgins
Trustee, James E. (Jim) Holman, age 66
Trustee, Michael Novak
Trustee, Paul R. Roney
Trustee, Kevin Ryan
Trustee, Glory L. Sullivan
Trustee, Michael T. O. Timmis
Trustee, John V. Tippmann Sr.

LOCATIONS

HQ: Ave Maria University
5050 Ave Maria Blvd., Ave Maria FL 34142-9505
Phone: 239-280-2556   **Fax:** 239-280-2559
Web: www.avemaria.edu

PRODUCTS/OPERATIONS

Selected Academic Departments
Biology & Chemistry
Classics & Early Christian Literature
Economics
History
Literature
Mathematics & Physics
Philosophy
Politics
Sacred Music
Theology

HISTORICAL FINANCIALS
Company Type: School

Income Statement
FYE: June 30

	REVENUE ($ mil.)	NET INCOME ($ mil.)	NET PROFIT MARGIN	EMPLOYEES
06/11	48	(4)	—	195
06/08	1	0	—	0
06/05	164	145	88.5%	0
06/04	0	0	—	0
Annual Growth	—	—	—	—

2011 Year-End Financials

Debt ratio: ——
Return on equity: (-9.00)%
Cash ($ mil.): 2
Current ratio: —
Long-term debt ($ mil.): —

Dividends
Yield: —
Payout: —
Market value ($ mil.): —

AVERA HEALTH

Avera Health provides health care services to eastern South Dakota as well as parts of Iowa Minnesota Nebraska and North Dakota. The health care system operates an extensive network of facilities including some 28 hospitals (totaling 1450 acute-care beds) and 140 primary care community clinics. Other facilities include nursing homes hospices urgent care clinics and home health offices. These operations are divided into five regions: Avera St. Luke's Avera Queen of Peace Avera Marshall Avera McKennan and Avera Sacred Heart. The system also operates a health care plan and Avera PACE a hospital purchasing organization. Avera Health is sponsored by the Benedictine Sisters and Presentation Sisters.

EXECUTIVES

President and CEO, John T. Porter
CFO, Jim Breckenridge
SVP Avera Health, Richard Thompson
SVP Governance and Strategic Planning, Jean Reed
President and CEO Avera St. Luke's Hospital, Ron L. Jacobson
SVP Medical Affairs Avera McKennan Hospital, David Kapaska
SVP Environmental Services, Richard Molseed
Regional President Avera McKennan Hospital, Fred Slunecka
President and CEO Avera Sacred Heart Hospital, Pamela (Pam) Rezac
President and CEO Avera Queen of Peace Health Services, Thomas P. (Tom) Rasmusson, age 65
SVP Finance Avera McKenna Hospital and University Center, Ron Farr
SVP Hospital Operations, Judy Blauwet
SVP Clinic Operations Avera McKennan Hospital, David Flicek
President and CEO Avera Holy Family Health, Bill Bumgarner
President and CEO Avera St. Anthony's Hospital, Ronald (Ron) Cork
President and CEO Avera Heart Hospital of South Dakota, Jon C. Soderholm
President and CEO Avera St. Benedict Health Center, Gale Walker
Director Marketing and Public Relations, Daryl Thuringer
Executive Director Avera PACE, Mary Kuper

SVP Information Systems, Jim Veline
Director Health Information Management, Kathy
 Dorale
Executive Director Information Systems
 Administrative Support, Steve Yates
President Avera McKennan Foundation, Joe Orsak
SVP Managed Facilities, Curt Hohman
SVP Strategic Marketing and Communications,
 Michelle Lavallee
Controller Avera McKenna Hospital and
 University Health Center, Julie Norton
Director Risk Management, Christopher (Chris)
 Specht
CEO and Administrator Hegg Memorial Health
 Center Avera, Glenn Zevenbergen
CEO and Administrator Avera De Smet Memorial
 Hospital, Janice Schardin
Chairman, Rodney (Rod) Fouberg
SVP Mission Avera McKennan Hospital &
 University Health Center, Mary Thomas
Marketing and Public Relations, Clare Willrodt
Medical Director Avera Center for
 MindBodySpirit, Michael McVay
SVP and Chief Medical Officer, David Erickson
President and CEO Avera Marshall Regional
 Medical Center, Mary Maertens

LOCATIONS

HQ: Avera Health
 3900 W. Avera Dr., Sioux Falls SD 57108
Phone: 605-322-4700   Fax: 605-322-4799
Web: www.avera.org

Selected Facilities

Iowa
 Avera Holy Family Health (Estherville)
 Floyd Valley Hospital (Le Mars)
 Hegg Memorial Health Center (Rock Valley)
 Osceola Community Hospital (Sibley)
 Sioux Center Community Hospital & Health Center
  (Sioux Center)
Nebraska
 Avera Sacred Heart Medical Clinic (Crofton)
 Avera St. Anthony's Hospital (O'Neill)
Minnesota
 Avera Marshall Regional Medical Center (Marshall)
 Beckering Clinic (Edgerton)
 Pipestone County Medical Center (Pipestone)
 Southwestern Mental Health Center (Luverne)
 United Medical Clinic (Windom)
South Dakota
 Avera Gregory Healthcare Center (Gregory)
 Avera McKennan Hospital & University Health Center
  (Sioux Falls)
 Avera Queen of Peace Hospital (Mitchell)
 Avera Sacred Heart Hospital (Yankton)
 Avera St. Benedict Health Center (Parkston)
 Avera St. Luke's (Aberdeen)
 Avera Weskota Memorial Medical Center (Wessington
  Springs)
 Flandreau Medical Center (Flandreau)
 Hand County Memorial Hospital & Clinic (Miller)
 Heart Hospital of South Dakota (Sioux Falls)
 Landmann-Jungman Memorial Hospital (Scotland)
 Milbank Area Hospital (Milkbank)
 St. Michael's Hospital & Nursing Home
  (Tyndall)
 Wagner Community Memorial Hospital (Wagner)

COMPETITORS

Altru Health
Catholic Health
 Initiatives
First Care
Iowa Health System
Mercy Health Network

Rapid City Regional
 Hospital
Sanford
 Health-MeritCare
St. Alexius Medical
 Center

HISTORICAL FINANCIALS

Company Type: Private - Not-for-Profit

Income Statement

FYE: June 30

	REVENUE ($ mil.)	NET INCOME ($ mil.)	NET PROFIT MARGIN	EMPLOYEES
06/11	74	11	14.8%	2,450
06/05	9	4	51.2%	0
06/04	5	1	19.8%	0
06/03	1,061	0	0.0%	0
Annual Growth	(58.8%)	4183.3%	—	—

2011 Year-End Financials

Debt ratio: ——
Return on equity: 14.80%
Cash ($ mil.): 15
Current ratio: 0.10
Long-term debt ($ mil.): —

Dividends
 Yield: —
 Payout: —
Market value ($ mil.): —

AVERITT EXPRESS INC.

Small loads add up at Averitt Express. The company provides less-than-truckload (LTL) freight transportation service. (LTL carriers combine freight from multiple shippers into a single trailer.) It operates a fleet of about 3700 tractors and 12000 trailers from a network of some 80 terminals. Averitt Express directly serves the southern US and Mexico and it provides service elsewhere in North America through partnerships with other carriers such as Lakeville Motor Express and DATS. The company also offers truckload and expedited freight transportation along with logistics warehousing and international freight forwarding. Customers have included Home Depot Shoe Carnival and V.F. Corporation.

Geographic Reach

Averitt Express has trucking facilities in Alabama Arkansas California Florida Georgia Illinois Kentucky Louisiana Mississippi Missouri North Carolina Ohio Oklahoma South Carolina Tennessee Texas Virginia and Wisconsin.

Strategy

The company aims to grow from solely a LTL carrier based in the Southeast to an international transportation and logistics company. To this end it continues to strategically broaden its geographic reach and range of services. Averitt Express in 2012 launched a new business unit zeroing in on retailers in need of distribution services. The new unit Averitt Retail Distribution Services offers customized delivery services catering to the unique requirements of retailers and is targeting retailers needing delivery in large Southern markets.

During 2010 Averitt Express responded to customer demand by expanding its flatbed operation launched early in the year. The move built upon the company's decision to bundle its full-load transportation offerings with national intermodal service. It has partnered with railroads in several key regions Union Pacific and BNSF in the West Norfolk Southern and CSX in the East and Midwest and Florida East Coast in Florida and Georgia.

Ownership

CEO Gary Sasser owns Averitt Express which was founded by Thurman Averitt as Livingston Merchants Co-op in 1958. Sasser bought the company from Averitt in 1971.

EXECUTIVES

President and CEO, Gary D. Sasser
EVP and COO, Wayne Spain
EVP Sales and Marketing, Phil Pierce
EVP and CFO, George Johnson

LOCATIONS

HQ: Averitt Express Inc.
 Perimeter Place One 1415 Neal St., Cookeville TN
 38501-4328
Phone: 931-526-3306   Fax: 402-479-2075
Web: www.cretecarrier.com

PRODUCTS/OPERATIONS

Selected Services

Cross-border/domestic offshore (Canada Mexico Puerto
 Rico/Virgin Islands)
Dedicated
Expedited
Intermodal
International ocean/air (ocean/air Asia-Memphis
 Express)
LTL (regional nationwide distribution/consolidation)
Portside
Retail specialized services
Transportation management
Truckload (dry van flatbed brokerage)
Warehousing

COMPETITORS

AAA Cooper
 Transportation
Arkansas Best
C.H. Robinson
 Worldwide
Con-way Freight
Estes Express
FedEx Freight
J.B. Hunt

Old Dominion Freight
R+L Carriers
Schneider National
Southeastern Freight
 Lines
Swift Transportation
UPS Freight
YRC Worldwide

HISTORICAL FINANCIALS

Company Type: Private

Income Statement

FYE: December 31

	REVENUE ($ mil.)	NET INCOME ($ mil.)	NET PROFIT MARGIN	EMPLOYEES
12/11	917	30	3.3%	8,208
12/10	819	18	2.2%	0
12/09	766	5	0.7%	0
12/08	966	15	1.6%	0
Annual Growth	(1.7%)	24.9%	—	—

2011 Year-End Financials

Debt ratio: ——
Return on equity: 3.30%
Cash ($ mil.): 207
Current ratio: 4.80
Long-term debt ($ mil.): —

Dividends
 Yield: —
 Payout: —
Market value ($ mil.): —

AVITA HEALTH SYSTEM

LOCATIONS

HQ: AVITA HEALTH SYSTEM
269 PORTLAND WAY S, GALION, OH 44833-2312
Phone: 419-468-4841

HISTORICAL FINANCIALS

Company Type: Private

Income Statement

FYE: June 30

	REVENUE ($ mil.)	NET INCOME ($ mil.)	NET PROFIT MARGIN	EMPLOYEES
06/11	83	8	10.1%	800
Annual Growth	—	—	—	—

2011 Year-End Financials

Debt ratio: ——
Return on equity: 10.10%
Cash ($ mil.): 4
Current ratio: 1.50
Long-term debt ($ mil.): —

Dividends
Yield: —
Payout: —
Market value ($ mil.): —

AVIV HEALTHCARE PROPERTIES LIMITED PARTNERSHIP

LOCATIONS

HQ: AVIV HEALTHCARE PROPERTIES LIMITED PARTNERSHIP
303 W MADISON ST, CHICAGO, IL 60606-3309
Phone: 312-855-0930

HISTORICAL FINANCIALS

Company Type: Private

Income Statement

FYE: September 30

	REVENUE ($ mil.)	NET INCOME ($ mil.)	NET PROFIT MARGIN	EMPLOYEES
09/12*	91	11	12.4%	2
12/11	104	11	10.8%	0
Annual Growth	(12.3%)	0.7%	—	—

*Fiscal year change

2012 Year-End Financials

Debt ratio: ——
Return on equity: 12.40%
Cash ($ mil.): 12
Current ratio: ——
Long-term debt ($ mil.): —

Dividends
Yield: —
Payout: —
Market value ($ mil.): —

AVOMEX INC.

LOCATIONS

HQ: AVOMEX INC.
300 BURLINGTON RD, SAGINAW, TX 76179-1304
Phone: 817-509-0626

HISTORICAL FINANCIALS

Company Type: Private

Income Statement

FYE: July 2

	REVENUE ($ mil.)	NET INCOME ($ mil.)	NET PROFIT MARGIN	EMPLOYEES
07/11	148	3	2.4%	50
Annual Growth	—	—	—	—

2011 Year-End Financials

Debt ratio: ——
Return on equity: 2.40%
Cash ($ mil.): 1
Current ratio: 1.10
Long-term debt ($ mil.): —

Dividends
Yield: —
Payout: —
Market value ($ mil.): —

AXEL JOHNSON INC.

The Johnson family of Stockholm Sweden has an investment arm that stretches across the ocean. Axel Johnson owns and operates North American businesses on behalf of the Johnson dynasty. The investment firm focuses on several industries such as energy distribution medical device manufacturing and water treatment. Its portfolio includes Sprague Energy Parkson Corp. and Kinetico Incorporated. Axel Johnson's companies boast about $4 billion in annual revenues. Axel Johnson along with Axel Johnson AB and AXFast are all affiliated with Sweden-based Axel Johnson Group but are independent. Established in 1873 the Johnson family of companies is in its fifth generation of family ownership.

Operations

Axel Johnson which was formed in 1920 is a long-term investor that typically holds on to its companies for about 20 years. Some companies have been a part of Axel Johnson's portfolio for more than 40 years. Two of its holdings Parkson and Kinetico are part of Axel Johnson's AxWater Group which was formed in 2000.

Strategy

Through NewtrAX Axel Johnson makes minority investments in smaller businesses. NewtrAX has stakes in Cadence a manufacturer of cutting and piercing instruments used for the medical and industrial applications. It also owns portions of wood reclamation company Mountain Lumber Co. and Walk2Campus a real estate management and acquisition company. The company in late 2011 invested some $15 million in ConforMIS which develops and markets customized medical devices for the treatment of osteoarthritis and joint damage.

The company's Sprague subsidiary acquired an oil terminal in Rensselaer New York for $3.4 million. The 2011 deal also included $4.4 million in inventory that was stored at the terminal.

Financial Performance

Following the economic downturn the company has seen sales increase for several years. Axel Johnson's revenue rose by 33% in 2011 as compared to 2010. Energy product sales generated the largest portion of the company's revenue.

Company Ownership

Axel Johnson operates as an independently owned investment firm that's affiliated with Axel Johnson AB AXFast and Axel Johnson Group.

EXECUTIVES

President and CEO Kinetico, Shamus Hurley, age 51
President and CEO, Michael D. (Mike) Milligan, age 48
President and CEO Sprague Energy, David C. (Dave) Glendon, age 46
EVP and CFO, Ben J. Hennelly, age 41
VP Corporate Development, Grant A.H. Brown
Manager Corporate Development, Erika M. Cafarella
EVP, John C Pascale
Auditors: CajNackstadandPerBergman

LOCATIONS

HQ: Axel Johnson Inc.
155 Spring St. 6th Fl., New York NY 10012
Phone: 646-291-2445   **Fax:** 212-966-9546
Web: www.axeljohnson.com

PRODUCTS/OPERATIONS

Selected Portfolio Companies
Cadence Incorporated
Kinestico Incorporated
Mountain Lumber Company
Parkson Corporation
Sprague Energy Corp.
Walk2Campus Holdings LLC

COMPETITORS

CCMP Capital
Court Square Capital Partners
Enterprise Partners

KKR
Menlo Ventures
Sevin Rosen

HISTORICAL FINANCIALS

Company Type: Private

Income Statement

FYE: December 31

	REVENUE ($ mil.)	NET INCOME ($ mil.)	NET PROFIT MARGIN	EMPLOYEES
12/11	3,954	22	0.6%	1,200
12/10	2,982	15	0.5%	0
12/09	2,598	11	0.5%	0
12/08	4,312	8	0.2%	0
Annual Growth	(2.9%)	39.9%	—	—

2011 Year-End Financials

Debt ratio: ——
Return on equity: 0.60%
Cash ($ mil.): 41
Current ratio: 0.60
Long-term debt ($ mil.): —

Dividends
Yield: —
Payout: —
Market value ($ mil.): —

AZUSA PACIFIC UNIVERSITY

An evangelical Christian institution Azusa Pacific University (APU) has an enrollment of more than 8500 undergraduate graduate and doctoral students. It offers approximately 60 fields of undergraduate study and about 30 graduate programs. Undergraduate students are required to complete ministry and service credits every semester; options include participating in ministries international service experience and doing volunteer work. APU traces its roots to 1899 and the Training School for Christian Workers the West Coast's first bible college. In addition to its main campus the university has seven regional centers in Southern California.

EXECUTIVES

President CEO and Trustee, Jon R. Wallace
EVP and Chief Development Officer, David E. Bixby
VP Legal Affairs and Community Relations and General Counsel, Mark S. Dickerson
SVP Student Life and Dean of Students, Terry A. Franson
Vice Provost Graduate and Adult Programs, Rosemary M. Liegler
Provost, Michael M. Whyte
Vice Provost Undergraduate Programs, Diane J. Guido
SVP People and Organizational Development, Deana L. Porterfield
EVP, John C. Reynolds
Director Alumni Relations, Craig Wallace
Dean School of Business and Management, Ilene Smith-Bezjian
Assistant Provost, Pamela M. Christian
Dean School of Music, Duane A. Funderburk
Dean Center for Adult and Professional Studies, Fred Garlett
Dean School of Nursing, Aja Tulleners Lesh
Vice Provost Academic Programs and Research and Dean Library Services, Paul W. Gray
Dean College of Liberal Arts and Sciences, David Weeks
Dean School of Education, Helen E. Williams
Senior Director Strategic Communications, Maureen Taylor
Undergraduate Registrar, Jennifer Moore
VP People and Organizational Development, Gary Lemaster
Provost, Mark E. Stanton
Acting Dean School of Theology, Russell Duke
Director Undergraduate Admissions, Dave Burke
Director Graduate Admissions, L. Jo White
Web Services Librarian, Kimberley Wilcox
Interim Director Facilities Management, Dennis Robbins
SVP and CFO, Bob Johansen
Controller, Tom Harris
Purchasing Coordinator, Dana Langley
Director Career Services, Lynn Pearson
Trustee, Nickolas W. Vande Steeg, age 69
President CEO and Trustee, Jon R. Wallace
Trustee, Faye Bert
Trustee, Sally Colace
Trustee, Evan R. Collins
Trustee, Gregory Dixon
Trustee, Howard Kazanjian
Trustee, Tom Kobayashi
Trustee, Michael Lizarraga
Trustee, David Le Shana

Trustee, Kenneth Ogden
Trustee, Jeannie Pascale
Trustee, Sheryl Patton
Trustee, Earl Schamehorn
Trustee, Paul Szeto
Trustee, Dolly Warren
Trustee, Raleigh Washington
Trustee, David Dias
Trustee, Robyn Dillon
Trustee, Ray Johnston
Trustee, Ray Rood
Trustee, David Axene
Auditors: KPMGLLP

LOCATIONS

HQ: Azusa Pacific University
901 E. Alosta Ave., Azusa CA 91702
Phone: 626-969-3434   **Fax:** 626-334-5766
Web: www.apu.edu

Selected Locations

Azusa CA
Los Angeles CA
Murrieta CA
Orange CA
Oxnard CA
San Bernardino CA
San Diego CA
Victorville CA

PRODUCTS/OPERATIONS

Selected Schools and Departments

American Language and Cultural Institute
Center for Academic Service Learning and Research
Center for Adult and Professional Studies
Center for Research in Ethics and Values
Center for Research in Science
College of Liberal Arts and Sciences
Institute of Faith Integration
Noel Academy for Strengths-Based Leadership and Education
School of Behavioral and Applied Sciences
School of Business and Management
School of Education
School of Music
School of Nursing
School of Theology

HISTORICAL FINANCIALS

Company Type: School

Income Statement

	REVENUE ($ mil.)	NET INCOME ($ mil.)	NET PROFIT MARGIN	EMPLOYEES
06/11	270	26	9.7%	1,344
06/10	227	8	3.8%	0
06/09	203	0	—	0
06/08	195	8	4.3%	0
Annual Growth	11.4%	46.5%	—	—

2011 Year-End Financials

Debt ratio: ——
Return on equity: 9.70%
Cash ($ mil.): 31
Current ratio: —
Long-term debt ($ mil.): —
Dividends
Yield: —
Payout: —
Market value ($ mil.): —

AZUSA UNIFIED SCHOOL DISTRICT

LOCATIONS

HQ: AZUSA UNIFIED SCHOOL DISTRICT
546 S CITRUS AVE, AZUSA, CA 91702-5932
Phone: 626-967-6211
Web: www.ausd-ca.schoolloop.com

HISTORICAL FINANCIALS

Company Type: Private

Income Statement

FYE: June 30

	REVENUE ($ mil.)	NET INCOME ($ mil.)	NET PROFIT MARGIN	EMPLOYEES
06/11	103	(1)	—	1,500
06/05	99	0	—	0
06/03	0	0	—	0
06/02	84	1	1.9%	0
Annual Growth	6.8%	—	—	—

2011 Year-End Financials

Debt ratio: ——
Return on equity: (-1.60)%
Cash ($ mil.): 21
Current ratio: 3.10
Long-term debt ($ mil.): —
Dividends
Yield: —
Payout: —
Market value ($ mil.): —

BABSON COLLEGE

Babson —with an enrollment of some 3400 students on its campus in Wellesley Massachusetts — is lauded as one of the nation's leading business schools. The school's undergraduate programs combine liberal arts with business curriculum; The Arthur M. Blank Center for Entrepreneurship offers graduate and undergraduate courses in entrepreneurial leadership. Babson students in their first year receive the practical experience of creating for-profit ventures. Babson's entrepreneurship program has been ranked at the top of such programs in publications including Entrepreneur and U.S. News & World Report. Babson was founded in 1908 (as Babson Institute) by philanthropist educator and businessman Roger Babson.

EXECUTIVES

Chairman, Thomas T. (Tom) Stallkamp, age 66
Vice Chairman, Robert E. Weissman, age 71
President and Trustee, Leonard A. (Len) Schlesinger, age 59
Director Public Relations, Michael J. Chmura
Vice Provost Academic Affairs, Henry N. Deneault
Associate VP Financial Services and Controller, Richard Bowman
Chief of Staff and Associate VP Planning, Carol Hacker
VP Administration and CIO, Mary Rose
Vice Provost Entrepreneurship and Global Management, Stephen Spinelli Jr., age 57
VP College Marketing, Scott Timmins
VP Advancement, Richard Voos
Provost, Patricia Greene
Associate VP Human Resources, Adele Langevin

College Registrar, Linda E. Kean
Vice Chairman, N. Lyle Howland
Treasurer and Trustee, Ronald G. Weiner
Vice Chairman, Anthony C. Woodruff
VP Finance and CFO, Philip N. (Phil) Shapiro
Manager Collection Management Library, Martha Burk
Web Services Librarian, Anna Burke
Director Libraries, Hope Tillman
Murata Dean F.W. Olin Graduate School of Business, Mark Rice
Director Public Safety, John Jackson
Associate Director Public Relations, Barbara Spies Blair
Director Budget, Jeffrey Dubois
Dean Babson Executive Education, Elaine Eisenman
Dean Undergraduate School, Dennis Hanno
VP Development, Eric Graage
Director Student Financial Services and Associate Dean Undergraduate School, Melissa Shaak
Associate VP and Director Human Resources, Charles J. Anderson
Dean Faculty, Shahid Ansari
EVP and Executive Dean, Robert Fogel
Director Strategic Communications, Diane Fulman
VP and General Counsel, Jonathan Moll
Dean Student Affairs, Betsy Newman
Chief Diversity Officer, Elizabeth Thornton
Trustee, Andronico A. Luksic
Vice Chairman, Robert E. Weissman, age 71
Trustee, Joseph L. Winn
Trustee, Francis P. Jenkins Jr., age 68
President and Trustee, Leonard A. (Len) Schlesinger, age 59
Trustee, Edsel B. Ford II, age 63
Trustee, Joseph P. (Joe) Campanelli, age 56
Trustee, Cleve L. Killingsworth Jr., age 60
Trustee, David F. (Dave) Lamere, age 51
Trustee, Delia H. (Bina) Thompson, age 62
Trustee, Myra M. Hart, age 71
Trustee, Thomas F. (Tom) Gilbane Jr., age 64
Trustee, William G. Burrill
Trustee, Karen K. Chandor
Trustee, Stephen Cutler
Trustee, Everett R. Dowling
Trustee, Gloria M. Gutierrez
Trustee, Muhammad H. Habib
Vice Chairman, N. Lyle Howland
Trustee, Estefano E. Isaias Sr.
Trustee, Eric G. Johnson
Trustee, Kathryn D. Karlic
Trustee, Richard K. Miller
Trustee, Jeremiah J. Noonan
Trustee, Richard A. Renwick
Trustee, Thomas N. (Tom) Riley
Trustee, Gobind Sahney
Trustee, James W. Taylor
Trustee, Aaron M. Walton
Trustee, Lawrence Weber
Treasurer and Trustee, Ronald G. Weiner
Vice Chairman, Anthony C. Woodruff
Trustee, Kelly A. Ayotte
Trustee, Thom J. Blischok
Trustee, Craig R. Benson
Trustee, William D. Bygrave
Trustee, Theodore A. Clark
Trustee, Patrick McGonagle
Trustee, Bruce T. Herring
Trustee, Ann B. Hutchins
Trustee, Gary Zwerling
Auditors: PricewaterhouseCoopersLLP

LOCATIONS

HQ: Babson College
231 Forest St., Babson Park MA 02457-0310
Phone: 781-235-1200   Fax: 781-239-5618
Web: www.babson.edu

HISTORICAL FINANCIALS

Company Type: School

Income Statement

FYE: June 30

	REVENUE ($ mil.)	NET INCOME ($ mil.)	NET PROFIT MARGIN	EMPLOYEES
06/12	170	4	2.5%	750
06/11	202	14	7.1%	0
06/10	176	0	0.4%	0
06/09	174	0	—	0
Annual Growth	(0.8%)	—	—	—

2012 Year-End Financials

Debt ratio: ——
Return on equity: 2.50%
Cash ($ mil.): 37
Current ratio: ——
Long-term debt ($ mil.): —

Dividends
Yield: —
Payout: —
Market value ($ mil.): —

BALDWIN WALLACE UNIVERSITY

LOCATIONS

HQ: BALDWIN WALLACE UNIVERSITY
275 EASTLAND RD, BEREA, OH 44017-2005
Phone: 440-826-2900
Web: www.bw.edu

HISTORICAL FINANCIALS

Company Type: Private

Income Statement

FYE: June 30

	REVENUE ($ mil.)	NET INCOME ($ mil.)	NET PROFIT MARGIN	EMPLOYEES
06/12	90	3	3.7%	1,108
06/11	119	4	3.5%	0
06/10	127	16	12.9%	0
06/09	89	(28)	—	0
Annual Growth	0.4%	—	—	—

2012 Year-End Financials

Debt ratio: ——
Return on equity: 3.70%
Cash ($ mil.): 3
Current ratio: —
Long-term debt ($ mil.): —

Dividends
Yield: —
Payout: —
Market value ($ mil.): —

BALTIMORE CITY PUBLIC SCHOOL SYSTEMS (INC)

LOCATIONS

HQ: BALTIMORE CITY PUBLIC SCHOOL SYSTEMS (INC)
200 E NORTH AVE, BALTIMORE, MD 21202-5910
Phone: 410-396-8700

HISTORICAL FINANCIALS

Company Type: Private

Income Statement

FYE: June 30

	REVENUE ($ mil.)	NET INCOME ($ mil.)	NET PROFIT MARGIN	EMPLOYEES
06/12	1,480	(18)	—	12,000
06/02	988	(23)	—	0
Annual Growth	49.7%	—	—	—

2012 Year-End Financials

Debt ratio: ——
Return on equity: (-1.30)%
Cash ($ mil.): 183
Current ratio: —
Long-term debt ($ mil.): —

Dividends
Yield: —
Payout: —
Market value ($ mil.): —

BAPTIST HEALTH SYSTEM INC.

LOCATIONS

HQ: BAPTIST HEALTH SYSTEM INC.
3201 4TH AVE S, BIRMINGHAM, AL 35222-1723
Phone: 205-715-5000
Web: www.baptisthealthsystem.org

PRODUCTS/OPERATIONS

Selected facilities

Baptist Medical Center Beaches (Jacksonville Beach Florida)
Baptist Medical Center Downtown (Jacksonville Florida)
Baptist Medical Center Nassau (Fernandina Beach Florida)
Baptist Medical Center South (Jacksonville Florida)
Wolfson Children's Hospital (Jacksonville Florida)

HISTORICAL FINANCIALS

Company Type: Private

Income Statement

FYE: December 31

	REVENUE ($ mil.)	NET INCOME ($ mil.)	NET PROFIT MARGIN	EMPLOYEES
12/11*	587	(34)	—	4,300
06/10	602	15	2.6%	0
06/09	482	(4)	—	0
06/08	496	22	4.4%	0
Annual Growth	5.8%	—	—	—

*Fiscal year change

2011 Year-End Financials

Debt ratio: —
Return on equity: (-5.80)%
Cash ($ mil.): 1
Current ratio: 0.50
Long-term debt ($ mil.): —

Dividends
Yield: —
Payout: —
Market value ($ mil.): —

BAPTIST MEMORIAL HOSPITAL-GOLDEN TRIANGLE INC.

LOCATIONS

HQ: BAPTIST MEMORIAL HOSPITAL-GOLDEN TRIANGLE INC.
2520 5TH ST N, COLUMBUS, MS 39705-2008
Phone: 662-244-1000
Web: www.baptistonline.org

HISTORICAL FINANCIALS

Company Type: Private

Income Statement

FYE: September 30

	REVENUE ($ mil.)	NET INCOME ($ mil.)	NET PROFIT MARGIN	EMPLOYEES
09/11	147	8	5.7%	1,083
09/10	149	14	9.6%	0
09/09	146	12	8.9%	0
09/08	145	9	6.9%	0
Annual Growth	0.6%	(5.6%)	—	

2011 Year-End Financials

Debt ratio: —
Return on equity: 5.70%
Cash ($ mil.): 2
Current ratio: 0.60
Long-term debt ($ mil.): —

Dividends
Yield: —
Payout: —
Market value ($ mil.): —

BARD COLLEGE

Although Shakespeare might appreciate the curriculum Bard College is not named for the Bard of Avon. Founded in 1860 by John Bard the school grants liberal arts degrees and provides a classical education. Bard's total enrollment of 1600 includes some 200 graduate students. First-year students are required to take a three-week Workshop in Language and Thinking that emphasizes the connection between expression and thought. Students must also complete a year-long senior project that is reviewed by faculty members. Donald Fagen and Walter Becker of the band Steely Dan both attended Bard (Fagen is an alum; Becker did not graduate) and penned the song "My Old School" as a sardonic tribute to their alma mater.

EXECUTIVES

President, Leon Botstein
VP Student Affairs, Mary Backlund
VP Administration, James (Jim) Brudvig
VP Academic Affairs and Director Bard Conservatory of Music, Robert L. Martin
Director Communications, Mark Primoff
EVP President Levy Economics Institute and Executive Director The Bard Center, Dimitri B. Papadimitriou
Dean Information Services and Director Libraries, Jeffrey (Jeff) Katz
Director Career Development, April Kinser
VP Development and Alumni Affairs, Debra R. Pemstein
Director Safety and Security, Ken Cooper
Director Financial Aid, Denise Ackerman
Bursar, Viki Papadimitriou

LOCATIONS

HQ: Bard College
30 Campus Rd., Annandale-on-Hudson NY 12504
Phone: 845-758-6822   **Fax:** 845-758-5208
Web: www.bard.edu

HISTORICAL FINANCIALS

Company Type: School

Income Statement

FYE: June 30

	REVENUE ($ mil.)	NET INCOME ($ mil.)	NET PROFIT MARGIN	EMPLOYEES
06/11	278	76	27.4%	525
06/10	181	(5)	—	0
06/09	164	0	—	0
06/08	126	17	13.7%	0
Annual Growth	29.9%	63.5%	—	

2011 Year-End Financials

Debt ratio: —
Return on equity: 27.40%
Cash ($ mil.): 1
Current ratio: —
Long-term debt ($ mil.): —

Dividends
Yield: —
Payout: —
Market value ($ mil.): —

BARFIELD INC.

LOCATIONS

HQ: BARFIELD INC.
4101 NW 29TH ST, MIAMI, FL 33142-5617
Phone: 305-894-5375
Web: www.barfieldinc.com/

HISTORICAL FINANCIALS

Company Type: Private

Income Statement

FYE: December 31

	REVENUE ($ mil.)	NET INCOME ($ mil.)	NET PROFIT MARGIN	EMPLOYEES
12/11	88	1	1.9%	220
12/10	75	2	2.7%	0
12/09	63	2	3.5%	0
Annual Growth	18.0%	(11.7%)	—	

2011 Year-End Financials

Debt ratio: —
Return on equity: 1.90%
Cash ($ mil.): 3
Current ratio: 0.60
Long-term debt ($ mil.): —

Dividends
Yield: —
Payout: —
Market value ($ mil.): —

BARRY UNIVERSITY INC.

Barry University is a Catholic institution of Dominican heritage based in South Florida. With a student-faculty ratio of about 14:1 the liberal arts university annually enrolls about 2740 undergraduate students and almost 4200 graduate students. The university's academic division includes two colleges (the College of Arts and Sciences and the College of Health Sciences) and seven schools. It offers more than 100 specializations and programs for undergraduate graduate and doctoral studies. Barry University also offers about 35 non-degree and certificate programs. Barry University was founded by the Adrian Dominican Sisters in 1940.

EXECUTIVES

President and Trustee, Sister Linda Bevilacqua, age 71
Assistant VP Administrative Information Systems, Traci A. Simpson
Chairperson, William J. Heffernan
Associate VP and University Budget Officer, Nicole Diez
Director Accounts Payable, Nancy Perez
Assistant Director Cashier and Business Office, Ronald LaBarrie
Director Alumni Programs, Renee Glover-Hodge
Assistant VP Communications and Marketing, Michael S. Laderman
Director Campus Ministry, Sister Arlene Scott
Director University Sponsorships, Caridad MacNamara
VP Institutional Advancement, Ann Paton
Assistant Vice Provost Enrollment, Angela M. Scott
Senior Director Graduate Admissions, Dave C. Fletcher
Director Undergraduate Admissions, Laura Antczack
Trustee; President Barry University Alumni Association, Maura O'Shea-Owens
SVP Business and Finance, Bruce Edwards
Associate VP Finance and Chief Accounting Officer, Susan Kirkland
Controller, Judith Penate
Assistant Dean Information Systems and Technology, Yolairis Barranco
Assistant Dean and Director Financial Aid, Howard D. Humeston
Director Purchasing, Sandra Madison
VP Human Resources and General Counsel, John A. Walker
Assistant VP Alumni Relations, Sean Kramer
VP Student Affairs, Michael J. Griffin
Associate VP Student Affairs and Dean Students, Maria Luisa Alvarez
Director Career Services, Amy Diepenbrock
Executive Director Public Safety, Stanley A. Young
Provost, Linda M. Peterson
Vice Provost Planning Assessment and Institutional Research, Christopher Starratt
Director Institutional Research, Shaunette Grant
Interim CTO, Yvette A-M Brown
Dean Academic Records and University Registrar, Debra D. Weyman
Trustee, Joseph P. Klock Jr., age 63
Trustee, Nelson L. Adams III
Trustee, Gregory F. (Greg) Greene, age 52
President and Trustee, Sister Linda Bevilacqua, age 71
Trustee, Alejandro Aguirre
Trustee, John M. Bussel
Trustee, Sister Mary Ann Caulfield
Trustee, Sister Rosemary T. Finnegan
Trustee, Robert B. Galt III

LOCATIONS

HQ: Barry University
  11300 NE 2nd Ave., Miami Shores FL 33161-6695
Phone: 305-899-3100   **Fax:** 305-899-2971
Web: www.barry.edu

Selected Program Locations

Alachua County
Bahamas
Brevard County
Broward County
Collier County
Hillsborough County
Lake County
Lee County
Leon County
Marion County
Miami-Dade County (Main Campus)
Miami-Dade County (Other Locations)
Orange County
Palm Beach County
Pasco County
Pinellas County
Polk County
Sarasota County
St. Lucie/Indian River/Martin Counties

PRODUCTS/OPERATIONS

Selected Colleges and Schools

Adrian Dominican School of Education
College of Arts and Sciences
College of Health Sciences
D. Inez Andreas School of Business
Dwayne O. Andreas School of Law
Ellen Whiteside McDonnell School of Social Work
Frank J. Rooney School of Adult and Continuing
  Education
School of Human Performance and Leisure Sciences
School of Podiatric Medicine

HISTORICAL FINANCIALS

Company Type: School

Income Statement

FYE: June 30

	REVENUE ($ mil.)	NET INCOME ($ mil.)	NET PROFIT MARGIN	EMPLOYEES
06/11	203	10	5.2%	1,407
06/10	151	12	8.1%	0
06/09	147	8	5.7%	0
06/08	144	10	6.9%	0
Annual Growth	12.1%	1.9%	—	—

2011 Year-End Financials

Debt ratio: —
Return on equity: 5.20%
Cash ($ mil.): 38
Current ratio: —
Long-term debt ($ mil.): —

Dividends
Yield: —
Payout: —
Market value ($ mil.): —

BARRY-WEHMILLER GROUP INC.

With Barry-Wehmiller you get the whole package. The company manufactures and supplies packaging corrugating paper converting filling and labeling automation equipment for a broad range of industries. It conducts business around the world through a group of 50 companies including Accraply (labeling machinery) Barry-Wehmiller Company (bottle washers and pasteurizers); HayssenSandiacre and Thiele Technologies (packaging systems); PneumaticScaleAngelus (bottle fillers and cappers); and FleetwoodGoldcoWyard (conveyor systems). Other divisions manufacture paper converting machinery and offer engineering/design consulting services. Chairman and CEO Bob Chapman and his family hold majority control the company.

Geographic Reach

Barry Wehmiller has operations in more than 50 locations spanning Asia Australia and the Americas.

Strategy

Barry Wehmiller's mantra is expansion through organic growth and acquisitions. The company has purchased more than 40 companies over approximately 20 years creating a mosaic of time and money-saving products and services in locations around the globe. In the same vein its businesses' operations are built upon lean manufacturing practices whereby employees are empowered and resources optimized to contribute to the end product's value.

Company Background

Originally a provider of conveying equipment to St. Louis malt houses Barry-Wehmiller Companies was founded by Thomas Barry and Alfred Wehmiller in 1885. Ownership passed from the Wehmiller family to the Chapman family in 1963 and the Chapmans continue as the majority owners.

EXECUTIVES

Chairman and CEO, Robert H. (Bob) Chapman, age 66
VP CFO and Director, James W. (Jim) Lawson
CIO; Group Director Barry-Wehmiller International Resources, Craig Hergenroether
Treasurer, Micheal (Mike) Zaccarello
Director Organizational Empowerment, Rhonda Spencer
Director Corporate Communications, Kim Hutton
Director, Brian W. Hotarek, age 66
Director, William D. (Bill) Smithburg, age 74
Director, Richard F. (Dick) Ford, age 76
Director, Peter C. Wallace, age 58
VP CFO and Director, James W. (Jim) Lawson
Director, Eric L. Motley
Director, John Morton III, age 68
Director, Marjorie E. (Marge) Abernathy
Director, Louis F. Umsted
Director, W.W. (Chet) Walker
Director, John S. Stroup, age 46

LOCATIONS

HQ: Barry-Wehmiller Group Inc.
  8020 Forsyth Blvd., St. Louis MO 63105
Phone: 314-862-8000   **Fax:** 314-862-8858
Web: www.barry-wehmiller.com

PRODUCTS/OPERATIONS

Selected Operations

Engineering/Consulting
  Barry-Wehmiller Design Group Inc. (high-speed complex automated manufacturing and packaging system design)
  Barry-Wehmiller International Resources (IT consulting and engineering services)
Converting equipment
  Paper Converting Machine Company (PCMC)
    Coaters
    Narrow web in-line printing systems
    Nonwovens converting equipment
    Tissue converting equipment
    Wide web flexo printing coating and laminating
Corrugating equipment
  MarquipWardUnited Inc. (corrugating sheeting and finishing equipment)
Packaging equipment
  Accraply Inc. (packaging label machinery)
  FleetwoodGoldcoWyard (conveyer systems)
  HayssenSandiacre (form/fill/seal packaging machinery)
  PneumaticScaleAngelus (fillers cappers seamers and labelers)
  Thiele Technologies Inc. (packaging systems)

Selected Markets

Corrugated paperboard and folded carton
Dairy
Food and beverage
Household
Medical and biotech
Packaging
Personal care
Pharmaceutical
Tissue and nonwovens

COMPETITORS

Bradman Lake
Gilbreth
Industria Macchine
Automatiche
Klockner-Werke
Semco Technologies
Sencorp Inc
Tetra Laval
Traco Manufacturing

HISTORICAL FINANCIALS

Company Type: Private

Income Statement

FYE: September 30

	REVENUE ($ mil.)	NET INCOME ($ mil.)	NET PROFIT MARGIN	EMPLOYEES
09/11	1,240	0	—	4,500
09/10	1,097	0	—	0
09/09	976	0	—	0
09/06	785	0	—	0
Annual Growth	16.5%	—	—	—

2011 Year-End Financials

Debt ratio: —
Return on equity: —
Cash ($ mil.): 222
Current ratio: 1.20
Long-term debt ($ mil.): —

Dividends
Yield: —
Payout: —
Market value ($ mil.): —

BARTON MALOW ENTERPRISES INC.

LOCATIONS

HQ: BARTON MALOW ENTERPRISES INC.
26500 AMERICAN DR, SOUTHFIELD, MI 48034-2252
Phone: 248-436-5000
Web: www.bartonmalow.com

HISTORICAL FINANCIALS

Company Type: Private

Income Statement   FYE: March 31

	REVENUE ($ mil.)	NET INCOME ($ mil.)	NET PROFIT MARGIN	EMPLOYEES
03/12	1,164	(14)	—	1,415
03/11	0	0	—	0
03/09	0	0	—	0
03/08	0	0	—	0
Annual Growth	—	—	—	—

2012 Year-End Financials

Debt ratio: ——
Return on equity: (-1.20)%
Cash ($ mil.): 84
Current ratio: 1.10
Long-term debt ($ mil.): —

Dividends
  Yield: —
  Payout: —
Market value ($ mil.): —

BASTIAN SOLUTIONS LLC

LOCATIONS

HQ: BASTIAN SOLUTIONS LLC
9820 ASSOCIATION CT, INDIANAPOLIS, IN
46280-1962
Phone: 317-575-9992
Web: www.bmhcorp.com

HISTORICAL FINANCIALS

Company Type: Private

Income Statement   FYE: December 31

	REVENUE ($ mil.)	NET INCOME ($ mil.)	NET PROFIT MARGIN	EMPLOYEES
12/11	98	3	3.4%	320
12/08	80	3	4.4%	0
12/07	65	0	1.1%	0
12/06	76	3	4.0%	0
Annual Growth	8.8%	2.6%	—	—

2011 Year-End Financials

Debt ratio: ——
Return on equity: 3.40%
Cash ($ mil.): 1
Current ratio: 0.70
Long-term debt ($ mil.): —

Dividends
  Yield: —
  Payout: —
Market value ($ mil.): —

BATTELLE MEMORIAL INSTITUTE INC

When you use a copier hit a golf ball or listen to a CD you're using technologies developed by Battelle Memorial Institute. The not-for-profit is one of the world's largest research enterprises with more than 22000 scientists engineers and staff serving corporate and government clients. Research areas include national security energy and health and life sciences. Battelle owns 130 locations in the US Asia and Europe and manages four Department of Energy-sponsored labs: Brookhaven National Laboratory Oak Ridge National Laboratory Idaho National Laboratory and Pacific Northwest National Laboratory. The institute was established by the family of steel industry pioneer Gordon Battelle in 1929.

While contract research and development remains the core activity of the company Battelle is becoming more and more involved in managing operations for about a half-dozen laboratories for the government. Battelle operates Idaho National Laboratory through Battelle Energy Alliance a partnership formed with BWX Technologies Washington Group International Electric Power Research Institute and a consortium of universities including MIT Ohio State and the University of Idaho. Battelle also manages the Lawrence Livermore National Laboratory the National Nuclear Laboratory UK the National Biodefense Analysis and Countermeasures Center and the National Renewable Energy Laboratory.

Through its Battelle Ventures subsidiary the company also serves as a nesting ground for new businesses formed to commercialize discoveries and technologies Battelle owns or to which it has rights.

Originally formed to promote metallurgy and related industries the institute —which conducts nearly $6 billion in research and development each year —has diversified into researching other areas such as agriculture energy software and medicine. Among other notable milestones Battelle's research was instrumental in developing the photocopy machine optical digital recording (used with compact discs) and bar codes.

Battelle is led by CEO and president Jeffrey Wadsworth a former metallurgist who started at Battelle in 2002 and served as director of Oak Ridge National Laboratory. Wadsworth took over as CEO in 2009 replacing Carl Kohrt who retired.

HISTORY

Battelle Memorial Institute was founded with a $1.5 million trust willed by Gordon Battelle who died in 1923. Battelle was a champion of research for the advancement of humankind and before taking his father's place as president of several Ohio steel mills he had funded a former university professor's successful work to extract useful chemicals from mine waste. Battelle's mother upon her death in 1925 left the institute an additional $2.1 million. The institute opened in 1929.

The institute took on perhaps the most important project in its history in 1944 when it helped an electronics company's patent lawyer Chester Carlson find practical uses for his invention called xerography. Eventually Battelle developed the first photocopy machine and in 1955 it sold the patent rights for the machine to Haloid (now Xerox) in exchange for royalties.

During WWII Battelle worked on uranium refining for the Manhattan Project and in the early 1950s it established the world's first private nuclear research facility. The company also set up operations in Germany and Switzerland.

The tax man came knocking in 1961 questioning the tax-free status of some of Battelle's activities. The organization eventually had to pay $47 million. In 1965 Battelle developed a coin with a copper core and a copper-and-nickel-alloy cladding for the US Treasury.

As the result of a ruling that reinterpreted a clause in Gordon Battelle's will in 1975 the institute gave $80 million to philanthropic enterprises. This ruling coupled with the taxes that the organization was still unaccustomed to paying forced Battelle to re-examine its strategy.

Battelle co-developed the Universal Product Code (the bar code symbol found today on nearly all consumer goods packaging) in the 1970s. The institute also landed a lucrative contract from the US Department of Energy (DOE) to manage its commercial nuclear waste isolation program.

In 1987 Battelle chose Douglas Olesen —a 20-year veteran of the institute —to replace retiring CEO Ronald Paul. The company signed an extension with the DOE in 1992 to run its Pacific Northwest Laboratory (which it has operated since 1965).

An Ohio court in 1997 approved a seven-page agreement with the institute outlining the key principles that must be followed according to Gordon Battelle's will. This agreement replaced the 1975 decree and ended more than 20 years of scrutiny by the state attorney general's office.

In 1998 the DOE contracted Brookhaven Science Associates —a partnership between the State University of New York and Battelle —to operate Brookhaven National Laboratory. That year a Battelle contract to dispose of Vietnam War-era napalm drew national attention when subcontractor Pollution Control Industries backed out of the project citing safety concerns. Under Battelle's direction Houston-based GNI Group took the 3.4 million gallons of napalm off the US Navy's hands.

Battelle and the University of Tennessee in 1999 won a five-year contract to operate the US government's Oak Ridge National Laboratory. That year the institute made several breakthroughs in cancer research including FDA approval to test an inhalation delivery system for treating lung cancer.

In 2000 the company spun off OmniViz (data mining software) and Battelle Pulmonary Therapeutics (pulmonary and drug delivery technology) as wholly owned subsidiaries. In 2001 Battelle chose former Kodak EVP and CTO Carl Kohrt to replace Olesen. (Kohrt retired in January 2009 and was replaced by Jeffrey Wadsworth who has worked for the company since 2002.)

Battelle and several partners including BWX Technologies Washington Group International and Electric Power Research Institute won a 10-year contract in 2004 to operate Idaho National Laboratory a research facility established to focus on nuclear energy research and related technologies.

With offices in Japan and South Korea Battelle expanded its international reach to include India in 2008. The company formed a partnership in 2007 with oil and gas company PETRONAS to operate a renewable energy lab in Kuala Lumpur Malaysia.

Battelle underwent a leadership change in 2009 when Jeffrey Wadsworth took over as CEO replacing Carl Kohrt who retired.

EXECUTIVES

SVP Organizational Development, Robert W. Smith Jr.

SVP Energy Technology Global Business, Donald P. McConnell

SVP International Partnerships, Richard C. Adams

Chairman, John B. McCoy Jr.

SVP National Security Global Business, Stephen E. Kelly

President and CEO, Jeffrey (Jeff) Wadsworth, age 62

Assistant Treasurer and Assistant Secretary, Daniel W. O'Bryan

Controller and Assistant Treasurer, Stephen H. Valentine

Manager National Media Relations, Katy Delaney, age 46

EVP and CFO, I. Martin Inglis

SVP; Director Global Laboratory Operations Pacific Northwest National Laboratory, Michael Kluse

SVP Corporate Relations, Anthony T. Hebron

SVP; Director Global Laboratory Operations Idaho National Laboratory, Vice Adm. John J. Grossenbacher

Treasurer, Gwendolyn C. VonHolten

Assistant Treasurer, Judith L. Mobley

SVP General Counsel and Secretary, Russell P. (Russ) Austin

corporate Senior Vice President President of Battelle ?s, Barbara L. Kunz

SVP; Director Global Laboratory Operations Oak Ridge National Laboratory, Thomas E. Mason

EVP Global Laboratory Operations, Ronald D. (Ron) Townsend

SVP Business and Economic Development, Alexander R. Fischer

VP Education and Philanthropy, Richard D. Rosen

SVP Carbon Management, Donald P. (Chuck) McConnell

VP Energy Infrastructure, Mani Vadari

VP Strategy Development, Michael A. Aimone

VP and Manager Industrial and International Markets., Spencer Pugh

VP Education and STEM Learning, Eric D. Fingerhut

VP Navy and Special Operations Market Sector, Adm. Fred Byus

SVP, Thomas D. Snowberger

Director, John K. Welch, age 62

Director, Michael G. (Mike) Morris, age 65

Director, Robert D. (Bob) Walter, age 66

Director, Bernadine P. Healy, age 67

Director, Gen. Lester L. Lyles, age 65

Director, Vicky A. Bailey, age 59

Director, Sean O'Keefe

Director, Russell A. Hulse

Auditors: Deloitte&ToucheLLP

LOCATIONS

HQ: Battelle Memorial Institute
505 King Ave., Columbus OH 43201-2693
Phone: 614-424-6424   **Fax:** 704-551-2799
Web: www.bekbuildinggroup.com

PRODUCTS/OPERATIONS

Selected Laboratories and Research Facilities

Battelle Biomedical Research Center (West Jefferson OH)
Battelle Eastern Science and Technology Center (Aberdeen MD)
Battelle Frederick Operations (Maryland)
Battelle Geneva Operations (Switzerland)
Brookhaven National Laboratory (Upton NY)
Human Factors Transportation Center (Seattle)
Idaho National Laboratory (Idaho Falls)
Lawrence Livermore National Laboratory (Livermore CA)
Marine Science Laboratory (Sequim WA)
National Renewable Energy Laboratory (Golden CO)
Oak Ridge National Laboratory (Tennessee)
Battelle Duxbury Operations (Massachusetts)
Pacific Northwest National Laboratory (Richland WA)

Selected Inventions

Exploded-tip paintbrush (nylon brush for Wooster Brush Co. 1950)
Golf ball coatings (1965)
Heat Seat (microwaveable stadium cushion 1990s)
Holograms (work began in the 1970s)
Insulin injection pen (for Eli Lilly 1990s)
Oil spill outline monitor (1992)
PCB-cleaning chemical process (1992)
Photocopy machine (with Haloid 1940s)
Plastic breakdown process (1990s)
"Sandwich" coins (copper/copper-and-nickel-alloy cladding design for US Treasury 1965)
SenSonic toothbrush (with Teledyne/WaterPik 1990s)
Smart cards (cards embedded with tiny computer chips that store information 1980s)
Universal Product Code (co-creator; bar code 1970s)

COMPETITORS

Argonne National Laboratory
Berkeley Lab
Charles Stark Draper Laboratory
Institute for Defense Analyses
SwRI

HISTORICAL FINANCIALS

Company Type: Private - Not-for-Profit

Income Statement

FYE: September 30

	REVENUE ($ mil.)	NET INCOME ($ mil.)	NET PROFIT MARGIN	EMPLOYEES
09/11	5,499	27	0.5%	7,457
09/10	5,547	0	0.0%	0
09/09	4,878	31	0.6%	0
09/07	4,180	8	0.2%	0
Annual Growth	9.6%	48.8%	—	—

2011 Year-End Financials

Debt ratio: ——
Return on equity: 0.50%
Cash ($ mil.): 55
Current ratio: 1.40
Long-term debt ($ mil.): —
Dividends
Yield: —
Payout: —
Market value ($ mil.): —

BAY AREA HEALTH DISTRICT INC.

LOCATIONS

HQ: BAY AREA HEALTH DISTRICT INC.
1775 THOMPSON RD, COOS BAY, OR 97420-2125
Phone: 541-269-8111
Web: www.bayareahospital.org

HISTORICAL FINANCIALS

Company Type: Private

Income Statement

FYE: June 30

	REVENUE ($ mil.)	NET INCOME ($ mil.)	NET PROFIT MARGIN	EMPLOYEES
06/12	127	9	7.2%	1,020
06/11	121	2	2.3%	0
06/10	125	10	8.3%	0
06/09	118	2	1.8%	0
Annual Growth	2.4%	61.9%	—	—

2012 Year-End Financials

Debt ratio: ——
Return on equity: 7.20%
Cash ($ mil.): 7
Current ratio: 1.10
Long-term debt ($ mil.): —
Dividends
Yield: —
Payout: —
Market value ($ mil.): —

BAY AREA MEDICAL CENTER INC.

LOCATIONS

HQ: BAY AREA MEDICAL CENTER INC.
3100 SHORE DR, MARINETTE, WI 54143-4297
Phone: 715-735-6621
Web: www.bamc.org

HISTORICAL FINANCIALS

Company Type: Private

Income Statement

FYE: December 31

	REVENUE ($ mil.)	NET INCOME ($ mil.)	NET PROFIT MARGIN	EMPLOYEES
12/11	125	5	4.3%	800
12/10*	120	9	7.8%	0
10/10	97	4	4.2%	0
12/09	0	(0)		0
Annual Growth	865.9%	—	—	—

*Fiscal year change

2011 Year-End Financials

Debt ratio: ——
Return on equity: 4.30%
Cash ($ mil.): 9
Current ratio: 2.20
Long-term debt ($ mil.): —
Dividends
Yield: —
Payout: —
Market value ($ mil.): —

BAY REGIONAL MEDICAL CENTER

McLaren Bay Region provides a full range of medical services for the residents of Bay County located at the tip of Saginaw Bay in eastern Michigan. A part of McLaren Health Care the hospital's main campus has more than 400 beds and provides general medical and surgical care as well as specialty care in areas such as cardiovascular disease neuroscience oncology rehabilitation orthopedics and women's health. It also features an emergency room and Level II trauma center and provides home health and hospice care. A second campus McLaren-Bay Special Care Hospital is a long-term acute care hospital serving patients requiring hospital stays of longer than 25 days.

The hospital system is one of the largest multidisciplinary research programs in the state it works with international medical/pharmaceutical and other healthcare companies as well as universities foundations agencies to create new more effective treatments for illnesses such as infectious diseases cancer and a whole spectrum of other ailments.

Going hand-in-hand with clinical trials is teaching and being a teaching hospital McLaren-Bay Region offers up-and-coming medical professionals a roster of residency programs from which to choose. The hospital works with Michigan State University's colleges of Human Medicine and Osteopathic Medicine keep the hospital's residency program fresh and full of eager young interns.

McLaren-Bay Region was formed after the merging of four hospitals during the 1970s and 1980s with the idea of developing a full continuum of health services for Northeast Michigan. It changed its name to McLaren-Bay Region from Bay Regional Medical Center in 2012.

EXECUTIVES

President and CEO McLaren Health Care, Philip A. Incarnati, age 58
President and CEO, Alice Gerard
VP Finance and CFO, Brian Kay
VP Human Resources, Joe Lyons
VP Administration, Jack Mills
Director Marketing and Public Relations, Kurt Miller
VP Patient Care Services, Ellen Talbott
Director Support Services and Facilities Management, Jim Bourdon
Corporate Compliance and Privacy Officer, Mike Jamrog
VP Medical Affairs, Jay Summer

LOCATIONS

HQ: McLaren Bay Region
  1900 Columbus Ave., Bay City MI 48708
Phone: 989-894-3000   **Fax:** 989-894-3808
Web: www.baymed.org/bayregion/BayRegion.aspx

COMPETITORS

Ascension Health	Hurley Medical Center
Covenant Medical	Munson Healthcare
Center	Select Medical
Crittenton Hospital	Sparrow Health System
Detroit Medical Center	St. John Health
Genesys Health System	University of Michigan
Genesys Regional	Health System
Medical Center	
Henry Ford Health	
System	

HISTORICAL FINANCIALS
Company Type: Subsidiary

Income Statement   FYE: February 29

	REVENUE ($ mil.)	NET INCOME ($ mil.)	NET PROFIT MARGIN	EMPLOYEES
02/12*	113	5	4.6%	2,000
09/11	271	(6)	—	0
09/10	272	19	7.3%	0
09/09	263	2	0.9%	0
Annual Growth	(24.5%)	29.2%	—	—

*Fiscal year change

2012 Year-End Financials

Debt ratio: ——
Return on equity: 4.60%
Cash ($ mil.): 4
Current ratio: 1.50
Long-term debt ($ mil.): —

Dividends
  Yield: —
  Payout: —
Market value ($ mil.): —

BAYHEALTH MEDICAL CENTER INC.

LOCATIONS

HQ: BAYHEALTH MEDICAL CENTER INC.
  640 SOUTH ST, DOVER, DE 19901
Phone: 302-674-4700

HISTORICAL FINANCIALS
Company Type: Private

Income Statement   FYE: June 30

	REVENUE ($ mil.)	NET INCOME ($ mil.)	NET PROFIT MARGIN	EMPLOYEES
06/12	490	22	4.7%	2,790
06/11	442	108	24.4%	0
06/10	411	32	8.0%	0
06/09	376	(33)	—	0
Annual Growth	9.2%	—	—	—

2012 Year-End Financials

Debt ratio: ——
Return on equity: 4.70%
Cash ($ mil.): 27
Current ratio: 0.90
Long-term debt ($ mil.): —

Dividends
  Yield: —
  Payout: —
Market value ($ mil.): —

BC INTERNATIONAL GROUP INC.

LOCATIONS

HQ: BC INTERNATIONAL GROUP INC.
  922 RIVERVIEW DR, TOTOWA, NJ 07512-1127
Phone: 973-826-1140
Web: www.birgerusa.com

HISTORICAL FINANCIALS
Company Type: Private

Income Statement   FYE: January 29

	REVENUE ($ mil.)	NET INCOME ($ mil.)	NET PROFIT MARGIN	EMPLOYEES
01/11	108	3	2.9%	800
01/10	112	1	1.5%	0
Annual Growth	(3.6%)	79.0%	—	—

2011 Year-End Financials

Debt ratio: ——
Return on equity: 2.90%
Cash ($ mil.): 2
Current ratio: 0.50
Long-term debt ($ mil.): —

Dividends
  Yield: —
  Payout: —
Market value ($ mil.): —

BCCI CONSTRUCTION COMPANY

LOCATIONS

HQ: BCCI CONSTRUCTION COMPANY
  185 BERRY ST STE 1200, SAN FRANCISCO, CA 94107-1794
Phone: 415-817-5100
Web: www.bcciconst.com

HISTORICAL FINANCIALS
Company Type: Private

Income Statement   FYE: December 31

	REVENUE ($ mil.)	NET INCOME ($ mil.)	NET PROFIT MARGIN	EMPLOYEES
12/11	133	0	0.4%	140
12/10	109	0	0.0%	0
12/09	91	(2)	—	0
12/08	165	3	2.1%	0
Annual Growth	(6.8%)	(47.7%)	—	—

2011 Year-End Financials

Debt ratio: ——
Return on equity: 0.40%
Cash ($ mil.): 10
Current ratio: 0.30
Long-term debt ($ mil.): —

Dividends
  Yield: —
  Payout: —
Market value ($ mil.): —

BEARD IMPLEMENT CO (INC)

LOCATIONS

HQ: BEARD IMPLEMENT CO (INC)
  216 W FREDERICK ST, ARENZVILLE, IL 62611-3588
Phone: 217-997-5514
Web: www.beardimplement.com

HISTORICAL FINANCIALS
Company Type: Private

Income Statement
FYE: March 31

	REVENUE ($ mil.)	NET INCOME ($ mil.)	NET PROFIT MARGIN	EMPLOYEES
03/12	88	0	0.4%	40
03/11	69	0	0.4%	0
03/10	64	0	0.4%	0
03/09	54	0	0.4%	0
Annual Growth	17.5%	10.8%	—	—

2012 Year-End Financials
Debt ratio: ——
Return on equity: 0.40%
Cash ($ mil.): 1
Current ratio: 0.10
Long-term debt ($ mil.): —

Dividends
Yield: —
Payout: —
Market value ($ mil.): —

BEATTIE FARMERS UNION COOPERATIVE ASSN INC

LOCATIONS

HQ: BEATTIE FARMERS UNION COOPERATIVE ASSN INC
203 HAMILTON ST, BEATTIE, KS 66406
Phone: 785-353-2237
Web: www.beattiecoop.com

HISTORICAL FINANCIALS
Company Type: Private

Income Statement
FYE: August 31

	REVENUE ($ mil.)	NET INCOME ($ mil.)	NET PROFIT MARGIN	EMPLOYEES
08/12	81	1	1.9%	42
08/11	60	1	2.8%	0
08/10	63	0	1.2%	0
08/09	59	2	4.0%	0
Annual Growth	10.8%	(13.3%)	—	—

2012 Year-End Financials
Debt ratio: ——
Return on equity: 1.90%
Cash ($ mil.): 0
Current ratio: 0.10
Long-term debt ($ mil.): —

Dividends
Yield: —
Payout: —
Market value ($ mil.): —

BEAUTY ENTERPRISES INC.

LOCATIONS

HQ: BEAUTY ENTERPRISES INC.
150 MEADOW ST, HARTFORD, CT 06114-1593
Phone: 860-296-9303
Web: www.beautyenterprises.com

HISTORICAL FINANCIALS
Company Type: Private

Income Statement
FYE: September 30

	REVENUE ($ mil.)	NET INCOME ($ mil.)	NET PROFIT MARGIN	EMPLOYEES
09/11	87	1	1.6%	350
09/10	85	(0)		0
09/09	85	1	1.4%	0
09/07	85	(0)		0
Annual Growth	0.7%	—	—	—

2011 Year-End Financials
Debt ratio: ——
Return on equity: 1.60%
Cash ($ mil.): 0
Current ratio: 0.80
Long-term debt ($ mil.): —

Dividends
Yield: —
Payout: —
Market value ($ mil.): —

BEAVER DAM COMMUNITY HOSPITALS INC

Beaver Dam Community Hospitals (BDCH) provides medical services for the residents of south central Wisconsin. The non-profit medical center includes the 60-bed Beaver Dam Community Hospital as well as its Hillside Manor skilled nursing facility. Other facilities include an assisted living retirement center community-based residential facilities home health care services and a wellness center. BDCH also operates FastCare clinics in two towns and a dialysis center. BDCH has invested in an electronic medical records system and upgrades to its dialysis services.

Geographic Reach

Located at Beaver Dam Wisconsin the company's service area extends across the greater Dodge Columbia and Fond du Lac County region.

Operations

The hospital system offers preventive programs such as health education screenings or physical fitness hospital-based services long-term care through nursing home community-based residential facilities and home health care programs.

Financial Performance

BDCH's revenues grew by 5% in 2011. It income (revenues in excess of expenses) increased by 144% that year.

Company Background

BDCH was formed in 1972. It was one of the first hospitals in the country and the first in the state of Wisconsin to merge a Catholic Hospital and a Lutheran Hospital.

EXECUTIVES

Chief Patient Care Officer, Patricia (Pat) Tuckwell
CFO, K. Scott Abrams
Treasurer and Director, Ken O'Connell
Secretary and Director, Sue Sutter
COO, Mark Monson
Chairman, Jim Kirsh
President and CEO, Kim Miller
Vice Chairman, Karla Chase
Chief Human Resources Officer, Bridget Sheridan
Chief Strategy Officer, Amy Nyberg
Director, Daniel Klossner
Treasurer and Director, Ken O'Connell
Secretary and Director, Sue Sutter
President and CEO, Kim Miller
Vice Chairman, Karla Chase
Director, Craig Haberman
Director, Terry O'Connor
Director, Wade Fletcher
Director, David Hechimovich
Director, Beth Koepsell-Zeamer
Director, Daniel Landdeck
Director, Peter Jung
Director, Timothy Rentmeester

LOCATIONS

HQ: Beaver Dam Community Hospitals Inc.
707 S. University Ave., Beaver Dam WI 53916
Phone: 920-887-7181   **Fax:** 920-887-4101
Web: www.bdch.com

PRODUCTS/OPERATIONS

Selected Services
Breast Health
Cancer
Cardiac Rehab
Cardiovascular
Emergency Services
ENT
Heart Failure Zones
Joint Replacement
Massage and Wellness
Massage Specialties
Medical Imaging
Ophthalmology
Orthopaedics
Pain Management
Rehabilitation
Sleep Center
Sports Fitness Center
Surgery Center
Surgical Services
Therapy Services
Womens Health

COMPETITORS

Meriter Health Services
Ministry Health Care
ProHealth Care
University of Wisconsin Hospital and Clinics

Company Type: Private - Not-for-Profit

Income Statement
FYE: June 30

	REVENUE ($ mil.)	NET INCOME ($ mil.)	NET PROFIT MARGIN	EMPLOYEES
06/12	103	5	5.1%	830
06/11	97	2	2.2%	0
06/10	88	1	2.0%	0
06/09	85	7	8.5%	0
Annual Growth	6.6%	(9.8%)	—	—

2012 Year-End Financials

Debt ratio: ——
Return on equity: 5.10%
Cash ($ mil.): 4
Current ratio: 2.20
Long-term debt ($ mil.): —

Dividends
Yield: —
Payout: —
Market value ($ mil.): —

BEAVER STREET FISHERIES INC.

After more than 60 years Beaver Street Fisheries can tell a tale or two of the one that got away. It's a top supplier of fish and other seafood products to wholesalers retailers and food service operators. Sourcing its products from more than 50 countries Beaver Street Fisheries offers one of the largest selections of seafood in the US. It boasts a variety of fresh and frozen seafood –including octopus shrimp and turtle –sold under the Sea Best and Admiral Jacks names. Beaver Street Fisheries also imports lamb from New Zealand and sells Silver Fern-brand pork and beef via its Florida-New Zealand Lamb & Meat unit. Alfred and Hans Frisch started the family-owned business as a retail fish shop in 1950.

Beaver Street Fisheries has expanded its products portfolio in recent years through the efforts of its sister companies Bahamas Food Service and Tropic Seafood. Based in Nassau Bahamas the company's food service operation specializes in food distribution as one of the largest full-line food service distributors in the Bahamas. In 2012 the unit is working to double the size of its warehouse in Nassau while also fine-tuning the company's automation labor and transportation processes. Beaver Street Fisheries hopes to automate the workforce management processes in Nassau so that it can boost order volume without greatly expanding its employee count there. The company's Tropic Seafood business concentrates on lobster tail and seafood processing in the Bahamas. Specifically it processes lobster tails conch and other seafood items under the Island Queen and Island Prince brand names for sale worldwide.

EXECUTIVES

Chairman, Harry Frisch
CFO, Jeff Edwards
General Manager, Jim O'Brien
Buying Director Seafood, Charles Trager
President, Benjamin P. (Ben) Frisch
Manager Human Resources and Safety, Nick Malie
Director Sales Purchasing and Quality Assurance, Carlos Sanchez
EVP, Hans Frisch

VP and Director Sales, Mark Frisch

LOCATIONS

HQ: Beaver Street Fisheries Inc.
1741 W. Beaver St., Jacksonville FL 32203-1430
Phone: 904-354-8533   **Fax:** 904-633-7271
Web: www.beaverfish.com

PRODUCTS/OPERATIONS

Selected Products
Fish and other seafood
  Albacore tuna
  Black cod
  Bluefish
  Calamari
  Catfish
  Clams
  Cod
  Conch
  Crab
  Crawfish
  Flounder
  Grouper
  Haddock
  Halibut
  Lake perch
  Langostinos
  Lobster
  Mackerel
  Mahi mahi
  Marlin
  Mullet
  Mussels
  Ocean catfish
  Ocean perch
  Orange roughy
  Oysters
  Pollock
  Salmon
  Scallops
  Sea bass
  Sea trout
  Shark
  Shrimp
  Snails/escargot
  Snapper
  Sole
  Squid
  Surimi
  Swordfish
  Tilapia
  Whiting
  Yellowfin tuna
Value-added
  Breaded seafood
  Crab cakes
  Crab patties
  Crabmeat stuffing
  Deviled crab
  Lobster tails
  Paella mix
  Salted fish
  Smoked fish
Other
  Alligator
  Beef
  Frog legs
  Lamb
  Octopus
  Pork
  Turtle

COMPETITORS

American Seafoods
Brown Packing Company
Colorado Boxed Beef
Del Monte Capitol Meat
Fishhawk Fisheries
Florida Fresh Seafood Corp.
Fossil Farms
Mims Meat
Niman Ranch
North Pacific Seafoods
Ocean Beauty Seafoods
Pacific Seafood Group
Pioneer Wholesale Meat
Red Chamber Co.
Ronald A. Chisholm

Freedman Meats
Gorton's
Harvest Meat Company
High Liner Foods
Icelandic Group
JBS USA
Maid-Rite Steak Company
Limited
Smithfield Foods
SYSCO Newport Meat Company
Trident Seafoods
Wolverine Packing

Company Type: Private

Income Statement
FYE: May 28

	REVENUE ($ mil.)	NET INCOME ($ mil.)	NET PROFIT MARGIN	EMPLOYEES
05/11	450	13	3.0%	200
05/10	442	19	4.4%	0
05/09	468	17	3.7%	0
05/08	423	23	5.6%	0
Annual Growth	2.1%	(17.3%)	—	—

2011 Year-End Financials

Debt ratio: ——
Return on equity: 3.00%
Cash ($ mil.): 19
Current ratio: 1.80
Long-term debt ($ mil.): —

Dividends
Yield: —
Payout: —
Market value ($ mil.): —

BEEBE MEDICAL CENTER INC.

Sea shells on the sea shore can be found near Beebe Medical Center. The health care provider offers emergency inpatient long-term care women's health and other medical services to residents of Sussex County Delaware. The hospital is located in the town of Lewes near Rehoboth Beach. It has approximately 210 beds and offers specialized services including cardiology orthopedic rehabilitation and oncology treatments. Beebe Medical Center offers outpatient services including wound care diabetes management surgery radiology and sleep disorder diagnosis. It also operates senior care centers home health agencies medical laboratories and a nursing school.

Operations

Beebe Medical Center has a staff of some 1400 health professionals including about 300 doctors. It handles some 50000 emergency room visits per year. In addition to the primary hospital facilities the health care provider operates the Beebe Health Campus (outpatient services) and the nearby Millville Emergency Center (a summertime clinic near Bethany Beach).

Strategy

Beebe Medical Center has expanded its facilities over the years to better serve area residents. It began an expansion aiming to double enrollment of the nursing school in 2012. Construction efforts at the main hospital facility include a new emergency and critical care wing added in 2008.

Company Background

Beebe Medical Center was founded in 1916 by two brothers Dr. James Beebe and Dr. Richard Beebe. The Beebe School of Nursing opened in 1921 and the outpatient Beebe Health Campus was completed in 2003.

EXECUTIVES

President CEO and Secretary, Jeffrey M. (Jeff) Fried
VP Corporate Affairs, Wallace E. Hudson
VP and CFO, James Bartle
VP Human Resources, Catherine C. Halen
Director Physician Services, Marilyn Hill
Chair, Janet B. McCarty
Treasurer, Paul H. Mylander
Vice Chair, William S. Lee
VP Operations, Donna A Streletzky
VP and CIO, Barbara P. Vugrinec
EVP and COO, Thomas K. Steiner
VP Patient Care Services, Vendla A. Esler
Interim VP Medical Affairs, Andrejs Strauss
Executive Director Beebe Medical Foundation,
  Alex Sydnor
Trustee, James D. Barr
Trustee, James Beebe Jr.
Trustee, Steven D. Berlin
Trustee, William L. Berry
Trustee, Eugene D. Bookhammer
Trustee, Joseph W. Booth
Trustee, Stephen M. Fanto
Trustee, Thomas L. King
Trustee, Halsey G. Knapp
Vice Chair, William S. Lee
Trustee, Robert H. Moore
Trustee, Esthelda R. Parker-Selby
Trustee, Anis K. Saliba
Trustee, Patricia D. Shreeve
Trustee, Robert J. White
Trustee, Jacquelyn O. Wilson
Trustee, Joseph R. Hudson
Trustee, Habib Bolourchi
Trustee, Michael L. Wilgus

LOCATIONS

HQ: Beebe Medical Center
  424 Savannah Rd., Lewes DE 19958
Phone: 302-645-3300   **Fax:** 302-645-3466
Web: www.beebemed.org

Selected Delaware Locations
Beebe Health Campus (Rehoboth Beach)
Beebe Lab Express (Milton)
Beebe School of Nursing (Lewes)
Diabetes Management and Wound Care Center (Long
  Neck)
Georgetown Professional Park (Georgetown)
Gull House Adult Activities Center (Lewes)
Home Health Agency (Lewes)
Millville Walk-in Health Center (Millville)
Sleep Disorders Center (Rehoboth Beach)
Tunnell Cancer Center (Rehoboth Beach)

PRODUCTS/OPERATIONS

Selected Services
Bariatric
Cancer care
Cardiac & vascular
Community health
Diabetes management
Emergency
Home health
Hospitalist program
Imaging
Integrative health
Orthopedics
Rehabilitation
Senior care
Sleep Disorder
Surgical
Walk-in Healthcare
Wellness
Women's Health
Wound Care

COMPETITORS

Anne Arundel Medical
  Center
AtlantiCare
Catholic Health East
Christiana Care
Crozer-Keystone Health
  System

Shore Memorial
  Hospital
South Jersey
  Healthcare

HISTORICAL FINANCIALS
Company Type: Private - Not-for-Profit

Income Statement
FYE: June 30

	REVENUE ($ mil.)	NET INCOME ($ mil.)	NET PROFIT MARGIN	EMPLOYEES
06/11	260	8	3.4%	1,600
06/10	259	15	5.9%	0
06/09*	234	0	—	0
04/09	0	0	3.6%	0
Annual Growth	757.6%	735.1%		

*Fiscal year change

2011 Year-End Financials

Debt ratio: ——
Return on equity: 3.40%
Cash ($ mil.): 20
Current ratio: 0.30
Long-term debt ($ mil.): —

Dividends
  Yield: —
  Payout: —
  Market value ($ mil.): —

BELCAN SERVICES GROUP LIMITED PARTNERSHIP

LOCATIONS

HQ: BELCAN SERVICES GROUP LIMITED
  PARTNERSHIP
  10200 ANDERSON WAY, BLUE ASH, OH 45242-4718
Phone: 513-891-0972
Web: www.belcantechnical.com

HISTORICAL FINANCIALS
Company Type: Private

Income Statement
FYE: December 31

	REVENUE ($ mil.)	NET INCOME ($ mil.)	NET PROFIT MARGIN	EMPLOYEES
12/11	273	8	3.0%	3,500
12/10	249	6	2.8%	0
12/09	205	2	1.1%	0
12/08	231	4	2.1%	0
Annual Growth	5.7%	19.1%		

2011 Year-End Financials

Debt ratio: ——
Return on equity: 3.00%
Cash ($ mil.): 0
Current ratio: 3.40
Long-term debt ($ mil.): —

Dividends
  Yield: —
  Payout: —
  Market value ($ mil.): —

BELLIN HEALTH SYSTEMS INC.

LOCATIONS

HQ: BELLIN HEALTH SYSTEMS INC.
  744 S WEBSTER AVE, GREEN BAY, WI 54301-3505
Phone: 920-433-3500
Web: www.bellin.org

HISTORICAL FINANCIALS
Company Type: Private

Income Statement
FYE: September 30

	REVENUE ($ mil.)	NET INCOME ($ mil.)	NET PROFIT MARGIN	EMPLOYEES
09/11	389	27	7.1%	2,300
09/10	348	30	8.8%	0
09/09	323	13	4.0%	0
09/08	284	(19)	—	0
Annual Growth	11.1%	—	—	—

2011 Year-End Financials

Debt ratio: ——
Return on equity: 7.10%
Cash ($ mil.): 53
Current ratio: 2.60
Long-term debt ($ mil.): —

Dividends
  Yield: —
  Payout: —
  Market value ($ mil.): —

BELLINGHAM PUBLIC SCHOOLS

LOCATIONS

HQ: BELLINGHAM PUBLIC SCHOOLS
  1306 DUPONT ST, BELLINGHAM, WA 98225-3118
Phone: 360-676-6400
Web: www.bellinghamschools.org

HISTORICAL FINANCIALS
Company Type: Private

Income Statement
FYE: August 31

	REVENUE ($ mil.)	NET INCOME ($ mil.)	NET PROFIT MARGIN	EMPLOYEES
08/11	100	2	2.9%	1,300
08/10	122	14	11.6%	0
08/09	115	(2)	—	0
08/08	109	(16)	—	0
Annual Growth	(3.1%)	—	—	—

2011 Year-End Financials

Debt ratio: ——
Return on equity: 2.90%
Cash ($ mil.): 0
Current ratio: ——
Long-term debt ($ mil.): —

Dividends
  Yield: —
  Payout: —
  Market value ($ mil.): —

BELOIT COLLEGE

Beloit College home of the famed Beloit Poetry Journal is a liberal arts and sciences college with an enrollment of about 1200 students. The school offers more than 50 majors and has some 100 full-time faculty members. Academic fields include anthropology health and society and philosophy. Beloit College also offers pre-professional programs in medicine law engineering and environmental management. The town of Beloit (population 36500) is home to a Frito-Lay cheese powder plant and incoming freshman are warned about the "cheese breeze" prevalent in winter months. Founded in 1846 when Wisconsin was still a territory Beloit College is the state's oldest college.

EXECUTIVES

Interim President, Richard M. (Dick) Niemiec
VP External Affairs, Francis C. (Frank) McGovern
VP Student Affairs and Dean Students, William J. Flanagan
Director Admissions, James S. Zielinski
Director Business Services and Risk Manager, Jeff A. Finger
Controller, Rick A. Lemke
Director Human Resources, Lori J. Rhead
Director Alumni Affairs, P. Jane Armitage
Director Financial Aid, Jane H. Hessian
Director Information Services and Resources, Charlotte Slocum Patriquin
Director Public Affairs, Ron Nief
Registrar, Mary M. Boros-Kazai
VP Academic Affairs and Dean College, Lynn Franken
VP Administration and Treasurer, John M. Nicholas
VP Enrollment Services, Nancy L. Benedict

LOCATIONS

HQ: Beloit College
   700 College St., Beloit WI 53511
Phone: 608-363-2000   **Fax:** 608-363-2075
Web: www.beloit.edu

HISTORICAL FINANCIALS
Company Type: School

Income Statement
FYE: May 31

	REVENUE ($ mil.)	NET INCOME ($ mil.)	NET PROFIT MARGIN	EMPLOYEES
05/11	68	0	1.3%	450
05/10	69	1	2.5%	0
05/09	59	0	—	0
05/08	42	(3)	—	0
Annual Growth	17.9%	—	—	—

2011 Year-End Financials
Debt ratio: —
Return on equity: 1.30%
Cash ($ mil.): 11
Current ratio: —
Long-term debt ($ mil.): —
Dividends
   Yield: —
   Payout: —
Market value ($ mil.): —

BEN HILL GRIFFIN INC.

LOCATIONS

HQ: BEN HILL GRIFFIN INC.
   700 S SCENIC HWY, FROSTPROOF, FL 33843-2443
Phone: 863-635-2251

HISTORICAL FINANCIALS
Company Type: Private

Income Statement
FYE: August 31

	REVENUE ($ mil.)	NET INCOME ($ mil.)	NET PROFIT MARGIN	EMPLOYEES
08/12	125	11	9.4%	300
08/11	115	13	11.6%	0
08/10	105	7	6.7%	0
08/09	99	0	0.4%	0
Annual Growth	8.3%	216.4%	—	—

2012 Year-End Financials
Debt ratio: —
Return on equity: 9.40%
Cash ($ mil.): 2
Current ratio: 0.10
Long-term debt ($ mil.): —
Dividends
   Yield: —
   Payout: —
Market value ($ mil.): —

BENEDICT COLLEGE

Benedict College is a private Baptist-affiliated liberal arts college in an urban environment. It has an annual enrollment of about 3140 students from across the US and abroad and its student-faculty ratio is 18:1. Students may choose from 29 majors offered through a dozen academic departments including business education social sciences technology and more. Benedict College is also part of the NCAA II athletic conference. The historically black school began in 1870 when the American Baptist Home Mission Society created Benedict Institute setting as its goal to train emancipated slaves to teach and preach. The school name was changed to Benedict College in 1894.

The most popular majors at Benedict College in 2010 included business administration and management criminal justice/law enforcement administration biology and biological sciences human development and family studies and mass communication/media studies.

In 2012 the college partnered with the US Environmental Protection Agency to support and sustain green initiatives in policy and on campus. Provisions of the partnership include the EPA's commitment to enhance the school's science curricula and provide opportunities for environmentally career-minded students and improve the school's environmental policy.

Benedict College invests in campus improvements that include purchasing land and buildings renovating existing facilities and constructing new facilities. Recent new construction has included residence halls and an athletics complex.

EXECUTIVES

EVP Institutional Effectiveness, Love Collins III
President, David H. Swinton
VP Academic Affairs, Janeen P. Witty

EVP, Ruby W. Watts
VP Institutional Services and Major Gifts, Barbara C. Moore
VP Student Affairs, Gary E. Knight
VP Institutional Effectiveness and Sponsored Programs, Stacey F. Jones
VP Community Development, Jabari Simama
VP Academic Affairs, Burnett C. Joiner
VP Business and Finance, Brenda Walker

LOCATIONS

HQ: Benedict College
   1600 Harden St., Columbia SC 29204
Phone: 803-253-5000   **Fax:** 803-253-5167
Web: www.benedict.edu

HISTORICAL FINANCIALS
Company Type: School

Income Statement
FYE: June 30

	REVENUE ($ mil.)	NET INCOME ($ mil.)	NET PROFIT MARGIN	EMPLOYEES
06/12	69	2	3.7%	600
06/11	83	7	8.6%	0
06/10	61	2	4.0%	0
06/09	55	1	3.0%	0
Annual Growth	7.5%	15.1%	—	—

2012 Year-End Financials
Debt ratio: —
Return on equity: 3.70%
Cash ($ mil.): 0
Current ratio: —
Long-term debt ($ mil.): —
Dividends
   Yield: —
   Payout: —
Market value ($ mil.): —

BENEDICTINE COLLEGE

Benedictine College is a Roman Catholic liberal arts school that provides instruction to nearly 1200 students. It offers bachelor's degrees in nearly 40 major fields as well as three graduate degree programs. The school's Atchison Kansas campus overlooks the Missouri River. The college which opened its doors in 1859 is sponsored by brothers and sisters of the Benedictine monastic order.

EXECUTIVES

Chairman, James T. (Jim) O'Brien, age 73
VP and Dean of the College, Kimberly C. Shankman
VP Institutional Advancement, Kelly J. Vowels
Secretary, Abbot Barnabas Senecal
President, Stephen D. Minnis
CFO, Ronald J. (Ron) Olinger
Vice Chair, Sister Anne Shepard
VP College Relations Marketing and Communications, Phil Baniewicz

LOCATIONS

HQ: Benedictine College
   1020 N. 2nd St., Atchison KS 66002
Phone: 913-367-5340   **Fax:** 913-367-5462
Web: www.benedictine.edu

HISTORICAL FINANCIALS
Company Type: School

Income Statement
FYE: June 30

	REVENUE ($ mil.)	NET INCOME ($ mil.)	NET PROFIT MARGIN	EMPLOYEES
06/11	53	8	15.8%	184
06/10	50	9	18.6%	0
06/09	0	0	—	0
06/08	38	4	10.7%	0
Annual Growth	10.9%	26.2%	—	—

2011 Year-End Financials

Debt ratio: ——
Return on equity: 15.80%
Cash ($ mil.): 3
Current ratio: —
Long-term debt ($ mil.): —
Dividends
  Yield: —
  Payout: —
  Market value ($ mil.): —

BENEDICTINE UNIVERSITY

LOCATIONS

HQ: BENEDICTINE UNIVERSITY
  5700 COLLEGE RD, LISLE, IL 60532-0900
Phone: 630-829-6000
Web: www.ben.edu

HISTORICAL FINANCIALS
Company Type: Private

Income Statement
FYE: May 31

	REVENUE ($ mil.)	NET INCOME ($ mil.)	NET PROFIT MARGIN	EMPLOYEES
05/12	85	(0)	—	350
05/11	118	11	10.0%	0
05/10	100	7	7.4%	0
05/09	53	(4)	—	0
Annual Growth	17.2%	—	—	—

2012 Year-End Financials

Debt ratio: ——
Return on equity: (-1.00)%
Cash ($ mil.): 9
Current ratio: 1.00
Long-term debt ($ mil.): —
Dividends
  Yield: —
  Payout: —
  Market value ($ mil.): —

BENTLEY UNIVERSITY

Bentley University formerly known as Bentley College offers undergraduate graduate and doctoral degree programs to its nearly 5600 enrolled students from around the world. It also offers professional development and certificate programs for executives and corporations. The focus at Bentley is on business; the school was a pioneer in integrating information technology into the business curriculum. In the belief that businesspeople need a broad education Bentley requires a liberal arts core of classes in behavioral and social sciences English and other subjects in the humanities math and natural sciences. Harry Bentley founded the institution as a school of accounting and finance in 1917.

Bentley University is situated on about 165 acres in Waltham west of Boston. The university supports a student-faculty ratio of 12:1 with more than 80% of its faculty holding doctoral degrees.

Bentley offers numerous on-campus activities outside its academic and research functions. These include cultural events athletics the arts volunteering and more than 100 student organizations.

In partnership with Bahrain Institute of Banking and Finance Bentley launched its "Bentley in Bahrain" degree program in 2002 expanding its campus to students in Bahrain and surrounding Gulf States in the Middle East.

Bentley's university designation and name change occurred in 2008.

EXECUTIVES

VP Business and Finance and Treasurer, Paul Clemente
VP Academic Affairs and Provost, Robert D. (Bob) Galliers
COO and VP Information Technology, Traci A. Logan
VP Development and Corporate and Alumni Relations, Robert H. (Bob) Minetti
VP Student Affairs, Kathleen L. Yorkis
VP Marketing Communication and Public Affairs, Sandra T. King
VP Enrollment Management, Joann C. McKenna
Chairman, J. Terence Carleton
Executive Director Marketing Communication, Katherine H. Blake
Director Web Services, Rob Condit
Executive Director Human Resources, Barbara J. Addison Reid
Executive Director Facilities Management, John J. Shenette
Director Public and Media Relations, Michele M. Walsh
Chairman, Steven P. Manfredi
President and Trustee, Gloria Cordes Larson
General Counsel and Secretary, Judith Malone
VP Academic Affairs and Provost, Michael J. Page
Managing Director University Career Services, Susan Brennan
Trustee, Robert P. (Bob) Badavas, age 58
Trustee, Andrew J. Hajducky III, age 58
Trustee, Mark B. Skaletsky, age 64
Trustee, Robert F. Smith, age 79
Trustee, Francis J. Aguilar, age 79
Trustee, William C. Freda
Trustee, George W. Carmany III, age 72
Trustee, David H. Weener
Trustee, R. Marcelo Claure
Trustee, Kenneth H. Colburn
Trustee, Cynthia M. Deysher
Trustee, Tanya Hairston Whitner
Trustee, Daniel A. (Dan) Keshian
Trustee, Francis F. Kingsley
Trustee, Deborah A. Leitch
Trustee, Norman I. Massry
Trustee, Elkin B. McCallum
Trustee, Olaperi Onipede
Vice Chairman, Steven P. Manfredi
Trustee, Nathan R. Miller
President and Trustee, Gloria Cordes Larson
Trustee, Kevin Armata
Auditors: KPMGLLP

LOCATIONS

HQ: Bentley University
  175 Forest St., Waltham MA 02452-4705
Phone: 781-891-2000   **Fax:** 312-729-5600
Web: www.worldbook.com

HISTORICAL FINANCIALS
Company Type: School

Income Statement
FYE: June 30

	REVENUE ($ mil.)	NET INCOME ($ mil.)	NET PROFIT MARGIN	EMPLOYEES
06/12	185	(21)	—	911
06/11	183	34	18.9%	0
06/10	227	(2)	—	0
06/09	216	0	—	0
Annual Growth	(5.1%)	—	—	—

2012 Year-End Financials

Debt ratio: ——
Return on equity: (-11.30)%
Cash ($ mil.): 11
Current ratio: —
Long-term debt ($ mil.): —
Dividends
  Yield: —
  Payout: —
  Market value ($ mil.): —

BEREA COLLEGE

Founded in 1855 by abolitionist John G. Fee Berea College was the first interracial and coeducational school in the South. The Christian school provides a private tuition-free liberal arts education to about 1500 students each year most of whom come from Kentucky and the Appalachian region. In lieu of tuition Berea has a work program that requires its students to work in on-campus jobs for at least 10 hours each week in their choice of some 130 different departments. Berea offers about 30 majors leading to Bachelor of Arts and Bachelor of Science degrees and each student is required to attend seven convocations (guest lectures concerts or other cultural events) each term.

EXECUTIVES

President, Larry D. Shinn
VP Alumni and College Relations, William A. (Bill) Laramee
VP Finance, Jeff Amburgey
VP Labor and Student Life, Gail W. Wolford
Academic VP and Provost, Carolyn R. Newton
VP Business and Administration, Steve Karcher

LOCATIONS

HQ: Berea College
  101 Chestnut St., Berea KY 40404
Phone: 859-985-3000   **Fax:** 760-727-9041
Web: www.plitho.com

HISTORICAL FINANCIALS
Company Type: School

Income Statement
FYE: June 30

	REVENUE ($ mil.)	NET INCOME ($ mil.)	NET PROFIT MARGIN	EMPLOYEES
06/12	81	(30)	—	550
06/11	79	148	188.0%	0
06/10	77	65	84.8%	0
06/09	77	(244)	—	0
Annual Growth	1.6%	—	—	—

2012 Year-End Financials
Debt ratio: ——
Return on equity: (-36.90)%
Cash ($ mil.): 50
Current ratio: 3.50
Long-term debt ($ mil.): —

Dividends
Yield: —
Payout: —
Market value ($ mil.): —

BERGELECTRIC CORP.

One of the nation's top electrical contractors Bergelectric provides design/build and design/assist services on projects that include office buildings public-sector facilities bioscience labs entertainment complexes hotels data centers and hospitals. Its projects also consist of parking garages water treatment plants residential towers and correctional facilities. The company boasts expertise in building information modeling fire alarms and security and telecommunications and data infrastructure. Established in 1946 Bergelectric operates mainly in the western and southeastern US from about a dozen offices in Arizona California Colorado Florida Nevada North Carolina Texas and Oregon.

Geographic Reach

From its headquarters in Los Angeles Bergelectric maintains a presence in California through a handful of offices in San Diego Los Angeles Orange County Sacramento and Ventura. It also serves as an electrical contractor in half a dozen cities: Austin (Texas) Denver (Colorado) Las Vegas (Nevada) Orlando (Florida) Phoenix (Arizona) Portland (Oregon) and Raleigh (North Carolina).

Operations

The electrical company keeps a lengthy list of projects past and current. More recent projects have included the University of Oregon Basketball Arena Children's Hospital Central California Visitors Center at King Gillette Ranch the Northwest Reclamation Facility and Lackland Ambulatory Care Center.

The company is also focused on green initiatives completing Leadership in Energy and Environmental Design (LEED) construction projects for the likes of Sony the FBI the EPA and the University of Oregon.

Strategy

Bergelectric has extended the reach of its traditional electrical contracting operations by expanding into new markets including sustainable building structures and renewable energy systems such as wind farms. Through a partnership with telecommunications firm Teo inked in 2011 Bergelectric provides communications services to wind energy producers. As part of the agreement Bergelectric designs and installs fiber connections and equipment while Teo supplies phones switches and other hardware.

EXECUTIVES
CEO, John R. Briscoe
President, Donald L. (Don) Briscoe
CFO, Steve Buhr
EVP, Tom Anderson
SVP Sales and Marketing, Alan Mashburn
SVP Construction San Diego, Ken Bertalan
SVP Construction Los Angeles, Eddie Billig

LOCATIONS
HQ: Bergelectric Corp.
5650 W. Centinela Ave., Los Angeles CA 90045
Phone: 310-337-1377   **Fax:** 310-337-2663
Web: www.bergelectric.com

Selected Locations
Agoura Hills CA
Austin TX
Costa Mesa CA
Denver
Durham NC
Escondido CA
Los Angeles
North Las Vegas NV
Orlando FL
Portland OR
Rancho Cordova CA
Tempe AZ

COMPETITORS
Cupertino Electric	Morrow-Meadows
EMCOR	MYR Group
Fisk Electric	Rex Moore
Henkels & McCoy	Rosendin Electric
Integrated Electrical Services	Sachs Electric

HISTORICAL FINANCIALS
Company Type: Private

Income Statement
FYE: January 31

	REVENUE ($ mil.)	NET INCOME ($ mil.)	NET PROFIT MARGIN	EMPLOYEES
01/12	394	23	6.0%	1,900
01/11	403	6	1.6%	0
01/10	423	7	1.9%	0
01/08	454	64	14.1%	0
Annual Growth	(4.6%)	(28.1%)	—	—

2012 Year-End Financials
Debt ratio: ——
Return on equity: 6.00%
Cash ($ mil.): 11
Current ratio: 1.70
Long-term debt ($ mil.): —

Dividends
Yield: —
Payout: —
Market value ($ mil.): —

BERKEL & COMPANY CONTRACTORS INC.

LOCATIONS
HQ: BERKEL & COMPANY CONTRACTORS INC.
2649 S 142ND ST, BONNER SPRINGS, KS 66012-9459
Phone: 913-422-5125
Web: www.berkelandcompany.com

HISTORICAL FINANCIALS
Company Type: Private

Income Statement
FYE: December 31

	REVENUE ($ mil.)	NET INCOME ($ mil.)	NET PROFIT MARGIN	EMPLOYEES
12/11*	164	7	4.4%	600
01/10	164	11	7.2%	0
12/08	251	26	10.6%	0
12/07	255	30	12.0%	0
Annual Growth	(13.5%)	(38.2%)	—	—

*Fiscal year change

2011 Year-End Financials
Debt ratio: ——
Return on equity: 4.40%
Cash ($ mil.): 0
Current ratio: 1.70
Long-term debt ($ mil.): —

Dividends
Yield: —
Payout: —
Market value ($ mil.): —

BERKELEY COUNTY BOARD OF EDUCATION

LOCATIONS
HQ: BERKELEY COUNTY BOARD OF EDUCATION
401 S QUEEN ST, MARTINSBURG, WV 25401-3233
Phone: 304-267-3500
Web: www.berkeleycountyschools.org

HISTORICAL FINANCIALS
Company Type: Private

Income Statement
FYE: June 30

	REVENUE ($ mil.)	NET INCOME ($ mil.)	NET PROFIT MARGIN	EMPLOYEES
06/12	210	15	7.4%	2,000
06/11	202	(22)	—	0
06/10	233	39	16.9%	0
06/09	170	1	0.6%	0
Annual Growth	7.2%	148.9%	—	—

2012 Year-End Financials
Debt ratio: ——
Return on equity: 7.40%
Cash ($ mil.): 36
Current ratio: ——
Long-term debt ($ mil.): —

Dividends
Yield: —
Payout: —
Market value ($ mil.): —

BESTSWEET HOLDINGS INC.

LOCATIONS
HQ: BESTSWEET HOLDINGS INC.
288 MAZEPPA RD, MOORESVILLE, NC 28115-7928
Phone: 704-664-4300
Web: www.bestsweet.com

HISTORICAL FINANCIALS

Company Type: Private

Income Statement

FYE: December 31

	REVENUE ($ mil.)	NET INCOME ($ mil.)	NET PROFIT MARGIN	EMPLOYEES
12/11	104	4	4.2%	601
12/10*	94	8	8.6%	0
08/07	0	0	—	0
Annual Growth	—	—	—	—

*Fiscal year change

2011 Year-End Financials

Debt ratio: ——
Return on equity: 4.20%
Cash ($ mil.): 0
Current ratio: 0.90
Long-term debt ($ mil.): —

Dividends
Yield: —
Payout: —
Market value ($ mil.): —

HISTORICAL FINANCIALS

Company Type: Private - Not-for-Profit

Income Statement

FYE: December 31

	REVENUE ($ mil.)	NET INCOME ($ mil.)	NET PROFIT MARGIN	EMPLOYEES
12/11	274	2	1.0%	3,000
12/10	225	0	0.1%	0
12/09	213	2	1.0%	0
12/08	191	0	0.0%	0
Annual Growth	12.7%	529.0%	—	—

2011 Year-End Financials

Debt ratio: ——
Return on equity: 1.00%
Cash ($ mil.): 8
Current ratio: 0.30
Long-term debt ($ mil.): —

Dividends
Yield: —
Payout: —
Market value ($ mil.): —

HISTORICAL FINANCIALS

Company Type: Private

Income Statement

FYE: August 31

	REVENUE ($ mil.)	NET INCOME ($ mil.)	NET PROFIT MARGIN	EMPLOYEES
08/11	193	(27)	—	2,000
08/10	219	22	10.1%	0
08/09	204	(8)	—	0
08/08	176	(21)	—	0
Annual Growth	3.1%	—	—	—

2011 Year-End Financials

Debt ratio: ——
Return on equity: (-14.20)%
Cash ($ mil.): 9
Current ratio: —
Long-term debt ($ mil.): —

Dividends
Yield: —
Payout: —
Market value ($ mil.): —

BETH ABRAHAM HEALTH SERVICES

EXECUTIVES

COO, Paul Rosenfeld
COO Managed Care for Comprehensive Care Management, Joseph M. Healy Jr.
President and CEO, Michael S. Fassler
SVP Finance and CFO, Stephen Mann
Program Director Comprehensive Care Management, Karen Humphrey
EVP, Clari Gilbert
VP Marketing and Public Affairs, Connie Tejeda
VP Medical Services, Sandra Selikson
Director Human Resources, Celeste Smith
Executive Director Center for Nursing and Rehabilitation, Randy Palmaira
Executive Director Margaret Tietz Nursing and Rehabilitation Center, Gerald H. Hart
VP Music Therapy and Director Institute for Music and Neurologic Function, Concetta M. Tomaino
Medical Director Center for Nursing and Rehabilitation, Saka A. Kazeem

LOCATIONS

HQ: Beth Abraham Family of Health Services
612 Allerton Ave., Bronx NY 10467
Phone: 718-519-4000   **Fax:** 718-519-4230
Web: www.bethabe.org

COMPETITORS

Catholic Healthcare System
Eger Health Care
NewYork-Presbyterian Healthcare

BETHCO CORPORATION

LOCATIONS

HQ: BETHCO CORPORATION
612 ALLERTON AVE, BRONX, NY 10467-7404
Phone: 718-519-5937

HISTORICAL FINANCIALS

Company Type: Private

Income Statement

FYE: December 31

	REVENUE ($ mil.)	NET INCOME ($ mil.)	NET PROFIT MARGIN	EMPLOYEES
12/11	551	(5)	—	2
12/10	484	10	2.2%	0
12/09	5	2	46.3%	0
12/07	5	1	25.5%	0
Annual Growth	379.5%	—	—	—

2011 Year-End Financials

Debt ratio: ——
Return on equity: (-0.90)%
Cash ($ mil.): 37
Current ratio: 0.60
Long-term debt ($ mil.): —

Dividends
Yield: —
Payout: —
Market value ($ mil.): —

BETHEL SCHOOL DISTRICT 403

LOCATIONS

HQ: BETHEL SCHOOL DISTRICT 403
516 176TH ST E, SPANAWAY, WA 98387-8335
Phone: 253-683-6000
Web: www.jimboyce.com

BETHEL UNIVERSITY

LOCATIONS

HQ: BETHEL UNIVERSITY
3900 BETHEL DR, SAINT PAUL, MN 55112-6902
Phone: 651-638-6400
Web: www.bethelcollege.com

HISTORICAL FINANCIALS

Company Type: Private

Income Statement

FYE: May 31

	REVENUE ($ mil.)	NET INCOME ($ mil.)	NET PROFIT MARGIN	EMPLOYEES
05/11	132	9	7.2%	720
05/10*	126	0	0.5%	0
12/08	0	0	—	0
04/06	4	3	73.2%	0
Annual Growth	205.6%	41.1%	—	—

*Fiscal year change

2011 Year-End Financials

Debt ratio: ——
Return on equity: 7.20%
Cash ($ mil.): 12
Current ratio: —
Long-term debt ($ mil.): —

Dividends
Yield: —
Payout: —
Market value ($ mil.): —

BETHESDA LUTHERAN COMMUNITIES INC.

LOCATIONS

HQ: BETHESDA LUTHERAN COMMUNITIES INC.
600 HOFFMANN DR, WATERTOWN, WI 53094-6223
Phone: 920-261-3050
Web: www.bethesdalutherancommunities.org

HISTORICAL FINANCIALS
Company Type: Private

Income Statement
FYE: August 31

	REVENUE ($ mil.)	NET INCOME ($ mil.)	NET PROFIT MARGIN	EMPLOYEES
08/11	117	(16)	—	3,106
08/10	115	(20)	—	0
08/09	68	(9)	—	0
08/08	10	6	64.1%	0
Annual Growth	**121.1%**	—	—	—

2011 Year-End Financials
Debt ratio: ——
Return on equity: (-14.10)%
Cash ($ mil.): 5
Current ratio: 0.40
Long-term debt ($ mil.): —

Dividends
Yield: —
Payout: —
Market value ($ mil.): —

BETTY FORD CENTER AT EISENHOWER

Quite possibly the most famous of California's addiction treatment facilities The Betty Ford Center provides a variety of drug and alcohol rehabilitation services for all members of a family affected by addiction. Services include a children's program outpatient and inpatient treatment programs and clinical diagnostic evaluation. The not-for-profit organization also offers professional education programs to keep its medical providers up-to-date on the latest treatment options. Its primary facility is on the grounds of the Eisenhower Medical Center; it also has children's centers in Colorado and Texas. Betty Ford the wife of the late President Gerald Ford along with Leonard Firestone started the center in 1982.

Betty Ford got involved with addiction work after getting treatment for alcoholism herself at the US Naval Hospital in Long Beach California. She recognized the need for gender-specific treatment and opened her center with the help of then Ambassador Leonard Firestone. The Betty Ford Center treats both men and women who live in separate residence halls and attend gender-specific programs.

Ford has also established the Betty Ford Foundation which operates independently from the center to focus on recovery-related education advocacy and the dissemination of research.

EXECUTIVES
CEO, John T. Schwarzlose
Secretary Treasurer and Director, Dennie Jagger
VP Human Resources, Charlene Montgomery
Vice Chairman, James R. Greenbaum
Chairwoman, Mary Turner Pattiz
Chief Medical Officer and Director, Anthony S. Tornay
Treasurer and CFO, Jim Onorato
President Betty Ford Recovery Hospital, Michael S. Neatherton
President Betty Ford Center Foundation, John M. Boop
President Betty Ford Institute, Garrett O'Connor
Director, Betty Ford
Secretary Treasurer and Director, Dennie Jagger

Director, G. Aubrey Serfling
Vice Chairman, James R. Greenbaum
Director, Lois U. Horvitz
Director, Geoffrey S. Mason
Director, Cini Gannon Robb
Chief Medical Officer and Director, Anthony S. Tornay
Director, Linda Q. Hahn
Director, Michael J. Martella
Director, Joan O'Neil
Director, Ed Monarch
Director, Madeline M. Redstone

LOCATIONS
HQ: The Betty Ford Center At Eisenhower
39000 Bob Hope Dr., Rancho Mirage CA 92270
Phone: 760-773-4100   **Fax:** 760-773-4141
Web: www.bettyfordcenter.org

COMPETITORS
CIGNA Behavioral Health
Crossroads Antigua
Hazelden
Horizon Health
Los Angeles County Health Department
Mental Health Network
ValueOptions

HISTORICAL FINANCIALS
Company Type: Private - Not-for-Profit

Income Statement
FYE: June 30

	REVENUE ($ mil.)	NET INCOME ($ mil.)	NET PROFIT MARGIN	EMPLOYEES
06/11	38	1	3.0%	260
06/10	32	(1)	—	0
06/09	27	0	—	0
06/08	38	2	6.6%	0
Annual Growth	**(0.1%)**	**(23.2%)**	—	—

2011 Year-End Financials
Debt ratio: ——
Return on equity: 3.00%
Cash ($ mil.): 1
Current ratio: 0.10
Long-term debt ($ mil.): —

Dividends
Yield: —
Payout: —
Market value ($ mil.): —

BI-RITE RESTAURANT SUPPLY CO. INC.

Bi-Rite Restaurant Supply which does business as BiRite Foodservice Distributors is a leading foodservice supplier serving the San Francisco area and Northern California. The company distributes a full line of food equipment and supplies including meat and dairy items frozen foods dry groceries cleaning supplies and disposables. Its customers include restaurant operators hotels schools and healthcare facilities. A member of the UniPro Foodservice cooperative the family-owned company was founded in 1966 by cousins Victor and John Barulich.

EXECUTIVES
President, Steve Barulich
CEO, William (Bill) Barulich
Director Finance, Roger Mackin
General Manager, Dennis Collins

VP Purchasing, Phyllis Sarratt
VP Sales and Marketing, Michael Pendergast

LOCATIONS
HQ: Bi-Rite Restaurant Supply Co. Inc.
123 S. Hill Dr., Brisbane CA 94005
Phone: 415-656-0213   **Fax:** 415-656-0767
Web: www.biritefoodservice.com

COMPETITORS
Dot Foods
Golden State Foods
Jacmar
MAINES
McLane Foodservice
Performance Food
Sysco
US Foods

HISTORICAL FINANCIALS
Company Type: Private

Income Statement
FYE: December 31

	REVENUE ($ mil.)	NET INCOME ($ mil.)	NET PROFIT MARGIN	EMPLOYEES
12/11	255	4	1.8%	230
12/10	271	4	1.8%	0
12/09	285	5	1.9%	0
12/08	290	2	0.7%	0
Annual Growth	**(4.3%)**	**31.0%**	—	—

2011 Year-End Financials
Debt ratio: ——
Return on equity: 1.80%
Cash ($ mil.): 8
Current ratio: 3.50
Long-term debt ($ mil.): —

Dividends
Yield: —
Payout: —
Market value ($ mil.): —

BIBB COUNTY BOARD OF EDUCATION

LOCATIONS
HQ: BIBB COUNTY BOARD OF EDUCATION
484 MULBERRY ST STE 310, MACON, GA 31201-7928
Phone: 478-765-8711
Web: www.schools.bibb.k12.ga.us

HISTORICAL FINANCIALS
Company Type: Private

Income Statement
FYE: June 30

	REVENUE ($ mil.)	NET INCOME ($ mil.)	NET PROFIT MARGIN	EMPLOYEES
06/11	265	44	16.7%	3,800
06/10	252	2	0.9%	0
06/07	0	0	—	0
06/05	0	0	—	0
Annual Growth	—	—	—	—

2011 Year-End Financials
Debt ratio: ——
Return on equity: 16.70%
Cash ($ mil.): 30
Current ratio: —
Long-term debt ($ mil.): —

Dividends
Yield: —
Payout: —
Market value ($ mil.): —

BIG BROTHERS BIG SISTERS OF AMERICA

These siblings wrote the book on youth mentoring. Big Brothers Big Sisters of America establishes and supervises mentoring relationships between adults and children ages five to 18. Its network of some 400 local agencies serves more than 250000 youths. It pairs at-risk youth with adults for casual interactions like going to movies sporting events parks and just being together. Adults or "Bigs" are interviewed screened trained and approved by the parent or guardian of the "Littles." Agency staff makes matches and a caseworker stays in touch with the pair to make sure everything works well. The group is funded by federal state and local government as well as individuals foundations and companies.

Big Brothers Big Sisters caters to children in all 50 states Puerto Rico and Guam. The group spends about 80% of its revenues on programs and has measurable results to show for it. A national independent study showed that children who participated in the group were 52% less likely to skip school and 46% less likely to start using drugs than children who didn't participate.

In addition to the community-based program where Littles and Bigs interact on their own the organization offers supervised activities usually at a school where adults and kids have lunch play sports or use school computers together. The organization also offers the Amachi Big Brothers Big Sisters program which matches the child of an incarcerated parent with a member of a church in that child's community. In 2007 more than 25000 of the group's Littles had a mother or father in prison.

Crediting US President Barack Obama and First Lady Michelle Obama Big Brothers Big Sisters points to a 25% rise in potential-mentor inquiries in January 2009. Obama had designated January "mentoring month."

Karen Mathis became CEO in September 2009 soon after CEO Judy Vredenburgh retired after 10 years with Big Brothers Big Sisters.

EXECUTIVES

Chairman, Gregory R. (Greg) Page, age 60
VP Finance and Operations, Michael Lewis
EVP and COO, Mack Koonce
President and CEO, Karen J. Mathis
VP Marketing and Communications, Kay Keenan
VP Human Resources, Diane M. Maguire
VP Mentoring Programs, Joseph R. Radelet
VP Information Technology, Stu Zeiger
VP Philanthropy, Nick Booth
VP Agency Development, Cindy Mesko
Chair Elect, Brian Jackson
Chief Diversity Officer and National Director Hispanic Mentoring, Hector Cortez
Director, Paul S. Pressler, age 55
Director, Donald J. (Don) Carty Jr., age 65
Director, William W. (Bill) Hanna
Director, Roger Goodell
Director, William J. Hybl, age 70
Director, Robert N. (Bob) Taylor, age 58
Director, Lynn C. Swann, age 60
Director, Robert L. Wood, age 57
Director, Jody L. Bilney, age 50
Director, Edward B. (Ed) Rudner, age 61
Director, Richard Georgi
Chair Elect, Brian Jackson
Director, James J. O'Brien

Director, Frances Rubacha
Director, Steven L. Schwartz
Director, James F. Singleton
Director, Kate Snow
Director, Beverly Benz-Treuille
Director, Fernando Vigil
Director, Kevin Warren

LOCATIONS

HQ: Big Brothers Big Sisters of America
230 N. 13th St., Philadelphia PA 19107
Phone: 215-567-7000   **Fax:** 215-567-0394
Web: www.bbbsa.org

HISTORICAL FINANCIALS

Company Type: Private - Not-for-Profit

Income Statement

FYE: June 30

	REVENUE ($ mil.)	NET INCOME ($ mil.)	NET PROFIT MARGIN	EMPLOYEES
06/11	37	1	4.9%	85
06/10*	6	(5)	—	0
12/09	18	(4)	—	0
12/08	32	5	16.3%	0
Annual Growth	4.7%	(30.0%)	—	—

*Fiscal year change

2011 Year-End Financials

Debt ratio: —
Return on equity: 4.90%
Cash ($ mil.): 4
Current ratio: 0.40
Long-term debt ($ mil.): —
Dividends
Yield: —
Payout: —
Market value ($ mil.): —

BIG RIVER RESOURCES GALVA LLC

LOCATIONS

HQ: BIG RIVER RESOURCES GALVA LLC
211 N GEAR AVE STE 200, WEST BURLINGTON, IA 52655-1027
Phone: 309-932-9977
Web: www.bigriverresources.com

HISTORICAL FINANCIALS

Company Type: Private

Income Statement

FYE: December 31

	REVENUE ($ mil.)	NET INCOME ($ mil.)	NET PROFIT MARGIN	EMPLOYEES
12/11	371	31	8.5%	60
12/10	244	20	8.6%	0
12/09	156	10	6.9%	0
12/08	78	1	2.2%	0
Annual Growth	67.5%	162.4%	—	—

2011 Year-End Financials

Debt ratio: —
Return on equity: 8.50%
Cash ($ mil.): 1
Current ratio: 0.40
Long-term debt ($ mil.): —
Dividends
Yield: —
Payout: —
Market value ($ mil.): —

BIG RIVER RESOURCES LLC.

LOCATIONS

HQ: BIG RIVER RESOURCES LLC.
211 N GEAR AVE STE 200, WEST BURLINGTON, IA 52655-1027
Phone: 319-753-1100

HISTORICAL FINANCIALS

Company Type: Private

Income Statement

FYE: December 31

	REVENUE ($ mil.)	NET INCOME ($ mil.)	NET PROFIT MARGIN	EMPLOYEES
12/11	1,162	71	6.1%	202
12/10	742	52	7.1%	0
12/09	448	25	5.6%	0
12/08	343	24	7.1%	0
Annual Growth	50.1%	42.7%	—	—

2011 Year-End Financials

Debt ratio: —
Return on equity: 6.10%
Cash ($ mil.): 27
Current ratio: 0.60
Long-term debt ($ mil.): —
Dividends
Yield: —
Payout: —
Market value ($ mil.): —

BIG-D CONSTRUCTION CORP.

Big-D builds big things. With offices in Utah Arizona California and Wyoming the construction firm offers design/build services to customers in about 20 states. Big-D focuses on projects for clients in such industries as manufacturing health care hospitality food processing and distribution manufacturing and retail. The company's Signature Group builds high-end luxury homes as well as and condominiums spas and other special projects in resort communities. Clients have included SYSCO and Marriott. The company also operates a concrete division devoted to architectural structural and parking garage projects. Big-D was founded in 1967 by Dee Livingood. His family continues to lead the company.

Big-D has been courting more government projects as a way to weather the economic downturn which has put a halt on many commercial jobs. Among those public projects is the Utah Museum of Natural History at The University of Utah and the Wallace F. Bennett Federal Building in Salt Lake City. Big-D also is focusing on developing its eco-friendly construction business.

EXECUTIVES

Chairman and CEO, Jack Livingood
SVP and CFO, Larry Worrell
VP Field Operations, Kim O'Dell
SVP, Dale Satterthwait
SVP Operations, Forrest McNabb
President Big-D Construction, Rob Moore

VP and Project Executive, Jim Allison
VP and Project Executive, Blaine Nimer
VP Food Industry Focus, Doug Rowe
VP and Regional Manager, Greg Fix
President Big-D Pacific, Ken Mitchell
Chief Estimator, Brandon Briggs
Subcontractor Manager, Jana Cochell
VP, Greg Dean
VP, Oscar Yousefi
VP, Ryan Carter
VP, Cory Moore

LOCATIONS

HQ: Big-D Construction Corporation
404 W. 400 South, Salt Lake City UT 84101
Phone: 801-415-6000   **Fax:** 801-415-6900
Web: www.big-d.com

Selected Markets

Arizona
Arkansas
California
Colorado
Georgia
Hawaii
Idaho
Montana
Nevada
New Mexico
North Carolina
North Dakota
Oklahoma
Oregon
South Dakota
Tennessee
Texas
Utah
Washington

PRODUCTS/OPERATIONS

Selected Services

Construction management
Design/build
Field services
 Architectural concrete
 Finish carpentry
 Rough framing
 Structural concrete
General contracting
Green and Leadership in Energy and Environmental
 Design

Selected Industry Specializations

Commercial/public spaces (governmental educational
 and office complexes; mixed-use projects)
Food processing and distribution
Health care
Hospitality and resort
Manufacturing

Retail

COMPETITORS

Bechtel	Jaynes Companies
Hensel Phelps	Layton
Construction	Okland Construction
J.F. Shea	Swinerton
Jacobsen Construction	

HISTORICAL FINANCIALS

Company Type: Private

Income Statement

FYE: December 31

	REVENUE ($ mil.)	NET INCOME ($ mil.)	NET PROFIT MARGIN	EMPLOYEES
12/11	554	0	—	433
12/10	259	0	—	0
12/09	0	0	—	0
12/08	0	0	—	0
Annual Growth	—	—	—	—

2011 Year-End Financials

Debt ratio: —
Return on equity: —
Cash ($ mil.): 28
Current ratio: 1.10
Long-term debt ($ mil.): —

Dividends
 Yield: —
 Payout: —
Market value ($ mil.): —

BILL CURRIE FORD INC.

LOCATIONS

HQ: BILL CURRIE FORD INC.
5815 N DALE MABRY HWY, TAMPA, FL 33614-5697
Phone: 813-872-5555
Web: www.billcurrie.com

HISTORICAL FINANCIALS

Company Type: Private

Income Statement

FYE: December 31

	REVENUE ($ mil.)	NET INCOME ($ mil.)	NET PROFIT MARGIN	EMPLOYEES
12/11	82	1	1.5%	312
12/10	70	2	3.9%	0
12/09	70	0	0.7%	0
12/08	77	(0)	—	0
Annual Growth	2.1%	—	—	—

2011 Year-End Financials

Debt ratio: ——
Return on equity: 1.50%
Cash ($ mil.): 2
Current ratio: 0.20
Long-term debt ($ mil.): —

Dividends
 Yield: —
 Payout: —
Market value ($ mil.): —

BILLINGS CLINIC

Billings Clinic is an integrated health care system that serves the residents of Big Sky Country. Through a group of more than 320 doctors and other providers the clinic caters to some 570000 people in Billings Montana and in surrounding communities. It offers 45-plus specialties such as emergency and trauma cancer orthopedics birthing cardiovascular neurosciences dialysis and pediatrics. Its operations include a more than 270-bed hospital and the organization's main clinic. Additionally Billings Clinic operates the 90-bed Aspen Meadows Retirement Community and provides support services to several regional community

hospitals. The not-for-profit health care system is owned by the community.
 Geographic Reach
 As the largest health care organization in the area Billings Clinic's service area comprises 40 counties and extends more than 120000 miles in Montana Wyoming and the western Dakotas.
 Operations
 With its vast service area the health care system provides a MedFlight advanced life support fixed-wing aircraft service that transports critically ill or injured patients from rural communities. The service averages 700 flights per year.
 As part of its operations Billings Clinic runs a Level II emergency and trauma center 14-suite family birthing center Level III neonatal intensive care unit inpatient cancer care unit and a 15-bed transitional care unit. The health care system's cancer center provides both inpatient and outpatient care in Billings and the surrounding four-state region.
 Billings Clinic is governed by a 12-member board consisting of mostly community members but also a pair of doctors and a physician CEO.
 Strategy
 Billings Clinic works with pharmaceutical sponsors on a variety of clinical research trials in various phases and indications. To this end it operates a research center with more than 20 years of experience in the areas of basic and clinical research. The center has participated in more than 200 clinical research studies with the help of some 5000 volunteer subjects since 1988.
 The health care system has been growing. It expanded its capacity for infusions in 2012 when its Billings Clinic Cody location opened an infusion center. In late 2012 the organization also opened a new Stillwater Billings Clinic medical facility which combines Stillwater Community Hospital and Billings Clinic Columbus and integrates the billing process for the two health care facilities.

EXECUTIVES

Vice Chairman, Lyle R. Knight, age 66
CEO and Director, Nicholas J. Wolter
VP and CIO, Chris Stevens
**VP Strategic Development and Corporate
 Compliance Officer,** Kristianne Wilson
Physician in Chief, Mark C. Rumans
COO, Jon D. Ness
VP Research, Howard Knapp
President Billings Clinic Foundation, Jim Duncan
Secretary and Director, Linda Overstreet
Chairman, J. Scott Millikan
Chairman, Mike Schaer
VP Hospital Operations, Lu Byrd
VP People Resources, Kellee J. Fisk
VP Facility Services, Mitch Goplen
VP and Regional CFO, Kyle Gee
Vice Chairman, David Brown
VP Clinic Operations, Peggy Wharton
CFO, Connie F. Prewitt
Vice Chairman, Lyle R. Knight, age 66
CEO and Director, Nicholas J. Wolter
Director, Joy N. Ott
Director, William W. Ballard
Secretary and Director, Linda Overstreet
Director, Tim Hathaway
Director, Julie Lovell
Treasurer and Director, J. Scott Millikan
Vice Chairman, David Brown
Director, C. H. (Tersh) McCracken III
Director, Penni Nance

LOCATIONS

HQ: BILLINGS CLINIC
2800 10TH AVE N, BILLINGS, MT 59101-0703
Phone: 406-657-4000
Web: www.billingsclinic.org

PRODUCTS/OPERATIONS

Selected Services

Advance Medical Directives
Allergy Asthma Immunology
Aspen Meadows - Skilled Nursing and Assisted Living
Anticoagulation Clinic
Breast Center
Cancer Center
Cardiovascular Services
Cardiovascular Surgery
Children' s Services
Continence Center
Community Training Center
Cosmetic Surgery
da Vinci Surgical System
Dermatology Center
Diabetes Management Center
Diagnostic Imaging
Diabetes
Dialysis Center
Eldercare Solutions
Emergency & Trauma Center
Emmi Educational Videos
Employer Services - Occupational Health
Endocrinology
Eye Center
Facial Plastic Surgery
Family Medicine
Family Birth Center
Gastroenterology
General Surgery
Genetic Counseling
Geriatric Assessment Program
Gynecologic Cancer
Heart Services
Heart Surgery
Home Oxygen & Medical Equipment
Hospitalist Program
Infectious Diseases
Insurance Finder
Internal Medicine
Laboratory Services
LifeFit
Maternal-Fetal Medicine
MedFlight Air Ambulance
Mental Health Services
Metabolism Center
Mohs Surgery
Nutrition Services
Neurosciences
Obstetrics & Gynecology
Occupational Health - Employer Services
Ophthalmology
Orthopedics & Sports Medicine
Palliative Care
Pediatrics
  Pediatric Center
  Pediatric Cancer
  Pediatric Diabetes
  Pediatric Gastroenterology
  Pediatric Pulmonology
  Rehabilitation (Therapy)
Pharmacy
Physical Medicine & Rehabilitation
Plastic Surgery
Primary Care for Adults
Pulmonary Rehabilitation Program
Radiology Services
Reproductive Medicine and Fertility Care
Robotic Surgery
SameDay Care
Senior Services
Sleep Disorders Center
Sports Medicine
Sports Specific Camps
Stroke Care
Surgery Center
Transitional Care Unit

Urology Services
Vascular Surgery
Vein Clinic
Women's Free Screenings
Women' s and Children' s Services

Selected Affiliate Hospitals and Clinics

Beartooth Billings Clinic - Red Lodge
Colstrip Medical Center - Colstrip
Daniels Memorial Healthcare - Scobey
Livingston HealthCare - Livingston
North Big Horn Hospital - Lovell
Pioneer Medical Center - Big Timber
Roundup Memorial Healthcare - Roundup
Sheridan Memorial Hospital Association
Stillwater Billings Clinic

COMPETITORS

Glendive Medical Center
St. Alexius Medical Center
St. James Healthcare
St. Patrick Hospital
Wyoming Medical Center

HISTORICAL FINANCIALS

Company Type: Private - Not-for-Profit

Income Statement

FYE: June 30

	REVENUE ($ mil.)	NET INCOME ($ mil.)	NET PROFIT MARGIN	EMPLOYEES
06/11	533	28	5.4%	3,300
06/10	494	25	5.2%	0
06/09	461	(11)	—	0
06/08	433	(9)	—	0
Annual Growth	7.1%	—	—	—

2011 Year-End Financials

Debt ratio: —
Return on equity: 5.40%
Cash ($ mil.): 31
Current ratio: 0.50
Long-term debt ($ mil.): —
Dividends
Yield: —
Payout: —
Market value ($ mil.): —

BIOURJA TRADING LLC

LOCATIONS

HQ: BIOURJA TRADING LLC
757 N ELDRIDGE PKWY, HOUSTON, TX 77079-4527
Phone: 832-775-9000
Web: www.biourja.com

HISTORICAL FINANCIALS

Company Type: Private

Income Statement

FYE: December 31

	REVENUE ($ mil.)	NET INCOME ($ mil.)	NET PROFIT MARGIN	EMPLOYEES
12/11	3,842	13	0.4%	32
12/10	2,157	10	0.5%	0
12/09	1,163	10	0.9%	0
12/08	1,276	5	0.4%	0
Annual Growth	44.4%	33.6%	—	—

2011 Year-End Financials

Debt ratio: —
Return on equity: 0.40%
Cash ($ mil.): 1
Current ratio: 0.70
Long-term debt ($ mil.): —
Dividends
Yield: —
Payout: —
Market value ($ mil.): —

BLACK & VEATCH HOLDING COMPANY

LOCATIONS

HQ: BLACK & VEATCH HOLDING COMPANY
8400 WARD PKWY, KANSAS CITY, MO 64114-2031
Phone: 913-458-2000
Web: www.bv.com

HISTORICAL FINANCIALS

Company Type: Private

Income Statement

FYE: December 30

	REVENUE ($ mil.)	NET INCOME ($ mil.)	NET PROFIT MARGIN	EMPLOYEES
12/11	2,560	104	4.1%	7,017
12/10	2,265	34	1.5%	0
12/08	2,714	32	1.2%	0
Annual Growth	(2.9%)	79.7%	—	—

2011 Year-End Financials

Debt ratio: —
Return on equity: 4.10%
Cash ($ mil.): 540
Current ratio: 1.00
Long-term debt ($ mil.): —
Dividends
Yield: —
Payout: —
Market value ($ mil.): —

BLACK ELK ENERGY OFFSHORE OPERATIONS LLC

LOCATIONS

HQ: BLACK ELK ENERGY OFFSHORE OPERATIONS LLC
11451 KATY FWY STE 500, HOUSTON, TX 77079-2005
Phone: 281-598-8600
Web: www.blackelkenergy.com

HISTORICAL FINANCIALS

Company Type: Private

Income Statement

FYE: September 30

	REVENUE ($ mil.)	NET INCOME ($ mil.)	NET PROFIT MARGIN	EMPLOYEES
09/12*	239	(16)	—	10
12/11	339	15	4.4%	0
Annual Growth	(29.4%)	—	—	—

*Fiscal year change

2012 Year-End Financials

Debt ratio: —
Return on equity: (7.00)%
Cash ($ mil.): 17
Current ratio: 0.60
Long-term debt ($ mil.): —
Dividends
Yield: —
Payout: —
Market value ($ mil.): —

BLACK GOLD POTATO SALES INC.

LOCATIONS

HQ: BLACK GOLD POTATO SALES INC.
4575 32ND AVE S STE 2A, GRAND FORKS, ND
58201-3305
Phone: 701-772-2620
Web: www.blackgoldpotato.com

HISTORICAL FINANCIALS
Company Type: Private

Income Statement				FYE: July 31
	REVENUE ($ mil.)	NET INCOME ($ mil.)	NET PROFIT MARGIN	EMPLOYEES
07/11	81	0	0.2%	11
07/10	76	0	0.4%	0
07/09	61	0	0.4%	0
07/08	43	0	0.6%	0
Annual Growth	23.2%	(20.7%)	—	—

2011 Year-End Financials

Debt ratio: ——
Return on equity: 0.20%
Cash ($ mil.): 0
Current ratio: 1.40
Long-term debt ($ mil.): —

Dividends
Yield: —
Payout: —
Market value ($ mil.): —

BLANCHARD VALLEY FARMERS COOPERATIVE INC.

Supporting local farmers gives Blanchard Valley Farmers Cooperative (BVFC) roots and reach. Founded in 1989 BVFC has about 1700 area members. The co-op owns more than a dozen locations including four agronomy stations two seasonal grain facilities a farm and garden store and two petroleum sites. Member-farmers benefit from the co-op's array of products and services including seed feed fertilizer grain crop storage crop applications and farming equipment sales and rental. The feed store also sells mulch birdseed and pet supplies as well as conducts soil testing and arranges seeding and fertilizer programs. BVFC's petroleum locations offer gasoline and home-heating oil among several products.

BVFC's terminal elevator at Fostoria is one of Ohio's largest grain facilities. Its installation and capacity weighing in at 8.77 million bushels allows farmers depositing grain to get through the facility more quickly and store more grain until markets are favorable for selling. In 2011 the co-op handled nearly 27 million bushels throughout all locations.

BVFC's capacity is the result of an expansion during 2010 and 2011 that added two new receiving pits a 30000-bph Hawthorne-Servingleg several massive enclosed-belt conveyors a new 73000-bushel grain bin and new scalehouse and probe.

The probe allows the facility to reroute and expedite truck traffic.

Financially BVFC has reportedly averaged a 5% increase through grain marketing. Its cost of operation takes a 1% cut out of total revenue; the remaining revenue is distributed to members. Since 2004 BVFC has averaged more than nine cents per bushel to members.

The co-op's future faces increased competition from large and small rivals such as ADM and Cargill ethanol plants and neighbor co-op Central Ohio Farmers. At the same time farmers who have had better yields at high higher prices have purchased more efficient equipment to plant and harvest crops. As a result the co-op's facilities are pressured to handle more bushels faster. Few growers are also accounting for a higher percentage of business making investment decisions that serve members in far-flung areas more difficult. BVFC in early 2012 began mulling a merger with another cooperative Luckey Farmers. A merger is anticipated to strengthen the co-ops' product offerings and marketing opportunities and provide a more stable cost structure.

EXECUTIVES

General Manager, Jerry Silveus
Assistant Manager; Manager Agronomy, Michael (Mike) Tobe
Controller, Deborah (Debbie) Boger
Manager Petroleum Division, Steve Rodman
President Board of Directors, Thomas E. (Tom) Wise, age 47
Grain Manager, Mitch Welty
Office Manager, Jean Drerup
Treasurer Board of Directors, Steven Cramer
Secretary Board of Directors, Ronald D. Cornwell
Vice President Board of Directors, William Tong
Risk Coordinator, Joe Hochstettler
Stock Coordinator, Coleen Wright
Grain Accounting, Melissa Curtis
Chemical Sales Manager, Don Boehm
Agronomy Seed and Sales Manager, Mike McBride
Accounts Payable and Accounts Receivable, Sam Clark
Treasurer Board of Directors, Steven Cramer
Secretary Board of Directors, Ronald D. Cornwell
Vice President Board of Directors, William Tong
Director, Marvin Tuttle
Director, Mark Brian
Director, Shawn Beucler
Director, David Roberts
Director, Mike Stacy

LOCATIONS

HQ: Blanchard Valley Farmers Cooperative Inc.
6566 County Rd. 236, Findlay OH 45840
Phone: 419-423-2611　　　**Fax:** 419-423-9706
Web: www.bvfcoop.com

PRODUCTS/OPERATIONS

Selected Services
Customer accounting
Feed
Grain
Petroleum
Seasonal grain

COMPETITORS

ADM　　　　　　　　CHS
Ag Processing Inc.　　GROWMARK
Cargill　　　　　　　Luckey Farmers

HISTORICAL FINANCIALS
Company Type: Private - Cooperative

Income Statement				FYE: December 31
	REVENUE ($ mil.)	NET INCOME ($ mil.)	NET PROFIT MARGIN	EMPLOYEES
12/11	292	7	2.5%	122
12/10	196	4	2.5%	0
12/09	168	6	3.9%	0
12/08	210	6	3.1%	0
Annual Growth	11.7%	4.4%	—	—

2011 Year-End Financials

Debt ratio: ——
Return on equity: 2.50%
Cash ($ mil.): 2
Current ratio: —
Long-term debt ($ mil.): —

Dividends
Yield: —
Payout: —
Market value ($ mil.): —

BLOODSOURCE INC.

LOCATIONS

HQ: BLOODSOURCE INC.
10536 PETER A MCCUEN BLVD, MATHER, CA
95655-4128
Phone: 916-456-1500

HISTORICAL FINANCIALS
Company Type: Private

Income Statement				FYE: September 30
	REVENUE ($ mil.)	NET INCOME ($ mil.)	NET PROFIT MARGIN	EMPLOYEES
09/11	90	3	4.0%	595
09/10	83	1	1.2%	0
09/09	85	0	0.5%	0
09/08	105	23	22.1%	0
Annual Growth	(5.3%)	(46.5%)	—	—

2011 Year-End Financials

Debt ratio: ——
Return on equity: 4.00%
Cash ($ mil.): 11
Current ratio: 0.60
Long-term debt ($ mil.): —

Dividends
Yield: —
Payout: —
Market value ($ mil.): —

BLUE TEE CORP.

Handling a variety of steel products and scrap materials suits Blue Tee to a tee. The holding company which operates through two primary subsidiaries distributes steel building materials and scrap metal. Blue Tee's Brown-Strauss Steel subsidiary is one of the largest distributors of wide flange beam and structural structural steel products (beams pipe and tubing) in the US. The metal distributor's other primary business is Azcon a leading scrap processor broker and mill services management company which handles scrap metal sales rail cars and other steel parts.

Geographic Reach

Brown-Strauss Steel has operations in Arkansas California Colorado Kansas Utah and Washington. Azcon has operations in Illinois Minnesota Pennsylvania and Texas.

Strategy

In 2011 Blue Tee divested subsidiaries GEFCO (an OEM of portable drilling rigs and other industrial equipment) and STECO (transfer and dump-truck trailers) to Astec Industries for about $30.8 million.

The move to axe its GEFCO and STECO subsidiaries followed another sale. Blue Tee sold off its pump parts subsidiary Texas-based Standard Alloys to German pump manufacturer KSB in mid-2010.

The sales reflect Blue Tee's effort to focus its resources on its more lucrative businesses Azcon and Brown-Strauss Steel.

Ownership

Blue Tee is owned by its employees.

EXECUTIVES

Chairman, Richard A. Secrist
President and CEO, William M. Kelly, age 63
EVP Finance and Secretary, David P. Alldian
Group VP Metals Operations, Richard A. Secrist Jr.
Controller and Assistant Secretary, Thomas Caruso
Executive Director Benefit Plans, Annette Marino D'Arienzo

LOCATIONS

HQ: BLUE TEE CORP.
250 PARK AVE S RM 203, NEW YORK, NY 10003-1495
Phone: 212-598-0880
Web: www.gefco.com

PRODUCTS/OPERATIONS

Selected Subsidiaries

Azcon Corporation (ferrous and nonferrous scrap; rail cars locomotives and parts; relay and reroll rail)
Brown-Strauss Steel (steel distribution including angles beams channels pipe and tubing)

Selected Azcon Services

Barge Services
Brokerage Services
Demolition Services
Foundries - Scrap Management
Industrial Plants - Scrap Management
Mill Service
Mine Services
Railroad Industry Services
Steel Mills - Scrap Management

Selected Brown-Strauss Steel Products and Services

Products:
Structural Angle
Structural Channels
Structural Pipe
Structural Tubing
Wide Flange Beams
Services:
Cambering
Inventory Stocking program
Length/cutting optimization program
Mill Brokerage
Saw Cutting
Track Torch Cutting

COMPETITORS

A. M. Castle	Russel Metals
APi Group	Trinity Industries
Dover Corp.	TTX
OmniSource	Wescast Industries
Reliance Steel	
RTI International	

Metals

HISTORICAL FINANCIALS
Company Type: Private

Income Statement
FYE: December 31

	REVENUE ($ mil.)	NET INCOME ($ mil.)	NET PROFIT MARGIN	EMPLOYEES
12/11	964	10	1.1%	900
12/10	809	14	1.8%	0
12/09	564	(10)	—	0
12/08	1,549	33	2.1%	0
Annual Growth	(14.6%)	(31.7%)	—	—

2011 Year-End Financials
Debt ratio: ——
Return on equity: 1.10%
Cash ($ mil.): 29
Current ratio: 1.10
Long-term debt ($ mil.): —
Dividends
Yield: —
Payout: —
Market value ($ mil.): —

BOARD OF EDUCATION FOR THE CITY OF VALDOSTA

LOCATIONS

HQ: BOARD OF EDUCATION FOR THE CITY OF VALDOSTA
1204 WILLIAMS ST, VALDOSTA, GA 31601-4043
Phone: 229-333-8500
Web: www.gocats.org

HISTORICAL FINANCIALS
Company Type: Private

Income Statement
FYE: June 30

	REVENUE ($ mil.)	NET INCOME ($ mil.)	NET PROFIT MARGIN	EMPLOYEES
06/11	81	3	3.8%	819
06/09	77	8	10.9%	0
06/08	78	(14)	—	0
06/07	73	16	22.0%	0
Annual Growth	3.6%	(42.4%)	—	—

2011 Year-End Financials
Debt ratio: ——
Return on equity: 3.80%
Cash ($ mil.): 3
Current ratio: —
Long-term debt ($ mil.): —
Dividends
Yield: —
Payout: —
Market value ($ mil.): —

BOARD OF EDUCATION OF CARROLL COUNTY

LOCATIONS

HQ: BOARD OF EDUCATION OF CARROLL COUNTY
125 N COURT ST STE 101, WESTMINSTER, MD 21157-5192
Phone: 410-751-3000
Web: www.carrollk12.org

HISTORICAL FINANCIALS
Company Type: Private

Income Statement
FYE: June 30

	REVENUE ($ mil.)	NET INCOME ($ mil.)	NET PROFIT MARGIN	EMPLOYEES
06/12	375	10	2.7%	2,500
06/07	0	0	—	0
06/06	298	0	0.2%	0
06/05	63	14	23.6%	0
Annual Growth	80.9%	(12.5%)	—	—

2012 Year-End Financials
Debt ratio: ——
Return on equity: 2.70%
Cash ($ mil.): 16
Current ratio: 0.40
Long-term debt ($ mil.): —
Dividends
Yield: —
Payout: —
Market value ($ mil.): —

BOARD OF EDUCATION OF FREDERICK COUNTY MD (INC)

LOCATIONS

HQ: BOARD OF EDUCATION OF FREDERICK COUNTY MD (INC)
191 S EAST ST, FREDERICK, MD 21701-5918
Phone: 301-662-4068

HISTORICAL FINANCIALS
Company Type: Private

Income Statement
FYE: June 30

	REVENUE ($ mil.)	NET INCOME ($ mil.)	NET PROFIT MARGIN	EMPLOYEES
06/12	543	(5)	—	3,500
06/05	0	0	—	0
06/03	0	0	—	0
06/02	0	0	—	0
Annual Growth	—	—	—	—

BOARD OF EDUCATION OF ST MARY'S COUNTY

LOCATIONS

HQ: BOARD OF EDUCATION OF ST MARY' S COUNTY
23160 MOAKLEY ST, LEONARDTOWN, MD
20650-2922
Phone: 301-475-5511
Web: www.smcps.k12.md.us

HISTORICAL FINANCIALS

Company Type: Private

Income Statement

	REVENUE ($ mil.)	NET INCOME ($ mil.)	NET PROFIT MARGIN	EMPLOYEES
06/12	209	(3)	—	220
06/11	210	(4)	—	0
06/10	209	(8)	—	0
06/08	206	8	4.2%	0
Annual Growth	0.4%	—	—	—

FYE: June 30

2012 Year-End Financials

Debt ratio: ——
Return on equity: (-1.60)%
Cash ($ mil.): 23
Current ratio: —
Long-term debt ($ mil.): —

Dividends
Yield: —
Payout: —
Market value ($ mil.): —

BOARD OF EDUCATION-MEMPHIS CITY SCHOOLS

LOCATIONS

HQ: BOARD OF EDUCATION-MEMPHIS CITY
SCHOOLS
2597 AVERY AVE, MEMPHIS, TN 38112-4818
Phone: 901-416-5300
Web: www.treadwellhigh.com

HISTORICAL FINANCIALS

Company Type: Private

Income Statement

	REVENUE ($ mil.)	NET INCOME ($ mil.)	NET PROFIT MARGIN	EMPLOYEES
06/11*	1,173	(5)	—	12,015
12/09	449	(64)	—	0
06/08	1,161	53	4.6%	0
06/07	1,082	21	2.0%	0
Annual Growth	2.7%	—	—	—

FYE: June 30

*Fiscal year change

2011 Year-End Financials

Debt ratio: ——
Return on equity: (-0.50)%
Cash ($ mil.): 175
Current ratio: —
Long-term debt ($ mil.): —

Dividends
Yield: —
Payout: —
Market value ($ mil.): —

BOARD OF WATER SUPPLY

LOCATIONS

HQ: BOARD OF WATER SUPPLY
630 S BERETANIA ST, HONOLULU, HI 96843-0001
Phone: 808-748-5100

HISTORICAL FINANCIALS

Company Type: Private

Income Statement

	REVENUE ($ mil.)	NET INCOME ($ mil.)	NET PROFIT MARGIN	EMPLOYEES
06/12	159	19	12.2%	589
06/11	149	12	8.3%	0
06/10	152	17	11.5%	0
06/09	139	(2)	—	0
Annual Growth	4.5%	—	—	—

FYE: June 30

2012 Year-End Financials

Debt ratio: ——
Return on equity: 12.20%
Cash ($ mil.): 14
Current ratio: 1.20
Long-term debt ($ mil.): —

Dividends
Yield: —
Payout: —
Market value ($ mil.): —

BOB ROSS BUICK INC.

The Bob Ross Dealerships sells new and used cars made by Buick GMC and Mercedes Benz at in Centerville Ohio. Bob Ross also provides financing parts service and collision repair. The company's bobrossauto.com Web site allows customers to search new and used inventory as well as schedule service order parts and apply for financing. Bob Ross ranks near the top of many categories (Buick sales customer satisfaction GMC truck sales) for Buick dealerships in Ohio. The company was founded in 1979 by the late Bob Ross Sr. and his wife president and CEO Norma Ross (daughter Jenell is owner). It was the first African-American owned Mercedes-Benz dealership in the world.

EXECUTIVES

President and CEO, Norma Ross
VP and Dealer Principal, Jenell Ross
Controller and Secretary, Linda Carter

LOCATIONS

HQ: BOB ROSS BUICK INC.
85 LOOP RD, DAYTON, OH 45459-2199
Phone: 937-433-0990
Web: www.bobrossbuick.com

COMPETITORS

AutoNation	Penske Automotive
CarMax	Group
Columbus Fair Auto Auction	Ricart Automotive
	Serra Automotive
Germain Motor	Sonic Automotive
Jeff Wyler Automotive	Spitzer

March/Hodge
Martin Management
Group

Sterling Autobody

HISTORICAL FINANCIALS

Company Type: Private

Income Statement

	REVENUE ($ mil.)	NET INCOME ($ mil.)	NET PROFIT MARGIN	EMPLOYEES
12/11	48	0	1.0%	89
12/10	49	1	2.2%	0
12/09	45	0	0.7%	0
12/08	54	(1)	—	0
Annual Growth	(3.8%)	—	—	—

FYE: December 31

2011 Year-End Financials

Debt ratio: ——
Return on equity: 1.00%
Cash ($ mil.): 0
Current ratio: 0.10
Long-term debt ($ mil.): —

Dividends
Yield: —
Payout: —
Market value ($ mil.): —

BODDIE-NOELL ENTERPRISES INC.

Boddie-Noell Enterprises (BNE) is a hearty competitor in the fast-food business. The company is one of the largest franchise operators of Hardee's a fast-food chain owned by CKE Restaurants with about 340 locations in four southeastern states. BNE also operates 10 Moe's Southwest Grill quick-Mex units franchised from FOCUS Brands. In addition the company owns restaurant concepts such as the Cafe Carolina & Bakery and The Highway Diner. BNE is also involved in real estate development through BNE Land & Development. The family-owned company was started in 1962 by Carleton Noell and his nephews Nick and Mayo Boddie.

The company also owns the Texas Steakhouse & Saloon concept but it is selling that operation to CB Holding owner of Charlie Brown's Steakhouse. CB Holding is using the purchase to add nearly 20 Texas Steakhouse locations in three states to its existing portfolio of 20 steakhouse restaurants in New Jersey New York and Pennsylvania. There are currently 10 Texas Steakhouse locations in North Carolina five in Virginia and four in West Virginia. Charlie Brown's will continue to operate the restaurants as Texas Steakhouse and plans to grow the concept throughout the region.

EXECUTIVES

Senior Chairman, Mayo Boddie Sr., age 82
President and CEO, William L. (Bill) Boddie, age 58
President Restaurant Operations, Mike Boddie, age 55
VP Purchasing and Product Development, Tim Lane
Director Corporate Accounting, Debra Baker White
SVP and CFO, Craig Worthy
VP and Corporate Controller, Dave Schmitt
SVP Human Resources, Robert Crumley
SVP and Chief Marketing Officer, Jerry Allsbrook
Vice Chairman, Nick B. Boddie

EVP Restaurant Development, Michael (Mike) Hancock
President BNE Land and Development, Doug Anderson
VP Information Services, Bob Larimar
Director of Operations, Don Mack
vice Chairman Chief Administrative Officer of Boddie-Noell, James H. Waters
Auditors: Ernst&YoungLLP

LOCATIONS

HQ: Boddie-Noell Enterprises Inc.
1021 Noell Ln., Rocky Mount NC 27804
Phone: 252-937-2800   **Fax:** 252-937-2978
Web: www.bneinc.com

PRODUCTS/OPERATIONS

Selected Operations
Restaurants
Cafe Carolina and Bakery
Hardee's
Highway Diner
Moe's Southwest Grill
Texas Steakhouse
Other
BNE Land & Development (commercial and resort real estate development)
Rose Hill Conference Center (Rocky Mount NC)

COMPETITORS

Biglari Holdings
Bojangles'
Burger King
Carolina Restaurant
 Group
Carrols

Chick-fil-A
DavCo Restaurants
McDonald' s
Sonic Corp.
Wendy' s
YUM!

HISTORICAL FINANCIALS
Company Type: Private

Income Statement				FYE: December 26
	REVENUE ($ mil.)	NET INCOME ($ mil.)	NET PROFIT MARGIN	EMPLOYEES
12/11	395	(9)	—	13,000
12/10	389	(49)	—	0
12/09	388	(6)	—	0
12/08	401	(26)	—	0
Annual Growth	(0.5%)	—	—	—

2011 Year-End Financials
Debt ratio: ——
Return on equity: (-2.40)%
Cash ($ mil.): 22
Current ratio: 0.50
Long-term debt ($ mil.): —

Dividends
Yield: —
Payout: —
Market value ($ mil.): —

BOGOPA ENTERPRISES INC.

LOCATIONS

HQ: BOGOPA ENTERPRISES INC.
650 FOUNTAIN AVE, BROOKLYN, NY 11208-5306
Phone: 718-346-6500

HISTORICAL FINANCIALS
Company Type: Private

Income Statement				FYE: December 31
	REVENUE ($ mil.)	NET INCOME ($ mil.)	NET PROFIT MARGIN	EMPLOYEES
12/11	452	10	2.4%	1,200
12/10	312	6	2.1%	0
12/06	294	6	2.1%	0
12/04	39	(0)	—	0
Annual Growth	124.9%	—	—	—

2011 Year-End Financials
Debt ratio:
Return on equity: 2.40%
Cash ($ mil.): 5
Current ratio: 0.20
Long-term debt ($ mil.): —

Dividends
Yield:
Payout:
Market value ($ mil.): —

BOLTON OIL CO LTD

LOCATIONS

HQ: BOLTON OIL CO LTD
1316 54TH ST, LUBBOCK, TX 79412-3206
Phone: 806-747-1629
Web: www.boltonoil.com

HISTORICAL FINANCIALS
Company Type: Private

Income Statement				FYE: December 31
	REVENUE ($ mil.)	NET INCOME ($ mil.)	NET PROFIT MARGIN	EMPLOYEES
12/11	80	(0)	—	60
12/10	66	1	2.5%	0
12/09	58	0	0.6%	0
12/08	0	0	—	0
Annual Growth	—	—	—	—

2011 Year-End Financials
Debt ratio: ——
Return on equity: (-0.70)%
Cash ($ mil.): 0
Current ratio: 0.70
Long-term debt ($ mil.): —

Dividends
Yield: —
Payout: —
Market value ($ mil.): —

BON SECOURS HOSPITAL BALTIMORE INC.

LOCATIONS

HQ: BON SECOURS HOSPITAL BALTIMORE INC.
2000 W BALTIMORE ST, BALTIMORE, MD 21223-1558
Phone: 410-362-3000
Web: www.bonsecoursbaltimore.com

HISTORICAL FINANCIALS
Company Type: Private

Income Statement				FYE: August 31
	REVENUE ($ mil.)	NET INCOME ($ mil.)	NET PROFIT MARGIN	EMPLOYEES
08/11	140	3	2.2%	1,120
08/10	137	1	1.0%	0
08/09*	126	(10)	—	0
06/09	116	(13)	—	0
Annual Growth	6.3%	—	—	—

*Fiscal year change

2011 Year-End Financials
Debt ratio: ——
Return on equity: 2.20%
Cash ($ mil.): 0
Current ratio: 1.40
Long-term debt ($ mil.): —

Dividends
Yield: —
Payout: —
Market value ($ mil.): —

BONITZ FLOORING GROUP INC.

LOCATIONS

HQ: BONITZ FLOORING GROUP INC.
645 ROSEWOOD DR, COLUMBIA, SC 29201-4699
Phone: 803-799-0181
Web: www.bonitz.com

HISTORICAL FINANCIALS
Company Type: Private

Income Statement				FYE: December 31
	REVENUE ($ mil.)	NET INCOME ($ mil.)	NET PROFIT MARGIN	EMPLOYEES
12/11	126	6	5.4%	178
12/02	0	0	—	0
12/01	0	0	—	0
Annual Growth	—	—	—	—

2011 Year-End Financials
Debt ratio: ——
Return on equity: 5.40%
Cash ($ mil.): 28
Current ratio: 3.40
Long-term debt ($ mil.): —

Dividends
Yield: —
Payout: —
Market value ($ mil.): —

BONITZ INC.

Bonitz is a veteran US acoustical ceiling and drywall contractor. Founded by chairman Bill Rogers in 1954 the company got a humble start in South Carolina and has grown to operate in more than a dozen US locations primarily in the Southeast including Alabama Colorado Georgia Tennessee Virginia and the Carolinas. Through its operating divisions Bonitz also offers commercial and residential flooring contracting roofing contracting and manufacturing of prefabricated light gage metal wall panels and trusses for educational institutional and commercial buildings. Its clients include architects interior designers general contractors and building owners. Bonitz is employee owned.

EXECUTIVES

Chairman, George W. (Bill) Rogers
President, Tom Edens
Manager Access Flooring, Andy Miarka
Manager Raleigh, Justin Douglas
Sales and Estimating Charleston, Anna De Wein
Manager Charleston, Teddy Sykes
Safety Manager, Doug Beard
SVP Contracting, Rhett Seel
VP Human Resources, Phyllis Barnhardt
VP Bonitz Contracting, Paul Justice
President and CEO Bonitz Flooring Group, Harold Chapman
Manager Information Systems, Jay Anderson

LOCATIONS

HQ: Bonitz Inc.
645 Rosewood Dr., Columbia SC 29201-4603
Phone: 803-799-0181   **Fax:** 803-748-9223
Web: www.bonitz.us

PRODUCTS/OPERATIONS

Selected Products
Contracting
  Access floors
  Acoustical ceilings and walls
  Contamination and cleanroom products
  Metal framing and drywall partitions
  Movable wall systems
  Surfacing
Flooring
  Access floors
  Church interiors and flooring
  Coatings
  Commercial flooring
  Maintenance
  Renovation and replacement
  Residential flooring
  Specialty flooring
Manufacturing
  Load-bearing panels
  Masonry support panels
  Synthetic stucco panels
  TrusSteel steel trusses
Roofing
  Insulating concrete
  Metal roof decks
  Precast gypsum plank
  Steel edge concrete plank
  Wood fiber plank

COMPETITORS

Acousti Engineering	Pickens Roofing
Acoustics Incorporated	
Performance	
Contracting	

HISTORICAL FINANCIALS

Company Type: Private

Income Statement

FYE: December 31

	REVENUE ($ mil.)	NET INCOME ($ mil.)	NET PROFIT MARGIN	EMPLOYEES
12/11	126	6	5.4%	850
12/10	139	1	1.1%	0
12/09	154	3	2.2%	0
12/08	192	8	4.4%	0
Annual Growth	(13.1%)	(7.1%)	—	—

2011 Year-End Financials

Debt ratio: ——
Return on equity: 5.40%
Cash ($ mil.): 28
Current ratio: 3.40
Long-term debt ($ mil.): —

Dividends
  Yield: —
  Payout: —
  Market value ($ mil.): —

BOSSIER PARISH SCHOOL BOARD INC

LOCATIONS

HQ: BOSSIER PARISH SCHOOL BOARD INC
316 SIBLEY ST, BENTON, LA 71006-8351
Phone: 318-549-5000
Web: www.bentonhighschool.com

HISTORICAL FINANCIALS

Company Type: Private

Income Statement

FYE: June 30

	REVENUE ($ mil.)	NET INCOME ($ mil.)	NET PROFIT MARGIN	EMPLOYEES
06/11	222	(17)	—	2,300
06/07	177	1	0.7%	0
06/06	161	21	13.4%	0
06/05	0	0		0
Annual Growth	—	—	—	—

2011 Year-End Financials

Debt ratio: ——
Return on equity: (-7.70)%
Cash ($ mil.): 35
Current ratio: ——
Long-term debt ($ mil.): —

Dividends
  Yield: —
  Payout: —
  Market value ($ mil.): —

BOSTON FOUNDATION INC.

LOCATIONS

HQ: BOSTON FOUNDATION INC.
75 ARLINGTON ST FL 10, BOSTON, MA 02116-3992
Phone: 617-338-1700
Web: www.tbf.org

HISTORICAL FINANCIALS

Company Type: Private

Income Statement

FYE: June 30

	REVENUE ($ mil.)	NET INCOME ($ mil.)	NET PROFIT MARGIN	EMPLOYEES
06/11	88	(1)	—	64
06/10	87	(4)	—	0
06/09	67	0	—	0
06/08	130	35	27.3%	0
Annual Growth	(12.2%)	—	—	—

2011 Year-End Financials

Debt ratio: ——
Return on equity: (-1.20)%
Cash ($ mil.): 24
Current ratio: 2.50
Long-term debt ($ mil.): —

Dividends
  Yield: —
  Payout: —
  Market value ($ mil.): —

BOSTON SYMPHONY ORCHESTRA INC.

If you want to venture out for some live music but are not in the mood for rock or pop then a performance by The Boston Symphony Orchestra (BSO) might strike the right chord with you. Featuring compositions by composers like Beethoven Mozart and Stravinsky the BSO performs more than 100 concerts during the regular season at Symphony Hall. The BSO also performs during the summer at the Tanglewood music center; other BSO-related performances are given by the smaller and lighter Boston Pops orchestra. One of the more prominent orchestras in the US the BSO was founded in 1881 by businessman Henry Lee Higginson. Current music director James Levine is the BSO's first America-born conductor.

EXECUTIVES

Managing Director Eunice and Julian Cohen Managing Directorship, Mark Volpe
Conductor Boston Pops, Keith Lockhart
Director Public Relations, Bernadette M. Horgan
CFO, Thomas D. May
Artistic Administrator, Anthony Fogg
Director Human Resources, Marion Gardner-Saxe
Director Tanglewood Music Center, Ellen Highstein
Director Sales Marketing and Communications, Kim Noltemy
Development Director Campaign and Individual Giving, Elizabeth P. Roberts
Orchestra Manager, Ray F. Wellbaum
Development Director Institutional and Special Event Fundraising and Administration, Bart Reidy
Director Information Technology, Timothy James

LOCATIONS

HQ: The Boston Symphony Orchestra Inc.
Symphony Hall 301 Massachusetts Ave., Boston MA 02115
Phone: 617-266-1492   **Fax:** 202-393-1025
Web: www.nawj.org

HISTORICAL FINANCIALS
Company Type: Private - Not-for-Profit

Income Statement
FYE: August 31

	REVENUE ($ mil.)	NET INCOME ($ mil.)	NET PROFIT MARGIN	EMPLOYEES
08/11	38	41	109.1%	350
08/10	39	12	32.1%	0
08/09	43	(75)	—	0
08/08	43	142	325.2%	0
Annual Growth	(4.3%)	(33.5%)	—	—

2011 Year-End Financials
Debt ratio: —
Return on equity: 109.10%
Cash ($ mil.): 22
Current ratio: 0.40
Long-term debt ($ mil.): —
Dividends
Yield: —
Payout: —
Market value ($ mil.): —

BOWDEN OIL COMPANY INC.

LOCATIONS
HQ: BOWDEN OIL COMPANY INC.
40865 US HIGHWAY 280, SYLACAUGA, AL 35150-6837
Phone: 256-245-5611
Web: www.bowdenoil.com

HISTORICAL FINANCIALS
Company Type: Private

Income Statement
FYE: December 31

	REVENUE ($ mil.)	NET INCOME ($ mil.)	NET PROFIT MARGIN	EMPLOYEES
12/11	103	0	0.1%	130
12/10	84	0	0.2%	0
12/09	70	0	0.0%	0
12/08	102	0	0.3%	0
Annual Growth	0.3%	(27.0%)	—	—

2011 Year-End Financials
Debt ratio: —
Return on equity: 0.10%
Cash ($ mil.): 3
Current ratio: 2.10
Long-term debt ($ mil.): —
Dividends
Yield: —
Payout: —
Market value ($ mil.): —

BOY SCOUTS OF AMERICA

Scouts enter dens as Tigers and eventually take flight as Eagles. Boy Scouts of America (BSA) one of the nation's largest youth organizations has about 2.8 million youth members and about 1 million adult leaders in its ranks. BSA offers educational and character-building programs emphasizing leadership citizenship personal development and physical fitness. In addition to traditional scouting programs (Tiger Cub Webelos and Boy Scouts ranging up to Eagle rank) it offers the Venturing program for boys and girls ages 14-21. BSA generates revenue through membership and council fees supply and magazine sales and contributions. The organization was founded by Chicago publisher William Boyce in 1910.

Operations

BSA's group membership is supported through 300 local Boy Scout councils. Additionally it hosts a National Scout Jamboree each year to bring all scouts together. The organization also operates a high-adventure base in West Virginia. The bases offer scouts a range of outdoor activities including backpacking camping canoeing and diving. The West Virginia location serves as the organization's permanent location for its Jamboree. BSA operates also bases in Florida Minnesota and New Mexico.

BSA also publishes Boys' Life monthly magazine which boasts more than 1 million subscribers and Scouting magazine for adults registered in Cub Scouting Boy Scouting Varsity Scouting and Venturing.

Financial Analysis

BSA's revenue in 2011 declined 35% vs. 2010. The steep drop off resulted from a drop off in fees (48% of total revenue) primarily due to the 2010 National Scout Jamboree partially offset by fees from the world jamboree and an increase in high-adventure base fees. Membership revenue increased in 2011 due to a membership fee increase offset by a small decline in membership. Revenue from Supply operations fell as did proceeds from magazine publications. Contributions and bequests declined as well in 2011 vs. 2010.

Strategy

BSA boasts programs that remain popular but in recent years membership growth has slowed with the recession and other societal forces. Indeed the group competes with popular gaming devices such as the Nintendo's Wii system for the attention of young boys through its more-wholesome outdoor and community activities.

In 2011 Cub Scout membership (which accounts for more than 50% of total youth membership) dipped by about 1% vs. 2010 while the ranks of the Boy Scouts grew by just over 1%. Overall total youth membership declined by less than 1% for the year continuing its downward trend. To boost membership and grow its organization BSA developed a strategic plan that involves reaching out to new groups of parents and students. To this end it has developed and maintained relationships with civic religious and fraternal organizations across the US including those that serve African-American Asian and Latino families. It has also analyzed Generation X and Millennial parents to determine how to best bring scouting to their communities.

EXECUTIVES
Assistant Treasurer, R. Thomas (Tom) Buffenbarger, age 61
VP, Drayton McLane Jr., age 76
VP, Richard L. (Rick) Burdick
VP, Henry A. Rosenberg Jr.
VP, Earl G. Graves Sr., age 77
VP Supply, O. Temple Sloan Jr., age 73
National President, Rex W. Tillerson, age 59
Treasurer, Aubrey B. Harwell Jr., age 69
Group Director Supply, Michael (Mike) Ashline
National Commissioner, Tico A. Perez
VP, Donald D. Belcher
VP Council Solutions, Terrence P. (Terry) Dunn
International Commissioner, James S. Turley
International Commissioner, Wayne Perry
VP Marketing, Nathan O. Rosenberg
CFO and Assistant Chief Scout Executive, Jim Terry
Chief Scout Executive, Robert J. (Bob) Mazzuca
VP Outdoor Adventures, Jack Furst
VP Finance, Randall Stephenson
Chief Scout Executive, Wayne Brock
Group Director Innovation and Strategy, Fred Meijering
Group Director Marketing, Stephen Medlicott
Group Director Outdoor Adventures, John Green
Assistant Chief Scout Executive?Council Operations, Gary P. Butler
Group Director Administration, Nate Langston
Group Director Human Resources, Al Morin
Legal, David Park
Team Leader Health and Safety, Richard Bourlon
Scout Executive Great Lakes Council, John Reesor
Media Contact, David L. Harkins
VP Human Resources, Lyle R. Knight
CFO, Alf Tuggle
Chief Scout Executive - Development, Bradley D. Farmer
Auditors: PricewaterhouseCoopersLLP

LOCATIONS
HQ: Boy Scouts of America
1325 W. Walnut Hill Ln., Irving TX 75015
Phone: 972-580-2000   **Fax:** 972-580-7870
Web: www.scouting.org

PRODUCTS/OPERATIONS

2011 Youth Membership

	No.
Cub	1,583,166
Boy	848,291
Venturers	231,127
Explorers	112,783
Varsity	61,285
Total	**2,836,652**

2011 Revenue

	$ mil.	% of total
Fees	96	48
Supply operations	24	12
Magazines	1	1
Contributions & bequests	61	30
Net investment gain	8	4
Other (includes trading post sales)	9	5
Total	**201**	**100**

HISTORICAL FINANCIALS
Company Type: Private - Not-for-Profit

Income Statement
FYE: December 31

	REVENUE ($ mil.)	NET INCOME ($ mil.)	NET PROFIT MARGIN	EMPLOYEES
12/11	201	(2)	—	50
12/09	0	(0)	—	0
12/02	4	(1)	—	0
12/01	5	16	280.1%	0
Annual Growth	225.3%	—	—	—

2011 Year-End Financials
Debt ratio: —
Return on equity: (-1.10)%
Cash ($ mil.): 73
Current ratio: —
Long-term debt ($ mil.): —
Dividends
Yield: —
Payout: —
Market value ($ mil.): —

BOY SCOUTS OF AMERICA

Scouts enter dens as Tigers and eventually take flight as Eagles. Boy Scouts of America (BSA) one of the nation's largest youth organizations has about 2.8 million youth members and about 1 million adult leaders in its ranks. BSA offers educational and character-building programs emphasizing leadership citizenship personal development and physical fitness. In addition to traditional scouting programs (Tiger Cub Webelos and Boy Scouts ranging up to Eagle rank) it offers the Venturing program for boys and girls ages 14-21. BSA generates revenue through membership and council fees supply and magazine sales and contributions. The organization was founded by Chicago publisher William Boyce in 1910.

Operations

BSA's group membership is supported through 300 local Boy Scout councils. Additionally it hosts a National Scout Jamboree each year to bring all scouts together. The organization also operates a high-adventure base in West Virginia. The bases offer scouts a range of outdoor activities including backpacking camping canoeing and diving. The West Virginia location serves as the organization's permanent location for its Jamboree. BSA operates also bases in Florida Minnesota and New Mexico.

BSA also publishes Boys' Life monthly magazine which boasts more than 1 million subscribers and Scouting magazine for adults registered in Cub Scouting Boy Scouting Varsity Scouting and Venturing.

Financial Analysis

BSA's revenue in 2011 declined 35% vs. 2010. The steep drop off resulted from a drop off in fees (48% of total revenue) primarily due to the 2010 National Scout Jamboree partially offset by fees from the world jamboree and an increase in high-adventure base fees. Membership revenue increased in 2011 due to a membership fee increase offset by a small decline in membership. Revenue from Supply operations fell as did proceeds from magazine publications. Contributions and bequests declined as well in 2011 vs. 2010.

Strategy

BSA boasts programs that remain popular but in recent years membership growth has slowed with the recession and other societal forces. Indeed the group competes with popular gaming devices such as the Nintendo's Wii system for the attention of young boys through its more-wholesome outdoor and community activities.

In 2011 Cub Scout membership (which accounts for more than 50% of total youth membership) dipped by about 1% vs. 2010 while the ranks of the Boy Scouts grew by just over 1%. Overall total youth membership declined by less than 1% for the year continuing its downward trend. To boost membership and grow its organization BSA developed a strategic plan that involves reaching out to new groups of parents and students. To this end it has developed and maintained relationships with civic religious and fraternal organizations across the US including those that serve African-American Asian and Latino families. It has also analyzed Generation X and Millennial parents to determine how to best bring scouting to their communities.

EXECUTIVES

Assistant Treasurer, R. Thomas (Tom) Buffenbarger, age 61
VP, Drayton McLane Jr., age 76
VP, Richard L. (Rick) Burdick
VP, Henry A. Rosenberg Jr.
VP, Earl G. Graves Sr., age 77
VP Supply, O. Temple Sloan Jr., age 73
National President, Rex W. Tillerson, age 59
Treasurer, Aubrey B. Harwell Jr., age 69
Group Director Supply, Michael (Mike) Ashline
National Commissioner, Tico A. Perez
VP, Donald D. Belcher
VP Council Solutions, Terrence P. (Terry) Dunn
International Commissioner, James S. Turley
International Commissioner, Wayne Perry
VP Marketing, Nathan O. Rosenberg
CFO and Assistant Chief Scout Executive, Jim Terry
Chief Scout Executive, Robert J. (Bob) Mazzuca
VP Outdoor Adventures, Jack Furst
VP Finance, Randall Stephenson
Chief Scout Executive, Wayne Brock
Group Director Innovation and Strategy, Fred Meijering
Group Director Marketing, Stephen Medlicott
Group Director Outdoor Adventures, John Green
Assistant Chief Scout Executive?Council Operations, Gary P. Butler
Group Director Administration, Nate Langston
Group Director Human Resources, Al Morin
Legal, David Park
Team Leader Health and Safety, Richard Bourlon
Scout Executive Great Lakes Council, John Reesor
Media Contact, David L. Harkins
VP Human Resources, Lyle R. Knight
CFO, Alf Tuggle
Chief Scout Executive - Development, Bradley D. Farmer
Auditors: PricewaterhouseCoopersLLP

LOCATIONS

HQ: Boy Scouts of America
1325 W. Walnut Hill Ln., Irving TX 75015
Phone: 972-580-2000   **Fax:** 972-580-7870
Web: www.scouting.org

PRODUCTS/OPERATIONS

2011 Youth Membership

	No.
Cub	1,583,166
Boy	848,291
Venturers	231,127
Explorers	112,783
Varsity	61,285
Total	**2,836,652**

2011 Revenue

	$ mil.	% of total
Fees	96	48
Supply operations	24	12
Magazines	1	1
Contributions & bequests	61	30
Net investment gain	8	4
Other (includes trading post sales)	9	5
Total	**201**	**100**

HISTORICAL FINANCIALS
Company Type: Private - Not-for-Profit

Income Statement
FYE: December 31

	REVENUE ($ mil.)	NET INCOME ($ mil.)	NET PROFIT MARGIN	EMPLOYEES
12/11	201	(2)	—	2,800
12/10	310	90	29.0%	0
12/09	287	145	50.5%	0
12/08	302	39	12.9%	0
Annual Growth	**(12.7%)**	—	—	—

2011 Year-End Financials

Debt ratio: —
Return on equity: (-1.10)%
Cash ($ mil.): 73
Current ratio: 0.30
Long-term debt ($ mil.): —

Dividends
Yield: —
Payout: —
Market value ($ mil.): —

BOYER'S FOOD MARKETS INC.

LOCATIONS

HQ: BOYER' S FOOD MARKETS INC.
301 S WARREN ST, ORWIGSBURG, PA 17961-2119
Phone: 570-366-1477
Web: www.boyersfood.com

HISTORICAL FINANCIALS
Company Type: Private

Income Statement
FYE: December 31

	REVENUE ($ mil.)	NET INCOME ($ mil.)	NET PROFIT MARGIN	EMPLOYEES
12/11	120	1	1.0%	900
12/10	0	0	—	0
12/09	112	1	1.2%	0
12/08	116	1	1.2%	0
Annual Growth	**1.2%**	**(3.4%)**	—	—

2011 Year-End Financials

Debt ratio: —
Return on equity: 1.00%
Cash ($ mil.): 2
Current ratio: 0.40
Long-term debt ($ mil.): —

Dividends
Yield: —
Payout: —
Market value ($ mil.): —

BRAD LANIER OIL CO. INC.

LOCATIONS

HQ: BRAD LANIER OIL CO. INC.
611 W ROOSEVELT AVE, ALBANY, GA 31701-2150
Phone: 229-436-0131

HISTORICAL FINANCIALS

Company Type: Private

Income Statement — FYE: February 29

	REVENUE ($ mil.)	NET INCOME ($ mil.)	NET PROFIT MARGIN	EMPLOYEES
02/12	127	(0)	—	85
02/11	97	(0)	—	0
02/10	77	(0)	—	0
02/09	110	0	0.1%	0
Annual Growth	4.9%	—	—	—

2012 Year-End Financials

Debt ratio: —
Return on equity: (-0.20)%
Cash ($ mil.): 0
Current ratio: —
Long-term debt ($ mil.): —

Dividends
Yield: —
Payout: —
Market value ($ mil.): —

BRADLEY UNIVERSITY

Bradley University is a private university offering a wide breadth of higher education opportunites. The school provides 100 undergraduate programs in fields ranging from art science and education to business media and health. Bradley also confers graduate degrees in more than 30 academic fields including a Doctorate of Physical Therapy. With a student-to-teacher ratio of 12:1 the university has an enrollment of approximately 6000 students —more than 5000 of whom are undergraduates - that receive instruction from some 350 full-time faculty members.

Operations

Bradley offers courses through five colleges: Foster College of Business Administration Slane College of Communications and Fine Arts College of Education and Health Sciences Caterpillar College of Engineering and Technology and College of Liberal Arts and Sciences. The university has a 90% success rate for students who start careers or pursue additional degrees within six months of graduation.

Financial Performance

Bradley University increased revenues by 7% to $152 million in fiscal 2011 from increased tuition and fees as well as higher levels of government grants and appropriations. Tuition runs at about $28000 per year. Net income also increased 17% to $36 million in 2011 due to higher investment income.

Bradley has an endowment of some $237 million (as of mid-2012).

Company Background

The university was founded in 1897 as Bradley Polytechnic Institute by Lydia Moss Bradley as a memorial to her children and husband.

EXECUTIVES

Chairman Board of Trustees, Gerald L. (Gerry) Shaheen, age 67
President and Trustee, Joanne K. Glasser
Controller, Pratima N. Gandhi
VP Business Affairs, Gary M. Anna
Secretary Board of Trustees, Kay W. McCurdy, age 61
Dean College of Liberal Arts and Sciences, Claire Etaugh
Director Athletic Development, Richard D. (Rick) Gaa
Manager Bookstore, Paul Kroenke
Dean Foster College of Business Administration, Robert (Rob) Baer
Associate Dean Foster College of Business Administration and Economics, Edward L. Sattler
Executive Director Smith Career Center, Jane C. Linnenburger
Director Career Development, Rick R. Smith
Executive Director Cullom-Davis Library, Barbara A. Galik
Director Human Resources, Nena M. Peplow
Senior Director Public Relations, M. Kathleen (Kath) Conver
Director Pre-Law Center, Maria L. Vertuno
Interim Provost and VP Academic Affairs, Robert (Bob) Bolla
VP Student Affairs, Alan G. Galsky
VP Advancement, Pat Vickerman
Assistant VP Communications, Shelley Epstein
Interim Athletic Director, Virnette House-Browning
Director Admissions, Rodney San Jose
Director Residential Living, Ryan Bair
Chief University Police, David A. Baer
Director Facilities Management, Ronald Doerzaph
Director Food Services, Ron Gibson
Registrar, Katherine M. Beaty
Director Employer Relations, Kelly Harris
Purchasing Accounts Administrator, Diane Smith
Vice Chairman Board of Trustees, Michael A. McCord
Assistant Athletic Director/Communications, Bobby Parker
Benefit Administrator, Dayna Fico
Director Conference Facilities, Charmin Hibberd
Director Student Center Operations, Pegi Meyer
Executive Director Alumni Relations, Lori W. Fan
Associate Provost Information Resources and Technology, Chuck Ruch
Executive Director Computing Services, Sandra H. Bury
Executive Director Instructional Technology and Media Services, Nial L. Johnson
Trustee, Robert J. (Bob) Clanin, age 68
Trustee, Rajesh K. (Raj) Soin, age 64
Trustee, Judson C. Mitchell
President and Trustee, Joanne K. Glasser
Trustee, David P. (Dave) Ransburg
Secretary Board of Trustees, Kay W. McCurdy, age 61
Trustee, Rex K. Linder
Trustee, Robert E. Turner
Vice Chairman Board of Trustees, Michael A. McCord
Trustee, Keith L. Alm
Trustee, Wayne E. Baum
Trustee, Carl M. Birkelbach
Trustee, Cheryl D. Corley
Trustee, Michael N. Cullinan
Trustee, Georgina E. Heard-Labonne
Trustee, William P. Heidrich
Trustee, Joan L. Janssen
Trustee, Wayne G. Klasing
Trustee, Michael A. Landwirth
Trustee, Harry L. Puterbaugh
Trustee, Michele J. Richey

Trustee, Mel J. Smith
Trustee, Thomas E. Spurgeon
Trustee, Douglas S. Stewart
Trustee, Donald L. Ullman
Trustee, W. Philip Wilmington
Auditors: PricewaterhouseCoopersLLP

LOCATIONS

HQ: Bradley University
1501 W. Bradley Ave., Peoria IL 61625
Phone: 309-676-7611 **Fax:** 309-677-2797
Web: www.bradley.edu

PRODUCTS/OPERATIONS

Selected Colleges

Caterpillar College of Engineering and Technology
College of Education and Health Sciences
College of Liberal Arts and Sciences
Foster College of Business Administration
Slane College of Communications and Fine Arts

HISTORICAL FINANCIALS

Company Type: School

Income Statement — FYE: May 31

	REVENUE ($ mil.)	NET INCOME ($ mil.)	NET PROFIT MARGIN	EMPLOYEES
05/12	155	(18)	—	1,000
05/11	151	36	23.8%	0
05/10	141	30	21.8%	0
05/09	139	(63)	—	0
Annual Growth	3.6%	—	—	—

2012 Year-End Financials

Debt ratio: —
Return on equity: (-11.90)%
Cash ($ mil.): 1
Current ratio: —
Long-term debt ($ mil.): —

Dividends
Yield: —
Payout: —
Market value ($ mil.): —

BRAHMA GROUP INC.

LOCATIONS

HQ: BRAHMA GROUP INC.
1132 S 500 W, SALT LAKE CITY, UT 84101-3018
Phone: 801-521-5200
Web: www.brahmagroupinc.com

HISTORICAL FINANCIALS

Company Type: Private

Income Statement — FYE: October 31

	REVENUE ($ mil.)	NET INCOME ($ mil.)	NET PROFIT MARGIN	EMPLOYEES
10/11	81	2	2.7%	400
10/10	55	0	0.5%	0
10/09	62	0	1.2%	0
10/08	72	2	3.3%	0
Annual Growth	4.3%	(2.5%)	—	—

2011 Year-End Financials

Debt ratio: —
Return on equity: 2.70%
Cash ($ mil.): 0
Current ratio: 1.30
Long-term debt ($ mil.): —

Dividends
Yield: —
Payout: —
Market value ($ mil.): —

BRAINERD PUBLIC SCHOOLS

LOCATIONS

HQ: BRAINERD PUBLIC SCHOOLS
804 OAK ST, BRAINERD, MN 56401-3755
Phone: 218-454-6900

HISTORICAL FINANCIALS

Company Type: Private

Income Statement			FYE: June 30
	REVENUE ($ mil.)	NET INCOME ($ mil.)	NET PROFIT MARGIN	EMPLOYEES
06/11	85	(1)	—	25
06/10	83	5	6.1%	0
06/09	83	5	6.1%	0
06/08	83	2	3.0%	0
Annual Growth	1.1%	—	—	—

BRANCH & ASSOCIATES INC.

Branch & Associates is no twig in the Branch Group family tree. The employee-owned subsidiary offers general contracting design/build and construction management services for commercial and industrial construction projects in the Carolinas Tennessee Virginia and West Virginia. The company builds retail health care educational multi-unit residential government hospitality and industrial facilities. Billy Branch founded the company in 1963. It was reorganized and became Branch Associates under the Branch Group in 1985. Other Branch Group subsidiaries include Branch Highways E.V. Williams and G.J. Hopkins.

The Branch Group expanded into northern Virginia in 2007 by acquiring general contractor R.E. Daffan. The general contractor and construction management firm focuses on building projects in and around Manassas Virginia.

Branch & Associates' projects include construction of exhibition space at the Roanoke Civic Center Complex in Virginia and renovations and additions at Ferrum College in Ferrum Virginia the Central Academy of Technology & Arts in Monroe North Carolina and residence halls at Virginia Tech. Other projects include a Volvo Assembly plant an EchoStar call center and a lodge at Snowshoe Mountain Resort.

EXECUTIVES

President, Stephen Aud
VP; Business Development Virginia, Lawrence Dickenson
VP Estimating, Tony Brown
Director of Operations, Michael Quinn
Business Development North Carolina, Mike Undseth

LOCATIONS

HQ: Branch & Associates Inc.
5732 Airport Rd. NW, Roanoke VA 24012
Phone: 540-989-5215   **Fax:** 540-989-0883
Web: www.branch-associates.com

COMPETITORS

Hitt	SMCI
KBS	W.M. Jordan
Parsons Brinckerhoff	

HISTORICAL FINANCIALS

Company Type: Subsidiary

Income Statement			FYE: December 31
	REVENUE ($ mil.)	NET INCOME ($ mil.)	NET PROFIT MARGIN	EMPLOYEES
12/11	108	0	—	90
12/10	90	0	—	0
Annual Growth	19.4%	—	—	—

2011 Year-End Financials

Debt ratio: —
Return on equity: —
Cash ($ mil.): 36
Current ratio: 1.50
Long-term debt ($ mil.): —
Dividends
Yield: —
Payout: —
Market value ($ mil.): —

BRANDENBURG INDUSTRIAL SERVICE COMPANY

LOCATIONS

HQ: BRANDENBURG INDUSTRIAL SERVICE COMPANY
2625 S LOOMIS ST, CHICAGO, IL 60608-5400
Phone: 630-956-7200
Web: www.brandenburg.com

HISTORICAL FINANCIALS

Company Type: Private

Income Statement			FYE: December 31
	REVENUE ($ mil.)	NET INCOME ($ mil.)	NET PROFIT MARGIN	EMPLOYEES
12/11	180	3	2.0%	750
12/08	211	12	5.8%	0
12/07	194	11	5.9%	0
12/06	136	5	3.7%	0
Annual Growth	9.6%	(10.9%)	—	—

2011 Year-End Financials

Debt ratio: —
Return on equity: 2.00%
Cash ($ mil.): 0
Current ratio: —
Long-term debt ($ mil.): —
Dividends
Yield: —
Payout: —
Market value ($ mil.): —

BRIDGEWATER-RARITAN REGIONAL SCHOOL DISTRICT

LOCATIONS

HQ: BRIDGEWATER-RARITAN REGIONAL SCHOOL DISTRICT
836 NEWMANS LN, BRIDGEWATER, NJ 08807
Phone: 908-685-2777

HISTORICAL FINANCIALS

Company Type: Private

Income Statement			FYE: June 30
	REVENUE ($ mil.)	NET INCOME ($ mil.)	NET PROFIT MARGIN	EMPLOYEES
06/11	145	2	1.6%	1,000
Annual Growth	—	—	—	—

2011 Year-End Financials

Debt ratio: —
Return on equity: 1.60%
Cash ($ mil.): 9
Current ratio: —
Long-term debt ($ mil.): —
Dividends
Yield: —
Payout: —
Market value ($ mil.): —

BRIGHAM YOUNG UNIVERSITY-IDAHO

LOCATIONS

HQ: BRIGHAM YOUNG UNIVERSITY-IDAHO
525 S CENTER ST, REXBURG, ID 83460-0004
Phone: 208-496-1144
Web: www.byui.edu

HISTORICAL FINANCIALS

Company Type: Private

Income Statement			FYE: December 31
	REVENUE ($ mil.)	NET INCOME ($ mil.)	NET PROFIT MARGIN	EMPLOYEES
12/11	208	(32)	—	2,129
12/10	0	0	—	0
12/09	0	0	—	0
12/08	203	99	48.9%	0
Annual Growth	0.7%	—	—	—

2011 Year-End Financials

Debt ratio: —
Return on equity: (-15.70)%
Cash ($ mil.): 17
Current ratio: —
Long-term debt ($ mil.): —
Dividends
Yield: —
Payout: —
Market value ($ mil.): —

BROADWAY AUTOMOTIVE - GREEN BAY INC.

LOCATIONS

HQ: BROADWAY AUTOMOTIVE - GREEN BAY INC.
2700 S ASHLAND AVE, GREEN BAY, WI 54304-5303
Phone: 920-498-6666
Web: www.broadwayautomotive.com

HISTORICAL FINANCIALS
Company Type: Private

Income Statement

FYE: December 31

	REVENUE ($ mil.)	NET INCOME ($ mil.)	NET PROFIT MARGIN	EMPLOYEES
12/11	85	1	1.6%	170
12/10	69	0	0.5%	0
12/07	71	1	2.2%	0
12/06	75	1	2.2%	0
Annual Growth	4.2%	(6.7%)	—	—

2011 Year-End Financials

Debt ratio: ——
Return on equity: 1.60%
Cash ($ mil.): 0
Current ratio: 0.20
Long-term debt ($ mil.): ——

Dividends
　Yield: —
　Payout: —
　Market value ($ mil.): —

BROADWAY FORD JEEP INC.

LOCATIONS

HQ: BROADWAY FORD JEEP INC.
1010 S MILITARY AVE, GREEN BAY, WI 54304-2117
Phone: 920-499-3131
Web: www.broadwayautomotive.com

HISTORICAL FINANCIALS
Company Type: Private

Income Statement

FYE: December 31

	REVENUE ($ mil.)	NET INCOME ($ mil.)	NET PROFIT MARGIN	EMPLOYEES
12/11	90	2	2.4%	110
12/10	76	0	1.2%	0
12/06	86	0	0.2%	0
12/05	76	(1)	—	0
Annual Growth	5.8%	—	—	—

2011 Year-End Financials

Debt ratio: ——
Return on equity: 2.40%
Cash ($ mil.): 0
Current ratio: 0.10
Long-term debt ($ mil.): ——

Dividends
　Yield: —
　Payout: —
　Market value ($ mil.): —

BROOKDALE COMMUNITY COLLEGE INC

LOCATIONS

HQ: BROOKDALE COMMUNITY COLLEGE INC
765 NEWMAN SPRINGS RD, LINCROFT, NJ 07738-1599
Phone: 732-842-1900
Web: www.wbjb.org

HISTORICAL FINANCIALS
Company Type: Private

Income Statement

FYE: June 30

	REVENUE ($ mil.)	NET INCOME ($ mil.)	NET PROFIT MARGIN	EMPLOYEES
06/11	85	3	4.1%	800
06/10	83	7	9.3%	0
06/09	0	0	—	0
06/06	52	4	8.5%	0
Annual Growth	17.1%	(7.9%)	—	—

2011 Year-End Financials

Debt ratio: ——
Return on equity: 4.10%
Cash ($ mil.): 24
Current ratio: 1.90
Long-term debt ($ mil.): ——

Dividends
　Yield: —
　Payout: —
　Market value ($ mil.): —

BROOKLYN LAW SCHOOL

LOCATIONS

HQ: BROOKLYN LAW SCHOOL
250 JORALEMON ST, BROOKLYN, NY 11201-3798
Phone: 718-625-2200

HISTORICAL FINANCIALS
Company Type: Private

Income Statement

FYE: June 30

	REVENUE ($ mil.)	NET INCOME ($ mil.)	NET PROFIT MARGIN	EMPLOYEES
06/11	80	5	6.8%	230
06/10	73	1	2.4%	0
06/09	63	0	—	0
06/08	69	9	13.1%	0
Annual Growth	5.4%	(15.3%)	—	—

2011 Year-End Financials

Debt ratio: ——
Return on equity: 6.80%
Cash ($ mil.): 7
Current ratio: ——
Long-term debt ($ mil.): ——

Dividends
　Yield: —
　Payout: —
　Market value ($ mil.): —

BROOKLYN PUBLIC LIBRARY

LOCATIONS

HQ: BROOKLYN PUBLIC LIBRARY
10 GRAND ARMY PLZ, BROOKLYN, NY 11238-5619
Phone: 718-230-2100
Web: www.brooklynpubliclibrary.org

HISTORICAL FINANCIALS
Company Type: Private

Income Statement

FYE: June 30

	REVENUE ($ mil.)	NET INCOME ($ mil.)	NET PROFIT MARGIN	EMPLOYEES
06/11	103	3	3.8%	1,700
06/10	105	(1)	—	0
06/09	105	(4)	—	0
06/08	110	7	7.0%	0
Annual Growth	(2.1%)	(20.0%)	—	—

2011 Year-End Financials

Debt ratio: ——
Return on equity: 3.80%
Cash ($ mil.): 55
Current ratio: 3.20
Long-term debt ($ mil.): ——

Dividends
　Yield: —
　Payout: —
　Market value ($ mil.): —

BROOKS TROPICALS HOLDING INC.

Brooks Tropicals offers exotic tastes with every bite. The company is a producer importer and supplier of tropical fruits and vegetables. Brooks product line consists of about 25 fruits and vegetables —some familiar some virtually unknown to American palates. They include avocados boniato calabaza chayote coconut ginger key lime kumquat lime malanga mamey sapote mango papaya Scotch bonnet pepper star fruit sugar cane and yuca. Brooks' produce is grown on its more than 6000 acres located in Florida as well as growing operations in Belize. The company was founded in 1928 by J.R. Brooks and is still owned and managed by his son and company president Neal (Pal) Brooks.

EXECUTIVES

President, Neal Palmer (Pal) Brooks
CEO, Craig Wheeling
VP Sales Management, Bill Brindle
VP Packaging Operations, Billy Pritchett
VP Tropicals Operations, Kevin Bryan
Director Marketing, Mary Ostlund
Director National Sales, Jose Rossignoli
Assistant to the CEO, Luis Laya
Controller, Janice Kolar
Manager Purchasing, William Brown
Assistant Controller, Marie Simard
Manager Avocado Production, Jeff Crawford

LOCATIONS

HQ: Brooks Tropicals Inc.
18400 SW 256th St., Homestead FL 33090
Phone: 305-247-3544 **Fax:** 305-246-5827
Web: www.brookstropicals.com

PRODUCTS/OPERATIONS

Selected Products

Aloe
Boniato
Calabaza
Chayote
Coconut
Eddo
Ginger
Guava
Keylime
Kumquat
Lime
Malanga
Mamey sapote
Mango
Papaya
Plantain
Scotch bonnet pepper
Star fruit
Sugar cane
Uniq fruit
Water coconut
Yam
Yuca

COMPETITORS

Calavo Growers	Pro-Fac
Chiquita Brands	River Ranch Fresh
Dole Food	Foods
Fresh Del Monte	Sun World
Produce	International
Jamaica Producers	Sunsweet Growers
Group	Tanimura & Antle
Naturipe Farms	

HISTORICAL FINANCIALS

Company Type: Private

Income Statement

FYE: December 31

	REVENUE ($ mil.)	NET INCOME ($ mil.)	NET PROFIT MARGIN	EMPLOYEES
12/11	51	3	7.2%	200
12/10	48	2	5.9%	0
12/09	42	(1)	—	0
12/08	44	(1)	—	0
Annual Growth	5.0%	—	—	—

2011 Year-End Financials

Debt ratio: ——
Return on equity: 7.20%
Cash ($ mil.): 7
Current ratio: 3.20
Long-term debt ($ mil.): ——

Dividends
  Yield: —
  Payout: —
Market value ($ mil.): —

BRUCKNER TRUCK SALES INC.

LOCATIONS

HQ: BRUCKNER TRUCK SALES INC.
9471 E INTERSTATE 40, AMARILLO, TX 79118-6960
Phone: 806-376-6273

HISTORICAL FINANCIALS

Company Type: Private

Income Statement

FYE: June 30

	REVENUE ($ mil.)	NET INCOME ($ mil.)	NET PROFIT MARGIN	EMPLOYEES
06/11	295	7	2.5%	550
06/10	200	2	1.1%	0
06/09	229	4	1.9%	0
06/08	325	6	2.0%	0
Annual Growth	(3.2%)	4.3%	—	—

2011 Year-End Financials

Debt ratio: ——
Return on equity: 2.50%
Cash ($ mil.): 18
Current ratio: 0.40
Long-term debt ($ mil.): —

Dividends
  Yield: —
  Payout: —
Market value ($ mil.): —

BRUNSWICK COUNTY BOARD OF EDUCATION

LOCATIONS

HQ: BRUNSWICK COUNTY BOARD OF EDUCATION
35 REFERENDUM DR NE, BOLIVIA, NC 28422-7578
Phone: 910-253-2900

HISTORICAL FINANCIALS

Company Type: Private

Income Statement

FYE: June 30

	REVENUE ($ mil.)	NET INCOME ($ mil.)	NET PROFIT MARGIN	EMPLOYEES
06/11	110	1	1.1%	1,500
06/09	109	2	2.1%	0
06/08	110	1	1.5%	0
06/07	0	0	—	0
Annual Growth	—	317.0%	—	—

2011 Year-End Financials

Debt ratio: ——
Return on equity: 1.10%
Cash ($ mil.): 17
Current ratio: —
Long-term debt ($ mil.): —

Dividends
  Yield: —
  Payout: —
Market value ($ mil.): —

BRUNSWICK ELECTRIC MEMBERSHIP CORPORATION

LOCATIONS

HQ: BRUNSWICK ELECTRIC MEMBERSHIP
CORPORATION
795 OCEAN HWY W, SUPPLY, NC 28462
Phone: 910-754-4391
Web: www.bemc.org

HISTORICAL FINANCIALS

Company Type: Private

Income Statement

FYE: December 31

	REVENUE ($ mil.)	NET INCOME ($ mil.)	NET PROFIT MARGIN	EMPLOYEES
12/11	156	6	4.1%	150
12/10	152	9	6.2%	0
12/09	143	7	4.9%	0
12/01	85	2	3.1%	0
Annual Growth	22.7%	34.0%	—	—

2011 Year-End Financials

Debt ratio: ——
Return on equity: 4.10%
Cash ($ mil.): 10
Current ratio: 1.00
Long-term debt ($ mil.): —

Dividends
  Yield: —
  Payout: —
Market value ($ mil.): —

BRYANT UNIVERSITY

LOCATIONS

HQ: BRYANT UNIVERSITY
1150 DOUGLAS PIKE, SMITHFIELD, RI 02917-1291
Phone: 401-232-6000
Web: www.bryantbulldogs.com

HISTORICAL FINANCIALS

Company Type: Private

Income Statement

FYE: June 30

	REVENUE ($ mil.)	NET INCOME ($ mil.)	NET PROFIT MARGIN	EMPLOYEES
06/12	129	(4)	—	575
06/11	159	(2)	—	0
06/10	158	5	3.4%	0
06/09	145	0	—	0
Annual Growth	(3.7%)	—	—	—

2012 Year-End Financials

Debt ratio: ——
Return on equity: (-3.50)%
Cash ($ mil.): 45
Current ratio: —
Long-term debt ($ mil.): —

Dividends
  Yield: —
  Payout: —
Market value ($ mil.): —

BRYN MAWR COLLEGE

These Mawrters aren't sacrificing anything especially when it comes to their education. Bryn Mawr is a college for women often referred to as Mawrters who hail from 60 countries. Its undergraduate programs including biology English math political science and psychology enroll 1300 students. Bryn Mawr also offers degrees through its co-educational Graduate School of Arts and Sciences and Graduate School of Social Work and Social Research which enrolls some 425 students. The college pools resources with Haverford Swarthmore and The University of Pennsylvania. Founded in 1885 Bryn Mawr is one of the nation's oldest women's colleges and the first to offer women an education through the Ph.D. level.

Geographic Reach

Located in Bryn Mawr Pennsylvania the college operates through a campus that consists of some 40 buildings.

Strategy

Bryn Mawr offers programs for 37 majors and 38 minors. Through its partnership with The University of Pennsylvania the college in 2012 launched a program that allows Bryn Mawr students who are majoring in math and science to earn a master's degree from The University of Pennsylvania's School of Engineering and Applied Science with one additional year of study. The college also added an International Studies major to its roster of major programs bringing its total to 37.

Sales and Marketing

Bryn Mawr sources its student population from about 45 US states and nearly 60 countries. About 33% of the university's students come from the Mid-Atlantic region. Another 45% arrive from other US regions while foreign countries account for the remaining 22% of Bryn Mawr's undergraduate student population. Additionally some 73% of its student body receives grant aid.

Financial Performance

The women's college reported revenue of more than $108 million in fiscal year 2012. Bryn Mawr generates revenue through tuition and fees private contributions government grants and a formula of endowment payout after spending.

EXECUTIVES

Chief Administrative Officer, Jerry Berenson
Director Human Resources, Joseph (Joe) Bucci
CIO and Director Constance A. Jones Libraries and Professor of History, Prof Elliott Shore
President, Jane Dammen McAuliffe
Director of Law and Social Policy Program, Raymond Albert
Director Development, Martha Dean
Executive Director Alumn? Association, Wendy Greenfield
Associate CIO Library and Equal Opportunity Officer, Florence Goff
Director Graduate School of Social Work and Social Research, Marcia Martin
Director Facilities Services, Glenn Smith
Dean Undergraduate College, Karen Tidmarsh
Director Career Development, Liza Jane Bernard
Director Library Collections and Symour Adelman Head of Special Collections, Eric Pumroy
Director Purchasing, Paul Vassallo
Provost, Kimberly E. Cassidy
Director Publications, Al Dorof
Interim Dean of the Graduate School of Arts and Sciences, Elizabeth McCormack

Chief Enrollment and Communications Officer, Jennifer Rickard
Controller, Betsy Stewart
Registrar, Kristen O'Beirne
Director Student Services, Mary Beth Horvath
CFO and Treasurer, John Griffith
Chief Development Officer, Donna Hooven Frithsen

LOCATIONS

HQ: Bryn Mawr College
101 N. Merion Ave., Bryn Mawr PA 19010-2899
Phone: 610-526-5000 **Fax:** 610-526-7471
Web: www.brynmawr.edu

PRODUCTS/OPERATIONS

Selected Graduate and Postbaccalaureate Programs

Graduate School of Arts and Sciences
Graduate School of Social Work and Social Research
Postbaccalaureate Premedical Program

HISTORICAL FINANCIALS
Company Type: School

Income Statement
FYE: May 31

	REVENUE ($ mil.)	NET INCOME ($ mil.)	NET PROFIT MARGIN	EMPLOYEES
05/12	108	(42)		777
05/11	163	23	14.3%	0
05/10	131	0	0.3%	0
05/09	116	0		0
Annual Growth	(2.5%)	—	—	—

2012 Year-End Financials

Debt ratio: —
Return on equity: (-38.90)%
Cash ($ mil.): 29
Current ratio: —
Long-term debt ($ mil.): —

Dividends
Yield: —
Payout: —
Market value ($ mil.): —

BUCHANAN TECHNOLOGIES INC.

CSSI The Support Group (which does business as Buchanan Associates) hopes that you come to associate it with good service. The company provides a variety of IT services such as consulting application development managed network services network design and implementation systems integration training and support. Buchanan Associates also resells and distributes a variety of computer hardware and software. Clients come from fields such as education electronics financial services government health care manufacturing retail and transportation. Jim Buchanan founded Buchanan Associates in 1988.

Geographic Reach

Buchanan Associates has operations in Canada London and the US.

Operations

Branded products include its ARIES Asset Management System. Buchanan Associates also offers automated testing systems and call tracking tools. To offer these products the company partners with companies such as Dell IBM Microsoft Peak 10 Oki and Cyrus One.

EXECUTIVES

President and CEO, James H. (Jim) Buchanan
CFO, Robert Venable
Regional VP, Sally Dixon
Regional VP; President Buchanan Associates Canada, Stephen Sweett
VP Automotive and Field Service Delivery, Roger Edwards

LOCATIONS

HQ: CSSI The Support Group Inc.
125 E. John Carpenter Fwy. Ste. 1200, Irving TX 76052
Phone: 972-869-3966 **Fax:** 972-869-3975
Web: www.buchanan.com

PRODUCTS/OPERATIONS

Selected Industries Served

Automotive
Education
Financial
Government
Healthcare
Non-Profit
Professional Services
Retail
Telecommunications
Transportation

Selected Products and Services

ARIES Asset Management System
Automated Testing System
Call Tracking System
Creative Web Design
Desktop Services
Enterprise Resource Planning (ERP)
IT Assessments and Planning
Messaging/Email
Near Shore Application Development
Network Services
Security
Service Desk Support Services
Software Development
Technology Lifecycle Management
Technology Migration/Upgrade and Transformation Services

COMPETITORS

Computer Sciences Corp.
HP Enterprise Services
IBM Global Services

HISTORICAL FINANCIALS
Company Type: Private

Income Statement
FYE: December 31

	REVENUE ($ mil.)	NET INCOME ($ mil.)	NET PROFIT MARGIN	EMPLOYEES
12/11	44	1	2.3%	310
12/10	43	(1)		0
12/09	36	1	4.4%	0
12/06	38	7	18.7%	0
Annual Growth	4.8%	(47.9%)	—	—

2011 Year-End Financials

Debt ratio: —
Return on equity: 2.30%
Cash ($ mil.): 0
Current ratio: 0.70
Long-term debt ($ mil.): —

Dividends
Yield: —
Payout: —
Market value ($ mil.): —

BUCKNELL UNIVERSITY

Just getting into Bucknell University is an accomplishment. The highly selective private liberal arts school accepts only about 10% of applicants each year. Students who do get in some 3400 of them from around the world have the option to specialize in more than 50 majors and 60 minors. Bucknell confers both undergraduate and master's degrees in the liberal arts sciences engineering and music. It also offers programs in pre-law and pre-med. Bucknell tuition and fees total about $48000; more than half of the student body typically receives financial aid. The school's student-to-faculty ratio is 11-to-1. Bucknell was founded in 1846 as the University at Lewisburg.

EXECUTIVES

General Counsel, Wayne A. Bromfield
President and Trustee, Brian Christopher Mitchell
VP Finance and Administration, David J. Surgala
VP Enrollment Management, Kurt M. Thiede
Associate Provost Dean of Graduate Studies, James Powers Rice
Director Information Integration, Nancy Schroeder Dagle
Director IT Service Integration, Jean Margaret Zappe
Assistant VP Planning and Institutional Research, Jerome Samuel (Jerry) Rackoff
Director University Press, Greg Clingham
Director Financial Aid, Andrea C.A. Leithner Stauffer
Associate VP Facilities, Dennis Wayne Hawley
Director Financial Services, Kathy M. Guyer
Director University Bookstore, Vicki Morris Benion
Director Campus Activities and Programs Associate Dean of Students and Judicial Administrator, Kari Marie Conrad
Instructional Technologist Digital Media, Meredith Paige Field
Associate Dean of Students, Gerald William Commerford
Associate Registrar, Dennis M. Hopple
Director Facility Services, Michael Joseph (Mike) Patterson
Director of Business Operations Provost's Office, Pamela A. Benfer
Provost, Michael A. (Mick) Smyer
Chief of Staff and Secretary of the University, Richard David Myers
Instructional Design Librarian, Brody Ryan Selleck
Auditors: KPMGLLP

LOCATIONS

HQ: Bucknell University
701 Moore Ave., Lewisburg PA 17837-2029
Phone: 570-577-2000   **Fax:** 570-577-3683
Web: www.bucknell.edu

HISTORICAL FINANCIALS
Company Type: School

Income Statement

	REVENUE ($ mil.)	NET INCOME ($ mil.)	NET PROFIT MARGIN	EMPLOYEES
06/12	189	(28)	—	1,500
06/11	184	119	64.9%	0
06/06	151	52	35.0%	0
06/05	139	43	30.8%	0
Annual Growth	10.6%			

FYE: June 30

2012 Year-End Financials
Debt ratio: —
Return on equity: (-15.30)%
Cash ($ mil.): 12
Current ratio: —
Long-term debt ($ mil.): —
Dividends
Yield: —
Payout: —
Market value ($ mil.): —

2011 Year-End Financials
Debt ratio: —
Return on equity: (-0.10)%
Cash ($ mil.): 0
Current ratio: 0.30
Long-term debt ($ mil.): —
Dividends
Yield: —
Payout: —
Market value ($ mil.): —

BUCKS COUNTY INTERMEDIATE UNIT 22

LOCATIONS

HQ: BUCKS COUNTY INTERMEDIATE UNIT 22
705 N SHADY RETREAT RD, DOYLESTOWN, PA 18901-2507
Phone: 215-348-2940
Web: www.bucksiu.org

HISTORICAL FINANCIALS
Company Type: Private

Income Statement

	REVENUE ($ mil.)	NET INCOME ($ mil.)	NET PROFIT MARGIN	EMPLOYEES
06/11	127	0	0.5%	1,755
06/10	129	1	0.8%	0
06/09	117	1	1.3%	0
Annual Growth	4.3%	(33.3%)	—	—

FYE: June 30

2011 Year-End Financials
Debt ratio: —
Return on equity: 0.50%
Cash ($ mil.): 40
Current ratio: 1.30
Long-term debt ($ mil.): —
Dividends
Yield: —
Payout: —
Market value ($ mil.): —

BUFFALO SERVICES INC.

LOCATIONS

HQ: BUFFALO SERVICES INC.
747 S BROADWAY ST, MCCOMB, MS 39648-5131
Phone: 601-684-7702
Web: www.buffaloservices.com

HISTORICAL FINANCIALS
Company Type: Private

Income Statement

	REVENUE ($ mil.)	NET INCOME ($ mil.)	NET PROFIT MARGIN	EMPLOYEES
12/11	103	(0)	—	150
12/10	85	0	0.0%	0
12/09	71	(0)	—	0
12/08	105	(0)	—	0
Annual Growth	(0.7%)	—	—	—

FYE: December 31

BUILDING PLASTICS INC.

LOCATIONS

HQ: BUILDING PLASTICS INC.
3263 SHARPE AVE, MEMPHIS, TN 38111-3700
Phone: 901-744-6200
Web: www.bpidecosurf.com

HISTORICAL FINANCIALS
Company Type: Private

Income Statement

	REVENUE ($ mil.)	NET INCOME ($ mil.)	NET PROFIT MARGIN	EMPLOYEES
01/12	176	0	0.3%	403
01/11	174	0	0.2%	0
01/10*	184	(0)	—	0
12/08	221	(2)	—	0
Annual Growth	(7.4%)	—	—	—

FYE: January 1

*Fiscal year change

2012 Year-End Financials
Debt ratio: —
Return on equity: 0.30%
Cash ($ mil.): 0
Current ratio: 0.60
Long-term debt ($ mil.): —
Dividends
Yield: —
Payout: —
Market value ($ mil.): —

BURKETT OIL COMPANY INC.

LOCATIONS

HQ: BURKETT OIL COMPANY INC.
6788 BEST FRIEND RD, NORCROSS, GA 30071-2919
Phone: 770-447-8030
Web: www.burkettoil.com

HISTORICAL FINANCIALS
Company Type: Private

Income Statement

	REVENUE ($ mil.)	NET INCOME ($ mil.)	NET PROFIT MARGIN	EMPLOYEES
12/11	103	0	0.5%	18
12/10	93	0	0.6%	0
12/09	83	0	0.8%	0
12/08	119	0	0.8%	0
Annual Growth	(4.7%)	(18.4%)	—	—

FYE: December 31

2011 Year-End Financials

Debt ratio: —
Return on equity: 0.50%
Cash ($ mil.): 1
Current ratio: 0.90
Long-term debt ($ mil.): —

Dividends
Yield: —
Payout: —
Market value ($ mil.): —

BURTON LUMBER & HARDWARE CO.

Family-owned-and-run Burton Lumber & Hardware designs makes and installs truss and floor packages wall panels and doors (interior and exterior) from its facility in Salt Lake City. It also sells and installs Heatilator-brand fireplaces and building materials made by Trex James Hardie and other companies. Burton Lumber & Hardware operates half a dozen locations in Utah and offers delivery services throughout the state. Its customers have included contractors home builders and government agencies. The company was founded in 1911 by Willard C. Burton.

EXECUTIVES

President and CEO, Daniel Burton
CFO and Controller, JoAnn Hall
VP Sales, Jeff Burton
Director Human Resources, Jake Conrad
General Counsel, Robert Burton
VP Operations, Steve Hawkes

LOCATIONS

HQ: Burton Lumber & Hardware Co.
1170 S. 4400 West, Salt Lake City UT 84103
Phone: 801-952-3700   **Fax:** 801-952-3701
Web: www.burtonlumber.com

COMPETITORS

84 Lumber   Lowe's
Ace Hardware   Stock Building Supply
HD Supply   Sutherland Lumber

HISTORICAL FINANCIALS

Company Type: Private

Income Statement				FYE: December 31
	REVENUE ($ mil.)	NET INCOME ($ mil.)	NET PROFIT MARGIN	EMPLOYEES
12/11	70	1	1.7%	250
12/09	63	(0)	—	0
12/08	91	0	1.0%	0
12/06	179	16	9.4%	0
Annual Growth	(26.7%)	(58.3%)	—	—

2011 Year-End Financials

Debt ratio: —
Return on equity: 1.70%
Cash ($ mil.): 9
Current ratio: 3.30
Long-term debt ($ mil.): —

Dividends
Yield: —
Payout: —
Market value ($ mil.): —

BUSY BEAVER BUILDING CENTERS INC.

They're busy as well you know what kind of animals at Busy Beaver Building Centers. The company has 15 stores in Ohio Pennsylvania and West Virginia selling ceilings flooring lumber plumbing fixtures and other building materials along with garden supplies hardware power equipment and tools. Busy Beaver serves the professional contractor as well as the do-it-yourselfer. The regional home improvement center chain was founded in 1962. A management group led by chairman and former CEO Charles Bender acquired the company in 1988 and now owns about one-quarter of Busy Beaver which is facing heavyweight competition from big-box chains such as Home Depot and Lowe's.

The company closed two stores in 2008 citing a housing slump. New stores will be located far from its big-box rivals and within two hours of the company's headquarters to keep costs down.

From 1972 to 1988 Busy Beaver was a subsidiary of SILO Inc. (formerly Cyclops Corporation).

Busy Beaver voluntarily filed for Chapter 11 protection from creditors in 1990. Under a reorganization plan confirmed by the US Bankruptcy Court in 1992 unsecured creditors received an equity stake of 25%. The company emerged from Chapter 11 in 1992.

EXECUTIVES

President, Frank Filmeck
CFO, Nicholas (Nick) Demayo
VP Merchandising, Arthur (Art) Sand
CIO, Robert Cain
Controller, Brian Walsh
Human Resources and Payroll Administrator,
Joyce Palmer

LOCATIONS

HQ: Busy Beaver Building Centers Inc.
3130 William Pitt Way, Pittsburgh PA 15238
Phone: 412-828-2323   **Fax:** 412-828-2430
Web: www.busybeaver.com

COMPETITORS

84 Lumber   Home Depot
ABC Supply   Lowe's
Ace Hardware   Menard
HD Supply   True Value

HISTORICAL FINANCIALS

Company Type: Private

Income Statement				FYE: December 31
	REVENUE ($ mil.)	NET INCOME ($ mil.)	NET PROFIT MARGIN	EMPLOYEES
12/11	40	0	1.1%	350
12/10	41	0	0.9%	0
12/09	42	0	0.7%	0
Annual Growth	(1.8%)	17.1%	—	—

2011 Year-End Financials

Debt ratio: —
Return on equity: 1.10%
Cash ($ mil.): 0
Current ratio: 0.10
Long-term debt ($ mil.): —

Dividends
Yield: —
Payout: —
Market value ($ mil.): —

BUTLER HEALTHCARE PROVIDERS

LOCATIONS

HQ: BUTLER HEALTHCARE PROVIDERS
1 HOSPITAL WAY, BUTLER, PA 16001-4670
Phone: 724-283-6666
Web: www.butlerhealthsystem.org

HISTORICAL FINANCIALS

Company Type: Private

Income Statement				FYE: June 30
	REVENUE ($ mil.)	NET INCOME ($ mil.)	NET PROFIT MARGIN	EMPLOYEES
06/11	218	4	2.0%	1,300
06/10	205	18	8.8%	0
06/09	185	12	6.7%	0
06/08	491	15	3.2%	0
Annual Growth	(23.7%)	(35.0%)	—	—

2011 Year-End Financials

Debt ratio: —
Return on equity: 2.00%
Cash ($ mil.): 25
Current ratio: 2.60
Long-term debt ($ mil.): —

Dividends
Yield: —
Payout: —
Market value ($ mil.): —

BUTLER UNIVERSITY

LOCATIONS

HQ: BUTLER UNIVERSITY
4600 SUNSET AVE, INDIANAPOLIS, IN 46208-3487
Phone: 317-940-8000
Web: www.butlermba.com

HISTORICAL FINANCIALS

Company Type: Private

Income Statement				FYE: May 31
	REVENUE ($ mil.)	NET INCOME ($ mil.)	NET PROFIT MARGIN	EMPLOYEES
05/12	182	6	3.5%	805
05/11	141	34	24.7%	0
05/10	124	10	8.5%	0
05/09	114	(60)	—	0
Annual Growth	16.8%	—	—	—

2012 Year-End Financials

Debt ratio: —
Return on equity: 3.50%
Cash ($ mil.): 14
Current ratio: —
Long-term debt ($ mil.): —

Dividends
Yield: —
Payout: —
Market value ($ mil.): —

BVU AUTHORITY

LOCATIONS

HQ: BVU AUTHORITY
 15022 LEE HWY, BRISTOL, VA 24202-4256
Phone: 276-669-4112
Web: www.bvub.com

HISTORICAL FINANCIALS
Company Type: Private

Income Statement

	REVENUE ($ mil.)	NET INCOME ($ mil.)	NET PROFIT MARGIN	EMPLOYEES
06/11	81	10	13.1%	180
06/09	78	6	8.1%	0
06/08	67	10	15.5%	0
06/07	57	3	6.0%	0
Annual Growth	12.3%	45.9%	—	—

FYE: June 30

2011 Year-End Financials

Debt ratio: —
Return on equity: 13.10%
Cash ($ mil.): 18
Current ratio: 1.50
Long-term debt ($ mil.): —

Dividends
 Yield: —
 Payout: —
Market value ($ mil.): —

BYCOR GENERAL CONTRACTORS INC.

Bycor General Contractors provides construction services for a variety of commercial retail institutional civic and leisure facilities in the San Diego area. Its offerings include tenant improvements shell construction build-to-suit and LEED-certified services and projects range from church sanctuaries to auto dealerships. The company has served clients including Western University of Health Sciences Northrop Grumman and San Diego National Bank. President Rich Byer CEO Scott Kaats and Van Smith founded co-founded Bycor General Contractors in 1981.

EXECUTIVES

President, Rich Byer
CEO, Scott Kaats
Controller, Janette A. Young

LOCATIONS

HQ: Bycor General Contractors Inc.
 6490 Marindustry Dr. Ste. A, San Diego CA 92121-2563
Phone: 858-587-1901   **Fax:** 858-587-1903
Web: www.bycor.com

COMPETITORS

Fullmer Construction	Moorefield
Good & Roberts	Construction
Grant General	Pacific Building Group
Contractors	Reno Contracting
Johnson & Jennings	Staples Construction
Ledcor	TSA Contracting

HISTORICAL FINANCIALS
Company Type: Private

Income Statement

	REVENUE ($ mil.)	NET INCOME ($ mil.)	NET PROFIT MARGIN	EMPLOYEES
12/11	58	2	3.7%	80
12/10	46	0	1.2%	0
12/09	80	1	1.7%	0
12/07	108	2	2.4%	0
Annual Growth	(18.7%)	(5.3%)	—	—

FYE: December 31

2011 Year-End Financials

Debt ratio: —
Return on equity: 3.70%
Cash ($ mil.): 1
Current ratio: 1.10
Long-term debt ($ mil.): —

Dividends
 Yield: —
 Payout: —
Market value ($ mil.): —

C C 1 LIMITED PARTNERSHIP

LOCATIONS

HQ: C C 1 LIMITED PARTNERSHIP
 URB IND MINILLAS LOTE, BAYAMON, PR 00959
Phone: 787-288-6400
Web: www.coca-colapr.com

HISTORICAL FINANCIALS
Company Type: Private

Income Statement

	REVENUE ($ mil.)	NET INCOME ($ mil.)	NET PROFIT MARGIN	EMPLOYEES
12/11	306	14	4.7%	816
12/10	301	25	8.5%	0
12/09	293	26	8.9%	0
12/08	279	20	7.5%	0
Annual Growth	3.2%	(11.8%)	—	—

FYE: December 31

C. STEIN INC.

LOCATIONS

HQ: C. STEIN INC.
 4719 S MARKET ST STE 100, BOISE, ID 83705-5415
Phone: 208-378-0550

HISTORICAL FINANCIALS
Company Type: Private

Income Statement

	REVENUE ($ mil.)	NET INCOME ($ mil.)	NET PROFIT MARGIN	EMPLOYEES
12/11	116	5	5.1%	160
12/10	112	5	4.6%	0
12/09	57	6	10.7%	0
12/08	107	4	4.3%	0
Annual Growth	2.7%	8.0%	—	—

FYE: December 31

2011 Year-End Financials

Debt ratio: —
Return on equity: 5.10%
Cash ($ mil.): 2
Current ratio: 0.60
Long-term debt ($ mil.): —

Dividends
 Yield: —
 Payout: —
Market value ($ mil.): —

C.R. ENGLAND INC.

London might have its cool foggy days but the England of C.R. England is always chilly. Truckload freight carrier C.R. England hauls refrigerated and dry cargo throughout the US. The company also serves parts of Canada and through alliances points in Mexico. C.R. England's fleet includes more than 2800 Freightliner Peterbilt Volvo and International tractors and 4100 trailers. Besides for-hire freight hauling C.R. England offers dedicated contract carriage in which drivers and equipment are assigned to a customer long-term; logistics services including freight brokerage; and intermodal railroad service. C.R. England was founded in 1920 by Chester Rodney England and is run by his descendants.

Under family management the company leverages its logistics operations to provide end-to-end services thereby enabling C.R. England to retain and gain market share. In addition to freight brokerage England Logistics offers intermodal service for refrigerated cargo in which customers' containerized freight is shuttled between truck and railroad facility. The logistics unit also arranges the transportation of less-than-truckload quantities of freight and provides ground transportation of ocean containers for shipping lines.

England Logistics gained momentum in 2007 when it acquired Trans-Man Logistics and Traffic Management Services both third-party logistics companies headquartered in Michigan. The next year it bought a controlling stake in Los Angeles-based Dynalink Systems a provider of supply chain management and freight-forwarding services that has offices in China as well as in the US. The purchase paves the way for acquiring a Chinese company through which C.R. England plans to operate a cold chain network and capture a share of the country's market for handling perishable food.

England North American C.R. England's truck-load division has beefed up its operations too. In 2010 it added a temperature-controlled container-on-flatcar transport mode TempStack. The offering enables England North American to double-stack refrigerated containers on the flatcars of its partner railroads. Benefits include reduced customer costs increased shipping capacity and efficiency as well as decreased fuel usage and a lighter carbon footprint. Simultaneously C.R. England boosted its regional division by introducing short haul transportation services centered in Chicago. The office targets customers within a 250 mile radius of Chicago and several cities beyond.

C.R. England's business also benefits from operating four truck driving schools in the US and a course on becoming a freight broker. The school helps improve driver safety as well as provides a pool of qualified truck drivers for hire.

The company in 2011 shifted senior management roles; chairman Dan England is serving a one-year stint as chairman of the American Trucking Association. Covering his absence CEO Dean England has taken over as company president. Concurrently Wayne Cederholm former chief operating officer succeeds Dean England as CEO.

EXECUTIVES

VP Mexico, David Akers
Chairman, Daniel E. (Dan) England, age 64
President, Dean D. England
EVP Maintenance, Todd D. England
EVP Operations Support, Corey D. England
Chief Sales Officer, Mike Bunnell
CEO, Wayne Cederholm
SVP and CFO, Keith Wallace
VP Technology, Dirk Anderson
Corporate Counsel, Nelson Hayes
VP Safety and Compliance, Gordon Lambert
VP LTL Services England Logistics, Joe Finney
VP National Account Sales, Earnie Seibert
COO, Chad England
President England Logistics, Josh England
VP TL Services England Logistics, Jason Beardall
VP Recruiting Training and Safe Driving, Thom Pronk
VP Dedicated, Kirk Freimuth
VP National, Brandon Harrison
EVP Corporate Sales and Business Development, David A. Kramer
Director Human Resources, Dennis Hanson
Director Management Services and Assistant to the Chairman/CEO/COO, David Allred
VP Intermodal, Zach England
VP Regional, Bill Champine
Director Accident Prevention, Mark Fillmore
VP Safety Compliance, Dustin England
Vice President Intermodal, Coby Bullard
Vice President Supply Chain, Jim Monkmeyer
Vice President Finance & Business Development, Philip May

LOCATIONS

HQ: C.R. England Inc.
4701 W. 2100 South, Salt Lake City UT 84120
Phone: 801-972-2712   **Fax:** 801-977-6703
Web: www.crengland.com

PRODUCTS/OPERATIONS

Selected Services
Dedicated service
Expedited priority rail service
Long haul truckload service
Mexico service

Short haul regional service

COMPETITORS

C.H. Robinson Worldwide
Central Refrigerated Service
Covenant Transportation
Crete Carrier
Frozen Food Express
J.B. Hunt
KLLM Transport Services

Landstar System
Marten Transport
Menlo Worldwide
Navajo Shippers
Prime Inc.
Stevens Transport
Swift Transportation
Willis Shaw Express

HISTORICAL FINANCIALS
Company Type: Private

Income Statement

	REVENUE ($ mil.)	NET INCOME ($ mil.)	NET PROFIT MARGIN	EMPLOYEES
12/11	1,315	55	4.3%	4,500
12/07	829	41	5.0%	0
12/06	708	51	7.3%	0
12/05	609	34	5.6%	0
Annual Growth	**29.2%**	**17.8%**	**—**	**—**

FYE: December 31

2011 Year-End Financials

Debt ratio: —
Return on equity: 4.30%
Cash ($ mil.): 28
Current ratio: 1.20
Long-term debt ($ mil.): —

Dividends
Yield: —
Payout: —
Market value ($ mil.): —

CACHE COUNTY SCHOOL DISTRICT

LOCATIONS

HQ: CACHE COUNTY SCHOOL DISTRICT
2063 N 1200 E, NORTH LOGAN, UT 84341-2099
Phone: 435-752-3925
Web: www.ccsdut.org

HISTORICAL FINANCIALS
Company Type: Private

Income Statement

	REVENUE ($ mil.)	NET INCOME ($ mil.)	NET PROFIT MARGIN	EMPLOYEES
06/12	113	0	0.4%	2,300
06/11	114	(3)	—	0
06/10	109	(15)	—	0
06/09	113	15	13.8%	0
Annual Growth	**(0.1%)**	**(70.3%)**	**—**	**—**

FYE: June 30

2012 Year-End Financials

Debt ratio: —
Return on equity: 0.40%
Cash ($ mil.): 6
Current ratio: —
Long-term debt ($ mil.): —

Dividends
Yield: —
Payout: —
Market value ($ mil.): —

CADENCE MCSHANE CONSTRUCTION COMPANY LLC

With a certain cadence Cadence McShane Construction has been right in step with the top contractors in the US. A part of development and construction group The McShane Companies it provides general construction construction management and design/build services for commercial institutional and industrial projects in Texas and the central US. The firm is known for its school and community projects throughout Texas. It also provides services to the manufacturing office multifamily residential government hospitality and retail markets. Recent projects include a 730000 sq. ft Port of Houston distribution center for First Industrial Realty. Cadence McShane was founded in 1995.

EXECUTIVES

CEO, James A. (Jim) McShane
President, Neal L. Harper
VP Operations, John H. Heim Jr.
VP Finance, Shawn Pyatt

LOCATIONS

HQ: Cadence McShane Construction LLC
14860 Montfort Dr. Ste. 270, Dallas TX 75254
Phone: 972-239-2336   **Fax:** 972-239-1214
Web:
www.mcshane.com/companyOverview.asp?site=mc&division=cmc
Cadence McShane has offices Austin Houston and Dallas Texas.

PRODUCTS/OPERATIONS

Selected Project Areas
Community/Religious (churches)
Cultural (museums libraries)
Educational (K-12 schools and higher education)
Health care (medical centers labs medical suites and offices)
Hospitality (hotels)
Industrial (distribution assembly manufacturing)
Institutional (federal state county and municipal)
Offices (single-story to mid-rise)
Parking structures
Residential (multi-residence condominium complexes townhomes senior living)
Retail (shopping centers parking structures)

COMPETITORS

Austin Industries
Beck Group
FaulknerUSA
Gilbane Building Company
Harvey Builders
Hensel Phelps Construction

Hunt Construction
Manhattan Construction
Spawglass Holding
Structure Tone Southwest
Turner Corporation

HISTORICAL FINANCIALS
Company Type: Private

Income Statement
FYE: September 30

	REVENUE ($ mil.)	NET INCOME ($ mil.)	NET PROFIT MARGIN	EMPLOYEES
09/11	133	1	0.8%	120
09/10	158	1	0.8%	0
09/09	259	4	1.9%	0
09/07	237	7	3.3%	0
Annual Growth	(17.6%)	(47.6%)	—	—

2011 Year-End Financials
Debt ratio: —
Return on equity: 0.80%
Cash ($ mil.): 7
Current ratio: 1.20
Long-term debt ($ mil.): —

Dividends
Yield: —
Payout: —
Market value ($ mil.): —

CALCASIEU PARISH SCHOOL BOARD

LOCATIONS
HQ: CALCASIEU PARISH SCHOOL BOARD
3310 BROAD ST, LAKE CHARLES, LA 70615-3808
Phone: 337-217-4000

HISTORICAL FINANCIALS
Company Type: Private

Income Statement
FYE: June 30

	REVENUE ($ mil.)	NET INCOME ($ mil.)	NET PROFIT MARGIN	EMPLOYEES
06/11	345	(23)	—	4,500
06/04	249	(16)	—	0
06/03	234	(3)	—	0
06/02	222	15	6.8%	0
Annual Growth	15.8%	—	—	—

2011 Year-End Financials
Debt ratio: —
Return on equity: (-6.80)%
Cash ($ mil.): 71
Current ratio: —
Long-term debt ($ mil.): —

Dividends
Yield: —
Payout: —
Market value ($ mil.): —

CALIFORNIA AMMONIA CO.

LOCATIONS
HQ: CALIFORNIA AMMONIA CO.
1776 W MARCH LN STE 420, STOCKTON, CA 95207-6427
Phone: 209-982-1000
Web: www.calamco.com

HISTORICAL FINANCIALS
Company Type: Private

Income Statement
FYE: October 31

	REVENUE ($ mil.)	NET INCOME ($ mil.)	NET PROFIT MARGIN	EMPLOYEES
10/11	130	14	10.9%	35
10/10	89	8	9.1%	0
10/09	78	10	13.0%	0
10/08	147	8	5.6%	0
Annual Growth	(4.0%)	20.1%	—	—

2011 Year-End Financials
Debt ratio: —
Return on equity: 10.90%
Cash ($ mil.): 9
Current ratio: 1.00
Long-term debt ($ mil.): —

Dividends
Yield: —
Payout: —
Market value ($ mil.): —

CALIFORNIA BAPTIST UNIVERSITY

LOCATIONS
HQ: CALIFORNIA BAPTIST UNIVERSITY
8432 MAGNOLIA AVE, RIVERSIDE, CA 92504-3297
Phone: 951-689-5771
Web: www.calbaptist.edu

HISTORICAL FINANCIALS
Company Type: Private

Income Statement
FYE: June 30

	REVENUE ($ mil.)	NET INCOME ($ mil.)	NET PROFIT MARGIN	EMPLOYEES
06/11	142	13	9.2%	300
06/10	113	6	5.3%	0
06/09	101	0	—	0
06/08	92	0	0.0%	0
Annual Growth	15.6%	606.4%	—	—

2011 Year-End Financials
Debt ratio: —
Return on equity: 9.20%
Cash ($ mil.): 41
Current ratio: —
Long-term debt ($ mil.): —

Dividends
Yield: —
Payout: —
Market value ($ mil.): —

CALIFORNIA COMMUNITY FOUNDATION

California Community Foundation supports not-for-profit organizations and public institutions in the Los Angeles area. The organization performs its function by offering funding for health and human services affordable housing early childhood education and community arts and culture. The 24th Street Theatre Antelope Valley Hospital and Community Arts Partnership are among the organizations to have received the foundation's grant funding. In times of emergency it has also pitched in to help groups in other areas. California Community Foundation was founded in 1915.

By 2015 the foundation hopes to have helped others find affordable housing and quality education access health care and discover the arts and culture.

EXECUTIVES
President and CEO, Antonia Hernandez
VP and CFO, Steve Cobb
Director Human Resources, Silvana Miller
SVP Programs, Alvertha Bratton Penny
Chair, Reveta Bowers
Chair Emeritus, Jane B. Eisner
EVP and COO, John E. Kobara
Director Communications, Namju Cho
Deputy Field Director Preschool Advocacy Initiative, Sandy Escobedo
Project Coordinator Community Foundation Land Trust, Rosie Diaz
President Community Foundation Land Trust, Ann Sewill
Director Project Management, Lynn Hansen
VP External and Donor Relations, Carol Bradford
Manager Donor and Prospect Research, Patrice Cablayan
Manager Scholarships, Kerry L. Franco
Charitable Business Development Officer, Mia Gorman
Director Donor Relations, Terri Mosqueda
Estate and Gift Planning Officer, Edward Mullen
Director Charitable Business Development, Barry Peterson
Controller, Carolyn Steffen
Network Coordinator, Teresita Vega
Director, David C. Bohnett
Director, James M. Rosser, age 72
Director, Sheldon M. Stone, age 59
Director, Quan Phung
Director, Tom Unterman
Director, Dennis Gertmenian
Director, Cynthia A. Telles, age 59
Chair, Reveta Bowers
Chair Emeritus, Jane B. Eisner
Director, Carolina Reyes
Director, Joanne Corday Kozberg
Director, David W. Fleming
Director, Preston Johnson
Director, Melanie Staggs
Director, Paul Schulz
Director, Jean Bixby Smith
Director, Catherine L. Unger
Director, Sonia Marie De Leon de Vega
Director, Ronald T. Vera
Auditors: KPMGLLP

LOCATIONS
HQ: CALIFORNIA COMMUNITY FOUNDATION
221 S FIGUEROA ST STE 400, LOS ANGELES, CA 90012-2524
Phone: 213-413-4130
Web: www.calfund.org

HISTORICAL FINANCIALS

Company Type: Private - Foundation

Income Statement

FYE: June 30

	REVENUE ($ mil.)	NET INCOME ($ mil.)	NET PROFIT MARGIN	EMPLOYEES
06/11	255	139	54.6%	47
06/10	222	85	38.4%	0
06/09	17	(182)	—	0
06/08	141	(87)	—	0
Annual Growth	21.8%	—	—	—

2011 Year-End Financials

Debt ratio: ——
Return on equity: 54.60%
Cash ($ mil.): 15
Current ratio: ——
Long-term debt ($ mil.): —

Dividends
  Yield: —
  Payout: —
Market value ($ mil.): —

CALIFORNIA IRONWORKERS FIELD WELFARE PLAN

LOCATIONS

HQ: CALIFORNIA IRONWORKERS FIELD WELFARE PLAN
131 N EL MOLINO AVE # 330, PASADENA, CA 91101-1873
Phone: 626-792-7337

HISTORICAL FINANCIALS

Company Type: Private

Income Statement

FYE: May 31

	REVENUE ($ mil.)	NET INCOME ($ mil.)	NET PROFIT MARGIN	EMPLOYEES
05/11	111	(11)	—	3
Annual Growth	—	—	—	—

2011 Year-End Financials

Debt ratio: ——
Return on equity: (-10.00)%
Cash ($ mil.): 34
Current ratio: 0.30
Long-term debt ($ mil.): —

Dividends
  Yield: —
  Payout: —
Market value ($ mil.): —

CALNET INC.

CALNET provides information technology (IT) consulting and services for businesses and public sector agencies. The company's IT services include application development and testing; e-commerce consulting; network management and security; and technical staffing. Industries served include technology telecommunications and financial services. In addition CALNET provides intelligence analysis including linguist services in a variety of languages for the US military. Customers have included the Food and Drug Administration Cisco Systems and Intel. The company has offices in Reston Virginia and San Diego. CALNET was founded in 1989 by president Kaleem Shah.

EXECUTIVES

President, Kaleem S. Shah
SVP, Helena Robinette
SVP West Coast Division, Feizal Mohideen
Facility Security Officer, Kimberly Scott
SVP Business Development, Kris Menon
CTO, Anthony Scolaro

LOCATIONS

HQ: CALNET Inc.
12359 Sunrise Valley Dr. Ste. 270, Reston VA 20191
Phone: 703-547-6800   **Fax:** 703-547-6806
Web: www.calnet.com

COMPETITORS

Computer Sciences Corp.
HP Enterprise Services
IBM Global Services

HISTORICAL FINANCIALS

Company Type: Private

Income Statement

FYE: December 31

	REVENUE ($ mil.)	NET INCOME ($ mil.)	NET PROFIT MARGIN	EMPLOYEES
12/11	82	14	17.4%	350
12/10	0	0	—	0
12/08	83	(0)	—	0
12/06	27	6	22.3%	0
Annual Growth	43.7%	32.3%	—	—

2011 Year-End Financials

Debt ratio: ——
Return on equity: 17.40%
Cash ($ mil.): 20
Current ratio: 1.50
Long-term debt ($ mil.): —

Dividends
  Yield: —
  Payout: —
Market value ($ mil.): —

CALVARY HOSPITAL INC.

Calvary Hospital rallies its nurses around advanced cancer patients hoping to keep them as comfortable as possible. The facility founded in 1899 specializes in palliative care the practice of relieving the pain and symptoms associated with an illness (not curing the illness itself). Calvary Hospital offers both inpatient and outpatient services to adult patients in the advanced stages of cancer through two campuses; the main hospital has about 200 beds and a satellite location in Brooklyn has about 25 beds. In addition the hospital operates home health and hospice agencies and provides case management and family support services.

Operations

Calvary Hospital's home health and hospice divisions provide services to patients in the Bronx Manhattan Queens and Brooklyn as well as in Nassau Westchester and Rockland counties. The Calvary Nursing Home Hospice agency administers palliative care at about 30 nursing homes in the service territory.

Financial Analysis

Higher net patient service earnings led to a 4% increase in overall revenues for Calvary Hospital to some $103 million in 2011. In addition to patient revenues and support from its Catholic sponsors the hospital receives some funding from other charitable organizations such as the Altman Foundation and the United Hospital Fund.

Strategy

Calvary Hospital is expanding its home and hospice services. In 2011 it added two new locations where its nursing home hospice unit provides services.

Ownership

The not-for-profit organization is sponsored by the Archdiocese of New York.

EXECUTIVES

President and CEO, Frank A. Calamari
SVP and Executive Medical Director, Michael J. Brescia
Director Palliative Care Institute, Robert A. Brescia
VP and COO, Richard Kutilek
Director Public Affairs and Community Relations, Barbara J. Nitzberg
Chairman, Thomas J. Fahey Jr.
Medical Director, Christopher P. Comfort
VP Community Patient Services, Nancy S. D'Agostino
Executive Secretary, Susan Garry
Executive Secretary, Jenny Jassey
Director Human Resources, Mary Ann Lane
VP Patient Hospital Services, Sally Umbro
CFO, Andrew Greco
EVP Calvary Fund, Vincent J. Spinelli
Director, Minto L. Soares, age 75
Director, Manfred Altstadt
Director, John P. Bertsch
Director, John A. Decina
Director, Thomas G. Ferrara
Director, Terence Gallagher
Director, Edward D. Heben
Director, James E. Introne
Director, Ralph V. Johnson
Director, Richard E. Meyer
Director, Rena M. Murtha
Director, Amit Sikdar
Director, Joseph A. Tarantino
Director, Anne Cote Taylor
Director, Rev Edward M. Barry

LOCATIONS

HQ: Calvary Hospital Inc.
1740 Eastchester Rd., Bronx NY 10461
Phone: 718-518-2000   **Fax:** 803-256-7500
Web: www.nmrs.com

PRODUCTS/OPERATIONS

Selected Services

Bereavement support
Calvary@Home
Center for Curative and Palliative Wound Care
Family care/social work
Home Care and Hospice Division
  Calvary Nursing Home Hospice
Inpatient care
Music therapy
Nutrition
Palliative Care Institute
Pastoral care
Therapeutic recreation

COMPETITORS

Cancer Care
Dana-Farber
NewYork-Presbyterian Hospital

Johns Hopkins Medicine
Mayo Clinic Rochester
Memorial
  Sloan-Kettering
New York City Health
  and Hospitals
NewYork-Presbyterian
  Healthcare

Roswell Park Cancer
  Institute
SUNY Upstate Medical
  University
Winthrop-University
  Hospital

HISTORICAL FINANCIALS
Company Type: Private - Not-for-Profit

Income Statement — FYE: December 31

	REVENUE ($ mil.)	NET INCOME ($ mil.)	NET PROFIT MARGIN	EMPLOYEES
12/11	103	(2)	—	900
Annual Growth	—	—	—	—

2011 Year-End Financials

Debt ratio: —
Return on equity: (-2.40)%
Cash ($ mil.): 4
Current ratio: 1.40
Long-term debt ($ mil.): —

Dividends
  Yield: —
  Payout: —
  Market value ($ mil.): —

CAMCO MANUFACTURING INC.

LOCATIONS

HQ: CAMCO MANUFACTURING INC.
  121 LANDMARK DR, GREENSBORO, NC 27409-9626
Phone: 336-668-7661
Web: www.camco.net

HISTORICAL FINANCIALS
Company Type: Private

Income Statement — FYE: December 31

	REVENUE ($ mil.)	NET INCOME ($ mil.)	NET PROFIT MARGIN	EMPLOYEES
12/11	119	11	9.6%	250
12/10	116	13	11.3%	0
12/09*	100	11	10.9%	0
09/08	76	4	6.5%	0
Annual Growth	16.1%	32.3%	—	—

*Fiscal year change

2011 Year-End Financials

Debt ratio: —
Return on equity: 9.60%
Cash ($ mil.): 0
Current ratio: 1.30
Long-term debt ($ mil.): —

Dividends
  Yield: —
  Payout: —
  Market value ($ mil.): —

CAMDEN-CLARK MEMORIAL HOSPITAL CORPORATION

LOCATIONS

HQ: CAMDEN-CLARK MEMORIAL HOSPITAL
  CORPORATION
  800 GARFIELD AVE, PARKERSBURG, WV 26101-5340
Phone: 304-424-2111
Web: www.ccmh.org

HISTORICAL FINANCIALS
Company Type: Private

Income Statement — FYE: June 30

	REVENUE ($ mil.)	NET INCOME ($ mil.)	NET PROFIT MARGIN	EMPLOYEES
06/11	224	25	11.5%	1,600
06/10	171	(4)	—	0
06/09	153	(8)	—	0
06/08	178	3	2.2%	0
Annual Growth	7.8%	87.1%	—	—

2011 Year-End Financials

Debt ratio: —
Return on equity: 11.50%
Cash ($ mil.): 5
Current ratio: 2.00
Long-term debt ($ mil.): —

Dividends
  Yield: —
  Payout: —
  Market value ($ mil.): —

CAMERON DICKINSON CONSTRUCTION COMPANY INC

LOCATIONS

HQ: CAMERON DICKINSON CONSTRUCTION
  COMPANY INC
  6184 INNOVATION WAY, CARLSBAD, CA 92009-1728
Phone: 760-438-9114
Web: www.dickinsoncameron.com

HISTORICAL FINANCIALS
Company Type: Private

Income Statement — FYE: December 31

	REVENUE ($ mil.)	NET INCOME ($ mil.)	NET PROFIT MARGIN	EMPLOYEES
12/11	81	6	7.5%	25
12/10	36	2	6.8%	0
12/09	47	2	6.2%	0
12/08	65	2	4.0%	0
Annual Growth	7.6%	32.6%	—	—

2011 Year-End Financials

Debt ratio: —
Return on equity: 7.50%
Cash ($ mil.): 1
Current ratio: 0.90
Long-term debt ($ mil.): —

Dividends
  Yield: —
  Payout: —
  Market value ($ mil.): —

CAMPBELL COUNTY SCHOOL DISTRICT 1

LOCATIONS

HQ: CAMPBELL COUNTY SCHOOL DISTRICT 1
  1000 W 8TH ST, GILLETTE, WY 82716-3423
Phone: 307-682-5171
Web: www.campbellcountyschools.net

HISTORICAL FINANCIALS
Company Type: Private

Income Statement — FYE: June 30

	REVENUE ($ mil.)	NET INCOME ($ mil.)	NET PROFIT MARGIN	EMPLOYEES
06/12	154	(9)	—	1,360
06/11	140	(11)	—	0
06/10	142	(7)	—	0
06/09	151	5	3.7%	0
Annual Growth	0.6%	—	—	—

2012 Year-End Financials

Debt ratio: —
Return on equity: (-6.40)%
Cash ($ mil.): 3
Current ratio: —
Long-term debt ($ mil.): —

Dividends
  Yield: —
  Payout: —
  Market value ($ mil.): —

CAMPBELL UNIVERSITY INC

LOCATIONS

HQ: CAMPBELL UNIVERSITY INC
  148 MAIN ST, BUIES CREEK, NC 27506
Phone: 910-893-1240

HISTORICAL FINANCIALS
Company Type: Private

Income Statement — FYE: May 31

	REVENUE ($ mil.)	NET INCOME ($ mil.)	NET PROFIT MARGIN	EMPLOYEES
05/12	114	4	3.6%	1,000
05/11	101	31	31.5%	0
05/10	92	22	24.4%	0
05/09	95	(11)	—	0
Annual Growth	6.2%	—	—	—

2012 Year-End Financials

Debt ratio: ——
Return on equity: 3.60%
Cash ($ mil.): 46
Current ratio: ——
Long-term debt ($ mil.): ——

Dividends
Yield: —
Payout: —
Market value ($ mil.): —

2011 Year-End Financials

Debt ratio: ——
Return on equity: 110.70%
Cash ($ mil.): 78
Current ratio: 2.80
Long-term debt ($ mil.): ——

Dividends
Yield: —
Payout: —
Market value ($ mil.): —

HISTORICAL FINANCIALS

Company Type: Private

Income Statement

FYE: December 31

	REVENUE ($ mil.)	NET INCOME ($ mil.)	NET PROFIT MARGIN	EMPLOYEES
12/11	105	6	6.0%	125
12/10	101	4	4.0%	0
12/09	87	2	2.6%	0
12/08	105	3	3.3%	0
Annual Growth	(0.2%)	22.1%	—	—

2011 Year-End Financials

Debt ratio: ——
Return on equity: 6.00%
Cash ($ mil.): 0
Current ratio: 1.50
Long-term debt ($ mil.): ——

Dividends
Yield: —
Payout: —
Market value ($ mil.): —

CANUSA HERSHMAN RECYCLING LLC

LOCATIONS

HQ: CANUSA HERSHMAN RECYCLING LLC
45 NE INDUSTRIAL RD, BRANFORD, CT 06405-6801
Phone: 203-488-0887
Web: www.chrecycling.com

HISTORICAL FINANCIALS

Company Type: Private

Income Statement

FYE: December 31

	REVENUE ($ mil.)	NET INCOME ($ mil.)	NET PROFIT MARGIN	EMPLOYEES
12/11	240	34	14.3%	150
12/10	212	10	5.0%	0
12/09	132	3	2.4%	0
12/08	161	4	3.0%	0
Annual Growth	14.2%	92.9%	—	—

2011 Year-End Financials

Debt ratio: ——
Return on equity: 14.30%
Cash ($ mil.): 3
Current ratio: 1.90
Long-term debt ($ mil.): ——

Dividends
Yield: —
Payout: —
Market value ($ mil.): —

CAPITAL REGION MEDICAL CENTER

LOCATIONS

HQ: CAPITAL REGION MEDICAL CENTER
1125 MADISON ST, JEFFERSON CITY, MO 65101-5200
Phone: 573-632-5000
Web: www.crmc.org

HISTORICAL FINANCIALS

Company Type: Private

Income Statement

FYE: June 30

	REVENUE ($ mil.)	NET INCOME ($ mil.)	NET PROFIT MARGIN	EMPLOYEES
06/11	163	4	2.5%	1,200
06/10	163	10	6.3%	0
06/09*	152	7	4.7%	0
12/08	1	0	—	0
Annual Growth	392.6%	—	—	—

*Fiscal year change

2011 Year-End Financials

Debt ratio: ——
Return on equity: 2.50%
Cash ($ mil.): 7
Current ratio: 1.10
Long-term debt ($ mil.): ——

Dividends
Yield: —
Payout: —
Market value ($ mil.): —

CARIBBEAN PRODUCE EXCHANGE INC

LOCATIONS

HQ: CARIBBEAN PRODUCE EXCHANGE INC
4TH ST BLDG D MRCADO CNTL, SAN JUAN, PR 00920
Phone: 787-793-0750

HISTORICAL FINANCIALS

Company Type: Private

Income Statement

FYE: December 30

	REVENUE ($ mil.)	NET INCOME ($ mil.)	NET PROFIT MARGIN	EMPLOYEES
12/11	93	3	3.7%	234
12/10	96	3	3.9%	0
12/09	91	5	5.6%	0
12/08	94	4	4.9%	0
Annual Growth	(0.6%)	(9.7%)	—	—

2011 Year-End Financials

Debt ratio: ——
Return on equity: 3.70%
Cash ($ mil.): 1
Current ratio: 0.80
Long-term debt ($ mil.): ——

Dividends
Yield: —
Payout: —
Market value ($ mil.): —

CAPITAL IMPROVEMENT BOARD OF MANAGERS

LOCATIONS

HQ: CAPITAL IMPROVEMENT BOARD OF MANAGERS
100 S CAPITOL AVE STE 100, INDIANAPOLIS, IN 46225-1003
Phone: 317-262-3400
Web: www.iccrd.com

HISTORICAL FINANCIALS

Company Type: Private

Income Statement

FYE: December 31

	ASSETS ($ mil.)	NET INCOME ($ mil.)	INCOME AS % OF ASSETS	EMPLOYEES
12/11	1,493	30	2.0%	291
12/10	1,473	18	1.3%	0
12/09	1,402	10	0.8%	0
12/08	1,287	86	6.7%	0
Annual Growth	5.1%	(29.5%)	—	—

CAREER SYSTEMS DEVELOPMENT CORPORATION

LOCATIONS

HQ: CAREER SYSTEMS DEVELOPMENT CORPORATION
75 THRUWAY PARK DR # 100, WEST HENRIETTA, NY 14586-9793
Phone: 585-334-8080
Web: www.csdis.com

CARING PEOPLE ALLIANCE

LOCATIONS

HQ: CARING PEOPLE ALLIANCE
8 PENN CTR 1628 JOHN F KE ST 8 PENN C, PHILADELPHIA, PA 19103
Phone: 215-545-5230
Web: www.caringpeoplealliance.org

HISTORICAL FINANCIALS

Company Type: Private

Income Statement

FYE: June 30

	REVENUE ($ mil.)	NET INCOME ($ mil.)	NET PROFIT MARGIN	EMPLOYEES
06/11	105	(0)	—	300
06/10	111	0	0.0%	0
06/09	118	0	—	0
06/08	110	(1)	—	0
Annual Growth	(1.5%)	—	—	—

2011 Year-End Financials

Debt ratio: —
Return on equity: (-0.70)%
Cash ($ mil.): 3
Current ratio: —
Long-term debt ($ mil.): —

Dividends
  Yield: —
  Payout: —
  Market value ($ mil.): —

CARL BOLANDER & SONS CO.

LOCATIONS

HQ: CARL BOLANDER & SONS CO.
251 STARKEY ST STE 1, SAINT PAUL, MN
55107-1824
Phone: 651-224-6299
Web: www.bolander.com

HISTORICAL FINANCIALS

Company Type: Private

Income Statement

FYE: December 31

	REVENUE ($ mil.)	NET INCOME ($ mil.)	NET PROFIT MARGIN	EMPLOYEES
12/11	85	14	16.7%	142
12/10	58	7	12.9%	0
12/09	52	4	8.7%	0
12/08	69	5	8.0%	0
Annual Growth	7.3%	37.0%	—	—

2011 Year-End Financials

Debt ratio: —
Return on equity: 16.70%
Cash ($ mil.): 1
Current ratio: 1.30
Long-term debt ($ mil.): —

Dividends
  Yield: —
  Payout: —
  Market value ($ mil.): —

CARNEGIE MELLON UNIVERSITY

If you can't act maybe Carnegie Mellon University can help. The university is known around the world for churning out award-winning actors from its highly regarded drama school. Drama isn't all Carnegie teaches though the school has seven colleges and schools that offer academic programs in areas such as psychology computer science engineering biology and public policy. It has more than 12000 students and 5000 faculty and staff and it has a relatively small student-teacher ratio of 10:1. Carnegie Mellon was founded by philanthropist and industrialist Andrew Carnegie who established the Carnegie Technical Schools in 1900 for the sons and daughters of Pittsburgh's blue-collar workers.

Geographic Reach

The school has locations in Pittsburgh (its main campus); Australia; Japan; Silicon Valley California; Singapore; Mexico; Greece; Portugal; and Doha Qatar.

Operations

Along with its undergraduate and graduate degree programs Carnegie offers working adults a chance to continue their learning through the Professional & Distance Learning arm of the school. Students there can hone their international business management skills and bone up on information technology health systems and human resources among other topics.

Carnegie prides itself on its innovation efforts and to support them operates about 120 research institutes and centers across its campus. Carnegie's CyLab is one of the largest university-based cybersecurity education and research centers in the country. Cylab focuses on seven primary areas of research and development spanning a wide range of technologies and systems and users.

Carnegie in 2012 established the Wilton E. Scott Institute for Energy Innovation a research and education initiative focused on improving energy efficiency and developing new clean and affordable energy sources. It also launched Initiative for Digital Entertainment Analytics which conducts research into questions raised by the emergence of digital distribution channels for entertainment content.

Financial Performance

The university experienced growth of 11% in 2012 due to increased retention in undergraduate programs and growth in graduate program tuition and international programs. The growth was also due to increase in investment income and income from auxiliary service.

However Carnegie experienced a 84% decline in net income in 2012 due to increases in operating expenses dining vendor expenses and software and maintenance licenses. Its bottom line was also hurt by a decrease in revenue from non-operating activities.

Company Background

Carnegie Tech merged with the Mellon Institute of Research to become Carnegie Mellon University in 1967.

EXECUTIVES

Chairman, Raymond J. (Ray) Lane, age 65
President and Trustee, Jared L. Cohon, age 64
EVP and Provost, Mark S. Kamlet
VP and General Counsel, Mary Jo Dively
VP and CFO, Deborah Moon
Vice Chairman, E. Kears Pollock
VP Research, Richard D. (Rick) McCullough
VP University Advancement, Robbee Baker Kosak
Chief Investment Officer, Charles A Kennedy
Life Trustee, Attila Molnar, age 64
Trustee, Dina Dublon, age 59
Trustee, Murry S. Gerber, age 59
Emeritus Life Trustee, Edward E. Lucente, age 72
Emeritus Life Trustee, Paul A. Allaire, age 68
Life Trustee, Philip L. Dowd
Emeritus Life Trustee, T. Jerome Holleran
Life Trustee, Robert W. Dunlap
Life Trustee, David S. (Dave) Shapira, age 70

Trustee, Louis R. Bucalo, age 53
Trustee, John R. Bertucci, age 72
Emeritus Life Trustee, Raymond W. Smith
Trustee, Yoshiaki Fujimori, age 61
Trustee, Bruce M. McWilliams, age 56
Emeritus Life Trustee, David M. Roderick, age 87
Trustee, William S. Dietrich II, age 74
Emeritus Life Trustee, Claire W. Gargalli, age 69
Emeritus Life Trustee, Douglas D. Danforth
Trustee, William B. Ellis, age 72
President and Trustee, Jared L. Cohon, age 64
Emeritus Life Trustee, Thomas A. McConomy, age 78
Emeritus Life Trustee, Charles J. Queenan Jr., age 81
Emeritus Life Trustee, Vincent A. Sarni, age 83
Trustee, Joel P. Adams, age 54
Emeritus Life Trustee, William Goldsmith, age 92
Emeritus Life Trustee, Konrad M. Weis, age 83
Trustee, Manoj P. Singh
Emeritus Life Trustee, George A. Roberts, age 90
Emeritus Life Trustee, Carol R. Brown, age 78
Trustee, Frank Brunckhorst
Emeritus Life Trustee, John G. Rangos Sr.
Emeritus Life Trustee, Anthony J. A. Bryan
Emeritus Life Trustee, Lucian Caste
Emeritus Life Trustee, Robert A. Charpie
Emeritus Life Trustee, Linda A. Dickerson
Trustee, W. Logan Dickerson
Emeritus Life Trustee, Edward Donley
Trustee, John Ghaznavi
Emeritus Life Trustee, Stanley R. Gumberg
Trustee, Richard D. Hamilton
Trustee, Oscar L. Harris Jr.
Emeritus Life Trustee, Wilton A. Hawkins
Trustee, Teresa Heinz
Emeritus Life Trustee, Orion L. Hoch
Emeritus Life Trustee, W. Lee Hoskins
Life Trustee, Torrence M. Hunt Jr.
Trustee, Larry Jennings
Trustee, Patricia Askwith Kenner
Emeritus Life Trustee, Hans W. Lange
Trustee, Glenn Meakem
Emeritus Life Trustee, Lindsay J. Morgenthaler
Emeritus Life Trustee, Theodore D. Nierenberg
Emeritus Life Trustee, Alessandro Ovi, age 68
Emeritus Life Trustee, Norman F. Parker
Vice Chairman, E. Kears Pollock
Trustee, Henry Posner Jr.
Trustee, Barrie Dinkins Simpson
Emeritus Life Trustee, William P. Snyder III
Emeritus Life Trustee, Alexander C. Speyer Jr.
Life Trustee, W. Lowell Steinbrenner
Trustee, Donald E. Stingle
Emeritus Life Trustee, James W. Taylor
Emeritus Life Trustee, James M. Walton
Emeritus Life Trustee, S. Donald Wiley
Trustee, Candace S. Matthews, age 53
Emeritus Life Trustee, William H. Knoell
Trustee, J. Lea Hillman Simonds
Trustee, David A. Tepper
Trustee, Paula Kaufman Wagner
Trustee, Johnathan M Rothberg
Trustee, Ronald P Bianchini
Trustee, Marco Delgado
Trustee, Sulajja Firodia Motwani
Trustee, Howard Ellin
Auditors: Deloitte&ToucheLLP

LOCATIONS

HQ: CARNEGIE MELLON UNIVERSITY
5000 FORBES AVE, PITTSBURGH, PA 15213-3890
Phone: 412-268-8746
Web: www.theasa.net

Selected Locations
Adelaide Australia

Athens Greece
Aveiro and Coimbra Portugal
Doha Qatar
Kobe Japan
Lisbon Portugal
Los Angeles
Madeira Portugal
Minho and Porto Portugal
Mexico
Silicon Valley
Singapore

PRODUCTS/OPERATIONS

Selected Schools
Carnegie Institute of Technology
School of Computer Science
College of Fine Arts
College of Humanities & Social Sciences
H. John Heinz III College
Mellon College of Science
Tepper School of Business

HISTORICAL FINANCIALS
Company Type: School

Income Statement				FYE: June 30
	REVENUE ($ mil.)	NET INCOME ($ mil.)	NET PROFIT MARGIN	EMPLOYEES
06/12	1,061	44	4.2%	4,913
06/11	956	278	29.1%	0
06/10	899	97	10.8%	0
06/09	864	(366)	—	0
Annual Growth	7.1%	—	—	—

2012 Year-End Financials
Debt ratio: —
Return on equity: 4.20%
Cash ($ mil.): 162
Current ratio: —
Long-term debt ($ mil.): —
Dividends
Yield: —
Payout: —
Market value ($ mil.): —

CAROLINA CARPORTS INC.

LOCATIONS
HQ: CAROLINA CARPORTS INC.
187 CARDINAL RIDGE LN, DOBSON, NC 27017-8652
Phone: 336-367-6400
Web: www.carolinacarportsinc.com

HISTORICAL FINANCIALS
Company Type: Private

Income Statement				FYE: December 31
	REVENUE ($ mil.)	NET INCOME ($ mil.)	NET PROFIT MARGIN	EMPLOYEES
12/11	91	1	1.4%	147
12/09	84	0	0.0%	0
12/07	86	1	1.3%	0
12/06	73	0	0.7%	0
Annual Growth	7.9%	32.3%	—	—

2011 Year-End Financials
Debt ratio: —
Return on equity: 1.40%
Cash ($ mil.): 0
Current ratio: 0.10
Long-term debt ($ mil.): —
Dividends
Yield: —
Payout: —
Market value ($ mil.): —

CARRICO IMPLEMENT CO. INC.

LOCATIONS
HQ: CARRICO IMPLEMENT CO. INC.
3160 US 24 HWY, BELOIT, KS 67420-1577
Phone: 785-738-5744
Web: www.carricoimplement.com

HISTORICAL FINANCIALS
Company Type: Private

Income Statement				FYE: October 31
	REVENUE ($ mil.)	NET INCOME ($ mil.)	NET PROFIT MARGIN	EMPLOYEES
10/11	116	4	4.1%	62
10/10	99	4	4.6%	0
10/09	87	3	4.5%	0
10/08	70	9	13.3%	0
Annual Growth	18.1%	(20.4%)	—	—

2011 Year-End Financials
Debt ratio: —
Return on equity: 4.10%
Cash ($ mil.): 0
Current ratio: —
Long-term debt ($ mil.): —
Dividends
Yield: —
Payout: —
Market value ($ mil.): —

CARROLL HOSPITAL CENTER INC.

LOCATIONS
HQ: CARROLL HOSPITAL CENTER INC.
200 MEMORIAL AVE, WESTMINSTER, MD 21157-5726
Phone: 410-848-3000
Web: www.cbgh.com

HISTORICAL FINANCIALS
Company Type: Private

Income Statement				FYE: June 30
	REVENUE ($ mil.)	NET INCOME ($ mil.)	NET PROFIT MARGIN	EMPLOYEES
06/11	206	16	8.1%	1,100
06/10	196	(0)	—	0
06/09	187	(12)	—	0
06/08	2	0	32.3%	0
Annual Growth	365.5%	193.6%	—	—

2011 Year-End Financials
Debt ratio: —
Return on equity: 8.10%
Cash ($ mil.): 28
Current ratio: 2.10
Long-term debt ($ mil.): —
Dividends
Yield: —
Payout: —
Market value ($ mil.): —

CARTER LUMBER INC

LOCATIONS
HQ: CARTER LUMBER INC
601 TALLMADGE RD, KENT, OH 44240-7331
Phone: 330-673-6100
Web: www.carterlumber.com

HISTORICAL FINANCIALS
Company Type: Private

Income Statement				FYE: December 31
	REVENUE ($ mil.)	NET INCOME ($ mil.)	NET PROFIT MARGIN	EMPLOYEES
12/11	105	(1)	—	425
12/10	95	(3)	—	0
12/09	96	(2)	—	0
12/08	96	(2)	—	0
Annual Growth	2.8%	—	—	—

2011 Year-End Financials
Debt ratio: —
Return on equity: (-1.50)%
Cash ($ mil.): 0
Current ratio: 0.20
Long-term debt ($ mil.): —
Dividends
Yield: —
Payout: —
Market value ($ mil.): —

CARTER-JONES COMPANIES INC

LOCATIONS
HQ: CARTER-JONES COMPANIES INC
601 TALLMADGE RD, KENT, OH 44240-7331
Phone: 330-673-6100
Web: www.carterlumber.com

HISTORICAL FINANCIALS
Company Type: Private

Income Statement				FYE: December 31
	REVENUE ($ mil.)	NET INCOME ($ mil.)	NET PROFIT MARGIN	EMPLOYEES
12/11	671	1	0.3%	3,225
12/10	652	(6)	—	0
12/09	583	(8)	—	0
Annual Growth	7.3%	—	—	—

Debt ratio: —
Return on equity: 0.30%
Cash ($ mil.): 12
Current ratio: 0.10
Long-term debt ($ mil.): —

Dividends
Yield: —
Payout: —
Market value ($ mil.): —

CASH-WA DISTRIBUTING CO. OF KEARNEY INC.

This company keeps the Quik-E Marts in merchandise. Cash-Wa Distributing supplies food produce beverages equipment cleaning supplies and more to foodservice operators and convenience stores throughout Nebraska and in parts of nine other Upper Plains states. It operates three distribution centers and serves more than 3500 customers. The family owned and operated company was formed in 1934 as a candy and tobacco wholesaler and was purchased by the Henning family in 1957. Cash-Wa Distributing is a member of the UniPro distribution cooperative.

EXECUTIVES

Chairman and President, Thomas J. (Tom) Henning
SVP Sales, James H. Kindig
VP Multi Unit Sales, Rick Meyer
Secretary and Treasurer, Gary Henning
Director Personnel, Leonard Wintermote
Controller, Edward J. Bloomfield

LOCATIONS

HQ: Cash-Wa Distributing Company
401 W. 4th St., Kearney NE 68845-7825
Phone: 308-237-3151   **Fax:** 308-234-6018
Web: www.cashwa.com

COMPETITORS

Affiliated Foods	MAINES
Midwest	McLane
AMCON Distributing	Meadowbrook Meat
Associated Wholesale	Company
Grocers	Nash-Finch
C&S Wholesale	Performance Food
Core-Mark	Performance Food Group
Farner-Bocken	Reinhart FoodService
Hawkeye Foodservice	Sysco
Distribution	US Foods

HISTORICAL FINANCIALS

Company Type: Private

Income Statement

FYE: December 3

	REVENUE ($ mil.)	NET INCOME ($ mil.)	NET PROFIT MARGIN	EMPLOYEES
12/11	306	5	1.8%	539
Annual Growth	—	—	—	—

2011 Year-End Financials

Debt ratio: —
Return on equity: 1.80%
Cash ($ mil.): 0
Current ratio: 0.90
Long-term debt ($ mil.): —

Dividends
Yield: —
Payout: —
Market value ($ mil.): —

CASSIDY TURLEY INC.

LOCATIONS

HQ: CASSIDY TURLEY INC.
7700 FORSYTH BLVD STE 900, SAINT LOUIS, MO
63105-1826
Phone: 314-862-7100
Web: www.cassidyturley.com

PRODUCTS/OPERATIONS

Selected Services

Auction services
Capital markets
Corporate services
Distressed asset services
Financial advisory
Practices and specialties
Project and development services
Project leasing
Sustainability services
Tenant representation

HISTORICAL FINANCIALS

Company Type: Private

Income Statement

FYE: December 31

	ASSETS ($ mil.)	NET INCOME ($ mil.)	INCOME AS % OF ASSETS	EMPLOYEES
12/11	248	1	0.6%	2,120
Annual Growth	—	—	—	—

2011 Year-End Financials

Debt ratio: —
Return on equity: 0.40%
Cash ($ mil.): 17
Current ratio: 1.20
Long-term debt ($ mil.): —

Dividends
Yield: —
Payout: —
Market value ($ mil.): —

CATAWBA VALLEY MEDICAL CENTER

LOCATIONS

HQ: CATAWBA VALLEY MEDICAL CENTER
810 FAIRGROVE CHURCH RD, HICKORY, NC
28602-9617
Phone: 828-326-3000
Web: www.catawbavalleymedical.org

HISTORICAL FINANCIALS

Company Type: Private

Income Statement

FYE: June 30

	REVENUE ($ mil.)	NET INCOME ($ mil.)	NET PROFIT MARGIN	EMPLOYEES
06/11	192	12	6.4%	1,450
06/10	188	10	5.8%	0
06/09	187	9	4.9%	0
06/06	151	4	3.0%	0
Annual Growth	8.4%	39.5%	—	—

Debt ratio: —
Return on equity: 6.40%
Cash ($ mil.): 75
Current ratio: 2.60
Long-term debt ($ mil.): —

Dividends
Yield: —
Payout: —
Market value ($ mil.): —

CATHOLIC COMMUNITY SERVICES OF WESTERN WASHINGTON

LOCATIONS

HQ: CATHOLIC COMMUNITY SERVICES OF WESTERN
WASHINGTON
100 23RD AVE S, SEATTLE, WA 98144-2302
Phone: 206-323-6336
Web: www.catholiccharitiesseattlearch.org

HISTORICAL FINANCIALS

Company Type: Private

Income Statement

FYE: June 30

	REVENUE ($ mil.)	NET INCOME ($ mil.)	NET PROFIT MARGIN	EMPLOYEES
06/11	99	2	2.3%	80
06/10	98	2	2.9%	0
06/09	90	1	2.2%	0
06/08	85	3	3.9%	0
Annual Growth	5.0%	(12.8%)	—	—

2011 Year-End Financials

Debt ratio: —
Return on equity: 2.30%
Cash ($ mil.): 6
Current ratio: 1.20
Long-term debt ($ mil.): —

Dividends
Yield: —
Payout: —
Market value ($ mil.): —

CATHOLIC MEDICAL CENTER

Catholic Medical Center is a 230-bed hospital serving southern New Hampshire. Services include cancer treatment surgery rehabilitation treatments for sleep disorders and emergency medical services. Catholic Medical Center (CMC) includes The Mom's Place a birthing facility and the New England Heart Institute. CMC has partnered with its community to extend health care and dental care to the uninsured and the homeless and has established a health clinic geared to help refugees being resettled in the area. In 2011 CMC canceled plans to merge with Dartmouth-Hitchcock Medical Center although the hospitals continue to collaborate at CMC's Special Care Nursery and D-H's Norris Cotton Cancer Center.
Strategy

CMC and Dartmouth-Hitchcock cited evolving changes in health care reforms behind their decision not to merge. The partnership had been opposed by the New Hampshire attorney general on the grounds that it would violate state law and needed court approval.

EXECUTIVES

President and CEO, Alyson Pitman Giles
VP Human Resources, Margo Compagna
VP Business Development and COO, Allen Ericson
VP Clinical Services and Chief Quality Officer, Tina Legere
Chief Medical Officer, Joseph Pepe
VP Marketing Corporate Communication and Philanthropy, Gail Winslow-Pine
CFO, Kevin Kilday
Chairman, Jeffrey Eisenberg
Vice Chairman, Maria Mongan
CIO, Brian Tew
EVP and Chief Compliance Officer, Raymond Bonito

LOCATIONS

HQ: Catholic Medical Center
100 McGregor St., Manchester NH 03102
Phone: 603-668-3545   **Fax:** 603-663-6929
Web: www.catholicmedicalcenter.org
Affiliated primary care practices
Amoskeag Primary Care (Manchester
Dartmouth-Hitchcock Bedford Internal Medicine (Bedford)
Family Health & Wellness Center (Bedford)
Family Physicians of Manchester (Manchester
Goffstown Primary Care (Goffstown
Granite State Internal Medicine (Manchester
Hooksett Primary Care (Hooksett)
Medical Group of Manchester (Manchester
Queen City Medical Associates (Manchester
Webster Street Internal Medicine (Manchester
Willowbend Family Practice (Bedford)

PRODUCTS/OPERATIONS

Selected services
Arthritis Clinic
Behavioral Health Services
Breast Care Center
Cancer Care
Critical & Intensive Care
Diabetes Resource Institute
Diagnostic Imaging & Radiology
Emergency Services
Gynecology
Laboratory
Nutrition Services
Obesity Treatment Center
Orthopedics
Surgical Care Group
Vascular Services
Women's Health
Wound Care

COMPETITORS

Beth Israel Deaconess Medical Center	Concord Hospital
Boston Medical Center	Elliot Health System
Brigham and Women's Hospital	Exeter Health Resources
Cambridge Health Alliance	Frisbie Memorial Hospital
CareGroup	HealthSouth
Caritas Holy Family Hospital	Southern New Hampshire Medical Center

HISTORICAL FINANCIALS
Company Type: Private

Income Statement   FYE: June 30

	REVENUE ($ mil.)	NET INCOME ($ mil.)	NET PROFIT MARGIN	EMPLOYEES
06/11	315	14	4.7%	1,536
06/10	277	11	4.2%	0
06/09	241	(1)	—	0
06/08	228	14	6.2%	0
Annual Growth	11.4%	2.0%		

2011 Year-End Financials

Debt ratio: ——
Return on equity: 4.70%
Cash ($ mil.): 51
Current ratio: —
Long-term debt ($ mil.): —

Dividends
  Yield: —
  Payout: —
Market value ($ mil.): —

CATOOSA COUNTY BOARD OF EDUCATION INC

LOCATIONS

HQ: CATOOSA COUNTY BOARD OF EDUCATION INC
307 CLEVELAND ST, RINGGOLD, GA 30736-2057
Phone: 706-965-2297
Web: www.ringgoldmiddleschool.org

HISTORICAL FINANCIALS
Company Type: Private

Income Statement   FYE: June 30

	REVENUE ($ mil.)	NET INCOME ($ mil.)	NET PROFIT MARGIN	EMPLOYEES
06/11	111	14	13.3%	1,900
06/10	106	(0)	—	0
06/09	109	1	1.2%	0
06/08	112	(23)	—	0
Annual Growth	(0.5%)	—	—	—

2011 Year-End Financials

Debt ratio: ——
Return on equity: 13.30%
Cash ($ mil.): 38
Current ratio: —
Long-term debt ($ mil.): —

Dividends
  Yield: —
  Payout: —
Market value ($ mil.): —

CDM FEDERAL PROGRAMS CORPORATION

LOCATIONS

HQ: CDM FEDERAL PROGRAMS CORPORATION
3201 JERMANTOWN RD # 400, FAIRFAX, VA 22030-2883
Phone: 703-691-6500
Web: www.cdmsmith.com

HISTORICAL FINANCIALS
Company Type: Private

Income Statement   FYE: December 31

	REVENUE ($ mil.)	NET INCOME ($ mil.)	NET PROFIT MARGIN	EMPLOYEES
12/11*	117	1	1.2%	525
01/11	119	2	2.2%	0
01/09	96	1	1.3%	0
01/04	75	0	1.1%	0
Annual Growth	15.9%	21.2%	—	—

*Fiscal year change

2011 Year-End Financials

Debt ratio: ——
Return on equity: 1.20%
Cash ($ mil.): 0
Current ratio: 2.60
Long-term debt ($ mil.): —

Dividends
  Yield: —
  Payout: —
Market value ($ mil.): —

CEDAR RAPIDS COMMUNITY SCHOOL DISTRICT FOUNDATION

LOCATIONS

HQ: CEDAR RAPIDS COMMUNITY SCHOOL DISTRICT FOUNDATION
907 15TH ST SW, CEDAR RAPIDS, IA 52404-1700
Phone: 319-558-2964
Web: www.cr.k12.ia.us

HISTORICAL FINANCIALS
Company Type: Private

Income Statement   FYE: June 30

	REVENUE ($ mil.)	NET INCOME ($ mil.)	NET PROFIT MARGIN	EMPLOYEES
06/11	217	15	7.0%	2,540
06/10	204	(33)	—	0
06/09	206	(15)	—	0
06/08	195	11	5.8%	0
Annual Growth	3.7%	10.5%	—	—

2011 Year-End Financials

Debt ratio: ——
Return on equity: 7.00%
Cash ($ mil.): 62
Current ratio: 0.50
Long-term debt ($ mil.): ——

Dividends
  Yield: ——
  Payout: ——
Market value ($ mil.): ——

CEDARS-SINAI MEDICAL CARE FOUNDATION

LOCATIONS

HQ: CEDARS-SINAI MEDICAL CARE FOUNDATION
200 N ROBERTSON BLVD # 101, BEVERLY HILLS, CA
90211-1769
Phone: 310-385-3200

HISTORICAL FINANCIALS

Company Type: Private

Income Statement

FYE: June 30

	REVENUE ($ mil.)	NET INCOME ($ mil.)	NET PROFIT MARGIN	EMPLOYEES
06/11	145	6	4.2%	4
06/10	129	4	3.5%	0
06/09	119	3	3.1%	0
06/08	89	(15)	——	0
Annual Growth	17.3%	——	——	——

2011 Year-End Financials

Debt ratio: ——
Return on equity: 4.20%
Cash ($ mil.): 12
Current ratio: 1.40
Long-term debt ($ mil.): ——

Dividends
  Yield: ——
  Payout: ——
Market value ($ mil.): ——

CEDARS-SINAI MEDICAL CENTER

Many a star has been born literally at Cedars-Sinai Medical Center. The 895-bed teaching and research hospital is located right where Los Angeles meets Beverly Hills and West Hollywood and has tended to the medical needs of a number of celebrities since its founding in 1902. However the center is also a major teaching hospital for UCLA's David Geffen School of Medicine and is engaged in hundreds of research programs in areas such as cancer neuroscience and genetics. It also includes two multi-specialty physician associations Cedars-Sinai Medical Group and Ceders-Sinai Health Associates and operates a number of community health centers and outreach programs (such as mobile health clinics).

Operations

The not-for-profit hospital's 2100 staff physicians represent just about every clinical specialty out there. Cedars-Sinai is consistently listed as a top-ranked hospital by U.S. News & World Report in such specialties as cancer cardiology endocrinol-

ogy gastrointestinal disorders gynecology heart surgery kidney disease neurology orthopaedics and respiratory disorders.

Cedars-Sinai is the only private hospital with a Level 1 trauma center in Los Angeles County; as such the hospital sees about 1600 trauma patients a year. The hospital also provides a number of outpatient services.

Financial Analysis

Revenues from patient care and other sources totaled nearly $2.75 billion in fiscal 2012 (ends June) while net income amounted to $132.6 million.

Strategy

To meet increasing patient demand as well as to expand its capacity for research projects Cedars-Sinai is constructing a $600 million outpatient and research center (the Advanced Health Sciences Pavilion) that is scheduled to open in summer 2013. The hospital conducts some $100 million in medical and clinical research each year.

EXECUTIVES

President and CEO, Thomas M. (Tom) Priselac
SVP Finance and CFO, Edward M. Prunchunas
SVP Human Resources and Organization Development, Jeanne Flores
SVP Clinical Care Services and COO, Mark R. Gavens
SVP Community Relations, Arthur J. Ochoa
SVP Academic Affairs and Chief Academic Officer, Shlomo Melmed
SVP Medical Affairs and Chief Medical Officer, Michael L. Langberg
SVP System Development and Chief Strategy Officer, Richard B. Jacobs
SVP Medical Delivery Network, Thomas D. Gordon
SVP Legal Affairs, Peter E. Braveman
Chief of Staff and Director, William W. Brien
Secretary, Robert M. Eller
Chairman, Lawrence B. Platt
Chairman, Mark S. Siegel
SVP Enterprise Information Systems and CIO, Darren Dworkin
Senior Development Officer Foundation Relations, Sharon Friedman
Vice Chairman, Vera Guerin
VP Nursing and Chief Nursing Officer, Linda Burnes Bolton
Director, Jay S. Wintrob, age 54
Director, Jeffrey Katzenberg, age 61
Director, Andy Heyward
Director, John M. Bendheim, age 57
Director, John G. Harold
Director, John C. Law
Director, James A. Nathan
Chief of Staff and Director, William W. Brien
Director, Steven D. Broidy
Director, Irving Feintech
Director, Julian A. Gold
Director, Mark S. Greenfield
Director, Sue Neuman Hochberg
Director, Thomas J. Leanse
Director, John W. Mack
Director, Edward Meltzer
Director, Todd M. Morgan
Director, Richard Powell
Vice Chairman, Lawrence B. Platt
Director, Marc Rapaport
Director, Mark S. Siegel
Director, Robert Silverstein
Director, Steven Spielberg
Director, Theodore Stein
Director, Leslie Vermut
Director, Walter Zifkin
Director, Paul Silka

Director, Robert Davidson
Vice Chairman, Vera Guerin
Director, Sheila Kar
Director, Beth Karlan
Director, Steven B. Nichols
Director, Luis Nogales
Director, Lynda Oschin
Director, Steven Romick
Director, David Saperstein
Director, Zab Mosenifar

LOCATIONS

HQ: Cedars-Sinai Medical Center
  8700 Beverly Blvd., Los Angeles CA 90048
Phone: 310-423-3277   **Fax:** 248-863-3100
Web: www.homedics.com

PRODUCTS/OPERATIONS

Selected Centers and Services

Ambulatory Care Center
Cedars-Sinai Center for Chest Disease
Cedars-Sinai Center for Digestive Diseases
Cedars-Sinai Heart Institute
Cedars-Sinai Institute Spine Center
Cedars-Sinai Health Associates (affiliated independent physician association)
Cedars-Sinai Medical Group (multi-specialty physicians group)
Cedars-Sinai Orthopedic Center
Diagnostic imaging center
Emergency department and trauma center
Hospice services
Kidney and pancreas transplant center
Neuroscience services
Pediatric services
Psychiatry and mental health services
Samuel Oschin Comprehensive Cancer Institute
Surgical services
Organ and bone marrow transplantation
Radiation therapy
Radiology
Stroke program
Pain management services
Women's health services

COMPETITORS

Adventist Health
Brotman Medical Center
Childrens Hospital Los Angeles
City of Hope
Community Health Systems
Dignity Health
Eisenhower Medical Center
Glendale Adventist Medical Center
Glendale Memorial Hospital
Golden State Health Centers
Good Samaritan Hospital (IN)
HCA
Hollywood Presbyterian Medical Center
Kaiser Permanente
Little Company of Mary
Los Angeles County Health Department
Newhall Memorial Hospital
Pasadena Hospital Association
Providence Saint Joseph Medical Center
Scripps health
Tenet Healthcare
UCSF Medical
White Memorial Medical Center

HISTORICAL FINANCIALS

Company Type: Private - Not-for-Profit

Income Statement

FYE: June 30

	REVENUE ($ mil.)	NET INCOME ($ mil.)	NET PROFIT MARGIN	EMPLOYEES
06/11	2,658	210	7.9%	8,000
06/10	2,309	152	6.6%	0
06/09	1,962	88	4.5%	0
06/08	2,037	246	12.1%	0
Annual Growth	9.3%	(5.1%)	—	—

2011 Year-End Financials

Debt ratio: ——
Return on equity: 7.90%
Cash ($ mil.): 303
Current ratio: 0.40
Long-term debt ($ mil.): —

Dividends
Yield: —
Payout: —
Market value ($ mil.): —

CEDARVILLE UNIVERSITY INC

LOCATIONS

HQ: CEDARVILLE UNIVERSITY INC
251 N MAIN ST, CEDARVILLE, OH 45314-8564
Phone: 937-766-7700
Web: www.cedarvillesife.com

HISTORICAL FINANCIALS

Company Type: Private

Income Statement

FYE: June 30

	REVENUE ($ mil.)	NET INCOME ($ mil.)	NET PROFIT MARGIN	EMPLOYEES
06/11	104	8	8.5%	500
06/10	93	1	2.0%	0
06/09	85	0	—	0
06/08	88	6	6.9%	0
Annual Growth	5.7%	13.2%	—	—

2011 Year-End Financials

Debt ratio: ——
Return on equity: 8.50%
Cash ($ mil.): 12
Current ratio: —
Long-term debt ($ mil.): —

Dividends
Yield: —
Payout: —
Market value ($ mil.): —

CEDARWOOD-YOUNG COMPANY

LOCATIONS

HQ: CEDARWOOD-YOUNG COMPANY
14620 JOANBRIDGE ST, BALDWIN PARK, CA
91706-1750
Phone: 626-962-4047
Web: www.allancompany.com

HISTORICAL FINANCIALS

Company Type: Private

Income Statement

FYE: December 31

	REVENUE ($ mil.)	NET INCOME ($ mil.)	NET PROFIT MARGIN	EMPLOYEES
12/11	456	4	1.1%	275
12/10	391	7	2.0%	0
12/09	296	4	1.7%	0
12/08	399	7	1.9%	0
Annual Growth	4.6%	(13.9%)	—	—

2011 Year-End Financials

Debt ratio: ——
Return on equity: 1.10%
Cash ($ mil.): 4
Current ratio: 2.10
Long-term debt ($ mil.): —

Dividends
Yield: —
Payout: —
Market value ($ mil.): —

CENTEGRA HEALTH SYSTEM

Centegra Health System seeks integrity in the health care services realm. The health network serves residents of the greater McHenry County region in northern Illinois and southern Wisconsin. The company operates two main medical centers Centegra Hospital-McHenry and Centegra Hospital-Woodstock with a total of some 350 beds. They offer emergency and trauma care as well as general medicine surgery and obstetrics services. Centegra has dedicated cancer diabetes and heart centers and also offers rehabilitation behavioral health and fitness services. In addition the community-based health system operates a network of primary care and specialty outpatient clinics.

Company Background

Centegra Health System became a "system" when two northern Illinois area hospitals Memorial Medical Center and Northern Illinois Medical Center joined forces in 1995. Memorial Medical Center was founded in 1914 and is now named Centegra Hospital-Woodstock while Northern Illinois Medical Center was established in 1956 and is called Centegra Hospital-McHenry.

EXECUTIVES

President CEO and Director, Michael S. Eesley
SVP Human Resources Development, Barbara Jo Johnson
Senior Media and Public Relations Coordinator, Melissa Matusek
SVP Chief Quality Officer and Corporate Counsel, Aaron Shepley
SVP Women's Health, Angela McAuley
VP Centegra Primary Care, Robert J. Turngren
Chairman, Christian Newkirk
VP Medical Affairs, Z. Thaddeus (Ted) Lorenc
Vice Chairman, Charlie Zanck
EVP and COO, Jason Sciarro
SVP and CFO, Robert M. Rosenberger
VP Strategic Marketing and Planning, Susan Milford
VP System Operations, Joseph (Joe) Hurshe
VP Development, Gail D. Bauersachs
Secretary, William Cox
Treasurer, Pat Morehead

VP Clinical Ancillary Services, David Tomlinson
VP and Chief Nursing Officer Centegra Hospital McHenry, Sue Murphy
VP and Chief Nursing Officer Centegra Hospital Woodstock, Laura Walczak
President CEO and Director, Michael S. Eesley
Director, Amir Heydari
Director, James Hooker
Director, Luke Johnsos
Director, Sanjukta Mitra
Director, D. Michael Splitt
Director, Laurence Gott
Director, Paul Hills
Director, Patrick Morehead
Director, Parmod Narang
Director, Katherine Powell
Vice Chairman, Charlie Zanck
Director, William Cox
Director, Tom Carey

LOCATIONS

HQ: Centegra Health System
385 Millennium Dr., Crystal Lake IL 60012
Phone: 815-788-5800   **Fax:** 678-947-3368
Web: www.sawnee.com

PRODUCTS/OPERATIONS

Selected Medical Services
Anticoagulation Management
Bone and Joint Services
Cancer Services
Centegra Clinical Laboratories
Centegra Immediate Care
Centegra Physician Care
Corporate Health Services
Diabetes Services
Emergency and Trauma Services
Family Birth Centers
Heart Services
Home Health Services
Medical Imaging/X-Ray
Mental Health Services
Nursing
Nutrition
Orthopedic Services
Outpatient Services
Rehabilitation Services
Respiratory Care Services
Screenings
Sleep Services
Surgical Services
Weight-Loss Surgery
Wellness Services
Women's Services
Wound Care and Hyperbaric Services

COMPETITORS

Advocate Health Care
Alexian Brothers
 Health System
KishHealth
NorthShore University
 HealthSystem
Northwest Community
 Healthcare
Northwestern Memorial
 HealthCare

OSF Healthcare System
Rockford Health System
Rush System for Health
Sherman Health Systems
Silver Cross Hospital
SwedishAmerican Health
 System
University of Chicago
 Medical Center

HISTORICAL FINANCIALS

Company Type: Private - Not-for-Profit

Income Statement
FYE: September 30

	REVENUE ($ mil.)	NET INCOME ($ mil.)	NET PROFIT MARGIN	EMPLOYEES
09/12*	98	9	9.5%	3,700
06/12	427	(13)	—	0
06/11	0	0	—	0
06/10	80	(11)	—	0
Annual Growth	6.7%	—	—	—

*Fiscal year change

2012 Year-End Financials

Debt ratio: ——
Return on equity: 9.50%
Cash ($ mil.): 29
Current ratio: 0.90
Long-term debt ($ mil.): —

Dividends
Yield: —
Payout: —
Market value ($ mil.): —

CENTER FOR CREATIVE LEADERSHIP INC

The Center for Creative Leadership (CCL) is a not-for-profit organization that provides coaching in management training to public private nonprofit government and education sectors worldwide. the center is headquartered in Greensboro North Carolina and offers its programs through open enrollment courses and customized training at its campuses and affiliates across North America Europe Africa and Asia. Virtual learning through webinars podcasts and eBooks also is available. CCL serves some 20000 individuals and 2000 organizations each year with clients such as Wells Fargo Time Warner Cable and the US Army.

Operations

CCL provides an array of customized organizational solutions assessment instruments and feedback services leadership coaching publications. and online resources.

In fiscal year 2012 it funded 255 scholarships at a value of more than $1 million for leaders of nonprofit organizations to attend CCL educational programs.

CCL partners include UNC Kenan-Flagler Business School Jossey-Bass SHRM and the Singapore Economic Development Board.

Geographic Reach

CCL is headquartered in North Carolina and has offices in California and Colorado as well as in Belgium China Ethiopia India Russia and Singapore.

Financial Performance

In fiscal year 2012 CCL reported $99.2 million in total operating revenues of which about 85% was generated by tuition program and coaching fees.

Strategy

While it is already reaching clients in more than 120 countries the company is looking to expand internationally develop new programs and expand its language offerings.

In 2013 CCL launched its first China office (in Shanghai). A year earlier it set up its first Africa office (in Addis Ababa Ethiopia).

Company Background

CCL was founded in 1970.

EXECUTIVES

EVP Chief Financial and Administrative Officer and Treasurer, Bradley E. Shumaker
President CEO and Member Board of Governors, Vice Adm. John R. Ryan, age 66
Chairman Board of Governors, Ingar O. Skaug, age 65
EVP Research Innovation and Product Development, David G. Altman
Media Contact, Stephen Martin
VP Global Marketing, Portia Mount
VP and Chief Talent Officer, Paul Draeger
VP Chief of Staff and Secretary Board of Governors, Mona Edwards
Global Public Relations, Flontina Miller
VP Americas, Bruce Byington
SVP Global Organizational Leadership Development, Bill Pasmore
VP and Managing Director Europe Middle East and Africa, Rudi Plettinx
VP Asia/Pacific, Sureish D. Nathan

LOCATIONS

HQ: The Center for Creative Leadership
 1 Leadership Place, Greensboro NC 27438-6300
Phone: 336-545-2810   **Fax:** 336-282-3284
Web: www.ccl.org

PRODUCTS/OPERATIONS

2012 Sales

	% of total
Tuition program & coaching	85
Products &	6
Grants & research	6
Licensee royalties &	2
Donations & other	1
Total	**100**

COMPETITORS

Accenture	Linkage
Dale Carnegie	McKinsey & Company
Development Dimensions	Mission Control
International	Productivity
Franklin Covey	Nightingale-Conant
Interaction Associates	The Forum Corporation
Kepner-Tregoe	The Innovative Edge
Korn/Ferry	Viewpoint Learning
Learning Key	

HISTORICAL FINANCIALS

Company Type: Private - Not-for-Profit

Income Statement
FYE: March 31

	REVENUE ($ mil.)	NET INCOME ($ mil.)	NET PROFIT MARGIN	EMPLOYEES
03/11	92	3	4.0%	600
03/10	86	7	9.3%	0
03/09	69	(29)	—	0
03/08	92	(0)	—	0
Annual Growth	0.1%	—	—	—

2011 Year-End Financials

Debt ratio: ——
Return on equity: 4.00%
Cash ($ mil.): 10
Current ratio: 1.30
Long-term debt ($ mil.): —

Dividends
Yield: —
Payout: —
Market value ($ mil.): —

CENTER FOR NURSING & REHABILITATION INC.

LOCATIONS

HQ: CENTER FOR NURSING & REHABILITATION INC.
 520 PROSPECT PL, BROOKLYN, NY 11238-4205
Phone: 718-519-4226

HISTORICAL FINANCIALS

Company Type: Private

Income Statement
FYE: December 31

	REVENUE ($ mil.)	NET INCOME ($ mil.)	NET PROFIT MARGIN	EMPLOYEES
12/11	90	(2)	—	635
12/10	89	(1)	—	0
12/09	88	1	1.4%	0
12/08	89	3	3.4%	0
Annual Growth	0.3%	—	—	—

2011 Year-End Financials

Debt ratio: ——
Return on equity: (-2.90)%
Cash ($ mil.): 8
Current ratio: 1.20
Long-term debt ($ mil.): —

Dividends
Yield: —
Payout: —
Market value ($ mil.): —

CENTER OF SPECIAL CARE INC.

LOCATIONS

HQ: CENTER OF SPECIAL CARE INC.
 2150 CORBIN AVE, NEW BRITAIN, CT 06053-2266
Phone: 860-223-2761

HISTORICAL FINANCIALS

Company Type: Private

Income Statement
FYE: March 31

	REVENUE ($ mil.)	NET INCOME ($ mil.)	NET PROFIT MARGIN	EMPLOYEES
03/11	122	7	5.8%	0
03/10	0	0	—	0
03/09	0	0	—	0
Annual Growth	18832.7%	—	—	—

2011 Year-End Financials

Debt ratio: ——
Return on equity: 5.80%
Cash ($ mil.): 9
Current ratio: 1.70
Long-term debt ($ mil.): —

Dividends
Yield: —
Payout: —
Market value ($ mil.): —

CENTIMARK CORPORATION

Shout it from the rooftops CentiMark is one of the largest commercial and industrial roofing contractors in North America. The company provides roof installation inspection repair and emergency leak service. CentiMark typically works on flat roofs using EPDM rubber thermoplastic bitumen metal and coatings. Top customers include NASA and the US Army Corps of Engineers. Its QuestMark division offers commercial industrial and retail flooring do-it-yourself products and floor maintenance and cleaning products. Chairman and CEO Edward Dunlap founded CentiMark as an industrial cleaning business in 1967. The company which has about 70 offices throughout North America is owned by its employees.

Geographic Reach

Pittsburgh Pennsylvania-based CentiMark also does business in Canada through subsidiary CentiMark Ltd. which has offices in Calgary Edmonton Toronto and Vancouver.

Financial Performance

CentiMark's 2011 sales totaled more than $474 million a 17% increase vs. 2010.

Strategy

In response to customer demand for more energy-efficient options CentiMark has been increasing its use of spray polyurethane foam (which adds insulation and a waterproof barrier to roofs). The company also installs electricity-producing photovoltaic solar panels onto roofs. Other green options available from CentiMark include skylights and garden roofs.

The company also tries to stay ahead of the pack with technological innovations such as its MyCentiMark service. The online resource allows property owners to view invoices work authorizations before-and-after photos and recommendations for future roof maintenance.

Ownership

CentiMark is owned by its employees.

EXECUTIVES

Chairman and CEO, Edward B. Dunlap
President and COO, Timothy M. Dunlap
EVP and Group Director North and Canada, Robert Rudzik
EVP and Group Director East, Robert Fulton
EVP and Group Director West, Steve Ferencz
EVP National and Regional Sales, John Godwin
EVP and CFO, John Heisey
EVP and Group Director South, Sherman Gaskins
VP and Controller, Robert zovko
VP Advertising and Creative, John Zivkovich
VP Compensation and Benefits, Laura Kickbusch
VP Human Resources, Barbara Felton
VP and General Counsel, Thor DiCesare
SVP and CIO, Greg Wilson
SVP Purchasing, James Patterson

LOCATIONS

HQ: CentiMark Corporation
12 Grandview Circle, Canonsburg PA 15317
Phone: 724-514-8700   **Fax:** -12879
Web: www.wind.it

PRODUCTS/OPERATIONS

Selected Operations
CentiMark (roofing)
CentiMark ltd. (Canada roofing)
QuestMark (flooring)

COMPETITORS

Armstrong World Industries
Cabral Roofing & Waterproofing
D. C. Taylor
Duro-Last Roofing
Garcia Roofing
Holland Roofing
Pickens Roofing
Tecta America

HISTORICAL FINANCIALS
Company Type: Private

Income Statement
FYE: April 30

	REVENUE ($ mil.)	NET INCOME ($ mil.)	NET PROFIT MARGIN	EMPLOYEES
04/12	474	38	8.1%	1,900
04/11	404	31	7.8%	0
04/10	363	29	8.1%	0
04/09	404	31	7.9%	0
Annual Growth	5.5%	6.3%	—	—

2012 Year-End Financials
Debt ratio: —
Return on equity: 8.10%
Cash ($ mil.): 65
Current ratio: 2.50
Long-term debt ($ mil.): —
Dividends
Yield: —
Payout: —
Market value ($ mil.): —

CENTRAL ARKANSAS RADIATION THERAPY INSTITUTE INC.

LOCATIONS

HQ: CENTRAL ARKANSAS RADIATION THERAPY INSTITUTE INC.
4 SAINT VINCENT CIR, LITTLE ROCK, AR 72205-5402
Phone: 501-664-8573
Web: www.irmagailhatcher.com

HISTORICAL FINANCIALS
Company Type: Private

Income Statement
FYE: June 30

	REVENUE ($ mil.)	NET INCOME ($ mil.)	NET PROFIT MARGIN	EMPLOYEES
06/11	136	8	5.9%	175
06/10	139	5	4.1%	0
06/09	128	0	—	0
06/08	0	0	—	0
Annual Growth	—	—	—	—

2011 Year-End Financials
Debt ratio: —
Return on equity: 5.90%
Cash ($ mil.): 2
Current ratio: 1.90
Long-term debt ($ mil.): —
Dividends
Yield: —
Payout: —
Market value ($ mil.): —

CENTRAL ELECTRIC POWER COOPERATIVE INC

LOCATIONS

HQ: CENTRAL ELECTRIC POWER COOPERATIVE INC
2106 JEFFERSON ST, JEFFERSON CITY, MO 65109-2066
Phone: 573-634-2454
Web: www.cepc.net

HISTORICAL FINANCIALS
Company Type: Private

Income Statement
FYE: December 31

	REVENUE ($ mil.)	NET INCOME ($ mil.)	NET PROFIT MARGIN	EMPLOYEES
12/11	196	0	—	110
12/10	183	12	6.9%	0
12/09	176	12	7.2%	0
12/08	157	16	10.7%	0
Annual Growth	7.6%	—	—	—

2011 Year-End Financials
Debt ratio: —
Return on equity: —
Cash ($ mil.): 21
Current ratio: 0.30
Long-term debt ($ mil.): —
Dividends
Yield: —
Payout: —
Market value ($ mil.): —

CENTRAL ILLINOIS AG INC.

LOCATIONS

HQ: CENTRAL ILLINOIS AG INC.
200 E SHARON ST, ATLANTA, IL 61723-8741
Phone: 217-648-2307
Web: www.schmidt-marcotte.com

HISTORICAL FINANCIALS
Company Type: Private

Income Statement
FYE: December 31

	REVENUE ($ mil.)	NET INCOME ($ mil.)	NET PROFIT MARGIN	EMPLOYEES
12/11	90	3	3.7%	50
12/10	90	3	3.7%	0
12/09	80	2	2.7%	0
12/08	58	3	5.5%	0
Annual Growth	15.8%	1.8%	—	—

CENTRAL KITSAP SCHOOL DISTRICT 401

LOCATIONS

HQ: CENTRAL KITSAP SCHOOL DISTRICT 401
9210 SILVERDALE WAY NW, SILVERDALE, WA
98383-9197
Phone: 360-662-1610
Web: www.cksd.wednet.edu

HISTORICAL FINANCIALS

Company Type: Private

Income Statement

	REVENUE ($ mil.)	NET INCOME ($ mil.)	NET PROFIT MARGIN	EMPLOYEES
08/11	117	(8)	—	1,286
08/10	130	0	0.4%	0
08/09	132	(1)	—	0
08/08	127	3	2.7%	0
Annual Growth	(2.8%)	—	—	—

FYE: August 31

2011 Year-End Financials

Debt ratio: ——
Return on equity: (-7.50)%
Cash ($ mil.): 1
Current ratio: ——
Long-term debt ($ mil.): ——

Dividends
Yield: —
Payout: —
Market value ($ mil.): —

CENTRAL MICHIGAN UNIVERSITY

Academic advancement is central at Central Michigan University (CMU). It offers undergraduate graduate and professional coursework in eight academic divisions including business communication and fine arts medicine and education and human services. The university enrolls about 28000 students most of which attend the main campus in Mt. Pleasant. The institution also offers off-campus courses online and from more than 60 locations throughout North America. Notable alumni include former US Senator Robert P. Griffin and actor Jeff Daniels. CMU was founded in 1892 as a teachers' college.

CMU is the only university in the US to offer a bachelor's degree in microscopy.

EXECUTIVES

Dean Students, Bruce Roscoe
Associate VP Human Resources, Lori Hella
Associate VP Financial Services and Reporting and Controller, Barrie J. Wilkes
VP Government Relations and Public Affairs, Kathleen M. (Kathy) Wilbur
Vice Chair, Sam R. Kottamasu
Vice Chair, Marilyn French Hubbard
Chair, Stephanie Comai
VP Technology and CIO, Roger Rehm
Director Financial Planning and Budgets, Carol Haas

VP Finance and Administrative Services, David A. Burdette
EVP and Provost, E. Gary Shapiro
Director Administration, Dave Bunting
Associate VP Facilities Management, Stephen (Steve) Lawrence
Associate VP Residences and Auxiliary Services, John Fisher
Associate VP University Communications, Renee Walker
Executive Director Alumni Relations, Marcie Otteman
Interim VP Research Office of Research and Sponsored Programs, Ian Davison
Interim Dean College of Graduate Studies, Roger Coles
Dean Libraries, Thomas Moore
President, George E. Ross
Trustee, Brian W. Fannon, age 63
Trustee, Gail F. Torreano
Vice Chair, Sam R. Kottamasu
Vice Chair, Marilyn French Hubbard
President, George E. Ross
Trustee, John D. Hurd
Trustee, Sarah R. Opperman
Trustee, Robert F. Wardrop II
Auditors: AndrewsHooper&PavlikP.L.C.

LOCATIONS

HQ: CENTRAL MICHIGAN UNIVERSITY
1200 S FRANKLIN ST, MOUNT PLEASANT, MI
48859-0001
Phone: 989-774-4000
Web: www.ccfa.cmich.edu

PRODUCTS/OPERATIONS

Selected Areas of Study

Bilingual/Bicultural - Spanish/Ojibwe
Biology
Business Teacher Education
Chemistry
Chemistry/Physics
Dance
Earth Science
English
English as a Second Language (ESL)
Family Studies: Life Management Education
French
General Business
Geography
German
History
Industrial Education
Mathematics
Music Education
Outdoor and Environmental Education
Physical Education
Physics
School Health Education
Science Integrated
Secondary Education
Social Studies
Spanish
Special Education
Speech
Visual Arts Education

HISTORICAL FINANCIALS

Company Type: School

Income Statement

	REVENUE ($ mil.)	NET INCOME ($ mil.)	NET PROFIT MARGIN	EMPLOYEES
06/12	321	6	1.9%	2,388
06/11	329	90	27.4%	0
06/10	293	54	18.4%	0
06/09	276	33	12.2%	0
Annual Growth	5.1%	(43.4%)	—	—

FYE: June 30

2012 Year-End Financials

Debt ratio: ——
Return on equity: 1.90%
Cash ($ mil.): 73
Current ratio: 1.10
Long-term debt ($ mil.): ——

Dividends
Yield: —
Payout: —
Market value ($ mil.): —

CENTRAL PENINSULA GENERAL HOSPITAL INC.

LOCATIONS

HQ: CENTRAL PENINSULA GENERAL HOSPITAL INC.
250 HOSPITAL PL, SOLDOTNA, AK 99669-6999
Phone: 907-714-4404
Web: www.cpgh.org

HISTORICAL FINANCIALS

Company Type: Private

Income Statement

	REVENUE ($ mil.)	NET INCOME ($ mil.)	NET PROFIT MARGIN	EMPLOYEES
06/11	162	5	3.4%	611
06/10	89	2	3.0%	0
06/09	84	2	2.7%	0
06/08	118	1	1.5%	0
Annual Growth	11.4%	46.0%	—	—

FYE: June 30

2011 Year-End Financials

Debt ratio: ——
Return on equity: 3.40%
Cash ($ mil.): 21
Current ratio: 4.20
Long-term debt ($ mil.): ——

Dividends
Yield: —
Payout: —
Market value ($ mil.): —

CENTRAL REFRIGERATED SERVICE INC.

No matter the weather conditions trucking company Central Refrigerated Service stays cool when it's on the move. The carrier provides temperature-controlled transportation and dry cargo services for major food suppliers and retailers across the US. It specializes in providing a wide array of transportation requests from inner city and solo driver deliveries to long haul truckload transportation services. Central Refrigerated Service operates a fleet of about 1800 tractors and 2700 refrigerated trailers or reefers. The company is owned by Jerry Moyes who also owns less-than-truckload carrier Central Freight Lines and truckload carrier Swift Transportation.

Something of a one trick pony Central Refrigerated Service estimates that 95% of its loads are food products. Through its Central Logistics division the company provides truckload capacity brokerage and dedicated fleet services.

Founded in 2002 as a unit of Central Freight Lines Central Refrigerated Service expanded that year by buying the assets of bankrupt Simon Transportation Services another Moyes-controlled company. Central Refrigerated Service was spun off from Central Freight Lines at the end of 2002.

EXECUTIVES

CEO, Jon F. Isaacson
VP Sales and Pricing, Tork A. Fulton
Director Information Systems, Kevin Harper
Director Risk Management, Allan Lowry
Director Fleet, Carl Dicharo
Director Brokerage and Logistics, Lee Garbett
Southern California and Southwest Sales Manager, Brian Kilpatrick
Director Sales West, Brad Culy
Rocky Mountain Sales Manager, Alan Bird
Director Sales East, John Bohn
Director Sales National Accounts, Charlie Bringle
Southeast Sales Manager, Mike Bailey
Director Brokerage and National Accounts Customer Service, Amy Dickinson
Director Customer Service, Mike Cafarelli
Receivables Manager, Trudi Shutt
OS&D (Over Short and Damaged) Manager, Pat Edwards
Receivables Manager, Colette Read
Rate Department, Gary Thomas
CFO, Bob Baer

LOCATIONS

HQ: Central Refrigerated Service Inc.
5175 W. 2100 S., West Valley City UT 84120
Phone: 801-924-7000   **Fax:** 801-924-7337
Web: www.centralref.com

COMPETITORS

C.R. England
Covenant
  Transportation
Crete Carrier
Frozen Food Express
KLLM Transport
  Services

Marten Transport
Prime Inc.
Stevens Transport
Werner Enterprises
Willis Shaw Express

HISTORICAL FINANCIALS

Company Type: Private

Income Statement

FYE: December 31

	REVENUE ($ mil.)	NET INCOME ($ mil.)	NET PROFIT MARGIN	EMPLOYEES
12/11	419	0	—	1,650
12/08	406	9	2.4%	0
12/07	361	6	1.8%	0
12/06	775	0	0.0%	0
Annual Growth	(18.5%)	—	—	—

CENTRAL TEXAS COLLEGE

LOCATIONS

HQ: CENTRAL TEXAS COLLEGE
6200 W CENTRAL TEXAS EXPY, KILLEEN, TX 76549-1272
Phone: 254-526-1331

HISTORICAL FINANCIALS

Company Type: Private

Income Statement

FYE: August 31

	REVENUE ($ mil.)	NET INCOME ($ mil.)	NET PROFIT MARGIN	EMPLOYEES
08/12	99	17	17.5%	2,853
08/11	98	13	14.2%	0
08/10	98	15	15.6%	0
08/09	95	11	12.0%	0
Annual Growth	1.4%	14.8%	—	—

2012 Year-End Financials

Debt ratio: ——
Return on equity: 17.50%
Cash ($ mil.): 104
Current ratio: 3.50
Long-term debt ($ mil.): —

Dividends
  Yield: —
  Payout: —
Market value ($ mil.): —

CENTRAL WASHINGTON HEALTH SERVICES ASSOCIATION

LOCATIONS

HQ: CENTRAL WASHINGTON HEALTH SERVICES ASSOCIATION
1201 S MILLER ST, WENATCHEE, WA 98801-3201
Phone: 509-662-1511
Web: www.cwhs.com

HISTORICAL FINANCIALS

Company Type: Private

Income Statement

FYE: December 31

	REVENUE ($ mil.)	NET INCOME ($ mil.)	NET PROFIT MARGIN	EMPLOYEES
12/11	182	(7)	—	1,231
12/10	182	8	4.4%	0
12/09	177	19	10.9%	0
12/08	177	(15)	—	0
Annual Growth	0.8%	—	—	—

2011 Year-End Financials

Debt ratio: ——
Return on equity: (-4.30)%
Cash ($ mil.): 2
Current ratio: 1.40
Long-term debt ($ mil.): —

Dividends
  Yield: —
  Payout: —
Market value ($ mil.): —

CENTRE COLLEGE OF KENTUCKY

Centre College's name reflects its location in the geographic center of Kentucky (near Lexington) as well as its founders' preponderance for British spellings. The private liberal arts school enrolls some 1200 students majoring in about 30 academic areas. Some 85% of students participate in study-abroad opportunities which cost little more than regular tuition. Centre boasts a fraternity that carries an oil portrait of alum former Supreme Court Chief Justice Fred Vinson (Dead Fred) to all home football games. Living alums seem to like the place too: The school is ranked #1 in the nation in terms of percentage of alumni making annual contributions. Centre College was founded in 1819 by Presbyterian leaders.

EXECUTIVES

President, John A. Roush
Director Human Resources and Administrative Services, Kay Drake
VP Finance and Treasurer, John E. Cuny
Controller, Steve A. Jamison
VP and Dean Student Life, Randy Hays
Registrar, Timothy P. (Tim) Culhan
Director Communications, C. Michael Norris
Director Information Technology Services, Arthur L. Moore
Director Public Safety, Gary D. Bugg
Director Public Safety, Kevin Milby
VP College Relations, Richard W. Trollinger
Associate VP Development and Alumni Affairs, Shawn Lyons
VP Enrollment and Student Planning Services, J. Carey Thompson
Director Student Financial Planning, Elaine E. Larson
Director Purchasing and Campus Interiors, Dorothy C. Rinehart
VP Academic Affairs and Dean College, Stephanie L. Fabritius

LOCATIONS

HQ: Centre College
600 W. Walnut St., Danville KY 40422
Phone: 859-238-5200   **Fax:** 859-238-5723
Web: www.centre.edu

HISTORICAL FINANCIALS

Company Type: School

Income Statement

FYE: June 30

	REVENUE ($ mil.)	NET INCOME ($ mil.)	NET PROFIT MARGIN	EMPLOYEES
06/11	85	14	16.4%	325
06/10	58	(6)	—	0
06/09	57	53	93.8%	0
06/08	62	1	2.7%	0
Annual Growth	11.0%	103.1%	—	—

2011 Year-End Financials

Debt ratio: ——
Return on equity: 16.40%
Cash ($ mil.): 19
Current ratio: —
Long-term debt ($ mil.): —

Dividends
  Yield: —
  Payout: —
Market value ($ mil.): —

CERES SOLUTIONS LLP

Ceres Solutions is a growth business. The agricultural partnership provides farmers in about a dozen Indiana counties with crop farming support services and supplies. It sells stores and distributes such goods as fertilizers and fuel (gasoline propane home-heating). The company's agronomy services include field mapping crop and pest management soil sampling and yield analysis. Ceres Solutions also offers crop-financing programs sells crop insurance and provides marketing services. Its Green Notes newsletter offers the state's farmers market and technical advice and analysis.

Ceres Solutions which was formed in 2007 through the merger of three agricultural cooperatives –Westland Growers and AgroKey. It operates primarily in the western region of Indiana through about 30 agronomy office locations an energy office and its main office which is located in Crawfordsville Indiana.

EXECUTIVES

VP Agronomy, Dan Weber
CEO, Jeffrey (Jeff) Troike
Chairman, Shan Del Unger
VP Energy and Special Projects, Howard Jones
Secretary and Director, Bob Hall
Vice Chairman, Dale Johnson
Director, Rex Marchino
Director, Alan Meyer
Secretary and Director, Bob Hall
Vice Chairman, Dale Johnson
Director, Alan McDonald
Director, John Taylor
Director, Randy Waling
Director, Dennis Foster
Director, Joe Irwin
Director, Allan Clauser Jr.
Director, Mark Nesbitt

LOCATIONS

HQ: Ceres Solutions LLP
2112 Indianapolis Rd., Crawfordsville IN 47933
Phone: 765-362-6700   **Fax:** 765-362-7010
Web: www.ceresllp.com

COMPETITORS

ADM	CHS
Ag Processing Inc.	GROWMARK
Cargill	Premier AG Co-Op Inc.

HISTORICAL FINANCIALS
Company Type: Private

Income Statement
FYE: July 31

	REVENUE ($ mil.)	NET INCOME ($ mil.)	NET PROFIT MARGIN	EMPLOYEES
07/12	399	22	5.6%	125
07/11	329	16	5.1%	0
07/10	285	13	4.9%	0
07/09	325	9	2.9%	0
Annual Growth	**7.1%**	**33.4%**	—	—

2012 Year-End Financials

Debt ratio: ——
Return on equity: 5.60%
Cash ($ mil.): 11
Current ratio: 0.60
Long-term debt ($ mil.): ——

Dividends
Yield: —
Payout: —
Market value ($ mil.): ——

CFA INSTITUTE

LOCATIONS

HQ: CFA INSTITUTE
560 RAY C HUNT DR, CHARLOTTESVILLE, VA 22903-2981
Phone: 434-951-5236

HISTORICAL FINANCIALS
Company Type: Private

Income Statement
FYE: August 31

	REVENUE ($ mil.)	NET INCOME ($ mil.)	NET PROFIT MARGIN	EMPLOYEES
08/11	220	9	4.5%	230
08/10	200	13	6.5%	0
08/09	182	(0)	—	0
08/08	175	5	3.3%	0
Annual Growth	**7.9%**	**19.2%**	—	—

2011 Year-End Financials

Debt ratio: ——
Return on equity: 4.50%
Cash ($ mil.): 40
Current ratio: 1.30
Long-term debt ($ mil.): ——

Dividends
Yield: —
Payout: —
Market value ($ mil.): ——

CGH MEDICAL CENTER

LOCATIONS

HQ: CGH MEDICAL CENTER
100 E LE FEVRE RD, STERLING, IL 61081-1279
Phone: 815-625-0400
Web: www.nicancer.com

HISTORICAL FINANCIALS
Company Type: Private

Income Statement
FYE: April 30

	REVENUE ($ mil.)	NET INCOME ($ mil.)	NET PROFIT MARGIN	EMPLOYEES
04/12	193	8	4.3%	837
04/11	143	5	3.9%	0
04/10	117	4	4.1%	0
04/09	104	5	4.8%	0
Annual Growth	**22.9%**	**18.2%**	—	—

2012 Year-End Financials

Debt ratio: ——
Return on equity: 4.30%
Cash ($ mil.): 3
Current ratio: 1.20
Long-term debt ($ mil.): ——

Dividends
Yield: —
Payout: —
Market value ($ mil.): ——

CHAPMAN UNIVERSITY

Chapman University enrolls 7000 students at campuses throughout California as well as in Washington State. From its main campus in Orange California the university offers traditional undergraduate graduate and professional programs at seven colleges and schools. It also confers bachelor and master's degrees and teaching credentials to non-traditional students at its two-dozen satellite campuses. The university offers some 50 undergraduate majors and 40 graduate programs. It has 650 faculty members and a student-to-teacher ratio of 15:1. Chapman University includes Brandman University a distance learning program for some 10000 working adults that operates two dozen locations and offers online courses.

Financial Performance

Chapman University reported a 9% increase in revenues to $304 million in 2011 due to higher income from tuition fees gifts grants and bequests. Net income also increased 27% to $70 million due to increased endowment returns offset slightly by increased general educational and auxiliary expenses.

Strategy

Chapman University is expanding programs to widen opportunities for students. In 2011 the School of Law launched a new business law program and in 2013 the Argyros School of Business and Economics opened a new financial center for real-time student investor trading and portfolio management training. Facilities expansions include the construction of a new center for the arts and a new health sciences campus; both projects were launched in 2012.

Company Background

Chapman University was founded in 1861 as Hesperian College; it was re-named Chapman College in 1934 in honor of philanthropist Charles C. Chapman.

EXECUTIVES

President, James L. (Jim) Doti, age 65
Associate VP Legal Affairs and University Counsel, Janine P. DuMontelle
Chancellor, Gary Brahm
Dean George L. Argyros School of Business and Economics, Arthur Kraft
EVP University Advancement, Sheryl A. Bourgeois
Director Institutional Research, Marisol Arredondo
Director Purchasing and University Services, Pamela Ames
Director Career Development Center, Barbara Hubert
Director Athletics, David Currey
Chancellor, Daniele Struppa
EVP and COO, Harold W. Hewitt Jr.
VP Finance and CFO, Janna Bersi
VP Campus Planning and Operations, Kris E. Olsen
Dean Leatherby Libraries, Charlene Baldwin
Dean Lawrence and Kristina Dodge College of Film and Media Arts, Robert Bassett
Dean School of Education, Donald N. Cardinal
Director Center for Global Education, James Coyle
Dean School of Law, John Eastman
Director Sponsored Research, Ronald DiMelfi
Dean Chapel, Ronald Farmer
Vice Chancellor Institutional Planning and Assessment, David Fite
Vice Chancellor Faculty Affairs, Karen R. Graham
Vice Chancellor Undergraduate Education, Jeanne Gunner
Dean College of Performing Arts, William D. Hall
Interim Dean College of Science, Janeen Hill
Dean Wilkinson College of Humanities and Social Sciences, Roberta Lessor
Vice Chancellor Enrollment Management, Mike Pelly
Manager Financial Operations, Kristofer Pitman
Vice Chancellor and Dean Students, Jerry Price

Vice Chancellor Academic Administration,
Raymond Sfeir
Director Financial Aid, Gregory Ball
Assistant Vice Chancellor Enrollment Services and Chief Admission Officer, Michael Drummy
Registrar, John Snodgrass
Controller, Behzad Binesh
Chief Public Safety, Randy Burba
Director Human Resources, Brenda Dunbar
Equal Opportunity Officer, Eduardo A. Monge
Director Budget Planning, Michael C. Price
CIO, Shari Waters
Director Development Education New Initiatives, Carol Bonner
Director Foundation and Corporate Relations, Ganka Brown
Director Parent and Alumni Relations, David Moore
Director Communication and Media Relations, Mary Platt

LOCATIONS

HQ: Chapman University
1 University Dr., Orange CA 92866
Phone: 714-997-6815   **Fax:** 714-997-6986
Web: www.chapman.edu

PRODUCTS/OPERATIONS

Selected Colleges and Schools
College of Educational Studies
College of Performing Arts
George L. Argyros School of Business and Economics
Lawrence and Kristina Dodge College of Film and Media Arts
Schmid College of Science and Technology
School of Law
Wilkinson College of Humanities and Social Sciences

HISTORICAL FINANCIALS

Company Type: School

Income Statement   FYE: May 31

	REVENUE ($ mil.)	NET INCOME ($ mil.)	NET PROFIT MARGIN	EMPLOYEES
05/11	303	70	23.1%	3,300
05/10	276	38	13.8%	0
05/09	196	0	—	0
05/05	222	38	17.4%	0
Annual Growth	11.0%	22.1%	—	—

2011 Year-End Financials

Debt ratio: ——
Return on equity: 23.10%   Dividends
Cash ($ mil.): 50   Yield: —
Current ratio: 0.90   Payout: —
Long-term debt ($ mil.): —   Market value ($ mil.): —

CHARLES C PARKS CO INC

The Charles C. Parks Company is a grocery distributor that primarily supplies convenience stores in more than half a dozen Southern states. It distributes a variety of food items and dry goods as well as beverages cigarettes candy and general merchandise. The company also offers support programs for in-store delis and other quick-serv-

ice food operations. Carl C. Parks Jr. started the family-run business in 1934.

EXECUTIVES

SVP Sales, Gary Pickett
President, Crockett Parks III
Warehouse Manager, Donnie Vaughn
Manager Transportation, Jamie Davenport
CFO, Tom Cripps
EVP and COO, Bo Lanier
Sales Manager, Chris Pizzini
Food Service Director, Chuck Watkins
Purchasing Manager, Tim Flick
Information Technology Manager, David Lowery
Novelty Manager, Mike Pike

LOCATIONS

HQ: Charles C. Parks Company
500 Belvedere Dr., Gallatin TN 37066
Phone: 615-452-2406   **Fax:** 615-451-4212
Web: www.charlescparks.com

COMPETITORS

Alex Lee	H. T. Hackney
Atlantic Dominion	McLane
Core-Mark	S. Abraham & Sons
Eby-Brown	SUPERVALU

HISTORICAL FINANCIALS

Company Type: Private

Income Statement   FYE: April 30

	REVENUE ($ mil.)	NET INCOME ($ mil.)	NET PROFIT MARGIN	EMPLOYEES
04/12	268	(0)	—	145
04/11	264	0	0.1%	0
04/10	292	1	0.5%	0
04/09	257	1	0.5%	0
Annual Growth	1.4%	—	—	—

2012 Year-End Financials

Debt ratio: ——
Return on equity: (-0.20)%   Dividends
Cash ($ mil.): 0   Yield: —
Current ratio: 1.60   Payout: —
Long-term debt ($ mil.): —   Market value ($ mil.): —

CHATHAM UNIVERSITY

Men need not apply to Chatham University at least not for its undergraduate program. The university consists of Chatham College for Women which offers bachelor's degrees to women only; Chatham College for Graduate Studies which offers graduate degrees and teaching certificates to both men and women; and Chatham College for Continuing and Professional Studies its co-educational online school. Undergraduate students can choose from more than 30 majors in such areas as the sciences humanities arts environmental studies and pre-professional studies. Chatham has an enrollment of more than 2000 students. The private liberal arts school was founded in 1869 as Pennsylvania Female College.

EXECUTIVES

Vice Chairman, Sigo Falk

President, Esther L. Barazzone
VP Academic Affairs, Laura S. Armesto
VP Public and Community Relations, Paul A. Kovach
Director Human Resources, Frank M. Greco
Director Financial Aid, Jennifer A. Burns
CIO and Director Information Technology, Paul D. Steinhaus
Director Development Information Systems, Gary A. McKillop
Director Library, Jill Ausel
Athletic Director, Amy M. Buxbaum
Treasurer, Mary B. Templeton, age 65
Registrar, Jennifer Bronson
VP Finance and Administration, Walter Fowler
Controller, Scott Dillon
Director Prospect Research, Alisa Braho
Director Corporate/Foundation Relations, Kate Freed
Chairman, S. Murray Rust III
Secretary, W. Duff McCrady
Manager Internet Services, Hana Morris
Head Technical Services, Dan Nolting
Manager Instructional Technology and Media Services, Lauren Panton

LOCATIONS

HQ: Chatham University
Mellon Center Woodland Rd., Pittsburgh PA 15232
Phone: 412-365-1100   **Fax:** 412-365-1644
Web: www.chatham.edu

HISTORICAL FINANCIALS

Company Type: School

Income Statement   FYE: June 30

	REVENUE ($ mil.)	NET INCOME ($ mil.)	NET PROFIT MARGIN	EMPLOYEES
06/11	59	4	8.1%	300
06/09	26	(16)	—	0
06/08	41	0	1.9%	0
06/07	744	0	0.0%	0
Annual Growth	(56.9%)	566.1%	—	—

2011 Year-End Financials

Debt ratio: ——
Return on equity: 8.10%   Dividends
Cash ($ mil.): 8   Yield: —
Current ratio: ——   Payout: —
Long-term debt ($ mil.): —   Market value ($ mil.): —

CHENEGA CORPORATION

An Alaska Native Corporation Chenega Corporation has gone from landowner to business titan. Founded in 1974 to represent the Chenega people residing in the central Alaskan Prince William Sound region it operates mostly through its subsidiaries. Chenega Integrated Systems and Chenega Technology Services offer information technology security training manufacturing research and development network engineering and military operation support services. Chenega Corporation whose clients have included the Department of Defense Department of Homeland Security and EPA is owned by about 140 Native Alaskan shareholders.

In late 2008 Chenega Corporation expanded its technical and management consulting services offerings by acquiring Time Solutions Corp. whose clients included government private industry national laboratories and universities.

Chenega Corporation also owns the site of the original village of Chenega the oldest continually inhabited community in the area before it was destroyed by a tsunami in 1964. With some 80000 acres of land in the Prince William Sound region Chenega Corporation was the largest private landowner affected by the Exxon Valdez oil spill of 1989. It released about 60000 acres of land to federal and state agencies for environmental restoration in exchange for some $34 million. It retained ownership of some 20000 acres as well as some 10 land parcels held for tourism development.

EXECUTIVES

VP and Director, Lloyd Kompkoff
President CEO and Director, Charles W. Totemoff
Secretary Treasurer and Director, Paul T. Selanoff
Manager Shareholder Services, Patricia J. Andrews
Director Human Resources, Peggy O'Keefe
VP and Director, Lloyd Kompkoff
President CEO and Director, Charles W. Totemoff
Secretary Treasurer and Director, Paul T. Selanoff
Director, Joyce Kompkoff
Director, Paul Kompkoff

LOCATIONS

HQ: Chenega Corporation
  3000 C St. Ste. 301, Anchorage AK 99503
Phone: 907-277-5706   **Fax:** 907-277-5700
Web: www.chenega.com

PRODUCTS/OPERATIONS

Selected Services

Base operations and maintenance
Environmental management
Information technology
Intel and military operations
Light manufacturing
Logistics support
Telecommunications
Tourism and hospitality
Training services
Security services

COMPETITORS

Akal Security	Halliburton
Arctic Slope Regional	HP Enterprise Services
Corporation	IBM Global Services
chugach alaska	Parsons Corporation
Computer Sciences	TKC Communications
Corp.	

HISTORICAL FINANCIALS

Company Type: Private

Income Statement   FYE: September 30

	ASSETS ($ mil.)	NET INCOME ($ mil.)	INCOME AS % OF ASSETS	EMPLOYEES
09/11	375	28	7.6%	4,500
09/10	370	28	7.7%	0
09/09	325	25	7.9%	0
09/08	314	16	5.1%	0
Annual Growth	6.1%	20.8%	—	—

2011 Year-End Financials

Debt ratio: ——
Return on equity: 2.60%
Cash ($ mil.): 54
Current ratio: 1.70
Long-term debt ($ mil.): —

Dividends
  Yield: —
  Payout: —
Market value ($ mil.): —

CHENEGA FEDERAL SYSTEMS LLC

LOCATIONS

HQ: CHENEGA FEDERAL SYSTEMS LLC
10505 FURNACE RD STE 205, LORTON, VA 22079-2636
Phone: 703-493-9880
Web: www.chenegafederal.com

HISTORICAL FINANCIALS

Company Type: Private

Income Statement   FYE: September 30

	REVENUE ($ mil.)	NET INCOME ($ mil.)	NET PROFIT MARGIN	EMPLOYEES
09/11	94	7	8.4%	450
09/10	139	11	8.0%	0
09/09	219	18	8.6%	0
09/08	126	13	10.3%	0
Annual Growth	(9.3%)	(15.3%)	—	—

CHERRY BEKAERT & HOLLAND L.L.P.

Life's a bowl of accounting and consulting services at Cherry Bekaert (formerly Cherry Bekaert & Holland). The firm provides financial and management consulting services in the southeastern US. It specializes in serving sectors such as government financial services not-for-profit higher education healthcare retail and manufacturing. In addition to tax and accounting services Cherry Bekaert provides business valuations litigation support M&A advisory and other services. It also has a wealth management arm for well-to-do families. The firm has an international reach through its affiliation with Baker Tilly International.

Geographic Reach Cherry Bekaert operates in Florida Georgia North Carolina South Carolina and Virginia.

Financial Performance Although privately held the firm reports annual revenue of some $130 million.

Strategy In early 2013 the company rebranded as Cherry Bekaert and launched a new website that includes mobile access to better serve growing middle-market clients.

Mergers and Acquisitions Cherry Bekaert has grown through acquisition. In 2010 it bought Atlanta firm Braver Schimler Pierce Jenkins expanding its presence in Georgia. It also purchased McLeod & Company a Roanoke Virginia accountancy. Previously it had acquired Tampa firm Aidman Piser to become the largest accounting firm in that area. Other purchases include Florida's Rex Meighen and Virginia's Soza Associates.

EXECUTIVES

Partner Director of Risk Management group Raleigh North Carolina, Michelle L. Thompson

Firm Managing Partner, Howard J. Kies, age 59
Partner-in-Charge Director of Government Contracting or Services Group Vienna Virginia, Susan J. Moser
Partner-in-Charge Virginia Beach Virginia, Kurt W. Taves
Partner-In-Charge Raleigh North Carolina, Paul D. Fedorkowicz
Pricipal Director of Marketing and Business Development, August P. (Augie) Keller III
Partner-in-Charge Orlando Florida, C. A. (Tony) Morris
Partner-in-Charge Augusta Georgia, J. Douglass (Doug) Cates IV
Partner-in-Charge Charlotte and Gastonia North Carolina, James E. (Jim) Ratchford
Partner-in-Charge SC Upstate practice South Carolina, J. Bradley (Brad) Campbell
Partner Spartanburg South Carolina, L. Eddie Dutton
Partner-in-Charge Low County practice South Carolina, Raymond E. (Ray) Warco
Partner-in-Charge Richmond Virginia, Jerry P. Fox
Partner West Palm Beach Florida, Edward C. (E.C.) Blackburn
Partner Director of State & Local Government group Ricmond Virginia, John B. Montoro
Director of Tax Partner Richmond Virginia, Brooks E. Nelson
Partner-in-charge Atlanta Georgia, Kent M. (Kip) Plowman
Partner Director of Transaction Services group Charlotte North Carolina, Scott M. Moss
CFO, Ray Christopher
Director of State and Local Tax (SALT) Services, Catherine Shaw Stanton

LOCATIONS

HQ: Cherry Bekaert & Holland L.L.P.
1700 Bayberry Ct. Ste. 300, Richmond VA 23226
Phone: 804-673-4224   **Fax:** 804-673-4290
Web: www.cbh.com

PRODUCTS/OPERATIONS

Selected Services

Assurance and Accounting
  Audit & attestation
  Accounting
  Employee benefit plan audit
  SSAE 16 services
  SEC audit
  IFRS reporting
Tax
  Corporate Tax Solutions
  Specialty Tax Services
Advisory
  Risk advisory services
  Transaction advisory services
  Valuation services
  Fraud & forensics
  Litigation support
  Government contractor consulting services
  Entrepreneurial services
  Collateral review services
Wealth Management

COMPETITORS

BDO Seidman	PricewaterhouseCoopers
Deloitte & Touche	US
Dixon Hughes Goodman	Reznick Group
Ernst & Young LLP	RSM McGladrey
Grant Thornton	UHY Advisors
KPMG L.L.P.	

HISTORICAL FINANCIALS

Company Type: Private - Partnership

Income Statement

FYE: April 30

	REVENUE ($ mil.)	NET INCOME ($ mil.)	NET PROFIT MARGIN	EMPLOYEES
04/11	111	25	23.2%	850
04/10	98	24	24.4%	0
04/07	77	16	20.7%	0
04/05	66	0	—	0
Annual Growth	18.5%	—	—	—

2011 Year-End Financials

Debt ratio: ——
Return on equity: 23.20%
Cash ($ mil.): 0
Current ratio: 1.50
Long-term debt ($ mil.): —

Dividends
  Yield: —
  Payout: —
  Market value ($ mil.): —

CHERRY CENTRAL COOPERATIVE INC.

Serving as a central hub for cherry pickers' crops Cherry Central Cooperative is a fruit marketing co-operative that consists of more than a dozen member cooperatives representing hundreds of growers in Michigan New York Utah Washington and Wisconsin. It processes cherries cranberries apples and other fruit products including the Indian Summer and Wilderness brands of apple and cherry juices and ciders. Its Oceana Foods unit makes dried fruit sold under the Traverse Bay label while its Dunkley International subsidiary makes fruit-processing equipment. Cherry Central's products are sold to retail foodservice and ingredient customers. The cooperative was formed in 1973.

Geographic Reach

From its base in Traverse City Michigan Cherry Central Cooperative directs fruit-growing activities in Michigan New York Utah Washington and Wisconsin serving customers nationwide in Canada and globally.

Operations

Besides its namesake cherry operations Cherry Central supplies customers with apples blueberries cranberries strawberries pomegranate arils and asparagus. The company makes Traverse Bay-brand dried fruit through its Shelby Michigan based Oceana Foods business. The cooperative makes equipment to process fruit at its Dunkley International subsidiary headquartered in Kalamazoo Michigan.

Strategy

To entice customers to continue to buy its products Cherry Central has been working to go to market with new shelf-stable and alternative products. Through a partnership inked in mid-2012 with Vancouver-based EnWave Corporation Cherry Central is evaluating and testing EnWave's Radiant Energy Vacuum (REV) technology. The cooperative anticipates that the collaboration will fuel the development and subsequent launch of a premium dehydrated cherry snack product as well as cherry and apple powders marketed as an alternative to conventional fruit purees. As part of the agreement Cherry Central licenses the REV technology for commercial distribution of these products.

Sales and Marketing

The cooperative organization sells products to retailers foodservice operators and ingredient customers.

EXECUTIVES

President and General Manager, Richard L. (Dick) Bogard
VP Ingredient Sales, Jim Giannestras
Marketing Manager Ingredient Sales (Rocky Mountain and Western States Western Canada and Offshore Exports), James (Jim) Bryant
Marketing Manager Ingredient Sales (States East of the Rocky Mountains and Eastern Canada), Chris Olsen
National Sales Manager Retail Brands, Brent Tackett
National Sales Manager Foodservice, David Barger
National Sales Manager Private Label, Frank Wolff
Manager Customer Service and Logistics Ingredients Division, Cheryl Saxton
Manager Customer Service and Logistics Retail Division, Heidi Musser
General Manager Dunkley International, Ernie Kenneway
General Manager Oceana Foods, Jeff Tucker
VP Operations, Steve Eiseler

LOCATIONS

HQ: Cherry Central Cooperative Inc.
1771 N. US Hwy. 31 South, Traverse City MI 49684
Phone: 231-946-1860   **Fax:** 231-941-4167
Web: www.cherrycentral.com

PRODUCTS/OPERATIONS

Selected Frozen Ingredients

Apples
Blueberries
Cranberries
Damson Plums
Dark Sweet Cherries
Red Tart Cherries

Selected Frozen Fruit Varieties

Diced
Juice concentrate
IQF (Individually Quick Frozen)
Pitted or punch pitted
Pureed
Sliced
Solid or sugar pack
Whole

Selected Private Label and Co-pack Products

Applesauce
Formulas
Juice Flavors
Packaging

Selected Brands

Indian Summer
Traverse Bay Fruit Co.

COMPETITORS

Allens	Pacific Coast
California Giant	Producers
Chiquita Brands	Pro-Fac
Dole Food	Red Jacket Orchards
Donio Produce	Seneca Foods
Encore Fruit Marketing	Shoreline Fruit
Fazio Marketing	Sun World
Fresh Del Monte	International
Produce	Sun-Maid
Graceland Fruit	SunnyRidge Farm
Greenridge Fruit	SunOpta
Jasper Wyman & Son	Sunsweet Growers
Knouse Foods	Tree Top

Naturipe Farms   Welch's

HISTORICAL FINANCIALS

Company Type: Private - Cooperative

Income Statement

FYE: April 30

	REVENUE ($ mil.)	NET INCOME ($ mil.)	NET PROFIT MARGIN	EMPLOYEES
04/11	144	0	0.1%	115
04/10	136	0	0.2%	0
04/09	137	0	0.0%	0
04/08	120	0	0.3%	0
Annual Growth	6.3%	(18.9%)	—	—

2011 Year-End Financials

Debt ratio: ——
Return on equity: 0.10%
Cash ($ mil.): 0
Current ratio: 0.40
Long-term debt ($ mil.): —

Dividends
  Yield: —
  Payout: —
  Market value ($ mil.): —

CHESHIRE MEDICAL CENTER

LOCATIONS

HQ: CHESHIRE MEDICAL CENTER
580 COURT ST, KEENE, NH 03431-1729
Phone: 603-352-5400
Web: www.danielreading.com

HISTORICAL FINANCIALS

Company Type: Private

Income Statement

FYE: June 30

	REVENUE ($ mil.)	NET INCOME ($ mil.)	NET PROFIT MARGIN	EMPLOYEES
06/12*	118	3	2.9%	1,000
09/11	151	(5)	—	0
09/10	156	(8)	—	0
09/09	150	(6)	—	0
Annual Growth	(7.6%)	—	—	—

*Fiscal year change

2012 Year-End Financials

Debt ratio: ——
Return on equity: 2.90%
Cash ($ mil.): 26
Current ratio: 2.00
Long-term debt ($ mil.): —

Dividends
  Yield: —
  Payout: —
  Market value ($ mil.): —

CHESHIRE OIL COMPANY INC.

Cheshire Oil is confident that the smile it has put on customers' faces in Southern New Hampshire and Vermont won't suddenly disappear. The company's services (under the Cheshire Oil and T-Bird

Fuel brands) to residential and commercial clients include heating oil delivery oil and propane furnace and boiler installation service and repair fleet fueling and central air-conditioning installation and repair. Cheshire Oil also operates gas stations and convenience stores under the T-Bird Mini-Marts moniker. The company is owned and managed by members of the founding Robertson family.

Local resident George Robertson founded Cheshire Oil in 1921 as a chain of gas stations. Following WWII the moved into home heating oil delivery and later HVAC installation and service.

EXECUTIVES

President, James E. Robertson
VP, G. Bryant Robertson
Service Manager, Edward MacPhail
IT Systems Manager, Philip Chase
Air Conditioning Manager, Thomas Hinz
T-Bird Mini Marts Operations, Peter Kenniston
Service Manager T-Bird Fuel, Bernie Ferland
VP, JoJi Robertson
Marketing and Merchandising Manager, Katrina Babbitt
Office Manager, Jean Wright
Assistant Human Resources, Patricia Cook
Credit and Accounting, Jane Derosier
Inventory Control, Sandra Lafreniere
Office Manager T-Bird Fuel, Kristel Desmond
Assistant Office Manager, Kay Alderman
Accounting Keene Mini Storage, Lori Metcalf
Fuel Oil Delivery T-Bird Fuel, Scott Ruethe

LOCATIONS

HQ: Cheshire Oil Company Inc.
678 Marlborough St., Keene NH 03431
Phone: 603-352-0001 **Fax:** 603-357-3115
Web: www.cheshireoil.com

COMPETITORS

Getty Petroleum Golub
Marketing Shaw's
Global Partners

HISTORICAL FINANCIALS

Company Type: Private

Income Statement

FYE: October 31

	REVENUE ($ mil.)	NET INCOME ($ mil.)	NET PROFIT MARGIN	EMPLOYEES
10/11	92	0	0.8%	175
10/10	77	0	0.3%	0
10/09	69	0	1.0%	0
10/08	93	0	0.8%	0
Annual Growth	(0.2%)	0.2%	—	—

2011 Year-End Financials

Debt ratio: ——
Return on equity: 0.80%
Cash ($ mil.): 3
Current ratio: 0.70
Long-term debt ($ mil.): ——
Dividends
Yield: —
Payout: —
Market value ($ mil.): —

CHI-IOWA CORP

LOCATIONS

HQ: CHI-IOWA CORP
1111 6TH AVE, DES MOINES, IA 50314-2613
Phone: 515-247-3121

HISTORICAL FINANCIALS

Company Type: Private

Income Statement

FYE: June 30

	REVENUE ($ mil.)	NET INCOME ($ mil.)	NET PROFIT MARGIN	EMPLOYEES
06/11	738	40	5.5%	6,100
06/10	691	39	5.8%	0
06/08	577	36	6.3%	0
06/02	5,900	260	4.4%	0
Annual Growth	(50.0%)	(46.0%)	—	—

2011 Year-End Financials

Debt ratio: ——
Return on equity: 5.50%
Cash ($ mil.): 30
Current ratio: 0.60
Long-term debt ($ mil.): ——
Dividends
Yield: —
Payout: —
Market value ($ mil.): —

CHICKASAW DISTRIBUTORS INC.

LOCATIONS

HQ: CHICKASAW DISTRIBUTORS INC.
800 BERING DR STE 330, HOUSTON, TX 77057-2184
Phone: 713-974-2905
Web: www.chickasawdistributors.com

HISTORICAL FINANCIALS

Company Type: Private

Income Statement

FYE: September 30

	REVENUE ($ mil.)	NET INCOME ($ mil.)	NET PROFIT MARGIN	EMPLOYEES
09/11	304	2	0.7%	13
09/10	240	1	0.7%	0
09/09	288	5	1.8%	0
09/08	222	3	1.4%	0
Annual Growth	11.1%	(12.1%)	—	—

2011 Year-End Financials

Debt ratio: ——
Return on equity: 0.70%
Cash ($ mil.): 5
Current ratio: 0.60
Long-term debt ($ mil.): ——
Dividends
Yield: —
Payout: —
Market value ($ mil.): —

CHICKASAW HOLDING COMPANY

Chickasaw Holding's family of businesses keeps south central Oklahoma connected. The company's original business Chickasaw Telephone Company was founded in 1909 and offers local phone service to about 9000 business and residential customers. Its other subsidiaries provide such services as long-distance (Chickasaw Long Distance) Internet access (BrightNet Oklahoma) wireless service (Chickasaw Cellular) and wholesale fiber-optic networking for business customers and other communications carriers (Indian Nations Fiber Optics). The group also installs telecommunications equipment including private branch exchange (PBX) and voice mail systems through its Telco Supply Company subsidiary.

EXECUTIVES

Chairman and CEO, Royce E. Gauntt
President, Sonny Bright
VP, Jack O. Hester

LOCATIONS

HQ: Chickasaw Holding Company
5 N. McCormick St., Oklahoma City OK 73127
Phone: 405-946-1200 **Fax:** 405-946-4200
Web: www.brightok.net/chickasaw/Chickasaw

COMPETITORS

AT&T Telephone & Data
Sprint Nextel Systems
T-Mobile USA Verizon

HISTORICAL FINANCIALS

Company Type: Private

Income Statement

FYE: December 31

	REVENUE ($ mil.)	NET INCOME ($ mil.)	NET PROFIT MARGIN	EMPLOYEES
12/11	81	14	17.4%	600
12/10	93	18	19.4%	0
12/09	93	5	5.7%	0
12/08	92	10	11.3%	0
Annual Growth	(4.1%)	10.8%	—	—

2011 Year-End Financials

Debt ratio: ——
Return on equity: 17.40%
Cash ($ mil.): 34
Current ratio: 4.50
Long-term debt ($ mil.): ——
Dividends
Yield: —
Payout: —
Market value ($ mil.): —

CHILDFUND INTERNATIONAL USA

ChildFund International (CFI) serves the little ones. The worldwide non-profit organization provides education medical care food and safe water to more than 13 million children —of all faiths —in about 30 countries in Africa Asia the Caribbean

Eastern Europe Latin America and the US. It works in areas of early childhood development education family income generation nutrition and sanitation. The group also tries to get child soldiers away from the military and reintegrated into daily life. Founded in 1938 as China's Children Fund the group changed its name to Christian Children's Fund in 1951. In 2009 it again renamed itself ChildFund International.

Since its founding as an organization focused on orphans and orphanages CFI has become an international child development organization. More than 500000 sponsored children receive monthly contributions through the group; about 350000 of those sponsorships are supported by donors in the US. CFI also publishes newsletters booklets and studies on the effects of poverty and violence on children.

EXECUTIVES

VP Communications and Public Affairs, Cheri W. Dahl
President and CEO, Anne Lynam Goddard
CFO, James M. Tuite
Secretary and Director, Louis B. Weeks
Chairman, Charles M. Caravati Jr.
VP Africa, Isam M. Ghanim
Interim VP Global Programs, Dula C. James
VP People and Culture, Diane H. Willis
Treasurer and Director, A. Scott Andrews
VP Marketing and Strategic Resources, Mike Pressendo
VP Global Programs, Anne Scott
Director Communications, Cynthia Price
Manager Communications, Ellie Whinnery
Secretary and Director, Louis B. Weeks
Director, Jesus M. Amadeo
Treasurer and Director, A. Scott Andrews
Director, A. Hugh Ewing III
Director, Roger L. Gregory
Director, Karen Hein
Director, Darrell D. Martin
Director, Maureen Denlea-Massey
Director, Velma McBride Murry
Director, Peter J. Tanous
Director, John C. Purnell Jr.
Director, Masood Z. Rehmani
Director, Brian Wilcox
Director, Lynne Vernon-Feagans
Director, Marilyn Grist
Director, Sarah Hanson
Director, Barbara Joynes
Director, Robert F. Norfleet Jr.
Director, Thomas A. Siegfried
Director, Thomas Weisner
Director, Paul Hirschbiel
Auditors: Ernst&YoungLLP

LOCATIONS

HQ: ChildFund International USA
2821 Emerywood Pkwy., Richmond VA 23294-3726
Phone: 804-756-2700   **Fax:** 804-756-2718
Web: www.childfund.org

HISTORICAL FINANCIALS
Company Type: Private - Not-for-Profit

Income Statement
FYE: June 30

	REVENUE ($ mil.)	NET INCOME ($ mil.)	NET PROFIT MARGIN	EMPLOYEES
06/11	228	12	5.3%	160
06/10	215	4	2.2%	0
06/09	217	12	5.7%	0
06/08	230	7	3.4%	0
Annual Growth	(0.4%)	15.8%	—	—

2011 Year-End Financials

Debt ratio: ——
Return on equity: 5.30%
Cash ($ mil.): 30
Current ratio: 1.70
Long-term debt ($ mil.): —

Dividends
Yield: —
Payout: —
Market value ($ mil.): —

CHILDREN'S HEALTH CARE ASSOCIATES INC

LOCATIONS

HQ: CHILDREN' S HEALTH CARE ASSOCIATES INC
100 N 20TH ST STE 301, PHILADELPHIA, PA
19103-1454
Phone: 215-977-9779

HISTORICAL FINANCIALS
Company Type: Private

Income Statement
FYE: June 30

	REVENUE ($ mil.)	NET INCOME ($ mil.)	NET PROFIT MARGIN	EMPLOYEES
06/11	189	1	0.6%	75
06/10	194	11	5.8%	0
06/09	165	(1)	—	0
06/08	164	0	0.2%	0
Annual Growth	4.7%	40.8%	—	—

2011 Year-End Financials

Debt ratio: ——
Return on equity: 0.60%
Cash ($ mil.): 16
Current ratio: 0.80
Long-term debt ($ mil.): —

Dividends
Yield: —
Payout: —
Market value ($ mil.): —

CHILDREN'S HOSPITAL MEDICAL CENTER

Cincinnati Children's Hospital Medical Center has a special place in its heart for kids —and vice versa. The pediatric health care facility offers specialty treatments for children and adolescents suffering from just about any malady including those of the heart and liver as well as blood diseases and cancer. Cincinnati Children's Hospital has some 520 beds and operates nearly a dozen outpatient

care centers. Founded in 1883 the not-for-profit hospital runs the only Level 1 pediatric trauma center in the region and serves as a teaching and research facility for the University of Cincinnati College of Medicine.

Reaching beyond Cincinnati the hospital also provides services to communities in southeastern Indiana and northern Kentucky through its network of outpatient clinics. These centers include community urgent and emergency care facilities and general and specialty physician practices as well as laboratory radiology dentistry and physical therapy clinics. The hospital expanded its outpatient network by opening a Cincinnati center for kids with special needs and chronic ailments in 2010.

The Cincinnati Children's Research Foundation conducts research and clinical trials of pediatric medical innovations including new vaccines and surgical techniques. It has research partnerships with hospitals in Africa Asia Latin America and the Middle East. The hospital and research foundation's contributions to pediatric medicine include the rotavirus vaccine (approved in for use in the US in 2008) and Albert Sabin's discovery of the oral polio vaccine (first tested in 1960). In order to more closely align its research and clinical operations Cincinnati Children's Medical Center formed three new institutes in 2009: The Heart Institute the Perinatal Institute and the Cancer and Blood Diseases Institute.

Cincinnati Children's Medical Center has remained on the forefront of the digital revolution that has swept the health care industry. In recent years the organization has linked its emergency inpatient radiology pharmacy and specialty department patient data together to create an electronic medical record (EHR). The move toward an integrated EMR system is meant to reduce patient errors (such as dispensing the wrong medications to patients) and provide efficiencies and improved communication between departments.

EXECUTIVES

Chair, Thomas G. Cody, age 70
President and CEO, Michael Fisher, age 53
SVP Planning and Business Development, Dwight E. Ellingwood
Chief-of-Staff, Michael K. Farrell
CFO and Chief Adminsitrative Officer, Scott J. Hamlin
SVP Infrastructure and Operations, William M. Kent
SVP Information Services and CIO, Marianne F. James
SVP Quality and Transformation, Uma Kotagal
SVP and General Counsel, Elizabeth A. Stautberg
Anesthesiologist-in-Chief and Director Anesthesia, C. Dean Kurth
SVP Patient Services, Cheryl Hoying
Physician-in-Chief, Arnold W. Strauss
SVP Human Resources, Elisabeth Baldock
Trustee, Michael S. Cambron
Trustee, Thomas F. Boat
Trustee, Lee A. Carter
Trustee, Sharry Addison
Trustee, Robert D. H. Anning
Trustee, John P. Zanotti
Trustee, Lynwood Battle
Trustee, Katharine DeWitt
Trustee, Todd M. Duncan
Trustee, Nancy Krieger-Eddy
Trustee, Barbara Fitch
Trustee, Vallie Comisar Geier
Trustee, Louis D. George
Trustee, Deborah Henretta

LOCATIONS

HQ: Cincinnati Children's Hospital Medical Center
3333 Burnet Ave., Cincinnati OH 45229-3026
Phone: 513-636-4200   **Fax:** 513-636-2460
Web: www.cincinnatichildrens.org

PRODUCTS/OPERATIONS

2010 Revenues

Patient services	1,093	70
Professional services	214	13
Other	153	8

COMPETITORS

Bethesda North	Nemours Foundation
Catholic Health Partners	Premier Health Partners
Children's Hospital of Philadelphia	Shriners Hospitals For Children
Christ Hospital	St. Elizabeth Healthcare
Deaconess Associations	St. Jude Children's Research Hospital
Kettering Health Network	TriHealth
Nationwide Children's Hospital	UC Health

HISTORICAL FINANCIALS

Company Type: Private - Not-for-Profit

Income Statement				FYE: June 30
	REVENUE ($ mil.)	NET INCOME ($ mil.)	NET PROFIT MARGIN	EMPLOYEES
06/11	1,693	53	3.2%	7,700
06/10	1,590	78	4.9%	0
06/09	1,487	(281)	—	0
06/05	912	19	2.2%	0
Annual Growth	22.9%	39.3%	—	—

2011 Year-End Financials

Debt ratio: ——
Return on equity: 3.20%
Cash ($ mil.): 97
Current ratio: 1.40
Long-term debt ($ mil.): —

Dividends
Yield: —
Payout: —
Market value ($ mil.): —

CHILDRENSWEAR LLC

LOCATIONS

HQ: CHILDRENSWEAR LLC
1333 BROADWAY RM 700, NEW YORK, NY
10018-7207
Phone: 212-863-2400

HISTORICAL FINANCIALS

Company Type: Private

Income Statement				FYE: January 28
	REVENUE ($ mil.)	NET INCOME ($ mil.)	NET PROFIT MARGIN	EMPLOYEES
01/12	261	7	2.7%	400
01/11	269	10	3.8%	0
01/09	299	4	1.6%	0
Annual Growth	(6.6%)	22.2%	—	—

2012 Year-End Financials

Debt ratio: ——
Return on equity: 2.70%
Cash ($ mil.): 0
Current ratio: 0.40
Long-term debt ($ mil.): —

Dividends
Yield: —
Payout: —
Market value ($ mil.): —

CHINA MANUFACTURERS ALLIANCE LLC

LOCATIONS

HQ: CHINA MANUFACTURERS ALLIANCE LLC
406 E HUNTINGTON DR # 200, MONROVIA, CA
91016-3638
Phone: 626-301-9575

HISTORICAL FINANCIALS

Company Type: Private

Income Statement				FYE: December 31
	REVENUE ($ mil.)	NET INCOME ($ mil.)	NET PROFIT MARGIN	EMPLOYEES
12/11	207	4	2.0%	26
Annual Growth	—	—	—	—

2011 Year-End Financials

Debt ratio: ——
Return on equity: 2.00%
Cash ($ mil.): 1
Current ratio: 0.50
Long-term debt ($ mil.): —

Dividends
Yield: —
Payout: —
Market value ($ mil.): —

CHINA SUTONG TIRE RESOURCES INC

LOCATIONS

HQ: CHINA SUTONG TIRE RESOURCES INC
4849 CRANSWICK RD, HOUSTON, TX 77041-7721
Phone: 713-690-5500

HISTORICAL FINANCIALS

Company Type: Private

Income Statement				FYE: December 31
	REVENUE ($ mil.)	NET INCOME ($ mil.)	NET PROFIT MARGIN	EMPLOYEES
12/11	103	1	1.1%	25
12/07	59	1	1.9%	0
Annual Growth	74.7%	(0.1%)	—	—

2011 Year-End Financials

Debt ratio: ——
Return on equity: 1.10%
Cash ($ mil.): 0
Current ratio: 0.50
Long-term debt ($ mil.): —

Dividends
Yield: —
Payout: —
Market value ($ mil.): —

CHMC ANESTHESIA FOUNDATION INC.

LOCATIONS

HQ: CHMC ANESTHESIA FOUNDATION INC.
300 LONGWOOD AVE, BOSTON, MA 02115-5724
Phone: 617-734-5748

HISTORICAL FINANCIALS

Company Type: Private

Income Statement				FYE: June 30
	REVENUE ($ mil.)	NET INCOME ($ mil.)	NET PROFIT MARGIN	EMPLOYEES
06/11	88	7	8.0%	80
06/10	82	17	20.9%	0
06/09	0	0	—	0
06/08	65	5	7.7%	0
Annual Growth	10.4%	12.1%	—	—

2011 Year-End Financials

Debt ratio: ——
Return on equity: 8.00%
Cash ($ mil.): 12
Current ratio: 0.30
Long-term debt ($ mil.): —

Dividends
Yield: —
Payout: —
Market value ($ mil.): —

CHRISTIAN AID MINISTRIES

LOCATIONS

HQ: CHRISTIAN AID MINISTRIES
4464 STATE ROUTE 39, MILLERSBURG, OH
44654-9677
Phone: 330-893-2428
Web: www.caminulfelix.org

HISTORICAL FINANCIALS

Company Type: Private

Income Statement

	REVENUE ($ mil.)	NET INCOME ($ mil.)	NET PROFIT MARGIN	EMPLOYEES
12/11	188	47	25.3%	204
12/10	156	4	3.1%	0
12/08	186	0	—	0
12/07	185	49	26.9%	0
Annual Growth	0.5%	(1.5%)	—	—

FYE: December 31

2011 Year-End Financials

Debt ratio: —
Return on equity: 25.30%
Cash ($ mil.): 11
Current ratio: —
Long-term debt ($ mil.): —

Dividends
Yield: —
Payout: —
Market value ($ mil.): —

CHRISTIAN BROTHERS INVESTMENT SERVICES INC.

LOCATIONS

HQ: CHRISTIAN BROTHERS INVESTMENT SERVICES INC.
20 N WACKER DR STE 2000, CHICAGO, IL
60606-3002
Phone: 312-526-3343

HISTORICAL FINANCIALS

Company Type: Private

Income Statement

	REVENUE ($ mil.)	NET INCOME ($ mil.)	NET PROFIT MARGIN	EMPLOYEES
12/11	114	100	87.1%	45
12/10	81	68	83.5%	0
12/09	0	0	—	0
12/05	0	0	—	0
Annual Growth	—	—	—	—

FYE: December 30

2011 Year-End Financials

Debt ratio: —
Return on equity: 87.10%
Cash ($ mil.): 0
Current ratio: —
Long-term debt ($ mil.): —

Dividends
Yield: —
Payout: —
Market value ($ mil.): —

CHRISTOPHER NEWPORT UNIVERSITY

LOCATIONS

HQ: CHRISTOPHER NEWPORT UNIVERSITY
1 AVENUE OF THE ARTS, NEWPORT NEWS, VA
23606-3072
Phone: 757-594-7354
Web: www.cnuhockey.com

HISTORICAL FINANCIALS

Company Type: Private

Income Statement

	REVENUE ($ mil.)	NET INCOME ($ mil.)	NET PROFIT MARGIN	EMPLOYEES
06/12	85	47	54.9%	767
06/11	89	40	45.3%	0
06/09	4	1	37.1%	0
06/06	59	6	11.2%	0
Annual Growth	13.0%	91.9%	—	—

FYE: June 30

2012 Year-End Financials

Debt ratio: —
Return on equity: 54.90%
Cash ($ mil.): 25
Current ratio: 0.80
Long-term debt ($ mil.): —

Dividends
Yield: —
Payout: —
Market value ($ mil.): —

CHRISTUS HEALTH

In CHRISTUS there is no east or west but plenty of care nonetheless. The not-for-profit Catholic health care system operates about 350 medical facilities from its more than 40 hospitals including general hospitals and long-term acute care facilities to clinics and outpatient centers. It operates mostly in Louisiana and Texas but also has facilities in Arkansas Georgia Missouri and New Mexico and in five states in Mexico. In addition to its acute care facilities CHRISTUS Health runs medical groups home health and hospice agencies and senior living facilities. Specialized services include oncology pediatrics rehabilitation and women's and children's health care.

Over the past several years CHRISTUS Health has engaged in cutting some of its operations and reining in costs to generate positive growth. In fiscal 2011 the health care system made modest gains ending the year with a more than 2% operating margin (compared to 1.6% the previous year) with its net operating income coming in at just under $1 billion up more than 40% from fiscal 2010.

CHRISTUS Health formed its CHRISTUS Continuing Care division in 2009 to advance the organization's plan to increase its non-acute care operations and house all of its non-acute care services. These services include home care hospice long-term care services residential senior services and its long-term acute care hospitals (many of which operate under the Dubuis brand name).

Another goal of CHRISTUS Health is to reduce overcrowding and such misuses as patients being seen for routine illnesses in its emergency rooms.

To that end and to make primary care a bit more accessible the company has opened immediate care clinics in a number of Texas Wal-Mart stores. CHRISTUS Health has plans to expand the clinics into Wal-Marts in Louisiana.

Like many hospital companies the organization has struggled financially as a result of providing care (usually in the emergency room) for the indigent and for the growing ranks of uninsured especially in the hard-hit economic environment of 2008 and 2009. During that period the health care system's charity care (defined as unpaid services provided to the uninsured and indigent) was up nearly 35%.

As a result CHRISTUS Health has had to sell some money-losing facilities such as the St. Joseph Hospital in Houston which it sold to Hospital Partners of America (HPA) a company that allows doctors to take an ownership stake in its hospitals.

It also sold the CHRISTUS Medical Group-Southwest Community Health Center in Houston to Legacy Community Health Services in 2010 because Legacy is designated as a federally qualified health center (FQHC) and can operate the clinic as such (meaning it is eligible for more public-sector funding). FQHCs are not-for-profit or public entity community-owned health care providers serving low-income and medically underserved communities.

CHRISTUS Health has taken other steps to try to offset some costs of indigent care including pushing for the establishment of hospital districts to pay for charity care costs in some of its markets.

The organization has been focused on growing its operations in Mexico where it operates about a dozen hospitals and clinics in six states. CHRISTUS Health's Mexico operations are a majority-owned partnership with Monterrey-based Muguerza. The organization's main Monterrey facility became the first Mexican hospital to win accreditation from the Joint Commission International a unit of the organization that certifies US hospitals.

Because Mexican citizens overwhelmingly rely on public hospitals run by the national health care system CHRISTUS Muguerza markets itself as a "medical tourism" destination where Americans can go for cheaper and lower-hassle medical care. Services include acute and primary care dental care urgent care and post-surgical rehabilitation.

CHRISTUS Health was formed through the 1999 merger of Incarnate Word Health System and Sisters of Charity Health System. Both systems have their roots in the religious order Sisters of Charity of the Incarnate Word founded when three French nuns arrived in Texas in 1866 to care for the poor and sick.

EXECUTIVES

SVP and Chief Medical Officer, John Gillean
SVP Human Resource Services, Mary Lynch
SVP and CFO, Jay Herron
President and CEO CHRISTUS Santa Rosa Health Care, Patrick B. Carrier
President and CEO, Ernie W. Sadau
SVP Communications and Public Affairs, Linda McClung
SVP and CIO, George Conklin
SVP Business Strategy and Corporate Development, Peter Maddox
Chairman, Catherine Dulle
President and CEO CHRISTUS Health Gulf Coast and CHRISTUS Health Southeast Texas (CHRISTUS Hospital St. Elizabeth; CHRISTUS Hospital St. Mary and CHRISTUS Jasper Memorial Hospital), Ellen Jones

System Senior Director Strategic Marketing and Communications, Teri Cardenas
Senior Writer, Christie J. Fortune
President and CEO CHRISTUS Health Ark-La-Tex (CHRISTUS St. Michael Health System), Chris Karam
President and CEO CHRISTUS Health Central Louisiana (includes CHRISTUS Health Northern Louisiana CHRISTUS Health Central Louisiana and CHRISTUS Health Southwestern Louisiana), Stephen Wright
President and CEO CHRISTUS Health Utah (includes CHRISTUS St. Joseph Villa), Galen Ewer
Chairman, Richard L. (Dick) Clarke
Administrator CHRISTUS St. Joseph Village, Kim Bomgardner
President and CEO CHRISTUS Medical Group, Donna Mikulecky
Corporate VP Business Development and Managed Care, Jeff Puckett
Communications Specialist, Abby Lowe
Human Resources, Sandy York
Director, Sister Kathleen Coughlin
Director, Robert Z. (Bob) Gussin
Director, Pedro Martin
Director, Mary Jo Potter
Director, Celina Garza Ridge
Director, Dennis Stine
Director, Sister Celeste Trahan
Director, Father Charles E. Bouchard
Director, Richard L. (Dick) Clarke
Director, Kenneth D. Wells
Director, Phyllis A. Cowling
Director, Sister Walter Maher
Director, Sister Hannah O'Donoghue

LOCATIONS

HQ: CHRISTUS Health
Las Colinas Corporate Center II 6363 N. Hwy. 161 Ste. 450, Irving TX 75038
Phone: 214-492-8500   **Fax:** 858-731-5301
Web: www.packetvideo.com

PRODUCTS/OPERATIONS

2011 Revenues

	$ mil.	% of total
Patient services	3,410	90
Premium revenue	164	4
Other revenue	172	5
Equity in income of unconsolidated organizations	33	1
Total	**3,781**	**100**

2011 Payor Mix

	% of total
Managed care	37
Medicare	25
Self-pay	16
Medicaid	5
Commercial	4
Others	13
Total	**100**

2011 Payor Mix

	% of total
Managed care	37
Medicare	25
Self-pay	16
Medicaid	5
Commercial	4
Others	13
Total	**100**

Selected Facilities in Texas

CHRISTUS HomeCare - Corpus Christi
CHRISTUS HomeCare - Texarkana
CHRISTUS Hospital - St. Elizabeth
CHRISTUS Hospital - St. Mary

CHRISTUS Jasper Memorial Hospital
CHRISTUS Santa Rosa Alamo Heights Imaging Center
CHRISTUS Santa Rosa Ambulatory Surgery Center
CHRISTUS Santa Rosa Cancer Center
CHRISTUS Santa Rosa Children's Hospital
CHRISTUS Santa Rosa Hospital - City Centre
CHRISTUS Santa Rosa Hospital - Medical Center
CHRISTUS Santa Rosa Hospital New Braunfels
CHRISTUS Santa Rosa Hospital Westover Hills
CHRISTUS Santa Rosa Imaging Center
CHRISTUS Santa Rosa Outpatient Rehabilitation Center
CHRISTUS Santa Rosa Rehabilitation Hospital
CHRISTUS Santa Rosa Rehabilitation Services - Downtown
CHRISTUS Santa Rosa Rehabilitation Services - Medical Center
CHRISTUS Santa Rosa Wound Care and Hyperbaric Center - Downtown
CHRISTUS Santa Rosa Wound Care and Hyperbaric Center - Medical Center
CHRISTUS Spohn Family Center Northside
CHRISTUS Spohn Family Health Center
CHRISTUS Spohn Family Health Center Falfurrias
CHRISTUS Spohn Family Health Center Padre Island
CHRISTUS Spohn Family Health Center Robstown
CHRISTUS Spohn Family Health Center San Diego
CHRISTUS Spohn Family Health Center Westside
CHRISTUS Spohn Health System
CHRISTUS Spohn Hospital Alice
CHRISTUS Spohn Hospital Beeville
CHRISTUS Spohn Hospital Corpus Christi - Memorial
CHRISTUS Spohn Hospital Corpus Christi - Shoreline
CHRISTUS Spohn Hospital Corpus Christi - South
CHRISTUS Spohn Hospital Kleberg
CHRISTUS Spohn Medical Group - Obstetrics and Gynecology Associates
CHRISTUS St. Catherine Hospital
CHRISTUS St. John Hospital
CHRISTUS St. Michael Health System
CHRISTUS St. Michael Rehabilitation Hospital
CHRISTUS Transplant Institute
CHRISTUS Visiting Nurse Association - Houston
CHRISTUS Visiting Nurse Association - Nassau Bay
CHRISTUS Visiting Nurse Association - San Antonio
David Christopher Goldsbury Center for Children and Families
Dubuis Hospital of Beaumont
Dubuis Hospital of Bryan Texas
Dubuis Hospital of Corpus Christi
Dubuis Hospital of Houston Texas (long-term acute care)
Dubuis Hospital of Paris
Dubuis Hospital of Port Arthur Texas (long-term acute care)
Dubuis Hospital of Texarkana

Selected Other US Facilities

Advance Care Hospital of Fort Smith (Arkansas)
Advance Care Hospital of Hot Springs (Arkansas)
CHRISTUS Coushatta Health Care Center (Coushatta Louisiana)
CHRISTUS HomeCare - Jennings (Louisiana)
CHRISTUS HomeCare - Lake Charles (Louisiana)
CHRISTUS HomeCare - Shreveport (Louisiana)
CHRISTUS Hospice and Palliative Care - Alexandria (Louisiana)
CHRISTUS Schumpert Health System (Shreveport Louisiana)
CHRISTUS Schumpert Highland (Shreveport Louisiana)
CHRISTUS Schumpert St. Mary Place (Shreveport Louisiana)
CHRISTUS St. Frances Cabrini Hospital (Alexandria Louisiana)
CHRISTUS St. Patrick Hospital (Lake Charles Louisiana)
CHRISTUS St. Vincent (Santa Fe New Mexico)
Dubuis Hospital of Alexandria (Louisiana)
Dubuis Hospital of Lake Charles (Louisiana)
Dubuis Hospital of Shreveport (Louisiana)
Dubuis Hospital of St. Louis (Chesterfield Missouri)
Natchitoches Parish Hospital (Louisiana)
Southern Crescent Hospital for Specialty Care (Riverdale Georgia)

Selected Facilities in Mexico

CHRISTUS MUGUERZA Hospital Alta Especialidad (Monterrey Nuevo Leon)

CHRISTUS MUGUERZA Hospital Conchita (Monterrey Nuevo Leon)
CHRISTUS MUGUERZA Hospital Del Parque (Chihuahua)
CHRISTUS MUGUERZA Hospital Reynosa (Tamaulipas C.P.)
CHRISTUS MUGUERZA Hospital Saltillo (Coahuila)
CHRISTUS MUGUERZA Hospital Sur (Monterrey Nuevo Leon)
CHRISTUS MUGUERZA Hospital UPAEP (Puebla)

COMPETITORS

Ascension Health
Baylor Health
Catholic Health Initiatives
Community Health Systems
HCA
Health Management Associates
Iasis Healthcare
Intermountain Health Care
LifePoint Hospitals
MD Anderson Cancer Center
Memorial Health Services
Memorial Hermann Healthcare
Mercy Health
Methodist Hospital System
St. Luke's Episcopal Hospital
Tenet Healthcare
Texas Children's Hospital
Universal Health Services
University of Utah Hospitals & Clinics
Vanguard Health Systems

HISTORICAL FINANCIALS

Company Type: Private - Not-for-Profit

Income Statement

FYE: June 30

	REVENUE ($ mil.)	NET INCOME ($ mil.)	NET PROFIT MARGIN	EMPLOYEES
06/11	3,780	263	7.0%	25,000
06/10	3,653	55	1.5%	0
06/09	3,466	(411)	—	0
06/08	3,167	(144)	—	0
Annual Growth	**6.1%**	**—**	**—**	**—**

2011 Year-End Financials

Debt ratio: ——
Return on equity: 7.00%
Cash ($ mil.): 418
Current ratio: 1.10
Long-term debt ($ mil.): —

Dividends
    Yield: —
    Payout: —
Market value ($ mil.): —

CHRISTUS HEALTH CENTRAL LOUISIANA

CHRISTUS St. Frances Cabrini Hospital provides a wide range of medical services to the denizens of Alexandria Louisiana. If you're ailing down south there's not much the hospital can't do to help especially in the area of cancer. Founded in 1950 the 240-bed St. Frances Cabrini Hospital has a staff of more than 320 physicians providing services that include emergency care women's health surgery and cardiology. For the insomniacs among us the hospital provides specialized care through its sleep center. St. Francis Cabrini's parent company is one of the nation's major hospital operators —with about 50 facilities located around the country.

CHRISTY SPORTS L.L.C.

Christy Sports isn't some girly group of pony-tailed cheerleaders. It's the largest specialty ski and snowboard retailer in the Rocky Mountains. With more than 40 retail stores in skiing hot spots like Snowmass Crested Butte Steamboat Springs and Vail the company sells skiing snowboarding snow-shoeing mountain biking and golf equipment along with shoes shirts gloves and bags to carry it all. Stores also carry patio furniture grills hammocks and other accessories for the outdoor life and rent skiing and snowboarding gear. Christy's staff are all serious skiers and snowboarders who use the equipment they sell. The company was founded in 1958 by avid skiers Ed and Gale Crist.

Demand for Christy's offerings has improved in recent years; revenues bottomed in 2009 on account of the recession. The challenging economic conditions have given Christy's perspective on right-sizing its retail network. To this end the retailer in early 2011 opened a new store in Park City Utah and shuttered an underperforming mall location in Colorado Springs Colorado (there is one other location in the city).

Christy Sports' Smart Rentals system allows members to rent sports equipment at a 20% discount by reserving online. Those rentals can then be delivered to a customer's doorstep through the company's Door 2 Door delivery service which expanded in 2010 to include retail purchases.

LOCATIONS

HQ: Christy Sports LLC
875 Parfet St., Lakewood CO 80215-5780
Phone: 303-237-6321   **Fax:** 303-233-5946
Web: www.christysports.com

COMPETITORS

Big 5
Dick's Sporting Goods
Lands' End
Patagonia Inc.

Pelican Sport Center
REI
Sports Authority

HISTORICAL FINANCIALS
Company Type: Private

Income Statement
FYE: April 30

	REVENUE ($ mil.)	NET INCOME ($ mil.)	NET PROFIT MARGIN	EMPLOYEES
04/12	55	1	2.6%	450
04/11	56	2	4.2%	0
04/10	50	0	1.4%	0
04/08	58	1	2.8%	0
Annual Growth	(1.2%)	(3.9%)	—	—

2012 Year-End Financials

Debt ratio: ——
Return on equity: 2.60%
Cash ($ mil.): 0
Current ratio: 0.10
Long-term debt ($ mil.): —

Dividends
  Yield: —
  Payout: —
Market value ($ mil.): —

CHUGACH WORLD SERVICES INC.

LOCATIONS

HQ: CHUGACH WORLD SERVICES INC.
3800 CENTERPOINT DR # 700, ANCHORAGE, AK 99503-5801
Phone: 907-563-8866
Web: www.chugach-ak.com

HISTORICAL FINANCIALS
Company Type: Private

Income Statement
FYE: December 31

	REVENUE ($ mil.)	NET INCOME ($ mil.)	NET PROFIT MARGIN	EMPLOYEES
12/11	148	0	0.1%	1,115
12/10	176	5	3.1%	0
12/09	48	(0)	—	0
12/08	0	0	—	0
Annual Growth	—	—	—	—

CHURCH SCHOOLS IN THE DIOCESE OF VIRGINIA

LOCATIONS

HQ: CHURCH SCHOOLS IN THE DIOCESE OF VIRGINIA
8727 RIVER RD, RICHMOND, VA 23229-8303
Phone: 804-643-8451
Web: www.thediocese.net

HISTORICAL FINANCIALS
Company Type: Private

Income Statement
FYE: June 30

	REVENUE ($ mil.)	NET INCOME ($ mil.)	NET PROFIT MARGIN	EMPLOYEES
06/12	96	(2)	—	650
06/11	117	25	21.3%	0
06/10	108	17	16.1%	0
06/09	0	0	9.2%	0
Annual Growth	426.2%	—	—	—

2012 Year-End Financials

Debt ratio: ——
Return on equity: (-2.40)%
Cash ($ mil.): 15
Current ratio: 0.30
Long-term debt ($ mil.): —

Dividends
  Yield: —
  Payout: —
Market value ($ mil.): —

CIMC USA INC

LOCATIONS

HQ: CIMC USA INC
289 WATER TOWER DR, MONON, IN 47959-8160
Phone: 219-253-2054

HISTORICAL FINANCIALS
Company Type: Private

Income Statement
FYE: December 31

	REVENUE ($ mil.)	NET INCOME ($ mil.)	NET PROFIT MARGIN	EMPLOYEES
12/11	268	8	3.2%	1
Annual Growth	—	—	—	—

2011 Year-End Financials

Debt ratio: ——
Return on equity: 3.20%
Cash ($ mil.): 9
Current ratio: 0.50
Long-term debt ($ mil.): —

Dividends
  Yield: —
  Payout: —
Market value ($ mil.): —

CITATION OIL & GAS CORP.

Citation Oil & Gas plans to write a ticket to profits in the petroleum industry. The oil and gas development and production company has interests in nearly 14000 wells with 209 million barrels of proved reserves. Its oil fields are in the Mid-Continent Permian Basin and Rocky Mountain regions - the central US. Citation seeks out properties with high levels of crude oil declining production with long reserve life and low risk. The company uses a variety of techniques to recover oil and gas including waterflood and infill drilling. Subsidiary Citation Crude Marketing sells the company's products to refiners. Formed in 1981 Citation has offices in Midland Texas; Gillette Wyoming; and Oklahoma City.

EXECUTIVES

SVP and CFO, Christopher A. Phelps, age 41
President and CEO, Curtis F. Harrell, age 48
Chairman, Forrest E. (Eddie) Harrell Sr.
VP Marketing and President CCMI, Forrest E. Harrell Jr.
SVP Engineering, Steve K. Anna
SVP Business Development and Land, Robert T. (Bobby) Kennedy
SVP CCMI, Jerry C. Martin
SVP Operations, Steven C. Pearson
SVP General Counsel and Secretary, Wayne Wiesen
VP Information Systems, Mark A. Anchondo
VP Administration, Nancy A. Anglin
VP Commercial Activities and Business Development, Scott A. Loosley
VP Taxation, Thomas E. Patrick

LOCATIONS

HQ: Citation Oil & Gas Corp.
14077 Cutten Rd., Houston TX 77069-2212
Phone: 281-891-1000   **Fax:** -6401
Web: www.cathaybiotech.com

COMPETITORS

Adams Resources
Anadarko Petroleum
Apache
BP
Cabot Oil & Gas
Chesapeake Energy
Chevron
Cimarex
ConocoPhillips
Devon Energy

EOG
Exxon Mobil
Hunt Consolidated
Jones Energy
Key Energy
National Fuel Gas
Noble Energy
Pioneer Natural Resources
Royal Dutch Shell

HISTORICAL FINANCIALS
Company Type: Private

Income Statement
FYE: December 31

	REVENUE ($ mil.)	NET INCOME ($ mil.)	NET PROFIT MARGIN	EMPLOYEES
12/11	449	251	56.0%	507
12/09	233	99	42.6%	0
12/08	364	219	60.1%	0
12/07	260	136	52.4%	0
Annual Growth	19.9%	22.6%	—	—

2011 Year-End Financials

Debt ratio: ——
Return on equity: 56.00%
Cash ($ mil.): 28
Current ratio: 0.60
Long-term debt ($ mil.): ——

Dividends
Yield: ——
Payout: ——
Market value ($ mil.): ——

CITIZENS ENERGY GROUP

Hoosiers are happy to have their homes provided with gas and water services by Public Utilities of the City of Indianapolis (dba Citizens Energy and CWA Authority public charitable trusts). Its Citizens Water unit provides water and wastewater services to 300000 customers in Indianapolis; Citizens Gas serves more than 265000 gas customers. Citizens Energy also provides steam heating and chilled water cooling services to about 250 customers through Citizens Thermal Energy. The regional utility also has a small oil production unit (Citizens Oil Division). Its Citizens Resources unit has joint venture stakes in some companies not regulated by the Indiana Utility Regulatory Commission such as ProLiance Energy.

Citizens Energy operates six business segments: Citizens Gas Water Steam Chilled Water Oil and Citizens Resources Steam and Chilled Water. Citizen Resources holds affiliate joint venture interests including ProLiance Energy and a number of subsidiaries including Westfield Gas a regulated natural gas distribution utility. Citizens Oil has produced more than 6 million barrels of oil since 1969 from Greene County Indiana. CWA Authority provides wastewater services.

Boosted by the acquisition of Indianapolis' water utility the company reported a growth in revenues of 5% in 2011 despite weaker natural gas commodity prices that dragged down gas sales. A gain of $46 million led by the reduction of the legacy post-retirement benefit costs associated with the water utility purchase did cut Citizens Energy's expenses allowing the company to post a $32.4 million for the year compared to a $1.9 million loss in 2010.

Responding to the company's efficient operation of its gas utility in 2010 the Indianapolis City/County Council voted to sell its debt-laden water and wastewater utility (CWA Authority) to Citizens Energy in a $1.9 billion deal pending regulatory approval. The deal completed in 2011 reshaped the utility's business organization and transformed Citizens Energy into a multi-utility.

The company was first organized as a public charitable trust in 1887. In a 2008 rebranding Citizens Gas & Coke Utility changed its operating name to Citizens Energy Group to reflect the company's closing of its old smokestack industry (coke manufacturing operations for steelmakers and smelter) and its new strategic emphasis on energy conservation.

EXECUTIVES

President and CEO, Carey B. Lykins
SVP and Chief Administrative Officer, M. Jean Richcreek
SVP Corporate and Legal Affairs, John R. Whitaker
VP Human Resources, Robert J. Hummel
VP Gas and Steam Operations, Lindsay C. Lindgren

VP Customer and Information Services, Andrew J. Proctor
SVP Operations, William A. (Bill) Tracy
Board President, Martha D. Lamkin
Board Secretary, Dorothy J. Jones
Board President, James A. Wade
SVP and CFO, John Brehm
VP Customer Relationships, Michael Strohl
VP Community Relations, Yvonne Perkins
VP Engineering and Facilities Management, Jeffrey Harrison
Director, Anne Nobles, age 55
Director, Anita J. Harden
Board Secretary, Dorothy J. Jones
Board Treasurer, Lawrence A. O'Connor Jr.
Director, James M. McClelland
Board President, James A. Wade
Auditors: PricewaterhouseCoopersLLP

LOCATIONS

HQ: Public Utilities of the City of Indianapolis
2020 N. Meridian St., Indianapolis IN 46202-1393
Phone: 317-327-3311   **Fax:** 604-682-4768
Web: www.hastingsresourcescorp.com

PRODUCTS/OPERATIONS

2011 Sales

	$ mil.	% of total
Utility	418	90
Non-utility	44	10
Total	**463**	**100**

2011 Sales

	% of total
Citizens	67
Steam	15
Chilled	8
Water	5
Wastewater	3
Oil	1
Resources	1
Total	**100**

COMPETITORS

American States Water
Duke Energy
Indiana Municipal Power Agency
NIPSCO
Vectren
Veolia Environnement

HISTORICAL FINANCIALS

Company Type: Government-owned

Income Statement

FYE: September 30

	REVENUE ($ mil.)	NET INCOME ($ mil.)	NET PROFIT MARGIN	EMPLOYEES
09/11	463	32	7.0%	1,090
09/10	440	(1)	—	0
09/09	555	(6)	—	0
09/08	542	19	3.7%	0
Annual Growth	**(5.1%)**	**17.7%**	**—**	**—**

2011 Year-End Financials

Debt ratio: ——
Return on equity: 7.00%
Cash ($ mil.): 391
Current ratio: 1.30
Long-term debt ($ mil.): ——

Dividends
Yield: ——
Payout: ——
Market value ($ mil.): ——

CITIZENS MEDICAL CENTER

LOCATIONS

HQ: CITIZENS MEDICAL CENTER
2701 HOSPITAL DR, VICTORIA, TX 77901-5749
Phone: 361-573-9181
Web: www.citizensmedicalcenter.org

HISTORICAL FINANCIALS

Company Type: Private

Income Statement

FYE: June 30

	REVENUE ($ mil.)	NET INCOME ($ mil.)	NET PROFIT MARGIN	EMPLOYEES
06/11	134	4	3.5%	1,200
06/07	131	25	19.7%	0
06/05	112	10	9.5%	0
06/04	103	5	5.6%	0
Annual Growth	**9.2%**	**(6.5%)**	**—**	**—**

2011 Year-End Financials

Debt ratio: ——
Return on equity: 3.50%
Cash ($ mil.): 100
Current ratio: 12.80
Long-term debt ($ mil.): ——

Dividends
Yield: ——
Payout: ——
Market value ($ mil.): ——

CITIZENS MEMORIAL HOSPITAL DISTRICT OF POLK COUNTY

LOCATIONS

HQ: CITIZENS MEMORIAL HOSPITAL DISTRICT OF POLK COUNTY
1500 N OAKLAND AVE, BOLIVAR, MO 65613-3011
Phone: 417-326-6000
Web: www.citizensmemorialhealthcare.com

HISTORICAL FINANCIALS

Company Type: Private

Income Statement

FYE: May 31

	REVENUE ($ mil.)	NET INCOME ($ mil.)	NET PROFIT MARGIN	EMPLOYEES
05/12	102	2	2.2%	659
05/05	25	0	1.1%	0
05/03	0	0	—	0
05/02	35	1	5.3%	0
Annual Growth	**42.0%**	**5.4%**	**—**	**—**

2012 Year-End Financials

Debt ratio: ——
Return on equity: 2.20%
Cash ($ mil.): 7
Current ratio: 1.10
Long-term debt ($ mil.): ——

Dividends
Yield: ——
Payout: ——
Market value ($ mil.): ——

CITY OF LA CROSSE

LOCATIONS

HQ: CITY OF LA CROSSE
400 LA CROSSE ST, LA CROSSE, WI 54601-3374
Phone: 608-789-7567
Web: www.lacrossecenter.com

HISTORICAL FINANCIALS

Company Type: Private

Income Statement

FYE: December 31

	REVENUE ($ mil.)	NET INCOME ($ mil.)	NET PROFIT MARGIN	EMPLOYEES
12/11	88	(20)	—	1,500
12/10	94	31	33.7%	0
12/09	103	8	8.5%	0
12/08	0	9		0
Annual Growth	—	—	—	—

CITY OF SURPRISE

LOCATIONS

HQ: CITY OF SURPRISE
16000 N CIVIC CENTER PLZ, SURPRISE, AZ
85374-7470
Phone: 623-222-1000
Web: www.surpriseaz.gov

HISTORICAL FINANCIALS

Company Type: Private

Income Statement

FYE: June 30

	REVENUE ($ mil.)	NET INCOME ($ mil.)	NET PROFIT MARGIN	EMPLOYEES
06/11	89	0	0.9%	600
Annual Growth	—	—	—	—

2011 Year-End Financials

Debt ratio: ——
Return on equity: 0.90%
Cash ($ mil.): 67
Current ratio: ——
Long-term debt ($ mil.): ——

Dividends
  Yield: —
  Payout: —
Market value ($ mil.): —

CITY PUBLIC SERVICES OF SAN ANTONIO

And the award for being the energy distributor for the seventh-largest city in the US goes to City Public Service of San Antonio (also known as CPS Energy). Serving 717000 electricity customers and 325000 natural gas customers the utility operates in a 1514-sq.-mi. service territory. CPS Energy also has a generating capacity of more than 5000 MW from its 16 fossil-fueled power plants and its ownership interests in the South Texas Nuclear Project and wind power and solar power projects. As a municipally owned utility CPS Energy is exempt from retail competition in Texas.

CPS Energy serves customers in Bexar County and portions of Atascosa Bandera Comal Guadalupe Kendall Medina and Wilson counties.

In 2012 CPS Energy reported a 10% jump in revenues (despite a slump in gas sales due to low commodity prices) thanks to brutally hot summer weather driving up demand for electricity. Income dropped by 65% that year primarily due to higher fuel purchased power and distribution gas costs coupled with higher conservation operating pension and regulatory expenses.

Pushing renewables to reduce green house gas emissions to meet state and federal standards CPS Energy is now leading in wind-energy capacity among municipally owned utilities across the US with almost 860 MW of wind energy under contract in 2012 and more planned to come on line that year. The company has a goal of getting 20% of its power from renewable sources by 2020 including 100 MW from solar power. In 2011 CPS Energy announced the proposed closure of its older Deely coal plant units which will be replaced by a cleaner-burning natural gas plant.

Looking to reduce both power use and its carbon footprint CPS Energy is retrofitting more than 1 million electric and gas meters (including 40000 in 2011) in order to bring them into a smart technology grid to help customers save money and conserve power. It is also encouraging customers to switch to compact fluorescent lights and has a goal of reducing power demand by 771 MW by 2020.

A venerable company CPS Energy traces its roots to the 1860s when its predecessor opened a manufactured gas plant on Houston Street.

EXECUTIVES

EVP Energy Delivery Services, John Moore, age 54
Chairman, Charles E. Foster, age 75
VP Retail Energy, John M. Saenz
SVP Energy Development, Michael K. Kotara
President and CEO, Doyle N. Beneby, age 52
EVP and CFO, Paula Gold-Williams
Chairman, Derrick Howard
EVP and Chief Administrative Officer, Jelynne L. Burley
EVP CTO and Chief Strategy Officer, Cris Eugster
Chief Audit and Ethics Officer, Helen Madison
Trustee, Stephen S. Hennigan
Trustee, Derrick Howard
Trustee, Homer Guevara
Trustee, Julian Castro
Auditors: BakerTillyVirchowKrauseLLP

LOCATIONS

HQ: City Public Service of San Antonio
145 Navarro St., San Antonio TX 78205
Phone: 210-353-2000   **Fax:** 920-303-7020
Web: www.perfecseal.com

PRODUCTS/OPERATIONS

2012 Fuel Mix

% of total	
Coal	47
Nuclear	32
Natural gas & purchased	12
Renewables	9
Total	**100**

2012 Sales

% of total	
Electric	89
Gas	9
Other	2
Total	**100**

COMPETITORS

AEP	Energy Future
AES	NextEra Energy
Duke Energy	ONEOK

HISTORICAL FINANCIALS

Company Type: Government-owned

Income Statement

FYE: January 31

	REVENUE ($ mil.)	NET INCOME ($ mil.)	NET PROFIT MARGIN	EMPLOYEES
01/11	2,068	78	3.8%	3,743
01/10	1,930	107	5.6%	0
01/09	2,151	81	3.8%	0
01/08	1,860	110	5.9%	0
Annual Growth	3.6%	(10.6%)	—	—

2011 Year-End Financials

Debt ratio: ——
Return on equity: 3.80%
Cash ($ mil.): 156
Current ratio: 0.60
Long-term debt ($ mil.): ——

Dividends
  Yield: —
  Payout: —
Market value ($ mil.): —

CITY UTILITIES OF SPRINGFIELD MO

This Springfield is not Homer Simpson's hometown or Abe Lincoln's. City Utilities of Springfield Missouri supplies electricity natural gas and water for residents and businesses in the southwestern Missouri town. The utility which has about 1870 miles of power lines and 1300 miles of natural gas mains serves about 109560 electric customers more than 82560 natural gas customers and more than 76760 water customers. It also operates the municipal bus system which has 25 regular street buses and five demand/response buses and serves 213 broadband customers through SpringNet Telecommunications. City Utilities of Springfield has a service region of 320 sq. ml. and serves a base population of 229000.

In addition to its regular electricity supplies the utility offers its customers the option of using renewable wind-generated electricity imported to Springfield from a Kansas wind farm (the 50 MW Smoky Hills Wind Farm in Salina).

The company reported an 11% jump in revenues in 2011. This was due to hotter-than-usual weather spurring power demand and increased capacity driving up off-system sales volumes. Low rainfall during the year also resulted in increased water usage by customers. City Utilities of Springfield reported an 8% increase in operating expenses which was kept to single digits by lower natural gas prices.

The utility traces its origins to the gas works of Springfield Gas Lighting Company which opened in 1874. In 1945 Springfield Gas and Electric was bought by the City of Springfield resulting in the creation of City Utilities of Springfield.

EXECUTIVES

Associate General Manager Operations, Wade Stinson
General Manager, John Twitty
Associate General Manager Administration, Robin House
Senior Manager Pricing, Cathy Meyer
Associate General Manager and Chief Internal Auditor, Brenda Putnam
Associate General Manager and CFO, Jim Shuler
Associate General Manager Electric Supply, Scott Miller
Associate General Manager and General Counsel, John Black
Supervisor Communications, Joel Alexander
Auditors: BKDLLP

LOCATIONS

HQ: City Utilities of Springfield Missouri
301 E. Central St., Springfield MO 65801
Phone: 417-863-9000   **Fax:** 417-831-8377
Web: www.cityutilities.net/index.htm

PRODUCTS/OPERATIONS

2011 Sales

	% of total
Electric	65
Natural	23
Water	8
Telco/Broadband	4
Transporation	-
Total	**100**

HISTORICAL FINANCIALS

Company Type: Government-owned

Income Statement — FYE: September 30

	REVENUE ($ mil.)	NET INCOME ($ mil.)	NET PROFIT MARGIN	EMPLOYEES
09/11	402	18	4.5%	1,020
09/10	359	28	8.0%	0
09/09	344	16	4.9%	0
09/08	393	24	6.2%	0
Annual Growth	**0.7%**	**(9.3%)**	**—**	**—**

2011 Year-End Financials

Debt ratio: ——
Return on equity: 4.50%
Cash ($ mil.): 53
Current ratio: 1.10
Long-term debt ($ mil.): —
Dividends
Yield: —
Payout: —
Market value ($ mil.): —

CIVISTA HEALTH FOUNDATION INC.

Civista Health sees a civic vista wherever it looks. The organization brings medical care to the residents of Charles County and surrounding areas in southern Maryland. The regional not-for-profit hospital system includes acute care facility Civista Medical Center Civista Women's Health Center Civista Surgery Center (an outpatient facility) and

Civista OB/GYN Associates. Civista Health's services include emergency care rehabilitation surgery and cancer treatment offered by more than 230 physicians. The system also offers a chronic pain program radiology and laboratory services. Nearly half the system's revenue comes from Medicare payments.

EXECUTIVES

Interim CEO and CFO, Noel A. Cervino
Secretary and Treasurer, Louis P. Jenkins Jr., age 39
Chair, James Burke
Vice Chair, Sara Middleton
Chief of Staff, Sanjeeb Mishra
COO, Gary Herbek
VP Patient Care Services and Nurse Executive, Cathy Delligatti
Director Marketing and Planning, Linda Kandel
Director Human Resources, Stacey Cook
Practice Administrator, Ivette Montes De Ocaa
Chief Medical Officer, Mark Dumais
Director, Gregory V. Billups
Director, Barbara Stepura
Director, Seetaramayya Nagula
Director, Wayne Cooper
Director, C. Devadason
Vice Chair, Sara Middleton
Director, Suryakant J. Patel
Director, Khadar Baig
Director, Delores C. Datcher
Director, Van T. Mitchell
Director, Richard A. Winkler

LOCATIONS

HQ: Civista Health Inc.
701 E. Charles St., La Plata MD 20646
Phone: 301-609-4000   **Fax:** 301-609-4191
Web: www.civista.org

COMPETITORS

Adventist HealthCare
MedStar Health
Washington County Health System

HISTORICAL FINANCIALS

Company Type: Private - Not-for-Profit

Income Statement — FYE: June 30

	REVENUE ($ mil.)	NET INCOME ($ mil.)	NET PROFIT MARGIN	EMPLOYEES
06/11	105	4	4.4%	668
06/10	102	1	1.8%	0
06/09	0	0	—	0
06/06	77	0	1.1%	0
Annual Growth	**10.6%**	**74.3%**	**—**	**—**

2011 Year-End Financials

Debt ratio: ——
Return on equity: 4.40%
Cash ($ mil.): 33
Current ratio: —
Long-term debt ($ mil.): —
Dividends
Yield: —
Payout: —
Market value ($ mil.): —

CLAFLIN UNIVERSITY

Independent liberal arts institution Claflin University offers undergraduate degree programs select graduate programs internships and other career-focused and continuing education programs

to students from some 25 states and over 15 countries. Enrollment is about 1800 with a student/faculty ratio of 12-to-1. About 96% of the students receive tuition and financial assistance. It is South Carolina's oldest historically black college or university tracing its roots to 1866 and its founding to 1869. (The university awarded its first bachelor's degree in 1882.) Claflin University is affiliated with the United Methodist Church.

To better prepare its students Claflin has adopted a strategic plan that provides for academic programs that emphasize research scholarly contributions and creative activity. The university is working to gain national accreditation for all of its academic programs. In 2005 The National Association of Schools of Music (NASM) awarded associate membership to the Claflin University Department of Music and the Association of Collegiate Business Schools and Program (ACBSP) awarded national accreditation to Claflin's MBA program. Claflin also has achieved accreditation for their teacher education programs by the National Council for Accreditation of Teacher Education (NCATE).

Among Comprehensive Colleges in the South for students pursuing bachelor's degrees Claflin University received "Top 10" and "Best Value" rankings by U.S. News and World Report in its "2006 Guidebook to America's Best Colleges and Universities."

EXECUTIVES

President, Henry N. Tisdale
Director Research Development, Rebecca Bullard-Dillard
Chief Accountant, Albernel J. Jones
Associate VP Fiscal Affairs, Leon A. Brunson
Staff Accountant, Gelane Dantzler
VP Student Development and Services, Leroy A. Durant
Director Sponsored Programs, Veronica Goodman
Student Accounts Manager, Hattie Harmon
Administrative Assistant Student Development and Services, Claudette M. Hopkins
Grants Administrator Sponsored Programs, Janice E. McCollom
VP Academic Affairs and Executive Assistant Government Relations and Research, George E. Miller III
Director Testing and Assessment Services, Sri Sitharaman
Accounts Payable Manager, Margaret D. Stokes
Administrative Assistant to VP Fiscal Affairs, Patricia Sweat
Director Internal Audit, Priscilla T. Anderson

LOCATIONS

HQ: Claflin University
400 Magnolia St., Orangeburg SC 29115-9970
Phone: 803-535-5000   **Fax:** 803-531-2860
Web: www.claflin.edu/index.html

COMPETITORS

Clark Atlanta University
Fisk University
Florida A&M University
Howard University
Morehouse College
Morris College
South Carolina State University
Spelman College
University of South Carolina
Xavier University

HISTORICAL FINANCIALS

Company Type: School

Income Statement

FYE: June 30

	REVENUE ($ mil.)	NET INCOME ($ mil.)	NET PROFIT MARGIN	EMPLOYEES
06/11	46	4	10.0%	340
06/09	48	0	—	0
06/08	44	2	5.7%	0
06/07	38	1	5.1%	0
Annual Growth	6.4%	33.0%	—	—

2011 Year-End Financials

Debt ratio: —
Return on equity: 10.00%
Cash ($ mil.): 1
Current ratio: —
Long-term debt ($ mil.): —

Dividends
Yield: —
Payout: —
Market value ($ mil.): —

CLARE ROSE INC.

Clare Rose has risen to the top with help from The King of Beers. The company a top beer wholesaler in the US primarily markets Anheuser-Busch products including Budweiser Michelob Bacardi and Busch branded products. Clare Rose dominates distribution of the US beer maker's brands on New York's Long Island and Staten Island. The firm also carries other products including those of Heineken Redhook Ale and Widmer Brothers (both owned by Craft Brewers Alliance) Kona Brewing China's Harbin and Japan's Kirin. Founded in 1936 by Clare Rose the company is still owned and operated by the Rose family.

A longtime resident of Patchogue the company pulled up stakes in fall 2010 and moved into a new 265000 sq.-ft. facility in Yaphank New York. Clare Rose has proposed bulldozing its old Patchogue facility and replacing it with a 200-unit condo project worth $80 million as part of the town's efforts to revitalize the downtown area and add centrally located housing.

Founder Clare Rose died in 2010 at the age of 98.

EXECUTIVES

President and CEO, Lisa Rose, age 44
Chairman, Sean Rose
Sales Manager, George MacDonald
Director Safety and Health, Pat Costanzo
Director Human Resources, Christine Dunne
VP Operations and Procurement, Darwin Thomas
VP Information Technology, Gary Neumen
SVP, Kenneth (Ken) Meyer
VP Finance, Monica Wray

LOCATIONS

HQ: Clare Rose Inc.
72 Clare Rose Blvd., Patchogue NY 11772
Phone: 631-475-1840   **Fax:** 631-475-1837
Web: www.clarerose.com

COMPETITORS

Empire Merchants
Manhattan Beer Distributors

Phoenix Beverages
Yuengling & Son

HISTORICAL FINANCIALS

Company Type: Private

Income Statement

FYE: December 31

	REVENUE ($ mil.)	NET INCOME ($ mil.)	NET PROFIT MARGIN	EMPLOYEES
12/11	199	8	4.2%	267
12/10	200	5	2.6%	0
12/08	194	7	4.0%	0
12/07	187	8	4.4%	0
Annual Growth	2.1%	0.1%	—	—

2011 Year-End Financials

Debt ratio: —
Return on equity: 4.20%
Cash ($ mil.): 2
Current ratio: 0.70
Long-term debt ($ mil.): —

Dividends
Yield: —
Payout: —
Market value ($ mil.): —

CLAREMONT GRADUATE UNIVERSITY

Claremont Graduate University (CGU) offers sunshine as well as strong academics to students. About 35 miles from Los Angeles the university provides master's and doctoral degrees in 22 disciplines including education mathematics and psychology. A member of the Claremont University Consortium the university is made up of nine academic schools including arts and humanities educational studies and politics and economics. The Peter F. Drucker Graduate School of Management also is housed on the Claremont Graduate University campus. The relatively small university with an enrollment of about 2000 focuses on giving its students individualized attention. CGU was founded in 1925.

EXECUTIVES

Vice Provost Student Services and Dean Students, James (Jim) Whitaker
Director Office of Student Financing, Jack Millis
President, Robert Klitgaard
Associate VP Human Resources, Brenda Leswick
VP Academic Affairs and Provost, Yi Feng
Vice Provost and Director Research, Dean R. Gerstein
SVP Finance and Administration, Steven N. Garcia
CIO, Travis Wynberry
VP Advancement, Gregory P. Cox
Director University Communications, Esther Wiley
Director Alumni Services, Monika Moore
Senior Secretary, Nancy Cavin
Assistant Vice President Director of Development, Mike Avila
Executive Vice President, Jacob Adams
President, Deborah A. Freund
Assistant Director, Brendan Babish
Director Institutional Effectiveness and WASC Accreditation Liaison Officer, Alana Olschwang
Vice President of Advancement, Bedford McIntosh
Assistant Director Corporate and Foundation Relations, Kevin Riel
Assistant Director Media and Online Relations, Rod Leveque

LOCATIONS

HQ: Claremont Graduate University
150 E. 10th St., Claremont CA 91711
Phone: 909-621-8000   **Fax:** 909-607-7285
Web: www.cgu.edu

PRODUCTS/OPERATIONS

Academic Schools
Peter F. Drucker and Masatoshi Graduate School of Management
School of the Arts and Humanities
School of Community and Global Health
School of Behavioral and Organizational Sciences
School of Educational Studies
School of Information Systems and Technology
School of Mathematical Sciences
School of Politics and Economics
School of Religion

HISTORICAL FINANCIALS

Company Type: School

Income Statement

FYE: June 30

	REVENUE ($ mil.)	NET INCOME ($ mil.)	NET PROFIT MARGIN	EMPLOYEES
06/11	87	11	13.3%	250
06/10	59	(16)	—	0
06/09	57	(15)	—	0
06/08	58	(19)	—	0
Annual Growth	14.4%	—	—	—

2011 Year-End Financials

Debt ratio: —
Return on equity: 13.30%
Cash ($ mil.): 13
Current ratio: —
Long-term debt ($ mil.): —

Dividends
Yield: —
Payout: —
Market value ($ mil.): —

CLAREMONT UNIVERSITY CONSORTIUM

Claremont University Consortium (CUC) provides administrative and support services to The Claremont Colleges a group of independent colleges located on adjoining campuses in Claremont California. The colleges collectively serve some 6300 students and include Claremont McKenna (public affairs) Harvey Mudd (science engineering and math) Pitzer (social science) Pomona and Claremont Graduate University (liberal arts) Scripps (women's college) and Keck Graduate Institute (applied life sciences). The consortium operates the campus facilities including the bookstore libraries labs and health centers. CUC was founded in 1925 and modeled after the University of Oxford.

EXECUTIVES

CEO, Robert A. Walton
Chief Administrative Officer, John F. Beckman
Director Information Technology, Rene Yang
VP and Treasurer, James (Jim) Dunkelman
Director Advancement, Barbara Jefferson
Director Human Resources, Cynthia Beckwith

LOCATIONS

HQ: Claremont University Consortium
150 E. 8th St., Claremont CA 91711
Phone: 909-621-8000 **Fax:** 909-621-8517
Web: www.cuc.claremont.edu

HISTORICAL FINANCIALS

Company Type: Private - Consortium

Income Statement

FYE: June 30

	REVENUE ($ mil.)	NET INCOME ($ mil.)	NET PROFIT MARGIN	EMPLOYEES
06/12	36	(4)	—	500
06/11	35	6	18.7%	0
06/10	35	3	11.1%	0
06/08	37	(0)	—	0
Annual Growth	(1.3%)	—	—	—

2012 Year-End Financials

Debt ratio: ——
Return on equity: (-12.80)%
Cash ($ mil.): 0
Current ratio: —
Long-term debt ($ mil.): —

Dividends
Yield: —
Payout: —
Market value ($ mil.): —

CLARK PEST CONTROL OF STOCKTON INC.

LOCATIONS

HQ: CLARK PEST CONTROL OF STOCKTON INC.
555 N GUILD AVE, LODI, CA 95240-0809
Phone: 209-368-7152
Web: www.clarkpest.com

HISTORICAL FINANCIALS

Company Type: Private

Income Statement

FYE: December 31

	REVENUE ($ mil.)	NET INCOME ($ mil.)	NET PROFIT MARGIN	EMPLOYEES
12/11	103	1	1.7%	1,000
12/10	100	6	6.1%	0
12/09	100	5	5.1%	0
12/08	106	6	6.3%	0
Annual Growth	(1.0%)	(35.9%)	—	—

2011 Year-End Financials

Debt ratio: ——
Return on equity: 1.70%
Cash ($ mil.): 7
Current ratio: 4.70
Long-term debt ($ mil.): —

Dividends
Yield: —
Payout: —
Market value ($ mil.): —

CLASSIC DISTRIBUTING AND BEVERAGE GROUP INC.

LOCATIONS

HQ: CLASSIC DISTRIBUTING AND BEVERAGE GROUP INC.
120 PUENTE AVE, CITY OF INDUSTRY, CA 91746-2301
Phone: 626-934-3700

HISTORICAL FINANCIALS

Company Type: Private

Income Statement

FYE: December 31

	REVENUE ($ mil.)	NET INCOME ($ mil.)	NET PROFIT MARGIN	EMPLOYEES
12/11	127	16	13.2%	261
12/10	133	5	3.8%	0
12/09	132	5	4.2%	0
12/08	112	3	3.0%	0
Annual Growth	4.4%	70.2%	—	—

2011 Year-End Financials

Debt ratio: ——
Return on equity: 13.20%
Cash ($ mil.): 0
Current ratio: 0.60
Long-term debt ($ mil.): —

Dividends
Yield: —
Payout: —
Market value ($ mil.): —

CLAY ELECTRIC COOPERATIVE INC.

Clay Electric Cooperative covers a lot of ground in Florida. The utility distributes electricity to 14 counties in the northeastern part of the state including the suburbs of Jacksonville and Gainesville. It delivers power to about 165000 residential commercial and industrial members over more than 12900 miles of distribution and transmission lines. The consumer-owned utility offers electronic funds transfer average billing and a seniors' payment plan to residential customers and backup diesel power generation and special rate plans to businesses. The consumer-owned utility has a stake in Seminole Electric Cooperative which provides generation services to Clay Electric and nine other cooperatives.

To encourage conservation and green energy use the coop also supports customers' installation of small photovoltaic solar displays on their own homes through an arrangement whereby Seminole Electric purchases electricity generated and delivered to Clay Electric from any of its members' qualifying solar power systems.

Like other non-profit cooperatives Clay Electric refunds any annual profits to its members as credit refunds. In 2012 the company made $5.25 million in refunds available to its members or about $19 a customer.

That year Clay Electric announced that it would further cut its members' bills due to weak natural gas prices lowering the costs of power production from its gas-fired plants.

EXECUTIVES

General Manager and CEO, Bill Phillips
Director Member and Public Relations, Henry Barrow
Director Engineering, Herman Dyal
Director Finance and Administration, Mark Maxwell
Director Information and Communication Technology, Bruce McHollan
Manager Energy Services, Sherman Phillips
Manager Communications, Larry E. Horne
Editor, Wayne Mattox
Video Services Coordinator, Tom Whitney
District Manager, Howard Mott
District Manager, Tommy Tomlinson
Director Operations, Ricky Davis
Director District Operations, Bill Thompson
District Manager, Kerry Page
District Manager, Jim Beeler
Communications Specialist, Amanda Hernandez
Manager Safety and Training, Lee Hicks
Safety and Training Coordinator, Mark Mosley
Director Human Resources, Chip Gray

LOCATIONS

HQ: Clay Electric Cooperative Inc.
225 W. Walker Dr., Keystone Heights FL 32656
Phone: 352-473-4917 **Fax:** 352-473-1403
Web: www.clayelectric.com

COMPETITORS

Florida Power & Light	Gainesville Regional Utilities
Florida Public Utilities	JEA

HISTORICAL FINANCIALS

Company Type: Private - Cooperative

Income Statement

FYE: December 31

	REVENUE ($ mil.)	NET INCOME ($ mil.)	NET PROFIT MARGIN	EMPLOYEES
12/11	356	20	5.7%	444
12/10	376	15	4.0%	0
Annual Growth	(5.3%)	32.6%	—	—

2011 Year-End Financials

Debt ratio: ——
Return on equity: 5.70%
Cash ($ mil.): 0
Current ratio: 0.30
Long-term debt ($ mil.): —

Dividends
Yield: —
Payout: —
Market value ($ mil.): —

CLAYCO INC.

Clayco is a top US general building contractor that offers real estate architecture design and construction services. The privately owned company serves a range of industries with a focus on industrial corporate government residential institutional and financial facilities. Projects include distribution and logistics centers industrial facilities and food and beverage industry warehouses and plants. Clayco also has constructed headquarters and operation centers call and data centers sports and education facilities and retail centers. Its Clayco Realty Group provides land development site selection and project financing. Clayco was founded in 1984 by CEO Robert Clark.

Geographic Reach

Clayco has offices in Chicago from St. Louis. The firm which is seeking to grow its global presence has major projects in 43 states and three countries.

Operations

Other subsidiaries include Forum Studio an architecture/planning/interior design firm and Concrete Strategies a general contracting firm that specializes in concrete design.

Financial Performance

Clayco's revenues exceeded $820 million in 2011.

Strategy

Clayco vaulted to the top ranks of US general building contractors by developing its own building technique of tilt-up a process of concrete building construction. The group specializes in building distribution/warehouse facilities and sports headquarters and training facilities –it has designed facilities for the Dow Chemical Company Amazon Caterpillar Procter and Gamble 3M and Chevron.

Clayco which weathered the downturn in the construction business by relying on its diverse service offerings in a variety of geographic markets and taking on government-funded projects is seeking new projects in new markets across the country and abroad. To support its growth the firm in 2013 announced that it is moving its corporate headquarters to Chicago where it plans to double the number of employees there over the next several years from 280 at present. Clayco plans to hire new architects designers and project managers and expand its concrete and infrastructure business in Illinois. It's also seeking to make acquisitions including a municipal engineering firm.

EXECUTIVES

Chairman and CEO, Robert G. (Bob) Clark, age 52
EVP Logistic/Distribution and Partner, C. David (Dave) Moses
SVP and COO, Steven R. Sieckhaus
Principal Clayco Realty Group, Tom Schroyer
President Forum Studio, Chris Cedergreen
SVP and Director Construction Chicago, Kevin McKenna
SVP and CFO, Greg Beck
SVP and Director Business Development St. Louis, P. Kirk Warden
VP Financial Facilities, Paul Barrath
VP Residential, Paul Giacoletto
VP Self Perform Concrete, Perry Esslinger
General Counsel, Caroline Saunders
President, Russ Burns
Government Construction and Design, Scott Higgins
Shop Manager Clayco Shop St. Louis, Kevin Schulte
SVP and Partner, Tom Sieckhaus
Executive Director Chicago, Cassandra Francis
Auditors: Ernst&YoungLLP

LOCATIONS

HQ: CLAYCO INC.
2199 INNERBELT BUS CTR DR, SAINT LOUIS, MO 63114-5721
Phone: 314-429-5100
Web: www.claycorp.com

PRODUCTS/OPERATIONS

Selected Subsidiaries

Clayco Realty Group
Concrete Strategies
Forum Studio Inc.

COMPETITORS

AECOM	KHS&S
Alberici	Kinsley Construction
Alter Group	Korte
Amusement Leisure	M. A. Mortenson
Baker Concrete	McCarthy Building
Barton Malow	Populous Inc.
Bechtel	Skanska USA Building
H&M Company	The Austin Company
Hensel Phelps Construction	Turner Corporation
Hunt Construction	Whiting-Turner
James G. Davis Construction	

HISTORICAL FINANCIALS

Company Type: Private

Income Statement

FYE: December 31

	REVENUE ($ mil.)	NET INCOME ($ mil.)	NET PROFIT MARGIN	EMPLOYEES
12/11	511	2	0.5%	500
12/10	443	4	1.0%	0
12/09	450	6	1.3%	0
12/08	374	(0)	—	0
Annual Growth	10.9%	—	—	—

2011 Year-End Financials

Debt ratio: ——
Return on equity: 0.50%
Cash ($ mil.): 17
Current ratio: 1.00
Long-term debt ($ mil.): —
Dividends
Yield: —
Payout: —
Market value ($ mil.): —

CLEANNET U.S.A. INC.

If Mr. Clean himself can't make a personal appearance at your office building CleanNet USA will happily come to your rescue. The company provides commercial building cleaning services to clients nationwide through franchises in more than 115 cities across the US. Its clients' properties include commercial buildings and facilities as well as retail properties such as Wachovia. CleanNet USA was founded in 1987 by president Mark Salek.

EXECUTIVES

President, Mark Salek
Human Resources Director, Kelly Wiseman
VP Sales, Jim Marek
Franchise Development, Ed Lugo

LOCATIONS

HQ: CleanNet U.S.A. Inc.
9861 Broken Land Pkwy. Ste. 208, Columbia MD 21046
Phone: 410-720-6444   **Fax:** 410-720-5307
Web: www.cleannetusa.com

COMPETITORS

ABM Industries	Jani-King

Bonus of America	Rentokil Initial
Coverall	ServiceMaster
Ecolab	UGL Services UNICCO

HISTORICAL FINANCIALS

Company Type: Private

Income Statement

FYE: December 31

	REVENUE ($ mil.)	NET INCOME ($ mil.)	NET PROFIT MARGIN	EMPLOYEES
12/11	64	5	8.4%	150
12/10	61	5	8.2%	0
12/08	52	4	9.0%	0
12/07	36	3	9.7%	0
Annual Growth	21.3%	15.6%	—	—

2011 Year-End Financials

Debt ratio: ——
Return on equity: 8.40%
Cash ($ mil.): 4
Current ratio: 7.30
Long-term debt ($ mil.): —
Dividends
Yield: —
Payout: —
Market value ($ mil.): —

CLEARFIELD HOSPITAL

Clearly if you are looking for health care in Clearfield Pennsylvania the place to go is Clearfield Hospital. Operated by Clearfield Area Health Services the rural acute care hospital has about 100 beds and provides emergency surgical diagnostic and general inpatient services. Specialized care centers focus on pediatrics obstetrics cardiac care wound healing cancer treatment rehabilitation and home care. Clearfield Hospital –which operates a number of rural primary and specialty care clinics –also provides educational programs classes and community outreach testing and screening services.

Strategy

The medical center which opened its doors in 1901 is conducting renovation and upgrade efforts at its facilities to keep pace with the needs of residents in Clearfield and surrounding communities. Clearfield Hospital also conducts a number of community outreach programs including education health screening and preventative care projects to help keep a finger on the pulse of the area's health care needs.

EXECUTIVES

Corporate Communications, Terri Polachek
Secretary and Treasurer, Michael F. Lezzer, age 51
President Clearfield Hospital Medical Staff, Gregory S. Sheffo
VP Support Services Clearfield Hospital, Jon R. Steen
President and CEO; President and CEO Clearfield Hospital, David J. (Dave) McConnell
Chairman, C. Alan Walker, age 68
CFO Clearfield Hospital, Robert H. Locke
Chief Nursing Officer Clearfield Hospital, Kathy Bedger

LOCATIONS

HQ: Clearfield Area Health Services
809 Turnpike Ave., Clearfield PA 16830
Phone: 814-765-5341   **Fax:** 814-768-2445
Web: www.clearfieldhosp.org

PRODUCTS/OPERATIONS

Selected Facilities Divisions and Services

Ambulatory Care Unit (Same-Day Surgery)
Better Breathing Center (Pulmonary Rehabilitation)
Bright Horizons Center for Emotional Wellness
Cancer Center (Nathaniel D. Yingling M.D. Cancer Center)
Cardiac Rehabilitation
Cardiopulmonary
Chemotherapy Clinic
Clear-Care Corporation
Clearfield Center for Children's Care
Clearfield Community Surgical Care
Clear-Med Clearfield Family Medical Center
Clear-Med Orthopedics - Clearfield
Clear-Med Primary Care - Clearfield
Clear-Med Primary Care - Philipsburg
Clear-Med Specialty Services - Urology
Curwensville Family Medical Services
Dialysis
Diagnostic Imaging
Education Services
Emergency Department
Hospice
Home Health
Houtzdale Family Medicine
Intensive Care Unit (ICU)
In-Patient Surgery (Peri-Operative Suite)
Labor and Delivery (Obstetrics)
Laboratory
Lifeline
Lithotripsy (Kidney Stone Removal)
Moshannon Valley Surgical Clinic
Occupational Therapy
Pediatrics Unit
Philipsburg Medical Services
Philipsburg Outpatient Services
Phlebotomy Services - Curwensville
Physical Therapy
Radiation Oncology
Rehabilitation Services
Sleep Studies
Social Work
Speech Therapy
Surgical Services
Wound Care Clinic

COMPETITORS

Altoona Regional
Conemaugh Health
  System
J. C. Blair Memorial
  Hospital

Kane Community
  Hospital
Lewistown Hospital
UPMC

HISTORICAL FINANCIALS

Company Type: Private - Not-for-Profit

Income Statement

FYE: June 30

	REVENUE ($ mil.)	NET INCOME ($ mil.)	NET PROFIT MARGIN	EMPLOYEES
06/11	67	(0)	—	700
06/10	70	(0)	—	0
06/09	69	(0)	—	0
06/08	71	4	5.8%	0
Annual Growth	(2.0%)	—	—	—

2011 Year-End Financials

Debt ratio: —
Return on equity: (-0.70)%
Cash ($ mil.): 1
Current ratio: 1.00
Long-term debt ($ mil.): —

Dividends
  Yield: —
  Payout: —
  Market value ($ mil.): —

CLEVELAND CONSTRUCTION INC.

Cleveland Construction Inc. (CCI) has ventured beyond Cleveland to offer its services nationwide and abroad. The company offers construction management services for commercial and institutional projects. It also is a top interior contractor in the US installing finishes such as drywall acoustic wall panels and specialty ceilings. Projects have included hospitals universities correctional facilities hotels convention centers sports complexes retail outlets and government buildings such as the Ohio State Stadium the George Bush Intercontinental Airport in Houston and Wal-Mart superstores in Florida. Founded in 1980 by CEO Richard Small and his sons the company remains family-owned.

EXECUTIVES

CEO, Richard G. Small
President, Jon Small
Information Systems, Jan Bjorksten
Purchasing, Steve Williams
CFO and VP Project Management, Mark T. Small
Estimating Interiors, Neal Keller
Apprenticeships and Human Resources, Jack Quinif
Estimating General Contracts, Edward Paradise
Project Management, Keith Ziegler
Sales and Marketing, Matthew Young

LOCATIONS

HQ: Cleveland Construction Inc.
  8620 Tyler Blvd., Mentor OH 44060
Phone: 440-255-8000   **Fax:** 440-255-7443
Web: www.clevelandconstruction.com

COMPETITORS

Albert M. Higley
The Austin Company

The Haskell Company
URS

HISTORICAL FINANCIALS

Company Type: Private

Income Statement

FYE: December 31

	REVENUE ($ mil.)	NET INCOME ($ mil.)	NET PROFIT MARGIN	EMPLOYEES
12/11	218	4	2.2%	800
12/09	217	25	11.9%	0
12/08	186	24	12.9%	0
12/07	227	16	7.2%	0
Annual Growth	(1.4%)	(33.9%)	—	—

2011 Year-End Financials

Debt ratio: —
Return on equity: 2.20%
Cash ($ mil.): 10
Current ratio: 1.20
Long-term debt ($ mil.): —

Dividends
  Yield: —
  Payout: —
  Market value ($ mil.): —

CLINICA SIERRA VISTA

LOCATIONS

HQ: CLINICA SIERRA VISTA
  1430 TRUXTUN AVE STE 400, BAKERSFIELD, CA 93301-5220
Phone: 661-635-3050
Web: www.clinicasierravista.org

HISTORICAL FINANCIALS

Company Type: Private

Income Statement

FYE: March 31

	REVENUE ($ mil.)	NET INCOME ($ mil.)	NET PROFIT MARGIN	EMPLOYEES
03/12	80	6	8.0%	910
03/11	72	6	9.5%	0
03/10	69	5	8.0%	0
03/09	57	2	4.6%	0
Annual Growth	12.1%	34.5%	—	—

2012 Year-End Financials

Debt ratio: —
Return on equity: 8.00%
Cash ($ mil.): 15
Current ratio: 1.90
Long-term debt ($ mil.): —

Dividends
  Yield: —
  Payout: —
  Market value ($ mil.): —

CNL LIFESTYLE PROPERTIES INC.

LOCATIONS

HQ: CNL LIFESTYLE PROPERTIES INC.
  450 S ORANGE AVE, ORLANDO, FL 32801-3383
Phone: 407-650-1000
Web: www.cnl.com

HISTORICAL FINANCIALS

Company Type: Private

Income Statement

FYE: September 30

	ASSETS ($ mil.)	NET INCOME ($ mil.)	INCOME AS % OF ASSETS	EMPLOYEES
09/12*	2,983	(21)	—	4
12/11	2,893	(69)	—	0
12/10	2,673	(81)	—	0
12/09	2,672	(19)	—	0
Annual Growth	3.7%	—	—	—

*Fiscal year change

2012 Year-End Financials

Debt ratio: —
Return on equity: (-5.40)%
Cash ($ mil.): 92
Current ratio: —
Long-term debt ($ mil.): —

Dividends
  Yield: —
  Payout: —
  Market value ($ mil.): —

COACHELLA VALLEY WATER DISTRICT PUBLIC FACILITIES CORPORATION

LOCATIONS

HQ: COACHELLA VALLEY WATER DISTRICT PUBLIC FACILITIES CORPORATION
85995 AVENUE 52, COACHELLA, CA 92236-2568
Phone: 760-398-2651
Web: www.cvwd.org

HISTORICAL FINANCIALS

Company Type: Private

Income Statement

FYE: June 30

	REVENUE ($ mil.)	NET INCOME ($ mil.)	NET PROFIT MARGIN	EMPLOYEES
06/11	164	82	50.2%	500
06/10	138	45	33.2%	0
06/09	134	63	47.5%	0
06/08	118	113	96.4%	0
Annual Growth	11.7%	(10.1%)	—	—

2011 Year-End Financials

Debt ratio: ——
Return on equity: 50.20%
Cash ($ mil.): 264
Current ratio: 12.70
Long-term debt ($ mil.): —

Dividends
  Yield: —
  Payout: —
  Market value ($ mil.): —

COAST PRODUCE COMPANY

LOCATIONS

HQ: COAST PRODUCE COMPANY
1791 BAY ST, LOS ANGELES, CA 90021-1655
Phone: 213-955-4900
Web: www.coastproduce.com

HISTORICAL FINANCIALS

Company Type: Private

Income Statement

FYE: June 29

	REVENUE ($ mil.)	NET INCOME ($ mil.)	NET PROFIT MARGIN	EMPLOYEES
06/12*	130	0	0.6%	180
07/11	136	(0)		0
06/09	146	0	0.4%	0
06/08	144	1	1.3%	0
Annual Growth	(3.3%)	(25.4%)	—	—

*Fiscal year change

2012 Year-End Financials

Debt ratio: ——
Return on equity: 0.60%
Cash ($ mil.): 3
Current ratio: 0.90
Long-term debt ($ mil.): —

Dividends
  Yield: —
  Payout: —
  Market value ($ mil.): —

COASTAL CAROLINA UNIVERSITY

It's hard for students at Coastal Carolina University not to be cocky. The university (whose rooster mascot Chanticleer appears in Chaucer's Canterbury Tales) offers bachelor's degrees in about 50 fields of study and 40 undergraduate minors. It also offers master's degrees in business administration education and coastal marine and wetland studies. The school has an enrollment of roughly 8400 students from 45 states and 40 countries. Coastal Carolina University was founded in 1954 as Coastal Carolina Junior College. Originally a branch of the College of Charleston it was later affiliated with the University of South Carolina. Coastal Carolina became an independent institution in 1993.

EXECUTIVES

EVP and COO, Edgar L. (Eddie) Dyer III
Chairman, William H. (Billy) Alford
Vice Chairman, Samuel J. Swad
Director International Programs, Geoffrey J. Parsons
VP Enrollment Services, Judy W. Vogt
Director Enrollment Planning, Timothy J. McCormick
Interim Associate Provost Grants and Sponsored Research, Valgene L. Dunham
Associate Director Finance, Linda P. Lyerly
Director Procurement, Randall F. Cox
Director University Projects and Planning, Thomas R. Mungo
Director Facility Operations, James A. Hendrick Jr.
Director Risk Management, Janice A. Cannan
Special Projects Coordinator, Marvin F. Marozas
Director Administrative Computing Services, Fadi N. Baroody
Executive Director Information Technology Services, Abdallah S. Haddad
Manager Network Services, John J. Hanna
Manager Application Services, Mike A. McClellan
Director Athletics, Warren D. Koegel
Director Compensation and Operations, Kimberly B Sherfesee
Director Employee Services, Lamonica L. Yates
Special Projects Coordinator, Lynette Willett
Director Campus Recreation and Intramurals, Jody H. Davis
Director Residence Life, Paula D. Drummond
Associate VP and Executive Director Foundations, Stanyarne R. Godshall
Director Special Projects Human Resources and Equal Opportunity, Jacob E. Locklair III
VP Student Affairs, Deborah K. Conner
Assistant VP Marketing Communications, Anne T. Monk
Manager Printing Services, Dennis Roakes
Head of Public Services Kimel Library, Margaret A. Fain
President, David A. (Dave) DeCenzo, age 57
SVP Finance and Administration, Wilbur L. Garland
Secretary Treasurer and Trustee, Tommy M. Stringer
Director Alumni Relations, Jean A. Brakefield
Registrar, Daniel M. Lawless
Head of Collection Management and Systems Kimbel Library, Michael M. Lackey
Associate Director Library Services Kimbel Library, Charmaine B. Tomczyk
Director Academic Advising and First Year Experience, Agatha O'Brien-Gayes
Director Enrollment Events, Amanda E. Craddock
Director Financial Aid, Dawn Hitchcock
Vice Chairman, Gary W. Brown
SVP and Provost, Robert Sheehan
Interim Associate VP Student Affairs and Dean Students, Haven L. Hart
Director Environmental Health and Safety, Greg Weisner
Chairman, D. Wyatt Henderson
VP and CFO, Stacie Ann Bowie
Trustee, Charles J. Hodge
Trustee, Daniel W. R. Moore Sr.
Trustee, Joseph L. Carter
Trustee, Samuel L. Frink
Trustee, William L. Lyles Jr.
Trustee, Robert L. Rabon
Trustee, Oran P. Smith
Trustee, Eugene C. Spivey
Trustee, Samuel J. Swad
Secretary Treasurer and Trustee, Tommy M. Stringer
Trustee, William S. Biggs
Trustee, J. Wayne George
Trustee, Mark Sanford
Vice Chairman, Gary W. Brown
Trustee, R. Duke Brown
Trustee, Robert G. Templeton

LOCATIONS

HQ: Coastal Carolina University
755 Hwy. 544, Conway SC 29526
Phone: 843-347-3161   **Fax:** 843-349-2909
Web: www.coastal.edu

HISTORICAL FINANCIALS

Company Type: School

Income Statement

FYE: June 30

	REVENUE ($ mil.)	NET INCOME ($ mil.)	NET PROFIT MARGIN	EMPLOYEES
06/12	128	29	23.1%	900
06/11	116	29	25.2%	0
06/10	106	30	28.8%	0
06/09	106	14	14.0%	0
Annual Growth	6.6%	26.0%	—	—

2012 Year-End Financials

Debt ratio: ——
Return on equity: 23.10%
Cash ($ mil.): 67
Current ratio: 2.50
Long-term debt ($ mil.): —

Dividends
  Yield: —
  Payout: —
  Market value ($ mil.): —

COASTAL INTERNATIONAL SECURITY INC.

LOCATIONS

HQ: COASTAL INTERNATIONAL SECURITY INC.
6101 FALLARD DR, UPPER MARLBORO, MD
20772-3878
Phone: 703-339-0233
Web: www.coastalinternationalsecurity.com

HISTORICAL FINANCIALS
Company Type: Private

Income Statement				FYE: December 31
	REVENUE ($ mil.)	NET INCOME ($ mil.)	NET PROFIT MARGIN	EMPLOYEES
12/11	133	0	0.3%	5,003
12/10	142	1	0.8%	0
12/07	121	0	0.0%	0
12/06	0	0	—	0
Annual Growth	—	—	—	—

COASTAL PACIFIC FOOD DISTRIBUTORS INC.

Coastal Pacific Food Distributors (CPF) fuels the military forces from facility to fork. The company is a leading wholesale food distributor that primarily serves the US armed forces across the Western US and in the Far East. As part of its business CPF provides a full line of groceries to military bases run by the US Army Navy Air Force and Marines. It delivers a variety of products from distribution centers located in California Washington and Hawaii. CPF also offers information system programming services for its customers to track sales and shipping as well as procurement and logistics through partnerships in Iraq Kuwait and Saudi Arabia. The company was founded in 1986.
Geographic Reach
CPF caters to the Western US as well as Alaska Hawaii Guam Japan Okinawa Korea Singapore Kwajalein and the Philippines. Its business extends to the Middle East through partnerships for procurement and logistics with other companies. These additional areas include Iraq Kuwait and Saudi Arabia.
Operations
As part of its business CPF operates distribution centers in California Washington and Hawaii. In California its largest Stockton facility spans more than 500000 sq. ft. while its Ontario center boasts 429000 sq. ft. Its distribution center in Fife Washington is 153000 sq. ft. A 45000-sq.-ft. facility in Hawaii delivers food to four military commissaries.
Sales and Marketing
Industry partners that keep CPF busy include the Defense Logistics Agency the Defense Commissary Agency Air Force NAF Purchasing Office

Navy Exchange (NEXCOM) Army and Air Force Exchange Service (AAFES) and the American Logistics Association to name a few.

EXECUTIVES

Chairman, Jerry Jared
COO, Terrance Wood
Treasurer, John Payne III
Vice Chairman, David Jared
VP Finance, Monika Bertke
President, Frank Pecoraro
CFO, William Ungerman
VP Business Development, Jeffrey King
VP Distribution Systems, Timothy Tveitnes

LOCATIONS

HQ: Coastal Pacific Food Distributors Inc.
1015 Performance Dr., Stockton CA 95206
Phone: 209-983-2454   **Fax:** 209-983-8009
Web: www.cpfd.com

PRODUCTS/OPERATIONS

Selected Brokers
Acosta Sales & Marketing
Alder Foods Inc.
Bisek & Co. Inc.
Dixon Marketing Inc.
Dunham & Smith Agencies
Elite Brands
Finnegan International Sales
First Wave Sales
Gateway Military LLC
Global Office Building
HI-PAC Ltd
Mid Valley
Overseas Service Corporation
Otis McAllister
Parra Sales Inc
Reese Group
S&K
S. Schwartz Sales Inc.
Turnkey Management
WEBCO General Partnership

COMPETITORS

AdvancePierre	Richmond Wholesale
JTM Provisions	Meat
Nash-Finch	

HISTORICAL FINANCIALS
Company Type: Private

Income Statement				FYE: December 31
	REVENUE ($ mil.)	NET INCOME ($ mil.)	NET PROFIT MARGIN	EMPLOYEES
12/11*	1,162	25	2.2%	459
01/11	1,113	17	1.6%	0
01/10	1,119	17	1.6%	0
12/08	1,101	20	1.9%	0
Annual Growth	1.8%	6.6%	—	—

*Fiscal year change

2011 Year-End Financials
Debt ratio: —
Return on equity: 2.20%
Cash ($ mil.): 4
Current ratio: 1.30
Long-term debt ($ mil.): —
Dividends
Yield: —
Payout: —
Market value ($ mil.): —

COBALT CONSTRUCTION COMPANY

LOCATIONS

HQ: COBALT CONSTRUCTION COMPANY
2259 WARD AVE STE 200, SIMI VALLEY, CA
93065-1880
Phone: 805-577-6222

HISTORICAL FINANCIALS
Company Type: Private

Income Statement				FYE: December 31
	REVENUE ($ mil.)	NET INCOME ($ mil.)	NET PROFIT MARGIN	EMPLOYEES
12/11	87	1	1.6%	70
12/09	46	1	3.6%	0
12/08	105	2	2.7%	0
12/07	105	2	2.5%	0
Annual Growth	(6.1%)	(20.0%)	—	—

2011 Year-End Financials
Debt ratio: —
Return on equity: 1.60%
Cash ($ mil.): 10
Current ratio: 0.50
Long-term debt ($ mil.): —
Dividends
Yield: —
Payout: —
Market value ($ mil.): —

COBORN'S INCORPORATED

Coborn's hopes you'll shop at your convenience. The company runs about 40 Coborn's and Cash Wise Foods stores in Minnesota and the Dakotas another 35 shops under the Holiday Little Dukes and Save-A-Lot banners and online grocery shopping service CobornDelivers. It supplies its stores with baked goods deli items and meat from its own central bakery and manufacturing plant. Along with its grocery stores the firm owns and operates convenience liquor hardware and video stores and pharmacies. Founded in 1921 when Chester Coborn started a single produce market the company opened its first Cash Wise Foods store in 1979 and its first convenience store in 1986. Coborn's is owned by its employees.
Financial Analysis
Across its 90 retail stores Coborn's rang up $1.2 billion in sales in 2011 compared with $1 billion in 2010.
Strategy
Independently-owned Corborn's is building a sizable empire in the Upper Midwest through acquisitions and organic growth. In spring 2012 it purchased a partial interest in JK Foods a Williston North Dakota operator of three stores under the Economart and Food Pride banners as well as a flower shop. The company is also building its own stores: five new Coborn's and Cash Wise locations in North Dakota are slated to debut through 2014. (North Dakota's economy is growing rapidly thanks to the oil boom.)

The regional retailer is growing its discount Cash Wise Foods chain with the acquisition of two independently-owned Cub Foods stores in St. Cloud Minnesota that reopened under the Cash Wise banner in 2010. The purchase coincided with increased price competition in the local grocery market and the recent entry of the limited-assortment deep-discount chain ALDI and a Wal-Mart Supercenter and Sam's Club in September 2010. Discounter Target is also expanding its grocery offering in its area stores. Like ALDI shoppers at Cash Wise Foods stores bag their own groceries. Coborn's also operates several limited-assortment Save-A-Lot deep-discount grocery stores. (The company bought the rights to the Save-A-Lot name from SUPERVALU in 2002.)

EXECUTIVES

COO, Bob Thueringer
Controller, Jerome Schumacher
Director Human Resources, Greg Koenig
President and CEO, Chris Coborn
CFO, Curt Tillotson
Director Communications and Consumer Affairs, Steve Gottwalt

LOCATIONS

HQ: COBORN' S INCORPORATED
1445 HIGHWAY 23 E BLDG A, SAINT CLOUD, MN 56304-0952
Phone: 320-252-4222
Web: www.cashwise.com

PRODUCTS/OPERATIONS

2011 Grocery Stores

	No.
Coborn's	29
Little	18
Holiday	15
Cash Wise	10
Save-A-Lot	3
Total	**75**

Selected Store Formats

Convenience stores (Little Dukes Holiday Stationstores)
Hardware stores (Ace)
Liquor stores
Pharmacies
Restaurants (Subway)
Supermarkets (Coborn's Cash Wise Foods Save-A-.Lot)
Video stores

COMPETITORS

ALDI	Kroger
Couche-Tard	Lunds
Cub Foods	Target Corporation
Kowalski' s Markets	Wal-Mart

HISTORICAL FINANCIALS
Company Type: Private

Income Statement

FYE: December 31

	REVENUE ($ mil.)	NET INCOME ($ mil.)	NET PROFIT MARGIN	EMPLOYEES
12/11	1,191	29	2.4%	6,695
12/10	1,103	23	2.1%	0
12/09	1,024	15	1.5%	0
12/08	1,019	11	1.1%	0
Annual Growth	5.3%	35.8%	—	—

2011 Year-End Financials

Debt ratio: ——
Return on equity: 2.40%
Cash ($ mil.): 26
Current ratio: 0.50
Long-term debt ($ mil.): ——
Dividends
  Yield: ——
  Payout: ——
  Market value ($ mil.): ——

COC PROPERTIES INC.

LOCATIONS

HQ: COC PROPERTIES INC.
110 MACKENAN DR STE 300, CARY, NC 27511-7901
Phone: 919-462-1100
Web: www.caryoil.com

HISTORICAL FINANCIALS
Company Type: Private

Income Statement

FYE: December 31

	ASSETS ($ mil.)	NET INCOME ($ mil.)	INCOME AS % OF ASSETS	EMPLOYEES
12/11	76	2	2.7%	100
12/09	67	0	1.2%	0
12/08	60	6	10.3%	0
12/07	73	4	6.0%	0
Annual Growth	1.5%	(22.5%)	—	—

2011 Year-End Financials

Debt ratio: ——
Return on equity: 0.10%
Cash ($ mil.): 4
Current ratio: 1.00
Long-term debt ($ mil.): ——
Dividends
  Yield: ——
  Payout: ——
  Market value ($ mil.): ——

CODALE ELECTRIC SUPPLY INC.

Codale Electric Supply distributes lighting fixtures electrical supplies and datacomm products to wholesale customers through 11 locations in Nevada Utah Idaho and Wyoming. It stocks products from such manufacturers as Brad Harrison Chromalox Greenlee Philips Lighting Southwire and Western Tube & Conduit. The company sells to the aerospace construction mining healthcare schools government and utility markets. Codale Electric also offers consulting and training energy and safety audits and inventory management services. The company was founded in 1975 by CEO Dale Holt who owns nearly all of Codale Electric's equity.

In addition to expanding its service offerings beyond traditional wholesale distribution the company has added a division that provides modification and assembly of power substations for the utility industry.

HISTORY

odale

EXECUTIVES

President, Dale P. Holt, age 61
Purchasing, Roger Earle
Director Human Resources, Glen Brown

LOCATIONS

HQ: Codale Electric Supply Inc.
5225 W. 2400 South, Salt Lake City UT 84120
Phone: 801-975-7300   **Fax:** 801-977-8833
Web: www.codale.com

COMPETITORS

Allied Electronics	W.W. Grainger
Graybar Electric	WESCO International
MRC Global	

HISTORICAL FINANCIALS
Company Type: Private

Income Statement

FYE: December 25

	REVENUE ($ mil.)	NET INCOME ($ mil.)	NET PROFIT MARGIN	EMPLOYEES
12/11	220	12	5.4%	220
12/10	175	6	3.4%	0
12/09	175	6	3.6%	0
12/08	235	16	6.9%	0
Annual Growth	(2.2%)	(9.8%)	—	

2011 Year-End Financials

Debt ratio: ——
Return on equity: 5.40%
Cash ($ mil.): 0
Current ratio: 0.90
Long-term debt ($ mil.): ——
Dividends
  Yield: ——
  Payout: ——
  Market value ($ mil.): ——

COE COLLEGE

Coe College is a private liberal arts college with a residential campus in Cedar Rapids Iowa. The school offers more than 40 academic majors and grants undergraduate degrees (Bachelor of Arts Bachelor of Music and Bachelor of Science in Nursing) as well as a Master of Arts in Teaching. It has an annual enrollment of more than 1200 students who are required to participate in an internship student research project practicum or study abroad program as they matriculate. Approximately half of the school's students go on to post-graduate studies. Coe College was founded in 1851.

EXECUTIVES

President, James R. Phifer
VP Student Affairs, Lou Stark
Director Marketing and Public Relations, Rod Pritchard
VP Advancement, Richard Meisterling
Controller, Rich Rheinschmidt
VP Enrollment and Administration, Michael White
Dean Admissions, John Grundig
Director Financial Aid, Barbara Hoffman
Director Alumni Programs, Jean Johnson
Manager Administrative Computer Services and Programmer/Analyst, Michael C. Vance
VP Academic Affairs and Dean Faculty, Marie Baehr
Registrar, Evelyn Moore

Director Internships and Career Services, Diana
Patten

LOCATIONS

HQ: Coe College
1220 1st Ave. NE, Cedar Rapids IA 52402
Phone: 319-399-8500   **Fax:** 319-399-8816
Web: www.coe.edu

HISTORICAL FINANCIALS

Company Type: School

Income Statement

	REVENUE ($ mil.)	NET INCOME ($ mil.)	NET PROFIT MARGIN	EMPLOYEES
06/12	41	8	20.8%	272
06/11	37	3	9.6%	0
06/10	39	4	12.0%	0
06/09	27	(7)	—	0
Annual Growth	**15.3%**	—	—	—

FYE: June 30

2012 Year-End Financials

Debt ratio: ——
Return on equity: 20.80%
Cash ($ mil.): 5
Current ratio: —
Long-term debt ($ mil.): —
Dividends
Yield: —
Payout: —
Market value ($ mil.): —

COLBY COLLEGE

Colby College is one of the oldest liberal arts colleges in the US. The school was founded in 1813 as the Maine Literary and Theological Institution and in 1871 it became the first previously all-male college in New England to admit women. Colby offers bachelor of arts degrees in more than 50 majors and has an enrollment of approximately 1800 students. Its most popular majors are biology economics English government history and international studies. Not only is Colby one of the oldest liberal arts colleges in the US it is also one of the most pricey: Annual tuition room and board and fees total more than $46000.

EXECUTIVES

Director Communications, Stephen B. (Steve) Collins
Special Assistant to President External Affairs, Janice Armo Kassman
President and Trustee, William D. Adams, age 64
VP College Relations, Richard A. Ammons
Director Information Technology Services, Raymond B. Philips
VP Administration and Treasurer, W. Arnold Yasinski
VP Academic Affairs and Dean of Faculty, Edward H. Yeterian
Assistant Director Alumni Relations, Karin R. Weston
Director Annual Giving, Kelly L. Dodge
Director Operations and Analysis, Joseph M. (Joe) Medina
Director College Relations Technology Services, Patricia A. (Trisha) Ayers-Miller
Managing Editor Communications, Gerard E. (Gerry) Boyle
Associate Director Corporate and Foundation Relations, Bets Brown

Director Alumni and Donor Relations, Lisa B. Tessler
Director Major Gifts, Avrum R. (Ave) Vinick
Director College Research, Julie Macksoud
Chair, Joseph F. Boulos
Director Counseling Services, Patti Newmen
VP Administration, Douglas C. Terp
Director Safety, Bruce A. McDougal
Benefits Specialist, Mary A. Nelson
Dean Admissions and Financial Aid, Parker J. Beverage
Vice Chair, William H. Goldfarb
VP and Secretary, Sally A. Baker
VP Student Affairs and Dean of Students, James S. Terhune
Trustee, James E. (Jamie) Cowie
Trustee, Todd W. Halloran, age 47
Trustee, Colleen A. Khoury
Trustee, Michael L. Gordon
President and Trustee, William D. Adams, age 64
Trustee, James B. Crawford, age 69
Trustee, Michael S. Sylvester
Trustee, Richard R. Schmaltz
Vice Chair, William H. Goldfarb
Trustee, William L. Alfond
Trustee, Susan Comeau
Trustee, Ann Marie Connolly
Trustee, Rebecca Littleton Corbett
Trustee, William R. Cotter
Trustee, John B. Devine Jr.
Trustee, Robert E. Diamond Jr.
Trustee, Gerald Dorros
Trustee, Diana J. Fuss
Trustee, Robert Sidney Gelbard
Trustee, Timothy B. Hussey
Trustee, Emma J. James
Trustee, Seth W. Lawry
Trustee, Paula Crane Lunder
Trustee, William J. Montgoris
Trustee, William A. Oates Jr.
Trustee, M. Jane Powers
Trustee, Lawrence R. Pugh
Trustee, David Pulver
Trustee, Robert A. Rudnick
Trustee, Paul G. Spillane Jr.
Trustee, Paul G. Spillane
Trustee, Robert E. L. Strider II
Trustee, Charles Terrell
Trustee, Richard Y. Uchida
Trustee, Nancy Greer Weiland
Trustee, Anne Clarke Wolff
Auditors: PricewaterhouseCoopersLLP

LOCATIONS

HQ: Colby College
4000 Mayflower Hill Dr., Waterville ME 04901-8840
Phone: 207-859-4000   **Fax:** 207-872-3227
Web: www.colby.edu

HISTORICAL FINANCIALS

Company Type: School

Income Statement

	REVENUE ($ mil.)	NET INCOME ($ mil.)	NET PROFIT MARGIN	EMPLOYEES
06/12	115	(13)	—	580
06/11	112	124	111.0%	0
06/10	108	68	62.7%	0
06/08	184	57	31.1%	0
Annual Growth	**(14.6%)**	—	—	—

FYE: June 30

2012 Year-End Financials

Debt ratio: ——
Return on equity: (-12.00)%
Cash ($ mil.): 35
Current ratio: —
Long-term debt ($ mil.): —
Dividends
Yield: —
Payout: —
Market value ($ mil.): —

COLE CREDIT PROPERTY TRUST II INC.

LOCATIONS

HQ: COLE CREDIT PROPERTY TRUST II INC.
2555 E CAMELBACK RD # 400, PHOENIX, AZ 85016-4258
Phone: 602-778-8700

HISTORICAL FINANCIALS

Company Type: Private

Income Statement

	REVENUE ($ mil.)	NET INCOME ($ mil.)	NET PROFIT MARGIN	EMPLOYEES
09/12*	212	23	11.2%	2
12/11	279	53	19.3%	0
Annual Growth	**(23.9%)**	**(55.8%)**	—	—

FYE: September 30

*Fiscal year change

2012 Year-End Financials

Debt ratio: ——
Return on equity: 11.20%
Cash ($ mil.): 47
Current ratio: —
Long-term debt ($ mil.): —
Dividends
Yield: —
Payout: —
Market value ($ mil.): —

COLLEGE ENTRANCE EXAMINATION BOARD

There are three letters every high school student must learn: S A and T. Who is responsible for making those letters so infamous? Why The College Board of course. The not-for-profit association owns and administers the Scholastic Assessment Test (SAT) College-Level Examination Program (CLEP) and the Advanced Placement Program (AP) at high schools nationwide. It also offers guidance counseling financial aid student assessment standardized testing and professional development courses. The College Board was founded in 1900; its members include nearly 6000 schools colleges universities and other educational institutions.

Geographic Reach

The College Board has main offices in New York City; Reston Virginia; and Washington DC. It also has six regional offices scattered across the US; these offices handle administrative duties for testing administrations in their respective regions. The organization's member institutions include schools in more than 60 countries; College Board exams are administered in more than 180 countries and territories worldwide.

Operations

The College Board's services reach more than 7 million students at 23000 high schools and 3800 colleges in the US and abroad. In 2012 the association administered some 3 million SAT exams. It also serves some 130000 AP teachers and administers 3.2 million AP exams annually. Some of the College Board's tests such as the SAT are administered at schools with support from third parties such as Educational Testing Services.

Strategy

In 2010 The College Board launched the College Board Advocacy & Policy Center to improve academic standards and support educators through a number of measures. It also seeks ways to improve college affordability and increase awareness of financial aid options among students and their families. In 2012 the center launched an affinity network designed to strengthen connections between K-12 and postsecondary education organizations and help students transition from high school to college.

Company Background

The College Board was created by a group of colleges as a way to expand access to higher education. The SAT (originally called the College Boards) was formed to help colleges and universities identify "deserving" students through shared entrance exams.

EXECUTIVES

SVP Region and Account Services and College Readiness Systems, Eric Cantor
President and Trustee, W. Gaston Caperton III, age 72
COO, Herbert Elish, age 77
SVP and CFO, Thomas (Tom) Higgins
VP Research and Development, Wayne J. Camara
SVP Region and Account Services, Andrea Mainelli
Chair, Youlonda Copeland-Morgan
Chairman, Paul W. Sechrist, age 52
SVP Operations and SAT Program, Laurence Bunin
SVP Relationship Development, Peter Negroni
SVP Government Relations Grants Advocacy, Thomas Rudin
SVP, Hal Higginbotham
SVP College Readiness Products, Lee Jones
SVP Administration and General Counsel, Neil Lane
Treasurer, Steven (Steve) Titan
VP Organizational Effectiveness, Juliet Weissman
VP and Secretary, Dorothy Sexton
VP Membership, Mary C. Scott
Vice Chairman, Maghan Keita
SVP Communications and Marketing, Edna Johnson
SVP AP and College Readiness, Trevor Packer
VP Communications, Peter Kauffmann
SVP and CIO, Diane Duggan
VP and Chief of Staff, Kanika Lichthardt
President and Trustee, W. Gaston Caperton III, age 72
Trustee, Michael R. Heintze
Trustee, Sheldon Ekland-Olson
Trustee, JoAnn W. Haysbert
Trustee, Scott C. Kelley
Trustee, Jerome A. (Jerry) Lucido
Trustee, Shirley A. Ort
Trustee, Roderick Chu
Trustee, Lester P. Monts
Trustee, Donald Saleh
Vice Chairman, Paul W. Sechrist, age 52
Trustee, Robert J. Weintraub
Trustee, Donald M. Honeman

Trustee, Evelyn Hu-DeHart
Trustee, Allison G. Jones
Trustee, Michael E. Malone
Trustee, Raymund A. Paredes
Trustee, Beverly A. Richardson
Trustee, Susan M. Rusk
Trustee, Mabel Freeman
Trustee, Ann Guzman
Vice Chairman, Maghan Keita
Trustee, Carolyn Lindley
Trustee, Peggy O'Neill Skinner
Trustee, Patricia Z. Smith
Trustee, Frank B Ashley III
Trustee, Catharine B Hill
Trustee, Mildred R Johnson
Trustee, Arthur L Williams

LOCATIONS

HQ: College Entrance Examination Board
45 Columbus Ave., New York NY 10023
Phone: 212-713-8000 **Fax:** 212-713-8143
Web: www.collegeboard.org

PRODUCTS/OPERATIONS

Selected services

Advanced Placement (college readiness)
Big Future (college planning)
CLEP (College-Level Examination Program)
CollegeEd (college planning career guidance)
College Search (college readiness)
CSS/Financial Aid PROFILE (financial aid application service)
EXCELerator (school district consultation services college readiness)
PSAT/NMSQT (practice for SAT National Merit Scholarship Qualifying Test)
ReadiStep (middle school assessment high school readiness)
SAT SAT Subject Tests and SAT Readiness Tools
Scholarship Search (scholarship aid)
SpringBoard (pre-AP college readiness)
Student Search Service (sends student testing information to colleges and scholarship programs)

COMPETITORS

ACT Inc.	Kaplan
Bridges Transitions	McGraw-Hill
College Coach	PLATO Learning
Educate	Questar Assessment
ETS	The Princeton Review

HISTORICAL FINANCIALS

Company Type: Private - Not-for-Profit

Income Statement   FYE: June 30

	REVENUE ($ mil.)	NET INCOME ($ mil.)	NET PROFIT MARGIN	EMPLOYEES
06/11	705	102	14.5%	1,130
06/10	668	78	11.7%	0
06/09	623	0	—	0
06/08	621	39	6.3%	0
Annual Growth	4.3%	37.8%	—	—

2011 Year-End Financials

Debt ratio: —
Return on equity: 14.50%
Cash ($ mil.): 159
Current ratio: 2.40
Long-term debt ($ mil.): —

Dividends
  Yield: —
  Payout: —
  Market value ($ mil.): —

COLLEGE OF NEW JERSEY

LOCATIONS

HQ: COLLEGE OF NEW JERSEY
2000 PENNINGTON RD, EWING, NJ 08618-1100
Phone: 609-771-1855
Web: www.tcnj.pages.tcnj.edu

HISTORICAL FINANCIALS

Company Type: Private

Income Statement   FYE: June 30

	REVENUE ($ mil.)	NET INCOME ($ mil.)	NET PROFIT MARGIN	EMPLOYEES
06/12	151	9	6.6%	1,075
06/11	145	12	8.8%	0
06/10	136	10	7.8%	0
06/09	130	13	10.2%	0
Annual Growth	5.0%	(9.0%)	—	—

2012 Year-End Financials

Debt ratio: —
Return on equity: 6.60%
Cash ($ mil.): 59
Current ratio: 2.10
Long-term debt ($ mil.): —

Dividends
  Yield: —
  Payout: —
  Market value ($ mil.): —

COLLEGE OF SAINT ROSE

LOCATIONS

HQ: COLLEGE OF SAINT ROSE
432 WESTERN AVE, ALBANY, NY 12203-1490
Phone: 518-454-5111
Web: www.library.strose.edu

HISTORICAL FINANCIALS

Company Type: Private

Income Statement   FYE: June 30

	REVENUE ($ mil.)	NET INCOME ($ mil.)	NET PROFIT MARGIN	EMPLOYEES
06/12	87	(4)	—	525
06/11	87	11	12.7%	0
06/10	84	6	7.4%	0
06/09	80	(2)	—	0
Annual Growth	3.1%	—	—	—

2012 Year-End Financials

Debt ratio: —
Return on equity: (-5.40)%
Cash ($ mil.): 4
Current ratio: —
Long-term debt ($ mil.): —

Dividends
  Yield: —
  Payout: —
  Market value ($ mil.): —

COLLEGE OF SOUTHERN IDAHO

LOCATIONS

HQ: COLLEGE OF SOUTHERN IDAHO
315 FALLS AVE, TWIN FALLS, ID 83301-3389
Phone: 208-733-9554
Web: www.herrett.csi.edu

HISTORICAL FINANCIALS
Company Type: Private

Income Statement

	REVENUE ($ mil.)	NET INCOME ($ mil.)	NET PROFIT MARGIN	EMPLOYEES
				FYE: June 30
06/11	127	7	5.5%	716
06/10	98	18	18.5%	0
06/09	0	(1)	—	0
06/08	53	11	20.8%	0
Annual Growth	33.8%	(14.1%)	—	—

COLLEGE OF THE HOLY CROSS

College of The Holy Cross has some real Crusaders. The college with sports teams nicknamed the Crusaders is a liberal arts undergraduate institution in central Massachusetts with some 2900 students. Some of the school's more popular areas of study include liberal arts' favorites such as English history and political science but also multidisciplinary concentrations and specialty programs including biochemistry Latin American studies and women's studies. The school has more than 300 full- and part-time faculty with a 10:1 student-to-faculty ratio. Founded in 1843 by the Society of Jesus (Jesuits) Holy Cross is the oldest Catholic college in New England.

Geographic Reach

College of The Holy Cross is located on a 170-acre campus in Worcester Massachusetts. Its students come from throughout the US and more than 20 countries.

Financial Performance

College of the Holy Cross reported a 2% revenue increase to some $154 million in 2012 due to increased income from student tuition and fees auxiliary enterprises including living and dining services and external contributions. Tuition is the largest revenue contributor and falls at around $44000 annually per student. Net income fell into the red in 2012 however due to higher operating expenses and lower returns on investments.

EXECUTIVES

President, Rev Michael C. McFarland
Treasurer and Chief Investment Officer, William R. Durgin
VP Development and Alumni Relations, Paul E. Sheff
Director Human Resources, Donna C. Wrenn
Controller, Robert E. Grenon
SVP, Frank Vellaccio
VP Student Affairs and Dean Students, Jacqueline D. Peterson
Chair, Michael F. Collins
VP Administration and Finance, Michael J. Lochhead
Director Public Safety, Christine Bernard-NcNamara
Manager Purchasing, Joan E. Anderson
Director Academic Services and Learning Resources, Christina Bi Chen
Bursar, Sheila E. Coakley
Director Library Services, James E. Hogan
Director Information Technology Services, Ellen J. Keohane
Director Athletics, Richard M. Regan Jr.
Director Public Affairs, Ellen Ryder
Head of Acquisitions and Cataloging, Nancy G. Singleton
Director Career Planning, John J. Winters Jr.
Director Development, Timm M. Zolkos
VP Academic Affairs and Dean College, Timothy R. Austin
General Counsel, Timothy F. Mines
Director Administrative Services and Acting Affirmative Action Officer, William J. Conley
Director Alumni Relations, Kristyn M. Dyer
Auditors: KPMGLLP

LOCATIONS

HQ: College of the Holy Cross
1 College St., Worcester MA 01610
Phone: 508-793-2011   **Fax:** 508-793-2347
Web: www.holycross.edu

PRODUCTS/OPERATIONS

Selected Programs
Anthropology
Art History
Biology
Chemistry
Chinese
Classics
Computer Science
Economics
Economics and Accounting
Education
English
French
German
History
Italian
Mathematics
Modern Languages & Literatures
Music
Philosophy
Physics
Political Science
Psychology
Religious Studies
Russian
Sociology
Spanish
Studies in World Literature
Studio Art
Theatre
Career Programs
  Business
  Engineering
  Health Professions
  Law
  Teacher Education Program
Multidisciplinary and Specialty Programs
  Africana Studies
  Asian Studies
  Biochemistry
  Biological Psychology
  Education
  Environmental Studies
  Latin American and Latino Studies
Naval Science
Peace and Conflict Studies
Women's and Gender Studies

COMPETITORS

Boston College
Fairfield University
Fordham University
Molloy College

HISTORICAL FINANCIALS
Company Type: School

Income Statement

	REVENUE ($ mil.)	NET INCOME ($ mil.)	NET PROFIT MARGIN	EMPLOYEES
				FYE: June 30
06/12	154	(16)	—	949
06/11	151	96	63.6%	0
06/10	149	35	23.9%	0
06/09	144	(140)	—	0
Annual Growth	2.3%	—	—	—

2012 Year-End Financials

Debt ratio: —	
Return on equity: (-10.60)%	Dividends
Cash ($ mil.): 34	Yield: —
Current ratio: —	Payout: —
Long-term debt ($ mil.): —	Market value ($ mil.): —

COLOMER BEAUTY BRANDS USA INC.

LOCATIONS

HQ: COLOMER BEAUTY BRANDS USA INC.
1515 WAZEE ST STE 200, DENVER, CO 80202-1674
Phone: 303-292-4850

HISTORICAL FINANCIALS
Company Type: Private

Income Statement

	REVENUE ($ mil.)	NET INCOME ($ mil.)	NET PROFIT MARGIN	EMPLOYEES
				FYE: December 31
12/11	203	19	9.3%	60
Annual Growth	—	—	—	—

COLONIAL SAVINGS F.A.

LOCATIONS

HQ: COLONIAL SAVINGS F.A.
2600 WEST FWY, FORT WORTH, TX 76102-7109
Phone: 817-390-2000
Web: www.colonialsavings.com

HISTORICAL FINANCIALS

Company Type: Private

Income Statement

FYE: September 30

	ASSETS ($ mil.)	NET INCOME ($ mil.)	INCOME AS % OF ASSETS	EMPLOYEES
09/11	927	38	4.2%	650
09/10	1,037	17	1.7%	0
09/09	920	(11)	—	0
09/08	865	4	0.6%	0
Annual Growth	2.3%	98.9%	—	—

2011 Year-End Financials

Debt ratio: ——
Return on equity: 25.30%
Cash ($ mil.): 40
Current ratio: —
Long-term debt ($ mil.): —

Dividends
Yield: —
Payout: —
Market value ($ mil.): —

COLORADO COLLEGE

Colorado College does things a little differently but it shares its mission with other institutions of higher learning. The private liberal arts and sciences college in 1970 adopted the Block Plan which divides the school year into eight three-and-a-half week blocks. Students take one course per three-and-a-half week block allowing them to focus on a single subject at a time. Its class size averages about 15 students with most classes capped at 25. Colorado College's 12000 students can choose from more than 40 majors and 30-plus minors. They are required to live on campus the first three years. Established in 1874 the Colorado Springs school boasts a 10:1 student-faculty ratio.

Operations

The college's revenues are predominately earned from tuition and fees contributions auxiliary enterprises and investments. Colorado College raised its comprehensive fee by 4.6% for the 2012-13 academic year resulting in a tuition of $41332.

To assist its students and faculty Colorado College in late 2012 opened a new 9000-sq.-ft. Children's Center. The facility doubles the previous capacity to 64 children –from infants to preschoolers –or up to 74 children for after-school.

Financial Performance

Colorado College logged revenue increases of 5% in 2011 vs. 2010 thanks to tuition and fee increases contributions government grants and contracts and other investment income. Rising educational and general expenses boosted operating expenses resulting in increases in net income by some 61% during the same reporting period. Net income growth also came from a bump in non-operating activities from increases in investment return on endowment reinvested and absence of loss on retirement of debt. Investments and land building and equipment purchases contributed to a cash flow decrease of $23.7 million in 2011 as compared to 2010.

Sales and Marketing

Some 85% of Colorado College's student body graduates within five years. Within five years of graduating 71% of its students begin graduate work. The educational institution ranks 7th nationwide for the number of alumni who serve in the Peace Corps.

Company Background

Civil War veteran Gen. William Jackson Palmer founder of the Rio Grande and Denver Railroads founded Colorado College. It was established as a coeducational institution some two years before Colorado became a state.

EXECUTIVES

President, Richard F. Celeste, age 74
Director Tutt Library, Carol Dickerson
External Relations, Lisa Ellis
Chair, Suzanne Woolsey
Co-Vice-Chair, Nancy Woodrow
Director Office of the President, Beth Brooks
Director Institutional Research and Planning, Margi Duncombe
Director Financial Aid, James M. Swanson
Director Alumni Relations, Karrie Williams
College and Faculty Dean, Susan A. Ashley
VP Finance and Administration, Robert Moore
Registrar, Phil Apodaca
Co-Vice-Chair, Robert Manning
Co-Vice-Chair, Nancy Woodrow
Co-Vice-Chair, Robert Manning

LOCATIONS

HQ: Colorado College
14 E. Cache La Poudre St., Colorado Springs CO 80903
Phone: 719-389-6000 **Fax:** 719-389-6933
Web: www.coloradocollege.edu

PRODUCTS/OPERATIONS

Selected Services

Disability Services
International Programs
Quantitative Reasoning Center
Reading and Rhetoric Specialist
Tutt Library
Writing Center

HISTORICAL FINANCIALS

Company Type: School

Income Statement

FYE: June 30

	REVENUE ($ mil.)	NET INCOME ($ mil.)	NET PROFIT MARGIN	EMPLOYEES
06/11	119	89	74.9%	800
06/10	114	55	48.7%	0
06/09	16	(90)	—	0
06/07	169	66	39.3%	0
Annual Growth	(11.0%)	10.3%	—	—

2011 Year-End Financials

Debt ratio: ——
Return on equity: 74.90%
Cash ($ mil.): 24
Current ratio: —
Long-term debt ($ mil.): —

Dividends
Yield: —
Payout: —
Market value ($ mil.): —

COLORADO SEMINARY

Want a mile-high education? Colorado Seminary which does business as University of Denver (DU) offers graduate and undergraduate degrees in more than 100 fields of study including law government humanities education engineering and psychology. About 12000 undergraduate and graduate students from across the US and more than 90 countries are enrolled at the school. Former Secretary of State Condoleezza Rice former Interior Secretary Gale Norton and former Coors Brewing CEO Peter Coors attended DU. Founded in 1864 the university has a staff of some 650 faculty members; its student-to-faculty ratio is 10:1. DU is located on a 125-acre campus.

Strategy

DU has added about 20 buildings since 1997 to enhance its academic administrative athletic and residential capacities. Projects have included a soccer stadium and a center for international security and diplomacy within the School of International Studies. In 2011 DU began construction of a new Academic Commons building which will house the school's Penrose Library.

EXECUTIVES

Executive Director Newman Center for the Performing Arts, Stephen (Steve) Seifert
Chancellor, Robert D. (Bob) Coombe
Dean Josef Korbel School of International Studies, Christopher R. Hill
Vice Chancellor Business and Financial Affairs, Craig W. Woody
Director University Business Services Purchasing Services Department, Joe Benson
Assistant Vice Chancellor Business and Financial Affairs, Neil D. Krauss
Director Risk Management, Ellen M. Shew Holland
Director Campus Safety, Don Enloe
Controller and Assistant Treasurer, Margaret Henry
Dean Women's College, Lynn Gangone
Provost, Gregg Kvistad
Director Alumni Relations and Special Events Korbel School of International Studies, Alicia O. Kirkeby
Senior Director Advancement Services Office of University Advancement, Ben Storck
Bursar, Kathleen M. (Kathy) Shoemaker
Manager Technology and Security Services Department of Campus Safety, Steven J. Fay
Director Administrative Information Services University Technology Services, Susan L. Lutz
Director Computer Operations University Technology Services Department, Cindy Crouch
Chief Information Security Officer University Technology Services Department, Arlen M. Fletcher
Registrar, Dennis M. Becker
Dean Divisions of Arts Humanities and Social Sciences, Anne E. McCall
Dean and Professor of Management Daniels College of Business, Christine M. (Chris) Riordan
Dean and Professor Graduate School of Professional Psychology, Peter Buirski
Dean Graduate School of Social Work, James H. Williams
Dean Division of Natural Sciences and Mathematics, L. Alayne Parson
Dean and Director Penrose Library, Nancy H. Allen
Dean and Professor School of Engineering and Computer Science, Rahmat A. Shoureshi
Dean University College, Jim Davis
Dean Sturm College of Law, Martin J. (Marty) Katz
Senior Public Affairs Specialist News and Public Affairs, Chase Squires
Interim Vice Chancellor University Communications and Executive Director News and Public Affairs, Jim Berscheidt
Director News and Public Affairs, Kim DeVigil
Adjunct and Executive Director of Homeland Security Program Josef Korbel School of International Studies, Greg Moser
Director Advising and Orientation, Niki Latino

Manager Information Technology Office of **Admission,** Bryan David Axtman
Director Career Center, Mary Michael Hawkins
Dean Morgridge College of Education, Gregory M. (Greg) Anderson
Director Center for Teaching and Learning, Julanna V. Gilbert
Human Resources Coordinator, Sarah B. Childs
Human Resources Coordinator, Ashley N. Gross
Executive Director Institute for Human-Animal Connection, Frank Ascione
Director Institutional Compliance and Internal Audits, Sandy Kasahara
Executive Director Intermodal Transportation Institute, Cathryne C. Johnson
Director International Human Rights Advocacy Center, Robert Golten

LOCATIONS

HQ: Colorado Seminary
2199 S. University Blvd., Denver CO 80208
Phone: 303-871-2000 **Fax:** 303-871-3301
Web: www.du.edu

PRODUCTS/OPERATIONS

Selected Schools and Programs

Undergraduate Schools and Colleges
  Daniels College of Business
  Division of Natural Sciences & Mathematics
  Division of Arts Humanities and Social Sciences
  Josef Korbel School of International Studies
  Morgridge College of Education
  School of Engineering and Computer Science
  University College
  Women's College
Graduate and Professional Programs
  Daniels College of Business
  Divisions of Arts Humanities and Social Sciences
  Divisions of Natural Sciences and Mathematics
  Graduate School of Professional Psychology (GSPP)
  Graduate School of Social Work (GSSW)
  Graduate Tax Program
  Interdisciplinary Degree Programs
  Josef Korbel School of International Studies
  Morgridge College of Education (MCE)
  School of Engineering and Computer Science
  The Sturm College of Law
  University College

HISTORICAL FINANCIALS

Company Type: School

Income Statement

	REVENUE ($ mil.)	NET INCOME ($ mil.)	NET PROFIT MARGIN	EMPLOYEES
06/12	367	56	15.5%	2,770
06/11	398	96	24.2%	0
06/10	469	48	10.3%	0
06/09	429	21	5.0%	0
Annual Growth	(5.1%)	38.3%	—	—

2012 Year-End Financials

Debt ratio: ——
Return on equity: 15.50%
Cash ($ mil.): 42
Current ratio: ——
Long-term debt ($ mil.): —
Dividends
  Yield: —
  Payout: —
Market value ($ mil.): —

COLSA CORPORATION

COLSA doesn't mind being called a little defensive. The company provides advanced technology systems and services to US government agencies such as the Missile Defense Agency and NASA. COLSA which specializes in radar and guidance system technology offers services including engineering and testing developing war games simulations analyzing radar technology and virtual prototyping. Its information systems services include integration maintenance and administration for large computer centers. COLSA also offers a software system for nuclear power plants and a gateway for sending simulation data to remote systems. COLSA was founded in 1980.

COLSA has offices in Alabama Arizona California Colorado Florida and Washington DC. About a third of COLSA's employees work directly at Redstone Arsenal home to the U.S. Army Aviation and Missile Command the Space and Missile Defense Command and components of the Defense Intelligence Agency and the Missile Defense Agency.

Primarily working with defense agencies COLSA has sought to diversify its client base by adding other government bodies such as the Department of Justice. COLSA also plans to pursue international clients.

EXECUTIVES

EVP Business Management, Richard (Dick) Carter
EVP and CTO, Anthony (Tony) DiRienzo
VP West Coast Operations, Kearney Bennett
VP Advanced Research Center, John Welt
VP Army and Intelligence Programs, Ivan Garcia
VP Planning and Proposal Development, Penny Chilton
VP North Florida Operations, Joe Anderson
President, Richard Amos
VP Business Development, Timothy (Tim) Mango
Deputy CEO, Van Corum
CEO, Francisco J. Collazo
VP NASA Programs, Phil Hodges
VP MDA Programs, Jim Hunter

LOCATIONS

HQ: COLSA Corporation
6728 Odyssey Dr., Huntsville AL 35806
Phone: 256-964-5555 **Fax:** 510-893-3681
Web: www.worldmarket.com

PRODUCTS/OPERATIONS

Selected Services

Information services
  Computer center design and engineering
  Computer center operation and maintenance
  Information assurance/security
Programmatic support
  Acquisition management
  Independent assessment
  Test support
System engineering
  Configuration management
  Modeling and simulation
  Software engineering
  Test engineering
  Testbed design development and operation
System integration
  Command control communications computers and intel (C4I) systems
  Hardware/software systems
  Security systems

COMPETITORS

CACI International
Computer Sciences Corp.
GTSI
HP Enterprise Services
Northrop Grumman
Raytheon
SM&A

HISTORICAL FINANCIALS

Company Type: Private

Income Statement

FYE: December 31

	REVENUE ($ mil.)	NET INCOME ($ mil.)	NET PROFIT MARGIN	EMPLOYEES
12/11	152	11	7.8%	890
12/10	155	11	7.3%	0
12/09	151	8	5.8%	0
12/08	140	8	6.0%	0
Annual Growth	2.7%	11.8%	—	—

2011 Year-End Financials

Debt ratio: —
Return on equity: 7.80%
Cash ($ mil.): 12
Current ratio: 1.00
Long-term debt ($ mil.): —
Dividends
  Yield: —
  Payout: —
Market value ($ mil.): —

COLUMBIA COLLEGE CHICAGO

Columbia College Chicago revels in its creative reputation. Specializing in arts and media the private school offers undergraduate and graduate degrees in the visual performing media and communication arts. The college offers more than 120 academic programs including architecture and interior design photography dance television theater film music composition journalism and marketing communication. Comedian Andy Richter and Wheel of Fortune host Pat Sajak number among the school's notable alumni. Founded in 1890 Columbia College is located in various buildings in downtown Chicago and has about 12000 students. Average teacher to student ratio is 20:1.

Columbia College is planning to open its first new-construction academic building in 2010. The Media Production Center will include two sound stages a motion-capture studio an animation lab and classrooms. The school's most popular majors are Film & Video Art & Design and Arts Entertainment & Media Management in that order.

Many of the college's students live on campus. About 2200 students live in four residence centers helping to make Columbia the second largest college for out of state students in Illinois.

The school is in the midst of a $100 million campaign with three parts: student scholarships support of building projects and to build its endowment. Student scholarships are number one. Although the school has worked to hold down costs of the institution - and its tuition is still more approachable than some private institutions - it's still a hefty amount of money. The school wants to support students who want to follow in the footsteps of its alums but can't afford it. Consequently Columbia College Chicago made scholarships its number-one priority.

EXECUTIVES

Vice Chair, Richard P. (Dick) Kiphart, age 70
Secretary and Trustee, John R. Gehron, age 66
VP Administration Research and Planning, Anne E. Foley
SVP Academic Affairs and Provost, Steven (Steve) Kapelke
President and Trustee, Warrick L. Carter
VP Student Affairs, Mark Kelly
VP Business Affairs and CFO, Michael DeSalle
Associate VP Information Technology and CIO, Bernadette McMahon
Associate VP Business Affairs and Controller, Kevin Doherty
VP and General Counsel, Annice M. Kelly
Associate VP Academic Research and Dean of the Library, Jo Cates
Manager Benefits, Gabina Mora
Director Human Resources, Patricia Olalde
VP Business Affairs and CFO, Kenneth C. (Ken) Gotsch
Chairman, Allen M. Turner
Associate VP and Chief of Staff President's Office, Paul Chiaravalle
Director Purchasing, Thomas Russell
Associate Director Administrative Services, Theresa Kerr
National Director Alumni Relations, Joshua Culley-Foster
VP Academic Affairs and Interim Provost, Louise Love
Director Office of Budget and Reporting, Paula Scheiwe
Director Business Systems and Applications, Ann Kennedy
Director Enrollment Management Services, Maureen Herlehy
Associate VP Enrollment Management, Debra McGrath
Associate VP Facilities and Construction, John Kavouris
Executive Director Facilities and Operations, Katherine Dwyer
Associate VP and Dean of Students, Sharon Wilson-Taylor
VP Human Resources, Ellen Krutz
Director Telecommunications and Networking, Billy Cole
Director User Support, Dorothy Dare
Director Business Processes, Marsha J. Heizer
Executive Director of Development Institutional Advancement, Michael Anderson
Director Annual Giving Institutional Advancement, Dawn Baity
Associate VP Institutional Advancement, Kim Clement
Associate VP Public Relations Marketing and Advertising, Diane Doyne
Director Marketing, Brenda Berman
Director Internal Auditing, Greg Narlow
Director Payroll Office, Tracy Cargo
Director and Registrar Records Office, Marvin Cohen
Associate VP Safety and Security, Robert Koverman
VP Campus Environment, Alicia Berg
VP Institutional Advancement, Eric Winston
Vice Chair, Ellen Stone Belic
Vice Chair, Warren King Chapman
Vice Chair, Marcia Lazar
Vice Chair, Don Jackson
Treasurer and Trustee, Ralph W. Gidwitz
Vice Chair, Sylvia Neil
Secretary and Trustee, Madeleine Moore Burrell
Trustee, William F. Cellini Jr., age 77
Trustee, Lerone Bennett Jr.
Vice Chair, Richard P. (Dick) Kiphart, age 70
Trustee, Arthur M. Sussman

Secretary and Trustee, John R. Gehron, age 66
Trustee, Raymond J. Spencer, age 61
Trustee, Barry A. Mayo, age 59
President and Trustee, Warrick L. Carter
Trustee, Robert A. Wislow
Trustee, Andrew Alexander
Trustee, Barry M. Sabloff
Vice Chair, Ellen Stone Belic
Vice Chair, Warren King Chapman
Vice Chair, Marcia Lazar
Vice Chair, Don Jackson
Treasurer and Trustee, Ralph W. Gidwitz
Trustee, Lester Coney
Trustee, Steve Devick
Trustee, Susan Downing
Trustee, Allan R. Drebin
Trustee, Loranne Ehlenbach
Trustee, Brent W. Felitto
Trustee, Georgia Fogelson
Trustee, Sydney Smith Gordon
Trustee, Mary Louise Haddad
Trustee, Bill Hood
Trustee, Chester T. Kamin
Trustee, Pamela Kendall-Rijos
Trustee, Paul R. Knapp
Trustee, Bill Kurtis
Trustee, Averill Leviton
Trustee, Daniel E. McLean
Trustee, Howard Mendelsohn
Vice Chair, Sylvia Neil
Trustee, Joseph F. Peyronnin III
Trustee, Samuel E. Pfeffer
Trustee, Stephen H. Pugh
Trustee, Madeline Murphy Rabb
Trustee, Michelle Rosen
Trustee, Arlen Rubin
Trustee, Victor Skrebneski
Trustee, Lawrence K. Snider
Trustee, David S. Solomon
Trustee, Nancy Tom
Trustee, Helena Chapellin Wilson
Secretary and Trustee, Madeleine Moore Burrell
Auditors: KPMGLLP

LOCATIONS

HQ: Columbia College Chicago
600 S. Michigan Ave., Chicago IL 60605
Phone: 312-663-1600   **Fax:** 312-369-8039
Web: www.colum.edu

HISTORICAL FINANCIALS
Company Type: School

Income Statement

FYE: August 31

	REVENUE ($ mil.)	NET INCOME ($ mil.)	NET PROFIT MARGIN	EMPLOYEES
08/11	260	17	6.7%	1,000
08/10	244	18	7.6%	0
08/09	246	23	9.7%	0
08/08	232	(7)	—	0
Annual Growth	4.0%	—	—	—

2011 Year-End Financials

Debt ratio: ——
Return on equity: 6.70%
Cash ($ mil.): 37
Current ratio: ——
Long-term debt ($ mil.): —

Dividends
    Yield: —
    Payout: —
    Market value ($ mil.): —

COLUMBIA ST MARYS HOSPITAL OZAUKEE INC

LOCATIONS

HQ: COLUMBIA ST MARYS HOSPITAL OZAUKEE INC
4425 N PORT WASHINGTON RD, GLENDALE, WI 53212-1082
Phone: 414-326-2230

HISTORICAL FINANCIALS
Company Type: Private

Income Statement

FYE: June 30

	REVENUE ($ mil.)	NET INCOME ($ mil.)	NET PROFIT MARGIN	EMPLOYEES
06/11	198	19	9.9%	0
06/10	216	29	13.5%	0
Annual Growth	(8.2%)	(32.7%)	—	—

2011 Year-End Financials

Debt ratio: ——
Return on equity: 9.90%
Cash ($ mil.): 6
Current ratio: 2.60
Long-term debt ($ mil.): —

Dividends
    Yield: —
    Payout: —
    Market value ($ mil.): —

COLUMBIA ST. MARY'S INC.

LOCATIONS

HQ: COLUMBIA ST. MARY' S INC.
4425 N PORT WASHINGTON RD STO, MILWAUKEE, WI 53212-1082
Phone: 414-326-1771
Web: www.columbia-stmarys.org

HISTORICAL FINANCIALS
Company Type: Private

Income Statement

FYE: June 30

	REVENUE ($ mil.)	NET INCOME ($ mil.)	NET PROFIT MARGIN	EMPLOYEES
06/11	163	16	10.1%	5,000
06/10	27	2	8.9%	0
06/09	18	3	20.3%	0
06/08	194	41	21.3%	0
Annual Growth	(5.5%)	(26.4%)	—	—

2011 Year-End Financials

Debt ratio: ——
Return on equity: 10.10%
Cash ($ mil.): 24
Current ratio: ——
Long-term debt ($ mil.): —

Dividends
    Yield: —
    Payout: —
    Market value ($ mil.): —

COMMISSIONER OF PUBLIC WORKS

LOCATIONS

HQ: COMMISSIONER OF PUBLIC WORKS
103 SAINT PHILIP ST, CHARLESTON, SC 29403-6101
Phone: 843-727-6800
Web: www.charlestonwater.com

HISTORICAL FINANCIALS

Company Type: Private

Income Statement

FYE: December 31

	REVENUE ($ mil.)	NET INCOME ($ mil.)	NET PROFIT MARGIN	EMPLOYEES
12/11	106	21	20.4%	400
12/10	101	17	17.6%	0
12/09	94	20	21.7%	0
12/08	91	29	32.5%	0
Annual Growth	5.3%	(9.8%)	—	—

2011 Year-End Financials

Debt ratio: ——
Return on equity: 20.40%
Cash ($ mil.): 103
Current ratio: 3.30
Long-term debt ($ mil.): —

Dividends
Yield: —
Payout: —
Market value ($ mil.): —

COMMON FUND NON-PROFIT ORGANIZATION THE (INC)

LOCATIONS

HQ: COMMON FUND NON-PROFIT ORGANIZATION THE (INC)
15 OLD DANBURY RD STE 200, WILTON, CT 06897-2531
Phone: 203-563-5000
Web: www.commonfund.org

HISTORICAL FINANCIALS

Company Type: Private

Income Statement

FYE: June 30

	ASSETS ($ mil.)	NET INCOME ($ mil.)	INCOME AS % OF ASSETS	EMPLOYEES
06/11	7,362	508	6.9%	220
06/10	7,469	126	1.7%	0
06/09	8,832	0	—	0
06/08	12,483	830	6.7%	0
Annual Growth	(16.1%)	(15.1%)	—	—

2011 Year-End Financials

Debt ratio: ——
Return on equity: 92.00%
Cash ($ mil.): 157
Current ratio: —
Long-term debt ($ mil.): —

Dividends
Yield: —
Payout: —
Market value ($ mil.): —

COMMONWEALTH HEALTH CORPORATION INC

For care in Kentucky Bluegrass Staters can turn to Commonwealth Health Corporation. The holding company houses a full spectrum of health care facilities and services including The Medical Center a 525-bed regional health care system comprised of four hospitals long-term health care providers and senior care among other services. Commonwealth's outpatient offerings include nutrition therapy a women's center diabetes programs and adult day care. The corporation's Center Care Health Benefits Program supplies employers with products and services to support the distribution and administration of employee benefits and healthcare services.

Operations

The company's four hospitals include Commonwealth Regional Specialty Hospital (28 beds); The Medical Center (Bowling Green) (337 beds); The Medical Center at Franklin (25 beds) critical access acute care hospital providing both inpatient and outpatient services including a 24-hour full service emergency room; and The Medical Center (Scottsville) (135 beds).

Commonwealth also runs two companies designed to help health care providers get paid. Commonwealth Financial Services supplies medical billing services for hospitals physicians and other care givers while Hillcrest Credit Agency operates as a collection agency assisting providers in recouping payment for medical services.

The Commonwealth Health Free Clinic operates two programs designed to accommodate patients who are employed but do not have insurance or other forms of social assistance and cannot otherwise afford healthcare. The Medical Clinic offers free medical services to the working uninsured while The Dental Clinic offers a low cost alternative to locals in need of basic dental care.

Company Background

The corporation started out in 1926 as a 35-bed hospital. In 1984 Commonwealth Health Corporation was formed as a not-for-profit holding company for The Medical Center at Bowling Green Franklin and Scottsville Commonwealth Regional Specialty Hospital and other health related businesses.

EXECUTIVES

Chairman, Floyd H. Ellis, age 85
President and CEO, John C. Desmarais
COO, Connie Smith
EVP and CIO, Jean Cherry
EVP and CFO, Ron Sowell
VP Marketing and Development, Doris C. Thomas
Director Health Information Management The Medical Center, Georgena Brackett
Corporate Director Pharmacy, Melinda C. Joyce
Auditors: Ernst&YoungLLP

LOCATIONS

HQ: Commonwealth Health Corporation
800 Park St., Bowling Green KY 42101
Phone: 270-745-1500   **Fax:** 270-745-1498
Web: www.chc.net

PRODUCTS/OPERATIONS

Selected Operations (Kentucky)

Barren River Adult Day Care (Bowling Green)
Barren River Regional Cancer Center (Glasgow)
Bluegrass Outpatient Center (Bowling Green)
Bone & Joint Center (Bowling Green)
Cal Turner Extended Care Pavilion (Bowling Green)
Center Care Health Benefit Programs (Bowling Green)
Commonwealth Health Free Clinic (Bowling Green)
Commonwealth Regional Specialty Hospital (Bowling Green)
Corpcare (Bowling Green)
MedEquip (Bowling Green)
The Medical Center at Bowling Green
The Medical Center at Franklin
The Medical Center at Scottsville
Quick Care Clinic (Bowling Green)
Scottsville Medical Plaza (Scottsville)
Urgentcare (Bowling Green)
Women's Health Specialists (Bowling Green)

COMPETITORS

Baptist Health
Cookeville Regional Medical Center
Deaconess Health System
Essent Healthcare
Hardin Memorial Hospital
HCA
Iasis Healthcare
Jewish Hospital & St. Mary's HealthCare
Kindred Healthcare

HISTORICAL FINANCIALS

Company Type: Private - Not-for-Profit

Income Statement

FYE: March 31

	REVENUE ($ mil.)	NET INCOME ($ mil.)	NET PROFIT MARGIN	EMPLOYEES
03/11	59	6	10.2%	2,700
03/10	61	9	14.7%	0
03/09	2	0	—	0
Annual Growth	443.8%	—	—	—

2011 Year-End Financials

Debt ratio: ——
Return on equity: 10.20%
Cash ($ mil.): 23
Current ratio: 1.60
Long-term debt ($ mil.): —

Dividends
Yield: —
Payout: —
Market value ($ mil.): —

COMMUNITY DEVELOPMENT INSTITUTE HEAD START

LOCATIONS

HQ: COMMUNITY DEVELOPMENT INSTITUTE HEAD START
10065 E HARVARD AVE # 700, DENVER, CO 80231-5915
Phone: 720-747-5100
Web: www.cditeam.org

HISTORICAL FINANCIALS

Company Type: Private

Income Statement
FYE: June 30

	REVENUE ($ mil.)	NET INCOME ($ mil.)	NET PROFIT MARGIN	EMPLOYEES
06/12	159	(0)	—	3,272
06/11	159	(0)	—	0
06/10	159	0	0.1%	0
06/09	118	0	0.8%	0
Annual Growth	10.3%	—	—	—

2012 Year-End Financials

Debt ratio: ——
Return on equity: (-0.10)%
Cash ($ mil.): 0
Current ratio: 25.40
Long-term debt ($ mil.): ——

Dividends
Yield: —
Payout: —
Market value ($ mil.): —

COMMUNITY FOOD BANK OF NEW JERSEY INC

LOCATIONS

HQ: COMMUNITY FOOD BANK OF NEW JERSEY INC
31 EVANS TERMINAL, HILLSIDE, NJ 07205-2400
Phone: 908-355-3663
Web: www.njfoodbank.org

HISTORICAL FINANCIALS

Company Type: Private

Income Statement
FYE: June 30

	REVENUE ($ mil.)	NET INCOME ($ mil.)	NET PROFIT MARGIN	EMPLOYEES
06/12	88	0	0.2%	180
06/11	96	14	15.2%	0
06/10	76	0	0.4%	0
06/09	70	1	1.7%	0
Annual Growth	8.1%	(51.7%)	—	—

2012 Year-End Financials

Debt ratio: ——
Return on equity: 0.20%
Cash ($ mil.): 0
Current ratio: 0.60
Long-term debt ($ mil.): ——

Dividends
Yield: —
Payout: —
Market value ($ mil.): —

COMMUNITY LIVING SERVICES INC.

LOCATIONS

HQ: COMMUNITY LIVING SERVICES INC.
35425 W MICHIGAN AVE # 1, WAYNE, MI 48184-1600
Phone: 734-467-7600
Web: www.comlivserv.com

HISTORICAL FINANCIALS

Company Type: Private

Income Statement
FYE: September 30

	REVENUE ($ mil.)	NET INCOME ($ mil.)	NET PROFIT MARGIN	EMPLOYEES
09/11	129	4	3.7%	240
09/10	128	0	0.8%	0
09/09	128	0	0.7%	0
09/08	123	4	3.9%	0
Annual Growth	1.8%	(0.3%)	—	—

2011 Year-End Financials

Debt ratio: ——
Return on equity: 3.70%
Cash ($ mil.): 5
Current ratio: 0.80
Long-term debt ($ mil.): ——

Dividends
Yield: —
Payout: —
Market value ($ mil.): —

COMMUNITY MEMORIAL HEALTH CENTER

LOCATIONS

HQ: COMMUNITY MEMORIAL HEALTH CENTER
125 BUENA VISTA CIR, SOUTH HILL, VA 23970-1431
Phone: 434-447-3151
Web: www.cmh-sh.org

HISTORICAL FINANCIALS

Company Type: Private

Income Statement
FYE: June 30

	REVENUE ($ mil.)	NET INCOME ($ mil.)	NET PROFIT MARGIN	EMPLOYEES
06/11	92	(0)	—	750
06/10	88	1	1.6%	0
06/09	88	1	1.4%	0
06/08	86	3	4.0%	0
Annual Growth	2.4%	—	—	—

2011 Year-End Financials

Debt ratio: ——
Return on equity: (-0.20)%
Cash ($ mil.): 13
Current ratio: 2.00
Long-term debt ($ mil.): ——

Dividends
Yield: —
Payout: —
Market value ($ mil.): —

COMMUNITY MEMORIAL HOSPITAL OF MENOMONEE FALLS INC.

LOCATIONS

HQ: COMMUNITY MEMORIAL HOSPITAL OF MENOMONEE FALLS INC.
W 180TH N 8085 TOWN HL, MENOMONEE FALLS, WI 53051
Phone: 262-251-1000
Web: www.communitymemorial.com

HISTORICAL FINANCIALS

Company Type: Private

Income Statement
FYE: June 30

	REVENUE ($ mil.)	NET INCOME ($ mil.)	NET PROFIT MARGIN	EMPLOYEES
06/11	197	6	3.4%	1,500
06/10	183	8	4.7%	0
06/09	171	(12)	—	0
06/08	87	5	6.7%	0
Annual Growth	31.0%	4.1%	—	—

2011 Year-End Financials

Debt ratio: ——
Return on equity: 3.40%
Cash ($ mil.): 10
Current ratio: 2.90
Long-term debt ($ mil.): ——

Dividends
Yield: —
Payout: —
Market value ($ mil.): —

COMP-VIEW INC.

CompView rents and sells audio-visual computer peripherals (primarily projectors and conferencing systems) to corporations educational organizations and government agencies; it also provides system installation and integration services. Its CompView Medical subsidiary specializes in providing audio-visual equipment for medical applications such as projectors for surgical operating rooms. CompView has facilities in California Minnesota Oregon Utah and Washington state. The company was started in 1987 by Paul White who is the majority owner.

EXECUTIVES

VP Technical Services, Mark Madison
President and CEO, Scott Birdsall
Chairman, Paul White
Manager Education Program, Robert H. (Bob) Friedler
Inside Sales Customer Service Manager, Brad Thomas
Inside Sales Representative, Carolyn Berlin
Inside Sales Representative, Cynthia Washburn
Manager Human Resources, Pam Grater
CFO, Terry Hillier

LOCATIONS

HQ: CompView Inc.
10035 SW Arctic Dr., Beaverton OR 97005
Phone: 503-641-8439   **Fax:** 503-626-8439
Web: www.compview.com

COMPETITORS

CDW   Ricoh USA
Global Imaging Systems

HISTORICAL FINANCIALS
Company Type: Private

Income Statement
FYE: December 31

	REVENUE ($ mil.)	NET INCOME ($ mil.)	NET PROFIT MARGIN	EMPLOYEES
12/11	55	0	1.6%	129
12/01	36	0	0.2%	0
12/00	38	(0)	—	0
12/99	28	0	2.3%	0
Annual Growth	25.7%	11.2%	—	—

2011 Year-End Financials

Debt ratio: —
Return on equity: 1.60%
Cash ($ mil.): 0
Current ratio: 1.90
Long-term debt ($ mil.): —

Dividends
  Yield: —
  Payout: —
  Market value ($ mil.): —

COMPASSION INTERNATIONAL INC

LOCATIONS

HQ: COMPASSION INTERNATIONAL INC
12290 VOYAGER PKWY, COLORADO SPRINGS, CO
80921-3694
Phone: 719-487-7000
Web: www.compassion.com

HISTORICAL FINANCIALS
Company Type: Private

Income Statement
FYE: June 30

	REVENUE ($ mil.)	NET INCOME ($ mil.)	NET PROFIT MARGIN	EMPLOYEES
06/11	551	31	5.7%	1,000
06/10	506	34	6.9%	0
06/09	402	6	1.6%	0
06/08	368	364	98.9%	0
Annual Growth	14.4%	(55.8%)	—	—

2011 Year-End Financials

Debt ratio: —
Return on equity: 5.70%
Cash ($ mil.): 78
Current ratio: 1.60
Long-term debt ($ mil.): —

Dividends
  Yield: —
  Payout: —
  Market value ($ mil.): —

COMPREHENSIVE HEALTH HOLDINGS INC.

LOCATIONS

HQ: COMPREHENSIVE HEALTH HOLDINGS INC.
10701 PARKRIDGE BLVD # 200, RESTON, VA
20191-4359
Phone: 703-288-5449

HISTORICAL FINANCIALS
Company Type: Private

Income Statement
FYE: December 31

	REVENUE ($ mil.)	NET INCOME ($ mil.)	NET PROFIT MARGIN	EMPLOYEES
12/11	121	4	3.7%	0
Annual Growth	—	—	—	—

2011 Year-End Financials

Debt ratio: —
Return on equity: 3.70%
Cash ($ mil.): 0
Current ratio: 1.10
Long-term debt ($ mil.): —

Dividends
  Yield: —
  Payout: —
  Market value ($ mil.): —

COMPUTER SECURITY SOLUTIONS INC.

LOCATIONS

HQ: COMPUTER SECURITY SOLUTIONS INC.
1350 BEVERLY RD 115-312, MC LEAN, VA 22101-3961
Phone: 703-917-0274

HISTORICAL FINANCIALS
Company Type: Private

Income Statement
FYE: December 31

	REVENUE ($ mil.)	NET INCOME ($ mil.)	NET PROFIT MARGIN	EMPLOYEES
12/11	102	3	3.3%	14
12/10	93	4	4.9%	0
12/09	75	3	5.0%	0
12/08	66	4	6.6%	0
Annual Growth	15.7%	(8.2%)	—	—

2011 Year-End Financials

Debt ratio: —
Return on equity: 3.30%
Cash ($ mil.): 4
Current ratio: 1.10
Long-term debt ($ mil.): —

Dividends
  Yield: —
  Payout: —
  Market value ($ mil.): —

CONCORD HOSPITAL INC.

Concord Hospital is agreeably an acute care regional hospital serving central New Hampshire. The hospital has some 300 licensed beds admits more than 18000 patients each year and offers centers for cardiology orthopedics cancer care urology and women's health. Concord Hospital also operates other medical facilities in the region including surgery imaging sleep diagnostic and rehabilitation facilities and its affiliated physician groups operate family health and physician practice offices. With roots reaching back to 1884 Concord Hospital is an affiliate of Capital Region Health Care which also offers mental health and home health care services.

As part of Capital Region Health Care Concord Hospital shares education purchasing and outpatient service functions (and expenses) with its affiliates while retaining its independence. In 2011 Concord Hospital formed another collaborative network the Granite Healthcare Network with four regional New Hampshire health care providers: Elliot Health System (which operates the Elliot Hospital) LRGHealthcare (consisting of Lakes Region General Hospital and Franklin Regional Hospital) Southern New Hampshire Health System (operating the Southern New Hampshire Medical Center) and Wentworth-Douglass Hospital.

To help control the spiraling costs of medical care in the US as well as to meet health reform mandates the affiliated facilities are launching programs to share technology and administrative resources such as claims management software data storage linen service liability insurance pooling and Medicare patient management. The hospitals in the newly formed network will remain independently managed and owned and have the option to participate or not participate in each of the group efforts.

With annual operating revenues of some $480 million Concord Hospital spends about $37 million annually on community care efforts including charity medical care for low-income and uninsured patients. The medical center has also launched initiatives to improve quality and patient safety programs including putting infection reduction protocols in place consolidating electronic health record (EHR) consolidation efforts and enacting medication management practices.

After a financially challenging year in 2010 (due to changes in state tax regulations for hospitals) Concord Hospital's cost-control and improvement efforts helped increase profits to some $27 million in 2011 (up more than 80% from 2010).

EXECUTIVES

President CEO and ex officio Trustee, Michael B. Green
SVP Medical Affairs and Chief Medical Officer, David F. Green
SVP and COO, Joe Conley
SVP CFO and ex officio Trustee, Bruce Burns
CIO, Deane Morrison
VP Operations Chief Nursing Officer and Trustee, Diane E. Wood Allen
VP Finance, Scott Sloane
VP Operations, Kevin McCarthy
VP Physician Services, Marjo Mitchell
VP Philanthropy and Public Affairs, Pamela Puleo
VP Operations, Kristine Terrio
VP Operations, James Thorne

LOCATIONS

HQ: Concord Hospital Inc.
  250 Pleasant St., Concord NH 03301
Phone: 603-225-2711   Fax: 254-771-0827
Web: www.sagusi.com

COMPETITORS

Cambridge Health Alliance	Frisbie Memorial Hospital
Catholic Medical Center	HCA
Elliot Health System	Partners HealthCare
Exeter Health Resources	Southern New Hampshire Medical Center
	Steward Health Care

HISTORICAL FINANCIALS

Company Type: Private - Not-for-Profit

Income Statement

FYE: September 30

	REVENUE ($ mil.)	NET INCOME ($ mil.)	NET PROFIT MARGIN	EMPLOYEES
09/11	442	(9)	—	2,000
09/10	369	18	5.1%	0
09/09	349	0	—	0
09/08	331	16	4.9%	0
Annual Growth	10.1%	—	—	—

2011 Year-End Financials

Debt ratio: ——
Return on equity: (-2.10)%
Cash ($ mil.): 8
Current ratio: 0.80
Long-term debt ($ mil.): —

Dividends
  Yield: —
  Payout: —
  Market value ($ mil.): —

CONCORDIA LUTHERAN MINISTRIES

LOCATIONS

HQ: CONCORDIA LUTHERAN MINISTRIES
  134 MARWOOD RD, CABOT, PA 16023-2245
Phone: 724-352-1571
Web: www.rebeccaresidence.com

HISTORICAL FINANCIALS

Company Type: Private

Income Statement

FYE: June 30

	REVENUE ($ mil.)	NET INCOME ($ mil.)	NET PROFIT MARGIN	EMPLOYEES
06/11	95	35	37.5%	1,500
06/10	85	17	20.8%	0
06/09	75	(8)	—	0
06/08	58	3	6.1%	0
Annual Growth	17.4%	115.5%	—	—

2011 Year-End Financials

Debt ratio: ——
Return on equity: 37.50%
Cash ($ mil.): 10
Current ratio: 2.70
Long-term debt ($ mil.): —

Dividends
  Yield: —
  Payout: —
  Market value ($ mil.): —

CONCORDIA UNIVERSITY WISCONSIN INC.

LOCATIONS

HQ: CONCORDIA UNIVERSITY WISCONSIN INC.
  12800 N LAKE SHORE DR, MEQUON, WI 53097-2418
Phone: 262-243-5700

HISTORICAL FINANCIALS

Company Type: Private

Income Statement

FYE: June 30

	REVENUE ($ mil.)	NET INCOME ($ mil.)	NET PROFIT MARGIN	EMPLOYEES
06/11	90	9	10.1%	350
06/10	71	16	23.2%	0
06/09	53	2	5.0%	0
06/06	53	2	4.6%	0
Annual Growth	18.8%	54.5%	—	—

2011 Year-End Financials

Debt ratio: ——
Return on equity: 10.10%
Cash ($ mil.): 10
Current ratio: —
Long-term debt ($ mil.): —

Dividends
  Yield: —
  Payout: —
  Market value ($ mil.): —

CONEMAUGH HEALTH SYSTEM INC.

Medical provider Conemaugh Health System serves the residents of western Pennsylvania through three hospitals and a rehabilitation center. Its operations include Memorial Medical Center Meyersdale Medical Center Miners Medical Center and Crichton Rehabilitation Center. Altogether its facilities boast about 600 beds. Conemaugh Health System also operates a network of community health care facilities. It offers such services as regional cancer cardiovascular and neurosciences centers; home health care and home medical equipment; general care facilities; and specialized facilities for managing pain and wounds. Conemaugh also operates Penn Highlands Health Plan a PPO.

Geographic Reach

Focused on west-central Pennsylvania Conemaugh Health System serves a five-county region.

Operations

Memorial Medical Center Conemaugh's 545-bed flagship hospital is a tertiary care teaching hospital with a Level I trauma center and Level III Neonatal Intensive Care Unit. As the largest teaching hospital in the region Memorial Medical Center offers eight medical residency programs a pharmaceutical residency program a school of nursing and a school of allied health. For trauma patients Memorial Medical Center provides Medstar Aeromedical Helicopter Transport.

Its Conemaugh Physician Group and Conemaugh Home Health provide care throughout the health system's 11-county service area.

Through a partnership with Northrop Grumman and the Department of Defense Conemaugh Health System installed an electronic medical records system at the Memorial Medical Center.

EXECUTIVES

CFO, Edward H. DePasquale
VP Clinical Programs and Special Projects,
  Thomas M. Kurtz
President Meyersdale Medical Center, Mary
  Libengood
VP Business Development and Marketing, John M.
  Moryken
President Memorial Medical Center and Good
  Samaritan Medical Center, Steven E. Tucker
President Conemaugh Health Foundation, Susan
  M. Mann
Director Public Affairs, Amy Bradley
VP; Director Office of Community Health,
  Matthew (Matt) Masiello
CEO and Director; CEO Memorial Medical Center,
  Scott A. Becker
CIO, Joseph Dado
President Miners Medical Center, William R. Crowe
Vice Chairman, James Hargreaves
Chairman, Rt. Hon. Norman Krumenacker
Chief Medical Officer, David J. Carlson
VP Patient Care Services Memorial Medical
  Center, Claudia Rager
VP Memorial Medical Center, Kathy S. Knoll
President Conemaugh Health Initiatives, Elaine M.
  Lambert
VP Human Resources, Wesley Schmidt
Director, Daniel R. (Dan) DeVos, age 69
CEO and Director; CEO Memorial Medical Center,
  Scott A. Becker
Director, Robert A. Gleason Jr.
Director, James Hargreaves

Director and Board Treasurer, Samuel McClure
Director, John Saracena
Director, Sally Sargent
Director, Michael Smith
Director, Ron Vickroy
Director and Board Secretary, J. Michael Moses
Director, Kristin Brant
Director, James Cascio
Director, Kim Craig
Director, Adib Khouzami
Director, Brian Lieb
Director, Tom Morino
Director, Roberta Ream

LOCATIONS

HQ: Conemaugh Health System Inc.
  1086 Franklin St., Johnstown PA 15905
Phone: 814-534-9000   **Fax:** 814-539-0264
Web: www.conemaugh.org

Selected Facilities

Crichton Rehabilitation Center-Johnstown
Conemaugh Memorial Medical Center-Johnstown
Conemaugh Meyersdale Medical Center-Meyersdale
Conemaugh Miners Medical Center-Hastings
Conemaugh Physicians Group

PRODUCTS/OPERATIONS

Selected Services

Cancer Care
Emergency and Trauma
Family Medicine
Heart and Vascular
Rehabilitation
Surgical Services
Women/Child Services

COMPETITORS

Allegheny General Hospital
Altoona Regional
Bon Secours Health
Butler Health System
Excela Health
Heritage Valley Health
Jefferson Regional Medical Center of Pennsylvania
Ohio Valley General
Saint Vincent Health System
Sharon Regional Health System
St. Clair Health
UPMC
West Penn Allegheny Health System

HISTORICAL FINANCIALS

Company Type: Private - Not-for-Profit

Income Statement

FYE: June 30

	REVENUE ($ mil.)	NET INCOME ($ mil.)	NET PROFIT MARGIN	EMPLOYEES
06/12	509	5	1.2%	3,500
06/11	519	59	11.4%	0
06/10	6	0	—	0
06/09	460	(47)	—	0
Annual Growth	3.4%	—	—	—

2012 Year-End Financials

Debt ratio: ——
Return on equity: 1.20%
Cash ($ mil.): 39
Current ratio: 1.00
Long-term debt ($ mil.): —

Dividends
  Yield: —
  Payout: —
Market value ($ mil.): —

CONNECTICUT CHILDREN'S MEDICAL CENTER

When their tiny tykes needs some TLC Nutmeg Staters turn to Connecticut Children's Medical Center (CCMC). CCMC's centerpiece is its children's hospital that cares for children from babyhood to adulthood with a variety of services including surgery behavioral care and emergency medicine. The critical care department houses a Level I Pediatric Intensive Care Unit (PICU) that receives referral patients from more than 30 hospitals throughout the region. The center also conducts clinical research and provides pediatric training to health professionals. CCMC is home to more than 10 outpatient facilities throughout Connecticut and a 120-student school for children with physical and behavioral challenges.

Additionally CCMC operates the Faculty Practice Plan an integrated full-service multi-specialty pediatric practice providing care to children and their families. The practice employs about 170 physicians and mid-level practitioners.

CCMC is the only academic medical center dedicated exclusively to pediatric care in western New England and is home to the University of Connecticut's Department of Pediatrics and their Division of Pediatric Surgery. Along with conducting clinical research and providing pediatric training the department offers several two-year fellowships in pediatric subspecialties and a three-year fellowship in pediatric emergency medicine.

CCMC was founded in 1996 and is led by former insurance executive CEO Martin Gavin.

EXECUTIVES

Vice Chairman, Charles W. (Chuck) Shivery, age 66
VP Human Resources, Elizabeth A. (Betsy) Rudden
Surgeon-in-Chief, Fernando A. Ferrer
Director Corporate Communications, Robert J. (Bob) Fraleigh
Secretary, Barbara McGrath
SVP Finance and CFO, Gerald J. Boisvert Jr.
Media Relations Manager, Christopher (Chris) Boyle
VP Strategy and Regional Development, Leonard Banco
Physician-In-Chief, Paul H. Dworkin
VP Quality and Patient Safety, Robert Englander
VP Clinical Services and Chief Nursing Officer, Theresa Hendricksen
Chairman, Thomas O. Barnes
Vice Chairman, H. Mark Lunenburg, age 52
General Counsel, Ann Taylor
President CEO and Director, Martin J. (Marty) Gavin
SVP and COO, Wendy E. Warring
VP Connecticut Children's Medical Center Foundation, Martha E. Schall
Vice Chairman, Charles W. (Chuck) Shivery, age 66
Director, Louis Hernandez Jr., age 45
Director, Thomas M. (Tom) Marra, age 54
Director, William C. Popik, age 66
Director, Robert M. (Bobby) Le Blanc, age 45
Secretary, Barbara McGrath
SVP Finance and CFO, Gerald J. Boisvert Jr.
Vice Chairman, H. Mark Lunenburg, age 52
Director, Jeffrey Hoffman
Director, Stephen J. Sills
Director, Lynda B. Smith
Director, John S. Stout
Director, Doris Sugarman

President CEO and Director, Martin J. (Marty) Gavin
Director, Anne P. Sargent
Director, Cato T. Laurencin, age 53
Director, Marilyn Bacon
Director, E. Clayton Gengras III
Director, Robert Shanfield

LOCATIONS

HQ: Connecticut Children' s Medical Center
  282 Washington St., Hartford CT 06106
Phone: 860-545-9000   **Fax:** 860-545-8560
Web: www.connecticutchildrens.org

COMPETITORS

Backus
Baystate Health
Baystate Medical Center
Bridgeport Hospital
Bristol Hospital
Day Kimball Hospital
Griffin Health
Harrington Memorial Hospital
Hartford Health Care
Lawrence & Memorial Hospital
MidState Medical Center
New Milford Hospital
Saint Francis Hospital and Medical Center
St. Raphael Healthcare
St. Vincent' s Health Services
Yale-New Haven Hospital

HISTORICAL FINANCIALS

Company Type: Private - Not-for-Profit

Income Statement

FYE: September 30

	REVENUE ($ mil.)	NET INCOME ($ mil.)	NET PROFIT MARGIN	EMPLOYEES
09/11	267	(2)	—	1,117
09/10	210	10	4.8%	0
09/09	192	6	3.6%	0
09/08	187	5	2.7%	0
Annual Growth	12.7%	—	—	—

2011 Year-End Financials

Debt ratio: ——
Return on equity: (-0.90)%
Cash ($ mil.): 4
Current ratio: 0.60
Long-term debt ($ mil.): —

Dividends
  Yield: —
  Payout: —
Market value ($ mil.): —

CONNECTICUT COLLEGE

With its picturesque campus overlooking Long Island Sound Connecticut College (CC) strives to be the quintessential New England college. It is a private co-educational liberal arts college in New London which is close to Providence Hartford and New Haven. The college offers approximately 55 majors has an enrollment of 1900 and a reputation as one of the most selective schools in the nation. Top majors include biology English government international relations and psychology. CC is known for its interdisciplinary studies. The school has a 9-to-1 student-faculty ratio. The comprehensive fee (tuition room board and fees) for the 2009-10 academic year is just over $51000. CC was founded in 1911.

EXECUTIVES

President, Leo I. (Lee) Higdon Jr., age 65
VP College Relations, Patricia M. Carey

VP Finance, Paul Maroni
VP Information Services and Librarian, Lee Hisle
VP Administration, Ulysses Hammond
Registrar, Beth S. Labriola
Financial Aid Director, Elaine F. Solinga
Director Campus Safety, Stewart Smith
Assistant VP Human Resources and Professional Development, Cheryl Miller

LOCATIONS

HQ: Connecticut College
270 Mohegan Ave., New London CT 06320
Phone: 860-447-1911 **Fax:** 860-439-2101
Web: www.conncoll.edu

HISTORICAL FINANCIALS

Company Type: School

Income Statement

FYE: June 30

	REVENUE ($ mil.)	NET INCOME ($ mil.)	NET PROFIT MARGIN	EMPLOYEES
06/11	139	15	10.9%	0
06/10	123	4	3.3%	0
06/09	109	0	—	0
06/08	139	31	22.5%	0
Annual Growth	(0.1%)	(21.5%)	—	—

2011 Year-End Financials

Debt ratio: ——
Return on equity: 10.90%
Cash ($ mil.): 17
Current ratio: —
Long-term debt ($ mil.): —

Dividends
Yield: —
Payout: —
Market value ($ mil.): —

CONSERV FS INC.

LOCATIONS

HQ: CONSERV FS INC.
1110 MCCONNELL RD, WOODSTOCK, IL 60098-7310
Phone: 815-334-5950
Web: www.home.conservfs.com

HISTORICAL FINANCIALS

Company Type: Private

Income Statement

FYE: August 31

	REVENUE ($ mil.)	NET INCOME ($ mil.)	NET PROFIT MARGIN	EMPLOYEES
08/12	221	4	1.9%	140
08/11	188	4	2.2%	0
08/10	142	3	2.5%	0
08/09	23	5	24.8%	0
Annual Growth	111.8%	(9.6%)	—	—

2012 Year-End Financials

Debt ratio: ——
Return on equity: 1.90%
Cash ($ mil.): 0
Current ratio: 0.80
Long-term debt ($ mil.): —

Dividends
Yield: —
Payout: —
Market value ($ mil.): —

CONSOLIDATED FABRICATORS CORPORATION

LOCATIONS

HQ: CONSOLIDATED FABRICATORS CORPORATION
14620 ARMINTA ST, VAN NUYS, CA 91402-5902
Phone: 818-901-1005
Web: www.con-fab.com

HISTORICAL FINANCIALS

Company Type: Private

Income Statement

FYE: December 31

	REVENUE ($ mil.)	NET INCOME ($ mil.)	NET PROFIT MARGIN	EMPLOYEES
12/11	108	1	1.5%	373
12/10	81	0	0.1%	0
12/08	105	5	5.1%	0
12/07	100	0	1.0%	0
Annual Growth	2.8%	20.1%	—	—

2011 Year-End Financials

Debt ratio: ——
Return on equity: 1.50%
Cash ($ mil.): 0
Current ratio: 0.50
Long-term debt ($ mil.): —

Dividends
Yield: —
Payout: —
Market value ($ mil.): —

CONSORTIUM FOR OCEAN LEADERSHIP INC.

LOCATIONS

HQ: CONSORTIUM FOR OCEAN LEADERSHIP INC.
1201 NEW YORK AVE NW # 420, WASHINGTON, DC 20005-3917
Phone: 202-332-0063
Web: www.coreocean.org

HISTORICAL FINANCIALS

Company Type: Private

Income Statement

FYE: September 30

	REVENUE ($ mil.)	NET INCOME ($ mil.)	NET PROFIT MARGIN	EMPLOYEES
09/11	173	0	0.1%	26
09/10	134	(0)	—	0
09/09	103	0	0.2%	0
09/08	91	(0)	—	0
Annual Growth	23.5%	—	—	—

2011 Year-End Financials

Debt ratio: —
Return on equity: 0.10%
Cash ($ mil.): 2
Current ratio: —
Long-term debt ($ mil.): —

Dividends
Yield: —
Payout: —
Market value ($ mil.): —

CONSUMERS UNION OF UNITED STATES INC

Consumers Union of United States (CU) inspires both trust and fear. Best known for publishing "Consumer Reports" magazine the independent not-for-profit organization also serves as a consumer watchdog through other print publications and the Web (ConsumerReports.org). Its subscription site rates products ranging from candy bars to cars. CU tests and rates thousands of products annually through its National Testing and Research Center. CU accepts no advertising and derives income from the sale of Consumer Reports and other services and from non-commercial contributions grants and fees. CU traces its roots to 1926 when engineer Frederick Schlink organized a "consumer club" to rate products.

In addition to its Consumer Reports publication CU publishes ShopSmart a magazine aimed at women who want a quick read on consumer items such as food beauty products and home and yard products. CU also covers health information through its ConsumerReportsHealth.org website and the Consumer Reports Health Ratings Center. It has a presence in the blogging world with Consumerist.com which provides snarky coverage of retail markups and shopper complaints. Rounding out its portfolio of offerings the organization delivers ratings of product categories to smart phones via its Consumer Reports Mobile service.

CU's magazines websites and newsletters have a combined subscription base of more than 8 million. Its staff of lobbyists and activists work to change legislation and the marketplace in favor of the consumer interest. Coinciding with a public weary of corporate practices during a faltering economy in 2011 the organization reported an increase in revenues thanks to higher sales of its products and more contributions from donors. That year CU helped advocate against Bank of America's unpopular introduction of a monthly $5 debit card fee; the bank eventually ended the practice.

At its headquarters in Yonkers New York CU houses the Testing and Research Center which consists of 50 labs and offices. The organization also has an Auto Test Center in East Haddam Connecticut; and three advocacy offices in Washington DC; Austin Texas; and San Francisco. CU testifies before legislative and regulatory entities and files lawsuits on behalf of consumers. The organization is governed by an 18-member board. Board members are elected by CU members and meet three times a year. To preserve its independence CU does not permit its ratings or comments to be used commercially.

HISTORY

In 1926 engineer Frederick Schlink organized a "consumer club" (in White Plains New York) which distributed lists of recommended and non-recommended products. The lists led to the founding of Consumers' Research and a magazine devoted to testing products.

Schlink moved the group to Washington New Jersey in 1933. In 1935 three employees formed a union. Schlink fired them. Faced with another strike that year Schlink accused the strikers of being "Red" and responded with strikebreakers and armed detectives. The next year the strikers set up their own organization the Consumers Union of United States (CU).

CU's first magazine "Consumers Union Reports" came out three months later and rated products that the fledgling organization could afford to test such as soap and breakfast cereals. Subsequent issues focused on food and drug regulation and working conditions for women in textile mills.

The organization drew the wrath of both "Reader's Digest" and "Good Housekeeping" (which accused it in 1939 of prolonging the Depression). The next year the House Un-American Activities Committee put CU on its list of suspect organizations. CU cut staff and dropped "Union" from its magazine title but circulation remained low until after WWII.

By 1950 however Americans began consuming again helping to boost circulation to almost 400000. During the 1950s CU published a series of reports on the health hazards of smoking.

In 1960 CU helped found the International Organization of Consumers Unions (now Consumers International) to foster the consumer movement worldwide. Rhoda Karpatkin was hired as publisher in 1974. During the 1970s CU established consumer advocacy offices in California Texas and Washington DC.

Recession and an increase in not-for-profit mailing rates caused the organization to lose money in the early 1980s. CU looked to its readers who donated more than $3 million. The organization was hit by a 13-week strike in 1984 by union members calling for more say in management.

In 1996 CU slapped "not acceptable" ratings on the Isuzu Trooper and the Acura SLX. The next year the National Highway Traffic Safety Administration declared that CU's testing procedure of the Trooper was flawed but CU stood by its tests of the vehicle.

CU hit another bump in 1998 when it was compelled to retract a story on the nutritional value of Iams and Eukanuba pet food. Admitting its test results were incorrect CU's retraction of the story was something of a rarity —its last retraction had occurred almost 20 years earlier when the organization retracted a story on condoms.

A legal dispute broke out in 1999 between CU and automakers Isuzu and Suzuki which claimed negative reviews by Consumer Reports constituted defamation. The following year a jury found CU guilty of falsely reporting on the Isuzu but declined to impose fines on the publisher. (Suzuki eventually settled its case out of court in 2004.)

Karpatkin announced she would step down as president in 2001 and was replaced by chairman James Guest. That same year CU agreed to license its content to Internet portal Yahoo! Retailer Sharper Image (later TSIC) sued CU over an article unflattering to the company's popular air purifier device but a judge threw out the suit in late 2004.

In 2006 CU launched ShopSmart a shopping magazine geared at women aged 30 to 45. The next year it launched ConsumerReportsHealth.org and the Consumer Reports Health Ratings Center. In 2009 the company entered the blogging world with Consumerist.com which it purchased from Gawker Media.

The following year it introduced its Consumer Reports Mobile service which delivers product ratings to cell phones. Feats for CU in 2010 include discoveries of a potential safety hazard of Toyota's Lexus GX460 and a signal-loss problem with Apple's phone 4 which resulted in a recall from Toyota and Apple's announcement of a free remedy.

EXECUTIVES

Director Food Policy Initiatives, Jean Halloran
VP Administration and Human Resources, Richard (Rick) Lustig
President and CEO, James A. (Jim) Guest
Director Policy Outreach and Southwest Office, Reggie James
VP and CFO, Richard B. (Rich) Gannon
Chairman, Walter D. Bristol Jr.
VP and CIO, Rahul Belani
VP Human Resources, Linda Tepedino
VP and Technical Director, Jeffrey A. (Jeff) Asher
VP Executive Operations and Chief of Staff, Michael (Mike) D'Alessandro
Senior Director Strategic Planning and Information Services Publishing, Elena Falcone
SVP Information Products, John J. Sateja
VP Publishing, Jerry Steinbrink
Associate Technical Director, Carolyn Clifford-Ferrara
Director Appliances Recreation and Home Improvement Technical, Mark Connelly
Senior Director Product Safety and Technical Public Policy, Donald Mays
VP Health Programs, Paige Amidon
Director Special Projects, Elizabeth (Betsy) Imholz
Director Consumer Reports WebWatch, Beau Brendler
Manager Development Consumer WebWatch Publishing, Rob Drucker
Director Business Planning and Analysis, JoAnne Boyd
Senior Director External Relations, Milca Esdaille
Programs Director, Charles Bell
COO and Director, Laurence Bunin
VP External Affairs, Christopher (Chris) Meyer
Director West Coast and State Campaigns, Elisa Odabashian
Director External Relations, Rob Schneider
VP and General Counsel, Eileen B. Hershenov
VP and Editorial Director, Kevin McKean
Media Director, Michael McCauley
Director Federal Policy, Ellen Bloom
VP Communications, Ken Weine
Media Director, Susan Herold
Foundation Grants Officer, Robbin Blaine
Evaluation Director Consumers Union Best Buy Drugs, Maria Botello
Esther Peterson Fellow, J. Alex Chasick
Senior Policy Analyst, Elena Chavez
Senior Counsel, Janell M. Duncan
Research Professor, Kennerly H. Digges
Managing Director Consumer Reports Best Buy Drugs, Steve Findlay
Policy Counsel Product Food and Auto Safety, Ami Gadhia
Senior Attorney, Norma P. Garcia
Senior Attorney and Program Manager, Adrienne Hahn
Senior Staff Scientist, Michael Hansen
Staff Attorney, Michelle Jun
Policy Analyst, Joel Kelsey
Project Director StopHospitalInfections.org, Lisa McGiffert
Senior Attorney, Mark Savage
Director Health Policy Analysis, Gail Shearer

Senior Attorney and Manager Financial Services Campaign, Gail Hillebrand
Senior Attorney, Laurie Sobel
Science and Policy Analyst, Kristi Wiedemann
Director Strategic Resource and HearUsNow.org, Bob Williams
Senior Producer Consumer Reports WebWatch, J?rgen Wouters
Staff Attorney, Lauren Zeichner
Campaign Organizer, Meg Bohne
Campaign Organizer PrescriptionForChange.org, Liz Foley
Campaign Organizer StopHospitalInfections.org, Suzanne Henry
Grassroots Organizer, Blake Hutson
Grassroots Organizer, Tim Marvin
Grassroots Organizer, Daniela Nu?ez
Campaign Organizer Not in my Cart, Jamie Schaefer-Wilson
Web Developer, Gregory Foster
Web Administrator and Art Director, Amanda Frayer
Advocacy Outreach Strategy, Morgan Jindrich
Advocacy Web Site Coordinator, Minerva Novoa
Activist Development Specialist, Melissa Trevino
DIrector, Norman I. Silber
Vice Chairman, Thomas A. Wathen
Director, Craig A. Newmark, age 59
Director, Marcia Aronoff
COO and Director, Laurence Bunin
DIrector, Norman I. Silber
Director, Barbara S. Friedmann
Director, Robert E. Baensch
Director, Robert S. Alder
Director, Clarence M. Ditlow
Director, Jean Ann Fox
Director, Karen Hein
Director, Steven R. Hill
Director, Carol Izumi
Director, Burnele V. Powell
Vice Chairman, Thomas A. Wathen
Auditors: KPMGLLP

LOCATIONS

HQ: Consumers Union of United States Inc.
101 Truman Ave., Yonkers NY 10703-1057
Phone: 914-378-2000 **Fax:** 914-378-2900
Web: www.consumersunion.org

PRODUCTS/OPERATIONS

2011 Sales

	$ mil.	% of total
Subscriptions newsstand & other sales	229	91
Contributions	17	7
Other	5	2
Total	**252**	**100**

Content Areas
Autos
Food
Health Care
Money
Phones and Media
Product Safety

Selected Offerings

Magazines and newsletters
  Consumer Reports Magazine
  Consumer Reports Money Advisor (newsletter)
  Consumer Reports on Health (newsletter)
  ShopSmart
Websites
  ConsumerReports.org
  ConsumerReportsHealth.org
  Consumerist.com

HISTORICAL FINANCIALS

Company Type: Private - Not-for-Profit

Income Statement				FYE: May 31
	REVENUE ($ mil.)	NET INCOME ($ mil.)	NET PROFIT MARGIN	EMPLOYEES
05/11	252	32	12.9%	480
05/10	242	9	3.7%	0
05/09	253	6	2.8%	0
05/07	255	10	4.1%	0
Annual Growth	(0.4%)	46.3%	—	—

2011 Year-End Financials

Debt ratio: ——
Return on equity: 12.90%
Cash ($ mil.): 18
Current ratio: 0.20
Long-term debt ($ mil.): —

Dividends
Yield: —
Payout: —
Market value ($ mil.): —

CONTINENTAL PAPER GRADING CO.

LOCATIONS

HQ: CONTINENTAL PAPER GRADING CO.
1623 S LUMBER ST, CHICAGO, IL 60616-1192
Phone: 312-226-2010
Web: www.cpgco.com

HISTORICAL FINANCIALS

Company Type: Private

Income Statement				FYE: December 31
	REVENUE ($ mil.)	NET INCOME ($ mil.)	NET PROFIT MARGIN	EMPLOYEES
12/11	218	2	1.0%	50
12/10	213	3	1.6%	0
12/09	138	1	0.9%	0
12/08	230	11	5.0%	0
Annual Growth	(1.8%)	(42.6%)	—	—

2011 Year-End Financials

Debt ratio: ——
Return on equity: 1.00%
Cash ($ mil.): 3
Current ratio: 1.70
Long-term debt ($ mil.): —

Dividends
Yield: —
Payout: —
Market value ($ mil.): —

CONTRACK INTERNATIONAL INC.

LOCATIONS

HQ: CONTRACK INTERNATIONAL INC.
6862 ELM ST STE 500, MC LEAN, VA 22101-3838
Phone: 703-358-8800
Web: www.contrack.com

HISTORICAL FINANCIALS

Company Type: Private

Income Statement				FYE: December 31
	REVENUE ($ mil.)	NET INCOME ($ mil.)	NET PROFIT MARGIN	EMPLOYEES
12/11	328	31	9.5%	6,200
12/09	181	15	8.8%	0
12/08	166	18	10.9%	0
12/07	1,042	0	0.0%	0
Annual Growth	(31.9%)	1141.8%	—	—

2011 Year-End Financials

Debt ratio: ——
Return on equity: 9.50%
Cash ($ mil.): 6
Current ratio: 0.70
Long-term debt ($ mil.): —

Dividends
Yield: —
Payout: —
Market value ($ mil.): —

CONTRACTORS STEEL COMPANY

Steel service center operator Contractors Steel provides products such as bars (cold-rolled and hot-rolled) pipe plate sheet structural members (angles beams and channels) and tubing. The company's fabricating and processing services include burning grinding plasma cutting sawing and shearing. Contractors Steel operates from facilities in Michigan and Ohio. The company maintains its own fleet of delivery trucks. Chairman president and CEO Donald Simon founded Contractors Steel in 1960.

EXECUTIVES

Chairman President CEO and Treasurer, Donald R. (Don) Simon
Director Purchasing, Cynthia Wagner
General Manager, Mark Bokus Jr.
Director Marketing and Advertising, Ralph Hartzoe
Controller, Robert Simon

LOCATIONS

HQ: Contractors Steel Company
36555 Amrhein Rd., Livonia MI 48150
Phone: 734-464-4000   **Fax:** 734-452-3939
Web: www.contractorssteel.com

COMPETITORS

Alro	Peerless Steel
Mill Steel	

HISTORICAL FINANCIALS

Company Type: Private

Income Statement				FYE: October 31
	REVENUE ($ mil.)	NET INCOME ($ mil.)	NET PROFIT MARGIN	EMPLOYEES
10/11	253	14	5.6%	250
10/10	184	6	3.5%	0
10/09	153	(24)	—	0
10/08	316	37	11.9%	0
Annual Growth	(7.1%)	(27.6%)	—	—

2011 Year-End Financials

Debt ratio: ——
Return on equity: 5.60%
Cash ($ mil.): 9
Current ratio: 2.70
Long-term debt ($ mil.): —

Dividends
Yield: —
Payout: —
Market value ($ mil.): —

CONWAY HOSPITAL INC.

Conway Medical Center (CMC) finds a way to provide a wide range of health care services to residents of eastern South Carolina. The private not-for-profit 210-bed hospital (served by a medical staff of 200) provides services including primary diagnostic emergency surgical maternal and pediatric and rehabilitative care. CMC specializes in heart health hospice care and occupational health. Additionally CMC operates the Kingston Nursing Center an about 90-bed long-term nursing and rehabilitative care facility and the Conway Physicians Group which is home to about 10 physician practices offering a range of specialties.

Geographic Reach

The hospital system serves patients in eastern South Carolina.

Financial Analysis

CMC receives financial support in part through donations to the Conway Medical Center Foundation which was founded in 1988 to provide financial and voluntary staffing support to the hospital.

Company Background

The center expanded its operations in 2009 with the completion of a new patient tower with about 65 patient beds new nurses stations for streamlined patient care and updated technology.

EXECUTIVES

CEO, Philip A. (Phil) Clayton
VP Fiscal Services, Bret Barr
VP Nursing Services, Annamarie Sheffield
VP Human Resources, Craig Hyman
Administrator Kingston Nursing Center/Medstar, Laura Fowler
VP Ancillary Services, Dwight Gentry
Executive Director Foundation, Berns Massey
VP Facility Management, Kevin Lovett

LOCATIONS

HQ: Conway Medical Center
300 Singleton Ridge Rd., Conway SC 29526
Phone: 843-347-7111   **Fax:** 843-347-8181
Web: www.conwayhospital.com

PRODUCTS/OPERATIONS

Selected Departments and Services
Center for Wound Healing
Critical Care Services
Diabetes Management
Diagnostic
Endoscopy
Heart Center
Hospice
Joint Replacement Center
Laboratory Services
Long Term Care
Mammography
Medical Services Center
Palliative Care
Pediatric Center
Pulmonary Rehabilitation
Rehabilitation
Senior Privileges Club
Sleep Disorders Center
Subacute
Surgical Services
The Birthplace
Weight Loss Surgery
Wellness & Fitness Center

COMPETITORS

Carolinas Hospital
  System
Georgetown Hospital
  System
Grand Strand Regional
  Medical Center
McLeod Health

Medical University of
  South Carolina
New Hanover Regional
  Medical Center
Roper St. Francis
  Healthcare

HISTORICAL FINANCIALS

Company Type: Private - Not-for-Profit

Income Statement
FYE: September 30

	REVENUE ($ mil.)	NET INCOME ($ mil.)	NET PROFIT MARGIN	EMPLOYEES
09/11	149	13	8.9%	1,200
09/09	149	14	10.0%	0
09/06	126	3	2.4%	0
09/05	132	17	13.1%	0
Annual Growth	4.1%	(8.5%)	—	—

2011 Year-End Financials
Debt ratio: ——
Return on equity: 8.90%
Cash ($ mil.): 19
Current ratio: 1.80
Long-term debt ($ mil.): —
Dividends
  Yield: —
  Payout: —
Market value ($ mil.): —

COOK & BOARDMAN INC.

LOCATIONS

HQ: COOK & BOARDMAN INC.
  9347 D DUCKS LN STE A, CHARLOTTE, NC
  28273-4553
Phone: 704-334-8683
Web: www.cookandboardman.com

HISTORICAL FINANCIALS

Company Type: Private

Income Statement
FYE: September 30

	REVENUE ($ mil.)	NET INCOME ($ mil.)	NET PROFIT MARGIN	EMPLOYEES
09/11	168	0	—	135
09/10	94	0	—	0
09/09	53	0	—	0
09/08	54	0	—	0
Annual Growth	46.0%	—	—	—

2011 Year-End Financials
Debt ratio: ——
Return on equity: —
Cash ($ mil.): 1
Current ratio: 1.60
Long-term debt ($ mil.): —
Dividends
  Yield: —
  Payout: —
Market value ($ mil.): —

COOPER COMMUNITIES INC.

Feeling cooped up in your cookie-cutter house with its bare minimum of surrounding green space? Cooper Communities develops master-planned communities and resorts in the southeastern US. Some properties feature golf courses and lakes with 20-30% of their land set aside for natural landscape. Subsidiaries include custom builder Cooper Homes Cooper Land Development and Escapes! which sells timeshare options for Cooper's resorts. Cooper Realty Investments acquires and manages commercial properties. The largest homebuilder in Arkansas Cooper Communities also has developments in eight other states. Cooper Communities was founded by John Cooper in 1954 and builds about 1300 new homes each year.

EXECUTIVES

Chairman, John A. Cooper Jr., age 70
President, John A. Cooper III
SVP and CFO, Kent Burger
SVP, Neff Basore
SVP and General Counsel, William H. Kennedy III
VP, Patrick Samples

LOCATIONS

HQ: COOPER COMMUNITIES INC.
  903 N 47TH ST, ROGERS, AR 72756-9622
Phone: 479-246-6500
Web: www.cooperhomes.com

PRODUCTS/OPERATIONS

Selected Communities
Bella Vista Village (Bella Vista Arkansas)
Creekmoor (Raymore Missouri)
Cross Creek (Rogers Arkansas)
Glade Springs Village (West Virginia)
Hot Springs Village (Arkansas)
StoneBridge Village (Branson Missouri)
Sienna Lake (Little Rock Arkansas)
Tellico Village (Loudon Tennessee)
Escapes! Resorts
  Escapes! to Bella Vista Village
  Escapes! to Cherokee Village
  Escapes! to the Gulf at Galveston
  Escapes! to Hot Springs Village
  Escapes! to the Gulf at Orange Beach
  Escapes! to StoneBridge Village
  Escapes! to Tropical Breeze
  Escapes! to the Branson Yacht Club

COMPETITORS

Bonita Bay Group
D.R. Horton
KB Home
Lennar
PulteGroup

St. Joe
Toll Brothers
WCI Communities
Woodbridge Holdings

HISTORICAL FINANCIALS

Company Type: Private

Income Statement
FYE: December 31

	ASSETS ($ mil.)	NET INCOME ($ mil.)	INCOME AS % OF ASSETS	EMPLOYEES
12/11	156	(20)	—	400
12/10	228	(65)	—	0
12/08	398	(29)	—	0
12/07	469	14	3.0%	0
Annual Growth	(30.7%)	—	—	—

2011 Year-End Financials
Debt ratio: ——
Return on equity: (-50.10)%
Cash ($ mil.): 8
Current ratio: 0.50
Long-term debt ($ mil.): —
Dividends
  Yield: —
  Payout: —
Market value ($ mil.): —

COOPERATIVE ELEVATOR CO.

Cooperative Elevator represents and serves northern Michigan bean and grain farmers. The agricultural cooperative is made up of approximately 900 member/owners. It operates storage facilities and processing plants offers crop marketing and agronomy services and provides farm supplies to its members including seed feed fertilizer herbicides fuel and agricultural chemicals. The co-op's bean farmers grow black red pinto and navy beans which are distributed in bulk throughout the US as well as in Africa and the Caribbean. Cooperative Elevator's grain farmers produce wheat soy corn barley and oats and the co-op provides storage and market services such as price updates for these commodities.

EXECUTIVES

President and CEO, Pat Anderson
VP Information Technology and Assistant Board Secretary, Barry Albrecht
VP Bean and Grain Divisions, Mike Janowicz
VP Finance and Board Treasurer, Mike Wehner
Chairman, Kurt Ewald
Vice Chairman, Doug Houghtaling
VP Petroleum, Tim Sielaff
VP Agronomy, Mark Boyne

LOCATIONS

HQ: Cooperative Elevator Co.
  7211 E. Michigan Ave., Pigeon MI 48755
Phone: 989-453-4500   Fax: 989-453-3942
Web: www.coopelev.com

COMPETITORS

ADM	Kelley Bean
Cargill	Organic Bean &
Chippewa Valley Bean	Grain
CHS	Star of the West
Della Natura	United Producers
Commodities	Zeeland Farm

HISTORICAL FINANCIALS

Company Type: Private - Cooperative

Income Statement

FYE: January 31

	REVENUE ($ mil.)	NET INCOME ($ mil.)	NET PROFIT MARGIN	EMPLOYEES
01/12	242	13	5.4%	136
01/11	166	11	6.8%	0
01/10	163	7	4.6%	0
01/09	176	7	4.5%	0
Annual Growth	11.1%	18.0%	—	—

2012 Year-End Financials

Debt ratio: ——
Return on equity: 5.40%
Cash ($ mil.): 0
Current ratio: —
Long-term debt ($ mil.): —

Dividends
Yield: —
Payout: —
Market value ($ mil.): —

COOPERATIVE ENERGY COMPANY

LOCATIONS

HQ: COOPERATIVE ENERGY COMPANY
1708 PIERCE AVE, SIBLEY, IA 51249-7091
Phone: 712-754-2586

HISTORICAL FINANCIALS

Company Type: Private

Income Statement

FYE: May 31

	REVENUE ($ mil.)	NET INCOME ($ mil.)	NET PROFIT MARGIN	EMPLOYEES
05/11	82	1	2.1%	52
05/10*	26	1	3.9%	0
12/09	46	1	3.5%	0
12/07	35	1	3.3%	0
Annual Growth	32.7%	13.6%	—	—

*Fiscal year change

2011 Year-End Financials

Debt ratio: ——
Return on equity: 2.10%
Cash ($ mil.): 0
Current ratio: 0.70
Long-term debt ($ mil.): —

Dividends
Yield: —
Payout: —
Market value ($ mil.): —

COOPERATIVE FOR ASSISTANCE AND RELIEF EVERYWHERE INC.

The Cooperative for Assistance and Relief Everywhere (CARE) strives to be the beginning of the end of poverty. The organization works to reduce poverty in more than 70 countries by helping communities in areas such as health education economic development emergency relief and agriculture. CARE supports more than 1000 projects to combat poverty. It also operates a small economic activity development (SEAD) unit that supports moneymaking activities. Through SEAD CARE provides technical training and savings and loans programs to help people —particularly women — open or expand small businesses. CARE was founded in 1945 to give aid to WWII survivors.

About 90% of the funds that CARE receives go toward its aid efforts. The organization helps people in the poorest communities of developing nations; it does not provide assistance in the US. CARE is supported by donations from thousands of individuals and dozens of corporations foundations and other charitable organizations in the US. The group also receives funding and supplies from government agencies including the United Nations and European Union. Amid the global economic downturn CARE has been working to raise contribution levels as governments businesses and individuals cut back their spending including charitable donations.

In addition to its Atlanta headquarters CARE maintains field offices in about 10 US cities including Boston Chicago Miami New York and Washington DC. The group's international field offices are located in more than 55 countries.

EXECUTIVES

General Counsel, Kent B. Alexander, age 53
Treasurer and Director, Dean C. Kehler, age 55
Secretary, Carol Hudson
Chair, W. Bowman (Bo) Cutter III
President CEO and Director, Helene D. Gayle, age 56
SVP Global Support Services, Patrick Solomon
SVP Finance and CFO, Vickie J. Barrow-Klein
Vice Chair, Doris Meissner
Director Poilcy Communications CARE USA, Julie Bernstein
Media Officer CARE USA, Brian Feagans
Regional Communications Manager Central Region CARE USA, Kathy Lane
Director Strategic Communications CARE USA, Stephanie Libby
Regional Communications Manager Western Region CARE USA, Sarah Moser
Media Officer CARE International, Melanie Brooks
VP Program Partnerships Learning and Advocacy, Nick Osborne
COO, Jonathan (Jon) Mitchell
VP International Programs and Operations, Abby Maxman
VP Individual Fundraising and Marketing, Lee Taliaferro (Tolli) Love
Director, Deidra Wager, age 57
Director, Susan M. Crown, age 53
Director, Kenneth A. (Ken) Lehman

Treasurer and Director, Dean C. Kehler, age 55
Director, Eduardo Castro-Wright, age 57
Director, Richard A. (Rich) Marin
Director, Ranvir K. Trehan
Director, Katharin S. (Kathy) Dyer
Director, Bruce C. Tully
President CEO and Director, Helene D. Gayle, age 56
Director, Virginia (Ginger) Sall
Director, K. Y. Amoako
Director, Richard J. Almeida
Director, Gilles Concordel
Director, Maria Echaveste
Director, Paul J. Jansen
Vice Chair, Doris Meissner
Director, Afaf I. Meleis
Director, Randall E. (Randy) Pond
Director, William D. (Bill) Unger
Director, Monica Vachher
Auditors: PricewaterhouseCoopersLLP

LOCATIONS

HQ: Cooperative for Assistance and Relief Everywhere Inc.
151 Ellis St., Atlanta GA 30303-2440
Phone: 404-681-2552   **Fax:** 404-589-2650
Web: www.care.org

PRODUCTS/OPERATIONS

2010 Revenues

	$ mil.	% of total
Private support	285	49
Government and agency grants	282	48
Other	17	3
Total	**586**	**100**

HISTORICAL FINANCIALS

Company Type: Private - Not-for-Profit

Income Statement

FYE: June 30

	REVENUE ($ mil.)	NET INCOME ($ mil.)	NET PROFIT MARGIN	EMPLOYEES
06/11	589	10	1.7%	10,000
06/08	713	40	5.6%	0
06/05	624	66	10.6%	0
06/04	300	0	0.0%	0
Annual Growth	25.1%	5214.7%	—	—

2011 Year-End Financials

Debt ratio: ——
Return on equity: 1.70%
Cash ($ mil.): 72
Current ratio: 0.50
Long-term debt ($ mil.): —

Dividends
Yield: —
Payout: —
Market value ($ mil.): —

COOPERATIVE HOUSING FOUNDATION

LOCATIONS

HQ: COOPERATIVE HOUSING FOUNDATION
8601 GEORGIA AVE STE 800, SILVER SPRING, MD 20910-3440
Phone: 301-587-4700
Web: www.chfinternational.org

HISTORICAL FINANCIALS
Company Type: Private

Income Statement
FYE: September 30

	REVENUE ($ mil.)	NET INCOME ($ mil.)	NET PROFIT MARGIN	EMPLOYEES
09/11	257	59	22.9%	1,300
09/10	227	8	3.5%	0
09/09	218	(24)	—	0
09/08	376	19	5.1%	0
Annual Growth	(11.9%)	45.1%	—	—

2011 Year-End Financials
Debt ratio: ——
Return on equity: 22.90%
Cash ($ mil.): 39
Current ratio: —
Long-term debt ($ mil.): —

Dividends
Yield: —
Payout: —
Market value ($ mil.): —

COPLEY MEMORIAL HOSPITAL INC.

LOCATIONS
HQ: COPLEY MEMORIAL HOSPITAL INC.
2000 OGDEN AVE, AURORA, IL 60504-7222
Phone: 630-978-6200
Web: www.rushcopley.com

HISTORICAL FINANCIALS
Company Type: Private

Income Statement
FYE: June 30

	REVENUE ($ mil.)	NET INCOME ($ mil.)	NET PROFIT MARGIN	EMPLOYEES
06/12	268	14	5.5%	1,100
06/11	274	27	10.1%	0
06/10	265	24	9.1%	0
06/09	254	17	6.7%	0
Annual Growth	1.8%	(4.4%)	—	—

2012 Year-End Financials
Debt ratio: ——
Return on equity: 5.50%
Cash ($ mil.): 32
Current ratio: 1.00
Long-term debt ($ mil.): —

Dividends
Yield: —
Payout: —
Market value ($ mil.): —

COPPERAS COVE INDEPENDENT SCHOOL DISTRICT

LOCATIONS
HQ: COPPERAS COVE INDEPENDENT SCHOOL DISTRICT
703 W AVENUE D, COPPERAS COVE, TX 76522-2000
Phone: 254-547-1227
Web: www.specialeducationprogram.com

HISTORICAL FINANCIALS
Company Type: Private

Income Statement
FYE: August 31

	REVENUE ($ mil.)	NET INCOME ($ mil.)	NET PROFIT MARGIN	EMPLOYEES
08/12	80	5	6.8%	1,172
08/11	86	(2)	—	0
08/09	78	5	7.0%	0
08/08	75	0	0.5%	0
Annual Growth	2.1%	139.5%	—	—

2012 Year-End Financials
Debt ratio: ——
Return on equity: 6.80%
Cash ($ mil.): 0
Current ratio: 0.10
Long-term debt ($ mil.): —

Dividends
Yield: —
Payout: —
Market value ($ mil.): —

CORE CONSTRUCTION INC.

CORE Construction fits into the core clique of contractors in the southwestern US. The company formerly Targent General is one of the top contractors in the region; it also has offices in Florida and Illinois. CORE offers construction management general contracting and design/build services for municipal educational health care office residential retail sports institutional and industrial projects. It has worked on projects as diverse as Phoenix's Chase Field Ballpark Dodge Theatre and Lower Buckeye Jail. German immigrant Otto Baum founded the company in 1937.

CORE Construction is the seventh largest builder of schools in the US. The company is focusing its efforts on commercial developments affordable housing and senior care facilities.

CORE Construction has regional offices in Arizona Florida Illinois Nevada and Texas

ARIG (Al Rajhi Investment Group) owns a majority stake in the company.

EXECUTIVES
President, Howard L. Maurer
EVP, Shawn L. Maurer
VP Administration, JoAnn Dean
VP Finance, Dennis Barber
Treasurer, Steve Roeschley

Estimator, Marshall Wtizig
Director Business Development, Dennis Montague

LOCATIONS
HQ: CORE CONSTRUCTION INC.
3036 E GREENWAY RD, PHOENIX, AZ 85032-4414
Phone: 602-494-0800
Web: www.coreconstructaz.com

COMPETITORS
DPR Construction
Jaynes Companies
Kitchell
McCarthy Building
Summit Builders
Sundt
Tutor Perini

HISTORICAL FINANCIALS
Company Type: Private

Income Statement
FYE: December 31

	REVENUE ($ mil.)	NET INCOME ($ mil.)	NET PROFIT MARGIN	EMPLOYEES
12/11	206	0	—	60
12/10	244	0	—	0
12/09	0	0	—	0
12/08	0	0	—	0
Annual Growth	—	—	—	—

2011 Year-End Financials
Debt ratio: ——
Return on equity: —
Cash ($ mil.): 4
Current ratio: 0.10
Long-term debt ($ mil.): —

Dividends
Yield: —
Payout: —
Market value ($ mil.): —

CORRECTIONAL HEALTHCARE COMPANIES INC.

LOCATIONS
HQ: CORRECTIONAL HEALTHCARE COMPANIES INC.
6200 S SYRACUSE WAY # 440, GREENWOOD VILLAGE, CO 80111-4737
Phone: 720-622-8079

HISTORICAL FINANCIALS
Company Type: Private

Income Statement
FYE: December 31

	REVENUE ($ mil.)	NET INCOME ($ mil.)	NET PROFIT MARGIN	EMPLOYEES
12/11	178	(1)	—	2,110
12/10	115	2	2.4%	0
Annual Growth	54.0%	—	—	—

2011 Year-End Financials
Debt ratio: ——
Return on equity: (-0.70)%
Cash ($ mil.): 3
Current ratio: 0.90
Long-term debt ($ mil.): —

Dividends
Yield: —
Payout: —
Market value ($ mil.): —

COTTAGE CARE CORPORATION

LOCATIONS

HQ: COTTAGE CARE CORPORATION
695 N KELLOGG ST, GALESBURG, IL 61401-2807
Phone: 309-343-8131

HISTORICAL FINANCIALS

Company Type: Private

Income Statement

FYE: December 31

	REVENUE ($ mil.)	NET INCOME ($ mil.)	NET PROFIT MARGIN	EMPLOYEES
12/11	84	16	20.1%	59
Annual Growth	—	—	—	—

COUNCIL BLUFFS COMMUNITY SCHOOL DISTRICT

LOCATIONS

HQ: COUNCIL BLUFFS COMMUNITY SCHOOL DISTRICT
12 SCOTT ST, COUNCIL BLUFFS, IA 51503-0782
Phone: 712-328-6446

HISTORICAL FINANCIALS

Company Type: Private

Income Statement

FYE: June 30

	REVENUE ($ mil.)	NET INCOME ($ mil.)	NET PROFIT MARGIN	EMPLOYEES
06/11	113	(8)	—	1,200
06/10	102	27	27.0%	0
06/09	102	(12)	—	0
06/08	97	(1)	—	0
Annual Growth	4.9%	—	—	—

2011 Year-End Financials

Debt ratio: ——
Return on equity: (-7.60)%
Cash ($ mil.): 36
Current ratio: —
Long-term debt ($ mil.): —

Dividends
Yield: —
Payout: —
Market value ($ mil.): —

COUNCIL ON FOREIGN RELATIONS INC.

The Council on Foreign Relations was established in 1921 with support from the Rockefeller family to provide a forum for government officials corporate executives journalists students and other interested parties to study and discuss world issues and the related impact on American foreign policy. The council publishes Foreign Affairs a magazine that comes out six times a year along with books and studies by its own scholars. Former president Leslie H. Gelb once a columnist and editor at The New York Times retired in 2003 after 10 years in the post and was succeeded by diplomat Richard Haass. Prospective members must be US citizens (native-born or naturalized) and are nominated by an existing member.

The Council on Foreign Relations also operates the David Rockefeller Studies Program which functions as the council's think tank. The Studies Program has three interdisciplinary centers: Center for Preventive Action; the Maurice R. Greenberg Center for Geoeconomic Studies; and the Center for Universal Education.

EXECUTIVES

Co-Chairman, Robert E. (Bob) Rubin, age 74
Co-Chairman, Carla A. Hills, age 78
President and Director, Richard N. Haass, age 59
SVP COO and Treasurer, Janice L. Murray
Editor, James F. (Jim) Hoge Jr.
Secretary, Lilita V. Gusts
VP Communications and Marketing, Lisa Shields
SVP and Publisher, David Kellogg
VP National Program and Academic Outreach, Irina A. Faskianos
Deputy COO, Jan Mowder Hughes
Chief of Staff to the President, Jeffrey A. Reinke
Director Publishing, Patricia Lee Dorff
Director Facility and Event Operations, Neftali Frank Alvarez
Director Special Events, Valerie Post
Senior Fellow and Director of International Economics, Benn Steil
Vice Chairman, Richard E. Salomon
VP Meetings, Nancy D. Bodurtha
VP Development, Suzanne E. Helm
VP Washington Program, Kay King
VP Membership Fellowship and Corporate Affairs, L. Camille Massey
Honorary Vice Chairman, Maurice R. Greenberg
VP Director of Studies, Gary Samore
Director Web Management and Development, Tom Davey
CFO, Kenneth Castiglia
Director, James W. (Jim) Owens, age 66
Director, Henry S. Bienen, age 72
Director, Ann M. Fudge, age 60
Co-Chairman, Robert E. (Bob) Rubin, age 74
President and Director, Richard N. Haass, age 59
Director, Madeleine K. Albright, age 75
Vice Chairman, Richard E. Salomon
Director, Fouad Ajami
Director, Colin L. Powell
Honorary Vice Chairman, Maurice R. Greenberg
Director, Fareed Zakaria
Director, Peter Ackerman
Director, Charlene Barshefsky
Director, Tom Brokaw
Director, Richard N. Foster
Director, Vin Weber
Director, Stephen Friedman

Director, Anne-Marie Slaughter
Director, Jami Miscik
Director, J. Tomilson Hill
Director, Alan S. Blinder
Director, George E. Rupp
Director, Joseph S. Nye Jr.
Director, Stephen W. Bosworth
Director, Frank J. Caufield
Director, Ronald L. Olson
Director, Joan E. Spero, age 66
Director, Shirley Ann Jackson
Director, David M. Rubenstein
Director, Kenneth M. Duberstein
Director, Sylvia Mathews Burwell
Director, Christine Todd Whitman
Director, Richard C. Holbrooke
Director, Alberto Ibarguen, age 68
Auditors: Ernst&Young

LOCATIONS

HQ: COUNCIL ON FOREIGN RELATIONS INC.
58 E 68TH ST, NEW YORK, NY 10065-5953
Phone: 212-434-9400
Web: www.foreignaffairs.org

PRODUCTS/OPERATIONS

2011 Revenues

	% of revenues
Gifts & grants	34
Investment income	24
Foreign Affairs	14
Corporate membership & other	13
Membership dues	11
Rental income	4
Total	**0** **100**

HISTORICAL FINANCIALS

Company Type: Private - Foundation

Income Statement

FYE: June 30

	REVENUE ($ mil.)	NET INCOME ($ mil.)	NET PROFIT MARGIN	EMPLOYEES
06/11	59	6	11.5%	200
06/10	42	(8)	—	0
06/09	28	0	—	0
06/08	86	40	47.0%	0
Annual Growth	(11.6%)	(44.6%)	—	—

2011 Year-End Financials

Debt ratio: ——
Return on equity: 11.50%
Cash ($ mil.): 24
Current ratio: 0.30
Long-term debt ($ mil.): —

Dividends
Yield: —
Payout: —
Market value ($ mil.): —

COUNTRY PRIDE COOPERATIVE INC.

The Country Pride Cooperative has provided assistance to farmers in south central South Dakota since 1935. Country Pride offers it members an agronomy center seed sales grain storage and merchandising a feed mill and an equipment-rental center as well as finance programs and farm supply stores an auto-service center and bulk refined fuel delivery. It also operates five convenience stores under the Cenex name. The co-op was created through the 2000 merger of two area cooperatives Freeman Oil Cooperative (formed in 1935) and Dakota Pride Cooperative.

EXECUTIVES

President and General Manager, Carl Dickinson
Manager Human Resources, Laura Root
Controller, Marsha Lowry
Manager Energy and Safety, Mike Barfuss
Manager Feed and Grain Division, Rod Farley
Manager Retail Operations West, Ritch Hawranek
Manager Agronomy and Operations East, Bill Pape
Manager Progressive Marketing, Steve Koenig
Board President, Ross Plucker

LOCATIONS

HQ: Country Pride Cooperative
648 W. 2nd St., Winner SD 57580
Phone: 605-842-2711   **Fax:** 605-842-2715
Web: www.countrypridecoop.com

COMPETITORS

ADM
Cargill
CHS
North Central Farmers
  Elevator
Northern Growers
South Dakota Wheat
  Growers

HISTORICAL FINANCIALS

Company Type: Private - Cooperative

Income Statement

FYE: June 30

	REVENUE ($ mil.)	NET INCOME ($ mil.)	NET PROFIT MARGIN	EMPLOYEES
06/12	170	3	2.0%	200
06/11	139	2	1.6%	0
06/10	109	1	1.2%	0
06/09	141	0	0.2%	0
Annual Growth	6.4%	125.7%	—	—

2012 Year-End Financials

Debt ratio: ——
Return on equity: 2.00%
Cash ($ mil.): 3
Current ratio: 0.60
Long-term debt ($ mil.): —
Dividends
  Yield: —
  Payout: —
  Market value ($ mil.): —

COUNTY OF BERKELEY

LOCATIONS

HQ: COUNTY OF BERKELEY
1003 HIGHWAY 52, MONCKS CORNER, SC
29461-3007
Phone: 843-761-6900
Web: www.sangareesubdivision.com

HISTORICAL FINANCIALS

Company Type: Private

Income Statement

FYE: June 30

	REVENUE ($ mil.)	NET INCOME ($ mil.)	NET PROFIT MARGIN	EMPLOYEES
06/11	96	10	10.7%	700
06/09	0	0	—	0
06/08	66	1	1.9%	0
06/07	64	2	3.3%	0
Annual Growth	14.7%	69.9%	—	—

2011 Year-End Financials

Debt ratio: ——
Return on equity: 10.70%
Cash ($ mil.): 51
Current ratio: 0.80
Long-term debt ($ mil.): —
Dividends
  Yield: —
  Payout: —
  Market value ($ mil.): —

COVENANT HOUSE

Young people rely on Covenant House to keep its promises. The not-for-profit group offers outreach and crisis centers for homeless and runaway youths. Its centers offer food shelter clothing and medical and counseling services as well as job skills and substance abuse and parenting programs. There are about 15 centers in the US two in Canada and one each in Mexico Honduras and Nicaragua. Its Rights of Passage Programs and Covenant House Crisis Shelters served more than 15000 people and the entire organization reaches some 71000 homeless kids annually. The group also operates the Nineline (1-800-999-9999) for runaways. Covenant House was founded in 1972 by Franciscan priest Father Bruce Ritter.

Covenant House is on the other end of the line for those in crisis in the US and Central America. Its Nineline received and responded to more than 48000 crisis calls from US youth. In Mexico Covenant House operates Acercatel its 24-hour national crisis hotline. Acercatel assisted with more than 13000 crisis calls.

EXECUTIVES

SVP, Virginia S. Bauer
Executive Director Florida, James M. Gress
EVP COO and Secretary, James M. (Jim) White, age 51
Executive Director California, George R. Lozano
Executive Director Toronto, Ruth daCosta
Executive Director Texas, Ronda G. Robinson
Executive Director Alaska, Deirdre Cronin
Executive Director Michigan, Sam Joseph
National Director Honduras, Jose Manuel Capellin
Executive Director New Orleans, Stacy Horn Koch
Executive Director Vancouver, Krista Thompson
SVP and Special Assistant to COO, Robert R. Cardany Jr.
SVP Program Development and Acting Executive Director Georgia, Thomas (Tom) Kennedy
SVP Administration and Human Resources, Thomas J. Potenza
President and CEO, Kevin M. Ryan
Executive Director Mexico, Sofia Almazan Argumedo
Executive Director Missouri, Suzanne Wagener
Executive Director New Jersey, Jill Rottmann
Executive Director Nicaragua (Casa Alianza Nicaragua), Grethel Lopez

Executive Director Pennsylvania, Cordella Hill
Executive Director New York, Jerry Kilbane
Executive Director Washington, Daniel J. Brannen
SVP CFO and Treasurer, Daniel C. McCarthy
SVP, Diane S. Milan
SVP Direct Marketing, Joan H.S. Dengler

LOCATIONS

HQ: Covenant House
346 W. 17th St., New York NY 10011-5002
Phone: 212-727-4000   **Fax:** 212-727-4992
Web: www.covenanthouse.org

PRODUCTS/OPERATIONS

Selected Programs & Services

Advocacy
Crisis centers
Healthcare services
Job training and education
Mother/child
Substance abuse counseling
Rights of Passage
Pastoral ministry
Nineline hotline

HISTORICAL FINANCIALS

Company Type: Private - Not-for-Profit

Income Statement

FYE: June 30

	REVENUE ($ mil.)	NET INCOME ($ mil.)	NET PROFIT MARGIN	EMPLOYEES
06/11	56	(5)	—	1,860
06/10	54	(10)	—	0
06/09	56	0	—	0
06/05	34	0	—	0
Annual Growth	18.5%	—	—	—

2011 Year-End Financials

Debt ratio: ——
Return on equity: (-9.60)%
Cash ($ mil.): 14
Current ratio: —
Long-term debt ($ mil.): —
Dividends
  Yield: —
  Payout: —
  Market value ($ mil.): —

COVENANT MEDICAL CENTER INC

Covenant Medical Center (operating as Covenant HealthCare) has made a pact with Wolverine Staters to try to keep them in good health. The healthcare provider operates more than 20 inpatient and outpatient care facilities including its two main Covenant Medical Center campuses. It serves residents in a 20-county area of east-central Michigan with additional facilities in Bay City Frankenmuth and Midland. Specialized care services include cardiovascular health cancer treatment and obstetrics. The regional health care system has more than 620 beds.

Operations

Covenant Medical Center has more than 20 inpatient and outpatient facilities and a trauma/emergency department that provides 80000 visits per year. The system employs more than 500 physicians from 52 medical specialties.

Company Background

Covenant HealthCare was formed in 1998 through the merger of Saginaw General and St. Luke's Hospitals.

EXECUTIVES

President CEO and Chief Administrative Officer, Spencer T. (Spence) Maidlow
EVP, Edward Bruff
CFO, Mark Gronda
Corporate Compliance Officer, W. Lee Morrill
VP Medical Affairs, John Kosanavich
Media Relations, Leslie Perry
Director Human Resources, Al VanArsdal

LOCATIONS

HQ: Covenant Medical Center Inc.
1447 N. Harrison St., Saginaw MI 48602
Phone: 989-583-0000   **Fax:** 989-583-6457
Web: www.covenanthealthcare.com

PRODUCTS/OPERATIONS

Selected services

Bariatrics
Birth Center
Cancer Care
Cardiology - Center for the Heart
Childbirth Classes
da Vinci Robotic Surgery
Diabetes Self-Management Program
Emergency Care Center
Imaging and Diagnostics
Neonatal Intensive Care
Neurology
Osteoporosis
Orthopaedics
Pediatrics
Physical Medicine and Rehab.
Pulmonary/Respiratory Care
Sleep Center
Surgical Services
Trauma
Urologic Surgery
Women's Health
Wound Healing Center

COMPETITORS

Genesys Health System
Genesys Regional
  Medical Center
Hurley Medical Center
McLaren Bay

McLaren Health Care
Munson Healthcare
Sparrow Health System
University of Michigan
  Health System

HISTORICAL FINANCIALS

Company Type: Private - Not-for-Profit

Income Statement

FYE: June 30

	REVENUE ($ mil.)	NET INCOME ($ mil.)	NET PROFIT MARGIN	EMPLOYEES
06/11	530	36	6.8%	3,900
06/10	508	28	5.5%	0
06/09	467	(14)	—	0
06/08	443	2	0.5%	0
Annual Growth	6.2%	160.1%	—	—

2011 Year-End Financials

Debt ratio: ——
Return on equity: 6.80%
Cash ($ mil.): 29
Current ratio: 1.50
Long-term debt ($ mil.): —

Dividends
  Yield: —
  Payout: —
  Market value ($ mil.): —

COVENANT MEDICAL CENTER INC.

LOCATIONS

HQ: COVENANT MEDICAL CENTER INC.
3421 W 9TH ST, WATERLOO, IA 50702-5401
Phone: 319-272-7296
Web: www.wheatoniowa.org

PRODUCTS/OPERATIONS

Selected services

Bariatrics
Birth Center
Cancer Care
Cardiology - Center for the Heart
Childbirth Classes
da Vinci Robotic Surgery
Diabetes Self-Management Program
Emergency Care Center
Imaging and Diagnostics
Neonatal Intensive Care
Neurology
Osteoporosis
Orthopaedics
Pediatrics
Physical Medicine and Rehab.
Pulmonary/Respiratory Care
Sleep Center
Surgical Services
Trauma
Urologic Surgery
Women's Health
Wound Healing Center

HISTORICAL FINANCIALS

Company Type: Private

Income Statement

FYE: June 30

	REVENUE ($ mil.)	NET INCOME ($ mil.)	NET PROFIT MARGIN	EMPLOYEES
06/12	253	22	8.9%	2,300
06/11	244	11	4.6%	0
06/10	238	40	16.9%	0
06/09	247	2	1.0%	0
Annual Growth	0.9%	108.5%	—	—

2012 Year-End Financials

Debt ratio: ——
Return on equity: 8.90%
Cash ($ mil.): 84
Current ratio: 4.90
Long-term debt ($ mil.): —

Dividends
  Yield: —
  Payout: —
  Market value ($ mil.): —

COVENANT RETIREMENT COMMUNITIES WEST INC

LOCATIONS

HQ: COVENANT RETIREMENT COMMUNITIES WEST INC
5700 OLD ORCHARD RD # 100, SKOKIE, IL 60077-1036
Phone: 773-878-2294
Web: www.covenantretirement.com

HISTORICAL FINANCIALS

Company Type: Private

Income Statement

FYE: January 31

	REVENUE ($ mil.)	NET INCOME ($ mil.)	NET PROFIT MARGIN	EMPLOYEES
01/11	84	6	7.8%	825
01/06	13	1	12.9%	0
01/05	160	2	1.2%	0
01/03	807	0	0.0%	0
Annual Growth	(53.0%)	2357.6%	—	—

2011 Year-End Financials

Debt ratio: ——
Return on equity: 7.80%
Cash ($ mil.): 0
Current ratio: 0.10
Long-term debt ($ mil.): —

Dividends
  Yield: —
  Payout: —
  Market value ($ mil.): —

COX OIL COMPANY INC.

LOCATIONS

HQ: COX OIL COMPANY INC.
623 PERKINS ST, UNION CITY, TN 38261-3949
Phone: 731-885-6444

HISTORICAL FINANCIALS

Company Type: Private

Income Statement

FYE: August 31

	REVENUE ($ mil.)	NET INCOME ($ mil.)	NET PROFIT MARGIN	EMPLOYEES
08/11	147	1	0.7%	435
08/10	125	0	0.6%	0
08/09	112	0	0.4%	0
08/08	124	15	12.2%	0
Annual Growth	5.7%	(59.5%)	—	—

2011 Year-End Financials

Debt ratio: ——
Return on equity: 0.70%
Cash ($ mil.): 3
Current ratio: 0.70
Long-term debt ($ mil.): —

Dividends
  Yield: —
  Payout: —
  Market value ($ mil.): —

CREATIVE GROUP INC.

Creative Group has devoted its energy towards business improvement. The company provides a variety of marketing services specializing in building and managing incentive programs and planning corporate meetings and events. The company's incentive programs target sales reseller and employees offering travel merchandise and gift certificates as rewards for good performance. Creative Group also offers personal travel services including travel planning and emergency services that benefit from the company's large corporate travel business. Clients have included Abbott Laboratories Mutual of Omaha and Johnson Controls. The company which has offices in Wisconsin and Illinois was founded in 1970.

EXECUTIVES

CFO, Martin Van Stippen
Chairman and CEO, Ronald D. Officer
President and COO, Brad Langley
SVP Sales, Janet Traphagen

LOCATIONS

HQ: Creative Group Inc.
619 N. Lynndale Dr., Appleton WI 54914
Phone: 920-739-8850   **Fax:** 920-739-8817
Web: www.creativegroupinc.com

COMPETITORS

Alcone Marketing	ITAGroup
All Star Incentive	Pitney Bowes Marketing
Marketing	Solutions
Balboa Travel	Schoeneckers
CA Short	

HISTORICAL FINANCIALS

Company Type: Private

Income Statement   FYE: September 30

	REVENUE ($ mil.)	NET INCOME ($ mil.)	NET PROFIT MARGIN	EMPLOYEES
09/11	80	0	—	173
09/10	80	0	—	0
09/09	80	0	—	0
09/08	80	0	—	0
Annual Growth	(0.0%)	—	—	—

2011 Year-End Financials

Debt ratio: ——
Return on equity: —
Cash ($ mil.): 4
Current ratio: 0.90
Long-term debt ($ mil.): —

Dividends
Yield: —
Payout: —
Market value ($ mil.): —

CREATIVE MANAGEMENT INC

LOCATIONS

HQ: CREATIVE MANAGEMENT INC
935 ROUTE 34 STE 3A, MATAWAN, NJ 07747-3282
Phone: 732-696-2201

HISTORICAL FINANCIALS

Company Type: Private

Income Statement   FYE: December 31

	REVENUE ($ mil.)	NET INCOME ($ mil.)	NET PROFIT MARGIN	EMPLOYEES
12/11	532	1	0.3%	50
12/98	4	0	2.4%	0
Annual Growth	12002.1%	1436.4%	—	—

2011 Year-End Financials

Debt ratio: ——
Return on equity: 0.30%
Cash ($ mil.): 3
Current ratio: 0.80
Long-term debt ($ mil.): —

Dividends
Yield: —
Payout: —
Market value ($ mil.): —

CREIGHTON ALEGENT HEALTH

Alegent Creighton Health (formerly Alegent Health) pledges allegiance to medical wellbeing in its corner of the Midwest. The not-for-profit health care system operates ten full-service hospitals with about 1500 beds in Omaha and surrounding communities in eastern Nebraska and southwestern Iowa including Bergan Mercy Medical Center and Immanuel Medical Center. Alegent Creighton Health's hospitals provide specialty services including cardiovascular orthopedic and cancer care; it also operates psychiatric retirement housing home health and outpatient centers. The health system is sponsored by Catholic Health Initiatives and Immanuel Healthcare System and is affiliated with Creighton University.

The company changed its name to Alegent Creighton Health in 2012 after it acquired the 400-bed Creighton University Medical Center (CUMC) in Omaha from its former owners Tenet Healthcare (which owned 74% of CUMC) and Creighton University (26%) for around $60 million to expand its hospital network and educational programs. Alegent Creighton Health already provided a number of academic programs in partnership with the university in areas such as psychiatry women's health nursing and pharmacy; through the purchase the company became the primary provider of teaching locations for the Creighton University School of Medicine.

In addition to CUMC the transaction with Tenet and Creighton University added a physician practice organization Creighton Medical Associates (CMA) which was combined with the Alegent Health Clinic organization under the new Alegent Creighton Health Clinics name. The facilities pro-

vide primary care via a network of doctors in Omaha and surrounding areas. There are also two Express Care clinics that offer urgent care for non-life-threatening ailments and six Quick Care clinics in Omaha (located in Hy-Vee retail stores) that provide minor medical ailment treatment as well as sports physicals and vaccinations. The idea behind the clinics is to divert patients who might otherwise end up at ERs with non-emergency symptoms (thus lowering hospital expenses).

In addition to expanding its facilities the transaction also helped Alegent Creighton create a more unified regional health network that will be better able to compete and thrive in the changing US health care landscape. The purchase of CUMC and CMA as well as the stronger alliance with Creighton University will have a direct impact on Alegent Creighton Health's long-term goal of providing meaningful quality care and integrated health management services —while simultaneously lowering medical expenses —within its regional service territories.

Alegent Creighton Health is a joint venture between Catholic Health Initiatives which counts the Sisters of Mercy of Omaha among its sponsors and the Immanuel Healthcare System an organization sponsored by the Nebraska Synod of the Evangelical Lutheran Church in America. Alegent Creighton Health was formed in 1996 when Immanuel Medical Center and Bergan Mercy Medical Center chose to join forces. In 2012 however Immanuel Healthcare System agreed to transfer full sponsorship duties of Alegent Creighton Health to CHI.

EXECUTIVES

President CEO and Director, Richard A. (Rick) Hachten II
SVP Strategy and Technology, Ken Lawonn
SVP and CFO, Scott Wooten
Chairman, Leslie R. Andersen
Secretary Treasurer and Director, Anthony L. Hatcher
Chairman, John C. Hewitt
Director Operations Public Relations, Kelly Grinnell
Communications Strategist, Jodi Hoatson
SVP and COO, Joan Neuhaus
Communications Specialist, Jennifer Homann
Vice Chairman, Michael T. DeFreece
General Counsel, Charles Sederstrom
SVP; President and CEO Alegent Creighton Clinic, Richard Rolston
SVP and Chief Quality Officer, Richard Miller
President CEO and Director, Richard A. (Rick) Hachten II
Director, Leslie R. Andersen
Director, Paul W. Edgett III
Secretary Treasurer and Director, Anthony L. Hatcher
Vice Chairman, John C. Hewitt
Director, Martin Mancuso
Director, Sister Lillian Murphy
Director, Richard J. Vierk
Vice Chairman, Michael T. DeFreece
Director, Eric N. Gurley
Director, Guillermo Huerta
Director, H. Keith Schmode

LOCATIONS

HQ: Alegent Creighton Health
12809 W. Dodge Rd., Omaha NE 68154
Phone: 402-343-4300   **Fax:** 513-682-8602
Web: www.totes-isotoner.com

PRODUCTS/OPERATIONS

Selected Facilities and Operations

Alegent Creighton Health Clinics (primary care multiple locations in Iowa and Nebraska)

Alegent Creighton Health Express Care clinics (urgent care two locations in Nebraska)

Alegent Creighton Health Quick Care (minor care clinics; six locations in Omaha Nebraska in Hy-Vee stores)

Alegent Health at Home (home health care)

Bergan Mercy Medical Center (Omaha Nebraska; 300 beds)

Community Memorial Hospital (Missouri Valley Iowa; 20 beds)

Creighton University Medical Center (Omaha Nebraska; 400 beds)

Immanuel Communities (independent and assisted living in Omaha and Lincoln)

Immanuel Fontenelle (nursing home in Omaha)

Immanuel Medical Center (Omaha Nebraska; 280 beds)

Lakeside Hospital (Omaha Nebraska; 160 beds)

Lasting Hope Recovery Center (Omaha Nebraska; psychiatric hospital with 120 beds)

Memorial Community Hospital (minority owned; Blair Nebraska; 25 beds)

Memorial Hospital (Schuyler Nebraska; 25 beds)

Mercy Corning Hospital (Corning Iowa; 20 beds)

Mercy Hospital (Council Bluffs Iowa; 160 beds)

Midlands Hospital (Papillion Nebraska; 50 beds)

COMPETITORS

BryanLGH Medical Center
Children's Hospital & Medical Center
Fremont Area Medical Center
Heartland Health
Iowa Health System
Madonna Rehabilitation Hospital
Mercy Health Network
Methodist Health System
Nebraska medical center
Saint Elizabeth Regional Medical Center
Tenet Healthcare
UNMC Physicians

HISTORICAL FINANCIALS

Company Type: Joint Venture

Income Statement

FYE: June 30

	REVENUE ($ mil.)	NET INCOME ($ mil.)	NET PROFIT MARGIN	EMPLOYEES
06/11	262	26	10.2%	8,600
06/10	285	23	8.4%	0
06/09	3	0	—	0
06/08	5	(0)	—	0
Annual Growth	268.7%	—		—

2011 Year-End Financials

Debt ratio: ——
Return on equity: 10.20%
Cash ($ mil.): 25
Current ratio: 0.10
Long-term debt ($ mil.): —

Dividends
Yield: —
Payout: —
Market value ($ mil.): —

CREIGHTON UNIVERSITY

Consistently ranked among the top universities in the Midwest Creighton University is a Jesuit Catholic university with an enrollment of approximately 7500 undergraduate graduate and professional students. With a student-to-faculty ratio of 11-to-1 it offers more than 70 majors through nine schools and colleges including colleges of arts and sciences business law medicine dentistry pharmacy and nursing. Its 108-acre campus is adjacent to the downtown business district of Omaha Nebraska. Creighton University was founded in 1878 and named after Omaha businessman Edward Creighton.

In addition to teaching about 200 international students from about 45 countries at its Omaha campus Creighton University offers hands-on service and learning programs in the Dominican Republic and the Middle East. It also has international affiliate or exchange programs with institutions in about 55 countries.

The university also has a long history of providing medical education. Many of its on-site medical training programs programs are provided at the facilities of medical care provider Alegent Creighton Health (formerly Alegent Health). Creighton University strengthened its partnership with the health network in 2012 when it sold its 26% stake in the 400-bed Creighton University Medical Center (CUMC) in Omaha to Alegent. (Tenet Healthcare owned a majority stake in the hospital which was also acquired by Alegent.) The transaction also made Alegent's network of care centers the primary teaching sites for Creighton University's School of Medicine and other health-related schools.

Creighton University already partnered with Alegent on a number of health-related professional education programs prior to the deal and the university believes that its students will benefit from the expanded relationship with Alegent. In addition CUMC has been recognized for its cancer and bone disease research programs and the university's extensive medical research programs will continue in partnership with Alegent Health. Creighton University also has a partnership with the St. Joseph's Hospital and Medical Center in Phoenix Arizona.

EXECUTIVES

Vice Chairman, Bruce C. Rohde, age 63
President and Director, Rev John P. Schlegel
SVP Operations and Treasurer, Daniel E. Burkey
Controller, Michael A. Pille
VP Information Technology, Brian A. Young
VP Student Services and Dean Students, John C. Cernech
VP University Relations, Lisa D. Calvert
Senior General Counsel and Corporate Secretary, Greg D. Jahn
VP University Ministry, Rev Andrew F. Alexander
Director Career Center, Jim Bretl
Dean College of Business Administration, Anthony R. Hendrickson
Director Budget, Fred J. Nesler
Assistant VP Public Relations and Marketing, Kim B. Manning
Assistant VP Alumni Relations, Diane H. Dougherty Crowley
VP Institutional Relations, Patricia R. (Pat) Callone
Senior Associate VP Development and Campaign Director, Laura C. Simic
CEO Creighton Medical Associates, Todd Carlon
VP Academic Affairs and Interim Dean School of Law, Patrick J. Borchers
VP Health Services, Donald R. Frey
Associate VP Enrollment Management, Mary E. Chase
Director Environmental Health and Safety, John T. Baxter
University Registrar, John A. Krecek
Dean University College and Summer Sessions, Barbara J. Braden
Dean College of Arts and Sciences, Robert J. Lueger

Director Financial Aid, Robert D. Walker
Associate VP Faculty Development and Dean Graduate School, Gail M. Jensen
Dean School of Dentistry, Wayne W. Barkmeier
Dean School of Medicine, Rowen K. Zetterman
Dean School of Nursing, Eleanor V. Howell
Dean School of Pharmacy and Health Professions, J. Christopher Bradberry
Director Purchasing, Joseph J. Zaborowski
Associate VP Administration and Director Operational Planning, John L. Wilhelm
Director Human Resources, Jeffrey C. Branstetter
VP for General Counsel, Amy S. Bones
VP Research, Robert P. Heaney
Chairman, William A. Fitzgerald
Vice Chairman, Bruce C. Rohde, age 63
Director, James R. (Jim) Young, age 59
Director, Mogens C. Bay, age 63
Director, Patrick J. (Pat) Zenner, age 64
Director, Ronald B. (Ron) Gartlan
Director, W. Gary Gates, age 61
Director, Jane E. Miller, age 47
Director, Mark H. Rauenhorst, age 59
Director, Bruce E. Grewcock, age 57
Director, Joseph H. (Joe) Moglia, age 62
Director, George F. Haddix, age 73
Director, Michael R. (Mike) McCarthy, age 61
Director, Alan D. Simon
Director, Daniel P. (Dan) Neary, age 60
Director, Howard L. Hawks
Director, Robert A. Reed Sr.
Director, Richard T. (Dick) Kizer
President and Director, Rev John P. Schlegel
Director, Floyd J. Malveaux
Director, Rev Ned H. Cassem
Director, Mary E. Walton Conti
Director, Mimi A. Feller
Director, Frank L. Hayes
Director, Mark D. Huber
Director, Susan M. Jacques
Director, Melissa C. Kean
Director, Michael E. Kelly
Director, Rev Peter J. Klink
Director, Terry J. Kroeger
Director, Bruce R. Lauritzen
Director, Deborah A. Macdonald
Director, Chris J. Murphy
Director, Rev Roc O'Connor
Director, Rev Philip J. Rossi
Director, Constance M. Ryan
Director, Rev Gerard L. Stockhausen
Director, Gail Werner-Robertson
Auditors: Deloitte&ToucheLLP

LOCATIONS

HQ: Creighton University
2500 California Plaza, Omaha NE 68178
Phone: 402-280-2700   **Fax:** 402-280-2549
Web: www.creighton.edu

HISTORICAL FINANCIALS

Company Type: School

Income Statement

FYE: June 30

	REVENUE ($ mil.)	NET INCOME ($ mil.)	NET PROFIT MARGIN	EMPLOYEES
06/12	419	(28)	—	5,000
06/11	414	79	19.2%	0
06/10	405	36	8.9%	0
06/09	392	(79)	—	0
Annual Growth	2.2%	—		—

2012 Year-End Financials

Debt ratio: —
Return on equity: (-6.80)%
Cash ($ mil.): 32
Current ratio: —
Long-term debt ($ mil.): —
Dividends
Yield: —
Payout: —
Market value ($ mil.): —

CROSSLAND CONSTRUCTION COMPANY INC.

Crossland Construction has crossed the prairie going from a local player in Columbus Kansas to a firm with a strong regional base. The company designs builds and manages construction of government education healthcare retail and other buildings from four offices in Kansas Arkansas Oklahoma and Texas. Customers have included Harley-Davidson SAM'S CLUB McCune Brooks Hospital Embassy Suites and a variety of school districts and municipalities. Crossland builds everything from office buildings and warehouses to veteran's memorials and airports. The company which often works in partnership with PBA Architects was founded by Ivan Crossland Sr. in 1978.

Crossland Construction ensures it will always have a solid workforce by investing in education at two levels. The company's Crossland Academy offers current employees the chance to earn certificates in concrete welding heavy equipment operation and storm water protection in addition to a complete curriculum laid out by the National Center for Construction Education and Research (NCCER). Its Crossland Connection program helps elementary through high school students learn about careers in construction. High school students are offered the same NCCER curriculum as employees to prepare for a trade apprenticeship or to enter a college construction trades program.

EXECUTIVES

CEO, Ivan Crossland Jr.
President, Bennie Crossland
VP Texas Division, Mike Crossland
VP Design/Build Division, Curt Crossland
VP Business Development and Real Estate, Christopher Crossland
VP Special Projects, Patrick Crossland

LOCATIONS

HQ: Crossland Construction Company Inc.
833 S. East Ave., Columbus KS 66725
Phone: 620-429-1414   **Fax:** 620-429-1412
Web: www.crosslandconstruction.com

PRODUCTS/OPERATIONS

Selected Areas of Work

Distribution Centers
Educational
Healthcare
Hospitality
Meeting Spaces
Municipal
Office
Retail
Sporting Facilities

COMPETITORS

Austin Commercial
Austin Industries
Baldwin & Shell
C.F. Jordan
Cadence McShane
CDI Contractors
Dean Word
Fluor
Gilbane Building Company
Harvey Builders
JC General Contractors
KBR
Spawglass Holding
Structure Tone Southwest
Tellepsen Builders
Turner Construction
W.S. Bellows

CROZER-KEYSTONE HEALTH SYSTEM

Crozer-Keystone Health System provides a full range of health care in the Philadelphia metropolitan area. The health system's facilities include five acute care hospitals four outpatient care centers and a sports science and technology center. Combined its not-for-profit member hospitals have about 840 beds. The hospitals' specialty units include trauma cardiac cancer orthopedic wound healing obesity sleep disorder and women's and children's health centers. The system also operates family occupational and diagnostic health clinics as well as home health and hospice agencies.

Geographic Reach

Crozer-Keystone Health System serves residents of Delaware County Pennsylvania and portions of northern Delaware and western New Jersey.

Operations

The Crozer-Keystone Health System's five hospitals include Community Hospital Crozer-Chester Medical Center Delaware County Memorial Hospital Springfield Hospital and Taylor Hospital. The health system's medical staff —consisting of about 1100 physicians and 3000 nurses –provides wellness and preventative care acute and long-term care and rehabilitative and restorative care. Altogether its hospitals handle some 140000 emergency room visits per year.

The system's subsidiary hospitals educate future physicians through residencies in family practice internal medicine women's health pediatrics and a variety of osteopathic and allied health training programs. Most residency training takes place at the 460-bed Crozer-Chester Medical Center through the system's affiliation with the Temple University Medical School. Crozer-Keystone residents are able to use the system's facilities as well as those of its educational affiliates as they train.

Strategy

In 2011 the health system adopted what is known as a "medical home" model in an effort to develop strong patient relationships. The model engages primary care practices to serve as central sources for all of a patient's health care needs by coordinating with specialists maintaining electronic medical records and prompting follow-up visits.

Crozer-Keystone also partners with other area providers and charitable organizations to conduct community outreach and medical research programs.

Company Background

Crozer-Keystone was created in 1990 through the partnership of Delaware County Memorial Hospital Springfield Hospital and Crozer-Chester Medical Center. Later Sacred Heart Hospital joined the system and was renamed Community Hospital. Then came Springfield Hospital and the system's newest member Taylor Hospital which joined the system in 1997.

EXECUTIVES

President and CEO, Joan K. Richards
COO, Richard I. Bennett
VP Public Relations and Marketing, Kathy Scullin
Director Public Relations and Marketing, Grant Gegwich
VP Quality and Patient, Eric Dobkin
Assistant Director of Public Relations and Marketing, Katie Stier
Auditors: PricewaterhouseCoopersLLP

LOCATIONS

HQ: Crozer-Keystone Health System
100 W. Sproul Rd. Pavillion 2, Springfield PA 19064
Phone: 610-328-8200   **Fax:** 610-447-2820
Web: www.crozer.org

PRODUCTS/OPERATIONS

Selected Facilities in Pennsylvania

Hospitals
  Community Hospital (Chester)
  Crozer-Chester Medical Center (Upland)
  Delaware County Memorial Hospital (Drexel Hill)
  Springfield Hospital (Springfield)
  Taylor Hospital (Ridley Park)
Outpatient Centers
  Crozer Brinton Lake (Glen Mills)
    Crozer Health Pavilion at Brinton Lake
    Crozer Medical Plaza at Brinton Lake
    Crozer-Keystone Cancer Center at Brinton Lake
  Delaware County Memorial Hospital (DCMH) Health Pavilion (Drexel Hill)
  Media Medical Plaza (Media)
  Philadelphia CyberKnife
Sports Club
  The Healthplex Sports Club (Springfield)
Other Facilities
  Centers for Occupational Health
  Community Health and Wellness Services
  Crozer-Keystone Health Network of Physicians

COMPETITORS

Abington Memorial Hospital
Albert Einstein Healthcare Network
AtlantiCare
Children' s Hospital of Philadelphia
Christiana Care
Doylestown Hospital
Jefferson Health System
Johns Hopkins Health System
Lancaster General

HISTORICAL FINANCIALS

Company Type: Private

Income Statement

FYE: July 31

	REVENUE ($ mil.)	NET INCOME ($ mil.)	NET PROFIT MARGIN	EMPLOYEES
07/11	363	2	0.6%	715
07/08	434	10	2.4%	0
07/07	336	11	3.4%	0
07/04	176	2	1.3%	0
Annual Growth	27.3%	(4.7%)	—	—

2011 Year-End Financials

Debt ratio: —
Return on equity: 0.60%
Cash ($ mil.): 34
Current ratio: 1.10
Long-term debt ($ mil.): —
Dividends
Yield: —
Payout: —
Market value ($ mil.): —

Lehigh Valley Health Network
Memorial Hospital (PA)
Mercy Health System
North Philadelphia Health System
Shore Memorial Hospital
South Jersey Healthcare
TUHS
University of Maryland Medical System
University of Pennsylvania Health System
Virtua Health

HISTORICAL FINANCIALS

Company Type: Private - Not-for-Profit

Income Statement

FYE: June 30

	REVENUE ($ mil.)	NET INCOME ($ mil.)	NET PROFIT MARGIN	EMPLOYEES
06/11	52	2	5.6%	7,100
06/10	50	0	1.6%	0
06/09	49	(1)		0
06/08	51	0	1.8%	0
Annual Growth	0.8%	46.8%	—	—

2011 Year-End Financials

Debt ratio: ——
Return on equity: 5.60%
Cash ($ mil.): 19
Current ratio: 0.20
Long-term debt ($ mil.): —

Dividends
Yield: —
Payout: —
Market value ($ mil.): —

CRYSTAL FINISHING SYSTEMS INC.

LOCATIONS

HQ: CRYSTAL FINISHING SYSTEMS INC.
2610 ROSS AVE, SCHOFIELD, WI 54476-1864
Phone: 715-355-5351

HISTORICAL FINANCIALS

Company Type: Private

Income Statement

FYE: September 30

	REVENUE ($ mil.)	NET INCOME ($ mil.)	NET PROFIT MARGIN	EMPLOYEES
09/11*	86	2	2.5%	520
06/10	0	0		0
09/08	74	0	0.1%	0
05/02	6	0	5.2%	0
Annual Growth	136.2%	84.5%	—	—

*Fiscal year change

2011 Year-End Financials

Debt ratio: ——
Return on equity: 2.50%
Cash ($ mil.): 0
Current ratio: 0.70
Long-term debt ($ mil.): —

Dividends
Yield: —
Payout: —
Market value ($ mil.): —

CRYSTAL STAIRS INC.

LOCATIONS

HQ: CRYSTAL STAIRS INC.
5110 W GOLDLEAF CIR # 150, LOS ANGELES, CA 90056-1282
Phone: 323-299-8998
Web: www.crystalstairs.org

HISTORICAL FINANCIALS

Company Type: Private

Income Statement

FYE: June 30

	REVENUE ($ mil.)	NET INCOME ($ mil.)	NET PROFIT MARGIN	EMPLOYEES
06/11	109	0	0.6%	356
06/10	124	0	0.0%	0
Annual Growth	(12.4%)	1164.0%	—	—

2011 Year-End Financials

Debt ratio: ——
Return on equity: 0.60%
Cash ($ mil.): 2
Current ratio: 0.20
Long-term debt ($ mil.): —

Dividends
Yield: —
Payout: —
Market value ($ mil.): —

CUBIX LATIN AMERICA LLC

LOCATIONS

HQ: CUBIX LATIN AMERICA LLC
2841 NW 107TH AVE, DORAL, FL 33172-2130
Phone: 305-599-2742

HISTORICAL FINANCIALS

Company Type: Private

Income Statement

FYE: December 31

	REVENUE ($ mil.)	NET INCOME ($ mil.)	NET PROFIT MARGIN	EMPLOYEES
12/11	129	1	1.1%	31
12/10	96	1	1.1%	0
12/09	119	1	1.2%	0
12/08	98	1	1.1%	0
Annual Growth	9.6%	8.1%	—	—

2011 Year-End Financials

Debt ratio: ——
Return on equity: 1.10%
Cash ($ mil.): 3
Current ratio: 1.10
Long-term debt ($ mil.): —

Dividends
Yield: —
Payout: —
Market value ($ mil.): —

CULLMAN ELECTRIC COOPERATIVE

LOCATIONS

HQ: CULLMAN ELECTRIC COOPERATIVE
1749 EVA RD NE, CULLMAN, AL 35055-6031
Phone: 256-737-3200
Web: www.cullmanec.com

HISTORICAL FINANCIALS

Company Type: Private

Income Statement

FYE: June 30

	REVENUE ($ mil.)	NET INCOME ($ mil.)	NET PROFIT MARGIN	EMPLOYEES
06/12	107	6	5.8%	90
06/11	108	9	8.7%	0
06/10	94	4	4.5%	0
06/09	99	3	3.7%	0
Annual Growth	2.4%	18.6%	—	—

2012 Year-End Financials

Debt ratio: ——
Return on equity: 5.80%
Cash ($ mil.): 10
Current ratio: 0.90
Long-term debt ($ mil.): —

Dividends
Yield: —
Payout: —
Market value ($ mil.): —

CULLMAN REGIONAL MEDICAL CENTER INC.

LOCATIONS

HQ: CULLMAN REGIONAL MEDICAL CENTER INC.
1912 AL HIGHWAY 157, CULLMAN, AL 35058-0609
Phone: 256-737-2741
Web: www.crmchospital.com

HISTORICAL FINANCIALS

Company Type: Private

Income Statement

FYE: June 30

	REVENUE ($ mil.)	NET INCOME ($ mil.)	NET PROFIT MARGIN	EMPLOYEES
06/11	96	(2)	—	1,006
06/10	124	5	4.8%	0
06/09	89	(5)	—	0
06/08	102	(3)	—	0
Annual Growth	(2.0%)	—	—	—

2011 Year-End Financials

Debt ratio: ——
Return on equity: (-2.30)%
Cash ($ mil.): 1
Current ratio: 0.20
Long-term debt ($ mil.): —

Dividends
Yield: —
Payout: —
Market value ($ mil.): —

CUMBERLAND COUNTY SCHOOLS

LOCATIONS

HQ: CUMBERLAND COUNTY SCHOOLS
2465 GILLESPIE ST, FAYETTEVILLE, NC 28306-3053
Phone: 910-678-2300

HISTORICAL FINANCIALS
Company Type: Private

Income Statement
FYE: June 30

	REVENUE ($ mil.)	NET INCOME ($ mil.)	NET PROFIT MARGIN	EMPLOYEES
06/11	444	3	0.8%	6,210
06/09	454	0	0.1%	0
06/06	0	0	—	0
06/05	0	0	—	0
Annual Growth	—	—		

2011 Year-End Financials
Debt ratio: ——
Return on equity: 0.80%
Cash ($ mil.): 69
Current ratio: ——
Long-term debt ($ mil.): —

Dividends
Yield: —
Payout: —
Market value ($ mil.): —

CUNNINGHAM HOLDINGS LLC

LOCATIONS

HQ: CUNNINGHAM HOLDINGS LLC
41707 WINCHESTER RD # 206, TEMECULA, CA
92590-4867
Phone: 877-329-3835
Web: www.apexfuels.com

HISTORICAL FINANCIALS
Company Type: Private

Income Statement
FYE: December 31

	REVENUE ($ mil.)	NET INCOME ($ mil.)	NET PROFIT MARGIN	EMPLOYEES
12/11	303	3	1.0%	11
Annual Growth	—	—	—	—

2011 Year-End Financials
Debt ratio: ——
Return on equity: 1.00%
Cash ($ mil.): 6
Current ratio: 1.70
Long-term debt ($ mil.): —

Dividends
Yield: —
Payout: —
Market value ($ mil.): —

D'ARRIGO BROS CO OF NEW YORK INC

LOCATIONS

HQ: D' ARRIGO BROS CO OF NEW YORK INC
315 ROW C HUNTS POINT TER, BRONX, NY 10474
Phone: 718-991-5900
Web: www.darrigony.com

HISTORICAL FINANCIALS
Company Type: Private

Income Statement
FYE: April 30

	REVENUE ($ mil.)	NET INCOME ($ mil.)	NET PROFIT MARGIN	EMPLOYEES
04/12	179	1	0.8%	205
04/11	0	0	—	0
04/10	165	1	0.8%	0
04/09	181	1	0.6%	0
Annual Growth	(0.3%)	13.5%		

2012 Year-End Financials
Debt ratio: ——
Return on equity: 0.80%
Cash ($ mil.): 4
Current ratio: 1.30
Long-term debt ($ mil.): —

Dividends
Yield: —
Payout: —
Market value ($ mil.): —

D-PATRICK INC.

LOCATIONS

HQ: D-PATRICK INC.
200 N GREEN RIVER RD, EVANSVILLE, IN
47715-2486
Phone: 812-473-6500
Web: www.dpat.com

HISTORICAL FINANCIALS
Company Type: Private

Income Statement
FYE: June 30

	REVENUE ($ mil.)	NET INCOME ($ mil.)	NET PROFIT MARGIN	EMPLOYEES
06/12	145	0	0.5%	250
06/11	128	0	0.4%	0
06/07	118	0	0.4%	0
06/06	115	0	0.2%	0
Annual Growth	8.0%	39.7%	—	—

2012 Year-End Financials
Debt ratio: ——
Return on equity: 0.50%
Cash ($ mil.): 2
Current ratio: 0.20
Long-term debt ($ mil.): —

Dividends
Yield: —
Payout: —
Market value ($ mil.): —

D. C. TAYLOR CO.

D. C. Taylor is one of the largest commercial and industrial roofing contractors in the US providing roof installation repair and maintenance services. It has some 60 service and roofing crews that operate from offices in Arizona California Georgia Illinois and Iowa. Dudley C. Taylor started Taylor Tuckpointing a tuckpointing (cosmetic brick finishing commonly found on Federation houses and Californian bungalows) and masonry repair company in Chicago in 1949; the company's name was changed to D. C. Taylor in 1954 and the firm was formally incorporated in 1960. Chairman and CEO Bill Taylor is the company's majority shareholder.

EXECUTIVES

Chairman and CEO, William W. (Bill) Taylor
President and COO, Philip J. (Phil) Suess
VP Preferred Accounts, Todd M. Kaska
VP and Regional Manager West Service Area, Bo Meyersieck
VP Operations, Gary S. Rickert
VP Regional Operations, Brian Higgins
VP Contract Administration, Greg Thirnbeck
Manager IT, Rob Moore
VP Business Development, Eric Hasselbusch
Director Environmental Health and Safety, Brad Richardson
Assistant VP Purchasing, Bob Pence
Director Human Resources, Jessica Dungan
Operations Manager Southwest Service Area, Pete Butch
Secretary and Treasurer, Jenny Steuri

LOCATIONS

HQ: D. C. Taylor Co.
312 29th St. NE, Cedar Rapids IA 52406
Phone: 319-363-2073   **Fax:** 319-363-8311
Web: www.dctaylorco.com

COMPETITORS

CentiMark	Pickens Roofing
Duro-Last Roofing	Tecta America
Holland Roofing	THL Enterprises

HISTORICAL FINANCIALS
Company Type: Private

Income Statement
FYE: December 31

	REVENUE ($ mil.)	NET INCOME ($ mil.)	NET PROFIT MARGIN	EMPLOYEES
12/11	41	0	1.1%	350
12/10	40	1	4.7%	0
12/09	8	1	14.8%	0
12/08	56	2	4.1%	0
Annual Growth	(9.6%)	(41.5%)	—	—

2011 Year-End Financials
Debt ratio: ——
Return on equity: 1.10%
Cash ($ mil.): 0
Current ratio: 0.10
Long-term debt ($ mil.): —

Dividends
Yield: —
Payout: —
Market value ($ mil.): —

D.E.W. CONSTRUCTION CORP.

LOCATIONS

HQ: D.E.W. CONSTRUCTION CORP.
277 BLAIR PARK RD STE 130, WILLISTON, VT
05495-7885
Phone: 802-872-0505
Web: www.dewcorp.com

HISTORICAL FINANCIALS
Company Type: Private

Income Statement
FYE: December 31

	REVENUE ($ mil.)	NET INCOME ($ mil.)	NET PROFIT MARGIN	EMPLOYEES
12/11	149	2	1.3%	165
12/10	58	0	1.3%	0
12/09	77	0	0.8%	0
12/08	60	0	1.0%	0
Annual Growth	35.3%	49.1%	—	—

2011 Year-End Financials
Debt ratio: —
Return on equity: 1.30%
Cash ($ mil.): 8
Current ratio: 1.10
Long-term debt ($ mil.): —
Dividends
Yield: —
Payout: —
Market value ($ mil.): —

D/L COOPERATIVE INC.

Yes the farmer takes a wife then hi-ho the dairy-o the farmer takes membership in milk-marketing organizations such as Dairylea Cooperative. Owned by more than 2000 dairy farmers in the northeastern US Dairylea processes and markets 6 billion pounds of milk for its farmers annually to dairy-product customers including food manufacturers. Its Agri-Services holding company provides members with a full range of financial and farm-management services as well as insurance. Its Empire Livestock Marketing unit operates regional livestock auction locations. Dairylea established in 1907 by New York dairy farmers has a joint marketing venture (Dairy Marketing Services or DMS) with Dairy Farmers of America.

Through its DMS partnership with Dairy Farmers of America Dairylea sells and distributes raw milk. DMS serves both organizations as well as independent producers and cooperatives that produce 16 billion pounds of milk each year.

EXECUTIVES

CEO, Gregory I. (Greg) Wickham
Chairman and President, Clyde E. Rutherford
CFO and Director Human Resources, Edward Bangel
VP Finance, Ellen Gall
Second VP Board of Directors and Secretary, William Beeman
Treasurer and Director, David R. Chamberlain
First VP Board of Directors, Raymond J. Diebold
Assistant Treasurer and Director, Calvin Wood
Public Relations, Jennifer Huson

Media Contact, Karen Cartier
COO Dairy Marketing Services, Brad Keating
Second VP Board of Directors and Secretary, William Beeman
Treasurer and Director, David R. Chamberlain
First VP Board of Directors, Raymond J. Diebold
Assistant Treasurer and Director, Calvin Wood
Director, Todd Hathorn
Director, G. Douglas Young
Director, James Madigan
Director, Sanford Stauffer
Director, Glen Gasstrom
Director, Lawrence Woodruff Jr.
Director, Edgar A. King
Director, Dale Van Erden
Director, Arnold Dueppengiesser
Director, Donald Risser
Director, Richard Baldwin

LOCATIONS

HQ: Dairylea Cooperative Inc.
5001 Brittonfield Pkwy., East Syracuse NY 13057
Phone: 315-433-0100   **Fax:** 417-885-9252
Web: www.aeci.org

PRODUCTS/OPERATIONS

Selected Affiliates & Subsidiaries
Agri-Edge Development
Agri-Max Financial Services
Agri-Services Agency
Dairy Risk Management Services
Eagle Dairy Direct
Empire Livestock Marketing Services

COMPETITORS
Agri-Mark
Associated Milk Producers
Dairy Farmers of America
Dean Foods
Foremost Farms
Garelick Farms
Keller' s Creamery
Land O' Lakes
Maryland & Virginia Milk Producers
Quality Chekd

HISTORICAL FINANCIALS
Company Type: Private - Cooperative

Income Statement
FYE: March 31

	REVENUE ($ mil.)	NET INCOME ($ mil.)	NET PROFIT MARGIN	EMPLOYEES
03/12	1,584	2	0.1%	107
03/11	1,333	1	0.1%	0
03/10	1,066	1	0.1%	0
03/09	1,201	1	0.2%	0
Annual Growth	9.7%	3.6%	—	—

2012 Year-End Financials
Debt ratio: —
Return on equity: 0.10%
Cash ($ mil.): 39
Current ratio: 0.60
Long-term debt ($ mil.): —
Dividends
Yield: —
Payout: —
Market value ($ mil.): —

DAEHAN SOLUTION ALABAMA L.L.C.

LOCATIONS

HQ: DAEHAN SOLUTION ALABAMA L.L.C.
9101 COUNTY ROAD 26, HOPE HULL, AL 36043-6222
Phone: 334-404-5000

HISTORICAL FINANCIALS
Company Type: Private

Income Statement
FYE: December 31

	REVENUE ($ mil.)	NET INCOME ($ mil.)	NET PROFIT MARGIN	EMPLOYEES
12/11	95	0	1.0%	228
12/10	88	1	1.3%	0
Annual Growth	8.3%	(16.0%)	—	—

2011 Year-End Financials
Debt ratio: —
Return on equity: 1.00%
Cash ($ mil.): 2
Current ratio: 0.40
Long-term debt ($ mil.): —
Dividends
Yield: —
Payout: —
Market value ($ mil.): —

DAEMEN COLLEGE

Daemen College is a private liberal arts university located in Amherst New York. The college offers more than than three dozen undergraduate major programs about 15 graduate and accelerated courses of study and a handful of professional certifications. It has an enrollment of about 3000 students and a student-faculty ratio of 15:1. The school was established in 1947 as Rosary Hill College by the Sisters of St. Francis of Penance and Christian Charity whose founder was Magdalene Daemen a Dutch woman dedicated to working with the poor. Originally a liberal arts college for women Daemen became coeducational in 1971.

EXECUTIVES

President, Martin J. Anisman
VP Business Affairs and Treasurer, Robert C. Beiswanger Jr.
Director Financial Aid, Jeffrey M. Pagano
Director Personnel, Pamela R. Neumann
President Wel, Edwin G. Clausen
Controller and Assistant Treasurer, Michael Looker
Director Cooperative Education and Career Development, Maureen E. Huber
Director College Relations, Michael G. Andrei
Director Information Technology Services, James J. Bachraty
Director Annual Giving and Alumni Relations, Shawn Schlifke
Dean Enrollment Management, Patricia Ruppert Brown
VP External Affairs, David A. Cristantello
VP Student Affairs and Dean Students, Richanne C. Mankey
Director Security and Fire Safety, Craig Hughes
Director Purchasing and Central Services, Gwendolyn Walker

Dean Admissions, Donna Shaffner
Director Marketing, Linda A. Koller
Registrar, Paulette A. Anzelone
Director Senior Women ?s Administrator, Katie
 Bishop
Associate, Mike Miranto
Administrative Assistant, Karen Cash
Head Coach, Dave Skolen
Assistant Director of Residence Life, Dan Nilsson
Director for Recreation & Facilities, Dan Dolan
Director of Leadership Giving, Pat Smith
Director of Athletics, William Morris
Director of Residence Life, Sara Alexanderson
Head Athletic Trainer, Jeff Sage
Head Coach, Mark Parisi
Head Coach, Mark Spacone
Head Coach, Matt Pokigo

LOCATIONS

HQ: Daemen College
 4380 Main St., Amherst NY 14226
Phone: 716-839-8225 **Fax:** 716-839-8343
Web: www.daemen.edu

HISTORICAL FINANCIALS

Company Type: School

Income Statement

FYE: May 31

	REVENUE ($ mil.)	NET INCOME ($ mil.)	NET PROFIT MARGIN	EMPLOYEES
05/12	42	(2)	—	0
05/11	41	2	7.0%	0
05/10	38	2	5.4%	0
05/09	36	(1)	—	0
Annual Growth	5.9%	—	—	—

2012 Year-End Financials

Debt ratio: ——
Return on equity: (-6.10)%
Cash ($ mil.): 12
Current ratio: ——
Long-term debt ($ mil.): ——

Dividends
 Yield: —
 Payout: —
Market value ($ mil.): —

DAIEI PAPERS (USA) CORP.

LOCATIONS

HQ: DAIEI PAPERS (USA) CORP.
 505 INDEPENDENCE PKWY # 200, CHESAPEAKE, VA
 23320-5178
Phone: 757-523-2100
Web: www.daieipapers.com

HISTORICAL FINANCIALS

Company Type: Private

Income Statement

FYE: December 31

	REVENUE ($ mil.)	NET INCOME ($ mil.)	NET PROFIT MARGIN	EMPLOYEES
12/11	89	0	0.7%	23
12/10	97	0	0.5%	0
12/09	88	0	0.6%	0
12/08	107	0	0.5%	0
Annual Growth	(5.9%)	4.2%	—	—

2011 Year-End Financials

Debt ratio: ——
Return on equity: 0.70%
Cash ($ mil.): 0
Current ratio: 0.70
Long-term debt ($ mil.): ——

Dividends
 Yield: —
 Payout: —
Market value ($ mil.): —

DALHART CONSUMERS FUEL ASSOCIATION INC

LOCATIONS

HQ: DALHART CONSUMERS FUEL ASSOCIATION INC
 1300 N HIGHWAY 87, DALHART, TX 79022
Phone: 806-249-5695
Web: www.dalhartconsumers.com

HISTORICAL FINANCIALS

Company Type: Private

Income Statement

FYE: July 31

	REVENUE ($ mil.)	NET INCOME ($ mil.)	NET PROFIT MARGIN	EMPLOYEES
07/11	142	3	2.6%	40
07/10*	36	2	7.0%	0
02/10	106	2	2.5%	0
02/08	108	4	4.5%	0
Annual Growth	9.6%	(8.6%)	—	—

*Fiscal year change

2011 Year-End Financials

Debt ratio: ——
Return on equity: 2.60%
Cash ($ mil.): 2
Current ratio: ——
Long-term debt ($ mil.): —

Dividends
 Yield: —
 Payout: —
Market value ($ mil.): —

DALLAS BAPTIST UNIVERSITY

LOCATIONS

HQ: DALLAS BAPTIST UNIVERSITY
 3000 MOUNTAIN CREEK PKWY, DALLAS, TX
 75211-6700
Phone: 214-333-5160
Web: www.dbu.edu

HISTORICAL FINANCIALS

Company Type: Private

Income Statement

FYE: May 31

	REVENUE ($ mil.)	NET INCOME ($ mil.)	NET PROFIT MARGIN	EMPLOYEES
05/12	80	6	8.7%	620
05/11	99	7	7.2%	0
05/10	76	10	13.6%	0
05/09	55	(5)	—	0
Annual Growth	13.0%	—	—	—

2012 Year-End Financials

Debt ratio: ——
Return on equity: 8.70%
Cash ($ mil.): 14
Current ratio: ——
Long-term debt ($ mil.): ——

Dividends
 Yield: —
 Payout: —
Market value ($ mil.): ——

DALLASTOWN AREA SCHOOL DISTRICT

LOCATIONS

HQ: DALLASTOWN AREA SCHOOL DISTRICT
 700 NEW SCHOOL LN, DALLASTOWN, PA
 17313-9242
Phone: 717-244-4021
Web: www.dallastown.net

HISTORICAL FINANCIALS

Company Type: Private

Income Statement

FYE: June 30

	REVENUE ($ mil.)	NET INCOME ($ mil.)	NET PROFIT MARGIN	EMPLOYEES
06/11	89	(5)	—	575
06/10	84	(34)	—	0
06/07	75	1	2.6%	0
06/06	0	0	—	0
Annual Growth	—	—	—	—

2011 Year-End Financials

Debt ratio: ——
Return on equity: (-6.40)%
Cash ($ mil.): 13
Current ratio: 0.20
Long-term debt ($ mil.): ——

Dividends
 Yield: —
 Payout: —
Market value ($ mil.): —

DANA-FARBER CANCER INSTITUTE INC.

 The Dana-Farber Cancer Institute fights cancer
on two fronts: It provides treatment to cancer patients young and old and researches new cancer
diagnostics treatments and preventions. The organization's scientists also research AIDS treatments
and cures for a host of other deadly diseases. Patients receive treatment from Dana-Farber through

its cancer centers operated in conjunction with Brigham and Women's Hospital Children's Hospital Boston and Massachusetts General Hospital. The institute is also a principal teaching affiliate of Harvard Medical School. Dana-Farber is funded by the National Cancer Institute the National Institute of Allergy and Infectious Diseases and private contributions.

Strategy

When it comes to patient care Dana-Farber emphasizes the importance of forming research and treatment partnerships with other health care organizations. To that end the institute has opened a handful of treatment clinics on other medical campuses including one at Faulkner Hospital in southwest Boston and another at Milford Regional Medical Center in Massachusetts.

Along with expanding on other campuses Dana-Farber built a new cancer care center on its main campus in Boston. The Yawkey Center for Cancer Care named in honor of long-time contributor The Yawkey Foundation opened in 2011 to serve a growing number of patients. The 275000-sq.-ft center's 14-stories house most of Dana-Farber's adult outpatient care. The building has more than 100 exam rooms about 140 infusion chairs and a number of consultation rooms for family and patients. It also connects Dana-Farber to other campus buildings and to its clinical partners Brigham and Women's Hospital and Children's Hospital Boston.

Although Dana-Farber directs its research efforts toward saving lives from deadly diseases some of its discoveries also bring in a tidy income as the company and its research partners occasionally license out their drug discoveries to pharmaceutical companies. For example in 2010 Dana-Farber and the Sanford-Burnham Medical Research Institute licensed the manufacturing and marketing rights to their newly discovered monoclonal antibody vaccine to treat and protect against influenza viruses to Genentech.

Company Background

Dana-Farber Cancer Institute was founded as a children's cancer research foundation in 1947 by Dr. Sidney Farber. The institute later expanded its services to provide programs for adults as well as children.

EXECUTIVES

SVP Human Resources, Deborah Hicks
EVP CFO and Assistant Treasurer, Dorothy E. Puhy, age 59
President and CEO, Edward J. Benz Jr.
Chair Department of Radiation Oncology, Jay R. Harris
SVP Communications, Steven R. Singer
Chief Quality Officer, Joseph Jacobson
SVP and General Counsel, Richard S. Boskey
Chair Department of Medical Oncology, James D. Griffin
VP External Affairs, Anne L. Levine
SVP Experimental Medicine, Lee M. Nadler, age 65
Chair Department of Pediatric Oncology, Stuart H. Orkin
SVP Development, Susan S. Paresky
SVP Patient Care Services and Chief Nursing Officer, Patricia Reid Ponte
Chief Scientific Officer, Barrett J. Rollins
Chief of Staff, Stephen E. Sallan
SVP Medical Affairs and Chief Medical Officer, Lawrence N. Shulman
EVP and COO, Janet E. Porter
SVP Research, Beverly R. Ginsburg
Chief Clinical Research Officer, Philip Kantoff
SVP Finance, Karen Bird

Chief Department of Imaging, Annick D. Van den Abbeele

LOCATIONS

HQ: Dana-Farber Cancer Institute Inc.
450 Brookline Ave., Boston MA 02215
Phone: 617-632-3000   **Fax:** 617-632-4421
Web: www.dana-farber.org

PRODUCTS/OPERATIONS

Selected Clinical Affiliations

Dana-Farber/Brigham and Women's Cancer Center (outpatient services for adult cancer patients provided by Dana-Farber; and inpatient care provided by Brigham and Women's Hospital)
Dana-Farber/Children's Hospital Cancer Center (Dana-Farber Cancer Institute and Children's Hospital Boston outpatient care for children provided at Dana-Farber's Jimmy Fund Clinic)
Dana-Farber/Harvard Cancer Center (Beth Israel Deaconess Medical Center Brigham and Women's Hospital Children's Hospital Boston and Massachusetts General Hospital collaborate on research cancer prevention and treatments and therapies for cancer
Dana-Farber/Partners Cancer Care (consolidated adult oncology programs and clinical research of Dana-Farber Cancer Institute Brigham and Women's Hospital and Massachusetts General Hospital)

Selected Satellite Centers

Dana-Farber/Brigham and Women's Cancer Center at Faulkner Hospital in Jamaica Plain (southwest Boston area)
Dana-Farber/Brigham and Women's Cancer Center at Milford Regional Medical Center (Massachusetts)
Dana-Farber/Brigham and Women's Cancer Center in clinical affiliation with South Shore Hospital (South Weymouth Massachusetts)
Dana-Farber/New Hampshire Oncology-Hematology (Londonderry)

COMPETITORS

Baystate Health	Mayo Clinic
Beth Israel Deaconess Medical Center	MD Anderson Cancer Center
Boston Medical Center	Memorial
Brigham and Women's Hospital	Sloan-Kettering
Care New England	Partners HealthCare
CareGroup	Roswell Park Cancer Institute
Children's National Medical Center	St. Elizabeth's Medical Center
Emory Healthcare	St. Jude Children's Research Hospital
Fox Chase Cancer Center	St. Luke's-Roosevelt Hospital
Johns Hopkins Medicine	

HISTORICAL FINANCIALS

Company Type: Private - Not-for-Profit

Income Statement

FYE: September 30

	REVENUE ($ mil.)	NET INCOME ($ mil.)	NET PROFIT MARGIN	EMPLOYEES
09/11	1,002	37	3.7%	3,000
09/10	894	16	1.9%	0
09/09	816	28	3.5%	0
09/08	808	85	10.5%	0
Annual Growth	7.4%	(24.0%)	—	—

2011 Year-End Financials

Debt ratio: ——
Return on equity: 3.70%
Cash ($ mil.): 13
Current ratio: 0.20
Long-term debt ($ mil.): ——

Dividends
Yield: —
Payout: —
Market value ($ mil.): —

DANSK INVESTMENT GROUP INC.

LOCATIONS

HQ: DANSK INVESTMENT GROUP INC.
6591 COLLINS DR STE E11, MOORPARK, CA 93021-1493
Phone: 805-299-8200

HISTORICAL FINANCIALS

Company Type: Private

Income Statement

FYE: December 31

	ASSETS ($ mil.)	NET INCOME ($ mil.)	INCOME AS % OF ASSETS	EMPLOYEES
12/11	47	(1)	—	25
12/10	63	11	17.6%	0
12/09	70	(9)	—	0
12/08	67	(30)	—	0
Annual Growth	(11.0%)	—	—	—

2011 Year-End Financials

Debt ratio: ——
Return on equity: (-1.20)%
Cash ($ mil.): 5
Current ratio: 1.80
Long-term debt ($ mil.): —

Dividends
Yield: —
Payout: —
Market value ($ mil.): —

DASCO INCORPORATED

LOCATIONS

HQ: DASCO INCORPORATED
9785 MAROON CIR STE 110, ENGLEWOOD, CO 80112-2692
Phone: 303-350-5050
Web: www.dascoinc.com

HISTORICAL FINANCIALS

Company Type: Private

Income Statement

FYE: June 30

	REVENUE ($ mil.)	NET INCOME ($ mil.)	NET PROFIT MARGIN	EMPLOYEES
06/12	198	1	1.0%	18
06/11	160	3	1.9%	0
06/10	78	1	1.3%	0
06/09	118	2	1.8%	0
Annual Growth	18.7%	(3.5%)	—	—

2012 Year-End Financials

Debt ratio: ——
Return on equity: 1.00%
Cash ($ mil.): 8
Current ratio: 1.60
Long-term debt ($ mil.): —

Dividends
Yield: —
Payout: —
Market value ($ mil.): —

DATA VISION COMPUTER VIDEO INC.

LOCATIONS

HQ: DATA VISION COMPUTER VIDEO INC.
445 5TH AVE, NEW YORK, NY 10016-0133
Phone: 212-689-1111

HISTORICAL FINANCIALS

Company Type: Private

Income Statement

FYE: December 31

	REVENUE ($ mil.)	NET INCOME ($ mil.)	NET PROFIT MARGIN	EMPLOYEES
12/11	83	1	2.1%	90
12/10	59	0	1.3%	0
12/08	53	0	1.0%	0
12/06	56	1	1.8%	0
Annual Growth	13.7%	19.4%	—	—

2011 Year-End Financials

Debt ratio: ——
Return on equity: 2.10%
Cash ($ mil.): 2
Current ratio: 0.50
Long-term debt ($ mil.): —

Dividends
Yield: —
Payout: —
Market value ($ mil.): —

DAUGHERTY SYSTEMS INC.

LOCATIONS

HQ: DAUGHERTY SYSTEMS INC.
3 CITYPLACE DR STE 400, SAINT LOUIS, MO
63141-7087
Phone: 314-432-8200
Web: www.daugherty.com

HISTORICAL FINANCIALS

Company Type: Private

Income Statement

FYE: December 31

	REVENUE ($ mil.)	NET INCOME ($ mil.)	NET PROFIT MARGIN	EMPLOYEES
12/11	86	3	3.7%	475
12/10	77	3	4.7%	0
12/09	71	1	2.7%	0
12/05	0	0	—	0
Annual Growth	—	—	—	—

2011 Year-End Financials

Debt ratio: ——
Return on equity: 3.70%
Cash ($ mil.): 1
Current ratio: 1.70
Long-term debt ($ mil.): —

Dividends
Yield: —
Payout: —
Market value ($ mil.): —

DAVENPORT COMMUNITY SCHOOL DISTRICT

LOCATIONS

HQ: DAVENPORT COMMUNITY SCHOOL DISTRICT
1606 BRADY ST STE 100, DAVENPORT, IA
52803-4709
Phone: 563-336-5000
Web: www.davenportschools.org

HISTORICAL FINANCIALS

Company Type: Private

Income Statement

FYE: June 30

	REVENUE ($ mil.)	NET INCOME ($ mil.)	NET PROFIT MARGIN	EMPLOYEES
06/11	192	0	0.4%	2,450
06/10	177	(4)	—	0
06/09	182	5	3.2%	0
06/07	169	7	4.2%	0
Annual Growth	4.3%	(53.9%)		

DAVENPORT UNIVERSITY

Couch potatoes need not apply to Davenport. A private not-for-profit school Davenport University offers its 13000 students (many of whom are working adults) associate's bachelor's and master's degrees as well as certification and diploma programs. Founded in 1866 Davenport offers some 70 majors in business health and technology plus an MBA program. With nearly 20 campuses in Michigan two more in Indiana online offerings and a study abroad program Davenport is the largest independent university system in Michigan and northern Indiana.

Dr. Richard J. Passas was named the new president of Davenport University in 2009. He was formerly the president of National-Louis Univeristy in Chicago and has 35 years experience in higher education.

EXECUTIVES

EVP Finance and CFO, Michael Volk
EVP Human and Organizational Development, David Veneklase
SVP Major Gifts, Barbara A. Mieras
EVP Enrollment and Student Services, Kevin O'Halla
Chairman, Kenneth C. Bovee
EVP Advancement, Kim Bruyn
EVP Academics and Provost, David W. Fleming
President, Richard J. Pappas
Vice Chairman, Tracy D. Graham
Trustee, James B. (Jim) Meyer, age 65
Trustee, Robert L. Hetzler, age 66
Trustee, Frank H. Merlotti Jr., age 61
Trustee, Kimberly K. (Kim) Horn
Vice Chairman, Tracy D. Graham
Trustee, James N. DeBoer Jr.
Trustee, Rami A. Fawaz
Trustee, Dayle Hayes
Trustee, Wilbur A. Lettinga
Trustee, Michelle Van Dyke
Trustee, Norma Wallis
Trustee, Kenneth Yerrick

LOCATIONS

HQ: Davenport University
6191 Kraft Ave. Southeast, Grand Rapids MI 49512
Phone: 616-698-7111   **Fax:** 616-698-0333
Web: www.davenport.edu

HISTORICAL FINANCIALS

Company Type: School

Income Statement

FYE: June 30

	REVENUE ($ mil.)	NET INCOME ($ mil.)	NET PROFIT MARGIN	EMPLOYEES
06/11	137	9	6.9%	927
06/10	132	12	9.5%	0
06/05	1	0	25.4%	0
06/04	96	2	3.0%	0
Annual Growth	12.3%	47.5%	—	—

2011 Year-End Financials

Debt ratio: ——
Return on equity: 6.90%
Cash ($ mil.): 7
Current ratio: —
Long-term debt ($ mil.): —

Dividends
Yield: —
Payout: —
Market value ($ mil.): —

DAVID A. CAMPBELL CORPORATION

LOCATIONS

HQ: DAVID A. CAMPBELL CORPORATION
3060 ADAMS ST, RIVERSIDE, CA 92504-4014
Phone: 951-785-4444

HISTORICAL FINANCIALS

Company Type: Private

Income Statement

FYE: December 31

	REVENUE ($ mil.)	NET INCOME ($ mil.)	NET PROFIT MARGIN	EMPLOYEES
12/11	130	1	1.1%	150
12/10	120	1	1.4%	0
12/09	107	1	1.3%	0
12/08	118	1	1.7%	0
Annual Growth	3.3%	(10.9%)	—	—

2011 Year-End Financials

Debt ratio: ——
Return on equity: 1.10%
Cash ($ mil.): 5
Current ratio: 0.30
Long-term debt ($ mil.): —

Dividends
Yield: —
Payout: —
Market value ($ mil.): —

DAVIS CONSTRUCTORS & ENGINEERS INC.

LOCATIONS

HQ: DAVIS CONSTRUCTORS & ENGINEERS INC.
740 BONANZA AVE, ANCHORAGE, AK 99518-1705
Phone: 907-562-2336
Web: www.davisconstructors.com

HISTORICAL FINANCIALS

Company Type: Private

Income Statement

FYE: August 31

	REVENUE ($ mil.)	NET INCOME ($ mil.)	NET PROFIT MARGIN	EMPLOYEES
08/11	118	0	0.2%	150
08/10	120	1	0.9%	0
08/09	151	1	1.2%	0
08/08	178	21	12.1%	0
Annual Growth	(12.6%)	(76.1%)	—	—

2011 Year-End Financials

Debt ratio: ——
Return on equity: 0.20%
Cash ($ mil.): 38
Current ratio: 1.10
Long-term debt ($ mil.): —
Dividends
Yield: —
Payout: —
Market value ($ mil.): —

DAY KIMBALL HEALTHCARE INC.

With more than 100 beds Day Kimball Hospital is a non-profit acute-care facility that caters primarily to Connecticut with an extended reach into parts of Massachusetts and Rhode Island. The health care provider founded in 1894 offers general medical and surgical care along with the option of home care services. Logging an average of nearly 29000 emergency department visits and 550 births Day Kimball offers specialized services such as pediatrics gynecology emergency medicine and psychiatric health care. It also provides hospice and palliative care for terminally ill patients. Outpatient surgery and other medical services are provided through the facility's Ambulatory Care Unit.

Operations

The Ambulatory Care Unit offers endoscopic procedures one-day surgery outpatient IV therapy a pain clinic pre-surgery interviews and testing and a wound care clinic.

Through a partnership with the University of Massachusetts Memorial Medical Center in Worcester Massachusetts Day Kimball provides cardiac care and works to stabilize and transport these specialized patients for further treatment at the university medical center.

Day Kimball Hospital operates additional outpatient medical centers in Connecticut in the cities of Danielson Dayville Plainfield Putnam and Thompson. The clinics provide a range of services such as diagnostic imaging physical therapy and cardiac rehabilitation. In late 2012 Day Kimball Healthcare broke ground on the construction of a new emergency department. The project is valued at some $10 million.

Geographic Reach

Day Kimball Hospital not only serves the residents of northeastern Connecticut the health care facility caters to some regions of Massachusetts and Rhode Island to altogether serve a community of some 90000 members.

EXECUTIVES

President CEO and Director, Robert E. (Bob) Smanik
VP Finance and CFO, Julie Drouin
Director Quality Risk Management and Security, Sharon Sawyer
Director Patient Accounts, Sarah Ginnetti
Co-Director Management Information System, Odile Romanick
VP Medical Affairs and Quality, Doug Waite
Chairman, John Miller
Director Human Resources, Nancy Contillo
VP Patient Services, Carol Howland
Director Communications, Charlene Leith-Bushey
Co-Director Management Information System, Marilyn Rath

LOCATIONS

HQ: Day Kimball Hospital
320 Pomfret St., Putnam CT 06260
Phone: 860-928-6541 **Fax:** 860-928-5341
Web: www.daykimball.org

PRODUCTS/OPERATIONS

Selected Services

Bone densitometry
Cancer services
Cardiac rehabilitation
Endocrinology
Endoscopic procedures
Inpatient nutritional services
Intensive care unit
Mammography
Neurology
One-day surgery
Outpatient IV therapy
Pain clinic
Pediatrics
Pharmacy
Pre-surgery interviews and testing
Pulmonary rehabilitation
Rehabilitation services
Surgery
  Dental
  ENT
  General
  Obstetrical/gynecological
  Ophthalmic
  Orthopedic
  Podiatric
  Urological
Wellness programs
Wound care clinic

COMPETITORS

Backus
Care New England
Connecticut Children's Medical Center
Harrington Memorial Hospital
Kent Hospital
Lifespan Corporation
Memorial Hospital of Rhode Island
Milford Regional Medical Center
Roger Williams Medical Center
Sturdy Memorial

HISTORICAL FINANCIALS

Company Type: Private - Not-for-Profit

Income Statement

FYE: September 30

	REVENUE ($ mil.)	NET INCOME ($ mil.)	NET PROFIT MARGIN	EMPLOYEES
09/11	119	(0)	—	900
09/10	110	(3)	—	0
09/08	158	(3)	—	0
09/05	150	0	—	0
Annual Growth	(7.3%)	—	—	—

2011 Year-End Financials

Debt ratio: ——
Return on equity: (-0.70)%
Cash ($ mil.): 3
Current ratio: 1.00
Long-term debt ($ mil.): —
Dividends
Yield: —
Payout: —
Market value ($ mil.): —

DAYTON BOARD OF EDUCATION

LOCATIONS

HQ: DAYTON BOARD OF EDUCATION
115 S LUDLOW ST, DAYTON, OH 45402-1812
Phone: 937-461-3000
Web: www.dps.com

HISTORICAL FINANCIALS

Company Type: Private

Income Statement

FYE: June 30

	REVENUE ($ mil.)	NET INCOME ($ mil.)	NET PROFIT MARGIN	EMPLOYEES
06/11*	306	(49)	—	3,500
12/05	0	0	—	0
06/02	267	32	12.0%	0
06/01	234	13	5.7%	0
Annual Growth	9.3%	—	—	—

*Fiscal year change

2011 Year-End Financials

Debt ratio: ——
Return on equity: (-16.10)%
Cash ($ mil.): 129
Current ratio: —
Long-term debt ($ mil.): —
Dividends
Yield: —
Payout: —
Market value ($ mil.): —

DCR WORKFORCE INC.

LOCATIONS

HQ: DCR WORKFORCE INC.
7815 NW BCN SQR BLVD # 224, BOCA RATON, FL 33487-1345
Phone: 561-998-3737
Web: www.dcrworkforce.com

HISTORICAL FINANCIALS
Company Type: Private

Income Statement
FYE: December 31

	REVENUE ($ mil.)	NET INCOME ($ mil.)	NET PROFIT MARGIN	EMPLOYEES
12/11	464	2	0.6%	82
12/01	12	0	6.3%	0
12/00	9	1	12.4%	0
Annual Growth	598.5%	50.6%		

2011 Year-End Financials
Debt ratio: ——
Return on equity: 0.60%
Cash ($ mil.): 2
Current ratio: 3.30
Long-term debt ($ mil.): ——
Dividends
Yield: ——
Payout: ——
Market value ($ mil.): ——

DE PAUL UNIVERSITY

In the land of da Bulls and da Bears there's DePaul. One of the largest private not-for-profit universities in the US DePaul has a total of about 25000 students attending classes at its five Chicago-area campuses. Also one of the country's largest Catholic institutions of higher learning the university offers more than 300 undergraduate and graduate programs through about a dozen colleges and schools including the Kellstadt Graduate School of Business and the College of Communication. It has a student teacher ratio of 17 to 1. DePaul was founded in 1898 by the Vincentian religious community and is named after 17th century French priest St. Vincent de Paul.

Geographic Reach

DePaul's five Chicago-area campuses are located in Lincoln Park the Loop Naperville Oak Forest and the O'Hare area.

EXECUTIVES

VP Teaching and Learning Resources; Senior Executive University Mission; and Secretary, Rev Edward R. Udovic
Chancellor, Rev John T. Richardson
VP Student Affairs, James R. (Jim) Doyle
SVP Enrollment Management and Marketing, David H. Kalsbeek
EVP, Robert L. (Bob) Kozoman
VP Finance, Bonnie Frankel
VP Facility Operations, Robert (Bob) Janis
President, Rev Dennis H. Holtschneider, age 50
VP Human Resources, William Seithel
SVP Advancement, Mary C. Finger
VP and General Counsel, Jose D. Padilla
Provost, Helmut P. Epp
Dean College of Commerce and Kellstadt Graduate School of Business, Ray Whittington
VP Institutional Diversity and Equity, Elizabeth F. Ortiz
Dean School for New Learning, Marisa Alicea
Dean School of Music, Donald E. Casey
Dean The Theatre School, John Culbert
Dean College of Computing and Digital Media, David Miller
Dean College of Liberal Arts and Sciences, Charles S. (Chuck) Suchar
Dean College of Communication, Jacqueline Taylor
Treasurer, Jeffrey (Jeff) Bethke
Chief of Staff and Senior Executive Presidential Administration, Jay Braatz

VP Development, David A. Lively
Dean School of Education, Paul Zionts
Interim Dean College of Law, Warren D. Wolfson
Controller, Mark Hawkins
VP Alumni Outreach and Engagement, Patricia O'Donoghue
VP Public Relations and Communications, Cheryl Procter-Rogers
Director Information Services, Bob McCormick
VP Community Government and International Affairs, J.D. Bindenagel

LOCATIONS

HQ: DePaul University
1 E. Jackson Blvd., Chicago IL 60604
Phone: 312-362-8000 **Fax:** 312-362-6639
Web: www.depaul.edu

HISTORICAL FINANCIALS
Company Type: School

Income Statement
FYE: June 30

	REVENUE ($ mil.)	NET INCOME ($ mil.)	NET PROFIT MARGIN	EMPLOYEES
06/12	546	39	7.2%	3,895
06/11	535	94	17.7%	0
06/10	510	81	16.0%	0
06/09	477	(45)	—	0
Annual Growth	4.6%	—	—	—

2012 Year-End Financials
Debt ratio: ——
Return on equity: 7.20%
Cash ($ mil.): 56
Current ratio: ——
Long-term debt ($ mil.): ——
Dividends
Yield: ——
Payout: ——
Market value ($ mil.): ——

DEALERS SUPPLY COMPANY INC.

Dealers Supply Company (DSC) strives to keep cool during those long Southern summers. Through about 15 locations in Georgia and North Carolina the company distributes air conditioning and heating products to residential customers contractors and small businesses. Products include air conditioners heaters motors insulation lifts sealants and other items from such brands as Airgas Honeywell RUUD Trion and WeatherKing. DSC sells the tools needed to install and maintain all the heating and cooling equipment it sells and it offers classes and reference guides. The company's Web site includes an online catalog and searchable database of licensed conditioned air contractors.

EXECUTIVES

President and CEO, Richard Laurens
VP Information Services, Rob Pierce
VP Sales, Mark Fields
Financial Manager, Yvonne Boles
Regional Manager Region 1, Greg Wilkes
Director Logistics, Stephen Smith
Manager Programs, Laura Buehl
Manager Warehouse Operations Forest Park, Jerry Van Pelt Sr.
Regional Manager Region 3, Ryan Sheckter
Regional Manager Region 2, Joseph Buehl

Manager Credit, Karl Pike
Manager Human Resources, Renee Lewis
Office Manager, Veronica Bailey
Accounts Payable, Carol Warner

LOCATIONS

HQ: Dealers Supply Company Inc.
82 Kennedy Dr., Forest Park GA 30297
Phone: 404-361-6800 **Fax:** 404-361-2852
Web: www.dealerssupply.net

COMPETITORS

84 Lumber	Lowe's
Ferguson Enterprises	Watsco
HD Supply	WinWholesale

HISTORICAL FINANCIALS
Company Type: Private

Income Statement
FYE: March 31

	REVENUE ($ mil.)	NET INCOME ($ mil.)	NET PROFIT MARGIN	EMPLOYEES
03/12	40	0	1.3%	126
03/11	41	0	1.7%	0
03/10	38	0	1.5%	0
03/09	47	0	1.7%	0
Annual Growth	(5.0%)	(12.6%)	—	—

2012 Year-End Financials
Debt ratio: ——
Return on equity: 1.30%
Cash ($ mil.): 0
Current ratio: 1.90
Long-term debt ($ mil.): ——
Dividends
Yield: ——
Payout: ——
Market value ($ mil.): ——

DECATUR CITY BOARD OF EDUCATION

LOCATIONS

HQ: DECATUR CITY BOARD OF EDUCATION
302 4TH AVE NE, DECATUR, AL 35601-1972
Phone: 256-552-3000
Web: www.ahsfccla.org

HISTORICAL FINANCIALS
Company Type: Private

Income Statement
FYE: September 30

	REVENUE ($ mil.)	NET INCOME ($ mil.)	NET PROFIT MARGIN	EMPLOYEES
09/11	95	10	10.6%	1,285
09/10	92	0	0.1%	0
09/09	91	(5)	—	0
09/08	102	2	2.7%	0
Annual Growth	(2.4%)	53.0%	—	—

2011 Year-End Financials
Debt ratio: ——
Return on equity: 10.60%
Cash ($ mil.): 27
Current ratio: ——
Long-term debt ($ mil.): ——
Dividends
Yield: ——
Payout: ——
Market value ($ mil.): ——

DECO INC

LOCATIONS

HQ: DECO INC
13850 BLUESTEM CT STE 100, BAXTER, MN
56425-6028
Phone: 218-824-3326
Web: www.deco-inc.com

HISTORICAL FINANCIALS
Company Type: Private

Income Statement
FYE: December 31

	REVENUE ($ mil.)	NET INCOME ($ mil.)	NET PROFIT MARGIN	EMPLOYEES
12/11	94	1	1.2%	2
Annual Growth	—	—	—	—

2011 Year-End Financials

Debt ratio: ——
Return on equity: 1.20%
Cash ($ mil.): 0
Current ratio: 1.50
Long-term debt ($ mil.): —

Dividends
Yield: —
Payout: —
Market value ($ mil.): —

DECO INC.

This DECO has nothing to do with art and everything to do with security. The private Native American-owned firm provides professional security services including anti-terrorism training armed and unarmed guards escorts and patrols security system monitoring security consulting and administrative staffing support to federal corporate and tribal clients. Security services account for about 90% of the firm's revenue. The remainder comes from its contracting division which offers construction services for large-scale remodeling projects and electrical and security system installations. DECO counts the US Department of Homeland Security FAA and US Environmental Protection Agency among its clients.

DECO supports these federal government agencies with specialized security training programs that involve anti-terrorism measures counter-intelligence crisis management physical defense surveillance tactical operations and weapons.

EXECUTIVES

President and CEO, Robert A. Dorr
President Contracting Services, Derek J. Dorr
Business Development, Stephanie Semanko

LOCATIONS

HQ: DECO INC.
11140 ZEALAND AVE N, CHAMPLIN, MN 55316-3594
Phone: 763-576-9572
Web: www.deco-inc.com

COMPETITORS

Academi
Brink' s
DynCorp International
G4S Secure Solutions
Securitas Security Services North America

Tri-S Security

HISTORICAL FINANCIALS
Company Type: Private

Income Statement
FYE: December 31

	REVENUE ($ mil.)	NET INCOME ($ mil.)	NET PROFIT MARGIN	EMPLOYEES
12/11	94	1	1.2%	1,600
12/10	82	0	0.8%	0
12/09	62	0	0.7%	0
12/08	55	1	2.6%	0
Annual Growth	19.7%	(6.9%)	—	—

2011 Year-End Financials

Debt ratio: ——
Return on equity: 1.20%
Cash ($ mil.): 0
Current ratio: 1.50
Long-term debt ($ mil.): —

Dividends
Yield: —
Payout: —
Market value ($ mil.): —

DEKALB COUNTY BOARD OF EDUCATION

LOCATIONS

HQ: DEKALB COUNTY BOARD OF EDUCATION
3770 N DECATUR RD BLDG AB, DECATUR, GA
30032-1099
Phone: 678-676-1200
Web: www.oakgrovepta.org

HISTORICAL FINANCIALS
Company Type: Private

Income Statement
FYE: June 30

	REVENUE ($ mil.)	NET INCOME ($ mil.)	NET PROFIT MARGIN	EMPLOYEES
06/11	1,106	(78)	—	16,000
06/07	1,128	350	31.1%	0
06/06	1,055	10	0.9%	0
Annual Growth	2.4%	—	—	—

2011 Year-End Financials

Debt ratio: ——
Return on equity: (-7.10)%
Cash ($ mil.): 128
Current ratio: —
Long-term debt ($ mil.): —

Dividends
Yield: —
Payout: —
Market value ($ mil.): —

DEKALB MEDICAL CENTER INC.

As far as DeKalb is concerned da healthier da better! Beginning as a rural hospital DeKalb Regional Health System now serves all of the Atlanta metropolitan area. The health system operating as DeKalb Medical is home to two acute-care hospitals DeKalb Medical at North Decatur and DeKalb

---

Medical at Hillandale that have a combined total of about 550 beds. It also operates a 75-bed long-term rehabilitation hospital DeKalb Medical at Downtown Decatur. Specialty hospital services include oncology cardiology orthopedics and diabetes care. The health system which was founded in 1961 also operates primary specialty and mobile health care clinics partly through the DeKalb Medical Physicians Group.

Operations

The health network of three hospitals staffs about 775 physicians who represent about 55 medical specialties including neurosurgery interventional radiology sports medicine endovascular surgery gynecology emergency medicine and infectious disease.

DeKalb Medical is a self-supporting not-for-profit community hospital that does not receive tax dollars as part of its funding. The hospital system's operating budget comes solely from patient fees; DeKalb Medical reinvests any excess income into expanding or updating its services and facilities to meet Atlanta's growing population. The DeKalb Medical Foundation was established in 1991 and since then has funded improvements in facilities technology and community outreach programs.

EXECUTIVES

President CEO and Director, Eric P. Norwood
EVP and COO, John A. Shelton Jr.
VP Patient Relations and Compliance, Lynne Anderson
VP Physician Support Services, C. Duane Barclay
VP Human Resources, Tom Crawford
SVP and CFO, Diane Harden
SVP and Chief Quality Officer, Cathleen Wheatley
VP and Administrator DeKalb Medical at Hillandale, J. Clay Fowler
Assistant Administrator and Director Nursing DeKalb Medical at Hillandale, Philida Seda
VP Patient Care Services and Chief Nursing Officer DeKalb Medical, Jan Gannon
Chairman, Oliver Lee
Vice Chairman, Terry E. Duis
Secretary and Director, Robert E. Wilson
Treasurer and Director, David L. Jollay
Director Quality and Care Management DeKalb Medical, Jackie Paynter
Media Relations Coordinator DeKalb Medical, Tori Vogt
Executive Director The DeKalb Medical Foundation, Leigh Minter
Director Materials Management DeKalb Medical, Joe Jackson
President CEO and Director, Eric P. Norwood
Director, Peter Gordon
Director, Susan Parry
Vice Chairman, Terry E. Duis
Secretary and Director, Robert E. Wilson
Treasurer and Director, David L. Jollay
Director, Gulshan Harjee
Director, Gregory B. Levett Sr.
Director, Tyrone Malloy
Director, Michael Quinones
Director, Donald E. Smith Jr.
Director, Daniel J. Thompson

LOCATIONS

HQ: DeKalb Regional Health System Inc.
2701 N. Decatur Rd., Decatur GA 30033
Phone: 404-501-1000   **Fax:** 404-501-5761
Web: www.drhs.org

PRODUCTS/OPERATIONS

Selected Specialties

Cancer Center
Community Programs
Corporate Health Services
Emergency Department
Heart and Vascular Services
Orthopedic Services
Podiatry
Radiology and Medical Imaging
Rehabilitation Services
Senior Services
Sleep Center
Surgical Weight Loss
Volunteers
Wellness Center
Women's Services
Workswell Services
Wound Care

COMPETITORS

Children' s Healthcare of Atlanta	Northside Hospital
	Piedmont Healthcare
Emory Healthcare	Saint Joseph' s Health
Grady Health System	System
Gwinnett Health System	St. Mary' s Health Care
HCA	WellStar Health System

HISTORICAL FINANCIALS

Company Type: Private

Income Statement

FYE: June 30

	REVENUE ($ mil.)	NET INCOME ($ mil.)	NET PROFIT MARGIN	EMPLOYEES
06/11	422	0	0.2%	2,700
06/10	397	(15)	—	0
06/09	390	0	—	0
06/08	370	(11)	—	0
Annual Growth	4.5%	—	—	—

2011 Year-End Financials

Debt ratio: —
Return on equity: 0.20%
Cash ($ mil.): 21
Current ratio: 0.30
Long-term debt ($ mil.): —

Dividends
Yield: —
Payout: —
Market value ($ mil.): —

DEL VALLE GROUP S P

LOCATIONS

HQ: DEL VALLE GROUP S P
CARR 865 KM 06 BO CMPNLLA ST CA, TOA BAJA, PR 00949
Phone: 787-794-0927
Web: www.delvallegroup.net

HISTORICAL FINANCIALS

Company Type: Private

Income Statement

FYE: June 30

	REVENUE ($ mil.)	NET INCOME ($ mil.)	NET PROFIT MARGIN	EMPLOYEES
06/12	97	2	2.7%	400
06/11	64	1	2.5%	0
06/10	73	3	4.5%	0
06/09	116	7	6.4%	0
Annual Growth	(5.5%)	(29.2%)	—	—

2012 Year-End Financials

Debt ratio: —
Return on equity: 2.70%
Cash ($ mil.): 6
Current ratio: 1.60
Long-term debt ($ mil.): —

Dividends
Yield: —
Payout: —
Market value ($ mil.): —

DELAWARE STATE UNIVERSITY

One of the top historically black colleges and universities in the US Delaware State University (DSU) offers more than 50 bachelor's degree programs 25 graduate degree programs and five doctoral degree programs through more than 20 academic departments and five colleges. In addition to its main 400-acre campus in Dover the university has satellite locations in Georgetown and Wilmington. The school began as a land-grant educational institution founded in 1891 as the State College for Colored Students. It became known as Delaware State College in 1947 and gained university status in 1993. The university has a student-teacher ratio of 14:1 and enrolls more than 3800 students each year.

While proud of its black heritage DSU has grown to be a diverse campus with a fourth of its student body represented by Caucasian Asian Hispanic and other cultures. It has also grown from its agricultural roots to expand its offerings from the development of its nationally acclaimed business school to its advanced state-of-the-art research and technology labs.

DSU's most popular majors (as measured by degrees awarded) are business administration psychology mass communications criminal justice and sociology sport management social work biological sciences nursing and education programs. The university also operates the mid-Atlantic region's only university-based full-service flight school.

Outside the classroom the school sponsors athletic teams and activities about 20 student organizations and student support services. The main campus is within several hours driving distance to Philadelphia Baltimore and Washington DC and New York City is within a three-hour drive.

EXECUTIVES

President, Allen L. Sessoms
VP Academic Affairs and Interim Provost, Kenneth W. Bell
Chairman, Claibourne D. Smith
Head Librarian and Division Head of Reference Services, Rebecca E. Batson
Assistant VP Academic Affairs, Hector Figueroa
Director Alumni Affairs, Lorene K. Robinson
VP Student Affairs, Paul A. Bryant
Vice Chairman, John Land
Trustee, Bennie L. Smith
Vice Chairman, John Land
Trustee, Jose F. Echeverri
Trustee, Calvin T. Wilson II
Trustee, James Stewart
Trustee, Charles McDowell
Trustee, Wesley E. Perkins
Trustee, Matthew Mackie
Trustee, Lillian M. Lowery
Trustee, A. Richard Barros
Trustee, Willa M. Jordan

Trustee, David G. Turner
Trustee, Marvin E. Lawrence

LOCATIONS

HQ: Delaware State University
1200 N. DuPont Hwy., Dover DE 19901
Phone: 302-857-6060   Fax: 908-526-0253
Web: www.raritanval.edu

PRODUCTS/OPERATIONS

Selected Colleges

College of Agriculture and Related Sciences
College of Arts Humanities and Social Sciences
College of Business
College of Education Health and Public Policy
College of Mathematics Natural Sciences and Technology

HISTORICAL FINANCIALS

Company Type: School

Income Statement

FYE: June 30

	REVENUE ($ mil.)	NET INCOME ($ mil.)	NET PROFIT MARGIN	EMPLOYEES
06/12	82	10	12.3%	600
06/11	75	9	13.0%	0
06/10	67	1	1.6%	0
06/09	65	0	0.4%	0
Annual Growth	8.0%	247.2%	—	—

2012 Year-End Financials

Debt ratio: —
Return on equity: 12.30%
Cash ($ mil.): 24
Current ratio: 1.30
Long-term debt ($ mil.): —

Dividends
Yield: —
Payout: —
Market value ($ mil.): —

DELAWARE VALLEY COLLEGE

Delaware Valley College serves about 2000 undergraduate and graduate students. The school offers associate's bachelor's and master's degrees in fields such as agriculture biology business administration chemistry computer science and criminal justice. Delaware Valley's campus is located on 550 acres 30 miles north of Philadelphia. The college was founded in 1896.

EXECUTIVES

President, Joseph S. Brosnan
Director Technology Services, Donna L. Doan
Director Communications and Public Relations, Sean A. Dallas
VP Academic Affairs and Dean Faculty, Dorothy A. Prisco
Dean Business Education and Arts and Sciences, Benjamin E. Rusiloski
Interim Dean Agriculture and Environmental Sciences, Lawrence D. Hepner
VP Enrollment Management, Robert Yapsuga
Director Admissions, Steve Zenko
Director Financial Aid, Robert M. Sauer
VP Technology and CIO, William A. Brichta
VP Institutional Advancement, Joseph T. Erckert

Associate VP Business and Finance, Patricia
  Benson
Controller, Virginia A. Altmann
Director Purchasing, William Lyle
Registrar, Adam Wichryk
Interim Director Security and Public Safety, Linda
  Fluck

LOCATIONS

HQ: Delaware Valley College
  700 E. Butler Ave., Doylestown PA 18901
Phone: 215-489-2203   Fax: 334-288-5485
Web: www.normentsecurity.com/

HISTORICAL FINANCIALS

Company Type: School

Income Statement

	REVENUE ($ mil.)	NET INCOME ($ mil.)	NET PROFIT MARGIN	EMPLOYEES
06/12	52	(0)	—	405
06/11	72	37	51.5%	0
06/10	47	2	4.7%	0
06/09	46	(2)	—	0
Annual Growth	4.1%	—	—	—

FYE: June 30

2012 Year-End Financials

Debt ratio: —
Return on equity: (-1.20)%
Cash ($ mil.): 1
Current ratio: —
Long-term debt ($ mil.): —
Dividends
  Yield: —
  Payout: —
  Market value ($ mil.): —

DELTA COLLEGE

Delta can help ya prepare for a career. Founded in 1961 Delta College is a community college offering one-year certificate programs and two-year applied associate degree programs. In addition to its main campus the college has satellite centers in Bay Midland and Saginaw counties in central Michigan. It also runs a public radio station a public television station a planetarium and a small business and technology development center. Delta College has an enrollment of approximately 11000; about two-thirds of students are 20 or older and most of them take a combination of day and evening classes.

EXECUTIVES

Executive Director Communication Technology,
  Barry G. Baker
VP Business and Finance, Debra Lutz
VP Instruction and Learning Services, Donald B.
  (Don) Halog
Executive Director Corporate Services, Paul F.
  Seidel
President, Jean Goodnow
Director Business Services, Barbara Webb
Director Facilities Management, Larry Ramseyer
VP Student and Educational Services, Trevor A.
  Kubatzke
Executive Director Institutional Advancement,
  Pamela N. Clark
Director Financial Aid, Kim Donat
Associate Director Enrollment Services, Gary
  Brasseur
Registrar and Veteran Services, Duff Zube

Director Marketing and Public Information,
  Leanne Govitz
Manager Public Safety, Kim S. Bickel

LOCATIONS

HQ: Delta College
  1961 Delta Rd., University Center MI 48710
Phone: 989-686-9000   Fax: 989-686-8736
Web: www.delta.edu

HISTORICAL FINANCIALS

Company Type: School

Income Statement

	REVENUE ($ mil.)	NET INCOME ($ mil.)	NET PROFIT MARGIN	EMPLOYEES
06/12	38	5	15.3%	2,000
06/11	41	6	16.8%	0
06/10	41	6	15.0%	0
06/09	37	2	6.8%	0
Annual Growth	0.6%	31.5%	—	—

FYE: June 30

2012 Year-End Financials

Debt ratio: —
Return on equity: 15.30%
Cash ($ mil.): 22
Current ratio: 3.10
Long-term debt ($ mil.): —
Dividends
  Yield: —
  Payout: —
  Market value ($ mil.): —

DENISON UNIVERSITY

Denizens of Denison University have a desire to dedicate themselves to higher learning. The university is a private undergraduate school with an enrollment of about 2100. It has an especially low student-to-teacher ratio of approximately 10-to-1. It offers some 60 majors concentrations and pre-professional programs in both liberal arts and science fields including a pre-medical program and an athletic training program as well as social science and humanities programs. The small-town college includes a 350-acre main campus and a 550-acre biological reserve in Granville Ohio (a suburb of Columbus).

Denison was founded in 1831 by the Ohio Baptist Education Society as the Granville Literary and Theological Institution. Most of the school's students live on campus. It's current name is in honor of benefactor William S. Denison. Alumni of Denison (Denisonians) include US Senator Richard Lugar former Walt Disney CEO Michael Eisner and actor Steve Carell.

The university has an endowment of some $670 million. It provides some $43 million in scholarships annually.

EXECUTIVES

President, Dale T. Knobel
VP Finance and Management, Seth H. Patton
Director Information Technology Services, Lisa M.
  Bazley
VP Student Affairs, Samuel J. (Sam) Thios
VP Institutional Advancement, Julia Beyer Houpt
Associate VP and Director Planned Giving, Marcia
  D. Koester
Controller, Cathy M. Untied
Director Financial Aid, Nancy Hoover
Director Administrative Services, Veronica M.
  (Ronni) Hintz

Administrative Director University
  Communications, Jack Hire
Provost, Bradley Bateman
Registrar, Yadi Collins
Director Alumni Relations, Steve Crawford
Director Security Safety and Risk Management,
  Garret Moore
Director Human Resources, Jim Ables
Auditors: Ernst&YoungLLP

LOCATIONS

HQ: Denison University
  100 W. College St., Granville OH 43023
Phone: 740-587-0810   Fax: 740-587-6364
Web: www.denison.edu

HISTORICAL FINANCIALS

Company Type: School

Income Statement

	REVENUE ($ mil.)	NET INCOME ($ mil.)	NET PROFIT MARGIN	EMPLOYEES
06/12	112	(14)	—	220
06/11	110	110	100.7%	0
06/10	122	(13)	—	0
06/09	104	(154)	—	0
Annual Growth	2.3%	—	—	—

FYE: June 30

2012 Year-End Financials

Debt ratio: —
Return on equity: (-12.90)%
Cash ($ mil.): 0
Current ratio: —
Long-term debt ($ mil.): —
Dividends
  Yield: —
  Payout: —
  Market value ($ mil.): —

DES MOINES INDEPENDENT SCHOOL DISTRICT

LOCATIONS

HQ: DES MOINES INDEPENDENT SCHOOL DISTRICT
  901 WALNUT ST, DES MOINES, IA 50309-3501
Phone: 515-242-7911
Web: www.edcocu.com

HISTORICAL FINANCIALS

Company Type: Private

Income Statement

	REVENUE ($ mil.)	NET INCOME ($ mil.)	NET PROFIT MARGIN	EMPLOYEES
06/11*	409	1	0.3%	4,000
12/09	1	0	11.4%	0
05/09	0	(0)	—	0
06/06	0	0	—	0
Annual Growth	—	—	—	—

FYE: June 30

*Fiscal year change

2011 Year-End Financials

Debt ratio: —
Return on equity: 0.30%
Cash ($ mil.): 107
Current ratio: 0.60
Long-term debt ($ mil.): —

Dividends
Yield: —
Payout: —
Market value ($ mil.): —

DET DISTRIBUTING COMPANY

LOCATIONS

HQ: DET DISTRIBUTING COMPANY
301 GREAT CIRCLE RD, NASHVILLE, TN 37228-1789
Phone: 615-244-4113
Web: www.detdist.com

HISTORICAL FINANCIALS

Company Type: Private

Income Statement — FYE: December 31

	REVENUE ($ mil.)	NET INCOME ($ mil.)	NET PROFIT MARGIN	EMPLOYEES
12/11	95	0	0.2%	150
12/10	92	0	0.5%	0
Annual Growth	3.6%	(61.0%)	—	—

2011 Year-End Financials

Debt ratio: —
Return on equity: 0.20%
Cash ($ mil.): 0
Current ratio: —
Long-term debt ($ mil.): —

Dividends
Yield: —
Payout: —
Market value ($ mil.): —

DEVCON CONSTRUCTION INCORPORATED

Devcon Construction is devoted to building in the Bay Area. One of the area's top general building contractors Devcon has constructed more than 35 million sq. ft. of office industrial and commercial space mainly in the San Francisco Bay Area and Silicon Valley. The company provides engineering design/build and interior design services. It specializes in high-tech projects including data centers and industrial research and development facilities. In addition to building company facilities and offices Devcon works on such projects as hotels restaurants parking structures retail stores sports facilities and schools.

Although most of Devcon's work is in California the company also has completed projects in Nevada Oregon Idaho Texas Massachusetts and Florida. Recent projects in the San Francisco Forty Niners Stadium in Santa Clara San Jose Sharks Ice Center in Pleasanton and the Stanford Research Computing Facility.

EXECUTIVES

VP and Controller, Bret Sisney
President, Gary Filizetti
Safety Officer, Ken Sullivan
CIO, Jeremy Holland
Secretary, Justine Pereira

LOCATIONS

HQ: Devcon Construction Incorporated
690 Gibraltar Dr., Milpitas CA 95035
Phone: 408-942-8200   **Fax:** 408-262-2342
Web: www.devcon-const.com

COMPETITORS

Charles Pankow Builders	KPRS Construction
DPR Construction	Obayashi
Hathaway Dinwiddie Construction	Rudolph & Sletten
Hensel Phelps Construction	Structure Tone
	Swinerton
	Turner Corporation
	Webcor Builders

HISTORICAL FINANCIALS

Company Type: Private

Income Statement — FYE: December 31

	REVENUE ($ mil.)	NET INCOME ($ mil.)	NET PROFIT MARGIN	EMPLOYEES
12/11	434	1	0.3%	350
12/10	469	1	0.2%	0
12/09	381	10	2.7%	0
12/08	915	13	1.4%	0
Annual Growth	(22.0%)	(55.5%)	—	—

2011 Year-End Financials

Debt ratio: —
Return on equity: 0.30%
Cash ($ mil.): 1
Current ratio: 0.80
Long-term debt ($ mil.): —

Dividends
Yield: —
Payout: —
Market value ($ mil.): —

DEVERE CONSTRUCTION COMPANY INC

LOCATIONS

HQ: DEVERE CONSTRUCTION COMPANY INC
1030 DEVERE DR, ALPENA, MI 49707-8163
Phone: 989-356-4411
Web: www.devere.tv

HISTORICAL FINANCIALS

Company Type: Private

Income Statement — FYE: December 31

	REVENUE ($ mil.)	NET INCOME ($ mil.)	NET PROFIT MARGIN	EMPLOYEES
12/11	101	0	0.7%	175
12/10	58	0	1.3%	0
12/09	52	(1)	—	0
12/08	122	0	0.3%	0
Annual Growth	(5.8%)	33.3%	—	—

2011 Year-End Financials

Debt ratio: —
Return on equity: 0.70%
Cash ($ mil.): 8
Current ratio: 0.40
Long-term debt ($ mil.): —

Dividends
Yield: —
Payout: —
Market value ($ mil.): —

DEVEREUX FOUNDATION

Devereux Foundation endeavors to make a difference in the lives of people with behavioral psychological intellectual or neurological problems. A not-for-profit organization Devereux serves children adolescents and adults and their families through about 20 centers in about a dozen states. Its offerings include hospitalization group homes respite care family counseling and vocational training. Devereux also conducts behavioral health research and provides consulting services for other organizations with similar concerns. The group's work began in 1912 when Philadelphia educator Helena Devereux began working with three special education students in her parents' home.

The organization's Institute of Clinical Training and Research was founded in 1938. It provides professional training in psychology psychiatry social work and special education.

Devereux Foundation maintains facilities in Arizona California Colorado Connecticut Florida Georgia Massachusetts New Jersey New York Pennsylvania and Texas.

Devereux's revenue increased by a little over 1% in 2011 to $395.2 million compared to $389.4 million in 2010. Its net income increased to $2.6 million compared to its loss of $0.9 million in 2010. That year the foundation provided $17.9 million in charity care representing a 3% decrease from 2010 for clients who were unable to pay.

In 2012 as the foundation entered its second century of operation it began working on a comprehensive plan to set its strategic direction that would take into account not only new challenges but new opportunities present in the world today. Devereux is examining its centers and corporate departments while it continues to place the highest value on building relationships with the people and public agencies that use its services. Key elements to its strategic plan include quality management national branding and maintaining fiscal responsibility to ensure a strong balance sheet. The foundation is also looking to expand opportunities for its intellectual properties and services through partnerships with school systems and universities and through expanded services for people with autism and added community-based adult services.

EXECUTIVES

President and CEO, Robert Q. (Bob) Kreider
COO, Margaret (Maggie) McGill
SVP Operations and Business Development, James Colvin
VP and CIO, Peter Della Porta
VP Operations and Organizational Development, Sarah E. Lenahan
VP and General Counsel, Lori McLaughlin
VP and Secretary Planned Giving and Real Estate, Allen F. Thomas
VP Audit and Compliance, Lawrence W. Williams
Treasurer, Steven H. Mansh
Assistant Secretary, Roberta M. Lewis

Vice Chairman, Thomas C. Hays
SVP External Affairs, Beth Chadwick
Vice Chairman, Samuel G. Coppersmith
Chairman, Francis (Skip) Genuardi
VP Operations, L. Gail Atkinson
VP Human Resources, Timothy Dillon
SVP CFO and Controller, Robert C. Dunne
VP Product Development, Martha Lindsay
SVP and Chief Clinical Officer, Marilyn Benoit
Vice Chairman, Thomas C. Hays
Vice Chairman, Samuel G. Coppersmith
Trustee, Charles S. Ackerman
Trustee, K. Lisa Yang
Trustee, John C. Taylor
Trustee, James H. Schwab
Trustee, Peter Haje
Trustee, Marilyn Benoit
Trustee, Christopher D. Butler
Trustee, Larry J. Overton
Trustee, William Christopher
Trustee, Thomas F. Donovan
Trustee, Robert D. Ellis
Trustee, Elva B. Ferrari
Trustee, Marguerite D. Hark
Trustee, John R. Gunn
Trustee, Robert Gottlieb

LOCATIONS

HQ: The Devereux Foundation
444 Devereux Dr., Villanova PA 19085
Phone: 610-520-3000 **Fax:** 818-752-9339
Web: www.artistviewent.com

PRODUCTS/OPERATIONS

2011 Revenue

	$ mil.	% of total
Client revenue	367	93
Investment income	8	2
Gifts & bequests	7	2
Other revenue	11	3
Total	**395**	**100**

Selected Services

After care programs
Community-based group homes
Family counseling and therapy
Foster care homes
Hospital inpatient and outpatient settings
Partial hospitalization
Preventive and post-discharge services
Residential and day treatment programs
Respite care programs
Special education day schools
Supervised apartments
Transitional living arrangements
Vocational and pre-vocational training

COMPETITORS

CIGNA Behavioral Health
CRC Health
Diakon Lutheran Social Ministries
FHC Health Systems
Hazelden
HealthSouth
Magellan Health
Mental Health Network
Northwestern Human Services
Physiotherapy Associates
Providence Service
Select Medical
UBH
Universal Health Services
Watson Institute
YAI National Institute for People with Disabilitie

HISTORICAL FINANCIALS

Company Type: Private - Foundation

Income Statement
FYE: June 30

	REVENUE ($ mil.)	NET INCOME ($ mil.)	NET PROFIT MARGIN	EMPLOYEES
06/11	395	17	4.5%	6,000
06/08	384	5	1.4%	0
06/07	400	22	5.6%	0
06/06	388	6	1.7%	0
Annual Growth	**0.6%**	**39.6%**	**—**	**—**

2011 Year-End Financials

Debt ratio: —
Return on equity: 4.50%
Cash ($ mil.): 5
Current ratio: 0.90
Long-term debt ($ mil.): —
Dividends
Yield: —
Payout: —
Market value ($ mil.): —

DIALYSIS CLINIC INC.

Dialysis Clinic Inc. or DCI is dedicated to caring for patients with end-stage renal disease (ESRD). The not-for-profit company which operates a network of more than 210 dialysis centers serving more than 13000 patients in 27 states also provides kidney transplant assistance services. Affiliate DCI Donor Services is an organ and tissue procurement agency. DCI also funds kidney-related research and educational programs and is affiliated with various universities and teaching hospitals throughout the US including Tufts University the University of Arizona and Tulane University.

Geographic Reach

The company has its locations in Alabama Arizona Arkansas California Colorado Connecticut Florida Georgia Indiana Iowa Kentucky Louisiana Maine Massachusetts Missouri Montana Nebraska Nevada New Jersey New Mexico New York North Carolina Ohio Pennsylvania South Carolina Tennessee and Texas.

Strategy

DCI grows its network of facilities by forming partnerships with health care providers and other organizations. The company provides funding for construction and operation of the facility and it provides clinic support services including supply procurement and central laboratory services (through its DCI Lab subsidiary).

In 2012 the company opened a dialysis clinic in Albuquerque its first dialysis clinic in the South Valley region of New Mexico.

Company Background

DCI was established in 1971 by nephrologist Keith Johnson.

EXECUTIVES

Chairman, H. Keith Johnson
President and Trustee, James Perry
Director Operations and Assistant Treasurer, William E. (Bill) Wood
Secretary and Treasurer, Ed Attrill
Director Human Resources, David (Dave) Hagewood
Corporate Controller, Mark Penick
Director Corporate Contracts Sales and Marketing, Hal Whetstone
Corporate Counsel, Gina Zylstra
Director Reimbursement and Managed Care, Joe Swearingen

Corporate Director Budgeting, Gigi Abston
Director Quality Management and Education, Pam Havermann

Director Risk Management, Mark S. Likos
Director Internal Audit, Andy Parker
Assistant Controller, LaVerne Pope
President and Trustee, James Perry
Trustee, Nancy N. Johnson
Trustee, Douglas S. Johnson

LOCATIONS

HQ: Dialysis Clinic Inc.
1633 Church St. Ste. 500, Nashville TN 37203
Phone: 615-327-3061 **Fax:** 615-329-2513
Web: www.dciinc.org

COMPETITORS

DaVita
FMCNA
Fresenius
Renal Advantage
U.S. Renal Care

HISTORICAL FINANCIALS

Company Type: Private - Not-for-Profit

Income Statement
FYE: September 30

	REVENUE ($ mil.)	NET INCOME ($ mil.)	NET PROFIT MARGIN	EMPLOYEES
09/11	642	48	7.5%	5,000
09/10	654	21	3.2%	0
09/09	631	(3)	—	0
09/08	608	(4)	—	0
Annual Growth	**1.8%**	**—**	**—**	**—**

2011 Year-End Financials

Debt ratio: —
Return on equity: 7.50%
Cash ($ mil.): 163
Current ratio: 4.10
Long-term debt ($ mil.): —
Dividends
Yield: —
Payout: —
Market value ($ mil.): —

DICKINSON COLLEGE

Dickinson College is a private liberal arts college with an enrollment of about 2400 students. The school's campus is in Carlisle a pre-Revolutionary town of 20000 people founded in 1756 located in the Cumberland Valley of central Pennsylvania. Academic offerings include programs in arts and humanities social sciences and natural sciences. The school also offers minors in fields including astronomy creative writing film studies and Latin American studies. Dickinson College was created in 1783 by Benjamin Rush the famed Philadelphia physician and patriot and is named for John Dickinson who signed the US Constitution and was known as "The Penman of the [American] Revolution."

More than half of the student body of Dickinson College comes from Pennsylvania New York and New Jersey.

EXECUTIVES

President, William G. Durden, age 75
VP Financial Operations and Treasurer, Annette S. Parker, age 61
Director Media Relations, Christine M. Dugan

VP Library and Information Services and CIO, Robert Renaud
VP Enrollment and College Relations, Robert J. Massa
Director Planning and Budget, L. Jill Hans
Provost and Dean College, Neil B. Weissman
Director Alumni Programs, Rick Delgiorno
Bursar, Thomas B. Meyer
Controller, Sean M. Witte
VP Human Resource Services, John Weis
Registrar, Karen Weikel
Chief and Director Public Safety, Dolores Danser
Dean Admissions and Financial Aid, Stephanie Balmer
Auditors: Deloitte&ToucheLLP

LOCATIONS

HQ: Dickinson College
55 N. West St., Carlisle PA 17013
Phone: 717-243-5121   Fax: 717-245-1534
Web: www.dickinson.edu

HISTORICAL FINANCIALS
Company Type: School

Income Statement

	REVENUE ($ mil.)	NET INCOME ($ mil.)	NET PROFIT MARGIN	EMPLOYEES
				FYE: June 30
06/12	115	(0)	—	632
06/11	159	51	32.2%	0
06/10	39	(69)	—	0
06/09	39	(69)	—	0
Annual Growth	42.9%	—	—	—

2012 Year-End Financials

Debt ratio: ——
Return on equity: (-0.60)%
Cash ($ mil.): 9
Current ratio: —
Long-term debt ($ mil.): —
Dividends
Yield: —
Payout: —
Market value ($ mil.): —

DIMEO CONSTRUCTION COMPANY

Dimeo Construction has built a reputation in New England. The company provides general contracting design/build and construction management services ranging from pre-planning to post-construction commissioning. It focuses on commercial education health care residential and public projects such as schools hospitals corporate headquarters research and development facilities and shopping centers. It also has worked on renovation projects such as The Mark Twain House & Museum and the Ocean House. The family-owned company was established in 1930 by Joseph Dimeo. Current CEO Brad Dimeo represents the third generation to lead the firm.

Dimeo Construction has offices in Boston; New Haven Connecticut; and Providence Rhode Island. The company has completed work for several of the region's Fortune 500 companies including CIGNA Hasbro and United Technologies Corporation. Its green side has emerged as well as it has completed eco-friendly projects for the likes of IKEA CVS Caremark and Yale University.

EXECUTIVES
President, Bradford S. Dimeo
Project Manager, Douglas (Doug) Peckham
VP Corporate Development, Anthony F. Dematteo
EVP and COO, Stephen F. Rutledge
VP Operations, Paul G. Aballo
CFO, Steven B. Avery
VP and Project Executive, Kosta Bitsis
VP Preconstruction Services, Michael J. Fuchs
Marketing Manager, Claudine A. Lajoie
Auditors: Ernst&YoungLLP

LOCATIONS
HQ: Dimeo Construction Company
75 Chapman St., Providence RI 02905
Phone: 401-781-9800   Fax: 401-461-4580
Web: www.dimeo.com

COMPETITORS
Gilbane Building Company
Heery
Imperial Construction Group
Konover Properties
Skanska USA Building
Turner Construction
Walsh Brothers

HISTORICAL FINANCIALS
Company Type: Private

Income Statement

	REVENUE ($ mil.)	NET INCOME ($ mil.)	NET PROFIT MARGIN	EMPLOYEES
				FYE: June 30
06/12	373	6	1.7%	300
06/11	300	9	3.1%	0
06/10	356	9	2.7%	0
06/09	567	8	1.5%	0
Annual Growth	(13.0%)	(9.7%)	—	—

2012 Year-End Financials

Debt ratio: ——
Return on equity: 1.70%
Cash ($ mil.): 78
Current ratio: 1.20
Long-term debt ($ mil.): —
Dividends
Yield: —
Payout: —
Market value ($ mil.): —

DIVINE PROVIDENCE HOSPITAL OF THE SISTERS OF CHRISTIAN CHARITY

LOCATIONS

HQ: DIVINE PROVIDENCE HOSPITAL OF THE SISTERS OF CHRISTIAN CHARITY
1100 GRAMPIAN BLVD, WILLIAMSPORT, PA 17701-1995
Phone: 570-321-1000

HISTORICAL FINANCIALS
Company Type: Private

Income Statement

	REVENUE ($ mil.)	NET INCOME ($ mil.)	NET PROFIT MARGIN	EMPLOYEES
				FYE: June 30
06/11	87	4	5.2%	332
06/10	86	5	6.1%	0
06/09	82	0	—	0
06/08	71	5	8.3%	0
Annual Growth	7.1%	(8.4%)	—	—

2011 Year-End Financials

Debt ratio: ——
Return on equity: 5.20%
Cash ($ mil.): 7
Current ratio: 2.50
Long-term debt ($ mil.): —
Dividends
Yield: —
Payout: —
Market value ($ mil.): —

DLT SOLUTIONS LLC

DLT Solutions provides information technology products and services primarily to local state and federal government clients in the US. The company sells and integrates enterprise applications from such vendors as Autodesk Oracle NetApp Red Hat and Symantec. It also offers consulting network design application development training and other professional services. The company's areas of expertise include cloud computing data center consolidation cybersecurity and computer-aided design. DLT 's customers have included the US Department of Defense the City of Los Angeles the FBI and the States of Texas and New Mexico.

Strategy As government budgets are tightened DLT is looking to higher-margin professional services as an avenue for future growth. In early 2013 the company announced it was boosting its DLT Professional Services division with more subject matter experts and engineers (specializing in Oracle technology) as well as a new unit leader.

EXECUTIVES

EVP and CFO, Craig Adler
President and CEO, Rick Marcotte
VP Human Resources, Chris Laggini
VP Enterprise Platform Sales, Russ Holmes
VP Marketing, Christine Schaefer

VP Autodesk Sales, Jim Helou
Director Infrastructure and Peripherals Sales,
 Chris Dewey
Director Information Technology, Bob Nayak
Senior Contracts Administrator, Edward A. Abbot
 III
SVP, Ed Jones
VP General Counsel and Secretary, Kathryn Harris
VP Enterprise Data Management (EDM), Brian
 Strosser
CTO, Van Ristau

LOCATIONS

HQ: DLT Solutions Inc.
 13861 Sunrise Valley Dr. Ste. 400, Herndon VA 20170
Phone: 703-709-7172 **Fax:** 703-709-8450
Web: www.dlt.com

PRODUCTS/OPERATIONS

Selected Product Vendors
Akamai
Amazon Web Services
Autodesk
Blue Coat Systems
BMC Software
Google
Informatica
Quest Software
NetApp
Oracle
Red Hat
SolarWinds
Solera Networks
Symantec

COMPETITORS

Accenture
Apptis
CACI International
CDW
ComGlobal Systems
Computer Sciences
 Corp.
GTSI
HP Enterprise Services

IBM Global Services
Lockheed Martin
 Information Systems
Melillo Consulting
Northrop Grumman Info
 Systems
SAIC
Unisys

HISTORICAL FINANCIALS
Company Type: Private

Income Statement
FYE: December 31

	REVENUE ($ mil.)	NET INCOME ($ mil.)	NET PROFIT MARGIN	EMPLOYEES
12/11	354	14	4.1%	253
12/10	447	13	2.9%	0
12/09	87	(1)	—	0
12/08	271	8	3.2%	0
Annual Growth	**9.3%**	**18.8%**	—	—

2011 Year-End Financials

Debt ratio: —
Return on equity: 4.10%
Cash ($ mil.): 10
Current ratio: 0.70
Long-term debt ($ mil.): —

Dividends
 Yield: —
 Payout: —
Market value ($ mil.): —

DOCTOR'S ASSOCIATES INC.

You're more likely to catch a sub than a train at these Subway stations. Doctor's Associates owns the Subway chain of sandwich shops the world's largest quick-service restaurant chain having recently surpassed burger giant McDonald's. It boasts about 34500 locations in almost 100 countries. Virtually all Subway restaurants are franchised and offer such fare as hot and cold sub sandwiches turkey wraps and salads. The eateries are located in freestanding buildings as well as in airports convenience stores sports facilities and other locations. Doctor's Associates is owned by co-founders Fred DeLuca and Peter Buck who opened the first Subway in 1965.

In surpassing the mighty McDonald's the Subway chain has succeeded where few in the quick-service industry have dared. The company's network of eateries stretching from Afghanistan to Zambia is a testament to how effectively the franchising model can be used to expand a dining concept. Local operators who own the individual restaurants use the Subway name in exchange for royalties and other fees. This allows Doctor's Associates to expand its sandwich business without the cost of construction and operation. (Domiciled in Florida the company operates its franchising business largely through Connecticut-based affiliate World Franchise Headquarters.)

Part of the reason for Subway's success is the portability and adaptability of the dining concept. The sandwich restaurants can be found in a vast array of locations including shopping center food courts suburban strip malls and even military bases. With the ability to fit one of its restaurants almost anywhere Subway can offer franchisees lower startup costs as compared to other concepts that require large areas for food preparation or dining space. The company is particularly focused on expanding its international presence in Asia and Central Europe. Many of Subway's franchisees operate just a single location but a few like Florida-based DiPasqua Enterprises oversee a large estate.

The Subway chain has also tapped into the weight loss zeitgeist in the US prominently featuring in its advertising Jared Fogle a man who famously lost nearly 250 lbs. by switching to a Subway sandwich diet. The chain continues to tout the health benefits of its sandwiches over traditional burgers and fries by introducing new low-fat menu items. Like its fast-food brethren Subway relies heavily on continuous television advertising to promote itself. It appropriately has a marketing partnership with the weight loss competition program The Biggest Loser on NBC.

With success though comes increasing competition. Subway is itself being doggedly pursued by #2 sub sandwich chain Quiznos. Other fast-food chains including pizza delivery giant Domino's have added sub-style sandwiches to their menu while McDonald's and Wendy's have focused on adding salads and other low-calorie items to their menus to attract business from health conscious consumers. Striking back Subway launched a breakfast menu in 2010.

In 2011 Subway began developing an upscale concept called Subway Cafe. The new format conceived for office buildings and other high-end locations will be larger than the average Subway restaurant and will feature coffee espresso lattes

and hot chocolate along with an expanded breakfast menu.

HISTORY

In 1965 17-year-old Fred DeLuca dreamed of becoming a doctor while working as a stock boy in a Bridgeport Connecticut hardware store to earn college tuition. It wasn't enough so he cornered family friend Peter Buck at a backyard barbecue and asked for advice. Buck a nuclear physicist suggested DeLuca open a submarine sandwich shop and put up $1000 to get him started.

As the summer of 1965 was coming to an end DeLuca rented a small location in a remote area of Bridgeport opened Pete's Super Submarines and there he sold foot-long sandwiches. On the first day the sandwiches were so popular that DeLuca hired his own customers to work behind the counter; by the end of the day he had sold out of all his supplies. The sandwiches continued to be popular for a while but within a few months the shop started losing money and DeLuca and Buck found that selling submarine sandwiches was a seasonal business. They decided they could create an illusion of success by opening a second location and then a third. The third store was finally successful partly because of its more visible location and increased marketing and partly because of a new name —Subway.

DeLuca and Buck had set a goal of 32 shops opened by 1975 but they had only 16 by 1974. They realized that the only way they could reach their goal in one year was to license the Subway name. The first franchise opened that year in Wallingford Connecticut and they opened 32 by the end of 1975. The partners hit 100 by 1978 then 200 by 1983 and DeLuca set a new goal: 5000 Subway shops by 1994. The first international Subway opened in Bahrain in 1984 and DeLuca achieved his goal of 5000 shops by 1990.

During the 1990s DeLuca experimented with several other franchise concepts including We Care Hair (budget styling salons) Cajun Joe's (spicy fried chicken) and Q Burgers. But none of these ventures fared as well as his sandwich empire. As Subway grew however controversy surrounding its treatment of franchisees began to surface. A Federal Trade Commission investigation of the company was dropped in 1993 but Subway continued to battle franchisees complaining about broken contracts market over-saturation (and therefore too much competition and self-cannibalization) and what the franchisees viewed as unreasonably high royalty fees.

In spite of its franchising troubles Subway kept growing. It expanded into Russia and China in the mid-1990s and opened its 11000th restaurant in 1995. In 1997 Subway inked deals with the Army Navy and Air Force exchange services to bring Subway units to military bases. Two years later the company opened its 14000th restaurant in Mount Gambier Australia an event that coincided with Subway's renewed push to expand internationally.

The company got some unexpected publicity in 1999 when 22-year-old Jared Fogle claimed that he dropped 245 pounds from his 425-pound frame by subsisting on a diet of Subway turkey sandwiches. Subway helped Fogle extend his 15 minutes of fame by featuring him and his oversized pants in a TV commercial. (The company has since built an entire campaign around Fogle that features other weight watchers attributing their success to Jared and Subway.) Subway introduced its largest menu initiative ever in 2000 when it unveiled its Subway Selects Gourmet Sandwiches adding 13 items to the menu. In April 2001 the company opened its 15000th store.

Also that year Buck retired as chairman but stayed on as a member of the board of directors. Becoming one of the fastest-growing franchises in the world Subway expanded from 16000 locations in 2002 to more than 22000 stores by the end of 2004.

All US Subway outlets switched from Pepsi to Coke products in 2005. Two years later the chain surpassed 21000 locations in the US.

EXECUTIVES

Chief Development Officer, Don Fertman
President, Frederick A. (Fred) DeLuca, age 64
Coordinator Public Relations, Les Winograd
Controller, David Worroll
Chief Marketing Officer, Bill Schettini
Director Research and Development, Suzanne Greco
VP Development Subway Development Corporation of Washington, John A. Filipiak
Manager Public Relations, Kevin Kane
Supervisor Public Relations Subway Franchisee Advertising Fund Trust, Mack Bridenbaker
VP Operations, Millie Shinn
CEO Subway Franchisee Advertising Trust, Jeff Moody
VP Purchasing, Dennis Clabby
Director Brand Management, Michelle Cordial
SVP and Chief Marketing Officer Subway Franchisee Advertising Fund Trust, Tony Pace
President and CEO Subway Independent Purchasing Cooperative, Jan Risi
Director Retail Technology, Marina O'Rourke
CTO, Thys Van Hout
President Subway Development Corporation of Washington, Alan Warmund
CEO Subway Development Corporation of Washington, Larry Feldman
Brand Manager Subway Franchisee Advertising Trust Fund, Louise Jasmin
Director Marketing Subway UK, Manaaz Akhtar

LOCATIONS

HQ: Doctor's Associates Inc.
325 Bic Dr., Milford CT 06461-3059
Phone: 203-877-4281 **Fax:** 818-379-7405
Web: www.sunkist.com

COMPETITORS

AFC Enterprises	Panda Restaurant Group
Burger King	Panera Bread
Chick-fil-A	Papa John's
Chipotle	Quiznos
Church's Chicken	Sonic Corp.
CKE Restaurants	Starbucks
Dairy Queen	Tim Hortons
Domino's	Wendy's
Jack in the Box	YUM!
McDonald's	

HISTORICAL FINANCIALS
Company Type: Private

Income Statement

FYE: December 31

	ASSETS ($ mil.)	NET INCOME ($ mil.)	INCOME AS % OF ASSETS	EMPLOYEES
12/11	117	7	6.8%	650
12/10	114	7	6.5%	0
12/08	95	6	6.6%	0
12/07	73	5	7.7%	0
Annual Growth	17.1%	12.2%	—	—

2011 Year-End Financials

Debt ratio: —
Return on equity: 0.70%
Cash ($ mil.): 20
Current ratio: 0.50
Long-term debt ($ mil.): —

Dividends
Yield: —
Payout: —
Market value ($ mil.): —

DOCTORS' HOSPITAL INC.

Doctors Community Hospital is an acute care and surgical hospital serving the Washington DC area. The not-for-profit medical center admits 12000 patients each year and has some 220 beds and offers standard and specialty services such as diagnostics emergency and cardiac care diagnostics rehabilitation wound care and neurology. Comprising of 600 doctors the hospital also includes a women's health center a sleep therapy division and the Joslin Diabetes Center. Established in 1975 Doctors Community Hospital also provides community health services such as educational programs and support groups for specific medical conditions.

EXECUTIVES

President, Philip B. Down
EVP, Thomas Crowley
VP Finance, Dennis Scanlon
VP Nursing and Patient Care Services, Paula L. Bruening
VP Human Resources, Charlene Lundgren
VP Medical Affairs, Gabriel Jaffe
VP Operations, Eric L. Conley
VP Business Development, Scott B. Gregerson

LOCATIONS

HQ: Doctors Community Hospital
8118 Good Luck Rd., Lanham MD 20706
Phone: 301-552-8118 **Fax:** 301-552-8597
Web: www.dchweb.org

PRODUCTS/OPERATIONS

Selected Services

Bariatric services
Breast health
Cancer services
Cardiac services
Diabetes services
Diagnostic service
Emergency services
Neurosciences
Orthopedic services
Robotic surgery
Sleep center
Surgical services
Sears/nose/throat
Support groups
Therapy services
Wound care

COMPETITORS

Adventist HealthCare	Johns Hopkins Medicine
Bon Secours Health	MedStar Health
Calvert Memorial Hospital	Providence Hospital (Washington DC)
Civista Health	Suburban Hospital
Dimensions Healthcare	

HISTORICAL FINANCIALS
Company Type: Private

Income Statement

FYE: June 30

	REVENUE ($ mil.)	NET INCOME ($ mil.)	NET PROFIT MARGIN	EMPLOYEES
06/11	211	16	7.9%	1,200
06/10	198	(1)	—	0
06/09	179	(12)	—	0
06/08	0	0	38.4%	0
Annual Growth	576.1%	298.4%	—	—

2011 Year-End Financials

Debt ratio: —
Return on equity: 7.90%
Cash ($ mil.): 24
Current ratio: 1.20
Long-term debt ($ mil.): —

Dividends
Yield: —
Payout: —
Market value ($ mil.): —

DOMESTIC AND FOREIGN MISSIONARY SOCIETY OF THE PROTESTANT EPISCO

LOCATIONS

HQ: DOMESTIC AND FOREIGN MISSIONARY SOCIETY OF THE PROTESTANT EPISCO
815 2ND AVE RM 301, NEW YORK, NY 10017-4509
Phone: 212-716-6000
Web: www.stpeterschool.com

HISTORICAL FINANCIALS
Company Type: Private

Income Statement

FYE: December 31

	REVENUE ($ mil.)	NET INCOME ($ mil.)	NET PROFIT MARGIN	EMPLOYEES
12/11	83	(21)	—	298
12/09	88	25	29.3%	0
12/05	100	25	25.0%	0
12/01	43	(28)	—	0
Annual Growth	24.5%	—	—	—

2011 Year-End Financials

Debt ratio: —
Return on equity: (-26.20)%
Cash ($ mil.): 22
Current ratio: 0.30
Long-term debt ($ mil.): —

Dividends
Yield: —
Payout: —
Market value ($ mil.): —

DOMINICAN UNIVERSITY OF CALIFORNIA

LOCATIONS

HQ: DOMINICAN UNIVERSITY OF CALIFORNIA
50 ACACIA AVE, SAN RAFAEL, CA 94901-2298
Phone: 415-457-4440
Web: www.mendocino.edu

HISTORICAL FINANCIALS
Company Type: Private

Income Statement
FYE: June 30

	REVENUE ($ mil.)	NET INCOME ($ mil.)	NET PROFIT MARGIN	EMPLOYEES
06/11	82	9	11.9%	300
06/10	66	1	2.0%	0
06/09	60	0	—	0
06/08	59	3	5.4%	0
Annual Growth	11.6%	45.3%	—	—

2011 Year-End Financials

Debt ratio: ——
Return on equity: 11.90%
Cash ($ mil.): 14
Current ratio: —
Long-term debt ($ mil.): —

Dividends
Yield: —
Payout: —
Market value ($ mil.): —

DON FORD SANDERSON INC

LOCATIONS

HQ: DON FORD SANDERSON INC
6400 N 51ST AVE, GLENDALE, AZ 85301-4600
Phone: 623-842-8600
Web: www.fordxplanarizona.com

HISTORICAL FINANCIALS
Company Type: Private

Income Statement
FYE: December 31

	REVENUE ($ mil.)	NET INCOME ($ mil.)	NET PROFIT MARGIN	EMPLOYEES
12/11	510	3	0.7%	416
12/09	301	1	0.3%	0
12/07	531	2	0.5%	0
12/06	497	3	0.6%	0
Annual Growth	0.9%	1.9%	—	—

2011 Year-End Financials

Debt ratio: ——
Return on equity: 0.70%
Cash ($ mil.): 1
Current ratio: 0.30
Long-term debt ($ mil.): —

Dividends
Yield: —
Payout: —
Market value ($ mil.): —

DOT GREEN PUBLIC SCHOOLS

LOCATIONS

HQ: DOT GREEN PUBLIC SCHOOLS
1149 S HILL ST FL 6, LOS ANGELES, CA 90015-2218
Phone: 323-565-1600

HISTORICAL FINANCIALS
Company Type: Private

Income Statement
FYE: June 30

	REVENUE ($ mil.)	NET INCOME ($ mil.)	NET PROFIT MARGIN	EMPLOYEES
06/11	89	6	7.5%	800
06/10	90	(2)	—	0
06/05	0	0	—	0
Annual Growth	—	—	—	—

2011 Year-End Financials

Debt ratio: ——
Return on equity: 7.50%
Cash ($ mil.): 32
Current ratio: —
Long-term debt ($ mil.): —

Dividends
Yield: —
Payout: —
Market value ($ mil.): —

DOMINO FOOD AND FUEL INC.

LOCATIONS

HQ: DOMINO FOOD AND FUEL INC.
HWY 183 S, CLINTON, OK 73601
Phone: 580-323-2929

HISTORICAL FINANCIALS
Company Type: Private

Income Statement
FYE: December 31

	REVENUE ($ mil.)	NET INCOME ($ mil.)	NET PROFIT MARGIN	EMPLOYEES
12/11	98	1	1.7%	150
12/10	72	1	1.8%	0
12/09	59	0	1.2%	0
12/08	0	0	—	0
Annual Growth	—	—	—	—

2011 Year-End Financials

Debt ratio: ——
Return on equity: 1.70%
Cash ($ mil.): 0
Current ratio: 0.20
Long-term debt ($ mil.): —

Dividends
Yield: —
Payout: —
Market value ($ mil.): —

DOOLEY'S PETROLEUM INC.

LOCATIONS

HQ: DOOLEY' S PETROLEUM INC.
304 MAIN AVE, MURDOCK, MN 56271-8033
Phone: 320-875-2641

HISTORICAL FINANCIALS
Company Type: Private

Income Statement
FYE: December 31

	REVENUE ($ mil.)	NET INCOME ($ mil.)	NET PROFIT MARGIN	EMPLOYEES
12/11	359	2	0.6%	110
12/10	250	1	0.7%	0
12/09	205	2	1.3%	0
12/08	253	3	1.3%	0
Annual Growth	12.3%	(14.7%)	—	—

2011 Year-End Financials

Debt ratio: ——
Return on equity: 0.60%
Cash ($ mil.): 1
Current ratio: 0.70
Long-term debt ($ mil.): —

Dividends
Yield: —
Payout: —
Market value ($ mil.): —

DOUGLAS COUNTY BOARD OF EDUCATION

LOCATIONS

HQ: DOUGLAS COUNTY BOARD OF EDUCATION
9030 HIGHWAY 5, DOUGLASVILLE, GA 30134-1539
Phone: 770-651-2000
Web: www.beulah.dce.schoolinsites.com

HISTORICAL FINANCIALS
Company Type: Private

Income Statement
FYE: June 30

	REVENUE ($ mil.)	NET INCOME ($ mil.)	NET PROFIT MARGIN	EMPLOYEES
06/11	272	(8)	—	3,200
06/08	131	31	23.6%	0
06/06	213	(12)	—	0
06/05	0	0	—	0
Annual Growth	—	—	—	—

2011 Year-End Financials

Debt ratio: ——
Return on equity: (-3.30)%
Cash ($ mil.): 97
Current ratio: —
Long-term debt ($ mil.): —

Dividends
Yield: —
Payout: —
Market value ($ mil.): —

DOWNERS GROVE IMPORTS LTD.

LOCATIONS

HQ: DOWNERS GROVE IMPORTS LTD.
2020 OGDEN AVE, DOWNERS GROVE, IL 60515-2620
Phone: 630-964-9500
Web: www.pugi.com

HISTORICAL FINANCIALS

Company Type: Private

Income Statement

FYE: December 31

	REVENUE ($ mil.)	NET INCOME ($ mil.)	NET PROFIT MARGIN	EMPLOYEES
12/11	87	1	1.3%	0
12/10	64	0	0.4%	0
12/09	52	0	0.3%	0
12/08	48	(0)	—	0
Annual Growth	**22.3%**	—	—	—

2011 Year-End Financials

Debt ratio: ——
Return on equity: 1.30%
Cash ($ mil.): 1
Current ratio: 0.40
Long-term debt ($ mil.): —

Dividends
Yield: —
Payout: —
Market value ($ mil.): —

DOWNTOWN BRONX MEDICAL ASSOCIATES P.C.

LOCATIONS

HQ: DOWNTOWN BRONX MEDICAL ASSOCIATES P.C.
234 E 149TH ST STE 8D-200, BRONX, NY 10451-5504
Phone: 718-579-6200

HISTORICAL FINANCIALS

Company Type: Private

Income Statement

FYE: June 30

	REVENUE ($ mil.)	NET INCOME ($ mil.)	NET PROFIT MARGIN	EMPLOYEES
06/11	99	4	4.9%	318
06/10	101	5	5.8%	0
06/09	86	1	1.5%	0
Annual Growth	**7.4%**	**91.7%**	—	—

2011 Year-End Financials

Debt ratio: ——
Return on equity: 4.90%
Cash ($ mil.): 6
Current ratio: 0.90
Long-term debt ($ mil.): —

Dividends
Yield: —
Payout: —
Market value ($ mil.): —

DPR CONSTRUCTION

From bio labs to wafer fabs DPR Construction runs the gamut for its high tech and health care clients. The employee-owned firm provides general contracting and construction management services for the advanced technology/mission critical life sciences healthcare higher education and corporate office markets. It specializes in retail stores hospitals data centers clean rooms laboratories manufacturing facilities and green buildings. The firm has more than 15 regional offices in Arizona California Florida Georgia Texas Virginia and Washington DC. Company head Doug Woods former CEO Peter Nosler and secretary/treasurer Ron Davidowski (the D P and R in DPR Construction) founded the firm in 1990.

Geographic Reach

To maintain a presence near customers DPR boasts more than 15 regional offices. Its operations span more than half a dozen states including Arizona California Florida Georgia Texas Virginia and Washington DC.

Strategy

DPR has been focusing on eco-friendly construction. More than 40% of its projects incorporate green building techniques or products and approximately one in four of its employees are Leadership in Energy and Environmental Design (LEED) certified.

Clients have included the American Red Cross Banner Health eBay Hewlett-Packard Kaiser Permanente Visa and the University of Texas.

EXECUTIVES

Head National Advanced Technology Core Market Group, Mark Thompson, age 59
EVP, Jim Dolen
Secretary and Treasurer, Ron J. Davidowski
EVP, Peter A. Salvati
President, Douglas E. (Doug) Woods
EVP, Eric Lamb
Marketing and Corporate Communications, Yumi Clevenger
Director Human Resources, Jorinne Jackson
Head National Life Sciences Core Market Group, Michael Lynch
CFO, Gary Wohl
Director Sustainable Construction, Ted van der Linden
Regional Manager Redwood City, Jody Quinton
Regional Manager Raleigh-Durham NC, Greg Haldeman
Project Executive, George Hurley
VP, George Pfeffer
VP, Mike Ford
Regional Manager Atlanta, Andy Andres
Regional Manager West Palm Beach, Deborah Beetson
Head National Healthcare Core Market Group, Hamilton Espinosa
Director Construction Technologies, Atul Khanzode
National Special Services Group Leader, Rocky Moss
Regional Manager Washington DC, Jeff Vertucci
Regional Manager Austin, Gary Nauert
Regional Manager Phoenix, David Elrod
Regional Manager San Diego, Jay Leopold
Director of Innovation, Jim Washburn
Regional Manager Sacramento, Mark Cirksena
Regional Manager San Jose, Scott Greubel
CFO, Michele Leiva
Regional Manager San Francisco, Mike Humphrey
Regional Manager Southern California, David Seastrom
Director Lean Construction, Dean Reed
Regional Manager Richmond VA, Lisa Lingerfelt

LOCATIONS

HQ: DPR Construction Inc.
1450 Veterans Blvd., Redwood City CA 94063
Phone: 650-474-1450   **Fax:** 650-474-1451
Web: www.dprinc.com

Selected Offices

Atlanta
Austin TX
Denver
Houston
Newport Beach CA
Pasadena CA
Phoenix
Raleigh-Durham NC
Redwood City CA
Richmond VA
Sacramento CA
San Diego CA
San Francisco CA
San Jose CA
Washington DC
West Palm Beach FL

COMPETITORS

Austin Industries	Jacobs Engineering
Bechtel	M. A. Mortenson
Bovis Lend Lease	PC Construction
Devcon Construction	Skanska USA Building
Fluor	Swinerton
Hensel Phelps Construction	Turner Corporation
Hoffman Corporation	Whiting-Turner

HISTORICAL FINANCIALS

Company Type: Private

Income Statement

FYE: December 31

	REVENUE ($ mil.)	NET INCOME ($ mil.)	NET PROFIT MARGIN	EMPLOYEES
12/11	2,111	41	2.0%	2,300
12/08	1,836	68	3.7%	0
12/00	1,958	25	1.3%	0
12/99	62,586	0	—	0
Annual Growth	—	**1247.9%**	—	—

2011 Year-End Financials

Debt ratio: ——
Return on equity: 2.00%
Cash ($ mil.): 161
Current ratio: 1.10
Long-term debt ($ mil.): —

Dividends
Yield: —
Payout: —
Market value ($ mil.): —

DREXEL UNIVERSITY

These dragons don't need slaying just a good education. Drexel University (home of the Drexel Dragons) is a private coeducational institution of higher learning with an enrollment of more than 25000 undergraduate and graduate students and a student-teacher ratio of about 17:1. It operates more than a dozen schools and colleges in the US; the Drexel University College of Medicine is the one of the country's largest private medical schools. Drexel runs a mandatory co-operative education program that helps students gain real-world experience while supplying local employers with trained workers. Philadelphia financier and philanthropist Anthony Drexel founded the university in 1891.

Financial Performance

Drexel's fiscal 2012 (ends June) revenue increased nearly 3% vs. the prior year while net income fell by 43% over the same period. The revenue gain was driven by increased net revenue per student and an increase in investment income. Rising education and general expenses and a decrease in its endowment and other gifts led to decline in net income.

Strategy

Drexel is looking to expand on a 3.6 acre lot in Philadelphia acquired in 2011 for $21.8 million. Farther afield the university opened the Drexel-SARI Center in Shanghai China in mid-2012. Drexel signed an agreement with the Shanghai Advanced Research Institute (SARI) Chinese Academy of Sciences to launch the Drexel-SARI Center in fall 2011. The center will house Drexel's research collaborations and educational partnerships with SARI and other institutes of the Chinese Academy of Sciences. The university also has an international research partnership in Israel.

Mergers and Acquisitions

In September 2012 Drexel acquired the Academy of Natural Sciences of Philadelphia (ANS) establishing it as a not-for-profit subsidiary of the university.

EXECUTIVES

President, John A. Fry, age 51
President and CEO Academy of Natural Sciences of Drexel University, George W. Gephart Jr.
Comptroller, Susan Wilmer
Vice Provost Academic Affairs, N. John DiNardo
SVP and Dean Sacramento Center for Graduate Studies, Carl (Tobey) Oxholm III
SVP Enrollment Management, Joan T. McDonald
VP Information Resources and Technology, John A. Bielec
SVP and Executive Director Office of the President, Brian T. Keech
VP University Relations, Philip Terranova
Dean College of Arts and Sciences, Donna Murasko
Dean Bennett S. LeBow College of Business, George P. Tsetsekos
Dean College of Engineering, Selcuk Guceri
Dean College of Information Science and Technology, David E. Fenske
Dean College of Nursing and Health Professions, Gloria F. Donnelly
Provost, Mark L. Greenberg
Director School of Biomedical Engineering Science and Health Systems, Banu Onaral
Dean School of Public Health, Marla J. Gold
Dean Goodwin College of Professional Studies, William F. Lynch
Dean Students, David A. Ruth
Senior Associate; VP Career Education, Peter J. Franks
Senior Vice Provost Budget Planning Administration, Janice (Jan) Biros
VP Financial Planning and Student Financial Services; Interim Bursar, Amy A. Bosio
SVP Student Life and Administrative Services, James R. Tucker
SVP Institutional Advancement, Elizabeth A. Dale
Dean Antoinette Westphal College of Media Arts and Design, Allen Sabinson
Dean Earle Mack College of Law, Roger J. Dennis
SVP and General Counsel Drexel University and Drexel University College of Medicine, Michael J. Exler
Dean Pennoni Honors College, D. B. Jones

Vice Provost Institutional Research, Bernard F. Lentz
Athletic Director, Eric Zillmer
VP Internal Audit and Management Consulting Services, James K. (Jim) Seaman
Dean University Libraries, Danuta Nitecki
Director Finance and Administration, Thomas J. Quinn
University Registrar, Joseph J. Salomone
VP Human Resources, Deborah Glenn
Senior Associate VP Public Safety, Domenic Ceccanecchio
Vice Provost Research, Deborah Crawford
SVP Finance CFO and Treasurer, Helen Y. Bowman
SVP University Communications, Lori N. Doyle
SVP Health Affairs and Interim Dean College of Medicine, Daniel V. Schidlow
President Drexel e-Learning Inc., Kenneth E. Hartman
VP University Facilities, Robert (Bob) Francis
VP Institutional Advancement, Peter Frisko
VP Human Resources, Deborah Eskridge Glenn
VP Finance and Associate Treasurer, Eric J. Olson
VP Government and Community Relations, David E. Wilson
VP Drexel University College of Medicine Institutional Advancement, John Zabinski
Dean College of Engineering, Joseph Hughes
Ombuds, David Flood
Auditors: Deloitte&ToucheLLP

LOCATIONS

HQ: Drexel University
3141 Chestnut St., Philadelphia PA 19104
Phone: 215-895-2000   **Fax:** 416-694-1869
Web: www.hpaulin.com

PRODUCTS/OPERATIONS

Selected Schools and Colleges

Antoinette Westphal College of Media Arts & Design
Bennett S. Lebow College of Business
College of Arts and Sciences
College of Engineering
The College of Information Science and Technology
College of Law
College of Nursing and Health Professions
Drexel University College of Medicine
Earle Mack School of Law
Pennoni Honors College
Richard C. Goodwin College of Professional Studies
School of Biomedical Engineering Science and Health Systems
School of Education
School of Public Health

HISTORICAL FINANCIALS

Company Type: School

Income Statement

FYE: June 30

	REVENUE ($ mil.)	NET INCOME ($ mil.)	NET PROFIT MARGIN	EMPLOYEES
06/11*	896	166	18.6%	2,868
12/08	0	0	—	0
06/05	471	50	10.7%	0
Annual Growth	37.9%	81.8%	—	—

*Fiscal year change

2011 Year-End Financials

Debt ratio: ——
Return on equity: 18.60%
Cash ($ mil.): 63
Current ratio: —
Long-term debt ($ mil.): —
Dividends
  Yield: —
  Payout: —
  Market value ($ mil.): —

DRUGPLACE INC.

LOCATIONS

HQ: DRUGPLACE INC.
2201 W SAMPLE RD BLDG 9S, POMPANO BEACH, FL 33073-3082
Phone: 954-990-2204
Web: www.drugplace.com

HISTORICAL FINANCIALS

Company Type: Private

Income Statement

FYE: December 31

	REVENUE ($ mil.)	NET INCOME ($ mil.)	NET PROFIT MARGIN	EMPLOYEES
12/11*	145	8	5.8%	140
06/08	56	0	1.0%	0
Annual Growth	158.9%	1341.7%	—	—

*Fiscal year change

2011 Year-End Financials

Debt ratio: ——
Return on equity: 5.80%
Cash ($ mil.): 0
Current ratio: 0.80
Long-term debt ($ mil.): —
Dividends
  Yield: —
  Payout: —
  Market value ($ mil.): —

DSI VIDEO SYSTEMS LLC

LOCATIONS

HQ: DSI VIDEO SYSTEMS LLC
363 MARKET ST, KENILWORTH, NJ 07033-2033
Phone: 908-245-4833
Web: www.divsystems.com

HISTORICAL FINANCIALS

Company Type: Private

Income Statement

FYE: December 31

	REVENUE ($ mil.)	NET INCOME ($ mil.)	NET PROFIT MARGIN	EMPLOYEES
12/11	93	3	3.2%	122
12/08	77	5	7.0%	0
12/07	67	2	3.0%	0
12/06	1,917	0	—	0
Annual Growth	—	470.1%	—	—

2011 Year-End Financials

Debt ratio: ——
Return on equity: 3.20%
Cash ($ mil.): 11
Current ratio: 1.20
Long-term debt ($ mil.): —
Dividends
  Yield: —
  Payout: —
  Market value ($ mil.): —

DUBOIS REGIONAL MEDICAL CENTER INC

LOCATIONS

HQ: DUBOIS REGIONAL MEDICAL CENTER INC
100 HOSPITAL AVE, DU BOIS, PA 15801-1499
Phone: 814-371-2200
Web: www.drmc.org

HISTORICAL FINANCIALS

Company Type: Private

Income Statement   FYE: June 30

	REVENUE ($ mil.)	NET INCOME ($ mil.)	NET PROFIT MARGIN	EMPLOYEES
06/11	213	0	0.0%	1,400
06/10	240	10	4.4%	0
06/09	188	(2)	—	0
06/08	181	7	4.0%	0
Annual Growth	5.5%	(79.0%)	—	—

2011 Year-End Financials

Debt ratio: ——
Return on equity: —
Cash ($ mil.): 9
Current ratio: 1.50
Long-term debt ($ mil.): —

Dividends
Yield: —
Payout: —
Market value ($ mil.): —

DUCK RIVER ELECTRIC MEMBERSHIP CORPORATION

LOCATIONS

HQ: DUCK RIVER ELECTRIC MEMBERSHIP CORPORATION
1411 MADISON ST, SHELBYVILLE, TN 37160-3629
Phone: 931-684-4621
Web: www.dremc.com

HISTORICAL FINANCIALS

Company Type: Private

Income Statement   FYE: June 30

	REVENUE ($ mil.)	NET INCOME ($ mil.)	NET PROFIT MARGIN	EMPLOYEES
06/12	172	5	3.0%	166
06/11	179	3	2.2%	0
06/10	155	3	2.2%	0
06/09	164	2	1.7%	0
Annual Growth	1.6%	21.7%	—	—

2012 Year-End Financials

Debt ratio: ——
Return on equity: 3.00%
Cash ($ mil.): 3
Current ratio: 0.40
Long-term debt ($ mil.): —

Dividends
Yield: —
Payout: —
Market value ($ mil.): —

DUNCAN-WILLIAMS INC.

Duncan-Williams raises its capital by helping others raise theirs. An investment banking firm Duncan-Williams offers research sales and trading of fixed income securities (bonds) and equities (stock) to individual and institutional investors including banks credit unions corporations and public entities (e.g. municipalities housing authorities school districts). Other services include underwriting financial analysis bond structuring for public entities and equity capital market research of emerging growth companies in the health care and financial technology sectors. Founded in 1969 by the late A. Duncan Williams the firm operates 16 offices across the eastern US and in Texas and California.

Since its founding Duncan-Williams has been expanding its presence beyond its core southeastern US market and into other US regions. In addition to geographic expansion the firm has also been expanding its service offerings beyond its traditional fixed income securities to include the research and sale of equities. Financially the firm's growth efforts have paid off in a big way in recent years. It has watched its revenues and profits spike as it has taken in more and more income from account management fees underwriting and trading activities associated with fixed-income securities.

Duncan-Williams is owned by A. Duncan Williams' wife Carolyn Williams who assumed control of the firm in 1989 after Mr. Williams' death. The couple's son Duncan F. Williams is the firm's president.

EXECUTIVES

Co-Chair, Carolyn Williams
President, Duncan F. Williams
Co-Chair, Donald A. Malmo
Senior Adviser to the President, Demetri Patikas
COO, Don B. Clanton
CFO, Frank Reid
EVP Operations, Jim Pauline
Managing Director and Head Sales and Trading, Jack Schlifer
Managing Director Private Client Group, Henry M. ((Trey)) Fyfe III
Managing Director Equity Capital Markets, Benjamin C. (Ben) Labry
Chief Compliance Officer, Brad Ziemba
Managing Director and Head Public Finance, Wayne T. Breunig
CTO, Alex P. Tartera Jr.
Managing Director Southeast Region Public Finance, A.O. (Buddy) Crihfield
VP Marketing and Communications, Gary W. Lendermon
Managing Director Municipal Trading, Johnny Lessley
Auditors: DixonHughesGoodmanLLP

LOCATIONS

HQ: Duncan-Williams Inc.
6750 Poplar Ave. Ste. 300, Memphis TN 38138
Phone: 901-260-6800   **Fax:** 214-778-0880
Web: www.tts-us.com

COMPETITORS

Charles Schwab	Morgan Keegan
First Horizon	Piper Jaffray
Gleacher & Company	Raymond James & Associates
Janney Montgomery Scott	Wells Fargo Advisors

HISTORICAL FINANCIALS

Company Type: Private

Income Statement   FYE: December 31

	REVENUE ($ mil.)	NET INCOME ($ mil.)	NET PROFIT MARGIN	EMPLOYEES
12/11	53	3	5.7%	65
12/10	49	2	5.5%	0
12/09	56	7	12.7%	0
12/08	27	0	3.2%	0
Annual Growth	24.2%	50.5%	—	—

2011 Year-End Financials

Debt ratio: ——
Return on equity: 5.70%
Cash ($ mil.): 0
Current ratio: —
Long-term debt ($ mil.): —

Dividends
Yield: —
Payout: —
Market value ($ mil.): —

DUQUESNE UNIVERSITY OF THE HOLY SPIRIT

Duquesne University of The Holy Ghost keeps a keen eye on the spiritual as well as the academic. The school offers more than 100 undergraduate degree programs about 65 graduate and professional degree programs and more than 20 doctoral programs at schools of business education law liberal arts nursing pharmacy health sciences natural and environmental sciences music and leadership and professional advancement. Duquesne was founded in 1878 as the Pittsburgh Catholic College of the Holy Ghost. It has an annual enrollment of more than 10000 undergraduate graduate and law students.

EXECUTIVES

Chancellor, John E. Murray Jr., age 79
President, Charles J. Dougherty, age 63
VP Academics and Provost, Ralph L. Pearson
VP Business and Management, Stephen Schillo
EVP Student Life, Rev Sean M. Hogan
General Counsel, Linda S. Drago
Executive Director Mission and Identity, Rev Timothy J. Hickey
Dean School of Nursing, Eileen Zungolo
Dean Rangos School of Health Sciences, Gregory Frazer
Dean School of Natural and Environmental Science, David Seybert
Dean School of Music, Edward Kocher
Assistant VP Student Life, Alice Sivulich
Associate VP Financial Affairs, David Grousosky
Director Learning Skills Center, Judith Griggs
Librarian, Laverna Saunders
Associate VP Enrollment Management, Paul-James Cukanna
Director University Press, Susan Wadworth-Booth
Director Post-Bac Pre-Med Program, Kyle Selcer
Executive Director Office of International Programs, Roberta Aronson
Dean School of Pharmacy, J. Douglas Bricker
Director English as a Second Language, Frank Giannotta
Director Judicial Affairs, Susan Monahan
Director Commuter Affairs, Tim Lewis
Director Career Services, James McClenahan

Director Freshman Development, Frederick
Lorensen
Director Residence Life, Sharon Oelschlager
Director Health Services, Barbara Galderise
Director Counseling, John Nelson
Director WDUQ, Rev Francis Hanley
Managing Director Tamburitzans, Paul Stafura
Director Public Affairs, Bridget Fare
Director Purchasing, Cynthia A. Vinarski
Director Public Safety, James J. Caputo
Executive Director Auxilliary Services, David
DiPetro
Executive Director Facilities Management, George
Fecik
Director Environmental Health and Safety, Paul
M. King
Internal Auditor, Kevin Wolbert
Executive Director CTS, John Ziegler
Chairman, P. David Pappert
Vice Chair, Marie M. Jones
VP University Advancement, John P. Plante
Acting Dean College of Liberal Arts, Albert
Labriola
Dean School of Law, Donald Guter
Dean Palumbo Donahue School of Business, Alan
Miciak
Dean School of Education, Olga Welch
Dean School of Leadership and Professional
Advancement, Dorothy Bassett
Registrar, Kimberly J. Hoeritz
Director Honors College, Michael Cahall
Director Financial Aid, Richard Esposito
Associate VP Development, James Miller
Director Alumni Relations, Julie Shepard
Director Human Resources, Mary Ellen Baney
Director Athletics, Greg Amodio
Director, James F. McGuirk II
Director, Irene M. Qualters, age 62
Director, Joseph C. (Joe) Guyaux, age 61
Director, John W. McGonigle, age 73
Director, William J. Lyons, age 63
Director, Gregory S. (Greg) Babe, age 55
Director, Robert Z. Gussin, age 74
Director, James N. Crutchfield
Director, Sister Mary Dacey
Director, Thomas R. Donahue
Vice Chair, Marie M. Jones
Director, Samuel P. Kamin
Director, Patricia D. Yoder
Director, Rev John P. Skaj
Director, Thaddeus J. Senko
Director, Winston Pittman Sr.
Director, Mary Grealy
Director, Rev John Fogarty
Director, Anthony J. Carfang
Auditors: KPMGLLP

LOCATIONS

HQ: Duquesne University of The Holy Ghost
600 Forbes Ave., Pittsburgh PA 15282
Phone: 412-396-6000   Fax: 412-396-5780
Web: www.duq.edu

HISTORICAL FINANCIALS
Company Type: School

Income Statement   FYE: June 30

	REVENUE ($ mil.)	NET INCOME ($ mil.)	NET PROFIT MARGIN	EMPLOYEES
06/11	333	21	6.6%	2,836
06/10	290	0	—	0
06/09	290	0	—	0
06/08	293	17	5.9%	0
Annual Growth	4.3%	7.9%	—	—

2011 Year-End Financials

Debt ratio: ——
Return on equity: 6.60%
Cash ($ mil.): 30
Current ratio: ——
Long-term debt ($ mil.): —
Dividends
Yield: —
Payout: —
Market value ($ mil.): —

DURHAM PUBLIC SCHOOLS SCHOLARSHIP FOUNDATION INC.

LOCATIONS

HQ: DURHAM PUBLIC SCHOOLS SCHOLARSHIP
FOUNDATION INC.
511 CLEVELAND ST, DURHAM, NC 27701-3334
Phone: 919-560-2000
Web: www.dpsnc.net

HISTORICAL FINANCIALS
Company Type: Private

Income Statement   FYE: June 30

	REVENUE ($ mil.)	NET INCOME ($ mil.)	NET PROFIT MARGIN	EMPLOYEES
06/11	398	20	5.2%	4,500
06/10	331	7	2.3%	0
06/09	359	0	0.2%	0
06/08	331	(0)	—	0
Annual Growth	6.3%	—	—	—

2011 Year-End Financials

Debt ratio: ——
Return on equity: 5.20%
Cash ($ mil.): 51
Current ratio: 1.60
Long-term debt ($ mil.): —
Dividends
Yield: —
Payout: —
Market value ($ mil.): —

DURVET INC.

LOCATIONS

HQ: DURVET INC.
100 SE MAGELLAN DR, BLUE SPRINGS, MO
64014-5909
Phone: 816-229-9101
Web: www.durvet.com

HISTORICAL FINANCIALS
Company Type: Private

Income Statement   FYE: November 30

	REVENUE ($ mil.)	NET INCOME ($ mil.)	NET PROFIT MARGIN	EMPLOYEES
11/11	133	6	5.1%	30
11/10	116	5	4.5%	0
11/09	103	4	4.7%	0
11/08	105	4	4.3%	0
Annual Growth	8.3%	14.5%	—	—

2011 Year-End Financials

Debt ratio: ——
Return on equity: 5.10%
Cash ($ mil.): 0
Current ratio: 0.70
Long-term debt ($ mil.): —
Dividends
Yield: —
Payout: —
Market value ($ mil.): —

DUSTIN CONSTRUCTION INC.

LOCATIONS

HQ: DUSTIN CONSTRUCTION INC.
2510 URBANA PIKE STE 201, IJAMSVILLE, MD
21754-8609
Phone: 301-810-4320
Web: www.dustinconstruction.com

HISTORICAL FINANCIALS
Company Type: Private

Income Statement   FYE: December 31

	REVENUE ($ mil.)	NET INCOME ($ mil.)	NET PROFIT MARGIN	EMPLOYEES
12/11	88	1	1.5%	75
12/10	88	1	1.2%	0
12/09*	0	0	—	0
06/05	66	0	—	0
Annual Growth	10.1%	—	—	—

*Fiscal year change

2011 Year-End Financials

Debt ratio: ——
Return on equity: 1.50%
Cash ($ mil.): 3
Current ratio: 1.20
Long-term debt ($ mil.): —
Dividends
Yield: —
Payout: —
Market value ($ mil.): —

DUVAL COUNTY PUBLIC SCHOOLS

LOCATIONS

HQ: DUVAL COUNTY PUBLIC SCHOOLS
1701 PRUDENTIAL DR, JACKSONVILLE, FL
32207-8152
Phone: 904-390-2000
Web: www.seabreezepta.org

HISTORICAL FINANCIALS

Company Type: Private

Income Statement

FYE: June 30

	REVENUE ($ mil.)	NET INCOME ($ mil.)	NET PROFIT MARGIN	EMPLOYEES
06/11	1,187	17	1.5%	13,000
06/07	1,189	27	2.3%	0
06/06	1,063	(22)	—	0
06/05	982	59	6.0%	0
Annual Growth	6.5%	(33.3%)	—	—

2011 Year-End Financials

Debt ratio: ——
Return on equity: 1.50%
Cash ($ mil.): 35
Current ratio: —
Long-term debt ($ mil.): —

Dividends
Yield: —
Payout: —
Market value ($ mil.): —

DYNAMIX GROUP INC

Dynamix Group understands that business technology never sits still. The company provides information technology (IT) products and services including the implementation and configuration of software and hardware as well as network systems maintenance and technical support from its offices throughout the southeastern US. The company's core business is centered around IBM products but it also has product partnerships with other business software vendors including Oracle and VMware. Additional data network services include disaster recovery and storage management. Dynamix was founded in 1995 by CEO Chuck Hawkins and COO Dave DeLong both veterans of IBM.

EXECUTIVES

Technical Services Manager, Rick Scott
President, Charles E. (Chuck) Hawkins Jr., age 57
CFO and COO, David A. (Dave) DeLong, age 61
Director Marketing, John Sousa
Director Sales, Fred Duckett
Director Sales, Nicky Hobbs
Maintenance and Support Manager, Paul Reams
Controller, Scott McKelvey

LOCATIONS

HQ: Dynamix Group Inc.
1905 Woodstock Rd. Ste. 4150, Roswell GA 30075-5625
Phone: 770-643-8877   **Fax:** 770-643-8331
Web: www.dynamixgroup.com

COMPETITORS

Agilysys	Unisys
CDW	Ventyx
Pomeroy IT	
ProSys Information Systems	

HISTORICAL FINANCIALS

Company Type: Private

Income Statement

FYE: December 31

	REVENUE ($ mil.)	NET INCOME ($ mil.)	NET PROFIT MARGIN	EMPLOYEES
12/11	120	10	8.7%	90
12/10	84	5	6.7%	0
Annual Growth	43.1%	84.1%	—	—

2011 Year-End Financials

Debt ratio: ——
Return on equity: 8.70%
Cash ($ mil.): 16
Current ratio: 2.40
Long-term debt ($ mil.): —

Dividends
Yield: —
Payout: —
Market value ($ mil.): —

DYNASTY FARMS INC.

LOCATIONS

HQ: DYNASTY FARMS INC.
740 AIRPORT BLVD, SALINAS, CA 93901-4510
Phone: 831-755-1398

HISTORICAL FINANCIALS

Company Type: Private

Income Statement

FYE: December 31

	REVENUE ($ mil.)	NET INCOME ($ mil.)	NET PROFIT MARGIN	EMPLOYEES
12/11	282	0	0.0%	100
12/10	257	4	1.9%	0
Annual Growth	9.4%	(97.6%)	—	—

2011 Year-End Financials

Debt ratio: ——
Return on equity: —
Cash ($ mil.): 6
Current ratio: 1.10
Long-term debt ($ mil.): —

Dividends
Yield: —
Payout: —
Market value ($ mil.): —

DYNETICS INC.

LOCATIONS

HQ: DYNETICS INC.
1002 EXPLORER BLVD NW, HUNTSVILLE, AL
35806-2806
Phone: 256-922-9230
Web: www.dynetics.com

HISTORICAL FINANCIALS

Company Type: Private

Income Statement

FYE: July 1

	REVENUE ($ mil.)	NET INCOME ($ mil.)	NET PROFIT MARGIN	EMPLOYEES
07/12	266	17	6.5%	1,400
07/11*	273	21	7.9%	0
06/10	235	13	5.6%	0
06/09	263	16	6.3%	0
Annual Growth	0.4%	1.4%	—	—

*Fiscal year change

2012 Year-End Financials

Debt ratio: —
Return on equity: 6.50%
Cash ($ mil.): 35
Current ratio: 2.40
Long-term debt ($ mil.): —

Dividends
Yield: —
Payout: —
Market value ($ mil.): —

E & J LAWRENCE CORP.

LOCATIONS

HQ: E & J LAWRENCE CORP.
85 METRO WAY, SECAUCUS, NJ 07094-1905
Phone: 201-210-5577
Web: www.jimmyjazzstores.com

HISTORICAL FINANCIALS

Company Type: Private

Income Statement

FYE: December 31

	REVENUE ($ mil.)	NET INCOME ($ mil.)	NET PROFIT MARGIN	EMPLOYEES
12/11	204	3	1.9%	2,000
12/10*	184	3	1.9%	0
06/09	62	0	1.0%	0
Annual Growth	80.9%	151.1%	—	—

*Fiscal year change

2011 Year-End Financials

Debt ratio: ——
Return on equity: 1.90%
Cash ($ mil.): 5
Current ratio: 0.10
Long-term debt ($ mil.): —

Dividends
Yield: —
Payout: —
Market value ($ mil.): —

EA ENGINEERING SCIENCE AND TECHNOLOGY INC.

EA Engineering Science and Technology wants to stop pollution before it starts by offering environmental consulting services. The company's specialties include brownfields and urban redevelopment environmental compliance management and natural resources management. Its more than 450 professionals have completed more than 100000 environmental projects worldwide (more than $1 billion of services). Customers include government agencies and industrial manufacturers. EA Engineering operates from more than 25 offices —23 in the US (including facilities in Alaska and Hawaii) and one in Guam.

Client loyalty is a major factor in EA Engineering's business development plan. Some 80% of the company's business comes from its existing client base. EA Engineering's strategy is to approach the marketplace and its clients with openness towards towards ideas and information the judicious use of resources a balanced method and a collaborative approach to problem-solving.

In 2010 EA Engineering reported revenues of $92 million with net income of almost $4 million.

The company (which has operated in Guam since 1994) secured a $400 million contract in 2010 from the US Department of Transportation's Maritime Administration to provide program management services for the remodeling and expansion of Guam's major port.

Also that year EA Engineering acquired Blumen Consulting Group of Kirkland Washington. The 12-member professional services firm provides state and national Environmental Policy Act compliance land use permitting community planning project/team coordination and management services. the deal will expand EA Engineering's environmental planning and compliance services.

The company was established in 1973. A partnership between founder and chairman Loren Jensen and engineering firm Louis Berger Group took EA Engineering private in 2001.

EXECUTIVES

Chairman, Loren D. Jensen
CFO, Peter Ney
President and CEO, Ian D. MacFarlane
SVP Operations, Michael Battle
Chief Scientist, Christine Papageorgis
Director IT, Joe Haggerty
Marketing Manager, Catherine Kuwabara
Auditors: PricewaterhouseCoopersLLP

LOCATIONS

HQ: EA Engineering Science and Technology Inc.
11019 McCormick Rd., Hunt Valley MD 21031
Phone: 410-584-7000 **Fax:** 410-771-1625
Web: www.eaest.com

PRODUCTS/OPERATIONS

Selected Services

Air resources management
Brownfields and urban redevelopment
Construction management and inspection
Environmental compliance management
Information technology
Infrastructure engineering
Natural resources management
Site characterization
Site remediation
Solid waste management
Water resources management

COMPETITORS

BioMedical Technology Solutions	GZA GeoEnvironmental
	MWH Global
Black & Veatch	Tetra Tech
Brown and Caldwell	TRC Companies
Ecology and Environment	URS
	Weston Solutions

HISTORICAL FINANCIALS

Company Type: Private

Income Statement

FYE: June 30

	REVENUE ($ mil.)	NET INCOME ($ mil.)	NET PROFIT MARGIN	EMPLOYEES
06/12	59	3	6.0%	440
06/11	99	4	4.1%	0
06/09	85	4	4.9%	0
06/07	46	3	8.3%	0
Annual Growth	**8.5%**	**(2.5%)**	**—**	**—**

2012 Year-End Financials

Debt ratio: ——
Return on equity: 6.00%
Cash ($ mil.): 5
Current ratio: 1.20
Long-term debt ($ mil.): —
Dividends
Yield: —
Payout: —
Market value ($ mil.): —

EARLY LEARNING COALITION OF PALM BEACH COUNTY INC.

LOCATIONS

HQ: EARLY LEARNING COALITION OF PALM BEACH COUNTY INC.
2300 HIGH RIDGE RD # 115, BOYNTON BEACH, FL 33426-8795
Phone: 561-214-7420

HISTORICAL FINANCIALS

Company Type: Private

Income Statement

FYE: June 30

	REVENUE ($ mil.)	NET INCOME ($ mil.)	NET PROFIT MARGIN	EMPLOYEES
06/11	89	0	0.1%	2
06/10	85	(0)	—	0
06/09	75	0	—	0
Annual Growth	**9.3%**	**—**	**—**	**—**

2011 Year-End Financials

Debt ratio: ——
Return on equity: 0.10%
Cash ($ mil.): 1
Current ratio: 0.30
Long-term debt ($ mil.): —
Dividends
Yield: —
Payout: —
Market value ($ mil.): —

EARNHARDT FORD SALES COMPANY INC

LOCATIONS

HQ: EARNHARDT FORD SALES COMPANY INC
7300 W ORCHID LN, TEMPE, AZ 85284
Phone: 480-893-0000
Web: www.nobull.com

HISTORICAL FINANCIALS

Company Type: Private

Income Statement

FYE: December 31

	REVENUE ($ mil.)	NET INCOME ($ mil.)	NET PROFIT MARGIN	EMPLOYEES
12/11	97	0	0.2%	520
12/10	97	0	0.2%	0
12/09	0	0	—	0
12/08	97	0	0.2%	0
Annual Growth	**(0.0%)**	**(0.0%)**	**—**	**—**

2011 Year-End Financials

Debt ratio: ——
Return on equity: 0.20%
Cash ($ mil.): 14
Current ratio: 1.00
Long-term debt ($ mil.): —
Dividends
Yield: —
Payout: —
Market value ($ mil.): —

EAST BATON ROUGE PARISH SCHOOL DISTRICT

LOCATIONS

HQ: EAST BATON ROUGE PARISH SCHOOL DISTRICT
1050 S FOSTER DR, BATON ROUGE, LA 70806-7221
Phone: 225-922-5618
Web: www.ebrschools.org

HISTORICAL FINANCIALS

Company Type: Private

Income Statement

FYE: June 30

	REVENUE ($ mil.)	NET INCOME ($ mil.)	NET PROFIT MARGIN	EMPLOYEES
06/12	96	(72)	—	6,800
06/07	427	393	92.0%	0
06/05	427	34	8.0%	0
06/03	419	0	—	0
Annual Growth	**(38.7%)**	**—**	**—**	**—**

2012 Year-End Financials

Debt ratio: ——
Return on equity: (-74.70)%
Cash ($ mil.): 207
Current ratio: ——
Long-term debt ($ mil.): —
Dividends
Yield: —
Payout: —
Market value ($ mil.): —

EAST CENTRAL IOWA COOPERATIVE

LOCATIONS

HQ: EAST CENTRAL IOWA COOPERATIVE
602 WASHINGTON ST, HUDSON, IA 50643-7751
Phone: 319-988-3257
Web: www.ecicoop.com

HISTORICAL FINANCIALS

Company Type: Private

Income Statement

	REVENUE ($ mil.)	NET INCOME ($ mil.)	NET PROFIT MARGIN	EMPLOYEES
08/12	172	1	0.8%	54
08/11	131	1	0.9%	0
08/10	86	1	1.6%	0
08/09	117	1	1.3%	0
Annual Growth	13.4%	(2.7%)	—	—

FYE: August 31

2012 Year-End Financials

Debt ratio: —
Return on equity: 0.80%
Cash ($ mil.): 1
Current ratio: 0.20
Long-term debt ($ mil.): —
Dividends
  Yield: —
  Payout: —
Market value ($ mil.): —

EAST COAST DISTRIBUTORS INC.

LOCATIONS

HQ: EAST COAST DISTRIBUTORS INC.
1705 BROAD ST, CRANSTON, RI 02905-2724
Phone: 401-780-8800
Web: www.eastcoastdistributors.com

HISTORICAL FINANCIALS

Company Type: Private

Income Statement

	REVENUE ($ mil.)	NET INCOME ($ mil.)	NET PROFIT MARGIN	EMPLOYEES
12/11	160	1	1.1%	10
12/10	128	1	1.2%	0
12/09	111	1	1.2%	0
12/08	111	1	1.1%	0
Annual Growth	12.9%	14.3%	—	—

FYE: December 31

EAST TENNESSEE CHILDREN'S HOSPITAL ASSOCIATION INC.

ETCH has made a permanent mark on the lives of countless children over the years. Knoxville-based East Tennessee Children's Hospital (ETCH) with more than 150 beds provides a full range of health care services to children from eastern Tennessee and nearby portions of Kentucky North Carolina and Virginia. Among its 90 specialized services are cardiology neonatal care orthopedics and psychiatry. The hospital also offers several outside support services including those for families of children stricken by cancer. Its emergency department treats some 70000 patients each year. The hospital's roots are in the foundation of Knox County Crippled Children's Hospital in 1937 with less than 50 beds.

EXECUTIVES

President CEO and Director, Keith D. Goodwin, age 57
VP Operations, Rudy McKinley
VP Human Resources, Paul Bates
VP Medical Services, Joe Childs
VP Patient Care, Laura Barnes
Chief of Staff, John Buchheit
VP Finance and CFO, Zane Goodrich
Chief of Medicine, Lori Patterson
Chief of Surgery, Alfred P. Kennedy Jr.

LOCATIONS

HQ: East Tennessee Children's Hospital
2018 Clinch Ave., Knoxville TN 37901
Phone: 865-541-8000   **Fax:** 865-541-8696
Web: www.etch.com

COMPETITORS

Akron Children's Hospital
All Children's Hospital
Children's Hopsital of Chicago
Children's Hospital and Health System
Children's Hospital Boston
Children's Hospital Colorado
Children's Hospital of Philadelphia
Children's Hospital of Richmond
Children's Mercy Hospital
Cincinnati Children's Hospital
Covenant Health
Dell Children's Medical Center
Nationwide Children's Hospital
Shriners Hospitals For Children
Tennova Healthcare
University Health System Inc.

HISTORICAL FINANCIALS

Company Type: Private - Not-for-Profit

Income Statement

	REVENUE ($ mil.)	NET INCOME ($ mil.)	NET PROFIT MARGIN	EMPLOYEES
06/12	209	29	14.2%	1,500
06/11	183	19	10.5%	0
06/10	170	11	6.5%	0
06/09	158	(5)	—	0
Annual Growth	9.7%	—	—	—

FYE: June 30

2012 Year-End Financials

Debt ratio: —
Return on equity: 14.20%
Cash ($ mil.): 32
Current ratio: 2.80
Long-term debt ($ mil.): —
Dividends
  Yield: —
  Payout: —
Market value ($ mil.): —

EASTERN LOS ANGELES REGIONAL CENTER FOR THE DEVELOPMENTALLY DISA

LOCATIONS

HQ: EASTERN LOS ANGELES REGIONAL CENTER FOR THE DEVELOPMENTALLY DISA
1000 S FREMONT AVE # 23, ALHAMBRA, CA 91803-8800
Phone: 626-299-4700

HISTORICAL FINANCIALS

Company Type: Private

Income Statement

	REVENUE ($ mil.)	NET INCOME ($ mil.)	NET PROFIT MARGIN	EMPLOYEES
06/11	149	(0)	—	287
06/10	144	(0)	—	0
06/09	144	0	0.0%	0
06/08	125	0	0.0%	0
Annual Growth	6.0%	—	—	—

FYE: June 30

2011 Year-End Financials

Debt ratio: —
Return on equity: —
Cash ($ mil.): 8
Current ratio: 0.60
Long-term debt ($ mil.): —
Dividends
  Yield: —
  Payout: —
Market value ($ mil.): —

EASTERN MICHIGAN UNIVERSITY

Eastern Michigan University (known affectionately as just plain Eastern) has long been an affordable place to study your way into a better career. The university began as a teachers' college in 1849 and it still graduates one out of every four teachers in Michigan. Eastern has an enrollment of some 23000 students (90% are Michigan residents) who attend college on its campus in the southeastern part of the state. Its 143 undergraduate and 136 graduate program offerings include arts and sciences business education technology and health and human services. The university operates continuing education campuses in Brighton Detroit Flint Jackson Livonia Monroe and Traverse City.

Eastern knows its student base well and has created accelerated Continuing Education programs with classes held on weekends and evenings. It is also steadily adding online coursework and seeks to attract military personnel. Its Return to Learn program is specifically geared to serve displaced workers who need additional education to rejoin the workforce.

EXECUTIVES

Chair Board of Regents, Thomas W. (Tom) Sidlik, age 62
Executive Director Public Safety, Greg O'Dell
Chief Government Relations Officer Office of Government Relations and Special Projects, Freman Hendrix
EVP Academic Affairs and Provost, Donald M. (Don) Loppnow
General Counsel and University Attorney, Kenneth A. (Ken) McKanders
Vice Chair Board of Regents, Roy E. Wilbanks
Interim Associate VP Human Resources, Karen Simpkins
President, Susan W. Martin, age 61
Director Office of Diversity and Affirmative Action, Sharon Abraham
Associate VP Facilities, John Donegan
Athletic Director Intercollegiate Athletics, Derrick Gragg
Interim CFO Business and Finance, John Lumm
Interim VP Enrollment Management, Bernice Lindke
Member Board of Regents, James F. Stapleton
Member Board of Regents, Philip A. Incarnati, age 58
Member Board of Regents, Gary D. Hawks
Member Board of Regents, Francine (Fran) Parker, age 57
Member Board of Regents, Floyd Clack
Vice Chair Board of Regents, Roy E. Wilbanks
Member Board of Regents, Mohamed Okdie
Auditors: PricewaterhouseCoopersLLP

LOCATIONS

HQ: Eastern Michigan University
1000 College Place, Ypsilanti MI 48197
Phone: 734-487-1849   **Fax:** 808-956-5286
Web: www.hawaii.edu

PRODUCTS/OPERATIONS

Selected Colleges Schools and Departments

College of Arts and Sciences
  African American Studies
  Art
  Biology
  Chemistry
  Communications and Theatre Arts
  Computer Science
  Economics
  English Language and Literature
  Foreign Languages and Bilingual Studies
  Geography and Geology
  History and Philosphy
  Mathematics
  Music and Dance
  Physic and Astronomy
  Political Science
  Psychology
  Sociology Anthropology and Criminology
College of Business
  Accounting and Finance
  Computer Information Systems
  Management
  Marketing
College of Education
  Leadership and Counseling
  Special Education

Teacher Education
College of Health and Human Services
  School of Health Promotion and Human Performance
  School of Health Sciences
  School of Nursing
  School of Social Work
College of Technology
  Military Science and Leadership
  School of Engineering Technology
  School of Technology Studies

HISTORICAL FINANCIALS

Company Type: School

Income Statement   FYE: June 30

	REVENUE ($ mil.)	NET INCOME ($ mil.)	NET PROFIT MARGIN	EMPLOYEES
06/11	221	24	11.2%	2,000
06/10	217	(1)	—	0
06/09	211	5	2.5%	0
06/08	201	3	1.5%	0
Annual Growth	3.2%	101.3%	—	—

2011 Year-End Financials

Debt ratio: —
Return on equity: 11.20%
Cash ($ mil.): 4
Current ratio: 0.40
Long-term debt ($ mil.): —
Dividends
  Yield: —
  Payout: —
  Market value ($ mil.): —

EASTERN UNIVERSITY

LOCATIONS

HQ: EASTERN UNIVERSITY
1300 EAGLE RD, WAYNE, PA 19087-3617
Phone: 610-341-5800
Web: www.easternuniversity.com

HISTORICAL FINANCIALS

Company Type: Private

Income Statement   FYE: June 30

	REVENUE ($ mil.)	NET INCOME ($ mil.)	NET PROFIT MARGIN	EMPLOYEES
06/11	91	4	4.7%	0
06/10	94	9	9.8%	0
06/09	81	0	—	0
06/08	77	2	3.5%	0
Annual Growth	5.6%	16.5%	—	—

2011 Year-End Financials

Debt ratio: —
Return on equity: 4.70%
Cash ($ mil.): 19
Current ratio: —
Long-term debt ($ mil.): —
Dividends
  Yield: —
  Payout: —
  Market value ($ mil.): —

EASTERN VIRGINIA MEDICAL SCHOOL

Eastern Virginia Medical School (EVMS) sends graduated physicians down the Hampton Roads. The school offers medical and doctoral degrees residencies and specialty programs such as reproductive medicine. The community-oriented school does not have a teaching hospital but rather partners with about a dozen regional hospitals. Its main campus is part of the Eastern Virginia Medical Center which is also home to Sentara Norfolk General Hospital and Children's Hospital of The King's Daughters located in the Hampton Roads region of southeastern Virginia. The south campus hosts pediatric and diabetes research programs. EVMS also has research programs devoted to cancer infectious diseases and heart disease.

The school was established in 1973. EVMS operates under a state charter and operates as a public institution. Its governing board is comprised of representatives from surrounding communities as well as appointees from the EVMS Foundation which conducts fundraising activities for the school.

In 2012 EVMS entered discussions with the College of William & Mary over a possible merger or affiliation agreement. Under proposed terms of the deal which must be approved by Virginia's governing entities EVMS would join the College of William & Mary organization becoming known as the William & Mary School of Medicine. The two schools have worked together on projects in the past including conducting research collaborations.

In addition EVMS has been working to improve its facilities so that it can increase its enrollment numbers in both the physician assistant and medical doctorate programs. A new medical education and research building that meets this need was opened in mid-2011.

EXECUTIVES

VP Administration and Finance, Mark Babashanian
Dean and Provost, Gerald J. Pepe
President, Harry T. Lester
Director News, Doug Gardner
Director of Events Planning and Management, Ashlyn Brandt
VP External Affairs, Claudia Keenan Hough
General Counsel and Compliance Officer, Stacy Purcell
Director Office of Alumni Affairs, Melissa Lang
Director Office of Development, Connie Hetrick
Director Office of Marketing and Communications, Vincent Rhodes

LOCATIONS

HQ: Eastern Virginia Medical School
358 Mowbray Arch, Norfolk VA 23507
Phone: 757-446-5600   **Fax:** 757-446-5896
Web: www.evms.edu

HISTORICAL FINANCIALS
Company Type: School

Income Statement
FYE: June 30

	REVENUE ($ mil.)	NET INCOME ($ mil.)	NET PROFIT MARGIN	EMPLOYEES
06/12	226	17	7.5%	1,500
06/11	238	47	20.0%	0
06/10	211	15	7.2%	0
06/07	9	5	58.4%	0
Annual Growth	185.2%	44.0%	—	—

2012 Year-End Financials

Debt ratio: ——
Return on equity: 7.50%
Cash ($ mil.): 2
Current ratio: 1.00
Long-term debt ($ mil.): —

Dividends
Yield: —
Payout: —
Market value ($ mil.): —

EASTERN WASHINGTON UNIVERSITY INC

Eagles —the mascot kind at any rate —soar around Eastern Washington University (EWU). The university serves about 10000 students in the area around metropolitan Spokane Washington. Most students study at EWU's Cheney campus but the school includes other learning centers around the state. EWU boasts small classes and a 20 to 1 student-to-faculty ratio. More than 100 fields of study are offered through colleges that include Arts and Letters Business and Public Administration Education and Human Development and Science Mathematics and Technology. The school was founded in 1882 as the Benjamin P. Cheney Academy

EXECUTIVES

VP Business and Finance, Mary Voves
Associate VP and CFO, Toni Habegger
Associate VP Enrollment Management, Lawrence (Larry) Briggs
Vice Provost Graduate Education Research Academic Planning and Evaluation, Ronald (Ron) Dalla
President, Rodolfo Arevalo
Provost, John B. Mason
VP Student Affairs, Dorothy Zeisler-Vralsted
CIO, Gary Pratt
Director Public Safety and Chief of Police, Timothy Walters
VP University Advancement, Michael Westfall
Director University Relations, David Sonntag

LOCATIONS

HQ: Eastern Washington University
526 5th St., Cheney WA 99004
Phone: 509-359-6200   **Fax:** 509-359-6692
Web: www.ewu.edu

HISTORICAL FINANCIALS
Company Type: School

Income Statement
FYE: June 30

	REVENUE ($ mil.)	NET INCOME ($ mil.)	NET PROFIT MARGIN	EMPLOYEES
06/11	122	11	9.5%	1,550
06/08	110	4	4.4%	0
06/05	4	0	6.7%	0
06/04	101	22	21.8%	0
Annual Growth	6.3%	(19.4%)	—	—

2011 Year-End Financials

Debt ratio: ——
Return on equity: 9.50%
Cash ($ mil.): 32
Current ratio: 2.00
Long-term debt ($ mil.): —

Dividends
Yield: —
Payout: —
Market value ($ mil.): —

EASTERNS AUTOMOTIVE GROUP

LOCATIONS

HQ: EASTERNS AUTOMOTIVE GROUP
4809 SAINT BARNABAS RD, TEMPLE HILLS, MD 20748-4603
Phone: 301-702-6565

HISTORICAL FINANCIALS
Company Type: Private

Income Statement
FYE: December 31

	REVENUE ($ mil.)	NET INCOME ($ mil.)	NET PROFIT MARGIN	EMPLOYEES
12/11	82	5	6.6%	2
Annual Growth	—	—	—	—

2011 Year-End Financials

Debt ratio: ——
Return on equity: 6.60%
Cash ($ mil.): 0
Current ratio: 0.10
Long-term debt ($ mil.): —

Dividends
Yield: —
Payout: —
Market value ($ mil.): —

EBP SUPPLY SOLUTIONS

Eastern Bag & Paper is a leading distributor of paper products in the northeastern US. In addition to disposable tableware and packaging the company offers food service products (including china and glassware) restaurant equipment (can openers refrigerators) personal care items (bath mats roll towels) and cleansers and maintenance supplies (air fresheners vacuums). Its products are used by the industrial health care food service and janitorial industries. Eastern Bag & Paper is a family-operated company founded in 1918 by Samuel Baum.

The company operates three distribution centers in Connecticut Massachusetts and New Jersey and

it maintains a fleet of more than 70 trucks and trailers.

EXECUTIVES

President, James Sugarman
CEO, Meredith Baum Reuben
VP Marketing, Ken Rosenberg
VP and General Manager Tewksbury Division, John Mahon
CFO, William O'Donnell
VP Operations, Don Burton
Director Purchasing, Dave Epstein
CIO, Jack Jurkowski
VP Human Resources, Joseph F. Lopresti
VP and Sales Manager Healthcare Services, Dan Colcord
VP and Sales Manager Redistribution, Richard Lipp
VP and Sales Manager Food Services, Alan Schachter
VP and Sales Manager Cleaning Services, Derek Wallace
Director Customer Service and Telesales, Kathy Carbonella
Manager Customer Service Tewksbury, Sherry Benham
VP Sales New Jersey Division, Matthew Sugarman
VP Purchasing, Eric Liebeskind

LOCATIONS

HQ: Eastern Bag and Paper Company Incorporated
200 Research Dr., Milford CT 06460
Phone: 203-878-1814   **Fax:** 203-878-0438
Web: www.easternbag.com

COMPETITORS

AFFLINK	Perkins Paper
MAINES	RDA Advantage
Penn Jersey	Sysco

HISTORICAL FINANCIALS
Company Type: Private

Income Statement
FYE: December 31

	REVENUE ($ mil.)	NET INCOME ($ mil.)	NET PROFIT MARGIN	EMPLOYEES
12/11	174	0	—	285
12/08	0	0	—	0
Annual Growth	—	—	—	—

ECKERD COLLEGE INC.

What better place to study marine science than on nearly 200 acres of Florida waterfront? Eckerd College is a private co-educational college located in St. Petersburg. The school has more than 1800 students and 160 faculty members and it offers about 40 majors for students to earn bachelor of arts and bachelor of science degrees. Areas of study include marine science psychology economics biology biochemistry international studies literature and art. The school also operates a Program for Experienced Learners where about 700 adult students can earn a bachelor's degree in about a dozen areas as well as study abroad offerings. Eckerd College is affiliated with the Presbyterian Church (U.S.A.).

Company Background

Eckerd College was founded in 1958 as the Florida Presbyterian College and changed its name in 1972 after being saved from financial crisis by Jack Eckerd the founder of Florida-based drugstore chain Eckerd.

EXECUTIVES

President, Donald R. Eastman III
VP and Dean Faculty, Lloyd W. Chapin
VP Advancement, Mathew S. Bisset
VP Student Life and Dean Students, James J. Annarelli
Director Alumni Relations and Advancement Programming, E. Grace Lager
CFO and Treasurer, Chris Brennan
Controller, Gerald (Jerry) Ganz
Bursar, Angie Noronow
Director Information Technology Services, John Duff
Dean Admission and Financial Aid, John Sullivan
Director Financial Aid, Pat G. Watkins
Registrar, Linda Swindall
Director Campus Safety and Security, Sylvia Chillcott
Director Career Resources, Jane G. Colson
Director Community and Media Relations, Alizza T. Punzalan-Hall

LOCATIONS

HQ: Eckerd College
4200 54th Ave. South, St. Petersburg FL 33711
Phone: 727-867-1166   **Fax:** 610-865-9832
Web: www.phoenixtube.com

PRODUCTS/OPERATIONS

Selected Programs

American Studies
Ancient Studies
Anthropology
Art (Visual Arts)
Biochemistry
Biology
Business Administration
Chemistry
Communication
Comparative Literature
Computer Science
Creative Writing
East Asian Studies
Economics
English
Environmental Studies
French
Geosciences
History
Humanities
Human Development
Interdisciplinary Arts
International Business
International Relations & Global Affairs
International Studies
Literature
Management
Marine Science
Mathematics
Music
Philosophy
Physics
Political Science
Psychology
Religious Studies
Sociology
Spanish
Theatre
Visual Arts
Women's and Gender Studies

HISTORICAL FINANCIALS

Company Type: School

Income Statement

FYE: June 30

	REVENUE ($ mil.)	NET INCOME ($ mil.)	NET PROFIT MARGIN	EMPLOYEES
06/11	110	19	17.9%	377
06/10	95	9	10.1%	0
06/09	90	0	—	0
06/08	89	4	5.1%	0
Annual Growth	7.0%	62.4%	—	—

2011 Year-End Financials

Debt ratio: —
Return on equity: 17.90%
Cash ($ mil.): 38
Current ratio: —
Long-term debt ($ mil.): —
Dividends
    Yield: —
    Payout: —
Market value ($ mil.): —

ECKERD YOUTH ALTERNATIVES INC.

Eckerd Youth Alternatives (EYA) provides early intervention and prevention wilderness education residential and day treatment and re-entry and aftercare programs for at-risk youths. The not-for-profit organization has worked to help more than 80000 kids through its operations in about 10 states located primarily in the eastern US. Many of EYA's some 40 programs are offered under contract with state juvenile justice agencies. EYA was established in 1968 by Jack Eckerd the founder of the Eckerd drugstore chain and his wife Ruth Eckerd. During the past few years the company has been focused on expanding its community-based support programs.

In 2007 the organization launched its Eckerd Community and Home Outreach Program (ECHO) program in Louisiana's Region 3 area to serve youth and their families there. It also established the Eckerd Multi-Systemic Therapy program in Tallahassee Florida to provide in-home intensive therapy and support to youth and their families.

EYA in 2008 debuted a pair of therapeutic programs in Texas. Both community-based support programs they include the Eckerd Community Supervision Program and the Eckerd Functional Family Therapy Program.

EXECUTIVES

Director Admissions, Francene Hazel
Chairman, Ken O'Herron
President CEO and Director, David Dennis
Chief Administrative Officer, Pamela Griffin
COO, Kimberly O'Brien
VP Community-Based Services, Ron Zychowski
Director Marketing and Communications, Karen Bonsignori
Chief Development Officer, Cynthia A. Smith
Director, Peter M. Scott III, age 61
Director, Kathleen M. Shanahan, age 52
Director, James T. Swann III
Director, Nancy Eckerd Hart
Director, V. Raymond Ferrara
President CEO and Director, David Dennis
Director, Nick Dewan
Director, Jay B. (Trey) Starkey

LOCATIONS

HQ: Eckerd Youth Alternatives
100 N. Starcrest Dr., Clearwater FL 33758-7450
Phone: 727-461-2990   **Fax:** 727-442-5911
Web: www.eckerd.org

HISTORICAL FINANCIALS

Company Type: Private - Not-for-Profit

Income Statement

FYE: June 30

	REVENUE ($ mil.)	NET INCOME ($ mil.)	NET PROFIT MARGIN	EMPLOYEES
06/11	99	1	2.0%	1,400
06/10	100	(0)	—	0
06/09*	120	(5)	—	0
12/08	81	(2)	—	0
Annual Growth	7.1%	—	—	—

*Fiscal year change

2011 Year-End Financials

Debt ratio: —
Return on equity: 2.00%
Cash ($ mil.): 11
Current ratio: 1.20
Long-term debt ($ mil.): —
Dividends
    Yield: —
    Payout: —
Market value ($ mil.): —

EDEN TOWNSHIP HOSPITAL DISTRICT INC

LOCATIONS

HQ: EDEN TOWNSHIP HOSPITAL DISTRICT INC
20103 LAKE CHABOT RD, CASTRO VALLEY, CA 94546-5305
Phone: 510-727-2700

HISTORICAL FINANCIALS

Company Type: Private

Income Statement

FYE: December 31

	REVENUE ($ mil.)	NET INCOME ($ mil.)	NET PROFIT MARGIN	EMPLOYEES
12/11	317	(3)	—	968
12/09*	311	16	5.2%	0
06/08	2	1	69.0%	0
12/02	146	2	1.8%	0
Annual Growth	29.4%	—	—	—

*Fiscal year change

2011 Year-End Financials

Debt ratio: —
Return on equity: (-0.90)%
Cash ($ mil.): 12
Current ratio: 0.60
Long-term debt ($ mil.): —
Dividends
    Yield: —
    Payout: —
Market value ($ mil.): —

EDPA USA INC.

LOCATIONS

HQ: EDPA USA INC.
350 5TH AVE STE 5010, NEW YORK, NY 10118-5010
Phone: 212-714-0644
Web: www.edpausa.com

HISTORICAL FINANCIALS

Company Type: Private

Income Statement
FYE: June 30

	REVENUE ($ mil.)	NET INCOME ($ mil.)	NET PROFIT MARGIN	EMPLOYEES
06/11	87	0	0.8%	28
06/10	63	0	0.9%	0
06/08	66	0	0.3%	0
06/07	59	0	0.4%	0
Annual Growth	13.5%	38.1%	—	—

2011 Year-End Financials

Debt ratio: ——
Return on equity: 0.80%
Cash ($ mil.): 1
Current ratio: 0.80
Long-term debt ($ mil.): —

Dividends
Yield: —
Payout: —
Market value ($ mil.): —

EDUCATION DEVELOPMENT CENTER INC.

LOCATIONS

HQ: EDUCATION DEVELOPMENT CENTER INC.
43 FOUNDRY AVE, WALTHAM, MA 02453-8313
Phone: 617-969-7100
Web: www.childrenssafetynetwork.org

HISTORICAL FINANCIALS

Company Type: Private

Income Statement
FYE: September 30

	REVENUE ($ mil.)	NET INCOME ($ mil.)	NET PROFIT MARGIN	EMPLOYEES
09/11	200	3	1.7%	600
09/10	179	1	0.7%	0
09/08	145	1	0.8%	0
09/06	120	3	2.6%	0
Annual Growth	18.3%	2.5%	—	—

2011 Year-End Financials

Debt ratio: ——
Return on equity: 1.70%
Cash ($ mil.): 19
Current ratio: 1.20
Long-term debt ($ mil.): —

Dividends
Yield: —
Payout: —
Market value ($ mil.): —

EDWARD HOSPITAL

LOCATIONS

HQ: EDWARD HOSPITAL
801 S WASHINGTON ST, NAPERVILLE, IL 60540-7499
Phone: 630-355-0450

HISTORICAL FINANCIALS

Company Type: Private

Income Statement
FYE: June 30

	REVENUE ($ mil.)	NET INCOME ($ mil.)	NET PROFIT MARGIN	EMPLOYEES
06/11	493	31	6.3%	2,500
06/10	481	24	5.2%	0
06/09	450	(16)	—	0
06/08	494	35	7.1%	0
Annual Growth	(0.1%)	(4.0%)	—	—

2011 Year-End Financials

Debt ratio: ——
Return on equity: 6.30%
Cash ($ mil.): 9
Current ratio: 1.60
Long-term debt ($ mil.): —

Dividends
Yield: —
Payout: —
Market value ($ mil.): —

EDWARD W. SPARROW HOSPITAL ASSOCIATION

LOCATIONS

HQ: EDWARD W. SPARROW HOSPITAL ASSOCIATION
1215 E MICHIGAN AVE, LANSING, MI 48912-1896
Phone: 517-364-1000

HISTORICAL FINANCIALS

Company Type: Private

Income Statement
FYE: March 31

	REVENUE ($ mil.)	NET INCOME ($ mil.)	NET PROFIT MARGIN	EMPLOYEES
03/12*	187	24	13.1%	3,000
12/07	617	27	4.4%	0
12/06	566	(12)	—	0
12/05	524	11	2.1%	0
Annual Growth	(29.0%)	30.6%	—	—

*Fiscal year change

2012 Year-End Financials

Debt ratio: ——
Return on equity: 13.10%
Cash ($ mil.): 17
Current ratio: 1.20
Long-term debt ($ mil.): —

Dividends
Yield: —
Payout: —
Market value ($ mil.): —

EIDE BAILLY LLP

Eide Bailly is how the West was audited. The company which was founded in 1917 provides clients with audit accounting tax and consulting services from more than 20 offices in 10 western and central US states. Eide Bailly's target industries include construction agricultural processing oil and gas real estate renewable energy government financial services manufacturing health care and not-for-profit organizations. Additional services are provided by subsidiaries and affiliates including Eide Bailly Technology Consulting. International services are provided through Eide Bailly's affiliation with HLB International. The firm serves some 40000 clients annually.

Geographic Reach

Fargo North Dakota-based Eide Bailly has offices in Arizona Colorado Idaho Iowa Minnesota Montana Oklahoma Utah and the Dakotas.

Financial Performance

Edie Bailly's net fees amounted to $158 million in fiscal 2012 (ends April) with the firm's audit and assurance and tax services businesses accounting for 43% and 38% of the total respectively.

Strategy

Edie Bailly is growing its business through the acquisition of regional accounting firms to better compete with larger national firms. The company expanded into Utah in 2012 with the purchase of Schmitt Griffiths Smith & Co. adding about $6 million in revenue to Edie Bailly's total. More significantly Edie Bailly announced plans to merge with fellow accountancy Milwaukee-based Wipfli in 2012. However the deal was called off later that year when the two firms could not reach an agreement on key terms.

Mergers and Acquisitions

Other recent purchases include Williston North Dakota-based CPA firm Voller Lee Seuss & Associates. The purchase which closed in December 2012 expands Edie Bailly's resources and services to clients in the rapidly-growing Bakken Oil Region in western North Dakota. Also in late 2012 the firm acquired Clark & Srsich LLC a boutique tax firm in Littleton Colorado. In 2010 the firm bought Denver-based R T Higgins & Associates boosting its oil and gas industry business an area of focus for the company.

EXECUTIVES

Managing Partner and CEO, Jerry A. Topp
Partner Management and Tax, Darrell D. Strivens
Director Operations, LaRae E. Langerud
Partner amd Director Professional Practice, Jeff S. Strand
Partner Management and Tax, Gary G. Ness
Director Finance, Karla R. Wilson
Director Communications, Elizabeth (Liz) Stabenow
Director Leadership Development, Candace Kane
COO, David L. (Dave) Stende
Director Human Resources, Lisa R. Fitzgerald
Director Corporate Learning, Jason S. McKeever

LOCATIONS

HQ: Eide Bailly LLP
4310 17th Ave. S., Fargo ND 58103
Phone: 701-239-8500   **Fax:** 701-239-8611
Web: www.eidebailly.com

PRODUCTS/OPERATIONS

2012 Services by Category

% of total	
Assurance	43
Tax	38
Affiliates	2
Consulting and	17
Total	**100**

Selected Services

Accounting
Audit & assurance
Employee benefits
Enterprise risk management
Financial services
Forensic & valuation
International services
Tax
Technology consulting
Transaction services
Wealth management

COMPETITORS

BDO Seidman	Grant Thornton
BKD LLP	KPMG L.L.P.
CliftonLarsonAllen	PricewaterhouseCoopers
Crowe Horwath	US
Deloitte & Touche	RSM McGladrey
Ernst & Young LLP	

HISTORICAL FINANCIALS

Company Type: Private - Partnership

Income Statement

FYE: April 30

	REVENUE ($ mil.)	NET INCOME ($ mil.)	NET PROFIT MARGIN	EMPLOYEES
04/12	148	51	34.5%	1,161
04/11	142	51	36.2%	0
04/10	144	48	33.6%	0
04/09	134	44	32.9%	0
Annual Growth	**3.2%**	**4.8%**	**—**	**—**

2012 Year-End Financials

Debt ratio: ——
Return on equity: 34.50%
Cash ($ mil.): 1
Current ratio: 1.20
Long-term debt ($ mil.): ——

Dividends
  Yield: —
  Payout: —
  Market value ($ mil.): —

EISENHOWER MEDICAL CENTER

The Eisenhower Medical Center is perhaps less known by its presidential name than by the name of a first lady: The not-for-profit medical campus is the home of the Betty Ford Center. In addition to the renowned alcohol and drug rehabilitation center Eisenhower Medical Center comprises the about 540-bed Eisenhower Memorial Hospital the Barbara Sinatra Children's Center and the Annenberg Center for Health Sciences. The center's facilities are all located on its main campus in Rancho Mirage California. In addition to medical surgical and emergency services the hospital offers cancer care neurology orthopedics cardiology and rehabilitation. It also operates outpatient clinics in surrounding areas.

The late entertainer Bob Hope and his wife were the hospital's biggest benefactors having donated the original land for the hospital and continuing to help fundraising efforts until his death in 2003. The Eisenhower Medical Center maintains the leading market share in its service location representing nearly 50% of the area.

The medical center has been working to maintain that share by launching a number of expansion campaigns in recent years. For instance in 2010 it completed construction of a $213 million addition to its main hospital that included 160 patient beds a cafeteria information systems and other departments. The addition is named the Eisenhower Walter and Leonore Annenberg Pavilion.

Also in 2010 it completed a $55 million outpatient center in La Quinta the Argyros Health Center which includes an urgent-care clinic imaging center breast health center and primary care offices among other services. In addition the hospital has opened new community clinics and emergency centers in the Palm Springs area.

The medical center is also working towards becoming a teaching hospital by adding residency programs in family medicine and internal medicine. It hopes to launch the programs in 2013.

Eisenhower Medical Center faces some financial challenges due to a high volume of elderly Medicare patients. As a result it has made efforts to attract more self-pay patients to its facilities. In addition the hospital has incurred substantial debt due to its construction efforts; however it aims to recoup through increased revenues from the added facilities and through its successful fundraising efforts.

EXECUTIVES

President and CEO, G. Aubrey Serfling
VP Human Resources, Liz Guignier
VP and CIO, David Perez
President Eisenhower Medical Center Foundation, Michael D. Landes
VP Business Development, Mary Ellen Fontana
Assistant Vice President Clinic Nursing, Lynn Hart
Assistant VP Inpatient Nursing, Mary Ann McLaughlin
VP Patient Care Services and Chief Nursing Officer, Louise White
EVP and COO, Martin J. Massiello
VP Medical Affairs, Alan Williamson
VP Patient Care and Chief Nursing Officer, Ann Mostofi
General Counsel, Michael Appelhans
VP Express Clinics, Thomas Johnston
VP Primary Care, Joseph Scherger
VP Facility Planning and Construction, Ali Tourkaman
VP and CFO, Kimberly Osborne
VP Quality and Resource Management, Lynn Hart
Auditors: Ernst&YoungLLP

LOCATIONS

HQ: Eisenhower Medical Center
  39000 Bob Hope Dr., Rancho Mirage CA 92270
Phone: 760-340-3911   **Fax:** 201-525-0805
Web: www.filippoberio.com

PRODUCTS/OPERATIONS

Selected Facilities

Annenberg Center for Health Sciences (continuing education for health professionals)
Barbara Sinatra Children's Center
Betty Ford Center (alcohol and substance abuse)

Eisenhower George and Julia Argyros Health Center (La Quinta)
Eisenhower Health Centers in Palm Springs

COMPETITORS

Anaheim Regional Medical Center	HCA
Arrowhead Medical Center	HealthSouth
Cedars-Sinai Medical Center	Kaiser Permanente
Citrus Valley Health Partners	Memorial Health Services
Community Hospital of San Bernardino	Palomar Health
Dignity Health	Providence Health & Services
Grossmont Hospital	Scripps health
	Southwest Healthcare
	Tenet Healthcare
	UCSD Medical

HISTORICAL FINANCIALS

Company Type: Private - Not-for-Profit

Income Statement

FYE: June 30

	REVENUE ($ mil.)	NET INCOME ($ mil.)	NET PROFIT MARGIN	EMPLOYEES
06/11	455	(26)	—	2,200
06/10	411	6	1.7%	0
06/09	394	25	6.4%	0
06/08	408	47	11.6%	0
Annual Growth	**3.7%**			

2011 Year-End Financials

Debt ratio: ——
Return on equity: (-5.80)%
Cash ($ mil.): 58
Current ratio: 1.60
Long-term debt ($ mil.): —

Dividends
  Yield: —
  Payout: —
  Market value ($ mil.): —

EISNERAMPER LLP

Need help getting amped up to crunch numbers? EisnerAmper (formed by the 2010 merger of Eisner LLP and Amper Politziner & Mattia) provides accounting and consulting services for clients (typically middle-market businesses) in the northeastern US. It specializes in industries and sectors including health sciences sports and entertainment not-for-profit financial services and technology. EisnerAmper provides auditing and accounting services tax planning legal support bankruptcy consulting corporate finance employee benefits plan services and IT consulting. Services outside the US are provided through Eisner's Cayman Islands office as well as through its affiliation with PKF International.

Operations

As part of its services EisnerAmper specializes in structuring organizing and managing its clients' businesses as well as heading up their reporting requirements. It enlists the help of cross-border specialists who support the needs of multinational companies with a US presence. The company also serves wealthy clients providing them with services such as wealth management asset protection planning and tax advisory. EisnerAmper boasts more than 600 hedge funds among other institutional clients.

Geographic Reach

Among its operations EisnerAmper counts about a dozen offices along the New York/New

Jersey/Philadelphia corridor as well as in the Cayman Islands.

Change in Company Type

EisnerAmper was created in 2010 through the combination of Eisner and Amper Politziner & Mattia similar accounting firms based in New Jersey. Now under one umbrella the company enjoys enhanced service capabilities and geographic reach.

EXECUTIVES

CEO, Charles (Charly) Weinstein
Managing Partner, Theodore (Ted) Levine
CFO, Brett James
Audit Partner Sports and Entertainment Services Group, Richard S. Nachmias
Partner-in-Charge Internal Audit and Risk Management, Neil Goldenberg
Partner-in-Charge Real Estate Practice, Kenneth (Ken) Weissenberg, age 55
Partner-in-Charge Financial Services Group, Stanley J. (Stan) Goldberg
Partner-in-Charge Not-For-Profit Industry Group, D. Edward (Ed) Martin
Director Operations Management Consulting Services Group, Victor Albanese
President Eisner Retirement Solutions, Peter Alwardt
Principal Corporate Finance Group, Joel Barth
Partner-in-Charge Technical Services Department, David Einhorn
Partner-in-Charge Human Resources, Richard (Rick) Fisher
Partner-in-Charge Business Services Group, Joel Gensler
General Counsel, Lawrence (Larry) Goodman
Partner Internal Audit and Risk Management, Arthur Drucker
Director Recruiting Operations and Diversity, Ronald E. (Ron) Taylor
Chairman, Howard Cohen
Partner-in-charge Professional Development, Robert Levine

LOCATIONS

HQ: EisnerAmper LLP
750 3rd Ave., New York NY 10017
Phone: 212-949-8700   **Fax:** 212-891-4100
Web: www.eisneramper.com

PRODUCTS/OPERATIONS

Selected Services

Audit & accounting
Bankruptcy & insolvency
Business services
Corporate finance
Employee benefits plan services
Human resource strategies
Internal audit & risk management
Litigation consulting & forensic accounting
Resource staffing
Retirement solutions
Tax advisory
Wealth advisory

Selected Areas of Specialization

Automotive
Employee benefits
Financial services
Health care
Health sciences
Law firms
Litigation
Not-for-profit
Real estate
Sports media & entertainment
Technology industries

Wealth management

COMPETITORS

Anchin Block & Anchin
Citrin Cooperman
Crowe Horwath
Ernst & Young Global
Grant Thornton
Heffler Radetich & Saitta
KPMG L.L.P.
PricewaterhouseCoopers US
RSM McGladrey

HISTORICAL FINANCIALS
Company Type: Private - Partnership

Income Statement
FYE: January 31

	REVENUE ($ mil.)	NET INCOME ($ mil.)	NET PROFIT MARGIN	EMPLOYEES
01/12	230	59	25.9%	1,895
01/11	173	40	23.4%	0
Annual Growth	32.7%	46.5%	—	—

2012 Year-End Financials

Debt ratio: ——
Return on equity: 25.90%
Cash ($ mil.): 31
Current ratio: 5.00
Long-term debt ($ mil.): —

Dividends
　Yield: —
　Payout: —
Market value ($ mil.): —

EL DORADO FURNITURE CORP

The road to El Dorado Furniture is covered in sand. The company sells home furnishings in South Florida through about 10 retail showrooms and a pair of outlets in Broward Dade and Palm Beach counties. El Dorado Furniture stores offer wood upholstered and leather furniture for every room in the house as well as mattresses bedding and decorative accents. Stores are designed to look like small towns with building facades situated along a main street; locations also feature cafes. El Dorado one of the largest Hispanic-owned retail enterprises in the US was founded in 1967 and is still operated by the Capo family.

As Florida's real estate market beings to rebound after the recession El Dorado Furniture announced in 2012 that it would extend its reach in Florida by purchasing a shopping center on Florida's Gulf Coast. The purchase will include a 179000-sq.-ft. shopping center which will house a 70000-sq.-ft. El Dorado showroom. The company estimates the store will generate sales between $10 million to $12 million.

EXECUTIVES

President and CEO, Luis Capo
Chief Merchandising Officer, Carlos Capo
VP Finance, Ivan Trabal
VP Human Resources, Henry E. Hererro

LOCATIONS

HQ: El Dorado Furniture Corporation
4200 NW 167th St., Miami FL 33054-6112
Phone: 305-624-9700   **Fax:** 305-624-8772
Web: www.eldoradofurniture.com

2011 Stores

	No.
Dade	7
Broward	3
Palm	2
Total	**12**

COMPETITORS

Baer's Furniture
Carls Furniture
City Furniture
Havertys
La-Z-Boy
Leader's Casual Furniture
Rooms To Go
W.S. Badcock

HISTORICAL FINANCIALS
Company Type: Private

Income Statement
FYE: December 31

	REVENUE ($ mil.)	NET INCOME ($ mil.)	NET PROFIT MARGIN	EMPLOYEES
12/11	152	23	15.5%	705
12/10	131	16	12.2%	0
12/09	126	14	11.7%	0
12/08	133	15	11.6%	0
Annual Growth	4.6%	14.9%	—	—

2011 Year-End Financials

Debt ratio: ——
Return on equity: 15.50%
Cash ($ mil.): 2
Current ratio: 0.20
Long-term debt ($ mil.): —

Dividends
　Yield: —
　Payout: —
Market value ($ mil.): —

EL PASO WATER UTILITIES PUBLIC SERVICE BOARD

LOCATIONS

HQ: EL PASO WATER UTILITIES PUBLIC SERVICE BOARD
1154 HAWKINS BLVD, EL PASO, TX 79925-6436
Phone: 915-594-5500
Web: www.elpasowaterutilities.com

HISTORICAL FINANCIALS
Company Type: Private

Income Statement
FYE: February 29

	REVENUE ($ mil.)	NET INCOME ($ mil.)	NET PROFIT MARGIN	EMPLOYEES
02/12	190	31	16.5%	99
02/11	182	29	16.1%	0
02/08	149	10	7.3%	0
02/07	139	34	25.0%	0
Annual Growth	11.1%	(3.3%)	—	—

2012 Year-End Financials

Debt ratio: ——
Return on equity: 16.50%
Cash ($ mil.): 22
Current ratio: 0.50
Long-term debt ($ mil.): —

Dividends
　Yield: —
　Payout: —
Market value ($ mil.): —

ELECTRIC POWER BOARD OF CHATTANOOGA

Pardon me .... is that the Electric Power Board (EPB) of Chattanooga? EPB keeps on choochooin' along by providing electricity to more than 169000 residents and businesses. The utility (a non-profit agency of the City of Chattanooga) distributes energy in a 600 sq.-ml. area that includes greater Chattanooga as well as parts of surrounding counties in Georgia and Tennessee. It gets its wholesale power supply from the Tennessee Valley Authority. EPB also provides telecommunications (telephone and Internet) services to area homes and businesses through its EPB Fiber Optics unit.

EPB serves greater Chattanooga and parts of surrounding counties (Bledsoe Bradley Marion Rhea and Sequatchie) and North Georgia (parts of Catoosa Dade and Walker counties).

The company saw its operating revenues jump by 17% in 2011 thanks to the pass through of $40 million in TVA fuel cost adjustments an increase of $20 million in Fiber Optics residential services sales and the full effects of a 2009 TVA rate increase. However the higher cost of TVA-purchased power increased fiber optic costs and higher maintenance expenses (due to a major storm) took EFB's operating income from $5.3 million in 2010 to a loss of more than $1 million in 2011.

EFB is pushing technological innovation and the modernization of its systems as a way to increase value and efficiency. Its all-fiber Internet product gives businesses and residences access to up to 500 Mbps of bandwidth a capacity 300 times faster than standard DSL cable or T1 connections. This service completed in 2011 gives all EFB customers internet bandwidth capacity and service on a par with or superior to that offered in Atlanta Chicago and Los Angeles.

During 2009 the company received a $111 million federal stimulus grant to build and operate a Smart Grid (an automated electric system with communication capabilities to help improve response time reduce outages cut down on theft and help clients take charge of their own power use). In 2012 EFB completed the installation of the 1170 IntelliRupter? PulseCloser ("smart switches") making EPB's Smart Grid the most automated system of its size in the US.

The utility was established in 1935 to provide electric power to the people of the greater Chattanooga area.

EXECUTIVES

President and CEO, Harold E. DePriest
VP Stratetic Systems, Steven (Steve) Clark
VP Economic Development and Government Relations, Diana Bullock
SVP Finance and CFO, Greg Eaves
SVP Electric System, David Wade
VP Legal Services, Aldous McCrory
Chairman, L. Joe Ferguson
Vice Chairman, Warren E. Logan Jr.
VP Corporate Communications, Danna B. Cannon
VP Communications System, Katie Espeseth
VP Human Resources, Marcellus Scott
SVP Customer Relations, Kathy Burns
VP Strategic Planning, Jim Ingraham

VP Culture and Development, Pamper G. Crangle
Director, John N. Foy, age 68
Director, Vicky B. Gregg, age 57
Vice Chairman, Warren E. Logan Jr.
Director, Harold Cooker
Auditors: HazlettLewis&BieterPLLC

LOCATIONS

HQ: The Electric Power Board of Chattanooga
10 West M.L. King Blvd., Chattanooga TN 37402
Phone: 423-756-2706   **Fax:** 423-648-3576
Web: www.epb.net

PRODUCTS/OPERATIONS

2011 Sales

% of total	
Electric	91
Fiber	7
Other	2
Total	**100**

2011 Sales

% of total	
Electric	
Large commercial &	44
Residential	39
Small commercial &	7
Outdoor lighting	1
Fiber Optics &	9
Total	**100**

COMPETITORS

AGL Resources
AT&T

Constellation Energy Group

HISTORICAL FINANCIALS

Company Type: Government-owned

Income Statement

FYE: February 29

	REVENUE ($ mil.)	NET INCOME ($ mil.)	NET PROFIT MARGIN	EMPLOYEES
02/12*	385	4	1.3%	400
06/11	589	(16)	—	0
06/10	504	(6)	—	0
06/09	544	8	1.6%	0
Annual Growth	**(10.9%)**	**(18.1%)**	**—**	**—**

*Fiscal year change

2012 Year-End Financials

Debt ratio: ——
Return on equity: 1.30%
Cash ($ mil.): 59
Current ratio: 0.80
Long-term debt ($ mil.): —

Dividends
  Yield: —
  Payout: —
Market value ($ mil.): —

ELIXIR INDUSTRIES

Key ingredients of Elixir Industries' product mix include doors and windows for manufactured housing and recreational vehicles. Elixir units make a variety of extruded aluminum fabricated metal and plastic products including roofing siding roof vents and domes range hoods and cargo trailers. Other products include tapes sealants tool boxes and hockey and lacrosse goals. The company maintains about 15 manufacturing facilities throughout the US. Roland Sahm grandfather of

company president and COO Christopher Sahm founded what is now Elixir Industries in 1948.

EXECUTIVES

President and CEO, Christopher A. Sahm
Director International Sales, Julie Cameron
National Credit, Pat Hoeg
CFO, Bob Cuthbertson
VP Human Resources, Barbara Wright
VP Operations, Dwight Knowles
Director New Business Development, John T. Willis
Director Information Technology, Roger Grant
National Accounts Coordinator, Bob Powers

LOCATIONS

HQ: Elixir Industries Inc.
24800 Chrisanta Dr. Ste. 210, Mission Viejo CA 92691
Phone: 949-860-5000   **Fax:** 949-860-5011
Web: www.elixirind.com

PRODUCTS/OPERATIONS

Selected Brands
Alum-A-Form
Custom Aluminum
Club Wholesale
Eurovent
Instant-Bond
Ironwood
G & L Steel
Mobile Trim
Mobilastic
Northwest Mobile Products
Plas-T-Cote
Rixile Mobile Components
RVCA RV Centers of America
Spraymatic
Trav' ler
Travel Trim
Tru Seal
Ultra Vent
Venturi Vent
Ward & Son

COMPETITORS

CertainTeed
Drew Industries

MW Manufacturers
Nortek

HISTORICAL FINANCIALS

Company Type: Private

Income Statement

FYE: December 31

	REVENUE ($ mil.)	NET INCOME ($ mil.)	NET PROFIT MARGIN	EMPLOYEES
12/11	145	14	9.9%	700
12/05	221	0	—	0
Annual Growth	**(34.0%)**	**—**	**—**	**—**

2011 Year-End Financials

Debt ratio: ——
Return on equity: 9.90%
Cash ($ mil.): 7
Current ratio: 1.40
Long-term debt ($ mil.): —

Dividends
  Yield: —
  Payout: —
Market value ($ mil.): —

ELLIOT HOSPITAL OF THE CITY OF MANCHESTER

Elliot Health System provides medical care to southern New Hampshire. The health care organization operates Elliot Hospital an acute care hospital with nearly 300 beds that is home to a regional cancer center a designated regional trauma center and a Level 3 neonatal intensive care unit (NICU). In addition to general and surgical care the hospital offers rehabilitation behavioral health obstetrics cardiology and lab services. The system also operates the Elliot Physician Network which operates primary care centers specialty clinics and surgery centers in various regional communities. Elliot Hospital was founded in 1890.

Strategy

Elliot Health System has expanded throughout the region by constructing new outpatient care centers in nearby towns. Most recently Elliot Health completed construction of satellite facilities including an ambulatory care center and a senior health center.

EXECUTIVES

President CEO and Trustee, Douglas (Doug) Dean
SVP and CFO, Rick Elwell
Chief Nurse Executive, Deb Baker
Treasurer, John C. Miles
VP Medical Staff and Trustee, Peter Kachavos
Chairman, John Hession
Medical Director Elliot Occupational Health Services, John A. Devine
VP Public Affairs and Marketing, Tiffany Nelson
President Medical Staff and Trustee, Martin Ginsberg
President CEO and Trustee, Douglas (Doug) Dean
Trustee, William G. Steele Jr.
Trustee Emeritus, Mark Stebbins
Trustee Emeritus, Richard I. Winneg
Trustee, Wayne Robinson
Trustee, Barbara A. Rand
Trustee, Karl E. Norwood
Trustee, Robert J. Normandeau
Trustee, Selma Naccach-Hoff
Trustee, Rochelle H. Lindner
Trustee, Robert Lavery
VP Medical Staff and Trustee, Peter Kachavos
Trustee, Richard A. Gustafson
Trustee Emeritus, William S. Green
Trustee Emeritus, Raymond E. Closson
Trustee, Peter Cheung
Trustee, Sidney Baines
President Medical Staff and Trustee, Martin Ginsberg
Trustee, Scott Bacon
Trustee, Ethel Chaput
Trustee, James Hood
Trustee, Richard Marcucci
Trustee, John C. Miles
Trustee, Edward Mitchell
Trustee, Robert Provencher Jr.
Trustee, Ann Remus
Trustee, Malcolm Widness

LOCATIONS

HQ: Elliot Health System
1 Elliot Way, Manchester NH 03103
Phone: 603-669-5300   **Fax:** 603-663-2110
Web: www.elliothospital.org

PRODUCTS/OPERATIONS

Selected Centers and Services

Aeronautics Medicine
Adult Day Programs
Bariatric Surgery
Behavioral Health
Breast Health Center
Cardiology Services
Center for Sleep Evaluation
Center for Wound Care & Hyberbaric Medicine
Childbirth And Family Education
Community Health and Wellness
Critical Care at The Elliot
Diabetes and Outpatient Nutrition Services
Diagnostic Imaging
Elliot 1-Day Surgery Center
The Elliot at Hooksett
Elliot Behavioral Health Services
Elliot Endocrinology Associates
Elliot Gastroenterology
Elliot General Surgical Specialists
Elliot Maternal Fetal Medicine
Elliot Medical Center at Londonderry
Elliot Neurology Associates
Elliot Obstetrics and Gynecology
Elliot Orthopaedic Surgical Specialists
Elliot Physician Network
Elliot Regional Cancer Center
Elliot Sports Medicine
Elliot Trauma Center
Elliot Wellness Center
Endoscopy Center
Health Education Library
Home Medical Equipment
Hospitalist Program
Infection Control Department
Inpatient Care/Nursing Units
Laboratory Services
Max K. Willscher Urology Center
Neurophysiology
New England EMS Institute
New Hampshire Arthritis Center
Nursing Units/Inpatient Care
Nutrition Services
Occupational Health & Wellness
Oral Maxillofacial Surgery Center
Oxygen Therapy
Pain Management Center
Pediatric Surgery
Pharmacy Services
Pulmonary Medicine
Pulmonary Rehabilitation
Physical Therapy
Rehabilitation
Respiratory Care
Senior Health Center
Sports Medicine
Surgery
Speech Therapy
Urgent Care - Londonderry
Urgent Care - Manchester
Visiting Nurse Association of Manchester & So. NH Inc.
Weight Management
Wellness Center
Women's & Children's Services
Wound Center

COMPETITORS

Caritas Holy Family Hospital
Catholic Medical Center
Concord Hospital
Exeter Health Resources
Frisbie Memorial Hospital
HCA
Lahey Clinic
Southern New Hampshire Medical Center

HISTORICAL FINANCIALS

Company Type: Private - Not-for-Profit

Income Statement

FYE: June 30

	REVENUE ($ mil.)	NET INCOME ($ mil.)	NET PROFIT MARGIN	EMPLOYEES
06/11	344	6	1.8%	2,000
06/10	324	7	2.4%	0
06/09	288	0	—	0
06/08	0	0	8.1%	0
Annual Growth	662.8%	358.6%	—	—

2011 Year-End Financials

Debt ratio: —
Return on equity: 1.80%
Cash ($ mil.): 25
Current ratio: 0.20
Long-term debt ($ mil.): —
Dividends
  Yield: —
  Payout: —
Market value ($ mil.): —

ELMER SMITH OIL COMPANY

LOCATIONS

HQ: ELMER SMITH OIL COMPANY
HWY 183 S, CLINTON, OK 73601
Phone: 580-323-2929

HISTORICAL FINANCIALS

Company Type: Private

Income Statement

FYE: December 31

	REVENUE ($ mil.)	NET INCOME ($ mil.)	NET PROFIT MARGIN	EMPLOYEES
12/11	190	0	0.0%	162
12/10	136	0	0.2%	0
12/09	107	0	0.5%	0
12/08	241	0	0.4%	0
Annual Growth	(7.6%)	(62.1%)	—	—

2011 Year-End Financials

Debt ratio: —
Return on equity: —
Cash ($ mil.): 1
Current ratio: 0.20
Long-term debt ($ mil.): —
Dividends
  Yield: —
  Payout: —
Market value ($ mil.): —

ELMHURST COMMUNITY UNIT SCHOOL DIST 205

LOCATIONS

HQ: ELMHURST COMMUNITY UNIT SCHOOL DIST 205
162 S YORK ST, ELMHURST, IL 60126-3417
Phone: 630-834-4530
Web: www.field-elmhurstcusd205-il.schoolloop.com

HISTORICAL FINANCIALS
Company Type: Private

Income Statement
FYE: June 30

	REVENUE ($ mil.)	NET INCOME ($ mil.)	NET PROFIT MARGIN	EMPLOYEES
06/11	122	4	3.4%	926
06/07	97	(6)	—	0
06/06	84	41	49.5%	0
06/05	80	(2)	—	0
Annual Growth	15.1%	—	—	—

EMBREE CONSTRUCTION GROUP INC.

The Embree Construction Group develops designs and builds free-standing buildings for business chains across the US. The group serves as a general contractor or construction manager primarily for major national companies. It is active throughout the US. Ground-up and remodeling projects include retail properties restaurants gas stations convenience stores automotive service centers and correctional facilities. Operating companies include Embree Healthcare Group which develops assisted-living and specialty medical projects and Embree Asset Group which develops build-to-suit single-tenant buildings and leases them back to clients. Owner and chairman Jim Embree founded the firm in 1979 in Kansas City.

EXECUTIVES

EVP; President Embree Asset, Philip Annis
President; EVP Embree Asset, Frank Krenek
EVP and CFO Embree Asset, Rocky Hardin
Chairman and CEO, Jim Embree
VP Design Services, Bob Thomas
VP Pre-Construction Services, Glenn McDonald
Vice Chairman and General Counsel, Rick Crowe
VP Operations, Mark Henderson
VP Remodel/Tenant Improvement, Bill Paetznick

LOCATIONS

HQ: Embree Construction Group Inc.
4747 Williams Dr., Georgetown TX 78628
Phone: 512-819-4700   **Fax:** 512-863-6357
Web: www.embreegroup.com

COMPETITORS

American Constructors	FaulknerUSA
Austin Commercial	Fisher Development
Bovis Lend Lease	H.J. Russell
Charles Pankow Builders	McCarthy Building
Colson & Colson	Schlosser Development
EMJ	Venture Construction
	Workman Commercial

HISTORICAL FINANCIALS
Company Type: Private

Income Statement
FYE: December 31

	REVENUE ($ mil.)	NET INCOME ($ mil.)	NET PROFIT MARGIN	EMPLOYEES
12/11	106	0	0.8%	110
12/10	64	0	0.7%	0
12/09	51	0	0.8%	0
12/08	82	1	1.2%	0
Annual Growth	8.9%	(6.7%)	—	—

2011 Year-End Financials

Debt ratio: ——
Return on equity: 0.80%
Cash ($ mil.): 4
Current ratio: 1.10
Long-term debt ($ mil.): —

Dividends
Yield: —
Payout: —
Market value ($ mil.): —

EMBRY-RIDDLE AERONAUTICAL UNIVERSITY INC.

Embry-Riddle Aeronautical University (ERAU) helps students solve the mysteries of space and flying. The not-for-profit corporation teaches aviation aerospace and engineering to about 24000 students a year (and a student-teacher ratio of about 15:1). ERAU which offers hands-on training through a fleet of 90 instructional aircraft has residential campuses in Daytona Beach Florida and Prescott Arizona. Its Embry-Riddle Worldwide program provides learning through more than 150 teaching centers and online training in the US Canada Europe and Middle East. It offers bachelor's master's and doctoral degrees in 35 areas.

Geographic Reach

ERAU's campuses provide instruction through more than 150 locations in Asia Canada Europe and the US through online learning.

Operations

The school has been adding non-degree programs to its curriculum in recent years in order to reach a broader range of students (such as working adults). Its worldwide campus houses the Center for Professional Education (CPE) which provides professional certification experience and training to corporate and professional adult learners. Many CPE programs are administered online; the school also offers a variety of seminars and workshops. ERAU's non-degree programs include English language training and aviation safety and security short courses.

Its fleet of more than 90 instructional aircraft includes American Champion Decathlon Cessna 150 Cessna 162 Cessna 172 G1000 Cessna 172R Cessna 172S Cessna 172S Nav III Cessna 182RG Diamond DA42 Diamond DA42NG Piper PA28R and Piper PA44. Embry-Riddle also has roughly 40 simulators at both campuses.

ERAU students enroll from 50 states and 120 nations with 14% of international students at the Daytona Beach campus and 4% at the Prescott campus.

Financial Performance

The annual operating budget of ERAU is about $297 million. From 2011 to 2012 it enjoyed a 6% increase in revenue due to a jump in tuition fees. However it posted a 4% decrease in net income in 2012 due to a spike in expenses related to student services flight instructions and auxiliary enterprises expenses. The decline was also due to a decrease in non-operating activities. Its net cash flow dipped by $20 million as a result of lower student deposits and advance payments.

Strategy

ERAU's growth strategy involves adding additional degree programs to its curriculum in order to increase the amount of tuitions. In 2013 it launched three new degree programs: astronomy; cyber intelligence; and security software engineering.

Also benefiting from additional offices ERAU opened a new location in the Fort Worth Alliance Airport in Texas in 2012. ERAU in 2011 expanded its Joint-Degree Pact with two Chinese universities to absorb growth in China's aviation sector.

Company Background

ERAU was founded to train pilots in 1925 by barnstormer John Paul Riddle and entrepreneur T. Higbee Embry.

EXECUTIVES

Chairman, Jim W. Henderson, age 65
SEVP and CFO, Eric B. Weekes
Trustee, Eleanor Baum, age 72
President, John P. Johnson
CIO, Cindy Bixler
Associate VP Safety, Daniel (Dan) McCune
Director Board Operations, Deborah Praver
EVP and Chief Academic Officer Daytona Beach Campus, Richard H. Heist
VP Institutional Advancement, Daniel (Dan) Montplaisir
VP Human Resources, Irene C. McReynolds
SEVP Academics and Research, Christina M. Frederick-Recascino
Trustee, Karen A. Holbrook
EVP and Chief Academic Officer Prescott Campus, Frank Ayers Jr.
University Controller, Linda Manning
Executive Director Career Services, Lisa Scott-Kollar
EVP and Chief Academic Officer Worldwide Campus, John R. Watret
Dean College of Arts and Sciences Daytona Beach Campus, Bill Grams
Dean College of Aviation Daytona Beach Campus, Tim Brady
Dean College of Business Daytona Beach Campus, Michael Williams
Dean College of Engineering Daytona Beach Campus, Maj Mirmirani
Dean College of Arts and Sciences Prescott Campus, Archie Dickey
Dean College of Aviation Prescott Campus, Gary Northam
Dean College of Engineering Prescott Campus, Ron Madler
University Attorney, Charles Sevastos
Associate VP University Relations, Karen Jans
Trustee, James (Jim) Hagedorn, age 56
Trustee, Joseph R. (Joe) Martin, age 64
Trustee, Lawrence W. Clarkson, age 74
Trustee, Eleanor Baum, age 72
Trustee, Karen A. Holbrook
Trustee, Kenneth M. Dufour
Trustee, Jeffrey Feasel
Trustee, Mori Hosseini
Trustee, John E. O'Brien
Trustee, Glenn S. Ritchey

LOCATIONS

HQ: Embry-Riddle Aeronautical University Inc.
600 S. Clyde Morris Blvd., Daytona Beach FL 32114-3900
Phone: 386-226-6000 **Fax:** 386-226-6158
Web: www.erau.edu

HISTORICAL FINANCIALS

Company Type: School

Income Statement

FYE: June 30

	REVENUE ($ mil.)	NET INCOME ($ mil.)	NET PROFIT MARGIN	EMPLOYEES
06/12	318	24	7.6%	4,719
06/11	359	46	12.9%	0
06/10	276	25	9.2%	0
06/09	270	3	1.4%	0
Annual Growth	5.5%	86.2%	—	—

2012 Year-End Financials

Debt ratio:
Return on equity: 7.60%
Cash ($ mil.): 120
Current ratio: 2.20
Long-term debt ($ mil.): —
Dividends
Yield: —
Payout: —
Market value ($ mil.): —

EMERSON COLLEGE

Emerson College specializes in teaching subjects in the fields of communication and the arts in a liberal arts context. Areas of study include journalism; marketing; organizational and political communication; performing arts; visual and media arts; and writing literature and publishing. Its also has an acclaimed communication sciences and disorders program. The college enrolls about 3200 full-time undergraduates and 1000 full and part-time graduate students on its Boston-based campus. Among its alumni are producer Norman Lear talk show host Jay Leno and journalist Morton Dean. The college has additional facilities in Los Angeles and in the Netherlands. Emerson was founded in 1880 as a school of oratory.

EXECUTIVES

Executive Director Department of Professional Studies and Special Programs, Hank W. Zappala
President, Lee Pelton
VP Institutional Advancement, Robert Ashton
VP Information Technology, William Gilligan
VP Development and Alumni Relations, Jeffrey Schoenherr
Dean of Students, Ronald Ludman
VP Academic Affairs, Linda Moore
Associate VP Finance, John Donohoe
VP Administration and Finance, Maureen Murphy
VP and General Counsel, Christine Hughes
Executive Director College Library, Robert Fleming
Associate VP Human Resources, Alexa Jackson
Associate VP Government and Community Relations, Margaret Ann Ings
Associate VP Institutional Advancement and Director Alumni Relations, Barbara Rutberg
Associate VP Academic Affairs, Richard Zauft

Senior Associate VP Financial Affairs, Michelle DeAngeles
Dean School of Communication, Janis Andersen
VP Enrollment, MJ Knoll Finn
VP Communications and Marketing, Andrew Tiedemann

LOCATIONS

HQ: Emerson College
120 Boylston St., Boston MA 02116-4624
Phone: 617-824-8500 **Fax:** 604-684-2902
Web: www.rocamines.com

HISTORICAL FINANCIALS

Company Type: School

Income Statement

FYE: June 30

	REVENUE ($ mil.)	NET INCOME ($ mil.)	NET PROFIT MARGIN	EMPLOYEES
06/11	170	6	4.1%	425
06/10	154	17	11.6%	0
06/09	147	15	10.8%	0
06/08	139	15	10.7%	0
Annual Growth	6.7%	(22.5%)	—	—

2011 Year-End Financials

Debt ratio: —
Return on equity: 4.10%
Cash ($ mil.): 16
Current ratio: —
Long-term debt ($ mil.): —
Dividends
Yield: —
Payout: —
Market value ($ mil.): —

EMPLOYERS RESOURCE MANAGEMENT COMPANY

LOCATIONS

HQ: EMPLOYERS RESOURCE MANAGEMENT COMPANY
1301 S VISTA AVE STE 200, BOISE, ID 83705-2576
Phone: 208-376-3000
Web: www.employersresource.com

HISTORICAL FINANCIALS

Company Type: Private

Income Statement

FYE: June 30

	REVENUE ($ mil.)	NET INCOME ($ mil.)	NET PROFIT MARGIN	EMPLOYEES
06/11	357	0	0.1%	95
06/08	425	1	0.3%	0
06/07	412	0	0.1%	0
06/06	1,287	0	—	0
Annual Growth	(34.8%)	1931.0%	—	—

2011 Year-End Financials

Debt ratio: ——
Return on equity: 0.10%
Cash ($ mil.): 5
Current ratio: 0.30
Long-term debt ($ mil.): —
Dividends
Yield: —
Payout: —
Market value ($ mil.): —

EMS USA INC.

LOCATIONS

HQ: EMS USA INC.
2000 BERING DR STE 600, HOUSTON, TX 77057-3835
Phone: 713-595-7600
Web: www.emsusainc.com

HISTORICAL FINANCIALS

Company Type: Private

Income Statement

FYE: December 31

	REVENUE ($ mil.)	NET INCOME ($ mil.)	NET PROFIT MARGIN	EMPLOYEES
12/11	145	(4)	—	41
Annual Growth	—	—	—	—

2011 Year-End Financials

Debt ratio: —
Return on equity: (-3.10)%
Cash ($ mil.): 0
Current ratio: 0.40
Long-term debt ($ mil.): —
Dividends
Yield: —
Payout: —
Market value ($ mil.): —

ENDICOTT COLLEGE

LOCATIONS

HQ: ENDICOTT COLLEGE
376 HALE ST, BEVERLY, MA 01915-2096
Phone: 978-927-0585
Web: www.catalog.endicott.edu

HISTORICAL FINANCIALS

Company Type: Private

Income Statement

FYE: June 30

	REVENUE ($ mil.)	NET INCOME ($ mil.)	NET PROFIT MARGIN	EMPLOYEES
06/11	92	9	10.7%	0
06/10	85	12	14.1%	0
06/09	78	10	13.2%	0
06/08	70	9	13.1%	0
Annual Growth	9.4%	2.3%	—	—

2011 Year-End Financials

Debt ratio: ——
Return on equity: 10.70%
Cash ($ mil.): 0
Current ratio: —
Long-term debt ($ mil.): —
Dividends
Yield: —
Payout: —
Market value ($ mil.): —

ENSCO INC.

LOCATIONS

HQ: ENSCO INC.
3110 FRVIEW PK DR STE 300, FALLS CHURCH, VA
22042
Phone: 703-321-9000
Web: www.ensco.com

HISTORICAL FINANCIALS

Company Type: Private

Income Statement				FYE: June 29
	REVENUE ($ mil.)	NET INCOME ($ mil.)	NET PROFIT MARGIN	EMPLOYEES
06/12*	94	5	5.6%	700
07/11	88	4	5.1%	0
07/10	83	4	5.3%	0
07/09	100	3	3.5%	0
Annual Growth	(1.9%)	14.8%	—	—

*Fiscal year change

2012 Year-End Financials

Debt ratio: ——
Return on equity: 5.60%
Cash ($ mil.): 4
Current ratio: 0.30
Long-term debt ($ mil.): ——

Dividends
Yield: —
Payout: —
Market value ($ mil.): —

ENTERPRISE ELECTRIC LLC

Enterprise Electric welcomes the power hungry. The full service electrical firms specializes in construction and design of electrical systems for institutional commercial industrial and services projects from planning through construction. The company completes projects large and small and has completed design and installation of wiring and electrical systems for health care correctional commercial and industrial clients. Services include temporary power installations voice data and fiber optic cabling systems emergency generator and substation installations maintenance services. Headquartered in Nashville Tennessee the company serves clients throughout the US.

The company was formed in 1945 under the name Sullivan Electric it changed its name to Encompass Electrical Technologies Central Tennessee in 2001 before settling on the Enterprise Electric name in 2004.

EXECUTIVES

CEO, James C. Seabury III
COO and Chief Safety Officer, Michael W. Campbell
President, Jeffrey C. Hendrix

LOCATIONS

HQ: Enterprise Electric LLC
1300 Fort Negley Blvd., Nashville TN 37203
Phone: 615-350-7270   **Fax:** 615-350-7242
Web: www.enterprisellc.com

COMPETITORS

Bergelectric   Mass Electric
EMCOR
Integrated Electrical
  Services

HISTORICAL FINANCIALS

Company Type: Private

Income Statement				FYE: December 31
	REVENUE ($ mil.)	NET INCOME ($ mil.)	NET PROFIT MARGIN	EMPLOYEES
12/11	86	6	7.2%	400
12/10	69	0	0.2%	0
Annual Growth	24.9%	3934.2%	—	—

2011 Year-End Financials

Debt ratio: ——
Return on equity: 7.20%
Cash ($ mil.): 0
Current ratio: 1.00
Long-term debt ($ mil.): ——

Dividends
Yield: —
Payout: —
Market value ($ mil.): —

EPISCOPAL SENIOR COMMUNITIES

LOCATIONS

HQ: EPISCOPAL SENIOR COMMUNITIES
2185 N CALIF BLVD STE 575, WALNUT CREEK, CA
94596-7323
Phone: 925-956-7400
Web: www.jtm-esc.org

HISTORICAL FINANCIALS

Company Type: Private

Income Statement				FYE: March 31
	REVENUE ($ mil.)	NET INCOME ($ mil.)	NET PROFIT MARGIN	EMPLOYEES
03/12	103	2	2.5%	800
03/11	97	5	5.2%	0
03/10	105	16	15.2%	0
03/09	83	0	—	0
Annual Growth	7.4%			

2012 Year-End Financials

Debt ratio: ——
Return on equity: 2.50%
Cash ($ mil.): 14
Current ratio: 0.60
Long-term debt ($ mil.): ——

Dividends
Yield: —
Payout: —
Market value ($ mil.): —

ERB EQUIPMENT CO. INC.

LOCATIONS

HQ: ERB EQUIPMENT CO. INC.
200 ERB INDUSTRIAL DR, FENTON, MO 63026-4640
Phone: 636-349-0200
Web: www.erbequipment.com

HISTORICAL FINANCIALS

Company Type: Private

Income Statement				FYE: December 31
	REVENUE ($ mil.)	NET INCOME ($ mil.)	NET PROFIT MARGIN	EMPLOYEES
12/11	111	9	8.2%	120
12/10	54	1	2.6%	0
12/09	46	0	1.3%	0
12/08	52	0	1.0%	0
Annual Growth	28.8%	162.2%	—	—

2011 Year-End Financials

Debt ratio: ——
Return on equity: 8.20%
Cash ($ mil.): 0
Current ratio: 0.10
Long-term debt ($ mil.): ——

Dividends
Yield: —
Payout: —
Market value ($ mil.): —

ERM-WEST INC.

LOCATIONS

HQ: ERM-WEST INC.
1277 TREAT BLVD STE 500, WALNUT CREEK, CA
94597-7989
Phone: 925-946-0455

HISTORICAL FINANCIALS

Company Type: Private

Income Statement				FYE: March 31
	REVENUE ($ mil.)	NET INCOME ($ mil.)	NET PROFIT MARGIN	EMPLOYEES
03/12	91	4	4.6%	270
03/04	28	(0)	—	0
03/03	22	(0)	—	0
03/01	23	(2)	—	0
Annual Growth	58.5%	—	—	—

ESTES EXPRESS LINES INC.

Estes Express makes a business out of beating expectations. Founded during the Depression with a Chevy truck the company has grown into a multiregional less-than-truckload (LTL) freight hauler. (LTL carriers consolidate freight from multiple shippers into a single trailer.) Its fleet of some 7700 tractors and 22760 trailers operates via a network of 210 terminals dotting the US. Service in Canada is provided by TST Overland Express an ExpressLINK partner. Estes Express works with designated carriers to offer door-to-door delivery in the Caribbean and in Mexico. Subsidiary Estes Forwarding Worldwide services ocean/air freight forwarding. The company is owned and run by the family of founder W.W. Estes.

Financial Analysis

As the economy gradually recovers Estes Express has recognized between $1 billion to $2 billion in annual revenues. From 2010 to 2011 its total sales increased by 15%. It attributes the growth to cost-balancing programs and new technology helping to optimize the pricing and capacity of its trucking services.

Strategy

Estes Express has continued to build out its LTL business by offering expedited delivery volume truckload transportation supply chain management nationwide brokerage services warehousing services and equipment leasing. The latter has provided such rental services as laundry trucks for the Department of Veterans Affairs. Its slate of services are supported by an upgraded wireless onboard pickup and delivery system implemented in 2010 featuring real-time data enabling terminals and drivers to process freight more efficiently.

The company also responds to growth by adding new locations. Estes Express in 2010 opened new offices in San Francisco Los Angeles Dallas Chicago Miami and New York. In 2012 it opened additional terminals in Ohio and Texas. Estes Express has also formed a Mexico third-party logistics subsidiary Estes Logistica for managing freight consolidation and transportation to points south of the US border.

EXECUTIVES

President and CEO, Rob W. Estes Jr., age 60
EVP and COO, William T. (Billy) Hupp
Corporate Secretary, Stephen E. Hupp
CFO and Treasurer, Gary D. Okes
VP Pricing and Traffic, Paul J. Dugent
VP Information Services, Hugh Camden
VP Corporate Communications, Trish Garland
VP Corporate Sales, Chuck Parker
VP Human Resources, Thomas Donahue
President and CEO Estes Forwarding Worldwide, Scott Fisher
VP Operations, Al Bucher
VP Sales, Pat Martin
Regional VP Estes Southeast, Legree Oswald
Manager Strategic Communications, Paula Evans
VP Operations Estes Air Forwarding, Steve Mulloy
Managing Director International Estes Air Forwarding, Gary Weekley
VP Sales and Marketing Estes Forwarding Worldwide, Mark Molloy
Manager Pricing and Yeild Management, Jarrett Williams
Manager International Ocean and Customs Brokerage, Christine Smith
Manager Purchased Transportation and Regulatory Affairs, John McKeon
Manager Call Center, Tanya Williams
Supervisor Customer Engagement and Quality Control, Dale Batkins
Supervisor Inside Sales, Sara Batkins
Supervisor Forwarder Team, Shanna Gomez-Harrison
Supervisor Sales Support, Sue Reed

Supervisor Evening and Night Operations, Dave Abbott
Director Operations Technology, Michael Lackey
District Operations Manager, R. J. Collins
District Operations Manager, Max Thierer
Terminal Manager Hope, Scot Sellers
Terminal Manager San Antonio, Woody Woodall
Auditors: JoynerKirkhamKeel&RobertsonP.C.

LOCATIONS

HQ: Estes Express Lines Inc.
  3901 W. Broad St., Richmond VA 23230
Phone: 804-353-1900   **Fax:** 804-353-8001
Web: www.estes-express.com

PRODUCTS/OPERATIONS

Selected Services

Global (airfreight ocean international consolidation/deconsolidation customs brokerage international freight forwarding)
Less-than-truckload (regional national international/offshore)
Time critical (expedited guaranteed time/date definite)
Volume & truckload (LTL full loads backhaul services truckload brokerage dedicated truckload)

COMPETITORS

AAA Cooper Transportation	Penske Truck Leasing
Arkansas Best	R+L Carriers
Averitt Express	Ryder System
Con-way Freight	Saia
FedEx Freight	UPS Freight
Old Dominion Freight	Vitran
	YRC Worldwide

HISTORICAL FINANCIALS

Company Type: Private

Income Statement				FYE: December 31
	REVENUE ($ mil.)	NET INCOME ($ mil.)	NET PROFIT MARGIN	EMPLOYEES
12/11	1,738	52	3.0%	13,000
12/10	1,506	24	1.6%	0
12/09	1,309	(6)	—	0
12/08	1,489	11	0.7%	0
Annual Growth	5.3%	68.4%	—	—

2011 Year-End Financials

Debt ratio: ——
Return on equity: 3.00%   Dividends
Cash ($ mil.): 39   Yield: —
Current ratio: 1.10   Payout: —
Long-term debt ($ mil.): — Market value ($ mil.): —

ETNA DISTRIBUTORS LLC

Unlike the volcano in Sicily that shares its name Etna Supply spews out water not fire. The company distributes equipment and supplies for residential and commercial plumbing hydronic heating waterworks and sewage facilities and fire protection. It operates through about 15 locations in Michigan Indiana and Ohio. The company also offers related services such as custom pipe flaring and threading welding valve and hydrant mainte-

nance and meter reading. Customers include architects engineers contractors and homeowners. Etna Supply was founded in 1965.

EXECUTIVES

President, R. David Potgeter
CEO, Russ Visner
Human Resources Manager, Angela Visner
Auditors: BDOSeidmanLLP

LOCATIONS

HQ: Etna Supply Company
  529 32nd St. SE, Grand Rapids MI 49548-2303
Phone: 616-241-5414   **Fax:** 616-241-4786
Web: www.etnasupply.com

COMPETITORS

Fastenal	Noland
Ferguson Enterprises	Sid Harvey Industries
Hajoca Corporation	Inc.
HD Supply	W.W. Grainger
Lowe' s	Watsco
MSC Industrial Direct	WinWholesale

HISTORICAL FINANCIALS

Company Type: Private

Income Statement				FYE: December 31
	REVENUE ($ mil.)	NET INCOME ($ mil.)	NET PROFIT MARGIN	EMPLOYEES
12/11	132	0	0.6%	285
12/10	130	2	2.2%	0
12/09	126	3	2.7%	0
12/08	161	3	2.3%	0
Annual Growth	(6.3%)	(39.7%)	—	—

2011 Year-End Financials

Debt ratio: ——
Return on equity: 0.60%   Dividends
Cash ($ mil.): 1   Yield: —
Current ratio: 1.10   Payout: —
Long-term debt ($ mil.): — Market value ($ mil.): —

EURAMAX HOLDINGS INC.

Euramax Holdings is into metal and vinyl but it's not involved in the music industry. Operating through Euramax International and other subsidiaries Euramax produces metal fabricated products used in residential repair and remodeling commercial construction and RV markets in North America and Europe. Core lines include preformed drainage systems for roofs metal roofing and siding roll-coated aluminum and aluminum siding for RVs. Most of Euramax's products are fabricated from aluminum but the company also manufactures materials out of vinyl steel and copper. Customers include contractors and home improvement retailers distributors and RV OEMs. In mid-2010 Euramax filed to go public.

The company's decision to make a public offering of stock is indicative of the global recession's impact on Euramax's core markets in recent years. After dropping in 2008 and 2009 the company's sales rebounded in 2010; Euramax's profits while still in the red also improved that year. The company hopes to raise approximately $175 million from the initial public offering. Proceeds raised will be used mostly to reduce debt.

Euramax attributes its improvements in 2010 to mild economic recovery in the US and cost-cutting measures it implemented in 2008. Among other measures the company has reduced its workforce closed manufacturing facilities and restructured its debt. (Between 2008 and 2011 it reduced its facilities from 70 to 41. Most of the affected plants were in the US.)

Founded in 1996 the company has evolved from its initial acquisition of the fabricated products business of Alumax Inc. an aluminum producer. Euramax continued to expand its market presence through a series of complementary business acquisitions.

EXECUTIVES

Chairman, Michael D. Lundin, age 52
VP CFO and Secretary, R. Scott Vansant, age 50, $255,417 total compensation
President CEO and Director, Mitchell B. Lewis, age 50, $306,500 total compensation
VP U.S. Residential Building Products, Scott R. Anderson, age 49
President Amerimax Building Products, Nick E. Dowd, age 54
VP Human Resources, Jeffrey C. Hummel, age 48
VP Operations, Ronald Slahetka
Director, James G. Bradley, age 67
Director, Jeffrey A. Brodsky, age 53
Director, Marjorie L. Bowen, age 47
Director, J. David Smith, age 63
President CEO and Director, Mitchell B. Lewis, age 50
Director, G. Fulton Collins, age 45
Director, Alvo M. Oddis, age 56
Auditors: Ernst&YoungLLP

LOCATIONS

HQ: Euramax Holdings Inc.
5445 Triangle Pkwy. Ste. 350, Norcross GA 30092
Phone: 770-449-7066   **Fax:** 770-449-7354
Web: www.euramax.com

2010 Sales

	$ mil.	% of total
North America	592	67
Europe	291	33
Total	**883**	**100**

PRODUCTS/OPERATIONS

2010 Sales

	$ mil.	% of total
US Residential Building Products	244	28
European Roll Coated Aluminum	210	24
US Non-Residential Building Products	203	23
US RV and Specialty Building Products	146	16
European Engineered Products	79	9
Total	**883**	**100**

Selected Products

Bath and shower enclosures (aluminum)
Doors (aluminum vinyl)
Patio products
Railing (vinyl)
Rain carrying systems (metal vinyl)
Recreational vehicle aluminum doors windows sidewalls
Roof systems (metal)
Roofing accessories
Snow retention
Solar systems (photovoltaic solar laminate)
Soffit and fascia systems
Specialty coated coils
Walls (metal)
Windows (aluminum vinyl)

COMPETITORS

American Buildings
Atwood Mobile
Butler Manufacturing
Design Components
Gibraltar Industries
NCI Building Systems

HISTORICAL FINANCIALS

Company Type: Private

Income Statement

FYE: September 28

	REVENUE ($ mil.)	NET INCOME ($ mil.)	NET PROFIT MARGIN	EMPLOYEES
09/12*	641	(24)	—	2,300
12/11	933	(62)	—	0
Annual Growth	**(31.3%)**	—	—	

*Fiscal year change

2012 Year-End Financials

Debt ratio: ——
Return on equity: (-3.90)%
Cash ($ mil.): 9
Current ratio: 0.90
Long-term debt ($ mil.): ——
Dividends
  Yield: —
  Payout: —
Market value ($ mil.): —

EUROMOTORS INC.

LOCATIONS

HQ: EUROMOTORS INC.
500 8TH ST, SAN FRANCISCO, CA 94103-4409
Phone: 415-673-2000
Web: www.mercedesbenzofsanfrancisco.com

HISTORICAL FINANCIALS

Company Type: Private

Income Statement

FYE: August 31

	REVENUE ($ mil.)	NET INCOME ($ mil.)	NET PROFIT MARGIN	EMPLOYEES
08/11	108	0	0.5%	125
08/10	94	4	5.2%	0
08/09*	84	(1)	—	0
12/08	0	0	—	0
Annual Growth	—	—	—	—

*Fiscal year change

2011 Year-End Financials

Debt ratio: ——
Return on equity: 0.50%
Cash ($ mil.): 2
Current ratio: 0.20
Long-term debt ($ mil.): ——
Dividends
  Yield: —
  Payout: —
Market value ($ mil.): ——

EVANGELICAL COMMUNITY HOSPITAL

Evangelical Community Hospital brings the good news of community health to residents in central Pennsylvania. Evangelical Community Hospital provides a wide range of medical services to the residents of Susquehanna Valley. Among its specialized services are home health care and hospice maternity oncology rehabilitation and pediatrics. The hospital delivers more than 1000 babies annually and treats more than 30000 patients in its emergency department each year. Its outreach network includes family practice offices and other medical services. Despite its name the hospital has no affiliation with any religious organization.

Geographic Reach

Evangelical Community Hospital serves patients in Northumberland Snyder and Union counties in Pennsylvania.

Operations

The hospital has 127 patient beds and 18 bassinets about 200 physicians on medical staff and about 900 clinical employees including lab technicians nurses therapists and radiology technicians.

Financial Performance

Evangelical Community Hospital reported a 9% increase in revenues in 2011 due to an increase an in patients visits investment income and funds raised.

Company Background

The hospital was established in 1926.

EXECUTIVES

President and CEO, Michael N. O'Keefe
Public Relations, Lizz Hendricks
VP Medical Affairs, J. Lawrence Ginsburg
VP Human Resources, Michael P. Pierce
Assistant Director Public Relations, Angela L. Brouse
Chair, Karen L. Hackman
Vice Chair, Martha A. Barrick
VP Community Relations and Chief Development Officer, Tami Radecke
VP Subsidiary Operations, Kendra A. Aucker
Director Planning, Linda Boose
VP Information Services and CIO, Scott Peterson
VP Nursing Administration, Paul E. Tarves
COO, Richard E. Smith Jr.
VP Finance and CFO, James Stopper
Director, Norman S. Rich, age 74
Director, Michael M. Apfelbaum, age 50
Director, James W. Morgan Jr.
Director, James G. Apple
Vice Chair, Martha A. Barrick
Director, Carol A. Graybeal
Director, John D. Griffith
Director, Robert L. Gronlund
Director, Roger S. Haddon Jr.
Director, Fredrik B. Paulsen Jr.
Director, W. Gale Reish
Director, Susan Forgett Rheam
Director, Douglas A. Spotts
Director, Michael R. Wimer Sr.
Director, Julie Barna
Director, Kristine Perle
Director, Hank Truslow Jr.
Director, Charles Zaleski

LOCATIONS

HQ: Evangelical Community Hospital
1 Hospital Dr., Lewisburg PA 17837
Phone: 570-522-2000   **Fax:** 570-522-2500
Web: www.evanhospital.com

COMPETITORS

Geisinger Health System
Lewistown Hospital
Mercy Health Partners Toledo
PinnacleHealth System

HISTORICAL FINANCIALS
Company Type: Private - Not-for-Profit

Income Statement
FYE: June 30

	REVENUE ($ mil.)	NET INCOME ($ mil.)	NET PROFIT MARGIN	EMPLOYEES
06/12	154	9	6.2%	1,360
06/11	142	18	12.6%	0
06/10	122	13	10.8%	0
06/09	112	7	6.3%	0
Annual Growth	11.3%	10.7%	—	—

2012 Year-End Financials

Debt ratio: ——
Return on equity: 6.20%
Cash ($ mil.): 15
Current ratio: 1.30
Long-term debt ($ mil.): —

Dividends
Yield: —
Payout: —
Market value ($ mil.): —

EVANS OIL COMPANY L.L.C.

LOCATIONS

HQ: EVANS OIL COMPANY L.L.C.
8450 MILLHAVEN RD, MONROE, LA 71203-8927
Phone: 318-345-1502

HISTORICAL FINANCIALS
Company Type: Private

Income Statement
FYE: December 31

	REVENUE ($ mil.)	NET INCOME ($ mil.)	NET PROFIT MARGIN	EMPLOYEES
12/11	194	2	1.3%	27
12/10	160	0	0.1%	0
12/09	128	0	0.0%	0
12/08	201	4	2.1%	0
Annual Growth	(1.3%)	(17.2%)	—	—

2011 Year-End Financials

Debt ratio: ——
Return on equity: 1.30%
Cash ($ mil.): 7
Current ratio: 1.70
Long-term debt ($ mil.): —

Dividends
Yield: —
Payout: —
Market value ($ mil.): —

EVERGREEN FS INC

Evergreen FS is an agricultural cooperative serving the needs of northern Illinois farmers. The co-op provides a full range of farm supplies and services including agronomy feed seed fertilizer fuel financing and marketing advice and products. The group also operates a handful of grain elevators as part of its operations. It specializes in the production of corn soybeans and wheat. The co-op boasts some 13000 member/owners that operate businesses on farmland in the counties of McLean Woodford and Livingston. Evergreen FS is a member of the GROWMARK system.

EXECUTIVES

President of the Board, Daniel T. (Dan) Kelley
Vice President of the Board, Rick Dickinson
General Manager, Kendall Miller
Manager Operations, Bob Eichelerger
Assistant Manager Marketing, Keith Hufendick
Manager Grain Department, Steve Dennis
Manager Human Resources Agri-Finance and Credit, Laura Winterland
Manager FAST STOP, Nancy Koopman
Assistant Controller, David Neill
Assistant Controller, Steve Conard
Manager Agronomy Marketing, Ervin Caselton
Manager Energy Marketing, Don Herring
Manager Information Technology, Scott Plato
Vice President of the Board, Rick Dickinson
Secretary, Darwin Builta
Treasurer, Paul Duzan
Director, Irvin Bane
Director, Kent Hodel
Director, Russell Johnson
Director, William Ruestman
Director, Bill Masching
Director, Mark Neumann
Director, Lynn Rader
Director, Gary Swartz
Director, Jerry Wisted
Director, Forrest Woods
Regional Manager, Jim Hoyt

LOCATIONS

HQ: Evergreen FS Inc.
402 N. Hershey Rd., Bloomington IL 61702
Phone: 309-663-2392   **Fax:** 309-663-0494
Web: www.evergreen-fs.com

PRODUCTS/OPERATIONS

2009 Sales

	$ mil.	% of total
Merchandise sales	177	66
Grain sales	93	34
Total	270	100

COMPETITORS

ADM	Cargill
ADM Alliance Nutrition	Land O' Lakes Purina
Ag Processing Inc.	Feed

HISTORICAL FINANCIALS
Company Type: Private - Cooperative

Income Statement
FYE: August 31

	REVENUE ($ mil.)	NET INCOME ($ mil.)	NET PROFIT MARGIN	EMPLOYEES
08/11	307	10	3.4%	240
08/10	246	7	3.1%	0
08/09	0	0	—	0
08/07	204	3	1.9%	0
Annual Growth	14.5%	39.5%	—	—

2011 Year-End Financials

Debt ratio: ——
Return on equity: 3.40%
Cash ($ mil.): 0
Current ratio: —
Long-term debt ($ mil.): —

Dividends
Yield: —
Payout: —
Market value ($ mil.): —

EVERGREEN STATE COLLEGE

Puget Sounders can earn their sheepskins at The Evergreen State College. The public liberal arts and sciences college the largest of its type in Washington state offers a variety of undergraduate degrees as well as graduate-level programs in environmental studies public administration and education. Evergreen is known for its unusual approach to learning; students enroll in comprehensive programs rather than a series of separate classes and courses are taught by teams of two to four professors. Students then receive "narrative" evaluations rather than traditional letter grades. Student enrollment is approximately 4500 with tuition at about $4000 per year. Evergreen State College was founded in 1967.

EXECUTIVES

President, Thomas L. (Les) Purce
VP Student Affairs, Art Costantino
VP Finance and Administration, John Hurley
Academic VP and Provost, Don Bantz
Director Computing and Communications, Aaron Powell
Dean Library and Media Services, Gregg Sapp

LOCATIONS

HQ: The Evergreen State College
2700 Evergreen Pkwy. NW, Olympia WA 98505-0002
Phone: 360-867-6000   **Fax:** 360-867-6577
Web: www.evergreen.edu

HISTORICAL FINANCIALS
Company Type: School

Income Statement
FYE: June 30

	REVENUE ($ mil.)	NET INCOME ($ mil.)	NET PROFIT MARGIN	EMPLOYEES
06/11	61	3	5.5%	580
06/08	56	20	36.8%	0
06/07	56	6	11.7%	0
06/06	322	0	—	0
Annual Growth	—	1786.9%	—	—

2011 Year-End Financials

Debt ratio: ——
Return on equity: 5.50%
Cash ($ mil.): 30
Current ratio: 2.50
Long-term debt ($ mil.): —

Dividends
Yield: —
Payout: —
Market value ($ mil.): —

EX-STUDENTS ASSOCIATION OF THE UNIVERSITY OF TEXAS

All these Exes may have lived in Texas during college but today they are spread throughout the world. The Ex-Students' Association is the alumni association for The University of Texas at Austin.

The group has more than 83000 members (Texas Exes) and some 140 chapters around the globe though about half of those are in Texas. In addition to facilitating social gatherings for former students the Ex-Students' Association offers career services and awards more than $2 million in scholarships annually. The group was established as the UT Alumni Association in 1885.

EXECUTIVES

Executive Director, James C. (Jim) Boon
CFO and Director Administration, Michael Ryan
Director Accounting and Human Resources, Janice Garcia
Director Marketing, Kimberly Gundersen
Director Communications; Editor The Alcalde, Avrel B. Seale
Managing Editor The Alcalde, Cora O. Bullock
Director Information Systems, David Reeves
Executive Assistant and Council Coordinator, Gina Schrader
Associate Executive Director, Susan Kessler
Director Alumni Records and Membership, Tracey Shultz
Associate Director, Carol Barrett
Director Travel, Betty Cotten
Director Accounting, Brigid McCormack
Director Campus Relations, Erin Crook
Director Career Services, Jennifer Duncan
General Manager, Tracie Hutchins
Director Public Policy, Leticia Acosta
Director Scholarships, Eleanor Moore
Executive Director, James C. (Jim) Boon
Treasurer/ Finance Chair, I. Craig Hester
Secretary, Lareatha Clay
President, John Adkins
President Elect, Sonia Perez

LOCATIONS

HQ: The Ex-Students' Association
2110 San Jacinto Blvd., Austin TX 78712
Phone: 512-471-8839   **Fax:** 512-471-8832
Web: www.texasexes.org

HISTORICAL FINANCIALS

Company Type: Private - Not-for-Profit

Income Statement

FYE: April 30

	REVENUE ($ mil.)	NET INCOME ($ mil.)	NET PROFIT MARGIN	EMPLOYEES
04/11	30	21	71.7%	36
04/10	11	(22)	—	0
04/09	0	0	—	0
04/98	4	8	184.3%	0
Annual Growth	87.9%	37.2%	—	—

2011 Year-End Financials

Debt ratio: ——
Return on equity: 71.70%
Cash ($ mil.): 3
Current ratio: 2.50
Long-term debt ($ mil.): —
Dividends
  Yield: —
  Payout: —
  Market value ($ mil.): —

EXCELITAS TECHNOLOGIES CORP.

LOCATIONS

HQ: EXCELITAS TECHNOLOGIES CORP.
200 WEST ST FL 1, WALTHAM, MA 02451-1195
Phone: 781-522-5900

HISTORICAL FINANCIALS

Company Type: Private

Income Statement

FYE: January 1

	REVENUE ($ mil.)	NET INCOME ($ mil.)	NET PROFIT MARGIN	EMPLOYEES
01/12	322	(38)	—	3,200
Annual Growth	—	—	—	—

2012 Year-End Financials

Debt ratio: ——
Return on equity: (-11.90)%
Cash ($ mil.): 14
Current ratio: 1.00
Long-term debt ($ mil.): —
Dividends
  Yield: —
  Payout: —
  Market value ($ mil.): —

EXETER HOSPITAL INC.

LOCATIONS

HQ: EXETER HOSPITAL INC.
5 ALUMNI DR, EXETER, NH 03833-2160
Phone: 603-778-7311
Web: www.exeterhospital.com

HISTORICAL FINANCIALS

Company Type: Private

Income Statement

FYE: September 30

	REVENUE ($ mil.)	NET INCOME ($ mil.)	NET PROFIT MARGIN	EMPLOYEES
09/11	207	11	5.7%	740
09/10	218	19	8.8%	0
09/09	210	0	—	0
09/08	205	20	10.2%	0
Annual Growth	0.3%	(17.3%)	—	—

2011 Year-End Financials

Debt ratio: ——
Return on equity: 5.70%
Cash ($ mil.): 56
Current ratio: 4.00
Long-term debt ($ mil.): —
Dividends
  Yield: —
  Payout: —
  Market value ($ mil.): —

EXIT 76 CORPORATION

LOCATIONS

HQ: EXIT 76 CORPORATION
2696 CHICAGO DR SW, GRAND RAPIDS, MI 49519-1628
Phone: 616-534-2181

HISTORICAL FINANCIALS

Company Type: Private

Income Statement

FYE: June 30

	REVENUE ($ mil.)	NET INCOME ($ mil.)	NET PROFIT MARGIN	EMPLOYEES
06/12	234	3	1.6%	450
06/11	204	1	1.0%	0
06/10	161	1	0.8%	0
06/09	156	2	1.5%	0
Annual Growth	14.3%	18.1%	—	—

2012 Year-End Financials

Debt ratio: ——
Return on equity: 1.60%
Cash ($ mil.): 1
Current ratio: 1.40
Long-term debt ($ mil.): —
Dividends
  Yield: —
  Payout: —
  Market value ($ mil.): —

EXPERIENCE WORKS INC.

Experience Works makes experience pay. The not-for-profit organization helps low-income individuals 55 years of age and older find jobs. It provides training as well as community service and employment opportunities for more than 125000 mature workers in 30 states and Puerto Rico. The group offers annual local state and national awards computer and technology skills services targeted to local markets and Senior Community Service Employment Program funded by the Older Americans Act to help low-income seniors. Experience Works was created in 1965. The company was called Green Thumb before it was renamed in 2002.

EXECUTIVES

Co-Acting CEO VP Operations and Assistant Secretary, Sally Boofer
Assistant Treasurer and Controller, Florie Munz
Director Human Resources and Supportive Services and Assistant Secretary, William (Bill) Dodson
Director Information Technology, Susan Lattanzi
VP External Affairs, Lita Levine-Kleger
Co-Acting CEO and CFO, Shane Bateman
Director Training and Staff Development, Marvin Jones
Director Operations East, Michi McNeace
Director Operations West, Jean Bennett
Auditors: Deloitte&ToucheLLP

LOCATIONS

HQ: Experience Works Inc.
2200 Clarendon Blvd. Ste. 1000, Arlington VA 22201
Phone: 703-522-7272   **Fax:** 703-522-0141
Web: www.experienceworks.org

HISTORICAL FINANCIALS

Company Type: Private - Not-for-Profit

Income Statement

FYE: June 30

	REVENUE ($ mil.)	NET INCOME ($ mil.)	NET PROFIT MARGIN	EMPLOYEES
06/11	181	0	0.2%	400
06/10	166	(1)	—	0
06/09	130	0	—	0
06/08	112	(0)	—	0
Annual Growth	17.1%	—	—	—

2011 Year-End Financials

Debt ratio: ——
Return on equity: 0.20%
Cash ($ mil.): 1
Current ratio: 0.20
Long-term debt ($ mil.): —

Dividends
Yield: —
Payout: —
Market value ($ mil.): —

EXPERT GLOBAL SOLUTIONS INC.

EXECUTIVES

President and CEO, Ronald A. (Ron) Rittenmeyer, age 65
EVP and General Counsel, Joshua Gindin, age 55, $316,860 total compensation
EVP and CIO, Stephen W. Elliott, age 50, $316,860 total compensation
EVP and CFO, John R. Schwab, $300,830 total compensation
EVP, Albert Zezulinski
EVP and COO, Jack Jones
President and CEO, Ronald A. (Ron) Rittenmeyer, age 65
EVP and General Counsel, Joshua Gindin, age 55, $316,860 total compensation
EVP and CIO, Stephen W. Elliott, age 50, $316,860 total compensation
EVP and CFO, John R. Schwab, $300,830 total compensation
EVP, Albert Zezulinski
EVP and COO, Jack Jones
Auditors: PricewaterhouseCoopersLLP

LOCATIONS

HQ: NCO Group Inc.
507 Prudential Rd., Horsham PA 19044
Phone: 215-441-3000   **Fax:** 724-867-1614
Web: www.emclairefinancial.com

2011 Sales

	$ mil.	% of total
US	1,436	93
Canada	44	3
Australia	33	2
UK	15	1
Mexico	10	1
Panama	1	-
Total	1,541	100

PRODUCTS/OPERATIONS

2011 Sales

	$ mil.	% of total
Accounts receivable management	1,203	78
Customer relationship management	338	22
Total	1,541	100

2011 Sales

	$ mil.	% of total
Services	1,216	79
Reimbursable costs & fees	325	21
Total	1,541	100

COMPETITORS

Asset Acceptance Capital	GC Services
	iQor
Asset Acceptance Capital	iQor
Asta Funding	Nationwide Recovery Systems
Asta Funding	Nationwide Recovery Systems
Banc of America Merchant Services	Portfolio Recovery
Banc of America Merchant Services	Portfolio Recovery
	Sitel Worldwide
Convergys	Sitel Worldwide
Convergys	Sykes Enterprises
Encore Capital Group	Sykes Enterprises
Encore Capital Group	TeleTech
Equifax	TeleTech
Equifax	West Corporation
GC Services	West Corporation

HISTORICAL FINANCIALS

Company Type: Private

Income Statement

FYE: December 31

	REVENUE ($ mil.)	NET INCOME ($ mil.)	NET PROFIT MARGIN	EMPLOYEES
12/11	1,541	(281)	—	26,900
12/10	1,602	(155)	—	0
12/09	1,563	(88)	—	0
12/08	1,513	(337)	—	0
Annual Growth	0.6%	—	—	—

2011 Year-End Financials

Debt ratio: ——
Return on equity: (-18.30)%
Cash ($ mil.): 17
Current ratio: 1.10
Long-term debt ($ mil.): —

Dividends
Yield: —
Payout: —
Market value ($ mil.): —

EXPLORER PIPELINE SERVICES COMPANY

LOCATIONS

HQ: EXPLORER PIPELINE SERVICES COMPANY
6846 S CANTON AVE STE 300, TULSA, OK 74136-3415
Phone: 918-493-5100
Web: www.expl.com

HISTORICAL FINANCIALS

Company Type: Private

Income Statement

FYE: December 31

	REVENUE ($ mil.)	NET INCOME ($ mil.)	NET PROFIT MARGIN	EMPLOYEES
12/11	221	42	19.0%	185
12/10	225	57	25.4%	0
12/09	219	53	24.4%	0
12/08	238	41	17.6%	0
Annual Growth	(2.4%)	0.1%	—	—

2011 Year-End Financials

Debt ratio: ——
Return on equity: 19.00%
Cash ($ mil.): 27
Current ratio: 0.30
Long-term debt ($ mil.): —

Dividends
Yield: —
Payout: —
Market value ($ mil.): —

EYAK CORPORATION

LOCATIONS

HQ: EYAK CORPORATION
901 LEFEVRE ST, CORDOVA, AK 99574
Phone: 907-424-7161
Web: www.eyakcorporation.com

HISTORICAL FINANCIALS

Company Type: Private

Income Statement

FYE: December 31

	REVENUE ($ mil.)	NET INCOME ($ mil.)	NET PROFIT MARGIN	EMPLOYEES
12/11	264	8	3.2%	270
Annual Growth	—	—	—	—

2011 Year-End Financials

Debt ratio: ——
Return on equity: 3.20%
Cash ($ mil.): 21
Current ratio: 0.80
Long-term debt ($ mil.): —

Dividends
Yield: —
Payout: —
Market value ($ mil.): —

F & M MAFCO INC.

LOCATIONS

HQ: F & M MAFCO INC.
9149 DRY FORK RD, HARRISON, OH 45030-1901
Phone: 513-367-2151
Web: www.fmmafco.com

HISTORICAL FINANCIALS
Company Type: Private

Income Statement
FYE: September 30

	REVENUE ($ mil.)	NET INCOME ($ mil.)	NET PROFIT MARGIN	EMPLOYEES
09/11	90	4	5.2%	272
09/10	82	3	4.3%	0
09/09	83	1	2.0%	0
09/08	105	8	8.0%	0
Annual Growth	(4.9%)	(17.4%)	—	—

2011 Year-End Financials

Debt ratio: ——
Return on equity: 5.20%
Cash ($ mil.): 0
Current ratio: 0.90
Long-term debt ($ mil.): ——

Dividends
Yield: —
Payout: —
Market value ($ mil.): —

FABIAN OIL INC.

LOCATIONS

HQ: FABIAN OIL INC.
15 OAK ST, OAKLAND, ME 04963-5013
Phone: 207-465-2000
Web: www.fabianoil.com

HISTORICAL FINANCIALS
Company Type: Private

Income Statement
FYE: December 31

	REVENUE ($ mil.)	NET INCOME ($ mil.)	NET PROFIT MARGIN	EMPLOYEES
12/11	90	0	0.2%	40
12/10	69	0	0.4%	0
12/09	54	0	1.5%	0
12/08	65	0	0.2%	0
Annual Growth	11.3%	4.9%	—	—

2011 Year-End Financials

Debt ratio: ——
Return on equity: 0.20%
Cash ($ mil.): 0
Current ratio: 0.70
Long-term debt ($ mil.): ——

Dividends
Yield: —
Payout: —
Market value ($ mil.): —

FACULTY PRACTICE FOUNDATION INC AND AFFILIATES

LOCATIONS

HQ: FACULTY PRACTICE FOUNDATION INC AND AFFILIATES
660 HARRISON AVE, BOSTON, MA 02118-2304
Phone: 617-638-8923

HISTORICAL FINANCIALS
Company Type: Private

Income Statement
FYE: June 30

	REVENUE ($ mil.)	NET INCOME ($ mil.)	NET PROFIT MARGIN	EMPLOYEES
06/11	331	(1)	—	4
06/10	281	(2)	—	0
Annual Growth	17.6%	—	—	—

2011 Year-End Financials

Debt ratio: ——
Return on equity: (-0.30)%
Cash ($ mil.): 19
Current ratio: 1.90
Long-term debt ($ mil.): ——

Dividends
Yield: —
Payout: —
Market value ($ mil.): —

FAIRFIELD UNIVERSITY

Fairfield University is a private Jesuit school with an enrollment of more than 5000 undergraduate and graduate students. It offers about 40 undergraduate majors as well as 40 graduate degree programs through six schools and colleges: College of Arts and Sciences; School of Nursing; School of Engineering; Dolan School of Business; Graduate School of Education and Allied Professions; and University College. With a faculty of about 550 professionals Fairfield University has one campus in Fairfield Connecticut and offers about 60 study abroad programs. The university was established by the Society of Jesus in 1942.

Geographic Reach

Fairfield University offers a variety of study abroad programs including courses in Italy Ireland Australia Brazil and Nicaragua. It also engages about 200 international students at its Connecticut campus.

Financial Performance

Fairfield University reported $187 million in revenues during fiscal 2012 an increase of about 6% over 2011. Most of the institution's earnings come from student tuition and fees. Net income dipped slightly into the red in 2012 (-$534000) down from $44 million in profits in 2011.

Strategy

The university aims to prepare students to take on leadership and service roles developing creativity and intelligence while fostering social responsibility and ethical and religious values. As part of its mission to create new opportunities for its students in 2011 Fairfield University added a new study abroad program in Brazil. In addition in 2012 it formed a partnership with Bridgeport Hospital to transition hospital RNs into the School of Nursing's Bachelor of Science degree program.

EXECUTIVES

VP Finance and Administration and Treasurer, William J. Lucas
Director Human Resources, Mark J. Guglielmoni
President, Rev Jeffrey P. von Arx, age 64
VP Information Services and University Librarian, James A. Estrada
Associate VP Academic Affairs, Mary Frances A. H. Malone
Associate Academic VP Enrollment Management, Judith Dobai
Associate VP Finance, Michael S. Maccarone
Controller, Kenneth R. Fontaine
Director Alumni Relations, Janet Canepa
VP Finance, Julie Dolan
Bursar, Raymond M. Bourdeau
University Registrar, Robert C. Russo
VP Advancement, Stephanie B. Frost
EVP and Chief of Staff., William H. (Billy) Weitzer
University Chaplain, Father Gerald R. Blaszczak
Chairman, Paul J. Huston
SVP Academic Affairs, Paul J. Fitzgerald
VP Marketing and Communications, Rama Sudhakar
Associate VP Global Relationships and Community Engagement and Dean University College, Edna F. Wilson
Associate VP Individual Giving, Michael Boyd
VP Administration and Chief of Staff, Mark C. Reed
VP Student Affairs, Thomas C. Pellegrino
Trustee, Ned C. Lautenbach, age 68
Trustee, David H. Chafey Jr., age 58
Trustee, Joseph F. Berardino, age 61
Trustee, William L. (Bill) Atwell, age 61
Trustee, Michele M. Macauda
Trustee, Kevin M. Conlisk, age 67
Trustee, Timothy J. Conway, age 57
Trustee, Michael E. McGuinness
Trustee, John F. Baldovin
Trustee, Terrence A. Baum
Trustee, Thomas G. Benz
Trustee, Stephen E. Bepler
Trustee, Joseph R. Bronson
Trustee, Frank J. Carroll III
Trustee, Thomas A. Franko
Trustee, Michael Garanzini
Trustee, Peter Gillen
Trustee, Patricia Glassford
Trustee, Brian Hull
Trustee, Jack L. Kelly
Trustee, Susan R. King
Trustee, Stephen M. Lessing
Trustee, William K. Lisecky
Trustee, William A. Malloy
Trustee, John C. Meditz
Trustee, Elner L. Morrell
Trustee, Rev George B. Murry
Trustee, Christopher C. Quick
Trustee, Lawrence C. Rafferty
Trustee, Eileen Rominger
Trustee, Rosellen Schnurr
Trustee, Jeffrey P. von Arx
Auditors: PricewaterhouseCoopersLLP

LOCATIONS

HQ: Fairfield University
1073 N. Benson Rd., Fairfield CT 06824
Phone: 203-254-4000   **Fax:** 806-474-1168
Web: www.indmolding.com

HISTORICAL FINANCIALS

Company Type: School

Income Statement

FYE: June 30

	REVENUE ($ mil.)	NET INCOME ($ mil.)	NET PROFIT MARGIN	EMPLOYEES
06/12	187	(0)	—	883
06/11	176	44	25.0%	0
06/10	172	26	15.6%	0
06/09	173	(64)	—	0
Annual Growth	2.7%	—	—	—

2012 Year-End Financials

Debt ratio: ——
Return on equity: (-0.30)%
Cash ($ mil.): 29
Current ratio: ——
Long-term debt ($ mil.): ——

Dividends
Yield: —
Payout: —
Market value ($ mil.): —

FAIRLEIGH DICKINSON UNIVERSITY

It's fair to say that Fairleigh Dickinson University (FDU) is one of the largest private universities in New Jersey. It has an enrollment of approximately 12000 students and 360 full-time faculty members. It has a student-teacher ratio of 12:1 and offers more than 100 undergraduate and graduate degree programs as well as doctoral programs in clinical psychology and school psychology. In addition to its main Metropolitan Campus in Teaneck New Jersey; the university also offers degree programs at the College at Florham in Madison New Jersey; at FDU-Vancouver in Canada; and at Wroxton College in Oxfordshire England. Fairleigh Dickinson was founded in 1942.

Some of the school's many disciplines include business education engineering hotel and restaurant management liberal arts (including communication criminal justice film and animation psychology and theater) nursing and allied health and the sciences.

The school also offers combined degree programs that allow students to earn a master's or professional degree at an accelerated pace in more than a dozen disciplines. FDU introduced an interdisciplinary studies program in sports administration began in 2009.

EXECUTIVES

Chair, Patrick J. (Pat) Zenner, age 64
President and Trustee, J. Michael Adams
Executive Director Online Programs, David F. Epstein
General Counsel, Wayne M. Richardson
VP Administration, Richard A. Riccio
Trustee and Interim President, Sheldon Drucker
VP Finance and Treasurer, Hania Ferrara
VP and CIO, Neal Sturm
Associate VP Communications and Marketing, Arthur E. (Art) Petrosemolo
SVP University Advancement, Richard P. Reiss
Associate VP Institutional Research and Assessment, Indira Govindan
Assistant VP Facilities, Michael Holland
Senior Development Officer University Advancement, Karen Lewis

Assistant VP Administration, Robert Valenti
Director University Advancement, Marilyn Adamczyk
Director Student Life, Sarah Azavedo
Executive Director Rothman Institute, James Barrood
Senior Program Director Continuing Education, Richard Bettencourt
Director Publications, Carol Black
Director Communications and Special Projects, Angelo Carfagna
Director School of Education, Vicki Cohen
Director Financial Aid, Theresa Coll
University Director Enrollment Services, Carol Creekmore
University Director Undergraduate Admissions, Coleen Curtis
Director Information Systems and Technology, Brian Domenick
Director MFA in Creative Writing Program and Special Assistant to the President, Martin Donoff
Director Continuing Education, Jennifer Dudley
Director Bi-Campus Facilities, William Dyer
Director Office of Global Learning, Stuart Eisenstadt
Director Athletics and Administration, Scott Fisher
Director Internal Auditing, Peter Forman
Director Payroll and HRIS, Julie Friedman
Director Center for Student Academic Services, Rachel Friend
Director Academic Support Center, Patricia Geehr
Director University College Dean, June Anne Giardina
Director Sports Information, William Giglio
Director Freshman Intensive Studies, William Gillard
Director Vpia-Development, Christopher Groff
Director The EOF Program, Marjorie Hall-Jacques
Director Institute for Global Business Education, Karin Hamilton
Executive Director Human Resources, Gregory Hammill
Director Adult Education, Denise Hart
Director Aquatics, Tracy Holt
Executive Director Global Partnerships, Irwin Isquith
Director Public Relations, Gretchen Johnson
Director Transfer Students, Roger Kane
Executive Director Online Programs, Malavika Khullar
Director Management Information Systems, Saul Kleinman
Director Athletics, William Klika
Director Computing Services, Ralph Knapp
Director Telecommunications, Carl Kraus
Director Budgeting Service, Frank Lawson
Program Director Continuing Education, Joan Leder
Director Enhanced Freshman Experience, Rendell Mabey
Director Student Health Services, Ann Mahan
Director Petrocelli College, Anthony Mastropietro
Executive Director Development, Susan McConville
Director Financial Aid, Margaret McGrail
Director Vpia-Development, Andrew McKay
Director International Student Services, Jessica McMillan
Co-Director Student Counseling and Psychology Services, David Mednick
Director Campus Public Safety, David Miles
Co-Director Student Counseling and Psychology Services, Alice Mills
Director Residence Life, Bernard Montgomery
Senior Program Director Continuing Education, Diane Mora
Director Student Life, Craig Mourton

Director Adult and Part-time Studies, Andrew Nelson
Director Purchasing, Susan O'Connor
Director Computing Services, Robert Pelech
Director Operations, Helene Pier
Director Academic Advising Center, Deborah Pilipie
Director Donor Relations, Laura Reynolds
Director Educational Technology, Sandra Selick
Director International and Graduate Admissions, Thomas Shea
Director Grants and Sponsored Projects, Laurie Treleven
Budget Manager and Assistant to the Dean Petrocelli College, Denise Wisniewski
Accounts Payable Manager, Gregory Sarajian
Research and Records Manager, Dora Rodriguez
Print Shop Manager, Charlotte Morey
Manager Human Resources, Maureen Curry
Manager Software and Databases, Joseph Brancone
Systems Manager University Systems and Security, Christopher Bland
Campus Property Manager, Sal Vacirca
Executive Associate Dean Petrocelli College Administrative Science, Ronald Calissi
Assistant Dean Becton College, Elizabeth Feeley
Interim Campus Provost Metropolitan College, Robert Greenfield
Director Special Student Services, Brenda Jackson
Assistant Dean Students, Michelle McCroy Heins
Assistant Dean Students, Nestor Melendez
Associate Dean University College, Albert Schielke
Assistant Dean Silberman College, Janette Shurdom
Dean University College, John Snyder
Associate Dean Petrocelli College, Thomas Swanzey
Dean Petrocelli College, Kenneth Vehrkens
Campus Provost College at Florham, Kenneth Greene
SVP and Interim University Provost, Joseph J. Kiernan
Associate VP Human Resources, Rose D'Ambrosio
Associate Provost Academic Administration, Bonnie Diehl
SVPand Assistant to the University Provost, Shealine Meyers
Director Office of Government and Community Affairs, Richard D. Bronson
Campus Provost Fairleigh Dickinson University Vancouver, Ian Haslam
VP Enrollment Management, Jonathan Wexler
SVP Academic Affairs and Provost, Christopher A. Capuano
Dean Students, Brian Mauro
Dean Silberman College of Business, William M. Moore
Dean Maxwell Becton College of Arts and Sciences, Geoffrey Weinman
Trustee, Ronald J. Doerfler, age 71
Trustee, Cheryl K. Beebe, age 56
Trustee, Vincent J. Naimoli
Trustee, Stewart Krentzman
President and Trustee, J. Michael Adams
Trustee and Interim President, Sheldon Drucker
Trustee, John E. Bailye
Trustee, Kenneth Brier
Trustee, Guy F. Budinscak
Trustee, Anthony J. Cuti
Trustee, Robert Hallenbeck
Trustee, Gregory H. Olsen
Trustee, Robert Saltarelli
Trustee, Paul Santucci
Trustee, George Sella
Trustee, Mary Kay Stratis
Trustee, Skippy Weinstein
Trustee, Molly Easo Smith
Trustee, Nick Agostino

LOCATIONS

HQ: Fairleigh Dickinson University
1000 River Rd., Teaneck NJ 07666-1995
Phone: 201-692-2000   Fax: 201-692-2030
Web: www.fdu.edu

HISTORICAL FINANCIALS

Company Type: School

Income Statement

	REVENUE ($ mil.)	NET INCOME ($ mil.)	NET PROFIT MARGIN	EMPLOYEES
				FYE: June 30
06/12	204	7	3.9%	1,505
06/11	202	22	11.3%	0
06/10*	191	13	7.2%	0
12/09	0	(0)	—	0
Annual Growth	612.0%	—	—	—

*Fiscal year change

2012 Year-End Financials

Debt ratio: —
Return on equity: 3.90%
Cash ($ mil.): 60
Current ratio: —
Long-term debt ($ mil.): —
Dividends
  Yield: —
  Payout: —
Market value ($ mil.): —

FAITH TECHNOLOGIES INC.

Keeping the faith in technology is a basic commitment of Faith Technologies one of the largest privately held electrical and specialty systems contractors in the US. The company's specialties include electrical contracting and service automated controls lighting security technology and preconstruction. It primarily serves clients in the commercial government industrial institutional health care manufacturing power residential retail transportation and data center sectors. The company has worked on a range of projects such as airports bridges correctional facilities government agencies hospitals restaurants and shopping centers.

Established in 1972 employee-owned Faith Technologies has around 15 locations in Georgia Kansas Minnesota Missouri Oklahoma and Wisconsin and is licensed to do business in some 45 states. In 2009 its Faith Technologies Tulsa division in Oklahoma merged with Alpha Electrical Services. Also that year the company completed the final phase of a nationwide transition by converting all 10 of its Town & Country Electric locations in Wisconsin under the Faith Technologies banner.

Faith Technologies opened its 15th location in Minneapolis in 2010.

EXECUTIVES

CEO, Roland G. (Rollie) Stephenson, age 66
President, Richard A. Schinke Jr.
CFO, Donald M. Stachowiak

VP Human Resources, Amy Sabourin
VP Operations, George Van Der Linden
Chief Learning Officer, Terri Luebke
VP Business Development Northern Region, Jim Schlater
VP Business Development Southern Region, Mike Stewart

LOCATIONS

HQ: Faith Technologies Inc.
225 Main St., Menasha WI 54952
Phone: 920-225-6500   Fax: 858-535-0312
Web: www.helixelectric.com

COMPETITORS

Aldridge Electric	Guarantee Electrical
EEI	Sachs Electric
EMCOR	

HISTORICAL FINANCIALS

Company Type: Private

Income Statement

	REVENUE ($ mil.)	NET INCOME ($ mil.)	NET PROFIT MARGIN	EMPLOYEES
				FYE: December 31
12/11	248	4	1.9%	1,480
12/10	228	2	1.0%	0
12/09	219	5	2.6%	0
12/08	227	15	6.8%	0
Annual Growth	3.0%	(33.3%)	—	—

2011 Year-End Financials

Debt ratio: —
Return on equity: 1.90%
Cash ($ mil.): 0
Current ratio: 1.10
Long-term debt ($ mil.): —
Dividends
  Yield: —
  Payout: —
Market value ($ mil.): —

FALASCA MECHANICAL INC

LOCATIONS

HQ: FALASCA MECHANICAL INC
3329 N MILL RD, VINELAND, NJ 08360-1525
Phone: 856-794-2010

HISTORICAL FINANCIALS

Company Type: Private

Income Statement

	REVENUE ($ mil.)	NET INCOME ($ mil.)	NET PROFIT MARGIN	EMPLOYEES
				FYE: December 31
12/11	130	23	17.9%	80
12/10	47	5	10.5%	0
12/09	85	13	16.1%	0
12/08	95	11	12.4%	0
Annual Growth	11.0%	25.3%	—	—

2011 Year-End Financials

Debt ratio: —
Return on equity: 17.90%
Cash ($ mil.): 9
Current ratio: 0.40
Long-term debt ($ mil.): —
Dividends
  Yield: —
  Payout: —
Market value ($ mil.): —

FALMOUTH HOSPITAL ASSOCIATION INC.

LOCATIONS

HQ: FALMOUTH HOSPITAL ASSOCIATION INC.
100 TER HEUN DR, FALMOUTH, MA 02540-2599
Phone: 508-548-5300
Web: www.capecodhealth.org

HISTORICAL FINANCIALS

Company Type: Private

Income Statement

	REVENUE ($ mil.)	NET INCOME ($ mil.)	NET PROFIT MARGIN	EMPLOYEES
				FYE: September 30
09/11	146	10	7.0%	950
09/08*	131	(5)	—	0
12/07	32	(0)	—	0
09/07	1,890	0	—	0
Annual Growth	—	3774.5%	—	—

*Fiscal year change

2011 Year-End Financials

Debt ratio: —
Return on equity: 7.00%
Cash ($ mil.): 10
Current ratio: 1.00
Long-term debt ($ mil.): —
Dividends
  Yield: —
  Payout: —
Market value ($ mil.): —

FAMILY CENTRAL INC.

LOCATIONS

HQ: FAMILY CENTRAL INC.
840 SW 81ST AVE, NORTH LAUDERDALE, FL 33068-2001
Phone: 954-724-3874
Web: www.familycentral.org

HISTORICAL FINANCIALS

Company Type: Private

Income Statement

	REVENUE ($ mil.)	NET INCOME ($ mil.)	NET PROFIT MARGIN	EMPLOYEES
				FYE: June 30
06/12	197	0	0.0%	428
06/11	203	0	0.1%	0
06/10	199	0	0.2%	0
06/09	184	0	0.1%	0
Annual Growth	2.4%	(50.8%)	—	—

FAR NORTHERN COORDINATING COUNCIL ON DEVELOPMENTAL DISABILITIES

LOCATIONS

HQ: FAR NORTHERN COORDINATING COUNCIL ON DEVELOPMENTAL DISABILITIES
1900 CHURN CREEK RD # 31, REDDING, CA 96002-0292
Phone: 530-222-4791
Web: www.farnorthernrc.org

HISTORICAL FINANCIALS
Company Type: Private

Income Statement
FYE: June 30

	REVENUE ($ mil.)	NET INCOME ($ mil.)	NET PROFIT MARGIN	EMPLOYEES
06/12	110	0	0.0%	180
06/11	109	(0)	—	0
06/10	105	0	0.0%	0
06/09	106	(0)	—	0
Annual Growth	1.3%	—	—	—

2012 Year-End Financials

Debt ratio: ——
Return on equity: —
Cash ($ mil.): 2
Current ratio: 0.10
Long-term debt ($ mil.): —

Dividends
Yield: —
Payout: —
Market value ($ mil.): —

FARGO PUBLIC SCHOOLS DISTRICT NO. 1

LOCATIONS

HQ: FARGO PUBLIC SCHOOLS DISTRICT NO. 1
415 4TH ST N, FARGO, ND 58102-4514
Phone: 701-446-1000
Web: www.fargo.k12.nd.us

HISTORICAL FINANCIALS
Company Type: Private

Income Statement
FYE: June 30

	REVENUE ($ mil.)	NET INCOME ($ mil.)	NET PROFIT MARGIN	EMPLOYEES
06/12	145	(10)	—	1,600
06/09	0	(0)	—	0
06/08	127	46	36.8%	0
06/07	121	(3)	—	0
Annual Growth	6.4%	—	—	—

FARM CREDIT SERVICES ILLINOIS ACA

LOCATIONS

HQ: FARM CREDIT SERVICES ILLINOIS ACA
1100 FARM CREDIT DR, MAHOMET, IL 61853-8532
Phone: 217-590-2200

HISTORICAL FINANCIALS
Company Type: Private

Income Statement
FYE: December 31

	ASSETS ($ mil.)	NET INCOME ($ mil.)	INCOME AS % OF ASSETS	EMPLOYEES
12/11	2,843	56	2.0%	165
12/10	2,607	61	2.4%	0
12/09	2,230	36	1.7%	0
12/08	2,079	36	1.8%	0
Annual Growth	11.0%	15.5%	—	—

FARMERS CO-OPERATIVE ELEVATOR COMPANY

LOCATIONS

HQ: FARMERS CO-OPERATIVE ELEVATOR COMPANY
1972 510TH ST, HANLEY FALLS, MN 56245
Phone: 507-768-3448
Web: www.farmerscoopelevator.com

HISTORICAL FINANCIALS
Company Type: Private

Income Statement
FYE: December 31

	REVENUE ($ mil.)	NET INCOME ($ mil.)	NET PROFIT MARGIN	EMPLOYEES
12/11	354	2	0.8%	56
12/10	243	2	0.9%	0
12/09	162	1	1.0%	0
12/08	255	4	1.7%	0
Annual Growth	11.6%	(12.2%)	—	—

2011 Year-End Financials

Debt ratio: ——
Return on equity: 0.80%
Cash ($ mil.): 11
Current ratio: 0.10
Long-term debt ($ mil.): —

Dividends
Yield: —
Payout: —
Market value ($ mil.): —

FARMERS CO-OPERATIVE OF HANSKA

LOCATIONS

HQ: FARMERS CO-OPERATIVE OF HANSKA
103 E 1ST ST, HANSKA, MN 56041-7706
Phone: 507-439-6244
Web: www.hanskaco.com

HISTORICAL FINANCIALS
Company Type: Private

Income Statement
FYE: July 31

	REVENUE ($ mil.)	NET INCOME ($ mil.)	NET PROFIT MARGIN	EMPLOYEES
07/12	101	0	0.1%	58
07/11	106	0	0.6%	0
07/10	82	0	1.1%	0
07/09	108	1	1.3%	0
Annual Growth	(2.0%)	(56.1%)	—	—

2012 Year-End Financials

Debt ratio: ——
Return on equity: 0.10%
Cash ($ mil.): 11
Current ratio: 0.60
Long-term debt ($ mil.): —

Dividends
Yield: —
Payout: —
Market value ($ mil.): —

FARMERS COOP SUPPLY & SHIPPING ASSOCIATION

LOCATIONS

HQ: FARMERS COOP SUPPLY & SHIPPING ASSOCIATION
570 COMMERCE ST, WEST SALEM, WI 54669-1155
Phone: 608-786-1100
Web: www.fcoopssassn.com

HISTORICAL FINANCIALS
Company Type: Private

Income Statement
FYE: July 31

	REVENUE ($ mil.)	NET INCOME ($ mil.)	NET PROFIT MARGIN	EMPLOYEES
07/12	81	5	6.4%	51
07/11	59	3	5.6%	0
07/10	44	2	5.6%	0
07/09	46	2	5.7%	0
Annual Growth	20.9%	25.8%	—	—

2012 Year-End Financials

Debt ratio: ——
Return on equity: 6.40%
Cash ($ mil.): 1
Current ratio: 0.10
Long-term debt ($ mil.): —

Dividends
Yield: —
Payout: —
Market value ($ mil.): —

FARMERS COOPERATIVE COMPANY

LOCATIONS

HQ: FARMERS COOPERATIVE COMPANY
196 E RAILROAD ST, AFTON, IA 50830-7715
Phone: 641-347-8428

HISTORICAL FINANCIALS
Company Type: Private

Income Statement
FYE: December 31

	REVENUE ($ mil.)	NET INCOME ($ mil.)	NET PROFIT MARGIN	EMPLOYEES
12/11	120	2	2.4%	120
12/10	70	1	2.5%	0
12/09	65	1	2.5%	0
12/07	63	0	1.4%	0
Annual Growth	24.2%	46.7%	—	—

2011 Year-End Financials

Debt ratio: ——
Return on equity: 2.40%
Cash ($ mil.): 2
Current ratio: 0.20
Long-term debt ($ mil.): —

Dividends
Yield: —
Payout: —
Market value ($ mil.): —

FARMERS COOPERATIVE SOCIETY

When farmers cooperate society benefits. Through its seven centers in northwest Iowa Farmers Cooperative Society offers its member/farmers a full range of agricultural growing and marketing products and services including crop-storage facilities and business consulting. Its feedlot with room for some 5500 head of cattle helps members buy and care for feeder cattle and provides discounts on grain for members. The co-op also operates a member-only How-To Building Store in Sioux Center Iowa that sells hardware lawn-care products lumber and paint as well as brand-name home appliances. Farmers Cooperative Society has roots dating back to 1907.

To provide the right product for its members the co-op's How-To Building store uses over 40 suppliers such as Andersen CertainTeed Toro and Weber-Stephen Products. The co-op also sells pork producers with products through suppliers like AP Valco and Chore-time. The co-op also supplies pork producers through suppliers such as AP Valco and Chore-time.

EXECUTIVES

General Manager, Ken Ehrp
Manager Administration and Finance, Carol Koops
Board President, Leon Schuiteman
Secretary, Dave Hofland
Manager Feed Division, Brad De Vries
Manager Feed Mill, Kevin Hulstein
Manager Lumber Division, Ron Boon
Location Manager Boyden (IA), Leon Blanchet
Location Manager Ireton (IA), Doug Shurr
Location Manager Little Rock (IA), Ed Mayland
Location Manager Melvin (IA), Brad Knock
Manager Agronomy Department, Stan Feekes
Manager Purchasing, Kevin Sandbulte
Location Manager Sanborn, Buzz Tourangeau
Location Manager Ritter, Chris Blair
VP, Marvin Wynia

LOCATIONS

HQ: Farmers Cooperative Society
317 3rd St. NW, Sioux Center IA 51250
Phone: 712-722-2671   **Fax:** 712-722-2674
Web: www.farmerscoopsociety.com

COMPETITORS

AGRI Industries	Miles Enterprises
Five Star Co-op	Premier AG Co-Op Inc.
Gold-Eagle Cooperative	Sears
Heartland Co-op	True Value
Home Depot	Wal-Mart
Lowe's	West Central Co-op

HISTORICAL FINANCIALS
Company Type: Private - Cooperative

Income Statement
FYE: December 31

	REVENUE ($ mil.)	NET INCOME ($ mil.)	NET PROFIT MARGIN	EMPLOYEES
12/11*	380	7	2.1%	200
07/11	380	7	2.1%	0
07/10	249	4	1.6%	0
07/09	288	4	1.5%	0
Annual Growth	9.7%	21.3%	—	—

*Fiscal year change

2011 Year-End Financials

Debt ratio: ——
Return on equity: 2.10%
Cash ($ mil.): 1
Current ratio: ——
Long-term debt ($ mil.): —

Dividends
Yield: —
Payout: —
Market value ($ mil.): —

FARMERS ELECTRIC COOPERATIVE INC.

LOCATIONS

HQ: FARMERS ELECTRIC COOPERATIVE INC.
2000 INTERSTATE HWY 30 E, GREENVILLE, TX 75402-9084
Phone: 903-455-1715
Web: www.farmerselectric.coop

HISTORICAL FINANCIALS
Company Type: Private

Income Statement
FYE: December 31

	REVENUE ($ mil.)	NET INCOME ($ mil.)	NET PROFIT MARGIN	EMPLOYEES
12/11	105	10	9.9%	130
12/10	106	10	9.7%	0
12/09	103	8	8.5%	0
12/08	113	9	8.5%	0
Annual Growth	(2.4%)	2.8%	—	—

2011 Year-End Financials

Debt ratio: ——
Return on equity: 9.90%
Cash ($ mil.): 1
Current ratio: 0.30
Long-term debt ($ mil.): —

Dividends
Yield: —
Payout: —
Market value ($ mil.): —

FARMERS GRAIN TERMINAL INC.

LOCATIONS

HQ: FARMERS GRAIN TERMINAL INC.
1977 HARBOR FRONT RD, GREENVILLE, MS 38701-9588
Phone: 662-332-0987
Web: www.fgtcoop.com

HISTORICAL FINANCIALS
Company Type: Private

Income Statement
FYE: July 31

	REVENUE ($ mil.)	NET INCOME ($ mil.)	NET PROFIT MARGIN	EMPLOYEES
07/12	615	12	2.1%	82
07/11	471	8	1.8%	0
07/10	303	(5)	—	0
07/09	416	7	1.7%	0
Annual Growth	13.9%	20.9%	—	—

2012 Year-End Financials
Debt ratio: ——
Return on equity: 2.10%
Cash ($ mil.): 51
Current ratio: 0.60
Long-term debt ($ mil.): —

Dividends
Yield: —
Payout: —
Market value ($ mil.): —

HISTORICAL FINANCIALS
Company Type: Private - Cooperative

Income Statement
FYE: June 30

	REVENUE ($ mil.)	NET INCOME ($ mil.)	NET PROFIT MARGIN	EMPLOYEES
06/11	136	14	10.7%	418
06/10	131	8	6.6%	0
06/08	83	2	2.7%	0
06/07	0	0	—	0
Annual Growth	—	—	—	—

2011 Year-End Financials
Debt ratio: ——
Return on equity: 10.70%
Cash ($ mil.): 28
Current ratio: 1.70
Long-term debt ($ mil.): —

Dividends
Yield: —
Payout: —
Market value ($ mil.): —

HISTORICAL FINANCIALS
Company Type: Private

Income Statement
FYE: June 30

	REVENUE ($ mil.)	NET INCOME ($ mil.)	NET PROFIT MARGIN	EMPLOYEES
06/11	231	14	6.3%	3,500
06/10*	243	21	9.0%	0
07/09	0	0	7.2%	0
06/06	206	(15)	—	0
Annual Growth	3.9%	—	—	—

*Fiscal year change

2011 Year-End Financials
Debt ratio: ——
Return on equity: 6.30%
Cash ($ mil.): 14
Current ratio: —
Long-term debt ($ mil.): —

Dividends
Yield: —
Payout: —
Market value ($ mil.): —

FARMERS TELEPHONE COOPERATIVE INC.

Farmers Telephone Cooperative (FTC) is the incumbent local-exchange carrier (ILEC) in Williamsburg Lee Sumter Clarendon and Florence counties in eastern South Carolina. Serving more than 60000 customers in a 3000 mile area the company provides traditional phone services including local-exchange access and long-distance as well as dial-up and DSL Internet access. The company also offers wireless phone service through a partnership with AT&T Mobility as well as security services and enterprise communications services. In operation since 1951 FTC claims to be the second-largest co-op in the US and should not be confused with the Farmers Telephone Cooperative serving the Rainsville Alabama area.

Among its business telecommunications services FTC resells communications and networking equipment. The company deals in products from such vendors as ADTRAN Mitel and Cisco Systems. In addition to equipment phone wireless and Internet service FTC also offers enterprise customers data services such as T-1 asynchronous transfer mode data transport frame relay and Ethernet services.

EXECUTIVES
CEO, F. Bradley (Brad) Erwin
CFO, Jeff Lawrimore
Chief Regulatory Officer, Ronald K. Nesmith
Chief Marketing Officer, Robin Coker
Manager Human Resources, William I. (Nicky) Nexsen III

LOCATIONS
HQ: Farmers Telephone Cooperative Inc.
1101 E. Main St., Kingstree SC 29556
Phone: 843-382-2333   **Fax:** 843-382-3909
Web: www.ftc-i.net

COMPETITORS
AT&T	Sprint Nextel
AT&T Mobility	tw telecom
EarthLink	Verizon

FARMINGTON PUBLIC SCHOOL DISTRICT

LOCATIONS
HQ: FARMINGTON PUBLIC SCHOOL DISTRICT
32500 SHIAWASSEE RD, FARMINGTON, MI 48336-2338
Phone: 248-489-3300

HISTORICAL FINANCIALS
Company Type: Private

Income Statement
FYE: June 30

	REVENUE ($ mil.)	NET INCOME ($ mil.)	NET PROFIT MARGIN	EMPLOYEES
06/12	160	(6)	—	1,639
06/11	170	2	1.3%	0
06/10	171	(8)	—	0
06/09	174	(3)	—	0
Annual Growth	(2.7%)	—	—	—

2012 Year-End Financials
Debt ratio: ——
Return on equity: (-4.20)%
Cash ($ mil.): 27
Current ratio: —
Long-term debt ($ mil.): —

Dividends
Yield: —
Payout: —
Market value ($ mil.): —

FAYETTE COUNTY BOARD OF EDUCATION

LOCATIONS
HQ: FAYETTE COUNTY BOARD OF EDUCATION
210 STONEWALL AVE W, FAYETTEVILLE, GA 30214-1518
Phone: 770-460-3535
Web: www.fayettemiddle.org

FCL BUILDERS LLC

LOCATIONS
HQ: FCL BUILDERS LLC
1150 SPRING LAKE DR, ITASCA, IL 60143-2066
Phone: 630-773-0050
Web: www.fclbuilders.com

HISTORICAL FINANCIALS
Company Type: Private

Income Statement
FYE: December 31

	REVENUE ($ mil.)	NET INCOME ($ mil.)	NET PROFIT MARGIN	EMPLOYEES
12/11	81	0	0.0%	50
12/10	60	(2)	—	0
12/03	128	5	4.3%	0
12/02	120	2	2.4%	0
Annual Growth	(12.4%)	(80.2%)	—	—

2011 Year-End Financials
Debt ratio: ——
Return on equity: —
Cash ($ mil.): 3
Current ratio: 0.30
Long-term debt ($ mil.): —

Dividends
Yield: —
Payout: —
Market value ($ mil.): —

FEDCAP REHABILITATION SERVICES INC.

LOCATIONS
HQ: FEDCAP REHABILITATION SERVICES INC.
211 W 14TH ST, NEW YORK, NY 10011-7157
Phone: 212-727-4200
Web: www.fedcap.org

Income Statement

FYE: September 30

	REVENUE ($ mil.)	NET INCOME ($ mil.)	NET PROFIT MARGIN	EMPLOYEES
09/11	82	0	0.0%	1,500
09/10	69	0	0.0%	0
09/09	70	0	0.3%	0
09/08	66	1	2.0%	0
Annual Growth	7.2%	(79.5%)	—	—

2011 Year-End Financials

Debt ratio: ——
Return on equity: —
Cash ($ mil.): 8
Current ratio: 2.50
Long-term debt ($ mil.): —

Dividends
Yield: —
Payout: —
Market value ($ mil.): —

FEDERAL HOME LOAN BANK OF INDIANAPOLIS

Federal Home Loan Bank of Indianapolis (FHLB Indianapolis) is one of a dozen regional banks in the Federal Home Loan Bank System established by Congress in 1932. It provides funding for residential mortgages and community development loans to about 420 member financial institutions including banks credit unions insurance companies and thrifts in Indiana and Michigan. (Community development financial institutions are also eligibile to become members of FHLB Indianapolis.) It also provides support services such as risk management securities safekeeping and funds transfers. FHLB Indianapolis is a government-sponsored enterprise that is cooperatively owned by its member financial institutions.

FHLB Indianapolis operates through two primary segments: Traditional which provides credit services invests in securities and provides correspondent services; and MPP which comprises mortgage loans acquired from its members.

FHLB Indianapolis' financial performance is closely tied with that of its members and the overall economy. In particular demand for loans is a determining factor for how well the bank does. Not unexpectedly its earnings have been falling in the economic downturn. Its 2011 revenues fell 14% to $670.2 million while net income fell nearly 1% to $110.1 million. The decline was primarily due to lower interest earnings as well as net losses on investment activities. Asset levels also declined by 10% that year.

EXECUTIVES

SVP and Director Marketing, Douglas J. (Doug) Iverson, age 54
Vice Chairman, Jeffrey A. Poxon, age 65
VP and Director Sales, William S. McDowell
SVP and Chief Banking Officer, Gregory L. Teare, age 58, $231,552 total compensation
President and CEO, Milton J. Miller II, age 56, $538,461 total compensation
EVP and COO Business Operations, Jonathan R. West, age 55, $296,892 total compensation
VP and Director of Human Resources, LaVonne C. Cate

VP and Funding Manager, Laura L. DiCioccio
VP and Senior Marketing Representative, James B. Eibel
First VP, Jonathan W. Griffin
EVP COO and CFO, Cindy L. Konich, age 55, $323,082 total compensation
VP and Underwriting Manager, Dennis M. Haworth
VP and Network and Support Services Manager, Ronald L. Malone
First VP and Director Internal Audit, Gregory J. McKee
SVP and Chief Risk Officer, Sunil U. Mohandas, age 52, $256,257 total compensation
First VP, William R. Nicksin
First VP, Jeffrey A. Sanders
VP and Business Information Manager, Daniel C. Weeden
VP and Community Investment Officer, MaryBeth Wott
VP and Communications and Media Relations Manager, Barbara K. Hembree
Chair, Paul C. Clabuesch, age 63
VP, David B. Cross
VP, Charles A. Rainey
VP and Director Mortgage Purchase Program, Donald C. Erwin
First VP and Controller, Bradley A. Burnett, age 37
SVP and Chief Accounting Officer, K. Lowell Short Jr., age 55
Director, Maurice F. Winkler III, age 55
Director, Matthew P. (Matt) Forrester, age 55
Vice Chairman, Jeffrey A. Poxon, age 65
Director, Thomas R. (Tom) Sullivan, age 61
Director, John L. Skibski, age 47
Director, Timothy P. Gaylord, age 52
Director, Christopher A. (Chris) Wolking, age 52
Director, Paul D. Borja, age 50
Director, James D. MacPhee
Director, Jonathan P. Bradford, age 62
Director, Christine A. Coady, age 48
Director, Michael J. Hannigan Jr., age 67
Director, Prof Carl E. Liedholm, age 71
Director, James L. Logue III, age 59
Director, Robert D. Long, age 57
Director, Elliot A. Spoon, age 61
Director, Larry A. Swank, age 70
Director, Dan L. Moore, age 61
Director, Christine Coady Narayanan, age 48
Auditors: PricewaterhouseCoopersLLP

LOCATIONS

HQ: Federal Home Loan Bank of Indianapolis
8250 Woodfield Crossing Blvd., Indianapolis IN 46240
Phone: 317-465-0200   **Fax:** 512-370-1920
Web: www.planetcse.com

PRODUCTS/OPERATIONS

2011 Sales

	$ mil.	% of total
Interest		
Mortgages held for portfolio net	299	42
Held-to-maturity securities	178	25
Advances to members	161	23
Available-for-sale securities	48	7
Other	14	2
Noninterest	7	1
Adjustments	(40.5)	
Total	**670**	**100**

Income Statement

FYE: September 30

	ASSETS ($ mil.)	NET INCOME ($ mil.)	INCOME AS % OF ASSETS	EMPLOYEES
09/12*	41,231	107	0.3%	175
12/11	40,375	110	0.3%	0
12/10	44,929	110	0.2%	0
12/09	46,599	120	0.3%	0
Annual Growth	(4.0%)	(3.6%)	—	—

*Fiscal year change

2012 Year-End Financials

Debt ratio: ——
Return on equity: 22.30%
Cash ($ mil.): 2,858
Current ratio: —
Long-term debt ($ mil.): —

Dividends
Yield: —
Payout: —
Market value ($ mil.): —

FEDERAL HOME LOAN BANK OF NEW YORK

Federal Home Loan Bank of New York (FHLBNY) provides funds for residential mortgages and community development to more than 330 member banks savings and loans credit unions and life insurance companies in New York New Jersey Puerto Rico and the US Virgin Islands. One of a dozen Federal Home Loan Banks (FHLBs) in the US it is cooperatively owned by its member institutions and supervised by the Federal Housing Finance Agency. FHLBNY like the others in the system is privately capitalized; it receives no taxpayer funding. The bank instead raises funds mainly by issuing debt instruments in the capital markets.

FHLBNY is a secured lender that requires collateral for its advances which are typically used by members to underwrite residential mortgages or to invest in US Treasury and agency securities mortgage-backed securities and other real estate-related assets. The bank has remained consistently profitable by keeping very low overhead and investing in relatively low-risk loans and securities. Loan demand (along with corresponding revenue and net income) declined in 2010 however as member institutions grew their deposit bases giving them a bigger pool of money to lend.

Credit unions are a possible area of growth for FHLBNY. The bank has identified more than 50 credit unions and banks that are not members but are eligible. To be under consideration an institution must have more than $50 million in assets ($100 million for banks) be an established wholesale lender maintain a high deposit-to-loan ratio and have management that has done business with an FHLB in the past.

EXECUTIVES

Vice Chairman, Jose R. Gonzalez, age 57
Chairman, Michael M. (Mike) Horn, age 72
President and CEO, Alfred A. DelliBovi, age 66, $649,494 total compensation
Director Compliance, Steve S. Christatos
SVP and Head Member Services, Paul B. Heroux, age 53, $300,980 total compensation

SVP and Head Asset Liability Management, Craig
E. Reynolds, age 63, $270,443 total compensation

SVP and CFO, Patrick A. Morgan, age 71, $319,154
total compensation

SVP and Chief Risk Officer, Peter S. Leung Jr., age
57, $423,294 total compensation

VP and Director Collateral Operations, Michael A.
Volpe

**SVP and Head Strategy and Business
Development,** Kevin M. Neylan, age 54, $310,415
total compensation

VP, Backer Ali

SVP and Director Bank Relations, Eric P. Amig,
age 53

VP, Edwin Artuz

**VP and Director Credit and Correspondent
Services,** James Bernard

VP, Sean Borde

VP and Director Acquired Member Assets, Thomas
J. Doyle

VP, John Edelen

VP, Paul Friend

VP, G. Robert Fusco

**VP Director Community Investment and
Community Investment Officer,** Joseph Gallo

SVP and Head Marketing and Sales, Adam
Goldstein, age 38

Director Credit Policy, Susan Isquith

VP Sales and Calling Officer, Maureen Kalena

Director Operations Risk, Rebecca Logan

VP, Walter Moran

VP Sales and Calling Officer, Alfred O'Connell

VP, Agnes Olah

VP Funds Transfer and Deposit Services, Aida
Polanco

VP Sales and Calling Officer, Facundo (Frank)
Saenz de Viteri

VP, Grace Sit

VP and Director Funding and Derivatives, Louis
Solimine

VP, Barbara Sperrazza

VP, John Surre

Director Risk Analytics, M. Hampton Tunis

VP, Barbara Way

**VP and Community Investment Operations
Officer,** Edwin Bird

VP Sales and Manager Sales, James Feeney

VP and Director Investment Portfolio, Diahann
Rothstein

VP and Senior Trader Analyst, Phil Scott

VP and Director Marketing Communications,
Candice Soldano

**Internet Services Specialist Funds Transfer and
Deposit Services,** Shirley Hemphill

VP and Director Loan Review Analysis, Cynthia
Palladino

VP and Collateral Valuations, Bryan Gallagher

SVP and Chief Audit Officer, Stephen Angelo

Director, Joseph R. Ficalora, age 65

Director, James W. (Jim) Fulmer, age 60

Director, George Strayton, age 68

Director, Ronald E. Hermance Jr., age 64

Director, John R. Buran, age 62

Director, Joseph J. (Joe) Melone, age 80

Vice Chairman, Jose R. Gonzalez, age 57

Director, C. Cathleen (Cathi) Raffaeli, age 55

Director, Thomas M. O'Brien, age 61

Director, Anne Evans Estabrook, age 67

Director, Katherine J. Liseno, age 67

Director, Kevin J. Lynch, age 65

Director, Richard S. Mroz, age 50

Director, Rev Edwin C. Reed, age 58

Director, Jay M. Ford, age 62

Director, DeForest B. Soaries Jr., age 60

Vice Chairman, Jose R. Gonzalez, age 57

Chairman, Michael M. (Mike) Horn, age 72

President and CEO, Alfred A. DelliBovi, age 66,
$649,494 total compensation

Director Compliance, Steve S. Christatos

SVP and Head Member Services, Paul B. Heroux,
age 53, $300,980 total compensation

SVP and Head Asset Liability Management, Craig
E. Reynolds, age 63, $270,443 total compensation

SVP and CFO, Patrick A. Morgan, age 71, $319,154
total compensation

SVP and Chief Risk Officer, Peter S. Leung Jr., age
57, $423,294 total compensation

VP and Director Collateral Operations, Michael A.
Volpe

**SVP and Head Strategy and Business
Development,** Kevin M. Neylan, age 54, $310,415
total compensation

VP, Backer Ali

SVP and Director Bank Relations, Eric P. Amig,
age 53

VP, Edwin Artuz

**VP and Director Credit and Correspondent
Services,** James Bernard

VP, Sean Borde

VP and Director Acquired Member Assets, Thomas
J. Doyle

VP, John Edelen

VP, Paul Friend

VP, G. Robert Fusco

**VP Director Community Investment and
Community Investment Officer,** Joseph Gallo

SVP and Head Marketing and Sales, Adam
Goldstein, age 38

Director Credit Policy, Susan Isquith

VP Sales and Calling Officer, Maureen Kalena

Director Operations Risk, Rebecca Logan

VP, Walter Moran

VP Sales and Calling Officer, Alfred O'Connell

VP, Agnes Olah

VP Funds Transfer and Deposit Services, Aida
Polanco

VP Sales and Calling Officer, Facundo (Frank)
Saenz de Viteri

VP, Grace Sit

VP and Director Funding and Derivatives, Louis
Solimine

VP, Barbara Sperrazza

VP, John Surre

Director Risk Analytics, M. Hampton Tunis

VP, Barbara Way

**VP and Community Investment Operations
Officer,** Edwin Bird

VP Sales and Manager Sales, James Feeney

VP and Director Investment Portfolio, Diahann
Rothstein

VP and Senior Trader Analyst, Phil Scott

VP and Director Marketing Communications,
Candice Soldano

**Internet Services Specialist Funds Transfer and
Deposit Services,** Shirley Hemphill

VP and Director Loan Review Analysis, Cynthia
Palladino

VP and Collateral Valuations, Bryan Gallagher

SVP and Chief Audit Officer, Stephen Angelo

Director, Joseph R. Ficalora, age 65

Director, James W. (Jim) Fulmer, age 60

Director, George Strayton, age 68

Director, Ronald E. Hermance Jr., age 64

Director, John R. Buran, age 62

Director, Joseph J. (Joe) Melone, age 80

Vice Chairman, Jose R. Gonzalez, age 57

Director, C. Cathleen (Cathi) Raffaeli, age 55

Director, Thomas M. O'Brien, age 61

Director, Anne Evans Estabrook, age 67

Director, Katherine J. Liseno, age 67

Director, Kevin J. Lynch, age 65

Director, Richard S. Mroz, age 50

Director, Rev Edwin C. Reed, age 58

Director, Jay M. Ford, age 62

Director, DeForest B. Soaries Jr., age 60

Auditors: PricewaterhouseCoopersLLP

LOCATIONS

HQ: Federal Home Loan Bank of New York
101 Park Ave., New York NY 10178-0599
Phone: 212-681-6000 **Fax:** 212-441-6890
Web: www.fhlbny.com

PRODUCTS/OPERATIONS

2010 Sales

	$ mil.	% of total
Interest		
Advances	614	56
Long-term securities	352	32
Mortgage loans held for portfolio	65	6
Available-for-sale securities	31	3
Other	14	1
Noninterest	16	2
Total	**1,095**	**100**

HISTORICAL FINANCIALS

Company Type: Private - Member-Owned Banking Authority

Income Statement — FYE: September 30

	ASSETS ($ mil.)	NET INCOME ($ mil.)	INCOME AS % OF ASSETS	EMPLOYEES
09/12*	107,130	276	0.3%	271
12/11	97,662	244	0.3%	0
12/10	100,212	275	0.3%	0
12/09	114,460	570	0.5%	0
Annual Growth	(2.2%)	(21.4%)	—	—

*Fiscal year change

2012 Year-End Financials

Debt ratio: ——
Return on equity: 38.80%
Cash ($ mil.): 12,846
Current ratio: —
Long-term debt ($ mil.): —

Dividends
Yield: —
Payout: —
Market value ($ mil.): —

FEDERAL HOME LOAN BANK OF SAN FRANCISCO

The city by the bay is the home to the Federal
Home Loan Bank of San Francisco one of a dozen
regional banks in the Federal Home Loan Bank
System chartered by Congress in 1932 to provide
credit to residential mortgage lenders. The government-sponsored enterprise is privately owned by its
members which include some 400 commercial
banks credit unions industrial loan companies savings and loans insurance companies and housing
associates headquartered in Arizona California and
Nevada. The bank links members to worldwide
capital markets which provide them with low-cost
funding. Members then pass these advances along
to their customers in the form of affordable home
mortgage and economic development loans.

FHLB San Francisco and its counterparts
around the country are governed by the Federal
Housing Finance Agency which recently gave eli-

gible community development financial institutions approval to become FHLB members. In addition to providing its member institutions with advances the bank also acquires residential mortgage-backed securities (RMBS) from its members.

Although FHLB San Francisco has remained profitable through the economic downturn it has been dealing with the ill effects of the crash which has severely impacted the states of Arizona California and Nevada in particular. In 2011 the bank's revenues fell 35% to $1.1 billion while net income fell 46% to $216 million. Demand for loans remains low in the stagnant economy and FHLB San Francisco's interest earnings fell 20% that year. Additionally the value of its RMBS portfolio has declined in the downturn.

EXECUTIVES

Chairman, Timothy R. Chrisman, age 65
Vice Chairman, John F. Luikart, age 62
President and CEO, Dean Schultz, age 65, $725,000 total compensation
SVP and Chief Capital Markets Officer, Steven T. Honda, age 60, $330,000 total compensation
EVP and COO, Lisa B. MacMillen, age 52, $466,500 total compensation
SVP Financial Services and Community Investment, Stephen P. Traynor, age 55, $282,800 total compensation
SVP and Chief Risk Officer, David H. Martens, age 59, $345,230 total compensation
SVP Controller and Operations Officer, Vera Maytum, age 62
SVP and CFO, Kenneth C. Miller, age 59, $345,000 total compensation
SVP External and Legislative Affairs, Lawrence H. Parks, age 50, $394,823 total compensation
SVP General Counsel and Corporate Secretary, Suzanne Titus-Johnson, age 54
SVP and Chief Corporate Securities Counsel, Kevin A. Gong, age 52
SVP Mortgage Finance Sales and Product Development, Patricia M. Remch, age 59
VP Corporate Communications, Amy Stewart
VP Marketing, Cynthia Lopez
SVP and Director Human Resources, Gregory P. Fontenot, age 53
SVP and Director Internal Audit, Mark J. Watson, age 50
SVP Credit and Collateral Risk Management, Robert M. (Rob) Shovlowsky, age 53
SVP and CIO, Elena Andreadakis, age 50
Director, Craig G. Blunden, age 64
Vice Chairman, John F. Luikart, age 62
Director, John F. Robinson, age 64
Director, Douglas H. (Tad) Lowrey, age 59
Director, W. Douglas (Doug) Hile, age 59
Director, Kenneth A. (Ken) Vecchione, age 57
Director, J. Benson Porter, age 46
Director, Paul R. Ackerman, age 50
Director, David A. Funk, age 68
Director, Scott C. Syphax, age 48
Director, Melinda Guzman, age 48
Director, John T. Wasley, age 50
Director, Kevin G. Murray, age 51
Director, Reginald Chen, age 51
Director, Robert F. Nielsen, age 65
Chairman, Timothy R. Chrisman, age 65
Vice Chairman, John F. Luikart, age 62
President and CEO, Dean Schultz, age 65, $725,000 total compensation
SVP and Chief Capital Markets Officer, Steven T. Honda, age 60, $330,000 total compensation
EVP and COO, Lisa B. MacMillen, age 52, $466,500 total compensation

SVP Financial Services and Community Investment, Stephen P. Traynor, age 55, $282,800 total compensation
SVP and Chief Risk Officer, David H. Martens, age 59, $345,230 total compensation
SVP Controller and Operations Officer, Vera Maytum, age 62
SVP and CFO, Kenneth C. Miller, age 59, $345,000 total compensation
SVP External and Legislative Affairs, Lawrence H. Parks, age 50, $394,823 total compensation
SVP General Counsel and Corporate Secretary, Suzanne Titus-Johnson, age 54
SVP and Chief Corporate Securities Counsel, Kevin A. Gong, age 52
SVP Mortgage Finance Sales and Product Development, Patricia M. Remch, age 59
VP Corporate Communications, Amy Stewart
VP Marketing, Cynthia Lopez
SVP and Director Human Resources, Gregory P. Fontenot, age 53
SVP and Director Internal Audit, Mark J. Watson, age 50
SVP Credit and Collateral Risk Management, Robert M. (Rob) Shovlowsky, age 53
SVP and CIO, Elena Andreadakis, age 50
Director, Craig G. Blunden, age 64
Vice Chairman, John F. Luikart, age 62
Director, John F. Robinson, age 64
Director, Douglas H. (Tad) Lowrey, age 59
Director, W. Douglas (Doug) Hile, age 59
Director, Kenneth A. (Ken) Vecchione, age 57
Director, J. Benson Porter, age 46
Director, Paul R. Ackerman, age 50
Director, David A. Funk, age 68
Director, Scott C. Syphax, age 48
Director, Melinda Guzman, age 48
Director, John T. Wasley, age 50
Director, Kevin G. Murray, age 51
Director, Reginald Chen, age 51
Director, Robert F. Nielsen, age 65
Auditors: PricewaterhouseCoopersLLP

LOCATIONS

HQ: Federal Home Loan Bank of San Francisco
600 California St., San Francisco CA 94108
Phone: 415-616-1000   **Fax:** 415-616-2626
Web: www.fhlbsf.com

PRODUCTS/OPERATIONS

2011 Sales

	$ mil.	% of total
Interest		
Advances	692	38
Held-to-maturity securities	679	37
Available-for-sale securities	238	13
Mortgage loans held for portfolio	113	6
Other	64	3
Noninterest	55	3
Adjustments	(700)	-
Total	**1,141**	**100**

HISTORICAL FINANCIALS

Company Type: Private - Member-Owned Banking Authority

Income Statement				FYE: June 30
	ASSETS ($ mil.)	NET INCOME ($ mil.)	INCOME AS % OF ASSETS	EMPLOYEES
06/12*	102,662	260	0.3%	304
12/11	113,552	216	0.2%	0
12/10	152,423	399	0.3%	0
12/09	192,862	515	0.3%	0
Annual Growth	**(19.0%)**	**(20.4%)**	**—**	**—**

*Fiscal year change

SVP Financial Services and Community Investment, Stephen P. Traynor, age 55, $282,800 total compensation
SVP and Chief Risk Officer, David H. Martens, age 59, $345,230 total compensation
SVP Controller and Operations Officer, Vera Maytum, age 62
SVP and CFO, Kenneth C. Miller, age 59, $345,000 total compensation
SVP External and Legislative Affairs, Lawrence H. Parks, age 50, $394,823 total compensation
SVP General Counsel and Corporate Secretary, Suzanne Titus-Johnson, age 54
SVP and Chief Corporate Securities Counsel, Kevin A. Gong, age 52
SVP Mortgage Finance Sales and Product Development, Patricia M. Remch, age 59

2012 Year-End Financials

Debt ratio: —
Return on equity: 32.80%
Cash ($ mil.): 6,388
Current ratio: —
Long-term debt ($ mil.): —
Dividends
Yield: —
Payout: —
Market value ($ mil.): —

FEDERAL INTERNATIONAL INC.

LOCATIONS

HQ: FEDERAL INTERNATIONAL INC.
7935 CLAYTON RD, SAINT LOUIS, MO 63117-1369
Phone: 800-972-7277
Web: www.federalinternational.com

HISTORICAL FINANCIALS

Company Type: Private

Income Statement			FYE: December 31
	REVENUE ($ mil.)	NET INCOME ($ mil.)	NET PROFIT MARGIN	EMPLOYEES
12/11	164	2	1.5%	322
12/10	135	(0)	—	0
12/09	93	1	1.7%	0
12/08	126	3	2.4%	0
Annual Growth	**9.2%**	**(7.8%)**	**—**	**—**

2011 Year-End Financials

Debt ratio: —
Return on equity: 1.50%
Cash ($ mil.): 3
Current ratio: 1.70
Long-term debt ($ mil.): —
Dividends
Yield: —
Payout: —
Market value ($ mil.): —

FERMI RESEARCH ALLIANCE LLC

LOCATIONS

HQ: FERMI RESEARCH ALLIANCE LLC
PINE ST KIRK RD STE 213, BATAVIA, IL 60510
Phone: 630-406-7901

HISTORICAL FINANCIALS

Company Type: Private

Income Statement			FYE: September 30
	REVENUE ($ mil.)	NET INCOME ($ mil.)	NET PROFIT MARGIN	EMPLOYEES
09/11	437	(0)	—	5
09/10	424	1	0.4%	0
09/08	339	1	0.4%	0
Annual Growth	**13.5%**			

2011 Year-End Financials

Debt ratio: —
Return on equity: —
Cash ($ mil.): 2
Current ratio: 1.50
Long-term debt ($ mil.): —

Dividends
Yield: —
Payout: —
Market value ($ mil.): —

2012 Year-End Financials

Debt ratio: —
Return on equity: 2.70%
Cash ($ mil.): 4
Current ratio: 1.50
Long-term debt ($ mil.): —

Dividends
Yield: —
Payout: —
Market value ($ mil.): —

FERREIRA CONSTRUCTION CO. INC.

LOCATIONS

HQ: FERREIRA CONSTRUCTION CO. INC.
31 TANNERY RD, SOMERVILLE, NJ 08876-6001
Phone: 908-534-8655
Web: www.ferreiraconstruction.com

HISTORICAL FINANCIALS

Company Type: Private

Income Statement

FYE: December 31

	REVENUE ($ mil.)	NET INCOME ($ mil.)	NET PROFIT MARGIN	EMPLOYEES
12/11	112	1	1.3%	225
12/10	78	0	0.3%	0
12/09	104	2	2.5%	0
Annual Growth	3.9%	(24.1%)	—	—

2011 Year-End Financials

Debt ratio: —
Return on equity: 1.30%
Cash ($ mil.): 4
Current ratio: 0.80
Long-term debt ($ mil.): —

Dividends
Yield: —
Payout: —
Market value ($ mil.): —

FERROUS PROCESSING AND TRADING COMPANY

LOCATIONS

HQ: FERROUS PROCESSING AND TRADING COMPANY
3400 E LAFAYETTE ST, DETROIT, MI 48207-4962
Phone: 313-582-2910
Web: www.fpt1.com

HISTORICAL FINANCIALS

Company Type: Private

Income Statement

FYE: May 31

	REVENUE ($ mil.)	NET INCOME ($ mil.)	NET PROFIT MARGIN	EMPLOYEES
05/12	1,506	40	2.7%	425
05/11	1,272	41	3.3%	0
05/10	915	23	2.6%	0
05/09	1,001	(20)	—	0
Annual Growth	14.6%	—	—	—

FETCH LOGISTICS INC.

Don't just throw this company a ball –tell it you want a truckload of balls hauled to your customer's warehouse ASAP. Fetch Logistics provides freight transportation management services for businesses with items to ship throughout North America. The company doesn't own transportation assets; instead by working through a network of more than 20000 carriers Fetch Logistics can arrange truckload less-than-truckload and intermodal freight hauling. It serves companies in the beverage bottled water building materials consumer goods food paper and plastics industries. Fetch Logistics was founded in 1997.

In 2010 Fetch Logistics opened an office in Chicago a city typically counted among the largest freight destinations in the US. The company plans for the new office to be a springboard for additional client growth throughout the Midwest. In addition to Chicago and its headquarters in New York Fetch Logistics has an office in Atlanta.

EXECUTIVES

President, Robert Closs II
VP, Bob Atwater
VP, William (Will) Wilcox
VP National Accounts, Tom Cloen
VP Sales, Dave Bryk
VP Operations, Gary M. Zoldos
Head Accounting, Irene Closs

LOCATIONS

HQ: Fetch Logistics Inc.
25 Northpointe Pkwy. Ste. 200, Amherst NY 14228
Phone: 716-689-4556   **Fax:** 716-689-9676
Web: www.fetchlogistics.com

COMPETITORS

APL Logistics
C.H. Robinson Worldwide
Menlo Worldwide
Pacer Transportation Solutions
Transplace
UPS Supply Chain Solutions
UTi Worldwide

HISTORICAL FINANCIALS

Company Type: Private

Income Statement

FYE: December 31

	REVENUE ($ mil.)	NET INCOME ($ mil.)	NET PROFIT MARGIN	EMPLOYEES
12/11*	34	1	3.0%	47
11/10	24	0	3.0%	0
12/03	17	0	4.2%	0
12/02	11	0	3.7%	0
Annual Growth	44.4%	34.2%	—	—

*Fiscal year change

FIELD MUSEUM OF NATURAL HISTORY

The Field Museum is one of the world's leading natural history museums. Founded as the Columbian Museum of Chicago in 1893 the institution adopted the Field name in 1905 in honor of major benefactor (and department store mogul) Marshall Field. The museum houses enormous biological and anthropological collections —more than 20 million specimens in all —along with a quarter-million-volume natural history library. It is also home to Sue the largest most complete and best preserved Tyrannosaurus rex fossil discovered to date. The Field Museum conducts basic research in anthropology and biology as well as an extensive program of public education.

EXECUTIVES

President and CEO, John W. McCarter Jr., age 74
EVP, James W. (Jim) Croft
SVP Public Museum, Laura M. Sadler
VP Operations, Diane White
CIO and General Counsel, Joe Brennan
SVP Collections and Research, Lance Grande
VP Human Resources and Administration, Shawn VanDerziel
President and CEO, Richard W. Lariviere
VP Auxiliary Groups and Board Relations, Melissa Hilton
Provost Academic Affairs, Neil L. Shubin, age 48
VP Institutional Advancement, Sheila Cawley
SVP Environment Culture and Conservation, Debra K. Moskovits
Manager Public Relations, Nancy O'Shea
VP Institutional Advancement, Laura Biddle Clarke

LOCATIONS

HQ: The Field Museum of Natural History
1400 S. Lake Shore Dr., Chicago IL 60605-2496
Phone: 312-922-9410   **Fax:** 312-665-7101
Web: www.fieldmuseum.org

HISTORICAL FINANCIALS

Company Type: Private - Not-for-Profit

Income Statement

FYE: December 31

	REVENUE ($ mil.)	NET INCOME ($ mil.)	NET PROFIT MARGIN	EMPLOYEES
12/11	67	(25)	—	600
12/09	46	(25)	—	0
12/03	66	38	58.5%	0
12/02	64	2	4.3%	0
Annual Growth	1.4%	—	—	—

2011 Year-End Financials

Debt ratio: —
Return on equity: (-37.20)%
Cash ($ mil.): 1
Current ratio: —
Long-term debt ($ mil.): —

Dividends
Yield: —
Payout: —
Market value ($ mil.): —

FINANCIAL INDUSTRY REGULATORY AUTHORITY INC.

FINRA is one of the long arms of the law for the securities industry. A non-governmental regulatory authority FINRA regulates all securities firms (roughly 4300) that conduct business in the US. Its activities include writing and enforcing rules; enforcing federal securities laws; licensing and registering brokerages and private equity firms; and providing educational information and arbitration services to investors. The regulator works with the SEC and the Fed and possesses the authority to issue fines and bar violators among other punitive actions. FINRA was formed in 2007 from the consolidation of the National Association of Securities Dealers and certain regulatory and enforcement elements of the NYSE.

Geographic Reach

FINRA operates from Washington DC and New York with 20 regional offices around the US. It also has more than 160000 branch offices and some 635000 registered securities representatives.

Financial Analysis

FINRA obviously benefits when lawmakers and regulators crack down on fraud and the breaking of securities laws that led up to the Great Recession. As such the bulk of its revenues (about 85%) come from the collection of regulatory user and contract service fees.

Total revenues for the organization increased by almost 4% from 2010 to 2011. The growth was attributed to a rise in the number of fines it collected along with higher contract services fees affiliated with market regulation services.

FINRA suffered a net loss of $84 million for 2011 mostly as a result of non-recurring costs related to the development of new data center facilities in New York and Maryland. The net loss was also due to increased integration expenses used to extend FINRA's cross market surveillance capabilities.

EXECUTIVES

Vice Chairman, Stephen I. Luparello
EVP and Chief Technology Officer, Martin P. Colburn
EVP and General Counsel, T. Grant Callery
EVP Corporate Communications and Government Relations, Howard M. Schloss
EVP and General Counsel for Regulation, Marc Menchel
EVP Regulatory Policy, Thomas M. (Tom) Selman
EVP Business Services and CIO, Samuel H. Gaer, age 45
EVP Member Regulation, Grace B. Vogel
Chairman and CEO, Richard G. Ketchum
EVP and CFO, Todd Diganci
SVP and Corporate Secretary, Marcia E. Asquith
EVP Member Regulation Sales Practice, Susan F. Axelrod
EVP Enforcement, J. Bradley Bennett
SVP Human Resources, Tracy Johnson
President FINRA Investor Education Foundation; VP FINRA Investor Education, Gerri Walsh
Auditors: Ernst&YoungLLP

LOCATIONS

HQ: Financial Industry Regulatory Authority Inc.
1735 K St. NW, Washington DC 20006-1506
Phone: 202-728-8000   **Fax:** 860-566-7410
Web: www.ct.gov/cid/site/default.asp

PRODUCTS/OPERATIONS

2011 Sales

	$ mil.	% of total
Regulatory fees	407	50
User fees	157	20
Contract service fees	129	16
Transparency services fees	56	7
Dispute resolution fees	48	6
Other	11	1
Total	**808**	**100**

HISTORICAL FINANCIALS

Company Type: Private

Income Statement

FYE: December 31

	REVENUE ($ mil.)	NET INCOME ($ mil.)	NET PROFIT MARGIN	EMPLOYEES
12/11	880	(84)	—	3,300
12/10	849	54	6.4%	0
12/09	1,097	48	4.4%	0
12/07	724	(27)	—	0
Annual Growth	**6.7%**	—	—	—

2011 Year-End Financials

Debt ratio: —
Return on equity: (-9.50)%
Cash ($ mil.): 424
Current ratio: 0.70
Long-term debt ($ mil.): —
Dividends
  Yield: —
  Payout: —
  Market value ($ mil.): —

FIRSTHEALTH OF THE CAROLINAS INC.

FirstHealth of the Carolinas maintains a health care network that spans across 15 counties in the mid-Carolinas. The network includes three hospitals (Moore Regional Richmond Memorial and Montgomery Memorial) that provide emergency surgical acute care and diagnostic services and have a combined capacity of about 580 beds. Its largest hospital Moore Regional includes an inpatient rehabilitation center and a heart hospital. FirstHealth of the Carolinas also operates satellite facilities including family practice clinics fitness centers and dental practices. In addition the system provides home health and hospice services emergency care medical transportation and health insurance (FirstCarolinaCare).

Like most US hospital systems FirstHealth made some cost-control efforts in 2009 in response to the economic recession including minimal job cuts and adjustments to employee benefits. The health system did carry on with certain growth measures though including the opening of a new cardiology and neurology facility the Reid Heart Hospital in early 2011. The center is located on the Moore Regional campus and has about 60 beds.

To expand its services in Hoke County FirstHealth is building a medical campus consisting of an urgent care center diagnostic facilities and physician offices. It has also announced plans to build a new 65-bed acute care hospital in the area.

EXECUTIVES

President and CEO, Charles T. Frock
CEO, David J. Kilarski
Director Public Relations, Gretchen Kelly
Assistant Director Public Relations, Emily Sloan
Chairman, David Burns
COO Moore Regional Hospital, Brian T. Canfield

LOCATIONS

HQ: FirstHealth of the Carolinas Inc.
155 Memorial Dr., Pinehurst NC 28374
Phone: 910-715-1000   **Fax:** 574-522-0334
Web: www.conn-selmer.com

PRODUCTS/OPERATIONS

Selected Facilities

Montgomery Memorial Hospital (Troy North Carolina)
Moore Regional Hospital (Pinehurst North Carolina)
Richmond Memorial Hospital (Rockingham North Carolina)

COMPETITORS

Alamance Regional Medical Center
Carolinas HealthCare System
Cumberland County Hospital System
Duke University Health System
Health Management Associates
Morehead Memorial Hospital
Moses Cone Health
Novant Health
Rex Healthcare
Stanly Medical Center
UNC Hospitals
Vidant Health
Wake Forest University Baptist Medical Center
WakeMed

HISTORICAL FINANCIALS

Company Type: Private - Not-for-Profit

Income Statement

FYE: June 30

	REVENUE ($ mil.)	NET INCOME ($ mil.)	NET PROFIT MARGIN	EMPLOYEES
06/12*	429	49	11.5%	3,897
09/11	507	12	2.4%	0
09/09	462	(9)	—	0
09/08	438	(45)	—	0
Annual Growth	**(0.7%)**	—	—	—

*Fiscal year change

2012 Year-End Financials

Debt ratio: —
Return on equity: 11.50%
Cash ($ mil.): 55
Current ratio: 1.60
Long-term debt ($ mil.): —
Dividends
  Yield: —
  Payout: —
  Market value ($ mil.): —

FIVE STAR COOPERATIVE

If Old MacDonald actually had a farm he'd want to be a member of the Five Star Cooperative. Operating in north-central and northeast Iowa Five Star has operations in more than 15 small to mid-sized towns in the Hawkeye State. The cooperative is divided into five divisions according to the products and services offered —agronomy petroleum (diesel fuel and home heating oil) feed (for beef cattle and swine) grain and hardware —it operates a True Value hardware store in New Hampton that offers all the usual hardware products and services. Established in 1916 Five Star Cooperative provides a full complement for its member/farmers.

EXECUTIVES

General Manager, Ron Pumphrey, age 62
Assistant Manager and Controller, Robert Lynch
Location Manager and Agronomist Mason City, Tony Cockrell
Location Manager Dougherty, Rick Demaray
Region Grain Manager New Hampton, Judy Biwer
Manager Grain and Rockwell, Randy Park
Chairman, Steve Laures
Vice-Chairman, Leon Zeien
Board Secretary, Terry Thomas
Project Manager and IT, Laura Schwickerath
Manager Agronomy, Olin Amundson
Manager Hardware, Steve Breitback
Manager Feed Department, John Winter
Location Manager Lawler, Dennis Lau
Location Manager Nashua, Mike Wedemeier
Location Manager North Washington, Bill Goss
Manager Petroleum, Bruce Halvorson
Manager Operations/Safety, Wayne Steven
Location Manager Hanlontown, Jon Langan
Location Manager Ionia, Curt Koenigsfeld
Feed Mill Manager Klemme, Paul Larson
Location Manager Lake Mills, Paul Pederson
Agronomy Contact, Carmen Milliren
Location Manager Ventura, Dar Avery
Vice-Chairman, Leon Zeien
Director, Dave Newman
Director, John Eichenberger
Board Secretary, Terry Thomas
Director, Gary Gorman
Director, Larry Eden
Director, Randy Greiman
Director, Don Chambers

LOCATIONS

HQ: Five Star Cooperative
  1949 N. Linn Ave., New Hampton IA 50659
Phone: 641-394-3052   **Fax:** 641-394-2920
Web: www.fivestarcoop.com

PRODUCTS/OPERATIONS

Selected Office Locations

Burchinal
Dougherty
Hanlontown
Ionia
Joice
Klemme
Lake Mills
Lawler
Mason City
Nashua
New Hampton
North Washington
Rockwell
Ventura

COMPETITORS

ADM Alliance Nutrition	Heartland Co-op
DeBruce Grain	Orscheln Farm and Home
Farmers Cooperative	Rabo AgriFinance

Society   West Central Co-op
GROWMARK

HISTORICAL FINANCIALS

Company Type: Private - Cooperative

Income Statement
FYE: June 30

	REVENUE ($ mil.)	NET INCOME ($ mil.)	NET PROFIT MARGIN	EMPLOYEES
06/12	479	9	2.0%	190
06/11	376	2	0.7%	0
06/10	269	7	2.6%	0
06/09	368	11	3.2%	0
Annual Growth	9.1%	(6.1%)	—	—

2012 Year-End Financials

Debt ratio: —
Return on equity: 2.00%
Cash ($ mil.): 0
Current ratio: 0.20
Long-term debt ($ mil.): —

Dividends
  Yield: —
  Payout: —
  Market value ($ mil.): —

FLAGLER HEALTHCARE SYSTEMS INC

LOCATIONS

HQ: FLAGLER HEALTHCARE SYSTEMS INC
  400 HEALTH PARK BLVD, SAINT AUGUSTINE, FL 32086-5784
Phone: 904-819-4400
Web: www.flaglerhospital.org

HISTORICAL FINANCIALS

Company Type: Private

Income Statement
FYE: September 30

	REVENUE ($ mil.)	NET INCOME ($ mil.)	NET PROFIT MARGIN	EMPLOYEES
09/11	216	3	1.8%	1,600
09/09	0	(0)	—	0
09/07	178	10	5.7%	0
09/05	153	3	2.2%	0
Annual Growth	12.1%	5.3%	—	—

2011 Year-End Financials

Debt ratio: —
Return on equity: 1.80%
Cash ($ mil.): 5
Current ratio: 0.80
Long-term debt ($ mil.): —

Dividends
  Yield: —
  Payout: —
  Market value ($ mil.): —

FLEETWING CORPORATION

LOCATIONS

HQ: FLEETWING CORPORATION
  742 S COMBEE RD, LAKELAND, FL 33801-6314
Phone: 863-665-7557
Web: www.fleetwingoil.com

HISTORICAL FINANCIALS

Company Type: Private

Income Statement
FYE: March 31

	REVENUE ($ mil.)	NET INCOME ($ mil.)	NET PROFIT MARGIN	EMPLOYEES
03/12	143	0	0.5%	84
03/11	122	0	0.5%	0
03/10	101	0	0.2%	0
03/09	146	0	0.3%	0
Annual Growth	(0.8%)	15.5%	—	—

2012 Year-End Financials

Debt ratio: —
Return on equity: 0.50%
Cash ($ mil.): 3
Current ratio: 1.70
Long-term debt ($ mil.): —

Dividends
  Yield: —
  Payout: —
  Market value ($ mil.): —

FLEMING GANNETT INC

Engineering firm Gannett Fleming has waded through water waste and sludge for nearly a century. Founded in 1915 the company focuses on serving the transportation water and wastewater facilities technology and environmental industries. Gannett Fleming operates through about a dozen subsidiaries that offer a variety of services that range from design/build construction management ground testing and soil strengthening site remediation structural rehabilitation electrical and mechanical installation geophysical mapping and surveying and 3D visualization. The company works on projects around the world and has more than 60 offices throughout the US Canada Mexico and Middle East.

Gannett Fleming expanded its international presence in 2010 when it opened an office in Abu Dhabi. The office will coordinate the company's work in the Middle East. Gannett Fleming's projects in the region include infrastructure improvements to the Afghanistan National Logistics Compound.

The company's geographic diversity along with its long list of services provided has helped it endure dips in the economy. Its 25 lines of business include information technology civil transportation geotechnical infrastructure industrial/commercial structural geospatial technology mechanical/electrical and construction management services.

Gannett Fleming's transit and rail division has worked on many transit systems around the US including the Detroit People Mover in Michigan and the Dallas Area Rapid Transit system in Texas. The company is positioned to work on high speed rail systems as the US looks to enhance its mobility.

On the technology side of things Gannett Fleming's design practice GeoDecisions has been involved in developing master plans for highways railroads bridges and airports. It also has designed new dams and modifications on those needing repair. In 2010 Gannett Fleming further invested in that business when it acquired traffic engineering and intelligence transportation systems provider VANUS.

While the firm is heavily involved in traffic and transportation projects its water and wastewater infrastructure work is perhaps its hallmark. Gannett Fleming has worked on hundreds of treatment plants and pumping stations in addition to thousands of miles of water and sewer systems. It serves both the private and public sectors on such projects throughout the US and abroad. Clients have included JEA Washington Suburban Sanitary Commission and Chevron.

L.G. Hetager Drilling is Gannett Fleming's exploration and drilling arm. The company completes subsurface exploration for the construction of highways and bridges buildings and other facilities. It also provides soil sampling and supports mining and other construction projects. In 2009 Gannett Fleming expanded its geotechnical engineering services by acquiring Williams Earth Sciences which became Williams Geotechnical Group of Gannett Fleming. The group specializes in materials testing subsurface investigations and design/build services.

Gannett Fleming expanded its structural engineering capabilities in the western US with the 2011 acquisition of Nabar Stanley Brown now known as the NSB Group of Gannett Fleming. The new addition joins Gannett Fleming's structural practice which is involved in preliminary and final design of new structures repair and expansions.

EXECUTIVES

VP and Senior Associate; National Practice Manager Marketing and Business Development Practice Leadership Team, Judy L. Hricak
Vice Chairman President and COO, Robert M. Scaer
SVP and Secretary, Chester L. Allen
SVP; Regional Director Chicago IL, John G. Diviney
SVP, Gene C. Koontz
Chairman and CEO, William M. Stout
SVP; Regional Office Manager South Plainfield NJ, Paul D. Nowicki
SVP, John R. Kenny
VP; Office Manager Tampa FL Kansas City KS and LaPlace LA, Jay H. L. Calhoun
VP; Regional Office Manager Austin TX and Office Manager Mexico City Mexico, Matthew J. Schiemer
SVP and National Director Transit and Rail, David B. Thomas
Manager, Paul Lewis
President Quantum Geophysics, Richard K. Lee
General Manager Abu Dhabi United Arab Emirates, Abdulilah Z. Zineddin

LOCATIONS

HQ: Gannett Fleming Inc.
207 Senate Ave., Camp Hill PA 17011
Phone: 717-763-7211 **Fax:** 717-763-8150
Web: www.gannettfleming.com

PRODUCTS/OPERATIONS

Selected Subsidiaries & Affiliates
GANCOM (reprographics digital printing and graphic design)
Ganflec Architects & Engineers Inc. (general architectural and engineering design)
Gannett Fleming Pharmaceutical & Biotechnology Services (design and construction services on pharmaceutical and biotechnology facilities)
Gannett Fleming Project Development Corp. (design and construction management on commercial and industrial facilities)
Gannett Fleming Transit & Rail Systems (design and construction management on railway and rail transit systems)
Gannett Fleming Valuation and Rate Division (consulting to public utilities and railroads)
Gannett Fleming Williams Geotechnical Group (geotechnical engineering quality control testing construction inspection)
GeoDecisions (computerized mapping and database management services)
IT Services Division (computer consulting)
L.G. Hetager Drilling (exploratory drilling and testing services)
TerraSure (real estate remediation)
Vertical Transportation Excellence (consulting on elevator escalator moving walks material handling design and other specialty services)

COMPETITORS

AECOM	K&M Engineering
Bechtel	and Consulting
Black & Veatch	Louis Berger
Ltd.	MWH Global
CH2M HILL	Parsons Brinckerhoff
Jacobs Engineering	URS

HISTORICAL FINANCIALS
Company Type: Holding Company

Income Statement
FYE: December 31

	REVENUE ($ mil.)	NET INCOME ($ mil.)	NET PROFIT MARGIN	EMPLOYEES
12/11	286	4	1.6%	800
12/10	287	2	0.8%	0
12/09	283	13	4.8%	0
12/08	250	7	3.2%	0
Annual Growth	4.6%	(17.5%)	—	—

2011 Year-End Financials
Debt ratio: ——
Return on equity: 1.60%
Cash ($ mil.): 6
Current ratio: 1.90
Long-term debt ($ mil.): —
Dividends
Yield: —
Payout: —
Market value ($ mil.): —

FLORIDA CLINICAL PRACTICE ASSOCIATION INC.

LOCATIONS

HQ: FLORIDA CLINICAL PRACTICE ASSOCIATION INC.
1329 SW 16TH ST STE 4250, GAINESVILLE, FL 32608-1128
Phone: 352-265-8017

HISTORICAL FINANCIALS
Company Type: Private

Income Statement
FYE: June 30

	REVENUE ($ mil.)	NET INCOME ($ mil.)	NET PROFIT MARGIN	EMPLOYEES
06/11	379	0	0.2%	2
06/09	297	5	1.8%	0
06/08	276	2	0.8%	0
06/07	612	0	—	0
Annual Growth	(14.8%)	6520.1%	—	—

2011 Year-End Financials
Debt ratio: ——
Return on equity: 0.20%
Cash ($ mil.): 49
Current ratio: 7.20
Long-term debt ($ mil.): —
Dividends
Yield: —
Payout: —
Market value ($ mil.): —

FLORIDA INSTITUTE OF TECHNOLOGY INC.

LOCATIONS

HQ: FLORIDA INSTITUTE OF TECHNOLOGY INC.
150 W UNIVERSITY BLVD OFC, MELBOURNE, FL 32901-6975
Phone: 321-674-8000
Web: www.floridatechsports.com

HISTORICAL FINANCIALS
Company Type: Private

Income Statement
FYE: April 30

	REVENUE ($ mil.)	NET INCOME ($ mil.)	NET PROFIT MARGIN	EMPLOYEES
04/12*	163	8	5.1%	1,100
06/11	143	3	2.7%	0
04/10	177	6	3.4%	0
04/09	152	0	—	0
Annual Growth	2.5%	—	—	—

*Fiscal year change

2012 Year-End Financials
Debt ratio: ——
Return on equity: 5.10%
Cash ($ mil.): 17
Current ratio: —
Long-term debt ($ mil.): —
Dividends
Yield: —
Payout: —
Market value ($ mil.): —

FLORIDA MEMORIAL UNIVERSITY INC.

Florida Memorial University (formerly Florida Memorial College) offers some 40 undergraduate and graduate programs to some 2200 students in Miami-Dade County. A historically black college and Baptist institution the school introduced its graduate studies in 2004 with programs in elementary education special education and reading. The school is known as the birthplace of the Negro National Anthem "Lift Every Voice and Sing." In 1900 the song was composed by brothers James Weldon Johnson and J. Rosamond Johnson a former professor at the college. The school traces its roots to the 1879 founding of Florida Baptist Institute which later merged with Florida Baptist Academy to form Florida Memorial University.

EXECUTIVES

President, Karl S. Wright
Provost, Sandra T. Thompson
VP Student Affairs, Harold R. Clarke Jr.
Executive Assistant to President, Barbara J. Edwards
Director Grants and Sponsored Research, Langston T. (Trey) Coleman
Director Center for Urban Environmental Studies, William E. Hopper Jr.
Collections and Distance Services Librarian, Lucy Osemota
Interim Director Nathan W. Collier University Library Services, Gloria Oswald
Director Music Program, Alfred Pinkston
Director Residential Life, Jacklan Alexander
Director Lion Shop and Cafe, Hopeton N. Anderson
Reference Librarian, Daniel T. Buggs
Director Administrative Support Services, Alphonso Burnside
Director Church Relations, Patricia T. Carter
Library Assistant Nathan W. Collier University Library Services, Nehemy Cher-Frere
Public Services Technician College Library, Rosa Dominguez
Head of Library Systems Support, Balfour (George) Duncan
Library Assistant College Library, Michael Dysart
Campus Minister Campus Ministry, Rev Newton Fairweather
Director Academic Resource Center, Rabie Harris
Acquisitions Technician College Library, Reuben Hunter
Director Career Development Center, Athena Jackson
Director Athletics, Robert Smith
Manager Accounts Payable, Delores Joseph
Library Audio-Visual Media Coordinator, Desmond C. King
Director Entrepreneurial Institute, Phillip Mann
Director Student Activities, C. Vernon Martin Jr.
Director Admissions, Peggy K. Martin
Bursar, Archie L. Mobley
Director Broward Off-Site Campus, Shirley Paremore
Director Financial Aid, Brian Phillip
Manager Purchasing, Cheryl Phillip
Library Technician College Library, Sadie Reyes
Director Pre-Student Teaching Division of Education, Gwendolyn Robinson
Director Health Clinic, Patricia Seabrooks
Cataloging Technician College Library, Pomona Seay
Periodicals Librarian, Bernice Smith

Director Enrollment Management, Roscoe Warren
Library Systems and Technology Technician, Keith Webb
Director Student Support Services, Argerine Williams
Director Counseling Center, Woodrow Wilson
VP Institutional Advancement, Sumner Hutcheson III
VP Business and Fiscal Affairs, Tony Valentine
CIO, Harriette Haynes
Interim Director Human Resources, Valerie Williams
Director Alumni Affairs, J. Walter Hale
Director Facilities, Jaime Cruz
Interim Registrar, Lelia Efford
Director Campus Safety, John Watson

LOCATIONS

HQ: FLORIDA MEMORIAL UNIVERSITY INC.
15800 NW 42ND AVE, OPA LOCKA, FL 33054-6155
Phone: 305-626-3600
Web: www.fmuniv.edu

HISTORICAL FINANCIALS
Company Type: School

Income Statement
FYE: June 30

	REVENUE ($ mil.)	NET INCOME ($ mil.)	NET PROFIT MARGIN	EMPLOYEES
06/11	44	1	4.4%	300
06/10	42	1	3.7%	0
06/09	39	0	1.0%	0
06/08	35	1	5.5%	0
Annual Growth	8.1%	0.6%	—	—

2011 Year-End Financials

Debt ratio: ——
Return on equity: 4.40%
Cash ($ mil.): 17
Current ratio: —
Long-term debt ($ mil.): —

Dividends
Yield: —
Payout: —
Market value ($ mil.): —

FLORIM USA INC.

LOCATIONS

HQ: FLORIM USA INC.
300 INTERNATIONAL BLVD, CLARKSVILLE, TN 37040-5307
Phone: 931-553-7548
Web: www.classic-tile.com

HISTORICAL FINANCIALS
Company Type: Private

Income Statement
FYE: December 31

	REVENUE ($ mil.)	NET INCOME ($ mil.)	NET PROFIT MARGIN	EMPLOYEES
12/11	89	15	17.4%	367
Annual Growth	—	—	—	—

2011 Year-End Financials

Debt ratio: ——
Return on equity: 17.40%
Cash ($ mil.): 0
Current ratio: 0.40
Long-term debt ($ mil.): —

Dividends
Yield: —
Payout: —
Market value ($ mil.): —

FLOURNOY DEVELOPMENT COMPANY

LOCATIONS

HQ: FLOURNOY DEVELOPMENT COMPANY
900 BROKSTONE CENTRE PKWY, COLUMBUS, GA 31904-2987
Phone: 706-324-4000
Web: www.flournoycompanies.com

HISTORICAL FINANCIALS
Company Type: Private

Income Statement
FYE: December 31

	ASSETS ($ mil.)	NET INCOME ($ mil.)	INCOME AS % OF ASSETS	EMPLOYEES
12/11	263	(1)	—	550
12/09	396	(3)	—	0
12/08	392	(9)	—	0
12/07	52	(0)	—	0
Annual Growth	70.9%	—	—	—

2011 Year-End Financials

Debt ratio: ——
Return on equity: (-1.40)%
Cash ($ mil.): 3
Current ratio: 0.10
Long-term debt ($ mil.): —

Dividends
Yield: —
Payout: —
Market value ($ mil.): —

FLOWERS FOODS SPECIALTY GROUP LLC

LOCATIONS

HQ: FLOWERS FOODS SPECIALTY GROUP LLC
5087 S ROYAL ATLANTA DR, TUCKER, GA 30084-3019
Phone: 770-723-0173

HISTORICAL FINANCIALS
Company Type: Private

Income Statement
FYE: January 1

	REVENUE ($ mil.)	NET INCOME ($ mil.)	NET PROFIT MARGIN	EMPLOYEES
01/11	2,573	137	5.3%	30
Annual Growth	—	—	—	—

2011 Year-End Financials

Debt ratio: ——
Return on equity: 5.30%
Cash ($ mil.): 6
Current ratio: —
Long-term debt ($ mil.): —

Dividends
Yield: —
Payout: —
Market value ($ mil.): —

FLOYD HEALTHCARE MANAGEMENT INC.

If your heart needs help in the Heart of Dixie Floyd Healthcare Management is there for what ails you. Its main hospital Floyd Medical Center has more than 300 beds and serves northwestern Georgia and northeastern Alabama. In addition to medical surgical and emergency care (including a Level II trauma center and neonatal intensive care unit) the hospital offers rehabilitation programs home health care and psychiatric care through Floyd Behavioral Health Center a freestanding facility with more than 50 beds. Floyd Healthcare Management and its affiliates include about 20 primary care centers and five urgent care locations. The organization was founded in 1942.

In partnership with the Floyd County Commission Floyd County Department of Family and Children Services (DFCS) and physicians in the community Floyd sponsors the Floyd County Clinic where low-income uninsured residents of Floyd County can receive free primary medical care services through the faculty and resident medical students enrolled in the Floyd Family Medicine Residency program.

Floyd Medical Center also provides community outreach programs through its mobile mammography vans and a range of other outreach services aimed at improving access to health care throughout the service area.

EXECUTIVES

President and CEO, Kurt Stuenkel
Chief Medical Affairs, Dee B. Russell
SVP and COO, Warren A. (Sonny) Rigas
VP and CFO, Rick Sheerin
Director Public Relations, Haley Crider
VP, Alison Land
Director Human Resources, Rick Tew
CIO, Brian Barnette
Public Relations Specialist, Bill Fortenberry
VP, Greg Polley
VP Market Development, Dan Sweitzer
VP and Compliance Officer, Mary Maire
VP and Chief Nursing Officer, Shelia Bennett
General Counsel, Wade Monk
Senior Public Relations Specialist, Donna Braden
Director Planning, Matt Gorman
Chief Medical Officer, Joe Biuso
Corporate Compliance Officer, Julie Rogers

LOCATIONS

HQ: Floyd Healthcare Management Inc.
304 Turner McCall Blvd., Rome GA 30165
Phone: 706-509-5000 **Fax:** 765-298-5848
Web: www.communityanderson.com

COMPETITORS

Gadsden Regional Medical Center
Hutcheson Medical
Redmond Regional Medical Center
WellStar Kennestone Hospital

HISTORICAL FINANCIALS
Company Type: Private - Not-for-Profit

Income Statement
FYE: June 30

	REVENUE ($ mil.)	NET INCOME ($ mil.)	NET PROFIT MARGIN	EMPLOYEES
06/11	332	11	3.4%	2,400
06/10	288	8	3.0%	0
06/08	237	11	4.8%	0
06/06	215	2	0.9%	0
Annual Growth	15.5%	78.4%	—	—

2011 Year-End Financials

Debt ratio: ——
Return on equity: 3.40%
Cash ($ mil.): 10
Current ratio: 0.40
Long-term debt ($ mil.): —
Dividends
Yield: —
Payout: —
Market value ($ mil.): —

FNS INC.

LOCATIONS

HQ: FNS INC.
18301 S BROADWICK ST, RANCHO DOMINGUEZ, CA 90220-6442
Phone: 310-667-4821
Web: www.fnsusa.com

HISTORICAL FINANCIALS
Company Type: Private

Income Statement
FYE: December 31

	REVENUE ($ mil.)	NET INCOME ($ mil.)	NET PROFIT MARGIN	EMPLOYEES
12/11	110	3	3.0%	114
12/10	0	0	—	0
12/09	54	1	3.6%	0
12/07	64	2	4.4%	0
Annual Growth	19.9%	6.2%	—	—

2011 Year-End Financials

Debt ratio: ——
Return on equity: 3.00%
Cash ($ mil.): 2
Current ratio: 0.60
Long-term debt ($ mil.): —
Dividends
Yield: —
Payout: —
Market value ($ mil.): —

FOODCOMM INTERNATIONAL

LOCATIONS

HQ: FOODCOMM INTERNATIONAL
4260 EL CAMINO REAL, PALO ALTO, CA 94306-4404
Phone: 650-813-1300
Web: www.austerra.com

HISTORICAL FINANCIALS
Company Type: Private

Income Statement
FYE: December 31

	REVENUE ($ mil.)	NET INCOME ($ mil.)	NET PROFIT MARGIN	EMPLOYEES
12/11	194	1	0.7%	30
12/10	168	1	1.2%	0
12/09	111	3	3.3%	0
12/07	147	1	1.1%	0
Annual Growth	9.6%	(4.7%)	—	—

2011 Year-End Financials

Debt ratio: ——
Return on equity: 0.70%
Cash ($ mil.): 0
Current ratio: 0.40
Long-term debt ($ mil.): —
Dividends
Yield: —
Payout: —
Market value ($ mil.): —

FOODMASTER SUPER MARKETS INC.

LOCATIONS

HQ: FOODMASTER SUPER MARKETS INC.
100 EVERETT AVE STE 12, CHELSEA, MA 02150-2374
Phone: 617-660-1300
Web: www.foodmasterinc.com

HISTORICAL FINANCIALS
Company Type: Private

Income Statement
FYE: December 29

	REVENUE ($ mil.)	NET INCOME ($ mil.)	NET PROFIT MARGIN	EMPLOYEES
12/11	117	1	1.1%	1,100
12/08	126	1	0.8%	0
12/07	120	1	1.1%	0
12/06	613	0	—	0
Annual Growth	—	1684.6%	—	—

2011 Year-End Financials

Debt ratio: ——
Return on equity: 1.10%
Cash ($ mil.): 1
Current ratio: 0.20
Long-term debt ($ mil.): —
Dividends
Yield: —
Payout: —
Market value ($ mil.): —

FORDHAM UNIVERSITY

A private Catholic university Fordham offers its 14700 students —hailing from all 50 states and 50 foreign countries —degree programs through 10 graduate and undergraduate schools. Called the Jesuit University of New York Fordham has four locations including the original Rose Hill campus in the Bronx (often the scene of location shooting for movies TV shows and commercials) the Westchester campus the Lincoln Center campus in Manhattan as well as a biological field station in Armonk New York and international centers in China and the UK. The school opened in 1841 as St. John's College. It officially changed its name to Fordham University in 1907.

The Rose Hill campus is located on 85 acres in the Bronx and offers studies in business liberal arts science and religion. The Lincoln Center campus provides education business administration social services and legal training while the Westchester campus provides graduate programs in a variety of subjects. The Armonk field station is the headquarters for a number of university research programs.

In 2008 Fordham University sold its Marymount College campus in Tarrytown to EF Schools Inc. a chain of private language instruction institutions for $27 million. Fordham officials said the campus had experienced dwindling enrollment and financial difficulties.

EXECUTIVES

President and Trustee, Rev Joseph M. McShane
SVP and CFO, John J. Lordan
SVP and Chief Academic Officer, Stephen Freedman
Director University Libraries, James P. McCabe
Secretary, Margaret T. Ball
VP Administration, Brian J. Byrne
VP Student Affairs, Jeffrey L. Gray
VP Enrollment, Peter A. Stace
VP Finance, Frank Simio
Director Labor and Employee Relations, Angela Cioffi
Assistant VP Student Financial Services, Angela Van Dekker
Director Career Planning and Placement Rose Hill, Angela Yorio
Controller, Anthony Grono
Campus Director Student Financial Services, Barbara Wakie
Administrative Director Institute of International Humanitarian Affairs, Brendan Cahill
Chief of Operations Fordham University Emergency Medical Service (FUEMS), Brendan Ryan
Director Budget Operations, Carol Murabito
Business Office Manager, Casimira M. Stricker
Director Athletic Administration, Charles Elwood
Director Internet Services, Charles-Henri Sanson
Director Employer Relations, Christina Meincke
Director Treasury Operations, Conrad J. Obregon
President and CEO Graduate School of Arts and Sciences, David Reed
Associate VP Academic Affairs, David Stuhr
Legal Secretary, Diane Pinero
Assisant Dean and Director Admissions, Elaine Gerald
Director MBA Admissions, Frank Fletcher
Director Technical Operations, George J. Evans
Director Assessment and Accreditation, Gilbert Stack
Director Computer Services and Operations, Jason Benedict
Assistant VP Academic Affairs, Jerome A. Contee
Associate VP Government Relations, Joseph P. Muriana
Assistant VP Budgets and Logistics, Kevin Munnelly
Assistant VP Government Relations and State Affairs, Lesley Massiah
Associate VP Administration and Facilities, Marc Valera
Provost Marymount College, Mary Ann Quaranta
Director Information Technology Services Libraries, Michael Considine

Associate VP Student Affairs and Dean of Students Marymount, Michele C. Burris
Associate VP Academic Affairs, Ron Jacobson
Assistant VP Enrollment Services, Stephen Bordas
Director Office of Academic Effectiveness, Kristen Wenzel
Director Experiential Education Program, Bernard Stratford
VP Mission and Ministry, Rev Patrick Ryan
VP Technology and CIO, Frank Sirianni
Associate VP Academic Affairs and Associate Chief Academic Officer, Joel Reidenbert
VP Goverment Relations and Urban Affairs, Thomas A. Dunne
General Counsel, Thomas E. DeJulio
Director of Equity and Equal Oportunity, Georgina Calia Arendacs
Executive Director Human Resources, Michael C. Mineo
Trustee, Richard J. Buoncore, age 55
Vice Chair, Patricia M. Nazemetz, age 62
Trustee, Frank J. Petrilli, age 61
Trustee, Thomas P. Salice, age 52
Trustee, James E. Buckman, age 67
Trustee, Steven E. Sanderson
Trustee, Joel I. Picket, age 73
Trustee, Winston J. Churchill Jr., age 71
Trustee, Christine F. Driessen
Trustee, Robert B. McKeon, age 58
Trustee, Rev Michael J. Garanzini
President and Trustee, Rev Joseph M. McShane
Trustee, Stephen E. Bepler
Trustee, Donna M. Carroll
Trustee, John J. Cook Jr.
Trustee, Vincent M. Cooke
Trustee, Michael J. Cosgrove
Trustee, John R. Costantino, age 65
Trustee, Carolyn N. Dolan
Trustee, Kathleen Fagan
Trustee, William P. Frank
Trustee, Gerold F. L. Klauer
Trustee, Gerdenio Manuel
Trustee, Sylvester D. McClearn
Trustee, Francis J. Morison
Trustee, Nicholas A. Romano
Trustee, John S. Wilcha
Trustee, Robert A. Ferris
Trustee, Peter W. Howe
Trustee and Secretary, John P. Kehoe
Trustee, V. John Kriss
Trustee, Paul C. Saunders
Trustee, Christopher F. Fitzmaurice
Trustee, Darelene L. Jordan
Trustee, J. Thomas McClain
Trustee, Robert J. O'Shea
Trustee, Regina M. Pitaro
Trustee, Loretta A. Preska

LOCATIONS

HQ: Fordham University
441 E. Fordham Rd., Bronx NY 10458-5149
Phone: 718-817-1000   **Fax:** 718-817-4965
Web: www.fordham.edu

PRODUCTS/OPERATIONS

Selected Colleges
Graduate and Professional
  Graduate School of Arts and Sciences
  Graduate School of Business Administration
  Graduate School of Education
  Graduate School of Religion and Religious Education
  Graduate School of Social Services
  School of Law
Undergraduate
  Fordham College at Lincoln Center
  Fordham College at Rose Hill

Fordham College of Liberal Studies
Gabelli School of Business

HISTORICAL FINANCIALS
Company Type: School

Income Statement   FYE: June 30

	REVENUE ($ mil.)	NET INCOME ($ mil.)	NET PROFIT MARGIN	EMPLOYEES
06/12	518	60	11.6%	4,070
06/11	494	283	57.4%	0
06/10	568	17	3.0%	0
06/09	432	(103)	—	0
Annual Growth	6.2%	—	—	—

2012 Year-End Financials

Debt ratio: —
Return on equity: 11.60%
Cash ($ mil.): 3
Current ratio: —
Long-term debt ($ mil.): —
Dividends
  Yield: —
  Payout: —
Market value ($ mil.): —

FOREST SNAVELY PRODUCTS INC

Snavely Forest Products hopes it's never out of the woods. The company wholesales appearance-grade lumber and other wood products through some 10 sales and distribution centers. Snavely Forest Products' operations span Arizona California Colorado Florida Maryland North Carolina Pennsylvania and Texas. Its products include doors engineered wood millwork molding and softwood as well as composite factory fire-retardant structural and treated lumber. The company sources much of its product from sustainable-yield forests. Founded in 1902 Snavely Forest Products is still owned by the Snavely family and is run by Chris Snavely its chairman.

During the past two years housing woes and a slumping economy have whittled away at Snavely Forest Products. The company logged a disappointing performance in 2007 with a more than 20% dip in revenue. Its concerns deepened in 2008 as the US slipped into recession.

Though the company is part of the lumber industry it supports sustainable forests doesn't sell endangered species and looks for suppliers that recycle and use alternative products.

The supplier to the lumber industry is active in its field. One of Snavely Forest Products' executives was named the first-ever chairwoman of the North American Wholesale Lumber Association. At the association's conference in Arizona Susan Fitzsimmons a VP of mass merchants was elected to the position.

EXECUTIVES

Chairman and CEO, Stephen V. Snavely
Chairman Emeritus, Chris M. Snavely
President and COO, John A. Stockhausen

LOCATIONS

HQ: Snavely Forest Products
600 Delwar Rd., Pittsburgh PA 15236
Phone: 412-885-4000   **Fax:** 412-885-6050
Web: www.snavelyforest.com

COMPETITORS

84 Lumber
ABC Supply
Builders FirstSource Southeast Group
Diamond Hill Plywood
E.C. Barton
Emco Corporation
Foxworth-Galbraith Lumber
Georgia-Pacific
Guardian Building Products Distribution
HD Supply
Hull Forest Products
Huttig Building Products
Jewett-Cameron Trading
Lumber Products
Pacific Coast Building Products
PrimeSource Building
Stock Building Supply
Weyerhaeuser

HISTORICAL FINANCIALS
Company Type: Private

Income Statement

	REVENUE ($ mil.)	NET INCOME ($ mil.)	NET PROFIT MARGIN	EMPLOYEES
12/11	116	(0)	—	145
12/10	128	(0)	—	0
12/09	125	0	0.6%	0
12/08	163	(1)	—	0
Annual Growth	(10.8%)	—	—	—

2011 Year-End Financials

Debt ratio: —
Return on equity: (-0.20)%
Cash ($ mil.): 0
Current ratio: 1.70
Long-term debt ($ mil.): —

Dividends
Yield: —
Payout: —
Market value ($ mil.): —

FORGOTTEN HARVEST INC.

LOCATIONS

HQ: FORGOTTEN HARVEST INC.
21800 GREENFIELD RD, OAK PARK, MI 48237-2507
Phone: 248-967-1500
Web: www.forgottenharvest.org

HISTORICAL FINANCIALS
Company Type: Private

Income Statement

FYE: June 30

	REVENUE ($ mil.)	NET INCOME ($ mil.)	NET PROFIT MARGIN	EMPLOYEES
06/12	80	(0)	—	71
06/11	48	3	7.8%	0
06/10	36	1	5.0%	0
06/09	23	1	5.9%	0
Annual Growth	50.5%	—	—	—

2012 Year-End Financials

Debt ratio: —
Return on equity: (-1.00)%
Cash ($ mil.): 3
Current ratio: 7.20
Long-term debt ($ mil.): —

Dividends
Yield: —
Payout: —
Market value ($ mil.): —

FORT HEALTHCARE INC.

LOCATIONS

HQ: FORT HEALTHCARE INC.
611 SHERMAN AVE E, FORT ATKINSON, WI
53538-1960
Phone: 920-568-5401
Web: www.forthealthcare.com

HISTORICAL FINANCIALS
Company Type: Private

Income Statement

FYE: September 30

	REVENUE ($ mil.)	NET INCOME ($ mil.)	NET PROFIT MARGIN	EMPLOYEES
09/11	132	3	2.6%	850
09/10	127	6	5.5%	0
09/09	118	(0)	—	0
09/08	116	4	4.0%	0
Annual Growth	4.6%	(10.2%)	—	—

2011 Year-End Financials

Debt ratio: —
Return on equity: 2.60%
Cash ($ mil.): 2
Current ratio: 0.30
Long-term debt ($ mil.): —

Dividends
Yield: —
Payout: —
Market value ($ mil.): —

FORWARD CORPORATION

LOCATIONS

HQ: FORWARD CORPORATION
219 N FRONT ST, STANDISH, MI 48658-9256
Phone: 989-846-4501
Web: www.qualityinn.com

HISTORICAL FINANCIALS
Company Type: Private

Income Statement

FYE: December 31

	REVENUE ($ mil.)	NET INCOME ($ mil.)	NET PROFIT MARGIN	EMPLOYEES
12/11	161	1	0.7%	600
12/10	143	1	1.0%	0
12/09	123	0	0.2%	0
12/08	140	0	0.3%	0
Annual Growth	4.7%	37.8%	—	—

2011 Year-End Financials

Debt ratio: —
Return on equity: 0.70%
Cash ($ mil.): 1
Current ratio: 0.60
Long-term debt ($ mil.): —

Dividends
Yield: —
Payout: —
Market value ($ mil.): —

FOX CHASE CANCER CENTER

Fox Chase Cancer Center looks at cancer from all angles. The 100-bed nonprofit medical center specializes in cancer research detection and treatment. Formed in 1974 as one of the few US institutions dedicated exclusively to cancer Fox Chase Cancer Center provides diagnostic radiation oncology pathology robotic and laser surgery and other cancer-centric medical services. Its research center supports clinical trials of possible new treatments as well as standard care for cancer patients. Much of its work is focused on cancer prevention and identifying risk levels in populations. The center also offers community outreach and patient support services including nutrition social work and support groups.

Fox Chase is a National Cancer Institute Comprehensive Cancer Center that serves more than 33500 patients annually. Most of its patients are seen through ourpatient visits. The center treats a wide range of cancers with the most prevalent being prostate breast and lung cancers which together acount for about 40% of the cancers treated there. Patient care revenue makes up about 75% of Fox Chase's total revenues.

The center has expanded its facilities by opening the region's first women's cancer center (2009) as well as a smaller radiation center in nearby Buckingham Pennsylvania. The organization has also increased the scope of a number of its clinical programs including at its breast evaluation center ovarian cancer research and diagnostic imaging. Through its division of molecular pathology the center is exploiting current state-of-the-art technology and information as well as exploring research and development in the field of genomic technology that within several years will become a standard part of care for cancer patients. The field of molecular medicine is also referred to as personalized medicine or targeted therapy.

In addition to operating its own facilities in Pennsylvania Fox Chase provides cancer care through partnerships with other regional hospitals. Its collaborators include AtlantiCare and PinnacleHealth. The hospital is also expanding its reach internationally through a partnership in China with 307 Hospital of the People's Liberation Army which houses China's first cancer center.

Fox Chase Cancer Center was formed through the 1974 union of American Oncologic Hospital (established in 1904) and the Institute for Cancer Research (founded in 1927).

The center is led by CEO Dr. Michael Seiden who succeeded Dr. Robert Young in 2009 when Young retired after 18 years in the position.

EXECUTIVES

SVP and Chief Scientific Officer, Jonathan Chernoff
Chief Network Officer and Associate Medical Director, Mark L. Sobczak
SVP Molecular Medicine, Jeffrey (Jeff) Boyd
SVP and CFO, Thomas S. (Tom) Albanesi Jr.
Chief Nursing Officer, Anne Jadwin
Director Public Affairs, Karen Mallet
Chief Anesthesiology and Medical Director Intensive-Care Unit, David J. Fish
Chairman Department of Medical Oncology and VP Translational Research, Louis M. Weiner
SVP and Chief Development Officer, Michael J. Burton

Chairman Department of Pathology, Arthur S. Patchefsky
Director Hematopathology and Flow Cytometry, Tahseen I. Al-Saleem
Vice Chairman Pathology and Chief Immunohistochemistry, Harry S. Cooper
Chief Cytopathology, Hormoz Ehya
Director Surgical Pathology, Douglas B. Flieder
SVP Patient Services, Joanne Hambleton
Chairman, David G. Marshall
Chairman Radiation Oncology, Alan Pollack
Chairman Surgical Oncology, Monica Morrow
CFO, Theresa Larivee
Chairman Department of Surgery, Robert G. Uzzo
Vice Chairman, Louis Della Penna
President and CEO, Michael V. Seiden
SVP and Chief Academic Officer, J. Robert Beck
SVP COO and Chief Administrative Officer, Gary J. Weyhmuller

LOCATIONS

HQ: The Fox Chase Cancer Center
333 Cottman Ave., Philadelphia PA 19111-2497
Phone: 215-728-6900 **Fax:** 215-728-2682
Web: www.fccc.edu

PRODUCTS/OPERATIONS

2010 Revenues

	% of total
Patient-care	75
Research grants & commercial	17
Fundraising	4
Governmental	2
Investment & other	2
Total	**100**

Selected Technologies and Services

Diagnostic imaging services
  Colonoscopy
  CT
  Fluoroscopy
  Mammography
  MRI
  Nuclear medicine
  PET/CT
  Stereotactic breast biopsy
  Ultrasound
Radiation oncology services
  CT/MRI simulated 3-dimensional treatment planning
  Image-guided radiation therapy (IGRT)
  Intensity Modulated Radiation Therapy (IMRT)
  Low-dose-rate and high-dose-rate implants (brachytherapy)
Surgery
  Cryosurgery
  Laser surgery
  Robotic surgery (da Vinci)

Selected Partners

AtlantiCare
Crozer-Keystone
Easton Hospital
Hunterdon
Paoli
Pinnacle Health
Pottstown
South Jersey Healthcare
Virtua Cancer Program

COMPETITORS

Dana-Farber
H. Lee Moffitt Cancer Center & Research Institute
Johns Hopkins Medicine
Mayo Clinic
MD Anderson Cancer Center
Memorial Sloan-Kettering
Roswell Park Cancer Institute
Wistar Institute

HISTORICAL FINANCIALS

Company Type: Private - Not-for-Profit

Income Statement
FYE: June 30

	REVENUE ($ mil.)	NET INCOME ($ mil.)	NET PROFIT MARGIN	EMPLOYEES
06/11	44	(9)	—	1,900
06/10	49	(7)	—	0
06/09	55	(8)	—	0
06/08	54	(16)	—	0
Annual Growth	**(7.0%)**	—	—	—

2011 Year-End Financials

Debt ratio: —
Return on equity: (-21.60)%
Cash ($ mil.): 1
Current ratio: —
Long-term debt ($ mil.): —
Dividends
  Yield: —
  Payout: —
  Market value ($ mil.): —

FOXWORTH GALBRAITH LUMBER COMPANY

Foxworth-Galbraith Lumber Company is helping build the Southwest. It sells hardware lumber paint plumbing equipment tools and other building supplies through about 20 locations in Arizona Colorado New Mexico and Texas. Foxworth-Galbraith's main customers are residential and commercial builders; other clients include do-it-yourselfers specialty contractors and federal and state agencies. Foxworth-Galbraith is still owned and operated by the families of W.L. Foxworth and H.W. Galbraith who founded the company in Dalhart Texas in 1901 to take advantage of railroad construction.

The company's commercial division supplies materials manufactured components engineered wood and specialty and environmental products for certain special projects that have included government light commercial and Native American projects. Completed building projects include Cheddar's (Independence Missouri) Jack In The Box (Broken Arrow Oklahoma) McDonald's (Englewood Colorado) and Well Fargo bank (Waco Texas).

Foxworth-Galbraith also provides other services such as project support (cabinet design custom paint matching and special-order products) and truss services (manufacturers and engineers trusses and wall panels) for residential and commercial projects. The firm also provides installation and delivery services.

Amid the drop in new home construction and economic downturn in the US Foxworth-Galbraith has been closing its stores. By 2011 the company had slashed its store count by about 70% compared to its operations just five years prior. The company sold its headquarters building in 2011.

EXECUTIVES

President and CEO, Jimmy Galbraith III
EVP and Internet Director, Ted Galbraith
VP Finance and Administration, Jack Foxworth
Chairman, Walter L. Foxworth
VP Operations, Daniel Brunson
Director Human Resources, Jennifer Thedford
Controller, Rich Perkins

LOCATIONS

HQ: Foxworth-Galbraith Lumber Company
17111 Waterview Pkwy., Dallas TX 75252-8005
Phone: 972-437-6100 **Fax:** 972-454-4251
Web: www.foxgal.com

2011 Stores

	No.
Texas	9
New	6
Arizona	3
Colorado	2
Total	**20**

PRODUCTS/OPERATIONS

Selected Product Categories

Building materials
Cabinets
Electrical
Hardware
Lawn and garden
Lumber
Paint
Plumbing
Tools

COMPETITORS

84 Lumber	Home Depot
A.C. Houston Lumber	Lowe's
Ace Hardware	McCoy Corp.
Bison Building Materials	Sears
	Sherwin-Williams
BMC	Stock Building Supply
Builders FirstSource	Sutherland Lumber
Do it Best	True Value

HISTORICAL FINANCIALS

Company Type: Private

Income Statement
FYE: December 31

	REVENUE ($ mil.)	NET INCOME ($ mil.)	NET PROFIT MARGIN	EMPLOYEES
12/11	164	(3)	—	2,500
12/10	154	(10)	—	0
12/09	148	(8)	—	0
12/08	308	(17)	—	0
Annual Growth	**(18.9%)**	—	—	—

2011 Year-End Financials

Debt ratio: —
Return on equity: (-2.40)%
Cash ($ mil.): 0
Current ratio: 0.60
Long-term debt ($ mil.): —
Dividends
  Yield: —
  Payout: —
  Market value ($ mil.): —

FPL FOOD LLC

LOCATIONS

HQ: FPL FOOD LLC
1301 NEW SAVANNAH RD, AUGUSTA, GA 30901-3843
Phone: 706-922-5513
Web: www.fplfood.com

HISTORICAL FINANCIALS
Company Type: Private

Income Statement
FYE: January 1

	REVENUE ($ mil.)	NET INCOME ($ mil.)	NET PROFIT MARGIN	EMPLOYEES
01/11	261	4	1.5%	800
Annual Growth	—	—	—	—

2011 Year-End Financials
Debt ratio: —
Return on equity: 1.50%
Cash ($ mil.): 1
Current ratio: 0.50
Long-term debt ($ mil.): —
Dividends
  Yield: —
  Payout: —
  Market value ($ mil.): —

HISTORICAL FINANCIALS
Company Type: Private - Not-for-Profit

Income Statement
FYE: June 30

	REVENUE ($ mil.)	NET INCOME ($ mil.)	NET PROFIT MARGIN	EMPLOYEES
06/11	423	48	11.4%	1,500
06/10	369	34	9.3%	0
06/09	313	(3)	—	0
06/08	0	0	83.8%	0
Annual Growth	665.9%	293.8%	—	—

2011 Year-End Financials
Debt ratio: —
Return on equity: 11.40%
Cash ($ mil.): 40
Current ratio: 0.40
Long-term debt ($ mil.): —
Dividends
  Yield: —
  Payout: —
  Market value ($ mil.): —

HISTORICAL FINANCIALS
Company Type: School

Income Statement
FYE: May 31

	REVENUE ($ mil.)	NET INCOME ($ mil.)	NET PROFIT MARGIN	EMPLOYEES
05/11	68	5	7.9%	320
05/10	63	1	3.0%	0
05/09	56	0	—	0
05/06	55	11	20.8%	0
Annual Growth	7.5%	(22.2%)	—	—

2011 Year-End Financials
Debt ratio: —
Return on equity: 7.90%
Cash ($ mil.): 7
Current ratio: —
Long-term debt ($ mil.): —
Dividends
  Yield: —
  Payout: —
  Market value ($ mil.): —

FRANCIS SAINT MEDICAL CENTER

It may be guided by Catholic principles but you don't have to be a saint to get medical care at Saint Francis Medical Center. The hospital serves a five-state region from Missouri (its home base) to Arkansas with about 250 beds. Services include emergency medicine orthopedics rehabilitation and women's health care. It also offers heart and neurosciences institutes as well as diabetes education and wound healing centers. The health care provider which was established in 1875 partners with Poplar Bluff Medical Partners to provide outpatient care at Poplar Bluff Medical Complex. Services include family practice OB-GYN and pain management.

Saint Francis Medical Center also partners with Landmark Holdings of Missouri to provide long-term acute care services through the 30-bed Landmark Hospital. The only facility of its kind between St. Louis and Memphis the hospital provides long-term care for patients who need complex medical care from catastrophic accidents or chronic diseases.

EXECUTIVES
President and CEO, Steven C. Bjelich
CFO, Tony Balsano

LOCATIONS
HQ: Saint Francis Medical Center
  211 St. Francis Dr., Cape Girardeau MO 63703
Phone: 573-331-3000   **Fax:** 573-331-5010
Web: www.sfmc.net

COMPETITORS
Barnes-Jewish Hospital
Memorial Hospital (Illinois)
Southeast Missouri State University
Southern Illinois Healthcare
St. Anthony's Medical Center
St. John's Hospital (Illinois)

FRANCISCAN UNIVERSITY OF STEUBENVILLE

Franciscan University of Steubenville is a Roman Catholic school that provides instruction to more than 2300 students. It offers more than 30 undergraduate majors as well as master's degrees in six separate fields. The college was established in 1946 when Steubenville Ohio's first bishop John King Mussio invited Franciscan friars to establish a college to serve the needs of local students especially veterans of WWII.

EXECUTIVES
President, Rev Terence Henry
VP Finance, David M. Skiviat
VP Enrollment, Joel Recznik
Registrar, Kathy Reehl
Director Public Relations, Lisa Ferguson
Chancellor, Rev Michael Scanlan
EVP, Robert Filby
VP Academic Affairs, Max Bonilla
VP Community Relations and Religious Administrator, Rev Richard Davis
VP Student Life, David Schmiesing
Director Alumni and Constituent Relations, Timothy (Tim) Delaney
Director Information Technology, Kevin Sebolt
Director Career Planning and Services, Nancy Ronevich
VP Advancement, Michael Hernon
VP Human Resources and Legal Counsel, Adam Scurti

LOCATIONS
HQ: Franciscan University of Steubenville
  1235 University Blvd., Steubenville OH 43952
Phone: 740-283-3771   **Fax:** 212-593-5194
Web: www.leadersmag.com

FRANKLIN AND MARSHALL COLLEGE

When Ben & Jerry say "dip" think ice cream. When Ben & John say "dip" think diplomat. Franklin & Marshall College named after Benjamin Franklin and John Marshall is a private liberal arts institution serving approximately 2000 students. It offers academic and research programs in areas including English mathematics political science art sociology and environmental studies. The school was created in 1853 through the merger of Franklin College (founded in 1787 with a contribution from Ben Franklin) and Marshall College (opened in 1836 and named after Chief Justice John Marshall).

EXECUTIVES
Interim President and Trustee, John F. Burness
VP Administrative Services and External Affairs, Keith Orris
Associate Provost and Chief Information Officer, Jonathan C. Enos
Provost and Dean of the Faculty, Ann R. Steiner
VP College Advancement, Lewis E. Thayne
Director Human Resources, Nancy A. Eshleman
VP Finance and Treasurer, Helen Y. Bowman
VP Enrollment Management and Dean of Admission, Sara S. Harberson

LOCATIONS
HQ: Franklin & Marshall College
  638 College Ave., Lancaster PA 17603
Phone: 717-291-3911   **Fax:** 717-291-4370
Web: www.fandm.edu

HISTORICAL FINANCIALS
Company Type: School

Income Statement
FYE: June 30

	REVENUE ($ mil.)	NET INCOME ($ mil.)	NET PROFIT MARGIN	EMPLOYEES
06/11	114	46	40.7%	722
06/10	141	10	7.3%	0
06/08	110	(6)	—	0
06/07	107	64	60.3%	0
Annual Growth	2.2%	(10.4%)	—	—

2011 Year-End Financials
Debt ratio: —
Return on equity: 40.70%
Cash ($ mil.): 24
Current ratio: —
Long-term debt ($ mil.): —

Dividends
Yield: —
Payout: —
Market value ($ mil.): —

FRANKLIN TOWNSHIP PUBLIC SCHOOL DISTRICT OF SOMERSET

LOCATIONS
HQ: FRANKLIN TOWNSHIP PUBLIC SCHOOL
DISTRICT OF SOMERSET
1755 AMWELL RD, SOMERSET, NJ 08873-2746
Phone: 732-873-2400
Web: www.franklinboe.org

HISTORICAL FINANCIALS
Company Type: Private

Income Statement
FYE: June 30

	REVENUE ($ mil.)	NET INCOME ($ mil.)	NET PROFIT MARGIN	EMPLOYEES
06/12	149	2	1.5%	1,000
06/11	144	(0)	—	0
06/10	143	(1)	—	0
06/09	136	(4)	—	0
Annual Growth	3.0%	—	—	—

2012 Year-End Financials
Debt ratio: —
Return on equity: 1.50%
Cash ($ mil.): 6
Current ratio: —
Long-term debt ($ mil.): —

Dividends
Yield: —
Payout: —
Market value ($ mil.): —

FRAZIER INDUSTRIAL

This company's racket is structural steel storage systems. Frazier Industrial Co. is a leading manufacturer of structural as opposed to roll-formed steel storage racks at about a dozen production centers in the US Canada and Mexico. These facilities can adapt production to demand and receive just-in-time delivery of raw materials. Customers use Frazier Industrial's storage racks in warehouses factories farms and other industrial and commercial facilities. Among the company's storage products is the Glide 'N Pick pallet cart that automatically rolls out for greater ease in retrieving items. Founded in 1949 Frazier Industrial is owned by CEO William Mascharka.

Geographic Reach

Frazier Industrial has manufacturing locations in Idaho New Jersey New York Pennsylvania South Carolina and Wisconsin. Outside the US it has plants in Mexicali and Monterrey Mexico and in Ontario Canada.

Strategy

Frazier is taking a stand for environmentally sound business practices as green initiatives become a focal point for customers such as Nestle Procter & Gamble and Unilever. Frazier sources all of its steel sections from North American minimills which only use recycled scrap material. Fittingly all of Frazier's scrap raw material is fully recyclable. Because the company receives preformed structural sections energy output is minimal; these structural parts require only cutting punching and welding. The location of Frazier's production centers helps to keep travel time and fuel expenses under control. They are all within 400 miles of the company's raw material suppliers and within 500 miles of major population centers in North America.

EXECUTIVES
CEO, William L. Mascharka
President, Carlos Oliver
CFO, Walter Budzinski

LOCATIONS
HQ: Frazier Industrial Company Inc.
91 Fairview Ave., Long Valley NJ 07853
Phone: 908-876-3001   **Fax:** 908-876-3615
Web: www.frazier.com

PRODUCTS/OPERATIONS

Selected Products
Drive-In/Drive-Thru Storage
Frazier Design-Build
Glide-In Push-Back Storage
Glide N' Pick Order Picking Cart
Klamp-Fast Cantilever Rack
Pick-to-Belt Systems
Rack Supported Buildings
Safety Accessories
SelecDeck Carton Flow System
Sentinel Selective Pallet Rack
The Pallet Mole

COMPETITORS
Actionrack
Edsal Manufacturing
Interlake Mecalux

Lyon Workspace
Products
Steel of West Virginia

HISTORICAL FINANCIALS
Company Type: Private

Income Statement
FYE: December 31

	REVENUE ($ mil.)	NET INCOME ($ mil.)	NET PROFIT MARGIN	EMPLOYEES
12/11	178	4	2.7%	750
12/10	133	3	2.8%	0
12/09	169	7	4.4%	0
12/08	221	7	3.5%	0
Annual Growth	(7.0%)	(14.9%)	—	—

2011 Year-End Financials
Debt ratio: —
Return on equity: 2.70%
Cash ($ mil.): 3
Current ratio: 0.70
Long-term debt ($ mil.): —

Dividends
Yield: —
Payout: —
Market value ($ mil.): —

FREDERICK COUNTY SCHOOL DISTRICT

LOCATIONS
HQ: FREDERICK COUNTY SCHOOL DISTRICT
1415 AMHERST ST, WINCHESTER, VA 22601-3009
Phone: 540-662-3888

HISTORICAL FINANCIALS
Company Type: Private

Income Statement
FYE: June 30

	REVENUE ($ mil.)	NET INCOME ($ mil.)	NET PROFIT MARGIN	EMPLOYEES
06/11	132	1	1.3%	1,600
Annual Growth	—	—	—	—

2011 Year-End Financials
Debt ratio: —
Return on equity: 1.30%
Cash ($ mil.): 15
Current ratio: —
Long-term debt ($ mil.): —

Dividends
Yield: —
Payout: —
Market value ($ mil.): —

FREDERICKSBURG FARMERS COOPERATIVE

LOCATIONS
HQ: FREDERICKSBURG FARMERS COOPERATIVE
110 N JEFFERSON AVE, FREDERICKSBURG, IA
50630-7757
Phone: 563-237-5324
Web: www.fburgcoop.com

HISTORICAL FINANCIALS

Company Type: Private

Income Statement

FYE: July 31

	REVENUE ($ mil.)	NET INCOME ($ mil.)	NET PROFIT MARGIN	EMPLOYEES
07/12	138	3	2.5%	42
07/11	110	2	2.4%	0
07/10	71	1	2.7%	0
07/09	89	1	1.7%	0
Annual Growth	15.6%	29.3%	—	—

2012 Year-End Financials

Debt ratio: —
Return on equity: 2.50%
Cash ($ mil.): 0
Current ratio: 0.10
Long-term debt ($ mil.): —

Dividends
Yield: —
Payout: —
Market value ($ mil.): —

FREEDOM OIL COMPANY

LOCATIONS

HQ: FREEDOM OIL COMPANY
814 W CHESTNUT ST, BLOOMINGTON, IL
61701-2816
Phone: 309-828-7750
Web: www.freedomoil.com

HISTORICAL FINANCIALS

Company Type: Private

Income Statement

FYE: December 31

	REVENUE ($ mil.)	NET INCOME ($ mil.)	NET PROFIT MARGIN	EMPLOYEES
12/11	146	0	0.6%	250
12/10	126	0	0.5%	0
12/09	105	(0)		0
12/07	127	0	0.7%	0
Annual Growth	4.6%	(0.1%)	—	—

2011 Year-End Financials

Debt ratio: —
Return on equity: 0.60%
Cash ($ mil.): 0
Current ratio: 0.50
Long-term debt ($ mil.): —

Dividends
Yield: —
Payout: —
Market value ($ mil.): —

FREESE AND NICHOLS INC.

Freese and Nichols (FNI) keeps water in the Lone Star State flowing in the right direction. The consulting firm specializes in water management engineering but offers other services including architecture environmental science and construction management to clients in the Southwest primarily Texas. The company has designed more than 150 dams and reservoirs and also works on such projects as municipal waterworks water treatment facilities and highways. Freese and Nichols serves the private and public sectors including clients from all levels of government. The company has offices in about a dozen Texas cities and traces its roots to a Ft. Worth firm founded in 1894 by John B. Hawley.

Strategy

The prolonged drought in Texas has spurred renewed interest in water infrastructure projects positioning FNI for future growth. Clients have included multiple Texas municipalities (including Temple Killeen Mansfield) the Dallas/Fort Worth International Airport and the Texas A&M University System.

EXECUTIVES

Chairman Emeritus, James R. Nichols, age 73
Chairman, Robert L. (Bob) Herchert, age 69
President and CEO, Robert F. (Bob) Pence
SVP COO and Director, Ron M. Lemons
SVP and Director, Michael L. Nichols
VP, Alan D. Greer
SVP CFO CAO and Treasurer, Cindy P. Milrany
VP and Engineer VIII, Lee B. Freese
VP Engineer VIII and Secretary, Thomas C. Gooch
VP and Engineer VIII, Michael G. Morrison
VP Group Manager and Principal, Barbara A. Nickerson
President Emeritus, Robert L. Nichols
VP, Will McDonald
SVP COO and Director, Ron M. Lemons
SVP and Director, Michael L. Nichols

LOCATIONS

HQ: Freese and Nichols Inc.
4055 International Plaza Ste. 200, Fort Worth TX
76109-4895
Phone: 817-735-7300   **Fax:** 817-735-7491
Web: www.freese.com

PRODUCTS/OPERATIONS

Selected Services

Architectural
  Architectural design
  Historical restoration and preservation
  Interior design
  Master planning
  3-D visualization
Engineering
  Dam design and rehabilitation
  Geotechnical engineering
  Mechanical engineering
  Plumbing engineering
  Storm water management
  Streets and highways
  Water and wastewater system planning
  Water storage tanks
  Water treatment
Environmental science
  Contamination assessments and remediation
  Environmental impact assessments
  Geographic information systems/remote sensing
  Pollution prevention and permitting

COMPETITORS

AECOM	Sunland Group
Barnes Gromatzky	Swinerton
Kosarek Architects	URS
Huitt-Zollars	Walter P. Moore and
Molzen-Corbin &	Associates
Associates	WS Atkins

HISTORICAL FINANCIALS

Company Type: Private

Income Statement

FYE: December 31

	REVENUE ($ mil.)	NET INCOME ($ mil.)	NET PROFIT MARGIN	EMPLOYEES
12/11	105	1	1.5%	487
Annual Growth	—	—	—	—

2011 Year-End Financials

Debt ratio: —
Return on equity: 1.50%
Cash ($ mil.): 5
Current ratio: 0.90
Long-term debt ($ mil.): —

Dividends
Yield: —
Payout: —
Market value ($ mil.): —

FREIGHTQUOTE.COM INC.

Where should one go on the Web to find quotes for freight carriers? Freightquote.com silly. The company rates schedules and tracks all types of freight comparing numerous carriers in seconds through its free service. Freightquote serves customers across North America who use its services to schedule and track their shipments entirely on the Web. It also offers free online freight shipping quotes. Modes of freight transport include trucks airplanes and ships. The company moves more than one million shipments across North America per year. Freightquote was founded in 1998 by Timothy Barton. It has received funding from investment firms such as Menlo Ventures and Morgan Stanley Venture Partners.

Operations

Freightquote organizes its freight solutions in categories that meet customer's different needs including truckload (TL) less than truckload (LTL freight) expedited LTL or intermodal (shipping by rail). The firm also offers custom logistics solutions such as project freight (a solution for projects with multiple-shipments) and freight spend analysis.

The company also operates subsidiary Rockwell Transportation Services a Pennsylvania-based transportation brokerage provider specializing in truckload less than truckload and intermodal solutions for shippers. Its transportation management system Freightview allows customers to streamline and automate the shipping process.

Strategy

To accomodate the company's recent growth Freightquote is moving its corporate headquarters to a larger facility in Kansas City Missouri. The new building will be 200000 square feet and is set to open in 2013. The move is a response to increased demand.

Financials

Freightquote continues to maintain growth with a 24% year-over-year revenue increase since 2004. In 2011 annual sales increased to more than $500 million up from $400 million in 2010.

EXECUTIVES

Chairman and CEO, Timothy A. (Tim) Barton
VP Enterprise Sales, Jason Beer
COO and CIO, Shawn McCarrick
VP Human Resources, Luanne Eskew

VP and General Manager Rockwell Transportation Services, Lori Wittman
CFO, Matt Druten
VP Business Solutions, Doug Grojean
VP Sales, Trent Flanary
VP Customer Service Operations, Lance Huggins
VP Finance, Abbey Caton

LOCATIONS

HQ: Freightquote.com Inc.
16025 W. 113th St., Lenexa KS 66219
Phone: 913-642-4700   **Fax:** 913-642-6773
Web: www.freightquote.com

PRODUCTS/OPERATIONS

Selected Services
Truckload freight
Less-than-truckload (LTL) freight
Expedited LTL freight
Intermodal (rail) freight
Project freight (multiple shipments)
Dry van freight
Flatbed trucking
Refrigerated shipping
Air freight
Free online quotes

COMPETITORS

Expeditors   UBM Global Trade
Phoenix International
Freight Services

HISTORICAL FINANCIALS

Company Type: Private

Income Statement   FYE: December 31

	REVENUE ($ mil.)	NET INCOME ($ mil.)	NET PROFIT MARGIN	EMPLOYEES
12/11	385	0	—	1,200
12/10	0	0	—	0
12/09	359	0	—	0
12/08	0	0	—	0
Annual Growth	—	—	—	—

2011 Year-End Financials
Debt ratio: ——
Return on equity: —
Cash ($ mil.): 15
Current ratio: 1.20
Long-term debt ($ mil.): —

Dividends
Yield: —
Payout: —
Market value ($ mil.): —

FREMONT CONTRACT CARRIERS INC.

Truckload carrier Fremont Contract Carriers (FCC) hauls general and non-hazardous freight throughout the US and Canada. Its fleet consists of some 315 trucks 550 high-cubed dry van trailers and 100 flatbed curtain-side and step-deck trailers. The company's FCC Transportation Services unit provides freight brokerage and logistics services in which customers' freight is matched with carriers' capacity. In addition to offering traditional trucking services the company provides online load tracking and reporting on its Web site. FCC was founded in 1966.

EXECUTIVES

President and CEO, Mike Herre
VP Safety, Ann Dostal
VP Maintenance, Todd Miles
COO, Tim McCormick
Director Logistics, Elaine Asper
VP Sales, Guy Mumford
VP Operations, Erik Andry
Manager Flatbed Operations, Rob Musson
Driver Recruiting, Tom Hostetler
VP Information Technology, Chris Mayer
Director Training and Development, Susan Hilgenkamp

LOCATIONS

HQ: Fremont Contract Carriers Inc.
865 S. Bud Blvd., Fremont NE 68025
Phone: 402-721-3020   **Fax:** 402-727-8712
Web: www.fcc-inc.com

COMPETITORS

C.H. Robinson   Landstar System
Worldwide   Schneider National
Crete Carrier   Swift Transportation
J.B. Hunt   Werner Enterprises

HISTORICAL FINANCIALS

Company Type: Private

Income Statement   FYE: December 31

	REVENUE ($ mil.)	NET INCOME ($ mil.)	NET PROFIT MARGIN	EMPLOYEES
12/11	61	0	0.3%	91
12/10	55	(0)	—	0
12/09	50	0	1.2%	0
12/08	58	0	0.9%	0
Annual Growth	1.5%	(29.6%)	—	—

2011 Year-End Financials
Debt ratio: ——
Return on equity: 0.30%
Cash ($ mil.): 1
Current ratio: 2.70
Long-term debt ($ mil.): —

Dividends
Yield: —
Payout: —
Market value ($ mil.): —

FRESNO COMMUNITY HOSPITAL AND MEDICAL CENTER

LOCATIONS

HQ: FRESNO COMMUNITY HOSPITAL AND MEDICAL CENTER
2823 FRESNO ST, FRESNO, CA 93721-1324
Phone: 559-228-5312
Web: www.communitymedical.org

HISTORICAL FINANCIALS

Company Type: Private

Income Statement   FYE: August 31

	REVENUE ($ mil.)	NET INCOME ($ mil.)	NET PROFIT MARGIN	EMPLOYEES
08/11	1,207	114	9.5%	5,045
08/10	1,027	9	0.9%	0
08/09	1,010	65	6.5%	0
08/06	625	(9)	—	0
Annual Growth	24.5%	—	—	—

2011 Year-End Financials
Debt ratio: ——
Return on equity: 9.50%
Cash ($ mil.): 83
Current ratio: 2.30
Long-term debt ($ mil.): —

Dividends
Yield: —
Payout: —
Market value ($ mil.): —

FRICK COLLECTION

The Frick Collection consists of hundreds of works of art including paintings sculpture furniture and porcelains clocks and textiles that are housed in a Manhattan mansion built by steel and railroad tycoon Henry Clay Frick. Upon his death in 1919 Frick bequeathed his vast collection of Western European art (from the Renaissance through the end of the 19th century) to the public. In addition to its permanent collection of more than 1100 works of art and other exhibitions The Frick Collection offers public programs such as lectures and concerts. An affiliated facility the Frick Art Reference Library offers books and photographic materials for scholars.

EXECUTIVES

Manager Media Relations and Marketing, Heidi Rosenau
Controller and Assistant Treasurer, Michael J. Paccione
Manager Human Resources, Diane Winfield
Director, Anne Litle Poulet
Chief Conservator, Joseph Godla
Vice Director External Affairs, Jessica W. London
Media Relations and Marketing Coordinator, Geetha Natarajan
Associate Director, Colin Bailey
Chief Curator, Peter Jay Sharp
Chairman, Margot Bogert
Media Relations and Marketing Coordinator, Alexis Light
Director, Stephen A. Schwarzman, age 65
Director, Franklin W. (Fritz) Hobbs IV, age 64
Director, John P. Birkelund
Director, Walter A. Eberstadt
Director, George Wachter
Director, Aso O. Tavitian

LOCATIONS

HQ: The Frick Collection
1 E. 70th St., New York NY 10021-4967
Phone: 212-288-0700   **Fax:** 212-628-4417
Web: www.frick.org

HISTORICAL FINANCIALS
Company Type: Private

Income Statement
FYE: June 30

	REVENUE ($ mil.)	NET INCOME ($ mil.)	NET PROFIT MARGIN	EMPLOYEES
06/11	37	16	45.3%	240
06/10	17	(7)	—	0
06/09	2	0	—	0
06/08	25	2	10.7%	0
Annual Growth	13.2%	83.2%	—	—

2011 Year-End Financials
Debt ratio: —
Return on equity: 45.30%
Cash ($ mil.): 14
Current ratio: —
Long-term debt ($ mil.): —

Dividends
Yield: —
Payout: —
Market value ($ mil.): —

FRISBIE MEMORIAL HOSPITAL

Frisbie Memorial Hospital hopes to maintain a high-flying reputation as it serves southeastern New Hampshire and southern Maine. The acute-care facility has nearly 90 beds and about 250 physicians on staff. The not-for-profit community hospital offers patients a variety of services including emergency radiology cardiology neurology and respiratory and surgical care. Frisbie Memorial also operates outpatient and primary medical care facilities and it provides oncology services through a partnership with the Dartmouth-Hitchcock Medical Center in Lebanon New Hampshire.

Operations

Frisbie Memorial Hospital provides a range of preventive and advanced diagnostic and surgical services with more than 20 hospital services primary care medical offices in five greater Rochester communities nearly 30 different specialty care services two walk-in care centers and an occupational health center.

Strategy

Upgrading its technology in 2012 Frisbie Memorial Hospital acquired the latest in magnetic respnance imaging technology by installing the new Vantage TitanTM from Toshiba. That year it also expanded its clinical affiliation to include cancer services.

Company Background

The hospital was established in 1919.

EXECUTIVES

President COO and CEO, Alvin D. (Al) Felgar
CFO, John Marzinzik
VP Human Resources, Carol Themelis
Marketing Specialist, Michelle Landry

LOCATIONS

HQ: Frisbie Memorial Hospital
11 Whitehall Rd., Rochester NH 03867
Phone: 603-332-5211   Fax: 603-332-2699
Web: www.frisbiehospital.com

COMPETITORS

Catholic Medical   Partners HealthCare

Center
Concord Hospital
Elliot Health System
Exeter Health
Resources

Southern New Hampshire
Medical Center

HISTORICAL FINANCIALS
Company Type: Private - Not-for-Profit

Income Statement
FYE: September 30

	REVENUE ($ mil.)	NET INCOME ($ mil.)	NET PROFIT MARGIN	EMPLOYEES
09/11	130	3	2.8%	900
09/10	136	3	2.6%	0
09/09	126	(0)	—	0
09/08	120	(4)	—	0
Annual Growth	2.7%			

2011 Year-End Financials
Debt ratio: —
Return on equity: 2.80%
Cash ($ mil.): 5
Current ratio: 1.50
Long-term debt ($ mil.): —

Dividends
Yield: —
Payout: —
Market value ($ mil.): —

FROEDTERT MEMORIAL LUTHERAN HOSPITAL INC

Patients in southeastern Wisconsin count on Froedtert Memorial Lutheran Hospital for a full range of health services including trauma transplant sports medicine and senior care. The 500-bed hospital also known as Froedtert & The Medical College of Wisconsin is part of the Froedtert Health system (pronounced "fray-dert"). Specialty units include cancer dermatology neuroscience birthing fertility urology and vein clinics. The hospital also serves as a teaching facility for the Medical College of Wisconsin and it partners with the Children's Hospital of Wisconsin to provide pediatric services. Froedtert Hospital which was founded in 1980 operates the only adult Level One trauma center in the region.

Operations

Froedtert Health offers medical practice care in roughly 35 specialties and subspecialties. Beyond the hospital's walls it operates four diagnostic imaging centers as well as rehabilitation facilities and a handful of primary care clinics in the community. The Froedtert Health system also includes Community Memorial Hospital in Menomonee Falls; St. Joseph's Hospital in West Bend Wisconsin; and Froedtert Health Medical Group.

Strategy

In 2010 Froedtert Health acquired ProHealth Care Medical Associates practices in six Germantown Hartford and Menomonee Falls locations. The practices now operating as Froedtert Health included three general clinics specialty services behavioral health rehabilitation and a physician practice.

EXECUTIVES

Chief Strategy Officer, David Olson

Vice Chairman, Edward J. Zore, age 66
President CEO and Director, William D. (Bill) Petasnick
President Froedtert Hospital, Catherine (Cathy) Buck
CFO Froedtert Health, Jeffrey Van De Kreeke
President and CEO Froedtert Health, Catherine A. Jacobson
Chief Medical Officer Froedtert Hospital, Lee Biblo
Media Relations Supervisor, Kathy Sieja
Media Relations Specialist, Kimberly Wick
Media Relations Specialist, Brian Dorrington
Chairman, P. Michael Mahoney
Treasurer, Roger D. Peirce
Chairman Froedtert Hospital Foundation, Geneva B. Johnson, age 82
President St. Joseph's Hospital, Allen Ericson
Secretary, David Lubar
SVP and Chief Human Resources Officer, Keith Allen
VP Marketing, Kathleen Perlewitz
VP and Chief Diversity Officer, Joseph Hill
COO Froedtert Health and President Community Memorial Hospital, Dennis Pollard
VP Information Technology and CIO, Robert DeGrand
Vice Chairman, Edward J. Zore, age 66
President CEO and Director, William D. (Bill) Petasnick
Auditors: KPMGPeatMarwickLLP

LOCATIONS

HQ: FROEDTERT MEMORIAL LUTHERAN HOSPITAL INC
9200 W WISCONSIN AVE, MILWAUKEE, WI 53226-3522
Phone: 414-259-3000
Web: www.froedtert.com

PRODUCTS/OPERATIONS

Selected Departments Centers and Programs

Clinical Cancer Center
  Blood and Lymph Node Cancer Program
  Blood and Marrow Transplant Program
  Bone and Connective Tissue Cancer Program
  Brain and Spine Tumor Program
  Breast Cancer Program
  Cancer Genetics Screening Program
  Colorectal Cancer Program
  Endocrine Cancer Program
  Eye/Orbital Cancer Program
  Geriatric Oncology
  Gynecologic Cancer Program
  Head and Neck Cancer Program
  Liver Pancreas and Bile Duct Cancer Program
  Neuro-oncology Cognitive Clinic
  Palliative Care Program
  Plastic Surgery Center
  Prostate and Urologic Cancer Program
  Skin Cancer Center
  Thoracic Cancer Program (Lung and Esophageal Cancers)
Heart and Vascular Center
  Adult Congenital Heart Disease
  Advanced Heart Failure and Cardiac Transplantation
  Aortic Disease
  Arrhythmia and Atrial Fibrillation
  Coronary Artery Disease (CAD)
  Hereditary Hemorrhagic Telangiectasia (HHT)
  Hypertrophic Cardiomyopathy (HCM)
  Preventive Cardiology and Lipid Therapy
  Peripheral Arterial Disease (PAD)
  Pulmonary Hypertension
  Valvular Disease
  Venous Thrombotic Disease
  Venous and Vein Disease
  Women and Heart Disease
Neurosciences Center
  Brain Injury Program
  Brain and Spine Tumor Program

Comprehensive Epilepsy Program
Comprehensive Spasticity Management Program
Memory Disorders Program
Neuro-Oncology Cognitive Clinic
Normal Pressure Hydrocephalus
Parkinson's and Movement Disorders Program
Sleep Disorders Program
SpineCare Program
Spinal Cord Injury Center
Stroke and Neurovascular Program

COMPETITORS

Children's Hospital and Health System	Rockford Health System
Columbia St. Mary's	Waukesha Memorial
Ministry Health Care	Wheaton Franciscan Services
ProHealth Care	

HISTORICAL FINANCIALS

Company Type: Private - Not-for-Profit

Income Statement
FYE: June 30

	REVENUE ($ mil.)	NET INCOME ($ mil.)	NET PROFIT MARGIN	EMPLOYEES
06/11	980	79	8.1%	3,459
06/10	894	59	6.7%	0
06/09	810	(28)	—	0
06/08	22	0	0.1%	0
Annual Growth	252.7%	1774.9%		

2011 Year-End Financials

Debt ratio: ——
Return on equity: 8.10%
Cash ($ mil.): 41
Current ratio: 3.10
Long-term debt ($ mil.): —

Dividends
Yield: —
Payout: —
Market value ($ mil.): —

FRUIT GROWERS SUPPLY COMPANY INC

Shipping cartons are the real fruit of Fruit Growers Supply Co.'s labor (FGS). The non-profit cooperative association supplies affiliate Sunkist Growers and other agricultural businesses with packing materials fertilizer and related implements. Offerings include a range of equipment used to grow pick package and transport many commodity cash crops. FSG also provides packing services and custom design and installation of irrigation systems. It owns and operates some 335000 acres of timberland along the West coast (a source of box material and income) a carton manufacturing and supply plant and retail operations centers. Founded in 1907 FGS is owned by 6000-plus citrus growers and shippers in the US.

Most FSG products and services support members of Sunkist's marketing organization. To this end in a typical year its plant will produce 80 million citrus containers. FGS sells to non-member vineyards and ranch owners too enabling it to defray plant operating costs. Its operations centers provide over-the-counter sales customer service and support for irrigation systems as well as wind machines used to protect fruit crops from cold damage.

In addition to cartons FGS operates a pallet-manufacturing subsidiary United Wholesale Lumber which is supplied by its timberland resources.

The association is one of the largest landowners in California; its timberland (which also spans Oregon and Washington) is overseen by a forestry-trained staff that manages timber sales logging and reforestation. Although the association branched out to corrugated cardboard cartons it maintains timberland as a renewable resource to help reduce overhead expenses. This investment allows FGS to operate without additional capital investment from its members.

HISTORY

The company was formed in 1907 by the members of California Fruit Growers Exchange (now Sunkist Growers) and has grown with the expansion of citrus production in California.

EXECUTIVES

Chairman, Nicholas L. Bozick
President and CEO, Nazir Khan
VP Finance Accounting and Information Technology, John Striff
VP Supply Division and Strategic Planning Member Business, Mark Lindgren
VP Northern Operations and Strategic Planning Timberlands, Charles Brown
VP Legal Affairs and Administration, Willam Knox

LOCATIONS

HQ: Fruit Growers Supply Company
14130 Riverside Dr., Sherman Oaks CA 91423-2313
Phone: 818-986-6480   **Fax:** 818-783-1941
Web: www.fruitgrowers.com

PRODUCTS/OPERATIONS

Selected Products and Services
Agricultural Equipment
Cartons
Fertilizers and Pesticides
Grower Supplies
Harvesting Supplies
Irrigation Design and Installation
Lawn and Garden Supplies
Packaging
Packinghouse Supplies
Packing Services
Pallets
Powered Equipment
Small Engine Repair

COMPETITORS

Caraustar	Pro-Fac
Gibraltar Packaging	Rock-Tenn
Green Bay Packaging	

HISTORICAL FINANCIALS

Company Type: Private - Cooperative

Income Statement
FYE: December 31

	REVENUE ($ mil.)	NET INCOME ($ mil.)	NET PROFIT MARGIN	EMPLOYEES
12/11	177	6	3.9%	240
12/10	151	3	2.6%	0
12/09	118	10	8.6%	0
12/08	150	1	0.8%	0
Annual Growth	5.5%	80.9%	—	—

2011 Year-End Financials

Debt ratio: ——
Return on equity: 3.90%
Cash ($ mil.): 0
Current ratio: 0.70
Long-term debt ($ mil.): —

Dividends
Yield: —
Payout: —
Market value ($ mil.): —

FULLER THEOLOGICAL SEMINARY

Looking for a fuller life experience? Fuller Theological Seminary one of the largest multidenominational seminaries in the world offers just that through its schools of theology psychology and intercultural studies. It offers about 20 master's and doctoral degree programs and seven certificate programs to more than 4000 students from some 70 countries. In addition to its main campus in Pasadena California the seminary operates six regional campuses as well as online classes. It also offers degree programs in Spanish and Korean. Fuller Theological Seminary was founded in 1947 by radio evangelist Charles E. Fuller and pastor Harold John Ockenga.

The seminary offers a range of certificate programs through its Schools of Theology Intercultural Studies and Psychology. There is also a joint degree which combines the academic resources of all three schools.

Fuller Theological Seminary has campuses in California in Menlo Park Irvine and Pasadena and in Houston Phoenix Seattle and Colorado Springs Colorado.

EXECUTIVES

Chair, David L. (Dave) Bere, age 59
President, Richard J. Mouw
Associate Provost and CIO, Grant C. Millikan
SVP and Provost, Sherwood G. Lingenfelter
EVP Administration, Howard G. Wilson
VP Finance, H. Lee Merritt
Assistant VP Finance, David R. Adams
Manager Human Resources, Teresa A. Lewis
Treasurer, Warren Van Genderen
Vice Chair, Daniel L. Villanueva
Director Management Information Services, William P. Roberts
Dean Students, Ruth Vuong
Registrar, David E. Kiefer
Dean School of Theology, Howard J. Loewen
Dean School of Intercultural Studies, C. Douglas (Doug) McConnell
Dean School of Psychology, Winston E. Gooden
Controller, Christine Hong
Director Purchasing and Copy Services, Rick Steiner
Legal Counsel, Rita Rowland
Director Publications, Randall Cole
Executive Director The Fuller Foundation, Samuel L. Delcamp
VP Seminary Advancement, Joseph (Joe) Webb
Director Development Horner Center for Lifelong Learning and the School of Theology, Rolf Geying
Executive Director Brehm Center for Worship Theology and the Arts, Fred Davison
Director Doctor of Ministry, Kurt Fredrickson
Associate VP Alumni(ae) and Church Relations, Mary H. Given

LOCATIONS

HQ: Fuller Theological Seminary
  135 N. Oakland Ave., Pasadena CA 91182
Phone: 626-584-5200   **Fax:** 626-584-5449
Web: www.fuller.edu

PRODUCTS/OPERATIONS

Selected Certificate Programs

Joint Certificate
  Certificate in Urban Youth Ministry
School of Intercultural Studies
  Certificate in Global Christian Worship
  Certificate of Christian Studies
School of Psychology
  Certificate in Family and Marriage Enrichment
School of Theology
  Brehm Center Certificate in Theology and the Arts
  Certificate in Recovery Ministry
  Certificate in Youth Ministry
  Certificate of Christian Studies

Selected Centers and Institutes

African American Church Studies
Brehm Center
Center for Advanced Theological Studies
Center for Missiological Research
Depree Leadership Center
Fuller Institute for Recovery Ministry
Fuller Youth Institute
Global Research Institute
Hispanic Church Studies
Fuller Psychological and Family Services (FPFS)
Travis Research Institute
Thrive Center

HISTORICAL FINANCIALS

Company Type: School

Income Statement

	REVENUE ($ mil.)	NET INCOME ($ mil.)	NET PROFIT MARGIN	EMPLOYEES
06/11	70	10	15.5%	700
06/10	60	4	7.6%	0
06/09	66	0	—	0
06/08	58	2	4.0%	0
Annual Growth	6.6%	67.8%	—	—

2011 Year-End Financials

Debt ratio: —
Return on equity: 15.50%
Cash ($ mil.): 2
Current ratio: —
Long-term debt ($ mil.): —

Dividends
  Yield: —
  Payout: —
Market value ($ mil.): —

FULLERTON FARMERS ELEVATOR

LOCATIONS

HQ: FULLERTON FARMERS ELEVATOR
  202 MINNEAPOLIS AVE, FULLERTON, ND
  58441-4023
Phone: 701-375-7251

HISTORICAL FINANCIALS

Company Type: Private

Income Statement

	REVENUE ($ mil.)	NET INCOME ($ mil.)	NET PROFIT MARGIN	EMPLOYEES
02/12	123	(0)	—	20
02/11	83	1	1.8%	0
02/10	80	1	1.3%	0
02/09	90	1	1.5%	0
Annual Growth	10.9%	—	—	—

2012 Year-End Financials

Debt ratio: —
Return on equity: (-0.10)%
Cash ($ mil.): 0
Current ratio: —
Long-term debt ($ mil.): —

Dividends
  Yield: —
  Payout: —
Market value ($ mil.): —

FUNKHOUSER AND CO. H. N.

LOCATIONS

HQ: FUNKHOUSER AND CO. H. N.
  2150 S LOUDOUN ST, WINCHESTER, VA 22601-3615
Phone: 540-662-0833
Web: www.hnfunkhouser.com

HISTORICAL FINANCIALS

Company Type: Private

Income Statement

	REVENUE ($ mil.)	NET INCOME ($ mil.)	NET PROFIT MARGIN	EMPLOYEES
06/12	157	0	0.5%	350
06/11	146	0	0.3%	0
06/10	18	0	1.9%	0
06/09	17	0	0.4%	0
Annual Growth	108.5%	131.5%	—	—

2012 Year-End Financials

Debt ratio: —
Return on equity: 0.50%
Cash ($ mil.): 0
Current ratio: 0.40
Long-term debt ($ mil.): —

Dividends
  Yield: —
  Payout: —
Market value ($ mil.): —

FURMAN UNIVERSITY

The school's slogan could be "Go Further than Furman." More than 70% of Furman University's graduates go on to law medical or other graduate schools. The private school offers an undergraduate liberal arts curriculum and a graduate program focused on teaching and education. Furman offers more than 40 majors through more than 25 departments to some 2700 undergraduate and 200 graduate students from 45 states and close to 50 foreign countries. It also offers internship and study away programs. The student-faculty ratio is 11:1. Its 750-acre campus features a lake bell tower amphitheater and rose and Japanese gardens and is regarded as one of the most beautiful campuses in the US. Furman was founded in 1826.

Furman has formulated a strategic plan articulating its aspirations to guide the university through 2020. In a nutshell the plan which is considered a framework for its ongoing processes attempts to align the university's mission with its resources.

Key elements of the plan include reaffirming its commitment to academic excellence; maintaining competitive faculty and staff compensation levels; fostering growth of both mind and spirit through enhanced mentoring advising academic assistance and personal career and vocational counseling; renovating residence halls and the University Center; investing in development of student athletes and athletic programs; revamping admissions and financial aid policies; supporting diversity; growing the size of its student body investing in sustainability and stewardship creating a strategic information technology plan and addressing administrative and employment practices.

Furman's endowment funds for fiscal 2011 were $572 million reflecting an almost 15% increase from 2010 levels. The university receives research grants from The Library of Congress NASA the Mellon Foundation the Howard Hughes Medical Institute and other funding agencies.

The university is named for minister Richard Furman president of the first Baptist Convention in America. It wasn't until 1992 that Furman became fully independent severing formal ties with the South Carolina Baptist Convention.

EXECUTIVES

President and Trustee, David E. Shi, age 61
VP Marketing and Public Relations, Gregory A. (Greg) Carroll
VP Business Affairs, Mary Lou Merkt
VP Development, Donald J. (Don) Lineback
Provost, Tom Kazee
Accounting Manager and Bursar, Jane B. Burton
CIO, Fred Miller
VP Student Services, Connie Carson

LOCATIONS

HQ: Furman University
3300 Poinsett Hwy., Greenville SC 29613
Phone: 864-294-2000   **Fax:** 864-294-3479
Web: www.furman.edu

PRODUCTS/OPERATIONS

Selected Departments

Arts
  Art
  Music
  Theatre Arts
Business Disciplines
  Business and Accounting
Education
  Education
Humanities
  Classics
  Communication Studies
  English
  Modern Languages and Literatures
  History
  Philosophy
  Religion
Multi-Disciplinary Majors
  Asian Studies
  Neuroscience
  Sustainability Science
Sciences and Mathematics
  Biology
  Chemistry
  Computer Science
  Earth and Environmental Sciences
  Mathematics
  Physics
Social Sciences
  Economics
  Health Sciences
  Political Science
  Psychology
  Sociology
Other
  Military Science (ROTC)

Selected Student Activities

Academic organizations (33)
Athletics
  Inramural and club teams (17)
  NCAA Division I teams (17)
Community/Political organizations (28)
Fraternities (7)
Media organizations (4)
Organizations for the arts (12)
Religious organizations (15)
Sororities (8)

HISTORICAL FINANCIALS

Company Type: School

Income Statement

FYE: June 30

	REVENUE ($ mil.)	NET INCOME ($ mil.)	NET PROFIT MARGIN	EMPLOYEES
06/12	142	(5)	—	759
06/11	132	83	62.7%	0
06/10	158	(3)	—	0
06/08	142	33	23.8%	0
Annual Growth	(0.0%)	—	—	—

2012 Year-End Financials

Debt ratio: —
Return on equity: (-3.90)%
Cash ($ mil.): 20
Current ratio: —
Long-term debt ($ mil.): —

Dividends
  Yield: —
  Payout: —
  Market value ($ mil.): —

2011 Year-End Financials

Debt ratio: —
Return on equity: 0.50%
Cash ($ mil.): 2
Current ratio: 0.90
Long-term debt ($ mil.): —

Dividends
  Yield: —
  Payout: —
  Market value ($ mil.): —

FURNITURE MART USA INC.

LOCATIONS

HQ: FURNITURE MART USA INC.
140 E HINKS LN, SIOUX FALLS, SD 57104-0465
Phone: 605-336-5000
Web: www.furnitureoutletsusa.com

HISTORICAL FINANCIALS

Company Type: Private

Income Statement

FYE: December 31

	REVENUE ($ mil.)	NET INCOME ($ mil.)	NET PROFIT MARGIN	EMPLOYEES
12/11	115	5	4.5%	800
12/09	98	2	2.6%	0
12/08	108	0	—	0
12/07	119	1	1.0%	0
Annual Growth	(1.1%)	61.6%	—	—

2011 Year-End Financials

Debt ratio: —
Return on equity: 4.50%
Cash ($ mil.): 0
Current ratio: 0.20
Long-term debt ($ mil.): —

Dividends
  Yield: —
  Payout: —
  Market value ($ mil.): —

FURST-MCNESS COMPANY

LOCATIONS

HQ: FURST-MCNESS COMPANY
120 E CLARK ST, FREEPORT, IL 61032-3300
Phone: 815-235-6151
Web: www.mcness.com

HISTORICAL FINANCIALS

Company Type: Private

Income Statement

FYE: December 31

	REVENUE ($ mil.)	NET INCOME ($ mil.)	NET PROFIT MARGIN	EMPLOYEES
12/11	243	1	0.5%	245
12/10	176	(6)	—	0
Annual Growth	38.1%	—	—	—

FUTURE FOAM INC.

LOCATIONS

HQ: FUTURE FOAM INC.
1610 AVENUE N, COUNCIL BLUFFS, IA 51501-1071
Phone: 712-323-9122
Web: www.futurefoam.com

HISTORICAL FINANCIALS

Company Type: Private

Income Statement

FYE: January 31

	REVENUE ($ mil.)	NET INCOME ($ mil.)	NET PROFIT MARGIN	EMPLOYEES
01/12	379	6	1.6%	1,000
01/11	307	6	2.0%	0
01/10	282	13	4.7%	0
Annual Growth	15.8%	(32.7%)	—	—

2012 Year-End Financials

Debt ratio: —
Return on equity: 1.60%
Cash ($ mil.): 25
Current ratio: 1.40
Long-term debt ($ mil.): —

Dividends
  Yield: —
  Payout: —
  Market value ($ mil.): —

G M T CORP

LOCATIONS

HQ: G M T CORP
CARR 175 KM 27 2 SOLA ST CA, CAGUAS, PR 00725
Phone: 787-783-1988

HISTORICAL FINANCIALS

Company Type: Private

Income Statement

FYE: March 31

	REVENUE ($ mil.)	NET INCOME ($ mil.)	NET PROFIT MARGIN	EMPLOYEES
03/12	89	3	4.0%	160
03/11	86	3	3.6%	0
03/10	84	2	3.2%	0
03/09	79	2	3.0%	0
Annual Growth	3.9%	13.7%	—	—

2012 Year-End Financials

Debt ratio: —
Return on equity: 4.00%
Cash ($ mil.): 22
Current ratio: 2.50
Long-term debt ($ mil.): —

Dividends
  Yield: —
  Payout: —
  Market value ($ mil.): —

G. E. JOHNSON CONSTRUCTION COMPANY INC.

LOCATIONS

HQ: G. E. JOHNSON CONSTRUCTION COMPANY INC.
25 N CASCADE AVE STE 400, COLORADO SPRINGS, CO 80903-1647
Phone: 719-473-5321
Web: www.gejohnson.com

HISTORICAL FINANCIALS

Company Type: Private

Income Statement			FYE: September 30
	REVENUE ($ mil.)	NET INCOME ($ mil.)	NET PROFIT MARGIN	EMPLOYEES
09/11	224	1	0.8%	300
09/10	250	3	1.2%	0
09/09	307	8	2.7%	0
09/08	350	10	3.0%	0
Annual Growth	(13.8%)	(45.1%)	—	—

2011 Year-End Financials

Debt ratio: ——
Return on equity: 0.80%
Cash ($ mil.): 14
Current ratio: 0.30
Long-term debt ($ mil.): —

Dividends
Yield: —
Payout: —
Market value ($ mil.): —

G.A. WEST & CO. INC.

LOCATIONS

HQ: G.A. WEST & CO. INC.
12526 CELESTE RD, CHUNCHULA, AL 36521-3578
Phone: 251-679-1965
Web: www.gawest.com

HISTORICAL FINANCIALS

Company Type: Private

Income Statement			FYE: December 31
	REVENUE ($ mil.)	NET INCOME ($ mil.)	NET PROFIT MARGIN	EMPLOYEES
12/11	114	3	2.9%	1,000
12/10	129	8	6.2%	0
12/09	130	7	5.9%	0
12/08	116	3	3.1%	0
Annual Growth	(0.3%)	(2.7%)	—	—

2011 Year-End Financials

Debt ratio: ——
Return on equity: 2.90%
Cash ($ mil.): 0
Current ratio: —
Long-term debt ($ mil.): —

Dividends
Yield: —
Payout: —
Market value ($ mil.): —

G.S.E. CONSTRUCTION COMPANY INC.

GSE Construction Company provides heavy construction for government agencies public utilities and the private sector. The general engineering contractor specializes in building water and wastewater infrastructure. GSE provides services such as new construction renovation work and upgrades and construction labor. Projects range from retrofitting old systems and expanding capacity to constructing storage tanks treatment facilities and pump stations. The company also often teams with fellow engineering firm Applied Technologies to complete waste-to-energy conversion projects. GSE performs most of its work in California and Nevada. President and CEO Orlando Gutierrez founded GSE Construction in 1980.

EXECUTIVES

President and CEO, Orlando Gutierrez
Director Marketing Communications and Business Development, Cynthia Gutierrez
Estimator, Paul Havlicek
VP Field Operations and Project Manager, Steve Mazza
Manager Human Resources, Carol Meyer
Assistant Secretary, Dennis Gutierrez

LOCATIONS

HQ: GSE Construction Company Inc.
6950 Preston Ave., Livermore CA 94551
Phone: 925-447-0292   **Fax:** 925-447-0962
Web: www.gseconstruction.com

COMPETITORS

I.E.-Pacific
Ortiz Enterprises
Perera Construction & Design

Reyes Construction
Top Grade Construction
Western Summit Constructors

HISTORICAL FINANCIALS

Company Type: Private

Income Statement			FYE: December 31
	REVENUE ($ mil.)	NET INCOME ($ mil.)	NET PROFIT MARGIN	EMPLOYEES
12/11	58	(0)	—	245
12/10	63	0	0.5%	0
12/09	69	2	3.0%	0
12/08	76	3	5.0%	0
Annual Growth	(8.2%)	—	—	—

2011 Year-End Financials

Debt ratio: ——
Return on equity: (-0.60)%
Cash ($ mil.): 4
Current ratio: 0.60
Long-term debt ($ mil.): —

Dividends
Yield: —
Payout: —
Market value ($ mil.): —

GADSDEN INDEPENDENT SCHOOL DISTRICT

LOCATIONS

HQ: GADSDEN INDEPENDENT SCHOOL DISTRICT
4950 MCNUTT RD, SANTA TERESA, NM 88008-9621
Phone: 575-882-6200
Web: www.dves.hermiston.k12.or.us

HISTORICAL FINANCIALS

Company Type: Private

Income Statement			FYE: June 30
	REVENUE ($ mil.)	NET INCOME ($ mil.)	NET PROFIT MARGIN	EMPLOYEES
06/11	151	6	4.6%	2,000
06/05	6	(51)	—	0
06/04	115	1	1.0%	0
06/03	0	0	—	0
Annual Growth	—	—	—	—

2011 Year-End Financials

Debt ratio: ——
Return on equity: 4.60%
Cash ($ mil.): 17
Current ratio: 1.20
Long-term debt ($ mil.): —

Dividends
Yield: —
Payout: —
Market value ($ mil.): —

GAFFNEY-KROESE ELECTRICAL SUPPLY CORPORATION

LOCATIONS

HQ: GAFFNEY-KROESE ELECTRICAL SUPPLY CORPORATION
50 RANDOLPH RD, SOMERSET, NJ 08873-1240
Phone: 732-885-9000

HISTORICAL FINANCIALS

Company Type: Private

Income Statement			FYE: December 31
	REVENUE ($ mil.)	NET INCOME ($ mil.)	NET PROFIT MARGIN	EMPLOYEES
12/11	204	4	2.4%	260
12/10	155	3	2.1%	0
12/09	190	3	1.8%	0
12/08	280	9	3.5%	0
Annual Growth	(10.0%)	(21.0%)	—	—

2011 Year-End Financials

Debt ratio: ——
Return on equity: 2.40%
Cash ($ mil.): 1
Current ratio: 0.70
Long-term debt ($ mil.): —

Dividends
Yield: —
Payout: —
Market value ($ mil.): —

GALLUP INC.

More than a pollster Gallup draws from its research and behavioral studies to offer consulting services related to performance management. Other specialties include branding marketing and recruiting. The company delivers its services on the Web through its Gallup University campuses and through more than 40 global offices. It draws customers from a variety of industries including automotive business services health care hospitality manufacturing and retail. Despite its diversified business offerings the company is still most famous for its Gallup Poll surveys. It is owned by its employees.

Operations

In addition to its famous polls and research surveys (conducted in 160 countries) the company's Gallup Consulting division provides expertise in measuring employee satisfaction and engagement and in teaching managers and workers how to develop their strengths in order to be the best at their jobs.

Strategy

Gallup consultants help private and public sector organizations boost organic growth through measurement tools strategic advice and education. It has a staff of 2000 professionals who deliver services at client organizations through the Web and in more than 40 offices around the world.

The company's reputation for accuracy took a hit in 2012 when its polling showed Republican US Presidential contender Mitt Romney with a significant lead among likely voters just 10 days before the November 6 US Presidential election and slightly ahead of the incumbent (Barack Obama) on the eve of the election. Obama won the election by more than 3 percentage points prompting Gallup to reexamine its modeling data and presuppositions.

Ownership

Gallup is an employee-owned company.

Company Background

The company was founded in 1935 by Dr. George Gallup a pioneer in the science of polling.

EXECUTIVES

CIO, Phil Ruhlman
Vice Chairman; Dean Gallup University, Connie Rath
Vice Chairman Research and Development, Gale D. Muller
General Counsel and Executive Publisher Gallup, Steve D. O'Brien
Director Corporate Communications, Sarah Van Allen
EVP and COO, Jane E. Miller, age 47
Chief Marketing Officer; Executive Publisher Gallup Press, Lawrence M. (Larry) Emond
Chairman and CEO, Jim Clifton
Vice Chairman and CFO, James (Jim) Krieger
Editor-in-Chief Gallup, Frank M. Newport
Regional Managing Partner-East, Kevin McConville
Chief Global Talent Resources, Matt Mosser
Chief Economist, Dennis Jacobe
Regional Director Middle East and North Africa, Richard W. Burkholder Jr.
Regional Director Former Soviet Union Countries, Neli Esipova
Regional Director Latin America, Johanna Godoy
Senior Analyst and Executive Director Gallup Center for Muslim Studies, Dalia Mogahed
Regional Director Europe, Zsolt Nyiri
Regional Director Latin America, Jesus Rios
Regional Director Asia, Rajesh Srinivasan

Regional Director Sub-Saharan Africa, Robert D. Tortora
Chief Scientist, Jim Asplund
Chief Scientist, John H. Fleming
Chief Scientist, James K. Harter
Global Practice Leader Brand Engagement, William J. McEwen
Global Practice Leader Workplace and Leadership, Tom Rath
Senior Director Media Strategies, Eric Nielsen
Regional Managing Partner-Midwest, Randy Beck
Global Practice Leader Brand and Customer Engagement, Ed O'Boyle
Executive Director Gallup University, Timothy D. Hodges
Editorial Director Gallup Press, Geoffrey Brewer
Vice Chairman; Dean Gallup University, Connie Rath
Vice Chairman and CFO, James (Jim) Krieger
Auditors: KPMG

LOCATIONS

HQ: Gallup Inc.
901 F St. NW, Washington DC 20004
Phone: 202-715-3030   **Fax:** 202-715-3045
Web: www.gallup.com

PRODUCTS/OPERATIONS

Selected Consulting Practice Areas

Customer relationship management
Employee development and training
Employee performance measurement
Employee relationship management
Executive coaching
Performance strategy analysis
Sales force training
Succession planning
Talent-based hiring

Selected Gallup Poll Topics

Business
Economics
Education
Government and public affairs
Healthcare
Lifestyle issues
Politics and elections
Religion and values
Other Products and Services
Books
Gallup University (management education)
Subscription publications

COMPETITORS

Abt Associates	IBOPE Zogby
Bain & Company	International
Booz Allen	International
Boston Consulting	Demographics
Development Dimensions	J.D. Power
International	Kantar Group
Edison Media Research	Maritz
Harris Interactive	McKinsey & Company
Hay Group	ORC International

HISTORICAL FINANCIALS

Company Type: Private

Income Statement   FYE: December 31

	REVENUE ($ mil.)	NET INCOME ($ mil.)	NET PROFIT MARGIN	EMPLOYEES
12/11	303	34	11.2%	2,000
12/09	264	6	2.6%	0
12/08	300	21	7.0%	0
12/07	271	20	7.6%	0
Annual Growth	3.7%	18.2%	—	—

2011 Year-End Financials

Debt ratio: ——
Return on equity: 11.20%
Cash ($ mil.): 35
Current ratio: 0.90
Long-term debt ($ mil.): —

Dividends
Yield: —
Payout: —
Market value ($ mil.): —

GANNETT FLEMING AFFILIATES INC

LOCATIONS

HQ: GANNETT FLEMING AFFILIATES INC
207 SENATE AVE, CAMP HILL, PA 17011-2316
Phone: 717-763-7211
Web: www.gannettfleming.com

HISTORICAL FINANCIALS

Company Type: Private

Income Statement   FYE: December 31

	REVENUE ($ mil.)	NET INCOME ($ mil.)	NET PROFIT MARGIN	EMPLOYEES
12/11	290	5	1.8%	1,550
12/10	290	3	1.1%	0
12/09	285	12	4.4%	0
12/08	253	6	2.4%	0
Annual Growth	4.6%	(5.4%)	—	—

2011 Year-End Financials

Debt ratio: ——
Return on equity: 1.80%
Cash ($ mil.): 0
Current ratio: 1.50
Long-term debt ($ mil.): —

Dividends
Yield: —
Payout: —
Market value ($ mil.): —

GASTON COUNTY SCHOOL DISTRICT

LOCATIONS

HQ: GASTON COUNTY SCHOOL DISTRICT
943 OSCEOLA ST, GASTONIA, NC 28054-5482
Phone: 704-866-6100

HISTORICAL FINANCIALS

Company Type: Private

Income Statement   FYE: June 30

	REVENUE ($ mil.)	NET INCOME ($ mil.)	NET PROFIT MARGIN	EMPLOYEES
06/12	262	4	1.6%	3,824
06/11	269	8	3.0%	0
06/10	264	2	0.9%	0
06/09	276	2	0.9%	0
Annual Growth	(1.7%)	19.4%	—	—

Debt ratio: —
Return on equity: 1.60%
Cash ($ mil.): 28
Current ratio: —
Long-term debt ($ mil.): —

Dividends
Yield: —
Payout: —
Market value ($ mil.): —

GASTON MEMORIAL HOSPITAL INC

LOCATIONS

HQ: GASTON MEMORIAL HOSPITAL INC
2525 COURT DR, GASTONIA, NC 28054-2182
Phone: 704-834-2000
Web: www.caromonthealth.org

HISTORICAL FINANCIALS

Company Type: Private

Income Statement

	REVENUE ($ mil.)	NET INCOME ($ mil.)	NET PROFIT MARGIN	EMPLOYEES
06/11	410	32	8.0%	1,849
06/10	383	25	6.7%	0
06/08	0	(0)	—	0
06/06	340	64	18.8%	0
Annual Growth	6.4%	(20.0%)	—	—

FYE: June 30

GBS CORP.

LOCATIONS

HQ: GBS CORP.
7233 FREEDOM AVE NW, CANTON, OH 44720-7123
Phone: 330-494-5330
Web: www.gbsohio.com

HISTORICAL FINANCIALS

Company Type: Private

Income Statement

FYE: December 31

	REVENUE ($ mil.)	NET INCOME ($ mil.)	NET PROFIT MARGIN	EMPLOYEES
12/11	87	8	9.6%	315
12/10	82	7	9.2%	0
12/09	76	5	6.9%	0
12/08	83	4	5.8%	0
Annual Growth	1.7%	20.1%	—	—

2011 Year-End Financials

Debt ratio: —
Return on equity: 9.60%
Cash ($ mil.): 1
Current ratio: 1.00
Long-term debt ($ mil.): —

Dividends
Yield: —
Payout: —
Market value ($ mil.): —

GEL SPICE CO. INC.

LOCATIONS

HQ: GEL SPICE CO. INC.
48 HOOK RD, BAYONNE, NJ 07002-5007
Phone: 201-339-0700
Web: www.gel-spice.com

HISTORICAL FINANCIALS

Company Type: Private

Income Statement

FYE: June 30

	REVENUE ($ mil.)	NET INCOME ($ mil.)	NET PROFIT MARGIN	EMPLOYEES
06/12	92	1	1.1%	200
06/11	81	0	1.2%	0
06/10	76	(3)	—	0
06/09	72	0	1.0%	0
Annual Growth	8.3%	10.8%	—	—

GENESIS CORP.

Genesis Corp.'s raison d'etre is business and technology consulting. Focused on helping organizations streamline processes manage employees and minimize costs the company (doing business as Genesis10) provides services in areas such as project management application development enterprise systems integration staffing and management support. Genesis10 which employs more than 2000 consultants operates from more than 10 offices in the US and Canada; it has served customers in the insurance (UnitedHealth Group) financial services (Citigroup) and entertainment (Caesars Entertainment) industries among others. CEO Harley Lippman established Genesis10 in 1999.

The company's managed service program assists businesses in managing its workforce as well as outsourced work. Genesis10 helps organizations in hiring compliance and change management issues.

EXECUTIVES

CFO, Glenn Klein
Director IT, Vinny Ruallo
Director Human Resources, Sarah Cernohous
SVP Sales, Angie Brekke
CEO, Harley Lippman

LOCATIONS

HQ: GENESIS CORP.
950 3RD AVE STE 2702, NEW YORK, NY 10022-2874
Phone: 212-688-5522
Web: www.genesis10.com

COMPETITORS

Accenture	Boston Consulting
Bain & Company	Deloitte Consulting
Booz Allen	McKinsey & Company

HISTORICAL FINANCIALS

Company Type: Private

Income Statement

FYE: December 31

	REVENUE ($ mil.)	NET INCOME ($ mil.)	NET PROFIT MARGIN	EMPLOYEES
12/11	218	11	5.5%	2,105
12/10	173	10	6.1%	0
12/08	122	2	2.2%	0
12/07	130	3	2.5%	0
Annual Growth	18.6%	53.7%	—	—

2011 Year-End Financials

Debt ratio: —
Return on equity: 5.50%
Cash ($ mil.): 6
Current ratio: 1.30
Long-term debt ($ mil.): —

Dividends
Yield: —
Payout: —
Market value ($ mil.): —

GENESIS HEALTH INC.

Brooks helps people get back on their feet — often literally. Brooks Health System operates Brooks Rehabilitation Hospital a 160-bed facility dedicated to helping patients recover from injury and illness. Rehabilitation services include physical occupational speech aquatic and recreational therapy. The not-for-profit hospital also helps patients coping with chronic pain cognitive disorders and other long-term disabilities. Brooks Health System provides outpatient care through a network of more than two dozen rehab clinics a nursing home and a home health care agency in northern Florida and southeastern Georgia. The system is a research affiliate of the Health Science Center at the University of Florida.

Operations

Brooks Rehabilitation Hospital offers specialized programs for patients recovering from such incidents as stroke traumatic brain injury and limb amputation. As part of its continuum of care the hospital operates the Brooks Home Care Advantage agency which provides a range of home care services to its patients including skilling nursing infusion therapy and advanced cardiac care. The Brooks Health System's affiliated nursing home Brooks San Marco Terrace provides traditional skilled nursing as well as rehabilitation services.

The Brooks Clinical Research Center conducts clinical trials for new medicines and medical devices in the rehabilitation therapy market through partnerships with manufacturers and other research entities. Specific fields of research include stroke recovery spinal cord and brain injuries and communication and cognitive skills recovery.

EXECUTIVES

Vice Chairman, Bruce M. Johnson, age 64
President and CEO, Douglas M. (Doug) Baer
Chief Medical Officer; Medical Director Brooks Rehabilitation Hospital, Deborah Stewart
President Brooks Clinical Research and External Affairs, Charles Schauer
Chairman, Gary W. Sneed
Clinical Coordinator Brooks Center, Floris (Flo) Singletary
Associate Medical Director; Medical Director Spinal Cord Injury Center of Excellence, Jeff Johns

212

Medical Director Admitting Consulting Physician, Kerry Maher

Medical Director Stroke Center of Excellence, Trevor Paris

Co-Medical Director Pediatric Center of Excellence, Connie Prudencio

Medical Director Orthopedic Center of Excellence, Howard Weiss

COO, Michael Spigel

CFO, Odin Berg

VP Human Resources and Learning, Karen Gallagher

SVP Clinical Services Hospital Administrator, Patricia (Pattie) deBear

SVP Brooks Home Care Advantage, Karen Wright-Bennett

Secretary, Stanley Carter

Executive Director Community Health, Marion Anderson

Interim Director Brooks Center, Alan Berger

Brooks Rehabilitation Research Director, Holly Morris

Marketing Manager, Jill Matejcek

Executive Director Business Development and Planning, Brian Fuller

Director Information Technology Operations, Michael Helinsky

VP Outpatient Operations, Ramsey Carol

Controller and Director Accounting, Pat Rausch

LOCATIONS

HQ: Brooks Health System
3599 University Blvd. South, Jacksonville FL 32216
Phone: 904-858-7600 **Fax:** 904-858-7619
Web: www.brookshealth.org

PRODUCTS/OPERATIONS

Selected Medical Services

Adaptive Sports and Recreation
Amputee Rehabilitation
Aphasia Program
Aquatic (Pool) Therapy
Behavioral Medicine
Biofeedback
Brain Injury Rehabilitation
Brain Injury Wellness
Case Management
Certified Rehabilitation Nursing
Chaplain Services
Clinical Research Center
Cognitive Rehabilitation Therapy
Clubhouse
Community Health Programs
Community Re-entry
Counseling Services
Clinical Education
Dietitian Services
Driver Rehabilitation
Environmental Control Lab
Fellowship Programs
Functional Capacity Evaluations
Hip Fracture Rehabilitation
Home Safety Assessment
Independent Exercise
Industrial Rehabilitation
Integrated Care
Neurological Disorders Rehabilitation
Neuropsychology
Neuro Recovery Center
Neuro Rehab Day Treatment
Occupational Therapy
Orthopedic Rehabilitation
Pain Rehabilitation
Parastep System
Peer Mentoring
Pediatric Rehabilitation

Physiatry
Physical Therapy
Psychology

Recreational Therapy
Research
Residency Programs
Response Evaluation
SaeboFlex
School Re-entry
Spasticity Management
Speech-Language Pathology
Spinal Cord Injury Rehabilitation
Sports Therapy
Stroke Rehabilitation
Stroke Wellness Program
Support Groups
Swallowing Disorders Program
Therapy Dogs
Vestibular and Balance Rehabilitation
VitalStim Swallowing
Volunteer Services
Wheelchair Clinic
Women's Health
Worker's Compensation
Zero G

COMPETITORS

Baptist Health System
HealthSouth
Kindred Healthcare
Orange Park Medical
RehabCare
Select Medical

St. Vincent' s Health System
Sun Healthcare
U.S. Physical Therapy
UF&Shands

HISTORICAL FINANCIALS

Company Type: Private - Not-for-Profit

Income Statement
FYE: December 31

	REVENUE ($ mil.)	NET INCOME ($ mil.)	NET PROFIT MARGIN	EMPLOYEES
12/11	123	(19)	—	1,400
12/10	119	27	23.1%	0
12/09	98	36	36.9%	0
12/08	68	(107)	—	0
Annual Growth	21.5%	—	—	—

2011 Year-End Financials

Debt ratio: ——
Return on equity: (-15.80)%
Cash ($ mil.): 5
Current ratio: 0.30
Long-term debt ($ mil.): —

Dividends
Yield: —
Payout: —
Market value ($ mil.): —

GENESIS HEALTH SYSTEM

Genesis Health System operates three acute care hospitals in Iowa and Illinois that have more than 660 beds total and employ some 600 doctors. Genesis Medical Center in Davenport Iowa with more than 500 beds is the system's flagship facility; the hospital offers a range of general surgical and specialist health services. The system's Illini Campus in Silvis Illinois features an assisted-living center. The Genesis Medical Center Dewitt Campus serves that Iowa town and the surrounding area with its 13-bed hospital nursing home and related care facilities. Genesis Health System also operates physician practices outpatient centers and a home health agency.

Strategy In mid-2012 Genesis Health System joined with Wellmark Blue Cross and Blue Shield of Iowa to create an accountable care organization (ACO) in an effort to improve the quality and slow the costs of healthcare. In an ACO provider reimbursements are related to the quality of the care.

Company Background Genesis Health System had its genesis in 1869 with the establishment of Mercy Hospital (one of the first hospitals west of the Mississippi) and in the 1895 founding of St. Luke's Hospital. The two hospitals merged in 1994 to form the health system.

EXECUTIVES

VP Information Systems and CIO, Robert (Rob) Frieden

VP; CEO Genesis Medical Center DeWitt, Jeffrey M. (Jeff) Cooper

VP Strategic Development, Robert (Bob) Travis

VP Quality, James Lehman

VP Human Resources, Jerry McCormick

VP Corporate Communications and Marketing, Kenneth (Ken) Croken

President and CEO, Douglas P. Cropper

VP Medical Staff Affairs, Frank Claudy

VP Clinical Services, Rob Nelson

Medical Director, Bill Langley

VP Legal Affairs, Judith Mondello

Interim VP Patient Services, Judy Pranger

VP Finance and CFO, Mark Rogers

VP Support Services, Mike Sharp

VP; Interim President Genesis Medical Center Illini, Florence (Flo) Spyrow

LOCATIONS

HQ: Genesis Health System
1227 E. Rusholme St., Davenport IA 52803
Phone: 563-421-1000 **Fax:** 563-421-6500
Web: www.genesishealth.com

PRODUCTS/OPERATIONS

Selected Services

Bariatric Surgery
Behavioral Health
Birthing Services
Cancer
Cardiology
Home Health/Hospice
Neuroscience
Nursing Homes
Physical Medicine & Rehab
Senior Services

COMPETITORS

Blessing Hospital
Catholic Health Initiatives
Iowa Health System
McDonough District Hospital
Mercy Health Network
ORHC
OSF Healthcare System
University of Iowa Hospitals and Clinics

HISTORICAL FINANCIALS

Company Type: Private - Not-for-Profit

Income Statement
FYE: June 30

	REVENUE ($ mil.)	NET INCOME ($ mil.)	NET PROFIT MARGIN	EMPLOYEES
06/11	446	11	2.6%	5,000
06/10	461	16	3.5%	0
06/09	993	0	—	0
06/08	3	1	46.3%	0
Annual Growth	424.9%	100.6%	—	—

2011 Year-End Financials

Debt ratio: ——
Return on equity: 2.60%
Cash ($ mil.): 53
Current ratio: 0.80
Long-term debt ($ mil.): ——

Dividends
Yield: ——
Payout: ——
Market value ($ mil.): ——

GEORGETOWN HOSPITAL SYSTEM

LOCATIONS

HQ: GEORGETOWN HOSPITAL SYSTEM
4070 HIGHWAY 17, MURRELLS INLET, SC
29576-5033
Phone: 843-652-1315
Web: www.georgetownhospitalsystem.org

PRODUCTS/OPERATIONS

Selected Services
Bone joint spine
Cancer
Diagnostic imaging
Heart/stroke
Hospital
Primary care
Surgical
Women's/obstetrics

HISTORICAL FINANCIALS

Company Type: Private

Income Statement

FYE: September 30

	REVENUE ($ mil.)	NET INCOME ($ mil.)	NET PROFIT MARGIN	EMPLOYEES
09/11	274	9	3.5%	4
09/10	262	11	4.3%	0
09/09	0	0	——	0
Annual Growth	——	——	——	——

2011 Year-End Financials

Debt ratio: ——
Return on equity: 3.50%
Cash ($ mil.): 53
Current ratio: 2.50
Long-term debt ($ mil.): ——

Dividends
Yield: ——
Payout: ——
Market value ($ mil.): ——

GEORGETOWN MEMORIAL HOSPITAL

Georgetown Hospital System may be set amidst the Antebellum grace of the South but its health care services are far from antiquated. The system on the southeast coast of South Carolina operates Georgetown Memorial Hospital an acute-care facility with more than 130 beds and Waccamaw Community Hospital which operates with more than 170 beds. Georgetown Memorial Hospital features an ICU cardiac and surgical services labor and delivery and a pediatric wing. Waccamaw Commu-

nity Hospital covering the northern part of the system's service area provides 24-hour emergency services rehabilitation obstetrics and inpatient and outpatient surgery. The organization is led by CEO Bruce Bailey.

Operations

Along with the two hospitals Georgetown Hospital System operates numerous outpatient facilities including wound care diagnostic imaging rehabilitation cancer treatment and breast health centers. The system employs about 350 physicians and handles about 58000 emergency room visits each year. It also provides about $30 million in charity care to uninsured or under-insured patients each year.

Strategy

Georgetown Hospital System works to improve care through measures including adding new resources and services upgrading its facilities and enhancing its technology systems. In 2012 the system completed an expansion project on the Waccamaw Community Hospital campus adding a 90000 sq. ft. medical office housing physician practices and centers for endoscopy rehabilitation pain management and other specialty services.

EXECUTIVES

CIO, Frank Scafidi
President and CEO, Bruce P. Bailey
VP and CFO, Terry L. Kiser
Chief Nursing Officer and Associate Administrator Patient Care Services Georgetown Memorial Hospital, Ann Waters
Administrator Operations Georgetown Memorial Hospital, Suzanne Doscher
Administrator Operations Waccamaw Community Hospital, Oscar K. Weinmeister III
Administrator Patient Care Services Waccamaw Community Hospital, Pam Maxwell
Assistant Administrator ? NextStep Services, John LaRochelle
VP Medical Affairs, Roy E. (Reg) Gilbreath
Chief of Staff Georgetown Memorial Hospital, Joseph J. Gammel
Vice-Chief of Staff Georgetown Memorial Hospita, Walter L. Frank
Chief of Staff Waccamaw Community Hospital, David G. Thomas
Vice-Chief of Staff Waccamaw Community Hospita, E. Victor Archambeau

LOCATIONS

HQ: Georgetown Hospital System
606 Black River Rd., Georgetown SC 29442
Phone: 843-527-7000   **Fax:** 843-527-7025
Web: www.gmhsc.com

PRODUCTS/OPERATIONS

Selected Services
Bone joint spine
Cancer
Diagnostic imaging
Heart/stroke
Hospital
Primary care
Surgical
Women's/obstetrics

COMPETITORS

Carolinas HealthCare
  System
Carolinas Hospital
  System
Greenville Hospital
  System
Laurens County
  Hospital

Grand Strand Regional
  Medical Center
Palmetto Health

HISTORICAL FINANCIALS

Company Type: Private - Not-for-Profit

Income Statement

FYE: September 30

	REVENUE ($ mil.)	NET INCOME ($ mil.)	NET PROFIT MARGIN	EMPLOYEES
09/11	120	8	6.7%	1,300
09/09	125	(4)	——	0
09/08	118	(11)	——	0
09/07	120	22	18.5%	0
Annual Growth	(0.0%)	(28.9%)	——	——

2011 Year-End Financials

Debt ratio: ——
Return on equity: 6.70%
Cash ($ mil.): 49
Current ratio: 2.80
Long-term debt ($ mil.): ——

Dividends
Yield: ——
Payout: ——
Market value ($ mil.): ——

GEORGIA ENERGY COOPERATIVE (AN ELECTRIC MEMBERSHIP CORPORATION)

LOCATIONS

HQ: GEORGIA ENERGY COOPERATIVE (AN ELECTRIC MEMBERSHIP CORPORATION)
2100 E EXCH PL STE 300, TUCKER, GA 30084
Phone: 770-270-7500

HISTORICAL FINANCIALS

Company Type: Private

Income Statement

FYE: December 31

	REVENUE ($ mil.)	NET INCOME ($ mil.)	NET PROFIT MARGIN	EMPLOYEES
12/11	214	0	0.4%	4
12/10	113	1	0.9%	0
12/09	80	0	0.7%	0
12/08	33	0	——	0
Annual Growth	86.0%	——	——	——

2011 Year-End Financials

Debt ratio: ——
Return on equity: 0.40%
Cash ($ mil.): 2
Current ratio: 0.90
Long-term debt ($ mil.): ——

Dividends
Yield: ——
Payout: ——
Market value ($ mil.): ——

GEORGIA SOUTHERN UNIVERSITY

Georgia Southern University shows students that higher education can be just peachy. Georgia Southern offers more than 100 bachelor master and doctoral programs from eight colleges; academic fields include business education science and public health. One of 35 colleges and universities in the University System of Georgia it enrolls more than 17000 students most of which hail from Georgia. Georgia Southern has graduate centers in Augusta Brunswick Dublin and Savannah; it also offers distance learning programs. Founded as a district agricultural school in 1906 the institution became a university in 1990.

EXECUTIVES

President, Bruce Grube
VP Business and Finance, Ronald J. Core
Controller, Kim Thompson
VP Academic Affairs and Provost, Linda M. Bleicken
VP Student Affairs and Enrollment Management, Teresa E. Thompson
VP University Advancement, William I. Griffis
Associate VP Center for International Studies, Nancy W. Shumaker
Director Administrative Office of Alumni Relations, Frank Hook III
Director Business and Finance, Keith Roughton
Director Student Affairs Office of Career Services, Warren Riles
Director Office of Financial Accounting, William C. Bird
Director Administrative Department of Procurement and Contract Services, George A. Horn
Registrar, Thomas M. Deal
Director Student Affairs and Enrollment Management Technical Services, Theodore E. Williams
Director Advancement Services, Jodi R. Collins
Director Admissions, Susan Braxton Davies
Controller, Georj L. Lewis
Director Student Affairs Office of Financial Aid, Connie Griggs Murphey
Associate Director Human Resources, Melanee Jo Morales
VP Information Technology Services, Steve Burrell
Associate Dean Library, Ann H. Hamilton
Director Administrative Office of Marketing and Communications, Christian H. Flathman
Dean College of Business Administration, Ronald E. Shiffler
Dean College of Education, Lucindia Chance
Dean College of Graduate Studies, Timothy P. Mack
Dean College of Health and Human Services, Frederick K. Whitt
Dean Jiann-Ping Hsu College of Public Health, Charles J. Hardy
Dean College of Liberal Arts and Social Sciences, Sue M. Moore
Dean College Science and Technology, Bret S. Danilowicz
Director Center for Sustainability, Lissa Leege

LOCATIONS

HQ: GEORGIA SOUTHERN UNIVERSITY
1582 SOUTHERN DR, STATESBORO, GA 30458
Phone: 912-681-5224
Web: www.gsustore.com

HISTORICAL FINANCIALS
Company Type: School

Income Statement

	REVENUE ($ mil.)	NET INCOME ($ mil.)	NET PROFIT MARGIN	EMPLOYEES
06/11	177	10	5.8%	1,700
06/10	151	9	6.0%	0
06/09	6	(0)	—	0
06/08	125	6	5.2%	0
Annual Growth	12.3%	16.9%	—	—

FYE: June 30

2011 Year-End Financials

Debt ratio: —
Return on equity: 5.80%
Cash ($ mil.): 30
Current ratio: 2.30
Long-term debt ($ mil.): —

Dividends
Yield: —
Payout: —
Market value ($ mil.): —

GEORGIA TECH APPLIED RESEARCH CORPORATION

LOCATIONS

HQ: GEORGIA TECH APPLIED RESEARCH CORPORATION
505 10TH ST NW, ATLANTA, GA 30318-5775
Phone: 404-894-4819
Web: www.gtrc.gatech.edu

HISTORICAL FINANCIALS
Company Type: Private

Income Statement

	REVENUE ($ mil.)	NET INCOME ($ mil.)	NET PROFIT MARGIN	EMPLOYEES
06/12	239	0	0.0%	1,100
06/11	208	0	0.1%	0
06/10	196	(0)	—	0
06/09	162	0	—	0
Annual Growth	13.7%	—	—	—

FYE: June 30

2012 Year-End Financials

Debt ratio: —
Return on equity: —
Cash ($ mil.): 21
Current ratio: 1.40
Long-term debt ($ mil.): —

Dividends
Yield: —
Payout: —
Market value ($ mil.): —

GERALD H. PHIPPS INC.

LOCATIONS

HQ: GERALD H. PHIPPS INC.
5995 GREENWOOD STE 100, GREENWOOD VILLAGE, CO 80111
Phone: 303-571-5377
Web: www.geraldhphipps.com

HISTORICAL FINANCIALS
Company Type: Private

Income Statement

	REVENUE ($ mil.)	NET INCOME ($ mil.)	NET PROFIT MARGIN	EMPLOYEES
10/11	131	(0)	—	350
10/10	203	1	0.5%	0
10/09	179	0	0.2%	0
10/08	283	1	0.6%	0
Annual Growth	(22.6%)	—	—	—

FYE: October 31

2011 Year-End Financials

Debt ratio: —
Return on equity: (-0.70)%
Cash ($ mil.): 17
Current ratio: 1.30
Long-term debt ($ mil.): —

Dividends
Yield: —
Payout: —
Market value ($ mil.): —

GETTYSBURG COLLEGE

Four score and many years ago Gettysburg College opened its doors. The private four-year liberal arts and sciences college offers about 65 academic programs and about 40 majors to 2600 students who come from more than 40 states and 35 countries. Gettysburg's student-faculty ratio is 10:1. The campus is adjacent to the Gettysburg National Military Park in Pennsylvania. The college was founded in 1832; its first building Pennsylvania Hall served during and after the Battle of Gettysburg as a hospital for the wounded. In 1863 students and faculty of Gettysburg College walked from Pennsylvania Hall to the national cemetery in Gettysburg to hear President Lincoln deliver his legendary Gettysburg Address.

The historic setting for the college places students in close proximity to other national treasures in the cities Baltimore (one hour away) Washington DC (an hour and a half away) and Philadelphia (two hours away).

Gettysburg College has a 100% tenured faculty all holding either PhD or terminal degrees. Student-faculty collaboration at Gettysburg College is supported in part by a $500000 grant from The Andrew W. Mellon Foundation.

Other learning opportunities include the college's study abroad programs. Nearly half of Gettysburg's students spend at least one semester abroad some as interns some conducting research studying languages or pursuing other academic experiences.

EXECUTIVES

Associate VP Communications and Public Relations, Patricia A. Lawson
EVP, Jane D. North
Co-Director Human Resources and Risk Management, Regina Z. Campo
Co-Director Human Resources and Risk Management, Jennifer R. (Jen) Lucas
Director Alumni Relations, Joe Lynch
Director Financial Aid, Christine L. Gormley
Associate Director Financial Aid, Jean M. Stone
VP Information Technology, Rodney S. (Rod) Tosten
Assistant Dean Director Security and Director Greek Organization, William J. (Bill) Lafferty
Interim President, Janet Morgan Riggs
Acting Provost, Jay White
Acting Vice Provost, Kathleen Cain

Director Environmental Health and Safety,
William Shoemaker
Registrar, Michael E. Maysilles
VP Finanace and Administration, Daniel Konstalid

LOCATIONS

HQ: Gettysburg College
300 N. Washington St., Gettysburg PA 17325
Phone: 717-337-6300   **Fax:** 717-337-6666
Web: www.gettysburg.edu

PRODUCTS/OPERATIONS

Selected Departments and Programs

Africana Studies (Major Minor)
Anthropology (Major Minor)
Art and Art History (Major Minor)
Asian Studies
    Chinese Studies (Major)
    East Asian Studies (Minor)
    Japanese Studies (Major Minor)
Biology (Major Minor)
    Biochemistry and Molecular Biology (Major)
    Neuroscience (Minor)
    Nursing Articulation Agreement (Program)
    Optometry Articulation Agreements (Program)
    Physical Therapy Articulation Agreement (Program)
    Pre-Health Professions Advising (Program)
Chemistry (Major Minor)
    Biochemistry and Molecular Biology (Major)
    Neuroscience (Minor)
    Nursing Articulation Agreement (Program)
    Optometry Articulation Agreements (Program)
    Physical Therapy Articulation Agreement (Program)
    Pre-Health Professions Advising (Program)
Civil War Era Studies (Minor)
    History (Major Minor)
Classics (Major Minor)
    Greek (Minor)
    Latin (Minor)
Computer Science (Major Minor)
    Mathematics (Major Minor)
Conservatory of Music
    Music/Sunderman Conservatory of Music (Major Minor)
Economics (Major Minor)
    Public Policy (Major Dual Major)
Education (Minor)
English (Major Minor)
    Writing (Minor)
Environmental Studies (Major Minor)
    Public Policy (Major Dual Major)
French (Major Minor)
German (Major Minor)
Globalization Studies (Major)
Health Sciences (Major Minor)
    Nursing Articulation Agreement (Program)
    Optometry Articulation Agreements (Program)
    Physical Therapy Articulation Agreement (Program)
    Pre-Health Professions Advising (Program)
History Major (Minor)
    Civil War Era Studies (Minor)
Interdisciplinary Studies
    Film Studies (Minor)
    Individual (Self-designed Major)
    Interdisciplinary studies (Program)
    Peace and Justice Studies (Minor)
    Pre-Law Advising (Program)
International Affairs (Major Dual Major)
Italian Studies (Major Minor)
Latin American Studies (Minor)
    Latin American Studies/(Spanish Major)
Management
    Business (Minor)
    Organization and Management Studies (Major)
    Computer Science (Major Minor)
Mathematics (Major Minor)
Peace and Justice Studies (Minor)
Philosophy (Major Minor)
Physics
    Engineering (Dual Degree Program)
    Physics (Major Minor)
Political Science
    International Affairs (Major Dual Major)

Political Science (Major Minor)
    Public Policy (Major Dual Major)
Psychology
    Neuroscience (Minor)
    Psychology (Major)
Public Policy (Major Dual Major)
Religious Studies
    Judaic Studies (Minor)
    Religious Studies (Major Minor)
Sociology (Major Minor)
Spanish
    Latin American Studies (Minor)
    Latin American Studies/Spanish (Major)
    Spanish (Major Minor)
Theatre Arts (Major Minor)
Women Gender and Sexuality Studies (Major Minor)

HISTORICAL FINANCIALS

Company Type: School

Income Statement   FYE: May 31

	REVENUE ($ mil.)	NET INCOME ($ mil.)	NET PROFIT MARGIN	EMPLOYEES
05/12	122	(4)	—	0
05/11	115	32	27.7%	0
05/10	112	23	20.7%	0
05/09	110	(66)	—	0
Annual Growth	3.3%	—	—	—

2012 Year-End Financials

Debt ratio: ——
Return on equity: (-3.70)%
Cash ($ mil.): 46
Current ratio: ——
Long-term debt ($ mil.): ——

Dividends
    Yield: ——
    Payout: ——
Market value ($ mil.): ——

GIBSON ELECTRIC MEMBERSHIP CORPORATION

LOCATIONS

HQ: GIBSON ELECTRIC MEMBERSHIP CORPORATION
1207 S COLLEGE ST, TRENTON, TN 38382-3605
Phone: 731-855-4740

HISTORICAL FINANCIALS

Company Type: Private

Income Statement   FYE: December 31

	REVENUE ($ mil.)	NET INCOME ($ mil.)	NET PROFIT MARGIN	EMPLOYEES
12/11*	84	4	5.5%	85
06/11	87	5	5.8%	0
06/10	77	5	6.6%	0
06/08	71	3	5.4%	0
Annual Growth	5.7%	6.3%	—	—

*Fiscal year change

2011 Year-End Financials

Debt ratio: ——
Return on equity: 5.50%
Cash ($ mil.): 0
Current ratio: ——
Long-term debt ($ mil.): ——

Dividends
    Yield: ——
    Payout: ——
Market value ($ mil.): ——

GIBSON OVERSEAS INC.

Not to be confused with the popular guitars under a similar name this Gibson concentrates on place sets rather than music sets. Established in 1979 Gibson Overseas manufactures dinnerware flatware and glassware. The company makes and markets its products under the Cuisine Select Gibson Everyday Gibson Elite brand names as well as under licenses Sunbeam and Oster. Gibson Overseas sells its wares (including combination sets which put dinnerware flatware and glassware all in one box) to large retailers the likes of Pier 1 Imports and Crate & Barrel. The company is owned by the Gabbay family and today is run by founder Nejat Gabbay's three sons.

EXECUTIVES

Principal, Solomon Gabbay
Principal, Sal Gabbay
Principal, Dar Gabbay

LOCATIONS

HQ: Gibson Overseas Inc.
2410 Yates Ave., Commerce CA 90040
Phone: 323-832-8900   **Fax:** 312-443-0567
Web: www.doblin.com

COMPETITORS

ARC International   WKI Holding
Lenox Corp   WWRD Holdings
Lifetime Brands

HISTORICAL FINANCIALS

Company Type: Private

Income Statement   FYE: December 31

	REVENUE ($ mil.)	NET INCOME ($ mil.)	NET PROFIT MARGIN	EMPLOYEES
12/11	141	8	6.0%	3
Annual Growth	—	—	—	—

2011 Year-End Financials

Debt ratio: ——
Return on equity: 6.00%
Cash ($ mil.): 0
Current ratio: 0.80
Long-term debt ($ mil.): ——

Dividends
    Yield: ——
    Payout: ——
Market value ($ mil.): ——

GINSBERG'S INSTITUTIONAL FOODS INC.

LOCATIONS

HQ: GINSBERG'S INSTITUTIONAL FOODS INC.
29 GINSBURG LN, HUDSON, NY 12534-3431
Phone: 518-828-4004
Web: www.ginsbergs.com

HISTORICAL FINANCIALS

Company Type: Private

Income Statement

FYE: December 31

	REVENUE ($ mil.)	NET INCOME ($ mil.)	NET PROFIT MARGIN	EMPLOYEES
12/11	122	1	1.0%	225
12/10	111	1	1.1%	0
12/09	109	1	1.4%	0
12/07	102	1	1.6%	0
Annual Growth	5.9%	(7.9%)	—	—

2011 Year-End Financials

Debt ratio: ——
Return on equity: 1.00%
Cash ($ mil.): 1
Current ratio: 0.90
Long-term debt ($ mil.): —

Dividends
  Yield: —
  Payout: —
  Market value ($ mil.): —

GLENN O. HAWBAKER INC.

For Glenn O. Hawbaker (GOH) it's all about making the grade. Founded as an excavating and grading company GOH provides heavy construction concrete construction utility work asphalt production and heavy equipment rentals and sales. From its home base in Pennsylvania the company serves customers in the north-central portion of the state. As part of its business GOH operates two dozen quarries and eight asphalt production facilities in Pennsylvania New York and eastern Ohio (since 2012). Its Hawbaker Engineering subsidiary provides civil engineering services and site designs. The family-owned company was founded in 1952 by Glenn and Thelma Hawbaker the parents of president and CEO Daniel Hawbaker.

Geographic Reach

GOH targets customers in north-central Pennsylvania where it is headquartered. In Pennsylvania New York and eastern Ohio it operates quarries asphalt production facilities and four regional operations centers.

Operations

Besides its core operations GOH runs a construction materials recycling center in State College Pennsylvania that reuses and resells materials such as concrete asphalt wood bricks and yard waste. It also operates subsidiary Hawbaker Engineering a civil engineering and site design provider and Northeast Prestressed Products a unit that offers prestressed concrete bridge beams and precast products for transportation projects in eight northeastern states.

Strategy

GOH has been involved with the development of the Marcellus Shale gas reserve in central Pennsylvania. Drilling for gas trapped beneath layers of shale created a boom for the area and for GOH. It has built roads sold aggregates and performed other services for gas companies as they explore there. To boot the company opened a new quarry to service the gas industry. The project helped GOH weather the economic crisis as road projects and other construction projects ground to a halt. Government stimulus-funded infrastructure projects also helped the company make it through the recession.

Company Ownership

The company is owned by the Glenn and Thelma Hawbaker family.

EXECUTIVES

President and CEO, Daniel R. (Dan) Hawbaker, age 72
CFO Secretary and Treasurer, Alan G. Hawbaker
CIO, Robert (Bob) Hocutt
Benefits Administrator, Kristin Wright
Manager Personnel, Dawn Davidson

LOCATIONS

HQ: Glenn O. Hawbaker Inc.
  1952 Waddle Rd., State College PA 16803-1649
Phone: 814-237-1444   **Fax:** 814-237-5348
Web: www.goh-inc.com

Selected Locations

Eastern region
  Montoursville office
Northeast region
  Greens Landing office
Northern region
  Turtle Point office
Ohio region
  New Philadelphia office
Pleasant Gap office
State College Pennsylvania
Western region
  Dubois office
  Grove City office

PRODUCTS/OPERATIONS

Selected Services

Bridge Construction
Environmental Services
Equipment Rental
Equipment sales
Gas Field Services
Portadam Impoundments
Recycle Center State College
Roads & Highways
Sheeting Shoring & Piling
Site Development
Soil Stabilization
Utilities
Wetlands Remediation

Selected Locations

Eastern region
  Montoursville office
Northeast region
  Greens Landing office
Northern region
  Turtle Point office
Ohio region
  New Philadelphia office
Pleasant Gap office
State College Pennsylvania
Western region
  Dubois office
  Grove City office

COMPETITORS

A & L
American Asphalt
  Paving
Balfour Beatty
  Infrastructure
Community Asphalt
  Corp.
Eastern Industries
Glasgow Inc.

Gohmann Asphalt &
  Construction
Kinsley Construction
Lane Construction
New Enterprise Stone
  & Lime
Peter Kiewit Sons'
Skanska USA Civil

HISTORICAL FINANCIALS

Company Type: Private

Income Statement

FYE: December 31

	REVENUE ($ mil.)	NET INCOME ($ mil.)	NET PROFIT MARGIN	EMPLOYEES
12/11	326	20	6.4%	1,300
12/10	337	25	7.5%	0
12/09	220	7	3.6%	0
12/08	239	8	3.4%	0
Annual Growth	10.9%	36.0%	—	—

2011 Year-End Financials

Debt ratio: ——
Return on equity: 6.40%
Cash ($ mil.): 0
Current ratio: 1.10
Long-term debt ($ mil.): —

Dividends
  Yield: —
  Payout: —
  Market value ($ mil.): —

GLOBAL TRADING ENTERPRISES LLC

LOCATIONS

HQ: GLOBAL TRADING ENTERPRISES LLC
  504 SHARPTOWN RD, SWEDESBORO, NJ 08085-3161
Phone: 856-223-9966

HISTORICAL FINANCIALS

Company Type: Private

Income Statement

FYE: January 1

	REVENUE ($ mil.)	NET INCOME ($ mil.)	NET PROFIT MARGIN	EMPLOYEES
01/11*	247	3	1.5%	150
12/09	319	8	2.7%	0
12/08	253	5	2.3%	0
12/07	237	2	1.1%	0
Annual Growth	1.5%	10.2%	—	—

*Fiscal year change

2011 Year-End Financials

Debt ratio: ——
Return on equity: 1.50%
Cash ($ mil.): 0
Current ratio: 1.00
Long-term debt ($ mil.): —

Dividends
  Yield: —
  Payout: —
  Market value ($ mil.): —

GODBERSEN-SMITH CONSTRUCTION CO INC

LOCATIONS
HQ: GODBERSEN-SMITH CONSTRUCTION CO INC
121 E HIGHWAY 175, IDA GROVE, IA 51445
Phone: 712-364-3347

HISTORICAL FINANCIALS
Company Type: Private

Income Statement
FYE: September 30

	REVENUE ($ mil.)	NET INCOME ($ mil.)	NET PROFIT MARGIN	EMPLOYEES
09/11	81	4	5.5%	450
09/10	75	4	6.2%	0
09/09	97	4	4.6%	0
09/08	89	5	5.9%	0
Annual Growth	(3.4%)	(5.6%)	—	—

2011 Year-End Financials
Debt ratio: ——
Return on equity: 5.50%
Cash ($ mil.): 25
Current ratio: 3.00
Long-term debt ($ mil.): —
Dividends
Yield: —
Payout: —
Market value ($ mil.): —

GOLDEN ALUMINUM INC.

LOCATIONS
HQ: GOLDEN ALUMINUM INC.
1405 14TH ST, FORT LUPTON, CO 80621-2718
Phone: 303-659-9767
Web: www.goldenaluminum.com

HISTORICAL FINANCIALS
Company Type: Private

Income Statement
FYE: December 31

	REVENUE ($ mil.)	NET INCOME ($ mil.)	NET PROFIT MARGIN	EMPLOYEES
12/11*	115	10	9.2%	153
11/09	79	5	7.3%	0
12/06	112	2	2.0%	0
12/04	23	0	2.0%	0
Annual Growth	69.3%	183.4%	—	—

*Fiscal year change

2011 Year-End Financials
Debt ratio: ——
Return on equity: 9.20%
Cash ($ mil.): 0
Current ratio: 1.50
Long-term debt ($ mil.): —
Dividends
Yield: —
Payout: —
Market value ($ mil.): —

GOLDEN GATE NATIONAL PARKS CONSERVANCY

San Francisco open your Golden Gate —National Parks that is. The Golden Gate National Parks Conservancy is dedicated to preserving and enhancing the national parks in the San Francisco Bay area. The not-for-profit organization is a co-operating association authorized by the US Congress to assist and support the National Park Service in operating more than 30 national park sites in and around the City by the Bay. The Golden Gate National Recreation Area includes such sites as Alcatraz Island Fort Point Muir Woods in nearby Marin County and the Presidio of San Francisco (a former US Army base that was decommissioned in 1994). The conservancy was established in 1981.

The Golden Gate National Parks Conservancy is financially supported by donations from corporate foundation and individual donors as well as income from operating park bookstores selling merchandise providing educational materials and conducting interpretive tours.

Alcatraz Island may be the best known of sites in the Golden Gate National Recreational Area. Accessible by ferry from the docks of Fisherman's Wharf in San Francisco the island was the site of a federal penitentiary from 1934 to 1963 and a military prison from 1907 to 1933. The most notorious and incorrigible federal prisoners were sent to Alcatraz including Al Capone and George "Machine Gun" Kelly. Alcatraz is the locale of more than a dozen Hollywood movies such as The Rock and Escape From Alcatraz.

The conservancy's biggest project has been the restoration of Crissy Field 100 acres within the Presidio of San Francisco that overlook the Golden Gate with its iconic bridge. Once an airfield Crissy Field has been transformed into urban parkland for the public with an interpretive center.

EXECUTIVES
President CEO, Greg Moore
Vice President Marketing and Communications, David Shaw
Vice President Human Resources, Jane Chin

LOCATIONS
HQ: Golden Gate National Parks Conservancy
Bldg. 201 Fort Mason, San Francisco CA 94123
Phone: 415-561-3000   **Fax:** 415-561-3003
Web: www.parksconservancy.org

HISTORICAL FINANCIALS
Company Type: Private - Not-for-Profit

Income Statement
FYE: September 30

	REVENUE ($ mil.)	NET INCOME ($ mil.)	NET PROFIT MARGIN	EMPLOYEES
09/11	33	(1)	—	219
09/08	32	3	9.5%	0
09/05	17	2	16.1%	0
09/04	13	1	10.6%	0
Annual Growth	34.6%	—	—	—

2011 Year-End Financials
Debt ratio: ——
Return on equity: (-3.50)%
Cash ($ mil.): 1
Current ratio: 1.50
Long-term debt ($ mil.): —
Dividends
Yield: —
Payout: —
Market value ($ mil.): —

GOLDER ASSOCIATES INC.

LOCATIONS
HQ: GOLDER ASSOCIATES INC.
3730 CHAMBLEE TUCKER RD, ATLANTA, GA 30341-4414
Phone: 770-496-1893
Web: www.golder.com

HISTORICAL FINANCIALS
Company Type: Private

Income Statement
FYE: December 31

	REVENUE ($ mil.)	NET INCOME ($ mil.)	NET PROFIT MARGIN	EMPLOYEES
12/11	165	0	0.6%	1,200
12/10	225	(0)	—	0
12/09	135	(0)	—	0
12/07	124	1	1.4%	0
Annual Growth	9.9%	(17.2%)	—	—

2011 Year-End Financials
Debt ratio: ——
Return on equity: 0.60%
Cash ($ mil.): 0
Current ratio: 0.60
Long-term debt ($ mil.): —
Dividends
Yield: —
Payout: —
Market value ($ mil.): —

GOLDSMITH & EGGLETON INC.

LOCATIONS
HQ: GOLDSMITH & EGGLETON INC.
300 1ST ST, WADSWORTH, OH 44281-2084
Phone: 330-336-6616
Web: www.goldsmith-eggleton.com

HISTORICAL FINANCIALS
Company Type: Private

Income Statement
FYE: June 30

	REVENUE ($ mil.)	NET INCOME ($ mil.)	NET PROFIT MARGIN	EMPLOYEES
06/11	88	11	12.9%	108
06/10	71	7	10.2%	0
06/09	56	(2)	—	0
06/08	62	4	7.1%	0
Annual Growth	12.1%	36.7%	—	—

2011 Year-End Financials

Debt ratio: —
Return on equity: 12.90%
Cash ($ mil.): 4
Current ratio: 1.30
Long-term debt ($ mil.): —

Dividends
Yield: —
Payout: —
Market value ($ mil.): —

GOOD SAMARITAN HOSPITAL

Good Samaritan Hospital provides a full slate of health care services to southwest Indiana and southeast Illinois. Services include cardiology emergency care orthopedics women's health and pediatrics. The 230-bed hospital is located a few blocks from the Wabash River that forms the border between the Hoosier and Prairies States. It operates specialty units including same day surgery breast care behavioral health radiology sleep cancer care and rehabilitation centers. It also provides home health and hospice services. Established in 1908 with 25 beds Good Samaritan was Indiana's first county hospital.

EXECUTIVES

SVP, Gerald Waldroup
President and CEO, Robert McLin
VP Nursing Service, Carol Olson
VP Medical Affairs, Charles C. Hedde
VP Professional and Support Services, Fred J. England
Chairman, Mary Cay Martin
VP Financial Services, Jerry Stump
Media Contact, Sandra Hatton

LOCATIONS

HQ: GOOD SAMARITAN HOSPITAL
520 S 7TH ST, VINCENNES, IN 47591-1038
Phone: 812-882-5220

COMPETITORS

Daviess Community
Hospital
Deaconess Health
System
IU Health
Southern Illinois
Healthcare

St. John's Hospital
(Illinois)
St. Mary's Medical
Center of Evansville
Wabash County Hospital

HISTORICAL FINANCIALS

Company Type: Private - Not-for-Profit

Income Statement

FYE: December 31

	REVENUE ($ mil.)	NET INCOME ($ mil.)	NET PROFIT MARGIN	EMPLOYEES
12/11	175	8	4.8%	1,700
12/10	156	10	6.4%	0
12/09	143	9	6.8%	0
12/08	145	(3)	—	0
Annual Growth	6.2%	—	—	—

2011 Year-End Financials

Debt ratio: —
Return on equity: 4.80%
Cash ($ mil.): 37
Current ratio: 3.30
Long-term debt ($ mil.): —

Dividends
Yield: —
Payout: —
Market value ($ mil.): —

GOOD SHEPHERD HEALTH CARE SYSTEM

LOCATIONS

HQ: GOOD SHEPHERD HEALTH CARE SYSTEM
610 NW 11TH ST, HERMISTON, OR 97838-6601
Phone: 541-567-6483
Web: www.gshealth.org

HISTORICAL FINANCIALS

Company Type: Private

Income Statement

FYE: June 30

	REVENUE ($ mil.)	NET INCOME ($ mil.)	NET PROFIT MARGIN	EMPLOYEES
06/11	81	13	16.7%	450
06/10	78	12	16.2%	0
06/09	68	7	10.6%	0
06/08	59	6	11.4%	0
Annual Growth	11.0%	25.9%	—	—

2011 Year-End Financials

Debt ratio: —
Return on equity: 16.70%
Cash ($ mil.): 4
Current ratio: 0.70
Long-term debt ($ mil.): —

Dividends
Yield: —
Payout: —
Market value ($ mil.): —

GOODIN COMPANY

LOCATIONS

HQ: GOODIN COMPANY
2700 N 2ND ST, MINNEAPOLIS, MN 55411-1679
Phone: 612-588-7811
Web: www.goodinco.com

HISTORICAL FINANCIALS

Company Type: Private

Income Statement

FYE: December 31

	REVENUE ($ mil.)	NET INCOME ($ mil.)	NET PROFIT MARGIN	EMPLOYEES
12/11	145	1	1.2%	314
12/10	132	1	0.8%	0
12/09	125	0	0.7%	0
12/08	156	5	3.2%	0
Annual Growth	(2.4%)	(30.4%)	—	—

2011 Year-End Financials

Debt ratio: —
Return on equity: 1.20%
Cash ($ mil.): 0
Current ratio: 1.90
Long-term debt ($ mil.): —

Dividends
Yield: —
Payout: —
Market value ($ mil.): —

GOODWILL INDUSTRIES OF SOUTH FLORIDA INC.

LOCATIONS

HQ: GOODWILL INDUSTRIES OF SOUTH FLORIDA INC.
2121 NW 21ST ST, MIAMI, FL 33142-7382
Phone: 305-325-9114
Web: www.goodwillsouthflorida.org

HISTORICAL FINANCIALS

Company Type: Private

Income Statement

FYE: December 31

	REVENUE ($ mil.)	NET INCOME ($ mil.)	NET PROFIT MARGIN	EMPLOYEES
12/11	105	3	3.8%	2,300
12/10	109	8	7.8%	0
12/09	18	0	3.7%	0
12/08	67	1	2.6%	0
Annual Growth	15.7%	31.4%	—	—

2011 Year-End Financials

Debt ratio: —
Return on equity: 3.80%
Cash ($ mil.): 8
Current ratio: 0.30
Long-term debt ($ mil.): —

Dividends
Yield: —
Payout: —
Market value ($ mil.): —

GOODWILL INDUSTRIES OF SOUTHERN CALIFORNIA

LOCATIONS

HQ: GOODWILL INDUSTRIES OF SOUTHERN CALIFORNIA
342 N SAN FERNANDO RD, LOS ANGELES, CA 90031-1730
Phone: 323-223-1211
Web: www.goodwillsb.org

HISTORICAL FINANCIALS

Company Type: Private

Income Statement

FYE: December 31

	REVENUE ($ mil.)	NET INCOME ($ mil.)	NET PROFIT MARGIN	EMPLOYEES
12/11*	130	7	6.1%	2,100
07/11	130	7	6.1%	0
12/10	130	7	6.1%	0
12/09	111	3	3.2%	0
Annual Growth	5.4%	30.9%	—	—

*Fiscal year change

2011 Year-End Financials

Debt ratio: —
Return on equity: 6.10%
Cash ($ mil.): 10
Current ratio: 0.80
Long-term debt ($ mil.): —

Dividends
Yield: —
Payout: —
Market value ($ mil.): —

2012 Year-End Financials

Debt ratio: —
Return on equity: 6.10%
Cash ($ mil.): 10
Current ratio: 0.90
Long-term debt ($ mil.): —

Dividends
Yield: —
Payout: —
Market value ($ mil.): —

2012 Year-End Financials

Debt ratio: —
Return on equity: (-2.60)%
Cash ($ mil.): 4
Current ratio: —
Long-term debt ($ mil.): —

Dividends
Yield: —
Payout: —
Market value ($ mil.): —

GOODWILL RETAIL SERVICES INC.

LOCATIONS

HQ: GOODWILL RETAIL SERVICES INC.
5300 N 118TH CT, MILWAUKEE, WI 53225-3084
Phone: 414-847-4200
Web: www.amazinggoodwill.com

HISTORICAL FINANCIALS

Company Type: Private

Income Statement

FYE: December 31

	REVENUE ($ mil.)	NET INCOME ($ mil.)	NET PROFIT MARGIN	EMPLOYEES
12/11	96	6	6.6%	1,000
12/09	66	17	26.1%	0
12/05	58	6	11.4%	0
Annual Growth	28.7%	(2.3%)	—	—

2011 Year-End Financials

Debt ratio: —
Return on equity: 6.60%
Cash ($ mil.): 1
Current ratio: 0.40
Long-term debt ($ mil.): —

Dividends
Yield: —
Payout: —
Market value ($ mil.): —

GOODWILL SOUTHERN CALIFORNIA

LOCATIONS

HQ: GOODWILL SOUTHERN CALIFORNIA
8120 PALM LN, SAN BERNARDINO, CA 92410-4961
Phone: 323-223-1211
Web: www.goodwillsocal.org

HISTORICAL FINANCIALS

Company Type: Private

Income Statement

FYE: August 31

	REVENUE ($ mil.)	NET INCOME ($ mil.)	NET PROFIT MARGIN	EMPLOYEES
08/12*	130	7	6.1%	200
04/11	0	0	—	0
12/10	130	7	6.1%	0
12/08	95	0	1.0%	0
Annual Growth	10.9%	105.8%	—	—

*Fiscal year change

GORDON COLLEGE

Gordon College a New England non-denominational Christian liberal arts college offers nearly 40 majors and has about 1800 students. A demonstrated Christian commitment is required for admission. Undergraduate tuition is approximately $20000. In 1985 Gordon merged with Barrington College with the combined school retaining Gordon College's name. Gordon College was founded in 1889 by Reverend Dr. A.J. Gordon as a missionary training institute.

EXECUTIVES

Director Human Resources, Nancy Anderson
President, R. Judson Carlberg
Provost, Mark L. Sargent
VP Student Development and Dean Students, Barry J. Loy
VP Development, Robert Grinnell
College Counsel, Stephen McLeod
EVP, Dan Tymann
Chair, Kurt Keilhacker
Interim Academic Dean, Dan Russ
Vice Chair, Herman J. Smith Jr.
Treasurer Clerk and Trustee, David C. Schultz
Assistant Clerk and Trustee, Bronwyn E. (Bonny) Loring
VP Finance and Administration, Michael (Mike) Ahearn
VP Enrollment and Marketing, Brook Berry
Dean Chapel, Greg Carmer
Assistant Dean and Registrar, Carol Herrick
Athletic Director, Jon Tymann
Associate Director College Communications, Cyndi McMahon
Vice Chair, Herman J. Smith Jr.
Treasurer Clerk and Trustee, David C. Schultz
Assistant Clerk and Trustee, Bronwyn E. (Bonny) Loring

LOCATIONS

HQ: Gordon College
255 Grapevine Rd., Wenham MA 01984
Phone: 978-927-2300   **Fax:** 978-524-3704
Web: www.gordon.edu

HISTORICAL FINANCIALS

Company Type: School

Income Statement

FYE: June 30

	REVENUE ($ mil.)	NET INCOME ($ mil.)	NET PROFIT MARGIN	EMPLOYEES
06/12	51	(1)	—	496
06/11	52	7	13.9%	0
06/10	48	(1)	—	0
06/09	0	0	—	0
Annual Growth	—	—	—	—

GOVERNMENT SCIENTIFIC SOURCE INC.

LOCATIONS

HQ: GOVERNMENT SCIENTIFIC SOURCE INC.
12351 SUNRISE VALLEY DR, RESTON, VA 20191-3415
Phone: 703-734-1805
Web: www.govsci.com

HISTORICAL FINANCIALS

Company Type: Private

Income Statement

FYE: December 31

	REVENUE ($ mil.)	NET INCOME ($ mil.)	NET PROFIT MARGIN	EMPLOYEES
12/11	125	2	1.9%	65
12/09	99	2	2.6%	0
12/08	92	1	2.0%	0
12/07	76	1	1.7%	0
Annual Growth	18.1%	22.3%	—	—

2011 Year-End Financials

Debt ratio: —
Return on equity: 1.90%
Cash ($ mil.): 6
Current ratio: 2.20
Long-term debt ($ mil.): —

Dividends
Yield: —
Payout: —
Market value ($ mil.): —

GRAEBEL COMPANIES INC.

Graebel can move your table ... and just about anything else you need relocated. Offering both domestic and international household and commercial relocation services most of the company's business comes from firms transferring employees but it also provides individual household moving services and storage as well as freight forwarding. Graebel operates from service centers throughout the US and from international forwarding offices at major ports. It provides transportation services in Asia Europe the Middle East and Africa through hubs in Prague and Singapore and elsewhere in the world via a network of partners. Chairman Dave Graebel founded the family-run company in 1950.

Geographic Reach

Graebel has operations in Colorado and other locations throughout the US; it provides moving services in more than 150 countries and maintains an international presence in the Czech Republic Prague Singapore and Shanghai.

Operations

In addition to providing its moving services the company offers storage services freight forwarding and move management. Because the company insists on tight background checks and security measures Graebel serves specialized industries as well as high-end customers.

Additionally Graebel handles relocations for libraries hotels health care facilities and the entertainment industry. To serve its customers better the company offers its Graebel Relocation app (application) which gives clients their relocation facts and status of their transfers via an iPhone or iPad tablet computer; in 2011 it added an Android app.

EXECUTIVES

CEO, William (Bill) Graebel
Chairman, David (Dave) Graebel
President Continental Moving Services Move Management Graebel Van Lines Graebel Movers and Graebel Forwarders, Craig Broback
CFO, Brad Siler
SVP Marketing and Public Relations, Carolyn White
SVP Procurement, Phil Burton
SVP Commercial Services Workplace Services, Scott Snead
SVP Human Resources, Mary Dymond
President Graebel Movers International Inc., Jim Petzel
COO, Tim Callahan

LOCATIONS

HQ: Graebel Companies Inc.
16346 Airport Cir., Aurora CO 80011
Phone: 303-214-6683   **Fax:** 303-214-2156
Web: www.graebel.com

PRODUCTS/OPERATIONS

Selected Services

Bar-coded inventory and asset management
Corporate headquarters office and one-time office relocation
Healthcare industry relocation project services
High density filing systems storage solutions
Hospitality industry furniture fixtures and equipment (FF&E) services
Just-In-Time deliveries
MAC management
Project management
Records storage and disposal
Relocation services
Single-source logistic services and management
Sub-contractor data telephony electrical coordination
Systems furniture transport delivery installation and reconfiguration
Warehouse and distribution services
Worldwide air ocean transportation including less-than-truckload truckload / padded van services

COMPETITORS

ALTAIR Global Relocation	Seino Transportation Co
Arpin Van Lines	SIRVA
Atlas World Group	Suddath
Bekins	TheMIGroup
Brookfield Global Relocation	UniGroup
National Van Lines	Weichert Relocation Resources
Prudential	Wheaton Van Lines

HISTORICAL FINANCIALS
Company Type: Private

Income Statement
FYE: December 31

	REVENUE ($ mil.)	NET INCOME ($ mil.)	NET PROFIT MARGIN	EMPLOYEES
12/11	322	3	0.9%	1,771
12/09	260	(3)	—	0
12/06	334	0	0.1%	0
12/05	29	(3)	—	0
Annual Growth	123.3%	—	—	—

2011 Year-End Financials
Debt ratio: —
Return on equity: 0.90%
Cash ($ mil.): 5
Current ratio: 0.50
Long-term debt ($ mil.): —
Dividends
  Yield: —
  Payout: —
Market value ($ mil.): —

GRAINLAND COOPERATIVE

LOCATIONS

HQ: GRAINLAND COOPERATIVE
927 COUNTY HIGHWAY 3, EUREKA, IL 61530-9457
Phone: 309-467-2355
Web: www.grainlandcooperative.com

HISTORICAL FINANCIALS
Company Type: Private

Income Statement
FYE: June 30

	REVENUE ($ mil.)	NET INCOME ($ mil.)	NET PROFIT MARGIN	EMPLOYEES
06/12	95	3	3.4%	50
06/11	67	2	3.2%	0
06/10	46	2	5.1%	0
06/09	60	0	1.4%	0
Annual Growth	16.3%	55.1%	—	—

2012 Year-End Financials
Debt ratio: —
Return on equity: 3.40%
Cash ($ mil.): 5
Current ratio: 1.00
Long-term debt ($ mil.): —
Dividends
  Yield: —
  Payout: —
Market value ($ mil.): —

GRAND VIEW HEALTH FOUNDATION

LOCATIONS

HQ: GRAND VIEW HEALTH FOUNDATION
700 LAWN AVE, SELLERSVILLE, PA 18960-1548
Phone: 215-453-4000
Web: www.gvh.org

HISTORICAL FINANCIALS
Company Type: Private

Income Statement
FYE: June 30

	REVENUE ($ mil.)	NET INCOME ($ mil.)	NET PROFIT MARGIN	EMPLOYEES
06/12	173	(26)	—	67
06/11	183	44	24.1%	0
06/10	182	4	2.2%	0
06/09	187	(41)	—	0
Annual Growth	(2.5%)	—	—	—

2012 Year-End Financials
Debt ratio: —
Return on equity: (-15.40)%
Cash ($ mil.): 16
Current ratio: 1.40
Long-term debt ($ mil.): —
Dividends
  Yield: —
  Payout: —
Market value ($ mil.): —

GRAND VIEW HOSPITAL

Grand View Hospital (GVH) hopes to give patients a glimpse of great health care. The hospital provide emergency inpatient surgery and specialty services including cardiology orthopedics sleep diagnostic rehabilitation women's and children's care and other medical services to the Bucks County region of Pennsylvania. GVH's oncology program is affiliated with the Fox Chase Cancer Center in Philadelphia. The medical center also operates primary care and outpatient clinics in the region and it provides home health hospice fitness and community outreach programs. Founded in 1913 the hospital has about 200 beds.

Geographic Reach

In addition to its main hospital in Sellersville Pennsylvania GVH operates outpatient centers in Sellersville Harleysville and Pennsburg as well as a cancer center in Chalfont.

Financial Performance

In 2012 GVH reported revenues of some $175 million up 2% from 2011. About 80% of the company's earnings came from commercial managed care insurance and Medicare reimbursements. Other patient revenues come from self-pay customers. Operating expenses in 2012 were about $168 million.

Strategy

GVH has grown in recent years by expanding its medical facilities and services. In 2010 it opened a new labor and delivery unit and in 2012 it began offering neonatology services through a partnership with the Children's Hospital of Philadelphia.

EXECUTIVES

Secretary, William S. Aichele, age 61
CEO, Stuart H. Fine
SVP and General Counsel, Jean M. Keeler
Chairman, Thomas J. Hipp
VP and CIO, Jane D. Loveless
VP Quality, Darla Weaver
VP Medical Affairs, Linda S. Lavin
SVP Clinical and Support Services, J. Mark Horne
Vice Chairman, Jeffrey Landis
Treasurer, Walter Cressman
VP Nursing, Kathleen Burkey

LOCATIONS

HQ: Grand View Hospital
   700 Lawn Ave., Sellersville PA 18960
Phone: 215-453-4000   **Fax:** 215-453-9151
Web: www.gvh.org

PRODUCTS/OPERATIONS

Selected Services and Centers

Acute Rehabilitation Unit
Ambulance/Transport Services
Case Management
Child Immunization Clinic
Children's Center - Daycare
Clinical Research
Diabetes Education
Emergency Department
Grand View Information Line
Health Promotion and Wellness
Healthy Beginnings Plus
Home Health Care Services
Industrial Medicine
Laboratory (Blood Work) Services at Grand View
   Hospital
Lifestyle Fitness Center
Medical Equipment and Supplies
Men's Health
Nutritional Counseling Services
Pediatric Weight Management (Grand New Youth)
Physical Medicine & Rehabilitation
Pulmonary Rehabilitation
Radiology Services (X-ray) Senior Services
Stoneridge Sleep Center
Sports Medicine
Support Groups & Consultations
Weight Management (Grand New You)
Wound Care Center

COMPETITORS

Abington Memorial Hospital
Children' s Hospital of Philadelphia
Doylestown Hospital
Jefferson Health System
Lehigh Valley Health Network
North Philadelphia Health System
St. Luke' s University Health Network
Tenet Healthcare
University of Pennsylvania Health System

HISTORICAL FINANCIALS

Company Type: Private - Not-for-Profit

Income Statement

FYE: June 30

	REVENUE ($ mil.)	NET INCOME ($ mil.)	NET PROFIT MARGIN	EMPLOYEES
06/12	169	(26)	—	1,600
06/11	177	10	5.7%	0
06/10	182	7	4.1%	0
06/09	176	(16)	—	0
Annual Growth	**(1.4%)**	**—**	**—**	**—**

2012 Year-End Financials

Debt ratio: ——
Return on equity: (-15.60)%
Cash ($ mil.): 14
Current ratio: 1.30
Long-term debt ($ mil.): —
Dividends
   Yield: —
   Payout: —
   Market value ($ mil.): —

GREAT LAKES EDUCATIONAL LOAN SERVICES INC.

LOCATIONS

HQ: GREAT LAKES EDUCATIONAL LOAN SERVICES
   INC.
   2401 INTERNATIONAL LN, MADISON, WI 53704-3121
Phone: 608-246-1800
Web: www.mygreatlakes.com

HISTORICAL FINANCIALS

Company Type: Private

Income Statement

FYE: December 31

	ASSETS ($ mil.)	NET INCOME ($ mil.)	INCOME AS % OF ASSETS	EMPLOYEES
12/11	67	13	20.3%	725
12/10	65	15	23.6%	0
12/09	70	13	19.2%	0
12/08	52	7	14.6%	0
Annual Growth	**8.3%**	**20.8%**	**—**	

2011 Year-End Financials

Debt ratio: ——
Return on equity: 9.50%
Cash ($ mil.): 27
Current ratio: 1.30
Long-term debt ($ mil.): —
Dividends
   Yield: —
   Payout: —
   Market value ($ mil.): —

GREAT RIVER MEDICAL CENTER

LOCATIONS

HQ: GREAT RIVER MEDICAL CENTER
   1221 S GEAR AVE, WEST BURLINGTON, IA
   52655-1681
Phone: 319-768-1000
Web: www.greatrivermedical.org

HISTORICAL FINANCIALS

Company Type: Private

Income Statement

FYE: June 30

	REVENUE ($ mil.)	NET INCOME ($ mil.)	NET PROFIT MARGIN	EMPLOYEES
06/11	147	12	8.4%	1,400
06/10	159	15	9.6%	0
06/09	153	13	8.7%	0
06/08	15	15	99.1%	0
Annual Growth	**111.5%**	**(7.2%)**	**—**	**—**

2011 Year-End Financials

Debt ratio: ——
Return on equity: 8.40%
Cash ($ mil.): 6
Current ratio: 1.30
Long-term debt ($ mil.): —
Dividends
   Yield: —
   Payout: —
   Market value ($ mil.): —

GREATER BALTIMORE MEDICAL CENTER INC.

Greater Baltimore Medical Center also known as GBMC operates an integrated health system for residents of Baltimore and surrounding counties. The 300-bed medical center provides psychiatry surgery women's health oncology and other specialty and general medical services. The hospital provides inpatient and outpatient services and its emergency room treats about 60000 patients every year. In addition it provides teaching services through an affiliation with Johns Hopkins University. GBMC also includes the Greater Baltimore Medical Associates physician practices and the Gilchrist Hospice Care agency. The GBMC Foundation coordinates fundraising for the health network.

GBMC was born out of two hospitals. The Hospital for the Women of Maryland of Baltimore City was the nation's second hospital for women's care when it opened in 1882. The Presbyterian Eye Ear and Throat Charity Hospital began in 1887 as a clinic run by a civil war surgeon in his carriage house. The two joined to create GBMC in 1960; the hospital opened five years later.

In 2010 the hospital opened a palliative care unit in its Berman Cancer Institute. The unit funded through Gilchrist Hospice Care offers guidance and support to cancer patients and their families; it also serves as an in-hospital end-of-life care option. Another hospice option launched in 2010 was Gilchrist Kids the state's only hospice program exclusively for children.

EXECUTIVES

President CEO and Director, Lawrence M. Merlis
EVP and CFO, Eric L. Melchior
VP and CIO, Tressa Springmann
EVP and Chief Medical Officer, Rodney Williams
Chief of Staff Greater Baltimore Medical Center and Director, John R. Saunders Jr.
President Gilchrist Hospice Care, Catherine J. Boyne
VP Facilities and Support Services, Michael A. Forthman
VP Government and External Relations, Wynee E. Hawk
SVP Patient Care Services and Chief Nurse Executive, Jody Porter
President Greater Baltimore Medical Center Foundation, Douglas G. Smith
Manager Media Relations, Michael Schwartzberg
Chairman, Charles C. Fenwick Jr.
Vice Chair, Harry S. Johnson
Secretary and Director, Thomas M. Kane
Vice Chair, Patricia J. Mitchell
Vice Chair, Stephen T. Scott
VP Organization Development and Human Resources, Mark R. Thomas
VP Greater Baltimore Medical Associates, Steven K. Twaddle
VP Finance, George Bayless
SVP Corporate Strategy and Business Development, John W. Ellis
EVP and COO, Keith Poisson
President CEO and Director, Lawrence M. Merlis
Chief of Staff Greater Baltimore Medical Center and Director, John R. Saunders Jr.
Director, Kenneth P. Barksdale
Director, Herbert J. Belgrad
Director, William H. Conkling Jr.
Vice Chair, Harry S. Johnson

Secretary and Director, Thomas M. Kane
Director, William A. Kroh
Director, Thomas H. Maddux
Vice Chair, Patricia J. Mitchell
Vice Chair, Stephen T. Scott
Director, Harold Tucker
Director, Rt. Hon. Vicki Ballou-Watts
Director, Frederick M. (Fred) Hudson, age 66
Director, Douglas Huether
Director, Robert A. Shelton
Director, Bernard Siegel
Director, Howard L. Siegel
Director, Stuart O. Simms
Director, Marion G. Thompson
Director, Ronald F. Tutrone
Director, Mary B Wieler

LOCATIONS

HQ: Greater Baltimore Medical Center Inc.
6701 N. Charles St., Baltimore MD 21204
Phone: 443-849-2000   **Fax:** 701-947-2105
Web: tenderbison.ndnatural.com

COMPETITORS

Anne Arundel Medical
  Center
Bon Secours Health
Dimensions Healthcare
Franklin Square
  Hospital Center
Harbor Hospital
Johns Hopkins Health
  System

Johns Hopkins Medicine
LifeBridge Health
University of Maryland
  Medical System
Upper Chesapeake
  Health

HISTORICAL FINANCIALS

Company Type: Private - Not-for-Profit

Income Statement

	REVENUE ($ mil.)	NET INCOME ($ mil.)	NET PROFIT MARGIN	EMPLOYEES
06/11	416	25	6.1%	0
06/10	403	20	5.1%	0
06/09	388	0	—	0
06/08	392	8	2.1%	0
Annual Growth	2.0%	45.7%	—	—

2011 Year-End Financials

Debt ratio: ——
Return on equity: 6.10%
Cash ($ mil.): 44
Current ratio: 0.40
Long-term debt ($ mil.): —

Dividends
  Yield: —
  Payout: —
  Market value ($ mil.): —

GREATER CHICAGO FOOD DEPOSITORY

LOCATIONS

HQ: GREATER CHICAGO FOOD DEPOSITORY
4100 W ANN LURIE PL, CHICAGO, IL 60632-3920
Phone: 773-247-3663
Web: www.chicagosfoodbank.org

HISTORICAL FINANCIALS

Company Type: Private

Income Statement   FYE: June 30

	REVENUE ($ mil.)	NET INCOME ($ mil.)	NET PROFIT MARGIN	EMPLOYEES
06/12	85	1	2.2%	95
06/11	83	4	5.0%	0
06/10	77	1	1.9%	0
06/09	67	0	—	0
Annual Growth	8.0%	—	—	—

2012 Year-End Financials

Debt ratio: ——
Return on equity: 2.20%
Cash ($ mil.): 15
Current ratio: 4.80
Long-term debt ($ mil.): —

Dividends
  Yield: —
  Payout: —
  Market value ($ mil.): —

GREATER HAZELTON HEALTH ALLIANCE

LOCATIONS

HQ: GREATER HAZELTON HEALTH ALLIANCE
700 E BROAD ST, HAZLETON, PA 18201-6835
Phone: 570-501-4000
Web: www.ghha.org

HISTORICAL FINANCIALS

Company Type: Private

Income Statement   FYE: December 31

	REVENUE ($ mil.)	NET INCOME ($ mil.)	NET PROFIT MARGIN	EMPLOYEES
12/11	118	11	9.4%	1
Annual Growth	—	—	—	—

2011 Year-End Financials

Debt ratio: ——
Return on equity: 9.40%
Cash ($ mil.): 20
Current ratio: 1.30
Long-term debt ($ mil.): —

Dividends
  Yield: —
  Payout: —
  Market value ($ mil.): —

GREEN LINE EQUIP. INC.

LOCATIONS

HQ: GREEN LINE EQUIP. INC.
3990 W US HIGHWAY 30, GRAND ISLAND, NE 68803-5039
Phone: 308-384-8777
Web: www.greenlineequip.com

HISTORICAL FINANCIALS

Company Type: Private

Income Statement   FYE: June 30

	REVENUE ($ mil.)	NET INCOME ($ mil.)	NET PROFIT MARGIN	EMPLOYEES
06/11	150	4	3.1%	110
06/07	60	1	2.5%	0
06/06	54	1	2.0%	0
06/05	49	1	2.4%	0
Annual Growth	45.1%	58.2%	—	—

2011 Year-End Financials

Debt ratio: ——
Return on equity: 3.10%
Cash ($ mil.): 2
Current ratio: 0.10
Long-term debt ($ mil.): —

Dividends
  Yield: —
  Payout: —
  Market value ($ mil.): —

GREENWOOD FARMERS COOPERATIVE

LOCATIONS

HQ: GREENWOOD FARMERS COOPERATIVE
304 S 3RD ST, ELMWOOD, NE 68349-6114
Phone: 402-994-2585
Web: www.nehawkacoop.com

HISTORICAL FINANCIALS

Company Type: Private

Income Statement   FYE: August 31

	REVENUE ($ mil.)	NET INCOME ($ mil.)	NET PROFIT MARGIN	EMPLOYEES
08/11	187	3	2.1%	70
08/10	153	3	2.4%	0
08/09	147	4	2.8%	0
08/08	143	3	2.3%	0
Annual Growth	9.2%	6.5%	—	—

2011 Year-End Financials

Debt ratio: ——
Return on equity: 2.10%
Cash ($ mil.): 1
Current ratio: 0.30
Long-term debt ($ mil.): —

Dividends
  Yield: —
  Payout: —
  Market value ($ mil.): —

GSMA LTD

LOCATIONS

HQ: GSMA LTD
1000 ABERNATHY RD NE # 450, ATLANTA, GA 30328-5623
Phone: 678-281-6600
Web: www.gsma.com

HISTORICAL FINANCIALS

Company Type: Private

Income Statement

FYE: March 31

	REVENUE ($ mil.)	NET INCOME ($ mil.)	NET PROFIT MARGIN	EMPLOYEES
03/11	97	30	31.4%	105
03/10	80	21	26.6%	0
Annual Growth	21.2%	43.1%	—	—

2011 Year-End Financials

Debt ratio: ——
Return on equity: 31.40%
Cash ($ mil.): 24
Current ratio: ——
Long-term debt ($ mil.): ——

Dividends
  Yield: —
  Payout: —
  Market value ($ mil.): ——

GUADALUPE VALLEY TELEPHONE COOPERATIVE INC.

Guadalupe Valley Telephone Cooperative (GVTC) offers telecommunications services to residential and business customers in the Hill Country area of south Texas. Founded in 1951 the cooperative local exchange carrier provides an 11-county area covering about 2000 square miles with traditional local and long-distance telephone services Internet access digital cable television and high-speed fiber-to-the-home (FTTH) converged service packages. GVTC also installs and monitors residential and commercial security systems and provides additional enterprise services such as its ID Vault information security service.

Revenues eked up nearly a percent and a half in 2010 largely due to non-telephone operations. Revenue for its telephone business dropped a mere 0.6% but expenses brought that income down by 8% ultimately making total operating income more than 13% lower than 2009. Non-operating income however picked up the slack by improving more than 55% while non-operating expenses decreased leaving the company with a net improvement of nearly 11% on its bottom line to $16.3 million. GVTC also knocked its long-term debt (net of current portion) down from $8.2 million to $193000.

GVTC sold a record number of cable TV services in 2010 thanks to its continuing fiber optic build-out. Also its security services customer base increased by 10% to nearly 4500. Those services are typically sold under a 36-month term contract. Non-packaged local telephone service sales waned but packages containing local service ramped up to 2.5 times that of 2009. Long distance subscribers also grew 5%. Enterprise customers climbed 14% in the competitive local exchange carrier (LEC) territory more than making up for a 3% shortfall in the incumbent LEC territory.

FTTH is a key component GVTC's growth strategy. In 2008 the company began a five-year $35 million fiber optic expansion project. It spent $112 million on network expansions and upgrades from 2006 through 2010.

Like many companies in the industry GVTC aims to be the one-stop shop of converged communications for its customers. In 2011 it introduced desktop security remote online backup and additional service and content integration.

EXECUTIVES

Chairman, Charles J. (Chuck) Knibbe
President and CEO, Ritchie Sorrells
CFO, Mark J. Gitter
VP Sales and Marketing, Jeffrey J. (Jeff) Mnick
VP Human Resources, Kathy Young
Vice President Vice President Regulatory Affairs and Business Operations, Robert Hunt
VP Network Services, George O'Neal
Manager Communications, Bruce Forey
VP Product Development, Josh Pettiette
Manager Public Relations, Paula White
Vice President - Network Services, George ONeal
Secretary Treasurer, Bette Wehner
Auditors: CurtisBlakely&Co.PC

LOCATIONS

HQ: Guadalupe Valley Telephone Cooperative Inc.
  36101 FM 3159, New Braunfels TX 78132
Phone: 830-885-4411   **Fax:** 830-885-2400
Web: gvtc.com

COMPETITORS

ABM Security Services	DISH Network
AT&T	Garda World Security
Birch Communications	Grande Communications
Brink' s	Time Warner Cable
DIRECTV	Verizon Southwest

HISTORICAL FINANCIALS

Company Type: Private - Cooperative

Income Statement

FYE: December 31

	REVENUE ($ mil.)	NET INCOME ($ mil.)	NET PROFIT MARGIN	EMPLOYEES
12/11	60	18	30.1%	135
12/10	59	16	27.7%	0
12/09	59	14	24.9%	0
Annual Growth	1.1%	11.2%	—	—

2011 Year-End Financials

Debt ratio: ——
Return on equity: 30.10%
Cash ($ mil.): 3
Current ratio: 0.60
Long-term debt ($ mil.): ——

Dividends
  Yield: —
  Payout: —
  Market value ($ mil.): ——

GUARANTEE ELECTRICAL COMPANY

Guarantee Electrical has been powering up St. Louis since it "guaranteed" to electrify the World's Fair in 1904. (It delivered on the guarantee). Now a major US electrical contractor the company offers commercial institutional and industrial services including construction design/build communications/data and maintenance. Guarantee Electrical operates throughout the country and has worked on such varied projects as the MGM Grand in Las Vegas and several post office and prison facilities. Its GECO Systems division installs and services intercom closed-circuit television and other audio-vi-sual systems. The Oertli family owns and operates the firm.

Guarantee Electrical is headquartered in St. Louis with offices in Granite City Illinois; Denver; and Benicia California. As a member of Federated Electrical Contractors the firm has more than 30 joint venture partners operating in 60 cities across North America Europe and Asia.

EXECUTIVES

CEO, Rick Oertli
Chairman, Charles W. (Chuck) Oertli
Vice Chairman, Fred G. Oertli Jr.
COO, Roger Oertli
CFO, Douglas (Doug) Mertzlufft
Director Human Resources, Linda McGillis
Industrial Director, David Banford
Business Development and Marketing, Julie TenEyck
VP Preconstruction, Steve Juan
VP and Senior Project Manager, Dipak Kapadia
Director Construction, Steve Kellenberger
Manager Critical Power Group, John Gray
VP Operations GECO Systems/TelVi, Patrick McSalley
President GECO Engineering, Gary Schaeffer

LOCATIONS

HQ: Guarantee Electrical Company
  3405 Bent Ave., St. Louis MO 63116
Phone: 314-772-5400   **Fax:** 314-772-9261
Web: www.geco.com

COMPETITORS

Conti Electric	MDU Construction
Dycom	Services
Integrated Electrical	Quanta Services
Services	

HISTORICAL FINANCIALS

Company Type: Private

Income Statement

FYE: September 30

	REVENUE ($ mil.)	NET INCOME ($ mil.)	NET PROFIT MARGIN	EMPLOYEES
09/11	119	0	—	700
09/10	135	0	—	0
09/09	0	0	—	0
09/05	106	0	—	0
Annual Growth	4.1%	—	—	—

2011 Year-End Financials

Debt ratio: ——
Return on equity: —
Cash ($ mil.): 4
Current ratio: 1.60
Long-term debt ($ mil.): ——

Dividends
  Yield: —
  Payout: —
  Market value ($ mil.): ——

GUEST SERVICES INC.

Guest Services satisfies hungry and sleepy patrons. The company provides contract food services and hospitality-management services nationwide. It operates cafeterias and onsite restaurants and offers catering to businesses hotels hospitals conference centers and government operations including the US Supreme Court the US House of Representatives and the National Park Service. For leisure and resort facilities Guest Services also provides special-event catering and offers management services such as marketing human resources procurement quality-assurance and information technology services. Guest Services was founded in 1917 as a private company to serve governmental agencies.

Geographic Reach

Guest Services serves customers nationwide in several sectors.

Operations

As part of its business Guest Services serves some 250 facilities across the US and more than 25 million guests each year. It operates Lancaster Foods one of the largest wholesale produce companies in the mid-Atlantic region as a wholly owned subsidiary.

Sales and Marketing

Guest Services serves several clients including government and business dining facilities museums hotels resorts conference centers luxury condominiums senior living centers health care systems state and national park recreation school and university dining facilities specialty retail stores and full-service restaurants.

EXECUTIVES

General Counsel and Secretary, Douglas H. Verner
President and CEO, Gerard T. Gabrys
CFO, Jeffrey A. (Jeff) Marquis
VP Human Resources, Richard Hirsch
President Lancaster Foods, John Gates
VP Hotel Operations South, Barry G. Trice
VP Operations Division, Beverly Frazer

LOCATIONS

HQ: Guest Services Inc.
3055 Prosperity Ave., Fairfax VA 22031
Phone: 703-849-9300   **Fax:** 703-641-4690
Web: www.guestservices.com

PRODUCTS/OPERATIONS

Selected Management Services
Audits
Corporate Support Services
Financial Accounting Systems
Food Safety and Health
Human Resources
Maintenance Support
Management Information Systems
Marketing
PeopleSoft Processing
Procurement
Quality Assurance
Security
Test Kitchen
Training

COMPETITORS

ARAMARK	Delaware North
Centerplate	Sodexo USA
Compass Group USA	Valley Services

HISTORICAL FINANCIALS
Company Type: Private

Income Statement
FYE: December 31

	REVENUE ($ mil.)	NET INCOME ($ mil.)	NET PROFIT MARGIN	EMPLOYEES
12/11	369	0	0.0%	3,500
12/10	346	0	0.3%	0
12/09	332	0	0.1%	0
12/08	333	1	0.3%	0
Annual Growth	3.4%	(81.2%)	—	—

2011 Year-End Financials

Debt ratio: —
Return on equity: —
Cash ($ mil.): 3
Current ratio: 1.10
Long-term debt ($ mil.): —
Dividends
Yield: —
Payout: —
Market value ($ mil.): —

GUILFORD COUNTY SCHOOL SYSTEM

LOCATIONS

HQ: GUILFORD COUNTY SCHOOL SYSTEM
712 N EUGENE ST, GREENSBORO, NC 27401-1622
Phone: 336-370-8100

HISTORICAL FINANCIALS
Company Type: Private

Income Statement
FYE: June 30

	REVENUE ($ mil.)	NET INCOME ($ mil.)	NET PROFIT MARGIN	EMPLOYEES
06/11	692	(0)	—	8,000
06/09	0	(0)	—	0
06/03	0	0	—	0
06/02	546	69	12.8%	0
Annual Growth	8.2%	—	—	—

2011 Year-End Financials

Debt ratio: —
Return on equity: (-0.10)%
Cash ($ mil.): 28
Current ratio: 0.70
Long-term debt ($ mil.): —
Dividends
Yield: —
Payout: —
Market value ($ mil.): —

GULF EQUIPMENT CORPORATION A CLOSE CORPORATION

LOCATIONS

HQ: GULF EQUIPMENT CORPORATION A CLOSE CORPORATION
5540 BUSINESS PARK WAY, THEODORE, AL 36582-1616
Phone: 251-653-5075
Web: www.gulfequipment.net

HISTORICAL FINANCIALS
Company Type: Private

Income Statement
FYE: December 31

	REVENUE ($ mil.)	NET INCOME ($ mil.)	NET PROFIT MARGIN	EMPLOYEES
12/11	122	26	21.5%	60
12/10	107	15	14.6%	0
Annual Growth	13.4%	66.9%	—	—

2011 Year-End Financials

Debt ratio: —
Return on equity: 21.50%
Cash ($ mil.): 51
Current ratio: 10.00
Long-term debt ($ mil.): —
Dividends
Yield: —
Payout: —
Market value ($ mil.): —

GULF INTERSTATE ENGINEERING COMPANY

LOCATIONS

HQ: GULF INTERSTATE ENGINEERING COMPANY
16010 BARKERS POINT LN # 600, HOUSTON, TX 77079-9000
Phone: 713-850-3400
Web: www.postoakgraphics.net

HISTORICAL FINANCIALS
Company Type: Private

Income Statement
FYE: December 31

	REVENUE ($ mil.)	NET INCOME ($ mil.)	NET PROFIT MARGIN	EMPLOYEES
12/11	152	5	3.7%	350
12/10	94	0	0.7%	0
12/03	52	(0)	—	0
12/02	85	3	4.1%	0
Annual Growth	21.4%	17.6%	—	—

2011 Year-End Financials

Debt ratio: —
Return on equity: 3.70%
Cash ($ mil.): 1
Current ratio: 1.30
Long-term debt ($ mil.): —
Dividends
Yield: —
Payout: —
Market value ($ mil.): —

GUSTAVUS ADOLPHUS COLLEGE

You don't have to enter the Pearly Gates to get into this St. Peter Minnesota university. However Gustavus Adolphus College is deeply rooted in its Evangelical Lutheran Church heritage. The private liberal arts coeducational school offers some 70 majors in about two dozen academic departments including education fine arts humanities and social sciences. It has a student population of about 2500 and a student/faculty ratio of 12-to-1. Gustavus Adolphus College was founded in 1862 by Swedish Lutheran immigrant and pastor Eric Norelius. It is named after 17th-century Swedish king Gustav II Adolf.

EXECUTIVES

VP Finance and Treasurer, Kenneth C. Westphal
Assistant VP College Relations, Stacia Senne
Controller, Kelly Waldron
Registrar, Kristianne Reinholtzen
Director Alumni Relations, Randall Stuckey
Director Human Resources, Kirk Beyer
Director Safety and Security, Raymond H. Thrower Jr.
Director Gustavus Technology Services, Bruce Aarsvold
Academic Dean, Eric Eliason
Academic Dean, Mariangela McGuire
President, Jack R. Ohle
VP Academic Affairs and Provost, Mary E. Morton Strey
VP College Relations, Gwendolyn Freed
VP Institutional Advancement, Thomas Young
VP Admission and Student Financial Assistance, Mark Anderson
VP Student Affairs and Dean Students, Henry Toutain

LOCATIONS

HQ: Gustavus Adolphus College
800 W. College Ave., St. Peter MN 56082
Phone: 507-933-8000   **Fax:** 507-933-7474
Web: gustavus.edu

HISTORICAL FINANCIALS

Company Type: School

Income Statement

	REVENUE ($ mil.)	NET INCOME ($ mil.)	NET PROFIT MARGIN	EMPLOYEES
05/11	97	19	20.0%	700
05/10	106	(1)	—	0
05/09	40	(34)	—	0
05/07	90	21	23.4%	0
Annual Growth	2.8%	(2.4%)	—	—

FYE: May 31

2011 Year-End Financials

Debt ratio: ——
Return on equity: 20.00%
Cash ($ mil.): 16
Current ratio: —
Long-term debt ($ mil.): —
Dividends
Yield: —
Payout: —
Market value ($ mil.): —

GUTHRIE CLINIC LTD.

LOCATIONS

HQ: GUTHRIE CLINIC LTD.
1 GUTHRIE SQ, SAYRE, PA 18840-1699
Phone: 570-888-5858
Web: www.guthrie.org

HISTORICAL FINANCIALS

Company Type: Private

Income Statement

	REVENUE ($ mil.)	NET INCOME ($ mil.)	NET PROFIT MARGIN	EMPLOYEES
06/11	280	49	17.7%	1,600
06/10	210	(19)	—	0
06/08	191	(20)	—	0
06/05	155	(6)	—	0
Annual Growth	21.7%	—	—	—

FYE: June 30

2011 Year-End Financials

Debt ratio: ——
Return on equity: 17.70%
Cash ($ mil.): 6
Current ratio: —
Long-term debt ($ mil.): —
Dividends
Yield: —
Payout: —
Market value ($ mil.): —

GUTHRIE HEALTHCARE SYSTEM

Guthrie Healthcare System is a community health care organization serving residents of the Twin Tiers region of northern Pennsylvania and southern New York through a network of hospitals community clinics physicians' practices and specialty care facilities. The flagship facility is Robert Packer Hospital in Sayre Pennsylvania a 238-bed tertiary care teaching hospital (affiliated with Pennsylvania's Mansfield University) that provides a comprehensive range of health services including emergency/trauma care pediatric care orthopedics and rehabilitative care. The system also includes two additional hospitals nursing homes a senior care community a hospice care program and a home health agency.

Operations Corning Hospital which serves Steuben and Chemung Counties in New York is a 99-bed community hospital and state-designated stroke center. Troy Community Hospital offers traditional inpatient and outpatient services including diagnostic testing rehabilitation surgery and emergency services.

Strategy Guthrie Healthcare System grows through new construction as well as expansion of existing facilities. New facilities to replace both Corning and Troy are currently in development. In addition in 2011 and 2012 Guthrie has opened an endocrine and bariatric center a new pediatric center and new facilities in Wellsboro PA and Owego NY.

EXECUTIVES

President and CEO, Mark Stensager
CFO Guthrie Health, Craig Faerber

President and COO Robert Packer Hospital, Mary N. Mannix
Administrator Troy Community Hospital, Staci Covey
Co-CEO; President and CEO Guthrie Clinic, Joseph Scopelliti
VP Corporate Affairs Guthrie Clinic, Lynn Smaha
President and COO Corning Hospital, Shirley Magana

LOCATIONS

HQ: Guthrie Healthcare System
1 Guthrie Sq., Sayre PA 18840-1625
Phone: 570-888-6666   **Fax:** 570-882-5463
Web: www.guthrie.org

PRODUCTS/OPERATIONS

Selected Facilities

Corning Hospital
Guthrie Hospice
Robert Packer Hospital
Sayre House Nursing Home
Tioga Nursing Facility
Tioga Senior Care Community
Troy Community Hospital

COMPETITORS

Ascension Health
Community Health Systems
Golden Horizons
HCR ManorCare
United Health Services Hospitals

HISTORICAL FINANCIALS

Company Type: Private - Not-for-Profit

Income Statement

	REVENUE ($ mil.)	NET INCOME ($ mil.)	NET PROFIT MARGIN	EMPLOYEES
06/11	50	14	29.0%	2,575
06/10	56	24	43.3%	0
06/08	52	17	33.6%	0
Annual Growth	(1.9%)	(8.9%)	—	—

FYE: June 30

2011 Year-End Financials

Debt ratio: ——
Return on equity: 29.00%
Cash ($ mil.): 0
Current ratio: —
Long-term debt ($ mil.): —
Dividends
Yield: —
Payout: —
Market value ($ mil.): —

GWINNETT HEALTH SYSTEM INC.

Gwinnett Health System provides a gamut of medical services in northern Georgia. The 553-bed hospital system consists of the Gwinnett Medical Center-Lawrenceville and the Gwinnett Medical Center-Duluth. Both hospitals are located northeast of Atlanta and offer acute care day surgery emergency care and rehabilitation. The system also includes the Gwinnett Women's Pavilion (maternity and neonatal care) and the Gwinnett Extended Care Center. The Glancy Rehabilitation Center offers intensive inpatient and outpatient rehabilitation. Other facilities provide diagnostic imaging and general physician care.

Geographic Reach

The hospital system serves patients in northern Georgia.

Operations

Gwinnett Medical Center-Lawrenceville offers single incision laparoscopic surgery and home to a Level II trauma center while Gwinnett Medical Center-Duluth offers an array of specialty services including surgical weight management da Vinci? robotic surgery and sports medicine.

Gwinnett's 800 affiliated physicians serve more than 400000 patients annually.

Strategy

The hospital system has undergone expansion efforts to strengthen its service offerings and increase its market share. In 2011 the Lawrenceville campus opened the Gwinnett Breast Center to provide better breast health services. (In 2009 Gwinnett completed construction of a new 8-story patient tower at the Lawrenceville campus that increased the hospital's capacity by adding 155 private patient beds).

Company Background

Gwinnett also occasionally divests assets that are not core to its growth strategies. For instance the company sold its SummitRidge psychiatric hospital to Universal Health Services in 2008.

EXECUTIVES

SVP and CFO, Thomas Y. McBride III
President CEO and Director, Philip R. (Phil) Wolfe, age 58
VP and CIO, Ed Brown
VP Human Resources, Steve Nadeau
VP Marketing and Development, John Riddle
VP Operations Facility Administrator, Lea Bay
VP Physician and Community Alliances, Janet Schwalbe
Corporate Controller, Scott Orem
Chairman, Steven Boyd
VP Clinical Services, Ron Corder
Legal Counsel, Chip Wheeler
Planning Coordinator Planning and Development, Mark Mullin
VP Support Services, Pam Kauffman
VP Managed Care, Tom Lynch
President CEO and Director, Philip R. (Phil) Wolfe, age 58
Director, Wayne Sykes
Director, Jay Desai
Director, Joseph C. Finley
Director, Willard C. Hearin III
Director, Eric Kreimer
Director, Chung H. Lee
Director, Miles H. Mason III
Director, David McCleskey
Director, Kathryn Parsons Willis
Director, Carolyn Hill
Director, Edward Radford
Director, Jock Connell
Director, Tom Martin
Director, Manfred Sandler
Auditors: Ernst&YoungLLP

LOCATIONS

HQ: Gwinnett Health System Inc.
1000 Medical Center Blvd., Lawrenceville GA 30045
Phone: 678-442-4321   **Fax:** 450-746-4438
Web: www.qit.com

PRODUCTS/OPERATIONS

Selected Services
Bariatrics
Cancer Care

Cardiac Services
Cosmetic Surgery
Diabetes Education
Emergency Department
Endoscopy
Fitness
Imaging Services
Inpatient Medical Group
Laboratory Services
Mobile Mammography
Neurology
Nutrition & Weight Management
Orthopedics
Pain Management Center
Respiratory Care
Rehabilitation
Robotic Surgery
Sinus Services
Skilled Nursing and Extended Care
Sleep Lab
Stroke Care
Surgical Services
Trauma Services
Women's Services
Wound Treatment Center

COMPETITORS

AnMed Health
Athens Regional
  Medical Center
DeKalb Medical
Emory Healthcare
HCA
Northside Hospital

Piedmont Fayette
  Hospital
Regency Hospital
Saint Joseph' s Health
  System
St. Mary' s Health Care

HISTORICAL FINANCIALS
Company Type: Private - Not-for-Profit

Income Statement
FYE: June 30

	REVENUE ($ mil.)	NET INCOME ($ mil.)	NET PROFIT MARGIN	EMPLOYEES
06/11	599	53	8.9%	2,050
06/10	0	0	—	0
06/06	517	38	7.5%	0
06/05	473	56	12.0%	0
Annual Growth	8.2%	(2.2%)	—	—

2011 Year-End Financials

Debt ratio: —
Return on equity: 8.90%
Cash ($ mil.): 96
Current ratio: 2.90
Long-term debt ($ mil.): —
Dividends
  Yield: —
  Payout: —
Market value ($ mil.): —

H. LEE MOFFITT CANCER CENTER AND RESEARCH INSTITUTE HOSPITAL INC

LOCATIONS

HQ: H. LEE MOFFITT CANCER CENTER AND RESEARCH INSTITUTE HOSPITAL INC
12902 USF MAGNOLIA DR, TAMPA, FL 33612-9416
Phone: 813-745-4673
Web: www.moffitt.org

HISTORICAL FINANCIALS
Company Type: Private

Income Statement
FYE: June 30

	REVENUE ($ mil.)	NET INCOME ($ mil.)	NET PROFIT MARGIN	EMPLOYEES
06/12	771	(7)	—	3,700
06/11	744	22	3.0%	0
06/10	676	19	2.9%	0
06/09	599	(20)	—	0
Annual Growth	8.8%	—	—	—

2012 Year-End Financials

Debt ratio: —
Return on equity: (-1.00)%
Cash ($ mil.): 31
Current ratio: 1.10
Long-term debt ($ mil.): —
Dividends
  Yield: —
  Payout: —
Market value ($ mil.): —

H. W. LOCHNER INC.

LOCATIONS

HQ: H. W. LOCHNER INC.
20 N WACKER DR STE 1200, CHICAGO, IL 60606-2901
Phone: 312-372-7346
Web: www.hwlochner.com

HISTORICAL FINANCIALS
Company Type: Private

Income Statement
FYE: April 30

	REVENUE ($ mil.)	NET INCOME ($ mil.)	NET PROFIT MARGIN	EMPLOYEES
04/11	96	0	0.4%	400
04/10	53	1	2.4%	0
04/09	75	1	1.9%	0
04/08	70	2	3.0%	0
Annual Growth	10.8%	(42.5%)	—	—

2011 Year-End Financials

Debt ratio: —
Return on equity: 0.40%
Cash ($ mil.): 5
Current ratio: 1.40
Long-term debt ($ mil.): —
Dividends
  Yield: —
  Payout: —
Market value ($ mil.): —

HALEY & ALDRICH INC.

LOCATIONS

HQ: HALEY & ALDRICH INC.
70 BLANCHARD RD STE 204, BURLINGTON, MA 01803-5100
Phone: 617-886-7400
Web: www.haleyaldrich.com

HISTORICAL FINANCIALS
Company Type: Private

Income Statement
FYE: December 31

	REVENUE ($ mil.)	NET INCOME ($ mil.)	NET PROFIT MARGIN	EMPLOYEES
12/11*	105	0	0.9%	498
09/06	92	0	0.4%	0
09/05	74	0	0.5%	0
09/04	75	0	0.1%	0
Annual Growth	11.9%	145.3%	—	—

*Fiscal year change

2011 Year-End Financials

Debt ratio: —
Return on equity: 0.90%
Cash ($ mil.): 2
Current ratio: 0.90
Long-term debt ($ mil.): —

Dividends
Yield: —
Payout: —
Market value ($ mil.): —

HALMAR INTERNATIONAL LLC

LOCATIONS

HQ: HALMAR INTERNATIONAL LLC
421 E ROUTE 59, NANUET, NY 10954-2908
Phone: 845-735-3511
Web: www.halmarinternational.com

HISTORICAL FINANCIALS
Company Type: Private

Income Statement
FYE: December 31

	REVENUE ($ mil.)	NET INCOME ($ mil.)	NET PROFIT MARGIN	EMPLOYEES
12/11	130	11	9.0%	120
12/09	25	2	11.1%	0
Annual Growth	416.2%	318.2%	—	—

2011 Year-End Financials

Debt ratio: —
Return on equity: 9.00%
Cash ($ mil.): 4
Current ratio: 0.30
Long-term debt ($ mil.): —

Dividends
Yield: —
Payout: —
Market value ($ mil.): —

HALO LLC

LOCATIONS

HQ: HALO LLC
9820 ASSOCIATION CT, INDIANAPOLIS, IN 46280-1962
Phone: 317-575-9992

HISTORICAL FINANCIALS
Company Type: Private

Income Statement
FYE: December 31

	REVENUE ($ mil.)	NET INCOME ($ mil.)	NET PROFIT MARGIN	EMPLOYEES
12/11	105	3	3.6%	321
12/08	95	4	4.3%	0
12/06	81	3	4.0%	0
12/05	69	13	18.7%	0
Annual Growth	15.1%	(33.8%)	—	—

2011 Year-End Financials

Debt ratio: —
Return on equity: 3.60%
Cash ($ mil.): 1
Current ratio: 0.70
Long-term debt ($ mil.): —

Dividends
Yield: —
Payout: —
Market value ($ mil.): —

HAMLINE UNIVERSITY

LOCATIONS

HQ: HAMLINE UNIVERSITY
1536 HEWITT AVE, SAINT PAUL, MN 55104-1284
Phone: 651-523-2202
Web: www.hamline.edu

HISTORICAL FINANCIALS
Company Type: Private

Income Statement
FYE: June 30

	REVENUE ($ mil.)	NET INCOME ($ mil.)	NET PROFIT MARGIN	EMPLOYEES
06/12	92	1	1.3%	563
06/11	91	12	13.9%	0
06/09	86	(17)	—	0
06/08	96	(6)	—	0
Annual Growth	(1.3%)	—	—	—

2012 Year-End Financials

Debt ratio: —
Return on equity: 1.30%
Cash ($ mil.): 9
Current ratio: —
Long-term debt ($ mil.): —

Dividends
Yield: —
Payout: —
Market value ($ mil.): —

HANCOCK REGIONAL HOSPITAL

LOCATIONS

HQ: HANCOCK REGIONAL HOSPITAL
801 N STATE ST, GREENFIELD, IN 46140-1270
Phone: 317-462-5544
Web: www.hancockregionalhospital.org

HISTORICAL FINANCIALS
Company Type: Private

Income Statement
FYE: December 31

	REVENUE ($ mil.)	NET INCOME ($ mil.)	NET PROFIT MARGIN	EMPLOYEES
12/11	96	(0)	—	620
12/10	94	6	7.2%	0
Annual Growth	3.0%	—	—	—

2011 Year-End Financials

Debt ratio: —
Return on equity: (-0.10)%
Cash ($ mil.): 12
Current ratio: 1.50
Long-term debt ($ mil.): —

Dividends
Yield: —
Payout: —
Market value ($ mil.): —

HANOVER HOSPITAL INC.

LOCATIONS

HQ: HANOVER HOSPITAL INC.
300 HIGHLAND AVE, HANOVER, PA 17331-2297
Phone: 717-637-3711
Web: www.hanoverhospital.org

HISTORICAL FINANCIALS
Company Type: Private

Income Statement
FYE: June 30

	REVENUE ($ mil.)	NET INCOME ($ mil.)	NET PROFIT MARGIN	EMPLOYEES
06/12	141	1	1.2%	1,400
06/11	140	10	7.4%	0
06/10	127	(6)	—	0
06/09	135	0	0.1%	0
Annual Growth	1.4%	106.9%	—	—

2012 Year-End Financials

Debt ratio: —
Return on equity: 1.20%
Cash ($ mil.): 9
Current ratio: 1.10
Long-term debt ($ mil.): —

Dividends
Yield: —
Payout: —
Market value ($ mil.): —

HARBISON-MAHONY-HIGGINS BUILDERS INC.

LOCATIONS

HQ: HARBISON-MAHONY-HIGGINS BUILDERS INC.
15 BUSINESS PKWY STE 101, SACRAMENTO, CA 95828
Phone: 916-383-4825
Web: www.hmh.com

HISTORICAL FINANCIALS
Company Type: Private

Income Statement
FYE: December 31

	REVENUE ($ mil.)	NET INCOME ($ mil.)	NET PROFIT MARGIN	EMPLOYEES
12/11	105	0	—	150
12/10	128	0	—	0
12/09	0	0	—	0
12/08	380	10	2.8%	0
Annual Growth	(34.8%)	—	—	—

2011 Year-End Financials
Debt ratio: ——
Return on equity: —
Cash ($ mil.): 15
Current ratio: 1.30
Long-term debt ($ mil.): —
Dividends
 Yield: —
 Payout: —
Market value ($ mil.): —

HARBOR BUNKERING CORPORATION

LOCATIONS

HQ: HARBOR BUNKERING CORPORATION
404 AVE FERNANDEZ JUNCOS, SAN JUAN, PR 00901-3223
Phone: 787-723-1182
Web: www.harborbunkering.com

HISTORICAL FINANCIALS
Company Type: Private

Income Statement
FYE: September 30

	REVENUE ($ mil.)	NET INCOME ($ mil.)	NET PROFIT MARGIN	EMPLOYEES
09/11	131	1	0.8%	43
09/10	91	1	1.2%	0
09/09	75	0	0.0%	0
09/08	121	0	0.7%	0
Annual Growth	2.8%	9.0%	—	—

2011 Year-End Financials
Debt ratio: ——
Return on equity: 0.80%
Cash ($ mil.): 1
Current ratio: 0.90
Long-term debt ($ mil.): —
Dividends
 Yield: —
 Payout: —
Market value ($ mil.): —

HARBOR DEVELOPMENTAL DISABILITIES FOUNDATION INC

LOCATIONS

HQ: HARBOR DEVELOPMENTAL DISABILITIES FOUNDATION INC
21231 HAWTHORNE BLVD, TORRANCE, CA 90503-5501
Phone: 310-540-1711
Web: www.harborrc.org

HISTORICAL FINANCIALS
Company Type: Private

Income Statement
FYE: June 30

	REVENUE ($ mil.)	NET INCOME ($ mil.)	NET PROFIT MARGIN	EMPLOYEES
06/11	127	(0)	—	225
06/10	122	(0)	—	0
06/09	123	0	0.0%	0
06/08	116	0	0.0%	0
Annual Growth	3.0%	—	—	—

2011 Year-End Financials
Debt ratio: ——
Return on equity: —
Cash ($ mil.): 16
Current ratio: 0.90
Long-term debt ($ mil.): —
Dividends
 Yield: —
 Payout: —
Market value ($ mil.): —

HARBOUR PETROLEUM CORP. OF BREVARD INC.

LOCATIONS

HQ: HARBOUR PETROLEUM CORP. OF BREVARD INC.
21 W FEE AVE STE F, MELBOURNE, FL 32901-4478
Phone: 321-724-0641
Web: www.harbourpetro.com

HISTORICAL FINANCIALS
Company Type: Private

Income Statement
FYE: December 31

	REVENUE ($ mil.)	NET INCOME ($ mil.)	NET PROFIT MARGIN	EMPLOYEES
12/11	108	0	0.2%	7
12/10	83	0	0.1%	0
12/09	73	0	0.2%	0
12/08	103	0	0.3%	0
Annual Growth	1.8%	(7.9%)	—	—

2011 Year-End Financials
Debt ratio: ——
Return on equity: 0.20%
Cash ($ mil.): 1
Current ratio: 0.90
Long-term debt ($ mil.): —
Dividends
 Yield: —
 Payout: —
Market value ($ mil.): —

HARDIN COUNTY BOARD OF EDUCATION

LOCATIONS

HQ: HARDIN COUNTY BOARD OF EDUCATION
65 W A JENKINS RD, ELIZABETHTOWN, KY 42701-8452
Phone: 270-769-8800

HISTORICAL FINANCIALS
Company Type: Private

Income Statement
FYE: June 30

	REVENUE ($ mil.)	NET INCOME ($ mil.)	NET PROFIT MARGIN	EMPLOYEES
06/12	169	23	14.2%	2,700
06/11	165	23	13.9%	0
06/10*	112	17	15.5%	0
12/09	0	0	—	0
Annual Growth	—	—	—	—

*Fiscal year change

2012 Year-End Financials
Debt ratio: ——
Return on equity: 14.20%
Cash ($ mil.): 23
Current ratio: —
Long-term debt ($ mil.): —
Dividends
 Yield: —
 Payout: —
Market value ($ mil.): —

HARDING UNIVERSITY INC.

LOCATIONS

HQ: HARDING UNIVERSITY INC.
900 E CENTER AVE, SEARCY, AR 72149-0002
Phone: 501-279-4000
Web: www.hugsr.edu

HISTORICAL FINANCIALS
Company Type: Private

Income Statement
FYE: June 30

	REVENUE ($ mil.)	NET INCOME ($ mil.)	NET PROFIT MARGIN	EMPLOYEES
06/12	111	4	4.1%	1,445
06/11	98	13	13.8%	0
06/10	95	7	8.0%	0
06/09	95	(20)	—	0
Annual Growth	5.3%	—	—	—

2012 Year-End Financials

Debt ratio: —
Return on equity: 4.10%
Cash ($ mil.): 10
Current ratio: —
Long-term debt ($ mil.): —

Dividends
Yield: —
Payout: —
Market value ($ mil.): —

2011 Year-End Financials

Debt ratio: —
Return on equity: 14.00%
Cash ($ mil.): 0
Current ratio: 1.70
Long-term debt ($ mil.): —

Dividends
Yield: —
Payout: —
Market value ($ mil.): —

EXECUTIVES

President, Mike Hamilton
VP Sales, Dick Veale
Office Manager Finance, Karen Thareererg
Controller, Brian Jung
Documentation Assistant, Christine Cho
Production Supervisor Manufacturing, Sergio Novo
Logistics Manager, Brenda A. Ho
General Manager, Roland Sebastian
Quality Control Operator, Gene Beenders
Sales Manager, Rene Buchhammer
Sales Assistant, Chad Robertson
Logistics Documentation, Derek Wu
Documentation Supervisor, Ryan Tang

LOCATIONS

HQ: Harland M. Braun & Co. Inc.
4010 Whiteside St., Los Angeles CA 90063
Phone: 323-263-9275   **Fax:** 323-263-3010
Web: www.braunexp.com

COMPETITORS

Danier Leather   Prime Tanning Co.
Pittards   S. B. Foot Tanning

HISTORICAL FINANCIALS

Company Type: Private

Income Statement

FYE: October 31

	REVENUE ($ mil.)	NET INCOME ($ mil.)	NET PROFIT MARGIN	EMPLOYEES
10/11	290	0	0.0%	30
10/10	212	0	0.2%	0
10/09	136	0	0.1%	0
10/05	107	0	0.1%	0
Annual Growth	39.2%	(41.5%)	—	—

2011 Year-End Financials

Debt ratio: —
Return on equity: —
Cash ($ mil.): 1
Current ratio: 1.00
Long-term debt ($ mil.): —

Dividends
Yield: —
Payout: —
Market value ($ mil.): —

HARDWOOD PRODUCTS COMPANY LP

Hardwood Products Company manufactures woodenware items for applications in the dairy foodservice and crafts markets as well as for medical and industrial uses. Its food and craft products include skewers sticks spoons and other items produced under the Gold Bond and Trophy brands. The company markets its single-use swabs applicators tongue depressors and specialty products for medical and diagnostic applications under the Puritan brand. It also offers critical-environment cleaning applicators. Hardwood Products Company was founded in 1919.

EXECUTIVES

General Manager and COO, Terry N. Young
EVP Global and Diagnostic Sales, Timothy Templet
VP Medical Sales, Garrett Byrnes
CFO, Scott Wellman
VP Operations Hardwood, James Cartwright
Director of Manufacturing Puritan, Paul Dube
VP Sales South Region, Elaine Maliff
SVP Sales, David Perkins
VP Sales West Region, Susan Shrader
VP Purchasing, Joseph Cartwright
Human Resources Manager, Nancy Lovell
Director of Information Technology, Heidi Thompson
VP Quality Assurance and Regulatory Affairs, William Young
Auditors: MacdonaldPage&CoLLC

LOCATIONS

HQ: Hardwood Products Company LLC
31 School St., Guilford ME 04443-0149
Phone: 207-876-3311   **Fax:** 207-876-3130
Web: www.hwppuritan.com

COMPETITORS

Johnson & Johnson   Unilever
Kimberly-Clark Health

HISTORICAL FINANCIALS

Company Type: Private

Income Statement

FYE: December 31

	REVENUE ($ mil.)	NET INCOME ($ mil.)	NET PROFIT MARGIN	EMPLOYEES
12/11	44	6	14.0%	382
12/10	35	5	16.3%	0
12/09	34	5	16.0%	0
Annual Growth	13.2%	5.8%	—	—

HARFORD COUNTY BOARD OF EDUCATION

LOCATIONS

HQ: HARFORD COUNTY BOARD OF EDUCATION
102 S HICKORY AVE, BEL AIR, MD 21014-3731
Phone: 410-838-7300
Web: www.acps.org

HISTORICAL FINANCIALS

Company Type: Private

Income Statement

FYE: June 30

	REVENUE ($ mil.)	NET INCOME ($ mil.)	NET PROFIT MARGIN	EMPLOYEES
06/12	536	1	0.3%	5,400
06/08	572	(0)	—	0
06/07	481	6	1.4%	0
06/06	339	0	—	0
Annual Growth	16.5%	—	—	—

2012 Year-End Financials

Debt ratio: —
Return on equity: 0.30%
Cash ($ mil.): 11
Current ratio: —
Long-term debt ($ mil.): —

Dividends
Yield: —
Payout: —
Market value ($ mil.): —

HARLAND M. BRAUN & CO. INC.

Hide (the raw material) and seek (find a buyer) are all in a day's work for Harland M. Braun & Co. Operating through its subsidiary Braun Export the company supplies raw hide goods primarily cattle hides and skins and to a lesser extent pigskin and kipskins to tanners. A slate of services is provided for leather (wet blue and crust) hide and skin manufacturing as well as brokering exporting and importing. Dotting the US Braun & Co.'s processing facilities tie in with several suppliers of Holstein steer hides. Partnerships are sealed with such meat packers as JBS Packerland Group Central Valley Meat Creekstone Farms Premium Beef Manning Beef Nebraska Beef and American Beef Packers.

Established more than 45 years ago Harland M. Braun is a frequent recipient of the "Good Corporate Citizens" award given by the Sanitation Districts of Los Angeles County. The "Atta Boy!" recognizes businesses that meet the County's environmental wastewater discharge requirements.

HARNETT COUNTY BOARD OF EDUCATION

LOCATIONS

HQ: HARNETT COUNTY BOARD OF EDUCATION
1008 11TH ST, LILLINGTON, NC 27546
Phone: 910-893-8151
Web: www.westernharnett.com

HISTORICAL FINANCIALS
Company Type: Private

Income Statement
FYE: June 30

	REVENUE ($ mil.)	NET INCOME ($ mil.)	NET PROFIT MARGIN	EMPLOYEES
06/12	154	4	2.9%	2,105
06/11	151	4	2.6%	0
06/10	170	3	1.9%	0
Annual Growth	(5.0%)	15.8%	—	—

2012 Year-End Financials
Debt ratio: —
Return on equity: 2.90%
Cash ($ mil.): 19
Current ratio: —
Long-term debt ($ mil.): —

Dividends
Yield: —
Payout: —
Market value ($ mil.): —

HISTORICAL FINANCIALS
Company Type: Private

Income Statement
FYE: April 30

	REVENUE ($ mil.)	NET INCOME ($ mil.)	NET PROFIT MARGIN	EMPLOYEES
04/12	345	(22)	—	2,400
04/11	363	15	4.2%	0
04/10	343	37	10.9%	0
04/09	297	9	3.3%	0
Annual Growth	5.1%	—	—	—

2012 Year-End Financials
Debt ratio: —
Return on equity: (-6.60)%
Cash ($ mil.): 21
Current ratio: 1.40
Long-term debt ($ mil.): —

Dividends
Yield: —
Payout: —
Market value ($ mil.): —

---

by the Claremont University Consortium. The group shares resources and offers dual degree programs. HMC alums include Jonathan Gay creator of Flash software and Unison founder Rick Sontag.

EXECUTIVES
VP Administration and Finance and Treasurer, Andrew R. Dorantes
President, Maria M. Klawe, age 60
VP College Advancement, Marc L. Archambault
VP Admission and Financial Aid, Thyra L. Briggs
VP Academic Affairs and Dean Faculty, Robert J. Cave
VP Student Affairs and Dean Students, Marguerite A. (Maggie) Browning
VP Computing and Information Services and CIO, Joseph Vaughan

LOCATIONS
HQ: HARVEY MUDD COLLEGE
301 E 12TH ST, CLAREMONT, CA 91711-5901
Phone: 909-621-8000
Web: www.hmc.edu

HISTORICAL FINANCIALS
Company Type: School

Income Statement
FYE: June 30

	REVENUE ($ mil.)	NET INCOME ($ mil.)	NET PROFIT MARGIN	EMPLOYEES
06/12	69	(3)	—	235
06/11	65	1	2.4%	0
06/10	56	(5)	—	0
06/08	74	16	22.4%	0
Annual Growth	(2.4%)	—	—	—

2012 Year-End Financials
Debt ratio: —
Return on equity: (-5.60)%
Cash ($ mil.): 0
Current ratio: —
Long-term debt ($ mil.): —

Dividends
Yield: —
Payout: —
Market value ($ mil.): —

HARPEL OIL COMPANY

LOCATIONS
HQ: HARPEL OIL COMPANY
5480 BRIGHTON BLVD, COMMERCE CITY, CO 80022-3607
Phone: 303-294-0767
Web: www.harpeloil.com

HISTORICAL FINANCIALS
Company Type: Private

Income Statement
FYE: December 31

	REVENUE ($ mil.)	NET INCOME ($ mil.)	NET PROFIT MARGIN	EMPLOYEES
12/11	102	0	0.3%	16
12/10	64	0	0.3%	0
12/08	22	(0)	—	0
12/07	27	0	0.6%	0
Annual Growth	55.2%	17.2%	—	—

2011 Year-End Financials
Debt ratio: —
Return on equity: 0.30%
Cash ($ mil.): 0
Current ratio: 0.90
Long-term debt ($ mil.): —

Dividends
Yield: —
Payout: —
Market value ($ mil.): —

HARRISON MEDICAL CENTER

LOCATIONS
HQ: HARRISON MEDICAL CENTER
2520 CHERRY AVE, BREMERTON, WA 98310-4229
Phone: 360-744-6510
Web: www.harrisonmedical.org

HARVEST LAND COOPERATIVE

LOCATIONS
HQ: HARVEST LAND COOPERATIVE
711 FRONT ST, MORGAN, MN 56266
Phone: 507-249-3196
Web: www.harvestland.com

HISTORICAL FINANCIALS
Company Type: Private

Income Statement
FYE: August 31

	REVENUE ($ mil.)	NET INCOME ($ mil.)	NET PROFIT MARGIN	EMPLOYEES
08/11	226	6	2.9%	150
08/10	183	7	4.1%	0
08/09	221	10	4.7%	0
08/08	198	6	3.1%	0
Annual Growth	4.5%	1.6%	—	—

2011 Year-End Financials
Debt ratio: —
Return on equity: 2.90%
Cash ($ mil.): 2
Current ratio: —
Long-term debt ($ mil.): —

Dividends
Yield: —
Payout: —
Market value ($ mil.): —

HARVEY MUDD COLLEGE

Mudders get down and dirty with math and science. More than 700 undergraduate students (called "Mudders") attend Harvey Mudd College (HMC) a private liberal arts school that specializes in engineering mathematics and the sciences. The college was established in 1955 by mining engineer Harvey S. Mudd co-founder of one of the richest copper mines in the world Cyprus Mines. HMC is a member of The Claremont Colleges a confederation of five independent undergraduate colleges and two graduate schools that is managed

---

HAWAI I PACIFIC HEALTH

Hawaii may be paradise but even paradise's residents get sick sometimes. That's when Hawai'i Pacific Health (HPH) surfs in to save the day. HPH is a not-for-profit health care system consisting of four hospitals (Kapi'olani Medical Center for Women & Children Pali Momi Medical Center Straub Clinic & Hospital and Wilcox Memorial Hospital) across the islands with a combined capacity of 550 beds. The system offers a full array of tertiary specialty and acute care services through its hospitals which also serve as teaching and research centers as well as about 50 outpatient centers. Specialized services offered by HPH include cardiac care maternity services oncology orthopedics and pediatric care.

Operations

HPH supplies a wide range of primary and specialty medical services through its physician organizations. The Kapi'olani Medical Specialists group for instance comprises more than 100 physicians and partners with Kapi'olani Medical Center for Women & Children to care for patients from infancy through adulthood. The center also functions as the women's health and pediatric teaching hospital for the University of Hawaii School of Medicine. Its Visiting Specialists group provides care to the islands where HPH doesn't have primary care facilities.

The system has partnered with Surgical Care Affiliates to build an outpatient surgical center in Honolulu in an effort to meet growing demand there. The center dubbed Surgicare of Hawai'i offers an array of medical services including orthopedics pain management ophthalmology general surgery and podiatry; the facility opened in 2010.

Also in 2010 the hospital system embarked on a 6-year $580 million master facility plan to make expansion and improvement efforts at some of its primary hospital locations. The first stage includes new intensive care units and parking capacity at the Kapi'olani Medical Center.

Company Background

The organization was formed through the 2001 merger of three entities: Kapi'olani Health Straub Clinic & Hospital and Wilcox Health System.

EXECUTIVES

Director Philanthropy Wilcox Health Foundation, Jill Lowry

President and CEO, Chuck Sted

COO Straub Hospital, Art Gladstone, age 48

EVP Human Resources and Organizational Development, Gail Lerch

Director Philanthropy and Community Relations Wilcox Memorial Hospital, Lani Yukimura

EVP and Chief Medical Officer, Kenneth B. Robbins

EVP and CEO Hospital Operations; CEO Kapi'olani Medical Center for Women & Children, Raymond P. Vara Jr.

EVP and CFO, David Okabe

EVP and General Counsel, Bob Ching

EVP Strategic Business Development, Ginny Pressler

COO Kapi'olani Medical Center at Pali Momi, Jen Chahanovich

COO Kapi'olani Medical Center for Women & Children, Martha Smith

President and CEO Wilcox Memorial Hospital, Kathy Clark

EVP Revenue Management and Information Technology and CIO, Steve Robertson

Chief Medical Officer Kapi'olani Medical Specialist, Kenneth Nakamura

Director Communications and Marketing, Claire Tong

COO Kauai Medical Clinic, Lynn Joseph

Chief Medical Officer Kauai Medical Clinic, Geri Young

Chief Medical Officer Straub Clinic & Hospital, Yvonne Kwan

LOCATIONS

HQ: Hawai'i Pacific Health
55 Merchant St. 27th Fl., Honolulu HI 96813
Phone: 808-535-7401 **Fax:** 808-535-7411
Web: www.hawaiipacifichealth.org

PRODUCTS/OPERATIONS

Selected Facilities

Kapi'olani Medical Center for Women & Children (Honolulu)
Kaua'i Medical Clinics (Kaua'i)
Pali Momi Medical Center (Aiea)

Straub Clinic & Hospital (Honolulu)
Straub Family Health Centers (Honolulu)
Visiting Specialists (Hilo Kaua'i Lana'i Maui Moloka'i Walmea)
Wilcox Memorial Hospital (Lihue Kaua'i)

COMPETITORS

Adventist Health
Kuakini Health System
Queen's Medical Center
Rehabilitation Hospital of the Pacific

HISTORICAL FINANCIALS

Company Type: Private - Not-for-Profit

Income Statement

FYE: June 30

	REVENUE ($ mil.)	NET INCOME ($ mil.)	NET PROFIT MARGIN	EMPLOYEES
06/11	901	75	8.4%	5,400
06/10	112	1	1.5%	0
06/09	812	(8)	—	0
06/08	716	(2)	—	0
Annual Growth	8.0%	—	—	—

2011 Year-End Financials

Debt ratio: —
Return on equity: 8.40%
Cash ($ mil.): 66
Current ratio: 1.20
Long-term debt ($ mil.): —
Dividends
 Yield: —
 Payout: —
Market value ($ mil.): —

HAWKINS CONSTRUCTION INC.

LOCATIONS

HQ: HAWKINS CONSTRUCTION INC.
1430 L AND R INDUS BLVD, TARPON SPRINGS, FL 34689-6807
Phone: 727-938-9719

HISTORICAL FINANCIALS

Company Type: Private

Income Statement

FYE: December 31

	REVENUE ($ mil.)	NET INCOME ($ mil.)	NET PROFIT MARGIN	EMPLOYEES
12/11	86	0	1.1%	110
Annual Growth	—	—	—	—

2011 Year-End Financials

Debt ratio: —
Return on equity: 1.10%
Cash ($ mil.): 5
Current ratio: 1.50
Long-term debt ($ mil.): —
Dividends
 Yield: —
 Payout: —
Market value ($ mil.): —

HAY HOUSE INC.

Self-help publisher Hay House publishes books and sells audio and video content covering topics such as self-help sociology philosophy psychology alternative health and environmental issues. It has more than 300 print books and 350 audio programs from some 130 authors including TV psychic John Edward talk show host Montel Williams and radio personality Tavis Smiley. In addition to its eponymous imprint the company publishes under the New Beginnings Press Princess Books and Smiley Books labels; the firm has international divisions in Australia the UK India and South Africa. Hay House was founded in 1984 by Louise Hay to self-publish her first two books "Heal Your Body" and "You Can Heal Your Life."

EXECUTIVES

Director Publicity, Jacqui Clark
President and CEO, Reid Tracy
Director Sales, Jeannie Liberati
Director Marketing and Advertising, Margarete Nielsen
Creative Director, Christy Salinas
Editorial Director, Jill Kramer
Internet Marketing Specialist, Roberta Gallagher
Event Director, Nancy Levin
Controller, Greg Davis

LOCATIONS

HQ: Hay House Inc.
2776 Loker Ave. West, Carlsbad CA 92010
Phone: 760-431-7695 **Fax:** 760-431-6948
Web: www.hayhouse.com

COMPETITORS

Hachette Book Group
HarperCollins
Health Communications
New Harbinger Publications
Nightingale-Conant
Perseus Books Group
Random House
Simon & Schuster
Sourcebooks Inc.
Sterling Publishing
Workman Publishing

HISTORICAL FINANCIALS

Company Type: Private

Income Statement

FYE: December 31

	REVENUE ($ mil.)	NET INCOME ($ mil.)	NET PROFIT MARGIN	EMPLOYEES
12/11	44	1	2.4%	92
12/08	60	0	1.5%	0
12/06	57	1	2.6%	0
12/05	723	0	0.0%	0
Annual Growth	(60.6%)	304.9%	—	—

2011 Year-End Financials

Debt ratio: —
Return on equity: 2.40%
Cash ($ mil.): 0
Current ratio: 0.40
Long-term debt ($ mil.): —
Dividends
 Yield: —
 Payout: —
Market value ($ mil.): —

HAYS MEDICAL CENTER INC.

Hays Medical Center brings big city health care to rural Kansas. The not-for-profit hospital which has more than 220 beds provides both acute and tertiary medical care to the Midwestern plains serving more than 13000 emergency patients each year. In addition to medical surgical and pediatric care Hays Medical Center offers home care hospice skilled nursing rehabilitation and behavioral health services. It operates centers for cardiac care (the DeBakey Heart Institute) and cancer treatment (the Dreiling/Schmidt Cancer Center). The organization also operates specialty and rural health clinics.

Strategy

The medical center has grown its business through selective acquisitions and hospital expansion projects. At the tune of $18.5 million Hays Medical Center in 2011 began to add about 65000 sq. ft. of both office and clinical space to the hospital's main building while also remodeling a handful of exisiting departments. Due to be completed in 2013 the plan includes the $3.8 million expansion of the Dreiling/Schmidt Cancer Institute and Breast Care Center which began construction in 2012.

Hays Medical Center has also added reconstructive surgery services with the addition of a cosmetic surgeon and expanded its surgical capabilities by agreeing to assist with operations at nearby St. Joseph Memorial Hospital.

Sales and Marketing

Hays Medical Center maintains a local market share of nearly 90% with total primary/secondary/tertiary service at 25%.

Company Background

The medical center was formed in 1991 through the merger of a pair of religiously affiliated facilities.

EXECUTIVES

President and CEO, John H. Jeter
Chief Development Officer, Jodi A. Schmidt
COO, Bryce Young
VP Human Resources, D. Bruce Whittington
Executive Director Hays Medical Center Foundation, Ruth Heffel
Chief Nursing Officer, Terry J. Siek
SVP CFO and CIO, William J. (Bill) Overbey
VP Support Services, Dale A. Montgomery
Chief Medical Officer, Ken Lindsey
Media Contact, Tammy Jacobs

LOCATIONS

HQ: Hays Medical Center
2220 Canterbury Dr., Hays KS 67601
Phone: 785-623-5000   **Fax:** 785-623-2291
Web: www.haysmed.com

PRODUCTS/OPERATIONS

Selected Departments

Billing/Financial
Dietary
Education
Emergency Department
Fitness Center
Hospice
Hospitalists
Imaging

Lifeline
Occupational Therapy
Palliative Care
Pharmacy
Rehabilitation
  In-Patient
  Out Patient
Respiratory Therapy
Senior Focused Care
Sexual Assault Response Team
Sleep and Neurodiagnostic
Special Nursing Services
Sports Medicine
Volunteer Services
Wound Healing and Hyperbaric Center
Weight Loss Surgery
WorkSMART

COMPETITORS

Adventist Health System   Sunbelt Healthcare
Sisters of Charity of Leavenworth
Stormont-Vail HealthCare
University of Kansas Medical Center
Via Christi Health System

HISTORICAL FINANCIALS
Company Type: Private - Not-for-Profit

Income Statement
FYE: June 30

	REVENUE ($ mil.)	NET INCOME ($ mil.)	NET PROFIT MARGIN	EMPLOYEES
06/12	209	17	8.1%	1,178
06/11	189	9	4.8%	0
06/10	184	9	5.1%	0
06/09	159	5	3.7%	0
Annual Growth	9.4%	42.8%	—	—

2012 Year-End Financials

Debt ratio: ——
Return on equity: 8.10%
Cash ($ mil.): 11
Current ratio: 2.00
Long-term debt ($ mil.): —
Dividends
  Yield: —
  Payout: —
Market value ($ mil.): —

HAYSSEN INC.

LOCATIONS

HQ: HAYSSEN INC.
225 SPARTANGREEN BLVD, DUNCAN, SC 29334-9400
Phone: 864-486-4000
Web: www.hayssen.com

HISTORICAL FINANCIALS
Company Type: Private

Income Statement
FYE: September 30

	REVENUE ($ mil.)	NET INCOME ($ mil.)	NET PROFIT MARGIN	EMPLOYEES
09/11	80	0	—	280
09/10	72	0	—	0
09/09	74	0	—	0
09/06	56	0	—	0
Annual Growth	12.8%	—	—	—

HAZLETON AREA SCHOOL DISTRICT (INC)

LOCATIONS

HQ: HAZLETON AREA SCHOOL DISTRICT (INC)
1515 W 23RD ST, HAZLE TOWNSHIP, PA 18202-1647
Phone: 570-459-3111
Web: www.hasdk12.org

HISTORICAL FINANCIALS
Company Type: Private

Income Statement
FYE: June 30

	REVENUE ($ mil.)	NET INCOME ($ mil.)	NET PROFIT MARGIN	EMPLOYEES
06/11	118	17	14.4%	1,400
06/06	0	0	—	0
06/01	68	(8)	—	0
Annual Growth	31.7%	—	—	—

2011 Year-End Financials

Debt ratio: ——
Return on equity: 14.40%
Cash ($ mil.): 34
Current ratio: 1.60
Long-term debt ($ mil.): —
Dividends
  Yield: —
  Payout: —
Market value ($ mil.): —

2011 Year-End Financials

Debt ratio: ——
Return on equity: —
Cash ($ mil.): 1
Current ratio: 0.70
Long-term debt ($ mil.): —
Dividends
  Yield: —
  Payout: —
Market value ($ mil.): —

HEARTLAND HEALTH

Heartland Health provides medical care in the heart of the Midwest. The integrated health care system serves residents of northwest Missouri as well as bordering areas of Kansas and Nebraska. Its flagship facility is Heartland Regional Medical Center a 350-bed acute-care hospital that features an emergency room and Level II trauma center as well as specialty care programs in heart disease cancer and obstetrics. Heartland Health also provides primary care through a multi-specialty medical practice (Heartland Clinic) and it offers home health hospice and long-term care services from the primary medical center facility. The company's Community Health Improvement Solutions unit is an HMO health insurer.

Strategy In 2012 Heartland Health joined the Mayo Clinic Care Network which will enable to it to tap the knowledge and expertise of Mayo Clinic physicians to better serve its patients.

Company Background Heartland Health was formed in 1984 through the merger of two St. Joseph Missouri hospital: Methodist Medical Center and St. Joseph's Hospital. The two facilities trace their roots back to 1924 and 1861 respectively.

EXECUTIVES

COO, Curt Kretzinger
CFO, John Wilson
Chief Administrative Officer, Rudolph F. (Rudy) Wacker II
Vice Chairman, Carol Roever
Chairman, Alfred L. Purcell
Chairman, David Salanski
Chief Business Development, Dirck Clark
Chief Communications Officer, Charlie Shields
Coordinator Media and Communications, Marcy George
President and CEO, Mark Laney
President and CEO, Lowell C. Kruse
Chief Brand Officer, Tama Wagner
Chief Human Resources Officer, Michael Pulido
Director, Carol Roever
Director, Robert C. Johnson
Vice Chairman, Al Purcell
Director, David Cathcart
Director, James Scanlon
Director, Barbara Wurtzler
Director, Chuck Hamilton
Director, Frank Leone
Director, John T. Olson

LOCATIONS

HQ: Heartland Health
5325 Faraon St., St. Joseph MO 64506
Phone: 816-271-6000   **Fax:** 206-215-9777
Web: www.pinnaclerealty.com

PRODUCTS/OPERATIONS

Selected Affiliates

Atchison Hospital (Atchison KS)
Community Hospital (Fairfax MO)
Community Medical Center (Falls City NE)
Dental Clinic (St. Joseph MO)
Laser Cosmedic Center (Platte City MO)
North Kansas City Hospital (North Kansas City MO)
The Surgery Center (St. Joseph MO)

COMPETITORS

Ascension Health
BJC HealthCare
Blue Cross and Blue Shield of Kansas City
Catholic Health Initiatives
Children's Mercy Hospital
CoxHealth
HCA
Mercy Health
Mercy Hospital Springfield
Saint Luke's Health System
Shawnee Mission Medical Center
Sisters of Charity of Leavenworth
St. John's Health System
Truman Medical Centers
University of Kansas Medical Center

HISTORICAL FINANCIALS

Company Type: Private - Not-for-Profit

Income Statement

FYE: June 30

	REVENUE ($ mil.)	NET INCOME ($ mil.)	NET PROFIT MARGIN	EMPLOYEES
06/12	584	10	1.8%	32,000
06/11	528	69	13.1%	0
06/03	309	5	1.6%	0
06/02	297	(5)	—	0
Annual Growth	25.3%	—	—	—

2012 Year-End Financials

Debt ratio: ——
Return on equity: 1.80%
Cash ($ mil.): 19
Current ratio: 1.10
Long-term debt ($ mil.): —

Dividends
Yield: —
Payout: —
Market value ($ mil.): —

HEARTLAND REGIONAL MEDICAL CENTER

Heartland Regional Medical Center strives for healthy hearts minds and bodies in the US heartland. The acute care hospital a subsidiary of Heartland Health provides medical services to residents of St. Joseph Missouri and some 20 surrounding counties in northwest Missouri southeast Nebraska and northeast Kansas. Heartland Regional Medical Center encompasses specialty centers for trauma and long-term care acute rehabilitation cancer heart disease and birthing. Other services include arthritis pain and wound treatments as well as home health and hospice care.

EXECUTIVES

COO, Curt Kretzinger
CFO, John Wilson
Marketing Research, Steve Wenger
Chief Human Resources Officer, Mike Pulido
Vice Chairman, Karen Baker
Chairman, Steve Schram
Media and Community Relations Coordinator, Marcy George
HRMC Medical Director, Philip Fracica
President, Mark Laney
Purchasing Secretary, Sharon Erickson
Vice Chairman, Karen Baker
Director, James Graves
Director, Michael Nellestein
Director, Maureen Boyle
Director, David Howery
Director, John Jarrett
Director, Dennis Dobyan
Director, Andrew McCrea
Director, Dan Hegeman
Auditors: KPMGLLP

LOCATIONS

HQ: Heartland Regional Medical Center
5325 Faraon St., St. Joseph MO 64506-3373
Phone: 816-271-6000   **Fax:** 816-271-6656
Web: www.heartland-health.com

COMPETITORS

Ascension Health
BJC HealthCare
Catholic Health Initiatives
Children's Mercy Hospital
CoxHealth
Mercy Health
Saint Luke's Health System

Shawnee Mission Medical Center
Sisters of Charity of Leavenworth
St. John's Health System
Truman Medical Centers
University of Kansas Medical Center

HISTORICAL FINANCIALS

Company Type: Subsidiary

Income Statement

FYE: June 30

	REVENUE ($ mil.)	NET INCOME ($ mil.)	NET PROFIT MARGIN	EMPLOYEES
06/12	564	11	2.0%	2,600
06/11	514	72	14.0%	0
06/10	483	50	10.4%	0
06/09	476	(27)	—	0
Annual Growth	5.8%	—	—	—

2012 Year-End Financials

Debt ratio: ——
Return on equity: 2.00%
Cash ($ mil.): 16
Current ratio: 1.00
Long-term debt ($ mil.): —

Dividends
Yield: —
Payout: —
Market value ($ mil.): —

HEIFER PROJECT INTERNATIONAL INC

It's not just a handout; it's a new way of life. Heifer Project International (known as Heifer International) runs more than 925 projects that help millions of impoverished families become self-sufficient. Current recipients are located in more than 50 countries around the world including about 28 US states. The non-profit organization provides more than 25 different kinds of breeding livestock and other animals (bees rabbits ducks) that can be used for food income or plowing power in addition to training in sustainable agriculture techniques. In exchange the family agrees to pass on not only the animals' first female offspring to another needy family but their knowledge too.

The international development and education group draws support from individuals businesses and organizations and congregations: individual contributions account for more than two-thirds of its total revenue.

Despite a $42 million grant from the Bill & Melinda Gates Foundation (the largest single grant in the group's history) in 2008 Heifer International saw a decline in donations that year as well as in 2009. As a result the organization initiated cost-cutting measures and in mid-2009 laid off 20% of its staff in the US and abroad. Heifer International cited declining donations as a result of the deep recession in the US as the reason for the layoffs.

Following the streamlining efforts the group named Pierre Ferrari as CEO in late 2010. Ferrari has more than 40 years' experience in the corporate world and with social organizations serving Coca-Cola USA CARE and the Small Enterprise Assistance Fund. Ferrari succeeded president and CEO Jo Luck who stepped down earlier that year to write her memoir. (Former Heifer International chairman Charles Stewart served as interim CEO before Ferrari was chosen.)

Heifer International was established in 1944 by Dan West who had worked helping feed the hungry during the Spanish Civil War.

EXECUTIVES

EVP Programs and Secretary, James (Jim) De Vries
EVP Global Learning and Action, Tanya Wright

Director Finance, Kit Smith
Senior Director Marketing, Mike Matchett
EVP Finance and Administration CFO and Treasurer, James Neal
COO, Steve Denne
EVP Marketing and Resource Development, Steve Stirling
Chair, C. Douglas Smith
CEO, Pierre Ferrari, age 62
Director, Efrain Diaz Arrivillaga
Director, Andrew Bartlett
Director, Kathleen Campanella
Director, Fu Changxiu
Director, Susan B. Fulton
Director, Julia Hall-Wilson
Director, Don Hammond
Director, Ladislav Hetenyi
Director, James Howell
Director, Franklin Ishida
Director, Stephen A. (Steve) Mondora
Director, Ron McLean
Director, Johnson Nkuuhe
Director, Susan Sanders
Director, Charles Stewart
Director, Gary Tabaskinske
Director, Arlene Falk Withers
Auditors: BKDLLP

LOCATIONS

HQ: Heifer Project International
1 World Ave., Little Rock AR 72202
Phone: 586-416-9090   **Fax:** 586-416-9091
Web: www.orrandboss.com

PRODUCTS/OPERATIONS

2009

	$ mil.	% of total
Program services (includes international development & education programs)	95 76	
Fundraising	22	18
Management & general	7	6
Total	**125**	**100**

HISTORICAL FINANCIALS

Company Type: Private - Not-for-Profit

Income Statement

FYE: June 30

	REVENUE ($ mil.)	NET INCOME ($ mil.)	NET PROFIT MARGIN	EMPLOYEES
06/11	127	9	7.8%	304
06/10	118	4	3.9%	0
06/09	98	(28)	—	0
06/08	139	15	10.9%	0
Annual Growth	**(2.9%)**	**(13.1%)**	**—**	**—**

2011 Year-End Financials

Debt ratio: ——
Return on equity: 7.80%
Cash ($ mil.): 58
Current ratio: —
Long-term debt ($ mil.): —

Dividends
Yield: —
Payout: —
Market value ($ mil.): —

HELEN KELLER INTERNATIONAL

Helen Keller International (HKI) has vision. The organization fights blindness by working with doctors government agencies partner groups and individuals in 22 countries citing that 80% of all blindness is avoidable. Its core areas of focus are eye health overall health and nutrition and poverty reduction. HKI distributes antibiotics performs cataract surgery and provides eye screenings glasses and education. The group works to combat malnutrition by promoting prenatal care supplying Vitamin A and helping others set up sustainable gardens and nutrition programs. It aims to reduce poverty through projects for literacy preschool and clean water and offers entrepreneurial support for women.

HKI generated more than $162 million in revenue in 2011 up from $112 million in 2010. Of this government grants comprised some 64% with contributions from individuals corporations and foundations (including gifts in kind) accounting for the balance. The group spends 84% of its funds on programs to prevent blindness and malnutrition 14% on management and 2% on fundraising.

In recent years HKI has expanded its ChildSight program which makes it easier for struggling school children to get prescription eyeglasses. Already active in the US for nearly two decades and having reached 1.4 million students the program is now getting traction in Indonesia's underserved communities. In Indonesia ChildSight has trained more than 1500 teachers who've conducted vision screenings for 85000 children —16500 of which have received eyeglasses. To leverage the successes of the ChildSight program a similar program has since been rolled out in Vietnam.

Headquartered in New York City HKI has extended its reach and its services to regional offices in Africa's Senegal and in Cambodia; it has an office in France through affiliate Helen Keller International Europe.

HKI began in 1915 as an organization to help soldiers blinded in World War I. Focus on prevention including nutritional causes of blindness didn't come until 1966.

EXECUTIVES

President and CEO, Kathy Spahn
VP and Regional Director Africa, Shawn K. Baker
VP Eye Health, Nicholas Kourgialis
SVP Finance Operations and CFO, Elspeth E. Taylor
Chairman, L. Bradford Perkins
VP and Regional Director Asia-Pacific, Nancy Haselow
SVP Programs, Victoria Quinn
VP Development and Communications, Jennifer S. Klopp
SVP and COO, Lori Tiller
Managing Director Helen Keller International Europe, Alix de Nicolay
Vice Chair and Secretary, Nancy Smith Lione

LOCATIONS

HQ: Helen Keller International
352 Park Ave. South 12th Fl., New York NY 10010
Phone: 212-532-0544   **Fax:** 212-532-6014
Web: www.hki.org

PRODUCTS/OPERATIONS

2011 Revenue

	$ mil.	% of total
Gifts in kind	121	75
Grants from US government agencies	19	12
Contributions from individuals corporations & foundations	13	8
Grants from other government agencies	6	4
Legacies and trusts	1	1
Dividends and interest income	—	—
Program and other revenue	—	—
Total	**162**	**100**

HISTORICAL FINANCIALS

Company Type: Private - Not-for-Profit

Income Statement

FYE: June 30

	REVENUE ($ mil.)	NET INCOME ($ mil.)	NET PROFIT MARGIN	EMPLOYEES
06/11	162	(0)	—	600
06/10	94	(2)	—	0
06/09	39	0	1.5%	0
06/08	91	0	0.9%	0
Annual Growth	**21.3%**	**—**	**—**	**—**

2011 Year-End Financials

Debt ratio: ——
Return on equity: (-0.20)%
Cash ($ mil.): 18
Current ratio: —
Long-term debt ($ mil.): —

Dividends
Yield: —
Payout: —
Market value ($ mil.): —

HENRICKSEN & COMPANY INC.

Henricksen & Company wants your company to be comfortable. The firm is an office furniture distributor selling mid- and high-end office furnishings such as desks chairs and partitions from manufacturers including Allsteel Falcon Gunlocke HONand Trendway. Henricksen also offers furniture warehousing installation maintenance and cleaning as well as reconfiguration design and space planning services. It leases furniture as well. Customers have included Cray Huron Consulting Restaurant Technologies SXC Health Solutions and Roundy's.The company is owned by the founding Henricksen family who started the business in the 1960s.

Henricksen has locations in Brookfield and Madison Wisconsin; Minneapolis; Peoria Illinois and the surrounding parts of Chicago.

EXECUTIVES

President, Stephen E. (Steve) McPartlin
Director Human Resources, Michelle Addari
CFO, Tim Osborne
VP, Russell Frees
VP Sales and Marketing, Rick Fallia
Director Business Development, Mark Dalton
Director Project Management, Carol Hess
Controller, Juellen Longhurst
VP and General Manager Minneapolis, Dick Nash
VP and General Manager Wisconsin, Steve Kuehl

LOCATIONS

HQ: Henricksen & Company Inc.
1070 W. Ardmore Ave., Itasca IL 60143
Phone: 630-250-9090 **Fax:** 630-250-9112
Web: www.henricksen.com

COMPETITORS

Aaron's Inc.	OfficeMax
Corporate Concepts	Staples
OEC Business Interiors	Target Commercial
Office Concepts	Interiors
Office Depot	

HISTORICAL FINANCIALS

Company Type: Private

Income Statement

FYE: April 30

	REVENUE ($ mil.)	NET INCOME ($ mil.)	NET PROFIT MARGIN	EMPLOYEES
04/12	147	0	0.1%	197
04/11	129	0	0.2%	0
04/10	114	0	0.1%	0
04/09	116	0	0.1%	0
Annual Growth	8.1%	2.2%	—	—

2012 Year-End Financials

Debt ratio: ——
Return on equity: 0.10%
Cash ($ mil.): 0
Current ratio: 1.30
Long-term debt ($ mil.): —

Dividends
Yield: —
Payout: —
Market value ($ mil.): —

HENRY AVOCADO CORPORATION

LOCATIONS

HQ: HENRY AVOCADO CORPORATION
2355 E LINCOLN AVE, ESCONDIDO, CA 92027-1298
Phone: 760-745-6632
Web: www.henryavocado.com

HISTORICAL FINANCIALS

Company Type: Private

Income Statement

FYE: September 30

	REVENUE ($ mil.)	NET INCOME ($ mil.)	NET PROFIT MARGIN	EMPLOYEES
09/11	129	2	2.2%	88
09/10	90	2	2.7%	0
09/09	92	0	1.1%	0
09/08	97	2	2.1%	0
Annual Growth	9.7%	10.2%	—	—

2011 Year-End Financials

Debt ratio: ——
Return on equity: 2.20%
Cash ($ mil.): 2
Current ratio: 1.80
Long-term debt ($ mil.): —

Dividends
Yield: —
Payout: —
Market value ($ mil.): —

HENRY MEDICAL CENTER INC.

LOCATIONS

HQ: HENRY MEDICAL CENTER INC.
1133 EAGLES LANDING PKWY, STOCKBRIDGE, GA 30281-5099
Phone: 678-604-1001
Web: www.piedmonthenry.org

HISTORICAL FINANCIALS

Company Type: Private

Income Statement

FYE: June 30

	REVENUE ($ mil.)	NET INCOME ($ mil.)	NET PROFIT MARGIN	EMPLOYEES
06/11	181	(18)	—	1,083
06/10	170	(9)	—	0
06/09	174	(6)	—	0
06/08	162	(5)	—	0
Annual Growth	3.8%	—	—	—

2011 Year-End Financials

Debt ratio: ——
Return on equity: (-10.30)%
Cash ($ mil.): 3
Current ratio: 0.20
Long-term debt ($ mil.): —

Dividends
Yield: —
Payout: —
Market value ($ mil.): —

HENRY MODELL & COMPANY INC.

Longtime retailer Henry Modell & Company sells sporting goods fitness equipment apparel and brand-name athletic footwear as America's oldest family-owned and -operated sporting goods retailer. Established in 1889 it also ensures it has local team apparel on hand. Through 150-plus stores that operate under the Modell's Sporting Goods banner the company serves more than 10 East Coast states and the District of Columbia. Known for its reasonably priced branded products Modell's locates its stores in malls regional shopping centers and busy urban areas. It also boasts an online presence at Modells.com. The retail chain is run by the fourth generation of Modell management.

Geographic Reach

Henry Modell & Company operates its business in nearly a dozen US states. It has a retail presence in New York New Jersey Pennsylvania Connecticut Rhode Island Massachusetts New Hampshire Delaware Maryland Virginia and the District of Columbia.

Strategy

To ensure it has all its bases covered Henry Modell & Company offers licensed products from nearly 30 sports leagues. Also during recent years Henry Modell & Company has focused on designing more appealing and accessible stores. To this end most Modell's locations have been renovated to provide improved accommodations for shoppers. Also the retailer opened three stores in New York City including its redesigned 20000-sq.-ft. flagship store in Times Square. Renovations come at a price however. When Modell's kicked off renovations in 2010 the company reported revenues of $567 million that year 10% lower than 2009.

Company Background

Hungarian immigrant Morris Modell first sold menswear from a Lower East Side pushcart in New York City before he founded Henry Modell & Company in 1889.

EXECUTIVES

SVP Human Resources and Loss Prevention, Thomas Tilley
CEO, Mitchell B. (Mitch) Modell, age 58
VP Information Technology, Hans Kantor
VP Real Estate and General Counsel, Douglas (Doug) Epstein
Director Planning and Allocation, Richard (Rich) Taub
VP and General Merchandise Manager Sporting Goods, Roger Kitch, age 44
EVP and CFO, Eric J. Spiel
Director Promotions and Public Relations, Rich Lampmann
EVP Stores and Operations, David Hoodis
SVP Marketing, Jed Berger
VP and General Merchandise Manager Licensed Products, William (Bill) Hackett
VP and General Merchandise Manager Apparel, William (Willy) Kaplan
VP and General Merchandise Manager Footwear, Jason (Jay) O'Brien
VP Logistics, Steve Ondrejack

LOCATIONS

HQ: Henry Modell & Company Inc.
498 7th Ave. 20th Fl., New York NY 10018
Phone: 212-822-1000 **Fax:** 212-822-1025
Web: www.modells.com

PRODUCTS/OPERATIONS

Selected Product Categories
Accessories
Apparel
Baseball
Basketball
Boxing/martial arts
Camping/hiking
Cycling
Electronics/optics
Fan shop-pro/college
Field hockey
Fishing
Fitness
Football
Footwear
Games
Golf
Ice/roller hockey
In-Line/roller skating
Lacrosse
Optics/telescopes
Outdoor recreation
Paintball
Pilates
Racquetball/squash
Roller hockey
Rugby
Running
Scooters
Skateboarding
Snow sports
Soccer
Softball
Tennis
Water recreation
Winter recreation

Wrestling
Yoga

COMPETITORS

Athleta	Hat World
Dick's Sporting Goods	Olympia Sports
Dunham's	Sears
Eastern Mountain	Sports Authority
Sports	Target Corporation
Foot Locker	Wal-Mart

HISTORICAL FINANCIALS

Company Type: Private

Income Statement
FYE: January 28

	REVENUE ($ mil.)	NET INCOME ($ mil.)	NET PROFIT MARGIN	EMPLOYEES
01/12	570	(3)	—	5,430
01/11	558	(7)	—	0
01/10	567	4	0.7%	0
01/09	636	4	0.6%	0
Annual Growth	(3.6%)	—	—	—

2012 Year-End Financials

Debt ratio: —
Return on equity: (-0.60)%
Cash ($ mil.): 4
Current ratio: —
Long-term debt ($ mil.): —
Dividends
Yield: —
Payout: —
Market value ($ mil.): —

HERITAGE FS INC.

LOCATIONS

HQ: HERITAGE FS INC.
1381 S CRESCENT ST, GILMAN, IL 60938-6128
Phone: 815-265-4751
Web: www.home.heritagefs.com

HISTORICAL FINANCIALS

Company Type: Private

Income Statement
FYE: July 31

	REVENUE ($ mil.)	NET INCOME ($ mil.)	NET PROFIT MARGIN	EMPLOYEES
07/12	171	10	5.8%	79
07/11	195	5	2.7%	0
07/10	25	5	22.5%	0
07/09	173	5	3.1%	0
Annual Growth	(0.4%)	23.3%		

2012 Year-End Financials

Debt ratio: —
Return on equity: 5.80%
Cash ($ mil.): 2
Current ratio: 0.10
Long-term debt ($ mil.): —
Dividends
Yield: —
Payout: —
Market value ($ mil.): —

HERITAGE VALLEY HEALTH SYSTEM INC.

Heritage Valley Health System has a legacy of serving the health care needs of residents of southwestern Pennsylvania eastern Ohio and the West Virginia Panhandle. The two hospital system includes the flagship Heritage Valley Beaver hospital in Beaver Pennsylvania with about 360 beds and a smaller facility in nearby Sewickley with roughly 185 beds. In addition to its acute-care facilities the system operates several satellite facilities and provides primary care through a network of three affiliated physician groups. Heritage Valley Health System was formed in 1996 when the two hospitals merged but it has roots going back to 1894.

Strategy

The health system expands its service offerings and increases its geographic reach in part by forming collaborative relationships with health care providers and other organizations. For example it operates immediate care clinics at local Wal-Mart stores to offer patients routine care such as immunizations screenings and treatment of minor injuries and illnesses. Heritage Valley also partners with UPMC to offer radiation therapy and medical oncology services at Heritage Valley Beaver. Additionally Heritage Valley and UPMC Health Plan operate LifeSmart which identifies patients at risk for diabetes connects them with a primary care physician and provides them with lifestyle intervention programs.

Heritage Valley Health System entered an alliance in 2011 with Good Samaritan Hospice (GSH) that allowed it to serve more individuals in need of hospice care in the southwestern Pennsylvania region. Under the agreement Heritage Valley Health System gained partial share in GSH which includes the Good Samaritan House in Wexford and the Good Samaritan Cabot Unit in Cabot Pennsylvania.

Along with increasing its medical offerings through partnerships Heritage Valley hires specialists and adds new services to meet community demand. Some areas of focus include infectious disease endocrinology inpatient rehabilitation and wound care.

EXECUTIVES

President CEO and Director, Norman F. Mitry
COO and Chief Nursing Officer, Rosemary Nolan
Chairperson, Laura A. Vassamillet
Emeritus Chair, Timothy (Tim) Merrill Jr.
VP Community Health Services, Daniel Brooks
VP and Chief Human Resources Officer, Bruce Edwards
VP Quality and Support Services, Richard Beaver
VP Patient Care Services Heritage Valley Sewickley, Anne Hitchak
CIO, David Carleton
Chief Medical Officer, Oliver Hayes
VP and CFO, Bryan J. Randall
Director Finance, Mark Schneider
Vice Chair, Joseph Becherer
Treasurer, Gary Chace
Secretary, Johannah M. Robb
VP Institutional Advancement, Daniel Murphy
VP Physician Practices, Laura Wagner
VP and Chief Medical Officer, John T. Cinicola
Vice President Surgical Services, Kathleen Harley
VP and Deputy General Counsel, Sharon Loftus
President CEO and Director, Norman F. Mitry

Chairperson, Laura A. Vassamillet
Vice Chair, Joseph Becherer
Director, Kathy Adelman
Director, Donald A. Flick
Director, Richard C. Hogan
Director, Thomas Johnson
Director, Peter G. Manolukas
Director, Jack S. Mustoe
Director, Daniel J. Nadler
Director, G. R. Orr III
Director, Dennis Pegden
Director, David Rafalko
Director, Ian G. Rawson
Director, James P. Scibilia
Director, Donald Spalding
Director, John C. Y. Wright Jr.
Director, Allen I. Wolfert
Director, David Motley

LOCATIONS

HQ: Heritage Valley Health System Inc.
1000 Dutch Ridge Rd., Beaver PA 15009
Phone: 724-728-7000   **Fax:** 724-728-5322
Web: www.heritagevalley.org

PRODUCTS/OPERATIONS

Selected Medical Services

Advanced Cardiology
Bariatric Surgery
Behavioral Health
Breast Imaging
Cancer Treatment
Cardiac Computed Tomography (Cardiac CT)
Cardiology
Community Advanced Illness Program (CAIP)
Community Health Services
Diabetes Radiology
Diagnostic Centers
Emergency
Endoscopy Center
Family Planning
Heart and Vascular Center
Inpatient Rehabilitation
Laboratory
LIFE Beaver and Lawrence County
Maternity
MRI Services
Neurology
Nutrition Counseling
Occupational Medicine
Orthopedics Services
Osteoporosis
Pediatric Asthma
Pharmacy retail
Pulmonary Services
Signature BusinessCare
Signature Rehab
Signature SportsCare
Sleep Lab
Surgery Centers
VeinCare
Weight Loss
WoundCare

COMPETITORS

Butler Health System
Children's Hospital of Pittsburgh
Conemaugh Health System
Excela Health
Jefferson Regional Medical Center of Pennsylvania
Kindred Healthcare
Ohio Valley General
Sharon Regional Health System
St. Clair Health
Trinity Health System
UPMC
Weirton Medical Center
West Penn Allegheny Health System

HISTORICAL FINANCIALS

Company Type: Private - Not-for-Profit

Income Statement

FYE: June 30

	REVENUE ($ mil.)	NET INCOME ($ mil.)	NET PROFIT MARGIN	EMPLOYEES
06/12	453	(53)	—	4,291
06/11	449	40	9.0%	0
06/10	445	13	2.9%	0
06/09	432	(65)	—	0
Annual Growth	1.6%	—	—	—

2012 Year-End Financials

Debt ratio: ——
Return on equity: (-11.90)%
Cash ($ mil.): 22
Current ratio: 1.10
Long-term debt ($ mil.): —

Dividends
 Yield: —
 Payout: —
 Market value ($ mil.): —

HERMAN GOLDNER COMPANY INC

LOCATIONS

HQ: HERMAN GOLDNER COMPANY INC
7777 BREWSTER AVE, PHILADELPHIA, PA
19153-3298
Phone: 215-365-5400
Web: www.goldner.com

HISTORICAL FINANCIALS

Company Type: Private

Income Statement

FYE: May 31

	REVENUE ($ mil.)	NET INCOME ($ mil.)	NET PROFIT MARGIN	EMPLOYEES
05/12	102	0	1.0%	275
05/11	87	0	1.1%	0
05/10	72	1	1.4%	0
05/09	83	1	1.6%	0
Annual Growth	7.0%	(10.2%)	—	—

2012 Year-End Financials

Debt ratio: ——
Return on equity: 1.00%
Cash ($ mil.): 6
Current ratio: 1.30
Long-term debt ($ mil.): —

Dividends
 Yield: —
 Payout: —
 Market value ($ mil.): —

HERON LAKE BIOENERGY LLC

LOCATIONS

HQ: HERON LAKE BIOENERGY LLC
91246 390TH AVE, HERON LAKE, MN 56137-3175
Phone: 507-793-0077
Web: www.heronlakebioenergy.com

HISTORICAL FINANCIALS

Company Type: Private

Income Statement

FYE: July 31

	REVENUE ($ mil.)	NET INCOME ($ mil.)	NET PROFIT MARGIN	EMPLOYEES
07/12*	121	(2)	—	48
10/11	164	0	0.3%	0
10/10	110	1	1.5%	0
10/09	88	(11)	—	0
Annual Growth	11.1%	—	—	—

*Fiscal year change

2012 Year-End Financials

Debt ratio: ——
Return on equity: (-2.40)%
Cash ($ mil.): 1
Current ratio: 0.40
Long-term debt ($ mil.): —

Dividends
 Yield: —
 Payout: —
 Market value ($ mil.): —

HESS CONSTRUCTION + ENGINEERING SERVICES INC.

LOCATIONS

HQ: HESS CONSTRUCTION + ENGINEERING SERVICES INC.
804 W DIAMOND AVE STE 300, GAITHERSBURG, MD 20878-1411
Phone: 301-670-9000

HISTORICAL FINANCIALS

Company Type: Private

Income Statement

FYE: December 31

	REVENUE ($ mil.)	NET INCOME ($ mil.)	NET PROFIT MARGIN	EMPLOYEES
12/11	224	3	1.4%	100
Annual Growth	—	—	—	—

2011 Year-End Financials

Debt ratio: ——
Return on equity: 1.40%
Cash ($ mil.): 14
Current ratio: 0.30
Long-term debt ($ mil.): —

Dividends
 Yield: —
 Payout: —
 Market value ($ mil.): —

HIGH COUNTRY FUSION COMPANY INC.

High Country Fusion Company (HCFC) makes its path to success through its pipes. HCFC manufactures high-density polyethylene pipes (HDPE) and pipe fittings for use in industrial marine municipal wastewater and other types of projects. The company's HDPE pipes (in essence dense plastic-based pipes) are capable of transporting water and wastewater chemicals compressed gases and other substances. HCFC's customers include municipal and government agencies as well as US and international construction companies. Based in a small town in Idaho the company operates a 21000-sq.-ft. facility as well as a smaller facility in Utah. HCFC was founded in 1994 by president Steve Wilson and VP David Hanks.

EXECUTIVES

President and CEO, Steve Wilson
VP COO and CIO, David Hanks
VP Sales, John Bjorkman
Equipment Rentals Repairs and Sales Manager, Bryan Obland
Salt Lake Branch Manager, Tom Hutchinson
Boise Branch Manager, Scott Peters

LOCATIONS

HQ: High Country Fusion Company Inc.
 20 North Poly Fusion Pl., Fairfield ID 83327
Phone: 208-764-2000   **Fax:** 208-764-2094
Web: www.hcfusion.com

COMPETITORS

Advanced Drainage Systems
Hancor
J-M Manufacturing

HISTORICAL FINANCIALS

Company Type: Private

Income Statement

FYE: December 31

	REVENUE ($ mil.)	NET INCOME ($ mil.)	NET PROFIT MARGIN	EMPLOYEES
12/11	30	0	2.0%	49
12/09	13	0	2.7%	0
12/08	13	0	2.7%	0
12/07	16	0	2.3%	0
Annual Growth	23.5%	17.1%	—	—

2011 Year-End Financials

Debt ratio: ——
Return on equity: 2.00%
Cash ($ mil.): 0
Current ratio: 0.70
Long-term debt ($ mil.): —

Dividends
 Yield: —
 Payout: —
 Market value ($ mil.): —

HIGH POINT REGIONAL HEALTH SYSTEM

Hospital stays are usually not the high point of one's life but High Point Regional Health System aims to make patients comfortable. Its main facility is High Point Regional Hospital a medical/surgical facility with nearly 400 beds serving the Piedmont Triad region of North Carolina. The private not-for-profit health care system also operates the Carolina Regional Heart Center The Neuroscience Center Piedmont Joint Replacement Center and centers devoted to cancer care diabetes treatment mental health sleep disorders and women's health care. The hospital was founded in 1904.

Other services offered through the Health System include the Rehab Center the Millis Regional Health Education Center the Regional Wound

Center the Diabetes Self Care Management Center The Vascular Center and High Point Behavioral Health.

In 2010 the Hayworth Cancer Center received accreditation by the American College of Surgeons Commission on Cancer and was one of 80 centers nationwide to achieve a perfect score on the accreditation standards. In addition the U.S. News & World Report ranked the Hayworth Cancer Center as number one in the Triad for the 3rd consecutive year.

That same year the hospital provided more than $7 million in uncompensated care to the community. Regardless of government reimbursement shortfalls the health system continues to provide uncompensated care to people whose health care is subsidized by programs such as Medicare Medicaid and other non-negotiated government programs partially through its various endowment programs.

EXECUTIVES

President and CEO, Jeffrey S. (Jeff) Miller
SVP, Linda M. Roney, age 62
COO, Gregory W. Taylor
Chief Medical Officer, Dale Williams
Director Medical Staff, Jane Campbell
VP and Chief Nursing Officer, Tammi Mengel
Director Development, Courtney Best
VP and CFO, Kimberly Crews
CIO, Diana Sharkey
VP People Services, Katherine Burns
VP Foundation Public Relations and Marketing, Denise Potter
Director Medical and Risk Services, Max Herrington
Auditors: PricewaterhouseCoopersLLP

LOCATIONS

HQ: High Point Regional Health System
601 N. Elm St., High Point NC 27262
Phone: 336-878-6000   **Fax:** 336-878-6158
Web: www.highpointregional.com

COMPETITORS

Alamance Regional Medical Center
Carolinas HealthCare System
Health Management Associates
Moses Cone Health
Tenet Healthcare
UNC Hospitals
Wake Forest University Baptist Medical Center

HISTORICAL FINANCIALS

Company Type: Private - Not-for-Profit

Income Statement

	REVENUE ($ mil.)	NET INCOME ($ mil.)	NET PROFIT MARGIN	EMPLOYEES
09/11	276	(13)	—	2,338
09/10	296	0	0.3%	0
09/09	302	(1)	—	0
09/08	252	(16)	—	0
Annual Growth	3.1%	—	—	—

2011 Year-End Financials

Debt ratio: ——
Return on equity: (-4.70)%
Cash ($ mil.): 0
Current ratio: 0.60
Long-term debt ($ mil.): —

Dividends
Yield: —
Payout: —
Market value ($ mil.): —

HIGH POINT UNIVERSITY

LOCATIONS

HQ: HIGH POINT UNIVERSITY
833 MONTLIEU AVE, HIGH POINT, NC 27262-4260
Phone: 336-841-9000
Web: www.highpointpanthers.com

HISTORICAL FINANCIALS

Company Type: Private

Income Statement
FYE: May 31

	REVENUE ($ mil.)	NET INCOME ($ mil.)	NET PROFIT MARGIN	EMPLOYEES
05/11	151	36	24.5%	500
05/10	90	12	13.5%	0
05/09	71	8	11.8%	0
05/08	63	8	14.1%	0
Annual Growth	33.6%	60.7%		

2011 Year-End Financials

Debt ratio: ——
Return on equity: 24.50%
Cash ($ mil.): 10
Current ratio: ——
Long-term debt ($ mil.): —

Dividends
Yield: —
Payout: —
Market value ($ mil.): —

HIGHLAND CORPORATION

LOCATIONS

HQ: HIGHLAND CORPORATION
108 MILL AVE, HOHENWALD, TN 38462-1533
Phone: 931-796-2274
Web: www.highlandcorp.com

HISTORICAL FINANCIALS

Company Type: Private

Income Statement
FYE: December 31

	REVENUE ($ mil.)	NET INCOME ($ mil.)	NET PROFIT MARGIN	EMPLOYEES
12/11	131	0	0.2%	150
12/10	107	(0)	—	0
12/09	87	0	0.2%	0
12/08	120	0	0.5%	0
Annual Growth	2.9%	(18.6%)	—	—

2011 Year-End Financials

Debt ratio: ——
Return on equity: 0.20%
Cash ($ mil.): 1
Current ratio: 1.00
Long-term debt ($ mil.): —

Dividends
Yield: —
Payout: —
Market value ($ mil.): —

HILL COUNTRY MEMORIAL HOSPITAL

Hill Country Memorial takes care of the peaks and valleys in the wellness of area residents. The health system provides medical services to eight counties near Fredericksburg in Central Texas. Its hospital Hill Country Memorial Hospital has about 85 beds and a staff of close to 100 physicians. Specialties include cardiology obstetrics oncology orthopedics and emergency medicine. The health system also operates a wellness center that offers locals yoga stress management weight loss and massage. Other community services include hospice and home care and the administration of state-funded services for low income women infants children (WIC).

Geographic Reach

While the health system provides medical services to eight counties near Fredericksburg in Central Texas the Hill Country Memorial Hospice service area casts its net wider and includes the counties of Bandera Blanco Burnet Comal Gillespie Hays Kendall Kerr Kimble Llano Mason Medina and San Saba and portions of Travis.

Company Background

Hill Country Memorial was established in 1971.

EXECUTIVES

Executive Director Hill Country Memorial Hospital Foundation, Sandy Goff
Marketing Specialist, Carolyn Rose
Director Marketing and Public Relations, Barry Cheshier
Director Wellness Center, Dawn Bourgeois
Executive Assistant to the CEO, Jaydean Young
Director Human Resources, Erin Cates
CFO, Robert (Bob) Smelser
CIO, Fred Evans
SVP Administration and Executive Director Quality, Debbye Wallace
CEO Hill Country Memorial Hospital, Michael R. (Mike) Williams
Chairman, Chris Avery
Community Relations, Linda Davis
Marketing Specialist, Troy Sifford
Secretary Hill Country Memorial Hospital Foundation, Ron Woellhof
Chief Nursing Officer, Robin Duderstat

LOCATIONS

HQ: Hill Country Memorial Health System
1020 S. State Hwy.16, Fredericksburg TX 78624
Phone: 830-997-4353   **Fax:** 830-990-1595
Web: www.hillcountrymemorial.com

PRODUCTS/OPERATIONS

Selected Services
Women's Health Services
Breast Center
OB
Women's Services
Virtual Nursery
Orthopedic Services
The HCM orthopedic program features a comprehensive approach to treating injuries and diseases of bones joints ligaments tendons muscles and nerves.
Rehab Center
Physical Therapy
Occupational Therapy
Speech Therapy

Cardiac Rehab
Pulmonary Rehab
Wound Healing
Home Health Care
Homemaker Services (private pay)
Medical Social Worker Care
Nursing Services
Physical Therapy Services
Speech Therapy
Occupational Therapy Services
Lifeline
Tele-Health
Hospice
Cancer Resource Center
The HCM Cancer Resource Center (CRC) offers
visitors an opportunity to learn more about cancer
for themselves or their loved ones.
HCM Wellness Center
Wildflower Run
Indoor Heated Pools
Personal Training

COMPETITORS

Dell Children' s Medical Center
HCA
Methodist Healthcare System
Scott & White
Seton Healthcare Network
Shriners Hospitals For Children
St. David' s Health Care
St. David' s Round Rock Medical Center
St. David' s South Austin Medical Center
Texas Children' s Hospital
University Health System

HISTORICAL FINANCIALS

Company Type: Private

Income Statement

FYE: December 31

	REVENUE ($ mil.)	NET INCOME ($ mil.)	NET PROFIT MARGIN	EMPLOYEES
12/11	63	(9)	—	626
Annual Growth	—	—	—	—

2011 Year-End Financials

Debt ratio: ——	
Return on equity: (-15.30)%	Dividends
Cash ($ mil.): 18	Yield: —
Current ratio: 1.90	Payout: —
Long-term debt ($ mil.): —	Market value ($ mil.): —

HINES GLOBAL REIT INC.

LOCATIONS

HQ: HINES GLOBAL REIT INC.
2800 POST OAK BLVD # 5000, HOUSTON, TX
77056-6178
Phone: 888-220-6121
Web: www.hines.com

HISTORICAL FINANCIALS

Company Type: Private

Income Statement

FYE: September 30

	ASSETS ($ mil.)	NET INCOME ($ mil.)	INCOME AS % OF ASSETS	EMPLOYEES
09/12*	2,005	(32)	—	2
12/11	1,381	(58)	—	0
Annual Growth	45.2%	—	—	—

*Fiscal year change

2012 Year-End Financials

Debt ratio: ——	
Return on equity: (-24.90)%	Dividends
Cash ($ mil.): 72	Yield: —
Current ratio: —	Payout: —
Long-term debt ($ mil.): —	Market value ($ mil.): —

HISTORIC TOURS OF AMERICA INC.

LOCATIONS

HQ: HISTORIC TOURS OF AMERICA INC.
201 FRONT ST STE 224, KEY WEST, FL 33040-8348
Phone: 305-296-3609
Web: www.historeum.com

HISTORICAL FINANCIALS

Company Type: Private

Income Statement

FYE: March 31

	REVENUE ($ mil.)	NET INCOME ($ mil.)	NET PROFIT MARGIN	EMPLOYEES
03/12	80	2	3.2%	850
03/11	72	1	1.8%	0
03/10	68	(3)	—	0
03/09	69	1	1.9%	0
Annual Growth	4.7%	24.5%	—	—

2012 Year-End Financials

Debt ratio: ——	
Return on equity: 3.20%	Dividends
Cash ($ mil.): 3	Yield: —
Current ratio: 0.40	Payout: —
Long-term debt ($ mil.): —	Market value ($ mil.): —

HOG INC.

LOCATIONS

HQ: HOG INC.
RR 2 BOX 8, GREENFIELD, IL 62044-9603
Phone: 217-368-2888
Web: www.hoginc.org

HISTORICAL FINANCIALS

Company Type: Private

Income Statement

FYE: February 29

	REVENUE ($ mil.)	NET INCOME ($ mil.)	NET PROFIT MARGIN	EMPLOYEES
02/12	81	0	0.3%	26
02/11	68	0	0.2%	0
02/10	63	0	0.7%	0
02/06	45	2	4.6%	0
Annual Growth	21.5%	(50.4%)	—	—

2012 Year-End Financials

Debt ratio: ——	
Return on equity: 0.30%	Dividends
Cash ($ mil.): 0	Yield: —
Current ratio: 0.10	Payout: —
Long-term debt ($ mil.): —	Market value ($ mil.): —

HOLLINS UNIVERSITY CORPORATION

Hollins University was founded in 1842 as the first chartered women's college in Virginia. It has about 800 female undergraduates as well as nearly 300 students in its graduate school which is coeducational. A private institution emphasizing the liberal arts Hollins offers undergraduate majors and graduate degrees (MFAs and MAs) in subjects such as creative writing liberal studies children's literature teaching and film studies. Notable alumni include the first woman publisher at Time (Elizabeth Valk Long '72) and the first woman to be named a White House correspondent (Ann Compton '69).

EXECUTIVES

VP Finance and Administration, Richard Alvarez
University Registrar, Thomas H. (Tom) Mesner
Director Media Relations, Jeffrey Hodges
President, Nancy Oliver Gray
Dean Academic Services, Alison Ridley
Director Campus Safety, David Carlson
Director Career Center, Tina Rolen
Dean Admissions and Financial Assistance, Rebecca Eckstein
VP Academic Affairs, Jeanine Silveira Stewart
Dean Students, Patty O'Toole
Executive Director Administration and Human Resources, Kerry J. Edmonds
CIO, Carol Reed
University Controller and Accounts Receivable, Laurie Gearheart
VP External Relations, Meredith Pierce Hunter
Director Alumnae Relations, Ann Cassell
Executive Director Marketing, Jean C. Holzinger

LOCATIONS

HQ: Hollins University
7916 Williamson Rd., Roanoke VA 24019
Phone: 540-362-6000   **Fax:** 540-362-6642
Web: www.hollins.edu

HISTORICAL FINANCIALS

Company Type: School

Income Statement

FYE: June 30

	REVENUE ($ mil.)	NET INCOME ($ mil.)	NET PROFIT MARGIN	EMPLOYEES
06/12	31	(0)	—	380
06/11	31	21	68.7%	0
06/10	32	21	66.2%	0
06/09	32	(10)	—	0
Annual Growth	(1.3%)	—	—	—

2012 Year-End Financials

Debt ratio: ——
Return on equity: (-1.60)%
Cash ($ mil.): 10
Current ratio: ——
Long-term debt ($ mil.): —

Dividends
Yield: —
Payout: —
Market value ($ mil.): —

HOLTEC INTERNATIONAL

LOCATIONS

HQ: HOLTEC INTERNATIONAL
1001 N US HIGHWAY 1 # 204, JUPITER, FL 33477-4482
Phone: 856-797-0900
Web: www.holtecinternational.com

HISTORICAL FINANCIALS

Company Type: Private

Income Statement

FYE: December 31

	REVENUE ($ mil.)	NET INCOME ($ mil.)	NET PROFIT MARGIN	EMPLOYEES
12/11	256	86	33.7%	700
12/10	266	77	29.2%	0
12/09	257	77	29.9%	0
12/07	165	66	40.1%	0
Annual Growth	15.6%	9.1%	—	—

2011 Year-End Financials

Debt ratio: ——
Return on equity: 33.70%
Cash ($ mil.): 34
Current ratio: 0.90
Long-term debt ($ mil.): —

Dividends
Yield: —
Payout: —
Market value ($ mil.): —

HOLY CROSS HOSPITAL

LOCATIONS

HQ: HOLY CROSS HOSPITAL
2701 W 68TH ST, CHICAGO, IL 60629-1882
Phone: 773-884-9000
Web: www.holycrosshospital.org

HISTORICAL FINANCIALS

Company Type: Private

Income Statement

FYE: June 30

	REVENUE ($ mil.)	NET INCOME ($ mil.)	NET PROFIT MARGIN	EMPLOYEES
06/11	117	1	1.6%	1,600
06/10	111	0	0.6%	0
06/09	100	13	13.2%	0
06/08	126	5	4.1%	0
Annual Growth	(2.5%)	(28.9%)	—	—

2011 Year-End Financials

Debt ratio: ——
Return on equity: 1.60%
Cash ($ mil.): 14
Current ratio: 1.60
Long-term debt ($ mil.): —

Dividends
Yield: —
Payout: —
Market value ($ mil.): —

HOLY CROSS HOSPITAL OF SILVER SPRING INCORPORATED

LOCATIONS

HQ: HOLY CROSS HOSPITAL OF SILVER SPRING INCORPORATED
1500 FOREST GLEN RD, SILVER SPRING, MD 20910-1483
Phone: 301-754-7000
Web: www.holycrosshealth.org

HISTORICAL FINANCIALS

Company Type: Private

Income Statement

FYE: June 30

	REVENUE ($ mil.)	NET INCOME ($ mil.)	NET PROFIT MARGIN	EMPLOYEES
06/12	414	22	5.4%	2,600
06/11	416	33	8.1%	0
06/10	394	29	7.4%	0
06/09	0	0	—	0
Annual Growth	1076.3%	—	—	—

2012 Year-End Financials

Debt ratio: ——
Return on equity: 5.40%
Cash ($ mil.): 46
Current ratio: 1.50
Long-term debt ($ mil.): —

Dividends
Yield: —
Payout: —
Market value ($ mil.): —

HOLY SPIRIT HOSPITAL OF THE SISTERS OF CHRISTIAN CHARITY

Holy Spirit Health tends to the health of the incarnate. The Holy Spirit Health System (HSHS) provides cardiology women's health care pediatric care and other acute and emergency medical services to the residents of greater Harrisburg and Cumberland County in south-central Pennsylvania. HSHS was established in 1963 and is operated by the Sisters of Christian Charity. The flagship Holy Spirit Hospital has more than 330 beds as well as a level III neonatal intensive care unit. The hospital also operates an adjoining cardiac treatment facility and it has a network of affiliated family practice and specialty health clinics.

HSHS has undergone a number of expansions in recent years opening more than ten outpatient centers in the past five years to deliver care closer to home in the communities in which it serves. Also many hospitals are growing their outpatient services because they tend to bring in more income and help compensate for downward pricing on inpatient hospital stays from private and public health care payers.

Some of its centers include an endoscopy clinic family medicine center a hyperbaric wound healing unit and women's post-surgical recovery unit (in the hospital). Also within the hospital administrators are adding room for robotic surgeries and more endovascular procedures.

HSHS employs a number of hospitalists who can be thought of as patient liaisons. The hospitalists follow the patient's progress from the moment they are admitted to the moment they are discharged and to ensure follow-up care; hospitalists cared for more than 80% of all general medical admissions at HSHS in 2010.

The hospital also provides free community health seminars to educate the public on topics such as breast cancer prostate cancer heart disease diabetes minimally invasive surgery Crohn's disease ulcerative colitis and childhood depression. By giving these seminars patients are more likely to head to HSHS should the need arise for them to receive healthcare.

Holy Spirit Health System provided nearly $60 million in charity care in 2010 to benefit the communities in which it serves. That total includes uncompensated care charity care and subsidies for Medicare (government programs that typically pay less than it costs to provide services) as well as subsidies for behavioral health services.

EXECUTIVES

President and CEO, Sister Romaine Niemeyer
SVP Strategic and Business Development, Richard E. LaVanture
VP Patient Services and Chief Nursing Officer, Lisa Lewis
Director Marketing, Scott Dugan
Public Relations Specialist, Lori P. Moran
SVP and CFO, Manuel J. Evans
Director Quality and Organizational Performance, Karen G. Sloan
Chairman, Leon Feinerman
COO, Richard A. (Rick) Schaffner Jr.
Director Volunteer Services, Kristi Ondo
CIO, Edith Hunter

SVP Human Resources, William Shartle
Vice Chairman, Bruce J. Brown

LOCATIONS

HQ: Holy Spirit Health System
503 N. 21st St., Camp Hill PA 17011-2288
Phone: 717-763-2100   Fax: 717-763-2183
Web: www.hsh.org

PRODUCTS/OPERATIONS

Selected Facilities

Broad Street Family Health Center
Devonshire Family Health Center
Dillsburg Family Health Center
Duncannon Family Health Center
Grandview Surgery and Laser Center
Green Hill Family Health Center
Holy Spirit Hospital
Holy Spirit Imaging Center East
John R. Dietz Emergency Center
OakWood Center Radiation Oncology
Ortenzio Heart Center at Holy Spirit Hospital
Silver Creek Family Health Center

COMPETITORS

Hershey Medical Center
PinnacleHealth System
Pocono Health System
Saint Vincent Health System
Sharon Regional Health System
University of Pennsylvania Health System
WellSpan Health

HISTORICAL FINANCIALS

Company Type: Private - Not-for-Profit

Income Statement

FYE: June 30

	REVENUE ($ mil.)	NET INCOME ($ mil.)	NET PROFIT MARGIN	EMPLOYEES
06/11	294	8	3.0%	2,698
06/10	271	11	4.2%	0
06/09	5	0	—	0
06/08	660	10	1.5%	0
Annual Growth	(23.7%)	(4.8%)	—	—

2011 Year-End Financials

Debt ratio: —
Return on equity: 3.00%
Cash ($ mil.): 8
Current ratio: 1.40
Long-term debt ($ mil.): —

Dividends
Yield: —
Payout: —
Market value ($ mil.): —

HOMEWOOD RETIREMENT CENTERS OF THE UNITED CHURCH OF CHRIST INC.

LOCATIONS

HQ: HOMEWOOD RETIREMENT CENTERS OF THE UNITED CHURCH OF CHRIST INC.
16107 ELLIOTT PKWY, WILLIAMSPORT, MD 21795-4084
Phone: 301-582-1626
Web: www.homewood.com

HISTORICAL FINANCIALS

Company Type: Private

Income Statement

FYE: December 31

	REVENUE ($ mil.)	NET INCOME ($ mil.)	NET PROFIT MARGIN	EMPLOYEES
12/11	83	6	8.3%	1,075
12/10	77	6	8.5%	0
12/08	78	(2)		0
12/07	74	5	7.7%	0
Annual Growth	3.7%	6.3%	—	—

2011 Year-End Financials

Debt ratio: —
Return on equity: 8.30%
Cash ($ mil.): 5
Current ratio: 0.80
Long-term debt ($ mil.): —

Dividends
Yield: —
Payout: —
Market value ($ mil.): —

HOOPER CORPORATION

LOCATIONS

HQ: HOOPER CORPORATION
2030 PENNSYLVANIA AVE, MADISON, WI 53704-4746
Phone: 608-249-0451
Web: www.hoopercorp.com

HISTORICAL FINANCIALS

Company Type: Private

Income Statement

FYE: December 31

	REVENUE ($ mil.)	NET INCOME ($ mil.)	NET PROFIT MARGIN	EMPLOYEES
12/11	150	0	—	350
12/10	115	0	—	0
12/08	0	0	—	0
12/07	0	0	—	0
Annual Growth	—	—	—	—

2011 Year-End Financials

Debt ratio: —
Return on equity: —
Cash ($ mil.): 7
Current ratio: 1.40
Long-term debt ($ mil.): —

Dividends
Yield: —
Payout: —
Market value ($ mil.): —

HOOSIER ENERGY RURAL ELECTRIC COOPERATIVE INC

Who's yer daddy? In terms of providing electricity for many Indianans (and some residents of Illinois) that would be Hoosier Energy Rural Electric Cooperative which provides wholesale electric power to 18 member distribution cooperatives in 48 central and southern Indiana counties and 11 counties in southeastern Illinois. These electric cooperatives serve 800000 residents businesses industries and farms in a 15000 sq. ml. service area. Hoosier Energy operates six power plants and a 1700-mile transmission system and maintains the Tuttle Creek Reservoir in Southwest Indiana. Hoosier Energy is part of the Touchstone Energy network of electric cooperatives.

Hoosier Energy operates coal- natural gas- and renewable energy-generation plants. It delivers electricity via a 1700-mile transmission network including 21 major substations and more than 350 delivery points.

The company delivers power to member distribution cooperatives in central and southern Indiana and southeastern Illinois.

Lower sales to nonmembers dragged down revenues by about 1% in 2011 and the lower revenues and higher fuel costs cut Hoosier Energy's operating margins by more than 3%.

To advance its push for more renewable sources in 2010 Hoosier Energy announced plans to quadruple the production of renewable energy. In 2011 it was operating a 2.5 MW landfill methane generation facility in addition to buying 25 MW of wind energy.

Expanding its geographic coverage in 2011 Hoosier Energy began to supply power to the Wayne-White Counties Electric Cooperative when that coop's contract with an independent power supplier ended. The distribution coop serves 13500 residential farm and business consumers in 11 counties in southeastern Illinois.

Hoosier Energy was formed in 1948 as part of the nationwide rural electrification drive started under the Roosevelt administration in the 1930s.

EXECUTIVES

President and CEO, J. Steven (Steve) Smith
SVP Planning and Projects, Thomas L. (Tom) Bernardi
SVP Marketing and Business Development, R. M. (Mike) Rampley
Director Public Affairs, Randy Haymaker
Chairman, Eugene Roberts
Vice Chairman, Dale Walther
VP Management Services, Robert I. Richhart
VP Power Supply, David W. Sandefur
VP Finance, Donna L. Snyder
Secretary and Director, August A. Bauer
Treasurer and Director, Darin Duncan
Attorney, Christopher Goffinet
Director, Jerry C. Jackle
Director, Charles Meier
Vice Chairman, Dale Walther
Director, Harry Althoff
Secretary and Director, August A. Bauer
Director, Herbert C. (Herb) Haggard
Director, Emil Page
Director, Larry Peters
Director, Robert D. Stroup

Director, Vaughn Tucker
Treasurer and Director, Darin Duncan
Director, Jerry Pheifer
Director, Donald Braun
Director, James Weimer
Director, Donald Cross
Director, Larry Hosselton
Director, James L. (Jimmie) Sanders
Auditors: Deloitte&ToucheLLP

LOCATIONS

HQ: Hoosier Energy Rural Electric Cooperative Inc.
7398 N. State Rd. 37, Bloomington IN 47404
Phone: 812-876-2021   **Fax:** 812-876-3476
Web: www.hepn.com

PRODUCTS/OPERATIONS

2011 Sales

	$ mil.	% of total
Members	514	79
Nonmembers	135	21
Other	0	-
Total	**649**	**100**

Member Cooperativ
Bartholomew County REMC
Clark County REMC
Decatur County REMC
Daviess-Martin County REMC
Dubois REC Inc.
Harrison REMC
Henry County REMC
Jackson County REMC
Johnson County REMC
Orange County REMC
RushShelby Energy
South Central Indiana REMC
Southeastern Indiana REMC
Southern Indiana Power
Utilities District of Western Indiana REMC
Wayne-White Counties Electric Cooperativ
WIN Energy REMC
Whitewater Valley REMC

COMPETITORS

Indiana Michigan Power   IPALCO Enterprises
Indiana Municipal
   Power Agency

HISTORICAL FINANCIALS

Company Type: Private - Cooperative

Income Statement   FYE: December 31

	REVENUE ($ mil.)	NET INCOME ($ mil.)	NET PROFIT MARGIN	EMPLOYEES
12/11	649	30	4.7%	450
12/09	575	16	2.9%	0
12/08	566	19	3.5%	0
12/07	512	26	5.2%	0
Annual Growth	8.2%	4.1%	—	—

2011 Year-End Financials

Debt ratio: ——
Return on equity: 4.70%
Cash ($ mil.): 139
Current ratio: 1.10
Long-term debt ($ mil.): —

Dividends
Yield: —
Payout: —
Market value ($ mil.): —

HORIZON CONSTRUCTION GROUP INC.

LOCATIONS

HQ: HORIZON CONSTRUCTION GROUP INC.
5201 E TERRACE DR STE 300, MADISON, WI 53718-8362
Phone: 608-354-0900
Web: www.horizondbm.com

HISTORICAL FINANCIALS

Company Type: Private

Income Statement   FYE: December 31

	REVENUE ($ mil.)	NET INCOME ($ mil.)	NET PROFIT MARGIN	EMPLOYEES
12/11	106	3	3.3%	44
12/10	15	0	0.8%	0
Annual Growth	569.5%	2538.7%	—	—

2011 Year-End Financials

Debt ratio: ——
Return on equity: 3.30%
Cash ($ mil.): 5
Current ratio: 1.00
Long-term debt ($ mil.): —

Dividends
Yield: —
Payout: —
Market value ($ mil.): —

HOSPITAL CENTRAL SERVICES INC.

LOCATIONS

HQ: HOSPITAL CENTRAL SERVICES INC.
2171 28TH ST SW, ALLENTOWN, PA 18103-7093
Phone: 610-791-2222
Web: www.hcsc.org

HISTORICAL FINANCIALS

Company Type: Private

Income Statement   FYE: June 30

	REVENUE ($ mil.)	NET INCOME ($ mil.)	NET PROFIT MARGIN	EMPLOYEES
06/12	102	0	0.1%	1,200
06/11	99	0	0.5%	0
06/10	98	2	3.0%	0
06/09	95	3	4.0%	0
Annual Growth	2.4%	(66.1%)	—	—

2012 Year-End Financials

Debt ratio: ——
Return on equity: 0.10%
Cash ($ mil.): 7
Current ratio: 2.10
Long-term debt ($ mil.): —

Dividends
Yield: —
Payout: —
Market value ($ mil.): —

HOSPITAL FOR SPECIAL CARE

LOCATIONS

HQ: HOSPITAL FOR SPECIAL CARE
2150 CORBIN AVE, NEW BRITAIN, CT 06053-2298
Phone: 860-223-2761
Web: www.hospitalforspecialcare.com

HISTORICAL FINANCIALS

Company Type: Private

Income Statement   FYE: March 31

	REVENUE ($ mil.)	NET INCOME ($ mil.)	NET PROFIT MARGIN	EMPLOYEES
03/11	93	7	7.5%	40
03/10	144	4	3.3%	0
03/09	119	(7)	—	0
Annual Growth	(11.4%)	—	—	—

2011 Year-End Financials

Debt ratio: ——
Return on equity: 7.50%
Cash ($ mil.): 5
Current ratio: 1.60
Long-term debt ($ mil.): —

Dividends
Yield: —
Payout: —
Market value ($ mil.): —

HOSPITAL SISTERS HEALTH SYSTEM

These sisters want their big family to benefit everyone in the community. Hospital Sisters Health System (HSHS) a Catholic ministry of the Hospital Sisters of the Third Order of St. Francis operates more than a dozen hospitals located throughout Wisconsin and Illinois. Its facilities have a total of more than 2500 beds and range from large-scale acute care facilities such as St. John's Hospital (Springfield Illinois) St. Elizabeth's Hospital (Bellevue Illinois) and St. Vincent Hospital (Green Bay Wisconsin) to small community hospitals; it also operates regional outpatient clinics. While the organization was incorporated in 1978 the health care ministry of the HSHS goes back to 1875.

HSHS' primary function is to provide support and consultation services to its local hospital ministries including planning system development and mission implementation. It also provides accounting finance procurement human resources IT philanthropy and construction management services. The main HSHS office is located next to the St. Francis Convent in Springfield Illinois.

In addition to its 2000 hospital physicians the provider partners with doctors in the affiliated HSHS Medical Group a growing network of primary and multi-specialty care providers in Illinois and Wisconsin. The two organizations have a symbiotic relationship in that the physicians may refer more complicated patients to one of HSHS' hospitals when necessary and vice versa; they also share patient data partly through electronic health record (EHR) systems facilitated by IT provider Medicity. HSHS also partners with other area physician practice organizations to coordinate care in the region.

HSHS is a not-for-profit organization operating under a Catholic doctrine and therefore has a community benefit expense budget that has been increasing in recent years due to economic conditions. In 2011 the company spent some $166 million on community care (up from some $150 million in 2010) including $37 million in charity health care provisions and another $100 million on shortfalls from care provided to low-income patients (mostly from unreimbursed care to Medicaid members). Outside of the community budget HSHS also records expenses from excess services for Medicare patients and uncollectable accounts.

To meet growing patient populations and replace aging equipment and buildings HSHS is conducting some construction projects. For instance the company broke ground on a $100 million replacement facility for its 25-bed St. Joseph's Hospital in Highland Illinois in 2012. The project includes new ER and surgery centers increased diagnostic and technological capabilities a larger rehabilitation unit private inpatient rooms and an adjacent outpatient center. HSHS also launched a $161 million project to rebuild or renovate the 430-bed St. John's Hospital's surgery and patient towers in Springfield in 2011.

The company is also investing in the implementation of its EHR system at all of its hospitals. Its facilities in northeast Wisconsin launched a system in early 2012 to connect the hospitals' records and also coordinate care with area physicians including the affiliated Prevea physician practice organization.

EXECUTIVES

President and CEO, Mary C. Starmann-Harrison
COO, Larry Schumacher, age 54
SVP Sponsorship and Governance, Sister Marybeth Culnan
CFO, Michael W. Cottrell
VP Chief People Officer, Jay D. Justice
SVP and Treasury, Leo A. Lenn
VP Mission Integration, Sister Monica Laws
Chief Physician Executive, Frank Mikell

LOCATIONS

HQ: HOSPITAL SISTERS HEALTH SYSTEM
4936 LAVERNA RD, SPRINGFIELD, IL 62707-9797
Phone: 217-523-4747

Selected Facilities
Southern Illinois
  St. Elizabeth Hospital (340 beds Belleville)
  St. Joseph's Hospital (Breese)
  St. Joseph's Hospital (Highland)
Central Illinois
  St. Anthony's Memorial Hospital (150 beds Effingham)
  St. Francis Hospital (Litchfield)
  St. John's Hospital (430 beds Springfield)
  St. Mary's Hospital (355 beds Decatur)
  St. Mary's Hospital (130 beds Streator)
Eastern Wisconsin
  St. Mary's Hospital (Green Bay)
  St. Nicholas Hospital (Sheboygan)
  St. Vincent Hospital (550 beds Green Bay)
Western Wisconsin
  Sacred Heart Hospital (340 beds Eau Claire)
  St. Joseph's Hospital (190 beds Chippewa Falls)

COMPETITORS

Advocate BroMenn
Advocate Health Care
Ascension Health
BJC HealthCare

Blessing Hospital
Carle Hospital
Community Health Systems
Dean Health Systems Inc.
Decatur Memorial Hospital
Franciscan Skemp Healthcare

McDonough District Hospital
Memorial Health System
Memorial Health System (Colorado)
Memorial Hospital (Illinois)
Memorial Medical Center
Mercy Hospital and Medical Center
Meriter Health Services
Ministry Health Care
ProHealth Care
Rockford Health System
Rush System for Health
Sarah Bush Lincoln Health Center
Southern Illinois Healthcare
SSM Health Care
St. John's Hospital (Illinois)
SwedishAmerican Health System
University of Wisconsin Hospital and Clinics
Wheaton Franciscan Services

HISTORICAL FINANCIALS

Company Type: Private - Not-for-Profit

Income Statement

FYE: June 30

	REVENUE ($ mil.)	NET INCOME ($ mil.)	NET PROFIT MARGIN	EMPLOYEES
06/11	131	35	27.2%	14,000
06/10	92	10	11.3%	0
06/09	60	(7)	—	0
06/08	12	(4)	—	0
Annual Growth	**120.9%**	**—**	**—**	**—**

2011 Year-End Financials

Debt ratio: ——
Return on equity: 27.20%
Cash ($ mil.): 3
Current ratio: 0.30
Long-term debt ($ mil.): —
Dividends
  Yield: —
  Payout: —
  Market value ($ mil.): —

HOSPITAL THE UNIONTOWN INC

LOCATIONS

HQ: HOSPITAL THE UNIONTOWN INC
500 W BERKELEY ST, UNIONTOWN, PA 15401-5596
Phone: 724-430-5000
Web: www.uniontownhospital.com

HISTORICAL FINANCIALS

Company Type: Private

Income Statement

FYE: June 30

	REVENUE ($ mil.)	NET INCOME ($ mil.)	NET PROFIT MARGIN	EMPLOYEES
06/11	130	(2)	—	1,050
06/10	121	(2)	—	0
06/09	110	0	0.4%	0
06/08	118	2	2.0%	0
Annual Growth	**3.2%**	**—**	**—**	**—**

2011 Year-End Financials

Debt ratio: ——
Return on equity: (-1.50)%
Cash ($ mil.): 9
Current ratio: 1.00
Long-term debt ($ mil.): —
Dividends
  Yield: —
  Payout: —
  Market value ($ mil.): —

HOURIGAN CONSTRUCTION CORP.

LOCATIONS

HQ: HOURIGAN CONSTRUCTION CORP.
4429 BONNEY RD STE 200, VIRGINIA BEACH, VA 23462-3877
Phone: 757-499-3434
Web: www.houriganconstruction.com

HISTORICAL FINANCIALS

Company Type: Private

Income Statement

FYE: December 31

	REVENUE ($ mil.)	NET INCOME ($ mil.)	NET PROFIT MARGIN	EMPLOYEES
12/11	88	0	0.3%	99
12/10	122	7	5.8%	0
12/09	0	0	—	0
12/08	124	2	1.8%	0
Annual Growth	**(10.9%)**	**(53.0%)**	**—**	**—**

2011 Year-End Financials

Debt ratio: ——
Return on equity: 0.30%
Cash ($ mil.): 9
Current ratio: 1.70
Long-term debt ($ mil.): —
Dividends
  Yield: —
  Payout: —
  Market value ($ mil.): —

HOUSTON FOOD BANK

LOCATIONS

HQ: HOUSTON FOOD BANK
535 PORTWALL ST, HOUSTON, TX 77029-1332
Phone: 713-223-3700
Web: www.endhungernetwork.org

HISTORICAL FINANCIALS

Company Type: Private

Income Statement

FYE: June 30

	REVENUE ($ mil.)	NET INCOME ($ mil.)	NET PROFIT MARGIN	EMPLOYEES
06/11	148	16	11.4%	108
06/10	138	22	16.0%	0
06/09	115	6	5.9%	0
06/08	54	(1)	—	0
Annual Growth	**39.9%**	**—**	**—**	**—**

2011 Year-End Financials

Debt ratio: —
Return on equity: 11.40%
Cash ($ mil.): 6
Current ratio: 1.60
Long-term debt ($ mil.): —
Dividends
Yield: —
Payout: —
Market value ($ mil.): —

HOUSTON SAM STATE UNIVERSITY

Part of the Texas State University System Sam Houston University has an enrollment of some 17000 students. It consists of six schools: Business Administration Criminal Justice Education Fine Arts and Mass Communications Humanities and Social Sciences and Sciences. The university offers some 130 undergraduate and master programs as well as doctoral programs in counselor education criminal justice educational leadership reading and clinical psychology. Sam Houston State was founded as Sam Houston Normal Institute in 1879 and is named after Texas hero General Sam Houston.

EXECUTIVES

President, James F. (Jim) Gaertner, age 69
VP Finance and Operations, Jack C. Parker
Director Human Resources, Ted Michael
Director Purchasing and HUB Coordinator, John Hitzeman
VP Academic Affairs and Provost, David E. Payne
VP University Advancement, Frank R. Holmes
VP Student Services, Frank Parker
Associate VP Academic Affairs, Richard Eglsaer
Associate VP Academic Affairs and Dean Graduate Studies, Mitchell Muehsam
Associate VP Research and Special Programs, Jerry Cook
Dean College of Arts and Sciences, Jaimie Hebert
Dean College of Business Administration, R. Dean Lewis
Dean College of Criminal Justice, Vincent Webb
Dean College of Education, Genevieve Brown
Dean College of Humanities and Social Sciences, John de Castro
Director Newton Gresham Library, Ann Holder
Director Business Office, Anne Heartfield
Associate VP Finance and Operations, Jacque Gilliam
Associate VP Information Resources, Mark Adams
Director Public Safety, Kevin H. Morris
Executive Director Development, Thelma Mooney
Director Financial Aid, Lisa Tatom
Director Admissions, Trevor Thorn
Executive Director Alumni Relations, Charlie Vienne
Assistant Director Membership and Marketing, Kristle Castillo
Director Career Services, Pam Laughlin
VP Enrollment Management, Heather Crowson

LOCATIONS

HQ: Sam Houston State University
1803 Ave. I, Huntsville TX 77341
Phone: 936-294-1111   **Fax:** 936-294-3776
Web: www.shsu.edu

HISTORICAL FINANCIALS

Company Type: School

Income Statement

FYE: August 31

	REVENUE ($ mil.)	NET INCOME ($ mil.)	NET PROFIT MARGIN	EMPLOYEES
08/11	160	29	18.4%	2,200
08/08	136	63	46.5%	0
08/07	128	14	11.6%	0
08/06	255	0	—	0
Annual Growth	(14.4%)	16033.5%		

2011 Year-End Financials

Debt ratio: —
Return on equity: 18.40%
Cash ($ mil.): 66
Current ratio: 0.90
Long-term debt ($ mil.): —
Dividends
Yield: —
Payout: —
Market value ($ mil.): —

HOUSTON-GALVESTON AREA COUNCIL

LOCATIONS

HQ: HOUSTON-GALVESTON AREA COUNCIL
3555 TIMMONS LN STE 120, HOUSTON, TX 77027-6466
Phone: 713-627-3200
Web: www.hgacbuy.org

HISTORICAL FINANCIALS

Company Type: Private

Income Statement

FYE: December 31

	ASSETS ($ mil.)	NET INCOME ($ mil.)	INCOME AS % OF ASSETS	EMPLOYEES
12/11	43	3	7.7%	200
12/10	63	0	0.5%	0
Annual Growth	(32.4%)	1035.7%	—	—

2011 Year-End Financials

Debt ratio: —
Return on equity: 1.20%
Cash ($ mil.): 15
Current ratio: —
Long-term debt ($ mil.): —
Dividends
Yield: —
Payout: —
Market value ($ mil.): —

HOWARD COMMUNITY COLLEGE

Howard Community College (HCC) provides academic programs to students in Maryland's Howard County. More than 7900 of its students pursue studies leading to immediate employment upon graduation or transfer to four year colleges (many go to the University System of Maryland's University of Maryland College Park; University of Maryland Baltimore County; and Towson State University). Another 17000 students take HCC courses for personal or professional development. Founded by the Board of Education of Howard County HCC was formally authorized by the Howard County Commissioners and approved by the State of Maryland in 1966.

EXECUTIVES

VP Administration and Finance, Lynn C. Coleman
VP Academic Affairs, Ronald X. (Ron) Roberson
Director Public Relations and Marketing, Randall (Randy) Bengfort
VP Information Technology, Thomas (Tom) Glaser
President, Kathleen Hetherington
Executive Director Planning Research and Organizational Development, Zoe Irvin
Security, Gavalian Hailey
Manager Benefits, Sharon Heckler
Chairperson Arts and Humanities Division, Valerie Lash
Chairperson Business and Computers Systems Division, Sharon Schmickley
Executive Director Workforce Development, Patty Keeton
Chair English and World Languages Division, Tara Hart
Chair Mathmatics Division, Bernadette Sandruck
Chair Science and Technology, Daniel (Dan) Friedman
Chair Social Sciences Division, Jerrold I. Casway
Director User and Network Services, Michael (Mike) Heinmuller
Manager Marketing, Jane Sharp
Executive Assistant to the President, Farida Guzdar
Director Student Life, Llatetra D. Brown
Director Records and Registration, Judi Bulliner
Analyst, Carol A. Egan
Director Teaching and Learning Services, Lucy K. Gardner
Associate VP Enrollment Services, Barbara C. Greenfeld
Director Educational Technology, Quent Kardos
Director Music, Deborah P. Kent
Associate VP Student Development, Janice L. Marks
Director Development and Executive Director Foundation, Missy Mattey
VP Academic Affairs, Sharon J. Pierce
Director Children's Learning Center, Kim Pins
Director Athletics, Diane E. Schumacher
Director Financial Aid Services, Katherine M. Allen
Director Auxiliary Services, Arla J. Webb
Director Administrative Information Systems, Linda C. Wu
VP Student Services, Cindy Peterka
Director Board Relations and Special Projects, Erin Yun
Acting Director Human Resources, Karlyn K. Young
Interim Director Mediation and Conflict Resolution Center, Kathryn B. Rockefeller
Director, Patrick Huddie
Director, Roberta E. Dillow
Director, Kevin J. Doyle
Director, Louis G. Hutt Jr.
Director, Mary Beth Tung

LOCATIONS

HQ: Howard Community College
10901 Little Patuxent Pkwy., Columbia MD 21044
Phone: 443-518-1000   **Fax:** 443-518-4803
Web: www.howardcc.edu

HISTORICAL FINANCIALS

Company Type: School

Income Statement

FYE: June 30

	REVENUE ($ mil.)	NET INCOME ($ mil.)	NET PROFIT MARGIN	EMPLOYEES
06/12	33	26	77.9%	659
06/11	32	6	21.2%	0
06/10	31	5	18.0%	0
06/09	30	21	70.0%	0
Annual Growth	3.2%	7.0%	—	—

2012 Year-End Financials

Debt ratio: —
Return on equity: 77.90%
Cash ($ mil.): 25
Current ratio: 1.70
Long-term debt ($ mil.): —

Dividends
Yield: —
Payout: —
Market value ($ mil.): —

HOWARD UNIVERSITY INC.

How hard is it to find a good education in our nation's capital? Not too hard thanks to Howard University. The predominantly African-American university enrolls about 10500 students and has a low student-teacher ratio of about 8:1. The school offers undergraduate graduate and professional degrees in areas such as engineering education divinity dentistry law medicine history political science music and social work. Howard University's endowment is about $400 million. Its operating budget is nearly $885 million. Established in 1867 the school was named after one of its founders General Oliver O. Howard a Civil War hero who was commissioner of the Freedman's Bureau.

Medical students at Howard University have the convenience of using Howard University Hospital (located right on the school's campus) for their training and residency programs. The not-for-profit hospital offers students training in a full range of medical specialties including Level 1 Trauma care. The hospital is also a research facility giving students the opportunity to participate in clinical and research work.

Notable alumni at Howard University include choreographer Debbie Allen former US Supreme Court Justice Thurgood Marshall former New York City mayor David Dinkins Nobel laureate Toni Morrison and singer Roberta Flack.

EXECUTIVES

President, Sidney A. Ribeau, age 63
VP and General Counsel, Kurt L. Schmoke, age 62
SVP and Secretary, Artis G. Hampshire-Cowan
General Counsel, Norma Leftwich
VP University Advancement, Virgil E. Ecton
VP Student Affairs, Barbara L.J. Griffin
Founder President CEO, Harold P. Freeman
Dean School of Education, Leslie T. Fenwick
EVP and Chief Human Resources Officer, Jimmy Jones
SVP Strategic Planning and External Affairs, Hassan Minor
VP Development and Alumni Relations, Nesta H. Bernard

Assistant VP Alumni Relations, Raymond W. Archer III
Assistant VP University Communications, Jennifer James-Pryor
Executive Communications Manager, Grace Virtue
Program Manager Alumni Relations, Jeraldene Shorter
Special Events Manager, Natalie K. Meyers
Vice Chairwoman, Renee Higginbotham-Brooks
Director Risk Estate and Asset Management, Leonard A. Williams Jr.
Director Compliance Athletics, A. B. Williamson
Director Sports Information, Edward Hill Jr.
Director Center for Excellence in Teaching Learning and Assessment (CETLA), Teresa Redd
Director Howard University Continuing Education (HUCE), Peggy A. Berry
Interim Executive Director Physical Facilities Management (PFM), Steven G. Johnson
Director Student Financial Services, Sevester Bell
Manager Student Loans Student Financial Services, Brenda Hughes
Chairman, A. Barry Rand, age 67
Dean College of Arts and Sciences, James Donaldson
Dean College of Business, Barron Harvey
Dean School of Communications, Jannette L. Dates
Dean College of Dentistry, Leo E. Rouse
Dean College of Engineering Architecture and Computer Sciences, James H. Johnson
Dean Graduate School, Orlando L. Taylor
Interim Dean College of Medicine, Robert E. Taylor
Interim Dean College of Pharmacy Nursing and Allied Health Services, Beatrice Adderley-Kelly
Dean School of Social Work, Cudore L. Snell
SVP CFO and Treasurer, Sidney H. Evans Jr.
Media Relations Manager, Stacie Royster
Athletic Director, Dwight Datcher
Dean School of Divinity, Alton B. Pollard III
Acting Dean and Director Counseling and Career Development, Ayana Watkins-Northern
Dean Residence Life, Charles J. Gibbs
Dean Student Life and Activities, Tonya L. Guillory
Director Admissions, Linda Sanders-Hawkins
Associate VP and Controller, Clarence A. Jones
Acting VP Research and Compliance, Florence Bonner
SVP Health and Sciences, Donald E. Wilson
Associate Director Career Services, Joan M. Browne
President Alumni Association, Kimberly Singleton
Associate Dean Division of Allied Health Sciences, Allan A. Johnson
Director Annual Giving, Christie Davis
Provost and Chief Academic Officer, Wayne A.I. Frederick
Senior Vice President Chief Financial Officer Treasurer, Robert Tarola
Director of Communications, Ron Harris
Trustee, Wayman F. Smith III
Trustee, Stacey J. Mobley, age 67
Trustee, Robert L. Lumpkins, age 68
Trustee, John A. Thain, age 56
Trustee, Vernon E. Jordan Jr., age 76
Trustee, John D. Zeglis, age 64
Trustee, Richard D. (Dick) Parsons, age 64
Trustee, Earl G. Graves Sr., age 77
Trustee Emeritus, Gabrielle K. McDonald, age 70
Trustee, Floretta D. McKenzie
Trustee, Gerald D. Prothro, age 69
Trustee Emeritus, Martin D. Payson, age 74
Trustee, Marie C. Johns
Trustee, Renetta McCann, age 53
Trustee, Harold P. Freeman
Trustee, Charisse R. Lillie, age 60
Trustee, Starmanda Bullock
Trustee, Elizabeth G. Early

Trustee, Aprille J. Ericsson
Vice Chairwoman, Renee Higginbotham-Brooks
Trustee, Charles J. McDonald
Trustee, Cornell Leverette Moore
Trustee, Jessye Norman
Trustee, M. Kasim Reed
Trustee, James E. Silcott
Trustee, Gregory A. White
Trustee, L. Douglas Wilder, age 81
Trustee, Anita D. Stearns Mayo
Trustee, Victoria D. Kirby

LOCATIONS

HQ: Howard University Inc.
2400 6th St. NW, Washington DC 20059
Phone: 202-806-6100   Fax: 604-677-5856
Web: www.westcanuranium.com

HISTORICAL FINANCIALS

Company Type: School

Income Statement

FYE: June 30

	REVENUE ($ mil.)	NET INCOME ($ mil.)	NET PROFIT MARGIN	EMPLOYEES
06/12	851	(148)	—	5,600
06/11	989	11	1.2%	0
06/10	941	10	1.1%	0
06/09	844	835	98.9%	0
Annual Growth	0.2%	—	—	—

2012 Year-End Financials

Debt ratio: —
Return on equity: (-17.50)%
Cash ($ mil.): 35
Current ratio: —
Long-term debt ($ mil.): —

Dividends
Yield: —
Payout: —
Market value ($ mil.): —

HSS INC.

LOCATIONS

HQ: HSS INC.
900 S BROADWAY STE 100, DENVER, CO 80209-4269
Phone: 303-603-3000
Web: www.hospitalshared.com

HISTORICAL FINANCIALS

Company Type: Private

Income Statement

FYE: December 31

	REVENUE ($ mil.)	NET INCOME ($ mil.)	NET PROFIT MARGIN	EMPLOYEES
12/11	102	1	1.4%	2,600
12/07	77	1	1.9%	0
12/01	49	0	0.4%	0
12/00	135	0	—	0
Annual Growth	—	2553.3%	—	—

2011 Year-End Financials

Debt ratio: —
Return on equity: 1.40%
Cash ($ mil.): 6
Current ratio: 2.40
Long-term debt ($ mil.): —

Dividends
Yield: —
Payout: —
Market value ($ mil.): —

HUMAN RIGHTS WATCH INC.

Human Rights Watch (HRW) is watching out for everyone. The organization's mission is to prevent discrimination uphold political freedom protect people during wartime and bring offenders to justice. HRW researches human rights violations around the world and publishes its findings to help generate publicity about the atrocities it uncovers. It also meets with national and international governing officials to help steer policy change. Along with partner organizations HRW won the 1997 Nobel Peace Prize for its International Campaign to Ban Landmines. HRW is an independent organization; all funds come from private contributors. The group was founded in 1978.

EXECUTIVES

Vice Chair, John J. Studzinski, age 56
Vice Chair, Bruce J. Klatsky
Executive Director, Kenneth Roth
Associate Director, Carroll Bogert
Director Development and Outreach, Michele Alexander
Director Finance and Administration, Barbara Guglielmo
Director Global Advocacy, Peggy Hicks
COO, Suzanne Nossel
General Counsel, Dinah PoKempner
Program Director, Iain Levine
Director Legal and Policy, James Ross
Program Director Asia, Brad Adams
Program Director Europe and Central Asia, Holly Cartner
Program Director Americas, Jose Miguel Vivanco
Program Director Middle East and North Africa, Sarah L. Whitson
Program Director United States, David Fathi
Program Director HIV/AIDS, Joseph Amon
Program Director Emergencies, Peter Bouckaert
Program Director International Justice, Richard Dicker
Program Director Refugee Policy, Bill Frelick
Program Director Business and Human Rights, Arvind Ganesan
Program Director Arms, Steve Goose
Program Director Lesbian Gay Bisexual and Transgender Rights, Scott Long
Program Director Terrorism and Counterterrorism, Joanne Mariner
Program Director Children's Rights, Lois Whitman
Director Information Technology, Walid Ayoub
Director Human Resources, Maria Pignataro Nielsen
Director Communications, Emma Daly
Director Media, Minky Worden
Chair, Jane Olson
Vice Chair, Sid Sheinberg
Senior Legal Advisor, Clive Baldwin
Senior Legal Advisor, Aisling Reidy
Deputy Program Director, Joe Saunders
Program Director Africa, Georgette Gagnon
Program Director International Film Festival, John Biaggi
Program Director Women's Rights, Liesl Gerntholtz
Director Leadership Gifts and Planned Giving, Matthew Collins-Gibson
Associate Director European Operations, Akila Lingham
Associate Director Administration, David Bragg
Controller, Suzanna Davidson
Associate Director Finance and Strategy, Jay Schwartz

Director, Barry M. Meyer
Director, James F. (Jim) Hoge Jr.
Vice Chair, John J. Studzinski, age 56
Director, Lloyd Axworthy
Director, Richard J. Goldstone
Director, Robert Kissane
Vice Chair, Bruce J. Klatsky
Director, Susan Manilow
Director, Kati Marton
Director, Sigrid Rausing
Director, Kevin P. Ryan
Director, Louise Arbour
Vice Chair, Sid Sheinberg
Director, David M. Brown
Director, Jorge Casta?eda
Director, Geoffrey Cowan
Director, Tony Elliott
Director, Hassan Elmasry
Director, Michael G. Fisch
Director, Michael E. Gellert
Director, Wendy Keys
Director, Joanne Leedom-Ackerman
Director, Linda Mason
Director, Pat Mitchell
Director, Joel Motley
Director, Samuel K. Murumba
Director, Catherine Powell
Director, Victoria Riskin
Director, Shelley Rubin
Director, Jean-Louis Servan-Schreiber
Director, Darian W. Swig
Director, John R. Taylor
Director, Shibley Telhami
Director, Catherine Zennstrom

LOCATIONS

HQ: Human Rights Watch
350 5th Ave. 34th Fl., New York NY 10118-3299
Phone: 212-290-4700   **Fax:** 212-736-1300
Web: www.hrw.org

Selected Regions of Operation

Africa
Americas
Asia
Europe and Central Asia
Middle East and North Africa

PRODUCTS/OPERATIONS

Selected Global Issues

Arms
Business
Children's rights
Counterterrorism
Economic social and cultural rights
Health and human rights
HIV/AIDS
International justice
LGBT rights
Migrants
Press freedom
Refugees
United Nations
Women's rights

HISTORICAL FINANCIALS
Company Type: Private - Not-for-Profit

Income Statement
FYE: June 30

	REVENUE ($ mil.)	NET INCOME ($ mil.)	NET PROFIT MARGIN	EMPLOYEES
06/11	151	101	66.6%	260
06/10	42	(0)	—	0
06/09	31	(12)	—	0
06/07	55	19	35.7%	0
Annual Growth	40.1%	72.4%	—	—

2011 Year-End Financials

Debt ratio: ——
Return on equity: 66.60%
Cash ($ mil.): 24
Current ratio: 7.70
Long-term debt ($ mil.): —

Dividends
Yield: —
Payout: —
Market value ($ mil.): —

HUMAX USA INC.

Humax USA prefers to connect with its customers through its products. The company develops and manufactures flat-panel TV sets and digital set-top boxes for satellite cable and terrestrial connections. Humax USA is the US-based subsidiary of Korean consumer electronics manufacturing firm Humax Co. which was founded in 1989. The brand has become one of the most popular worldwide among set-top boxes. Humax's products are available in more than 90 countries as well as in the US. The company primarily serves customers in Asia and Europe.

To expand its presence in the US market Humax USA has partnered with the likes of DIRECTV and TiVo to offer products integrated with their technology.

EXECUTIVES

Chairman and CEO, Dae Gyu Byun
President Humax USA, T.H. Kim
SVP Sales and Marketing Humax USA, Christopher C. Cudina

LOCATIONS

HQ: Humax USA Inc.
17501 Von Karman Ave., Irvine CA 92614
Phone: 817-498-6000   **Fax:** 817-577-2376
Web: www.andrews-transport.com

COMPETITORS

DIRECTV
Samsung Electronics
SANYO
Sony USA
TiVo

HISTORICAL FINANCIALS
Company Type: Private

Income Statement
FYE: December 31

	REVENUE ($ mil.)	NET INCOME ($ mil.)	NET PROFIT MARGIN	EMPLOYEES
12/11	347	1	0.4%	22
12/10	268	0	0.1%	0
12/09	116	0	0.2%	0
12/08	68	0	0.1%	0
Annual Growth	71.7%	153.0%	—	—

Debt ratio: ——
Return on equity: 0.40%
Cash ($ mil.): 1
Current ratio: 0.60
Long-term debt ($ mil.): ——

Dividends
Yield: ——
Payout: ——
Market value ($ mil.): ——

HUNTSVILLE MEMORIAL HOSPITAL AUXILIARY

LOCATIONS

HQ: HUNTSVILLE MEMORIAL HOSPITAL AUXILIARY
110 MEMORIAL HOSPITAL DR, HUNTSVILLE, TX
77340-4940
Phone: 936-291-3411
Web: www.huntsvillememorial.com

HISTORICAL FINANCIALS
Company Type: Private

Income Statement
FYE: June 30

	REVENUE ($ mil.)	NET INCOME ($ mil.)	NET PROFIT MARGIN	EMPLOYEES
06/11	84	11	13.7%	500
06/10*	76	1	2.5%	0
05/10	0	0	16.5%	0
10/08	47	5	10.7%	0
Annual Growth	21.2%	31.7%	—	—

*Fiscal year change

2011 Year-End Financials

Debt ratio: ——
Return on equity: 13.70%
Cash ($ mil.): 23
Current ratio: 2.70
Long-term debt ($ mil.): ——

Dividends
Yield: ——
Payout: ——
Market value ($ mil.): ——

HUSKER AG LLC

LOCATIONS

HQ: HUSKER AG LLC
54048 HIGHWAY 20, PLAINVIEW, NE 68769-4072
Phone: 402-582-4446
Web: www.huskerag.com

HISTORICAL FINANCIALS
Company Type: Private

Income Statement
FYE: December 31

	REVENUE ($ mil.)	NET INCOME ($ mil.)	NET PROFIT MARGIN	EMPLOYEES
12/11	237	20	8.5%	52
12/10	146	9	6.3%	0
12/09	116	13	11.7%	0
12/08	169	(40)	—	0
Annual Growth	11.8%	—	—	—

Debt ratio: ——
Return on equity: 8.50%
Cash ($ mil.): 0
Current ratio: 0.40
Long-term debt ($ mil.): ——

Dividends
Yield: ——
Payout: ——
Market value ($ mil.): ——

HUTCHENS PETROLEUM CORPORATION

LOCATIONS

HQ: HUTCHENS PETROLEUM CORPORATION
22 PERFORMANCE DR, STUART, VA 24171-5150
Phone: 276-694-7000
Web: www.hutchenspetro.com

HISTORICAL FINANCIALS
Company Type: Private

Income Statement
FYE: December 31

	REVENUE ($ mil.)	NET INCOME ($ mil.)	NET PROFIT MARGIN	EMPLOYEES
12/11	100	0	0.6%	36
12/10	75	0	0.2%	0
12/09	52	0	0.4%	0
12/08	76	0	0.8%	0
Annual Growth	9.6%	3.6%	—	—

2011 Year-End Financials

Debt ratio: ——
Return on equity: 0.60%
Cash ($ mil.): 0
Current ratio: 0.50
Long-term debt ($ mil.): ——

Dividends
Yield: ——
Payout: ——
Market value ($ mil.): ——

HY-VEE INC.

Give Hy-Vee a high five for being one of the largest privately owned US supermarket chains despite serving some modestly sized towns in the Midwest. The company runs some 235 stores in eight Midwestern states: Illinois Iowa Kansas Minnesota Missouri Nebraska South Dakota and Wisconsin. About half of its supermarkets are in Iowa as are most of its nearly two dozen Hy-Vee drugstores. It distributes products to its stores through several subsidiaries including Lomar Distributing (specialty foods) and Perishable Distributors of Iowa (fresh foods). Charles Hyde and David Vredenburg founded the employee-owned firm in 1930. It takes its name from a combination of its founders' names.

Operations

In addition to its food and drug retail operations Hy-Vee offers customers financial products. Adding to its menu of financial services Hy-Vee subsidiary Midwest Heritage Bank in 2011 acquired Iowa-based L&K Insurance a full-line insurance agency. L&K changed its name to Midwest Heritage Insurance Services post sale.

Financial Anaylsis

Hy-Vee's 235 stores rang up more than $7.3 billion in sales in fiscal 2011 (ends September) vs. about $6.9 billion the previous year.

Strategy

Hy-Vee is gradually expanding in several key markets in the Midwest including Chicago Minneapolis and Madison Wisconsin. To that end the regional grocery chain opened its first supermarket in Madison in 2009 marking its entry into a new state for the first time in nearly 20 years. To cater to local tastes the company says the 92000-sq.-ft. Madison store has the largest cheese selection of any Hy-Vee supermarket. Hy-Vee is also testing a smaller-format store (about 20000-25000 sq. ft. with no pharmacies) in select locations. The chain is also growing in existing markets. In 2010 it purchased a pair of stores in South Dakota and another in Minnesota from local rival Sunshine Foods.

Going beyond traditional grocery fare Hy-Vee has teamed up with specialty pharmacy operator Amber Pharmacy to form a new company (called Hy-Vee Pharmacy Solutions) to provide services for patients with complex and chronic health problems including Crohn's disease hemophilia psoriasis and other chronic ailments. The grocery chain has also been focusing on adding Hy-Vee Gas convenience units (some 80 locations include these) wine and spirits stores pharmacies and Hy-Vee HealthMarket departments.

Ric Jurgens in 2012 retired as chairman and CEO after 43-years with Hy-Vee. He was succeeded by president and COO Randy Edeker.

EXECUTIVES

Chairman Emeritus, Ronald D. (Ron) Pearson, age 71
President Perishable Distributors of Iowa, Andy McCann
EVP and Chief Administrative Officer, Ronald P. (Ron) Taylor
Chairman President and CEO, Richard N. (Ric) Jurgens
SVP Marketing, Jon S. Wendel, age 48
Assistant VP Pharmacy and Drug Town Operations, Gary A. Goodhall
Assistant VP Information Technology, Cevin R. Anderson
Assistant VP Media Relations, Ruth Comer
VP Management Information Systems, Eric Smith
Assistant Director Communications, Chris Friesleben
VP Western Region, Paula K. Correy, age 45
VP Eastern Region, Thomas E. (Tom) Watson
Assistant VP Food Service, Gregory L. (Greg) Frampton
Director Benefit Plan, Kristine Garms
VP Distribution, Tod B. Hockenson
Store Manager Madison Wisconsin, Rob Budd
Chairman President and CEO, Randall B. (Randy) Edeker, age 49
SVP and Secretary, Stephen P. Meyer
Assistant Secretary, Michael P. Jurgens
Controller, Kevin A. Reeve
VP Human Resources, Sheila Laing
CFO and Treasurer, Mike Skokan
Auditors: McGladreyLLP

LOCATIONS

HQ: Hy-Vee Inc.
5820 Westown Pkwy., West Des Moines IA 50266-8223
Phone: 515-267-2800   **Fax:** 515-267-2817
Web: www.hy-vee.com

PRODUCTS/OPERATIONS

2012 Stores

	No.
Supermarkets	212
Drugstores	23
Total	**235**

Selected Subsidiaries

D & D Foods Inc. (salads dips and meats)
Florist Distributing Inc. (flowers plants and florist supplies)
Hy-Vee Pharmacy Solutions (specialty pharmacy services)
Hy-Vee Weitz Construction L.C. (construction)
Lomar Distributing Inc. (specialty foods)
Midwest Heritage Bank FSB (banking)
Perishable Distributors of Iowa Ltd. (meat fish seafood and ice cream)

COMPETITORS

ALDI	Nash-Finch
Associated Wholesale Grocers	Niemann Foods
	Rite Aid
Ball' s Food	Roundy' s
Casey' s General Stores	Save-A-Lot Food Stores
CVS Caremark	SUPERVALU
Dahl' s Foods	Target Corporation
Fareway Stores	Wal-Mart
Kmart	Walgreen
Kroger	

HISTORICAL FINANCIALS

Company Type: Private

Income Statement

FYE: September 30

	REVENUE ($ mil.)	NET INCOME ($ mil.)	NET PROFIT MARGIN	EMPLOYEES
09/12*	7,682	0	—	58,000
10/11	0	0	—	0
10/10	0	0	—	0
09/09	0	0	—	0
Annual Growth	—	—	—	—

*Fiscal year change

2012 Year-End Financials

Debt ratio: ——
Return on equity: —
Cash ($ mil.): 7
Current ratio: 0.20
Long-term debt ($ mil.): —

Dividends
  Yield: —
  Payout: —
Market value ($ mil.): —

HYSTERIA PRODUCTIONS

LOCATIONS

HQ: HYSTERIA PRODUCTIONS
203 ROSE MORROW RD, SUSSEX, NJ 07461-3838
Phone: 973-702-8978

HISTORICAL FINANCIALS

Company Type: Private

Income Statement

FYE: December 31

	REVENUE ($ mil.)	NET INCOME ($ mil.)	NET PROFIT MARGIN	EMPLOYEES
12/11	420	19	4.6%	2
Annual Growth	—	—	—	—

ICI CONSTRUCTION INC.

LOCATIONS

HQ: ICI CONSTRUCTION INC.
24715 W HARDY RD, SPRING, TX 77373-5764
Phone: 281-355-5151
Web: www.icidallas.com

HISTORICAL FINANCIALS

Company Type: Private

Income Statement

FYE: June 30

	REVENUE ($ mil.)	NET INCOME ($ mil.)	NET PROFIT MARGIN	EMPLOYEES
06/12	91	0	0.2%	102
06/11	112	0	0.4%	0
06/10	111	0	0.5%	0
06/09	175	1	0.9%	0
Annual Growth	(19.4%)	(49.2%)	—	—

2012 Year-End Financials

Debt ratio: ——
Return on equity: 0.20%
Cash ($ mil.): 7
Current ratio: 0.30
Long-term debt ($ mil.): —

Dividends
  Yield: —
  Payout: —
Market value ($ mil.): —

ICIMS INC.

Who says good help is hard to find? iCIMS provides Web-based applicant tracking and recruiting management software for corporate human resources professionals and third-party recruiters. The company's iCIMS Talent Platform which is designed to help businesses make their hiring processes more efficient includes software for screening and storing applicant information enabling online job applications tracking candidates monitoring performance after recruitment and managing post-employment processes. It sells its applications on a Software-as-a-Service basis. iCIMS targets recruiters midsized companies and large corporations. The company was founded in 1999 by Colin Day and George Lieu.

Geographic Reach

iCIMS' domestic locations reside in Boston; Dallas; Denver; New York; Portland Maine; Portland Oregon; San Diego; Tampa; and Vancouver Washington. International headquarters are located in Beijing and London.

Sales and Marketing

iCIMS has customers in such industries as financial services consumer electronics food retail and clothing. Its clients have included The Hershey Company Whole Foods Market Esurance and Canon.

Strategy

In addition to international clients in the UK and Asia iCIMS is targeting small and midsized businesses in North America and Europe to fuel growth in its core regions. It is also considering acquisitions to build its product portfolio and its business.

Mergers and Acquisitions

iCIMS acquired social recruiting software maker Jobmagic in 2012 to expand its selection of recruiting tools. Jobmagic specialized in recruiting applications that incorporated social media functionality.

EXECUTIVES

Chairman, George Liou
President and CEO, Colin Day
Director Research and Development and CIO, Chris Bartholomew
Director Sales, Adam Feigenbaum
Director MIS, Chris Young
Director Customer Services, Andrew Curtis
Director Technology, Paul Melici
Director Finance, Daniel Bovarnick
Director Human Resources, John Teehan
Director Marketing, Susan Vitale
Director, Bradley E. Sparks
Director, Sincia Liu
Director, Stephen Day
Director, Andy Ferrentino

LOCATIONS

HQ: iCIMS.com Inc.
90 Matawan Rd. Pkwy 120 5th Fl., Matawan NJ 07747-2623
Phone: 732-847-1941   **Fax:** 732-876-0422
Web: www.icims.com

COMPETITORS

ERC Dataplus	Talent Technology
Kenexa	Taleo
Lawson Software	Ultimate Software
Peopleclick Authoria	Workscape
SilkRoad technology	

Income Statement FYE: December 31

	REVENUE ($ mil.)	NET INCOME ($ mil.)	NET PROFIT MARGIN	EMPLOYEES
12/11	30	3	12.0%	240
12/10	25	3	14.5%	0
12/09	21	2	10.2%	0
12/08	18	2	13.2%	0
Annual Growth	17.9%	14.0%	—	—

2011 Year-End Financials

Debt ratio: ——
Return on equity: 12.00%
Cash ($ mil.): 8
Current ratio: 1.80
Long-term debt ($ mil.): —

Dividends
Yield: —
Payout: —
Market value ($ mil.): —

HISTORICAL FINANCIALS
Company Type: Private

Income Statement FYE: December 31

	REVENUE ($ mil.)	NET INCOME ($ mil.)	NET PROFIT MARGIN	EMPLOYEES
12/11	112	9	8.2%	450
12/09	116	3	3.2%	0
12/05	83	0	—	0
12/04	83	0	—	0
Annual Growth	10.6%	—	—	—

2011 Year-End Financials

Debt ratio: ——
Return on equity: 8.20%
Cash ($ mil.): 0
Current ratio: 0.90
Long-term debt ($ mil.): —

Dividends
Yield: —
Payout: —
Market value ($ mil.): —

HISTORICAL FINANCIALS
Company Type: Private

Income Statement FYE: December 31

	REVENUE ($ mil.)	NET INCOME ($ mil.)	NET PROFIT MARGIN	EMPLOYEES
12/11	121	1	0.9%	126
12/09	111	3	3.2%	0
12/08	88	2	2.5%	0
12/07	95	1	1.9%	0
Annual Growth	8.2%	(17.2%)	—	—

2011 Year-End Financials

Debt ratio: ——
Return on equity: 0.90%
Cash ($ mil.): 7
Current ratio: 1.20
Long-term debt ($ mil.): —

Dividends
Yield: —
Payout: —
Market value ($ mil.): —

ICON IDENTITY SOLUTIONS INC.

Icon Identity Solutions helps its customers avoid identity crises. The firm provides a variety of services related to the building of a company's brand through the use of signs and exterior graphics. Icon can help clients manage multiple sign projects on a global scale if needed. Its services include sign design permitting and manufacturing. Icon Identity Solutions is one arm of Icon Companies which also operates subsidiaries East Coast Sign Advertising and ImageCare Maintenance Services (IMS). IMS provides sign repair and maintenance. Past clients have included BMW's Mini unit and Citigroup.

HISTORY

update per web site

EXECUTIVES

CFO, John Callan
EVP Human Resources, Larry S. Brigman
President and CEO, Kurt W. Ripkey, age 43
EVP Sales and Marketing, John Noonan
EVP Operations, Doug Long
EVP Program Management, Thomas Hunt
EVP IMS, Melanee Jech
SVP Marketing and Business Development, Matt Czyl

LOCATIONS

HQ: Icon Identity Solutions Inc.
1418 Elmhurst Rd., Elk Grove Village IL 60007
Phone: 847-364-2250 **Fax:** 847-364-1517
Web: www.iconid.com

COMPETITORS

3M Digital Signage
Everbrite
IDS Menus

Image Works
Young Electric Sign

IDAHO STATE UNIVERSITY FOUNDATION INC.

LOCATIONS

HQ: IDAHO STATE UNIVERSITY FOUNDATION INC.
921 S 8TH AVE, POCATELLO, ID 83201-5377
Phone: 208-282-3470
Web: www.isu.edu

HISTORICAL FINANCIALS
Company Type: Private

Income Statement FYE: June 30

	REVENUE ($ mil.)	NET INCOME ($ mil.)	NET PROFIT MARGIN	EMPLOYEES
06/12	129	11	8.6%	1
06/10	8	(2)	—	0
Annual Growth	1442.2%	—	—	—

2012 Year-End Financials

Debt ratio: ——
Return on equity: 8.60%
Cash ($ mil.): 1
Current ratio: —
Long-term debt ($ mil.): —

Dividends
Yield: —
Payout: —
Market value ($ mil.): —

IGNITED LLC

LOCATIONS

HQ: IGNITED LLC
2221 PARK PL, EL SEGUNDO, CA 90245-4909
Phone: 310-773-3100
Web: www.ignitedminds.com

ILLINOIS INSTITUTE OF TECHNOLOGY

Chicago has some cool architecture due in part to the Illinois Institute of Technology (IIT). The school offers more than 100 undergraduate and graduate degree programs in engineering science psychology architecture business law humanities and design. In addition to three campuses in Chicago IIT also has locations in Summit-Argo (Moffet campus) and Wheaton (Daniel F. and Ada L. Rice campus). The institute has an enrollment of some 8000 undergraduate graduate business school and law school students with a student-to-faculty ratio of 8:1. IIT was created in 1940 by the merger of Armour Institute (founded in 1893) with Lewis Institute (established in 1895).

Operations

IIT's heritage includes the innovative Bauhaus tradition that set up shop at the university in the 1930's. These days its innovation is expressed in the form of interdisciplinary research on such themes as Energy and Sustainability Improving the Quality of Life and Perfect Power. IIT maintains about 30 research institutes with major centers focused on the study of sustainable energy electricity innovation and biomedical science and engineering and food safety and health.

Financial Performance

IIT reported $250 million in revenues in fiscal 2012 up 1% over results in 2011 as the university met its growth targets for tuition and enrollment. However net income fell into the red in 2012 as the university reported a loss of about $7 million down from profits of nearly $32 million in 2011.

Strategy

IIT regularly evaluates its offerings and adds new degree programs to meet the needs of a changing society. In 2011 it added five new degree programs in fields including biology physics and sociology and in 2012 it introduced a Master's degree program for cyber forensics and security majors.

In addition to expand its research capacity and reflect the growing importance of food safety research IIT opened a new center for food safety and technology research in 2011 upgrading the previous nutritional research center's status to institute. The move will help the university increase services to government and industry partners. IIT also opened a new startup business center that year to help transition research discoveries into commercial business stages.

EXECUTIVES

Vice Chair, David J. Vitale, age 66
Vice Chair, Craig J. Duchossois, age 67
VP and CFO, Susan H. Wallace
CIO, Ophir Trigalo
Chair, John W. Rowe, age 66
Vice Provost New Initiatives, Dennis A. Roberson, age 63
Director Human Resources, Beverly Perret
VP External Affairs, David Baker
VP Business and Operations, John P. Collins
SVP and Director IIT Research Institute, David McCormick
VP Enrollment Management, Mary Ann Rowan
VP and General Counsel, Mary Anne Smith
VP International Affairs, Darsh Wasan
President, John L. Anderson
SVP Academic Affairs and Provost, Alan W. Cramb
VP Institutional Advancement, Elizabeth J. Hughes
Manager Accounts Payable and Fixed Assets, Donna Taylor
Manager Payroll, Sharon Muldrow-Thomas
Manager Regional Alumni Programs, Marian Quirk
VP Community Affairs and Outreach Programs, Leroy Kennedy
Director Educational Services, Carol Orze
Director Athletics, Lee Hitchen
Director Enterprise Systems, Wesley Matthews
Director Programming and Customer Service, James Meyer
Director Technology Infrastructure, Ibukun Oyewole
Director Foundation Relations, Doris McGee
Dean Libraries, Christopher Stewart
Head of Collection Management Galvin Library, Charles Uth
Acquisitions Specialist Galvin Library, L'Argent Humphrey
Director Finance, Patricia A. Grow
VP Research and Dean Graduate College, Ali Cinar
Associate Provost Undergraduate Affairs, Michael R. Gosz
Director Alumni Relations, Tara L. Anderson
Associate Controller and Bursar, Geneva Harris
Vice Provost Undergraduate Admission and Financial Aid, Gerald P. Doyle
Director Public Safety, Steven Horton
Assistant Director Public Safety Administration, Gina Shelton
Assistant Director Public Safety Operations, Ramos Tolbert
Vice President for Marketing and Communications, Jeanne Hartig
Dean of IIT Armour College of Engineering, Natacha DePaola
VP Finance and Administration, Patricia Laughlin
Associate Director, Faye Bulaclac
Senior Director of Communications, Evan Venie
Director of Admissions and Special Projects, Maya Suraj
Associate Director, Ryan Nelson
Vice Chair, David J. Vitale, age 66
Vice Chair, Craig J. Duchossois, age 67
Auditors: KPMGPeatMarwickLLP

LOCATIONS

HQ: Illinois Institute of Technology
3300 S. Federal St., Chicago IL 60616-3793
Phone: 312-567-3000   **Fax:** 312-567-3004
Web: www.iit.edu

PRODUCTS/OPERATIONS

Selected Schools and Colleges

Armour College of Engineering
ChicagoKent College of Law
College of Architecture
College of Psychology
College of Science and Letters
Institute of Design
School of Applied Technology (SAT)
Stuart School of Business

HISTORICAL FINANCIALS

Company Type: School

Income Statement

FYE: May 31

	REVENUE ($ mil.)	NET INCOME ($ mil.)	NET PROFIT MARGIN	EMPLOYEES
05/12	249	(6)	—	1,662
05/11	305	8	2.9%	0
05/10	333	41	12.4%	0
05/09	190	0	—	0
Annual Growth	9.4%	—	—	—

2012 Year-End Financials

Debt ratio: ——
Return on equity: (-2.80)%
Cash ($ mil.): 18
Current ratio: —
Long-term debt ($ mil.): —

Dividends
Yield: —
Payout: —
Market value ($ mil.): —

ILLINOIS MUNICIPAL ELECTRIC AGENCY (INC)

LOCATIONS

HQ: ILLINOIS MUNICIPAL ELECTRIC AGENCY (INC)
3400 CONIFER DR, SPRINGFIELD, IL 62711-8301
Phone: 217-789-4632
Web: www.imea.org

HISTORICAL FINANCIALS

Company Type: Private

Income Statement

FYE: April 30

	REVENUE ($ mil.)	NET INCOME ($ mil.)	NET PROFIT MARGIN	EMPLOYEES
04/12	280	18	6.4%	27
04/11	176	12	7.3%	0
04/10	159	1	1.2%	0
04/09	150	3	2.3%	0
Annual Growth	23.2%	74.7%	—	—

ILLINOIS WESLEYAN UNIVERSITY

The Fightin' Titans of Illinois Wesleyan University cannot be accused of having a one-track mind.

The small private university offers 50 majors and programs and is organized into three colleges: liberal arts fine arts and the school of nursing. As an undergraduate university Illinois Wesleyan which has about 2100 students enrolled also offers pre-engineering pre-law and pre-medical professional programs. Traditionally about 85% of the student population is enrolled in the College of Liberal Arts. The school was founded in 1850 by civic an Methodist Church leaders.

EXECUTIVES

President, Richard F. Wilson
VP Business and Finance, Daniel P. Klotzbach
Controller, John Bryant
VP Student Affairs and Dean of Students, Kathryn Cavins
Director Career Center, Warren Kistner
Provost and Dean of the Faculty, Beth Cunningham
Registrar and Assistant Provost, Jeff Frick
Director Alumni Relations, Ann Harding
VP Public Relations, Matt Kurz
Director University Communications, Sharlyn (Sherry) Wallace
Dean of Admissions, Tony Bankston

LOCATIONS

HQ: ILLINOIS WESLEYAN UNIVERSITY
1312 PARK ST, BLOOMINGTON, IL 61701-1773
Phone: 309-556-1000
Web: www.iwu.edu

HISTORICAL FINANCIALS

Company Type: School

Income Statement

FYE: July 31

	REVENUE ($ mil.)	NET INCOME ($ mil.)	NET PROFIT MARGIN	EMPLOYEES
07/12	77	2	3.6%	500
07/11	97	23	24.3%	0
07/10*	77	6	8.5%	0
12/09	0	0	2.6%	0
Annual Growth	814.7%	915.4%	—	—

*Fiscal year change

2012 Year-End Financials

Debt ratio: ——
Return on equity: 3.60%
Cash ($ mil.): 16
Current ratio: 0.80
Long-term debt ($ mil.): —

Dividends
Yield: —
Payout: —
Market value ($ mil.): —

IMPER COU OFF OF EDUC FOUND

LOCATIONS

HQ: IMPER COU OFF OF EDUC FOUND
1398 SPERBER RD, EL CENTRO, CA 92243-9621
Phone: 760-312-6464
Web: www.icoe.org

Company Type: Private

Income Statement FYE: June 30

	REVENUE ($ mil.)	NET INCOME ($ mil.)	NET PROFIT MARGIN	EMPLOYEES
06/11	82	(0)	—	530
06/10	0	0	75.2%	0
06/09	73	2	2.8%	0
06/08	74	2	3.5%	0
Annual Growth	3.2%	—	—	—

2011 Year-End Financials

Debt ratio: ——
Return on equity: (-1.10)%
Cash ($ mil.): 35
Current ratio: 2.70
Long-term debt ($ mil.): —

Dividends
Yield: —
Payout: —
Market value ($ mil.): —

IN-Q-TEL INC

Just where do spies go to get their toys? Well James Bond had "Q" and the CIA has In-Q-Tel. While it doesn't deal in exploding pens or cars equipped with missiles this not-for-profit venture capital firm does keep the CIA and the broader US intelligence community equipped with the latest in information technology by investing in innovative high-tech companies. Originally named "Peleus" and renamed after the above-mentioned "007" series character In-Q-Tel was formed in 1999 to help the CIA keep pace with the rapid technological advances of the private sector an increasingly daunting task.

The firm's investments are funded by taxpayer dollars and approved by an independent board of trustees; investment proceeds are reinvested in technologies and other programs on behalf of the CIA.

In-Q-Tel has invested in more than 100 companies and 10 universities and research labs since its founding. The firm's typical investments range from $1 million to $3 million.

Portfolio companies develop a range of innovative products and services such as inflatable satellite antennas and automatic license plate readers. In-Q-Tel also invested in Keyhole which created the 3-D mapping software now used by Google Earth.

EXECUTIVES

EVP and Managing Partner, Stephen C. (Steve) Bowsher, age 43
Chairman, Michael M. Crow, age 56
President and CEO, Christopher A. R. (Chris) Darby
EVP Architecture and Engineering, Troy M. Pearsall
EVP IC Support, Patrick Ciganer
EVP and CFO, Matthew Strottman

LOCATIONS

HQ: In-Q-Tel Inc.
P.O. Box 749, Arlington VA 22219
Phone: 703-248-3000   **Fax:** 703-248-3001
Web: www.in-q-tel.com

PRODUCTS/OPERATIONS

Selected Investments

3VR Security (searchable surveillance systems services)
AdaptiveEnergy (miniature piezo actuators and generators)
Adapx (field data management)
Arcxis (molecular diagnostic technologies)
Asankya (real-time content delivery)
Basis Technology (foreign language document and media exploitation)
Bay Microsystems (internetworking processor)
CallMiner (conversation analytics)
Carnegie Speech (language instruction)
CopperEye (enterprise data management)
Destineer (videogames and 3-D training simulations)
Elemental Technologies (parallel processing solutions for video applications)
Ember Corporation (ZigBee-compliant wireless semiconductor systems)
Endeca (information retrieval and analysis)
Etherstack (wireless communications software)
febit (DNA analysis)
FireEye (cybersecurity platform)
Fluidigm (integrated fluidic circuits for high-throughput bioassays)
FMS (COTS link analysis software)
FortiusOne (browser-based visual intelligence)
GATR Technologies (deployable satellite communications)
Geosemble (fusion of geospatial datasets)
iMove (immersive imaging for wide area and geospatial surveillance)
Infinite Power Solutions (battery technologies)
Innocentive (open innovation collaboration platform)
IntegenX (bioprocessing technology)
KZO Innovations (streaming video platform)
Language Weaver (statistical machine translation software)
LensVector (autofocus camera lenses)
Lingotek (translation technology)
MotionDSP (video software)
Nanosys (nanotechnology-enabled systems)
Nextreme Thermal Solutions (technologies for converting heat to electrical energy and for emplaced sensors and equipment)
NovoDynamics (document exploitation and OCR)
OpGen (molecule DNA analysis technology)
Paratek (RF circuitry for multi-function multi-frequency wireless devices)
Pixim (imaging technology for security cameras)
piXlogic (image segmentation and search engine)
Polychromix (miniature and portable analysis tools)
QD Vision (quantum-dot products)
Qynergy (power technologies)
Recorded Future (extraction and analysis of Web-based information)
Rhevision Technology (optics technology)
Seventh Sense Biosystems (medical diagnostics)
SkyBuilt Power (mobile renewable energy power station)
StreamBase Systems (complex event processing software platform)
T2 Biosystems (medical diagnostic products)
Tendril (operating platform for ZigBee applications)
TerraGo Technologies (technologies for GIS professionals)
Thetus (knowledge modeling and discovery software)
Traction Software (software for user-generated content)
Veracode (on-demand application security testing)
Visible Technologies (social media monitoring and analysis)
VSEE (video conferencing)
WiSpry (tunable RF silicon solutions)

COMPETITORS

Accel Partners
Benchmark Capital
Draper Fisher Jurvetson
Garage Technology Ventures
Hummer Winblad
Kleiner Perkins
Newtek Business Services
Sequoia Capital

Company Type: Private - Not-for-Profit

Income Statement FYE: March 31

	REVENUE ($ mil.)	NET INCOME ($ mil.)	NET PROFIT MARGIN	EMPLOYEES
03/11	57	11	20.0%	60
03/10*	69	17	25.4%	0
05/99	0	0	—	0
Annual Growth	—	—	—	—

*Fiscal year change

2011 Year-End Financials

Debt ratio: ——
Return on equity: 20.00%
Cash ($ mil.): 96
Current ratio: 9.50
Long-term debt ($ mil.): —

Dividends
Yield: —
Payout: —
Market value ($ mil.): —

INDEPENDENCE EXCAVATING INC.

LOCATIONS

HQ: INDEPENDENCE EXCAVATING INC.
5720 E SCHAAF RD, INDEPENDENCE, OH 44131-1396
Phone: 216-524-1700
Web: www.indexc.com

HISTORICAL FINANCIALS

Company Type: Private

Income Statement FYE: December 31

	REVENUE ($ mil.)	NET INCOME ($ mil.)	NET PROFIT MARGIN	EMPLOYEES
12/11	107	1	1.5%	350
12/09*	63	5	9.0%	0
03/09	74	1	2.3%	0
03/08	107	3	3.1%	0
Annual Growth	(0.1%)	(22.5%)	—	—

*Fiscal year change

2011 Year-End Financials

Debt ratio: ——
Return on equity: 1.50%
Cash ($ mil.): 16
Current ratio: 1.50
Long-term debt ($ mil.): —

Dividends
Yield: —
Payout: —
Market value ($ mil.): —

INDEPENDENT AGRIBUSINESS PROFESSIONALS COOPERATIVE INC.

LOCATIONS

HQ: INDEPENDENT AGRIBUSINESS PROFESSIONALS COOPERATIVE INC.
7108 N FRESNO ST STE 150, FRESNO, CA 93720-2960
Phone: 559-440-1980
Web: www.iapros.com

HISTORICAL FINANCIALS

Company Type: Private

Income Statement

FYE: December 31

	REVENUE ($ mil.)	NET INCOME ($ mil.)	NET PROFIT MARGIN	EMPLOYEES
12/11	139	0	0.0%	8
12/10	133	(0)	—	0
12/01	37	4	12.8%	0
12/98	4	0	1.1%	0
Annual Growth	225.9%	(93.0%)	—	—

2011 Year-End Financials

Debt ratio: ——
Return on equity: —
Cash ($ mil.): 15
Current ratio: 1.00
Long-term debt ($ mil.): —
Dividends
Yield: —
Payout: —
Market value ($ mil.): —

INDEPENDENT PHARMACY COOPERATIVE

LOCATIONS

HQ: INDEPENDENT PHARMACY COOPERATIVE
1550 COLUMBUS ST, SUN PRAIRIE, WI 53590-3901
Phone: 608-825-9556

HISTORICAL FINANCIALS

Company Type: Private

Income Statement

FYE: December 31

	REVENUE ($ mil.)	NET INCOME ($ mil.)	NET PROFIT MARGIN	EMPLOYEES
12/11	806	1	0.2%	65
12/10	869	1	0.2%	0
12/09	642	0	0.1%	0
12/07	717	0	0.0%	0
Annual Growth	4.0%	1985.7%	—	—

2011 Year-End Financials

Debt ratio: ——
Return on equity: 0.20%
Cash ($ mil.): 14
Current ratio: 0.40
Long-term debt ($ mil.): —
Dividends
Yield: —
Payout: —
Market value ($ mil.): —

INDEPENDENT SCHOOL DISTRICT 1 OF TULSA COUNTY

LOCATIONS

HQ: INDEPENDENT SCHOOL DISTRICT 1 OF TULSA COUNTY
3027 S NEW HAVEN AVE, TULSA, OK 74114-6131
Phone: 918-746-6800
Web: www.tulsaschools.org

HISTORICAL FINANCIALS

Company Type: Private

Income Statement

FYE: June 30

	REVENUE ($ mil.)	NET INCOME ($ mil.)	NET PROFIT MARGIN	EMPLOYEES
06/11	403	(10)	—	6,115
06/08	388	9	2.4%	0
06/07	373	(17)	—	0
06/06	0	0		0
Annual Growth	—	—	—	—

2011 Year-End Financials

Debt ratio: ——
Return on equity: (-2.60)%
Cash ($ mil.): 167
Current ratio: 1.60
Long-term debt ($ mil.): —
Dividends
Yield: —
Payout: —
Market value ($ mil.): —

INDEPENDENT SCHOOL DISTRICT 194

LOCATIONS

HQ: INDEPENDENT SCHOOL DISTRICT 194
8670 210TH ST W, LAKEVILLE, MN 55044-7000
Phone: 952-232-2000

HISTORICAL FINANCIALS

Company Type: Private

Income Statement

FYE: June 30

	REVENUE ($ mil.)	NET INCOME ($ mil.)	NET PROFIT MARGIN	EMPLOYEES
06/12	134	21	16.0%	1,600
06/08	127	(23)	—	0
06/06	111	(8)	—	0
06/05	103	32	31.9%	0
Annual Growth	9.1%	(13.4%)	—	—

2012 Year-End Financials

Debt ratio: ——
Return on equity: 16.00%
Cash ($ mil.): 31
Current ratio: —
Long-term debt ($ mil.): —
Dividends
Yield: —
Payout: —
Market value ($ mil.): —

INDEPENDENT SCHOOL DISTRICT 271

LOCATIONS

HQ: INDEPENDENT SCHOOL DISTRICT 271
1350 W 106TH ST, BLOOMINGTON, MN 55431-4152
Phone: 952-681-6400
Web: www.mindquest.org

HISTORICAL FINANCIALS

Company Type: Private

Income Statement

FYE: June 30

	REVENUE ($ mil.)	NET INCOME ($ mil.)	NET PROFIT MARGIN	EMPLOYEES
06/11*	180	4	2.6%	2,200
08/09	0	(0)	—	0
06/09	142	(14)	—	0
06/06	129	46	35.9%	0
Annual Growth	11.7%	(53.7%)	—	—

*Fiscal year change

2011 Year-End Financials

Debt ratio: ——
Return on equity: 2.60%
Cash ($ mil.): 86
Current ratio: —
Long-term debt ($ mil.): —
Dividends
Yield: —
Payout: —
Market value ($ mil.): —

INDEPENDENT SCHOOL DISTRICT 9 TULSA COUNTY OK

LOCATIONS

HQ: INDEPENDENT SCHOOL DISTRICT 9 TULSA
COUNTY OK
8506 E 61ST ST, TULSA, OK 74133-1926
Phone: 918-459-5432
Web: www.unionps.org

HISTORICAL FINANCIALS
Company Type: Private

Income Statement
FYE: June 30

	REVENUE ($ mil.)	NET INCOME ($ mil.)	NET PROFIT MARGIN	EMPLOYEES
06/11	124	9	7.4%	1,250
06/10	120	8	7.2%	0
06/09	118	3	2.8%	0
06/08	109	1	1.3%	0
Annual Growth	4.5%	86.2%	—	—

2011 Year-End Financials

Debt ratio: —
Return on equity: 7.40%
Cash ($ mil.): 28
Current ratio: 0.80
Long-term debt ($ mil.): —
Dividends
Yield: —
Payout: —
Market value ($ mil.): —

INDEPENDENT SCHOOL DISTRICT NO 77

LOCATIONS

HQ: INDEPENDENT SCHOOL DISTRICT NO 77
10 CIVIC CENTER PLZ STE 1, MANKATO, MN
56001-7795
Phone: 507-387-1868
Web: www.mankatocougars.com

HISTORICAL FINANCIALS
Company Type: Private

Income Statement
FYE: June 30

	REVENUE ($ mil.)	NET INCOME ($ mil.)	NET PROFIT MARGIN	EMPLOYEES
06/12	86	(1)	—	1,200
06/11	88	(4)	—	0
06/10	82	(10)	—	0
06/09	79	27	33.9%	0
Annual Growth	2.9%	—	—	—

INDIANA AUTOMOTIVE FASTENERS INC.

LOCATIONS

HQ: INDIANA AUTOMOTIVE FASTENERS INC.
1300 ANDERSON BLVD, GREENFIELD, IN
46140-7934
Phone: 317-467-0100
Web: www.iafi.com

HISTORICAL FINANCIALS
Company Type: Private

Income Statement
FYE: June 30

	REVENUE ($ mil.)	NET INCOME ($ mil.)	NET PROFIT MARGIN	EMPLOYEES
06/12	138	(1)	—	401
06/11	105	(6)	—	0
06/10	111	(6)	—	0
06/06	102	9	8.9%	0
Annual Growth	10.3%	—	—	—

2012 Year-End Financials

Debt ratio: —
Return on equity: (-1.20)%
Cash ($ mil.): 11
Current ratio: 0.30
Long-term debt ($ mil.): —
Dividends
Yield: —
Payout: —
Market value ($ mil.): —

INDIANA REGIONAL MEDICAL CENTER INC.

LOCATIONS

HQ: INDIANA REGIONAL MEDICAL CENTER INC.
835 HOSPITAL RD, INDIANA, PA 15701-3629
Phone: 724-357-7000
Web: www.indianahospital.net

HISTORICAL FINANCIALS
Company Type: Private

Income Statement
FYE: June 30

	REVENUE ($ mil.)	NET INCOME ($ mil.)	NET PROFIT MARGIN	EMPLOYEES
06/11	140	4	3.1%	1,100
06/10	129	2	1.7%	0
06/09	127	(22)	—	0
06/08	118	8	6.7%	0
Annual Growth	5.7%	(18.4%)	—	—

2011 Year-End Financials

Debt ratio: —
Return on equity: 3.10%
Cash ($ mil.): 5
Current ratio: 0.40
Long-term debt ($ mil.): —
Dividends
Yield: —
Payout: —
Market value ($ mil.): —

INDIANA UNIVERSITY HEALTH BLOOMINGTON INC

Bloomington Hospital wants to put a bloom back in patients' cheeks. The facility operating as IU Health Bloomington provides care in a ten-county region in south central Indiana. The not-for-profit hospital –which includes a 350-bed main campus in Bloomington and a 25-bed rural hospital in Paoli –provides care in a number of medical specialties including cardiovascular disease cancer orthopedics and neuroscience. It also runs home health and hospice urgent care lab and specialty care facilities as well as physician practices under the name Southern Indiana Physicians. IU Health Bloomington part of the Indiana University Health (IU Health) system also conducts research and educational programs.

Geographic Reach

IU Health Bloomington has a customer base of about 400000 patients in a 10-county area in south central Indiana. The hospital serves as a regional referral center for other hospitals in the area.

Strategy

In 2011 when parent IU Health changed its name from Clarian Health Partners Bloomington Hospital began operating as IU Health Bloomington to align with the parent's identity. The Paoli facility formerly known as Bloomington Hospital of Orange County began operating as IU Health Paoli.

IU Health Bloomington plans to build a replacement facility for its aging main campus medical center by 2015.

Ownership

After several years of negotiations IU Health Bloomington officially became an integrated part of the Clarian network at the start of 2010. Then at the beginning of 2011 Clarian changed its name to IU Health to clarify its relationship with Indiana University and to provide a unified brand to connect all of its facilities.

EXECUTIVES

President and CEO, Mark E. Moore
COO, Larry Bailey
CFO, James (Jim) Myers
Medical Director Emergency Department, Owen Slaughter
CIO, Mark McMath
VP Human Resources, Steve Deckard
VP Support Services, Mark Crain
Director Professional Relations, John Lee
VP Fund Development; Executive Director Bloomington Hospital Foundation, Chris Molloy
VP Patient Care Services, Ruth Ann Morris
VP; CEO Bloomington Hospital Orange County, Gene Perry
VP Marketing Business Development and Community Relations, F. Brian Whitman
Director Development, Diane Ballard
Director Volunteer Services, Connie Hill
Manager Special Events, Michelle Farmer
Manager VIM Fund Raising, Heather Allen
Manager Grants Development and Research, Jill Nielsen-Farrell
Donor Relations Specialist, Tara Gahlinger
COO BHOC, Candace Isom
Director Internal Audit, Tim Brown
Director Laboratory, Dan Grecek

Director Ambulance Service, David DeGroote
Director Community Health Education and Services, Carol Weiss-Kennedy
Director Allied Health, Ed Getts Sr.
Director Occ Health and Promptcare, Thomas Kuhn
Director Pharmacy, Michael Melby
Executive Director Regional Orthopedics Center and Regional Neuroscience Institute, Myron Lewis
Director Radiology, Bruce Riley
Director Radiation Oncology Physics, William Van de Reit
Executive Director Regional Cancer Institute, Sonya Zeller
Director Risk Management, Valynda Laird
Executive Director Regional Heart and Vascular Institute, Vickie Franck
Director Environmental Services, John Freeman
Director of Purchasing, Stephen Boyle
Director Security, Don Miller
Director Food and Nutrition Services, Randy Sparrow
Manager Clinical Engineering, Mike Cherbak
Manager Plant Operations, Kenny Gilbert
Manager Construction, Mike Harding
Plant Engineer and Property Management, Rusty Rozelle
Director Accounting, Pat Stahly
Director Case Management, Kathy Bennett
Director Health Information Management, Dennis Heller
Director Managed Care, Mary Ann Valenta
Director Patient Access, Kathy Blickenstaff
Director Patient Accounts, Geri Geringer
Director Reimbursement and Financial Planning, Mike Craig
Director Revenue Cycle Management, Evelyn Alwine
Director Information Services, Ellen Snyder
Director Telecommunications, Nancy Jacobs
Manager Project Management Office, Justin Grant
Director Organizational Effectiveness and Education, Rick Barton
Supervisor Media Services, Tim Pittman
Coordinator Medical Education, Patty Booker
Director Human Resources, Bruce Wade
Manager Staff Scheduling, Jill Trinkle
Director Kid's Club, Marsha Tailon
Director Clinical Education and Practice, Deb Wellman
Director for Med-Surg and ICU, Michele Ridge
Director Home Health and Hospice, Ellen Surburg
Interim Director Clinical Informatics, Suzy Vaughn
Director Pastoral Services, John VanderZee
Administrative Director Behavioral Health Services, Scott Branam
Director Quality Improvement and Medical Staff Services, LeAnne Horn
Administrative Director Surgical Services, Sharon Ormstedt
Executive Director Regional Center for Women and Children, Dana Watters
Coordinator Media Relations, Amanda Roach
Coordinator Communication, Todd Curtis
Coordinator Communication, Peter Poletti
Coordinator Communication, Chris Rice
Service and Market Analyst, Claire Tempel
Coordinator Service Excellence, Chris Rudolf
Business Development Liaison, Barbara Kissel
Graphic Design and Art Direction, Ellen Houghton
Visual Production Specialist, Junetta Wineinger

LOCATIONS

HQ: Bloomington Hospital Inc.
601 W. 2nd St., Bloomington IN 47402
Phone: 812-353-6821   **Fax:** 812-353-9339
Web: www.iuhealthbloomington.org

PRODUCTS/OPERATIONS

Selected Services

Anticoagulation Center
Assisted Medical Transportation
Behavioral Health
Cancer
Cardiovascular
Children's Therapy Center
Diabetes Center
Emergency
Home Care
Home Medical Equipment
Hospice
Laboratory
Neuroscience
Occupational
Orthopedics
Pain Center
Primary Care
Radiology
Rehabilitation
Sleep Lab
Surgical
Urgent Care Centers
Women and Children's
Wound Center

COMPETITORS

Ascension Health
Community Hospitals of Indiana
Daviess Community Hospital
Franciscan Alliance
Henry County Memorial Hospital
Memorial Hospital (Logansport)
Riverview Hospital
Saint John's Health System
Union Hospital (Indiana)
Wabash County Hospital

HISTORICAL FINANCIALS

Company Type: Private - Not-for-Profit

Income Statement

FYE: December 31

	REVENUE ($ mil.)	NET INCOME ($ mil.)	NET PROFIT MARGIN	EMPLOYEES
12/11	391	22	5.7%	3,200
12/10	359	30	8.4%	0
12/09	346	31	9.1%	0
12/08	321	(5)	—	0
Annual Growth	6.8%	—	—	—

2011 Year-End Financials

Debt ratio: ——
Return on equity: 5.70%
Cash ($ mil.): 69
Current ratio: 2.50
Long-term debt ($ mil.): —
Dividends
Yield: —
Payout: —
Market value ($ mil.): —

INDIANA UNIVERSITY HEALTH LA PORTE HOSPITAL INC.

LOCATIONS

HQ: INDIANA UNIVERSITY HEALTH LA PORTE HOSPITAL INC.
1007 LINCOLNWAY, LA PORTE, IN 46350-3201
Phone: 219-326-1234

HISTORICAL FINANCIALS

Company Type: Private

Income Statement

FYE: September 30

	REVENUE ($ mil.)	NET INCOME ($ mil.)	NET PROFIT MARGIN	EMPLOYEES
09/12*	173	11	6.9%	1,500
12/11	231	(0)	—	0
06/11	113	0	0.8%	0
12/10	222	15	6.9%	0
Annual Growth	(7.9%)	(7.9%)	—	—

*Fiscal year change

2012 Year-End Financials

Debt ratio: ——
Return on equity: 6.90%
Cash ($ mil.): 18
Current ratio: 0.70
Long-term debt ($ mil.): —
Dividends
Yield: —
Payout: —
Market value ($ mil.): —

INDUSTRIAL AIR TOOL L.P. L.L.P.

LOCATIONS

HQ: INDUSTRIAL AIR TOOL L.P. L.L.P.
1305 W JACKSON AVE, PASADENA, TX 77506-1709
Phone: 713-477-3144
Web: www.industrialairtool.com

HISTORICAL FINANCIALS

Company Type: Private

Income Statement

FYE: December 31

	REVENUE ($ mil.)	NET INCOME ($ mil.)	NET PROFIT MARGIN	EMPLOYEES
12/11	121	13	10.7%	108
12/10	94	4	4.7%	0
12/09	91	2	2.2%	0
12/07	133	22	17.2%	0
Annual Growth	(3.1%)	(17.2%)	—	—

2011 Year-End Financials

Debt ratio: ——
Return on equity: 10.70%
Cash ($ mil.): 1
Current ratio: 1.50
Long-term debt ($ mil.): —
Dividends
Yield: —
Payout: —
Market value ($ mil.): —

INDUSTRIAL CHEMICALS INC.

LOCATIONS

HQ: INDUSTRIAL CHEMICALS INC.
2042 MONTREAT DR, VESTAVIA, AL 35216-4040
Phone: 205-823-7330
Web: www.sweetlakechem.com

HISTORICAL FINANCIALS

Company Type: Private

Income Statement

FYE: December 31

	REVENUE ($ mil.)	NET INCOME ($ mil.)	NET PROFIT MARGIN	EMPLOYEES
12/11	91	1	1.2%	130
12/10	73	2	3.0%	0
12/09	60	4	7.6%	0
12/08	80	3	4.5%	0
Annual Growth	4.2%	(32.8%)	—	—

2011 Year-End Financials

Debt ratio: —
Return on equity: 1.20%
Cash ($ mil.): 0
Current ratio: 0.60
Long-term debt ($ mil.): —
Dividends
Yield: —
Payout: —
Market value ($ mil.): —

INDUSTRIAL TURNAROUND CORPORATION

Facility builder Industrial TurnAround Corporation (ITAC) makes sure that wheels turn and conveyors churn at industrial plants around the world. ITAC provides architectural and design expertise construction management and electrical and mechanical engineering to clients whose facilities are based on heavy production such as biofuels chemical metal pharmaceutical power pulp and paper and tobacco. It also offers on-site staffing (for clients who need temporary project managers draftsmen CAD operators and other support staff) as well as hazard and fall prevention assessment equipment and training. Clients include Amtrak Honeywell International and NASA.

The renewable energy market represents a key growth area for ITAC as it pursues projects involved in the industrial production of cleaner burning sources of fuel including ethanol biodiesels and wood pellets (an alternative to petroleum). The company designs plants that are intended to reduce harmful emissions. Its projects include one of the largest wood pellet plants and one of the largest biodiesel plants in the US.

EXECUTIVES

Director Projects and Business Development, Walt Johnson
Manager Human Resources, Teresa Meade

Director Projects and Business Development, Rick Stames
Manager Mechanical and Process Engineering, Michael (Mike) Pitek
Senior Process Engineer, Art Sinclair
VP Construction, Glenn Harper
Director Engineering, John Moody
Director Construction, William Smyth
CEO, Sidney Harrison
President, Jon Loftis
VP BioEnergy, Steve Gordon
Director Fall Production, Bruce Simms
Manager On-Site Services, Martin Puckett
Manager Electrical and Controls Engineering, Scott Garner
Manager Electrical and Controls Engineering, Michael (Mike) Jones
Manager C.S.A. Engineering, Jeff Stotesberry
Manager Machine Division, James Young
Director Design and Build Construction and Regional Manager, Michael (Mike) Winchell
Manager Electrical Plant Services Division, Lewis Irving
Manager Mechanical Plant Services Division, Robert (Bob) Rushing

LOCATIONS

HQ: Industrial TurnAround Corporation
13203 N. Enon Church Rd., Chester VA 23836
Phone: 804-414-1100   **Fax:** 804-414-1295
Web: www.itac.us.com

PRODUCTS/OPERATIONS

Selected Services

Civil and structural engineering
Construction management
Electrical engineering
Fall protection assessment equipment & training
Machine design
Mechanical engineering
Piping design
Procurement
Project management
Project staffing

COMPETITORS

Austin Industries	Fluor
Bechtel	Kiewit Power Engineers
Black & Veatch	Stellar Group
Facility Group	

HISTORICAL FINANCIALS

Company Type: Private

Income Statement

FYE: December 31

	REVENUE ($ mil.)	NET INCOME ($ mil.)	NET PROFIT MARGIN	EMPLOYEES
12/11	43	0	1.1%	250
12/10	52	1	1.9%	0
12/09	44	0	0.6%	0
12/08	55	7	13.2%	0
Annual Growth	(8.2%)	(60.4%)	—	—

2011 Year-End Financials

Debt ratio: —
Return on equity: 1.10%
Cash ($ mil.): 2
Current ratio: 1.20
Long-term debt ($ mil.): —
Dividends
Yield: —
Payout: —
Market value ($ mil.): —

INDYNE INC.

InDyne offers out-of-this-world technology expertise. The company provides information technology science and engineering and technical and administrative services primarily to US government agencies including NASA. It develops custom software designs Web sites and builds computer networks. InDyne's science and engineering division designs aerospace systems provides space mission support and crew training and offers structural and fluid analysis. Its technical and administrative services unit handles imagery operations data management media services and operations support. The company's project have included the development of custom database software for the CDC and the Department of Transportation.

EXECUTIVES

President, C. Donald Bishop
Manager Business Development, Candace Solomon
Director Human Resources, Margaret James
CFO, Robert (Bob) Miller
VP Strategic Programs, Jeff Riemer
Director Washington Operations, JuliAnna Potter

LOCATIONS

HQ: InDyne Inc.
11800 Sunrise Valley Dr. Ste. 250, Reston VA 20191
Phone: 703-903-6900   **Fax:** 703-903-4997
Web: www.indyneinc.com

COMPETITORS

Affiliated Computer Services
Alion
CACI International
Computer Sciences Corp.
Dynamics Research
General Dynamics Information Technology
GTSI
HP Enterprise Services
IBM Global Services
Lockheed Martin Information Systems
ManTech
Northrop Grumman Info Systems
Raytheon IIS
SAIC
SRA International
Unisys

HISTORICAL FINANCIALS

Company Type: Private

Income Statement

FYE: December 31

	REVENUE ($ mil.)	NET INCOME ($ mil.)	NET PROFIT MARGIN	EMPLOYEES
12/11	240	6	2.8%	1,700
12/10	260	6	2.6%	0
12/09	255	7	3.0%	0
12/08	288	8	3.1%	0
Annual Growth	(5.8%)	(8.9%)	—	—

2011 Year-End Financials

Debt ratio: —
Return on equity: 2.80%
Cash ($ mil.): 3
Current ratio: 0.20
Long-term debt ($ mil.): —
Dividends
Yield: —
Payout: —
Market value ($ mil.): —

INFINITY CONSTRUCTION SERVICES LP

LOCATIONS

HQ: INFINITY CONSTRUCTION SERVICES LP
622 COMMERCE ST, CLUTE, TX 77531-5612
Phone: 979-388-8579
Web: www.inf-grp.com

HISTORICAL FINANCIALS

Company Type: Private

Income Statement

	REVENUE ($ mil.)	NET INCOME ($ mil.)	NET PROFIT MARGIN	EMPLOYEES
12/11	138	10	7.4%	1,100
12/10	122	4	3.3%	0
12/09	113	(2)	—	0
12/08	164	11	7.0%	0
Annual Growth	(5.7%)	(3.9%)	—	—

2011 Year-End Financials

Debt ratio: —
Return on equity: 7.40%
Cash ($ mil.): 7
Current ratio: 1.50
Long-term debt ($ mil.): —
Dividends
Yield: —
Payout: —
Market value ($ mil.): —

INGERSOLL MACHINE TOOLS INC.

At Ingersoll Machine Tools folks want to talk shop. The company leads the conversation in global production churning out advanced machine tools for other industries' goods. Products include general purpose equipment (vertical turning lathes scalpers and horizontal boring centers) to one-of-a-kind machines that produce aluminum and hard metal components and structures from composite materials. Ingersoll's contract manufacturing services offer prototype machining and short production runs of windmill hubs to small engine parts. Customers include most of the world's aerospace transportation energy and heavy industry OEMs from Caterpillar to Lockheed Martin. Ingersoll is a company of Italy's Camozzi Group.

The machine tool maker formerly known as Ingersoll Milling was originally a division of Ingersoll International. Following its parent company's demise through bankruptcy Ingersoll gained new life in October 2003 when federal regulators approved a buyout by the Camozzi Group. The industrial group bolted on Ingersoll to its other business units.

EXECUTIVES

President and CEO, Tino Oldani
Manager Machining and Engineering Services, Steven (Steve) Saichek
CFO, Larry Mocadlo
Director Sales and Marketing, Michael (Mike) Reese

LOCATIONS

HQ: Ingersoll Machine Tools Inc.
707 Fulton Ave., Rockford IL 61103
Phone: 815-987-6000   **Fax:** 815-987-6725
Web: www.ingersoll.com

PRODUCTS/OPERATIONS

Selected Products and Services

Composites
Automated composite layup systems
Automated fiber placement
Composite machining/drilling
Contract manufacturing
Assembly
Machining
Machine tools
Horizontal boring centers
Rotor slotters
Scalpers
Vertical turning lathes
Rebuilds and retrofits
Controls retrofits
Mechanical upgrades

COMPETITORS

BuhlerPrince	MAG Giddings &
GILDEMEISTER	Lewis
Hardinge	Makino
Harrington Tool	Mazak
Hurco	Seco Tools
Kuhl Machine Shop	Toyoda Machinery USA

HISTORICAL FINANCIALS

Company Type: Subsidiary

Income Statement

	REVENUE ($ mil.)	NET INCOME ($ mil.)	NET PROFIT MARGIN	EMPLOYEES
12/11	65	0	0.0%	331
12/09	56	0	0.6%	0
12/08	81	0	0.3%	0
12/07	86	0	0.9%	0
Annual Growth	(9.0%)	(82.0%)	—	—

2011 Year-End Financials

Debt ratio: —
Return on equity: —
Cash ($ mil.): 1
Current ratio: —
Long-term debt ($ mil.): —
Dividends
Yield: —
Payout: —
Market value ($ mil.): —

INNOSPEC FUEL SPECIALTIES LLC

LOCATIONS

HQ: INNOSPEC FUEL SPECIALTIES LLC
8375 WILLOW ST FL 5, LITTLETON, CO 80124-2846
Phone: 303-792-5554
Web: www.octel-starreon.com

HISTORICAL FINANCIALS

Company Type: Private

Income Statement

	REVENUE ($ mil.)	NET INCOME ($ mil.)	NET PROFIT MARGIN	EMPLOYEES
12/11	212	22	10.8%	100
12/10	193	26	13.5%	0
Annual Growth	9.8%	(12.7%)	—	—

2011 Year-End Financials

Debt ratio: —
Return on equity: 10.80%
Cash ($ mil.): 1
Current ratio: 0.30
Long-term debt ($ mil.): —
Dividends
Yield: —
Payout: —
Market value ($ mil.): —

INNOVIS HEALTH LLC

LOCATIONS

HQ: INNOVIS HEALTH LLC
3000 32ND AVE S, FARGO, ND 58103-6132
Phone: 701-364-3300

HISTORICAL FINANCIALS

Company Type: Private

Income Statement

	REVENUE ($ mil.)	NET INCOME ($ mil.)	NET PROFIT MARGIN	EMPLOYEES
06/11	259	(1)	—	4
06/10	252	1	0.4%	0
Annual Growth	2.8%	—	—	—

2011 Year-End Financials

Debt ratio: —
Return on equity: (-0.50)%
Cash ($ mil.): 11
Current ratio: 0.30
Long-term debt ($ mil.): —
Dividends
Yield: —
Payout: —
Market value ($ mil.): —

INTER AMERICAN UNIVERSITY OF PUERTO RICO INC

LOCATIONS

HQ: INTER AMERICAN UNIVERSITY OF PUERTO RICO INC

399 CALLE GALILEO, SAN JUAN, PR 00927-4517

Phone: 787-766-1912

HISTORICAL FINANCIALS

Company Type: Private

Income Statement

FYE: June 30

	REVENUE ($ mil.)	NET INCOME ($ mil.)	NET PROFIT MARGIN	EMPLOYEES
06/12	267	11	4.3%	4,306
06/11	291	49	16.8%	0
06/10	267	35	13.3%	0
06/09	210	(17)	—	0
Annual Growth	8.4%	—	—	—

2012 Year-End Financials

Debt ratio: ——
Return on equity: 4.30%
Cash ($ mil.): 41
Current ratio: —
Long-term debt ($ mil.): —

Dividends
Yield: —
Payout: —
Market value ($ mil.): —

INTERMOUNTAIN HEALTH CARE INC

If you whoosh down the side of one of Idaho's majestic mountains and take a nasty spill Intermountain Health Care (dba Intermountain Healthcare) will pick you up and put you back together. From air ambulance services to urgent care clinics and general hospitals Intermountain has all the tools to mend skiers (and non-skiers alike) in Utah and southern Idaho. The not-for-profit health system operates 22 hospitals and more than 185 physician and urgent care clinics home health care agencies and rehabilitation centers. The company was formed in 1975 when the Church of Jesus Christ of Latter Day Saints donated 15 hospitals to local communities. Its hospitals have a combined total of about 2700 licensed beds.

Its hospitals range from general surgical to specialty care including orthopedic and pediatric facilities. Along with the full spectrum of physical health care services Intermountain also offers comprehensive mental health and substance abuse programs for patients of all ages. The organization's spectrum of care includes acute inpatient residential treatment day treatment chemical dependency inpatient/detoxification and intensive outpatient programs. To serve the the region's uninsured and low-income residents Intermountain owns or supports 18 community and school primary care clinics.

The organization conducts cancer research through its partnership with Huntsman Cancer Institute at the University of Utah. The two share data best practices funding and co-conduct clinical trials. They also operate a number of cancer-specific treatment centers including multi-disciplinary tumor-specific clinics designed to provide one-stop service for cancer patients to meet with different cancer specialists on the same day for a more comprehensive treatment plan. Other areas of research include cardiovascular intensive medicine surgical care and behavioral health.

On the physician side the Intermountain Medical Group administers multi-specialty health care services through more than 800 doctors in clinics located throughout the region. The group also operates urgent care clinics under the ExpressCare InstaCare and KidsCare banners.

Entering itself into the "what doesn't Intermountain do?" category the health system also provides health and dental insurance plans through its SelectHealth division. SelectHealth provides coverage for large and small employer groups runs the state Children's Health Insurance Program and administers a high-risk insurance pool for the state of Utah.

With increases in every service category except births which were down by about 2% Intermountain Health Care's revenues in 2011 increased to $4.7 billion representing an almost 4% increase over 2010. The largest changes were in the number of homecare patients served (up more than 6%) and the number of acute admissions (up almost 5%).

Strategically Intermountain strives to improve clinical quality and establish efficiency enhancements to manage costs. For example in 2011 the company joined such peers as the Mayo Clinic Cleveland Clinic and others to form the High Value Healthcare Collaborative to share information to improve health care manage and save costs and extend best practices out to physicians clinics and hospitals throughout the US. By streamlining its purchasing storage and distribution processes the company was also able to save about $56 million in supply chain costs. The company is also collaborating with the Centers for Medicare and Medicaid Services and other health systems to examine ways to improve health care safety and reduce costs by preventing patient injuries and complications.

EXECUTIVES

Chair Park City Medical Center Foundation, Bill Johnson

Chair Dixie Regional Medical Center, Suzanne Allen

Trustee; Chair Intermountain Healthcare Foundation, Merrill Gappmayer

CEO Intermountain Medical Group and Trustee, Linda C. Leckman

Media Contact, Daron Cowley

Chairman, Kem C. Gardner

Co-Chair Primary Children's Medical Center Foundation, E. J. (Jake) Garn

Chair Park City Medical Center, Rebecca (Becky) Kearns, age 54

Vice Chairman, Douglas C. Black

Trustee; Chair SelectHealth, Thomas B. Morgan

Trustee; Chair Intermountain Medical Group, Daniel W. Davis

Chair Bear River Valley Hospital Urban North Region, Jay Hardy

Chair Delta and Fillmore Community Medical Centers, Kenneth Day

Chair Garfield Memorial Hospital and Clinics, Maloy Dodds

Chair McKay-Dee Hospital Center Urban North Region, Karen Fairbanks

Chair Intermountain Community Care Foundation, Dominic Albo

Trustee; Chair Urban South Region, Jane Carlile

Chair Bear River Valley Hospital Foundations, Marlene Berger

Chair Deseret Foundation, J. Howard Van Boerum

President Tri-County Health Foundation and Sevier Valley Medical Center, Jamie Robinson

President Cassia Healthcare Foundation, Bruce Beck

Co-Chair Primary Children's Medical Center Foundation, Kathleen Garn

Chair Utah Valley Healthcare Foundation, Henry E. Heilesen

CIO, Marc Probst

Chair Heber Valley Medical Center, Shauna VanWagoner

Chair McKay-Dee Hospital Foundation, Dwight Baldwin

President Garfield Memorial HealthCare Foundation, Garry Holbrook

Chair Sanpete Valley Healthcare Foundation, Dale Lewis

President CEO and Trustee, Charles W. Sorenson

Medical Director Intermountain Medical Group Weber/North Davis and Trustee, Brett T. Muse

Medical Director Intermountain Medical Group North Salt Lake/South Davis and Trustee, Brent J. Christensen

Chair The Foundation of Dixie Regional Medical Center, Cyndi W. Gilbert

Chair Intermountain Homecare, JoAnn E. Bott

Chair Sanpete Valley Hospital, Earl Clark

Chair Valley View Medical Center, Wayne Clark

Chair Cassia Regional Medical Center, Clay Handy

Chair Sevier Valley Medical Center, Eugene Beck

Chair Logan Regional Hospital Urban North Region, Larry W. Carter

Chair Foundation of Homecare and Hospice, Daniel Nelsen

Chair The Foundation of Valley View Medical Center, Nate Esplin

Chair Logan Regional Hospital Foundation, Rod Hunter

VP Clinical Operations and Chief Nursing Officer, Nancy Nowak

Chief Purchasing Officer, Brent Johnson

CEO Dixie Regional Medical Center, Terri Kane

Director Social Work McKay-Dee Hospital Center, Rod Fifield

VP Medical Research and Chief Quality Officer; Executive Director Intermountain Institute for Healthcare Delivery Research, Brent C. James

President and CEO SelectHealth, Pat Richards

Administrator and Director Operations Orem Community Hospital and Utah Valley Regional medical Center, Ron Liston

Chief Medical Informaticist, Stan Huff

Trustee, Teresa Beck, age 57

Trustee, Spencer F. Eccles, age 75

Trustee, Clark D. Ivory

Trustee, F. Ann Millner

Trustee, Bruce T. Reese

Trustee; Chair Intermountain Healthcare Foundation, Merrill Gappmayer

CEO Intermountain Medical Group and Trustee, Linda C. Leckman

Vice Chairman, Douglas C. Black

Trustee; Chair SelectHealth, Thomas B. Morgan

Trustee; Chair Intermountain Medical Group, Daniel W. Davis

Trustee, Edward G. Kleyn

Trustee; Chair Urban South Region, Jane Carlile

LOCATIONS

HQ: Intermountain Health Care Inc.
36 S. State St., Salt Lake City UT 84111-1486
Phone: 801-442-2000   **Fax:** 801-442-3327
Web: www.ihc.com

PRODUCTS/OPERATIONS

2011 Revenues

	$ mil.	% of total
Patient services	3,577	71
Non-patient activities (health insurance premiums contributions & other)	1,393	29
Investment income	19	-
Charity services	(276.8)	-
Total	**4,713**	**100**

Selected Hospitals

Alta View Hospital (Sandy UT)
American Fork Hospital (Utah)
Bear River Valley Hospital (Tremonton UT)
Cassia Regional Medical Center (Burley ID)
Delta Community Medical Center (Utah)
Dixie Regional Medical Center (St. George UT)
Fillmore Community Medical Center (Utah)
Garfield Memorial Hospital (Panguitch UT)
Heber Valley Medical Center (Heber City UT)
Intermountain Medical Center (Murray UT)
LDS Hospital (Salt Lake City)
Logan Regional Hospital (Orem UT)
McKay-Dee Hospital Center (Ogden UT)
  McKay-Dee Behavioral Health Institute
Orem Community Hospital (Utah)
Park City Medical Center (Park City UT)
Primary Children's Medical Center (Salt Lake City)
Riverton Hospital (Riverton UT)
Sanpete Valley Hospital (Mt. Pleasant UT)
Sevier Valley Hospital (Richfield UT)
TOSH - The Orthopedic Specialty Hospital (Murray UT)
Utah Valley Regional Medical Center (Provo UT)
Valley View Medical Center (Cedar City UT)

Selected Other Facilities

Northern Idaho and Utah
  Clinics
    Bear River Clinic
    Budge Clinic
    Canyon View Orthopedics & Associates
    Isom Plastic Surgery
    Logan Clinic
    South Cache Valley Clinic
    Summit Clinic
  Home Health Hospice and Home Medical Equipment
    Cassia
    Logan
    Tremonton
  InstaCare and KidsCare
    Logan InstaCare
  WorkMed
    Burley
    Logan
    Tremonton
Davis - Weber
  Clinics
    Bountiful Clinic
    Calton/Harrison Orthopedic Clinic
    Endocrine Diabetes
    Herefordshire Clinic
    Layton Clinic
    McKay-Dee Cardiology Clinic

McKay-Dee Dermatology & Plastic Surgery
McKay-Dee ENT Clinic
McKay-Dee Foot and Ankle Clinic
McKay-Dee Internal Medicine Clinic
McKay-Dee Rheumatology Clinic
McKay-Dee Urogynecology Clinic
North Ogden Clinic
Northern Utah Pediatrics
Northern Utah Surgeons
Ogden Cardiovascular Associates
South Ogden Clinic
Sports Medicine Specialists - Bountiful
Summit Orthopedics
Syracuse Clinic
Wasatch OB/GYN
  Home Health Hospice and Home Medical Equipment
    Ogden
  InstaCare and KidsCare
    Bountiful InstaCare
    Bountiful KidsCare
    Herefordshire InstaCare
    Layton InstaCare
    Layton KidsCare
    North Ogden InstaCare
    North Ogden KidsCare
    South Ogden InstaCare
    Syracuse InstaCare
  ExpressCare
    Smith's Food & Drug - Farmington
  WorkMed
    Layton
    Ogden
Greater Salt Lake Valley
  Clinics
    Alta View Specialty Clinic
    Avenues Specialty Clinic
    Bryner Clinic
    Central Valley ENT Head & Neck Surgery
    Central Valley Thyroid & Parathyroid Clinic
    Cottonwood Endocrine & Diabetes Center
    Cottonwood Family Practice
    Cottonwood Internal Medicine
    Gorang Family Practice
    Heart and Lung Surgical Associates
    Hillcrest Pediatrics
    Holladay Clinic
    Holladay Pediatrics
    Holladay Pediatrics - North
    Internal Medicine Associates
    Medical Tower Family Practice
    Memorial Clinic
    Mountain View Pediatrics
    Noyes Surgical Oncology
    Obstetrics & Gynecology Specialists
    Orthopedic Specialty Group Clinics
    Park City Specialty Clinic
    Plastic Surgery Center
    Pulmonology Clinic
    Salt Lake Clinic
    Sandy Clinic
    Sandy OB/GYN
    South Jordan Clinic
    South Sandy Clinic
    Southridge Clinic
    Southridge OB/GYN
    Southridge Pediatrics
    Surgical Specialists
    Taylorsville Clinic
    Utah Heart Clinic
    Urological Institute Clinics
    West Jordan Clinic
  Home Health Hospice and Home Medical Equipment
    Salt Lake City
  InstaCare and KidsCare
    Holladay InstaCare
    Memorial InstaCare
    Memorial KidsCare
    Mountain View Pediatrics KidsCare
    Murray InstaCare
    Sandy InstaCare
    Southridge InstaCare
    Southridge KidsCare
    Taylorsville InstaCare
    Taylorsville KidsCare
    West Jordan InstaCare
    West Jordan KidsCare
  ExpressCare

Smith's Food & Drug - Draper
Smith's Food & Drug - Salt Lake City
  WorkMed
    Murray
    Salt Lake City
Greater Utah Valley
  Clinics
    American Fork Internal Medicine & Dermatology
    American Fork Pulmonary Clinic
    American Fork Surgical Associates
    Central Orem Clinic
    Heber Valley Clinic
    Highland Clinic
    Legacy OB/GYN Clinic
    North Canyon Family Practice
    North Orem Clinic
    North Valley Pediatrics
    Physical Medicine & Rehabilitation
    Provo Neurological Clinic
    Saratoga Springs Clinic
    Springville Clinic
    Utah Valley Ear Nose & Throat
    Utah Valley Heart & Lung Surgical Associates
    Utah Valley Internal Medicine Clinic
    Utah Valley Orthopaedics & Sports Medicine
    Utah Valley Pediatric Specialists
    Utah Valley Pulmonary Clinic
    Utah Valley Vein Clinic
  Home Health Hospice and Home Medical Equipment
    Heber City
    Orem
  Urgent Care
    Highland InstaCare
    North Orem InstaCare
    Provo InstaCare
    Saratoga Springs InstaCare
    Springville InstaCare
  WorkMed
    Orem
    Springville
Central Utah
  Clinics
    Ephraim Clinic
    Fillmore Clinic
    Manti Family Clinic
    Moroni Clinic
    Mt. Pleasant Clinic
    North Sevier Medical Clinic
    Richfield Family Practice
    Sevier Valley Family Practice
  Home Health Hospice and Home Medical Equipment
    Delta
    Fillmore
    Mt. Pleasant
    Richfield
  WorkMed
    Moroni
    Mt. Pleasant
Southern Utah
  Clinics
    Canyon View Family Practice
    Cardiovascular & Thoracic Surgery St. George
    Cedar City Clinic
    Dixie Plastic & Reconstructive Surgery
    Hurricane Valley Clinic
    Pulmonary Medicine Clinic - St. George
    Redrock Pediatrics
    Rim Rock Orthopaedics & Sports Medicine
    River Road Family Practice
    River Road Internal Medicine
    Southern Utah Behavioral Health
    Southern Utah Surgical Associates
    Southwest Cardiology - St. George
    Southwest Neurology Associates
    Southwest Regional Cancer Clinic
    Southwest Rheumatology Associates
    Southwest Spine & Pain Center
    Sunset Clinic
    Valley View Heart Clinic
    Women's Health Specialists
    Zion Orthopaedics & Sports Medicine
  Home Health Hospice and Home Medical Equipment
    Cedar City
    St. George
  InstaCare and KidsCare
    Cedar City InstaCare
    Hurricane Valley InstaCare

River Road InstaCare
Sunset InstaCare
WorkMed
Cedar City
St. George

COMPETITORS

CHRISTUS Health
HCA
HealthSouth
Iasis Healthcare
LifePoint Hospitals
Ogden Regional Medical Center
Regence BlueCross BlueShield of Utah
St. Mark' s
University of Utah Hospitals & Clinics

HISTORICAL FINANCIALS

Company Type: Private - Not-for-Profit

Income Statement

FYE: December 31

	REVENUE ($ mil.)	NET INCOME ($ mil.)	NET PROFIT MARGIN	EMPLOYEES
12/11	4,049	6	0.2%	23,000
12/10	4,381	716	16.3%	0
12/09	3,568	1,032	28.9%	0
12/07	3,048	298	9.8%	0
Annual Growth	9.9%	(72.4%)	—	—

2011 Year-End Financials

Debt ratio: ——
Return on equity: 0.20%
Cash ($ mil.): 175
Current ratio: 0.60
Long-term debt ($ mil.): —

Dividends
Yield: —
Payout: —
Market value ($ mil.): —

INTERNATIONAL BROTHERHOOD OF ELECTRICAL WORKERS - PENSION BENEFI

LOCATIONS

HQ: INTERNATIONAL BROTHERHOOD OF ELECTRICAL WORKERS - PENSION BENEFI
900 7TH ST NW, WASHINGTON, DC 20001-3886
Phone: 202-728-6200

HISTORICAL FINANCIALS

Company Type: Private

Income Statement

FYE: June 30

	REVENUE ($ mil.)	NET INCOME ($ mil.)	NET PROFIT MARGIN	EMPLOYEES
06/11	171	36	21.1%	3
06/10	182	53	29.1%	0
Annual Growth	(6.0%)	(31.8%)	—	—

2011 Year-End Financials

Debt ratio: ——
Return on equity: 21.10%
Cash ($ mil.): 72
Current ratio: 1.60
Long-term debt ($ mil.): —

Dividends
Yield: —
Payout: —
Market value ($ mil.): —

INTERNATIONAL RESCUE COMMITTEE INC.

LOCATIONS

HQ: INTERNATIONAL RESCUE COMMITTEE INC.
122 E 42ND ST FL 12, NEW YORK, NY 10168-1299
Phone: 212-551-3000
Web: www.womenscommission.org

HISTORICAL FINANCIALS

Company Type: Private

Income Statement

FYE: September 30

	REVENUE ($ mil.)	NET INCOME ($ mil.)	NET PROFIT MARGIN	EMPLOYEES
09/11	397	11	2.9%	6,500
09/10	316	10	3.3%	0
09/09	281	(6)	—	0
09/08	260	(19)	—	0
Annual Growth	15.1%	—	—	—

2011 Year-End Financials

Debt ratio: ——
Return on equity: 2.90%
Cash ($ mil.): 47
Current ratio: 0.70
Long-term debt ($ mil.): —

Dividends
Yield: —
Payout: —
Market value ($ mil.): —

INTERNATIONAL AID INC.

LOCATIONS

HQ: INTERNATIONAL AID INC.
17011 HICKORY ST, SPRING LAKE, MI 49456-9795
Phone: 616-846-7490
Web: www.internationalaid.org

HISTORICAL FINANCIALS

Company Type: Private

Income Statement

FYE: June 30

	REVENUE ($ mil.)	NET INCOME ($ mil.)	NET PROFIT MARGIN	EMPLOYEES
06/12	162	0	0.1%	20
06/11	133	0	0.4%	0
06/10	73	0	0.3%	0
06/09	61	(2)	—	0
Annual Growth	37.8%	—	—	—

2012 Year-End Financials

Debt ratio: ——
Return on equity: 0.10%
Cash ($ mil.): 0
Current ratio: 5.00
Long-term debt ($ mil.): —

Dividends
Yield: —
Payout: —
Market value ($ mil.): —

INTERNATIONAL MEDICAL CORPS

LOCATIONS

HQ: INTERNATIONAL MEDICAL CORPS
1919 SANTA MONICA BLVD, SANTA MONICA, CA 90404-1954
Phone: 310-826-7800
Web: www.internationalmedicalcorps.org

HISTORICAL FINANCIALS

Company Type: Private

Income Statement

FYE: June 30

	REVENUE ($ mil.)	NET INCOME ($ mil.)	NET PROFIT MARGIN	EMPLOYEES
06/12	107	(0)	—	35
06/11	134	(1)	—	0
06/10	133	9	6.8%	0
06/09	115	(9)	—	0
Annual Growth	(2.4%)	—	—	—

2012 Year-End Financials

Debt ratio: ——
Return on equity: (-0.70)%
Cash ($ mil.): 10
Current ratio: 0.70
Long-term debt ($ mil.): —

Dividends
Yield: —
Payout: —
Market value ($ mil.): —

IONA COLLEGE

LOCATIONS

HQ: IONA COLLEGE
715 NORTH AVE, NEW ROCHELLE, NY 10801-1890
Phone: 914-633-2000
Web: www.iona.edu

HISTORICAL FINANCIALS

Company Type: Private

Income Statement

FYE: June 30

	REVENUE ($ mil.)	NET INCOME ($ mil.)	NET PROFIT MARGIN	EMPLOYEES
06/11	133	8	6.7%	750
06/10	129	10	8.0%	0
06/09	126	11	9.5%	0
06/08	121	11	9.9%	0
Annual Growth	3.2%	(9.2%)	—	—

2011 Year-End Financials

Debt ratio: ——
Return on equity: 6.70%
Cash ($ mil.): 10
Current ratio: 0.70
Long-term debt ($ mil.): —

Dividends
Yield: —
Payout: —
Market value ($ mil.): —

IOWA HEALTH SYSTEM

The land where the tall corn grows is also the land of Iowa Health System (IHS). The integrated health care system operates some 15 acute care hospitals that serve large communities throughout Iowa as well as parts of western Illinois and eastern Nebraska. IHS also supports about a dozen rural hospitals and it manages more than 200 physician clinics located in rural and suburban areas. The system's hospitals provide general medical-surgical care as well as care in a number of medical specialties such as cardiovascular disease and home health services. Founded in 1993 HIS has about 3100 licensed beds some 630 physicians and 235 mid-level medical professionals.

Strategy IHS expands its network through affiliations. In late 2012 it brought Stewart Memorial Community Hospital in Lake City into its network just as it had done the previous year with Methodist Health Services operator of the 330-bed Methodist Medical Center of Illinois located in Peoria. IHS also committed $175 million to help Methodist-Illinois enhance its technologies and its service offerings. The health system operates many of its member hospitals through similar affiliation agreements; IHS provides administration contracting billing legal recruitment information technology and other central services.

EXECUTIVES

President and CEO, Bill Leaver
VP Public Relations and Communications, Cheri Bustos
VP and General Counsel, Denny Drake
Secretary and Director, Paul Brandt
Vice Chair, Paula Arnell
Chair, Jim Hoffman
Treasurer and Director, Bruce Sherman
VP and CIO, Joy M. Grosser
VP and Chief Medical Officer, Alan S. Kaplan
EVP and CFO, Kevin Vermeer
Director, Donald F. (Don) Ross
Director, Peg Armstrong-Gustafson
Director, Craig Bainbridge
Director, David Oman
Director, Mark Parise
Director, Gene Blanc
Director, Pryce Boeye
Director, Bill Prowell
Secretary and Director, Paul Brandt
Director, Kevin Schminke
Director, Kathy Eno
Vice Chair, Paula Arnell
Director, Mark Baldwin
Director, Terri Christoffersen
Director, Ronald Klosterman
Director, Larry Liebscher
Treasurer and Director, Bruce Sherman
Director, John Gleeson
Director, Kurt Pittner
Auditors: Deloitte&ToucheLLP

LOCATIONS

HQ: Iowa Health System
1200 Pleasant St., Des Moines IA 50309
Phone: 515-241-6161　　**Fax:** 515-241-6220
Web: www.ihs.org

PRODUCTS/OPERATIONS

Selected Facilities
Metropolitan Hospitals
Allen Memorial Hospital Corporation (Waterloo Iowa)

Iowa Lutheran Hospital (Des Moines Iowa)
Iowa Methodist Medical Center (Des Moines Iowa)
　Blank Children's Hospital (Des Moines Iowa)
Methodist Medical Center of Illinois (Peoria Illinois)
Methodist West Hospital (West Des Moines Iowa)
St. Luke's Hospital (Cedar Rapids Iowa)
St. Luke's Regional Medical Center (Sioux City Iowa)
Jones Regional Medical Center (Anamosa Iowa)
The Finley Hospital (Dubuque Iowa)
Trinity Bettendorf (Bettendorf Iowa)
Trinity Moline (Moline Illinois)
Trinity Muscatine (Muscatine Iowa)
Trinity Regional Medical Center (Fort Dodge Iowa)
Trinity Rock Island (Rock Island Illinois)
Rural Hospitals
Buena Vista Regional Medical Center (Storm Lake Iowa)
Clarke County Hospital (Osceola Iowa)
Community Memorial Hospital (Sumner Iowa)
Greater Regional Medical Center (Creston Iowa)
Greene County Medical Center (Jefferson Iowa)
Grundy County Memorial Hospital (Grundy Center Iowa)
Guthrie County Hospital (Guthrie Center Iowa)
Guttenberg Municipal Hospital (Guttenberg Iowa)
Humboldt County Memorial Hospital (Humboldt Iowa)
Loring Hospital (Sac City Iowa)
Pocahontas Community Hospital (Pocahantas Iowa)

COMPETITORS

Alegent Creighton Health
Avera Health
Blessing Hospital
Genesis Health System
McDonough District Hospital
Mercy Health Network
Methodist Health System
ORHC
OSF Healthcare System
University of Iowa Hospitals and Clinics

HISTORICAL FINANCIALS
Company Type: Private - Not-for-Profit

Income Statement
FYE: December 31

	REVENUE ($ mil.)	NET INCOME ($ mil.)	NET PROFIT MARGIN	EMPLOYEES
12/11	2,380	159	6.7%	18,923
12/09*	109	(51)	—	0
09/09	0	0	—	0
12/07	1,874	108	5.8%	0
Annual Growth	8.3%	13.7%	—	—

*Fiscal year change

2011 Year-End Financials

Debt ratio: ——
Return on equity: 6.70%
Cash ($ mil.): 96
Current ratio: 1.00
Long-term debt ($ mil.): —

Dividends
　Yield: —
　Payout: —
Market value ($ mil.): —

IPS-INTEGRATED PROJECT SERVICES INC.

LOCATIONS

HQ: IPS-INTEGRATED PROJECT SERVICES INC.
2001 JOSHUA RD, LAFAYETTE HILL, PA 19444-2431
Phone: 610-828-4090
Web: www.ipsdb.com

HISTORICAL FINANCIALS
Company Type: Private

Income Statement
FYE: December 31

	REVENUE ($ mil.)	NET INCOME ($ mil.)	NET PROFIT MARGIN	EMPLOYEES
12/11	116	4	3.5%	375
12/10	75	3	4.2%	0
12/07*	75	2	2.7%	0
06/06	38	1	2.6%	0
Annual Growth	44.5%	58.4%	—	—

*Fiscal year change

2011 Year-End Financials

Debt ratio: —
Return on equity: 3.50%
Cash ($ mil.): 6
Current ratio: 1.00
Long-term debt ($ mil.): —

Dividends
　Yield: —
　Payout: —
Market value ($ mil.): —

IRA HIGDON GROCERY COMPANY

LOCATIONS

HQ: IRA HIGDON GROCERY COMPANY
150 IGA WAY NE, CAIRO, GA 39828
Phone: 229-377-1272
Web: www.irahigdongc.com

HISTORICAL FINANCIALS
Company Type: Private

Income Statement
FYE: December 31

	REVENUE ($ mil.)	NET INCOME ($ mil.)	NET PROFIT MARGIN	EMPLOYEES
12/11	100	2	2.3%	100
12/10	106	3	2.8%	0
12/09	113	2	2.4%	0
12/08	106	3	2.9%	0
Annual Growth	(1.8%)	(8.8%)	—	—

2011 Year-End Financials

Debt ratio: —
Return on equity: 2.30%
Cash ($ mil.): 5
Current ratio: 3.10
Long-term debt ($ mil.): —

Dividends
　Yield: —
　Payout: —
Market value ($ mil.): —

IREDELL-STATESVILLE SCHOOLS

LOCATIONS

HQ: IREDELL-STATESVILLE SCHOOLS
549 N RACE ST, STATESVILLE, NC 28677-3915
Phone: 704-924-2000

HISTORICAL FINANCIALS
Company Type: Private

Income Statement
FYE: June 30

	REVENUE ($ mil.)	NET INCOME ($ mil.)	NET PROFIT MARGIN	EMPLOYEES
06/12*	165	4	2.5%	3,300
12/05	0	0	14.4%	0
06/04	122	(0)	—	0
06/03	114	4	3.8%	0
Annual Growth	13.0%	(1.3%)	—	—

*Fiscal year change

2012 Year-End Financials

Debt ratio: ——
Return on equity: 2.50%
Cash ($ mil.): 18
Current ratio: ——
Long-term debt ($ mil.): ——

Dividends
Yield: —
Payout: —
Market value ($ mil.): —

ISEC INCORPORATED

LOCATIONS

HQ: ISEC INCORPORATED
33 INVERNESS DR E, ENGLEWOOD, CO 80112-5412
Phone: 303-790-1444
Web: www.isecinc.com

HISTORICAL FINANCIALS
Company Type: Private

Income Statement
FYE: June 30

	REVENUE ($ mil.)	NET INCOME ($ mil.)	NET PROFIT MARGIN	EMPLOYEES
06/12	211	2	1.0%	1,150
06/11	252	2	0.9%	0
06/10	263	3	1.1%	0
06/09	278	4	1.5%	0
Annual Growth	(8.7%)	(19.6%)	—	—

2012 Year-End Financials

Debt ratio: ——
Return on equity: 1.00%
Cash ($ mil.): 18
Current ratio: 1.50
Long-term debt ($ mil.): ——

Dividends
Yield: —
Payout: —
Market value ($ mil.): —

ITA GROUP INC

ITA Group (doing business as ITAGroup) bets it can make your company better. Specializing in performance marketing ITAGroup (standing for "Ideas to Action") builds and manages programs that help clients increase sales and customer satisfaction through incentives and training. The company's services include research and program design administration fulfillment and measurement for employee recognition and rewards programs business-to-business loyalty programs and sales incentive programs. ITAGroup also provides business meeting and event planning services. It was founded in 1963 and has a dozen sales offices located across the US.

EXECUTIVES

Chairman, Steven G. Chapman, age 60
Jr. President Chief Executive Officer, Thomas J. Mahoney Jr.
President and CEO, Tom Mahoney
Senior Vice President Chief Financial Officer, Richard Rue
Vice President Controller, Brent VanderWaal
Senior Vice President - Sales, Doug Stine
Vice President Chief Information Officer, John Rose
Senior Vice President Event Management, Mary Z. Bussone

LOCATIONS

HQ: ITA Group Inc.
4800 Westown Pkwy. Ste. 300, West Des Moines IA 50266-6700
Phone: 515-326-3400   **Fax:** 972-852-9074
Web: www.cbapex.com

COMPETITORS

All Star Incentive Marketing
Alliance Data Systems
Korman Marketing Group
LoyaltyOne
Loyaltyworks
Maritz Loyalty & Motivation
Marketing Innovators
Motivcom
Pitney Bowes Marketing Solutions
Points International
Schoeneckers
TharpeRobbins

HISTORICAL FINANCIALS
Company Type: Private

Income Statement
FYE: August 31

	REVENUE ($ mil.)	NET INCOME ($ mil.)	NET PROFIT MARGIN	EMPLOYEES
08/11	233	0	—	500
08/10	0	0	—	0
08/09	0	0	—	0
08/08	0	0	—	0
Annual Growth	—	—	—	—

2011 Year-End Financials

Debt ratio: ——
Return on equity: —
Cash ($ mil.): 49
Current ratio: 1.10
Long-term debt ($ mil.): ——

Dividends
Yield: —
Payout: —
Market value ($ mil.): —

ITI TROPICALS INC.

ITI Tropicals packs a lot of fruity flavor into not very itty-bitty packages. The company imports tropical fruit purees concentrates waters essences and other products focusing on banana coconut guava mango papaya and passion fruit. It also carries more exotic fruits such as mangosteen moraberry acerola lulo tamarind and guanabana. ITI distributes its products which come in frozen or aseptic packaging and range in size from 5-gallon pails to 220-gallon drums to food manufacturers throughout the US. Founded in 1988 ITI Tropicals is owned by president Gert Van Manen.

EXECUTIVES

President, Gert Van Manen
VP, Don Giampeitro
National Sales Manager, John Salzano
Manager Operations, Pete Coiante
Senior Research and Development Technologist, Tony Cantu
Accounting, Irina Belovsky

LOCATIONS

HQ: ITI TROPICALS INC.
30 GORDON AVE, LAWRENCEVILLE, NJ 08648-1033
Phone: 609-987-0550
Web: www.thetropicalsource.com

COMPETITORS

Al-Rite Fruits and Syrups
Del Monte Foods
Encore Fruit Marketing
Hayward Enterprises Inc.
Kendall Frozen Fruits national fruit flavor company
Sabroso

HISTORICAL FINANCIALS
Company Type: Private

Income Statement
FYE: December 5

	REVENUE ($ mil.)	NET INCOME ($ mil.)	NET PROFIT MARGIN	EMPLOYEES
12/11	37	0	—	16
12/09	35	0	1.9%	0
12/07	31	0	—	0
12/06	28	0	—	0
Annual Growth	9.3%	—	—	—

2011 Year-End Financials

Debt ratio: ——
Return on equity: —
Cash ($ mil.): 0
Current ratio: 0.40
Long-term debt ($ mil.): ——

Dividends
Yield: —
Payout: —
Market value ($ mil.): —

IVCI LLC

IVCi screens its calls. The company resells and installs cameras video servers speaker phones and other equipment used for video audio and Web conferences. It supplies and supports equipment made by such industry leaders as Cisco and Polycom. In addition to installation IVCi's Audio/Visual Division offers conference room design consulting project management on-site technical assistance maintenance and training services. Its private video communications network enables 24-hour access to a secure managed conferencing environment. Customers range from the education to health care industries as well as from the legal and federal and state government industries. IVCi was founded in 1995 by president Robert Swing.

The CTS (custom telepresence solutions) unit designs installs and supports customized telepresence rooms for corporate clients as well as government agencies and educational institutions. Applications for these customer premises-located audio visual conferencing facilities include training and remote meetings.

While privately-owned IVCi doesn't report its financial results the company rang up an estimated $80 million revenues in fiscal 2011 (ends December) up from some $75 million in 2010.

In order to target the $2 trillion dollar health care industry in 2012 the company created and introduced a cloud-based video service that allows the doctor and patient to communicate in real-time over its private cloud network. As part of the cloud-based video service products and services can be utilized between such platforms like Cisco Google Talk Microsoft Lync Polycom and Skype.

EXECUTIVES

CEO, Robert (Bob) Swing
President, Charles Macli
SVP Managed Conferencing Services, Chris Bottger
VP Human Resources, Andrea Conzo
SVP Audio Visual Integrated Services, Tim Hennen
VP Purchasing and Order Management, Karen Cantalupo
VP Engineering and Technology Management, Tom E. Nyhus
SVP Business Operations, Curtis Heath
VP Audio Visual Integration Services, Cliff Frankenberger
VP Strategic Accounts, Brett Busch
VP Sales and Service, David Lemperle
VP Sales South Central Region, Paul Fragalle
VP Sales Northeastern Region, Tom Bottini

LOCATIONS

HQ: IVCi LLC
601 Old Willets Path, Hauppauge NY 11788
Phone: 631-273-5800   **Fax:** 631-273-7277
Web: www.ivci.com

COMPETITORS

ACT Teleconferencing	ClearOne
AT Conference	Eagle Teleconferencing
AVI Systems	Expedite
AVI-SPL	Glowpoint
BT Conferencing	Interactive Solutions
Cisco WebEx	ViewCast.com

HISTORICAL FINANCIALS
Company Type: Private

Income Statement

	REVENUE ($ mil.)	NET INCOME ($ mil.)	NET PROFIT MARGIN	EMPLOYEES
12/11	76	3	4.9%	180
12/10	74	2	3.3%	0
12/09	63	1	2.4%	0
12/08	66	2	3.6%	0
Annual Growth	5.2%	16.8%	—	—

2011 Year-End Financials

Debt ratio: —
Return on equity: 4.90%
Cash ($ mil.): 2
Current ratio: 1.10
Long-term debt ($ mil.): —

Dividends
Yield: —
Payout: —
Market value ($ mil.): —

IVIE & ASSOCIATES INC.

LOCATIONS

HQ: IVIE & ASSOCIATES INC.
601 SILVERON STE 200, FLOWER MOUND, TX 75028-4030
Phone: 972-899-5000
Web: www.ivieinc.com

HISTORICAL FINANCIALS
Company Type: Private

Income Statement

	REVENUE ($ mil.)	NET INCOME ($ mil.)	NET PROFIT MARGIN	EMPLOYEES
12/11	171	0	—	225
12/09	0	0	—	0
12/08	171	0	—	0
12/06	111	0	—	0
Annual Growth	15.3%	—	—	—

2011 Year-End Financials

Debt ratio: —
Return on equity: —
Cash ($ mil.): 8
Current ratio: 1.00
Long-term debt ($ mil.): —

Dividends
Yield: —
Payout: —
Market value ($ mil.): —

J C BLAIR MEMORIAL HOSPITAL

J. C. Blair Memorial Hospital serves Huntingdon County in central Pennsylvania. With more than 100 beds the community hospital has about 40 physicians on staff representing a variety of specialties including cancer care pediatrics cardiology and orthopedics. J. C. Blair also offers patients a range of hospital services including emergency behavioral health diagnostic birthing and surgical care as well as ambulatory outpatient services. The hospital was established in 1911 by Kate Fisher Blair in memory of her husband John Chalmers Blair.

EXECUTIVES

VP Human Relations, Michael F. Hubert
Director Marketing and Public Relations, Christine Gildea
President and CEO, Joseph J. Peluso
VP Finance and CFO, Nancy W. Glidden
VP Quality Improvement, Marlene Pierce
VP Patient Care and Chief Nursing Officer, Pamela Matthias

Director Management Information System, Steve Gildea
Director Patient Financial Services, Sandie Mitchell
Director Engineering, Timothy Davis

LOCATIONS

HQ: J C BLAIR MEMORIAL HOSPITAL
1225 WARM SPRINGS AVE, HUNTINGDON, PA 16652-2398
Phone: 814-643-2290
Web: www.jcblair.org

COMPETITORS

Altoona Regional	Guthrie Healthcare
Ascension Health	Hershey Medical Center
Geisinger Health System	Lewistown Hospital
	PinnacleHealth System

HISTORICAL FINANCIALS
Company Type: Private - Not-for-Profit

Income Statement
FYE: June 30

	REVENUE ($ mil.)	NET INCOME ($ mil.)	NET PROFIT MARGIN	EMPLOYEES
06/11	44	(1)	—	479
06/10	41	0	1.1%	0
06/09	34	(1)	—	0
06/08	38	(0)	—	0
Annual Growth	4.3%	—	—	—

2011 Year-End Financials

Debt ratio: —
Return on equity: (-4.20)%
Cash ($ mil.): 0
Current ratio: 0.90
Long-term debt ($ mil.): —

Dividends
Yield: —
Payout: —
Market value ($ mil.): —

J. D. STREETT & COMPANY INC.

Word on the street is that J. D. Streett tries to stay streets ahead of its rivals as it supplies its customers with a wide range of fuels oxygenates lubricants transmission fluids and antifreezes. The company operates more than 20 retail locations (convenience stores and gas stations) under its own ZX label and/or BP brand in Missouri and Illinois. J. D. Streett also serves more than 10 international markets. In addition the company offers terminalling services for distillate ethanol and oil products and owns and operates a chain of discount cigarette shops (most that also sell beer) across Missouri.

Its seven-acre petroleum terminal complex in St. Louis has a total capacity or more than of 485000 barrels and is capable of handling more than 25000 barrels a day. It also has a 252000 barrel terminal in Lemay Missouri. The terminals are centrally located and easily accessible by highway river rail and pipeline enabling the company to control costs.

J. D. Streett has a long track record of keeping the wheels of vehicles turning. It was formed in 1884 to make grease for wagon wheels.

EXECUTIVES

Chairman, Newell A. Baker Sr.
President and CEO, Newell A. Baker Jr.
CFO Treasurer and Controller, Jim Schuering
Export Sales Manager, Stewart Dahlberg
Auditors: BKDLLP

LOCATIONS

HQ: J.D. Streett & Company Inc.
144 Weldon Pkwy., Maryland Heights MO 63043
Phone: 314-432-6600 **Fax:** 314-432-4248
Web: www.jdstreett.com

COMPETITORS

BP Lubricants USA
Fuchs Lubricants
Lubrizol

PetroLiance
U.S. Venture
Vesco Oil

HISTORICAL FINANCIALS

Company Type: Private

Income Statement

FYE: December 31

	REVENUE ($ mil.)	NET INCOME ($ mil.)	NET PROFIT MARGIN	EMPLOYEES
12/11	366	3	0.8%	340
12/10	313	3	1.0%	0
12/09	270	6	2.5%	0
12/08	448	5	1.2%	0
Annual Growth	(6.5%)	(17.0%)	—	—

2011 Year-End Financials

Debt ratio: —
Return on equity: 0.80%
Cash ($ mil.): 1
Current ratio: 0.90
Long-term debt ($ mil.): —

Dividends
Yield: —
Payout: —
Market value ($ mil.): —

VP Operations, Mike Dillis
VP Administration, Tim Stadelman
Auditors: McGladreyLLP

LOCATIONS

HQ: J.H. Findorff & Son Inc.
300 S. Bedford St., Madison WI 53703
Phone: 608-257-5321 **Fax:** 608-257-5306
Web: www.findorff.com

COMPETITORS

Boldt
C. G. Schmidt
C.D. Smith
Hunt Construction
Hunzinger Construction

Market & Johnson
Miron Construction
Walsh Group
Weis Builders

HISTORICAL FINANCIALS

Company Type: Private

Income Statement

FYE: September 30

	REVENUE ($ mil.)	NET INCOME ($ mil.)	NET PROFIT MARGIN	EMPLOYEES
09/11	209	0	0.1%	500
09/08	322	3	1.2%	0
09/06	248	5	2.1%	0
09/05	1,092	0	0.0%	0
Annual Growth	(42.4%)	1473.2%	—	—

2011 Year-End Financials

Debt ratio: —
Return on equity: 0.10%
Cash ($ mil.): 49
Current ratio: 1.20
Long-term debt ($ mil.): —

Dividends
Yield: —
Payout: —
Market value ($ mil.): —

EXECUTIVES

EVP and CFO, Gordon E. Lansford III
President and CEO, Terrence P. (Terry) Dunn
Chairman, Stephen D. (Steve) Dunn
EVP Operations, James R. (Jim) Miller
EVP, Bernard Jacquinot
Chairman Emeritus, William H. (Bill) Dunn Sr.
Corporate Communications Specialist, Danna Guffey
President and CEO, Daniel A. (Dan) Euston

LOCATIONS

HQ: J.E. Dunn Construction Company
1001 Locust St., Kansas City MO 64106
Phone: 816-474-8600 **Fax:** 816-391-2510
Web: www.jedunn.com

COMPETITORS

Adolfson & Peterson Inc.
Barnhart
Boran Craig Barber Engel
C.F. Jordan
Clarkson Construction
CORE Construction
Flintco

H.J. Russell
Hensel Phelps Construction
Korte
M. A. Mortenson
MEDCO Construction
Skanska USA Building
The Weitz Company LLC
Turner Corporation

HISTORICAL FINANCIALS

Company Type: Subsidiary

Income Statement

FYE: December 31

	REVENUE ($ mil.)	NET INCOME ($ mil.)	NET PROFIT MARGIN	EMPLOYEES
12/11	1,937	16	0.8%	1,635
12/10	1,931	0	—	0
12/09	1,829	0	—	0
12/08	1,313	0	—	0
Annual Growth	13.8%	—	—	—

2011 Year-End Financials

Debt ratio: —
Return on equity: 0.80%
Cash ($ mil.): 39
Current ratio: 0.90
Long-term debt ($ mil.): —

Dividends
Yield: —
Payout: —
Market value ($ mil.): —

J. H. FINDORFF & SON INC.

J.H. Findorff & Son has been building its resume since the 19th century. The company constructs commercial and institutional projects in the US Midwest. It provides general contracting design/build and construction management services. Projects include schools government buildings health care centers hotels condos offices and shopping complexes. Findorff also self-performs trade work including carpentry concrete masonry drywall and steel erection. Among its projects is Madison Wisconsin's Overture Center for the Arts. It also is building the Wisconsin Institutes for Discovery at The University of Wisconsin-Madison. John Findorff founded the company as J.H. Findorff in 1890.

In 1917 Milton Findorff joined his father and the company J. H. Findorff & Son became Madison's first general contractor. The company is now owned by directors and employees.

EXECUTIVES

Chairman, Curt Hastings
President, Richard M. (Rich) Lynch
VP Finance and CFO, Daniel L. (Dan) Petersen
EVP, Dave Beck-Engel

J.E. DUNN CONSTRUCTION COMPANY

J. E. Dunn Construction can help you make your building plans a done deal. Operating as JE Dunn the contractor offers general construction services construction management and design/build services throughout the US. JE Dunn works on projects in sectors including multifamily residential office and health care. Its portfolio of projects includes the Mizzou Arena at the University of Missouri the H&R Block world headquarters and the new National Nuclear Security Administration campus. JE Dunn is Kansas City's top commercial construction firm and one of the nation's top 10 general building companies. John Dunn founded the company which is still family-owned as a residential contractor in 1924.

The company has grown through acquisitions including the purchases of RJ Griffin & Co. (Atlanta) Witcher Construction (Minneapolis) and Drake Construction (Portland Oregon). RJ Griffin continues to operate under that name and serves the southeast US. JE Dunn has nearly 20 offices throughout the US and brings in more than $2 billion in revenue each year.

J.E. KINGHAM CONSTRUCTION COMPANY LTD.

LOCATIONS

HQ: J.E. KINGHAM CONSTRUCTION COMPANY LTD.
312 OLD TYLER RD, NACOGDOCHES, TX 75961-4879
Phone: 936-564-3329
Web: www.jekingham.com

HISTORICAL FINANCIALS
Company Type: Private

Income Statement
FYE: December 31

	REVENUE ($ mil.)	NET INCOME ($ mil.)	NET PROFIT MARGIN	EMPLOYEES
12/11	134	7	5.4%	80
12/10	187	8	4.3%	0
12/09	131	7	5.8%	0
12/08	108	6	6.1%	0
Annual Growth	7.3%	2.8%	—	—

2011 Year-End Financials
Debt ratio: ——
Return on equity: 5.40%
Cash ($ mil.): 14
Current ratio: 1.30
Long-term debt ($ mil.): —

Dividends
Yield: —
Payout: —
Market value ($ mil.): —

J.F. ELECTRIC INCORPORATED

LOCATIONS
HQ: J.F. ELECTRIC INCORPORATED
100 LAKE FRONT PKWY, EDWARDSVILLE, IL
62025-2900
Phone: 618-797-5353
Web: www.jfelectric.com

HISTORICAL FINANCIALS
Company Type: Private

Income Statement
FYE: June 30

	REVENUE ($ mil.)	NET INCOME ($ mil.)	NET PROFIT MARGIN	EMPLOYEES
06/11	88	0	—	550
06/08	89	0	—	0
06/07	53	3	5.7%	0
06/06	1,206	0	—	0
Annual Growth	—	—	—	—

2011 Year-End Financials
Debt ratio: ——
Return on equity: —
Cash ($ mil.): 2
Current ratio: 2.30
Long-term debt ($ mil.): —

Dividends
Yield: —
Payout: —
Market value ($ mil.): —

JAC. VANDENBERG INC.

LOCATIONS
HQ: JAC. VANDENBERG INC.
100 CORPORATE DR, YONKERS, NY 10701-6807
Phone: 914-964-5900

HISTORICAL FINANCIALS
Company Type: Private

Income Statement
FYE: December 31

	REVENUE ($ mil.)	NET INCOME ($ mil.)	NET PROFIT MARGIN	EMPLOYEES
12/11	168	3	2.1%	30
12/10	164	3	2.2%	0
12/09	138	2	1.8%	0
12/08	145	1	1.2%	0
Annual Growth	5.0%	26.4%	—	—

2011 Year-End Financials
Debt ratio: ——
Return on equity: 2.10%
Cash ($ mil.): 5
Current ratio: 0.70
Long-term debt ($ mil.): —

Dividends
Yield: —
Payout: —
Market value ($ mil.): —

JACKSON ENERGY AUTHORITY

Jackson Energy Authority has the power and the authority to provide for all of Jackson Tennessee's energy needs. The municipal utility distributes electricity natural gas and water and provides wastewater services to about 40000 residential commercial and industrial customers in Jackson and surrounding areas. Jackson Energy also sells propane and offers broadband telecommunications services (cable Internet and telephone). Other services provided by Jackson Energy Authority include the sale of outdoor security lights surge protection systems gas grills and decorative lights.

As part of its strategy to reduce carbon emission conserve energy and help its customers cut costs Jackson Energy Authority's Wise Energy program provides practical energy saving advice to gas power and water users.

The company was formed by the City of Jackson in 1959 to combine its three separate utilities (natural gas electricity and water/wastewater) under one utility operation. A five-member Board of Directors appointed by the Mayor and City Council of Jackson governs Jackson Energy Authority.

EXECUTIVES
President and CEO, Danny Wheeler
VP Engineering, George Flew
VP Corporate Relations, Kyle Spurgeon
VP Human Resources, Ann Lewis
SVP Gas Division, Charlie Crockarell
SVP Telecommunications, Kim Kersey
SVP Electric Division, Tommy Nanney
SVP Wastewater Division, Truman Murray
SVP and COO, Jim Watson

General Counsel, Teresa Cobb
Corporate Secretary, Vicky Wright
VP Distribution, David Middlebrooks
SVP Gas Division, Randy Nipp
SVP Water and Wastewater Division, Steve Raper
VP Internal Control, Mechele Williams
VP Information Technology, Michael Johnston
Chair, Ken Marston Sr.
Vice Chair, Howard Bond
SVP and CFO, Nancy Nanney
VP Operations, Jim Ferrell
VP Customer Service, Rowland Fisher
Director, Bob Campbell
Vice Chair, Howard Bond

LOCATIONS
HQ: Jackson Energy Authority
119 E. College St., Jackson TN 38301
Phone: 731-422-7500   **Fax:** 731-422-7307
Web: www.jaxenergy.com

HISTORICAL FINANCIALS
Company Type: Government-owned

Income Statement
FYE: December 31

	REVENUE ($ mil.)	NET INCOME ($ mil.)	NET PROFIT MARGIN	EMPLOYEES
12/11*	243	22	9.4%	425
06/10	218	10	5.0%	0
06/09	237	4	1.8%	0
06/08	210	9	4.4%	0
Annual Growth	4.9%	35.2%	—	—

*Fiscal year change

2011 Year-End Financials
Debt ratio: ——
Return on equity: 9.40%
Cash ($ mil.): 49
Current ratio: 2.20
Long-term debt ($ mil.): —

Dividends
Yield: —
Payout: —
Market value ($ mil.): —

JACKSON PARK HOSPITAL FOUNDATION

LOCATIONS
HQ: JACKSON PARK HOSPITAL FOUNDATION
7531 S STONY ISLAND AVE # 1, CHICAGO, IL
60649-3954
Phone: 773-947-7500
Web: www.jacksonparkhospital.com

HISTORICAL FINANCIALS
Company Type: Private

Income Statement
FYE: March 31

	REVENUE ($ mil.)	NET INCOME ($ mil.)	NET PROFIT MARGIN	EMPLOYEES
03/11	128	10	7.8%	700
03/10	117	9	7.8%	0
03/09	117	12	10.6%	0
03/08	105	10	9.7%	0
Annual Growth	6.7%	(0.6%)	—	—

2011 Year-End Financials

Debt ratio: —
Return on equity: 7.80%
Cash ($ mil.): 11
Current ratio: 3.20
Long-term debt ($ mil.): —

Dividends
Yield: —
Payout: —
Market value ($ mil.): —

2011 Year-End Financials

Debt ratio: —
Return on equity: 0.20%
Cash ($ mil.): 2
Current ratio: —
Long-term debt ($ mil.): —

Dividends
Yield: —
Payout: —
Market value ($ mil.): —

JACKSONVILLE UNIVERSITY

If you think you don't know jack you might want to head to Jacksonville University. The private university offers about 70 majors and a handful of graduate programs. Jacksonville University has roughly 3400 students and is comprised of the Colleges of Arts & Sciences Business and Fine Arts. Its Adult Degree Program designed for adults to complete a bachelor's degree without putting their career or family on hold offers degrees in business and social sciences. The school was founded in 1934 as a two year community college. Jacksonville Junior College expand to a four year program when it became Jacksonville University in 1956.

EXECUTIVES

VP Student Life, John A. Balog
President, Kerry Romesburg
Athletic Director, C. Alan Verlander Jr.
Manager Accounting, Ralph C. Morris
Executive Director Budgets and Business Operations, Ellen M. Paige
Director Financial Aid, Catherine N. Huntress
Director Human Resources, James V. William Jr.
VP Institutional Advancement, Grady B. Jones
Director Purchasing, Michael J. Bobbin
Registrar, Carolyn A. Barrett
VP Information Technology and CIO, Thomas Hall

LOCATIONS

HQ: Jacksonville University
2800 University Blvd. North, Jacksonville FL 32211
Phone: 904-256-8000   **Fax:** 810-762-9837
Web: www.kettering.edu

COMPETITORS

Bethune-Cookman University	Rollins College
Florida A&M University	Stetson University
Florida State University	University of Florida
	University of Miami
	University of North Florida

HISTORICAL FINANCIALS

Company Type: School

Income Statement

FYE: June 30

	REVENUE ($ mil.)	NET INCOME ($ mil.)	NET PROFIT MARGIN	EMPLOYEES
06/11	104	0	0.2%	450
06/10	96	2	2.1%	0
06/09	78	0	—	0
06/08	75	(9)	—	0
Annual Growth	11.4%			

JACO OIL COMPANY

Jaco Oil Company is jockeying for its piece of the convenience store pie. The company's Fastrip Food Stores subsidiary operates about 35 convenience stores and gas stations primarily in and around Bakersfield California but also in Arizona. The Fastrip chain offers in-store financial service centers which provide check cashing payday loans wire transfer services via The Western Union Company and other services at many locations. Jaco Oil Company was founded in 1970.

EXECUTIVES

President and CEO, Thomas J. Jamieson
CFO, Brian Busacca
VP, Charles McCan
President Real Estate Division, Lee Jamieson
Human Resources Manager, Alissa Thome

LOCATIONS

HQ: Jaco Oil Company
3101 State Rd., Bakersfield CA 93308
Phone: 661-393-7000   **Fax:** 661-393-8738
Web: www.fastrip.com

2008 Stores

	No.
California	30
Arizona	4
Total	**34**

COMPETITORS

7-Eleven	Ralphs Grocery
Chevron	Stater Bros.
Couche-Tard	Vons
Exxon Mobil	

HISTORICAL FINANCIALS

Company Type: Private

Income Statement

FYE: December 31

	REVENUE ($ mil.)	NET INCOME ($ mil.)	NET PROFIT MARGIN	EMPLOYEES
12/11	794	20	2.6%	350
12/10	644	10	1.6%	0
12/08	517	7	1.5%	0
12/07	323	(0)	—	0
Annual Growth	35.0%	—	—	—

2011 Year-End Financials

Debt ratio: —
Return on equity: 2.60%
Cash ($ mil.): 41
Current ratio: 1.80
Long-term debt ($ mil.): —

Dividends
Yield: —
Payout: —
Market value ($ mil.): —

JAMES MADISON UNIVERSITY INC.

James Madison is known as the Father of the Constitution and America's fourth president but he also has a public institution of higher education named after him. James Madison University (JMU) offers some 70 undergraduate and 40 graduate degrees through more than a half-dozen colleges including arts and letters business education visual and performing arts and science and mathematics. The university enrolls about 20000 students mostly undergrads with a faculty of 1200 teachers and a student-to-faculty ratio of 16:1. JMU also has extensive men's and women's athletic programs. JMU was established in 1908 in Harrisonburg Virginia.

Geographic Reach

James Madison University is located on on a 470-acre campus in Harrisonburg located in the Shenandoah Valley of Virginia. Altogether the university operates more than 112 building on 720 acres. More than 70% of its students are residents of Virginia while the rest pay out-of-state tuition fees.

Strategy

In 2012 James Madison University increased the number of colleges from seven to eight (including the graduate school) when it broke up its College of Integrated Science and Technology into two new schools. The new College of Health and Behavioral Studies includes the psychology health sciences nursing social work and communication disorders programs while the College of Integrated Science and Engineering includes computer science integrated science and technology engineering programs. The move helps the university meet the growing need for education programs for health and human behavior professionals.

EXECUTIVES

President, Linwood H. Rose
Provost and VP Academic Affairs, Douglas T. Brown
SVP Administration and Finance, Charles W. King Jr.
SVP Student Affairs and University Planning, Mark Warner
SVP University Advancement, Joanne Carr
Dean College of Education, Phillip M. Wishon
Dean College of Science and Mathematics, David F. Brakke
Dean University Studies, Linda Cabe Halpern
Dean Libraries and Educational Technologies, Ralph A. Alberico
Dean College of Business, Robert D. Reid
Director Athletics, Jeffrey T. Bourne
Rector Board of Visitors, Meredith Strohm Gunter
Secretary and Member Board of Visitors, Donna L. Harper
Vice Rector Board of Visitors, James E. (Jim) Hartman
Dean The Graduate School, Reid Linn
Dean College of Arts and Letters, David K. Jeffrey
Speaker Faculty Senate and Faculty Representative to Board of Visitors, Steven Garren
Dean College of Integrated Science and Technology, Sharon Lovell
Dean College of Visual and Performing Arts, George E. Sparks
Director Public Affairs and University Spokesman, Don Egle
Media Relations Manager, Bill Wyatt

Community Affairs Manager, Rachael Walters
Member Board of Visitors, Charles H. (Charlie) Foster Jr., age 69
Member Board of Visitors, Stephen R. Leeolou, age 52
Member Board of Visitors, Fred Thompson
Member Board of Visitors, Joseph F. Damico, age 58
Rector Board of Visitors, Meredith Strohm Gunter
Secretary and Member Board of Visitors, Donna L. Harper
Member Board of Visitors, Mark T. Bowles
Vice Rector Board of Visitors, James E. (Jim) Hartman
Member Board of Visitors, Wharton B. (Zie) Rivers Jr., age 63
Member Board of Visitors, Larry M. Rogers
Member Board of Visitors, Judith (Judy) Strickler
Speaker Faculty Senate and Faculty Representative to Board of Visitors, Steven Garren
Member Board of Visitors, Robert Cellucci
Member Board of Visitors, Elizabeth V. Lodal
Member Board of Visitors, Joseph K. Funkhouser II
Member Board of Visitors, Lois Forbes
Member Board of Visitors, Vanessa M. Evans
Member Board of Visitors, Ronald C. Devine

LOCATIONS

HQ: James Madison University
800 S. Main St., Harrisonburg VA 22807
Phone: 540-568-6211   Fax: 540-568-3634
Web: www.jmu.edu

PRODUCTS/OPERATIONS

Selected Schools

College of Arts and Letters
College of Business
College of Education
College of Health and Behavioral Studies
College of Integrated Science and Engineering
College of Science and Mathematics
College of Visual and Performing Arts
The Graduate School

Selected Degrees

Bachelor of Arts (BA)
Bachelor of Science (BS)
Bachelor of Music Education (BMEd)
Bachelor of Business Administration (BBA)
Bachelor of General Studies (BGS)
Bachelor of Music (BM)
Bachelor of Social Work (BSW)
Bachelor of Science in Nursing (BSN)
Doctor of Psychology (PsyD)
Master of Arts (MA)
Master of Fine Arts (MFA)
Master of Science (MS)
Master of Business Administration (MBA)
Master of Science in Education (MSEd)
Master of Arts in Teaching (MAT)
Master of Education (MEd)
Master of Music (MM)
Master of Public Administration (MPA)
Educational Specialist (EdS)
Doctor of Audiology (AUD)
Doctor of Philosophy (PhD)
Doctor of Musical Arts (DMA)
Master o Science in Nursing (MSN)
Master of Occupational Therapy (MOT)
Master of Physician Assistant Studies (MPAS)

HISTORICAL FINANCIALS

Company Type: School

Income Statement

FYE: June 30

	REVENUE ($ mil.)	NET INCOME ($ mil.)	NET PROFIT MARGIN	EMPLOYEES
06/11	323	56	17.5%	1,700
06/08	270	69	25.6%	0
06/07	248	78	31.5%	0
06/06	1,980	0	—	0
Annual Growth	(45.3%)	—	—	—

2011 Year-End Financials

Debt ratio: ——
Return on equity: 17.50%
Cash ($ mil.): 117
Current ratio: 1.50
Long-term debt ($ mil.): —

Dividends
Yield: —
Payout: —
Market value ($ mil.): —

JAMESON MEMORIAL HOSPITAL

LOCATIONS

HQ: JAMESON MEMORIAL HOSPITAL
1211 WILMINGTON AVE, NEW CASTLE, PA 16105-2595
Phone: 724-658-9001
Web: www.jamesonhealth.org

HISTORICAL FINANCIALS

Company Type: Private

Income Statement

FYE: June 30

	REVENUE ($ mil.)	NET INCOME ($ mil.)	NET PROFIT MARGIN	EMPLOYEES
06/11	109	4	4.1%	1,063
06/10	111	(0)	—	0
06/09	111	(6)	—	0
06/08	111	(6)	—	0
Annual Growth	(0.5%)	—	—	—

2011 Year-End Financials

Debt ratio: ——
Return on equity: 4.10%
Cash ($ mil.): 5
Current ratio: 1.40
Long-term debt ($ mil.): —

Dividends
Yield: —
Payout: —
Market value ($ mil.): —

JAMIESON-HILL A GENERAL PARTNERSHIP

LOCATIONS

HQ: JAMIESON-HILL A GENERAL PARTNERSHIP
3101 STATE RD, BAKERSFIELD, CA 93308-4931
Phone: 661-393-7000

HISTORICAL FINANCIALS

Company Type: Private

Income Statement

FYE: December 31

	REVENUE ($ mil.)	NET INCOME ($ mil.)	NET PROFIT MARGIN	EMPLOYEES
12/11	197	4	2.0%	50
12/08	171	3	2.2%	0
12/07	145	(0)	—	0
12/06	123	1	1.2%	0
Annual Growth	16.9%	38.1%	—	—

2011 Year-End Financials

Debt ratio: ——
Return on equity: 2.00%
Cash ($ mil.): 3
Current ratio: 6.30
Long-term debt ($ mil.): —

Dividends
Yield: —
Payout: —
Market value ($ mil.): —

JEFFERSON HOSPITAL ASSOCIATION INC.

Jefferson Regional Medical Center (JRMC) provides acute care and other health services to residents of Pine Bluff and an 11-county area of southern Arkansas. The not-for-profit community-owned hospital has about 470 acute care beds and offers general medical and surgical care as well as services in a range of specialties including urology orthopedics cardiology and oncology. It also has a 25-bed skilled nursing unit that cares for patients transitioning to long-term care or home care. A network of clinics offers outpatient surgery diagnostic imaging wound care and other ambulatory health services. Additionally the health system operates a nursing school and home health and hospice agencies.

To bring its operations up to speed with modern technology requirements in the health care industry JRMC has implemented an electronic health record (EHR) system and is employing that system to comply with meaningful use guidelines from the US government. In fact JRMC was a frontrunner in the movement to bring medical records online first moving to install EHR systems in 2003.

The hospital also expanded its services for the southern Arkansas region by becoming certified as a Level II trauma center in 2010. JRMC has also expanded and upgraded its wellness centers to serve the exercise needs of the community.

EXECUTIVES

President CEO and Director, Robert P. (Bob) Atkinson

EVP, Tomas (Tom) Harbuck

SVP and COO, Walter Johnson

Director Marketing and Community Outreach, Julie Bridgforth

VP Patient Care Services, Louise Hickman

VP and CFO, Nathan Van Genderen

Administrative Director Human Resources, Daryl Scott

Chairman, Jerrel Boast

Vice Chairman, Chuck Morgan

Secretary, David Brown

Chief of Staff and Director, Omar Attiq

Manager Marketing and Community Outreach, Rebecca Pittillo

Director Nursing Administration, Rebekah Davis

Director Nursing Administration, Rosemary K. Taliaferro

President CEO and Director, Robert P. (Bob) Atkinson

Director, Marty D. Casteel, age 60

Vice Chairman, Chuck Morgan

Director, Frank Anthony

Director, Drew Atkinson

Director, James A. Campbell Jr.

Director, Ed Copeland

Director, Lee A. Forestiere

Chief of Staff and Director, Omar Attiq

Director, Annette Kline

Director, Joe Ratliff

Director, Clifton Roaf

Director, George Roberson

LOCATIONS

HQ: Jefferson Regional Medical Center
1600 W. 40th Ave., Pine Bluff AR 71603
Phone: 870-541-7100   **Fax:** 870-541-7204
Web: www.jrmc.org

COMPETITORS

Arkansas Heart Hospital
Baptist Health (Arkansas)
Conway Regional Health System
Medical Park Hospital
Sparks Health System
St. Vincent Health System
University of Arkansas
Weirton Medical Center
White County Medical Center

HISTORICAL FINANCIALS

Company Type: Private - Not-for-Profit

Income Statement
FYE: June 30

	REVENUE ($ mil.)	NET INCOME ($ mil.)	NET PROFIT MARGIN	EMPLOYEES
06/11	190	11	6.0%	1,800
06/10	198	11	5.6%	0
06/09	5	(4)	—	0
06/07	177	4	2.7%	0
Annual Growth	2.5%	34.0%	—	—

2011 Year-End Financials

Debt ratio: ——
Return on equity: 6.00%
Cash ($ mil.): 60
Current ratio: 2.50
Long-term debt ($ mil.): —

Dividends
 Yield: —
 Payout: —
 Market value ($ mil.): —

JEFFERSON UNIVERSITY PHYSICIANS

LOCATIONS

HQ: JEFFERSON UNIVERSITY PHYSICIANS
1020 WALNUT ST, PHILADELPHIA, PA 19107-5543
Phone: 215-955-6000
Web: www.jefferson.edu

HISTORICAL FINANCIALS

Company Type: Private

Income Statement
FYE: June 30

	REVENUE ($ mil.)	NET INCOME ($ mil.)	NET PROFIT MARGIN	EMPLOYEES
06/11	337	(2)	—	4
06/10	300	8	2.7%	0
06/09	259	24	9.3%	0
Annual Growth	13.9%	—	—	—

2011 Year-End Financials

Debt ratio: ——
Return on equity: (-0.80)%
Cash ($ mil.): 65
Current ratio: 1.10
Long-term debt ($ mil.): —

Dividends
 Yield: —
 Payout: —
 Market value ($ mil.): —

JERNIGAN OIL CO. INC.

LOCATIONS

HQ: JERNIGAN OIL CO. INC.
109 DR MRTN LTHER KING JR, AHOSKIE, NC 27910-7612
Phone: 252-332-2131
Web: www.jerniganoil.com

HISTORICAL FINANCIALS

Company Type: Private

Income Statement
FYE: December 31

	REVENUE ($ mil.)	NET INCOME ($ mil.)	NET PROFIT MARGIN	EMPLOYEES
12/11	218	0	0.1%	350
12/10	168	0	0.1%	0
12/09	138	0	0.1%	0
12/08	193	0	0.1%	0
Annual Growth	4.2%	(0.8%)	—	—

2011 Year-End Financials

Debt ratio: ——
Return on equity: 0.10%
Cash ($ mil.): 0
Current ratio: 0.60
Long-term debt ($ mil.): —

Dividends
 Yield: —
 Payout: —
 Market value ($ mil.): —

JEWISH CHILD CARE ASSOCIATION OF NEW YORK

LOCATIONS

HQ: JEWISH CHILD CARE ASSOCIATION OF NEW YORK
120 WALL ST FL 12, NEW YORK, NY 10005-3909
Phone: 212-425-3333
Web: www.jccany.org

HISTORICAL FINANCIALS

Company Type: Private

Income Statement
FYE: June 30

	REVENUE ($ mil.)	NET INCOME ($ mil.)	NET PROFIT MARGIN	EMPLOYEES
06/11	81	(1)	—	600
06/10	78	(4)	—	0
06/09	62	(15)	—	0
06/08	65	(3)	—	0
Annual Growth	7.8%	—	—	—

2011 Year-End Financials

Debt ratio: ——
Return on equity: (-2.00)%
Cash ($ mil.): 1
Current ratio: 0.60
Long-term debt ($ mil.): —

Dividends
 Yield: —
 Payout: —
 Market value ($ mil.): —

JFK HEALTH SYSTEM INC.

JFK Health System provides medical services a tri-county area in central New Jersey through flagship facility JFK Medical Center. The hospital has about 500 acute care beds and is one of the Garden State's major health care facilities. Included in the medical center complex are JFK Johnson Rehabilitation Institute JFK New Jersey Neuroscience Institute and a number of outpatient care and imaging centers. A separate site Muhlenberg Campus consists of a satellite emergency room and outpatient care facilities as well as schools of nursing and medicine. Other JFK Health System facilities provide primary and specialty services as well as senior living home health and hospice care.

Geographic Reach

JFK Health System serves patients in the central New Jersey counties of Middlesex Union and Somerset.

Operations

JFK Health System's Muhlenberg Campus educational programs offer degrees in nursing radiography radiation therapy nuclear medicine and diagnostic medical sonography. Students have access to JFK's equipment and clinical facilities.

Another set of the system's facilities the JFK Hartwyck Nursing Convalescent and Rehabilitation Centers are located at three other separate sites. Combined they house more than 500 beds for nursing home subacute rehabilitation and respite-care patients. One of the units is the only center in the state and one of very few in the country offering specialty care for Huntington's disease patients.

Financial Performance

JFK Health System showed a 2% increase in revenues in 2011 to some $510 million largely due to a 2% increase in patient service revenues (which account for 95% of earnings). The system also saw a 48% rise in net income to nearly $11 million.

Strategy

JFK Health System regularly expands and upgrades its facilities and its medical equipment to keep pace with modern health care needs. For instance in 2011 JFK Medical Center began construction of a three-story ER pavilion on top of its existing emergency department.

Company Background

Formerly Solaris Health the not-for-profit system took the JFK Health System name in 2011 to align with its flagship facility. It previously took on the Solaris name in 1997 when JFK Medical Center (founded in 1967) and Muhlenberg Regional Medical Center (founded in 1894) merged. The Muhlenberg inpatient operations were discontinued in 2008 victim of an economically declining population base.

EXECUTIVES

COO JFK Medical Center, J. Scott Gebhard
President and CEO, John P. McGee
Chief Medical Officer, William Oser
President and CEO, Raymond F. Fredericks
CIO, Louis (Lou) Hermans
VP Human Resources, Shirley Higgins-Bowers
VP Strategic Planning Public Relations and Marketing, Thomas Casey
SVP and CFO, Richard C. Smith
Director Public Relations and Marketing, Steven Weiss
Manager Public Relations and Marketing, Robert (Rob) Cavanaugh
Public Relations Assistant, Elizabeth Dobis
SVP and Chief Nurse Executive, Ann P. Logan
Chair, Michael Kleiman

LOCATIONS

HQ: JFK Health System Inc.
80 James St., Edison NJ 08820
Phone: 732-321-7000 **Fax:** 732-632-1549
Web: www.jfkhealthsystem.org

Selected Facilities

JFK At Home
JFK Hartwyck Nursing and Rehabilitation Centers
JFK Johnson Rehabilitation Institute
JFK Medical Center
JFK MediPlex Surgery Center
JFK Muhlenberg Campus
JFK Muhlenberg Harold B. & Dorothy A. Snyder Schools
JFK New Jersey Neuroscience Institute
Whispering Knoll Assisted Living

COMPETITORS

Atlantic Health	Robert Wood Johnson
Barnabas Health	University Hospital
Catholic Health East	Saint Peter' s
CentraState Healthcare	University Hospital
System	Somerset Medical
Continuum Health	Center
Partners	St. Joseph' s
East Orange General	Healthcare System
Hospital	Staten Island
Newark Beth Israel	University Hospital
Medical Center	Trinitas Regional
NewYork-Presbyterian	Medical Center
Healthcare	
Raritan Bay Medical	
Center	

HISTORICAL FINANCIALS

Company Type: Private - Not-for-Profit

Income Statement

FYE: December 31

	REVENUE ($ mil.)	NET INCOME ($ mil.)	NET PROFIT MARGIN	EMPLOYEES
12/11	509	11	2.2%	6,735
12/10	500	(12)	—	0
12/09	488	3	0.8%	0
12/07	0	0	—	0
Annual Growth	—	—	—	—

2011 Year-End Financials

Debt ratio: ——
Return on equity: 2.20%
Cash ($ mil.): 53
Current ratio: 1.50
Long-term debt ($ mil.): —

Dividends
Yield: —
Payout: —
Market value ($ mil.): —

JOHN BROWN UNIVERSITY

You won't find that John Brown's body at John Brown University. You will find a student body some 1900 strong working toward undergraduate and graduate degrees in a non-denominational Christian environment. (Enrollment is comprised of about 1200 undergrads some 380 graduate students and some 500 adult degree completion students.) Popular majors include digital media arts engineering construction management education business and communications. The school was founded in northwest Arkansas in 1919 by evangelist and broadcaster John E. Brown Sr.

EXECUTIVES

VP Student Development, Stephen (Steve) Beers
VP Enrollment Management, Don Crandall
VP Academic Affairs, Ed Ericson III
VP Finance and Administration, Patricia R. Gustavson, age 66
VP University Advancement, James (Jim) Krall
President, Charles W. Pollard
Financial Aid, Kim Eldridge
Director Alumni and Parent Relations, Jerry Rollene
Coordinator Campus Safety, Mike O'Neal
Coordinator Public Relations, Rachel Fiet
Registrar, Becky Lambert

LOCATIONS

HQ: John Brown University
2000 W. University St., Siloam Springs AR 72761
Phone: 479-524-9500 **Fax:** 650-358-2790
Web: www.laszlosystems.com

COMPETITORS

Arkansas State	University of the
University	Ozarks
Lyon College	

HISTORICAL FINANCIALS

Company Type: School

Income Statement

FYE: June 30

	REVENUE ($ mil.)	NET INCOME ($ mil.)	NET PROFIT MARGIN	EMPLOYEES
06/11	63	8	13.2%	242
06/10	68	16	23.9%	0
06/09	60	0	—	0
06/05	31	(0)	—	0
Annual Growth	26.1%	—	—	—

2011 Year-End Financials

Debt ratio: ——
Return on equity: 13.20%
Cash ($ mil.): 18
Current ratio: —
Long-term debt ($ mil.): —

Dividends
Yield: —
Payout: —
Market value ($ mil.): —

JOHN CARROLL UNIVERSITY (INC)

John Carroll University is a Roman Catholic school that offers degree programs in more than 40 fields of the liberal arts social sciences natural sciences business and interdisciplinary studies at the undergraduate level and in selected areas at the master's level. Operated by the Society of Jesus — the Jesuits —it provides instruction to more than 4000 students. The school was founded in 1886 as St. Ignatius College then renamed in 1923 in honor of the first Catholic archbishop in the US. Women were admitted to John Carroll for the first time in 1968.

EXECUTIVES

VP Finance and Treasurer, Richard F. Mausser
President, Rev Robert L. Niehoff
VP Enrollment, Brian G. Williams
VP University Advancement, Doreen K. Riley
Chairman, Allyn R. Adams
VP Student Affairs, Mark McCarthy
VP Academic, John T. Day
VP and Executive Assistant to the President, Jonathan E. Smith
General Counsel, Maria G. Alfaro-Lopez
Secretary, Laurie A. Frantz
CIO, Michael Bestul
Director Human Resources, Charles Stuppy

LOCATIONS

HQ: John Carroll University
1 John Carroll Blvd., University Heights OH 44118
Phone: 216-397-1886 **Fax:** 216-397-4675
Web: www.jcu.edu

HISTORICAL FINANCIALS

Company Type: School

Income Statement

FYE: May 31

	REVENUE ($ mil.)	NET INCOME ($ mil.)	NET PROFIT MARGIN	EMPLOYEES
05/12	88	(5)	—	2,343
05/11	83	22	26.9%	0
05/10	82	17	21.4%	0
05/09	86	(49)	—	0
Annual Growth	0.6%	—	—	—

2012 Year-End Financials

Debt ratio: —
Return on equity: (-6.40)%
Cash ($ mil.): 8
Current ratio: —
Long-term debt ($ mil.): —

Dividends
Yield: —
Payout: —
Market value ($ mil.): —

JOHN SNOW INCORPORATED

LOCATIONS

HQ: JOHN SNOW INCORPORATED
44 FARNSWORTH ST FL 7, BOSTON, MA 02210-1223
Phone: 617-482-9485
Web: www.jsi.com

HISTORICAL FINANCIALS

Company Type: Private

Income Statement

FYE: December 31

	REVENUE ($ mil.)	NET INCOME ($ mil.)	NET PROFIT MARGIN	EMPLOYEES
12/11	435	7	1.8%	297
12/10	321	4	1.5%	0
12/09	220	5	2.3%	0
12/08	159	5	3.3%	0
Annual Growth	39.7%	13.6%	—	—

2011 Year-End Financials

Debt ratio: —
Return on equity: 1.80%
Cash ($ mil.): 22
Current ratio: 4.10
Long-term debt ($ mil.): —

Dividends
Yield: —
Payout: —
Market value ($ mil.): —

JOHNSON & WALES UNIVERSITY INC

Things are a little "upside-down" at Johnson & Wales University and that's just the way they like it. The private not-for-profit accredited institution provides what it calls an upside-down curriculum allowing students to take courses in their major during the first year so they learn right away if their career choice is right for them. At the end of two years of study students earn an associate's degree

and the opportunity to go on to earn a bachelor's degree. Founded in 1914 the school enrolls more than 16000 students on four campuses in Colorado Florida North Carolina and Rhode Island. It offers degrees in business education foodservice hospitality culinary arts and technology.

EXECUTIVES

Chairman, John A. Yena, age 71
Director Human Resources, Diane D'Ambra
Chancellor, John J. Bowen
Vice Chancellor, Thomas L. G. Dwyer
SVP Emeritus University Relations, Manuel Pimentel Jr.
SVP Special Projects, Kenneth R. Levy
President Providence Campus, Irving Schneider
SVP Facilities Management, Merlin A. DeConti Jr.
SVP Administration, Robin Krakowsky
President Charlotte Campus, Arthur J. Gallagher
VP Enrollment Management, Kenneth F. DiSaia
VP Career Development, Donna J. Yena
President and COO Providence Campus, Mim L. Runey
Corporate Secretary and General Counsel, Barbara L. Bennett
CFO and Treasurer, William F. McArdle
VP Finance and Assistant Treasurer, Joseph J. Greene Jr.
SVP University Affairs, Charles M. Cook
Dean Academic Administration, Louis A. D'Abrosca
Dean International Recruitment and Training, Manny Tavares
Director International Admissions, Rita Mulligan
Director Career Development, Sheri L. Ispir
VP Facilities Management, Christopher O. Placco
University Controller, Alan Restivo
Director University Budget, Eileen Haskins
VP Information Technology and CIO, John A. Smithers
Executive Director Information Technology Operations, Deborah J. Towey
Registrar, Gail Nevadonski
Director Community Relations, Everett Brooks
Director University Communications, Piya A. Sarawgi
Manager Operations Career Development, Donna Remington
Executive Director Student Financial Services, Lynn M. Robinson
President Denver Campus, Bette Matkowski
President North Miami Campus, Loreen Chant, age 44
Director Communications and Media Relations, Lisa Pelosi
Provost, Veera S. Gaul
SVP Institutional Advancement, Patricia A. McLaughlin
Chief Diversity Officer, Toni D. Green
Executive Director Campus Safety and Security, Michael P. Quinn
Executive Director Alumni Relations, Jeffrey M. Cartee
Executive Director University Information Systems, Bill Prew
University Compliance Officer, Sandra Lawrence
VP Student Affairs and Dean Students, Ronald Martel
Director University Marketing, Greg DiStefano
VP Student Services and University Registrar, Marie Bernardo-Sousa
Trustee, Don W. Hubble, age 72
Trustee, Richard L. Bready, age 68
Trustee, Peter H. (Pete) Coors, age 65
Trustee, James H. (Jim) Hance Jr., age 67
Trustee, Merrill W. Sherman, age 63
President and Trustee, John J. Bowen

Trustee, Walter L. Isenberg
Trustee, John H. White Jr.
Trustee, Edward P. Grace III, age 61
Trustee, Sylvia E. Robinson
Trustee, Gerald A. Fernandez
Trustee, Emeril J. Lagasse
Trustee, Edward P. Triangolo Jr.
Trustee, David F. Brochu
Trustee, Michele Bailey DiMartino
Trustee, Laura Freid
Trustee, William E. Trueheart
Auditors: MayerHoffmanMcCannP.C.

LOCATIONS

HQ: Johnson & Wales University
8 Abbott Park Place, Providence RI 02903
Phone: 401-598-1000   Fax: 401-598-1833
Web: www.jwu.edu

PRODUCTS/OPERATIONS

Selected Colleges and Majors

College of Business
Accounting
Advertising & Marketing Communications
Criminal Justice
Entrepreneurship
Equine Business Management
Fashion Merchandising & Retail Marketing
Financial Services Management
Food Marketing
Food Service Entrepreneurship
International Business
Management
Marketing
Paralegal Studies
College of Culinary Arts
Baking & Pastry Arts
Culinary Arts & Food Service Management
Culinary Nutrition
Food Marketing
Food Service Entrepreneurship
Pastry Arts & Food Service Management
The Hospitality College
Culinary Arts & Food Service Management
Hotel & Lodging Management
International Hotel and Tourism Management
Pastry Arts & Food Service Management
Restaurant Food & Beverage Management
Sports/Entertainment/Event Management
Travel Tourism & Hospitality Management
School of Technology
Business/Information Systems Analysis
Computer Programming
Computerized Drafting
Computing Technology Services
Electronics Engineering
Engineering Design & Configuration Management
Graphic Design & Digital Media
Network Engineering
Robotic Engineering Technology
Software Engineering
Technology Services Management
School of Education
Master of Education in Teaching and Learning (M.Ed)
Master of Arts in Teaching (M.A.T.)

HISTORICAL FINANCIALS

Company Type: School

Income Statement

FYE: June 30

	REVENUE ($ mil.)	NET INCOME ($ mil.)	NET PROFIT MARGIN	EMPLOYEES
06/11	343	75	22.0%	1,400
06/10	427	33	7.8%	0
06/09	407	10	2.7%	0
06/08	404	48	12.1%	0
Annual Growth	(5.3%)	15.6%	—	—

2011 Year-End Financials

Debt ratio: ——
Return on equity: 22.00%
Cash ($ mil.): 35
Current ratio: ——
Long-term debt ($ mil.): ——

Dividends
Yield: ——
Payout: ——
Market value ($ mil.): ——

JOHNSON C. SMITH UNIVERSITY INCORPORATED

Founded as Biddle Memorial Institute Johnson C. Smith University has historically benefited from generous benefactors like the Biddles and the Smiths. The independent private coeducational institution of higher learning enrolls about 1400 students a year. It confers bachelor's degrees to hundreds of students each year in 32 different majors. The historically African-American university aims to provide an outstanding educational experience for a diverse group of students from various ethnic socioeconomic and geographical backgrounds.It offers a liberal education curriculum in conjunction with focused study in specialized fields in preparation for advanced study and careers.

The educational institution was set up in 1867 under the auspices of the Committee on Freedmen of the Presbyterian Church U.S.A. The university took its first name from the late Major Henry Biddle whose wife (Mary) was a generous fundraiser and donor. The campus took its present name in 1923 when Mrs. Jane Smith endowed the school in memory of her late husband Johnson C. Smith.

EXECUTIVES

Director Public Relations, Benny L. Smith
Director Human Resources, Latrelle P. McAllister
VP Finance, Gerald Hector
VP Institutional Advancement, Kenneth Westary
Dean Students, Cathy Jones
Dean University Records and Financial Aid, Moses W. Jones
Director Alumni Affairs, Ron Matthews
Director Campus Police, John O. Williams
Director Career Planning and Placement, Barbara Wilks
Director Financial Aid, Cynthia Anderson
Director Information Technology, John Norris
Interim Director Institutional Planning Assessment Effectiveness and Research, Kelli S. Rainey
President, Ronald L. (Ron) Carter, age 63
Chief of Staff, Brian Johnson

LOCATIONS

HQ: Johnson C. Smith University
100 Beatties Ford Rd., Charlotte NC 28216
Phone: 704-378-1000　　**Fax:** 704-372-5746
Web: www.jcsu.edu

HISTORICAL FINANCIALS

Company Type: School

Income Statement

FYE: June 30

	REVENUE ($ mil.)	NET INCOME ($ mil.)	NET PROFIT MARGIN	EMPLOYEES
06/11	42	(2)	—	280
06/10	42	(0)	—	0
06/09	43	(0)	—	0
06/08	43	4	9.9%	0
Annual Growth	(1.2%)	—	—	—

2011 Year-End Financials

Debt ratio: ——
Return on equity: (-6.90)%
Cash ($ mil.): 15
Current ratio: ——
Long-term debt ($ mil.): ——

Dividends
Yield: —
Payout: —
Market value ($ mil.): —

JOHNSON MIRMIRAN & THOMPSON INC.

LOCATIONS

HQ: JOHNSON MIRMIRAN & THOMPSON INC.
72 LOVETON CIR, SPARKS, MD 21152-9202
Phone: 410-329-3100
Web: www.jmt-engineering.com

HISTORICAL FINANCIALS

Company Type: Private

Income Statement

FYE: December 31

	REVENUE ($ mil.)	NET INCOME ($ mil.)	NET PROFIT MARGIN	EMPLOYEES
12/11	104	1	1.0%	760
12/10	106	5	4.9%	0
12/09	95	5	5.4%	0
12/08	0	0	—	0
Annual Growth	—	—	—	—

2011 Year-End Financials

Debt ratio: ——
Return on equity: 1.00%
Cash ($ mil.): 3
Current ratio: 3.80
Long-term debt ($ mil.): ——

Dividends
Yield: —
Payout: —
Market value ($ mil.): —

JOHNSTON ENTERPRISES INC.

Johnston Enterprises serves the harvesters of America's amber waves of grain. The company offers farmers in Oklahoma and other Midwestern states grain-processing and storage facilities and inland water transportation services through its Johnston Grain and Johnston Port Terminals divisions. Its Johnston Seed subsidiary sells wildflower and turf wild forage and native grass seed and

wildlife feed. The company was founded in 1893 by W. B. Johnston and is owned and operated by the founder's descendants president Lew Meibergen and COO Butch Meibergen.

EXECUTIVES

Chairman, J. L. (Lew) Meibergen II
President and CEO, J. L. (Butch) Meibergen III, age 56
COO, Dennis Craig
VP, Joey Meibergen

LOCATIONS

HQ: Johnston Enterprises Inc.
411 W. Chestnut Ave., Enid OK 73701
Phone: 580-233-5800　　**Fax:** 580-234-8712
Web: www.jeinc.com

COMPETITORS

ADM	CHS
Ag Processing Inc.	DeBruce Grain
Andersons	Owensboro Grain
Bartlett and Company	Scoular
Cargill	Stewart Grain
CGC	

HISTORICAL FINANCIALS

Company Type: Private

Income Statement

FYE: April 30

	REVENUE ($ mil.)	NET INCOME ($ mil.)	NET PROFIT MARGIN	EMPLOYEES
04/12	297	1	0.5%	280
04/11	289	1	0.5%	0
04/10	140	0	0.2%	0
04/09	287	1	0.5%	0
Annual Growth	1.2%	6.6%	—	—

2012 Year-End Financials

Debt ratio: ——
Return on equity: 0.50%
Cash ($ mil.): 1
Current ratio: 0.40
Long-term debt ($ mil.): —

Dividends
Yield: —
Payout: —
Market value ($ mil.): —

JOINT COMMISSION ON ACCREDITATION OF HEALTHCARE ORGANIZATIONS

Its not really about joints per se unless they are aching and in need of repair. The Joint Commission on Accreditation of Health Care Organizations is a nonprofit that provides accreditation and certification services to more than 18000 health care providers in the US. Its board of commissioners includes doctors nurses consumers and administrators. They evaluate hospitals health care networks nursing homes and other long-term care facilities laboratories and health-related groups. The Joint Commission's Quality Check website includes each accredited organization's quality review. The group also known simply as The Joint Commission was founded in 1951.

The commission's corporate members include the American College of Physicians the American College of Surgeons the American Dental Association the American Hospital Association and the American Medical Association.

EXECUTIVES

CFO, Paige A. Rodgers
SVP, Paul M. Schyve
General Counsel, Harold J. Bressler
EVP Quality Measurement and Research Division, Jerod M. Loeb
EVP Business Development Government and External Relations, Charles A. (Chuck) Mowll
VP Human Resources, Lynn B. Dragisic
VP Public Policy and Government Relations, Margaret A. VanAmringe
VP Standards Division and Survey Methods, Robert A. Wise
Director Policy and Administration, Gail Weinberger
Executive Director Behavioral Health Care Accreditation, Mary Cesare-Murphy
Project Director Bureau of Primary Health Care, Lon Berkeley
Chief Communications Officer, Cathy Barry-Ipema
Executive Director State and External Relations, Mark Crafton
Associate Director Custom Education and Conferences, Karen Hoffner
Associate Director Federal and State Accreditation Survey Contracts, Janet Malkiewicz
Senior Associate Director Disease-Specific Care Certification and Health Care Staffing Services Certification, M.J. Hampel
Associate Director Distance Learning, George Riccio
Meeting Planner Program Logistics Continuing Education Credits and Cancellations, Claire Galiardo
Conference Specialist Program Logistics Continuing Education Credits and Cancellations, Renata Raudys
Executive Director Education Management, Pamela (Pam) Steinbach
Program Manager National Conferences and Public Policy Symposia, Alma Harrell
Project Coordinator Eisenberg Patient Safety and Quality Awards, Kristine Donofrio
Associate Director Employment Opportunities, Ruth Metsch
VP Consulting Services Joint Commission Resources and Joint Commission International, Anne Rooney
Executive Director Standards Development and Interpretation International Accreditation Services Development, Paul vanOstenberg
President and CEO Joint Commission Resources and Joint Commission International, Karen H. Timmons
Laboratory Performance Measurement Analyst, Eileen Stawczyk
Director Legal Issues Relating to Accreditation, Eleanor Wagner
Senior Executive Director Business Development Network Accreditation Services and Long Term Care Accreditation, Gina Val Zimmerman
Editor Ambulatory Advisor DSC Update and Home Care Bulletin, Alice Brown
Editor BHC News Lab Focus and LTC Update, Pamela Schumacher
Manager Sentinel Event Alert and Joint Commission Online, Caron Wong

Executive Editor The Environment of Care News, Kristine Miller
Executive Editor Joint Commission on Quality and Patient Safety and Joint Commission on Quality and Safety, Steve Berman
Executive Director Ambulatory Accreditation, Michael T. Kulczycki
Senior Associate Director Business Development Policy and Administration and Associate Director Ambulatory Surgery Centers, Mike Dye
Associate Director ORYX, Frank Zibrat
Associate Director ORYX Performance Measurement Systems, Mary K. Bowie
Director Public Affairs Office of President, Terri Tye
Director Board of Commissioners and Liaison Network, Kim Andersen
Executive Director Publications, Catherine C. Hinckley
Manager Accreditation and Certification Editorial Unit, Diane Bell
Director Department of Quality Measurement, Linda Hanold
Director Department of Health Policy Research, Richard Koss
Director Operations Quality Measurement and Research, Mary Fialkowski
Associate Director State and External Relations Payor Relations, Jennifer Hoppe
Director Standards Interpretation Group, Pat Adamski
Manager Refunds and Reimbursements, Pat Hall
Field Director Hospital Accreditation Services, Nancy Wuggazer
DIVACO Education Director Surveyor Management and Development, Kimo Hemmes
Commissioner, Jonathan B. (Jon) Perlin, age 51
Executive Director Disease Specific Care Certification, Jean E. Range
Executive Director Health Care Staffing Services Certification, Michele M. Sacco
President and Commissioner, Mark R. Chassin
EVP Support Operations and Chief of Staff, Anne Marie Benedicto
EVP Accreditation and Certification Operations, Ann Scott Blouin
Senior Specialist Business Development Policy and Administration, Darrell Anderson
Executive Director US Consulting and Continuous Service Readiness, Lucille Skuteris
Business Development Senior Specialist Disease Specific Care Certification and Health Care Staffing Services Certification, Stacy Veitengruber
Associate Director Behavioral Health Care Accreditation and Long Term Care Accreditation, Peggy Lavin
Business Development Specialist Behavioral Health Care Accreditation and Long Term Care Accreditation, Evelyn Choi
Associate Director Core Measures, Ann Watt
Associate Director Disease-Specific Care Certification, Caroline Isbey
Director Federal Relations Federal Legislative and Regulatory Affairs, Trisha Kurtz
Executive Director International Services, Sherry Kaufield
Executive Director International Consulting, Ann Jacobson
Ad Sales and Manager International Editorial Unit, Paul Reis
Senior Secretary Ambulatory Care PTAC, Jacqueline Franklin
Executive Secretary Legal Issues Relating to Accreditation, Veronica Goffer
Manager Media Relations, Ken Powers
Corporate Compliance and Privacy Officer, Fran Carroll

LMS Administrator eLearning Products, Jamie Cunningham
Senior HR Consultant, Sharon Kusen
Chair Board of Commissioners, David A. Whiston
Vice Chair Board of Commissioners, Isabel V. Hoverman
Executive Director Home Care Program, Margherita C. Labson
Executive Director Hospital Programs and Accreditation and Certification Services, Mark G. Pelletier
Admisitrative Secretary Communications, Terri Argumosa
Executive Secretary Human Resources, Jan Burgess
Executive Director CLIA Certification, Jennifer F. Rhamy
Associate Director Marketing, Donna Rutkowski
Executive Director The Joint Commission Perspectives, Helen Fry
Executive Editor The Joint Commission: The Source, Janet Pimentel
Senior Editor The Perspectives on Patient Safety, Jim Parker
Senior Editor The Joint Commission: Benchmark, Audrie Bretl-Roelf
Executive Assistant to President, Olivia Trippi
Manager Books and Acquisitions Editorial Unit, Vicki Smith-Gaudette
Executive Secretary Quality Measurement and Research, Sharon Weidenbach
Associate Director Research, Scott Williams
Director Standards and Survey Methods, Amy Panagolpoulos
Chief of Staff and CFO Joint Commission Resources and Joint Commission International, Jean Courtney
Information Technology Director Joint Commission Resources and Joint Commission International, Mike DeGraff
Executive Director Software Joint Commission Resources and Joint Cimmission International, James Eduljee
EVP and Chief Medical Officer, Ana Pujols-McKee
Commissioner, Benjamin K. Chu, age 59
Commissioner, R. Timothy (Tim) Rice
Commissioner, Ralph W. Muller
Commissioner, David L. Bronson
Commissioner, Kurt D. Newman
Commissioner, Jonathan B. (Jon) Perlin, age 51
President and Commissioner, Mark R. Chassin
Commissioner, Josie R. Williams
Commissioner, Nancy Howell Agee
Vice Chair Board of Commissioners, Isabel V. Hoverman
Commissioner, Charles R. Buck Jr.
Commissioner, Alexander M. Capron
Commissioner, Marilyn P. Chow
Commissioner, Ilene Corina
Commissioner, T. Anthony Denton
Commissioner, Joseph M. Heyman
Cimmissioner, M. Nicole Jamali
Commissioner, Craig W. Jones
Commissioner, Edward L. Langston
Commissioner, Eric B. Larson
Commissioner, Mary Anne McCaffree
Commissioner, LaMar S. McGinnis Jr.
Commissioner, Mary H. McGrath
Commissioner, Rebecca J. Patchin
Commissioner, Christopher J. Queram
Commissioner, Gerald M. Shea
Commissioner, J. B. Silvers
Copmmissioner, Michael F. Hogan
Commissioner, Connie S. March
Commissioner, Kristy Wright

LOCATIONS

HQ: Joint Commission on Accreditation of Healthcare Organizations
1 Renaissance Blvd., Oakbrook Terrace IL 60181
Phone: 630-792-5000   **Fax:** 630-792-5005
Web: www.jointcommission.org/

HISTORICAL FINANCIALS

Company Type: Private - Not-for-Profit

Income Statement
FYE: December 31

	REVENUE ($ mil.)	NET INCOME ($ mil.)	NET PROFIT MARGIN	EMPLOYEES
12/11	180	8	4.6%	936
12/02	115	12	10.8%	0
12/01*	122	8	7.2%	0
03/01	1,045	0	0.0%	0
Annual Growth	(44.3%)	2777.7%	—	—

*Fiscal year change

2011 Year-End Financials

Debt ratio: ——
Return on equity: 4.60%
Cash ($ mil.): 31
Current ratio: 1.70
Long-term debt ($ mil.): ——

Dividends
Yield: —
Payout: —
Market value ($ mil.): —

JOLIET TOWNSHIP HIGH SCHOOL DISTRICT 204

LOCATIONS

HQ: JOLIET TOWNSHIP HIGH SCHOOL DISTRICT 204
300 CATERPILLAR DR, JOLIET, IL 60436-1047
Phone: 815-727-6890
Web: www.jths.org

HISTORICAL FINANCIALS

Company Type: Private

Income Statement
FYE: June 30

	REVENUE ($ mil.)	NET INCOME ($ mil.)	NET PROFIT MARGIN	EMPLOYEES
06/11	96	(5)	—	640
06/02	50	(6)	—	0
06/01	47	13	28.0%	0
06/00	46	1	3.0%	0
Annual Growth	26.9%	—	—	—

2011 Year-End Financials

Debt ratio: ——
Return on equity: (-5.30)%
Cash ($ mil.): 23
Current ratio: 0.50
Long-term debt ($ mil.): ——

Dividends
Yield: —
Payout: —
Market value ($ mil.): —

JONES-ONSLOW ELECTRIC MEMBERSHIP CORPORATION

LOCATIONS

HQ: JONES-ONSLOW ELECTRIC MEMBERSHIP CORPORATION
259 WESTERN BLVD, JACKSONVILLE, NC 28546-5736
Phone: 910-353-1940
Web: www.joemc.com

HISTORICAL FINANCIALS

Company Type: Private

Income Statement
FYE: December 31

	REVENUE ($ mil.)	NET INCOME ($ mil.)	NET PROFIT MARGIN	EMPLOYEES
12/11	117	5	5.0%	151
12/10	120	6	5.7%	0
12/09	109	7	6.5%	0
12/08	103	7	7.7%	0
Annual Growth	4.3%	(9.5%)	—	—

2011 Year-End Financials

Debt ratio: ——
Return on equity: 5.00%
Cash ($ mil.): 1
Current ratio: 0.40
Long-term debt ($ mil.): ——

Dividends
Yield: —
Payout: —
Market value ($ mil.): —

JORDAN CF CONSTRUCTION LLC

LOCATIONS

HQ: JORDAN CF CONSTRUCTION LLC
7700 CF JORDAN DR, EL PASO, TX 79912-8808
Phone: 915-877-3333
Web: www.cfjordan.com

HISTORICAL FINANCIALS

Company Type: Private

Income Statement
FYE: December 31

	REVENUE ($ mil.)	NET INCOME ($ mil.)	NET PROFIT MARGIN	EMPLOYEES
12/11	299	0	0.2%	500
12/10	214	2	1.0%	0
12/09	0	0	—	0
12/08	300	5	1.8%	0
Annual Growth	(0.1%)	(52.0%)	—	—

2011 Year-End Financials

Debt ratio: ——
Return on equity: 0.20%
Cash ($ mil.): 4
Current ratio: 0.90
Long-term debt ($ mil.): ——

Dividends
Yield: —
Payout: —
Market value ($ mil.): —

JORDAN CF INVESTMENTS LLP

A high-flier in construction services C.F. Jordan is a top building contractor that offers preconstruction design/build development and project management services. The company has traditionally built hotels and resorts but has diversified into military residential highway and school construction. Its contracts include projects for the Immigration and Naturalization Service for border patrol stations health care centers and detention centers. Other works have included Sea World in San Antonio the Insights Science Museum in El Paso and the Pearl Harbor Commissary and Exchange in Hawaii. Chairman Charles "Paco" Jordan started the Texas-based firm in 1988.

C.F. Jordan has worked throughout Texas as well as 30 other states and in Mexico. Its civil construction division works extensively on Texas Department of Transportation projects in West Texas and builds other highway and road construction projects in New Mexico. Its concrete division pours slabs and builds concrete garages in Texas and southern New Mexico.

EXECUTIVES

President and CEO, Darren G. Woody, age 52
Chairman, Charles F. (Paco) Jordan III
EVP El Paso, Paul Bauer
Secretary and CFO, J. Robert (Rob) Hutchison
EVP Dallas Commercial Division, Denis E. Gee
Executive Vice President Commercial Operations, David E. Baer
President of the Residential Group, Mark Lear
VP Risk and Safety Management, Patricia Kagerer
EVP Civil and Concrete Divisions, John Goodrich
EVP, Mike Miller
Executive Vice President of Corporate Business Development, Jay F. Nelson
VP Corporate Estimating, James M. Roach
Chief Financial Officer, Cynthia Rogers
Director of Preconstruction, Pete Galyean
Executive Vice President Houston, Bob Richardson
Director of Business Development, Joe Gomez
Director of Business Development, John Riggins
Executive Vice President Central South Texas, Leland Rocchio

LOCATIONS

HQ: C.F. Jordan L.P.
7700 C F Jordan Dr., El Paso TX 79912
Phone: 915-877-3333   **Fax:** 915-877-3999
Web: www.cfjordan.com

COMPETITORS

D.R. Horton	JC General Contractors
Harvey Builders	Manhattan Construction
Hensel Phelps Construction	Structure Tone Southwest
Hunt Companies	Summit Builders
Hunt Construction	Turner Corporation
J.D. Abrams	Tutor Perini

HISTORICAL FINANCIALS

Company Type: Private

Income Statement

FYE: December 31

	REVENUE ($ mil.)	NET INCOME ($ mil.)	NET PROFIT MARGIN	EMPLOYEES
12/11	299	0	0.3%	500
12/09	337	3	1.1%	0
12/08	337	3	1.1%	0
12/05	259	2	1.0%	0
Annual Growth	4.9%	(29.4%)	—	—

2011 Year-End Financials

Debt ratio: —
Return on equity: 0.30%
Cash ($ mil.): 7
Current ratio: 0.20
Long-term debt ($ mil.): —

Dividends
Yield: —
Payout: —
Market value ($ mil.): —

JOURNEYMAN CONSTRUCTION INC.

LOCATIONS

HQ: JOURNEYMAN CONSTRUCTION INC.
7701 N LAMAR BLVD STE 100, AUSTIN, TX 78752-1012
Phone: 512-247-7000
Web: www.journeymanco.com

HISTORICAL FINANCIALS

Company Type: Private

Income Statement

FYE: December 31

	REVENUE ($ mil.)	NET INCOME ($ mil.)	NET PROFIT MARGIN	EMPLOYEES
12/11	126	5	4.2%	55
12/10	70	0	0.7%	0
12/09	85	5	6.6%	0
12/08	88	5	5.9%	0
Annual Growth	12.7%	1.2%	—	—

2011 Year-End Financials

Debt ratio: —
Return on equity: 4.20%
Cash ($ mil.): 16
Current ratio: 1.10
Long-term debt ($ mil.): —

Dividends
Yield: —
Payout: —
Market value ($ mil.): —

JOYCE LESLIE INC.

Club-hoppers (and high schoolers) hoping to look like Paris Hilton without spending like her do their shopping at Joyce Leslie. The northeastern retail chain specializes in trendy and inexpensive women's and junior's clothing aimed primarily at teens and tweens. It operates about 50 shops filled with high-fashion knockoffs in Connecticut New Jersey New York and Pennsylvania. Joyce Leslie named after the daughter of the company's founder Julius Gewirtz was established in Brooklyn in 1945 and originally sold women's dresses.

EXECUTIVES

President, Joyce G. Segal, age 66
Treasurer, Hermine Gewirtz
VP Store Operations, Nancy Shapiro, age 64
Human Resources, Cheryl O'Reilly

LOCATIONS

HQ: Joyce Leslie Inc.
135 W. Commercial Ave., Moonachie NJ 07074
Phone: 201-804-7800   **Fax:** 877-253-5060
Web: www.joyceleslie.com/

2011 Stores

	No.
New	24
New	19
Pennsylvania	5
Connecticut	3
Total	**51**

COMPETITORS

A & E Stores	H&M
Ascena Retail	Pacific Sunwear
Big M	Target Corporation
Cato	TJX Companies
Charlotte Russe	Urban Outfitters
Deb Shops	Wet Seal
dELiA*s	Zara
Forever 21	

HISTORICAL FINANCIALS

Company Type: Private

Income Statement

FYE: January 28

	REVENUE ($ mil.)	NET INCOME ($ mil.)	NET PROFIT MARGIN	EMPLOYEES
01/12	104	1	1.4%	900
01/10	101	1	1.3%	0
01/09	100	1	1.2%	0
01/08	94	1	1.3%	0
Annual Growth	3.2%	5.2%	—	—

2012 Year-End Financials

Debt ratio: —
Return on equity: 1.40%
Cash ($ mil.): 8
Current ratio: 0.90
Long-term debt ($ mil.): —

Dividends
Yield: —
Payout: —
Market value ($ mil.): —

JSI RESEARCH AND TRAINING INSTITUTE INC.

LOCATIONS

HQ: JSI RESEARCH AND TRAINING INSTITUTE INC.
44 FARNSWORTH ST FL 7, BOSTON, MA 02210-1206
Phone: 617-482-9485

HISTORICAL FINANCIALS

Company Type: Private

Income Statement

FYE: September 30

	REVENUE ($ mil.)	NET INCOME ($ mil.)	NET PROFIT MARGIN	EMPLOYEES
09/11	151	3	2.1%	135
09/10	163	1	1.1%	0
09/09	150	1	1.2%	0
09/08	142	1	1.3%	0
Annual Growth	2.0%	21.3%	—	—

2011 Year-End Financials

Debt ratio: —
Return on equity: 2.10%
Cash ($ mil.): 30
Current ratio: 1.40
Long-term debt ($ mil.): —

Dividends
Yield: —
Payout: —
Market value ($ mil.): —

JUNIATA COLLEGE

Brothers and sisters are welcome at Juniata College an independent co-educational school affiliated with the Church of the Brethren. The college offers bachelor of arts and bachelor of science degrees in nearly 100 programs in some two dozen academic departments. Students are encouraged to design their own majors or "programs of emphasis" (POEs); nearly half do just that. Its most popular POEs include biology and pre-health accounting business education environmental science psychology chemistry and sociology. Founded in 1876 Juniata College enrolls approximately 1500 students each year about two-thirds of whom are from Pennsylvania.

EXECUTIVES

President, Thomas R. Kepple Jr.
EVP Student Development and Provost, James (Jim) Lakso
EVP Avancement and Marketing, John S. Hille
Director Human Resources, Gail Leiby Ulrich
Registrar, Athena Frederick
Associate VP and CIO, Dave Fusco
Director Administrative Information Services, Barbara (Barb) Hughes
Director Campus Security and Safety, Rocco Panosetti Jr.
Director Media Relations, John T. Wall
VP Finance and Operations, Robert E. Yelnosky
Director Student Financial Planning, Valerie Rennell

Director Campus Network and Security, Anne Wood
Director Environmental Health and Safety, Roy D. Nagle
Dean Students, Kris R. Clarkson
Dean Enrollment, Michelle M. Bartol
Vice President for Marketing and Advancement, Gabe Welsch
Chief Information Officer Vice President of Information Technology, Francis M. Richards
Chief Financial Officer, Matthew A. Cassidy
Vice President for University Operations, Maurice C. Taylor

LOCATIONS

HQ: Juniata College
1700 Moore St., Huntingdon PA 16652
Phone: 814-641-3000   **Fax:** 814-641-3199
Web: www.juniata.edu

HISTORICAL FINANCIALS
Company Type: School

Income Statement
FYE: May 31

	REVENUE ($ mil.)	NET INCOME ($ mil.)	NET PROFIT MARGIN	EMPLOYEES
05/12	49	(1)	—	500
05/11	61	11	19.4%	0
05/10	46	(1)	—	0
05/09	41	(17)	—	0
Annual Growth	6.6%	—	—	—

2012 Year-End Financials

Debt ratio: ——
Return on equity: (-3.20)%
Cash ($ mil.): 24
Current ratio: —
Long-term debt ($ mil.): —

Dividends
  Yield: —
  Payout: —
Market value ($ mil.): —

JUSTICE RESOURCE INSTITUTE INC.

LOCATIONS

HQ: JUSTICE RESOURCE INSTITUTE INC.
160 GOULD ST STE 300, NEEDHAM, MA 02494-2300
Phone: 781-559-4900
Web: www.jri.org

HISTORICAL FINANCIALS
Company Type: Private

Income Statement
FYE: June 30

	REVENUE ($ mil.)	NET INCOME ($ mil.)	NET PROFIT MARGIN	EMPLOYEES
06/11	97	3	3.8%	1,600
06/10	88	9	10.3%	0
06/09	87	(6)	—	0
06/08	87	(4)	—	0
Annual Growth	3.9%	—	—	—

JUVENILE DIABETES RESEARCH FOUNDATION INTERNATIONAL

LOCATIONS

HQ: JUVENILE DIABETES RESEARCH FOUNDATION INTERNATIONAL
26 BROADWAY FL 14, NEW YORK, NY 10004-1838
Phone: 212-785-9500
Web: www.jdrfdetroit.org

HISTORICAL FINANCIALS
Company Type: Private

Income Statement
FYE: June 30

	REVENUE ($ mil.)	NET INCOME ($ mil.)	NET PROFIT MARGIN	EMPLOYEES
06/12	193	(11)	—	600
06/11	220	16	7.5%	0
06/10	207	16	7.8%	0
Annual Growth	(3.5%)	—	—	—

2012 Year-End Financials

Debt ratio: ——
Return on equity: (-6.00)%
Cash ($ mil.): 13
Current ratio: 0.30
Long-term debt ($ mil.): —

Dividends
  Yield: —
  Payout: —
Market value ($ mil.): —

JWM VENTURES LLC

LOCATIONS

HQ: JWM VENTURES LLC
376 E WARM SPRINGS RD, LAS VEGAS, NV 89119-4262
Phone: 702-434-6400

HISTORICAL FINANCIALS
Company Type: Private

Income Statement
FYE: December 31

	REVENUE ($ mil.)	NET INCOME ($ mil.)	NET PROFIT MARGIN	EMPLOYEES
12/11	455	455	100.0%	11
12/09*	0	0	—	0
05/09	0	0	—	0
Annual Growth	—	—	—	—

*Fiscal year change

2011 Year-End Financials

Debt ratio: ——
Return on equity: 3.80%
Cash ($ mil.): 7
Current ratio: 0.90
Long-term debt ($ mil.): —

Dividends
  Yield: —
  Payout: —
Market value ($ mil.): —

2011 Year-End Financials

Debt ratio: ——
Return on equity: 100.00%
Cash ($ mil.): 12
Current ratio: 920.50
Long-term debt ($ mil.): —

Dividends
  Yield: —
  Payout: —
Market value ($ mil.): —

K & M TIRE INC.

LOCATIONS

HQ: K & M TIRE INC.
965 SPENCERVILLE RD, DELPHOS, OH 45833-2351
Phone: 419-695-1061
Web: www.kmtire.com

HISTORICAL FINANCIALS
Company Type: Private

Income Statement
FYE: September 30

	REVENUE ($ mil.)	NET INCOME ($ mil.)	NET PROFIT MARGIN	EMPLOYEES
09/11	220	13	6.1%	250
09/10	149	8	5.4%	0
Annual Growth	47.5%	66.3%	—	—

2011 Year-End Financials

Debt ratio: ——
Return on equity: 6.10%
Cash ($ mil.): 0
Current ratio: 0.80
Long-term debt ($ mil.): —

Dividends
  Yield: —
  Payout: —
Market value ($ mil.): —

K.S.I. TRADING CORP.

LOCATIONS

HQ: K.S.I. TRADING CORP.
100A WADE AVE, SOUTH PLAINFIELD, NJ 07080-1311
Phone: 908-754-7154
Web: www.ksiautoparts.com

HISTORICAL FINANCIALS
Company Type: Private

Income Statement
FYE: December 31

	REVENUE ($ mil.)	NET INCOME ($ mil.)	NET PROFIT MARGIN	EMPLOYEES
12/11	95	0	0.8%	100
12/10*	77	0	0.9%	0
09/09	52	2	4.1%	0
12/01	18	(0)	—	0
Annual Growth	73.5%	—	—	—

*Fiscal year change

2011 Year-End Financials

Debt ratio: ——
Return on equity: 0.80%
Cash ($ mil.): 0
Current ratio: 0.20
Long-term debt ($ mil.): —

Dividends
  Yield: —
  Payout: —
Market value ($ mil.): —

KAMO ELECTRIC COOPERATIVE INC.

LOCATIONS
HQ: KAMO ELECTRIC COOPERATIVE INC.
500 S KAMO DR, VINITA, OK 74301-4613
Phone: 918-256-5551

HISTORICAL FINANCIALS
Company Type: Private

Income Statement
FYE: December 31

	REVENUE ($ mil.)	NET INCOME ($ mil.)	NET PROFIT MARGIN	EMPLOYEES
12/11	361	19	5.3%	154
12/10	332	14	4.2%	0
12/09	338	14	4.1%	0
12/08	300	18	6.2%	0
Annual Growth	6.3%	0.8%	—	—

2011 Year-End Financials
Debt ratio: ——
Return on equity: 5.30%
Cash ($ mil.): 7
Current ratio: 0.30
Long-term debt ($ mil.): —
Dividends
Yield: —
Payout: —
Market value ($ mil.): —

KANDY KISS OF CALIFORNIA INC.

LOCATIONS
HQ: KANDY KISS OF CALIFORNIA INC.
14761 CALIFA ST, VAN NUYS, CA 91411-3107
Phone: 818-833-6360
Web: www.kandykiss.com

HISTORICAL FINANCIALS
Company Type: Private

Income Statement
FYE: December 31

	REVENUE ($ mil.)	NET INCOME ($ mil.)	NET PROFIT MARGIN	EMPLOYEES
12/11	104	0	0.7%	132
12/10	83	(0)	—	0
12/09*	91	0	0.3%	0
07/07	63	3	5.0%	0
Annual Growth	17.9%	(39.7%)	—	—

*Fiscal year change

2011 Year-End Financials
Debt ratio: ——
Return on equity: 0.70%
Cash ($ mil.): 0
Current ratio: —
Long-term debt ($ mil.): —
Dividends
Yield: —
Payout: —
Market value ($ mil.): —

KEENAN HOPKINS SCHMIDT AND STOWELL CONTRACTORS INC.

Business is always looking up for KHS&S Contractors which specializes in wall and ceiling construction including interior exterior acoustical and insulation work. KHS&S is also one of the largest theme park contractors in the US and provides water feature and rockwork technology and concrete/tilt-up construction through its d2i venture. Founded in 1984 the specialty contractor has worked on projects for Universal Studios Islands of Adventure and for Walt Disney Parks & Resorts. KHS&S also works on convention centers health care facilities office buildings laboratories and other commercial projects.

In 2010 the company's Innovative Modular Pre-Frabrication affiliate acquired assets of Eggrock Modular Solutions which manufactures prefabricated bathrooms.

EXECUTIVES
Director Marketing and Communications, Janet Puglisi
SVP KHS&S-West Coast, John Platon
President KHS&S-East Coast, Michael Cannon
President KHS&S-West Coast, David Suder
EVP KHS&S-West Coast, Philip Cherne
Group President KHS&S-Northern California, Mark Gill
CFO KHS&S Contractors, Steven Ehrlich
SVP U.S. East Coast, Pete Costello

LOCATIONS
HQ: KHS&S Contractors
5422 Bay Center Dr., Tampa FL 33609
Phone: 813-628-9330   **Fax:** 813-628-4339
Web: www.khss.com
KHS&S Contractors operates throughout the US from offices in California (Anaheim Concord and San Diego) Florida (Orlando and Tampa) Nevada (Las Vegas and Reno) New Jersey (Atlantic City) Texas (Dallas) and Washington (Seattle).

COMPETITORS
Acousti Engineering
Acoustics Incorporated
Baker Triangle
Clayco
Hunt Construction
Jacobson & Company Inc.
Performance Contracting
Tri-City Electrical Contractors
Tutor Perini

HISTORICAL FINANCIALS
Company Type: Private

Income Statement
FYE: December 31

	REVENUE ($ mil.)	NET INCOME ($ mil.)	NET PROFIT MARGIN	EMPLOYEES
12/11	73	0	1.1%	1,400
12/10	28	(3)	—	0
12/09	30	(0)	—	0
12/08	85	6	7.7%	0
Annual Growth	(4.7%)	(50.1%)	—	—

2011 Year-End Financials
Debt ratio: ——
Return on equity: 1.10%
Cash ($ mil.): 2
Current ratio: 0.10
Long-term debt ($ mil.): —
Dividends
Yield: —
Payout: —
Market value ($ mil.): —

KENAI PENINSULA BOROUGH SCHOOL DISTRICT

LOCATIONS
HQ: KENAI PENINSULA BOROUGH SCHOOL DISTRICT
148 N BINKLEY ST, SOLDOTNA, AK 99669-7520
Phone: 907-714-8888
Web: www.kpbsd.k12.ak.us

HISTORICAL FINANCIALS
Company Type: Private

Income Statement
FYE: June 30

	REVENUE ($ mil.)	NET INCOME ($ mil.)	NET PROFIT MARGIN	EMPLOYEES
06/12	155	(3)	—	1,104
06/09	137	5	3.9%	0
06/06	103	0	0.8%	0
06/05	1,091	0	0.0%	0
Annual Growth	(47.8%)	—	—	—

2012 Year-End Financials
Debt ratio: ——
Return on equity: (-2.50)%
Cash ($ mil.): 0
Current ratio: —
Long-term debt ($ mil.): —
Dividends
Yield: —
Payout: —
Market value ($ mil.): —

KENNEDY/JENKS CONSULTANTS INC.

LOCATIONS
HQ: KENNEDY/JENKS CONSULTANTS INC.
303 2ND ST STE 300, SAN FRANCISCO, CA 94107-1366
Phone: 415-243-2150
Web: www.kennedyjenks.com

HISTORICAL FINANCIALS
Company Type: Private

Income Statement

	REVENUE ($ mil.)	NET INCOME ($ mil.)	NET PROFIT MARGIN	EMPLOYEES
12/11	87	(1)	—	450
12/10	94	0	0.2%	0
12/09	92	0	0.9%	0
12/08	106	1	0.9%	0
Annual Growth	(6.2%)			

2011 Year-End Financials

Debt ratio: —
Return on equity: (-1.30)%
Cash ($ mil.): 0
Current ratio: 1.00
Long-term debt ($ mil.): —

Dividends
Yield: —
Payout: —
Market value ($ mil.): —

KENSINGTON PUBLISHING CORP.

Kensington Publishing holds court with readers. The independent publisher sells hardcover trade and mass market fiction and non-fiction books through its Kensington Zebra Pinnacle and Citadel imprints. The company publishes about 600 titles a year and has a backlist of more than 3000. Romance and women's fiction account for more than half of its titles published each year. Other niche topics covered include wicca gambling gay & lesbian and military history. Readers can turn to the company's Rebel Base Books Web site to order titles such as I Hope They Serve Beer in Hell by Tucker Max which sold more than 70000 copies its first year and made the New York Times Bestseller list in 2006 2007 and 2008.

The company's Los Angeles-based Kensington Media division (formed in 2007) focuses on selling the film and TV rights for the company's books and producing low-budget films primarily in genres such as romance African-American subject matter and fratire (a term used to describe politically incorrect overtly masculine literature such as I Hope They Serve Beer in Hell). The division's first book-to-film project is The Company We Keep based on a book by Mary Monroe.

The company was founded in 1974 by Chairman Emeritus Walter Zacharius. His son Stephen is president and CEO; grandson Adam is also an executive.

EXECUTIVES

Founder and Chairman Emeritus, Walter Zacharius
President and CEO, Steven (Steve) Zacharius
VP and Publisher, Laurie Perkin

LOCATIONS

HQ: Kensington Publishing Corp.
119 W. 40th St., New York NY 10018
Phone: 212-407-1500 **Fax:** 212-935-0699
Web: www.kensingtonbooks.com

PRODUCTS/OPERATIONS

Selected Imprints
Aphrodesia
Brava
Citadel
Dafina
Kensington
Pinnacle
Zebra

COMPETITORS

Bloomsbury
Hachette Book Group
Harlequin Enterprises
HarperCollins
Random House
Simon & Schuster

HISTORICAL FINANCIALS
Company Type: Private

Income Statement
FYE: September 30

	REVENUE ($ mil.)	NET INCOME ($ mil.)	NET PROFIT MARGIN	EMPLOYEES
09/11	64	3	4.9%	80
09/06	56	1	3.4%	0
09/05	47	1	2.3%	0
09/04	47	45	97.3%	0
Annual Growth	11.1%	(59.1%)		

2011 Year-End Financials

Debt ratio: —
Return on equity: 4.90%
Cash ($ mil.): 22
Current ratio: 0.60
Long-term debt ($ mil.): —

Dividends
Yield: —
Payout: —
Market value ($ mil.): —

KENT INTERMEDIATE SCHOOL DISTRICT

LOCATIONS

HQ: KENT INTERMEDIATE SCHOOL DISTRICT
2930 KNAPP ST NE, GRAND RAPIDS, MI 49525-7006
Phone: 616-364-1333
Web: www.kentisd.org

HISTORICAL FINANCIALS
Company Type: Private

Income Statement
FYE: June 30

	REVENUE ($ mil.)	NET INCOME ($ mil.)	NET PROFIT MARGIN	EMPLOYEES
06/12	231	0	0.2%	1,000
06/11	243	0	0.2%	0
06/10	249	1	0.5%	0
06/09	234	(8)	—	0
Annual Growth	(0.4%)			

2012 Year-End Financials

Debt ratio: —
Return on equity: 0.20%
Cash ($ mil.): 6
Current ratio: 0.20
Long-term debt ($ mil.): —

Dividends
Yield: —
Payout: —
Market value ($ mil.): —

KENTUCKY LAKE OIL COMPANY INC.

LOCATIONS

HQ: KENTUCKY LAKE OIL COMPANY INC.
620 S 4TH ST, MURRAY, KY 42071-2680
Phone: 270-753-1323

HISTORICAL FINANCIALS
Company Type: Private

Income Statement
FYE: December 31

	REVENUE ($ mil.)	NET INCOME ($ mil.)	NET PROFIT MARGIN	EMPLOYEES
12/11	121	0	0.2%	170
12/10	98	0	0.5%	0
12/09	80	0	0.0%	0
12/08	90	0	0.9%	0
Annual Growth	10.4%	(30.9%)		

2011 Year-End Financials

Debt ratio: —
Return on equity: 0.20%
Cash ($ mil.): 0
Current ratio: 0.40
Long-term debt ($ mil.): —

Dividends
Yield: —
Payout: —
Market value ($ mil.): —

KENTUCKY MEDICAL SERVICES FOUNDATION INC.

Does the mailbox at your old Kentucky home contain doctors' bills? They might be from Kentucky Medical Services Foundation. The physician's practice group provides billing and other administrative services for the more than 600 physicians and other health care providers affiliated with the University of Kentucky's health system UK HealthCare. The network provides more than 80 specialty services offers educational programs and operates acute medical centers including Chandler Hospital Good Samaritan Hospital and Kentucky Children's Hospital.

EXECUTIVES

Executive Director, Darrell Griffith
IT Manager, Jamie Tillett
Associate Director Business Operations, Peggy Halcomb
Human Resources Manager, Garland Strang

LOCATIONS

HQ: Kentucky Medical Services Foundation Inc.
138 Leader Ave., Lexington KY 40508
Phone: 859-257-7910 **Fax:** 859-257-7960

COMPETITORS

Appalachian Regional Healthcare
Baptist Health

Catholic Health Initiatives
Jewish Hospital & St. Mary' s HealthCare
Norton Healthcare

HISTORICAL FINANCIALS
Company Type: Private - Not-for-Profit

Income Statement
FYE: June 30

	REVENUE ($ mil.)	NET INCOME ($ mil.)	NET PROFIT MARGIN	EMPLOYEES
06/11	203	(2)	—	150
06/10	196	(4)	—	0
06/09	189	2	1.4%	0
06/08	177	1	0.7%	0
Annual Growth	4.7%	—	—	—

2011 Year-End Financials

Debt ratio: —
Return on equity: (-1.20)%
Cash ($ mil.): 38
Current ratio: 0.60
Long-term debt ($ mil.): —

Dividends
Yield: —
Payout: —
Market value ($ mil.): —

KERN REGIONAL CENTER

LOCATIONS

HQ: KERN REGIONAL CENTER
3200 N SILLECT AVE, BAKERSFIELD, CA 93308-6333
Phone: 661-327-8531
Web: www.kernrc.org

HISTORICAL FINANCIALS
Company Type: Private

Income Statement
FYE: June 30

	REVENUE ($ mil.)	NET INCOME ($ mil.)	NET PROFIT MARGIN	EMPLOYEES
06/11	140	(0)	—	178
06/10	136	0	0.0%	0
06/09	136	0	—	0
06/08	125	(0)	—	0
Annual Growth	4.0%	—	—	—

2011 Year-End Financials

Debt ratio: —
Return on equity: —
Cash ($ mil.): 3
Current ratio: 0.50
Long-term debt ($ mil.): —

Dividends
Yield: —
Payout: —
Market value ($ mil.): —

KETTERING UNIVERSITY

Sometimes referred to as the "West Point of Industry" Kettering University specializes in engineering science and mathematics programs. Other academic fields include business pre-law pre-med and computer gaming. The private school offers undergraduate and graduate degrees to a small student body of about 2000. Kettering University was founded in 1919 as the School of Automotive Trades. It later became the General Motors Institute. In 1998 the school was renamed in honor of Charles F. "The Boss" Kettering founder of Delco Electronics which was acquired by General Motors in 1936 and absorbed by auto parts manufacturer (and GM spin-off) Delphi in 1997.

Prior to 1982 GM fully supported the college and set the stage for Kettering to attain the reputation as one of the preeminent cooperative education institutions in the country. Today students co-op in aerospace CPA government law medical not-for-profit and research firms in addition to traditional co-ops in the manufacturing sector.

EXECUTIVES

President, Stan R. Liberty
VP Administration and Finance, Susan K. Bolt
Director Marketing, Julie A. Ulseth
VP Human Resources, Linda K. Peterson
SVP Academic Affairs and Provost, Robert L. Simpson
VP Graduate Studies Corporate Connections and Business Graduate Studies and Extension Services, Tony Hain
VP Information Technology and CIO, James A. (Jim) Hamilton
Director of External Affairs and Associate to the President, Robert M. (Bob) Nichols
Chief Public Relations Officer, Patricia A. (Pat) Mroczek
Director of Publications and Communications and Lecturer of Communications, Gary J. Erwin
Director Media Relations, Dawn M. Hibbard
Director Recreation Services, David (Dave) Stewart
Controller, Beth Covers
Associate VP Individual Gifts, Judy Howald
Corporate Relations Manager, Venetia Chaney
Director Human Resources Environment Health and Safety, Nadine L. Thor
Director Information Systems Technology, Donald J. Vantine
VP University Advancement, Dennis Washington
Director Academic Services, Carol Brooks
Academic Advisor, Ella Derricks
Director Annual Giving, Michele Loper
Assistant to the President, Susan Reynolds
Provost and VP Academic Affairs, Michael Harris
Website Content Administrator, Deena J. Hosmer
Director Pre-College Programs, Ricky Brown
Chief Great Court Campus Center, Jim Benford
Director Wellness Center, Deborah Williams-Roberts
Housing Secretary, Fran Webster
Manager Human Resources, Elizabeth Ewald
Manager Corporate Relations, Darren Heartwell
President, Robert K. McMahan
VP Administration and Finance, Tom Ayers
VP Instructional Administrative and Information Technology, Viola Sprague

LOCATIONS

HQ: KETTERING UNIVERSITY
1700 UNIVERSITY AVE, FLINT, MI 48504-4898
Phone: 810-762-9925
Web: www.kettering.edu

HISTORICAL FINANCIALS
Company Type: School

Income Statement
FYE: June 30

	REVENUE ($ mil.)	NET INCOME ($ mil.)	NET PROFIT MARGIN	EMPLOYEES
06/12	49	(5)	—	425
06/11	54	9	17.9%	0
06/10	59	5	9.0%	0
06/09	41	(15)	—	0
Annual Growth	6.2%	—	—	—

2012 Year-End Financials

Debt ratio: —
Return on equity: (-10.30)%
Cash ($ mil.): 9
Current ratio: —
Long-term debt ($ mil.): —

Dividends
Yield: —
Payout: —
Market value ($ mil.): —

KEY FOOD STORES CO-OPERATIVE INC.

LOCATIONS

HQ: KEY FOOD STORES CO-OPERATIVE INC.
1200 SOUTH AVE, STATEN ISLAND, NY 10314-3413
Phone: 718-370-4200
Web: www.keyfoodstores.com

HISTORICAL FINANCIALS
Company Type: Private

Income Statement
FYE: April 28

	REVENUE ($ mil.)	NET INCOME ($ mil.)	NET PROFIT MARGIN	EMPLOYEES
04/12	578	(0)	—	66
04/11	537	(0)	—	0
04/10	0	0	—	0
Annual Growth	—	—	—	—

2012 Year-End Financials

Debt ratio: —
Return on equity: —
Cash ($ mil.): 10
Current ratio: 0.80
Long-term debt ($ mil.): —

Dividends
Yield: —
Payout: —
Market value ($ mil.): —

KEYSTONE SERVICE SYSTEMS INC.

LOCATIONS

HQ: KEYSTONE SERVICE SYSTEMS INC.
124 PINE ST, HARRISBURG, PA 17101-1208
Phone: 717-232-7509
Web: www.keystonehumanservices.org

HISTORICAL FINANCIALS
Company Type: Private

Income Statement
FYE: June 30

	REVENUE ($ mil.)	NET INCOME ($ mil.)	NET PROFIT MARGIN	EMPLOYEES
06/11	89	0	0.9%	2,200
06/10	88	1	1.8%	0
06/09	85	1	1.5%	0
06/08	0	(0)	—	0
Annual Growth	425.3%	—	—	—

2011 Year-End Financials
Debt ratio: ——
Return on equity: 0.90%
Cash ($ mil.): 0
Current ratio: 0.90
Long-term debt ($ mil.): —

Dividends
Yield: —
Payout: —
Market value ($ mil.): —

KIC HOLDINGS INC.

LOCATIONS
HQ: KIC HOLDINGS INC.
3800 FRUIT VALLEY RD, VANCOUVER, WA 98660-1220
Phone: 360-823-4440

HISTORICAL FINANCIALS
Company Type: Private

Income Statement
FYE: December 31

	REVENUE ($ mil.)	NET INCOME ($ mil.)	NET PROFIT MARGIN	EMPLOYEES
12/11	105	3	3.0%	15
12/10	50	0	1.9%	0
12/09	29	(0)	—	0
12/08	36	0	2.0%	0
Annual Growth	42.3%	63.4%	—	—

KILLIAN CONSTRUCTION CO.

LOCATIONS
HQ: KILLIAN CONSTRUCTION CO.
2664 E KEARNEY ST, SPRINGFIELD, MO 65803-4913
Phone: 417-883-1204
Web: www.killco.com

HISTORICAL FINANCIALS
Company Type: Private

Income Statement
FYE: September 30

	REVENUE ($ mil.)	NET INCOME ($ mil.)	NET PROFIT MARGIN	EMPLOYEES
09/11	101	0	0.5%	80
09/10	33	0	0.0%	0
Annual Growth	200.4%	7153.1%		

2011 Year-End Financials
Debt ratio: ——
Return on equity: 0.50%
Cash ($ mil.): 13
Current ratio: 0.40
Long-term debt ($ mil.): —

Dividends
Yield: —
Payout: —
Market value ($ mil.): —

KINGSTON HEALTHCARE COMPANY

LOCATIONS
HQ: KINGSTON HEALTHCARE COMPANY
1 SEAGATE STE 1960, TOLEDO, OH 43604-1592
Phone: 419-247-2880
Web: www.kingstonhealthcare.com

HISTORICAL FINANCIALS
Company Type: Private

Income Statement
FYE: December 31

	REVENUE ($ mil.)	NET INCOME ($ mil.)	NET PROFIT MARGIN	EMPLOYEES
12/11	86	9	11.1%	565
12/10	83	7	9.5%	0
Annual Growth	3.8%	22.1%	—	—

2011 Year-End Financials
Debt ratio: ——
Return on equity: 11.10%
Cash ($ mil.): 18
Current ratio: 1.80
Long-term debt ($ mil.): —

Dividends
Yield: —
Payout: —
Market value ($ mil.): —

KIRBY RISK CORPORATION

Kirby Risk sees nothing risky about helping harness a little electrical energy. The company named after one of its co-founders supplies electrical products (process automation products drives and motors lighting fuses wire and cable) and services to the Midwestern US. The company operates through four business units comprising Electrical Supply Service Center Mechanical Solutions and Service and Precision Machining. The Electrical Supply distribution unit handles more than 20000 products from some 500 manufacturers including GE Thomas & Betts and Rockwell Automation.

Other operations include ARCO Electric Products (phase converters). CEO James Risk III owns the company that was founded in 1926.

Operations

The company's Electrical Supply division stocks lighting and power instruments while the Kirby Risk Service Center makes custom wiring harnesses control panels subassemblies and kits for industrial customers. Mechanical Solutions and Service is the repair end of the business it also sells motors power transmissions and generators.

Kirby Risk Precision Machining offers precision machining using CNC (computer numerical control) technology. ARCO manufactures roto-phase converters which are rotary-type generators (different from static phase converters) as well as power factor correction capacitors.

Sales and Marketing

The company has roughly 35 customer service locations throughout Illinois Indiana and Ohio.

Company Background

Otto Keiffer and J. Kirby Risk founded the company as the Keiffer-Risk Battery Company in 1926 in an abandoned blacksmith shop in Lafayette Indiana.

EXECUTIVES
CEO, James K. Risk III
VP and CFO, Jason Bricker
President, John Burke
President and COO Manufacturing Group, Douglas A. Mansfield
Manager Sales Administration and Pricing, Edgar Cyr

LOCATIONS
HQ: Kirby Risk Corporation
1815 Sagamore Pkwy. N., Lafayette IN 47904
Phone: 765-448-4567   **Fax:** 765-447-3621
Web: www.kirbyrisk.com

PRODUCTS/OPERATIONS

Selected Divisions
Arco Electric Products
Electrical supply
Mechanical solutions and service
Precision machining
Service center

COMPETITORS

Anixter International	Premier Farnell
Consolidated	Rexel Inc.
Electrical	Skyworks
Graybar Electric	SUMMIT Electric Supply
Hagemeyer North	W.W. Grainger
America	WESCO International

HISTORICAL FINANCIALS
Company Type: Private

Income Statement
FYE: December 31

	REVENUE ($ mil.)	NET INCOME ($ mil.)	NET PROFIT MARGIN	EMPLOYEES
12/11	377	0	—	950
12/10	399	0	—	0
12/09	0	0	—	0
12/08	399	0	—	0
Annual Growth	(1.8%)	—	—	—

Debt ratio: —
Return on equity: —
Cash ($ mil.): 6   Dividends
Current ratio: 2.00   Yield: —
Long-term debt ($ mil.): —   Payout: —
                                    Market value ($ mil.): —

KNIGHTS OF COLUMBUS

Good Knight! The Knights of Columbus is a formidable volunteer group boasting about 14000 councils made up of 1.8 million Roman Catholic male members in the US Canada Mexico Cuba the Philippines Poland and several other countries. The organization is also a force to be reckoned with in the insurance world providing life insurance annuities and long-term care insurance to its members and their families. In addition the group manages the Knights of Columbus Museum in New Haven Connecticut featuring exhibits of religious art and history. The Knights of Columbus was founded in New Haven by Father Michael J. McGivney in 1882 and has been selling insurance since its founding.

Geographic Reach

The Knights of Columbus comprises more than 14000 local councils throughout the US Canada Mexico Puerto Rico Guam and the U.S.Virgin Islands. It also has councils in the Bahamas Cuba the Dominican Republic Guatemala Panama the Philippines Poland and Saipan.

Operations

The Knights of Columbus is also engaged in religious education the support of public policy issues (including immigration reform marriage protection opposing abortion) and charitable activities such as disaster relief. Indeed The Gulf States relief efforts led the Knights to a record year of charitable giving with more than 64 million hours and $139 million dollars donated overall. Also the organization underwrote the cost of restoration work done on the gravesite of President John F. Kennedy in Arlington National Cemetery in 2010.

Financial Performance

During the past decade the charity has raised more than $1.4 billion. Total charitable contributions totaled $154.6 million in 2011 exeeding 2010's total by more than $3.4 million.

EXECUTIVES

Supreme Knight, Carl A. Anderson
EVP Agencies and Marketing, Thomas P. (Tom) Smith Jr.
VP Information Systems, Robert (Bob) Blanchette
CIO, Gary Wood
Supreme Chaplain, Bishop William E. Lori
Deputy Supreme Knight, Dennis Savoie
Supreme Advocate, Paul R. Devin
VP Communications, Patrick Korten
Director Media Relations, Andrew Walther
Director Public Relations, Peter Sonski
Supreme Treasurer, John W. O'Reilly Jr.
Supreme Secretary, Donald R. Kehoe
Supreme Treasurer, Logan T. Ludwig
Supreme Secretary, Charles E. Maurer Jr.
Supreme Advocate and General Counsel, John A. Marrella

LOCATIONS

HQ: Knights of Columbus
 1 Columbus Plaza, New Haven CT 06510
Phone: 203-752-4000   **Fax:** 203-752-4100
Web: www.kofc.org

PRODUCTS/OPERATIONS

2011 Charitable Contributions

	$ mil.	% of total
State and local affiliates	125	81
Supreme Council	29	19
Total	**154**	**100**

HISTORICAL FINANCIALS
Company Type: Private - Not-for-Profit

Income Statement   FYE: December 31

	REVENUE ($ mil.)	NET INCOME ($ mil.)	NET PROFIT MARGIN	EMPLOYEES
12/11	2,059	81	3.9%	2,300
12/10*	1,937	86	4.5%	0
06/09	0	(0)	—	0
12/99	1,335	109	8.2%	0
Annual Growth	**15.5%**	**(9.4%)**	—	—

*Fiscal year change

2011 Year-End Financials

Debt ratio: —
Return on equity: 3.90%
Cash ($ mil.): 389   Dividends
Current ratio: —   Yield: —
Long-term debt ($ mil.): —   Payout: —
                                 Market value ($ mil.): —

KNUST-SBO LTD.

LOCATIONS

HQ: KNUST-SBO LTD.
 8625 MEADOWCROFT DR, HOUSTON, TX 77063-5011
Phone: 713-785-1060
Web: www.knust.com

HISTORICAL FINANCIALS
Company Type: Private

Income Statement   FYE: December 31

	REVENUE ($ mil.)	NET INCOME ($ mil.)	NET PROFIT MARGIN	EMPLOYEES
12/11	81	14	17.3%	178
12/10	68	12	17.7%	0
12/08	122	31	26.1%	0
12/07	108	26	24.3%	0
Annual Growth	**(9.2%)**	**(18.9%)**	—	—

2011 Year-End Financials

Debt ratio: —
Return on equity: 17.30%
Cash ($ mil.): 22   Dividends
Current ratio: 7.10   Yield: —
Long-term debt ($ mil.): —   Payout: —
                                 Market value ($ mil.): —

KONIAG DEVELOPMENT CORPORATION

LOCATIONS

HQ: KONIAG DEVELOPMENT CORPORATION
 4300 B ST STE 408, ANCHORAGE, AK 99503-5933
Phone: 907-261-4040
Web: www.koniagdevelopment.com

HISTORICAL FINANCIALS
Company Type: Private

Income Statement   FYE: March 31

	REVENUE ($ mil.)	NET INCOME ($ mil.)	NET PROFIT MARGIN	EMPLOYEES
03/12	120	(3)	—	820
03/11	122	9	8.0%	0
03/10	136	3	2.4%	0
03/09	112	1	1.3%	0
Annual Growth	**2.2%**	—	—	—

2012 Year-End Financials

Debt ratio: —
Return on equity: (-2.60)%
Cash ($ mil.): 4   Dividends
Current ratio: 0.10   Yield: —
Long-term debt ($ mil.): —   Payout: —
                                 Market value ($ mil.): —

KONIAG INC.

LOCATIONS

HQ: KONIAG INC.
 4300 B ST STE 407, ANCHORAGE, AK 99503-5961
Phone: 907-561-2668
Web: www.koniag.com

HISTORICAL FINANCIALS
Company Type: Private

Income Statement   FYE: March 31

	ASSETS ($ mil.)	NET INCOME ($ mil.)	INCOME AS % OF ASSETS	EMPLOYEES
03/12	145	5	4.0%	834
03/11	160	8	5.4%	0
03/10	143	6	4.5%	0
03/09	145	6	4.2%	0
Annual Growth	**(0.0%)**	**(1.3%)**	—	—

2012 Year-End Financials

Debt ratio: —
Return on equity: 4.60%
Cash ($ mil.): 0   Dividends
Current ratio: 0.60   Yield: —
Long-term debt ($ mil.): —   Payout: —
                                 Market value ($ mil.): —

KONVISSER CUSTOM SOFTWARE

LOCATIONS

HQ: KONVISSER CUSTOM SOFTWARE
5109 DEER RUN CIR, ORCHARD LAKE, MI
48323-1510
Phone: 248-682-3009

HISTORICAL FINANCIALS

Company Type: Private

Income Statement
FYE: December 31

	REVENUE ($ mil.)	NET INCOME ($ mil.)	NET PROFIT MARGIN	EMPLOYEES
12/11	214	17	8.1%	2
Annual Growth	—	—	—	—

2011 Year-End Financials

Debt ratio: —
Return on equity: 8.10%
Cash ($ mil.): 0
Current ratio: 1.00
Long-term debt ($ mil.): —

Dividends
Yield: —
Payout: —
Market value ($ mil.): —

KORTE CONSTRUCTION COMPANY

The Korte Company provides design/build design/build/furnish construction management and interior design services for a variety of commercial and industrial construction projects. The group works on projects that include warehouse/distribution centers recreational centers schools office complexes churches and facilities for local state and federal government agencies including Department of Defense. The Korte Company which was founded in 1958 operates from offices in Las Vegas St. Louis and Highland Illinois.

In 2007 the company won contracts for naval projects from the US Navy totalling some $50 million. It also won an $18 million contract from the US Air Force.

That year Chairman Ralph Korte donated a St. Louis building worth $1 million to the Center for Emerging Technologies a nonprofit business incubator that launches medical and high-tech startups.

EXECUTIVES

President and CEO, Todd Korte
SVP and President Las Vegas Operations, Greg Korte
EVP Production, Thomas Korte
New Business Specialist, Ted Giza
Permit Expediter, Bobbi Davis

LOCATIONS

HQ: The Korte Company
The Annex - Ste. 200 700 St. Louis Union Station, St. Louis MO 63103
Phone: 314-231-3700   **Fax:** 314-231-4682
Web: www.korteco.com

COMPETITORS

Berglund Construction	J.E. Dunn Construction
Bulley & Andrews	Leopardo
Clarkson Construction	Ragnar Benson
George Sollitt Construction	West Coast Contractors of Nevada
HOK	

HISTORICAL FINANCIALS

Company Type: Private

Income Statement
FYE: December 31

	REVENUE ($ mil.)	NET INCOME ($ mil.)	NET PROFIT MARGIN	EMPLOYEES
12/11	240	1	0.7%	170
12/10	267	13	5.0%	0
12/09	264	11	4.2%	0
12/08	362	10	3.0%	0
Annual Growth	(12.7%)	(45.6%)	—	—

2011 Year-End Financials

Debt ratio: —
Return on equity: 0.70%
Cash ($ mil.): 4
Current ratio: 0.70
Long-term debt ($ mil.): —

Dividends
Yield: —
Payout: —
Market value ($ mil.): —

KQED INC.

Public interest is a big concern for this West Coast broadcasting company. Publicly financed TV and radio broadcaster KQED serves the Northern California area through its flagship KQED Public Television 9 station. KQED produces and broadcasts educational programming focused on arts science and the humanities as well as public interest shows highlighting local national and international issues. It creates most of its own programming but also specializes in broadcasting independent films and programs from PBS and other distributors. In addition KQED Public Radio broadcasts to listeners across San Francisco and Sacramento and its website provides event listings resources polls podcasts and blogs.

EXECUTIVES

President and CEO, John L. Boland
EVP Marketing and Communications, Donald W. (Don) Derheim
Chief Development Officer, Traci A. Eckels
VP Human Resources and Labor Relations, Joanne Carder
VP KQED Public Radio General Manager, Jo Anne Wallace
VP Television Content, Michael Isip
VP Engineering and Technology, Steve Welch
Chief Content Officer, Linda O'Bryon
VP Digital Media and Education, Tim Olson
Executive Director Communications, Scott Walton
Vice Chair, Anne Avis
Chair, Willa Seldon
Executive Director and Executive Producer KTEH Public Television, Becca King Reed
Interim CFO, Mitzie Kelley
Interim General Counsel and Corporate Secretary, William L. Lowery
Director and Board Treasurer, Elizabeth (Betsy) Hambrecht, age 49
Director, David L. Mahoney, age 58

Director, Tom Epstein
Director, David Lee
Vice Chair, Anne Avis
Director, John Sobrato
Director, Brenda Boudreaux
Director, Lee Caraher
Director, Dianne Harrison
Director, Yogen Dalal
Director and Board Secretary, Scott Dettmer
Director, Warren Hellman
Director, Marie Jorajuria
Director, Heidi Locke Simon
Director, Michael Billeci
Director, Chuck Kissner
Director, Daphne Li
Director, Srini Madala
Director, Charley Moore
Director, Mike Ramsay
Director, Jay Yamada
Auditors: Hood&Strong

LOCATIONS

HQ: KQED Inc.
2601 Mariposa St., San Francisco CA 94110
Phone: 415-864-2000   **Fax:** 978-952-8065
Web: www.doversaddlery.com

COMPETITORS

A&E Networks	Discovery
ABC Inc.	Communications
CBS	Entercom
CBS Radio	NBC
Citadel Broadcasting	New Young Broadcasting
Clear Channel	Pacifica
Cox Enterprises	Spanish Broadcasting
Cumulus Media	Univision
Current Media	

HISTORICAL FINANCIALS

Company Type: Private - Not-for-Profit

Income Statement
FYE: September 30

	REVENUE ($ mil.)	NET INCOME ($ mil.)	NET PROFIT MARGIN	EMPLOYEES
09/11	62	1	3.0%	266
09/10	56	3	6.4%	0
09/09	62	0	1.5%	0
09/08	63	(5)	—	0
Annual Growth	(0.6%)	—	—	—

2011 Year-End Financials

Debt ratio: —
Return on equity: 3.00%
Cash ($ mil.): 13
Current ratio: 1.90
Long-term debt ($ mil.): —

Dividends
Yield: —
Payout: —
Market value ($ mil.): —

KRUEGER INTERNATIONAL INC.

Krueger International can be found in cubicles classrooms cafeterias and college dorms. The company which does business as KI makes ergonomic seating cabinets and other furniture used by businesses health care organizations government agencies and educational institutions. The company offers everything from benches and beds to desks and tables not to mention shelving filing systems movable walls and trash bins. KI markets its products through sales representatives furniture dealers architects and interior designers worldwide. Founded in 1941 KI was purchased in the 1980s by its managers who later allowed employees to buy stock. Today KI is 100% employee owned.

Geographic Reach

KI operates manufacturing facilities and sales offices in the US Canada China and India as well as throughout Europe Latin America and Asia. It has subsidiaries based in the UK Canada India and Malaysia.

Operations

KI is well-regarded in the classroom furniture market and is a leading supplier for both K-12 schools and universities. The company has outfitted classrooms lecture halls administrative offices computer labs media centers residence halls and student unions. KI has been a government vendor for more than six decades and provided furnishings for an assortment of federal agencies including all branches of the military. KI's corporate offerings are ergonomically designed to help individuals work more comfortably and efficiently and its health care furniture allows for comfort. In addition to these core customer groups KI has also installed its furnishings in outdoor public spaces sports arenas conference centers and airports.

Strategy

The company has been expanding its network of showrooms both in the US and abroad. KI added a showroom in Houston in 2010 adding to its existing US presence which includes about 10 locations in half a dozen states. To better serve its Asian and European customers the company operates through a showroom in Shanghai China. KI has international showrooms in London Malaysia Mexico Puerto Rico and Toronto. As its showroom presence grows KI has also formed new sales partnerships. The company tapped Heartland Furniture Group (HFG) a contract furniture representative in 2011 to take care of existing customer accounts and broker sales in Kansas Missouri and southern Illinois. It's also looking to acquisitions to extend the reach of its business. In late 2012 KI agreed to purchase Sebel Furniture Limited from GWA Group Ltd. a top supplier of building fixtures in Australia. The $24 million deal gives KI a foothold in the commercial furniture business in Australia New Zealand the UK and Hong Kong.

EXECUTIVES

CFO and Treasurer, Mark Olsen
President and CEO, Richard J. Resch
VP Education Markets, Nat Porter
VP Healthcare, Debbie Breunig
Senior Product Manager Architectural Walls, Andy Kopish
Product Manager Movable Walls, Rob Wittl
VP Sales Eastern Region, John Duffy
Seating Product Manager, Leo Welter
VP National Accounts, Mike Watson
Dealer Representative Southern California, Gregg Kent
VP Business Markets, Jonathan Webb
VP Sales, Richard Butrym
EVP, Brian Krenke
Manager Government Marketing, Randy Hoople
Corporate Communications, Ken Burkard

LOCATIONS

HQ: Krueger International Inc.
1330 Bellevue St., Green Bay WI 54302
Phone: 920-468-8100   **Fax:** 920-468-0280
Web: www.ki.com

PRODUCTS/OPERATIONS

Selected Products

Auditorium seating
Beds
Benches
Bookcases
Carrels
Chairs
Desks
File cabinets
Lecterns
Movable walls
Planters
Power and data connections
Receptacles
Recliners
Residence hall furniture
Sleepers
Special events seating
Stools
Tables

COMPETITORS

ABCO Office Furniture	Kewaunee Scientific
Allsteel	Kimball International
Bretford	Knoll Inc.
CFGroup	La-Z-Boy
Columbia Manufacturing	Norstar Office
Edsal Manufacturing	Products
Global Group	Royal Seating
Haworth Inc.	Sagus
Herman Miller	Steelcase
HNI	Trendway
Inscape corp	Virco Mfg.

HISTORICAL FINANCIALS

Company Type: Private

Income Statement

FYE: December 31

	REVENUE ($ mil.)	NET INCOME ($ mil.)	NET PROFIT MARGIN	EMPLOYEES
12/11	649	56	8.8%	2,300
12/10	615	59	9.6%	0
12/08	665	36	5.4%	0
12/06	610	33	5.4%	0
Annual Growth	2.1%	19.8%	—	—

2011 Year-End Financials

Debt ratio: ——
Return on equity: 8.80%
Cash ($ mil.): 3
Current ratio: 0.80
Long-term debt ($ mil.): —

Dividends
Yield: —
Payout: —
Market value ($ mil.): —

KUAKINI HEALTH SYSTEM

Say aloha to better health! Kuakini Health System operates the non-profit Kuakini Medical Center a 250-bed acute care hospital that provides specialty services including cancer treatment cardiac care and orthopedic surgery. The hospital serves as a teaching center for the University of Hawaii's John A. Burns School of Medicine. Kuakini Health System also operates the 234-bed Kuakini Geriatric Care facility which offers nursing home and adult day care for Honolulu's senior citizens. The system also maintains two medical office buildings. The Kuakini Health System was founded by Japanese immigrants in 1900. It is a member of the Premier group purchasing alliance.

EXECUTIVES

President and CEO, Gary K. Kajiwara
VP Medical Affairs, Nobuyuki Miki
SVP and COO, Greg Oishi
CFO, Quin Ogawa
VP Clinical Services, June Drumeller
Manager Human Resources and Payroll, Ann Choy
Director Surgical Services, Ka`imi Maka
Nursing Director Long Term Care, Laurene Chun
Managing Director Facilities, Hubert Biete
Cardiac Catheterization Services Manager, Stephen Foster
Patient Care Coordinator Emergency Services, Carlene Peterson
Chief of Staff, Michael Nagoshi
Marketing and Public Relations Manager, Donda D. Spiker
Medical Director Emergency Medicine, Myo Nwe
Medical Director Nuclear Medicine, Michael Ling
Medical Director Pathology, Eugene T. Yanagihara
Medical Director Radiation Therapy, Charles H. Yamashiro
Medical Director Radiology, Matthew I. Yuh
Auditors: Deloitte&ToucheLLP

LOCATIONS

HQ: Kuakini Health System
347 N. Kuakini St., Honolulu HI 96817
Phone: 808-536-2236   **Fax:** 808-547-9547
Web: www.kuakini.org

COMPETITORS

Hawai' i Pacific Health
Queen' s Medical Center
Rehabilitation Hospital of the Pacific

HISTORICAL FINANCIALS

Company Type: Private

Income Statement

FYE: June 30

	REVENUE ($ mil.)	NET INCOME ($ mil.)	NET PROFIT MARGIN	EMPLOYEES
06/11	149	(12)	—	1,400
06/10	1	0	0.0%	0
06/09	1	0	22.0%	0
06/08	1	0	2.2%	0
Annual Growth	408.4%	—	—	—

2011 Year-End Financials

Debt ratio: ——
Return on equity: (-8.50)%
Cash ($ mil.): 21
Current ratio: 1.50
Long-term debt ($ mil.): —

Dividends
Yield: —
Payout: —
Market value ($ mil.): —

KUAKINI MEDICAL CENTER

LOCATIONS

HQ: KUAKINI MEDICAL CENTER
347 N KUAKINI ST, HONOLULU, HI 96817-2381
Phone: 808-547-9231
Web: www.kuakini.org

HISTORICAL FINANCIALS
Company Type: Private

Income Statement				FYE: June 30
	REVENUE ($ mil.)	NET INCOME ($ mil.)	NET PROFIT MARGIN	EMPLOYEES
06/11	126	(3)	—	1,216
06/10*	124	(0)	—	0
12/09	1	0	3.4%	0
06/09	132	2	2.0%	0
Annual Growth	**(1.6%)**	**—**	**—**	**—**

*Fiscal year change

2011 Year-End Financials
Debt ratio: ——
Return on equity: (-3.10)%
Cash ($ mil.): 5
Current ratio: 2.30
Long-term debt ($ mil.): —
Dividends
  Yield: —
  Payout: —
  Market value ($ mil.): —

KUNA MEAT COMPANY INC.

LOCATIONS

HQ: KUNA MEAT COMPANY INC.
704 KUNA INDUSTRIAL CT, DUPO, IL 62239-1823
Phone: 618-286-4000
Web: www.kunafoodservice.com

HISTORICAL FINANCIALS
Company Type: Private

Income Statement				FYE: December 31
	REVENUE ($ mil.)	NET INCOME ($ mil.)	NET PROFIT MARGIN	EMPLOYEES
12/11*	96	0	0.9%	105
01/11	79	1	1.4%	0
01/10	70	(0)	—	0
01/09	71	(0)	—	0
Annual Growth	**10.6%**	**—**	**—**	**—**

*Fiscal year change

L & M TRANSPORTATION SERVICES INC.

LOCATIONS

HQ: L & M TRANSPORTATION SERVICES INC.
2925 HUNTLEIGH DR STE 104, RALEIGH, NC 27604-3373
Phone: 919-876-5942
Web: www.lmts.com

HISTORICAL FINANCIALS
Company Type: Private

Income Statement				FYE: December 31
	REVENUE ($ mil.)	NET INCOME ($ mil.)	NET PROFIT MARGIN	EMPLOYEES
12/11	93	0	0.9%	45
12/10	87	0	0.8%	0
12/98	42	1	2.6%	0
Annual Growth	**47.7%**	**(14.0%)**	**—**	**—**

LA BODEGA MEAT INC.

LOCATIONS

HQ: LA BODEGA MEAT INC.
2600 MCCREE RD STE 99, GARLAND, TX 75041-3901
Phone: 972-926-6129
Web: www.labodegacorp.com

HISTORICAL FINANCIALS
Company Type: Private

Income Statement				FYE: December 31
	REVENUE ($ mil.)	NET INCOME ($ mil.)	NET PROFIT MARGIN	EMPLOYEES
12/11	128	6	5.0%	99
12/10	102	7	7.4%	0
12/09	83	4	5.6%	0
Annual Growth	**23.7%**	**17.4%**	**—**	**—**

2011 Year-End Financials
Debt ratio: ——
Return on equity: 5.00%
Cash ($ mil.): 1
Current ratio: 0.70
Long-term debt ($ mil.): —
Dividends
  Yield: —
  Payout: —
  Market value ($ mil.): —

LA PLATA ELECTRIC ASSOCIATION INC.

LOCATIONS

HQ: LA PLATA ELECTRIC ASSOCIATION INC.
45 STEWART ST, DURANGO, CO 81303-7915
Phone: 970-247-5786
Web: www.lpea.com

HISTORICAL FINANCIALS
Company Type: Private

Income Statement				FYE: December 31
	REVENUE ($ mil.)	NET INCOME ($ mil.)	NET PROFIT MARGIN	EMPLOYEES
12/11	110	6	5.9%	113
12/10	113	7	6.8%	0
12/09	110	10	9.8%	0
12/08	94	12	13.3%	0
Annual Growth	**5.4%**	**(19.6%)**	**—**	**—**

2011 Year-End Financials
Debt ratio: ——
Return on equity: 5.90%
Cash ($ mil.): 10
Current ratio: 1.40
Long-term debt ($ mil.): —
Dividends
  Yield: —
  Payout: —
  Market value ($ mil.): —

LAFAYETTE COLLEGE

Lafayette College has a revolutionary background. The school offers bachelor's degrees in about 45 areas of study in engineering sciences and the arts. Some 2400 students –all undergraduates–are enrolled on the campus located about 70 miles west of New York City and 60 miles north of Philadelphia. All 206 full-time faculty have a PhD or equivalent degree. The college was founded in 1826 by the citizens of Easton Pennsylvania and named in honor of the Marquis de Lafayette a French-born hero of the American Revolution and associate of George Washington and Thomas Jefferson. The college has an endowment of more than $780 million.

EXECUTIVES

Director College Communications, Roger B. Clow
President, Daniel H. Weiss
Director Admissions, Carol A. Rowlands
Director Career Services, Linda N. Arra
VP Student Affairs, James F. Krivoski
VP Development and College Relations, James W. Dicker
Director Development Communications, Ann R. Carter
Director Financial Aid, Arlina B. DeNardo
VP Human Resources and General Counsel, Leslie F. Muhlfelder
Dean Libraries and Information Technology, Neil J. McElroy
Director Public Safety, Hugh W. Harris
Registrar, Francis A. Benginia
Provost and Dean Faculty, Wendy L. Hill
Manager Procurement, Linda Jroski

VP Business Affairs and Treasurer, Mitchell L. Wein
Dean Enrollment Services, Roberto Noya
Director Alumni Affairs, Sherri I. Jones

LOCATIONS

HQ: Lafayette College
316 Markle Hall, Easton PA 18042
Phone: 610-330-5000   **Fax:** 610-330-5700
Web: www.lafayette.edu

HISTORICAL FINANCIALS
Company Type: School

Income Statement
FYE: June 30

	REVENUE ($ mil.)	NET INCOME ($ mil.)	NET PROFIT MARGIN	EMPLOYEES
06/12	134	(25)	—	675
06/08	191	41	21.6%	0
06/07	113	87	77.7%	0
06/06	106	64	60.7%	0
Annual Growth	8.2%	—	—	—

2012 Year-End Financials
Debt ratio: ——
Return on equity: (-19.20)%
Cash ($ mil.): 46
Current ratio: —
Long-term debt ($ mil.): —
Dividends
Yield: —
Payout: —
Market value ($ mil.): —

LAFAYETTE PARISH SCHOOL BOARD (INC)

LOCATIONS

HQ: LAFAYETTE PARISH SCHOOL BOARD (INC)
113 CHAPLIN DR, LAFAYETTE, LA 70508-2101
Phone: 337-236-6800
Web: www.lhsband.net

HISTORICAL FINANCIALS
Company Type: Private

Income Statement
FYE: June 30

	REVENUE ($ mil.)	NET INCOME ($ mil.)	NET PROFIT MARGIN	EMPLOYEES
06/11	328	17	5.3%	3,400
06/10	322	8	2.7%	0
06/09	326	15	4.9%	0
06/08	312	21	7.0%	0
Annual Growth	1.7%	(7.3%)	—	—

2011 Year-End Financials
Debt ratio: ——
Return on equity: 5.30%
Cash ($ mil.): 155
Current ratio: —
Long-term debt ($ mil.): —
Dividends
Yield: —
Payout: —
Market value ($ mil.): —

LAIRD & COMPANY

The North American settlers may have had a bit of applejack for breakfast but don't think it was a sweet cereal. Applejack is a brandy distilled from —you guessed it —apples and Robert Laird was among the first to make it in the New World. (Laird fought in the Revolutionary War under George Washington and supplied the Colonial troops with applejack.) He formally established the Laird distillery in 1780 and today the ninth generation of the Laird family continues to make applejack — which is aged from four to eight years. The firm also imports (mostly Italian and French) wine and hard spirits (vodka gin grappa tequila). Laird's beverages are distributed throughout the US.

EXECUTIVES

Chairman, John E. Laird III
President and CEO, Larrie W. Laird, age 71
EVP and CFO, John E. Laird IV, age 63
VP Advertising and Public Relations, Lisa Laird Dunn, age 50
VP Sales and Marketing, Tom Alberico
VP Production, Janice Custer
Sales Administrator, Susan Herrmann

LOCATIONS

HQ: Laird & Company Inc.
1 Laird Rd., Eatontown NJ 07724
Phone: 732-542-0312   **Fax:** 732-542-2244
Web: www.lairdandcompany.com

COMPETITORS

Bacardi	Jackson Family Wines
Beam Global Spirits	Korbel
& Wine	Louis Vuitton North
Brown-Forman	America
Constellation Brands	Maxxium
Diageo	Pernod Ricard
Heaven Hill	Remy Cointreau
Distilleries	Smith Bowman
Hood River	Distillery

HISTORICAL FINANCIALS
Company Type: Private

Income Statement
FYE: December 31

	REVENUE ($ mil.)	NET INCOME ($ mil.)	NET PROFIT MARGIN	EMPLOYEES
12/11	44	0	1.1%	56
12/10	47	0	1.9%	0
Annual Growth	(5.9%)	(43.2%)	—	—

2011 Year-End Financials
Debt ratio: ——
Return on equity: 1.10%
Cash ($ mil.): 2
Current ratio: 3.90
Long-term debt ($ mil.): —
Dividends
Yield: —
Payout: —
Market value ($ mil.): —

LAKE ERIE COLLEGE OF OSTEOPATHIC MEDICINE INC.

LOCATIONS

HQ: LAKE ERIE COLLEGE OF OSTEOPATHIC MEDICINE INC.
1858 W GRANDVIEW BLVD, ERIE, PA 16509-1025
Phone: 814-866-6641
Web: www.lecomsga.com

HISTORICAL FINANCIALS
Company Type: Private

Income Statement
FYE: June 30

	REVENUE ($ mil.)	NET INCOME ($ mil.)	NET PROFIT MARGIN	EMPLOYEES
06/12	88	32	36.5%	180
06/11	86	35	41.0%	0
06/10	79	29	37.3%	0
06/09	56	13	24.2%	0
Annual Growth	16.1%	33.2%	—	—

2012 Year-End Financials
Debt ratio: ——
Return on equity: 36.50%
Cash ($ mil.): 37
Current ratio: 1.40
Long-term debt ($ mil.): —
Dividends
Yield: —
Payout: —
Market value ($ mil.): —

LAKE REGION HEALTHCARE CORPORATION

LOCATIONS

HQ: LAKE REGION HEALTHCARE CORPORATION
712 S CASCADE ST, FERGUS FALLS, MN 56537-2913
Phone: 218-736-8000
Web: www.lrhc.org

HISTORICAL FINANCIALS
Company Type: Private

Income Statement
FYE: September 30

	REVENUE ($ mil.)	NET INCOME ($ mil.)	NET PROFIT MARGIN	EMPLOYEES
09/11	102	1	1.1%	850
09/10	78	1	1.7%	0
09/09*	59	0	—	0
08/09	0	0	—	0
Annual Growth	1257.2%	—	—	—

*Fiscal year change

2011 Year-End Financials
Debt ratio: —
Return on equity: 1.10%
Cash ($ mil.): 10
Current ratio: 2.70
Long-term debt ($ mil.): —
Dividends
Yield: —
Payout: —
Market value ($ mil.): —

2011 Year-End Financials
Debt ratio: —
Return on equity: 5.50%
Cash ($ mil.): 18
Current ratio: 1.60
Long-term debt ($ mil.): —
Dividends
Yield: —
Payout: —
Market value ($ mil.): —

Barshinger Cancer Center which is scheduled to open in mid-2013.

EXECUTIVES

SVP Business Development, Susan Wynne
EVP Lancaster General Health; President Lancaster General Hospital, Marion A. McGowan
SVP and CFO, F. Joseph Byorick III
President and CEO, Thomas E. (Tom) Beeman
Chairperson, Jeffrey F. Lehman
EVP Strategic Implementation and Chief Mission Officer, Jan L. Bergen
SVP Chief Administrative and Legal Officer and Corporate Secretary, Robert P. Macina
SVP Ambulatory Care; President Lancaster General Services Business Trust, Andre W. Renna
VP Home Care Services, William V. Dunstan
VP Legal Services and Associate General Counsel, Margaret F. Costella
VP Risk Management, Margaret M. Klecha
VP Human Resources, Mary B. Miskey
Assistant VP Finance, Douglas W. Rinehart
Assistant VP Finance, Denise A. Kennedy
SVP Post-Acute Care; SVP Operations Lancaster General Hospital, Geoffrey W. Eddowes
Director Community Relations, John Lines
SVP and Chief Physician Executive, Lee M. Duke II
SVP Chief Quality Officer and Chief Marketing Officer, Norma J. Ferdinand
SVP Physician Practices; President Lancaster General Medical Group, Jerome I. Gottlieb
SVP Human Resources and Chief Leadership Officer, Regina Mingle
Vice Chairperson, Alexander Henderson III
President Lancaster General Health Foundation, Jay Bucher

LAKE STEVENS SCHOOL DISTRICT 4

LOCATIONS

HQ: LAKE STEVENS SCHOOL DISTRICT 4
12309 22ND ST NE, LAKE STEVENS, WA 98258-9500
Phone: 425-335-1500

HISTORICAL FINANCIALS

Company Type: Private

Income Statement

FYE: August 31

	REVENUE ($ mil.)	NET INCOME ($ mil.)	NET PROFIT MARGIN	EMPLOYEES
08/11	80	1	2.4%	1,000
08/10	80	(2)	—	0
08/09	84	(5)	—	0
08/07	58	1	2.4%	0
Annual Growth	11.2%	11.0%	—	—

2011 Year-End Financials
Debt ratio: —
Return on equity: 2.40%
Cash ($ mil.): 0
Current ratio: —
Long-term debt ($ mil.): —
Dividends
Yield: —
Payout: —
Market value ($ mil.): —

LANCASTER COUNTY SCHOOL DISTRICT

LOCATIONS

HQ: LANCASTER COUNTY SCHOOL DISTRICT
300 S CATAWBA ST, LANCASTER, SC 29720-2458
Phone: 803-286-6972
Web: www.lancasterscschools.org

HISTORICAL FINANCIALS

Company Type: Private

Income Statement

FYE: June 30

	REVENUE ($ mil.)	NET INCOME ($ mil.)	NET PROFIT MARGIN	EMPLOYEES
06/11	103	5	5.5%	1,600
06/10	106	(2)	—	0
06/09	105	(4)	—	0
06/08	105	(9)	—	0
Annual Growth	(0.7%)	—	—	—

2011 Year-End Financials
Debt ratio: —
Return on equity: 5.50%
Cash ($ mil.): 18
Current ratio: —
Long-term debt ($ mil.): —
Dividends
Yield: —
Payout: —
Market value ($ mil.): —

LOCATIONS

HQ: The Lancaster General Hospital
555 N. Duke St., Lancaster PA 17604
Phone: 717-544-5511   **Fax:** 800-390-5351
Web: www.starite.com

PRODUCTS/OPERATIONS

Selected Specialties
Cardiology
Emergency medical
Intensive care
Neurology
Oncology
Radiology
Rehabilitation
Urology

COMPETITORS

Altoona Regional
Ascension Health
Catholic Health Initiatives
Evangelical Community Hospital
Hanover Healthcare
Holy Spirit
Jefferson Health System
Lewistown Hospital
Memorial Hospital (PA)
PinnacleHealth System
Saint Vincent Health System
St. Luke's University Health Network
University of Pennsylvania Health System
WellSpan Health

LAKEVIEW CENTER INC.

LOCATIONS

HQ: LAKEVIEW CENTER INC.
1221 W LAKEVIEW AVE, PENSACOLA, FL 32501-1836
Phone: 850-432-1222
Web: www.elakeviewcenter.org

HISTORICAL FINANCIALS

Company Type: Private

Income Statement

FYE: September 30

	REVENUE ($ mil.)	NET INCOME ($ mil.)	NET PROFIT MARGIN	EMPLOYEES
09/11	155	8	5.5%	1,900
09/10	143	8	6.0%	0
09/09	131	4	3.8%	0
09/08	128	2	1.8%	0
Annual Growth	6.6%	53.9%	—	—

LANCASTER GENERAL HOSPITAL INC

Lancaster General Health (LG Health) is a 623-bed integrated health care delivery system serving residents of Lancaster County Pennsylvania and surrounding areas. Its flagship Lancaster General Hospital (LGH) - opened in 1893 - is known for its cardiology orthopedic and intensive care specialties. A separate Women & Babies hospital cares for those just making it into the world. The system also includes multiple outpatient clinics a rehab hospital home care services and a nursing center and healthcare college as well as a medical group of more than 100 physicians operating from 20 offices throughout the area.

Strategy LG Health continues to make strategic investments to better serve its patients and the community. In 2010 it began a $100 million electronic records initiative which included the launch of the MyLGHealth online program for accessing records communicating with doctors and requesting appointments. The following year the health system began construction on the Ann B.

HISTORICAL FINANCIALS

Company Type: Private - Not-for-Profit

Income Statement

FYE: June 30

	REVENUE ($ mil.)	NET INCOME ($ mil.)	NET PROFIT MARGIN	EMPLOYEES
06/12	852	31	3.7%	5,000
06/11	838	(113)	—	0
06/10	828	31	3.8%	0
06/09	815	48	5.9%	0
Annual Growth	1.5%	(13.2%)	—	—

2012 Year-End Financials

Debt ratio: —
Return on equity: 3.70%
Cash ($ mil.): 5
Current ratio: 1.20
Long-term debt ($ mil.): —

Dividends
Yield: —
Payout: —
Market value ($ mil.): —

LANE COLLEGE

For Lane College the past is prologue. The small private liberal arts school was established in 1882 by the Christian Methodist Episcopal (C.M.E.) Church to provide educational opportunities –particularly in the areas of teaching and preaching – for newly-freed slaves. Originally called C.M.E. High School it was renamed Lane College (after its founder Bishop Isaac Lane) in 1896. Throughout its history the preparation of professional educators has been a primary focus; however the college also offers undergraduate degrees in such disciplines as computer science business and criminal justice. Lane College enrolls 800-1000 students annually.

EXECUTIVES

Chairman, Rev William H. Graves, age 75
President and Trustee, Wesley Cornelious McClure
Director Financial Aid, Ursula Singleton
Director Information Technology, Ernest Mitchell III
Assistant to the Director of Information Technology and Registrar, Tiffany Young
Help Desk Coordinator and Technician, Linda Ragland
Computer Services Technician Academics, Elgenor Douglas
Director Athletics, J.L. Perry
Vice Chairman, Cynthia Rawls Bond
Assistant Professor Physics, Reda Abraham
Assistant Professor Spanish, Blanca Acosta
Chair Natural Sciences, Tade Adedokun
Instructor History, Olayinka Agbetuyi
Assistant Professor Biology, Samir Alsadi
Residence Counselor Student Affairs, Cedric Anderson
Financial Aid Staff Assistant Business, Regina Anderson
Assistant Professor Criminal Justice, Bede Anyanwu
Assistant Professor English, C.O.T. Appiah
Instructor English, Unoma Azuah
Professor Sociology, Patrick Bamwine
Assistant Professor Chemistry, Joseph Bariyanga
Residence Counselor Student Affairs, Christine Bell
Secretary Student Affairs, Katherine Bell
Residence Counselor Student Affairs, Sharyn Bell
Secretary Institutional Advancement, Charlise Bingham
Assistant to Registrar Academics, Terry Blackmon

Admissions Counselor Academics, Angela Bond
Residence Counselor Student Affairs, Joe Bond
Instructor Physical Education, Gregory Bormann
Residence Counselor Student Affairs, Ernest Boyd
Director Loan Management Business, Kelly Boyd
Technology Specialist Academics, Ned Boyland
Residence Counselor Student Affairs, Robert Brand
ETS Advisor Academics, Travis Brint
Adjunct Professor Academics, Ernest Brooks
Residence Counselor Student Affairs, Necol Brooks
Assistant Professor English, Samone Brooks
Director Admissions Academics, Evelyn Brown
Director Hamlett Hall Student Affairs, Gloria Brown
EVP, Sharron Burnett
Assistant Director Financial Aid Business, Tony Calhoun
Assistant Professor Religion, David Carefoot
Associate Professor Religion, Nathaniel Carter
Residence Counselor Student Affairs, Jason Clark
Residence Counselor Student Affairs, Eugene Cole
Residence Counselor Student Affairs, Linda Cole
Admissions Counselor Academics, Robbie Coleman
ETS Secretary Academics, Zekydia Collier
Residence Counselor Student Affairs, Carsandra Cooper
Residence Counselor Student Affairs, Evelyn Craft
Residence Counselor Student Affairs, Fredrick Crawford
Band Director Music, Kenneth Curry
Professor History, Arthur David
Residence Counselor Student Affairs, Carola Davis
Executive Assistant to the President, Shelia Deadmon
Chair Business, Nirmalendu Debnath
Security Officer Business, Freddie Donnell
VP Institutional Advancement, Richard Donnell Sr.
Instructor English, Eugenia Eberhart
Assistant Professor Education, Rodney Echols
Director Institutional Research and Director Testing and Assessment Academics, Nicole Edwards
Residence Counselor Student Affairs, Antonio Ellison
Professor Chemistry, Clarence Epps
Assistant Professor Mathematics, Nooraldin Fattahi
Adjunct Professor Business, Richard Finney
Residence Counselor Student Affairs, Christine Franklin
Advisor to the President, Shirley Friar
Administrative Assistant Academics - TRIO, Linda Godwin
Assistant Football Coach Athletics, John Gore
College Historian, Ameera Graves
Library Assistant Academics, Connie Gray
Residence Counselor Student Affairs, Willie Green
Maintenance Physical Plant, Robert Greer
Student Accounts Business and Finance, Donna Hamlett
VP Business, Melvin Hamlett Sr.
Assistant Professor History, Peggy Hardman
Head Women's Basketball Coach Athletics, Anita Harris
Residence Counselor Student Affairs, Freddie Harris
Residence Counselor Student Affairs, James Harris
Head Football Coach Athletics, Darrin Hayes
Residence Counselor Student Affairs, Elaine Haynes
Residence Counselor Student Affairs, Ty Haynes
Associate Professor Education, Stephen Herr
Director TRIO Academics, Clara Hewitt
Residence Counselor Student Affairs, Auvshandria Hicks
Maintenance Physical Plant, Carl Hill
Residence Counselor Student Affairs, Cynthia Hill

Accounting Assistant Business, Katrina Hill
Residence Counselor Student Affairs, Lane Hodges
Residence Counselor Student Affairs, Alfronte Holliday
Residence Counselor Student Affairs, Vanesa House
Secretary Academics, Bettye Hunter
Assistant Professor Business, Oz Inanli
Assistant Football Coach Athletics, Michael Jackson
Copy Center Coordinator Auxiliary Enterprise, Mary Jarrett
Associate Librarian Library, John Johnson
Director Freshman Studies Academics, Monique Johnson
Physical Plant Engineer Physical Plant, Bobby Jones
College Nurse Student Affairs, Cynedra Jones
Dean of Campus Student Affairs, Stefan Jones
Assistant Professor History, Brucella Jordan
Professor Mass Communication, Musa Kamara
Assistant Professor Mathematics, Jongchul Kim
TLC Coordinator Academics, L. Kapel Kirkendoll
Instructor English, Clifton Laird
ETS Advisor Academics, Jacqueline Lee
Instructor Computer Science, Jingwei Lin
Admissions Counselor Academics, Darrell Listenbee
Switchboard and Mail Clerk Business, Winnie Lofton
VP Academics and Provost, Vicki Lott
Residence Counselor Student Affairs, Vernon Love
Compliance and Budget Officer Business, Paula Love
Director Academic Computing Academics, Sibin Lu
Professor Biology and Faculty Trustee, Satish Mahajan
Assistant Secretary, Maya Manns
Director Campus Center Student Affairs, Charles Marshall
Assistant to the VP of Business, Juanita Marshall
Assistant Professor Computer Science, Rolf Martin
Residence Counselor Student Affairs, Bruce Mayo
Residence Counselor Student Affairs, Diane Mayo
Residence Counselor Student Affairs, Felicia McCarley
Library Assistant Library, Erika McClain
Assistant Professor Education, Sherre McClain
Residence Counselor Student Affairs, Ursula McClenden
Internal Auditor Business, Carter McClure
Director Counseling Student Affairs, Karla McClure
Assistant Director CDC, Marsha McClure
Associate VP Institutional Advancement and Research and Development, Wesley McClure II
Payroll and Purchasing Business, Tammy McDougal
Security Officer Business, Ernest Meadows
Library Assistant Library, Neivine Michael
ETS Advisor Academics, Ebony Milam
SSS Counselor Academics, Melissa Miller
TLC Coordinator Academics, Penny Minter
ETS Advisor Academics, Teri Moore
SSS Coordinator Academics, Anna Morrison
Residence Counselor Student Affairs, Pam Moses
Assistant Professor English, Makim Mputubwele
Dean of Campus Student Affairs, Matthew Nwokoji
ETS Advisor Academics, LaFonda Payne
Assistant Director Physical Plant Business, Cynthia Pearson
Director Physical Plant Business, Joe Person
Assistant Professor Mathematics, Regon Peterson
Director Security Business, Thomas Pillow
Director ETS Program Academics, Patricia Porter
Residence Counselor Student Affairs, Bobby Poston
Director Planning and Safety, Sammie Potts

Residence Counselor Student Affairs, Doris Price
Admissions Counselor Academics, Angela Rainey
Assistant Professor French, Mary Randall
Instructor Art, Earl Raney
Residence Counselor Student Affairs, Columbus Reid
Residence Counselor Student Affairs, TeHisha Richardson
Residence Counselor Student Affairs, James Rimmer
Chief Accountant Business, Duan Robinson
Residence Counselor Student Affairs, Jimmy Robinson
Director Writing Center English, Gabrielle Ross
Associate Professor Music, Kenneth Sampson
Executive Assistant to the President, Darlette Samuels
Residence Counselor Student Affairs, Adrian Sanders
TLC Assistant Academics, Ian Scott
VP Student Affairs, Sherrill Scott
Physical Plant Engineer Physical Plant, William Scott
Instructor Mathematics, Ahmad Shafiee
Professor Business, Stephen Shanklin
Assistant Professor Music, Jung-Won Shin
Assistant Director Research, Mary Sipes
Professor Criminal Justice, Sherri Smith
Professor English, William Smith
Admissions Counselor Academics, William Smith III
Residence Counselor Student Affairs, Willie Springfield
Residence Counselor Student Affairs, Kimberly Stigger
Secretary Athletics, Sherry Stokes
Residence Counselor Student Affairs, Rachel Strayhorn
Assistant Basketball Coach Athletics, Frederick (Fred) Summers
Registrar Academics, Ragan Summers
Residence Counselor Student Affairs, Steve Tallie
Choir Director Music, Allen Todd
Executive Assistant Admissions and Institutional Advancement, Soneya Verser
Accounts Receivable Clerk Business, Willie Walker
Head Librarian Library, Lan Wang
Director Cleaves Hall Student Affairs, Hattie Watkins
Residence Counselor Student Affairs, Donald Wilkes
Athletic Trainer Athletics, Roger Wilkes
Residence Counselor Student Affairs, Kelvin Williams
Instructor Physical Education, Timothy Williams
Assistant Professor Spanish, Karla Wilmath
Instructor Speech, Cicely Wilson
Instructor Business, Craig Wright
Residence Counselor Student Affairs, Sylvia Wynn
Residence Counselor Student Affairs, Maxine Yarbrough
Assistant Professor Computer Science, Saeed Yazdani
Director Mathematics Lab Mathematics, Yusuf Yildirim
Assistant Professor Mathematics, Huasong Yin
TLC Operations Staff Academics, Robin Young
Assistant Professor Sociology, Sherri Zazueta
Trustee, Olin Morris
President and Trustee, Wesley Cornelious McClure
Secretary of the Board, Charles E. Carpenter
Trustee, Kenny W. Armstrong
Trustee, Jeannie Bond
Trustee, Harold W. Byrd
Trustee, Carmichael Crutchfield
Trustee, Ronald M. Cunningham
Trustee, Rev Albert Davidson
Trustee, Daniel Lee Fitten

Trustee, Clarence Gooch
Trustee, Elnora Palmer Hamb
Vice Chairman, Cynthia Rawls Bond
Trustee, William Hamilton
Trustee, Nancy Lane
Trustee, J.C. Mclin
Trustee, John Miller
Trustee, Joseph Neal
Trustee, Rev Louis T. Purham
Trustee, Dan Shaw Jr.
Trustee, Haywood Strickland
Trustee, Melvin Wright
Student Trustee, Kelvin Pearson
Professor Biology and Faculty Trustee, Satish Mahajan

LOCATIONS

HQ: Lane College
545 Lane Ave., Jackson TN 38301
Phone: 731-426-7500   **Fax:** 731-426-7652
Web: www.lanecollege.edu/

HISTORICAL FINANCIALS
Company Type: School

Income Statement
FYE: June 30

	REVENUE ($ mil.)	NET INCOME ($ mil.)	NET PROFIT MARGIN	EMPLOYEES
06/11	44	1	3.4%	165
06/10	41	1	2.8%	0
06/09	41	0	2.3%	0
06/08	41	0	2.3%	0
Annual Growth	1.9%	15.2%	—	—

2011 Year-End Financials

Debt ratio: ——
Return on equity: 3.40%
Cash ($ mil.): 5
Current ratio: ——
Long-term debt ($ mil.): ——
Dividends
Yield: ——
Payout: ——
Market value ($ mil.): ——

LANE COMMUNITY COLLEGE

LOCATIONS

HQ: LANE COMMUNITY COLLEGE
4000 E 30TH AVE, EUGENE, OR 97405-0640
Phone: 541-463-3000
Web: www.lanecc.edu

HISTORICAL FINANCIALS
Company Type: Private

Income Statement
FYE: June 30

	REVENUE ($ mil.)	NET INCOME ($ mil.)	NET PROFIT MARGIN	EMPLOYEES
06/11	185	7	4.3%	1,888
06/09	130	(14)	—	0
06/08	97	13	13.9%	0
06/07	87	2	3.0%	0
Annual Growth	28.5%	45.5%	—	—

2011 Year-End Financials

Debt ratio: ——
Return on equity: 4.30%
Cash ($ mil.): 51
Current ratio: 1.80
Long-term debt ($ mil.): ——
Dividends
Yield: ——
Payout: ——
Market value ($ mil.): ——

LANGSTON SNYDER L P

No Snyder Langston isn't the name of a "wacky neighbor" sitcom character but it might have built the property next door. Snyder Langston develops and builds commercial industrial and multifamily residential properties. Serving business clients ranging from start-ups to Fortune 500 firms the company provides a range of services such as planning design financing government relations general contracting and construction management. Some of the properties that Snyder Langston has developed include business parks retail centers office buildings manufacturing facilities parking garages car dealerships condominiums churches schools and hotels.

Snyder Langston operates throughout the western US but concentrates on Southern California. The firm was founded in 1959 by Donald Snyder and William Langston.

EXECUTIVES

Chairman Emeritus, William E. (Bill) Langston
Risk Manager Snyder Langston Optym, William J. Romay
President and COO, John Rochford
Chairman and CEO, Stephen Jones
Treasurer, Paul Pfeiffer
SVP and Chief Estimator, Steve Nelson
VP, Matt Vujovich
Project Manager William H. Hannon Library, Jonathan Bagnall
Project Executive Optym, John Gunther

LOCATIONS

HQ: Snyder Langston L.P.
17962 Cowan, Irvine CA 92614
Phone: 949-863-9200   **Fax:** 949-863-1087
Web: www.snyder-langston.com

COMPETITORS

DPR Construction
Hathaway Dinwiddie Construction
Hensel Phelps Construction
KPRS Construction
MPG Office Trust

HISTORICAL FINANCIALS
Company Type: Private

Income Statement
FYE: December 31

	REVENUE ($ mil.)	NET INCOME ($ mil.)	NET PROFIT MARGIN	EMPLOYEES
12/11	53	(0)	—	65
12/10	56	(1)	—	0
12/09	78	(1)	—	0
12/07	342	5	1.5%	0
Annual Growth	(46.1%)			

2011 Year-End Financials

Debt ratio: ——
Return on equity: (-1.00)%
Cash ($ mil.): 5
Current ratio: 0.40
Long-term debt ($ mil.): ——

Dividends
Yield: ——
Payout: ——
Market value ($ mil.): ——

LARROC INC.

LOCATIONS

HQ: LARROC INC.
6420 BOEING DR, EL PASO, TX 79925-1007
Phone: 915-772-3733
Web: www.larroc.com

HISTORICAL FINANCIALS

Company Type: Private

Income Statement

	REVENUE ($ mil.)	NET INCOME ($ mil.)	NET PROFIT MARGIN	EMPLOYEES
FYE: April 30				
04/12	127	1	1.4%	25
04/11	118	1	1.3%	0
04/10	90	1	1.6%	0
04/09	97	1	1.8%	0
Annual Growth	9.3%	(0.3%)	—	—

2012 Year-End Financials

Debt ratio: ——
Return on equity: 1.40%
Cash ($ mil.): 9
Current ratio: 1.80
Long-term debt ($ mil.): ——

Dividends
Yield: ——
Payout: ——
Market value ($ mil.): ——

LARSEN COOPERATIVE CO.

LOCATIONS

HQ: LARSEN COOPERATIVE CO.
8290 COUNTY HWY T, LARSEN, WI 54947-9701
Phone: 920-982-1111
Web: www.larsen.coop

HISTORICAL FINANCIALS

Company Type: Private

Income Statement

	REVENUE ($ mil.)	NET INCOME ($ mil.)	NET PROFIT MARGIN	EMPLOYEES
FYE: August 31				
08/11	179	3	2.0%	150
08/10	110	5	4.8%	0
08/09	115	0	0.5%	0
08/08	142	2	1.7%	0
Annual Growth	8.0%	13.0%	—	—

2011 Year-End Financials

Debt ratio: ——
Return on equity: 2.00%
Cash ($ mil.): 2
Current ratio: 0.10
Long-term debt ($ mil.): ——

Dividends
Yield: ——
Payout: ——
Market value ($ mil.): ——

LARSON GRAIN COMPANY

LOCATIONS

HQ: LARSON GRAIN COMPANY
103 1ST ST NE, LAMOURE, ND 58458-7206
Phone: 701-883-5201
Web: www.larsongrain.com

HISTORICAL FINANCIALS

Company Type: Private

Income Statement

	REVENUE ($ mil.)	NET INCOME ($ mil.)	NET PROFIT MARGIN	EMPLOYEES
FYE: December 31				
12/11	90	1	2.0%	36
12/10	52	0	0.1%	0
12/09	57	1	3.2%	0
Annual Growth	25.8%	(2.2%)	—	—

2011 Year-End Financials

Debt ratio: ——
Return on equity: 2.00%
Cash ($ mil.): 0
Current ratio: ——
Long-term debt ($ mil.): ——

Dividends
Yield: ——
Payout: ——
Market value ($ mil.): ——

LASALLE UNIVERSITY

La Salle University is an independent Catholic institution of higher learning with an enrollment of some 7500 students. It offers about 40 undergraduate majors 15 minors about a dozen graduate programs (including a doctoral program in Clinical Psychology) and more than 30 certificate programs. The university consists of three schools: arts and sciences business and nursing and health sciences plus a College of Professional and Continuing Studies. Nursing psychology education and communications are among the school's most popular undergraduate areas of study. La Salle University was founded in 1863.

EXECUTIVES

President, Michael J. McGinniss
Provost, Richard A. Nigro
Dean School of Business, Paul R. Brazina
VP Business Affairs, Matthew S. McManness
Director Accounts Payable and Purchasing, Nancylee D. Moore
Director Administrative Services, Jeffrey S. Hershberger
Assistant VP Alumni Relations, James K. Gulick

Director Intercollegiate Athletics and Recreation, Thomas M. Brennan
Manager Athletic Services, Michael Murphy
Director Human Resources, Margurete Walsh
Associate Director Human Resources, Christine Mickel
Manager Training, Paul R. Roden
Assistant Director for Benefits, Tara Feeney
Dean of Students, Joseph J. Cicala
Director Career Services, Louis A. Lamorte Jr.
Director Library, John Baky
Reference Librarian Online Services, Eithne C. Bearden
Registrar, Dominic J. Galante
VP University Advancement, Brian R. Elderton
Director Advancement Services, Elizabeth R. Lochner
Programming Analyst University Advancement, Yuan (Joyce) Bei
Information Technology Officer, Rob Fischer
Assistant VP Development, Theresa Travis
Assistant VP Government and Community Relations, Edward A. Turzanski
Assistant VP Marketing and Communications, Joseph W. Donovan
Director Media Relations, Jon C. Caroulis
Executive Assistant to the President, William J. DeVito
Director Information Management Group, Kathryn-Mary E. Payne
Operations Manager Information Technology, Anthony F. Walker
Director Information Technology, Edward A. Nickerson
Administrative Assistant, John Coyle
Associate Director of Career Services Center, Genevieve M. Carlton
Administrative Assistant, Jeanine Cohill
Assistant Director Student, Andrea Okagawa
Secretary, Cassandra Sims
Administrative Assistant, Elizabeth Wilson
Associate Director, Mike Nielsen
Executive Director Career and Employment Services, Steve McGonigle
Executive Secretary, Maryanne Taylor
Executive Assistant President, Alice L. Hoersch
Services Director, Kyra Spoto
Director of Off-Campus Communities, TiRease Holmes
Executive Assistant President, Joseph J. Willard
Director Student Counseling Center, Suzanne Boyll

LOCATIONS

HQ: La Salle University
1900 W. Olney Ave., Philadelphia PA 19141
Phone: 215-951-1000   **Fax:** 215-951-1086

Web: www.lasalle.edu

HISTORICAL FINANCIALS

Company Type: School

Income Statement

	REVENUE ($ mil.)	NET INCOME ($ mil.)	NET PROFIT MARGIN	EMPLOYEES
FYE: May 31				
05/12	132	(0)	—	900
05/11*	134	15	11.5%	0
06/10	0	(0)	—	0
05/09	163	0	—	0
Annual Growth	(6.7%)	—	—	—

*Fiscal year change

2012 Year-End Financials

Debt ratio: ——
Return on equity: (-0.50)%
Cash ($ mil.): 13
Current ratio: ——
Long-term debt ($ mil.): ——

Dividends
Yield: ——
Payout: ——
Market value ($ mil.): ——

2011 Year-End Financials

Debt ratio: ——
Return on equity: ——
Cash ($ mil.): 1
Current ratio: 1.00
Long-term debt ($ mil.): ——

Dividends
Yield: ——
Payout: ——
Market value ($ mil.): ——

Brand Manager, Jody Lee
VP Business Development, Lee Moore
General Manager Fabrication and Industrial Services, Gary Milligan
VP Engineering, Clint Rosenbaum

LOCATIONS

HQ: Lauren Engineers & Constructors Inc.
901 S. 1st St., Abilene TX 79602-1502
Phone: 325-670-9660   **Fax:** 325-670-9663
Web: www.laurenec.com

PRODUCTS/OPERATIONS

Selected Services
Construction
Engineering
EPC
Fabrication
Field Services
Modularization
Procurement
Project Management
Safety

Selected Markets
Chemical
Polymers
Power
Pulp & Paper
Refining
Solar Power
Special Metals

COMPETITORS

Bechtel	Gemma Power Systems
CH2M HILL	Jacobs Engineering
Fluor	KBR Building Group
ForeRunner Corporation	MYR Group
Foster Wheeler	Shaw Group

HISTORICAL FINANCIALS

Company Type: Private

Income Statement

FYE: December 31

	REVENUE ($ mil.)	NET INCOME ($ mil.)	NET PROFIT MARGIN	EMPLOYEES
12/11	249	(0)	—	1,000
12/10	162	21	13.4%	0
12/09	217	15	7.2%	0
12/08	375	13	3.5%	0
Annual Growth	(12.7%)	—	—	—

2011 Year-End Financials

Debt ratio: ——
Return on equity: (-0.10)%
Cash ($ mil.): 6
Current ratio: 0.20
Long-term debt ($ mil.): ——

Dividends
Yield: ——
Payout: ——
Market value ($ mil.): ——

LASSUS BROS OIL INC

LOCATIONS

HQ: LASSUS BROS OIL INC
1800 MAGNAVOX WAY, FORT WAYNE, IN 46804-1540
Phone: 260-436-1415
Web: www.lassus.com

HISTORICAL FINANCIALS

Company Type: Private

Income Statement

FYE: September 30

	REVENUE ($ mil.)	NET INCOME ($ mil.)	NET PROFIT MARGIN	EMPLOYEES
09/11	209	0	0.2%	325
09/10	0	0	21.9%	0
09/09	0	(0)	—	0
09/08	201	1	0.6%	0
Annual Growth	1.4%	(36.2%)	—	—

2011 Year-End Financials

Debt ratio: ——
Return on equity: 0.10%
Cash ($ mil.): 0
Current ratio: 0.40
Long-term debt ($ mil.): ——

Dividends
Yield: ——
Payout: ——
Market value ($ mil.): ——

LAUGHLIN-CARTRELL INC.

LOCATIONS

HQ: LAUGHLIN-CARTRELL INC.
12850 NE HENDRICKS RD, CARLTON, OR 97111
Phone: 503-852-7151
Web: www.lciglove.com

HISTORICAL FINANCIALS

Company Type: Private

Income Statement

FYE: December 31

	REVENUE ($ mil.)	NET INCOME ($ mil.)	NET PROFIT MARGIN	EMPLOYEES
12/11	102	(0)	—	13
12/10	76	(0)	—	0
12/09	87	0	0.1%	0
12/08	116	0	0.1%	0
Annual Growth	(4.2%)	—	—	—

LAUREN HOLDINGS INC.

Lauren Engineers & Constructors is a contractor that targets the power chemical special metals and oil refining industries. In addition to its core engineering procurement and construction capabilities the company offers fabrication project management and mechanical and electrical maintenance services. With offices in Georgia Tennessee and Texas Lauren Engineers & Constructors serves nearly 40 states. It also operates in Canada with a presence in Calgary. Some of its power and chemical customers include Flying J Florida Power & Light General Electric Company and Procter & Gamble. The company was originally established in 1984 as a subsidiary of Comstock Mechanical.

Geographic Reach

Lauren Engineers & Constructors which is licensed in nearly 40 states maintains offices in the US in Georgia Tennessee and Texas as well as in Canada through subsidiary Kamtech Services Inc. (KSI). It operates a joint venture in India.

Operations

Boasting more than 1000 employees companywide the contractor operates its business through three entities. Lauren Concise an EPC contractor serves Canada's oil and gas sector. Leveraging its parent's strengths Lauren Concise offers turnkey engineering procurement and construction services in the country. Another subsidiary Kamtech Services Inc. (KSI) is based in Canada and caters to the industrial sector with its building trades expertise in mechanical construction services. Lauren CCL Engineers Private Limited a leader in Concentrated Solar Power (CSP) provides India with engineering procurement management and construction services for the country's thermal solar power facilities. Headquartered in Navi Mumbai Lauren CCL is a joint venture of CCL Optoelectronics Pvt. Ltd. and Lauren Engineers & Constructors.

Sales and Marketing

Lauren Engineers & Constructors serves a variety of customers. Typical clients –large and small –include Florida Power & Light Bosque Power General Electric Calpine Siemens Westinghouse Eastman Chemical DAK Americas Buhler Flying J Murphy Oil and Alon among others.

Company Ownership

The Lauren Corporation owns Lauren Engineers & Constructors.

EXECUTIVES

VP Major Projects, Ron Johnson
President and CEO, C. Cleve Whitener III
VP Construction, Mike Breed
VP Estimating, Brian Rogers
VP Product Management, John Hyland
VP, Roy Milne
Director Marketing, Nancy Abel
CFO, Leslie Hammond
Human Resources Administrator, Gayle Crain
COO, Bill King
EVP Human Resources, Kevin Porter

LAW ENFORCEMENT HEALTH BENEFITS INC

LOCATIONS

HQ: LAW ENFORCEMENT HEALTH BENEFITS INC
2233 SPRING GARDEN ST, PHILADELPHIA, PA
19130-3511
Phone: 215-763-8290
Web: www.lehb.org

HISTORICAL FINANCIALS
Company Type: Private

Income Statement
FYE: June 30

	REVENUE ($ mil.)	NET INCOME ($ mil.)	NET PROFIT MARGIN	EMPLOYEES
06/11	107	3	3.4%	10
Annual Growth	—	—	—	—

2011 Year-End Financials

Debt ratio: —
Return on equity: 3.40%
Cash ($ mil.): 4
Current ratio: 1.40
Long-term debt ($ mil.): —

Dividends
Yield: —
Payout: —
Market value ($ mil.): —

LAWRENCE & MEMORIAL HOSPITAL INC.

Lawrence & Memorial Hospital (L&M) connects residents of Connecticut with health care whether they're near the Rhode Island border or enjoying the Connecticut River. The not-for-profit hospital founded in 1912 provides services to a ten-town region on the Connecticut shoreline and neighboring areas in the Northeast. L&M has roughly 280 beds and provides general acute care including medical surgical rehabilitative pediatric psychiatric and obstetrical services. Its facilities include a cardiac catheterization lab a cancer center a sleep disorder unit and a the region's only neonatal ICU. The hospital also runs about a dozen community physician practices and specialty clinics.

The changing economy and health care landscape in the US has prompted many independent hospitals to seek affiliations with other medical providers as a means of controlling spending and enhancing care and L&M is no exception. The hospital intends to acquire neighboring 125-bed community hospital Westerly Hospital in Westerly Rhode Island. The two hospitals began their negotiations in 2011 but were suspended briefly when Westerly Hospital filed for receivership. In mid-2012 the deal resumed when L&M submitted a bid to acquire Westerly Hospital for some $69 million. The bid had cleared one regulatory hurdle but must still pass another before its anticipated closure in 2013.

Westerly Hospital already has a network agreement with Yale New Haven Health which allows the facility to participate in payer contract negotiations as part of a larger health network. However Westerly Hospital began looking for additional af-filiation options in 2011 after experiencing several years of operating losses; Westerly Hospital entered into receivership (similar to bankruptcy) proceedings later that year and L&M entered a bid for to purchase the hospital as part of Westerly's receivership proceedings.

In addition L&M is planning to grow its service offerings through other means. The care provider has announced plans to build a $35 million cancer center in Waterford Rhode Island.

EXECUTIVES

VP Finance, Elwin Bresette
Director Public Relations, Kelly Anthony
President CEO and Director, Bruce D. Cummings
VP Nursing and Clinical Services, Frances S. Bonardi
Secretary and Director, Marilynn R. (Lynn) Malerba, age 59
VP Chief Medical & Clinical Operations Officer, Daniel Rissi
VP Human Resources, Peter Fraser
VP Medical Affairs, Alan Bier
VP and CIO, Kimberly Kalajainen
VP Development and Community Relations, William A. Stanley
Director Information Services, Donna Baker
Director Emergency and Surgical Services, Jo Aldred
Director Human Resources, Gary Cass
Director Financial Services, Tina DiCioccio
VP and Chief HR Officer, Donna Epps
Director Information Services, Helen Favello
Chairman, Ulysses B. Hammond
Vice Chairman, Granville Morris
VP and General Counsel, Maureen Anderson
President Medical Staff, Henry Amdur
VP Medical Staff and Director, Donald Felitto
Treasurer and Director, Fred Conti
VP and Chief Financial and Support Services Officer, Lou Inzana
Director, Leon J. (Lee) Olivier, age 63
Director, Scott D. Bates
President CEO and Director, Bruce D. Cummings
Secretary and Director, Marilynn R. (Lynn) Malerba, age 59
Director, Timothy D. Bates
Vice Chairman, Granville Morris
VP and General Counsel, Maureen Anderson
VP Medical Staff and Director, Donald Felitto
Director, John E. Allen
Director, L. James Carroll
Treasurer and Director, Fred Conti
Director, Toni Hoover
Director, R. Alan Hunter
Director, Mary Ellen Jukoski
Director, Robert Keltner
Director, Daniel P. O?Shea
Director, Carol Ridgway
Director, Kathy Steamer
Auditors: Ernst&YoungLLP

LOCATIONS

HQ: Lawrence & Memorial Hospital Inc.
365 Montauk Ave., New London CT 06320
Phone: 860-442-0711   **Fax:** 516-775-2407
Web: www.harborseafood.com

COMPETITORS

Backus
Care New England
Connecticut Children' s Medical Center
Day Kimball Hospital
Harrington Memorial Hospital
Hartford Health Care

Hospital of Central Connecticut
Kent Hospital
Roger Williams Medical Center
Saint Francis Hospital and Medical Center
Sturdy Memorial
University of Connecticut Health Center
Waterbury Hospital
Yale New Haven Health Services Corporation

HISTORICAL FINANCIALS
Company Type: Private - Not-for-Profit

Income Statement
FYE: September 30

	REVENUE ($ mil.)	NET INCOME ($ mil.)	NET PROFIT MARGIN	EMPLOYEES
09/11	336	3	1.0%	2,200
09/10	324	8	2.6%	0
09/09	293	(11)	—	0
09/08	278	(17)	—	0
Annual Growth	6.6%	—	—	—

2011 Year-End Financials

Debt ratio: —
Return on equity: 1.00%
Cash ($ mil.): 41
Current ratio: 1.40
Long-term debt ($ mil.): —

Dividends
Yield: —
Payout: —
Market value ($ mil.): —

LB STEEL LLC

LOCATIONS

HQ: LB STEEL LLC
15700 LATHROP AVE, HARVEY, IL 60426-5118
Phone: 708-331-2600
Web: www.protectivedoor.com

HISTORICAL FINANCIALS
Company Type: Private

Income Statement
FYE: December 31

	REVENUE ($ mil.)	NET INCOME ($ mil.)	NET PROFIT MARGIN	EMPLOYEES
12/11	99	5	5.4%	350
12/09	31	(2)	—	0
12/08	81	5	6.6%	0
12/07	61	4	7.9%	0
Annual Growth	17.4%	3.2%	—	—

2011 Year-End Financials

Debt ratio: —
Return on equity: 5.40%
Cash ($ mil.): 0
Current ratio: 0.60
Long-term debt ($ mil.): —

Dividends
Yield: —
Payout: —
Market value ($ mil.): —

LE MOYNE COLLEGE

Le Moyne College offers more than 700 courses leading to Bachelor of Arts or Bachelor of Science degrees in 24 different majors. A Jesuit Catholic school Le Moyne has approximately 2200 under-graduate students and 700 students in the graduate program which offers degrees in business administration and education. It has a 13-1 ratio of students to faculty. Le Moyne was founded in 1946.

EXECUTIVES

Director of Communications, Joe Della Posta
President, Fred P. Pestello
VP Enrollment Management, Dennis DePerro
VP Student Development, Shawn Ward
VP Information Technology, Robert Clapp
Director of Human Resources, Lynn McMartin
Director Admission, Dennis J. (Denny) Nicholson
VP Academic Affairs, Linda LeMura
VP Finance and Admininstration, Roger Stackpoole
President Le Moyne Student Government, Kate Van Etten
Chairman, Mary Cotter
Interim VP Institutional Advancement, Juliahn (Julie) Simms
Assistant Director of Admission, Tom Muench

LOCATIONS

HQ: Le Moyne College
1419 Salt Springs Rd., Syracuse NY 13214
Phone: 315-445-4100   **Fax:** 315-445-4711
Web: www.lemoyne.edu

HISTORICAL FINANCIALS
Company Type: School

Income Statement
FYE: May 31

	REVENUE ($ mil.)	NET INCOME ($ mil.)	NET PROFIT MARGIN	EMPLOYEES
05/11	102	10	10.0%	500
05/10	99	11	11.5%	0
05/09	130	0	—	0
05/07	62	11	18.2%	0
Annual Growth	17.7%	(3.5%)	—	—

2011 Year-End Financials

Debt ratio: ——
Return on equity: 10.00%
Cash ($ mil.): 12
Current ratio: —
Long-term debt ($ mil.): —

Dividends
Yield: —
Payout: —
Market value ($ mil.): —

LEE SUPPLY COMPANY INC.

LOCATIONS

HQ: LEE SUPPLY COMPANY INC.
305 1ST ST, CHARLEROI, PA 15022-1427
Phone: 724-483-3543
Web: www.leesupply.com

HISTORICAL FINANCIALS
Company Type: Private

Income Statement
FYE: September 30

	REVENUE ($ mil.)	NET INCOME ($ mil.)	NET PROFIT MARGIN	EMPLOYEES
09/11	111	8	7.2%	112
09/10	80	3	4.8%	0
09/09	76	3	5.0%	0
09/08	85	4	5.4%	0
Annual Growth	9.5%	20.6%	—	—

LEESBURG REGIONAL MEDICAL CENTER INC.

LOCATIONS

HQ: LEESBURG REGIONAL MEDICAL CENTER INC.
600 E DIXIE AVE, LEESBURG, FL 34748-5999
Phone: 352-323-5000
Web: www.leesburgregional.org

HISTORICAL FINANCIALS
Company Type: Private

Income Statement
FYE: June 30

	REVENUE ($ mil.)	NET INCOME ($ mil.)	NET PROFIT MARGIN	EMPLOYEES
06/11	246	9	3.9%	1,900
06/10	241	5	2.2%	0
06/09	264	(6)	—	0
06/08	337	5	1.6%	0
Annual Growth	(10.0%)	21.5%	—	—

2011 Year-End Financials

Debt ratio: ——
Return on equity: 3.90%
Cash ($ mil.): 58
Current ratio: 0.60
Long-term debt ($ mil.): —

Dividends
Yield: —
Payout: —
Market value ($ mil.): —

LEGACY EMANUEL HOSPITAL & HEALTH CENTER

Legacy Emanuel Hospital and Health Center part of the Legacy Health System provides acute and specialized health care to residents of Portland Oregon and surrounding communities. The 400-bed teaching hospital's operations include centers devoted to trauma treatment burn care oncology birthing neurosurgery orthopedics and cardiology. It also houses the Legacy Emanuel Children's Hospital a 160-bed pediatric facility located on the same campus and the area Life Flight Network which is owned by a consortium of local hospitals.

Legacy Emanuel Hospital was established in 1912 by the Lutheran Church.

The hospital is undergoing massive expansion efforts. The Emanuel Children's Hospital is getting a new seven-story patient tower and the Emanuel Hospital is also getting new acute and intensive care capacity. Construction started in 2008 and is scheduled for completion by the end of 2010.

EXECUTIVES

SVP CFO and and System Office Chief Administrative Officer, Pamela S. (Pam) Vukovich, age 57
SVP Chief Legal Officer and Compliance Officer, P. Campbell (Cam) Groner III
SVP and Chief Medical Officer, George A. (Jack) Cioffi, age 51
SVP and CIO, Richard (Dick) Gibson, age 57
Chief Administrative Officer, Lori Morgan

LOCATIONS

HQ: Legacy Emanuel Hospital and Health Center
2801 N. Gantenbein Ave., Portland OR 97227
Phone: 503-413-2200   **Fax:** 503-415-5200
Web: www.legacyhealth.org

COMPETITORS

Adventist Health
Asante Health System
Dignity Health
Kadlec Regional
  Medical Center
Kaiser Permanente

PeaceHealth
PeaceHealth Southwest
  Medical Center
Providence Health
  & Services
Salem Hospital

HISTORICAL FINANCIALS
Company Type: Subsidiary

Income Statement
FYE: March 31

	REVENUE ($ mil.)	NET INCOME ($ mil.)	NET PROFIT MARGIN	EMPLOYEES
03/12	571	(6)	—	3,619
03/10*	573	13	2.4%	0
04/05	0	0	—	0
03/04	383	12	3.2%	0
Annual Growth	14.2%	—	—	—

*Fiscal year change

2012 Year-End Financials

Debt ratio: ——
Return on equity: (-1.10)%
Cash ($ mil.): 0
Current ratio: 1.30
Long-term debt ($ mil.): —

Dividends
Yield: —
Payout: —
Market value ($ mil.): —

LEGACY MOUNT HOOD MEDICAL CENTER

LOCATIONS

HQ: LEGACY MOUNT HOOD MEDICAL CENTER
24800 SE STARK ST, GRESHAM, OR 97030-3378
Phone: 503-674-1122
Web: www.legacyhealth.org

LEHIGH VALLEY HEALTH NETWORK INC.

They may be closing all the factories down in Allentown (at least according to Billy Joel) but the city along with nearby Bethlehem can claim world class medical facilities in Lehigh Valley Health Network (LVHN). The not-for-profit health care provider operates through three hospital campuses (two in Allentown and one in Bethlehem) housing a total of about 1000 licensed beds. The medical center serves as a regional referral center for trauma and burn care and organ transplantation as well as specialty care in numerous areas such as cardiology women's health and pediatric surgery. LVHN also boasts a 400-member physician group several community health centers and a hospice agency.

LVHN performs research in a range of different areas including cancer cardiovascular and infectious disease.

LVHN is also building the first pediatric emergency department in the Lehigh Valley and surrounding area also at its Cedar Crest campus. The project which is expected to be completed in 2011 will house about a dozen beds and be staffed by dedicated pediatric emergency medicine physicians pediatric emergency nurses and a child life specialist to assist children and their families visiting the emergency room.

The health organization has an alliance with the Sacred Heart Hospital of Allentown through which it provides Sacred Heart with certain services in the areas of cardiac care primary care telehealth services and mental health care. The two hospitals discussed but ultimately dismissed the possibility of a formal merger settling on being affiliated instead.

LVHN's 40 community clinics administer primary and specialty care for people who are uninsured or underinsured. For patients (insured or not) who need care for minor ailments and routine tests LVHN operates a handful of retail health clinics under the Careworks brand. The clinics' physician assistants and nurse practitioners treat illnesses and injuries such as bronchitis ear infections sprains and strains flu symptoms and pinkeye. They also provide health screenings administer immunizations and perform physicals.

EXECUTIVES

SVP and CIO, Harry F. Lukens
SVP Quality and Patient Safety, Anthony J. Ardire
President CEO and Trustee, Ronald W. Swinfard
COO, Terry A. Capuano
Chief Strategy Officer, Brian A. Nester
Chairman, J.B. Reilly
SVP External Affairs, Charles G. Lewis
SVP Health Systems Research and Innovation; Chairman Community Health and Health Studies, Jeff Etchason
Chairman Department of Pathology and Laboratory Medicine, Peter E. Fisher
SVP Operations, James Geiger
Chair Department of Obstetrics/Gynecology, Thomas A. Hutchinson
Chair Department of Psychiatry, Michael W. Kaufmann
Chair Department of Radiology, Robert Kricun
Chair Department of Anesthesiology, Thomas M. McLoughlin Jr.
Chair Department of Family Medicine, William L. Miller
Assistant Chief Medical Officer; Medical Director Lehigh Valley Hospital Muhlenberg, Robert X. Murphy Jr.
Chair Department of Pediatrics, John D. Van Brakle
Chief Medical Officer, Thomas V. Whalen
Director Media Relations, Brian Downs
President-Elect Lehigh Valley Health Network Medical Staff and Trustee, Robert J. Motley
Interim Chair Department of Emergency Medicine, David B. Burmeister
Interim CFO, Edward O?Dea
Associate Dean Educational Affairs, J. Alan Otsuki
SVP Patient Care Services and Chief Nursing Officer, Anne Panik
Chair Department of Surgery, Michael D. Pasquale
VP Human Resources, Debby Patrick
President Medical Staff, Michael J. Pistoria
Chair Department of Medicine, Debbie Salas-Lopez
SVP Operations, Keith Weinhold
Trustee, William F. Hecht, age 69
Trustee, Arnold H. Kaplan, age 64
Trustee, James H. (Jim) Miller, age 63
Trustee, Marvin L. Woodall
Trustee, Jeffrey P. (Jeff) Feather, age 69
Trustee, Richard J. Green
President CEO and Trustee, Ronald W. Swinfard
Trustee, Daniel H. Weiss
Trustee, Susan C. Yee
Trustee, Martin K. Till
Trustee, Kathryn P. Taylor
Trustee, Robert J. Dillman
President-Elect Lehigh Valley Health Network Medical Staff and Trustee, Robert J. Motley

LOCATIONS

HQ: LEHIGH VALLEY HEALTH NETWORK INC.
1247 CEDAR CREST BLVD, ALLENTOWN, PA 18105
Phone: 610-402-8000

PRODUCTS/OPERATIONS

Selected Facilities
Community Health Centers
Hamburg Community Health Center
Lehigh Valley Health Center at Bath
Lehigh Valley Health Center at Bethlehem Township
Lehigh Valley Health Center at Hellertown
Lehigh Valley Health Center at Kutztown
Lehigh Valley Health Center at Saucon Valley
Lehigh Valley Health Center at Trexlertown
Upper Bucks Health & Diagnostic Center (in partnership with Grand View Hospital Quakertown)
Hospitals

Lehigh Valley Hospital - 17th and Chew (short-stay hospital Allentown)
Lehigh Valley Hospital - Cedar Crest (Allentown)
Lehigh Valley Hospital - Muhlenberg (Bethlehem)

COMPETITORS

Abington Memorial Hospital
Ascension Health
Community Health Systems
Doylestown Hospital
Grand View
Jefferson Health System
Mercy Health System
Moses Taylor Hospital
North Philadelphia Health System
Pennsylvania Hospital
Reading Hospital and Medical Center
Sacred Heart Hospital of Allentown
Shore Memorial Hospital
St. Luke's University Health Network
Tenet Healthcare
University of Pennsylvania Health System
Wyoming Valley Health Care System

HISTORICAL FINANCIALS
Company Type: Private - Not-for-Profit

Income Statement
FYE: June 30

	REVENUE ($ mil.)	NET INCOME ($ mil.)	NET PROFIT MARGIN	EMPLOYEES
06/12	1,620	(63)	—	7,000
06/11	1,524	314	20.6%	0
06/10	1,399	58	4.2%	0
06/09	1,291	(177)	—	0
Annual Growth	7.8%	—	—	—

2012 Year-End Financials

Debt ratio: —
Return on equity: (-3.90)%
Cash ($ mil.): 26
Current ratio: 1.40
Long-term debt ($ mil.): —

Dividends
Yield: —
Payout: —
Market value ($ mil.): —

LENMORE INC.

LOCATIONS

HQ: LENMORE INC.
401 PENN AVE, PITTSBURGH, PA 15221-2135
Phone: 412-243-8000

HISTORICAL FINANCIALS
Company Type: Private

Income Statement
FYE: December 31

	REVENUE ($ mil.)	NET INCOME ($ mil.)	NET PROFIT MARGIN	EMPLOYEES
12/11	177	0	—	28
12/10	179	0	—	0
12/09	141	1	0.9%	0
12/08	0	0	—	0
Annual Growth	—	—	—	—

2011 Year-End Financials

Debt ratio: —
Return on equity: —
Cash ($ mil.): 4
Current ratio: 1.90
Long-term debt ($ mil.): —

Dividends
Yield: —
Payout: —
Market value ($ mil.): —

LESLEY UNIVERSITY

LOCATIONS

HQ: LESLEY UNIVERSITY
29 EVERETT ST, CAMBRIDGE, MA 02138-2702
Phone: 617-868-9600
Web: www.aiboston.edu

HISTORICAL FINANCIALS

Company Type: Private

Income Statement

FYE: June 30

	REVENUE ($ mil.)	NET INCOME ($ mil.)	NET PROFIT MARGIN	EMPLOYEES
06/12	110	(3)	—	800
06/11	105	21	20.2%	0
06/10	103	9	9.0%	0
06/09	100	(47)	—	0
Annual Growth	3.3%	—	—	—

2012 Year-End Financials

Debt ratio: ——
Return on equity: (-3.30)%
Cash ($ mil.): 6
Current ratio: —
Long-term debt ($ mil.): —

Dividends
Yield: —
Payout: —
Market value ($ mil.): —

LEWIS UNIVERSITY

LOCATIONS

HQ: LEWIS UNIVERSITY
1 UNIVERSITY PKWY, ROMEOVILLE, IL 60446-1832
Phone: 815-838-0500
Web: www.lewisuniversityonline.com

HISTORICAL FINANCIALS

Company Type: Private

Income Statement

FYE: June 30

	REVENUE ($ mil.)	NET INCOME ($ mil.)	NET PROFIT MARGIN	EMPLOYEES
06/12	146	5	4.1%	500
06/11	144	15	10.5%	0
06/10	127	5	3.9%	0
06/09	108	(4)	—	0
Annual Growth	10.6%	—	—	—

2012 Year-End Financials

Debt ratio: ——
Return on equity: 4.10%
Cash ($ mil.): 15
Current ratio: —
Long-term debt ($ mil.): —

Dividends
Yield: —
Payout: —
Market value ($ mil.): —

LEWISTOWN HOSPITAL

Lewistown may have been named after a Quaker but Lewistown Hospital has no qualms about using the latest technology to care for its patients. The acute-care rural hospital has a great dependency on its small physician staff causing it to be particularly vulnerable to physician turnover. As a result the hospital included an aggressive physician recruitment plan in its 2007-2011 business plan which includes making the latest health information technology available to new recruits. Family Health Associates the hospital's affiliated group of 21 physicians offer a range of specialties from pediatrics to pulmonary medicine to the 80000 residents of Mifflin and Juniata counties.

EXECUTIVES

VP Finance and CFO, Randy E. Tewksbury
VP Human Resources, N. Sue Reinke
VP Marketing and Community Affairs, Phyllis K. Mitchell
VP Information Management and CIO, Ronald M. (Ron) Cowan
President and CEO, Kay A. Hamilton
VP Family Health Associates (FHA) Operations, Crista L. Bobb
Director Engineering and Support Services, Joseph F. Gagliardo
VP Nursing Services, Christine W. Mathews
VP Operations, Kirk E. Thomas

LOCATIONS

HQ: Lewistown Hospital
400 Highland Ave., Lewistown PA 17044
Phone: 717-248-5411   **Fax:** 717-242-7132
Web: www.lewistownhospital.org

COMPETITORS

Ascension Health
Guthrie Healthcare
J. C. Blair Memorial Hospital
Mercy Health Partners
Toledo

HISTORICAL FINANCIALS

Company Type: Private - Not-for-Profit

Income Statement

FYE: June 30

	REVENUE ($ mil.)	NET INCOME ($ mil.)	NET PROFIT MARGIN	EMPLOYEES
06/11	95	2	2.5%	900
06/10	91	1	2.0%	0
06/09	86	1	2.0%	0
06/08	91	(2)	—	0
Annual Growth	1.7%	—	—	—

2011 Year-End Financials

Debt ratio: ——
Return on equity: 2.50%
Cash ($ mil.): 13
Current ratio: 0.90
Long-term debt ($ mil.): —

Dividends
Yield: —
Payout: —
Market value ($ mil.): —

LEXA INTERNATIONAL CORPORATION

LOCATIONS

HQ: LEXA INTERNATIONAL CORPORATION
1 LANDMARK SQ STE 407, STAMFORD, CT 06901-2601
Phone: 203-326-5200
Web: www.axeljohnson.com

HISTORICAL FINANCIALS

Company Type: Private

Income Statement

FYE: December 31

	REVENUE ($ mil.)	NET INCOME ($ mil.)	NET PROFIT MARGIN	EMPLOYEES
12/11	3,954	18	0.5%	1,204
12/09	2,598	6	0.2%	0
12/08	4,312	4	0.1%	0
12/07	4,003	(21)	—	0
Annual Growth	(0.4%)	—	—	—

2011 Year-End Financials

Debt ratio: ——
Return on equity: 0.50%
Cash ($ mil.): 90
Current ratio: 0.60
Long-term debt ($ mil.): —

Dividends
Yield: —
Payout: —
Market value ($ mil.): —

LGS SPECIALTY SALES LTD.

LOCATIONS

HQ: LGS SPECIALTY SALES LTD.
1 RADISSON PLZ, NEW ROCHELLE, NY 10801-5766
Phone: 718-542-2200

HISTORICAL FINANCIALS

Company Type: Private

Income Statement

FYE: August 31

	REVENUE ($ mil.)	NET INCOME ($ mil.)	NET PROFIT MARGIN	EMPLOYEES
08/12	117	2	2.0%	15
08/11	116	1	1.7%	0
08/10	105	1	1.6%	0
Annual Growth	5.3%	19.9%	—	—

2012 Year-End Financials

Debt ratio: ——
Return on equity: 2.00%
Cash ($ mil.): 5
Current ratio: 4.60
Long-term debt ($ mil.): —

Dividends
Yield: —
Payout: —
Market value ($ mil.): —

LIBERTY PROPERTY LIMITED PARTNERSHIP

LOCATIONS

HQ: LIBERTY PROPERTY LIMITED PARTNERSHIP
500 CHESTERFIELD PKWY, MALVERN, PA
19355-8707
Phone: 610-648-1700
Web: www.libertyproperty.com

HISTORICAL FINANCIALS

Company Type: Private

Income Statement

FYE: September 30

	REVENUE ($ mil.)	NET INCOME ($ mil.)	NET PROFIT MARGIN	EMPLOYEES
09/12*	509	107	21.0%	443
12/11	667	210	31.6%	0
Annual Growth	(23.7%)	(49.1%)	—	—

*Fiscal year change

2012 Year-End Financials

Debt ratio: ——
Return on equity: 21.00%
Cash ($ mil.): 34
Current ratio: ——
Long-term debt ($ mil.): ——
Dividends
Yield: —
Payout: —
Market value ($ mil.): —

LICKING MEMORIAL HEALTH SYSTEMS

Here to help Buckeye Staters lick disease is Licking Memorial Health Systems. The health care provider operates the 230-bed Licking Memorial Hospital and a multi-specialty physician group called Licking Memorial Health Professionals. Specialty services at the hospital include cancer care home health occupational health rehabilitation and cardiology. Licking Memorial Hospital administers behavioral health care (including substance abuse treatments) through its Shepard Hill department. The physicians' group operates through about 40 practices with 90 doctors spanning over about a seven-town area. Licking Memorial Health Systems was founded in 1898 by the Newark Hospital Association.

EXECUTIVES

President CEO and Director, Rob Montagnese
VP Human Resources and Support Services, Anne Peterson
VP Development and Public Relations, Veronica Link
VP Information Systems, Sallie Arnett
VP Medical Affairs, Craig Cairns
VP Patient Care Services, Deborah Young
VP Corporate Compliance, Ann Hubbuch
VP Physician Practices, Christine McGee
Vice Chairman, William Mann
Secretary Treasurer and Director, John Hinderer
Chairman, Gordon Wilken
VP Finance, Thomas Poulson

VP Financial Services, Cindy Webster
President CEO and Director, Rob Montagnese
Vice Chairman, William Mann
Secretary Treasurer and Director, John Hinderer
Director, David Shull
Director, Walter Gemmell
Director, Prof Louis Mollica
Director, Judith Pierce
Diretor, Patrick M. Jeffries

LOCATIONS

HQ: Licking Memorial Health Systems
1320 W. Main St., Newark OH 43055
Phone: 740-348-4000   **Fax:** 740-348-4026
Web: www.lmhealth.org

COMPETITORS

Fairfield Medical Center
Genesis HealthCare System (Ohio)
Mount Carmel Health
Nationwide Children' s Hospital
OhioHealth

HISTORICAL FINANCIALS

Company Type: Private - Not-for-Profit

Income Statement

FYE: December 31

	REVENUE ($ mil.)	NET INCOME ($ mil.)	NET PROFIT MARGIN	EMPLOYEES
12/11	184	(7)		1,600
12/10	198	4	2.2%	0
12/09	199	12	6.1%	0
12/08	34	0		0
Annual Growth	75.3%	—	—	—

2011 Year-End Financials

Debt ratio: ——
Return on equity: (-4.20)%
Cash ($ mil.): 11
Current ratio: 1.30
Long-term debt ($ mil.): —
Dividends
Yield: —
Payout: —
Market value ($ mil.): —

LIFESPACE COMMUNITIES INC.

LOCATIONS

HQ: LIFESPACE COMMUNITIES INC.
100 E GRAND AVE STE 200, DES MOINES, IA
50309-1835
Phone: 515-288-5805
Web: www.abbeydelray.com

HISTORICAL FINANCIALS

Company Type: Private

Income Statement

FYE: December 31

	REVENUE ($ mil.)	NET INCOME ($ mil.)	NET PROFIT MARGIN	EMPLOYEES
12/11	194	15	8.0%	1,875
12/10	159	8	5.0%	0
12/09	166	7	4.5%	0
12/08	167	7	4.6%	0
Annual Growth	5.2%	26.4%	—	—

2011 Year-End Financials

Debt ratio: ——
Return on equity: 8.00%
Cash ($ mil.): 26
Current ratio: 0.50
Long-term debt ($ mil.): —
Dividends
Yield: —
Payout: —
Market value ($ mil.): —

LIMSON TRADING INC.

LOCATIONS

HQ: LIMSON TRADING INC.
1045 GEZON PKWY SW, GRAND RAPIDS, MI
49509-9542
Phone: 616-530-3110
Web: www.limsontrading.com

HISTORICAL FINANCIALS

Company Type: Private

Income Statement

FYE: December 31

	REVENUE ($ mil.)	NET INCOME ($ mil.)	NET PROFIT MARGIN	EMPLOYEES
12/11	118	8	7.6%	12
Annual Growth	—	—	—	—

2011 Year-End Financials

Debt ratio: ——
Return on equity: 7.60%
Cash ($ mil.): 4
Current ratio: 1.80
Long-term debt ($ mil.): —
Dividends
Yield: —
Payout: —
Market value ($ mil.): —

LIN R. ROGERS ELECTRICAL CONTRACTORS INC.

LOCATIONS

HQ: LIN R. ROGERS ELECTRICAL CONTRACTORS INC.
2050 MARCONI DR STE 200, ALPHARETTA, GA
30005-5202
Phone: 770-772-3400
Web: www.lrogerselectric.com

HISTORICAL FINANCIALS

Company Type: Private

Income Statement

FYE: December 31

	REVENUE ($ mil.)	NET INCOME ($ mil.)	NET PROFIT MARGIN	EMPLOYEES
12/11	105	6	6.1%	1,100
12/09	94	5	6.1%	0
12/08	132	16	12.2%	0
12/07	115	7	6.4%	0
Annual Growth	(3.1%)	(4.4%)	—	—

LINCOLN CENTER FOR THE PERFORMING ARTS INC.

One of the world's largest cultural hubs Lincoln Center presents live music theater dance and opera performances from its 16-acre complex in New York City. The Center also offers educational programming and provides a home base for such organizations as the School of American Ballet the New York Philharmonic the Metropolitan Opera and The Film Society of Lincoln Center. More than 5000 performances and educational programs are presented and more than 5 million people visit each year. The Lincoln Center was conceived by New York City movers and shakers including Robert Moses Robert F. Wagner Jr. and John D. Rockefeller III; construction of the complex took place between 1959 and 1972.

The organization has made some $900 million in renovations to the facility and in recent years. The Center paid for the improvements through fundraising efforts including $240 million pledged by New York City.

The renovations opened up Broadway to more pedestrians and made the Lincoln Center grounds more welcoming to tourists.

EXECUTIVES

Treasurer, Harvey Golub, age 73
Chair, Katherine G. Farley, age 62
President, Reynold Levy
Chief Administrative Officer, Liza Parker
VP Programming, Jane S. Moss
VP Planning and Development, Tamar C. Podell
VP Public Relations, Betsy Vorce
Executive Producer Live from Lincoln Center Media, John Goberman
Executive Director Lincoln Center Institute, Scott Noppe-Brandon
Director Lincoln Center Festival, Nigel Redden
VP General Counsel and Secretary, Lesley F. Rosenthal
Senior Campaign Officer Campaign for Lincoln Center, Sue Mellin
Deputy Executive Director Bravo Campaign, Paula Kascel
Chief Government Relations Officer, Melissa Thornton
Director Music Programming, Hanako Yamaguchi
Director Contemporary Programming, Jon Nakagawa
Producer Contemporary Programming, Charles Cermele
Senior Producer Lincoln Center Festival, Carmen Kovens
General Manager Lincoln Center Festival, Erica D. Zielinski
Production Manager Lincoln Center Festival, Paul E. King

Producer Lincoln Center Festival, Boo Froebel
Supervising Producer Media, Marc Bauman
Senior Director Special Events, Mary Callaghan
Senior Director Sponsorship and Corporate Relations, Polly W. Rua
Director Development Operations Planning and Development, Christine A. Donato
VP Creative Services, Peter Duffin
Associate Director Creative Services, Celie Fitzgerald
Director Programs and Services for People with Disabilities, Bobbi Wailes
Senior Director Publicity and Public Relations, Eileen McMahon
Senior Manager Communication Services, Marian Skokan
Editorial Manager, Joy Chutz
Senior Director Financial Planning and Analysis, Farang Azari
Senior Financial Analyst, Yuliya Bukhman
Assistant Director Payroll, James (Jim) McGivney
Senior Director Human Resources, Marina Sgroi
Manager Human Resources, Stacey Tunks
Mailroom Assistant, Mark Council
VP Finance and CFO, Daniel Rubin
VP Concert Halls and Operations, Kerry A. Madden
Director Executive Strategy and Business, Kara M. Barnett
Assistant Strategy and Business, Leah Day
Controller, Elaine Ruiz
Government and Community Relations Officer, Maureen McCormack
CTO, Robert Tarleton
Manager Publicity, Kate Merlino
Director Security, Susan Bick
Director Facilities and Operations, Michael Powers
Manager Marketing, Mara Forbes
Manager Marketing Services, Michael DeFroda
Director Administration Concert Halls, John Tiebout
Manager Marketing and Bookings Concert Halls, Alison Walters
Head Treasurer Alice Tully Hall Box Office, Anne Reda
Head Treasurer Avery Fisher Hall Box Office, Peter Meyers Jr.
Deputy Director Ticketing Systems Information Technology, Paul Bair
Network Administrator Information Technology, Don Chan
Senior Publicity Manager, Eva Chien
Director Public Programming, Bill Bragin
Manager Corporate Relations, Jack Trinco
Manager Corporate Relations, Monika La Nuez
Manager Donor Relations Planning and Development, Alexandra Olin
Assistant Director Sponsorship and Corporate Relations, Lisa Ueki
Manager Human Resources, Michele Louhisdon
Performance Manager Concert Halls, Domingo Cabrera
Performance Manager Concert Halls, Megan Thorne
Director Information Resources, Judith Johnson

LOCATIONS

HQ: Lincoln Center for the Performing Arts Inc.
70 Lincoln Center Plaza, New York NY 10023-6583
Phone: 212-875-5000   **Fax:** 212-875-5275
Web: www.lincolncenter.org

HISTORICAL FINANCIALS

Company Type: Private - Not-for-Profit

Income Statement   FYE: June 30

	REVENUE ($ mil.)	NET INCOME ($ mil.)	NET PROFIT MARGIN	EMPLOYEES
06/11	169	(17)	—	525
06/10	205	(28)	—	0
06/09	246	0	—	0
06/06	196	78	40.0%	0
Annual Growth	(4.7%)	—	—	—

2011 Year-End Financials

Debt ratio: —
Return on equity: (-10.10)%
Cash ($ mil.): 44
Current ratio: 0.10
Long-term debt ($ mil.): —

Dividends
Yield: —
Payout: —
Market value ($ mil.): —

LINCOLN PUBLIC SCHOOLS INC

LOCATIONS

HQ: LINCOLN PUBLIC SCHOOLS INC
5901 O ST, LINCOLN, NE 68510-2235
Phone: 402-436-1000
Web: www.lps.org

HISTORICAL FINANCIALS

Company Type: Private

Income Statement   FYE: August 31

	REVENUE ($ mil.)	NET INCOME ($ mil.)	NET PROFIT MARGIN	EMPLOYEES
08/12	427	(39)	—	6,950
08/11	419	(38)	—	0
08/10	442	(10)	—	0
08/09	515	39	7.6%	0
Annual Growth	(6.0%)	—	—	—

2012 Year-End Financials

Debt ratio: —
Return on equity: (-9.10)%
Cash ($ mil.): 0
Current ratio: —
Long-term debt ($ mil.): —

Dividends
Yield: —
Payout: —
Market value ($ mil.): —

LIQUID INVESTMENTS INC.

Liquid Investments has nothing to do with your bank accounts your retirement fund or your broker. The company supplies beer malt beverages soda energy drinks and water to customers in parts of California and Colorado. It owns the Mesa Beverage Co. in Santa Rosa California which handles over 1500 accounts in Sonoma and Marin counties. It also serves 475 accounts in the western slope area of Colorado through Colorado Beverage Distribution which has locations in Grand Junction and Montrose Colorado. Liquid distributes imported domestic and craft beers. It also offers regional and local beers along with soda and bottled water. Its latest addition to its craft labels is Victoria lagers.

Through Mesa Beverage the company distributes more than 4 million cases annually from suppliers like Boston Beer Crown Imports Heineken USA and MillerCoors. Mesa Beverage also distributes local beers from brewers such as Lagunitas based in Petaluma California.

Colorado Beverage Distributing distributes a wide range of national imported and craft beers from brewers like Anchor Brewing Big Sky Brewing Duvel New Belgium Beer and Scottish & Newcastle.

EXECUTIVES

Chairman and CEO, Ronald L. (Ron) Fowler, age 67
VP Marketing, Patrick (Pat) Connors
VP Finance, Terry L. Harris
Legal Counsel, Jack Studebaker
VP Operations, Mitch Morgan
President Mesa Beverage Co, Mark Herculson
General Sales Manager Mesa Beverage, Tony Amaral
Operations Manager Mesa Beverage, Shane Hilkey
Human Resources Manager Mesa Beverage, Lisa Burleson
VP; General Manager Colorado Beverage Distributing, Ron Foster
General Sales Manager Colorado Beverage Distributing, Cody Carlson
Operations Manager Colorado Beverage Distributing, Lance Williams
Distribution Logistics Manager, Greg Newhouse

LOCATIONS

HQ: Liquid Investments Co. Inc.
8870 Liquid Ct., San Diego CA 92121-2234
Phone: 858-509-8510 **Fax:** 858-509-8511
Web: www.lqdinv.com
Liquid Investments has locations in California (Sacramento Santa Rosa San Diego) and Colorado (Grand Junction and Montrose).

PRODUCTS/OPERATIONS

Selected Suppliers
Anchor Brewing
Asahi USA
Bartles & James
Big Sky Brewing
Binding Brauerei USA
Boston Beer
Boulder Brewing
Breckenridge Brewery
Crown Imports
Crystal Geyser
Diageo-Guinness USA
Dogfish Head Brewery
Flying Dog Brewing
Gambrinus Company
Gordon Biersch Brewery
Grand Teton Brewing
Heineken USA
Heineken-CCM
Henry Weinhard Soda
Jackson Hole Soda
King Fisher
Lagunitas Brewing
Mendocino Brewing
Mike's Hard Beverages
MillerCoors Brewing Co.
New Belgium Brewing
Oskar Blues Brewery
Pabst Brewing

Palisade Brewing
Pyramid Ales
Red Bull
Rockies Brewing
Sapporo USA
Scottish & Newcastle
Sierra Nevada
Thomas Kemper Soda

COMPETITORS

Beauchamp Distributing
Beverage Distributors Company
Coca-Cola
Constellation Brands
Danone Water
Dr Pepper Snapple Group
Harbor Distributing
Jordano' s
Nestle Waters North America
PepsiCo
Southern Wine & Spirits
The Charmer Sunbelt Group
Young' s Market

HISTORICAL FINANCIALS

Company Type: Private

Income Statement

FYE: December 31

	REVENUE ($ mil.)	NET INCOME ($ mil.)	NET PROFIT MARGIN	EMPLOYEES
12/11	93	1	1.3%	629
12/10	91	(0)	—	0
12/09	93	0	0.4%	0
12/08	95	128	134.4%	0
Annual Growth	(0.5%)	(79.0%)	—	—

2011 Year-End Financials

Debt ratio: —
Return on equity: 1.30%
Cash ($ mil.) 0
Current ratio: 0.90
Long-term debt ($ mil.): —
Dividends
Yield: —
Payout: —
Market value ($ mil.): —

LITTLE COMPANY OF MARY HOSPITAL OF INDIANA INC.

LOCATIONS

HQ: LITTLE COMPANY OF MARY HOSPITAL OF INDIANA INC.
800 W 9TH ST, JASPER, IN 47546-2514
Phone: 812-482-2345
Web: www.mhhcc.org

HISTORICAL FINANCIALS

Company Type: Private

Income Statement

FYE: June 30

	REVENUE ($ mil.)	NET INCOME ($ mil.)	NET PROFIT MARGIN	EMPLOYEES
06/12	163	4	2.5%	950
06/11	150	16	10.8%	0
06/10	143	8	6.2%	0
06/09	142	(5)	—	0
Annual Growth	4.7%	—	—	—

2012 Year-End Financials

Debt ratio: —
Return on equity: 2.50%
Cash ($ mil.): 44
Current ratio: 3.40
Long-term debt ($ mil.):
Dividends
Yield: —
Payout: —
Market value ($ mil.): —

LITTLE SIOUX CORN PROCESSORS LLC

Pursuing the corny American Heartland dream of profitable renewable energy Little Sioux Corn Processors operates an ethanol plant in northwest Iowa. (It actually owns a 60% interest in the limited partnership that owns the ethanol facility.) The company converts bushels of corn into ethanol distiller grains (used as feed for the dairy and beef industries) and corn oil. Ethanol is used as an additive to gasoline as well as a fuel enhancer for high-octane motors and it burns more cleanly than normal gasoline thereby reducing carbon monoxide emissions. Little Sioux's production capacity is about 90 million gallons of ethanol annually more than double its orginal capacity after successive expansions.

EXECUTIVES

Chairman, Ron Wetherell, age 67
Secretary and Director, Timothy (Tim) Ohlson, age 61
Vice Chairman, Myron Pingel, age 72
President and CEO, Stephen (Steve) Roe, age 58, $161,519 total compensation
CFO, Gary Grotjohn, age 61, $97,289 total compensation
Plant Manager, Chris Williams
Grain Merchandiser, Jake Wetter
Director, Daryl Haack, age 68
Secretary and Director, Timothy (Tim) Ohlson, age 61
Director, Doug Lansink, age 54
Director, Verdell Johnson, age 75
Vice Chairman, Myron Pingel, age 72
Director, Darrell Downs, age 74
Director, Vincent (Vince) Davis, age 60
Director, Dale Arends, age 57
Auditors: BoulayHeutmakerZibell&Co.P.L.L.P.

LOCATIONS

HQ: Little Sioux Corn Processors LLC
4808 F Ave., Marcus IA 51035
Phone: 712-376-2800 **Fax:** 712-376-2815
Web: www.littlesiouxcornprocessors.com

COMPETITORS

Abengoa Bioenergy
ADM
Badger State Ethanol
Cargill
GreenField Ethanol
Lake Area Corn Processors
POET

HISTORICAL FINANCIALS
Company Type: Private

Income Statement
FYE: September 30

	REVENUE ($ mil.)	NET INCOME ($ mil.)	NET PROFIT MARGIN	EMPLOYEES
09/11*	329	9	2.9%	45
06/08	0	0	—	0
09/03	31	4	12.8%	0
Annual Growth	221.9%	52.6%	—	—

*Fiscal year change

2011 Year-End Financials
Debt ratio: ——
Return on equity: 2.90%
Cash ($ mil.): 14
Current ratio: 1.10
Long-term debt ($ mil.): —
Dividends
Yield: —
Payout: —
Market value ($ mil.): —

LITTLEJOHN GRAIN INC.

LOCATIONS
HQ: LITTLEJOHN GRAIN INC.
8801 E US HWY 40, MARTINSVILLE, IL 62442
Phone: 217-382-4158
Web: www.littlejohngrain.com

HISTORICAL FINANCIALS
Company Type: Private

Income Statement
FYE: August 31

	REVENUE ($ mil.)	NET INCOME ($ mil.)	NET PROFIT MARGIN	EMPLOYEES
08/12	82	0	0.2%	21
08/11	100	1	1.0%	0
08/10	48	0	0.5%	0
08/09	60	0	1.2%	0
Annual Growth	10.9%	(39.3%)	—	—

2012 Year-End Financials
Debt ratio: ——
Return on equity: 0.20%
Cash ($ mil.): 6
Current ratio: 0.30
Long-term debt ($ mil.): —
Dividends
Yield: —
Payout: —
Market value ($ mil.): —

LIVERPOOL CENTRAL SCHOOL DISTRICT

LOCATIONS
HQ: LIVERPOOL CENTRAL SCHOOL DISTRICT
195 BLACKBERRY RD, LIVERPOOL, NY 13090-3047
Phone: 315-622-7148
Web: www.srm.liverpool.k12.ny.us

HISTORICAL FINANCIALS
Company Type: Private

Income Statement
FYE: June 30

	REVENUE ($ mil.)	NET INCOME ($ mil.)	NET PROFIT MARGIN	EMPLOYEES
06/12	141	(3)	—	1,300
06/11	136	(23)	—	0
06/10*	142	(2)	—	0
12/09	1	0	19.4%	0
Annual Growth	386.4%	—	—	—

*Fiscal year change

2012 Year-End Financials
Debt ratio: ——
Return on equity: (-2.80)%
Cash ($ mil.): 23
Current ratio: 0.60
Long-term debt ($ mil.): —
Dividends
Yield: —
Payout: —
Market value ($ mil.): —

LIVINGSTONE COLLEGE

Livingstone College is one of the more than 100 Historically Black Colleges and Universities (HBCUs) in the US. The school which is affiliated with the African Methodist Episcopal Zion Church offers undergraduate degrees in business education and social work liberal arts and math and sciences. Academic programs include accounting sports management political science and chemistry. Livingstone College also offers accelerated degree programs for non-traditional students with online coursework and evening and weekend classes. HBCUs collectively grant about one-fifth of the undergraduate degrees earned by African-Americans. Dr. Joseph Charles Price founded the school in 1879.

EXECUTIVES
Director Public Relations, Mai Li Mu?oz Adams
VP Advancement and Director Public Affairs, Rev Anthony Davis
President, Jimmy R. Perkins Sr.
Director of Human Resources, Sharon M. Thompson
Associate Director of Human Resources, Kerri Moore

LOCATIONS
HQ: Livingstone College
701 W. Monroe St., Salisbury NC 28144
Phone: 704-216-6000   Fax: 704-216-6795
Web: www.livingstone.edu

HISTORICAL FINANCIALS
Company Type: School

Income Statement
FYE: June 30

	REVENUE ($ mil.)	NET INCOME ($ mil.)	NET PROFIT MARGIN	EMPLOYEES
06/11	30	2	7.5%	140
06/10*	25	2	11.5%	0
08/09	0	0	—	0
06/08	29	3	11.8%	0
Annual Growth	1.5%	(12.8%)	—	—

*Fiscal year change

2011 Year-End Financials
Debt ratio: ——
Return on equity: 7.50%
Cash ($ mil.): 1
Current ratio: —
Long-term debt ($ mil.): —
Dividends
Yield: —
Payout: —
Market value ($ mil.): —

LODGING RLJ TRUST L P

LOCATIONS
HQ: LODGING RLJ TRUST L P
3 BETHESDA METRO CTR, BETHESDA, MD 20814-5330
Phone: 301-280-7777
Web: www.rljlodgingtrust.com

HISTORICAL FINANCIALS
Company Type: Private

Income Statement
FYE: September 30

	REVENUE ($ mil.)	NET INCOME ($ mil.)	NET PROFIT MARGIN	EMPLOYEES
09/12*	631	27	4.3%	2
12/11	758	11	1.5%	0
Annual Growth	(16.8%)	134.0%	—	—

*Fiscal year change

2012 Year-End Financials
Debt ratio: ——
Return on equity: 4.30%
Cash ($ mil.): 192
Current ratio: 1.30
Long-term debt ($ mil.): —
Dividends
Yield: —
Payout: —
Market value ($ mil.): —

LODI MEMORIAL HOSPITAL ASSOCIATION INC.

LOCATIONS
HQ: LODI MEMORIAL HOSPITAL ASSOCIATION INC.
975 S FAIRMONT AVE, LODI, CA 95240-5118
Phone: 209-334-3411
Web: www.lodihealth.org

HISTORICAL FINANCIALS
Company Type: Private

Income Statement
FYE: December 31

	REVENUE ($ mil.)	NET INCOME ($ mil.)	NET PROFIT MARGIN	EMPLOYEES
12/11	156	(7)	—	1,050
12/10	198	(7)	—	0
12/09	167	4	2.5%	0
12/08	154	6	4.4%	0
Annual Growth	0.3%	—	—	—

2011 Year-End Financials

Debt ratio: ——
Return on equity: (-4.70)%
Cash ($ mil.): 5
Current ratio: 1.20
Long-term debt ($ mil.): ——

Dividends
Yield: ——
Payout: ——
Market value ($ mil.): ——

LOEBER MOTORS INC.

Want to buy a car from a son of a son of a salesman? Go to Loeber Motors family-owned and -operated for three generations. The company sells Mercedes-Benz Porsche and smart cars vans and trucks from its dealerships in Lincolnwood Illinois. Loeber Motors also sells used cars and maintains parts and service departments. Loeber's Web site allows visitors to get quick quotes on new cars schedule service appointments order parts apply for finance and search for used vehicles. The site also provides a forum for owners to chat about their cars. Martin Loeber founded Loeber Motors in 1938.

EXECUTIVES

VP, George Loeber
President, Michael Loeber
Controller, Jen Koller
New Car Sales Manager, Gary Jones

LOCATIONS

HQ: Loeber Motors Inc.
4255 W. Touhy Ave., Lincolnwood IL 60712
Phone: 847-675-1000   **Fax:** 847-675-5212
Web: www.loebermotors.com

COMPETITORS

AutoNation
Bob Rohrman Auto
Continental Motors
Jordan Automotive
Motor Werks of
Barrington

Penske Automotive
Group
Steve Foley

HISTORICAL FINANCIALS

Company Type: Private

Income Statement

FYE: December 31

	REVENUE ($ mil.)	NET INCOME ($ mil.)	NET PROFIT MARGIN	EMPLOYEES
12/11	138	2	1.6%	110
12/10	120	0	0.8%	0
12/09	75	1	1.4%	0
12/08	101	1	1.8%	0
Annual Growth	10.9%	6.1%	——	——

2011 Year-End Financials

Debt ratio: ——
Return on equity: 1.60%
Cash ($ mil.): 5
Current ratio: 1.40
Long-term debt ($ mil.): ——

Dividends
Yield: ——
Payout: ——
Market value ($ mil.): ——

LOGICALIS INC.

Logicalis believes that your enterprise technology should operate in a straightforward fashion. The company provides a variety of information technology (IT) services such as consulting implementation systems integration staffing network design and training. Logicalis also offers managed services for tasks such as network security IT infrastructure management and monitoring and application management. The company's customers come from a variety of fields including manufacturing financial services and health care. The company is the US operating subsidiary of UK-based Logicalis Group.

As part of its broader global expansion effort parent company Logicalis Group acquired Phoenix-based Network Infrastructure Corporation (NIC) to boost its profile in the southwestern US in late 2010. NIC specialized in network consulting and IT services for the education gaming and hospitality markets as well as state and local government agencies.

Logicalis Group is a unit of South Africa-based network equipment reseller Datatec Limited. Datatec acquired UK-based Logical Networks in 1997 and shortly followed up that deal by buying more than 20 additional companies around the globe that became the Logicalis Group.

EXECUTIVES

Chairman, Michael B. (Mike) Cox
President and CEO, Terrence (Terry) Flood
EVP and General Counsel, Robert A. Maxwell
EVP and General Manager STG Division, Jeffrey J. Teeter
SVP Sales, Kirk P. Zaranti
VP Business Relations Cisco Solutions, Bob Hankins
EVP and General Manager Solutions Services, Brian Nogar
SVP Solutions Services North American Managed Services Division, Eric Linxweiler
VP Marketing and Business Development, Lisa Dreher
CFO, Greg Baker
COO Argentina Chile Paraguay Peru and Uruguay, Rodrigo Parreira, age 46
VP Operations, Bill Kole
EVP Managed Services Group, Wayne Kiphart
VP Application Services, Shaun Olsen
VP Consulting Services, Chris Rafter
VP Services Operations, Bob Verheyen
VP Business Relations HP Solutions, Brandon Harris
VP Business Relations IBM Solutions, John Iffert

LOCATIONS

HQ: Logicalis Inc.
34505 W. 12 Mile Rd. Ste. 210, Farmington Hills MI 48331
Phone: 248-957-5600   **Fax:** 248-957-5601
Web: www.us.logicalis.com

COMPETITORS

Accenture
Affiliated Computer
Services
Agilysys
Black Box

Computer Sciences
Corp.
HP Enterprise Services
IBM Global Services
Unisys

HISTORICAL FINANCIALS

Company Type: Subsidiary

Income Statement

FYE: February 29

	REVENUE ($ mil.)	NET INCOME ($ mil.)	NET PROFIT MARGIN	EMPLOYEES
02/12	384	4	1.1%	595
02/11	357	5	1.4%	0
02/10	338	0	0.2%	0
02/09	409	8	2.1%	0
Annual Growth	(2.1%)	(21.3%)	——	——

2012 Year-End Financials

Debt ratio: ——
Return on equity: 1.10%
Cash ($ mil.): 1
Current ratio: 0.50
Long-term debt ($ mil.): ——

Dividends
Yield: ——
Payout: ——
Market value ($ mil.): ——

LOGISTICS HOLLINGSWORTH GROUP LLC

LOCATIONS

HQ: LOGISTICS HOLLINGSWORTH GROUP LLC
14225 W WARREN AVE, DEARBORN, MI 48126-1456
Phone: 313-768-1400
Web: www.hlgllc.com

HISTORICAL FINANCIALS

Company Type: Private

Income Statement

FYE: December 31

	REVENUE ($ mil.)	NET INCOME ($ mil.)	NET PROFIT MARGIN	EMPLOYEES
12/11	184	0	——	700
12/10	123	0	——	0
12/09	0	0	——	0
Annual Growth	——	——	——	——

2011 Year-End Financials

Debt ratio: ——
Return on equity: ——
Cash ($ mil.): 0
Current ratio: 0.70
Long-term debt ($ mil.): ——

Dividends
Yield: ——
Payout: ——
Market value ($ mil.): ——

LONESTAR FREIGHTLINER GROUP LLC

LOCATIONS

HQ: LONESTAR FREIGHTLINER GROUP LLC
2051 HUGHES RD, GRAPEVINE, TX 76051-7317
Phone: 817-428-9736
Web: www.lonestartruckgroup.com

HISTORICAL FINANCIALS
Company Type: Private

Income Statement
FYE: December 31

	REVENUE ($ mil.)	NET INCOME ($ mil.)	NET PROFIT MARGIN	EMPLOYEES
12/11	117	3	3.1%	350
Annual Growth	—	—	—	—

2011 Year-End Financials
Debt ratio: —
Return on equity: 3.10%
Cash ($ mil.): 1
Current ratio: 0.10
Long-term debt ($ mil.): —
Dividends
Yield: —
Payout: —
Market value ($ mil.): —

LONG ISLAND UNIVERSITY

Long Island University (LIU) helps students see a long future in professional fields including medicine and business. LIU has an enrollment of more than 24000 students at multiple locations in New York State. The university employs more than 600 full-time faculty members and has a 12:1 student-to-teacher ratio. LIU offers 575 degree programs and certificates in fields including pharmacy nursing health sciences education liberal arts sciences business and information studies. The school traces its roots to 1886 when the Brooklyn College of Pharmacy was founded.

Geographic Reach

LIU has eight campuses in New York located in Brooklyn Brookville Brentwood Riverhead Rockland and Westchester). Internationally LIU Global offers study abroad programs in Asia Australia the Middle East and South America.

Strategy

LIU has expanded its offerings in recent years to meet current demands. It has added degree programs in fields such as digital game design computer information systems health sciences and human resource management.

EXECUTIVES

President, David J. Steinberg
VP University Relations, Richard W. Gorman
VP Academic Affairs, Jeffrey Kane
VP Finance and Treasurer, Robert N. (Rob) Altholz
Director Purchasing, Margaret Natalie

Provost LIU Brooklyn, Gale Stevens Haynes
Chairman, Edward Travaglianti
VP Information Technology, George Baroudi
VP Legal Services and University Counsel, Lynette Phillips
Senior Vice Chair, Thomas L. Pulling
Secretary and Trustee, Steven J. Kumble
Provost LIU Post, Paul H. Forestell
VP Planning and Human Resources, Daniel J. Rodas
Associate VP Marketing and Public Relations, Paola Curcio-Kleinman
University Director Public Relations, Kim Volpe-Casalino
Associate VP Academic Affairs, Lori Knapp
Director Foundation Relations, Patricia E. (Pat) Carson
Assistant VP Academic Planning and Instructional Development, Elizabeth (Liz) Ciabocchi
University Director Assessment, Kathleen (Kathy) Morley
Academic Budget Officer, Peggy Riggs
Assistant VP Sponsored Research, Kathryn S. (Kitty) Rockett
Trustee, Roland A. DeSilva
Trustee, John A. Kanas, age 64
Trustee, George L. Engelke Jr., age 73
Trustee, Howard M. Lorber, age 63
Trustee, Martin L. Sperber, age 80
Trustee, Byron E. Lewis
Trustee, John R. Bransfield Jr.
Trustee, Les Goodstein
Trustee, Richard P. (Rich) Nespola, age 67
Trustee, William R. (Bill) Nuti, age 48
Trustee, Donald H. Elliott
Trustee, Eric J. Tveter, age 53
Trustee, Brian J. Madocks, age 56
Trustee, Stanley F. Barshay, age 72
Trustee, William L. Zeckendorf
Trustee, Salvatore (Sal) Iannuzzi, age 58
Trustee, Michael Melnicke
Trustee, Steven A. Klar
Trustee, William Lynch Jr.
Trustee, Edward E. Shorin
Trustee, Harvey Simpson
Trustee, Richard O. Ullman
Senior Vice Chair, Thomas L. Pulling
Secretary and Trustee, Steven J. Kumble
Trustee, Michael N. Emmerman
Trustee, Alfred R. Kahn
Trustee, Eric Krasnoff
Trustee, Leon Lachman
Trustee, Theresa Mall Mullarkey
Trustee, Joel Press
Trustee, Ronald J. Sylvestri
Trustee, Rosalind P. Walter
Trustee, Mark A. Boyar
Trustee, James P. Breslawski
Trustee, Michael Devine
Trustee, Angelo Mangia
Trustee, Salvatore Naro
Director, David Sterling
Trustee, Sharon Sternheim

LOCATIONS

HQ: Long Island University
700 Northern Blvd., Brookville NY 11548-1327
Phone: 516-299-2535   **Fax:** 515-221-9947
Web: www.american-equity.com

HISTORICAL FINANCIALS
Company Type: School

Income Statement
FYE: August 31

	REVENUE ($ mil.)	NET INCOME ($ mil.)	NET PROFIT MARGIN	EMPLOYEES
08/11	468	2	0.5%	3,300
08/10	370	(1)	—	0
08/09	363	(26)	—	0
08/08	364	(12)	—	0
Annual Growth	8.7%	—	—	—

2011 Year-End Financials
Debt ratio: —
Return on equity: 0.50%
Cash ($ mil.): 55
Current ratio: —
Long-term debt ($ mil.): —
Dividends
Yield: —
Payout: —
Market value ($ mil.): —

LOS ANGELES COUNTY DEVELOPMENTAL SERVICES FOUNDATION

LOCATIONS

HQ: LOS ANGELES COUNTY DEVELOPMENTAL SERVICES FOUNDATION
3303 WILSHIRE BLVD FL 700, LOS ANGELES, CA 90010-4000
Phone: 213-383-1300
Web: www.lanterman.org

HISTORICAL FINANCIALS
Company Type: Private

Income Statement
FYE: June 30

	REVENUE ($ mil.)	NET INCOME ($ mil.)	NET PROFIT MARGIN	EMPLOYEES
06/11	119	0	0.1%	180
06/10	124	0	0.0%	0
06/09	135	(0)	—	0
06/08	127	0	0.1%	0
Annual Growth	(2.0%)	(2.9%)	—	—

2011 Year-End Financials
Debt ratio: —
Return on equity: 0.10%
Cash ($ mil.): 13
Current ratio: 0.90
Long-term debt ($ mil.): —
Dividends
Yield: —
Payout: —
Market value ($ mil.): —

LOS ANGELES COUNTY OFFICE OF EDUCATION

LOCATIONS

HQ: LOS ANGELES COUNTY OFFICE OF EDUCATION
9300 IMPERIAL HWY, DOWNEY, CA 90242-2813
Phone: 562-922-6111
Web: www.lacoe.edu

HISTORICAL FINANCIALS

Company Type: Private

Income Statement

FYE: June 30

	REVENUE ($ mil.)	NET INCOME ($ mil.)	NET PROFIT MARGIN	EMPLOYEES
06/12	863	(25)	—	4,000
06/08	6	0	1.4%	0
Annual Growth	12259.9%	—	—	—

LOS ANGELES DEPARTMENT OF WATER AND POWER

The Los Angeles Department of Water and Power (LADWP) keeps the movie cameras running and the swimming pools full. The largest municipally owned utility in the US LADWP provides electricity to more than 1.4 million residential and business customers and water to 640000 customers. The company has power plant interests that give it more than 7220 MW of generating capacity; it also buys and sells wholesale power. Most of the city's water supply is transported through two aqueduct systems from the Sierra Nevada Mountains; other water sources include wells and local groundwater basins. Because LADWP is city-owned its retail monopoly status was unaffected by utility deregulation in California.

Residential customers form the largest client group of the utility's water service unit; commercial customers the largest customer class of the power segment. To enhance operating efficiencies and conserve energy the department has launched a 10-year $1 billion Smart Grid program to automate and upgrade the City's grid.

It is also pushing to increase the amount of energy it generates from renewable sources (mainly wind and solar power) to meet state and federal clean air goals. LADWP got only 5% of it power from renewables in 2005 but by 2010 had upped that amount to 20%. In 2010 only 39% of its power generation came from coal. LADWP plans to sell its Navajo Generating Station in Arizona (by 2014) which will cut carbon emissions by a further 26%

LADWP's operations are entirely financed by the sale of water and electric services. The multiutility transfers about 7% of its annual electric revenues and 5% of its water revenues to the City of Los Angeles general fund.

As the Western states battle a prolonged drought the utility is negotiating with water agencies across the region to ensure a reliable future supply for its citizens.

EXECUTIVES

Interim General Manager, S. David Freeman, age 86
Generation, Eric Tharp
CFO, Ronald O. Vazquez
Director Economic Development, Bernadette S. Kirkwood
Chief Administrative Officer, Cecilia K. T. Weldon
Assistant General Manager, Pamela T. Porter
Manager Water Conservation, Tom Gackstetter
Manager Media and Community Relations, Darlene Battle
Resource Planning Procurement and Development, Randy S. Howard
Manager Environmental Communications and Educational Services Affairs, Walter Zeisl
City Attorney Water and Power, Richard Brown
Assistant General Manager Employee Relations, Hal D. Lindsey
Manager Risk Management, Avery Neaman
Senior Assistant General Manager Water System, James (Jim) McDaniel
COO, Raman Raj
Director Public Affairs, Joseph M. (Joe) Ramallo
Environmental Affairs, James H. Caldwell Jr.
Senior Assistant General Manager Power System, Aram Benyamin
CIO, Mathew M. Lampe
Engineering Services, Marvin Moon
Power Operation and Maintenance, Michael A. Coia
Power Transmission and Distribution, Darrell G. Mathis
Power System Planning and Development, Mo Beshir
Power Control and Business Systems, Ali Morabbi
Water Resources, Thomas M. Erb
Water Distribution, Steven Malinoski
Water Engineering and Technical Services, Glen C. Singley
Director Water Quality and Operations, Martin L. Adams
President Board of Commissioners, Lee K. Alpert
CFO, Jeffery L. Peltola
Chief Investment Officer, Jeremy Wolfson
Executive Director Customer Service, John X. Chen
Commissioner, Thomas S. (Tom) Sayles, age 61
VP Board of Water and Power Commissioners, Edith Ramirez
Commissioner, Forescee Hogan-Rowles
President Board of Commissioners, Lee K. Alpert
Auditors: KPMGLLP

LOCATIONS

HQ: Los Angeles Department of Water and Power
111 N. Hope St., Los Angeles CA 90012
Phone: 213-367-4211 **Fax:** 213-367-1455
Web: www.ladwp.com

PRODUCTS/OPERATIONS

2010 Sales

	$ mil.	% of total
% of total		
Electric		80
Water		20
Total		**100**

COMPETITORS

AES	Edison International

American States Water
Avista
California Water Service
Calpine
Duke Energy
PG&E Corporation
Sacramento Municipal Utility
Sempra Energy
SouthWest Water

HISTORICAL FINANCIALS

Company Type: Government-owned

Income Statement

FYE: June 30

	REVENUE ($ mil.)	NET INCOME ($ mil.)	NET PROFIT MARGIN	EMPLOYEES
06/11	3,125	57	1.8%	8,000
06/10	812	67	8.3%	0
Annual Growth	284.8%	(14.4%)	—	—

2011 Year-End Financials

Debt ratio: —	
Return on equity: 1.80%	Dividends
Cash ($ mil.): 630	Yield: —
Current ratio: 0.80	Payout: —
Long-term debt ($ mil.): —	Market value ($ mil.): —

LOUDOUN COUNTY PUBLIC SCHOOL DISTRICT

LOCATIONS

HQ: LOUDOUN COUNTY PUBLIC SCHOOL DISTRICT
21000 EDUCATION CT, BROADLANDS, VA 20148-5526
Phone: 571-252-1000

HISTORICAL FINANCIALS

Company Type: Private

Income Statement

FYE: June 30

	REVENUE ($ mil.)	NET INCOME ($ mil.)	NET PROFIT MARGIN	EMPLOYEES
06/11	783	(26)	—	8,000
06/05	0	0	25.6%	0
Annual Growth	244810.9%	—	—	—

2011 Year-End Financials

Debt ratio: —	
Return on equity: (-3.40)%	Dividends
Cash ($ mil.): 226	Yield: —
Current ratio: —	Payout: —
Long-term debt ($ mil.): —	Market value ($ mil.): —

LOUISIANA WHOLESALE DRUG COMPANY INC.

LOCATIONS

HQ: LOUISIANA WHOLESALE DRUG COMPANY INC.
2085 I 49 S SERVICE RD, SUNSET, LA 70584
Phone: 337-662-1040

HISTORICAL FINANCIALS

Company Type: Private

Income Statement				FYE: July 27
	REVENUE ($ mil.)	NET INCOME ($ mil.)	NET PROFIT MARGIN	EMPLOYEES
07/12	386	4	1.1%	52
07/11	373	4	1.2%	0
07/10	372	4	1.2%	0
07/09	344	4	1.3%	0
Annual Growth	3.9%	(1.4%)	—	—

2012 Year-End Financials

Debt ratio: ——
Return on equity: 1.10%
Cash ($ mil.): 14
Current ratio: 0.60
Long-term debt ($ mil.): —

Dividends
Yield: —
Payout: —
Market value ($ mil.): —

LOWELL GENERAL HOSPITAL

LOCATIONS

HQ: LOWELL GENERAL HOSPITAL
295 VARNUM AVE, LOWELL, MA 01854-2193
Phone: 978-937-6000
Web: www.lowellgeneral.org

HISTORICAL FINANCIALS

Company Type: Private

Income Statement				FYE: September 30
	REVENUE ($ mil.)	NET INCOME ($ mil.)	NET PROFIT MARGIN	EMPLOYEES
09/11	254	9	3.7%	1,400
09/10	235	14	6.0%	0
09/09*	217	(10)	—	0
11/08	35	(9)	—	0
Annual Growth	93.6%	—	—	—

*Fiscal year change

2011 Year-End Financials

Debt ratio: ——
Return on equity: 3.70%
Cash ($ mil.): 17
Current ratio: 0.80
Long-term debt ($ mil.): —

Dividends
Yield: —
Payout: —
Market value ($ mil.): —

LOYOLA UNIVERSITY MARYLAND INC.

Loyola University in Maryland is a Jesuit Catholic university that offers studies in liberal arts and sciences. In addition to its undergraduate programs Loyola has graduate degree programs in education speech pathology finance psychology modern studies pastoral counseling and engineering science. The university annually enrolls about 3500 undergraduate and some 2600 graduate students. The school has more than 300 full-time faculty and a student-teacher ratio of about 12:1. Loyola was founded in 1852 by Father John Early and eight other Jesuits.

EXECUTIVES

Dean College of Arts and Sciences, James Buckley
VP Finance and Treasurer, Randall D. Gentzler
President, Rev Brian Linnane, age 57
VP Administration, Terrence Sawyer
EVP, Susan Donovan
Director Library, John McGinty
Assistant VP Administration, Joan Flynn
Assistant VP Human Resources, George (Skip) Casey
Director Admissions-Undergraduate, Elena Hicks
Interim Director Admissions-Graduate, Maureen Faux
VP Advancement, Megan Gillick
Dirtector Alumni Relations, Brian M. Oakes
Assistant VP and CIO, Louise Finn
Assistant VP Facilitites and Campus Services, Helen Schneider
Director The Career Center, CreSaundra Sills
Controller, Kelly Nelson
Dean Sellinger School of Business and Management, Karyl B. Leggio
Director Facilities Operations, Charles Riordan
Director and Assistant VP Financial Aid, Mark Lindenmeyer
Digital Access Librarian, Danielle Whren
Assistant VP Marketing and Communications, Sharon Higgins
VP Academic Affairs, Timothy Law Snyder
VP Enrollment Management and Communications, Marc M. Camille

LOCATIONS

HQ: Loyola University Maryland Inc.
4501 N. Charles St, Baltimore MD 21210-2699
Phone: 410-617-2000   **Fax:** 210-226-8395
Web: www.coxsmith.com

HISTORICAL FINANCIALS

Company Type: School

Income Statement				FYE: May 31
	REVENUE ($ mil.)	NET INCOME ($ mil.)	NET PROFIT MARGIN	EMPLOYEES
05/12	185	(2)	—	2,066
05/11	238	11	5.0%	0
05/10	221	9	4.1%	0
05/09	196	0	—	0
Annual Growth	(2.0%)	—	—	—

2012 Year-End Financials

Debt ratio: ——
Return on equity: (-1.20)%
Cash ($ mil.): 34
Current ratio: —
Long-term debt ($ mil.): —

Dividends
Yield: —
Payout: —
Market value ($ mil.): —

LOYOLA UNIVERSITY MEDICAL CENTER

LOCATIONS

HQ: LOYOLA UNIVERSITY MEDICAL CENTER
2160 S 1ST AVE, MAYWOOD, IL 60153-3328
Phone: 708-216-9000

HISTORICAL FINANCIALS

Company Type: Private

Income Statement				FYE: June 30
	REVENUE ($ mil.)	NET INCOME ($ mil.)	NET PROFIT MARGIN	EMPLOYEES
06/11	938	14	1.6%	4
06/10	917	8	0.9%	0
Annual Growth	2.3%	75.7%	—	—

2011 Year-End Financials

Debt ratio: ——
Return on equity: 1.60%
Cash ($ mil.): 65
Current ratio: 0.30
Long-term debt ($ mil.): —

Dividends
Yield: —
Payout: —
Market value ($ mil.): —

LUCILE SALTER PACKARD CHILDREN'S HOSPITAL AT STANFORD

LOCATIONS

HQ: LUCILE SALTER PACKARD CHILDREN' S HOSPITAL AT STANFORD
725 WELCH RD, PALO ALTO, CA 94304-1601
Phone: 650-497-8000
Web: www.lpch.org

HISTORICAL FINANCIALS

Company Type: Private

Income Statement				FYE: August 31
	REVENUE ($ mil.)	NET INCOME ($ mil.)	NET PROFIT MARGIN	EMPLOYEES
08/11	942	110	11.8%	1,100
08/10	794	48	6.1%	0
08/09	772	76	9.9%	0
08/08	757	119	15.7%	0
Annual Growth	7.5%	(2.4%)	—	—

2011 Year-End Financials

Debt ratio: —
Return on equity: 11.80%
Cash ($ mil.): 90
Current ratio: 2.20
Long-term debt ($ mil.): —

Dividends
  Yield: —
  Payout: —
  Market value ($ mil.): —

2011 Year-End Financials

Debt ratio: —
Return on equity: 2.40%
Cash ($ mil.): 6
Current ratio: 0.50
Long-term debt ($ mil.): —

Dividends
  Yield: —
  Payout: —
  Market value ($ mil.): —

LUTHERAN CHURCH-MISSOURI SYNOD

LOCATIONS

HQ: LUTHERAN CHURCH-MISSOURI SYNOD
1333 S KIRKWOOD RD, SAINT LOUIS, MO
63122-7295
Phone: 314-965-9000
Web: www.allabouthope.org

HISTORICAL FINANCIALS

Company Type: Private

Income Statement

FYE: June 30

	REVENUE ($ mil.)	NET INCOME ($ mil.)	NET PROFIT MARGIN	EMPLOYEES
06/11	137	14	10.3%	525
06/06	98	0	—	0
06/05	1	0	29.5%	0
06/04	640	0	—	0
Annual Growth	—	4303.3%	—	—

2011 Year-End Financials

Debt ratio: —
Return on equity: 10.30%
Cash ($ mil.): 39
Current ratio: 1.70
Long-term debt ($ mil.): —

Dividends
  Yield: —
  Payout: —
  Market value ($ mil.): —

LUTHERAN SOCIAL SERVICES OF MICHIGAN

LOCATIONS

HQ: LUTHERAN SOCIAL SERVICES OF MICHIGAN
8131 E JEFFERSON AVE, DETROIT, MI 48214-2691
Phone: 313-823-7700
Web: www.lssm.org

HISTORICAL FINANCIALS

Company Type: Private

Income Statement

FYE: December 31

	REVENUE ($ mil.)	NET INCOME ($ mil.)	NET PROFIT MARGIN	EMPLOYEES
12/11	86	2	2.4%	1,250
12/10	88	2	2.3%	0
12/09	83	1	1.8%	0
12/08	78	(0)	—	0
Annual Growth	3.1%	—	—	—

LVI SERVICES INC.

Asbestos lead-based paint nuclear materials and toxic mold don't scare LVI Services one of the top environmental contractors in the US with more than 30 offices across the country. The privately-held company provides integrated facility services such as remediation of hazardous materials decontamination and demolition. It caters to clients in a wide range of business segments from hotels and retail to commercial industrial and institutional. It also serves government and education segments. Customers have included AT&T IBM Marriott Prudential and Raytheon.

Geographic Reach

Headquartered in New York City the company works in all 50 US states. It has more than 30 offices nationwide.

Strategy

In 2012 the company acquired Washington State-based Randolph Construction Services which provides design-build contracting services for commercial industrial and government clients. It recently provided services to aid in detecting and interdicting nuclear and radioactive threats for three federal agencies: the US Department of Homeland Security the US Department of Energy and the US Customs and Border Protection Agency.

In 2012 LVI Services completed the decommissioning of the University of Arizona's 52-year-old Nuclear Reactor Laboratory.

Major stockholder CHS Capital moved in 2010 to merge LVI Services with another of its companies Penhall International which specializes in highway excavations. However Penhall ran into debt problems which squelched the deal and sent LVI Services to the bond market to restructure its debt.

Ownership

CHS Capital is the majority equity investor in LVI Services. Apollo Investments also owns a stake in the company.

Company Background

LVI Services was founded in 1986.

EXECUTIVES

President and CEO, Scott E. State, age 49
Branch Manager LVI Environmental Services Fort Lauderdale, George White
General Manager LVI Environmental Services Indianapolis, William Foss
Chairman, Burton T. Fried
VP and Co-COO, John Leonard
Co-COO, David P. Pearson
SVP National Accounts, Mark Canessa
President LVI Environmental Services Chicago, Dave Fracassi
Regional Manager New York / New Jersey, Frank Aiello
Branch Manager LVI Environmental Services Pittsburgh, Darrin Dewitt
President LVI Environmental Services San Leandro, John McKnight

President LVI Environmental Services Las Vegas, Joe Catania
Branch Manager LVI Environmental Services Rochester, Sean Miller
Branch Manager LVI Facility Services San Antonio, Mark Buescher
Branch Manager LVI Environmental Services Massena, James (Hank) Berry
Director Health and Safety, Gary Thibodeaux
President LVI Environmental Services Hawaii, Lisa Cooper
VP LVI Environmental Services San Diego, Ryan Crowe
Branch Manager LVI Environmental Services Cincinnati, Albert C. Meininger
Treasurer, Joseph M. Annarumma
VP Payroll and System Administration, Kamal Sookram
Branch Manager Boston, Peter Scopa
President TEG / LVI Environmental Services Los Angeles, Mike Johnston
President LVI Environmental Services Maryland, David M. Rymers
President LVI Environmental Services Denver, Daniel Dunlap
VP NorthStar Recovery Services, Tami Casey
Director LVI Restoration, Alfred C. Draper III
Branch Manager LVI Environmental Services Downingtown, Gary Bowman
Director National Sales, Matthew Dembin
Claims Administrator, Kendra Matte
VP LVI Facility Services Dallas, Joe Hinkson
President NorthStar Recovery Services, Lloyd E. Swiggum
VP and CFO, Paul S. Cutrone
Regional Manager Washington D.C., James L. Mooney
Regional Manager West, Chad Maddock
President LVI Environmental Services Oakland, John E. Weber
VP Industrial Demolition Division, Richard McManus
VP Nuclear Decontamination and Decommissioning and Regional Manager, Thomas W. Gilmore
VP LVI Environmental Services Tampa, John Skinner
LVI Environmental Services Fort Lauderdale, Gregory Marcello
VP LVI Environmental Services Indianapolis, Robert Seamon
President LVI Environmental Services Connecticut, Matt Fay
President LVI Facility Services Houston, James McNeely
Branch Manager LVI Environmental Services Azusa, Ken Plachy
President LVI Environmental Services Virginia, Van Lewis
VP LVI Environmental Services Wisconsin, Gregory Marenda
President LVI Environmental Services New Jersey, Peter Demeropoulos
President LVI Environmental Services New Orleans, Rick Crider
VP Sales Western Region, Thomas Sandoval
VP and Co-COO, J. David Eads
Regional Manager Southeastern Region, John E. Kling
General Manager Connecticut, Richard Meahan
President LIV Facility Services Dallas, Jerry Fields
President LVI Environmental Services Denver, William Deadman
Branch Manager LVI Environmental Services Hawaii, Michael Moore
Branch Manager LVI Facility Services Houston, Michael Luczak

Branch Manager ICONCO/LVI Demolition
  Services, Jeff Droubay
President LVI/Mazzocchi Wrecking Inc., Grace
  Mazzocchi
General Manager LVI Environmental Services
  Albany NY, Art Cody
Branch Manager ICONCO/LVI Demolition
  Services Seattle, Reef Anderson
Branch Manager LVI Environmental Services
  Tampa, Frank Donovan
VP Preconstruction Services, Michael Marcheschi

LOCATIONS

HQ: LVI Services Inc.
  80 Broad St. 3rd Fl., New York NY 10004
Phone: 212-951-3664   Fax: 212-481-9895
Web: www.lviservices.com

PRODUCTS/OPERATIONS

Selected Services

Asbestos abatement
Demolition
Emergency/disaster response
Drying and dehumidification
Biological and chemical decontamination
Mold remediation
Infection control
Lead abatement
Decontamination and decommissioning
Fireproofing
Power and Petroleum

Selected Industries

Commercial
Government
Industrial
Retail
Health care
Education
Hospitality

COMPETITORS

Bechtel	ERM
CH2M HILL	Fluor
Controlled Demolition	Native Environmental
Corvera Abatement	Parsons Corporation
Dallas Contracting	URS
ENSR International	

HISTORICAL FINANCIALS

Company Type: Private

Income Statement

	REVENUE ($ mil.)	NET INCOME ($ mil.)	NET PROFIT MARGIN	EMPLOYEES
				FYE: March 31
03/12*	65	5	7.8%	3,500
12/11	339	(6)	—	0
12/10	250	65	26.1%	0
12/09	265	0	—	0
Annual Growth	(37.3%)	—	—	—

*Fiscal year change

2012 Year-End Financials

Debt ratio: ——
Return on equity: 7.80%   Dividends
Cash ($ mil.): 3   Yield: —
Current ratio: 1.00   Payout: —
Long-term debt ($ mil.): —   Market value ($ mil.): —

LYNCHBURG COLLEGE

In Lynchburg Tennessee they make whiskey. In Lynchburg Virginia they make graduates. Lynchburg College is an independent residential college with about 160 full-time faculty members and 2600 undergraduate and graduate students in some 40 majors. It consists of six schools: Business and Economics Communication and Fine Arts Education and Human Development Health Sciences and Human Performance Humanities and Social Sciences and Sciences. Tuition is about $14000 per semester; however virtually all students receive financial aid. The college was founded in 1903 by Dr. Josephus Hopwood a Christian Church (Disciples of Christ) minister and his wife Sarah.

EXECUTIVES

President, Kenneth R. Garren
Dean, Vernon Miles Jr.
VP Community Advancement, Ed Polloway
Director Technology Support Services, Wendall
  Russell
Director Personnel Services, Shirley Bates

LOCATIONS

HQ: Lynchburg College
  1501 Lakeside Dr., Lynchburg VA 24501-3199
Phone: 434-544-8100   Fax: 434-544-8220
Web: www.lynchburg.edu

HISTORICAL FINANCIALS

Company Type: School

Income Statement

	REVENUE ($ mil.)	NET INCOME ($ mil.)	NET PROFIT MARGIN	EMPLOYEES
				FYE: June 30
06/12	61	(2)	—	1,077
06/11	87	4	5.1%	0
06/10	76	(3)	—	0
06/09	71	0	—	0
Annual Growth	(4.9%)	—	—	—

2012 Year-End Financials

Debt ratio: ——
Return on equity: (-4.10)%   Dividends
Cash ($ mil.): 3   Yield: —
Current ratio: —   Payout: —
Long-term debt ($ mil.): —   Market value ($ mil.): —

LYNTEGAR ELECTRIC COOPERATIVE INC.

Lyntegar Electric Cooperative is based in the agricultural heart of the Texas Panhandle where the summer heat sizzles and the winter ice storms freeze. The rural power cooperative provides electric utility services to customers in Borden Dawson Gaines Garza Hockley Lynn Martin Terry and Yoakum counties. The cooperative also sells electric grills and provides internet and television services. In addition Lyntegar Electric Cooperative produces Typically Texas Cookbooks which share collections of recipes used by cooperative member-consumers.

Lyntegar Electric Cooperative was organized in 1938 in response to the Roosevelt administration's national drive to bring affordable electric power to rural areas.

EXECUTIVES

General Manager, Wilton J. Payne
Comptroller, Raydon (Ray) Box
Benefits Administration, Jana Bishop
Billing, Sherry Tilley
Purchasing, Richard Lopez
Engineering, Shane McMin
Safety Coordinator, Mark Wuensche
Data Processing, Roy Hinkle
Data Processing, Jerry Reno
Director, Earl J. Brown
Director, Ben Franklin
Director, Billy Weaver
Director, Ricky Day
Director, Troy Howard
Director, Gonzell Hogg
Director, Leonard Nettles

LOCATIONS

HQ: Lyntegar Electric Cooperative Inc.
  1807 Main St., Tahoka TX 79373
Phone: 806-561-4588   Fax: 806-561-4724
Web: www.lyntegar.coop

HISTORICAL FINANCIALS

Company Type: Private - Cooperative

Income Statement

	REVENUE ($ mil.)	NET INCOME ($ mil.)	NET PROFIT MARGIN	EMPLOYEES
				FYE: December 31
12/11	72	10	13.8%	103
12/10	58	6	11.2%	0
12/09	54	2	3.8%	0
12/08	70	5	8.4%	0
Annual Growth	0.9%	19.0%	—	—

2011 Year-End Financials

Debt ratio: ——
Return on equity: 13.80%   Dividends
Cash ($ mil.): 1   Yield: —
Current ratio: 0.20   Payout: —
Long-term debt ($ mil.): —   Market value ($ mil.): —

LYONS SPECIALTY CO. L.L.C.

LOCATIONS

HQ: LYONS SPECIALTY CO. L.L.C.
  2800 LA HIGHWAY 1 N, PORT ALLEN, LA 70767-3417
Phone: 225-356-1319
Web: www.lyons-aav.com

Income Statement

FYE: September 30

	REVENUE ($ mil.)	NET INCOME ($ mil.)	NET PROFIT MARGIN	EMPLOYEES
09/11	108	0	0.5%	80
09/08	85	0	0.3%	0
09/06	91	6	7.6%	0
09/05	1,867	0	0.0%	0
Annual Growth	(61.3%)	1520.4%	—	—

2011 Year-End Financials

Debt ratio: ——
Return on equity: 0.50%
Cash ($ mil.): 0
Current ratio: 0.70
Long-term debt ($ mil.): ——

Dividends
Yield: —
Payout: —
Market value ($ mil.): —

HISTORICAL FINANCIALS
Company Type: Private

Income Statement

FYE: November 30

	REVENUE ($ mil.)	NET INCOME ($ mil.)	NET PROFIT MARGIN	EMPLOYEES
11/11*	119	1	1.2%	140
12/10	168	1	0.9%	0
12/09	165	1	1.1%	0
12/08	353	6	1.8%	0
Annual Growth	(30.4%)	(38.5%)	—	—

*Fiscal year change

2011 Year-End Financials

Debt ratio: ——
Return on equity: 1.20%
Cash ($ mil.): 6
Current ratio: 0.70
Long-term debt ($ mil.): ——

Dividends
Yield: —
Payout: —
Market value ($ mil.): —

M & H ENTERPRISES INC.

What M & H Enterprises builds in Vegas stays in Vegas. Also known as Martin-Harris Construction the company provides design/build general construction and construction management services to commercial institutional and industrial projects throughout the Southwest. In addition to its home state Martin-Harris also provides general contracting services in New Mexico Texas Colorado and Utah. Martin-Harris has completed office retail hospitality entertainment high-rise condominium and public works projects for clients such as Neiman Marcus Embassy Suites and US Air Force. The company was founded in 1976 by president and CEO Frank Martin. It has offices in Las Vegas and Phoenix.

EXECUTIVES

President and CEO, Frank Martin
VP Pre-Construction Services, Ray C. Newmiller
CFO, Steve Lords
Manager Human Resources, Lauri Ross-de Vera
SVP Operations, Kevin Zahm
VP Estimating, Frank (Guy) Martin
Public Relations Contact, Ellie Shattuck
Safety Contact, Tyson Hollis
Las Vegas Contact, Paul Toplak
Phoenix Contact, Mike Orr
Austin Contact, Ernie Beltz

LOCATIONS

HQ: M & H Enterprises Inc.
3030 S. Highland Dr., Las Vegas NV 89109-1047
Phone: 702-385-5257   **Fax:** 702-474-8257
Web: www.martinharris.com

COMPETITORS

Balfour Construction
Bovis Lend Lease
Turner Corporation

M. A. MORTENSON COMPANY

M. A. Mortenson Company leaves its footprints all over the country. The general contractor performs construction development and design-build services for a variety of projects. Sectors served include aviation corporate education electronics and semiconductors entertainment health care hospitality manufacturing and retail; the firm also has groups devoted to federal contracting sports venues facilities operations and renewable energy including wind farms and biofuel facilities. Active throughout the US the company also has operations in China helping its domestic clients to expand into markets there. The company was founded in 1954 by the late M.A. Mortenson Sr. His son is now its chairman.

Geographic Reach

Headquartered in Minneapolis Mortenson has 10 offices across the US Canada and China.

Operations

Health care and power projects account for a majority of the company's activity. Other notable projects have included the FedExForum home of the Memphis Grizzlies; the Frank Gehry-designed Walt Disney Concert Hall home of the Los Angeles Philharmonic; and the Minnesota Twins' Target Field which opened in 2010.

Financial Performance

Mortenson's revenue approached $2.5 billion in 2011 an essentially flat comparison with 2010. The firm's revenue topped $2.8 billion in 2008 but has yet to recover.

Strategy

Mortenson is growing along with its multinational clients. In 2012 it partnered with industrial conglomerate Honeywell to perform construction management of two Honeywell facilities in China.

EXECUTIVES

Chairman, M. A. Mortenson Jr.
President and CEO, Thomas F. (Tom) Gunkel
VP Estimating, Gregory M. Clark
SVP, Robert J. (Bob) Nartonis
VP Risk Management, Jacqueline P. Sirany
SVP Administration, Paul V. Campbell

SVP Operations, Bradley C. (Brad) Funk
COO, Daniel L. (Dan) Johnson
EVP, David C. Mortenson
SVP, John V. Wood
SVP, Paul I. Cossette
Senior Communications Specialist, Kim Kaisler
Corporate Secretary, Mark A. Mortenson
VP and General Manager, Mark A. Sherry
VP and General Manager, Gregory (Greg) Werner
SVP, Thomas W. (Tom) Wacker
VP and General Manager, Craig W. Southorn
Manager Communications, Cameron Snyder
VP and General Manager, Kenneth L. (Ken) Sorensen
VP Strategic Marketing, James P. Lesinski
VP Controller and Chief Accounting Officer, William Patt
VP Business Development, Patrick A. Burns
SVP and CFO, Sandra G. (Sandy) Sponem
VP and General Manager, Timothy L. Maag
VP and General Manager, James J. Yowan
VP and CIO, Cole Orndorff
VP Operations, Robert A. (Bob) Leonard
VP and General Manager, Mark W. Ruffino
VP and Treasurer, Jennifer Facciani
VP Operations, John T. Martin
VP and General Manager, Derek J. Cunz
VP and General Manager, Mark E. Donahue
VP and General Manager, Kendall Griffith
VP Project Development, Maja E. Rosenquist
VP Preconstruction, Mark G. Schmidt
VP Operations, John J. Nowoj
VP Operations, Stephen L. DeGroote
Auditors: Deloitte&ToucheLLP

LOCATIONS

HQ: M. A. Mortenson Company
700 Meadow Ln. North, Minneapolis MN 55422-4899
Phone: 763-522-2100   **Fax:** 763-287-5430
Web: www.mortenson.com

Selected Regional Offices
Chicago
Colorado Springs Colorado
Denver
Madison Wisconsin
Milwaukee
Minneapolis
Phoenix
Portland
Seattle
Shanghai China
Toronto Canada

PRODUCTS/OPERATIONS

Selected Services
Construction
  Cost control
  Insurance administration
  Owner move-in planning and management
  Scheduling
Design/build delivery
Development
  Feasibility analysis
  Property and facility management
  Site acquisition
Diverse workforce planning
Facility operations
Preconstruction
  Building information modeling
  Constructability analysis
  Design management
  Schedule development
  SWMBE participation
Program management
Virtual design and construction

COMPETITORS

Barton Malow
McCarthy Building

Bechtel
Bovis Lend Lease
C. G. Schmidt
Fluor
Gilbane
Hensel Phelps
  Construction
Hunt Construction
KBR

Miron Construction
Parsons Corporation
Pepper Construction
The Haskell Company
Turner Corporation
Tutor Perini
Walsh Group
Whiting-Turner

HISTORICAL FINANCIALS
Company Type: Private

Income Statement

FYE: December 31

	REVENUE ($ mil.)	NET INCOME ($ mil.)	NET PROFIT MARGIN	EMPLOYEES
12/11	2,257	0	—	1,730
12/06	0	0	—	0
12/04	0	0	—	0
12/03	1,121	13	1.2%	0
Annual Growth	26.3%	—	—	—

2011 Year-End Financials

Debt ratio: ——
Return on equity: —
Cash ($ mil.): 123
Current ratio: 0.70
Long-term debt ($ mil.): —

Dividends
  Yield: —
  Payout: —
  Market value ($ mil.): —

M. B. KAHN CONSTRUCTION CO. INC.

One of the largest construction companies in the southeastern US M. B. Kahn Construction Co. works on commercial institutional and industrial projects including hospitals airports shopping centers and manufacturing plants. Additionally it is rated as one of the top builders in the nation's education market. The company provides general contracting and design/build delivery services as well as construction management and program management services. Russian immigrant Myron B. Kahn founded the company in 1927. It is now chaired by Alan Kahn his grandson. The group operates through divisions in South Carolina and Georgia.

The purchase of South Carolina-based general contractor Chancel Construction increased the company's customer base in the Carolina's. Since then M.B. Kahn has been busy building and designing business parks arts centers and jails in the region.

EXECUTIVES

Chairman, Allan B. Kahn
President and CEO, William H. Neely
Director Human Resources, John Gorsage
SEVP, Rick Ott
SVP, Harry A. (Buzz) Pleming
VP Finance, Robert A. Chisholm

LOCATIONS

HQ: M. B. Kahn Construction Co. Inc.
  101 Flintlake Dr., Columbia SC 29202
Phone: 803-736-2950   **Fax:** 803-736-5833
Web: www.mbkahn.com

PRODUCTS/OPERATIONS

Selected Projects and Customers

Commercial
  Blue Cross/Blue Shield South Carolina
  South Carolina Bank & Trust
  Hilton Hotel
  South Carolina Bank and Trust headquarters
Education
  Barbara Bush Center at Columbia College
  Camden High School
  New Marietta High School
  West Ashley High School
Health Care
  Hollings Cancer Institute
  Roper Hospital
  Steadman Hawkins Clinic of the Carolinas
Industrial
  Bose Corporation
  Caterpillar
  Fruit of the Loom
  John Deere
  Komatsu America
Public Sector
  Greenville County Detention Center
  Horry County Courthouse
  Lexington County Judicial Center
  Pamlico County Detention Center
Religous
  Riverland Hills Baptist Church
  Pelham Road Baptist Church
  Saxe Gotha Presbyterian Church Facility
Water Works
  Columbia Wastewater Treatment Plant
  Hartwell Water Treatment Plant

COMPETITORS

Brasfield & Gorrie
Choate Construction
Gilbane Building
  Company
Hardin Construction
Parsons Infrastructure
  & Technology

Rodgers Builders
Shelco
Skanska USA Building
Tetra Tech Tesoro
Turner Corporation

HISTORICAL FINANCIALS
Company Type: Private

Income Statement

FYE: December 31

	REVENUE ($ mil.)	NET INCOME ($ mil.)	NET PROFIT MARGIN	EMPLOYEES
12/11	248	3	1.6%	570
12/10	184	8	4.7%	0
Annual Growth	34.4%	(55.1%)	—	—

2011 Year-End Financials

Debt ratio: ——
Return on equity: 1.60%
Cash ($ mil.): 19
Current ratio: 1.10
Long-term debt ($ mil.): —

Dividends
  Yield: —
  Payout: —
  Market value ($ mil.): —

M. M. FOWLER INC.

LOCATIONS

HQ: M. M. FOWLER INC.
  4220 NEAL RD, DURHAM, NC 27705-2322
Phone: 919-309-2925

HISTORICAL FINANCIALS
Company Type: Private

Income Statement

FYE: December 31

	REVENUE ($ mil.)	NET INCOME ($ mil.)	NET PROFIT MARGIN	EMPLOYEES
12/11	542	14	2.7%	28
12/10	407	9	2.4%	0
12/09	332	6	2.1%	0
12/08	404	15	3.9%	0
Annual Growth	10.3%	(2.0%)	—	—

2011 Year-End Financials

Debt ratio: ——
Return on equity: 2.70%
Cash ($ mil.): 24
Current ratio: 1.40
Long-term debt ($ mil.): —

Dividends
  Yield: —
  Payout: —
  Market value ($ mil.): —

M. O. DION & SONS INC.

LOCATIONS

HQ: M. O. DION & SONS INC.
  1543 W 16TH ST, LONG BEACH, CA 90813-1210
Phone: 562-432-3946
Web: www.fandl.com

HISTORICAL FINANCIALS
Company Type: Private

Income Statement

FYE: September 30

	REVENUE ($ mil.)	NET INCOME ($ mil.)	NET PROFIT MARGIN	EMPLOYEES
09/11	106	0	0.6%	90
09/10	71	0	0.5%	0
09/09	56	0	0.4%	0
09/08	69	0	0.6%	0
Annual Growth	15.4%	16.3%	—	—

2011 Year-End Financials

Debt ratio: ——
Return on equity: 0.60%
Cash ($ mil.): 0
Current ratio: 0.80
Long-term debt ($ mil.): —

Dividends
  Yield: —
  Payout: —
  Market value ($ mil.): —

M.G. OIL COMPANY

LOCATIONS

HQ: M.G. OIL COMPANY
1002 W MAIN ST, RAPID CITY, SD 57701-2651
Phone: 605-342-0527

HISTORICAL FINANCIALS

Company Type: Private

Income Statement
FYE: December 31

	REVENUE ($ mil.)	NET INCOME ($ mil.)	NET PROFIT MARGIN	EMPLOYEES
12/11	328	0	0.2%	450
12/10	253	2	1.2%	0
12/09	231	2	1.1%	0
12/08	279	3	1.3%	0
Annual Growth	5.5%	(46.8%)	—	—

2011 Year-End Financials

Debt ratio: ——
Return on equity: 0.20%
Cash ($ mil.): 1
Current ratio: 0.50
Long-term debt ($ mil.): —

Dividends
Yield: —
Payout: —
Market value ($ mil.): —

M3 ENGINEERING & TECHNOLOGY CORPORATION

LOCATIONS

HQ: M3 ENGINEERING & TECHNOLOGY CORPORATION
2051 W SUNSET RD STE 101, TUCSON, AZ 85704-1722
Phone: 520-293-1488
Web: www.m3eng.com

HISTORICAL FINANCIALS

Company Type: Private

Income Statement
FYE: December 31

	REVENUE ($ mil.)	NET INCOME ($ mil.)	NET PROFIT MARGIN	EMPLOYEES
12/11	82	9	11.9%	470
12/10	63	6	9.9%	0
12/09	62	8	13.8%	0
12/08	71	11	16.0%	0
Annual Growth	4.9%	(4.8%)	—	—

2011 Year-End Financials

Debt ratio: ——
Return on equity: 11.90%
Cash ($ mil.): 10
Current ratio: 2.30
Long-term debt ($ mil.): —

Dividends
Yield: —
Payout: —
Market value ($ mil.): —

MACALESTER COLLEGE

Macalester College is a private liberal arts school that serves more than 1900 students. The college is supported by an endowment of more than $675 million. Macalester has a student-faculty ratio of 10 to 1 and charges about $41900 in tuition and fees. It was founded in 1874 by the Rev. Edward Duffield as a Presbyterian-related but non-sectarian college and was named after Charles Macalester a prominent Philadelphia businessman and philanthropist.

EXECUTIVES

President, Brian C. Rosenberg
Chief Investment Officer, Craig H. Aase
VP Student Affairs, Laurie B. Hamre
Dean Admissions and Financial Aid, Lorne T. Robinson
VP Administration and Finance, David Wheaton
Director Employment Services, Charles H. Standfuss
VP Advancement, Thomas P. Bonner
Assistant VP Advancement Operations, Kathleen D. (Kate) Abbott
Dean Students, James C. Hoppe
Director Media Services, Brian C. Longley
Associate VP Information Technology Services, Jerry R. Sanders
Assistant VP Finance and Business Services, Kate Walker
Provost and Dean Faculty, Kathleen M. Murray

LOCATIONS

HQ: Macalester College
1600 Grand Ave., St. Paul MN 55105
Phone: 651-696-6000   **Fax:** 651-696-6241
Web: www.macalester.edu

HISTORICAL FINANCIALS

Company Type: School

Income Statement
FYE: May 31

	REVENUE ($ mil.)	NET INCOME ($ mil.)	NET PROFIT MARGIN	EMPLOYEES
05/12	96	(38)	—	0
05/11	129	(3)	—	0
05/10*	131	6	4.6%	0
06/09	0	0	11.6%	0
Annual Growth	788.3%	—	—	—

*Fiscal year change

2012 Year-End Financials

Debt ratio: ——
Return on equity: (-39.50)%
Cash ($ mil.): 30
Current ratio: —
Long-term debt ($ mil.): —

Dividends
Yield: —
Payout: —
Market value ($ mil.): —

MACOMB OAKLAND REGIONAL CENTER INC

Michigan's disabled citizens have more than a friend in MORC. The Macomb-Oakland Regional Center (MORC) advocates for adults and children with developmental physical or psychiatric disabilities hoping to improve the lives of its clients. In addition to finding homes and jobs and coordinating recreational activities for the disabled the not-for-profit organization helps connect customers with support services including psychology nursing and medical care. It also holds community education seminars and it provides home health visitation and rehabilitation therapy services through its MORC Home Care and MORC Rehab divisions. Founded in 1972 MORC serves over 4000 clients in the state.

EXECUTIVES

President and Executive Director, Gerald (Jerry) Provencal
Secretary and Director, Thomas (Tom) Marchand
Director Clinical Operations, Diane Lindsay
Chief Human Resources Officer, Peter Lynch
Administration, Dennis Bott
Manager Human Resources, Cathy Gibson
Medical Director, Robert Lechy
CFO Treasurer and Director, Richard Stone
Chairman, Joseph Erwin
Development and Communications Manager, Lindsay Calcatera
President and Executive Director, Gerald (Jerry) Provencal
Secretary and Director, Thomas (Tom) Marchand
CFO Treasurer and Director, Richard Stone
Director, Mark Stilwell
Director, Lynda Wolf
Director, Michael Switalski
Auditors: GrantThorntonLLP

LOCATIONS

HQ: Macomb-Oakland Regional Center Inc.
16200 Nineteen Mile Rd., Clinton Township MI 48038-0070
Phone: 586-263-8700   **Fax:** 586-412-7889
Web: www.morcinc.org

COMPETITORS

Gentiva
HealthSouth
Magellan Health
NHC
Sun Healthcare

HISTORICAL FINANCIALS

Company Type: Private - Not-for-Profit

Income Statement
FYE: September 30

	REVENUE ($ mil.)	NET INCOME ($ mil.)	NET PROFIT MARGIN	EMPLOYEES
09/11	190	0	0.2%	300
09/10	186	0	0.2%	0
09/09	181	0	0.1%	0
09/08	178	0	0.4%	0
Annual Growth	2.3%	(20.0%)	—	—

2011 Year-End Financials

Debt ratio: ——
Return on equity: 0.20%
Cash ($ mil.): 9
Current ratio: 0.60
Long-term debt ($ mil.): —

Dividends
Yield: —
Payout: —
Market value ($ mil.): —

MADISON ELECTRIC COMPANY

Founded by Morris and Max Blumberg Madison Electric broke ground in a rented room in Detroit in 1914. The company has grown from pushing light bulbs fuses wire and conduit to rival the top 200 electrical and electronics distributors in the US. Joined by affiliate Standard Electric Co. Madison Electric distributes electrical supplies industrial automation commercial lighting and network communication components. Branches dotting Michigan cater to a swath of commercial industrial utility and defense activities. Supply options tout brands by 3M Brady Federal Signal Leviton Panduit Square D/Schneider Electric and Thomas & Betts. The family-owned company is led by the Blumberg's fourth generation.

EXECUTIVES

President, Joseph Schneider
VP and CIO, Richard Sonenklar
VP and General Manager Electronics Division, Scott Leemaster
Secretary and Treasurer, Benjamin Rosenthal
VP Product Management, Brett Schneider
VP Contractor Sales, Jon Waitz
Quality Manager, Ron Simpson
Marketing, Deanna Klisz
Product Manager Wire/Cable/Conduit, Marcel Done
Product Manager Commercial Lighting, Ted Fleszar
Credit Manager, Jim Ivers
Credit Manager, Robin Krist
Warehouse Manager, Brad Schneider

LOCATIONS

HQ: Madison Electric Company
31855 Van Dyke Ave., Warren MI 48093
Phone: 586-825-0200   **Fax:** 586-825-0225
Web: www.madisonelectric.com

COMPETITORS

Electro-Matic	Medler Electric
Graybar Electric	Sonepar USA
McNaughton-McKay	Werner Electric Supply

HISTORICAL FINANCIALS

Company Type: Private

Income Statement

FYE: January 31

	REVENUE ($ mil.)	NET INCOME ($ mil.)	NET PROFIT MARGIN	EMPLOYEES
01/12	77	1	1.3%	200
01/11	66	(0)	—	0
01/10	52	(1)	—	0
01/09	75	(0)	—	0
Annual Growth	0.7%	—	—	—

2012 Year-End Financials

Debt ratio: —
Return on equity: 1.30%
Cash ($ mil.): 0
Current ratio: 0.70
Long-term debt ($ mil.): —
Dividends
Yield: —
Payout: —
Market value ($ mil.): —

MADONNA REHABILITATION HOSPITAL

No this hospital was not named after the pop chanteuse but it does have a lot of fans. Located in Lincoln Nebraska Madonna Rehabilitation Hospital has more than 250 beds and provides acute and long-term rehabilitation as well as subacute care. The hospital treats patients with a variety of orthopedic musculoskeletal and neurological conditions such as cancer cerebral palsy arthritis and multiple sclerosis. Each patient has a full team of physicians to help integrate and treat all symptoms. Madonna Rehabilitation Hospital was founded as a geriatric hospital by the the Benedictine Sisters of Yankton South Dakota in 1958.

Not content to be known as simply a local rehabilitation provider Madonna Rehabilitation Hospital is expanding its reach outside Nebraska into Missouri Iowa South Dakota and Kansas. In 2008 more than 20% of the hospital's referrals came from outside Lincoln.

The hospital intends to continue to increase its geographic reach through clinical education outreach programs and by sending nurse liaisons to out-of-state hospitals with the goal of drumming up referrals.

Madonna Rehabilitation Hospital operates four business segments: the hospital long-term care its TherapyPlus outpatient services and ProActive a medically-based health and fitness center that offers physical therapy sports medicine and wellness programs.

EXECUTIVES

Chairperson, Angie Muhleisen
President CEO and Director, Marsha Lommel
SVP and CFO, Victor Witkowicz
EVP and COO, Paul Dongilli
Director Human Resources, Lou Ann Manske
VP Medical Affairs, Tom Stalder
VP Long Term Care, Paul Nathenson
VP Patient Care, Susan Klanecky
VP Rehabilitation, Christopher Lee
VP Referral Development, Linda Sullivan
Director Strategic Planning and Marketing, Molly Nance
Vice Chairperson, Jim Schultz
VP and Director, John Folda
Secretary and Director, Rich Bailey
Treasurer and Director, Rich Herink
Director, David E. Lechner
President CEO and Director, Marsha Lommel
Director, Frank H. Hilsabeck
Vice Chairperson, Jim Schultz
VP and Director, John Folda
Secretary and Director, Rich Bailey
Treasurer and Director, Rich Herink
Director, Carol Beran
Director, Jan Connolly
Director, John Hanigan
Director, Matt Harris
Director, Bill Johnson
Director, Lori McClurg
Director, Elizabeth Noordhoek
Director, Tom Smith
Director, Dan Tomes
Director, Rick Wallace

LOCATIONS

HQ: Madonna Rehabilitation Hospital
5401 South St., Lincoln NE 68506
Phone: 402-489-7102   **Fax:** 402-483-9589
Web: www.madonna.org

COMPETITORS

Bethesda Hospital
BryanLGH Medical Center
Nebraska medical center
Saint Elizabeth Regional Medical Center

HISTORICAL FINANCIALS

Company Type: Private - Not-for-Profit

Income Statement

FYE: June 30

	REVENUE ($ mil.)	NET INCOME ($ mil.)	NET PROFIT MARGIN	EMPLOYEES
06/11	93	9	9.7%	1,465
06/10	92	8	9.4%	0
06/09	85	0	—	0
06/08	81	3	4.2%	0
Annual Growth	4.5%	37.8%	—	—

2011 Year-End Financials

Debt ratio: —
Return on equity: 9.70%
Cash ($ mil.): 12
Current ratio: 2.00
Long-term debt ($ mil.): —
Dividends
Yield: —
Payout: —
Market value ($ mil.): —

MAGIC COIL PRODUCTS LLC

LOCATIONS

HQ: MAGIC COIL PRODUCTS LLC
4143 COUNTY ROAD 61, BUTLER, IN 46721-9562
Phone: 260-868-2645
Web: www.magiccoilproducts.com

HISTORICAL FINANCIALS

Company Type: Private

Income Statement

FYE: December 31

	REVENUE ($ mil.)	NET INCOME ($ mil.)	NET PROFIT MARGIN	EMPLOYEES
12/11	111	4	3.9%	50
12/09	61	2	3.9%	0
12/08	100	3	3.2%	0
12/07	96	3	3.3%	0
Annual Growth	5.0%	11.3%	—	—

2011 Year-End Financials

Debt ratio: —
Return on equity: 3.90%
Cash ($ mil.): 0
Current ratio: 0.50
Long-term debt ($ mil.): —
Dividends
Yield: —
Payout: —
Market value ($ mil.): —

MAGNECO/METREL INC.

Magneco/Metrel makes ceramics but you won't find any artistic pieces at this company's plant! Magneco/Metrel uses the world's largest blast furnace to produce high-temperature refractory ceramics. The lineup serves as a lining in pipes and molds carrying molten iron and steel. The heat of molten steel would erode the pipes and molds without the ceramic barrier. Magneco/Metrel also makes a spray-on nano-particulate refractory line that can be used to create a liner for constructing or repairing steel-making molds and pipe. Its ceramics line is sold largely to steel foundries; other applications include ironmaking glass and copper. Magneco/Metrel was established in 1979 and is owned by CEO Charles Connors.

EXECUTIVES

CEO, Charles W. Connors Sr.
President and COO, Charles W. Connors Jr.
SVP Marketing Technology and Engineering, Majid Soofi
VP Industrial Sales, Roger Timberlake
VP Finance and Treasurer, Susan C. Malloy
VP Research and Quality Assurance, Michael Anderson
VP and General Counsel, Colleen Connors
VP Sales, Thomas Colander
VP Industrial Sales, Curtis Rothman
VP Marketing, Thomas E. Wank
VP Engineering, Albert J. Dzermejko

LOCATIONS

HQ: Magneco/Metrel Inc.
223 W. Interstate Rd., Addison IL 60101
Phone: 630-543-6660   **Fax:** 630-543-1479
Web: www.magneco-metrel.com

PRODUCTS/OPERATIONS

Selected Products
Abrasion resistant
Aluminum industry
Blast furnace reprofile
Casthouse products
Copper industry
Delta products
Ferro alloy
Glass industry
Reheat furnace pumpables
Reheat furnace shotcretes

COMPETITORS

Carpenter Technology   Minerals Technologies
Cookson Group   RHI
Imerys   Shinagawa Refractories

HISTORICAL FINANCIALS
Company Type: Private

Income Statement
FYE: December 31

	REVENUE ($ mil.)	NET INCOME ($ mil.)	NET PROFIT MARGIN	EMPLOYEES
12/11	66	3	5.1%	145
12/10	62	2	3.6%	0
12/08	63	0	1.1%	0
12/07	60	1	1.9%	0
Annual Growth	3.4%	44.4%	—	—

2011 Year-End Financials
Debt ratio: ——
Return on equity: 5.10%
Cash ($ mil.): 0
Current ratio: 1.20
Long-term debt ($ mil.): ——
Dividends
Yield: —
Payout: —
Market value ($ mil.): —

MAIN BROTHERS OIL COMPANY INC

LOCATIONS

HQ: MAIN BROTHERS OIL COMPANY INC
1 BOOTH LN, ALBANY, NY 12205-1403
Phone: 518-438-4195
Web: www.maincareenergy.com

HISTORICAL FINANCIALS
Company Type: Private

Income Statement
FYE: June 30

	REVENUE ($ mil.)	NET INCOME ($ mil.)	NET PROFIT MARGIN	EMPLOYEES
06/12	85	1	1.3%	150
06/11	84	1	1.5%	0
06/10	71	0	1.4%	0
06/09	85	1	1.2%	0
Annual Growth	(0.2%)	2.6%	—	—

2012 Year-End Financials
Debt ratio: ——
Return on equity: 1.30%
Cash ($ mil.): 5
Current ratio: 0.70
Long-term debt ($ mil.): ——
Dividends
Yield: —
Payout: —
Market value ($ mil.): —

MAIN LINE HEALTH INC.

Part of the Jefferson Health System Main Line Health serves constituents in the Philadelphia area. The health system consists of four acute-care facilities (Bryn Mawr Hospital Lankenau Hospital Paoli Hospital and Riddle Memorial Hospital) with a total of more than 1100 beds. It also operates physician practices a research institute a 150-bed rehabilitation hospital (Bryn Mawr Rehab Hospital) an addiction recovery facility (Mirmont Treatment Center) and various other facilities. Main Line Health provides home health care services and care for the elderly through senior programs. It operates several ambulatory-care centers and provides occupational health as well.

EXECUTIVES

President and CEO, John J. (Jack) Lynch III
Chairman, George W. Gephart Jr.
Chairman, Frank P. Slattery Jr., age 74
VP and CIO, Karen Thomas
SVP Human Resources, Eileen McAnally
EVP and CFO, Michael J. (Mike) Buongiorno, age 53
President Bryn Mawr Hospital, Andrea F. (Andi) Gilbert, age 58
SVP and General Counsel, Brian T. Corbett
President Lankenau Hospital, Elaine C. Thompson, age 56
President Paoli Hospital, Barbara J. Tachovsky
SVP Marketing and Public Affairs, Sarah A. Peterson
President Bryn Mawr Rehab Hospital and Affiliates, Donna M. Phillips
SVP Development, Kenneth E. Kirby
SVP Facilities Design and Construction, JoAnn M. Magnatta
VP Planning and Business Development, Joel A. Port
President and CEO Lankenau Institute of Medical Research, George C. Prendergast
Chief Nursing Officer, Nancy Valentine
Manager Public Relations, Frieda Schmidt
President and CEO Riddle Memorial Hospital, Daniel E. Kennedy
SVP Medical Affairs and Chief Medical Officer, Donald C. Arthur
VP and Chief Medical Information Officer, Harm J. Scherpbier
Assistant Manager Public Relations, Bridget Therriault

LOCATIONS

HQ: Main Line Health Inc.
130 S. Bryn Mawr Ave., Bryn Mawr PA 19010
Phone: 484-337-3000   **Fax:** 604-515-7978
Web: www.cryopak.com

PRODUCTS/OPERATIONS

Selected Operations
Bryn Mawr Hospital (Bryn Mawr PA)
Bryn Mawr Rehab Hospital (Malvern PA)
Lankenau Hospital (Wynnewood PA)
Mirmont Treatment Center (Lima PA)
Paoli Hospital (Paoli PA)
Riddle Memorial Hospital (Media PA)

COMPETITORS

Abington Memorial Hospital
Christiana Care
Crozer-Keystone Health System
Doylestown Hospital
Kennedy Health System
Mercy Health System
North Philadelphia Health System
The Cooper Health System
University of Pennsylvania Health System

HISTORICAL FINANCIALS
Company Type: Subsidiary

Income Statement
FYE: June 30

	REVENUE ($ mil.)	NET INCOME ($ mil.)	NET PROFIT MARGIN	EMPLOYEES
06/11	1,405	112	8.0%	5,840
06/10	1,361	111	8.2%	0
06/08	1,224	118	9.6%	0
06/06	9	2	23.5%	0
Annual Growth	436.7%	275.0%	—	—

2011 Year-End Financials
Debt ratio: ——
Return on equity: 8.00%
Cash ($ mil.): 109
Current ratio: 1.30
Long-term debt ($ mil.): ——
Dividends
Yield: —
Payout: —
Market value ($ mil.): —

MAINEGENERAL HEALTH

If you're aching or ailing within shouting distance of the Kennebec River in Maine then MaineGeneral Health is the place to head. The comprehensive health care organization features acute care hospitals outpatient clinics and physicians' practices long-term care centers and home health and hospice agencies. Its flagship facilities are the three main campuses (in state capital Augusta and Waterville farther north) of MaineGeneral Medical Center together featuring about 290 inpatient beds. MaineGeneral Health also runs nursing homes with some 270 beds in all as well as senior living apartments lab and imaging centers and inpatient rehabilitation and mental health facilities.

Operations MaineGeneral has a number of operations aimed at reaching underserved populations in rural parts of its service area. For instance the organization includes a small rural facility in northern Somerset County with an emergency room outpatient center and nursing home. And its HealthReach Network works with area hospitals and health care providers to ensure that some services (particularly home health care substance abuse treatment and mental health services) reach rural residents. Similarly the health care system hosts periodic specialty clinics that bring in doctors in medical specialties not represented on its own staff. Strategy In 2009 MaineGeneral announced plans to build a new 225-bed medical center in north Augusta that would consolidate the inpatient operations of its hospital campuses. Two of the medical center campuses would close (Augusta Campus and Seton Campus) while the third (Thayer Campus) would become an outpatient/emergency care facility. Construction of the $322 million hospital began in 2011 with a completion date in late 2013.

EXECUTIVES

President CEO and Director, Scott B. Bullock, age 60
President and CEO MaineGeneral Medical Center, Charles Hays
SVP Marketing and Strategy, Gail Evans
VP Human Resources, Rebecca Lamey
CFO, Mike Koziol
Chair, Barbara Mayer
Vice Chair, Robert Marden
President CEO and Director, Scott B. Bullock, age 60
Director, Conrad L. Ayotte, age 57
Vice Chair, Robert Marden
Director, William (Bro) Adams
Director, Charles Danielson
Director, Jeffrey Hubert
Director, Gordon Pow
Director, William Sprague
Director, Peter Alfond
Director, Diane Campbell
Director, Margaret Griffin
Director, Frederick (Ted) LaRochelle
Director, Roy Miller
Director, Brian Rines
Director, Kenneth Viens
Director, Douglas Cutchin
Director, Peter Guzzetti
Director, Elizabeth Mitchell
Director, Tobi Schneider
Director, Barbara Woodlee
Auditors: PricewaterhouseCoopersLLP

LOCATIONS

HQ: MaineGeneral Health
6 E. Chestnut St., Augusta ME 04330
Phone: 207-626-1000   **Fax:** 207-852-1594
Web: www.mainegeneral.org

COMPETITORS

Eastern Maine Healthcare Systems	MaineHealth
Franklin Community Health Network	Mercy Health System of Maine
Maine Coast Memorial Hospital	Parkview Hospital
	St. Joseph Healthcare

HISTORICAL FINANCIALS

Company Type: Private - Not-for-Profit

Income Statement

FYE: June 30

	REVENUE ($ mil.)	NET INCOME ($ mil.)	NET PROFIT MARGIN	EMPLOYEES
06/12	440	(2)	—	3,800
06/11	421	46	10.9%	0
06/10	401	15	3.8%	0
06/09	378	(35)	—	0
Annual Growth	5.2%	—	—	—

2012 Year-End Financials

Debt ratio: ——
Return on equity: (-0.50)%
Cash ($ mil.): 19
Current ratio: 0.70
Long-term debt ($ mil.): —
Dividends
Yield: —
Payout: —
Market value ($ mil.): —

MAINEGENERAL MEDICAL CENTER

LOCATIONS

HQ: MAINEGENERAL MEDICAL CENTER
6 E CHESTNUT ST, AUGUSTA, ME 04330-5717
Phone: 207-626-1000
Web: www.mainegeneral.org

HISTORICAL FINANCIALS

Company Type: Private

Income Statement

FYE: June 30

	REVENUE ($ mil.)	NET INCOME ($ mil.)	NET PROFIT MARGIN	EMPLOYEES
06/12	395	(35)	—	2,200
06/11	372	39	10.7%	0
06/10	336	10	3.2%	0
06/09	315	(27)	—	0
Annual Growth	7.7%	—	—	—

2012 Year-End Financials

Debt ratio: ——
Return on equity: (-8.90)%
Cash ($ mil.): 14
Current ratio: 0.60
Long-term debt ($ mil.): —
Dividends
Yield: —
Payout: —
Market value ($ mil.): —

MAINLINE INFORMATION SYSTEMS INC.

LOCATIONS

HQ: MAINLINE INFORMATION SYSTEMS INC.
1700 SUMMIT LAKE DR, TALLAHASSEE, FL 32317-7942
Phone: 850-219-5000
Web: www.mainline.com

HISTORICAL FINANCIALS

Company Type: Private

Income Statement

FYE: December 31

	REVENUE ($ mil.)	NET INCOME ($ mil.)	NET PROFIT MARGIN	EMPLOYEES
12/11	567	26	4.6%	528
12/10	576	26	4.7%	0
12/09	592	25	4.2%	0
12/08	514	7	1.5%	0
Annual Growth	3.3%	49.5%	—	—

2011 Year-End Financials

Debt ratio: ——
Return on equity: 4.60%
Cash ($ mil.): 13
Current ratio: 1.10
Long-term debt ($ mil.): —
Dividends
Yield: —
Payout: —
Market value ($ mil.): —

MAKE-A-WISH FOUNDATION OF AMERICA

The Make-A-Wish Foundation of America's mission is to grant the wishes of children with life-threatening medical conditions. The charitable organization grants wishes to ailing kids between the ages of two-and-a-half and 18 from more than 60 chapters in the US and its territories. Funded through donations in-kind contributions grants chapter fees and corporate donations the not-for-profit foundation boasts a volunteer network of some 25000 people and has granted more than 200000 wishes to children since its creation in 1980. The foundation was originally named the Chris Greicius Make-A-Wish Memorial after the first boy to receive his wish: becoming an honorary Arizona state trooper.

More wishes were granted in fiscal year 2010 than in any other year in the organization's history: 13580 wishes in all. The foundation estimates that each wish costs it approximately $7200. Typically children wish to visit a theme park (Disneyland is a popular choice) and travel shop for something such as a new computer or electronics and visit with a pro athlete or other celebrity. The Walt Disney Company and Macys are the largest corporate sponsors of Make-A-Wish Foundation.

The organization works with more than 35 international affiliates to grant wishes across the globe through about 30000 volunteers.

EXECUTIVES

President and CEO, David A. Williams
Chairman, Robert J. (Bob) Bigler
VP National Operations and COO, Phillip M. (Phil) Boudreau
Vice Chairman, Suzanne Y. Allen
Director, Charles A. James, age 57
Director, Elizabeth (Liz Ann) Sonders
Director, Matthew A. (Matt) Ouimet, age 53
Director, Salil Mehta
Director, Bonnie W. Gwin
Director, Craig A. Coffey
Director, Lawrence J. (Larry) Byar
Director, Daniel L. (Dan) Beem
Director, James D. (Jim) Fielding
Director, Thomas M. (Tom) McAlpin, age 53
Director, Robert L. (Bob) Paglia
Vice Chairman, Suzanne Y. Allen
Director, Andrea S. Hunt
Director, Robert K. (Bob) Jordan
Director, John K. Round
Director, Liza Wright
Auditors: GrantThorntonLLP

LOCATIONS

HQ: Make-A-Wish Foundation of America
4742 N. 24th St. Ste. 400, Phoenix AZ 85016-4862
Phone: 602-279-9474   **Fax:** 602-279-0855
Web: www.wish.org

PRODUCTS/OPERATIONS

2010 Revenue

	$ mil.	% of total
Public support		
Contributions	102	45
In-kind contributions	66	29
Grants	6	3
Special events	44	20
Investment income	8	3
Other income	0	-
Total	**229**	**100**

2010 Expenses

	$ mil.	% of total
Program services		
Wish granting	134	60
Public information	24	11
Chapter support	5	2
Program-related support	4	2
Training and development	1	1
Support services		
Fundraising	34	15
Management & general	19	9
Total	**225**	**100**

HISTORICAL FINANCIALS

Company Type: Private - Not-for-Profit

Income Statement

FYE: August 31

	REVENUE ($ mil.)	NET INCOME ($ mil.)	NET PROFIT MARGIN	EMPLOYEES
08/11	64	3	6.0%	118
08/10	60	2	4.1%	0
08/09	57	0	—	0
08/08	58	9	16.9%	0
Annual Growth	**3.8%**	**(26.5%)**	**—**	**—**

2011 Year-End Financials

Debt ratio: ——
Return on equity: 6.00%
Cash ($ mil.): 9
Current ratio: 1.40
Long-term debt ($ mil.): —
Dividends
  Yield: —
  Payout: —
  Market value ($ mil.): —

MANAGEMENT & TRAINING CORPORATION

Management & Training Corporation (MTC) prepares prison inmates for re-entry into society. It provides a variety of academic vocational and social-skills training in rehabilitation-oriented private prisons. Its holistic education model offers programs to help inmates avoid substance abuse as they also boost their engagement in community service find work and increase their cognitive skills. As part of its services MTC operates about two dozen correctional facilities in eight states including Arizona California Florida Idaho Ohio New Mexico Mississippi and Texas. The company is also a contractor for the US Department of Labor. Founded in 1981 MTC operates facilities that house some 25000 inmates.

Operations

The company has held contracts with the US Agency for International Development the African Development Bank UNICEF and other organizations. It is the largest single operator of Job Corps a government funded job-training program for 16-to-24-year-old children and adults. The company's MTC Institute performs research into forming best practices related to addressing issues facing those who work with Job Corps youth and prison inmates. The company also provides subcontracted health care services by employing a range of medical providers including dentists optometrists psychiatrists and psychologists and physicians.

Geographic Reach

MTC operates internationally providing governments NGOs ministries and private entities with customized training programs designed to help develop workforces.

EXECUTIVES

Chairman, Robert Marquardt
President and CEO, R. Scott Marquardt
CFO, Lyle J. Parry
SVP Training, John Pederson
VP Human Resources, Teresa Aramaki
Director Communications, Carl Stuart
VP Corrections Marketing, Mike Murphy
VP Regional Corrections, J. C. Conner
VP Corrections, Al Murphy
VP Communication, Celeste McDonald
VP Information Systems, Rich Skeen
VP and General Counsel, Dawn Call
SVP Corrections, Odie Washington
VP Corrections Programming, Anita Dutson
Director Corrections, Mark Lee

LOCATIONS

HQ: Management & Training Corporation
500 N. Marketplace Dr., Centerville UT 84014
Phone: 801-693-2600   **Fax:** 801-693-2900
Web: www.mtctrains.com

PRODUCTS/OPERATIONS

Selected Services

Communicate through formal and informal channels
Develop custom training for students clients & offenders
Manage facilities
Provide community connections
Provide data solutions

COMPETITORS

Avalon Correctional Services
Community Education Centers
Corrections Corporation of America
GEO Group

HISTORICAL FINANCIALS

Company Type: Private

Income Statement

FYE: December 31

	REVENUE ($ mil.)	NET INCOME ($ mil.)	NET PROFIT MARGIN	EMPLOYEES
12/11	687	30	4.4%	7,800
12/10	667	24	3.6%	0
12/09	672	20	3.0%	0
12/08	596	13	2.2%	0
Annual Growth	**4.8%**	**32.3%**	**—**	

2011 Year-End Financials

Debt ratio: ——
Return on equity: 4.40%
Cash ($ mil.): 2
Current ratio: —
Long-term debt ($ mil.): —
Dividends
  Yield: —
  Payout: —
  Market value ($ mil.): —

MANCHESTER COLLEGE

LOCATIONS

HQ: MANCHESTER COLLEGE
604 E COLLEGE AVE, NORTH MANCHESTER, IN 46962-1232
Phone: 260-982-5000
Web: www.manchester.edu

HISTORICAL FINANCIALS

Company Type: Private

Income Statement

FYE: June 30

	REVENUE ($ mil.)	NET INCOME ($ mil.)	NET PROFIT MARGIN	EMPLOYEES
06/11	89	41	46.3%	250
06/10	47	2	5.9%	0
06/09	38	(4)	—	0
06/07	26	2	11.2%	0
Annual Growth	**49.3%**	**140.1%**	**—**	**—**

2011 Year-End Financials

Debt ratio: ——
Return on equity: 46.30%
Cash ($ mil.): 1
Current ratio: —
Long-term debt ($ mil.): —
Dividends
  Yield: —
  Payout: —
  Market value ($ mil.): —

MANHATTAN SCHOOL OF MUSIC INC

Music is on the minds of students at the Manhattan School of Music in New York. The school is dedicated to the study of jazz and classical music.

Majors range from orchestral instruments and voice to piano composition and jazz. It has more than 800 students and nearly 275 faculty. The school provides undergraduate graduate and doctoral programs. Manhattan School of Music also offers distance learning and a Global Conservatory which provides video conferencing to institutions throughout the world. Famous alumni include Harry Connick Jr. Herbie Hancock and Yusef Lateef. Pianist and philanthropist Janet D. Schenck founded the Manhattan School of Music as as the Neighborhood Music School in 1917.

EXECUTIVES

Director Administration and Human Relations, Carol Matos
Controller, Pat Zumaran
Director Public Relations Marketing and Publications, Debra Kinzler
VP External Affairs, Susan Ebersole
Associate Dean for Enrollment Management, Amy A. Anderson
Director Alumni Affairs, John Blanchard
Director Facilities, Frank J. Graupe
Director Library Services, Peter Caleb
Dean of Students, Elsa Jean Davidson
President, Robert Sirota
Dean of Performance, David Geber
VP Finance and Administration, Paul Kelleher
Dean of Precollege Division, Joanne Polk
Assistant Dean for Doctoral Studies, Jeffrey Langford
Registrar, David McDonagh

LOCATIONS

HQ: Manhattan School of Music
120 Claremont Ave., New York NY 10027
Phone: 212-749-2802   **Fax:** 212-749-5571
Web: www.msmnyc.edu

HISTORICAL FINANCIALS
Company Type: School

Income Statement

	REVENUE ($ mil.)	NET INCOME ($ mil.)	NET PROFIT MARGIN	EMPLOYEES
06/11	38	3	9.7%	450
06/10	34	2	6.1%	0
06/09	31	0	—	0
06/08	35	2	6.1%	0
Annual Growth	2.6%	19.6%	—	—

FYE: June 30

2011 Year-End Financials

Debt ratio: ——
Return on equity: 9.70%
Cash ($ mil.): 4
Current ratio: 0.10
Long-term debt ($ mil.): —

Dividends
Yield: —
Payout: —
Market value ($ mil.): —

MANHATTANVILLE COLLEGE

Manhattanville College is a private liberal arts institution offering undergraduate and masters degree programs in more than 40 fields. Manhattanville is home to about 1500 undergraduate students. In addition to college degree programs the school also offers in-house and on-site corporate training programs in such areas as business writing project management and diversity. Manhattanville was founded in 1841 in New York City by the Religous of the Sacred Heart. It relocated in 1847 to an area just north of New York City on a hill overlooking the village of Manhattanville. The school has been coeducational and non-denominational since 1971.

EXECUTIVES

VP and CIO, Larry Arps
VP Operations, J. Gregory Palmer
Controller, Norma Bass
Manager Purchasing Services, Marsha Kirchoff
President, Molly Easo Smith
VP Finance and Treasurer, Marvin Suchoff
General Counsel, Maureen Bateman
Dean Students, Brandon Dawson
Director Human Resources, Don Dean
VP Enrollment Management, Jose Flores
Director Financial Aid, Maria Barlaam
Director Marketing and Communications, Daniel Preniszni
Interim Provost, Edgar Schick
Registrar, Joseph Redington
Director Security and Safety, Joe Hinchey

LOCATIONS

HQ: Manhattanville College
2900 Purchase St., Purchase NY 10577-2131
Phone: 914-694-2200   **Fax:** 914-694-2386
Web: www.mville.edu

COMPETITORS

Briarcliffe College   Marymount Manhattan
CUNY

HISTORICAL FINANCIALS
Company Type: School

Income Statement

	REVENUE ($ mil.)	NET INCOME ($ mil.)	NET PROFIT MARGIN	EMPLOYEES
06/11	98	(0)	—	420
06/10	98	0	0.2%	0
06/09	96	0	—	0
06/08	63	(0)	—	0
Annual Growth	15.8%	—	—	—

FYE: June 30

2011 Year-End Financials

Debt ratio: ——
Return on equity: (-0.10)%
Cash ($ mil.): 0
Current ratio: —
Long-term debt ($ mil.): —

Dividends
Yield: —
Payout: —
Market value ($ mil.): —

MARICOPA HEALTH FOUNDATION

LOCATIONS

HQ: MARICOPA HEALTH FOUNDATION
2502 E UNIVERSITY DR, PHOENIX, AZ 85034-6930
Phone: 602-344-5011
Web: www.mihs.org

HISTORICAL FINANCIALS
Company Type: Private

Income Statement

	REVENUE ($ mil.)	NET INCOME ($ mil.)	NET PROFIT MARGIN	EMPLOYEES
06/11*	607	29	4.9%	25
12/09	1	0	31.1%	0
Annual Growth	34135.3%	5267.3%	—	—

FYE: June 30

*Fiscal year change

2011 Year-End Financials

Debt ratio: ——
Return on equity: 4.90%
Cash ($ mil.): 1
Current ratio: 0.70
Long-term debt ($ mil.): —

Dividends
Yield: —
Payout: —
Market value ($ mil.): —

MARIETTA CORPORATION

Marietta makes miniatures –those little personal care amenities found in hotels and bed-and-breakfast inns. The manufacturer rolls out soaps shampoos lotions and the like. Its products are distributed to hospitality and institutional customers including hotels spas military bases and correctional facilities. Using its sample-size packaging know-how Marietta also provides contract manufacturing for consumer products companies. It has worked with leading firms such as Estee Lauder Procter & Gamble and Pfizer. Marietta's manufacturing and warehousing network spans the US Canada Europe and Asia. Founded as Marietta Packaging Company in 1976 the firm has been owned by Ares Management since 2004.

Marietta's offerings are produced under both private labels and well-known brands. Its private-label portfolio includes Lord & Mayfair Aromae Botanicals Earth's Accents Hydro Basics and Sun & Sand. The company has turned out personal care products carrying name brands such as Aveda Pantene Pro-V Jergens Vaseline philosophy and Finesse. Marietta has grown its business over the years by expanding its slate of partnerships with large consumer products companies including Johnson & Johnson Unilever and L'Oreal.

The company has also focused on eco-friendly initiatives. Some of its efforts have included using wind-generated electricity for manufacturing processes recycled materials and soy-based inks in packaging and sourcing supplies from local vendors (which reduces transportation emissions).

HISTORY

The company was founded in 1976 by New York cabbage farmer Manny Siegle after a trip to Europe during which he received shampoo packets in hotels. He returned to the US and decided to go into the shampoo business using his sauerkraut packaging equipment. The company's first job was packaging shampoo for a hotel in Salt Lake City. Just two years later the company began packaging personal-care products for Holiday Inn. Through the years it added other contracts with major hotels including Howard Johnson Radisson and Sheraton. In 1989 Marietta acquired manufacturer American Soap Co. and began making some of its own soaps.

In 1995 former Marietta CFO Thomas Blair was sentenced to a year in federal prison for embezzling over $400000 in 1991. Blair cooperated in an investigation that led to Nadolski's conviction on charges that he manipulated information to inflate Marietta's stock prices. Nadolski was sentenced to 21 months in federal prison and fined $50000 for securities fraud. In 1996 the company merged with BFMA Holding a shell owned by Barry Florescue and went private again. The firm did not change its name and Florescue became Marietta's chairman and CEO.

In 1999 Marietta signed a seven-year contract with Cendant Corp. to supply amenities to Cendant's hotel holdings. In 2002 Marietta purchased the 430000 square-foot former Rubbermaid plant in Cortland (plus machinery and equipment to make soap) for about $14 million.

In late 2004 parent company BFMA sold itself and subsidiary Marietta to Ares Management LLC.

Marietta acquired Packaging Advantage Corp. (PAC) in late 2005. The purchase added to the company's US capabilities with manufacturing operations in California Illinois Mississippi and New York.

EXECUTIVES

VP Quality Assurance, David P. Hempson
Director Business, John Samman
Operations Australia New Zealand and Pacific Islands, John Riley
CFO, Perry Morgan
Operations North and South America, Donna Southworth
Director Human Resources, Beth Corl
CEO, Donald Sturdivant
Vice President Sales and Marketing, Stephan Heldt
VP Contract Sales, Rob Chichester
National Accounts Manager, Arkady Sokolov
Director Business, April Rabago
Vice President Global Accounts, Michael Stokoe
Customer Service Manager - International Markets, Carlotta Bertagna
Sales Director East Coast plus LongHouse, Melissa Walters
SVP Sales and Marketing, John Watson
Regional Sales Manager NYC Metro, Elizabethe Manzi
Regional Sales Manager, Bill Matson
VP Business Development, Bill Carley
SVP Operations, Brian Oneil
Director Business, Dana McElroy
Regional Sales Manager Midwest, Laura Atkinson
Sales Director, Rudy Baker
Regional Sales Manager, Sean Ferreira

LOCATIONS

HQ: Marietta Corporation
37 Huntington St., Cortland NY 13045
Phone: 607-756-0650   **Fax:** 607-756-0658
Web: www.mariettacorp.com

PRODUCTS/OPERATIONS

Selected Products

Conditioners
Fragrances
Laundry detergent
Lotions
Shampoos
Soaps

COMPETITORS

American Hotel Register	Henkel
Bristol-Myers Squibb	Johnson & Johnson
Colgate-Palmolive	Procter & Gamble
Flexpaq Corporation	S.C. Johnson
Guest Supply	Unilever
	Xela Pack

HISTORICAL FINANCIALS

Company Type: Private

Income Statement

FYE: October 1

	REVENUE ($ mil.)	NET INCOME ($ mil.)	NET PROFIT MARGIN	EMPLOYEES
10/11*	163	0	0.5%	1,500
09/10	0	0	—	0
Annual Growth	—	—	—	—

*Fiscal year change

2011 Year-End Financials

Debt ratio: ——
Return on equity: 0.50%
Cash ($ mil.): 20
Current ratio: 1.70
Long-term debt ($ mil.): —
Dividends
  Yield: —
  Payout: —
  Market value ($ mil.): —

MARION GENERAL HOSPITAL

LOCATIONS

HQ: MARION GENERAL HOSPITAL
441 N WABASH AVE, MARION, IN 46952-2690
Phone: 765-662-1441
Web: www.mgh.net

HISTORICAL FINANCIALS

Company Type: Private

Income Statement

FYE: June 30

	REVENUE ($ mil.)	NET INCOME ($ mil.)	NET PROFIT MARGIN	EMPLOYEES
06/12	157	1	1.1%	1,212
06/11	144	39	27.5%	0
06/10	133	16	12.4%	0
06/09	132	3	2.5%	0
Annual Growth	5.9%	(19.6%)	—	—

2012 Year-End Financials

Debt ratio: ——
Return on equity: 1.10%
Cash ($ mil.): 36
Current ratio: 3.50
Long-term debt ($ mil.): —
Dividends
  Yield: —
  Payout: —
  Market value ($ mil.): —

MARIST COLLEGE

Marist College is a gem among small private US colleges. The liberal arts college has a enrollment of some 6300 students and a student-faculty ratio of 15-to-1. It offers more than 40 bachelor's and a dozen master's programs as well as some 20 certificate programs. It seven schools specialize in communication and the arts computer science and math continuing education liberal arts management science and social and behavioral sciences. In addition to its main 220-acre campus along the shores of the Hudson River the college has several off-campus extension sites that mainly cater to adult students. Marist College was founded in 1929 as a training center for the brothers of the Roman Catholic Marist order.

Marist College has recently been recognized by publications including Kiplinger's Private Finance magazine which named Marist as one of the best value private college in the US. It has also been on the Princeton Review's best colleges list with a special recognition for its extensive study abroad programs (including a branch campus in Florence Italy) as well as its business teaching criminal justice fashion and communication programs. Marist College also offers advanced IT resources to its students through a partnership with IBM which is also located in southeastern New York State.

The college has an endowment of some $44 million and an annual operating budget of $153 million. In 2011 Marist College reported operating revenues of some $155 million primarily attributed to student tuition and fees.

EXECUTIVES

Dean School of Communication and the Arts, Steven Ralston
President, Dennis J. Murray
EVP, Roy H. Merolli
Chief Public Affairs Officer, Timmian C. (Tim) Massie
VP; Dean for Student Affairs, Deborah (Deb) DiCaprio
Dean School of Social and Behavioral Sciences, Margaret R. Calista
VP Admission and Enrollment Planning, Sean P. Kaylor
Director Institutional Research and Planning, Victoria Mullen
Dean School of Computer Science and Mathematics and Associate Professor, Roger L. Norton
Associate VP Academic Affairs; Dean of Academic Programs, John T. Ritschdorff
VP Academic Affairs; Dean of Faculty, Thomas S. Wermuth
Library Director James A. Cannavino Library, Verne Newton
Dean School of Management, Elmore R. Alexander
Administrative Assistant to the President; Secretary Board of Trustees, Eileen Sico
Presidential Fellow, Edward (Eddie) Summers

Special Assistant to the President, Elisabeth Tavarez
VP and CIO, William (Bill) Thirsk
VP Business Affairs and CFO, Jeanne T. Plecenik
Assistant VP Human Resources, Michael Silvestro
Dean School of Liberal Arts, Martin B. Shaffer
Dean School of Global and Professional Programs, Lauren Mounty

LOCATIONS

HQ: MARIST COLLEGE
3399 NORTH RD, POUGHKEEPSIE, NY 12601-1387
Phone: 845-575-3000
Web: www.marist.edu

HISTORICAL FINANCIALS
Company Type: School

Income Statement
FYE: June 30

	REVENUE ($ mil.)	NET INCOME ($ mil.)	NET PROFIT MARGIN	EMPLOYEES
06/11	196	19	10.2%	750
06/10	211	47	22.3%	0
06/09	159	0	—	0
06/08	119	(2)	—	0
Annual Growth	17.9%	—	—	—

2011 Year-End Financials
Debt ratio: ——
Return on equity: 10.20%
Cash ($ mil.): 48
Current ratio: ——
Long-term debt ($ mil.): —

Dividends
Yield: —
Payout: —
Market value ($ mil.): —

MARJAM SUPPLY CO. INC.

LOCATIONS

HQ: MARJAM SUPPLY CO. INC.
885 CONKLIN ST, FARMINGDALE, NY 11735-2400
Phone: 631-249-4900
Web: www.marjam.com

HISTORICAL FINANCIALS
Company Type: Private

Income Statement
FYE: December 31

	REVENUE ($ mil.)	NET INCOME ($ mil.)	NET PROFIT MARGIN	EMPLOYEES
12/11	258	2	1.2%	614
12/10	202	3	1.9%	0
12/09	204	(1)	—	0
Annual Growth	12.5%	—	—	—

2011 Year-End Financials
Debt ratio: ——
Return on equity: 1.20%
Cash ($ mil.): 0
Current ratio: 1.60
Long-term debt ($ mil.): —

Dividends
Yield: —
Payout: —
Market value ($ mil.): —

MARKET & JOHNSON INC.

Market & Johnson provides commercial construction and general contracting services in western Wisconsin. It offers a full range of services ranging from the planning and preliminary design stages through delivery and maintenance. The company operates in the industrial commercial government health care religion and education markets. Projects range from large buildings to small remodeling jobs. Juel Market and Milt Johnson founded the company as a home builder in 1948. Today Market & Johnson is owned by a group of five principal managers including CEO Dan Market.

EXECUTIVES

President and CEO, Dan R. Market
VP Finance, Steve Breitenfeldt
VP Operations, Donald (Don) Carlson
VP, Jerry Shea
CFO, Kevin Monson
Director Business Development, Jason Plante
Senior Project Manager, Matthew (Matt) Faulkner
Auditors: WipfliUllrichBertelsonLLP

LOCATIONS

HQ: Market & Johnson Inc.
2350 Galloway St., Eau Claire WI 54701
Phone: 715-834-1213   **Fax:** 715-834-2331
Web: www.market-johnson.com

COMPETITORS

Boldt	Hunzinger Construction
C. G. Schmidt	J.H. Findorff &
C.D. Smith	Son
F.A. Wilhelm	Tutor Perini
Hill International	Weis Builders
Hunt Construction	

HISTORICAL FINANCIALS
Company Type: Private

Income Statement
FYE: December 31

	REVENUE ($ mil.)	NET INCOME ($ mil.)	NET PROFIT MARGIN	EMPLOYEES
12/11	84	1	1.8%	250
12/10	116	6	5.4%	0
Annual Growth	(27.6%)	(75.8%)	—	—

2011 Year-End Financials
Debt ratio: ——
Return on equity: 1.80%
Cash ($ mil.): 3
Current ratio: 1.20
Long-term debt ($ mil.): —

Dividends
Yield: —
Payout: —
Market value ($ mil.): —

MARYLAND AND VIRGINIA MILK PRODUCERS COOPERATIVE ASSOCIATION INC

LOCATIONS

HQ: MARYLAND AND VIRGINIA MILK PRODUCERS COOPERATIVE ASSOCIATION INC
1985 ISAAC NEWTON SQ W # 200, RESTON, VA 20190-5031
Phone: 703-742-6800
Web: www.mdvamilk.com

HISTORICAL FINANCIALS
Company Type: Private

Income Statement
FYE: December 31

	REVENUE ($ mil.)	NET INCOME ($ mil.)	NET PROFIT MARGIN	EMPLOYEES
12/11	1,362	(2)	—	550
12/10	1,219	8	0.7%	0
12/09	865	14	1.7%	0
12/06	894	2	0.3%	0
Annual Growth	15.0%	—	—	—

2011 Year-End Financials
Debt ratio: ——
Return on equity: (-0.20)%
Cash ($ mil.): 0
Current ratio: 0.90
Long-term debt ($ mil.): —

Dividends
Yield: —
Payout: —
Market value ($ mil.): —

MARYLAND GENERAL HOSPITAL INC.

LOCATIONS

HQ: MARYLAND GENERAL HOSPITAL INC.
827 LINDEN AVE, BALTIMORE, MD 21201-4606
Phone: 410-225-8000
Web: www.marylandgeneral.com

HISTORICAL FINANCIALS
Company Type: Private

Income Statement
FYE: June 30

	REVENUE ($ mil.)	NET INCOME ($ mil.)	NET PROFIT MARGIN	EMPLOYEES
06/11	186	8	4.4%	1,200
06/10	180	5	3.3%	0
06/09*	185	1	0.8%	0
04/09	0	0	76.5%	0
Annual Growth	1835.6%	646.5%	—	—

2011 Year-End Financials

Debt ratio: ——
Return on equity: 4.40%
Cash ($ mil.): 14
Current ratio: 1.10
Long-term debt ($ mil.): —

Dividends
Yield: —
Payout: —
Market value ($ mil.): —

MARYMOUNT MANHATTAN COLLEGE

Marymount Manhattan College is a four-year undergraduate liberal arts college in the middle of New York City with an enrollment of more than 2000 students. The school offers 17 major programs of study. It was originally was founded by the Religious of the Sacred Heart of Mary in Tarrytown New York and was independently chartered in 1961 as Marymount Manhattan College.

EXECUTIVES

President, Judson R. Shaver
EVP Administration and Finance, Paul Ciraulo
Associate VP Administration and Finance and Controller, Wayne Santucci
Director Human Resources, Christina Flanagan
Manager Human Resources Information Systems and Benefits, Kevin Ng
Director Information Technology, Patricia Hansen
Director Security, Richard Barbakoff
Director Administrative Services, Maria C. Marzano
Director Corporations Foundations and Planned Giving, Jean Wilhelm
Dean Admissions, James (Jim) Rogers
VP Institutional Research and Planning, Peter H. Baker
VP Student Affairs and Enrollment Management, Michael Cappeto
VP Academic Affairs and Dean Faculty, David Podell
Director Financial Aid, Christina Bennett
Registrar, Regina Chan
VP Institutional Advancement, Betty Heinig
Director Publications and Communication, Manuel Romero
Manager Alumni Relations, Linda Sada
Dean Students, Ron Jackson

LOCATIONS

HQ: Marymount Manhattan College
221 E. 71st St., New York NY 10021
Phone: 212-517-0400   **Fax:** 212-517-0465
Web: marymount.mmm.edu

COMPETITORS

CUNY
Metropolitan College
of New York

New School

MARYMOUNT UNIVERSITY

LOCATIONS

HQ: MARYMOUNT UNIVERSITY
2807 N GLEBE RD, ARLINGTON, VA 22207-4299
Phone: 703-284-1500
Web: www.marymount.edu

HISTORICAL FINANCIALS

Company Type: Private

Income Statement

FYE: June 30

	REVENUE ($ mil.)	NET INCOME ($ mil.)	NET PROFIT MARGIN	EMPLOYEES
06/11	84	4	5.8%	625
06/10	76	4	5.4%	0
06/09	75	0	—	0
06/08	64	6	9.3%	0
Annual Growth	9.2%	(6.8%)	—	—

2011 Year-End Financials

Debt ratio: ——
Return on equity: 5.80%
Cash ($ mil.): 23
Current ratio: —
Long-term debt ($ mil.): —

Dividends
Yield: —
Payout: —
Market value ($ mil.): —

MASSACHUSETTS HIGHER EDUCATION ASSISTANCE CORPORATION

Don't know how you're going to pay for college? You might want to consult ASA ASAP. The Mas-

HISTORICAL FINANCIALS

Company Type: School

Income Statement

FYE: June 30

	REVENUE ($ mil.)	NET INCOME ($ mil.)	NET PROFIT MARGIN	EMPLOYEES
06/11	58	1	1.9%	630
06/10	49	0	1.9%	0
06/09	56	4	7.3%	0
06/08	51	3	6.8%	0
Annual Growth	3.9%	(32.1%)	—	—

2011 Year-End Financials

Debt ratio: ——
Return on equity: 1.90%
Cash ($ mil.): 13
Current ratio: —
Long-term debt ($ mil.): —

Dividends
Yield: —
Payout: —
Market value ($ mil.): —

sachusetts Higher Education Assistance Corporation which does business as American Student Assistance or ASA is a federal student loan guarantor one of the first in the country. The not-for-profit company provides Federal Family Education Loan Program (FFELP) guarantee origination fund delivery and default prevention services to students schools and lenders. ASA guarantees more than $2 billion in student loans each year and manages a student loan portfolio worth more than $45 billion. The company was established in 1955.

ASA utilizes a "wellness" approach to borrowing which involves less emphasis on traditional loan collection and more on the "health" of each loan. With such practices the company keeps its default and delinquency rates below the national average.

EXECUTIVES

VP Systems and CIO, Elisabeth P. (Betsy) Nietsch
President and CEO, Paul Combe
EVP and COO, Michael Finn
VP Lender and School Services, Susan Nathan
VP Strategic Services, Shelley Saunders
VP and Ombudsman, Grace Bartini
VP Business Development, Debra Chromy
VP Human Resources, Lauren Rolfe
VP Borrower Services, Michael Ryan
CFO, Barbara Matez
Auditors: GrantThorntonLLP

LOCATIONS

HQ: Massachusetts Higher Education Assistance Corporation
100 Cambridge St. Ste. 1600, Boston MA 02114
Phone: 617-728-4200   **Fax:** 719-632-5175
Web: www.taeus.com

COMPETITORS

Access Group
Bank of America
Discover
First Marblehead
JPMorgan Chase
Nelnet
Pennsylvania Higher Education Assistance Agency
Sallie Mae

HISTORICAL FINANCIALS

Company Type: Private - Not-for-Profit

Income Statement

FYE: June 30

	ASSETS ($ mil.)	NET INCOME ($ mil.)	INCOME AS % OF ASSETS	EMPLOYEES
06/11	235	73	31.4%	650
06/10	170	34	20.0%	0
06/09	148	0	—	0
06/08	164	46	28.1%	0
Annual Growth	12.7%	17.0%	—	—

2011 Year-End Financials

Debt ratio: ——
Return on equity: 37.30%
Cash ($ mil.): 95
Current ratio: —
Long-term debt ($ mil.): —

Dividends
Yield: —
Payout: —
Market value ($ mil.): —

MASSACHUSETTS MEDICAL SOCIETY INC

The Massachusetts Medical Society (MMS) is a professional organization of physicians and medical students with more than 23000 members. The organization an advocate for patients and physicians promotes a code of ethics for medical professions as well as the training research and education of physicians. It also helps to develop health care policy and publishes the New England Journal of Medicine. The Massachusetts Medical Society was founded in 1781 and is the oldest continuously operating medical society in the nation.

Membership increased by just over 1% in 2011 to around 23000. Membership among young physicians increased close to 3% among women by about 4% and residents by almost 15% in 2011.

In 2011 revenues for the society's publishing experienced stable returns due to economic instability in the US. The society's remaining channels grew in 2011 with pharmaceutical-based and online advertising and permissions taking the lead. Print subscriptions declined as customers/members moved toward online subscriptions.

EXECUTIVES

EVP, Corinne Broderick
President-Elect, Alice A. Tolbert Coombs
Speaker of the House of Delegates, Richard S. Pieters
President, Mario E. Motta
VP, Lynda M. Young
Secretary and Treasurer, Richard V. Aghababian
Assistant Secretary and Treasurer, Deanna P. Ricker
Vice-Speaker of the House of Delegates, Jesse M. Ehrenfeld
Auditors: Deloitte&ToucheLLP

LOCATIONS

HQ: Massachusetts Medical Society
860 Winter St., Waltham MA 02451
Phone: 781-893-4610   **Fax:** 781-893-5003
Web: www.massmed.org

HISTORICAL FINANCIALS
Company Type: Private - Not-for-Profit

Income Statement

	REVENUE ($ mil.)	NET INCOME ($ mil.)	NET PROFIT MARGIN	EMPLOYEES
05/11	118	19	16.5%	700
Annual Growth	—	—	—	—

FYE: May 31

2011 Year-End Financials
Debt ratio: ——
Return on equity: 16.50%
Cash ($ mil.): 10
Current ratio: 0.30
Long-term debt ($ mil.): —
Dividends
 Yield: —
 Payout: —
 Market value ($ mil.): —

MATTESON-RIDOLFI INC.

Matteson-Ridolfi distributes chemicals such as catalysts pigments resins solvents surfactants and thickening agents to companies in the adhesives and sealants automotive glass and refractory paints and coatings pharmaceuticals pulp and paper and soaps and detergents industries. The company maintains facilities in Cleveland; Detroit; and Louisville Kentucky. Customers include Cabot and other major chemical manufacturers. The family of company president Scot Westerbeek owns Matteson-Ridolfi which was founded in 1932.

EXECUTIVES

President and CEO, Scot Westerbeek
Manager Operations, John Wloch
Controller, Bill Riggs
VP, Gary Westerbeek
Quality Assurance Coordinator, Ray Grix
CTO, J. R. Maskeny

LOCATIONS

HQ: Matteson-Ridolfi Inc.
14450 King Rd., Riverview MI 48192-7939
Phone: 734-479-4500   **Fax:** 734-479-1630
Web: www.mattrid.com

COMPETITORS

Brenntag North America   Univar USA
Gallade Chemical

HISTORICAL FINANCIALS
Company Type: Private

Income Statement

	REVENUE ($ mil.)	NET INCOME ($ mil.)	NET PROFIT MARGIN	EMPLOYEES
12/11	36	2	7.9%	18
12/10	34	3	8.8%	0
12/09	28	1	6.6%	0
12/08	33	1	4.5%	0
Annual Growth	2.8%	23.8%	—	—

FYE: December 31

2011 Year-End Financials
Debt ratio: ——
Return on equity: 7.90%
Cash ($ mil.): 3
Current ratio: 2.20
Long-term debt ($ mil.): —
Dividends
 Yield: —
 Payout: —
 Market value ($ mil.): —

MAV6 LLC

LOCATIONS

HQ: MAV6 LLC
800 CHERRY ST, VICKSBURG, MS 39183-2507
Phone: 703-340-1304

HISTORICAL FINANCIALS
Company Type: Private

Income Statement

	REVENUE ($ mil.)	NET INCOME ($ mil.)	NET PROFIT MARGIN	EMPLOYEES
12/11	116	7	6.5%	150
Annual Growth	—	—	—	—

FYE: December 31

2011 Year-End Financials
Debt ratio: ——
Return on equity: 6.50%
Cash ($ mil.): 1
Current ratio: 1.80
Long-term debt ($ mil.): —
Dividends
 Yield: —
 Payout: —
 Market value ($ mil.): —

MAXIM HEALTHCARE SERVICES INC.

Good health as the maxim goes is one of life's greatest blessings and Maxim Healthcare Services aims to promote that principle by offering medical staffing and home health care as well as immunizations and other wellness services to clients nationwide. The company provides medical and administrative personnel for hospitals school systems nursing homes and correctional facilities. The company's staffing division offers contract per diem and travel assignments. Maxim Healthcare's consultants are available 24 hours a day seven days a week to provide assistance for clients. The company which operates from more than 360 locations worldwide was established in 1988.

Operations

The company's Maxim Health Systems division established in 1996 provides immunizations health screenings and health fairs. Each year the division's immunization program is responsible for vaccinating millions of people across more than 40000 clinics.

Other major Maxim Healthcare divisions include Maxim Staffing Solutions (Nurse Allied Health Administrative Staffing) Maxim Government Services Maxim Physician Resources Timeline Recruiting Maxim Coders Maxim Pediatric Services; Logix Healthcare Search Partners and StaffAssist.

EXECUTIVES

VP and Chief Culture Officer, Timothy Kuhn
VP Human Resources, Kathleen (Kathy) Ayres
COO, Chris Powell
CFO, David (Dave) Franchak
VP and CIO, Gregory (Greg) Ericson
CEO, W. Bradley (Brad) Bennett
VP Strategy and Development, Steve Wright
President Maxim Staffing Solutions, Patrick (Pat) Lamon

VP and Chief Clinical Officer, Paula Sotir
Chief Medical Officer and Chief Quality Officer,
  W. John Langley
VP and General Counsel, Toni-Jean (TJ) Lisa
VP and Chief Compliance Officer, Jacqueline
  (Jackie) Baratian
VP Human Resources, David Sloan

LOCATIONS

HQ: Maxim Healthcare Services Inc.
  7227 Lee Deforest Dr., Columbia MD 21046
Phone: 410-910-1500   **Fax:** 410-910-1600
Web: www.maxhealth.com

PRODUCTS/OPERATIONS

Selected Services

Allied Health staffing
Facility nurse staffing
Flu and wellness services
Government services
Health information services
International nursing
Home healthcare
HME/pharmacy services
Habilitation services
Physician services
Travel nursing

Selected Divisions

CareFocus
CareFocus Companion Services
Centrus Premier Homecare
Logix Healthcare Search Partners
Maxim Coders
Maxim Government Services
Maxim Health Information Services
Maxim Health Systems
Maxim Healthcare Services (Homecare)
Maxim Home Health Resources
Maxim Pediatric Services
Maxim Physician Resources
Maxim Staffing Solutions - Administrative Staffing
Maxim Staffing Solutions - Allied Health
Maxim Staffing Solutions - Nurse Staffing
Orbis Clinical
Reflectx Services
StaffAssist
TimeLine Recruiting
TravelMax

COMPETITORS

American HomePatient   MedStaff
Apria Healthcare   PHS Correctional
Cross Country   Healthcare
  Healthcare   Team Health
Medical Staffing   TeamStaff
  Network
Medsearch Staffing
  Services

HISTORICAL FINANCIALS

Company Type: Private

Income Statement

	REVENUE ($ mil.)	NET INCOME ($ mil.)	NET PROFIT MARGIN	EMPLOYEES
12/11	1,341	(12)	—	35,000
12/10	1,390	51	3.7%	0
12/09	1,369	(62)	—	0
12/08	1,293	70	5.4%	0
Annual Growth	1.2%	—	—	—

FYE: December 31

MAXYIELD COOPERATIVE

LOCATIONS

HQ: MAXYIELD COOPERATIVE
  313 3RD AVE NW, WEST BEND, IA 50597-8572
Phone: 515-887-7211
Web: www.westbendelev.com

HISTORICAL FINANCIALS

Company Type: Private

Income Statement

FYE: July 31

	REVENUE ($ mil.)	NET INCOME ($ mil.)	NET PROFIT MARGIN	EMPLOYEES
07/12	387	6	1.8%	157
07/11	241	5	2.1%	0
07/10	242	4	1.7%	0
07/09	348	9	2.7%	0
Annual Growth	3.6%	(10.3%)	—	—

2012 Year-End Financials

Debt ratio: ——
Return on equity: 1.80%   Dividends
Cash ($ mil.): 0   Yield: —
Current ratio: 0.10   Payout: —
Long-term debt ($ mil.): —   Market value ($ mil.): —

MAYVILLE ENGINEERING CO INC

Sometimes it's all right to get loaded. Mayville Engineering Company (MEC) manufactures shotshell reloading machinery and equipment used by hunters sport shooting enthusiasts and sporting goods stores. MEC also provides coating welding riveting painting manufacturing prototyping and mechanical assembly services. Its operations are divided across five main divisions: MEC Shotshell Reloaders MEC Contract MEC Prototype/Service Phoenix Coaters and Fabricating Specialists. Overall these divisions cater to the agricultural construction military medical and industrial markets. Cousins Leo and Ted Bachhuber founded the employee-owned company in 1945 inside a rented garage in Mayville Wisconsin.

In addition to MEC's manufacturing processes its Phoenix Coaters division offers coating services which include electrocoating shot blasting alodine conversion coating and liquid painting for military and other diverse commercial applications.

The company has partnered with the National Rifle Association to provide training to NRA instructors on the operations of their MEC reloaders. Reloading is an environmentally friendly prac-

---

2011 Year-End Financials

Debt ratio: ——
Return on equity: (-0.90)%   Dividends
Cash ($ mil.): 10   Yield: —
Current ratio: 1.50   Payout: —
Long-term debt ($ mil.): —   Market value ($ mil.): —

---

tice since the hulls and brass are recycled in the process.

MEC operates through eight facilities spanning the state of Wisconsin.

EXECUTIVES

Chairman President and CEO, Robert Kamphuis
Director Sales and Marketing, Jim Sokoly
Manager Estimating, Rick Hartwig
Manager New Product Development, Tom Williams
VP Operations, Doug Smith
Director Information Services, Brian Post
VP Administration, Barry Hoops
Benefits Coordinator, Marleen Lechner
Controller, Glenn Helmbrecht

LOCATIONS

HQ: Mayville Engineering Company Inc.
  715 South St., Mayville WI 53050
Phone: 920-387-4500   **Fax:** 920-387-2682
Web: www.mayvl.com

COMPETITORS

Kuhl Machine Shop   Smith & Wesson
Kurt Manufacturing   Holding
MetoKote   Valmont Industries

HISTORICAL FINANCIALS

Company Type: Private

Income Statement

FYE: December 31

	REVENUE ($ mil.)	NET INCOME ($ mil.)	NET PROFIT MARGIN	EMPLOYEES
12/11	177	6	3.9%	1,100
12/10*	153	15	10.3%	0
03/10	131	15	11.6%	0
12/09	123	12	10.2%	0
Annual Growth	12.9%	(18.2%)	—	—

*Fiscal year change

2011 Year-End Financials

Debt ratio: ——
Return on equity: 3.90%   Dividends
Cash ($ mil.): 7   Yield: —
Current ratio: 1.20   Payout: —
Long-term debt ($ mil.): —   Market value ($ mil.): —

MBF INSPECTION SERVICES INC.

LOCATIONS

HQ: MBF INSPECTION SERVICES INC.
  805 N RICHARDSON AVE, ROSWELL, NM 88201-4920
Phone: 575-625-0599
Web: www.mbfservices.com

HISTORICAL FINANCIALS

Company Type: Private

Income Statement
FYE: December 31

	REVENUE ($ mil.)	NET INCOME ($ mil.)	NET PROFIT MARGIN	EMPLOYEES
12/11	83	2	3.1%	30
12/10	48	4	10.1%	0
12/09	45	3	8.2%	0
Annual Growth	35.8%	(17.1%)	—	—

2011 Year-End Financials

Debt ratio: ——
Return on equity: 3.10%
Cash ($ mil.): 1
Current ratio: 18.30
Long-term debt ($ mil.): —

Dividends
Yield: —
Payout: —
Market value ($ mil.): —

MC NEESE STATE UNIVERSITY

Founded in 1938 as Lake Charles Junior College McNeese State is one of eight schools in the University of Louisiana System. Its more than 8000 enrolled students can choose from approximately 75 associate bachelor master and specialist degree programs offered at colleges of business education engineering and technology liberal arts nursing and science the Division of General and Basic Studies and the Dore School of Graduate Studies. Its campus includes a 500-plus acre farm and nearly 1600 acres of donated farm property for research farming and ranching. The university is named for Louisiana educator John McNeese.

EXECUTIVES

President, Robert D. Hebert
VP Administration and Student Affairs, Kalil P. Ieyoub
Chief Information Technology Officer, Michael Graham
VP Academic Affairs and Provost, Jeanne Daboval
VP Development and Public Affairs, Richard H. Reid
VP Special Services and Equity, Rosemary Gray
VP Business Affairs, Eddie P. Meche
Director Financial Aid, Taina Savoit
Director Human Resources, Charlene Abbott
Director Career Services, Kathy E. Bond
Registrar, April Millett
Director Alumni Affairs, Joyce Patterson
Director Development Operations and Special Events, Melissa Northcutt
Director Admissions and Recruiting, Kara Smith
Director Purchasing and Property Control, Pamela L. Watkins
Comptroller, Mona White
Director Library, Debbie Johnson-Houston

LOCATIONS

HQ: McNeese State University
4205 Ryan St., Lake Charles LA 70609
Phone: 337-475-5000   **Fax:** 337-475-5938
Web: www.mcneese.edu

HISTORICAL FINANCIALS

Company Type: School

Income Statement
FYE: June 30

	REVENUE ($ mil.)	NET INCOME ($ mil.)	NET PROFIT MARGIN	EMPLOYEES
06/12	48	0	1.2%	894
06/11	47	10	21.7%	0
06/10	49	3	6.8%	0
06/09	42	(1)	—	0
Annual Growth	5.0%			

2012 Year-End Financials

Debt ratio: ——
Return on equity: 1.20%
Cash ($ mil.): 29
Current ratio: 4.50
Long-term debt ($ mil.): —

Dividends
Yield: —
Payout: —
Market value ($ mil.): —

MCCALL PATTERN COMPANY

If you've got your eye on the runway you best start from scratch with a little help from this company. The McCall Pattern Company makes sewing patterns and instructions for women's men's and children's fashions as well as accessories costumes crafts and home decor. Its patterns are sold under the brand names McCall's (contemporary) Butterick (classic) and Vogue (couture). The company produces do-it-yourself wall treatments such as wallpaper borders cutouts and murals under the Wallies brand. It publishes catalogs for the three pattern brands as well as consumer magazine Vogue Patterns. The company was founded in 1870.

EXECUTIVES

President, Robin Davies
CFO, John W. Kobiskie

LOCATIONS

HQ: The McCall Pattern Company
11 Penn Plaza, New York NY 10001
Phone: 212-465-6800   **Fax:** 212-465-6831
Web: www.mccall.com

PRODUCTS/OPERATIONS

Selected Patterns

Accessories
  Aprons
  Hats
  Purses
  Scarves
Clothing
  Bridal
  Eveningwear
  Kids
  Maternity
  Sleepwear
Crafts
  Doll clothes
  Dolls
  Holiday
Home Fashions
  Pillows
  Slipcovers

Tablecloths
Window coverings

COMPETITORS

Conso International
Dynamic Resource Group
Harris Publications
Keepsake Quilting
Kwik Sew

Leisure Arts
Martha Stewart Living
Simplicity Pattern
Taunton Press

HISTORICAL FINANCIALS

Company Type: Private

Income Statement
FYE: December 31

	REVENUE ($ mil.)	NET INCOME ($ mil.)	NET PROFIT MARGIN	EMPLOYEES
12/11	39	24	63.0%	288
Annual Growth	—	—	—	—

2011 Year-End Financials

Debt ratio: ——
Return on equity: 63.00%
Cash ($ mil.): 2
Current ratio: 0.50
Long-term debt ($ mil.): —

Dividends
Yield: —
Payout: —
Market value ($ mil.): —

MCMILLIN COMPANIES LLC

LOCATIONS

HQ: MCMILLIN COMPANIES LLC
2750 WOMBLE RD STE 200, SAN DIEGO, CA 92106-6114
Phone: 619-477-4117
Web: www.mcmillinrealty.com

HISTORICAL FINANCIALS

Company Type: Private

Income Statement
FYE: December 31

	ASSETS ($ mil.)	NET INCOME ($ mil.)	INCOME AS % OF ASSETS	EMPLOYEES
12/11	209	(17)		300
12/10	257	11	4.6%	0
12/09	331	(32)	—	0
12/08	471	(29)	—	0
Annual Growth	(23.7%)	—	—	—

2011 Year-End Financials

Debt ratio: ——
Return on equity: (-14.80)%
Cash ($ mil.): 23
Current ratio: —
Long-term debt ($ mil.): —

Dividends
Yield: —
Payout: —
Market value ($ mil.): —

MCNAUGHTON-MCKAY ELECTRIC CO.

Getting connected at work has a completely different meaning at McNaughton-McKay. Its more than 10000 customers can buy electrical supplies sensors and controls and automation and security software online or through 22 branches in five US states and a location in Germany. One of the largest employee-owned companies in the US Mc-Naughton-McKay distributes some 300 product lines from manufacturers such as Hubbell GE Brady Belden Coleman Cable Leviton Thomas & Betts Cognex Specter Instruments and Rockwell Automation. It sells to the construction commercial government and industrial automation markets.

Geographic Reach

The company has 22 locations in five US states (Georgia Ohio Michigan North Carolina and South Carolina) and a European location in Krefeld Germany.

Sales and Marketing

McNaughton-McKay's customers include supplyFORCE Vanguard National Alliance and Vantage Group.

Strategy

McNaughton-McKay —informally known as Mc-Mc —has grown by expanding its product lineup and increasing its purchasing power through buying and marketing groups such as Affiliated Distributors supplyFORCE and Vantage Group. The distributor has also added a group dedicated to green products primarily energy-efficient lighting and power distribution products along with an Engineered Solutions Group that sells and installs solar and wind energy through partnerships with companies that include Schletter and Ohio Green Wind.

Ownership

McNaughton-McKay is owned by its employees.

Company Background

Founded in 1910 the Bull and McNaughton families ran McNaughton-McKay until 2006. It established a sales office in Germany in 2004.

EXECUTIVES

President and CEO, Donald D. (Don) Slominski Jr.
VP Human Resources, Kathleen M. (Kathy) Gollin
EVP and COO, John R. (Jack) McNaughton III
EVP Sales and Marketing, Richard (Rick) Dahlstrom
Director Supplier Relations, Jeffrey W. (Jeff) Brittain
VP Information Technology, Gregory H. (Greg) Chun
VP Finance, John D. Kuczmanski
VP Operations, Scott Sellers
General Manager S&D Service & Distribution GmbH, Werber Schuepfer
Sales & Engineering S&D Service & Distribution GmbH, Matthias Kistler
General Manager Charleston SC; Fayetteville New Bern and Wilmington NC; and Savannah GA, Douglas Cooper
General Manager Charlotte and Gastonia NC and Greenville and Spartanburg SC, Christopher Majni
Operations Manager Ann Arbor MI, Glen S. Ewald
Operations Manager Flint MI, Kelly Kurtiak
Operations Manager Madison Heights MI, Marc E. Kuiper
General Manager Carrollton Cartersville Covington and Norcross GA, Bryan Hays
General Manager Columbus Defiance Findlay Hebron Mansfield and Toledo OH, William Parsons

LOCATIONS

HQ: McNaughton-McKay Electric Company
1357 E. Lincoln Ave., Madison Heights MI 48071-4134
Phone: 248-399-7500   **Fax:** 248-399-6828
Web: www.mc-mc.com

PRODUCTS/OPERATIONS

Selected Products

Bar code scanners and systems
Communication input/output (I/O) networks
Computers and peripherals
Convenience panels (cables and equipment)
Cordsets
Data-collection terminals and software
Drives and motor controllers
Engineered products
I/O products (AC/DC modules)
Motion-control products
   CNC controls
   Servos
   Spindles
Motors (AC)
PLC processors
Radio-frequency identification (RFID) products
Safety products
   Gate switches
   Light curtains
   Mats
   Relays
Sensors
Software
Vision products (inspection equipment)

COMPETITORS

Anixter International	Hite Company
Border States Electric	Kendall Electric
Central Wholesale	Madison Electric
Electrical	Medler Electric
Consolidated	OneSource Distributors
Electrical	Rexel Inc.
Crescent Electric	Steiner Electric
Supply	Stuart C. Irby
Dealers Electrical	SUMMIT Electric Supply
Electrocomponents	W.W. Grainger
Graybar Electric	WESCO International

HISTORICAL FINANCIALS

Company Type: Private

Income Statement

FYE: December 31

	REVENUE ($ mil.)	NET INCOME ($ mil.)	NET PROFIT MARGIN	EMPLOYEES
12/11	603	0	—	725
12/10	493	0	—	0
12/09	389	0	—	0
12/08	507	0	—	0
Annual Growth	5.9%	—	—	—

2011 Year-End Financials

Debt ratio: —
Return on equity: —
Cash ($ mil.): 2   Dividends
Current ratio: 1.20   Yield: —
Long-term debt ($ mil.): —   Payout: —
   Market value ($ mil.): —

MCNEEL INTERNATIONAL CORPORATION

LOCATIONS

HQ: MCNEEL INTERNATIONAL CORPORATION
5401 W KENNEDY BLVD # 751, TAMPA, FL 33609-2428
Phone: 813-286-8680
Web: www.olefinas.com

HISTORICAL FINANCIALS

Company Type: Private

Income Statement

FYE: December 31

	REVENUE ($ mil.)	NET INCOME ($ mil.)	NET PROFIT MARGIN	EMPLOYEES
12/11	133	(4)	—	500
12/10	122	(0)	—	0
12/09	100	5	5.9%	0
12/08	108	1	0.9%	0
Annual Growth	7.1%	—	—	—

2011 Year-End Financials

Debt ratio: —
Return on equity: (-3.00)%
Cash ($ mil.): 2   Dividends
Current ratio: 0.70   Yield: —
Long-term debt ($ mil.): —   Payout: —
   Market value ($ mil.): —

MCNEILUS STEEL INC.

LOCATIONS

HQ: MCNEILUS STEEL INC.
702 2ND AVE SE, DODGE CENTER, MN 55927-8903
Phone: 507-374-6336
Web: www.mcneilus.com

HISTORICAL FINANCIALS

Company Type: Private

Income Statement

FYE: September 30

	REVENUE ($ mil.)	NET INCOME ($ mil.)	NET PROFIT MARGIN	EMPLOYEES
09/11	360	22	6.3%	400
09/10	245	9	4.0%	0
09/08	323	21	6.6%	0
09/07	264	14	5.5%	0
Annual Growth	10.9%	16.5%	—	—

MCPHEE ELECTRIC LTD

McPhee Electric is energized about its work. The company which is a unit of Phalcon provides electrical construction and data and communications installation services (including cellular towers) throughout New England. Services include conceptual planning feasibility studies budgeting design development installation maintenance and service. McPhee Electric's clients come from a wide variety of industries including education financial services government health care manufacturing pharmaceuticals retail and utilities. The company's projects include utility substations Foxwoods Resort Casino a Bristol-Myers Squibb research facility and Cordon Bleu Culinary Institute.

McPhee Electric was founded by Ted McPhee Jr. in 1974. His sons continue to the lead the company which has locations in Boston and Stratford Connecticut. The company was acquired by Xcelecom in 2000 and then sold to Phalcon in early 2007. Sister companies include J.E. Richards and JBL Electric which have offices New Jersey and Maryland.

EXECUTIVES

President and CEO, Michael E. McPhee
EVP, Marcus W. McPhee
VP Construction, Ron Stawecki
Branch Manager Stratford CT, Ken Spodnik
Operations Manager Building Services, Erik Robinson
Operations Manager Communications, Brian Parent
VP Utilities, Mark Howard
Operations Manager Wireless, Doug Barker
Operations Manager Estimating, Julie Blum
Operations Manager Maintenance and Service, Chip Ware
Branch Manager Boston MA, Thomas (Tom) Lombardo
CFO, John Conroy
Operations Manager Safety, Mike Stanczyk

LOCATIONS

HQ: McPhee Electric Ltd.
505 Main St., Farmington CT 06032
Phone: 860-677-9797   **Fax:** 860-674-9385
Web: www.mcpheeusa.com

COMPETITORS

ADCO Electrical	EMCOR
Allan Electric	Nead
E-J Electric	
Installation Co.	

HISTORICAL FINANCIALS

Company Type: Private

Income Statement
FYE: December 31

	REVENUE ($ mil.)	NET INCOME ($ mil.)	NET PROFIT MARGIN	EMPLOYEES
12/11	87	9	11.0%	500
12/10	77	5	7.2%	0
12/09	63	13	21.5%	0
12/08	173	18	10.9%	0
Annual Growth	**(20.3%)**	**(20.0%)**	—	—

2011 Year-End Financials

Debt ratio: ——
Return on equity: 11.00%
Cash ($ mil.): 8
Current ratio: 0.50
Long-term debt ($ mil.): ——
Dividends
Yield: —
Payout: —
Market value ($ mil.): —

MECCA ELECTRONICS INDUSTRIES INC.

LOCATIONS

HQ: MECCA ELECTRONICS INDUSTRIES INC.
1016 44TH DR, LONG ISLAND CITY, NY 11101-7014
Phone: 718-361-9001
Web: www.meccaelect.com

HISTORICAL FINANCIALS

Company Type: Private

Income Statement
FYE: December 31

	REVENUE ($ mil.)	NET INCOME ($ mil.)	NET PROFIT MARGIN	EMPLOYEES
12/11	207	7	3.4%	25
12/10	223	8	3.6%	0
12/09	228	7	3.5%	0
12/08	272	12	4.6%	0
Annual Growth	**(8.8%)**	**(17.3%)**	—	—

2011 Year-End Financials

Debt ratio: ——
Return on equity: 3.40%
Cash ($ mil.): 21
Current ratio: 1.20
Long-term debt ($ mil.): ——
Dividends
Yield: —
Payout: —
Market value ($ mil.): —

MEDAILLE COLLEGE

Medaille College is a private liberal arts college in Buffalo New York that provides career-oriented education. It also has branch campuses in Amherst and Rochester. With a student enrollment of nearly 3000 the school offers bachelor's master's and associate degrees in a range of subjects through day evening and weekend programs. Medaille traces its roots to 1875 when it was founded by the Sisters of St. Joseph as an institute to educate teachers. In 1937 the institute received a charter from New York State and was named Mount St. Joseph Teachers College. The school expanded its mission and earned its current name in 1968.

EXECUTIVES

Director Human Resources, Barbara J. Bilotta
VP Student Affairs, Holly J. McCarthy
Director Campus Public Safety, Ronald J. Christopher
Director Career Planning and Placement, Carol Cullinan
Director Alumni Affairs and Athletic Fundraising, Keith Koch
VP Academic Affairs, Douglas W. Howard
President and CEO, Richard T. Jurasek
Interim VP Business and Finance, Matthew J. Carver
CIO, Cheryl J. Thompson
Director Financial Aid, Catherine Buzanski
Registrar, Kathleen Lazar

LOCATIONS

HQ: Medaille College
18 Agassiz Cir., Buffalo NY 14214
Phone: 716-880-2000   **Fax:** 716-884-0291
Web: www.medaille.edu

HISTORICAL FINANCIALS

Company Type: School

Income Statement
FYE: June 30

	REVENUE ($ mil.)	NET INCOME ($ mil.)	NET PROFIT MARGIN	EMPLOYEES
06/12	41	1	4.0%	693
06/11	41	2	6.6%	0
06/10	43	5	11.7%	0
06/09	42	3	7.3%	0
Annual Growth	**(0.7%)**	**(18.9%)**	—	—

2012 Year-End Financials

Debt ratio: ——
Return on equity: 4.00%
Cash ($ mil.): 10
Current ratio: ——
Long-term debt ($ mil.): ——
Dividends
Yield: —
Payout: —
Market value ($ mil.): ——

MEDICAL INFORMATION TECHNOLOGY INC.

Medical Information Technology knows what to prescribe for the operational disorders of health care information systems. The company which does business as MEDITECH provides software used mainly by hospitals in the management of clinical and financial departments ambulatory care centers long-term care facilities nursing homes and home health care programs. Its applications include products tailored for patient identification and scheduling care management clinical data management long-term and ambulatory care behavioral health and financial and reimbursement management. The company's core market is the US but Canada accounts for nearly 10% of sales.

After a 1% dip in revenues in 2009 MEDITECH has seen double digit sales growth each year since. Although product revenues have outpaced service revenues replacing it as the larger segment in 2011 both have grown since 2009. The sales increases have come through both existing and new customers. Net income has likewise rebounded after its own more severe 60% drop in 2009. Positive year-end balance sheet metrics include nearly $340 million in cash equivalents and marketable securities as well as having no long term debt.

In 2011 MEDITECH acquired partner LSS Data Systems a provider of ambulatory information systems applications for physicians. Based in a suburb of Minneapolis LSS expands MEDITECH's expertise beyond the acute home and continuing care products enhancing its ability to offer a cohesive interoperable set of hospital information system software.

The company continues to focus strictly on software only offering suggestions on the hardware side as to configuration and vendors. Among vendors that have designed products to work with MEDITECH software are Dell and VMware. It sells its software through a regionally-based direct sales staff. MEDITECH customers have included Johns

Hopkins Bayview Medical Center Poudre Valley Health System SISU Medical Systems and White River Health System.

Founder chairman and CEO Neil Pappalardo controls nearly 39% of the company's shares which includes the roughly 13% stake held by MEDITECH Profit Sharing Trust of which he is the sole trustee. Director Morton Ruderman a co-founder owns more than 12% of the company.

Founded in 1969 MEDITECH has several offices in Massachusetts one in Atlanta and after the acquisition of LSS two near Minneapolis.

EXECUTIVES

Chairman, A. Neil Pappalardo, age 69, $360,000 total compensation

Vice Chairman, Lawrence A. (Larry) Polimeno, age 70, $180,000 total compensation

President and CEO, Howard Messing, age 59, $264,000 total compensation

CFO Treasurer and Clerk, Barbara A. Manzolillo, age 59, $228,000 total compensation

SVP Product Development, Robert G. Gale, age 65

VP Technology, Christopher (Chris) Anschuetz, age 59

VP Implementation, Steven B. (Steve) Koretz, age 60

SVP Client Services, Joanne Wood, age 58

VP Sales, Stuart N. (Stu) Lefthes, age 59, $216,000 total compensation

VP Marketing, Hoda Sayed-Friel, age 54

Marketing and Public Relations, Paul Berthiaume

VP Product Development, Michelle O'Connor, age 46

VP Client Services, Leah Farina

Director, Louis P. (Dan) Valente, age 81

Director, Edward B. (Ed) Roberts, age 76

Vice Chairman, Lawrence A. (Larry) Polimeno, age 70

Director, Roland L. Driscoll, age 83

Director, Morton E. Ruderman, age 75

Auditors: Ernst&YoungLLP

LOCATIONS

HQ: Medical Information Technology Inc.
MEDITECH Circle, Westwood MA 02090
Phone: 781-821-3000   **Fax:** 781-821-2199
Web: www.meditech.com

2011 Sales

	$ mil.	% of total
% of total		
US		90
Canada		8
Other		2
Total		**100**

PRODUCTS/OPERATIONS

2011 Sales

	$ mil.	% of total
Product	288	53
Service	256	47
Total	**545**	**100**

Selected Software Products

Ambulatory care applications
  Emergency department management
  Prescription management
Behavioral health applications
Clinical applications
  Anatomical pathology
  Blood bank
  Imaging and therapeutic services
  Laboratory
  Microbiology
  Pharmacy
Decision support applications

Budgeting and forecasting
Cost accounting
Data archiving
Data repository
Executive support system
Faxing
Integrated communication system
Financial management applications
  Accounts payable
  Fixed assets
  General ledger
  Materials management
  Payroll/personnel
  Staffing and scheduling
Long-term care information system
Patient care management applications
  Patient care system
  Patient education suite
  Physician care manager
  Physician practice management
Patient identification and scheduling applications
  Case mix management
  Community-wide scheduling
  Enterprise patient index and medical records
  Operating room management
  Registration
Reimbursement applications
  Authorization and referral management
  Billing/accounts receivable

COMPETITORS

3M HIS	McKesson
Allscripts	MedAssets
Alteer	Mediware
Cerner	MedPlus
CPSI	Misys
Epic Systems	QuadraMed
GE Healthcare	Quality Systems
Health Management	Siemens Healthcare
Systems	TriZetto
iSOFT Group	

HISTORICAL FINANCIALS

Company Type: Private

Income Statement

FYE: September 30

	REVENUE ($ mil.)	NET INCOME ($ mil.)	NET PROFIT MARGIN	EMPLOYEES
09/12*	446	98	22.0%	3,845
12/11	545	124	22.7%	0
12/10	459	108	23.7%	0
12/09	393	81	20.8%	0
Annual Growth	**4.4%**	**6.4%**	**—**	**—**

*Fiscal year change

2012 Year-End Financials

Debt ratio: ——
Return on equity: 22.00%
Cash ($ mil.): 43
Current ratio: 1.30
Long-term debt ($ mil.): —

Dividends
  Yield: —
  Payout: —
  Market value ($ mil.): —

MEDICAL TEAMS INTERNATIONAL

LOCATIONS

HQ: MEDICAL TEAMS INTERNATIONAL
  14150 SW MILTON CT, TIGARD, OR 97224-8024
Phone: 503-624-1000
Web: www.disasterteams.net

HISTORICAL FINANCIALS

Company Type: Private

Income Statement

FYE: June 30

	REVENUE ($ mil.)	NET INCOME ($ mil.)	NET PROFIT MARGIN	EMPLOYEES
06/12	154	(2)	—	91
06/11	146	0	0.1%	0
06/10	211	4	2.2%	0
06/09	138	(6)	—	0
Annual Growth	**3.5%**	**—**	**—**	**—**

2012 Year-End Financials

Debt ratio: ——
Return on equity: (-1.60)%
Cash ($ mil.): 0
Current ratio: 0.70
Long-term debt ($ mil.): —

Dividends
  Yield: —
  Payout: —
  Market value ($ mil.): —

MEDICALODGES INC.

LOCATIONS

HQ: MEDICALODGES INC.
  201 W 8TH ST, COFFEYVILLE, KS 67337-5807
Phone: 620-251-6700
Web: www.medicalodges.com

HISTORICAL FINANCIALS

Company Type: Private

Income Statement

FYE: October 31

	REVENUE ($ mil.)	NET INCOME ($ mil.)	NET PROFIT MARGIN	EMPLOYEES
10/11	99	7	7.3%	2,500
10/10	91	3	4.1%	0
10/09	91	1	1.8%	0
10/08	102	(0)	—	0
Annual Growth	**(0.9%)**	**—**	**—**	**—**

2011 Year-End Financials

Debt ratio: ——
Return on equity: 7.30%
Cash ($ mil.): 17
Current ratio: 2.00
Long-term debt ($ mil.): —

Dividends
  Yield: —
  Payout: —
  Market value ($ mil.): —

MEDLER ELECTRIC COMPANY

No meddlers here; this company just wants to help customers. Medler Electric Company is a distributor of electrical parts and supplies; it gets the majority of its business from companies in the construction market. Medler Electric carries products (ranging from motors and heaters to lighting and much more) from such manufacturers as 3M Cooper Lighting Daniel Woodhead Ferraz Shawmut Littelfuse and Square D Company. The employee-owned company was established in 1918 by W. W. Medler and operates through 14 branch offices in the state of Michigan.

EXECUTIVES

President, Ron Heine
Purchasing Manager, Bob Mead
IT and Operations Manager, Jeremy Hamlin
Controller, Doug Dietlein
VP Inside Sales, Dave Gott
VP Central Quotes, Chuck McPhall
Human Resources Manager, Dave Simon
VP Sales, Kelly Vliet
ISO Manager, Doug Duffy

LOCATIONS

HQ: Medler Electric Company
2155 Redman Dr., Alma MI 48801
Phone: 989-463-3308 **Fax:** 989-463-4522
Web: www.medlerelectric.com

COMPETITORS

Kendall Electric
Madison Electric
McNaughton-McKay
Standard Electric

Utility Supply and Construction
Werner Electric Supply

HISTORICAL FINANCIALS

Company Type: Private

Income Statement

FYE: December 31

	REVENUE ($ mil.)	NET INCOME ($ mil.)	NET PROFIT MARGIN	EMPLOYEES
12/11	37	0	0.1%	111
12/10	34	0	0.2%	0
12/09	29	(0)	—	0
12/08	36	0	0.1%	0
Annual Growth	1.4%	(26.3%)	—	—

2011 Year-End Financials

Debt ratio: —
Return on equity: 0.10%
Cash ($ mil.): 0
Current ratio: 1.10
Long-term debt ($ mil.): —

Dividends
Yield: —
Payout: —
Market value ($ mil.): —

MEDSTAR FRANKLIN SQUARE MEDICAL CENTER INC

Franklin Square Hospital Center has made a declaration to care for the residents of eastern Baltimore County Maryland. The facility offers a wide range of specialties through some 700 doctors and about 375 beds. Since 1998 the hospital has been part of MedStar Health the region's largest integrated health system. As a teaching hospital Franklin Square offers a number of residency programs including internal and family medicine OB-GYN and surgery. The not-for-profit hospital's medical services are provided via six primary service lines: Medicine Surgery Women's and Children's Care Oncology Behavioral Health and Community Health and Wellness.

Geographic Reach

The only one of its kind in the region Franklin Square's Cancer Institute serves oncology patients by offering education and prevention services research and diagnostic treatment.

Strategy

The hospital which logs one of the highest numbers of cancer admissions in Maryland is working to expand its cancer services as it anticipates admissions to grow.

In fact the company is expanding other services as well also in anticipation of future patient demand. The hospital built a 300-bed patient tower on the campus which opened in 2010. Components of the new tower include an expanded emergency department dedicated pediatric and inpatient suites and an expanded 50-bed critical care unit.

EXECUTIVES

President and Director, Carl J. Schindelar
SVP Operations, Glenn A. Visbeen
CFO, Bob Lally
Director Planning, Eric Slechter
VP Development and Community Relations, Janet Rafky
Assistant VP Public Relations Marketing and Community Affairs, Trina Adams
VP Medical Affairs, Anthony Sclama
VP Human Resources, Karen Robertson-Keck
VP Patient Care and Chief Nursing Officer, Larry Strassner
Chairman, G. Scott Barhight
Vice Chairman, Debra B. Doyle
Chief Pathology and Laboratory Medicine, Jerry J. Marty
Secretary and Treasurer, Vincent Martorana
President and Director, Carl J. Schindelar
Director, John Gontrum
Vice Chairman, Debra B. Doyle
Director, Hatem Abdo
Director, Khalid Al-Talib
Director, Michael Dietrich
Director, John B. Franzone
Director, George J. Jabaji
Director, Patricia Norman
Director, Alexander (Bob) Page III
Director, Dennis F. Rasmussen
Director, Richard W. Single Sr.
Director, Michael D. Suter
Director, Deborah M. Turner
Director, Kenneth A. Samet, age 54

LOCATIONS

HQ: Franklin Square Hospital Center
9000 Franklin Square Dr., Baltimore MD 21237-3998
Phone: 443-777-7000 **Fax:** 443-777-7910
Web: www.franklinsquare.org

COMPETITORS

Anne Arundel Medical Center
Bon Secours Health
GBMC
Good Samaritan Hospital of Maryland
Harbor Hospital
Johns Hopkins Bayview Medical Center
Johns Hopkins Health System
Johns Hopkins Medicine

LifeBridge Health
Sinai Hospital of Baltimore
St. Agnes HealthCare
St. Joseph Medical Center
Union Memorial Hospital
University of Maryland Medical System
Upper Chesapeake Health

HISTORICAL FINANCIALS

Company Type: Subsidiary

Income Statement

FYE: June 30

	REVENUE ($ mil.)	NET INCOME ($ mil.)	NET PROFIT MARGIN	EMPLOYEES
06/11	452	18	4.0%	3,019
06/10*	439	31	7.1%	0
04/09	0	0	—	0
06/08	1	0	34.2%	0
Annual Growth	512.4%	199.3%	—	—

*Fiscal year change

2011 Year-End Financials

Debt ratio: —
Return on equity: 4.00%
Cash ($ mil.): 0
Current ratio: 1.50
Long-term debt ($ mil.): —

Dividends
Yield: —
Payout: —
Market value ($ mil.): —

MEHARRY MEDICAL COLLEGE

LOCATIONS

HQ: MEHARRY MEDICAL COLLEGE
1005 DR DB TODD JR BLVD, NASHVILLE, TN 37208-3501
Phone: 615-327-6111

HISTORICAL FINANCIALS

Company Type: Private

Income Statement

FYE: June 30

	REVENUE ($ mil.)	NET INCOME ($ mil.)	NET PROFIT MARGIN	EMPLOYEES
06/12	139	12	9.1%	1,100
06/11	161	22	14.0%	0
06/10	152	16	11.0%	0
06/09	127	0	—	0
Annual Growth	3.1%	—	—	—

2012 Year-End Financials

Debt ratio: —
Return on equity: 9.10%
Cash ($ mil.): 18
Current ratio: —
Long-term debt ($ mil.): —

Dividends
Yield: —
Payout: —
Market value ($ mil.): —

MEIER OIL SERVICE INC.

LOCATIONS

HQ: MEIER OIL SERVICE INC.
405 N SECOND ST, ASHKUM, IL 60911-6033
Phone: 815-698-2343
Web: www.meieroil.com

HISTORICAL FINANCIALS

Company Type: Private

Income Statement

FYE: July 31

	REVENUE ($ mil.)	NET INCOME ($ mil.)	NET PROFIT MARGIN	EMPLOYEES
07/12	139	0	0.3%	30
07/11	111	0	0.5%	0
07/10	84	0	0.3%	0
07/09	86	(0)	—	0
Annual Growth	17.5%	—	—	—

2012 Year-End Financials

Debt ratio: —
Return on equity: 0.30%
Cash ($ mil.): 0
Current ratio: 0.50
Long-term debt ($ mil.): —

Dividends
Yield: —
Payout: —
Market value ($ mil.): —

MEMORIAL HEALTH SERVICES CORPORATION

Where do you go after you get sick riding the tea cups at Disneyland? Not-for-profit Memorial Health Services (MHS) owns hospitals in Southern California including Long Beach Memorial Medical Center Miller Children's Hospital Orange Coast Memorial Medical Center and Saddleback Memorial Medical Center. The facilities have a total of more than 1300 beds and offer a full spectrum of medical services including rehabilitation diagnostic/radiology and emergency services. MHS also operates women's health facilities and other specialty and general practice clinics as well as home health and hospice programs. The organization was founded in 1907.

MHS is joining the growing trend of hospitals partnering with retailers to open in-store retail clinics that offer basic after-hours medical care through physicians and nurse practitioners. MHS intends to open a range of MemorialCare clinics throughout its service area and is up to more than a dozen as of early 2012.

MHS has been chosen to participate in the Western Health Information Network that will connect a minimum of 10 Los Angeles County community clinics to an existing health information exchange network.The network is expected to cover more than 120000 patients and 4000 hospital beds. Participating clinics will have access to network members' patient data including admission diagnosis treatment medication physician notes demographic information. and laboratory results. The idea behind sharing such data is to help improve quality of care reduce duplication of tests and services and help providers become more comfortable using the technology that will inevitably be used in the majority of the nation's hospitals.

The network is also expanding to meet continued demand throughout its service area. It has several projects either going on or recently completed that have added operating rooms neonatal beds more advanced technology and centers of excellence in imaging cardiac cancer and obesity at several of its hospitals.

MemorialCare spent the past few years hard at work implementing inpatient and outpatient electronic medical record systems that seamlessly connect its hospitals' patient data. With the launch of MemorialCare's EMR system Epic at Orange Coast Memorial in 2010 all major MemorialCare sites are successfully deployed; making the health system available for certain financial incentives from the government.

EXECUTIVES

President and CEO, Barry Arbuckle
CFO, Rick Graniere
CIO, Scott Joslyn
Interim CEO Anaheim Memorial Medical Center, Bryon Schweigert
CEO Saddleback Memorial Medical Center, Steve Geidt
CEO Orange Coast Memorial Medical Center, Marcia Manker
CEO Long Beach Memorial Community Hospital Long Beach and Miller Children?s Hospital Long Beach, Diana Hendel
EVP and COO, Tammie McMann Brailsford
Media Contact, Rhoda Weiss
Chair, Barbara Enlow
Chairman, Keith Nelson
Director, Anthony J. Abbate
Director, Barry Arbuckle
Director, Rakesh Bhola
Director, Thomas Collins
Director, Santos Cortez
Director, Chris Downey
Director, Barbara Enlow
Director, Eric Feldman
Director, Robert Hernandez
Director, Peter Knudson
Director, David Lagrew Jr.
Director, Larry Lambert
Director, Susan Melvin
Director, Keith Nelson
Director, Tom Rogers
Director, Haydee V. Tillotson

LOCATIONS

HQ: Memorial Health Services
17360 Brookhurst St., Fountain Valley CA 92708
Phone: 714-377-2900 **Fax:** 954-355-4966
Web: www.browardhealth.org

Selected Facilities

Long Beach Memorial (Long Beach California)
Miller Children's Hospital (Long Beach California)
Community Hospital (Long Beach California)

Orange Coast Memorial (Fountain Valley California)
Saddleback Memorial (San Clemente California)
Saddleback Memorial (Laguna Hills California)
MemorialCare Medical Group (Regional)
MemorialCare HealthExpress (Regional)
MemorialCare Imaging Centers (Regional)
Laboratories (Regional)

COMPETITORS

Adventist Health
Cedars-Sinai Medical Center
Childrens Hospital Los Angeles
Community Health Systems
Dignity Health
Good Samaritan Hospital (IN)
Good Samaritan Hospital (Los Angeles)
HCA
HealthCare Partners
Hollywood Presbyterian Medical Center
Kaiser Permanente
LifePoint Hospitals
Los Angeles County Health Department
Methodist Hospital of Southern California
Pasadena Hospital Association
Prospect Medical
Providence Health & Services
St. Joseph Health System
St. Jude Medical Center
Sutter Health
Tenet Healthcare
Trinity Health (Novi)
Western Medical Center - Santa Ana

HISTORICAL FINANCIALS

Company Type: Private - Not-for-Profit

Income Statement

FYE: June 30

	REVENUE ($ mil.)	NET INCOME ($ mil.)	NET PROFIT MARGIN	EMPLOYEES
06/11	1,788	334	18.7%	2,000
06/10	113	6	5.4%	0
06/09	90	0	—	0
06/08	88	5	5.7%	0
Annual Growth	172.4%	305.6%	—	—

2011 Year-End Financials

Debt ratio: —
Return on equity: 18.70%
Cash ($ mil.): 150
Current ratio: 1.00
Long-term debt ($ mil.): —

Dividends
Yield: —
Payout: —
Market value ($ mil.): —

MEMORIAL HOSPITAL CORP

LOCATIONS

HQ: MEMORIAL HOSPITAL CORP
718 N MACOMB ST, MONROE, MI 48162-7815
Phone: 734-240-8400
Web: www.mercymemorial.org

HISTORICAL FINANCIALS
Company Type: Private

Income Statement
FYE: June 30

	REVENUE ($ mil.)	NET INCOME ($ mil.)	NET PROFIT MARGIN	EMPLOYEES
06/12	171	(11)		1,300
06/11	180	20	11.5%	0
06/10	182	21	11.9%	0
06/08	149	(4)		0
Annual Growth	4.6%	—	—	—

2012 Year-End Financials

Debt ratio: ——
Return on equity: (-6.80)%
Cash ($ mil.): 12
Current ratio: 1.40
Long-term debt ($ mil.): —

Dividends
Yield: —
Payout: —
Market value ($ mil.): —

HISTORICAL FINANCIALS
Company Type: Private

Income Statement
FYE: December 31

	REVENUE ($ mil.)	NET INCOME ($ mil.)	NET PROFIT MARGIN	EMPLOYEES
12/11	142	3	2.7%	800
12/10	63	1	2.7%	0
12/09	61	2	4.0%	0
12/08	60	2	3.8%	0
Annual Growth	33.2%	18.9%	—	—

2011 Year-End Financials

Debt ratio: ——
Return on equity: 2.70%
Cash ($ mil.): 29
Current ratio: 4.30
Long-term debt ($ mil.): —

Dividends
Yield: —
Payout: —
Market value ($ mil.): —

MERCHANTS GROCERY COMPANY INCORPORATED

LOCATIONS

HQ: MERCHANTS GROCERY COMPANY INCORPORATED
800 MADDOX DR, CULPEPER, VA 22701-4156
Phone: 540-825-0786
Web: www.merchants-grocery.com

HISTORICAL FINANCIALS
Company Type: Private

Income Statement
FYE: July 31

	REVENUE ($ mil.)	NET INCOME ($ mil.)	NET PROFIT MARGIN	EMPLOYEES
07/12	131	0	0.6%	135
07/11	125	1	1.0%	0
07/10	132	1	1.5%	0
07/09	130	1	1.0%	0
Annual Growth	0.3%	(16.3%)	—	—

2012 Year-End Financials

Debt ratio: ——
Return on equity: 0.60%
Cash ($ mil.): 0
Current ratio: 1.40
Long-term debt ($ mil.): —

Dividends
Yield: —
Payout: —
Market value ($ mil.): —

MEMORIAL HOSPITAL OF SOUTH BEND INC

LOCATIONS

HQ: MEMORIAL HOSPITAL OF SOUTH BEND INC
615 N MICHIGAN ST, SOUTH BEND, IN 46601-1087
Phone: 574-647-1000

HISTORICAL FINANCIALS
Company Type: Private

Income Statement
FYE: December 31

	REVENUE ($ mil.)	NET INCOME ($ mil.)	NET PROFIT MARGIN	EMPLOYEES
12/11	374	29	7.8%	3,700
12/09	418	67	16.0%	0
12/07	368	13	3.8%	0
12/06	348	46	13.5%	0
Annual Growth	2.4%	(14.6%)	—	—

2011 Year-End Financials

Debt ratio: ——
Return on equity: 7.80%
Cash ($ mil.): 47
Current ratio: 2.40
Long-term debt ($ mil.): —

Dividends
Yield: —
Payout: —
Market value ($ mil.): —

MENNONITE GENERAL HOSPITAL INC

LOCATIONS

HQ: MENNONITE GENERAL HOSPITAL INC
CARR 14 KM 131 SCTOR LMAS ST CA, CAYEY, PR 00737
Phone: 787-535-1001
Web: www.hospitalmenonita.com

HISTORICAL FINANCIALS
Company Type: Private

Income Statement
FYE: March 31

	REVENUE ($ mil.)	NET INCOME ($ mil.)	NET PROFIT MARGIN	EMPLOYEES
03/11	157	12	8.1%	1,172
03/10	147	7	4.8%	0
03/09	153	6	4.0%	0
03/06	109	4	4.0%	0
Annual Growth	13.0%	42.5%	—	—

2011 Year-End Financials

Debt ratio: ——
Return on equity: 8.10%
Cash ($ mil.): 19
Current ratio: 3.60
Long-term debt ($ mil.): —

Dividends
Yield: —
Payout: —
Market value ($ mil.): —

MERCY HEALTH CENTER INC.

LOCATIONS

HQ: MERCY HEALTH CENTER INC.
4300 W MEMORIAL RD, OKLAHOMA CITY, OK 73120-8362
Phone: 405-755-1515
Web: www.lovecountyems.com

HISTORICAL FINANCIALS
Company Type: Private

Income Statement
FYE: June 30

	REVENUE ($ mil.)	NET INCOME ($ mil.)	NET PROFIT MARGIN	EMPLOYEES
06/11	337	22	6.7%	2,300
06/10	312	16	5.2%	0
06/09	287	7	2.7%	0
06/08	1	0	34.7%	0
Annual Growth	453.4%	219.1%	—	—

2011 Year-End Financials

Debt ratio: ——
Return on equity: 6.70%
Cash ($ mil.): 22
Current ratio: 3.00
Long-term debt ($ mil.): —

Dividends
Yield: —
Payout: —
Market value ($ mil.): —

MEMORIAL HOSPITAL OF UNION COUNTY

LOCATIONS

HQ: MEMORIAL HOSPITAL OF UNION COUNTY
500 LONDON AVE, MARYSVILLE, OH 43040-1594
Phone: 937-644-6115
Web: www.johnrevans.com

MERCY HOSPITAL AND MEDICAL CENTER

Chicagoans in the loop know Mercy Hospital and Medical Center is the place to go for health care. The Catholic hospital located near Chicago's Loop (the historic downtown commercial district) has about 485 beds and operates a network of community clinics and occupational health facilities providing employment-related services such as drug screening executive physicals and physical therapy. Other services include a cancer treatment center an inpatient hospice care unit an eye care center and inpatient and outpatient chemical dependence recovery programs.

Operations

The hospital's two on-site clinics the Doctors Office Center and the Mercy Family Health Center get about 65000 patient visits each year in every major specialty. Mercy's satellite clinics located throughout the Chicago area see upwards of 100000 patient visits a year. Mercy plans to expand its critical care unit and gastrointestinal laboratory suites to accommodate increased patient demand.

Strategy

Mercy Hospital and Medical Center has agreed to consider affiliation with Trinity Health. The two organizations began a relationship in 2009 when Mercy joined Trinity's group purchasing organization and began receiving information services support.

Company Background

The hospital became Chicago's first chartered health care facility when it opened in 1852.

EXECUTIVES

President CEO and Director, Sister Sheila Lyne
Director Materials Management, John Scalfani
COO, Rick Cerceo
CFO, Tom Garvey
VP Business Development, Barbara Townsend
VP Spirituality and Mission, Rev Martin Hebda
VP Human Resources and Risk Management, Nancy Hill
VP Public Relations and Marketing, Constance (Connie) Murphy
Vice Chair and Secretary, Susan G. Gallagher
Chief Nursing Officer, Jill Roemer
Chief Medical Officer, Warren Furey
Chairman, John McCarthy
Treasurer, Joe Reger
Secretary and Director, William A. Brown
Administration and Director, Sister Lenore Mulvihill
Program Director Department of Internal Medicine and Director, Steven Potts
Treasurer and Director, Raymond J. Spaeth II
Department of Neonatology and Director, Rohitkumar Vasa
Chief Nursing Officer, Carla Campbell
President Medical Staff, Pierre Noisette
President CEO and Director, Sister Sheila Lyne
Vice Chair and Secretary, Susan G. Gallagher
Secretary and Director, William A. Brown
Director, William Kressee
Director, James J. McDonough
Administration and Director, Sister Lenore Mulvihill
Director, Michelle Murphy
Director, Langdon Neal
Director, D. Dirk Nelson
Program Director Department of Internal Medicine and Director, Steven Potts
Director, Sister Betty Smith
Treasurer and Director, Raymond J. Spaeth II

Department of Neonatology and Director, Rohitkumar Vasa
Director, Gavin Weir
Auditors: Ernst&YoungLLP

LOCATIONS

HQ: Mercy Hospital and Medical Center
2525 S. Michigan Ave., Chicago IL 60616-2477
Phone: 312-567-2000   **Fax:** 312-567-5562
Web: www.mercy-chicago.org

PRODUCTS/OPERATIONS

Selected specialty care centers
ADDP-Behavioral Health
Diagnostic Imaging/Radiology
Dizziness & Balance Center
Eye Center
Family Health Center
Gastroenterology
Laboratory & Pathology
Lap-Band Program
Occupational Health
Pain Management
Pediatric
Pre-Birth Center
Sleep Center
Urinary Health
Vitas Hospice
Wound Management

COMPETITORS

Covenant Ministries
MacNeal Hospital
NorthShore University HealthSystem
Northwestern Memorial HealthCare
Rush System for Health
Silver Cross Hospital
Sinai Health System
St. Bernard Hospital and Health Care Center
Swedish Covenant
SwedishAmerican Health System
University of Chicago Medical Center
Weiss Memorial Hospital

HISTORICAL FINANCIALS

Company Type: Private - Not-for-Profit

Income Statement

FYE: June 30

	REVENUE ($ mil.)	NET INCOME ($ mil.)	NET PROFIT MARGIN	EMPLOYEES
06/11	257	13	5.2%	1,550
06/10	250	9	3.6%	0
06/09	235	2	1.1%	0
06/08	2	0	29.7%	0
Annual Growth	**353.8%**	**154.5%**	—	—

2011 Year-End Financials

Debt ratio: ——
Return on equity: 5.20%
Cash ($ mil.): 30
Current ratio: 2.00
Long-term debt ($ mil.): —

Dividends
  Yield: —
  Payout: —
  Market value ($ mil.): —

MERCY HOSPITAL SPRINGFIELD

Mercy Hospital Springfield (formerly St. John's Regional Health Center) is an 890-bed acute-care hospital in the Mercy Health system (formerly the Sisters of Mercy Health System). The facility provides health care to Southwest Missouri and Northwest Arkansas and includes the Mercy Children's Hospital Springfield. Other hospital specialties include cardiology and stroke care as well as women's and seniors' health cancer emergency trauma neuroscience rehabilitation and sports medicine. In addition to its hospital in Springfield Mercy Hospital Springfield operates a number of community clinics and specialty care centers in the area.

EXECUTIVES

CEO St. John's Health System, Kim Day
VP Information Systems, Mark Pasquale
COO, Michele Schaefer

LOCATIONS

HQ: Mercy Hospital Springfield
1235 E. Cherokee St., Springfield MO 65804-2203
Phone: 417-820-2000   **Fax:** 417-820-7780
Web: www.stjohns.com

COMPETITORS

Allina Hospitals	Heartland Health
Ascension Health	Liberty Hospital
Baxter Regional Medical Center	OhioHealth
	Tenet Healthcare
Boone Hospital Center	UC Health
Catholic Health Initiatives	Universal Health Services
Christian Hospital	

HISTORICAL FINANCIALS

Company Type: Business Segment

Income Statement

FYE: June 30

	REVENUE ($ mil.)	NET INCOME ($ mil.)	NET PROFIT MARGIN	EMPLOYEES
06/11	880	86	9.8%	4,400
06/10	68	5	8.1%	0
06/09	644	98	15.3%	0
06/08	387	0	—	0
Annual Growth	**31.5%**	—	—	—

2011 Year-End Financials

Debt ratio: ——
Return on equity: 9.80%
Cash ($ mil.): 19
Current ratio: 1.10
Long-term debt ($ mil.): —

Dividends
  Yield: —
  Payout: —
  Market value ($ mil.): —

MERCY HOUSING INC.

LOCATIONS

HQ: MERCY HOUSING INC.
1999 BROADWAY STE 1000, DENVER, CO 80202-5704
Phone: 303-830-3300
Web: www.mercyhousing.org

HISTORICAL FINANCIALS
Company Type: Private

Income Statement — FYE: December 31

	REVENUE ($ mil.)	NET INCOME ($ mil.)	NET PROFIT MARGIN	EMPLOYEES
12/11	172	(42)	—	1,200
12/10	345	4	1.4%	0
12/09	0	(0)	—	0
12/08	332	(3)	—	0
Annual Growth	(19.6%)	—	—	—

2011 Year-End Financials

Debt ratio: —
Return on equity: (-24.80)%
Cash ($ mil.): 31
Current ratio: 0.30
Long-term debt ($ mil.): —

Dividends
Yield: —
Payout: —
Market value ($ mil.): —

MERCY MEDICAL CENTER - CLINTON INC.

LOCATIONS

HQ: MERCY MEDICAL CENTER - CLINTON INC.
1410 N 4TH ST, CLINTON, IA 52732-2940
Phone: 563-244-5555
Web: www.mercysiouxcity.com

HISTORICAL FINANCIALS
Company Type: Private

Income Statement — FYE: June 30

	REVENUE ($ mil.)	NET INCOME ($ mil.)	NET PROFIT MARGIN	EMPLOYEES
06/11	101	15	15.3%	1,057
06/10	95	6	6.6%	0
06/09	83	(6)	—	0
06/08	88	5	5.9%	0
Annual Growth	4.7%	43.6%	—	—

2011 Year-End Financials

Debt ratio: —
Return on equity: 15.30%
Cash ($ mil.): 1
Current ratio: 0.40
Long-term debt ($ mil.): —

Dividends
Yield: —
Payout: —
Market value ($ mil.): —

MERCY MEDICAL CENTER INC.

LOCATIONS

HQ: MERCY MEDICAL CENTER INC.
301 SAINT PAUL PL, BALTIMORE, MD 21202-2165
Phone: 410-332-9000
Web: www.overleadocs.com

HISTORICAL FINANCIALS
Company Type: Private

Income Statement — FYE: June 30

	REVENUE ($ mil.)	NET INCOME ($ mil.)	NET PROFIT MARGIN	EMPLOYEES
06/11	413	22	5.5%	2,139
06/10	387	36	9.3%	0
06/09	374	0	—	0
06/08	355	31	8.9%	0
Annual Growth	5.2%	(10.5%)	—	—

2011 Year-End Financials

Debt ratio: —
Return on equity: 5.50%
Cash ($ mil.): 68
Current ratio: 1.60
Long-term debt ($ mil.): —

Dividends
Yield: —
Payout: —
Market value ($ mil.): —

MERCYHURST UNIVERSITY

LOCATIONS

HQ: MERCYHURST UNIVERSITY
501 E 38TH ST, ERIE, PA 16546-0002
Phone: 814-824-2000
Web: www.mercyhurst.edu

HISTORICAL FINANCIALS
Company Type: Private

Income Statement — FYE: May 31

	REVENUE ($ mil.)	NET INCOME ($ mil.)	NET PROFIT MARGIN	EMPLOYEES
05/12	86	3	4.4%	615
05/11*	81	10	13.5%	0
06/10	79	5	6.9%	0
06/09	69	(0)	—	0
Annual Growth	7.8%	—	—	—

*Fiscal year change

2012 Year-End Financials

Debt ratio: —
Return on equity: 4.40%
Cash ($ mil.): 14
Current ratio: —
Long-term debt ($ mil.): —

Dividends
Yield: —
Payout: —
Market value ($ mil.): —

MERRICK & COMPANY

LOCATIONS

HQ: MERRICK & COMPANY
2450 S PEORIA ST STE 125, AURORA, CO 80014-5472
Phone: 303-751-0741
Web: www.merrick.com

HISTORICAL FINANCIALS
Company Type: Private

Income Statement — FYE: March 31

	REVENUE ($ mil.)	NET INCOME ($ mil.)	NET PROFIT MARGIN	EMPLOYEES
03/11	126	2	2.2%	501
03/10	73	1	2.6%	0
03/09	60	1	2.3%	0
03/08	49	0	1.5%	0
Annual Growth	37.2%	54.7%	—	—

2011 Year-End Financials

Debt ratio: —
Return on equity: 2.20%
Cash ($ mil.): 7
Current ratio: 0.80
Long-term debt ($ mil.): —

Dividends
Yield: —
Payout: —
Market value ($ mil.): —

MERRIMACK COLLEGE

LOCATIONS

HQ: MERRIMACK COLLEGE
315 TURNPIKE ST, NORTH ANDOVER, MA 01845-5800
Phone: 978-837-5000
Web: www.merrimackathletics.com

HISTORICAL FINANCIALS
Company Type: Private

Income Statement — FYE: June 30

	REVENUE ($ mil.)	NET INCOME ($ mil.)	NET PROFIT MARGIN	EMPLOYEES
06/11	84	(0)	—	600
06/10*	76	(1)	—	0
12/09	0	(0)	—	0
06/08	78	5	7.0%	0
Annual Growth	2.5%	—	—	—

*Fiscal year change

2011 Year-End Financials

Debt ratio: —
Return on equity: (-0.90)%
Cash ($ mil.): 3
Current ratio: —
Long-term debt ($ mil.): —

Dividends
Yield: —
Payout: —
Market value ($ mil.): —

MERS/MISSOURI GOODWILL INDUSTRIES

LOCATIONS

HQ: MERS/MISSOURI GOODWILL INDUSTRIES
1727 LOCUST ST, SAINT LOUIS, MO 63103-1703
Phone: 314-241-3464
Web: www.mersgoodwill.org

HISTORICAL FINANCIALS

Company Type: Private

Income Statement

FYE: December 31

	REVENUE ($ mil.)	NET INCOME ($ mil.)	NET PROFIT MARGIN	EMPLOYEES
12/11	120	2	2.5%	1,300
12/10	110	5	5.4%	0
12/09	99	5	5.2%	0
12/08	82	0	0.0%	0
Annual Growth	13.3%	361.2%		

2011 Year-End Financials

Debt ratio: ——
Return on equity: 2.50%
Cash ($ mil.): 7
Current ratio: 1.80
Long-term debt ($ mil.): —

Dividends
Yield: —
Payout: —
Market value ($ mil.): —

METALLIX REFINING INC.

LOCATIONS

HQ: METALLIX REFINING INC.
59 AVENUE AT THE CMN # 201, SHREWSBURY, NJ
07702-4806
Phone: 732-936-0050
Web: www.metallixrefining.com

HISTORICAL FINANCIALS

Company Type: Private

Income Statement

FYE: December 31

	REVENUE ($ mil.)	NET INCOME ($ mil.)	NET PROFIT MARGIN	EMPLOYEES
12/11	175	0	—	64
12/10	0	0	—	0
12/09	0	0	—	0
12/08	0	0	—	0
Annual Growth	—	—		

2011 Year-End Financials

Debt ratio: ——
Return on equity: —
Cash ($ mil.): 0
Current ratio: 0.70
Long-term debt ($ mil.): —

Dividends
Yield: —
Payout: —
Market value ($ mil.): —

METHODIST HOSPITALS OF DALLAS INC

Methodist Hospitals of Dallas serves the health care needs of North Texas —from Mansfield to McKinney. The church-affiliated organization which does business as Methodist Health System operates more than a dozen hospitals clinics and medical facilities in and around the area deemed by locals as Big D. The original hospital Methodist Dallas Medical Center opened in 1927. The 515-bed teaching and referral hospital boasts a Level II trauma center and an organ transplant program. Other facilities include the 300-bed Methodist Charlton Medical Center the 80-bed Methodist Mansfield Medical Center and the 200-bed Methodist Richardson Medical Center.

Geographic Reach

Methodist Hospitals of Dallas serves the residents of several communities located in and around the North Dallas area such as Midlothian Grand Prairie Cedar Hill Richardson Plano Garland Wylie and McKinney.

Operations

The Methodist Dallas liver kidney and pancreas transplant program is one of the largest and most active transplant centers in the southwestern part of the country performing hundreds of kidney pancreas and liver transplants each year.

Both Methodist Hospital for Special Surgery and Methodist McKinney are part of two separate joint venture agreements made between Methodist Health System and Nueterra Healthcare a health care facilities management and development company.

Strategy

In recent years Methodist Health System has grown through a series of acquisitions (such as the Methodist Mansfield Medical Center and the Methodist Richardson Medical Center) as well as through organic expansion efforts such as the construction of about 50 rooms and new surgery suites in the Methodist Charlton hospital.

In late 2012 the health care provider began to expand its Methodist Richardson Medical Center - Bush/Renner hospital. Scheduled to open in fall 2014 the new 125-bed hospital will reach four stories high and serve the northeast Dallas communities of Richardson Garland Murphy Plano Sachse Wylie and other surrounding areas. It will boast a women's pavilion level III neonatal intensive care unit advanced neurosciences program outpatient surgical services such as the robotic da Vinci surgical system and other specialty services.

EXECUTIVES

Chairman, John Ford
SVP and Chief Human Resources Officer, Deanna Kenard
President and CEO, Stephen L. (Steve) Mansfield
EVP and CFO, Michael J. Schaefer, age 61, $370,759 total compensation
VP Public Relations and Marketing, Kathleen Beathard
EVP and Chief Legal Officer, Michael O. (Mickey) Price, $219,359 total compensation
SVP Planning and Marketing, Leslie A. Barden
SVP; President and CEO Methodist Health System Foundation, April B. Box Chamberlain
SVP and CIO, Pamela G. McNutt
President Methodist Dallas Medical Center, Michael A. Mayo
President Methodist Dallas Medical Center, Laura Irvine
EVP and COO, Pamela (Pam) Stoyanoff
SVP and Chief Development Officer, Michael W. Arvin
EVP System Alignment and Integration, Tim B. Kirby
SVP Human Resources, John F. Lacy
President Methodist Charlton Medical Center, Jonathan S. Davis
President Methodist Richardson Medical Center, E. Kenneth Hutchenrider Jr.
SVP and Chief Medical Officer, Adam L. Myers
SVP and Chief Nursing Officer; Chief Nursing Officer Methodist Dallas Medical Center, Nancy E. Simon
VP HR Operations, Jackie Middleton
SVP Development and Strategy, Scott Siemer

LOCATIONS

HQ: Methodist Hospitals of Dallas
1441 N. Beckley Ave., Dallas TX 75203
Phone: 214-947-8181   **Fax:** 214-947-4632
Web: www.methodisthealthsystem.org

PRODUCTS/OPERATIONS

Selected Services

Back and Spine
Behavioral Health and Addiction Recovery
Cancer Services
Cardiovascular
da Vinci Surgical System
Diabetes
Digestive Diseases
Ear Nose & Throat (ENT) Services & Allergy Treatments
Emergency and Trauma Care
Fitness Programs
Home Health
Imaging and Radiology
The Liver Institute
Neurosurgery and Neurology
Ophthalmology
Orthopedics
Pain Management
Palliative Care
Physical Therapy and Rehabilitation
Prostate Screening and Awareness Program
Sleep Disorders
Transplant
Urology
Weight Management
Women and Children's Services
Women's Imaging and Mammography
Wound Care and Hyperbaric Center

Selected Facilities

Golden Cross Academic Clinic
Methodist Dallas Medical Center
Methodist Charlton Medical Center
Methodist Family Health Centers
  Cedar Hill
  Central Grand Prairie
  Dallas
  Midlothian
  South Grand Prairie
Methodist Hospital for Surgery
Methodist Mansfield Medical Center
Methodist McKinney Hospital
Methodist Midlothian Health Center (imaging)
Methodist Richardson Medical Center
Methodist Richardson Medical Center Bush/Renner
Methodist Rehabilitation Hospital

COMPETITORS

Baylor Health	Hunt Memorial
Children's Medical Center of Dallas	JPS Health Network
	NW Texas Healthcare
CHRISTUS Health	Parkland Health &
Community Health	Hospital System

Systems
Cook Children' s Health
Care System
Harris Methodist Fort
Worth Hospital
HCA
Health Management
Associates

Presbyterian Hospital
of Dallas
Southwestern Medical
Center
Tenet Healthcare
Texas Health Denton
Texas Health Resources

HISTORICAL FINANCIALS
Company Type: Private - Not-for-Profit

Income Statement
FYE: September 30

	REVENUE ($ mil.)	NET INCOME ($ mil.)	NET PROFIT MARGIN	EMPLOYEES
09/11	985	51	5.3%	4,804
09/10	889	88	10.0%	0
09/09	747	37	5.0%	0
09/08	660	112	17.0%	0
Annual Growth	14.2%	(22.7%)	—	—

2011 Year-End Financials
Debt ratio: —
Return on equity: 5.30%
Cash ($ mil.): 42
Current ratio: 1.60
Long-term debt ($ mil.): —

Dividends
Yield: —
Payout: —
Market value ($ mil.): —

METRO BUSINESS SYSTEMS INC.

LOCATIONS
HQ: METRO BUSINESS SYSTEMS INC.
11 LARGO DR S, STAMFORD, CT 06907-2337
Phone: 203-967-3435
Web: www.metropc.com

HISTORICAL FINANCIALS
Company Type: Private

Income Statement
FYE: December 31

	REVENUE ($ mil.)	NET INCOME ($ mil.)	NET PROFIT MARGIN	EMPLOYEES
12/11	85	1	1.4%	45
12/10	114	2	2.3%	0
12/07	85	1	1.9%	0
12/06	64	0	0.4%	0
Annual Growth	9.6%	72.0%	—	—

2011 Year-End Financials
Debt ratio: —
Return on equity: 1.40%
Cash ($ mil.): 2
Current ratio: 1.40
Long-term debt ($ mil.): —

Dividends
Yield: —
Payout: —
Market value ($ mil.): —

METROPOLITAN UTILITIES DISTRICT OF OMAHA

The Metropolitan Utilities District distributes natural gas and water in the Omaha Nebraska metropolitan area. The company serves more than 200000 natural gas customers and more than 190000 water customers. It also collects sewer and trash fees for municipalities. The Metropolitan Utility District is a political subdivision of the State of Nebraska and says it is the fifth-largest public gas utility in the US. The district's board members are elected by residents of its service territory.

The Metropolitan Water District was created by the Nebraska Legislature in 1913. In 1918 state legislators authorized the City of Omaha to take charge of the gas system and the Metropolitan Water District subsequently was renamed as the Metropolitan Utilities District.

EXECUTIVES
President Secretary and Director, Thomas A. (Tom) Wurtz
SVP Administration and Treasurer, Ronald E. (Ron) Bucher
SVP and General Counsel, Daniel G. (Dan) Crouchley
VP Water Operations, Joel G. Christensen
VP Human Resources, John Hemschemeyer
SVP Operations, Scott L. Keep
VP Purchasing, James B. Goodwin
Chairman, Jack C. Frost
Vice Chairman, David J. Friend
VP Rates and Regulatory Affairs, Rhonda S. Chantry
VP Accounting, Roger A. Burmeister
VP Governmental Affairs and Marketing, Douglas R. (Doug) Clark
SVP and CIO, Mark W. Weiss
VP Gas Operations, James J. (Jim) Knight
VP Customer Services, Lisa R. Hale
Media Relations, Mari Matulka
Internal Auditor, J. W. Tiarks
VP Engineering and Construction, Ronald K. Reisner
VP IT Business Systems, Evan C. Osborn
VP IT Infrastructure, Bruce G. Burton
VP Safety and Security, Peter H. Neddo
Director, Michael W. (Mike) McGowan
President Secretary and Director, Thomas A. (Tom) Wurtz
Vice Chairman, David J. Friend
Director, Tim Cavanaugh
Director, Thomas F. Dowd
Director, Mark Doyle
Director, Amy Lindsay
Auditors: KPMGLLP

LOCATIONS
HQ: Metropolitan Utilities District
1723 Harney St., Omaha NE 68102-1960
Phone: 402-554-6666   **Fax:** 402-504-7020
Web: www.mudomaha.com

PRODUCTS/OPERATIONS

2007 Sales

	$ mil.	% of total
Gas	312	84
Total	370	100

HISTORICAL FINANCIALS
Company Type: Government Agency

Income Statement
FYE: December 31

	REVENUE ($ mil.)	NET INCOME ($ mil.)	NET PROFIT MARGIN	EMPLOYEES
12/11	311	15	4.9%	852
12/09	308	4	1.3%	0
12/08	407	13	3.4%	0
12/07	370	15	4.2%	0
Annual Growth	(5.6%)	(0.5%)	—	—

2011 Year-End Financials
Debt ratio: —
Return on equity: 4.90%
Cash ($ mil.): 10
Current ratio: 0.70
Long-term debt ($ mil.): —

Dividends
Yield: —
Payout: —
Market value ($ mil.): —

MIAMI-LUKEN INC.

LOCATIONS
HQ: MIAMI-LUKEN INC.
265 S PIONEER BLVD, SPRINGBORO, OH 45066-3307
Phone: 937-743-7775
Web: www.miamiluken.com

HISTORICAL FINANCIALS
Company Type: Private

Income Statement
FYE: June 30

	REVENUE ($ mil.)	NET INCOME ($ mil.)	NET PROFIT MARGIN	EMPLOYEES
06/11	144	0	0.3%	275
06/09	138	1	0.9%	0
06/08	138	0	0.4%	0
06/07	146	1	1.2%	0
Annual Growth	(0.6%)	(34.9%)	—	—

2011 Year-End Financials
Debt ratio: —
Return on equity: 0.30%
Cash ($ mil.): 1
Current ratio: 0.10
Long-term debt ($ mil.): —

Dividends
Yield: —
Payout: —
Market value ($ mil.): —

MICHIGAN BLUEBERRY GROWERS ASSOCIATION

LOCATIONS
HQ: MICHIGAN BLUEBERRY GROWERS ASSOCIATION
O4726 CR 215, GRAND JUNCTION, MI 49056
Phone: 269-434-6791
Web: www.mbggrower.com

Company Type: Private

Income Statement FYE: February 29

	REVENUE ($ mil.)	NET INCOME ($ mil.)	NET PROFIT MARGIN	EMPLOYEES
02/12	165	0	0.3%	28
02/11	143	114	79.9%	0
02/10	126	0	0.1%	0
02/09	131	0	0.1%	0
Annual Growth	8.2%	71.9%	—	—

2012 Year-End Financials

Debt ratio: ——
Return on equity: 0.30%
Cash ($ mil.): 0
Current ratio: 0.60
Long-term debt ($ mil.): —

Dividends
Yield: —
Payout: —
Market value ($ mil.): —

MICROTECHNOLOGIES LLC

MicroTechnologies is a US small business dishing up tech services to some big clients. Also known as MicroTech the Hispanic- and veteran-owned company focuses on delivering IT reseller products technical support systems integration and management consulting services to clients ranging from Fortune 500 companies to the federal government. It also serves state city and local agencies. For the US General Services Administration it has provided and set up personal computers Web access data voice and video communications and teleconferencing systems for President Obama's staff.

Geographic Reach

The company maintains offices in Alabama and North Carolina and in Virginia where it's headquartered.

Operations

MicroTech is a Service-Disabled Veteran-Owned Business and Minority Supplier Development Council certified supplier. It is a prime contractor on more than 100 Federal projects and holds more than 25 procurement vehicles offering access to 2500 vendors and more than a million technology products and services to the US government and state and local authorities.

Sales and Marketing

In addition to calling the Army DoD and GSA clients MicroTech serves as a prime contractor for other federal agencies under the Government-wide Acquisition Contract (GWAC) program. Regarded for its ability to take on large-scale government technology support projects it maintains more than 100 federal contracts with clients including the Social Security Administration Department of Agriculture and the Navy Coast Guard and Air Force service branches of the military.

Strategy

Through partnerships with leading manufacturers and brands MicroTech resells hardware and software products from the likes of Adobe Cisco Dell HP and Microsoft. It also works with product vendors to procure less toxic and energy-efficient options in hardware and software to stay in step with enterprises undertaking green initiatives.

Company Background

MicroTech was founded in 2004 by CEO Anthony Jimenez a US Army vet and former US Department of Defense executive. Since its launch in 2004 MicroTech's revenues have grown more than 4000% and it has been incrementally moving up the Inc. 500 fastest-growing US private business list. It is also one of the top five fastest-growing Hispanic-owned businesses in the US.

EXECUTIVES

President and CEO, Anthony R. (Tony) Jimenez
SVP and Executive Director MicroTech International, Tomas Esterrich
EVP and COO, Steve Truitt
SVP Technology Services and Solutions, Dave Coker
SVP Federal and Civilian Programs, Randy Moulton
SVP Unified Communications and Collaboration (UCC) Installation and Services, Bob Otto
SVP Engineering and Chief Product Officer, Joseph (Joe) Staehly
SVP Sales and Product Solutions, Steve Pace
SVP Business Development DoD Programs, Richard Solomon
SVP Capture DoD Programs, Thomas (Tom) Hodges
SVP Business Development Federal and Civilian Programs, Byron (By) Athan
SVP Enterprise IDIQ and GWAC, Bill Lytle
SVP Contracts and General Counsel, Aaron Drabkin
SVP and Chief Administrative Officer, Paul Price
SVP Business Development and Chief Information Officer, Preston Quick
SVP Strategic Partnerships, Rod McKinley
SVP Infrastructure Cloud and Mobility Solutions, Tim Dioquino
SVP Unified Communications and Collaboration, Jeff Bomkamp
SVP Product Sales and Solutions, Ray Miles
SVP Channels and Alliances, Scott Kaye
SVP and CTO, Roger Channing
SVP and CFO, Vineet Puri

LOCATIONS

HQ: MicroTechnologies LLC
8330 Boone Blvd. Ste. 600, Tysons Corner VA 22182
Phone: 703-891-1073   **Fax:** 703-891-1074
Web: www.microtechllc.com

PRODUCTS/OPERATIONS

Selected Services
Audio/visual telecommunications
  Enterprise telecommunications
    Audio & video bridging
    Configurations
    Customized software
  Integrated audio/visual design
    3-D room animation
    Acoustic modeling
    Control systems design
    Digital signage
    Streaming content storage & delivery
    Telepresence
  Secure conferencing
    Audio & video bridging
    Switching
Consulting
  Business process
    Business process improvement
    Change management
    Enterprise architecture design & integration
    Strategy planning
  Knowledge management
    Finance administration
    Human Resources
    Logistics management
    Network support
  Lifecycle
    Analysis reporting
    Design & integration
    Implementation
    Testing & evaluation
    Training
IT
  Software & value-added services
    Application development
    Lifecycle management
    Server visualization
  Technical support
    Database administration
    Help desk assistance
    Network engineering management & administration
    System engineering management & administration
    Technical architecture development

Selected Partnerships
ADOBE
Autonomy
ca Technologies
CISCO
CITRIX
DELL
EMC2
HITACHI
HP
Microsoft
NET APP
Polycom
sgi
SYMANTEC
VMWare

COMPETITORS

American Information Technology Solutions	HP Enterprise Group
Avaya Government Solutions	IBM Global Services
CACI International	Keane
Computer Sciences Corp.	SAIC
	SHI International
	STG Inc.
	The CENTECH GROUP

HISTORICAL FINANCIALS
Company Type: Private

Income Statement FYE: December 31

	REVENUE ($ mil.)	NET INCOME ($ mil.)	NET PROFIT MARGIN	EMPLOYEES
12/11	117	3	2.8%	425
12/10	93	7	7.9%	0
12/08	39	2	6.3%	0
12/07	12	0	—	0
Annual Growth	111.6%	—	—	—

2011 Year-End Financials

Debt ratio: ——
Return on equity: 2.80%
Cash ($ mil.): 0
Current ratio: —
Long-term debt ($ mil.): —

Dividends
Yield: —
Payout: —
Market value ($ mil.): —

MIDDLE TENNESSE MEDICAL CENTER

LOCATIONS

HQ: MIDDLE TENNESSE MEDICAL CENTER
1700 MEDICAL CENTER PKWY, MURFREESBORO, TN 37129-2245
Phone: 615-396-4459
Web: www.mtmc.org

HISTORICAL FINANCIALS

Company Type: Private

Income Statement

FYE: June 30

	REVENUE ($ mil.)	NET INCOME ($ mil.)	NET PROFIT MARGIN	EMPLOYEES
06/11	253	(10)	—	0
06/10	217	19	9.2%	0
Annual Growth	16.9%	—	—	—

2011 Year-End Financials

Debt ratio: —
Return on equity: (-4.30)%
Cash ($ mil.): 16
Current ratio: 0.20
Long-term debt ($ mil.): —

Dividends
Yield: —
Payout: —
Market value ($ mil.): —

MIDMICHIGAN HEALTH

LOCATIONS

HQ: MIDMICHIGAN HEALTH
4000 WELLNESS DR, MIDLAND, MI 48670-2000
Phone: 989-839-3000
Web: www.midmichiganhealth.com

HISTORICAL FINANCIALS

Company Type: Private

Income Statement

FYE: September 30

	REVENUE ($ mil.)	NET INCOME ($ mil.)	NET PROFIT MARGIN	EMPLOYEES
09/12*	145	2	1.9%	6,500
06/12	576	6	1.2%	0
06/11	565	89	15.8%	0
09/10	273	60	22.1%	0
Annual Growth	(18.9%)	(64.1%)	—	—

*Fiscal year change

2012 Year-End Financials

Debt ratio: —
Return on equity: 1.90%
Cash ($ mil.): 11
Current ratio: 1.20
Long-term debt ($ mil.): —

Dividends
Yield: —
Payout: —
Market value ($ mil.): —

MIKE SHANNON AUTOMOTIVE INC.

LOCATIONS

HQ: MIKE SHANNON AUTOMOTIVE INC.
321 N ROLLING MEADOWS DR, FOND DU LAC, WI 54937-9726
Phone: 920-921-8898
Web: www.holidayautomotive.com

HISTORICAL FINANCIALS

Company Type: Private

Income Statement

FYE: December 31

	REVENUE ($ mil.)	NET INCOME ($ mil.)	NET PROFIT MARGIN	EMPLOYEES
12/11	117	4	3.9%	175
12/10	113	4	4.2%	0
12/09	93	2	3.1%	0
Annual Growth	11.9%	25.5%	—	—

2011 Year-End Financials

Debt ratio: —
Return on equity: 3.90%
Cash ($ mil.): 0
Current ratio: 0.10
Long-term debt ($ mil.): —

Dividends
Yield: —
Payout: —
Market value ($ mil.): —

MIDDLETOWN CITY SCHOOL DISTRICT

LOCATIONS

HQ: MIDDLETOWN CITY SCHOOL DISTRICT
1515 GIRARD AVE, MIDDLETOWN, OH 45044-4364
Phone: 513-423-0781
Web: www.middletowncityschools.com

HISTORICAL FINANCIALS

Company Type: Private

Income Statement

FYE: June 30

	REVENUE ($ mil.)	NET INCOME ($ mil.)	NET PROFIT MARGIN	EMPLOYEES
06/11	84	(4)	—	675
06/05	60	(4)	—	0
Annual Growth	40.3%	—	—	—

2011 Year-End Financials

Debt ratio: —
Return on equity: (-5.00)%
Cash ($ mil.): 10
Current ratio: —
Long-term debt ($ mil.): —

Dividends
Yield: —
Payout: —
Market value ($ mil.): —

MIDWAY CO-OP ASSOCIATION

LOCATIONS

HQ: MIDWAY CO-OP ASSOCIATION
210 W HARRISON ST, OSBORNE, KS 67473
Phone: 785-346-5451
Web: www.midwaycoop.com

HISTORICAL FINANCIALS

Company Type: Private

Income Statement

FYE: March 31

	REVENUE ($ mil.)	NET INCOME ($ mil.)	NET PROFIT MARGIN	EMPLOYEES
03/12	156	9	6.3%	90
03/11	91	6	7.4%	0
03/10	100	6	6.7%	0
03/09	122	6	5.0%	0
Annual Growth	8.4%	17.4%	—	—

2012 Year-End Financials

Debt ratio: —
Return on equity: 6.30%
Cash ($ mil.): 1
Current ratio: 0.10
Long-term debt ($ mil.): —

Dividends
Yield: —
Payout: —
Market value ($ mil.): —

MILLARD PUBLIC SCHOOLS

LOCATIONS

HQ: MILLARD PUBLIC SCHOOLS
5606 S 147TH ST, OMAHA, NE 68137-2647
Phone: 402-715-8200
Web: www.centralmiddleschool.com

HISTORICAL FINANCIALS

Company Type: Private

Income Statement

FYE: August 31

	REVENUE ($ mil.)	NET INCOME ($ mil.)	NET PROFIT MARGIN	EMPLOYEES
08/12	233	(4)	—	2,500
08/09	214	(11)	—	0
08/08	212	(5)	—	0
08/07	197	(21)	—	0
Annual Growth	5.7%	—	—	—

2012 Year-End Financials

Debt ratio: —
Return on equity: (-2.10)%
Cash ($ mil.): 27
Current ratio: —
Long-term debt ($ mil.): —

Dividends
Yield: —
Payout: —
Market value ($ mil.): —

MILLER'S INC.

LOCATIONS

HQ: MILLER' S INC.
610 E JEFFERSON ST, PITTSBURG, KS 66762-5913
Phone: 620-231-8050
Web: www.millerslab.com

HISTORICAL FINANCIALS

Company Type: Private

Income Statement

FYE: December 31

	REVENUE ($ mil.)	NET INCOME ($ mil.)	NET PROFIT MARGIN	EMPLOYEES
12/11	111	23	21.6%	500
12/10	102	24	24.0%	0
12/09	90	21	23.4%	0
12/08	80	18	23.1%	0
Annual Growth	11.3%	8.7%	—	—

2011 Year-End Financials

Debt ratio: —
Return on equity: 21.60%
Cash ($ mil.): 13
Current ratio: 2.30
Long-term debt ($ mil.): —
Dividends
Yield: —
Payout: —
Market value ($ mil.): —

MILLS COLLEGE

LOCATIONS

HQ: MILLS COLLEGE
5000 MACARTHUR BLVD, OAKLAND, CA 94613-1000
Phone: 510-430-2255
Web: www.mills.edu

HISTORICAL FINANCIALS

Company Type: Private

Income Statement

FYE: June 30

	REVENUE ($ mil.)	NET INCOME ($ mil.)	NET PROFIT MARGIN	EMPLOYEES
06/11	86	(3)	—	0
06/10	73	(12)	—	0
06/09	79	0	—	0
06/08	54	(8)	—	0
Annual Growth	16.4%	—	—	—

2011 Year-End Financials

Debt ratio: —
Return on equity: (-4.60)%
Cash ($ mil.): 16
Current ratio: —
Long-term debt ($ mil.): —
Dividends
Yield: —
Payout: —
Market value ($ mil.): —

MILLS-PENINSULA HEALTH SERVICES

With health facilities south of San Francisco Mills-Peninsula Health Services provides care to communities in and around Burlingame California. The group includes Mills-Peninsula Medical Center an acute-care hospital in Burlingame; Mills Health Center an outpatient diagnostic surgery and rehabilitation facility in San Mateo; and a skilled nursing center in Burlingame. The facilities have more than 400 beds and provide specialty services such as cancer care cardiovascular therapy behavioral health radiology respiratory care and senior services. The health system's inpatient rehabilitation program is part of the Mills Health Center. Mills-Peninsula Health Services is part of the Sutter Health network.

Mills-Peninsula opened the doors on its newly constructed Burlingame medical center in 2011. The $490 million project added a new main hospital facility (to replace the previous Peninsula Medical Center) medical offices and a parking garage. The new hospital is compliant with California's new earthquake safety requirements.

The company's physician organization Mills-Peninsula Medical Group formed an affiliation agreement with another Sutter Health member Palo Alto Medical Foundation (PAMF) in 2009. The two physician organizations plan to combine certain operations over time; the first step was the formation of a new group the Peninsula Medical Clinic consisting of about 40 Mills-Peninsula doctors that began operating as part of PAMF.

Founded in 1908 the Mills hospital was named for philanthropist Elizabeth Mills Reid who helped to fund the medical facility. The Peninsula facility was founded as a public hospital district in 1954. The two hospitals merged in 1985 and became part of Sutter Health the following year.

EXECUTIVES

CEO, Robert W. (Bob) Merwin
Chief of Staff, Michael Wood
CFO, Jeff Gerard
Director Marketing, Margie O'Clair
Director Human Resources, Judy DiPaolo

LOCATIONS

HQ: Mills-Peninsula Health Services
1501 Trousdale Dr., Burlingame CA 94010
Phone: 650-696-5400   **Fax:** 650-696-5374
Web: www.mills-peninsula.org

COMPETITORS

Alta Bates Summit
  Medical Center
California Pacific
  Medical Center
Dignity Health
Marin General Hospital
Sequoia Healthcare
  District
The Palo Alto Medical
  Foundation
UCSF Medical

HISTORICAL FINANCIALS

Company Type: Private - Not-for-Profit

Income Statement

FYE: December 31

	REVENUE ($ mil.)	NET INCOME ($ mil.)	NET PROFIT MARGIN	EMPLOYEES
12/11	572	(34)	—	2,200
12/09	533	56	10.6%	0
12/02	274	18	6.6%	0
12/01	267	20	7.5%	0
Annual Growth	28.9%	—	—	—

2011 Year-End Financials

Debt ratio: —
Return on equity: (-5.90)%
Cash ($ mil.): 25
Current ratio: 1.50
Long-term debt ($ mil.): —
Dividends
Yield: —
Payout: —
Market value ($ mil.): —

MILWAUKEE PUBLIC SCHOOLS

LOCATIONS

HQ: MILWAUKEE PUBLIC SCHOOLS
5225 W VLIET ST, MILWAUKEE, WI 53208-2698
Phone: 414-475-8288
Web: www.milwaukeehighschoolofthearts.org

HISTORICAL FINANCIALS

Company Type: Private

Income Statement

FYE: June 30

	REVENUE ($ mil.)	NET INCOME ($ mil.)	NET PROFIT MARGIN	EMPLOYEES
06/11	1,292	(2)	—	14,154
06/09	1,237	(5)	—	0
06/05	1,122	(19)	—	0
06/04	0	0	—	0
Annual Growth	—	—	—	—

MIRAGE APPLIANCES INC.

LOCATIONS

HQ: MIRAGE APPLIANCES INC.
6700 GATEWAY PARK DR # 6, SAN DIEGO, CA 92154-7533
Phone: 619-426-0033
Web: www.airesmirage.com

HISTORICAL FINANCIALS
Company Type: Private

Income Statement
FYE: December 31

	REVENUE ($ mil.)	NET INCOME ($ mil.)	NET PROFIT MARGIN	EMPLOYEES
12/11	91	0	0.5%	14
12/10	70	0	0.5%	0
12/09	38	0	0.9%	0
12/08	41	0	1.0%	0
Annual Growth	29.6%	3.4%	—	—

2011 Year-End Financials

Debt ratio: ——
Return on equity: 0.50%
Cash ($ mil.): 0
Current ratio: 5.60
Long-term debt ($ mil.): —

Dividends
  Yield: —
  Payout: —
  Market value ($ mil.): —

HISTORICAL FINANCIALS
Company Type: Private

Income Statement
FYE: September 30

	REVENUE ($ mil.)	NET INCOME ($ mil.)	NET PROFIT MARGIN	EMPLOYEES
09/12*	37	2	7.2%	34
12/11	46	(1)	—	0
12/10	39	(4)	—	0
12/09	33	(2)	—	0
Annual Growth	3.3%	—	—	—

*Fiscal year change

2012 Year-End Financials

Debt ratio: ——
Return on equity: 7.20%
Cash ($ mil.): 0
Current ratio: 0.20
Long-term debt ($ mil.): —

Dividends
  Yield: —
  Payout: —
  Market value ($ mil.): —

HISTORICAL FINANCIALS
Company Type: Private

Income Statement
FYE: September 30

	REVENUE ($ mil.)	NET INCOME ($ mil.)	NET PROFIT MARGIN	EMPLOYEES
09/12	112	0	0.5%	850
09/11	114	2	2.0%	0
09/10*	117	0	0.2%	0
06/10	87	(0)	—	0
Annual Growth	8.6%	—	—	—

*Fiscal year change

2012 Year-End Financials

Debt ratio: ——
Return on equity: 0.50%
Cash ($ mil.): 4
Current ratio: 1.70
Long-term debt ($ mil.): —

Dividends
  Yield: —
  Payout: —
  Market value ($ mil.): —

MISSION BROADCASTING INC.

TV is the purpose of this company. Mission Broadcasting owns broadcasting licenses for 16 television stations serving small and medium-sized markets mostly in Texas Missouri and Pennsylvania. It generates most of its revenue through local service agreements with TV stations owned by Nexstar Broadcasting under which Nexstar operates the stations and provides programming sales and other services. The company's portfolio of stations includes affiliates of all the major broadcasting networks as well as a couple stations affiliated with mini-network MyNetworkTV. President David Smith who owns the company started Mission Broadcasting in 1998.

EXECUTIVES

VP and Secretary, Nancie J. Smith, age 59, $3,120 total compensation
President Treasurer and Director, David S. Smith, age 57, $305,000 total compensation
EVP and COO, Dennis Thatcher, age 65, $139,600 total compensation
Auditors: PricewaterhouseCoopersLLP

LOCATIONS

HQ: Mission Broadcasting Inc.
  30400 Detroit Rd. Ste. 304, Westlake OH 44145-1855
Phone: 440-526-2227   **Fax:** 877-268-6040

PRODUCTS/OPERATIONS

Selected Television Stations

KAMC (ABC; Lubbock TX)
KCIT (FOX; Amarillo TX)
KHMT (FOX; Billings MT)
KJTL (FOX; Wichita Falls TX)
KODE (ABC; Joplin MO)
KOLR (CBS; Springfield MO)
KRBC (NBC; Abilene-Sweetwater TX)
KSAN (NBC; San Angelo TX)
KTVE (NBC; Monroe LA)
WFXP (FOX; Erie PA)
WFXW (FOX; Terre Haute IN)
WTVO (ABC; Rockford IL)
WUTR (ABC; Utica NY)
WYOU (CBS; Wilkes Barre-Scranton PA)

MISSION HOSPITAL INC.

LOCATIONS

HQ: MISSION HOSPITAL INC.
  900 S BRYAN RD, MISSION, TX 78572-6613
Phone: 956-580-9000
Web: www.missionhospital.com

PRODUCTS/OPERATIONS

Surgical Services
General Surgery
Minimally Invasive Surgery
Outpatient Surgery
Prepare for Surgery
Robotic Surgery
Surgery at Mission Hospital
Surgery Guide
Programs of Service
Endoscopy
Genetics
Integrative Healthcare
Mother and Baby
Outpatient Care Centers
Sleep Center
Urology
Weight Management Center
Wound Healing and Hyperbaric
Support Services
Chronic Medical Conditions
Long-Term Acute Care
Laboratory
Pastoral Care Services
Pharmacy
Psychiatric Services
Radiology (Imaging) Services
Rehabilitation Services
Research Institute
Respiratory Therapy
Senior Services and Geriatrics

MISSION PHARMACAL COMPANY

Mission Pharmacal's purpose objective and undertaking if you will is to make you feel better. The company makes prescription and over-the-counter (OTC) remedies for infection kidney stones and arthritis as well as nutritional supplements. Mission's products include muscle ointment Thera-Gesic Fosfree multivitamin supplement kidney stone preventer Urocit-K parasitic and bacterial infection fighter Tindamax and CitraNatal prescription prenatal vitamins. The company also offers third-party OTC nutritional and prescription manufacturing packaging and inventory management to pharmaceutical companies. Mission Pharmacal was founded in 1946 by the Walsdorf family which still owns and runs the business.

Geographic Reach

The company operates nationwide and distributes some products overseas through partnerships with pharmaceutical companies in markets it sees as desirable.

Mission has a partnership agreement with Paladin Labs granting the Canadian pharmaceutical company distribution rights to Urocit-K in that country as well as a number of African countries. Mission has similar marketing agreements in Australia Asia Europe and South America.

Operations

The company's corporate headquarters are located in San Antonio Texas. Mission researches and develops new products at its facility in Boerne Texas (northwest of San Antonio). The Texas facility is also where Mission provides its outsourcing services.

Mission has the capability to manufacture and package powders tablets solutions creams lotions gels and suspensions. Packaging capabilities include cartoning shrink wrapping tray packaging and bundling.

The company also offers third-party OTC nutritional and prescription manufacturing packaging and inventory management to pharmaceutical companies.

In addition to its Texas facilities Mission also operates a research and development facility in the state of Washington and a commercial office in the

Northeast corridor where there is a high concentration of companies in the pharmaceutical industry.

Strategy

Along with growing its product lines through acquisitions and licensing the company conducts extensive research. Mission's research is focused on the areas of osteoporosis urolithiasis and cardiovascular disease.

Mission considers its women's health offerings to be a key part of its product roster and works to add to that portfolio through licensing agreements and acquisitions. In 2012 Mission Pharmacal launched Alamo Pharma Services as a wholly-owned subsidiary to operate its women's health urology pediatrics and dermatology sales teams.

Two of Mission's key products are Ferralet an iron supplement treatment for anemia and migraine treatment Cambia which the company sells as part of its women's health lineup through a co-marketing agreement with drugmaker Nautilus Neurosciences.

In 2012 the company acquired the prescription barrier cream Eletone Cream from Ferndale Healthcare. The product strengthened Mission's pediatric product offerings.

Company Background

The company was founded in 1946 by the Walsdorf family. The family still owns and operates the business.

EXECUTIVES

EVP, James K. Walsdorf
President and CEO, Neil B. Walsdorf Jr.
Director Human Resources, Georgia Kubasak
CFO, Thomas J. Dooley
COO, Max Martin
Controller, Leonard A. Koehl
Secretary, Benjamin Youngblood III
IT Project Manager, Tom Johnson

LOCATIONS

HQ: Mission Pharmacal Company
   10999 IH-10 West Ste. 1000, San Antonio TX 78278
Phone: 210-696-8400   **Fax:** 210-696-6010
Web: www.missionpharmacal.com

PRODUCTS/OPERATIONS

Selected Products

Calcet (calcium supplements)
CitraNatal (prenatal vitamins)
Compete (multivitamin)
Dr. Smith's (diaper rash ointment)
Ferralet 90 (iron supplement)
Fosfree (phosphorous-free iron calcium multivitamin supplement)
Heat Guard (salt tablets)
Iromin-G (iron supplement)
Lithostat (kidney stones)
Magtrate (magnesium supplement)
Maxilube (personal lubricant)
Mission Prenatal
Oncovite (multivitamin)
Thera-Gesic (topical analgesic for muscle pain)
Thiola (kidney stones)
Tindamax (bacterial vaginosis)
Urocit-K (kidney stones)

COMPETITORS

Alere	Nature's Sunshine
Bayer AG	Nutraceutical
Chattem	International
Contract Pharmacal	Perrigo
Depomed	Sandoz International
Eli Lilly	GmbH

Endo	Teva
GlaxoSmithKline	Upsher-Smith
HealthTronics	Warner Chilcott
Hi-Tech Pharmacal	Watson Pharmaceuticals
Johnson & Johnson	Xanodyne
Mylan	Pharmaceuticals

HISTORICAL FINANCIALS

Company Type: Private

Income Statement
FYE: April 30

	REVENUE ($ mil.)	NET INCOME ($ mil.)	NET PROFIT MARGIN	EMPLOYEES
04/12	118	18	15.5%	495
04/11	95	5	6.0%	0
04/10	75	(2)	—	0
04/09	61	(7)	—	0
Annual Growth	24.4%	—	—	—

2012 Year-End Financials

Debt ratio: ——
Return on equity: 15.50%
Cash ($ mil.): 7
Current ratio: 0.50
Long-term debt ($ mil.): —

Dividends
   Yield: —
   Payout: —
Market value ($ mil.): —

MISSOURI STATE UNIVERSITY

When Missouri students say "show me" Missouri State University happily obliges. It is the state's second-largest university (after University of Missouri) with an enrollment of more than 21000 students. The school offers about 150 undergraduate and 50 graduate programs including coursework in accounting biology criminology and physical geography. In addition to its main campus in Springfield the university also has campuses in Mountain Grove and West Plains. The school was founded in 1905 as the Fourth District Normal School a teacher training institution; it changed its name to Missouri State University 100 years later.

EXECUTIVES

President, Michael T. (Mike) Nietzel, age 61
VP Administrative and Information Services, Greg Burris
VP Research and Economic Development, Jim Baker
Dean College of Business Administration, Ron Bottin
Provost, Belinda R. McCarthy
General Counsel, Clif Smart
Assistant VP Enrollment Management and Services and Director Admissions, Don Simpson
Registrar and Veteran Certifying Official, Nicole Rovig
Executive Director Alumni Relations, Julie Ebersold
VP University Advancement, Brent Dunn
Associate Dean of Library Services, Neosha Mackey
Director Facilities Management, Bob Eckels
Acting Dean of Students, Mike Jungers
Director Career Center, Jack Hunter
CFO, Nila Hayes
Board Member, Michael J. (Mike) Duggan, age 61
VP Board of Governors, Mary Sheid

Board Member, Phyllis Washington
Board Member, Ryan Sivill
Board Member, James H. Buford
Board Member, John L. Winston
Board Member, Brian Hammons

LOCATIONS

HQ: Missouri State University
   901 S. National Ave., Springfield MO 65897
Phone: 417-836-5000   **Fax:** 417-836-7669
Web: www.missouristate.edu

HISTORICAL FINANCIALS

Company Type: School

Income Statement
FYE: June 30

	REVENUE ($ mil.)	NET INCOME ($ mil.)	NET PROFIT MARGIN	EMPLOYEES
06/11	190	33	17.7%	2,066
06/10	189	30	16.0%	0
06/09	177	12	6.9%	0
06/08	186	25	13.8%	0
Annual Growth	0.7%	9.5%	—	—

2011 Year-End Financials

Debt ratio: ——
Return on equity: 17.70%
Cash ($ mil.): 159
Current ratio: 4.00
Long-term debt ($ mil.): —

Dividends
   Yield: —
   Payout: —
Market value ($ mil.): —

MMR CONSTRUCTORS INC.

LOCATIONS

HQ: MMR CONSTRUCTORS INC.
   15961 AIRLINE HWY, BATON ROUGE, LA 70817-7412
Phone: 225-756-5090

HISTORICAL FINANCIALS

Company Type: Private

Income Statement
FYE: December 31

	REVENUE ($ mil.)	NET INCOME ($ mil.)	NET PROFIT MARGIN	EMPLOYEES
12/11	233	12	5.1%	2,500
12/01	0	0	—	0
Annual Growth	—	—	—	—

2011 Year-End Financials

Debt ratio: ——
Return on equity: 5.10%
Cash ($ mil.): 5
Current ratio: 1.00
Long-term debt ($ mil.): —

Dividends
   Yield: —
   Payout: —
Market value ($ mil.): —

MMR GROUP INC.

That murmur you hear could be the gentle hum of a properly functioning power system. MMG Group provides specialty contracting services for clients in the oil and gas manufacturing chemical and power generation industries around the world. It also offers services in offshore marine and platform environments. Its Power Solutions division constructs onsite power-generation systems in industrial plants and other facilities. The group primarily operates in the Gulf of New Mexico. MMG has served such clients as Chevron Shell BP Merck Air Liquide DuPont and 3M. The company was founded in 1990.

Arizona-based division Southwestern Power Group specializes in the development and operation of gas-fired power plants. It is working on a 500-mile transmission line spanning Arizona and New Mexico. Named the SunZia Southwest Transmission Project the line will provide 3000 megawatts of capacity generated from wind solar and geothermal energy sources. It is expected to be complete in 2013 and is designed to meet the growing need for clean renewable energy. Another project the $1 billion Bowie Power Station in Arizona will utilize clean-burning natural gas.

EXECUTIVES

CEO, James R. Rutland
EVP, Allen R. Boudreaux
VP Marketing, Grady Saucier

LOCATIONS

HQ: MMR Group Inc.
15961 Airline Hwy., Baton Rouge LA 70817
Phone: 225-756-5090   **Fax:** 225-753-7012
Web: www.mmrgrp.com

PRODUCTS/OPERATIONS

Selected Services
Instrumentation
  Air supply installation
  Control room equipment installation
  Instrument installation
  Process leads
  Panel fabrication
  Signal wiring
Electrical
  Controls
  Electrical equipment setting
  Grounding
  Lighting
  Power distribution
Technical
  Calibration
  Commissioning
  Detail design
  High voltage testing
  Instrument procurement
  Loop check
  Maintenance
  Start up assistance
  System analysis

Selected Divisions
MMR Constructors
MMR International
MMR Power Solutions
MMR Offshore Services
MMR Technical Services
Southwestern Power Group

COMPETITORS

Alberici   Matrix Service

EMCOR   MYR Group
Fisk Electric   Turner Industries
Industrial Specialty
  Contractors

HISTORICAL FINANCIALS
Company Type: Private

Income Statement
FYE: December 31

	REVENUE ($ mil.)	NET INCOME ($ mil.)	NET PROFIT MARGIN	EMPLOYEES
12/11	254	11	4.4%	2,500
12/10	0	0	—	0
12/09	0	0	—	0
12/08	314	0	—	0
Annual Growth	(6.7%)	—	—	—

2011 Year-End Financials
Debt ratio: ——
Return on equity: 4.40%
Cash ($ mil.): 6
Current ratio: 0.80
Long-term debt ($ mil.): —
Dividends
  Yield: —
  Payout: —
  Market value ($ mil.): —

MNJ TECHNOLOGIES DIRECT INC.

LOCATIONS

HQ: MNJ TECHNOLOGIES DIRECT INC.
1025 BUSCH PKWY, BUFFALO GROVE, IL 60089-4504
Phone: 847-634-0700
Web: www.mnjtech.com

HISTORICAL FINANCIALS
Company Type: Private

Income Statement
FYE: December 31

	REVENUE ($ mil.)	NET INCOME ($ mil.)	NET PROFIT MARGIN	EMPLOYEES
12/11	91	2	2.2%	78
12/10	86	2	2.5%	0
12/09	61	0	0.1%	0
12/08	61	0	1.3%	0
Annual Growth	14.1%	37.5%	—	—

2011 Year-End Financials
Debt ratio: ——
Return on equity: 2.20%
Cash ($ mil.): 3
Current ratio: 1.20
Long-term debt ($ mil.): —
Dividends
  Yield: —
  Payout: —
  Market value ($ mil.): —

MOBILE INFIRMARY ASSOCIATION

LOCATIONS

HQ: MOBILE INFIRMARY ASSOCIATION
5 MOBILE INFIRMARY CIR, MOBILE, AL 36607-3513
Phone: 251-435-2400
Web: www.mimc.com

HISTORICAL FINANCIALS
Company Type: Private

Income Statement
FYE: March 31

	REVENUE ($ mil.)	NET INCOME ($ mil.)	NET PROFIT MARGIN	EMPLOYEES
03/11	394	24	6.3%	2,938
03/10	351	12	3.5%	0
03/08	332	0	0.2%	0
03/07	314	27	8.8%	0
Annual Growth	7.9%	(3.6%)	—	—

2011 Year-End Financials
Debt ratio: ——
Return on equity: 6.30%
Cash ($ mil.): 58
Current ratio: 0.60
Long-term debt ($ mil.): —
Dividends
  Yield: —
  Payout: —
  Market value ($ mil.): —

MOLINE PUBLIC SCHOOL DISTRICT 40

LOCATIONS

HQ: MOLINE PUBLIC SCHOOL DISTRICT 40
1619 11TH AVE, MOLINE, IL 61265-3143
Phone: 309-757-3500
Web: www.molineschools.org

HISTORICAL FINANCIALS
Company Type: Private

Income Statement
FYE: June 30

	REVENUE ($ mil.)	NET INCOME ($ mil.)	NET PROFIT MARGIN	EMPLOYEES
06/12	86	1	1.5%	1,450
06/11	85	(3)	—	0
06/10	82	7	9.5%	0
06/09	82	(6)	—	0
Annual Growth	1.8%	—	—	—

2012 Year-End Financials
Debt ratio: ——
Return on equity: 1.50%
Cash ($ mil.): 61
Current ratio: —
Long-term debt ($ mil.): —
Dividends
  Yield: —
  Payout: —
  Market value ($ mil.): —

MOLLOY COLLEGE

Molloy College is a Catholic school on the South Shore of Long Island. In addition to a variety of undergraduate majors the college offers graduate degrees in business criminal justice education nursing and social work. Molloy College has an enrollment of more than 2000 students. It was founded in 1955 by the Sisters of St. Dominic of the Congregation of the Holy Cross with the support of Archbishop Thomas E. Molloy Bishop of Brooklyn.

EXECUTIVES

President, Drew Bogner
VP Academic Affairs and Dean of Faculty, Valerie Collins
VP Finance and Treasurer, Michael McGovern
VP Student Affairs, Robert C. Houlihan
VP Information Technology Planning and Research, Robert Paterson
Director Library and Media Services, Robert Martin
Director Human Resources, Lisa Miller

LOCATIONS

HQ: Molloy College
1000 Hempstead Ave., Rockville Centre NY 11571-5002
Phone: 516-678-5000   **Fax:** 516-255-4832
Web: www.molloy.edu

HISTORICAL FINANCIALS

Company Type: School

Income Statement

FYE: June 30

	REVENUE ($ mil.)	NET INCOME ($ mil.)	NET PROFIT MARGIN	EMPLOYEES
06/11	93	10	10.8%	700
06/10	79	4	6.0%	0
06/09	68	0	—	0
06/08	63	1	2.6%	0
Annual Growth	**13.9%**	**82.9%**	**—**	**—**

2011 Year-End Financials

Debt ratio: ——
Return on equity: 10.80%
Cash ($ mil.): 16
Current ratio: ——
Long-term debt ($ mil.): —

Dividends
Yield: —
Payout: —
Market value ($ mil.): —

MON-VALE HEALTH RESOURCES INC.

LOCATIONS

HQ: MON-VALE HEALTH RESOURCES INC.
1163 COUNTRY CLUB RD, MONONGAHELA, PA 15063-1013
Phone: 724-258-1000

HISTORICAL FINANCIALS

Company Type: Private

Income Statement

FYE: June 30

	REVENUE ($ mil.)	NET INCOME ($ mil.)	NET PROFIT MARGIN	EMPLOYEES
06/12	140	(12)	—	1,024
06/11	0	0	57.1%	0
06/10	116	(1)	—	0
06/09	113	(13)	—	0
Annual Growth	**7.4%**	**—**	**—**	**—**

2012 Year-End Financials

Debt ratio: ——
Return on equity: (-9.10)%
Cash ($ mil.): 31
Current ratio: 2.20
Long-term debt ($ mil.): —

Dividends
Yield: —
Payout: —
Market value ($ mil.): —

MONMOUTH UNIVERSITY

Students looking for a monumental education might want to head to Monmouth University. The private institution offers more than 30 undergraduate programs through eight schools that include business administration education humanities and social sciences and nursing and health sciences among others. Monmouth University —located in West Long Branch New Jersey —also operates graduate and honors schools. Founded in 1933 as the Monmouth Junior College Monmouth University has an enrollment of roughly an 6500 graduate and undergraduate students. The school's student-teacher ratio is about 15:1.

EXECUTIVES

Treasurer and Trustee, John R. Garbarino, age 62
President and Trustee, Paul G. Gaffney II, age 65
VP Academic Affairs and Provost, Thomas Pearson
VP Finance, William G. Craig
VP and General Counsel, Grey J. Dimenna
VP Student Services, Mary Anne Nagy
VP University Advancement, Jeffery N. Mills
Associate VP Enrollment Management and Director Financial Aid, Claire Alasio
VP Administrative Services, Patricia Swannack
Director Affirmative Action Human Relations and Compliance, Raymond Rodriguez
Associate VP Academic Administration and Registrar, Susan J. O'Keefe
Director Registration and Records, Laura Papa Babbin
Director Institutional Research, Eleanor C. Swanson
Associate VP Academic Program Initiatives, Saliba Sarsar
Dean Graduate School and Continuing Education, Datta V. Naik
Director Kislak Real Estate Institute, Donald M. Moliver
Associate Director Kislak Real Estate Institute, Theresa Guyer
Chairman, Alfred J. Schiavetti Jr.
Secretary and Trustee, Deborah B. Larrison
Chairman, Robert B. Sculthorpe
VP Enrollment Management, Robert D. McCaig
VP and Director Athletics, Marilyn McNeil
Dean School of Business Administration, Frederick (Fred) Kelly
Dean School of Education, Lynn Romeo
Dean School of Social Work, Robin S. Mama
Dean McMurray School of Humanities and Social Sciences, Stanton Green
Dean Marjorie K. Unterberg School of Nursing and Health Studies, Marilyn M. Lauria
Dean School of Science Technology and Engineering, Michael A. Palladino
Dean The Honors School, Brian Garvey
Director Public Affairs, Petra Ludwig
Director Purchasing, Mark Miranda
Bursar, Linda Pulcrano
VP Information Management, Edward Christensen
Treasurer and Trustee, John R. Garbarino, age 62
President and Trustee, Paul G. Gaffney II, age 65
Trustee, Rudolph J. Borneo, age 71
Trustee, Stephen M. Parks
Secretary and Trustee, Deborah B. Larrison
Vice Chairman, Robert B. Sculthorpe
Trustee, Marcia Sue Clever
Trustee, Marti S. Egger
Trustee, Alfred L. Ferguson
Director, Michael Gooch
Trustee, Jan Greenwood
Trustee, John H. Kessler
Trustee, Robert E. McAllan
Trustee, Thomas A. Porskievies
Trustee, Steven J. Pozycki
Trustee, Robert B. Rumsby
Trustee, Ann Unterberg
Trustee, Harold L. Hodes
Trustee, Jerome P. Amedeo
Trustee, Peter R. Bruckmann
Trustee, Rose Chaviano-Moran
Trustee, Dennis M. Coleman
Trustee, William P. Dioguardi Jr.
Trustee, Marianne Hesse
Trustee, Kenneth W. Hitchner III
Trustee, Thomas J. Michelli
Trustee, H. William Mullaney
Trustee, Tavit O. Najarian
Trustee, M. Monica Sweeney

LOCATIONS

HQ: Monmouth University
400 Cedar Ave., West Long Branch NJ 07764-1898
Phone: 732-571-3400   **Fax:** 732-263-5117
Web: www.monmouth.edu

HISTORICAL FINANCIALS
Company Type: School

Income Statement
FYE: June 30

	REVENUE ($ mil.)	NET INCOME ($ mil.)	NET PROFIT MARGIN	EMPLOYEES
06/11	196	10	5.6%	1,000
06/10	145	18	12.6%	0
06/08	166	14	8.9%	0
06/07	132	26	19.7%	0
Annual Growth	14.2%	(25.0%)	—	—

2011 Year-End Financials
Debt ratio: —
Return on equity: 5.60%
Cash ($ mil.): 2
Current ratio: —
Long-term debt ($ mil.): —
Dividends
Yield: —
Payout: —
Market value ($ mil.): —

MONOGRAM FOOD SOLUTIONS LLC

Monogram Food Solutions makes its products out of the letters M E A and T. A manufacturer of meat and meat snack products the company produces beef jerky sausage hot dogs bacon and other processed products. Its brands include Circle B King Cotton and Trail's Best Meat Snacks; through special licensing agreements Monogram also sells Jeff Foxworthy Jerky Products NASCAR Jerky and Steak Strips and Bass Pro Uncle Buck's Licensed Products. The company operates facilities in Chandler Minnesota; Muncie Indiana; and Martinsville Virginia and distributes its products nationally. Founded in 2004 Monogram was formed through the merger of assets (King Cotton and Circle B) previously owned by Sara Lee Corp.

Beginning in 2010 the company began manufacturing and selling meat snacks for the energy drink maker DNA Beverages Corporation under the DNA brand. Geared toward a younger consumer the DNA beef products gives Monogram a larger demographic for its products.

Since its founding the company has quickly built itself up by buying established meat product manufacturers and processing plants. In 2009 it acquired three companies including beef jerky maker Wild Bill's Foods and Al Pete's Meats (and the Pete's Pride brand name). It also acquired the Hannah's Bull's O'Brien's and Dakota meat snack brands from meat processing company American Foods Group.

EXECUTIVES
Chief People Officer, Raymond R. Stitle
VP Finance, Jeff Combs
Chairman and CEO, Karl A. Schledwitz
CFO, David (Dave) Dunavant
President, Wes Jackson
COO, Don Brunson
VP Business Development, Mark Olivito
VP and General Manager Monogram Brands, Kirk Harris
VP Marketing, Kathy Mullins
President and COO Monogram Meat Snacks, Ches Jackson

VP Sales North Monogram Meat Snacks, Bill Schneider
VP Operations Monogram Meat Snacks, Jeff Johnson
VP and General Manager Monogram Comfort Foods, Steve Hofford

LOCATIONS
HQ: Monogram Food Solutions LLC
930 S. White Station Rd., Memphis TN 38117
Phone: 901-685-7167   **Fax:** 901-259-6671
Web: www.monogramfoods.com

COMPETITORS
Bridgford Foods
Carl Buddig
Clemens Family Corporation
ConAgra
Hormel
Jerky Snack Brands
Link Snacks
Oberto Sausage Company
Weaver Meats

HISTORICAL FINANCIALS
Company Type: Private

Income Statement
FYE: December 31

	REVENUE ($ mil.)	NET INCOME ($ mil.)	NET PROFIT MARGIN	EMPLOYEES
12/11	173	3	1.8%	790
Annual Growth	—	—	—	—

2011 Year-End Financials
Debt ratio: —
Return on equity: 1.80%
Cash ($ mil.): 0
Current ratio: 1.00
Long-term debt ($ mil.): —
Dividends
Yield: —
Payout: —
Market value ($ mil.): —

MONONGAHELA VALLEY HOSPITAL INC

LOCATIONS
HQ: MONONGAHELA VALLEY HOSPITAL INC
1163 COUNTRY CLUB RD, MONONGAHELA, PA 15063-1095
Phone: 724-258-1000
Web: www.monvalleyhospital.com

HISTORICAL FINANCIALS
Company Type: Private

Income Statement
FYE: June 30

	REVENUE ($ mil.)	NET INCOME ($ mil.)	NET PROFIT MARGIN	EMPLOYEES
06/12	124	(12)	—	1,000
06/11	123	1	1.4%	0
06/10	111	(2)	—	0
06/09	108	(12)	—	0
Annual Growth	4.9%	—	—	—

2012 Year-End Financials
Debt ratio: —
Return on equity: (-9.70)%
Cash ($ mil.): 23
Current ratio: 2.00
Long-term debt ($ mil.): —
Dividends
Yield: —
Payout: —
Market value ($ mil.): —

MONONGALIA COUNTY GENERAL HOSPITAL COMPANY

LOCATIONS
HQ: MONONGALIA COUNTY GENERAL HOSPITAL COMPANY
1200 J D ANDERSON DR, MORGANTOWN, WV 26505-3494
Phone: 304-598-1200
Web: www.mongeneral.com

HISTORICAL FINANCIALS
Company Type: Private

Income Statement
FYE: June 30

	REVENUE ($ mil.)	NET INCOME ($ mil.)	NET PROFIT MARGIN	EMPLOYEES
06/11	220	13	6.0%	1,100
06/10	205	13	6.7%	0
06/09	368	6	1.8%	0
06/08	3	1	55.4%	0
Annual Growth	303.6%	92.6%	—	—

2011 Year-End Financials
Debt ratio: —
Return on equity: 6.00%
Cash ($ mil.): 33
Current ratio: 4.40
Long-term debt ($ mil.): —
Dividends
Yield: —
Payout: —
Market value ($ mil.): —

MONTGOMERY COLLEGE FOUNDATION INC.

LOCATIONS
HQ: MONTGOMERY COLLEGE FOUNDATION INC.
900 HUNGERFORD DR, ROCKVILLE, MD 20850-1728
Phone: 240-567-5000
Web: www.montgomerycollege.edu

HISTORICAL FINANCIALS
Company Type: Private

Income Statement
FYE: June 30

	REVENUE ($ mil.)	NET INCOME ($ mil.)	NET PROFIT MARGIN	EMPLOYEES
06/12	123	10	8.6%	3,600
06/11	118	33	28.3%	0
06/10	112	45	40.7%	0
06/09	105	46	43.6%	0
Annual Growth	5.2%	(38.8%)	—	—

2012 Year-End Financials
Debt ratio: —
Return on equity: 8.60%
Cash ($ mil.): 49
Current ratio: 1.40
Long-term debt ($ mil.): —
Dividends
Yield: —
Payout: —
Market value ($ mil.): —

MONTGOMERY GENERAL HOSPITAL INCORPORATED

LOCATIONS

HQ: MONTGOMERY GENERAL HOSPITAL INCORPORATED
18101 PRINCE PHILIP DR, OLNEY, MD 20832-1512
Phone: 301-774-8882
Web: www.montgomerygeneral.org

HISTORICAL FINANCIALS

Company Type: Private

Income Statement

FYE: June 30

	REVENUE ($ mil.)	NET INCOME ($ mil.)	NET PROFIT MARGIN	EMPLOYEES
06/11	143	7	4.9%	1,500
06/10	138	5	3.8%	0
06/09	127	0	0.3%	0
06/08	125	6	5.4%	0
Annual Growth	**4.5%**	**0.9%**	**—**	**—**

2011 Year-End Financials

Debt ratio: —
Return on equity: 4.90%
Cash ($ mil.): 22
Current ratio: 2.70
Long-term debt ($ mil.): —
Dividends
Yield: —
Payout: —
Market value ($ mil.): —

MOORE INDEPENDENT SCHOOL DISTRICT NO 2

LOCATIONS

HQ: MOORE INDEPENDENT SCHOOL DISTRICT NO 2
1500 SE 4TH ST, MOORE, OK 73160-8266
Phone: 405-735-4200

HISTORICAL FINANCIALS

Company Type: Private

Income Statement

FYE: June 30

	REVENUE ($ mil.)	NET INCOME ($ mil.)	NET PROFIT MARGIN	EMPLOYEES
06/11	177	(4)	—	2,000
06/10	166	9	5.8%	0
06/08	160	(7)	—	0
06/07	150	0	0.2%	0
Annual Growth	**5.7%**	**—**	**—**	**—**

2011 Year-End Financials

Debt ratio: —
Return on equity: (-2.60)%
Cash ($ mil.): 77
Current ratio: —
Long-term debt ($ mil.): —
Dividends
Yield: —
Payout: —
Market value ($ mil.): —

MOREHEAD MEMORIAL HOSPITAL INC

Morehead Memorial Hospital is a not-for-profit community hospital that provides health care services to residents of Rockingham County in north-central North Carolina. The hospital has about 110 acute care beds and provides general medical-surgical care including emergency services obstetrical care outpatient surgery and cancer treatment. It also provides home health care services and operates several ancillary facilities such as a freestanding diagnostic imaging facility and a physical rehabilitation center. The hospital's main campus (built in 1960) includes Morehead Nursing Center a long-term care facility with about 135 beds. Madison Morehead Memorial Hospital traces its origin back to 1924.

Drs. C. V. Tyner Kenan Casteen and H. Carlyle Dixon founded a 24-bed hospital in 1924 that in 1953 became a publicly owned community hospital named Tri-City Hospital. Through a series of expansions and support from the community the current hospital evolved and was renamed Morehead Memorial Hospital.

Today the hospital has its main campus and two off-campus sites: the Wright Diagnostic Center and Morehead Physical Rehabilitation. The diagnostic center provides laboratory and diagnostic imaging and houses a wound healing center the Lou McMichael Miracle Breast Imaging suite the Morehead Memorial Hospital Foundation and patient financial services.

Morehead Physical Rehabilitation provides a range of therapies from physical and occupational therapy to speech and language and massage therapy. It also provides for functional capacity evaluations.

The hospital also has three office buildings for physicians. Modernization efforts have included implementation of an electronic medical records system and adoption of such technologies and services as CT and MRI scanning lithotripsy laser surgery angiography digital mammography and stereotactic breast biopsy procedures. It also has a vascular laboratory.

EXECUTIVES

VP Human Resources, Tom Stevens
VP Finance, Dan Elmer
VP, Amanda Currin
VP, Mark Twilla
Administrator Morehead Nursing Center, Kathy McLawhorn
VP Nursing, Michele Pilon
Director Marketing and Public Relations, Kerry Faunce
President and CEO, W. Carl Martin, age 58
VP Practice Management, Tamara Hunt
Director Nursing Morehead Nursing Center, Daphyne Anderson
Director Physical Rehabilitation, Bruce Richardson
VP Operations, Steven Kleckowski

LOCATIONS

HQ: Morehead Memorial Hospital
117 E. Kings Hwy., Eden NC 27288
Phone: 336-623-9711   **Fax:** 336-623-7660
Web: www.morehead.org

COMPETITORS

Danville Regional Medical Center
Duke University Health System
FirstHealth of the Carolinas
Moses Cone Health
Novant Health
UNC Hospitals
Wake Forest University Baptist Medical Center
Wesley Long Community Hospital

HISTORICAL FINANCIALS

Company Type: Private - Not-for-Profit

Income Statement

FYE: September 30

	REVENUE ($ mil.)	NET INCOME ($ mil.)	NET PROFIT MARGIN	EMPLOYEES
09/11	103	(3)	—	850
09/10	100	5	5.6%	0
09/09	0	0	—	0
09/06	82	3	3.8%	0
Annual Growth	**7.6%**	**—**	**—**	**—**

2011 Year-End Financials

Debt ratio: —
Return on equity: (-3.20)%
Cash ($ mil.): 10
Current ratio: 2.50
Long-term debt ($ mil.): —
Dividends
Yield: —
Payout: —
Market value ($ mil.): —

MOREHOUSE COLLEGE (INC.)

Morehouse College is the largest private liberal arts college for African-American men. Located three miles from downtown Atlanta the college has an enrollment of nearly 3000 students. Facilities include the Leadership Center at Morehouse College Morehouse Research Institute and Andrew Young Center for International Affairs. The school has courses of study in business and economics humanities and social sciences and science and mathematics. It also offers a degree in engineering in conjunction with Georgia Institute of Technology. Notable alumni include civil rights activist Dr. Martin Luther King Jr. filmmaker Shelton "Spike" Lee and actor Samuel L. Jackson. Morehouse College was founded in 1867.

Morehouse College is home to the Martin Luther King Jr. Collection —a 10000-piece collection of original papers and documents written by the school's most iconic alumnus. Scholarly access to the collection was made available in 2009. In 2006 a group of business leaders helped raise some $32 million to purchase the documents which were bound for the auction block. The documents are now held at the Robert W. Woodruff Library and also available to view digitally.

EXECUTIVES

Vice Chair, Robert C. (Bob) Davidson Jr., age 66
Director Public Relations, Toni O'Neal Mosley
VP Campus Operations, Andre Bertrand
Chief Audit Officer Department of Internal Auditing and Advisory Services, C. O. Hollis Jr.
Associate VP Student Financial Services, Margaret Jackson

LOCATIONS

HQ: Morehouse College
830 Westview Dr. SW, Atlanta GA 30314
Phone: 404-681-2800 **Fax:** 208-773-7467
Web: www.commandlabor.com

HISTORICAL FINANCIALS
Company Type: School

Income Statement

	REVENUE ($ mil.)	NET INCOME ($ mil.)	NET PROFIT MARGIN	EMPLOYEES
				FYE: June 30
06/11	104	(12)	—	700
06/10*	99	16	16.2%	0
04/10	93	30	33.1%	0
06/08	79	(6)	—	0
Annual Growth	9.5%	—	—	—

*Fiscal year change

2011 Year-End Financials

Debt ratio: ——
Return on equity: (-12.40)%
Cash ($ mil.): 18
Current ratio: ——
Long-term debt ($ mil.): —

Dividends
Yield: —
Payout: —
Market value ($ mil.): —

MORRIS HOLDINGS INC

LOCATIONS

HQ: MORRIS HOLDINGS INC
1650 COUNTY ROAD 210 W, JACKSONVILLE, FL 32259-2011
Phone: 904-829-3946

HISTORICAL FINANCIALS
Company Type: Private

Income Statement

	REVENUE ($ mil.)	NET INCOME ($ mil.)	NET PROFIT MARGIN	EMPLOYEES
				FYE: March 31
03/11	93	0	0.2%	350
03/07	83	0	1.0%	0
03/06	82	0	0.4%	0
03/05	76	0	1.2%	0
Annual Growth	6.6%	(43.5%)	—	—

2011 Year-End Financials

Debt ratio: ——
Return on equity: 0.20%
Cash ($ mil.): 0
Current ratio: 0.30
Long-term debt ($ mil.): —

Dividends
Yield: —
Payout: —
Market value ($ mil.): —

MORRIS ROBERT UNIVERSITY ILLINOIS

LOCATIONS

HQ: MORRIS ROBERT UNIVERSITY ILLINOIS
401 S STATE ST FL 2, CHICAGO, IL 60605-1234
Phone: 312-935-6800

HISTORICAL FINANCIALS
Company Type: Private

Income Statement

	REVENUE ($ mil.)	NET INCOME ($ mil.)	NET PROFIT MARGIN	EMPLOYEES
				FYE: June 30
06/12	114	(10)	—	800
06/11	120	(0)	—	0
06/10	119	8	6.9%	0
06/09	0	0	—	0
Annual Growth	—	—	—	—

2012 Year-End Financials

Debt ratio: ——
Return on equity: (-8.90)%
Cash ($ mil.): 2
Current ratio: ——
Long-term debt ($ mil.): —

Dividends
Yield: —
Payout: —
Market value ($ mil.): —

MORTGAGE INVESTORS CORPORATION

LOCATIONS

HQ: MORTGAGE INVESTORS CORPORATION
6090 CENTRAL AVE, SAINT PETERSBURG, FL 33707-1622
Phone: 727-347-1930
Web: www.mortgageinvestors.com

HISTORICAL FINANCIALS
Company Type: Private

Income Statement

	ASSETS ($ mil.)	NET INCOME ($ mil.)	INCOME AS % OF ASSETS	EMPLOYEES
				FYE: December 31
12/11	165	6	4.1%	700
12/10	120	23	19.5%	0
12/09	73	36	50.2%	0
12/08	12	4	34.2%	0
Annual Growth	135.2%	15.9%	—	—

2011 Year-End Financials

Debt ratio: ——
Return on equity: 2.40%
Cash ($ mil.): 15
Current ratio: —
Long-term debt ($ mil.): —

Dividends
Yield: —
Payout: —
Market value ($ mil.): —

MOSAIC

Mosaic creates color in the lives of the disadvantaged. The not-for-profit organization provides individualized support and advocacy services living facilities education and employment for people with disabilities. The Christian organization serves some 3500 clients through 40 agencies in 250 communities. Its operations are located in more than a dozen states across the US as well as in Latvia and the UK. Services include case management foster care vocational training and supervised living arrangements. Mosaic also offers senior independent living services and support at select facilities in Iowa and Wisconsin.

The organization has been expanding its international efforts both on its own (Latvia and Great Britain) and through its participation in international Lutheran network IMPACT. Through the alliance Mosaic also offers support in Romania and Tanzania.

US expansion has also been part of the plan in 2009. After problems at a state-funded residential facility in Nebraska led the state to relocate many residents to local hospitals Mosaic said it would open nearly a dozen new small homes to handle the medically dependent individuals. The organization is looking for growth opportunities in other areas as well.

Also in 2009 Mosaic began a cost-cutting program in response to financial challenges brought on by economic difficulties state budget cuts and reductions in Medicaid reimbursements. (Medicaid is a major source of funding for Mosaic.) Restructuring efforts included a hiring freeze and a reshuffling of regional organizations. The group is also working to attract new charitable donors and volunteers to support its organization.

Mosaic is affiliated with the Evangelical Lutheran Church in America and came into being when Bethpage Inner Mission Association and Martin Luther Homes consolidated in 2003.

EXECUTIVES

EVP, David A. Jacox
SVP and CFO, Cynthia L. Schroeder
SVP Human Resources and Chief Integrity Officer, Raul Saldivar
President and CEO, Linda M. Timmons
SVP Mission Advancement, Keith Schmode
SVP Business Development, Gary Lee
Chairperson, Richard Toftness
SVP Operations and Public Policy, Anne Starr
Director, David Bailey
Director, Joseph Derdzinski
Director, Susan Flack
Director, John Fullenkamp
Director, Karen Hawkins
Director, Rev Kevin Kanouse
Director, Mark Klever
Director, Rev Walter May Jr.
Director, Billie McMiller
Director, Julie Schlueter
Director, Jenna Schrack
Director, Jack Stark

LOCATIONS

HQ: Mosaic
4980 S. 118th St., Omaha NE 68137-2220
Phone: 402-896-3884   **Fax:** 402-896-1511
Web: www.mosaicinfo.org

COMPETITORS

Brookdale Senior Living
Care UK
Elwyn
GEO Group
HCR ManorCare
Kindred Healthcare
Life Care Centers
Magellan Health
Providence Service
Res-Care
Sun Healthcare
Sunrise Senior Living

HISTORICAL FINANCIALS
Company Type: Private - Not-for-Profit

Income Statement
FYE: June 30

	REVENUE ($ mil.)	NET INCOME ($ mil.)	NET PROFIT MARGIN	EMPLOYEES
06/12	212	4	1.9%	3,500
06/11	212	11	5.3%	0
06/10	197	7	4.0%	0
06/09	185	1	0.6%	0
Annual Growth	4.6%	51.5%	—	—

2012 Year-End Financials
Debt ratio: —
Return on equity: 1.90%
Cash ($ mil.): 17
Current ratio: 0.50
Long-term debt ($ mil.): —
Dividends
Yield: —
Payout: —
Market value ($ mil.): —

MOTHER FRANCES HOSPITAL REGIONAL HEALTH CARE CENTER

LOCATIONS

HQ: MOTHER FRANCES HOSPITAL REGIONAL HEALTH CARE CENTER
800 E DAWSON ST, TYLER, TX 75701-2093
Phone: 903-593-8441

HISTORICAL FINANCIALS
Company Type: Private

Income Statement
FYE: June 30

	REVENUE ($ mil.)	NET INCOME ($ mil.)	NET PROFIT MARGIN	EMPLOYEES
06/11*	533	65	12.3%	2,747
03/10	314	50	16.1%	0
06/08	376	18	4.8%	0
06/06	350	315	89.8%	0
Annual Growth	15.0%	(40.7%)	—	—

*Fiscal year change

2011 Year-End Financials
Debt ratio: —
Return on equity: 12.30%
Cash ($ mil.): 78
Current ratio: 0.40
Long-term debt ($ mil.): —
Dividends
Yield: —
Payout: —
Market value ($ mil.): —

MOUNT NITTANY MEDICAL CENTER

LOCATIONS

HQ: MOUNT NITTANY MEDICAL CENTER
1800 E PARK AVE, STATE COLLEGE, PA 16803-6797
Phone: 814-231-7000
Web: www.mountnittany.org

HISTORICAL FINANCIALS
Company Type: Private

Income Statement
FYE: June 30

	REVENUE ($ mil.)	NET INCOME ($ mil.)	NET PROFIT MARGIN	EMPLOYEES
06/12	260	(7)	—	902
06/11	235	18	7.8%	0
06/10	209	27	13.1%	0
06/09	190	17	9.2%	0
Annual Growth	11.0%	—	—	—

2012 Year-End Financials
Debt ratio: —
Return on equity: (-3.00)%
Cash ($ mil.): 25
Current ratio: 2.10
Long-term debt ($ mil.): —
Dividends
Yield: —
Payout: —
Market value ($ mil.): —

MOUNT ST MARY'S COLLEGE

LOCATIONS

HQ: MOUNT ST MARY' S COLLEGE
12001 CHALON RD, LOS ANGELES, CA 90049-1599
Phone: 310-954-4000
Web: www.msmc.la.edu

HISTORICAL FINANCIALS
Company Type: Private

Income Statement
FYE: June 30

	REVENUE ($ mil.)	NET INCOME ($ mil.)	NET PROFIT MARGIN	EMPLOYEES
06/11	91	10	11.3%	350
06/10	77	7	9.4%	0
06/09	67	0	—	0
06/08	72	10	15.0%	0
Annual Growth	7.9%	(1.9%)	—	—

2011 Year-End Financials
Debt ratio: —
Return on equity: 11.30%
Cash ($ mil.): 10
Current ratio: —
Long-term debt ($ mil.): —
Dividends
Yield: —
Payout: —
Market value ($ mil.): —

MOUNTAIN STATES HEALTH ALLIANCE

Mountain States Health Alliance (MSHA) believes in teamwork when it comes to providing health care to the good people living in Tennessee and Virginia. Along with MSHA's dozen acute care hospitals the integrated healthcare delivery system operates more than 20 primary and preventive care centers and numerous outpatient care sites including First Assist Urgent Care MedWorks Same Day Surgery and Rehab Plus. It also operates the Mountain States Medical group of about 180 doctors who administer care at dozens of locations throughout the region. Formed in 1998 MSHA is home to roughly 1500 beds; its largest facility is the Johnson City Medical Center with 500 beds.

Operations

MSHA is the region's largest healthcare system with 13 hospitals and 21 primary/preventive care centers and numerous outpatient care sites including First Assist Urgent Care MedWorks Same Day Surgery and Rehab Plus.

Geographic Reach

The company serves 29 counties in Kentucky North CarolinaTennessee and Virginia.

Strategy

Deep cuts to the Medicare reimbursement rates paid to hospitals in Tennessee (and the rest of the nation) have led MSHA to implement a number of cost-cutting measures across the system. The organization put into action a program to standardize its clinical and non-clinical processes based on the adoption of best practices throughout MSHA. It also eliminates duplicate services by centralizing certain services. For example it stopped providing psychiatric care at its Indian Path Pavilion and consolidated those services into the Woodridge Hospital.

In 2012 MSHA partnered with LMU (Lincoln Memorial University) to expand the university's Medical Laboratory Science program to Kingsport to address a staffing shortage of medical laboratory scientists that has been a problem for a number of years.

In addition the Smyth County Community Hospital got a $66 million facelift to increase its size and to make the facility an all-private-room (higher revenue-generating) hospital. The hospital's 44 private rooms include 30 acute care beds and 14 rehab beds. The upgrade completed in 2012 also increased the emergency department by 75%.

EXECUTIVES

President CEO and Director, Dennis Vonderfecht
SVP and CFO, Marvin Eichorn
VP, Edward (Ed) Herbert
VP, Jamie Parsons
VP and CIO, Richard Eshbach
SVP and Chief Medical Officer, Ken Marshall
VP and Chief Nursing Executive, Kathryn W. Wilhoit
VP and CEO Indian Path Medical Center, Monty McLaurin
SVP and CEO North Side Hospital, John Melton
Administrator Director of Nursing Johnson County Health Center-JCHC, Lisa A. Heaton
VP Human Resources, June Pieschel
VP, Lisa Smithgall
VP and President BRMMC, Steve Kilgore
VP; CFO Washington County Operations, Kerry Vermillion
VP, Cindy Salyer

Chairman, Joanne Gilmer
Vice Chairman, W.E. Hawkins Jr.
VP; CEO Sycamore Shoals Hospital, Dwayne Taylor
SVP Strategic Service Units, Ann L. Fleming
VP and CEO Norton Community Hospital and Dickenson Community Hospital, Craig James
VP and COO Washington County Operations, Candace Jennings
VP and CEO Smyth County Community Hospital, Lindy White
President Mountain States Foundation, Pat Holtsclaw
CEO Indian Path Pavilion, Jeff Dykes
Director James H. and Cecile C. Quillen Rehabilitaiton Hospital, Tammy Bishop
CFO Russell County Medical Center, Mike Widener
CEO Woodridge Hospital, Jeff Dice
Assistant VP Administration Russell County Medical Center, Eddie Greene
President CEO and Director, Dennis Vonderfecht
Vice Chairman, W.E. Hawkins Jr.
Director, Don Jeanes
Director, Jeff Farrow
Director, Robert Feathers
Director, Maureen MacIver
Director, Cameron Perry
Director, William Walker
Director, Sandra Brooks
Director, Thomas J. Burleson
Director, John Campbell

LOCATIONS

HQ: Mountain States Health Alliance
400 N. State of Franklin Rd., Johnson City TN 37604-6094
Phone: 423-431-6111   **Fax:** 423-431-2856
Web: www.msha.com

PRODUCTS/OPERATIONS

Selected Facilities
Tennessee
  Indian Path Medical Center (Kingsport)
  James H. and Cecile C. Quillen Rehabilitation Hospital (Johnson City)
  Johnson City Medical Center (Johnson City)
  Johnson County Community Hospital (Mountain City)
  Niswonger Community Hospital (Johnson City)
  North Side Hospital (Johnson City)
  Sycamore Shoals Hospital (Elizabethton)
  Woodridge Hospital (Johnson City)
Virginia
  Dickenson Community Hospital (Clintwood)
  Johnston Memorial Hospital (Abingdon)
  Norton Community Hospital (Norton)
  Russell County Medical Center (Lebanon)
  Smyth County Community Hospital (Marion)

COMPETITORS

Baptist Hospital
Baptist Memorial Health Care
Community Health Systems
Cookeville Regional Medical Center
Erlanger Health System
HCA
Health Management Associates
Kindred Healthcare
LifePoint Hospitals
Middle Tennessee Medical Center
Shelby County Health Care
Southern Hills
Vanderbilt University Medical Center

HISTORICAL FINANCIALS
Company Type: Private

Income Statement
FYE: June 30

	REVENUE ($ mil.)	NET INCOME ($ mil.)	NET PROFIT MARGIN	EMPLOYEES
06/11	729	49	6.8%	5,978
06/10	701	43	6.2%	0
06/08	0	0	0.2%	0
06/05	513	9	1.9%	0
Annual Growth	12.4%	72.9%	—	—

2011 Year-End Financials
Debt ratio: —
Return on equity: 6.80%
Cash ($ mil.): 94
Current ratio: —
Long-term debt ($ mil.): —
Dividends
  Yield: —
  Payout: —
  Market value ($ mil.): —

MUHLENBERG COLLEGE

LOCATIONS

HQ: MUHLENBERG COLLEGE
2400 CHEW ST, ALLENTOWN, PA 18104-5586
Phone: 484-664-3100
Web: www.muhlenberg.edu

HISTORICAL FINANCIALS
Company Type: Private

Income Statement
FYE: June 30

	REVENUE ($ mil.)	NET INCOME ($ mil.)	NET PROFIT MARGIN	EMPLOYEES
06/12	89	(1)	—	491
06/11	88	23	26.8%	0
06/10	85	15	17.8%	0
06/09	81	(10)	—	0
Annual Growth	3.0%	—	—	—

2012 Year-End Financials
Debt ratio: —
Return on equity: (-2.10)%
Cash ($ mil.): 20
Current ratio: —
Long-term debt ($ mil.): —
Dividends
  Yield: —
  Payout: —
  Market value ($ mil.): —

MULTNOMAH COUNTY SCHOOL DISTRICT U2-20 JT

LOCATIONS

HQ: MULTNOMAH COUNTY SCHOOL DISTRICT U2-20 JT
1331 NW EASTMAN PKWY, GRESHAM, OR 97030-3825
Phone: 503-618-2470

HISTORICAL FINANCIALS

Company Type: Private

Income Statement

FYE: June 30

	REVENUE ($ mil.)	NET INCOME ($ mil.)	NET PROFIT MARGIN	EMPLOYEES
06/12	109	(5)	—	1,003
06/11	111	(0)	—	0
06/10	113	3	3.0%	0
06/09	110	(3)	—	0
Annual Growth	(0.3%)	—	—	—

2012 Year-End Financials

Debt ratio: —
Return on equity: (-4.90)%
Cash ($ mil.): 21
Current ratio: —
Long-term debt ($ mil.): —
Dividends
  Yield: —
  Payout: —
Market value ($ mil.): —

MUNICIPAL UTILITIES BOARD OF DECATUR MORGAN COUNTY ALABAMA

LOCATIONS

HQ: MUNICIPAL UTILITIES BOARD OF DECATUR MORGAN COUNTY ALABAMA
1002 CENTRAL PKWY SW, DECATUR, AL 35601-4848
Phone: 256-552-1440
Web: www.decaturutilities.com

HISTORICAL FINANCIALS

Company Type: Private

Income Statement

FYE: September 30

	REVENUE ($ mil.)	NET INCOME ($ mil.)	NET PROFIT MARGIN	EMPLOYEES
09/11	141	4	2.9%	157
09/10	135	1	1.4%	0
09/09	141	0	0.3%	0
09/08	145	1	1.1%	0
Annual Growth	(0.8%)	35.6%	—	—

2011 Year-End Financials

Debt ratio: —
Return on equity: 2.90%
Cash ($ mil.): 28
Current ratio: 2.60
Long-term debt ($ mil.): —
Dividends
  Yield: —
  Payout: —
Market value ($ mil.): —

MUSCULAR DYSTROPHY ASSOCIATION INC.

The Muscular Dystrophy Association (MDA) is a not-for-profit health agency that supports research into more than 40 neuromuscular diseases including including muscular dystrophy and Lou Gehrig's disease (also known as ALS). MDA believes more than one million Americans have some form of muscular dystrophy. The organization operates more than 200 health care clinics across the US runs summer camps for kids provides funding for research publishes educational materials and engages in national advocacy. It also sponsors more than 200 hospital-affiliated clinics and funds some 330 research projects globally. Founded in 1950 MDA is funded by private contributions.

Along with private contributions MDA is also funded by corporate sponsorships such as 7-Eleven Burger King CITGO Harley Davidson and Safeway.

The organization also publishes print and online magazines such as Quest and MDA/ALS Newsmagazine.Both Quest and MDA/ALS published quarterly and a subscribership of over 130000 provides important stories and facts to people with neurological diseases like tips for better independent living resources available to people with disabilities medical treatment and procedures and and new medical treatments.

After serving 49 years as the host and fundraiser for the MDA the organization parted ways with comedian Jerry Lewis in 2011.

EXECUTIVES

Treasurer, Suzanne Lowden, age 58
VP Public Information, Bob Mackle
President and CEO, Gerald C. (Jerry) Weinberg
National VP, Jerry Allsbrook
National Chairman, Jerry Lewis
VP Community Programs, Michael A. Blishak
VP Western Divisions, Brad Barghols
VP Information Technology, Rod E. Brandon
Chairman, R. Rodney Howell
Vice Chairman, Lois R. West
Secretary, Timmi Masters
SVP, Valerie Cwik
SVP, Kevin Moran
SVP, Pete Morgan
SVP and General Counsel, Gail Schmertz
President and CEO, Steven M. (Steve) Derks
Vice Chairman, Lois R. West
Director, Stanley H. Appel
Director, Robert M. Bennett
Director, Leon I. Charash
Director, Bart Conner
Director, Harold C. Crump
Director, Benjamin F. Cumbo
Director, Joseph S. DiMartino
Director, Daniel G. Fries
Director, R. Rodney Howell
Director, Louis M. Kunkel

Director, Dave Hutton
Director, Maureen McGovern
Director, Ed McMahon
Director, Olin F. Morris
Director, Christopher J. Rosa
Director, Charles D. Schoor
Auditors: Ernst&YoungLLP

LOCATIONS

HQ: Muscular Dystrophy Association
3300 E. Sunrise Dr., Tucson AZ 85718
Phone: 520-529-2000   **Fax:** 520-529-5300
Web: www.mda.org

HISTORICAL FINANCIALS

Company Type: Private - Not-for-Profit

Income Statement

FYE: December 31

	REVENUE ($ mil.)	NET INCOME ($ mil.)	NET PROFIT MARGIN	EMPLOYEES
12/11	159	(53)	—	1,150
12/10	178	(7)	—	0
12/09	190	5	2.9%	0
12/08	164	0	—	0
Annual Growth	(1.1%)	—	—	—

2011 Year-End Financials

Debt ratio: —
Return on equity: (-33.90)%
Cash ($ mil.): 12
Current ratio: 0.20
Long-term debt ($ mil.): —
Dividends
  Yield: —
  Payout: —
Market value ($ mil.): —

MUSEUM OF FINE ARTS

In a city known for its erudite inhabitants the The Museum of Fine Arts (MFA) Boston seeks to entertain and educate. The MFA Boston offers a wide range of collections such as Art of Americas Art of Europe Art of the Ancient World Contemporary Art Textile and Fashion Arts and Musical Instruments. The museum also provides public programs for children and adults including art classes and workshops. With approximately 75000 members the MFA Boston attracts about one million visitors annually. Founded in 1870 the museum through a partnership opened the Nagoya/Boston Museum of Fine Arts in 1999.

The MFA is in the midst of a major ongoing renovation project that includes the erection of a new American Wing slated to reopen in late 2010 and the Ruth and Carl J. Shapiro Family Courtyard. The building project is being paid for with $504 million raised in a campagn that concluded in fall 2008.

In 2007 the MFA acquired the Forsyth Institute property a Boston landmark adjacent to the museum on the Fenway.

EXECUTIVES

Deputy Director and CFO, Mark Kerwin
Ann and Graham Gund Director, Malcolm Rogers
Public Relations Associate, Amelia Kantrovitz
Director Public Relations, Dawn Griffin
Chairman, Stokley P. Towles
President Board of Trustees, Barbara Alfond

LOCATIONS

HQ: Museum of Fine Arts Boston
465 Huntington Ave., Boston MA 02115-5597
Phone: 617-267-9300 **Fax:** 617-247-6880
Web: www.mfa.org

HISTORICAL FINANCIALS
Company Type: Private

Income Statement				FYE: June 30
	REVENUE ($ mil.)	NET INCOME ($ mil.)	NET PROFIT MARGIN	EMPLOYEES
06/11	157	12	7.8%	1,000
06/10	122	7	5.9%	0
06/09	69	(49)	—	0
06/08	226	64	28.5%	0
Annual Growth	(11.5%)	(42.5%)	—	—

2011 Year-End Financials

Debt ratio: ——
Return on equity: 7.80%
Cash ($ mil.): 71
Current ratio: 0.40
Long-term debt ($ mil.): ——
Dividends
Yield: ——
Payout: ——
Market value ($ mil.): ——

NAI GROUP LLC

LOCATIONS

HQ: NAI GROUP LLC
7975 N HAYDEN RD STE D105, SCOTTSDALE, AZ
85258-3247
Phone: 480-556-6066
Web: www.nai-group.com

HISTORICAL FINANCIALS
Company Type: Private

Income Statement				FYE: December 31
	REVENUE ($ mil.)	NET INCOME ($ mil.)	NET PROFIT MARGIN	EMPLOYEES
12/11	96	2	2.8%	1,500
12/09	56	0	1.3%	0
12/08	67	0	1.0%	0
Annual Growth	19.4%	105.0%	—	—

2011 Year-End Financials

Debt ratio: ——
Return on equity: 2.80%
Cash ($ mil.): 0
Current ratio: 0.70
Long-term debt ($ mil.): ——
Dividends
Yield: ——
Payout: ——
Market value ($ mil.): ——

NAPERVILLE COMMUNITY UNIT SCHOOL DISTRICT 203

LOCATIONS

HQ: NAPERVILLE COMMUNITY UNIT SCHOOL
DISTRICT 203
203 W HILLSIDE RD, NAPERVILLE, IL 60540-6500
Phone: 630-420-6300
Web: www.naperville203.org

HISTORICAL FINANCIALS
Company Type: Private

Income Statement				FYE: June 30
	REVENUE ($ mil.)	NET INCOME ($ mil.)	NET PROFIT MARGIN	EMPLOYEES
06/12	283	6	2.4%	2,000
06/11	273	(22)	—	0
06/10	263	0	0.2%	0
06/09	0	0	—	0
Annual Growth	630.4%	—	—	—

NATIONAL BOARD OF MEDICAL EXAMINERS INC

LOCATIONS

HQ: NATIONAL BOARD OF MEDICAL EXAMINERS INC
3750 MARKET ST, PHILADELPHIA, PA 19104-3190
Phone: 215-590-9525
Web: www.nbme.org

HISTORICAL FINANCIALS
Company Type: Private

Income Statement				FYE: December 31
	REVENUE ($ mil.)	NET INCOME ($ mil.)	NET PROFIT MARGIN	EMPLOYEES
12/11	111	116	104.1%	300
12/09	103	(4)	—	0
12/08	96	(73)	—	0
12/07	97	(3)	—	0
Annual Growth	4.7%	—	—	—

2011 Year-End Financials

Debt ratio: ——
Return on equity: 104.10%
Cash ($ mil.): 6
Current ratio: 0.30
Long-term debt ($ mil.): ——
Dividends
Yield: ——
Payout: ——
Market value ($ mil.): ——

NATIONAL BRONZE AND METALS INC.

LOCATIONS

HQ: NATIONAL BRONZE AND METALS INC.
2929 W 12TH ST, HOUSTON, TX 77008-6113
Phone: 713-869-9600
Web: www.nbm-houston.com

HISTORICAL FINANCIALS
Company Type: Private

Income Statement				FYE: June 30
	REVENUE ($ mil.)	NET INCOME ($ mil.)	NET PROFIT MARGIN	EMPLOYEES
06/12	112	2	2.1%	159
06/11	94	2	2.5%	0
06/10	65	(1)	—	0
06/09	74	(2)	—	0
Annual Growth	14.6%	—	—	—

2012 Year-End Financials

Debt ratio: ——
Return on equity: 2.10%
Cash ($ mil.): 0
Current ratio: 1.20
Long-term debt ($ mil.): ——
Dividends
Yield: ——
Payout: ——
Market value ($ mil.): ——

NATIONAL CHRISTIAN CHARITABLE

LOCATIONS

HQ: NATIONAL CHRISTIAN CHARITABLE
11625 RAINWATER DR # 500, ALPHARETTA, GA
30009-8674
Phone: 404-252-0100
Web: www.nationalchristian.com

HISTORICAL FINANCIALS
Company Type: Private

Income Statement				FYE: December 31
	REVENUE ($ mil.)	NET INCOME ($ mil.)	NET PROFIT MARGIN	EMPLOYEES
12/11	665	141	21.3%	2
12/09	396	50	12.7%	0
Annual Growth	68.0%	181.9%	—	—

2011 Year-End Financials

Debt ratio: ——
Return on equity: 21.30%
Cash ($ mil.): 302
Current ratio: 42.00
Long-term debt ($ mil.): ——
Dividends
Yield: ——
Payout: ——
Market value ($ mil.): ——

NATIONAL DEMOCRATIC INSTITUTE FOR INTERNATIONAL AFFAIRS (INC.)

LOCATIONS

HQ: NATIONAL DEMOCRATIC INSTITUTE FOR INTERNATIONAL AFFAIRS (INC.)
455 MDCCHSTTS AVE NW FL 8, WASHINGTON, DC 20001
Phone: 202-728-5500

HISTORICAL FINANCIALS

Company Type: Private

Income Statement

FYE: September 30

	REVENUE ($ mil.)	NET INCOME ($ mil.)	NET PROFIT MARGIN	EMPLOYEES
09/11	148	(0)	—	1,300
09/10	130	0	0.1%	0
09/09	118	0	0.2%	0
09/08	117	(0)	—	0
Annual Growth	**8.2%**	—	—	—

2011 Year-End Financials

Debt ratio: ——
Return on equity: (-0.10)%
Cash ($ mil.): 18
Current ratio: 1.10
Long-term debt ($ mil.): —

Dividends
Yield: —
Payout: —
Market value ($ mil.): —

NATIONAL EDUCATION ASSOCIATION OF THE UNITED STATES

The National Education Association (NEA) is dedicated to promoting the cause of public education and the teaching profession. The organization boasts a membership of 3.2 million elementary and secondary teachers support professionals administrators higher education faculty and student teachers. The group's key issues include the No Child Left Behind Act professional pay education funding minority community outreach dropout prevention achievement gaps and other matters facing America's schools. NEA also hosts Read Across America a one-day reading event held on Dr. Seuss' birthday. The group was founded in 1857.

The organization also puts on regional leadership conferences American Education Week and National Teacher Day.

Among the magazines newsletters and journals it publishes are NEA Today This Active Life and The NEA Almanac of Higher Education. The group's Web site provides links to its publications as well as to lesson plans articles on classroom management and instruction methods professional development resources and additional online tools.

In 1966 the NEA merged with the American Teachers Association. It serves as the nation's largest teachers union followed by the American Federation of Teachers with 1.5 million members.

EXECUTIVES

President, Dennis Van Roekel
VP, Lily Eskelsen
Executive Director, John I. Wilson, age 65
Secretary and Treasurer, Rebecca Pringle

LOCATIONS

HQ: National Education Associations Staff Organization
1201 16th St. Northwest, Washington DC 20036-3290
Phone: 202-833-4000   **Fax:** 202-822-7974
Web: www.nea.org

HISTORICAL FINANCIALS

Company Type: Private - Not-for-Profit

Income Statement

FYE: August 31

	REVENUE ($ mil.)	NET INCOME ($ mil.)	NET PROFIT MARGIN	EMPLOYEES
08/11	376	3	0.9%	735
08/10*	376	16	4.3%	0
12/08	0	0	—	0
08/08	392	18	4.6%	0
Annual Growth	**(1.4%)**	**(43.4%)**	—	—

*Fiscal year change

2011 Year-End Financials

Debt ratio: ——
Return on equity: 0.90%
Cash ($ mil.): 59
Current ratio: 2.20
Long-term debt ($ mil.): —

Dividends
Yield: —
Payout: —
Market value ($ mil.): —

NATIONAL ENDOWMENT FOR DEMOCRACY INC

LOCATIONS

HQ: NATIONAL ENDOWMENT FOR DEMOCRACY INC
1025 F ST NW STE 800, WASHINGTON, DC 20004-1432
Phone: 202-378-9700
Web: www.wmd.org

HISTORICAL FINANCIALS

Company Type: Private

Income Statement

FYE: September 30

	REVENUE ($ mil.)	NET INCOME ($ mil.)	NET PROFIT MARGIN	EMPLOYEES
09/11	135	0	0.1%	99
09/10	136	(0)	—	0
09/08	135	(0)	—	0
09/06	110	0	0.8%	0
Annual Growth	**7.2%**	**(41.6%)**	—	—

2011 Year-End Financials

Debt ratio: ——
Return on equity: 0.10%
Cash ($ mil.): 3
Current ratio: —
Long-term debt ($ mil.): —

Dividends
Yield: —
Payout: —
Market value ($ mil.): —

NATIONAL FISH & WILDLIFE FOUNDATION

LOCATIONS

HQ: NATIONAL FISH & WILDLIFE FOUNDATION
1133 15TH ST NW FL 11, WASHINGTON, DC 20005-2708
Phone: 202-857-0166
Web: www.nfwf.org

HISTORICAL FINANCIALS

Company Type: Private

Income Statement

FYE: September 30

	REVENUE ($ mil.)	NET INCOME ($ mil.)	NET PROFIT MARGIN	EMPLOYEES
09/11	108	(0)	—	85
09/10	108	23	21.6%	0
09/09	73	0	1.1%	0
09/06	65	7	11.1%	0
Annual Growth	**18.6%**	—	—	—

2011 Year-End Financials

Debt ratio: ——
Return on equity: (-0.10)%
Cash ($ mil.): 93
Current ratio: 0.80
Long-term debt ($ mil.): —

Dividends
Yield: —
Payout: —
Market value ($ mil.): —

NATIONAL GRAPE CO-OPERATIVE ASSOCIATION INC.

Well of course grape growers want to hang out in a bunch! The more than 1090 grower/owner-members of the National Grape Cooperative harvest Concord and Niagara grapes from almost 50000 acres of vineyards. The plucked produce supplies the coop's wholly owned subsidiary Welch Foods. Welch Foods makes and sells fruit-based juices jams jellies and spreads under the Welch's and Bama brands in the US and nearly 50 other countries. Offerings include fresh eating grapes distributed by C.H. Robinson Worldwide as well as dried fruit and frozen juice pops. The grape growers own vineyards in Pennsylvania Michigan New York Ohio Washington and Ontario Canada which produce some 300000 tons of grapes annually.

The entire business from growing to processing grapes is highly competitive and the difference between sales and cost of goods sold often so slim that earning a profit is challenging. Despite the economic downturn and soaring commodity costs in 2011 Welch's sustained less than a 10% decline in net income on a small slip in sales. The results reflect new value-priced product introductions coupled with an initiative started in 2009 to slash costs through concentrating production and distribution. Welch's initiative included adding a new bottle production facility to its plant in 2011 and cutting its workforce by 17% in early 2010.

The coop also realized a smaller crop in 2011 in part due to a decline in family-farmer owners. The 10% decrease in tons sold modestly reduced total net proceeds. Nonetheless net income on patron business grew boosted by a sizeable increase in distributable proceeds per ton.

HISTORY

Looking for a steady supply of grapes for his processing plant in 1945 Russian immigrant Jack Kaplan convinced 900 grape growers to join the newly formed National Grape Cooperative. Also that year Welch Foods' parent company decided to spin off its purple fruit interests and Kaplan purchased a controlling interest. Welch's –a competitor at the time –had been started in 1869 when Dr. Thomas Welch a tee totaling dentist created an unfermented Concord grape wine to be used for nonalcoholic communions. The juice was coolly received at first but the advent of Prohibition helped push the company to the forefront of the fruit-drink industry.

While Kaplan had purchased his interest in Welch's with the intention of combining it with the National Grape Co-op it wasn't until the mid-1950s that the two could agree on the acquisition. Welch's product line grew throughout the 1960s and 1970s including the 1972 introduction of red grape and white grape juices. A glut of grapes depressed prices in the 1980s but the co-op rebounded by the 1990s.

In 1994 the co-op acquired jam and jelly maker BAMA Foods from Borden. Daniel Dillon became CEO of Welch's in 1995 and Fredrick Kalian was named president of the co-op the next year. Yakima Valley Grape Producers joined National Grape Co-op in 1997 adding new growers and more grapes to meet a growing demand spurred in part by newly discovered health benefits of purple and white grape juice. (Welch's helped fund the research.)

New products and increased advertising helped boost juice sales dramatically in 1998 and 1999. Fresh table grapes distributed by C.H. Robinson Worldwide were also introduced in 1999 and by 2000 were available nationwide. In 2001 the company announced it would be cutting up to 100 jobs –its first layoffs in more than two decades –due to slowing sales.

In 2003 the company introduced new variations of its products including single-serving juices (Welsh Squeezables). This along with increased marketing and new packaging have seen its sales growing during the last two years. Expansion in grocery channels and the introduction of low-calorie items and shrink-pack products led to further sales gains in 2004.

EXECUTIVES

President and CEO Welch Foods, David J. Lukiewski, age 58
President and Director, Joseph C. Falcone
Chief Legal Officer and Assistant Secretary, Vivian S. Y. Tseng

General Manager COO and Treasurer, Brent J. Roggie
Secretary and Assistant Treasurer, Timothy A. Buss
First VP and Director, Timothy E. Grow
Assistant Treasurer, Thomas A. Bockhorst
Assistant Secretary, Mathew A. Aufman
Third VP and Director, Jon B. Hinkelman
Second VP and Director, Anthony J. Falcone Jr.
Financial and Accounting Officer, Michael J. Perda
President and Director, Joseph C. Falcone
Director, Richard A. Boushey
Director, Douglas R. Forraht
Director, Randolph H. Graham
Director, Jerry A. Czebotar
First VP and Director, Timothy E. Grow
Director, Jon B. Hinkelman
Director, Marvin D. Vining
Director, Gary R. Youngs
Director, William G. (Bill) Barker III, age 53
Third VP and Director, Jon B. Hinkelman
Director, Dennis C. Vacco
Second VP and Director, Anthony J. Falcone Jr.
Director, Thomas G. Wilkinson
Director, Ned R. Totzke
Auditors: KPMGLLP

LOCATIONS

HQ: National Grape Cooperative Association Inc.
2 S. Portage St., Westfield NY 14787
Phone: 716-326-5200   **Fax:** 716-326-5494
Web: www.nationalgrape.com

PRODUCTS/OPERATIONS

Selected Products
Food and snacks
  Dried fruit
  Fresh grapes
  Fruit 'N Yogurt
  Fruit snacks mixed
  Welch's frozen pops
  Welch's soda
Jams jellies and spreads
Juice
  100% juices
  Concentrates
  Essentials fruit blends
  Fruit fizz sparkling juice beverage
  Light lower calorie
  Sparkling grape cocktails
  Refrigerator cocktails

COMPETITORS

B&G Foods	Hornell Brewing
Chiquita Brands	IZZE
Coca-Cola	Mondelez International
Constellation Brands	Monster Beverage
Cranberries Limited	Nestle USA
Del Monte Foods	Ocean Spray
Dole Food	PepsiCo
Dr Pepper Snapple	Procter & Gamble
Group	Ralcorp
Fresh Del Monte	Smucker
Produce	Snapple
Goya	Tropicana

HISTORICAL FINANCIALS

Company Type: Private - Cooperative

Income Statement

FYE: August 31

	REVENUE ($ mil.)	NET INCOME ($ mil.)	NET PROFIT MARGIN	EMPLOYEES
08/12	649	74	11.5%	1,325
08/11	640	74	11.6%	0
08/10	658	82	12.6%	0
08/09	673	81	12.0%	0
Annual Growth	(1.2%)	(2.8%)	—	—

2012 Year-End Financials

Debt ratio: ——
Return on equity: 11.50%   Dividends
Cash ($ mil.): 4   Yield: —
Current ratio: 0.70   Payout: —
Long-term debt ($ mil.): —   Market value ($ mil.): —

NATIONAL RETAIL FEDERATION INC.

The National Retail Federation (NRF) wants everyone to shop 'til they drop. The group is a trade association representing the retail industry that works through four divisions addressing technology in retail chain restaurants advertising and marketing and online retail. It functions as both an advocacy group and an informational network for its members lobbying government hosting conferences and seminars and publishing newsletters and books. The NRF magazine Stores is published monthly. NRF includes more than 100 US national state and international retail associations and more than 1.6 million US retailers with about 25 million employees.

In early 2011 the NRF reorganized its executive staff and made some new hires to achieve the priorities outlined in a new strategic plan recently approved by its board. The trade association aims to sharpen its focus on advocacy communications and education for its retail industry members. Executive changes included the appointment of a new COO several promotions and the creation of new senior-level positions.

EXECUTIVES

First Vice Chairman, Stephen I. (Steve) Sadove, age 61
Chairman, Terry J. Lundgren, age 60
COO and CFO, Carleen C. Kohut
SVP Retail Operations and CIO, David (Dave) Hogan
VP Industry Public Relations, Scott Krugman
VP Retail Operations, Dan Butler
SVP and General Counsel, Mallory Duncan
VP International Trade Counsel, Erik Autor
VP Supply Chain and Customs Policy, Jonathan Gold
Executive Assistant to President and Assistant Secretary, Peggy Blackwell
VP Tax Counsel, Rachelle Bernstein
SVP Conferences, Susan Newman
VP Government and Industry Relations Counsel, Maureen Riehl
VP Government Affairs Public Relations, J. Craig Shearman

SVP Member Relations, Mike Gatti
VP Strategic Partnerships, Lisa Marzetti
VP Public Relations, Ellen Davis
VP and Assistant General Counsel, Monica
Anderson
SVP Retail Advertising and Marketing
Association, Kelly Gilmore
VP Government and Political Affairs, Robert J.
(Rob) Green
VP Strategic Marketing, Libby Landen
Executive Director NRF Foundation, Kathy Mance
Controller, Kathy Murphy
VP Applications Development, Karen Shunk
VP Employee Benefits Policy Counsel, E. Neil
Trautwein
Secretary and Director, Robert M. Benham
Second Vice Chairman, Kip Tindell
President CEO and Director, Matthew (Matt) Shay
Director Media Relations, Kathy Grannis
Manager Communications, Margaret Case Little
VP Shop.org, Larry Joseloff
VP STORES Media, Harry Lister
VP Education Strategies, Eric Olson
VP National Council of Chain Restaurants, Scott
Vinson
SVP Government Relations, David French
SVP Communications and Public Affairs, Tita
Freeman
Director Sales and Advertising STORES and
LPinformation, Mike Gribbin
Senior Director Speaker Management, Tonya
Brigham
Manager Customer Data, Diane Collins
Senior Director Membership Administration,
Jannise Corry
Senior Director Attendee Services, Daryl Everett
Director Member Relations, Steven Glover
Project Coordinator Customer Data, Wanda Powell
Senior Director Internet Strategies, Sara Rand
Editor STORES Media, Susan Reda
Senior Director Loss Prevention, Angelica
Rodriguez
Director Retail Finance and Accounting, Rachel
Ryan
Director Membership Development, Jessica Viator
First Vice Chairman, Stephen I. (Steve) Sadove, age
61
Director, Karen W. Katz, age 55
Director, M. Farooq Kathwari, age 68
Director, Elliot S. Jaffe, age 86
Director, Philip L. (Phil) Francis, age 65
Director, Arnold B. Zetcher, age 71
Director, Brian K. Devine
Director, Trudy F. Sullivan, age 62
Director, Marty P. Albertson, age 58
Director, Edward W. (Ed) Stack, age 57
Director, Claudio Del Vecchio, age 54
Director, Lovro Mandac
Director, Roger N. Farah, age 59
Director, Mindy Grossman, age 54
Director, James F. (Jim) Wright, age 62
Director, Byron L. (Bud) Bergren, age 65
Director, Matthew E. (Matt) Rubel, age 54
Director, Kim C. Goodman, age 47
Director, William L. McComb, age 49
Director, Robert M. (Bob) Beall II
Director, H. James Baum
Director, Thomas G. Bata Jr.
Director, Artem Bektemirov
Secretary and Director, Robert M. Benham
Director, Cem Boyner
Director, William Dombrowski
Director, Joseph A. Flannery
Director, Philippe Houze
Director, Daniel S. C. Koo
Director, Kay Lawther Krill
Director, Keith Lipert

Director, Chris McCormick
Director, Mitchell B. Modell
Director, Jorge Pont
Director, Daryl Routzahn
Director, Gordon I. Segal
Director, J. Hill Stockton
Second Vice Chairman, Kip Tindell
President CEO and Director, Matthew (Matt) Shay
Director, Ron Sacino
Director, Bill Gonzalez
Director, Karen Lowe
Director, Bob Myers

LOCATIONS

HQ: National Retail Federation Inc.
325 7th St. NW Ste. 1100, Washington DC 20004
Phone: 202-783-7971   Fax: 202-737-2849
Web: www.nrf.com

PRODUCTS/OPERATIONS

2009 Membership

% of total	
Apparel &	46
Consumables	12
Department	9
Hardware home centers &	8
Jewelry	3
Sporting	3
Consumer	2
Entertainment	2
Discount	2
Miscellaneous (auto books gifts office pet &	13
Total	100

HISTORICAL FINANCIALS

Company Type: Private - Association

Income Statement

FYE: February 29

	REVENUE ($ mil.)	NET INCOME ($ mil.)	NET PROFIT MARGIN	EMPLOYEES
02/12	38	1	2.8%	96
02/11	34	4	14.1%	0
02/10	29	2	8.8%	0
02/09	35	(6)	—	0
Annual Growth	2.7%	—	—	—

2012 Year-End Financials

Debt ratio: ——
Return on equity: 2.80%   Dividends
Cash ($ mil.): 6   Yield: —
Current ratio: 0.70   Payout: —
Long-term debt ($ mil.): —   Market value ($ mil.): —

NATIONAL SEPTEMBER 11 MEMORIAL AND MUSEUM AT THE WORLD TRADE CEN

LOCATIONS

HQ: NATIONAL SEPTEMBER 11 MEMORIAL AND
MUSEUM AT THE WORLD TRADE CEN
1 LIBERTY PLZ LBBY 220, NEW YORK, NY
10006-1443
Phone: 212-312-8800
Web: www.911memorial.org

HISTORICAL FINANCIALS

Company Type: Private

Income Statement

FYE: December 31

	REVENUE ($ mil.)	NET INCOME ($ mil.)	NET PROFIT MARGIN	EMPLOYEES
12/11	85	48	56.8%	15
12/09	94	84	89.9%	0
Annual Growth	(9.2%)	(42.6%)	—	—

2011 Year-End Financials

Debt ratio: ——
Return on equity: 56.80%   Dividends
Cash ($ mil.): 33   Yield: —
Current ratio: 0.60   Payout: —
Long-term debt ($ mil.): —   Market value ($ mil.): —

NATIONAL UNIVERSITY

If you can read this thank your reading teacher.
You might also thank National University. The
flagship school of the National University System
offers about 100 undergraduate and graduate degrees and teacher credential and certificate programs. A not-for-profit institution National University also offers programs in business engineering
education media and human services. The university enrolls 22000 students at some 30 campuses
throughout California and one in Nevada; it also
offers about 50 online degree programs (and more
than 1200 online courses). The school conducts research through the National University Community
Research Institute (NUCRI). National University
was founded in 1971.

EXECUTIVES

Chair, Gerald M. Czarnecki, age 72
Chancellor National University System and
President Emeritus National University, Jerry C.
Lee
President, Kevin B. Casey
EVP, David Waller
Director of Financial Aid, Lida Lida Castillo
Director Admissions, Shelly Mitchell
Registrar, Jonathon Osorio
Vice Chancelor for Marketing and System
Advancement, Virginia E. Beneke

General Counsel, Michael W. Prairie
Chancellor National University System and
  President Emeritus National University, Jerry C.
  Lee
Director, Michael B. Wilkes
Trustee, John Bucher
Director, Stacy Allison
Director, Felipe Becerra
Director, Richard Chisholm
Director, John Collins
Director, Robert Freelen
Director, Cheryl Kendrick
Vice Chair, Jacqueline Townsend Konstanturos
Director, Donald Kripke
Director, Jean Leonard
Director, Carlos Rodriguez
Director, Judith Sweet
Director, Doreen Tyburski
Auditors: KPMGLLP

LOCATIONS

HQ: NATIONAL UNIVERSITY
11255 N TORREY PINES RD, LA JOLLA, CA
92037-1011
Phone: 858-642-8000
Web: www.nu.edu

HISTORICAL FINANCIALS

Company Type: School

Income Statement

FYE: June 30

	REVENUE ($ mil.)	NET INCOME ($ mil.)	NET PROFIT MARGIN	EMPLOYEES
06/11	203	25	12.4%	1,954
06/10	178	18	10.3%	0
06/09	165	5	3.1%	0
06/02	126	20	16.4%	0
Annual Growth	**17.2%**	**6.7%**	**—**	**—**

2011 Year-End Financials

Debt ratio: ——
Return on equity: 12.40%
Cash ($ mil.): 38
Current ratio: ——
Long-term debt ($ mil.): —

Dividends
Yield: —
Payout: —
Market value ($ mil.): —

NATURAL RESOURCES DEFENSE COUNCIL INC.

Natural Resource Defense Council (NRDC) may be Mother Nature's strongest advocate. It is a nonprofit environmental action organization comprising 1.3-million members dedicated to preserving wildlife and the wilderness. To that end the NRDC's mission takes aim at curbing global warming; creating a future fueled by clean energy; restoring the Earth's oceans; saving endangered wildlife and wild places; stemming the tide of pollutants that endanger heath; and accelerating the greening of communities. In addition press releases and blog posts it publishes Nature's Voice a bulletin on environmental campaigns; OnEarth its quarterly magazine; and periodic NRDC Reports on specific issues.

The NRDC operates through a staff of more than 400 attorneys scientists and other environmental specialists. Once a small law firm it now takes on environmental issues not only through the courtroom but on many other fronts ranging from media outreach to scientific programs and public policy campaigns. Along with the support of volunteer members online activists and major foundations it claims a presence in strategic seats of government finance and manufacturing. A subsidiary the NRDC Action Fund advocates clean energy economy and public health improvement through legislative efforts; as such it serves as a watchdog to monitor the activities of elected officials.

NRDC conducts its work from its New York headquarters and regional offices in Los Angeles San Francisco Chicago and Washington DC and Montana. Beyond the US it has an office in Beijing China. Its influence extends across the Americas China and India.

In 2011 the NRDC reported roughly a 10% increase in program services atop a 5% rise in revenues over the prior year. Although membership and contributions slipped they accounted for more than half of all revenues. Return on investments and foundation grants helped to offset the decline by jumping more more than 76% and 27% respectively. Topping the list of program services clean energy future and wildlife and wildlands programs accounted for 42% and 15% respectively of all expenses. However programs for reviving the ocean and protecting health received the largest funding increases. NRDC also posted significant upticks in fundraising and membership recruitment expenses.

The NRDC's strategy for advancing its cause is reflected in its 5-year fundraising Partnership for Earth campaign. Coming to a close in December 2010 NRDC raised close to $532 million exceeding its goal of $400 million. The campaign's success supports the council's work in a number of critical areas. Among them it has recruited a formidable staff of energy talent to deliver on its goal of an 80% reduction in America's global warming pollution by 2050. A Center for Market Innovation was launched to document and demonstrate the economic potential of clean energy. In addition a Science Center was created to add technical expertise to the council's litigation and advocacy work. The council has meanwhile opened a new office in the Midwest to fight for renewable energy standards in the region as well as fend off invasive species. A new office in Beijing is anticipated to foster collaboration between government and the private sector on a range of energy efficiency programs and environmental laws. The NRDC also points to future growth through harnessing digital and social media to raise activist awareness.

EXECUTIVES

Chair, Daniel R. (Dan) Tishman, age 56
Vice Chair, Alan F. Horn
Vice Chair, Robert J. (Bob) Fisher, age 57
President, Frances G. Bainecke
Chair Emeritus, Adrian W. DeWind
Deputy Executive Director, Patricia F. Sullivan
Director of Programs, Wesley Warren
Director of Finance and Operations, Judith Keefer
Director of Development, John Murray
Director of Major Gifts, Priscilla Bayley
Co-Director of Special Projects, Jennifer Iselin
  Chapin
Director of Foundation Relations, Robert Ferguson
Director of Membership and Public Education,
  Linda Lopez
Program Director Litigation, Mitch Bernard
Program Director Land & Forests, Sharon Buccino
Program Director International, S. Jacob Scherr
Program Director Health, Linda Greer

Program Director Oceans, Lisa Speer
Co-Program Director Urban, Eric Goldstein
Co-Program Director Urban, Joel Reynolds
Director Gift Planning, Michelle Mulia-Howell
Campaign Director Center for Advocacy
  Campaigns, Robert (Rob) Perks
Executive Director, Peter Lehner
Program Director Air and Energy, Ashok Gupta
Program Director Nuclear, Christopher E. Paine
Program Director Science Center, Gabriela
  Chavarria
Legislative Director, Karen Wayland
Co-Program Director Water, David S. Beckman
Co-Program Director Water, Nancy Stoner
Director Climate Programs, David Hawkins
Director Climate Center, Daniel Lashof
Director Midwest, Henry Henderson
Co-Director Special Projects, Annie Weis
Director Communications, Phil Gutis
Chair Emeritus, Frederick A. O. Schwarz Jr.
Vice Chair, Adam Albright
Vice Chair, Patricia Bauman
Director Government Affairs, David Goldston
Vice Chair, Alan F. Horn
Chair Emeritus, Adrian W. DeWind
Chair Emeritus, Frederick A. O. Schwarz Jr.
Vice Chair, Adam Albright
Vice Chair, Patricia Bauman

LOCATIONS

HQ: Natural Resources Defense Council
  40 W. 20th St., New York NY 10011
Phone: 212-727-2700   Fax: 212-727-1773
Web: www.nrdc.org

PRODUCTS/OPERATIONS

2011 Donor Support

% of total	
Membership &	56
Foundations	19
Investment	14
Awarded attorneys'	4
Bequests	3
In-kind	3
Government	-
Other	1
Total	**100**

2011 Expenses

% of total	
Program services	
Clean energy	42
Wildlife &	15
Revive our	7
Protect our	7
Safe & sufficient	6
Sustainable	3
Membership	5
Supporting services	
Management &	7
Fundraising	6
Member	2
Total	**100**

Selected Priority Issues

Creating the clean energy future
Curbing global warming
Defending endangered wildlife and wild places
Ensuring safe and sufficient water
Fostering sustainable communities
Protecting our health by preventing pollution
Reviving the world's oceans

HISTORICAL FINANCIALS
Company Type: Private - Not-for-Profit

Income Statement

	REVENUE ($ mil.)	NET INCOME ($ mil.)	NET PROFIT MARGIN	EMPLOYEES
				FYE: June 30
06/11	97	(1)	—	500
06/10	96	7	8.2%	0
06/08	0	0	—	0
06/07	112	42	37.6%	0
Annual Growth	(4.8%)	—	—	—

2011 Year-End Financials

Debt ratio: —
Return on equity: (-1.10)%
Cash ($ mil.): 15
Current ratio: 0.40
Long-term debt ($ mil.): —

Dividends
Yield: —
Payout: —
Market value ($ mil.): —

NBHX TRIM USA CORPORATION

For those car owners who can't bear to be without the best things in life Behr Industries is there to satisfy those needs. The company manufactures interior wood trim components for OEM automotive heavy-duty truck and marine suppliers across North America. It is the only US-based full-service wood component supplier with a domestic production plant. The Michigan-based facility neighbors the Detroit Big Three production plants. Behr Industries has captured more than 70% of the US market for center consoles instrument panels side door panels and similar wood components. Its fortunes have been closely tied to those of GM's. The company is a subsidiary of Erwin Behr GmbH of Wedlingen Germany.

Behr Industries' parent Erwin Behr GmbH was founded in 1912 as a maker of furniture and fine cabinetry. In 1949 the company ventured into making wood products for the automotive industry in Europe. In the early 1990s the company opened its first US plant in Comstock Park Michigan.

EXECUTIVES

Managing Director, Norb Dieterle
VP Operations, Mike Homrich

LOCATIONS

HQ: Behr Industries Corporation
1020 Seven Mile Rd., Comstock Park MI 49321
Phone: 616-785-9400   **Fax:** 616-785-9520
Web: www.BehrIndustries.com

COMPETITORS

Lacks Enterprises
Magna International

Trim Masters

HISTORICAL FINANCIALS
Company Type: Private

Income Statement

	REVENUE ($ mil.)	NET INCOME ($ mil.)	NET PROFIT MARGIN	EMPLOYEES
				FYE: December 31
12/11	40	1	2.8%	500
Annual Growth	—	—	—	—

NCH CORPORATION

NCH has been cleaning up for years and like everyone else it's been using soaps and detergents to do so. The company makes and sells about 450 chemical maintenance repair and supply products including all kinds of cleaners for customers in more than 50 countries throughout the world. NCH markets its products through a direct sales force to companies in the agricultural home-improvement industrial recreational and utility markets. Other products include fasteners welding supplies pet care supplies plumbing parts lubricants and metal-working fluids.

The company's major areas of focus include producing products for the industrial cleaning and maintenance pet care plumbing specialty industries supply and water treatment and remediation markets.

NCH's cleaning products include hand cleaners industrial cleaners and housekeeping supplies. Specialty chemical products including cleaning and water treatment chemicals deodorizers lubricants paints and paint strippers patching compounds and flooring and carpet treatments account for the majority of sales.

It operates almost 40 separate business units. Subsidiary Supply Line Direct offers safety and maintenance products such as janitorial supplies safety signs first aid kits spills kits storage cabinets for hazardous chemicals and protective apparel. Its plumbing products group has plumbing supplies for OEM and retail consumer markets. Other subsidiaries include Pure Solve a parts washing service TERRA Services (which reduces hazardous chemicals used in the hydraulic fracturing process) and X-Chem an oil field services division.

Descendants of founder Milton Levy own the company which was established in 1919.

HISTORY

Salesman Milton Levy founded National Disinfectant Co. in Dallas in 1919 to make disinfectants insecticides and soaps. The company's offerings grew in the 1930s to include Everbrite a top-selling industrial floor wax. Levy's sons Irvin Lester and Milton Jr. worked for the company as teenagers and took over its management after their father's death in 1946.

National Disinfectant expanded geographically in the 1950s and 1960s opening its first branch office in St. Louis in 1956. The company changed its name to National Chemsearch in 1960 to reflect its diversity. It also expanded into Europe and Latin America. National Chemsearch went public in 1965. Acquisitions boosted its product line to about 250 items by 1970. The company shortened its name to NCH in 1978.

NCH expanded its marketing to include catalog sales direct mail and telemarketing in 1986. It opened a South Korean plant in 1992. Troubled economies in Mexico and Venezuela hurt profits in 1994 and the next year NCH began work on a long-term business strategy that envisioned third-generation Levy family members moving into higher executive ranks.

Softened currency rates in Europe and Asia contributed to a decrease in profits for fiscal 1999. That year NCH focused on strengthening its customer relationships by boosting sales staff training and implementing an Internet-based corporate network.

In 2000 Irvin Levy became the company's chairman and NCH sold its electronic components business. The next year the company shut down its direct broadcast satellite equipment operations. In February 2002 the Levys took the company private by purchasing the 43% of the company that they didn't already own. The brothers originally offered a 20% premium to buy the shares but were greeted by lawsuits from shareholders who claimed they were taking advantage of a depressed market. The Levys settled the suits by upping the offer by $120 million.

EXECUTIVES

Chairman, Irvin L. Levy
Co-President and Director, Lester A. Levy Jr.
Co-President and Director, Robert M. Levy
Co-President and Director, Walter M. Levy
Co-President and Director, John I. Levy
Director Marketing Supply Line Direct, David Wilson
Director Product Development, Mike Benton
General Counsel, Rich Robinson
VP Research and Development, John Roheim
VP Sales, Tony Lewis
CEO NCH Europe, Charles Gile
CFO, Tom Hetzer
General Manager Supply Line Direct, Kent LeeMaster
Marketing Specialist Supply Line Direct, Andrea Berg
Co-President and Director, Lester A. Levy Jr.
Co-President and Director, Robert M. Levy
Co-President and Director, Walter M. Levy
Co-President and Director, John I. Levy
Auditors: GrantThorntonLLP

LOCATIONS

HQ: NCH Corporation
2727 Chemsearch Blvd., Irving TX 75062
Phone: 972-438-0211   **Fax:** 972-438-0707
Web: www.nch.com

PRODUCTS/OPERATIONS

Selected Operations & Products

Chemical Specialties
 Cleaning chemicals
 Deodorizers
 Floor and carpet care products
 HVAC products
 Lubricants
 Oil production facility chemicals
 Paint
 Paint removers
 Water-treatment chemicals
Landmark Direct
 First-aid supplies
 Workplace signage and productivity products
Pet Care
 Training pads
 Stain & odor removers
 Housebreaking aids

Grooming products
Partsmaster Group
  Cutting tools
  Electrical products
  Fasteners
  Welding alloys
Plumbing Products Group
  Plumbing products for new construction
  Plumbing repair and replacement parts

COMPETITORS

Church & Dwight	H.B. Fuller
Cintas	Illinois Tool Works
Clariant	Pioneer Corporation
Danaher	Quaker Chemical
Detrex	Safety-Kleen
Ecolab	WD-40

HISTORICAL FINANCIALS
Company Type: Private

Income Statement
FYE: April 30

	REVENUE ($ mil.)	NET INCOME ($ mil.)	NET PROFIT MARGIN	EMPLOYEES
04/12	1,045	6	0.6%	8,500
04/11	952	6	0.7%	0
04/10	885	16	1.9%	0
04/09	923	10	1.2%	0
Annual Growth	4.2%	(14.9%)	—	—

2012 Year-End Financials
Debt ratio: ——
Return on equity: 0.60%
Cash ($ mil.): 9
Current ratio: 1.30
Long-term debt ($ mil.): —
Dividends
  Yield: —
  Payout: —
  Market value ($ mil.): —

NCH HEALTHCARE SYSTEM INC.

NCH Healthcare System provides a comprehensive range of health care services to residents of Collier County and the surrounding area of southwest Florida. The system includes two acute care hospitals (NCH Downtown Naples Hospital and NCH North Naples Hospital) with a combined 715-bed capacity and regional institutes which specialize in orthopedics and the treatment of cancer heart ailments and women's and children's health issues. NCH includes an area network of more than 650 primary care and specialist physicians as well as numerous outpatient and ambulatory care facilities that provide services ranging from diagnostics to rehabilitative care to surgery and emergency care.

Operations

In 2011 NCH reported 37284 admissions 87100 emergency room visits 3033 births 416 open heart surgeries 11282 surgical procedures and 3000 employee colleagues. NCH is a member of the Mayo Clinic Care Network.

Financial Analysis

NCH's revenues increased by 16% in 2011. Net patient service revenues increased by 16% and accounted for approximately 96% of NCH's total revenues that year. Its net income decreased by 66% in 2011.

Strategy

In 2012 Mayo Clinic and NCH signed a collaboration deal whereby NCH became the first member of the Mayo Clinic Care Network in Florida and the Southeast region of the US. Among other things the deal gives NCH access to the expertise and resources of the much larger Mayo Clinic operations.

NCH is streamlining its information technology systems to free up resources and focus on patient care operations. In 2010 the health network outsourced its medical records department (including billing and patient registration operations) to reduce internal hospital administrative functions. It outsourced its computer support department the previous year.

Company Background

In a move to focus on the provision of medical care in 2007 the company sold its DSI Laboratories subsidiary which provided medical reference and toxicology services to national laboratory services provider LabCorp.

EXECUTIVES

First Vice Chairman, Mariann T. MacDonald, age 64
President CEO and Trustee, Alan S. Weiss
Chief Nursing Officer, Linda Gipson
COO North Naples Hospital Campus, Gail A. Dolan
General Counsel and Chief of Staff, Kevin D. Cooper
Second Vice Chair, Ambassador Francis Rooney, age 58
Secretary Treasurer and Trustee, Edwin Stedem
CIO, Susan Wolff
Chief Human Resources Officer, Brian Settle
Chief Medical Officer, Aurora Estevez
COO, Phillip Dutcher
CFO and Assistant Treasurer, Vicki Hale Orr
Chief Development Officer, Jim Martin
Chairman, Joseph Perkovich
Chief Human Resources Officer, John McGirl
First Vice Chairman, Mariann T. MacDonald, age 64
Trustee, Jay H. Baker, age 77
President CEO and Trustee, Alan S. Weiss
Trustee, Carl E. Westman
Second Vice Chair, Ambassador Francis Rooney, age 58
Secretary Treasurer and Trustee, Edwin Stedem
Trustee, William Allyn
Trustee, Susan Dalton
Auditors: PricewaterhouseCoopersLLP

LOCATIONS

HQ: NCH Healthcare System Inc.
  350 7th St. North, Naples FL 34102
Phone: 239-436-5000   **Fax:** 239-436-5914
Web: www.nchmd.org

PRODUCTS/OPERATIONS

2011 Sales

% of total	
Net patient service	96
Other	4
Total	**100**

Selected Subsidiaries and Facilities
Bonita Community Health Center
Collier Health Care Inc.
Community Home Services Inc.
Isabel Collier Read Healthpark
Marco Island Hospital Inc. (dba Marco Healthcare Center)
Naples Community Hospital Inc.
  NCH Naples Downtown Hospital
  NCH North Naples Hospital

COMPETITORS

Adventist Health System Sunbelt Healthcare
Baptist Health South Florida
Broward Health
HCA
Lakeland Regional Medical Center
Lee Memorial
Miami Children's Hospital
Mount Sinai Medical Center of Florida
Public Health Trust
South Broward Hospital District
University of Miami Hospital

HISTORICAL FINANCIALS
Company Type: Private

Income Statement
FYE: September 30

	REVENUE ($ mil.)	NET INCOME ($ mil.)	NET PROFIT MARGIN	EMPLOYEES
09/11	483	7	1.5%	3,500
09/08	456	25	5.6%	0
09/07	524	49	9.5%	0
09/06	475	35	7.5%	0
Annual Growth	0.5%	(41.1%)	—	

2011 Year-End Financials
Debt ratio: ——
Return on equity: 1.50%
Cash ($ mil.): 57
Current ratio: 2.10
Long-term debt ($ mil.): —
Dividends
  Yield: —
  Payout: —
  Market value ($ mil.): —

NCS TECHNOLOGIES INC.

NCS Technologies makes enterprise computing needs personal. The company makes and supplies PC products to clients large and small. NCS Technologies offers personal computers mobile computing thin client computing servers and Internet appliances to clients in the government educational and private sectors. Products include desktops notebooks rugged tablets and servers. In addition to providing built-to-order hardware the company also provides software customizations and installation and technical support services. Founded in 1996 the company's single facility in Washington DC serves clients from across the world.

EXECUTIVES

President, An V. Nguyen
EVP and CFO, Mark Christopher
CIO, John Eldred
Group VP Thin Client Products, Manoj Thomas
Executive Director Marketing, John Callahan
Controller, Laura Brashier
VP Operations, Doug Eacker
VP Engineering, Brian Gentry
Director Army Sales, Stephen Yosh
Director Air Force Sales, Joseph Guest
Director Navy and Marine Sales, Scott Sinclair
Director Customer Service, Chris Nguyen
Director Product Management, Mike Turicchi
Director Program Management, Rick Goodman
Director Account Management, George Brooks
Program Manager, Latrece Quander

LOCATIONS

HQ: NCS Technologies Inc.
7669 Limestone Dr., Gainesville VA 20155-4038
Phone: 703-743-8500 **Fax:** 703-621-1701
Web: www.ncst.com

COMPETITORS

Acer	Hewlett-Packard
Apple Inc.	IBM
Dell	Toshiba
Gateway Inc.	

HISTORICAL FINANCIALS
Company Type: Private

Income Statement
FYE: December 31

	REVENUE ($ mil.)	NET INCOME ($ mil.)	NET PROFIT MARGIN	EMPLOYEES
12/11	139	1	1.0%	150
12/10	117	0	0.6%	0
12/09*	80	1	1.7%	0
09/06	35	1	3.1%	0
Annual Growth	58.4%	8.2%	—	—

*Fiscal year change

2011 Year-End Financials

Debt ratio: ——
Return on equity: 1.00%
Cash ($ mil.): 0
Current ratio: 0.80
Long-term debt ($ mil.): ——
Dividends
Yield: —
Payout: —
Market value ($ mil.): —

NECA IBEW WELFARE TRUST FUND

LOCATIONS

HQ: NECA IBEW WELFARE TRUST FUND
2120 HUBBARD AVE, DECATUR, IL 62526-2871
Phone: 800-765-4239
Web: www.neca-ibew.org

HISTORICAL FINANCIALS
Company Type: Private

Income Statement
FYE: June 30

	REVENUE ($ mil.)	NET INCOME ($ mil.)	NET PROFIT MARGIN	EMPLOYEES
06/11	104	8	8.5%	40
06/10	88	(1)	—	0
06/09	95	0	—	0
06/08	100	19	19.3%	0
Annual Growth	1.1%	(23.1%)	—	—

2011 Year-End Financials

Debt ratio: ——
Return on equity: 8.50%
Cash ($ mil.): 9
Current ratio: 6.20
Long-term debt ($ mil.): ——
Dividends
Yield: —
Payout: —
Market value ($ mil.): —

NEW DIXIE OIL CORPORATION

LOCATIONS

HQ: NEW DIXIE OIL CORPORATION
1501 MARSHALL ST, ROANOKE RAPIDS, NC 27870-4415
Phone: 252-537-4118
Web: www.newdixieoil.com

HISTORICAL FINANCIALS
Company Type: Private

Income Statement
FYE: March 31

	REVENUE ($ mil.)	NET INCOME ($ mil.)	NET PROFIT MARGIN	EMPLOYEES
03/12	137	0	0.6%	195
03/11	93	0	0.6%	0
03/10	61	0	0.8%	0
03/09	68	0	0.6%	0
Annual Growth	25.8%	20.0%	—	—

2012 Year-End Financials

Debt ratio: ——
Return on equity: 0.60%
Cash ($ mil.): 1
Current ratio: 0.70
Long-term debt ($ mil.): ——
Dividends
Yield: —
Payout: —
Market value ($ mil.): —

NEBRASKALAND TIRE INC.

LOCATIONS

HQ: NEBRASKALAND TIRE INC.
SOUTH283 I 80 # 283, LEXINGTON, NE 68850
Phone: 308-324-6374
Web: www.thetirestore.com

HISTORICAL FINANCIALS
Company Type: Private

Income Statement
FYE: October 31

	REVENUE ($ mil.)	NET INCOME ($ mil.)	NET PROFIT MARGIN	EMPLOYEES
10/11	95	0	0.5%	340
10/10	78	0	0.5%	0
10/09	68	0	0.2%	0
10/06	47	0	0.4%	0
Annual Growth	26.3%	44.1%	—	—

2011 Year-End Financials

Debt ratio: ——
Return on equity: 0.50%
Cash ($ mil.): 5
Current ratio: 0.70
Long-term debt ($ mil.): ——
Dividends
Yield: —
Payout: —
Market value ($ mil.): —

NEW DISTRIBUTING CO. INC.

LOCATIONS

HQ: NEW DISTRIBUTING CO. INC.
4102 US HIGHWAY 59 N, VICTORIA, TX 77905-5592
Phone: 361-575-1981
Web: www.newdistributing.com

HISTORICAL FINANCIALS
Company Type: Private

Income Statement
FYE: December 31

	REVENUE ($ mil.)	NET INCOME ($ mil.)	NET PROFIT MARGIN	EMPLOYEES
12/11	142	1	1.2%	25
12/10	88	0	1.0%	0
12/09	60	0	0.8%	0
12/08	11	1	11.8%	0
Annual Growth	133.0%	9.8%	—	—

2011 Year-End Financials

Debt ratio: ——
Return on equity: 1.20%
Cash ($ mil.): 2
Current ratio: 1.20
Long-term debt ($ mil.): ——
Dividends
Yield: —
Payout: —
Market value ($ mil.): —

NEW HAMPSHIRE ELECTRIC COOPERATIVE INC

The granite in the Granite State won't keep the folks in New Hampshire warm in winter but New Hampshire Electric Cooperative will. The utility provides electricity to about 80000 residential and business customers (who are also member-owners of the cooperative) in 115 New Hampshire towns and cities. The enterprise operates 5400 miles of distribution lines and is seeking to become a complete energy solutions organization offering energy saving options such as equipment retrofits at local schools and selling energy-efficient compact fluorescent light bulbs. Most of New Hampshire Electric Cooperative's revenues comes from residential customers and the balance form small businesses.

Looking to conserve energy and promote green energy options the cooperative is offering rebates (up to $4000) to its customers for installing renewable energy systems and energy efficient heating systems in its service territory. Options include solar hot water heaters solar panels small wind turbines and low temperature heat pumps.

New Hampshire Electric Cooperative was founded in 1939 as part of the federal Rural Electrification Administration's push to bring affordable electricity to the rural areas of the US.

EXECUTIVES

President and CEO, Fredrick C. (Fred) Anderson, age
  60
EVP Strategy and Government Relations, William
  R. (Ray) Gosney Jr.
VP Power Resources and Access, Stephen E.
  (Steve) Kaminski
VP Corporate and Member Services and CFO,
  Dena Lee DeLucca
VP Operations and Engineering, James (Jim) Bakas
Chair, Earl Hansen
Treasurer and Director, David C. Talbot
Secretary and Director, Gail F. Paine
Assistant Treasurer and Director, Sharon L. Davis
Vice Chair, Jerry Hopkins
Treasurer and Director, David C. Talbot
Secretary and Director, Gail F. Paine
Director, Charles R. (Chuck) Braxton
Assistant Treasurer and Director, Sharon L. Davis
Vice Chair, Jerry Hopkins
Director, George (Chip) Kimball
Director, Georgie A. Thomas
Director, Robert V. Johnson II
Director, Bob Reals
Director, Kenneth Colburn
Auditors: BerryDunnMcNeil&Parker

LOCATIONS

HQ: New Hampshire Electric Cooperative Inc.
  579 Tenney Mountain Hwy., Plymouth NH 03264-3154
Phone: 603-536-1800   **Fax:** 603-536-8687
Web: www.nhec.com

HISTORICAL FINANCIALS

Company Type: Private - Cooperative

Income Statement

	REVENUE ($ mil.)	NET INCOME ($ mil.)	NET PROFIT MARGIN	EMPLOYEES
12/11	124	12	10.2%	199
12/10	130	8	6.8%	0
12/09	130	6	4.8%	0
12/08	145	5	3.9%	0
Annual Growth	(5.1%)	30.8%	—	—

2011 Year-End Financials

Debt ratio: ——
Return on equity: 10.20%
Cash ($ mil.): 2
Current ratio: 0.70
Long-term debt ($ mil.): ——
Dividends
  Yield: —
  Payout: —
Market value ($ mil.): —

NEW HANOVER COUNTY SCHOOLS

LOCATIONS

HQ: NEW HANOVER COUNTY SCHOOLS
  6410 CAROLINA BEACH RD, WILMINGTON, NC
  28412-2908
Phone: 910-254-4252
Web: www.nhcs.net

HISTORICAL FINANCIALS

Company Type: Private

Income Statement

FYE: June 30

	REVENUE ($ mil.)	NET INCOME ($ mil.)	NET PROFIT MARGIN	EMPLOYEES
06/12	220	5	2.5%	3,500
06/09	267	(1)	—	0
Annual Growth	(17.8%)	—	—	—

2012 Year-End Financials

Debt ratio: ——
Return on equity: 2.50%
Cash ($ mil.): 36
Current ratio: —
Long-term debt ($ mil.): —
Dividends
  Yield: —
  Payout: —
Market value ($ mil.): —

NEW HANOVER REGIONAL MEDICAL CENTER

Sometimes when you're sick you just have to hand over your health to a professional. Enter New Hanover Regional Medical Center (NHRMC). The integrated health system serves the Wilmington and Cape Fear area of North Carolina through its flagship 635-bed New Hanover Regional Medical Center the 130-bed Cape Fear Hospital and the 85-bed Pender Memorial Hospital. NHRMC is also home to a rehabilitation center a behavioral health facility hospice services home health care EMS transport services physicians practices and outpatient clinics. The not-for-profit health network is affiliated with the UNC-Chapel Hill School of Medicine.

Geographic Reach

New Hanover Regional Medical Center's hospitals serve Southeastern North Carolina. NHRMC's main campus is in Wilmington. The health network also offers general hospital services at Cape Fear Hospital in Wilmington and Pender Memorial Hospital in Burgaw North Carolina.

Operations

NHRMC has about 5400 employees including 565 physicians and 800 active volunteers. The medical network is governed by a board of trustees consisting of members appointed by the New Hanover County commissioners and representatives from the neighboring Pender County.

Financial Analysis

Total revenue increased about 9% to $674.3 million in fiscal 2011 compared to the $616.6 million the network brought in during fiscal 2010. The increase was primarily attributable to the expansion of the NHRMC physician network along with increased utilization of inpatient and outpatient services.

NHRMC provides more than $83 million every year in uncompensated care mostly to those who would not otherwise have access to healthcare.

Strategy

NHRMC is part of the Coastal Carolinas Health Alliance a cooperative of regional hospitals that use their combined buying size to negotiate lower prices for hospital equipment and supplies. The group also works together to increase community access to health care and promote continuing medical education amongst its peers.

EXECUTIVES

VP and CIO, Avery Cloud
Secretary and Trustee, Gayle P. Van Velsor
EVP and CFO, Edwin J. (Ed) Ollie
Director Marketing and Public Relations, Martha
  Harlan
President and CEO, Jack Barto
VP Human Resources, Keith Strawn
Director Government Affairs, Scott Whisnant
Chairman, John D. (Jack) Fuller
SVP and Chief Nurse Executive, Mary Ellen
  Bonczek
Treasurer and Trustees, Lawrence S. (Larry) Clark
Chairman, David B. Sims Jr.
Chief of Staff, George (Van) Huffmon
Compliance and Privacy Officer, Pat Wheeler
Chief of Staff, Robert E. Lubanski Jr.
Secretary and Trustee, Gayle P. Van Velsor
Trustee, Bruce M. Prouty
Trustees, Ronald J. (Ron) Isyk
Trustee, Patricia L. Leonard
Vice Chairman, John D. (Jack) Fuller
Trustee, Nancy S. Marks
Trustee, Robert G. (Bobby) Greer
Trustee, Elizabeth J. Griffin
Trustee, Carl D. Brown
Treasurer and Trustees, Lawrence S. (Larry) Clark
Trustees, Helyn R. Lofton
Trustee, Michael G. Rallis
Trustee, F. D. Rivenbark
Trustee, Sylvia H. Rountree
Trustee, James E. Vann
Trustee, Clarence L. Wilson II

LOCATIONS

HQ: New Hanover Regional Medical Center
  2131 S. 17th St., Wilmington NC 28401
Phone: 910-343-7000   **Fax:** 910-343-2135
Web: www.nhrmc.org/

PRODUCTS/OPERATIONS

Selected Locations

Betty H. Cameron Women's & Children's
  Hospital (Wilmington NC)
Brunswick Forest (health diagnostics Leland NC)
Cape Fear Hospital (Wilmington NC)
New Hanover Regional Medical Center (Wilmington NC)
NHRMC Urgent Care (Wilmington NC)
Zimmer Cancer Center (Wilmington NC)

COMPETITORS

Blue Ridge HealthCare	Health Management
Carolinas HealthCare	Associates
System	High Point Regional
Community Health	Health System
Systems	Mission Hospitals
Conway Medical Center	Novant Health
Grand Strand Regional	UNC Hospitals
Medical Center	

HISTORICAL FINANCIALS

Company Type: Private - Not-for-Profit

Income Statement

FYE: June 30

	REVENUE ($ mil.)	NET INCOME ($ mil.)	NET PROFIT MARGIN	EMPLOYEES
06/12*	602	24	4.0%	3,692
09/11	674	26	3.9%	0
06/10	528	19	3.6%	0
06/09	514	15	3.1%	0
Annual Growth	5.5%	15.0%	—	—

*Fiscal year change

2012 Year-End Financials

Debt ratio: ——
Return on equity: 4.00%
Cash ($ mil.): 27
Current ratio: 0.90
Long-term debt ($ mil.): —

Dividends
Yield: —
Payout: —
Market value ($ mil.): —

NEW JERSEY CITY UNIVERSITY

LOCATIONS

HQ: NEW JERSEY CITY UNIVERSITY
2039 JOHN F KENNEDY BLVD, JERSEY CITY, NJ 07305-1596
Phone: 201-200-2000
Web: www.njcu.org

HISTORICAL FINANCIALS

Company Type: Private

Income Statement

FYE: June 30

	REVENUE ($ mil.)	NET INCOME ($ mil.)	NET PROFIT MARGIN	EMPLOYEES
06/12	94	2	3.0%	900
06/11	91	(0)	—	0
06/10	85	1	1.4%	0
06/09	79	(2)	—	0
Annual Growth	5.8%	—	—	—

2012 Year-End Financials

Debt ratio: ——
Return on equity: 3.00%
Cash ($ mil.): 7
Current ratio: 0.40
Long-term debt ($ mil.): —

Dividends
Yield: —
Payout: —
Market value ($ mil.): —

NEW JERSEY INSTITUTE OF TECHNOLOGY

A public research university New Jersey Institute of Technology (NJIT) offers about 100 undergraduate and graduate programs including about 20 doctoral programs in fields including architecture engineering computer science and liberal arts. The school also offers continuing education and dis-

tance courses. With some 500 full-time faculty members NJIT boasts a student-faulty ratio of 16:1. Its Albert Dorman Honors College provides students with individualized curricula and honors colloquia including travel and featured speakers. About 10000 students attend the NJIT which operates a single campus in Newark. NJIT was founded in 1881 as the Newark Technical School.

Operations

Newark's NJIT has some 7125 undergraduate and 2825 graduate students. Master's programs are offered across 56 specialties. The school also offers some 46 baccalaureate degree programs.

Strategy

Looking to provide additional capacity for students to reside on campus NJIT focuses on campus and area development. Through the efforts of three ongoing projects the university is working to enhance campus life for its students and increase its residential student numbers on campus by 600.

Financial Performance

Thanks to organic growth the university has logged revenue increases during the past three years. NJIT's revenue rose some 11% in 2011 vs. 2010 due to increases in tuition and fees and auxiliary enterprise revenues attributable to a boost in occupancy and residence hall charges and increases in federal state and other grants and contracts. Net income during the same reporting period increased by 61%. NJIT points to income from realized net gains on the sale of investments (partially offset by a decrease in interest and dividends) for the increases. Cash generated from tuition and fees and auxiliary enterprises contributed toward a cash flow bump of more than $20 million in 2011 vs. 2010.

EXECUTIVES

Chairperson, Kathleen Wielkopolski
President, Robert A. Altenkirch
SVP Administration Treasurer and Trustee, Henry A. Mauermeyer
SVP Research and Development, Donald H. Sebastian
President, Joel S. Bloom
VP University Advancement, Charles R. Dees Jr.
VP Human Resources and Executive Director Compliance Training and Community Relations, Theodore T. Johnson
Provost and SVP Academic Affairs, Ian Gatley
General Counsel and Secretary Board of Trustees, Holly Stern
Associate VP Enrollment Services and Dean of Admissions, Kathryn Kelly
Executive Director University Communications, Jean Llewellyn
University Librarian, Richard T. (Rich) Sweeney
Associate Provost for Information Services and Technology and Chief Information Officer, David F. Ullman
University Registrar, Joseph F. Thompson
Executive Director Alumni Relations, Robert A. Boynton
Chief of Staff, Henry J. Ross
Co-Vice Chairperson, Vincent DeCaprio
Co-Vice Chairperson, Stephen De Palma
Dean Newark College of Engineering, Sunil Saigal
Dean College of Science and Liberal Arts, Fadi Deek
Dean College of Architecture and Design, Urs P. Gauchat
Dean School of Management, Pius J. Egbelu
Dean College of Computing Sciences, Narain Gehani
Executive Director Career Development Services, Gregory Mass

Interim VP Academic and Student Services, Jack Gentul
Director Financial Aid, Ivon Nunez
Director Institutional Research and Planning, Eugene P. Deess
Director Reference NJIT University Library, Davida Scharf
Co-Vice Chairperson, Anthony R. Slimowicz
SVP Administration Treasurer and Trustee, Henry A. Mauermeyer
General Counsel and Secretary Board of Trustees, Holly Stern
Co-Vice Chairperson, Vincent DeCaprio
Trustee, Stephen De Palma
Co-Vice Chairperson, Anthony R. Slimowicz
Auditors: KPMGLLP

LOCATIONS

HQ: New Jersey Institute of Technology
323 Martin Luther King Jr. Blvd., Newark NJ 07102-1982
Phone: 973-596-3000   **Fax:** 305-591-5607
Web: www.andeschem.com

PRODUCTS/OPERATIONS

Selected Colleges

Newark College of Engineering
College of Architecture and Design
College of Science and Liberal Arts
School of Management
Albert Dorman Honors College
College of Computing Sciences

HISTORICAL FINANCIALS

Company Type: School

Income Statement

FYE: June 30

	REVENUE ($ mil.)	NET INCOME ($ mil.)	NET PROFIT MARGIN	EMPLOYEES
06/11	184	19	10.4%	1,047
06/09	162	(13)	—	0
06/08	149	(2)	—	0
06/06	9	3	37.1%	0
Annual Growth	168.9%	75.6%	—	—

2011 Year-End Financials

Debt ratio: ——
Return on equity: 10.40%
Cash ($ mil.): 32
Current ratio: 0.80
Long-term debt ($ mil.): —

Dividends
Yield: —
Payout: —
Market value ($ mil.): —

NEW PRIME INC.

Check out this Prime number –more than 5800 remotely monitored temperature-controlled trailers. Specialized carrier New Prime (which does business simply as Prime) provides refrigerated flatbed and liquid bulk tanker trucking services throughout North America. The company operates in the US and Canada and serves Mexico through arrangements with other carriers. A subsidiary Prime Floral uses the parent company's refrigerated equipment and facilities to serve the flower industry. In addition to its freight-hauling operations Prime provides logistics services including freight brokerage.

Geographic Reach

The company serves customers in Canada Mexico and the US.

Operations

It operates through three divisions: Prime's liquid bulk fleet (Tanker Division) consists of 6800-gallon Walker Stainless MC407 trailers with air ride suspensions. The company's Refrigerated Division has a fleet of remotely monitored temperature-controlled trailers and serves businesses whose needs include transportation of fresh produce fresh cut floral produce pharmaceuticals fresh or frozen meats or any other dry or temperature controlled freight. Prime also has a Flatbed Division.

Sales and Marketing

Prime has hauled goods for such blue chip consumer goods makers as ConAgra Foods Kraft Foods and General Mills.

Strategy

Prime is shifting its strategy to align with customer preferences for shortening supply chain mileage and delivery time all of which is intended to offset lower consumer demand and volatile fuel costs.

It is also using technology to enhance its position as an industry leader in the safe cost-effective transport of temperature-sensitive goods. The company has embraced modern technology like the QUALCOMM satellite system which benefits shippers by providing continuous communication from initial dispatch to final delivery. This option helps to monitor load temperatures set points alarm conditions connect and disconnect times and uses the QUALCOMM link present in every Prime tractor to transfer this important data.

Prime Position Tracking enables the company to locate tractors in real-time within a 600 foot radius at all times. Prime Mapping and Routing provides detailed Rand McNally and PC*Miler directions to driver associates to ensure that loads get to their destination in the quickest safest and most efficient manner.

Company Background

Prime was founded in 1970 by Robert Low who continues to serve as Prime's president.

EXECUTIVES

Founder, Robert E. Low
General Counsel, Steve Crawford
Manager Success Leasing Program, Fred Ege
Director Logistics, Rick Gallagher
Director Operations, Pat Leonard
Director Driver Personnel, Barbara Mayhew
Manager Credit, Zach Whitehead
Director Flatbed Operations, Jim Wilkins
VP Sales and Marketing, Steve Wutke
Director Marketing, Keith McCoy
Director Payroll, John Moore
VP Risk Management, Jim Owen
Director Finance, Dean Hoedl
Director Leasing, Darrel Hopkins
Director Safety, Don Lacy
Director Tanker Division, Kirk Erickson
Director Training and Driver Recruiting, John Hancock
Director Maintenance, Bill Taylor
Manager National Pricing, David Pfitzner
Manager Taxes and Permits, Patricia Hicks
Manager Prime Plaza, Paul Higgins
Facility Engineer, Johnny Madison
Director Technology, Rodney Rader
Director Security, James (Jamie) Morton

LOCATIONS

HQ: New Prime Inc.
2740 N. Mayfair, Springfield MO 65803
Phone: 417-521-6886   **Fax:** 417-521-6878
Web: www.primeinc.com

COMPETITORS

Boyd Bros.   Comcar
   Transportation   Frozen Food Express
C.H. Robinson   KLLM Transport
   Worldwide   Services
C.R. England   Marten Transport
Central Refrigerated   Quality Distribution
   Service   Stevens Transport

HISTORICAL FINANCIALS

Company Type: Private

Income Statement
FYE: April 1

	REVENUE ($ mil.)	NET INCOME ($ mil.)	NET PROFIT MARGIN	EMPLOYEES
04/11*	941	47	5.0%	4,600
03/10	844	91	10.8%	0
03/09	849	76	9.0%	0
03/08	784	76	9.7%	0
Annual Growth	6.3%	(14.6%)	—	—

*Fiscal year change

2011 Year-End Financials

Debt ratio: ——
Return on equity: 5.00%
Cash ($ mil.): 0
Current ratio: 0.80
Long-term debt ($ mil.): —
Dividends
Yield: —
Payout: —
Market value ($ mil.): —

NEW RIVER ELECTRICAL CORPORATION

LOCATIONS

HQ: NEW RIVER ELECTRICAL CORPORATION
15 CLOVERDALE PL, CLOVERDALE, VA 24077-3124
Phone: 540-966-1650
Web: www.newriverelectrical.com

HISTORICAL FINANCIALS

Company Type: Private

Income Statement
FYE: December 31

	REVENUE ($ mil.)	NET INCOME ($ mil.)	NET PROFIT MARGIN	EMPLOYEES
12/11	135	6	4.8%	500
12/10	119	30	25.2%	0
12/09	109	8	7.9%	0
12/08	149	12	8.3%	0
Annual Growth	(3.1%)	(19.0%)	—	—

2011 Year-End Financials

Debt ratio: ——
Return on equity: 4.80%
Cash ($ mil.): 32
Current ratio: 5.90
Long-term debt ($ mil.): —
Dividends
Yield: —
Payout: —
Market value ($ mil.): —

NEW YORK BLOOD CENTER INC.

New York Blood Center (NYBC) holds a very literal interpretation of the meaning of life. It is a not-for-profit blood distribution and research organization serving New York City and its environs in New York State and New Jersey as well as parts of Connecticut and Pennsylvania. As one of the largest blood centers in the US NYBC provides nearly 1 million blood components to some 200 hospitals each year. The center's facilities collect blood from more than 2000 donors each day. It also operates the nation's oldest and largest public cord blood bank. In addition its Kimball Research Institute includes more than a dozen research laboratories which study the prevention and treatment of blood-related illnesses.

Operations Areas of research in the Kimball Research Institute include virology molecular genetics cell biology and signaling viral immunology and infectious disease prevention. It has been responsible for the development and licensing of solvent and detergent technology used to deactivate the potency of viruses in blood and blood products (such as plasma and platelets used in transfusions). NYBC's clinical services division acts as an adjunct and resource to hospitals throughout its service areas by providing expertise in transfusion medicine as well as delivering more than 8500 specialized procedures each year. In addition the center maintains a bone marrow donor registry for the New York area provides hemophilia services to some 1500 patients and offers screening and education programs for cholesterol high blood pressure and cardiovascular disease.

EXECUTIVES

Trustee, Harriet Edelman, age 56
CIO, Michele Scaggiante
VP and CFO, Lawrence J. Hannigan
Chairman, Howard P. Milstein
SVP and Chief Administrative Officer, Michael J. Monahan
VP Strategic Planning and Marketing, Margi Gandolfi
VP and Executive Director Medical Programs and Services, Pascal George
VP Quality Assurance, Donald N. Kender
VP Corporate and Community Relations, Rolf Kovenetsky
VP Blood Services, James E. Louie
SVP and COO, Elizabeth J. McQuail
VP and Director Lindsley F. Kimball Research Institute, Mohandas Narla
VP Customer Service, Robert Purvis
VP External Affairs, Kathleen Reichert
VP and Executive Director Hudson Valley Blood Services, Michele Shenfeld
VP and Executive Director Long Island Blood Services, Harvey Schaffler
VP and Chief Medical Officer, Beth Shaz
VP and General Counsel, David Whitescarver
Acting VP and Executive Director Brooklyn/Staten Island Blood Services, Marc Bertman
VP and Executive Director New Jersey Blood Services, Charles Grossenbacher
Director Corporate Communications, Jim Fox
Director National Cord Blood Program, Pablo Rubinstein
President and CEO, Christopher D. Hillyer

LOCATIONS

HQ: NEW YORK BLOOD CENTER INC.
310 E 67TH ST, NEW YORK, NY 10065-6273
Phone: 212-570-3010
Web: www.projectachieve.org

COMPETITORS

Blood Systems Inc.	Red Cross
Daxor	SeraCare Life Sciences
HemaCare	

HISTORICAL FINANCIALS

Company Type: Private - Not-for-Profit

Income Statement

FYE: March 31

	REVENUE ($ mil.)	NET INCOME ($ mil.)	NET PROFIT MARGIN	EMPLOYEES
03/11	348	(11)	—	1,500
03/10	375	20	5.4%	0
03/09	329	(13)	—	0
03/06	327	67	20.5%	0
Annual Growth	2.1%	—	—	—

2011 Year-End Financials

Debt ratio: —
Return on equity: (-3.40)%
Cash ($ mil.): 38
Current ratio: 1.00
Long-term debt ($ mil.): —

Dividends
Yield: —
Payout: —
Market value ($ mil.): —

NEW YORK COMMUNITY TRUST AND COMMUNITY FUNDS INC

LOCATIONS

HQ: NEW YORK COMMUNITY TRUST AND COMMUNITY FUNDS INC
909 3RD AVE FL 22, NEW YORK, NY 10022-4752
Phone: 212-686-0010

HISTORICAL FINANCIALS

Company Type: Private

Income Statement

FYE: December 31

	REVENUE ($ mil.)	NET INCOME ($ mil.)	NET PROFIT MARGIN	EMPLOYEES
12/11	170	17	10.3%	65
12/10	290	137	47.5%	0
12/09	363	230	63.2%	0
12/08	89	0	—	0
Annual Growth	24.0%	—	—	—

2011 Year-End Financials

Debt ratio: —
Return on equity: 10.30%
Cash ($ mil.): 68
Current ratio: —
Long-term debt ($ mil.): —

Dividends
Yield: —
Payout: —
Market value ($ mil.): —

NEW YORK LAW SCHOOL

LOCATIONS

HQ: NEW YORK LAW SCHOOL
185 W BROADWAY, NEW YORK, NY 10013-2921
Phone: 212-431-2100
Web: www.nyls.edu

HISTORICAL FINANCIALS

Company Type: Private

Income Statement

FYE: June 30

	REVENUE ($ mil.)	NET INCOME ($ mil.)	NET PROFIT MARGIN	EMPLOYEES
06/11	118	37	31.7%	208
06/10	115	33	28.6%	0
Annual Growth	2.4%	13.4%	—	—

2011 Year-End Financials

Debt ratio: —
Return on equity: 31.70%
Cash ($ mil.): 1
Current ratio: —
Long-term debt ($ mil.): —

Dividends
Yield: —
Payout: —
Market value ($ mil.): —

NEW YORK MEDICAL COLLEGE

It doesn't take a brain surgeon to figure out this school's specialty. New York Medical College (NYMC) confers advanced degrees to those preparing for careers in the medical and health professions. The institution's three divisions (the School of Medicine the School of Public Health and the Graduate School of Basic Medical Sciences) offer programs in more than 20 disciplines. NYMC has an enrollment of more than 1600 students who practice at nearby Westchester Medical Center and Saint Vincent Catholic Medical Centers' Manhattan location. Founded in 1860 the college has been affiliated with the Archdiocese of New York since 1978. NYMC is part of Touro College.

EXECUTIVES

President and CEO, Karl P. Adler
SVP Finance CFO and Vice Provost Administration and Finance, Stephen J. Piccolo Jr.
CIO, John C. Hammond
Vice Provost and Senior Associate Dean Academic Administration, William A. Steadman II
Provost and Dean School of Medicine, Ralph A. O'Connell
Dean Graduate School of Basic Medical Sciences, Francis L. Belloni
Vice Dean Westchester Medical Center, Renee Garrick
Vice Dean School of Public Health, James J. O'Brien
VP General Counsel and Institutional Compliance Officer, Waldemar A. (Tony) Comas
Chairman Department of Rehabilitation Medicine, Maria P. deAraujo
Dean School of Public Health, Robert W. Amler
Associate VP and Director Human Resources, Peter M. Brown
Controller, George Nestler
Associate Provost and University Registrar, Judith A. Ehren
University Bursar, Diane Alexander
Chief Affiliation Officer, Howard Nelson
Director Environmental Health and Safety, William Collesano
Director Web Communications, Kevin R. Cummings
Director Internal Audit, Redmond Jacobsen Jr.
VP Development and Alumni Relations, Julie A. Kabaska
Associate Director Information Services, Luis Montes
Physician-in-Chief and Vice Dean, William G. Bithoney
Associate General Counsel and Compliance Director, Dana H. Lee
University Budget Officer, Bonnie Gurran-Heindl
Director Security, William Allison
Assistant Dean and Director Admissions and Recruitment, Marian F. McGowan
Vice Dean Medical Education, Martha S. Grayson
Vice Dean Clinical Affairs and Graduate Medical Education, Richard McCarrick
Senior Associate Dean Student Affairs, Gladys M. Ayala
Senior Associate Dean Fifth Pathway Program, Saverio S. Bentivegna
Senior Associate Dean, C. Gene Cayten
Senior Associate Dean Academic Administration and Research Development, Rosemary A. Martino
Senior Associate Dean NYMC Danbury Hospital, Pierre F. Saldinger

Senior Associate Dean and Medical Director
  Metropolitan Hospital Center, Richard K. Stone
Senior Associate Dean Westchester Medical
  Center, Paul K. Woolf
Director Advancement Services, Dee Demling
Director Annual Giving, David K. Berkner
Director Research Information and Development,
  Lea Emmett
Director Corporate and Foundation Relations, Lisa
  Koch
Director Development Communications and
  Donor Relations, Monica Maye
Senior Director Communications, Donna Moriarty
Director Purchasing, John Stein
Associate Director Information Services, Douglas
  Daly
Associate Director Human Resources, Theresa
  Gelchie
Associate Director Human Resources, Theresa
  Haviland
Associate Director Information Services, Chao-Chi
  Tien
Auditors: PricewaterhouseCoopersLLP

LOCATIONS

HQ: New York Medical College
  Administration Bldg., Valhalla NY 10595
Phone: 914-594-4000   Fax: 914-594-4328
Web: www.nymc.edu

PRODUCTS/OPERATIONS

Selected Departments

Anesthesiology
Biochemistry and Molecular Biology
Cell Biology and Anatomy
Dental Medicine
Dermatology
Emergency Medicine
Family and Community Medicine
Medicine
Microbiology and Immunology
Neurology
Obstetrics and Gynecology
Ophthalmology
Otolaryngology
Pathology
Pediatrics
Pharmacology
Physiology
Psychiatry and Behavioral Science
Radiation Medicine
Radiology
Rehabilitation Medicine
Surgery
Urology

HISTORICAL FINANCIALS

Company Type: School

Income Statement

FYE: June 30

	REVENUE ($ mil.)	NET INCOME ($ mil.)	NET PROFIT MARGIN	EMPLOYEES
06/11	245	32	13.2%	1,600
06/10	215	(1)	—	0
Annual Growth	**14.2%**	—	—	—

2011 Year-End Financials

Debt ratio: —
Return on equity: 13.20%
Cash ($ mil.): 38
Current ratio: —
Long-term debt ($ mil.): —

Dividends
  Yield: —
  Payout: —
Market value ($ mil.): —

NEW YORK POWER AUTHORITY

The hydropower generated by the mighty Niagara Falls is the real authority behind the New York Power Authority (NYPA). The company generates and transmits more than 20% of New York's electricity making it the largest state-owned public power provider in the US. It is also New York's only statewide electricity supplier. NYPA owns hydroelectric and fossil-fueled generating facilities (17 in total) that produce about 5700 MW of electricity and it operates more than 1400 circuit-miles of transmission lines.

The authority sells power to government agencies municipal systems rural cooperatives private companies private utilities (for resale) and neighboring states. Its clients include some of the largest electricity users in the US including the New York City government and the Metropolitan Transportation Authority. NYPA receives no state funds or tax credits. Instead it finances new projects through bond sales.

Following its shift from a regulated monopoly to a competitor in an open power market NYPA is aiming to grow by reducing the cost of the energy it provides and by developing electric transportation (such as electric cars) and other energy-efficiency projects including installing emergency power generators in metropolitan buildings. It is also working to improve the state's transmission grid increase its generating capacity and help support the state's directive to get 45% of its power from clean energy sources by 2015 (include 100 MW of power from solar arrays at buildings across the state). Participating in the green energy push by 2010 NYPA's fleet of more than 1200 electric vehicles had logged more than 11 million miles of service.

Low commodity prices and depressed demand prompted by the global recession hurt NYPA's revenue performance in 2009. In 2010 revenues and income were down further largely due to lower power generation from its main Niagara plant (because of lower lake levels) which in turn limited the power volumes that the NYPA was able to sell.

To improve its delivery of power is pursuing the development of a new cross-Hudson transmission line that will connect New York City customers to the PJM Interconnection power grid.

HISTORY

The Power Authority of the State of New York (aka New York Power Authority or NYPA) was established in 1931 by Gov. Franklin Roosevelt to gain public control of New York's hydropower resources. The utility's major power plants came on line with the opening of the St. Lawrence-Franklin D. Roosevelt Power Project (1958) and the Niagara Power Project (1961). The Blenheim-Gilboa Pumped Storage Power Project opened in 1973.

In the mid-1970s NYPA shifted to nuclear power when it opened the James A. FitzPatrick Nuclear Power Plant (1975) and the Indian Point 3 Nuclear Power Plant (1976). The company then opened gas- and oil-powered plants: the Charles Poletti Power Project (1977) and the Richard M. Flynn Power Plant (1994).

In 1998 the authority allocated low-cost electricity to five companies that planned to invest $104 million in business expansions in western New York. The company suffered a loss in 1999 in part

from reduced hydro generation and a drop in investment earnings. In 2000 NYPA sold its two nuclear plants (1800 MW of capacity) to utility holding company Entergy for $967 million.

The company completed the installation of 11 gas-powered turbines at various locations in New York City and on Long Island in 2001; the program was initiated to prevent expected energy shortages that summer but it also helped maintain power in areas of the city during the September 11 terrorist attacks.

EXECUTIVES

SVP Energy Resource Management and Strategic
  Planning, William J. Nadeau
VP and Controller, Arnold M. Bellis
President and CEO, Richard M. Kessel
EVP and CFO, Donald A. Russak
EVP and CFO, Joseph M. Del Sindaco
Chairman, Michael J. Townsend
SVP Energy Services and Technology, Angelo S.
  Esposito
Director Media Relations, Michael A. Saltzman
SVP Transmission, Steven J. DeCarlo
COO, Edward A. Welz
Vice Chairman, Jonathan F. (Jon) Foster, age 51
President and CEO, Gil C. Quiniones
SVP Corporate Support Services, Joan Tursi
SVP Economic Development and Efficiency, James
  F. Pasquale
SVP Public and Governmental Affairs, Paul F.
  Finnegan
EVP and General Counsel, Terryl Brown Clemons
Acting SVP Energy Services, Paul W. Belnick
EVP and General Counsel, Judith C. McCarthy
Chief of Staff and Director Energy Policy, Jill C.
  Anderson
VP Community and Government Relations, Joseph
  Leary
Vice Chairman, Jonathan F. (Jon) Foster, age 51
Trustee, D. Patrick Curley
Trustee, Eugene L. Nicandri
Auditors: KPMGLLP

LOCATIONS

HQ: NEW YORK POWER AUTHORITY
  123 MAIN ST STE 1600, WHITE PLAINS, NY
  10601-3132
Phone: 914-681-6200
Web: www.nypa.gov

PRODUCTS/OPERATIONS

2010 Sales

	$ mil.	% of total
Power sales	1,889	74
Wheeling charges	528	20
Transmission charges	151	6
Total	**2,568**	**100**

Selected Operations

Transmission Control Facility
  Frederick R. Clark Energy Center (Oneida County)
Fossil-Fueled Plants
  Charles Poletti Power Project (New York City)
  Richard M. Flynn Power Plant (Suffolk County)
  PowerNow! Turbines (11 units in New York City and
    Long Island)
Hydropower Plants
  Blenheim-Gilboa Pumped Storage Power Project
    (Schoharie County)
  Niagara Power Project (Niagara County)
  St. Lawrence-Franklin D. Roosevelt Power Project (St.
    Lawrence County)
Small Hydropower Plants
  Ashokan Project (Ulster County)
  Crescent Plant (Albany and Saratoga Counties)

Gregory B. Jarvis Plant (Oneida County)
Kensico Project (Westchester County)
Vischer Ferry Plant (Saratoga and Schenectady counties)

COMPETITORS

CH Energy	Iberdrola USA
Con Edison	National Grid USA
Dynegy	Rochester Gas and
Enbridge	Electric
Entergy	TransCanada

HISTORICAL FINANCIALS
Company Type: Government-owned

Income Statement
FYE: December 31

	REVENUE ($ mil.)	NET INCOME ($ mil.)	NET PROFIT MARGIN	EMPLOYEES
12/11*	2,655	294	11.1%	4,450
02/10	454	415	91.5%	0
12/08	3,185	299	9.4%	0
12/07	2,906	235	8.1%	0
Annual Growth	(3.0%)	7.8%	—	—

*Fiscal year change

2011 Year-End Financials
Debt ratio: —
Return on equity: 11.10%
Cash ($ mil.): 65
Current ratio: 0.30
Long-term debt ($ mil.): —

Dividends
Yield: —
Payout: —
Market value ($ mil.): —

NEW YORK STATE INDUSTRIES FOR THE DISABLED INC.

LOCATIONS
HQ: NEW YORK STATE INDUSTRIES FOR THE DISABLED INC.
11 COLUMBIA CIR, ALBANY, NY 12203-5156
Phone: 518-463-9706
Web: www.nysid.org

HISTORICAL FINANCIALS
Company Type: Private

Income Statement
FYE: September 30

	REVENUE ($ mil.)	NET INCOME ($ mil.)	NET PROFIT MARGIN	EMPLOYEES
09/11	174	0	0.5%	50
09/10	154	0	0.3%	0
09/09	159	0	—	0
09/08	5	0	8.0%	0
Annual Growth	218.6%	24.6%	—	—

2011 Year-End Financials
Debt ratio: —
Return on equity: 0.50%
Cash ($ mil.): 1
Current ratio: 1.20
Long-term debt ($ mil.): —

Dividends
Yield: —
Payout: —
Market value ($ mil.): —

NEWARK BOARD OF EDUCATION

LOCATIONS
HQ: NEWARK BOARD OF EDUCATION
85 E MAIN ST, NEWARK, OH 43055-5605
Phone: 740-670-7000
Web: www.newarkcityschools.com

HISTORICAL FINANCIALS
Company Type: Private

Income Statement
FYE: June 30

	REVENUE ($ mil.)	NET INCOME ($ mil.)	NET PROFIT MARGIN	EMPLOYEES
06/11	101	1	1.6%	1,046
06/10	92	10	11.4%	0
06/09	82	2	2.5%	0
06/08	70	(11)	—	0
Annual Growth	12.8%	—	—	—

2011 Year-End Financials
Debt ratio: —
Return on equity: 1.60%
Cash ($ mil.): 50
Current ratio: —
Long-term debt ($ mil.): —

Dividends
Yield: —
Payout: —
Market value ($ mil.): —

NEWAYGO COUNTY GENERAL HOSPITAL ASSOCIATION

Gerber Memorial Health Services (GMHS) provides acute medical services for the rural county of Newaygo County Michigan. The not-for-profit hospital operating as Spectrum Health Gerber Memorial has about 60 licensed beds. Services include cancer care cardiac rehabilitation orthopedics surgery emergency medicine and women's health. It also provides general practice and home health services. GMHS was founded in 1918. GMHS was acquired by western Michigan health network Spectrum Health in 2010; GMHS had already been affiliated with Spectrum through its membership in the Spectrum Health Regional Hospital Network.

EXECUTIVES
President and CEO, Randall J. (Randy) Stasik, age 61
VP Finance, John Sella

LOCATIONS
HQ: NEWAYGO COUNTY GENERAL HOSPITAL ASSOCIATION
212 S SULLIVAN AVE, FREMONT, MI 49412-1548
Phone: 231-924-3300

COMPETITORS

Holland Community	Mercy Health Hackley

Hospital   Trinity Health (Novi)

HISTORICAL FINANCIALS
Company Type: Subsidiary

Income Statement
FYE: June 30

	REVENUE ($ mil.)	NET INCOME ($ mil.)	NET PROFIT MARGIN	EMPLOYEES
06/11	72	3	4.9%	600
06/10	65	(2)	—	0
06/09	62	(4)	—	0
06/08	62	(2)	—	0
Annual Growth	5.2%	—	—	—

2011 Year-End Financials
Debt ratio: —
Return on equity: 4.90%
Cash ($ mil.): 6
Current ratio: 1.60
Long-term debt ($ mil.): —

Dividends
Yield: —
Payout: —
Market value ($ mil.): —

NEWTON HEALTHCARE CORPORATION

LOCATIONS
HQ: NEWTON HEALTHCARE CORPORATION
600 MEDICAL CENTER DR, NEWTON, KS 67114-8780
Phone: 316-283-2700
Web: www.newtonmedicalcenter.com

HISTORICAL FINANCIALS
Company Type: Private

Income Statement
FYE: June 30

	REVENUE ($ mil.)	NET INCOME ($ mil.)	NET PROFIT MARGIN	EMPLOYEES
06/11	136	3	2.4%	539
06/10	131	4	3.8%	0
06/09*	118	0	—	0
03/08	41	2	5.3%	0
Annual Growth	48.6%	14.3%	—	—

*Fiscal year change

2011 Year-End Financials
Debt ratio: —
Return on equity: 2.40%
Cash ($ mil.): 4
Current ratio: 0.50
Long-term debt ($ mil.): —

Dividends
Yield: —
Payout: —
Market value ($ mil.): —

NEWTRON INC

LOCATIONS

HQ: NEWTRON INC
8183 W EL CAJON DR, BATON ROUGE, LA
70815-8093
Phone: 225-927-8921
Web: www.thenewtrongroup.com

HISTORICAL FINANCIALS

Company Type: Private

Income Statement

FYE: June 30

	REVENUE ($ mil.)	NET INCOME ($ mil.)	NET PROFIT MARGIN	EMPLOYEES
06/12	173	2	1.3%	750
06/11	129	2	1.7%	0
06/10	174	3	1.8%	0
06/09	204	3	1.8%	0
Annual Growth	(5.3%)	(14.8%)	—	—

2012 Year-End Financials

Debt ratio: ——
Return on equity: 1.30%
Cash ($ mil.): 1
Current ratio: 1
Long-term debt ($ mil.): —

Dividends
Yield: —
Payout: —
Market value ($ mil.): —

NEXTSOURCE INC.

LOCATIONS

HQ: NEXTSOURCE INC.
3 PARK AVE RM 1503, NEW YORK, NY 10016-5930
Phone: 212-736-5870
Web: www.consultingdirect.com

HISTORICAL FINANCIALS

Company Type: Private

Income Statement

FYE: December 31

	REVENUE ($ mil.)	NET INCOME ($ mil.)	NET PROFIT MARGIN	EMPLOYEES
12/11	129	0	0.6%	2,300
12/10	99	1	1.1%	0
Annual Growth	29.8%	(27.0%)	—	—

2011 Year-End Financials

Debt ratio: ——
Return on equity: 0.60%
Cash ($ mil.): 2
Current ratio: 0.80
Long-term debt ($ mil.): —

Dividends
Yield: —
Payout: —
Market value ($ mil.): —

NGL ENERGY PARTNERS LP

Animated propane salesman Hank Hill would be proud of this company. NGL Energy Partners retails wholesales and stores propane and other natural gas liquids. Wholesale operations which account for a majority of sales deliver propane to third-party storage and transportation facilities. Retail operations include leasing propane tanks and other equipment and propane delivery to residential agricultural and commercial customers. The company also has about 50 propane stations in Georgia Illinois Indiana and Kansas. The midstream business includes three terminal facilities in the US and Canada that store and distribute propane. Formed in late 2010 NGL Energy Partners went public in 2011.

The company plans to use the $74 million proceeds from the IPO to repay debt from acquisitions and purchase additional propane and midstream assets or businesses. It has no specific acquisition plans.

NGL Energy Partners is part of NGL Energy Holdings which is owned by company management and NGL Holdings. Silverthorne Operating holds the company's operating subsidiaries. The multi-layer structure is common among energy companies. NGL Holdings owned about 27% of the company pre-IPO. Brothers and co-presidents Shawn and Todd Coady together owned 38% through Hicks Oil & Hicksgas Incorporated.

Expanding its midstream business in 2011 the company bought SemGroup's SemStream unit for about $282 million.

In 2012 it acquired Downeast Energy's Maine and New Hampshire distribution assets (50000 customers and annual deliveries of 12 million gallons of retail propane and 28 million gallons of distillate.)

That year the company continued its buying spree with the acquisition of Denver-based High Sierra Energy LP and its general partner High Sierra Energy GP LLC for about $693 million. High Sierra Energy has crude oil gathering water treatment and natural gas liquids (NGL) operations.

EXECUTIVES

VP Business Development, Bradley K. Atkinson, age 55
CEO and Director, H. Michael Krimbill, age 58
CFO Secretary and Treasurer, Craig S. Jones, age 59
Co-President and COO Retail Division and Director, Shawn W. Coady, age 50
Co-President Retail Division, Todd M. Coady, age 53
COO Midstream Division, Brian K. Pauling, age 61
President Midstream Division, Stephen D. Tuttle, age 64
VP and Comptroller, Sharra Straight, age 48
CEO and Director, H. Michael Krimbill, age 58
Co-President and COO Retail Division and Director, Shawn W. Coady, age 50
VP Business Development, Bradley K. Atkinson, age 55
CEO and Director, H. Michael Krimbill, age 58
CFO Secretary and Treasurer, Craig S. Jones, age 59
Co-President and COO Retail Division and Director, Shawn W. Coady, age 50

Co-President Retail Division, Todd M. Coady, age 53
COO Midstream Division, Brian K. Pauling, age 61
President Midstream Division, Stephen D. Tuttle, age 64
VP and Comptroller, Sharra Straight, age 48
CEO and Director, H. Michael Krimbill, age 58
Co-President and COO Retail Division and Director, Shawn W. Coady, age 50
Auditors: GrantThorntonLLP

LOCATIONS

HQ: NGL ENERGY PARTNERS LP
6120 S YALE AVE STE 805, TULSA, OK 74136-4233
Phone: 918-481-1119

COMPETITORS

AmeriGas Partners	Equistar Chemicals
AmeriGas Partners	Equistar Chemicals
Crestwood Midstream Partners LP	Exxon Mobil
Crestwood Midstream Partners LP	Exxon Mobil
Duke Energy	Ferrellgas Partners
Duke Energy	Ferrellgas Partners
Dynegy	Huntsman International
Dynegy	Huntsman International
Energy Transfer	Occidental Petroleum
Energy Transfer	Occidental Petroleum
Enterprise Products	Spectra Energy
Enterprise Products	Spectra Energy
	Williams Companies
	Williams Companies

HISTORICAL FINANCIALS

Company Type: Public

Income Statement

FYE: September 30

	REVENUE ($ mil.)	NET INCOME ($ mil.)	NET PROFIT MARGIN	EMPLOYEES
09/12*	1,461	(14)		353
03/12	1,310	7	0.6%	0
03/11	622	12	2.0%	0
Annual Growth	53.3%	—	—	—

*Fiscal year change

2012 Year-End Financials

Debt ratio: ——
Return on equity: (-1.00)%
Cash ($ mil.): 26
Current ratio: 0.60
Long-term debt ($ mil.): —

Dividends
Yield: —
Payout: —
Market value ($ mil.): —

NIBCO INC.

A more-than-a-century-old maker and distributor of plumbing supplies NIBCO makes a living by (in its own words) staying ahead of the flow. Its flow-control products include pipes fittings actuators and valves made from bronze copper stainless steel plastic and other materials. NIBCO DURA-PEX piping systems Chemtrol flow-control fittings radiant heating equipment and press-to-connect fittings and ball valves are used in commercial construction irrigation residential environmental as well as industrial applications around the world. Founded by Casper Schweitzer NIBCO is owned by his descendants the Martin family and company employees.

Geographic Reach

Serving a global marketplace NIBCO operates 10 manufacturing plants throughout the US an in Mexico and Poland.

Operations

NIBCO is a leading provider of valves fittings and flow control products for commercial industrial and institutional construction as well as residential and irrigation markets. Through its TOLCO subsidiary the company also manufactures seismic bracings strut fittings and custom fabricated supports. The TOLCO line has shored up such projects as John Hopkins Hospital Yankee Stadium the Las Vegas City Center and the Bay Bridge of San Francisco.

Strategy

The company's storied business however faces tough competition from Chinese and other low-cost producers. NIBCO preserves its market share by pushing to increase productivity and improve customer service. NIBCO's focus includes new products launches such as a Universal Sway Brace Attachment (a drill- and weld-free connection); the Fast Clamp attachment (TOLCO seismic bracing line); BlazeMaster fire sprinkler fittings; NIBCO cast bronze Y-strainers and lead-free products to keep up with new lead-free legislation. In 2012 it launched its Coil-Connec manual and automatic balancing valves combination ball valves unions and valve kits.

The company has web-enabled its offerings via a 3D CAD digital parts catalog. The capability reduces its customers' design time and costs increasing NIBCO's sales opportunities. NIBCO has long used computer networks to improve its efficiency in handling orders for customers and suppliers; almost all orders are digitally automated. In 2012 it redesigned its customer-centric website (NIBCO.com) to offer customers easy and quick access to NIBCO's expansive offering of valves fittings PEX and industrial plastics.

Ownership

NIBCO is owned by the Martin family (the descendants of the company's founder) and by employees.

EXECUTIVES

Chairman and CEO, Rex Martin, age 60
SVP Chief Legal Officer and Secretary, Thomas L. (Tom) Eisele
SVP and CTO, Gerald L. (Gary) Wilson
President and COO, Steven E. (Steve) Malm
VP International Sales, Clyde Hayes
Manager Marketing Communications, Sally Boyer
Director Product Development, Rick Noel
VP and General Manager TOLCO, Scott S. Beutler
Vice Chairman and Chief People Officer, Alice A. Martin
VP Finance CFO and Treasurer, Christopher (Chris) Wynne
VP Wholesale Sales, Jeff Shreiner
VP Supply Chain, David L. (Dave) Goodling
VP Supply Management, Christopher (Chris) Mason
VP Retail Sales, Jim Hilfinger
General Manager PEX, Randy Doering
General Manager Chemtrol, Doug Kieper
Director Marketing, Bill Geers
Director Pricing and Profitability, Steve Kemp
Director Information Services, Mike Sajdak

LOCATIONS

HQ: NIBCO INC.
1516 Middlebury St., Elkhart IN 46516-4740
Phone: 574-295-3000   **Fax:** 574-295-3307
Web: www.nibco.com

PRODUCTS/OPERATIONS

Selected Products

Chemtrol thermoplastic valves fittings pipe
Fire protection
  BlazeMaster CPVC fittings
  NIBCO fire protection valves
  TOLCO support systems
Fittings (metal & plastic)
Industrial pressure plastics
Lead-free fittings & valves
PEX NIBCO DURA-PEX piping systems
Pipe support systems (TOLCO)
  Fabricate-to-order pipe supports
  Hangers & supports
  Seismic bracing
  Strut fittings & accessories
Press-to-connect valve system
Valves & actuation
  Actuation
  Angle valves
  Ball valves
  Butterfly valves
  Check valves
  Circuit balancing valves
  Gate valves
  Globe valves
  Irrigation valves
  Multi-turn valves
  Plumbing specialty products
  Press valves
  Strainers

COMPETITORS

Anvil International	Hayward Industries
Asahi/America	Henry Technologies
BrassCraft	KSB AG
Campbell Manufacturing	Mueller Industries
Dixon Valve	Tyco
Elkhart Products	Watts Water
Flowserve	Technologies
Gerber Plumbing	
Fixtures	

HISTORICAL FINANCIALS

Company Type: Private

Income Statement

FYE: December 31

	REVENUE ($ mil.)	NET INCOME ($ mil.)	NET PROFIT MARGIN	EMPLOYEES
12/11	487	23	4.8%	2,420
12/09	436	20	4.6%	0
12/08	570	17	3.1%	0
12/07	417	0	—	0
Annual Growth	—	5107.2%	—	—

2011 Year-End Financials

Debt ratio: ——
Return on equity: 4.80%
Cash ($ mil.): 59
Current ratio: 1.40
Long-term debt ($ mil.): —

Dividends
  Yield: —
  Payout: —
Market value ($ mil.): —

NIKKEN INTERNATIONAL INC.

LOCATIONS

HQ: NIKKEN INTERNATIONAL INC.
52 DISCOVERY, IRVINE, CA 92618-3105
Phone: 949-789-2000
Web: www.nikken.com

HISTORICAL FINANCIALS

Company Type: Private

Income Statement

FYE: December 31

	REVENUE ($ mil.)	NET INCOME ($ mil.)	NET PROFIT MARGIN	EMPLOYEES
12/11	149	4	3.1%	480
12/10	167	6	4.0%	0
12/09	170	8	5.1%	0
12/08	210	14	6.8%	0
Annual Growth	(10.8%)	(31.1%)	—	—

2011 Year-End Financials

Debt ratio: ——
Return on equity: 3.10%
Cash ($ mil.): 24
Current ratio: 1.60
Long-term debt ($ mil.): —

Dividends
  Yield: —
  Payout: —
Market value ($ mil.): —

NINYO & MOORE GEOTECHNICAL & ENVIRONMENTAL SCIENCES CONSULTANTS

Need more engineering services than are immediately at your disposal? Ninyo & Moore provides geological and technical engineering and consulting services for public and private projects throughout the western US. Its offerings include earthquake and fault studies hydrogeologic and geologic hazard evaluations air quality services and environmental consultations for site developments. The company serves a variety of clients including school districts property developers transportation agencies and the military. Past projects include the Las Vegas monorail and the Emporium redevelopment project in San Francisco. Ninyo & Moore was founded in 1986 and today operates about a dozen offices.

EXECUTIVES

President, Avram Ninyo
Manager IT, Mark Morud

LOCATIONS

HQ: Ninyo & Moore Geotechnical & Environmental Sciences Consultants
5710 Ruffin Rd., San Diego CA 92123
Phone: 858-576-1000   **Fax:** 858-576-9600
Web: www.ninyoandmoore.com

PRODUCTS/OPERATIONS

Selected Services

Asbestos and lead paint surveys
Asphalt batch plant inspection
Contaminated site evaluation and remediation
Coring of concrete and masonry
Feasibility studies
Geophysical studies
Hydrologic and hydrogeologic evaluations
Liquefaction studies
Pavement design
Slope stability studies
Steel shop fabrication inspection

COMPETITORS

AMEC Geomatrix	Jacobs Engineering
ARCADIS US	The Kleinfelder Group
Bureau Veritas	Inc.
Fuscoe Engineering	URS
Geotechnics	Willdan Group
Huitt-Zollars	

HISTORICAL FINANCIALS

Company Type: Private

Income Statement

FYE: December 31

	REVENUE ($ mil.)	NET INCOME ($ mil.)	NET PROFIT MARGIN	EMPLOYEES
12/11	55	3	7.2%	350
12/10	52	2	5.3%	0
12/09	53	3	6.4%	0
12/08	58	5	9.1%	0
Annual Growth	(2.3%)	(9.6%)	—	—

2011 Year-End Financials

Debt ratio: ——
Return on equity: 7.20%
Cash ($ mil.): 0
Current ratio: 4.70
Long-term debt ($ mil.): —

Dividends
Yield: —
Payout: —
Market value ($ mil.): —

NISSAN ROSEN INC

LOCATIONS

HQ: NISSAN ROSEN INC
5505 S 27TH ST, MILWAUKEE, WI 53221-4105
Phone: 414-282-9300
Web: www.rosennissan.com

HISTORICAL FINANCIALS

Company Type: Private

Income Statement

FYE: December 31

	REVENUE ($ mil.)	NET INCOME ($ mil.)	NET PROFIT MARGIN	EMPLOYEES
12/11	91	1	1.2%	87
12/10	71	0	0.6%	0
12/09	58	0	0.7%	0
12/08	63	0	0.8%	0
Annual Growth	12.7%	27.5%		

2011 Year-End Financials

Debt ratio: ——
Return on equity: 1.20%
Cash ($ mil.): 2
Current ratio: 0.20
Long-term debt ($ mil.): —

Dividends
Yield: —
Payout: —
Market value ($ mil.): —

NJVC LLC

LOCATIONS

HQ: NJVC LLC
8614 WESTWOOD CENTER DR # 100, VIENNA, VA 22182-2233
Phone: 703-556-0110
Web: www.njvc.com

HISTORICAL FINANCIALS

Company Type: Private

Income Statement

FYE: September 30

	REVENUE ($ mil.)	NET INCOME ($ mil.)	NET PROFIT MARGIN	EMPLOYEES
09/11	542	44	8.1%	1,300
09/10	495	31	6.3%	0
Annual Growth	9.4%	41.5%		

2011 Year-End Financials

Debt ratio: ——
Return on equity: 8.10%
Cash ($ mil.): 0
Current ratio: 1.30
Long-term debt ($ mil.): —

Dividends
Yield: —
Payout: —
Market value ($ mil.): —

NOBLIS INC.

Noblis' noble pursuit is through its offering of science-related strategic and technology consulting services. The not-for-profit company which pledges to serve the public interest helps various government entities and other clients evaluate technology options and vendors as well as solve complex technical problems. Noblis provides strategic planning decision analysis and acquisition support services. The company addresses problems in areas such as criminal justice environment and energy health care homeland security public safety and transportation. Noblis has worked with such clients as the US Air Force Army Navy and Departments of Commerce and Defense.

The company's product suite includes RASMAS a Web-based service allowing health care providers and suppliers to respond more efficiently to product recalls and AcquTrak an acquisitions support tool aimed at helping government entities reduce costs and schedule times.

In 2012 Noblis acquired ElanTech Systems a provider of government systems engineering program management and acquisition services to the intelligence community. The two companies made the deal because of the complementary strengths of their businesses; the acquisition expands Nobils' portfolio giving the firm a broader knowledge base and the ability to capitalize on emerging technology trends and bring innovative new capabilities to clients.

The company was formed in 1996 as Mitretek Systems; it changed its name to Noblis in 2007.

EXECUTIVES

President CEO and Trustee, Amr A. ElSawy
Chairman, Togo Dennis West Jr., age 69
Director Transportation Systems Concepts and Planning, Steven (Steve) Zaidman
Director Center for Sustainability:Earth Energy and Climate, David L. Evans
SVP CFO Chief Administrative Officer and Treasurer, Mark A. Simione
Corporate VP and CTO, H. Gilbert Miller
Corporate VP Corporate Mission Development, Robert J. Clerman
Corporate VP Center for National Security Intelligence, L. Roger Mason Jr.
VP General Counsel Secretary Chief Ethics and Compliance Officer, Sherry L. Rhodes
Director Transportation Systems, Daniel J. Brudnicki
Director Energy and Environmental Sustainability, Daniel J. Casagrande
Director Private Sector Healthcare Center for Health Innovation, Susanna E. Krentz
Director Enterprise Services, Robert R. Menna
Director Health Innovation, Diane Hartingh Price
Corporate Communications, Edna Davis
President CEO and Trustee, Amr A. ElSawy
Trustee, Kathryn D. Sullivan, age 60
Trustee, Alan B. Salisbury, age 75
Trustee, Ronald R. Blanck, age 70
Trustee, John E. McLaughlin
Trustee, Edward C. Meyer

LOCATIONS

HQ: NOBLIS INC.
3150 FAIRVIEW PARK DR, FALLS CHURCH, VA 22042-4504
Phone: 703-610-2000
Web: www.noblis.org

COMPETITORS

Accenture	HP Enterprise Services
Bain & Company	IBM
Boston Consulting	McKinsey & Company
Deloitte Consulting	

HISTORICAL FINANCIALS
Company Type: Private

Income Statement
FYE: October 2

	REVENUE ($ mil.)	NET INCOME ($ mil.)	NET PROFIT MARGIN	EMPLOYEES
10/11	151	4	3.0%	804
10/10	144	8	6.0%	0
10/09	145	(10)	—	0
10/08	142	(13)	—	0
Annual Growth	2.1%	—	—	—

2011 Year-End Financials
Debt ratio: ——
Return on equity: 3.00%
Cash ($ mil.): 0
Current ratio: 1.00
Long-term debt ($ mil.): ——
Dividends
  Yield: —
  Payout: —
  Market value ($ mil.): —

NOLAND HEALTH SERVICES INC.

LOCATIONS
HQ: NOLAND HEALTH SERVICES INC.
600 CORPORATE PKWY # 100, BIRMINGHAM, AL 35242-5450
Phone: 205-783-8440

HISTORICAL FINANCIALS
Company Type: Private

Income Statement
FYE: June 30

	REVENUE ($ mil.)	NET INCOME ($ mil.)	NET PROFIT MARGIN	EMPLOYEES
06/11	119	14	11.7%	1,100
06/10	111	7	6.7%	0
06/09	116	22	19.3%	0
06/08	105	8	8.5%	0
Annual Growth	4.3%	16.3%	—	—

2011 Year-End Financials
Debt ratio: ——
Return on equity: 11.70%
Cash ($ mil.): 6
Current ratio: 0.10
Long-term debt ($ mil.): ——
Dividends
  Yield: —
  Payout: —
  Market value ($ mil.): —

NOONAN BROTHERS PETROLEUM PRODUCTS INC.

LOCATIONS
HQ: NOONAN BROTHERS PETROLEUM PRODUCTS INC.
415 WEST ST, WEST BRIDGEWATER, MA 02379-1030
Phone: 508-588-8026

HISTORICAL FINANCIALS
Company Type: Private

Income Statement
FYE: September 30

	REVENUE ($ mil.)	NET INCOME ($ mil.)	NET PROFIT MARGIN	EMPLOYEES
09/11	133	0	0.1%	14
09/10	96	0	0.1%	0
09/09	80	0	0.1%	0
09/08	122	0	0.1%	0
Annual Growth	3.0%	2.1%	—	—

2011 Year-End Financials
Debt ratio: ——
Return on equity: 0.10%
Cash ($ mil.): 0
Current ratio: 1.70
Long-term debt ($ mil.): —
Dividends
  Yield: —
  Payout: —
  Market value ($ mil.): —

NORTH AMERICAN FAMILY INSTITUTE INC.

LOCATIONS
HQ: NORTH AMERICAN FAMILY INSTITUTE INC.
26 HOWLEY ST STE 2, PEABODY, MA 01960-8634
Phone: 978-538-0286

HISTORICAL FINANCIALS
Company Type: Private

Income Statement
FYE: June 30

	REVENUE ($ mil.)	NET INCOME ($ mil.)	NET PROFIT MARGIN	EMPLOYEES
06/12	85	(0)	—	1,600
06/11	87	0	0.5%	0
06/10	91	0	0.7%	0
06/09	25	0	—	0
Annual Growth	50.0%	—	—	—

2012 Year-End Financials
Debt ratio: ——
Return on equity: (-0.90)%
Cash ($ mil.): 7
Current ratio: 1.20
Long-term debt ($ mil.): —
Dividends
  Yield: —
  Payout: —
  Market value ($ mil.): —

NORTH AMERICAN POWER GROUP LTD.

LOCATIONS
HQ: NORTH AMERICAN POWER GROUP LTD.
8480 E ORCHARD RD # 4000, GREENWOOD VILLAGE, CO 80111-5014
Phone: 303-796-8600
Web: www.napg-ltd.com

HISTORICAL FINANCIALS
Company Type: Private

Income Statement
FYE: December 31

	REVENUE ($ mil.)	NET INCOME ($ mil.)	NET PROFIT MARGIN	EMPLOYEES
12/11	91	(0)	—	16
12/10	91	(0)	—	0
12/09	95	0	0.0%	0
12/08	100	(1)	—	0
Annual Growth	(3.0%)	—	—	—

2011 Year-End Financials
Debt ratio: ——
Return on equity: (-0.60)%
Cash ($ mil.): 4
Current ratio: 1.00
Long-term debt ($ mil.): —
Dividends
  Yield: —
  Payout: —
  Market value ($ mil.): —

NORTH CENTRAL TEXAS COUNCIL OF GOVERNMENTS

LOCATIONS
HQ: NORTH CENTRAL TEXAS COUNCIL OF GOVERNMENTS
616 SIX FLAGS DR, ARLINGTON, TX 76011-6347
Phone: 817-640-3300
Web: www.developmentexcellence.com

HISTORICAL FINANCIALS
Company Type: Private

Income Statement
FYE: September 30

	REVENUE ($ mil.)	NET INCOME ($ mil.)	NET PROFIT MARGIN	EMPLOYEES
09/11	162	(13)	—	331
09/08	159	13	8.4%	0
09/07	172	40	23.7%	0
09/06	481	0	—	0
Annual Growth	—	—	—	—

2011 Year-End Financials
Debt ratio: ——
Return on equity: (-8.50)%
Cash ($ mil.): 0
Current ratio: —
Long-term debt ($ mil.): —
Dividends
  Yield: —
  Payout: —
  Market value ($ mil.): —

NORTH DAKOTA UNIVERSITY SYSTEM

LOCATIONS

HQ: NORTH DAKOTA UNIVERSITY SYSTEM
600 E BOULEVARD AVE # 215, BISMARCK, ND
58505-0601
Phone: 701-328-2960
Web: www.ndus.edu

HISTORICAL FINANCIALS
Company Type: Private

Income Statement
FYE: June 30

	REVENUE ($ mil.)	NET INCOME ($ mil.)	NET PROFIT MARGIN	EMPLOYEES
06/11	626	75	12.0%	26
06/09	571	27	4.9%	0
06/08	616	31	5.1%	0
06/07	584	96	16.4%	0
Annual Growth	2.3%	(7.8%)	—	—

2011 Year-End Financials

Debt ratio: ——
Return on equity: 12.00%
Cash ($ mil.): 89
Current ratio: 1.10
Long-term debt ($ mil.): —

Dividends
Yield: —
Payout: —
Market value ($ mil.): —

NORTH KANSAS CITY HOSPITAL

LOCATIONS

HQ: NORTH KANSAS CITY HOSPITAL
2800 CLAY EDWARDS DR, NORTH KANSAS CITY, MO
64116-3220
Phone: 816-691-2000
Web: www.nkch.org

HISTORICAL FINANCIALS
Company Type: Private

Income Statement
FYE: June 30

	REVENUE ($ mil.)	NET INCOME ($ mil.)	NET PROFIT MARGIN	EMPLOYEES
06/11	419	22	5.3%	3,100
06/09	370	36	9.9%	0
06/08	353	31	8.9%	0
06/07	131	0	0.0%	0
Annual Growth	47.1%	4527.6%	—	—

2011 Year-End Financials

Debt ratio: ——
Return on equity: 5.30%
Cash ($ mil.): 28
Current ratio: 1.50
Long-term debt ($ mil.): —

Dividends
Yield: —
Payout: —
Market value ($ mil.): —

Director, Al Tidwell
Director, Bo Gibens
Director, Hughes Milam
Director, Robin McGraw
Director, Jim Kelley
Director, Scott Reed
Director, Robert Irwin
Director, Richard Heyer
Director, Zell Long
Auditors: KPMGLLP

LOCATIONS

HQ: North Mississippi Medical Center Inc.
830 S. Gloster St., Tupelo MS 38801
Phone: 662-377-3000   **Fax:** 978-683-1713
Web: www.bakingbusiness.com/images/ads/bnj.asp

COMPETITORS

Community Health Systems
Delta Regional Medical Center
Forrest General Hospital
HCA
Memorial Hospital at Gulfport
Natchez Regional Medical Center
Southwest Mississippi Regional Medical Center

HISTORICAL FINANCIALS
Company Type: Subsidiary

Income Statement
FYE: September 30

	REVENUE ($ mil.)	NET INCOME ($ mil.)	NET PROFIT MARGIN	EMPLOYEES
09/11	614	4	0.8%	6,000
09/10	585	51	8.8%	0
09/09	559	54	9.8%	0
09/08	535	23	4.4%	0
Annual Growth	4.7%	(41.3%)	—	—

2011 Year-End Financials

Debt ratio: ——
Return on equity: 0.80%
Cash ($ mil.): 81
Current ratio: 1.00
Long-term debt ($ mil.): —

Dividends
Yield: —
Payout: —
Market value ($ mil.): —

NORTH GEORGIA ELECTRIC MEMBERSHIP FOUNDATION INC.

LOCATIONS

HQ: NORTH GEORGIA ELECTRIC MEMBERSHIP
FOUNDATION INC.
1850 CLEVELAND HWY, DALTON, GA 30721-8315
Phone: 706-259-9441
Web: www.ngemc.com

HISTORICAL FINANCIALS
Company Type: Private

Income Statement
FYE: June 30

	REVENUE ($ mil.)	NET INCOME ($ mil.)	NET PROFIT MARGIN	EMPLOYEES
06/11	243	4	1.8%	192
06/10	217	4	2.3%	0
06/09	238	4	1.9%	0
06/08	217	10	4.7%	0
Annual Growth	3.7%	(24.5%)	—	—

2011 Year-End Financials

Debt ratio: ——
Return on equity: 1.80%
Cash ($ mil.): 2
Current ratio: 0.20
Long-term debt ($ mil.): —

Dividends
Yield: —
Payout: —
Market value ($ mil.): —

NORTH MISSISSIPPI MEDICAL CENTER INC.

At North Mississippi Medical Center you might get some Mississippi Mud ice cream after your tonsils are removed. The full-service 650-bed regional referral hospital in Tupelo is part of the North Mississippi Health Services system an affiliation of hospitals and clinics serving northern Mississippi northwestern Alabama and parts of Tennessee. Specialty services at North Mississippi Medical Center include cancer treatment women's health care cardiology and behavioral health care. The hospital also includes a skilled-nursing facility and home health and hospice organizations.

EXECUTIVES

EVP External Affairs, Gerald D. (Joe) Wages
VP and CIO, Tommy Bozeman
VP and Legal Counsel, Bruce Toppin
Administrator Surgical Services North Mississippi Health Services, Michael (Mike) Denham
CFO, Joe Reppert
VP Managed Care, Wally Davis
VP Professional Services and Chief Nurse Executive, Laura Brower
Director Marketing and Public Relations, Marsha Tapscott
VP Facility Management, Bruce Ridgway
Chief Quality Officer, Michael L. O'Dell
President, Steve Altmiller
Chief Medical Officer, Mark Williams
Chairman, C.K. White

NORTH SOUTH FOODS GROUP INC.

LOCATIONS

HQ: NORTH SOUTH FOODS GROUP INC.
3373 STERLING RIDGE CT, LONGWOOD, FL
32779-3183
Phone: 407-805-3290
Web: www.northsouthmeats.com

HISTORICAL FINANCIALS
Company Type: Private

Income Statement
FYE: December 31

	REVENUE ($ mil.)	NET INCOME ($ mil.)	NET PROFIT MARGIN	EMPLOYEES
12/11	208	1	0.7%	7
12/10	176	1	0.6%	0
12/09	185	0	0.3%	0
12/08	207	0	0.1%	0
Annual Growth	0.1%	64.7%	—	—

NORTH SYRACUSE CENTRAL SCHOOL DISTRICT

LOCATIONS

HQ: NORTH SYRACUSE CENTRAL SCHOOL DISTRICT
5355 W TAFT RD, NORTH SYRACUSE, NY 13212-2796
Phone: 315-218-2123
Web: www.allen.a2schools.org

HISTORICAL FINANCIALS
Company Type: Private

Income Statement
FYE: June 30

	REVENUE ($ mil.)	NET INCOME ($ mil.)	NET PROFIT MARGIN	EMPLOYEES
06/12	150	(8)	—	1,400
06/11	148	(10)	—	0
06/10	152	3	2.5%	0
06/09	149	(2)	—	0
Annual Growth	0.2%	—	—	—

2012 Year-End Financials

Debt ratio: ——
Return on equity: (-5.40)%
Cash ($ mil.): 18
Current ratio: 0.60
Long-term debt ($ mil.): —

Dividends
Yield: —
Payout: —
Market value ($ mil.): —

NORTH WIND INC.

"The North wind doth blow and we shall have".... clean air and water. North Wind works to keep the air clean the ground fresh and the water clear in North America. The environmental consulting firm's services include site assessment soil and groundwater remediation geographic information system (GIS) data hazardous and nonhazardous waste management and project engineering and construction. North Wind has expanded by buying South Carolina-based Pinnacle Consulting Group which offers engineering environmental and information technology consulting services.

North Wind maintains a staff of archaeologists as well as a laboratory and has 19 offices across

the US. The woman-owned minority-owned business targets niche (primarily Federal Government sponsored) contracts in the environmental engineering technical service and construction industries.

In 2007 the company announced that it was part of a team that secured a $100 million Environmental Remediation Services contract from the Naval Facilities Engineering Command Southwest Division.

In 2009 North Wind secured a multiyear contract with Los Alamos National Security LLC which operates national security research institution Los Alamos National Laboratory.

EXECUTIVES

President, Sylvia M. Medina
ESVP, Charlie Marcinkiewicz
Director Human Resources, Tara Gartrell
VP National Repository Programs, Joan Connolly
Controller, Phil Peterson
Manager Alaska Operations, Joey Gillespie
Project Manager Alaska, Don Haas
Manager Alaska Construction Division, Bob Weber
Staff Geologist, Jim Daigle
Senior Geologist, Ron Paulling
COO, John E. Law

LOCATIONS

HQ: North Wind Inc.
1425 Higham St., Idaho Falls ID 83405
Phone: 208-528-8718   **Fax:** 208-528-8714
Web: www.nwindenv.com

COMPETITORS

Shaw Environmental & Infrastructure	Tetra Tech URS

HISTORICAL FINANCIALS
Company Type: Private

Income Statement
FYE: December 31

	REVENUE ($ mil.)	NET INCOME ($ mil.)	NET PROFIT MARGIN	EMPLOYEES
12/11	75	4	5.3%	86
12/10	85	4	5.0%	0
12/09	120	6	5.3%	0
12/08	65	2	3.9%	0
Annual Growth	4.9%	16.3%	—	—

2011 Year-End Financials

Debt ratio: ——
Return on equity: 5.30%
Cash ($ mil.): 3
Current ratio: 1.20
Long-term debt ($ mil.): —

Dividends
Yield: —
Payout: —
Market value ($ mil.): —

NORTHEAST ARC INC.

LOCATIONS

HQ: NORTHEAST ARC INC.
64 HOLTEN ST, DANVERS, MA 01923-1973
Phone: 978-762-4878
Web: www.ne-arc.org

HISTORICAL FINANCIALS
Company Type: Private

Income Statement
FYE: June 30

	REVENUE ($ mil.)	NET INCOME ($ mil.)	NET PROFIT MARGIN	EMPLOYEES
06/11	104	0	0.8%	1,000
06/10	93	0	0.6%	0
06/09	83	0	—	0
06/06	54	0	0.2%	0
Annual Growth	24.4%	103.7%	—	—

2011 Year-End Financials

Debt ratio: ——
Return on equity: 0.80%
Cash ($ mil.): 9
Current ratio: —
Long-term debt ($ mil.): —

Dividends
Yield: —
Payout: —
Market value ($ mil.): —

NORTHEAST OKLAHOMA ELECTRIC COOPERATIVE INC.

LOCATIONS

HQ: NORTHEAST OKLAHOMA ELECTRIC COOPERATIVE INC.
443857 E HIGHWAY 60, VINITA, OK 74301
Phone: 918-256-6405
Web: www.rectec.net

HISTORICAL FINANCIALS
Company Type: Private

Income Statement
FYE: December 31

	REVENUE ($ mil.)	NET INCOME ($ mil.)	NET PROFIT MARGIN	EMPLOYEES
12/11	83	7	8.8%	184
12/10	76	4	6.2%	0
12/09	69	3	4.5%	0
12/08	65	0	1.0%	0
Annual Growth	8.4%	126.7%	—	—

2011 Year-End Financials

Debt ratio: ——
Return on equity: 8.80%
Cash ($ mil.): 9
Current ratio: 1.00
Long-term debt ($ mil.): —

Dividends
Yield: —
Payout: —
Market value ($ mil.): —

NORTHEASTERN SUPPLY INC.

Northeastern Supply keeps its little corner of the world cozy. Through more than 30 locations in Delaware Maryland Pennsylvania Virginia and West Virginia the company distributes air conditioning heating plumbing ventilation and water system equipment along with fixtures and hardware to contractors and other building professionals. Major suppliers include American Standard Bradford White Delta Elkay Jacuzzi and Moen. Northeastern also offers online credit applications electronic funds transfers and e-mail invoicing to its customers. Founded in 1945 the company is owned by the family of president Steve Cook.

EXECUTIVES

Chairman President and CEO, Steve Cook
VP Operations, Mike Combrooks
VP Purchasing, R.J. Kline
VP Residential Sales, Rick Tomaschefsky
VP Business Development, Steve Coppage
Manager Regional Sales, Don Bartsch
Regional Sales Manager, Bill Pritchett
Manager Regional Sales, Alan Cowan
Manager Regional Sales, Andy Kemp
Director Information Technology, Frank Collacchi
VP HVAC, Russ Everson
Commercial Plumbing Sales, Rick Yost
Controller, Bob Kahmer
Human Resources, Helene Headrick
Accounts Receivable, Lori Everson
Accounts Payable, Trina Wilson
Manager CDC, Norman Houck
Central Receiving, Richard Lazzara
Manager Commercial Plumbing Sales, Mike Tagliaferri
Human Resource Administrator, Martha Weaver
Director Inventory Management, Tony Gonclaves
Accounts Payable, Noel Blosser

LOCATIONS

HQ: Northeastern Supply Inc.
  8323 Pulaski Hwy., Baltimore MD 21237
Phone: 410-574-0010   **Fax:** 410-687-5723
Web: www.northeastern.com

2011 Locations

	No.
Maryland	16
Virginia	6
Pennsylvania	3
Delaware	3
West	1
Total	**29**

COMPETITORS

Ferguson Enterprises	Lowe's
HD Supply	Watsco
Johnstone Supply	WinWholesale

HISTORICAL FINANCIALS
Company Type: Private

Income Statement
FYE: December 31

	REVENUE ($ mil.)	NET INCOME ($ mil.)	NET PROFIT MARGIN	EMPLOYEES
12/11	106	1	1.0%	285
12/09	100	2	2.6%	0
12/08	113	2	1.9%	0
12/07	117	3	3.3%	0
Annual Growth	(3.3%)	(34.4%)	—	—

2011 Year-End Financials
Debt ratio: ——
Return on equity: 1.00%
Cash ($ mil.): 2
Current ratio: 1.60
Long-term debt ($ mil.): ——
Dividends
  Yield: —
  Payout: —
Market value ($ mil.): —

NORTHERN ARIZONA REGIONAL BEHAVIORAL HEALTH AUTHORITY INC.

LOCATIONS

HQ: NORTHERN ARIZONA REGIONAL BEHAVIORAL HEALTH AUTHORITY INC.
  1300 S YALE ST, FLAGSTAFF, AZ 86001-6328
Phone: 928-774-7128

HISTORICAL FINANCIALS
Company Type: Private

Income Statement
FYE: June 30

	REVENUE ($ mil.)	NET INCOME ($ mil.)	NET PROFIT MARGIN	EMPLOYEES
06/12	148	5	3.9%	120
06/11	149	1	0.7%	0
06/10	146	2	1.4%	0
06/09	141	3	2.7%	0
Annual Growth	1.6%	14.8%	—	—

2012 Year-End Financials
Debt ratio: ——
Return on equity: 3.90%
Cash ($ mil.): 27
Current ratio: 2.40
Long-term debt ($ mil.): ——
Dividends
  Yield: —
  Payout: —
Market value ($ mil.): —

NORTHERN FRUIT COMPANY

LOCATIONS

HQ: NORTHERN FRUIT COMPANY
  220 2ND ST NE, EAST WENATCHEE, WA 98802-4851
Phone: 509-884-6651
Web: www.northernfruit.com

HISTORICAL FINANCIALS
Company Type: Private

Income Statement
FYE: April 30

	REVENUE ($ mil.)	NET INCOME ($ mil.)	NET PROFIT MARGIN	EMPLOYEES
04/12	87	9	10.5%	30
04/11	70	5	7.9%	0
04/10	69	4	6.9%	0
04/09	70	3	5.0%	0
Annual Growth	7.3%	37.6%	—	—

2012 Year-End Financials
Debt ratio: ——
Return on equity: 10.50%
Cash ($ mil.): 9
Current ratio: 1.50
Long-term debt ($ mil.): ——
Dividends
  Yield: —
  Payout: —
Market value ($ mil.): —

NORTHERN PRIDE INC.

Northern Pride helps northern US turkey farmers take pride in their efforts. The agricultural cooperative processes some 20000 turkeys a day (or 40 million live pounds of turkey a year) and sells whole bird bone-in breast and turkey parts (drums wings necks gizzards tails and thighs) under the Snowland Northern Pride Harvest Gold and Premium Specialty brand names throughout the US and in several foreign countries. It also sells a line of free-range and antibiotic turkeys; and offers private-label services. Northern Pride's customers include food retailers foodservice operators and food manufacturers.

Grower-owned the co-op serves 25 member/farmers located in northern Minnesota and North Dakota and operates a single processing plant in Thief River Falls Minnesota. Northern Pride was founded in 1989 when it took over a former Land O'Lakes facility.

EXECUTIVES

General Manager, Russel (Russ) Christianson
President, Glen Jaenicke
Secretary, John Stauffenecker
Purchasing, Troy Stauffenecker
VP, Doug Headland
Transportation, Terry Tureson
Controller, Peggy Genereux
Director Personnel, Sue Nelson

LOCATIONS

HQ: Northern Pride Inc.
  401 Conley Ave. South, Thief River Falls MN 56701
Phone: 218-681-1201   **Fax:** 218-681-7183
Web: www.northernprideinc.com

COMPETITORS

Butterball	Perdue Incorporated
Cargill	Pilgrim's Pride
Cooper Farms	Plainville Farms
Empire Kosher Poultry	Raeford Farms
Foster Farms	Tyson Foods
Hormel	West Liberty Foods
Jennie-O	Zacky Farms
Mondelez International	

HISTORICAL FINANCIALS
Company Type: Private - Cooperative

Income Statement
FYE: December 31

	REVENUE ($ mil.)	NET INCOME ($ mil.)	NET PROFIT MARGIN	EMPLOYEES
12/11	35	0	0.2%	210
12/10	30	0	0.3%	0
12/09	25	0	0.3%	0
12/08	27	0	0.3%	0
Annual Growth	9.6%	5.7%	—	—

NORTHWEST EVALUATION ASSOCIATION

LOCATIONS

HQ: NORTHWEST EVALUATION ASSOCIATION
121 NW EVERETT ST, PORTLAND, OR 97209-4049
Phone: 503-624-1951

HISTORICAL FINANCIALS

Company Type: Private

Income Statement

FYE: June 30

	REVENUE ($ mil.)	NET INCOME ($ mil.)	NET PROFIT MARGIN	EMPLOYEES
06/12	84	(4)	—	510
06/11	73	1	1.7%	0
06/10	64	4	6.4%	0
06/09	54	0	0.9%	0
Annual Growth	15.4%	—	—	—

2012 Year-End Financials

Debt ratio: ——
Return on equity: (-5.90)%
Cash ($ mil.): 5
Current ratio: 0.40
Long-term debt ($ mil.): ——

Dividends
Yield: ——
Payout: ——
Market value ($ mil.): ——

NORTHWEST FARM CREDIT SERVICES ACA

Northwest Farm Credit Services is an agricultural lender that provides financial services to farmers ranchers agribusinesses commercial fishermen timber producers and rural home owners in Alaska Idaho Montana Oregon and Washington. The co-operatively-owned company has a network of around 50 branches and offers a broad range of flexible loan programs to meet the needs of people in the agriculture business. Farm Credit also provides leasing services appraisal services and life mortgage disability and crop insurance as well as legal advocacy and assistance to customers in need. The company is part of the Farm Credit System a network of lenders serving the US agriculture industry.

Congress created the Farm Credit System in 1916 to meet the financial needs of farmers ranchers and cooperatives who invest as well as borrow from the institutions within the system. All Farm Credit System members are regulated by the Farm Credit Administration.

EXECUTIVES

President and CEO, Jay B. Penick, $500,000 total compensation
EVP Credit, Dan Stainbrook
EVP Financial Services, Fred (Fred) DePell
EVP and General Counsel, Thomas (Tom) Tracy
EVP Corporate Administration and Secretary, Joan E. Haynes
EVP Human Resources and Marketing, Kathy Payne
EVP CFO and CIO, Tom Nakano
Chairman, Drew Eggers, $41,250 total compensation
SVP Loan Processing, Wendy Vail
SVP Agribusiness, Marnie Vandenberg
SVP Commercial Lending, John Phelan
SVP Agribusiness, Jeff Hattori
SVP Community Lending, Brent Fetsch
SVP Capital Markets, Jim D. Allen
Vice Chairman, Kevin Riel, $45,000 total compensation
Director, Christy M. Burmeister-Smith, age 55
Director, Edward S. (Ed) Malesich
Director, Bruce Nelson
Director, David (Dave) Hedlin
Director, Herb Karst
Director, David (Dave) Nisbet
Vice Chairman, Kevin Riel
Director, Karen Schott
Director, Julie Shiflett
Director, Rick Barnes
Director, Jim Farmer
Director, Mark Gehring
Director, Shawn Walters
Auditors: PricewaterhouseCoopersLLP

LOCATIONS

HQ: Northwest Farm Credit Services ACA
1700 S. Assembly St., Spokane WA 99220
Phone: 509-340-5300   **Fax:** 416-572-2201
Web: www.clinemining.com

PRODUCTS/OPERATIONS

Sales 2008

	$ mil.	% of total
$ in mil. % of total		
Interest income	438	88
Non interest income		
Patronage income	34	7
Loan and other fees	17	3
Other	7	2
Total	**497**	**100**

COMPETITORS

Bank of America
First Interstate
Idaho Independent Bank
KeyCorp
Northwest Bancorporation

U.S. Bancorp
Wells Fargo
Zions Bancorporation

HISTORICAL FINANCIALS

Company Type: Private - Member-Owned Banking Authority

Income Statement

FYE: December 31

	ASSETS ($ mil.)	NET INCOME ($ mil.)	INCOME AS % OF ASSETS	EMPLOYEES
12/11	8,696	159	1.8%	500
12/10	8,705	150	1.7%	0
12/09	8,579	106	1.2%	0
12/08	8,326	124	1.5%	0
Annual Growth	1.5%	8.6%	—	—

2011 Year-End Financials

Debt ratio: ——
Return on equity: 38.90%
Cash ($ mil.): 62
Current ratio: ——
Long-term debt ($ mil.): ——

Dividends
Yield: ——
Payout: ——
Market value ($ mil.): ——

NORTHWEST HOSPITAL CENTER INC.

LOCATIONS

HQ: NORTHWEST HOSPITAL CENTER INC.
5401 OLD COURT RD, RANDALLSTOWN, MD 21133-5103
Phone: 410-521-2200
Web: www.nwhospctr.org

HISTORICAL FINANCIALS

Company Type: Private

Income Statement

FYE: June 30

	REVENUE ($ mil.)	NET INCOME ($ mil.)	NET PROFIT MARGIN	EMPLOYEES
06/11	222	16	7.5%	981
06/10	210	14	6.8%	0
06/09	194	3	1.9%	0
06/08	203	21	10.6%	0
Annual Growth	3.0%	(8.1%)	—	—

2011 Year-End Financials

Debt ratio: ——
Return on equity: 7.50%
Cash ($ mil.): 45
Current ratio: 2.00
Long-term debt ($ mil.): ——

Dividends
Yield: ——
Payout: ——
Market value ($ mil.): ——

NORTHWEST LOCAL SCHOOL DISTRICT

LOCATIONS

HQ: NORTHWEST LOCAL SCHOOL DISTRICT
3240 BANNING RD, CINCINNATI, OH 45239-5207
Phone: 513-923-1000
Web: www.nwlsd.org

HISTORICAL FINANCIALS
Company Type: Private

Income Statement
FYE: June 30

	REVENUE ($ mil.)	NET INCOME ($ mil.)	NET PROFIT MARGIN	EMPLOYEES
06/11	100	1	1.8%	1,300
06/10	100	1	1.8%	0
Annual Growth	(0.0%)	(0.0%)	—	—

2011 Year-End Financials
Debt ratio: ——
Return on equity: 1.80%
Cash ($ mil.): 23
Current ratio: —
Long-term debt ($ mil.): —

Dividends
Yield: —
Payout: —
Market value ($ mil.): —

NORTHWESTERN COLLEGE

LOCATIONS
HQ: NORTHWESTERN COLLEGE
3003 SNELLING AVE N, SAINT PAUL, MN 55113-1598
Phone: 651-631-5100
Web: www.nwc.edu

HISTORICAL FINANCIALS
Company Type: Private

Income Statement
FYE: June 30

	REVENUE ($ mil.)	NET INCOME ($ mil.)	NET PROFIT MARGIN	EMPLOYEES
06/11	80	2	3.2%	400
06/10	77	2	2.6%	0
06/09	74	0	—	0
Annual Growth	4.1%	—	—	—

2011 Year-End Financials
Debt ratio: ——
Return on equity: 3.20%
Cash ($ mil.): 11
Current ratio: —
Long-term debt ($ mil.): —

Dividends
Yield: —
Payout: —
Market value ($ mil.): —

NORTHWESTERN SELECTA INC

LOCATIONS
HQ: NORTHWESTERN SELECTA INC
AVENIDA MATADERO ST AVENIDA MATADE, SAN JUAN, PR 00920
Phone: 787-781-1950
Web: www.northwesternselecta.com

HISTORICAL FINANCIALS
Company Type: Private

Income Statement
FYE: July 31

	REVENUE ($ mil.)	NET INCOME ($ mil.)	NET PROFIT MARGIN	EMPLOYEES
07/12	158	4	2.6%	300
07/11	146	3	2.5%	0
07/06	82	0	0.3%	0
07/05	91	1	2.1%	0
Annual Growth	19.9%	28.1%	—	—

2012 Year-End Financials
Debt ratio: ——
Return on equity: 2.60%
Cash ($ mil.): 0
Current ratio: 0.50
Long-term debt ($ mil.): —

Dividends
Yield: —
Payout: —
Market value ($ mil.): —

NORWEGIAN AMERICAN HOSPITAL INC.

LOCATIONS
HQ: NORWEGIAN AMERICAN HOSPITAL INC.
1044 N FRANCISCO AVE, CHICAGO, IL 60622-2743
Phone: 773-292-8200
Web: www.nahospital.org

HISTORICAL FINANCIALS
Company Type: Private

Income Statement
FYE: September 30

	REVENUE ($ mil.)	NET INCOME ($ mil.)	NET PROFIT MARGIN	EMPLOYEES
09/11	111	2	2.1%	800
09/10	109	(1)	—	0
09/09	117	1	1.2%	0
09/08	102	(5)	—	0
Annual Growth	2.9%	—	—	—

2011 Year-End Financials
Debt ratio: ——
Return on equity: 2.10%
Cash ($ mil.): 19
Current ratio: 3.30
Long-term debt ($ mil.): —

Dividends
Yield: —
Payout: —
Market value ($ mil.): —

NORWICH UNIVERSITY

Whether military man or regular old citizen Norwich University could be the perfect place to learn the ropes. As both a traditional and a military college Norwich accepts military and civilian students. The coeducational school has an enrollment of about 2100. It offers 30 on-campus bachelor's programs a teacher lincensure program and four ROTC programs. The university is the birthplace of the nation's Reserve Officers' Training Corps (ROTC) program. The oldest private military college in the US Norwich University was founded in 1819 by Captain Alden Partridge.

EXECUTIVES
Chairman, Gordon R. Sullivan, age 74
CFO and Treasurer, Richard E. Rebmann
Chief Administrative Officer, David Magida
VP Strategic Partnerships, Philip T. Susmann
VP Development and Alumni Relations, David J. Whaley
VP Student Affairs and Commandant, Michael B. Kelley
Dean Enrollment and Communications Management, Karen P. McGrath
Vice Chairman, Frederick M. Haynes

LOCATIONS
HQ: Norwich University
158 Harmon Dr., Northfield VT 05663
Phone: 802-485-2001   **Fax:** 802-485-2032
Web: www.norwich.edu

HISTORICAL FINANCIALS
Company Type: School

Income Statement
FYE: May 31

	REVENUE ($ mil.)	NET INCOME ($ mil.)	NET PROFIT MARGIN	EMPLOYEES
05/12	93	(25)	—	510
05/11	92	29	32.4%	0
05/10	89	17	19.8%	0
05/09	85	(50)	—	0
Annual Growth	3.0%	—	—	—

2012 Year-End Financials
Debt ratio: ——
Return on equity: (-27.40)%
Cash ($ mil.): 22
Current ratio: —
Long-term debt ($ mil.): —

Dividends
Yield: —
Payout: —
Market value ($ mil.): —

NOTRE DAME OF MARYLAND UNIVERSITY INC.

While College of Notre Dame of Maryland remains rooted to its foundation as a four-year women's college it also offers Weekend College classes for working professionals of both genders as well as a graduate studies program. As the first Catholic college for women in the US to award the four-year baccalaureate degree the College of Notre Dame of Maryland provides roughly 30 undergraduate majors and 10 Weekend College degrees in fields including nursing education pharmacy and arts and sciences. The school has some 3000 students and a student to teacher ratio of about 12:1. College of Notre Dame of Maryland was founded in 1873 by the School Sisters of Notre Dame.

Geographic Reach

College of Notre Dame of Maryland has its main campus in northern Baltimore; it also operates satellite centers throughout Maryland (including sites in Anne Arundel Calvert Cecil Charles Frederick Harford Howard Montgomery Prince Georges St. Mary's Talbot and Washington counties). Many of these satellite centers are located at area hospitals.

To provide study abroad opportunities College of Notre Dame of Maryland has partnerships with universities in Australia China Italy Japan and the UK.

Strategy

College of Notre Dame of Maryland has invested some $120 million in capital improvement projects over the last decade. It is working to form centers of excellence in adult education scientific education liberal arts professional programs and other fields of study. It is also working to address sustainability concerns through its campus improvement projects.

In 2012 the college broke ground on a new academic building that will house its School of Education and the School of Nursing.

EXECUTIVES

President, Mary P. Seurkamp
Director Information Systems and Technology, Warren Szelistowski
VP Finance and Administration, Richard L. (Rick) Staisloff II
Director Human Resources, Suzanne Boyer
Director Media Relations, Theresa Wiseman
VP Student Development, Irene Ferguson
Associate VP Enrollment Management and Registrar, Sharon Bogdan
VP Academic Affairs, Sally White

LOCATIONS

HQ: College of Notre Dame of Maryland
4701 N. Charles St., Baltimore MD 21210-2404
Phone: 410-435-0100   **Fax:** 410-532-5785
Web: www.ndm.edu

PRODUCTS/OPERATIONS

Selected Schools

College of Adult Undergraduate Studies
College of Graduate Studies
International Programs
Renaissance Institute
School of Arts and Sciences
School of Education
School of Nursing
School of Pharmacy
Women's College

HISTORICAL FINANCIALS

Company Type: School

Income Statement

FYE: June 30

	REVENUE ($ mil.)	NET INCOME ($ mil.)	NET PROFIT MARGIN	EMPLOYEES
06/12	39	(1)	—	440
06/11	51	6	12.5%	0
06/10	34	6	17.7%	0
06/09	33	(13)	—	0
Annual Growth	**6.1%**	—	—	—

2012 Year-End Financials

Debt ratio: ——
Return on equity: (-4.80)%
Cash ($ mil.): 1
Current ratio: ——
Long-term debt ($ mil.): —

Dividends
Yield: —
Payout: —
Market value ($ mil.): —

NOVA SOUTHEASTERN UNIVERSITY INC.

Nova Southeastern University (NSU) gives a whole new meaning to "school of sharks." NSU whose mascot is the deep sea predator has an enrollment of more than 28000 students and offers a variety of undergraduate graduate and professional academic programs. NSU offers degrees in several medical disciplines (osteopathic medicine pharmacy optometry nursing) marine biology business law education and computer sciences. The not-for-profit independent school operates four campuses in the Miami-Fort Lauderdale area several health centers and an oceanographic center. Founded in 1964 Nova University merged with Southeastern University of the Health Sciences in 1994 to become Nova Southeastern University.

Geographic Reach

NSU is a distance education pioneer (it was the first US university to offer graduate programs online) offering classes on the Internet as well as at dozens of offsite centers in more than 20 states and about 15 international countries.

Operations

In addition to its undergraduate and graduate programs NSU also operates The University School a pre-K through 12th grade college preparatory day school that draws part of its staff from NSU's School of Education and Human services. The university's Mailman Segal Institute for Early Childhood Studies serves the local community with programming for parents and educators.

Finance

Continuing a trend of earnings growth over the last five years from organic growth measures NSU reported a 4% rise in revenues in 2012 to some $630 million. The growth was attributed to increased tuition and fee income as well as revenues from auxiliary enterprises and government grants. Net income fell 35% however to $46 million due to increased operating expenses (program managed and general expenses).

Strategy

As universities do NSU regularly invests in facility upgrades to meet the growing needs of its students. NSU got hold of some $15 million in federal economic stimulus money in 2010 added $15 million of its own reserves and put the money to building a coral reef research center (construction began in 2011). In addition the university expanded its Student Educational Center (by relocating it to a new facility in Palm Beach) and its nursing school facilities during 2011.

EXECUTIVES

Chair, Ronald G. Assaf
Dean H. Wayne Huizenga School of Business and Entrepreneurship, Randolph A. (Randy) Pohlman
Chancellor Health Professions Division, Frederick Lippman
CEO President and Trustee, George L. Hanbury II
VP Legal Affairs, Joel S. Berman
VP Finance, W. David Heron
VP Institutional Effectiveness, Ronald J. (Ron) Chenail
VP Facilities Management, John J. Santulli
Dean Student Affairs, Brad Williams
Executive Director University Relations, David C. Dawson
Associate VP Business Services, Marc M. Crocquet
Vice Chair, Barry J. Silverman

Executive Director Protective Services, Bronson S. Bias
Controller, Roger T. Lacasse
Director Internal Auditing, Ron Midei
Executive Director Student Educational Centers, Deo Nellis
Associate VP Human Resources, Mark A. Jones
VP Community and Governmental Affairs, Larry A. Calderon
Associate VP Enrollment and Student Services, Stephanie Brown
Director Office of Public Affairs, Julie Spechler
Executive Director Office of Grants and Contracts, Barbara Sterry
Director Purchasing, Mike Corominas
Director Career Development, Shari Saperstein
VP Information Services and University Librarian, Lydia M. Acosta
Dean Shepard Broad Law Center, Athornia Steele
University Provost and EVP Academic Affairs, Frank DePiano
Secretary, W. Tinsley Ellis
VP Institutional Advancement, Joanne Ferchland-Parella
University Budget Officer, Virginia C. Pardo
University Registrar, Elaine Poff
Director Public Safety, Jim Ewing
Director Alumni Relations, Sara DuCuennois
Dean University School, Jerome Chermak
Dean College of Allied Health and Nursing, Richard Davis
Dean Oceanographic Center, Richard E. Dodge
Dean Center for Psychological Studies, Karen Grosby
Dean College of Medical Sciences, Harold E. Laubach
Dean Mailman Segal Institute for Early Childhood Studies, Roni Leiderman
Dean Graduate School of Computer and Information Sciences, Edward Lieblein
Dean College of Optometry, David S. Loshin
Dean College of Pharmacy, Andres Malave
Dean Farquhar College of Arts and Sciences, Don Rosenblum
Dean College of Osteopathic Medicine, Anthony J. Silvagni
Dean Fischler School of Education and Human Services, H. Wells Singleton
Dean College of Dental Medicine, Robert A. Uchin
Dean Graduate School of Humanities and Social Sciences, Honggang Yang
EVP and COO, Jacqueline A. Travisano
Trustee, Richard D. Segal, age 48
Trustee, Alan B. Levan, age 67
Trustee, H. Wayne Huizenga, age 74
Trustee, Paul M. Sallarulo
CEO President and Trustee, George L. Hanbury II
Trustee, R. Douglas Donn, age 63
Vice Chair, Barry J. Silverman
Trustee, Albert J. Miniaci
Trustee, Mitchell W. Berger
Trustee, Keith A. Brown
Trustee, Rick Case
Trustee, Andrew J. DiBattista
Trustee, Arthur J. Falcone
Trustee, Silvia M. Flores
Trustee, David W. Horvitz
Trustee, Royal F. Jonas
Trustee, Milton Jones
Trustee, Nell McMillan Lewis
Trustee, Joseph R. Millsaps
Trustee, Samuel F. Morrison
Trustee, E. Clay Shaw
Trustee, Franklin L. Smith
Trustee, J. Kenneth Tate
Trustee, Zachariah P. Zachariah
Auditors: Ernst&YoungLLP

LOCATIONS

HQ: Nova Southeastern University Inc.
3301 College Ave., Fort Lauderdale-Davie FL 33314-7796
Phone: 954-262-7300   **Fax:** 954-262-3954
Web: www.nova.edu

PRODUCTS/OPERATIONS

2012 Revenues

	$ mil.	% of total
Tuition & fees	521	83
Government grants	37	6
Auxiliary operations	36	6
Contributions	14	2
Investment income	3	1
Other	17	2
Total	**630**	**100**

COMPETITORS

Florida Atlantic University
Florida International University
University of Florida

HISTORICAL FINANCIALS

Company Type: School

Income Statement

FYE: June 30

	REVENUE ($ mil.)	NET INCOME ($ mil.)	NET PROFIT MARGIN	EMPLOYEES
06/11	661	64	9.8%	2,500
06/10	612	22	3.7%	0
06/09	595	17	2.9%	0
06/08	512	24	4.8%	0
Annual Growth	**8.9%**	**38.5%**	**—**	**—**

2011 Year-End Financials

Debt ratio: —
Return on equity: 9.80%
Cash ($ mil.): 98
Current ratio: —
Long-term debt ($ mil.): —
Dividends
Yield: —
Payout: —
Market value ($ mil.): —

NOVAK CONSTRUCTION COMPANY

LOCATIONS

HQ: NOVAK CONSTRUCTION COMPANY
3423 N DRAKE AVE, CHICAGO, IL 60618-5449
Phone: 773-278-1100
Web: www.novakconstruction.com

HISTORICAL FINANCIALS

Company Type: Private

Income Statement

FYE: December 31

	REVENUE ($ mil.)	NET INCOME ($ mil.)	NET PROFIT MARGIN	EMPLOYEES
12/11	112	4	4.3%	100
12/10	114	4	4.2%	0
12/09	91	2	3.1%	0
12/08	153	6	4.0%	0
Annual Growth	**(9.8%)**	**(7.4%)**	**—**	**—**

2011 Year-End Financials

Debt ratio: —
Return on equity: 4.30%
Cash ($ mil.): 5
Current ratio: 0.20
Long-term debt ($ mil.): —
Dividends
Yield: —
Payout: —
Market value ($ mil.): —

NOVO CONSTRUCTION INC.

LOCATIONS

HQ: NOVO CONSTRUCTION INC.
1460 OBRIEN DR, MENLO PARK, CA 94025-1445
Phone: 650-701-1500
Web: www.novoconstruction.com

HISTORICAL FINANCIALS

Company Type: Private

Income Statement

FYE: October 31

	REVENUE ($ mil.)	NET INCOME ($ mil.)	NET PROFIT MARGIN	EMPLOYEES
10/11	230	2	1.1%	155
10/10	91	1	1.2%	0
10/09	85	0	0.8%	0
10/08	148	3	2.5%	0
Annual Growth	**16.0%**	**(13.3%)**	**—**	**—**

2011 Year-End Financials

Debt ratio: —
Return on equity: 1.10%
Cash ($ mil.): 8
Current ratio: 1.00
Long-term debt ($ mil.): —
Dividends
Yield: —
Payout: —
Market value ($ mil.): —

NYACK COLLEGE

Nyack College is a Christian liberal arts college of the Christian and Missionary Alliance with nearly 1000 students enrolled at its main campus located in Nyack New York (twenty miles north of New York City). The university has additional campuses in New York City Washington DC and Miami Valley Ohio and offers graduate programs through the Alliance Theological Seminary. Nyack College was founded in New York City in 1882 as the Missionary Training Institute the first Bible college in America by missionary Dr. A.B. Simpson.

EXECUTIVES

President, Michael G. Scales
EVP and Treasurer, David C. Jennings
Provost and VP Academic Affairs, David F. Turk
Director Athletics, Keith Davie
VP Enrollment and Marketing, Andrea Hennessy
Director Information Technologies, Kevin Buell
Director Human Resources, Karen Davie
VP Advancement, Jeffrey Cory
Director Admissions NYC, Leslie Rosado
Director Student Financial Services, Isaac Foster

Director Student Life and Spiritual Formation, Rev Charles Hammond
Director Library Services and Assistant Professor Research Methods, Cheryl Felmlee

LOCATIONS

HQ: NYACK COLLEGE
1 S BOULEVARD, NYACK, NY 10960-3698
Phone: 845-358-1710
Web: www.nyack.edu

COMPETITORS

Marymount Manhattan   St. Joseph's College
Mercy College

HISTORICAL FINANCIALS

Company Type: School

Income Statement

FYE: June 30

	REVENUE ($ mil.)	NET INCOME ($ mil.)	NET PROFIT MARGIN	EMPLOYEES
06/11	60	0	1.6%	300
06/10	59	1	3.1%	0
06/09	52	0	—	0
06/08	53	(0)	—	0
Annual Growth	**4.2%**	**—**	**—**	**—**

2011 Year-End Financials

Debt ratio: —
Return on equity: 1.60%
Cash ($ mil.): 9
Current ratio: —
Long-term debt ($ mil.): —
Dividends
Yield: —
Payout: —
Market value ($ mil.): —

NYPRO INC.

Nypro is a real pro when it comes to injection molding. The company makes plastic parts used in devices that range from cell phones and electric razors to inkjet printer cartridges and personal computers. Nypro's three global units include Consumer & Electronics Packaging and Healthcare (medical devices such as single-use fluid and drug management components). Although custom-precision plastic-injection molding is Nypro's core business the company also offers assembly services to other manufacturers. Major customers include Dell Nokia and Procter & Gamble. Established in 1955 Nypro agreed to be acquired by electronics manufacturing services provider Jabil Circuit in early 2013.

Change of Company Type

In early 2013 electronics manufacturing services provider Jabil Circuit agreed to buy Nypro. Jabil is buying Nypro in order to expand its materials manufacturing operations into the healthcare market.

Geographic Reach

Nypro comprises more than 40 businesses throughout 15 countries in Asia/Pacific Europe and the US.

Financial Performance

Nypro generated $1.2 billion in total sales for its most recent fiscal year.

Strategy

One of the challenges Nypro has faced is getting its many business operations to work together smoothly. During the worldwide recession the company decentralized its operations by creating three global business units each with its own group president to focus on customers in Nypro's primary markets. The three units ensure a revenue balance in which no market accounts for more than 50%.

Nypro continues to push for an ever larger share of the medical plastics market. In early 2011 the company completed its purchase of Schlosser Medizintechnik a medical device manufacturer in Germany. Nypro has also bumped up its investment in new ventures and strategic companies — which tap new emerging markets —including New Ventures Group (NVG) and Radius Product Development Group as well as Nypro-branded NP Medical and Union Street Brand Packaging.

Company Background

In 1962 chairman Gordon Lankton joined Nypro (then known as Nylon Products Inc.) as general manager and co-owner. In 1969 he acquired the remainder of the company he didn't already own. In 1998 Lankton sold the firm to Nypro's employee stock ownership plan (ESOP).

EXECUTIVES

SVP CFO and Director, Greg G. Adams
Chairman, Gordon B. Lankton
CFO Chief Strategy Officer and Director, James R. (Jim) Buonomo
President CEO and Director, Theodore E. (Ted) Lapres III
Corporate VP Human Resources and Organizational Development, Ann S. Liotta
Director Corporate Communications, Al Cotton
President Nypro Healthcare, Boris Levin
President Nypro Healthcare, Raymond S. (Ray) Grupinski
Corporate VP General Counsel and Secretary, James W. (Jim) Peck
President Nypro Consumer and Electronics, Nelson Ngai
President Nypro Packaging, Paul Kayser
VP Human Resources and Organizational Development, Pat Davies
Director, Thomas E. Moloney, age 68
Director, Aaron Lazare
Director, Charles A. (Charlie) Dickinson, age 89
SVP CFO and Director, Greg G. Adams
Director, Nelson S. Gifford
Director, Woodie C. Flowers
Director, Frank J. Pipp
Director, Richard A. Wiley
CFO Chief Strategy Officer and Director, James R. (Jim) Buonomo
President CEO and Director, Theodore E. (Ted) Lapres III
Director, Cynthia P. Danaher
Auditors: PricewaterhouseCoopersLLP

LOCATIONS

HQ: NYPRO INC.
101 UNION ST, CLINTON, MA 01510-2935
Phone: 978-365-9721
Web: www.nypro.com

PRODUCTS/OPERATIONS

Selected Markets

Consumer and Electronics
Consumer/industrial
Adhesives
Electrical components
Fasteners
Fitness
Lawn and garden
Photography
Small and large appliances
Sporting goods
Storage
Tools
Electronics/telecommunications
Assemblies and disposable cartridges
Consumer electronic products
Hard disk drive components
Laptop computer components and assemblies
Mechanical printer components
Mobile phones
Health care
Collection containers
Contact lenses
Drug containers
Drug syringes
Inhalers
Lancing devices
Petri dishes
Pipettes
Surgical instruments
Test tubes
Packaging
Beverage containers
Cosmetics
Food storage
Hair and personal care
Kitchen and bath products

Selected Services

Assembly
Automation
Contract manufacturing
Decoration & finishing technologies
Injection molding
Mold design and fabrication
Product design and development
Program management

COMPETITORS

Berry Plastics	MXL Industries
Blue Star Plastics	Omni Industries
Deswell	Holdings
Hoffer Plastics	Protomold Company

HISTORICAL FINANCIALS

Company Type: Private

Income Statement

FYE: June 30

	REVENUE ($ mil.)	NET INCOME ($ mil.)	NET PROFIT MARGIN	EMPLOYEES
06/12*	1,144	(6)	—	16,000
07/11	1,169	9	0.8%	0
07/10	1,234	29	2.4%	0
06/09	1,089	2	0.2%	0
Annual Growth	1.6%	—	—	—

*Fiscal year change

2012 Year-End Financials

Debt ratio: —
Return on equity: (-0.50)%
Cash ($ mil.): 44
Current ratio: 0.80
Long-term debt ($ mil.): —
Dividends
Yield: —
Payout: —
Market value ($ mil.): —

NYSARC INC.

LOCATIONS

HQ: NYSARC INC.
393 DELAWARE AVE, DELMAR, NY 12054-3094
Phone: 518-439-8311
Web: www.nysarc.org

HISTORICAL FINANCIALS

Company Type: Private

Income Statement

FYE: December 31

	REVENUE ($ mil.)	NET INCOME ($ mil.)	NET PROFIT MARGIN	EMPLOYEES
12/11	1,788	68	3.8%	28,000
12/09	1,746	55	3.2%	0
12/08	0	0	—	0
12/07	1,561	9	0.6%	0
Annual Growth	4.6%	92.1%	—	—

2011 Year-End Financials

Debt ratio: —
Return on equity: 3.80%
Cash ($ mil.): 187
Current ratio: 0.60
Long-term debt ($ mil.): —
Dividends
Yield: —
Payout: —
Market value ($ mil.): —

O'BRIEN & GERE ENGINEERS INC.

LOCATIONS

HQ: O' BRIEN & GERE ENGINEERS INC.
333 W WASHINGTON ST # 400, SYRACUSE, NY 13202-5253
Phone: 315-956-6100

HISTORICAL FINANCIALS

Company Type: Private

Income Statement

FYE: December 31

	REVENUE ($ mil.)	NET INCOME ($ mil.)	NET PROFIT MARGIN	EMPLOYEES
12/11	187	2	1.5%	343
12/06	89	89	99.8%	0
12/05	77	19	24.6%	0
12/03	62	2	3.9%	0
Annual Growth	44.3%	4.0%	—	—

2011 Year-End Financials

Debt ratio: —
Return on equity: 1.50%
Cash ($ mil.): 9
Current ratio: 0.90
Long-term debt ($ mil.): —
Dividends
Yield: —
Payout: —
Market value ($ mil.): —

O'BRIEN & GERE LIMITED

O'Brien & Gere provides a range of engineering consulting and project management services throughout the US including wastewater management and water resources environmental compliance and remediation civil and facilities engineering and utility services. It also provides contract operations and maintenance. O'Brien & Gere serves municipal environmental manufacturing and federal clients. The company which employs hundreds of scientists engineers construction and other personnel operates some 30 offices located throughout the eastern half of the US. Employee-owned O'Brien & Gere was formed by Earl O'Brien William Gere and Glenn Holmes as a water and wastewater engineering partnership in 1945.

The company has made several acquisitions through the years in order to expand its geographic reach and grow its capabilities. In 2012 O'Brien & Gere acquired the remaining 55% of South Carolina-based architecture/engineering company Lindgergh & Associates.

O'Brien & Gere weathered the economic downturn rather well and enjoyed increases in its gross revenue in 2010 and 2011 ($170 million and $187 million respectively). The company is focused on making strategic investments in its energy environmental facilities and water programs. O'Brien & Gere also launched a new manufacturing and technology development facility. O'Brien & Gere plans to extend its core business and develop emerging markets in order to grow business.

EXECUTIVES

Chairman, Terry L. Brown
CFO Treasurer and Director, Joseph M. McNulty
Chairman and CEO, James A. (Jim) Fox
Director Emeritus; SVP Environmental Business Unit, Steven J. (Steve) Roland
Senior Vice President - OBrien & Gere, Timothy J. Barry
Director, Elizabeth A. Fessenden, age 57
SVP Secretary and Director, Thomas A. Nowlan
President COO and Director, R. Leland (Lee) Davis
SVP and Municipal Business Unit Leader, George B. Rest
Manager Corporate Quality, Lynette A. Paduano
CEO, Andy Seidel
CFO Treasurer and Director, Joseph M. McNulty
CEO and Director, James A. (Jim) Fox
SVP and Director, Timothy J. Barry
Director, Elizabeth A. Fessenden, age 57
SVP Secretary and Director, Thomas A. Nowlan
President COO and Director, R. Leland (Lee) Davis
Director, Andy Seidel

LOCATIONS

HQ: O' Brien & Gere Limited
333 West Washington St., Syracuse NY 13202
Phone: 315-437-6100   **Fax:** 315-463-7554
Web: www.obg.com

COMPETITORS

CH2M HILL   Parsons Corporation
ENVIRON

HISTORICAL FINANCIALS
Company Type: Private

Income Statement				FYE: December 31
	REVENUE ($ mil.)	NET INCOME ($ mil.)	NET PROFIT MARGIN	EMPLOYEES
12/11	187	2	1.5%	800
12/06	125	1	1.1%	0
12/00	123	(4)	—	0
12/99	132	(5)	—	0
Annual Growth	12.2%	—	—	—

2011 Year-End Financials

Debt ratio: —
Return on equity: 1.50%
Cash ($ mil.): 9
Current ratio: 0.90
Long-term debt ($ mil.): —

Dividends
 Yield: —
 Payout: —
Market value ($ mil.): —

O-AT-KA MILK PRODUCTS COOPERATIVE INCORPORATED

LOCATIONS

HQ: O-AT-KA MILK PRODUCTS COOPERATIVE INCORPORATED
CEDAR & ELLICOTT STS, BATAVIA, NY 14020
Phone: 585-343-0536
Web: www.oatkamilk.com

HISTORICAL FINANCIALS
Company Type: Private

Income Statement				FYE: December 31
	REVENUE ($ mil.)	NET INCOME ($ mil.)	NET PROFIT MARGIN	EMPLOYEES
12/11	274	12	4.6%	302
12/10	236	14	6.2%	0
12/09	203	20	9.9%	0
12/08	231	13	5.9%	0
Annual Growth	5.9%	(2.3%)	—	—

2011 Year-End Financials

Debt ratio: —
Return on equity: 4.60%
Cash ($ mil.): 15
Current ratio: 1.00
Long-term debt ($ mil.): —

Dividends
 Yield: —
 Payout: —
Market value ($ mil.): —

OAK PARK & RIVER FOREST HIGH SCHOOL DIST 200

LOCATIONS

HQ: OAK PARK & RIVER FOREST HIGH SCHOOL DIST 200
201 N SCOVILLE AVE, OAK PARK, IL 60302-2264
Phone: 708-383-0700
Web: www.oprfhs.org

HISTORICAL FINANCIALS
Company Type: Private

Income Statement				FYE: June 30
	REVENUE ($ mil.)	NET INCOME ($ mil.)	NET PROFIT MARGIN	EMPLOYEES
06/12	85	12	14.8%	438
06/11	83	13	15.6%	0
06/10	85	15	18.6%	0
06/09	74	11	14.9%	0
Annual Growth	4.6%	4.4%	—	—

2012 Year-End Financials

Debt ratio: —
Return on equity: 14.80%
Cash ($ mil.): 123
Current ratio: —
Long-term debt ($ mil.): —

Dividends
 Yield: —
 Payout: —
Market value ($ mil.): —

OAK WHITE MANOR INC

LOCATIONS

HQ: OAK WHITE MANOR INC
130 E MAIN ST, SPARTANBURG, SC 29306-5113
Phone: 864-582-7503
Web: www.whiteoakmanor.com

HISTORICAL FINANCIALS
Company Type: Private

Income Statement				FYE: September 30
	REVENUE ($ mil.)	NET INCOME ($ mil.)	NET PROFIT MARGIN	EMPLOYEES
09/11	144	3	2.7%	2,300
09/10	134	1	1.1%	0
09/09	130	3	2.7%	0
09/08	124	3	2.9%	0
Annual Growth	5.1%	2.7%	—	—

2011 Year-End Financials

Debt ratio: —
Return on equity: 2.70%
Cash ($ mil.): 4
Current ratio: 1.20
Long-term debt ($ mil.): —

Dividends
 Yield: —
 Payout: —
Market value ($ mil.): —

OBERG INDUSTRIES INC.

With a product range to die for Oberg Industries manufactures high precision stamping dies and die components such as progressive dies primary and secondary scroll dies punches and die inserts. The company pioneered the use of tungsten carbide components in the manufacture of high-speed stamping dies. Oberg Industries which has manufacturing plants in Pennsylvania Mexico and Costa Rica also provides insert molding design support plastic injection and custom designed automation equipment. Oberg serves a number of industries including automotive aerospace medical device telecommunications and appliances.

Though Oberg has realized over $110 million per year in sales it has seen orders drop almost 45% during 2008 and 2009. The company is looking to reduce its workforce and also to restructure its operations; however it will continue to invest in new equipment and technology. As an example in 2010 the company merged its First Latin American Corporation (FLAC) with Oberg Industries to create Oberg Mexico.

A little farther to the South the Oberg Costa Rica unit added about 6000 square feet of manufacturing space to its facility in mid-2010. The factory expansion is part of the company's plan to expand its position in the medical device market. The company currents produces surgical instruments trauma plates and implants for joint replacement and spinal procedures.

The company is a prime source for replacement carbide die components. It stocks thousands of standard semi-finished forms and operates more than 50 stamping presses and over 30 machining centers. Oberg Industries was founded in 1948 by Donald Oberg.

EXECUTIVES

Chairman, Eric Oberg
Director Quality, Michael Truman
Director Human Resources, Lou Proviano
Manager Corporate Communications, David R. (Dave) Getty
President and CEO, Robert Wagner
VP Sales Marketing and Quality Control, David Rugaber

LOCATIONS

HQ: Oberg Industries Inc.
2301 Silverville Rd., Freeport PA 16229-0315
Phone: 724-295-2121   **Fax:** 724-295-2588
Web: www.oberg.com

PRODUCTS/OPERATIONS

Selected Markets and Capabilities

Aerospace & Defense
    Engineering
    Machining
    Materials knowledge
    Solid modeling
Automotive
    Engineering
    Precision manufacturing (milling prototyping lamination stamping reel-to-reel stamping precious metal electroplating)
Consumer products
    Machining and turning
    Metal stamping
    Tooling
Housing & Construction
    Design engineering
Interconnect
    Lead-free plating process
    Precision metal stamping
Medical
    Materials knowledge with metals and plastics (machining titanium titanium carbide aluminum cobalt chrome nitinol platinum acetal ceramic ultem celcon and other specialty alloys and composites)
    Orthopedic instruments implants and trial components
    Pace maker and stent components
    Surgical instrument components
    Titanium and stainless steel trauma plates
Metals Packaging
    Cupper tooling
    Curling rings and segments
    Draw/redraw tooling
    Necking and flanging dies
    Primary and secondary scroll dies

Score tooling

Shell and end tooling
Wave shear grinding
Oil & Gas Exploration
    Directional drilling components
    Flow control components
    Specialized processes for difficult-to-machine materials

COMPETITORS

Anchor Mfg. Group
Atlantic Tool & Die
Defiance Metal Products
Exact Tool

Laird Technologies
Loades
Robb-Jack
Superior Production
United Plastics

HISTORICAL FINANCIALS

Company Type: Private

Income Statement

FYE: June 30

	REVENUE ($ mil.)	NET INCOME ($ mil.)	NET PROFIT MARGIN	EMPLOYEES
06/12*	54	0	—	650
12/11	109	0	—	0
12/10	98	0	—	0
12/09	0	0	—	0
Annual Growth	—	—	—	—

*Fiscal year change

2012 Year-End Financials

Debt ratio: —
Return on equity: —
Cash ($ mil.): 0
Current ratio: 1.20
Long-term debt ($ mil.): —

Dividends
    Yield: —
    Payout: —
Market value ($ mil.): —

OCCIDENTAL COLLEGE

It's no accident that Occidental College is a liberal arts school. With more than 2000 students an average class size of 19 and a 10:1 student-to-faculty ratio the school (nicknamed "Oxy") offers a hands-on approach to higher education. Its campus located in Eagle Rock is surrounded by the metropolis of Los Angeles. The college has 180 faculty members and offers about 30 majors including a number of interdisciplinary programs. Occidental students can also take classes at Caltech or the Art Center College of Design and earn joint degrees at Columbia University Keck Graduate Institute and Caltech. Occidental students can also participate in service-learning and study abroad programs.

Geographic Reach

Occidental's students come from more than 40 states and 25 foreign countries. In addition to its main campus and collaborations in California Occidental College has study abroad programs with affiliates in 30 countries in Europe Asia Latin America Africa the Middle East and the Asia/Pacific region.

Financial Performance

In 2012 Occidental College increased operating revenues by 5% to some $106 million due to higher student revenues (tuition and fees). Operating income also increased 56% to nearly $5.2 million.

About two-thirds of the company's operating revenues come from net student revenues. Other sources include investment income; private gifts grants and contracts; and federal and state grants and contracts. Tuition and fees total about $45000 per year plus $12000 in room and board (about three-fourths of students live on campus).

Company Background

The college was founded as The Occidental University of Los Angeles California in 1887 by a group of Presbyterians.

EXECUTIVES

VP Admission and Financial Aid, William Tingley
Dean Admission, Vince Cuseo
Director Communications, Jim Tranquada
VP Legal Affairs and General Counsel, Sandra Cooper
VP Acadmic Affairs and Dean College, Eric Frank
Registrar and Director Advising, Victor T. Egitto
Controller, Barbara Valienta
Director Campus Safety, Hollis B. Nieto
Director Human Resources, Richard Ledwin
Director Financial Aid, Maureen McRae Levy
Director Alumni Relations, James A. Jacobs
President, Jonathan Veitch
VP Administration and Finance, Michael P. Groener
VP Information Resources, Pamela McQuesten
VP Institutional Advancement, Tom Tomlinson
VP Student Affairs and Dean Students, Barbara Avery

LOCATIONS

HQ: Occidental College
1600 Campus Rd., Los Angeles CA 90041-3341
Phone: 323-259-2500   **Fax:** 323-259-2907
Web: www.oxy.edu

PRODUCTS/OPERATIONS

Selected Academic Majors

American Studies
Art History and the Visual Arts
Athletics and Physical Activities
Biochemistry
Biology
Chemistry
Classical Studies
Cognitive Science
Computer Science
Core Program
Critical Theory and Social Justice
Diplomacy and World Affairs
East Asian Languages and Cultures
Economics
Education
English and Comparative Literary Studies
English Writing
Geology
German Russian and Classical Studies
Group Language
History
Kinesiology
Latino/a and Latin American Studies
Mathematics
Music
Philosophy
Physics
Politics
Psychology
Religious Studies
Sociology
Spanish and French Studies
Theater
Urban and Environmental Policy

COMPETITORS

UC Davis

University of

UC Irvine California
UC Santa Barbara USC
UCLA

HISTORICAL FINANCIALS
Company Type: School

Income Statement
FYE: June 30

	REVENUE ($ mil.)	NET INCOME ($ mil.)	NET PROFIT MARGIN	EMPLOYEES
06/11	146	10	7.4%	610
06/10	115	(9)	—	0
06/09	87	0	—	0
06/08	129	19	15.2%	0
Annual Growth	4.1%	(17.9%)	—	—

2011 Year-End Financials
Debt ratio: ——
Return on equity: 7.40%
Cash ($ mil.): 44
Current ratio: ——
Long-term debt ($ mil.): ——

Dividends
Yield: —
Payout: —
Market value ($ mil.): —

OCEAN DUKE CORPORATION

Ocean Duke maintains a regal demeanor in a fishy environment. The company is a seafood wholesaler offering a variety of frozen raw fish shrimp mollusks and crustaceans. Ocean Duke also sells breaded fish shrimp and squid. The company imports its products and serves foodservice food processing distribution and wholesale companies throughout the US.

EXECUTIVES
President and CEO, Duke Lin
COO, Roger Lin
CFO, Alice Lin

LOCATIONS
HQ: Ocean Duke Corporation
3450 Fujita St., Torrance CA 90505-4019
Phone: 310-326-3198 **Fax:** 310-784-8848
Web: www.oceanduke.com

COMPETITORS
Arista Industries
Caspian Trading
Company

Florida Fresh Seafood
Corp.
Orca Bay Seafoods

HISTORICAL FINANCIALS
Company Type: Private

Income Statement
FYE: March 31

	REVENUE ($ mil.)	NET INCOME ($ mil.)	NET PROFIT MARGIN	EMPLOYEES
03/11	158	2	1.4%	25
03/02	191	0	0.5%	0
03/01	196	1	0.5%	0
03/00	0	0	—	0
Annual Growth	—	—	—	—

2011 Year-End Financials
Debt ratio: ——
Return on equity: 1.40%
Cash ($ mil.): 1
Current ratio: 0.50
Long-term debt ($ mil.): ——

Dividends
Yield: —
Payout: —
Market value ($ mil.): —

OCLC ONLINE COMPUTER LIBRARY CENTER INCORPORATE

OCLC Online Computer Library Center is a membership cooperative that provides access to the world's information and works to reduce information costs. The organization provides services and tools to some 72000 member libraries in about 170 countries. Services include computer-based cataloging preservation and library management. OCLC additionally facilitates interlibrary loan services administers the Dewey Decimal Classification system and operates the WorldCat database an online resource for finding library materials. OCLC was founded in 1967 by presidents of the colleges and universities in Ohio; its first location was in the Main Library at Ohio State. (OCLC stands for Ohio College Library Center.)

In 2010 the organization sold its NetLibrary division a provider of eBooks and audio books to database aggregator EBSCO Industries. The sale resulted in more than 60 job cuts. The previous year OCLC sold its Preservation Service Center which offered digitization retrospective conversion and cataloging services to libraries to Backstage Library Works a provider of microfilming and digital preservation services to libraries. OCLC is using the proceeds from the divestitures to pay down debt and focus on expanding WorldCat. It is building out the WorldCat service as a platform for libraries to manage and provide access to their entire collection.

EXECUTIVES
Vice Chairman, David P. Lauer, age 69
President CEO and Director, Robert L. (Jay) Jordan
VP OCLC Research and Chief Strategist, Lorcan Dempsey
VP for the Americas and Global VP Marketing, Catherine K. (Cathy) De Rosa
VP and General Counsel, James T. (Jim) Houfek
VP Member Services, George M. Needham
EVP CFO and Treasurer, Rick J. Schwieterman
Managing Director OCLC Europe Middle East and Africa, Rein van Charldorp
Chairman, Larry Alford
Senior Public Relations Specialist The Americas Northern Africa the Middle East and Asia/Pacific, Bob Murphy
Marketing Coordinator Europe and Southern Africa, Gillian McLeod
VP RLG Programs Development, Jim Michalko
VP Business Development, William (Chip) Nilges
VP Human Resources, Tammi Spayde
VP Global Product Architecture, Michael A. (Mike) Teets
VP Digital Collection Services, Greg Zick
VP WorldCat and Metadata Services, Karen Calhoun
VP Library Services for the Americas, Bruce Crocco
VP Global Product Management, Robin Murray
VP Asia Pacific, Andrew H. Wang
Vice Chairman, David P. Lauer, age 69
Director, David P. Roselle, age 72
Director, Jane N. Ryland, age 67
President CEO and Director, Robert L. (Jay) Jordan
Director, Lizabeth A. (Betsy) Wilson
Director, Elisabeth Niggemann
Director, Edward W. Barry
Director, Robert A. Seal
Director, Ralph K. Frasier
Director, Maggie Farrell
Director, Bruce Newell
Director, Anthony (Tony) Ferguson
Director, Kathleen R. T. Imhoff
Director, Sandra (Sandy) Yee

LOCATIONS
HQ: OCLC Online Computer Library Center Inc.
6565 Kilgour Pl., Dublin OH 43017-3395
Phone: 614-764-6000 **Fax:** 614-764-6096
Web: www.oclc.org

PRODUCTS/OPERATIONS

Selected Products
Connexion (online cataloging tool)
CONTENTdm (digital collection management software)
Dewey Services (Dewey Decimal classification)
Digital Archive (storage for digital preservation)
FirstSearch (online reference)
WorldCat (global network of library content)

COMPETITORS
American Library
EBSCO
FactSet
Google

Informa
LexisNexis
ProQuest

HISTORICAL FINANCIALS
Company Type: Private - Not-for-Profit

Income Statement
FYE: June 30

	REVENUE ($ mil.)	NET INCOME ($ mil.)	NET PROFIT MARGIN	EMPLOYEES
06/12	203	(2)	—	1,227
06/11	205	30	14.6%	0
06/10	228	32	14.2%	0
06/09	240	(34)	—	0
Annual Growth	(5.4%)	—	—	—

2012 Year-End Financials
Debt ratio: ——
Return on equity: (-1.50)%
Cash ($ mil.): 17
Current ratio: 0.20
Long-term debt ($ mil.): ——

Dividends
Yield: —
Payout: —
Market value ($ mil.): —

ODESSA PUMPS AND EQUIPMENT INC.

LOCATIONS

HQ: ODESSA PUMPS AND EQUIPMENT INC.
3209 N COUNTY RD W, ODESSA, TX 79764-6402
Phone: 432-333-2817
Web: www.odessapumps.com

HISTORICAL FINANCIALS
Company Type: Private

Income Statement
FYE: December 31

	REVENUE ($ mil.)	NET INCOME ($ mil.)	NET PROFIT MARGIN	EMPLOYEES
12/11	102	6	6.2%	135
12/10	72	3	5.1%	0
12/09	57	2	3.5%	0
12/98	12	0	2.5%	0
Annual Growth	102.8%	174.5%	—	—

2011 Year-End Financials

Debt ratio: ——
Return on equity: 6.20%
Cash ($ mil.): 4
Current ratio: 1.90
Long-term debt ($ mil.): —

Dividends
  Yield: —
  Payout: —
Market value ($ mil.): —

OEC BUSINESS INTERIORS INC.

Success at OEC Business Interiors is an inside job. The company supplies office equipment in the Chicago area and throughout the Midwest. Products include furniture panel systems lighting floor coverings and textiles from major manufacturers. It also provides services such as refinishing rentals brokerage warehouse storage and physical asset management. OEC Business Interiors was founded in 1955 by president Raymond Riha his wife and two partners as Riha Petersen & Vail. In 1961 the company purchased Office Equipment Company which had been in business since 1929 and later changed its name.

EXECUTIVES

President, Raymond R. Riha Sr.
CFO, Tom O'Malley
VP Sales and Marketing, Sherrie Riha

LOCATIONS

HQ: OEC Business Interiors Inc.
900 N. Church Rd., Elmhurst IL 60126
Phone: 630-589-5500   **Fax:** 630-589-5637
Web: www.oecbusinessinteriors.com

COMPETITORS

Aaron's Inc.	Office Concepts
Corporate Concepts	Office Depot
Henricksen &	OfficeMax
Company	Staples

HISTORICAL FINANCIALS
Company Type: Private

Income Statement
FYE: September 30

	REVENUE ($ mil.)	NET INCOME ($ mil.)	NET PROFIT MARGIN	EMPLOYEES
09/11	54	0	0.3%	135
09/10	47	(0)	—	0
09/09	55	(0)	—	0
09/08	70	0	0.5%	0
Annual Growth	(8.1%)	(21.2%)	—	—

2011 Year-End Financials

Debt ratio: ——
Return on equity: 0.30%
Cash ($ mil.): 5
Current ratio: 2.70
Long-term debt ($ mil.): —

Dividends
  Yield: —
  Payout: —
Market value ($ mil.): —

OHIO NORTHERN UNIVERSITY INC

LOCATIONS

HQ: OHIO NORTHERN UNIVERSITY INC
525 S MAIN ST UNIT 1, ADA, OH 45810-1599
Phone: 419-772-2000
Web: www.law.onu.edu

HISTORICAL FINANCIALS
Company Type: Private

Income Statement
FYE: May 31

	REVENUE ($ mil.)	NET INCOME ($ mil.)	NET PROFIT MARGIN	EMPLOYEES
05/12	94	(14)	—	700
05/07	110	53	48.3%	0
05/06	84	18	22.5%	0
05/05	71	14	20.4%	0
Annual Growth	9.8%	—	—	—

2012 Year-End Financials

Debt ratio: ——
Return on equity: (-15.10)%
Cash ($ mil.): 0
Current ratio: —
Long-term debt ($ mil.): —

Dividends
  Yield: —
  Payout: —
Market value ($ mil.): —

OHIO STATE UNIVERSITY RESEARCH FOUNDATION

The Ohio State University Research Foundation was established in 1936 to function as a central agency for supporting research and development through grants management and information technology for Ohio State University one of the largest public universities in the US. The not-for-profit corporation provides administrative services for research programs including submitting support requests managing equipment and governmental and university compliance oversight. Ohio State University's total awards reached more than $37 million by July 2007 with some 330 awards.

EXECUTIVES

Senior Director Financial Services and Procurement, Jeffrey H. (Jeff) Kemper
President Board of Directors, Robert T. McGrath
Deputy Executive Director, Anne J.M. Moffat
Executive Director and Associate VP Research Administration, Robert A. Killoren

LOCATIONS

HQ: The Ohio State University Research Foundation
1960 Kenny Rd., Columbus OH 43210-1063
Phone: 614-292-3815   **Fax:** 614-292-5913
Web: www1.rf.ohio-state.edu

HISTORICAL FINANCIALS
Company Type: Private - Foundation

Income Statement
FYE: June 30

	REVENUE ($ mil.)	NET INCOME ($ mil.)	NET PROFIT MARGIN	EMPLOYEES
06/11	485	0	0.1%	105
06/10	437	0	0.2%	0
06/09	411	0	—	0
06/08	387	0	0.1%	0
Annual Growth	7.8%	50.9%	—	—

2011 Year-End Financials

Debt ratio: ——
Return on equity: 0.10%
Cash ($ mil.): 52
Current ratio: 2.90
Long-term debt ($ mil.): —

Dividends
  Yield: —
  Payout: —
Market value ($ mil.): —

OHIO VALLEY GENERAL HOSPITAL

Ohio Valley General Hospital is a full service 120-bed community hospital serving residents of Pennsylvania's Allegheny County and the western suburbs of Pittsburgh. The hospital's staff of about 300 doctors (representing more than 35 medical specialties) provides emergency acute diagnostic and specialty care and a variety of inpatient and outpatient care services. Ohio Valley General's programs include cardiology occupational medicine pain treatment rehabilitation sleep disorder diagnosis ophthalmic surgery and wound care. The facility founded in 1901 also operates senior living communities and sponsors a school of nursing and a school of radiography.

EXECUTIVES

Chairman, Edward A. Nicholson, age 72
President and CEO, William F. (Bill) Provenzano
Vice Chairman, Richard V. Sica
COO, David Scott
VP Human Resources, Vicki Mell
Chairman of Surgery; Medical Director Wound Care Center, David Catalane
Treasurer, Mark R. Scholl
Secretary, Margery H. Lawrence

Medical Director Pain Treatment Center, David A. Provenzano
CFO, Tad Tefera
Media Relations, Kasey Goodman
VP Patient Care Services and Chief Nursing Officer, Gaye Falletta
Executive Director Ohio Valley General Hospital Foundation, Lynne M. Scanga

LOCATIONS

HQ: Ohio Valley General Hospital
25 Heckel Rd. Kennedy Township, McKees Rocks PA 15136-1694
Phone: 412-777-6161   **Fax:** 412-777-6804
Web: www.ohiovalleyhospital.org

COMPETITORS

Butler Health System
Conemaugh Health System
Heritage Valley Health
UPMC
West Penn Allegheny Health System

HISTORICAL FINANCIALS

Company Type: Private - Not-for-Profit

Income Statement

FYE: June 30

	REVENUE ($ mil.)	NET INCOME ($ mil.)	NET PROFIT MARGIN	EMPLOYEES
06/11	66	(0)	—	570
06/10	64	(0)	—	0
06/09	61	(10)	—	0
06/08	65	2	3.5%	0
Annual Growth	0.8%	—	—	—

2011 Year-End Financials

Debt ratio: ——
Return on equity: (-0.20)%
Cash ($ mil.): 2
Current ratio: 0.20
Long-term debt ($ mil.): —
Dividends
  Yield: —
  Payout: —
Market value ($ mil.): —

OHIOHEALTH CORPORATION

Operating throughout the central part of the state OhioHealth aims to keep Buckeyes healthy. The not-for-profit system runs eight acute care hospitals and is affiliated with another nine community hospitals and area health systems. All told OhioHealth has about 2000 staffed beds in and around Columbus. Additional facilities offer urgent care physical rehabilitation diagnostic imaging and sleep diagnostics services. Subsidiary HomeReach provides home health care and hospice care. Its WorkHealth program offers workers' compensation care management and occupational rehabilitation services. OhioHealth Group OhioHealth's joint venture with The Medical Group of Ohio operates the HealthReach PPO.

In addition to offering patient care OhioHealth also operates the The OhioHealth Research & Innovation Institute which coordinates research throughout the health system including conducting clinical trials of new drugs and medical devices. The system also operates The Center for Medical Education and Innovation a medical training facility that among other technologies offers human patient simulators on which medical professionals can practice new procedures in various clinical situations.

The health system traces its roots back to 1892 when Protestant Hospital (now known as Riverside Methodist Hospital) opened. The system initially organized as U.S. Health Corporation in 1984 later took on the OhioHealth name in 1997.

EXECUTIVES

President and CEO, David P. Blom, age 57
SVP Oncology Services, Steven (Steve) Garlock
EVP and CFO, Michael W. (Mike) Louge
VP Mission and Ministry, Rev Keith R. Vesper
Regional Executive; President Dublin Methodist Hospital and Grady Memorial Hospital, Bruce Hagen
EVP and COO, Robert P. (Bob) Millen, age 59
SVP Clinical Support Services, Cheryl Herbert
Director Media Relations, Mark Hopkins
Communications and Media Relations Associate Doctors Hospital and Dublin Methodist Hospital, Lara Lindsay
Communications and Media Relations Associate Grant Medical Center, Colin Yoder
Communications and Media Relations Associate Riverside Methodist Hospital, Christina Fitzer
Chief Medical Officer, Bruce Vanderhoff
SVP and Chief Strategy Officer, Michael Bernstein
SVP and Chief Communications Officer, Sue Jablonski
SVP and CIO, Michael Krouse
SVP External Affairs; President OhioHealth Foundation, Karen Jefferson Morrison
SVP General Counsel and Assistant Secretary, Frank T. Pandora II
VP Government Relations, Shawna L. Bosse
VP Regional System Development, Larry Thornhill
SVP and Chief Ethics and Compliance Officer, Andrew S. Quinn
President Medical Specialty Foundation, Hugh Thornhill
President HomeReach, James P. Newbrough

LOCATIONS

HQ: OhioHealth
180 E. Broad St., Columbus OH 43215
Phone: 614-544-4455   **Fax:** 614-566-6938
Web: www.ohiohealth.com

PRODUCTS/OPERATIONS

Selected Facilities

Owned
  Doctors Hospital (Columbus)
  Doctors Hospital Nelsonville (Nelsonville)
  Dublin Methodist Hospital (Dublin)
  Grady Memorial Hospital (Delaware)
  Grant Medical Center (Columbus)
  Hardin Memorial Hospital (Kenton)
  Marion General Hospital (Marion)
  Riverside Methodist Hospital (Columbus)
Affiliated
  Blanchard Valley Medical Center
  Galion Community Hospital (Galion)
  Genesis Healthcare System (Zanesville)
  Knox Community Hospital
  Morrow County Hospital (Mt. Gilead)
  Samaritan Regional Health System (Ashland)
  O'Bleness Memorial Hospital (Athens)
  Southern Ohio Medical Center (Portsmouth)

COMPETITORS

Adena Health System
Catholic Health Partners
Mount Carmel Health
Nationwide Children's Hospital

Fairfield Medical Center
Licking Memorial Health Systems
Regency Hospital
Select Medical

HISTORICAL FINANCIALS

Company Type: Private - Not-for-Profit

Income Statement

FYE: June 30

	REVENUE ($ mil.)	NET INCOME ($ mil.)	NET PROFIT MARGIN	EMPLOYEES
06/11	2,328	412	17.7%	15,000
06/10	1,967	221	11.3%	0
06/09	1,794	0	—	0
06/08	1,753	140	8.0%	0
Annual Growth	9.9%	43.3%	—	—

2011 Year-End Financials

Debt ratio: ——
Return on equity: 17.70%
Cash ($ mil.): 190
Current ratio: 1.30
Long-term debt ($ mil.): —
Dividends
  Yield: —
  Payout: —
Market value ($ mil.): —

OKLAHOMA CITY UNIVERSITY

LOCATIONS

HQ: OKLAHOMA CITY UNIVERSITY
2501 N BLACKWELDER AVE, OKLAHOMA CITY, OK 73106-1493
Phone: 405-521-5000

HISTORICAL FINANCIALS

Company Type: Private

Income Statement

FYE: June 30

	REVENUE ($ mil.)	NET INCOME ($ mil.)	NET PROFIT MARGIN	EMPLOYEES
06/11	81	7	8.8%	503
06/10	83	11	13.3%	0
06/08	98	8	8.4%	0
06/06	73	21	28.9%	0
Annual Growth	3.8%	(30.1%)	—	—

2011 Year-End Financials

Debt ratio: ——
Return on equity: 8.80%
Cash ($ mil.): 3
Current ratio: —
Long-term debt ($ mil.): —
Dividends
  Yield: —
  Payout: —
Market value ($ mil.): —

OKLAHOMA STATE UNIVERSITY FOUNDATION

LOCATIONS

HQ: OKLAHOMA STATE UNIVERSITY FOUNDATION
400 S MONROE ST, STILLWATER, OK 74074-3322
Phone: 405-385-5100
Web: www.osustufu.net

HISTORICAL FINANCIALS
Company Type: Private

Income Statement

	REVENUE ($ mil.)	NET INCOME ($ mil.)	NET PROFIT MARGIN	EMPLOYEES
06/11	103	47	45.5%	47
06/10	162	75	46.4%	0
06/09	31	(67)	—	0
06/08	310	205	66.1%	0
Annual Growth	(30.6%)	(38.7%)	—	—

2011 Year-End Financials
Debt ratio: ——
Return on equity: 45.50%
Cash ($ mil.): 3
Current ratio: 0.30
Long-term debt ($ mil.): —

Dividends
Yield: —
Payout: —
Market value ($ mil.): —

OLAM AMERICAS INC

LOCATIONS

HQ: OLAM AMERICAS INC
25 UNION PL STE 3, SUMMIT, NJ 07901-3603
Phone: 908-988-1960
Web: www.olamonline.com

HISTORICAL FINANCIALS
Company Type: Private

Income Statement

	REVENUE ($ mil.)	NET INCOME ($ mil.)	NET PROFIT MARGIN	EMPLOYEES
06/11	9,870	171	1.7%	0
Annual Growth	—	—	—	—

2011 Year-End Financials
Debt ratio: ——
Return on equity: 1.70%
Cash ($ mil.): 502
Current ratio: 0.20
Long-term debt ($ mil.): —

Dividends
Yield: —
Payout: —
Market value ($ mil.): —

OLDHAM COUNTY BOARD OF EDUCATION

LOCATIONS

HQ: OLDHAM COUNTY BOARD OF EDUCATION
6165 W HIGHWAY 146, CRESTWOOD, KY 40014-9531
Phone: 502-241-3500
Web: www.oldhamcountyartscenter.com

HISTORICAL FINANCIALS
Company Type: Private

Income Statement
FYE: June 30

	REVENUE ($ mil.)	NET INCOME ($ mil.)	NET PROFIT MARGIN	EMPLOYEES
06/12	111	(5)	—	1,300
06/11	109	(1)	—	0
06/10	107	(7)	—	0
06/09	106	(28)	—	0
Annual Growth	1.7%	—	—	—

2012 Year-End Financials
Debt ratio: ——
Return on equity: (-4.70)%
Cash ($ mil.): 20
Current ratio: 1.40
Long-term debt ($ mil.): —

Dividends
Yield: —
Payout: —
Market value ($ mil.): —

OLIVER OIL COMPANY

LOCATIONS

HQ: OLIVER OIL COMPANY
1811 E 5TH ST, LUMBERTON, NC 28358-6107
Phone: 910-738-1401

HISTORICAL FINANCIALS
Company Type: Private

Income Statement
FYE: December 31

	REVENUE ($ mil.)	NET INCOME ($ mil.)	NET PROFIT MARGIN	EMPLOYEES
12/11	134	1	1.1%	80
12/10	81	0	0.9%	0
12/09	61	0	0.3%	0
12/08	101	1	1.0%	0
Annual Growth	9.7%	12.5%	—	—

2011 Year-End Financials
Debt ratio: ——
Return on equity: 1.10%
Cash ($ mil.): 4
Current ratio: 1.60
Long-term debt ($ mil.): —

Dividends
Yield: —
Payout: —
Market value ($ mil.): —

OMAHA TRUCK CENTER INC.

LOCATIONS

HQ: OMAHA TRUCK CENTER INC.
10550 I ST, OMAHA, NE 68127-1012
Phone: 402-592-2440
Web: www.omahatruck.com

HISTORICAL FINANCIALS
Company Type: Private

Income Statement
FYE: December 31

	REVENUE ($ mil.)	NET INCOME ($ mil.)	NET PROFIT MARGIN	EMPLOYEES
12/11	166	6	4.1%	398
12/10	127	4	3.7%	0
12/09	134	3	2.5%	0
12/08	150	4	2.9%	0
Annual Growth	3.4%	16.2%	—	—

2011 Year-End Financials
Debt ratio: ——
Return on equity: 4.10%
Cash ($ mil.): 1
Current ratio: 0.20
Long-term debt ($ mil.): —

Dividends
Yield: —
Payout: —
Market value ($ mil.): —

OMNI CABLE CORPORATION

Omni Cable has it down to the wire. The company distributes electrical and electronic cables to wholesale customers in the US through 10 warehouses and distribution centers. Omni Cable also offers custom bundling coloring striping lashing twisting and imprinting of wires and cables. The employee-owned company was founded in 1977. Omni Cable has locations in Atlanta Boston Chicago Denver Houston Los Angeles Philadelphia St. Louis San Francisco and Tampa. It is expanding its facilities within the regions served and has relocated and upgraded its San Francisco branch to serve the Bay Area better.

EXECUTIVES

President and CEO, William J. (Jeff) Siegfried
Branch Manager Georgia, Steve Sweat
EVP Sales and Marketing, Peter J. Comber
Regional Manager Rocky Mountains Division, Adam DiCola
Branch Manager West Chester, Chris Regan
Director Supply Chain, Chris Bertolami
VP St. Louis, Mark Serafino
Manager Facilities, Keith Stewart
Manager Marketing, Janet Krause
EVP Sales Operations, Greg Donato
Corporate Marketing, Matthew (Matt.) Brady
CFO, Mike Schafer

LOCATIONS

HQ: Omni Cable Corporation
2 Hagerty Blvd., West Chester PA 19382
Phone: 610-701-0100   **Fax:** 610-701-0199
Web: www.omnicable.com

COMPETITORS

Gexpro
Premier Farnell
Sonepar USA

HISTORICAL FINANCIALS

Company Type: Private

Income Statement

	REVENUE ($ mil.)	NET INCOME ($ mil.)	NET PROFIT MARGIN	EMPLOYEES
12/11	256	0	—	220
12/10	202	12	5.9%	0
12/09	148	8	5.8%	0
12/08	223	22	10.0%	0
Annual Growth	**4.6%**	**—**	**—**	**—**

2011 Year-End Financials

Debt ratio: ——
Return on equity: —
Cash ($ mil.): 14
Current ratio: 3.40
Long-term debt ($ mil.): —

Dividends
Yield: —
Payout: —
Market value ($ mil.): —

ONX ACQUISITION LLC

LOCATIONS

HQ: ONX ACQUISITION LLC
5910 LANDERBROOK DR, MAYFIELD HEIGHTS, OH
44124-6508
Phone: 440-569-2300

HISTORICAL FINANCIALS

Company Type: Private

Income Statement

FYE: April 30

	REVENUE ($ mil.)	NET INCOME ($ mil.)	NET PROFIT MARGIN	EMPLOYEES
04/12	255	(6)	—	300
Annual Growth	**—**	**—**	**—**	**—**

2012 Year-End Financials

Debt ratio: ——
Return on equity: (-2.70)%
Cash ($ mil.): 8
Current ratio: 0.90
Long-term debt ($ mil.): —

Dividends
Yield: —
Payout: —
Market value ($ mil.): —

OPTICSPLANET INC.

LOCATIONS

HQ: OPTICSPLANET INC.
3150 COMMERCIAL AVE, NORTHBROOK, IL
60062-1906
Phone: 847-513-6201
Web: www.opticsplanet.com

HISTORICAL FINANCIALS

Company Type: Private

Income Statement

FYE: December 31

	REVENUE ($ mil.)	NET INCOME ($ mil.)	NET PROFIT MARGIN	EMPLOYEES
12/11	101	1	1.5%	231
12/10	78	1	2.0%	0
12/09*	60	1	1.9%	0
06/08	20	1	8.1%	0
Annual Growth	**70.2%**	**(3.5%)**	**—**	**—**

*Fiscal year change

2011 Year-End Financials

Debt ratio: ——
Return on equity: 1.50%
Cash ($ mil.): 1
Current ratio: 0.10
Long-term debt ($ mil.): —

Dividends
Yield: —
Payout: —
Market value ($ mil.): —

OPTIONS CLEARING CORPORATION THE (DEL)

The Options Clearing Corporation (OCC) is the world's largest equity derivatives clearinghouse. The corporation clears transactions for call and put options on equities stock indices foreign currencies and interest rate products. It also performs clearing and settlement services on futures options on futures and securities lending transactions. The OCC serves about 120 members including broker-dealers US futures commission merchants and foreign securities firms. It handles some 4.5 billion transactions annually. Participating exchanges include Chicago Board Options Exchange Nasdaq OMX Nasdaq OMX PHLX and NYSE Amex.

Operations

The Options Clearing Corporation (OCC) derives nearly 95% of its revenue from clearing fees collected on each transaction processes. OCC also sells market data and statistics reports on options and futures volumes representing about 3% of its sales in 2011.

Financial Performance

OCC's 2011 revenue declined 5% vs. 2010 due to a drop its clearing fees and investment income. Net income fell 78% over the same period on higher expenses including employee and IT costs.

Company Background

Founded in 1973 the OCC operates under the jurisdiction of the Securities and Exchange Commission and the Commodities Futures Trading Commission. It also manages the Options Indus-

try Council a not-for-profit organization sponsored by several securities and options exchanges to educate investors and brokers about the options industry.

EXECUTIVES

Chairman and CEO, Wayne P. Luthringshausen
President and COO, Michael E. Cahill
EVP General Counsel Chief Legal Officer and Secretary, William H. Navin
SVP Risk Management and Membership, Michael Walinskas
EVP Industry Services, Gina McFadden
EVP Business Development and Operations, Michael McClain
SVP Government Relations and Communications, Susan Milligan
SVP CFO and Treasurer, Frank Larocca, age 57
Public Relations, Jim Bender
SVP and Deputy General Counsel, Jean Cawley
CIO, Raymond Tamayo
VP Enterprise Integration and Infrastructure Platforms, Tom Chatoney
VP Financial Surveillance, Dennis Woods
Director, William D. (Bill) Felder, age 54
Director, Philip A. (Phil) Pendergraft, age 52
Director, Meyer S. (Sandy) Frucher, age 65
Director, Paul J. Brody, age 51
Director, Edward J. Joyce, age 59
Director, Frank J. Bisignano, age 52
Director, Richard R. Lindsey
Director, Gary E. Yetman
Director, Gary Katz
Director, Edward G. (Ed) Boyle, age 49
Director, Gerard (Gerry) McGraw
Director, Andrew D. Kolinsky
Director, Thomas E. (Tom) Stern
Auditors: Deloitte&ToucheLLP

LOCATIONS

HQ: The Options Clearing Corporation
1 N. Wacker Dr. Ste. 500, Chicago IL 60606
Phone: 312-322-6200   **Fax:** 312-977-0611
Web: www.optionsclearing.com

PRODUCTS/OPERATIONS

2011 Sales

	$ mil.	% of total
Clearing fees	141	94
Data service fees	4	3
Investment income	0	1
Other	3	2
Total	**150**	**100**

COMPETITORS

Cowen Group
DTCC
GSEC
NYMEX Holdings
Pershing LLC
R.J. O' Brien
Rosenthal Collins
Susquehanna International Group LLP

HISTORICAL FINANCIALS
Company Type: Private

Income Statement
FYE: September 30

	ASSETS ($ mil.)	NET INCOME ($ mil.)	INCOME AS % OF ASSETS	EMPLOYEES
09/12*	3,062	16	0.5%	338
12/11	3,151	1	0.1%	0
12/10	3,315	8	0.2%	0
12/09	3,194	1	0.0%	0
Annual Growth	(1.4%)	149.7%	—	—

*Fiscal year change

ORANGE UNIFIED SCHOOL DISTRICT (INC)

LOCATIONS

HQ: ORANGE UNIFIED SCHOOL DISTRICT (INC)
1401 N HANDY ST, ORANGE, CA 92867-4434
Phone: 714-628-4000
Web: www.orangeusd.org

HISTORICAL FINANCIALS
Company Type: Private

Income Statement
FYE: June 30

	REVENUE ($ mil.)	NET INCOME ($ mil.)	NET PROFIT MARGIN	EMPLOYEES
06/11	265	27	10.5%	3,100
06/08	184	10	5.6%	0
06/01	231	20	8.8%	0
06/00	198	1	0.8%	0
Annual Growth	10.3%	159.6%	—	—

ORCA BAY SEAFOODS INC.

Icy waters produce a lot of frozen fish. Orca Bay Seafoods is a leading supplier of fresh frozen seafood sourcing products from oceans all over the world. The company buys flash-frozen fish from suppliers and keeps it frozen as it cuts individual portions for sale to foodservice companies supermarkets club stores and restaurants across the US. Its products include Ahi tuna Alaskan cod Pacific Ocean pearch sockeye salmon mahi mahi and tilapia as well as Mexican white shrimp. Orca Bay was founded by Mike Samsel in 1985; the giant Japanese seafood company Maruha Nichiro owns a minority interest in the company; Japanese conglomerate Tokusui Corporation owns the controlling interest.

EXECUTIVES

President and CEO, Ryan Mackey

LOCATIONS

HQ: Orca Bay Seafoods Inc.
900 Powell Ave. SW, Renton WA 98055-2907
Phone: 425-204-9100 **Fax:** 425-204-9200
Web: www.orcabayfoods.com

COMPETITORS

American Seafoods	Nippon Suisan
Arrowac Fisheries	Ocean Beauty Seafoods
High Liner Foods	Pacific Seafood Group
Icelandic Group	Red Chamber Co.
Icicle Seafoods	Trident Seafoods
ISF (USA)	

HISTORICAL FINANCIALS
Company Type: Subsidiary

Income Statement
FYE: February 28

	REVENUE ($ mil.)	NET INCOME ($ mil.)	NET PROFIT MARGIN	EMPLOYEES
02/11	143	1	1.2%	180
02/10	140	0	0.6%	0
02/09	156	1	0.9%	0
Annual Growth	(4.4%)	13.2%	—	—

2011 Year-End Financials

Debt ratio: —
Return on equity: 1.20%
Cash ($ mil.): 2
Current ratio: 0.30
Long-term debt ($ mil.): —

Dividends
Yield: —
Payout: —
Market value ($ mil.): —

ORDER OF ST. BENEDICT

LOCATIONS

HQ: ORDER OF ST. BENEDICT
ST JOHNS ABBEY, COLLEGEVILLE, MN 56321
Phone: 320-363-2100

HISTORICAL FINANCIALS
Company Type: Private

Income Statement
FYE: June 30

	REVENUE ($ mil.)	NET INCOME ($ mil.)	NET PROFIT MARGIN	EMPLOYEES
06/12	95	(0)	—	129
06/11	96	34	35.6%	0
06/10	92	20	22.4%	0
06/09	90	(48)	—	0
Annual Growth	2.0%	—	—	—

2012 Year-End Financials

Debt ratio: —
Return on equity: (-1.00)%
Cash ($ mil.): 13
Current ratio: 0.90
Long-term debt ($ mil.): —

Dividends
Yield: —
Payout: —
Market value ($ mil.): —

OREGON HEALTH & SCIENCE UNIVERSITY

Oregon Health & Science University (OHSU) gives a dam about medical education in the Beaver State. OHSU is the state's sole institution providing doctoral degrees in medicine dentistry and nursing. It's other two schools are science and engineering and in partnership with Oregon State University pharmacy. The university is also home to three hospitals (one a children's hospital) as well as specialty and primary care clinics research and interdisciplinary centers and community service programs. OHSU traces its roots to 1867 when members of the medical department at Willamette University began the first formal medical education program in Oregon.

OHSU's medical school has a small student-teacher ratio at just 4:1. The organization is renowned for its research initiatives. In 2010 OHSU received nearly $400 million in research funding (the most it ever received) including $70 million from the American Recovery and Reinvestment Act. The school engages in an array of multidisciplinary research projects including diseases of the central nervous system weight regulation cancer rare genetic disorders and infectious disease.

Researchers at OHSU's Stem Cell Center worked with the Oregon National Primate Research Center to pioneer the first successful cloned nonhuman primate embryonic stem cells. Such cells could help stem cell research gain acceptance as the human element that causes such controversy has been removed.

EXECUTIVES

CFO, Lawrence J. Furnstahl
VP and Chief Administrative Officer, Norwood W. Knight-Richardson
Chairman, Keith L. Thomson, age 73
VP and General Counsel, Amy M. Wayson
EVP and Executive Director OHSU Hospitals and Clinics, Peter F. Rapp
VP Research, Daniel M. Dorsa
VP Human Resources, Rick L. Bentzinger, age 58
Director Center for Research on Occupational and Environmental Toxicology, Peter S. Spencer
Chair School of Science & Engineering, Edward W. Thompson
Dean School of Dentistry, Jack Clinton
Dean College of Pharmacy, Wayne A. Kradjan
Director Vollum Institute, Richard H. Goodman
Director Child Development and Rehabilitation Center, Brian T. Rogers
President OSHU Foundation, Allan Price
President and Director, Joseph (Joe) Robertson Jr.
Dean School of Medicine, Mark Richardson
Chairman, Charles A. Wilhoite
Chief of Staff, Connie Seeley
Vice Chairman, C. Scott Gibson
Vice Chairman, Jay Waldron
EVP, Steven D. Stadium
Interim Provost, Robert Vieira
Interim Provost, David Robinson
Interim CFO, James Walker
Dean School of Nursing, Michael Bleich
Director Oregon National Primate Research Center, Nancy L Haigwood
University Librarian, Chris Shaffer
Cataloger and Systems Librarian, Carla Pealer
Provost, Jeanette Mladenovic
Director, Kirby A. Dyess, age 65

President and Director, Joseph (Joe) Robertson Jr.
Director, Charles A. Wilhoite
Vice Chairman, C. Scott Gibson
Director, Roman Hernandez
Vice Chairman, Jay Waldron
Director, Meredith Wilson
Director, R. Jon Yunker

LOCATIONS

HQ: Oregon Health & Science University
3181 SW Sam Jackson Park Rd., Portland OR 97239-3098
Phone: 503-494-8311   **Fax:** 510-839-8853
Web: www.summitbanking.com

PRODUCTS/OPERATIONS

Selected schools
School of Dentistry
School of Medicine
School of Nursing
School of Pharmacy (with Oregon State University)
School of Science & Engineering

HISTORICAL FINANCIALS
Company Type: School

Income Statement   FYE: June 30

	REVENUE ($ mil.)	NET INCOME ($ mil.)	NET PROFIT MARGIN	EMPLOYEES
06/12	1,975	78	4.0%	12,600
06/06	1,257	140	11.2%	0
06/05	1,078	114	10.6%	0
06/04	1,078	114	10.6%	0
Annual Growth	22.3%	(11.8%)	—	—

2012 Year-End Financials

Debt ratio: ——
Return on equity: 4.00%
Cash ($ mil.): 209
Current ratio: 1.30
Long-term debt ($ mil.): —

Dividends
  Yield: —
  Payout: —
  Market value ($ mil.): —

ORGANICALLY GROWN COMPANY

Started by health-conscious Oregon farmers Organically Grown is exactly what its name says it is. The company grows and sells certified organic fruits vegetables and herbs produced by small to medium family-owned farmers located throughout the US's Pacific Northwest. Its line of more than 100 seasonal produce items are sold under the LADYBUG brand to customers including independent retailers supermarket chains restaurants home-delivery services and wholesalers. Organically Grown which is owned by its employees and growers was founded in 1978.

The company's customers include more than 500 vendors and 250 natural and food stores and restaurants throughout western Oregon and Washington. It has distribution operations in Eugene and Portland Oregon and in Kent Washington.

Dedicated to greening agriculture and the planet it donates 2.5% of its previous year's net profit to organizations focused on organic agriculture and sustainability.

EXECUTIVES

Manager Operations Portland, Tyson Haworth
Director Finance, Robbie Vasilinda
Director Marketing, David Lively
National Sales, M. L. Davies
Director Human Resources, Glenda Goodrich
CEO, Josh Hinerfeld

LOCATIONS

HQ: Organically Grown Company
1800 B Prarie Rd., Eugene OR 97402
Phone: 541-689-5320   **Fax:** 541-689-8768
Web: www.organicgrown.com

COMPETITORS

Albert' s Organics	Natural Selection
Chiquita Brands	Foods
Dole Food	Pacific International
Dovex Fruit	Vegetable
Eden Foods	Veritable Vegetable
Fresh Del Monte	Willow Wind Organic
Produce	Farms
Jonathan Sprouts	

HISTORICAL FINANCIALS
Company Type: Private

Income Statement   FYE: December 31

	REVENUE ($ mil.)	NET INCOME ($ mil.)	NET PROFIT MARGIN	EMPLOYEES
12/11	107	1	1.6%	189
12/10	85	1	2.3%	0
12/09	70	0	1.2%	0
12/08	72	1	1.6%	0
Annual Growth	13.8%	14.8%	—	—

2011 Year-End Financials

Debt ratio: ——
Return on equity: 1.60%
Cash ($ mil.): 4
Current ratio: 1.50
Long-term debt ($ mil.): —

Dividends
  Yield: —
  Payout: —
  Market value ($ mil.): —

ORNA KOKOSING CONSTRUCTION COMPANY

Corna Kokosing provides general contracting services for commercial industrial institutional and health care construction projects primarily in central Ohio. Services include construction management design/build and finance services for new construction and renovations. The company also performs construction services ranging from carpentry and drywall installation to metal building erection and demolition. Stonemason Al Corna and carpenter Joe DiCesare co-founded the company in 1956. Midwest heavy construction group Kokosing Construction acquired Corna Kokosing 40 years later.

EXECUTIVES

President, Mark S. Corna
Director of Finance, Jim Graves
Executive Vice President, James Negron

LOCATIONS

HQ: Corna Kokosing Construction Company
6235 Westerville Rd., Westerville OH 43081-4046
Phone: 614-901-8844   **Fax:** 614-212-5599
Web: www.corna.com

PRODUCTS/OPERATIONS

Selected Services
Carpentry
Casework
Concrete
Demolition
Drywall
Masonry
Metal building erection
Steel erection

Selected Projects
Buckeye Hall of Fame Cafe (restaurant renovation)
Capital University (new athletic facility and stadium)
Eddie George' s Grille 27 (new restaurant construction)
Mother Angeline McCrory Manor (nursing facility construction)
Wendy' s International Headquarters (office renovation)

COMPETITORS

Aker Construction	Messer Construction
Albert M. Higley	Miller-Valentine
Danis	Ruhlin
Envoy Inc.	Ruscilli Construction
MBC Holding	Shook National

HISTORICAL FINANCIALS
Company Type: Subsidiary

Income Statement   FYE: March 31

	REVENUE ($ mil.)	NET INCOME ($ mil.)	NET PROFIT MARGIN	EMPLOYEES
03/11	676	36	5.4%	500
03/10	676	36	5.4%	0
03/09	0	0	—	0
03/08	0	0	—	0
Annual Growth	—	—	—	—

2011 Year-End Financials

Debt ratio: —
Return on equity: 5.40%
Cash ($ mil.): 7
Current ratio: 1.20
Long-term debt ($ mil.): —

Dividends
  Yield: —
  Payout: —
  Market value ($ mil.): —

OROVILLE HOSPITAL

LOCATIONS

HQ: OROVILLE HOSPITAL
2767 OLIVE HWY, OROVILLE, CA 95966-6118
Phone: 530-533-8500
Web: www.orovillehospital.com

Income Statement

FYE: November 30

	REVENUE ($ mil.)	NET INCOME ($ mil.)	NET PROFIT MARGIN	EMPLOYEES
11/11	150	3	2.4%	1,400
11/10	152	7	5.2%	0
11/09	126	5	4.6%	0
11/08	394	1	0.4%	0
Annual Growth	(27.4%)	31.1%	—	—

2011 Year-End Financials

Debt ratio: ——
Return on equity: 2.40%
Cash ($ mil.): 9
Current ratio: 0.90
Long-term debt ($ mil.): ——

Dividends
Yield: —
Payout: —
Market value ($ mil.): —

OSC SPORTS INC.

Olympia Sports may not make you an Olympian but they do feature the gear to go for gold. The sporting goods retailer offers sports equipment fitness gear and apparel athletic shoes casual wear and sports accessories under such brands as Columbia Louisville Slugger Bauer PUMA Reebok and Teva. It sells merchandise through more than 200 banner stores in many of the small towns dotting the Northeast and Mid-Atlantic and via a website. In addition to its retail business the company oversees the private nonprofit Olympia Sports Foundation. The foundation runs a clothing bank and collaborates on projects with local charities and schools within its retail region. Founder and CEO Ed Manganello owns Olympia.

EXECUTIVES

Chairman, Ed Manganello
Accounting Manager, Patty Zub
President, Dick Coffey
Human Resources Manager, T. Meschinelli
Training Coordinator, David Heath

LOCATIONS

HQ: Olympia Sports
5 Bradley Dr., Westbrook ME 04092
Phone: 207-854-2794 **Fax:** 207-854-4168
Web: www.olympiasports.net

2012 Stores

	No.
Massachusetts	62
New	53
Maine	29
New	21
Pennsylvania	15
Connecticut	14
Vermont	11
Rhode	5
Maryland	4
Virginia	1
West	1
Total	**216**

PRODUCTS/OPERATIONS

Selected Brands

Adidas
Brooks
Champion
Columbia
Converse
Crocs
Easton
Etnies
Fanatics
Fathead
Life Is Good
Mizuno
Moving Comfort
New Balance
Nike
Nike NFL
Oakley
Puma
Rawlings
Reebok
Saucony
Teva
UFC
Under Armour

COMPETITORS

Dick' s Sporting Goods
Dunham' s
Eastern Mountain Sports
Finish Line
Foot Locker
Hat World
Kmart
L.L. Bean
Modell' s
REI
Sears
Sports Authority
Target Corporation
Wal-Mart

HISTORICAL FINANCIALS

Company Type: Private

Income Statement

FYE: September 30

	REVENUE ($ mil.)	NET INCOME ($ mil.)	NET PROFIT MARGIN	EMPLOYEES
09/11	183	9	5.2%	2,000
09/09	165	0	0.2%	0
09/08	191	4	2.3%	0
09/07	172	3	1.8%	0
Annual Growth	2.1%	45.6%	—	—

2011 Year-End Financials

Debt ratio: ——
Return on equity: 5.20%
Cash ($ mil.): 0
Current ratio: 0.10
Long-term debt ($ mil.): ——

Dividends
Yield: —
Payout: —
Market value ($ mil.): —

OTTAWA AREA INTERMEDIATE SCHOOL DISTRICT

LOCATIONS

HQ: OTTAWA AREA INTERMEDIATE SCHOOL DISTRICT
13565 PORT SHELDON ST, HOLLAND, MI 49424-9241
Phone: 616-738-8940
Web: www.oaisd.org

HISTORICAL FINANCIALS

Company Type: Private

Income Statement

FYE: June 30

	REVENUE ($ mil.)	NET INCOME ($ mil.)	NET PROFIT MARGIN	EMPLOYEES
06/11	100	3	3.2%	350
06/07	70	(2)	—	0
06/06	43	1	2.9%	0
06/05	1,498	0	0.0%	0
Annual Growth	(59.3%)	2902.5%	—	—

2011 Year-End Financials

Debt ratio: ——
Return on equity: 3.20%
Cash ($ mil.): 24
Current ratio: 1.80
Long-term debt ($ mil.): ——

Dividends
Yield: —
Payout: —
Market value ($ mil.): —

OTTER PRODUCTS LLC

Otter Products' products keep your precious electronic devices safe and dry. The company which goes by OtterBox makes about 170 models of cases for cell phones smart phones tablet computers and other portable electronics from Apple Dell Nokia Samsung Motorola and other manufacturers. It outsources production and sells its impact and water resistant Defender Reflex Commuter and Impact cases and watertight boxes at Best Buy Target and other retailers. OtterBox was formed in 1998 by CEO Curt Richardson and his wife Nancy. She came up with the name because otter skin is water repellant and otters are known for being playful and creative something the company works to incorporate into its culture.

EXECUTIVES

CEO, Curt Richardson
President, Brian Thomas
PR Manager, Kristin Golliher
PR Specialist, Kelly Richardson
PR Coordinator Europe Middle East and Asia (EMEA), Rhona Cashman
Managing Director EMEA, Matt Clark

LOCATIONS

HQ: Otter Products LLC
1 Old Town Sq. Ste. 303, Fort Collins CO 80524
Phone: 970-493-8446 **Fax:** 970-490-2888
Web: www.otterbox.com

COMPETITORS

Apple Inc.
Coach Inc.
Eagle Creek Travel Gear
Forward Industries
SKB Corporation
Skullcandy
Tamrac
Tandy Brands
Tenba
Tumi
ZAGG

HISTORICAL FINANCIALS
Company Type: Private

Income Statement
FYE: December 31

	REVENUE ($ mil.)	NET INCOME ($ mil.)	NET PROFIT MARGIN	EMPLOYEES
12/11	347	104	30.1%	320
12/10	168	60	35.8%	0
12/09	48	15	31.7%	0
12/08	10	0	6.8%	0
Annual Growth	225.6%	434.2%	—	—

2011 Year-End Financials

Debt ratio: ——
Return on equity: 30.10%
Cash ($ mil.): 0
Current ratio: 1.30
Long-term debt ($ mil.): ——

Dividends
Yield: —
Payout: —
Market value ($ mil.): —

OTTERBEIN UNIVERSITY

LOCATIONS

HQ: OTTERBEIN UNIVERSITY
1 S GROVE ST, WESTERVILLE, OH 43081-2004
Phone: 614-890-3000
Web: www.trustees.otterbein.edu

HISTORICAL FINANCIALS
Company Type: Private

Income Statement
FYE: June 30

	REVENUE ($ mil.)	NET INCOME ($ mil.)	NET PROFIT MARGIN	EMPLOYEES
06/11	92	5	5.8%	490
06/08	90	13	15.3%	0
06/07	58	17	30.5%	0
06/06	1,640	0	0.0%	0
Annual Growth	(61.7%)	3531.9%	—	—

2011 Year-End Financials

Debt ratio: ——
Return on equity: 5.80%
Cash ($ mil.): 18
Current ratio: —
Long-term debt ($ mil.): —

Dividends
Yield: —
Payout: —
Market value ($ mil.): —

OUACHITA PARISH SCHOOL DISTRICT

LOCATIONS

HQ: OUACHITA PARISH SCHOOL DISTRICT
100 BRY ST, MONROE, LA 71201-8406
Phone: 318-432-5000
Web: www.wmrebels.net

HISTORICAL FINANCIALS
Company Type: Private

Income Statement
FYE: June 30

	REVENUE ($ mil.)	NET INCOME ($ mil.)	NET PROFIT MARGIN	EMPLOYEES
06/11	210	(18)	—	2,804
06/10	204	(2)	—	0
06/08	193	26	13.7%	0
06/07	171	(1)	—	0
Annual Growth	7.1%	—	—	—

2011 Year-End Financials

Debt ratio: ——
Return on equity: (-9.00)%
Cash ($ mil.): 36
Current ratio: —
Long-term debt ($ mil.): —

Dividends
Yield: —
Payout: —
Market value ($ mil.): —

OUR LADY OF BELLEFONTE HOSPITAL INC.

LOCATIONS

HQ: OUR LADY OF BELLEFONTE HOSPITAL INC.
ST CHRISTOPHER DR, ASHLAND, KY 41101
Phone: 606-833-3333
Web: www.careyoucantrust.com

HISTORICAL FINANCIALS
Company Type: Private

Income Statement
FYE: August 31

	REVENUE ($ mil.)	NET INCOME ($ mil.)	NET PROFIT MARGIN	EMPLOYEES
08/11	155	8	5.4%	1,100
08/10	153	7	5.1%	0
08/09	160	3	2.0%	0
Annual Growth	(1.5%)	61.3%	—	—

2011 Year-End Financials

Debt ratio: ——
Return on equity: 5.40%
Cash ($ mil.): 9
Current ratio: 1.90
Long-term debt ($ mil.): —

Dividends
Yield: —
Payout: —
Market value ($ mil.): —

OUR LADY OF THE LAKE HOSPITAL INC.

Our Lady of the Lake Regional Medical Center reaches out to Baton Rouge residents with a helping hand. Participating in teaching programs for LSU and Tulane medical schools the medical center has some 700 inpatient beds and includes emergency surgery general medical and specialty care centers for conditions including heart disease cancer orthopedics and ENT (ear nose and throat) disorders. Our Lady of the Lake also includes a Children's Hospital two nursing homes and an independent-living facility and it offers outpatient services at its main campus and at satellite facilities throughout the greater Baton Rouge area. Our Lady of the Lake was founded in 1923 by the Franciscan Missionaries of Our Lady.

As a major facility in the Baton Rouge area Our Lady of the Lake has been expanding its services in the region in recent years. In 2012 for instance the hospital constructed a freestanding emergency room facility in the suburban community of Livingston Louisiana. It is also building a new nine-story patient tower to the main hospital campus; the tower will house the heart and vascular center as well as an expanded ER and a new level 1 regional trauma center and will be completed in late 2013.

Our Lady of the Lake has also expanded its education programs. For instance it added a pediatric residency program in 2010. The hospital also moved to extend its relationship with LSU that year by agreeing to become the primary clinical site for the LSU medical school. The agreement came as LSU considered whether to build a replacement hospital for its aging teaching facility and coincides with the Our Lady of the Lake expansion projects. The partnership launched a new psychiatric residency program in 2012.

EXECUTIVES

Chief of Staff and Director, Walter L. Bringaze III
Director and Secretary, John S. McClelland
Chair, Eugene Owen
CEO and Director, K. Scott Wester
EVP and COO, Terrie Sterling
VP Medical Affairs, Richard Vath
Vice Chair, Charles Freeburgh
Vice Chief of Staff and Director, Daniel Butler
Director, Joel Silverberg
Chief of Staff and Director, Walter L. Bringaze III
Director, Renee S. Furr
Director, Sister Betty Lyons
Director and Secretary, John S. McClelland
Director, Sister Penny Prophit
Director, Donald H. Daigle
CEO and Director, K. Scott Wester
Vice Chair, Charles Freeburgh
Director, Timothy Andrus
Director, Van Mayhall Jr.
Director, Daniel D. Montelaro
Vice Chief of Staff and Director, Daniel Butler
Auditors: KPMGLLP

LOCATIONS

HQ: Our Lady of the Lake Regional Medical Center
5000 Hennessy Blvd., Baton Rouge LA 70808
Phone: 225-765-6565   **Fax:** 225-765-8305
Web: www.ololrmc.com

COMPETITORS

Ardent Health
Baton Rouge General
CHRISTUS St. Frances
  Cabrini Hospital
Dynacq Healthcare
General Health System

Lane Regional Medical
  Center
Our Lady of Lourdes
River Parishes
  Hospital
Woman's Hospital

HISTORICAL FINANCIALS

Company Type: Private - Not-for-Profit

Income Statement

FYE: June 30

	REVENUE ($ mil.)	NET INCOME ($ mil.)	NET PROFIT MARGIN	EMPLOYEES
06/11	826	214	26.0%	1,800
06/10	614	12	2.0%	0
06/08*	6	1	18.4%	0
12/05	0	0	3.9%	0
Annual Growth	1491.6%	2894.5%	—	—

*Fiscal year change

2011 Year-End Financials

Debt ratio: ——
Return on equity: 26.00%
Cash ($ mil.): 200
Current ratio: 2.90
Long-term debt ($ mil.): —

Dividends
Yield: —
Payout: —
Market value ($ mil.): —

OUR LADY OF THE LAKE UNIVERSITY OF SAN ANTONIO

Our Lady of the Lake University was founded in 1895 by the Sisters of the Congregation of Divine Providence not that lady of the lake. The Catholic college offers undergraduate and graduate education courses at its main campus in San Antonio Texas as well as satellite locations in Houston and the Rio Grande Valley. It offers night and weekend classes as well as online programs. Altogether its 2700 students may choose from a variety of liberal arts and science subject areas including business information technology education social work and psychology.

EXECUTIVES

President, Tessa M. Pollack
Chair, Michael S. Edelmann
Assistant Director Development and Alumni Relations, Carolyn Young
Chief Communications Officer, Susan Schleicher
Director Academic Technology, Laurel L. Dodds
Director Network Telecommunications, Dave Lytle
Director Administrative Technology, Roger Castro
Director Campus Activities and University Center, Mary F. Scotka
Director Campus Ministry, Wayne Romo
Director Career Services, Anita Reynolds
Director Counseling Services, Teresa Casta?o
Director Health Services, Sarah Gormican
Director Residence Life, James Villarreal
Director Campus Recreational Sports, Adrienne Gomez
VP Finance and Facilities, Allen R. Klaus
Director Finance and Services, Ann DeBarros
Director Physical Plant, William N. Gower
Director Human Resources, Jim Miranda
Director Bookstore, Christina Moreno
VP Institutional Advancement, Jim Eskin
Director Annual Giving, Susan McMahon
Director Office of Development, Peggy Prather
Vice Chair, Sister Imelda Gonzalez
Director Human Resources, Phillip J. Vargas

VP Enrollment Management, Michael Acosta
Registrar, Norma Anderson
EVP, David Estes
Director Financial Aid, Esmeralda Flores
VP Student Life, Jack Hank
CTO, Samuel Young
VP Marketing and Communications, Daniel Yoxall

LOCATIONS

HQ: Our Lady of the Lake University
411 SW 24th St., San Antonio TX 78207
Phone: 210-434-6711   **Fax:** 210-431-4036
Web: www.ollusa.edu

HISTORICAL FINANCIALS

Company Type: School

Income Statement

FYE: May 31

	REVENUE ($ mil.)	NET INCOME ($ mil.)	NET PROFIT MARGIN	EMPLOYEES
05/12	39	(2)	—	504
05/11	46	13	28.2%	0
05/10	43	5	12.9%	0
05/09	53	0	—	0
Annual Growth	(9.9%)	—	—	—

2012 Year-End Financials

Debt ratio: ——
Return on equity: (-6.70)%
Cash ($ mil.): 14
Current ratio: 0.40
Long-term debt ($ mil.): —

Dividends
Yield: —
Payout: —
Market value ($ mil.): —

OVERLAKE HOSPITAL MEDICAL CENTER

Over the lake and through the sound to Overlake Hospital Medical Center we go! The not-for-profit hospital provides health care services to residents of Bellevue Washington in the Puget Sound region. The nearly 350-bed facility provides comprehensive inpatient and outpatient services ranging from cancer care and surgery to specialized senior care. Overlake also operates a number of outpatient clinics providing primary care urgent care and specialty care such as weight loss surgery. The organization also provides patients with health and wellness programs addressing issues like women's and children's health. Overlake founded in 1960 is led by CEO Craig Hendrickson a veteran health care executive.

Geographic Reach

Overlake Hospital Medical Center provides health care services to residents of Bellevue Washington and the entire Puget Sound region. With the addition of the newest Bellevue clinic Overlake operates clinics on its main campus in Bellevue as well as in Issaquah and on Mercer Island.

Operations

The medical center has more than 1000 physicians on staff and runs Centers of Excellence in cardiac care cancer care surgical services women's and infants' care and emergency and trauma care. The facility is home to a 24-hour urgent care clinic an anticoagulation clinic and a breast screening center. Overlake also operates numerous outpatient clinics providing primary care urgent care and specialty care.

Strategy

Increasing demand in the region has led the hospital to invest in expansions and equipment upgrades that include more emergency treatment capabilities and an on-campus helistop for trauma patients being airlifted to the area.

Along with its expansion and construction projects Overlake is investing in new technology to keep the health system in line with its competitors and to improve patient care. In 2011 it began phase one of adding endoscopic video towers to its operating rooms to facilitate improved views of surgical procedures. It is also planning to digitize all of its facilities with electronic health records.

Mergers and Acquisitions

In late 2011 Overlake Hospital Medical Center acquired Issaquah Medical Group and renamed it Overlake Medical Clinics Gilman. The acquisition expanded the company's network of primary care medical clinics on the east side of Puget Sound. Overlake has focused on adding new primary care clinics and expanding its physician network to serve patients in locations closer to where they live and work.

EXECUTIVES

President CEO and Trustee, Craig L. Hendrickson
VP Finance and CFO, Gary McLaughlin
Chief of Staff and Trustee, Gregory Engel
Treasurer and Trustee, Tom Cleveland
Chairman, Larry Hebner
Chief of Staff Elect and Trustee, Walter Smith
VP Professional Services, T.D. Sam Baxter
VP Human Resources, Lisa Brock
VP Patient Experience, Dianna Reely
Secretary and Trustee, John Murphy
EVP and COO, David W. Schultz
VP Information Services and CIO, Jody Albright
VP Quality and Patient Safety and Chief Compliance Officer, Richard Bryan
VP Strategy and Marketing, Caitlin Hillary
Director Medical Staff Services and Health Information Management, Marlene Tuttle
Chief Medical Officer and VP Network Development, Alan Ertle
VP Fund Development and Executive Director Overlake Hospital Fund, Molly Stearns
Trustee, F. Kemper Freeman Jr., age 70
Trustee, Janine Florence, age 63
Trustee, James J. (Jim) Doud Jr., age 74
President CEO and Trustee, Craig L. Hendrickson
Trustee, Bertrand A. (Bert) Valdman, age 49
Chief of Staff and Trustee, Gregory Engel
Treasurer and Trustee, Tom Cleveland
Chief of Staff Elect and Trustee, Walter Smith
Trustee, Roger A. Stark
Trustee, Ken Johnsen
Trustee, Douglas T. (Doug) Martin
Secretary and Trustee, John Murphy
Trustee, Skip Rowley
Trustee, Cecily Hall
Trustee, Patricia Wangsness
Auditors: KPMGLLP

LOCATIONS

HQ: Overlake Hospital Medical Center
1035 116th Ave. NE, Bellevue WA 98004
Phone: 425-688-5000   **Fax:** 425-688-5959
Web: www.overlakehospital.org

Selected Locations

Overlake Bellevue Campus (Bellevue Washington)
Bellevue Senior Health Center (Bellevue Washington)

Mercer Island Senior Health Center (Mercer Island Washington)
Overlake Medical Center in Bellevue (Bellevue Washington)
Overlake Medical Center in Issaquah (Issaquah Washington)

PRODUCTS/OPERATIONS

Selected Mergers and Acquisitions
FY2011
Issaquah Medical Group (undisclosed price; Issaquah WA; primary care clinics)

COMPETITORS

Catholic Health Initiatives
Franciscan Health System
Group Health Cooperative (Puget Sound)
Harrison Medical Center
MultiCare Health System
PeaceHealth
Providence Health & Services
Seattle Children's Hospital
Swedish Health Services
University of Washington
Yakima Valley Memorial

HISTORICAL FINANCIALS
Company Type: Private - Not-for-Profit

Income Statement
FYE: June 30

	REVENUE ($ mil.)	NET INCOME ($ mil.)	NET PROFIT MARGIN	EMPLOYEES
06/12	427	18	4.4%	2,450
06/11	417	68	16.3%	0
06/10	397	33	8.4%	0
06/09	391	14	3.7%	0
Annual Growth	3.0%	9.4%	—	—

2012 Year-End Financials
Debt ratio: —
Return on equity: 4.40%
Cash ($ mil.): 21
Current ratio: 1.20
Long-term debt ($ mil.): —
Dividends
Yield: —
Payout: —
Market value ($ mil.): —

OWENSBORO MUNICIPAL UTILITIES ELECTRIC LIGHT & POWER SYSTEM

Owensboro Kentucky (named after Abraham Owen a Shelby County legislator killed in the Battle of Tippecanoe) is served by Owensboro Municipal Utilities which provides power to almost 26000 customers and water to 24500. The city-owned utility operates water treatment facilities and a power plant that uses coal and used tires for fuel. Its operating divisions are Elmer Smith power plant Engineering & Operations Water Production and Customer Service Center. It also offers telecommunications services. Owensboro Municipal Utilities is overseen by the five-member Owens-

boro Utility Commission which is appointed by the mayor of Owensboro.

Focusing on its core businesses in 2009 the company sold its OMUOnline wireless internet service to Norlight Inc which had been managing the company's internet service since 1999.

Owensboro Municipal Utilities traces its origins to 1895 when Owensboro citizens voted to start their own electric system. Power was generated from the city's first power plant in 1900. The city's first deep well water utility was established in 1906. The electric and water systems were combined in 1940 as Owensboro Municipal Utilities.

EXECUTIVES

Director of Administrative Services, Sue Napper
Director of Finance and Accounting, Jim Grise
Director of Information Services, Harvey Sopher
Director of Engineering and Operations, Dick Chapman
Director of Water, Herman Cecil
General Manager, Stan Conn

LOCATIONS

HQ: Owensboro Municipal Utilities
2070 Tamarack Rd., Owensboro KY 42301
Phone: 270-926-3200   **Fax:** 703-563-1601
Web: www.intersectsoft.com

PRODUCTS/OPERATIONS

2008 Sales

	$ mil.	% of total
% of total		
Electric		93
Water		7
Total		**100**

2007 Sales

		% of total
% of total		
Electric		92
Water		8
Total		**100**

HISTORICAL FINANCIALS
Company Type: Government-owned

Income Statement
FYE: May 31

	REVENUE ($ mil.)	NET INCOME ($ mil.)	NET PROFIT MARGIN	EMPLOYEES
05/12	141	0	0.6%	235
05/11	138	(0)	—	0
05/10	137	2	1.8%	0
05/09	127	(5)	—	0
Annual Growth	3.4%	—	—	—

2012 Year-End Financials
Debt ratio: —
Return on equity: 0.60%
Cash ($ mil.): 17
Current ratio: 0.80
Long-term debt ($ mil.): —
Dividends
Yield: —
Payout: —
Market value ($ mil.): —

P1 GROUP INC.

LOCATIONS

HQ: P1 GROUP INC.
16210 W 108TH ST, LENEXA, KS 66219-1346
Phone: 785-843-2910
Web: www.p1group.com

HISTORICAL FINANCIALS
Company Type: Private

Income Statement
FYE: December 31

	REVENUE ($ mil.)	NET INCOME ($ mil.)	NET PROFIT MARGIN	EMPLOYEES
12/11	149	0	—	825
12/10	0	0	—	0
12/09	173	3	2.3%	0
12/08	199	6	3.1%	0
Annual Growth	(9.1%)	—	—	—

2011 Year-End Financials
Debt ratio: —
Return on equity: —
Cash ($ mil.): 3
Current ratio: 0.10
Long-term debt ($ mil.): —
Dividends
Yield: —
Payout: —
Market value ($ mil.): —

PACE UNIVERSITY

If you want to keep pace with your peers chances are you'll need a higher education. Pace University offers certificate programs as well as undergraduate graduate and doctoral degrees through half a dozen schools: arts and sciences business computer science and information systems education law and nursing. Altogether the school is home to 100 undergraduate majors offering roughly 30 undergraduate and graduate degrees 50 master's programs and four doctoral programs. Nearly 13000 students attend the university's three New York campuses (Lower Manhattan Pleasantville-Briarcliff and White Plains). It has a student-faculty ratio of about 18:1.

Geographic Reach
Pace boasts campus locations in New York City and in Westchester County.

Operations
The school has an endowment of more than $100 million. Besides its three New York campuses the university also offers courses online and at a location in midtown Manhattan.

Financial Performance
The university logged a 3% increase in revenue in 2012 as compared to 2011 due to a boost in contributions as well as tuition and fees net government grants and contracts. Net income meanwhile dropped by 160% during the same reporting period thanks to rises in expenses and unrealized depreciation in fair value of derivative instruments in 2012 vs. appreciation in 2011.

Company Background
Pace was founded in 1906 by the brothers Homer and Charles Pace as a co-educational business school called Pace Institute. It wasn't until 42 years later under Robert Pace that it began its transformation into its current incarnation as a liberal arts and sciences college.

LOCATIONS

HQ: Pace University
1 Pace Plaza, New York NY 10038-1598
Phone: 212-346-1200   **Fax:** 212-346-1036
Web: www.pace.edu

PRODUCTS/OPERATIONS

Selected Colleges and Schools

Dyson College of Arts and Sciences
Lienhard School of Nursing
Lubin School of Business
School of Education
School of Law
Seidenberg School of Computer Science and Information Systems

HISTORICAL FINANCIALS

Company Type: School

Income Statement

FYE: June 30

	REVENUE ($ mil.)	NET INCOME ($ mil.)	NET PROFIT MARGIN	EMPLOYEES
06/12	310	(15)	—	1,862
06/11	300	26	8.9%	0
06/10	274	(14)	—	0
06/09	276	(41)	—	0
Annual Growth	3.9%	—	—	—

2012 Year-End Financials

Debt ratio: ——
Return on equity: (-5.10)%
Cash ($ mil.): 22
Current ratio: ——
Long-term debt ($ mil.): —

Dividends
Yield: —
Payout: —
Market value ($ mil.): —

PACIFIC BUILDING GROUP

Pacific Building Group pacifies its clients by taking care of their property construction needs. The general contractor provides services including pre-construction evaluation facility design/build tenant improvements and facilities maintenance. It is known for its work on health care facilities including laboratories and medical office buildings; the company also provides services for corporate hospitality and industrial clients. Pacific Building Group has handled major projects for such customers as IBM Sharp HealthCare Sony and United Airlines. The company operates mainly in Southern California primarily in San Diego County. CEO and owner Greg Rogers founded the group in 1984.

He established Pacific Building Group with an initial focus on tenant improvements. The company subsequently expanded into other areas of construction.

EXECUTIVES

CEO, Gregory (Greg) Rogers
President, James R. (Jim) Roherty
VP Field Operations, Ron Maize
VP Operations, Bill Hansen
Chief Estimator, Mark Irish
Director Medical Services, Hollis Gentry IV
Director Business Development, Allison Beall

Controller, Matt Parker

LOCATIONS

HQ: Pacific Building Group
9752 Aspen Creek Ct. Ste. 150, San Diego CA 92121
Phone: 858-552-0600   **Fax:** 858-552-0604
Web: www.pacificbuildinggroup.com

COMPETITORS

Bernards Brothers
Clark Construction Group
DPR Construction
Fullmer Construction
Hensel Phelps Construction

Reno Contracting
Rudolph & Sletten
Suffolk Construction
Sundt
Swinerton
Tutor Perini

HISTORICAL FINANCIALS

Company Type: Private

Income Statement

FYE: December 31

	REVENUE ($ mil.)	NET INCOME ($ mil.)	NET PROFIT MARGIN	EMPLOYEES
12/11	51	0	0.4%	190
12/10	43	0	0.8%	0
12/09	55	3	6.3%	0
12/08	59	3	5.1%	0
Annual Growth	(5.2%)	(58.4%)	—	—

2011 Year-End Financials

Debt ratio: ——
Return on equity: 0.40%
Cash ($ mil.): 3
Current ratio: 0.30
Long-term debt ($ mil.): —

Dividends
Yield: —
Payout: —
Market value ($ mil.): —

PACIFIC MARITIME ASSOCIATION INC

LOCATIONS

HQ: PACIFIC MARITIME ASSOCIATION INC
555 MARKET ST FL 3, SAN FRANCISCO, CA 94105-5801
Phone: 415-576-3200
Web: www.pmanet.org

HISTORICAL FINANCIALS

Company Type: Private

Income Statement

FYE: June 30

	REVENUE ($ mil.)	NET INCOME ($ mil.)	NET PROFIT MARGIN	EMPLOYEES
06/11	88	4	5.0%	172
06/10	79	(1)	—	0
06/05	37	0	—	0
Annual Growth	52.7%	—	—	—

2011 Year-End Financials

Debt ratio: ——
Return on equity: 5.00%
Cash ($ mil.): 318
Current ratio: 1.00
Long-term debt ($ mil.): —

Dividends
Yield: —
Payout: —
Market value ($ mil.): —

PACIFIC PACKAGING PRODUCTS INC.

LOCATIONS

HQ: PACIFIC PACKAGING PRODUCTS INC.
24 INDUSTRIAL WAY, WILMINGTON, MA 01887-3434
Phone: 978-657-9100
Web: www.pacificpkg.com

HISTORICAL FINANCIALS

Company Type: Private

Income Statement — FYE: December 31

	REVENUE ($ mil.)	NET INCOME ($ mil.)	NET PROFIT MARGIN	EMPLOYEES
12/11	81	0	0.0%	165
12/10	79	0	0.2%	0
12/09	81	0	0.2%	0
12/08	81	0	0.2%	0
Annual Growth	(0.4%)	(48.3%)	—	—

2011 Year-End Financials

Debt ratio: ——
Return on equity: —
Cash ($ mil.): 0
Current ratio: 0.80
Long-term debt ($ mil.): —

Dividends
Yield: —
Payout: —
Market value ($ mil.): —

PALM BEACH ATLANTIC UNIVERSITY INC.

LOCATIONS

HQ: PALM BEACH ATLANTIC UNIVERSITY INC.
901 S FLAGLER DR, WEST PALM BEACH, FL 33401-6505
Phone: 561-803-2000
Web: www.pba.edu

HISTORICAL FINANCIALS

Company Type: Private

Income Statement — FYE: June 30

	REVENUE ($ mil.)	NET INCOME ($ mil.)	NET PROFIT MARGIN	EMPLOYEES
06/11	90	6	7.7%	551
06/10	79	0	0.1%	0
06/09	55	(6)	—	0
06/08	77	0	0.7%	0
Annual Growth	5.7%	135.1%	—	—

2011 Year-End Financials

Debt ratio: ——
Return on equity: 7.70%
Cash ($ mil.): 15
Current ratio: —
Long-term debt ($ mil.): —

Dividends
Yield: —
Payout: —
Market value ($ mil.): —

PALO ALTO MEDICAL FOUNDATION FOR HEALTH CARE RESEARCH AND EDUCAT

LOCATIONS

HQ: PALO ALTO MEDICAL FOUNDATION FOR HEALTH CARE RESEARCH AND EDUCAT
795 EL CAMINO REAL, PALO ALTO, CA 94301-2302
Phone: 650-321-4121
Web: www.pamf.org

HISTORICAL FINANCIALS

Company Type: Private

Income Statement — FYE: December 31

	REVENUE ($ mil.)	NET INCOME ($ mil.)	NET PROFIT MARGIN	EMPLOYEES
12/11	1,434	3	0.2%	1,168
12/01*	322	5	1.6%	0
10/00	198	23	11.9%	0
08/99	0	0		0
Annual Growth	—	—	—	—

*Fiscal year change

2011 Year-End Financials

Debt ratio: ——
Return on equity: 0.20%
Cash ($ mil.): 60
Current ratio: 1.10
Long-term debt ($ mil.): —

Dividends
Yield: —
Payout: —
Market value ($ mil.): —

PAN AMERICAN HEALTH ORGANIZATION INC

LOCATIONS

HQ: PAN AMERICAN HEALTH ORGANIZATION INC
525 TWENTY THIRD ST NW, WASHINGTON, DC 20037
Phone: 202-974-3000
Web: www.paho.org

HISTORICAL FINANCIALS

Company Type: Private

Income Statement — FYE: December 31

	REVENUE ($ mil.)	NET INCOME ($ mil.)	NET PROFIT MARGIN	EMPLOYEES
12/11	838	2	0.3%	1,500
12/09	1,268	101	8.0%	0
12/06	541	84	15.7%	0
12/05	798	9	1.2%	0
Annual Growth	1.6%	(39.5%)	—	—

2011 Year-End Financials

Debt ratio: ——
Return on equity: 0.30%
Cash ($ mil.): 104
Current ratio: 0.80
Long-term debt ($ mil.) — —

Dividends
Yield: —
Payout: —
Market value ($ mil.): —

PANAMERICAN CHEMICAL MARKETING LTD.

LOCATIONS

HQ: PANAMERICAN CHEMICAL MARKETING LTD.
2000 WEST LOOP S STE 2020, HOUSTON, TX 77027-3591
Phone: 713-993-0900
Web: www.panachem.com

HISTORICAL FINANCIALS

Company Type: Private

Income Statement — FYE: December 31

	REVENUE ($ mil.)	NET INCOME ($ mil.)	NET PROFIT MARGIN	EMPLOYEES
12/11	108	0	0.0%	10
12/10	93	0	0.5%	0
12/03	32	0	1.3%	0
12/02	25	0	1.6%	0
Annual Growth	63.2%	(65.8%)	—	—

2011 Year-End Financials

Debt ratio: ——
Return on equity: —
Cash ($ mil.): 2
Current ratio: 0.10
Long-term debt ($ mil.): —

Dividends
Yield: —
Payout: —
Market value ($ mil.): —

PAPER CONVERTING MACHINE COMPANY

An empire built on paper: The Paper Converting Machine Company (PCMC) does just that — manufactures machinery for the converting packaging printing and laminating of paper. PCMC makes and sells equipment for tissue converting and packaging; wide-web flexo printing coating and laminating; coaters; roll engraving; and nonwoven converting. Its equipment is used by manufacturers of flexible packaging non-woven disposable products (wet wipes) and sanitary tissues. PCMC has three production hubs in the US UK and Italy as well as offices in Brazil Germany Italy China and Japan. In business since 1919 PCMC is a division of manufacturing technology supplier Barry-Wehmiller Companies.

EXECUTIVES

Manager Product Development, Dave Kessenich
Manager Product Development, Mark Gillis
Manager Product Development, Mike Reedy
President, Tim Sullivan
VP Sales and Marketing, Steve Kemp

LOCATIONS

HQ: Paper Converting Machine Company
2300 S. Ashland Ave., Green Bay WI 54307-9005
Phone: 920-494-5601   **Fax:** 920-494-8865
Web: www.pcmc.com

PRODUCTS/OPERATIONS

Selected Products

Nonwoven converting
Printing
  Flexible packaging
  Labels and labeling
  Flexo
  Flexo and gravure
  Package printing
  Paper film and foil converting
Roll engraving
Tissue converting
  Accumulators
  Coaters
  Core machines
  Embossers
  Facial tissue machinery
  Laminators
  Printers
  Rewinders
  Saws
  Tail sealers
  Unwinds
Tissue packaging
  Tissue bundlers
  Tissue wrappers

COMPETITORS

Andritz AG   Nordson
imagelinx   Polymer Group
James Cropper   Sandusky International
Norbord   Voith

HISTORICAL FINANCIALS

Company Type: Private

Income Statement

	REVENUE ($ mil.)	NET INCOME ($ mil.)	NET PROFIT MARGIN	EMPLOYEES
09/11	215	0	—	1,304
09/10	196	0	—	0
09/06*	194	0	—	0
10/03	0	0	—	0
Annual Growth	—	—	—	—

*Fiscal year change

2011 Year-End Financials

Debt ratio: ——
Return on equity: —   Dividends
Cash ($ mil.): 7   Yield: —
Current ratio: 0.50   Payout: —
Long-term debt ($ mil.): —   Market value ($ mil.): —

PARISH OF ST CHARLES

LOCATIONS

HQ: PARISH OF ST CHARLES
15045 RIVER RD, HAHNVILLE, LA 70057-2182
Phone: 985-783-5000
Web: www.stcharlesgov.net

HISTORICAL FINANCIALS

Company Type: Private

Income Statement

FYE: December 31

	REVENUE ($ mil.)	NET INCOME ($ mil.)	NET PROFIT MARGIN	EMPLOYEES
12/11	82	0	0.4%	477
12/10	72	(2)	—	0
12/09	72	(6)	—	0
12/07	63	9	15.7%	0
Annual Growth	9.3%	(66.9%)	—	—

2011 Year-End Financials

Debt ratio: ——
Return on equity: 0.40%   Dividends
Cash ($ mil.): 1   Yield: —
Current ratio: 0.10   Payout: —
Long-term debt ($ mil.): —   Market value ($ mil.): —

PARK UNIVERSITY

LOCATIONS

HQ: PARK UNIVERSITY
8700 NW RIVER PARK DR, PARKVILLE, MO
64152-3795
Phone: 816-741-2000
Web: www.park.edu

HISTORICAL FINANCIALS

Company Type: Private

Income Statement

FYE: June 30

	REVENUE ($ mil.)	NET INCOME ($ mil.)	NET PROFIT MARGIN	EMPLOYEES
06/12	80	8	10.4%	2,500
06/11	76	9	12.7%	0
06/10	80	5	6.6%	0
06/09	68	(4)	—	0
Annual Growth	5.5%	—	—	—

2012 Year-End Financials

Debt ratio: ——
Return on equity: 10.40%   Dividends
Cash ($ mil.): 9   Yield: —
Current ratio: —   Payout: —
Long-term debt ($ mil.): —   Market value ($ mil.): —

PARKS XANTERRA & RESORTS INC

LOCATIONS

HQ: PARKS XANTERRA & RESORTS INC
6312 S FIDDLERS GREEN CIR 600N, GREENWOOD
VILLAGE, CO 80111-4943
Phone: 303-600-3400
Web: www.maumeebayresort.com

HISTORICAL FINANCIALS

Company Type: Private

Income Statement

FYE: December 28

	REVENUE ($ mil.)	NET INCOME ($ mil.)	NET PROFIT MARGIN	EMPLOYEES
12/11	301	7	2.4%	3,500
12/10	305	8	2.6%	0
12/09	298	9	3.2%	0
12/08	310	6	2.0%	0
Annual Growth	(1.0%)	4.9%	—	—

2011 Year-End Financials

Debt ratio: ——
Return on equity: 2.40%   Dividends
Cash ($ mil.): 42   Yield: —
Current ratio: 0.60   Payout: —
Long-term debt ($ mil.): —   Market value ($ mil.): —

PARTNERS IN HEALTH A NONPROFIT CORPORATION

LOCATIONS

HQ: PARTNERS IN HEALTH A NONPROFIT
CORPORATION
888 COMMONWEALTH AVE FL 3, BOSTON, MA
02215-1205
Phone: 617-998-8922
Web: www.pih.org

HISTORICAL FINANCIALS

Company Type: Private

Income Statement

FYE: June 30

	REVENUE ($ mil.)	NET INCOME ($ mil.)	NET PROFIT MARGIN	EMPLOYEES
06/11	88	(27)	—	120
06/10	151	60	39.7%	0
06/09	59	(4)	—	0
06/08	53	3	6.1%	0
Annual Growth	18.2%	—	—	—

2011 Year-End Financials

Debt ratio: ——
Return on equity: (-30.90)%   Dividends
Cash ($ mil.): 7   Yield: —
Current ratio: 1.80   Payout: —
Long-term debt ($ mil.): —   Market value ($ mil.): —

PARTNERSHIP FOR SUPPLY CHAIN MANAGEMENT INC.

LOCATIONS

HQ: PARTNERSHIP FOR SUPPLY CHAIN MANAGEMENT INC.
1616 FORT MYER DR FL 12, ARLINGTON, VA 22209-3110
Phone: 571-227-8600
Web: www.pfscm.org

HISTORICAL FINANCIALS
Company Type: Private

Income Statement
FYE: September 30

	REVENUE ($ mil.)	NET INCOME ($ mil.)	NET PROFIT MARGIN	EMPLOYEES
09/11	517	(2)	—	120
09/10	389	1	0.4%	0
09/09	294	1	0.5%	0
09/08	203	(0)	—	0
Annual Growth	36.4%	—	—	—

2011 Year-End Financials
Debt ratio: ——
Return on equity: (-0.40)%
Cash ($ mil.): 61
Current ratio: 0.60
Long-term debt ($ mil.): —

Dividends
Yield: —
Payout: —
Market value ($ mil.): —

PATERSON PUBLIC SCHOOL DISTRICT

LOCATIONS

HQ: PATERSON PUBLIC SCHOOL DISTRICT
90 DELAWARE AVE, PATERSON, NJ 07503-1804
Phone: 973-881-6000
Web: www.patersonpublicschools.com

HISTORICAL FINANCIALS
Company Type: Private

Income Statement
FYE: June 30

	REVENUE ($ mil.)	NET INCOME ($ mil.)	NET PROFIT MARGIN	EMPLOYEES
06/11	541	7	1.3%	3,055
06/05*	0	0	—	0
12/00	300	2	0.7%	0
06/99	291	(2)	—	0
Annual Growth	22.9%	—	—	—

*Fiscal year change

2011 Year-End Financials
Debt ratio: ——
Return on equity: 1.30%
Cash ($ mil.): 21
Current ratio: —
Long-term debt ($ mil.): —

Dividends
Yield: —
Payout: —
Market value ($ mil.): —

PATHFINDER INTERNATIONAL

Pathfinder International finds a way to provide reproductive health and family planning information and services to people in developing nations. The organization works in some 25 countries in Africa Asia Latin America and the Caribbean. It partners with local governments and other groups to provide access to sexual health and family planning information HIV/AIDS prevention and treatment advocacy for reproductive health policies worldwide abortion support where it's legal and post care where it isn't. Pathfinder also publishes newsletters resource lists guides and training information. Founded in 1957 it gets support from the US and European governments the United Nations and private sources.

Pathfinder International receives most of its funds from grants and contracts. It spends about 90% of its revenues on programs and services with Latin America and Asia each using about 40%.

EXECUTIVES

President and CEO, Daniel E. Pellegrom
VP Finance and Administration, Beverly M. Armstrong
SVP, Caroline Crosbie
Director Public Affairs, Cara Hesse
VP Resource Development, Erin S. Majernik
Founder, Clarence J. Gamble
Founder, Sarah B. Gamble
VP Programs, Demet Gural
Country Representative Angola, Hirondina Cucubica
Country Representative Botswana (Project Manager), Sinah Chaba
Country Representative Brazil, Carlos Laudari
Country Representative Egypt (Chief of Party), Mohamed Abou Nar
Country Representative Ethiopia, Tilahun Giday
Country Representative Ghana, Moses Liyobe Nanang
Country Representative India, Rekha Masilamani
Country Representative Kenya, Linda Casey
Country Representative Moldova (Team Leader), Iurie Climasevschi
Country Representative Mozambique, Julio Pacca
Country Representative Papua New Guinea (Program Manager), Jelilah Umia
Country Representative Peru, Miguel Gutierrez Ramos
Country Representative South Africa, Sophia Ladha
Country Representative Uganda, Caroline Abeja-Apunyo
Country Representative Viet Nam, Laura Wedeen
Country Representative Yemen, Hamouda Hanafi
Director Human Resources, Shari Stier
Country Representatives Nigeria, Sir Mohammed Murtala Mai
Country Representatives Bangladesh, Shabnam Shahnaz
Country Representative Tanzania, Mustafa Kudrati
Auditors: McGladreyLLP

LOCATIONS

HQ: Pathfinder International
9 Galen St. Ste. 217, Watertown MA 02472-4501
Phone: 617-924-7200   **Fax:** 617-924-3833
Web: www.pathfind.org

HISTORICAL FINANCIALS
Company Type: Private - Not-for-Profit

Income Statement
FYE: June 30

	REVENUE ($ mil.)	NET INCOME ($ mil.)	NET PROFIT MARGIN	EMPLOYEES
06/12	101	0	0.2%	628
06/11	101	1	1.3%	0
06/10	99	(2)	—	0
06/09	100	(0)	—	0
Annual Growth	0.2%	—	—	—

2012 Year-End Financials
Debt ratio: ——
Return on equity: 0.20%
Cash ($ mil.): 11
Current ratio: 0.50
Long-term debt ($ mil.): —

Dividends
Yield: —
Payout: —
Market value ($ mil.): —

PAYNECREST ELECTRIC INC.

LOCATIONS

HQ: PAYNECREST ELECTRIC INC.
10411 BAUR BLVD, SAINT LOUIS, MO 63132-1904
Phone: 314-996-0400
Web: www.payneelectric.com

HISTORICAL FINANCIALS
Company Type: Private

Income Statement
FYE: December 31

	REVENUE ($ mil.)	NET INCOME ($ mil.)	NET PROFIT MARGIN	EMPLOYEES
12/11	87	2	2.9%	300
12/10*	48	0	0.0%	0
10/04	59	7	12.5%	0
12/03	64	0	—	0
Annual Growth	10.5%	—	—	—

*Fiscal year change

2011 Year-End Financials
Debt ratio: ——
Return on equity: 2.90%
Cash ($ mil.): 0
Current ratio: 1.30
Long-term debt ($ mil.): —

Dividends
Yield: —
Payout: —
Market value ($ mil.): —

PCL CONSTRUCTION ENTERPRISES INC

PCL Construction Enterprises is the contractor to call on for commercial and civil construction concerns. The company serves as the parent to half a dozen US construction companies: PCL Construction Services; PCL Civil Constructors; PCL Construction; PCL Industrial Services; PCL Industrial Construction; and Nordic PCL Construction.

The companies serve as the operating entities for PCL one of Canada's largest general contracting groups. Having completed projects in nearly every US state PCL Construction Enterprises is active in the commercial institutional multi-family residential heavy industrial and civil construction sectors. PCL first entered the US construction market in 1975.

Geographic Reach

PCL Construction Enterprises through its six operating units concentrates on commercial civil and industrial construction projects located in the US.

Operations

PCL Construction Enterprises and its subsidiaries work on a variety of projects. PCL Construction Enterprises has completed bridges water and wastewater systems manufacturing plants office buildings and restaurants nationwide.

Like many construction companies PCL was hit by the economic recession. Backlogs were lacking and new projects became tougher to win due to an increase in competition. Contracts with water wastewater and renewable energy projects and universities have helped PCL Construction Enterprises through the downturn.

Sales and Marketing

PCL caters to customers in three primary markets: commercial buildings civil infrastructure and heavy industrial construction.

Company Ownership

PCL is 100% employee-owned.

EXECUTIVES

EVP; President Construction Services, Alfred E. (Al) Troppmann, age 62
President and COO, Peter E. Beaupre, age 61
Senior Vice President, Shaun P. Yancey, age 53
VP Finance, Michael J. (Mike) Kehoe
Director Finance and Administration, Bruce Lowell
Director Corporate Development, Dale Kain
Manager Marketing, Laura Dolan

LOCATIONS

HQ: PCL Construction Enterprises Inc.
2000 S. Colorado Blvd. Tower 2 Ste. 2-500, Denver CO 80222
Phone: 303-365-6500 **Fax:** 303-365-6590
Web: www.pcl.com

PRODUCTS/OPERATIONS

Selected Operating Companies

Nordic PCL Construction
PCL Civil Constructors
PCL Construction
PCL Construction Services
PCL Industrial Construction
PCL Industrial Services

COMPETITORS

Adolfson &	M. B. Kahn
Peterson Inc.	Skanska USA Civil
Andersen Construction	Suffolk Construction
Brasfield & Gorrie	TIC Holdings
C.W. Driver	Torix General
Dimeo Construction	Contractors
FCI Constructors	Turner Corporation
Fluor	
Gilbane Building	
Company	

HISTORICAL FINANCIALS

Company Type: Subsidiary

Income Statement

FYE: October 31

	REVENUE ($ mil.)	NET INCOME ($ mil.)	NET PROFIT MARGIN	EMPLOYEES
10/11	1,689	8	0.5%	3,300
10/10	1,616	23	1.5%	0
10/09	2,182	52	2.4%	0
10/08	2,315	84	3.7%	0
Annual Growth	(10.0%)	(53.8%)	—	—

2011 Year-End Financials

Debt ratio: ——
Return on equity: 0.50%
Cash ($ mil.): 127
Current ratio: 1.00
Long-term debt ($ mil.): —

Dividends
Yield: —
Payout: —
Market value ($ mil.): —

PDS TECH INC.

Need an IT pro to assist with your company's computer needs? PDS Tech wants to help. The company provides temporary technical industrial and general staffing services through more than 25 offices across the US with a concentration in Texas and on the East Coast. PDS Tech's specialties include aviation architecture engineering information technology administration and maritime staffing. Its PDS Engineering division handles engineering placement for the aerospace mechanical and structural engineering industries while the Information Services division offers technical consulting services in the IT and telecommunication industries. The company was founded in 1977 by aerospace engineer Art Janes.

EXECUTIVES

President and CEO, Arthur R. (Art) Janes
EVP CFO and General Counsel, Steven Cash Nickerson
Controller, Bryan Betzer

LOCATIONS

HQ: PDS Tech Inc.
1925 W. John Carpenter Fwy. Ste. 550, Irving TX 75063
Phone: 214-647-9600 **Fax:** 214-647-9636
Web: www.pdstech.com

PRODUCTS/OPERATIONS

PDS Operating Divisions
PDS Engineerin
PDS Aviation
PDS Information Services
PDS Maritime
PDS Profession
Offload Engineerin
Northwest Technical Services - Alaska

COMPETITORS

Adecco	ManpowerGroup
Allegis Group	On Assignment
Butler America	SFN Group
CDI	StarTek
COMFORCE	Volt Information

HISTORICAL FINANCIALS

Company Type: Private

Income Statement

FYE: December 25

	REVENUE ($ mil.)	NET INCOME ($ mil.)	NET PROFIT MARGIN	EMPLOYEES
12/11	397	5	1.3%	10,000
12/10	338	2	0.6%	0
12/09	344	0	0.1%	0
12/08	418	0	0.2%	0
Annual Growth	(1.7%)	86.3%	—	—

2011 Year-End Financials

Debt ratio: ——
Return on equity: 1.30%
Cash ($ mil.): 14
Current ratio: 4.00
Long-term debt ($ mil.): —

Dividends
Yield: —
Payout: —
Market value ($ mil.): —

PEACE DINING CORPORATION

LOCATIONS

HQ: PEACE DINING CORPORATION
1500 JFK BLVD STE 725, PHILADELPHIA, PA 19102-1747
Phone: 215-523-5782

HISTORICAL FINANCIALS

Company Type: Private

Income Statement

FYE: January 1

	REVENUE ($ mil.)	NET INCOME ($ mil.)	NET PROFIT MARGIN	EMPLOYEES
01/12	81	1	2.1%	900
01/11*	71	0	0.1%	0
12/09	55	0	1.7%	0
12/08	57	0	0.6%	0
Annual Growth	12.2%	72.7%	—	—

*Fiscal year change

2012 Year-End Financials

Debt ratio: ——
Return on equity: 2.10%
Cash ($ mil.): 0
Current ratio: 0.30
Long-term debt ($ mil.): —

Dividends
Yield: —
Payout: —
Market value ($ mil.): —

PEASE & CURREN INCORPORATED

LOCATIONS

HQ: PEASE & CURREN INCORPORATED
75 PENNSYLVANIA AVE, WARWICK, RI 02888-3028
Phone: 401-739-6350
Web: www.peaseandcurren.com

HISTORICAL FINANCIALS
Company Type: Private

Income Statement
FYE: December 31

	REVENUE ($ mil.)	NET INCOME ($ mil.)	NET PROFIT MARGIN	EMPLOYEES
12/11	109	3	3.2%	40
12/10	83	4	5.2%	0
12/09	83	4	5.2%	0
12/08	97	4	4.6%	0
Annual Growth	3.8%	(8.0%)	—	—

2011 Year-End Financials

Debt ratio: ——
Return on equity: 3.20%
Cash ($ mil.): 5
Current ratio: 0.70
Long-term debt ($ mil.): —

Dividends
  Yield: —
  Payout: —
  Market value ($ mil.): —

PENNSYLVANIA HOSPITAL OF THE UNIVERSITY OF PENNSYLVANIA HEALTH S

LOCATIONS

HQ: PENNSYLVANIA HOSPITAL OF THE UNIVERSITY OF PENNSYLVANIA HEALTH S
  800 SPRUCE ST, PHILADELPHIA, PA 19107-6192
Phone: 215-829-3000

HISTORICAL FINANCIALS
Company Type: Private

Income Statement
FYE: June 30

	REVENUE ($ mil.)	NET INCOME ($ mil.)	NET PROFIT MARGIN	EMPLOYEES
06/11	521	30	5.9%	2,200
06/10	485	27	5.7%	0
06/09	453	0	—	0
06/08	439	24	5.6%	0
Annual Growth	5.9%	7.6%	—	—

2011 Year-End Financials

Debt ratio: ——
Return on equity: 5.90%
Cash ($ mil.): 89
Current ratio: 9.10
Long-term debt ($ mil.): —

Dividends
  Yield: —
  Payout: —
  Market value ($ mil.): —

PENN UNITED TECHNOLOGIES INC.

LOCATIONS

HQ: PENN UNITED TECHNOLOGIES INC.
  799 N PIKE RD, CABOT, PA 16023-2297
Phone: 724-352-1507
Web: www.pennunited.com

HISTORICAL FINANCIALS
Company Type: Private

Income Statement
FYE: March 31

	REVENUE ($ mil.)	NET INCOME ($ mil.)	NET PROFIT MARGIN	EMPLOYEES
03/12	106	12	12.2%	600
Annual Growth	—	—	—	—

2012 Year-End Financials

Debt ratio: ——
Return on equity: 12.20%
Cash ($ mil.): 3
Current ratio: 0.20
Long-term debt ($ mil.): —

Dividends
  Yield: —
  Payout: —
  Market value ($ mil.): —

PENNYRILE RURAL ELECTRIC COOPERATIVE CORPORATION

LOCATIONS

HQ: PENNYRILE RURAL ELECTRIC COOPERATIVE CORPORATION
  2000 HARRISON ST, HOPKINSVILLE, KY 42240-6000
Phone: 270-886-2555
Web: www.precc.com

HISTORICAL FINANCIALS
Company Type: Private

Income Statement
FYE: June 30

	REVENUE ($ mil.)	NET INCOME ($ mil.)	NET PROFIT MARGIN	EMPLOYEES
06/12	120	5	4.9%	127
06/11	121	4	3.6%	0
06/10	109	4	4.3%	0
06/09	115	3	3.1%	0
Annual Growth	1.2%	18.7%	—	—

2012 Year-End Financials

Debt ratio: ——
Return on equity: 4.90%
Cash ($ mil.): 13
Current ratio: 0.90
Long-term debt ($ mil.): —

Dividends
  Yield: —
  Payout: —
  Market value ($ mil.): —

PEPPER CONSTRUCTION GROUP LLC

Pepper Construction Group spices up the construction business with a little of this and a pinch of that. The company provides general contracting and construction management services for commercial office education entertainment health care and institutional clients as well as waterworks projects. (Health care projects account for about 50% of Pepper's revenue.) Its client list includes UBS Northwestern University University of Notre Dame Texas Heart Institute Loyola University Medical Center and NASA. Pepper Construction Group has divisions in Illinois Indiana Ohio and Texas. Stanley F. Pepper founded the company in Chicago in 1927. The group is owned by his family and employees of the firm.

Geographic Reach

Chicago-based Pepper Construction comprises four geographic divisions: Illinois; Indiana; Ohio; and Texas. Overall the company is active in about 20 states mostly in the central and northeastern states.

Operations

The company's Pepper Environmental Technologies unit provides environmental services. Green building has become a large part of Pepper Construction's operations. Its Green Team of certified professionals have helped construct more than 2.9 million sq. ft. of eco-friendly space. The Green Team has built the Apple Computer flagship store HSBC Chicago North and Kohl's Children's Museum.

The firm's Pepper-Lawson Waterworks group constructs water purification plants for municipal clients including Houston and Missouri City Texas.

EXECUTIVES

SVP Marketing and Secretary; President Pepper Environmental Technologies, Richard H. (Rich) Tilghman
Chairman and CEO, J. David (Dave) Pepper II, age 49
EVP and General Counsel, Thomas M. O'Leary
SVP and CFO, Joel D. Thomason
President Pepper Construction Company of Indiana, William J. (Bill) McCarthy

President Pepper-Lawson Construction in Texas,
Paul E. Lawson
President and COO Pepper Construction Company, Kenneth A. (Ken) Egidi
President Pepper Construction Company of Ohio, Paul Francois
SVP and Director Operations Pepper Construction Company, Jim Guyette
SVP and Senior Director Operations Pepper Construction Company, James A. Nissen
SVP Business Development and Marketing, J. Scot Pepper
SVP Pepper Construction Company, Richard D. Schuster
SVP and COO Pepper Construction Company of Indiana, Michael T. (Mike) McCann Sr.
VP and Director Operations Pepper Construction Company of Ohio, Jay Jocobsmeyer

LOCATIONS

HQ: Pepper Construction Group LLC
643 N. Orleans St., Chicago IL 60610-3690
Phone: 312-266-4700   **Fax:** 312-266-2792
Web: www.pepperconstruction.com

PRODUCTS/OPERATIONS

Selected Operations

Pepper Construction Group LLC (Chicago Illinois)
Pepper Construction Co. (Chicago Illinois)
Pepper Construction Co. of Indiana (Indianapolis Indiana)
Pepper Construction Co. of Ohio LLC (Dublin Ohio)
Pepper Environmental Technologies Inc. (Barrington Illinois)
Pepper-Lawson Construction LP (Houston Texas)
Pepper-Lawson Waterworks LLC (Houston Texas)

COMPETITORS

Barton Malow	Graycor
Bovis Lend Lease	M. A. Mortenson
Bulley & Andrews	McCarthy Building
C. G. Schmidt	Power Construction
Charles Pankow	Turner Corporation
Builders	Walbridge Aldinger
Clark Enterprises	Walsh Group
Gilbane	

HISTORICAL FINANCIALS
Company Type: Private

Income Statement
FYE: September 30

	REVENUE ($ mil.)	NET INCOME ($ mil.)	NET PROFIT MARGIN	EMPLOYEES
09/11	911	15	1.7%	1,100
09/10	911	15	1.7%	0
09/09	1,071	12	1.2%	0
09/08	1,352	22	1.7%	0
Annual Growth	(12.3%)	(11.4%)	—	—

2011 Year-End Financials

Debt ratio: ——
Return on equity: 1.70%
Cash ($ mil.): 1
Current ratio: 0.50
Long-term debt ($ mil.): —
Dividends
Yield: —
Payout: —
Market value ($ mil.): —

PEREZ TRADING COMPANY INC.

No matter how you say it paper or el papel Perez Trading has it. From its Miami warehouse the company distributes more than 15000 tons of paper and paperboard inventory including corrugated box equipment napkin paper printing paper and other printing and shipping equipment and supplies. Customers include commercial printers converters distributors and packaging manufacturers. Perez Trading imports and exports to nearly 30 countries encompassing the Caribbean Islands Central and South America Mexico and the US. Perez Trading has been family owned and operated since 1947.

EXECUTIVES

Chairman and CEO, John Perez
CFO, Carl A. Perez
VP Logistics, Jose Arenas
President, John D. Perez
Human Resources Manager, Alfred Parra
Paper Division Manager, Erick Bonilla
Converting Equipment Division Manager, Jose Rodriguez
Corrugated Box Equipment Division Manager, Jose Sanchez
Folding Carton Equipment Division Manager, Eladio Del Riego
Containerboard & Kraft Division Manager, Jose Sanchez
Printing Equipment & Supplies Division Manager, Noel Alcantara

LOCATIONS

HQ: PEREZ TRADING COMPANY INC.
3490 NW 125TH ST, MIAMI, FL 33167-2412
Phone: 305-769-0761
Web: www.pereztrading.com

COMPETITORS

Georgia-Pacific	MeadWestvaco
Howard Smith Paper	Unisource
International Paper	

HISTORICAL FINANCIALS
Company Type: Private

Income Statement
FYE: December 31

	REVENUE ($ mil.)	NET INCOME ($ mil.)	NET PROFIT MARGIN	EMPLOYEES
12/11	532	18	3.5%	135
12/10	492	24	5.1%	0
12/09	372	21	5.7%	0
12/08	410	46	11.4%	0
Annual Growth	9.0%	(26.5%)	—	—

2011 Year-End Financials

Debt ratio: ——
Return on equity: 3.50%
Cash ($ mil.): 0
Current ratio: 1.50
Long-term debt ($ mil.): —
Dividends
Yield: —
Payout: —
Market value ($ mil.): —

PERRY CHARLES PARTNERS INC

LOCATIONS

HQ: PERRY CHARLES PARTNERS INC
8200 NW 15TH PL, GAINESVILLE, FL 32606-5203
Phone: 352-333-9292
Web: www.cppi.com

HISTORICAL FINANCIALS
Company Type: Private

Income Statement
FYE: December 31

	REVENUE ($ mil.)	NET INCOME ($ mil.)	NET PROFIT MARGIN	EMPLOYEES
12/11	131	1	0.9%	167
Annual Growth	—	—	—	—

2011 Year-End Financials

Debt ratio: ——
Return on equity: 0.90%
Cash ($ mil.): 10
Current ratio: 0.40
Long-term debt ($ mil.): —
Dividends
Yield: —
Payout: —
Market value ($ mil.): —

PERRYTON EQUITY EXCHANGE

LOCATIONS

HQ: PERRYTON EQUITY EXCHANGE
202 S AMHERST ST, PERRYTON, TX 79070-2528
Phone: 806-435-4016
Web: www.perrytonequity.com

HISTORICAL FINANCIALS
Company Type: Private

Income Statement
FYE: January 31

	REVENUE ($ mil.)	NET INCOME ($ mil.)	NET PROFIT MARGIN	EMPLOYEES
01/12	126	3	2.4%	110
01/10*	54	2	4.8%	0
03/06	68	0	0.5%	0
03/05	53	(0)	—	0
Annual Growth	33.3%	—	—	—

*Fiscal year change

2012 Year-End Financials

Debt ratio: ——
Return on equity: 2.40%
Cash ($ mil.): 0
Current ratio: 0.50
Long-term debt ($ mil.): —
Dividends
Yield: —
Payout: —
Market value ($ mil.): —

PETERSBURG MOTOR COMPANY INC

LOCATIONS

HQ: PETERSBURG MOTOR COMPANY INC
777 MYERS DR, CHARLOTTESVILLE, VA 22901-1139
Phone: 434-978-3711

HISTORICAL FINANCIALS

Company Type: Private

Income Statement

				FYE: December 31
	REVENUE ($ mil.)	NET INCOME ($ mil.)	NET PROFIT MARGIN	EMPLOYEES
12/11	204	3	1.6%	100
12/09	129	2	1.8%	0
12/07	170	1	1.0%	0
12/06	162	2	1.3%	0
Annual Growth	8.1%	14.0%	—	—

2011 Year-End Financials

Debt ratio: —
Return on equity: 1.60%
Cash ($ mil.): 8
Current ratio: 0.60
Long-term debt ($ mil.): —

Dividends
Yield: —
Payout: —
Market value ($ mil.): —

PETERSEN ALUMINUM CORPORATION

LOCATIONS

HQ: PETERSEN ALUMINUM CORPORATION
1005 TONNE RD, ELK GROVE VILLAGE, IL 60007-4817
Phone: 847-228-7150
Web: www.petersonaluminum.com

HISTORICAL FINANCIALS

Company Type: Private

Income Statement

				FYE: June 30
	REVENUE ($ mil.)	NET INCOME ($ mil.)	NET PROFIT MARGIN	EMPLOYEES
06/12	104	0	0.2%	190
06/11	97	0	0.9%	0
06/10	91	0	0.8%	0
06/09	116	1	1.2%	0
Annual Growth	(3.5%)	(48.8%)	—	—

2012 Year-End Financials

Debt ratio: —
Return on equity: 0.20%
Cash ($ mil.): 5
Current ratio: 2.40
Long-term debt ($ mil.): —

Dividends
Yield: —
Payout: —
Market value ($ mil.): —

PETERSON FARMS INC.

LOCATIONS

HQ: PETERSON FARMS INC.
3104 W BASELINE RD, SHELBY, MI 49455-9633
Phone: 231-861-6333
Web: www.petersonfarmsinc.com

HISTORICAL FINANCIALS

Company Type: Private

Income Statement

				FYE: March 31
	REVENUE ($ mil.)	NET INCOME ($ mil.)	NET PROFIT MARGIN	EMPLOYEES
03/12	110	5	5.4%	400
03/11	102	3	3.4%	0
03/10	100	2	3.0%	0
03/09	107	4	3.9%	0
Annual Growth	0.9%	12.6%	—	—

2012 Year-End Financials

Debt ratio: —
Return on equity: 5.40%
Cash ($ mil.): 0
Current ratio: 0.10
Long-term debt ($ mil.): —

Dividends
Yield: —
Payout: —
Market value ($ mil.): —

PETR-ALL PETROLEUM CONSULTING CORP.

LOCATIONS

HQ: PETR-ALL PETROLEUM CONSULTING CORP.
6567 KINNE RD, DE WITT, NY 13214-1923
Phone: 315-446-0125
Web: www.expressmart.com

HISTORICAL FINANCIALS

Company Type: Private

Income Statement

				FYE: July 27
	REVENUE ($ mil.)	NET INCOME ($ mil.)	NET PROFIT MARGIN	EMPLOYEES
07/11*	400	2	0.7%	600
12/09	323	0	0.0%	0
12/08	368	2	0.6%	0
12/07	334	30	9.2%	0
Annual Growth	6.1%	(56.0%)	—	—

*Fiscal year change

2011 Year-End Financials

Debt ratio: —
Return on equity: 0.70%
Cash ($ mil.): 2
Current ratio: 0.30
Long-term debt ($ mil.): —

Dividends
Yield: —
Payout: —
Market value ($ mil.): —

PETRO VM INC

LOCATIONS

HQ: PETRO VM INC
2188 KIRBY LN, SYOSSET, NY 11791-9614
Phone: 516-921-7190

HISTORICAL FINANCIALS

Company Type: Private

Income Statement

				FYE: December 31
	REVENUE ($ mil.)	NET INCOME ($ mil.)	NET PROFIT MARGIN	EMPLOYEES
12/11	128	0	0.5%	2
12/10	77	0	0.5%	0
12/09	54	0	0.5%	0
12/08	74	0	0.5%	0
Annual Growth	19.9%	18.2%	—	—

2011 Year-End Financials

Debt ratio: —
Return on equity: 0.50%
Cash ($ mil.): 1
Current ratio: 1.20
Long-term debt ($ mil.): —

Dividends
Yield: —
Payout: —
Market value ($ mil.): —

PETROCARD INC.

LOCATIONS

HQ: PETROCARD INC.
730 CENTRAL AVE S, KENT, WA 98032-6109
Phone: 253-852-7801
Web: www.petrocard.com

HISTORICAL FINANCIALS

Company Type: Private

Income Statement

				FYE: March 31
	REVENUE ($ mil.)	NET INCOME ($ mil.)	NET PROFIT MARGIN	EMPLOYEES
03/12	1,173	0	0.1%	190
03/11	948	3	0.4%	0
03/10	791	3	0.4%	0
03/08	993	2	0.2%	0
Annual Growth	5.7%	(30.5%)	—	—

2012 Year-End Financials

Debt ratio: —
Return on equity: 0.10%
Cash ($ mil.): 1
Current ratio: 0.90
Long-term debt ($ mil.): —

Dividends
Yield: —
Payout: —
Market value ($ mil.): —

PETROLEUM MARKETERS INC.

No fancy name for this company. It is what it says it is. Petroleum Marketers is a full-service petroleum company serving customers in Kentucky Maryland North Carolina Tennessee West Virginia and Virginia. The company's PM Terminals unit supplies gasoline diesel fuel motor oil and antifreeze to customers in its service area from eight bulk fuel storage facilities in Virginia. PMI Lubricants operates a fleet of bulk transport trucks while PM Transport offers for-hire tanker truckers for the transportation of petroleum products. The company also runs a chain of about 70 convenience stores/gas stations in Virginia under the banner Stop In Food Stores.

Some locations have fast food eateries in Virginia (run by its PM Foods division) including four Burger Kings two Arbys and one Subway located within or next door to Stop In Food Stores.

In 2009 Petroleum Marketers launched an 85% ethanol/15% gas blend at its Albemarle County Shell station (the first E85 fuel blend in Central Virginia) as a prototype for use of the alternative fuel blend at other gas stations in the region.

Petroleum Marketers was founded in 1921 The company set up PM Terminals in 1949.

EXECUTIVES

Chairman President and CEO, Ronald R. (Ron) Hare
CFO, Annette A. Willis
VP; President StopIn Food Stores, John C. Newton

LOCATIONS

HQ: Petroleum Marketers Inc.
3000 Ogden Rd., Roanoke VA 24014
Phone: 540-772-4900   **Fax:** 540-772-6900
Web: www.petroleummarketers.com

PRODUCTS/OPERATIONS

Operating Divisions
PMI Lubricants
PM Foods
PM Terminals
PM Transport
Stop In Food Stores

COMPETITORS

Chevron   Gate Petroleum
Cumberland Farms   Racetrac Petroleum
Exxon Mobil   The Pantry

HISTORICAL FINANCIALS

Company Type: Private

Income Statement

FYE: June 30

	REVENUE ($ mil.)	NET INCOME ($ mil.)	NET PROFIT MARGIN	EMPLOYEES
06/12	1,081	1	0.2%	1,500
06/11	945	2	0.2%	0
06/10	797	4	0.6%	0
06/09	765	5	0.7%	0
Annual Growth	12.2%	(27.1%)	—	—

2012 Year-End Financials

Debt ratio: ——
Return on equity: 0.20%
Cash ($ mil.): 6   Dividends
Current ratio: 0.80   Yield: —
Long-term debt ($ mil.): ——   Payout: —
                        Market value ($ mil.): —

PETROLEUM TRADERS CORPORATION

Petroleum Traders Corporation barters with fuel. The company provides wholesale gasoline diesel fuel and heating oil to fuel distributors government agencies and other large consumers of fuel such as businesses with vehicle fleets. The largest pure wholesale fuel distributor in the country Petroleum Traders operates and trades in 39 US states. It supplies #1 and #2 low sulfur diesel fuels biodiesel high sulfur heating oil and kerosene and conventional ethanol and reformulated blends of gasoline in regular midgrade and premium octane ratings.

Petroleum Traders was founded in 1979. It parlays its hedging experience into fuel cost management for its customers via firm pricing cap programs collars and fuel swaps.

In 2007 it secured an $86 million contract to supply fuel to the Defense Logistics Agency.

EXECUTIVES

President, Michael B. Himes
VP, Vicki L. Himes
Operations Manager, Joe Jurczak
CFO, Linda Stephens
Distribution Manager, Rick Hauschild
Distribution Manager, Mayleen Brinker
Contract Sales Manager, Gayle Newton

LOCATIONS

HQ: Petroleum Traders Corporation
7120 Pointe Inverness Way, Fort Wayne IN 46804
Phone: 260-432-6622   **Fax:** 260-432-6564
Web: www.petroleumtraders.com

COMPETITORS

Petro Holdings   Sun Coast Resources
SMF Energy

HISTORICAL FINANCIALS

Company Type: Private

Income Statement

FYE: June 30

	REVENUE ($ mil.)	NET INCOME ($ mil.)	NET PROFIT MARGIN	EMPLOYEES
06/12	2,796	13	0.5%	95
06/11	2,470	13	0.5%	0
06/10	1,953	13	0.7%	0
06/09	1,681	30	1.8%	0
Annual Growth	18.5%	(22.8%)	—	—

2012 Year-End Financials

Debt ratio: ——
Return on equity: 0.50%
Cash ($ mil.): 2   Dividends
Current ratio: 1.60   Yield: —
Long-term debt ($ mil.): ——   Payout: —
                        Market value ($ mil.): —

PHE INC.

LOCATIONS

HQ: PHE INC.
302 MEADOWLANDS DR, HILLSBOROUGH, NC 27278-8502
Phone: 919-644-8100

HISTORICAL FINANCIALS

Company Type: Private

Income Statement

FYE: December 31

	REVENUE ($ mil.)	NET INCOME ($ mil.)	NET PROFIT MARGIN	EMPLOYEES
12/11*	86	8	10.2%	350
01/11	79	6	7.7%	0
12/07	86	6	7.2%	0
12/06	82	8	10.3%	0
Annual Growth	1.5%	1.2%	—	—

*Fiscal year change

2011 Year-End Financials

Debt ratio: ——
Return on equity: 10.20%
Cash ($ mil.): 3   Dividends
Current ratio: 0.90   Yield: —
Long-term debt ($ mil.): ——   Payout: —
                        Market value ($ mil.): —

PHELPS DUNBAR L.L.P.

A leading regional law firm Phelps Dunbar has more than 270 attorneys overall. The firm has represented public and private companies educational institutions governmental agencies health care systems estates and individuals. Clients have included T3 Technologies Louisiana Wholesale Drug Co. and Deutsche Schiffsbank. Among Phelps Dunbar's practice areas are admiralty; bankruptcy; commercial litigation; intellectual property; oil and gas; and product liability. Phelps Dunbar is especially focused on clients operating in the oil gas and energy industries.

Geographic Reach

Phelps Dunbar considers the Gulf Region a major commercial center - a "third coast." The firm operates from some 10 offices in Alabama Florida Louisiana Mississippi North Carolina and Texas. Phelps Dunbar also has one office outside of the US located in London UK.

Strategy

The firm is focused on helping US companies do business with the expanding economies of Latin America and the energy industry.

Company Background

Phelps Dunbar was founded in 1853.

EXECUTIVES

Chairman and Managing Partner New Orleans, Richard N. Dicharry
Administrator, Thomas W. (Tom) Mitchell
Director Marketing, Mann Deynoodt
Director Legal Personnel and Recruiting, Tory George Nieset
Director Human Resources, Deborah Langenhennig
Managing Partner Baton Rouge, H. Alston Johnson III

Managing Partner Tupelo, F.M. (Mike) Bush III
Managing Partner Gulfport, James G. (Jim) Wyly
Managing Partner Houston, Patricia (Patty) Hair
Managing Partner Tampa, Lawrence P. (Larry)
Ingram
Director Finance, Kevin Moffett
Auditors: Ernst&YoungLLP

LOCATIONS

HQ: PHELPS DUNBAR L.L.P.
365 CANAL ST STE 2000, NEW ORLEANS, LA
70130-6534
Phone: 504-566-1311
Web: www.phelpsdunbar.com

PRODUCTS/OPERATIONS

Selected Practices Areas
Admiralty
Antitrust and trade regulation
Appellate litigation
Bankruptcy and creditors' rights
Business and finance
Commercial litigation
Construction
Corporate and securities
Employee benefits/executive compensation
Energy and utilities
Environmental
Franchise and distribution
Gaming
Government contracts
Health care
HIPAA compliance
Insurance and reinsurance
Intellectual property
International
Labor and employment
Legislative and governmental relations
Municipal finance
Oil and gas energy and minerals
Petroleum marketing
Products liability
Railroad
Real estate
Regulatory and governmental matters
Tax
Tort litigation
Toxic tort litigation
Trusts and estates

COMPETITORS

Alston & Bird	Kean Miller
Fulbright &	King & Spalding
Jaworski	Vinson & Elkins

HISTORICAL FINANCIALS
Company Type: Private - Partnership

Income Statement
FYE: December 31

	REVENUE ($ mil.)	NET INCOME ($ mil.)	NET PROFIT MARGIN	EMPLOYEES
12/11	109	45	41.1%	611
12/10	109	46	42.4%	0
12/09	98	36	36.9%	0
12/08	98	36	37.2%	0
Annual Growth	3.9%	7.3%	—	—

2011 Year-End Financials
Debt ratio: ——
Return on equity: 41.10%
Cash ($ mil.): 2
Current ratio: 0.70
Long-term debt ($ mil.): —
Dividends
Yield: —
Payout: —
Market value ($ mil.): —

PHILADELPHIA CORPORATION FOR AGING INC

LOCATIONS

HQ: PHILADELPHIA CORPORATION FOR AGING INC
642 N BROAD ST FL 5, PHILADELPHIA, PA
19130-3424
Phone: 215-765-9000
Web: www.pcaphl.org

HISTORICAL FINANCIALS
Company Type: Private

Income Statement
FYE: June 30

	REVENUE ($ mil.)	NET INCOME ($ mil.)	NET PROFIT MARGIN	EMPLOYEES
06/11	98	0	0.6%	650
06/10	97	(0)	—	0
06/09	96	(4)	—	0
06/08	92	(0)	—	0
Annual Growth	2.2%	—	—	—

2011 Year-End Financials
Debt ratio: ——
Return on equity: 0.60%
Cash ($ mil.): 12
Current ratio: —
Long-term debt ($ mil.): —
Dividends
Yield: —
Payout: —
Market value ($ mil.): —

PHILADELPHIA HEALTH AND EDUCATION CORPORATION

LOCATIONS

HQ: PHILADELPHIA HEALTH AND EDUCATION
CORPORATION
245 N 15TH ST, PHILADELPHIA, PA 19102-1101
Phone: 215-762-8288

HISTORICAL FINANCIALS
Company Type: Private

Income Statement
FYE: June 30

	REVENUE ($ mil.)	NET INCOME ($ mil.)	NET PROFIT MARGIN	EMPLOYEES
06/11	231	(0)	—	1,600
Annual Growth	—	—	—	—

2011 Year-End Financials
Debt ratio: ——
Return on equity: (-0.10)%
Cash ($ mil.): 23
Current ratio: —
Long-term debt ($ mil.): —
Dividends
Yield: —
Payout: —
Market value ($ mil.): —

PHONETIME NETWORKS INC.

LOCATIONS

HQ: PHONETIME NETWORKS INC.
1250 E HALLANDALE BCH, HALLANDALE BEACH,
FL 33009-4634
Phone: 954-455-2749

HISTORICAL FINANCIALS
Company Type: Private

Income Statement
FYE: December 31

	REVENUE ($ mil.)	NET INCOME ($ mil.)	NET PROFIT MARGIN	EMPLOYEES
12/11	120	3	2.8%	1
Annual Growth	—	—	—	—

2011 Year-End Financials
Debt ratio: ——
Return on equity: 2.80%
Cash ($ mil.): 0
Current ratio: 0.70
Long-term debt ($ mil.): —
Dividends
Yield: —
Payout: —
Market value ($ mil.): —

PHYLWAY CONSTRUCTION L.L.C.

LOCATIONS

HQ: PHYLWAY CONSTRUCTION L.L.C.
1074A HIGHWAY 1, THIBODAUX, LA 70301-6192
Phone: 985-446-9644
Web: www.phylway.com

HISTORICAL FINANCIALS
Company Type: Private

Income Statement
FYE: December 31

	REVENUE ($ mil.)	NET INCOME ($ mil.)	NET PROFIT MARGIN	EMPLOYEES
12/11	86	12	14.3%	125
12/08	34	1	3.6%	0
12/07*	26	1	6.4%	0
09/06	1,286	0	0.0%	0
Annual Growth	(59.3%)	4936.5%	—	—

*Fiscal year change

2011 Year-End Financials
Debt ratio: ——
Return on equity: 14.30%
Cash ($ mil.): 16
Current ratio: 1.60
Long-term debt ($ mil.): —
Dividends
Yield: —
Payout: —
Market value ($ mil.): —

PIEDMONT AREA MENTAL HEALTH FOUNDATION INC.

LOCATIONS

HQ: PIEDMONT AREA MENTAL HEALTH FOUNDATION INC.
4855 MILESTONE AVE, KANNAPOLIS, NC 28081-4500
Phone: 704-939-7700

HISTORICAL FINANCIALS

Company Type: Private

Income Statement

	REVENUE ($ mil.)	NET INCOME ($ mil.)	NET PROFIT MARGIN	EMPLOYEES
06/11	162	8	5.0%	625
06/10	156	0	0.5%	0
06/08	146	0	0.1%	0
06/06	3	8	233.6%	0
Annual Growth	250.6%	(2.8%)	—	—

FYE: June 30

2011 Year-End Financials

Debt ratio: ——
Return on equity: 5.00%
Cash ($ mil.): 60
Current ratio: 3.60
Long-term debt ($ mil.): —

Dividends
Yield: —
Payout: —
Market value ($ mil.): —

PIGGLY WIGGLY ALABAMA DISTRIBUTING CO. INC.

LOCATIONS

HQ: PIGGLY WIGGLY ALABAMA DISTRIBUTING CO. INC.
2400 J TERRELL WOOTEN DR, BESSEMER, AL 35020-2272
Phone: 205-481-2300
Web: www.pwadc.com

HISTORICAL FINANCIALS

Company Type: Private

Income Statement

	REVENUE ($ mil.)	NET INCOME ($ mil.)	NET PROFIT MARGIN	EMPLOYEES
07/12	733	0	0.1%	500
07/11	772	0	0.1%	0
07/10	837	0	0.0%	0
07/09	830	0	0.0%	0
Annual Growth	(4.1%)	45.7%	—	—

FYE: July 27

2012 Year-End Financials

Debt ratio: ——
Return on equity: 0.10%
Cash ($ mil.): 6
Current ratio: 0.20
Long-term debt ($ mil.): —

Dividends
Yield: —
Payout: —
Market value ($ mil.): —

PILOT CORPORATION

Pilot offers a salve to those suffering from white-line fever. Its Pilot Flying J a joint venture between Pilot and CVC Capital Partners runs more than 550 truck stops and convenience stores across North America. Its truck stops feature restaurant chains such as Subway Pizza Hut and Taco Bell and offer hot showers. Pilot has fuel islands large enough to service several 18-wheelers. Pilot Truck Care Centers provide TLC (tender loving care) for big rigs while some 45 Pilot Food Marts (all in Tennessee) keep drivers fed. James Haslam II got Pilot off the ground in 1958 as a gas station that sold cigarettes and soft drinks; now his son CEO James Haslam III runs the firm. The Haslam family owns the company.

As a leading supplier of diesel fuel to the trucking industry Pilot Corp. supplies about 10% of the truck diesel fuel used in US.

Travel centers are the company's focus; Pilot has built a nationwide network through organic growth and acquisitions. In 2010 the company acquired the travel center business of rival Flying J and subsequently combined its former Pilot Travel Centers and Flying J as Pilot Flying J. Flying J which was in bankruptcy at the time of the takeover had more than 270 travel centers and fuel stops in some 40 US states and six Canadian provinces. CVC Capital Partners owns about 47% of Pilot Flying J. The private equity firm acquired its stake from Marathon Petroleum.

EXECUTIVES

EVP Direct Sales and Development, Mark A. Hazelwood
Chairman, James A. Haslam II
CEO; President Pilot Travel Centers LLC, James A. (Jimmy) Haslam III, age 58
CFO, Mitch D. Steenrod
Director Merchandising, Tim Purcell
SVP Operations, Ken Parent

LOCATIONS

HQ: Pilot Corporation
5508 Lonas Rd., Knoxville TN 37909
Phone: 865-588-7487   **Fax:** 865-450-2800
Web: www.pilotcorp.com

PRODUCTS/OPERATIONS

Selected Operations

Convenience stores (groceries gas and diesel and assorted merchandise)
Garages (truck repair and maintenance)
Travel centers (groceries showers gas and diesel restaurants and assorted merchandise)

COMPETITORS

7-Eleven	Royal Dutch Shell
Chevron	Starbucks
Couche-Tard	Stuckey's
Exxon Mobil	TravelCenters of

Love's Country Stores	America
Motiva Enterprises	Wawa Inc.

HISTORICAL FINANCIALS

Company Type: Private

Income Statement

	REVENUE ($ mil.)	NET INCOME ($ mil.)	NET PROFIT MARGIN	EMPLOYEES
12/11	402	365	91.0%	445
12/10	415	373	89.9%	0
Annual Growth	(3.2%)	(2.0%)	—	—

FYE: December 31

2011 Year-End Financials

Debt ratio: ——
Return on equity: 91.00%
Cash ($ mil.): 21
Current ratio: 2.50
Long-term debt ($ mil.): —

Dividends
Yield: —
Payout: —
Market value ($ mil.): —

PLACID REFINING COMPANY LLC

A calm presence in the volatile oil and gas industry Placid Refining owns and operates the Port Allen refinery in Louisiana which converts crude oil into a number of petroleum products including diesel ethanol gasoline liquid petroleum gas jet fuel and fuel oils. Placid Refining's refinery has the capacity to process 80000 barrels of crude oil per day. The company is one of the largest employers and taxpayers in West Baton Rouge Parish. Placid Refining which is controlled by Petro-Hunt distribute fuels across a dozen states in the southeastern US from Texas to Virginia and is a major supplier of jet fuel to the US military.

Placid Refining's refinery (purchased in 1975) is strategically located on a 80-plus acre lot near the Mississippi River and about two miles from Interstate Highway 10 and about 10 minutes by car from downtown Baton Rouge.

To meet growing demand the Placid Refining invested $300 million in the late 2000s to expand the Port Allen refinery's throughput capacity from 55000 barrels per day to 80000 barrels per day. As part of this process in 2009 the company completed a 20000 barrels per day fluidized catalytic cracker gasoline hydrotreater.

In 2011 Placid Refining agreed to reduce the nitrogen oxide and sulfur dioxide emissions from its Port Allen refinery and agreed to pay $675000 to the State of Louisiana to settle previous emission violations.

EXECUTIVES

President and CEO, Daniel R. (Dan) Robinson, age 64
VP and Secretary, Ronald D. (Ron) Hurst
Manager Marketing and Distribution, Matt Pfister
Refinery Manager Port Allen, Joey Hagmann
Contracts Administrator and Media Relations, Candace M. Weber
Sales Manager, Joe Hankins
Community Relations, Ron Hancock

LOCATIONS

HQ: PLACID REFINING COMPANY LLC
   1601 ELM ST STE 3400, DALLAS, TX 75201-7201
Phone: 214-880-8479

COMPETITORS

CITGO Refining and Chemicals	United Refining
NuStar Energy	Valero Energy

HISTORICAL FINANCIALS
Company Type: Subsidiary

Income Statement
FYE: December 31

	REVENUE ($ mil.)	NET INCOME ($ mil.)	NET PROFIT MARGIN	EMPLOYEES
12/11	4,699	4	0.1%	200
12/10	3,686	39	1.1%	0
12/06	2,925	128	4.4%	0
12/04	1,429	37	2.6%	0
Annual Growth	48.7%	(52.1%)	—	—

2011 Year-End Financials

Debt ratio: ——
Return on equity: 0.10%
Cash ($ mil.): 58
Current ratio: 0.80
Long-term debt ($ mil.): —

Dividends
  Yield: —
  Payout: —
  Market value ($ mil.): —

PLAINS COTTON COOPERATIVE ASSOCIATION

Plainly speaking most of the US cotton used by textile mills worldwide starts with the Plains Cotton Cooperative Association (PCCA). The farmer-owned co-op markets millions of bales annually for members in Oklahoma Kansas and Texas. To obtain a competitive price for their cotton PCCA takes advantage of Telmark LP's access to The Seam an online cotton marketplace that continually updates cotton prices buyer data and more. Along with marketing PCCA operates a denim mill (American Cotton Growers) an apparel manufacturing plant in Guatemala (DENIMATRIX) and cotton warehouses in Texas Oklahoma and Kansas. Formed in 1953 PCCA's apparel customers include Replay Urban Outfitters and Abercrombie & Fitch.

EXECUTIVES

Corporate Secretary, John Johnson
VP Information Systems, Joe Tubb
VP Administration and Human Resources, Jim Taylor
Personnel Manager, Lee Phenix
VP Finance and Treasurer, Sam Hill
Chairman, Eddie Smith
VP Fabric Sales and Product Development, Jack Mathews
President and CEO, Wallace L. (Wally) Darneille
VP Marketing, Lonnie Winters
Vice Chairman, David Pearson
VP TELMARK, Stan Kirby

VP Grower Services, Dean Church
VP Textile Manufacturing, Bryan Gregory
Domestic Sales Manager, Chris Ford
Director Sales, Grady Martin
Export Sales Manager, Carlos Garcia
Auditors: RobinsonBurdetteMartin&CowanL.L.P.

LOCATIONS

HQ: Plains Cotton Cooperative Association
   3301 E. 50th St., Lubbock TX 79404
Phone: 806-763-8011   **Fax:** 806-762-7400
Web: www.pcca.com

Selected Divisions Offices and Operations
Corporate Headquarters
  Texas —Lubbock
Field Offices
  Kansas —Liberal
  Oklahoma —Altus
  Texas —Corpus Christi Sweetwater and Taylor
Telmark LP
  Texas —Lubbock
Textile Division
  Apparel Manufacturing
    All American All Cotton Jeans Lubbock Texas
    DENIMATRIX Guatemala City Guatemala
  Denim Manufacturing
    American Cotton Growers Littlefield Texas
  Denim Sales/Marketing
    Los Angeles California
    New York New York
    San Francisco California
Warehousing Division
  Oklahoma —Altus Frederick Liberal and Memphis
  Texas Big Spring Lubbock Lovington Rule and Sweetwater

PRODUCTS/OPERATIONS

Selected Sales and Services
Apparel (finished jeans)
Buying cotton
Cotton gins
  Gin bookkeeping
  Gin patronage
  Marketing and invoicing
  Scale ticket software
  Support and training
  Technology solutions
Cotton producers
  Agent gins
  Cash marketing
  marketing contracts
  Pool marketing
  Textile division option
Textiles (denim fabric)
Warehousing

COMPETITORS

Alabama Farmers Cooperative	Jordache Enterprises
American Eagle Outfitters	L.L. Bean
Calcot	Levi Strauss
Calvin Klein	OshKosh B' Gosh
Dunavant Enterprises	Parkdale Mills
Greenwood Mills	Ralph Lauren
Guess?	Staplcotn
International Cotton Marketing	The Gap
J.G. Boswell Co.	Urban Outfitters
	Wal-Mart
	Weil Brothers Cotton
	Wet Seal

HISTORICAL FINANCIALS
Company Type: Private - Cooperative

Income Statement
FYE: June 30

	REVENUE ($ mil.)	NET INCOME ($ mil.)	NET PROFIT MARGIN	EMPLOYEES
06/12	793	8	1.1%	800
06/11	1,835	41	2.2%	0
06/10	1,003	25	2.6%	0
06/09	760	13	1.8%	0
Annual Growth	1.4%	(15.3%)	—	—

2012 Year-End Financials

Debt ratio: ——
Return on equity: 1.10%
Cash ($ mil.): 0
Current ratio: 0.60
Long-term debt ($ mil.): —

Dividends
  Yield: —
  Payout: —
  Market value ($ mil.): —

PLANNED PARENTHOOD FEDERATION OF AMERICA INC.

"He who fails to plan plans to fail" could refer to parenting. No fear the Planned Parenthood Federation Of America provides sexual health information as well as reproductive healthcare through 800 affiliated health centers to more than 5 million people each year. PPFA also lobbies for reproductive rights and reproductive health issues and works to extend access to family planning services for all. The not-for-profit organization is supported by private and corporate donations and patient fees as well as government grants. Founded in 1916 by Margaret Sanger PPFA has grown to 84 affiliates in all 50 US states and the District of Columbia and is part of the International Planned Parenthood Federation.

PPFA's operations consist of: The Planned Parenthood Foundation which is tasked with raising funds and making grants to PPFA affiliates; Planned Parenthood Action Fund an advocate for informed individual choice in reproductive healthcare; and Voxent (formerly known as NGHN) a provider of technology support to some of PPFA's affiliates.

To help spread its mission PPFA pursues affiliate relationships currently counting 84 independent medical and related organizations and 120 outside (referred to as ancillary) entities including four political action committees. PPFA affiliates provide expertise in the fields of medicine advocacy sexual health communications fundraising and law.

Geographically PPFA's offices in New York City and Washington D.C. head up its largely domestic program services created to support affiliates in defending reproductive rights of the women and families in the communities in which they are based. PPFA also operates three international offices which oversee programs advancing reproductive rights abroad.

In fiscal 2011 (ends June) revenues and other support more than doubled over the prior year driven by increases from all significant sources. Major donors foundations and corporations led the growth jumping more than three-fold to generate roughly 60% of all revenues. Contributions and grants from direct response efforts posted a nearly 50% uptick over 2010.

Approximately 75% of the expenses incurred by PPFA are attributable to a number of program services. In the wake of higher revenues total program services increased 23%. Among the programs about half of all expenses are tied to grants and services driven by affiliates in the US. Less than 20% of expenses are associated with the field of family planning including domestic programs for advocacy medical services and education. Outlays for fundraising (which increased by one-third over 2010) and management and general administration represented some 16% and 9% respectively of total expenses in 2011.

PPFA's strategy for growth rests on providing community-based heathcare with a focus on access to reproductive services. To this end it is taking steps to improve the Planned Parenthood outreach to Latino communities. PPFA also supports Green Choices an information initiative to promote a healthier and greener environment. Another key area is the PPFA Board of Advocates a volunteer membership of more than 400 leaders in the arts and entertainment field. Members participate in PPFA events and public service announcements as well as blog posts give their name to fundraising efforts and lobby elected officials.

EXECUTIVES

VP Medical Affairs, Vanessa Cullins
Chief Development Officer, Jon K. Gossett
VP Information Technology, Daniel Rutberg
CEO Planned Parenthood of Nassau County, Karen Pearl
President, Cecile Richards
COO, Doug Jackson
Chief Development Officer, Kim Meredith
Senior Director Public Policy Litigation and Law, Roger Evans
Deputy Director Public Policy Litigation and Law, Eve C. Gartner
Senior Director Government Relations, Chris M. Korsmo
National Chaplain, Rev Ignacio Castuera
Senior Director Clinical Services and Medical Education, Jeff Waldman
CFO, Julia Nelson
CEO Planned Parenthood Washington DC, Laura Meyers
VP Public Policy and Advocacy, Laurie Rubiner
VP Communications, Stuart Schear
President and CEO Planned Parenthood of Illinois, Carole Brite
President Planned Parenthood North Texas, Kenneth S. (Ken) Lambrecht
Chair, Valerie A. McCarthy
Chair, Cecilia Guthrie Boone
Auditors: KPMGLLP

LOCATIONS

HQ: PLANNED PARENTHOOD FEDERATION OF AMERICA INC.
434 W 33RD ST FL 12, NEW YORK, NY 10001-2600
Phone: 212-541-7800
Web: www.plannedparenthood.org

PRODUCTS/OPERATIONS

2011 Revenue

	$ mil.	% of total
Contributions		
Major donors foundation & corporations	126	63
Direct response	35	18
Affiliates	15	8

Bequests	10	5
Federated fund-raising organizations	1	-
Special events net of expenses .1 -		
Other	11	6
Total	**201**	**100**

2011 Expenses

	$ mil.	% of total
Program services		
Grants & service to affiliates - USA	53	51
Service to the field of family planning	18	18
International assistance - family planning	7	7
Supporting services		
Fund-raising	16	15
Management & general	9	9
Total	**104**	**100**

HISTORICAL FINANCIALS
Company Type: Private - Not-for-Profit

Income Statement
FYE: June 30

	REVENUE ($ mil.)	NET INCOME ($ mil.)	NET PROFIT MARGIN	EMPLOYEES
06/11	184	87	47.6%	210
06/10	85	5	6.6%	0
06/09	106	21	20.5%	0
06/08	9	0	9.2%	0
Annual Growth	**172.1%**	**371.4%**	—	—

2011 Year-End Financials

Debt ratio: ——
Return on equity: 47.60%
Cash ($ mil.): 2
Current ratio: ——
Long-term debt ($ mil.): ——

Dividends
  Yield: ——
  Payout: ——
  Market value ($ mil.): ——

PLANNED SYSTEMS INTERNATIONAL INC.

LOCATIONS

HQ: PLANNED SYSTEMS INTERNATIONAL INC.
10632 LITTLE PATUXENT PKW, COLUMBIA, MD 21044-3273
Phone: 410-964-8000
Web: www.plan-sys.com

HISTORICAL FINANCIALS
Company Type: Private

Income Statement
FYE: December 31

	REVENUE ($ mil.)	NET INCOME ($ mil.)	NET PROFIT MARGIN	EMPLOYEES
12/11	105	0	0.6%	375
12/10	102	6	6.5%	0
12/09	92	6	6.5%	0
12/08	77	5	7.3%	0
Annual Growth	**10.8%**	**(51.4%)**	—	—

2011 Year-End Financials

Debt ratio: ——
Return on equity: 0.60%
Cash ($ mil.): 0
Current ratio: 0.90
Long-term debt ($ mil.): ——

Dividends
  Yield: ——
  Payout: ——
  Market value ($ mil.): ——

POCONO MEDICAL CENTER

LOCATIONS

HQ: POCONO MEDICAL CENTER
206 E BROWN ST, EAST STROUDSBURG, PA 18301-3094
Phone: 570-421-4000
Web: www.pmclab.org

HISTORICAL FINANCIALS
Company Type: Private

Income Statement
FYE: June 30

	REVENUE ($ mil.)	NET INCOME ($ mil.)	NET PROFIT MARGIN	EMPLOYEES
06/11	273	26	9.7%	1,057
06/10	248	15	6.3%	0
06/09	209	13	6.4%	0
06/07	190	4	2.2%	0
Annual Growth	**12.8%**	**86.4%**	—	—

2011 Year-End Financials

Debt ratio: ——
Return on equity: 9.70%
Cash ($ mil.): 5
Current ratio: 0.30
Long-term debt ($ mil.): ——

Dividends
  Yield: ——
  Payout: ——
  Market value ($ mil.): ——

POGUE CONSTRUCTION CO. LP

LOCATIONS

HQ: POGUE CONSTRUCTION CO. LP
1512 BRAY CENTRAL DR # 300, MCKINNEY, TX 75069-8264
Phone: 972-529-9401
Web: www.pogueconstruction.com

HISTORICAL FINANCIALS
Company Type: Private

Income Statement
FYE: December 31

	REVENUE ($ mil.)	NET INCOME ($ mil.)	NET PROFIT MARGIN	EMPLOYEES
12/11	225	2	1.1%	110
12/10	0	0	—	0
12/09	346	8	2.3%	0
12/08	387	11	2.9%	0
Annual Growth	**(16.5%)**	**(39.1%)**	—	—

2011 Year-End Financials

Debt ratio: ——
Return on equity: 1.10%
Cash ($ mil.): 14
Current ratio: 0.70
Long-term debt ($ mil.): ——

Dividends
  Yield: ——
  Payout: ——
  Market value ($ mil.): ——

POINT LOMA NAZARENE UNIVERSITY

Point Loma Nazarene University (PLNU) intends to provide a rounded education for Christian students. PLNU offers liberal arts and professional programs in 60 areas of study on its main campus in San Diego and select graduate and professional programs at regional centers in the California towns of Bakersfield Inland Empire (Corona) and Mission Valley (San Diego). Areas of study include art science business administration teaching medicine and ministry. Some 3500 students (undergraduate and graduate) are enrolled at the school which has a 13-to-1 faculty-student ratio. PLNU dates back to 1902 when it was established by Dr. Phineas F. Bresee one of the founders of the Church of the Nazarene.

Financial Analysis

PLNU reported some $92 million in operating revenues in 2011. About 80% of the school's revenues come from tuition and fees while gifts and auxiliary activities bring in the remainder.

Strategy

PLNU's ultimate strategy is to combine education with faith and community to prepare its students for future careers in a rapidly changing world. The school continues to embrace the teachings of the Church of the Nazarene.

As a result of a faltering economy in recent years Point Loma Nazarene University has been working to reduce expenses. For instance in 2011 it announced plans to close its satellite campus in Arcadia and began winding down operations at the location.

EXECUTIVES

President, Bob Brower
VP Financial and Administrative Services, George R. Latter Jr.
Vice Provost Academic Administration, Keith R. Bell
Dean College of Social Sciences and Professional Studies, Rebecca A. Havens
Vice Provost Faculty Development, Hadley Wood
CIO, Robert D. Joslin
Director Physical Plant, Richard Schult
Director Discipleship Ministries, Sylvia L. Cortez
Director Church Relations, Ron Fay
Director Community Ministries, Becky Modesto
Director Athletics, Carroll B. Land
Director Public Safety, Archie Yates
Director Planned Giving, Steve Seelig
Director Alumni Relations, Sheryl Smee
VP External Relations, Joseph E. Watkins III
Provost and Chief Academic Officer, John W. Hawthorne
VP Student Development, Caye Barton Smith

LOCATIONS

HQ: Point Loma Nazarene University
3900 Lomaland Dr., San Diego CA 92106-2810
Phone: 619-849-2200　　**Fax:** 619-849-2579
Web: www.pointloma.edu

PRODUCTS/OPERATIONS

2011 Revenues

	$ mil.	% of total
Tuition & fees	73	80
Unrestricted & church gifts	2	2
Auxiliaries & other	16	18
Total	92	100

Selected Degrees Offered

Graduate
　Educational Specialist
　Master of Science and Master of Arts in biology
　Master of Business Administration (MBA)
　Master of Arts in education
　Master of Science in Nursing
　Master of Ministry
　Master of Arts in Teaching
　Teaching professional service and administrative credentials
Undergraduate
　Accounting
　Art & Design
　Art History
　Athletic training
　Biblical studies
　Biology
　Business Administration
　Chemistry
　Child Development
　Computer Science
　Economics
　Engineering
　Fashion
　Finance
　Graphic Design
　History
　Information systems
　Journalism
　Literature
　Management
　Marketing
　Mathematics
　Media and Film
　Music
　Nursing
　Philosophy
　Physicial Education
　Physics
　Political Science
　Pre-Dental
　Pre-Law
　Pre-Medicine
　Psychology
　Speech
　Theology
　Women's Studies
　Writing
　Youth Ministry

HISTORICAL FINANCIALS

Company Type: School

Income Statement

FYE: June 30

	REVENUE ($ mil.)	NET INCOME ($ mil.)	NET PROFIT MARGIN	EMPLOYEES
06/12	83	0	0.3%	688
06/11	83	8	10.1%	0
06/10	79	4	6.1%	0
06/09	64	(14)	—	0
Annual Growth	9.0%	—	—	—

2012 Year-End Financials

Debt ratio: ——
Return on equity: 0.30%
Cash ($ mil.): 13
Current ratio: —
Long-term debt ($ mil.): —

Dividends
　Yield: —
　Payout: —
　Market value ($ mil.): —

POINT PARK UNIVERSITY

LOCATIONS

HQ: POINT PARK UNIVERSITY
201 WOOD ST, PITTSBURGH, PA 15222-1912
Phone: 412-391-4100
Web: www.pointpark.edu

HISTORICAL FINANCIALS

Company Type: Private

Income Statement

FYE: August 31

	REVENUE ($ mil.)	NET INCOME ($ mil.)	NET PROFIT MARGIN	EMPLOYEES
08/11	99	8	8.4%	252
08/10	88	3	4.0%	0
08/09	82	0	—	0
08/08	73	4	6.0%	0
Annual Growth	10.8%	24.0%	—	—

2011 Year-End Financials

Debt ratio: ——
Return on equity: 8.40%
Cash ($ mil.): 18
Current ratio: —
Long-term debt ($ mil.): —

Dividends
　Yield: —
　Payout: —
　Market value ($ mil.): —

POLARIS SOFTWARE LAB LIMITED

LOCATIONS

HQ: POLARIS SOFTWARE LAB LIMITED
517 US HIGHWAY 1 S # 2103, ISELIN, NJ 08830-3011
Phone: 732-404-1199

2007 Sales

	$ mil.	% of total
% of total		
North		35
Europe Middle East		35
Asia		30
Total		100

PRODUCTS/OPERATIONS

2007 Sales

	$ mil.	% of total
% of total		
Software		93
Business Process		5
Other		2
Total		100

Selected Products

Intellect Cards
Intellect Front Office
Intellect Universal Banking
Intellect Consumer Finance
Intellect Cash & Liquidity
Intellect Risk & Treasury
Intellect Portals
Intellect Wealth Management

Intellect Securities Services

HISTORICAL FINANCIALS
Company Type: Private

Income Statement
FYE: March 31

	REVENUE ($ mil.)	NET INCOME ($ mil.)	NET PROFIT MARGIN	EMPLOYEES
03/12	82	1	1.9%	300
03/11	79	1	2.1%	0
Annual Growth	4.0%	(4.7%)	—	—

2012 Year-End Financials
Debt ratio: ——
Return on equity: 1.90%
Cash ($ mil.): 6
Current ratio: 1.80
Long-term debt ($ mil.): —

Dividends
Yield: —
Payout: —
Market value ($ mil.): —

POLYTECHNIC INSTITUTE OF NEW YORK UNIVERSITY

LOCATIONS
HQ: POLYTECHNIC INSTITUTE OF NEW YORK UNIVERSITY
6 METROTECH CTR, BROOKLYN, NY 11201-3840
Phone: 718-260-3600
Web: www.long-islandlocksmiths.com

HISTORICAL FINANCIALS
Company Type: Private

Income Statement
FYE: June 30

	REVENUE ($ mil.)	NET INCOME ($ mil.)	NET PROFIT MARGIN	EMPLOYEES
06/11	175	(2)	—	552
06/10	145	(9)	—	0
06/09	88	(36)	—	0
06/08	84	(25)	—	0
Annual Growth	27.8%	—	—	—

2011 Year-End Financials
Debt ratio: ——
Return on equity: (-1.60)%
Cash ($ mil.): 0
Current ratio: —
Long-term debt ($ mil.): —

Dividends
Yield: —
Payout: —
Market value ($ mil.): —

POMONA COLLEGE

Looking to get an education in sunny California? You might want to consider Pomona College. The school offers about 50 academic programs in areas such as art humanities biology psychology computer science and English. The liberal arts college enrolls about 1600 students and has a student to teacher ratio of 8:1. Pomona College was founded in 1887. It is the founding member of The Claremont Colleges an affiliated group of seven independent colleges located on adjoining campuses in Claremont California. The affiliated campuses are coordinated by one of the member institutions the Claremont University Consortium.

Financial Analysis
Pomona College reported revenues of some $156 million in 2011. The college's revenues come from investment income (returns from pooled investments) student tuition grants and contracts (from government and private entities) and charitable contributions. The college has some $2.4 billion in assets including endowment funds.

EXECUTIVES
Senior Director Communications, Mark G. Wood
Director Alumni Relations, Nancy Treser-Osgood
Director Career Development, Carl Martellino
President, David W. Oxtoby
President Pacific Basin Institute, Dru C. Gladney
Registrar, Margaret Adorno
Executive Director Information Technology Services, Kenneth E. Pflueger
VP and Dean Students, Miriam Feldblum
Assistant VP and Director Human Resources, Brenda Rushforth
VP Institutional Advancement, Christopher Ponce
VP and Dean Admissions, Bruce J. Poch
Director Campus Safety, Lena M. Robinson
Director Financial Aid, Patricia A. Coye

LOCATIONS
HQ: Pomona College
333 N. College Way, Claremont CA 91711
Phone: 909-621-8000 **Fax:** 909-621-8203
Web: www.pomona.edu

PRODUCTS/OPERATIONS

2011 Revenues

	$ mil.	% of total
Realized gains on investments	64	41
Student revenues	51	33
Private gifts & grants	36	23
Federal grants & contracts	2	1
Private contracts	1	1
Sales services & other	1	1
Total	**156**	**100**

HISTORICAL FINANCIALS
Company Type: School

Income Statement
FYE: June 30

	REVENUE ($ mil.)	NET INCOME ($ mil.)	NET PROFIT MARGIN	EMPLOYEES
06/11	156	282	180.3%	500
06/10	152	134	87.8%	0
06/09	152	(464)	—	0
06/08	134	39	29.7%	0
Annual Growth	5.1%	91.8%	—	—

2011 Year-End Financials
Debt ratio: ——
Return on equity: 180.30%
Cash ($ mil.): 3
Current ratio: —
Long-term debt ($ mil.): —

Dividends
Yield: —
Payout: —
Market value ($ mil.): —

POMONA VALLEY HOSPITAL MEDICAL CENTER

LOCATIONS
HQ: POMONA VALLEY HOSPITAL MEDICAL CENTER
1798 N GAREY AVE, POMONA, CA 91767-2918
Phone: 909-865-9500
Web: www.pvhmcresidency.com

HISTORICAL FINANCIALS
Company Type: Private

Income Statement
FYE: September 30

	REVENUE ($ mil.)	NET INCOME ($ mil.)	NET PROFIT MARGIN	EMPLOYEES
09/12*	364	25	7.1%	2,209
12/11	425	18	4.2%	0
12/10	482	24	5.1%	0
12/09	432	10	2.3%	0
Annual Growth	(5.6%)	36.5%	—	—

*Fiscal year change

2012 Year-End Financials
Debt ratio: ——
Return on equity: 7.10%
Cash ($ mil.): 10
Current ratio: 1.70
Long-term debt ($ mil.): —

Dividends
Yield: —
Payout: —
Market value ($ mil.): —

PORT HURON AREA SCHOOL DISTRICT

LOCATIONS
HQ: PORT HURON AREA SCHOOL DISTRICT
1925 LAPEER AVE, PORT HURON, MI 48060-4153
Phone: 810-984-3101
Web: www.port-huron.k12.mi.us

HISTORICAL FINANCIALS
Company Type: Private

Income Statement
FYE: June 30

	REVENUE ($ mil.)	NET INCOME ($ mil.)	NET PROFIT MARGIN	EMPLOYEES
06/12	95	(8)	—	1,000
06/11	104	21	20.5%	0
06/10	104	(4)	—	0
06/09	105	(4)	—	0
Annual Growth	(3.4%)	—	—	—

2012 Year-End Financials
Debt ratio: ——
Return on equity: (-9.00)%
Cash ($ mil.): 16
Current ratio: —
Long-term debt ($ mil.): —

Dividends
Yield: —
Payout: —
Market value ($ mil.): —

PORTLAND COMMUNITY COLLEGE

LOCATIONS

HQ: PORTLAND COMMUNITY COLLEGE
12000 SW 49TH AVE, PORTLAND, OR 97219-7198
Phone: 503-244-6111
Web: www.rockcreek185.com

HISTORICAL FINANCIALS

Company Type: Private

Income Statement   FYE: June 30

	REVENUE ($ mil.)	NET INCOME ($ mil.)	NET PROFIT MARGIN	EMPLOYEES
06/11	102	25	25.0%	3,000
06/10	99	74	75.0%	0
06/09	85	(40)	—	0
06/08	86	41	48.0%	0
Annual Growth	5.6%	(15.1%)		

2011 Year-End Financials

Debt ratio: ——
Return on equity: 25.00%
Cash ($ mil.): 70
Current ratio: 1.30
Long-term debt ($ mil.): —

Dividends
Yield: —
Payout: —
Market value ($ mil.): —

POTANDON PRODUCE L.L.C.

LOCATIONS

HQ: POTANDON PRODUCE L.L.C.
1210 PIER VIEW DR, IDAHO FALLS, ID 83402-4966
Phone: 208-524-1900
Web: www.potandon.com

HISTORICAL FINANCIALS

Company Type: Private

Income Statement   FYE: December 31

	REVENUE ($ mil.)	NET INCOME ($ mil.)	NET PROFIT MARGIN	EMPLOYEES
12/11	433	5	1.3%	100
12/10	350	4	1.3%	0
12/09	333	4	1.3%	0
Annual Growth	14.1%	12.7%	—	—

2011 Year-End Financials

Debt ratio: ——
Return on equity: 1.30%
Cash ($ mil.): 0
Current ratio: 0.80
Long-term debt ($ mil.): —

Dividends
Yield: —
Payout: —
Market value ($ mil.): —

POUDRE SCHOOL DISTRICT R-1

LOCATIONS

HQ: POUDRE SCHOOL DISTRICT R-1
2407 LA PORTE AVE, FORT COLLINS, CO 80521
Phone: 970-482-7420
Web: www.psdschools.org

HISTORICAL FINANCIALS

Company Type: Private

Income Statement   FYE: June 30

	REVENUE ($ mil.)	NET INCOME ($ mil.)	NET PROFIT MARGIN	EMPLOYEES
06/11	261	66	25.3%	907
06/10	256	5	2.1%	0
06/09	243	(7)	—	0
06/08	237	(11)	—	0
Annual Growth	3.3%	—	—	—

2011 Year-End Financials

Debt ratio: ——
Return on equity: 25.30%
Cash ($ mil.): 194
Current ratio: —
Long-term debt ($ mil.): —

Dividends
Yield: —
Payout: —
Market value ($ mil.): —

POWER DESIGN INC.

LOCATIONS

HQ: POWER DESIGN INC.
11600 DR M L KING JR ST N MARTIN, SAINT PETERSBURG, FL 33716
Phone: 727-210-0492
Web: www.powerdesigninc.us

HISTORICAL FINANCIALS

Company Type: Private

Income Statement   FYE: December 31

	REVENUE ($ mil.)	NET INCOME ($ mil.)	NET PROFIT MARGIN	EMPLOYEES
12/11	91	(10)	—	500
12/10	91	(10)	—	0
12/09	129	8	6.3%	0
12/08	205	9	4.6%	0
Annual Growth	(23.5%)	—	—	—

2011 Year-End Financials

Debt ratio: ——
Return on equity: (-10.90)%
Cash ($ mil.): 1
Current ratio: 0.10
Long-term debt ($ mil.): —

Dividends
Yield: —
Payout: —
Market value ($ mil.): —

POWER SOLUTIONS LLC

LOCATIONS

HQ: POWER SOLUTIONS LLC
17201 MELFO BLVD STE A-K, BOWIE, MD 20715
Phone: 301-794-0330
Web: www.powersolutions-llc.com

HISTORICAL FINANCIALS

Company Type: Private

Income Statement   FYE: December 31

	REVENUE ($ mil.)	NET INCOME ($ mil.)	NET PROFIT MARGIN	EMPLOYEES
12/11	152	27	17.7%	350
12/10	117	16	14.5%	0
12/09	66	8	12.4%	0
12/08	87	15	17.6%	0
Annual Growth	20.5%	20.8%	—	—

2011 Year-End Financials

Debt ratio: ——
Return on equity: 17.70%
Cash ($ mil.): 4
Current ratio: 0.20
Long-term debt ($ mil.): —

Dividends
Yield: —
Payout: —
Market value ($ mil.): —

POWERSOUTH ENERGY COOPERATIVE

Alabamans and Floridians come together in PowerSouth Energy Cooperative which provides wholesale power services to its member-owners (16 electric cooperatives and four municipal distribution utilities). Its distribution members provide electric services to almost 417200 customer meters in central and southern Alabama (39 counties) and western Florida (10 counties). PowerSouth Energy Cooperative operates a more than 2200-mile power transmission system and has more than 2100 MW of generating capacity from interests in six fossil-fueled and hydroelectric power plants. The company also provided propane but sold its Cooperative Propane unit in 2011 to focus on its core power businesses.

To meet future demand and tightening environmental regulations the company is looking to diversify and expand its power production assets with an emphasis on cleaner energy plants. In 2009 PowerSouth's long-term energy plans included a 20-year contract for 125 MW of nuclear power from two Vogtle Units being built by the Municipal Energy Authority of Georgia near Augusta and due to come onstream in 2016 and 2017. The purchase iwas PowerSouth's first foray into nuclear power. The company is also investing in windpower and biomass-to-energy initiatives.

The global recession lower commodity prices and weaker demand saw the company's revenues drop in 2009. However the downturn had an upside. The lower cost of and need for purchased power (wholesale acquisitions from outside generators) helped PowerSouth save on costs allowing it to post an improved operating margin.

Extreme summer heat forced up power demand across the company's service area and lifted its revenues in 2010. The increase in revenues outstripped expenses resulting in an improved net income that year.

Founded in 1941 as Alabama Electric Cooperative the coop promotes a strong economic development program aimed at bringing industry into both Alabama and Florida.

In 2008 Alabama Electric Cooperative changed its name to PowerSouth Energy Cooperative to better reflect its service territory (Alabama and Florida) and its opportunities for future growth.

EXECUTIVES

President and CEO, Gary L. Smith
VP External Affairs, Horace Horn
VP and CFO, Ferrell Walton
VP Power Delivery, Larry Avery
VP Power Production, Damon Morgan
VP Legal Affairs Corporate Affairs and Human Resources, Beth Woodard
Director Economic Development, Seth Hammett
Director Financial Operations, Rick Kyle
Manager Corporate Communications, Mark Ingram
Auditors: Deloitte&ToucheLLP

LOCATIONS

HQ: PowerSouth Energy Cooperative
2027 E. Three Notch St., Andalusia AL 36421
Phone: 334-427-3000   **Fax:** 334-427-3747
Web: www.powersouth.com

PRODUCTS/OPERATIONS

2010 Sales

	$ mil.	% of total
% of total		
Electric		
Cooperatives		91
Municipalities		6
Nonmenbers		1
Other		-
Propane &		2
Total		**100**

HISTORICAL FINANCIALS

Company Type: Private - Cooperative

Income Statement

FYE: December 31

	REVENUE ($ mil.)	NET INCOME ($ mil.)	NET PROFIT MARGIN	EMPLOYEES
12/11	640	28	4.4%	600
12/10	673	26	3.9%	0
12/09	649	23	3.6%	0
12/08	750	28	3.8%	0
Annual Growth	**(5.2%)**	**(0.1%)**	**—**	**—**

2011 Year-End Financials

Debt ratio: ——
Return on equity: 4.40%
Cash ($ mil.): 35
Current ratio: 0.50
Long-term debt ($ mil.): —
Dividends
Yield: —
Payout: —
Market value ($ mil.): —

PRAIRIE FARMS DAIRY INC.

Prairie Farms Dairy is very cooperative. With some 700 dairy farmer/members the cooperative offers a full line of retail and food service dairy products. It turns raw milk into fresh fluid cultured and frozen dairy products under the Prairie Farms label. It also makes juices and ice cream novelties. The company's customers include food drug and convenience stores mass merchandisers schools restaurants and other food service operators. Located in Carlinville Illinois it is the managing partner for joint ventures with smaller regional dairies. It makes its products at 24 Prairie Farms-owned plants and 13 joint-venture plants which are located throughout the midwestern and southern areas of the US.

Geographic Reach

Prairie Farms and its subsidiaries manufacture dairy products at 24 co-op-owned plants as 13 joint venture plants in Arkansas Illinois Indiana Iowa Kansas Kentucky Michigan Mississippi Missouri Nebraska Oklahoma Ohio and Tennessee.

Operations

To get its dairy products to market the co-op relies on subsidiaries Hawthorne-Mellody Distributors in Chicago and Tom David & Sons in Detroit.

In addition to manufacturing diary foods co-packing is a big part of Prairie Farms' operation. Approximately 50% of the co-operative's sales come from packing non-Prairie Farm brands. The co-op's PFD Supply and GMS Transportation non-dairy subsidiaries distribute products for fast-food chains including McDonald's Dairy Queen and Church's Chicken.

Company Background

The cooperative dates back to 1932 when Illinois farmers formed a statewide organization Illinois Producers Creameries to market and sell cream. In 1938 it became Prairie Farms Dairy.

EXECUTIVES

VP Procurement, Gary Lee
VP Engineering, David Lattan
Chairman, Fred Kuenstler
VP Finance Personnel and Payroll, Tom Weber
COO and President Joint Ventures, Gary L. Aggus
CEO and EVP, Ed Mullins
Director Information Services, Mark Harris
Fleet Manager, Jay Naples
VP Insurance and Risk, Mark Hopping

LOCATIONS

HQ: Prairie Farms Dairy Inc.
1100 N. Broadway St., Carlinville IL 62626
Phone: 217-854-2547   **Fax:** 217-854-6426
Web: www.prairiefarmsdairy.com

Selected Areas of Distribution

Arkansas
Illinois
Indiana
Iowa
Kansas
Kentucky
Michigan
Mississippi
Missouri
Nebraska
Ohio
Oklahoma
Tennessee

PRODUCTS/OPERATIONS

Branded Partners
Belfonte Ice Cream & Dairy Foods Company
Coleman Dairy
Hiland Dairy Foods Company
Hiland-Roberts Ice Cream Company
Ice Cream Specialtie
LuVel Dairy Products
Madison Farms Butter
Muller-Pinehurst Dairy
Roberts Dairy Company
Southern Belle Dairy
Swiss Valley Farms
Turner Dairy

Selected Products

Butter
Cultured dairy products
 Cottage cheese (regular low fat and fat-free; small and large curd)
 Dips
 Sour cream
 Yogurt (regular low fat and fat-free)
Fluid milk products
 Buttermilk
 Cream
 Egg nog (seasonal)
 Milk (regular low fat and fat-free)
 Flavored milk
Frozen desserts
 Frozen yogurt
 Ice cream (regular low fat and fat-free)
 Novelties
 Sherbet
Juices drinks and iced tea

COMPETITORS

Associated Milk Producers	Foremost Farms
Dairy Farmers of America	Friendly Ice Cream
Darigold Inc.	HP Hood
Dean Foods	Land O' Lakes
Dreyer's	Quality Chekd
Farmland Dairies	Rockview Dairies
	Wells' Dairy

HISTORICAL FINANCIALS

Company Type: Private - Cooperative

Income Statement

FYE: September 30

	REVENUE ($ mil.)	NET INCOME ($ mil.)	NET PROFIT MARGIN	EMPLOYEES
09/11	1,607	28	1.7%	1,965
09/10	1,504	38	2.5%	0
09/04	1,183	45	3.8%	0
09/02	1,058	54	5.1%	0
Annual Growth	**14.9%**	**(19.6%)**	**—**	**—**

2011 Year-End Financials

Debt ratio: ——
Return on equity: 1.70%
Cash ($ mil.): 22
Current ratio: 0.10
Long-term debt ($ mil.): —
Dividends
Yield: —
Payout: —
Market value ($ mil.): —

PRAIRIE HORIZON AGRI-ENERGY LLC

LOCATIONS

HQ: PRAIRIE HORIZON AGRI-ENERGY LLC
1664 E 100 RD, PHILLIPSBURG, KS 67661-8757
Phone: 785-543-6719
Web: www.prairiehorizon.com

HISTORICAL FINANCIALS
Company Type: Private

Income Statement

	REVENUE ($ mil.)	NET INCOME ($ mil.)	NET PROFIT MARGIN	EMPLOYEES
12/11	137	11	8.3%	31
12/09	79	9	12.2%	0
Annual Growth	72.5%	17.2%	—	—

2011 Year-End Financials
Debt ratio: ——
Return on equity: 8.30%
Cash ($ mil.): 11
Current ratio: 2.00
Long-term debt ($ mil.): —

Dividends
 Yield: —
 Payout: —
 Market value ($ mil.): —

FYE: December 31

PRAIRIE POWER INC.

LOCATIONS

HQ: PRAIRIE POWER INC.
2103 S MAIN ST, JACKSONVILLE, IL 62650
Phone: 217-245-6161
Web: www.ppi.coop

HISTORICAL FINANCIALS
Company Type: Private

Income Statement

	REVENUE ($ mil.)	NET INCOME ($ mil.)	NET PROFIT MARGIN	EMPLOYEES
12/11	118	4	3.8%	45
12/10	120	5	4.5%	0
12/09	110	3	3.3%	0
12/08	76	0	—	0
Annual Growth	15.6%	—	—	—

FYE: December 31

2011 Year-End Financials
Debt ratio: ——
Return on equity: 3.80%
Cash ($ mil.): 1
Current ratio: 0.10
Long-term debt ($ mil.): —

Dividends
 Yield: —
 Payout: —
 Market value ($ mil.): —

PRATT INSTITUTE

LOCATIONS

HQ: PRATT INSTITUTE
200 WILLOUGHBY AVE, BROOKLYN, NY 11205-3899
Phone: 718-636-3600
Web: www.prattstore.net

HISTORICAL FINANCIALS
Company Type: Private

Income Statement

	REVENUE ($ mil.)	NET INCOME ($ mil.)	NET PROFIT MARGIN	EMPLOYEES
06/11	188	15	8.1%	900
06/10	175	12	7.0%	0
06/09	156	1	1.2%	0
06/08	159	7	4.6%	0
Annual Growth	5.8%	28.2%	—	—

FYE: June 30

2011 Year-End Financials
Debt ratio: ——
Return on equity: 8.10%
Cash ($ mil.): 83
Current ratio: ——
Long-term debt ($ mil.): —

Dividends
 Yield: —
 Payout: —
 Market value ($ mil.): —

PREMIER AG CO-OP INC.

Premier AG Co-Op provides the agricultural communities in Bartholomew Decatur and Johnson counties of south-central Indiana with farming supplies services and marketing assistance. It operates four grain elevators that handle corn soybeans and wheat. The co-op operates Country-Mark gas stations as well as one Countrymart store in Greensburg Indiana. The store sells seed fertilizer and chemical treatments lawn and garden products hardware apparel pet food and supplies animal feed and plants (in season). Premier also owns Premier Energy and Heyob Energy suppliers of propane and home heating oil.

EXECUTIVES

General Manager, Harold Cooper
Grain Merchandiser, Gary Fischer
Crops Manager, Mark Canary
Manager Franklin Crops, Burk Admire
Manager St. Paul Crops and Greenberg Crops, Mike Schwering
Manager Trafalgar Crops, Mike Sisson
Grain Administrator, Jane Smith

LOCATIONS

HQ: PREMIER AG CO-OP INC.
785 S MARR RD, COLUMBUS, IN 47201-7490
Phone: 812-379-9501
Web: www.premierag.com

COMPETITORS

ADM	Farmers Cooperative
AGRI Industries	Society
Andersons	Heartland Co-op
Cargill	Orscheln Farm and Home
CHS	West Central Co-op

Farmers Cooperative
 Company

HISTORICAL FINANCIALS
Company Type: Private - Cooperative

Income Statement

	REVENUE ($ mil.)	NET INCOME ($ mil.)	NET PROFIT MARGIN	EMPLOYEES
07/12	159	3	2.2%	100
07/11	142	2	1.8%	0
07/10	122	2	1.8%	0
07/09	131	2	1.6%	0
Annual Growth	6.7%	19.4%	—	—

FYE: July 31

2012 Year-End Financials
Debt ratio: ——
Return on equity: 2.20%
Cash ($ mil.): 0
Current ratio: 1.40
Long-term debt ($ mil.): —

Dividends
 Yield: —
 Payout: —
 Market value ($ mil.): —

PRESBYTERIAN HOMES AND SERVICES

LOCATIONS

HQ: PRESBYTERIAN HOMES AND SERVICES
2845 HAMLINE AVE N # 200, SAINT PAUL, MN 55113-7127
Phone: 651-631-6100
Web: www.preshomes.org

HISTORICAL FINANCIALS
Company Type: Private

Income Statement

	REVENUE ($ mil.)	NET INCOME ($ mil.)	NET PROFIT MARGIN	EMPLOYEES
09/11	268	18	6.8%	4,750
09/09	7	(0)	—	0
09/08	5	1	25.7%	0
09/07	8	4	52.0%	0
Annual Growth	213.8%	59.6%	—	—

FYE: September 30

2011 Year-End Financials
Debt ratio: ——
Return on equity: 6.80%
Cash ($ mil.): 41
Current ratio: 1.20
Long-term debt ($ mil.): —

Dividends
 Yield: —
 Payout: —
 Market value ($ mil.): —

PRESBYTERIAN RETIREMENT COMMUNITIES INC.

LOCATIONS

HQ: PRESBYTERIAN RETIREMENT COMMUNITIES INC.
80 W LUCERNE CIR, ORLANDO, FL 32801-3779
Phone: 407-839-5050

HISTORICAL FINANCIALS

Company Type: Private

Income Statement

	REVENUE ($ mil.)	NET INCOME ($ mil.)	NET PROFIT MARGIN	EMPLOYEES
03/11	99	3	3.9%	1,700
03/10	106	16	15.4%	0
03/09	78	0	—	0
03/03	62	0	—	0
Annual Growth	16.5%	—	—	—

FYE: March 31

2011 Year-End Financials

Debt ratio: ——
Return on equity: 3.90%
Cash ($ mil.): 24
Current ratio: 0.10
Long-term debt ($ mil.): —

Dividends
Yield: —
Payout: —
Market value ($ mil.): —

PRESCRIPTION SUPPLY INC.

LOCATIONS

HQ: PRESCRIPTION SUPPLY INC.
2233 TRACY RD, NORTHWOOD, OH 43619-1302
Phone: 419-661-6600
Web: www.prescriptionsupply.com

HISTORICAL FINANCIALS

Company Type: Private

Income Statement

	REVENUE ($ mil.)	NET INCOME ($ mil.)	NET PROFIT MARGIN	EMPLOYEES
08/11	84	(1)	—	54
08/10	112	0	0.5%	0
08/09	116	0	0.5%	0
08/08	104	0	0.1%	0
Annual Growth	(6.9%)	—	—	—

FYE: August 31

2011 Year-End Financials

Debt ratio: ——
Return on equity: (-1.90)%
Cash ($ mil.): 0
Current ratio: 0.90
Long-term debt ($ mil.): —

Dividends
Yield: —
Payout: —
Market value ($ mil.): —

PRESIDENT & TRUSTEES OF WILLIAMS COLLEGE

Liberals need apply. Liberal arts majors that is! Williams College is a private liberal arts school with an enrollment of more than 2000 students at its main campus in the Berkshires of northwestern Massachusetts. It also offers programs in England (Williams-Exeter Programme at Oxford) Connecticut (Williams-Mystic Program) and Williams in New York. The majority of its students come from New York followed by Massachusetts and California. Williams College offers more than 30 undergraduate majors in three academic divisions: humanities sciences and social sciences. Founded in 1793 by Colonel Ephraim Williams the school also confers master's degrees in the history of art and in policy economics.

Founded in 1793 by Colonel Ephraim Williams the college is supported by an endowment of more than $1.8 billion. It is in the midst of a building boom having spent $50 million on a theater and dance center (opened in 2005) and $44 million on a new student center (opened in 2007). A renovation and construction project that includes two new classroom and office buildings and a library is scheduled to be completed in 2011.

EXECUTIVES

VP Operations, Stephen P. Klass
Interim President, William G. (Bill) Wagner
Director Communications for Alumni Relations and Development, Robert H. White
Controller, Susan S. Hogan
CTO, Dinny S. Taylor
Director Financial Aid, Paul J. Boyer
Director Admission, Richard L. Nesbitt
Director Career Counseling, John H. Noble
College Librarian, David M. Pilachowski
Registrar and Associate Dean, Charles R. Toomajian
VP Strategic Planning and Institutional Diversity, Michael E. Reed
Provost and Treasurer, William J. Lenhart
Director Alumni Relations, Brooks Foehl
Chief Investment Officer, Collette Chilton
Associate VP Facilities, D. Prideaux-Brune

LOCATIONS

HQ: Williams College
33 Stetson Ct., Williamstown MA 01267
Phone: 413-597-3131   **Fax:** 413-597-4192
Web: www.williams.edu

HISTORICAL FINANCIALS

Company Type: School

Income Statement

	REVENUE ($ mil.)	NET INCOME ($ mil.)	NET PROFIT MARGIN	EMPLOYEES
06/12	156	(16)	—	950
06/11	149	245	163.6%	0
06/10	146	92	62.9%	0
06/09	187	(419)	—	0
Annual Growth	(5.8%)	—	—	—

FYE: June 30

2012 Year-End Financials

Debt ratio: ——
Return on equity: (-10.30)%
Cash ($ mil.): 13
Current ratio: —
Long-term debt ($ mil.): —

Dividends
Yield: —
Payout: —
Market value ($ mil.): —

PRESIDENT AND FELLOWS OF MIDDLEBURY COLLEGE

President and Fellows of Middlebury College operates Middlebury College a private liberal arts school in Vermont that offers courses of study in the arts humanities literature foreign languages social sciences and natural sciences. About 2450 undergraduates are enrolled at Middlebury College. Founded in 1800 it is home to the Bread Loaf School of English known for its summer graduate courses in literature as well as instruction in writing creative writing and theatre. Bread Loaf is located in the Green Mountains a dozen miles east of Middlebury. Every summer Middlebury College also opens the Language Schools from which the college provides instruction in 10 languages to more than 2000 students.

Geographic Reach

The Vermont liberal arts college boasts a global footprint with schools located in China Egypt France Germany Israel Italy Japan Jordan Russia Spain Brazil Argentina Uruguay Chile and Mexico. Its summer programs are taught in Vermont New Mexico North Carolina and the UK.

Operations

Middlebury College offers its 2450 undergraduates more than 850 courses across some 45 majors. Its student-faculty ratio is 9:1. Nearly an equal number of students attend Middlebury College during the summer to take advantage of its foreign language courses in French German Italian Russian and Spanish offered at both the undergraduate and graduate levels. Undergraduate students also have access to Arabic Chinese Japanese Portuguese and Hebrew there.

For more than 40 years iconic author Robert Frost spent his summers at the Bread Loaf School of English. Outside Vermont Bread Loaf maintains satellite summer sessions in the US in New Mexico and North Carolina as well as in the UK at the University of Oxford.

Strategy

Middlebury College has earned a global presence through its alliances with other universities. Through a partnership established in 2011 with Brandeis University Middlebury College offers the only study-abroad program in Israel designed to be experienced in Hebrew. Based in the city of Beer Sheva the program is affiliated with Ben-Gurion University of the Negev and began offering classes in spring 2012.

The college entered South Asia in 2012 through its existing C.V. Starr-Middlebury School Abroad program. The program will begin offering classes in fall 2013 at the University of Delhi's St. Stephen's College or its Lady Shri Ram College for Women. Previously Middlebury College established a program at the University of Jordan that began offering classes in fall 2011.

Financial Performance

Thanks to an increase in operating revenues and other support and sponsored activities Middlebury College logged a 1% increase in 2012 revenue as compared to 2011. Net income however decreased some 119% during the same reporting period. The institution points to rising operating expenses due to increases in total educational and general expenses as well as auxiliary enterprises. Decreases in non-operating activities in 2012 vs.

2011 also contributed to the net income dip primarily due to endowment return declines net of distribution. Increases in cash used for operating activities caused cash flow during the reporting period to decrease some $2.3 million. This was partially offset by decreases in realized and unrealized gains on investments.

Sales and Marketing

The college sources its 2450 student population from across the US and from 70 countries. Some 70% of Middlebury College's students originate from outside the New England area. Additionally more than half of its students spend one semester or more off-campus typically outside the US.

EXECUTIVES

President, Ronald D. Liebowitz
VP Finance and Treasurer, Patrick J. Norton
Associate VP Human Resources and Organizational Development, Drew Macan
EVP and Treasurer, F. Robert Huth Jr.
Provost and EVP, Alison Byerly
VP College Advancement, James R. Keyes
Dean of Faculty, James (Maggie) Ralph
SVP and Chief Philanthropic Advisor, Michael D. Schoenfeld
Dean of Admissions, Gregory B. Buckles
VP Administration, Timothy Spears
Athletics Director, Erin Quinn

LOCATIONS

HQ: President and Fellows of Middlebury College
Middlebury College, Middlebury VT 05753
Phone: 802-443-5000   **Fax:** 802-443-2056
Web: www.middlebury.edu

Selected Locations
Center for the Comparative Study of Race and Ethnicity
Chellis House
Middlebury College Snow Bowl
Ralph Myhre Golf Course
Rikert Nordic Center
Rohatyn Center for International Affairs
Scott Center for Spiritual & Religious Life

HISTORICAL FINANCIALS
Company Type: School

Income Statement

	REVENUE ($ mil.)	NET INCOME ($ mil.)	NET PROFIT MARGIN	EMPLOYEES
06/12	233	(24)	—	1,000
06/08	278	50	18.3%	0
06/06	181	79	43.9%	0
06/05	0	0		0
Annual Growth	—	—	—	—

2012 Year-End Financials

Debt ratio: ——
Return on equity: (-10.60)%
Cash ($ mil.): 25
Current ratio: ——
Long-term debt ($ mil.): —

Dividends
  Yield: —
  Payout: —
  Market value ($ mil.): —

PRESONUS AUDIO ELECTRONICS INC.

PreSonus Audio Electronics makes digital audio equipment for amateur musicians and professionals alike. Its product lineup (designed for the purposes of broadcasting live sound reinforcement live streaming of audio and recording) includes items such as preamplifiers processors and equalizers. PreSonus sells through more than 800 specialty music retailers (Guitar Center Hermes) in the US as well as internationally. The company was founded in 1995.

EXECUTIVES

President and CEO, Jim Odom
VP Operations, Kurt Bueche
VP Sales and Marketing, Rick Naqvi
Director International Sales, Mark Williams
Director Marketing, Brad Zell
EVP, Paul Hugo
Customer Support Manager, Brandon Hays

LOCATIONS

HQ: PreSonus Audio Electronics Inc.
7257 Florida Blvd., Baton Rouge LA 70806
Phone: 225-216-7887   **Fax:** 225-926-8347
Web: www.presonus.com

HISTORICAL FINANCIALS
Company Type: Private

Income Statement
FYE: December 31

	REVENUE ($ mil.)	NET INCOME ($ mil.)	NET PROFIT MARGIN	EMPLOYEES
12/11	43	4	10.5%	115
12/10	28	1	3.9%	0
12/02	0	0	—	0
Annual Growth	—	—		

2011 Year-End Financials

Debt ratio: ——
Return on equity: 10.50%
Cash ($ mil.): 1
Current ratio: 0.80
Long-term debt ($ mil.): —

Dividends
  Yield: —
  Payout: —
  Market value ($ mil.): —

PRESSURE VESSEL SERVICE INC.

LOCATIONS

HQ: PRESSURE VESSEL SERVICE INC.
10900 HARPER AVE, DETROIT, MI 48213-3364
Phone: 313-921-1200
Web: www.pvschemicals.com

HISTORICAL FINANCIALS
Company Type: Private

Income Statement
FYE: December 31

	REVENUE ($ mil.)	NET INCOME ($ mil.)	NET PROFIT MARGIN	EMPLOYEES
12/11	461	12	2.6%	800
12/10	356	10	2.8%	0
12/09	334	11	3.5%	0
12/08	383	15	4.1%	0
Annual Growth	6.4%	(8.4%)	—	—

2011 Year-End Financials

Debt ratio: ——
Return on equity: 2.60%
Cash ($ mil.): 14
Current ratio: 0.30
Long-term debt ($ mil.): —

Dividends
  Yield: —
  Payout: —
  Market value ($ mil.): —

PRIDE INDUSTRIES

LOCATIONS

HQ: PRIDE INDUSTRIES
10030 FOOTHILLS BLVD, ROSEVILLE, CA 95747-7102
Phone: 916-788-2100
Web: www.prideindustries.com

HISTORICAL FINANCIALS
Company Type: Private

Income Statement
FYE: June 30

	REVENUE ($ mil.)	NET INCOME ($ mil.)	NET PROFIT MARGIN	EMPLOYEES
06/11	193	2	1.5%	4,300
06/10	114	2	2.2%	0
06/07	105	(1)	—	0
06/06	94	(4)	—	0
Annual Growth	26.9%	—	—	—

2011 Year-End Financials

Debt ratio: ——
Return on equity: 1.50%
Cash ($ mil.): 0
Current ratio: 0.90
Long-term debt ($ mil.): —

Dividends
  Yield: —
  Payout: —
  Market value ($ mil.): —

PRIMEX FARMS LLC

LOCATIONS

HQ: PRIMEX FARMS LLC
16070 WILDWOOD RD, WASCO, CA 93280-9210
Phone: 661-758-7790
Web: www.primexprocessing.com

HISTORICAL FINANCIALS
Company Type: Private

Income Statement
FYE: December 31

	REVENUE ($ mil.)	NET INCOME ($ mil.)	NET PROFIT MARGIN	EMPLOYEES
12/11	112	6	5.6%	130
Annual Growth	—	—	—	—

2011 Year-End Financials
Debt ratio: ——
Return on equity: 5.60%
Cash ($ mil.): 3
Current ratio: 0.40
Long-term debt ($ mil.): —

Dividends
Yield: —
Payout: —
Market value ($ mil.): —

HISTORICAL FINANCIALS
Company Type: Private

Income Statement
FYE: December 31

	REVENUE ($ mil.)	NET INCOME ($ mil.)	NET PROFIT MARGIN	EMPLOYEES
12/11	262	1	0.7%	30
12/01	57	0	0.3%	0
12/00	47	0	0.5%	0
12/99	836	0	—	0
Annual Growth	—	4021.3%	—	—

2011 Year-End Financials
Debt ratio: ——
Return on equity: 0.70%
Cash ($ mil.): 3
Current ratio: 1.00
Long-term debt ($ mil.): —

Dividends
Yield: —
Payout: —
Market value ($ mil.): —

HISTORICAL FINANCIALS
Company Type: Private

Income Statement
FYE: December 31

	REVENUE ($ mil.)	NET INCOME ($ mil.)	NET PROFIT MARGIN	EMPLOYEES
12/11	30	0	2.2%	150
12/10	29	0	1.5%	0
12/09	29	0	2.8%	0
12/08	29	0	2.5%	0
Annual Growth	1.7%	(3.0%)	—	—

2011 Year-End Financials
Debt ratio: ——
Return on equity: 2.20%
Cash ($ mil.): 0
Current ratio: 1.90
Long-term debt ($ mil.): —

Dividends
Yield: —
Payout: —
Market value ($ mil.): —

PRIMEX INTERNATIONAL TRADING CORP

Primex International Trading is a leading exporter and international trader that specializes in dried fruits and nuts. Through affiliate offices located around the world the company ships such products as almonds hazelnuts and pecans as well as apricots figs and raisins. Primex also has its own pistachio orchards and a processing plant in California. The company was founded in 1989 by Ali Amin whose family has been involved in producing pistachios for four generations. It first started planting pistachio orchards in 1990. In 2008 the company shipped about 30 million pounds of pistachios and more than 40 million pounds of almonds.

EXECUTIVES
President, Ali Amin
Treasurer and Controller, Andrik Sarkesians
COO, Mojgan Amin

LOCATIONS
HQ: Primex International Trading Corp.
5777 W. Century Blvd. Ste. 1485, Los Angeles CA 90045
Phone: 310-568-8855 **Fax:** 310-568-3336
Web: www.primex-usa.com

COMPETITORS

BALSU USA	Meridian Nut Growers
Blue Diamond Growers	ML Macadamia Orchards
Del Monte Foods	Santa Clara Nut Co.
Diamond Foods	Sun World
Dole Food	International
Golden Peanut	SunWest Foods
Green Valley Pecan	Texoma Peanut
John Sanfilippo & Son	Tropical Nut & Fruit
McCall Farms	Young Pecan

PRIMUS SOFTWARE CORPORATION

Primus Software believes that a primary goal should be to tame your technology. The company specializes in custom software development integration and programming services as well as on- and offshore staff augmentation. The company's vendor managed solutions segment supplies Web-enabled software and assistance programs for optimizing the use of temporary labor. Its clients come from a wide range of industries such as financial services health care manufacturing and retail. The company also provides professional services including consulting support and training. Primus Software was founded in 1996 and has offices in the US and India.

EXECUTIVES
President, Veena Kalale
CTO, Satish Anand
VP, Sangeeta Basandra
Business Development Manager, Kelli Pfister

LOCATIONS
HQ: Primus Software Corporation
3061 Peachtree Industrial Blvd. Ste. 110, Duluth GA 30097
Phone: 770-300-0004 **Fax:** 770-300-0005
Web: www.primussoft.com

COMPETITORS

Satyam	Wipro Technologies
Tata Consultancy	

PRINCETON COMMUNITY HOSPITAL

LOCATIONS
HQ: PRINCETON COMMUNITY HOSPITAL
12TH ST, PRINCETON, WV 24740
Phone: 304-487-7000
Web: www.pchonline.org

HISTORICAL FINANCIALS
Company Type: Private

Income Statement
FYE: June 30

	REVENUE ($ mil.)	NET INCOME ($ mil.)	NET PROFIT MARGIN	EMPLOYEES
06/11	116	5	4.4%	0
06/09	104	0	0.1%	0
Annual Growth	12.1%	4360.4%	—	—

2011 Year-End Financials
Debt ratio: ——
Return on equity: 4.40%
Cash ($ mil.): 12
Current ratio: 1.50
Long-term debt ($ mil.): —

Dividends
Yield: —
Payout: —
Market value ($ mil.): —

PRINCETON HEALTHCARE SYSTEM A NEW JERSEY NONPROFIT CORPORATION

LOCATIONS

HQ: PRINCETON HEALTHCARE SYSTEM A NEW JERSEY NONPROFIT CORPORATION
253 WITHERSPOON ST STE 1, PRINCETON, NJ 08540-3211
Phone: 609-497-4000

HISTORICAL FINANCIALS
Company Type: Private

Income Statement
FYE: December 31

	REVENUE ($ mil.)	NET INCOME ($ mil.)	NET PROFIT MARGIN	EMPLOYEES
12/11	338	10	3.2%	12
12/08	310	(26)	—	0
12/06	283	17	6.2%	0
Annual Growth	9.2%	(21.7%)	—	—

2011 Year-End Financials
Debt ratio: ——
Return on equity: 3.20%
Cash ($ mil.): 25
Current ratio: 0.70
Long-term debt ($ mil.): —
Dividends
Yield: —
Payout: —
Market value ($ mil.): —

PRINSBURG FARMERS CO-OP

LOCATIONS

HQ: PRINSBURG FARMERS CO-OP
404 RAILROAD AVE, PRINSBURG, MN 56281
Phone: 320-978-8100
Web: www.prccoop.com

HISTORICAL FINANCIALS
Company Type: Private

Income Statement
FYE: December 31

	REVENUE ($ mil.)	NET INCOME ($ mil.)	NET PROFIT MARGIN	EMPLOYEES
12/11	149	1	1.2%	50
12/10	91	3	3.4%	0
12/09	86	2	2.5%	0
12/08	114	2	2.5%	0
Annual Growth	9.5%	(12.8%)	—	—

2011 Year-End Financials
Debt ratio: ——
Return on equity: 1.20%
Cash ($ mil.): 19
Current ratio: 0.60
Long-term debt ($ mil.): —
Dividends
Yield: —
Payout: —
Market value ($ mil.): —

PRIORITY WIRE & CABLE INC.

LOCATIONS

HQ: PRIORITY WIRE & CABLE INC.
1800 E ROOSEVELT RD, LITTLE ROCK, AR 72206-2516
Phone: 501-372-5444
Web: www.prioritywire.com

HISTORICAL FINANCIALS
Company Type: Private

Income Statement
FYE: September 30

	REVENUE ($ mil.)	NET INCOME ($ mil.)	NET PROFIT MARGIN	EMPLOYEES
09/11	184	9	5.1%	130
09/10	111	5	5.0%	0
09/08	205	11	5.6%	0
09/07	180	14	7.7%	0
Annual Growth	0.7%	(12.6%)	—	—

2011 Year-End Financials
Debt ratio: ——
Return on equity: 5.10%
Cash ($ mil.): 0
Current ratio: 1.20
Long-term debt ($ mil.): —
Dividends
Yield: —
Payout: —
Market value ($ mil.): —

PRODUCE ALLIANCE LLC

LOCATIONS

HQ: PRODUCE ALLIANCE LLC
100 LEXINGTON DR STE 201, BUFFALO GROVE, IL 60089-6937
Phone: 847-808-3030
Web: www.producealliance.com

HISTORICAL FINANCIALS
Company Type: Private

Income Statement
FYE: December 31

	REVENUE ($ mil.)	NET INCOME ($ mil.)	NET PROFIT MARGIN	EMPLOYEES
12/11	154	0	0.1%	20
12/10	149	0	0.2%	0
12/09	131	0	0.3%	0
12/08	136	0	0.0%	0
Annual Growth	4.1%	85.1%	—	—

2011 Year-End Financials
Debt ratio: ——
Return on equity: 0.10%
Cash ($ mil.): 0
Current ratio: 1.00
Long-term debt ($ mil.): —
Dividends
Yield: —
Payout: —
Market value ($ mil.): —

PRODUCERS RICE MILL INC.

These producers aren't concerned with Broadway. They instead go with the grain. Producers Rice Mill dries mills and markets more than 50 million bushels of rice each year which it sells both domestically and overseas. The growers' cooperative is one of the largest private-label producers of rice in the US packaging more than 100 brands for the foodservice retail private label export and industrial industries. Its brands include ParExcellence LeGourmet Golden Harvest Classic Grains Granada Mandalay Bamboo 103 Calrose and Thai Orchard. It also processes rice for animal feeds such as Buck Grub deer feed and Equi-Jewel horse feed.

Along with bagged and bulk rice Producers also offers parboiled rice and seasoned rice mixes. In addition to its corporate headquarters and production facilities in Stuttgart Arkansas the cooperative has 12 receiving operations located throughout Arkansas and Mississippi.

The company has customers such as Ahold U.S.A. Federated Nash Finch and SUPERVALU which have been long-term customers ranging from 10 to 26 years.

About 15% of US milled grains like rice are exported to countries such as Canada Mexico Japan Haiti and Iraq. The USDA projects a demand in US rice exports over the next several years. Milled rice will have a higher demand which will directly benefit the US rice industry.

EXECUTIVES

President and CEO, Keith Glover
SVP Rice Sales and Marketing, Marvin (Butch) Baden
VP Finance and Administration, Kent Lockwood
VP Operations, Kenny Dryden
VP Marketing Consumer Products, Gary Reifeiss
Administrative Coordinator, Mary Fields
Director Management Information Systems, Annette Dierks
Assistant VP Finance and Administration, Mary Ratcliff
Director Human Resources, Karen Bagley
Traffic Manager, Jason Earney
Director Marketing Foodservice and Retail, Christy Kalder
Sales Manager Food Service National Accounts, Mike Cullen
Credit Supervisor, Vicki Baker
Accounting Supervisor, Michele Adamson
Secretary, Claudia Goacher
Chairman, Gary Sebree
Vice Chairman and VP, Jerry Hoskyn
Supervisor Customer Service, Ashley Parker
Assistant VP Rice Sales and Co-Products, Jason Chastain

General Sales Manager Food Service, Steve Nicholas
Retail Sales Manager, Tony Richmond

LOCATIONS

HQ: Producers Rice Mill Inc.
518 E. Harrison St., Stuttgart AR 72160
Phone: 870-673-4444　　**Fax:** 870-672-4482
Web: www.producersrice.com

COMPETITORS

ADM	Goya
American Rice	Mars Incorporated
Cargill	Mondelez International
Cereal Byproducts	PepsiCo
CHS	Riceland Foods
Farmers Rice Milling	RiceX
Farmers' Rice Cooperative	Specialty Rice

HISTORICAL FINANCIALS

Company Type: Private - Cooperative

Income Statement

FYE: July 31

	REVENUE ($ mil.)	NET INCOME ($ mil.)	NET PROFIT MARGIN	EMPLOYEES
07/12	478	302	63.3%	730
07/11	499	351	70.4%	0
07/10	482	343	71.2%	0
07/09	509	377	74.0%	0
Annual Growth	(2.1%)	(7.1%)	—	—

2012 Year-End Financials

Debt ratio: ——
Return on equity: 63.30%
Cash ($ mil.): 2
Current ratio: 0.90
Long-term debt ($ mil.): —
Dividends
Yield: —
Payout: —
Market value ($ mil.): —

PROFESSIONAL GOLFERS ASSOCIATION OF AMERICA INC

You have to be a real swinger to get into this organization. The Professional Golfers' Association of America (PGA) is the world's largest professional sports organization with more than 28000 members. PGA members are primarily club pros but most touring professionals are also members in addition to holding membership in the separate PGA TOUR organization. The PGA conducts some 40 tournaments and runs four major golf competitions: the Ryder Cup the PGA Championship the Senior PGA Championship and the PGA Grand Slam of Golf. It also operates the PGA Learning Center a golf instruction school in Port St. Lucie Florida. Rodman Wanamaker a Philadelphia department store tycoon organized the PGA in 1916.

EXECUTIVES

Managing Director Finance, Tim Shank
Honorary President, Brian Whitcomb
President, James (Jim) Remy
CEO, Joe Steranka

VP, Allen Wronowski
Director Human Resources and Employee Benefits, Diane Patz
Senior Director Business Development, Kevin Carter
Director Public Relations, Jamie Carbone
Director Communications and Publications, Kelly Elbin
Senior Director Communications and Media Relations, Julius Mason
Managing Director and General Counsel, Christine Garrity
Managing Director Championships and Business Development, Kerry Haigh
General Manager PGA Village, Bob Baldassari
Senior Director Business Financial Affairs, Kirk Pottinger
Senior Director Membership Services, Brad Sullivan
PGA Golf Exhibitions Group Vice President and General Manager, Ed Several
Rules Chairman, Brad Gregory
PGA General Manager PGA Golf Club, Bob Baladassari
Secretary, Ted Bishop
Senior Director Corporate Controller, Rosemarie Barr
Senior Director Association & Industry Services, Paul Metzler
Senior Director Business Development, Kevin Carter

LOCATIONS

HQ: PROFESSIONAL GOLFERS ASSOCIATION OF AMERICA INC
100 AVENUE OF CHAMPIONS, PALM BEACH GARDENS, FL 33418-3653
Phone: 561-624-8400
Web: www.newenglandpga.com

PRODUCTS/OPERATIONS

Selected Events

PGA Championship
PGA Grand Slam of Golf
Ryder Cup
Senior PGA Championship
PGA Championship Winners
Tommy Armour (1930)
Paul Azinger (1993)
Jerry Barber (1961)
James M. Barnes (1916 1919)
Rich Beem (2002)
Julius Boros (1968)
Mark Brooks (1996)
Jack Burke Jr. (1956)
Walter Burkemo (1953)
Tom Creavy (1931)
John Daly (1991)
Leo Diegel (1928-29)
Olin Dutra (1932)
Steve Elkington (1995)
Jim Ferrier (1947)
Dow Finsterwald (1958)
Raymond Floyd (1969 1982)
Doug Ford (1955)
Al Geiberger (1966)
Vic Ghezzi (1941)
Wayne Grady (1990)
David Graham (1979)
Hubert Green (1985)
Walter Hagen (1921 1924-27)
Bob Hamilton (1944)
Chick Harbert (1954)
Chandler Harper (1950)
Padraig Harrington (2008)
Jay Hebert (1960)
Lionel Hebert (1957)
Ben Hogan (1946 1948)
Jock Hutchison (1920)
Don January (1967)

Martin Kaymar (2010)
Davis Love III (1997)
John Mahaffey (1978)
Dave Marr (1965)
Shaun Micheel (2003)
Phil Mickelson (2005)
Byron Nelson (1940 1945)
Larry Nelson (1981 1987)
Bobby Nichols (1964)
Jack Nicklaus (1963 1971 1973 1975 1980)
Henry Picard (1939)
Gary Player (1962 1972)
Nick Price (1992 1994)
Johnny Revolta (1935)
Bob Rosburg (1959)
Paul Runyan (1934 1938)
Gene Sarazen (1922-23 1933)
Denny Shute (1936-37)
Vijay Singh (1998 2004)
Jeff Sluman (1988)
Sam Snead (1942 1949 1951)
Payne Stewart (1989)
Dave Stockton (1970 1976)
Hal Sutton (1983)
David Toms (2001)
Lee Trevino (1974 1984)
Jim Turnesa (1952)
Bob Tway (1986)
Lanny Wadkins (1977)
Tiger Woods (1999-2000 2006-07)
Yang Yong-eun (2009)

COMPETITORS

LPGA	Professional Bowlers
Major League Baseball	Association
NASCAR	The R&A
NBA	USGA
NFL	USTA
NHL	WTA Tour
PGA TOUR	

HISTORICAL FINANCIALS

Company Type: Private - Not-for-Profit

Income Statement

FYE: June 30

	REVENUE ($ mil.)	NET INCOME ($ mil.)	NET PROFIT MARGIN	EMPLOYEES
06/11	93	14	15.9%	178
06/10	56	(10)	—	0
06/09*	72	0	0.3%	0
12/08	0	0	—	0
Annual Growth	704.2%	—	—	—

*Fiscal year change

2011 Year-End Financials

Debt ratio: ——
Return on equity: 15.90%
Cash ($ mil.): 35
Current ratio: 2.30
Long-term debt ($ mil.): —
Dividends
Yield: —
Payout: —
Market value ($ mil.): —

PROGRAM FOR APPROPRIATE TECHNOLOGY IN HEALTH

LOCATIONS

HQ: PROGRAM FOR APPROPRIATE TECHNOLOGY IN HEALTH
2201 WESTLAKE AVE STE 200, SEATTLE, WA 98121-2767
Phone: 206-285-3500
Web: www.malariavaccines.com

HISTORICAL FINANCIALS

Company Type: Private

Income Statement

	REVENUE ($ mil.)	NET INCOME ($ mil.)	NET PROFIT MARGIN	EMPLOYEES
12/11	283	(29)	—	12,000
12/08	0	0	—	0
12/02	35	(37)	—	0
12/01	99	59	59.5%	0
Annual Growth	41.6%	—	—	—

FYE: December 31

2011 Year-End Financials

Debt ratio: —
Return on equity: (-10.40)%
Cash ($ mil.): 18
Current ratio: 0.30
Long-term debt ($ mil.): —
Dividends
Yield: —
Payout: —
Market value ($ mil.): —

PROMISE REGIONAL MEDICAL CENTER - HUTCHINSON INC.

LOCATIONS

HQ: PROMISE REGIONAL MEDICAL CENTER - HUTCHINSON INC.
1701 E 23RD AVE, HUTCHINSON, KS 67502-1105
Phone: 620-665-2000

HISTORICAL FINANCIALS

Company Type: Private

Income Statement

	REVENUE ($ mil.)	NET INCOME ($ mil.)	NET PROFIT MARGIN	EMPLOYEES
06/11	163	3	2.2%	1,000
06/10	168	7	4.6%	0
06/09	134	5	4.2%	0
06/08	126	3	2.8%	0
Annual Growth	8.9%	1.1%	—	—

FYE: June 30

2011 Year-End Financials

Debt ratio: —
Return on equity: 2.20%
Cash ($ mil.): 17
Current ratio: 1.70
Long-term debt ($ mil.): —
Dividends
Yield: —
Payout: —
Market value ($ mil.): —

PROSPECT CAPITAL CORPORATION

Prospect Capital is a closed-end investment fund with holdings in the consumer food health care and manufacturing sectors among others. The company targets privately held middle-market firms with annual revenues of less than $500 million; it also considers thinly traded public companies or turnaround situations. Prospect's portfolio includes interests in more than 80 companies mainly through senior loans and mezzanine debt. The company also makes equity and secured debt investments. Typically investing from $5 million to $75 million per transaction Prospect is a long-term investor that maintains regular contact with its portfolio company's management and participates in their board meetings.

Prospect has elected to be regulated as a business development company (BDC) a status which affords the firm certain tax benefits. Although it initially targeted on industrial and energy investments the company has broadened its focus in the past few years and minimized its holdings in the energy sector.

The company has been capitalizing on the tightened credit markets that have prevailed since the recession reared its head. The economic downturn has reduced competition and led larger rivals to pursue larger clients. Prospect's revenue and net income has increased each year since then. In fiscal 2012 the company's revenues grew 89% to $320.9 million while profits rose 61% to $190.9 million.

Fiscal 2012 proved an active year for Prospect which made nearly 40 new investments and about 20 follow-on investments. The company also sold five investments and wrote off its investment in Deb Shops (which went into bankruptcy). All said and done Prospect's investment portfolio grew by nearly half again that year.

EXECUTIVES

Chairman and CEO, John F. Barry III, age 60
President COO and Board Member, M. Grier Eliasek, age 39
CFO Chief Compliance Officer Treasurer and Secretary, Brian H. Oswald, age 51
Board Member, Andrew C. Cooper, age 51
President COO and Board Member, M. Grier Eliasek, age 39
Board Member, Eugene S. Stark, age 54
Board Member, William J. (Bill) Gremp
Chairman and CEO, John F. Barry III, age 60
President COO and Board Member, M. Grier Eliasek, age 39
CFO Chief Compliance Officer Treasurer and Secretary, Brian H. Oswald, age 51
Board Member, Andrew C. Cooper, age 51
President COO and Board Member, M. Grier Eliasek, age 39
Board Member, Eugene S. Stark, age 54
Board Member, William J. (Bill) Gremp
Auditors: BDOUSALLP

LOCATIONS

HQ: Prospect Capital Corporation
10 E. 40th St. 44th Fl., New York NY 10016
Phone: 212-448-0702 **Fax:** 212-448-9652
Web: www.prospectstreet.com

PRODUCTS/OPERATIONS

2012 Sales

	$ mil.	% of total
Interest	219	69
Dividends	64	20
Other	36	11
Total	**320**	**100**

Selected Investments

AIRMALL USA Inc. (property management)
Ajax Rolled Ring & Machine Inc. (manufacturing)
AWCNC (machinery)
Biotronic Neuronetwork (health care)
Borga Inc. (manufacturing)
Boxercraft (textiles and leather)
Clearwater Seafoods LP (food products)
Focus Products (consumer products)
H&M Oil & Gas LLC (oil and gas production)
Integrated Contract Services Inc. (contracting)
Iron Horse Coiled Tubing Inc. (productin services)
Manx Energy Inc. (oil and gas production)
NMMB (advertising media buying)
NRG Manufacturing Inc. (drilling rig components)
R-V Industries Inc. (metal fabrication)
Wind River (oil and gas production)

COMPETITORS

ACI Capital	Katalyst
ACI Capital	NGPC
Apollo Investment	NGPC
Apollo Investment	Stephens Group
First Reserve	Stephens Group
First Reserve	TPG
GFI Energy Ventures	TPG
GFI Energy Ventures	Venrock
Katalyst	Venrock

HISTORICAL FINANCIALS

Company Type: Public

Income Statement

	ASSETS ($ mil.)	NET INCOME ($ mil.)	INCOME AS % OF ASSETS	EMPLOYEES
09/12*	2,912	47	1.6%	129
06/12	2,255	190	8.5%	0
06/11	1,549	402	26.0%	0
06/10	832	18	2.3%	0
Annual Growth	51.8%	35.8%	—	—

FYE: September 30
*Fiscal year change

2012 Year-End Financials

Debt ratio: —
Return on equity: 38.20%
Cash ($ mil.): 2
Current ratio: —
Long-term debt ($ mil.): —
Dividends
Yield: —
Payout: —
Market value ($ mil.): —

PROVIDENCE COLLEGE

Students don't need divine intervention to get into Providence College they just need good grades and an interest in liberal arts. The Catholic institution of higher education offers undergraduate and graduate degrees at its four schools: Arts and Sciences Business Continuing Education and Professional Studies. It offers degrees in about 50 academic disciplines including biology business education marketing politics and psychology. It has a student-to-faculty ratio of 12:1 with students primarily coming from New England and the Midwest and Mid-Atlantic regions. Providence College was founded in 1917 by the Dominican Friars of the Province of St. Joseph and the Diocese of Providence.

EXECUTIVES

VP Finance and Business and CFO, Michael Frazier
SVP Finance and Business, John M. Sweeney
Associate VP Athletics, Robert Driscoll
Provost and SVP Academic Affairs, Hugh F. Lena
Dean Undergraduate and Graduate Studies, Rev Mark Nowel
Dean Professional Studies, Thomas Flaherty
Associate VP Admission and Enrollment Planning, Christopher Lydon
VP College Relations and Planning, Edward Caron
Assistant VP College Relations and Planning, Ann Manchester-Molak
Associate VP College Relations and Planning, Patricia Vieira
Associate VP Financial Services, Jacqueline White
Assistant VP Business Services, Warren Gray
Assistant VP Information Technology, Rebecca Ramos
Associate VP Human Resources, Kathleen Alvino
VP and General Counsel, Marifrances McGinn
Assistant VP Alumni Relations, Robert Ferreira
Director Career Planning and Internship Services, Kathleen Clarkin
President, Rev Brian J. Shanley
EVP and Treasurer, Rev Kenneth Sicard
VP Student Services, Rev Brendan Murphy
VP Institutional Advancement, David C. Wegrzyn
Director Phillips Memorial Library, D. Russell Bailey
VP Mission and Ministry, Rev Joseph J. Guido
Assistant VP Development, Lisa Bousquet

LOCATIONS

HQ: PROVIDENCE COLLEGE
  1 CUNNINGHAM SQ, PROVIDENCE, RI 02918-0001
Phone: 401-865-1000
Web: www.providence.edu

HISTORICAL FINANCIALS
Company Type: School

Income Statement   FYE: June 30

	REVENUE ($ mil.)	NET INCOME ($ mil.)	NET PROFIT MARGIN	EMPLOYEES
06/11	216	24	11.2%	800
06/10	145	24	16.5%	0
06/09	142	(15)	—	0
06/08	139	11	8.6%	0
Annual Growth	15.9%	26.7%	—	—

2011 Year-End Financials
Debt ratio: ——
Return on equity: 11.20%
Cash ($ mil.): 38
Current ratio: —
Long-term debt ($ mil.): —
Dividends
  Yield: —
  Payout: —
  Market value ($ mil.): —

PROVIDENCE HOSPITAL

LOCATIONS

HQ: PROVIDENCE HOSPITAL
  6801 AIRPORT BLVD, MOBILE, AL 36608-3785
Phone: 251-633-1000

Selected Facilities
Carroll Manor Nursing And Rehabilitation Center (Washington DC)
Congress Heights Senior Wellness Center (Washington DC)
Model Cities Senior Wellness Center (Washington DC)
Hattie Holmes Senior Wellness Center (Washington DC)
Fort Lincoln Family Medicine Center (Colmar Manor Maryland)
Perry Family Health Center (Washington DC)
Police and Fire Clinic (Washington DC)
Seton House (Washington DC; behavioral health services)
Wellington Pharmacy (Washington DC)
Wellness Institute (Washington DC)

HISTORICAL FINANCIALS
Company Type: Private

Income Statement   FYE: June 30

	REVENUE ($ mil.)	NET INCOME ($ mil.)	NET PROFIT MARGIN	EMPLOYEES
06/11	231	21	9.5%	2,000
06/10	227	21	9.5%	0
06/09*	189	(7)	—	0
04/09	0	0	—	0
Annual Growth	868.2%	—	—	—
*Fiscal year change

2011 Year-End Financials
Debt ratio: ——
Return on equity: 9.50%
Cash ($ mil.): 8
Current ratio: 1.20
Long-term debt ($ mil.): —
Dividends
  Yield: —
  Payout: —
  Market value ($ mil.): —

PROVIDENCE HOSPITAL

LOCATIONS

HQ: PROVIDENCE HOSPITAL
  1150 VARNUM ST NE, WASHINGTON, DC 20017-2104
Phone: 202-269-7000
Web: www.provhosp.org

Selected Facilities
Carroll Manor Nursing And Rehabilitation Center (Washington DC)
Congress Heights Senior Wellness Center (Washington DC)
Model Cities Senior Wellness Center (Washington DC)
Hattie Holmes Senior Wellness Center (Washington DC)
Fort Lincoln Family Medicine Center (Colmar Manor Maryland)
Perry Family Health Center (Washington DC)
Police and Fire Clinic (Washington DC)
Seton House (Washington DC; behavioral health services)
Wellington Pharmacy (Washington DC)
Wellness Institute (Washington DC)

HISTORICAL FINANCIALS
Company Type: Private

Income Statement   FYE: June 30

	REVENUE ($ mil.)	NET INCOME ($ mil.)	NET PROFIT MARGIN	EMPLOYEES
06/11	229	8	3.8%	2,517
06/10	235	8	3.5%	0
06/09	230	(13)	—	0
06/08	19	(3)	—	0
Annual Growth	125.8%	—	—	—

2011 Year-End Financials
Debt ratio: ——
Return on equity: 3.80%
Cash ($ mil.): 15
Current ratio: 1.30
Long-term debt ($ mil.): —
Dividends
  Yield: —
  Payout: —
  Market value ($ mil.): —

PROVO CITY SCHOOL DISTRICT

LOCATIONS

HQ: PROVO CITY SCHOOL DISTRICT
  280 W 940 N, PROVO, UT 84604-3326
Phone: 801-374-4800
Web: www.provo.edu

HISTORICAL FINANCIALS
Company Type: Private

Income Statement   FYE: June 30

	REVENUE ($ mil.)	NET INCOME ($ mil.)	NET PROFIT MARGIN	EMPLOYEES
06/11	113	(5)	—	1,670
06/10	112	11	10.4%	0
06/09	115	3	3.2%	0
06/07	96	27	28.6%	0
Annual Growth	5.5%	—	—	—

PUBLIC CONSULTING GROUP INC.

LOCATIONS

HQ: PUBLIC CONSULTING GROUP INC.
  148 STATE ST FL 10, BOSTON, MA 02109-2589
Phone: 617-426-2026
Web: www.publicconsultinggroup.com

HISTORICAL FINANCIALS
Company Type: Private

Income Statement
FYE: June 30

	REVENUE ($ mil.)	NET INCOME ($ mil.)	NET PROFIT MARGIN	EMPLOYEES
06/11	159	9	6.0%	815
06/10	134	6	5.1%	0
06/09	112	7	6.9%	0
06/08	88	20	22.8%	0
Annual Growth	21.6%	(22.1%)	—	—

2011 Year-End Financials

Debt ratio: ——
Return on equity: 6.00%
Cash ($ mil.): 43
Current ratio: 1.30
Long-term debt ($ mil.): —

Dividends
 Yield: —
 Payout: —
 Market value ($ mil.): —

PUBLIC UTILITY DISTRICT 1 OF BENTON COUNTY

LOCATIONS

HQ: PUBLIC UTILITY DISTRICT 1 OF BENTON COUNTY
 2721 W 10TH AVE, KENNEWICK, WA 99336-4813
Phone: 509-582-2175
Web: www.bentonpud.org

HISTORICAL FINANCIALS
Company Type: Private

Income Statement
FYE: December 31

	REVENUE ($ mil.)	NET INCOME ($ mil.)	NET PROFIT MARGIN	EMPLOYEES
12/11	134	8	6.2%	155
12/10	127	(0)	—	0
12/09	133	11	8.9%	0
12/07	138	4	2.9%	0
Annual Growth	(0.9%)	27.1%	—	—

2011 Year-End Financials

Debt ratio: ——
Return on equity: 6.20%
Cash ($ mil.): 8
Current ratio: 1.20
Long-term debt ($ mil.): —

Dividends
 Yield: —
 Payout: —
 Market value ($ mil.): —

PUGET SOUND BLOOD CENTER & PROGRAM

Residents of the Emerald City can go here to give red. Puget Sound Blood Center (PSBC) is a not-for-profit blood and tissue bank serving more than 70 hospitals and clinics in and around Seat-tle. The blood center collects and processes donated blood through about a dozen donation centers and several mobile units; it also registers bone marrow donors provides testing and training services to patients with hemophilia and collects cord blood for use in stem cell transplantation. Its PSBC Research Institute conducts research on improving transfusion and transplantation medicine. PSBC was formed in 1944.

Geographic Reach

PSBC serves health care facilities in 14 counties in western Washington plus the nearby San Juan Islands. The company also has cord blood bank partnerships with hospitals across Washington and in Oregon and Hawaii.

Operations

PSBC funds its activities including its research efforts by charging services fees to clients as well as through research grants research partnerships and philanthropic donations. It also sells blood derivatives and related products (such as plasma).

Research programs focus on improving transfusion and transplantation medicine for patients with ailments including leukemia cancer serious injuries and burns.

Financial Analysis

PSBC reported revenues of $151 million in 2012. The company's earnings reflected a little more than 1% increase over revenues in 2011.

Strategy

Growth in its service territory and customer base as well as the increasingly complex blood testing needs of its clients has led PSBC to expand its facilities in recent years. For instance in 2011 it opened a new blood lab dedicated to pediatric transfusion services. It also completed construction of a new facility for its research institute that year.

At the same time PSBC is also selling off some operations to focus on core services. In 2012 it agreed to sell its Northwest Tissue Services unit which conducts human tissue donation and processing to LifeNet Health. It also agreed to sell its donor testing unit which performs blood testing for external clients such as other blood banks to Creative Testing Solutions (CTS); PSBC will retain an equity stake in CTS through the deal.

EXECUTIVES

Chair, Bertrand A. (Bert) Valdman, age 49
EVP Finance, Robert J. Gleason
EVP Marketing and Community Relations, Maria E. Geyer
EVP Blood Services Laboratories, Sandy Linauts
EVP Research Division, Jose A. Lopez
Press Contact, Michael Young
President and CEO, James P. AuBuchon
Vice Chair, Alan W. Schulkin
EVP Quality and Organizational Effectiveness, Lynn Craig
EVP Medical Division, Thomas H. Price
EVP Human Resources, Sally Sullivan
Trustee, Robert C. Wallace
Trustee, Barbara C. Sherland
Trustee, Virginia Broudy
Vice Chair, Alan W. Schulkin
Trustee, Colleen Ferris
Trustee, A. Kent Fisher
Trustee, Leslie Giblett
Trustee, John B. Hayhurst
Trustee, Steve Hix
Trustee, Toni Hoffman
Trustee, Rayburn S. Lewis
Trustee, Penelope Lie
Trustee, Susan J. Naficy
Trustee, Steve Nicholes
Trustee, Marnie Roozen
Trustee, Jon Summers
Trustee, Mirtha Vaca-Wilkens

LOCATIONS

HQ: Puget Sound Blood Center
 921 Terry Ave., Seattle WA 98104
Phone: 206-292-6500   Fax: 206-292-8030
Web: www.psbc.org

Selected Washington Service Counties
Clallam
Clark
Cowlitz
Grays Harbor
Jefferson
King
Kitsap
Lewis
Mason
Pierce
San Juan Islands
Skagit
Snohomish
Thurston
Whatcom

PRODUCTS/OPERATIONS

Selected Services
Blood Services
Clinical Services
Clinical Trial Support
Cord Blood Program
Research Institute
Specialty Diagnostics Laboratories
 Genomics Testing Laboratory
 Hemostasis Reference Laboratory
 Immunogenetics/HLA Laboratory
 Platelet Immunology Laboratory
Transfusion Medicine
 Compatibility Testing Laboratory
 Donor Testing/Virology Laboratory
 Red Cell Reference Laboratory

COMPETITORS

Blood Systems Inc.	HemaCare
CSL Plasma	Red Cross
Daxor	SeraCare Life Sciences
Haemonetics	

HISTORICAL FINANCIALS
Company Type: Private - Not-for-Profit

Income Statement
FYE: June 30

	REVENUE ($ mil.)	NET INCOME ($ mil.)	NET PROFIT MARGIN	EMPLOYEES
06/12	150	(1)	—	750
06/11	164	9	6.0%	0
06/10	149	1	0.8%	0
06/09	152	(0)	—	0
Annual Growth	(0.6%)	—	—	—

2012 Year-End Financials

Debt ratio: ——
Return on equity: (-1.10)%
Cash ($ mil.): 5
Current ratio: 1.30
Long-term debt ($ mil.): —

Dividends
 Yield: —
 Payout: —
 Market value ($ mil.): —

PURCHASING POWER LLC

LOCATIONS

HQ: PURCHASING POWER LLC
1375 PEACHTREE ST NE # 500, ATLANTA, GA
30309-3173
Phone: 404-609-5100

HISTORICAL FINANCIALS

Company Type: Private

Income Statement

FYE: December 31

	REVENUE ($ mil.)	NET INCOME ($ mil.)	NET PROFIT MARGIN	EMPLOYEES
12/11	179	(4)	—	115
12/09	107	9	8.7%	0
12/08	75	6	8.9%	0
12/07	50	4	9.4%	0
Annual Growth	52.7%	—	—	—

2011 Year-End Financials

Debt ratio: —
Return on equity: (-2.40)%
Cash ($ mil.): 2
Current ratio: 0.10
Long-term debt ($ mil.): —
Dividends
  Yield: —
  Payout: —
  Market value ($ mil.): —

PVS TECHNOLOGIES INC.

PVS Chemicals sells undrinkable soda sulfur-based chemicals and acids that not even Timothy Leary would find palatable. The company's product list includes sulfuric and hydrochloric acids liquid caustic soda ferric chloride and ammonium thiosulfate. These chemicals are used in applications such as water treatment (wastewater process and municipal) electronics manufacture (including semiconductor etching) gold and copper mining and food and aluminum production. PVS Chemicals' subsidiaries include PVS Technologies (water treatment) Dynecol (transportation analysis treatment and recycling of chemicals) and PVS Nolwood (chemical distribution).

EXECUTIVES

President and CEO, James B. (Jim) Nicholson, age 68
VP, Allan F. Schlumberger
VP and CFO, Candee Saferian
VP and General Counsel, Jonathan S. Taub
VP, James M. Nicholson
VP, David A. Nicholson
Manager Benefits Risk and Employee Excellence, Grace Bayer
Treasurer, James DeVleeschouwer
CIO, Frank Lada

LOCATIONS

HQ: PVS Chemicals Inc.
10900 Harper Ave., Detroit MI 48213
Phone: 313-921-1200   **Fax:** 313-921-1378
Web: www.pvschemicals.com

PRODUCTS/OPERATIONS

Selected Subsidiaries

Dynecol
PVS Minibulk Distribution
PVS Nolwood
PVS Solutions
PVS Technologies
PVS Transportation

Selected Products

Ferric chloride (liquid and anhydrous)
Hydrochloric acid
Liquid caustic soda
Sulfuric acid (commercial and electrolyte grade semi-conductor/reagent grade oleum sulfur trioxide)
Sulfur-based products (sodium bisulfite liquid ammonium thiosulfate sodium-potassium bisulfite sodium thiosulfate)

COMPETITORS

Arch Chemicals   JCI Jones Chemicals
Ashland Inc.

HISTORICAL FINANCIALS

Company Type: Private

Income Statement

FYE: December 31

	REVENUE ($ mil.)	NET INCOME ($ mil.)	NET PROFIT MARGIN	EMPLOYEES
12/11	45	4	9.2%	60
12/10	35	4	13.3%	0
12/09	43	8	19.2%	0
12/08	31	1	4.4%	0
Annual Growth	12.1%	43.6%	—	—

2011 Year-End Financials

Debt ratio: —
Return on equity: 9.20%
Cash ($ mil.): 0
Current ratio: —
Long-term debt ($ mil.): —
Dividends
  Yield: —
  Payout: —
  Market value ($ mil.): —

PVS-NOLWOOD CHEMICALS INC.

LOCATIONS

HQ: PVS-NOLWOOD CHEMICALS INC.
10900 HARPER AVE STE 2, DETROIT, MI 48213-3364
Phone: 313-921-1200
Web: www.pvschemical.com

HISTORICAL FINANCIALS

Company Type: Private

Income Statement

FYE: December 31

	REVENUE ($ mil.)	NET INCOME ($ mil.)	NET PROFIT MARGIN	EMPLOYEES
12/11	131	4	3.2%	71
12/10	89	3	3.9%	0
12/09	97	4	4.8%	0
12/08	119	3	2.7%	0
Annual Growth	3.4%	8.5%	—	—

2011 Year-End Financials

Debt ratio: —
Return on equity: 3.20%
Cash ($ mil.): 0
Current ratio: —
Long-term debt ($ mil.): —
Dividends
  Yield: —
  Payout: —
  Market value ($ mil.): —

QUALSERV CORPORATION

QualServ serves up quality by providing everything to turn an empty building into a functioning restaurant. The turnkey company brings together everything —from design and construction to millwork equipment furniture and fixtures —for opening a restaurant or a wide variety of other businesses and institutions. QualServ also serves up installation maintenance and repair services. Don't need a complete restaurant? Customers may also order a la carte from QualServ's menu of products and services. QualServ's clientele has included the likes of Chipotle Mexican Grill Extended Stay America Papa John's and Red Robin Gourmet Burgers. QualServ partners with Direct Capital Corporation to offer financing.

The partnership was created in the midst of the economic recession. Many franchisees struggled to gain access to funding in order to support their remodel and expansion plans. Direct Capital which specilizes in franchise lending stepped in to pledge a substantial portion of its lending capacity to QualServ clients.

The company's clients weren't the only ones to struggle during the recession. In 2008 QualServe completed a restructuring process that included a recapitalization through a debt-for-equity swap with its lenders. The company which was lossing money and overleveraged also consolidated business units and relocated its headquarters from North Kansas City Missouri to Fort Smith Arkansas. In the process QualServe streamlined its operations by eliminating its Kansas City production facilities and cut back its South Carolina operations.

QualServ has three warehousing office and manufacturing facilities in Arkansas Missouri and South Carolina. One of the largest companies in the industry QualServ's size allows it to combine comprehensive in-house fabrication capacities with a nationwide distribution and servicing network. In addition to restaurants QualServ offers its services to big-box retailers schools and hospitals government organizations and hospitality and entertainment companies.

The company was formed through the consolidation of five separate foodservice equipment and supply companies in 1997 and 1998: Air Systems Food Service Supplies Remco Smith St. John and Tennessee Restaurant Equipment Sales.

EXECUTIVES

Senior Account Manager Burger King, David Kensinger
President and CEO, Jerry Frederiksen
Chairman, Dennis Smith
CFO, Gerry Maughn
VP Sales, Mike McCormick

LOCATIONS

HQ: QualServ Corporation
  7400 S 28th St., Fort Smith AR 72906
Phone: 800-643-2980   **Fax:** 479-646-5517
Web: www.qualservcorp.com

PRODUCTS/OPERATIONS

Selected Products and Services

Custom fabrication
  Powder coating
  Millwork
  Stainless steel fabrication
Financing
Project management
  Consolidation
  Installation
Retail fixtures
  Buying
  Consolidation
  Engineering
  Millwork
  Steel work
  Upholstery

COMPETITORS

Embree Construction	Lozier
Hill International	Madix Inc.
KPRS Construction	Thorco

HISTORICAL FINANCIALS

Company Type: Private

Income Statement

FYE: December 31

	REVENUE ($ mil.)	NET INCOME ($ mil.)	NET PROFIT MARGIN	EMPLOYEES
12/11	68	(0)	—	192
12/10	68	(0)	—	0
12/09	69	(0)	—	0
Annual Growth	(1.0%)	—	—	—

2011 Year-End Financials

Debt ratio: ——
Return on equity: (-0.40)%
Cash ($ mil.): 2
Current ratio: 1.20
Long-term debt ($ mil.): —

Dividends
  Yield: —
  Payout: —
  Market value ($ mil.): —

QUEEN OF THE VALLEY MEDICAL CENTER

The Queen of the Valley Medical Center reigns over the whole of Napa Valley. The 190-bed hospital provides acute and tertiary care to the residents of California's Napa County. It operates a level III trauma center and provides emergency surgery and wound care services as well as specialty family work health nutritional and rehabilitation services. "The Queen" as it is known colloquially operates regional cancer orthopedic women's and heart centers as well as the Napa Valley Imaging Center and the Napa Valley Women's Healthcare Center. Queen of the Valley Medical Center is part of St. Joseph Health.

Current expansion efforts at Queen of the Valley Medical Center include construction of a $30 million three-story diagnostic and surgical pavilion. The new center will add high-tech surgical suites

and diagnostic laboratory and imaging facilities as well as private ICU rooms. The hospital is also developing a new neuroscience center.

The medical center was founded in 1958 by the Sisters of St. Joseph of Orange. It expanded its facilities a number of times over the years. For instance in 2006 the hospital added a wellness center and a unit dedicated to maternal and infant care. These expansion efforts prompted a name change from Queen of the Valley Hospital to Queen of the Valley Medical Center in 2007 to reflect the facility's expanded offerings and its emphasis on not just medical care but also community-based outreach and prevention services.

EXECUTIVES

President and CEO, Dennis M. Sisto
VP Human Resources, Ron Scott
VP Foundation and Chief Development Officer, Richard P. (Dick) Green
VP Patient Care Services and Chief Nursing Officer, Barbara Eusebio
VP Medical Affairs and Chief Medical Officer, Vincent Morgese
VP Mission Integration, Sister Marian Schubert
VP Finance and CFO, Don Miller
Director Marketing and Communications, Jaime Penaherrera
Public Relations Program Manager, Juanita Ramos

LOCATIONS

HQ: Queen of the Valley Medical Center
  1000 Trancas St., Napa CA 94558-2941
Phone: 707-252-4411   **Fax:** 707-257-4032
Web: www.thequeen.org

COMPETITORS

Adventist Health
Community Hospital of the Monterey Peninsula
Dignity Health
HCA
John Muir Health
Kaiser Permanente
Providence Health & Services
Stanford Hospital and Clinics
Sutter Health
Tenet Healthcare
UCSF Medical
Western Medical Center - Santa Ana

HISTORICAL FINANCIALS

Company Type: Subsidiary

Income Statement

FYE: June 30

	REVENUE ($ mil.)	NET INCOME ($ mil.)	NET PROFIT MARGIN	EMPLOYEES
06/11	268	11	4.5%	1,070
06/10	276	25	9.1%	0
06/09	242	(5)	—	0
06/08	268	15	5.9%	0
Annual Growth	(0.0%)	(9.0%)	—	—

2011 Year-End Financials

Debt ratio: ——
Return on equity: 4.50%
Cash ($ mil.): 86
Current ratio: 1.40
Long-term debt ($ mil.): —

Dividends
  Yield: —
  Payout: —
  Market value ($ mil.): —

QUEST MEDIA & SUPPLIES INC.

Quest wants to help guide clients in their technology journeys. Quest Media & Supplies provides a wide range of IT consulting and management services to Fortune 5000 firms as well as educational institutions government agencies and small and midsized companies across the US. Its offerings include cloud hosting application development networking security and disaster recovery data storage telecommunications and transport services and technology staffing. Quest is Gold Certified in the US for Cisco Systems and also supplies products from Blue Coat Dell Hitachi IBM Microsoft Polycom VMware and Xerox among other vendors. The company was founded in 1982 by CEO Tim Burke with his wife Cindy.

Financial Performance Although privately held the company reports annual revenue of more than $80 million.

EXECUTIVES

CEO, Tim Burke
COO, Kathy Campbell
CFO, Francine (Fran) Walrath
Director Marketing, Barbara Klide
Director IT, Mike Dillon
Director Customer Service, Kerri Marshall
Manager Purchasing and Configuration, Toby Merlo
Account Manager, Angie McKoy

LOCATIONS

HQ: QUEST MEDIA & SUPPLIES INC.
  5822 ROSEVILLE RD, SACRAMENTO, CA 95842-3071
Phone: 916-338-7070
Web: www.questsys.com

PRODUCTS/OPERATIONS

Selected Services

Data/Voice Circuits
Infrastructure Services
Maintenance Contract Management
Managed Services
  Business Resumption Center
  Cloud Services
  DR/BCP
  Managed Security Services
  Network Health
  Service Delivery Centers
Professional Services
Technical Staffing
Technology Products

COMPETITORS

Computer Sciences Corp.	HP Enterprise Services
	IBM Global Services

HISTORICAL FINANCIALS

Company Type: Private

Income Statement

FYE: December 31

	REVENUE ($ mil.)	NET INCOME ($ mil.)	NET PROFIT MARGIN	EMPLOYEES
12/11	81	0	1.0%	130
12/10	81	0	0.4%	0
12/09	82	0	1.2%	0
12/08	84	0	0.2%	0
Annual Growth	(1.2%)	66.9%	—	—

2011 Year-End Financials

Debt ratio: —
Return on equity: 1.00%
Cash ($ mil.): 0
Current ratio: 0.60
Long-term debt ($ mil.): —

Dividends
Yield: —
Payout: —
Market value ($ mil.): —

QUINNIPIAC UNIVERSITY

At Quinnipiac University the first thing you may have to learn is how to pronounce it (for the record it's KWIN-uh-pe-ack). The private university offers a variety of liberal arts undergraduate programs as well as graduate programs in selected professional fields (business education health sciences communications and law) to some 8500 students. It often appears on lists of top colleges including those published by U.S. News & World Report. The university which is known to political junkies and others for its polling operation includes eight schools and colleges across three Connecticut campuses (Mount Carmel York Hill and North Haven).

Company Background Originally named the Connecticut College of Commerce the school was founded in 1929 by Samuel W. Tator as a small business college awarding associate's degrees. The college changed its name in 1951 to Quinnipiac College commemorating the early Indian settlers who made their home in and around the New Haven Connecticut harbor area.

EXECUTIVES

President and Trustee, John L. Lahey, age 65
SVP Finance and Administration, Patrick J. Healy, age 68
VP Athletic Marketing and External Relations, Val Belmonte
VP Public Affairs, Lynn M. Bushnell
VP and Dean of Students, Manuel Carreiro
SVP Academic and Student Affairs, Kathleen M. McCourt
VP and Dean of Admissions, Joan Isaac Mohr
Chairman, Terry W. Goodwin
Dean Academic Services and Research Support, Linda K. Broker
Manager Systems and Research in Admissions and Financial Aid, Roger E. Goulet
Director Admissions, Carla May Knowlton
Director Admissions for Transfer and Part-Time Students, Mary E. Wargo
Director Arnold Bernhard Library, Charles M. Getchell

Director Athletics and Recreation, John J. McDonald
SVP School of Business, Mark A. Thompson
Associate Dean School of Business, Charles M. Brooks
Dean School of Communications, David Donnelly
VP Development and Alumni Affairs, Donald J. Weinbach
Associate VP Development and Alumni Affairs, Dianna Pategas
Associate VP Facilities Administration, Joseph D. Rubertone
Associate Director Facilities, Keith Woodward
Director Administrative Services, John J. Meriano
Associate Director Administrative Services, Maria L. Bimonte-Yerganian
Associate Director Administrative Services, Robert Rickert
Director Human Resources, Anna M. Spragg
Associate Director Human Resources, Donna L. Veitch
Senior Director Financial Aid, Dominic R. Yoia
Senior Associate Director Financial Aid, Laurie Folsom
Director Graduate Admissions, Scott Farber
Director Marketing Communications for Admissions, Louise M. Howe
Director Graduate Financial Aid, Heather Hamilton
Director Student Health Services, Katheryn B. Macaione
VP CIO and CTO, Richard C. Ferguson
Director International Education, Patrick S. Frazier
Dean School of Law, Brad Saxton
Director Learning Center, Andrew Delohery
Dean College of Liberal Arts, Hans D. Bergmann
Registrar, Dorothy M. Lauria
Director Residential Life, Cindy Long Porter
Chief of Security and Safety, John R. Twining
Dean Academic Technology, John Paton
Bursar, Valerie Carbone
Controller, Daniel Johnson
Director Career Services, Deborah L. Daddio
Interim Dean School of Health Sciences, Edward R. O'Connor
Dean College of Professional Studies, Maxine Lentz
Dean Division of Education, Cynthia K. Dubea
Trustee, William G. Spears, age 73
Trustee, William C. (Bill) Weldon, age 63
Trustee, Carlton L. Highsmith, age 59
President and Trustee, John L. Lahey, age 65
Trustee, David R. Nelson
Trustee, William L. (Bill) Ayers Jr.
Trustee, Frederick J. Mancheski
Vice Chairman, Murray Lender
Secretary and Trustee, Robert J. Hauser Jr.
Trustee, Alexander Alexiades
Trustee, John R. Antonino
Trustee, Anthony J. Baudanza
Trustee, Patrick Baumgarten
Trustee, Donald P. Calcagnini
Trustee, Albert Canosa
Trustee, Peter R. DeGeorge
Trustee, Gabriel Ferrucci
Trustee, Dennis P. Flanagan
Trustee, Mary-Jane Foster, age 61
Trustee, Hugh F. Keefe
Trustee, Richard G. Kelley
Trustee, Marcus R. McCraven
Trustee, John F. Meuser
Trustee, Paula Moynahan
Trustee, Donald L. Perlroth
Trustee, Jonathan M. Reeves
Trustee, Arthur H. Rice
Trustee, Edward L. Scalone
Auditors: Deloitte&ToucheLLP

LOCATIONS

HQ: Quinnipiac University
275 Mt. Carmel Ave., Hamden CT 06518-1908
Phone: 203-582-8200   Fax: 203-582-5347
Web: www.quinnipiac.edu

HISTORICAL FINANCIALS

Company Type: School

Income Statement

FYE: June 30

	REVENUE ($ mil.)	NET INCOME ($ mil.)	NET PROFIT MARGIN	EMPLOYEES
06/11	349	68	19.5%	900
06/10	290	45	15.6%	0
06/09	235	(0)	—	0
06/08	3	1	38.5%	0
Annual Growth	385.8%	287.2%	—	—

2011 Year-End Financials

Debt ratio: —
Return on equity: 19.50%
Cash ($ mil.): 7
Current ratio: —
Long-term debt ($ mil.): —

Dividends
Yield: —
Payout: —
Market value ($ mil.): —

R. E. MICHEL COMPANY INC.

Blowing hot and cold is good for R.E. Michel. The company is one of the nation's largest wholesale distributors of heating air-conditioning and refrigeration (HVAC-R) equipment parts and supplies. The family-owned and operated firm offers more than 16000 items through about 225 sales offices located across the Southern Mid-Atlantic and Northeastern regions of the country. R.E. Michel ships more than 10000 items each day from its 900000-sq.-ft. distribution center in Maryland. Its Exclusive Supplier Partnership (ESP) program offers customers inventory control advertising and marketing support. R.E. Michel was founded in 1935 as a supplier to the home heating oil burner industry.

Geographic Reach
The HVAC wholesaler maintains some 225 offices to cater to customers located in the Southern US as well as in the Mid-Atlantic and Northeastern regions.

Strategy
R.E. Michel has grown its business by partnering with manufacturers and by boosting its distribution capacity. The company's alliance with manufacturer Nordyne inked in 2009 has given R.E. Michel the exclusive rights to market the Broan brand of heating and cooling equipment. As part of the move R.E. Michel has made several investment in its Virginia facilities such as purchasing a more than 20000-sq.-ft. warehouse and expanding another location from 5000 sq. ft. to 8000 sq. ft.

Sales and Marketing
R.E. Michel uses up to 50 trailers to ship its more than 10000 items each day. To this end the company also ships more than 3200 items via the United Parcel Service each week.

As part of its business it publishes a 1300 page catalog that includes 20000 catalog line items.

EXECUTIVES

President, John W. H. (Doc) Michel
VP Sales, Glen Baker
VP Marketing, J. V. (Mike) Michel Jr.
Director Human Resources, Sherry Atkinson
Director Information Technology, Phillip Woolford
Director Technical Services, Frank Schneider
Director Marketing, Stephen Neathery
Director Distribution, J. V. (Beau) Michel III
Director Credit, Tom Gannon
VP Operations, Gene Winters
ESP Coordinator, Erin Moore

LOCATIONS

HQ: R.E. Michel Company Inc.
1 R.E. Michel Dr., Glen Burnie MD 21060
Phone: 410-760-4000 **Fax:** 410-760-6425
Web: www.remichel.com

PRODUCTS/OPERATIONS

Selected Products and Services

Air conditioning & heating
Indoor air quality
Boilers
Water heating equipment
Hydronic & steam systems
Valves
Pipe & fittings
Fuel oil systems
Gas systems
Chemicals
Refrigeration equipment & supplies
Controls
Electrical supplies
Motors
Air handling products
Venting products
Duct registers & grilles
Tools & test instruments
O.E.M. Parts

COMPETITORS

Emco Corporation	Lowe's
Ferguson Enterprises	MSC Industrial Direct
Gensco	W.W. Grainger
HD Supply	WinWholesale

HISTORICAL FINANCIALS

Company Type: Private

Income Statement — FYE: December 31

	REVENUE ($ mil.)	NET INCOME ($ mil.)	NET PROFIT MARGIN	EMPLOYEES
12/11	606	8	1.4%	1,640
12/10	593	11	1.9%	0
12/09	527	8	1.6%	0
12/08	564	10	1.8%	0
Annual Growth	2.4%	(5.6%)	—	—

2011 Year-End Financials

Debt ratio: ——
Return on equity: 1.40%
Cash ($ mil.): 0
Current ratio: 0.70
Long-term debt ($ mil.): —
Dividends
Yield: —
Payout: —
Market value ($ mil.): —

R. H. WHITE COMPANIES INC.

LOCATIONS

HQ: R. H. WHITE COMPANIES INC.
41 CENTRAL ST, AUBURN, MA 01501-2304
Phone: 508-832-3295
Web: www.rhwhite.com

HISTORICAL FINANCIALS

Company Type: Private

Income Statement — FYE: April 30

	REVENUE ($ mil.)	NET INCOME ($ mil.)	NET PROFIT MARGIN	EMPLOYEES
04/12	85	0	1.0%	764
04/11	78	0	1.3%	0
04/10	78	0	1.3%	0
04/08	103	1	1.7%	0
Annual Growth	(6.1%)	(20.6%)	—	—

2012 Year-End Financials

Debt ratio: ——
Return on equity: 1.00%
Cash ($ mil.): 6
Current ratio: 1.20
Long-term debt ($ mil.): —
Dividends
Yield: —
Payout: —
Market value ($ mil.): —

R. M. PARKS INC.

LOCATIONS

HQ: R. M. PARKS INC.
1061 N MAIN ST, PORTERVILLE, CA 93257-1686
Phone: 559-784-2384

HISTORICAL FINANCIALS

Company Type: Private

Income Statement — FYE: October 31

	REVENUE ($ mil.)	NET INCOME ($ mil.)	NET PROFIT MARGIN	EMPLOYEES
10/11	583	0	0.1%	4
10/10	431	0	0.1%	0
10/09	325	0	0.1%	0
10/08	498	0	0.1%	0
Annual Growth	5.4%	(7.8%)	—	—

2011 Year-End Financials

Debt ratio: ——
Return on equity: 0.10%
Cash ($ mil.): 3
Current ratio: 0.80
Long-term debt ($ mil.): —
Dividends
Yield: —
Payout: —
Market value ($ mil.): —

R. P. LUMBER CO. INC.

LOCATIONS

HQ: R. P. LUMBER CO. INC.
514 E VANDALIA ST, EDWARDSVILLE, IL 62025-1855
Phone: 618-656-1514
Web: www.rplumber.com

HISTORICAL FINANCIALS

Company Type: Private

Income Statement — FYE: December 31

	REVENUE ($ mil.)	NET INCOME ($ mil.)	NET PROFIT MARGIN	EMPLOYEES
12/11	147	9	6.1%	500
12/10	142	6	4.7%	0
12/09	140	7	5.6%	0
12/08	142	3	2.7%	0
Annual Growth	1.1%	32.7%	—	—

2011 Year-End Financials

Debt ratio: ——
Return on equity: 6.10%
Cash ($ mil.): 1
Current ratio: 1.00
Long-term debt ($ mil.): —
Dividends
Yield: —
Payout: —
Market value ($ mil.): —

R.I.M. LOGISTICS LTD.

LOCATIONS

HQ: R.I.M. LOGISTICS LTD.
200 GARY AVE, ROSELLE, IL 60172-1681
Phone: 630-595-0610
Web: www.rimlogistics.com

HISTORICAL FINANCIALS

Company Type: Private

Income Statement — FYE: December 30

	REVENUE ($ mil.)	NET INCOME ($ mil.)	NET PROFIT MARGIN	EMPLOYEES
12/11	97	0	0.5%	250
12/10	76	0	1.1%	0
12/05*	36	7	20.8%	0
05/03	0	0	—	0
Annual Growth	—	—	—	—

*Fiscal year change

RADIANCE TECHNOLOGIES INC.

LOCATIONS

HQ: RADIANCE TECHNOLOGIES INC.
350 WYNN DR NW, HUNTSVILLE, AL 35805-1961
Phone: 256-704-3400
Web: www.radiancetechnologies.com

HISTORICAL FINANCIALS
Company Type: Private

Income Statement
FYE: December 31

	REVENUE ($ mil.)	NET INCOME ($ mil.)	NET PROFIT MARGIN	EMPLOYEES
12/11	138	6	4.6%	421
12/10	117	7	6.3%	0
12/09	106	3	3.7%	0
12/06	55	3	5.5%	0
Annual Growth	**35.5%**	**27.6%**	—	—

2011 Year-End Financials

Debt ratio: ——
Return on equity: 4.60%
Cash ($ mil.): 3
Current ratio: 0.20
Long-term debt ($ mil.): —

Dividends
Yield: —
Payout: —
Market value ($ mil.): —

RADY CHILDREN'S HOSPITAL-SAN DIEGO

Rady Children's Hospital-San Diego handles the big injuries of pint-sized patients. Serving as the region's only pediatric trauma center the nonprofit hospital boasts more than 460 beds. As part of its services Rady Children's Hospital-San Diego offers comprehensive pediatric care including surgical services convalescent care a neonatal intensive care unit and orthopedic services. Across its service area the hospital also operates about 25 satellite centers that provide such primary and specialized care services as physical therapy and hearing diagnostics. Rady Children's Hospital a teaching hospital affiliated with the University of California San Diego Medical School was founded in 1954.

Geographic Reach
Rady Children's Hospital serves as the pediatric medical center that caters to the California region of San Diego Imperial and southern Riverside counties. It provides care to more than 82% of the region's children.

Operations
Rady Children's operates its own 36-bed emergency department —The Sam S. and Rose Stein Emergency Care Center —that each day sees up to 300 patients. It is the only regional emergency center solely dedicated and equipped to care for children. The hospital also operates California's only pediatric skilled nursing facility —The Helen Bernardy Center —to provide 24-hour care to disabled and medically fragile children in a homelike environment.

For treating non-life-or-limb-threatening injuries and illnesses the hospital operates neighborhood urgent care centers in Escondido La Mesa Oceanside and San Diego.

Through its medical school affiliation Rady Children's engages in about 260 research studies and 170 clinical trials in all pediatric specialties. It collaborates with University of California San Diego the Sanford-Burnham Medical Research Institute The Scripps Research Institute the Salk Institute for Biological Studies and St. Jude Children's Research Hospital. Specialized research facilities on campus include the Autism Discovery Institute the Blair L. Sadler Center for Quality and the Child and Adolescent Services Research Center.

The hospital operates a LEED-certified Acute Care Pavilion which holds a neonatal intensive care unit the Peckham Center for Cancer and Blood Disorders and the Warren Family Surgical Center. It serves those suffering from eating disorders through its inpatient center (opened in 2011) to allow for intensive psychiatric therapy for patients with anorexia and bulimia and to aid families with home care.

Company Background
By Hospitals & Health Networks magazine Rady Children's Hospital was recognized in 2012 as one of the most wired hospitals in the nation. The hospital was recognized in U.S. News & World Report's 2011 ranking of the top 50 children's hospitals in 10 specialty areas. These included orthopedics urology neonatology diabetes and endocrinology and cancer. The hospital ranked in the top 25 in these specialties but also achieved rankings in the remaining categories: pulmonology nephrology cardiology and heart surgery gastroenterology and neurology and neurosurgery.

EXECUTIVES

SVP and CFO, Roger Roux
SVP and COO, Margareta E. (Meg) Norton
Public Information Officer, Ben Metcalf
President and CEO, Kathleen Sellick
Chairperson, Penny Dokmo
VP Human Resources, Mamoon Syed
Chief Medical Officer, Donald Kearns
VP and Chief Information Officer, Albert Oriol
VP and Chief Nursing Executive, Mary Fagan
Auditors: Deloitte&ToucheLLP

LOCATIONS

HQ: Rady Children' s Hospital-San Diego
3020 Children' s Way, San Diego CA 92123
Phone: 858-576-1700   **Fax:** 858-966-8531
Web: www.chsd.org

Selected Satellite Locations

Chula Vista
El Centro
Encinitas
Escondido
La Jolla
La Mesa
Murrieta
Oceanside
San Diego
Solana Beach

PRODUCTS/OPERATIONS

Selected Services

Allergy/Immunology
Attention Deficit Hyperactivity Disorder
Audiology/Hearing
Autism Discovery Institute
Behavioral Health
Brachial Plexus Clinic

Cancer & Blood Disorders
Cardiology
Cardiovascular Surgery
Celiac Disease Clinic
Center for Healthier Communities
Cerebral Palsy Center
Chadwick Center For Children & Families
Child & Adolescent Psychiatry Services (CAPS)
Child & Adolescent Services Research Center (CASRC)
Child Life Services
Children's Care Connection (C3)
Children's Hospital Emergency Transport (CHET)
Cleft Palate Clinic
Craniofacial Disorders
Critical Care
Cystic Fibrosis Center
Dental Surgery
Dermatology
Developmental Evaluation Clinic
Developmental-Behavioral Pediatrics
Developmental Screening & Enhancement Program (DSEP)
Developmental Services
Down Syndrome Center
Eating Disorders/ Medical-Behavioral Disorders Unit
Emergency Medicine
Endocrinology/Diabetes
Fatty Liver Clinic
Feeding Team
Gastroenterology Hepatology & Nutrition
Genetics/Dysmorphology
Heart Institute
Helen Bernardy Center for Medically Fragile Children
Hematology/Oncology
HomeCare
Hospice
Infectious Diseases
Kawasaki Disease Clinic
Kidney/Liver Tranplant Program
Kidney Disease
Laboratory Services/Pathology
Liver Disease
Liver Transplant
Muscle Disease Clinic
Metabolic Medicine
Neonatology
Nephrology
Neurology
Neurosurgery
Newborn Screening Program
Nutrition Clinic
Occupational Therapy
Ophthalmology
Orthopedics
Otolaryngology/ENT
Pain Services
Palliative Care
Pediatric Surgery
Pediatrics & Hospital Medicine
Pharmacy Services
Physical Therapy
Prader-Willi Syndrome Clinic
Psychiatry
Pulmonary/Respiratory Medicine
Radiology
Rehabilitation Medicine
Rheumatology
Sleep Center
Speech/Language Pathology
Spiritual Care
Sports Medicine
Surgery
Toddler School (Alexa's PLAYC)
Trauma Center
Urgent Care
Urology
Weight & Wellness Center

COMPETITORS

All Children' s Hospital
Children' s Health System
Children' s Hospital & Research Center at Oakland
Children' s Hospital of Orange County

Children's Hospital of Philadelphia
Children's Hospital of Richmond
Children's Specialized Hospital
Childrens Hospital Los Angeles
Cook Children's Health Care System
Dell Children's Medical Center
Nationwide Children's Hospital
Palomar Health
Scripps health
Seattle Children's Hospital
Sharp HealthCare
Shriners Hospitals For Children
St. Jude Children's Research Hospital
Sutter Health
Tri-City Healthcare District
UCSD Medical
UCSF Medical

HISTORICAL FINANCIALS
Company Type: Private - Not-for-Profit

Income Statement

	REVENUE ($ mil.)	NET INCOME ($ mil.)	NET PROFIT MARGIN	EMPLOYEES
06/11	756	96	12.7%	2,313
06/10	619	42	6.9%	0
06/09	490	(56)	—	0
06/08	511	69	13.7%	0
Annual Growth	14.0%	11.2%	—	—

FYE: June 30

2011 Year-End Financials

Debt ratio: ——
Return on equity: 12.70%
Cash ($ mil.): 47
Current ratio: 0.70
Long-term debt ($ mil.): —
Dividends
Yield: —
Payout: —
Market value ($ mil.): —

RALEY'S

Raley's has to stock plenty of fresh fruit and great wines —it sells to the people that produce them. The company operates about 125 supermarkets and superstores in California and Nevada. In addition to nearly 80 flagship Raley's Superstores the company operates about 20 Bel Air Markets (in the Sacramento area) Nob Hill Foods (an upscale Bay Area chain with about 20 locations) and nearly 10 discount warehouse stores under the Food Source banner in Northern California. Raley's stores typically offer groceries natural foods and liquor as well as in-store pharmacies. Founded during the Depression by Thomas Porter Raley the company is owned by Tom's daughter Joyce Raley Teel.

In addition to supermarkets Raley's operates about a dozen Aisle 1 full-service fuel stations in Northern California and Nevada.

Raley's three smaller chains serve different markets. Bel Air Markets are located in the greater Sacramento area. Nob Hill Foods stores are located along the Central Coast region of California and in the Bay Area. Food Source stores caters to customers in Hayward California the Sacramento area and northern Nevada.

The privately-owned company rang up an estimated $3 billion in sales in fiscal 2012 (ends June).

The company's store count is trending down as it struggles to compete. Indeed Raley's has announced the pending closure of two more stores in October which will bring to six the number of stores shuttered in 2012. Raley's is being squeezed

between non-traditional grocery operators such as Wal-Mart and WinCo Foods on the low end and more upscale chains like Whole Foods and grocery-giant Safeway. In a bid to cut costs the company has trimmed its executive ranks and cut health care coverage for retired hourly employees. The cost cutting has fueled speculation about Raley's future and led to strike threats by its unionized work force. The retailer has been closing conventional Raley's stores and in some cases converting them to its discount Food Source banner. The growing discount warehouse format caters to economically-stressed and value-seeking shoppers a growing niche in California and Nevada. Still the grocery chain's attempts to market itself as a value retailer haven't resonated with customers who increasingly are shopping elsewhere. Also Raley's has struggled to expand beyond its core market in California. It has a relatively small footprint in Nevada and exited New Mexico five years ago with the sale of its stores there to Albertsons.

EXECUTIVES

President and CEO, Michael J. Teel
Co-Chairman, James E. (Jim) Teel
Co-Chairman and Owner, Joyce Raley Teel, age 76
SVP Sales and Merchandising, Kevin Konkel
SVP and CIO, Gary Baumgartner
Communications Specialist, Amy Davis
Manager Community Relations, Jennifer (Jennie) Teel-Wolter
VP and Interim CFO, Ken Mueller
SVP Operations, Bob Abel
SVP Distribution and Logistics, Roger Bresnahan
Director Human Resources, Chris Clark
Senior Director Training and Performance, Susan Gilman
Senior Manager Human Resources Support, Wendy Campbell
Director Human Resources Project Management and Support, Deborah Curras

LOCATIONS

HQ: RALEY'S
500 W CAPITOL AVE, WEST SACRAMENTO, CA 95605-2696
Phone: 916-373-3333
Web: www.raleys.com

2012 Stores

	No.
California	115
Northern	13
Total	**128**

PRODUCTS/OPERATIONS

2012 Stores

	No.
Raley's	78
Nob	22
Bel	20
Food	8
Total	**128**

COMPETITORS

Andronico's Market	Safeway
Costco Wholesale	Save Mart
Food 4 Less Holdings	Trader Joe's
Grocery Outlet	Wal-Mart
Kroger	Whole Foods
Lunardi's Super Market	WinCo Foods
Ralphs Grocery	

HISTORICAL FINANCIALS
Company Type: Private

Income Statement

	REVENUE ($ mil.)	NET INCOME ($ mil.)	NET PROFIT MARGIN	EMPLOYEES
06/12	3,162	(1)	—	14,000
06/10	3,064	0	—	0
06/09	0	0	—	0
Annual Growth	—	—	—	—

FYE: June 30

2012 Year-End Financials

Debt ratio: ——
Return on equity: —
Cash ($ mil.): 26
Current ratio: 0.30
Long-term debt ($ mil.): —
Dividends
Yield: —
Payout: —
Market value ($ mil.): —

RANKEN TECHNICAL COLLEGE

Ranken Technical College offers postsecondary vocational education in a variety of technical and industrial fields. Students can gain certification or associate's degrees in automotive repair construction electronics information technology and industrial technology. The school is located in the Central West End of St. Louis. Irish-born David Ranken Jr. fulfilled his dream of founding a school for the teaching of mechanical trades when he established Ranken Technical College (then known as David Ranken Jr. School of Mechanical Trades) in 1907.

EXECUTIVES

President, Ben Ernst
VP Finance and Administration, Peter Murtaugh
VP Development, Timoth J. Willard
VP Education, Byron J. Gregery
Chairman, Robert W. Staley
Secretary Treasurer and Director, Dennis C. Donnelly
Director Annual Giving, Ken Meyer
Director Grants, Kent Hornberger
Director Major Gifts and Planned Giving, Tony Pisciotta
Director Alumni Relations, Kathy Fern
Coordinator Research and Records, Janna Greenwood
Records Specialist, Rose Crawford
Administrative Assistant, Pat Harting
Vice President of the Board, Lou Fusz Jr.
Secretary Treasurer and Director, Dennis C. Donnelly

LOCATIONS

HQ: Ranken Technical College
4431 Finney Ave., St. Louis MO 63113
Phone: 314-371-0236   **Fax:** 314-371-0241
Web: www.ranken.edu

Income Statement   FYE: June 30

	REVENUE ($ mil.)	NET INCOME ($ mil.)	NET PROFIT MARGIN	EMPLOYEES
06/11	39	16	40.4%	150
06/10	29	6	23.0%	0
Annual Growth	36.0%	139.0%	—	—

2011 Year-End Financials

Debt ratio: ——
Return on equity: 40.40%
Cash ($ mil.): 6
Current ratio: 0.30
Long-term debt ($ mil.): —

Dividends
Yield: —
Payout: —
Market value ($ mil.): —

RAPID CITY REGIONAL HOSPITAL INC.

Mt. Rushmore sightseers bikers and locals alike can seek medical care at Rapid City Regional Hospital. The medical facility is a general and psychiatric hospital with some 330 acute care beds and 50 psychiatric beds located in the Black Hills region of western South Dakota. In addition to emergency and acute care the not-for-profit hospital also offers a behavioral health center a rehabilitation facility a cancer care institute and women's and children's departments. Rapid City Regional Hospital which was established in 1973 is part of Regional Health a network of regional hospitals medical clinics and senior care centers.

Operations

In addition to Rapid City Regional Hospital the Regional Health group includes the Custer Regional Lead-Deadwood Regional Spearfish Regional and Sturgis Regional hospitals. It also operates area clinics and doctors' offices including a family medicine clinic that manages a physician residency program as well as retirement communities and nursing homes. Altogether Regional Health has a total of about 40 facilities in South Dakota's Black Hills region.

EXECUTIVES

Medical Staff Secretary and Treasurer and Director, Steve Frost
CEO and Director, Timothy H. (Tim) Sughrue
Media Relations Coordinator, Pamela Stillman-Rokusek
VP Medical Affairs, Robert Allen Jr.
Chief Medical Officer, James Keegan
Chairman, Edward H. (Ed) Yelick
Treasurer and Director, Jim Sorensen
Vice Chair, Sharon I. Lee
Secretary and Director, Raymond G. Burnett
Vice President of Operations, Suzanne Koehler
COO, Robert (Bob) Baxter
Chief of Staff and Director, Gary Bochna
Vice Chief of Staff and Director, Michael Statz
VP Patient Care, Rita Haxton
VP Professional Services, Heather Smith
VP Ancillary Services, Allan Berreth
Interim Director Volunteer Services, Konnie Sorensen

EVP and Chief Administrative Officer, Joseph Sluka
Medical Staff Secretary and Treasurer and Director, Steve Frost
Director, Charles E. Hart, age 62
CEO and Director, Timothy H. (Tim) Sughrue
Treasurer and Director, Jim Sorensen
Vice Chair, Sharon I. Lee
Director, Dale Bachwich
Secretary and Director, Raymond G. Burnett
Director, Steven (Steve) McCarthy
Director, Thomas Shortbull
Chief of Staff and Director, Gary Bochna
Director, Stephen Kovarik
Director, Tom Morrison
Director, Tamara Riddle-Schumacher
Vice Chief of Staff and Director, Michael Statz

LOCATIONS

HQ: Rapid City Regional Hospital Inc.
353 Fairmont Blvd., Rapid City SD 57701
Phone: 605-719-1000   **Fax:** 212-279-9171

PRODUCTS/OPERATIONS

Selected Services
Bariatrics and Weight Management
Behavioral Health
Bones Muscles and Joints
Brain and Spine
Cancer Care
Clinics (Primary and Speciality)
Diabetes
Heart and Vascular Care
Home Care
Home Medical Equipment
Hospice Care
Hospitalist
Hyperbaric Oxygen Therapy
Infusion Services
Intensive Care
Laboratory Services
Labor and Delivery
Lactation Services
Medical Imaging
Digital Mammography
Neonatal Care
Neurology
Nutrition Services
Pain Management
Pediatrics
Physical Therapy and Rehabilitation
Regional Health Research
Senior Care
Sepsis
Sports Medicine
Stroke Care
Telemedicine
Wound Care

COMPETITORS

Avera Health
Sanford
Health-MeritCare

St. Mary's Healthcare

HISTORICAL FINANCIALS
Company Type: Private - Not-for-Profit

Income Statement   FYE: June 30

	REVENUE ($ mil.)	NET INCOME ($ mil.)	NET PROFIT MARGIN	EMPLOYEES
06/11	142	39	27.6%	4,200
06/10	409	65	16.0%	0
06/09	381	42	11.0%	0
06/08	358	47	13.2%	0
Annual Growth	(26.4%)	(5.7%)	—	—

2011 Year-End Financials

Debt ratio: ——
Return on equity: 27.60%
Cash ($ mil.): 20
Current ratio: 1.80
Long-term debt ($ mil.): —

Dividends
Yield: —
Payout: —
Market value ($ mil.): —

RAPIDES PARISH SCHOOL DISTRICT

LOCATIONS

HQ: RAPIDES PARISH SCHOOL DISTRICT
619 6TH ST, ALEXANDRIA, LA 71301-8150
Phone: 318-487-0888

HISTORICAL FINANCIALS
Company Type: Private

Income Statement   FYE: June 30

	REVENUE ($ mil.)	NET INCOME ($ mil.)	NET PROFIT MARGIN	EMPLOYEES
06/11	232	10	4.5%	3,400
06/10	234	20	8.9%	0
06/08	217	(9)	—	0
06/07	202	(2)	—	0
Annual Growth	4.8%	—	—	—

2011 Year-End Financials

Debt ratio: ——
Return on equity: 4.50%
Cash ($ mil.): 67
Current ratio: —
Long-term debt ($ mil.): —

Dividends
Yield: —
Payout: —
Market value ($ mil.): —

RAPPAHANNOCK ELECTRIC COOPERATIVE

Like the river it's named after the Rappahannock Electric Cooperative (REC) keeps the power running smoothly. The consumer-owned cooperative provides electricity to homes businesses and industries in parts of 22 counties from the Blue Ridge Mountains to the mouth of the Rappahannock River in eastern Virginia. REC supplies power to 155000 members over more than 16000 miles of power line. REC offers surge protection internet services and home security plans to entice customers as competition from other suppliers arrives. Once rural in nature the cooperative's territory has seen large pockets of suburban growth.

Dramatically growing its business in 2010 the company and fellow co-op Shenandoah Valley Electric Cooperatives acquired Potomac Edison (Allegheny Energy's electric distribution operations in Virginia) for about $340 million. The expansion increased REC's coverage from 16 counties to 22 its customer base by about 50% and boosted the company's revenues and net income for the year.

REC is also pursuing ways to help its customers to become more energy efficient to help them save money and to help the cooperative trim its power capacity growth plans. Supported by a $16 million federal green energy grant awarded in 2010 the company is replacing customers' older meters with smart (automated efficient) ones. It installed some 4000 smart meters at business customer locations that year.

REC was formed when the Virginia Electric Cooperative in Bowling Green and the Northern Piedmont Electric Cooperative in Culpeper merged in 1980.

EXECUTIVES

President and CEO, Kent D. Farmer
VP Corporate Services, J. Bruce Barnett
VP Engineering and Operations, Robert A. Ellis
Treasurer and Director, Linda R. Gray
Vice Chairman, Richard C. Oliver
Secretary and Director, Frank B. Boxley
Chairman, A. Nash Johnston
Director, Darlene H. Carpenter, age 66
Director, Wickham B. Coleman
Director, William E. Lane
Treasurer and Director, Linda R. Gray
Vice Chairman, Richard C. Oliver
Director, William C. Frazier
Secretary and Director, Frank B. Boxley
Director, Lee S. Estes
Director, Frank D. Ashley
Director, William M. Alphin

LOCATIONS

HQ: Rappahannock Electric Cooperative
247 Industrial Ct., Fredericksburg VA 22408-7388
Phone: 540-898-8500   **Fax:** 540-891-5981
Web: www.myrec.coop/residential/index.cfm

PRODUCTS/OPERATIONS

2010 Sales

	$ mil.	% of total
% of total		
Residential		64
Large		28
Small		7
Public		1
Total		**100**

COMPETITORS

Pepco Energy Services   WGL Holdings
Virginia Electric and
Power

HISTORICAL FINANCIALS

Company Type: Private - Cooperative

Income Statement

FYE: December 31

	REVENUE ($ mil.)	NET INCOME ($ mil.)	NET PROFIT MARGIN	EMPLOYEES
12/11	410	17	4.2%	267
12/10	352	32	9.1%	0
12/09	276	31	11.3%	0
12/08	283	14	5.2%	0
Annual Growth	**13.2%**	**5.2%**	—	—

2011 Year-End Financials

Debt ratio: —	
Return on equity: 4.20%	Dividends
Cash ($ mil.): 3	Yield: —
Current ratio: 0.10	Payout: —
Long-term debt ($ mil.): —	Market value ($ mil.): —

RARITAN VALLEY COMMUNITY COLLEGE

Raritan Valley Community College provides more than 80 associate degree and certification programs to residents in central New Jersey's Somerset and Hunterdon counties. The school's academic departments include Business and Public Service Computer Science English Mathematics Science and Engineering and Visual and Performing Arts. The college also provides customized training programs and non-credit courses as well as job and career counseling services. More than 11000 students take classes at Raritan Valley Community College which was founded in 1965.

EXECUTIVES

Chairman, Richard D. Wellbrock
Dean of College Advancement, Jacki Belin
SVP Academic Affairs, Dehlly Porras
Dean of Student Services, Diane Lemcoe
Director Financial Aid, Leonard Mesonas
Director Library, Birthe Nebeker
President, Kathleen Crabill
Purchasing Coordinator, Michael DePinto
Director Transfer and Career Services, Paul Michaud
Registrar, Richard Cole
Director Facilities and Grounds, Brian O'Rourke

LOCATIONS

HQ: RARITAN VALLEY COMMUNITY COLLEGE
118 LAMINGTON RD, BRANCHBURG, NJ 08876-3315
Phone: 908-526-1200
Web: www.rvccarts.com

COMPETITORS

Bergen Community   Montclair State
College   New Jersey Institute
Fairleigh Dickinson   of Technology
University   Rutgers University

HISTORICAL FINANCIALS

Company Type: School

Income Statement

FYE: June 30

	REVENUE ($ mil.)	NET INCOME ($ mil.)	NET PROFIT MARGIN	EMPLOYEES
06/11	60	(3)	—	550
06/10	61	0	1.1%	0
06/08	56	3	6.4%	0
06/06	22	(0)	—	0
Annual Growth	**40.2%**	—	—	—

2011 Year-End Financials

Debt ratio: —	
Return on equity: (-5.00)%	Dividends
Cash ($ mil.): 9	Yield: —
Current ratio: 2.20	Payout: —
Long-term debt ($ mil.): —	Market value ($ mil.): —

RED APPLE SCHOOL INC

LOCATIONS

HQ: RED APPLE SCHOOL INC
6640 KENTUCKY AVE, NEW PORT RICHEY, FL 34653-2712
Phone: 727-847-2555
Web: www.redappleadt.org

HISTORICAL FINANCIALS

Company Type: Private

Income Statement

FYE: December 31

	REVENUE ($ mil.)	NET INCOME ($ mil.)	NET PROFIT MARGIN	EMPLOYEES
12/11	151	6	4.0%	2
12/10	1	0	5.3%	0
Annual Growth	**10308.4%**	**7866.6%**	—	—

2011 Year-End Financials

Debt ratio: —	
Return on equity: 4.00%	Dividends
Cash ($ mil.): 28	Yield: —
Current ratio: —	Payout: —
Long-term debt ($ mil.): —	Market value ($ mil.): —

REDAPT SYSTEMS INC.

LOCATIONS

HQ: REDAPT SYSTEMS INC.
12226 134TH CT NE BLDG D, REDMOND, WA 98052-2429
Phone: 425-882-0400
Web: www.redapt.com

HISTORICAL FINANCIALS

Company Type: Private

Income Statement

FYE: December 31

	REVENUE ($ mil.)	NET INCOME ($ mil.)	NET PROFIT MARGIN	EMPLOYEES
12/11	148	4	3.1%	45
12/06	24	0	3.4%	0
12/05	24	3	15.0%	0
12/04	25	(2)	—	0
Annual Growth	**80.7%**	—	—	—

2011 Year-End Financials

Debt ratio: —	
Return on equity: 3.10%	Dividends
Cash ($ mil.): 0	Yield: —
Current ratio: 1.00	Payout: —
Long-term debt ($ mil.): —	Market value ($ mil.): —

REDNER'S MARKETS INC.

Redner's Markets operates 40-plus warehouse club-style supermarkets under the Redner's Warehouse Markets banner and more than 15 Quick Shoppe convenience stores. Most of the company's stores are located in eastern Pennsylvania but the regional grocer also operates several locations in Maryland and Delaware having closed its one New York location. Redner's Warehouse Markets house bakery deli meat produce and seafood departments as well as in-store banks. The employee-owned company was founded by namesake Earl Redner in 1970. It is still operated by the Redner family including chairman and CEO Richard and COO Ryan Redner.

Financial Analysis

Redner's Markets rang up an estimated $859 million in sales in fiscal 2011 (ends September) compared with about $820 million in fiscal 2010.

Strategy

Redner's has been tinkering with its store portfolio shuttering underperforming locations including several in its core Pennsylvania market while building new stores in existing and new markets. Since entering Delaware with a store in Dover in 2008 a second store is slated for Dover in summer 2013 its fourth in the tiny state. It also added a store in Dundalk Maryland in 2011 after entering the market in 2005.

EXECUTIVES

Chairman President and CEO, Richard Redner
EVP Procurement and Director Wholesale Operations, Gary M. Redner
COO, Ryan S. Redner
VP Human Resources, Robert (Bob) McDonough
Consumer Communications Specialist, Eric B. White
VP Perishable Operations, Gary O'Brien
VP Grocery Operations, Frank Fiore
VP Information Technology, John Sweigart
VP and General Counsel, Jason Hopp
VP Construction Real Estate and Maintenance, Doug Emore
VP Finance, Michael McNaney

LOCATIONS

HQ: REDNER' S MARKETS INC.
3 QUARRY RD, READING, PA 19605-9787
Phone: 610-926-3700
Web: www.rednersmarkets.com

2011 Warehouse Market Stores

	No.
Pennsylvania	35
Maryland	3
Delaware	2
Total	**40**

PRODUCTS/OPERATIONS

2011 Stores

	No.
Redner's Warehouse	40
Quick	16
Total	**56**

COMPETITORS

7-Eleven	Wal-Mart

A&P	Wawa Inc.
Cumberland Farms	Wegmans
Giant Food Stores	Weis Markets
Sheetz	

HISTORICAL FINANCIALS

Company Type: Private

Income Statement

FYE: October 1

	REVENUE ($ mil.)	NET INCOME ($ mil.)	NET PROFIT MARGIN	EMPLOYEES
10/11	858	6	0.8%	4,200
10/10*	831	6	0.8%	0
09/09	807	8	1.0%	0
09/08	811	6	0.9%	0
Annual Growth	**1.9%**	**(1.6%)**	**—**	**—**

*Fiscal year change

2011 Year-End Financials

Debt ratio: —
Return on equity: 0.80%
Cash ($ mil.): 44
Current ratio: 1.40
Long-term debt ($ mil.): —

Dividends
Yield: —
Payout: —
Market value ($ mil.): —

REF-CHEM L.P.

LOCATIONS

HQ: REF-CHEM L.P.
1128 S GRANDVIEW AVE, ODESSA, TX 79761-7137
Phone: 432-332-8531
Web: www.ref-chem.com

HISTORICAL FINANCIALS

Company Type: Private

Income Statement

FYE: December 31

	REVENUE ($ mil.)	NET INCOME ($ mil.)	NET PROFIT MARGIN	EMPLOYEES
12/11	182	8	4.5%	1,000
12/10	100	3	3.3%	0
12/09	92	4	5.4%	0
12/08	104	5	5.6%	0
Annual Growth	**20.2%**	**12.1%**	**—**	**—**

2011 Year-End Financials

Debt ratio: —
Return on equity: 4.50%
Cash ($ mil.): 8
Current ratio: 1.50
Long-term debt ($ mil.): —

Dividends
Yield: —
Payout: —
Market value ($ mil.): —

REGENT UNIVERSITY

LOCATIONS

HQ: REGENT UNIVERSITY
1000 REGENT UNIVERSITY DR, VIRGINIA BEACH, VA 23464-9800
Phone: 757-352-4127
Web: www.regent.edu

HISTORICAL FINANCIALS

Company Type: Private

Income Statement

FYE: June 30

	REVENUE ($ mil.)	NET INCOME ($ mil.)	NET PROFIT MARGIN	EMPLOYEES
06/11	107	1	1.1%	450
06/10	91	(7)	—	0
06/09	60	0	—	0
06/08	102	(2)	—	0
Annual Growth	**1.4%**	**—**	**—**	**—**

2011 Year-End Financials

Debt ratio: —
Return on equity: 1.10%
Cash ($ mil.): 0
Current ratio: —
Long-term debt ($ mil.): —

Dividends
Yield: —
Payout: —
Market value ($ mil.): —

REGIONAL WEST HEALTH SERVICES INC

LOCATIONS

HQ: REGIONAL WEST HEALTH SERVICES INC
4021 AVENUE B, SCOTTSBLUFF, NE 69361-4602
Phone: 308-635-3711
Web: www.rwmc.net

HISTORICAL FINANCIALS

Company Type: Private

Income Statement

FYE: December 31

	REVENUE ($ mil.)	NET INCOME ($ mil.)	NET PROFIT MARGIN	EMPLOYEES
12/11	257	5	2.0%	1,500
12/09	6	3	49.6%	0
12/07	155	(4)	—	0
12/06	0	0	96.8%	0
Annual Growth	**630.8%**	**101.4%**	**—**	**—**

2011 Year-End Financials

Debt ratio: —
Return on equity: 2.00%
Cash ($ mil.): 9
Current ratio: 1.20
Long-term debt ($ mil.): —

Dividends
Yield: —
Payout: —
Market value ($ mil.): —

REI SYSTEMS INC.

No they don't sell hiking boots or kayaks. REI Systems provides information technology services and develops custom Web-based software used to automate the management of internal business communications contracts customer relationships and grants. Its Electronic Handbooks application is used to manage a variety of data collection and reporting functions; MaintenanceMax is an organizational tool for equipment maintenance providers. The company's IT services include database design software integration and network security. REI Systems' clientele is made up largely of US government agencies such as the Department of Energy and the Department of Defense; commercial clients have included Raytheon.

The company has sales and service partnerships with other software and IT service vendors including salesforce.com BEA Systems and Oracle. REI Systems is contracted by those companies to provide consulting implementation and support services related to their respective products.

Founded in 1989 the company's first customer was NASA.

EXECUTIVES

President and CEO, Veer Bhartiya
EVP and CTO, Shyam Salona
COO, Scott Fletcher
Technical Support, Sachin Kapoor
Human Resources, Lisa Chaboudy
VP, Subhash Kari
Marketing and Sales, Derek Sheets

LOCATIONS

HQ: REI Systems Inc.
200 Fairbrook Dr. Ste. 104, Herndon VA 20170
Phone: 703-480-9100   **Fax:** 703-689-4680
Web: www.reisys.com

COMPETITORS

Apptis
CACI International
Computer Sciences Corp.
General Dynamics Information Technology
HP Enterprise Services
IBM
Unisys
Wyle Information Systems

HISTORICAL FINANCIALS
Company Type: Private

Income Statement				FYE: December 31
	REVENUE ($ mil.)	NET INCOME ($ mil.)	NET PROFIT MARGIN	EMPLOYEES
12/11	66	4	6.4%	311
12/10	56	4	8.5%	0
12/09	38	3	8.0%	0
12/08	26	1	5.3%	0
Annual Growth	35.3%	44.5%	—	—

2011 Year-End Financials

Debt ratio: —
Return on equity: 6.40%
Cash ($ mil.): 4
Current ratio: 4.30
Long-term debt ($ mil.): —
Dividends
  Yield: —
  Payout: —
Market value ($ mil.): —

REID HOSPITAL & HEALTH CARE SERVICES INC.

LOCATIONS

HQ: REID HOSPITAL & HEALTH CARE SERVICES INC.
1100 REID PKWY, RICHMOND, IN 47374-1157
Phone: 765-983-3000
Web: www.reidhosp.com

HISTORICAL FINANCIALS
Company Type: Private

Income Statement				FYE: December 31
	REVENUE ($ mil.)	NET INCOME ($ mil.)	NET PROFIT MARGIN	EMPLOYEES
12/11	294	(47)	—	1,800
12/10	294	2	1.0%	0
12/09	282	25	8.9%	0
12/01	136	7	5.2%	0
Annual Growth	29.2%	—	—	—

2011 Year-End Financials

Debt ratio: —
Return on equity: (-16.00)%
Cash ($ mil.): 20
Current ratio: 2.10
Long-term debt ($ mil.): —
Dividends
  Yield: —
  Payout: —
Market value ($ mil.): —

RENO CONTRACTING INC.

Reno Contracting is building on its commercial state of mind in the southern part of the Golden State. The general contractor specializes in commercial construction projects primarily in its home region of San Diego County California. Projects include office retail and hospitality construction biotech and industrial facilities and hospitals. Reno develops properties from the ground up and also performs interior tenant improvements. Clients have included Diversa Corporation Biosite and Bridgepoint Education. Reno's green building division Reno ESP utilizes energy efficient products and technology in the construction process. The company was founded in 1993 by CEO Matt Reno.

EXECUTIVES

CEO, Matthew J. (Matt) Reno
President, Walter J. (Walt) Fegley
CFO, Linda Melemed
Project Director, Chris Heim
Chief Estimator and Senior Project Manager,
  Craig Hueners
Director of Field Operations, Erik Kissner
Senior Project Manager, Kevin Horst
Project Manager, Wade Richardson
Senior Project Manager, Rick Laferney
Project Manager, Rod Tower
Quality Assurance Manager, Robert (Bob) Buchanan

LOCATIONS

HQ: Reno Contracting Inc.
1450 Frazee Rd. Ste. 100, San Diego CA 92108
Phone: 619-220-0224   **Fax:** 619-220-0029
Web: www.renocon.com

COMPETITORS

Barnhart
Bycor General
  Contractors
Consolidated
  Contracting Services
Fullmer Construction
Grant General
  Contractors
Moorefield
  Construction
Pacific Building Group

HISTORICAL FINANCIALS
Company Type: Private

Income Statement				FYE: October 31
	REVENUE ($ mil.)	NET INCOME ($ mil.)	NET PROFIT MARGIN	EMPLOYEES
10/11	37	(1)	—	32
10/10	60	0	1.6%	0
10/08	213	1	0.7%	0
10/07	217	1	0.6%	0
Annual Growth	(44.5%)	—	—	—

2011 Year-End Financials

Debt ratio: —
Return on equity: (-3.90)%
Cash ($ mil.): 2
Current ratio: 0.20
Long-term debt ($ mil.): —
Dividends
  Yield: —
  Payout: —
Market value ($ mil.): —

RESEARCH FOD FOR MTAL HY INC.

LOCATIONS

HQ: RESEARCH FOD FOR MTAL HY INC.
150 BROADWAY STE 301, MENANDS, NY 12204-2726
Phone: 518-474-5661

HISTORICAL FINANCIALS
Company Type: Private

Income Statement				FYE: March 31
	REVENUE ($ mil.)	NET INCOME ($ mil.)	NET PROFIT MARGIN	EMPLOYEES
03/12	129	4	3.6%	1,250
03/11	129	4	3.8%	0
03/10	131	9	7.4%	0
03/09	113	(7)	—	0
Annual Growth	4.3%	—	—	—

2012 Year-End Financials

Debt ratio: —
Return on equity: 3.60%
Cash ($ mil.): 9
Current ratio: 0.30
Long-term debt ($ mil.): —
Dividends
  Yield: —
  Payout: —
Market value ($ mil.): —

RETAIL CONCEPTS INC.

LOCATIONS

HQ: RETAIL CONCEPTS INC.
10560 BTXONNET ST STE 100, HOUSTON, TX 77099
Phone: 281-340-5000
Web: www.sunandski.com

HISTORICAL FINANCIALS

Company Type: Private

Income Statement

FYE: March 25

	REVENUE ($ mil.)	NET INCOME ($ mil.)	NET PROFIT MARGIN	EMPLOYEES
03/12	85	1	1.8%	650
03/11	81	4	5.0%	0
03/10	75	2	2.8%	0
03/09	66	0	0.5%	0
Annual Growth	**8.8%**	**74.1%**	**—**	**—**

2012 Year-End Financials

Debt ratio: ——
Return on equity: 1.80%
Cash ($ mil.): 0
Current ratio: 0.10
Long-term debt ($ mil.): ——

Dividends
Yield: —
Payout: —
Market value ($ mil.): —

REX ELECTRIC & TECHNOLOGIES LLC

LOCATIONS

HQ: REX ELECTRIC & TECHNOLOGIES LLC
200 W MONROE ST STE 1700, CHICAGO, IL 60606-5072
Phone: 312-251-3620
Web: www.rexelectric.com

HISTORICAL FINANCIALS

Company Type: Private

Income Statement

FYE: December 31

	REVENUE ($ mil.)	NET INCOME ($ mil.)	NET PROFIT MARGIN	EMPLOYEES
12/11	80	1	1.5%	300
12/10	69	0	0.1%	0
12/09	69	0	0.2%	0
12/08	84	0	0.5%	0
Annual Growth	**(1.6%)**	**44.9%**	**—**	**—**

REX HEALTHCARE INC.

Rex is a king of health care in Raleigh. Part of the UNC HealthCare System Rex Healthcare is a not-for-profit health care provider that serves residents of Raleigh and the rest of Wake County North Carolina. Founded in 1894 Rex Healthcare includes the more than 430-bed acute-care Rex Hospital and two nursing homes with nearly 230 beds as well as primary and specialty care clinics throughout the area. Specialty centers and clinics provide services such as birthing cancer treatment same-day surgery heart and vascular care pain management and sleep disorder therapy. Rex also provides home health and mobile emergency medical services. UNC HealthCare also includes affiliate UNC Hospitals.

Operations

The healthcare system employs a medical staff of more than 1100 physicians and 1700 nurses. Its operations consist of an acute care hospital five wellness centers a pair of skilled nursing facilities (for rehabilitation and long-term nursing care) six suburban campuses and freestanding outpatient diagnostic urgent care and surgery centers.

Geographic Reach

Rex Healthcare operates facilities in Wake County North Carolina in the cities of Apex Cary Garner Holly Springs Knightdale Wakefield and Raleigh.

Strategy

Looking to provide the most promising innovations among new medical services tools and technologies Rex Healthcare in 2012 funded the newly launched Rex Strategic Innovations with an initial $10 million investment. Venture capital investment fund Rex Health Ventures plans to invest in researchers entrepreneurs and inventors and support start-up companies.

Company Background

In 2011 rival WakeMed offered to buy Rex Healthcare for about $750 million. WakeMed says the purchase would eliminate duplicate services from the regions the two health care providers serve. Rex Healthcare responded by saying it's not for sale and considers the offer "hostile." WakeMed previously filed a complaint with the state against Rex Healthcare saying it was creating duplicative services especially in the areas of surgery and cardiac care.

EXECUTIVES

President, David W. Strong
Vice President Ambulatory Services, Tom Williams
VP Support Services, Chad T. Lefteris
Associate VP Marketing Public Relations Community Relations and Government Affairs, Lisa Schiller
Community Relations Coordinator, Gloria Lopez
Senior Vice President Chief Financial Officer, Bernadette Spong
SVP Patient Services and Chief Nursing Officer, Mary Lou Powell
VP Human Resources, Sylvia Hackett
COO, Steve Burriss
VP Heart and Vascular Services UNC Health Care System, R. Erick Hawkins
VP Surgical Services, Jane Byrd
VP Rex Physician Services and Executive Operations Director University of North Carolina Physician Network, Bob Ricker
CIO, Novlet Bradshaw
VP Fundraising and Chief Development Officer, Emily Barbour
General Counsel, Don Esposito
Marketing Communications Coordinator, Jenny Johnson
Media Relations Manager, Melody Hunter-Pillion
Public Relations Manager, Kerry Grace Heckle
VP Post Acute Services UNC Health Care System, Tamie Stanton
VP Medical Affairs Chief Medical Officer and Chief Medical Information Officer, Linda Butler
Executive Director, Amy Daniels
Director Corporate, Carson Gilbert
Treasurer of Wake County Interact Board, Carolina Scout
Chairman, Dale Jenkins
Director Major Gifts, Katherine Stokes

LOCATIONS

HQ: Rex Healthcare Inc.
4420 Lake Boone Tr., Raleigh NC 27607
Phone: 919-784-3100   **Fax:** 207-783-4756
Web: www.swbconst.com

PRODUCTS/OPERATIONS

Selected Specialty Services

Oncology
Heart and vascular
Surgical Services: Bariatric Heartburn and GI
Orthopedic Neuro and Spine
Rehabilitation
Emergency and Urgent Care
Women's Services
Wound Healing

COMPETITORS

Carolinas HealthCare System
Cumberland County Hospital System
Danville Regional Medical Center
Duke University Health System
FirstHealth of the Carolinas
Morehead Memorial Hospital
Moses Cone Health
Novant Health
Vidant Health
Wake Forest University Baptist Medical Center
WakeMed

HISTORICAL FINANCIALS

Company Type: Private - Not-for-Profit

Income Statement

FYE: June 30

	REVENUE ($ mil.)	NET INCOME ($ mil.)	NET PROFIT MARGIN	EMPLOYEES
06/12	719	34	4.8%	5,500
06/11	628	69	11.0%	0
06/10	571	46	8.2%	0
06/09	513	(10)	—	0
Annual Growth	**11.9%**	**—**	**—**	**—**

2012 Year-End Financials

Debt ratio: ——
Return on equity: 4.80%
Cash ($ mil.): 70
Current ratio: 1.40
Long-term debt ($ mil.): ——

Dividends
Yield: —
Payout: —
Market value ($ mil.): —

RHODE ISLAND SCHOOL OF DESIGN INC

The Rhode Island School of Design (RISD pronounced RIZ-dee) is among the highest-rated fine arts colleges in the US. The private school enrolls about 1300 undergraduate and graduate students. It offers a variety of fine arts and design programs including art history apparel design architecture jewelry industrial design film printmaking textiles and painting. The college also offers continuing education through classes lectures workshops gallery talks and a six-week pre-college program designed for high schoolers. Notable alumni include David Byrne Tina Weymouth and Chris Frantz of the Talking Heads. RISD was founded in 1877.

EXECUTIVES

EVP Finance and Administration, W. Arnold Yasinski
Director Admissions and Financial Aid, Edward E. Newhall Jr.
President, John Maeda
Provost, E. Jessie Shefrin
VP Human Resources, Candace Baer
VP Media and Partners, Becky Bermont
Associate Provost Academic Affairs, David Bogen
Interim Associate Provost Student Affairs, Barbara Fienman
VP Institutional Engagement, Beth Garvin
Director Office of Public Engagement, Peter Hocking
Interim VP Finance and Administration, Kelly Morra
Director Media Relations, Jaime Marland
Interim Director RISD Museum of Art, Ann Woolsey
Auditors: PricewaterhouseCoopersLLP

LOCATIONS

HQ: Rhode Island School of Design
2 College St., Providence RI 02903
Phone: 401-454-6100 **Fax:** 401-454-6406
Web: www.risd.edu

HISTORICAL FINANCIALS
Company Type: School

Income Statement

	REVENUE ($ mil.)	NET INCOME ($ mil.)	NET PROFIT MARGIN	EMPLOYEES
06/11	141	12	8.8%	948
06/10	150	27	18.3%	0
06/09	101	(27)	—	0
06/08	133	13	9.7%	0
Annual Growth	1.8%	(1.5%)		

FYE: June 30

2011 Year-End Financials

Debt ratio: —
Return on equity: 8.80%
Cash ($ mil.): 28
Current ratio: —
Long-term debt ($ mil.): —
Dividends
Yield: —
Payout: —
Market value ($ mil.): —

RHODES COLLEGE

Rhodes College helps its students get further down the road to edification. A private liberal arts school in historic downtown Memphis Rhodes College enrolls about 1700 students in academic majors including biology English international studies and business administration. Rhodes College's students come from about 45 states and 15 countries. It additionally offers a Master's degree in accounting. In total Rhodes College offers more than 30 majors and 35 minors. The school also provides continuing education courses to the community. Founded in 1848 the college is supported by an endowment of more than $230 million. The stu-

dent-to-faculty ratio is about 10:1 and the average class size is just 13.

EXECUTIVES

Dean Admissions and Financial Aid, David J. Wottle
Director Communications, Daney D. Kepple
Associate VP Finance and Business Affairs and Comptroller, N. P. McWhirter II
Director Human Resources, Claire Revels Shapiro
Manager Employment and Training, Lori Von Bokel-Amin
Director Information Technology Services, L. Charles Lemond
President, William E. (Bill) Troutt
Bursar, Richard F. Huddleston
Associate VP College Relations, Warren A. (Bud) Richey
VP Finance and Business Affairs, James A. Boone Jr.
Director Career Services, Sandra George Tracy
Director Financial Aid, Forrest M. Stuart
VP Student and Information Services, Robert M. Johnson Jr.
VP Academic Affairs and Dean Faculty, Michael R. Drompp
VP Development, Jennifer Goodloe Wade
VP College Relations, Russell T. Wigginton
VP Academic Affairs and Provost, Charlotte G. Borst

LOCATIONS

HQ: Rhodes College
2000 N. Pkwy., Memphis TN 38112-1690
Phone: 901-843-3000 **Fax:** 901-843-3969
Web: www.rhodes.edu

HISTORICAL FINANCIALS
Company Type: School

Income Statement

	REVENUE ($ mil.)	NET INCOME ($ mil.)	NET PROFIT MARGIN	EMPLOYEES
06/12	66	(12)	—	400
06/11	64	32	50.6%	0
06/10	65	24	38.1%	0
06/09	61	(52)	—	0
Annual Growth	2.5%	—	—	—

FYE: June 30

2012 Year-End Financials

Debt ratio: —
Return on equity: (-18.70)%
Cash ($ mil.): 7
Current ratio: —
Long-term debt ($ mil.): —
Dividends
Yield: —
Payout: —
Market value ($ mil.): —

RIALTO UNIFIED SCHOOL DISTRICT

LOCATIONS

HQ: RIALTO UNIFIED SCHOOL DISTRICT
182 E WALNUT AVE, RIALTO, CA 92376-3598
Phone: 909-820-7700
Web: www.rialtoschools.org

HISTORICAL FINANCIALS
Company Type: Private

Income Statement

	REVENUE ($ mil.)	NET INCOME ($ mil.)	NET PROFIT MARGIN	EMPLOYEES
06/11	225	18	8.3%	2,833
06/06	231	(8)	—	0
06/05	226	(22)	—	0
06/04	1,534	0	—	0
Annual Growth	—	10906.7%	—	—

FYE: June 30

RICELAND FOODS INC.

Handling more than 125 million bushels of grain a year Riceland Foods is ingrained in its business. The agricultural cooperative processes and markets the rice soybeans and wheat grown by its 9000 member/owners who farm in Arkansas Louisiana Mississippi Missouri and Texas. One of the world's largest rice millers it sells white and brown rice plus flavored rices and meal kits under the Riceland and private-label brands. The co-op sells to food retailers and food service and food manufacturing companies worldwide. Riceland also makes cooking oils and processes soybeans bran and lecithin and offers rice bran and hulls to pet food makers and livestock farmers as feed and bedding.

Geographic Reach

Arkansas-based Riceland provides marketing services to farmers in its home state as well as Louisiana Mississippi Missouri and Texas.

Operations

A major rice exporter and edible oil producer Riceland markets its rice and oil products under the Riceland and Chefway (vegetable oil and shortening) labels. Its products are sold nationwide and to more than 75 foreign destinations.

In addition to being a leader in rice milling the cooperative is a major soybean processor. Indeed its soybean processing plant in Stuttgart Arkansas provides high-protein soybean meal and soybean mill run to poultry catfish and other livestock producers in the Mississippi Delta region and southwestern US.

Ownership

Riceland is a farmer-owned cooperative.

EXECUTIVES

VP and CFO, Harry E. Loftis
Chairman, Thomas C. (Tommy) Hoskyn
President and CEO, K. Daniel (Danny) Kennedy, age 53
VP Commodity Operations, Scott Gower
VP Corporate Communications and Public Affairs, Bill J. Reed
VP Soybean and Grain Procurement and Marketing, John B. Ruff
VP International Rice Marketing, Terry Harris
Director Marketing Food Ingredients, Dan Meins
VP Research, Don McCaskill
Manager Grain Terminal West Memphis (AR), David Hunt
District Manager Brinkley (AR), Opal Derrick
District Manager Des Arc and Griffithville (AR), Dwight Hill
District Manager Stuttgart (AR), Bill Free

Director New Madrid (MO) Operations, Ed
Williams

District Manager Gillett and Dumas (AR), David
Curtis

District Manager Newport and Tuckerman (AR),
Alvin Mullins

District Manager Jonesboro (AR), Freddie Gahr

Management Director Commodity Operations,
Bennie B. Lackey Jr.

LOCATIONS

HQ: Riceland Foods Inc.
2120 S. Park Ave., Stuttgart AR 72160
Phone: 870-673-5500   **Fax:** 870-673-3366
Web: www.riceland.com

PRODUCTS/OPERATIONS

Selected Products

Consumer
Saffron Yellow Rice Mix
Rice N Easy Mix Wild Rice
Long Grain & Wild Mix Rice N Easy Mix
Broccoli & Cheese Rice N Easy Mix
Spanish Rice Mix Rice N Easy Mix
Chicken Rice Mix Rice N Easy Mix
Long Grain Rice Riceland Extra Long Grain Rice
Riceland GOLD Perfected Rice
Riceland Jasmine Rice
Riceland Natural Brown Rice
Riceland Plump & Tender Medium Grain Rice
Food Service
Oil
Rice
Food Ingredients
Long grain milled rice
Long grain brown rice
Medium grain milled rice
Parboiled rice
Broken grains

COMPETITORS

AarhusKarlshamn	Goya
American Rice	JFC International
Cereal Byproducts	Lotus Foods
CHS	Louis Dreyfus Group
Connell Company	Producers Rice Mill
Ebro Foods	Riviana Foods
Farmers Rice Milling	Specialty Rice
Farmers' Rice Cooperative	

HISTORICAL FINANCIALS

Company Type: Private - Cooperative

Income Statement

FYE: July 31

	REVENUE ($ mil.)	NET INCOME ($ mil.)	NET PROFIT MARGIN	EMPLOYEES
07/12	1,159	1	0.1%	1,646
07/11	1,107	0	0.1%	0
07/10	1,131	4	0.4%	0
07/09	1,269	8	0.6%	0
Annual Growth	(3.0%)	(43.7%)	—	—

2012 Year-End Financials

Debt ratio: ——
Return on equity: 0.10%
Cash ($ mil.): 1
Current ratio: 0.30
Long-term debt ($ mil.): ——

Dividends
  Yield: —
  Payout: —
Market value ($ mil.): ——

RICHARD STOCKTON COLLEGE OF NEW JERSEY

LOCATIONS

HQ: RICHARD STOCKTON COLLEGE OF NEW JERSEY
101 VERA KING FARRIS DR, GALLOWAY, NJ
08205-9441
Phone: 609-652-1776
Web: www.intraweb.stockton.edu

HISTORICAL FINANCIALS

Company Type: Private

Income Statement

FYE: June 30

	REVENUE ($ mil.)	NET INCOME ($ mil.)	NET PROFIT MARGIN	EMPLOYEES
06/12	164	9	5.5%	1,360
06/11	117	8	7.2%	0
06/10	110	5	4.7%	0
06/09	107	1	1.8%	0
Annual Growth	15.3%	65.8%	—	—

2012 Year-End Financials

Debt ratio: ——
Return on equity: 5.50%
Cash ($ mil.): 13
Current ratio: 0.30
Long-term debt ($ mil.): ——

Dividends
  Yield: —
  Payout: —
Market value ($ mil.): ——

RICHMOND WHOLESALE COMPANY INC.

LOCATIONS

HQ: RICHMOND WHOLESALE COMPANY INC.
81 WINANT PL STE A, STATEN ISLAND, NY
10309-1334
Phone: 718-966-0800
Web: www.richwholesale.com

HISTORICAL FINANCIALS

Company Type: Private

Income Statement

FYE: December 31

	REVENUE ($ mil.)	NET INCOME ($ mil.)	NET PROFIT MARGIN	EMPLOYEES
12/11	126	0	0.2%	25
12/10	109	0	0.3%	0
12/08	64	0	0.3%	0
12/07	48	1	2.5%	0
Annual Growth	37.8%	(38.8%)	—	—

2011 Year-End Financials

Debt ratio: ——
Return on equity: 0.20%
Cash ($ mil.): 1
Current ratio: 0.60
Long-term debt ($ mil.): ——

Dividends
  Yield: —
  Payout: —
Market value ($ mil.): ——

RIDDLE MEMORIAL HOSPITAL

LOCATIONS

HQ: RIDDLE MEMORIAL HOSPITAL
1068 W BALTIMORE PIKE, MEDIA, PA 19063-5177
Phone: 610-566-9400
Web: www.mainlinehealth.org

HISTORICAL FINANCIALS

Company Type: Private

Income Statement

FYE: June 30

	REVENUE ($ mil.)	NET INCOME ($ mil.)	NET PROFIT MARGIN	EMPLOYEES
06/11	172	1	0.6%	1,350
06/10	171	(4)	—	0
06/07	165	1	1.1%	0
06/06	142	0	0.2%	0
Annual Growth	6.6%	63.5%	—	—

2011 Year-End Financials

Debt ratio: ——
Return on equity: 0.60%
Cash ($ mil.): 3
Current ratio: 1.20
Long-term debt ($ mil.): ——

Dividends
  Yield: —
  Payout: —
Market value ($ mil.): ——

RIDEOUT HEALTH

LOCATIONS

HQ: RIDEOUT HEALTH
989 PLUMAS ST, YUBA CITY, CA 95991-4012
Phone: 530-751-4010
Web: www.frhg.org

HISTORICAL FINANCIALS

Company Type: Private

Income Statement

FYE: June 30

	REVENUE ($ mil.)	NET INCOME ($ mil.)	NET PROFIT MARGIN	EMPLOYEES
06/11	305	45	14.9%	1,800
06/10*	254	(0)	—	0
12/05	0	(0)	—	0
06/04	199	27	13.8%	0
Annual Growth	15.2%	18.4%	—	—

*Fiscal year change

2011 Year-End Financials

Debt ratio: ——
Return on equity: 14.90%
Cash ($ mil.): 81
Current ratio: 1.80
Long-term debt ($ mil.): ——

Dividends
  Yield: —
  Payout: —
Market value ($ mil.): ——

RIDER UNIVERSITY A NEW JERSEY NON-PROFIT CORPORATION

LOCATIONS

HQ: RIDER UNIVERSITY A NEW JERSEY NON-PROFIT CORPORATION
2083 LAWRENCEVILLE RD, LAWRENCEVILLE, NJ 08648-3001
Phone: 609-896-5000
Web: www.rider.edu

HISTORICAL FINANCIALS
Company Type: Private

Income Statement
FYE: June 30

	REVENUE ($ mil.)	NET INCOME ($ mil.)	NET PROFIT MARGIN	EMPLOYEES
06/11	203	7	3.9%	740
06/10	190	0	0.2%	0
06/09	143	(4)	—	0
06/07	124	12	9.8%	0
Annual Growth	**17.9%**	**(13.6%)**	**—**	**—**

2011 Year-End Financials
Debt ratio: ——
Return on equity: 3.90%
Cash ($ mil.): 19
Current ratio: —
Long-term debt ($ mil.): —
Dividends
  Yield: —
  Payout: —
  Market value ($ mil.): —

RIP GRIFFIN TRUCK SERVICE CENTER INC.

Rip Griffin Truck Service Center tries to make sure you never go hungry again (in Scarlett O'Hara's words) at least when you're driving on the highways of North Texas. Rip Griffin's network of about 10 travel centers offers truckers tour buses and other travelers a smorgasbord of features such as convenience stores fuel game rooms laundry facilities restaurants and showers. Locations also offer truck maintenance and repair services. In addition to its travel center business Rip Griffin sells Freightliner trucks through two Texas dealerships and provides fuel transportation services. In 2004 CEO Rip Griffin sold the company to Ohio-based TravelCenters of America.

EXECUTIVES

Head Human Resources, Risa Barron
CFO, Don Hayden
CEO, B. R. (Rip) Griffin
President, Mark Griffin
VP Operations, Dallas Musgrave
Director Information Systems, Don Brooks
Director Shop Operations, Mark Thompson

LOCATIONS

HQ: Rip Griffin Truck Service Center Inc.
5202 4th St., Lubbock TX 79416
Phone: 806-795-8785   **Fax:** 806-795-6574
Web: www.ripgriffin.com

COMPETITORS

Allsup' s	Pilot Corporation
Chevron	Racetrac Petroleum
E-Z Mart Stores	Stuckey' s
Love' s Country Stores	Valero Energy

HISTORICAL FINANCIALS
Company Type: Subsidiary

Income Statement
FYE: December 31

	REVENUE ($ mil.)	NET INCOME ($ mil.)	NET PROFIT MARGIN	EMPLOYEES
12/11	260	3	1.2%	88
12/10	187	2	1.5%	0
12/08*	197	5	2.6%	0
01/08	190	1	0.8%	0
Annual Growth	**11.0%**	**28.3%**	**—**	**—**

*Fiscal year change

2011 Year-End Financials
Debt ratio: ——
Return on equity: 1.20%
Cash ($ mil.): 7
Current ratio: 1.10
Long-term debt ($ mil.): —
Dividends
  Yield: —
  Payout: —
  Market value ($ mil.): —

RIPON COLLEGE

Ripon College is a private institution that offers undergraduate degrees in the liberal arts and sciences. It has more than 30 different majors and nearly 40 minor fields of study. The college which guarantees on-campus housing for students for four years enrolls approximately 1000 undergraduates annually and employs more than 75 faculty members. Ripon College was founded in 1851 as a college preparatory school and converted to a four-year college in 1863. It boasts famous alumni such as Al Jarreau Harrison Ford and Spencer Tracy.

EXECUTIVES

President, David C. Joyce, age 55
VP Finance and Assistant Treasurer, Mary M. deRegnier
Director Corporate and Foundation Relations, David M. Minor
VP and Dean Students, Christophor M. (Chris) Ogle
VP Advancement, Linda J. (Lyn) Corder
Director Information Technology Services, Ronald I. Haefner
Director Development, Larry P. Malchow
VP and Dean Faculty, Gerald Seaman
VP Admission and Financial Aid, Steven M. Schuetz
Director Media and Public Relations, Cody Pinkston
Associate Dean Faculty and Registrar, Michele A. Wittler
Human Resource Administrator, Jennifer Franz
Controller, Lori A. Schulze

LOCATIONS

HQ: Ripon College
300 Seward St., Ripon WI 54971
Phone: 920-748-8115   **Fax:** 920-748-8707
Web: www.ripon.edu

HISTORICAL FINANCIALS
Company Type: School

Income Statement
FYE: June 30

	REVENUE ($ mil.)	NET INCOME ($ mil.)	NET PROFIT MARGIN	EMPLOYEES
06/11	43	15	36.7%	205
06/10	38	(3)	—	0
06/09	14	(13)	—	0
06/08	19	(5)	—	0
Annual Growth	**31.7%**	**—**	**—**	**—**

2011 Year-End Financials
Debt ratio: ——
Return on equity: 36.70%
Cash ($ mil.): 1
Current ratio: —
Long-term debt ($ mil.): —
Dividends
  Yield: —
  Payout: —
  Market value ($ mil.): —

RIVER CITY PETROLEUM INC.

LOCATIONS

HQ: RIVER CITY PETROLEUM INC.
840 DELTA LN, WEST SACRAMENTO, CA 95691-2801
Phone: 916-371-4960
Web: www.rcpfuel.com

HISTORICAL FINANCIALS
Company Type: Private

Income Statement
FYE: December 31

	REVENUE ($ mil.)	NET INCOME ($ mil.)	NET PROFIT MARGIN	EMPLOYEES
12/11	656	2	0.4%	75
12/10	488	4	0.8%	0
12/09	375	1	0.3%	0
12/04	78	3	3.9%	0
Annual Growth	**103.0%**	**(5.3%)**	**—**	**—**

2011 Year-End Financials
Debt ratio: ——
Return on equity: 0.40%
Cash ($ mil.): 7
Current ratio: 1.00
Long-term debt ($ mil.): —
Dividends
  Yield: —
  Payout: —
  Market value ($ mil.): —

RIVER COUNTRY COOPERATIVE

LOCATIONS

HQ: RIVER COUNTRY COOPERATIVE
425 CLINTON AVE, SOUTH SAINT PAUL, MN
55075-5910
Phone: 651-451-1151
Web: www.rivercountry.coop

HISTORICAL FINANCIALS

Company Type: Private

Income Statement

FYE: December 31

	REVENUE ($ mil.)	NET INCOME ($ mil.)	NET PROFIT MARGIN	EMPLOYEES
12/11	129	4	3.2%	100
12/10	104	4	4.0%	0
12/09	99	4	5.0%	0
12/07	101	4	4.0%	0
Annual Growth	8.5%	0.7%	—	—

2011 Year-End Financials

Debt ratio: ——
Return on equity: 3.20%
Cash ($ mil.): 9
Current ratio: 1.00
Long-term debt ($ mil.): —

Dividends
Yield: —
Payout: —
Market value ($ mil.): —

RIVER DISTRICT COMMUNITY HOSPITAL AUTHORITY

St. John River District runs deep in the communities it serves. Part of St. John Health the hospital serves Michigan's St. Clair and Macomb counties (the southern portion of the state's "thumb") with about 70 beds. The acute-care hospital operates five outpatient centers and offers a range of services including cardiology orthopedics and vascular diagnostics. St. John River District Hospital also runs a sleep study center and urinary incontinence center. In addition it has a bloodless treatment program for patients whose religious convictions preclude certain treatments. Since its inception in 1965 the hospital undergone seven major renovation programs including the reconstruction of emergency department.

The hospital provides emergency medical (ambulance and paramedic) services and magnetic resonance imaging diagnostic services through its partnership with two Port Huron facilities: TRI Hospital EMS and TRI Hospital MRI.

EXECUTIVES

President, Frank Poma
Controller, Phil Wild
Manager Media Relations, Brian Taylor
VP Medical Affairs, H. Lee Bacheldor
Manager Human Resources, Sue Gronbach

Board Chair, Bill Zweng
VP Patient Care, Cynthia Gregorich
Chief of Staff, Sridhar Reddy
Vice Chief of Staff, Bassam Nasr
Secretary and Treasurer Medical Staff, Mark O'Brien

LOCATIONS

HQ: St. John River District Hospital
4100 River Rd., East China Township MI 48054
Phone: 810-329-7111   **Fax:** 810-329-8920
Web: www.stjohn.org/RiverDistrict/

COMPETITORS

Beaumont Health System
Crittenton Hospital
Detroit Medical Center
Genesys Health System
Harper-Hutzel Hospital
Henry Ford Health System
Mount Clemens Regional Medical Center
Oakwood Healthcare
Providence Hospital and Medical Centers
Sinai-Grace Hospital
St. John conner creek village
Trinity Health (Novi)

HISTORICAL FINANCIALS

Company Type: Subsidiary

Income Statement

FYE: June 30

	REVENUE ($ mil.)	NET INCOME ($ mil.)	NET PROFIT MARGIN	EMPLOYEES
06/11	41	(4)	—	386
06/10	38	(4)	—	0
06/09*	38	0	—	0
03/09	0	0	18.9%	0
Annual Growth	621.1%	—	—	—

*Fiscal year change

2011 Year-End Financials

Debt ratio: ——
Return on equity: (-11.30)%
Cash ($ mil.): 0
Current ratio: 1.50
Long-term debt ($ mil.): —

Dividends
Yield: —
Payout: —
Market value ($ mil.): —

RIVERSIDE HEALTHCARE ASSOCIATION INC.

Extra! Extra! Read all about it! Residents of Newport News (and about a dozen other cities in Eastern Virginia) Turn to Riverside Health for Medical Care. The not-for-profit health care provider administers general emergency and specialty medical services from four hospitals Riverside Regional Medical Center Riverside Walter Reed Hospital Riverside Tappahannock Hospital and Riverside Shore Memorial Hospital as well as a psychiatric hospital a physical rehabilitation facility and retirement communities. Riverside also operates physician offices and medical training facilities. Specialty centers provide home and hospice care cancer treatment and dialysis.

The company plans to build another hospital the Doctors Hospital in Williamsburg. The hospital will have about 40 private rooms and provide acute and emergency care as well as specialty services including cardiology neurology and pulmonary care. It took five years before the state health depart-

---

ment finally gave Riverside Health approval in 2009 to build the hospital. Doctors Hospital in Williamsburg is set to open in 2012.

Riverside Health is also replacing the aging Shore Memorial Hospital with a new to-be-constructed facility. After determining that bringing the current hospital up-to-date would be "prohibitively expensive" Riverside and the governing body for Shore Memorial the Shore Health Services board of directors decided to build a new hospital and split up the services offered at Shore Memorial into two locations. Inpatient and support services will move to the new location; outpatient and physician services will remain in Northampton County. The health system is also investing a few million dollars in upgrading Shore Memorial's digital equipment.

Combined Riverside's hospitals (including rehabilitation and psychiatric) are home to nearly 1000 beds.

EXECUTIVES

EVP and COO, William B. Downey
President CEO and Director, Richard J. Pearce
Chairman, Alan S. Witt, age 56
SVP and Administrator Riverside Regional Medical Center, Patrick R. (Pat) Parcells
EVP Chief Medical Officer and Director, Barry L. Gross
EVP and CFO, Wade D. Broughman
Vice Chairman, McKinley Leonard Price
VP Strategic Development and Marketing, Faye Petro Gargiulo
Director, Thomas G. Snead Jr.
Director, Charles R. Revere
President CEO and Director, Richard J. Pearce
Director, Jerold W. (Jerry) Allen
EVP Chief Medical Officer and Director, Barry L. Gross
Director, John C. Jamison
Director, Kendall C. Jones
Director, Thomas J. Reagan
Vice Chairman, McKinley Leonard Price
Director, Thaddeus B. Holloman Sr.
Director, Julie Rautio
Director, Paul S. Trible Jr.
Director, Robert L. Gordon
Director, Robert L. Marble
Director, Conway H. Sheild III

LOCATIONS

HQ: Riverside Health System
701 Town Center Dr. Ste. 1000, Newport News VA
23606-4286
Phone: 757-534-7000   **Fax:** 757-534-7088
Web: www.riversideonline.com

Selected Facilities – Virginia

HOSPITALS
Riverside Behavioral Health Center (Hampton)
Riverside Regional Medical Center (Newport News)
Riverside Rehabilitation Institute (Williamsburg)
Riverside Tappahannock Hospital (Tappahannock)
Riverside Shore Memorial Hospital (Nassawadox)
Riverside Walter Reed Hospital (Gloucester)
RETIREMENT COMMUNITIES
Patriots Colony (Williamsburg)
Sanders (Gloucester)
Warwick Forest (Newport News)
SURGERY CENTERS
Doctors Surgery Center (Williamsburg)
Peninsula Surgery Center (Newport News)
Riverside Hampton Surgery Center (Hampton)

COMPETITORS

Alleghany Regional Hospital
Bon Secours Health

Carilion Clinic
Centra Health Inc.
Children' s Hospital of The King' s Daughters
Franklin Hospital Corp.
Novant Health
Sentara Healthcare
Wake Forest University Baptist Medical Center

HISTORICAL FINANCIALS
Company Type: Private - Not-for-Profit

Income Statement
FYE: December 31

	REVENUE ($ mil.)	NET INCOME ($ mil.)	NET PROFIT MARGIN	EMPLOYEES
12/11	952	(25)	—	7,050
12/10	872	7	0.8%	0
12/09	788	46	5.9%	0
12/08	703	(25)	—	0
Annual Growth	10.6%	—	—	—

2011 Year-End Financials
Debt ratio: ——
Return on equity: (-2.70)%
Cash ($ mil.): 18
Current ratio: 0.50
Long-term debt ($ mil.): —

Dividends
Yield: —
Payout: —
Market value ($ mil.): —

RIVERSIDE HOSPITAL INC.

Riverside Hospital operates as Riverside Regional Medical Center a 570-bed acute-care facility that serves the residents of Newport News Virginia. Founded in 1916 the hospital moved to its current 72-acre campus in 1963 providing more than 30 medical specialties including cancer treatment cardiology birthing and diagnostic imaging. It specializes in cardiovascular and neurological surgeries and provides radiosurgery (radiation surgery) through a partnership with the University of Virginia Health System. Its emergency department is a Level II Trauma Center that treats some 57000 patients each year. Riverside Hospital is part of the Riverside Health System.
Geographic Reach
Riverside Hospital serves the health care needs of those who reside in and around Newport News Virginia.
Operations
As part of its operations Riverside Hospital operates a heart center neonatal center 18-bed neonatal intensive care unit cancer care center and radiosurgery center through a partnership with Chesapeake Regional and the University of Virginia Health System. Riverside Hospital works to prevent diagnose and treat diseases of the stomach intestines esophagus pancreas gall bladder liver and biliary tract through its Peninsula Gastroenterology & Riverside Endoscopy Center.

EXECUTIVES
VP Medical Affairs, Christopher Stolle
SVP and Administrator, Patrick R. (Pat) Parcells
Director Human Resources, Ray Schmidt
Secretary and Treasurer Medical Staff, Kendall C. Jones
VP Ambulatory Services, Susan McAndrews

VP Patient Care Services; Chief Nursing Officer and Service Line Administrator Women's Health Services, Gwen Hartzog
VP Operations, Michael (Mike) Doucette
Service Line Chief Women's Health Services, Jeffrey Henke
Service Line Administrator Surgical Service Line, Justice Crain
Director Materials Management, Bob Hornsby
Director Facilities Engineering, Dave Pone
Director Information Systems, Dennis Loftus
Service Line Chief Surgical Service Line, Marshall Cross
Service Line Administrator Neurosciences Service Line, Sandra Snapp
Service Line Chief Neurosciences Service Line, Tom Reagan
Service Line Administrator Oncology Service Line, Carrie Schmidt
Service Line Chief Oncology Service Line, Mark Ellis
Service Line Chief Cardiac Service Line, Ed Chu
Service Line Administrator Cardiac Service Line, John Peterman
Service Line Administrator Inpatient Medical Services, Christine Woody
Service Line Chief Inpatient Medical Services, Chris Bosworth
Vice President Va International Terminals, Regina P. Brayboy
Senior Vice President Riverside, Michael Martin
Senior Vice President Chief Information Officer CIO, John T. Stanley
Senior Vice President and Chief Nursing Officer CNO, Terris Kennedy
Vice President, Scott Stabler
Chairman, Gordon L. Gentry
Senior Vice President Riverside, Rondra J. Matthews

LOCATIONS
HQ: Riverside Hospital Inc.
500 J. Clyde Morris Blvd., Newport News VA 23601
Phone: 757-594-2000   **Fax:** 757-594-2084
Web: www.riversideonline.com

PRODUCTS/OPERATIONS

Selected Services
Diagnostic Services
  Cardiac testing
  CT
  Digital mammography
  Electrocardiography
  Magnetic resonance imaging
  Nuclear medicine
  PET
  Ultrasound
Nutrition Services
  Radiosurgery Center
  Leksell Gamma Knife Synergy S Radiosurgery
  Gastroenterology Procedures
  Colonoscopy and polypectomy
  Flexible sigmoidoscopy
  Upper endoscopic exams and therapy
  Endoscopic retrograde cholangiopancreatography (ERCP)
  Percutaneous endoscopic gastrostomy (PEG)
  Capsule/Cam (M2A) study of the small intestine
  Esophageal dilation
  Esophageal and anal manometry
  BRAVO pH study of the esophagus
Pulmonary Rehabilitation
Surgical Services

COMPETITORS
Alleghany Regional Hospital
Bon Secours Health

Carilion Clinic
Centra Health Inc.
Children' s Hospital of The King' s Daughters
Franklin Hospital Corp.
Novant Health
Sentara Healthcare
Wake Forest University Baptist Medical Center

HISTORICAL FINANCIALS
Company Type: Private - Not-for-Profit

Income Statement
FYE: December 31

	REVENUE ($ mil.)	NET INCOME ($ mil.)	NET PROFIT MARGIN	EMPLOYEES
12/11	466	36	7.8%	3,500
12/10	429	20	4.9%	0
12/09	413	15	3.8%	0
12/07	333	13	4.1%	0
Annual Growth	11.8%	38.1%	—	—

2011 Year-End Financials
Debt ratio: ——
Return on equity: 7.80%
Cash ($ mil.): 177
Current ratio: 2.80
Long-term debt ($ mil.): —

Dividends
Yield: —
Payout: —
Market value ($ mil.): —

RIVERSIDE RESEARCH INSTITUTE

LOCATIONS
HQ: RIVERSIDE RESEARCH INSTITUTE
156 WILLIAM ST FL 9, NEW YORK, NY 10038-5325
Phone: 212-563-4545

HISTORICAL FINANCIALS
Company Type: Private

Income Statement
FYE: November 30

	REVENUE ($ mil.)	NET INCOME ($ mil.)	NET PROFIT MARGIN	EMPLOYEES
11/11	86	3	4.0%	300
11/08	65	2	3.3%	0
11/06	49	2	4.5%	0
11/05	39	1	2.8%	0
Annual Growth	30.2%	45.8%	—	—

2011 Year-End Financials
Debt ratio: ——
Return on equity: 4.00%
Cash ($ mil.): 18
Current ratio: 2.90
Long-term debt ($ mil.): —

Dividends
Yield: —
Payout: —
Market value ($ mil.): —

ROAD BUILDERS MACHINERY & SUPPLY CO INC

LOCATIONS

HQ: ROAD BUILDERS MACHINERY & SUPPLY CO INC
1001 S 7TH ST, KANSAS CITY, KS 66105-2007
Phone: 913-371-3822
Web: www.roadbuildersmachinery.com

HISTORICAL FINANCIALS

Company Type: Private

Income Statement

FYE: December 31

	REVENUE ($ mil.)	NET INCOME ($ mil.)	NET PROFIT MARGIN	EMPLOYEES
12/11	102	2	2.9%	103
12/10	85	1	2.1%	0
12/09	61	1	1.9%	0
12/08	101	2	2.3%	0
Annual Growth	0.5%	8.2%	—	—

2011 Year-End Financials

Debt ratio: —
Return on equity: 2.90%
Cash ($ mil.): 0
Current ratio: 0.50
Long-term debt ($ mil.): —
Dividends
Yield: —
Payout: —
Market value ($ mil.): —

ROADTEX TRANSPORTATION MANAGEMENT CORP.

LOCATIONS

HQ: ROADTEX TRANSPORTATION MANAGEMENT CORP.
13 JENSEN DR, SOMERSET, NJ 08873-1393
Phone: 908-686-8200

HISTORICAL FINANCIALS

Company Type: Private

Income Statement

FYE: September 30

	REVENUE ($ mil.)	NET INCOME ($ mil.)	NET PROFIT MARGIN	EMPLOYEES
09/11	235	3	1.7%	62
09/10	192	3	1.8%	0
09/07	84	2	3.2%	0
09/05	59	2	4.7%	0
Annual Growth	58.0%	11.8%	—	—

2011 Year-End Financials

Debt ratio: —
Return on equity: 1.70%
Cash ($ mil.): 3
Current ratio: 3.50
Long-term debt ($ mil.): —
Dividends
Yield: —
Payout: —
Market value ($ mil.): —

ROBERT WOOD JOHNSON UNIVERSITY HOSPITAL

Robert Wood Johnson University Hospital (RWJUH) is the flagship facility of the Robert Wood Johnson Health System and Network. The medical center offers patients acute and tertiary care including cardiovascular services organ and tissue transplantation pediatric care (at The Bristol-Myers Squibb Children's Hospital) Level 1 trauma care cancer treatment (at the Cancer Hospital of New Jersey) women's imaging maternal-fetal and emergency medicine and more. Founded in 1884 the 600-bed facility serves as a teaching center for the University of Medicine and Dentistry of New Jersey-Robert Wood Johnson Medical School. More than 1300 physicians affiliated with RWJUH treat some 200000 patients each year.

The hospital's cancer unit is the flagship partner of the Cancer Institute of New Jersey a research and treatment center located adjacent to RWJUH that is the only National Cancer Institute-designated cancer center in New Jersey.

For five straight years from 2007 through 2011 RWJUH has been listed among U.S. News & World Report's "America's Best Hospitals."

Other members of the Robert Wood Johnson Health System include Robert Wood Johnson University Hospital Rahway Robert Wood Johnson University Hospital Hamilton and the Children's Specialized Hospital. The Robert Wood Johnson Health Network is an affiliated group of health care providers including hospitals nursing homes and health clinics which are located throughout New Jersey.

The University of Medicine and Dentistry of New Jersey (UMNDJ) is facing an uncertain future as state officials made recommendations in 2011 that two of its schools –the Robert Wood Johnson Medical School and the School of Public Health –be given to Rutgers University. A task force led by former Governor Tom Keane also recommended that UMDNJ's remaining pieces be "fundamentally transformed." This latest recommendation is the third in eight years; previous attempts failed after a suggested merger with Rutgers was met with skepticism by the governing boards at Rutgers and UMDNJ. State officials believe a union between the two schools would raise New Jersey's profile as an academic destination.

The "fundamental changes" suggested (but not detailed) by the task force are most likely related to corruption investigations that occurred at the school in 2006. Federal regulators charged that the school billed Medicare and Medicaid millions in illegal fees; a task force was formed then that explored folding all or part of UMDNJ into Rutgers but the idea was eventually dropped. This time

around Rutgers is all for taking the two schools although UMNDJ remains skeptical.

EXECUTIVES

President and CEO, Stephen K. (Steve) Jones, age 64
SVP Corporate Services, Judith E. Burgis
SVP Development, Bruce D. Newman
VP Center for Disease Management and Clinical Outcomes, Maureen Bueno
VP Financial Services, Kevin Dunn
VP Strategic Planning, Lawrence Garinello
VP Information Systems, Robert G. Irwin
VP Administrative Services, Kevin J. McTernan
Assistant VP Operations, Renia Harris-Hellams
Assistant VP Business Planning and Development, Carl O'Brien
Assistant VP Nursing Education and Research Performance Improvement and Emergency Department, Joan Gleason
President Medical Staff, Andrew B. Covit
SVP Medical Affairs and Chief Medical Officer, Joshua Bershad
SVP Finance and CFO, Brian M. Reilly

LOCATIONS

HQ: Robert Wood Johnson University Hospital
1 Robert Wood Johnson Place, New Brunswick NJ 08901
Phone: 732-828-3000   **Fax:** 210-575-0443
Web: www.sahealth.com

COMPETITORS

Barnabas Health
Bergen Regional Medical
Capital Health System
JFK Health System
Princeton HealthCare
Raritan Bay Medical Center
Saint Peter's University Hospital
Somerset Medical Center
St. Joseph's Healthcare System

HISTORICAL FINANCIALS

Company Type: Private - Not-for-Profit

Income Statement

FYE: September 30

	REVENUE ($ mil.)	NET INCOME ($ mil.)	NET PROFIT MARGIN	EMPLOYEES
09/12*	622	65	10.5%	4,674
12/11	781	12	1.6%	0
12/10	737	67	9.1%	0
12/09	743	103	13.9%	0
Annual Growth	(5.7%)	(14.2%)	—	—

*Fiscal year change

2012 Year-End Financials

Debt ratio: —
Return on equity: 10.50%
Cash ($ mil.): 51
Current ratio: 1.20
Long-term debt ($ mil.): —
Dividends
Yield: —
Payout: —
Market value ($ mil.): —

ROBERTS WESLEYAN COLLEGE

At Roberts Wesleyan College getting a degree can be a spiritual experience. The Christian liberal arts college offers more than 50 undergraduate programs as well as graduate programs in counseling in ministry education management nursing school counseling school psychology and social work. It also offers undergraduate degree-completion programs in nursing and organizational management for working adults. Its Northeastern Seminary offers master's degrees in divinity and theological studies and a doctor of ministry degree. Wesleyan has an enrollment of more than 1800 students. It was founded in 1866 as Chili Seminary by Benjamin Titus Roberts the first bishop of the Free Methodist Church.

EXECUTIVES

President, John A. Martin
VP Academic Administration, Burton R. Jones
VP and Treasurer, James E. Cuthbert
VP Admissions and Marketing, Linda Kurtz Hoffman
VP Administration, Ruth Logan
Academic Dean, Nelson E. Hill
VP Advancement, William Bigham
VP Student Life, Barry M. Smith
Trustee, Larry F. Miller, age 73
Trustee, Norman P. Leenhouts, age 76
Trustee, Allen E. Busching
Trustee, Gilbert J. Chang
Trusteee, John D. Cooke
Trustee, Paul N. Crowell
Trustee, George P. Grace
Trustee, Allen T. Hawn
Trustee, David C. Hoselton
Trustee, Lorne W. Jackson
Trustee, John A. Kelley
Trustee, George A. Kimmich
Trustee, Roy W. King
Trustee, Duncan W. O'Dwyer
Trustee, Dwight M. (Kip) Palmer
Trustee, Stephen L. Pelton
Trustee, Neal J. Redmond
Trustee, David B. Rinker
Trustee, Ruth E. Simpkins
Trustee, Robert E. Smith
Trustee, Richard D. Snyder
Trustee, Terry R. Taber, age 57
Trustee, Merrin M. Thomson
Trustee, Mary-Frances Winters
Trustee, Lori A. Van Dusen

LOCATIONS

HQ: Roberts Wesleyan College
2301 Westside Dr., Rochester NY 14624-1997
Phone: 585-594-6000   **Fax:** 585-594-6371
Web: www.roberts.edu

HISTORICAL FINANCIALS
Company Type: School

Income Statement   FYE: June 30

	REVENUE ($ mil.)	NET INCOME ($ mil.)	NET PROFIT MARGIN	EMPLOYEES
06/11	36	6	16.4%	500
06/10	37	3	9.9%	0
06/09	35	(2)	—	0
06/08	34	(0)	—	0
Annual Growth	2.2%	—	—	—

2011 Year-End Financials

Debt ratio: ——
Return on equity: 16.40%
Cash ($ mil.): 11
Current ratio: ——
Long-term debt ($ mil.): ——

Dividends
 Yield: —
 Payout: —
 Market value ($ mil.): —

ROCHESTER CITY SCHOOL DISTRICT

LOCATIONS

HQ: ROCHESTER CITY SCHOOL DISTRICT
131 W BROAD ST, ROCHESTER, NY 14614-1103
Phone: 585-262-8100
Web: www.rcsdk12.org

HISTORICAL FINANCIALS
Company Type: Private

Income Statement   FYE: June 30

	REVENUE ($ mil.)	NET INCOME ($ mil.)	NET PROFIT MARGIN	EMPLOYEES
06/11	681	(19)	—	5,470
06/06	448	(2)	—	0
06/05	454	47	10.5%	0
06/03	516	0	0.1%	0
Annual Growth	9.7%	—	—	—

2011 Year-End Financials

Debt ratio: ——
Return on equity: (-2.80)%
Cash ($ mil.): 101
Current ratio: ——
Long-term debt ($ mil.): ——

Dividends
 Yield: —
 Payout: —
 Market value ($ mil.): —

ROCKEFELLER UNIVERSITY

LOCATIONS

HQ: ROCKEFELLER UNIVERSITY
1230 YORK AVE, NEW YORK, NY 10065-6399
Phone: 212-327-8000

HISTORICAL FINANCIALS
Company Type: Private

Income Statement   FYE: June 30

	REVENUE ($ mil.)	NET INCOME ($ mil.)	NET PROFIT MARGIN	EMPLOYEES
06/11	495	184	37.2%	1
Annual Growth	—	—	—	—

2011 Year-End Financials

Debt ratio: ——
Return on equity: 37.20%
Cash ($ mil.): 154
Current ratio: ——
Long-term debt ($ mil.): ——

Dividends
 Yield: —
 Payout: —
 Market value ($ mil.): —

ROCKHURST UNIVERSITY

Rockhurst University is a Jesuit institution serving approximately 3000 students from two campuses in Kansas City Missouri. The university offers more than 50 undergraduate and graduate programs. Approximately 30% of its students are graduate students —the university offers an Executive Fellows MBA program as well as graduate programs in occupational therapy physical therapy education and speech pathology. Rockhurst was founded by the Jesuits in 1910.

EXECUTIVES

VP Business and Finance, Guy Swanson
VP Academic Affairs and Student Development, William F. Haefele
Director Human Resources, Mary Burnett
Associate VP Administration, Matt Heinrich
Director Career Center, Michael J. Theobald
Registrar, Minda Thrower
President, Father Thomas B. Curran
Director Public Relations and Marketing, Katherine Frohoff
VP University Advancement, Jane Lampo
VP Mission and Ministry, Rev Kevin Cullen
Associate VP Enrollment, David Melton
Associate VP Student Development, Matt Quick
Director Financial Aid, Angela Karlin

LOCATIONS

HQ: Rockhurst University
1100 Rockhurst Rd., Kansas City MO 64110
Phone: 816-501-4000   **Fax:** 816-501-4293
Web: www.rockhurst.edu

HISTORICAL FINANCIALS
Company Type: School

Income Statement   FYE: June 30

	REVENUE ($ mil.)	NET INCOME ($ mil.)	NET PROFIT MARGIN	EMPLOYEES
06/12	86	(8)	—	250
06/11	89	5	6.1%	0
06/10	75	9	13.2%	0
06/09	61	0	—	0
Annual Growth	12.1%	—	—	—

2012 Year-End Financials

Debt ratio: ——
Return on equity: (-9.30)%
Cash ($ mil.): 2
Current ratio: ——
Long-term debt ($ mil.): ——

Dividends
 Yield: —
 Payout: —
 Market value ($ mil.): —

ROGER WILLIAMS UNIVERSITY

LOCATIONS

HQ: ROGER WILLIAMS UNIVERSITY
1 OLD FERRY RD, BRISTOL, RI 02809-2921
Phone: 401-253-1040
Web: www.scs.rwu.edu

HISTORICAL FINANCIALS
Company Type: Private

Income Statement
FYE: June 30

	REVENUE ($ mil.)	NET INCOME ($ mil.)	NET PROFIT MARGIN	EMPLOYEES
06/11	151	16	11.1%	425
06/10	157	(0)	—	0
06/09	141	0	—	0
06/08	161	14	9.1%	0
Annual Growth	(2.0%)	4.7%	—	—

2011 Year-End Financials

Debt ratio: —
Return on equity: 11.10%
Cash ($ mil.): 2
Current ratio: —
Long-term debt ($ mil.): —
Dividends
Yield: —
Payout: —
Market value ($ mil.): —

ROGERS PETROLEUM INC.

LOCATIONS

HQ: ROGERS PETROLEUM INC.
1634 W 1ST NORTH ST, MORRISTOWN, TN
37814-3709
Phone: 423-581-7460
Web: www.rogerspetro.com

HISTORICAL FINANCIALS
Company Type: Private

Income Statement
FYE: March 31

	REVENUE ($ mil.)	NET INCOME ($ mil.)	NET PROFIT MARGIN	EMPLOYEES
03/12	445	1	0.2%	200
03/11	371	0	0.1%	0
03/10	288	(0)	—	0
03/09	355	1	0.4%	0
Annual Growth	7.8%	(10.8%)	—	—

2012 Year-End Financials

Debt ratio: —
Return on equity: 0.20%
Cash ($ mil.): 3
Current ratio: 0.10
Long-term debt ($ mil.): —
Dividends
Yield: —
Payout: —
Market value ($ mil.): —

ROLLINS COLLEGE

Students get rolling at Rollins College. The school is a liberal arts college with an enrollment of some 3200 undergraduate students seeking associate bachelor and master's degrees. Rollins' core arts and sciences and professional studies programs offer about 30 majors. In addition its Crummer Graduate School of Business offers an MBA program and its Hamilton Holt School provides undergraduate and graduate evening degree and outreach programs in 10 major fields. The college has 200 faculty members and a student-to-teacher ratio of 10:1. Rollins was founded in 1885 by New England Congregationalists and is the oldest college in Florida. It is named for Chicago businessman and philanthropist Alonzo Rollins.

Sales and Marketing
Rollins spent some $892000 on advertising during fiscal 2012.

Financial Performance
Rollins increased revenues by 6% to $105 million in 2012 due to higher net tuition and student fee income as well as private grants and endowment releases. Net income declined to a loss of $27 million however due to increased operating expenses and lower endowment and investment income levels. Cash flow rose as the college borrowed nearly $30 million in higher educational bonds to fund renovation and expansion efforts.

Strategy
Construction and renovation efforts include expansion and improvement efforts on two existing academic buildings and the construction of two new residential halls as well as several infrastructure improvement projects.

To expand its educational programs Rollins launched an undergraduate college of professional studies in 2011. The new school division will focus on business management communications educational and legal studies. Three academic programs from the arts and sciences college —communication education and international business —were transferred to the new professional studies college. In addition the Rollins MBA division added a new executive MBA program featuring Saturday classes.

EXECUTIVES

VP Business and Finance and Treasurer, Jeffrey G. Eisenbarth
VP Institutional Advancement, Ronald J. Korvas
President, Lewis M. Duncan
Assistant VP Public Relations, Ann Marie Varga
Director Human Resources, Matt Hawks
Director Facilities Management, Scott Bitikofer
Director Athletics, Pennie Parker
Director Libraries, Jonathan Miller
VP Academic Affairs and Provost, Carol M. Bresnahan
VP Institutional Advancement, James S. Gerhardt
VP Strategic Marketing, Greg W. Marshall
Interim VP Academic Affairs and Provost, Laurie M. Joyner
Dean of Admission, David Erdmann
Interim Dean of Student Affairs, Karen Hater
Director Olin Library, Jonathan Miller
Director Rollins China Center, Ilan Alon
Director Winter Park Institute, Gail Sinclair
Dean Hamilton Holt School, Sharon Carrier
Dean Crummer Graduate School of Business, Craig McAllaster
Controller, Robert Cook
Director Environmental Health and Safety, Brad McKown

Director Campus Security, Kenneth Miller

LOCATIONS

HQ: Rollins College
1000 Holt Ave., Winter Park FL 32789
Phone: 407-646-2000   **Fax:** 407-646-1556
Web: www.rollins.edu

PRODUCTS/OPERATIONS

Selected Programs
Evening Undergraduate and Graduate Programs
  Hamilton Holt School
Full-Time Undergraduate Programs
  The College of Arts and Sciences
  The College of Professional Studies
MBA Programs
  Crummer Graduate School of Business

HISTORICAL FINANCIALS
Company Type: School

Income Statement
FYE: May 31

	REVENUE ($ mil.)	NET INCOME ($ mil.)	NET PROFIT MARGIN	EMPLOYEES
05/12	105	(27)	—	645
05/11	99	49	50.2%	0
05/10	100	22	22.1%	0
05/09	106	0	—	0
Annual Growth	(0.3%)	—	—	—

2012 Year-End Financials

Debt ratio: —
Return on equity: (-25.90)%
Cash ($ mil.): 47
Current ratio: —
Long-term debt ($ mil.): —
Dividends
Yield: —
Payout: —
Market value ($ mil.): —

ROOSEVELT CAPITAL LLC

Roosevelt Capital which does business as Promotions Unlimited provides advertising and promotional programs for 5500 retail stores. Its merchandising products include advertising circulars and coupon books as well as provide online merchandising guides for its clients. Promotions Unlimited also produces "buying shows" allowing retailers to view merchandise place orders and attend educational seminars on such topics as advertising merchandising and retail management. The family-owned company founded in 1973 by Ira Greenberg franchises the Ben Franklin variety and craft stores providing its merchandising and promotional services to the franchisees.

EXECUTIVES

President and CEO, Ira Greenberg
VP Sales, Scott Weaver

LOCATIONS

HQ: ROOSEVELT CAPITAL LLC
7601 DURAND AVE, MOUNT PLEASANT, WI
53177-1905
Phone: 262-681-7000
Web: www.promot.com

COMPETITORS

Acosta
nParallel
Premium Retail
  Services

Source Marketing

HISTORICAL FINANCIALS
Company Type: Private

Income Statement
FYE: December 31

	REVENUE ($ mil.)	NET INCOME ($ mil.)	NET PROFIT MARGIN	EMPLOYEES
12/11	40	0	0.8%	130
12/10	40	(1)	—	0
12/09	45	0	0.2%	0
12/08	51	0	1.3%	0
Annual Growth	(7.8%)	(21.9%)	—	—

2011 Year-End Financials

Debt ratio: ——
Return on equity: 0.80%
Cash ($ mil.): 0
Current ratio: 0.80
Long-term debt ($ mil.): —

Dividends
  Yield: —
  Payout: —
Market value ($ mil.): —

ROSALIND FRANKLIN UNIVERSITY OF MEDICINE AND SCIENCE

LOCATIONS

HQ: ROSALIND FRANKLIN UNIVERSITY OF MEDICINE
AND SCIENCE
3333 GREEN BAY RD, NORTH CHICAGO, IL
60064-3037
Phone: 847-578-3000
Web:
www.rosalindfranklinuniversityofmedicineandscience.c
o

HISTORICAL FINANCIALS
Company Type: Private

Income Statement
FYE: June 30

	REVENUE ($ mil.)	NET INCOME ($ mil.)	NET PROFIT MARGIN	EMPLOYEES
06/12	99	(1)	—	800
06/11	86	9	11.0%	0
06/10	80	0	0.5%	0
06/08	77	(10)	—	0
Annual Growth	8.9%			

2012 Year-End Financials

Debt ratio: ——
Return on equity: (-1.70)%
Cash ($ mil.): 19
Current ratio: —
Long-term debt ($ mil.): —

Dividends
  Yield: —
  Payout: —
Market value ($ mil.): —

ROSE-HULMAN INSTITUTE OF TECHNOLOGY INC.

LOCATIONS

HQ: ROSE-HULMAN INSTITUTE OF TECHNOLOGY
INC.
5500 WABASH AVE, TERRE HAUTE, IN 47803-3999
Phone: 812-877-1511
Web: www.rose-hulman.edu

HISTORICAL FINANCIALS
Company Type: Private

Income Statement
FYE: June 30

	REVENUE ($ mil.)	NET INCOME ($ mil.)	NET PROFIT MARGIN	EMPLOYEES
06/12	102	6	6.6%	460
06/11	73	21	29.3%	0
06/10	70	10	15.0%	0
06/09	81	0	—	0
Annual Growth	7.8%	—	—	—

2012 Year-End Financials

Debt ratio: ——
Return on equity: 6.60%
Cash ($ mil.): 21
Current ratio: —
Long-term debt ($ mil.): —

Dividends
  Yield: —
  Payout: —
Market value ($ mil.): —

ROSEN 9939 INC.

LOCATIONS

HQ: ROSEN 9939 INC.
9840 INTERNATIONAL DR, ORLANDO, FL
32819-8111
Phone: 407-996-9840
Web: www.rosenshinglecreek.com

HISTORICAL FINANCIALS
Company Type: Private

Income Statement
FYE: January 31

	REVENUE ($ mil.)	NET INCOME ($ mil.)	NET PROFIT MARGIN	EMPLOYEES
01/12	112	34	30.9%	1,401
01/11	108	34	32.0%	0
01/10	124	41	33.1%	0
01/09	124	41	33.1%	0
Annual Growth	(3.4%)	(5.6%)	—	—

2012 Year-End Financials

Debt ratio: ——
Return on equity: 30.90%
Cash ($ mil.): 1
Current ratio: 1.40
Long-term debt ($ mil.): —

Dividends
  Yield: —
  Payout: —
Market value ($ mil.): —

ROUSE'S ENTERPRISES L.L.C.

LOCATIONS

HQ: ROUSE' S ENTERPRISES L.L.C.
1301 SAINT MARY ST, THIBODAUX, LA 70301-6527
Phone: 985-447-5998
Web: www.shop.rouses.com

HISTORICAL FINANCIALS
Company Type: Private

Income Statement
FYE: December 28

	REVENUE ($ mil.)	NET INCOME ($ mil.)	NET PROFIT MARGIN	EMPLOYEES
12/11	739	31	4.2%	5,200
12/10	691	24	3.5%	0
12/09	689	21	3.1%	0
12/06	247	11	4.8%	0
Annual Growth	44.1%	38.5%	—	—

2011 Year-End Financials

Debt ratio: ——
Return on equity: 4.20%
Cash ($ mil.): 0
Current ratio: 0.10
Long-term debt ($ mil.): —

Dividends
  Yield: —
  Payout: —
Market value ($ mil.): —

RUMSEY ELECTRIC COMPANY

Passing on pi?a coladas Rumsey still gives companies a good buzz. Rumsey Electric distributes electrical construction equipment utility products and services and systems for relay and power and lighting for retailers. Operating through one central distribution facility and 12 branches the company caters to construction and industrial businesses and utilities as well as OEMs institutions and commercial Mid-Atlantic markets. Six of its branches are in Delaware; the rest reside in New Jersey and Philadelphia. It is the authorized distributor of Rockwell Automation a large industrial automation firm. Employee-owned Rumsey Electric has been in business for over 110 years.

EXECUTIVES

President and CEO, Gerald M. (Jerry) Lihota, age 64
CFO, Scott M. Cutler, age 61
VP Construction Sales, Jack Graham
EVP Sales, Fred Cubit
VP Operations and Logistics, Larry Haggerty
VP Utility Sales Mid-Atlantic, Chip Jones
VP Relay and Power Systems, Steven Cabibbo
Supervisor Credit and Collections, Ted Blucas
**Manager Business Development Greater
  Philadelphia and DE,** Fred Capanna
**Manager Business Development Greater
  Philadephia DE,** Shawn Huber
Purchasing Manager, Jim Napuda
SVP, Paul Esterheld
Manager Automation, Doug Metz

GSS Administrator Automation Training Service
Warranty and Repairs PA and NJ, Barbara Dever
GSS Administrator Automation Training Service
Warranty and Repairs Lehigh Valley South
Jersey, Nitza Colon
Lighting Specialist PA and NJ, Jon Morris
Lighting Specialist DE and MD, Chris Lewandowski
Switchgear Specialist PA and NJ, Chip Vandevere
Switchgear Specialist PA and NJ, Mike Karlson
Switchgear Specialist DE and MD, Steve McPhee
Manager Warehouse, Bill Johnson
Manager Information Technology, Matt Prior
Director Human Resources, Ned Clopton
Director Marketing, Jill Michener
QualityTraining and Technology, Jim Poach
General Manager Lighting Systems, Ralph
Giorondo

LOCATIONS

HQ: Rumsey Electric Company
15 Colwell Ln., Conshohocken PA 19428-1805
Phone: 610-832-9000   Fax: 610-941-8181
Web: www.rumsey.com

PRODUCTS/OPERATIONS

Selected Products

Automation and controls
Ballasts
Control panel components
Enclosures
Energy saving components
Fixtures
Lamps
Lighting
Lighting controls
Mechanical components
Metering
Power distribution
Process components
Protection and control products
Safety and supply parts
Switchgear
Tools
Transformers

COMPETITORS

Anixter International	Fromm Electric
Billows Electric	Gexpro
Supply	Graybar Electric
Colonial Electric	Rexel Inc.
Supply	United Electric Supply
Consolidated	WESCO International
Electrical	

HISTORICAL FINANCIALS

Company Type: Private

Income Statement

FYE: December 31

	REVENUE ($ mil.)	NET INCOME ($ mil.)	NET PROFIT MARGIN	EMPLOYEES
12/11	196	2	1.0%	284
12/10	187	10	5.7%	0
12/09	172	3	2.0%	0
12/08	201	7	3.6%	0
Annual Growth	(0.8%)	(34.7%)	—	—

2011 Year-End Financials

Debt ratio: ——
Return on equity: 1.00%
Cash ($ mil.): 0
Current ratio: 1.70
Long-term debt ($ mil.): —

Dividends
  Yield: —
  Payout: —
  Market value ($ mil.): —

RUSAL AMERICA CORP.

LOCATIONS

HQ: RUSAL AMERICA CORP.
550 MMARONECK AVE STE 301, HARRISON, NY 10528
Phone: 914-670-5771

HISTORICAL FINANCIALS

Company Type: Private

Income Statement

FYE: December 31

	REVENUE ($ mil.)	NET INCOME ($ mil.)	NET PROFIT MARGIN	EMPLOYEES
12/11	611	0	0.1%	12
12/10	525	0	0.1%	0
12/08	1,009	0	0.1%	0
12/03	628	0	0.1%	0
Annual Growth	(0.9%)	25.9%	—	—

2011 Year-End Financials

Debt ratio: ——
Return on equity: 0.10%
Cash ($ mil.): 3
Current ratio: 0.10
Long-term debt ($ mil.): —

Dividends
  Yield: —
  Payout: —
  Market value ($ mil.): —

RUSH UNIVERSITY MEDICAL CENTER

LOCATIONS

HQ: RUSH UNIVERSITY MEDICAL CENTER
1653 W CONGRESS PKWY, CHICAGO, IL 60612-3833
Phone: 312-942-5000
Web: www.cchaclib.org

HISTORICAL FINANCIALS

Company Type: Private

Income Statement

FYE: June 30

	REVENUE ($ mil.)	NET INCOME ($ mil.)	NET PROFIT MARGIN	EMPLOYEES
06/11	1,441	290	20.2%	8,000
06/10	1,395	52	3.8%	0
06/09	1,094	38	3.5%	0
06/06	1,068	207	19.4%	0
Annual Growth	10.5%	11.9%	—	—

2011 Year-End Financials

Debt ratio: ——
Return on equity: 20.20%
Cash ($ mil.): 127
Current ratio: 0.80
Long-term debt ($ mil.): —

Dividends
  Yield: —
  Payout: —
  Market value ($ mil.): —

RUSH-COPLEY MEDICAL CENTER INC.

People in a rush to get healthy can find help at Rush-Copley Medical Center. A member of the Rush System for Health family the medical center serves Illinois' Fox Valley area. The hospital has more than 180 beds and provides acute and tertiary medical services including cardiac care cancer treatment neurology women's services neonatal care and health education programs. Its Rush-Copley Surgery Center performs both day surgeries and inpatient procedures while its nearby Rush-Copley Healthcare Center houses doctors' offices and offers outpatient diagnostic imaging services. Other programs include a neuroscience center a home health care agency and its Healthplex fitness center.

The hospital has outlined a plan to expand its services in key areas by 2015. In addition to expanding its inpatient bed capacity Rush-Copley plans to expand its cardiovascular oncology neurology emergency and women's health departments as well as its outpatient care centers. It also plans to upgrade its technology systems to improve caregiver communication capabilities and qualify for meaningful use guidelines as outlined in the American Recovery and Reinvestment Act of 2009.

EXECUTIVES

Vice Chairman, William B. Skoglund, age 61
President and CEO, Barry C. Finn, age 52
SVP Strategy and Chief Strategy Officer, Lisa Brady
SVP Finance and CFO, Mac Salazar
SVP Operations and COO, John Diederich
Director Information Services, Beckie Coovert
VP Clinical Services and Patient Safety Officer, Mary Shilkaitis
VP Nursing Services and Chief Nursing Officer, Shawn Tyrrell
Director Human Resources, Darla Mullner
Director Marketing and Public Relations, Mary Zokan
VP Quality, Diane D. Homan
Chief of Staff, Bob Manam
Chairman, Ronald Hem
SVP Medical Affairs and Chief Medical Officer, Steven B. Lowenthal
VP Ancillary Services, Nancy J. Wilson
Assistant VP Patient Safety, Carrie Nelson
SVP Strategy, Gail Bumgarner
VP Information Technology and CIO, Dennis DeMasie
VP Finance, Brenda Van Wyhe
VP Philanthropy Chief Development Officer, Barbara A. Graham
VP Legal Affairs and General Counsel, Ryan Asmus

LOCATIONS

HQ: Rush-Copley Medical Center Inc.
2000 Ogden Ave., Aurora IL 60504
Phone: 630-978-6200   Fax: 606-874-9461
Web: www.thetruckpeople.com

COMPETITORS

Central DuPage	Resurrection Health
Hospital	Care
Dreyer Clinic	University of Chicago
Morris Hospital	Medical Center
Northwestern Memorial	Wheaton Franciscan

HISTORICAL FINANCIALS
Company Type: Subsidiary

Income Statement   FYE: June 30

	REVENUE ($ mil.)	NET INCOME ($ mil.)	NET PROFIT MARGIN	EMPLOYEES
06/12	296	17	6.0%	2,000
06/11	0	0	—	0
06/10	0	0	—	0
06/09	254	4	2.0%	0
Annual Growth	5.2%	52.6%	—	—

2012 Year-End Financials

Debt ratio: ——
Return on equity: 6.00%
Cash ($ mil.): 34
Current ratio: 1.10
Long-term debt ($ mil.): —

Dividends
Yield: —
Payout: —
Market value ($ mil.): —

RUSH-HENRIETTA CENTRAL SCHOOL DISTRICT

LOCATIONS

HQ: RUSH-HENRIETTA CENTRAL SCHOOL DISTRICT
2034 LEHIGH STATION RD, HENRIETTA, NY
14467-9616
Phone: 585-359-5000

HISTORICAL FINANCIALS
Company Type: Private

Income Statement   FYE: June 30

	REVENUE ($ mil.)	NET INCOME ($ mil.)	NET PROFIT MARGIN	EMPLOYEES
06/11	109	(0)	—	1,100
06/10	110	2	2.4%	0
06/09	0	0	—	0
06/06	0	0	—	0
Annual Growth	—	—	—	—

2011 Year-End Financials

Debt ratio: ——
Return on equity: (-0.10)%
Cash ($ mil.): 62
Current ratio: —
Long-term debt ($ mil.): —

Dividends
Yield: —
Payout: —
Market value ($ mil.): —

RUSKEN PACKAGING INC.

LOCATIONS

HQ: RUSKEN PACKAGING INC.
64 WALNUT ST NW, CULLMAN, AL 35055-5928
Phone: 256-734-0092
Web: www.rusken.com

HISTORICAL FINANCIALS
Company Type: Private

Income Statement   FYE: December 31

	REVENUE ($ mil.)	NET INCOME ($ mil.)	NET PROFIT MARGIN	EMPLOYEES
12/11	109	2	2.1%	330
12/10	82	1	2.1%	0
12/09	67	0	0.4%	0
12/08	99	1	1.3%	0
Annual Growth	3.1%	23.3%	—	—

RUSSELL & SMITH FORD INC.

LOCATIONS

HQ: RUSSELL & SMITH FORD INC.
3440 SOUTH LOOP W, HOUSTON, TX 77025-5296
Phone: 713-663-4111
Web: www.russellsmithford.com

HISTORICAL FINANCIALS
Company Type: Private

Income Statement   FYE: May 31

	REVENUE ($ mil.)	NET INCOME ($ mil.)	NET PROFIT MARGIN	EMPLOYEES
05/12	222	2	0.9%	310
05/11	194	0	0.4%	0
05/10	179	0	0.4%	0
05/08	214	(0)	—	0
Annual Growth	1.2%	—	—	—

2012 Year-End Financials

Debt ratio: ——
Return on equity: 0.90%
Cash ($ mil.): 5
Current ratio: 0.20
Long-term debt ($ mil.): —

Dividends
Yield: —
Payout: —
Market value ($ mil.): —

RUSSELL CHEVROLET CO

LOCATIONS

HQ: RUSSELL CHEVROLET CO
6100 LANDERS RD, NORTH LITTLE ROCK, AR
72117-1940
Phone: 501-835-8300
Web: www.russellchevrolet.com

HISTORICAL FINANCIALS
Company Type: Private

Income Statement   FYE: July 31

	REVENUE ($ mil.)	NET INCOME ($ mil.)	NET PROFIT MARGIN	EMPLOYEES
07/12	89	0	0.2%	156
07/11*	86	0	1.0%	0
04/10	18	0	1.7%	0
07/04	69	0	1.3%	0
Annual Growth	8.6%	(37.8%)	—	—

*Fiscal year change

2012 Year-End Financials

Debt ratio: ——
Return on equity: 0.20%
Cash ($ mil.): 6
Current ratio: 0.30
Long-term debt ($ mil.): —

Dividends
Yield: —
Payout: —
Market value ($ mil.): —

RUSSELL SIGLER INC.

Russell Sigler has built a business providing a cool service in a hot region. Through about 10 locations in Arizona California Idaho Nevada New Mexico and West Texas the company provides commercial and residential air conditioning contractors with equipment parts supplies and technical support. Its brands include Carrier Bryant and Payne. Russell Sigler has distributed Carrier products for about 60 years. The company also operates a residential and commercial distribution joint venture with Carrier; Russell Sigler owns a 60% stake while Carrier holds 40%.

While privately-owned Russell Sigler reported $390 million in sales in 2011.

EXECUTIVES

Chairman and CEO, Russell (Russ) Sigler
CFO, Robert Osborne
Credit Manager, Gary Goldberg
Human Resources Manager, Kathly Littler
IT Manager, Rich Unterbrink
Purchasing Manager, Matt Osborne
President Residential Division, Rod Martin
President Commercial Division, Don Reeves
Controls Manager, Tom Kohl
Commercial Technical Support, Larry Siller

LOCATIONS

HQ: Russell Sigler Inc.
9702 W. Tonto St., Tolleson AZ 85353
Phone: 623-388-5100   **Fax:** 623-388-5200
Web: www.siglers.com

COMPETITORS

Chas Roberts Air
  Conditioning
Ferguson Enterprises
Gustave A. Larson
  Company
HD Supply

Johnstone Supply
US Airconditioning
  Distributors
Watsco
WinWholesale

HISTORICAL FINANCIALS

Company Type: Private

Income Statement

FYE: December 31

	REVENUE ($ mil.)	NET INCOME ($ mil.)	NET PROFIT MARGIN	EMPLOYEES
12/11	393	(3)	—	550
12/09	140	(0)	—	0
12/08	176	1	0.8%	0
12/06	224	3	1.7%	0
Annual Growth	**20.6%**	—	—	—

2011 Year-End Financials

Debt ratio: ——
Return on equity: (-1.00)%
Cash ($ mil.): 0
Current ratio: 0.40
Long-term debt ($ mil.): —

Dividends
  Yield: —
  Payout: —
Market value ($ mil.): —

RYAN LLC

The professionals at Ryan aren't too concerned when clients notice their SALT-y language. One of the US's largest state and local tax (SALT) consulting firms Ryan provides tax advice preparation and planning for major corporations and other businesses. It also offers advice on federal and international tax issues. The firm specializes in audit defense dispute resolution strategic planning tax process efficiencies and tax recovery. Founded in 1991 in Texas Ryan serves customers through some 60 offices in more than 20 states as well as in Canada and Europe. Ryan traces its roots to a certified public accounting firm co-founded by CEO G. Brint Ryan in 1991. It bought a portion of Thomson Reuters in 2013.

Geographic Reach

Dallas-based Ryan has about 60 offices across the US and in Amsterdam Australia Canada India Singapore and the UK.

Strategy

The company often looks to form partnerships with other companies to broaden the scope of its services. To this end Ryan forged a strategic alliance with real estate giant Jones Lang LaSalle in 2010 to provide property tax services to commercial real estate clients. It has also teamed with recovery audit specialist PRG-Schultz International; US Tax Advantage which provides international tax services to US and foreign-based companies; and Associated Consultants an administrator of hiring tax credits.

Mergers and Acquisitions

Ryan has grown by adding new practices and making acquisitions. In 2013 the company purchased the Thomson Reuters Property Tax Services business adding 600 property tax and unclaimed property professionals. The move makes Ryan the largest global provider of property tax services and North America's largest indirect tax practice. As part of the agreement Ryan will operate a Center for Tax Excellence in India staffed by some 145 professionals. The center serves as a foundation for building Ryan's business in South Asia and extends the reach of its indirect tax practice to China's emerging markets.

In mid-2012 Ryan acquired The TAARP Group LLP the leading tax and penalty review firm in the US. The move added specialized federal income tax expertise and a number of Fortune 500 firms to Ryan's client roster. Other recent moves by Ryan to expand is business both geographically and by specialty include the launch of new groups devoted to fraud and forensic recovery and tax accounting risk services (2010) its entry into Canada by purchasing sales tax recovery firm Robert Brakel & Associates (2010) and the opening of a London office (2008).

Ryan spun off its tax software products including CertiSoft STS and Workflow in 2009 as an independent company called Second Decimal. The move has allowed it to focus its core tax services.

EXECUTIVES

SVP and Chief Human Resources Officer, Adrianne Court, age 41
Principal, John Sharp, age 57
EVP and Chief of Staff, Delta Emerson
CEO and Managing Principal, G. Brint Ryan, age 48
Principal in Charge Houston, Mark W. Bennett
Principal in Charge Los Angeles, Richard V. Carlson
Principal, Randy W. Donald
Principal in Charge El Paso, John R. Ferrell
Principal, Ginny Buckner Kissling
Principal in Charge New York, Jeremiah T. Lynch
EVP COO Treasurer and Principal, Gerry L. Ridgely Jr.
Principal in Charge Austin, Eric L. Stein
VP and Principal, Richard H. Thompson
VP and Principal, James M. Trester
Principal, John A. Walter
President Assistant Secretary and Principal, Tony G. Mills
Principal, Korey Kim
Principal in Charge Chicago, James (Jim) Kranjc
Principal, Trisha C. Fortune
Principal in Charge Pittsburgh, Helen Lemmon
Principal, William Samuels
SVP and CFO, David English, age 44
Principal, Richard D. (Rich) Fosburg
SVP Chief Legal Officer Secretary and Principal, Gregory S. (Greg) Weiss
Principal in Charge Atlanta, Douglas J. (Doug) DeRito
Principal, Michael Allen
Principal, Mark W. Eidman
Principal, Bruce Gibson
Principal, Stephen J. Allen
Principal, Karey W. Barton
Principal, Tony Chavez
Principal, Damon N. Chronis
Principal, Julie Chronis
Principal, Jim Crandall
Principal, Neil Fett
Principal, Leslie S. Hahn
Principal, Dena J. Hall
Principal, Noel E. Hall Jr.
Principal, Michael Henry
Principal in Charge St. Louis, Randy Hilger
Principal, Nigel Hoyle
Principal, Dennis J. Kolumber Jr.
Principal, Luke G. Krieger
Principal in Charge Cleveland, Nicholas Longo
EVP and Vice Chairman Global Corporate Development, Brendan F. Moore
Principal, Mark L. Nachbar
Principal, Dave Naney

Principal, Greg Odell
Principal in Charge Columbus Detroit and Lansing, John M. Polizzi
Principal, Kevin S. Powell
Principal, Gerard Quinlan
Principal, Lester C. Rhodes
Managing Principal Canadian Operations, Garry Round
EVP Chief Strategy Officer and Principal, Jon C. Sweet
SVP and Chief Marketing Officer, James R. Aubele
SVP and CIO, Blake K. Holman
SVP and Chief Real Estate Officer, Robert M. Wertz
VP Operations, Brooke A. Keene
Principal in Charge Boston, Janet L. Askenburg

LOCATIONS

HQ: Ryan Inc.
  3 Galleria Tower 13155 Noel Rd. Ste. 100, Dallas TX 75240-5090
Phone: 972-934-0022   **Fax:** 972-960-0613
Web: www.ryan.com

Selected Locations

Atlanta
Austin TX
Baton Rouge LA
Boston
Calgary AB
Charlotte NC
Chicago
Cleveland
Columbus
Dallas
Denver
Detroit
Downers Grove IL
El Paso TX
Ft. Lauderdale FL
Houston
Indianapolis
Jacksonville FL
Kansas City KS
Lansing MI
London
Los Angeles
Lubbock TX
Minneapolis
Montreal
Nashville TN
New Orleans
New York
Philadelphia
Pittsburgh
Providence RI
Sacramento CA
Salt Lake City
San Antonio
San Francisco
San Jose CA
Seattle
St. Louis
Tampa
Toronto
Washington DC

PRODUCTS/OPERATIONS

Selected Services

Alternative compliance procedures
Audit representation
Audit sampling analysis and evaluation
Captive insurance
Strategic planning
Tax compliance outsourcing
Tax refunds
Tax research
Tax systems implementation
Utility exemption studies
Voluntary disclosure and registration
Strategic alliances

COMPETITORS

CliftonLarsonAllen
Management Insights
Moss Adams LLP
Peisner Johnson &
 Company

SALT Group
SC&H Group
UHY Advisors TX

HISTORICAL FINANCIALS

Company Type: Private

Income Statement FYE: December 31

	REVENUE ($ mil.)	NET INCOME ($ mil.)	NET PROFIT MARGIN	EMPLOYEES
12/11	225	25	11.2%	925
12/10	212	24	11.6%	0
12/09	190	26	13.7%	0
12/08	176	17	10.1%	0
Annual Growth	8.4%	12.1%	—	—

2011 Year-End Financials

Debt ratio: ——
Return on equity: 11.20%
Cash ($ mil.): 2
Current ratio: 1.00
Long-term debt ($ mil.): —

Dividends
 Yield: —
 Payout: —
 Market value ($ mil.): —

S R M ALLIANCE HOSPITAL SERVICES

LOCATIONS

HQ: S R M ALLIANCE HOSPITAL SERVICES
 400 N MCDOWELL BLVD, PETALUMA, CA 94954-2339
Phone: 707-778-1111
Web: www.phcd.org

HISTORICAL FINANCIALS

Company Type: Private

Income Statement FYE: June 30

	REVENUE ($ mil.)	NET INCOME ($ mil.)	NET PROFIT MARGIN	EMPLOYEES
06/11	80	(2)	—	425
Annual Growth	—	—	—	—

2011 Year-End Financials

Debt ratio: ——
Return on equity: (-2.90)%
Cash ($ mil.): 3
Current ratio: 1.60
Long-term debt ($ mil.): —

Dividends
 Yield: —
 Payout: —
 Market value ($ mil.): —

S-N-GO STORES INC.

LOCATIONS

HQ: S-N-GO STORES INC.
 2701 UNIVERSITY DR S, FARGO, ND 58103-6027
Phone: 701-235-7531

HISTORICAL FINANCIALS

Company Type: Private

Income Statement FYE: May 31

	REVENUE ($ mil.)	NET INCOME ($ mil.)	NET PROFIT MARGIN	EMPLOYEES
05/12	100	(0)	—	300
05/11	93	1	1.4%	0
05/10	86	0	0.2%	0
05/09	84	(0)	—	0
Annual Growth	5.8%	—	—	—

2012 Year-End Financials

Debt ratio: ——
Return on equity: —
Cash ($ mil.): 0
Current ratio: 0.40
Long-term debt ($ mil.): —

Dividends
 Yield: —
 Payout: —
 Market value ($ mil.): —

SACRED HEART HEALTH SERVICES

LOCATIONS

HQ: SACRED HEART HEALTH SERVICES
 501 SUMMIT ST, YANKTON, SD 57078-3855
Phone: 605-665-9371
Web: www.averasacredheart.com

HISTORICAL FINANCIALS

Company Type: Private

Income Statement FYE: June 30

	REVENUE ($ mil.)	NET INCOME ($ mil.)	NET PROFIT MARGIN	EMPLOYEES
06/11	103	11	10.7%	794
06/10	88	7	8.0%	0
06/09	80	7	9.0%	0
06/08	4	(0)	—	0
Annual Growth	187.6%	—	—	—

2011 Year-End Financials

Debt ratio: ——
Return on equity: 10.70%
Cash ($ mil.): 0
Current ratio: 0.60
Long-term debt ($ mil.): —

Dividends
 Yield: —
 Payout: —
 Market value ($ mil.): —

SACRED HEART UNIVERSITY INCORPORATED

LOCATIONS

HQ: SACRED HEART UNIVERSITY INCORPORATED
 5151 PARK AVE, FAIRFIELD, CT 06825-1000
Phone: 203-371-7999
Web: www.livesmartedu.com

HISTORICAL FINANCIALS

Company Type: Private

Income Statement FYE: June 30

	REVENUE ($ mil.)	NET INCOME ($ mil.)	NET PROFIT MARGIN	EMPLOYEES
06/11	189	22	12.0%	600
06/10	176	17	9.9%	0
06/09	166	0	—	0
06/08	167	23	13.7%	0
Annual Growth	4.2%	(0.4%)	—	—

2011 Year-End Financials

Debt ratio: ——
Return on equity: 12.00%
Cash ($ mil.): 12
Current ratio: —
Long-term debt ($ mil.): —

Dividends
 Yield: —
 Payout: —
 Market value ($ mil.): —

SAINT AGNES MEDICAL CENTER

Protecting and caring for the vulnerable Saint Agnes continues to ward off death for the patients at Saint Agnes Medical Center. The medical center provides healthcare to Valley residents of Fresno California through a 436-bed acute care hospital. Along with general surgery the hospital offers a variety of services including asthma management bariatric surgery (for which it has scored state-wide accolades) cardiac rehabilitation hospice care and home care. The facility also has centers dedicated to cancer child development and women's health. The hospital —established in 1929 by nine Holy Cross Sisters —is part of Trinity Health the fourth-largest health care system in the US.

Geographic Reach
Saint Agnes Medical Center provides care to residents of the Fresno California area.

Operations
Saint Agnes Medical Center is a 436-bed medical campus that has 2705 staff members.

Strategy
Saint Agnes Medical Center recently launched a new state-of-the-art Electronic Medical Record (EMR) system. The new EMR system replaced paper medical records and streamlined patient care.

Company Background
Saint Agnes Medical Center also sponsors a number of community outreach programs

throughout the Valley including adult day care senior activity programs health care clinics for the uninsured and services for poor and homeless women.

EXECUTIVES

COO, Mark T. Bateman
CFO, Kathleen Cain
SVP Human Resources, Dan Camp
Acting President and CEO, Thomas E. Anderson
Acting Chief Operating Officer, Susan Ryan
President and CEO, Nancy Hollingsworth
Chief Administrative Officer, Stacy Vaillancourt
VP Foundation and Community Relations, Gregory Walaitis
General Counsel, Marie Paratto
Chairman, Craig Saladino
Chairman, Michael Martinez
CFO, Phil Robinson
Chief Nursing Officer, Debi Pasley
Vice President Foundation, Teri Amerine
President Chief Executive Officer, Jim Leonard
Executive Vice President COO, Rick OConnell
Trustee, Daniel G. (Dan) Hale
Trustee, Sister Veronique Wiedower
Vice Chairman, Michael Martinez
Trustee, Hilda C. Montoy
Trustee, Phillip Sanchez
Trustee, William Owen
Trustee, William Hadcock
Trustee, Lee Jay Kolligian
Trustee, Dianne Nury
Trustee, Sister Joan Marie Steadman
Trustee, Sister M. Corita Heid

LOCATIONS

HQ: Saint Agnes Medical Center
1303 E. Herndon Ave., Fresno CA 93720
Phone: 559-450-3000   **Fax:** 559-450-3990
Web: www.samc.com

COMPETITORS

Community Medical Centers	Memorial Hospitals Association
Dignity Health	Northern Inyo Hospital
HCA	Tenet Healthcare
Kaiser Permanente	

HISTORICAL FINANCIALS

Company Type: Subsidiary

Income Statement

FYE: June 30

	REVENUE ($ mil.)	NET INCOME ($ mil.)	NET PROFIT MARGIN	EMPLOYEES
06/11	487	6	1.2%	2,400
06/10	438	8	1.8%	0
06/09	394	(52)	—	0
06/08	420	24	5.8%	0
Annual Growth	5.1%	(37.2%)	—	—

2011 Year-End Financials

Debt ratio: ——
Return on equity: 1.20%
Cash ($ mil.): 0
Current ratio: 0.40
Long-term debt ($ mil.): —
Dividends
Yield: —
Payout: —
Market value ($ mil.): —

SAINT ALPHONSUS REGIONAL MEDICAL CENTER INC.

Saint Alphonsus Regional Medical Center makes medical care its primary mission. The hospital part of Trinity Health provides Boise Idaho and the surrounding region with general acute and specialized health care services. The medical center has some 380 beds and includes a trauma center an orthopedic spinal care unit an air transport service and a home health and hospice division. It also operates a secondary campus the 150-bed Saint Alphonsus Medical Center - Nampa and it provides general practice and specialty health services through the Saint Alphonsus Medical Group physician practice organization and through outpatient care clinics. The Sisters of the Holy Cross founded the hospital in 1894.

Geographic Reach

Saint Alphonsus Regional Medical Center serves a territory that includes portions of southwestern Idaho northern Nevada and eastern Oregon.

Operations

Saint Alphonsus Regional Medical Center provides outpatient services through the 70 affiliated physician practices that make up the Saint Alphonsus Medical Group. It also operates the Saint Alphonsus Health Plaza which provides urgent care and outpatient surgery laboratory rehabilitation and primary care services.

Strategy

Saint Alphonsus Regional Medical Center expands its facilities to improve medical care in its service territory. It recently added a new Center for Advanced Healing a nine-story patient tower that includes surgery and intensive care units. It is also working to upgrade its medical equipment and communication systems.

EXECUTIVES

Medical Director Physician Relations, Rick Turner
Chairman, George H. Juetten, age 64
Chief Strategy and Accountable Care Network Officer Saint Alphonsus Health System, Janelle Reilly
VP and General Counsel Saint Alphonsus Health System, Stephanie Westermeier
VP Finance and CFO, Kenneth (Ken) Fry
Chief Quality Officer Saint Alphonsus Health System, J. Robert Polk
Secretary and Trustee, Sam Haws
President CEO and Trustee, Sally E. Jeffcoat
VP Corporate Development and Marketing, Jean W. Basom
Public Relations Specialist, Jennifer Krajnik
VP Nursing and Chief Nursing Officer, Karen Hodge
Director Nursing, Sherry Parks
CEO Saint Alphonsus Medical Center Ontario Oregon - Saint Alphonsus Health System, Wes Colvin
CEO Saint Alphonsus Medical Center Nampa Idaho - Saint Alphonsus Health System, Karl Keeler
CEO Saint Alphonsus Medical Center Baker City Oregon - Saint Alphonsus Health System, H. Ray Gibbons
COO, Rodney Reider
VP Human Resources, Audra Pratt
Purchasing, Adrian Wengert

VP System Philanthropy Marketing/Communications and Advocacy Saint Alphonsus Health System, Linda Payne Smith
Director Communications Saint Alphonsus Health System, Kristen Micheletti
Director Marketing Saint Alphonsus Health System, Sarah Berg
Trustee, Richard (Rick) O'Connell
Trustee, Sister Jeanette Fettig
Secretary and Trustee, Sam Haws
Trustee, Mark Meier
Trustee, Diana Nicholson
Trustee, Kaye O'Riordan
President CEO and Trustee, Sally E. Jeffcoat
Trustee, Coyla Anderson
Trustee, Shauna Williams
Trustee, Sister Madeleine Marie Clayton

LOCATIONS

HQ: Saint Alphonsus Regional Medical Center
1055 N. Curtis Rd., Boise ID 83706
Phone: 208-367-2121   **Fax:** 208-367-3123
Web: www.saintalphonsus.org

COMPETITORS

Ascension Health	St. Luke' s Health
HCA	System
Intermountain Health Care	

HISTORICAL FINANCIALS

Company Type: Subsidiary

Income Statement

FYE: June 30

	REVENUE ($ mil.)	NET INCOME ($ mil.)	NET PROFIT MARGIN	EMPLOYEES
06/11	509	11	2.2%	3,500
06/10	449	13	3.1%	0
06/09	428	(8)	—	0
06/08	8	7	86.8%	0
Annual Growth	285.1%	13.4%	—	—

2011 Year-End Financials

Debt ratio: ——
Return on equity: 2.20%
Cash ($ mil.): 5
Current ratio: 0.30
Long-term debt ($ mil.): —
Dividends
Yield: —
Payout: —
Market value ($ mil.): —

SAINT ANSELM COLLEGE

It may be named after a philosopher and theologian but students of all types are welcome to study at Saint Anselm College. The Benedictine Catholic liberal arts college offers degrees in more than 30 majors as well as some 20 certificate programs. With an enrollment of 2000 and a full-time faculty of nearly 140 the school's student-teacher enrollment is 11:1. Saint Anselm College's core curriculum includes classes in English humanities philosophy foreign language science and theology. Located on a hill overlooking Manchester New Hampshire Saint Anselm College was founded in 1889 by monks of the Benedictine order.

EXECUTIVES

President, Rev Jonathan DeFelice
Dean of the College, Rev Augustine Kelly

Associate Dean of the College, Duane Bruce
EVP, Suzanne Mellon
Chancellor, Rev Matthew K. Leavy
Director Information Technology, Adam Albina
VP Finance and Treasurer, Rev Mark A. Cooper
Director Institutional Research, Julie L. Alig
Director Career and Employment Services, Samuel
 P. Allen
Director Student Activities, Shery Balzano
Assistant VP Finance and Assistant Treasurer,
 Margaret A. Bourque
Director Athletics, Edward F. Cannon
Director Financial Aid, Elizabeth Keuffel
Librarian, Joseph W. Constance
Assistant Dean of the College and Dean of
 Freshmen, Mark W. Cronin
Director Corporate and Foundations Relations,
 Kathleen D. Redmond
Registrar, Mary Ann Ericson
VP College Advancement, James F. Flanagan
VP Administration, Patricia R. Shuster
Assistant VP Facilities and Auxiliary Services,
 William Furlong
Assistant VP Public Relations, Tracy Manforte
 Sweet
Director Residence Life, Rebecca J. Gardzina
VP Enrollment Management, Nanci Tessier
Director Admission, Nancy Davis Griffin
Director Alumni Relations and Advancement
 Programming, Patricia Guanci Therrien
VP Student Affairs, Joseph M. Horton
Director Human Resources, Kathleen Parnell
Trustee, Joanne Pietrini-Smith
Trustee, Marie Chabot-Fletcher
Trustee, Michael J. Riegel

LOCATIONS

HQ: SAINT ANSELM COLLEGE
 100 SAINT ANSELM DR, MANCHESTER, NH
 03102-1310
Phone: 603-641-7000
Web: www.anselm.edu

HISTORICAL FINANCIALS
Company Type: School

Income Statement
FYE: June 30

	REVENUE ($ mil.)	NET INCOME ($ mil.)	NET PROFIT MARGIN	EMPLOYEES
06/12	66	(11)	—	700
06/11	65	20	31.6%	0
06/10	86	6	7.3%	0
06/09	60	(22)	—	0
Annual Growth	3.2%	—	—	—

2012 Year-End Financials

Debt ratio: —
Return on equity: (-18.00)%
Cash ($ mil.): 9
Current ratio: —
Long-term debt ($ mil.): —
Dividends
 Yield: —
 Payout: —
 Market value ($ mil.): —

SAINT CLARE'S HOSPITAL INC.

LOCATIONS

HQ: SAINT CLARE' S HOSPITAL INC.
 25 POCONO RD, DENVILLE, NJ 07834-2954
Phone: 973-625-6000
Web: www.saintclares.com

HISTORICAL FINANCIALS
Company Type: Private

Income Statement
FYE: June 30

	REVENUE ($ mil.)	NET INCOME ($ mil.)	NET PROFIT MARGIN	EMPLOYEES
06/11	305	(14)	—	4,916
06/09*	319	0	—	0
09/06	304	(3)	—	0
09/05	1,203	0	—	0
Annual Growth	—	—	—	—

*Fiscal year change

2011 Year-End Financials

Debt ratio: —
Return on equity: (-4.90)%
Cash ($ mil.): 29
Current ratio: 1.90
Long-term debt ($ mil.): —
Dividends
 Yield: —
 Payout: —
 Market value ($ mil.): —

SAINT CLARE'S HOSPITAL OF WESTON INC.

LOCATIONS

HQ: SAINT CLARE' S HOSPITAL OF WESTON INC.
 3400 MINISTRY PKWY, SCHOFIELD, WI 54476-5220
Phone: 715-393-3000

HISTORICAL FINANCIALS
Company Type: Private

Income Statement
FYE: September 30

	REVENUE ($ mil.)	NET INCOME ($ mil.)	NET PROFIT MARGIN	EMPLOYEES
09/11	91	(1)	—	580
09/10	92	(4)	—	0
09/09	90	(5)	—	0
09/08	94	(2)	—	0
Annual Growth	(1.0%)	—	—	—

2011 Year-End Financials

Debt ratio: —
Return on equity: (-1.70)%
Cash ($ mil.): 4
Current ratio: 0.50
Long-term debt ($ mil.): —
Dividends
 Yield: —
 Payout: —
 Market value ($ mil.): —

SAINT EDWARD'S UNIVERSITY INC.

St. Edward's University is a private Catholic liberal arts university in Austin Texas. With an enrollment of more than 5000 students and a student-to-faculty ratio of 14:1 the university offers undergraduate degrees in more than 60 areas of study at schools of behavioral and social sciences management and business the humanities education and natural sciences. St. Edward's also has about ten master's degree programs in fields including accounting business administration information systems and counseling. It offers numerous study abroad programs in Europe Latin America and Asia as well as continuing education programs through its New College.

Geographic Reach

St. Edwards has international study abroad and service learning programs in countries including Argentina China Costa Rica the Czech Republic Germany France India Japan and Peru. Its Austin Texas campus encompasses some 160 acres.

Sales and Marketing

In 2012 St. Edward's launched a new student recruitment initiative entitled "Take on Your World." The campaign highlights the school's global education initiatives and will appear on TV radio print online and social media avenues.

Strategy

St. Edward's is working to expand its international learning programs. It has a portal campus in France and partnerships with a dozen universities in 10 other countries and it is working to expand its learning network into new countries. The university is also working to double the number of undergraduates participating in study abroad programs by 2015. International student enrollment at St. Edward's Austin campus is also on the rise.

In addition St. Edward's is working to improve its curriculum through assessment of its existing activities. It aims to increase academic opportunities for students in areas including multidisciplinary collaborative and independent research projects. The university is also undertaking campus improvement projects; it has invested more than $150 million since 1999 on new or enhanced academic housing and recreation facilities.

Company Background

St. Edward's was founded in 1885 by the Very Rev. Edward Sorin superior general of the Congregation of Holy Cross; the priest also founded University of Notre Dame.

EXECUTIVES

Vice Chairperson, John H. Bauer, age 71
Associate Director Residence Life, Douglas F.
 McConkey
President and Trustee Ex Officio, George E. Martin,
 age 68
Controller, Paul R. Sintef
VP Marketing and Enrollment Management,
 Katherine P. (Paige) Booth
VP Information Technology, William H. (Bill) Cahill
EVP and Provost, Donna M. Jurick
VP Student Affairs, Sandra L. Pacheco
Registrar, Lance R. Hayes
Bursar, Peter J. Beilharz
Secretary and Trustee, F. Gary Valdez
Treasurer and Trustee, Margie D. Kintz
Chairperson, Kevin O'Connor
Associate Director Athletics, Scott J. Abel

Associate Director Instructional Technology, Brenda Adrian

Director Academic Affairs, Eileen Kay Altmiller

Director Sports Information, Naveen Boppana

Director Residence Hall, Christy L. Brown

Assistant Director Physical Plant, Brian Clark Burns

Assistant Director McNair Scholars, Marta I. Cantu

Director Residence Life, Jennifer Lynn Casey

Director Financial Services, Doris F. Constantine

Director Career Opportunity and Internships, Laura J. Cortez

Assistant Director Human Resources, Mary K. Dellinger

Director Development The Holy Cross Institute at St. Edward's New College and School of Natural Sciences, Jose Edward DeMedeiros

Director Fellowship, Shannon S. Duffy

Associate Director Advising, S. Rene Eakins

Director Development Human Resources School of Behavioral and Social Sciences and School of Education, Rachel Reitmeyer Elder

Assistant Director Student Life, Peter S. Erickson

Director Auxiliary Services, Laurelyn Elizabeth Gaede

Director Residence Hall, Karen Faye Gibson

Director Residence Hall, Michael S. Gilmer

Interim Director Center for Teaching Excellence, Jack Green Musselman

Director Alumni and Parent Programs, Kippi Renee Griffith

Director Prior Learning Center, Susan C. Gunn

Director CMP Career Planning, Donna Braun Hagey

Director Graduation Enhancement Program, Patricia Taber Hanks

Director Advancement Services, Cheri S. Hansen

Director Admission Operations, Kelly J. Hart

Director Career Planning, Barbara Jane Henderson

Assistant Director Editorial, Stacia Marie Hernstrom

Assistant Director Admission, Esmeralda Lozano Hoang

Assistant Director Admission, Paul F. Hopkinson

Director Instructional Technology, Mary Teresa Howerton

Assistant Director St. Edward's University Fund, John Griffith Hume III

Associate Director Residence Life, Ellisha Dawn Isom

Director Marketing Services, Carrie A. Johnson

Assistant Director Admission, Dinah Sbelgio Kinard

Director Campus Center, Stephan Gordon Langley

Director Student Life Programs, Sarah M. Leferink

Director Library, Thomas Wilburn Leonhardt

Associate Director Campus Ministry, Margarita Trejo Lohmeier

Director Art, Everett Lunning

Director Academic Support and Retention Program, Francis Gregory MacConnell

Director E-Marketing, Carmella A. Manges

Director PT3 Grant, Allison S. McKissack

Assistant Director Campus Ministry, Ann Francis Monedero

Associate Director Financial Services, Victor Monette

Director Student Life Programs, Jennifer Naman

Director Student Life Programs, Brian Obert

Assistant Director Alumni and Parent Programs, Manish Kiritkumar Pandya

Director Psychological Services, Willard J. Pannabecker

Assistant Director Advancement Services, Anil Jitendra Patel

Director Disabilities, Lorrain C. Perea

Director Campus Ministry Music, Gabriel Baudelio Perez

Associate Director Financial Services, Steven John Peterson

Director School of Management and Business, Constance D. Porter

Director School of Management and Business, Russell Rains

Director International Education, Erin J. Ray

Director Planned Giving, Diane Leach Riehs

Assistant Director Admission, Robyn C. Ross

Director Continuing Education, Lisa Hope Schwarzwald

Assistant Director Campus Ministry, Luis A. Serna

Assistant Director Counseling Center, Selia F. Servin-Guerrero Lopez

Director Math Lab, Matthew Edward Shirley

Director Residence Hall, Ashley A. Shopbell

Director St. Edward's University Fund, Renee Noel Silverthorne

Associate Director Admissions, Bridget M. Sowinski

Director Computer Services, Raymond J. Spinhirne

Director Theatre Technical, Buddy Bryan Staggs

Associate Director Foundations, Ann M. Starr

Director Residence Hall, Sean W. Steele

Director Human Resources, Haven Street-Allen

Director Student Life, Thomas B. Sullivan

Director Athletics, Debora Williamson Taylor

Office Specialist VI Registrar's Office, Erin Eileen Thomas

Director School of Humanities, Phillip M. Thompson

Director Residence Hall, Adam T. Tritt

Executive Director The Holy Cross Institute at St. Edward's, Stephen V. Walsh

Director Residence Hall, Jennifer A. Welles

Director Physical Plant, Michael W. Whitfield-Peterson

Director Campus Ministry, Richard S. (Rick) Wilkinson

Director Telecommunications, David John Wilmot

Assistant Director Admission, Jennifer Thornton Wood

Director Camp Program, Esther Q. Yacono

Career Manager of Adult Programs, Amy C. Bush

Bookstore Manager, Johnnie D. DeMoss

Systems Administration Manager, Alvin David Dobrowski

Technical Acquisitions Manager, Wayne Gaston Hebert II

Bookstore Assistant Manager, Mary P. Helton

Technology Manager IV, William K. Irvin

Access Services Manager, Claudia N. Kweder

Technology Manager IV, Michael R. Marks

Center for Academic Progress Operations Manager, Rhonda Lester McGaughey

Copy Center Manager, Pamela Gaye McGrew

Photocommunications Lab Manager, Lelania Keora Norris

Physical Plant Project Manager, Aubrey Southerland

Theatre Business Manager, Annie Suite

Web Site Manager, Ellen Ruth Sullivan

IT Training Manager, Joana R. Trimble

VP Academic Affairs, Robert Manzer

President Faculty Collegium and Trustee Ex Officio, Catherine Rainwater

Alumni Association and Trustee Ex Officio, Jesse Butler

VP Financial Affairs, Rhonda D. Cartwright

VP University Advancement, Jim Link

Director Communications, Mischelle Diaz

Director Design, Rick Ramos

Associate VP and Dean of Students, Lisa Kirkpatrick

Associate VP and Dean of Undergraduate Admission, Tracy Manier

Vice Chairperson, John H. Bauer, age 71

Trustee Emeritus, Isabella C. M. Cunningham, age 69

Trustee, Ian J. Turpin, age 67

President and Trustee Ex Officio, George E. Martin, age 68

Trustee, Rev Thomas J. O'Hara

Trustee Emeritus, Guy Bodine III

Trustee, Myra A. McDaniel

Secretary and Trustee, F. Gary Valdez

Treasurer and Trustee, Margie D. Kintz

Trustee, Donald Blauvelt

Trustee, Richard P. Daly

Trustee, Timothy F. Gavin

Trustee, Richard B. Gilman

Trustee, Elmer Holtman

Trustee Emeritus, Gregory A. (Greg) Kozmetsky

Trustee, Edward E. Leyden

Trustee, Victor Miramontes

Trustee, John E. Mooney

Trustee, Patricia Munday

Trustee, Theodore R. Popp

Trustee, J. William Sharman Jr.

Trustee, Jim Smith

Trustee, Donna VanFleet

Trustee, Melba Whatley

Trustee Emeritus, Charles A. Betts

Trustee Emeritus, Edward M. Block

Trustee Emeritus, Leslie Clement

Trustee Emeritus, Fred D. George

Trustee Emeritus, Lavon P. Philips

Trustee Emeritus, Bill Renfro

Trustee, James Branigan

Trustee, Linda Evans

Trustee, Kevin Koch

Trustee, Margaret M. Krasovec

Trustee, Sister Amata Miller

Trustee, Marilyn O'Neill

Trustee, Duncan K. Underwood

President Faculty Collegium and Trustee Ex Officio, Catherine Rainwater

Trustee Ex Officio, Austin Lytle

Alumni Association and Trustee Ex Officio, Jesse Butler

LOCATIONS

HQ: St. Edward' s University
3001 S. Congress Ave., Austin TX 78704
Phone: 512-448-8400   Fax: 512-464-8851
Web: www.stedwards.edu

PRODUCTS/OPERATIONS

Selected Undergraduate Schools

School of Behavioral and Social Sciences
School of Education
School of Humanities
School of Management and Business
School of Natural Sciences

Selected Graduate Programs

Accounting (MACT)
Business Administration (MBA)
College Student Development (MACSD)
Computer Information Systems (MSCIS)
Counseling (MAC)
Digital Media Management (DMBA)
Environmental Management and Sustainability (PSMEMS)
Liberal Arts (MLA)
Organization Development (MAOD)
Organizational Leadership and Ethics (MSOLE)

HISTORICAL FINANCIALS

Company Type: School

Income Statement

	REVENUE ($ mil.)	NET INCOME ($ mil.)	NET PROFIT MARGIN	EMPLOYEES
06/12	109	18	16.9%	964
06/11	105	18	17.2%	0
06/10	95	6	7.2%	0
06/09	90	(14)	—	0
Annual Growth	6.5%	—	—	—

FYE: June 30

2012 Year-End Financials

Debt ratio: —
Return on equity: 16.90%
Cash ($ mil.): 30
Current ratio: —
Long-term debt ($ mil.): —

Dividends
  Yield: —
  Payout: —
Market value ($ mil.): —

SAINT ELIZABETH REGIONAL MEDICAL CENTER

Saint Elizabeth Regional Medical Center a Catholic Health Initiatives (CHI) affiliate is a 260-bed acute care hospital that serves the Lincoln Nebraska area. The not-for-profit hospital's services include obstetrics bariatrics cancer care burn and wound care and cardiac and pulmonary care; some 400 physicians are affiliated with the facility. The hospital also operates community health clinics urgent care centers and physical therapy clinics as well as home health and hospice organizations. Saint Elizabeth Regional Medical Center was originally founded as a simple frontier hospital in 1889 by the Sisters of St. Francis of Perpetual Adoration.

SERMC is one of several affiliate and subsidiary hospitals of CHI operating in Nebraska. The national hospital operator has about half a dozen locations in the Cornhusker State including St. Mary's Community Hospital in Nebraska City Good Samaritan Hospital in Kearney and Saint Francis Medical Center in Grand Island as well as the Alegent Health network in Omaha.

As part of the CHI network these hospitals work together to coordinate administrative technology and clinical resources with the goal of increasing efficiency and quality of care in their respective communities. For instance in mid-2011 the Nebraska Heart Institute and Heart Hospital joined the CHI network and the following year Saint Elizabeth transferred all of its open-heart surgery operations to the heart hospital to eliminate duplication of services. In addition the Heart Hospital opened a clinic within Saint Elizabeth's cardiovascular department.

EXECUTIVES

CEO, Robert J. (Bob) Lanik
VP Strategic Planning and Business Development, Charlotte Liggett
CFO, Jeanette M. Wojtalewicz
VP Nursing and Chief Nursing Officer, Kim S. Moore

VP Mission and Human Resources, John G. Dumonceaux
Regional CIO, Tanya Arthur
VP Clinical and Support Services, Patrick Gilles
Chief Medical Officer, Cary Ward
Public Relations, Jo Miller

LOCATIONS

HQ: Saint Elizabeth Regional Medical Center
555 S. 70th St., Lincoln NE 68510
Phone: 402-219-8000   **Fax:** 402-219-8973
Web: www.saintelizabethonline.com

COMPETITORS

BryanLGH Medical Center
Children's Hospital & Medical Center
Fremont Area Medical Center
Madonna Rehabilitation Hospital

Methodist Health System
Nebraska medical center
Tenet Healthcare
University of Nebraska

HISTORICAL FINANCIALS

Company Type: Private - Not-for-Profit

Income Statement

	REVENUE ($ mil.)	NET INCOME ($ mil.)	NET PROFIT MARGIN	EMPLOYEES
06/11	253	75	30.0%	1,825
06/10	1	0	32.7%	0
06/09	251	(5)	—	0
06/08	1	0	18.9%	0
Annual Growth	418.9%	505.4%		

FYE: June 30

2011 Year-End Financials

Debt ratio: —
Return on equity: 30.00%
Cash ($ mil.): 82
Current ratio: 5.80
Long-term debt ($ mil.): —

Dividends
  Yield: —
  Payout: —
Market value ($ mil.): —

SAINT FRANCIS HOSPITAL AND MEDICAL CENTER

Saint Francis takes care of the hearts of Hartford Connecticut. The Saint Francis Hospital and Medical Center also known as Saint Francis Care is a regional medical center with some 620 beds. The hospital specializes in cardiology oncology neurology orthopedics and women's and children's health services. It also offers behavioral health weight management trauma care and injury rehabilitation programs. Saint Francis serves as a teaching hospital affiliated with the University of Connecticut Schools of Medicine and Dentistry. It also operates the nearby Mount Sinai Rehabilitation Hospital a 60-bed facility that provides brain trauma sports medicine and orthopedic care.

Operations

Saint Francis' on-campus specialty centers include the Hoffman Heart Institute which specializes in open-heart surgeries and catheterization procedures and the Saint Francis/Mount Sinai Regional

Cancer Center. In addition to its main campuses (Saint Francis and Mount Sinai Rehabilitation) Saint Francis operates health clinics and medical offices in about a dozen surrounding communities. The medical center also operates specialty clinics such as radiology and imaging centers and it maintains a medical laboratory in a joint venture with nearby Bristol Hospital.

In 2011 the Saint Francis campus completed construction of a 10-story addition. The John T. O'Connell Tower contains 135 private patient rooms 20 operating rooms and a two-floor orthopedic center (known as the Connecticut Joint Replacement Institute) as well as new emergency room and ambulance and helicopter facilities.

Financial Analysis

Saint Francis has initiated a number of internal cost-reduction efforts to keep its operations and finances healthy. It is also improving its internal information management systems to increase efficiencies at its facilities.

Strategy

As a sign of economic troubles and health care reform changes in the US market Saint Francis is exploring affiliations with other regional hospitals to improve care and control medical costs. As example: in 2012 Saint Francis established an affiliation with nearby Johnson Memorial Medical Center. It is also involved in efforts by the Connecticut legislature to form a UConn Health Network with the University of Connecticut Health Center and other area providers.

Company Background

Established in 1897 Saint Francis began an affiliation with Mount Sinai Hospital in 1990 and merged with it in 1995. Mount Sinai Hospital originally founded in 1923 was then converted from an acute care center into the Mount Sinai Rehabilitation Hospital.

EXECUTIVES

President and CEO, Christopher M. (Chris) Dadlez
VP Financial Management, Donald Straceski
VP Lean Redesign and Chief Compliance Officer, Jennifer S. Schneider
SVP Medical Affairs and Chief Medical Officer, Rolf W. Knoll
EVP and COO, Kathleen M. (Kate) Roche
Assistant Secretary and Board Administrator, Martha E. Hartle
Chief Development Officer; President Saint Francis Foundation, Paul F. Pendergast
VP and CIO, Kathleen A. DeMatteo
VP Facilities Support Services and Construction, Robert J. Falaguerra
VP Revenue Cycle, Nicole J. Schulz
VP Mission Integration, Judith A. Carey
President Medical Staff, Paul F. Mitchell
SVP Medical Affairs, Rebecca L. Burke
VP and Chief Compliance Officer, Kesha Boykin
Chairman and Director Department of Medicine, Bernard A. Clark III

LOCATIONS

HQ: Saint Francis Hospital and Medical Center
114 Woodland St., Hartford CT 06105-1208
Phone: 860-714-4000   **Fax:** 860-714-8048
Web: www.saintfranciscare.com

COMPETITORS

Backus
Bristol Hospital
Connecticut Children's Medical Center
Griffin Health
Hartford Health Care

Hospital of Central Connecticut
Lawrence & Memorial Hospital
MidState Medical Center
Stamford Health
University of Connecticut Health Center
Yale New Haven Health Services Corporation

HISTORICAL FINANCIALS
Company Type: Private - Not-for-Profit

Income Statement
FYE: September 30

	REVENUE ($ mil.)	NET INCOME ($ mil.)	NET PROFIT MARGIN	EMPLOYEES
09/11	674	(53)	—	3,270
09/10	651	(10)	—	0
09/09	638	(16)	—	0
09/08	616	(72)	—	0
Annual Growth	3.1%	—	—	—

2011 Year-End Financials

Debt ratio: —
Return on equity: (-7.90)%
Cash ($ mil.): 111
Current ratio: 2.00
Long-term debt ($ mil.): —

Dividends
Yield: —
Payout: —
Market value ($ mil.): —

SAINT FRANCIS UNIVERSITY

Saint Francis University is a Catholic liberal arts college with more than 2000 full- and part-time students. The university offers 25 undergraduate and seven graduate majors in areas such as business administration education medical science and human resource management. It also has a doctorate program in physical therapy. Saint Francis University was established when six Franciscan Friars from Ireland founded a boys' academy in the mountain hamlet of Loretto Pennsylvania in 1847. Now more than 60% of the student body are women. The former St. Francis College gained university status in 2001.

EXECUTIVES

Director Human Resources, Heather J. Meck
VP Finance, Robert Datsko
CIO, George Pyo
President, Father Gabriel Zeis
Dean Enrollment Management, Erin McCloskey
Director Alumni Relations, Anita Baumann
VP Advancement, Raymond Ponchione
Director Business Administration, Randy Frye
Director Career Services, Julie Barris
Director Purchasing, William Agosta
Provost, Wayne Powel
Director Marketing and Public Affairs, Ross Feltz
Bursar, Tom Kendziora
VP Mission Effectiveness, Father Daniel Sinisi
VP Student and Community Development, Frank Montecalvo Jr.
Registrar, Stephen Rombouts
Director Student Financial Aid, Jamie Kosh
University Police, Larry Wagner

LOCATIONS

HQ: Saint Francis University
117 Evergreen Dr., Loretto PA 15940
Phone: 814-472-3000   **Fax:** 814-472-3369
Web: www.francis.edu

COMPETITORS

Penn State
Pennsylvania State System of Higher Education
University of Pittsburgh

HISTORICAL FINANCIALS
Company Type: School

Income Statement
FYE: June 30

	REVENUE ($ mil.)	NET INCOME ($ mil.)	NET PROFIT MARGIN	EMPLOYEES
06/11	85	6	8.0%	420
06/10	59	6	10.8%	0
06/08	69	7	10.5%	0
06/05	41	2	5.4%	0
Annual Growth	26.7%	44.1%	—	—

2011 Year-End Financials

Debt ratio: —
Return on equity: 8.00%
Cash ($ mil.): 2
Current ratio: —
Long-term debt ($ mil.): —

Dividends
Yield: —
Payout: —
Market value ($ mil.): —

SAINT JOSEPH HOSPITAL

LOCATIONS

HQ: SAINT JOSEPH HOSPITAL
2900 N LAKE SHORE DR, CHICAGO, IL 60657-6274
Phone: 773-665-3000
Web: www.harborviewrecovery.com

HISTORICAL FINANCIALS
Company Type: Private

Income Statement
FYE: June 30

	REVENUE ($ mil.)	NET INCOME ($ mil.)	NET PROFIT MARGIN	EMPLOYEES
06/11	202	7	3.9%	1,600
06/10	193	(2)	—	0
06/09	192	5	2.8%	0
Annual Growth	2.5%	20.9%	—	—

SAINT JOSEPH'S COMMUNITY HOSPITAL

LOCATIONS

HQ: SAINT JOSEPH' S COMMUNITY HOSPITAL
3200 PLEASANT VALLEY RD, WEST BEND, WI 53095-9274
Phone: 262-836-5533
Web: www.stjosephswb.com

HISTORICAL FINANCIALS
Company Type: Private

Income Statement
FYE: June 30

	REVENUE ($ mil.)	NET INCOME ($ mil.)	NET PROFIT MARGIN	EMPLOYEES
06/11	81	3	4.4%	688
06/10	78	2	3.3%	0
06/09*	76	0	—	0
12/08	0	(0)	—	0
Annual Growth	1123.1%	—	—	—

*Fiscal year change

2011 Year-End Financials

Debt ratio: —
Return on equity: 4.40%
Cash ($ mil.): 7
Current ratio: 2.40
Long-term debt ($ mil.): —

Dividends
Yield: —
Payout: —
Market value ($ mil.): —

SAINT JOSEPH'S HOSPITAL INC.

LOCATIONS

HQ: SAINT JOSEPH' S HOSPITAL INC.
11705 MERCY BLVD, SAVANNAH, GA 31419-1791
Phone: 912-819-4100
Web: www.sjchs.org

HISTORICAL FINANCIALS
Company Type: Private

Income Statement
FYE: June 30

	REVENUE ($ mil.)	NET INCOME ($ mil.)	NET PROFIT MARGIN	EMPLOYEES
06/11	185	6	3.4%	0
06/10	215	9	4.5%	0
06/09	195	0	—	0
06/08	196	11	5.7%	0
Annual Growth	(1.8%)	(17.9%)	—	—

2011 Year-End Financials

Debt ratio: —
Return on equity: 3.40%
Cash ($ mil.): 0
Current ratio: 2.00
Long-term debt ($ mil.): —

Dividends
Yield: —
Payout: —
Market value ($ mil.): —

SAINT JOSEPH'S HOSPITAL OF MARSHFIELD INC.

LOCATIONS

HQ: SAINT JOSEPH' S HOSPITAL OF MARSHFIELD INC.
611 N SAINT JOSEPH AVE, MARSHFIELD, WI 54449-1832
Phone: 715-387-1713

HISTORICAL FINANCIALS
Company Type: Private

Income Statement

	REVENUE ($ mil.)	NET INCOME ($ mil.)	NET PROFIT MARGIN	EMPLOYEES
09/11	353	37	10.7%	2,200
09/10	348	31	9.2%	0
09/09	342	21	6.4%	0
09/08	316	22	7.1%	0
Annual Growth	3.7%	19.2%	—	—

FYE: September 30

2011 Year-End Financials

Debt ratio: ——
Return on equity: 10.70%
Cash ($ mil.): 56
Current ratio: 4.60
Long-term debt ($ mil.): —

Dividends
Yield: —
Payout: —
Market value ($ mil.): —

SAINT LEO UNIVERSITY INCORPORATED

LOCATIONS

HQ: SAINT LEO UNIVERSITY INCORPORATED
33701 STATE ROAD 52, SAINT LEO, FL 33574-9701
Phone: 352-588-8215

HISTORICAL FINANCIALS
Company Type: Private

Income Statement

	REVENUE ($ mil.)	NET INCOME ($ mil.)	NET PROFIT MARGIN	EMPLOYEES
06/11	151	22	14.9%	819
06/10	135	14	10.8%	0
06/09	116	0	—	0
06/08	106	0	0.6%	0
Annual Growth	12.7%	226.6%	—	—

FYE: June 30

2011 Year-End Financials

Debt ratio: ——
Return on equity: 14.90%
Cash ($ mil.): 14
Current ratio: —
Long-term debt ($ mil.): —

Dividends
Yield: —
Payout: —
Market value ($ mil.): —

SAINT MARY'S COLLEGE OF CALIFORNIA

LOCATIONS

HQ: SAINT MARY' S COLLEGE OF CALIFORNIA
1928 SAINT MARYS RD, MORAGA, CA 94556-2744
Phone: 925-631-4000

Web: www.stmarys-ca.edu

HISTORICAL FINANCIALS
Company Type: Private

Income Statement

	REVENUE ($ mil.)	NET INCOME ($ mil.)	NET PROFIT MARGIN	EMPLOYEES
06/12	117	(11)	—	1,000
06/10	97	(2)	—	0
06/09	100	(47)	—	0
06/08	97	(18)	—	0
Annual Growth	6.4%	—	—	—

FYE: June 30

2012 Year-End Financials

Debt ratio: ——
Return on equity: (-9.80)%
Cash ($ mil.): 3
Current ratio: 0.10
Long-term debt ($ mil.): —

Dividends
Yield: —
Payout: —
Market value ($ mil.): —

SAINT MARY'S UNIVERSITY OF MINNESOTA

Saint Mary's University of Minnesota is a private Roman Catholic institution that enrolls about 6000 students; approximately 20% are traditional undergraduates while the majority are adult learners in the Schools of Graduate and Professional Programs. The school which was founded in 1912 by Bishop Patrick R. Heffron has been administered by the brothers of the De La Salle order since 1933. It offers instruction in dozens of fields and has facilities in Minnesota and Wisconsin; in addition the school operates two institutes at Tangaza College in Nairobi Kenya.

EXECUTIVES

VP and Provost, Jeffrey R. Highland
Chair, John A. Ehlert
Vice Chair, Michael M. Gostomski
Director Library, Mary Moxness
Reference Librarian, Ruth Ann Schwartz
Library Acquisitions Associate, Lucille Smith
Dean School of Business, James M. Bedtke
Director Career Services, Renee Solberg
VP Student Development, Chris Kendall
Dean of Students, Mary Baumann
VP Admission, Tony Piscitello
President, William Mann, age 65

LOCATIONS

HQ: Saint Mary' s University of Minnesota
700 Terrace Heights, Winona MN 55987-1399
Phone: 507-452-4430   **Fax:** 507-453-5553
Web: www.smumn.edu

HISTORICAL FINANCIALS
Company Type: School

Income Statement

	REVENUE ($ mil.)	NET INCOME ($ mil.)	NET PROFIT MARGIN	EMPLOYEES
05/12	66	3	5.1%	1,000
05/11	68	8	12.2%	0
05/10	65	7	12.0%	0
05/09	50	(8)	—	0
Annual Growth	9.7%	—	—	—

FYE: May 31

2012 Year-End Financials

Debt ratio: ——
Return on equity: 5.10%
Cash ($ mil.): 11
Current ratio: —
Long-term debt ($ mil.): —

Dividends
Yield: —
Payout: —
Market value ($ mil.): —

SAINT NORBERT COLLEGE INC

St. Norbert College is a private Catholic liberal arts institution offering undergraduate and graduate programs to approximately 2000 students. The school offers more than 40 undergraduate programs of study in the natural sciences social sciences and humanities and fine arts. It also confers Master's degrees in Science in Education and Theological Studies. The college is one of only a handful of institutions in the US that offer a Peace Corps Preparatory Program. St. Norbert College was founded in 1898 by Abbot Bernard Pennings a Dutch immigrant priest as a school to ready men for the priesthood. It became coeducational in 1952.

EXECUTIVES

VP Enrollment Management and Communications, Bridget Krage O'Connor
VP Business and Finance, Eileen M. Jahnke
VP Student Affairs, Mary Oling-Sisay
Chief of Staff, Amy A. Sorenson
President, Thomas Kunkel
VP Mission and Heritage, Rev Jay Fostner
VP College Advancement, Phil Oswald

LOCATIONS

HQ: St. Norbert College
100 Grant St., De Pere WI 54115-2099
Phone: 920-403-3005   **Fax:** 920-403-4072
Web: www.snc.edu

HISTORICAL FINANCIALS

Company Type: School

Income Statement

FYE: May 31

	REVENUE ($ mil.)	NET INCOME ($ mil.)	NET PROFIT MARGIN	EMPLOYEES
05/12	58	6	11.5%	490
05/11	56	23	41.5%	0
05/10	54	10	20.1%	0
05/09	52	(16)	—	0
Annual Growth	3.8%	—	—	—

2012 Year-End Financials

Debt ratio: ——
Return on equity: 11.50%
Cash ($ mil.): 20
Current ratio: —
Long-term debt ($ mil.): —

Dividends
Yield: —
Payout: —
Market value ($ mil.): —

SAINT TAMMANY PARISH HOSPITAL SERVICE DISTRICT 1

St. Tammany Parish Hospital serves communities in St. Tammany Parish and Washington Parish along the northern shores of Lake Ponchartrain in eastern Louisiana. The not-for-profit hospital has about 240 beds and offers acute care diagnostic rehabilitation and community wellness services. It also includes centers and clinics specializing in surgery breast care cardiology and sleep disorders. In addition St. Tammany Parish Hospital operates a home health and hospice agency an outpatient services center and a primary care physicians' office. The company's facilities are served by doctors in St. Tammany Physicians Network.

Geographic Reach

The hospital serves patients in St. Tammany Parish and Washington Parish in eastern Louisiana.

Financial Performance

Some 42% of St. Tammany Parish Hospital's funding in 2011 came from individuals; 36% from companies and organizations; 12% from employees; and 10% from foundations.

Strategy

In respose to growing demand for primary care on the North Shore of Lake Ponchartrain in 2012 St. Tammany Physicians Network opened a new office in Madisonville expanding the reach of its primary care services. The new location specializes in family medicine including pediatrics and internal medicine. Services include acute care chronic illness and yearly physical exams for work school and sports.

Company Background

The hospital opened its doors in 1954.

EXECUTIVES

President and CEO, Patti Ellish
SVP and COO, Sharon A. Toups
SVP and Chief Medical Officer, Robert Capitelli
SVP and Chief Nursing Officer, Kerry Milton
VP Corporate Compliance, Midge Collett
VP Human Resources, Judy Gracia

SVP and CFO, Tim C. Lessing

LOCATIONS

HQ: St. Tammany Parish Hospital
1202 S. Tyler St., Covington LA 70433
Phone: 985-898-4000   **Fax:** 985-898-4360
Web: www.stph.org

PRODUCTS/OPERATIONS

Selected Services and Facilities

Adult Rehabilitation
Adult Rehabilitation Outpatient
Adult Weight Management
Angiography
Breast Center
Bronchoscopy
Cardiac Care (Heart)
Cardiac Cath Lab
Cardiac Rehab Outpatient
Cardiac Rehabilitation
Cardiology
Cardiology Non-Invasive
Center for Wound Care and Hyperbaric Medicine
Colonoscopy
Community Wellness Center
Coumadin Clinic
Covington Surgery Center
Critical Care
CT Scan
Diabetes Education Program
Diagnostic X-ray
EGD (Esophagogastroduodenoscopy)
Embolizations Emergency Services
Endoscopic Retrograde Cholangioancreatography
Endoscopy
ERCP
Esophageal Motility Studies
Family Medical Clinic Franklinton
Fluoroscopy
Gynecologic Surgery
Hospital Medicine
Hospitalist
Hyperbaric Medicine
Intensive Care Unit (ICU)
Interventional Radiology
Kyphoplasty
Labor & Delivery Suite
Lymphedema Management
Mammography
Mary Bird Perkins Cancer Center
MaternalChild Services
Medical Nutrition Therapy
Medical Surgical Nursing Care
MRI
Neonatal Intensive Care Unit
Nephrostograms
New Family Center
Nuclear Medicine
Occupational Therapy
Oncology Nursing Care
Outpatient Pavilion
Pacemaker Clinic
Parenting Center
Pediatric Care
Pediatric Rehabilitation Outpatient
Pediatric Unit
Physical Therapy
Post-Operative Care
Pre-Operative Care
Primary Care Physicians
Prostate Cancer
Prostatectomy
Pulmonary Rehab
Radio Frequency Ablation
Radiology/Imaging
Respiratory Services
Rehabilitation Services
Robotic Surgery
Sigmodoscopy
Sleep Disorders Center
Speech Therapy
St. Tammany Physician's Network Covington
St. Tammany Physician's Network Mandeville
St. Tammany Physician's Network Masonville
Surgery Inpatient
Surgery Outpatient
Ultrasound
Urologic Surgery
Vertebroplasty
Wellness Works
Women's Health
Wound Care

COMPETITORS

Baton Rouge General
Dynacq Healthcare
General Health System
MedCath
Medical Properties Trust

Our Lady of the Lake RMC
Regency Hospital
River Parishes Hospital
Woman' s Hospital

HISTORICAL FINANCIALS

Company Type: Private - Not-for-Profit

Income Statement

FYE: December 31

	REVENUE ($ mil.)	NET INCOME ($ mil.)	NET PROFIT MARGIN	EMPLOYEES
12/11	223	16	7.6%	1,520
12/09	200	8	4.2%	0
12/08	1	0	—	0
12/07	186	18	10.1%	0
Annual Growth	6.1%	(3.6%)	—	—

2011 Year-End Financials

Debt ratio: ——
Return on equity: 7.60%
Cash ($ mil.): 17
Current ratio: 1.80
Long-term debt ($ mil.): —

Dividends
Yield: —
Payout: —
Market value ($ mil.): —

SAINT TAMMANY PARISH SCHOOL BOARD

LOCATIONS

HQ: SAINT TAMMANY PARISH SCHOOL BOARD
321 N THEARD ST, COVINGTON, LA 70433-2835
Phone: 985-892-2276
Web: www.stpsb.org

HISTORICAL FINANCIALS

Company Type: Private

Income Statement

FYE: June 30

	REVENUE ($ mil.)	NET INCOME ($ mil.)	NET PROFIT MARGIN	EMPLOYEES
06/11	445	(44)	—	4,400
Annual Growth	—	—	—	—

2011 Year-End Financials

Debt ratio: ——
Return on equity: (-10.10)%
Cash ($ mil.): 128
Current ratio: —
Long-term debt ($ mil.): —

Dividends
Yield: —
Payout: —
Market value ($ mil.): —

SAINT THOMAS HOSPITAL

LOCATIONS

HQ: SAINT THOMAS HOSPITAL
4220 HARDING PIKE, NASHVILLE, TN 37205-2095
Phone: 615-222-5976
Web: www.saintthomashospital.com

HISTORICAL FINANCIALS

Company Type: Private

Income Statement

FYE: June 30

	REVENUE ($ mil.)	NET INCOME ($ mil.)	NET PROFIT MARGIN	EMPLOYEES
06/11	493	60	12.2%	99
06/10	455	60	13.3%	0
Annual Growth	8.4%	(0.2%)	—	—

2011 Year-End Financials

Debt ratio: ——
Return on equity: 12.20%
Cash ($ mil.): 35
Current ratio: 2.10
Long-term debt ($ mil.): —

Dividends
Yield: —
Payout: —
Market value ($ mil.): —

SAINT VINCENT HOSPITAL

LOCATIONS

HQ: SAINT VINCENT HOSPITAL
455 SAINT MICHAELS DR, SANTA FE, NM 87505-7663
Phone: 505-983-3361
Web: www.saraillustrates.com

HISTORICAL FINANCIALS

Company Type: Private

Income Statement

FYE: June 30

	REVENUE ($ mil.)	NET INCOME ($ mil.)	NET PROFIT MARGIN	EMPLOYEES
06/11	316	24	7.7%	1,555
06/10	299	21	7.1%	0
06/09*	288	18	6.5%	0
03/09	0	0	6.6%	0
Annual Growth	1326.6%	1396.2%	—	—

*Fiscal year change

2011 Year-End Financials

Debt ratio: ——
Return on equity: 7.70%
Cash ($ mil.): 12
Current ratio: 0.90
Long-term debt ($ mil.): —

Dividends
Yield: —
Payout: —
Market value ($ mil.): —

SALEM LEASING CORPORATION

LOCATIONS

HQ: SALEM LEASING CORPORATION
175 CHARLOIS BLVD, WINSTON SALEM, NC 27103-1521
Phone: 336-768-6800

HISTORICAL FINANCIALS

Company Type: Private

Income Statement

FYE: June 30

	REVENUE ($ mil.)	NET INCOME ($ mil.)	NET PROFIT MARGIN	EMPLOYEES
06/12	106	(2)	—	420
06/11	76	(2)	—	0
06/10	67	(2)	—	0
06/09	74	(0)	—	0
Annual Growth	12.7%	—	—	—

2012 Year-End Financials

Debt ratio: ——
Return on equity: (-2.60)%
Cash ($ mil.): 0
Current ratio: 0.10
Long-term debt ($ mil.): —

Dividends
Yield: —
Payout: —
Market value ($ mil.): —

SAINT VINCENT HEALTH CENTER INC

LOCATIONS

HQ: SAINT VINCENT HEALTH CENTER INC
232 W 25TH ST, ERIE, PA 16544-0001
Phone: 814-452-5000
Web: www.saintvincenthealth.com

HISTORICAL FINANCIALS

Company Type: Private

Income Statement

FYE: June 30

	REVENUE ($ mil.)	NET INCOME ($ mil.)	NET PROFIT MARGIN	EMPLOYEES
06/11	284	7	2.5%	3,000
06/10	269	(0)	—	0
06/09	252	4	1.8%	0
06/08	246	7	3.1%	0
Annual Growth	4.9%	(2.3%)	—	—

2011 Year-End Financials

Debt ratio: ——
Return on equity: 2.50%
Cash ($ mil.): 34
Current ratio: 1.20
Long-term debt ($ mil.): —

Dividends
Yield: —
Payout: —
Market value ($ mil.): —

SALEM COMMUNITY HOSPITAL

LOCATIONS

HQ: SALEM COMMUNITY HOSPITAL
1995 E STATE ST, SALEM, OH 44460-2400
Phone: 330-332-1551

HISTORICAL FINANCIALS

Company Type: Private

Income Statement

FYE: June 30

	REVENUE ($ mil.)	NET INCOME ($ mil.)	NET PROFIT MARGIN	EMPLOYEES
06/12	108	(18)	—	1,000
06/11	102	27	26.7%	0
06/10	104	9	9.1%	0
06/09	106	(20)	—	0
Annual Growth	0.7%	—	—	—

2012 Year-End Financials

Debt ratio: ——
Return on equity: (-17.40)%
Cash ($ mil.): 3
Current ratio: 1.10
Long-term debt ($ mil.): —

Dividends
Yield: —
Payout: —
Market value ($ mil.): —

SALEM STATE UNIVERSITY

LOCATIONS

HQ: SALEM STATE UNIVERSITY
352 LAFAYETTE ST, SALEM, MA 01970-5348
Phone: 978-542-6000
Web: www.enterprisectr.org

HISTORICAL FINANCIALS

Company Type: Private

Income Statement

FYE: June 30

	REVENUE ($ mil.)	NET INCOME ($ mil.)	NET PROFIT MARGIN	EMPLOYEES
06/12	97	23	24.3%	1,200
06/11	97	20	21.3%	0
06/08	2	1	58.7%	0
06/07	65	5	8.5%	0
Annual Growth	14.1%	62.0%	—	—

2012 Year-End Financials

Debt ratio: ——
Return on equity: 24.30%
Cash ($ mil.): 15
Current ratio: 0.70
Long-term debt ($ mil.): —

Dividends
Yield: —
Payout: —
Market value ($ mil.): —

SALINA REGIONAL HEALTH CENTER INC.

LOCATIONS

HQ: SALINA REGIONAL HEALTH CENTER INC.
400 S SANTA FE AVE, SALINA, KS 67401-4144
Phone: 785-452-7000
Web: www.srhc.com

HISTORICAL FINANCIALS

Company Type: Private

Income Statement

FYE: September 30

	REVENUE ($ mil.)	NET INCOME ($ mil.)	NET PROFIT MARGIN	EMPLOYEES
09/11	172	17	10.0%	1,500
09/10	159	11	7.0%	0
09/09	154	0	—	0
09/08	145	17	11.7%	0
Annual Growth	5.9%	0.7%	—	—

2011 Year-End Financials

Debt ratio: —
Return on equity: 10.00%
Cash ($ mil.): 94
Current ratio: 6.90
Long-term debt ($ mil.): —
Dividends
Yield: —
Payout: —
Market value ($ mil.): —

SALMON LEGACY CREEK HOSPITAL

LOCATIONS

HQ: SALMON LEGACY CREEK HOSPITAL
2211 NE 139TH ST, VANCOUVER, WA 98686-2742
Phone: 360-487-1000
Web: www.legacyhealth.org

HISTORICAL FINANCIALS

Company Type: Private

Income Statement

FYE: March 31

	REVENUE ($ mil.)	NET INCOME ($ mil.)	NET PROFIT MARGIN	EMPLOYEES
03/11	184	10	5.6%	700
03/10	182	0	0.2%	0
03/09	162	0	0.2%	0
Annual Growth	6.7%	531.9%	—	—

2011 Year-End Financials

Debt ratio: —
Return on equity: 5.60%
Cash ($ mil.): 0
Current ratio: 1.80
Long-term debt ($ mil.): —
Dividends
Yield: —
Payout: —
Market value ($ mil.): —

SALT LAKE COMMUNITY COLLEGE

Salt Lake Community College (SLCC) provides day night and weekend courses for early risers and night owls alike. SLCC serves more than 60000 students and has a student-to-teacher ratio of 20-to-1. The two-year school has about a dozen campuses and outreach centers in Salt Lake City Utah as well as online courses available to reach both traditional and non-traditional students. In addition to being a top US awarder of associate degrees in arts science applied science and pre-engineering the community college also has career and technical programs. More than half of SLCC's full-time students plan to graduate to a four-year school to pursue bachelor's degrees.

SLCC reported revenues of $201 million in 2011. The school's earnings come from a mix of tuition state funding appropriations and government contracts and grants. It also earns some revenues through auxiliary enterprises.

SLCC has had to reduce its budget through a number of programs in recent years in the face of economic challenges including reduced government funding. For instance the school has adjusted its class offerings and enrollment procedures to maximize teaching resources which resulted in a small decrease in its student numbers during 2011.

EXECUTIVES

Director Human Resources, Craig Gardner
VP Student Services, Deneece Huftalin
President, Cynthia A. Bioteau
VP Business Services, Dennis Klaus
VP Institutional Advancement, Tim Sheehan
Provost, Christopher Picard

LOCATIONS

HQ: Salt Lake Community College
4600 S. Redwood Rd., Salt Lake City UT 84123
Phone: 801-957-4111 **Fax:** 801-957-4961
Web: www.slcc.edu

PRODUCTS/OPERATIONS

2011 Sales

	$ mil.	% of total
State appropriations	64	32
Tuition & fees	58	29
Government contracts & grants	55	27
Auxiliary enterprises	14	7
Other sources	9	5
Total	201	100

HISTORICAL FINANCIALS

Company Type: School

Income Statement

FYE: June 30

	REVENUE ($ mil.)	NET INCOME ($ mil.)	NET PROFIT MARGIN	EMPLOYEES
06/11	90	3	3.5%	3,200
06/10	88	7	8.2%	0
06/09	76	(4)	—	0
06/08	73	10	13.8%	0
Annual Growth	7.5%	(31.7%)	—	—

2011 Year-End Financials

Debt ratio: —
Return on equity: 3.50%
Cash ($ mil.): 26
Current ratio: 1.30
Long-term debt ($ mil.): —
Dividends
Yield: —
Payout: —
Market value ($ mil.): —

SAM KANE BEEF PROCESSORS INC.

Sam Kane Beef Processors is a leading slaughterhouse that supplies beef products to customers throughout the country and in some foreign countries. Under the Kane's brand it markets a variety of traditional cuts of beef and portion-controlled steaks as well as such specialty products as liver hearts tongue and other exotic cuts. The company's warehouse facility has storage capacity for more than six million pounds of fresh and frozen meat. Sam Kane Beef is known for its ELECTRO-TENDER-aged process that uses an electrical current to accelerate the natural aging process. The family-owned company was founded in 1949.

EXECUTIVES

President and CEO, Jerry Kane
EVP and CFO, Harold Kane
VP and General Manager, Alfred H. Bausch
VP, Esther Kane
Director of Human Resources, Craig Reynolds

LOCATIONS

HQ: Sam Kane Beef Processors Inc.
9001 Leopard St., Corpus Christi TX 78409
Phone: 361-241-5000 **Fax:** 361-242-2999
Web: www.samkanebeef.com

COMPETITORS

American Foods	Loggins Meat
Cargill Meat Solutions	Meyer Natural Angus
Colorado Boxed Beef	National Beef Packing
Greater Omaha Packing	PM Beef Holdings
Hormel	Tyson Fresh Meats
JBS USA	

HISTORICAL FINANCIALS

Company Type: Private

Income Statement

FYE: January 1

	REVENUE ($ mil.)	NET INCOME ($ mil.)	NET PROFIT MARGIN	EMPLOYEES
01/12*	502	(4)	—	850
12/05	0	0	—	0
12/04	370	0	—	0
12/03	0	0	—	0
Annual Growth	—	—	—	—

*Fiscal year change

2012 Year-End Financials

Debt ratio: —
Return on equity: (-0.90%)
Cash ($ mil.): 0
Current ratio: 0.70
Long-term debt ($ mil.): —
Dividends
Yield: —
Payout: —
Market value ($ mil.): —

SAM LEVIN INC.

Founded in 1920 as a furniture and hardware store by the husband-and-wife team Sam and Jessie Levin Sam Levin (dba Levin Furniture) sells a wide variety of dining room bedroom living room and office furniture as well as mattresses at about a dozen retail locations in northeastern Ohio and southwestern Pennsylvania. It also operates a Sleep Center bedding store in Pennsylvania and a clearance outlet in Ohio. The family-owned-and-run-company offers self-service kiosks in its showrooms and creative exhibits that include sports-and Wizard of Oz-themed displays. Robert Levin Sam and Jessie's grandson is president of the company.

EXECUTIVES

President and CEO, Robert Levin
VP Finance, Basil Hawanchak
VP HR, Irene Fostyk
Director Operations, Paula Rojtas
VP Operations, Ward Dingman
VP Merchandising, Chris Pelcher

LOCATIONS

HQ: Sam Levin Inc.
301 Fitz Henry Rd., Smithton PA 15479-8715
Phone: 724-872-2055   **Fax:** 724-872-2060
Web: www.levinfurniture.com

2009 Stores

	No.
Ohio	7
Pennsylvania	7
Total	**14**

COMPETITORS

Ashley Furniture	J. C. Penney
Bassett Furniture	Macy' s
Havertys	Rooms To Go

HISTORICAL FINANCIALS

Company Type: Private

Income Statement

FYE: December 31

	REVENUE ($ mil.)	NET INCOME ($ mil.)	NET PROFIT MARGIN	EMPLOYEES
12/11	170	11	6.8%	400
12/10	145	4	2.9%	0
12/09	151	8	5.5%	0
12/08	149	7	5.3%	0
Annual Growth	4.3%	13.6%	—	—

2011 Year-End Financials

Debt ratio: —
Return on equity: 6.80%
Cash ($ mil.): 18
Current ratio: 1.30
Long-term debt ($ mil.): —
Dividends
  Yield: —
  Payout: —
Market value ($ mil.): —

SAMSUNG OPTO-ELECTRONICS AMERICA INC.

LOCATIONS

HQ: SAMSUNG OPTO-ELECTRONICS AMERICA INC.
100 CHALLENGER RD STE 700, RIDGEFIELD PARK, NJ 07660-2119
Phone: 201-325-6920
Web: www.samsung-security.com

HISTORICAL FINANCIALS

Company Type: Private

Income Statement

FYE: December 31

	REVENUE ($ mil.)	NET INCOME ($ mil.)	NET PROFIT MARGIN	EMPLOYEES
12/11	98	4	4.6%	81
Annual Growth	—	—	—	—

2011 Year-End Financials

Debt ratio: —
Return on equity: 4.60%
Cash ($ mil.): 2
Current ratio: 0.90
Long-term debt ($ mil.): —
Dividends
  Yield: —
  Payout: —
Market value ($ mil.): —

SAN ANDREAS REGIONAL CENTER

LOCATIONS

HQ: SAN ANDREAS REGIONAL CENTER
300 ORCHARD CY DR STE 170, CAMPBELL, CA 95008
Phone: 408-374-9960

HISTORICAL FINANCIALS

Company Type: Private

Income Statement

FYE: June 30

	REVENUE ($ mil.)	NET INCOME ($ mil.)	NET PROFIT MARGIN	EMPLOYEES
06/11	283	0	0.2%	272
06/10	276	(0)	—	0
06/09	257	0	—	0
06/08	226	0	0.0%	0
Annual Growth	7.7%	100.0%	—	—

2011 Year-End Financials

Debt ratio: —
Return on equity: 0.20%
Cash ($ mil.): 17
Current ratio: 0.20
Long-term debt ($ mil.): —
Dividends
  Yield: —
  Payout: —
Market value ($ mil.): —

SAN ANTONIO COMMUNITY HOSPITAL

LOCATIONS

HQ: SAN ANTONIO COMMUNITY HOSPITAL
999 SAN BERNARDINO RD, UPLAND, CA 91786-4920
Phone: 909-985-2811
Web: www.sach.org

HISTORICAL FINANCIALS

Company Type: Private

Income Statement

FYE: December 31

	REVENUE ($ mil.)	NET INCOME ($ mil.)	NET PROFIT MARGIN	EMPLOYEES
12/11	282	9	3.4%	2,000
12/10	305	35	11.6%	0
12/09	292	13	4.7%	0
12/08	287	(29)	—	0
Annual Growth	(0.6%)	—	—	—

2011 Year-End Financials

Debt ratio: —
Return on equity: 3.40%
Cash ($ mil.): 7
Current ratio: 1.30
Long-term debt ($ mil.): —
Dividends
  Yield: —
  Payout: —
Market value ($ mil.): —

SAN DIEGO UNIFIED PORT DISTRICT

The San Diego Unified Port District (better known as the Port of San Diego) brings in cash from land and sea. The agency manages two marine cargo facilities as well as a terminal used by cruise ships. Its real estate operations include leasing and managing land around the port including almost 20 bayfront parks and commercial property. In addition the Port of San Diego is charged with protecting San Diego Bay and adjoining tidelands from pollution. The agency which was created in 1962 is governed by a seven-member board appointed by the city councils of San Diego and four neighboring cities.

The Port of San Diego aims to capture more cruise ship business with a second terminal the Broadway Pier Cruise Ship Terminal opened in December 2010. The new terminal is able to accommodates cruise ships carrying 2600 passengers.

However a few months before the agency started building the new terminal Carnival announced it was changing the home port of the Elation from San Diego to Mobile Alabama in April 2010. The Elation was the Port of San Diego's only year-round cruise ship but the port still welcomes 190 cruise ships per year including cruises from Holland America and Celebrity Cruises which offer seasonal sailings from the port.

EXECUTIVES

VP Finance, Jeffrey B. McEntee

Director Human Resources, Karen G. Porteous
EVP, Dan E. Wilkens
VP Administration and Chief Administration Officer, Wayne K. Darbeau
Senior Director Organization Effectiveness, Jose M. Mesa
Director Marketing, Rita A. Vandergaw
Director Communications and Community Services, Irene McCormack
Chairman, Robert (Dukie) Valderrama
Senior Director Project Office, Marinus W. Baak
Director General Services, Pedro Cruz
Director Strategic Management Services, Brandy J. Christian
Director Financial Services, Janice Erickson
Senior Director Real Estate, Paul Fanfera
Director Engineering, Robert M. Frankel
Senior Director Facilities and Chief Engineer, Charles T. Heinrichs
Chief Harbor Police, Kirk Sanfilippo
Director Environmental Services, E. David Merk
Director Purchasing, Garnet (Dave) Thompson
Director Public Art, Catherine Sass
Director Audit Risk Management and Safety, Vilma Sevilla
Director Contracts and Quality Assurance, Gerald H. Wold
President and CEO, Vice Adm. Charles D. Wurster
Director Maritime Operations and Properties, Dick I. Mathiasen
Director Information Technology, Adolfo Segura
Senior Director Maritime, James R. Popham
Port Attorney, Duane E. Bennett
EVP, Ellen C. Born
Vice Chairman, Scott H. Peters
Commissioner, Robert J. (Rocky) Spane
Commissioner, Stephen P. Cushman
Commissioner, Sylvia C. Rios
Commissioner, Michael B. Bixler
Vice Chairman, Scott H. Peters
Auditors: KPMG

LOCATIONS

HQ: San Diego Unified Port District
  3165 Pacific Hwy., San Diego CA 92101-1128
Phone: 619-686-6200   Fax: 508-653-9538
Web: www.sterlingautobody.com

COMPETITORS

Port of Long Beach   Port of Seattle
Port of Los Angeles

HISTORICAL FINANCIALS

Company Type: Government Agency

Income Statement

	ASSETS ($ mil.)	NET INCOME ($ mil.)	INCOME AS % OF ASSETS	EMPLOYEES
				FYE: June 30
06/11	683	(1)	—	604
06/10	691	(7)	—	0
06/08	693	23	3.4%	0
06/07	673	38	5.7%	0
Annual Growth	0.5%	—	—	—

2011 Year-End Financials

Debt ratio: ——
Return on equity: (-1.40)%
Cash ($ mil.): 57
Current ratio: 2.90
Long-term debt ($ mil.): —

Dividends
  Yield: —
  Payout: —
Market value ($ mil.): —

SAN FELIPE DEL RIO CONSOLIDATED INDEPENDENT SCHOOL DISTRICT

LOCATIONS

HQ: SAN FELIPE DEL RIO CONSOLIDATED INDEPENDENT SCHOOL DISTRICT
  205 MEMORIAL DR, DEL RIO, TX 78840-2927
Phone: 830-778-4005
Web: www.sfdr-cisd.org

HISTORICAL FINANCIALS

Company Type: Private

Income Statement

FYE: August 31

	REVENUE ($ mil.)	NET INCOME ($ mil.)	NET PROFIT MARGIN	EMPLOYEES
08/11	99	6	6.5%	1,300
08/09	0	0	—	0
08/08	66	2	4.4%	0
08/05	3	0	5.1%	0
Annual Growth	204.8%	229.1%	—	—

2011 Year-End Financials

Debt ratio: ——
Return on equity: 6.50%
Cash ($ mil.): 56
Current ratio: 11.10
Long-term debt ($ mil.): —

Dividends
  Yield: —
  Payout: —
Market value ($ mil.): —

SAN FRANCISCO SYMPHONY INC.

LOCATIONS

HQ: SAN FRANCISCO SYMPHONY INC.
  201 VAN NESS AVE, SAN FRANCISCO, CA 94102-4585
Phone: 415-552-8000
Web: www.sfsymphony.org

HISTORICAL FINANCIALS

Company Type: Private

Income Statement

FYE: August 31

	REVENUE ($ mil.)	NET INCOME ($ mil.)	NET PROFIT MARGIN	EMPLOYEES
08/11	86	14	16.5%	400
08/10	59	(12)	—	0
08/09	35	(46)	—	0
08/08	59	(7)	—	0
Annual Growth	13.4%	—	—	—

2011 Year-End Financials

Debt ratio: ——
Return on equity: 16.50%
Cash ($ mil.): 1
Current ratio: 0.10
Long-term debt ($ mil.): —

Dividends
  Yield: —
  Payout: —
Market value ($ mil.): —

SAN JOAQUIN COMMUNITY HOSPITAL

LOCATIONS

HQ: SAN JOAQUIN COMMUNITY HOSPITAL
  2615 CHESTER AVE, BAKERSFIELD, CA 93301-2014
Phone: 661-395-3000
Web: www.sanjoaquinhospital.org

HISTORICAL FINANCIALS

Company Type: Private

Income Statement

FYE: September 30

	REVENUE ($ mil.)	NET INCOME ($ mil.)	NET PROFIT MARGIN	EMPLOYEES
09/12*	225	7	3.5%	900
12/11	317	16	5.1%	0
09/11	228	8	3.6%	0
12/10	285	27	9.6%	0
Annual Growth	(7.6%)	(33.8%)	—	—

*Fiscal year change

2012 Year-End Financials

Debt ratio: ——
Return on equity: 3.50%
Cash ($ mil.): 71
Current ratio: 2.10
Long-term debt ($ mil.): —

Dividends
  Yield: —
  Payout: —
Market value ($ mil.): —

SAN MIGUEL ELECTRIC COOPERATIVE INC.

LOCATIONS

HQ: SAN MIGUEL ELECTRIC COOPERATIVE INC.
  6200 FM 3387, CHRISTINE, TX 78012
Phone: 830-784-3411

HISTORICAL FINANCIALS

Company Type: Private

Income Statement

FYE: December 31

	REVENUE ($ mil.)	NET INCOME ($ mil.)	NET PROFIT MARGIN	EMPLOYEES
12/11	140	3	2.6%	183
12/10	136	3	2.6%	0
12/09	129	3	2.6%	0
12/08	124	1	1.4%	0
Annual Growth	4.1%	27.3%	—	—

2011 Year-End Financials

Debt ratio: —
Return on equity: 2.60%
Cash ($ mil.): 2
Current ratio: 0.40
Long-term debt ($ mil.): —
Dividends
Yield: —
Payout: —
Market value ($ mil.): —

SANFORD-BURNHAM MEDICAL RESEARCH INSTITUTE

Founded in 1976 as the La Jolla Cancer Research Foundation the Sanford-Burnham Medical Research Institute is a nonprofit organization that performs biomedical research in areas such as cellular biology cancer genetics degenerative diseases and developmental neurobiology. Known for its stem cell research and drug discovery technologies Sanford-Burnham houses five research centers including its Cancer Center which has been supported by National Cancer Institute (part of the NIH) since 1981. Sanford-Burnham's other centers include the Del E. Webb Neuroscience Aging and Stem Cell Research Center and the Sanford Children's Health Research Center.

EXECUTIVES

Chairman, Gregory T. (Greg) Lucier, age 47
CEO, John C. Reed, age 53
VP Human Resources, Beth Alton
SVP Business Development and Chief Business Officer, Paul K. Laikind, age 56
Director Safety, Larry Adelman
Corporate Secretary and Director Public Affairs, Nancy J. Beddingfield
Director Sponsored Research, Jean Freiser
Director Intellectual Property Management, Margaret Dunbar
Controller and Director Accounting, Michael Dollar
SVP External Relations, Ann Carollo
Director Purchasing, Jeanette Sansom
Director Facilities and Maintenance, David (Dave) Hassell
Business Development Director, Leslie Molony
President, Kristina Vuori
VP Finance and CFO, Eric Lofgren
VP Communications, Andrea Moser
Director Del E. Webb Neuroscience Aging and Stem Cell Research Center, Stuart Lipton
Director Infectious and Inflammatory Disease Center, Robert Liddington
Associate Scientific Director Technology, Jeffrey Smith
Program Director Professor Stem Cells and Regeneration, Evan Snyder
VP Drug Discovery and Development, Michael J. Jackson
EVP Chief Administrative Officer CFO and Treasurer, Gary F. Raisl

LOCATIONS

HQ: Sanford-Burnham Medical Research Institute
10901 N. Torrey Pines Rd., La Jolla CA 92037
Phone: 858-646-3100 **Fax:** 858-646-3199
Web: www.sanfordburnham.org

PRODUCTS/OPERATIONS

Selected Research Centers

Del E. Webb Neuroscience Aging and Stem Cell Research Center
Diabetes and Obesity Research Center
Infectious and Inflammatory Disease Center
NCI Cancer Center
Sanford Children's Health Research Center

COMPETITORS

Howard Hughes Medical Institute
Jackson Laboratory
Memorial Sloan-Kettering
Stowers Institute For Medical Research
The Palo Alto Medical Foundation
Whitehead Institute for Biomedical Research

HISTORICAL FINANCIALS

Company Type: Private - Not-for-Profit

Income Statement

FYE: June 30

	REVENUE ($ mil.)	NET INCOME ($ mil.)	NET PROFIT MARGIN	EMPLOYEES
06/12	162	0	0.5%	1,157
06/11	163	6	3.9%	0
06/10	152	3	2.0%	0
06/09	133	89	66.6%	0
Annual Growth	6.7%	(79.8%)	—	—

2012 Year-End Financials

Debt ratio: —
Return on equity: 0.50%
Cash ($ mil.): 9
Current ratio: —
Long-term debt ($ mil.): —
Dividends
Yield: —
Payout: —
Market value ($ mil.): —

SANTA CLARA VALLEY WATER DISTRICT

LOCATIONS

HQ: SANTA CLARA VALLEY WATER DISTRICT
5750 ALMADEN EXPY, SAN JOSE, CA 95118-3614
Phone: 408-265-2600
Web: www.valleywater.org

HISTORICAL FINANCIALS

Company Type: Private

Income Statement

FYE: June 30

	REVENUE ($ mil.)	NET INCOME ($ mil.)	NET PROFIT MARGIN	EMPLOYEES
06/12	124	2	1.9%	850
06/11	129	8	6.4%	0
06/10	117	12	10.4%	0
06/09	121	1	1.0%	0
Annual Growth	0.8%	23.6%	—	—

SANTA ROSA MEMORIAL HOSPITAL INC

LOCATIONS

HQ: SANTA ROSA MEMORIAL HOSPITAL INC
1165 MONTGOMERY DR, SANTA ROSA, CA 95405-4897
Phone: 707-546-3210
Web: www.stjosephhealth.org

HISTORICAL FINANCIALS

Company Type: Private

Income Statement

FYE: June 30

	REVENUE ($ mil.)	NET INCOME ($ mil.)	NET PROFIT MARGIN	EMPLOYEES
06/11	351	20	5.7%	2,100
06/10	357	(1)	—	0
06/09	319	5	1.8%	0
06/08	356	6	1.8%	0
Annual Growth	(0.5%)	46.0%	—	—

2011 Year-End Financials

Debt ratio: —
Return on equity: 5.70%
Cash ($ mil.): 23
Current ratio: 2.20
Long-term debt ($ mil.): —
Dividends
Yield: —
Payout: —
Market value ($ mil.): —

SARAH BUSH LINCOLN HEALTH CENTER

With the moniker of the Illinois' favorite son's stepmother (Sarah Bush Lincoln) who wouldn't want to go to this health center? And apparently the locals agree since Sarah Bush Lincoln Health Center (SBLHC) has a market share of about 44% in its seven-county service area in east central Illinois and an inpatient market share for Coles County of nearly 80%. SBLHC has 128 beds and provides a wide range of health care services including emergency medicine behavioral health care surgical services and cancer treatment. The center also offers support groups and continuing education classes.

Geographic Reach

The regional hospital is centrally located in East Central Illinois' Coles County and serves seven counties.

Operations

The health center has expanded its behavioral health services by joining forces with the Coles County Mental Health Center (now Life Links) and the Human Resources Center of Edgar and Clark to create the Regional Behavioral Health Network an organization that expands access to mental health care for people in crisis. Together the three firms respond to about 3000 crises inquires for behavioral health services annually. The collaborative effort is partially funded by grants.

SBLHC has also expanded its Lincolnland Home Care and Hospice services to cover nearly two dozen counties.

Strategy

To enhance care and convenience to people who are hospitalized SBLHC introduced a Hospitalist program in 2011. Jospitalists are more available throughout the day to talk with patients and their family members follow up on test results answer nurses' questions and respond quickly to issues that may arise.

As part of an ongoing expansion drive SBLHC opened a second medical office building at its main campus in 2011. The two-story clinic allows Orthopedics and Sports Medicine room to expand to accommodate the needs of the community. Physical and Occupational Therapy services are also housed in the new facility. The therapy area includes three therapy gyms a therapy pool locker room and a massage room. Lincolnland Home Care and Hospice Human Resources Employee and Organizational Development and Health Occupations occupy the building's second floor.

To better accommodate the community and keep up with changing technology and healthcare needs SBLHC also launched a $48 million expansion and renovation project in 2011. The three-year plan calls for the renovation and expansion of the Emergency Room surgical suites and the laboratory and the conversion of some units to private patient rooms.

Company Background

SBLHC opened its doors in 1977. It was named after President Abraham Lincoln's stepmother Sarah Bush Lincoln.

EXECUTIVES

President and CEO, Gary L. Barnett
VP Operations, James (Jim) Pierce

LOCATIONS

HQ: Sarah Bush Lincoln Health Center
1000 Health Center Dr., Mattoon IL 61938
Phone: 217-258-2525 **Fax:** 217-258-4175
Web: www.sarahbush.org

PRODUCTS/OPERATIONS

Selected Programs/Services

Advanced Wound Center
Audiology
Center for Interventional Pain
Emergency Department
EMS
Gastroenterology
Heart Center
Hospitalist Program
Laboratory
Lifeline
Lincolnland Hospice
Lincolnland Home Care
Orthopedics and Sports Medicine
Outpatient Surgery Center
Patient Care
Physical Medicine & Rehabilitation
Psychiatry and Counseling
Radiology
Regional Cancer Center
Women and Children's Center

COMPETITORS

Carle Hospital
Crawford Memorial Hospital
Decatur Memorial Hospital
Hospital Sisters Health System
Iroquois Memorial Hospital
Memorial Health System (Colorado)
Memorial Medical Center
St. John's Hospital (Illinois)

HISTORICAL FINANCIALS

Company Type: Private - Not-for-Profit

Income Statement

FYE: June 30

	REVENUE ($ mil.)	NET INCOME ($ mil.)	NET PROFIT MARGIN	EMPLOYEES
06/11	195	14	7.2%	1,543
06/09	132	(6)	—	0
06/08	0	(0)	—	0
06/05	0	0	—	0
Annual Growth	—	3791.5%	—	—

2011 Year-End Financials

Debt ratio: —
Return on equity: 7.20%
Cash ($ mil.): 47
Current ratio: 3.10
Long-term debt ($ mil.): —
Dividends
  Yield: —
  Payout: —
  Market value ($ mil.): —

SARAH LAWRENCE COLLEGE

Sarah Lawrence College (SLC) was founded in 1926 as an institution of higher education for young women. The private liberal arts school located on a 44-acre campus in suburban New York has been coeducational since 1968 and has an annual enrollment of some 1300 undergraduate and about 350 graduate students. Most of its courses are seminars limited to 15 students; the school has a student-to-faculty ratio of approximately 9-to-1 one of the lowest at any US university. SLC offers a wide range of academic concentrations including performing arts natural science history teaching and literature. It was founded by William Lawrence who named the school after his wife Sarah a supporter of women's suffrage.

EXECUTIVES

Director Development Operations, Janet Nelson, age 62
VP Finance and Planning, John Bernson
Controller, David Klein
Director Libraries and Academic Computing, Sha Fagan
Director Admissions, Stephen Schierloh
Director Alumni Relations, Cheryl Cipro
Director Media and Community Relations, Judith Schwartzstein
VP Operations, Michael W. Rengers
Director Information Systems, Sean Jameson
President, Karen R. Lawrence
College Dean, Pauline Watts
Director Financial Aid, Heather C. McDonnell
Registrar, Daniel Licht
VP Administration, Thomas Blum
VP Advancement, Robert Sweet

LOCATIONS

HQ: Sarah Lawrence College
1 Mead Way, Bronxville NY 10708-5999
Phone: 914-337-0700 **Fax:** 914-395-2669
Web: www.slc.edu

HISTORICAL FINANCIALS

Company Type: School

Income Statement

FYE: May 31

	REVENUE ($ mil.)	NET INCOME ($ mil.)	NET PROFIT MARGIN	EMPLOYEES
05/12	68	(16)	—	450
05/11	71	11	15.6%	0
05/10	76	7	10.0%	0
05/09	46	(28)	—	0
Annual Growth	13.5%	—	—	—

2012 Year-End Financials

Debt ratio: —
Return on equity: (-23.90)%
Cash ($ mil.): 1
Current ratio: —
Long-term debt ($ mil.): —
Dividends
  Yield: —
  Payout: —
  Market value ($ mil.): —

SARATOGA CITY SCHOOLS DISTRICT

LOCATIONS

HQ: SARATOGA CITY SCHOOLS DISTRICT
3 BLUE STREAK BLVD, SARATOGA SPRINGS, NY 12866-5952
Phone: 518-583-4700
Web: www.saratogaschools.org

HISTORICAL FINANCIALS

Company Type: Private

Income Statement

FYE: June 30

	REVENUE ($ mil.)	NET INCOME ($ mil.)	NET PROFIT MARGIN	EMPLOYEES
06/12	107	(0)	—	0
Annual Growth	—	—	—	—

2012 Year-End Financials

Debt ratio: —
Return on equity: (-0.60)%
Cash ($ mil.): 50
Current ratio: —
Long-term debt ($ mil.): —
Dividends
  Yield: —
  Payout: —
  Market value ($ mil.): —

SARGENTO FOODS INC.

Sargento Foods could be the biggest Cheesehead in Wisconsin. The company is one of the largest cheese manufacturers in the US offering a variety of block cheese and such value-added products as shredded cheese blends and sliced cheeses for sandwiches. Sargento Foods markets its products through supermarkets and other retail grocery stores nationwide. The manufacturer is also a leading supplier of custom cheese products to restaurants and other foodservice operators; its food ingredients division makes cheese items for other food manufacturers. The family-owned business was started in 1953 by Leonard Gentine Sr. and his business partner Joseph Sartori.

The Gentine family has controlled the company since 1965 when it bought out Sartori's stake. Today Sargento Foods operates its business through three divisions –consumer products foodservice and food ingredients –and four facilities all located in Wisconsin. The cheesemaker is looking to expand its primary Plymouth distribution center to meet growing demand for its shredded snack and specialty cheeses. The move would add some 50000 sq. ft. to the existing 416000-sq.-ft. distribution center.

Sargento Foods continues its effort to close the gap with industry leader Kraft Foods through new product releases designed to meet changing consumer needs. Catering to the reduced sodium push in 2010 it introduced a line of cheeses with 25% less sodium for both cooking and snacking. Varieties include Colby-Jack slices and snack sticks Provolone slices string snacks and Mild Cheddar and Mozzarella shredded cheeses. The move follows the company's launch in 2008 of a new line of toppings Sargento Salad Finishers and Potato Finishers that combine shredded cheese with other ingredients for topping potatoes and salads. Its foodservice operation meanwhile continues to develop new custom cheese products such as appetizers and sauces.

Loyal to its home state and the sports played therein Sargento is the official cheese of Lambeau Field home of the Green Bay Packers.

EXECUTIVES

EVP and COO, Mark W. Rhyan
Chairman and CEO, Louis P. (Lou) Gentine
SVP Human Resources, Karri Neils
EVP and CFO, George H. Hoff
VP Corporate and Marketing Communications, Barbara Gannon
President Consumer Products Division, Michael P. Pellegrino
VP Quality Systems, Janet Raddatz
SVP Innovation, Kristine M. Jankowski
VP New Business Development, Rod J. Hogan
VP Logistics, Dennis Roehrborn
President Food Ingredients, Michael A. McEvoy
President Food Service Division, Kevin G. Delahunt
VP Engineering, Karl Linck
SVP and Treasurer, Marcy Stanczyk
SVP and General Manager Sargento Culinary Solutions, David T. Vroom
VP Strategic Analysis, James (Jim) Birenbaum
VP Manufacturing, Lee McCollum
Senior Marketing Director Food Service, Jim Schafer
Senior Director Retail Merchandising, John Bottomley
VP Marketing, Daniel C. (Chip) Schuman
President and Chief Customer Officer, Louis P. (Louie) Gentine II
VP Sales Consumer Products Division, Mark D. Gumm
VP Sales Food Service Division, Michael P. Sokol
VP Information Technology, Suzanne M. Peterson
Senior Manager Market Research Established Products, Kate Krier
Director Pricing and Trade Management, Brian Rauch
Marketing Manager, Stephanie Scholz
Manager Research and Deveolpment, Paul Groth
Manager Sales Demand Planning, Jeff Bohman
Technology Principal, Craig Hackl
Manager Sales Support Food Service, Angie Colby
Manager Trade Promotion Consumer Products, Abbie Weber

Manager National Sales, Steve Harrison
Manager National Customer Business, Jim Besiada
Manager Marketing Core Business, Rob Krause
VP Procurement, Shawn Marcom
Senior Manager Pricing and Analysis Food Service, Brian Jenny
Associate Manager Marketing Refrigerated and Non-Refrigerated Snacks, Nicole Pauly
Senior Research Scientist, Mihir Sainani
Associate Marketing Manager Natural Sliced Cheese, Elizabeth Neils
Director Sales Food Ingredients, Douglas Marshall
Director Core Marketing, Chris Groom
Senior Manager Consumer Products Financial Analysis, Svetlana Tsygankova
Senior Manager Analytics, Ken Tobey
Senior Sales Analyst Walmart/Club Channel, Vince Juneau
Team Leader Safeway, Demetrius Carlton
Senior National Account Sales Manager Culinary Solutions Division, Kevin Greene
VP Logistics, Gary A. Vissers
VP Research & Development, Kati Fritz-Jung
VP Distribution Services, Keith Hartlaub

LOCATIONS

HQ: SARGENTO FOODS INC.
1 PERSNICKETY PL, PLYMOUTH, WI 53073-3544
Phone: 920-893-8484
Web: www.sargentofoodservice.com

PRODUCTS/OPERATIONS

Selected Cheeses
Asadero
Asiago
Blue cheese
Cheddar
Colby
Fontina
Monterrey Jack
Mozzarella
Parmesan
Provolone
Provolone
Queso gallego
Queso quesadilla
Ricotta
Romano

COMPETITORS

Associated Milk Producers	Land O' Lakes
California Dairies Inc.	Leprino Foods
	Michael Foods
Dairy Farmers of America	Mondelez International
	Saputo
Darigold Inc.	Schreiber Foods
Dean Foods	Tillamook County Creamery Association
Foremost Farms	

HISTORICAL FINANCIALS
Company Type: Private

Income Statement
FYE: January 1

	REVENUE ($ mil.)	NET INCOME ($ mil.)	NET PROFIT MARGIN	EMPLOYEES
01/12	980	0	—	1,550
01/11	980	0	—	0
01/10*	896	54	6.1%	0
12/08	905	0	—	0
Annual Growth	**2.7%**	—	—	—

*Fiscal year change

2012 Year-End Financials
Debt ratio: ——
Return on equity: —
Cash ($ mil.): 26
Current ratio: 1.20
Long-term debt ($ mil.): —
Dividends
Yield: —
Payout: —
Market value ($ mil.): —

SATTERFIELD AND PONTIKES CONSTRUCTION INC.

Satterfield & Pontikes Construction (S&P) provides general contracting consultation and construction management services primarily in the Gulf Coast region of Texas and Louisiana. The company often works on buildings for the commercial retail industrial educational entertainment and recreational sectors. High profile projects include the Texas A&M University Health Science Center and the expansion of the World War II Museum in New Orleans. S&P specializes in concrete work and early-stage site work as well as 3-D modeling and virtual design. The company was founded in 1989 and is headed by majority owner and CEO George Pontikes.

S&P works from offices in Houston Dallas/Fort Worth New Orleans San Antonio and Austin.

The firm has looked outside of the Gulf Region for work. In 2011 it was chosen by Delta Air Lines to work on the $1.2 billion expansion of a terminal and the demolition of another at JFK International airport in New York.

EXECUTIVES

President and CEO, George A. Pontikes Jr.
VP Contract Administration, Peter Lozada
CFO, Ron Byrd
CIO, Donald E. (Don) Watson Jr.
Human Resources, Charlotte Rosenauer
VP Business Development, John Marshall
VP Estimating, Art Theriot
VP Concrete Operations, Jesse Lopez
VP Special Projects, Laura Pontikes
EVP Houston Business Unit, Bud West
Corporate Safety Director, John Lott
Houston Business Unit, Jim Brown
Dallas and Ft. Worth Business Unit, George West
Auditors: Melton&MeltonLLP

LOCATIONS

HQ: Satterfield & Pontikes Construction Inc.
11000 Equity Dr. Ste. 100, Houston TX 77041
Phone: 713-996-1300   **Fax:** 713-996-1400
Web: www.satpon.com

PRODUCTS/OPERATIONS

Selected Services
Building information modeling
Construction
Construction management
Design build
Development
Green building
Practical Project Delivery

COMPETITORS

Balfour Construction
C.F. Jordan
Falkenberg
 Construction
Skanska USA Building
Spawglass Holding
Turner Corporation

HISTORICAL FINANCIALS

Company Type: Private

Income Statement

FYE: December 31

	REVENUE ($ mil.)	NET INCOME ($ mil.)	NET PROFIT MARGIN	EMPLOYEES
12/11	388	0	0.1%	300
12/10	445	8	1.9%	0
12/09	482	11	2.3%	0
12/08	345	8	2.5%	0
Annual Growth	4.0%	(66.2%)	—	—

2011 Year-End Financials

Debt ratio: ——
Return on equity: 0.10%
Cash ($ mil.): 32
Current ratio: 1.10
Long-term debt ($ mil.): —

Dividends
 Yield: —
 Payout: —
 Market value ($ mil.): —

SCAFF'S INC.

LOCATIONS

HQ: SCAFF' S INC.
 134 SE COLBURN AVE, LAKE CITY, FL 32025-4714
Phone: 386-752-7344
Web: www.scaffs.com

HISTORICAL FINANCIALS

Company Type: Private

Income Statement

FYE: December 29

	REVENUE ($ mil.)	NET INCOME ($ mil.)	NET PROFIT MARGIN	EMPLOYEES
12/11	211	1	0.8%	400
12/10	182	2	1.2%	0
12/09	166	1	0.7%	0
12/07	181	1	1.1%	0
Annual Growth	5.1%	(3.4%)	—	—

2011 Year-End Financials

Debt ratio: ——
Return on equity: 0.80%
Cash ($ mil.): 3
Current ratio: 0.70
Long-term debt ($ mil.): —

Dividends
 Yield: —
 Payout: —
 Market value ($ mil.): —

SCHEWEL FURNITURE COMPANY INCORPORATED

Schewel Furniture Company operates about 50 retail furniture and bedding stores in Virginia West Virginia and North Carolina. In addition to home furnishings the chain sells appliances electronics carpeting and related accessories. Typical store units average 18000 sq. ft. and primarily target the lower- and middle-income markets. Newer stores are larger in the 40000-55000 square foot range. Customers can also browse furniture collections and other items available at Schewel stores through the company's Web site. The family-run company now in its fourth generation of management got its start in 1897 when Elias Schewel began selling small furniture pieces out of his horse-drawn wagon.

EXECUTIVES

Chairman and CEO, Marc A. Schewel
CFO and Treasurer, William (Bill) Sprinkle
VP and Secretary, Donna Schewel Clark

LOCATIONS

HQ: Schewel Furniture Company Inc.
 1031 Main St., Lynchburg VA 24505
Phone: 434-522-0200   Fax: 434-522-0207
Web: www.schewels.com

COMPETITORS

Ashley Furniture
Bassett Furniture
Flooring America
Furnitureland South
Grand Home Furnishings
Havertys
Rooms To Go
Rowe Fine Furniture
Thomasville Furniture

HISTORICAL FINANCIALS

Company Type: Private

Income Statement

FYE: March 31

	REVENUE ($ mil.)	NET INCOME ($ mil.)	NET PROFIT MARGIN	EMPLOYEES
03/12	117	3	3.3%	850
03/11	111	3	3.2%	0
03/10	106	2	2.2%	0
03/09	114	4	4.1%	0
Annual Growth	1.1%	(5.8%)	—	—

2012 Year-End Financials

Debt ratio: ——
Return on equity: 3.30%
Cash ($ mil.): 6
Current ratio: 1.30
Long-term debt ($ mil.): —

Dividends
 Yield: —
 Payout: —
 Market value ($ mil.): —

SCHOLARSHIP AMERICA INC.

LOCATIONS

HQ: SCHOLARSHIP AMERICA INC.
 1 SCHOLARSHIP WAY, SAINT PETER, MN 56082-1693
Phone: 507-931-1682
Web: www.vantagescholar.com

HISTORICAL FINANCIALS

Company Type: Private

Income Statement

FYE: June 30

	REVENUE ($ mil.)	NET INCOME ($ mil.)	NET PROFIT MARGIN	EMPLOYEES
06/11	154	(7)	—	150
06/10*	154	(5)	—	0
12/09	28	9	32.7%	0
06/09	173	0	—	0
Annual Growth	(3.7%)			

*Fiscal year change

2011 Year-End Financials

Debt ratio: ——
Return on equity: (-4.90)%
Cash ($ mil.): 35
Current ratio: 0.90
Long-term debt ($ mil.): —

Dividends
 Yield: —
 Payout: —
 Market value ($ mil.): —

SCHOOL BOARD OF ORANGE COUNTY FLORIDA

LOCATIONS

HQ: SCHOOL BOARD OF ORANGE COUNTY FLORIDA
 445 W AMELIA ST, ORLANDO, FL 32801-1129
Phone: 407-317-3200

HISTORICAL FINANCIALS

Company Type: Private

Income Statement

FYE: June 30

	REVENUE ($ mil.)	NET INCOME ($ mil.)	NET PROFIT MARGIN	EMPLOYEES
06/11	1,895	24	1.3%	25,000
06/05	1,570	329	21.0%	0
06/04	1,393	1,389	99.6%	0
06/03	0	0		0
Annual Growth	—	753.2%	—	—

2011 Year-End Financials

Debt ratio: ——
Return on equity: 1.30%
Cash ($ mil.): 469
Current ratio: 3.10
Long-term debt ($ mil.): —

Dividends
 Yield: —
 Payout: —
 Market value ($ mil.): —

SCHOOL DISTRICT 1J MULTNOMAH COUNTY OREGON (INC)

LOCATIONS

HQ: SCHOOL DISTRICT 1J MULTNOMAH COUNTY OREGON (INC)
501 N DIXON ST, PORTLAND, OR 97227-1804
Phone: 503-916-2000
Web: www.skyline.pps.k12.or.us

HISTORICAL FINANCIALS

Company Type: Private

Income Statement

	REVENUE ($ mil.)	NET INCOME ($ mil.)	NET PROFIT MARGIN	EMPLOYEES
05/12*	527	5	1.1%	5,244
06/11	527	5	1.1%	0
06/10	0	0	—	0
06/09	520	(3)	—	0
Annual Growth	0.5%	—	—	—

FYE: May 17

*Fiscal year change

2012 Year-End Financials

Debt ratio: ——
Return on equity: 1.10%
Cash ($ mil.): 105
Current ratio: 0.90
Long-term debt ($ mil.): ——

Dividends
Yield: —
Payout: —
Market value ($ mil.): —

SCHOOL OF VISUAL ARTS INC.

LOCATIONS

HQ: SCHOOL OF VISUAL ARTS INC.
209 E 23RD ST, NEW YORK, NY 10010-3994
Phone: 212-592-2000
Web: www.adm.schoolofvisualarts.edu

HISTORICAL FINANCIALS

Company Type: Private

Income Statement

	REVENUE ($ mil.)	NET INCOME ($ mil.)	NET PROFIT MARGIN	EMPLOYEES
06/11	118	3	3.2%	1,400
06/10	105	0	0.3%	0
06/08	94	2	2.7%	0
06/05	71	1	2.0%	0
Annual Growth	18.2%	37.6%	—	—

FYE: June 30

2011 Year-End Financials

Debt ratio: ——
Return on equity: 3.20%
Cash ($ mil.): 24
Current ratio: 0.90
Long-term debt ($ mil.): ——

Dividends
Yield: —
Payout: —
Market value ($ mil.): —

SCHUYLKILL MEDICAL CENTER - SOUTH JACKSON STREET

LOCATIONS

HQ: SCHUYLKILL MEDICAL CENTER - SOUTH JACKSON STREET
420 S JACKSON ST, POTTSVILLE, PA 17901-3625
Phone: 570-621-5000
Web: www.pottsvillehospital.com

HISTORICAL FINANCIALS

Company Type: Private

Income Statement

	REVENUE ($ mil.)	NET INCOME ($ mil.)	NET PROFIT MARGIN	EMPLOYEES
06/11	92	(0)	—	99
06/10	85	(9)	—	0
Annual Growth	8.8%	—	—	—

FYE: June 30

2011 Year-End Financials

Debt ratio: ——
Return on equity: (-0.20)%
Cash ($ mil.): 5
Current ratio: 0.40
Long-term debt ($ mil.): —

Dividends
Yield: —
Payout: —
Market value ($ mil.): —

SCIENTIFIC RESEARCH CORP

Scientific Research Corporation (SRC) doesn't limit its services to the laboratory. The government contractor provides a wide variety of engineering and research services including consulting systems engineering project management network design hardware and software development prototyping testing and evaluation systems integration and training. Its expertise encompasses communications and intelligence systems electronic warfare simulation and instrumentation systems. In some cases SRC works as a subcontractor for larger companies. SRC's clients include the US government and military state agencies and private sector businesses.

Operations The company's integrated systems and solutions division specializes in software development network engineering systems automation digital signal processing production engineering and logistical support services for intelligence systems. It also provides other IT and wireless network support services. SRC's simulation test and instrumentation division offers products and engineering services to support surveillance radar and instrumentation systems. It also develops sensor systems and provides interoperability testing services for military weapons systems. The company's communications networks and electronics unit provides research and development systems integration design deployment and support services for military and commercial communications and network systems.

Geographic Reach SRC operates from about 15 offices located mainly in the southern and eastern US; it also has a few facilities in the Southwest and in California.

EXECUTIVES

Chairman, Charles K. Watt, age 75
President and CEO, Michael L. (Mike) Watt, age 49
EVP, Steven Watt, age 53
VP Wireless and Information Technology Division, Todd Marek
VP Business Development, David Chapman
Director of Operations, Mark Baseler

LOCATIONS

HQ: Scientific Research Corporation
2300 Windy Ridge Pkwy. Ste. 400 South, Atlanta GA 30339
Phone: 770-859-9161   **Fax:** 770-859-9315
Web: www.scires.com

COMPETITORS

Boeing	Northrop Grumman
CACI International	QinetiQ
Computer Sciences Corp.	Raytheon
HP Enterprise Services	Research Triangle Institute
Lockheed Martin	SAIC
Long Wave	Serco Inc.
ManTech	SRA International

HISTORICAL FINANCIALS

Company Type: Private

Income Statement

	REVENUE ($ mil.)	NET INCOME ($ mil.)	NET PROFIT MARGIN	EMPLOYEES
12/11	326	21	6.7%	1,006
12/10	322	22	6.9%	0
12/08	226	13	6.0%	0
12/07	171	11	6.5%	0
Annual Growth	24.0%	25.1%	—	—

FYE: December 31

2011 Year-End Financials

Debt ratio: ——
Return on equity: 6.70%
Cash ($ mil.): 27
Current ratio: 1.60
Long-term debt ($ mil.): —

Dividends
Yield: —
Payout: —
Market value ($ mil.): —

SCOTT AND WHITE MEMORIAL HOSPITAL AND SCOTT SHERWOOD AND BRINDLE

LOCATIONS

HQ: SCOTT AND WHITE MEMORIAL HOSPITAL AND SCOTT SHERWOOD AND BRINDLE
2401 S 31ST ST, TEMPLE, TX 76508-0001
Phone: 254-724-2111
Web: www.sw.org

HISTORICAL FINANCIALS

Company Type: Private

Income Statement				FYE: August 31
	REVENUE ($ mil.)	NET INCOME ($ mil.)	NET PROFIT MARGIN	EMPLOYEES
08/11	1,446	91	6.3%	8,000
08/10	902	41	4.6%	0
08/09	814	0	0.0%	0
08/06	804	0	—	0
Annual Growth	21.6%	—	—	—

2011 Year-End Financials

Debt ratio: —
Return on equity: 6.30%
Cash ($ mil.): 84
Current ratio: 1.50
Long-term debt ($ mil.): —
Dividends
  Yield: —
  Payout: —
Market value ($ mil.): —

SCOTT COOPERATIVE ASSOCIATION INC

LOCATIONS

HQ: SCOTT COOPERATIVE ASSOCIATION INC
410 E 1ST ST, SCOTT CITY, KS 67871-1065
Phone: 620-872-5823
Web: www.scottcoop.com

HISTORICAL FINANCIALS

Company Type: Private

Income Statement				FYE: October 31
	REVENUE ($ mil.)	NET INCOME ($ mil.)	NET PROFIT MARGIN	EMPLOYEES
10/11	134	5	3.8%	42
10/10	94	1	1.7%	0
10/09	74	1	2.5%	0
10/06	44	1	2.5%	0
Annual Growth	45.0%	66.2%	—	—

2011 Year-End Financials

Debt ratio: —
Return on equity: 3.80%
Cash ($ mil.): 0
Current ratio: 0.10
Long-term debt ($ mil.): 0
Dividends
  Yield: —
  Payout: —
Market value ($ mil.): —

SCOTT PET PRODUCTS INC.

Scott Pet Products wants it Pork Chomps to be the chew of choice for pets over rawhides. The company manufactures products for pets including collars feeding bowls kennels and pet crates sleeping mats and baked pork skin chews named Pork Chomps. Scott Pet Products makes and markets birdseed as well that accounts for about a quarter of the company sales. The family-owned firm was established to make sporting dog collars in 1975. Its founder T. E. Scott has since passed the reins on to his son-in-law and daughter Mike (CEO) and Kathy (marketing director) Bassett who run the company today.

EXECUTIVES

CEO, Michael (Mike) Bassett
Marketing Director, Kathleen (Kathy) Bassett
Human Resources, Tracey Lyons
Production Manager, Joe Blakey

LOCATIONS

HQ: Scott Pet Products Inc.
1543 N. US Hwy. 41, Rockville IN 47872
Phone: 765-569-4636   **Fax:** 765-569-4631
Web: www.scottpet.com

COMPETITORS

Del Monte Foods	Nutro Products
Hill' s Pet Nutrition	Procter & Gamble
Mars Incorporated	Royal Canin
Nestle Purina PetCare	

HISTORICAL FINANCIALS

Company Type: Private

Income Statement				FYE: December 31
	REVENUE ($ mil.)	NET INCOME ($ mil.)	NET PROFIT MARGIN	EMPLOYEES
12/11	31	0	0.5%	140
12/10	37	1	5.3%	0
12/09	0	0	—	0
12/08	37	0	1.6%	0
Annual Growth	(5.5%)	(37.1%)	—	—

SCOTWOOD INDUSTRIES INC.

LOCATIONS

HQ: SCOTWOOD INDUSTRIES INC.
12980 METCALF AVE STE 240, OVERLAND PARK, KS 66213-2646
Phone: 913-851-3500
Web: www.scotwoodindustries.com

HISTORICAL FINANCIALS

Company Type: Private

Income Statement				FYE: June 30
	REVENUE ($ mil.)	NET INCOME ($ mil.)	NET PROFIT MARGIN	EMPLOYEES
06/11	135	0	0.6%	50
06/05	69	1	2.3%	0
06/04	66	1	1.8%	0
06/03	53	0	1.7%	0
Annual Growth	36.5%	(3.8%)	—	—

2011 Year-End Financials

Debt ratio: —
Return on equity: 0.60%
Cash ($ mil.): 0
Current ratio: 0.40
Long-term debt ($ mil.): —
Dividends
  Yield: —
  Payout: —
Market value ($ mil.): —

SCULL CONSTRUCTION SERVICE INC.

LOCATIONS

HQ: SCULL CONSTRUCTION SERVICE INC.
803 INDUSTRIAL AVE, RAPID CITY, SD 57702-0337
Phone: 605-342-2379
Web: www.jscullconstruction.com

HISTORICAL FINANCIALS

Company Type: Private

Income Statement				FYE: December 31
	REVENUE ($ mil.)	NET INCOME ($ mil.)	NET PROFIT MARGIN	EMPLOYEES
12/11	104	2	2.0%	125
12/10	69	0	1.3%	0
12/09	53	0	0.8%	0
12/08	54	1	1.9%	0
Annual Growth	24.2%	25.6%	—	—

2011 Year-End Financials

Debt ratio: —
Return on equity: 2.00%
Cash ($ mil.): 4
Current ratio: 0.20
Long-term debt ($ mil.): —
Dividends
  Yield: —
  Payout: —
Market value ($ mil.): —

SEABROOK BROTHERS & SONS INC

Seabrook Brothers and Sons almost has an alphabet of products. From asparagus to water chestnuts the company grows processes and freezes a harvest of vegetables. In addition to producing items for retail sale under its Seabrook Farms label the company supplies vegetables to customers in the industrial ingredients foodservice and private-label retail sectors. It serves customers throughout the US as well as in internationally in Canada Chile Israel Puerto Rico Mexico and Saudi Arabia. Seabrook also makes such value-added products as frozen skillet meals creamed spinach and butter and cheese sauces. In business since 1978 the company is still run by the founding Seabrook family.

EXECUTIVES

Chairman, James Seabrook Sr.
President and CEO, James Seabrook Jr.
VP Sales and Marketing, Brian Seabrook
VP Quality Assurance, Barbara Michalkiewicz
VP Customer Service, Dixie Sickler
VP Procurement, Ivin Seabrook
VP Programming/IS, Peter Seabrook
CFO, Barbara Wiler
Plant Manager, Dave Deon
VP Customer Satisfaction, Beverly Crackovich

LOCATIONS

HQ: Seabrook Brothers & Sons Inc.
85 Finley Rd., Seabrook NJ 08302
Phone: 856-455-8080   **Fax:** -594
Web: www.bouygues-uk.com

COMPETITORS

Birds Eye	NORPAC
Del Monte Foods	Pictsweet
General Mills	Seneca Foods
JR Simplot	Smith Frozen Foods
Lakeside Foods	Twin City Foods
National Frozen Foods	

HISTORICAL FINANCIALS

Company Type: Private

Income Statement				FYE: May 26
	REVENUE ($ mil.)	NET INCOME ($ mil.)	NET PROFIT MARGIN	EMPLOYEES
05/12	102	4	4.1%	200
05/11	89	1	1.6%	0
05/10	93	0	0.4%	0
05/09	79	1	1.4%	0
Annual Growth	8.7%	54.7%	—	—

2012 Year-End Financials

Debt ratio: ——
Return on equity: 4.10%
Cash ($ mil.): 0
Current ratio: 0.70
Long-term debt ($ mil.): —
Dividends
  Yield: —
  Payout: —
Market value ($ mil.): —

SEALASKA CORPORATION

Sealaska Corporation is a native-owned investment firm active in natural resources manufacturing services and gaming. The holding company owns land in southeastern Alaska home to the Tlingit Haida and Tsimshian peoples. Sealaska core holdings include Sealaska Timber Corporation Alaska Coastal Aggregates Sealaska Constructors Sealaska Environmental Services and Colorado-based information technology services provider Managed Business Solutions. Sealaska's subsidiaries operate throughout North America and around the world. Its companies often win government contracts for construction environmental and engineering projects.

Sealaska owns about 290000 acres of timberland as well as the minerals rights to construction-grade aggregates on more than 565000 acres. The company also invests in stocks bonds and private equity.

The corporation has experienced a steady increase in its total revenues over the years (although there was a slight decline in 2008 due to the economic recession). Business diversity helped Sealaska weather the recession. Profits have been spotty as the corporation deals with market uncertainty and possible budget cuts in the federal government.

About 60% of Sealaska's revenues come from its services segment which includes subsidiary Sealaksa Environmental Services Sealaksa Constructors Synergy Systems and Managed Business Solutions. The services division expanded in 2010 with the acquisition of 70% of Flordia-based Security Alliance which provides guard and private investigation services.

More than 25% of Sealaska's revenues are earned from manufacturing activities. The manufacturing arm consists mainly of injection-molded plastics maker Nypro Kanaak which is a joint venture with Massachusetts-based Nypro. The division grew its revenue by 30% in 2011 after landing two major clients (Clorox and SC Johnson). Kraft also is another major client. In 2011 Sealaska shut down its mechanical parts manufacturer Olympic Fabrication.

Sealaska's natural resources division has experienced revenue growth over the years driven mostly by its timber operations. Demand in Asia and favorable prices have helped the timber segment maintain strong harvests. The company has worked to maintain sustainability and drive growth in that sector. Sealaska continues to seek custody of additional tribal lands in order to gain access to timber and is working on a Congressional bill that wound grant the tribes ownership to more land in southeast Alaska.

Sealaska's Alaska Coastal Aggregates subsidiary also is experiencing growth. The company supplies aggregate material for state and federal projects Alaska Coastal Aggregates is growing its cement and sand operations in southeast Alaska and developing a supply line to mines in the region.

The corporation is also looking to expand its reach on a global level. Its Sealaska Global Logistics arm ships freight internationally. In 2011 Sealaska Global Logistics entered the Asian market by establishing operations there. The logistics division also is looking the establish positions in emerging markets in Europe Mexico and South Africa.

Subsidiary Haa Aani (meaning "our land")was established in 2009 as a way to promote the culture social and economic viability of Southeast Alaska. Haa Aani has assisted tribal members with their efforts to establish businesses such as a new oyster farms in southeastern Alaska. Haa Aani also promotes renewable energy initiatives such as a biomass heating system for commercial buildings. In 2012 Haa Aani launched a non-profit community development financial institution in order to provide financing and promote economic development.

Sealaska's also is developing a gaming casino and resort in Cloverdale California. The corporation through its End-to-End Enterprises subsidiary is partners with the Pomo Indians of California on the project.

Sealaska is the largest of 13 corporations formed under the Alaska Native Claims Settlement Act (ANCSA) of 1971 which promised some 44 million acres of land to Alaska natives. The company is owned by some 21000 tribal member shareholders.

EXECUTIVES

EVP, Richard P. (Rick) Harris, $240,000 total compensation
President and CEO, Chris E. McNeil Jr., $350,000 total compensation
COO, Samuel (Sam) Landol, $250,000 total compensation
Manager Information Systems, Robert (Rob) Johnson
Director Corporate Communications, Todd P. Antioquia
Chairman, Albert M. Kookesh, age 63
Vice Chair, Rosita F. Worl, age 74
VP and CFO, Doug Morris
Director Business Development Sealaska Timber Corporation (STC), Ed Davis
Manager Shareholder Records, Ella D. Bennett
VP Corporate Secretary and VP Human Resources, Nicole D. Hallingstad
Manager Human Resources, Kenneth L. (Ken) Southerland
VP Corporate Development, Russell A. Dick
Corporate Counsel, E. Budd Simpson
Treasurer and Chief Investment Officer, Anthony Mallott
VP and General Counsel, Jaeleen Kookesh Araujo
Assistant to the President and CEO, Katherine Eldemar
Operations Controller, Nathan McCowan
Internal Auditor, Mark Shirley
Headquarters Controller, Vicki Soboleff
Manager Natural Resources, Ron Wolfe
Manager Records, Linda Wynne
President and CEO Sealaska Timber Corporation (STC), Wade Zammit
General Manager Nypro Kanaak Alabama, Kenneth Fair
General Manager Sealaska Environmental Services, Derik Frederiksen
COO Sealaska Environmental Services, Neil Hart
General Manager Alaska Coastal Aggregates, Dean McDonald
President and CEO Managed Business Solutions, Richard Noe, $293,119 total compensation
General Manager Nypro Kanaak Guadalajara, Julio Oropeza
President and General Manager Synergy Systems and Olympic Fabrication, Damon Pistulka
Director Sales and Marketing Nypro Kanaak, Ed Rivera
Director, Byron I. Mallott, age 69
Director, Patrick M. Anderson, age 58

Director, Clarence Jackson Sr., age 77
Director, Jacqueline L. (Jackie) Johnson Pata, age 56
Director, Edward K. Thomas, age 70
Vice Chair, Rosita F. Worl, age 74
Director, Joseph G. Nelson, age 41
Director, Sidney Edenshaw, age 48
Director, J. Tate London, age 50
Director, Jodi Mitchell, age 48
Director, William (Bill) Thomas, age 64
Director, Barbara Cadiente-Nelson, age 58
Auditors: KPMGLLP

LOCATIONS

HQ: SEALASKA CORPORATION
1 SEALASKA PLZ STE 400, JUNEAU, AK 99801-1276
Phone: 907-586-1512
Web: www.sealaska.com

PRODUCTS/OPERATIONS

2011 Sales

	$ mil.	% of total
Services	145	55
Manufacturing	72	28
Natural resources	45	17
Investments	(3.9)	-
Gaming	0	-
Corporate & other	0	-
Total	**259**	**100**

Selected Subsidiaries

Alaska Coastal Aggregates
Managed Business Solutions (majority owned)
Nypro Kanaak (joint venture)
Sealaska Constructors LLC
Sealaska Environmental Services
Sealaska Timber Corporation
Security Alliance

COMPETITORS

chugach alaska	Tembec
Plum Creek Timber	West Fraser Timber

HISTORICAL FINANCIALS

Company Type: Private

Income Statement

FYE: December 31

	REVENUE ($ mil.)	NET INCOME ($ mil.)	NET PROFIT MARGIN	EMPLOYEES
12/11	259	8	3.2%	1,400
12/10	223	17	7.8%	0
12/09	0	0	11.8%	0
12/08	0	(0)	—	0
Annual Growth	1173.0%	—	—	—

2011 Year-End Financials

Debt ratio: ——
Return on equity: 3.20%
Cash ($ mil.): 20
Current ratio: 0.30
Long-term debt ($ mil.): ——

Dividends
Yield: —
Payout: —
Market value ($ mil.): —

SEASIDE TRANSPORTATION SERVICES LLC

LOCATIONS

HQ: SEASIDE TRANSPORTATION SERVICES LLC
389 TERMINAL WAY, SAN PEDRO, CA 90731-7430
Phone: 310-241-1706

HISTORICAL FINANCIALS

Company Type: Private

Income Statement

FYE: December 31

	REVENUE ($ mil.)	NET INCOME ($ mil.)	NET PROFIT MARGIN	EMPLOYEES
12/11	184	2	1.5%	12
12/10	203	3	1.8%	0
12/09	156	2	1.4%	0
12/08	180	4	2.3%	0
Annual Growth	0.7%	(12.4%)	—	—

2011 Year-End Financials

Debt ratio: ——
Return on equity: 1.50%
Cash ($ mil.): 12
Current ratio: 2.00
Long-term debt ($ mil.): ——

Dividends
Yield: —
Payout: —
Market value ($ mil.): —

SEATTLE UNIVERSITY

Seattle University isn't very big but as one of 28 Jesuit universities in the US it is part of a Roman Catholic teaching legacy that spans the country and the world. With an enrollment of about 7500 students the school offers 64 undergraduate more than 35 graduate degree programs and 28 certificate programs through its eight schools (College of Arts and Sciences Albers School of Business and Economics College of Education School of Law Matteo Ricci College College of Nursing College of Science and Engineering and School of Theology and Ministry).

Operations

In 2012 Seattle University had 4589 undergraduate students and 1933 graduate students. Some 40% of the first year students were from Washington State and some 7% of all students were from outside the US.

The average class size is 19 and the faculty-to-student ratio is 1 to 13.

Financial Performance

In 2012 the university reported a 10% decrease in revenues due to a drop in investment income a loss incurred in net realized and unrealized losses on investments and a change in value of interest rate swap agreements.

Its net income declined by 90% in 2012 due to a decrease in revenues and an increase in expenses attributed largely to higher costs for instruction academic support and auxiliary enterprises.

Strategy

Growing its portfolio of degree programs in 2012 Seattle University's Albers School of Business and Economics added the Bridge MBA to its family of graduate degrees.

Company Background

Seattle University was founded in 1891 by two Jesuit priests.

EXECUTIVES

President, Father Stephen V. Sundborg
EVP, Timothy P. Leary
VP University Advancement, Mary Kay McFadden
Provost, Isiaah Crawford
Interim VP Finance, James Adolphson
VP Human Resources and University Services, Jerry Huffman
VP Student Development, Jacob Diaz
VP and University Counsel, Mary S. Peterson
VP University Planning and Vice Provost, Robert J. Dullea
Auditors: PricewaterhouseCoopersLLP

LOCATIONS

HQ: Seattle University
901 12th Ave., Seattle WA 98122-1090
Phone: 206-296-6000　　**Fax:** 206-296-6200
Web: www.seattleu.edu

PRODUCTS/OPERATIONS

Schools and Colleges
Albers School of Business and Economics
College of Arts and Sciences
College of Education
College of Nursing
College of Science and Engineerin
Matteo Ricci College
School of Law
School of Theology and Ministry

HISTORICAL FINANCIALS

Company Type: School

Income Statement

FYE: June 30

	REVENUE ($ mil.)	NET INCOME ($ mil.)	NET PROFIT MARGIN	EMPLOYEES
06/11	249	0	0.1%	1,100
06/10	236	11	4.9%	0
06/09	236	0	—	0
06/08	186	19	10.6%	0
Annual Growth	10.2%	(73.5%)	—	—

2011 Year-End Financials

Debt ratio: ——
Return on equity: 0.10%
Cash ($ mil.): 41
Current ratio: —
Long-term debt ($ mil.): ——

Dividends
Yield: —
Payout: —
Market value ($ mil.): —

SECOND HARVEST FOOD BANK OF SANTA CLARA & SAN MATEO COUNTIES

LOCATIONS

HQ: SECOND HARVEST FOOD BANK OF SANTA CLARA & SAN MATEO COUNTIES
750 CURTNER AVE, SAN JOSE, CA 95125-2118
Phone: 408-266-8866
Web: www.secondharvestfood.org

HISTORICAL FINANCIALS

Company Type: Private

Income Statement

FYE: June 30

	REVENUE ($ mil.)	NET INCOME ($ mil.)	NET PROFIT MARGIN	EMPLOYEES
06/12	92	8	9.6%	120
06/11	80	9	11.7%	0
06/10	71	3	5.4%	0
06/09	20	0	0.0%	0
Annual Growth	65.3%	2332.5%	—	—

2012 Year-End Financials

Debt ratio: ——
Return on equity: 9.60%
Cash ($ mil.): 9
Current ratio: 1.80
Long-term debt ($ mil.): ——

Dividends
Yield: —
Payout: —
Market value ($ mil.): —

SECOND HARVEST HEARTLAND

LOCATIONS

HQ: SECOND HARVEST HEARTLAND
1140 GERVAIS AVE, SAINT PAUL, MN 55109-2042
Phone: 651-484-5117

HISTORICAL FINANCIALS

Company Type: Private

Income Statement

FYE: September 30

	REVENUE ($ mil.)	NET INCOME ($ mil.)	NET PROFIT MARGIN	EMPLOYEES
09/11	105	1	1.4%	130
09/10	91	(0)	—	0
09/09	66	2	4.5%	0
09/08	51	1	2.6%	0
Annual Growth	27.6%	2.2%	—	—

2011 Year-End Financials

Debt ratio: ——
Return on equity: 1.40%
Cash ($ mil.): 1
Current ratio: 5.10
Long-term debt ($ mil.): ——

Dividends
Yield: —
Payout: —
Market value ($ mil.): —

SECURITY FINANCE CORPORATION OF SPARTANBURG

Folks looking for a little financial security just might turn to Security Finance Corporation of Spartanburg. Founded in 1955 the consumer loan company provides personal loans typically ranging from $100 to $600 (some states however allow loan amounts as high as $3000). Customers can also turn to Security Finance for credit reports and tax preparation services. The company operates approximately 800 offices in about 15 states that are marketed under the Security Finance Sunbelt Credit and PFS banner names. A subsidiary of Security Group the financial institution also has locations operating as Security Financial Services in North Carolina and Longhorn Finance in Texas.

Geographic Reach

From its headquarters in South Carolina Security Finance boasts offices in about 15 states across the US.

Strategy

Security Finance exited Colorado in 2010 after the state's attorney general general office filed a compliant that the company had been refinancing some consumer loans more than three times a year (the limit under Colorado law). The company agreed to repay acquisition fees that it had charged the customers for refinancing the loans.

Company Ownership

Security Finance is a subsidiary of Security Group Inc.

EXECUTIVES

President and COO, A.R. (Ray) Biggs, age 71
CFO and Treasurer, A. Greg Williams, age 50
Secretary, Marshall T. Walsh, age 60
Auditors: Deloitte&ToucheLLP

LOCATIONS

HQ: Security Finance Corporation of Spartanburg
181 Security Place, Spartanburg SC 29307
Phone: 864-582-8193   **Fax:** 864-582-2532
Web: www.security-finance.com

Selected Locations

Alabama
Florida
Georgia
Idaho
Illinois
Louisiana
Missouri
Nevada
New Mexico
North Carolina
Oklahoma
South Carolina
Tennessee
Texas
Utah
Wisconsin

PRODUCTS/OPERATIONS

Selected Banners

Longhorn Finance (Texas)
PFS
Security Finance
Security Financial Services (North Carolina)
Sunbelt Credit

COMPETITORS

1st Franklin Financial	DFC Global
ACE Cash Express	EZCORP
Advance America	First Cash Financial Services
Bank of America	
Capital One	GE Capital
Cash America	OneMain Financial
Cash Plus	Value Financial Services
Community Choice Financial	World Acceptance

HISTORICAL FINANCIALS

Company Type: Private

Income Statement

FYE: December 31

	ASSETS ($ mil.)	NET INCOME ($ mil.)	INCOME AS % OF ASSETS	EMPLOYEES
12/11	322	42	13.1%	2,500
12/10	495	41	8.4%	0
12/09	432	30	7.1%	0
12/08	383	22	5.8%	0
Annual Growth	(5.6%)	24.0%	—	—

2011 Year-End Financials

Debt ratio: ——
Return on equity: 12.00%
Cash ($ mil.): 7
Current ratio: ——
Long-term debt ($ mil.): —

Dividends
Yield: —
Payout: —
Market value ($ mil.): —

SEEMAC INCORPORATED

LOCATIONS

HQ: SEEMAC INCORPORATED
11350 N MERIDIAN ST # 450, CARMEL, IN 46032-4595
Phone: 317-844-3995
Web: www.seemac.com

HISTORICAL FINANCIALS

Company Type: Private

Income Statement

FYE: September 30

	REVENUE ($ mil.)	NET INCOME ($ mil.)	NET PROFIT MARGIN	EMPLOYEES
09/11	83	0	0.7%	20
09/10	81	0	0.7%	0
09/09	89	0	0.8%	0
09/08	151	(0)	—	0
Annual Growth	(18.1%)	—	—	—

2011 Year-End Financials

Debt ratio: ——
Return on equity: 0.70%
Cash ($ mil.): 6
Current ratio: 4.90
Long-term debt ($ mil.): ——

Dividends
Yield: —
Payout: —
Market value ($ mil.): —

SENTARA HEALTHCARE

Health care's a beach for Sentara Healthcare. The not-for-profit organization operates a network of hospitals and other health facilities primarily in the coastal Hampton Roads area of southeastern Virginia. The system includes 10 acute care hospitals housing a total of some 2400 beds; one of the hospitals Sentara Norfolk includes a dedicated cardiac hospital with more than 100 beds. In addition to its acute care facilities Sentara Healthcare operates several outpatient care facilities as well as nursing homes rehab centers medical practices imaging centers and home health agencies. Its Optima Health unit provides HMO PPO and other health insurance products to about 430000 Virginians.

The medical system's multi-specialty physicians group the Sentara Medical Group has more than 380 primary care and specialty physicians. Its Sentara Senior Services unit operates about 10 nursing and assisted living centers. Altogether Sentara Healthcare's facilities serve customers throughout southeastern and northern Virginia as well as in northeastern North Carolina.

Though it's already one of the largest health care organizations in the state Sentara is not resting on its laurels. The system continues to grow through acquisitions construction (both expansions and new buildings) and mergers. In mid-2009 the company expanded its home health services by acquiring Bath Community House Home Health and Hospice of the Highlands and subsequently gave it the less-lengthy moniker of Sentara Highlands Home Health. Following that acquisition Sentara operates home care offices in seven cities in Virginia and in Elizabeth North Carolina.

Sentara also acquired the 180-bed Potomac Hospital (now operating as Sentara Potomac Hospital) in Woodbridge through a merger transaction in 2009 expanding its hospital operations into northern Virginia. The agreement was made in part to keep Potomac Hospital from going under in the face of continuing economic pressure. As part of the agreement Sentara will invest in the hospital's infrastructure and establish a community health foundation to help address the medical needs of the area's residents.

In 2010 Sentara acquired two more Virginia medical centers starting with the purchase of RMH Healthcare which operates Rockingham Memorial Hospital in Harrisonburg Virginia. In addition to the 238-bed community hospital RMH operates a wellness center and physicians group. In mid-2011 Sentara completed the acquisition of Martha Jefferson Hospital (aka Martha Jefferson Health Services) adding a 175-bed acute care facility and a network of primary and specialty care clinics in central Virginia to its network.

Sentara has also completed construction of a new acute care hospital located on its existing Princess Anne outpatient campus in Virginia Beach. The facility named Sentara Princess Anne Hospital opened in mid-2011 and is operated through a 70%-owned joint venture with Bon Secours Health System. The 160-bed $145 million facility encompasses five stories and offers comprehensive surgical procedures intensive care advanced cardiac care and a maternity center.

Like any large health care system Sentara also occasionally must downsize operations at certain facilities to adjust to market needs. For instance following the completion of the new Princess Anne Hospital the company transitioned its older hospital facility in Virginia Beach Sentara Bayside Hospital to an outpatient facility.

EXECUTIVES

President and COO, Howard P. Kern
SVP and CIO, Bertram S. (Bert) Reese

CEO, David L. Bernd
SVP Human Resources, Michael V. (Mike) Taylor
SVP and CFO, Robert A. (Rob) Broerman
VP; Administrator Sentara Williamsburg Regional Medical Center, Robert L. (Bob) Graves
VP Materials Management, Carl Manley
President Healthcare Performance Improvement (HPI), Gary R. Yates
VP Reinventing and Decision Support, Douglas M. (Doug) Thompson
SVP Managed Care; President Sentara Health Plans, Michael M. Dudley
VP Peninsula, Mary L. Blunt
SVP; President Sentara Peninsula Region, Kenneth M. (Ken) Krakaur
VP; Administrator Sentara Leigh Hospital, Terrie Edwards
SVP System Development, Vicky G. Gray
Director Public Relations, Emma Inman
Director Government Relations and Advocacy, Sandra Miller
President Sentara CarePlex Hospital, Debra A. Flores
VP; Administrator Sentara Virginia Beach General Hospital, Raymond Troiano
Chief Neurology Sentara Medical Group, Richard M. Zweifler
Chief Nursing Officer, Genemarie McGee

LOCATIONS

HQ: Sentara Healthcare
6015 Poplar Hall Dr., Norfolk VA 23502
Phone: 757-455-7540   **Fax:** 757-455-7964
Web: www.sentara.com

Selected Virginia Locations

Martha Jefferson Hospital (Charlottesville)
Rockingham Memorial Hospital (RMH Healthcare Harrisonburg)
Sentara CarePlex Hospital (Hampton)
Sentara Leigh Hospital (Norfolk)
Sentara Norfolk General Hospital (Norfolk)
Sentara Heart Hospital (Norfolk)
Sentara Obici Hospital (Suffolk)
Sentara Potomac Hospital (Woodbridge)
Sentara Princess Anne Hospital (Virginia Beach)
Sentara Virginia Beach General Hospital (Virginia Beach)
Sentara Williamsburg Regional Medical Center (Williamsburg)

PRODUCTS/OPERATIONS

Selected Services

Cancer
Cardiac (Heart)
Digestive (Colorectal)
Home Care
Imaging
Maternity
Neurosciences
Rehabilitation
Seniors
Thoracic
Transplant
Trauma/Emergency Services
Urology
Vascular
Weight Loss Surgery
Women's

COMPETITORS

Aetna
Anthem Health Plans of Virginia
Bon Secours Health
Carilion Clinic
Centra Health Inc.
Children's Hospital of The King's Daughters
CIGNA

Franklin Hospital Corp.
HCA Capital Division
Humana
Inova
Kaiser Foundation Health Plan of the Mid-Atlantic
Norton Community Hospital
Novant Health
Riverside Health System (Virginia)
Twin County Regional Healthcare
UnitedHealth Group
Wake Forest University Baptist Medical Center

HISTORICAL FINANCIALS

Company Type: Private - Not-for-Profit

Income Statement

FYE: December 31

	REVENUE ($ mil.)	NET INCOME ($ mil.)	NET PROFIT MARGIN	EMPLOYEES
12/11	3,930	103	2.6%	22,000
12/10	3,385	316	9.4%	0
12/09	2,945	347	11.8%	0
12/08	2,776	(359)	—	0
Annual Growth	**12.3%**	**—**	**—**	**—**

2011 Year-End Financials

Debt ratio: ——
Return on equity: 2.60%
Cash ($ mil.): 860
Current ratio: 1.50
Long-term debt ($ mil.): —
Dividends
  Yield: —
  Payout: —
Market value ($ mil.): —

SERVCO PACIFIC INC.

Servco Pacific's business flows through an ocean's worth of enterprises. The company sells passenger vehicles (including Toyota Subaru Suzuki and Chevrolet models) and commercial trucks through dealerships in Hawaii and Australia. In addition Servco Home & Appliance wholesales kitchen and bath products to building professionals throughout the South Pacific; Servco Raynor Overhead Doors installs residential and commercial garage doors; Servco Insurance Services offers insurance coverage for businesses and individuals; and Servco School & Office Furniture outfits educational institutions and government agencies with desks seating and other furnishings. Servco Pacific was founded by Peter Fukunaga in 1919.

Geographic Reach
Servco Pacific has insurance offices in Seattle and Tacoma Washington. Its other businesses operate in Hawaii (Kauai Maui Oahu and the Big Island); and Australia (New South Wales Queensland).

Operations
The diversified firm sells insurance through Servco Insurance Services (SIS) in Washington state. It clients are in the fishing shipping and cargo industries in several states including Alaska. SIS also operates in Hawaii where sister chains Servco Home & Appliance Servco Forklift & Industrial Equipment and Servco Automotive also operate.

Strategy
Servco Pacific through its Australian subsidiary has been expanding its Toyota dealer operations in recent years. During 2010 the company acquired majority stakes in Sunshine Toyota of Queensland and Dubbo City Toyota of New South Wales. It also purchased Pacific Toyota in Cairns in 2009. The deals have significantly grown Servco

Pacific's business in Australia part of a bid to strengthen its international presence; altogether Servco Pacific owns five dealerships in the country. The firm started operating in Australia in late 2007 with the acquisition of a Toyota dealership in Brisbane.

EXECUTIVES

President and COO, Eric Fukunaga
Chairman and CEO, Mark H. Fukunaga, age 56
CFO, Jeffery Bell
VP Automotive Retail, Lance Ichimura
Director Fixed Operations Automotive Retail, Gary A. Hu
General Manager Service Motors Wahiawa, Keith Nakamura
General Manager Servco Auto Windward, Rod Saunders
VP and General Manager Servco Raynor Overhead Doors, Peter Eldridge
Auditors: Deloitte&Touche

LOCATIONS

HQ: Servco Pacific Inc.
2850 Pukoloa St. Ste. 300, Honolulu HI 96819
Phone: 808-564-1300   **Fax:** 808-523-3937
Web: www.servco.com

PRODUCTS/OPERATIONS

Selected Operations

Automotive
    Rex Tire and Supply
    Scion Dealers of Hawaii
    Subaru Dealers of Hawaii
    Suzuki Dealers of Hawaii
    Servco Australia
    Servco Chevy
    Servco Lexus
    Servco Truck & Commercial
    Toyota Dealers of Hawaii
Servco Home and Appliance Distribution
Servco Insurance Services
Servco Raynor Overhead Doors
Servco School and Office Furniture

COMPETITORS

AutoNation   HD Supply
Citigroup   Inchcape
Fletcher Jones

HISTORICAL FINANCIALS

Company Type: Private

Income Statement

	REVENUE ($ mil.)	NET INCOME ($ mil.)	NET PROFIT MARGIN	EMPLOYEES
12/11*	429	5	1.2%	925
06/11	791	10	1.4%	0
06/10	699	9	1.4%	0
06/09	547	(2)	—	0
Annual Growth	(7.8%)	—	—	—

*Fiscal year change

FYE: December 31

2011 Year-End Financials

Debt ratio: ——
Return on equity: 1.20%   Dividends
Cash ($ mil.): 24   Yield: —
Current ratio: 0.40   Payout: —
Long-term debt ($ mil.): —   Market value ($ mil.): —

SERVICE BY AIR INC.

LOCATIONS

HQ: SERVICE BY AIR INC.
222 CROSSWAYS PARK DR, WOODBURY, NY 11797-2015
Phone: 516-921-4101
Web: www.servicebyair.com

HISTORICAL FINANCIALS

Company Type: Private

Income Statement

FYE: August 31

	REVENUE ($ mil.)	NET INCOME ($ mil.)	NET PROFIT MARGIN	EMPLOYEES
08/11	119	0	0.1%	166
08/10	113	0	0.2%	0
08/08	117	0	0.3%	0
08/07	111	0	0.3%	0
Annual Growth	2.6%	(22.8%)	—	—

2011 Year-End Financials

Debt ratio: ——
Return on equity: 0.10%   Dividends
Cash ($ mil.): 4   Yield: —
Current ratio: 1.30   Payout: —
Long-term debt ($ mil.): —   Market value ($ mil.): —

SETON HALL UNIVERSITY

Seton Hall University is a Catholic institution with an enrollment of approximately 10000 students. The university offers about 150 undergraduate and graduate degree programs as well as more than a dozen doctoral programs at eight colleges and schools including the Whitehead School of Diplomacy and International Relations Stillman School of Business and Immaculate Conception Seminary School of Theology. It also offers degree and certificate programs online. With a history dating back to 1856 Seton Hall University was named after Mother Elizabeth Ann Seton the first American-born saint (and an aunt of school founder Bishop James Roosevelt Bayley).

EXECUTIVES

VP University Advancement, Joseph G. Sandman
VP Finance and Technology, Dennis J. Garbini
VP and General Counsel, Catherine A. Kiernan
VP; Interim Dean Whitehead School of Diplomacy and International Relations, Rev Paul A. Holmes
VP Student Affairs and Enrollment Services, Laura Wankel
Controller, John Passaro
EVP Administration, Paula Marie Buley
Director Athletics and Recreational, Joe Quinlan Jr.
Chair Board of Trustees and President Board of Regents, Rev John J. Myers
Vice Chair Board of Trustees, James M. Cafone
Rector and Dean Immaculate Conception Seminary/School of Theology and Trustee, Robert Coleman

Dean W. Paul Stillman School of Business, Karen Boroff
Dean College of Education and Human Services, Joseph DePierro
Director Seton World Wide, Philip DiSalvio
Dean Freshman Studies and Special Academic Programs, Tracy Gottlieb
Dean College of Nursing, Phyllis Shanley Hansell
Dean School of Law, Patricia E. Hobbs
Dean College of Arts and Sciences, Joseph Marbach
Dean University Libraries, Joseph F. McGinn
DeanWhitehead School of Diplomacy and International Relations, John K. Menzies
Dean School of Health and Medical Sciences, Brian B. Shulman
CIO; Project Manager Banner Implementation, Stephen Landry
Human Resources and Information Technology Administrator, Jane Hudson
Manager Training and Development Human Resources, Therese Chidiac
President Adelante, Julieta Caraballo
President Black Student Union, Kevaan Walton
President Interfraternity Council, Michael Kurlander
President International Students Association, Morella Mirabal
President Martin Luther King Scholars, Lauren Jackson
President Multicultural Greek Council, Charee Marquez
President Panhellenic Council, Nicole Fopeano
President Senior Class Council, Elizabeth Rathbun
President Student Activities Board, Richard Evans
President Student Government Association, Michael McLaughlin
Provost, A. Gabriel Esteban
Trustee, Patricia A. Cahill
Trustee, Patrick M. Murray, age 69
Vice Chair Board of Trustees, James M. Cafone
Trustee, Pamela M. Swartzberg
Trustee, Rev Arthur J. Serratelli
Trustee, Kurt T. Borowsky
Rector and Dean Immaculate Conception Seminary/School of Theology and Trustee, Robert Coleman
Trustee, John Doran
Trustee, Phillip Frese
Trustee, Joseph P. LaSala
Trustee, Joseph R. Reilly
Trustee, John J. Schimpf
Trustee, Bruce Tomason
Trustee, Robert Wister

LOCATIONS

HQ: Seton Hall University
400 S. Orange Ave., South Orange NJ 07079-2646
Phone: 973-761-9000   **Fax:** 973-275-2005
Web: www.shu.edu

PRODUCTS/OPERATIONS

Selected Schools & Colleges

College of Arts and Sciences
College of Education and Human Services
College of Nursing
Immaculate Conception Seminary School of Theology
School of Health and Medical Sciences
School of Law
Stillman School of Business
Whitehead School of Diplomacy & International Relations

HISTORICAL FINANCIALS
Company Type: School

Income Statement
FYE: June 30

	REVENUE ($ mil.)	NET INCOME ($ mil.)	NET PROFIT MARGIN	EMPLOYEES
06/12	256	(0)	—	1,050
06/11	256	39	15.4%	0
06/10	335	4	1.5%	0
06/09	232	(29)	—	0
Annual Growth	3.3%	—	—	—

2012 Year-End Financials

Debt ratio: ——
Return on equity: (-0.10)%
Cash ($ mil.): 38
Current ratio: —
Long-term debt ($ mil.): —

Dividends
 Yield: —
 Payout: —
 Market value ($ mil.): —

HISTORICAL FINANCIALS
Company Type: Private

Income Statement
FYE: June 30

	REVENUE ($ mil.)	NET INCOME ($ mil.)	NET PROFIT MARGIN	EMPLOYEES
06/12	100	2	2.4%	1,300
06/10	90	1	1.3%	0
06/09	85	0	0.9%	0
06/08	83	(0)	—	0
Annual Growth	6.2%	—	—	—

2012 Year-End Financials

Debt ratio: ——
Return on equity: 2.40%
Cash ($ mil.): 4
Current ratio: 0.50
Long-term debt ($ mil.): —

Dividends
 Yield: —
 Payout: —
 Market value ($ mil.): —

HISTORICAL FINANCIALS
Company Type: Private

Income Statement
FYE: December 31

	REVENUE ($ mil.)	NET INCOME ($ mil.)	NET PROFIT MARGIN	EMPLOYEES
12/11	142	0	0.4%	71
12/10	153	0	0.3%	0
12/09	130	0	0.3%	0
12/08	192	0	0.4%	0
Annual Growth	(9.5%)	(9.0%)	—	—

2011 Year-End Financials

Debt ratio: ——
Return on equity: 0.40%
Cash ($ mil.): 0
Current ratio: 0.50
Long-term debt ($ mil.): —

Dividends
 Yield: —
 Payout: —
 Market value ($ mil.): —

SETON MEDICAL CENTER

LOCATIONS

HQ: SETON MEDICAL CENTER
 1900 SULLIVAN AVE, DALY CITY, CA 94015-2229
Phone: 650-992-4000
Web: www.setoncoastside.org

HISTORICAL FINANCIALS
Company Type: Private

Income Statement
FYE: June 30

	REVENUE ($ mil.)	NET INCOME ($ mil.)	NET PROFIT MARGIN	EMPLOYEES
06/11	304	(16)	—	1,231
06/10	296	(14)	—	0
06/09	319	(1)	—	0
06/08	306	1	0.4%	0
Annual Growth	(0.1%)	—	—	—

2011 Year-End Financials

Debt ratio: ——
Return on equity: (-5.30)%
Cash ($ mil.): 34
Current ratio: —
Long-term debt ($ mil.): —

Dividends
 Yield: —
 Payout: —
 Market value ($ mil.): —

SEVIER COUNTY ELECTRIC SYSTEM (INC)

LOCATIONS

HQ: SEVIER COUNTY ELECTRIC SYSTEM (INC)
 315 E MAIN ST, SEVIERVILLE, TN 37862-3527
Phone: 865-453-2887
Web: www.sces.net

HISTORICAL FINANCIALS
Company Type: Private

Income Statement
FYE: June 30

	REVENUE ($ mil.)	NET INCOME ($ mil.)	NET PROFIT MARGIN	EMPLOYEES
06/12	142	6	4.8%	98
06/11	154	9	6.1%	0
06/09	145	7	4.9%	0
06/08	123	5	4.6%	0
Annual Growth	4.9%	6.7%	—	—

2012 Year-End Financials

Debt ratio: ——
Return on equity: 4.80%
Cash ($ mil.): 24
Current ratio: 1.00
Long-term debt ($ mil.): —

Dividends
 Yield: —
 Payout: —
 Market value ($ mil.): —

SHELBY COUNTY MEMORIAL HOSPITAL ASSOCIATION

LOCATIONS

HQ: SHELBY COUNTY MEMORIAL HOSPITAL ASSOCIATION
 915 MICHIGAN ST, SIDNEY, OH 45365-2401
Phone: 937-498-2311
Web: www.wilsonhospital.com

HISTORICAL FINANCIALS
Company Type: Private

Income Statement
FYE: December 31

	REVENUE ($ mil.)	NET INCOME ($ mil.)	NET PROFIT MARGIN	EMPLOYEES
12/11	86	75	87.3%	700
12/10	80	6	8.0%	0
12/09	78	3	4.8%	0
12/08	82	(0)	—	0
Annual Growth	1.9%	—	—	—

2011 Year-End Financials

Debt ratio: ——
Return on equity: 87.30%
Cash ($ mil.): 11
Current ratio: 2.70
Long-term debt ($ mil.): —

Dividends
 Yield: —
 Payout: —
 Market value ($ mil.): —

SEVEN COUNTIES SERVICES INC.

LOCATIONS

HQ: SEVEN COUNTIES SERVICES INC.
 101 W MUHAMMAD ALI BLVD, LOUISVILLE, KY 40202-1451
Phone: 502-589-8600
Web: www.cypressmd.com

SHAMROCK BUILDING MATERIALS INC.

LOCATIONS

HQ: SHAMROCK BUILDING MATERIALS INC.
 90422 HIGHWAY 99 N, EUGENE, OR 97402-9623
Phone: 541-688-5444
Web: www.shamrockbm.com

SHELTERING ARM HOSPITAL FOUNDATION INC

LOCATIONS

HQ: SHELTERING ARM HOSPITAL FOUNDATION INC
55 HOSPITAL DR, ATHENS, OH 45701-2302
Phone: 740-592-9300
Web: www.ohiopartnersinjustice.org

HISTORICAL FINANCIALS
Company Type: Private

Income Statement

	REVENUE ($ mil.)	NET INCOME ($ mil.)	NET PROFIT MARGIN	EMPLOYEES
06/11	82	3	4.8%	368
06/10	82	5	6.7%	0
06/09	79	0	0.2%	0
06/08	75	(6)	—	0
Annual Growth	2.9%	—	—	—

FYE: June 30

2011 Year-End Financials

Debt ratio: ——
Return on equity: 4.80%
Cash ($ mil.): 18
Current ratio: 2.50
Long-term debt ($ mil.): —

Dividends
Yield: —
Payout: —
Market value ($ mil.): —

SHEPHERD CENTER INC.

Here to shepherd those with catastrophic injuries back to good health is Shepherd Center. The not-for-profit hospital specializes in medical treatment research and rehabilitation for people with spinal cord and brain injuries as well as patients with neuromuscular disorders (such as spina bifida) and chronic pain. Shepherd Hospital boasts more than 150 beds including a 10-bed intensive care unit. Of its patients who have suffered injuries about 60% have been in car accidents. Founded in 1975 by James Shepherd (who was paralyzed in a bodysurfing accident) and his family the hospital conducts neurological and neuromuscular research through its Virginia C. Crawford Research Institute.

Operations

Aside from its primary Shepherd Hospital Shepherd Center operates the Shepherd Pain Institute and the Andrew C. Carlos Multiple Sclerosis Institute.

It's ranked by U.S. News & World Report magazine as one of the top 10 rehabilitation hospitals in the nation. Shepherd Center employs more than 1400 people. Seeing some 6600 people on an outpatient basis each year the center admits more than 960 patients to its inpatient programs and another 570 to its programs for day patients.

Geographic Reach

Based in Atlanta Shepherd Center serves not only its home state of Georgia but the entire nation as one of the leading rehabilitation hospitals in the US.

EXECUTIVES

Medical Director Emeritus and Board Member, David F. Apple Jr.
Chairman, James H. Shepherd Jr.
President CEO and Board Member, Gary R. Ulicny
VP Marketing and Managed Care, Mitchell J. (Mitch) Fillhaber
VP Facility Services, Wilma Bunch
CFO, Stephen B. Holleman
Director Public Relations, Larry Bowie
VP Research and Technology and CIO, Michael L. Jones
Medical Director and Board member, Donald P. Leslie
VP Development and Executive Director Shepherd Center Foundation, Scott H. Sikes
Chief Nurse Executive, Tamara King
Administrative Assistant, Teri Grimes
Board Member, Joseph R. (Joe) Moderow, age 62
Board Member, W. Clyde Shepherd III, age 51
Medical Director Emeritus and Board Member, David F. Apple Jr.
President CEO and Board Member, Gary R. Ulicny
Board Member, Goodloe H. Yancey III
Board Member and Secretary, Stephen B. Goot
Medical Director and Board member, Donald P. Leslie
Board Member and VP, Emory A. Schwall
Board Member and Treasurer, William C. Fowler
Board Member and Recording Secretary, Alana Shepherd
Board Member, Fred V. Alias
Board Member, Gregory P. Anderson
Board Member, James M. Caswell Jr.
Board Member, Sara S. Chapman
Board Member, John S. Dryman
Board Member, David H. Flint
Board Member, Bernie Marcus
Board Member, Julian B. Mohr
Board Member, Charles T. Nunnally III
Board Member, Sally D. Nunnally
Board Member, J. Harold Shepherd
Board Member, Jim Stephenson
Board Member, James D. Thompson

LOCATIONS

HQ: Shepherd Center Inc.
2020 Peachtree Rd. NW, Atlanta GA 30309-1465
Phone: 404-352-2020   **Fax:** 404-350-7346
Web: www.shepherd.org

PRODUCTS/OPERATIONS

Selected Facilities

Andrew C. Carlos Multiple Sclerosis Institute
Shepherd Hospital
Shepherd Pain Institute

COMPETITORS

DeKalb Medical
Emory Healthcare
Grady Health System
Northside Hospital
Piedmont Healthcare
Regency Hospital

Saint Joseph's Health System
Southern Regional Medical Center
WellStar Health System

HISTORICAL FINANCIALS
Company Type: Private - Not-for-Profit

Income Statement

	REVENUE ($ mil.)	NET INCOME ($ mil.)	NET PROFIT MARGIN	EMPLOYEES
03/12	159	23	14.8%	800
03/11	134	16	12.4%	0
03/10	127	33	26.2%	0
03/09	123	(22)	—	0
Annual Growth	8.8%	—	—	—

FYE: March 31

2012 Year-End Financials

Debt ratio: ——
Return on equity: 14.80%
Cash ($ mil.): 13
Current ratio: 2.40
Long-term debt ($ mil.): —

Dividends
Yield: —
Payout: —
Market value ($ mil.): —

SHEPPARD AND ENOCH PRATT FOUNDATION INC

LOCATIONS

HQ: SHEPPARD AND ENOCH PRATT FOUNDATION INC
6501 N CHARLES ST STE 242, BALTIMORE, MD 21204-6819
Phone: 410-938-3000
Web: www.sheppardpratt.org

HISTORICAL FINANCIALS
Company Type: Private

Income Statement

	REVENUE ($ mil.)	NET INCOME ($ mil.)	NET PROFIT MARGIN	EMPLOYEES
06/12	281	(17)	—	1,399
06/11	273	44	16.4%	0
06/10	264	3	1.3%	0
06/09	253	(16)	—	0
Annual Growth	3.6%	—	—	—

FYE: June 30

2012 Year-End Financials

Debt ratio: ——
Return on equity: (-6.30)%
Cash ($ mil.): 54
Current ratio: 1.90
Long-term debt ($ mil.): —

Dividends
Yield: —
Payout: —
Market value ($ mil.): —

SHI INTERNATIONAL CORP.

Businesses that need more than boxes of hardware and software can call SHI International. The company distributes scores of computer hardware and software products from suppliers such as Adobe Cisco HP Microsoft and McAfee. It resells PCs networking products data storage systems printers software and keyboards among other items. SHI offers a range of professional services including software licensing asset management managed desktop services systems integration and vocational training. The company serves corporate government and health care customers from nearly 30 offices across the US Canada the UK Germany France and Hong Kong. SHI was founded in 1989 by chairman Koguan Leo.

Strategy

SHI has invested some $20 million in a new data center that provided cloud services specifically what the company terms infrastructure-as-a-service (IaaS). The data center is one of six in the US that houses virtual machines for IT professionals to provide services such as application deployment disaster recovery software-as-a-service (SaaS). It also offers on-demand burst computing services where customers use the additional bandwidth to handle peaks in demand. HP Networking provides the network infrastructure for the data center which became operational in 2011. SHI's professional services unit is already provides some cloud services and data center consulting. SHI sees IaaS as a logical extension of the software asset management (SAM) service it already provides. Under the SAM program SHI handles software deployment licensing compliance and inventories across a business. SHI partners with Omaha Nebraska-based information security software specialist Solutionary to manage data security services using its ActiveGuard software product to block computer network security breaches as data center security is one of the biggest concerns for businesses in a cloud computing environment.

EXECUTIVES

President and CEO, Thai Lee, age 54
Director Human Resources, Michael Haluska
Chief Technologist Professional Services Organization, Henry Fastert
Corporate Sales Regional Director Canada, Adam Belzycki
Director Enterprise Account, Peter (Pete) Carufe
Warehouse Manager, Felipa Cousens
Director Enterprise Account, Anthony DeStefano
Director Enterprise Inside Sales, Frank Dilusto
VP Enterprise Sales, Al Fitzgerald
Director Enterprise Account, Jim Fogo
Training Program Manager, Ed Ford
Director Corporate Inside Sales, Ryan Ford
VP New Business Development, Melissa Graham
Director Software and Licensing, Patrick Hart
General Manager Corporate Sales, Hal Jagger
Corporate Sales Regional Director Western United States, Keith A. Joseph
Director Enterprise Account, Michael Kushner
VP New Business Development, Celeste Lee
Director Corporate Inside Sales Call Center, Jason E. Lee
Chairman, Koguan Leo
Controller, Akif Nizam
Director Public Sector Sales, Katie O'Kane
Corporate Sales Regional Director Eastern United States, Michael (Mike) Sampson
Corporate Sales Regional Director Central United States, Michael Schelbert
Director Marketing and Event Planning, Janet Valvano
Director Hardware and Advanced Solutions, Bill Wyckoff
Senior Director Professional Services Organization, Dave Hardy
Director Communications and Marketing, Ed McNamara
Lead Partner Cloud Services, Richard (Rich) Place

Corporate Sales Director Canada, Cheryl Stookes
Lead Partner Strategic Consulting, Richard (Rich) Taggart

LOCATIONS

HQ: SHI International Corp.
  290 Davidson Ave., Somerset NJ 08873
Phone: 732-764-8888   **Fax:** 732-764-8889
Web: www.shi.com

PRODUCTS/OPERATIONS

Selected Products

Accessories
Peripherals
Hardware
Memory
Software

Selected Services

Data services
Networking
Software asset management
Strategic consulting
Events
Webinars

COMPETITORS

Agilysys	Computacenter
Arrow Electronics	Ingram Micro
ASI Computer	Insight Enterprises
Technologies	PC Mall
Avnet	Softchoice
CDW	Tech Data
CompuCom	

HISTORICAL FINANCIALS

Company Type: Private

Income Statement

FYE: December 31

	REVENUE ($ mil.)	NET INCOME ($ mil.)	NET PROFIT MARGIN	EMPLOYEES
12/11	3,757	35	1.0%	1,700
12/08	0	0	—	0
Annual Growth	—	—	—	—

2011 Year-End Financials

Debt ratio: ——
Return on equity: 1.00%
Cash ($ mil.): 88
Current ratio: 1.10
Long-term debt ($ mil.): —

Dividends
  Yield: —
  Payout: —
  Market value ($ mil.): —

SHIEL SEXTON COMPANY INC.

LOCATIONS

HQ: SHIEL SEXTON COMPANY INC.
  902 N CAPITOL AVE, INDIANAPOLIS, IN 46204-1005
Phone: 317-423-6000

HISTORICAL FINANCIALS

Company Type: Private

Income Statement

FYE: September 30

	REVENUE ($ mil.)	NET INCOME ($ mil.)	NET PROFIT MARGIN	EMPLOYEES
09/11	288	(3)	—	380
09/10	293	2	0.9%	0
09/09	319	4	1.3%	0
09/08	253	4	1.8%	0
Annual Growth	4.4%	—	—	—

2011 Year-End Financials

Debt ratio: ——
Return on equity: (-1.20)%
Cash ($ mil.): 21
Current ratio: 1.00
Long-term debt ($ mil.): —

Dividends
  Yield: —
  Payout: —
  Market value ($ mil.): —

SHORE HEALTH SYSTEM INC.

LOCATIONS

HQ: SHORE HEALTH SYSTEM INC.
  219 S WASHINGTON ST, EASTON, MD 21601-2913
Phone: 410-822-1000
Web: www.shorehealth.org

HISTORICAL FINANCIALS

Company Type: Private

Income Statement

FYE: June 30

	REVENUE ($ mil.)	NET INCOME ($ mil.)	NET PROFIT MARGIN	EMPLOYEES
06/11	232	23	10.0%	1,800
06/10	213	11	5.4%	0
06/09	207	0	—	0
06/08	194	0	0.2%	0
Annual Growth	6.1%	316.9%	—	—

2011 Year-End Financials

Debt ratio: ——
Return on equity: 10.00%
Cash ($ mil.): 13
Current ratio: 0.10
Long-term debt ($ mil.): —

Dividends
  Yield: —
  Payout: —
  Market value ($ mil.): —

SILVER TOWNE L.P.

LOCATIONS

HQ: SILVER TOWNE L.P.
120 E UNION CITY PIKE, WINCHESTER, IN
47394-8383
Phone: 765-584-7481
Web: www.silvertowne.com

HISTORICAL FINANCIALS
Company Type: Private

Income Statement
FYE: December 31

	REVENUE ($ mil.)	NET INCOME ($ mil.)	NET PROFIT MARGIN	EMPLOYEES
12/11	509	4	0.8%	80
12/09	259	3	1.3%	0
12/07	126	2	2.0%	0
12/06	121	0	0.8%	0
Annual Growth	**61.4%**	**65.5%**	—	—

2011 Year-End Financials

Debt ratio: ——
Return on equity: 0.80%
Cash ($ mil.): 0
Current ratio: 0.70
Long-term debt ($ mil.): —

Dividends
Yield: —
Payout: —
Market value ($ mil.): —

SILVERTON HEALTH

LOCATIONS

HQ: SILVERTON HEALTH
342 FAIRVIEW ST, SILVERTON, OR 97381-1917
Phone: 503-873-1500
Web: www.silvertonhospital.org

HISTORICAL FINANCIALS
Company Type: Private

Income Statement
FYE: September 30

	REVENUE ($ mil.)	NET INCOME ($ mil.)	NET PROFIT MARGIN	EMPLOYEES
09/11	113	2	2.1%	642
09/10	104	3	2.9%	0
09/09	100	3	3.0%	0
09/06	62	2	3.8%	0
Annual Growth	**22.1%**	**0.3%**	—	—

2011 Year-End Financials

Debt ratio: ——
Return on equity: 2.10%
Cash ($ mil.): 2
Current ratio: 0.90
Long-term debt ($ mil.): —

Dividends
Yield: —
Payout: —
Market value ($ mil.): —

SIMON ROOFING AND SHEET METAL CORP.

LOCATIONS

HQ: SIMON ROOFING AND SHEET METAL CORP.
70 KARAGO AVE, YOUNGSTOWN, OH 44512-5949
Phone: 330-629-7663
Web: www.simonroofing.com

HISTORICAL FINANCIALS
Company Type: Private

Income Statement
FYE: December 31

	REVENUE ($ mil.)	NET INCOME ($ mil.)	NET PROFIT MARGIN	EMPLOYEES
12/11	82	1	1.2%	500
12/10	59	1	2.6%	0
12/09	67	2	4.4%	0
12/08	50	0	0.3%	0
Annual Growth	**17.3%**	**93.2%**	—	—

2011 Year-End Financials

Debt ratio: ——
Return on equity: 1.20%
Cash ($ mil.): 1
Current ratio: 1.00
Long-term debt ($ mil.): —

Dividends
Yield: —
Payout: —
Market value ($ mil.): —

SINAI HOSPITAL OF BALTIMORE INC

Sinai Hospital of Baltimore part of the LifeBridge Health network provides medical care in northwestern Baltimore. The 470-bed hospital is a not-for-profit medical center that includes such facilities as a heart center a children's hospital a cancer institute and a rehab center. Other specialties include orthopedics neurology and women's care. Medical students from Johns Hopkins University and the University of Maryland do some of their training at the hospital. Sinai Hospital of Baltimore was founded in 1866 as the Hebrew Hospital and Asylum and became a subsidiary of LifeBridge when it merged with other area providers in 1998.

Operations

The Sinai Hospital of Baltimore handles about 26000 inpatient admissions and some 75000 emergency room visits per year. It also conducts about 20000 inpatient and outpatient surgeries annually.

The medical center conducts a number of education and training programs including residencies and fellowships for about 400 medical students each year. It is a designated training site for the Johns Hopkins University's ambulatory and internal medicine clerkships.

Strategy

Sinai Hospital of Baltimore has completed several expansion efforts in recent years. In 2012 it opened a new dedicated inpatient hospice unit as well as a new center for geriatric surgery. In addition the 20-bed Friedman Neurological Rehabilitation Center was completed that year.

EXECUTIVES

President and COO, Neil M. Meltzer, $343,251 total compensation
SVP Finance and CFO, Charles (Chuck) Orlando
VP Marketing and Public Relations, Rudy Miller
Patient Safety Officer, Tina Gionet
VP Human Resources, Taylor Foss
Coordinator Auxiliary Services, Sharon Rosen
President Medical Staff, Joel Pleeter
Physician-in-Chief, Steven Gambert
VP, Barbara Epke
VP and Chief Nursing Officer, Diane Johnson
VP, Lorrie Liang
SVP Finance and CFO, Chuck Orlando
VP, Ida Samet
COO Practice Dynamics, Jeff Watson
Auditors: PricewaterhouseCoopersLLP

LOCATIONS

HQ: Sinai Hospital of Baltimore Inc.
2401 W. Belvedere Ave., Baltimore MD 21215
Phone: 410-601-9000   **Fax:** 410-601-8492
Web: www.lifebridgehealth.org/sinai.cfm

PRODUCTS/OPERATIONS

Selected Centers

Alvin & Lois Lapidus Cancer Institute at LifeBridge Health
Center for Joint Preservation and Replacement
Children's Hospital at Sinai
ER-7 Emergency Center
Heart Center at Sinai
International Center for Limb Lengthening
Krieger Eye Institute
Louis and Phyllis Friedman Neurological Rehabilitation Center
Rubin Institute for Advanced Orthopedics
Sandra and Malcolm Berman Brain & Spine Institute
Sinai Rehabilitation Center
The Spine Center at Sinai

Selected Services

Allergy and Immunology
Anesthesia
Cardiology
Cancer/Medical Oncology
Dermatology
Dialysis
Emergency Medicine
Endocrinology and Metabolism
Family Medicine
Gastroenterology
General Internal Medicine
Geriatric Medicine
Infectious Diseases
Nephrology (kidneys)
Pulmonary and Critical Care Medicine
Rheumatology (joints tendons)
Neurology
Neurosurgery
Obstetrics and Gynecology
Ophthalmology (eye care)
Oral and Maxillofacial Surgery and Dentistry
Orthopedic Surgery
Otolaryngology (ear nose & throat)
Pathology
Pediatrics
Pharmacy
Physical Medicine and Rehabilitation
Psychiatry
Radiation Oncology
Radiology
Surgery
Urology

COMPETITORS

Anne Arundel Medical Center	Johns Hopkins Health System
Ascension Health	MedStar Health
Bon Secours Health	University of Maryland
Franklin Square Hospital Center	Medical System
GBMC	Washington County Health System

HISTORICAL FINANCIALS

Company Type: Subsidiary

Income Statement   FYE: June 30

	REVENUE ($ mil.)	NET INCOME ($ mil.)	NET PROFIT MARGIN	EMPLOYEES
06/11	691	36	5.3%	1,403
06/10	665	14	2.1%	0
06/09	577	(3)	—	0
06/08	636	19	3.1%	0
Annual Growth	2.8%	22.5%	—	—

2011 Year-End Financials

Debt ratio: —
Return on equity: 5.30%
Cash ($ mil.): 88
Current ratio: 1.90
Long-term debt ($ mil.): —

Dividends
Yield: —
Payout: —
Market value ($ mil.): —

SINGER EQUIPMENT COMPANY INC.

LOCATIONS

HQ: SINGER EQUIPMENT COMPANY INC.
150 S TWIN VALLEY RD, ELVERSON, PA 19520-9387
Phone: 610-387-6400
Web: www.singerequipment.com

HISTORICAL FINANCIALS

Company Type: Private

Income Statement   FYE: January 1

	REVENUE ($ mil.)	NET INCOME ($ mil.)	NET PROFIT MARGIN	EMPLOYEES
01/11*	125	1	1.6%	240
12/05	98	1	1.3%	0
12/00	62	1	2.1%	0
Annual Growth	42.4%	24.5%	—	—

*Fiscal year change

2011 Year-End Financials

Debt ratio: —
Return on equity: 1.60%
Cash ($ mil.): 0
Current ratio: —
Long-term debt ($ mil.): —

Dividends
Yield: —
Payout: —
Market value ($ mil.): —

SINGLE SOURCE INC.

LOCATIONS

HQ: SINGLE SOURCE INC.
8160 S CASS AVE, DARIEN, IL 60561-5013
Phone: 630-985-6400

HISTORICAL FINANCIALS

Company Type: Private

Income Statement   FYE: December 31

	REVENUE ($ mil.)	NET INCOME ($ mil.)	NET PROFIT MARGIN	EMPLOYEES
12/11	106	0	0.7%	20
12/10	100	0	0.9%	0
12/09	110	1	1.1%	0
12/08	133	1	0.9%	0
Annual Growth	(7.2%)	(13.5%)	—	—

SISTEMA UNIVERSITARIO ANA G. MENDEZ INC.

LOCATIONS

HQ: SISTEMA UNIVERSITARIO ANA G. MENDEZ INC.
CARR 176 KM 0 3 CPEY LOWR ST CA, SAN JUAN, PR 00926
Phone: 787-751-0178
Web: www.suagm.edu

HISTORICAL FINANCIALS

Company Type: Private

Income Statement   FYE: July 31

	REVENUE ($ mil.)	NET INCOME ($ mil.)	NET PROFIT MARGIN	EMPLOYEES
07/12	259	(2)	—	5,387
07/11	262	31	12.2%	0
07/10	261	29	11.2%	0
07/09	225	7	3.4%	0
Annual Growth	4.7%	—	—	—

2012 Year-End Financials

Debt ratio: —
Return on equity: (-0.90)%
Cash ($ mil.): 4
Current ratio: —
Long-term debt ($ mil.): —

Dividends
Yield: —
Payout: —
Market value ($ mil.): —

SIVALLS INC.

LOCATIONS

HQ: SIVALLS INC.
2200 E 2ND ST, ODESSA, TX 79761-4910
Phone: 432-337-3571
Web: www.sivalls.com

HISTORICAL FINANCIALS

Company Type: Private

Income Statement   FYE: October 31

	REVENUE ($ mil.)	NET INCOME ($ mil.)	NET PROFIT MARGIN	EMPLOYEES
10/11	80	9	11.9%	422
10/10	46	2	5.3%	0
10/09	41	1	3.0%	0
10/08	56	4	8.8%	0
Annual Growth	12.7%	24.5%	—	—

2011 Year-End Financials

Debt ratio: —
Return on equity: 11.90%
Cash ($ mil.): 15
Current ratio: 2.70
Long-term debt ($ mil.): —

Dividends
Yield: —
Payout: —
Market value ($ mil.): —

SKAGIT FARMERS SUPPLY

LOCATIONS

HQ: SKAGIT FARMERS SUPPLY
1833 PARK LN, BURLINGTON, WA 98233
Phone: 360-757-6053
Web: www.skagitfarmers.com

HISTORICAL FINANCIALS

Company Type: Private

Income Statement   FYE: September 30

	REVENUE ($ mil.)	NET INCOME ($ mil.)	NET PROFIT MARGIN	EMPLOYEES
09/11	81	5	6.2%	200
09/10	71	4	5.9%	0
09/09	70	4	7.1%	0
09/03	40	2	5.4%	0
Annual Growth	26.5%	32.0%	—	—

2011 Year-End Financials

Debt ratio: —
Return on equity: 6.20%
Cash ($ mil.): 1
Current ratio: 1.20
Long-term debt ($ mil.): —

Dividends
Yield: —
Payout: —
Market value ($ mil.): —

SKIDMORE OWINGS & MERRILL LLP

Skidmore Owings & Merrill prefers a skyline view. One of the world's largest architectural and engineering firms Skidmore Owings & Merrill (or SOM) has earned its fame with innovative modernist designs and such high-profile projects as the John Hancock Building and Willis Tower (formerly the Sears Tower). Its portfolio of services includes graphics interior design and urban design and planning. Transportation planning infrastructure planning environmental engineering and geotechnical engineering are part of its structural and civil engineering offerings. The firm which has completed projects in more than 40 countries has offices in several major metropolitan US cities and in Europe and Asia.

SOM has been responsible for the look of some of the world's tallest buildings. Although it earned its reputation with its signature high-rises the firm also takes on institutional projects such as airports convention centers office buildings and schools. In addition it performs interior design work and renovation projects for older buildings. One of its most notable renovations was to the Smithsonian.

The company has designed headquarters in New York City for such blue-chip firms as Bear Stearns Random House and Time Warner. The group also was involved in designing the 1776-ft.-tall One World Trade Center tower at the site of the former World Trade Center. The National Museum of the US Army in Fairfax County Virginia is also a SOM creation.

The firm designed the Burj Khalifa the world's tallest building at some 2700 ft. in the United Arab Emirates. Similarly SOM planned Europe's tallest block of flats —two towers linked together and rising containing more than 700 apartments —in London's Docklands.

Sustainable design is a big part of the firm's offerings. It designed an office building in France that will be built to generate energy and have no carbon emissions. SOM also devised the eco-friendly master plans for an entire island off the coast of China.

SOM is calling for a 100-year plan for the Great Lakes and St. Lawrence River Region. The plan would improve water quality and the economies of the cities in the area.

One of the stalwarts of modernist design SOM has used its reputation for innovation to put its stamp on cities throughout Asia (though some critics say that it has lost its creative distinction to become the IBM of architectural firms). SOM leaders defend their style as innovative but not trendy.

HISTORY

"While studying and working in Paris in 1929 Louis Skidmore met two architects involved in planning the 1933-1934 Century of Progress Exposition in Chicago for the Chicago World's Fair. He arranged to be appointed chief designer for the exposition and asked Nathaniel Owings his brother-in-law to assist him thus beginning their professional association.

After the exposition the two pursued separate paths only to come together again in 1936 to found a small design firm in Chicago bearing their names. Trading on corporate relationships developed at the exposition the two men soon had enough work for three draftsmen.

The next year the firm opened a New York office and worked on the 1939 New York World's Fair. Gordon Bunshaft came on in 1937 and spent the next 42 years with the firm becoming one of its most famous and influential architects. By 1939 when architectural engineer John Merrill joined the firm it had developed a reputation for clean functional design.

In 1940 Skidmore & Owings won the contract that brought it to national prominence —designing the defense community of Oak Ridge Tennessee part of the Manhattan (atomic bomb) Project.

After WWII the firm now Skidmore Owings & Merrill grew rapidly opening a San Francisco office in 1946. The company's modernistic style was so distinctive by 1950 that Skidmore Owings & Merill became the first architectural firm to be granted an exhibition at New York's Museum of Modern Art. Two years later it had 14 partners and four offices.

The 1960s saw more noteworthy commissions and in 1961 Skidmore Owings & Merrill received the first architectural excellence award for firms given by the American Institute of Architects (it would win the recognition again in 1996 the only firm to win twice). It opened its Washington DC office in 1967 and was commissioned to develop the master plan for the Washington Mall. In the 1970s the firm's presence was keenly felt in Chicago where under the modernist influence of architect Bruce Graham its designs included the John Hancock building and the Sears Tower.

The group opened its first foreign office in London in 1986. That decade the firm's old-fashioned commitment to modernism in the face of postmodernism hurt its bottom line. By the time it had adapted the building boom of the 1980s had gone bust. Several offices closed and half of Skidmore Owings & Merrill's staff were laid off in 1990. To survive the firm's first chairman David Childs (appointed in 1991) cut costs and perks. He also steered the firm toward institutional work and integrating design services for clients instead of separating work by specialties. Meanwhile as some second-generation stars retired their retirement draws were a drain on company finances. Skidmore Owings & Merrill renegotiated with some retired partners but others (including John Merrill's son) sued in 1996.

The Asian financial crisis halted some projects in 1997 and the firm began focusing more on work in the US. In an ironic turn of events award-winning designer Joseph Gonzalez resigned after 20 years with the firm when it was learned that he was not licensed.

In 1999 China opened the Skidmore Owings & Merrill-designed 88-story Jin Mao Building in Shanghai China's tallest and the world's third-tallest structure behind the Petronas Twin Towers in Malaysia and the Sears Tower. The firm's plans to design the world's tallest building a 112-story Chicago skyscraper received a major setback in 2000 when financing for the project fell through.

The next year the group selected its first female chairman Marilyn Taylor who had served with the firm for more than 30 years. In 2002 the firm established the Center for Seismic Design in its San Francisco office. By 2003 the group had established offices in London and Shanghai.

Skidmore Owings & Merrill was selected to design One World Trade Center (formerly known as Freedom Tower) the primary building that will replace the fallen World Trade Center in New York City.

EXECUTIVES

General Counsel, Richard E. Viktora
Managing Partner Chicago, Jeffrey J. McCarthy
Managing Partner New York, Peter J. Magill
Design Partner New York, Gary P. Haney
Structural and Civil Engineering Partner, William F. Baker
Managing Partner New York, T. J. Gottesdiener
Managing Partner New York, Mark Regulinski
Managing Partner San Francisco, Gene Schnair
Managing Partner Chicago, Richard F. Tomlinson II
Managing Director San Francisco, Carrie Byles
Consulting Partner London, Roger Kallman
Chief Human Resources Officer, Suzanne Pennasilico
Consulting Partner Chicago, Peter G. Ellis
Director Structural Engineering San Francisco, Mark Sarkisian
Managing Partner New York, Anthony Vacchione
Technical Director San Francisco, Keith Boswell
Director China, Silas Chiow
Design Director London, Kent Jackson
Urban Design and Planning Director London, Daniel R Ringelstein
Managing Director London, Graham J Wiseman
Managing Director Washington DC, Rod Garrett
Human Resources Manager, Karen O'Doherty
Marketing Manager, Leslie Taylor
Auditors: Deloitte&ToucheLLP

LOCATIONS

HQ: Skidmore Owings & Merrill LLP
224 S. Michigan Ave. Ste. 1000, Chicago IL 60604
Phone: 312-554-9090   **Fax:** 312-360-4545
Web: www.som.com

PRODUCTS/OPERATIONS

Selected Services

Architecture
Graphics
Interiors
MEP (mechanical electrical & plumbing) engineering
Structural & civil engineering
Sustainable design
Urban design & planning

COMPETITORS

AECOM	Louis Berger
Callison Architecture	Parsons Brinckerhoff
Ellerbe Beckett	Perkins+Will
Epstein	RTKL Associates
Gensler	SmithGroupJJR
Heery	Takenaka
HOK	URS
Interior Architects	Wilbur Smith
Jacobs Engineering	Associates
Leo A Daly	
Loebl Schlossman & Hackl	

HISTORICAL FINANCIALS

Company Type: Private - Partnership

Income Statement

FYE: September 30

	REVENUE ($ mil.)	NET INCOME ($ mil.)	NET PROFIT MARGIN	EMPLOYEES
09/11*	236	48	20.6%	724
08/09	0	(0)	—	0
09/06	228	0	—	0
09/05	1,413	0	—	0
Annual Growth	(44.9%)	11286.4%	—	—

*Fiscal year change

2011 Year-End Financials
Debt ratio: ——
Return on equity: 20.60%
Cash ($ mil.): 19
Current ratio: 3.00
Long-term debt ($ mil.): ——

Dividends
Yield: ——
Payout: ——
Market value ($ mil.): ——

2011 Year-End Financials
Debt ratio: ——
Return on equity: 10.70%
Cash ($ mil.): 2
Current ratio: 0.30
Long-term debt ($ mil.): ——

Dividends
Yield: ——
Payout: ——
Market value ($ mil.): ——

SMILE TRAIN INC.

LOCATIONS

HQ: SMILE TRAIN INC.
41 MADISON AVE RM 2801, NEW YORK, NY 10010-2325
Phone: 212-689-9199
Web: www.smiletrainindonesia.com

HISTORICAL FINANCIALS
Company Type: Private

Income Statement
FYE: June 30

	REVENUE ($ mil.)	NET INCOME ($ mil.)	NET PROFIT MARGIN	EMPLOYEES
06/11	114	13	11.8%	16
06/10	105	19	18.4%	0
06/09	92	14	15.9%	0
06/08	109	22	20.6%	0
Annual Growth	1.6%	(15.8%)	—	—

2011 Year-End Financials
Debt ratio: ——
Return on equity: 11.80%
Cash ($ mil.): 25
Current ratio: 2.40
Long-term debt ($ mil.): ——

Dividends
Yield: ——
Payout: ——
Market value ($ mil.): ——

SLASHSUPPORT INC.

LOCATIONS

HQ: SLASHSUPPORT INC.
3031 TISCH WAY STE 300, SAN JOSE, CA 95128-2530
Phone: 408-985-4377
Web: www.slashsupport.com

HISTORICAL FINANCIALS
Company Type: Private

Income Statement
FYE: March 31

	REVENUE ($ mil.)	NET INCOME ($ mil.)	NET PROFIT MARGIN	EMPLOYEES
03/11	98	(0)		200
03/10	55	0	1.5%	0
03/09	55	0	1.0%	0
Annual Growth	33.2%	—	—	—

2011 Year-End Financials
Debt ratio: ——
Return on equity: (-0.80)%
Cash ($ mil.): 6
Current ratio: 1.30
Long-term debt ($ mil.): ——

Dividends
Yield: ——
Payout: ——
Market value ($ mil.): ——

SMART CIRCLE INTERNATIONAL LLC

LOCATIONS

HQ: SMART CIRCLE INTERNATIONAL LLC
19511 PAULING, FOOTHILL RANCH, CA 92610-2619
Phone: 949-587-9207

HISTORICAL FINANCIALS
Company Type: Private

Income Statement
FYE: January 28

	REVENUE ($ mil.)	NET INCOME ($ mil.)	NET PROFIT MARGIN	EMPLOYEES
01/12	202	16	7.9%	95
Annual Growth	—	—	—	—

2012 Year-End Financials
Debt ratio: ——
Return on equity: 7.90%
Cash ($ mil.): 12
Current ratio: 0.90
Long-term debt ($ mil.): ——

Dividends
Yield: ——
Payout: ——
Market value ($ mil.): ——

SMITH BAGLEY INC.

LOCATIONS

HQ: SMITH BAGLEY INC.
1500 S WHITE MOUNTAIN RD # 103, SHOW LOW, AZ 85901-7111
Phone: 928-537-0690
Web: www.cellularoneaz.com

HISTORICAL FINANCIALS
Company Type: Private

Income Statement
FYE: September 30

	REVENUE ($ mil.)	NET INCOME ($ mil.)	NET PROFIT MARGIN	EMPLOYEES
09/11	82	16	19.5%	180
09/10	74	4	6.2%	0
09/09	72	10	14.1%	0
09/08	73	7	10.3%	0
Annual Growth	4.0%	28.8%	—	—

2011 Year-End Financials
Debt ratio: ——
Return on equity: 19.50%
Cash ($ mil.): 1
Current ratio: 1.50
Long-term debt ($ mil.): ——

Dividends
Yield: ——
Payout: ——
Market value ($ mil.): ——

SMALL MINE DEVELOPMENT LLC

LOCATIONS

HQ: SMALL MINE DEVELOPMENT LLC
967 E PARKCENTER BLVD, BOISE, ID 83706-6721
Phone: 208-338-8880
Web: www.undergroundmining.com

HISTORICAL FINANCIALS
Company Type: Private

Income Statement
FYE: December 31

	REVENUE ($ mil.)	NET INCOME ($ mil.)	NET PROFIT MARGIN	EMPLOYEES
12/11	128	13	10.7%	250
12/09	80	16	20.3%	0
12/08	84	15	18.6%	0
12/07	0	0	—	0
Annual Growth	—	—	—	—

SMDC MEDICAL CENTER

LOCATIONS

HQ: SMDC MEDICAL CENTER
502 E 2ND ST, DULUTH, MN 55805-1913
Phone: 218-727-8762
Web: www.stmarysmedicalcenter.com

HISTORICAL FINANCIALS
Company Type: Private

Income Statement
FYE: June 30

	REVENUE ($ mil.)	NET INCOME ($ mil.)	NET PROFIT MARGIN	EMPLOYEES
06/11	373	13	3.7%	750
06/10	365	12	3.4%	0
06/09	208	(28)	—	0
06/08	0	0	—	0
Annual Growth	—	—	—	—

2011 Year-End Financials
Debt ratio: ——
Return on equity: 3.70%
Cash ($ mil.): 124
Current ratio: 3.50
Long-term debt ($ mil.): ——

Dividends
Yield: ——
Payout: ——
Market value ($ mil.): ——

SMITH POWER PRODUCTS INC.

LOCATIONS
HQ: SMITH POWER PRODUCTS INC.
3065 W CALIFORNIA AVE, SALT LAKE CITY, UT
84104-4586
Phone: 801-415-5000
Web: www.smithpowerproducts.com

HISTORICAL FINANCIALS
Company Type: Private

Income Statement				FYE: December 31
	REVENUE ($ mil.)	NET INCOME ($ mil.)	NET PROFIT MARGIN	EMPLOYEES
12/11	141	10	7.3%	275
12/10	104	6	6.0%	0
12/09	86	4	5.7%	0
12/08	107	8	8.2%	0
Annual Growth	9.5%	5.2%	—	—

2011 Year-End Financials
Debt ratio: ——
Return on equity: 7.30%
Cash ($ mil.): 0
Current ratio: 0.60
Long-term debt ($ mil.): —
Dividends
Yield: —
Payout: —
Market value ($ mil.): —

SNAKE RIVER SUGAR COMPANY

LOCATIONS
HQ: SNAKE RIVER SUGAR COMPANY
1951 S SATURN WAY STE 100, BOISE, ID 83709-2924
Phone: 208-383-6500
Web: www.srcoop.com

HISTORICAL FINANCIALS
Company Type: Private

Income Statement				FYE: August 31
	REVENUE ($ mil.)	NET INCOME ($ mil.)	NET PROFIT MARGIN	EMPLOYEES
08/11	876	13	1.5%	2,500
08/10	839	18	2.2%	0
08/09	658	22	3.4%	0
08/08	653	16	2.5%	0
Annual Growth	10.3%	(7.0%)	—	—

2011 Year-End Financials
Debt ratio: ——
Return on equity: 1.50%
Cash ($ mil.): 17
Current ratio: 0.30
Long-term debt ($ mil.): —
Dividends
Yield: —
Payout: —
Market value ($ mil.): —

SNAKEBITE LEASING INC.

LOCATIONS
HQ: SNAKEBITE LEASING INC.
821 S PACIFIC AVE, YUMA, AZ 85365-2117
Phone: 928-329-0777
Web: www.sellerspetroleum.com

HISTORICAL FINANCIALS
Company Type: Private

Income Statement				FYE: July 31
	REVENUE ($ mil.)	NET INCOME ($ mil.)	NET PROFIT MARGIN	EMPLOYEES
07/12	116	0	0.1%	42
07/11	0	(0)	—	0
07/10	100	0	0.0%	0
Annual Growth	7.9%	18.6%	—	—

2012 Year-End Financials
Debt ratio: ——
Return on equity: 0.10%
Cash ($ mil.): 0
Current ratio: 0.70
Long-term debt ($ mil.): —
Dividends
Yield: —
Payout: —
Market value ($ mil.): —

SNAPPING SHOALS ELECTRIC TRUST INC.

Named after a geographic area that sounds like an angler's dream Snapping Shoals Electric Membership Corporation (Snapping Shoals EMC) distributes electricity to 95000 residential commercial and industrial customers in an 8-county region in the southeastern portion of the Atlanta metropolitan area. The member-owned cooperative also provides competitive retail natural gas supply services to customers through Snapping Shoals Energy Management Company a partnership with SCANA. Snapping Shoals EMC also offers security systems surge protection services and security lighting options.

The cooperative is also a member of Green Power EMC which analyzes and negotiates power purchase agreements with Georgia-based renewable resource providers to allow member EMCs to access "greener" power supplies in order to conserve energy and help protect the environment.

Formed in 1938 as part of the national rural electrification drive Snapping Shoals EMC's service territory covers parts of Butts DeKalb Henry Jasper Morgan Newton Rockdale and Walton counties.

EXECUTIVES
President and CEO, Randall G. Meadows
VP Energy Services, Terry Clark
SVP Engineering and Operations, Brad Thomas
SVP Corporate and Energy Services, Randy Shaw
VP Engineering, Melvin Allen
VP Business Technology, Louise Blackman
Manager Member Services, Randy Price
Manager Economic Development, Danny Stone
Executive Assistant, Cathy Dyer
Chairman, James I. White
Vice Chairman, Anthony Norton
Secretary Treasurer and Director, Joseph Sharp
Accounting Supervisor, Katie Johnston
SVP Engineering and Operations, Brad Thomas
VP Line Services, Victor Hurst
Director Human Resources, Vicki Moon
Vice Chairman, Anthony Norton
Secretary Treasurer and Director, Joseph Sharp

LOCATIONS
HQ: Snapping Shoals Electric Membership Corporation
14750 Brown Bridge Rd., Covington GA 30016
Phone: 770-786-3484   **Fax:** 770-385-2720
Web: www.ssemc.com

HISTORICAL FINANCIALS
Company Type: Private - Not-for-Profit

Income Statement				FYE: December 31
	REVENUE ($ mil.)	NET INCOME ($ mil.)	NET PROFIT MARGIN	EMPLOYEES
12/11	176	2	1.6%	270
12/10	186	4	2.4%	0
12/09	179	4	2.5%	0
12/08	167	7	4.6%	0
Annual Growth	1.7%	(28.4%)	—	—

2011 Year-End Financials
Debt ratio: ——
Return on equity: 1.60%
Cash ($ mil.): 4
Current ratio: 0.60
Long-term debt ($ mil.): —
Dividends
Yield: —
Payout: —
Market value ($ mil.): —

SOCIEDAD ESPANOLA DE AUXILIO MUTUO & BENEFICENCIA DE PR

LOCATIONS
HQ: SOCIEDAD ESPANOLA DE AUXILIO MUTUO & BENEFICENCIA DE PR
AVE PONCE DE LEON, SAN JUAN, PR 00907-3907
Phone: 787-758-2000

HISTORICAL FINANCIALS
Company Type: Private

Income Statement				FYE: September 30
	REVENUE ($ mil.)	NET INCOME ($ mil.)	NET PROFIT MARGIN	EMPLOYEES
09/11	220	4	2.2%	2,100
09/10	27	1	5.8%	0
09/09	203	5	2.9%	0
09/08	29	2	7.5%	0
Annual Growth	95.9%	30.6%	—	—

2011 Year-End Financials

Debt ratio: ——
Return on equity: 2.20%
Cash ($ mil.): 29
Current ratio: 1.80
Long-term debt ($ mil.): ——

Dividends
Yield: ——
Payout: ——
Market value ($ mil.): ——

SOKA UNIVERSITY OF AMERICA INC

LOCATIONS

HQ: SOKA UNIVERSITY OF AMERICA INC
1 UNIVERSITY DR, ALISO VIEJO, CA 92656-8081
Phone: 949-297-4100
Web: www.soka.edu

HISTORICAL FINANCIALS

Company Type: Private

Income Statement

FYE: June 30

	REVENUE ($ mil.)	NET INCOME ($ mil.)	NET PROFIT MARGIN	EMPLOYEES
06/11	557	505	90.8%	100
06/10	38	(9)		0
06/09	70	21	30.4%	0
06/08	135	89	66.4%	0
Annual Growth	60.4%	78.0%	—	—

2011 Year-End Financials

Debt ratio: ——
Return on equity: 90.80%
Cash ($ mil.): 0
Current ratio: ——
Long-term debt ($ mil.): ——

Dividends
Yield: ——
Payout: ——
Market value ($ mil.): ——

SOMERSET TIRE SERVICE INC.

Somerset Tire Service (STS) operates nearly 140 tire and auto centers throughout New Jersey New York and Pennsylvania. The company primarily sells tires auto parts batteries and accessories under such top brand names as Bridgestone Firestone Michelin Toyo Pirelli Goodyear and Continental. Operating under the banner STS Tire & Auto Centers its locations feature a window between the store and service bays so customers can watch the work being done on their cars. STS has grown by acquiring other regional tire and service centers with hopes of saturating the Northeast before moving outside its home region. Founded in 1958 the company is employee-owned.

Geographic Reach

STS operates stores in the US states of New Jersey New York and Pennsylvania.

Operations

To support its distribution business STS in 2010 began operations at a 200000-sq.-ft. warehouse in Bridgewater Township New Jersey which today

represents its largest and boasts 20 loading docks and the capability of storing 325000 tires. The facility serves the company's retail stores and wholesale customers on the East Coast.

Strategy

In recent years STS has concentrated on expanding its retail footprint. In 2012 the company opened about 25 stores in its tri-state market of New York New Jersey and Pennsylvania.

Company Background

STS is recognized for its environmental commitment due to events that occurred many years ago. The company began work on a warehouse facility in 2005 having owned the land on which the facility was built since 1971. It had not started construction until decades later because the land was classified as "brownfield" (for high arsenic levels) and required substantial cleanup to be usable. (STS did not know the extent of the pollution at the time of purchase.) The cleanup efforts were substantial.

EXECUTIVES

President, William F. Caulin
VP Information Technology, Michael Cardali
VP Administration, Michael Ryan
VP Retail Operations, Kevin Traier
VP Real Estate, Ted Haase
Auditors: WithumSmith+Brown

LOCATIONS

HQ: Somerset Tire Service Inc.
400 W. Main St., Bound Brook NJ 08805
Phone: 732-356-8500   **Fax:** 732-356-8821
Web: www.ststire.com

2013 Stores

	No.
New	80
New	31
Pennsylvania	28
Total	**139**

PRODUCTS/OPERATIONS

Selected Services
Battery
General maintenance
Seasonal service
Tire services

Selected Brands
Bridgestone
Continental
Firestone
Goodyear
Michelin
Pirelli
Toyo Tires

COMPETITORS

Advance Auto Parts
AutoZone
Bridgestone Retail
  Operations
CARQUEST
Goodyear Tire &
  Rubber

Monro Muffler Brake
Pep Boys
Precision Auto
Sears
Wal-Mart

HISTORICAL FINANCIALS

Company Type: Private

Income Statement

FYE: December 31

	REVENUE ($ mil.)	NET INCOME ($ mil.)	NET PROFIT MARGIN	EMPLOYEES
12/11	201	8	4.3%	800
12/10	189	10	5.6%	0
12/09	174	9	5.2%	0
Annual Growth	7.5%	(2.4%)	—	—

2011 Year-End Financials

Debt ratio: ——
Return on equity: 4.30%
Cash ($ mil.): 4
Current ratio: 0.40
Long-term debt ($ mil.): ——

Dividends
Yield: ——
Payout: ——
Market value ($ mil.): ——

SOMERVILLE HOSPITAL

LOCATIONS

HQ: SOMERVILLE HOSPITAL
101 STATION LANDINGS 5TH # 5, MEDFORD, MA 02155
Phone: 781-306-8872

HISTORICAL FINANCIALS

Company Type: Private

Income Statement

FYE: June 30

	REVENUE ($ mil.)	NET INCOME ($ mil.)	NET PROFIT MARGIN	EMPLOYEES
06/11	119	0	—	0
06/10	106	0	—	0
Annual Growth	12.1%	—	—	—

SOUTH BAY UNION SCHOOL DISTRICT

LOCATIONS

HQ: SOUTH BAY UNION SCHOOL DISTRICT
601 ELM AVE, IMPERIAL BEACH, CA 91932-2029
Phone: 619-628-1600
Web: www.lpssanjose.org

HISTORICAL FINANCIALS

Company Type: Private

Income Statement

FYE: June 30

	REVENUE ($ mil.)	NET INCOME ($ mil.)	NET PROFIT MARGIN	EMPLOYEES
06/12	84	7	8.8%	1,200
06/05	65	(51)	—	0
06/04	20	(51)	—	0
06/03	75	(2)	—	0
Annual Growth	3.7%	—	—	—

2012 Year-End Financials

Debt ratio: ——
Return on equity: 8.80%
Cash ($ mil.): 36
Current ratio: —
Long-term debt ($ mil.): —

Dividends
Yield: —
Payout: —
Market value ($ mil.): —

SOUTH CAROLINA RESEARCH AUTHORITY INC

LOCATIONS

HQ: SOUTH CAROLINA RESEARCH AUTHORITY INC
1000 CATAWBA ST STE 100, COLUMBIA, SC
29201-5706
Phone: 843-760-3200

HISTORICAL FINANCIALS

Company Type: Private

Income Statement

FYE: June 30

	REVENUE ($ mil.)	NET INCOME ($ mil.)	NET PROFIT MARGIN	EMPLOYEES
06/12	194	1	0.7%	218
06/11	195	1	0.7%	0
06/10	172	0	0.4%	0
06/09	108	(2)	—	0
Annual Growth	21.6%	—	—	—

2012 Year-End Financials

Debt ratio: ——
Return on equity: 0.70%
Cash ($ mil.): 97
Current ratio: 1.20
Long-term debt ($ mil.): —

Dividends
Yield: —
Payout: —
Market value ($ mil.): —

SOUTH CAROLINA STATE PORTS AUTHORITY

Offering gateways for trade in the Palmetto State The South Carolina State Ports Authority (SCSPA) operates marine terminals at the ports in Charleston and Georgetown. The agency maintains its own container terminals at each port and provides container handling services; in addition space at the ports is leased to other terminal operators. The Port of Charleston provides services for cruise ships as well as for freight-carrying vessels including freight rail service. SCSPA is overseen by a nine-member board appointed by the governor along with the Secretaries of Transportation and Commerce. The agency which was founded in 1942 does not receive state money and is funded primarily by its operations.

EXECUTIVES

Chairman, David J. Posek
CFO, Peter N. Hughes
VP Operations, William A. McLean
CIO, Pamela A. Everitt
VP Terminal Development, Joe T. Bryant
VP Marketing and Sales, Fred N. Stribling
Director Planning and Business Development, Peter O. Lehman
VP Security Risk Management and Human Resources, Stephen E. Connor
Director Georgetown and Veterans, L. David Schronce
Director, Harry J. Butler Jr.
Treasurer and Director, Whitemarsh S. Smith III
Interim President and CEO; Director, John F. Hassell III
Vice Chairman, William H. Stern, age 55
General Manager Cargo Sales, J. Michael Westerfield
Manager National Accounts, S. Craig Lund
Manager Pricing and Tariffs, Ronald H. Chestnut
Manager Market Research Advertising and Publications, L. Marion Bull
Regional Sales Manager Atlanta, Matthew Pesavento
Manager International Carrier Sales, Victor Di Paolo
Regional Sales Manager New Jersey, Andrew Sallans
Director Japan Sales, Yukio (Yogi) Doi
Director Public Relations, Byron D. Miller
Manager Government Relations, Barbara L. Melvin
Director China Sales, Y. Z. Liu
Regional Sales Manager Charlotte, Sheila Cox
SVP and Chief Commercial Officer, Paul McClintock
Director, Colden R. Battey Jr., age 76
Director, Harry J. Butler Jr.
Treasurer and Director, Whitemarsh S. Smith III
Interim President and CEO; Director, John F. Hassell III
Vice Chairman, William H. Stern, age 55
Director, Karen K. Floyd
Director, S. Richard Hagins
Auditors: PricewaterhouseCoopersLLP

LOCATIONS

HQ: South Carolina State Ports Authority
176 Concord St., Charleston SC 29401
Phone: 843-723-8651 **Fax:** 406-238-2785
Web: www.billingsclinic.com

HISTORICAL FINANCIALS

Company Type: Government-owned

Income Statement

FYE: June 30

	REVENUE ($ mil.)	NET INCOME ($ mil.)	NET PROFIT MARGIN	EMPLOYEES
06/12	130	17	13.4%	493
06/11	124	21	17.0%	0
06/06	154	60	39.0%	0
06/05	138	45	32.6%	0
Annual Growth	(1.7%)	(26.9%)	—	—

2012 Year-End Financials

Debt ratio: ——
Return on equity: 13.40%
Cash ($ mil.): 5
Current ratio: 0.60
Long-term debt ($ mil.): —

Dividends
Yield: —
Payout: —
Market value ($ mil.): —

SOUTH CENTRAL COMMUNICATIONS CORPORATION

South Central Communications enjoys making waves in the central US radio market. The company owns and operates more than a dozen radio stations serving midsized and large markets in Tennessee and Indiana with a range of mostly music programming. In addition the company operates Muzak franchises (subscriber-based radio and voice services targeted to businesses) in seven states. Other operations include Dish Network installation services restaurant drive-thru intercoms and office paging systems. Its also owns Knoxville independent digital television station WMAK. The family-owned company was started in 1946 by John A. Engelbrecht.

EXECUTIVES

Chairman and President, John D. Engelbrecht, age 60
CEO and Director, JP Engelbrecht
CFO Secretary and Treasurer, Bob Shirel
President South Central Radio Group, Craig Jacobus
President South Central Sound, Bill Lyons
General Manager South Central Television, David Williams
Chief Financial Officer, Randy Champion
Director, John M. Dunn, age 74
CEO and Director, JP Engelbrecht
Director, Wendell Dixon
Director, Dave Knapp
Director, Andy Goebel
Director, Steve Sandford

LOCATIONS

HQ: South Central Communications Corp.
20 NW 3rd St., Evansville IN 47708-1200
Phone: 812-463-7950 **Fax:** 812-463-7915
Web: www.southcentralcommunications.net

Selected Radio Markets

Evansville IN
Knoxville TN
Nashville TN

PRODUCTS/OPERATIONS

Selected Operations

South Central Radio Group
South Central Sound
 Muzak digital music services
 Paging systems
 Restaurant intercom systems
 Satellite television installation
South Central Television (WMAK; Knoxville TN)

COMPETITORS

Citadel Broadcasting
Clear Channel
Cumulus Media
Journal Broadcast
Group

SIRIUS XM
Townsquare Media

HISTORICAL FINANCIALS

Company Type: Private

Income Statement				FYE: December 31
	REVENUE ($ mil.)	NET INCOME ($ mil.)	NET PROFIT MARGIN	EMPLOYEES
12/11	40	4	10.0%	285
12/10	38	3	8.2%	0
Annual Growth	5.8%	28.8%	—	—

2011 Year-End Financials

Debt ratio: ——
Return on equity: 10.00%
Cash ($ mil.): 4
Current ratio: 1.90
Long-term debt ($ mil.): —

Dividends
 Yield: —
 Payout: —
Market value ($ mil.): —

SOUTH CENTRAL LOS ANGELES REGIONAL CENTER FOR DEVELOPMENTALLY DI

LOCATIONS

HQ: SOUTH CENTRAL LOS ANGELES REGIONAL CENTER FOR DEVELOPMENTALLY DI
650 W ADAMS BLVD STE 200, LOS ANGELES, CA 90007-2579
Phone: 213-744-7000
Web: www.sclarc.org

HISTORICAL FINANCIALS

Company Type: Private

Income Statement				FYE: June 30
	REVENUE ($ mil.)	NET INCOME ($ mil.)	NET PROFIT MARGIN	EMPLOYEES
06/11	133	0	—	235
06/10	134	0	0.0%	0
06/06	119	0	0.0%	0
06/05	112	0	0.5%	0
Annual Growth	5.6%	(97.8%)	—	—

2011 Year-End Financials

Debt ratio: ——
Return on equity: ——
Cash ($ mil.): 20
Current ratio: ——
Long-term debt ($ mil.): —

Dividends
 Yield: —
 Payout: —
Market value ($ mil.): —

SOUTH COLONIE CENTRAL SCHOOLS DISTRICT

LOCATIONS

HQ: SOUTH COLONIE CENTRAL SCHOOLS DISTRICT
 102 LORALEE DR, ALBANY, NY 12205-2223
Phone: 518-869-3576
Web: www.southcolonieschools.org

HISTORICAL FINANCIALS

Company Type: Private

Income Statement				FYE: June 30
	REVENUE ($ mil.)	NET INCOME ($ mil.)	NET PROFIT MARGIN	EMPLOYEES
06/12	91	(3)	—	892
06/11	91	(2)	—	0
06/10	93	2	3.0%	0
06/09	91	4	5.0%	0
Annual Growth	(0.2%)	—	—	—

2012 Year-End Financials

Debt ratio: ——
Return on equity: (-3.40)%
Cash ($ mil.): 14
Current ratio: 1.10
Long-term debt ($ mil.): —

Dividends
 Yield: —
 Payout: —
Market value ($ mil.): —

SOUTH COUNTY HOSPITAL HEALTHCARE SYSTEM

LOCATIONS

HQ: SOUTH COUNTY HOSPITAL HEALTHCARE SYSTEM
 100 KENYON AVE, WAKEFIELD, RI 02879-4216
Phone: 401-782-8000
Web: www.schospital.com

HISTORICAL FINANCIALS

Company Type: Private

Income Statement				FYE: September 30
	REVENUE ($ mil.)	NET INCOME ($ mil.)	NET PROFIT MARGIN	EMPLOYEES
09/11	117	2	2.5%	600
09/08	98	(3)	—	0
09/05	86	0	0.2%	0
09/04	468	0	0.0%	0
Annual Growth	(37.0%)	1568.9%	—	—

2011 Year-End Financials

Debt ratio: ——
Return on equity: 2.50%
Cash ($ mil.): 6
Current ratio: 1.00
Long-term debt ($ mil.): —

Dividends
 Yield: —
 Payout: —
Market value ($ mil.): —

SOUTH DAKOTA SOYBEAN PROCESSORS LLC

Things are "soy-good" at South Dakota Soybean Processors. The agricultural cooperative turns the 30 million bushels per year of soybeans from its 2200 farmer/members into soybean oil soybean hulls and soybean meal. Its soybean meal is mainly sold to livestock feed companies and independent livestock producers. Most of South Dakota Soybean's crude soybean oil is processed into refined and bleached oil under the name Soyol which is sold to manufacturers of various consumer items (plastics and biodiesel manufacturers for example) who further process it for use in their products. The co-op owns 91% of Urethane Soy Systems Company (USSC) which it supplies with Soyol products.

Solyol is used in such products as household appliances building insulation carpet and carpet padding shoe soles roof coatings mattresses pillows and automobile bumpers and interiors

South Dakota Soybean's two main customers for soybean meal and hulls are Archer Daniels Midland and Commodity Specialists. Until 2008 its largest refined-oil customer was ACH with which the company had a supply agreement. However ACH and Archer Daniels formed a soybean-oil joint venture decreasing both companies' need for South Dakota's refined oil products; therefore South Dakota sells refined oil to ACH on a bid-only basis.

The co-op's facilities consist of facilities consist of one soybean processing plant a soybean oil refinery a bio-based polyurethane production facility a quality-control laboratory and administrative and operations buildings.

EXECUTIVES

CEO, Rodney G. Christianson, age 59, $322,917 total compensation
Commercial Manager, Thomas J. (Tom) Kersting, age 49, $188,333 total compensation
CFO, Mark Hyde, age 39, $92,000 total compensation
Director and Manager District 4, Paul Barthel, age 42
Director and Manager Distirct 5, Dean Christopherson, age 63
Director and Manager District 7, Wayne Enger, age 57
Director, Peter Kontz, age 69
Director, Bryce Loomis, age 69
Director and Manager District 2, Delbert Tschakert, age 55
Director and Manager District 3, Ardon Wek, age 54
Director, Ronald J. Gorder, age 49
Director, Robert Nelsen, age 67
Director, Jerome Jerzak, age 65

Director, David Driessen, age 57
Director and Manager District 6, Randy Tauer, age 50
Director, Alan Christensen, age 57
Director, Dan Fiege, age 57
Director, James H. Jepsen, age 56
Director, Maurice Odenbrett, age 67
Director, Lyle R. Trautman, age 58
Director, Gary Wertish, age 61
Director, Paul Dummer, age 58
Director and Manager District 1, Marvin Hope
Auditors: GordonHughes&BanksLLP

LOCATIONS

HQ: SOUTH DAKOTA SOYBEAN PROCESSORS LLC
100 CASPIAN AVE, VOLGA, SD 57071-9006
Phone: 605-647-9240
Web: www.sdsbp.com

2008 Sales

	$ mil.	% of total
US	332	92
Canada	28	8
Total	360	100

COMPETITORS

ACH Food Companies	DeBruce Grain
ADM	Dow Chemical
Ag Processing Inc.	Federated
BASF SE	Co-operatives
Bayer AG	Huntsman International
Bunge Limited	Minn-Dak Co-op
Bunge Milling	Procter & Gamble
Bunge North America	Scoular
Cargill	Smucker
ConAgra	

HISTORICAL FINANCIALS

Company Type: Private - Cooperative

Income Statement
FYE: September 30

	REVENUE ($ mil.)	NET INCOME ($ mil.)	NET PROFIT MARGIN	EMPLOYEES
09/12*	294	9	3.2%	80
12/11	397	(3)	—	0
12/10	287	(0)	—	0
12/09	268	(6)	—	0
Annual Growth	3.1%	—	—	—

*Fiscal year change

2012 Year-End Financials

Debt ratio: —
Return on equity: 3.20%
Cash ($ mil.): 0
Current ratio: 0.20
Long-term debt ($ mil.): —

Dividends
Yield: —
Payout: —
Market value ($ mil.): —

SOUTH LAKE HOSPITAL INC.

LOCATIONS

HQ: SOUTH LAKE HOSPITAL INC.
1900 DON WICKHAM DR LBBY, CLERMONT, FL 34711-1999
Phone: 352-394-4071
Web: www.southlakehospital.com

HISTORICAL FINANCIALS

Company Type: Private

Income Statement
FYE: September 30

	REVENUE ($ mil.)	NET INCOME ($ mil.)	NET PROFIT MARGIN	EMPLOYEES
09/11	142	15	11.1%	1,000
09/10	136	15	11.4%	0
09/09	131	15	11.8%	0
09/08	122	12	10.1%	0
Annual Growth	5.1%	8.3%	—	—

2011 Year-End Financials

Debt ratio: —
Return on equity: 11.10%
Cash ($ mil.): 33
Current ratio: 2.40
Long-term debt ($ mil.): —

Dividends
Yield: —
Payout: —
Market value ($ mil.): —

SOUTH NASSAU COMMUNITIES HOSPITAL INC

LOCATIONS

HQ: SOUTH NASSAU COMMUNITIES HOSPITAL INC
1 HEALTHY WAY, OCEANSIDE, NY 11572-1551
Phone: 516-632-3000
Web: www.southnassaurn.org

HISTORICAL FINANCIALS

Company Type: Private

Income Statement
FYE: December 31

	REVENUE ($ mil.)	NET INCOME ($ mil.)	NET PROFIT MARGIN	EMPLOYEES
12/11	386	(49)	—	2,400
12/10	383	39	10.4%	0
12/09	365	39	10.9%	0
12/08	323	(69)	—	0
Annual Growth	6.1%	—	—	—

2011 Year-End Financials

Debt ratio: —
Return on equity: (-12.70)%
Cash ($ mil.): 21
Current ratio: 0.80
Long-term debt ($ mil.): —

Dividends
Yield: —
Payout: —
Market value ($ mil.): —

SOUTH PENINSULA HOSPITALS INC.

South Peninsula Hospital provides a variety of medical services including home health care emergency medicine surgery orthopedics and ophthalmology for the residents of the Kenai Peninsula and surrounding areas in Alaska. The hospital also provides a 25-bed long-term facility that offers physical and occupational therapy services. In addition South Peninsula Hospital provides community and staff education classes.

EXECUTIVES

President and CEO, Robert Letson
Chief of Staff, Charles Burgess
Director Human Resources, Cindy Brinkerhoff
Secretary/Treasurer and Director, Pat Hartley
Interim CFO, Tom Davis
Controller, Lori Meyer
Chief of Staff, Randy Wiest
Director Patient Care Services, Christine Anderson
Chairman, Walt Partridge
Vice Chairman, Peg Coleman
Director Education, Ann Marie Bailey
Director Support Services, Larry Dallas
Director, William Marley
Secretary/Treasurer and Director, Pat Hartley
Director, Arthur Tilgner
Director, Terry Thompson
Vice Chairman, Peg Coleman

LOCATIONS

HQ: South Peninsula Hospital Inc.
4300 Bartlett St., Homer AK 99603
Phone: 907-235-8101   Fax: 907-235-0253
Web: www.sphosp.com

HISTORICAL FINANCIALS

Company Type: Private - Not-for-Profit

Income Statement
FYE: June 30

	REVENUE ($ mil.)	NET INCOME ($ mil.)	NET PROFIT MARGIN	EMPLOYEES
06/12	39	2	5.7%	350
06/11	34	(0)	—	0
06/10	41	1	4.6%	0
06/09	27	2	8.3%	0
Annual Growth	12.9%	(0.5%)	—	—

2012 Year-End Financials

Debt ratio: —
Return on equity: 5.70%
Cash ($ mil.): 7
Current ratio: 2.70
Long-term debt ($ mil.): —

Dividends
Yield: —
Payout: —
Market value ($ mil.): —

SOUTH PLAINS ELECTRIC COOPERATIVE INC.

LOCATIONS

HQ: SOUTH PLAINS ELECTRIC COOPERATIVE INC.
4727 S LOOP 289 STE 200, LUBBOCK, TX 79424-2263
Phone: 806-775-7732
Web: www.southplainselectric.com

HISTORICAL FINANCIALS
Company Type: Private

Income Statement
FYE: December 31

	REVENUE ($ mil.)	NET INCOME ($ mil.)	NET PROFIT MARGIN	EMPLOYEES
12/11	130	12	9.9%	144
12/10*	114	10	9.1%	0
11/10	105	3	3.7%	0
12/09	111	9	8.1%	0
Annual Growth	5.4%	12.6%	—	—

*Fiscal year change

2011 Year-End Financials
Debt ratio: ——
Return on equity: 9.90%
Cash ($ mil.): 10
Current ratio: 0.80
Long-term debt ($ mil.): ——
Dividends
Yield: —
Payout: —
Market value ($ mil.): —

HISTORICAL FINANCIALS
Company Type: Private

Income Statement
FYE: June 30

	REVENUE ($ mil.)	NET INCOME ($ mil.)	NET PROFIT MARGIN	EMPLOYEES
06/12	83	(7)	—	1,831
06/11	79	14	17.7%	0
06/10	80	(4)	—	0
06/09	74	(12)	—	0
Annual Growth	3.9%	—	—	—

2012 Year-End Financials
Debt ratio: ——
Return on equity: (-8.40)%
Cash ($ mil.): 32
Current ratio: 2.30
Long-term debt ($ mil.): ——
Dividends
Yield: —
Payout: —
Market value ($ mil.): —

HISTORICAL FINANCIALS
Company Type: Private

Income Statement
FYE: December 31

	REVENUE ($ mil.)	NET INCOME ($ mil.)	NET PROFIT MARGIN	EMPLOYEES
12/11*	86	2	2.7%	200
05/08	43	0	1.2%	0
05/07	29	(0)	—	0
05/06	18	(0)	—	0
Annual Growth	66.3%	—	—	—

*Fiscal year change

2011 Year-End Financials
Debt ratio: ——
Return on equity: 2.70%
Cash ($ mil.): 4
Current ratio: 0.60
Long-term debt ($ mil.): ——
Dividends
Yield: —
Payout: —
Market value ($ mil.): —

SOUTHCENTRAL FOUNDATION

LOCATIONS
HQ: SOUTHCENTRAL FOUNDATION
4501 DIPLOMACY DR, ANCHORAGE, AK 99508-5919
Phone: 907-729-4955
Web: www.southcentralfoundation.org

HISTORICAL FINANCIALS
Company Type: Private

Income Statement
FYE: September 30

	REVENUE ($ mil.)	NET INCOME ($ mil.)	NET PROFIT MARGIN	EMPLOYEES
09/11	206	12	6.2%	1,100
09/10	201	19	9.8%	0
09/08	157	10	6.6%	0
09/05	141	17	12.1%	0
Annual Growth	13.5%	(8.9%)	—	—

2011 Year-End Financials
Debt ratio: ——
Return on equity: 6.20%
Cash ($ mil.): 46
Current ratio: 1.60
Long-term debt ($ mil.): —
Dividends
Yield: —
Payout: —
Market value ($ mil.): —

SOUTHEASTERN REGIONAL MEDICAL CENTER

LOCATIONS
HQ: SOUTHEASTERN REGIONAL MEDICAL CENTER
300 W 27TH ST, LUMBERTON, NC 28358-3075
Phone: 910-671-5000
Web: www.srmc.org

HISTORICAL FINANCIALS
Company Type: Private

Income Statement
FYE: September 30

	REVENUE ($ mil.)	NET INCOME ($ mil.)	NET PROFIT MARGIN	EMPLOYEES
09/11	282	17	6.2%	2,000
09/10	288	10	3.7%	0
09/09	274	1	0.6%	0
09/08	248	(8)	—	0
Annual Growth	4.3%	—	—	—

2011 Year-End Financials
Debt ratio: ——
Return on equity: 6.20%
Cash ($ mil.): 12
Current ratio: 0.30
Long-term debt ($ mil.): —
Dividends
Yield: —
Payout: —
Market value ($ mil.): —

SOUTHERN BAPTIST HOSPITAL OF FLORIDA INC.

LOCATIONS
HQ: SOUTHERN BAPTIST HOSPITAL OF FLORIDA INC.
800 PRUDENTIAL DR, JACKSONVILLE, FL 32207-8202
Phone: 904-202-2000
Web: www.e-baptisthealth.com

HISTORICAL FINANCIALS
Company Type: Private

Income Statement
FYE: September 30

	REVENUE ($ mil.)	NET INCOME ($ mil.)	NET PROFIT MARGIN	EMPLOYEES
09/11	847	63	7.5%	4,000
09/09	793	(21)	—	0
09/08	1,007	82	8.1%	0
09/07	685	99	14.6%	0
Annual Growth	7.3%	(14.1%)	—	—

2011 Year-End Financials
Debt ratio: ——
Return on equity: 7.50%
Cash ($ mil.): 0
Current ratio: 1.10
Long-term debt ($ mil.): —
Dividends
Yield: —
Payout: —
Market value ($ mil.): —

SOUTHEASTERN LOUISIANA UNIVERSITY

LOCATIONS
HQ: SOUTHEASTERN LOUISIANA UNIVERSITY
500 NED MCGEHEE DR, HAMMOND, LA 70402-0001
Phone: 985-549-2068
Web: www.leadershipsttammany.org

SOUTHEASTRANS INC.

LOCATIONS
HQ: SOUTHEASTRANS INC.
4751 BEST RD STE 201, ATLANTA, GA 30337-5615
Phone: 678-510-4600
Web: www.southeastrans.com

SOUTHERN GRAPHIC SYSTEMS INC.

LOCATIONS

HQ: SOUTHERN GRAPHIC SYSTEMS INC.
626 W MAIN ST STE 500, LOUISVILLE, KY
40202-4269
Phone: 502-637-5443
Web: www.sgsintl.com

HISTORICAL FINANCIALS

Company Type: Private

Income Statement

FYE: December 31

	REVENUE ($ mil.)	NET INCOME ($ mil.)	NET PROFIT MARGIN	EMPLOYEES
12/11	265	9	3.4%	1,200
12/09	0	0	—	0
Annual Growth	—	—	—	—

2011 Year-End Financials

Debt ratio: ——
Return on equity: 3.40%
Cash ($ mil.): 4
Current ratio: 1.40
Long-term debt ($ mil.): —

Dividends
Yield: —
Payout: —
Market value ($ mil.): —

SOUTHERN ILLINOIS HEALTHCARE ENTERPRISES INC

Southern Illinois Healthcare a nonprofit health care system operates the flagship 140-bed tertiary-care Memorial Hospital of Carbondale as well as Herrin Hospital (with 114 beds) and St. Joseph Memorial Hospital (with 25 beds). The hospitals serve residents of a 16-county region across southern Illinois. The nearly 280-bed system provides services such as birthing cardiac cancer and emergency care as well as surgery and rehabilitation. Its cardiac care is offered through an affiliation with the Prairie Heart Institute at St. John's Hospital in Springfield Illinois. The medical school at Southern Illinois University conducts its Family Practice Residency Program at Memorial Hospital of Carbondale.

Operations

Across its health system Southern Illinois Healthcare employs more than 3000 people. Physicians at its primary hospital Memorial Hospital of Carbondale represent nearly 40 medical specialties. It maintains the only dedicated pediatric unit in the region as well as the largest birthing center with Level II Plus Special Care Nursery.

EXECUTIVES

President and CEO, Rex Budde
VP; Administrator St. Joseph Memorial Hospital, Scott Seaborn
VP and General Counsel, Bill Sherwood
VP; Administrator Ambulatory and Physician Services, Phil Schaefer
VP Human Resources, Pam Henderson
VP; Administrator Herrin Hospital Miners Memorial Health Center, Becky Ashton
VP Information Technology, David Holland
VP; Administrator Memorial Hospital of Carbondale, Bart Millstead
VP CFO and Treasurer, Mike Kasser
President and CEO Southern Illinois Healthcare Foundation, Larry McCulley
VP; Administrator Herrin Hospital and Miners Memorial Health Center, Terence Farrell
VP and Chief Nursing Officer, Julie Firman
Auditors: McGladreyLLP

LOCATIONS

HQ: Southern Illinois Healthcare Enterprises Inc.
1239 E. Main St., Carbondale IL 62902
Phone: 618-457-5200 **Fax:** 618-529-0563
Web: www.sih.net

PRODUCTS/OPERATIONS

Selected Facilities

Herrin Hospital
Memorial Hospital of Carbondale
St. Joseph Memorial Hospital

Selected Services

Birthing Center
Cancer
Senior Renewal
Heart
Infusion Therapy
Neurosciences
Occupational Health
Pediatrics
Rehabilitation
Robotic-assisted Surgery
Sleep Medicine
Stroke
Surgical Services
Weight Loss Surgery
Wound Healing

COMPETITORS

Community Health Systems
Heartland Health Memorial Hospital (Illinois)

Saint Francis Medical Center
St. John's Hospital (Illinois)

HISTORICAL FINANCIALS

Company Type: Private - Not-for-Profit

Income Statement

FYE: March 31

	REVENUE ($ mil.)	NET INCOME ($ mil.)	NET PROFIT MARGIN	EMPLOYEES
03/12	385	6	1.7%	1,600
03/11	394	52	13.2%	0
Annual Growth	(2.2%)	(87.6%)	—	—

2012 Year-End Financials

Debt ratio: ——
Return on equity: 1.70%
Cash ($ mil.): 8
Current ratio: 1.40
Long-term debt ($ mil.): —

Dividends
Yield: —
Payout: —
Market value ($ mil.): —

SOUTHERN MINNESOTA BEET SUGAR COOPERATIVE

Southern Minnesota Beet Sugar Cooperative (SMBSC) offers a sweet deal to its approximately 585 member/farmers. The co-op processes some 6500 sugar beets and 11250 cwt (hundredweight) sugar or more a day. Converted products include baker's sugar and fruit sugar as well as molasses beet pulp pellets and shreds and raffinate (liquid from desugaring molasses). The co-op also provides member services such as seed agronomy research farm support products and workers' compensation insurance. SMBSC's refined and liquid sugars are marketed through Cargill Sweeteners; the by-products (dried beet pulp and beet molasses for use in cattle feed) are marketed by Midwest Agri-Commodities in North American and Europe.

SMBSC's operations consist of a main factory with an annual processing capacity of about 2.6 million tons of sugar beets. The factory campus comprises settling ponds water-holding lagoons receiving strips off-site receiving stations and 1100 acres of land some of which is planted with grass and irrigated with waste water from the ponds and treatment plant. In addition the co-op has several silos to hold bulk granulated sugar a warehouse to store industrial-size bags of sugar and more than a dozen thick-juice storage tanks. Campus expansions since the factory's start in 1975 have included a molasses desugarization facility increases to processing capacity and new equipment.

SMBSC's performance is in large part at the mercy of nature. Planting season in 2011 was delayed due to heavy rainfall; more than 120000 acres were planted 80% of which was planted in late May and early June. Rain heat and humidity threatened to cause root rot and leafspot. August September and October posted low rainfall limiting growth and an early freeze damaged plants already under stress. As a result some 119000 acres were harvested yielding a disappointing 17 tons and some 16% sugar.

The co-op has grown both through investments in added capacity to attract new member/farmers and acquisitions. Acquired in 2005 subsidiary Spreckels Sugar Company operates a beet sugar factory in Brawley California. Sugar produced under the Spreckels Sugar brand is sold to markets in the western US. Based in Sheridan Wyoming SMBSC's Holly Seed a former subsidiary of Imperial Sugar also acquired in 2005 develops beet seed varieties to increase sucrose content and yields. Holly Seed partners with SESVanderHave to supply seeds adapted to growing sugar beets worldwide.

EXECUTIVES

VP Finance, Jeff Plathe
CEO and President, Kelvin P. Thompsen
Executive Secretary, Kathy Brunner
Agricultural Manager, Dan Bernhardson

LOCATIONS

HQ: Southern Minnesota Beet Sugar Cooperative
83550 County Rd. 21, Renville MN 56284
Phone: 320-329-8305 **Fax:** 320-329-3252
Web: www.smbsc.com

PRODUCTS/OPERATIONS

Selected Products

Ag liming material
Baker's sugar
Beet pulp pellets
Beet pulp shreds
Fruit sugar
Granulated sugar
Liquid sucrose
Liquid sugar
Molasses
Raffinates
Refined sugar

COMPETITORS

Amalgamated Sugar
American Crystal Sugar
C&H Sugar
Connell Company
Florida Crystals
Imperial Sugar
King Ranch
M. A. Patout
Michigan Sugar Company
Minn-Dak Co-op
Sterling Sugars
Sugar Cane Growers Cooperative of Florida
Sugar Foods
U.S. Sugar
United Sugars
Western Sugar Cooperative

HISTORICAL FINANCIALS

Company Type: Private - Cooperative

Income Statement

FYE: August 31

	REVENUE ($ mil.)	NET INCOME ($ mil.)	NET PROFIT MARGIN	EMPLOYEES
08/12	474	196	41.3%	610
08/11	509	214	42.2%	0
08/10	439	154	35.2%	0
08/08	380	120	31.7%	0
Annual Growth	7.7%	17.6%	—	—

2012 Year-End Financials

Debt ratio: ——
Return on equity: 41.30%
Cash ($ mil.): 1
Current ratio: 0.40
Long-term debt ($ mil.): —

Dividends
Yield: —
Payout: —
Market value ($ mil.): —

SOUTHERN NEW HAMPSHIRE MEDICAL CENTER

Southern New Hampshire Medical Center (SNHMC) provides medical care for the residents of the Nashua New Hampshire area and surrounding region. The two-campus hospital which has about 190 beds and is part of the Southern New Hampshire Health System offers centers for cancer treatment diabetes education fertility and childbirth obesity sleep disorders trauma and other programs. Outpatient and rehabilitation services are offered through several clinic locations. SNHMC is also affiliated with physician practice organization Foundation Medical Partners and it is a teaching facility for the Dartmouth Medical School.

Geographic Reach

SNHMC's main campus is located in the heart of downtown Nashua New Hampshire and serves patients in the Greater Nashua area.

Operations

The Medical Center has a medical staff of more than 500 primary and specialty care providers from Foundation Medical Partners Dartmouth-Hitchcock Nashua and local independent practices.

Strategy

SNHMC is expanding its network of medical facilities to keep pace wth demand. In 2012 Foundation Medical Partners opened Southern New Hampshire Health System at Pelham. In 2011 SNHMC opened Hudson and Merrimack locations to meet the growing needs of the greater Nashua community.

Company Background

The company was founded as an 8-bed emergency hospital in 1893

EXECUTIVES

President CEO and Trustee, Thomas E. (Tom) Wilhelmsen Jr.
VP Planning and Communications, Scott R. Westover
SVP; President and COO Foundation Medical Partners, Susan M. DeSocio
VP Medical Affairs; CMO Southern New Hampshire Medical Center, Stephanie Wolf-Rosenblum
VP Human Resources, Merryll Rosenfeld
VP Information Systems and CIO, Dwight C. Muller
VP Patient Care Services, Colette D. Tilton
VP Clinical and Support Services, Richard T. Duguay III
VP Administration, David E. Cawley
Associate VP Administration, Barbara J. Richards
Chief of Staff, Sean W. Fitzpatrick
Chairperson, John M. Mercier
Vice Chairperson, Praveen K. Suchdev
Chairman Leadership Steering Committee, George Rooney
SVP Finance and CFO, Michael S. Rose
Chief Medical Officer Foundation Medical Partners, Robert G. Dorf
VP Finance and Affiliated Practices Foundation Medical Partners, Erlene Washington
Vice Chief of Staff, Kenneth F. Howe
Secretary and Treasurer, Gary B. Friedman
Trustee, Bonalyn J. Hartley, age 67
Trustee, John R. Kreick, age 67
President CEO and Trustee, Thomas E. (Tom) Wilhelmsen Jr.
Trustee, John V. Dwyer Jr.
Trustee, Christine C. Hallock
Trustee, Holly J. Harmon-Morse
Trustee, Mary H. Jordan
Trustee, Peter J. McArdle
Trustee, Martha E. O'Neill
Trustee, Thomas A. Pursch
Vice Chairperson, Praveen K. Suchdev
Trustee, Sean W. Fitzpatrick
Trustee, Jame K. Steiner

LOCATIONS

HQ: Southern New Hampshire Medical Center
8 Prospect St., Nashua NH 03061
Phone: 603-577-2000   **Fax:** 603-577-2290
Web: www.snhmc.org

PRODUCTS/OPERATIONS

Selected Medical Services

Aesthetics
Allergy and Immunology
Anesthesia and Pain Management
Arthritis
Asthma
Audiology (Hearing Evaluations for Children)
Auditory Brainstem Response
Clinical Trials and Open Protocols
Ear Nose and Throat
Endocrinology
Family Practice
Genetic Counseling
Geriatric Medicine and Services
Hematology
Hospice Care
Hospitalist Program
Internal Medicine
Kidney Care
Maternity
Nephrology
Neurology
Neurosurgery
Nutrition
Pathology
Plastic Surgery
Podiatry
Pulmonary Medicine
Psychiatry
Pulmonary Rehab Program
Renal Dialysis
Rheumatology
Sleep Center
Sports Medicine
Stroke
Urology
Vascular Services
Specialty Medical Services
Behavioral Health
Cancer Care
Diabetes Care
Digestive Health
Dermatology
Emergency Department
Heart Care
Immediate Care
Laboratory Services
Orthopedics
Pediatric Services
Radiology Services
Rehabilitation Services
Spine and Brain Care
Surgical Services
Women's Services

COMPETITORS

Catholic Medical Center
Concord Hospital
Elliot Health System
Exeter Health Resources
Frisbie Memorial Hospital
Steward Health Care

HISTORICAL FINANCIALS

Company Type: Private - Not-for-Profit

Income Statement

FYE: September 30

	REVENUE ($ mil.)	NET INCOME ($ mil.)	NET PROFIT MARGIN	EMPLOYEES
09/11	274	(4)	—	1,200
09/10	214	7	3.7%	0
09/09	197	0	—	0
09/08	191	7	3.9%	0
Annual Growth	12.7%	—	—	—

SOUTHERN REGIONAL HEALTH SYSTEM INC.

Southern Regional Health System operates the Southern Regional Medical Center (SRMC) in a southern suburb of Atlanta. With more than 330 beds this hospital offers patients cardiac monitoring diagnostic imaging occupational and speech rehabilitation and an abundance of other services. Other facilities include the Women's Life Center which provides women's and newborn healthcare and a 30-bed long-term acute care hospital. The system's Spivey Station campus in Jonesboro includes a women's imaging center and surgery center. SRMC was established in 1971 to provide health care to residents of Clayton County and the surrounding areas.

Geographic Reach

SRMC serves patients in the Georgia counties of Clayton County Fulton Henry DeKalb Fayette among a few others.

Operations

SRMC owns the Advanced Primary Stroke Center and the Georgia Orthopedic Institute. It performs minimally-invasive robotic surgeries with the da Vinci Surgical System and a variety of rehabilitation services. In 2012 SRMC delivered 2975 babies and had 80035 emergency department visits.

Financial Performance

SRMC saw its net revenue decrease by 8% in 2012 over 2011 due to a sizable decrease in revenue from patient care. As a result it suffered a net loss of more than $13 million for 2012.

EXECUTIVES

VP Facilities and Support Services, James E. Crissey
Chairman, Ron Dodson
VP Operations, Therese Sucher
VP Information Technology, Karen Moore
VP Medical Affairs, Willie Cochran Jr.
Managing Director Marketing and Public Relations, William T. (Bill) Applegate
Managing Director Human Resources, Norma Adams
VP and Chief Nursing Officer, Cathy Kenney
President and CEO, Stephen W. Mahan
CFO, Steven L. (Lee) Boles Jr.
EVP and COO, John R. McLain

LOCATIONS

HQ: Southern Regional Health System
11 Upper Riverdale Rd. S.W., Riverdale GA 30274-2600
Phone: 770-991-8000   **Fax:** 770-991-8051
Web: www.southernregional.org

PRODUCTS/OPERATIONS

Selected Medical Services and Specialties
Georgia Orthopedic Joint Replacement

Heart and Vascular
Imaging
Surgery
Weight Management
Women's Health

COMPETITORS

DeKalb Medical
Emory Healthcare
Piedmont Healthcare
Shepherd Center
SunLink Health Systems

HISTORICAL FINANCIALS

Company Type: Private - Not-for-Profit

Income Statement

FYE: June 30

	REVENUE ($ mil.)	NET INCOME ($ mil.)	NET PROFIT MARGIN	EMPLOYEES
06/11	264	(3)	—	2,315
06/10	258	(10)	—	0
06/09	266	(30)	—	0
06/08	262	(5)	—	0
Annual Growth	0.2%	—	—	—

SOUTHERN RESEARCH INSTITUTE INC

Southern Research Institute performs contract research in areas such as drug development and discovery engineering and environmental and energy issues. The not-for-profit organization launched a life science R&D consulting firm BioSafety Solutions in 2008. Clients have included government agencies such as the National Institutes of Health the US Department of Defense and NASA as well as corporate clients Mercedes-Benz and Southern Company. SRI tests anti-influenza and anti-HIV drugs for NanoViricides Inc. Founded in 1941 the organization has been affiliated with the University of Alabama at Birmingham since 1999. SRI acquired the assets of BioCryst Pharmaceuticals in 2010.

EXECUTIVES

President and CEO Brookwood Pharmaceuticals, Arthur J. (Art) Tipton, age 54
Chair, Carol Z. Garrison
VP Human Resources and Administrative Services, Robert L. (Rob) McClure
Treasurer, Richard L. Margison
Manager Public Relations, Rhonda Jung
CFO, David A. Rutledge
Secretary, Shirley Salloway Kahn
President and CEO, John A. Secrist III
VP Engineering Division, Michael D. Johns
Director Contract Administration, Brenda H. Ehrensperger
Director Neuropharmacology Lab, Maurizio Grimaldi
VP Corporate Development, Nancy M. Gray
Interim VP Drug Development, William R. Waud

Director Power Systems and Environmental Research, Robert S. (Bob) Dahlin
VP Drug Discovery, Wilson B. Knight
Sales Manager, Michael Watson
Director Quality Assurance, Jim Ault
Director of Strategic Business Development, David Harris
Vice President, Andrew D. Penman
Vice President, Mark J. Suto
Director, Charles D. McCrary, age 60
Director, William W. Featheringill, age 69
Director, Malcolm Portera, age 65
Director, H. Corbin Day, age 73
Director, Fournier J. (Boots) Gale III, age 67
Director, Charles K. Porter

LOCATIONS

HQ: Southern Research Institute
2000 9th Ave. South, Birmingham AL 35205-5305
Phone: 205-581-2000   **Fax:** 205-581-2726
Web: www.southernresearch.org

COMPETITORS

Berkeley Lab
Momenta Pharmaceuticals
MRIGlobal
Ricerca Biosciences LLC
SwRI

HISTORICAL FINANCIALS

Company Type: Private - Not-for-Profit

Income Statement

FYE: December 30

	REVENUE ($ mil.)	NET INCOME ($ mil.)	NET PROFIT MARGIN	EMPLOYEES
12/11	89	3	3.9%	535
12/10*	89	13	15.5%	0
01/10	83	11	13.5%	0
01/09	79	(3)	—	0
Annual Growth	3.9%	—	—	—

*Fiscal year change

SOUTHFRESH AQUACULTURE LLC.

LOCATIONS

HQ: SOUTHFRESH AQUACULTURE LLC.
1792 MCFARLAND BLVD N B, TUSCALOOSA, AL 35406-2185
Phone: 205-247-4490
Web: www.southfresh.com

HISTORICAL FINANCIALS
Company Type: Private

Income Statement
FYE: July 31

	REVENUE ($ mil.)	NET INCOME ($ mil.)	NET PROFIT MARGIN	EMPLOYEES
07/11*	450	9	2.0%	250
12/08	0	0	—	0
05/03	54	1	2.4%	0
05/02	52	0	1.5%	0
Annual Growth	104.8%	126.5%	—	—

*Fiscal year change

2011 Year-End Financials
Debt ratio: —
Return on equity: 2.00%
Cash ($ mil.): 13
Current ratio: 0.70
Long-term debt ($ mil.): —
Dividends
 Yield: —
 Payout: —
Market value ($ mil.): —

SOUTHWEST RESEARCH INSTITUTE INC

If you're looking for research at an institute in the Southwest look no further. Founded in 1947 by oilman and rancher Thomas Slick Jr. Southwest Research Institute (SwRI) is an independent not-for-profit research and development institution that contracts to explore subjects in areas including automation and data systems applied physics space science and engineering and chemistry. SwRI has about 3000 scientists engineers and support staff at some 20 laboratories and offices in the US China and the UK. Customers include the private sector and government agencies. SwRI's Signature Science subsidiary researches national security environmental management and biotechnology.

Operations

SwRI provides contract research and development services to industrial and government clients. It keeps the scope of its work confidential and assigns patent rights arising from its sponsored research to the client. SwRI generally retains rights to Institute-funded advancements and holds more than 900 patents awarded to staff members.

The company operates through nearly a dozen technical divisions including Aerospace Electronics; Systems Engineering & Training; Applied Physics Chemistry & Chemical Engineering; Engine Emissions & Vehicl; Research; Geosciences & Engineering; Mechanical Engineering; and Space Science & Engineering.

Geographic Reach

The company is focused on expanding its presence in China. Examples of this strategy include a 2011 agreement with Beijing BSS Corrosion Protection Co. Ltd to promote its sensor nondestructive evaluation surface engineering and corrosion products and services to industries in China.

Strategy

In 2011 SwRI funded $6.1 million to its internally sponsored R&D program which is designed to encourage new ideas and innovative technologies. That year it initiated 67 new projects.

Examples of projects include cooperative research focusing on safe reliable cost-effective energy storage systems for electric and hybrid-electric vehicle applications. In addition it has formed

a consortium to conduct research and code development and apply advanced ROS (Robot Operating System)software to industrial applications.

EXECUTIVES
VP Geosciences and Engineering, Wesley C. Patrick
VP Space Science and Engineering, James L. Burch
VP Chemistry and Chemical Engineering, Michael G. MacNaughton
VP Aerospace Electronics and Information Technology, Richard D. Somers
VP Finance CFO and Secretary, Beth Ann Rafferty
EVP and Director, Walter D. Downing
President and Director, J. Dan Bates, age 67
VP Fuels and Lubricants Research, Lee J. Grant
VP Legal and Patent Office and General Counsel, John W. McLeod
Treasurer and Assistant Secretary, Jack S. Fernandi
VP Facilities and General Services, R. Pat Griffith Jr.
VP Special Programs, Katharine C. Golas
VP Signal Exploitation and Geolocation, William G. Guion
VP Applied Physics, Edward D. (Ed) Moore
VP Institute Environmental Safety and Quality Systems, Amos E. Holt
Chairman, John C. Korbell
Vice Chairman, Philip J. Pfeiffer
VP Applied Power, Bob Keys
VP Automation and Data Systems, Susan B. Crumrine
VP Engine Emissions and Vehicle Research, Bruce B. Bykowski
VP Mechanical Engineering, Danny M. Deffenbaugh
Director, Ricardo Romo
Director, Roger R. Hemminghaus, age 75
Director, H. Bartell Zachry Jr.
EVP and Director, Walter D. Downing
President and Director, J. Dan Bates, age 67
Director, Eugene L. Ames Jr.
Director, Milton B. Lee
Director, Mary Ann Rankin
Director, Wayne S. Alexander
Director, A. Baker Duncan
Director, Richard W. Calvert
Director, John B. Roberts
Director, Curtis Vaughan Jr.
Director, Richard B. Curtin
Vice Chairman, Philip J. Pfeiffer

LOCATIONS
HQ: Southwest Research Institute
 6220 Culebra Rd., San Antonio TX 78238-5166
Phone: 210-684-5111   Fax: 210-522-3547
Web: www.swri.edu

PRODUCTS/OPERATIONS

Selected Technical Divisions
Aerospace Electronics and Information Technology
Applied Physics
Applied Power
Automation and Data Systems
Chemistry and Chemical Engineering
Engine Emissions and Vehicle Research
Fuels and Lubricants Research
Geosciences and Engineering
Mechanical Engineering
Signal Exploitation and Geolocation
Space Science and Engineering
Training Simulation and Performance Improvement

COMPETITORS
Argonne National Laboratory	Lawrence Livermore Lab
Battelle Memorial	QinetiQ
	Southern Research

Berkeley Lab   Institute
Brookhaven Lab

HISTORICAL FINANCIALS
Company Type: Private - Not-for-Profit

Income Statement
FYE: September 30

	REVENUE ($ mil.)	NET INCOME ($ mil.)	NET PROFIT MARGIN	EMPLOYEES
09/11	581	28	4.9%	3,352
09/10	547	29	5.4%	0
09/09	563	22	4.1%	0
09/08	563	36	6.4%	0
Annual Growth	1.1%	(7.6%)	—	—

2011 Year-End Financials
Debt ratio: —
Return on equity: 4.90%
Cash ($ mil.): 5
Current ratio: 0.70
Long-term debt ($ mil.): —
Dividends
 Yield: —
 Payout: —
Market value ($ mil.): —

SOUTHWESTERN MOTOR TRANSPORT INC.

LOCATIONS
HQ: SOUTHWESTERN MOTOR TRANSPORT INC.
 4600 GOLDFIELD, SAN ANTONIO, TX 78218-4601
Phone: 210-661-6791
Web: www.smtl.com

HISTORICAL FINANCIALS
Company Type: Private

Income Statement
FYE: December 31

	REVENUE ($ mil.)	NET INCOME ($ mil.)	NET PROFIT MARGIN	EMPLOYEES
12/11	85	(1)	—	580
12/09	70	(1)	—	0
12/08	99	(4)	—	0
12/07	99	0	0.0%	0
Annual Growth	(4.9%)	—	—	—

2011 Year-End Financials
Debt ratio: —
Return on equity: (-1.30)%
Cash ($ mil.): 6
Current ratio: 2.20
Long-term debt ($ mil.): —
Dividends
 Yield: —
 Payout: —
Market value ($ mil.): —

SOUTHWESTERN UNIVERSITY

The first institution of higher learning in Texas Southwestern University was chartered by the Republic of Texas in 1840. The liberal arts university consists of The Brown College of Arts and Sciences and The Sarofim School of Fine Arts. It offers more than two-dozen undergraduate majors as well as pre-professional and certification programs and confers bachelor's degrees in arts music fine arts and science. Affiliated with The United Methodist Church Southwestern University has an enrollment of more than 1200 students. More than 80% of students live in residence halls on campus which is located on the edge of the Texas Hill Country in Georgetown Texas just north of Austin.

EXECUTIVES

President, Jake B. Schrum
VP Fiscal Affairs, Richard L. Anderson
Associate VP and Dean of Students, Michael (Mike) Leese
Provost and Faculty Dean, James W. Hunt
VP Institutional Advancement, C. Richard McKelvey
VP Student Life, Gerald D. Brody
Dean Library Services, Lynne Brody
Registrar, David H. Stones
Director Career Services, Roger Young
Associate VP Enrollment Services, Monty L. Curtis
VP Enrollment Services, Thomas J. Oliver
Director Financial Aid, James Gaeta
Associate VP Alumni Relations, Georgianne Hewett
Associate VP Finance, Gary L. Logan
Controller, Josie Rodriguez
Associate VP Human Resources, Elma F. Benavides
Associate VP Information Technology Services, Robert C. Paver
Purchasing Assistant, Paula Sutton
VP Innovation, W. Joseph King
Director Admisions, Michael G. Rossman
Auditors: Deloitte&ToucheLLP

LOCATIONS

HQ: Southwestern University
1001 E. University Ave., Georgetown TX 78626-6107
Phone: 512-863-6511   **Fax:** 512-863-5788
Web: www.southwestern.edu

HISTORICAL FINANCIALS
Company Type: School

Income Statement
FYE: June 30

	REVENUE ($ mil.)	NET INCOME ($ mil.)	NET PROFIT MARGIN	EMPLOYEES
06/12	46	(25)	—	357
06/10	62	(14)	—	0
06/09	0	(58)	—	0
06/08	18	(32)	—	0
Annual Growth	34.8%	—	—	—

2012 Year-End Financials
Debt ratio: ——
Return on equity: (-54.60)%
Cash ($ mil.): 41
Current ratio: 4.50
Long-term debt ($ mil.): —
Dividends
Yield: —
Payout: —
Market value ($ mil.): —

SPARTAN LIGHT METAL PRODUCTS INC.

LOCATIONS

HQ: SPARTAN LIGHT METAL PRODUCTS INC.
510 E MCCLURKEN AVE, SPARTA, IL 62286-1850
Phone: 618-443-4346
Web: www.spartanlmp.com

HISTORICAL FINANCIALS
Company Type: Private

Income Statement
FYE: December 31

	REVENUE ($ mil.)	NET INCOME ($ mil.)	NET PROFIT MARGIN	EMPLOYEES
12/11	93	0	—	600
12/10	0	0	—	0
12/09	65	0	—	0
12/08	93	0	—	0
Annual Growth	(0.0%)	—	—	—

2011 Year-End Financials
Debt ratio: ——
Return on equity: —
Cash ($ mil.): 12
Current ratio: 2.00
Long-term debt ($ mil.): —
Dividends
Yield: —
Payout: —
Market value ($ mil.): —

SPECIAL EDUCATION DISTRICT OF LAKE COUNTY

LOCATIONS

HQ: SPECIAL EDUCATION DISTRICT OF LAKE COUNTY
18160 W GAGES LAKE RD, GRAYSLAKE, IL 60030-1819
Phone: 847-548-8470
Web: www.sedol.k12.il.us

HISTORICAL FINANCIALS
Company Type: Private

Income Statement
FYE: June 30

	REVENUE ($ mil.)	NET INCOME ($ mil.)	NET PROFIT MARGIN	EMPLOYEES
06/12	85	7	8.7%	780
06/11	84	(10)	—	0
06/10	90	(7)	—	0
06/09	69	21	31.3%	0
Annual Growth	7.1%	(30.1%)	—	—

2012 Year-End Financials
Debt ratio: ——
Return on equity: 8.70%
Cash ($ mil.): 12
Current ratio: —
Long-term debt ($ mil.): —
Dividends
Yield: —
Payout: —
Market value ($ mil.): —

SPECIAL SCHOOL DISTRICT OF ST LOUIS COUNTY MO

LOCATIONS

HQ: SPECIAL SCHOOL DISTRICT OF ST LOUIS COUNTY MO
12110 CLAYTON RD, SAINT LOUIS, MO 63131-2516
Phone: 314-989-8100
Web: www.appliedtech-stl.com

HISTORICAL FINANCIALS
Company Type: Private

Income Statement
FYE: June 30

	REVENUE ($ mil.)	NET INCOME ($ mil.)	NET PROFIT MARGIN	EMPLOYEES
06/12	381	6	1.7%	5,500
06/11	391	7	1.8%	0
06/10	378	(2)	—	0
06/09	382	15	4.2%	0
Annual Growth	(0.1%)	(26.6%)	—	—

2012 Year-End Financials
Debt ratio: ——
Return on equity: 1.70%
Cash ($ mil.): 140
Current ratio: —
Long-term debt ($ mil.): —
Dividends
Yield: —
Payout: —
Market value ($ mil.): —

SPECIALTY FOODS HOLDINGS INC.

LOCATIONS

HQ: SPECIALTY FOODS HOLDINGS INC.
21 ENTERPRISE PKWY # 400, HAMPTON, VA 23666-6413
Phone: 757-952-1200
Web: www.specialtyfoodsgroup.com

HISTORICAL FINANCIALS
Company Type: Private

Income Statement
FYE: December 31

	REVENUE ($ mil.)	NET INCOME ($ mil.)	NET PROFIT MARGIN	EMPLOYEES
12/11*	324	11	3.6%	850
01/10	273	23	8.5%	0
12/08	258	13	5.4%	0
12/03	312	(8)	—	0
Annual Growth	1.2%	—	—	—

*Fiscal year change

2011 Year-End Financials
Debt ratio: ——
Return on equity: 3.60%
Cash ($ mil.): 13
Current ratio: 1.00
Long-term debt ($ mil.): —
Dividends
Yield: —
Payout: —
Market value ($ mil.): —

SPECIALTY PROMOTIONS INC.

LOCATIONS

HQ: SPECIALTY PROMOTIONS INC.
6019 W HOWARD ST, NILES, IL 60714-4801
Phone: 847-588-2580
Web: www.specialtyprintcomm.com

HISTORICAL FINANCIALS

Company Type: Private

Income Statement

	REVENUE ($ mil.)	NET INCOME ($ mil.)	NET PROFIT MARGIN	EMPLOYEES
06/11	80	1	1.9%	325
06/10	74	1	1.6%	0
06/09	60	(0)	—	0
06/08	61	0	0.1%	0
Annual Growth	9.4%	208.4%	—	—

FYE: June 30

2011 Year-End Financials

Debt ratio: —
Return on equity: 1.90%
Cash ($ mil.): 0
Current ratio: 0.90
Long-term debt ($ mil.): —

Dividends
Yield: —
Payout: —
Market value ($ mil.): —

SPECTRUM HEALTH PRIMARY CARE PARTNERS DBA

LOCATIONS

HQ: SPECTRUM HEALTH PRIMARY CARE PARTNERS DBA
1840 WEALTHY ST SE, GRAND RAPIDS, MI 49506-2921
Phone: 616-774-7322

HISTORICAL FINANCIALS

Company Type: Private

Income Statement

	REVENUE ($ mil.)	NET INCOME ($ mil.)	NET PROFIT MARGIN	EMPLOYEES
06/11	222	5	2.4%	4
06/10	75	3	4.7%	0
Annual Growth	193.4%	50.2%	—	—

FYE: June 30

2011 Year-End Financials

Debt ratio: —
Return on equity: 2.40%
Cash ($ mil.): 0
Current ratio: —
Long-term debt ($ mil.): —

Dividends
Yield: —
Payout: —
Market value ($ mil.): —

SPELMAN COLLEGE

Spelman College is a private historically African American college for women. The college enrolls some 2200 students from more than 40 states in the US and 15 countries. It offers majors in areas such as English economics mathematics music psychology art and religion. Spelman was founded in 1881 as Atlanta Baptist Female Seminary by Sophia B. Packard and Harriet E. Giles. The school's name was changed in 1884 to honor Mrs. Laura Spelman Rockefeller as well as her parents Harvey Buel and Lucy Henry Spelman activists involved in the antislavery movement. Tuition costs about $17250 and the student-faculty ratio is 12-to-1.

EXECUTIVES

President, Beverly D. Tatum
VP Business and Financial Affairs and Treasurer, Robert D. Flanigan Jr.
VP Academic Affairs and Provost, Johnnella E. Butler, age 62
Assistant Director Public Relations and Communications, Renita Mathis
Dean Undergraduate Studies Spring Semester, Desiree Pedescleaux
VP Enrollment Management, Arlene Cash
VP Institutional Advancement Fall Semester, Rosalyn Hines
VP College Relations, Eloise A. Alexis
CIO, Delores K. Barton
Dean Undergraduate Studies Fall Semester, Donna Akiba Harper
Director Communications, Tomika DePriest
Dean The Chapel, Rev Lisa Rhodes
Director International Affairs Center, Jeanne Meadows
Associate Dean Undergraduate Studies, Geneva Baxter
Associate VP Business and Financial Affairs, John Cunningham Jr.
Controller, April Austin
Director Human Resources, Judith Kenney
Dean Continuing Education and Community Outreach Ministries, Pauline E. Drake
Director Student Financial Services, Lenora Jackson
Director Career Planning and Development, Harold Bell
Associate Dean Students and Living Learning Programs, Teresa Ramey
VP Student Affairs, Sherry L. Turner
Registrar, Frederick Fresh
Associate VP Advancement Operations, Helga Greenfield
Dean of Students, Vera Dixon Rorie
Director Facilities Management, Arthur E. Frazier III
Auditors: KPMGLLP

LOCATIONS

HQ: Spelman College
350 Spelman Ln. SW, Atlanta GA 30314-4399
Phone: 404-681-3643   **Fax:** 404-270-5097
Web: www.spelman.edu

PRODUCTS/OPERATIONS

Selected Programs
Anthropology
Biology
Computer Science
Engineering

English
French
History
Mathematics
Physics
Psychology
Religious Studies
Spanish
Sociology

COMPETITORS

Bethune-Cookman University
Clark Atlanta University
Howard University
Morris College

HISTORICAL FINANCIALS

Company Type: School

Income Statement

	REVENUE ($ mil.)	NET INCOME ($ mil.)	NET PROFIT MARGIN	EMPLOYEES
06/12	86	(6)	—	550
06/11	103	0	0.8%	0
06/10	91	(8)	—	0
06/09	80	(73)	—	0
Annual Growth	2.4%	—	—	—

FYE: June 30

2012 Year-End Financials

Debt ratio: —
Return on equity: (-7.30)%
Cash ($ mil.): 13
Current ratio: —
Long-term debt ($ mil.): —

Dividends
Yield: —
Payout: —
Market value ($ mil.): —

SPF ENERGY INC.

Super-jobber SPF Energy is also a super-pumper of petroleum. The company's Super-pumper subsidiary runs a chain of about 15 convenience stores and gas stations in Minnesota Montana and North and South Dakota. Locations operate under the Conoco Exxon Sinclair and Tesoro banners. SPF Energy's Farstad Oil subsidiary offers bulk transportation of petroleum products including the distribution of about 250 million gallons of gas 20 million gallons of propane and 2.5 million gallons of lubricants a year. The Farstad fleet serves businesses and government agencies from Montana to eastern Minnesota and from northern Wyoming to the Canadian border.

Farstad Oil was founded in 1938 as a family-operated bulk oil business. Regional convenience store chain Superpumper was founded by John Havnvik in 1983.

EXECUTIVES

COO, Dennis Krueger
General Manager Superpumper, Kris Wolla
Secretary and Treasurer, Bruce Hest
Director Information Technology, Dan Olson
President and CEO, Jeff Farstad
Fargo Regional Manager, Jim Olson
Billings Regional Manager, Rick Roedocker

LOCATIONS

HQ: SPF Energy Inc.
  100 NE 27th St., Minot ND 58702-1847
Phone: 701-852-1194   **Fax:** 254-773-1661
Web: www.fsbcentex.com

COMPETITORS

BP   Wilson Oil
Redwood Coast
  Petroleum

HISTORICAL FINANCIALS

Company Type: Holding Company

Income Statement   FYE: December 31

	REVENUE ($ mil.)	NET INCOME ($ mil.)	NET PROFIT MARGIN	EMPLOYEES
12/11	1,078	4	0.4%	300
Annual Growth	—	—	—	—

2011 Year-End Financials

Debt ratio: ——
Return on equity: 0.40%
Cash ($ mil.): 2
Current ratio: 1.00
Long-term debt ($ mil.): —

Dividends
  Yield: —
  Payout: —
  Market value ($ mil.): —

SPRINGFIELD COLLEGE

LOCATIONS

HQ: SPRINGFIELD COLLEGE
  263 ALDEN ST, SPRINGFIELD, MA 01109-3788
Phone: 413-748-3000
Web: www.springfieldcollege.edu

HISTORICAL FINANCIALS

Company Type: Private

Income Statement   FYE: June 30

	REVENUE ($ mil.)	NET INCOME ($ mil.)	NET PROFIT MARGIN	EMPLOYEES
06/11	150	6	4.3%	579
06/10	127	0	—	0
06/09	127	0	—	0
06/08	121	3	2.9%	0
Annual Growth	7.4%	22.9%	—	—

2011 Year-End Financials

Debt ratio: ——
Return on equity: 4.30%
Cash ($ mil.): 24
Current ratio: —
Long-term debt ($ mil.): —

Dividends
  Yield: —
  Payout: —
  Market value ($ mil.): —

SRC TEC INC.

LOCATIONS

HQ: SRC TEC INC.
  5801 E TAFT RD STE 7, SYRACUSE, NY 13212-3273
Phone: 315-452-8700
Web: www.srctecinc.com

HISTORICAL FINANCIALS

Company Type: Private

Income Statement   FYE: September 30

	REVENUE ($ mil.)	NET INCOME ($ mil.)	NET PROFIT MARGIN	EMPLOYEES
09/11	452	35	7.8%	275
09/10	583	42	7.3%	0
09/09	365	19	5.4%	0
Annual Growth	11.3%	33.9%	—	—

2011 Year-End Financials

Debt ratio: ——
Return on equity: 7.80%
Cash ($ mil.): 77
Current ratio: 4.70
Long-term debt ($ mil.): —

Dividends
  Yield: —
  Payout: —
  Market value ($ mil.): —

SRT COMMUNICATIONS INC.

SRT Communications provides local-exchange access and long-distance telephone service to residents of north central North Dakota and Montana. The cooperative serves about 48000 access lines and operates 25 telephone exchanges including those in the towns of Minot Burlington and Surrey as well as the Minot Air Force Base. In addition to voice service the company sells Internet services (including broadband access and Web hosting) as well as PCS wireless service. SRT Communications also distributes business phone systems made by Avaya Mitel and 3Com and offers cable television to subscribers in nearly 20 cities and towns.

SRT added to its regional holdings in 2007 through its acquisition of Velva Telephone Exchange. The following year the company announced agreements with wireless providers Northwest Communications Cooperative and Nemont Telephone Cooperative that will allow SRT to resell wireless services in North Dakota and Montana respectively.

EXECUTIVES

General Manager and CEO, Steve D. Lysne
Assistant General Manager and COO, John A. Reiser
CFO, Perry G. Erdmann
Director Corporation Communications, Christine T. Morsfield
Director Network Technology, Shawn G. Grosz
Director Regulatory Affairs, Julie E. Lizotte
Director Field Operations, Tim A. Burckhard
Executive Secretary, Kim R. Weydahl

LOCATIONS

HQ: SRT Communications Inc.
  3615 N. Broadway, Minot ND 58703
Phone: 701-858-1200   **Fax:** 262-284-9333
Web: www.egginnovations.com

PRODUCTS/OPERATIONS

2007 Sales

	$ mil.	% of total
% of total		
Network access		46
Local network		17
PCS network		12
Internet		11
Long distance network		8
Nonregulated		2
Cable		1
Other		3
Total		100

COMPETITORS

AT&T   Sprint Nextel
Cellco   T-Mobile USA

HISTORICAL FINANCIALS

Company Type: Private - Cooperative

Income Statement   FYE: December 31

	REVENUE ($ mil.)	NET INCOME ($ mil.)	NET PROFIT MARGIN	EMPLOYEES
12/11	47	3	6.6%	221
12/10	47	4	9.9%	0
12/09	45	1	4.2%	0
12/08	45	3	8.7%	0
Annual Growth	2.0%	(7.0%)	—	—

2011 Year-End Financials

Debt ratio: ——
Return on equity: 6.60%
Cash ($ mil.): 2
Current ratio: 0.70
Long-term debt ($ mil.): —

Dividends
  Yield: —
  Payout: —
  Market value ($ mil.): —

SSI TECHNOLOGIES INC.

LOCATIONS

HQ: SSI TECHNOLOGIES INC.
  3200 PALMER DR, JANESVILLE, WI 53546-2308
Phone: 608-758-1500
Web: www.ssisintered.com

HISTORICAL FINANCIALS

Company Type: Private

Income Statement   FYE: December 31

	REVENUE ($ mil.)	NET INCOME ($ mil.)	NET PROFIT MARGIN	EMPLOYEES
12/11	87	0	—	525
12/10	0	0	—	0
12/09	0	0	—	0
12/08	0	0	—	0
Annual Growth	—	—	—	—

2011 Year-End Financials

Debt ratio: —
Return on equity: —
Cash ($ mil.): 1
Current ratio: 1.30
Long-term debt ($ mil.): —

Dividends
Yield: —
Payout: —
Market value ($ mil.): —

ST ANN'S HOSPITAL

LOCATIONS

HQ: ST ANN'S HOSPITAL
500 S CLEVELAND AVE, WESTERVILLE, OH
43081-8998
Phone: 614-546-4300
Web: www.mountcarmelhealth.com

HISTORICAL FINANCIALS

Company Type: Private

Income Statement

FYE: June 30

	REVENUE ($ mil.)	NET INCOME ($ mil.)	NET PROFIT MARGIN	EMPLOYEES
06/11	286	38	13.6%	0
06/10	249	27	11.0%	0
06/09	233	0	—	0
Annual Growth	10.8%	—	—	—

2011 Year-End Financials

Debt ratio: —
Return on equity: 13.60%
Cash ($ mil.): 0
Current ratio: 2.90
Long-term debt ($ mil.): —

Dividends
Yield: —
Payout: —
Market value ($ mil.): —

ST BERNARD HOSPITAL INC

Like a giant dog trudging through blinding snow to rescue a traveler in need St. Bernard Hospital is a powerhouse of betterment for the people it serves. St. Bernard Hospital and Health Care Center serves the residents of Chicago's south side neighborhood of Englewood. The facility has about 200 beds and its specialties include pediatrics psychiatry neurology orthopedics and cardiology services. The hospital also offers inpatient detoxification services for patients dependent on opiates or alcohol. St. Bernard has a separate nonprofit unit that takes care of south side residents' residences: Bernard Place Housing Development is a 90-unit affordable homes initiative in the Englewood neighborhood.

Bernard Place served as the first phase of New Englewood Crossings a community development endeavor in Englewood providing residents with single-family homes. The 1903 founders of St. Bernard Sisters of the Religious Hospitallers of St. Joseph in Montreal Canada provided a major contribution to the subsidiary to help get it off the ground.

St. Bernard's Comprehensive Health and Advocacy Network for the Children of Englewood (CHANCE) program provides health care (including dental) to underserved patients throughout the community. The Pediatric Mobile Health Unit (PMHU) is St. Bernard's clinic on wheels visiting elementary and secondary schools throughout South Side Chicago the PMHU provides school and sports physical exams immunizations and health referrals. The Dental Center at St. Bernard Hospital provides oral health care for the community's children and their parents.

EXECUTIVES

President CEO and Trustee, Sister Elizabeth Van Straten
EVP, Janet Nohos
CFO, Guy Alton
VP Quality and Corporate Compliance, Roland Abellera, age 46
VP Patient Care Services, Ronald Campbell
VP Government Relations and Hospital and Community Development, Charles Holland
Chief Nurse Officer, Evelyn Jones
Chairman, Gregory Whitehead
President CEO and Trustee, Sister Elizabeth Van Straten
Trustee, Sister Janet Wahleithner
Trustee, Leon Jackson
Trustee, Sister Margaret Morrissey
Trustee, Sister Mary Pokorny
Trustee, Sister Rosemarie Kugel
Trustee, Maria Ashley
Trustee, Henry Wiggins
Trustee, Sister Joanne Delehanty

LOCATIONS

HQ: St. Bernard Hospital and Health Care Center
326 W. 64th St., Chicago IL 60621
Phone: 773-962-3900   **Fax:** 773-962-0034
Web: www.stbernardhospital.com

COMPETITORS

Advocate Health Care
Alexian Brothers Health System
Ascension Health
Children's Hospital of Chicago
Ingalls Memorial Hospital
Mercy Hospital and Medical Center

Northwestern Memorial HealthCare
Resurrection Health Care
Rush System for Health
Sinai Health System
University of Chicago Medical Center
WellGroup HealthPartners

HISTORICAL FINANCIALS

Company Type: Private - Not-for-Profit

Income Statement

FYE: December 31

	REVENUE ($ mil.)	NET INCOME ($ mil.)	NET PROFIT MARGIN	EMPLOYEES
12/11	90	5	6.4%	875
12/09	94	11	12.5%	0
12/08	85	4	5.0%	0
12/06	78	3	4.4%	0
Annual Growth	4.7%	18.6%	—	—

2011 Year-End Financials

Debt ratio: —
Return on equity: 6.40%
Cash ($ mil.): 4
Current ratio: 0.90
Long-term debt ($ mil.): —

Dividends
Yield: —
Payout: —
Market value ($ mil.): —

ST JOSEPH HOSPITAL

LOCATIONS

HQ: ST JOSEPH HOSPITAL
172 KINSLEY ST, NASHUA, NH 03060-3688
Phone: 603-882-3000
Web: www.souheganhhc.org

HISTORICAL FINANCIALS

Company Type: Private

Income Statement

FYE: December 31

	REVENUE ($ mil.)	NET INCOME ($ mil.)	NET PROFIT MARGIN	EMPLOYEES
12/11	195	9	4.9%	1,200
12/09	171	19	11.5%	0
12/08	2	0	—	0
12/04	123	12	10.4%	0
Annual Growth	16.6%	(9.2%)	—	—

2011 Year-End Financials

Debt ratio: —
Return on equity: 4.90%
Cash ($ mil.): 9
Current ratio: 1.30
Long-term debt ($ mil.): —

Dividends
Yield: —
Payout: —
Market value ($ mil.): —

ST JOSEPH MEMORIAL HOSPITAL

LOCATIONS

HQ: ST JOSEPH MEMORIAL HOSPITAL
1907 W SYCAMORE ST, KOKOMO, IN 46901-5148
Phone: 765-452-5611

HISTORICAL FINANCIALS

Company Type: Private

Income Statement

FYE: June 30

	REVENUE ($ mil.)	NET INCOME ($ mil.)	NET PROFIT MARGIN	EMPLOYEES
06/11	137	21	15.3%	900
06/10	131	18	13.9%	0
06/09	111	1	1.0%	0
06/08	111	16	14.6%	0
Annual Growth	7.2%	8.9%	—	—

2011 Year-End Financials

Debt ratio: —
Return on equity: 15.30%
Cash ($ mil.): 7
Current ratio: 1.80
Long-term debt ($ mil.): —

Dividends
Yield: —
Payout: —
Market value ($ mil.): —

ST JOSEPH'S COLLEGE NEW YORK

St. Joseph's College is a liberal arts college with two locations in the metropolitan New York City area –one in Brooklyn and one in Long Island. St. Joseph's offers more than 20 undergraduate majors pre-professional and certificate programs and graduate degrees in management business and infant/toddler early childhood special education to over 5000 students. Its School of Adult and Professional Education provides adult students with certificate and degree programs in fields such as management computer information systems and health. Its Brooklyn campus also houses the Dillon Child Study Center a working preschool where child-study majors gain hands-on experience. St. Joseph's was founded in 1916.

EXECUTIVES

President, Sister Elizabeth A. Hill
VP Institutional Advancement, Nancy Connors
Provost, Sister Loretta McGrann
CFO, John Roth
VP Planning and VP and Dean School of Professional and Graduate Studies, Thomas G. Travis
CIO, Joseph Spadaro
VP Enrollment Management, Theresa LaRocca Meyer
Director Co-Curricular Programs Brooklyn, Sherrie Van Arnam
Director Co-Curricular Programs Long Island, Marian Russo
Executive Director Financial Aid, Carol Sullivan
Executive Registrar, Robert Pergolis
Dean Students, Susan Hudec
Associate VP Enrollment Management and Director Admissions Long Island, Gigi Lamens

LOCATIONS

HQ: St. Joseph's College
245 Clinton Ave., Brooklyn NY 11205
Phone: 718-636-6800   **Fax:** 718-636-6830
Web: www.sjcny.edu

HISTORICAL FINANCIALS

Company Type: School

Income Statement

	REVENUE ($ mil.)	NET INCOME ($ mil.)	NET PROFIT MARGIN	EMPLOYEES
06/11	93	0	0.6%	800
06/05	56	1	2.2%	0
06/04	50	0	2.0%	0
06/03	41	3	8.2%	0
Annual Growth	**30.7%**	**(45.9%)**	**—**	**—**

2011 Year-End Financials

Debt ratio: ——
Return on equity: 0.60%
Cash ($ mil.): 3
Current ratio: ——
Long-term debt ($ mil.): ——
Dividends
 Yield: ——
 Payout: ——
Market value ($ mil.): ——

ST LAWRENCE UNIVERSITY

St. Lawrence University is a four-year liberal arts college that also offers graduate degrees in education. The university has an enrollment of more than 2500 students as well as 200 faculty members and a student-to-teacher ratio of 12:1. Major fields of study include biology computer science economics history psychology foreign language and religious studies. Actors Kirk Douglas and Viggo Mortensen and US Senator Susan Collins are among the school's alumni. Founded in 1856 by members of the Universalist Church (now Unitarian Universalist) St. Lawrence is the oldest continuously coeducational institution of higher learning in New York State.

Geographic Reach

St. Lawrence is located in Canton New York. The school is named the river in upstate New York that separates the US and Canada. Students at St. Lawrence hail from across the US and about 45 international countries.

Operations

St. Lawrence provides degrees including Bachelor of Arts Bachelor of Science and Master of Education as well as a Certificate of Advanced Studies in Education Administration.

In addition to its core fields of study St. Lawrence has special programs in partnership with other institutions. For instance it conducts a collaborative MBA program with Clarkson University and Union College and a rural medicine program with SUNY Upstate. It also offers a nursing program in collaboration with NYU and semester study programs with institutions in Nashville; Washington DC; upstate New York; and New York City as well as in the Adirondacks.

Financial Performance

St. Lawrence University reported a 1% increase in revenue in 2012 to some $112 million due to higher income from tuition fees room and board (which total about $56000 per student per year) as well as auxiliary activities and private gifts. Net income dropped into the red in 2012 due to investment losses.

Strategy

To enhance student resources on campus St. Lawrence announced plans to build a new residence hall in 2012. The new building will house 150 students and will be completed in 2014.

EXECUTIVES

VP and Dean Division of Student Life and Co-Curricular Education, Joseph A. Tolliver
VP and Dean Academic Affairs, Grant H. Cornwell Jr.
Associate VP Human Resources and Special Assistant to the President for Equity Programs, Susan M. Cypert
VP Finance and Treasurer, Kathryn L. (Kathy) Mullaney
Vice Chair, Mary Fishel Bijur
Chair, Donald K. Rose
Director Institutional Research, Christine Zimmerman
Associate Dean Faculty Affairs and Director Academic Advising, Elizabeth A. Regosin
Director Academic Services for Students with Special Needs, John M. Meagher
Director The Center for Teaching and Learning, Kim M. Mooney
Associate Dean The First Year Program, Steven G. Horwitz
Director Community-Based Learning and Director Summerterm, Ronald J. Ortiz Flores
Director Athletics, Margaret F. Strait
Director Athletic Media Relations, Walter H. Johnson
Associate Dean International and Intercultural Studies, Patricia Ann Alden
VP Administrative Operations, Thomas F. Coakley
Bookstore Manager, Robert D. FitzRandolph
Director Dining and Conference Services, Cynthia Y. Atkins
Registrar, Carolyn R. Filippi
Director Facilities Operations, Daniel B. Seaman
Director Financial Aid, Patricia J.B. Farmer
Director Budget and Financial Planning, Peter D. Fieckert
Controller, Carol T. Gable
Manager Accounting and Accounts Payable, Richard A. Parks
Software Maintenance and Development Manager, Arthur Eddy
VP University Advancement and Secretary Board of Trustees, Michael P. Archibald
Director Corporate and Foundation Relations, Susan M. Pankey
Associate VP Development, Thomas R. Pynchon
Associate VP University Relations, Lisa M. Cania
President and Trustee, William L. (Bill) Fox
Director Contracts Compliance and Risk Management, Ted Coviello
Director Budget and Financial Planning, Peter Feickert
Trustee, Warren B. (Barry) Phelps III, age 65
Trustee, Peter Hunt
Vice Chair, Mary Fishel Bijur
Trustee, Jeffery H. Boyd

Trustee, Karen Diesl Bruett
Trustee, James B. Brush
Trustee, Michael W. Clark
Trustee, George N. Cochran
Trustee, Dekkers L. Davidson
Trustee, Sharee M. Freeman
Trustee, Peter F. Hunt
Trustee, Jay W. Ireland
Trustee, R. Sheldon Johnson Jr.
Trustee, David B. Laird Jr.
Trustee, Janet K. Langlois
Trustee, Katy B. MacKay
Trustee, Patrick D. Martin
Trustee, Allan P. Newell
Trustee, Derrick H. Pitts
Trustee, Sarah E. Johnson Redlich
Trustee, Marion Roach Smith
President and Trustee, William L. (Bill) Fox
Trustee, Jo Ann Campbell

LOCATIONS

HQ: St. Lawrence University
23 Romoda Dr., Canton NY 13617
Phone: 315-229-5011   **Fax:** 315-229-5818
Web: web.stlawu.edu

HISTORICAL FINANCIALS

Company Type: School

Income Statement

FYE: June 30

	REVENUE ($ mil.)	NET INCOME ($ mil.)	NET PROFIT MARGIN	EMPLOYEES
06/12	112	(13)	—	638
06/11	110	53	48.0%	0
06/10	112	13	12.2%	0
06/09	103	(69)	—	0
Annual Growth	2.7%	—	—	—

2012 Year-End Financials

Debt ratio: —
Return on equity: (-12.10)%
Cash ($ mil.): 15
Current ratio: —
Long-term debt ($ mil.): —

Dividends
Yield: —
Payout: —
Market value ($ mil.): —

ST MICHAELS HOSPITAL INC

LOCATIONS

HQ: ST MICHAELS HOSPITAL INC
900 ILLINOIS AVE, STEVENS POINT, WI 54481-3196
Phone: 715-346-5000

HISTORICAL FINANCIALS

Company Type: Private

Income Statement

FYE: September 30

	REVENUE ($ mil.)	NET INCOME ($ mil.)	NET PROFIT MARGIN	EMPLOYEES
09/11	181	20	11.2%	1,900
09/10	176	13	7.7%	0
09/09	173	8	4.8%	0
09/07	157	(1)	—	0
Annual Growth	4.9%	—	—	—

2011 Year-End Financials

Debt ratio: —
Return on equity: 11.20%
Cash ($ mil.): 51
Current ratio: 3.60
Long-term debt ($ mil.): —

Dividends
Yield: —
Payout: —
Market value ($ mil.): —

ST THOMAS AQUINAS COLLEGE

St. Thomas Aquinas College seeks to live up to its namesake by offering a wide range of liberal arts-based academic programs. The college's 2700 full and part-time students can choose from almost 100 different majors minors specializations and dual degree programs. St. Thomas Aquinas College confers both undergraduate and graduate degrees in the humanities business administration social sciences natural sciences and mathematics

and teacher education. The school has a student-teacher ratio of 18:1. It was founded in 1952 in New York's Hudson River Valley by the Dominican Order.

EXECUTIVES

President CEO and Trustee, Margaret M. Fitzpatrick
VP Academic Affairs and Provost, L. John Durney III
VP Enrollment Management and Campus Communications, Vincent (Vin) Crapanzano
Vice Chairman, Lanny Cohen
Executive Director Human Resources, Patricia Pacchiana
Director Athletics, Gerry Oswald
Registrar, Mildred Alexiou
VP and Dean of Student Affairs, Walter Schneider
VP Financial Affairs and Treasurer, Manuel D. Fernandes
Chairman, David Carroll
Secretary and Trustee, Eileen Clifford
Director Campus Ministry and Volunteer Services, Madeleine Murphy
Director Safety and Security, Edward Hanus
VP Institutional Advancement, Kevin P. Duignan
Director Foundation and Community Relations, Lois Jungman
Controller, Jennifer Mazza
Special Assistant to President, Anne Donini
Associate Director Computer Information Systems, Shwetank Anthwal
Associate Director Computer Information Systems, Siyong Yu
VP Administration, Joseph Donini
VP Student Life and Dean Student Development, Kirk Manning
Manager Facilities/Construction, Patrick Lambert
Assistant Director Enrollment Marketing and Campus Communications, Bridget F. Clark
Director Admissions, Danielle N. MacKay
President CEO and Trustee, Margaret M. Fitzpatrick
Vice Chairman, Lanny Cohen
Trustee, Carl Capuano
Secretary and Trustee, Eileen Clifford
Trustee, Frank J. Borelli Sr.
Trustee, John J. Casazza Jr.
Trustee, James Donaghy
Trustee, John J. Ferguson
Trustee, James Freeman Jr.
Trustee, Ursula Joyce
Trustee, Thomas G. Leahy
Trustee, Barbara Azarian-McCullough
Trustee, Catherine Moran
Trustee, Patricia A. Murphy
Trustee, Denis O'Leary
Trustee, Patrick O'Malley
Trustee, Margaret Ryan
Trustee, William R. Sichol Jr.
Trustee, Maryann Summa
Trustee, Jacques Tortoroli
Trustee, Mary B. Ritchey
Trustee, Avinash Sharma

LOCATIONS

HQ: St. Thomas Aquinas College
125 Rte. 340, Sparkill NY 10976-1050
Phone: 845-398-4100   **Fax:** 845-359-8136
Web: www.stac.edu

HISTORICAL FINANCIALS

Company Type: School

Income Statement

FYE: June 30

	REVENUE ($ mil.)	NET INCOME ($ mil.)	NET PROFIT MARGIN	EMPLOYEES
06/11	33	5	15.4%	280
06/10	32	4	14.9%	0
06/09	32	0	—	0
06/08	32	5	18.2%	0
Annual Growth	1.1%	(4.3%)	—	—

2011 Year-End Financials

Debt ratio: —
Return on equity: 15.40%
Cash ($ mil.): 0
Current ratio: —
Long-term debt ($ mil.): —

Dividends
Yield: —
Payout: —
Market value ($ mil.): —

ST VINCENT MEDICAL CENTER

LOCATIONS

HQ: ST VINCENT MEDICAL CENTER
2131 W 3RD ST, LOS ANGELES, CA 90057-1901
Phone: 213-484-7111
Web: www.stvincentmedicalcenter.org

HISTORICAL FINANCIALS

Company Type: Private

Income Statement

FYE: June 30

	REVENUE ($ mil.)	NET INCOME ($ mil.)	NET PROFIT MARGIN	EMPLOYEES
06/11	215	(19)	—	1,790
06/10	204	(5)	—	0
06/09	195	(7)	—	0
06/08	4	0	20.8%	0
Annual Growth	261.3%	—	—	—

2011 Year-End Financials

Debt ratio: —
Return on equity: (-9.20)%
Cash ($ mil.): 8
Current ratio: 0.30
Long-term debt ($ mil.): —

Dividends
Yield: —
Payout: —
Market value ($ mil.): —

ST. ALEXIUS MEDICAL CENTER

Established in 1885 St. Alexius Medical Center has been serving the health care needs of those who reside in the Dakotas and Montana longer than any other area hospital. The medical facility with more than 300 beds caters to central and western North Dakota and parts of South Dakota and Montana. Specialty services include cancer care trauma care geriatrics orthopedics and rehabilitation. As part of its operations the longtime hospital also owns and manages a handful of smaller regional hospitals and community clinics. St. Alexius Medical Center is part of the PrimeCare health group along with the Mid Dakota Cancer Treatment & Research Center The Bone & Joint Center and other medical providers.

Operations

St. Alexius Medical Center owns and operates hospitals and clinics in North Dakota (in Garrison and Turtle Lake) and manages the hospitals and clinics owned by Mobridge Regional Hospital in Mobridge South Dakota. Also part of its operations St. Alexius Medical Center owns and operates specialty and primary care clinics in Minot North Dakota and a primary care clinic in Mandan North Dakota.

Company Ownership

A Roman Catholic organization St. Alexius Medical Center is sponsored by the Sisters of St. Benedict of the Annunciation Monastery located in Bismarck North Dakota. The medical facility follows the Ethical and Religious Directives for Catholic Health Care Services as promulgated by the United States Conference of Catholic Bishops.

EXECUTIVES

SVP and CFO, Gary P. Miller
VP Government Relations and Marketing, Nancy R. Willis
SVP and Chief Nursing Officer, Linda Knodel
VP Human Resources, Wanda Pfaff
VP Material and Facility Resources, Frank Kilzer
VP Heart Vascular and Professional Services, Dewey Schlittenhard
VP Medical Affairs, S. Shiraz Hyder
President and CEO, Andrew Wilson
VP Behavioral Health and Inpatient Rehabilitation Services, Rosanne Schmidt
Chair, John Castleberry
VP Mission Effectiveness, Susan Lardy
VP Physician and Outreach Services, Kurt Waldbillig
Director St. Alexius Foundation, Jaclyn Bugbee
Director and Board President, Nancy Miller
Director and Board VP, Thomas Welder
Director and Board Secretary, Gerard Wald
Director and Board Treasurer, Rosanne Zastoupil
Director, Mariah Dietz
Director, Vern Dosch
Director, John Giese
Director, Nicholas Neumann
Director, Chuck Reichert
Director, Ken Ziegler
Director, Andrew L. Wilson

LOCATIONS

HQ: St. Alexius Medical Center
900 E. Broadway Ave., Bismarck ND 58501
Phone: 701-530-7000　　**Fax:** 701-530-8984
Web: www.st.alexius.org

PRODUCTS/OPERATIONS

Selected Services
Acceleration
Arthritis Clinic
Balance and Dizziness Center
Behavioral and Mental Health
Cardiac Rehabilitation
Clinical Research Services
Community Health
Community Pharmacy
Deep Brain Stimulation
Dialysis
EAP

Emergency & Trauma
Family Practice Clinic
Geriatrics (Older Adults)
Heart and Vascular Center
Home Care and Hospice
Human Performance Center
Kidney Dialysis
Mandan Clinic
Minot Medical Clinic
Neonatology Clinic
Nephrology Clinic
Neurology
Neuroscience
Neurosurgery
Occupational Health and Wellness
Occupational Therapy - Outpatient
Orthopedics
Pediatric Cardiology Clinic
Pediatric Neurology Clinic
Physical Medicine & Rehabilitation
Physical Therapy - Outpatient
Radiology Services
Rehabilitation Unit - Inpatient
Spine Center
Stroke Center
Surgical Services
Telemedicine and Videoconferencing Services
Therapy at HPC
Urology Clinic
Women's Health

COMPETITORS

Altru Health	Sanford
Avera Health	Health-MeritCare
Billings Clinic	
Catholic Health Initiatives	

HISTORICAL FINANCIALS

Company Type: Private - Not-for-Profit

Income Statement　　　　　　　　　FYE: June 30

	REVENUE ($ mil.)	NET INCOME ($ mil.)	NET PROFIT MARGIN	EMPLOYEES
06/12	294	11	3.7%	1,947
06/11	275	12	4.6%	0
06/10	243	6	2.6%	0
06/09	243	6	2.6%	0
Annual Growth	6.6%	20.3%	—	—

2012 Year-End Financials

Debt ratio: ——
Return on equity: 3.70%　　　　Dividends
Cash ($ mil.): 33　　　　　　　Yield: —
Current ratio: 1.50　　　　　　Payout: —
Long-term debt ($ mil.): —　　Market value ($ mil.): —

ST. ANTHONY'S MEDICAL CENTER

St. Anthony's Medical Center applies its skills to medical cases in the Midwest. The hospital serves residents in the areas surrounding St. Louis Missouri as well as portions of southwestern Illinois. With about 770 beds and more than 800 affiliated physicians the hospital provides a comprehensive offering including inpatient and outpatient medical surgical diagnostic and behavioral health care. The hospital also operates a level 2 trauma center cancer and chest pain units and a pediatric emergency center as well as several urgent care facilities. It

also offers home health hospice laboratory and pharmacy services. St. Anthony's Medical Center was founded in 1900 by the Franciscan Sisters of Germany.

Geographic Reach

St. Anthony's Medical Center is one of the largest hospitals in the St. Louis metropolitan area. It serves a population base of more than 900000 people in ten counties in Missouri and Illinois. It also operates four urgent care centers in surrounding communities of Arnold Big Bend Fenton and Lemay.

Operations

St. Anthony's Medical Center's ER is staffed by an independently-owned group of emergency physicians —in this case Emergency Physicians of St. Louis —who contract to provide services to the hospital. The physician-group model of employment aims to improve patient flow and reduce waiting times at the ER.

Strategy

St. Anthony's Medical Center completed a $90 million four-year redesign and expansion project in 2010 with the opening of its endovascular laboratory center which combined together catheterization radiology and electrophysiology units. Earlier phases included a new heart and surgical pavilion. To bring more cardiac physicians into the mix the medical center partnered with a physician practice association The Heart Specialty Associates in 2011.

To enhance patient convenience St. Anthony's Medical Center opened a new retail pharmacy in the lobby of its Medical Plaza building adjacent to the main hospital building.

EXECUTIVES

Chairman, David M. Sindelar, age 54
EVP Corporate Finance, John McGuire
Director St. Anthony's Hospice, Edward L. Burns
President and CEO, Thomas H. Rockers
Executive Director Physician Practice Management and Development, Dave Hinkle
VP Human Resources, Ann Bollone
VP Finance and CFO, John Skeans
EVP and COO, Robert Thames
VP Marketing and Communications, Tess Niehaus
President Medical Staff, Robert Beckman

LOCATIONS

HQ: St. Anthony' s Medical Center
10010 Kennerly Rd., St. Louis MO 63128
Phone: 314-525-1000　　**Fax:** 314-525-4040
Web: www.stanthonysmedcenter.com

PRODUCTS/OPERATIONS

Selected Services
Acute Rehabilitation
Audiology/Hearing
Behavioral Health
Breast Center
Cancer Care Center
Diabetes Education
Emergency/Trauma
Heart Specialty Center
Home Care
Hospice Field Program
Hyland Behavioral Health
Long-term Acute Care
Neuroscience and Stroke
Occupational Medicine
Oncology
Orthopedics
Ostomy Clinic
Outpatient Imaging
Pediatric Services

Physical Therapy
Pregnancy and Birth
Pharmacy
Pulmonary
Radiology/Imaging Centers
Rehabilitation (cardiac and acute)
Senior Services
Sleep Disorder Center
Social Services (Care Management)
Speech Therapy
Sports & Therapy
Stroke
Surgery
Urgent Care Centers
Urological Gynecology
Vestibular Rehab
Weight Management
Women's Medical/Surgical Unit
Wound Treatment

COMPETITORS

Ascension Health	RehabCare
Barnes-Jewish Hospital	Saint Francis Medical
BJC HealthCare	Center
Christian Hospital	SSM Health Care
CoxHealth	St. John's Health
HCA	System
Memorial Hospital	St. Luke's Hospital
(Illinois)	(MO)
Mercy Health	Tenet Healthcare
Mercy Hospital St.	
Louis	

HISTORICAL FINANCIALS

Company Type: Private - Not-for-Profit

Income Statement
FYE: June 30

	REVENUE ($ mil.)	NET INCOME ($ mil.)	NET PROFIT MARGIN	EMPLOYEES
06/12	467	(29)	—	3,900
06/11	473	53	11.3%	0
06/10	439	(10)	—	0
06/09	427	(4)	—	0
Annual Growth	3.0%	—	—	—

2012 Year-End Financials

Debt ratio: —
Return on equity: (-6.40)%
Cash ($ mil.): 2
Current ratio: 1.10
Long-term debt ($ mil.): —

Dividends
Yield: —
Payout: —
Market value ($ mil.): —

ST. ANTHONY'S MEMORIAL HOSPITAL OF THE HOSPITAL SISTERS OF THETH

LOCATIONS

HQ: ST. ANTHONY'S MEMORIAL HOSPITAL OF THE HOSPITAL SISTERS OF THETH
503 N MAPLE ST, EFFINGHAM, IL 62401-2099
Phone: 217-342-2121
Web: www.hshsmedicalgroup.com

HISTORICAL FINANCIALS

Company Type: Private

Income Statement
FYE: June 30

	REVENUE ($ mil.)	NET INCOME ($ mil.)	NET PROFIT MARGIN	EMPLOYEES
06/11	129	25	20.1%	900
06/10	117	20	17.1%	0
06/09	106	(0)	—	0
06/08	92	12	13.4%	0
Annual Growth	11.9%	28.0%	—	—

2011 Year-End Financials

Debt ratio: —
Return on equity: 20.10%
Cash ($ mil.): 3
Current ratio: 3.10
Long-term debt ($ mil.): —

Dividends
Yield: —
Payout: —
Market value ($ mil.): —

ST. CATHERINE HOSPITAL INC.

LOCATIONS

HQ: ST. CATHERINE HOSPITAL INC.
4321 FIR ST, EAST CHICAGO, IN 46312-3097
Phone: 219-392-1700
Web: www.comhs.org

HISTORICAL FINANCIALS

Company Type: Private

Income Statement
FYE: June 30

	REVENUE ($ mil.)	NET INCOME ($ mil.)	NET PROFIT MARGIN	EMPLOYEES
06/11	159	(7)	—	900
06/10	164	(1)	—	0
06/09	118	1	1.1%	0
06/08	154	11	7.2%	0
Annual Growth	1.2%	—	—	—

2011 Year-End Financials

Debt ratio: —
Return on equity: (-4.60)%
Cash ($ mil.): 5
Current ratio: 1.00
Long-term debt ($ mil.): —

Dividends
Yield: —
Payout: —
Market value ($ mil.): —

ST. CATHERINE UNIVERSITY

LOCATIONS

HQ: ST. CATHERINE UNIVERSITY
2004 RANDOLPH AVE, SAINT PAUL, MN 55105-1750
Phone: 651-690-6740
Web: www.stkate.edu

HISTORICAL FINANCIALS

Company Type: Private

Income Statement
FYE: May 31

	REVENUE ($ mil.)	NET INCOME ($ mil.)	NET PROFIT MARGIN	EMPLOYEES
05/11	115	10	9.1%	318
05/10	103	3	3.3%	0
05/09	89	0	—	0
05/05	57	(1)	—	0
Annual Growth	26.5%			

2011 Year-End Financials

Debt ratio: —
Return on equity: 9.10%
Cash ($ mil.): 8
Current ratio: —
Long-term debt ($ mil.): —

Dividends
Yield: —
Payout: —
Market value ($ mil.): —

ST. CLAIRE MEDICAL CENTER INC.

LOCATIONS

HQ: ST. CLAIRE MEDICAL CENTER INC.
222 MEDICAL CIR, MOREHEAD, KY 40351-1179
Phone: 606-783-6500
Web: www.fpresidency.org

HISTORICAL FINANCIALS

Company Type: Private

Income Statement
FYE: June 30

	REVENUE ($ mil.)	NET INCOME ($ mil.)	NET PROFIT MARGIN	EMPLOYEES
06/11	138	1	1.0%	2,527
06/10	129	1	1.5%	0
06/09	119	(2)	—	0
06/08	117	(1)	—	0
Annual Growth	5.6%	—	—	—

2011 Year-End Financials

Debt ratio: —
Return on equity: 1.00%
Cash ($ mil.): 7
Current ratio: 0.80
Long-term debt ($ mil.): —

Dividends
Yield: —
Payout: —
Market value ($ mil.): —

ST. ELIZABETH MEDICAL CENTER

LOCATIONS

HQ: ST. ELIZABETH MEDICAL CENTER
2209 GENESEE ST, UTICA, NY 13501-5999
Phone: 315-798-8100
Web: www.stelizabethmedicalcenter.com

HISTORICAL FINANCIALS

Company Type: Private

Income Statement				FYE: December 31
	REVENUE ($ mil.)	NET INCOME ($ mil.)	NET PROFIT MARGIN	EMPLOYEES
12/11	206	(15)	—	1,700
12/10	204	0	0.3%	0
12/09	205	6	3.3%	0
12/08	189	(7)	—	0
Annual Growth	2.9%	—	—	—

2011 Year-End Financials

Debt ratio: —
Return on equity: (-7.70)%
Cash ($ mil.): 4
Current ratio: 0.80
Long-term debt ($ mil.): —

Dividends
Yield: —
Payout: —
Market value ($ mil.): —

ST. FRANCIS HOSPITAL INC.

LOCATIONS

HQ: ST. FRANCIS HOSPITAL INC.
1 SAINT FRANCIS DR, GREENVILLE, SC 29601-3955
Phone: 864-255-1000
Web: www.stfrancishealth.com

HISTORICAL FINANCIALS

Company Type: Private

Income Statement				FYE: August 31
	REVENUE ($ mil.)	NET INCOME ($ mil.)	NET PROFIT MARGIN	EMPLOYEES
08/11	468	66	14.1%	2,105
Annual Growth	—	—	—	—

2011 Year-End Financials

Debt ratio: —
Return on equity: 14.10%
Cash ($ mil.): 234
Current ratio: 0.90
Long-term debt ($ mil.): —

Dividends
Yield: —
Payout: —
Market value ($ mil.): —

ST. FRANCIS MEDICAL CENTER INC.

LOCATIONS

HQ: ST. FRANCIS MEDICAL CENTER INC.
309 JACKSON ST, MONROE, LA 71201-7407
Phone: 318-966-4000
Web: www.stfran.com

HISTORICAL FINANCIALS

Company Type: Private

Income Statement				FYE: June 30
	REVENUE ($ mil.)	NET INCOME ($ mil.)	NET PROFIT MARGIN	EMPLOYEES
06/11	265	19	7.4%	99
Annual Growth	—	—	—	—

2011 Year-End Financials

Debt ratio: —
Return on equity: 7.40%
Cash ($ mil.): 44
Current ratio: 2.50
Long-term debt ($ mil.): —

Dividends
Yield: —
Payout: —
Market value ($ mil.): —

ST. JAMES SECURITY SERVICES INC.

LOCATIONS

HQ: ST. JAMES SECURITY SERVICES INC.
1604 AVE PONCE DE LEON, SAN JUAN, PR 00909
Phone: 787-754-8448
Web: www.stjamessecurity.com

HISTORICAL FINANCIALS

Company Type: Private

Income Statement				FYE: June 30
	REVENUE ($ mil.)	NET INCOME ($ mil.)	NET PROFIT MARGIN	EMPLOYEES
06/12	81	4	5.1%	3,400
06/11	83	3	4.5%	0
06/10	83	3	4.1%	0
Annual Growth	(1.2%)	10.5%	—	—

2012 Year-End Financials

Debt ratio: —
Return on equity: 5.10%
Cash ($ mil.): 3
Current ratio: 1.40
Long-term debt ($ mil.): —

Dividends
Yield: —
Payout: —
Market value ($ mil.): —

ST. JOHN HEALTH SYSTEM INC.

St. John Health System aims to bring health into the lives of the ill. The not-for-profit system provides health care services to residents of Tulsa and surrounding areas in northeastern Oklahoma and southern Kansas. In addition to flagship facility St. John Medical Center it owns or manages eight other community hospitals as well as urgent care and long-term care facilities. St. John Health System provides primary and specialty medical care through OMNI Medical Group and offers health insurance through CommunityCare health plan. Established in 1926 by the Sisters of the Sor-

rowful Mother the health system is part of Marian Health.

Operations

Facilities owned managed or sponsored by St. John Health System include hospitals Oklahoma State University Medical Center St. John Sapulpa St. John Owasso St. John Broken Arrow Pawhuska City Hospital Sedan City Hospital Nowata Hospital and Jane Phillips Medical Center. The company's senior living facilities include Franciscan Villa Frances Streitel Villa Heartsworth House and Rosewood Terrace.

Strategy

St. John Health System will periodically add services to its offerings to meet community demand. In early 2011 St. John Health opened the St. John Weight Management Institute to offer its patients weight loss options including bariatric surgery. The health system's newest hospital St. John Broken Arrow near Tulsa was constructed in 2009.

In 2012 Marian Health entered talks with another Catholic health system operator Ascension Health over the possibility of merging St. John Health System and other Marian organizations into the Ascension organization.

EXECUTIVES

COO, David Pynn
President and CEO, Sister M. Therese Gottschalk
President St. John Medical Center Foundation, Richard Boone
VP Medical Affairs, William Allred
CFO, Lex Anderson
CIO, Mike Reeves
VP Mission Services, Ann Meuser
Coordinator Media Relations, Cora Scott
Chairman, R. J. Sullivan Jr.
Media Relations, Joy McGill
CEO St. John Medical Center, Charles Anderson

LOCATIONS

HQ: St. John Health System Inc.
1923 S. Utica Ave., Tulsa OK 74104
Phone: 918-744-2345   Fax: 918-744-2716
Web: www.sjmc.org

PRODUCTS/OPERATIONS

Selected Facilities and Operations – Oklahoma

CommunityCare (health plan)
Jane Phillips Medical Center (Bartlesville)
Nowata Hospital
Oklahoma State University Medical Center (managed facility in Tulsa)
OMNI Medical Group (physicians group)
Pawhuska City Hospital
Regional Medical Laboratory (clinical lab testing)
Sedan City Hospital
St. John Broken Arrow Hospital
St. John Medical Center (Tulsa)
St. John Owasso Hospital
St. John Physicians
St. John Sapulpa Hospital

COMPETITORS

Ardent Health Services
Catholic Health Initiatives
CIGNA
Community Health Systems
Deaconess Health Care
HCA
Hillcrest Medical Center

Kindred Healthcare
Marian Health System
Norman Regional Health
Presbyterian Healthcare Services
Saint Francis Health System
SSM Health Care
UnitedHealth Group
WellPoint

HISTORICAL FINANCIALS
Company Type: Private

Income Statement
FYE: September 30

	ASSETS ($ mil.)	NET INCOME ($ mil.)	INCOME AS % OF ASSETS	EMPLOYEES
09/11	1,155	17	1.5%	4,011
09/10	1,132	41	3.7%	0
09/09	1,116	(9)	—	0
09/08	1,117	(95)	—	0
Annual Growth	1.1%	—	—	—

2011 Year-End Financials
Debt ratio: ——
Return on equity: 2.00%
Cash ($ mil.): 73
Current ratio: 1.60
Long-term debt ($ mil.): —

Dividends
Yield: —
Payout: —
Market value ($ mil.): —

ST. JOHN'S COLLEGE

St. John's College believes in the "Great Books" even as the canon is under attack elsewhere in academia. Students at the college study the classics in literature math philosophy and science. The curriculum starts with Aeschylus Aristotle Euclid and Plato taught freshman year; students work their way through the millennia of higher learning finishing with the works of contemporary thinkers and writers which are taught to seniors. St. John's (not to be confused with the university in New York City) is the third-oldest institution of higher learning in the US (after Harvard and William & Mary); it was founded in Maryland in 1696 and opened a Santa Fe campus in 1964. Each campus has about 450 students.

EXECUTIVES

President Santa Fe Campus, Michael P. (Mike) Peters
President Annapolis Campus, Christopher B. Nelson, age 64
Director Communications Annapolis Campus, Rosemary Harty
VP Advancement Santa Fe Campus, James W. Osterholt
Assistant Director Communications Annapolis Campus, Patricia Dempsey
Director Career Services Annapolis Campus, Shahrzad Arasteh
Dean Santa Fe Campus, Victoria Mora
Dean Annapolis Campus, Michael Dink
VP Advancement Annapolis Campus, Barbara Goyette
Director Communications and External Relations Santa Fe Campus, Anna Sochocky
Registrar, Jon Enriquez
Chief of Public Safety, Timon K. Linn
Director Student Services Annapolis Campus, Taylor Waters
Director Financial Aid Annapolis Campus, Paula Abernethy
Director Admissions Annapolis Campus, Jon Christensen
Auditors: MullenSondbergWimbish&StonePA

LOCATIONS
HQ: St. John' s College
60 College Ave., Annapolis MD 21401
Phone: 410-263-2371   **Fax:** 410-295-6937
Web: www.sjca.edu

HISTORICAL FINANCIALS
Company Type: School

Income Statement
FYE: June 30

	REVENUE ($ mil.)	NET INCOME ($ mil.)	NET PROFIT MARGIN	EMPLOYEES
06/12	42	(8)	—	250
06/11	34	6	20.1%	0
06/10	29	2	6.9%	0
Annual Growth	20.9%	—	—	—

2012 Year-End Financials
Debt ratio: ——
Return on equity: (-20.10)%
Cash ($ mil.): 11
Current ratio: —
Long-term debt ($ mil.): —

Dividends
Yield: —
Payout: —
Market value ($ mil.): —

ST. JOSEPH HEALTH SYSTEM

St. Joseph Health System has earned a medal for decades by caring for patients on the West Coast and more recently the South Plains. The health care network operates 14 acute care hospitals three home health agencies a half-dozen urgent care centers and other health care delivery organizations throughout California and in eastern New Mexico and West Texas. In its primary market of California the health system has some 2900 beds at 10 hospitals. Its Covenant Health System unit operates in Texas and New Mexico with about 1200 beds in its network of some 50 primary care facilities.

Geographic Reach

The network operates 14 acute care hospitals three home health agencies a half-dozen urgent care centers and other health care delivery organizations throughout California and in eastern New Mexico and West Texas.

Financial Analysis

St. Joseph Health System brought in $4.22 billion in revenue during fiscal 2011.

Strategy

Already one of the largest health systems on the West Coast St. Joseph continues to grow thanks principally to its proficient fundraising.

The system invests regularly in network and facility expansion efforts. In 2013 it formed an affiliation with Hoag Memorial Hospital Presbyterian which operates two hospitals in Orange County. The Hoag operations are being combined with five of St. Joseph's area hospitals to form a new network called Covenant Health Network. The affiliated facilities will provide comprehensive care in the region while retaining their respective identities and religious affiliations.

In 2011 the system spent $125 million to open a new tower on St. Jude Medical Center in Fullerton California.

That same year St. Joseph Health System invested in technology like the Computerized Provider order Entry (CPOE) which enhances patient care and safety by utilizing evidence-based order sets eliminating transcription errors reducing wait times and providing decisions support directly to providers. CPOE adoption was 67% across ministries including St Jude Medical Center Mission Hospital in Mission Viejo and Laguna Beach Santa Rosa Memorial Hospital and Queen of Valley Medical center.

Company Background

St. Joseph Health System traces its roots back to 1920 when St. Joseph Hospital in Eureka California was first established. The health care system was officially organized in 1982 as it expanded and took on additional health care facilities. The system is a ministry of The Sisters of St. Joseph of Orange which itself was organized in 1912.

EXECUTIVES

President CEO and Trustee, Deborah A. Proctor
EVP System Services, William J. (Bill) Murin
President and CEO St. Joseph Hospital Orange, Steven C. (Steve) Moreau
EVP and COO, Joseph (Joe) Randolph
President and CEO St. Jude Medical Center, Lee Penrose
SVP and General Counsel, Shannon Dwyer
SVP Theology and Ethics, John (Jack) Glaser
EVP Southern California Region and CFO, Darrin Montalvo
SVP Community Health, Azhar Qureshi
EVP Wellness and Health Improvement, Elliot B. Sternberg
SVP and CIO, Larry Stofko
SVP, Susan Whittaker
EVP, Sister Jayne Helmlinger
President and CEO Redwood Memorial Hospital and St. Joseph Hospital Eureka, Joe Mark
SVP Physician Practice, C. R. Burke
President and CEO Queen of the Valley Medical Center, Walt Mickens
EVP West Texas and Southern New Mexico, Richard H. Parks
Director Marketing and Communications Queen of the Valley Medical Center, Jaime Penaherrera
SVP Ministry Integrity, Margaret Hambleton
EVP Strategic Services, Annette M. Walker
VP Leadership Institute and Governance Support; Interim EVP Mission Integration, Jeff Thies
Chief Medical Officer, Clyde Wesp Jr.
Chairman, Walter W. (Bill) Noce
EVP Northern California Region, Kevin Klockenga
Manager Marketing and Media Relations System Office, Kellie Todd Griffin
Manager Marketing and Media Relations Covenant Health System, Michell Stephens
Manager Marketing and Media Relations Mission Hospital, Kelsey Martinez
Manager Marketing and Media Relations St. Mary Medical Center, Randy Bevilacqua
Manager Marketing and Media Relations SJHS-Humboldt County, Laurie Watson-Stone
Manager Marketing and Media Relations SJHS-Sonoma County, Katy Hillenmeyer
Manager Marketing and Media Relations St. Joseph Hospital Orange, Cathy Semar
Manager Marketing and Media Relations St. Jude Medical Center, Dru Ann Copping
Chair St. Joseph Hospital Orange, Sister Theresa LaMetterey
President and CEO St. Mary Medical Center, Alan H. Garrett
President and CEO Mission Hospital, Kenneth (Kenn) McFarland
Trustee, Dan S. Wilford, age 71
Trustee, Paula L. Woods

LOCATIONS

HQ: St. Joseph Health System
   500 S. Main St. Ste. 1000, Orange CA 92868-4533
Phone: 714-347-7500   **Fax:** 714-347-7540
Web: www.stjhs.org

Selected Operations

Northern California
   Petaluma Valley Hospital
   Queen of the Valley Medical Center (Napa)
   Redwood Memorial Hospital (Fortuna)
   St. Joseph Home Care Network (Sonoma)
   St. Joseph Hospital (Eureka)
   Santa Rosa Memorial Hospital
Southern California
   Mission Hospital (Mission Viejo)
   Mission Hospital Laguna Beach
   St. Joseph Hospital (Orange)
   St. Jude Medical Center (Fullerton)
   St. Mary Medical Center (Apple Valley)
West Texas/Eastern New Mexico
   Covenant Health System
      Artesia General Hospital (New Mexico)
      Covenant Hospital Levelland (Texas)
      Covenant Hospital Plainview (Texas)
      Covenant Medical Center (Lubbock TX)
      Nor-Lea General Hospital (Lovington NM)
      Roosevelt General Hospital (Portales NM)

COMPETITORS

Adventist Health	Loma Linda University
Arrowhead Medical	Medical Center
Center	Los Angeles County
Banner Health	Health Department
Catholic Health	Memorial Health
Initiatives	Services
Cedars-Sinai Medical	Pasadena Hospital
Center	Association
Citrus Valley Health	Prospect Medical
Partners	Scripps health
City of Hope	Sutter Health
Dignity Health	Tenet Healthcare
HCA	Western Medical Center
Kaiser Permanente	- Santa Ana

HISTORICAL FINANCIALS

Company Type: Private - Not-for-Profit

Income Statement

FYE: June 30

	REVENUE ($ mil.)	NET INCOME ($ mil.)	NET PROFIT MARGIN	EMPLOYEES
06/11	4,223	348	8.3%	21,500
06/10	4,268	268	6.3%	0
06/08	3,943	53	1.3%	0
06/07	3,668	302	8.2%	0
Annual Growth	4.8%	4.8%	—	—

2011 Year-End Financials

Debt ratio: ——
Return on equity: 8.30%
Cash ($ mil.): 250
Current ratio: 0.90
Long-term debt ($ mil.): —

Dividends
   Yield: —
   Payout: —
   Market value ($ mil.): —

ST. JOSEPH HOSPITAL OF ORANGE

If you're feeling green or blue in Orange County St. Joseph Hospital of Orange is there to help get back to feeling pink and rosy. The California hospital provides general medical and surgical services as well as specialty care such as women's health mental health services oncology cardiology and physical rehabilitation. Part of the St. Joseph Health System the hospital provides primary care and specialty outpatient services through a network of affiliated physician practices. It also operates low-income and mobile clinics. Founded in 1929 by the Sisters of St. Joseph of Orange the hospital has about 525 beds and a medical staff of some 1000.
   Geographic Reach
   St. Joseph Hospital serves Orange County California and the greater Los Angeles metropolitan area.
   Operations
   In addition to physician group affiliates St. Joseph Hospital Affiliated Physicians and St. Joseph Heritage Medical Group the hospital also partners with the Childrens Hospital of Orange County to help expand pediatric care throughout the region.
   Strategy
   St. Joseph Hospital has been working to expand its community outreach programs related to cancer through a number of projects including offering improved access to clinical trials; providing better overall access to cancer care; and implementing measures to garner support for the implementation of cancer electronic health records. St. Joseph Hospital is using stimulus money and about a $3 million award from the National Cancer Institute Community Cancer Centers Program to help fund its various projects.

EXECUTIVES

VP Sponsorship, Linda Simon
President and CEO, Larry Ainsworth
COO, Alan Garrett
CFO, Tina Mycroft
Chairman, James Harmon
Director Communications, Robert Cogswell
Auditors: Ernst&YoungLLP

LOCATIONS

HQ: St. Joseph Hospital of Orange
   1100 W. Stewart Dr., Orange CA 92868
Phone: 714-633-9111   **Fax:** 714-744-8668
Web: www.sjo.org

COMPETITORS

Anaheim Regional	Providence Health
Medical Center	& Services
Children' s Hospital of	Southwest Healthcare
Orange County	Sutter Health
Citrus Valley Health	Tenet Healthcare
Partners	Torrance Memorial
Hoag Memorial Hospital	Medical Center
Kaiser Permanente	Trinity Health (Novi)
Memorial Health	UC Irvine Medical
Services	Center
Pasadena Hospital	Western Medical Center
Association	- Santa Ana

HISTORICAL FINANCIALS

Company Type: Subsidiary

Income Statement

FYE: June 30

	REVENUE ($ mil.)	NET INCOME ($ mil.)	NET PROFIT MARGIN	EMPLOYEES
06/11	661	32	4.9%	3,300
06/10	638	26	4.2%	0
06/09	509	(14)	—	0
06/08	575	38	6.8%	0
Annual Growth	4.7%	(5.6%)	—	—

2011 Year-End Financials

Debt ratio: ——
Return on equity: 4.90%
Cash ($ mil.): 120
Current ratio: 1.90
Long-term debt ($ mil.): —

Dividends
   Yield: —
   Payout: —
   Market value ($ mil.): —

ST. JOSEPH MEDICAL CENTER

LOCATIONS

HQ: ST. JOSEPH MEDICAL CENTER
   1000 CARONDELET DR, KANSAS CITY, MO
   64114-4673
Phone: 816-942-4400
Web: www.stjosephkc.com

HISTORICAL FINANCIALS

Company Type: Private

Income Statement

FYE: June 30

	REVENUE ($ mil.)	NET INCOME ($ mil.)	NET PROFIT MARGIN	EMPLOYEES
06/11	204	14	7.1%	1,550
06/10	197	12	6.5%	0
06/09	184	(6)	—	0
06/08	178	10	5.7%	0
Annual Growth	4.6%	12.5%	—	—

2011 Year-End Financials

Debt ratio: ——
Return on equity: 7.10%
Cash ($ mil.): 7
Current ratio: 0.60
Long-term debt ($ mil.): —

Dividends
   Yield: —
   Payout: —
   Market value ($ mil.): —

ST. JOSEPH'S MEDICAL CENTER

LOCATIONS

HQ: ST. JOSEPH' S MEDICAL CENTER
   523 N 3RD ST, BRAINERD, MN 56401-3098
Phone: 218-829-2861
Web: www.sjmcmn.org

HISTORICAL FINANCIALS
Company Type: Private

Income Statement
FYE: June 30

	REVENUE ($ mil.)	NET INCOME ($ mil.)	NET PROFIT MARGIN	EMPLOYEES
06/11	159	(0)	—	1,400
06/10	143	2	2.0%	0
06/09	101	(7)	—	0
Annual Growth	25.3%	—	—	—

2011 Year-End Financials
Debt ratio: ——
Return on equity: (-0.10)%
Cash ($ mil.): 0
Current ratio: 0.70
Long-term debt ($ mil.): —

Dividends
Yield: —
Payout: —
Market value ($ mil.): —

ST. JUDE HOSPITAL

St. Jude Medical Center gets sickly Southern Californians on their feet again. The faith-based not-for-profit acute care facility with more than 370 beds serves the residents of Orange County. The medical center provides an onsite cancer center (the Virginia K. Crosson Cancer Center) and a heart institute that offers cardiac surgeries and rehabilitation programs. It also provides inpatient and outpatient physical rehabilitation services and a variety of community outreach programs. Established by the Sisters of St. Joseph of Orange religious order in the 1950s St. Jude Medical Center is part of the St. Joseph Health System.

Operations

Beyond the medical center's campus St. Jude operates its Heritage Medical Group with eight locations throughout its region. The medical group includes specialists in plastic surgery rheumatology and gastroenterology.

In October 2011 St. Jude Medical Center closed its 12-bed pediatric unit and redirected patients younger than 16 to nearby Children's Hospital of Orange County. St. Jude's NICU (neonatal intensive care unit) remains open and the hospital continues to provide emergency and outpatient services to children.

EXECUTIVES
President and CEO, Lee Penrose
Manager Guest Relations, Matt Foster
EVP and COO, Doreen Dann
Director Government and Community Relations, Burnie Dunlap
VP Medical Affairs, Joseph Lawton
VP Healthy Communities, Barry Ross
VP Resource Development, Susan Smith

LOCATIONS
HQ: St. Jude Medical Center
101 E. Valencia Mesa Dr., Fullerton CA 92835
Phone: 714-871-3280　　**Fax:** 713-740-8031
Web: www.apmdelivers.com

COMPETITORS
Anaheim Regional Medical Center
Children' s Hospital of Orange County
UC Irvine Medical Center
Western Medical Center - Santa Ana

Hoag Memorial Hospital
Memorial Health
Services

HISTORICAL FINANCIALS
Company Type: Subsidiary

Income Statement
FYE: June 30

	REVENUE ($ mil.)	NET INCOME ($ mil.)	NET PROFIT MARGIN	EMPLOYEES
06/11	496	56	11.4%	2,600
06/10	492	61	12.4%	0
06/09	412	0	—	0
06/08	419	40	9.7%	0
Annual Growth	5.8%	11.5%	—	—

2011 Year-End Financials
Debt ratio: ——
Return on equity: 11.40%
Cash ($ mil.): 93
Current ratio: 3.30
Long-term debt ($ mil.): —

Dividends
Yield: —
Payout: —
Market value ($ mil.): —

ST. MARY MEDICAL CENTER

LOCATIONS
HQ: ST. MARY MEDICAL CENTER
1201 LANGHORNE NEWTOWN RD, LANGHORNE, PA 19047-1295
Phone: 215-710-2000
Web: www.stmarymedicalcenter.com

HISTORICAL FINANCIALS
Company Type: Private

Income Statement
FYE: December 31

	REVENUE ($ mil.)	NET INCOME ($ mil.)	NET PROFIT MARGIN	EMPLOYEES
12/11	438	35	8.1%	2,400
12/09	372	44	11.9%	0
12/08	322	17	5.5%	0
12/05	1	(0)	—	0
Annual Growth	649.3%	—	—	—

2011 Year-End Financials
Debt ratio: ——
Return on equity: 8.10%
Cash ($ mil.): 137
Current ratio: 3.30
Long-term debt ($ mil.): —

Dividends
Yield: —
Payout: —
Market value ($ mil.): —

ST. MARY'S FOOD BANK ALLIANCE

LOCATIONS
HQ: ST. MARY' S FOOD BANK ALLIANCE
2831 N 31ST AVE, PHOENIX, AZ 85009-1518
Phone: 602-352-3640
Web: www.smfb.org

HISTORICAL FINANCIALS
Company Type: Private

Income Statement
FYE: June 30

	REVENUE ($ mil.)	NET INCOME ($ mil.)	NET PROFIT MARGIN	EMPLOYEES
06/11	125	(5)	—	76
06/10	126	2	2.3%	0
06/09	130	0	—	0
06/08	91	4	4.5%	0
Annual Growth	11.4%	—	—	—

2011 Year-End Financials
Debt ratio: ——
Return on equity: (-4.50)%
Cash ($ mil.): 2
Current ratio: 2.10
Long-term debt ($ mil.): —

Dividends
Yield: —
Payout: —
Market value ($ mil.): —

ST. MARY'S MEDICAL CENTER

LOCATIONS
HQ: ST. MARY' S MEDICAL CENTER
407 E 3RD ST, DULUTH, MN 55805-1984
Phone: 218-786-4000

PRODUCTS/OPERATIONS

Selected Services
Breast Center
Behavioral health
Emergency care
Home health care
Intensive care
Interventional radiology
Joslin Diabetes Center Affiliate
Maternity care
Occupational Health Center
Pain Relief Center
Pastoral care
Pharmacy
Regional Heart Institute
Regional Cancer Center
Regional Neuroscience Center
Regional Orthopedic Center
Regional Sleep Center
Regional Spine Center
Regional Stroke Center
Regional Orthopedic Center
Regional Wound Center
Rehabilitation
Skilled Nursing Care
Support groups
Weight Loss Surgery Center

HISTORICAL FINANCIALS

Company Type: Private

Income Statement

FYE: June 30

	REVENUE ($ mil.)	NET INCOME ($ mil.)	NET PROFIT MARGIN	EMPLOYEES
06/11	387	52	13.5%	4,209
06/10	365	39	10.9%	0
06/09	352	41	11.8%	0
06/08	343	28	8.4%	0
Annual Growth	4.1%	22.0%	—	—

2011 Year-End Financials

Debt ratio: ——
Return on equity: 13.50%
Cash ($ mil.): 29
Current ratio: 0.90
Long-term debt ($ mil.): —

Dividends
Yield: —
Payout: —
Market value ($ mil.): —

ST. MARY'S MEDICAL CENTER OF SAGINAW INC.

LOCATIONS

HQ: ST. MARY' S MEDICAL CENTER OF SAGINAW INC.
800 S WASHINGTON AVE, SAGINAW, MI 48601-2551
Phone: 989-907-8000
Web: www.stmarysofmichigan.org

HISTORICAL FINANCIALS

Company Type: Private

Income Statement

FYE: June 30

	REVENUE ($ mil.)	NET INCOME ($ mil.)	NET PROFIT MARGIN	EMPLOYEES
06/11	276	26	9.7%	1,869
06/10	271	14	5.2%	0
06/09	227	0	—	0
06/05	237	14	6.2%	0
Annual Growth	5.3%	22.3%	—	—

2011 Year-End Financials

Debt ratio: ——
Return on equity: 9.70%
Cash ($ mil.): 19
Current ratio: 0.30
Long-term debt ($ mil.): —

Dividends
Yield: —
Payout: —
Market value ($ mil.): —

ST. MARY'S UNIVERSITY OF SAN ANTONIO TEXAS

LOCATIONS

HQ: ST. MARY' S UNIVERSITY OF SAN ANTONIO TEXAS
3766 TUPELO LN APT 2904, SAN ANTONIO, TX 78229-2216
Phone: 210-436-3011
Web: www.stmarytx.edu

HISTORICAL FINANCIALS

Company Type: Private

Income Statement

FYE: May 31

	REVENUE ($ mil.)	NET INCOME ($ mil.)	NET PROFIT MARGIN	EMPLOYEES
05/12	94	(6)	—	806
05/07*	96	22	23.5%	0
06/05	75	3	4.3%	0
05/03	63	(3)	—	0
Annual Growth	14.0%	—	—	—

*Fiscal year change

2012 Year-End Financials

Debt ratio: ——
Return on equity: (-7.20)%
Cash ($ mil.): 47
Current ratio: —
Long-term debt ($ mil.): —

Dividends
Yield: —
Payout: —
Market value ($ mil.): —

ST. OLAF COLLEGE

The hills of Northfield Minnesota are alive with the sounds of St. Olaf College. The private liberal arts university offers undergraduate and pre-professional education to more than 3000 students offering degrees in about 45 academic focus areas. Popular majors include English psychology biology economics and chemistry. The school has a faculty of about 250 teachers and is recognized for its choral and orchestral music programs as well as its mathematics department. St. Olaf College was founded in 1874 by Norwegian immigrants and is affiliated with the Evangelical Lutheran Church of America.

EXECUTIVES

Controller, Linda Kuchinka
VP and Treasurer, Alan Norton
Assistant VP Finance Office and Chief Investment Officer, Mark Gelle
Provost and Dean College, James M. (Jim) May
Director Human Resources, Roger Loftus
Director Information and Instructional Technologies, Roberta Lembke
Assistant VP Facilities, Peter Sandberg
Director Public Safety, Fred Behr
VP and Dean Enrollment, Michael Kyle
President, David R. Anderson, age 60
VP and Liaison to the Board of Regents, Paula Carlson
VP Student Life and Dean Students, Greg Kneser
VP Advancement and College Relations, Michael Stitsworth

Registrar, Mary Cisar
Director Alumni and Parent Relations, Nathan Soland
Director Marketing and Communications, Steve Blodgett

LOCATIONS

HQ: St. Olaf College
1520 St. Olaf Ave., Northfield MN 55057
Phone: 507-786-2222   **Fax:** 507-786-3549
Web: www.stolaf.edu

HISTORICAL FINANCIALS

Company Type: School

Income Statement

FYE: May 31

	REVENUE ($ mil.)	NET INCOME ($ mil.)	NET PROFIT MARGIN	EMPLOYEES
05/12	124	(10)	—	800
05/11	121	60	49.7%	0
05/10	116	44	38.1%	0
05/09	141	0	—	0
Annual Growth	(4.1%)	—	—	—

2012 Year-End Financials

Debt ratio: ——
Return on equity: (-8.60)%
Cash ($ mil.): 23
Current ratio: —
Long-term debt ($ mil.): —

Dividends
Yield: —
Payout: —
Market value ($ mil.): —

ST. VINCENT HOSPITAL OF THE HOSPITAL SISTERS OF THE THIRD ORDER

LOCATIONS

HQ: ST. VINCENT HOSPITAL OF THE HOSPITAL SISTERS OF THE THIRD ORDER
835 S VAN BUREN ST, GREEN BAY, WI 54301-3575
Phone: 920-433-0111
Web: www.stvincenthospital.org

HISTORICAL FINANCIALS

Company Type: Private

Income Statement

FYE: June 30

	REVENUE ($ mil.)	NET INCOME ($ mil.)	NET PROFIT MARGIN	EMPLOYEES
06/11	424	26	6.3%	2,360
06/10	376	16	4.4%	0
06/09	247	0	—	0
06/08	261	13	5.1%	0
Annual Growth	17.5%	26.0%	—	—

2011 Year-End Financials

Debt ratio: ——
Return on equity: 6.30%
Cash ($ mil.): 21
Current ratio: 2.20
Long-term debt ($ mil.): —

Dividends
Yield: —
Payout: —
Market value ($ mil.): —

ST. VINCENT RANDOLPH HOSPITAL INC

LOCATIONS

HQ: ST. VINCENT RANDOLPH HOSPITAL INC
473 E GREENVILLE AVE, WINCHESTER, IN
47394-9436
Phone: 765-584-0004

HISTORICAL FINANCIALS

Company Type: Private

Income Statement
FYE: June 30

	REVENUE ($ mil.)	NET INCOME ($ mil.)	NET PROFIT MARGIN	EMPLOYEES
06/11	33,770	6,141	18.2%	251
06/10	30	0	2.5%	0
06/09	27	1	5.1%	0
06/08	22	1	6.7%	0
Annual Growth	1051.8%	1505.5%	—	—

2011 Year-End Financials

Debt ratio: —
Return on equity: 18.20%
Cash ($ mil.): 1
Current ratio: 0.90
Long-term debt ($ mil.): —

Dividends
Yield: —
Payout: —
Market value ($ mil.): —

STAND ENERGY CORPORATION

Stand Energy Corporation (SEC) took a stand in the 1980s when the US government deregulated the natural gas industry. The company markets natural gas to large commercial and industrial customers in nine states (Illinois Indiana Kentucky Maryland New York Ohio Pennsylvania Virginia and West Virginia) and the District of Columbia. SEC also constructs bypass pipelines for its customers (allowing companies to bypass the local utility) and designs and builds propane backup systems to take advantage of reduced gas rates. SEC was founded in 1984 by Chairman Matth Toebben and CEO Judith Phillips. Customers include Coors and the Ohio Hospital Association.

EXECUTIVES

Chairman, Matth Toebben
President and CEO, Judith A. Phillips

LOCATIONS

HQ: Stand Energy Corporation
1077 Celestial St. Ste. 110, Cincinnati OH 45202-1629
Phone: 513-621-1113   **Fax:** 513-621-3773
Web: www.standenergy.com

COMPETITORS

Columbia Gas of Ohio	Infinite Energy
Dominion East Ohio	ProLiance Energy
Duke Energy Ohio	Vectren Energy
Florida Gas	Delivery of Ohio

Transmission

HISTORICAL FINANCIALS

Company Type: Private

Income Statement
FYE: December 31

	REVENUE ($ mil.)	NET INCOME ($ mil.)	NET PROFIT MARGIN	EMPLOYEES
12/11	117	0	—	32
12/10	12	0	—	0
12/09	149	0	—	0
12/08	212	0	—	0
Annual Growth	(18.0%)	—	—	—

2011 Year-End Financials

Debt ratio: —
Return on equity: —
Cash ($ mil.): 7
Current ratio: 1.50
Long-term debt ($ mil.): —

Dividends
Yield: —
Payout: —
Market value ($ mil.): —

STANDARD ELECTRIC COMPANY

Standard Electric and its affiliates distribute electrical and electronic products and supplies to customers through about 30 locations in Michigan. The company was founded in 1929 by Samuel Cohen and brothers Morris and Max Blumberg. The Blumberg brothers earlier established another Michigan-based electrical distributor Madison Electric an affiliate of Standard Electric with 10 Michigan locations. Another affiliated firm U.P. Electric/Wittock Supply Co. is a distributor of electrical and mechanical products with four locations on the upper Michigan peninsula. The company is owned by its directors and their families.

EXECUTIVES

President, Laverne N. (Vern) Weber, age 76
Marketing Manager, Jeff Marner
Sales Manager Southern Regional, Dan Shimkos
Sales Manager, John Wisniewski
Sales Manager Northern Regional, Tim Schell
Sales Manager Grand Rapids Area, Dave LaGosh
Sales Manager U.P. Electric and Wittock, Mike Horton
Quality Manager, Ron Simpson
Vice President, Bill Gray

LOCATIONS

HQ: Standard Electric Company
2650 Trautner Dr., Saginaw MI 48603
Phone: 989-497-2100   **Fax:** 989-497-2101
Web: www.standardelectricco.com

COMPETITORS

Kendall Electric	Utility Supply and
McNaughton-McKay	Construction
Medler Electric	Werner Electric Supply

HISTORICAL FINANCIALS

Company Type: Private

Income Statement
FYE: February 29

	REVENUE ($ mil.)	NET INCOME ($ mil.)	NET PROFIT MARGIN	EMPLOYEES
02/12	155	1	1.1%	250
02/11	132	0	0.3%	0
02/10	102	(0)	—	0
02/09	129	0	0.5%	0
Annual Growth	6.2%	43.0%	—	—

2012 Year-End Financials

Debt ratio: —
Return on equity: 1.10%
Cash ($ mil.): 0
Current ratio: 0.80
Long-term debt ($ mil.): —

Dividends
Yield: —
Payout: —
Market value ($ mil.): —

STANLEY ELECTRIC US CO INC

LOCATIONS

HQ: STANLEY ELECTRIC US CO INC
420 E HIGH ST, LONDON, OH 43140-9799
Phone: 740-852-5200
Web: www.stanleyelectricus.com

HISTORICAL FINANCIALS

Company Type: Private

Income Statement
FYE: March 31

	REVENUE ($ mil.)	NET INCOME ($ mil.)	NET PROFIT MARGIN	EMPLOYEES
03/11	209	11	5.5%	780
Annual Growth	—	—	—	—

2011 Year-End Financials

Debt ratio: —
Return on equity: 5.50%
Cash ($ mil.): 61
Current ratio: 2.00
Long-term debt ($ mil.): —

Dividends
Yield: —
Payout: —
Market value ($ mil.): —

STANLEY STEEMER INTERNATIONAL INC.

Carpet stains don't startle this Stanley. Stanley Steemer International provides residential and commercial carpet and upholstery cleaning through almost 300 franchise and corporate locations. In addition to cleaning carpets the company provides cleaning services for tile and grout air ducts and cars boats and RVs. The company also offers water damage restoration for flooring. It sells its own branded cleaning products through an online store. Founded by Jack Bates in 1947 when he established his own one-man carpet cleaning business Stanley Steemer is owned by his descendants including CEO Wesley Bates and President Justin Bates.

EXECUTIVES

Chairman and CEO, Wesley C. Bates
CFO, Mark Bunner
EVP, Phillip P. Ryser
VP Human Resources, Eric Smith
Director MIS, Dale Bevins

LOCATIONS

HQ: Stanley Steemer International Inc.
5500 Stanley Steemer Pkwy., Dublin OH 43016
Phone: 614-764-2007   **Fax:** 614-764-1506
Web: www.stanleysteemer.com

PRODUCTS/OPERATIONS

Selected Products and Services
Air duct cleaning
Area rug cleaning
Auto boats and RVs interior cleaning
Carpet cleaning
Flooring sales and installation
Furniture cleaning
Leather cleaning
Tile and grout cleaning
Water damage restoration

COMPETITORS

Dwyer Group	ServiceMaster
Maid to Perfection	The BMS Enterprises
Molly Maid	

HISTORICAL FINANCIALS

Company Type: Private

Income Statement

	REVENUE ($ mil.)	NET INCOME ($ mil.)	NET PROFIT MARGIN	EMPLOYEES
12/11	191	11	6.3%	2,000
12/10	186	8	4.4%	0
12/09	172	3	2.3%	0
12/08	187	13	7.3%	0
Annual Growth	**0.6%**	**(4.2%)**	**—**	**—**

2011 Year-End Financials

Debt ratio: ——
Return on equity: 6.30%
Cash ($ mil.): 21
Current ratio: 1.30
Long-term debt ($ mil.): —

Dividends
Yield: —
Payout: —
Market value ($ mil.): —

STANLY REGIONAL MEDICAL CENTER

Nope it's not a typo. It really is Stanly without an "e." Stanly Regional Medical Center (SRMC) provides a wide range of general medical services to residents in and around Stanly County in North Carolina. Formed in 1950 the hospital has 120 beds and is under the management of Carolinas HealthCare which owns or manages about two dozen regional hospitals. The two organizations agreed to the management contract in 2009 to provide SRMC with more access to resources such as group purchasing help with physician recruitment and supply-chain management. SRMC is affiliated with a number of other organizations including about a dozen clinics a home health agency a medical equipment company and a nursing home.

The center's medical specialties include behavioral health care cancer and cardiology services hyperbaric medicine orthopedics and women's services.

SRMC and Carolinas HealthCare are attempting to open a 40-bed rehabilitation hospital called Carolinas Rehabilitation-NorthEast but have thus far been blocked by the North Carolina Division of Health Services. The state agency ruled that the two organizations have not shown significant need for the facility and have not shown that the project would be cost-effective. SRMC and Carolinas HealthCare are appealing the state's ruling.

EXECUTIVES

Legal Services, Ron Burris
Director Public Relations, Benjamin (Ben) Jolly
Director Stanly Regional Medical Center Foundation, Jane Boone
Customer Service, Sherry Dunevant
VP Facilities Management, Dale Burris
Facilities Management, Danny Dennis
Health Information Management, Kelly Hill
Biomedical Engineering, Jim Vick
Materials Management, Kerry Burris
SVP COO and Chief Nursing Officer, Debra B. Smith
President and CEO, Al Taylor, age 44
CFO, Nick Samilo
VP Ancillary Services and Information Systems, Brian Freeman
VP Human Resources, Paul Morlock
Director Marketing, Nicole Williams
VP Physician Network and Surgical Services, Brad Marino

LOCATIONS

HQ: Stanly Regional Medical Center
301 Yadkin St., Albermarle NC 28002
Phone: 704-984-4000   **Fax:** 704-983-3562
Web: www.stanly.org

PRODUCTS/OPERATIONS

Selected Affiliations
Alliance Medical (medical equipment —Albemarle North Carolina)
Home Care of the Carolinas (home health care —Albemarle Troy North Carolina)
Stanly Manor (100-bed nursing home —Albemarle North Carolina)
Stanly Medical Services (clinics —Stanly Montgomery counties)

COMPETITORS

Carolinas HealthCare System
Carolinas Medical Center-NorthEast
Davis Regional Medical Center
FirstHealth of the Carolinas
Forsyth Medical Center
High Point Regional Health System
MedCath
Novant Health
Presbyterian Healthcare
Rowan Regional Medical Center
Wake Forest University Baptist Medical Center

HISTORICAL FINANCIALS

Company Type: Private - Not-for-Profit

Income Statement

FYE: June 30

	REVENUE ($ mil.)	NET INCOME ($ mil.)	NET PROFIT MARGIN	EMPLOYEES
06/12*	78	8	11.2%	750
12/11	23	3	14.9%	0
09/11	103	6	6.8%	0
06/11	20	0	1.0%	0
Annual Growth	**56.4%**	**248.0%**	**—**	**—**

*Fiscal year change

2012 Year-End Financials

Debt ratio: ——
Return on equity: 11.20%
Cash ($ mil.): 8
Current ratio: 1.70
Long-term debt ($ mil.): —

Dividends
Yield: —
Payout: —
Market value ($ mil.): —

STAPLES CONSTRUCTION COMPANY INC.

Staples Construction Company uses sturdier material than staples to build with. The company specializes in commercial industrial and multi-family residential construction projects such as office buildings biotech campuses and public facilities. It built the $22 million corporate offices for A&R Distribution (a division of A&R Transport) in Morris Illinois; a $14 million renovation project for San Jose State University; and the $16 million Nexus University City Sciences Center in San Jose California. Staples Construction Company was founded in 1995 by President David Staples. It has regional offices in San Jose and San Diego California and Chicago Illinois.

EXECUTIVES

President, David Staples
Director of Construction Ventura, Lori Sayles
Director of Construction San Diego, Tracy Kistler
Director of Construction San Jose, Charles Terrazas
Director of Construction Mid West, James Fannin
Administration and Office Manager, Dee Falls
Director of Finance, Sue Pyne

LOCATIONS

HQ: Staples Construction Company Inc.
1501 Eastman Ave., Ventura CA 93003
Phone: 805-658-8786   **Fax:** 805-658-8785
Web: www.staplesconstruction.com

COMPETITORS

Bernards Brothers	Johnson & Jennings
Bycor General Contractors	R. J. Daum Construction
Fullmer Construction	Reno Contracting
Howard Building Corporation	

HISTORICAL FINANCIALS

Company Type: Private

Income Statement

FYE: December 31

	REVENUE ($ mil.)	NET INCOME ($ mil.)	NET PROFIT MARGIN	EMPLOYEES
12/11*	34	0	1.2%	35
09/10	19	0	2.6%	0
12/08	40	0	0.7%	0
12/07	54	1	1.9%	0
Annual Growth	(13.6%)	(25.1%)	—	—

*Fiscal year change

2011 Year-End Financials

Debt ratio: ——
Return on equity: 1.20%
Cash ($ mil.): 0
Current ratio: 1.10
Long-term debt ($ mil.): —

Dividends
Yield: —
Payout: —
Market value ($ mil.): —

STAR LUMBER & SUPPLY CO. INC.

LOCATIONS

HQ: STAR LUMBER & SUPPLY CO. INC.
325 S WEST ST, WICHITA, KS 67213-2177
Phone: 316-942-2221
Web: www.starlumber.com

HISTORICAL FINANCIALS

Company Type: Private

Income Statement

FYE: December 31

	REVENUE ($ mil.)	NET INCOME ($ mil.)	NET PROFIT MARGIN	EMPLOYEES
12/11	83	(0)	—	300
12/10*	84	(0)	—	0
03/09	2	(0)	—	0
12/07	113	3	3.2%	0
Annual Growth	(9.6%)	—	—	—

*Fiscal year change

2011 Year-End Financials

Debt ratio: ——
Return on equity: (-1.00)%
Cash ($ mil.): 0
Current ratio: 0.70
Long-term debt ($ mil.): —

Dividends
Yield: —
Payout: —
Market value ($ mil.): —

STAR OF THE WEST MILLING COMPANY

All hands are on the mill floor at Star of the West Milling. The company operates five flour mills in four US states and 10 storage elevators. The mills and elevators store and process wheat corn and soybeans. Its flour milling capacity is about 40000 lbs. per day. North Star Bean a division of Star of the West processes beans such as navy pinto kidney and black beans into dry commodity products. The company also owns Eastern Michigan Grain an elevator that offers grain handling and marketing services. Star of the West Milling sells its flour and beans worldwide to canning and packaging customers the likes of Kellogg General Mills Nabisco and Pepperidge Farm.

While the company has logged modest growth in recent years Star of the West Milling has grown steadily without any devastating blows to its bottom line during the economic slump. Also instead of setting aside cash for a rainy day or paying off debt Star of the West Milling has invested more than $8 million in new equipment and building additions in an effort to boost production and improve sales. The new machinery cleans and separates wheat and uses optical sorting to identify and remove imperfect kernels. Star of the West Milling in turn hopes to expand its capabilities further to include whole wheat production to cater to customer requests.

It has operations in Indiana Michigan Ohio New York and North Dakota.

Star of the West Milling was founded by the Hubinger family in 1870; its name was taken from a side-wheel merchant steamer of the same name that secretly transported soldiers and supplies to Fort Sumpter site of the first battle of the Civil War.

EXECUTIVES

President, Art Loeffler
VP Edible Bean Marketing, Joe Cramer
Controller, Eric Bushey
Director Information Technology, Jim Koski
VP Grain Marketing, Gary Kaufman
VP Flour Milling Division, Mike Fasserzke
VP Elevator Division, Jim Howe
Human Resources, Tim Brooks
Plant Manager, Mark Kern
Manager Maintenance, Frank Frysh
Manager Customer Service Flour Department, Janice Weiss
Director Safety, Wayne Bauer

LOCATIONS

HQ: Star of the West Milling Co.
121 E. Tuscola St., Frankenmuth MI 48734-1731
Phone: 989-652-9971   **Fax:** 989-652-6358
Web: www.starofthewest.com

PRODUCTS/OPERATIONS

Selected Products

Black beans
Cranberry beans
Dark red kidney beans
Great northern beans
Light red kidney beans
Navy beans (pea beans)
Pink beans
Pinto beans
Small reds
Small white beans
Yelloweye beans

COMPETITORS

Bay State Milling	Italgrani
Bunge Milling	Kelley Bean
C.H. Guenther & Son	North Dakota Mill
CGC	Seaboard
Chippewa Valley Bean	US Soy
DeBruce Grain	Washington Quality
Horizon Milling	Foods

HISTORICAL FINANCIALS

Company Type: Private

Income Statement

FYE: December 31

	REVENUE ($ mil.)	NET INCOME ($ mil.)	NET PROFIT MARGIN	EMPLOYEES
12/11	394	15	4.0%	202
12/10	294	13	4.5%	0
12/09	310	8	2.9%	0
12/08	376	6	1.7%	0
Annual Growth	1.6%	36.5%	—	—

2011 Year-End Financials

Debt ratio: ——
Return on equity: 4.00%
Cash ($ mil.): 14
Current ratio: 0.90
Long-term debt ($ mil.): —

Dividends
Yield: —
Payout: —
Market value ($ mil.): —

STAR SNACKS CO. LLC

LOCATIONS

HQ: STAR SNACKS CO. LLC
105 HARBOR DR, JERSEY CITY, NJ 07305-4505
Phone: 201-200-9820

HISTORICAL FINANCIALS

Company Type: Private

Income Statement

FYE: December 31

	REVENUE ($ mil.)	NET INCOME ($ mil.)	NET PROFIT MARGIN	EMPLOYEES
12/11	141	3	2.1%	430
12/10*	119	2	1.7%	0
06/09	0	0	—	0
Annual Growth	—	—	—	—

*Fiscal year change

2011 Year-End Financials

Debt ratio: ——
Return on equity: 2.10%
Cash ($ mil.): 0
Current ratio: 0.70
Long-term debt ($ mil.): —

Dividends
Yield: —
Payout: —
Market value ($ mil.): —

STATIC CONTROL COMPONENTS INC.

Static Control Components (SCC) isn't stuck on static cling. The company that made a name for itself by selling anti-static products has made an even greater impression by selling parts for rebuilt toner cartridges. Its Imaging Division which sells parts to recycle used printer cartridges has captured more than half of the world market. SCC also makes electrical testing tools. In 2006 Static Control Components sold its SCC Products affiliate to 3M. President and CEO Ed Swartz founded Static Control Components in 1987; the company is owned and operated by his family.

Static Control Components (SCC) sells its products worldwide through its website company offices as well authorized distributors. The company maintains some 20 manufacturing locations.

Rival Lexmark International sued SCC claiming its components and software for Lexmark toner cartridges violated both general copyright law and the federal Digital Millennium Copyright Act of 1998. Static Control ultimately prevailed in the federal appellate courts.

EXECUTIVES

VP, Michael L. Swartz
Chairman, Edwin H. (Ed) Swartz
President, William K. (Bill) Swartz
Secretary, Rhonda S. Coggins
Manager Corporate Account, Chad Golden
VP, Erwin Pijpers
VP North American Sales and Marketing, Richard Clemmer
Manager New Business Development, Elaine Holub
Manager International Business, Pete Martinez
Manager International Business, Michael Cox
Senior Account Executive, Melissa Campbell
Manager Country, Juan Bonell
Senior Account Executive, Erika Guerrero
Account Executive, Tannie Cummings
Sales Support Representative, Dawn Dean
Sales Support Representative, Bonnie Lowe
Sales Support Representative, Emma Laguna
Customer Service Representative, Jeri Latta
Technical Support, Carey Rosser
Account Manager Retail Networks, Debbie Smith
Account Manager Retail Networks, Danielle Wilson
Account Manager, Jay Williams
Sales Account Executive 9, Brandon Gaines
Account Executive 3 Retail Networks, Claudia Alston
Manager Customer Service, Lisa Moore
Manager Customer Service Assistant, Amber Canady
Customer Service Representative, Penny Marshburn
Technical Support Engineer, Javier Ventura
Technical Support Engineer, Michael Sawhney
Technical Support Regional, Travis Smith
Technical Support, Rob Elmore
Technical Support, Marcelo Sanchez
Technical Support, Jonin Hulings
Technical Support, Joey Saucier
Technical Support Engineer, David Thompson
Junior Business Manager, Nikko Adman
Unit Business Manager, Ed Snyder
Junior Business Manager, Jeff Jackson
Team Support, Diane Dickens
Team Support, Christy Oldham
Manager Unit Business, Brandon Atkins
Junior Business Manager, Johnny Carthens
Junior Business Manager, Kelly Rouse
Team Support, Cindy Stanley
Team Support, Jamie McArthur-White
Manager Unit Business, Paula Carter
Junior Business Manager, Shawn McGilberry
Junior Business Manager, Sai Taylor
Team Support, Pam Lee
Team Support, Ruth Walker
Manager Unit Business, Scott Conlon
Junior Business Manager, Jeff Morris
Junior Business Manager, Kathy Holiday
Team Support, Jennifer Woodham
Team Support, Samantha Puryear
Manager Unit Business, Chad Radomski
Manager Corporate Support, Teena Moore
Corporate Support, Dan Ahern
VP, William L. London
VP, Lynton R. Burchette
VP, Bryan Bonacum

LOCATIONS

HQ: Static Control Components Inc.
3010 Lee Ave., Sanford NC 27331
Phone: 919-774-3808   **Fax:** 919-774-1287
Web: www.scc-inc.com

COMPETITORS

3M	Illinois Tool Works
Canon	Lexmark
Clover Technologies	Wazana Brothers
Hewlett-Packard	

HISTORICAL FINANCIALS

Company Type: Private

Income Statement

FYE: December 31

	REVENUE ($ mil.)	NET INCOME ($ mil.)	NET PROFIT MARGIN	EMPLOYEES
12/11	191	7	4.1%	1,200
12/04	264	0	—	0
12/03	245	5	2.2%	0
12/02	238	3	1.5%	0
Annual Growth	(7.2%)	28.8%	—	—

2011 Year-End Financials

Debt ratio: ——
Return on equity: 4.10%
Cash ($ mil.): 0
Current ratio: 1.20
Long-term debt ($ mil.): —

Dividends
　Yield: —
　Payout: —
Market value ($ mil.): —

STAVROS CENTER FOR INDEPENDENT LIVING INC.

LOCATIONS

HQ: STAVROS CENTER FOR INDEPENDENT LIVING INC.
210 OLD FARM RD, AMHERST, MA 01002-2704
Phone: 413-256-0473
Web: www.stavros.org

HISTORICAL FINANCIALS

Company Type: Private

Income Statement

FYE: June 30

	REVENUE ($ mil.)	NET INCOME ($ mil.)	NET PROFIT MARGIN	EMPLOYEES
06/11	162	0	0.1%	100
06/10	155	0	0.1%	0
06/09	150	0	—	0
06/08	131	0	0.2%	0
Annual Growth	7.4%	(9.5%)	—	—

2011 Year-End Financials

Debt ratio: ——
Return on equity: 0.10%
Cash ($ mil.): 16
Current ratio: 3.10
Long-term debt ($ mil.): —

Dividends
　Yield: —
　Payout: —
Market value ($ mil.): —

STEEL AND PIPE SUPPLY COMPANY INC.

LOCATIONS

HQ: STEEL AND PIPE SUPPLY COMPANY INC.
555 POYNTZ AVE STE 122, MANHATTAN, KS 66502-0126
Phone: 785-587-5100
Web: www.spsci.com

HISTORICAL FINANCIALS

Company Type: Private

Income Statement

FYE: April 27

	REVENUE ($ mil.)	NET INCOME ($ mil.)	NET PROFIT MARGIN	EMPLOYEES
04/12*	744	0	—	587
05/08	0	0	—	0
04/07	528	14	2.7%	0
Annual Growth	18.7%	—	—	—

*Fiscal year change

2012 Year-End Financials

Debt ratio: ——
Return on equity: —
Cash ($ mil.): 0
Current ratio: 0.50
Long-term debt ($ mil.): —

Dividends
　Yield: —
　Payout: —
Market value ($ mil.): —

STEEL RESOURCES LLC

LOCATIONS

HQ: STEEL RESOURCES LLC
9155 S DADELAND BLVD # 1800, MIAMI, FL 33156-2737
Phone: 305-459-4000

HISTORICAL FINANCIALS

Company Type: Private

Income Statement

FYE: December 31

	REVENUE ($ mil.)	NET INCOME ($ mil.)	NET PROFIT MARGIN	EMPLOYEES
12/11	504	5	1.2%	36
12/10	418	5	1.3%	0
12/09	285	(2)	—	0
12/08	1,126	7	0.7%	0
Annual Growth	(23.5%)	(8.9%)	—	—

2011 Year-End Financials

Debt ratio: ——
Return on equity: 1.20%
Cash ($ mil.): 1
Current ratio: 3.70
Long-term debt ($ mil.): —

Dividends
　Yield: —
　Payout: —
Market value ($ mil.): —

STEINER ELECTRIC COMPANY

Steiner Electric electrifies Chicago by distributing electrical products and providing related supplies and services through eight locations in northern Illinois and northwest Indiana. Besides such standard electrical supplies as ballasts and fasteners the company's products include industrial supplies automation products motors and drives lighting products generators and bar code devices. Services include energy audits turnkey project management motor repair and electric vehicle charging. Customers purchase Steiner Electric's products for commercial construction residential and industrial applications. The founding family still owns the firm it began in 1916.

Steiner's Data Collection Group installs and supports bar code scanners radio-frequency identification (RFID) readers and wireless networks. Its Automation Products and Information Systems Group provides technology from Siemens and other vendors that track factory production data.

EXECUTIVES

Chairman and CEO, Harold M. Kerman
President and COO, Richard A. Kerman
CFO, Bernie Dost

LOCATIONS

HQ: Steiner Electric Company
1250 Touhy Ave., Elk Grove Village IL 60007
Phone: 847-228-0400 **Fax:** 847-228-1352
Web: https://www.steinerelectric.com

PRODUCTS/OPERATIONS

Selected Products

Automation products
  Industrial computers
  Motion control
  Pneumatics
  SCADA software
  Sensors
  Vision systems
Barcode products
  Barcode labels
  Printers
  Scanners
  Vehicle mounted computers
Electrical supplies
  Ballasts
  Cables
  Fasteners
  Fittings
  Heaters
  Lamps
  Lighting
  Motors
  Safety switches
  Tools
  Transformers
  Wires
Industrial supplies
  Indexable tooling
  Machine tool accessories
  Precision instruments
  Safety equipment
  Tapes
Generators
Lighting
Motors
Unlimited power supply

COMPETITORS

Consolidated Electrical	Rexel
Graybar Electric	Springfield Electric
McNaughton-McKay	Turtle & Hughes
Revere Electric	WESCO International

HISTORICAL FINANCIALS

Company Type: Private

Income Statement

FYE: December 31

	REVENUE ($ mil.)	NET INCOME ($ mil.)	NET PROFIT MARGIN	EMPLOYEES
12/11	181	0	—	500
12/10	181	0	—	0
12/09	0	0	—	0
12/08	239	0	—	0
Annual Growth	(8.8%)	—	—	—

2011 Year-End Financials

Debt ratio: ——
Return on equity: —
Cash ($ mil.): 0
Current ratio: 1.60
Long-term debt ($ mil.): —
Dividends
  Yield: —
  Payout: —
Market value ($ mil.): —

STEMCOR USA INC.

LOCATIONS

HQ: STEMCOR USA INC.
350 5TH AVE STE 1526, NEW YORK, NY 10118-7894
Phone: 212-563-0262

HISTORICAL FINANCIALS

Company Type: Private

Income Statement

FYE: December 31

	REVENUE ($ mil.)	NET INCOME ($ mil.)	NET PROFIT MARGIN	EMPLOYEES
12/11	1,019	10	1.0%	55
12/10	687	3	0.5%	0
12/08	1,378	64	4.7%	0
12/07	930	50	5.4%	0
Annual Growth	3.1%	(41.4%)	—	—

2011 Year-End Financials

Debt ratio: ——
Return on equity: 1.00%
Cash ($ mil.): 15
Current ratio: —
Long-term debt ($ mil.): —
Dividends
  Yield: —
  Payout: —
Market value ($ mil.): —

STEPHEN F AUSTIN STATE UNIVERSITY

Stephen F. Austin State University (SFA) is a public university located in the Pineywoods of East Texas. Its campus in the heart of Nacogdoches was part of the original homestead of Thomas J.

Rusk an early Texas patriot and US senator. The school's 11000-plus enrolled students may choose from more than 80 majors in some 120 study areas including business and nursing. The student-faculty ratio is 20 to 1. Stephen F. Austin also offers a number of undergraduate graduate and certification programs online or partially online. Notable alumni include former NFL coach Bum Phillips and Don Henley of the Eagles. Named for the founding father of Texas the university was created in 1923 as a teacher's college.

EXECUTIVES

Director Human Resources, Glenda F. Herrington
Controller, Annie Uhyrek
President, Baker Pattillo
Director Counseling and Career Services, Ralph Busby
Director Athletics, Robert Hill
Director Intramurals, Ray Worsham
VP University Affairs, Steven Westbrook
VP Advancement, Jill Still
General Counsel, Damon Derrick
Dean College of Business, Violet C. Rogers
Manager Benefits Human Resources, Billie Baggett
Director Libraries, Alvin Charles Cage
Head Reference Library, Lee Wayne Sullenger
Provost and VP Academic Affairs, Richard Berry
Associate VP Graduate Studies and Research, Tom Wheeler
VP Finance and Administration, Danny Gallant

LOCATIONS

HQ: Stephen F. Austin State University
1936 North St., Nacogdoches TX 75962
Phone: 936-468-2011 **Fax:** 936-468-1732
Web: www.sfasu.edu

HISTORICAL FINANCIALS

Company Type: School

Income Statement

FYE: August 31

	REVENUE ($ mil.)	NET INCOME ($ mil.)	NET PROFIT MARGIN	EMPLOYEES
08/11	120	1	1.5%	2,914
08/04	71	5	7.9%	0
08/03	78	3	4.1%	0
08/02	71	8	11.7%	0
Annual Growth	19.2%	(40.2%)	—	—

2011 Year-End Financials

Debt ratio: ——
Return on equity: 1.50%
Cash ($ mil.): 46
Current ratio: 0.50
Long-term debt ($ mil.): —
Dividends
  Yield: —
  Payout: —
Market value ($ mil.): —

STEPHEN GOULD CORPORATION

Others can worry about what's inside —Stephen Gould Corporation concentrates on the package. The company provides a full range of packaging-related printing services for customers worldwide. Its products include gift packaging point-of-purchase displays product merchandising and retail and industrial packaging. Stephen Gould Corporation also provides graphic design and package-engineering services as well as assembly and fulfillment. It operates from about 40 facilities; branches are located primarily in the US (more than 20 states) but also in China Ireland Malaysia and Mexico. Stephen Gould Corporation was founded in 1939 by Stephen Gould David Golden and Leonard Beckerman.

EXECUTIVES

President and CEO, Michael Golden
EVP, John Golden
VP, Dale Golden
CFO, Anthony Lupo

LOCATIONS

HQ: Stephen Gould Corporation
35 S. Jefferson Rd., Whippany NJ 07981
Phone: 973-428-1500   **Fax:** 973-428-5274
Web: www.stephengould.com

PRODUCTS/OPERATIONS

Selected Products and Services

Products
  Aerospace reusable cases
  Corrugated containers
  Gift packaging
  Industrial packaging
  Point of sale packaging
  Protective packaging
Services
  Creative services
  Logistics & facilities
  Package design & engineering

COMPETITORS

Consolidated	Gibraltar Packaging
Carqueville	Metro Packaging and
Focus Packaging &	Imaging
Display group	R.R. Donnelley
Fort Dearborn	WS Packaging Group

HISTORICAL FINANCIALS

Company Type: Private

Income Statement

	REVENUE ($ mil.)	NET INCOME ($ mil.)	NET PROFIT MARGIN	EMPLOYEES
12/11	519	4	0.8%	338
12/10	500	5	1.0%	0
12/09	428	1	0.3%	0
12/08	483	2	0.5%	0
Annual Growth	2.4%	17.3%	—	—

2011 Year-End Financials

Debt ratio: ——
Return on equity: 0.80%
Cash ($ mil.): 6
Current ratio: 1.50
Long-term debt ($ mil.): —
Dividends
  Yield: —
  Payout: —
Market value ($ mil.): —

STEPHENSON WHOLESALE COMPANY INC.

Buying a candy bar and a box of nails is made easier thanks to Stephenson Wholesale. Operating through subsidiaries Indian National Wholesale Company and GLC Marketing the company is a leading supplier of food and non-food goods to convenience stores and other retail outlets in Oklahoma and Texas. It also distributes goods to snack bars concessions operators and tribal smoke shops. The family-owned company was founded in 1953 by Ralphen Cross.

EXECUTIVES

President and CEO, Ronald R. (Ron) Cross
VP Administration, Dawn Laxson

LOCATIONS

HQ: Stephenson Wholesale Company Inc.
230 S. 22nd Ave., Durant OK 74701-5646
Phone: 580-920-0110   **Fax:** 408-629-7174
Web: www.osh.com

COMPETITORS

Associated Wholesale	GSC Enterprises
Grocers	H. T. Hackney
C&S Wholesale	McLane
Core-Mark	Nash-Finch
Eby-Brown	

HISTORICAL FINANCIALS

Company Type: Private

Income Statement

	REVENUE ($ mil.)	NET INCOME ($ mil.)	NET PROFIT MARGIN	EMPLOYEES
12/11	404	3	0.9%	315
12/10	401	2	0.7%	0
12/09	380	2	0.6%	0
12/08	354	3	0.9%	0
Annual Growth	4.5%	2.5%	—	—

2011 Year-End Financials

Debt ratio: ——
Return on equity: 0.90%
Cash ($ mil.): 3
Current ratio: 1.60
Long-term debt ($ mil.): —
Dividends
  Yield: —
  Payout: —
Market value ($ mil.): —

STERLING BOILER AND MECHANICAL INC.

LOCATIONS

HQ: STERLING BOILER AND MECHANICAL INC.
1420 KIMBER LN, EVANSVILLE, IN 47715-4025
Phone: 812-479-5447
Web: www.sterlingboiler.com

HISTORICAL FINANCIALS

Company Type: Private

Income Statement

	REVENUE ($ mil.)	NET INCOME ($ mil.)	NET PROFIT MARGIN	EMPLOYEES
12/11	203	0	0.3%	800
12/10	170	9	5.7%	0
12/08	359	20	5.6%	0
12/07	201	17	8.6%	0
Annual Growth	0.3%	(65.9%)	—	—

2011 Year-End Financials

Debt ratio: ——
Return on equity: 0.30%
Cash ($ mil.): 1
Current ratio: —
Long-term debt ($ mil.): —
Dividends
  Yield: —
  Payout: —
Market value ($ mil.): —

STETSON UNIVERSITY INC.

Not everyone at Stetson University wears a cowboy hat but there is a connection. The school offers undergraduate (60 majors and minors) and graduate degrees through its College of Arts and Sciences School of Business Administration School of Music and College of Law. The university enrolls about 2200 undergraduate students. Stetson has four campuses located in DeLand (main) Celebration (graduate degrees and continuing education) Tampa (law) and St. Petersburg/Gulfport (law). Florida's first private university Stetson was founded in 1883 by New York philanthropist Henry A. DeLand. The university's name was changed in 1889 to honor benefactor John B. Stetson the nationally-known hat manufacturer.

EXECUTIVES

President, H. Douglas (Doug) Lee
SVP Administration and COO, James R. Beasley
Executive Director Public Relations and Communications, Mary Anne Rogers
VP University Relations, Linda P. Davis
VP Finance, Sally A. Dowling
Associate VP University Relations, Susan P. Anderson
Director Public Safety, Robert (Bob) Matusick, age 54
VP Enrollment Management, Deborah Thompson
Director Technology Services, Richard Gaughran
Director Financial Aid and Institutional Research College of Law, Emily Attridge
Associate VP Legal Affairs and Human Resources, Deborah C. Brown
Director Risk Management, Terry Gordon
Director Public Safety, James D. Hess
Bursar, Brian L. Johnson
Director Media and Public Communications, Cheryl Downs
Associate VP and CTO, Robert Penney

LOCATIONS

HQ: Stetson University
 421 N. Woodland Blvd., DeLand FL 32723
Phone: 386-822-7100 **Fax:** 386-822-8925
Web: www.stetson.edu

HISTORICAL FINANCIALS
Company Type: School

Income Statement

	REVENUE ($ mil.)	NET INCOME ($ mil.)	NET PROFIT MARGIN	EMPLOYEES
06/12	110	3	3.2%	1,033
06/10	146	3	2.6%	0
06/09*	123	0	—	0
05/07	0	0	—	0
Annual Growth	—	—	—	—

FYE: June 30

*Fiscal year change

2012 Year-End Financials

Debt ratio: ——
Return on equity: 3.20%
Cash ($ mil.): 25
Current ratio: —
Long-term debt ($ mil.): —

Dividends
 Yield: —
 Payout: —
 Market value ($ mil.): —

STEUART INVESTMENT COMPANY

LOCATIONS

HQ: STEUART INVESTMENT COMPANY
 5454 WSCNSIN AVE STE 1600, CHEVY CHASE, MD 20815
Phone: 301-951-2700
Web: www.steuart.com

HISTORICAL FINANCIALS
Company Type: Private

Income Statement

	ASSETS ($ mil.)	NET INCOME ($ mil.)	INCOME AS % OF ASSETS	EMPLOYEES
12/11	404	19	4.9%	60
12/10	445	(11)	—	0
12/09	118	7	6.1%	0
12/08	478	(14)	—	0
Annual Growth	(5.5%)	—	—	—

FYE: December 31

2011 Year-End Financials

Debt ratio: ——
Return on equity: 19.80%
Cash ($ mil.): 13
Current ratio: —
Long-term debt ($ mil.): —

Dividends
 Yield: —
 Payout: —
 Market value ($ mil.): —

STEVE SILVER COMPANY

LOCATIONS

HQ: STEVE SILVER COMPANY
 1000 FM 548, FORNEY, TX 75126-6458
Phone: 972-564-2601
Web: www.ssilver.com

HISTORICAL FINANCIALS
Company Type: Private

Income Statement

	REVENUE ($ mil.)	NET INCOME ($ mil.)	NET PROFIT MARGIN	EMPLOYEES
12/11	117	2	1.9%	250
12/10	115	3	3.4%	0
12/09	101	1	1.9%	0
12/08	117	3	2.7%	0
Annual Growth	(0.3%)	(10.4%)	—	—

FYE: December 31

2011 Year-End Financials

Debt ratio: ——
Return on equity: 1.90%
Cash ($ mil.): 0
Current ratio: 0.50
Long-term debt ($ mil.): —

Dividends
 Yield: —
 Payout: —
 Market value ($ mil.): —

STEVENS ENGINEERS & CONSTRUCTORS INC.

LOCATIONS

HQ: STEVENS ENGINEERS & CONSTRUCTORS INC.
 7850 FREEWAY CIR STE 100, CLEVELAND, OH 44130-6317
Phone: 440-234-7888
Web: www.spcdmg.com

HISTORICAL FINANCIALS
Company Type: Private

Income Statement

	REVENUE ($ mil.)	NET INCOME ($ mil.)	NET PROFIT MARGIN	EMPLOYEES
04/12	135	(0)	—	270
04/11	164	1	0.8%	0
04/10	104	1	1.4%	0
04/09	162	2	1.4%	0
Annual Growth	(5.7%)	—	—	—

FYE: April 30

2012 Year-End Financials

Debt ratio: ——
Return on equity: (-0.10)%
Cash ($ mil.): 4
Current ratio: 1.10
Long-term debt ($ mil.): —

Dividends
 Yield: —
 Payout: —
 Market value ($ mil.): —

STEVENS INSTITUTE OF TECHNOLOGY (INC)

Even before the advent of the internal combustion engine Stevens Institute of Technology was educating students in science technology and engineering. Founded in 1870 through an endowment from engineer Edwin Stevens the college offers undergraduate master's and doctoral degrees in engineering science humanities computer science and technology management. More than 2150 undergraduates are enrolled and the school has some 3500 graduate students. Stevens teams up with corporate and military institutions to provide students with hands-on research experience; Stevens Technologies a for-profit subsidiary of the school licenses and sells the technological fruits of these partnerships.

Stevens collaborated with the University of Southern California to launch a new Systems Engineering Research Center (SERC) in 2008. The facility was established to develop and test complex defense systems for the Department of Defense. It also offers system engineering programs and workshops for DoD and intelligence community employees. Researchers from 16 universities from around the US will support SERC which is on Stevens' New Jersey campus.

EXECUTIVES

Chairman, Lawrence T. (Larry) Babbio Jr., age 67
Vice Chairman, Steven Shulman, age 70
VP Human Resources and Secretary, Mark L. Samolewicz
VP University Enrollment and Administration, Maureen P. Weatherall
Associate VP Information Technology and Administrative Computing, Eric Rosenberg
VP University Research and Enterprise Development, Helena S. Wisniewski, age 62
VP Facilities and Community Relations, Henry P. Dobbelaar Jr.
Vice Chairman, Kenneth W. DeBaun
Executive Assistant to the President and Assistant Secretary, Diana Colombo
Controller and Assistant Treasurer, Michael D'Onofrio
Chairman Emeritus, Frederick L. Bissinger
Executive Director Office Alumni, Anita Lang
Director Athletics, Russell Rogers
Dean Residence Life, Trina Ballantyne
Director Special Functions, Barbara Migliori
Dean University Admissions, Daniel G. Gallagher
Director International Admissions and Honors Programs, Edwina W. Fleming
Director International Student and Scholar Services, Jennifer Marsalis
Director Physical Plant, Kenneth Goldklang
Manager Campus Bookstore, Teresa Tridente
VP Research Enterprise, Joseph (Joe) Mitola
VP Finance Treasurer and CFO, Randy L. Greene
VP and Provost, George P. Korfiatis
Vice President for Advancement Chief Administrative Officer, Fred Regan
Professor & Dean Academic Administration, Prof Siva Thangam
Head Library Acquisitions and Collection Development, Scott Smith
Director Assessment & Academic Communications, Christine del Rosario
Executive Director Web Campus, Robert Ubell
Director Financial Aid, Adrienne Hynek
Director Procurement, Doris Schultz

LOCATIONS

HQ: Stevens Institute of Technology
Castle Point on Hudson, Hoboken NJ 07030-5991
Phone: 201-216-5000   **Fax:** 201-216-8250
Web: www.stevens.edu

HISTORICAL FINANCIALS

Company Type: School

Income Statement

FYE: June 30

	REVENUE ($ mil.)	NET INCOME ($ mil.)	NET PROFIT MARGIN	EMPLOYEES
06/11	215	2	1.0%	500
06/10	211	8	4.0%	0
06/08	168	(1)	—	0
06/07	129	24	18.6%	0
Annual Growth	18.6%	(55.6%)	—	—

2011 Year-End Financials

Debt ratio: ——
Return on equity: 1.00%
Cash ($ mil.): 20
Current ratio: —
Long-term debt ($ mil.): —

Dividends
Yield: —
Payout: —
Market value ($ mil.): —

STEVENS TRANSPORT INC.

Staying cool is a must for Stevens Transport. An irregular-route refrigerated truckload carrier (or reefer) Stevens hauls temperature-controlled cargo throughout the US covering the 48 contiguous states. Through alliances Stevens also covers every province in Canada and every state in Mexico. The company operates a fleet of about 2100 Kenworth and Peterbuilt tractors and 3050 Thermo King re-frigerated trailers from a network of more than a dozen service centers. Partnerships with railroads allow Stevens to arrange intermodal transport of temperature-controlled cargo. The company also provides third-party logistics services. Stevens Transport was founded in 1980.

Geographic Reach

Stevens Transport maintains its operations across Canada Mexico and the US through its partnerships with BNSF Norfolk Southern CSX and Union Pacific. It has 13 logistics offices located in Canada and throughout the US.

Sales and Marketing

Stevens has provided refrigerated shipping services for such big names as General Mills Kraft Foods M&M Mars Procter & Gamble and Wal-Mart.

Strategy

Even in a US economy ripe with unpredictable fuel costs and a decline in consumer confidence one thing has always worked in Stevens' favor: people will always need their food. The company has managed to maintain a steady growth rate by keeping costs down updating the technology of its trucking equipment and maintaining an efficient operating structure. Along these lines in 2012 it implemented new mobile computing platforms across its fleet of tractors to enhance its customer services and optimize productivity.

EXECUTIVES

VP Technical Services, J. D. Martin
President, Clay M. Aaron
EVP, Michael Richey
VP Logistic Sales, Daniel Bell
Vice Chairman, Todd S. Aaron
VP Risk Management, William Tallent
VP Administration Secretary Treasurer and Director, Bob Nelson
Chairman and CEO, Steven L. Aaron
VP Operations, Smokey Adams
VP Driver Resources, Angela A. Horowitz
Vice Chairman, Todd S. Aaron
VP Administration Secretary Treasurer and Director, Bob Nelson

LOCATIONS

HQ: Stevens Transport Inc.
9757 Military Pkwy., Dallas TX 75227
Phone: 972-216-9000   **Fax:** 305-630-3006
Web: www.adptotalsource.com

PRODUCTS/OPERATIONS

Selected Services

Intermodal
International
Logistics
Truckload

COMPETITORS

C.R. England
Central Refrigerated Service
Comcar
Covenant Transportation
Frozen Food Express
Henderson Trucking
Jim Palmer Trucking
KLLM Transport Services

Marten Transport
Navajo Shippers
Prime Inc.
Southern Refrigerated Transport
TransAm Trucking
Watkins Associated Industries
Willis Shaw Express

HISTORICAL FINANCIALS

Company Type: Private

Income Statement

FYE: December 31

	REVENUE ($ mil.)	NET INCOME ($ mil.)	NET PROFIT MARGIN	EMPLOYEES
12/11	566	76	13.5%	2,100
12/08	0	0	—	0
12/07	492	67	13.6%	0
12/06	461	0	0.0%	0
Annual Growth	7.1%	6305.9%	—	—

2011 Year-End Financials

Debt ratio: ——
Return on equity: 13.50%
Cash ($ mil.): 83
Current ratio: 1.90
Long-term debt ($ mil.): —

Dividends
Yield: —
Payout: —
Market value ($ mil.): —

STEVENSON UNIVERSITY INC.

Stevenson University is a career-focused liberal arts college with about 4000 undergraduate and graduate students. It has a student-faculty ratio of 13-to-1. The school has two locations in Stevenson and Owings Mills Maryland near Baltimore. It offers a wide range of bachelor's degree programs as well as master's degree programs in advanced information technologies business and technology management forensic science and forensic studies. Tuition and fees are almost $24000 a year. The school was founded as medical-secretarial training institute Villa Julie College in 1947; it became a university and changed its name to Stevenson in 2008.

EXECUTIVES

President, Kevin J. Manning, age 68
EVP Academic Affairs and Dean, Paul D. Lack
VP Marketing and Public Relations, Glenda LeGendre
EVP Financial Affairs and CFO, Timothy M. Campbell
Assistant VP Financial Affairs, Melanie M. Edmondson
Director Library Services, Maureen A. Beck
VP Enrollment Management, Mark Hergan
VP Student Affairs and Dean of Students, Claire Moore
Director Auxiliary Services, Robert A. Reed
Director Alumni Relations and Annual Giving, Jane Curley Hogge
Director Athletics, Brett Adams
Assistant VP Academic Affairs, Jo-Ellen Asbury
Registrar, Tracy Bolt
Dean Graduate and Professional Studies, Joyce K. Becker
Department Chair Humanities and Public History, Joseph G. McGraw Jr.
Department Chair Art, Lori L. Rubeling
Division Director Business and Legal Studies, Patricia M. Turnbaugh
Department Chair Psychology, Barbara A. Smith
VP Institutional Advancement, Steven W. Close Jr.
CIO, Thomas Allen
VP Human Resources, Brenda Balzer
Director Facilities, Jon W. Wells

LOCATIONS

HQ: Stevenson University
1525 Greenspring Valley Rd., Stevenson MD 21153-0641
Phone: 410-486-7000   **Fax:** 410-352-4400
Web: www.stevenson.edu

HISTORICAL FINANCIALS
Company Type: School

Income Statement
FYE: June 30

	REVENUE ($ mil.)	NET INCOME ($ mil.)	NET PROFIT MARGIN	EMPLOYEES
06/11	84	13	15.8%	550
06/10	87	0	1.0%	0
06/09	80	0	—	0
06/08	62	0	0.0%	0
Annual Growth	10.7%	731.9%	—	—

2011 Year-End Financials
Debt ratio: ——
Return on equity: 15.80%
Cash ($ mil.): 2
Current ratio: ——
Long-term debt ($ mil.): —
Dividends
Yield: —
Payout: —
Market value ($ mil.): —

STILLWATER MEDICAL CENTER AUTHORITY

LOCATIONS

HQ: STILLWATER MEDICAL CENTER AUTHORITY
1323 W 6TH AVE, STILLWATER, OK 74074-4399
Phone: 405-372-1480
Web: www.stillwater-medical.org

HISTORICAL FINANCIALS
Company Type: Private

Income Statement
FYE: December 31

	REVENUE ($ mil.)	NET INCOME ($ mil.)	NET PROFIT MARGIN	EMPLOYEES
12/11	98	11	11.8%	600
12/10	90	6	7.2%	0
12/09	79	4	5.9%	0
12/08	84	(0)	—	0
Annual Growth	5.3%	—	—	—

2011 Year-End Financials
Debt ratio: ——
Return on equity: 11.80%
Cash ($ mil.): 17
Current ratio: 3.00
Long-term debt ($ mil.): —
Dividends
Yield: —
Payout: —
Market value ($ mil.): —

STINKER STORES INC.

LOCATIONS

HQ: STINKER STORES INC.
300 N ORCHARD ST, BOISE, ID 83706-1627
Phone: 208-375-0942
Web: www.stinker.com

HISTORICAL FINANCIALS
Company Type: Private

Income Statement
FYE: May 31

	REVENUE ($ mil.)	NET INCOME ($ mil.)	NET PROFIT MARGIN	EMPLOYEES
05/12	256	2	0.9%	500
05/09	168	1	1.2%	0
05/08	192	3	1.8%	0
05/06	282	0	—	0
Annual Growth	—	1476.9%	—	—

2012 Year-End Financials
Debt ratio: ——
Return on equity: 0.90%
Cash ($ mil.): 8
Current ratio: 0.90
Long-term debt ($ mil.): —
Dividends
Yield: —
Payout: —
Market value ($ mil.): —

STOLLER INTERNATIONAL INC.

LOCATIONS

HQ: STOLLER INTERNATIONAL INC.
15521 E 1830 NORTH RD, PONTIAC, IL 61764-3183
Phone: 815-844-6197
Web: www.stollerinternational.com

HISTORICAL FINANCIALS
Company Type: Private

Income Statement
FYE: January 31

	REVENUE ($ mil.)	NET INCOME ($ mil.)	NET PROFIT MARGIN	EMPLOYEES
01/12	85	0	1.1%	68
01/10	62	0	0.3%	0
Annual Growth	36.8%	436.4%	—	—

2012 Year-End Financials
Debt ratio: ——
Return on equity: 1.10%
Cash ($ mil.): 0
Current ratio: 0.10
Long-term debt ($ mil.): —
Dividends
Yield: —
Payout: —
Market value ($ mil.): —

STONEHILL COLLEGE INC.

LOCATIONS

HQ: STONEHILL COLLEGE INC.
320 WASHINGTON ST, NORTH EASTON, MA 02357-0001
Phone: 508-565-1000
Web: www.stonehilldining.com

HISTORICAL FINANCIALS
Company Type: Private

Income Statement
FYE: June 30

	REVENUE ($ mil.)	NET INCOME ($ mil.)	NET PROFIT MARGIN	EMPLOYEES
06/11	123	4	4.0%	642
06/10	118	11	9.8%	0
06/09	102	(0)	—	0
06/08	78	(9)	—	0
Annual Growth	16.4%	—	—	—

2011 Year-End Financials
Debt ratio: ——
Return on equity: 4.00%
Cash ($ mil.): 17
Current ratio: —
Long-term debt ($ mil.): —
Dividends
Yield: —
Payout: —
Market value ($ mil.): —

STOUGHTON HOSPITAL ASSOCIATION

Stoughton Hospital is a 69-bed acute care hospital that serves the residents of south-central Wisconson. Specialty services include cardiac rehabilitation emergency medicine surgery and home health care. It also provides a sleep disorders center as well as community education programs. The hospital was established by Dr. Michael Iverson in 1904.

EXECUTIVES

President and CEO, Terrence J. (Terry) Brenney
CFO, Karen Myers
Manager Human Resources, Christopher (Chris) Schmitz
Manager Public Relations and Planning, Jane McGuire
Director Emergency Services, Warren Tripp
VP Patient Services, Kristi Hund
Chief of Staff, Richard Hill
Chairman, Randy Olson

LOCATIONS

HQ: STOUGHTON HOSPITAL ASSOCIATION
900 RIDGE ST, STOUGHTON, WI 53589-1864
Phone: 608-873-6611
Web: www.stoughtonhospital.com

HISTORICAL FINANCIALS
Company Type: Private

Income Statement
FYE: September 30

	REVENUE ($ mil.)	NET INCOME ($ mil.)	NET PROFIT MARGIN	EMPLOYEES
09/11	37	0	1.1%	450
09/10	37	2	6.1%	0
09/09	37	1	2.7%	0
09/08	35	1	4.9%	0
Annual Growth	2.2%	(37.6%)	—	—

2011 Year-End Financials
Debt ratio: ——
Return on equity: 1.10%
Cash ($ mil.): 6
Current ratio: 4.60
Long-term debt ($ mil.): —

Dividends
Yield: —
Payout: —
Market value ($ mil.): —

STRACK AND VAN TIL SUPER MARKET INC

One of Chicagoland's leading grocery chains Strack & Van Til operates about 30 supermarkets in and around Chicago and northern Indiana. Stores operate under the banners of Strack & Van Til Town & Country Food Market and Ultra Foods. The regional grocery chain offers fresh and packaged foods and has delicatessen and bakery divisions in each of its stores. Its websites offer weekly circulars and coupons as well as feature recipes cooking videos meal planners and food-related articles. The company is owned by Chicago-based grocery distributor Central Grocers which also operates supermarkets under the Berkot's and Key Market banners.

Strack & Van Til is facing increased competition from national chains moving into its market while taking advantage of the woes of smaller ones. While its store count has held relatively steady in recent years Stack & Van Til in 2012 will open a new 50000-square-foot store in Cedar Lake Indiana on the site of a former Wilco County Market. Strack & Van Til acquired the Cedar Lake site along with two other Wilco Stores in northwest Indiana in 2010. Strack & Van Til along with local rivals Safeway-owned Dominick's Supermarkets and Jewel-Osco is facing increased competition from supercenter operator Wal-Mart Stores. Wal-Mart which had been expanding aggressively in the Chicago suburbs has begun opening supercenters and smaller Walmart Express stores within the city limits. Its arrival has sparked fierce price competition among area grocers. Other relative newcomers to the Illinois grocery market include Roundy's and non-traditional grocery chains such as SuperTarget stores and limited-assortment ALDI. To take on nationwide retailers Strack & Van Til bands together with other independent stores as members of the Central Grocers cooperative. The combined buying power helps the stores to offer competitive pricing and product selection.

EXECUTIVES
President, David Wilkinson
VP Operations, Jeff Strack
VP Operations, Andrew (Andy) Raab

VP Finance, Keith Bruxvoort
Manager Frozen Dairy and Grocery, Terry Bickers
VP Grocery, Bob Wasiuta
Director Store Operations, Larry Moore
Director IT, Henry Bykerk
VP Human Resources, Rex Mudge

LOCATIONS
HQ: Strack & Van Til Super Market Inc.
2244 45th St., Highland IN 46322
Phone: 219-924-7588   Fax: 219-922-2756
Web: www.strackandvantil.com

PRODUCTS/OPERATIONS

2012 Stores

	No.
Strack & Van	15
Ultra	13
Town & Country Food	2
Total	**30**

COMPETITORS

ALDI	Roundy's
Dominick's	Target Corporation
Jewel Osco	Trader Joe's
Kmart	Wal-Mart
Meijer	Whole Foods

HISTORICAL FINANCIALS
Company Type: Subsidiary

Income Statement
FYE: July 31

	REVENUE ($ mil.)	NET INCOME ($ mil.)	NET PROFIT MARGIN	EMPLOYEES
07/11*	1,009	16	1.7%	2,300
08/10	961	15	1.7%	0
08/09	995	13	1.4%	0
08/08	963	204	21.2%	0
Annual Growth	1.6%	(56.6%)	—	—

*Fiscal year change

2011 Year-End Financials
Debt ratio: ——
Return on equity: 1.70%
Cash ($ mil.): 7
Current ratio: 0.20
Long-term debt ($ mil.): —

Dividends
Yield: —
Payout: —
Market value ($ mil.): —

STRASBURGER ENTERPRISES INC.

LOCATIONS
HQ: STRASBURGER ENTERPRISES INC.
4 N 3RD ST, TEMPLE, TX 76501-7617
Phone: 254-778-3547
Web: www.strasburger.net

HISTORICAL FINANCIALS
Company Type: Private

Income Statement
FYE: January 2

	REVENUE ($ mil.)	NET INCOME ($ mil.)	NET PROFIT MARGIN	EMPLOYEES
01/11*	165	1	1.0%	420
12/09	171	1	0.6%	0
12/08	139	(2)	—	0
12/07	159	0	0.3%	0
Annual Growth	1.4%	54.0%	—	—

*Fiscal year change

2011 Year-End Financials
Debt ratio: ——
Return on equity: 1.00%
Cash ($ mil.): 8
Current ratio: 0.70
Long-term debt ($ mil.): —

Dividends
Yield: —
Payout: —
Market value ($ mil.): —

STRONGWELL CORPORATION

Strong wells and a myriad of other products can be made by Strongwell a top pultruder of fiber-reinforced polymer composites. The company's primary division is its pultrusion manufacturing operation (comprised of 65 pultrusion machines) which makes structural shapes fabricates fiberglass structures and systems and builds pultrusion equipment and tooling. It primarily has expertise in making grating panels fencing products and stair treads. It serves such markets as energy automotive construction marine and leisure. Strongwell has three pultrusion manufacturing facilities in Virginia and Minnesota. Through these locations the company maintains about 647000 sq. ft. of total manufacturing space.

Strongwell serves many sectors within the leisure market. It makes enclosures handrails fencing walkways platforms decking profiles and other fabricated shapes for water parks restaurants and hotels.

The company traces its history to 1924 when as a furniture maker it built aircraft radio and TV cabinets. The company began using reinforced plastics and fiberglass after WWII.

EXECUTIVES
President, John D. Tickle
EVP and COO, A. Keith Liskey
CFO and Treasurer, Gene Delaney
Director Corporate Human Resources, Mitch Williams
Manager Corporate Marketing, Glenn Barefoot
Manager Corporate Information Systems, Dave Manahan
Corporate Health Safety and Environmental Manager, John Barker
Manager Purchasing, Ron Carrico
Manager Engineering and Quality, Clint Smith
Manager Strategic Business Development, Craig Seymour
Manager National Sales, Dave Faulkner
Manager International Business Group, John Ward

LOCATIONS

HQ: Strongwell Corporation
400 Commonwealth Ave., Bristol VA 24203
Phone: 276-645-8000 **Fax:** 276-645-8132
Web: www.strongwell.com

COMPETITORS

Harsco
Hexcel
Redman Fisher
  Engineering
Severstal North
  America
Zoltek

HISTORICAL FINANCIALS

Company Type: Private

Income Statement

FYE: December 31

	REVENUE ($ mil.)	NET INCOME ($ mil.)	NET PROFIT MARGIN	EMPLOYEES
12/11	96	2	2.7%	500
12/10	70	1	1.4%	0
12/09	84	2	3.1%	0
12/08	120	13	11.2%	0
Annual Growth	(7.1%)	(41.9%)	—	—

2011 Year-End Financials

Debt ratio: ——
Return on equity: 2.70%
Cash ($ mil.): 3
Current ratio: 2.40
Long-term debt ($ mil.): —

Dividends
  Yield: —
  Payout: —
  Market value ($ mil.): —

STURDY OIL COMPANY

LOCATIONS

HQ: STURDY OIL COMPANY
1511 ABBOTT ST, SALINAS, CA 93901-4599
Phone: 831-422-8801
Web: www.sturdyoil.com

HISTORICAL FINANCIALS

Company Type: Private

Income Statement

FYE: December 31

	REVENUE ($ mil.)	NET INCOME ($ mil.)	NET PROFIT MARGIN	EMPLOYEES
12/11	106	0	0.5%	85
12/07	79	0	0.4%	0
12/06	71	0	0.7%	0
12/05	1,796	0	0.0%	0
Annual Growth	(61.0%)	1382.5%	—	—

2011 Year-End Financials

Debt ratio: ——
Return on equity: 0.50%
Cash ($ mil.): 1
Current ratio: 1.00
Long-term debt ($ mil.): —

Dividends
  Yield: —
  Payout: —
  Market value ($ mil.): —

SUBURBAN HOSPITAL INC

Don't let the name fool you this hospital isn't just for big city expatriates. Suburban Hospital a member of the Johns Hopkins Medicine network is an acute-care medical-surgical hospital with about 235 beds that provides all major medical services except obstetrics to the residents of Montgomery County in Maryland. Specialized services include behavioral health cardiology cancer care home care and pediatrics. Founded in 1943 Suburban Hospital serves as the regional trauma center for the county and is equipped with a helipad. Other services include a center for sleep disorders 24-hour stroke team diagnostic pathology and radiology departments and a range of inpatient and outpatient programs.

Geographic Reach

Suburban Hospital is located in Bethesda Maryland. The facility primarily serves residents of Maryland's Montgomery County and the surrounding area.

Operations

Suburban Hospital has 233 beds more than 1000 medical staff and more than 500 nursing staff. The community-based not-for-profit hospital is an acute-care medical-surgical hospital featuring all major services except obstetrics. The hospital's admissions total more than 14000 annually.

The facility's major services include a comprehensive cancer and radiation oncology center NIH Heart Center at Suburban Hospital a designated Primary Stroke Center and senior care programs.

Suburban Hospital's other services include the NIH-Suburban MRI Center a center for sleep disorders and state-of-the-art diagnostic pathology and radiology departments.

Strategy

Suburban Hospital is in the midst of a $230 million upgrade and expansion at its existing campus that will create more private rooms larger operating rooms additional physician offices and improved access to the trauma center.

Suburban Hospital has formed joint ventures or affiliations with The National Institutes of Health NRH/Suburban Regional Rehab Potomac Home Health Care and Potomac Home Support (with Sibley Memorial Hospital) and Johns Hopkins Community Physicians among others.

Ownership

Regional health care provider Johns Hopkins Medicine acquired Suburban Hospital in 2009 to expand its operations in the Washington DC area.

EXECUTIVES

Corporate Compliance Officer Corporate Privacy Officer and Corporate Secretary, Nancy Miller
President and Trustee, Brian A. Gragnolati
Chairman, Christopher J. Doherty, age 52
SVP Finance and Treasurer, Marty Basso
SVP Human Resources, Dennis Parnell
SVP Clinical Operations and Chief Nursing Officer, Jacqueline (Jacky) Schultz, age 55
SVP Government and Community Relations; EVP Suburban Hospital Foundation, Leslie Ford Weber
Corporate Director Public Relations, Ronna Borenstein-Levy
VP Information Systems and CIO, Christopher T. Timbers
VP Medical Affairs, Robert Rothstein
Manager Communications, Debra Scheinberg
Trustee, Ronald R. Peterson, age 64

Trustee, Steven J. (Steve) Thompson, age 52
Trustee, William A. Baumgartner
President and Trustee, Brian A. Gragnolati
Trustee, Norman K. (Norm) Jenkins
Trustee, Barry K. Rogstad
Trustee, Diane Colgan
Trustee, William B. Dockser
Trustee, Ann S. Harrington
Trustee, Carolyn B. Hendricks
Trustee, Aris Mardirossian
Trustee, C. Alan Peyser
Trustee, David Silver
Trustee, Stanley H. Snow
Trustee, Patricia Stocker
Trustee, Sue Bailey
Trustee, Mary D. Kane
Trustee, Howard Gleckman
Trustee, Albert K. Lee
Trustee, Belle Brooks O'Brien

LOCATIONS

HQ: Suburban Hospital
8600 Old Georgetown Rd., Bethesda MD 20814
Phone: 301-896-3100 **Fax:** 301-897-1339
Web: www.suburbanhospital.org

COMPETITORS

Adventist HealthCare
Children's National
  Medical Center
Chindex International
Dimensions Healthcare
Doctors Community
  Hospital
Georgetown University
  Hospital
Inova Alexandria
  Hospital
MedStar Health
Providence Hospital
  (Washington DC)

HISTORICAL FINANCIALS

Company Type: Subsidiary

Income Statement

FYE: June 30

	REVENUE ($ mil.)	NET INCOME ($ mil.)	NET PROFIT MARGIN	EMPLOYEES
06/11	256	32	12.8%	1,550
06/10	240	15	6.4%	0
06/09	243	(5)	—	0
06/08	231	6	3.0%	0
Annual Growth	3.4%	68.3%	—	—

2011 Year-End Financials

Debt ratio: ——
Return on equity: 12.80%
Cash ($ mil.): 19
Current ratio: 1.00
Long-term debt ($ mil.): —

Dividends
  Yield: —
  Payout: —
  Market value ($ mil.): —

SUFFOLK UNIVERSITY

Suffolk University provides a well-rounded education around the Athens of America and abroad. Its main campus is located in Boston; the university also operates branch campuses in Spain and Senegal as well as offers degree programs at three satellite sites in Massachusetts. The university provides undergraduate and graduate degrees in more than 70 areas of study through the College of Arts and Sciences Sawyer Business School and Law School. Some 8900 students attend the private university which offers courses taught by about 880 faculty members. The university was founded in 1906 as the Suffolk School of Law. Students from all 50 states and more than 100 countries around the globe attend the university.

EXECUTIVES

Dean Sawyer Business School, William J. O'Neill Jr., age 70
President, David J. Sargent
VP and Treasurer, Francis X. Flannery
VP Enrollment and International Programs, Marguerite J. Dennis
Chair, Nicholas A. Macaronis
Director Athletics, James (Jim) Nelson
VP External Affairs, John A. Nucci
Director Suffolk University Political Research Center, David Paleologos
Vice Chair, Carol Sawyer Parks
Dean College of Arts and Sciences, Kenneth S. Greenberg
VP Student Affairs, Nancy Stoll
Registrar and Assistant VP Enrollment, Mary M. Lally
Registrar Law School, Lorraine D. Cove
Senior Marketing and Public Relations Strategist, Mariellen Norris
Director Public Affairs, Greg Gatlin, age 45
Provost, Barry Brown
VP Academics, Janice C. Griffith
Acting VP Advancement, Andrew Thompson
Dean Law School, Alfred C. Aman Jr.
Auditors: KPMGLLP

LOCATIONS

HQ: Suffolk University
8 Ashburton Place, Boston MA 02108-2770
Phone: 617-573-8000   **Fax:** 617-367-2250
Web: www.suffolk.edu

HISTORICAL FINANCIALS

Company Type: School

Income Statement   FYE: June 30

	REVENUE ($ mil.)	NET INCOME ($ mil.)	NET PROFIT MARGIN	EMPLOYEES
06/11	298	5	1.8%	800
06/10	282	4	1.7%	0
06/09	275	20	7.3%	0
06/08	205	(12)	—	0
Annual Growth	13.2%	—	—	—

2011 Year-End Financials

Debt ratio:
Return on equity: 1.80%
Cash ($ mil.): 0
Current ratio: —
Long-term debt ($ mil.): —

Dividends
Yield: —
Payout: —
Market value ($ mil.): —

SUMMIT ELECTRIC SUPPLY CO. INC

SUMMIT continues its ascent. SUMMIT Electric Supply founded in 1977 by the father-and-son team of Victor Jury Sr. and Victor Jr. (president and CEO) distributes goods from manufacturers such as Dialight Eaton Fluke and Thomas & Betts. Products include cable conduits switches fuses lamps light fixtures instruments and safety equipment. The company offers in-house marine cable braiding for offshore oil and gas customers. SUMMIT also sells to electrical contractors government agencies construction firms and public utilities. It has some 20 branches located in New Mexico Arizona Louisiana and Texas and a service center in Dubai. The Jury family continues to own a controlling interest in SUMMIT.

Geographic Reach

SUMMIT has locations in about 20 markets across Arizona Louisiana New Mexico and Texas. It also has a marine division based in New Orleans a Latin American sales office and a service center in Dubai UAE.

Financial Performance

SUMMIT's sales have rebounded from the drubbing they took during the global economic downturn when electrical wholesalers were hit hard as construction slowed and businesses cut back on expansion plans. Indeed SUMMIT's 2012 sales exceeded their pre-recession high. The $385 million in sales the electrical wholesaler rang up in 2012 was a 7% increase vs. the prior year. Strength in the MRO (maintenance repair and overhaul) and energy markets have buoyed sales. The company is also benefitting from its aggressive expansion in such growth markets as Latin America and the Middle East.

Strategy

In 2010 SUMMIT announced plans to expand its presence in the Middle East by opening a full-service branch in Dubai and actively developing a customer base across the region. The company initially opened a sales office in Dubai a region that has seen a boom in construction projects in 2007. SUMMIT is also actively working to expand sales in Latin America where it is focused on industrial construction projects in oil gas and mining across the region.

EXECUTIVES

VP Supplier and Product Strategy, Drew Ott
President and CEO, Victor R. Jury Jr.
VP Marketing, Sheila Hernandez
Service Center Leader Albuquerque, Wiley Shaw
Regional VP Southwest, Scott Cogan
Service Center Leader Farmington, Kenneth King
Service Center Leader Corpus Christi, Ted Mendoza
Service Center Leader Fort Worth, Richard Efurd
Service Center Leader Beaumont, Chris Rybacki
Service Center Leader Gonzales, W. Damain Kerek
VP Operations, Cole Harrison
Service Center Leader La Porte, Mike Mares
Marine Division Director, Ed Dowey
CFO and Treasurer, Russ Hiller
VP Associate Resources Chief Talent Officer and Corporate Counsel, Dan Long
VP Information Technologies, David Wascom
Regional VP Gulf Coast, Dan Ferrari
Service Center Leader Phoenix, Craig Rusk
Service Center Leader San Antonio, Allen O'Dell
Communications Director, Diane Velasco
Service Center Leader Austin, Matt Darling
Service Center Leader Clute, Steve Lincoln
Service Center Leader Dallas, Michael (Mike) Kizer
Service Center Leader El Paso, Chris Gallegos
Service Center Leader Houston, Rodney Ilseng
Service Center Leader New Orleans, Denny Wombles

LOCATIONS

HQ: SUMMIT Electric Supply Company Inc.
2900 Stanford Dr. NE, Albuquerque NM 87107
Phone: 505-346-9000   **Fax:** 505-346-1616
Web: www.summit.com

PRODUCTS/OPERATIONS

Selected Products

Ballasts
Box hangers
Brackets
Cable
Chemicals
Conduit
Drills
Enclosures
Fasteners
Fuses and fuse kits
Gaskets
Gloves
Goggles
Hand tools
Installation tools
Junction boxes
Lamps (HID and incandescent)
Light fixtures
Lubricants
Outlet boxes
PVC pipe
Power tools
Raceway
Receptacles
Safety equipment
Saws
Screws
Switches
Terminals
Test equipment
Transformers
Uninterruptible power supplies
Wire
Wire guards

COMPETITORS

Border States Electric
Consolidated Electrical
Crescent Electric Supply
Graybar Electric
Hisco
Kirby Risk
Rexel Inc.
Sonepar USA
Stuart C. Irby
W.W. Grainger
WESCO International

HISTORICAL FINANCIALS

Company Type: Private

Income Statement   FYE: December 31

	REVENUE ($ mil.)	NET INCOME ($ mil.)	NET PROFIT MARGIN	EMPLOYEES
12/11	358	7	2.1%	497
12/10	301	7	2.6%	0
12/06	337	5	1.6%	0
12/05	267	4	1.5%	0
Annual Growth	10.2%	21.9%	—	—

2011 Year-End Financials

Debt ratio: ——
Return on equity: 2.10%
Cash ($ mil.): 0
Current ratio: 1.20
Long-term debt ($ mil.): —

Dividends
Yield: —
Payout: —
Market value ($ mil.): —

SUMMIT HEALTH

LOCATIONS

HQ: SUMMIT HEALTH
112 N 7TH ST, CHAMBERSBURG, PA 17201-1720
Phone: 717-267-3000
Web: www.yellowpages.therecordherald.com

HISTORICAL FINANCIALS

Company Type: Private

Income Statement

FYE: June 30

	REVENUE ($ mil.)	NET INCOME ($ mil.)	NET PROFIT MARGIN	EMPLOYEES
06/11	401	53	13.4%	2,150
06/08	333	1	0.3%	0
06/07	310	33	10.7%	0
06/06	281	17	6.2%	0
Annual Growth	12.5%	45.4%	—	—

2011 Year-End Financials

Debt ratio: ——
Return on equity: 13.40%
Cash ($ mil.): 40
Current ratio: 1.30
Long-term debt ($ mil.): ——
Dividends
Yield: —
Payout: —
Market value ($ mil.): —

SUMTER SCHOOL DISTRICT

LOCATIONS

HQ: SUMTER SCHOOL DISTRICT
1345 WILSON HALL RD, SUMTER, SC 29150-1890
Phone: 803-469-6900
Web: www.district.sumterschools.net

HISTORICAL FINANCIALS

Company Type: Private

Income Statement

FYE: June 30

	REVENUE ($ mil.)	NET INCOME ($ mil.)	NET PROFIT MARGIN	EMPLOYEES
06/12	138	(3)	—	2,600
06/08	77	(4)	—	0
06/07	72	61	86.0%	0
06/06	22	1	7.1%	0
Annual Growth	84.2%	—	—	—

2012 Year-End Financials

Debt ratio: ——
Return on equity: (-2.50)%
Cash ($ mil.): 27
Current ratio: ——
Long-term debt ($ mil.): ——
Dividends
Yield: —
Payout: —
Market value ($ mil.): —

SUN AND SANDS ENTERPRISES LLC

LOCATIONS

HQ: SUN AND SANDS ENTERPRISES LLC
86705 AVENUE 54 STE A, COACHELLA, CA 92236-3814
Phone: 760-399-4278
Web: www.primetimeproduce.com

HISTORICAL FINANCIALS

Company Type: Private

Income Statement

FYE: December 31

	REVENUE ($ mil.)	NET INCOME ($ mil.)	NET PROFIT MARGIN	EMPLOYEES
12/11	97	5	5.7%	100
12/10	105	16	15.6%	0
12/09	95	10	10.5%	0
12/08	85	5	6.0%	0
Annual Growth	4.5%	3.0%	—	—

2011 Year-End Financials

Debt ratio: ——
Return on equity: 5.70%
Cash ($ mil.): 9
Current ratio: 0.90
Long-term debt ($ mil.): ——
Dividends
Yield: —
Payout: —
Market value ($ mil.): —

SUN COAST NURSING CENTERS INC

LOCATIONS

HQ: SUN COAST NURSING CENTERS INC
1675 PALM BCH LAKES BLVD, WEST PALM BEACH, FL 33401-2122
Phone: 561-801-7600

HISTORICAL FINANCIALS

Company Type: Private

Income Statement

FYE: June 30

	REVENUE ($ mil.)	NET INCOME ($ mil.)	NET PROFIT MARGIN	EMPLOYEES
06/11	236	11	4.9%	0
06/10	213	6	3.2%	0
Annual Growth	10.5%	72.2%	—	—

2011 Year-End Financials

Debt ratio: ——
Return on equity: 4.90%
Cash ($ mil.): 25
Current ratio: 2.20
Long-term debt ($ mil.): ——
Dividends
Yield: —
Payout: —
Market value ($ mil.): —

SUN-MAID GROWERS OF CALIFORNIA

The Sun-Maid's basket runneth over. Sun-Maid Growers is the producer of Sun-Maid Raisins. Packaged in the familiar red boxes with the smiling red-bonneted maid Lorraine Collett Petersen offering her basket laden with grapes the brand is seen in just about every food store in the US. In addition to offering every toddler's (and moms of toddlers) favorite little-red-boxed snack the grower-owned cooperative manufactures industrial and foodservice products and exports to more than 50 countries worldwide. The company's other dried fruits include pitted prunes currants apricots cranberries figs dates apples fruit bits and tropical fruit mixtures.

Sun-Maid whose growers harvest some 200 million pound of grapes every year also licenses its brand for products including raisin bread raisin muffins and raisin cookie mix as well as chocolate- and vanilla yogurt-covered raisins. Retail products make up about half of the co-op's sales; ingredient products comprise the rest.

EXECUTIVES

Chairman, Jon E. Marthedal
President, Barry F. Kriebel
VP Operations, James M. Henderson
VP Finance and CFO, Richard A. Emde
VP Sales, Harold F. Hilker
VP Sales, Michael K. Cassidy
VP Brand Management and Licensing, Rick C. Bruno
Secretary, Gary H. Marshburn
Vice Chairman, Nindy P. Sandhu
Manager Grower Relations, Rick Stark

LOCATIONS

HQ: Sun-Maid Growers of California
13525 S. Bethel Ave., Kingsburg CA 93631
Phone: 559-896-8000   **Fax:** 559-897-6209
Web: www.sun-maid.com

PRODUCTS/OPERATIONS

Selected Products
Bakery
  Oatmeal raisin cookie mix
  Raisin bread
  Raisin muffins
Dried apples
Dried California apricots
Dried Calimyrna figs
Dried chopped dates
Dried cranberries
Dried fruit bits
Dried golden raisins and cherries
Dried Mediterranean apricots
Dried mission figs
Dried mixed fruit
Dried pitted dates
Dried pitted plums
Dried tropical trio
Raisins
  Baking raisins
  Chocolate yogurt-covered raisins
  Chocolate-covered raisins
  Golden raisins
  Jumbo raisins
  Vanilla yogurt-covered raisins
  Zante currents

COMPETITORS

Cherry Central
  Cooperative Inc.
Dole Food
Encore Fruit Marketing
Florida Food Products
  Inc
Fresh Del Monte
  Produce
General Mills
Gold Harbor
Golden West Nuts
Graceland Fruit
Kendall Frozen Fruits
Lion Raisins
Meridian Nut Growers

Multiple Organics
National Raisin
Pinnacle Foods
Riviana Foods
Shoreline Fruit
SunOpta
Sunview Vineyards
Tree Top
Tropical Nut &
  Fruit
United Natural
Valley Fig Growers
Waymouth Farms
Welch' s

HISTORICAL FINANCIALS

Company Type: Private - Cooperative

Income Statement

FYE: July 31

	REVENUE ($ mil.)	NET INCOME ($ mil.)	NET PROFIT MARGIN	EMPLOYEES
07/12	360	8	2.3%	550
07/11	352	14	4.0%	0
07/10	322	16	5.0%	0
07/09	309	18	5.9%	0
Annual Growth	5.2%	(22.9%)	—	—

2012 Year-End Financials

Debt ratio: ——
Return on equity: 2.30%
Cash ($ mil.): 0
Current ratio: 0.30
Long-term debt ($ mil.): —

Dividends
  Yield: —
  Payout: —
Market value ($ mil.): —

SUNNYSIDE UNIFIED SCHOOL DISTRICT 12

LOCATIONS

HQ: SUNNYSIDE UNIFIED SCHOOL DISTRICT 12
2238 E GINTER RD, TUCSON, AZ 85706-5806
Phone: 520-545-2024

HISTORICAL FINANCIALS

Company Type: Private

Income Statement

FYE: June 30

	REVENUE ($ mil.)	NET INCOME ($ mil.)	NET PROFIT MARGIN	EMPLOYEES
06/11	138	3	2.7%	1,700
06/10	145	5	3.5%	0
06/06	134	0	0.2%	0
06/04	115	(0)	—	0
Annual Growth	6.1%	—	—	—

SUNSHINE BOUQUET COMPANY

LOCATIONS

HQ: SUNSHINE BOUQUET COMPANY
3 CHRIS CT STE A, DAYTON, NJ 08810-1543
Phone: 732-274-2900

HISTORICAL FINANCIALS

Company Type: Private

Income Statement

FYE: December 31

	REVENUE ($ mil.)	NET INCOME ($ mil.)	NET PROFIT MARGIN	EMPLOYEES
12/11	101	0	0.4%	200
12/10	82	0	0.7%	0
12/09	69	0	0.3%	0
Annual Growth	20.4%	39.2%	—	—

2011 Year-End Financials

Debt ratio: ——
Return on equity: 0.40%
Cash ($ mil.): 0
Current ratio: 1.20
Long-term debt ($ mil.): —

Dividends
  Yield: —
  Payout: —
Market value ($ mil.): —

SUNSWEET GROWERS INC.

Being all dried up is a good thing at Sunsweet Growers. The more than 400 member/grower-owned cooperative processes and markets dried fruit. Sunsweet produces one-third of the world's prunes (it processes more than 50000 tons of prunes each year). Its other fruit products include prune and other juices as well as dried apples apricots dates cranberries blueberries mangoes peaches pears pineapples and more. Sunsweet which has gotten into dietary supplement beverages supplies its products to retail food and food-service outlets worldwide. Sunsweet produces some 40000 cases of dried fruit products every day. The co-op was founded in 1917 as the California Prune and Apricot Growers Association.

Strategy

To diversify its business and give its bottom line a boost Sunsweet in 2011 acquired California-based Function Drinks known for making functional beverages that have added nutrition. As part of the transaction Sunsweet rolled Function Drinks into a newly formed subsidiary Disruptive Beverages Inc. (DBI). The cooperative is using DBI as the foundation for expanding its beverages portfolio.

EXECUTIVES

SVP Human Resources, Sharon K. Braun
Chairman, Gary S. Thiara
Vice Chairman, Tim D. Smith
President and CEO, Arthur Driscoll II
VP and CFO, Ana Spyres
VP Global Marketing and Sales, Dane L. Lance
VP Sales North America, Brad Schuller

VP Manufacturing, Gene Dodson
Vice Chairman, Tim D. Smith
Director, J. Michael Billiou III
Director, Joe Turkovich
Director, Brendon Flynn
Director, Ren L. Fairbanks
Director, Robert (Bob) Kolberg
Director, John Rehermann
Director, Hans F. Smith
Director, Phillip Filter
Director, Robert Amarel Jr.
Auditors: KPMGLLP

LOCATIONS

HQ: SUNSWEET GROWERS INC.
901 N WALTON AVE, YUBA CITY, CA 95993-9370
Phone: 530-674-5010
Web: www.sunsweet.com

PRODUCTS/OPERATIONS

Selected Products and Brands

Juices
  Amazing Prune Light
  Juicers
  PlumSmart
  PlumSmart Light
  Prune Juice
  Prune Juice with Pulp
Prunes
  60 CALORIE PACKS
  Amazins
  BITE SIZE PRUNES
  D' NOIR PRUNES
  ESSENCE
  Lighter Bake
  PREMIUM PRUNES
  WHOLE PRUNES
Specialty Fruits
  Antioxidant Blend
  Berry Blend
  Blueberries
  Cherries
  Cranberries
  Dates
  Jumbo Red Raisins
  Mediterranean Apricots
  Philippine Mangos
  Philippine Pineapple
  PlumSweets

COMPETITORS

Cherry Central
  Cooperative Inc.
Chiquita Brands
Del Monte Foods
Dole Food
Fresh Del Monte
  Produce
Graceland Fruit
Maui Land &
  Pineapple
Meridian Nut Growers
Naturipe Farms

Ocean Spray
Pro-Fac
Seneca Foods
Shoreline Fruit
Stewart & Jasper
  Orchards
Sunkist
Tropical Nut &
  Fruit
Valley Fig Growers
Waymouth Farms

HISTORICAL FINANCIALS

Company Type: Private - Cooperative

Income Statement

FYE: July 31

	REVENUE ($ mil.)	NET INCOME ($ mil.)	NET PROFIT MARGIN	EMPLOYEES
07/11	245	56	23.1%	700
07/09	262	80	30.6%	0
07/08	220	41	19.0%	0
07/07	293	124	42.4%	0
Annual Growth	(5.7%)	(23.0%)	—	—

Debt ratio: ——
Return on equity: 23.10%
Cash ($ mil.): 3
Current ratio: 0.40
Long-term debt ($ mil.): ——

Dividends
Yield: ——
Payout: ——
Market value ($ mil.): ——

SUPERIOR COMMUNICATIONS INC.

LOCATIONS

HQ: SUPERIOR COMMUNICATIONS INC.
5027 IRWINDALE AVE # 900, IRWINDALE, CA
91706-2187
Phone: 626-856-6020
Web: www.scp4me.com

HISTORICAL FINANCIALS

Company Type: Private

Income Statement

FYE: December 31

	REVENUE ($ mil.)	NET INCOME ($ mil.)	NET PROFIT MARGIN	EMPLOYEES
12/11	409	6	1.5%	325
12/10	432	13	3.1%	0
12/09	379	14	3.9%	0
12/08	432	13	3.1%	0
Annual Growth	(1.8%)	(23.1%)	—	—

2011 Year-End Financials

Debt ratio: ——
Return on equity: 1.50%
Cash ($ mil.): 6
Current ratio: 0.80
Long-term debt ($ mil.): ——

Dividends
Yield: ——
Payout: ——
Market value ($ mil.): ——

SUPERIOR OIL COMPANY INC.

Despite the name Superior Oil actually distributes industrial products and provides chemical and waste services. Superior's solvents and chemicals division supplies manufacturers of paints and coatings pharmaceuticals fabricated metal products and adhesives. The fiberglass and resins unit sells to clients that make products ranging from parts for recreational vehicles to bathtubs and showers. Superior Oil also provides blending solvent reclamation and hazardous waste removal services. The company has nine stocking facilities and a fleet of trucks trailers and tankers. The company is owned by members of its management team.

EXECUTIVES

CFO and Director Human Resources, Robert Andersen
Sales Manager Effingham Illinois Sales Distribution Center, Tom Edwards

FRP Sales Manager Elkhart Indiana Sales Distribution Center, Wes Nan
Sales Manager Nashville Tennessee Sales Distribution Center, Wade Childress
President, Ray Roembke
Sales Manager Springfield Missouri Sales Distribution Center, Bob Worthy
Sales Manager Indianapolis Indiana Sales Distribution Center, Bryan Teed
Sales Manager Louisville Kentucky Sales Distribution Center, Scott Bridges
Sales Manager Cincinnati Ohio Sales Distribution Center, Ken Smith
Solvents Sales Manager Elkhart Indiana Sales Distribution Center, Wayne Dixon
Sales Manager St. Louis Missouri Sales Distribution Center, Joel Zimmerman
Sales Manager Orrville Ohio Sales Distribution Center, Bill Garrett

LOCATIONS

HQ: Superior Oil Company Inc.
1402 North Capitol Ave. Ste. 100, Indianapolis IN 46202
Phone: 317-781-4400   **Fax:** 317-781-4401
Web: www.superioroil.com

PRODUCTS/OPERATIONS

Selected Products and Services

Acetate esters
Alcohols
Aliphatic naphthas
Aromatic hydrocarbons
Caustic soda
Chelating agents
Compliance management
Equipment programs
Glycol ethers
Glycols
Heat exchange fluids
Ketones
Lacquer thinners
Paint strippers
Plasticizers
Professional waste services
Recycling programs
Regulatory services
Silicones
Technical support
Terpenes
Transportation

COMPETITORS

Aceto
Brenntag North America
HallStar
Harcros Chemicals
ICC Chemical
Univar USA
Wego Chemical & Mineral

HISTORICAL FINANCIALS

Company Type: Private

Income Statement

FYE: December 31

	REVENUE ($ mil.)	NET INCOME ($ mil.)	NET PROFIT MARGIN	EMPLOYEES
12/11	191	0	—	250
12/10	167	0	—	0
12/09	132	0	—	0
12/08	178	0	—	0
Annual Growth	2.4%	—	—	—

2011 Year-End Financials

Debt ratio: ——
Return on equity: ——
Cash ($ mil.): 1
Current ratio: 1.30
Long-term debt ($ mil.): ——

Dividends
Yield: ——
Payout: ——
Market value ($ mil.): ——

SUPERIOR PETROLEUM COMPANY

LOCATIONS

HQ: SUPERIOR PETROLEUM COMPANY
8199 MCKNIGHT RD, PITTSBURGH, PA 15237-5749
Phone: 412-364-2200

HISTORICAL FINANCIALS

Company Type: Private

Income Statement

FYE: December 31

	REVENUE ($ mil.)	NET INCOME ($ mil.)	NET PROFIT MARGIN	EMPLOYEES
12/11	288	2	0.8%	250
12/10	219	1	0.8%	0
12/09	166	1	0.9%	0
12/06	106	0	0.1%	0
Annual Growth	39.4%	152.0%	—	—

2011 Year-End Financials

Debt ratio: ——
Return on equity: 0.80%
Cash ($ mil.): 1
Current ratio: 0.20
Long-term debt ($ mil.): ——

Dividends
Yield: ——
Payout: ——
Market value ($ mil.): ——

SUPERMERCADOS MR SPECIAL INC

LOCATIONS

HQ: SUPERMERCADOS MR SPECIAL INC
620 AVE SNTA TRESA JORNET, MAYAGUEZ, PR 00682-1342
Phone: 787-834-2695

HISTORICAL FINANCIALS

Company Type: Private

Income Statement

FYE: September 30

	REVENUE ($ mil.)	NET INCOME ($ mil.)	NET PROFIT MARGIN	EMPLOYEES
09/11	291	4	1.4%	1,150
09/10	277	5	1.9%	0
09/09	283	15	5.4%	0
09/08	260	8	3.1%	0
Annual Growth	3.9%	(20.9%)	—	—

2011 Year-End Financials

Debt ratio: ——
Return on equity: 1.40%
Cash ($ mil.): 5
Current ratio: 0.20
Long-term debt ($ mil.): ——

Dividends
Yield: ——
Payout: ——
Market value ($ mil.): ——

SUTTER CENTRAL VALLEY HOSPITALS

If you've stumbled from tasting too many fruits from the vines at nearby wineries keep your fingers crossed that someone will help you get to Memorial Medical Center. Not-for-profit Memorial Hospital Association runs the Memorial Medical Center which provides health care to the residents of Modesto California and the surrounding Stanislaus County. Specialized services include surgery pediatrics diagnostics cancer treatment home health and emergency medicine. Memorial Hospital Association also operates an air ambulance service. Founded in 1970 the Memorial Medical Center has more than 420 beds. It is a subsidiary of West Coast hospital giant Sutter Health.

An expansion project adding over 100 beds and nearly 20 operating rooms was completed in 2007. The new seven-story patient tower dubbed the North Tower includes capacity for the addition of future patient beds as well.

EXECUTIVES

COO, Steve Mitchell
CFO, C. Joseph (Joe) Hirt
VP Nursing Services, Sandra K. Proctor
Treasurer Memorial Hospitals Association Volunteers, Darleen Layman
Regional Marketing Director, Catherine Larsen
Regional Chief Information Officer, Patrick Anderson
CEO, James E. Conforti
Assistant Administrator Clinical Services, Jon Felton
Director Human Resources, Paula Rafala
President Memorial Hospital Foundation, Matthew Bruno
VP Memorial Hospital Foundation, Sean Carroll
Secretary Memorial Hospital Foundation, Michael West
President Memorial Hospitals Association Volunteers, Gladys Swagerty
Corresponding Secretary Memorial Hospitals Association Volunteers, Eleanor Rude
Recording Secretary Memorial Hospital Association Volunteers, Sandra Green
President, Lila Villierme
Chief Financial Officer, Eric Dalton

LOCATIONS

HQ: Memorial Hospitals Association
1700 Coffee Rd., Modesto CA 95355
Phone: 209-526-4500 **Fax:** 209-569-7417
Web: www.memorialmedicalcenter.org

COMPETITORS

Adventist Health	Stanford Hospital and
Dignity Health	Clinics
HCA	Tenet Healthcare
Kaiser Permanente	UCSF Medical
Saint Agnes Medical	
Center	

HISTORICAL FINANCIALS

Company Type: Subsidiary

Income Statement
FYE: December 31

	REVENUE ($ mil.)	NET INCOME ($ mil.)	NET PROFIT MARGIN	EMPLOYEES
12/11	701	32	4.6%	115
Annual Growth	—	—	—	—

2011 Year-End Financials

Debt ratio: ——
Return on equity: 4.60%
Cash ($ mil.): 19
Current ratio: 1.30
Long-term debt ($ mil.): —

Dividends
  Yield: —
  Payout: —
  Market value ($ mil.): —

SUTTER GOULD MEDICAL FOUNDATION

LOCATIONS

HQ: SUTTER GOULD MEDICAL FOUNDATION
1700 MCHENRY AVE STE 60B, MODESTO, CA 95350-4333
Phone: 209-526-4500

HISTORICAL FINANCIALS

Company Type: Private

Income Statement
FYE: December 31

	REVENUE ($ mil.)	NET INCOME ($ mil.)	NET PROFIT MARGIN	EMPLOYEES
12/11	305	(8)	—	4
12/09	288	(7)	—	0
Annual Growth	5.8%	—	—	—

2011 Year-End Financials

Debt ratio: ——
Return on equity: (-2.60)%
Cash ($ mil.): 23
Current ratio: 1.00
Long-term debt ($ mil.): —

Dividends
  Yield: —
  Payout: —
  Market value ($ mil.): —

SUTTER HEALTH

Whether you drink too much in Wine Country hit some rough waters off the Marin Headlands or trip during a hike through the redwood forest it's likely Sutter Health is just a stone's throw away. The Northern California not-for-profit health care system is one of the nation's largest. After being formed more than a decade ago through the merger of Sutter Health and California Healthcare System Sutter Health now caters to residents of more than 100 communities from the California Bay Area to the beaches of Hawaii. Its services are provided through affiliated doctors from a host of health care facilities including two dozen acute care hospitals home health networks and skilled nursing facilities.

Geographic Reach

Sutter Health's governance is structured into five geographic regions throughout Northern California. Each region has its own physician organization board to oversee all of the Sutter-affiliated medical facilities and hospitals in that area. The current structure was put in place to replace the more than 50 existing hospital and physician organization boards that were previously in place throughout the network. The regional boards also charter community-based boards to focus on local matters such as quality and community benefits.

Financial Analysis

Sutter Health's revenues increased by 3% in 2011 thanks to the growth in patient services sales (85% of total sales). Its 2011 operating performance included $69 million of net supplemental payments associated with California's temporary program to obtain federal matching dollars to partially offset underpayments in previous years for the care of Medi-Cal patients.

Strategy

Like most other health care organizations across the country Sutter Health is using technology to keep its patients informed about their medical care. The company is part of a national group participating in a program called Care Everywhere a technology that enables medical teams from separate hospitals and clinics to share a patient's medical records at the time he or she receives care. Through this technology Sutter Health is linked with UC Davis Health System Stanford and Santa Cruz County Health Services to share vital patient information.

Sutter Health invested $898 million in capital in 2011 and expects to invest $5.4 billion in capital between 2012 and 2016. Much of the company's investment supports advances in patient care technology. In 2011 Sutter Health implemented an electronic health record system in five hospitals within the Central Valley and Peninsula Coastal regions. The system enhances patient care linking doctors hospitals and patients throughout Northern California.

Sutter Health depends on philanthropy to keep some projects alive. It's currently using the $55 million it received in 2010 to help equip its facilities with more advanced technology; to increase OB-GYN services; fund research to help further disease prevention diagnosis and treatment; create innovative programs such as music therapy and outpatient pediatric diabetes clinics; and construct new facilities to deliver advanced efficient care to its thousands of patients.

EXECUTIVES

President and CEO, Patrick E. (Pat) Fry
Director and Secretary, Richard M. Levy, age 74
SVP and Chief Medical Officer, Gordon C. Hunt Jr.
SVP and CFO, Robert D. (Bob) Reed, age 59
President Sutter Health West Bay Region, Martin Brotman
Chair, Geraldine R. Brinton
President Sutter Health Central Valley Region, David P. Benn
VP Communications, Bill Gleeson
Director Communications, Karen Garner
President Sutter Health East Bay Region, Edward (Ed) Berdick
President Sutter Health East Bay Region, David Bradley
Chairman, Jim Gray, age 66
SVP and CIO, Jonathan (Jon) Manis
SVP; Executive Officer Sutter Medical Network, Jeffrey Burnich
President Sutter Health West Bay Region, Mike Cohill

President Sutter Health Sacramento Sierra Region, James E. Conforti
Communications Coordinator, Kami Lloyd
President Sutter Health Peninsula Coastal Region, Jeff Gerard
President CEO and Director, Patrick E. (Pat) Fry
Director and Secretary, Richard M. Levy, age 74
Director, Michael R. Gaulke, age 66
Director, Geraldine R. Brinton
Director, Gary L. Depolo, age 76
Director, Mary Brown
Director, Elizabeth Vilardo
Director, Todd Smith
Director, Jim Gray, age 67
Director, Alexander (Alex) Gonzalez
Director, David H. Jeppson
Director, Todd Murray
Director, Andrew Pansini
Director, Michael A. Roosevelt
Auditors: Ernst&YoungLLP

LOCATIONS

HQ: Sutter Health
2200 River Plaza Dr., Sacramento CA 95833
Phone: 916-733-8800   **Fax:** 847-483-7039
Web: www.alexianhealthsystem.org

Selected Hospitals

Alta Bates Summit Medical Center (Berkeley Oakland)
California Pacific Medical Center (San Francisco)
Eden Medical Center (Castro Valley)
Kahi Mohala (Ewa HI)
Marin General Hospital (Greenbrae)
Memorial Hospital Los Banos (Los Banos)
Memorial Medical Center (Modesto)
Menlo Park Surgical Hospital
Mills-Peninsula Health Services (Burlingame)
Novato Community Hospital (Novato)
Sutter Amador Hospital (Jackson)
Sutter Auburn Faith Hospital (Auburn)
Sutter Coast Hospital (Crescent City)
Sutter Davis Hospital (Davis)
Sutter Delta Medical Center (Antioch)
Sutter Lakeside Hospital (Lakeport)
Sutter Maternity & Surgery Center of Santa Cruz
Sutter Medical Center (Sacramento)
Sutter Medical Center of Santa Rosa
Sutter Roseville Medical Center
Sutter Solano Medical Center (Vallejo)
Sutter Tracy Community Hospital (Tracy)

PRODUCTS/OPERATIONS

Selected Operations (Northern California Southern Oregon and Hawaii)

Acute Care Hospitals
Neonatal Intensive Care Units
Cancer Centers
Cardiac Centers
Acute Rehabilitation Centers
Medical Foundations
Trauma Centers
Behavioral Health Services
Education Centers and Physician Training Programs
Express Medical Clinics
Home Health and Hospice Services
Long-term Care Centers
Medical Research Centers
Occupational Health Services
Long-Term Care Centers
Irene Swindells Alzheimer's Residential Care Center San Francisco
Sutter Oaks Nursing Center Sacramento
Sutter Senior Care PACE Program Sacramento
Cancer Centers
Alta Bates Summit Comprehensive Cancer Center Berkeley and Oakland
California Pacific Medical Center San Francisco
Dorothy E. Schneider Cancer Center at Mills-Peninsula Health Services Burlingame
Eden Medical Center Castro Valley
Memorial Regional Cancer Center Modesto

Sutter Auburn Faith Hospital Auburn
Sutter Cancer Center Sutter Medical Center Sacramento
Sutter Cancer Center Sutter Roseville Medical Center Roseville
Sutter Solano Cancer Center Vallejo
Programs listed above are approved by the American College of Surgeons' Commission on Cancer.
Research Institutes
California Pacific Medical Center San Francisco
Palo Alto Medical Foundation Research Institute Palo Alto
Sutter Health Institute for Research and Education San Francisco
Sutter Institute for Medical Research Sacramento
Home Health and Hospice Services
Coming Home Hospice
Cohen Cormier Home Attendant & Care Management
Sutter Auburn Faith VNA & Hospice
Sutter Care at Home
Sutter Coast Home Care
Sutter Infusion & Pharmacy Services / Emeryville and Sacramento
Sutter Lakeside Home Medical Services
Sutter Lifeline / Sacramento
Sutter North Home Health Agency
VNA of the Central Valley
VNA of Santa Cruz County
Express Medical Clinics
Sutter Express Care (Three locations in Sacramento & Placer counties)

COMPETITORS

Adventist Health
Alta Bates Summit Medical Center
Ascension Health
California Pacific Medical Center
Children' s Hospital & Research Center at Oakland
Dignity Health
Hawai' i Pacific Health
HCA
Kaiser Permanente
Kuakini Health System
Memorial Health Services
Odyssey HealthCare
Providence Health & Services
Rehabilitation Hospital of the Pacific
Stanford Hospital and Clinics
Tenet Healthcare
UCSF Medical

HISTORICAL FINANCIALS

Company Type: Private - Not-for-Profit

Income Statement

FYE: September 30

	REVENUE ($ mil.)	NET INCOME ($ mil.)	NET PROFIT MARGIN	EMPLOYEES
09/12*	7,179	761	10.6%	44,000
12/11	9,079	195	2.1%	0
12/10	9,116	978	10.7%	0
Annual Growth	(11.3%)	(11.8%)	—	—

*Fiscal year change

2012 Year-End Financials

Debt ratio: ——
Return on equity: 10.60%
Cash ($ mil.): 307
Current ratio: 1.00
Long-term debt ($ mil.): —

Dividends
Yield: —
Payout: —
Market value ($ mil.): —

SUTTER MEDICAL FOUNDATION

LOCATIONS

HQ: SUTTER MEDICAL FOUNDATION
2800 L ST FL 7, SACRAMENTO, CA 95816-5616
Phone: 916-454-6640

HISTORICAL FINANCIALS

Company Type: Private

Income Statement

FYE: December 31

	REVENUE ($ mil.)	NET INCOME ($ mil.)	NET PROFIT MARGIN	EMPLOYEES
12/11	705	(4)	—	700
12/09	505	(21)	—	0
12/02	111	(7)	—	0
12/01	189	(10)	—	0
Annual Growth	55.1%	—	—	—

2011 Year-End Financials

Debt ratio: ——
Return on equity: (-0.60)%
Cash ($ mil.): 44
Current ratio: 1.70
Long-term debt ($ mil.): —

Dividends
Yield: —
Payout: —
Market value ($ mil.): —

SUTTER WEST BAY HOSPITALS

Sutter West Bay Hospitals (doing business as California Pacific Medical Center or CPMC) is a health care complex located in the heart of hospital-heavy San Francisco. The private not-for-profit center's four area campuses (California Davies Pacific and St. Luke's) offer acute and specialty care including obstetrics and gynecology cardiovascular services pediatrics neurosciences orthopedics and organ transplantation. With more than 1300 beds between its campuses the center also conducts professional education and biomedical clinical and behavioral research. CPMC is part of the West Bay Region division of the Sutter Health hospital system.

Geographic Reach

CPMC serves patients from San Francisco Marin San Mateo Oakland Berkeley Palo Alto Santa Rosa San Jose. and the Bay Area.

Operations

CPMC's Sutter Health West Bay Region also includes Novato Community Hospital Sutter Lakeside Hospital and Sutter Medical Center of Santa Rosa. In addition to acute medical services CPMC also provides outpatient services at clinics in the San Francisco area operates home health and hospice organizations and conducts health education and charity care programs.

In 2011 CPMC's Research Institute conducted more than 200 clinical trials including studies on aging cancers epilepsy diabetes cardiovascular disease osteoporosis organ transplantation and more. That year CPMC's Kidney and Pancreas Transplant Program performed the first ever single-hospital five-way kidney swap transplant in California. CPMC's Joint Replacement Center is one of the leading joint replacement centers in the Bay Area performing roughly 1200 hip knee shoulder and elbow procedures per year. It has 1859 CPMC Medical Staff (including St. Luke's) and 109 medical residents and fellows.

That year the healthcare system reported about 619400 outpatient visits and 30300 inpatient cases.

Strategy

In order to meet California's seismic construction standards CPMC plans to renovate or rebuild most of its hospital campuses which are among the oldest medical centers in the San Francisco area. Its $2.5 billion reorganization plan includes the construction of a new 550-bed Cathedral Hill Campus that will include a full acute care hospital plus specialized women's and children's departments. CPMC also plans to rebuild and downsize the St. Luke's campus and convert the Pacific and California campuses into ambulatory care clinics. Reconstruction efforts at the Davies campus will include a new patient pavilion and a new Davies Neurosciences Institute for expanded neurological care. Major construction projects began in 2011 and will extend through 2015.

In 2010 the company sold its outpatient kidney dialysis operations to DaVita to focus on core operations.

Ownership

CPMC is part of the West Bay Region division of the Sutter Health hospital system.

Company Background

In 2007 parent Sutter Health merged St. Luke's Hospital into California Pacific to help keep the ailing St. Luke's afloat; St. Luke's provides care to many of San Francisco's low-income patients. CPMC had announced plans to turn St. Luke's into an outpatient facility in 2007; however the company rescinded those plans after San Franciscans objected to the proposal.

EXECUTIVES

President Sutter Health West Bay Region, Martin Brotman
Senior Director Communications Marketing and External Affairs, Cynthia Chiarappa
VP Finance and CFO; Region CFO Sutter Health West Bay Region, John B. Gates
VP Nursing and Chief Nursing Officer, Diana Karner
Regional VP Human Resources Sutter Health West Bay Region, Linda Isaacs
EVP and CEO North Bay Hospitals, Grant Davies
CEO, Warren Browner
CEO Sutter Pacific Medical Foundation, Morris Flaum
VP Post Acute Services; Chief Administrative Officer Davies Campus, Mary Lanier
Senior Director Surgical Services, Diane Petruzzella
VP Medical Affairs and Chief Medical Officer, Allan Pont
VP Service Excellence Organization and Personal Development, Wanda Roane
Presidio Administrator Presidio Surgery Center, Jessie Scott
Director Institute for Health and Healing, William B. Stewart
CFO, Henry Yu
Region VP Strategy and Business Development Sutter Health West Bay Region, Chris Willrich
Manager Media Relations, Kevin McCormack
Senior Director Accreditation and Regulatory Organizational Performance, Helen Helt

Region VP Health System Innovation and Community Benefit SWB, Judy Li
VP Clinical Services; Chief Administrative Officer St. Luke's Campus, Dionne Miller
COO, Craig Vercruysse
Chief Medical Officer Sutter Pacific Medical Foundation, Anabel Anderson Imbert
Director Research Operations; Administrator Brannan Campus, Lynne Day
VP Operations Support and Professional Services, Delvecchio Finley
President California Pacific Medical Center Foundation; Region VP Philanthropy Sutter Health West Bay Region, Mark Kimbell
VP Operations Specialty Services; Chief Administrative Officer Pacific Campus, Hamila Kownacki
VP Finance Sutter Pacific Medical Foundation, Marc Lamonica
Associate VP Nursing, Heather Sebanc
VP Support Services, Bud Schawl
VP Women and Children's Services; Chief Administrative Officer California Campus, Bernadette Smith
COO Sutter Pacific Medical Foundation, Lynne Tromble
VP Quality and Safety, Sean Townsend
CIO, Anne Barr

LOCATIONS

HQ: Sutter West Bay Hospitals
633 Folsom St., San Francisco CA 94107
Phone: 415-600-6000   **Fax:** 415-600-1137
Web: www.cpmc.org

PRODUCTS/OPERATIONS

Selected Hospitals

California Campus (aka Children's Hospital of San Francisco)
Davies Campus (aka Davies Medical Center or Franklin Hospital)
Pacific Campus (aka Presbyterian Medical Center)
St. Luke's Campus (aka St. Luke's Hospital)

COMPETITORS

Children' s Hospital & Research Center at Oakland
Dignity Health
HCA
John Muir Health
Kaiser Permanente
St. Joseph Health System
Stanford Hospital and Clinics
Tenet Healthcare
UCSF Medical
ValleyCare Health System

HISTORICAL FINANCIALS

Company Type: Subsidiary

Income Statement

FYE: December 31

	REVENUE ($ mil.)	NET INCOME ($ mil.)	NET PROFIT MARGIN	EMPLOYEES
12/11	1,616	67	4.1%	3,597
12/09	1,245	159	12.8%	0
12/08	830	168	20.3%	0
12/04	801	138	17.3%	0
Annual Growth	26.3%	(21.6%)	—	—

HOOVER'S HANDBOOK OF PRIVATE COMPANIES 2013

2011 Year-End Financials

Debt ratio: ——
Return on equity: 4.10%
Cash ($ mil.): 76
Current ratio: 0.90
Long-term debt ($ mil.): —

Dividends
Yield: —
Payout: —
Market value ($ mil.): —

SUZANO PULP AND PAPER AMERICA INC

LOCATIONS

HQ: SUZANO PULP AND PAPER AMERICA INC
800 CORPORATE DR STE 320, FORT LAUDERDALE, FL 33334-3618
Phone: 954-772-7716
Web: www.nemotrade.com

HISTORICAL FINANCIALS

Company Type: Private

Income Statement

FYE: December 31

	REVENUE ($ mil.)	NET INCOME ($ mil.)	NET PROFIT MARGIN	EMPLOYEES
12/11	291	0	0.3%	18
12/10	243	0	0.3%	0
Annual Growth	19.8%	54.6%	—	—

2011 Year-End Financials

Debt ratio: ——
Return on equity: 0.30%
Cash ($ mil.): 8
Current ratio: 0.60
Long-term debt ($ mil.): —

Dividends
Yield: —
Payout: —
Market value ($ mil.): —

SWARTHMORE COLLEGE

The Borough of Swarthmore southwest of Philadelphia was founded in 1893 and literally evolved around the College on the Hill aka Swarthmore College which had been founded nearly three decades earlier by the Religious Society of Friends more commonly known as the Quakers. With a student-teacher ratio of 8:1 the private co-educational liberal arts and engineering college offers more than 50 academic programs and bachelor's degrees in the arts and sciences. Swarthmore enrolls about 1550 students or nearly 25% of the town's population. Notable alumni include Pulitzer Prize-winning author James Michener and former governor of Massachusetts Michael Dukakis.

In 2012 the college initiated construction project plans to improve the campus and facilities as part of its long-term strategic goals. Initiatives underway include improving access for people with disabilities and making long-planned for renovations and repairs to facilities. More broadly Swarthmore has kicked off a master planning process requesting input from the community to develop the campus in a way that will support its future needs.

Students come to Swarthmore from all over the US (from every state and territory plus Washington DC) and about 50 foreign countries. All but a handful of the faculty (in physical education and athletics) have a Ph.D or terminal degree.

As a collaborating member of the Tri-College Consortium with Bryn Mawr and Haverford Swarthmore students may take courses at all three colleges and use combined online library catalogs and borrowing privileges. They may also cross-register for undergraduate courses at the University of Pennsylvania. Studying abroad for a semester or two is also encouraged at Swarthmore.

Swarthmore has an endowment valued at more than $1 billion. The college was named in honor of Swarthmoor Hall in England the home of George Fox the founder of the Religious Society of Friends.

EXECUTIVES

President, Alfred H. Bloom
Registrar, Martin O. Warner
VP Finance and Treasurer, Suzanne P. Welsh
VP Human Resources, Melanie Young
Provost, Constance Cain Hungerford
Dean of Admissions and Financial Aid, James L. Bock III
VP College and Community Relations and Executive Assistant to the President, Maurice G. Eldridge
Director Alumni and Gift Records, Ruth Krakower
Director Alumni Relations, Lisa Lee
Director Career Services, Nancy Burkett
VP Facilities and Services, C. Stuart Hain
College Librarian, Peggy Ann Seiden
Dean of Students, James A. Larimore
Associate Dean for Academic Affairs, Garikai Campbell
Director Communications, Nancy Nicely
Associate Provost, Lisa Smulyan
VP for Development and Alumni Relations, Stephen D. Bayer

LOCATIONS

HQ: Swarthmore College
500 College Ave., Swarthmore PA 19081
Phone: 610-328-8000   **Fax:** 610-328-8580
Web: www.swarthmore.edu

PRODUCTS/OPERATIONS

2010 Sources of Revenue

% of total	
Student	45
Endowment	43
Other	12
Total	**100**

HISTORICAL FINANCIALS

Company Type: School

Income Statement

FYE: June 30

	REVENUE ($ mil.)	NET INCOME ($ mil.)	NET PROFIT MARGIN	EMPLOYEES
06/12	122	(12)	—	700
06/11	117	264	224.7%	0
06/10	115	120	104.4%	0
06/09	124	(289)	—	0
Annual Growth	**(0.6%)**	**—**	**—**	**—**

2012 Year-End Financials

Debt ratio: ——
Return on equity: (-10.60)%
Cash ($ mil.): 32
Current ratio: —
Long-term debt ($ mil.): —
Dividends
Yield: —
Payout: —
Market value ($ mil.): —

SWEDISHAMERICAN HOSPITAL

LOCATIONS

HQ: SWEDISHAMERICAN HOSPITAL
1401 E STATE ST, ROCKFORD, IL 61104-2315
Phone: 815-968-4400
Web: www.swedishamerican.org

HISTORICAL FINANCIALS

Company Type: Private

Income Statement

FYE: May 31

	REVENUE ($ mil.)	NET INCOME ($ mil.)	NET PROFIT MARGIN	EMPLOYEES
05/11	450	15	3.5%	1,599
05/10	420	13	3.2%	0
05/09*	347	30	8.7%	0
09/05	217	10	4.9%	0
Annual Growth	**27.6%**	**13.9%**	**—**	**—**

*Fiscal year change

2011 Year-End Financials

Debt ratio: ——
Return on equity: 3.50%
Cash ($ mil.): 27
Current ratio: 1.90
Long-term debt ($ mil.): —
Dividends
Yield: —
Payout: —
Market value ($ mil.): —

SWEET PEOPLE APPAREL INC.

LOCATIONS

HQ: SWEET PEOPLE APPAREL INC.
4715 S ALAMEDA ST, VERNON, CA 90058-2014
Phone: 323-235-7303

HISTORICAL FINANCIALS

Company Type: Private

Income Statement

FYE: December 31

	REVENUE ($ mil.)	NET INCOME ($ mil.)	NET PROFIT MARGIN	EMPLOYEES
12/11	156	31	20.3%	93
12/10	112	24	22.1%	0
12/09	61	14	22.9%	0
12/08	37	5	14.3%	0
Annual Growth	**61.0%**	**80.9%**	**—**	**—**

2011 Year-End Financials

Debt ratio: ——
Return on equity: 20.30%
Cash ($ mil.): 3
Current ratio: 0.30
Long-term debt ($ mil.): —
Dividends
Yield: —
Payout: —
Market value ($ mil.): —

SWINERTON BUILDERS

Swinerton Builders a subsidiary of Swinerton provides a ton of services related to commercial and sustainable construction and renovation primarily in the western US. The company's interiors group offers interior tenant finishes and remodeling working on such projects as high-tech and lab renovations hospitals retail facilities and seismic upgrades. Its building group focuses on new construction and retrofitting. Projects include the San Francisco Museum of Modern Art a Lockheed Martin launch vehicle assembly plant in Colorado and the Bay Bridge toll operations building in San Francisco. Swinerton Builders operates from offices in California Colorado Hawaii Texas New Mexico and Washington.

Swinerton also constructs many buildings to meet environmental standards. Green projects have ranged from fire stations and retail outlets to college facilities and hotels. Swinertons' own corporate offices in California are solar powered.

EXECUTIVES

SVP and Southern California Regional Manager, Gary J. Rafferty
EVP and Northern California Regional Manager, Charles P. (Charlie) Kuffner
SVP and Division Manager, Frank Foellmer
VP and Division Manager, Steve Johnson
President, Michael (Mike) Re
VP and San Diego Division Manager, Don Adair
Chairman and CEO, Gordon W. Marks
SVP and General Manager Northern California, Eric Foster
VP and San Francisco Division Manager, Jeffrey D. (Jeff) Recob
VP and Denver Division Manager, Kevin Ott
Operations Manager San Francisco, Bill Krill
Business Development Manager Denver, Mike Mismash
Business Development Los Angeles, Cheryl Johnson
Business Development Manager Oakland, Linda Pearson
Operations Manager Oakland, Matt Kelly
Business Development Manager Orange County, Dave Pintar
Operations Manager Los Angeles, Gust Soteropulos
Operations Manager Los Angeles Special Projects Group, Kim Grant
Operations Manager Building Group, Jef Farrell
Operations Manager Special Projects Group, Mark Payne
Project Executive, Dennis Heine
VP Southern California, Chris Day
VP and Estimating Manager, Joe Urrutia
VP Preconstruction, Dan Beyer
VP and Division Manager, Dave Callis
VP and Division Manager, Barry Widen
VP and Division Manager, Ron Montoya
Head Information Technology, Larry Mathews

LOCATIONS

HQ: Swinerton Builders
260 Townsend St., San Francisco CA 94107
Phone: 415-421-2980   **Fax:** 415-984-1204
Web: www.swinerton.com

COMPETITORS

Andersen Construction	Hensel Phelps
Charles Pankow	Construction
Builders	J.F. Shea
Clark Builders Group	Jaynes Companies

Cordoba
Devcon Construction
DPR Construction
Gilbane Building
  Company
Hathaway Dinwiddie
  Construction

Kitchell
Torix General
  Contractors
Turner Corporation
W. L. Butler
Webcor Builders
Whiting-Turner

HISTORICAL FINANCIALS
Company Type: Subsidiary

Income Statement
FYE: December 31

	REVENUE ($ mil.)	NET INCOME ($ mil.)	NET PROFIT MARGIN	EMPLOYEES
12/11	948	0	—	900
12/10	796	0	—	0
12/09	0	0	—	0
12/08	1,287	37	2.9%	0
Annual Growth	(9.7%)	—	—	—

2011 Year-End Financials

Debt ratio: ——
Return on equity: —
Cash ($ mil.): 121
Current ratio: 1.20
Long-term debt ($ mil.): —

Dividends
Yield: —
Payout: —
Market value ($ mil.): —

SWINERTON INCORPORATED

Swinerton is building up the West just as it helped rebuild San Francisco after the 1906 earthquake. The construction group builds commercial industrial and government facilities including resorts subsidized housing public schools soundstages hospitals and airport terminals. Through its subsidiaries (including Swinerton Builders) Swinerton offers general contracting and design/build services as well as construction and program management. It also provides property management for conventional subsidized and assisted living residences. The employee-owned company traces its roots to 1888. Swinerton offices are located throughout California in Colorado Hawaii Texas Oregon and Washington.

Swinerton takes environmental stewardship to heart and has a special renewable energy division focused on solar and wind projects. As one of the top waste-reducing companies in California Swinerton employs green building construction and design practices to conserve resources reduce waste and create healthier environments. The company's own headquarters building in San Francisco received Gold LEED-EB (Leadership in Energy & Environmental Design for Existing Buildings) —a top certification from the U.S. Green Building Council. Swinerton also built the LEED platinum rated NASA Ames Research Center Sustainability Base the greenest government building in history.

In addition to a focus on sustainable design and renewable energy projects Swinerton established a division to handle government construction projects. The division delivers large-scale complex design and construction services for government agencies. Through the division Swinerton has worked on federal courthouses and administrative buildings training centers VA hospitals and military housing projects.

EXECUTIVES

EVP, Gary J. Rafferty
EVP and Co-COO, Charles P. (Charlie) Kuffner
SVP and Los Angeles Region Manager Swinerton Builders, Frank Foellmer
VP and Oakland Division Manager Swinerton Builders, Steve Johnson
EVP, Luke P. Argilla
Chairman and CEO, Michael (Mike) Re
VP San Diego, Christopher Day
SVP and General Manager Swinterton Builders San Diego, Don Adair
National Marketing Director, Mark Gudenas
President, Jeffrey C. (Jeff) Hoopes
President Harbison-Mahony-Higgins Builders (HMH), David Higgins Jr.
President Swinerton Property Services, Sue Twitchel
President Swinerton Management and Consulting, Terry Bush
SVP and CIO, Lucille (Luci) Morris-Tyndall
Marketing Manager Swinerton Builders, Will Cannell
VP and CFO, Linda G. Showalter
VP and San Francisco Division Manager Swinerton Builders, Jeffrey D. (Jeff) Recob
Building Division Manager Swinerton Builders San Francisco, Mike Neumann
VP and Denver Division Manager Swinerton Builders Colorado, Kevin Ott
Business Development Manager Swinerton Government Services, Cheryl Johnson
VP Business Development Northern California, Linda Pearson
Operations Manager Swinerton Builders Oakland, Matt Kelly
Business Development Manager Swinerton Builders Orange County, Dave Pintar
Assistant Corporate Controller, Brad Peterson
Business Development Manager Bud Bailey, Steve Kieffer
President Lyda Swinerton Builders, Jack Dysart
Business Development Representative Lyda Swinerton Builders, Leland Rocchio
Operations Manager Special Projects Lyda Swinerton Builders, David McKee
President William P. Young Construction, Jay Kuhre
VP and Hawaii Division Manager Swinerton Builders, George Ehara
Business Development Manager Swinerton Builders Denver, Mark Vogele
VP and Chief Estimator Swinerton Builders Colorado, Bob Vanderburg
Business Development Manager Swinerton Builders Portland, Randy Miller
SVP and Division Manager Swinerton Builders Washington, Andy Holden
Estimating Manager Swinerton Builders San Francisco, Joe Urrutia
Chief Estimator Swinerton Builders Santa Clara, Joe Magliulo
VP and Director Human Resources, Brenda Reimche
VP Community Relations, Charles (Rick) Moore
VP and Orange County Division Manager Swinerton Builders, Dave Callis
VP and Silicon Valley Division Manager, Barry Widen
VP and Seattle Division Manager, Ron Montoya
VP Business Development Harbison-Mahony-Higgins Builders (HMH), Cynthia Adamson
Auditors: PricewaterhouseCoopers

LOCATIONS

HQ: Swinerton Incorporated
  260 Townsend St., San Francisco CA 94107
Phone: 415-421-2980   **Fax:** 415-984-1204
Web: www.swinerton.com

PRODUCTS/OPERATIONS

Selected Companies and Divisions
Cameron Swinerton
Harbison-Mahony-Higgins Builders Inc. (HMH general contracting)
Swinerton Builders (general contracting)
Swinerton Government Services
Swinerton Management & Consulting (property assessment)
Swinerton Property Services (property management)
William P. Young Construction (engineering and civil construction)

COMPETITORS

A.G. Spanos	J.F. Shea
Bechtel	JCM Partners
Beck Group	Kitchell
Bovis Lend Lease	Menas Realty
Charles Pankow	Rudolph & Sletten
Builders	Skanska USA Building
Cordoba	Sundt
Devcon Construction	Turner Corporation
DPR Construction	Tutor-Saliba
Gilbane	Webcor Builders
Hathaway Dinwiddie	Western National Group
Construction	Whiting-Turner
Hensel Phelps	
Construction	

HISTORICAL FINANCIALS
Company Type: Private

Income Statement
FYE: December 31

	REVENUE ($ mil.)	NET INCOME ($ mil.)	NET PROFIT MARGIN	EMPLOYEES
12/11	1,080	0	—	900
12/10	981	0	—	0
12/09	1,215	0	—	0
12/08	1,892	14	0.8%	0
Annual Growth	(17.1%)	—	—	—

2011 Year-End Financials

Debt ratio: ——
Return on equity: —
Cash ($ mil.): 142
Current ratio: 1.20
Long-term debt ($ mil.): —

Dividends
Yield: —
Payout: —
Market value ($ mil.): —

SYCAMORE COMMUNITY SCHOOLS

LOCATIONS

HQ: SYCAMORE COMMUNITY SCHOOLS
  4881 COOPER RD, CINCINNATI, OH 45242-6902
Phone: 513-686-1780
Web: www.my.sycamoreschools.org

HISTORICAL FINANCIALS

Company Type: Private

Income Statement

FYE: June 30

	REVENUE ($ mil.)	NET INCOME ($ mil.)	NET PROFIT MARGIN	EMPLOYEES
06/11	86	20	24.3%	0
06/10	85	0	0.8%	0
Annual Growth	1.0%	2787.5%	—	—

SYSTEM STUDIES & SIMULATION INC

LOCATIONS

HQ: SYSTEM STUDIES & SIMULATION INC
615 DISCOVERY DR NW, HUNTSVILLE, AL
35806-2801
Phone: 256-539-1700
Web: www.s3inc.com

HISTORICAL FINANCIALS

Company Type: Private

Income Statement

FYE: December 31

	REVENUE ($ mil.)	NET INCOME ($ mil.)	NET PROFIT MARGIN	EMPLOYEES
12/11	93	11	12.1%	448
12/10	84	10	12.3%	0
12/09	67	8	12.0%	0
12/06	45	8	18.1%	0
Annual Growth	27.3%	11.1%	—	—

2011 Year-End Financials

Debt ratio: ——
Return on equity: 12.10%
Cash ($ mil.): 17
Current ratio: 2.10
Long-term debt ($ mil.): —

Dividends
Yield: —
Payout: —
Market value ($ mil.): —

SYSTEMS MADE SIMPLE INC.

LOCATIONS

HQ: SYSTEMS MADE SIMPLE INC.
149 NORTHERN CONCOURSE # 1, SYRACUSE, NY
13212-6000
Phone: 315-455-3200
Web: www.systemsmadesimple.com

HISTORICAL FINANCIALS

Company Type: Private

Income Statement

FYE: December 31

	REVENUE ($ mil.)	NET INCOME ($ mil.)	NET PROFIT MARGIN	EMPLOYEES
12/11	80	16	20.2%	118
12/10	40	5	12.9%	0
12/09	33	4	14.5%	0
12/08	17	1	11.4%	0
Annual Growth	67.3%	102.6%	—	—

2011 Year-End Financials

Debt ratio: ——
Return on equity: 20.20%
Cash ($ mil.): 9
Current ratio: 3.60
Long-term debt ($ mil.): —

Dividends
Yield: —
Payout: —
Market value ($ mil.): —

SYSTRAND MANUFACTURING CORP

Move over Rosie the Riveter a new woman is doing her part to keep American manufacturing humming. Led by Sharon Cannarsa Systrand is a maker of machined forged cast and powdered-metal automotive components. Operations include high-volume production of engine and transmission parts such as axle shafts cylinder heads differential cases engine blocks gear housings hubs and input shafts manifolds planetary gears and power steering housings. With production-run capabilities ranging from a few prototypes to hundreds of thousands of parts Systrand can supply components ranging in size from under a pound to several hundred pounds. Customers have included Chrysler General Motors Ford and Volkswagen.

EXECUTIVES

President and CEO, Sharon Cannarsa
VP Operations, Anthony Cannarsa Sr.
VP Finance, Alex Goralewski
VP Engineering, Anthony Kuczek
VP Quality, David Markovic
EVP, Anthony Cannarsa Jr.
VP Manufacturing, Michael Cannarsa

LOCATIONS

HQ: Systrand Manufacturing Corporation
19050 Allen Rd., Brownstown MI 48183
Phone: 734-479-8100   **Fax:** 734-479-8107
Web: www.systrand.com

COMPETITORS

Dana Holding	McLaren Performance
Linamar Corp.	Meritor
Magna International	

HISTORICAL FINANCIALS

Company Type: Private

Income Statement

FYE: December 31

	REVENUE ($ mil.)	NET INCOME ($ mil.)	NET PROFIT MARGIN	EMPLOYEES
12/11	42	(0)	—	160
12/10	39	0	2.5%	0
12/09	17	(5)	—	0
12/08	35	0	0.4%	0
Annual Growth	6.6%	—	—	—

2011 Year-End Financials

Debt ratio: ——
Return on equity: (-1.20)%
Cash ($ mil.): 2
Current ratio: 0.60
Long-term debt ($ mil.): —

Dividends
Yield: —
Payout: —
Market value ($ mil.): —

TACONIC FARMS INC.

Yes they are cute but Taconic Farms prefers that you don't pet their animals. The company provides research rodents and related products and services to pharmaceutical and biomedical companies government agencies and academic institutions in Asia Europe and North America through its facilities in Denmark Germany and the US. Taconic specially breeds rats and mice the workhorses of the biomedical industry to be disease-free or genetically modified to exhibit certain traits to help researchers develop new therapies for human disease. Other company units offer drug- and animal-safety testing and monoclonal antibody production. Family-owned Taconic was founded in 1952 by Robert Phelan.

Taconic operates a network of seven breeding facilities and three lab sites in the US and Europe. Besides providing precisely defined animal models the company offers supporting services that include generating custom models contract research compound profiling phenotyping imaging studies and surgical services. It also maintains an interactive library and provides a broad range of scientific presentations through webinars posted on its website.

Taconic grows its business to meet its clients' needs for innovative models and support services through facility expansions outright acquisitions and distribution agreements. Some of its major investments have included its acquisition of the Xenogen Biosciences business of Caliper Life Sciences for $11 million in 2009. The deal included a facility in New Jersey where in vivo preclinical contract research services are conducted. In 2010 Taconic struck a distribution agreement in with lab animal producer CLEA Japan to bring more of its products to researchers in that country. Also in 2010 Taconic entered a non-exclusive marketing and distribution agreement with Transposagen Biopharmaceuticals to produce and distribute Transposagen Biopharmaceutical's FatRat a genetically modified rat model that becomes obese because it lacks the "satiation gene" that inhibits overeating. The rat is being marketed to companies studying obesity treatments.

In 2007 Taconic acquired 80% of Cologne Germany-based Artemis Pharmaceuticals from its parent Exelixis as that company shifted its focus to drug development. (Artemis and Taconic had already collaborated for several years prior to the acquisition including the shared acquisition of technology from CGI Pharmaceuticals earlier in 2007.) The subsidiary which was renamed TaconicArtemis GmbH develops and commercializes genetically engineered mice and mouse stem cells including its ArteMice platform. In 2011 Taconic paid Exelixis approximately $2.3 million for its remaining 19.9% interest in TaconicArtemis after that company exercised its right to require Taconic to buy its remaining interest.

While Taconic remains in Phelan family control and Samuel Phelan serves as its vice chairman the company appointed Todd Little to the position of CEO in 2009 as the first non-family member to hold the job. The move signified the company's shift to bringing up non-family executives as part of its plan for executive development.

EXECUTIVES

Chairman, Joseph W. Phelan, age 67
CEO, Todd F. Little
SVP Scientific Affairs, James G. (Jim) Geistfeld
VP Finance, Richard Matacchiero
SVP Client Relations, Kevin Leak

LOCATIONS

HQ: Taconic Farms Inc.
 1 Hudson City Centre, Hudson NY 12534
Phone: 518-697-3900   **Fax:** 518-697-3905
Web: www.taconic.com

Selected Locations

US
  California
   Oxnard
  Indiana
   Cambridge City
  Maryland
   Rockville
  New Jersey
   Cranbury
  New York
   Albany
   Germantown
Europe
  Denmark
   Bomholt
   Borup
   Ejby
   Laven
  Germany
   Cologne

PRODUCTS/OPERATIONS

Selected Products and Services

Animal care products
Animal models
Contract research solutions
Custom breeding solutions
Custom model generation solutions
In Vivio compound efficacy evaluation
KinaseSwitch technology
Knockout repository
Phenotypic characterization
Research applications
Surgical modifications
Taconic Transgenic Exchange
Testing solutions
transADMET (co-developed with CXR Biosciences) mice

COMPETITORS

BioReliance	Deltagen
Charles River	Harlan Laboratories
Laboratories	Jackson Laboratory
Covance	

HISTORICAL FINANCIALS

Company Type: Private

Income Statement

FYE: December 31

	REVENUE ($ mil.)	NET INCOME ($ mil.)	NET PROFIT MARGIN	EMPLOYEES
12/11	144	(22)	—	720
12/10	151	1	0.8%	0
12/09	142	5	3.9%	0
12/08	134	2	2.2%	0
Annual Growth	2.5%	—	—	—

2011 Year-End Financials

Debt ratio: —
Return on equity: (-15.90)%
Cash ($ mil.): 2
Current ratio: 0.70
Long-term debt ($ mil.): —

Dividends
 Yield: —
 Payout: —
Market value ($ mil.): —

TAHOE FOREST HOSPITAL DISTRICT

LOCATIONS

HQ: TAHOE FOREST HOSPITAL DISTRICT
 10121 PINE AVE, TRUCKEE, CA 96161-4856
Phone: 530-587-6011
Web: www.tahoeforesthealth.org

HISTORICAL FINANCIALS

Company Type: Private

Income Statement

FYE: June 30

	REVENUE ($ mil.)	NET INCOME ($ mil.)	NET PROFIT MARGIN	EMPLOYEES
06/12	106	8	7.6%	600
06/11	100	6	6.5%	0
06/10	105	9	9.2%	0
06/09	103	6	6.7%	0
Annual Growth	1.0%	5.6%	—	—

2012 Year-End Financials

Debt ratio: —
Return on equity: 7.60%
Cash ($ mil.): 16
Current ratio: 1.40
Long-term debt ($ mil.): —

Dividends
 Yield: —
 Payout: —
Market value ($ mil.): —

TALEN'S MARINE & FUEL LLC

LOCATIONS

HQ: TALEN'S MARINE & FUEL LLC
 1707 EVANGELINE RD, JENNINGS, LA 70546-3923
Phone: 337-788-7100
Web: www.talensmarine.com

HISTORICAL FINANCIALS

Company Type: Private

Income Statement

FYE: December 31

	REVENUE ($ mil.)	NET INCOME ($ mil.)	NET PROFIT MARGIN	EMPLOYEES
12/11	441	(1)	—	225
12/09	234	2	0.9%	0
12/08	343	2	0.8%	0
Annual Growth	13.5%	—	—	—

2011 Year-End Financials

Debt ratio: —
Return on equity: (-0.30)%
Cash ($ mil.): 0
Current ratio: 0.80
Long-term debt ($ mil.): —

Dividends
 Yield: —
 Payout: —
Market value ($ mil.): —

TAMERON AUTOMOTIVE GROUP INC

LOCATIONS

HQ: TAMERON AUTOMOTIVE GROUP INC
 1675 MONTGOMERY HWY, BIRMINGHAM, AL 35216-4998
Phone: 205-823-3333
Web: www.tameronhonda.com

HISTORICAL FINANCIALS

Company Type: Private

Income Statement

FYE: December 31

	REVENUE ($ mil.)	NET INCOME ($ mil.)	NET PROFIT MARGIN	EMPLOYEES
12/11	87	3	3.9%	170
12/10	89	3	3.4%	0
12/09	78	2	2.9%	0
12/08	95	1	1.5%	0
Annual Growth	(2.9%)	33.0%	—	—

2011 Year-End Financials

Debt ratio: —
Return on equity: 3.90%
Cash ($ mil.): 1
Current ratio: 0.30
Long-term debt ($ mil.): —

Dividends
 Yield: —
 Payout: —
Market value ($ mil.): —

TAMPA ARMATURE WORKS INC.

LOCATIONS

HQ: TAMPA ARMATURE WORKS INC.
 6312 S 78TH ST, RIVERVIEW, FL 33578-8835
Phone: 813-621-5661
Web: www.tawinc.com

HISTORICAL FINANCIALS

Company Type: Private

Income Statement

FYE: December 31

	REVENUE ($ mil.)	NET INCOME ($ mil.)	NET PROFIT MARGIN	EMPLOYEES
12/11	135	4	3.1%	650
12/10	128	5	4.0%	0
12/09	124	2	1.9%	0
12/08	150	4	3.1%	0
Annual Growth	(3.5%)	(3.3%)	—	—

2011 Year-End Financials

Debt ratio: ——
Return on equity: 3.10%
Cash ($ mil.): 3
Current ratio: 2.30
Long-term debt ($ mil.): —

Dividends
Yield: —
Payout: —
Market value ($ mil.): —

TANADGUSIX CORPORATION

LOCATIONS

HQ: TANADGUSIX CORPORATION
615 E 82ND AVE STE 200, ANCHORAGE, AK
99518-3159
Phone: 907-278-2312

HISTORICAL FINANCIALS

Company Type: Private

Income Statement

FYE: September 30

	REVENUE ($ mil.)	NET INCOME ($ mil.)	NET PROFIT MARGIN	EMPLOYEES
09/11	116	3	3.0%	294
09/06	38	2	5.2%	0
09/03	22	0	2.2%	0
09/02	16	0	1.1%	0
Annual Growth	90.2%	162.7%	—	—

2011 Year-End Financials

Debt ratio: ——
Return on equity: 3.00%
Cash ($ mil.): 7
Current ratio: 0.40
Long-term debt ($ mil.): —

Dividends
Yield: —
Payout: —
Market value ($ mil.): —

TAOS HEALTH SYSTEMS INC.

Holy Cross Hospital provides general medical services for the residents of Taos and surrounding counties in New Mexico. The hospital opened its doors in 1937 and has expanded its facilities to include nearly 50 licensed beds. Among its specialty services are emergency medicine obstetrics orthopedics and women's health care. The hospital's active medical staff includes about 50 physicians.

EXECUTIVES

Chairman, Ron Burnham
Vice Chairman, Tim Martinez
Director Safety and Risk Management, Patty Hannigan
Chief Nursing Officer, Anna Abeyta
Treasurer and Director, Pamela Romero
Secretary and Director, Andy Torres
Chief of Staff and Director, Geilan Ismail
CEO, Peter A. Hofstetter
Director HCH Billing Office, Jose L. Guevara
Director Community Services and Planning, Marilyn Perryman
Department Chair Perinatal, Tim Moore
Department Chair Emergency Room, Oskar Moeller
Department Chair S&A, Jeb Reid
Director, Felix Duran
Director, Jeannie Masters
Vice Chairman, Tim Martinez
Director, Dan Guttmann
Director, Anna Martinez
Director, Bobby Duran
Director, Sylvia Villarreal
Treasurer and Director, Pamela Romero
Secretary and Director, Andy Torres
Chief of Staff and Director, Geilan Ismail
Director, Linda Aubrecht
Director, Beatriz Gonzales

LOCATIONS

HQ: Holy Cross Hospital
1397 Weimer Rd., Taos NM 87571
Phone: 575-758-8883   **Fax:** 575-751-5719
Web: www.taoshospital.org

HISTORICAL FINANCIALS

Company Type: Private - Not-for-Profit

Income Statement

FYE: May 31

	REVENUE ($ mil.)	NET INCOME ($ mil.)	NET PROFIT MARGIN	EMPLOYEES
05/11	57	(3)	—	412
05/10	59	(0)	—	0
05/09*	59	0	—	0
12/08	0	(0)	—	0
Annual Growth	532.8%	—	—	—

*Fiscal year change

2011 Year-End Financials

Debt ratio: ——
Return on equity: (-6.70)%
Cash ($ mil.): 4
Current ratio: 2.10
Long-term debt ($ mil.): —

Dividends
Yield: —
Payout: —
Market value ($ mil.): —

TEAM INDUSTRIES

It takes a team TEAM Industries to make the drivetrains that go into the vehicles you ride. The company designs tests manufacturers and assembles powertrain transmissions drivetrains gear sets and chassis components for snowmobile all-terrain vehicle lawn mowers and other vehicles through partnerships with CNH Ford Honda Ingersoll-Rand Kawasaki Textron Yamaha and other OEMs. TEAM maintains half a dozen facilities throughout Minnesota and North Carolina; its manufacturing capabilities run from ductile iron and shaft machining to aluminum die-casting and gear/spline mak-

ing. The company also offers engineering R&D and testing services. TEAM is owned by its founding family the Rickes.

Operations

TEAM Industries sells its products through six locations: TEAM Andrews acts as its precision machining gear manufacturing and metallurgical lab; TEAM Audubon specializes in gear cutting and heat treating; TEAM Bagley is its corporate headquarters; TEAM Detroit Lakes has expertise in aluminum die casting; TEAM Park Rapids works with CNC (computer numerical control) machining and loctite (a brand of adhesives) impregnation casting; and Motek-TEAM Industries is another metallurgical lab with a focus on induction hardening.

EXECUTIVES

President and CEO, David Ricke
Director Marketing, Stephen R. (Steve) Fagerlie
Director Finance, Steve Kast
Director Sales, Gene Bullis
Director Human Resources, Jim Russ
Senior Director Marketing and Strategic Planning, Tony Passanante
Public Relations, Kelly Mack
General Manager Motorsports, Dave Osterman

LOCATIONS

HQ: TEAM Industries Inc.
105 Park Ave. NW, Bagley MN 56621
Phone: 218-847-9582   **Fax:** 218-847-1052
Web: www.team-ind.com

PRODUCTS/OPERATIONS

Selected Products

Axle assemblies and housings (spiral straight bevel or hypoid gearing)
Continuously variable transmissions (10-200 horsepower & up to 10000 rpm)
Differentials (with a variety of traction control mechanisms)
Gear sets
Transaxles (for a variety of electric or gas powered vehicles)
Transmissions and gear boxes (using parallel axis gears crossed axis gears worm sets planetary)
Wet brake assemblies

Selected Market Applications

Agricultural
All-terrain vehicles
Alternative on-road vehicles
Automotive
Golf carts
Lawn & garden
Marine
Motorcycles
Off-highway construction & others
Personal watercraft
Snowmobiles
Turf care
Utility vehicles

COMPETITORS

American Axle & Manufacturing
Arctic Cat
BorgWarner
Dana Holding
Federal-Mogul

Lippert Components
Magna International
Meritor
Polaris Industries
Visteon

HISTORICAL FINANCIALS
Company Type: Private

Income Statement
FYE: September 24

	REVENUE ($ mil.)	NET INCOME ($ mil.)	NET PROFIT MARGIN	EMPLOYEES
09/11	251	22	9.1%	950
09/10	193	10	5.2%	0
09/09	165	(8)	—	0
09/08	229	1	0.7%	0
Annual Growth	3.1%	146.0%	—	—

2011 Year-End Financials
Debt ratio: ——
Return on equity: 9.10%
Cash ($ mil.): 15
Current ratio: 1.00
Long-term debt ($ mil.): —

Dividends
Yield: —
Payout: —
Market value ($ mil.): —

TEAM TECHNOLOGIES INC.

LOCATIONS
HQ: TEAM TECHNOLOGIES INC.
5949 COMMERCE BLVD, MORRISTOWN, TN 37814-8209
Phone: 423-587-2199
Web: www.teamtechinc.net

HISTORICAL FINANCIALS
Company Type: Private

Income Statement
FYE: December 31

	REVENUE ($ mil.)	NET INCOME ($ mil.)	NET PROFIT MARGIN	EMPLOYEES
12/11	129	10	7.8%	500
12/10	116	7	6.4%	0
12/09	103	7	7.3%	0
12/08	109	6	6.0%	0
Annual Growth	5.8%	15.3%	—	—

2011 Year-End Financials
Debt ratio: ——
Return on equity: 7.80%
Cash ($ mil.): 1
Current ratio: 1.70
Long-term debt ($ mil.): —

Dividends
Yield: —
Payout: —
Market value ($ mil.): —

TELCO 214 US INC.

LOCATIONS
HQ: TELCO 214 US INC.
2571 KIRBY CIR NE, MELBOURNE, FL 32905-3401
Phone: 321-956-0019

HISTORICAL FINANCIALS
Company Type: Private

Income Statement
FYE: June 30

	REVENUE ($ mil.)	NET INCOME ($ mil.)	NET PROFIT MARGIN	EMPLOYEES
06/11	82	2	2.6%	20
Annual Growth	—	—	—	—

2011 Year-End Financials
Debt ratio: ——
Return on equity: 2.60%
Cash ($ mil.): 17
Current ratio: 4.10
Long-term debt ($ mil.): —

Dividends
Yield: —
Payout: —
Market value ($ mil.): —

TEMPLE UNIVERSITY HEALTH SYSTEM INC.

Temple University Health System (TUHS) a network of academic and community hospitals associated with the Temple University School of Medicine provides primary secondary and tertiary care to residents in the Philadelphia County (Pennsylvania) area. TUHS' hospitals include 740-bed Temple University Hospital (a Level 1 trauma center) and two community-based hospitals providing acute and emergency care the Jeanes Hospital and TUHS Episcopal Hospital (home to a 120-bed behavioral health unit). TUHS supports programs in pediatric and adult cardiology organ transplantation oncology and pulmonary disease. Temple University Health System also includes a community-wide network of primary care physicians.

Along with its main hospitals TUHS operates a whole range of outpatient care facilities that offer everything from specialized cardiac care and spinal rehabilitation to a lung care center a burn center and stroke treatments.

In order to keep its hospitals well-staffed and its doctors up-to-date on the latest in continuing medical education TUHS operates a number of schools and universities including the aforementioned Temple University School of Medicine Temple University School of Pharmacy Temple University College of Health Professions Temple University School of Dentistry Temple University School of Podiatric Medicine and Northeastern Hospital School of Nursing.

EXECUTIVES
President and CEO, Joseph W. (Chip) Marshall III, age 59
VP and COO, Robert E. Pezzoli
VP Human Resources, Robert Birnbrauer
VP and CFO, Robert H. Lux
VP and CIO, Arthur Papacostas
VP Communications and External Affairs, David Newell
CEO and Executive Director Jeanes Hospital, Linda Grass
CEO and Executive Director Northeastern Hospital, John Buckley
Executive Director Temple University Hospital - Episcopal Campus, Kathleen Barron
CEO Temple Physicians, Eric Mankin
Director Public Relations, Rebecca Harmon
Chief Counsel, Beth Koob
Manager Internal Communications, Steve Bates
Coordinator Public Relations, Thomas Mitchell
VP and Chief Medical Officer, Calvin B. Johnson

LOCATIONS
HQ: Temple University Health System
3401 N. Broad St., Philadelphia PA 19140
Phone: 215-707-2000   **Fax:** 215-707-3494
Web: www.templehealth.org

PRODUCTS/OPERATIONS

Selected Facilities
Esther Boyer Pavilion (outpatient pediatric care)
Jeanes Hospital
Temple University Hospital
Temple University Hospital (TUH) Episcopal Campus

COMPETITORS
Albert Einstein Healthcare Network
Aria Health
Children's Hospital of Philadelphia
Community Health Systems
Crozer-Keystone Health System
Doylestown Hospital
Jefferson Health System
Mercy Health System
North Philadelphia Health System
Northwestern Human Services
Our Lady of Lourdes Medical Center
Pennsylvania Hospital
The Magee Memorial Hospital for Convalescents
Thomas Jefferson University Hospital
University of Pennsylvania Health System

HISTORICAL FINANCIALS
Company Type: Private - Not-for-Profit

Income Statement
FYE: June 30

	REVENUE ($ mil.)	NET INCOME ($ mil.)	NET PROFIT MARGIN	EMPLOYEES
06/11	994	45	4.6%	6,500
06/09	0	(0)	—	0
06/08*	0	0	—	0
12/06	0	(0)	—	0
Annual Growth	1202.4%	—	—	—

*Fiscal year change

2011 Year-End Financials
Debt ratio: ——
Return on equity: 4.60%
Cash ($ mil.): 140
Current ratio: 1.50
Long-term debt ($ mil.): —

Dividends
Yield: —
Payout: —
Market value ($ mil.): —

TEMPLE UNIVERSITY HOSPITAL INC.

LOCATIONS

HQ: TEMPLE UNIVERSITY HOSPITAL INC.
3401 N BROAD ST, PHILADELPHIA, PA 19140-5189
Phone: 215-707-2000
Web: www.wrti.org

HISTORICAL FINANCIALS

Company Type: Private

Income Statement

FYE: June 30

	REVENUE ($ mil.)	NET INCOME ($ mil.)	NET PROFIT MARGIN	EMPLOYEES
06/11	813	(2)	—	0
Annual Growth	—	—	—	—

2011 Year-End Financials

Debt ratio: ——
Return on equity: (-0.40)%
Cash ($ mil.): 164
Current ratio: 4.50
Long-term debt ($ mil.): ——

Dividends
 Yield: —
 Payout: —
 Market value ($ mil.): —

TEMPLE UNIVERSITY-OF THE COMMONWEALTH SYSTEM OF HIGHER EDUCATION

Where better to worship a good education than at Temple University? Part of Pennsylvania's Commonwealth System of Higher Education Temple has nine different campuses in the Philadelphia area as well as in Tokyo and Rome and educational programs in China Greece France Israel and the UK. More than 36000 students are enrolled in Temple's 320 academic programs. Temple's Health Sciences Center includes Temple University Hospital and schools that teach medicine and dentistry. The system has a student-teacher ratio of about 15:1. Dr. Russell Conwell founded Temple University in 1884; it was incorporated as Temple University in 1907.

Geographic Reach

Temple Univeristy operates nine distinct campuses. Seven are in and around Philadelphia. Farther afield Temple has campuses in Tokyo and Rome.

Operations

Temple's campus in suburban Ambler Pennsylvania offers programs in community and regional planning horticulture and landscape architecture. Together all of its campuses offer a combined total of about 140 bachelor's 125 master's 60 doctoral and nearly 10 professional degrees. Students can obtain professional degrees in dentistry law medicine pharmacy and podiatric medicine among others.

Financial Performance

Temple's revenue increased 2% in 2012 vs. 2011 driven by increasing tuition fees and patient care activities at the Temple's Health Sciences Center. Net income fell by 58% over the same period due to higher educational and general expenses among other factors.

EXECUTIVES

Chairman, Patrick J. (Pat) O'Connor
President, Ann Weaver Hart, age 63
VP Computing Financial Services and CIO, Timothy C. O'Rourke
Associate VP and Controller, Frank P. Annunziato
Director Purchasing, Theresa (Terry) Burt
SVP University Counsel and Secretary, George E. Moore
SVP Institutional Advancement, David Unruh
SVP Government Community and Public Affairs, Kenneth (Ken) Lawrence Jr.
SEVP Health Affairs; Dean and CEO School of Medicine, Larry R. Kaiser
VP Student Affairs, Theresa A. Powell
VP Human Resources, Deborah Hartnett
Director Communications, Ray Betzner
Vice Chair, Anthony J. Scirica
Provost, Richard M. (Dick) Englert
EVP Financial Affairs CFO and Treasurer, Anthony Wagner
Associate VP Human Resources, Harry A. Young
Senior Vice Provost Research and Graduate Education, Kenneth (Ken) Blank
Senior Vice Provost Enrollment Management, William N. Black
Senior Vice Provost International Affairs and Dean College of Science and Technology, Hai-Lung Dai
Senior Vice Provost Undergraduate Studies, Peter Jones
Vice Provost Academic Affairs and Assessment, Jodi Levine Laufgraben
Senior Vice Provost Faculty Development and Faculty Affairs, Diane Maleson
Vice Provost University College, Vicki Lewis McGarvey
Dean Boyer College of Music and Dance; Interim Dean Tyler School of Art; Vice Provost Arts, Robert T. Stroker
Senior Vice Provost Strategic Initiatives and Communications, Betsy Leebron Tutelman
Trustee, Jon A. Boscia, age 59
Trustee, Mitchell L. Morgan, age 57
Trustee, Joseph W. (Chip) Marshall III, age 59
President, Ann Weaver Hart, age 63
Trustee, William H. Cosby Jr.
Trustee, Frank Baldino Jr.
Trustee, Joan H. Ballots
Trustee, Leonard Barrack
Trustee, Theodore Z. Davis
Trustee, Nelson A. Diaz
Trustee, Ronald R. Donatucci
Trustee, Judith A. Felgoise
Trustee, Richard J. Fox
Trustee, Lewis F. Gould Jr.
Trustee, Lon R. Greenberg
Trustee, Lacy H. Hunt
Trustee, Ulrick P. Joseph
Trustee, Lewis Katz
Trustee, Adrian R. King Jr.
Trustee, Susanna E. Lachs
Trustee, Patrick V. Larkin
Trustee, Solomon C. Luo
Trustee, Scott Mazo
Trustee, Theodore A. McKee
Trustee, Christopher W. McNichol
Trustee, J. William Mills

Trustee, Daniel H. Polett
Trustee, Milton L. Rock
Trustee, Robert A. Rovner
Trustee, Jane Scaccetti
Vice Chair, Anthony J. Scirica
Trustee, Michael J. Stack III
Trustee, James S. White
Trustee, Michael P. Williams
Auditors: Deloitte&ToucheLLP

LOCATIONS

HQ: Temple University
1801 N. Broad St., Philadelphia PA 19122
Phone: 215-204-7000   **Fax:** 215-204-4403
Web: www.temple.edu

Selected Campuses

Philadelphia
 Ambler
 Center City
 Fort Washington
 Harrisburg
 Main
 Podiatric Medicine
  Health Sciences Center
International
 Japan
 Rome Italy

HISTORICAL FINANCIALS

Company Type: School

Income Statement

FYE: June 30

	REVENUE ($ mil.)	NET INCOME ($ mil.)	NET PROFIT MARGIN	EMPLOYEES
06/12	2,254	(37)	—	9,061
06/08	2,034	228	11.2%	0
06/07	1,902	118	6.2%	0
06/06	1,837	(1)	—	0
Annual Growth	7.1%	—	—	—

2012 Year-End Financials

Debt ratio: ——
Return on equity: (-1.70)%
Cash ($ mil.): 237
Current ratio: 0.40
Long-term debt ($ mil.): ——

Dividends
 Yield: —
 Payout: —
 Market value ($ mil.): —

TENNESSEE STATE UNIVERSITY

Tennessee State University (TSU) home to more than 8200 students is especially known for its programs in education nursing biology public administration and psychology. The university offers more than 45 undergraduate programs and more than 20 graduate programs through two campuses in Nashville. TSU was first organized as the Agricultural and Industrial State Normal School for black students in 1909; it began serving students in 1912. The school became a teacher's college in 1922 and in 1958 its name was changed to Tennessee State to reflect its status as a land-grant university. Famous alumni include Oprah Winfrey and Ed "Too Tall" Jones.

EXECUTIVES

VP Business and Finance, Cynthia Brooks

President, Melvin N. Johnson
VP Communication and Information Technologies, Dennis J. Gendron
Chancellor, Charles Manning
VP University Relations and Development, Sheriette Stokes
Interim VP Research and Sponsored Programs, Evelyn M. Thompson
EVP and Provost, Robert Hampton
VP Student Affairs, Michael Freeman
General Counsel, Christine Modisher

LOCATIONS

HQ: Tennessee State University
3500 John A. Merritt Blvd., Nashville TN 37209
Phone: 615-963-5000   Fax: 615-963-7407
Web: www.tnstate.edu

HISTORICAL FINANCIALS
Company Type: School

Income Statement

	REVENUE ($ mil.)	NET INCOME ($ mil.)	NET PROFIT MARGIN	EMPLOYEES
06/11	105	18	17.4%	1,234
06/08	1	0	27.4%	0
06/05	3	2	69.0%	0
06/01	808	0	—	0
Annual Growth	—	4411.5%		

FYE: June 30

2011 Year-End Financials

Debt ratio: —
Return on equity: 17.40%
Cash ($ mil.): 28
Current ratio: 1.30
Long-term debt ($ mil.): —

Dividends
Yield: —
Payout: —
Market value ($ mil.): —

TENNESSEE TECHNOLOGICAL UNIVERSITY

Tennessee Technological University (TTU or Tennessee Tech) takes on the task of providing academic education and career training services in the Volunteer State. The public university has six college divisions providing more than 60 undergraduate and graduate degrees in the areas of Agriculture and Human Sciences Arts and Sciences Business Education Engineering and Interdisciplinary Studies. The university has some 11000 students enrolled and a faculty of about 400 staff members. TTU opened in 1912 in Cookeville Tennessee and was originally named the University of Dixie.

EXECUTIVES

President, Robert (Bob) Bell
VP Academic Affairs and Provost, Marvin Barker
Associate VP Business and Fiscal Affairs, Linda Maxwell
Associate VP Academic Affairs, Leo McGee
VP Student Affairs, Marc Burnett
Associate VP Research and Graduate Studies, Francis Otuonye
Director Purchasing, Judy Hull

Director Athletics, Mark Wilson
Associate VP Information Technology Services, Danny Reese
Director University Libraries and Media Services, Winston Walden
Director Career Services, Alice K. Camuti
Interim Director Human Resources Services, Dorothy M. Nash
Chairman, Rt. Hon. Phil Bredesen, age 69
VP Business and Fiscal Affairs, Claire Stinson
VP University Advancement, J. Mark Hutchins
VP Extended Programs and Regional Development, Susan Elkins
Provost and VP Academic Affairs, Jack Armistead
Associate VP Academic Affairs, Mark Stephens
Associate VP University Development, Andy Wilson
Associate VP Communications and Marketing, Monica Greppin
Associate Vice President for Communications & Marketing, Karen Lykins
Associate Vice President for Facilities and Business Services, Jack Butler
Associate Vice President for Business and Fiscal Affairs, Jeff Young
Associate Vice President for Enrollment Management and Student Success, Robert Hodum

LOCATIONS

HQ: Tennessee Technological University
1 Derryberry Hall William L. Jones Dr., Cookeville TN 38505-0001
Phone: 931-372-3888   Fax: 931-372-3898
Web: www.tntech.edu

HISTORICAL FINANCIALS
Company Type: School

Income Statement

	REVENUE ($ mil.)	NET INCOME ($ mil.)	NET PROFIT MARGIN	EMPLOYEES
06/12	76	5	7.3%	1,096
06/11	65	23	35.7%	0
06/10	65	23	35.7%	0
Annual Growth	8.6%	(51.1%)	—	—

FYE: June 30

2012 Year-End Financials

Debt ratio: —
Return on equity: 7.30%
Cash ($ mil.): 31
Current ratio: 2.00
Long-term debt ($ mil.): —

Dividends
Yield: —
Payout: —
Market value ($ mil.): —

TENNESSEE TECHNOLOGICAL UNIVERSITY

Tennessee Technological University (TTU or Tennessee Tech) takes on the task of providing academic education and career training services in the Volunteer State. The public university has six college divisions providing more than 60 undergraduate and graduate degrees in the areas of Agriculture and Human Sciences Arts and Sciences Business Education Engineering and Interdisciplinary Studies. The university has some

11000 students enrolled and a faculty of about 400 staff members. TTU opened in 1912 in Cookeville Tennessee and was originally named the University of Dixie.

EXECUTIVES

President, Robert (Bob) Bell
VP Academic Affairs and Provost, Marvin Barker
Associate VP Business and Fiscal Affairs, Linda Maxwell
Associate VP Academic Affairs, Leo McGee
VP Student Affairs, Marc Burnett
Associate VP Research and Graduate Studies, Francis Otuonye
Director Purchasing, Judy Hull
Director Athletics, Mark Wilson
Associate VP Information Technology Services, Danny Reese
Director University Libraries and Media Services, Winston Walden
Director Career Services, Alice K. Camuti
Interim Director Human Resources Services, Dorothy M. Nash
Chairman, Rt. Hon. Phil Bredesen, age 69
VP Business and Fiscal Affairs, Claire Stinson
VP University Advancement, J. Mark Hutchins
VP Extended Programs and Regional Development, Susan Elkins
Provost and VP Academic Affairs, Jack Armistead
Associate VP Academic Affairs, Mark Stephens
Associate VP University Development, Andy Wilson
Associate VP Communications and Marketing, Monica Greppin
Associate Vice President for Communications & Marketing, Karen Lykins
Associate Vice President for Facilities and Business Services, Jack Butler
Associate Vice President for Business and Fiscal Affairs, Jeff Young
Associate Vice President for Enrollment Management and Student Success, Robert Hodum

LOCATIONS

HQ: Tennessee Technological University
1 Derryberry Hall William L. Jones Dr., Cookeville TN 38505-0001
Phone: 931-372-3888   Fax: 931-372-3898
Web: www.tntech.edu

HISTORICAL FINANCIALS
Company Type: School

Income Statement

	REVENUE ($ mil.)	NET INCOME ($ mil.)	NET PROFIT MARGIN	EMPLOYEES
06/11	69	32	46.4%	0
Annual Growth	—	—	—	—

FYE: June 30

2011 Year-End Financials

Debt ratio: —
Return on equity: 46.40%
Cash ($ mil.): 28
Current ratio: 2.60
Long-term debt ($ mil.): —

Dividends
Yield: —
Payout: —
Market value ($ mil.): —

TERMINIX SERVICE INC.

LOCATIONS

HQ: TERMINIX SERVICE INC.
3618 FERNANDINA RD, COLUMBIA, SC 29210-5221
Phone: 803-772-1783
Web: www.terminixsvc.com

HISTORICAL FINANCIALS

Company Type: Private

Income Statement				FYE: December 31
	REVENUE ($ mil.)	NET INCOME ($ mil.)	NET PROFIT MARGIN	EMPLOYEES
12/11	104	16	15.5%	1,125
12/10	101	16	15.9%	0
12/09	98	15	15.7%	0
12/08	94	13	14.2%	0
Annual Growth	3.5%	6.5%	—	—

2011 Year-End Financials

Debt ratio: —
Return on equity: 15.50%
Cash ($ mil.): 12
Current ratio: 0.70
Long-term debt ($ mil.): —

Dividends
Yield: —
Payout: —
Market value ($ mil.): —

TERRACON CONSULTANTS INC.

Employee-owned Terracon Consultants provides geotechnical environmental construction material evaluation pavement engineering and construction management and facilities engineering services. One of the nation's top design firms the company serves the agriculture energy telecommunications commercial development and transportation sectors as well as government clients. Founded in Iowa in 1965 Terracon began as a joint venture between Shive Hall and Hattery (civil consulting) Soil Testing Services (geotechnical testing) and Gerald Olson P.E. (the company's founder and a project engineer). The company now has more than 130 offices in some 40 states.

Geographic Reach

Kansas-based Terracon has operations throughout the US Canada Cuba and Mexico.

Strategy

Acquisitive Terracon is expanding its menu of services and geographic footprint via acquisitons of regional companies across the US.

Mergers and Acquisitions

Terracon has expanded its geotechnical environmental engineering and testing capabilities with a string of recent purchases. In 2012 it acquired California-based Earthtec Inc. a provider of geotechnical environmental special inspection and other services to clients in Northern California. Also in 2012 it purchased Utah-based IHI Environmental a provider of industrial hygiene occupational safety and environmental consulting services to public and private sector clients across the western US. Previously Terracon bought Colorado firm Geotechnical Engineering Group boosting its presence in the West; and Stafford Consulting Engi-

neers a building envelope system specialist with a presence in the Southeast. Also that year Terracon acquired Dressler Consulting Engineers a building forensics engineering firm based in Kansas and Nodarse & Associates a Florida-based environmental geotechnical and construction materials engineering firm.

Ownership

Terracon is owned by its employees. The firm was ranked 51st on the Employee Ownership 100 the list of the top 100 largest majority employee-owned companies in the US in 2012.

EXECUTIVES

President and CEO, David Gaboury
EVP and COO, Dennis E Whited
CFO, Roger R. Herting
VP Client Development, Kevin Langwell
Principal and Geotechnical Department Manager Las Vegas, Les C. Banas
Principal and Geotechnical Senior Project Manager Houston, Patrick Beecher
Principal and Construction Services Department Manager San Antonio, Laura Campa
Senior Principal and Senior Geotechnical Consultant Lenexa Kansas, Steve Levorson
Principal and Office Manager Lincoln Nebraska, Brad Levich
Principal and Office Manager Conroe Texas, Mark McClintock
Principal and Geotechnical Senior Project Manager Phoenix, Chuck Reynolds
Principal and Marketing and Communications Manager Olathe Kansas, Vanessa Zambo
VP General Counsel and Principal, Mike Yost
EVP and Director, Dan Israel
CIO, Frank Milano
National Director Federal Services, Frederick (Fritz) Heneman

LOCATIONS

HQ: Terracon Consultants Inc.
18001 W. 106th St. Ste. 300, Olathe KS 66061
Phone: 913-599-6886   **Fax:** 913-599-0574
Web: www.terracon.com

PRODUCTS/OPERATIONS

Selected Services

Construction Materials
  Construction quality control and quality assurance programs
  Deep foundation nondestructive testing
  Design and review of concrete grout and asphaltic concrete mixes
  Field and lab testing and analysis
  Forensic investigation and evaluation
  On-site observation and monitoring
  Special inspections
Geotechnical
  Subsurface exploration and testing
  Foundation analysis and design
  Soil stabilization
  Groundwater control
  Pavement design
Environmental
  Site assessment
  Industrial hygiene and occupational safety
  Regulatory compliance
  Solid waste planning and design
Construction Materials
  Quality control
  Testing
  Design and review of concrete
  Pavement engineering and construction management
Facilities
  Roof/waterproofing consulting
  Foundation/structural consulting

Life cycle cost analysis
Peer reviews
Seismic risk assessments
Construction administration

COMPETITORS

AECOM	Jacobs Engineering
Fluor	KBR
HNTB Companies	URS

HISTORICAL FINANCIALS

Company Type: Private

Income Statement				FYE: December 31
	REVENUE ($ mil.)	NET INCOME ($ mil.)	NET PROFIT MARGIN	EMPLOYEES
12/11	353	8	2.5%	2,753
12/10	319	6	2.0%	0
12/09	294	7	2.4%	0
12/08	334	5	1.5%	0
Annual Growth	1.8%	19.3%	—	—

2011 Year-End Financials

Debt ratio: —
Return on equity: 2.50%
Cash ($ mil.): 3
Current ratio: 1.00
Long-term debt ($ mil.): —

Dividends
Yield: —
Payout: —
Market value ($ mil.): —

TEXAS A&M ENGINEERING EXPERIMENT STATION

LOCATIONS

HQ: TEXAS A&M ENGINEERING EXPERIMENT STATION
1470 WILLIAM D FITCH PKWY, COLLEGE STATION, TX 77845-4645
Phone: 979-458-7643
Web: www.txtec.org

HISTORICAL FINANCIALS

Company Type: Private

Income Statement				FYE: August 31
	REVENUE ($ mil.)	NET INCOME ($ mil.)	NET PROFIT MARGIN	EMPLOYEES
08/12	122	10	8.3%	1,500
08/11	123	8	6.5%	0
08/10	126	7	5.7%	0
08/09	104	5	5.7%	0
Annual Growth	5.6%	20.2%	—	—

TEXAS AROMATICS LP

LOCATIONS

HQ: TEXAS AROMATICS LP
3555 TIMMONS LN STE 700, HOUSTON, TX
77027-6450
Phone: 713-520-2900

HISTORICAL FINANCIALS

Company Type: Private

Income Statement

FYE: December 31

	REVENUE ($ mil.)	NET INCOME ($ mil.)	NET PROFIT MARGIN	EMPLOYEES
12/11	928	10	1.2%	17
12/10	782	8	1.1%	0
12/09	414	10	2.4%	0
12/08	784	3	0.5%	0
Annual Growth	5.8%	42.1%	—	—

2011 Year-End Financials

Debt ratio: ——
Return on equity: 1.20%
Cash ($ mil.): 12
Current ratio: 0.90
Long-term debt ($ mil.): —

Dividends
Yield: —
Payout: —
Market value ($ mil.): —

TEXAS COUNTY AND DISTRICT RETIREMENT SYSTEM

LOCATIONS

HQ: TEXAS COUNTY AND DISTRICT RETIREMENT
SYSTEM
901 S MO PAC EXPY IV500, AUSTIN, TX 78746-5776
Phone: 512-328-8889

HISTORICAL FINANCIALS

Company Type: Private

Income Statement

FYE: December 31

	ASSETS ($ mil.)	NET INCOME ($ mil.)	INCOME AS % OF ASSETS	EMPLOYEES
12/11	17,828	(101)	—	108
12/10	18,116	2,178	12.0%	0
12/09	16,287	3,503	21.5%	0
12/08	12,833	0	—	0
Annual Growth	11.6%	—	—	—

2011 Year-End Financials

Debt ratio: ——
Return on equity: (-14.10)%
Cash ($ mil.): 15
Current ratio: —
Long-term debt ($ mil.): —

Dividends
Yield: —
Payout: —
Market value ($ mil.): —

TEXAS MEDICAL CENTER CENTRAL HEATING AND COOLING SERVICES CORPOR

LOCATIONS

HQ: TEXAS MEDICAL CENTER CENTRAL HEATING
AND COOLING SERVICES CORPOR
1615 BRAESWOOD BLVD, HOUSTON, TX 77030-3903
Phone: 713-791-6700

HISTORICAL FINANCIALS

Company Type: Private

Income Statement

FYE: August 31

	REVENUE ($ mil.)	NET INCOME ($ mil.)	NET PROFIT MARGIN	EMPLOYEES
08/12	83	4	5.0%	85
08/11	72	4	5.8%	0
08/10	72	25	35.0%	0
08/09	73	11	15.0%	0
Annual Growth	4.2%	(28.0%)	—	—

2012 Year-End Financials

Debt ratio: ——
Return on equity: 5.00%
Cash ($ mil.): 43
Current ratio: 2.70
Long-term debt ($ mil.): —

Dividends
Yield: —
Payout: —
Market value ($ mil.): —

TEXAS SOUTHERN UNIVERSITY

Texas Southern University (TSU) is a historically black public institution. The university located on a 150-acre campus in downtown Houston offers about 40 bachelor's degree programs and more than 30 master's and doctoral degree programs. Its 11 colleges and schools include the Thurgood Marshall School of Law and the Barbara Jordan Mickey Leland School of Public Affairs. (Jordan and Leland are both former US representatives and graduates of TSU.) The university has an enrollment of more than 9500 students and a staff of about 1000 faculty members and support personnel.

Financial Performance

TSU's revenues grew by 1% in 2012 due to the purchase of auxiliary enterprise housing units and the close out of existing bonds for the properties and the parking garage.

The 218% decrease in net income was due to an increase in non-operating expenses attributed to a 28% rise in the fair value of investments in 2012 and higher depreciation expenses due to housing units parking garage and gift-in-kind capital asset additions.

Tuition and fees accounted for 48% of TSU's total 2013 operating budget direct appropriations

from the State 35%. For 2013 there was an increase 10% in the overall budget primarily due to an increase in the capital budget.

Company Background

TSU was established in 1947 by the Texas Legislature.

EXECUTIVES

General Counsel, Gita Bolt
Associate Provost Student Services and Dean of Students, Willie Marshall
SVP Enrollment Management and Planning, Gayla B. Thomas
Provost and SVP Academic Affairs and Student Services, Bobby L. Wilson
SVP University Relations and Ombudsperson, Charlene T. Evans
Assistant VP Human Resources, Keffus S. Falls
Senior Benefits Manager, Jacqueline Columbus
President, John M. Rudley
SVP Administration, Bruce A. Wilson
VP Architectural Engineering and Construction Services, William E. Beckham
Associate Provost Academic Affairs and Dean of the Graduate School, Richard Pitre
Assistant VP Development, Nina W. Jones
Director Community Relations and Governmental Affairs, Dwight A. Boykins
VP Risk Management and Assurance Services, Terry Holderman
Associate Provost Research, Robert L. Ford
VP Strategic Development, Kimberly Williams
Director Marketing and Communications, Gayle Barge
Interim SVP Business and Finance, Carin Barth
Chief of Staff, Janis J. Newman
Auditors: TexasStateAuditor

LOCATIONS

HQ: Texas Southern University
3100 Cleburne St., Houston TX 77004
Phone: 713-313-7011   **Fax:** 713-313-7851
Web: www.tsu.edu

PRODUCTS/OPERATIONS

Schools & Colleges
Barbara Jordan Mickey Leland School of Public Affairs
College of Continuing Education
College of Liberal Arts & Behavioral Sciences
College of Education
College of Pharmacy & Health Sciences
College of Science & Technology
Graduate School
Jesse H. Jones School of Business
School of Communicat
Thomas F. Freeman Honors College
Thurgood Marshall School of Law

HISTORICAL FINANCIALS

Company Type: School

Income Statement

FYE: August 31

	REVENUE ($ mil.)	NET INCOME ($ mil.)	NET PROFIT MARGIN	EMPLOYEES
08/11	130	(6)	—	1,000
08/03	65	7	10.6%	0
08/02	0	0	—	0
08/01	96	4	4.8%	0
Annual Growth	10.5%	—	—	—

Predatory Lending
Reducing Gun Violence
Stroke Awareness
Supporting Minority Education
V-Chip Awareness
Wildfire Prevention
Youth Volunteerism

HISTORICAL FINANCIALS

Company Type: Private - Not-for-Profit

Income Statement

FYE: June 30

	REVENUE ($ mil.)	NET INCOME ($ mil.)	NET PROFIT MARGIN	EMPLOYEES
06/11	40	3	7.8%	105
06/10	39	2	7.0%	0
06/09	40	0	2.4%	0
06/08	36	0	1.4%	0
Annual Growth	3.9%	83.8%	—	—

2011 Year-End Financials

Debt ratio: —
Return on equity: 7.80%
Cash ($ mil.): 4
Current ratio: 1.30
Long-term debt ($ mil.): —

Dividends
Yield: —
Payout: —
Market value ($ mil.): —

TEXAS WOMAN'S UNIVERSITY

LOCATIONS

HQ: TEXAS WOMAN' S UNIVERSITY
305 ADMINISTRATION DR, DENTON, TX 76204
Phone: 940-898-2000
Web: www.twu.edu

HISTORICAL FINANCIALS

Company Type: Private

Income Statement

FYE: August 31

	REVENUE ($ mil.)	NET INCOME ($ mil.)	NET PROFIT MARGIN	EMPLOYEES
08/11	98	27	27.5%	1,200
08/10	90	25	28.0%	0
08/09	83	26	31.3%	0
08/08	85	18	21.3%	0
Annual Growth	5.0%	14.3%	—	—

2011 Year-End Financials

Debt ratio: —
Return on equity: 27.50%
Cash ($ mil.): 123
Current ratio: 2.40
Long-term debt ($ mil.): —

Dividends
Yield: —
Payout: —
Market value ($ mil.): —

THARPEROBBINS COMPANY INC.

LOCATIONS

HQ: THARPEROBBINS COMPANY INC.
149 CRAWFORD RD, STATESVILLE, NC 28625-8546
Phone: 704-872-5231
Web: www.tharperobbins.com

HISTORICAL FINANCIALS

Company Type: Private

Income Statement

FYE: December 31

	REVENUE ($ mil.)	NET INCOME ($ mil.)	NET PROFIT MARGIN	EMPLOYEES
12/11	82	2	3.2%	260
12/10	61	1	2.7%	0
Annual Growth	33.5%	58.9%	—	—

THE ADVERTISING COUNCIL INC

The birthplace of Rosie the Riveter and Smokey Bear The Advertising Council carries out pro bono ad campaigns on behalf of both government and private organizations. Using public service announcements the not-for-profit organization conducts about 50 campaigns each year aimed at areas such as children's issues health community the environment and family. The Advertising Council relies on volunteer efforts from advertising firms and receives about $2 billion in donated ad time and space annually. Founded in 1942 as the War Advertising Council the organization's success in promoting war bonds led President Franklin Roosevelt to ask it to continue applying its efforts to social issues.

EXECUTIVES

EVP Corporate Communications, Paula Veale
President CEO and Director, Peggy Conlon
EVP and Director Client Services, Priscilla Natkins
SVP Creative Services and Distribution, Danielle Linet
SVP Campaigns, Heidi Arthur
SVP and Director Group Campaign, Kathy Crosby
SVP Interactive Services, Barbara Shimaitis
EVP Development, Barbara Leshinsky
SVP Non-Profit and Governmental Affairs, Kate Emanuel
Executive Director Media, Charlie Rutman
SVP National Accounts and Media Marketing, James Baumann
SVP Research, Tony Foleno
SVP Development, Jennifer Mamlet
EVP and CFO, Jon Fish
Secretary, Nancy Hill
Auditors: PricewaterhouseCoopersLLP

LOCATIONS

HQ: The Advertising Council Inc.
261 Madison Ave. 11th Fl., New York NY 10016
Phone: 212-922-1500   **Fax:** 212-922-1676
Web: www.adcouncil.org

PRODUCTS/OPERATIONS

Selected Campaigns

Afterschool Participation
Breastfeeding Awareness
Childhood Obesity Prevention
Community Drug Prevention Campaign
Crime Prevention
Domestic Violence Prevention
Drunken Driving Prevention
Emergency Preparedness
Environmental Conservation
Family Literacy
Fatherhood Involvement
I am an American
Online Sexual Exploitation

THE AMALGAMATED SUGAR COMPANY LLC

The Amalgamated Sugar Company with roots reaching back to 1915 turns beets into sweets. As one of the nation's top sugar producers it processes sugar beets grown on about 180000 acres in Idaho Oregon and Washington. The company manufactures granulated coarse powdered and brown consumer sugar products marketed under the brand White Satin. It also makes products for retail grocery chains under private labels. The sugar company produces beet pulp molasses and other beet by-products for use by food and animal-feed manufacturers. Since 1997 Amalgamated Sugar has been owned by the Snake River Sugar Company a cooperative that comprises sugar beet growers in Idaho Oregon and Washington.

Geographic Reach

The company's sugar beets which are grown in Idaho Oregon and Washington are processed through the three sugar processing facilities it operates in Idaho. The Amalgamated Sugar Company also owns half a dozen storage facilities and distribution warehouses in the state.

Operations

The Amalgamated Sugar Company processes up to 1.6 billion pounds of sugar each year. Along with processing the cooperative's crops the company provides its owner-farmers with agronomy advice and services runs workshops and seminars operates a co-op store and sells used equipment.

The company's key management team is employed on a contract basis. A seven-member Management Committee oversees the management team. The committee comprises members of the cooperative's board of directors.

Strategy

The industry's return to the use of real sugar in soft drinks and other beverages has become a boon for The Amalgamated Sugar Company. To this end Pepsi Bottling Ventures has tapped the sugar beet processor to supply the bottler with granulated sugar. During the past few decades more beverage makers have moved to using lesser-expensive high fructose corn syrup to sweeten their beverages as a way to cut costs and boost profits but the shift spurred by consumers to return to sugar-sweetened drinks has become profitable for sugar processors the likes of The Amalgamated Sugar Company.

Sales and Marketing

The Amalgamated Sugar Company sells its sugar primarily in the nation's North Central Intermountain and Northwest regions.

Financial Performance

The Amalgamated Sugar Company generates some 90% of its annual sales through the sale of refined sugar. The balance of its revenue comes from animal feed derived from beet pulp and molasses and other by-products as a result of sugar beet procession.

Company Ownership

The company is owned by Snake River Sugar Company a sugar beet grower cooperative operating in three US states.

EXECUTIVES

President and CEO, Victor J. (Vic) Jaro, age 57
VP Finance, Wayne P. Neeley
Manager Employee Relations, Paul Lemieux
VP Operations, Joe Huff
VP Research and Quality Assurance, Dennis Costesso

LOCATIONS

HQ: The Amalgamated Sugar Company LLC
1951 S. Saturn Way Ste. 100, Boise ID 83709
Phone: 208-383-6500   **Fax:** 208-383-6688
Web: www.amalgamatedsugar.com

PRODUCTS/OPERATIONS

Selected Products

Bakers' special sugar
Brown sugar
Dark brown sugar
Extra-fine granulated sugar
Fine granulated sugar
Gel gran granulated sugar
Industrial coarse sugar
Powdered sugar 10x and 12x
Sugar packets
Sugar standards
Type 50 medium invert sugar
Type O liquid sucrose (66.5 brix)
Type O liquid sucrose (67.5 brix)

COMPETITORS

Alico Inc.
American Crystal Sugar
Associated British Foods
C&H Sugar
Cosun
Cumberland Packing
Eurosugar
Florida Crystals
Imperial Sugar
Ingredion
M. A. Patout
Merisant
Michigan Sugar Company
Minn-Dak Co-op
Nippon Beet Sugar
Nordzucker
NutraSweet
SMBSC

Sterling Sugars
Sudzucker
Sugar Cane Growers Cooperative of Florida
U.S. Sugar
Western Sugar Cooperative

HISTORICAL FINANCIALS

Company Type: Private

Income Statement

FYE: December 31

	REVENUE ($ mil.)	NET INCOME ($ mil.)	NET PROFIT MARGIN	EMPLOYEES
12/11	886	46	5.3%	1,500
12/10	841	2	0.3%	0
12/09	656	18	2.9%	0
12/08	605	(6)	—	0
Annual Growth	13.5%	—	—	—

2011 Year-End Financials

Debt ratio: ——
Return on equity: 5.30%
Cash ($ mil.): 6
Current ratio: ——
Long-term debt ($ mil.): —

Dividends
  Yield: —
  Payout: —
Market value ($ mil.): —

THE ARLINGTON AUTOMOTIVE GROUP INC

LOCATIONS

HQ: THE ARLINGTON AUTOMOTIVE GROUP INC
2095 N RAND RD, PALATINE, IL 60074-2596
Phone: 847-485-1200
Web: www.toyotaarlington.com

HISTORICAL FINANCIALS

Company Type: Private

Income Statement

FYE: December 31

	REVENUE ($ mil.)	NET INCOME ($ mil.)	NET PROFIT MARGIN	EMPLOYEES
12/11*	98	1	1.5%	136
03/11	22	0	1.3%	0
12/09	79	1	2.0%	0
12/08	75	1	1.8%	0
Annual Growth	9.4%	4.2%	—	—

*Fiscal year change

2011 Year-End Financials

Debt ratio: ——
Return on equity: 1.50%
Cash ($ mil.): 2
Current ratio: 0.20
Long-term debt ($ mil.): —

Dividends
  Yield: —
  Payout: —
Market value ($ mil.): —

THE ASIA FOUNDATION

LOCATIONS

HQ: THE ASIA FOUNDATION
465 CALIFORNIA ST FL 9, SAN FRANCISCO, CA 94104-1892
Phone: 415-982-4640
Web: www.asiafoundation.org

HISTORICAL FINANCIALS

Company Type: Private

Income Statement

FYE: September 30

	REVENUE ($ mil.)	NET INCOME ($ mil.)	NET PROFIT MARGIN	EMPLOYEES
09/11	146	(4)	—	700
09/09	141	2	1.5%	0
09/06	97	7	7.6%	0
09/05	96	(0)	—	0
Annual Growth	15.1%	—	—	—

2011 Year-End Financials

Debt ratio: ——
Return on equity: (-2.80)%
Cash ($ mil.): 12
Current ratio: 0.60
Long-term debt ($ mil.): —

Dividends
  Yield: —
  Payout: —
Market value ($ mil.): —

THE BARGAIN BARN INC

LOCATIONS

HQ: THE BARGAIN BARN INC
2924 LEE HWY, ATHENS, TN 37303-5063
Phone: 423-746-0022
Web: www.bargainbarn.com

HISTORICAL FINANCIALS

Company Type: Private

Income Statement

FYE: October 1

	REVENUE ($ mil.)	NET INCOME ($ mil.)	NET PROFIT MARGIN	EMPLOYEES
10/11	101	1	1.4%	700
10/10*	97	1	1.1%	0
09/09	100	2	2.0%	0
09/08	89	1	1.9%	0
Annual Growth	4.3%	(6.7%)	—	—

*Fiscal year change

2011 Year-End Financials

Debt ratio: ——
Return on equity: 1.40%
Cash ($ mil.): 4
Current ratio: 1.10
Long-term debt ($ mil.): —

Dividends
  Yield: —
  Payout: —
Market value ($ mil.): —

THE BERGQUIST COMPANY

LOCATIONS

HQ: THE BERGQUIST COMPANY
18930 W 78TH ST, CHANHASSEN, MN 55317-8728
Phone: 952-835-2322
Web: www.bergquistcompany.com

HISTORICAL FINANCIALS
Company Type: Private

Income Statement
FYE: October 28

	REVENUE ($ mil.)	NET INCOME ($ mil.)	NET PROFIT MARGIN	EMPLOYEES
10/11	173	0	—	824
10/10	162	0	—	0
10/09	113	0	—	0
10/08	0	0	—	0
Annual Growth	—	—	—	—

2011 Year-End Financials

Debt ratio: ——
Return on equity: —
Cash ($ mil.): 55
Current ratio: 2.90
Long-term debt ($ mil.): —

Dividends
Yield: —
Payout: —
Market value ($ mil.): —

THE BERND GROUP INC

The Bernd Group gets paid to shop for other companies. The supply chain management company distributes computer hardware software and a wide range of industrial and commercial equipment and supplies to companies in the aerospace construction manufacturing and transportation sectors. Customers include Johnson Controls Lockheed Martin Pratt & Whitney Tampa Electric United Technologies and other maintenance repair and operations (MRO) organizations and original equipment manufacturers (OEM). The Bernd Group draws upon a network of more than 18000 vendors and is able to rely on government-based contracts for women-owned companies. President Pilar Ricaurte-Bernd owns the company which she founded in 1989.

EXECUTIVES

President, Pilar Ricaurte Bernd
Comptroller, Gorman Lewis

LOCATIONS

HQ: The Bernd Group Inc.
1251 Pinehurst Rd., Dunedin FL 34698
Phone: 727-733-0122 **Fax:** 800-346-4717
Web: www.berndgroup.com

COMPETITORS

Arrow Electronics	Ingram Micro
Aviall	OpTech
Barnes Group	PartMiner
Duncan Industrial Solutions	Strategic Distribution
	TMX Aerospace

First Aviation

HISTORICAL FINANCIALS
Company Type: Private

Income Statement
FYE: December 31

	REVENUE ($ mil.)	NET INCOME ($ mil.)	NET PROFIT MARGIN	EMPLOYEES
12/11	55	1	1.9%	48
12/10	52	1	2.0%	0
12/09	51	1	2.0%	0
12/08	53	0	1.9%	0
Annual Growth	1.3%	2.8%	—	—

2011 Year-End Financials

Debt ratio: ——
Return on equity: 1.90%
Cash ($ mil.): 1
Current ratio: 1.40
Long-term debt ($ mil.): —

Dividends
Yield: —
Payout: —
Market value ($ mil.): —

THE BIG EAST CONFERENCE INC

LOCATIONS

HQ: THE BIG EAST CONFERENCE INC
15 PARK ROW W STE 1, PROVIDENCE, RI 02903-1115
Phone: 401-272-9108

HISTORICAL FINANCIALS
Company Type: Private

Income Statement
FYE: June 30

	REVENUE ($ mil.)	NET INCOME ($ mil.)	NET PROFIT MARGIN	EMPLOYEES
06/11	119	(0)	—	20
06/10	113	1	1.1%	0
06/09	103	1	1.0%	0
06/08	93	0	0.4%	0
Annual Growth	8.5%	—	—	—

2011 Year-End Financials

Debt ratio: ——
Return on equity: (-0.20)%
Cash ($ mil.): 9
Current ratio: 51.30
Long-term debt ($ mil.): —

Dividends
Yield: —
Payout: —
Market value ($ mil.): —

THE BIG TEN CONFERENCE INC

LOCATIONS

HQ: THE BIG TEN CONFERENCE INC
1500 HIGGINS RD, PARK RIDGE, IL 60068-5742
Phone: 847-696-1010
Web: www.bigten.org

HISTORICAL FINANCIALS
Company Type: Private

Income Statement
FYE: June 30

	REVENUE ($ mil.)	NET INCOME ($ mil.)	NET PROFIT MARGIN	EMPLOYEES
06/11	265	(0)	—	25
06/10	232	(4)	—	0
06/09	221	(1)	—	0
06/08	217	(1)	—	0
Annual Growth	6.8%	—	—	—

2011 Year-End Financials

Debt ratio: ——
Return on equity: (-0.10)%
Cash ($ mil.): 23
Current ratio: 0.80
Long-term debt ($ mil.): —

Dividends
Yield: —
Payout: —
Market value ($ mil.): —

THE BOARD OF EDUCATION OF HOWARD COUNTY

LOCATIONS

HQ: THE BOARD OF EDUCATION OF HOWARD COUNTY
10910 STATE ROUTE 108, ELLICOTT CITY, MD 21042-6106
Phone: 410-313-6600

HISTORICAL FINANCIALS
Company Type: Private

Income Statement
FYE: June 30

	REVENUE ($ mil.)	NET INCOME ($ mil.)	NET PROFIT MARGIN	EMPLOYEES
06/11	850	4	0.5%	5,456
Annual Growth	—	—	—	—

2011 Year-End Financials

Debt ratio: ——
Return on equity: 0.50%
Cash ($ mil.): 14
Current ratio: —
Long-term debt ($ mil.): —

Dividends
Yield: —
Payout: —
Market value ($ mil.): —

THE BROAD INSTITUTE INC

LOCATIONS

HQ: THE BROAD INSTITUTE INC
7 CAMBRIDGE CTR, CAMBRIDGE, MA 02142-1401
Phone: 617-714-7000
Web: www.broadinstitute.org

HISTORICAL FINANCIALS

Company Type: Private

Income Statement

	REVENUE ($ mil.)	NET INCOME ($ mil.)	NET PROFIT MARGIN	EMPLOYEES
06/11	343	63	18.5%	800
06/10	785	549	70.0%	0
Annual Growth	(56.2%)	(88.4%)	—	—

FYE: June 30

2011 Year-End Financials

Debt ratio: ——
Return on equity: 18.50%
Cash ($ mil.): 110
Current ratio: 1.30
Long-term debt ($ mil.): —

Dividends
  Yield: —
  Payout: —
  Market value ($ mil.): —

THE BROOKINGS INSTITUTION

The Brookings Institution may know an egghead or two (or 300). The non-partisan public policy organization is comprised of more than 300 resident and non-resident scholars who research and analyze emerging issues in areas such as economics foreign policy and governance. Its experts perform research; write books papers and articles; testify in front of congressional committees; and participate in public events every year. The non-profit organization which is financed by gifts and grants is named after one of its backers –businessman Robert S. Brookings a well-known civic leader and philanthropist. Founded in 1916 it is the first private organization devoted to analyzing national public policy issues.

Today The Brookings Institution's activities are focused on four priority initiatives: energy and climate growth through innovation global change and opportunity and well-being. In addition its research is designed to support recommendations that strengthen American democracy; foster the economic and social welfare security and opportunity of all Americans; and secure a more open safe prosperous and cooperative international system.

The think tank also publishes books such as The Arab Awakening through its Brookings Institution Press imprint while its Brookings Executive Education offers courses for corporate and government leaders through a partnership with Washington University in St. Louis. In addition to its Washington D.C. office Brookings also has an international presence in Qatar and Beijing.

EXECUTIVES

President, Strobe Talbott
VP Communications, Melissa Skolfield
Managing Director, William J. Antholis
VP and COO, Steven J. Bennett
VP and Director Brookings Press, Robert L. Faherty
VP and Director Metropolitan Policy Program, Bruce Katz
VP and Director Governance Studies, Darrell M. West
VP and Director Global Economy and Development, Kemal Dervis
VP and Director Foreign Policy, Martin Indyk
VP CFO and Treasurer, Stewart Uretsky
General Counsel, Ona Dosunmu
VP and Co-Director Economic Studies, Karen Dynan

LOCATIONS

HQ: The Brookings Institution
1775 Massachusetts Ave. NW., Washington DC 20036-2188
Phone: 202-797-6000   **Fax:** 202-797-6004
Web: www.brookings.edu

PRODUCTS/OPERATIONS

Selected Program Areas

Brookings Press
Economic studies
Executive Education
Foreign policy
Global economy and development
Governance studies
Metropolitan policy

HISTORICAL FINANCIALS

Company Type: Private

Income Statement

	REVENUE ($ mil.)	NET INCOME ($ mil.)	NET PROFIT MARGIN	EMPLOYEES
06/11	100	11	11.3%	400
06/10	67	(23)	—	0
06/09	75	0	—	0
06/08	91	8	9.7%	0
Annual Growth	3.0%	8.2%	—	—

FYE: June 30

2011 Year-End Financials

Debt ratio: ——
Return on equity: 11.30%
Cash ($ mil.): 20
Current ratio: 0.40
Long-term debt ($ mil.): —

Dividends
  Yield: —
  Payout: —
  Market value ($ mil.): —

THE BUDD GROUP INC

LOCATIONS

HQ: THE BUDD GROUP INC
2325 S STRATFORD RD, WINSTON SALEM, NC 27103-6223
Phone: 336-765-7690
Web: www.buddgroup.com

HISTORICAL FINANCIALS

Company Type: Private

Income Statement

	REVENUE ($ mil.)	NET INCOME ($ mil.)	NET PROFIT MARGIN	EMPLOYEES
12/11	93	1	1.2%	3,500
12/10	86	0	0.5%	0
12/09	76	1	2.0%	0
12/08	70	0	1.1%	0
Annual Growth	10.1%	15.6%	—	—

FYE: December 31

2011 Year-End Financials

Debt ratio: ——
Return on equity: 1.20%
Cash ($ mil.): 0
Current ratio: 0.90
Long-term debt ($ mil.): —

Dividends
  Yield: —
  Payout: —
  Market value ($ mil.): —

THE CADMUS GROUP INC

Drinking water protection is one of the areas of sage advice offered by The Cadmus Group. The environmental consulting firm (named after Cadmus the Phoenician prince and renowned wise man who founded the city of Thebes) provides research analytical and technical support services primarily to government agencies. Over time it has established itself as a lead contractor of the US Environmental Protection Agency). Other specialties include air quality energy conservation environmental risk assessment and regulatory support as well as marketing and public education related to environmental programs. Cadmus operates from 10 offices throughout the US.

The company has parlayed its role as a major support contractor to the EPA into a number of contracts with private-sector companies and non-profits.

Over the past two decades Cadmus has opened new offices from coast to coast and made a few strategic acquisitions. In 2008 the company acquired Portland Oregon-based Quantec a firm that specializes in research analysis and planning for the energy industry. In late 2011 the company acquired California-based Constructive Technologies Group (CTG). CTG consists of two consulting firms: CTG Energetics which focuses on sustainability and energy efficiency in buildings and communities and CTG Forensics which uses building science to reduce risk or respond to failures in building projects.

Chairman Gene Fax and Managing Director Ralph Jones cofounded the firm in 1983.

EXECUTIVES

CFO, Alan V. Seferian
Managing Director, Ralph T. Jones
Chairman, Gene E. Fax
VP Drinking Water and Water Quality Group, Chi Ho Sham
Principal Drinking Water and Water Quality Group, Vanessa M. Leiby
Principal, G. Tracy Mehan III
Principal, George Hallberg
Principal, Jo Anne Shatkin

Media, Melissa W. Saunders
VP Emerging Markets Group, Jane E. Obbagy
President and CEO, Ian Kline
Director Human Resources, Mary Raynard
VP and Group Manager, M. Sami Khawaja
VP, Ed Miller
Principal Energy Services Group, John H.
  Chamberlin
Principal Energy Services Group, Ben Bronfman
Principal Energy Services Group, Scott Dimetrosky
**Principal Capacity for Impacts Assessment and
  Management (CIAM) Emerging Markets Group,**
  Weston Fisher
Principal Energy Services Group, Hossein Haeri
Principal and Head of Environmental Solutions,
  Katharine Hastings
Principal Energy Services Group, Brian Hedman
**Principal Drinking Water and Water Quality
  Group,** Patricia Hertzler
Principal Voluntary Programs Group, Edouard
  Israel
Principal Water Quality Group, Donna Jensen
**Principal Clean Energy and Applied Technology
  Team Energy Services Group,** David Korn
**Principal Emerging Markets Group and Head of
  Data Collection and Analysis Practice,** Richard
  Krop
**Princippal Drinking Water and Water Quality
  Group,** Frank Letkiewicz
**Principal Drinking Water and Water Quality
  Group,** Laurie Potter
**Principal Voluntary Programs Group and Head of
  Green Building Practice,** Julio Rovi
Principal Energy Services Group, Ken Seiden
Auditors: GrantThorntonLLP

LOCATIONS

HQ: The Cadmus Group Inc.
  57 Water St., Watertown MA 02472
Phone: 617-673-7000   **Fax:** 617-673-7001
Web: www.cadmusgroup.com
The Cadmus Group has offices in Arlington Virginia; Chapel Hill North Carolina;
Chicago; Helena Montana; Santa Monica California; and Watertown Massa-
chuse

COMPETITORS

AECOM	Siemens Water
ARCADIS US	Technologies
Calgon Carbon	Tetra Tech
CH2M HILL	The Kleinfelder Group
ERM	Inc.
ICF International	Veolia Environnement
Shaw Group	Weston Solutions

HISTORICAL FINANCIALS

Company Type: Private

Income Statement   FYE: April 30

	REVENUE ($ mil.)	NET INCOME ($ mil.)	NET PROFIT MARGIN	EMPLOYEES
04/12	68	3	5.5%	350
04/11	66	4	6.2%	0
04/10	59	2	4.0%	0
04/09	45	1	3.2%	0
Annual Growth	15.0%	37.9%	—	—

2012 Year-End Financials

Debt ratio: ——
Return on equity: 5.50%
Cash ($ mil.): 3
Current ratio: 0.90
Long-term debt ($ mil.): —

Dividends
  Yield: —
  Payout: —
  Market value ($ mil.): —

THE CARROLL ELECTRIC MEMBERSHIP CORPORATION

LOCATIONS

HQ: THE CARROLL ELECTRIC MEMBERSHIP
  CORPORATION
  155 N HIGHWAY 113, CARROLLTON, GA 30117-7501
Phone: 770-830-3552
Web: www.cemc.com

HISTORICAL FINANCIALS

Company Type: Private

Income Statement   FYE: December 31

	REVENUE ($ mil.)	NET INCOME ($ mil.)	NET PROFIT MARGIN	EMPLOYEES
12/11	109	1	1.8%	134
12/10	110	1	1.8%	0
12/09*	105	4	4.6%	0
06/09	107	3	3.4%	0
Annual Growth	0.6%	(18.5%)	—	—

*Fiscal year change

2011 Year-End Financials

Debt ratio: ——
Return on equity: 1.80%
Cash ($ mil.): 1
Current ratio: 0.10
Long-term debt ($ mil.): —

Dividends
  Yield: —
  Payout: —
  Market value ($ mil.): —

THE CARTER CENTER INC

LOCATIONS

HQ: THE CARTER CENTER INC
  453 FREEDOM PKWY NE, ATLANTA, GA 30307-1406
Phone: 404-420-5100
Web: www.cartercenter.org

HISTORICAL FINANCIALS

Company Type: Private

Income Statement   FYE: August 31

	REVENUE ($ mil.)	NET INCOME ($ mil.)	NET PROFIT MARGIN	EMPLOYEES
08/11	235	15	6.4%	200
08/10	216	0	0.3%	0
08/09	109	38	35.2%	0
08/03	119	38	31.9%	0
Annual Growth	25.2%	(26.7%)	—	—

2011 Year-End Financials

Debt ratio: ——
Return on equity: 6.40%
Cash ($ mil.): 19
Current ratio: 2.80
Long-term debt ($ mil.): —

Dividends
  Yield: —
  Payout: —
  Market value ($ mil.): —

THE CARTER-JONES LUMBER COMPANY

Carter Lumber has the answer when new home construction has you hollering "timber!" The company owns more than 200 lumber and home improvement stores in 10 states from Michigan to South Carolina. The company caters to both contractors and do-it-yourselfers supplying them with lumber plywood roofing windows doors plumbing and electrical products heating equipment tools siding and other products. The home improvement retailer also owns Carter-Jones Lumber which runs a 17-acre lumberyard and custom millwork facilities in Ohio. The company was founded by Warren E. Carter in 1932 and it continues to be a family-owned business.

In addition to Carter-Jones Lumber the company operates half a dozen other divisions that also specialize in providing building materials. These include Ohio-based Holmes Lumber a building materials supplier with two stores in Ohio (acquired in 2004); Kight Home Centers with five stores in Indiana and Kentucky (acquired in 2005); Griggs Lumber with three locations along the Outer Banks of North Carolina; and Kempsville Building Materials with two locations in Virginia.

EXECUTIVES

President and CEO, Neil C. Sackett
SVP COO and CFO, Jeffrey S. (Jeff) Donley
VP Technology, Jeff Seder
VP Marketing and Director Human Resources,
  David McCafferty
VP Installed Sales, Don Morris
VP Holmes Lumber, Steve Miller
VP Product Management, Rollie Haring
VP Purchasing, Paul Barnaby

LOCATIONS

HQ: Carter Lumber
  601 Tallmadge Rd., Kent OH 44240
Phone: 330-673-6100   **Fax:** 330-678-6134
Web: www.carterlumber.com

PRODUCTS/OPERATIONS

Selected Subsidiaries

Carter-Jones Lumber Company
Griggs Lumber
Holmes Lumber
Kempsville Building Materials
Kight Home Center

COMPETITORS

84 Lumber
ABC Supply
BlueLinx
Guardian Building Products Distribution
HD Supply
Lowe' s
Menard
Pro-Build
Stock Building Supply
Weekes Forest Products

HISTORICAL FINANCIALS

Company Type: Private

Income Statement

FYE: December 31

	REVENUE ($ mil.)	NET INCOME ($ mil.)	NET PROFIT MARGIN	EMPLOYEES
12/11	339	3	1.0%	1,575
12/10	334	(4)	—	0
12/09	314	(4)	—	0
12/08	424	(1)	—	0
Annual Growth	(7.1%)	—	—	—

2011 Year-End Financials

Debt ratio: ——
Return on equity: 1.00%
Cash ($ mil.): 2
Current ratio: 0.40
Long-term debt ($ mil.): —

Dividends
Yield: —
Payout: —
Market value ($ mil.): —

THE CHARLES STARK DRAPER LABORATORY INC

The Charles Stark Draper Laboratory guides research into space under water and across continents. Founded in 1932 by MIT professor Charles Stark Draper as a teaching lab the not-for-profit corporation develops guidance navigation and control technologies for aircraft submarines missiles and spacecraft. It works with NASA the US Department of Defense and commercial businesses to develop technologies and fabricate prototypes. It also solves health care problems with its work in biomedical engineering. The lab has more than 850 engineers and scientists. Originally known as the Instrument Lab the laboratory was renamed in 1970 and became an independent institution three years later.

Draper Lab's innovations include a personal navigation system that allows soldiers to find their way in GPS-denied areas technology development for autonomous lunar landings for NASA's Constellation program and a micro-avionics system for a 20-gram nano air vehicle capable of flying in realistic wind conditions and equipped with a digital video recorder the size of a postage stamp.

In its growing biomedical engineering research area Draper is developing a device for the detection of tuberculosis and other respiratory disease by analyzing a patient's breath.

One of Draper Lab's major projects is working on the guidance system of the Navy's Trident D5 submarine-launched ballistic missile. In early 2009 the lab received a $157.3 million contract from Strategic Systems Programs and a $117.4 million contract from the US Department of Defense for its work on Trident.

Draper Lab has operations in Cape Canaveral Florida; Houston; Huntsville Alabama; Pittsfield Massachusetts; San Diego; Tampa Florida; and Washington DC.

EXECUTIVES

President CEO and Director, James D. (Jim) Shields
VP Programs, Darryl G. Sargent

Chairman, John A. Gordon, age 65
Assistant Secretary, Helen M. Gillis
VP Strategic Systems, John W. Stillwell
VP Finance and Administration and Treasurer, Elizabeth Mora
VP Engineering, John R. Dowdle
Secretary and General Counsel, Melinda J. Brown
President CEO and Director, James D. (Jim) Shields
Director, Franklin C. (Frank) Miller
Director, Sherwin Greenblatt
Director, Delores M. Etter
Director, Miriam E. John
Director, George M. Milne Jr.
Director, Malcolm R. O'Neil
Director, M. Elisabeth Pate-Cornell
Director, C. Bruce Tarter
Director, Peter B. Teets
Director, Richard D. White
Director, William F. Ballhaus Jr.
Auditors: PricewaterhouseCoopersLLP

LOCATIONS

HQ: The Charles Stark Draper Laboratory Inc.
555 Technology Sq., Cambridge MA 02139-3563
Phone: 617-258-1000   **Fax:** 617-258-1131
Web: www.draper.com

PRODUCTS/OPERATIONS

Selected Research Areas

Biomedical engineering
  Tissue engineering
  Sensor development
Space systems
  Military space systems
  Planetary exploration
  Scientific spacecraft
  Space transportation
Special operations
  Robotics
  Small low-power electronics
  Surveillance systems
Strategic systems
  Inertial guidance systems
Tactical systems
  Precision engagement systems
  Manned/unmanned systems
  Missile defense

COMPETITORS

Applied Research Associates
Institute for Defense Analyses
QinetiQ
Quantum Research

HISTORICAL FINANCIALS

Company Type: Private - Not-for-Profit

Income Statement

FYE: June 29

	REVENUE ($ mil.)	NET INCOME ($ mil.)	NET PROFIT MARGIN	EMPLOYEES
06/12*	514	(20)	—	1,134
07/11	0	40	—	0
07/10	493	12	2.6%	0
06/09	418	0	—	0
Annual Growth	7.1%	—	—	—

*Fiscal year change

2012 Year-End Financials

Debt ratio: ——
Return on equity: (-4.00)%
Cash ($ mil.): 46
Current ratio: 1.10
Long-term debt ($ mil.): —

Dividends
Yield: —
Payout: —
Market value ($ mil.): —

THE CHILDREN'S AID SOCIETY

LOCATIONS

HQ: THE CHILDREN'S AID SOCIETY
105 E 22ND ST FL 5, NEW YORK, NY 10010-5493
Phone: 212-949-4800
Web: www.rhinelandercenter.org

HISTORICAL FINANCIALS

Company Type: Private

Income Statement

FYE: June 30

	REVENUE ($ mil.)	NET INCOME ($ mil.)	NET PROFIT MARGIN	EMPLOYEES
06/11	111	0	0.5%	1,800
06/10	106	(1)	—	0
06/09	80	0	—	0
06/08	117	7	6.4%	0
Annual Growth	(1.7%)	(58.0%)	—	—

2011 Year-End Financials

Debt ratio: ——
Return on equity: 0.50%
Cash ($ mil.): 16
Current ratio: 0.80
Long-term debt ($ mil.): —

Dividends
Yield: —
Payout: —
Market value ($ mil.): —

THE CHILDREN'S HOSPITAL OF PHILADELPHIA FOUNDATION

LOCATIONS

HQ: THE CHILDREN'S HOSPITAL OF PHILADELPHIA FOUNDATION
34TH ST CIVIC CENTER BLVD, PHILADELPHIA, PA 19104
Phone: 215-590-1000

HISTORICAL FINANCIALS

Company Type: Private

Income Statement

FYE: June 30

	REVENUE ($ mil.)	NET INCOME ($ mil.)	NET PROFIT MARGIN	EMPLOYEES
06/11	112	23	20.9%	7,000
06/10	114	31	27.6%	0
06/08	17	(0)	—	0
06/03	722	10	1.5%	0
Annual Growth	(46.2%)	29.5%	—	—

THE CHILDREN'S MEDICAL CENTER DAYTON OHIO

LOCATIONS

HQ: THE CHILDREN' S MEDICAL CENTER DAYTON OHIO
1 CHILDRENS PLZ, DAYTON, OH 45404-1873
Phone: 937-641-3000
Web: www.childrensdayton.org

HISTORICAL FINANCIALS
Company Type: Private

Income Statement

	REVENUE ($ mil.)	NET INCOME ($ mil.)	NET PROFIT MARGIN	EMPLOYEES
06/11	216	39	18.4%	1,081
06/10	197	25	12.9%	0
06/08	196	31	16.0%	0
06/05	158	29	18.3%	0
Annual Growth	10.9%	10.9%	—	—

2011 Year-End Financials

Debt ratio: —
Return on equity: 18.40%
Cash ($ mil.): 29
Current ratio: 1.40
Long-term debt ($ mil.): —

Dividends
Yield: —
Payout: —
Market value ($ mil.): —

THE CHIMES INC

The sound of bells can induce a message of hope. The Chimes is a private agency serving the needs of about 10000 people of all ages with mental and physical disabilities. The organization offers a wide range of health education job training and placement housing and social services in the mid-Atlantic states of the US and in Tel Aviv Israel. The Chimes offers similar services through two subsidiaries Developmental Services of New Jersey and Holcomb Behavioral Health Systems. The agency was established in 1947 when a group of Baltimore parents used space in a church to found a school for their mentally disabled children.

EXECUTIVES

President CEO and Director, Terry Allen Perl
EVP COO and Assistant Secretary, Albert Bussone
VP Human Resources, Martha Loveman Perl
COO Holcomb Behavioral Health Systems, William DiFabio

Chairperson, Stephen S. Kramer
Vice Chairperson, Patrick Bagley
Vice Chairperson; Chairperson Chimes Maryland, Bobby G. Edmondson
Vice Chairperson, Julius B. Margolis
Vice Chairperson, Arthur C. George
CFO and CIO, Martin S. Lampner
Secretary and Director, Steven P. Alms
Treasurer and Director, Michael May
VP Organizational Advancement, Pat Dodd
COO Chimes District of Columbia, Johan (Hans) Rinecker
COO Chimes Delaware, Pete Dakunchak
COO Chimes Virginia, Sue Grigsby
COO Development Services of New Jersey, Steven Chafetz
President CEO and Director, Terry Allen Perl
Vice Chairperson, Patrick Bagley
Vice Chairperson; Chairperson Chimes Maryland, Bobby G. Edmondson
Vice Chairperson, Julius B. Margolis
Vice Chairperson, Arthur C. George
Secretary and Director, Steven P. Alms
Director, Ann W. Breihan
Treasurer and Director, Michael May

LOCATIONS

HQ: The Chimes Inc.
4815 Seton Dr., Baltimore MD 21215
Phone: 410-358-6400   **Fax:** 410-358-8546
Web: www.chimes.org

HISTORICAL FINANCIALS
Company Type: Private - Not-for-Profit

Income Statement

	REVENUE ($ mil.)	NET INCOME ($ mil.)	NET PROFIT MARGIN	EMPLOYEES
06/11	43	1	3.1%	581
06/10	42	1	2.7%	0
06/09	40	0	—	0
06/08	4	0	10.4%	0
Annual Growth	118.1%	45.2%	—	—

2011 Year-End Financials

Debt ratio: —
Return on equity: 3.10%
Cash ($ mil.): 8
Current ratio: 0.80
Long-term debt ($ mil.): —

Dividends
Yield: —
Payout: —
Market value ($ mil.): —

THE CHRISTIAN & MISSIONARY ALLIANCE FOUNDATION INC

LOCATIONS

HQ: THE CHRISTIAN & MISSIONARY ALLIANCE FOUNDATION INC
15000 SHELL POINT BLVD, FORT MYERS, FL 33908-1657
Phone: 239-466-1111
Web: www.shellpoint.org

HISTORICAL FINANCIALS
Company Type: Private

Income Statement
FYE: June 30

	ASSETS ($ mil.)	NET INCOME ($ mil.)	INCOME AS % OF ASSETS	EMPLOYEES
06/12	454	6	1.5%	750
06/11	457	5	1.3%	0
06/10	453	4	1.0%	0
06/09	456	2	0.6%	0
Annual Growth	(0.1%)	35.0%	—	—

2012 Year-End Financials

Debt ratio: —
Return on equity: 6.40%
Cash ($ mil.): 10
Current ratio: 0.90
Long-term debt ($ mil.): —

Dividends
Yield: —
Payout: —
Market value ($ mil.): —

THE CHRISTIAN BROADCASTING NETWORK INC

Standards & Practices probably won't find much wrong with these TV programs. The Christian Broadcasting Network (CBN) is one of the leading producers of religious television programming in the country offering news and entertainment shows with a spiritual message. Its centerpiece is The 700 Club a daily show featuring a mix of news and commentary interviews feature stories and Christian ministry co-hosted by CBN founder Pat Robertson. The company's programs are syndicated to broadcast and cable TV outlets that reach audiences in more than 200 countries. CBN generates most of its revenue through ministry donations. Robertson started the company with a single TV station in 1960.

EXECUTIVES

Chairman, M. G. (Pat) Robertson, age 82
President COO and Director, Michael D. Little
CEO, Gordon Robertson
Special Features Producer 700 Club, Kristi Watts
Producer 700 Club, Scott Ross
Controller, Jim Barr
Executive Director Human Resources, Malcolm Hedding

LOCATIONS

HQ: THE CHRISTIAN BROADCASTING NETWORK INC
977 CENTERVILLE TPKE, VIRGINIA BEACH, VA 23463-1001
Phone: 757-226-7000
Web: www.cbn.com

COMPETITORS

Eden Communications	Thomas Nelson
Guideposts	Trinity Broadcasting
Integrity Media	Zondervan
Salem Communications	

HISTORICAL FINANCIALS
Company Type: Private - Not-for-Profit

Income Statement
FYE: March 31

	REVENUE ($ mil.)	NET INCOME ($ mil.)	NET PROFIT MARGIN	EMPLOYEES
03/11	285	6	2.4%	941
03/10	283	8	3.0%	0
03/09	295	6	2.2%	0
03/08	547	(0)	—	0
Annual Growth	(19.5%)	—	—	—

2011 Year-End Financials

Debt ratio: ——
Return on equity: 2.40%
Cash ($ mil.): 18
Current ratio: 0.60
Long-term debt ($ mil.): —

Dividends
Yield: —
Payout: —
Market value ($ mil.): —

THE CITADEL

A state-supported military college The Citadel traces its roots back to the 1842 founding of the South Carolina Military Academy. Today's Citadel enrolls about 2000 undergraduate cadets who reside on the campus barracks. Cadets are given military and academic instruction in addition to physical training and a strict disciplinary regime; about a third of all graduates continue on to military careers. The Citadel enrolls another 1000 civilian graduate and undergraduate students who attend evening classes. With a student-to-faculty ratio of 13:1 the institution has schools in business education engineering the humanities and social sciences and science and mathematics.

Geographic Reach

Only about half of The Citadel's students hail from South Carolina giving it a higher-than-usual rate of students from out of state. Its enrollees come from more than 40 US states and 20 international countries.

Operations

Previously all-male The Citadel allowed its first female cadet in 1993. During 2012 its enrollment was 93% make and 7% female.

While evening classes are primarily held through The Citadel Graduate College the university also holds a number of evening undergraduate classes. The program has expanded to include partnerships with a number of South Carolina technical colleges which allow students to earn credits towards a bachelor's degree at The Citadel.

Sales and Marketing

The Citadel engages in several online enrollment initiatives including its Daretolead.com marketing campaign as well as through its primary website and social media channels including Facebook Twitter LinkedIn and Pinterest.

Strategy

The Citadel is expanding its programs to better meet the needs of its students. In 2012 for instance it launched a new criminal justice department. The university's criminal justice program was previously part of the political science department.

EXECUTIVES

Chairman The Citadel Foundation, Charles B. (Charlie) Coe, age 64

EVP Finance Administration and Operations, Thomas J. Elzey
President, John W. Rosa Jr., age 60
Director Information Technology Services, Richard Nelson
Controller, Lt. Col. Ralph P. Earhart
Manager Accounting, Sue Reynolds
Treasurer, Diana Lynne Shoaf
Director Human Resources, Col. Dennis D. Carpenter
Director Budget, Col. James N. Openshaw
Director Procurement, John Walker
Director Career Services, Brent A. Stewart
VP External Affairs, L. Jeffrey (Jeff) Perez
Marketing Director, Mark G. Danes
Provost and Dean of the College, Samuel M. (Sam) Hines Jr.
Commandant Cadets, Col. Leo A. Mercado
Assistant Commandant for Personnel and Logistics Cadets, Lt. Col. Kevin Dopf
Assistant Commandant for Discipline Cadets, Col. Christopher Moore
Assistant Commandant for Operations Training and Planning Cadets, Lt. Col. Pamela Barton
Director Athletics, Larry Leckonby
VP Finance and Business Affairs, Sue E. Mitchell
VP Facilities and Engineering, Col. G. Dewey Yeatts
Director Risk Management and Safety, Robert E. Williamson
Director Public Safety and Provost Marshal, Col. William A. (Bill) Fletcher Jr.
Deputy Director Human Resources and Chief Diversity Officer, Bridgette M. Beasley
Registrar, Sylvia L. Nesmith
Director Network Operations and Security, George Russ
Director Physical Plant, James P. (Jim) FitzGerald
Director Counseling Center, Lt. Col. Suzanne Bufano
Surgeon and Director Infirmary, Col. Carey M. Capell
Director Financial Aid, Lt. Col. Henry M. Fuller Jr.
President The Citadel Brigadier Foundation, Mark A. Nash
Director Cadet Activities, Lt. Col. Robert A. Sberna
Director Library Services, Col. Angie Le Clerq
Director Admissions, Lt. Col. John W. Powell Jr.
Director Alumni Affairs, Michael F. Rogers
Director Archives and Museum, Jane Yates
Associate Provost, Col. Mark Bebensee
Associate Dean The Citadel Graduate College, Raymond S. Jones
Director Staff, Col. Joseph W. Trez
Director Governmental and Community Affairs, Col. Cardon B. Crawford
Director Krause Center for Ethics and Leadership, Lt. Col. Jeffrey M. Weart
General Counsel, Mark Brandenburg

LOCATIONS

HQ: The Citadel
171 Moultrie St., Charleston SC 29409-0002
Phone: 843-225-3294   **Fax:** 843-953-6767
Web: www.citadel.edu

PRODUCTS/OPERATIONS

Selected Schools and Divisions
The Citadel Graduate College
The Citadel Honors Program
School of Business Administration
School of Education
School of Engineering
School of Humanities and Social Sciences
School of Science and Mathematics

HISTORICAL FINANCIALS
Company Type: School

Income Statement
FYE: June 30

	REVENUE ($ mil.)	NET INCOME ($ mil.)	NET PROFIT MARGIN	EMPLOYEES
06/12	67	2	4.0%	580
06/11	67	5	8.4%	0
06/10	64	5	8.0%	0
06/09	51	(12)	—	0
Annual Growth	9.3%	—	—	—

2012 Year-End Financials

Debt ratio: ——
Return on equity: 4.00%
Cash ($ mil.): 31
Current ratio: 2.30
Long-term debt ($ mil.): —

Dividends
Yield: —
Payout: —
Market value ($ mil.): —

THE COLBERT COUNTY-NORTHWEST ALABAMA HEALTH CARE AUTHORITY

LOCATIONS

HQ: THE COLBERT COUNTY-NORTHWEST ALABAMA HEALTH CARE AUTHORITY
1300 S MONTGOMERY AVE, SHEFFIELD, AL 35660-6334
Phone: 256-386-4196
Web: www.redbayhospital.com

HISTORICAL FINANCIALS
Company Type: Private

Income Statement
FYE: September 30

	REVENUE ($ mil.)	NET INCOME ($ mil.)	NET PROFIT MARGIN	EMPLOYEES
09/11	90	(1)	—	700
09/10	92	(1)	—	0
09/09	95	0	0.2%	0
09/08	84	(0)	—	0
Annual Growth	2.1%	—	—	—

2011 Year-End Financials

Debt ratio: ——
Return on equity: (-1.20)%
Cash ($ mil.): 1
Current ratio: 1.00
Long-term debt ($ mil.): —

Dividends
Yield: —
Payout: —
Market value ($ mil.): —

THE COLLEGE OF AMERICAN PATHOLOGISTS

LOCATIONS

HQ: THE COLLEGE OF AMERICAN PATHOLOGISTS
325 WAUKEGAN RD, NORTHFIELD, IL 60093-2750
Phone: 847-832-7000
Web: www.cap.org

HISTORICAL FINANCIALS

Company Type: Private

Income Statement

FYE: December 31

	REVENUE ($ mil.)	NET INCOME ($ mil.)	NET PROFIT MARGIN	EMPLOYEES
12/11	154	(16)	—	565
12/10	145	(0)	—	0
12/09	139	9	7.0%	0
12/08	130	(40)	—	0
Annual Growth	5.6%	—	—	—

2011 Year-End Financials

Debt ratio: ——
Return on equity: (-10.90)%
Cash ($ mil.): 22
Current ratio: 0.70
Long-term debt ($ mil.): —

Dividends
Yield: —
Payout: —
Market value ($ mil.): —

THE COLLEGIATE SCHOOL

This school may sound "college like" but it's really meant for Kindergartners through 12th graders. Collegiate School has some 1500 students enrolled in its lower school (grades K through 4th) middle school (grades 5th through 8th) and upper school (grades 9th through 12th). The private school's offerings include multiple foreign languages individual music instruction and community service and travel opportunities. Collegiate was founded in 1915 as Collegiate School for Girls in downtown Richmond Virginia by Helen Baker with help from Mary Carter Anderson. Just 13 years after its founding boys were admitted but just to the Kindergarten. The first group of boys actually graduated in 1963.

EXECUTIVES

President and Head of School, Keith A. Evans
VP Development, Alex Smith
Director Admission, Amanda L. Surgner
Associate Head of School, Lindy M. Williams
Head of Lower School, Jill S. Hunter
Director Information Technology Operations, Oscar Brinson
Manager Human Resources, Jill Aveson
Interim Head of Upper School, Patrick Loach
Head of Middle School, Charles L. (Charlie) Blair Jr.
Academic Dean, David Colon

Director Alumni, Anne Ahearn
Director Communications, Elizabeth Cogar
VP Finance and Treasurer, Phyllis Palmiero
Manager Campus Safety and Security, Harry Boyd

LOCATIONS

HQ: Collegiate School
N. Mooreland Rd., Richmond VA 23229
Phone: 804-740-7077   **Fax:** 804-741-9797
Web: www.collegiate-va.org

COMPETITORS

Edison Learning   The Gunnery
Imagine Schools

HISTORICAL FINANCIALS

Company Type: School

Income Statement

FYE: June 30

	REVENUE ($ mil.)	NET INCOME ($ mil.)	NET PROFIT MARGIN	EMPLOYEES
06/11	41	12	29.3%	0
06/10	35	0	0.3%	0
06/09	39	0	—	0
06/08	45	10	23.7%	0
Annual Growth	(3.0%)	4.2%	—	—

2011 Year-End Financials

Debt ratio: ——
Return on equity: 29.30%
Cash ($ mil.): 7
Current ratio: —
Long-term debt ($ mil.): —

Dividends
Yield: —
Payout: —
Market value ($ mil.): —

THE COMPUTING TECHNOLOGY INDUSTRY ASSOCIATION INC

Welcome to the IT club. The Computing Technology Industry Association (CompTIA) is a not-for-profit trade organization that provides research training networking and partnering services to its 2000-plus members. It serves more than 100 countries with international offices in Australia Canada China Germany Hong Kong India Japan South Africa South Korea Taiwan and the UK. CompTIA also helps companies implement best practices in relation to software convergence certification e-commerce and workforce development. Like the industry it serves CompTIA has grown dramatically since it was founded in 1982 by representatives of five micro-computer dealerships.

CompTIA develops and administers vendor-neutral IT certification exams in about a dozen areas including: cloud essentials green IT networks servers security printer and document imaging Linux and storage.

EXECUTIVES

Vice Chairman, Robert (Bob) Godgart
VP Industry Development, Jill L. Kerr
Chairman, Robert G. (Bob) O'Malley, age 66
President and CEO CompTIA Educational Foundation, John A. Venator

---

VP Industry Relations, Richard Rysiewicz
CFO, David Sommer
VP Channel Strategies, Annette Taber
President and CEO, Todd Thibodeaux, age 47
CIO, Randy Gross
SVP Skills Certification, Terry Erdle
VP Global Marketing and Communications, Ed Korenman
VP Industry Development, Brett Martin
VP Events and Conferences, Kelly Ricker
Senior Director Human Resources, Colleen Hughes
VP Public Advocacy, Elizabeth Hyman
SVP Industry Relations, L. Daniel (Dan) Liutikas
VP Research, Tim Herbert
Director Corporate Communications, Steven Ostrowski
Director Industry Communications, Matt Swanston
VP Strategic Relationships, Kirk Smallwood

LOCATIONS

HQ: The Computing Technology Industry Association Inc.
3500 Lacey Rd. Ste. 100, Downers Grove IL 60515
Phone: 630-678-8300   **Fax:** 630-678-8384
Web: www.comptia.org

HISTORICAL FINANCIALS

Company Type: Private - Association

Income Statement

FYE: December 31

	REVENUE ($ mil.)	NET INCOME ($ mil.)	NET PROFIT MARGIN	EMPLOYEES
12/11	46	(4)	—	150
12/09	48	6	14.2%	0
12/08	50	(9)	—	0
12/07	42	3	7.6%	0
Annual Growth	3.2%	—	—	—

2011 Year-End Financials

Debt ratio: ——
Return on equity: (-9.50)%
Cash ($ mil.): 14
Current ratio: 1.20
Long-term debt ($ mil.): —

Dividends
Yield: —
Payout: —
Market value ($ mil.): —

THE CONLAN COMPANY

LOCATIONS

HQ: THE CONLAN COMPANY
1800 PARKWAY PL SE # 1010, MARIETTA, GA 30067-8200
Phone: 770-423-8000
Web: www.conlancompany.com

HISTORICAL FINANCIALS

Company Type: Private

Income Statement

FYE: December 31

	REVENUE ($ mil.)	NET INCOME ($ mil.)	NET PROFIT MARGIN	EMPLOYEES
12/11	228	2	1.2%	150
12/10	156	1	1.2%	0
12/09	106	4	3.8%	0
12/08	313	12	3.9%	0
Annual Growth	(10.0%)	(38.7%)	—	—

THE COOPER UNION FOR THE ADVANCEMENT OF SCIENCE AND ART

The Cooper Union for the Advancement of Science and Art was founded in 1859 by inventor and industrialist Peter Cooper who created the US's first steam train engine and rose from poverty to build a fortune. Cooper's endowment continues to fund a full tuition scholarship for each of the 900 students who attend the college which is located in the East Village in downtown New York City. The Cooper Union offers degree programs in art architecture and engineering as well as a wide variety of lectures and continuing education courses for the public.

Thomas Edison and Felix Frankfurter were students at Cooper Union where Susan B. Anthony had her offices and where the Red Cross and NAACP were organized.

EXECUTIVES

Dean School of Art, Saskia Bos
Chairman Emeritus, Robert A. Bernhard, age 83
Chairman, Ronald W. Drucker, age 70
President, George Campbell Jr., age 66
VP External Affairs, Ronni Denes
VP Business Affairs and Treasurer, Robert E. Hawks
Assistant Secretary, Louise Baykash
Dean Albert Nerken School of Engineering, Eleanor Baum
Dean of Students, Linda Lemiesz
Dean Admissions and Records, Mitchell Lipton
Dean Irwin S. Chanin School of Architecture, Anthony Vidler
Vice Chairman, Mark Epstein
Dean Faculty of Humanities and Social Sciences, William Germano
Trustee, Vikas Kapoor
Chairman Emeritus, Robert A. Bernhard, age 83
Chairman, Ronald W. Drucker, age 70
Trustee, Moshe Safdi'e
Trustee, Martin Trust, age 77
Trustee, Jason H. Wright, age 51
Trustee, Philip P. Trahanas
Trustee, Bruce A. Pasternack, age 64
Trustee, Marc F. Appleton
Trustee, Robert M. Aquilina
Trustee, Lawrence B. Benenson
Trustee, Michael Borkowsky
Trustee, Francois deMenil
Vice Chairman, Mark Epstein
Trustee, Jeffrey Gural
Trustee, Douglas A.P. Hamilton
Trustee, Stanley N. Lapidus
Trustee, Charles S. Cohen
Trustee, Thomas R. Driscoll
Trustee, Edward Feiner
Trustee, Richard S. Lincer
Trustee, John C. Michaelson
Trustee, Sandra P. Rose
Trustee, William H. Sandholm
Trustee, Richard Schwartz
Trustee, Georgiana J. Slade
Trustee, Roger C. Tucker III
Trustee, Cynthia Weiler

LOCATIONS

HQ: The Cooper Union for the Advancement of Science and Art
Cooper Square, New York NY 10003-7120
Phone: 212-353-4100   **Fax:** 212-353-4327
Web: www.cooper.edu

HISTORICAL FINANCIALS

Company Type: School

Income Statement

FYE: June 30

	REVENUE ($ mil.)	NET INCOME ($ mil.)	NET PROFIT MARGIN	EMPLOYEES
06/11	51	16	31.9%	642
06/10	47	(18)	—	0
06/09	39	0	—	0
06/07	39	(10)	—	0
Annual Growth	9.5%	—	—	—

2011 Year-End Financials

Debt ratio: ——
Return on equity: 31.90%
Cash ($ mil.): 13
Current ratio: ——
Long-term debt ($ mil.): ——

Dividends
Yield: ——
Payout: ——
Market value ($ mil.): ——

THE CORPORATION OF GONZAGA UNIVERSITY

Gonzaga University provides instruction to more than 7500 undergraduate graduate doctoral and law students. The school offers about 75 undergraduate majors more than two dozen master's degree programs and a doctoral program in leadership studies. The university offers a Juris Doctor degree at its School of Law one of three in Washington State. The Roman Catholic university is run by the Society of Jesus —the Jesuits —and is named after a sixteenth-century Italian Jesuit Aloysius Gonzaga the patron saint of youth. The university was founded in 1887. In addition to its main campus in Spokane Washington Gonzaga University has a campus in Florence Italy where Aloysius Gonzaga lived as a student.

EXECUTIVES

Chancellor, Father Bernard J. Coughlin
VP Finance, Charles J. Murphy
VP University Relations, Margot J. Stanfield
VP Student Life, Sue D. Weitz
Corporate Counsel, Michael Casey
VP Mission, Father Patrick Lee
Interim President, Thayne M. McCulloh
University VP, Harry H. Sladich

LOCATIONS

HQ: Gonzaga University
502 E. Boone Ave., Spokane WA 99258-0102
Phone: 509-328-4220   **Fax:** 352-245-0726
Web: www.americanpanel.com

PRODUCTS/OPERATIONS

Selected Schools and Colleges
College of Arts and Sciences
School of Business Administration
School of Education
School of Engineering
School of Law
School of Professional Studies

HISTORICAL FINANCIALS

Company Type: School

Income Statement

FYE: May 31

	REVENUE ($ mil.)	NET INCOME ($ mil.)	NET PROFIT MARGIN	EMPLOYEES
05/11	186	36	19.8%	650
05/10	177	24	13.8%	0
05/09	165	(39)	—	0
05/08	155	(0)	—	0
Annual Growth	6.2%	—	—	—

2011 Year-End Financials

Debt ratio: ——
Return on equity: 19.80%
Cash ($ mil.): 43
Current ratio: ——
Long-term debt ($ mil.): ——

Dividends
Yield: ——
Payout: ——
Market value ($ mil.): ——

THE CORPORATION OF HAVERFORD COLLEGE

Haverford College is one of the nation's top 10 liberal arts colleges according to US News & World Report's 2007 annual ranking. The college is a private school located 10 miles away from Philadelphia that serves more than 1200 students. Haverford was founded in 1833 by members of the Religious Society of Friends (Quakers). Among its staff are more than 110 full-time faculty members; the student-faculty ratio is 10-to-1. The school boasts such notable alumni as former Time Warner CEO Gerald Levin Time editor-in-chief Norman Pearlstine and humorist Dave Barry.

EXECUTIVES

Controller and Assistant Treasurer, Stephen A. Tessino
Director Networking and Systems, Matthew Nocifore
Dean College, Gregory (Greg) Kannerstein
VP Finance and Administration and Treasurer, G. Richard Wynn
President, Stephen G. Emerson
Director Human Resources, Christopher P. Chandler
Provost, Linda Bell
Dean Admission and Financial Aid, Jess Lord
VP Institutional Advancement and Assistant Secretary, Michael Kiefer
Director Safety and Security, Thomas L. King
Director Financial Aid, David Hoy

Director Alumni Relations, Diane Wilder
Director Alumni Relations, Joanne Romano
Registrar, Lee Watkins
Director College Communications, Christopher Mills
Director Purchasing, Samuel A. Williams
Auditors: PricewaterhouseCoopersLLP

LOCATIONS

HQ: Haverford College
370 Lancaster Ave., Haverford PA 19041-1392
Phone: 610-896-1000   **Fax:** 610-896-1240
Web: www.haverford.edu

HISTORICAL FINANCIALS
Company Type: School

Income Statement
FYE: June 30

	REVENUE ($ mil.)	NET INCOME ($ mil.)	NET PROFIT MARGIN	EMPLOYEES
06/12	91	(17)	—	600
06/11	79	51	65.0%	0
06/10	76	13	17.4%	0
06/09	82	(198)	—	0
Annual Growth	**3.2%**	—	—	—

2012 Year-End Financials

Debt ratio: —
Return on equity: (-19.60)%
Cash ($ mil.): 10
Current ratio: —
Long-term debt ($ mil.): —

Dividends
Yield: —
Payout: —
Market value ($ mil.): —

LOCATIONS

HQ: Mercer University
1400 Coleman Ave., Macon GA 31207-0001
Phone: 478-301-2700   **Fax:** 478-301-2108
Web: www.mercer.edu

COMPETITORS

Baylor University
Benedict College
Clark Atlanta University
Georgia Southern University
Interdenominational Theological Center

Kennesaw State University
Morris College
Spelman College
University of Mobile
University of West Georgia

HISTORICAL FINANCIALS
Company Type: School

Income Statement
FYE: June 30

	REVENUE ($ mil.)	NET INCOME ($ mil.)	NET PROFIT MARGIN	EMPLOYEES
06/11	270	8	3.0%	1,658
06/10	255	0	0.2%	0
06/09	235	0	—	0
06/08	263	40	15.3%	0
Annual Growth	**0.8%**	**(41.6%)**	—	—

2011 Year-End Financials

Debt ratio: —
Return on equity: 3.00%
Cash ($ mil.): 28
Current ratio: —
Long-term debt ($ mil.): —

Dividends
Yield: —
Payout: —
Market value ($ mil.): —

Director Corporate Affairs, James E. Sailer
General Counsel and Secretary, Patricia C. Vaughan
Regional Director South and East Asia, Saroj Pachauri
Regional Director West Asia and North Africa, Safaa El-Kogali
CFO and Treasurer, Scott Newman
Trustee, Robert B. Millard, age 61
President and Trustee, Peter J. Donaldson
Trustee, Marc A. Bygdeman
Trustee, Lynn A. Foster
Trustee, Werner Holzer
Trustee, Anna Glasier
Trustee, Darcy Bradbury
Trustee, Wafaa El-Sadr
Trustee, Henry L. King
Trustee, Charles D. Klein
Trustee, Anna Mastroianni
Trustee, Jotham Musinguzi
Trustee, Anne R. Pebley
Trustee, Justin A. Rockefeller

LOCATIONS

HQ: The Population Council Inc.
1 Dag Hammarskjold Plaza 9th Fl., New York NY 10017
Phone: 212-339-0500   **Fax:** 212-755-6052
Web: www.popcouncil.org

HISTORICAL FINANCIALS
Company Type: Private - Not-for-Profit

Income Statement
FYE: December 31

	REVENUE ($ mil.)	NET INCOME ($ mil.)	NET PROFIT MARGIN	EMPLOYEES
12/11	64	(23)	—	603
12/10	64	(25)	—	0
12/09	100	6	6.9%	0
12/08	56	(21)	—	0
Annual Growth	**4.4%**	—	—	—

2011 Year-End Financials

Debt ratio: —
Return on equity: (-36.30)%
Cash ($ mil.): 10
Current ratio: 0.50
Long-term debt ($ mil.): —

Dividends
Yield: —
Payout: —
Market value ($ mil.): —

THE CORPORATION OF MERCER UNIVERSITY

Mercer University covers a lot of Georgia with one campus in Macon another in Atlanta and a third in Savannah. The main campus in Macon includes the Walter F. George School of Law (one of the nation's oldest law schools) while The Cecil B. Day Graduate and Professional campus in Atlanta includes schools of theology pharmacy and nursing. Savannah is home to a new four-year M.D. program at the Mercer School of Medicine at Memorial University Medical Center. The university which has a total enrollment of more than 8000 students also has educational centers in Douglas County Henry County and Eastman. Mercer was founded in 1833 by Jesse Mercer a prominent Georgia Baptist.

EXECUTIVES

President, William D. Underwood
SVP Marketing Communications and Chief of Staff, Larry D. Brumley
Administrative Assistant to SVP Marketing Communications, Debra Leahy
Administrative Assistant to President, Vonne Sheffield
Provost, Wallace L. Daniel

THE COUNCIL POPULATION INC

The Population Council is a not-for-profit organization that performs biomedical public health and social science research. The organization focuses on areas such as HIV and AIDS; poverty gender and youth; and reproductive health. Specifically it conducts research on sociological topics like gender inequality population trends and sexuality education; it also assists international governments with policy and program development as they pertain to these issues. The Population Council has more than 15 offices in more than 60 countries around the world. It is typically funded by governments foundations individuals and other organizations. The council was founded in 1952 by John D. Rockefeller III.

EXECUTIVES

Director Poverty Gender and Youth Program, Wendy Baldwin
President and Trustee, Peter J. Donaldson
Chairman, Mark A. Walker
VP and Distinguished Scholar, John Bongaarts
Director International Support, Mar Aguilar
Director Reproductive Health Program, John W. Townsend
VP HIV and AIDS Program, Naomi Rutenberg
VP Poverty Gender and Youth Program, Ann K. Blanc

THE CULINARY INSTITUTE OF AMERICA

At this CIA they work on countertops not counterterrorism. The Culinary Institute of America (CIA) offers bachelor's and associate degrees in Culinary Arts Management and Baking and Pastry Arts Management as well as continuing education conferences travel programs and e-learning. The independent not-for-profit educational organization enrolls some 2700 students and employs more than 125 chef-instructors and other faculty members representing 16 countries. The CIA operates campuses in Hyde Park New York; St. Helena California; and San Antonio Texas. Notable graduates include media personalities Anthony Bourdain and Rocco DiSpirito and Steven Ellis founder of Chipotle Mexican Grill.

The New York campus operates five award-winning student-staffed public restaurants including

St. Andrew's Cafe Ristorante Caterina de' Medici the Escoffier Restaurant American Bounty Restaurant and the Apple Pie Bakery Cafe.

Its California campus is home to 15 acres of Napa Valley vineyards the Rudd Center for Professional Wine Studies Sutter Home Organic Garden Cannard Herb Garden Wine Spectator Greystone Restaurant DeBaun Theater (a demonstration kitchen) and Ken and Grace De Baun Cafe. The San Antonio campus opened in 2008 with a focus on Latin cuisines.

The CIA was founded in 1946 as the New Haven Restaurant Institute a culinary school targeting WWII veterans.

EXECUTIVES

Chairman Emeritus, Fortunato N. (Nick) Valenti, age 64
Treasurer and Trustee, Frank J. Fahrenkopf Jr., age 70
Chairman, William C. Anton, age 71
President, L. Timothy Ryan
SVP Finance and Administration, Charles A. O'Mara
VP Marketing and Strategy, Bruce D. Hillenbrand
VP Human Resources, David Jaskiewicz
VP and Managing Director Greystone and Continuing Education, Mark Erickson
Dean Student Affairs, Alice-Ann Schuster
VP Enrollment Management, Drusilla Blackman
VP Academic Affairs, Peter Rainsford
Associate VP Planning Research and Accreditation, Ann A. Weeks
Media Relations Contact, Stephan Hengst
Registrar, Ted Witryk
Director Admissions, Rachel Birchwood
Director Regional Recruitment, Terri Ann Parks
Manager Communications, Lauren Cunningham
VP Advancement, Nancy D. Harvin
Media Relations Contact, Tyffani Peters
Director Career Services, Chet Koulik
Director Financial Aid, Pat Arcuri
Director Campus Safety, Rich Cullen
Vice Chairman, M. Cameron Mitchell
Secretary and Trustee, Richard Bradley
Trustee, Jon L. Luther, age 69
Trustee, Theodore J. (Ted) Kleisner, age 67
Trustee, Robert L. (Bob) Berenson
Chairman Emeritus, Fortunato N. (Nick) Valenti, age 64
Treasurer and Trustee, Frank J. Fahrenkopf Jr., age 70
Trustee, Melinda R. (Mindy) Rich, age 54
Vice Chairman, M. Cameron Mitchell
Secretary and Trustee, Richard Bradley
Trustee, Fred Carl Jr.
Trustee, Lee A. Cockerell
Trustee, Barry E. Colman
Trustee, Lori Daniel
Trustee, James Doherty
Trustee, John G. Giumarra
Trustee, Burton Hobson
Trustee, Michael Kaufman
Trustee, Takeshi Kohjima
Trustee, Barbara Lawrence
Trustee, Richard Mazer
Trustee, Charles Merinoff II
Trustee, Charlie Palmer
Trustee, Harold Rosser
Trustee, Roy Yamaguchi

LOCATIONS

HQ: The Culinary Institute of America
1946 Campus Dr., Hyde Park NY 12538-1499
Phone: 845-452-9600   **Fax:** 845-451-1067
Web: www.ciachef.edu

HISTORICAL FINANCIALS

Company Type: School

Income Statement

FYE: May 31

	REVENUE ($ mil.)	NET INCOME ($ mil.)	NET PROFIT MARGIN	EMPLOYEES
05/12	141	11	7.8%	810
05/11	129	24	18.8%	0
05/10	124	16	13.0%	0
05/09	123	(24)	—	0
Annual Growth	4.7%	—	—	—

2012 Year-End Financials

Debt ratio: ——
Return on equity: 7.80%
Cash ($ mil.): 11
Current ratio: —
Long-term debt ($ mil.): —
Dividends
Yield: —
Payout: —
Market value ($ mil.): —

THE CUSTOM COMPANIES INC

LOCATIONS

HQ: THE CUSTOM COMPANIES INC
317 W LAKE ST, NORTHLAKE, IL 60164-2433
Phone: 708-338-8888
Web: www.thecustomcompanies.com

HISTORICAL FINANCIALS

Company Type: Private

Income Statement

FYE: December 31

	REVENUE ($ mil.)	NET INCOME ($ mil.)	NET PROFIT MARGIN	EMPLOYEES
12/11	178	6	3.6%	350
12/10	141	1	0.8%	0
12/09	110	0	0.8%	0
12/08	143	1	0.9%	0
Annual Growth	7.6%	71.7%	—	—

2011 Year-End Financials

Debt ratio: ——
Return on equity: 3.60%
Cash ($ mil.): 3
Current ratio: 1.70
Long-term debt ($ mil.): —
Dividends
Yield: —
Payout: —
Market value ($ mil.): —

THE DEWEY CORPORATION

LOCATIONS

HQ: THE DEWEY CORPORATION
5500 HIGHWAY 80 W, JACKSON, MS 39209-3507
Phone: 601-922-8331
Web: www.millert.com

HISTORICAL FINANCIALS

Company Type: Private

Income Statement

FYE: December 31

	REVENUE ($ mil.)	NET INCOME ($ mil.)	NET PROFIT MARGIN	EMPLOYEES
12/11	96	0	0.3%	1,000
12/10	87	0	0.0%	0
12/09	80	(0)	—	0
12/08	99	0	0.4%	0
Annual Growth	(1.1%)	(3.6%)	—	—

2011 Year-End Financials

Debt ratio: ——
Return on equity: 0.30%
Cash ($ mil.): 0
Current ratio: 0.60
Long-term debt ($ mil.): —
Dividends
Yield: —
Payout: —
Market value ($ mil.): —

THE FIRST CHURCH OF CHRIST SCIENTIST IN BOSTON MASSACHUSETTS

LOCATIONS

HQ: THE FIRST CHURCH OF CHRIST SCIENTIST IN BOSTON MASSACHUSETTS
210 MASSACHUSETTS AVE, BOSTON, MA 02115-3012
Phone: 617-450-2000
Web: www.barringtoncs.org

HISTORICAL FINANCIALS

Company Type: Private

Income Statement

FYE: April 30

	REVENUE ($ mil.)	NET INCOME ($ mil.)	NET PROFIT MARGIN	EMPLOYEES
04/11	175	81	46.7%	544
04/08	132	30	22.7%	0
04/07	212	105	49.8%	0
04/06	317	0	0.0%	0
Annual Growth	(18.0%)	7817.0%	—	—

2011 Year-End Financials

Debt ratio: ——
Return on equity: 46.70%
Cash ($ mil.): 15
Current ratio: 0.20
Long-term debt ($ mil.): —
Dividends
Yield: —
Payout: —
Market value ($ mil.): —

THE FIRST DISTRICT ASSOCIATION

LOCATIONS

HQ: THE FIRST DISTRICT ASSOCIATION
101 S SWIFT AVE, LITCHFIELD, MN 55355-2800
Phone: 320-693-3236
Web: www.firstdistrict.com

HISTORICAL FINANCIALS

Company Type: Private

Income Statement

FYE: September 30

	REVENUE ($ mil.)	NET INCOME ($ mil.)	NET PROFIT MARGIN	EMPLOYEES
09/11	476	16	3.5%	150
09/10	391	15	4.0%	0
09/09	327	5	1.8%	0
09/08	494	14	3.0%	0
Annual Growth	(1.2%)	3.9%	—	—

THE FISHEL COMPANY

The Fishel Company reels in revenue by laying out lines. The company (also known as Team Fishel) provides consulting engineering construction management and maintenance services for electric and gas utility and communications infrastructure projects. The aerial and underground utility contractor designs and builds distribution networks for telecommunications cable and broadband television gas transmission and distribution and electric utilities throughout the US. It also counts municipalities state and federal agencies universities commercial building owners financial services companies health care proiders and residential real estate developers among its clients.

Geographic Reach

The Fishel Company is licensed to do business in some two dozen states. It operates from about 25 offices located in Arkansas Arizona California Florida Georgia Kentucky Nevada New Mexico Ohio Oklahoma Pennsylvania Tennessee Texas and Virginia.

Ownership

Kenneth Fishel founded the firm in 1936 as an underground contractor for telephone companies. It is owned by his daughter chairman Diane Fishel Keeler and family.

EXECUTIVES

President and CEO, John E. Phillips
VP and CFO, Paul R. Riewe
VP and General Counsel, Greg R. Grabovac
Vice Chairman, Eric C. Smith
EVP and COO, Randy Blair
VP Midwest Region, Scott Hornberger
VP Western Region, William E. (Bill) Pauley
Chairman, Diane Fishel Keeler
VP and CIO, Ken E. Katz

LOCATIONS

HQ: THE FISHEL COMPANY
1366 DUBLIN RD, COLUMBUS, OH 43215-1093
Phone: 614-274-8100
Web: www.columbusfibernet.com

PRODUCTS/OPERATIONS

Selected Services

Emergency restoration repair & maintenance
Fiber overbuilds
GPS survey
Network installation
Permitting
Project management
Right of way
Site Design
Utility construction

Selected Markets

Commercial industrial advanced logistics
Electric Distribution & Transmission
Financial & health care
Gas distribution & transmission pipeline
Telecom & broadband cable
Wireless backhaul

COMPETITORS

Dycom	MYR Group
EMCOR	Pike Electric
Integrated Electrical Services	Corporation
MasTec	Quanta Services
MDU Construction Services	

HISTORICAL FINANCIALS

Company Type: Private

Income Statement

FYE: December 31

	REVENUE ($ mil.)	NET INCOME ($ mil.)	NET PROFIT MARGIN	EMPLOYEES
12/11	174	7	4.5%	1,400
12/09	162	1	1.1%	0
12/08	182	1	0.6%	0
12/07	188	3	1.8%	0
Annual Growth	(2.5%)	32.0%	—	—

2011 Year-End Financials

Debt ratio: ——
Return on equity: 4.50%
Cash ($ mil.): 2
Current ratio: 0.10
Long-term debt ($ mil.): —
Dividends
  Yield: —
  Payout: —
Market value ($ mil.): —

THE FORD FOUNDATION

As one of the US's largest philanthropic organizations the Ford Foundation can afford to be generous. The foundation offers grants to individuals and institutions around the world that work to meet its goals of strengthening democratic values reducing poverty and injustice promoting international cooperation and advancing human achievement. The Ford Foundation's charitable giving has run the gamut from A (Association for Asian Studies) to Z (Zanzibar International Film Festival). The foundation has an endowment of about $10 billion. Established in 1936 by Edsel Ford whose father founded the Ford Motor Company the foundation

no longer owns stock in the automaker or has ties to the founding family.

Ford Foundation's programs address nine social justice issues including democratic and accountable government freedom of expression access to education economic fairness and opportunity sexuality and reproductive rights sustainable development social justice metropolitan opportunity and human rights.

The foundation is governed by an international board of trustees. It has offices in New York City as well as Beijing; Cairo; Jakarta Indonesia; Johannesburg; Lagos Nigeria; Mexico City; Nairobi Kenya; New Delhi; Rio de Janeiro; and Santiago Chile.

HISTORY

Henry Ford and his son Edsel gave $25000 to establish the Ford Foundation in Michigan in 1936 followed the next year by 250000 shares of nonvoting stock in the Ford Motor Company. The foundation's activities were limited mainly to Michigan until the deaths of Edsel (1943) and Henry (1947) made the foundation the owner of 90% of the automaker's nonvoting stock (catapulting the endowment to $474 million the US's largest).

In 1951 under a new mandate and president (Paul Hoffman former head of the Marshall Plan) the Ford Foundation made broad commitments to the promotion of world peace the strengthening of democracy and the improvement of education. Early education program grants overseen by University of Chicago chancellor Robert Maynard Hutchins ($100 million between 1951 and 1953) helped establish major international programs (e.g. Harvard's Center for International Legal Studies) and the National Merit Scholarships.

Under McCarthyite criticism for its experimental education grants the foundation in 1951 granted $550 million to noncontroversial recipients such as liberal arts colleges and not-for-profit hospitals. Public TV support became a foundation trademark that year when the organization's money set up the Radio and Television Workshop.

The Ford family and the Ford Foundation held sole ownership of the Ford company until 1956 when the company offered shares of its stock to the public. The foundation sold some 22% of its Ford Motor Company shares that year and shed the rest over the next 20-plus years.

The 1950s saw the beginning of international work; begun in Asia and the Middle East (1950) and extended to Africa (1958) and Latin America (1959) the programs focused on education and rural development. The foundation also supported the Population Council and research in high-yield agriculture with The Rockefeller Foundation.

The Ford Foundation targeted innovative approaches to employment and race relations in the early 1960s. McGeorge Bundy (former national security adviser to President John Kennedy) named president of the foundation in 1966 increased the activist trend with grants for direct voter registration; the NAACP; public-interest law centers serving consumer environmental and minority causes; and housing for the poor.

The early 1970s saw support for black colleges and scholarships child care and job training for women but by 1974 inflation weak stock prices and overspending had eroded assets. Programs were cut but continued support for social-justice issues led the conservative Henry Ford II to quit the board in 1976.

Under lawyer Franklin Thomas (named president in 1979) The Ford Foundation established the nation's largest community development support organization Local Initiatives Support. Thomas the first African-American to lead the foundation was a catalyst in a series of meetings between white and black South Africans in the mid-1980s.

Thomas stepped down in 1996 and new president Susan Berresford formerly EVP consolidated the foundation's grant programs into three areas: Asset Building and Community Development; Peace and Social Justice; and Education Media Arts and Culture. In the late 1990s Ford was surpassed by various other foundations and it had to relinquish its 30-year title as the biggest charitable organization in the US.

In 2000 the foundation announced its largest grant ever the 10-year $330 million International Fellowship Program to support graduate students studying in 20 countries.

After the September 11 2001 terrorist attacks the foundation joined other philanthropic organizations in providing disaster relief. It made grants of $10 million in New York and more than $1 million in Washington DC.

Berresford retired in early 2008 after 12 years as president of the foundation. She was succeeded by Luis Ubi?as formerly a director at McKinsey & Company.

EXECUTIVES

VP Education Creativity and Free Expression, Alison R. Bernstein
VP Treasurer and Chief Financial Officer, Nicholas M. Gabriel
EVP Secretary and General Counsel, Barron M. Tenny
VP Secretary and General Counsel, Nancy P. Feller
Chair, Kathryn S. Fuller, age 65
VP Economic Opportunity and Assets, Pablo J. Farias
VP Communications, Marta L. Tellado
Deputy VP Program Management, David B. Chiel
Deputy VP Global Initiative on HIV/AIDS, Jacob A. Gayle
Chair, Irene Y. Hirano Inouye
President and Trustee, Luis A. Ubi?as
VP Democracy Rights and Justice, Maya L. Harris
Chief Media Relations, Fiona Guthrie
Senior Communications Officer, Joseph (Joe) Voeller
VP and Chief Investment Officer, Eric W. Doppstadt, age 53
Trustee, Robert S. (Rob) Kaplan, age 54
Trustee, J. Clifford (Cliff) Hudson, age 57
Trustee, Richard Moe
Trustee, W. Richard (Rick) West Jr.
Trustee, Peter A. Nadosy
Trustee, Afsaneh M. Beschloss
Trustee, Anke A. Ehrhardt
Trustee, Juliet V. Garcia
Trustee, Yolanda Kakabadse
Chair, Irene Y. Hirano Inouye
Trustee, Cecile Richards
President and Trustee, Luis A. Ubi?as
Trustee, Kofi Appenteng
Trustee, Thurgood Marshall Jr.
Trustee, N. R. Narayana Murthy, age 66
Auditors: PricewaterhouseCoopersLLP

LOCATIONS

HQ: Ford Foundation
320 E. 43rd St., New York NY 10017
Phone: 212-573-5000   **Fax:** 212-351-3677
Web: www.fordfound.org

PRODUCTS/OPERATIONS

Selected Core Issues

Democratic and accountable government
Economic fairness
Education opportunity and scholarship
Freedom of expression
Human rights
Metropolitan opportunity
Sexuality and reproductive health rights
Social justice philanthropy
Sustainable development

HISTORICAL FINANCIALS

Company Type: Private - Foundation

Income Statement

FYE: September 30

	REVENUE ($ mil.)	NET INCOME ($ mil.)	NET PROFIT MARGIN	EMPLOYEES
09/11	559	(5)	—	556
09/09	0	0	—	0
09/06	0	0	—	0
09/05	1,008,992	16	—	0
Annual Growth	—	—	—	—

2011 Year-End Financials

Debt ratio: —
Return on equity: (-0.90)%
Cash ($ mil.): 391
Current ratio: —
Long-term debt ($ mil.): —

Dividends
Yield: —
Payout: —
Market value ($ mil.): —

THE FRESH CONNECTION

LOCATIONS

HQ: THE FRESH CONNECTION
914 DEWING AVE, LAFAYETTE, CA 94549-4209
Phone: 925-299-9939
Web: www.thefreshconnection.com

HISTORICAL FINANCIALS

Company Type: Private

Income Statement

FYE: December 31

	REVENUE ($ mil.)	NET INCOME ($ mil.)	NET PROFIT MARGIN	EMPLOYEES
12/11	133	2	1.8%	18
12/10	117	2	2.3%	0
12/09	88	2	2.8%	0
12/07	79	1	1.5%	0
Annual Growth	19.2%	28.3%	—	—

2011 Year-End Financials

Debt ratio: —
Return on equity: 1.80%
Cash ($ mil.): 0
Current ratio: 1.20
Long-term debt ($ mil.): —

Dividends
Yield: —
Payout: —
Market value ($ mil.): —

THE GARDEN CITY CO-OP INC

LOCATIONS

HQ: THE GARDEN CITY CO-OP INC
106 N 6TH ST, GARDEN CITY, KS 67846-5545
Phone: 620-275-6161
Web: www.gccoop.com

HISTORICAL FINANCIALS

Company Type: Private

Income Statement

FYE: August 31

	REVENUE ($ mil.)	NET INCOME ($ mil.)	NET PROFIT MARGIN	EMPLOYEES
08/11	347	6	1.8%	150
08/08	425	13	3.2%	0
08/07	237	5	2.4%	0
08/06	6	0	—	0
Annual Growth	—	3799.5%	—	—

2011 Year-End Financials

Debt ratio: —
Return on equity: 1.80%
Cash ($ mil.): 0
Current ratio: 0.20
Long-term debt ($ mil.): —

Dividends
Yield: —
Payout: —
Market value ($ mil.): —

THE GETTYSBURG HOSPITAL CORPORATION

Gettysburg Hospital serves the here-and-now sick and wounded residents of historic Gettysburg Pennsylvania Adams County and parts of northern Maryland. Specialized services include a maternity center emergency medicine and home health care. The facility is affiliated with nearby York Hospital through the regional WellSpan Health organization. In 2008 Gettysburg Hospital began work on an expansive project to increase ER capacity add new patient floors and build a new maternity center.

EXECUTIVES

VP Public Relations, Maria Royce
President, Kevin H. Mosser
VP Operations, Joseph H. Edgar
VP Patient Care Services, Kristen O'Shea
VP Medical Affairs, Charles Marley

LOCATIONS

HQ: The Gettysburg Hospital Inc.
147 Gettys St., Gettysburg PA 17325-0786
Phone: 717-334-2121   **Fax:** 717-337-4142
Web: www.wellspan.org/AboutUs/gettysburg.htm

COMPETITORS

Hanover Healthcare   Memorial Hospital (PA)

HISTORICAL FINANCIALS
Company Type: Subsidiary

Income Statement
FYE: June 30

	REVENUE ($ mil.)	NET INCOME ($ mil.)	NET PROFIT MARGIN	EMPLOYEES
06/11	136	18	13.7%	800
06/10	126	13	10.6%	0
06/09	114	(14)	—	0
06/08	99	(3)	—	0
Annual Growth	11.3%	—	—	—

2011 Year-End Financials

Debt ratio: ——
Return on equity: 13.70%
Cash ($ mil.): 3
Current ratio: 1.30
Long-term debt ($ mil.): —

Dividends
Yield: —
Payout: —
Market value ($ mil.): —

THE GOOD SAMARITAN HOSPITAL OF LEBANON PENNSYLVANIA

LOCATIONS

HQ: THE GOOD SAMARITAN HOSPITAL OF LEBANON PENNSYLVANIA
4TH AND WALNUT ST, LEBANON, PA 17042
Phone: 717-270-7500

HISTORICAL FINANCIALS
Company Type: Private

Income Statement
FYE: June 30

	REVENUE ($ mil.)	NET INCOME ($ mil.)	NET PROFIT MARGIN	EMPLOYEES
06/11	178	11	6.4%	99
06/10	168	(0)	—	0
06/09	157	0	—	0
Annual Growth	6.7%	—	—	—

2011 Year-End Financials

Debt ratio: ——
Return on equity: 6.40%
Cash ($ mil.): 2
Current ratio: 1.60
Long-term debt ($ mil.): —

Dividends
Yield: —
Payout: —
Market value ($ mil.): —

THE GOOD SAMARITAN HOSPITAL OF MD INC

Good Samaritan Hospital of Maryland provides emergency care and promotes good health in the Baltimore area. The 300-bed hospital operating as MedStar Good Samaritan provides acute medical and specialty services including rehabilitation (50-bed ward) transitional care (30-bed sub-acute ward) orthopedics cancer care cardiology dialysis and women's health as well as serving as a community teaching facility. The hospital founded in 1968 also operates nursing and assisted-living facilities for the elderly and it provides educational seminars diagnostic screening and preventative medical care through its Good Health Center. MedStar Good Samaritan of Maryland is part of the MedStar Health system.

Operations MedStar Good Samaritan has about 370 physicians on its medical staff. It serves about 16000 inpatients and handles some 140000 outpatient visits per year. The hospital's primary specialty centers include spine arthritis and joint replacement clinics.

Financial Performance
MedStar Good Samaritan reported some $327 million in net operating revenues in fiscal 2011. It also had assets of $177 million and stated community benefits (including outreach and charity care) at some $30 million.

Strategy
The hospital is working to provide an increasing variety of specialty services to patients in the Baltimore area. As such in 2012 MedStar Good Samaritan added a wound healing center for the treatment of chronic wounds. The hospital also expanded its community service provisions that year when it expanded its infant and toddler daycare center.

EXECUTIVES

Chairman Department of Medicine, Dana Frank
VP Medical Affairs, Martin L. Binstock
VP Finance, Deana L. Stout
VP Professional Services, Thomas J. Senker
Director Marketing and Communications, Kris Roeder
President, Jeffrey A. Matton
VP Human Resources, Laura E. O'Donnell
VP Patient Care Services Chief Nursing Officer, Shirley Roth
VP Strategic Planning and Business Development, Jennifer Weiss Wilkerson
Media Relations Manager, Debbie Bangledorf
VP Development, Geannine Darby
Chairman Department of Surgery, Dale Buchbinder
President of Medical Staff, Howard Freeland
Chief of Anesthesiology, Michael Sendak
Chairman Emergency Medicine, Kevin Scruggs
Chief of Radiology, Allen Weksberg
Chairman Department of Pathology, Moira Larsen
Chairman Deptartment of Physical Medicine and Rehabilitation, Kenneth Silver
Chairman, Anthony Read
Vice Chairman, Wilmot C. Ball Jr.
Assistant VP Information Services, Janet Decker
Director, Herbert Friedman
Director, Kenneth A. Samet, age 54
Vice Chairman, Wilmot C. Ball Jr.
Director, Charles L. Bauermann
Director, Kay G. Bee
Director, Rt. Hon. Ann Marie Doory
Director, Edmund J. Fick
Director, Sheldon M. Glusman
Director, W. Kenneth Gue
Director, Davis M. Hahn
Director, Rev Lawrence M. Johnson
Director, Jayne H. McGeehan
Director, W. Francis Malooly
Director, Earl Richardon
Director, T. Edgie Russell
Director, Kenneth L. Thompson

Director, James K. Smolev
Director, Jeremy P. Weiner
Auditors: PricewaterhouseCoopersLLP

LOCATIONS

HQ: Good Samaritan Hospital of Maryland Inc.
5601 Loch Raven Blvd., Baltimore MD 21239
Phone: 410-532-8000   **Fax:** 410-532-4599
Web: www.goodsam-md.org

PRODUCTS/OPERATIONS

Selected Services and Divisions

Belvedere Green (senior living)
Burn Reconstruction Center
Cancer Care/Oncology
Cardiology/Heart Care
Diabetes/Endocrinology
Diagnostic Imaging
Ear Nose and Throat
Emergency Services
Gastroenterology
Good Health Center
Kidney Care/Nephrology
MedStar Good Samaritan Nursing Center (senior living)
MedStar Pharmacy
Orthopedics
Pain Management
Pediatrics
Physical Therapy
Plastic Surgery
Primary Care Center
Pulmonary Services
Rehabilitation Services
Renal Dialysis
Rheumatology [Rheumatoid Arthritis/Sjgren's Syndrome]
Senior Living
Sleep Center
Sports Medicine
Stroke Rehabilitation
Surgical Services
Transitional Care
Urology
Vascular Services
Weight Management Good Weighs
Women's Health
Woodbourne Woods (senior living)
Wound Healing Center

COMPETITORS

Adventist HealthCare
Anne Arundel Medical Center
Ascension Health
Bon Secours Health
Catholic Health East
Children' s National Medical Center
Christiana Care
Civista Health
GBMC

Inova
Johns Hopkins Health System
Levindale Hospital
Novant Health
Sentara Healthcare
University of Maryland Medical System
Valley Health
Virginia Hospital Center

HISTORICAL FINANCIALS
Company Type: Subsidiary

Income Statement
FYE: June 30

	REVENUE ($ mil.)	NET INCOME ($ mil.)	NET PROFIT MARGIN	EMPLOYEES
06/11	331	14	4.2%	2,146
06/10	322	10	3.2%	0
06/09	314	0	—	0
06/08	281	(3)	—	0
Annual Growth	5.7%	—	—	—

2011 Year-End Financials

Debt ratio: ——
Return on equity: 4.20%
Cash ($ mil.): 0
Current ratio: 1.30
Long-term debt ($ mil.): ——

Dividends
Yield: —
Payout: —
Market value ($ mil.): —

THE HEALTH CARE AUTHORITY OF CULLMAN COUNTY

LOCATIONS

HQ: THE HEALTH CARE AUTHORITY OF CULLMAN
COUNTY
1912 AL HIGHWAY 157, CULLMAN, AL 35058-0609
Phone: 256-737-2000
Web: www.cullmanregionalmedicalcenter.com

HISTORICAL FINANCIALS

Company Type: Private

Income Statement

	REVENUE ($ mil.)	NET INCOME ($ mil.)	NET PROFIT MARGIN	EMPLOYEES
06/11	95	(2)	—	1,000
06/10	95	3	3.6%	0
06/08	88	(8)	—	0
Annual Growth	3.9%			

FYE: June 30

2011 Year-End Financials

Debt ratio: ——
Return on equity: (-2.40)%
Cash ($ mil.): 3
Current ratio: 1.60
Long-term debt ($ mil.): ——

Dividends
Yield: —
Payout: —
Market value ($ mil.): —

THE HENRY M JACKSON FOUNDATION FOR THE ADVANCEMENT OF MILITARY M

LOCATIONS

HQ: THE HENRY M JACKSON FOUNDATION FOR THE
ADVANCEMENT OF MILITARY M
6720A ROCKLEDGE DR # 100, BETHESDA, MD
20817-1888
Phone: 240-694-2000
Web: www.hjf.org

HISTORICAL FINANCIALS

Company Type: Private

Income Statement

	REVENUE ($ mil.)	NET INCOME ($ mil.)	NET PROFIT MARGIN	EMPLOYEES
09/11	428	16	3.8%	2,200
09/10	402	7	1.9%	0
09/08	268	2	1.0%	0
09/07	0	0	—	0
Annual Growth	—	—	—	—

FYE: September 30

2011 Year-End Financials

Debt ratio: ——
Return on equity: 3.80%
Cash ($ mil.): 129
Current ratio: 0.70
Long-term debt ($ mil.): ——

Dividends
Yield: —
Payout: —
Market value ($ mil.): —

THE HOSPITAL OF CENTRAL CONNETICUT

LOCATIONS

HQ: THE HOSPITAL OF CENTRAL CONNETICUT
50 GRISWOLD ST, NEW BRITAIN, CT 06052-2008
Phone: 860-224-5804

HISTORICAL FINANCIALS

Company Type: Private

Income Statement

	REVENUE ($ mil.)	NET INCOME ($ mil.)	NET PROFIT MARGIN	EMPLOYEES
09/11	260	24	9.2%	2
Annual Growth	—	—	—	—

FYE: September 30

2011 Year-End Financials

Debt ratio: ——
Return on equity: 9.20%
Cash ($ mil.): 20
Current ratio: 0.90
Long-term debt ($ mil.): ——

Dividends
Yield: —
Payout: —
Market value ($ mil.): —

THE JACKSON LABORATORY

The Jackson Laboratory was into genetics before genetics was cool. Founded in 1929 the not-for-profit organization is a leading researcher of human diseases their causes and their potential cures. Much of its research into mammalian genetics is focused on mice which share a similar genetic makeup to humans. In addition to its own research in areas such as cancer immunology and metabolic disease the organization maintains colonies of mice and supplies them under the brand name JAX to other laboratories around the globe. Additionally The Jackson Laboratory offers educational programs —including internships workshops and pre-doctoral programs —for both current and future scientists.

Geographic Reach

The company has locations in Sacramento California; Farmington Connecticut; and Bar Harbor Maine.

Financial Performance

The Jackson Laboratory receives operating revenue from public sector support in the form of federal grants private sector support in the form of private foundation grants philanthropic contributions and resource revenue in the form of cost and fees collected for JAX Mice & Services its service for supplying mice models used for research. The organization's operating revenue increased by 12% in 2011 over 2010 due to a 8% spike in government support and a 14% uptick in revenue from JAX Mice & Services.

Strategy

The Jackson Laboratory in 2012 finished its purchase of the former Lowe's building in Ellsworth Maine following a strategy of Ellsworth expansion and also launched a $27 million expansion of its JAX West facility in Sacramento.

EXECUTIVES

Treasurer, Daniel R. (Dan) Tishman, age 56
Chairman, Donald A. (Don) Stern
President and CEO, Richard P. (Rick) Woychik, age 59
Secretary, William Rudolf
Director Scientific Program Development, Barbara J. Tennent
VP and COO, Charles E. (Chuck) Hewett
Director Laboratory Animal Health Services, Peggy J. Danneman
Director Education Office, Jon Geiger
Associate Director and Chair for Research, Robert Braun
Chairman, Brian Wrueble
Director Genetic Resources and Senior Research Scientist, Leah Rae Donahue
VP Advancement and External Relations, Michael E. Hyde
CFO, Linda Jensen
VP Training Education and External Scientific Collaborations;, Barbara B. Knowles
Senior Director Scientific Services, Valerie Scott
President and CEO, Edison Liu
Chairman, Leo A. Holt

LOCATIONS

HQ: THE JACKSON LABORATORY
600 MAIN ST, BAR HARBOR, ME 04609-1500
Phone: 207-288-6051
Web: www.jax.org

COMPETITORS

Caliper Life Sciences
Charles River Laboratories
Deltagen
Harlan Laboratories
Howard Hughes Medical Institute
Taconic Farms
Whitehead Institute for Biomedical Research

HISTORICAL FINANCIALS
Company Type: Private - Not-for-Profit

Income Statement
FYE: May 31

	REVENUE ($ mil.)	NET INCOME ($ mil.)	NET PROFIT MARGIN	EMPLOYEES
05/11	231	49	21.3%	1,300
05/10	200	29	14.9%	0
05/09	166	(25)	—	0
05/08	160	(6)	—	0
Annual Growth	13.0%	—	—	—

2011 Year-End Financials

Debt ratio: ——
Return on equity: 21.30%
Cash ($ mil.): 99
Current ratio: 1.00
Long-term debt ($ mil.): ——

Dividends
Yield: —
Payout: —
Market value ($ mil.): —

THE JEWISH BOARD OF FAMILY AND CHILDREN'S SERVICES INC

LOCATIONS

HQ: THE JEWISH BOARD OF FAMILY AND
CHILDREN' S SERVICES INC
135 W 50TH ST FL 6, NEW YORK, NY 10020-1201
Phone: 212-582-9100
Web: www.jbfcs.org

HISTORICAL FINANCIALS
Company Type: Private

Income Statement
FYE: June 30

	REVENUE ($ mil.)	NET INCOME ($ mil.)	NET PROFIT MARGIN	EMPLOYEES
06/11	170	2	1.3%	2,000
06/10	156	2	1.5%	0
06/09	191	0	—	0
06/08	150	2	1.7%	0
Annual Growth	4.2%	(4.8%)	—	—

2011 Year-End Financials

Debt ratio: ——
Return on equity: 1.30%
Cash ($ mil.): 6
Current ratio: 0.50
Long-term debt ($ mil.): ——

Dividends
Yield: —
Payout: —
Market value ($ mil.): —

THE JEWISH FEDERATIONS OF NORTH AMERICA INC

From supporting food banks in the US to helping emigres fleeing Ethiopia for Israel The Jewish Federations of North America (formerly the United Jewish Communities) works to better Jewish life across the globe. One of North America's leading not-for-profit organizations the JFNA represents more than 150 Jewish federations and about 400 independent Jewish communities across the continent. The federation raises and distributes more than $3.5 billion annually for social welfare social services and educational needs in its effort to support Israel and Jews worldwide. The organization changed its name from United Jewish Communities to The Jewish Federations of North America in 2009.

The name change was adopted to project a stronger continental brand and market position for the Federation system.

EXECUTIVES

Secretary, Michael I. Lebovitz, age 48
SVP Operations, Robert Hyman
SVP Communications, Gail Hyman
Chair Financial Resources Development Pillar United Jewish Communities, S. Stephen Selig III
SVP Federation Services, Ron B. Meier
Director Human Resources, Gloria Nilsen
Chairman Executive Committee, Kathy E. Manning
SVP Campaign and Financial Resource Development, Victoria Agron
VP Public Policy UJC Washington, Diana Aviv
SVP Research and Development, Robert Hyfler
VP Planning and Special Projects, Richard Jacobs
VP Israel and Overseas, Doron Krakow
SVP and Director General UJC Israel, Nachman Shai
VP Instutional Advancement, Yitzchak Shavit
VP UJC Consulting Services, Barry Swartz
VP Jewish Renaissance and Renewal, Sheldon Zimmerman
President and CEO, Howard Rieger
Chairman, Joseph S. Kanfer
Treasurer, Michael Gelman
Chair Israel and Overseas Pillar, Arlene Kaufman
Chair Jewish Renaissance and Renewal Pillar, Marion Blumenthal
CEO United Jewish Federation of San Diego County (UJFSD), Steven J. Morris

LOCATIONS

HQ: The Jewish Federations of North America Inc.
25 Broadway Ste. 1700, New York NY 10004-1010
Phone: 212-284-6500   **Fax:** 212-284-6853
Web: www.jewishfederations.org

PRODUCTS/OPERATIONS

2008 Expenses

	$ mil.	% of total
Program services in Israel	301	74
Other programs	104	26
Total	**405**	**100**

HISTORICAL FINANCIALS
Company Type: Private - Not-for-Profit

Income Statement
FYE: June 30

	REVENUE ($ mil.)	NET INCOME ($ mil.)	NET PROFIT MARGIN	EMPLOYEES
06/11	47	(0)	—	200
06/10	43	1	2.8%	0
06/09	267	(61)	—	0
06/08	360	(14)	—	0
Annual Growth	(49.2%)	—	—	—

2011 Year-End Financials

Debt ratio: ——
Return on equity: (-1.20)%
Cash ($ mil.): 12
Current ratio: 0.60
Long-term debt ($ mil.): ——

Dividends
Yield: —
Payout: —
Market value ($ mil.): —

THE JUDGE GROUP INC

If your business requires staffing technology consulting or training services The Judge Group will be predisposed to render a verdict in your favor. The company offers temporary and permanent employee placement services in a wide variety of service and manufacturing sectors but specializes in technology staffing. The company's technology consulting services address such areas as enterprise content management and strategy. Through its Berkeley Training unit the company offers training for IT-related and other professional functions. The Judge Group operates from a network of more than 25 offices throughout the US and has locations in Asia and Canada. Martin Judge founded the company in 1970.

Strategy

The company's growth strategy revolves around the opening of offices in select markets and by entering alliances with other human resources services firms. In 2011 it launched offices in Houston Milwaukee and Phoenix. The following year it established an office in the important metropolitan area of Baltimore.

The Judge Group in 2010 took an important step in expanding its international reach inside a major emerging market when it launched a joint venture with Orchestrall Group Ltd. The endeavor Judge China provides clients with consulting expertise for accessing markets in the most populous country in the world through offices in Beijing and Shanghai.

EXECUTIVES

COO, Katy A. Wiercinski
Controller, John M. Work
EVP, Michael A. Dunn, $220,733 total compensation
CFO, Robert G. Alessandrini, $137,308 total compensation
CEO, Martin E. Judge Jr., $588,665 total compensation
General Counsel, Amy E. Feldman
President and COO Judge International, Raj Singh
President, Gary R. Morris
CIO and VP Training and Development, Kenneth F. Krieger
Chief Sales Officer, Brian T. Anderson
President Berkeley Training, Peter Pedone
Director Strategic Account Management, Janet Harbour

Director Technical Staffing Florida, Waine D. Cardinal
President Judge Audio Visual Solutions, James D. Miner
Managing Director Strategy, Scott O. Wilson
President Judge Consulting Group, Michael F. Ferreri
Head Accounting and Finance New York, Tim Lege
Director Technical Staffing Chicago, Robert Ruf
VP Recruiting Operations D.C. Metro, Eileen Lombardo
Director National Recruiting Center, Frank Santoro
VP Sales San Francisco Bay, Rick Iversen
Director DC Metro, Paul Brown
Director West Coast Operations, Justin Harless
VP Recruiting, Steven V. Joerg
Director IT Staffing Minnesota, Scott Labat
Auditors: McGladreyLLP

LOCATIONS

HQ: The Judge Group Inc.
300 Conshohocken State Rd. Ste. 300, West Conshohocken PA 19428-2949
Phone: 610-667-7700   **Fax:** 610-667-1058
Web: www.judge.com

PRODUCTS/OPERATIONS

Selected Services

Corporate training
  Custom content development
  Information technology training
  Professional development
  Project staffing and logistics
Enterprise-wide staffing
  Financial services
  Food/beverage
  Government
  Health care
  Insurance
  Manufacturing
  Pharmaceutical
  Retail/supermarkets
  Technology
  Utilities/telecom
  Wholesale distribution
Technology consulting
  Application design and development
  Audio visual design and implementation
  E-discovery and compliance
  Enterprise content management
  Research validation and compliance
  SAP implementation services
  Technology strategy and architecture

COMPETITORS

Accenture	Kelly Services
Adecco	Kenexa
Aquent	Kforce
Butler America	ManpowerGroup
CDI	RCM Technologies
IBM Global Services	Taleo
Keane	Unisys

HISTORICAL FINANCIALS

Company Type: Private

Income Statement

FYE: September 30

	REVENUE ($ mil.)	NET INCOME ($ mil.)	NET PROFIT MARGIN	EMPLOYEES
09/11	222	2	1.2%	570
09/08	188	2	1.5%	0
09/07	166	3	2.1%	0
09/06	129	2	2.3%	0
Annual Growth	19.8%	(4.5%)	—	—

2011 Year-End Financials

Debt ratio: ——
Return on equity: 1.20%
Cash ($ mil.): 0
Current ratio: 2.50
Long-term debt ($ mil.): ——
Dividends
  Yield: ——
  Payout: ——
Market value ($ mil.): ——

THE KLEINFELDER GROUP INC

The Kleinfelder Group isn't afraid to get its hands dirty. Since its start as a materials testing lab in 1961 the company has expanded to become one of the largest engineering consulting and design groups in the US. Kleinfelder's operating subsidiaries offer soils and materials testing geotechnical engineering construction management and environmental services. With about 50 domestic offices and locations in Australia and Guam the group targets the energy transportation water commercial/industrial government and education markets; projects run the gamut from building underground parking garages to establishing wind farms. Jim Kleinfelder who retired in 1993 founded the employee-owned company.

Geographic Reach

Kleinfelder has operations in the US and Calgary Canada. It opened offices in Australia and Guam in 2010.

Strategy

Kleinfelder is expanding at home and abroad though organic growth and frequent acquisitions of environmental services firms. It entered Canada in 2012 with an office in Calgary and continued its expansion in Australia (begun in 2010) with a pair of acquisitions there.

In 2011 the firm introduced a program to certify greenhouse gas emissions to help clients remain compliant in clean air regulations. Two years earlier it launched a nuclear services division to serve the uranium mining and milling power generation and spent-fuel storage sectors.

Mergers and Acquisitions

In 2012 Kleinfelder acquired two Australian environmental services firms: Ecobiological Group and Alliance Environmental Engineering and Consulting Pty Ltd.. The twin purchases strengthen Kleinfelder's position in the retail petroleum assessment and remediation market there and help the company grow its multinational client list throughout Australia and the Asia-Pacific Region.

Closer to home Kleinfelder in 2013 purchased Simon Wong Engineering (SWE) a San Diego-based firm providing project management structural and bridge engineering services construction management and inspection services and public relations support to the transportation and water markets in California to strengthen its resources to serve its global clients. The SWE purchase followed two domestic acquisitions: Omni Environmental in Princeton New Jersey and Houston-based Corrigan Consulting in 2012. In 2011 it purchased InSite Environmental in Stockton California.

Ownership

The Kleinfelder Group is owned by its employees.

EXECUTIVES

IT Director, Ed Rothenbaum
Director Ports and Harbors Practice, Bartlett (Bart) Patton
Chief Administrative Officer, Russell (Russ) Carey
SVP Sales and Marketing, Larry Peterson
VP Human Resources, Denise Howe
Chief Strategy Officer, Kevin E. Pottmeyer
President and CEO, William C. (Bill) Siegel
VP Corporate Marketing and Communications, Terry Reynolds
VP and CFO, John M. Pilkington
CTO, Russell E. (Russ) Erbes
Director Commercial/Industrial, Fred Schafer
Director Water Resources Program, Keith Ferguson
Manager Industrial Clients Program, Zene Bliss
Energy Program, Andy Flynn
Federal Program, Jeff Davis
SVP and Manager Energy Division, Michael Kesler
VP and General Counsel, Chuck Alpert

LOCATIONS

HQ: The Kleinfelder Group Inc.
5015 Shoreham Place, San Diego CA 92122
Phone: 858-320-2000   **Fax:** 858-320-2001
Web: www.kleinfelder.com

PRODUCTS/OPERATIONS

Selected Acquisitions

2013
  Simon Wong Engineering (San Diego CA; project management)
2012
  Alliance Environmental Engineering & Consulting Pty Ltd. (St. Kilda Victoria Australia; environmental engineering)
  Ecobiological Group (New South Wales Australia; ecological and brushfire consultancy)
  Omni Environmental (Princeton NJ; environmental consulting)
  Corrigan Consulting Inc. (Houston TX; environmental and professional engineering services)

Selected Services

Architecture
Chemical data management
Construction testing
Dewatering and infiltration
Due diligence
Ecological risk
Engineering geology
Environmental and process engineering design
Geotechnical engineering
GIS
Hydraulics
Hydrogeology
Materials laboratory testing
Numerical earthquake engineering
Pavement engineering
Regulatory compliance
Retaining walls
Risk assessment
Site development
Solid waste
Seismic earthquake engineering
Structural engineering
Tunneling and deep foundation engineering
Water/wastewater engineering

COMPETITORS

AECOM	Ninyo & Moore
ATC Associates	Precision Assessment
Cadmus Group	Technology
CH2M HILL	Professional Service
Dudek	Industries
Geocon Group	RECON Environmental
HNTB Companies	SCS Tracer
Holguin Fahan &	Environmental

Associates
Jacobs Engineering
LCS Constructors
Leighton Group

URS
USA Environmental
Willdan Geotechnical

HISTORICAL FINANCIALS
Company Type: Private

Income Statement

FYE: March 31

	REVENUE ($ mil.)	NET INCOME ($ mil.)	NET PROFIT MARGIN	EMPLOYEES
03/12	216	5	2.5%	1,522
03/11	222	8	3.7%	0
03/10	221	7	3.2%	0
03/09	230	9	4.0%	0
Annual Growth	(2.0%)	(16.8%)	—	—

2012 Year-End Financials

Debt ratio: ——
Return on equity: 2.50%
Cash ($ mil.): 6
Current ratio: 1.00
Long-term debt ($ mil.): ——

Dividends
Yield: —
Payout: —
Market value ($ mil.): —

THE KUIKEN BROTHERS COMPANY

LOCATIONS

HQ: THE KUIKEN BROTHERS COMPANY
6-02 FAIR LAWN AVE, FAIR LAWN, NJ 07410-1219
Phone: 201-796-2082
Web: www.kuikenbrothers.com

HISTORICAL FINANCIALS
Company Type: Private

Income Statement

FYE: December 31

	REVENUE ($ mil.)	NET INCOME ($ mil.)	NET PROFIT MARGIN	EMPLOYEES
12/11	100	2	2.2%	240
12/10	96	2	3.0%	0
12/09	90	4	4.8%	0
12/08	111	6	5.6%	0
Annual Growth	(3.3%)	(29.5%)	—	—

2011 Year-End Financials

Debt ratio: ——
Return on equity: 2.20%
Cash ($ mil.): 5
Current ratio: 2.40
Long-term debt ($ mil.): ——

Dividends
Yield: —
Payout: —
Market value ($ mil.): —

THE LUTHERAN UNIVERSITY ASSOCIATION INC

LOCATIONS

HQ: THE LUTHERAN UNIVERSITY ASSOCIATION INC
1700 CHAPEL DR, VALPARAISO, IN 46383-4520
Phone: 219-464-5000
Web: www.valpo.edu

HISTORICAL FINANCIALS
Company Type: Private

Income Statement

FYE: June 30

	REVENUE ($ mil.)	NET INCOME ($ mil.)	NET PROFIT MARGIN	EMPLOYEES
06/12	119	(0)	—	1,000
06/11	113	32	28.2%	0
06/10	105	(3)	—	0
06/09	107	(67)	—	0
Annual Growth	3.6%	—	—	—

2012 Year-End Financials

Debt ratio: ——
Return on equity: (-0.30)%
Cash ($ mil.): 11
Current ratio: ——
Long-term debt ($ mil.): ——

Dividends
Yield: —
Payout: —
Market value ($ mil.): —

THE MARFO COMPANY

LOCATIONS

HQ: THE MARFO COMPANY
799 N HAGUE AVE, COLUMBUS, OH 43204-1424
Phone: 614-276-3352

HISTORICAL FINANCIALS
Company Type: Private

Income Statement

FYE: December 31

	REVENUE ($ mil.)	NET INCOME ($ mil.)	NET PROFIT MARGIN	EMPLOYEES
12/11	85	0	—	120
12/10	85	0	—	0
12/09	85	0	—	0
12/08	85	0	—	0
Annual Growth	(0.0%)	—	—	—

2011 Year-End Financials

Debt ratio: ——
Return on equity: —
Cash ($ mil.): 1
Current ratio: 1.70
Long-term debt ($ mil.): ——

Dividends
Yield: —
Payout: —
Market value ($ mil.): —

THE MARYLAND INSTITUTE

LOCATIONS

HQ: THE MARYLAND INSTITUTE
1300 W MOUNT ROYAL AVE, BALTIMORE, MD 21217-4134
Phone: 410-669-9200
Web: www.mica.edu

HISTORICAL FINANCIALS
Company Type: Private

Income Statement

FYE: May 31

	REVENUE ($ mil.)	NET INCOME ($ mil.)	NET PROFIT MARGIN	EMPLOYEES
05/11	101	13	13.3%	400
05/10	83	2	2.7%	0
05/09	83	0	—	0
05/06	61	15	25.0%	0
Annual Growth	18.4%	(4.2%)	—	—

2011 Year-End Financials

Debt ratio: ——
Return on equity: 13.30%
Cash ($ mil.): 3
Current ratio: —
Long-term debt ($ mil.): ——

Dividends
Yield: —
Payout: —
Market value ($ mil.): —

THE MAY INSTITUTE INC

LOCATIONS

HQ: THE MAY INSTITUTE INC
41 PACELLA PARK DR, RANDOLPH, MA 02368-1755
Phone: 781-440-0400
Web: www.positiveschools.org

HISTORICAL FINANCIALS
Company Type: Private

Income Statement

FYE: June 30

	REVENUE ($ mil.)	NET INCOME ($ mil.)	NET PROFIT MARGIN	EMPLOYEES
06/11	104	2	2.6%	2,000
06/10	104	2	2.5%	0
06/09	100	0	—	0
06/08	93	0	0.5%	0
Annual Growth	3.7%	84.8%	—	—

2011 Year-End Financials

Debt ratio: ——
Return on equity: 2.60%
Cash ($ mil.): 6
Current ratio: 0.40
Long-term debt ($ mil.): ——

Dividends
Yield: —
Payout: —
Market value ($ mil.): —

THE MEDICAL CENTER INC

LOCATIONS

HQ: THE MEDICAL CENTER INC
710 CENTER ST, COLUMBUS, GA 31901-1547
Phone: 706-571-1000
Web: www.columbusregional.com

HISTORICAL FINANCIALS

Company Type: Private

Income Statement

FYE: June 30

	REVENUE ($ mil.)	NET INCOME ($ mil.)	NET PROFIT MARGIN	EMPLOYEES
06/11	329	11	3.4%	1,500
06/10	316	15	4.9%	0
06/08	283	12	4.5%	0
06/05	0	0	—	0
Annual Growth	—	—	—	—

2011 Year-End Financials

Debt ratio: ——
Return on equity: 3.40%
Cash ($ mil.): 44
Current ratio: 4.30
Long-term debt ($ mil.): ——

Dividends
Yield: —
Payout: —
Market value ($ mil.): —

THE MEDICAL COLLEGE OF WISCONSIN INC

LOCATIONS

HQ: THE MEDICAL COLLEGE OF WISCONSIN INC
8701 W WATERTOWN PLANK RD, MILWAUKEE, WI
53226-3548
Phone: 414-456-8296

HISTORICAL FINANCIALS

Company Type: Private

Income Statement

FYE: June 30

	REVENUE ($ mil.)	NET INCOME ($ mil.)	NET PROFIT MARGIN	EMPLOYEES
06/11	936	63	6.8%	4,700
06/10	839	20	2.5%	0
06/09	751	0	—	0
06/08	716	(75)	—	0
Annual Growth	9.3%	—	—	—

2011 Year-End Financials

Debt ratio: ——
Return on equity: 6.80%
Cash ($ mil.): 85
Current ratio: ——
Long-term debt ($ mil.): ——

Dividends
Yield: —
Payout: —
Market value ($ mil.): —

THE MEMORIAL HOSPITAL

The Memorial Hospital known as Memorial Hospital of Rhode Island brings a reminder of good health to the residents of the Blackstone Valley which encompasses parts of southern Massachusetts and northern Rhode Island. Founded in 1901 the not-for-profit hospital has some 300 beds and offers general medical and surgical care as well as specialty services in areas such as oncology cardiovascular care orthopedics rehabilitation women's health and home health care. It is also a teaching institution for Brown University's Warren Alpert Medical School. Through a handful of satellite clinics located throughout its service area Memorial Hospital of Rhode Island provides primary and preventive care.

Memorial Hospital of Rhode Island has an affiliation with the Brigham and Women's Hospital in Boston through which the facilities collaborate on emergency medicine services and quality improvement initiatives. The hospitals expanded the agreement to cover cardiovascular care in 2011.

Memorial Hospital of Rhode Island reported some $164 million in total patient revenues in 2011 down slightly from about $167 million in 2010.

EXECUTIVES

President CEO and Trustee, Francis R. Dietz
VP Strategic Planning and Business Development, Thomas J. Gough
Director Public Relations, Louise Paiva
SVP Administration, Elizabeth Girard
SVP Operations, Shelley MacDonald
SVP Financial Services, Michael J. Ryan
VP External Affairs, Marie K. Kessel
VP Environmental and Support Services, Thomas L. Ross
VP Professional Practice, Rosemary Wood
Chairman, Alfred P. Degen
Secretary and Trustee, Edna S. Poulin
Vice Chairman, Robert P. Andrade
Assistant Treasurer and Trustee, William M. Kapos
Public Relations and Marketing Specialist, Catherine (Cathy) Coffin
Vice Chairman, William J. Hunt
Assistant Secretary and Trustee, Robert K. MacKenzie
VP Human Resources, Lisa D. Pratt
President CEO and Trustee, Francis R. Dietz
Trustee, Gary E. Furtado
Secretary and Trustee, Edna S. Poulin
Vice Chairman, Robert P. Andrade
Assistant Treasurer and Trustee, William M. Kapos
Vice Chairman, William J. Hunt
Assistant Secretary and Trustee, Robert K. MacKenzie
Trustee, Donna Brady
Trustee, Arthur J. DeBlois III
Trustee, Rocco DeSimone Jr.
Trustee, Paul Keating
Trustee, Paul Mooney
Trustee, John J. Patridge
Trustee, Virginia Roberts
Trustee, Karl Sherry
Trustee, Kenneth W. Washburn
Trustee, Laurie White
Auditors: Deloitte&ToucheLLP

LOCATIONS

HQ: The Memorial Hospital
111 Brewster St., Pawtucket RI 02860
Phone: 401-729-2000 **Fax:** 401-722-0198
Web: www.mhri.org

COMPETITORS

Baystate Health
Care New England
Catholic Health East
Day Kimball Hospital
Kent Hospital
Lifespan Corporation
Partners HealthCare
Roger Williams Medical Center

Southcoast Health
Southcoast Hospitals Group
Sturdy Memorial
Yale New Haven Health Services Corporation

HISTORICAL FINANCIALS

Company Type: Private - Not-for-Profit

Income Statement

FYE: September 30

	REVENUE ($ mil.)	NET INCOME ($ mil.)	NET PROFIT MARGIN	EMPLOYEES
09/11	181	(4)	—	1,400
09/10	182	(1)	—	0
09/09	171	(6)	—	0
09/08	175	(1)	—	0
Annual Growth	1.0%	—	—	—

2011 Year-End Financials

Debt ratio: ——
Return on equity: (-2.80)%
Cash ($ mil.): 0
Current ratio: 1.60
Long-term debt ($ mil.): ——

Dividends
Yield: —
Payout: —
Market value ($ mil.): —

THE METHODIST HOSPITAL

Methodist Hospital provides care for Houstonians. The not-for-profit organization also known as Methodist Hospital System owns and operates several Houston-area medical centers including Methodist Hospital in Houston's Texas Medical Center complex and the suburban San Jacinto Methodist Methodist Sugar Land Methodist West Houston and Methodist Willowbrook hospitals. The system's flagship Methodist Hospital has 950 beds and is known for innovations in urology and neurosurgery among other specialties. The system also manages the Methodist Hospital Physician Organization.

Geographic Reach
The hospital system consists of five acute-care locations in the Houston Texas metropolitan area. The network added its fifth hospital in late 2010 when it completed construction of a new 200 bed community hospital on Houston's west side named Methodist West Houston Hospital.

Through its Methodist International unit the system serves international patients and provides consulting services worldwide.

Operations
The Methodist Hospital System's five hospitals together have about 1700 beds.

In addition the health system operates the Methodist Hospital Research Institute which conducts medical and clinical research. The research organization is based at the main Methodist Hospital location and works in partnership with the hospital's physicians to improve treatments for medical conditions. Construction of a new larger 12-story building to house the Research Institute was completed and opened in 2010.

The hospital has educational and research affiliations with Cornell University's Weil Cornell Medical College the New York-Presbyterian Hospital University of Houston Rice University Baylor College of Medicine and other organizations.

Strategy

To widen its capacity for medical care Methodist Hospital completed construction of a new 26-story Methodist Outpatient Center in mid-2010; the center is located near the flagship Methodist Hospital in Houston's Texas Medical Center complex.

The company also completed major expansion projects at its Sugar Land and Willowbrook hospitals in 2009 and 2010 more than doubling the capacity at both facilities. Other projects have included a new imaging and women's diagnostic center in the Houston's Upper Kirby neighborhood which opened in 2009.

EXECUTIVES

Assistant Secretary, Robert K. Moses Jr., age 70
President Methodist Willowbrook Hospital, Andy Cochrane
Chairman Neurology Methodist Hospital Neurological Institute, Stanley H. Appel
SVP and Chief Nursing Executive The Methodist Hospital, Ann Scanlon McGinity
President and CEO The Methodist Hospital System, Marc L. Boom
Director Public Relations, Stefanie Asin
SVP Human Resources, Lauren Rykert
CEO Methodist Sugar Land Hospital, Chris Siebenaler
Chairman, Ewing Werlein Jr.
VP Operations The Methodist Hospital, Karin Larson-Pollock
Chairman of Neurosurgery and Director Methodist Neurological Institute, Robert Grossman
EVP The Methodist Hospital, Roberta Schwartz
Director Eddy Scurlock Stroke Center Methodist Neurological Institute, David Chiu
President-elect Medical Staff, Wade Rosenberg
Secretary, D. Gibson Walton
Assistant Secretary, Emily A. Crosswell
Treasurer, Carlton E. Baucum
CEO San Jacinto Methodist Hospital, Donna Gares
Director Research Institute, Michael W. (Mike) Lieberman
VP Human Resources, Carole Hackett
VP Operations, Vicki Brownewell
VP Operations, Katherine Walsh
VP Operations, Bryan Croft
VP Operations, Clare Rose
VP Operations, Stephen Spielman
VP Operations, David Bernard
VP Research Institute, Ed Jones
EVP and CFO, Kevin Burns
CEO Methodist Willowbrook Hospital, Beryl Ramsey
CEO Research Institute, Mauro Ferrari
President Medical Staff, Victor Fainstein
CEO Methodist West Houston Hospital, Wayne Voss
Director, Morrie K. Abramson
Director, John F. Bookout III, age 58
Director, Lawrence W. (Larry) Kellner, age 53
Director, Gary W. Edwards
Assistant Secretary, Robert K. Moses Jr., age 70

Director, Gregory V. (Greg) Nelson
President-elect Medical Staff, Wade Rosenberg
Secretary, D. Gibson Walton
Assistant Secretary, Emily A. Crosswell
Treasurer, Carlton E. Baucum
Director, W. Earl Bledsoe
Director, Mary A. Daffin
Director, Connie M. Dyer
Director, James A. Elkins III
Director, Rev Richard W. Goodrich
Director, Robert E. Jackson
Director, Vidal G. Martinez
Director, Thomas J. Pace III
Director, Janice Riggle Huie
Director, Pliny C. Smith
Director, Joseph C. (Rusty) Walter III
Director, Elizabeth B. Wareing
Director, Stephen P. Wende
Director, Sandra Gayle Wright

LOCATIONS

HQ: THE METHODIST HOSPITAL
6565 FANNIN ST, HOUSTON, TX 77030-2707
Phone: 713-790-3311

PRODUCTS/OPERATIONS

Selected Houston-Area Hospitals
Methodist Hospital - Texas Medical Center (Houston)
Methodist Sugar Land Hospital
Methodist Willowbrook Hospital (Houston)
Methodist West Houston Hospital (Houston)
San Jacinto Methodist Hospital (Baytown)

COMPETITORS

CHRISTUS Health	St. Luke's Episcopal
Dynacq Healthcare	Health System
HCA	Tenet Healthcare
Johns Hopkins Medicine	Texas Children's
Mayo Clinic	Hospital
MD Anderson Cancer	Texas Health Resources
Center	Tomball Regional
Memorial Hermann	Universal Health
Healthcare	Services

HISTORICAL FINANCIALS

Company Type: Private - Not-for-Profit

Income Statement

FYE: December 31

	REVENUE ($ mil.)	NET INCOME ($ mil.)	NET PROFIT MARGIN	EMPLOYEES
12/11	2,284	101	4.4%	14,000
12/10	2,115	354	16.8%	0
12/09	2,086	655	31.4%	0
12/08	1,839	(232)	—	0
Annual Growth	7.5%	—	—	—

2011 Year-End Financials

Debt ratio: ——
Return on equity: 4.40%
Cash ($ mil.): 49
Current ratio: 0.20
Long-term debt ($ mil.): —

Dividends
Yield: —
Payout: —
Market value ($ mil.): —

THE MIDDLE TENNESSEE ELECTRIC MEMBERSHIP CORPORATION

Middle Tennessee Electric Membership Corporation's service territory is smack dab in the middle of Tennessee. The utility company distributes electricity to more than 185900 residential and business customers (member/owners) in four counties (Cannon Rutherford Williamson and Wilson) via more than 10390 miles of power lines connected to more than 30 electric distribution substations. Middle Tennessee Electric purchases its power supply from the Tennessee Valley Authority. The corporation is Tennessee's largest electric cooperative and the sixth largest in the US.

According to a US Census report three of Tennessee's five fastest growing counties (Rutherford Williamson and Wilson) are in Middle Tennessee Electric's service area.

To harness green energy as a way to limit fossil fuel power sources and reduce carbon emission the utility company is installing solar panels for customers. In 2012 the company completed a 850-panel solar field next to the City of Franklin's water plant. That year Middle Tennessee Electric had 70 solar projects operating across its service area and 30 more in the planning stages.

Formed in 1936 Middle Tennessee Electric's service area includes three of Tennessee's top five fastest-growing cities —LaVergne Smyrna and Franklin.

EXECUTIVES

Chairman, Gordon Bone
President, Frank Jennings
VP Engineering, Tom Suggs
VP Marketing and Communications, Chris Jones
VP Operations, Jeff Gill
VP Information Systems, John Florida
VP Human Resources and Corporate Services, Shannon Kaprive
VP Finance, Bernie Steen
Manager Franklin District, Dan Florida
Manager Lebanon District, Ken Throneberry
Manager Murfreesboro and Woodbury Districts, Ron Washington
Secretary Treasurer and Director, Will Jordan
Vice Chairman, Charlie Bowman
Director, Steve Seger
Director, Gloria O'Steen
Director, Bill Giddens
Director, David Lee
Director, Mike Woods
Secretary Treasurer and Director, Will Jordan
Vice Chairman, Charlie Bowman
Director, Luther Lenning
Director, Dan Smith
Director, Jim Mills

LOCATIONS

HQ: Middle Tennessee Electric Membership Corporation
555 New Salem Rd., Murfreesboro TN 37129
Phone: 615-890-9762   **Fax:** 615-494-1012
Web: www.mtemc.com

HISTORICAL FINANCIALS

Company Type: Private - Cooperative

Income Statement

FYE: June 30

	REVENUE ($ mil.)	NET INCOME ($ mil.)	NET PROFIT MARGIN	EMPLOYEES
06/12	510	19	3.8%	375
06/11*	525	31	6.0%	0
03/10	351	18	5.3%	0
06/08	426	18	4.4%	0
Annual Growth	6.2%	0.8%	—	—

*Fiscal year change

2012 Year-End Financials

Debt ratio: —
Return on equity: 3.80%
Cash ($ mil.): 57
Current ratio: 1.30
Long-term debt ($ mil.): —
Dividends
Yield: —
Payout: —
Market value ($ mil.): —

THE MITRE CORPORATION

Politicians try to engineer a better government but MITRE governs the country's best engineering. A private not-for-profit organization MITRE Corporation provides consulting engineering and technical research services primarily for agencies of the federal government. It employs more than 7000 scientists engineers and other specialists who work at primary research facilities in Massachusetts and Virginia. It also manages serveral federally funded research and development centers serving organizations such as the Department of Defense the Federal Aviation Administration the Internal Revenue Service and the Department of Veterans Affairs. MITRE was founded in 1958 by former MIT researchers.

Operations

MITRE also supports the Department of Homeland Security (DHS) and the Administrative Office of the US Courts. For the DHS MITRE provides systems engineering practices and acquisition expertise while it helps the US Courts with state-of-the-art technology to benefit the federal judicial system. The company has also assisted the Intelligence Community in safeguarding classified information.

In 2011 the company changed the name of The Department of Defense Command Control Communications and Intelligence Federally Funded Research and Development Center to National Security Engineering Center. It did so to reflect the various work programs —such as systems engineering information technology operational concepts and enterprise modernization —it conducts for the Department of Defense and the Intelligence Community and their partners.

Geographic Reach

In addition to primary research facilities in Bedford Massachusetts and McLean Virginia MITRE has international operations in Belgium Germany Japan the Netherlands South Korea Taiwan and the UK.

Strategy

The company is focusing on supporting the Department of Defense's operations and improving acquisition outcomes preserving an information advantage and addressing the government's enterprise IT consolidation. For the Intelligence Community it has been focusing on helping thwart cyber attacks to the nation's critical infrastructures.

In 2012 MITRE invested $51 million in research and development to advance military and civilian technologies. The investment is designed to provide more equipment and workspaces for the company's engineers and scientists. (Some 65% of its employees have advanced degrees.)

Financial Analysis

MITRE's revenue from operations increased 6% from $1.3 billion in fiscal year 2010 to about $1.4 billion illion in fiscal year 2011.The increase was primarily driven by the addition of work for the Departments of Veterans Affairs and Health and Human Services and the Federal Aviation Administration.

EXECUTIVES

SVP CFO and Treasurer, Mark W. Kontos
SVP and COO, David H. Lehman
VP General Counsel and Corporate Secretary, Sol Glasner
VP and Chief Human Resources Officer, Lisa R. Bender
President CEO and Trustee, Alfred Grasso
Corporate Chief Engineer and MITRE Fellow, Louis S. Metzger
SVP and General Manager Center for Integrated Intelligence Systems, Robert F. Nesbit
Chairman, James R. Schlesinger, age 83
Director SVP and General Manager Center for Advanced Aviation System Development and FAA Federally Funded Research and Development Center, Agam N. Sinha
SVP and Director National Security Engineering Center, Raymond Haller
VP and CTO, Stephen D. Huffman
Vice Chairman, Charles S. Robb, age 73
SVP and General Manager Command and Control Center (C2C), Richard J. Byrne
VP Center for Integrated Intelligence Systems and Corporate Director Cyber Security, Gary J. Gagnon
SVP and General Manager Center for Connected Government Director Homeland Security Systems Engineering and Development Institute DHS FFRDC, Jason F. Providakes
Executive Director Corporate Communications and Public Affairs, Catherine L. Crawford
Manager Media Corporate Citizenship and Branding, Jennifer J. Shearman
VP and Director Center for Enterprise Modernization, James E. (Jim) Cook
Media Relations, Karina H. Wright
VP and CIO, Joel Jacobs
VP Command and Control Center DoD C3I FFRDC, Peter Sherlock
Trustee, Nicholas M. (Nick) Donofrio, age 66
Trustee, Martin C. Faga, age 71
President CEO and Trustee, Alfred Grasso
Trustee, John J. Hamre, age 61
Trustee, William B. Mitchell, age 76
Trustee, Cleve L. Killingsworth Jr., age 60
Trustee, Cathy E. Minehan, age 63
Trustee, Victor A. DeMarines, age 75
Trustee, Adm. Edmund P. (Ed) Giambastiani Jr., age 63
Trustee, Jane C. Garvey, age 68
Trustee, John P. Stenbit, age 72
Trustee, Elizabeth J. Keefer
Trustee, Gen. Montgomery C. Meigs
Trustee, Gen. Ronald R. (Ron) Fogleman
Trustee, Donald M. Kerr

Trustee, William Happer Jr.
Vice Chairman, Charles S. Robb, age 73

LOCATIONS

HQ: The MITRE Corporation
202 Burlington Rd., Bedford MA 01730-1420
Phone: 781-271-2000 **Fax:** 781-271-2271
Web: www.mitre.org

PRODUCTS/OPERATIONS

Selected Practice Areas

Acquisition and systems analysis
Aviation systems safety and security
Command and control
Cybersecurity
Emerging technologies
Enterprise systems engineering
Global networking
Healthcare transformation
Homeland security
Information Technology
Intelligence surveillance and reconnaissance
Large-scale enterprise transformation
Systems engineering

COMPETITORS

Altarum	Sandia National
Battelle Memorial	Laboratories
Berkeley Lab	SITA
ComGlobal Systems	SRI International
EDSI	SwRI
General Atomics	The Scripps Research
Institute for Defense	Institute
Analyses	Wyle Information
QinetiQ	Systems
SAIC	

HISTORICAL FINANCIALS

Company Type: Private - Not-for-Profit

Income Statement

FYE: September 30

	REVENUE ($ mil.)	NET INCOME ($ mil.)	NET PROFIT MARGIN	EMPLOYEES
09/11*	1,389	21	1.5%	7,000
10/08	1,234	22	1.8%	0
10/07	1,113	23	2.1%	0
10/06	667,025	0	—	0
Annual Growth	—	374.6%	—	—

*Fiscal year change

2011 Year-End Financials

Debt ratio: —
Return on equity: 1.50%
Cash ($ mil.): 27
Current ratio: 0.90
Long-term debt ($ mil.): —
Dividends
Yield: —
Payout: —
Market value ($ mil.): —

THE MOODY BIBLE INSTITUTE OF CHICAGO

LOCATIONS

HQ: THE MOODY BIBLE INSTITUTE OF CHICAGO
820 N LA SALLE DR, CHICAGO, IL 60610-3263
Phone: 312-329-4000
Web: www.moodyministries.net

HISTORICAL FINANCIALS
Company Type: Private

Income Statement
FYE: June 30

	REVENUE ($ mil.)	NET INCOME ($ mil.)	NET PROFIT MARGIN	EMPLOYEES
06/12	107	(3)	—	605
06/11	97	24	25.5%	0
06/10	90	4	5.4%	0
06/09	82	(12)	—	0
Annual Growth	9.1%	—	—	—

2012 Year-End Financials

Debt ratio: ——
Return on equity: (-3.50)%
Cash ($ mil.): 8
Current ratio: ——
Long-term debt ($ mil.): —

Dividends
Yield: —
Payout: —
Market value ($ mil.): —

THE MOREHOUSE SCHOOL OF MEDICINE INC

LOCATIONS
HQ: THE MOREHOUSE SCHOOL OF MEDICINE INC
720 WESTVIEW DR SW, ATLANTA, GA 30310-1458
Phone: 404-752-1500
Web: www.web.msm.edu

HISTORICAL FINANCIALS
Company Type: Private

Income Statement
FYE: June 30

	REVENUE ($ mil.)	NET INCOME ($ mil.)	NET PROFIT MARGIN	EMPLOYEES
06/11	130	6	5.3%	700
06/10	124	7	6.2%	0
06/09	116	0	—	0
06/08	116	8	7.2%	0
Annual Growth	3.9%	(6.1%)	—	—

2011 Year-End Financials

Debt ratio: ——
Return on equity: 5.30%
Cash ($ mil.): 3
Current ratio: 1.60
Long-term debt ($ mil.): —

Dividends
Yield: —
Payout: —
Market value ($ mil.): —

THE MOSES H CONE MEMORIAL HOSPITAL

LOCATIONS
HQ: THE MOSES H CONE MEMORIAL HOSPITAL
1200 N ELM ST, GREENSBORO, NC 27401-1020
Phone: 336-832-7000
Web: www.nchealthcareers.com

HISTORICAL FINANCIALS
Company Type: Private

Income Statement
FYE: September 30

	REVENUE ($ mil.)	NET INCOME ($ mil.)	NET PROFIT MARGIN	EMPLOYEES
09/12*	1,096	99	9.1%	7,000
12/11	254	29	11.8%	0
09/11	976	38	3.9%	0
09/10	892	66	7.4%	0
Annual Growth	7.1%	14.6%	—	—

*Fiscal year change

2012 Year-End Financials

Debt ratio: ——
Return on equity: 9.10%
Cash ($ mil.): 29
Current ratio: 1.10
Long-term debt ($ mil.): —

Dividends
Yield: —
Payout: —
Market value ($ mil.): —

THE NATIONAL ASSOCIATION FOR THE EXCHANGE OF INDUSTRIAL RESOURCE

LOCATIONS
HQ: THE NATIONAL ASSOCIATION FOR THE
EXCHANGE OF INDUSTRIAL RESOURCE
560 MCCLURE ST, GALESBURG, IL 61401-4286
Phone: 309-343-0704
Web: www.naeir.org

HISTORICAL FINANCIALS
Company Type: Private

Income Statement
FYE: June 30

	REVENUE ($ mil.)	NET INCOME ($ mil.)	NET PROFIT MARGIN	EMPLOYEES
06/12	88	(7)	—	80
06/11	96	(22)	—	0
06/10	140	3	2.7%	0
06/09	138	12	8.9%	0
Annual Growth	(14.1%)	—	—	—

2012 Year-End Financials

Debt ratio: ——
Return on equity: (-9.00)%
Cash ($ mil.): 0
Current ratio: 0.10
Long-term debt ($ mil.): —

Dividends
Yield: —
Payout: —
Market value ($ mil.): —

THE NATIONAL CANCER COALITION

LOCATIONS
HQ: THE NATIONAL CANCER COALITION
333 FAYETTEVILLE ST # 1500, RALEIGH, NC
27601-1747
Phone: 919-821-4390
Web: www.nationalcancercoalition.org

HISTORICAL FINANCIALS
Company Type: Private

Income Statement
FYE: September 30

	REVENUE ($ mil.)	NET INCOME ($ mil.)	NET PROFIT MARGIN	EMPLOYEES
09/11	138	0	0.1%	3
09/10	180	0	0.1%	0
Annual Growth	(23.4%)	4.4%	—	—

2011 Year-End Financials

Debt ratio: ——
Return on equity: 0.10%
Cash ($ mil.): 0
Current ratio: 0.30
Long-term debt ($ mil.): —

Dividends
Yield: —
Payout: —
Market value ($ mil.): —

THE NEW SCHOOL

When James Lipton asks you what your favorite swear word is you know you've made it. The New School's drama department (formerly called The Actor's Studio) was made famous by the cable show Inside the Actors Studio which features Lipton interviewing movie and television stars. The school offers degrees in theater for playwriting directing and acting and has taught "Method" acting to grads such as Marlon Brando and Robert De Niro. It is also home to Parsons The New School for Design and has schools devoted to general studies liberal arts social research management and urban policy and music. More than 10500 traditional students and 5600 continuing education students are enrolled at The New School.

Operations

The New School offers more than 90 degree and diploma programs and majors to a population of undergraduate and graduate students who come from all 50 states and more than 100 foreign countries (about one-quarter of its students hail from international locations). It boasts small class sizes and a student-teacher ratio of about 10:1.

The New School for Public Engagement is the university's founding division and is composed of five schools: Milano School of International Affairs Management and Urban Policy; School of Language Learning and Teaching; School of Media Studies; School of Undergraduate Studies; and School of Writing. It has since added six divisions: Drama Jazz Lang Mannes Parsons and Social Research.

Financial Performance

The New School's 2011 revenue grew by more than 5% vs. 2010. Net income increased 13% over the same period.

Strategy

Parsons' new academic center in Paris is slated to open in fall 2013. The Paris site will offer students a program that addresses the global nature of contemporary art and design practice and reflects Europe's culture and philosophy.

The New School was founded in 1919 by a group of university professors and intellectuals in New York City as place for students wanting to explore their creativity and engage in deep thought while studying liberal arts. Dozens of years later The New School has gained a reputation for its unconventional teaching methods as well as for being the home of many world-renowned institutes including the think tank The World Policy Institute. It also hosts the annual National Book Awards which has helped establish the careers of some of the country's most recognized authors including Richard Powers and Jonathan Franzen.

EXECUTIVES

VP Communications and External Affairs, Nancy Donner, age 51
VP Communications and External Affairs, Peter Taback
President, J. Robert (Bob) Kerrey, age 68
SVP Student Services, Linda A. Reimer
SVP Development and Alumni Relations, Kristin Sorenson
SVP Finance and Business, Frank Barletta
SVP Human Resources and Labor Relations, Carol Cantrell
SVP Information Technology Services, Shelley Reed
EVP and COO, James Murtha
Director Community Services; Chair Techniques of Music Department, Elizabeth Aaron
Associate Dean for Academic Initiatives, Lisa Grocott
Assistant Dean Academic Affairs and Curriculum, Ellen Freeberg
VP and Controller, Jeanne Plecenik
Controller, Natalie Darrett
Senior Director Business Operations Services, Edward (Ed) Verdi
Manager Purchasing, John Giampiccolo
Director Admission Eugene Lang College, Nicole Curvin
VP Budget and Planning, Nancy Stier
Deputy Provost and SVP Academic Affairs, Bryna Sanger
Director Career Development and Placement Milano Graduate School, Carol R. Anderson
Director Career Services Parsons School of Design, Angie Wojak
SVP Enrollment and Career Services, Donald Resnick
Director Center for New York City Affairs Milano Graduate School, Andrew White
Senior Director Communications and Special Projects, Susan Heske
Assistant VP Enrollment Operations, Christy Kalan
Assistant Director Enrollment Operations, Elizabeth Diaz
Manager Systems and Operations, Sean Maguire

Director Acadmic Advising Eugene Lang College, Jonathan White
Director Executive Administration, Linda E. Adams
Director Campus Planning, Elizabeth Arcuri
VP Design Construction and Facilities Management, Lia Gartner
Director Graduate Program in International Affairs, Michael Cohen
Assistant VP Human Resources, Warren Petty
Director International Student Services, Monique Ngozi Nri
President, David E. Van Zandt
SVP International Affairs, Benjamin (Ben) Lee
VP Legal Affairs and General Counsel, Roy Moskowitz
VP and Secretary, Doris Suarez
VP Enrollment Management, Bob Gay
Dean The New School for General Studies, Linda Dunne
Dean Milano, Lisa Servon
Dean Mannes, Joel Lester
Director The New School for Drama, Pippin Parker
Provost and Chief Academic Officer, Tim Marshall
Executive Director The New School for Jazz and Contemporary Music, Martin Mueller
Dean The New School for Social Research, Michael Schober
Dean Eugene Lang College The New School for Liberal Arts, Stephanie Browner
Auditors: KPMGLLP

LOCATIONS

HQ: The New School
66 W. 12th St., New York NY 10011
Phone: 212-229-5600 **Fax:** 212-229-5648
Web: www.newschool.edu

PRODUCTS/OPERATIONS

Selected Schools

Eugene Lang College The New School for Liberal Arts
Mannes College The New School for Music
Milano The New School for Management and Urban Policy
The New School for Drama
The New School for General Studies
The New School for Jazz and Contemporary Music
The New School for Public Engagement
The New School for Social Research
Parsons The New School for Design

HISTORICAL FINANCIALS

Company Type: School

Income Statement

FYE: June 30

	REVENUE ($ mil.)	NET INCOME ($ mil.)	NET PROFIT MARGIN	EMPLOYEES
06/12	317	(3)	—	855
06/11	305	35	11.8%	0
06/10	288	31	11.0%	0
06/09	271	(32)	—	0
Annual Growth	**5.2%**	—	—	—

2012 Year-End Financials

Debt ratio: ——
Return on equity: (-1.10)%
Cash ($ mil.): 9
Current ratio: —
Long-term debt ($ mil.): —
Dividends
Yield: —
Payout: —
Market value ($ mil.): —

THE NEW YORK FOUNDLING HOSPITAL

LOCATIONS

HQ: THE NEW YORK FOUNDLING HOSPITAL
590 AVE OF THE AMERICAS, NEW YORK, NY 10011-2019
Phone: 212-633-9300
Web: www.stagathaalumni.org

HISTORICAL FINANCIALS

Company Type: Private

Income Statement

FYE: June 30

	REVENUE ($ mil.)	NET INCOME ($ mil.)	NET PROFIT MARGIN	EMPLOYEES
06/11	97	(3)	—	1,500
06/10	101	(1)	—	0
06/09	120	0	—	0
06/08	3	(5)	—	0
Annual Growth	**215.4%**	—	—	—

2011 Year-End Financials

Debt ratio: ——
Return on equity: (-3.20)%
Cash ($ mil.): 12
Current ratio: 1.00
Long-term debt ($ mil.): —
Dividends
Yield: —
Payout: —
Market value ($ mil.): —

THE NEWTRON GROUP L L C

Some contractors bomb but The Newtron Group keeps on ticking. Through subsidiaries The Newtron Group offers a variety of industrial electrical and other specialty construction and contracting services nationwide. Services include instrumentation and control systems installation and maintenance; fiber optic installation and testing; industrial pipe and panel fabrication; aviation services; and electrical heat tracing. Newtron serves clients in such industries as refining power generation mining pharmaceuticals and semiconductors. Subsidiaries include electrical contractor Triad Electric and Controls and fiber optics firm ComNet Services. The Newtron Group has offices in California Louisiana and Texas.

EXECUTIVES

President and CEO, Newton B. Thomas
VP Marketing, Duff Schempf
CFO, Tammi Misuraca

LOCATIONS

HQ: The Newtron Group L.L.C.
8183 W. El Cajon, Baton Rouge LA 70815
Phone: 225-927-8921 **Fax:** 305-681-7963
Web: www.pereztrading.com

PRODUCTS/OPERATIONS

Selected Subsidiaries

Com-Net Services Inc. (fiber optics)
Executive Aviation Inc. (hangar space fuel supplies)
Newtron Inc. (electrical and instrumentation)
Newtron Heat Trace (industrial heat tracing)
Newtron Mechanical (industrial mechanics)
Triad Electric and Controls Inc. (electrical and instrumentation)
Triad Control Systems Inc. (control panel fabrication)

Selected Industries

Cement
Electronics
Food processing
Gas transmission
Metals and mining
Petrochemical
Pharmaceuticals
Power generation
Pulp and paper
Refining
Semiconductors
Waste treatment

COMPETITORS

EMCOR	MMR Group
Fisk Electric	Motor City Electric
Industrial Specialty	Pike Electric
Contractors	Corporation
Jelec	

HISTORICAL FINANCIALS

Company Type: Private

Income Statement

FYE: June 30

	REVENUE ($ mil.)	NET INCOME ($ mil.)	NET PROFIT MARGIN	EMPLOYEES
06/12	296	2	0.7%	2,000
06/11	311	3	1.0%	0
06/10	362	5	1.5%	0
06/09	57	7	13.5%	0
Annual Growth	73.0%	(34.3%)	—	—

2012 Year-End Financials

Debt ratio: ——
Return on equity: 0.70%
Cash ($ mil.): 5
Current ratio: 0.10
Long-term debt ($ mil.): ——

Dividends
Yield: —
Payout: —
Market value ($ mil.): —

THE PENNSYLVANIA CYBER CHARTER SCHOOL

LOCATIONS

HQ: THE PENNSYLVANIA CYBER CHARTER SCHOOL
652 MIDLAND AVE, MIDLAND, PA 15059-1433
Phone: 724-643-1180

HISTORICAL FINANCIALS

Company Type: Private

Income Statement

FYE: June 30

	REVENUE ($ mil.)	NET INCOME ($ mil.)	NET PROFIT MARGIN	EMPLOYEES
06/11	109	0	0.2%	350
Annual Growth	—	—	—	—

2011 Year-End Financials

Debt ratio: ——
Return on equity: 0.20%
Cash ($ mil.): 3
Current ratio: 0.70
Long-term debt ($ mil.): —

Dividends
Yield: —
Payout: —
Market value ($ mil.): —

THE PHILLIPS EXETER ACADEMY

LOCATIONS

HQ: THE PHILLIPS EXETER ACADEMY
20 MAIN ST, EXETER, NH 03833-2460
Phone: 603-772-4311
Web: www.exeter.bkstore.com

HISTORICAL FINANCIALS

Company Type: Private

Income Statement

FYE: June 30

	REVENUE ($ mil.)	NET INCOME ($ mil.)	NET PROFIT MARGIN	EMPLOYEES
06/11	94	(3)	—	520
06/10	77	(11)	—	0
06/09	30	0	—	0
06/08	142	55	38.6%	0
Annual Growth	(12.9%)	—	—	—

2011 Year-End Financials

Debt ratio: ——
Return on equity: (-4.10)%
Cash ($ mil.): 44
Current ratio: ——
Long-term debt ($ mil.): —

Dividends
Yield: —
Payout: —
Market value ($ mil.): —

THE PLAZA GROUP INC

The Plaza Group (TPG) is an international distributor of petrochemical solvents and chemical intermediates. Established in 1994 TPG is the exclusive marketer of some products from companies such as Shell Oil and Frontier Oil. The company markets to FORTUNE 500 companies major international enterprises direct consumers and chemical distributors. Its products are used in the production of resins coatings and adhesives. TPG partners with global suppliers (like SABIC Innovative Plastics Total Petrochemicals and Alon) in Asia Australia Europe and the Americas. The company is owned by president Randy Velarde.

EXECUTIVES

VP, Wilfred J. (Wilf) Kimball
VP Sales, Roger R. Moyers
President, Randy E. Velarde
VP, Vicki Velarde
Director Business and Sales East and West Coasts and Europe, Steve Willett
Controller, Robert (Bob) Imm
Administrative Assistant, Mary Esquivel
Sales Manager Domestic and Mexican Sales, Jose Flores
Customer Service and Project Manager, Thaisla Courtney
Manager Customer Service, Teresa Hitt
VP Operations, Mark Hacas
VP Plastics, Giuseppe Maniscalco, age 62
Sales Director, Venere Vitiello
Controller, Ray Heinen
Commercial Manager, Erika Bernhardt
Customer Service, Michael S. Moyers
Director, Carmine Falcone, age 65
Director, Eugene R. Allspach, age 64
Director, Mario Concha, age 72
Director, John R. Yanney
Director, Graciela G. Saenz

LOCATIONS

HQ: The Plaza Group
10375 Richmond Ave. Ste. 1620, Houston TX 77042-4143
Phone: 713-266-1059   Fax: 713-266-8660
Web: www.theplazagrp.com

COMPETITORS

Cole Chemical	Sinochem
ICC Chemical	

HISTORICAL FINANCIALS

Company Type: Private

Income Statement

FYE: December 31

	REVENUE ($ mil.)	NET INCOME ($ mil.)	NET PROFIT MARGIN	EMPLOYEES
12/11	271	4	1.6%	18
12/10	198	2	1.2%	0
12/04	129	4	3.5%	0
12/03	76	1	2.0%	0
Annual Growth	52.3%	41.2%	—	—

2011 Year-End Financials

Debt ratio: ——
Return on equity: 1.60%
Cash ($ mil.): 1
Current ratio: 1.10
Long-term debt ($ mil.): —

Dividends
Yield: —
Payout: —
Market value ($ mil.): —

THE REED INSTITUTE

Reed College offers bachelor's degrees in more than 20 fields and a master of arts degree in liberal studies. Its special master's degree allows students to study both liberal arts and the sciences. The school enrolls more than 1400 students (called "Reedies") annually. It has an average of 15 students in its conference-style classes and has a student-to-faculty ratio of 10 to 1. It has produced more than 30 Rhodes Scholars. The college also has a nuclear reactor that is operated primarily by undergraduates. Reed College was founded in 1908 and is named for Oregon pioneers Simeon and Amanda Reed.

EXECUTIVES

Vice Chairman, Richard H. (Rick) Wollenberg, age 57
Director Strategic Communications, Kevin Myers
President and Trustee, Colin S. Diver, age 68
Chairman, Daniel B. Greenberg
Dean Faculty and Robert H. and Blanche Day Ellis Professor Political Science and Humanities, Peter Steinberger
Director Public Affairs, Jennifer Bates
Secretary, E. Randolph Labbe
VP and Treasurer, Edwin O. McFarlane
VP College Relations, Hugh Porter
College Librarian, Victoria L. Hanawalt
Registrar, Nora McLaughlin
Director Facilities Operations, Townsend Angell
Director Computer User Services, Ethan Benatan
Acting VP and Dean Student Services, Michael (Mike) Brody
Deputy CTO and Director Web and System Services, Marianne Colgrove
Director International Programs, Paul DeYoung
Director Research Reactor, Stephen Frantz
Director Corporate and Foundation Support, Diane Gumz
Director Administrative Computing Services, Gary Norbraten
CTO, Martin Ringle
Director Institutional Research, Jon Rivenburg
Director Technology Infrastructure Services, Gary Schlickeiser
Director Alumni and Parent Relations, Michael J. (Mike) Teskey
Acting Dean Admission, Kristine Sawicki
Director Human Resources, Anna Sestrich
Administrative Manager Community Safety, Monica Lobeck
Operations Manager Community Safety, Rick Fagerstrom
Network Security Administrator, Vincent Stoffer
Director Development, Jan Kurtz
Director Annual Fund, David Rubin
Acting Director Planned Giving, Kathy Saitas
Director Major Gifts, Chris Brentlinger
Interim Assistant Dean Multicultural Affairs, Rhea Combs
Director Physical Education and Athletics, Michael Lombardo
Director Learning Resources, Libby Rapkoch
Director Student Activities, Kristin Holmberg
Vice Chairman, Richard H. (Rick) Wollenberg, age 57
President and Trustee, Colin S. Diver, age 68

LOCATIONS

HQ: Reed College
3203 SE Woodstock Blvd., Portland OR 97202-8199
Phone: 503-771-1112   **Fax:** 503-777-7769
Web: web.reed.edu

HISTORICAL FINANCIALS

Company Type: School

Income Statement

FYE: June 30

	REVENUE ($ mil.)	NET INCOME ($ mil.)	NET PROFIT MARGIN	EMPLOYEES
06/11	124	54	44.0%	400
06/10	114	44	39.3%	0
06/09	0	0	—	0
06/08	51	(20)	—	0
Annual Growth	34.0%	—	—	—

2011 Year-End Financials

Debt ratio: ——
Return on equity: 44.00%
Cash ($ mil.): 10
Current ratio: 1.30
Long-term debt ($ mil.): —

Dividends
  Yield: —
  Payout: —
Market value ($ mil.): —

THE ROCKEFELLER UNIVERSITY FACULTY & STUDENTS CLUB INC

Rockefeller University sniffs out solid scientific evidence. The university is a leading US research institution and scientific graduate school providing training in biomedical and physical science fields such as biochemistry structural biology immunology neuroscience and human genetics. The university is centered around more than 70 research laboratories and a hospital and it runs M.D.-Ph.D. programs in conjunction with the Memorial Sloan-Kettering Cancer Center and the Weill Medical College at Cornell University. Rockefeller University's research is funded by entities such as the National Institutes of Health and the Howard Hughes Medical Institute as well as private gifts and endowments.

The school has been a university since 1955 although it was originally founded by John D. Rockefeller in 1901 as The Rockefeller Institute for Medical Research. The Rockefeller University Hospital the first research-focused medical center in the US opened in 1910. The university maintains a small enrollment with only about 200 Ph.D. students and some 550 research scientists on campus.

To promote collaboration and innovation Rockefeller University maintains an open structure with no formal departments. It also provides its Ph.D. students with amenities such as scholarships subsidized housing and annual research budgets to encourage independent study and creativity.

The university completed a $380 million renovation and construction program in 2010. The project included modernization of historical laboratory buildings and the construction of a new five-story Collaborative Research Center.

Rockefeller University's former president Paul Nurse resigned in March 2011 to take a job at the Royal Society of London which conducts scientific research for the UK prime minister. Nurse was replaced by Marc Tessier-Lavigne a former Genentech executive.

EXECUTIVES

Vice Chair, Henry R. Kravis, age 68
VP Human Resources, Virginia Huffman
Vice Chair, Richard E. Salomon, age 69
Vice Chair, David I. Hirsh, age 73
VP Development, Maren E. Imhoff
VP Medical Affairs, Barry S. Coller
Chair Institutional Review Board, Emil C. Gotschlich
President, Marc Tessier-Lavigne, age 51
VP Finance and Treasurer, James H. Lapple
Chair, Russell L. Carson
Assistant VP Finance and Assistant Treasurer, Robin Maloney
VP and General Counsel, Harriet Rabb
Corporate Secretary, Jane Rendall
VP Educational Affairs and Dean, Sidney Strickland
VP Academic Affairs, Michael W. Young
Vice Chair, Marnie S. Pillsbury
VP and Chief Investment Officer, Lisa Danzig
VP Scientific and Facility Operations, John Tooze
Director Communications and Public Affairs, Joseph Bonner
Director Information Technology, Anthony Popowicz
Director Information Technology Operations and Network Security, Armand Gazes
University Librarian, Carol A. Feltes
Honorary Chair and Life Trustee, David Rockefeller
Trustee, David H. Koch, age 72
Vice Chair, Henry R. Kravis, age 68
Trustee, James H. (Jim) Simons, age 71
Trustee, Anthony B. (Tony) Evnin, age 71
Trustee, Lewis A. (Lew) Sanders, age 65
Trustee, Robert M. Bass
Trustee, Sandra J. Horbach, age 51
Trustee, Paul B. Guenther, age 71
Vice Chair, Richard E. Salomon, age 69
Trustee, G. S. Beckwith Gilbert
Vice Chair, David I. Hirsh, age 73
Trustee, Willard J. (Mike) Overlock Jr., age 64
Trustee, Peter A. Flaherty, age 68
Vice Chair, Marnie S. Pillsbury
Trustee, Michael D. Fascitelli
Trustee, Lulu C. Wang, age 67
Honorary Chair and Life Trustee, David Rockefeller
Trustee, Allen R. Adler
Trustee, Edward J. Benz Jr.
Trustee, Judith Roth Berkowitz
Trustee, David Botstein
Trustee, Christopher H. Browne
Trustee, Andreas Dracopoulos
Trustee, Marlene Hess
Trustee, Nancy Maginnes Kissinger
Trustee, Thomas H. Lee
Trustee, Karen M. Levy
Trustee, Evelyn G. Lipper
Trustee, William E. Ford
Trustee, Robin Chemers Neustein
Trustee, Joseph L. Goldstein
Trustee, Neva R. Goodwin
Trustee, Peter T. Grauer
Trustee, Margaret A. Hamburg
Trustee, Don M. Randel
Trustee, Patricia P. Rosenwald
Trustee, Sydney R. Shuman
Auditors: KPMGLLP

LOCATIONS

HQ: The Rockefeller University
1230 York Ave., New York NY 10065
Phone: 212-327-8000   **Fax:** 212-327-7974
Web: www.rockefeller.edu

HISTORICAL FINANCIALS

Company Type: School

Income Statement

FYE: June 30

	REVENUE ($ mil.)	NET INCOME ($ mil.)	NET PROFIT MARGIN	EMPLOYEES
06/11	424	107	25.4%	1,700
06/06	413	271	65.5%	0
06/05	413	271	65.5%	0
06/04	285	61	21.4%	0
Annual Growth	14.1%	20.8%	—	—

2011 Year-End Financials

Debt ratio: ——
Return on equity: 25.40%
Cash ($ mil.): 154
Current ratio: 0.20
Long-term debt ($ mil.): —

Dividends
Yield: —
Payout: —
Market value ($ mil.): —

THE SAVANNAH COLLEGE OF ART AND DESIGN INC

With more than 9000 students Savannah College of Art and Design is one of the largest art and design schools in the US. It has undergraduate degrees in arts and fine arts as well as master's degrees from campuses in Atlanta and Lacoste France in addition to its namesake location. Courses of study include architecture interior and graphic design fashion film and television painting dance and art history. The school offers certificates in digital publishing digital publishing management historic preservation interactive design and typeface design. Annual tuition runs about $28000. The school was founded in 1978 and has taken an active role in restoring architectural landmarks in Savannah.

EXECUTIVES

COO, Brian Murphy
VP Information Management and Technology, Harley Lingerfelt
President, Paula S. Wallace
Chairman, Paul S. Bradley
VP Academic Services, Andy Fulp
VP Institutional Effectiveness, John Joseph Hoey IV
VP Student Services, Philip Alletto
Chief of Staff, Sharon Dwyer
VP Marketing, Anthony Dammicci
Chair Broadcast Design and Motion Graphics, Jeffery Boortz
Chief Academic Officer, Tom Fisher
Trustee, Chan Laiwa
Trustee, Nancy Herstand
Trustee, Alison Hopton
Trustee, Don Mondanaro
Trustee, May L. Poetter
Trustee, Sally Waranch Rajcic
Trustee, Andre Leon Talley
Truistee, Taras John Danyluk
Trustee, Ozlem P. Tascioglu

LOCATIONS

HQ: Savannah College of Art and Design
342 Bull St., Savannah GA 31401
Phone: 912-525-5100   **Fax:** 912-525-5986
Web: www.scad.edu

PRODUCTS/OPERATIONS

Degrees Offered
Bachelor of Arts (B.A.)
Bachelor of Fine Arts (B.F.A.)
Master of Architecture (M.Arch.)
Master of Arts (M.A.)
Master of Fine Arts (M.F.A.)
Master of Urban Design (M.U.D.)
Master of Arts in Teaching Art (M.A.)
Master of Arts in Teaching Drama (M.A.)

Selected Majors

Advertising Design
Animation
Architectural History
Architecture
Art History
Broadcast Design and Motion Graphics
Cinema Studies
Fashion
Fibers
Film and Television
Furniture Design
Graphic Design
Historic Preservation
Illustration
Industrial Design
Interactive Design and Game Development
Interior Design
Media and Performing Arts
Metals and Jewelry
Painting
Photography
Sequential Art
Sound Design
Visual Effects

HISTORICAL FINANCIALS

Company Type: School

Income Statement

FYE: June 30

	REVENUE ($ mil.)	NET INCOME ($ mil.)	NET PROFIT MARGIN	EMPLOYEES
06/11	331	30	9.3%	1,200
06/10	314	10	3.2%	0
06/09	283	21	7.7%	0
06/08	216	14	6.6%	0
Annual Growth	15.2%	28.8%	—	—

2011 Year-End Financials

Debt ratio: ——
Return on equity: 9.30%
Cash ($ mil.): 9
Current ratio: —
Long-term debt ($ mil.): —

Dividends
Yield: —
Payout: —
Market value ($ mil.): —

THE SOUTHEASTERN CONFERENCE

LOCATIONS

HQ: THE SOUTHEASTERN CONFERENCE
2201 RICHARD ARRINGTN JR, BIRMINGHAM, AL 35203-1103
Phone: 205-458-3000

HISTORICAL FINANCIALS

Company Type: Private

Income Statement

FYE: August 31

	REVENUE ($ mil.)	NET INCOME ($ mil.)	NET PROFIT MARGIN	EMPLOYEES
08/11	261	4	1.6%	30
08/10	244	5	2.1%	0
08/09	148	0	—	0
08/08	161	7	4.7%	0
Annual Growth	17.3%	(18.5%)	—	—

2011 Year-End Financials

Debt ratio: ——
Return on equity: 1.60%
Cash ($ mil.): 20
Current ratio: —
Long-term debt ($ mil.): —

Dividends
Yield: —
Payout: —
Market value ($ mil.): —

THE SPENCE SCHOOL

LOCATIONS

HQ: THE SPENCE SCHOOL
22 E 91ST ST, NEW YORK, NY 10128-0657
Phone: 646-943-6822
Web: www.spenceschool.org

HISTORICAL FINANCIALS

Company Type: Private

Income Statement

FYE: June 30

	REVENUE ($ mil.)	NET INCOME ($ mil.)	NET PROFIT MARGIN	EMPLOYEES
06/11	98	63	64.7%	160
06/10	0	0		0
Annual Growth	—	—	—	—

2011 Year-End Financials

Debt ratio: ——
Return on equity: 64.70%
Cash ($ mil.): 13
Current ratio: —
Long-term debt ($ mil.): —

Dividends
Yield: —
Payout: —
Market value ($ mil.): —

THE SUTPHEN CORPORATION

LOCATIONS

HQ: THE SUTPHEN CORPORATION
6450 EITERMAN RD, DUBLIN, OH 43016-8711
Phone: 614-889-1005
Web: www.sutpheneast.com

HISTORICAL FINANCIALS

Company Type: Private

Income Statement

FYE: February 29

	REVENUE ($ mil.)	NET INCOME ($ mil.)	NET PROFIT MARGIN	EMPLOYEES
02/12*	88	0	0.7%	230
12/07	72	0	0.5%	0
12/06	70	0	0.8%	0
12/05	827	0	0.0%	0
Annual Growth	(52.5%)	235.6%	—	—

*Fiscal year change

2012 Year-End Financials

Debt ratio: ——
Return on equity: 0.70%
Cash ($ mil.): 0
Current ratio: 0.30
Long-term debt ($ mil.): —

Dividends
  Yield: —
  Payout: —
  Market value ($ mil.): —

THE TASK FORCE FOR GLOBAL HEALTH INC

LOCATIONS

HQ: THE TASK FORCE FOR GLOBAL HEALTH INC
325 SWANTON WAY, DECATUR, GA 30030-3001
Phone: 404-592-1430

HISTORICAL FINANCIALS

Company Type: Private

Income Statement

FYE: August 31

	REVENUE ($ mil.)	NET INCOME ($ mil.)	NET PROFIT MARGIN	EMPLOYEES
08/11	1,160	(0)	—	55
08/10	1,149	4	0.4%	0
08/09	21	0	—	0
08/08	15	2	13.6%	0
Annual Growth	323.5%	—	—	—

2011 Year-End Financials

Debt ratio: ——
Return on equity: (-0.10)%
Cash ($ mil.): 38
Current ratio: 6.00
Long-term debt ($ mil.): —

Dividends
  Yield: —
  Payout: —
  Market value ($ mil.): —

THE TENNERGY CORPORATION

LOCATIONS

HQ: THE TENNERGY CORPORATION
250 N HIGHLAND AVE, JACKSON, TN 38301-6032
Phone: 731-422-7211

HISTORICAL FINANCIALS

Company Type: Private

Income Statement

FYE: June 30

	REVENUE ($ mil.)	NET INCOME ($ mil.)	NET PROFIT MARGIN	EMPLOYEES
06/12	114	0	0.8%	12
06/11	124	0	0.7%	0
06/10	136	1	0.8%	0
06/09	162	0	0.3%	0
Annual Growth	(11.1%)	26.5%	—	—

2012 Year-End Financials

Debt ratio: ——
Return on equity: 0.80%
Cash ($ mil.): 13
Current ratio: 0.10
Long-term debt ($ mil.): —

Dividends
  Yield: —
  Payout: —
  Market value ($ mil.): —

THE TRUSTEES OF DAVIDSON COLLEGE

The roughly 1700 students at Davidson College account for about a fifth of the population in the small North Carolina town with the same name. Located just north of Charlotte the liberal arts school offers more than 20 majors and about 14 minors in areas such as anthropology art economics history and philosophy. It also offers pre-professional programs in medicine law business ministerial and management. Students are bound by a strict honor code that allows self-scheduled unproctored exams and prohibits students from cheating and stealing. The school was founded in 1837 by Presbyterian ministers and named for Revolutionary War commander William Davidson.

Davidson College was one of the first liberal arts schools to eliminate student loans from its financial aid packages. All students have to rely on grants and student employment to cover their costs. The policy was created in an effort to reduce student debt. The college is supported by a more than $485 million endowment.

The school has a student-teacher ratio of just 11:1 which is relatively low compared to many colleges but the school is still pushing to lower it to 10:1. It also wants to increase its student population from where it is now to 2000. Davidson College intends to increase its physical size as well as its student and teacher population as part of a long-term master plan.

Davidson College's motto is Alenda Lux Ubi Orta Libertas: Translated it means "Let Learning Be Cherished Where Liberty Has Arisen" the motto reflects Davidson's roots in early American history.

There is speculation that the phrase refers to the Mecklenburg Declaration of Independence that was signed into effect in 1775.

EXECUTIVES

Director Planning and Institutional Research, Linda LeFauve
VP Academic Affairs and Dean of the Faculty, Clark G. Ross
Director Athletics, James E. Murphy III
Director Physical Plant, David Holthouser
Director Investments and Financial Planning, R. Burton Hudson Jr.
Director Business Services and Controller, Edward A. Kania
VP College Relations, Kristin Hills Bradberry
Director Donor Relations, Denise Howard
VP College Relations, Eileen Keeley
Director Alumni Relations, Matt Merrell
VP Student Life and Dean of Students, Thomas C. Shandley
Executive Director Information Technology Services, Mur Muchane
Director Communications, Stacey A. Schmeidel
VP Business and Finance, Karen L. Goldstein
President, Thomas W. Ross Sr.
Director Purchasing, Beth Christenbury
VP and Dean Admission and Financial Aid, Christopher J. Gruber
Development Director, Elizabeth Kiser
Director Public Safety and Police, Fountain Walker
Registrar, Hansford Epes
Diretor Human Resources, Kim Ball
Director Library, Jill Gremmels
Director Alumni Relations, Peter Wagner

LOCATIONS

HQ: Davidson College
209 Ridge Rd., Davidson NC 28035
Phone: 704-894-2000   **Fax:** 704-894-2502
Web: www.davidson.edu

PRODUCTS/OPERATIONS

Selected Academic Departments

Chambers Building —primary classroom building and the academic center of campus
E. H. Little Library
Baker-Watt Science Complex —facilities for biology psychology and physics departments
Martin Chemical Laboratory —home of the Chemistry Department
Carolina Inn —one of the oldest buildings in the town of Davidson the Carolina Inn serves as the home for the Center for Interdisciplinary Studies
Oak Row —faculty offices
Elm Row —faculty offices
Eumenean Hall —ceremonial meeting rooms and faculty offices
Philanthropic Hall —home to the Philanthropic Society
Hamilton House —Applied Psychology Building
McMillan Building —Physical Plant offices
Preyer Building —Medical Humanities Pre-Med Program

HISTORICAL FINANCIALS

Company Type: School

Income Statement

FYE: June 30

	REVENUE ($ mil.)	NET INCOME ($ mil.)	NET PROFIT MARGIN	EMPLOYEES
06/11	144	33	23.2%	800
06/10	100	71	71.5%	0
06/09	96	(137)	—	0
06/08	98	14	14.5%	0
Annual Growth	13.7%	33.1%	—	—

THE TRUSTEES OF GRINNELL COLLEGE

Ear to ear might be pushing it but the students at Grinnell College have reason to be happy. On the 120-acre campus in rural Iowa more than 1600 students choose from courses in social studies science and the humanities at this private liberal arts school. The college has an open curriculum allowing students to design their own academic programs. It also offers general literary studies and has campuses in London and Washington DC. Grinnell's endowment is about $1.4 billion. The college which was founded in 1846 is named after abolitionist minister Josiah Bushnell Grinnell.

EXECUTIVES

President, Russell K. Osgood
VP and Treasurer, David S. Clay
VP College and Alumni Relations, Michael J. (Mickey) Munley
VP College Services, John W. Kalkbrenner
Director Donor Relations, Margaret E. Jones Bair
Director Human Resources, Kristin K. Lovig
Director Corporate Foundation and Government Relations, Karen Wiese
Director Student Financial Aid, Arnold A. Woods Jr.
Director Information Technology Services, William D. Francis
Director Security, Stephen A. Briscoe
Controller, Nancy Combs
VP Institutional Planning, Marci Sortor
VP Academic Affairs and Dean College, Paula V. Smith
Dean Admission and Financial Aid, Christopher S. Allen
VP Student Affairs, W. Houston Dougharty
Auditors: Deloitte&ToucheLLP

LOCATIONS

HQ: Grinnell College
1121 Park St., Grinnell IA 50112
Phone: 641-269-4000   **Fax:** 641-269-4800
Web: www.grinnell.edu

HISTORICAL FINANCIALS

Company Type: School

Income Statement

FYE: June 30

	REVENUE ($ mil.)	NET INCOME ($ mil.)	NET PROFIT MARGIN	EMPLOYEES
06/12	99	(127)	—	535
06/11	93	239	254.9%	0
06/10	123	0	0.0%	0
06/09	0	0	—	0
Annual Growth	—	—	—	—

THE TRUSTEES OF WHEATON COLLEGE

Wheaton College located in Wheaton Illinois — not to be confused with a school of the same name in Massachusetts —is a interdenominational Christian college. The private school offers dozens of liberal arts programs of study including a Ph.D. in Biblical and Theological Studies to its undergraduate and graduate students. Liberal arts programs include literature music fine arts biology economics and psychology. Wheaton College has about 3000 students and a 12:1 student-teacher ratio. Wheaton College was founded in 1860 and is named after Warren L. Wheaton who donated land to the school.

Wheaton College is meant to be residential for undergraduates. Nearly 90% of students live on campus. The school has two underclass residence halls to house first and second year students. Williston Hall houses only second year students. McManis-Evans houses second third and fourth year students.

The school's graduates include 1500 business leaders 250 government & foreign service professionals 1000 in medical professionals nearly 400 scientists and researchers 30 college presidents or provosts more than 3000 in ministers and evangelists worldwide 550 in the arts plus more than 4800 teachers 560 attorneys and 2300 in business and commerce.

EXECUTIVES

President, Duane Litfin
VP Advancement and Alumni Relations, R. Mark Dillon
SVP and Treasurer, David E. (Dave) Johnston
Dean Graduate School and Provost, Stanton L. Jones
VP Student Development, Samuel A. Shellhammer
College Chaplain, Stephen B. Kellough
Registrar, Paul E. Johnson
Director Media Resources, J. R. Smith
Director Career Services, Ita Fischer
Dean Students, Richard J. Powers
Controller, Patrick T. Brooke
Director Public Safety, Robert F. Norris
Director Financial Aid, Donna J. Peltz
Director Human Resources, Christopher E. Woodard

LOCATIONS

HQ: Wheaton College (Illinois)
501 College Ave., Wheaton IL 60187-5593
Phone: 630-752-5000   **Fax:** 630-752-5285
Web: www.wheaton.edu

PRODUCTS/OPERATIONS

Selected Academics
Academics

Arts & Sciences B.A. B.S.
Ancient Languages
Anthropology
Applied Health Science
Art
Biblical Archaeology
Biblical & Theological Studies
Biology
Business/Economics
Chemistry
Christian Education & Ministry
Communication
Computer Science
Economics
Elementary Education
Engineering (Dual Degree)
English
Environmental Studies
French
Geology
German
History
History/Social Science
Interdisciplinary Studies
International Relations
Mathematics
Music (6 majors see Conservatory information)
Nursing (Liberal Arts)
Philosophy
Physics
Political Science
Psychology
Secondary Education (2nd major only)
Sociology
Spanish
Conservatory of Music
Composition
Education
History/Literature
Music with Elective Studies in an Outside Field
Music with Emphasis in a Music-Related Field
Performance
Undergraduate Certificates
Adventure Leadership Ministry
Christian Spirituality
Early Christian Studies
Gender Studies
HNGR - Human Needs and Global Resources (Development Studies)
Journalism
Military Science
Pre-Law
Urban Studies
Youth Ministry
Master of Arts Degrees M.A. M.A.T.
Biblical Archaeology
Biblical Exegesis
Biblical Studies
Christian Formation & Ministry
Clinical Psychology
Counseling Ministries
Evangelism and Leadership
Theology
History of Christianity
Intercultural Studies
Intercultural Studies & TESOL
Missions
Teaching Elementary or Secondary
Graduate Certificates
TESOL
Urban Evangelism
Urban Mission
Doctoral Degrees Ph.D. Psy. D.
Philosophy in Biblical & Theological Studies
Psychology in Clinical Psychology (Psy.D.)
Special Programs
Archaeological Excavation in Israel
Arts in London
HoneyRock
HNGR - Human Needs and Global Resources
International internship opportunities
Iron Sharpens Iron
Marine Biology in Belize
May in Asia
Music and Ministry in the Great Cities of Europe
Pre-Health Professions
Pre-Law Program

ROTC
Science Station
Wheaton in Chicago
Wheaton in East Africa
Wheaton in England
Wheaton in France
Wheaton in Germany
Wheaton in the Holy Lands
Wheaton in Latin America
Wheaton in Spain
Wheaton in Washington D.C.

HISTORICAL FINANCIALS
Company Type: School

Income Statement

	REVENUE ($ mil.)	NET INCOME ($ mil.)	NET PROFIT MARGIN	EMPLOYEES
				FYE: June 30
06/12	110	(9)	—	820
06/11	139	12	9.3%	0
06/10	140	16	11.6%	0
06/09	65	(57)	—	0
Annual Growth	19.0%	—	—	—

2012 Year-End Financials

Debt ratio: ——
Return on equity: (-8.50)%
Cash ($ mil.): 17
Current ratio: 1.30
Long-term debt ($ mil.): —

Dividends
Yield: —
Payout: —
Market value ($ mil.): —

THE UCLA FOUNDATION

Helping to make La-La Land a little more erudite The UCLA Foundation raises manages and disperses funds to help support the tripartite education research and service mission of UCLA. With more than $1 billion in assets the organization funds the aforementioned purposes as well as campus improvements and special programs. About half of the foundation's gifts received are provided by foundations; corporations and alumni each account for some 15% of gifts. The UCLA Progress Fund predecessor of the foundation was established in 1945 by the school's alumni association.

EXECUTIVES

VP Finance and Treasurer, Neal Axelrod
EVP, Rhea Turteltaub
Associate Executive Director, Jocelyn M. Smith
Investment Coordinator, George Letteney
VP Development, Tracie Christensen
Interim Executive Director, Steve Gamer
Auditors: PricewaterhouseCoopersLLP

LOCATIONS

HQ: The UCLA Foundation
10920 Wilshire Blvd. Ste. 900, Los Angeles CA 90024-6519
Phone: 310-794-3193 **Fax:** 310-794-8531
Web: https://island.fim.ucla.edu/foundation/index.asp

HISTORICAL FINANCIALS
Company Type: Private - Not-for-Profit

Income Statement

	REVENUE ($ mil.)	NET INCOME ($ mil.)	NET PROFIT MARGIN	EMPLOYEES
				FYE: June 30
06/11	351	447	127.3%	317
06/10	144	157	109.4%	0
06/09	128	(37)	—	0
06/00	0	0	—	0
Annual Growth	—	—	—	—

2011 Year-End Financials

Debt ratio: ——
Return on equity: 127.30%
Cash ($ mil.): 1
Current ratio: —
Long-term debt ($ mil.): —

Dividends
Yield: —
Payout: —
Market value ($ mil.): —

THE UNION HOSPITAL OF CECIL COUNTY INC

LOCATIONS

HQ: THE UNION HOSPITAL OF CECIL COUNTY INC
106 BOW ST, ELKTON, MD 21921-5544
Phone: 410-398-4000
Web: www.uhcc.com

HISTORICAL FINANCIALS
Company Type: Private

Income Statement

	REVENUE ($ mil.)	NET INCOME ($ mil.)	NET PROFIT MARGIN	EMPLOYEES
				FYE: June 30
06/11	141	1	1.3%	2,203
06/10	130	(4)	—	0
06/09	123	(6)	—	0
06/08	1	(0)	—	0
Annual Growth	376.6%	—	—	—

2011 Year-End Financials

Debt ratio: ——
Return on equity: 1.30%
Cash ($ mil.): 6
Current ratio: 2.00
Long-term debt ($ mil.): —

Dividends
Yield: —
Payout: —
Market value ($ mil.): —

THE UNION MEMORIAL HOSPITAL

Not quite for time immemorial but MedStar Union Memorial Hospital (formerly Union Memorial Hospital) has been caring for patients for a long time (since 1839). The Baltimore-area facility is a specialty acute-care hospital with 250 beds and more than 620 physicians. Areas of clinical research and expertise include cardiac care orthopedics and sports medicine. In addition it offers a range of inpatient and outpatient services including diabetes and endocrine center eye surgery center general surgery oncology and thoracic and vascular surgery. MedStar Union Memorial offers post-graduate programs orthopedic surgery residencies and hand surgery fellowships. The company is a part of MedStar Health.

Operations
MedStar Union Memorial offers a full array of diagnostic medical surgical and rehabilitative services. The hospital provides graduate medical education through residency programs and fellowship programs. MedStar Union Memorial offers 19 post-graduate first year positions in medicine; a surgical training program; and an orthopedic surgical program. MedStar's Online Clinical Library provides access both onsite and offsite to electronic resources for drug information evidence-based medicine point of care full-test textbooks and more the 400 full-text journals.

Strategy
To emphasize it parent's brand as part of its future growth strategy Union Memorial Hospital changed its name to MedStar Union Memorial Hospital in 2012.

Ownership
The company is a part of MedStar Health.

Company Background
As Union Memorial the company celebrated its sesquicentennial anniversary in 2004. The hospital has been repeatedly recognized as among "America's Best Hospitals" by U.S. News & World Report. It's also considered one of the top 100 hospitals for intensive care and cardiovascular services.

EXECUTIVES

VP Finance, Joseph B. Smith
President and Director, Bradley S. Chambers
VP Medical Affairs, Stuart B. Bell
VP Patient Care Services, Sharon Bottcher
VP Orthopedics Anesthesiology and Surgery, Steve Koenigsberg
VP Cardiovascular Services, Cheryl Lunnen
Assistant VP Information Technology, Mike W. Dailey
VP MedStar Sports Health, Lew Lyon
VP Operations, Neil MacDonald
VP Human Resources, Holly Phipps Adams
Chairman, Mark T. Jensen
Vice-Chair, Ebben D. Finney III
Assistant Treasurer, Joseph B. Smith Jr.
Assistant Secretary, Linda Heath
Manager Media Relations, Debra Schindler
VP Philanthropy, Michael C. Cather
President and Director, Bradley S. Chambers
Vice-Chair, Ebben D. Finney III
Director, Derrick A. Adams
Director, Philip C. Buescher
Director, Timothy D. A. Chriss
Director, Judith Feustle
Director, Alice Ann Finnerty
Director, Roger B. Hayden
Director, Matthew B. Hitt
Director, Lawrence A. La Motte
Director, Leslie Matthews
Director, George W. Moran
Director, Thomas B. O'Neill
Director, Michael Randolph
Director, Edward Rosenberg
Director, Kenneth A. Samet, age 54
Director, Peter Sloane
Director, David N. Willis
Director, Christopher G. Wunder

LOCATIONS

HQ: Union Memorial Hospital
201 E. University Pkwy., Baltimore MD 21218
Phone: 410-554-2000   **Fax:** 410-554-2110
Web: www.unionmemorial.org

PRODUCTS/OPERATIONS

Selected Facilities
Arnold Palmer SportsHealth Center
The Curtis National Hand Center
The Harry and Jeanette Weinberg Heart Institute
Union Memorial Orthopaedics and Sports Medicine
Vascular Institute

COMPETITORS

Anne Arundel Medical
  Center
Johns Hopkins Health
  System

LifeBridge Health
St. Agnes HealthCare
University of Maryland
  Medical System

HISTORICAL FINANCIALS
Company Type: Subsidiary

Income Statement
FYE: June 30

	REVENUE ($ mil.)	NET INCOME ($ mil.)	NET PROFIT MARGIN	EMPLOYEES
06/11	428	17	4.1%	2,500
06/09	438	0	—	0
06/08	424	28	6.7%	0
06/05	320	0	—	0
Annual Growth	10.1%	—	—	—

2011 Year-End Financials

Debt ratio: ——
Return on equity: 4.10%
Cash ($ mil.): 0
Current ratio: 1.20
Long-term debt ($ mil.): ——

Dividends
  Yield: —
  Payout: —
Market value ($ mil.): —

THE UNIVERSITY OF DAYTON

More than 10000 students make the University of Dayton one of the nation's largest Catholic universities and the largest private university in Ohio. The institution offers some 70 majors. UD was founded in 1850 by the Society of Mary (the Marianists). Well-known alumni include the late author and columnist Erma Bombeck and Super Bowl-winning NFL coaches Jon Gruden and Chuck Noll.

EXECUTIVES

Chair, Allen M. Hill, age 66
President, Daniel J. Curran
VP Research and Executive Director UDRI, Mickey V. McCabe
Associate Provost and CIO, Thomas D. (Tom) Skill
Dean University Libraries, Kathleen M. Webb
VP Finance and Administrative Services, Thomas E. Burkhardt
Director Government and Regional Relations, Ted Bucaro
Dean College of Arts and Science, Paul Benson
VP Human Resources, Joyce M. Carter
President Academic Senate, David W. Darrow
Interim Dean School of Engineering, Malcolm Daniels
Dean Graduate School, Thomas Eggemeier
VP Enrollment Management and Marketing, Sundar Kumarasamy
Dean School of Law, Lisa Kloppenberg
Dean School of Education and Allied Professions, Thomas J. Lasley
Interim VP University Advancement, Dave Harper
Associate VP Public Relations, Teri Rizvi
Provost, Joseph Saliba
VP Student Development, William Fischer
Associate Provost Faculty and Administrative Affairs, Joseph A. Untener
Dean School of Business Administration, Matthew Shank
VP and Director Athletics, Tim Wabler
Chief Accounting Officer, Lisa S. Mastrobuono
Director Purchases and Business Services, Ken Soucy
Chair, H. John (Jack) Proud
Vice Chair, Stephen M. Glodek
VP Mission and Rector, James F. Fitz
Executive Director International Center for Marianist Formation and Trustee, Thomas F. Giardino
Rector and Trustee, Rev Paul M. Marshall
VP Facilities Management, Beth H. Keyes
Trustee, Catherine V. Babington, age 59
Trustee, Allen M. Hill, age 66
Trustee, David P. Yeager, age 59
Trustee, Richard H. Finan, age 77
President Secretary and Trustee, Daniel J. Curran
Trustee, Robert J. (Bob) Froehlich
Trustee, H. John (Jack) Proud
Vice Chair, Stephen M. Glodek
Trustee, Edward M. Brink
Trustee, William J. Campbell
Trustee, Rev Thomas A. Cardone
Trustee, Annette Casella
Trustee, Margaret A. Cavanaugh
Trustee, Steven D. Cobb
Trustee, Rev James F. Fitz
Trustee, David P. Fitzgerald
Trustee, Frank P. Geraci
Executive Director International Center for Marianist Formation and Trustee, Thomas F. Giardino
Trustee, Francisco T. Gonzalez
Trustee, Darlene Gutmann
Trustee, John Haley
Trustee, George Hanley
Trustee, Susan Kettering
Trustee, Peter Luongo
Rector and Trustee, Rev Paul M. Marshall
Trustee, Richard Pfleger
Trustee, John Riazzi
Trustee, Kurtis (Kurt) Sanford
Trustee, Katharine Schipper
Trustee, Westina Matthews Shatteen
Trustee, Rev Ralph A. Siefert
Trustee, Sister Francis Marie Thrailkill
Trustee, Andrew F. Veres
Trustee, Rev Daryl Ward
Trustee, David C. Winch
Auditors: Ernst&YoungLLP

LOCATIONS

HQ: University of Dayton
300 College Park, Dayton OH 45469
Phone: 937-229-1000   **Fax:** 973-408-3068
Web: www.drew.edu

HISTORICAL FINANCIALS
Company Type: School

Income Statement
FYE: June 30

	REVENUE ($ mil.)	NET INCOME ($ mil.)	NET PROFIT MARGIN	EMPLOYEES
06/12	418	(21)	—	4,500
06/11	402	104	26.1%	0
06/10	396	54	13.7%	0
06/09	410	(103)	—	0
Annual Growth	0.7%	—	—	—

2012 Year-End Financials

Debt ratio: ——
Return on equity: (-5.10)%
Cash ($ mil.): 34
Current ratio: —
Long-term debt ($ mil.): —

Dividends
  Yield: —
  Payout: —
Market value ($ mil.): —

THE UNIVERSITY OF FINDLAY

LOCATIONS

HQ: THE UNIVERSITY OF FINDLAY
1000 N MAIN ST, FINDLAY, OH 45840-3653
Phone: 419-422-8313
Web: www.findlay.edu

HISTORICAL FINANCIALS
Company Type: Private

Income Statement
FYE: June 30

	REVENUE ($ mil.)	NET INCOME ($ mil.)	NET PROFIT MARGIN	EMPLOYEES
06/12	81	3	4.7%	800
06/11	84	14	17.5%	0
06/10	0	0	—	0
06/09	79	(1)	—	0
Annual Growth	0.8%	—	—	—

2012 Year-End Financials

Debt ratio: ——
Return on equity: 4.70%
Cash ($ mil.): 0
Current ratio: —
Long-term debt ($ mil.): —

Dividends
  Yield: —
  Payout: —
Market value ($ mil.): —

THE UNIVERSITY OF HARTFORD

This is a 50-year-old university with a 130-year legacy. If you can't do the math perhaps you need not apply to University of Hartford. While its roots date back to 1877 the university wasn't officially chartered until 1957 with the merger of the Hartford Art School the Hartt School of Music and Hillyer College. University of Hartford still has a strong arts program and its Museum of American

Political Life is home to what has been called the country's largest private collection of political memorabilia. The school which operates three campuses in West Hartford has about 7400 students enrolled in nearly 90 undergraduate and more than 30 graduate programs including business nursing and engineering.

EXECUTIVES

President, Walter Harrison
VP Student Affairs and Dean Students, J. Lee Peters
Human Resources Manager, Jen Conley
Associate VP and Treasurer, Thomas J. Perra
Associate Provost and Dean Undergraduate Studies, Guy C. Colarulli
Dean Admission, Richard A. Zeiser
VP Finance and Administration, Arosha Jayawickrema
Director Media Relations, David (Dave) Isgur
Executive Director Information Technology Services and CIO, George Brophy
VP Institutional Advancement, Christine Pina
Director Career Services, John Kniering
VP University Relations, John J. Carson, age 68
Director University Libraries, Randi Lynn Ashton-Pritting
Provost, Lynn Pasquerella
VP General Counsel and Secretary, Thomas Dorer
Assistant Provost and Dean Faculty Development, H. Frederick Sweitzer
Dean Graduate Studies, Peter Diffley
Provost, Sharon L. Vasquez

LOCATIONS

HQ: The University of Hartford
200 Bloomfield Ave., West Hartford CT 06117
Phone: 860-768-4100   **Fax:** 860-768-4070
Web: www.hartford.edu

HISTORICAL FINANCIALS
Company Type: School

Income Statement				FYE: June 30
	REVENUE ($ mil.)	NET INCOME ($ mil.)	NET PROFIT MARGIN	EMPLOYEES
06/12	165	(10)	—	950
06/11	165	19	11.6%	0
06/10	159	2	1.8%	0
06/09	167	(17)	—	0
Annual Growth	(0.3%)	—	—	—

2012 Year-End Financials
Debt ratio: —
Return on equity: (-6.30)%
Cash ($ mil.): 29
Current ratio: —
Long-term debt ($ mil.): —
Dividends
  Yield: —
  Payout: —
  Market value ($ mil.): —

THE UNIVERSITY OF THE ARTS

LOCATIONS
HQ: THE UNIVERSITY OF THE ARTS
320 S BROAD ST, PHILADELPHIA, PA 19102-4994
Phone: 215-717-6000

HISTORICAL FINANCIALS
Company Type: Private

Income Statement				FYE: June 30
	REVENUE ($ mil.)	NET INCOME ($ mil.)	NET PROFIT MARGIN	EMPLOYEES
06/11	105	4	4.4%	650
06/10	97	(0)	—	0
06/09	98	0	—	0
06/08	97	5	5.4%	0
Annual Growth	2.5%	(4.5%)	—	—

2011 Year-End Financials
Debt ratio: —
Return on equity: 4.40%
Cash ($ mil.): 13
Current ratio: —
Long-term debt ($ mil.): —
Dividends
  Yield: —
  Payout: —
  Market value ($ mil.): —

THE UNIVERSITY OF THE SOUTH

With more than two dozen Rhodes Scholars among its alumni The University of the South known as Sewanee is ranked among America's top private liberal arts colleges. Along with churning out brilliant graduates Sewanee is also home to a seminary of the Episcopal Church and a School of Letters —a summer Master's Degree program in English and creative writing. Sewanee offers more than 35 majors including computer science psychology mathematics theology and history. It also holds the copyrights to Tennessee Williams' body of work which was left to the school by the playwright. Sewanee traces its roots back to 1857 when Episcopal leaders from 10 southern states met to discuss the formation of the school.

EXECUTIVES

Provost, Linda Lankewicz
VP University Relations, Robert W. (Rob) Pearigen
Treasurer, Jerry Forster
Dean of Admission, David Lesesne
Associate Provost Information Technology Services and University Librarian, Vicki Sells
Dean of the School of Theology, William S. (Bill) Stafford
Dean of the College of Arts and Sciences, John J. Gatta Jr.
Dean of Students, Eric E. Hartman
Executive Director Alumni Association, Jay Fisher
Executive Director Marketing and Communications, Mark Kelly
Vice Chancellor and President, John M. McCardel Jr.

LOCATIONS

HQ: The University of the South
735 University Ave., Sewanee TN 37383
Phone: 931-598-1000   **Fax:** 931-598-3248
Web: www.sewanee.edu

COMPETITORS

Lane College
Lee University
Lipscomb University
Rhodes College
Tennessee Tech
Vanderbilt University

HISTORICAL FINANCIALS
Company Type: School

Income Statement				FYE: June 30
	REVENUE ($ mil.)	NET INCOME ($ mil.)	NET PROFIT MARGIN	EMPLOYEES
06/12	81	(1)	—	550
06/11	81	52	64.8%	0
06/10	80	32	40.4%	0
Annual Growth	0.5%	—	—	—

2012 Year-End Financials
Debt ratio: —
Return on equity: (-1.50)%
Cash ($ mil.): 2
Current ratio: —
Long-term debt ($ mil.): —
Dividends
  Yield: —
  Payout: —
  Market value ($ mil.): —

THE UNIVERSITY OF TULSA

If you're "Living on Tulsa Time" and looking for an education then the home of the Golden Hurricanes is the place to be. The University of Tulsa is a private university affiliated with the Presbyterian Church (USA) with an enrollment of more than 4000 students. The school offers nearly 60 undergraduate and more than 30 graduate programs including ten doctoral degree programs at colleges of arts and sciences business and engineering and natural sciences. The University of Tulsa was founded in Muskogee in 1882 as the Presbyterian School for Indian Girls and was chartered as Henry Kendall College in 1894. The school moved to Tulsa in 1907 and became The University of Tulsa in 1920.

EXECUTIVES

Associate VP and Controller, Mike Thesenvitz
General Counsel, Barbara F. Geffen
Associate VP Human Resources and Risk Management, Wayne A. Paulison
President, Steadman Upham
Associate VP University Relations, Barbara Sorochty
VP Academic Affairs and Provost, Roger Nathaniel Blais
Director Athletics, Lawrence Richard (Bubba) Cunningham
Assistant Director Institutional Reseach and Records, Carl H. Cunningham
EVP, Kevan C. Buck
VP Enrollment and Student Services, Roger W. Sorochty
SVP Planning and Outreach, Janis I. Zink

Dean Henry Kendall College of Arts and Sciences, Dale Thomas Benediktson

Dean College of Business Administration, Alfred Gale Sullenberger

Dean College of Engineering and Natural Sciences, Steven J. Bellovich

Dean Research and Graduate Studies, Janet A. Haggerty

Associate Dean McFarlin Library, Francine Fisk

Associate VP Information Services, Richard Paul Kearns

Director Networking Services, Tracia D. Moreland

VP Information Services and CIO, Dale A. Schoenefeld

Director Alumni Relations and Donor Relations, Sandy M. Willmann

Senior Administrative Associate to the President, Tia P. Creamer

Director New Student Programs and Services, Laura McNeese

Chair Management and Marketing, Ralph W. Jackson

Executive Assistant to the President, Jacqueline H. Caldwell

LOCATIONS

HQ: The University of Tulsa
600 S. Tucker Dr., Tulsa OK 74104-3126
Phone: 918-631-2000   Fax: 918-631-5003
Web: www.utulsa.edu

HISTORICAL FINANCIALS

Company Type: School

Income Statement

	REVENUE ($ mil.)	NET INCOME ($ mil.)	NET PROFIT MARGIN	EMPLOYEES
06/12	173	(23)	—	1,033
06/11	180	134	74.7%	0
06/10	163	74	45.8%	0
06/09	154	(197)	—	0
Annual Growth	4.1%	—	—	—

2012 Year-End Financials

Debt ratio: ——
Return on equity: (-13.40)%
Cash ($ mil.): 30   Dividends
Current ratio: 0.90   Yield: —
Long-term debt ($ mil.): —   Payout: —
     Market value ($ mil.): —

THE URBAN INSTITUTE

The Urban Institute is a not-for-profit economic and social policy research organization that oversees research projects in such areas as education health policy employment income and benefits housing and communities population studies poverty and judicial issues. Its Urban Institute Press publishes books and reports addressing social and economic issues from tax policy to prison reform. About three-fourths of the institution's funding comes from the federal government; most of the rest comes from foundations including The Aspen Institute and the California Endowment. The Urban Institute was established as a non-partisan research facility in 1968 by the Johnson Administration.

EXECUTIVES

Chairman, Joel L. Fleishman, age 78
President and Trustee, Robert D. Reischauer
EVP CFO and Treasurer, John R. Rogers
VP Communication, Kathleen Courrier
Assistant Treasurer and Director Administration, Everett Madden
Director Financial Planning and Analysis and Assistant Treasurer, Angela M. Keenan
Vice Chairman, Robert M. Solow
VP Research, Margery Austin Turner
Corporate Secretary, Maida Schifter
Trustee, Jamie S. Gorelick, age 61
Trustee, Richard C. (Rick) Green Jr., age 57
Trustee, Freeman A. Hrabowski III, age 61
President and Trustee, Robert D. Reischauer
Vice Chairman, Robert M. Solow
Trustee, Fernando A. Guerra
Trustee, Mary John Miller
Trustee, Melvin L. Oliver
Trustee, Judy Woodruff
Trustee, Afsaneh M. Beschloss
Trustee, Rebecca Blank
Trustee, Jeremy Travis

LOCATIONS

HQ: Urban Institute
2100 M St. NW, Washington DC 20037
Phone: 202-833-7200   Fax: 202-466-3982
Web: www.urban.org

PRODUCTS/OPERATIONS

2008 Expenditures

% of total	
Federal	62
Private	26
Other/state &	12
Total	**100**

HISTORICAL FINANCIALS

Company Type: Private - Not-for-Profit

Income Statement

FYE: December 31

	REVENUE ($ mil.)	NET INCOME ($ mil.)	NET PROFIT MARGIN	EMPLOYEES
12/11	71	(2)	—	350
12/09	67	12	18.6%	0
12/08	64	(28)	—	0
12/07	65	78	119.5%	0
Annual Growth	3.1%	—	—	—

2011 Year-End Financials

Debt ratio: ——
Return on equity: (-3.90)%
Cash ($ mil.): 14   Dividends
Current ratio: 1.30   Yield: —
Long-term debt ($ mil.): —   Payout: —
     Market value ($ mil.): —

THE VILLAGES TRI COUNTY MEDICAL CENTER INC

LOCATIONS

HQ: THE VILLAGES TRI COUNTY MEDICAL CENTER INC
1451 EL CAMINO REAL, LADY LAKE, FL 32159-0041
Phone: 352-751-8000
Web: www.cfhalliance.org

HISTORICAL FINANCIALS

Company Type: Private

Income Statement

FYE: June 30

	REVENUE ($ mil.)	NET INCOME ($ mil.)	NET PROFIT MARGIN	EMPLOYEES
06/11	142	8	5.9%	200
06/10	119	1	1.5%	0
06/09	94	(7)	—	0
06/08	74	(1)	—	0
Annual Growth	23.9%	—	—	—

2011 Year-End Financials

Debt ratio: ——
Return on equity: 5.90%
Cash ($ mil.): 28   Dividends
Current ratio: 2.60   Yield: —
Long-term debt ($ mil.): —   Payout: —
     Market value ($ mil.): —

THE WALDINGER CORPORATION

The Waldinger Corporation may actually do most of its work before the walls are even up. The company is an electrical mechanical and sheet metal contractor that primarily serves US customers across the Midwest and Southeast. Through its work in more than 40 states Waldinger designs fabricates installs and maintains HVAC refrigeration electrical plumbing and piping for commercial institutional and industrial clients. Waldinger also operates a division devoted to the food service industry. The company has offices in Iowa Kansas Missouri and Nebraska. Austrian tinsmith Harry Waldinger founded the company as Capital City Tin Shop in 1906.

Geographic Reach

From its headquarters in Des Moines Iowa Waldinger caters to clients nationwide through its offices in the Midwestern states of Iowa Kansas Missouri and Nebraska.

Operations

Waldinger has worked on projects throughout most of the US covering more than 40 states. Its projects portfolio includes a handful of nuclear power plants ethanol plants the Houston Astrodome the Louisiana Superdome and Cape Kennedy's Vehicle Assembly Building.

For commercial clients Waldinger works on corporate headquarters data centers office buildings and retail outlets. Industrial projects typically include alternative energy manufacturing water and waste water. Projects in the research and education sector include laboratories universities and schools and residence halls. Waldinger also serves the healthcare market through projects for hospitals and clinics and assisted living facilities as well as for arenas and casinos as part of the sports and entertainment market.

EXECUTIVES

CEO, Thomas (Tom) Koehn
Director Human Resources, Becky Buch
CFO, Mick Nordgren
Manager Information Technology, Barbara Steinbeck

LOCATIONS

HQ: The Waldinger Corporation
2601 Bell Ave., Des Moines IA 50321-1189
Phone: 515-284-1911　　**Fax:** 515-323-5150
Web: www.waldinger.com

PRODUCTS/OPERATIONS

Selected Sectors
Commercial
Healthcare
Hospitality
Industrial
Research and education
Sports and entertainment

COMPETITORS

ACCO	Market & Johnson
Duke Construction	MasTec
EMCOR	Siemens AG
F.A. Wilhelm	Yates Companies
Fluor	
Limbach Facility Services	

HISTORICAL FINANCIALS

Company Type: Private

Income Statement

FYE: December 31

	REVENUE ($ mil.)	NET INCOME ($ mil.)	NET PROFIT MARGIN	EMPLOYEES
12/11	160	0	—	900
12/10	155	0	—	0
12/09	174	0	—	0
12/08	193	0	—	0
Annual Growth	(6.0%)	—	—	—

2011 Year-End Financials

Debt ratio: ——
Return on equity: —
Cash ($ mil.): 26
Current ratio: 1.70
Long-term debt ($ mil.): —

Dividends
　Yield: —
　Payout: —
Market value ($ mil.): —

THE WARD MACHINERY COMPANY

LOCATIONS

HQ: THE WARD MACHINERY COMPANY
10615 BEAVER DAM RD, COCKEYSVILLE, MD 21030-2204
Phone: 410-584-7700

HISTORICAL FINANCIALS

Company Type: Private

Income Statement

FYE: September 30

	REVENUE ($ mil.)	NET INCOME ($ mil.)	NET PROFIT MARGIN	EMPLOYEES
09/11	90	0	—	652
09/10	78	0	—	0
Annual Growth	15.8%	—	—	—

2011 Year-End Financials

Debt ratio: ——
Return on equity: —
Cash ($ mil.): 4
Current ratio: 0.70
Long-term debt ($ mil.): —

Dividends
　Yield: —
　Payout: —
Market value ($ mil.): —

THE WASHINGTON HOSPITAL

LOCATIONS

HQ: THE WASHINGTON HOSPITAL
155 WILSON AVE, WASHINGTON, PA 15301-3398
Phone: 724-225-7000
Web: www.washingtonhospital.org

HISTORICAL FINANCIALS

Company Type: Private

Income Statement

FYE: June 30

	REVENUE ($ mil.)	NET INCOME ($ mil.)	NET PROFIT MARGIN	EMPLOYEES
06/11	249	20	8.1%	1,900
06/10	235	12	5.2%	0
06/09	228	(14)	—	0
06/08	4	2	49.9%	0
Annual Growth	274.4%	104.6%	—	—

2011 Year-End Financials

Debt ratio: ——
Return on equity: 8.10%
Cash ($ mil.): 19
Current ratio: 2.10
Long-term debt ($ mil.): —

Dividends
　Yield: —
　Payout: —
Market value ($ mil.): —

THE WASHINGTON UNIVERSITY

Washington University in St. Louis (WUSTL) is the gateway to higher education for more than 13000 students. Founded in 1853 the independent university offers 90 bachelor's master's and doctoral degrees and has about 3400 faculty members. It offers approximately 1500 courses in fields such as arts and sciences business design and visual arts engineering law medicine and social work. WUSTL which has multiple campuses in and near the city of St. Louis also offers associate degree and continuing education programs. The affiliated Washington University Medical Center is an acute-care hospital that also provides educational training and research services.

In addition to the main 170-acre Danforth Campus in St. Louis WUSTL's facilities include the nearby 165-acre Medical Campus (housing the School of Medicine and the hospital facilities). WUSTL also operates three smaller satellite academic campuses and music research and art centers in the greater St. Louis area.

The Medical Campus conducts extensive collaborative studies between students faculty and hospital staff as well as external institutions. Areas of research include genome sequencing of cancer patients and children's developmental studies. The 2000-acre Tyson Research Center outside the city is a biological field station that conducts environmental studies and research activities including renewable energy and sustainability programs some of which is coordinated with outside groups.

In 2011 WUSTL reported nearly $2.3 billion in revenues an increase of 5% over the previous year due to increased income from its patient care operations research grants and tuition segments. Nonoperational activities including interest on endowment investments and charitable gifts gave WUSTL's bottom line a boost in 2011 as well. The university has an endowment of some $5.4 billion.

WUSTL has made efforts to extend its collaborations with third parties which can help bring in academic and research funds. For instance in 2011 it formed a business school partnership with the Brookings Institution in Washington DC to offer courses on government and corporate policymaking and leadership development. In addition the university has worked to attract more government research grants in recent years. It is also upgrading some classroom and student facilities as well as hiring more experienced teachers and medical staff members to maintain its tuition auxiliary enterprise (lodging and vending) health services and research income expectations.

EXECUTIVES

Vice Chairman Board of Trustees, John F. McDonnell, age 73
Vice Chairman Board of Trustees, David W. Kemper, age 61
Executive Vice Chancellor for Administration, Henry S. Webber
Executive Vice Chancellor Alumni and Development Programs, David T. Blasingame
Provost and Executive Vice Chancellor Academic Affairs, Edward S. Macias
Vice Chancellor Scholarly Resources and Dean of Libraries, Shirley K. Baker
Executive Vice Chancellor and General Counsel, Michael R. Cannon

LOCATIONS

HQ: Washington University in St. Louis
1 Brookings Dr., St. Louis MO 63130
Phone: 314-935-5000   Fax: 314-935-7088
Web: www.wustl.edu

PRODUCTS/OPERATIONS

Selected Schools and Colleges

College of Arts & Sciences
  Graduate School of Arts & Sciences
  University College and Summer School (Arts & Sciences)
George Warren Brown School of Social Work
Sam Fox School of Design & Visual Arts
School of Engineering & Applied Science
School of Law
School of Medicine
Olin Business School

HISTORICAL FINANCIALS

Company Type: School

Income Statement

FYE: June 30

	REVENUE ($ mil.)	NET INCOME ($ mil.)	NET PROFIT MARGIN	EMPLOYEES
06/12	2,307	(49)	—	9,600
06/11	2,245	989	44.1%	0
06/10	2,129	682	32.0%	0
06/09	2,030	(1,351)	—	0
Annual Growth	4.4%	—	—	—

2012 Year-End Financials

Debt ratio: —
Return on equity: (-2.10)%
Cash ($ mil.): 148
Current ratio: —
Long-term debt ($ mil.): —

Dividends
  Yield: —
  Payout: —
Market value ($ mil.): —

THE WHITING-TURNER CONTRACTING COMPANY

Whiting-Turner Contracting provides construction management general contracting and design/build services primarily for large commercial institutional and infrastructure projects conducted across the US. A key player in retail construction the employee-owned company also undertakes such projects as biotech cleanrooms theme parks historical restorations senior living residences educational facilities stadiums and corporate headquarters. Clients past and present have included AT&T General Motors and Texas A&M University. Whiting-Turner Contracting operates some 30 locations nationwide. G.W.C. Whiting and LeBaron Turner founded the company in 1909 to build sewer lines.

Operations

Whiting-Turner Contracting's project portfolio includes the Joseph B. Whitehead Building at Emory University Vanderbilt Hall at Yale University projects at Universal Studios theme park and a vaccine facility at Chesapeake Biological Laboratories. Projects in the firm's hometown of Baltimore have included the city's convention center and the football stadium for the Baltimore Ravens. It completed about a dozen projects more recently. They include projects for the Horseshoe Casino Cleveland University of Maryland Baltimore County (UMBC) Performing Arts & Humanities Naval Facilities Engineering Command (NAVFAC) Jacksonville Sentara Princess Anne Hospital Norwalk Community College Texas A&M University at Galveston Mary Moody Northen Student Center renovation Opry Mills and College of Business & Economics.

Strategy

The company prefers to grow organically instead of making many acquisitions. It has been steadily expanding by opening new offices in places such as California Texas and Virginia.

EXECUTIVES

VP Richmond, Dani Niccolucci
Division VP Allentown, Jack DaSilva
Division VP Fort Lauderdale, Robert (Rob) Mitchell
VP Newark Delaware, James (Jim) Martini
SVP Bethesda, Richard L. Vogel Jr.
VP Pleasanton, Troy Caldwell
SVP Irvine, Len Cannatelli Jr.
SVP Baltimore, Gino J. Gemignani
VP Dallas and Houston, Espen S. Brooks
VP Bridgewater, Chris Martinson
SEVP Finance and CFO, Charles A. (Chuck) Irish
Division VP Atlanta, Keith Douglas
President and CEO, Willard Hackerman
SVP New Haven, Daniel (Dan) Bauer
VP Boston, Kevin Shields
VP Las Vegas, Paul Schmitt
VP Chantilly, Kempton C. Haile
VP Tampa, Brent A. Voyles
VP Denver, Mark Faul
VP San Diego, Steven Likins
VP Raleigh, Chris Carlson
VP Charlotte, Timothy Stevens
VP White Plains, David Brickley
VP Cambridge, John Nelson
VP Cleveland, Jeff Maeder
Recruiting Coordinator, Karen Lucas
Auditors: PricewaterhouseCoopersLLP

LOCATIONS

HQ: The Whiting-Turner Contracting Company
300 E. Joppa Rd., Baltimore MD 21286
Phone: 410-821-1100   Fax: 410-337-5770
Web: www.whiting-turner.com

Selected Locations

Maryland - Baltimore (Headquarters)
California - Irvine
California - Los Angeles
California - Pleasanton
California - Sacramento
California - San Diego
Colorado - Denver
Connecticut - New Haven
Delaware - Newark
District of Columbia
Florida - Ft. Lauderdale
Florida - Orlando
Florida - Tampa
Georgia - Atlanta
Maryland - Cambridge
Massachusetts - Boston
Missouri - Kansas City
Nevada - Las Vegas

New Jersey - Bridgewater
New York - White Plains
North Carolina - Charlotte
North Carolina - Raleigh
Ohio - Cleveland
Pennsylvania - Allentown
Texas - Dallas
Texas - Houston
Texas - San Antonio
Virginia - Chantilly
Virginia - Norfolk
Virginia - Richmond

PRODUCTS/OPERATIONS

Selected Services

Construction management
 Agency
 At-risk
Design/build
General contracting
Preconstruction

Selected Markets

Biotechnology and pharmaceutical
Cleanroom and high-technology
Education
Entertainment
Federal/military
Food/beverage distribution
Health care
Historical restoration
Industrial and manufacturing
Interiors
Life sciences
Lodging and hospitality
Mission critical facilities
Mixed use
Offices and headquarters
Parking garages
Restaurants
Retail
Senior living
Sports
Sustainable
Technology
 Microelectronics
 Nano
Theme parks
Utilities
Warehouse and distribution

COMPETITORS

Barton Malow	J.E. Dunn Construction
Bechtel	Group
Bovis Lend Lease	Jacobs Engineering
Choate Construction	Kitchell
Clark Construction	McCarthy Building
Group	Peter Kiewit Sons'
DPR Construction	Skanska
Fisher Development	Suffolk Construction
Fluor	Swinerton
Gilbane	The Weitz Company LLC
Hensel Phelps	Turner Corporation
Construction	Tutor Perini
Hoffman Corporation	

HISTORICAL FINANCIALS

Company Type: Private

Income Statement

FYE: December 31

	REVENUE ($ mil.)	NET INCOME ($ mil.)	NET PROFIT MARGIN	EMPLOYEES
12/11	3,897	57	1.5%	1,839
12/10	3,232	50	1.6%	0
12/09	3,504	48	1.4%	0
12/08	4,176	62	1.5%	0
Annual Growth	(2.3%)	(2.5%)	—	—

2011 Year-End Financials

Debt ratio: ——
Return on equity: 1.50%
Cash ($ mil.): 93
Current ratio: 0.70
Long-term debt ($ mil.): —

Dividends
 Yield: —
 Payout: —
Market value ($ mil.): —

THE WILLIAM PATERSON UNIVERSITY OF NEW JERSEY

Founded in 1855 as a normal school (teacher's college) for the city of Paterson New Jersey William Paterson University has evolved into a fully accredited liberal-arts university. William Paterson which has 1000 full-time faculty members enrolls about 10000 undergraduate and graduate students and offers more than 50 academic programs through five colleges. The university has a 370-acre campus with some 40 major buildings and other facilities including the David and Lorraine Cheng Library which boasts more than 350000 bound volumes. Tuition and fees are $10500 for full-time students who are residents. William Paterson is accredited by the Middle States Association of Colleges and Secondary Schools.

The university is named after statesman and patriot William Paterson (1745-1806). Paterson was New Jersey's first attorney general attendee at the 1787 Constitutional Convention in Philadelphia member of the first US Senate governor of New Jersey and chosen by George Washington as an associate justice of the US Supreme Court.

EXECUTIVES

Vice Chair, William J. (Will) Pesce, age 61
President and Trustee, Arnold Speert
VP Administration and Finance, Stephen Bolyai
VP Institutional Advancement, Sandra Deller
Provost and SVP Academic Affairs, Edward Weil
VP Student Development, John Martone
Associate Provost, Steve Hahn
Associate VP and Dean Graduate Studies and Research and Associate Professor Educational Leadership, Nina Jemmott
Associate VP Enrollment Management, William Anderson
Associate VP Administration, Timothy W. Fanning
Associate VP Institutional Advancement, Stuart Goldstein
Chief of Staff to the President and Board of Trustees, Marc Schaeffer
Executive Assistant to the Provost and SVP Academic Affairs and Associate Professor of Education, Robert Seal
Associate VP Capital Planning Design and Construction, Robert Bennett
Dean Christos M. Cotsakos College of Business and Professor of Economics Finance and Global Business, Sam Basu
Dean College of the Humanities and Social Sciences and Professor of History, Isabel Tirado
Dean College of Science and Health and Professor of Nursing, Sandra DeYoung
Executive Director for Continuing and Professional Education, Bernadette Tiernan

Associate VP and Dean of Student Development, Glen Sherman
Associate VP Campus Life, Roland Watts
Associate Dean College of Education and Associate Professor of Secondary and Middle School Education, Dorothy Feola
Associate Dean College of the Humanities and Social Sciences, Kara Rabbitt
Associate Dean College of Science and Health and Professor of Chemistry, Jean Fuller-Stanley
Secretary, Michael L. Jackson
Chair, Vincent J. Mazzola
Media Relations, Mary Beth Zeman
Associate VP for Human Resources, John Polding
Interim Associate Dean Christos M. Cotsakos College of Business and Associate Professor of Economics and Finance, Rajiv Kashyap
Interim Associate Dean College of the Arts and Communication and Professor of Art, Imafidon Olaye
Dean College of the Arts and Communication and Professor of Music, Raymond Torres-Santos
Interim Dean College of Education and Professor of Education, Ana Maria Schuhmann
Vice Chair, William J. (Will) Pesce, age 61
Trustee, Linda A. Niro, age 57
President and Trustee, Arnold Speert
Trustee, Stephen (Steve) Adzima
Trustee, Peter Fan
Trustee, Frederick L. Gruel
Trustee, Henry J. Pruitt Jr.
Trustee, Robert H. Taylor
Trustee, Jennifer Bauer
Trustee, Robert Guarasci
Trustee, Anna Marie Mascolo

LOCATIONS

HQ: William Paterson University
 300 Pompton Rd., Wayne NJ 07470
Phone: 973-720-2000   **Fax:** 215-233-3201
Web: www.coventry.com

PRODUCTS/OPERATIONS

Selected Academic Programs

Accounting
Anthropology
Art
Biology
Chemistry
Communication
Computer Science
Economics
English
Environmental Science
Geography
History
Languages and Culture
Mathematics
Music
Nursing
Philosophy
Political Science
Psychology

HISTORICAL FINANCIALS

Company Type: School

Income Statement

FYE: June 30

	REVENUE ($ mil.)	NET INCOME ($ mil.)	NET PROFIT MARGIN	EMPLOYEES
06/12	158	8	5.5%	1,300
06/09	0	0		0
06/08	118	17	15.1%	0
06/07	109	19	18.2%	0
Annual Growth	13.1%	(24.0%)	—	—

2012 Year-End Financials

Debt ratio: ——
Return on equity: 5.50%
Cash ($ mil.): 115
Current ratio: 4.10
Long-term debt ($ mil.): ——

Dividends
Yield: ——
Payout: ——
Market value ($ mil.): ——

THE WILLS GROUP INC

The Wills Group willingly delivers petroleum products and related products and services to its customer base in southern Maryland and adjacent areas. The family-owned company operates four business subsidiaries: Dash-In Convenience Stores (with 35 locations including 18 franchises); Delmarva Oil and Southern Maryland Oil (the largest home heating oil delivery service companies in the region); and Southern Maryland Oil (SMO) Motor Fuels (distribution of diesel gasoline and kerosene products). More than 90% of SMO's gasoline products are Shell-branded fuels. The Wills Group supplies more than 300 dealer-operated gas stations in Delaware southern Maryland and Washington DC.

The company has grown by building complementary businesses around its core fueling activities and by focusing on delivering services within a geographically limited area.

Expanding its network of gas stations in 2009 The Wills Group's SMO formed Potomac Energy Holdings a joint venture with Motiva to operate 73 Shell-branded gas stations in Maryland. SMO grew further in 2010 buying 16 dealer operated Exxon-branded gas stations in Delaware.

The company was founded in 1926 by Jim Wills and Harold Swann. In 1942 The Wills Group was the first principal fuel supplier to the newly built Patuxent Naval Air Station. In 1972 the company developed the first branded self-service station in Maryland. In 2012 Lock Wills was serving as the president of The Wills Group.

EXECUTIVES

President, Lock Wills
EVP Finance and Administration, Charles F. Boyers
EVP Retail Marketing and Director, Mel L. Strine
VP Human Resources, Stephen Niven
Manager Operations, Rich Morsberger
Director IT, Mike Adams

LOCATIONS

HQ: The Wills Group Inc.
6355 Crain Hwy., La Plata MD 20646
Phone: 301-932-3600   **Fax:** 301-932-3629
Web: www.willsgroup.com

COMPETITORS

Dixie Gas & Oil
Petroleum Marketers
Quarles Petroleum
SMF Energy
Weis Markets
Woodfin Oil

HISTORICAL FINANCIALS

Company Type: Private

Income Statement

FYE: September 30

	REVENUE ($ mil.)	NET INCOME ($ mil.)	NET PROFIT MARGIN	EMPLOYEES
09/11	1,052	17	1.7%	280
09/10	768	13	1.7%	0
09/09	614	11	1.9%	0
09/08	913	5	0.6%	0
Annual Growth	**4.8%**	**47.7%**	—	—

2011 Year-End Financials

Debt ratio: ——
Return on equity: 1.70%
Cash ($ mil.): 25
Current ratio: 0.80
Long-term debt ($ mil.): ——

Dividends
Yield: ——
Payout: ——
Market value ($ mil.): ——

THIRTEEN

You might say this broadcaster has some public appeal for New Yorkers. Educational Broadcasting Corporation (EBC) operates two public broadcasting stations serving the New York City area. Its flagship Thirteen/WNET the highest-rated public TV station in the US offers a wealth of locally produced content focused on the Big Apple as well as programming supplied by the Public Broadcasting Service (PBS). Thirteen/WNET is also a major producer of shows for PBS that are distributed to other public TV stations. In addition the non-profit corporation operates WLIW21 which serves audiences on Long Island as well as several digital channels and on-demand video services. Thirteen/WNET began broadcasting in 1962.

In 2007 EBC brought in former NBC News president Neal Shapiro to serve as president of the public broadcaster; he was appointed CEO the following year. Under his leadership Thirteen/WNET has been restructuring operations and making reductions in staff to cut costs. EBC has also beefed up its fundraising efforts.

EXECUTIVES

Chairman Emeritus, Henry R. Kravis, age 68
President and CEO, Neal B. Shapiro, age 54
VP Institutional Advancement, Barbara Bantivoglio
Vice Chairman, Catherine C. (Catie) Marron
Anchor, Rafael Pi Roman
Staff Announcer, Tom Stewart
Director Interactive Group, Anthony Chapman
Technical Director Interactive Group, Brian Patrick Lee
Director Production Interactive Group, Brian Brunius
Director Online Design Interactive Group, Sabina Daley
Department Coordinator Interactive Group, Diana Cofresi-Terrero
Director Educational Technologies Interactive Group, Brigitte Magar Matsuoka
Senior Content Producer Interactive Group, Sandra Goldberg
Technical Producer Interactive Group, Mikki Monkolchayut
VP CFO and Treasurer, Thomas A. Conway
VP Media Operations and CIO, Kenneth (Ken) Devine

VP and Director Communications and Brand Management, Stella Giammasi
VP Institutional Development, Deborah Cross MacFarlane
VP Business Affairs and Strategic Initiatives General Counsel and Secretary, Joshua C. Nathan
VP and Director Programming, Tamara E. Robinson
VP and Director Education, Ronald Thorpe
President and General Manager WLIW, Terrel L. Cass
VP National Productions WLIW, Roy A. Hammond
VP National Marketing and Content Development, Donn Rogosin
VP Marketing and Communications WLIW, Laura C. Savini
Vice Chairman, Barry R. Shapiro
Vice Chairman, Dirk Ziff
Chairman, James S. Tisch, age 57
Chairman Emeritus, William M. Ellinghaus
VP Acquisitions Co-Productions and Sales WLIW, Gillian Rose
Senior Publicist, Edward Gregory
VP National Productions, Stephen Segaller
VP and Acting General Manager, Roslyn Davis
Director, Barry S. Sternlicht, age 50
Director, James L. Dolan, age 56
Director, Philip A. (Phil) Laskawy, age 71
Director, D. Ronald Daniel, age 81
Chairman Emeritus, Henry R. Kravis, age 68
Director, Bernard L. Schwartz, age 83
Director, Albert R. Gamper Jr., age 70
Director, Morris W. Offit, age 75
Director, Michael I. Sovern, age 80
Director, Jeffrey L. (Jeff) Bewkes, age 59
Director, Barry Diller, age 70
Director, William F. Reilly, age 73
Director, Meredith Auld Brokaw
Director, Mario L. Baeza, age 61
Director, Aerin Lauder, age 42
Director, Steven Rattner, age 59
Vice Chairman, Catherine C. (Catie) Marron
Vice Chairman, Barry R. Shapiro
Vice Chairman, Dirk Ziff
Director, Charlotte N. Ackert
Director, Ralph M. Baruch
Director, Michael J. Bertuch
Director, Raymond G. Chambers
Director, Matthew T. Crosson
Director, Earl G. Graves Jr.
Director, Horace Hagedorn
Director, Thomas S. Johnson
Director, Mark M. Kaplan
Director, Bruce J. Klatsky
Director, Douglas W. Kurz
Director, Betsy Lack
Director, John A. Levin
Director, Betty Bao Lord
Director, James S. Marcus
Director, Thomas J. Moran
Director, Thomas A. Nicolette, age 59
Director, George D. O'Neill
Director, Ponchitta Pierce
Director, Judith Resnick
Director, Stephen Robert
Director, Marsha E. Simms
Director, A.J.C. Smith
Director, Scott M. Stuart
Director, Ann G. Tenenbaum
Director, Roger B. Tilles
Chairman, James S. Tisch, age 57
Director, Rosalind P. Walter
Director, Claude Becker Wasserstein
Director, Josh S. Weston
Director, Michael J. Wolf
Chairman Emeritus, William M. Ellinghaus

LOCATIONS

HQ: Educational Broadcasting Corporation
450 W. 33rd St., New York NY 10001
Phone: 212-560-2000   **Fax:** 212-560-1314
Web: www.thirteen.org

COMPETITORS

A&E Networks	ION Media Networks
ABC Inc.	NBC
CBS Corp	Scripps Networks
Discovery	Turner Broadcasting
Communications	Univision

HISTORICAL FINANCIALS

Company Type: Private - Not-for-Profit

Income Statement

FYE: June 30

	REVENUE ($ mil.)	NET INCOME ($ mil.)	NET PROFIT MARGIN	EMPLOYEES
06/11	105	12	11.6%	400
06/10	127	10	7.9%	0
06/09	146	(39)	—	0
06/08	170	3	1.9%	0
Annual Growth	(14.7%)	54.9%	—	—

2011 Year-End Financials

Debt ratio: ——
Return on equity: 11.60%
Cash ($ mil.): 1
Current ratio: 0.40
Long-term debt ($ mil.): —

Dividends
  Yield: —
  Payout: —
  Market value ($ mil.): —

THOMAS JEFFERSON SCHOOL OF LAW INC

If Thomas Jefferson ever wanted to sunbathe between bouts of shaping our nation this would have been the place. Thomas Jefferson School of Law (TJSL) offers a traditional program of legal education leading to the award of master's degrees and Juris Doctor degrees. The private school offers a three year full-time or a four year part-time program. Its campus is located in the historic Old Town section of San Diego. Thomas Jefferson School of Law has about 800 students and was founded in 1969 as the the Western State University College of Law. It achieved independence and accreditation with the American Bar Association in 1996. The school is building a new $40 million downtown campus.

The eight-story facility is expected to be complete by 2010. The school will then move from its Old Town location. The new campus will double the school's space and allow for an increase in enrollment.

EXECUTIVES

Dean and President, Rudolph Hasl
Communications Specialist, Chris Saunders
Assistant Dean Administration, Lori Wulfemeyer
Associate Dean Academic Affairs, Eric J. Mitnick
Associate Dean and General Counsel, Jeff Joseph
CFO, Nancy Vu
Assistant Dean Advancement and Alumni Relations, Karen Goyette

LOCATIONS

HQ: Thomas Jefferson School of Law
2121 San Diego Ave., San Diego CA 92110
Phone: 619-297-9700   **Fax:** 619-294-4713
Web: www.tjsl.edu/

HISTORICAL FINANCIALS

Company Type: School

Income Statement

FYE: June 30

	REVENUE ($ mil.)	NET INCOME ($ mil.)	NET PROFIT MARGIN	EMPLOYEES
06/11	42	0	0.1%	120
06/10	35	3	8.5%	0
06/09	29	0	—	0
06/08	29	3	12.6%	0
Annual Growth	13.0%	(81.9%)	—	—

2011 Year-End Financials

Debt ratio: ——
Return on equity: 0.10%
Cash ($ mil.): 5
Current ratio: —
Long-term debt ($ mil.): —

Dividends
  Yield: —
  Payout: —
  Market value ($ mil.): —

THOMAS JEFFERSON UNIVERSITY HOSPITALS INC.

Named after the "Man of the People" Thomas Jefferson University Hospital serves the people of the Keystone State with a medical staff of more than 1100 and some 970 beds. Part of the Jefferson Health System the hospital provides acute tertiary and specialty medical care. Aside from the main campus it operates through a Center City Campus Methodist Hospital Jefferson Voorhees and Jefferson Hospital for Neuroscience. The hospital also administers cardiac care at the Jefferson Heart Institute which provides everything from minimally invasive surgical procedures to heart transplants. It is also the teaching hospital for Thomas Jefferson University. Thomas Jefferson University Hospital was founded in 1825.

Geographic Reach

Through a handful of locations Thomas Jefferson University Hospital provides health care services to the residents of Philadelphia and the Delaware Valley. It shares a 13-acre campus with Thomas Jefferson University.

Operations

As part of its operations Thomas Jefferson University Hospital offers several premier programs to its patients as well as 35 different specialties. The hospital performed Delaware Valley's first liver transplant and designated a kidney transplant center for live and deceased donor transplants. In addition to transplantation the hospital provides surgical services heart and vascular digestive diseases and bones and joints in addition to its Kimmel Cancer Canter and Jefferson Hospital for Neuroscience. In fiscal year 2012 the health system logged more than 485000 outpatient visits.

EXECUTIVES

EVP and COO, David P. McQuaid
President CEO and Trustee, Thomas J. (Tom) Lewis, age 59
SVP Marketing Public Relations and Communications, Carmhiel J. (Caramel) Brown
SVP and CFO, Neil G. Lubarsky
SVP Special Programs, Janet E. Burnham
SVP Patient Care Services and Chief Nursing Officer, Mary Ann McGinley
SVP and General Counsel, Stacey Meadows
SVP and Chief Administrative Officer Methodist Hospital Division, James E. Robinson
SVP and Chief Medical Officer, Geno Merli
Chair, Robert S. Adelson
EVP Strategy and Organizational Development, Ronald P. Burd
SVP Clinical Services, Rebecca O'Shea
President Medical Staff and Trustee, John R. Cohn
Media Contact, Ed Federico
Media Contact, Emily Shafer
Trustee, Robert L. (Bob) Barchi, age 65
Trustee, Douglas J. MacMaster Jr., age 81
Trustee, Ira Brind Esq., age 71
President CEO and Trustee, Thomas J. (Tom) Lewis, age 59
Trustee, Brian G. Harrison
Trustee, Jack Farber
Trustee, Carter R. Buller
Trustee, Thomas B. Morris Jr.
President Medical Staff and Trustee, John R. Cohn
Trustee, Janice R. Bellace
Trustee, Andrew D. Freed
Trustee, Richard W. Hevner
Trustee, Paul Hondros
Trustee, Harold A. Honickman
Trustee, Hyman Kahn
Trustee, William A. Landman
Trustee, Carol Levin
Trustee, Caro U. Rock
Trustee, Michael J. Vergare
Trustee, Alex Wasilov
Trustee, R. Richard Williams
Auditors: PricewaterhouseCoopersLLP

LOCATIONS

HQ: Thomas Jefferson University Hospital
111 S. 11th St., Philadelphia PA 19107
Phone: 215-955-6000   **Fax:** 215-955-3745
Web: www.jeffersonhospital.org

PRODUCTS/OPERATIONS

Selected Services

Cancer
Diabetes & Endocrinology
Ear Nose & Throat
Gastroenterology
Geriatrics
Gynecology
Nephrology
Orthopedics
Pulmonology
Rehabilitation
Urology

Selected University Locations

Jefferson at the Navy Yard
Jefferson Medical College
Jefferson College of Graduate Studies
Jefferson Radiology
Jefferson School of Health Professions
Jefferson School of Nursing
Jefferson School of Pharmacy
Jefferson School of Population Health
Jefferson Voorhees

COMPETITORS

Albert Einstein Healthcare Network
Bryn Mawr Hospital
Catholic Health East
Community Health Systems
Doylestown Hospital
Main Line Health
Mercy Health System
North Philadelphia Health System
Our Lady of Lourdes Medical Center
Pennsylvania Hospital
TUHS
Universal Health Services
University of Pennsylvania Health System

HISTORICAL FINANCIALS

Company Type: Subsidiary

Income Statement

FYE: June 30

	REVENUE ($ mil.)	NET INCOME ($ mil.)	NET PROFIT MARGIN	EMPLOYEES
06/11	1,431	61	4.3%	4,701
06/10	1,250	49	4.0%	0
06/09	0	0		0
06/05	954	32	3.4%	0
Annual Growth	14.5%	23.3%	—	—

2011 Year-End Financials

Debt ratio: ——
Return on equity: 4.30%
Cash ($ mil.): 215
Current ratio: 2.00
Long-term debt ($ mil.): —

Dividends
Yield: —
Payout: —
Market value ($ mil.): —

THOMPSON CONSTRUCTION GROUP INC.

LOCATIONS

HQ: THOMPSON CONSTRUCTION GROUP INC.
100 N MAIN ST, SUMTER, SC 29150-4948
Phone: 803-934-0116

HISTORICAL FINANCIALS

Company Type: Private

Income Statement

FYE: December 31

	REVENUE ($ mil.)	NET INCOME ($ mil.)	NET PROFIT MARGIN	EMPLOYEES
12/11	95	5	5.9%	120
12/10	124	24	19.5%	0
12/09	122	6	5.5%	0
12/08	133	11	8.3%	0
Annual Growth	(10.6%)	(20.4%)	—	—

2011 Year-End Financials

Debt ratio: ——
Return on equity: 5.90%
Cash ($ mil.): 3
Current ratio: 1.20
Long-term debt ($ mil.): —

Dividends
Yield: —
Payout: —
Market value ($ mil.): —

THOMPSON HOSPITALITY

A side of diversity please: One of the largest minority-owned companies in the US Thompson Hospitality is a contract foodservice provider to businesses government agencies and educational institutions. The foodservice operator's clients include a number of historically black colleges and universities notably Delaware State and Norfolk State as well as institutions around Washington DC such as Walter Reed Army Hospital. Thompson Hospitality also owns a handful of chain restaurants including Austin Grill. Formed through an alliance with major food provider Compass Group Thompson Hospitality has a presence in more than 45 states and four foreign countries. The two companies still partner on contracts.

The company's core operation is contract foodservice to corporate and college campus cafeterias; it reportedly serves more than 100000 meals a day. Among its partnerships Thompson Hospitality teams up with Chartwells a division of Compass Group; Chartwells-Thompson Hospitality provides dining for students at Chicago Public Schools.

Beyond foodservice Thompson Hospitality is expanding its restaurant and retail business through small acquisitions. In addition to the Austin Grill Tex-Mex chain it owns Washington DC-based Marvelous Market a small chain of bakery cafes selling artisan breads pastries and sandwiches. In 2011 Thompson Hospitality invested in the build-out and push-button equipment for its first BRB Burger site a gourmet burger concept it hopes to duplicate at other locations. The company opened a third American Tap Room location that year too. Thompson Hospitality has also operated Ashburn Car Wash since 2004. Entered as a real estate opportunity the car wash turned into testing ground for matching facility design and services with customer demand.

Amid the economic downturn Thompson Hospitality's dual interest in foodservice and restaurant operations has buoyed revenues. The slump in restaurant sales has been offset by winning new foodservice contracts. The company has grown from generating $37 million in 1993 to more than $410 million in revenues in 2011.

President Warren Thompson founded the company in 1992 when he negotiated a $13.1 million buyout for 31 Bob's Big Boy restaurants many of which were converted to Shoney's from Marriott International. Following a stream of problems at Shoney's parent company Thompson Hospitality entered the contract food service market while selling off the Shoney's and Big Boys within nearly eight years.

EXECUTIVES

Chairman and President, Warren M. Thompson, age 52
Chief Administrative Officer, Fred Thompson
COO, Maurice Jenoure
CFO, Ali Azima
VP Joint Ventures, Benita Thompson-Byas
SVP Business Development, Shawn O'Quinn
VP Human Resources, Lydia Martinez
VP Restaurant Operations, Orson Williams
VP Culinary Development, Eric Reed

LOCATIONS

HQ: Thompson Hospitality Corporation
505 Huntmar Park Dr. Ste. 350, Herndon VA 20170
Phone: 703-964-5500   **Fax:** 703-964-0505
Web: www.thompsonhospitality.com

PRODUCTS/OPERATIONS

2010

% of sales

Business & Industry	37
College/University	30
K-12 Schools	14
Hospitals	7
Convention/Conference Centers	5
Museums/Perf. Art Centers	4
Arenas/Stadiums	3
Total	**0 100**

Selected Restaurant and Retail Brands
American Tap Room
Ashburn Car Wash
Austin Grill
Austin Grill Express
Be Right Burger (brb)
Marvelous Market

COMPETITORS

ABM Industries
ARAMARK
Autogrill Group
Bon Appetit Management
Crothall Healthcare
Delaware North
Healthcare Services
Sodexo USA
SSP America

HISTORICAL FINANCIALS

Company Type: Private

Income Statement

FYE: December 25

	REVENUE ($ mil.)	NET INCOME ($ mil.)	NET PROFIT MARGIN	EMPLOYEES
12/11	109	4	4.2%	3,000
12/10	101	10	9.9%	0
12/09	97	2	3.0%	0
12/08	93	2	2.9%	0
Annual Growth	5.4%	19.4%	—	—

2011 Year-End Financials

Debt ratio: ——
Return on equity: 4.20%
Cash ($ mil.): 8
Current ratio: 0.80
Long-term debt ($ mil.): —

Dividends
Yield: —
Payout: —
Market value ($ mil.): —

THUMANN INCORPORATED

LOCATIONS

HQ: THUMANN INCORPORATED
670 DELL RD STE 1, CARLSTADT, NJ 07072-2292
Phone: 201-935-3636
Web: www.thumanns.com

HISTORICAL FINANCIALS
Company Type: Private

Income Statement
FYE: December 31

	REVENUE ($ mil.)	NET INCOME ($ mil.)	NET PROFIT MARGIN	EMPLOYEES
12/11	95	0	0.6%	205
12/10	91	(0)	—	0
12/09	90	4	4.9%	0
12/08	100	2	2.2%	0
Annual Growth	(1.5%)	(35.4%)		

2011 Year-End Financials
Debt ratio: ——
Return on equity: 0.60%
Cash ($ mil.): 1
Current ratio: 0.70
Long-term debt ($ mil.): —

Dividends
Yield: —
Payout: —
Market value ($ mil.): —

TIDES FOUNDATION

LOCATIONS
HQ: TIDES FOUNDATION
PRESIDIO BLDG 1014, SAN FRANCISCO, CA 94129
Phone: 415-561-6400
Web: www.tides.org

HISTORICAL FINANCIALS
Company Type: Private

Income Statement
FYE: December 31

	REVENUE ($ mil.)	NET INCOME ($ mil.)	NET PROFIT MARGIN	EMPLOYEES
12/11	96	(9)	—	27
12/10	132	(24)	—	0
12/09	118	12	10.2%	0
12/08	100	(17)	—	0
Annual Growth	(1.3%)	—		

2011 Year-End Financials
Debt ratio: ——
Return on equity: (-9.80)%
Cash ($ mil.): 4
Current ratio: 0.30
Long-term debt ($ mil.): —

Dividends
Yield: —
Payout: —
Market value ($ mil.): —

TIDEWELL HOSPICE INC.

LOCATIONS
HQ: TIDEWELL HOSPICE INC.
5955 RAND BLVD, SARASOTA, FL 34238-5160
Phone: 941-552-7500
Web: www.hospice-swf.org

HISTORICAL FINANCIALS
Company Type: Private

Income Statement
FYE: June 30

	REVENUE ($ mil.)	NET INCOME ($ mil.)	NET PROFIT MARGIN	EMPLOYEES
06/11	102	10	9.9%	800
06/10	100	8	8.7%	0
06/09	93	0	—	0
06/08	92	4	5.4%	0
Annual Growth	3.8%	27.0%		

2011 Year-End Financials
Debt ratio: ——
Return on equity: 9.90%
Cash ($ mil.): 15
Current ratio: 3.10
Long-term debt ($ mil.): —

Dividends
Yield: —
Payout: —
Market value ($ mil.): —

TITUSVILLE AREA HOSPITAL

Titusville Area Hospital an acute care health facility provides diagnostic primary treatment and emergency health services to more than 30000 residents in the Crawford County Pennsylvania region. Specific services at Titusville include birthing home health care lithotripsy and pain management. Titusville Area Hospital opened its doors in 1901.

EXECUTIVES
President and CEO, Anthony J. (Tony) Nasralla
VP Patient Services, Linda Harris
VP Human Resources, Jeff Saintz
Director Nursing Services, Brenda Burnett
CFO, Jill Neely
CIO, Reice Altomare

LOCATIONS
HQ: Titusville Area Hospital
406 W. Oak St., Titusville PA 16354
Phone: 814-827-1851 **Fax:** 814-827-3099
Web: www.titusvillehospital.org

COMPETITORS
Sharon Regional Health System

HISTORICAL FINANCIALS
Company Type: Private - Not-for-Profit

Income Statement
FYE: June 30

	REVENUE ($ mil.)	NET INCOME ($ mil.)	NET PROFIT MARGIN	EMPLOYEES
06/11	31	1	3.2%	300
06/10	29	(1)	—	0
06/09	28	0	0.9%	0
06/08	39	(0)	—	0
Annual Growth	(7.4%)	—		

2011 Year-End Financials
Debt ratio: ——
Return on equity: 3.20%
Cash ($ mil.): 0
Current ratio: 0.90
Long-term debt ($ mil.): —

Dividends
Yield: —
Payout: —
Market value ($ mil.): —

TML INTERGOVERNMENTAL EMPLOYEE BENEFITS POOL

LOCATIONS
HQ: TML INTERGOVERNMENTAL EMPLOYEE BENEFITS POOL
1821 RUTHERFORD LN 300, AUSTIN, TX 78754-5197
Phone: 512-719-6500
Web: www.tmliebp.org

HISTORICAL FINANCIALS
Company Type: Private

Income Statement
FYE: September 30

	REVENUE ($ mil.)	NET INCOME ($ mil.)	NET PROFIT MARGIN	EMPLOYEES
09/11	122	2	2.4%	148
09/10	117	(3)	—	0
09/09	107	(0)	—	0
09/05	95	5	6.2%	0
Annual Growth	8.9%	(20.7%)	—	—

2011 Year-End Financials
Debt ratio: ——
Return on equity: 2.40%
Cash ($ mil.): 2
Current ratio: 0.20
Long-term debt ($ mil.): —

Dividends
Yield: —
Payout: —
Market value ($ mil.): —

TNEMEC COMPANY INC.

Tnemec (pronouced tah-KNEE-mick it is cement spelled backwards) makes more than 100 different paints and coatings that can be used as primers on concrete masonry steel and flooring materials. It also provides waterproofing corrosion prevention (for wastewater facilities) and exterior finishing products. Subsidiary Chemprobe Coating Systems specializes in masonry products while the company's StrataShield division focuses on floor and wall coatings. Tnemec has manufacturing and distribution facilities throughout the US. The family of founder Albert Bean still owns and runs the company.

In 2010 Tnemec purchased the Glass Armor epoxy lining technology for above-ground storage tanks from Bridgeport Chemical. The linings will be marketed by Tnemec under the Tank Armor name along with the company's other offerings of protective coatings and linings.

EXECUTIVES

Chairman, Albert C. Bean Jr.
VP Finance, Steve Eiserer
EVP, Chase Bean
VP Marketing, Mark Thomas
VP Human Resources, Gary Jones Jr.
President, Pete Cortelyou
VP Technical and Regulatory Affairs, Joe Davis
VP Sales, Terry Wallace
VP Research and Development, Remi Briand
Electronic Marketing Manager, Jessi Bixler

LOCATIONS

HQ: Tnemec Company Inc.
6800 Corporate Dr., Kansas City MO 64120-1372
Phone: 816-483-3400　　**Fax:** 816-483-3969
Web: www.tnemec.com

COMPETITORS

American Air Liquide　　PPG Industries
Ashland Inc.　　RPM International
Cohesant　　Structural Group
Insl-X

HISTORICAL FINANCIALS

Company Type: Private

Income Statement

	REVENUE ($ mil.)	NET INCOME ($ mil.)	NET PROFIT MARGIN	EMPLOYEES
12/11	124	4	3.7%	265
12/10	115	5	4.5%	0
12/09	112	5	4.7%	0
12/08	117	5	4.9%	0
Annual Growth	2.0%	(7.4%)	—	—

2011 Year-End Financials

Debt ratio: ——
Return on equity: 3.70%
Cash ($ mil.): 0
Current ratio: 1.20
Long-term debt ($ mil.): —

Dividends
　Yield: —
　Payout: —
Market value ($ mil.): —

TOM LANGE COMPANY INC.

Tom Lange Company wants you to eat your veggies. One of the largest purchasers and distributors of fresh fruits and vegetables in the US Tom Lange supplies its comestibles to clients in the retail wholesale and food service trades. The company also provides third party logistics services specializing in truckload freight movement. The company was founded in 1960 as a three-man operation in St. Louis Missouri Tom Lange has grown to encompass 35 offices in the US and Canada. Produce subsidiaries include Seven Seas M&M Marketing and Seven Seas Fruit.

EXECUTIVES

President and CEO, F. W. (Phil) Gumpert
EVP and CFO, Mike Smith

VP Sales Houston, Don Bertrand
VP Sales Houston, Mark Martino
VP Sales Dallas, Darrell Wolven
VP Sales Atlanta, Eric Hoffman
VP Sales Nashville, Wally Lampertz
VP Sales Midwest, Jeff Moore
VP Sales Chicago, Mike Patton
VP Sales Indianapolis, Rick Harsnett
VP Sales Pittsburgh, Tom Law
VP Sales Philadelphia, Bart Whitten
SVP, Jim Griswold
SVP, Bruce Rubin
Secretary and Treasurer, Hugh Seelbach
VP Sales Oklahoma City, Brian McGreevy

LOCATIONS

HQ: Tom Lange Company Inc.
755 Apple Orchard Rd., Springfield IL 62794-9261
Phone: 217-786-3300　　**Fax:** 217-786-2570
Web: www.tomlange.com

COMPETITORS

A. Duda & Sons　　FreshPoint
Caito Foods Service　　Get Fresh Produce
Coast Citrus　　The Oppenheimer Group
　Distributors　　Wilson Farms
Cristina Foods

HISTORICAL FINANCIALS

Company Type: Private

Income Statement

	REVENUE ($ mil.)	NET INCOME ($ mil.)	NET PROFIT MARGIN	EMPLOYEES
08/11	445	1	0.4%	110
08/08	407	3	0.8%	0
08/07	0	0	—	0
08/06	375	0	—	0
Annual Growth	5.9%	—	—	—

2011 Year-End Financials

Debt ratio: ——
Return on equity: 0.40%
Cash ($ mil.): 9
Current ratio: 1.30
Long-term debt ($ mil.): —

Dividends
　Yield: —
　Payout: —
Market value ($ mil.): —

TOMAH MEMORIAL HOSPITAL INC.

Tomah Memorial Hospital provides a wide range of medical services for the residents of western Wisconsin and southern Minnesota. The hospital's staff of about 100 health care professionals includes specialists in cardiology internal medicine oncology general and orthopedic surgery and emergency medicine. In 2005 the hospital completed a nearly $10 million construction and renovation project which included a new 20000 sq. ft. facility on its premises. With help and donations from many community residents Tomah Memorial opened its doors in 1952 with 29 beds.

EXECUTIVES

Administrator, Philip J. (Phil) Stuart
CFO, Joe Zeps

Chairman, Bob Fasbender
Marketing and Public Relations Coordinator, Eric Prise

LOCATIONS

HQ: Tomah Memorial Hospital
321 Butts Ave., Tomah WI 54660
Phone: 608-372-2181　　**Fax:** 608-374-0355
Web: www.tomahhospital.org

COMPETITORS

Dean Health Systems Inc.
Gundersen Lutheran Medical Center
University of Wisconsin Hospital and Clinics

HISTORICAL FINANCIALS

Company Type: Private - Not-for-Profit

Income Statement

FYE: September 30

	REVENUE ($ mil.)	NET INCOME ($ mil.)	NET PROFIT MARGIN	EMPLOYEES
09/11	34	1	4.1%	215
09/10	32	3	9.6%	0
09/09	31	2	6.5%	0
09/08	29	0	3.2%	0
Annual Growth	5.3%	14.3%	—	—

2011 Year-End Financials

Debt ratio: ——
Return on equity: 4.10%
Cash ($ mil.): 3
Current ratio: 2.10
Long-term debt ($ mil.): —

Dividends
　Yield: —
　Payout: —
Market value ($ mil.): —

TOP AG COOPERATIVE INC.

LOCATIONS

HQ: TOP AG COOPERATIVE INC.
702 S ELEVATOR ST, OKAWVILLE, IL 62271
Phone: 618-243-5293
Web: www.okawvillefarmerselevator.com

HISTORICAL FINANCIALS

Company Type: Private

Income Statement

FYE: August 31

	REVENUE ($ mil.)	NET INCOME ($ mil.)	NET PROFIT MARGIN	EMPLOYEES
08/12	135	0	0.2%	65
08/11	165	3	1.8%	0
08/10	95	1	1.9%	0
08/09	115	1	1.3%	0
Annual Growth	5.7%	(42.7%)	—	—

2012 Year-End Financials

Debt ratio: ——
Return on equity: 0.20%
Cash ($ mil.): 3
Current ratio: 0.30
Long-term debt ($ mil.): —

Dividends
　Yield: —
　Payout: —
Market value ($ mil.): —

TORRANCE MEMORIAL MEDICAL CENTER

Back in 1925 Jared Sydney Torrance founded Torrance Memorial Medical Center in the southern California town that also bears his name (also known as the South Bay of Los Angeles). The not-for-profit medical center complex now includes 400 beds clinical research facilities cancer and cardiology care It also operates a skilled nursing facility. It is one of three burn centers in Los Angeles. The medical center reaches beyond its walls and into the community with hospice care and home health care. It also provides nursing residency programs and staffing support services to physicians offices in the area.

In order to accommodate the area's growing population and increasing need for medical services the hospital is building a new tower featuring private rooms new medical technologies more beds and space and a modernized design. It houses seven stories more than 250 private rooms and about 20 surgical and interventional treatment rooms. The tower has become necessary with five area-hospital closures in recent years. It is expected to open in late 2015.

EXECUTIVES

President and CEO, Craig Leach
CFO, Doug Klebe
VP Human Resources, Lois Michael
SVP Patient Services, Peggy Berwald
SVP and Chief Medical Officer, John McNamara
VP Medical Staff Services and Performance Improvement, Robin Camrin
SVP Planning and Development, Sally Eberhard
VP Finance, Bill Larson
VP Information Technology, Bernadette Reid
VP Clinical Quality and Accreditation, Heather Shay

LOCATIONS

HQ: TORRANCE MEMORIAL MEDICAL CENTER
3330 LOMITA BLVD, TORRANCE, CA 90505-5002
Phone: 310-325-9110

PRODUCTS/OPERATIONS

Selected Services/Locations
Burn Center
Full-Service Emergency Department
Imaging ServicesDiagnostic and Interventional Radiology
Family Birth Center
Level III Neonatal Intensive Care Unit
Home Health & Hospice
Cancer Center
Lundquist Cardiovascular Institute
Thelma McMillen Center for Chemical Dependency Treatment
Designated Center of Excellence in Cardiac Care
Bariatric Surgery and Orthopedics

COMPETITORS

Brotman Medical Center
Cedars-Sinai Medical Center
Childrens Hospital Los Angeles
Dignity Health
Good Samaritan Hospital (Los Angeles)
HCA
Hollywood Presbyterian Medical Center
Kaiser Permanente
Little Company of Mary
Long Beach Memorial
Los Angeles County Health Department
Sisters of Charity of Leavenworth
Tenet Healthcare
Universal Health Services
White Memorial Medical Center

HISTORICAL FINANCIALS
Company Type: Private

Income Statement
FYE: September 30

	REVENUE ($ mil.)	NET INCOME ($ mil.)	NET PROFIT MARGIN	EMPLOYEES
09/12*	354	31	8.9%	2,000
06/12	222	20	9.2%	0
12/11	437	(17)	—	0
09/11	332	22	6.8%	0
Annual Growth	**2.2%**	**11.5%**	**—**	**—**

*Fiscal year change

2012 Year-End Financials

Debt ratio: ——
Return on equity: 8.90%
Cash ($ mil.): 11
Current ratio: 0.30
Long-term debt ($ mil.): —
Dividends
Yield: —
Payout: —
Market value ($ mil.): —

TOURO COLLEGE

Touro College is a Jewish university with sister institutions in France Germany Israel and Russia and branches in California Florida and Nevada. Some 17500 (Jewish and non-Jewish) students are enrolled in its various schools which offer associate bachelor's and master's degrees in business education and law as well as professional degrees in osteopathic medicine pharmacy law and other fields. Touro also operates New York Medical College. Dr. Bernard Lander a social behavior and Jewish studies scholar founded Touro College in 1971 to teach Jewish and secular subjects. The college is named after Judah and Isaac Touro who founded the Touro Synagogue in 1790.

Lander an orthodox rabbi died in 2010. He was one of the longest-serving college presidents in the country. Senior provost and medical doctor Alan Kadish was selected to replace Lander.

Under Lander's leadership Touro College grew quickly from a small school with 35 students to a multi-campus college with thousands of students. Touro continues to expand. It assumed control of New York Medical College in mid-2010. The Catholic-led medical school remains an independent institution. Some at the New York Medical College opposed the merger citing a well-publicized cash-for-grades scandal. In 2009 Touro's former director of admissions was found guilty of tampering with student transcripts and selling degrees. He was sentenced to two to eight years in prison. Nevertheless the deal went through and now New York Medical College is a member of the Touro College and University System.

EXECUTIVES

Data Manager, Michael J. Lee
Director Communications, Barbara Franklin
Senior Provost and CEO Global e-Learning Programs, Bernard J. Luskin
Chairman, Mark Hasten
President Chief Executive Officer of Touro College and Touro University, Alan Kadish
Executive Assistant, Annalene Antonio
Assistant Program Director, Yevgeny Komm
Assistant Director of Field Education and Advisement, Susan Brot
Director of Online Graduate Education and Special Education, Sandrine Lavallee
Director of Administrative Services, Elhanon Marvit
Director of Student Advancement, Allison Bobick
Director Forest Hills, Stephen Levy
Director of Admissions, Bradley Karasik
Director Resource Centers and Tutoring Program, Inna Goldstein
Director Academic Computing, Issac Herskowitz
Director of the Online Blended School Leadership Program, Joel Shapiro
Director of Social Work Professional Education and Online Learning, Melissa Earle
Director of Student Finances and Bursar, Myriam Elefant
Director of Field Education and Advisement, Roberta Shiffman
Director of the Online Blended Literacy Program, Sheldon Shuch

LOCATIONS

HQ: Touro College
27-33 W. 23rd St., New York NY 10010
Phone: 212-463-0400   **Fax:** 212-627-9144
Web: www.touro.edu

HISTORICAL FINANCIALS
Company Type: School

Income Statement
FYE: June 30

	REVENUE ($ mil.)	NET INCOME ($ mil.)	NET PROFIT MARGIN	EMPLOYEES
06/11	203	(9)	—	4,600
06/10	277	15	5.7%	0
06/09	145	0	—	0
06/08	0	0	—	0
Annual Growth	**—**	**—**	**—**	**—**

2011 Year-End Financials

Debt ratio: ——
Return on equity: (-4.50)%
Cash ($ mil.): 12
Current ratio: —
Long-term debt ($ mil.): —
Dividends
Yield: —
Payout: —
Market value ($ mil.): —

TOURO INFIRMARY

LOCATIONS

HQ: TOURO INFIRMARY
1401 FOUCHER ST, NEW ORLEANS, LA 70115-3593
Phone: 504-897-7011
Web: www.touro.com

HISTORICAL FINANCIALS
Company Type: Private

Income Statement
FYE: December 31

	REVENUE ($ mil.)	NET INCOME ($ mil.)	NET PROFIT MARGIN	EMPLOYEES
12/11	258	(3)	—	1,424
12/10	253	27	10.9%	0
12/09	213	5	2.5%	0
12/08	169	(39)	—	0
Annual Growth	**15.2%**	—	—	—

2011 Year-End Financials
Debt ratio: —
Return on equity: (-1.50)%
Cash ($ mil.): 2
Current ratio: 0.60
Long-term debt ($ mil.): —

Dividends
Yield: —
Payout: —
Market value ($ mil.): —

TOWN AND COUNTRY SUPPLY ASSOCIATION

LOCATIONS

HQ: TOWN AND COUNTRY SUPPLY ASSOCIATION
800 E MAIN ST, LAUREL, MT 59044-2866
Phone: 406-628-6314

HISTORICAL FINANCIALS
Company Type: Private

Income Statement
FYE: January 31

	REVENUE ($ mil.)	NET INCOME ($ mil.)	NET PROFIT MARGIN	EMPLOYEES
01/12	108	5	4.9%	123
Annual Growth	—	—	—	—

2012 Year-End Financials
Debt ratio: —
Return on equity: 4.90%
Cash ($ mil.): 1
Current ratio: 0.70
Long-term debt ($ mil.): —

Dividends
Yield: —
Payout: —
Market value ($ mil.): —

TOWNSEND OIL CORPORATION

LOCATIONS

HQ: TOWNSEND OIL CORPORATION
64 MAIN ST, LE ROY, NY 14482-1493
Phone: 585-768-8188
Web: www.townsendenergy.com

HISTORICAL FINANCIALS
Company Type: Private

Income Statement
FYE: September 30

	REVENUE ($ mil.)	NET INCOME ($ mil.)	NET PROFIT MARGIN	EMPLOYEES
09/11	125	0	0.1%	60
09/98	23	0	1.0%	0
Annual Growth	**441.6%**	**(24.2%)**	—	—

2011 Year-End Financials
Debt ratio: —
Return on equity: 0.10%
Cash ($ mil.): 1
Current ratio: 0.90
Long-term debt ($ mil.): —

Dividends
Yield: —
Payout: —
Market value ($ mil.): —

TOWNSHIP HIGH SCHOOL DISTRICT 211

Township High School District 211 is the largest high school district in Illinois with nearly 13000 students attending its five high schools (grades 9 to 12) —James B. Conant William Fremd Hoffman Estates Palatine and Schaumburg —and two special education academies. The district's student-teacher ratio is nearly 14-to-1 and serves several suburban communities 25 miles northwest of Chicago. The school district started as one school (Palatine High School) in the Palatine-Schaumburg Township area in 1875 with the first graduating class in 1877.

All schools in the district have been named among the top in the country in the US Department of Education's National Secondary School Recognition Program: Hoffman Estates in 1985 William Fremd in 1987 Palatine and Schaumburg in 1993 and James B. Conant in 1996.

HISTORY

All five district schools have been named among the top schools in the nation.

EXECUTIVES

Superintendent of Schools, Nancy N. Robb
Associate Superintendent for Instruction, Jeffery A. Butzen
Associate Superintendent Business, David S. Torres
Assistant Superintendent for Administrative Services and Special Programs, Daniel E. Cates
Assistant Superintendent for Personnel, Robert D. Grimm
Community Relations Coordinator, Thomas D. Petersen
Director Technology Services, Charles A. Peterson
Director Business Services, Christopher J. Kontney
Director Athletic Activities and Career Development, Otis G. Price
Director Special Education, James A. Britton
Director Food Service, Lauren C. Hummel

LOCATIONS

HQ: TOWNSHIP HIGH SCHOOL DISTRICT 211
1750 S ROSELLE RD STE 100, PALATINE, IL 60067-7302
Phone: 847-755-6600
Web: www.d211.org

PRODUCTS/OPERATIONS

Schools
High Schools
James B. Conant High School
William Fremd High School
Hoffman Estates High School
Palatine High School
Schaumburg High School
Special Education Schools
District 211 Academy North
District 211 Academy South

HISTORICAL FINANCIALS
Company Type: School

Income Statement
FYE: June 30

	REVENUE ($ mil.)	NET INCOME ($ mil.)	NET PROFIT MARGIN	EMPLOYEES
06/11	250	4	1.7%	1,909
06/10	0	0	41.7%	0
06/09	0	0	15.5%	0
06/06	210	15	7.5%	0
Annual Growth	**6.0%**	**(34.9%)**	—	—

2011 Year-End Financials
Debt ratio: —
Return on equity: 1.70%
Cash ($ mil.): 143
Current ratio: —
Long-term debt ($ mil.): —

Dividends
Yield: —
Payout: —
Market value ($ mil.): —

TOWNSHIP HIGH SCHOOL DISTRICT 214

LOCATIONS

HQ: TOWNSHIP HIGH SCHOOL DISTRICT 214
2121 S GOEBBERT RD, ARLINGTON HEIGHTS, IL 60005-4205
Phone: 847-718-7600
Web: www.d214.org

HISTORICAL FINANCIALS
Company Type: Private

Income Statement
FYE: June 30

	REVENUE ($ mil.)	NET INCOME ($ mil.)	NET PROFIT MARGIN	EMPLOYEES
06/12	259	15	6.0%	1,550
06/08	221	5	2.5%	0
06/07	212	23	10.8%	0
06/06	0	0		0
Annual Growth	—	**882.2%**	—	—

2012 Year-End Financials
Debt ratio: —
Return on equity: 6.00%
Cash ($ mil.): 5
Current ratio: —
Long-term debt ($ mil.): —

Dividends
Yield: —
Payout: —
Market value ($ mil.): —

TRANSAMMONIA INC.

Fertilizers liquefied petroleum gas (LPG) and petrochemicals form the lifeblood of international trader Transammonia. The company trades distributes and transports these commodities around the world. Transammonia's fertilizer business includes ammonia phosphates and urea. Its Sea-3 subsidiary imports and distributes propane to residential commercial and industrial customers in the northeastern US and Florida. The Trammochem unit trades in petrochemicals specializing in aromatics methanol methyltertiary butyl ether (MTBE) benzene and olefins. Its Trammo Gas trades LPG and propane as well as ethane butane and natural gas in the US. Formed in 1965 Transammonia is owned by founder Ronald Stanton.

Transammonia was founded in 1965 as an international ammonia trader. It branched into fertilizer merchandising and trading in 1967 LPG trading in 1978 and petrochemicals trading in 1987.

Since 2008 Transammonia has expanded its reach into the global market establishing merchandising and trading offices in Singapore China and the United Arab Emirates. Those offices complement its other global operations in Africa Asia Europe the Middle East and South America.

In 2010 the company's bulk carriers division entered the commodity shipping business. TA Bulk Carriers operates a fleet of 15 to 20 vessels which trade worldwide but focus on the handysize market (25000-35000 metric tons deadweight) in the Atlantic basin. In 2010 it transported about 2.9 million metric tons of cargo primarily fertilizers and grains.

EXECUTIVES

Director Human Resources, Marguerite Harrington
SVP and CFO, Edward G. Weiner
Chairman and CEO, Ronald P. Stanton
CIO, Benjamin Tan

LOCATIONS

HQ: Transammonia Inc.
 320 Park Ave., New York NY 10022-6987
Phone: 212-223-3200   **Fax:** 212-759-1410
Web: www.transammonia.com

PRODUCTS/OPERATIONS

Major Subsidiari
Sea-3 (liquefied propane)
Trammo Gas (LPG)
Trammo Petroleum (crude oil and oil products)
Trammochem (petrochem
Transammonia (fertilize

COMPETITORS

Cargill	HELM
CF Industries	Magellan Midstream
ConAgra	Yara
Dynegy	

HISTORICAL FINANCIALS

Company Type: Private

Income Statement

FYE: December 31

	REVENUE ($ mil.)	NET INCOME ($ mil.)	NET PROFIT MARGIN	EMPLOYEES
12/11	11,303	31	0.3%	320
12/10	8,414	35	0.4%	0
12/09	5,485	21	0.4%	0
12/08	11,214	68	0.6%	0
Annual Growth	0.3%	(22.9%)	—	—

2011 Year-End Financials

Debt ratio: ——
Return on equity: 0.30%
Cash ($ mil.): 207
Current ratio: 0.90
Long-term debt ($ mil.): —

Dividends
 Yield: —
 Payout: —
Market value ($ mil.): —

TRANSUNION CORP.

TransUnion helps credit scores transcend boundaries. The firm is one of the three major consumer credit reporting agencies (the others being Experian and Equifax) that lenders use to help determine a borrower's creditworthiness. The company maintains credit histories of more than 500 million people in more than 25 countries which it uses to help banks insurance providers retailers and others manage risk and reduce fraud. Subsidiary TransUnion Interactive provides online subscription-based credit management products to consumers. TransUnion is owned by Advent International and GS Capital Partners.

In 2012 Advent and GS Capital bought TransUnion from Madison Dearborn Partners and the Pritzker family. The deal valued TransUnion at around $3 billion.

TransUnion filed to go public in 2011. The company planned to raise up to $325 million in the initial public offering. However plans to go public were shelved as the IPO market stagnated that year.

TransUnion operates in three business segments: information services; international services; and consumer services. Its information services division (representing more than 60% of sales) provides credit reports analytical services and other services that help companies make decisions. TransUnion's international services arm helps domestic companies expand overseas and also assists international companies team with partners in other countries. The consumers services division gives people access to view and manage their credit health.

TransUnion has a presence in 25 countries around the world. Its geographic reach includes the Americas Europe Africa and the Asia-Pacific region.

The economic downturn sent TransUnion's revenues down from 2008 through 2010 as demand for its services fell. By 2010 and 2011 the economy began to improve and TransUnion's sales improved. Sales grew by about 7 % in 2011 exceeding the $1 billion mark.

Global expansion is a priority for TransUnion. In 2011 TransUnion acquired 80% of a software and services company in Brazil. The following year TransUnion expanded its presence in Africa when it acquired a majority share of CRBAfrica –a credit risk management firm. In recent years TransUnion also has targeted developing markets in Asia and today operates in nations including China India Hong Kong Singapore and Thailand.

TransUnion has been busy expanding its reach and growing its capabilities. The company is focused on penetrating industries that have low use of information-based analytics and decisioning technology such as insurance and health care. In line with that strategy TransUnion boosted its health care data in 2011 when it acquired the Denver-based Financial Healthcare Systems (FHS). FHS technology provides patients with real-time Internet-based data of out-of-pocket expenses for medical treatment. Previously TransUnion acquired North Carolina-based medical billing services provider MedData.

TransUnion also has a strategy to expand its interactive business. In 2010 TransUnion Interactive launched its streamlined zendough.com product to help consumers manage their credit.

TransUnion partnered with rivals Experian and Equifax to establish VantageScore an alternative to the FICO credit score system. FICO originator Fair Isaac challenged the VantageScore partners in an antitrust lawsuit which it lost in 2009. Although VantageScore and FICO are competing systems Fair Isaac continues to use TransUnion Experian and Equifax data so it remains a partner (as well as a competitor) of the credit bureaus.

EXECUTIVES

EVP Corporate General Counsel and Corporate Secretary, John W. Blenke, age 56
President CEO and Director, Siddharth N. (Bobby) Mehta, age 54
EVP Global Analytics Decision Services, Wilbert P. Noronha, age 53
EVP Human Resources, Mary K. Krupka, age 56
EVP Insurance, Kelley L. Buchanan, age 42
Chairwoman, Penny Pritzker, age 52
EVP and CFO, Samuel A. (Allen) Hamood, age 44
EVP U.S. Information Services, Jeffrey J. (Jeff) Hellinga, age 53
Senior Director Corporate Communications, Clifton M. O'Neal
EVP Interactive, Mark W. Marinko, age 50
EVP Healthcare Vertical, Milton G. Silva-Craig, age 44
Senior Director Corporate Communications, Steven R. Katz
EVP International, Andrew Knight, age 55
EVP CIO and CTO, Mohit Kapoor, age 48
Public Relations Manager Corporate Communications, Dave Blumberg
Director, John A. Canning Jr., age 67
President CEO and Director, Siddharth N. (Bobby) Mehta, age 54
Director, Nigel W. Morris, age 54
Director, Reuben Gamoran, age 51
Director, Timothy M. Hurd, age 42
Director, Vahe A. Dombalagian, age 38
Director, Edward M. Magnus, age 36
Director, Renu S. Karnad, age 59
Director, Matthew A. (Matt) Carey, age 47
Auditors: Ernst&YoungLLP

LOCATIONS

HQ: TRANSUNION CORP.
 555 W ADAMS ST FL 1, CHICAGO, IL 60661-3614
Phone: 312-258-1717
Web: www.transunion.com

PRODUCTS/OPERATIONS

2011 Sales
$ in mil. % of total

US information services	660	64
International	216	21
Interactive	147	15
Total	**1,024**	**100**

Selected Services
Business
  Collections
  Credit reporting
  Fraud and identity management
  Marketing
  Rental screening
  Risk management
Consumer
  Credit dispute investigation
  Credit monitoring
  Credit reports
  Fraud and identity theft

COMPETITORS

Acxiom	Global Payments
Advantage Credit	Harte-Hanks
Alliance Data Systems	Kroll Factual Data
Ceridian	Merrill
Convergys	MoneyGram
CreditRiskMonitor.com	International
D&B	Moody' s
Deluxe Corporation	Paychex
Discover	RealPage
DST Systems	Synovus
Equifax	TeleTech
Experian	Total System Services
Fair Isaac	Unisys
First Data	Valassis
Fiserv	

HISTORICAL FINANCIALS
Company Type: Private

Income Statement
FYE: September 30

	REVENUE ($ mil.)	NET INCOME ($ mil.)	NET PROFIT MARGIN	EMPLOYEES
09/12*	482	33	7.0%	3,908
12/11	1,024	48	4.8%	0
Annual Growth	**(52.9%)**	**(30.9%)**	**—**	**—**

*Fiscal year change

2012 Year-End Financials

Debt ratio: —
Return on equity: 7.00%
Cash ($ mil.): 127
Current ratio: 1.30
Long-term debt ($ mil.): —

Dividends
  Yield: —
  Payout: —
Market value ($ mil.): —

TRANSYSTEMS CORPORATION

LOCATIONS

HQ: TRANSYSTEMS CORPORATION
  2400 PERSHING RD STE 400, KANSAS CITY, MO
  64108-2526
Phone: 816-329-8700
Web: www.transystem.com

HISTORICAL FINANCIALS
Company Type: Private

Income Statement
FYE: December 31

	REVENUE ($ mil.)	NET INCOME ($ mil.)	NET PROFIT MARGIN	EMPLOYEES
12/11	211	5	2.4%	1,000
12/10	208	7	3.6%	0
12/09	156	7	4.7%	0
12/08	170	8	4.8%	0
Annual Growth	**7.5%**	**(14.9%)**	**—**	

2011 Year-End Financials

Debt ratio: —
Return on equity: 2.40%
Cash ($ mil.): 0
Current ratio: 0.60
Long-term debt ($ mil.): —

Dividends
  Yield: —
  Payout: —
Market value ($ mil.): —

TRAVEL AND TRANSPORT INC.

Travel and Transport can get you there and back. The company provides its business clients with travel management solutions such as air hotel vacation packages and meeting planning services. Its corporate travel services include travel policy development vendor negotiation analysis and reporting. Travel and Transport is able to support international travel through its membership in RADIUS a network of 90 US travel agencies with more than 3300 offices worldwide. Travel and Transport also has a travel agent school and works with leisure travelers. The company which was founded in 1946 is 100% owned by its employees.

In October 2011 the travel management firm acquired Sprayberry Travel in Atlanta Georgia as part of its bid to expand in the Southeastern US particularly Georgia and Florida. Sprayberry Travel which provided travel packages to businesses and leisure clients was integrated into Travel and Transport's operations. Previously in 2010 Travel and Transport acquired Eagle International Inc. a sports marketing company that provides group tour packages for the Masters Golf Tournament held yearly in Augusta Georgia.

EXECUTIVES

President and CEO, William H. (Bill) Tech
EVP Sales Operations and Client Services,
  Timothy J. (Tim) Fleming
VP and Director Human Resources, John F. Mock
EVP and CFO, Kevin M. O'Malley
SVP Information Services and CIO, Michael P. (Mike) Kubasik
SVP Strategic Business Development, John E. King
VP Operations, Nancy J. Miller
VP and Corporate Counsel, Michael J. (Mike) King
VP Client Services, Nancy L. Rissky

LOCATIONS

HQ: Travel and Transport Inc.
  2120 S. 72nd St., Omaha NE 68124-6310
Phone: 402-399-4500   **Fax:** 402-398-9290
Web: www.tandt.com

COMPETITORS

Alamo Travel	Ovation Travel Group
American Express	Thomas Cook
BCD Travel	Travel Solutions
Carlson Wagonlit	Travelport
Corporate Travel	TUI
Planners	Tzell Travel
Kuoni Travel	

HISTORICAL FINANCIALS
Company Type: Private

Income Statement
FYE: December 31

	REVENUE ($ mil.)	NET INCOME ($ mil.)	NET PROFIT MARGIN	EMPLOYEES
12/11*	57	3	6.0%	940
03/10	12	1	9.2%	0
12/08	48	2	5.0%	0
12/07	43	2	6.4%	0
Annual Growth	**9.5%**	**7.1%**	**—**	**—**

*Fiscal year change

2011 Year-End Financials

Debt ratio: —
Return on equity: 6.00%
Cash ($ mil.): 16
Current ratio: 1.60
Long-term debt ($ mil.): —

Dividends
  Yield: —
  Payout: —
Market value ($ mil.): —

TRAVERSE CITY AREA PUBLIC SCHOOLS

LOCATIONS

HQ: TRAVERSE CITY AREA PUBLIC SCHOOLS
  412 WEBSTER ST, TRAVERSE CITY, MI 49686-2650
Phone: 231-933-1700
Web: www.ci.traverse-city.mi.us

HISTORICAL FINANCIALS
Company Type: Private

Income Statement
FYE: June 30

	REVENUE ($ mil.)	NET INCOME ($ mil.)	NET PROFIT MARGIN	EMPLOYEES
06/12	103	2	2.5%	1,825
06/11	105	(14)	—	0
06/10	106	12	11.8%	0
06/09	108	(20)	—	0
Annual Growth	**(1.6%)**	**—**	**—**	**—**

2012 Year-End Financials

Debt ratio: —
Return on equity: 2.50%
Cash ($ mil.): 11
Current ratio: 0.50
Long-term debt ($ mil.): —

Dividends
  Yield: —
  Payout: —
Market value ($ mil.): —

TRI-GAS & OIL CO. INC.

LOCATIONS

HQ: TRI-GAS & OIL CO. INC.
3941 FEDERALSBURG HWY, FEDERALSBURG, MD
21632-2620
Phone: 410-754-2000
Web: www.trigas-oil.com

HISTORICAL FINANCIALS

Company Type: Private

Income Statement

FYE: March 31

	REVENUE ($ mil.)	NET INCOME ($ mil.)	NET PROFIT MARGIN	EMPLOYEES
03/12*	87	1	2.0%	119
09/11	156	1	1.0%	0
09/10	101	0	1.0%	0
09/09	81	1	1.4%	0
Annual Growth	2.5%	16.5%	—	—

*Fiscal year change

2012 Year-End Financials

Debt ratio: ——
Return on equity: 2.00%
Cash ($ mil.): 0
Current ratio: 0.60
Long-term debt ($ mil.): ——

Dividends
Yield: —
Payout: —
Market value ($ mil.): —

TRIAD ELECTRIC & CONTROLS INC

LOCATIONS

HQ: TRIAD ELECTRIC & CONTROLS INC
2288 N AIRWAY DR, BATON ROUGE, LA 70815-8132
Phone: 225-923-0604
Web: www.thenewtrongroup.com

HISTORICAL FINANCIALS

Company Type: Private

Income Statement

FYE: June 30

	REVENUE ($ mil.)	NET INCOME ($ mil.)	NET PROFIT MARGIN	EMPLOYEES
06/12	117	0	0.1%	750
06/11	170	1	0.7%	0
06/10	174	1	1.0%	0
06/09	165	3	1.9%	0
Annual Growth	(10.8%)	(70.9%)	—	—

2012 Year-End Financials

Debt ratio: ——
Return on equity: 0.10%
Cash ($ mil.): 2
Current ratio: 0.10
Long-term debt ($ mil.): ——

Dividends
Yield: —
Payout: —
Market value ($ mil.): —

TRIANGLE DISTRIBUTING CO.

LOCATIONS

HQ: TRIANGLE DISTRIBUTING CO.
12065 PIKE ST, SANTA FE SPRINGS, CA 90670-2964
Phone: 562-699-3424

HISTORICAL FINANCIALS

Company Type: Private

Income Statement

FYE: December 31

	REVENUE ($ mil.)	NET INCOME ($ mil.)	NET PROFIT MARGIN	EMPLOYEES
12/11	168	9	5.5%	270
12/10	163	8	4.9%	0
12/09	166	9	5.6%	0
12/08	160	19	12.2%	0
Annual Growth	1.5%	(22.2%)	—	—

2011 Year-End Financials

Debt ratio: ——
Return on equity: 5.50%
Cash ($ mil.): 8
Current ratio: 2.60
Long-term debt ($ mil.): ——

Dividends
Yield: —
Payout: —
Market value ($ mil.): —

TRIBALCO LLC

LOCATIONS

HQ: TRIBALCO LLC
4915 SAINT ELMO AVE # 501, BETHESDA, MD
20814-6019
Phone: 301-652-8450
Web: www.tribalco.com

HISTORICAL FINANCIALS

Company Type: Private

Income Statement

FYE: December 31

	REVENUE ($ mil.)	NET INCOME ($ mil.)	NET PROFIT MARGIN	EMPLOYEES
12/11	90	7	8.5%	105
12/10	85	6	7.2%	0
Annual Growth	6.5%	26.7%	—	—

2011 Year-End Financials

Debt ratio: ——
Return on equity: 8.50%
Cash ($ mil.): 0
Current ratio: 1.80
Long-term debt ($ mil.): ——

Dividends
Yield: —
Payout: —
Market value ($ mil.): —

TRIBUTE ENERGY INC.

LOCATIONS

HQ: TRIBUTE ENERGY INC.
2100 WEST LOOP S STE 1220, HOUSTON, TX
77027-3599
Phone: 281-768-5300

HISTORICAL FINANCIALS

Company Type: Private

Income Statement

FYE: December 31

	REVENUE ($ mil.)	NET INCOME ($ mil.)	NET PROFIT MARGIN	EMPLOYEES
12/11	209	1	0.8%	12
12/10	115	2	2.1%	0
12/09	51	1	3.5%	0
12/08	54	2	4.3%	0
Annual Growth	56.5%	(10.3%)	—	—

2011 Year-End Financials

Debt ratio: ——
Return on equity: 0.80%
Cash ($ mil.): 2
Current ratio: 0.80
Long-term debt ($ mil.): ——

Dividends
Yield: —
Payout: —
Market value ($ mil.): —

TRINITY HEALTH CORPORATION

Hospitals health centers and nursing homes make up Trinity Health. One of the largest Catholic health care systems in the US Trinity Health runs about 50 hospitals (with a total of 6900 beds) 30 long-term care centers (1700 beds) 400 outpatient facilities and numerous home health and hospice agencies. Of the hospitals it owns about 35 and manages another dozen for third parties. Its Trinity Senior Living Communities division operates its nursing homes and senior living facilities. Sponsored by the Catholic Health Ministries Trinity Health has facilities in 10 mostly Midwestern states and its Trinity Health International (THI) unit provides consulting and training to hospitals worldwide.

Geographic Reach

Trinity Health has locations in California Idaho Illinois Indiana Iowa Maryland Michigan and Ohio; the facilities also serve customers in Oregon and Nebraska. THI the company's international arm has conducted projects in more than 40 countries.

Operations

On both domestic and international soil Trinity Health conducts and supports a number of ministry projects to improve community health in poor or disaster-struck areas. THI's projects have included the management of infection control programs biomedical engineering training mental health training and feasibility and demand studies for other health care organizations.

Trinity Health also operates the Mount Carmel Health Plan which offers MediGold a Medicare Advantage program to seniors and others eligible for Medicare in Ohio. The program includes comprehensive health benefits and prescription drug coverage.

Altogether Trinity Health's facilities employ more than 9000 physicians discharge more than 350000 inpatients and handle more than 10 million emergency room and outpatient visits per year.

Financial Performance

Trinity Health reported a 21% increase in revenues to $8.9 billion in 2012 primarily due to growth from acquisitions and increased payment rates continuing a five-year trend of revenue growth. Net income fell 46% to some $367 million in 2012.

Strategy

To meet federal health reform guidelines Trinity Health is working to shape its organization into an accountable health network (AHN) by coordinating patient care across all regional facilities and providers both within and outside of the Trinity Health system. The company had already installed new information technology systems including the Genesis EHR (electronic health record) system and a new procurement platform at more than half of its facilities. In addition to improving the quality of care such measures aim to improve quality and lower costs for medical services.

As part of its AHN goals Trinity Health is forming collaborations with other area providers. Trinity Health announced in 2012 that it is exploring a merger with Pennsylvania-based Catholic Health East (CHE). The combination of CHE and Trinity would create a health system that serves people in 21 states from coast to coast with about 80 hospitals90 continuing care facilities and home health and hospice programs that provide nearly 2.8 million visits annually. The new system would have annual operating revenues of about $13.3 billion and assets of about $19.3 billion.

Trinity Health also expands its own network through construction efforts and by acquiring facilities. In 2010 the organization completed a new $355 million replacement hospital facility for the Saint Joseph Regional Medical Center in Indiana. It also constructed new senior living facilities and entered new home health contracts. In 2012 the company added eight new senior emergency rooms doubling the number of such facilities in the system.

Mergers and Acquisitions

In 2012 Trinity Health purchased the Mercy Hospital & Medical Center of Chicago. Mercy already participated in Trinity Health's group purchasing organization; the purchase expanded Trinity's presence in the Chicago area.

Trinity Health grew in 2011 through the acquisition of the Loyola University Health System which was previously owned by Loyola University Chicago. The purchase added the 570-bed Loyola University Medical Center (which continue to provide teaching programs with the university's medical school) the 250-bed Gottlieb Memorial Hospital and a number of specialty centers in Illinois.

In 2010 Trinity Health acquired three hospitals —Mercy Medical Center Holy Rosary Medical Center Saint Elizabeth Health Services —in Oregon and Idaho from Catholic Health Initiatives (CHI). The facilities were combined with Trinity Health's Saint Alphonsus Regional Medical Center to form a single local system called Saint Alphonsus Health System.

Company Background

The not-for-profit Trinity Health organization was formed through the 2000 merger of Mercy Health Services and Holy Cross Health System.

EXECUTIVES

SVP Organizational Integrity and Audit Services, Michael R. (Mike) Holper

President and CEO Mercy Medical Center - Sioux City, Paul Doherty

President Health Networks, Michael A. (Mike) Slubowski

SVP Governance and Sponsorship, Sister Catherine DeClercq

SVP Treasurer and Chief Investment Officer, James W. Bosscher

EVP Trinity Institute of Health and Community Benefits, Daniel G. (Dan) Hale

SVP Supply Chain and Capital Projects Management, Louis J. (Lou) Fierens II

President and CEO Mount Carmel Health System, Claus P. von Zychlin

SVP and CFO, Benjamin R. (Ben) Carter

President CEO and Director, Joseph R. Swedish, age 60

President and CEO St. Joseph Mercy Oakland, Jack Weiner, age 63

SVP Strategic Planning and Marketing, Preston Gee

President and CEO Saint Joseph Mercy Health System, Garry C. Faja

President and CEO Mercy Medical Center - North Iowa, James G. FitzPatrick

CEO Trinity Continuing Care Services, Jaclyn Harris

President and CEO Holy Cross Hospital, Kevin J. Sexton

CEO Mercy Hospital - Grayling, Stephanie Riemer-Matuzak

President and CEO Saint Mary's Mercy Medical Center, Philip H. McCorkle

CEO Trinity Home Health Services, Grace McCauley

CEO Mercy Hospital - Cadillac, John L. MacLeod

President and CEO Mercy Medical Center - Dubuque, Russell Knight

President and CEO St. Mary Mercy Hospital, David Spivey

President and CEO Mercy General Health Partners, Roger W. Spoelman, age 59

SVP Clinical Quality and Patient Safety, Paul F. Conlon

EVP and Chief Clinical Officer, P. Terrence (Terry) O'Rourke

EVP and Chief Administrative Officer, Debra A. (Deb) Canales

EVP and COO Hospital Networks, Richard (Rick) O'Connell

President and CEO Saint Joseph Regional Medical Center, Nancy Hellyer

President and CEO Mercy Hospital - Port Huron, Peter Karadjoff

SVP and General Counsel, Paul G. Neumann

SVP Integration Services, Paul Browne

President and CEO Mercy Medical Center - Clinton, Donna Oliver

SVP Diversity and Inclusion, VeLois Bowers

President and CEO Saint Alphonsus Regional Medical Center, Sally E. Jeffcoat

President Integrated Services, Kedrick D. Adkins Jr.

SVP Patient Care Services and Chief Nursing Officer, Gay Landstrom

SVP Mission Integration, Daniel P. Dwyer

Interim President and CEO Saint Agnes Medical Center, Thomas Anderson

President and CEO St. Joseph Mercy Hospital, Robert Casalou

EVP Health Networks, Michael (Mike) Murphy

SVP and Chief Development Officer, Maria Szymanski

SVP Insurance and Risk Management Services, Rebecca Havlisch

Chairperson, Sister Mary Mollison

SVP and Chief Medical Officer, Donald Bignotti

Director, Sarah Ladd Eames, age 54

Director, Suzanne R. Brennan, age 61

Director, Henry R. Autry, age 62

President CEO and Director, Joseph R. Swedish, age 60

Director, Angel R. (A. R.) Sales, age 62

Director, Melanie C. Dreher

Director, Sister Mary Kelly

Director, Sister Kathleen Moroney

Director, Norma Smith

Director, Mary Mollison

Director, Robert W. (Bob) Ladenburger

Director, Linda Werthman

Auditors: Deloitte&ToucheLLP

LOCATIONS

HQ: Trinity Health
27870 Cabot Dr., Novi MI 48377-2920
Phone: 248-489-6000 **Fax:** 513-639-2700
Web: www.health-partners.org

Selected Facilities

California
  Saint Agnes Medical Center (Fresno)
Idaho and Oregon
  Saint Alphonsus Medical Center - Baker City
  Saint Alphonsus Medical Center - Nampa
  Saint Alphonsus Medical Center - Ontario
  Saint Alphonsus Regional Medical Center (Boise)
Indiana
  Saint Joseph Regional Medical Center (South Bend)
  Saint Joseph Regional Medical Center (Plymouth)
Illinois
  Loyola University Health System (Chicago)
    Loyola University Medical Center
    Loyola Gottlieb Memorial Hospital
  Mercy Hospital & Medical Center (Chicago)
Iowa and Nebraska
  Mercy Health Network (Clinton Des Moines Dubuque Dyersville Mason City New Hampton and Sioux City Iowa; Oakland Nebraska)
Maryland
  Holy Cross Hospital (Silver Spring)
Michigan
  Mercy Health Partners (Muskegon)
  Mercy Hospital (Cadillac)
  Mercy Hospital (Grayling)
  Saint Joseph Mercy Health System (Ann Arbor)
  Saint Mary's Health Care (Grand Rapids)
Ohio
  Mount Carmel Health System (Columbus)

COMPETITORS

Advocate Health Care	Odyssey HealthCare
Amedisys	OhioHealth
Ascension Health	Resurrection Health
Beaumont Health System	Care
Community Health	St. Luke' s Health
Systems	System
HCA	Tenet Healthcare
Health Management	Universal Health
Associates	Services
HealthSouth	University of Chicago
Henry Ford Health	Medical Center
System	Vanguard Health
Hospice of Michigan	Systems
Johns Hopkins Medicine	VITAS Healthcare
Kindred Healthcare	Wheaton Franciscan
Mayo Clinic	Services
MedStar Health	
Memorial Hospital	
& Health System	

HISTORICAL FINANCIALS

Company Type: Private - Not-for-Profit

Income Statement

FYE: June 30

	REVENUE ($ mil.)	NET INCOME ($ mil.)	NET PROFIT MARGIN	EMPLOYEES
06/11	814	36	4.5%	51,100
06/10	738	50	6.8%	0
06/09	593	(59)	—	0
06/08	1	(0)	—	0
Annual Growth	700.0%	—	—	—

2011 Year-End Financials

Debt ratio: —
Return on equity: 4.50%
Cash ($ mil.): 2
Current ratio: —
Long-term debt ($ mil.): —

Dividends
Yield: —
Payout: —
Market value ($ mil.): —

TRINITY MOTHER FRANCES HEALTH SYSTEM FOUNDATION

Trinity Mother Frances Health System Foundation (dba Trinity Mother Frances Hospitals and Clinics) has a complicated name but a simple mission: to improve patient health. Consisting of three general hospitals several specialist facilities and a large physicians' group Trinity Mother Frances serves northeastern Texas. Its largest acute-care facility is Mother Frances Hospital-Tyler with more than 400 beds offering comprehensive medical surgical trauma and cardiovascular care. Two smaller hospitals in Jacksonville and Winnsboro provide emergency diagnostic surgery and select specialty services. The Trinity Clinic is a multi-specialty physician group that includes 300 doctors in 36 community clinics.

Operations

Trinity Mother Frances Hospitals and Clinics' specialty facilities include the freestanding Trinity Mother Frances Rehabilitation Hospital in Tyler which has 75 beds and is operated through a joint venture with HealthSouth. It also operates the Tyler ContinueCARE Hospital a long-term acute care hospital located within the Mother Frances Hospital-Tyler as well as several urgent care centers.

Strategy

In 2010 the network added the 35-bed Mother Frances Hospital-Winnsboro facility when it took over control of the Texas Health Presbyterian Hospital Winnsboro from Texas Health Resources. The transfer was made to align the Winnsboro hospital with the main Tyler facility where the majority of specialized cases from Winnsboro were already being transferred.

The network also added a freestanding 72-bed cardiac facility the Louis and Peaches Owen Heart Hospital in Tyler. The first phase of the center was added to the existing Mother Frances Hospital-Tyler facilities in 2010; the second stage is a six-story freestanding tower adjacent to the Tyler hospital. Construction on the tower started in early 2011 and was completed by the end of 2012.

Additionally Trinity Mother Frances Hospitals and Clinics is investing in information technology initiatives. It began installing electronic health record (EHR) systems at its facilities during 2012 as part of the US government's health care improvement initiatives.

Company Background

Trinity Mother Frances Hospitals and Clinics was established by the 1995 merger of Mother Frances Hospital and the Trinity Clinic both founded in the 1930s.

EXECUTIVES

President, J. Lindsey Bradley Jr.
President and Chief Medical Officer, David K. Teegarden
Administrative Director, Cindy Kidwell
Director Trauma/Surgical Critical Care, Luis G. Fernandez, age 54
VP Surgical Services, Chris Glenney
Medical Director Information, Tom Hargrove
VP Human Resources, Randy Perdue
EVP and COO, Ray Thompson
SVP Operations, Laura Owen
VP Finance, Joyce Hester
VP Regional Business Development, John Webb
VP Marketing, Mary Peterson
Public Information Officer, John Moore
VP Neuroscience, Rhonda Clawson
EVP, Steven P. Keuer
VP and CIO, Lee Portwood
Interim Chief Nursing Officer, Bobbie Ogg
Auditors: BKDLLP

LOCATIONS

HQ: Trinity Mother Frances Health System Foundation
800 E. Dawson St., Tyler TX 75701
Phone: 903-593-8441   **Fax:** 903-525-1201
Web: www.tmfhs.org

PRODUCTS/OPERATIONS

Selected Locations

DirectCARE (urgent care multiple sites)
Louis and Peaches Owen Heart Hospital Tyler
Mother Frances Hospital-Jacksonville
Mother Frances Hospital-Tyler
Mother Frances Hospital-Winnsboro
Trinity Clinics (physician practices multiple sites)
Trinity Mother Frances Rehabilitation Hospital-Tyler
Tyler ContinueCARE Hospital

Selected Services

Anesthesiology
Audiology
Bariatric Surgery Center
Cancer
Cardiac Services
Cardiothoracic Surgery
Critical Care Intensivists
Ear Nose & Throat
Emergency Medicine
Endocrinology
Gastroenterology Hepatology and Endoscopy
Family Medicine
General Surgeons
Genetics
Hospitalists
Imaging Radiology Mammography
Internal Medicine
Neonatology
Neuroscience Institute
Obstetrics & Gynecology
Occupational Medicine - Health At Work
Ophthalmology Optometry & Optical Services
Orthopedics
Pain Medicine
Pediatrics
Physical Medicine and Rehabilitation

Plastic Surgery
Podiatry
Psychiatry
Rehabilitation Hospital
Rheumatology
Sleep Medicine
Sports Medicine
Surgery Services
Trauma Services
Urgent Care
Urology Institute & Continence Center
Vascular Institute
Women & Children
WoundCARE

COMPETITORS

Baylor Health
Community Health Systems
East Texas Medical Center Regional Healthcare
Essent Healthcare
Good Shepherd Health System
HCA
Hunt Memorial
Memorial Health System of East Texas
Parkland Health & Hospital System
Southwestern Medical Center
Tenet Healthcare
The Methodist Health System
United Surgical Partners
Wadley Regional Medical Center
Woodland Heights Medical Center

HISTORICAL FINANCIALS

Company Type: Private - Not-for-Profit

Income Statement

FYE: June 30

	REVENUE ($ mil.)	NET INCOME ($ mil.)	NET PROFIT MARGIN	EMPLOYEES
06/11	674	73	10.9%	3,551
06/10	603	19	3.3%	0
06/09	562	(27)	—	0
06/08	530	(1)	—	0
Annual Growth	8.3%	—	—	—

2011 Year-End Financials

Debt ratio: —
Return on equity: 10.90%
Cash ($ mil.): 74
Current ratio: 1.40
Long-term debt ($ mil.): —

Dividends
Yield: —
Payout: —
Market value ($ mil.): —

TRINITY SENIOR LIVING COMMUNITY

LOCATIONS

HQ: TRINITY SENIOR LIVING COMMUNITY
17410 COLLEGE PKWY # 200, LIVONIA, MI 48152-2369
Phone: 734-542-8300
Web: www.stjosephshealthcare.com

HISTORICAL FINANCIALS

Company Type: Private

Income Statement

FYE: June 30

	REVENUE ($ mil.)	NET INCOME ($ mil.)	NET PROFIT MARGIN	EMPLOYEES
06/11	160	10	6.8%	1,800
06/10	158	6	4.3%	0
06/09	867	44	5.2%	0
06/08	36	1	3.4%	0
Annual Growth	63.5%	106.0%	—	—

2011 Year-End Financials

Debt ratio: ——
Return on equity: 6.80%
Cash ($ mil.): 64
Current ratio: 4.00
Long-term debt ($ mil.): ——

Dividends
Yield: ——
Payout: ——
Market value ($ mil.): ——

TRUE VALUE COMPANY

To survive against home improvement giants such as The Home Depot and Lowe's True Value (formerly TruServ) is relying on the true value of service. Formed by the 1997 merger of Cotter & Company (which supplied the True Value chain) and ServiStar Coast to Coast the retailer-owned hardware cooperative serves more than 5000 retail outlets in some 54 countries. Stores offer home improvement and garden supplies as well as appliances housewares sporting goods and pet food. In addition to the flagship True Value banner members operate under the names of Taylor Rental Grand Rental Station Home & Garden Showplace and Induserve Supply among others. True Value also manufactures its own brand of paints.

Operations

In addition to its main chain hardware stores True Value operates several specialty franchise businesses. Grand Rental Station and Taylor Rental Centers rent tools party and event supplies and equipment and contractor equipment to amateurs and professional contractors. Home and Garden Showplace is a garden center cooperative offering products for homes gardens and landscaping projects. Induserve Supply sells hand and power tools paint janitorial supplies and many more products to commercial and industrial customers. Party Central franchises rent supplies for weddings backyard parties. Its customers include caterers and event planners.

Financial Analysis

True Value's revenue increased by more than 3% in 2011 vs. 2010 to nearly $1.9 billion. Same-store sales grew nearly 5% and the international business reported double-digit sales growth. The modest improvement in sales followed an essentially flat previous annual comparison and nearly a 10% drop in sales in 2009 vs. the prior year. The company's net margins have narrowed over the past several years.

Strategy

Essential to the company's growth strategy has been the rollout of its Destination True Value (DTV) retail format which aims to simplify shopping in its hardware stores particularly for its female clientele (who hold sway when it comes to tackling home improvement projects). The format features a "racetrack" layout for easy navigation as well as color-coded signs brighter lighting and an expanded array of decorative hardware and paint. Also the format is relatively flexible and allows owners to customize their store layouts for their particular local markets. The DTV plan unveiled in 2007 had been adopted by about 230 store owners by the end of 2011. True Value estimates that stores operating under the DTV format average about 9% higher sales than their non-DTV counterparts. Another 100 DTV conversions are planned for 2012.

In addition to the DTV plan the company is working to woo younger do-it-yourselfers into its stores through the reach of digital marketing. Stores produce area-specific online circulars and True Value's website offers a project library product guides and bargains of the month. The co-op is taking its marketing efforts forward with social media and the development of an e-commerce site.

While the organization is focused on expanding its retail presence the weak housing market in the US has kept growth in check. Over the years its smaller in-town locations have taken a beating at the hands of the big-box hardware chains. To combat declining sales the company has implemented cost controls such staff reductions debt refinancing along with improving logistics and manufacturing infrastructures.

HISTORY

Noting that hardware retailers had begun to form wholesale cooperatives to lower costs John Cotter a traveling hardware salesman and associate Ed Lanctot started pitching the wholesale co-op idea in 1947 to small-town and suburban hardware retailers and by early 1948 they had enrolled 25 merchants for $1500 each. Cotter became chairman of the new firm Cotter & Company.

The co-op created the Value & Service (V&S) store trademark in 1951 to emphasize the advantages of an independent hardware store. Acquisitions included the 1963 purchase of Chicago-based wholesaler Hibbard Spencer Bartlett giving Cotter 400 new members and the well-known True Value trademark which soon replaced V&S signs. Four years later Cotter broadened its focus by buying the General Paint & Chemical Company (Tru-Test paint). The V&S name was revived in 1972 for a five-and-dime store co-op V&S Variety Stores.

In 1989 Cotter died and Lanctot retired. (Lanctot died in October 2003.) By 1989 there were almost 7000 True Value Stores. Cotter moved into Canada in 1992 by acquiring hardware distributor and store operator Macleod-Stedman (275 outlets).

Juggling variety-store and hardware merchandise and delivering very small amounts of merchandise to a lukewarm co-op membership did not allow for economies of scale so in 1995 the company quit its manufacturing operations and its US variety stores (though it still serves variety stores in Canada operating as C&S Choices) tightened membership requirements and introduced new services.

Two years later Cotter formed TruServ by merging with hardware wholesaler ServiStar Coast to Coast. ServiStar had its origins in the nation's first hardware co-op American Hardware Supply which was founded in Pittsburgh in 1910 by M. R. Porter John Howe and E. S. Corlett. By 1988 the year it changed its name to ServiStar the co-op topped $1 billion in sales.

ServiStar expanded in the upper Midwest and on the West Coast in 1990 when it acquired the assets of the Coast to Coast chain (founded in 1928 as a franchise hardware store in Minneapolis);

ServiStar brought Coast to Coast out of bankruptcy two years later making it a co-op. Merging its 1992 acquisition of Taylor Rental Center with its Grand Rental Station stores in 1993 made ServiStar the #1 general rental chain. In 1996 it consolidated Coast to Coast's operations into its own and changed its name to ServiStar Coast to Coast.

President Don Hoye became CEO of the company in 1999. That year TruServ slashed 1000 jobs and declared it would convert all its hardware store chains to the True Value banner. But TruServ lost $131 million in 1999 over bookkeeping gaffes and co-op members received no dividends. Of 2800 ServiStar dealers only 1900 raised the True Value flag. Others either declined to switch or were never offered the change because other True Value stores already shared their market area. In addition stores began deserting the co-op because of inventory and other problems. In late 2000 the company sold its lumber and building materials business.

As competition continued to increase in 2001 the company was facing falling sales lawsuits from shareholders and accusations by retailers of unfair practices intended to pressure them into adopting the cooperative's flagship True Value banner. TruServ also had to confront a $200 million loan default. It made cuts in its corporate staff and divested its Canadian interests. In July 2001 Hoye resigned. The company's CFO and COO Pamela Forbes Lieberman was named the new CEO that November.

In April 2002 the company reported a net loss of $50.7 million during 2001 which it attributed to restructuring charges inventory write-downs and finance fees. Also that month the company announced that it had received $200 million in long-term financing. TruServ under SEC investigation for alleged inventory accounting and other internal-control problems was one of several companies that failed in August 2002 to meet a government requirement to swear by their past financial results.

In January 2003 TruServ received about $125 million in financing from investment firm W. P. Carey & Co. in a sale-leaseback deal on seven of TruServ's distribution centers. In March TruServ settled the SEC's allegations without admitting or denying them and agreed to follow measures intended to ensure compliance with securities laws.

Lieberman resigned in November 2004. Director Thomas Hanemann was named interim CEO. TruServ changed its name to True Value in January 2005. That June Hanemann turned over the reins to Sears veteran Lyle Heidemann who joined True Value as its new president and CEO. In December the company sold its oil-based paint manufacturing operation in Chicago to Blackhawk/Halsted for about $10 million.

In 2007 True Value added more than 100 new stores in the US and experienced modest growth overseas. Also that year the company launched its new store format called Destination TrueValue.

The year 2008 marked the first time in over a decade that revenue from new stores exceeded lost revenue from terminated stores.

EXECUTIVES

President CEO and Director, Lyle G. Heidemann, age 67, $415,016 total compensation

VP Marketing and Chief Customer Officer, Blake A. Fohl, age 52

SVP and CFO, David A. (Dave) Shadduck, $317,750 total compensation

VP Specialty Businesses, Fred L. Kirst, age 57

VP Marketing, Carol Wentworth, age 51

VP and Corporate Treasurer, Barbara L. Wagner
SVP Human Resources General Counsel and
Secretary, Cathy C. Anderson, $312,250 total
compensation
Director; CEO Shively True Value Hardware
Saratoga WY, Michael S. Glode, age 60
Director; CEO Welch's True Value Hardware
South Royalton VT, Charles M. Welch, age 59
SVP and Chief Merchandising Officer, Michael
Clark
Director; CEO True Value Hardware House
Annapolis MD, Kenneth A. Niefeld, age 68
Chairman; CEO Krueger's True Value Neenah
Wis., Brian A. Webb
VP Specialty Businesses, Eric Lane
VP Retail Growth, Mark Flowers
VP Logistics, Donald J. (Don) Deegan
SVP Retail Operations, Stephen Poplawski
VP and CIO, Rosalee Hermens
Director; CEO Campbell's True Value Madison
Maine, Brent A. Burger
Merchandising Department Contact, Erika
Sandilands
Market Exhibitor Information Contact, Maureen
Feck
President CEO and Director, Lyle G. Heidemann,
age 67
Director, Gregory P. Josefowicz, age 58
Director, Cheryl A. Bachelder, age 55
Director, David Y. Schwartz, age 69
Director; CEO Shively True Value Hardware
Saratoga WY, Michael S. Glode, age 60
Director, Thomas S. (Tom) Hanemann, age 70
Director; CEO Welch's True Value Hardware
South Royalton VT, Charles M. Welch, age 59
Director; CEO True Value Hardware House
Annapolis MD, Kenneth A. Niefeld, age 68
Director, Richard E. George Jr., age 71
Director, M. Shan Atkins, age 55
Director; CEO Campbell's True Value Madison
Maine, Brent A. Burger
Auditors: PricewaterhouseCoopersLLP

LOCATIONS

HQ: True Value Company
8600 W. Bryn Mawr Ave., Chicago IL 60631-3505
Phone: 773-695-5000   Fax: 678-645-1079
Web: www.coxenterprises.com

PRODUCTS/OPERATIONS

Selected Operations

Grand Rental Station (general rental)
Home & Garden Showplace (nursery and giftware)
Induserve Supply (commercial and industrial)
Party Central (parties and corporate events)
Taylor Rental (general rental)
True Value (hardware)

COMPETITORS

84 Lumber	Menard
Ace Hardware	Northern Tool
Akzo Nobel	Orgill
Benjamin Moore	Sears
Do it Best	Sherwin-Williams
Fastenal	Stock Building Supply
Hertz	Sutherland Lumber
Home Depot	United Rentals
Kmart	Valspar
Lowe' s	Wal-Mart
McCoy Corp.	

HISTORICAL FINANCIALS

Company Type: Private - Cooperative

Income Statement

FYE: December 31

	REVENUE ($ mil.)	NET INCOME ($ mil.)	NET PROFIT MARGIN	EMPLOYEES
12/11*	1,864	60	3.2%	3,000
01/11	1,804	60	3.4%	0
01/10	1,823	65	3.6%	0
09/08	1,529	44	2.9%	0
Annual Growth	6.8%	10.9%	—	—

*Fiscal year change

2011 Year-End Financials

Debt ratio: ——
Return on equity: 3.20%
Cash ($ mil.): 3
Current ratio: 0.60
Long-term debt ($ mil.): —

Dividends
Yield: —
Payout: —
Market value ($ mil.): —

TRUMAN ARNOLD COMPANIES

It is not just jibber jabber —this jobber gets the job done by distributing wholesale petroleum across the US. Truman Arnold Companies (TAC) has more than 400 associates with fuel volume of more than 2 billion gallons a year and markets and distributes petroleum products to customers through its TAC Energy subsidiary. Its TAC Terminals unit operates two major petroleum terminals one in Arkansas and one in Texas which collectively have more than 1.3 million barrels of capacity. Through its TAC Air unit the company offers fixed-based operations (FBO) including aircraft fueling hangar and ground transportation services through 12 general aviation facilities located across the country.

The company also operates two Road Runner convenience stores and has interests in real estate.

TAC's four divisions —Aviation Services Wholesale Petroleum Marketing Branded Petroleum Marketing and Petroleum Terminal Services operate independently but take advantage of shared management and technical resources.

Aviation Services has been a growth area. The company opened its 13th FBO in 2009 in the Spirit of St. Louis Airport in Chesterfield Missouri. It opened an executive terminal (its first at any FBO location) at Blue Grass Airport in Kentucky in July 2010.

To raise cash in October 2010 TAC Air sold its Greenville South Carolina FBO operation to Greenville Jet Center for undisclosed terms.

TAC has also grown its wholesale energy segment. In 2009 TAC Energy acquired Fuel Managers (which has operation in 18 states) for an undisclosed price. The acquisition of the fuel wholesaler helped to boost TAC Energy's position in the supply market in the Central and Western US.

To keep up with the growth of the company TAC expanded its Dallas sale office. The company anticipates doubling in size by 2016 and sees Dallas as a key operational/sales hub for managing its growth.

The family-owned and -operated company was founded in 1964 by Texarkana businessman Truman Arnold. It once operated a chain of 125 Road Runner convenience stores in eight states before selling this network to Total Petroleum in 1989. TAC revived the brand in 2003.

EXECUTIVES

Chairman, Truman Arnold
President and CEO, Gregory A. (Greg) Arnold
SVP and CFO, Steve McMillen
VP and CIO, Michael Davis
SVP and General Counsel, James (Jim) Day
VP Aviation Division (TAC Air), Daniel A. (Danny)
Walsh
VP Trading and Supply, Tom Knight
Director Human Resources, Denny Peterson
VP Terminal Services (TAC Energy), Benny Webb
Director Marketing, Jennifer Green

LOCATIONS

HQ: Truman Arnold Companies
701 S. Robison Rd., Texarkana TX 75501
Phone: 903-794-3835   Fax: 903-831-4056
Web: www.trumanarnoldcompanies.com

COMPETITORS

Atlantic Aviation	Signature Flight
Getty Petroleum	SMF Energy
Marketing	Sun Coast Resources
Gulf Oil	Warren Equities
Million Air	

HISTORICAL FINANCIALS

Company Type: Private

Income Statement

FYE: September 30

	REVENUE ($ mil.)	NET INCOME ($ mil.)	NET PROFIT MARGIN	EMPLOYEES
09/11	3,023	9	0.3%	99
09/10	2,285	8	0.4%	0
09/09	1,271	9	0.7%	0
09/08	2,511	11	0.5%	0
Annual Growth	6.4%	(6.4%)	—	—

2011 Year-End Financials

Debt ratio: ——
Return on equity: 0.30%
Cash ($ mil.): 4
Current ratio: 0.70
Long-term debt ($ mil.): —

Dividends
Yield: —
Payout: —
Market value ($ mil.): —

TRUSTEES OF BOSTON COLLEGE

Students at Boston College (BC) get both academic excellence and the Red Sox. Located six miles from downtown Boston the university enrolls more than 14600 full- and part-time students (about a third of whom are graduate students) from every state in the US and 80 countries. It has a student-teacher ratio of 14:1. Founded in 1863 BC offers degrees in more than 55 fields of study through its schools and colleges on four campuses. The university also has more than 20 research centers including the Institute for Scientific Research and the Center for International Higher Education. BC is one of the oldest Jesuit Catholic universities in the nation and has the largest Jesuit community in the world.

About 70% of its undergraduate student body are self-identified as Catholic.

The university with campuses in Brighton Chestnut Hill Dover and Newton Massachusetts is also home to more than 20 centers and institutes designated for research and teaching. Research opportunities including participation in faculty research projects exist for both undergraduate and graduate students.

BC has enjoyed steady growth from voluntary giving by its alumni. Its endowment has grown to almost $2 billion placing it among the top 40 in the US.

Boston College's strategic plan includes adding 100 new faculty positions expanding research by faculty and graduate students increasing student financial aid to more than $128 million annually and extending undergraduate opportunities in international study internships and student formation.

During its first seven decades BC was an exclusively undergraduate institution that served sons of the Irish working class. Its liberal arts emphasis was on the Greek and Latin classics English and modern languages and philosophy and religion. Development into the college it is today did not begin until the 1920s when the Graduate School of Arts and Sciences the Law School and the Evening College (known today as the James A. Woods S.J. College of Advancing Studies) were inaugurated. All classes became co-educational in the 1970s and today BC has a fairly equal split among male and female students.

EXECUTIVES

President, William P. Leahy
VP Facilities Management, Thomas Devine
Chancellor, J. Donald Monan
VP University Mission And Ministry, Joseph A. Appleyard
Provost and Dean of Faculties, Cutberto (Bert) Garza
Vice Provost Faculties, Patricia DeLeeuw
Dean Carroll School of Management, Andrew C. Boynton
Dean Lynch School of Education, Joseph M. O'Keefe
Dean School of Nursing, Barbara Hazard
Co-Director Center on Aging and Work, Michael A. Smyer
Dean Graduate School of Social Work, Alberto Godenzi
University Librarian, Jerome Yavarkovsky
Dean of Enrollment Management, Robert Lay
Associate Academic VP Technology, Rita R. Owens
Associate VP Auxiliary Services, Patricia Bando
Executive Director Operations and Business Services, Linda J. Riley
Director Benefits, John R. Burke
Director Bookstore, Thomas McKenna
Director Career Center, Theresa A. Harrigan
Controller, Michael J. Driscoll
Director Employment and Human Resources, Anita E. Ulloa
EVP, Patrick J. Keating
Chairman Finance Carroll School of Management, Hassan Tehranian
VP Finance and Treasurer, Peter C. McKenzie
Director Weston Observatory, John E. Ebel
VP Human Resources, Leo V. Sullivan
Associate VP Applications and Systems Services, Michael Bourque
Director Network Services, Joseph E. Harrington

VP Information Technology Services, Marian G. Moore
Chairman Marketing Carroll School of Management, Gerald Smith
VP University Advancement, Jim Husson
Associate Academic VP Undergraduate Programs, J. Joseph Burns
Vice Provost Research, Kevin Bedell
Director Procurement Services, Paul McGowan
Director Student Services, Louise Lonabocker
Director Operations and University Bursar, Chris Cordella
Director Financial Aid, Mary McGranahan
Director Budget, Michael T. Callnan
Associate VP Human Resources, Robert J. Lewis
Vice President of Finance, Peter K. Markell
Auditors: PricewaterhouseCoopersLLP

LOCATIONS

HQ: TRUSTEES OF BOSTON COLLEGE
140 COMMONWEALTH AVE, CHESTNUT HILL, MA 02467-3800
Phone: 617-552-8000
Web: www.ajcunet.edu

PRODUCTS/OPERATIONS

Selected Colleges and Schools

Carolyn A. and Peter S. Lynch School of Education
College of Arts and Sciences
Graduate School of Arts and Sciences
Graduate School of Social Work
James A. Woods S.J. College of Advancing Studies
School of Law
School of Theology and Ministry
Wallace E. Carroll School of Management
William F. Connell School of Nursing

HISTORICAL FINANCIALS

Company Type: School

Income Statement

FYE: May 31

	REVENUE ($ mil.)	NET INCOME ($ mil.)	NET PROFIT MARGIN	EMPLOYEES
05/12	653	(76)	—	3,000
05/11	643	287	44.7%	0
05/10	628	177	28.2%	0
05/09	621	(318)	—	0
Annual Growth	1.7%	—	—	—

TRUSTEES OF CLARK UNIVERSITY

If you don't want to live in the dark get an education at Clark! Clark University is a private co-educational liberal arts university with an enrollment of more than 2200 undergraduate students and roughly 900 graduate students. It offers about 30 undergraduate majors (psychology is the most popular) and about two dozen master's degree programs. The university was founded in 1887 as the first all-graduate school in the US. Clark College began educating undergraduates in 1902 and was combined into the university in 1920. Clark University has been a pioneer in the academic study of geography; it has awarded more doctorates in the discipline than any other US school.

EXECUTIVES

Director Office of Financial Assistance, Mary Ellen Severance
CIO, Pennie S. Turgeon
Chief University Police, Stephen Goulet
Executive Assistant to the President, Shirley Granlund
President, David P. Angel
EVP, James Collins
VP Planning and Budget, Andrea Michaels
Director Study Abroad and Study Away Programs, Adrianne Van Gils
University Librarian, Gwen Arthur
Director Physical Plant, Paul Bottis
Associate Provost; Dean Graduate Studies and Research, Nancy Budwig
Controller, Katherine Cannon
Dean of Students, Denise Darrigrand
Director Office of Intercultural Affairs, Amy Daly
VP Government and Community Affairs and Campus Services, John Foley
Director Human Resources and Affirmative Action, Lynn Olson
Director Athletics, Linda Moulton
Dean Graduate School of Management and Associate Professor, Edward J. Ottensmeyer
Director Corporate and Foundation Relations, Jane Baker
Director Career Services, David McDonough
Dean Admissions and Financial Aid, Donald M. Honeman
Director The Clark Fund, Sarah C. Curtis
Director Academic Advancement, Wesaline Gadson
Director Residential Life and Housing, Kevin Forti
Director University Communications, Judith Jaeger
Dean College of Professional and Continuing Education (COPACE), Thomas P. Massey
VP University Advancement, C. Andrew McGadney
Office of Student Leadership and Programming, Michael McKenna
Director Admissions, Tricia Uber
University Registrar and Director Student Accounts, Linda Winslow
Associate Provost and Dean, Walter Wright
Director Planned Giving, Daniel Petrocelli
Director Alumni Affairs, Aixa L. Kidd
Director Advancement Services, Karen Doherty

LOCATIONS

HQ: Clark University
950 Main St., Worcester MA 01610
Phone: 508-793-7711   **Fax:** 508-793-7724
Web: www.clarku.edu

HISTORICAL FINANCIALS

Company Type: School

Income Statement

FYE: May 31

	REVENUE ($ mil.)	NET INCOME ($ mil.)	NET PROFIT MARGIN	EMPLOYEES
05/12	104	(14)	—	600
05/11	101	55	54.3%	0
05/10	149	9	6.5%	0
05/09	126	0	—	0
Annual Growth	(6.1%)	—	—	—

2012 Year-End Financials

Debt ratio: —
Return on equity: (-13.80)%
Cash ($ mil.): 41
Current ratio: —
Long-term debt ($ mil.): —
Dividends
Yield: —
Payout: —
Market value ($ mil.): —

TRUSTEES OF PHILLIPS ACADEMY

LOCATIONS

HQ: TRUSTEES OF PHILLIPS ACADEMY
180 MAIN ST, ANDOVER, MA 01810-4166
Phone: 978-749-4000
Web: www.phillipian.net

HISTORICAL FINANCIALS

Company Type: Private

Income Statement

FYE: June 30

	REVENUE ($ mil.)	NET INCOME ($ mil.)	NET PROFIT MARGIN	EMPLOYEES
06/11	136	33	24.3%	600
06/10	117	19	16.4%	0
06/09	78	(150)	—	0
06/08	75	(4)	—	0
Annual Growth	21.5%	—	—	—

2011 Year-End Financials

Debt ratio: ——
Return on equity: 24.30%
Cash ($ mil.): 22
Current ratio: ——
Long-term debt ($ mil.): ——

Dividends
Yield: —
Payout: —
Market value ($ mil.): —

TRUSTEES OF THE ESTATE OF BERNICE PAUAHI BISHOP

Kamehameha Schools provides an education fit for a king ... or queen. The private charitable trust was founded and endowed by Princess Bernice Pauahi Bishop great granddaughter and last royal descendant of Kamehameha the Great. One of the largest independent schools in the US Kamehameha educates more than 5000 elementary middle school and high school students many of whom board at one of its three Hawaii campuses. In addition it operates some 30 preschools with a total enrollment of about 1500. Kamehameha Schools is also the largest private property owner in the state of Hawaii and uses the proceeds from its real estate operations to support its schools.

The Kamehameha School for Boys was established in 1887 followed by the Kamehameha School for Girls which opened in 1894. By 1955 the schools consolidated onto a 600-acre campus with views of Honolulu that span from Pearl Harbor to Diamond Head.

To this day Kamehameha Schools gives preferential admissions treatment to students of Hawaiian decent a long-standing policy it is fighting to preserve despite the controversy it creates. The schools have successfully fought off several lawsuits aimed at opening its doors to other ethnicities including a close decision by an appeals court in 2009.

EXECUTIVES

VP Finance and Administration, Michael P. Loo
Secretary Treasurer and Trustee, Constance H. (Connie) Lau, age 60
VP Legal Services, Colleen I. Wong
VP Endowment, Kirk O. Belsby
CEO, Dee Jay A. Mailer
Headmaster Hawai'i Campus, Stan Fortuna
President and Headmaster Kapalama Campus, Michael J. Chun
VP Campus Strategies, D. Rodney Chamberlain
VP Community Relations and Communications, Ann Botticelli
VP Strategic Planning and Implementation, Christopher J. (Chris) Pating
Interim Head Community Outreach Education, Charlene Hoe
Head of Educational Support Services, Sylvia M. Hussey
Dean Extension Education Division, Juvenna Chang
Dean Community-Based Early Childhood Education, Theresa (Terry) Lock
Headmaster Maui Campus, Lee Ann DeLima
Executive Director Ke Ali'i Pauahi Foundation, Kalei Stern
Auditors: KPMGLLP

LOCATIONS

HQ: Kamehameha Schools
567 S. King St. Ste. 200, Honolulu HI 96813
Phone: 808-523-6200   **Fax:** 808-541-5305
Web: www.ksbe.edu

COMPETITORS

Edison Learning   Learning Care Group

HISTORICAL FINANCIALS

Company Type: School

Income Statement

FYE: June 30

	REVENUE ($ mil.)	NET INCOME ($ mil.)	NET PROFIT MARGIN	EMPLOYEES
06/11	524	159	30.5%	1,500
06/10	333	(21)	—	0
06/09	1	1	69.0%	0
06/08	1	1	69.0%	0
Annual Growth	554.0%	398.1%	—	—

2011 Year-End Financials

Debt ratio: ——
Return on equity: 30.50%
Cash ($ mil.): 31
Current ratio: ——
Long-term debt ($ mil.): ——

Dividends
Yield: —
Payout: —
Market value ($ mil.): —

TRUSTEES OF THE UNIVERSITY OF PENNSYLVANIA

The University of Pennsylvania was founded by Benjamin Franklin when he had a little down time between establishing a country and experimenting with lightning. Since opening its doors to students in 1751 the Ivy League university has accumulated a notable list of accomplishments including the creation of one of the first medical schools in the US. The university currently has a total of almost 25000 students who pursue their studies in four undergraduate schools and a dozen graduate and professional schools including the renowned Wharton School and the Annenberg School for Communications. Its student-teacher ratio is very low 6:1.

Geographic Reach

The University of Pennsylvania (commonly called Penn) is located in the heart of downtown Philadelphia.

Operations

The University of Pennsylvania's research staff includes more than 4300 faculty and 1100 postdoctoral fellows plus some 5600 academic support staff and graduate student trainees.

The university is also responsible for inventing the Electronic Numerical Integrator and Computer (ENIAC) the first general-purpose electronic computer. The ENIAC was constructed and operated at The Moore School of Electrical Engineering now part of the School of Engineering and Applied Science. The school still has on display four of the original 40 panels of ENIAC which represents one-tenth of its original size.

Financial Performance

The University of Pennsylvania has enjoyed an upward trend in revenue in recent years as a result of organic growth. The nominal increase of 2% in revenue for fiscal 2012 compared to 2011 came primarily from increases in tuition and fees. Undergraduate tuition is more than $39000 per year while annual fees cost students $4650.

The university has an annual budget of about $6 billion. Its endowment is about $5.7 billion. The University of Pennsylvania is heavily involved with research operating more than 165 research centers and institutes. Its research budget was $924 million in 2012 making it a nationally ranked research university.

Company Background

Former president Judith Rodin was the first female to head an Ivy League university.

EXECUTIVES

VP Human Resources, John J. (Jack) Heuer
EVP, Craig R. Carnaroli
President and Trustee, Amy Gutmann
VP Information Systems and Computing, Robin H. Beck
VP and Secretary, Leslie Laird Kruhly
VP Division of Public Safety, Maureen S. Rush
SVP and General Counsel University of Pennsylvania University of Pennsylvania Health System, Wendy S. White
CEO University of Pennsylvania Health System, Ralph W. Muller
VP Budget and Management Analysis, Bonnie Gibson
VP University Communications, Stephen J. (Steve) MacCarthy
Comptroller, John F. Horn
VP Institutional Affairs, Joann Mitchell
VP Development and Alumni Relations, John H. Zeller
Dean School of Arts and Sciences, Rebecca W. Bushnell
Dean Annenberg School for Communication, Michael X. Delli Carpini
Dean School of Law, Michael A. Fitts
Dean School of Social Policy and Practice, Richard Gelles

LOCATIONS

HQ: The University of Pennsylvania
3451 Walnut St., Philadelphia PA 19104
Phone: 215-898-5000   **Fax:** 215-898-9659
Web: www.upenn.edu

PRODUCTS/OPERATIONS

Selected Schools

Annenberg School for Communication
The College at Penn (School of Arts and Sciences)
Graduate School of Education
Graduate School of Fine Arts
Law School
School of Arts and Sciences
School of Dental Medicine
School of Engineering and Applied Science
School of Medicine
School of Nursing
School of Social Work
School of Veterinary Medicine
The Wharton School

HISTORICAL FINANCIALS

Company Type: School

Income Statement

FYE: June 30

	REVENUE ($ mil.)	NET INCOME ($ mil.)	NET PROFIT MARGIN	EMPLOYEES
06/11	5,330	643	12.1%	20,433
06/10	4	0	5.1%	0
06/09	5,221	(1,285)	—	0
06/08	5,092	133	2.6%	0
Annual Growth	1.5%	68.9%	—	—

2011 Year-End Financials

Debt ratio: ——
Return on equity: 12.10%
Cash ($ mil.): 947
Current ratio: ——
Long-term debt ($ mil.): —

Dividends
Yield: —
Payout: —
Market value ($ mil.): —

TUNNELL CONSULTING INC.

Tunnel vision can be a good thing in the life sciences. Tunnell Consulting helps clients in the biotech and pharmaceutical manufacturing industries achieve operational excellence. The company focuses on key areas such as regulation compliance and quality; technical services; operational improvement; and turnkey solutions. Specifically the firm can help start up facilities and reduce costs of established businesses. Abbott Labs IBM and 3M are among the company's customers. Tunnell Consulting was founded in 1962. It has been employee-owned since 1988.

EXECUTIVES

Managing Director and Principal, Richard A. (Rick) Winegar

SVP Operations, Joseph J. Villafranca, age 68

VP Quality and Regulatory Compliance, Gregory J. Sam, age 53

CFO and Treasurer, Joseph A. Hare

Managing Director Key Accounts, Susan C. Devane

Principal, Ted Shoneck

CEO, Conrad J. Heilman Jr.

Chairman, Joseph S. (Joe) Tempio

Corporate Secretary and Director, Marian Preston

VP and Process Analytical Technology (PAT) Leader, Philippe Cini

Principal, Jason Kamm

VP Chief Consulting Officer and Practice Director Organizational Excellence, Raymond E. (Ray) Schneider

VP and Business Development Operating Unit Leader, Michael Raquet

VP and Senior Managing Director Strategy Services, Raymond L. (Ray) Manganelli

VP Human Resources, Maria V. Butz

SVP Government Services and Strategy Leader, Mark R. Schroeder

Principal, William D. (Bill) Connell

Principal, Ronald D. (Ron) Snee

Principal, John S. Tegeris

Principal, J. Jaime Velez

Principal, William (Bill) Schmidt

Principal, Christopher S. Driscoll

Principal and Head West Coast Office, Siddharth J. (Sid) Advant

LOCATIONS

HQ: TUNNELL CONSULTING INC.
900 E 8TH AVE STE 106, KING OF PRUSSIA, PA 19406-1321
Phone: 610-337-0820
Web: www.tunnellconsulting.com

COMPETITORS

Advisory Board
Real Change Network
ReSearch Pharmaceutical Services

HISTORICAL FINANCIALS

Company Type: Private

Income Statement

FYE: December 31

	REVENUE ($ mil.)	NET INCOME ($ mil.)	NET PROFIT MARGIN	EMPLOYEES
12/11	42	0	0.4%	90
12/08	47	0	1.4%	0
12/06	37	0	0.6%	0
12/05	204	0	—	0
Annual Growth	—	794.4%	—	—

2011 Year-End Financials

Debt ratio: —
Return on equity: 0.40%
Cash ($ mil.): 1
Current ratio: 0.60
Long-term debt ($ mil.): —

Dividends
Yield: —
Payout: —
Market value ($ mil.): —

TURBANA CORPORATION

LOCATIONS

HQ: TURBANA CORPORATION
550 BILTMORE WAY STE 730, CORAL GABLES, FL
33134-5723
Phone: 305-445-1542
Web: www.turbana.com

HISTORICAL FINANCIALS

Company Type: Private

Income Statement

FYE: December 31

	REVENUE ($ mil.)	NET INCOME ($ mil.)	NET PROFIT MARGIN	EMPLOYEES
12/11	151	1	1.0%	33
12/10	153	1	1.2%	0
12/09	180	2	1.3%	0
12/08	170	3	1.9%	0
Annual Growth	(3.9%)	(21.1%)	—	—

2011 Year-End Financials

Debt ratio: —
Return on equity: 1.00%
Cash ($ mil.): 0
Current ratio: 3.40
Long-term debt ($ mil.): —

Dividends
Yield: —
Payout: —
Market value ($ mil.): —

TURN ON PRODUCTS INC.

LOCATIONS

HQ: TURN ON PRODUCTS INC.
270 W 38TH ST FL 19, NEW YORK, NY 10018-1696
Phone: 212-764-2121
Web: www.uniqueclothing.com

HISTORICAL FINANCIALS

Company Type: Private

Income Statement

FYE: December 31

	REVENUE ($ mil.)	NET INCOME ($ mil.)	NET PROFIT MARGIN	EMPLOYEES
12/11	150	0	0.4%	68
12/09*	88	1	2.2%	0
06/07	31	0	0.8%	0
06/06	48	0	0.7%	0
Annual Growth	45.4%	13.7%	—	—

*Fiscal year change

2011 Year-End Financials

Debt ratio: —
Return on equity: 0.40%
Cash ($ mil.): 0
Current ratio: 0.10
Long-term debt ($ mil.): —

Dividends
Yield: —
Payout: —
Market value ($ mil.): —

TURTLE & HUGHES INC

Founded in 1923 as an electrical supply house Turtle & Hughes demonstrates that slow and steady really does win the race to distributing electrical and industrial equipment. The company's exhaustive lineup is sold through three subsidiaries: Turtle & Hughes Integrated Supply Turtle Data (wire cable and power protection devices) and TurtleEnergy (energy systems). Its customers include industrial and construction companies electrical contractors telecommunications servers utilities and various government agencies. Family-owned the company is led by its fourth generation Jayne Millard its third female CEO. One-third of Turtle & Hughes is employee-owned. Its branches dot the northeastern US and Texas.

The company's newest branch in Long Island City –its ninth –neighbors several main arteries to Manhattan where a number of its major accounts are established. The location aims to boost Turtle & Hughes' marketplace presence as well as expand its geographic reach. Its projects in and around the city include the electrical power distribution contract for the new World Trade Center Transportation Hub and the power distribution equipment contract (to be installed by its customers) supplying the Freedom Tower and Tower Four.

The Garden State has been the home to Turtle & Hughes' solar projects in recent years thanks in part to state and local subsidies. In late 2010 the company was awarded a $30 million contract to install a photovoltaic system at a private school in Lawrenceville New Jersey. Turtle & Hughes can also boast the design and supply of the components and coordination of the contract work for installing a photovoltaic solar panel system on the roof of the New Jersey Institute of Technology's Student Center.

EXECUTIVES

CFO, Trevor Barnett
President Schlecter Industrial Division, Alan Schlecter
President Turtle & Hughes Integrated Supply (THIS), Jay Drummond
EVP, Frank Millard
Chairman, Suzanne Turtle Millard

President, Jack Sinagra
Operations Manager Bridgewater, Andrea Strong
Director Human Resources, Lucy Liana
CEO, Jayne Millard
Manager Corporate Operations, Chuck Noll
EVP; Branch Manager Bridgewater Distribution Center and Plainfield Branch, Rick Reffler
Controller, Cheryl Leonard
VP Finance, Kevin Doyle
Auditors: AmperPolitziner&MattiaP.C.

LOCATIONS

HQ: Turtle & Hughes Inc.
1900 Lower Rd., Linden NJ 07036
Phone: 732-574-3600   **Fax:** 732-574-3723
Web: www.turtle.com

PRODUCTS/OPERATIONS

Selected Products

Datacom categories
Anchors and fasteners
Burial products/innerduct
Cabinets and enclosures
Cable management
Cable tray/ladder rack
Category rated and coax cable
Connectivity
Fiber-optic cable
Hand tools
Outside plant
Power protection
Raceway and duct systems
Safety
Security fencing
Splices connectors and lugs
Tools testers and safety
Electrical categories
Alarms annunciators and signals
Anchors and plugs
Automation products
Ballasts and transformers
Batteries and flashlights
Box enclosures
Breakers panels and switchgears
Cable trays and struts
Conduit fittings
Cord connectors
Dimming controls
Electrical tools
Emergency lighting
Enclosures
Fans
Fluorescent lighting
Fuse holders and terminal blocks
Generators
Groundings
Heat shrink
Heating
High-bay lighting
Incandescent lighting
Lamps
Limit temp. and proximity switch
Lugs and terminals
Metering equipment
Motor control
Motors AC and DC drivers
Outdoor lighting
Pole line products
Programmable controls
Relays
Strut/channel
Test equipment
Time clocks
Transformers
Wire cable and cord
Wiring accessories
Wiring devices
Industrial categories
Adhesives and tapes
Brushes and brooms
Carbide tools
Cutting fluid/lubricant

Cutting tools
Fasteners
Hand tools
Hoist chain and accessories
Industrial abrasives
Janitorial paper supplies
Ladders
Locks
Lubricating devices
Material handling
MRO supplies
Paint/markets
Pipe hangers
Pipe valves and fittings
Pneumatics
Pneumatic tools
Power tools
Safety equipment
Saw blades
Shim/shim stock
Solenoid valves
Strut/channel
Tooling accessories

COMPETITORS

C. R. Laurence	Kennametal
Consolidated	MSC Industrial Direct
Electrical	Prime Advantage
CPAC	Rexel Inc.
Dillon Supply	Sonepar USA
Foster Wheeler	Steiner Electric
Graybar Electric	W.W. Grainger
Indoff	WESCO International
Interline Brands	

HISTORICAL FINANCIALS

Company Type: Private

Income Statement

FYE: September 30

	REVENUE ($ mil.)	NET INCOME ($ mil.)	NET PROFIT MARGIN	EMPLOYEES
09/11	452	17	4.0%	450
09/10	397	14	3.5%	0
09/09	376	11	3.1%	0
09/08	407	15	3.9%	0
Annual Growth	3.6%	4.5%	—	—

2011 Year-End Financials

Debt ratio: ——
Return on equity: 4.00%
Cash ($ mil.): 8
Current ratio: 1.50
Long-term debt ($ mil.): —
Dividends
 Yield: —
 Payout: —
 Market value ($ mil.): —

U. S. ENGINEERING COMPANY

LOCATIONS

HQ: U. S. ENGINEERING COMPANY
 3433 ROANOKE RD, KANSAS CITY, MO 64111-3778
Phone: 816-753-6969
Web: www.usengineering.com

Income Statement

FYE: September 30

	REVENUE ($ mil.)	NET INCOME ($ mil.)	NET PROFIT MARGIN	EMPLOYEES
09/11	210	0	—	800
09/10	172	0	—	0
09/09	201	0	—	0
09/08	0	0	—	0
Annual Growth	—	—	—	—

2011 Year-End Financials

Debt ratio: ——
Return on equity: —
Cash ($ mil.): 0
Current ratio: 1.10
Long-term debt ($ mil.): —
Dividends
 Yield: —
 Payout: —
 Market value ($ mil.): —

U.R.M. STORES INC.

URM Stores is a leading wholesale food distribution cooperative serving more than 160 grocery stores in the Northwest. Its member-owner stores operate under a variety of banners including Family Foods Harvest Foods Super 1 Foods Trading Co. Stores and Yoke's Fresh Market. It also owns the Rosauers Supermarkets chain. In addition to grocery stores URM supplies 1500-plus restaurants hotels and convenience stores; it also offers such services as merchandising store development consulting and technology purchasing. The cooperative was founded in 1921 as United Retail Merchants. The business is privately owned by its members.

Geographic Reach

Regional wholesaler URM Stores supplies stores and other customers in much of eastern Washington northern Idaho Oregon and Montana.

Operations

The company's Spokane Washington-based Peirone Produce distribution subsidiary supplies fresh produce including organic produce as well as specialty items source from Arizona California Florida Mexico and Texas. In addition to groceries and produce URM Stores sells insurance to its members and food service customers through URM Insurance Agency. Insurance products include business insurance for stores and personal lines of coverage for owns and their employees.

Financial Performance

URM Stores rings up sales of about $775 million employs more than 2700 people and has assets exceeding $100 million.

Strategy

In 2010 the company moved its Spokane Washington-based Peirone Produce distribution subsidiary into a larger facility boasting 70000 sq. ft. of warehouse space and 7000 sq. ft. of office space. It is equipped with about 15 docks for loading outgoing trucks and another dozen docks for unloading incoming trucks. The facility is more than twice the size of Peirone's previous building which had nearly 10 docks total. Because of the larger space and greater number of docks Peirone Produce said it has been able to improve its productivity.

EXECUTIVES

CFO, Laurie Bigej

President and CEO, Dean E. Sonnenberg
VP Information Technology, Jonathan Jennings
VP Purchasing and Profit Centers, Ray Sprinkle
Manager Grocery Procurement, Jon Roman
Controller, Brian Eldred
VP Human Resources, Linda Wilson
Manager URM Insurance Agency, Katherine E. (Kathy) Miotke
Director Marketing URM Food Service, Shary Blinzler
Director Food Service, Rick Jensen
Director Retail Systems, Mark Sutton
Manager Training, Barbara Baumann

LOCATIONS

HQ: URM Stores Inc.
 7511 N. Freya St., Spokane WA 99217
Phone: 509-467-2620   **Fax:** 604-515-7978
Web: www.cryopak.com

PRODUCTS/OPERATIONS

Selected Banners

CenterPlace Market
Family Foods
Harvest Foods
Trading Co. Stores
Rosauers Supermarkets
Super 1 Foods
Yoke's Fresh Market

COMPETITORS

Albertsons	Nash-Finch
AMCON Distributing	Safeway
Associated Food	SUPERVALU
C&S Wholesale	Sysco
Core-Mark	Unified Grocers
Farner-Bocken	US Foods
Fred Meyer Stores	Wal-Mart
McLane	

HISTORICAL FINANCIALS

Company Type: Private - Cooperative

Income Statement

FYE: July 30

	REVENUE ($ mil.)	NET INCOME ($ mil.)	NET PROFIT MARGIN	EMPLOYEES
07/11*	913	8	1.0%	2,100
08/08	932	8	0.9%	0
07/07	859	7	0.8%	0
07/06	799	4	0.6%	0
Annual Growth	4.6%	26.1%	—	—

*Fiscal year change

2011 Year-End Financials

Debt ratio: ——
Return on equity: 1.00%
Cash ($ mil.): 5
Current ratio: 0.50
Long-term debt ($ mil.): —
Dividends
 Yield: —
 Payout: —
 Market value ($ mil.): —

U.S. COMMODITIES LLC

LOCATIONS

HQ: U.S. COMMODITIES LLC
730 2ND AVE S STE 700, MINNEAPOLIS, MN
55402-2480
Phone: 612-486-3800
Web: www.uscommodities-ag.com

HISTORICAL FINANCIALS

Company Type: Private

Income Statement

FYE: September 30

	REVENUE ($ mil.)	NET INCOME ($ mil.)	NET PROFIT MARGIN	EMPLOYEES
09/11	481	0	—	55
09/10	357	0	—	0
Annual Growth	34.8%	—	—	—

U.S. VENTURE INC.

Smitten with the love of oil distribution the founding Schmidt family owns and operates U.S. Venture (formerly U.S. Oil). The company's U.S. Oil division (formerly U.S. Petroleum Operations) supplies refined oil products to residents in the Midwest and does a lot more. In addition to the wholesale distribution of oil products (its largest revenue generator) the company operates gas stations and installs gas pumps tanks and other petroleum-related equipment. U.S. Venture also provides plumbing and HVAC services (Design Air) collects used waste oil to be processed into burner fuel and has a metal custom manufacturing unit.

The company operates about 20 Express Convenience Centers with gas stations and convenience store operations. Under its U.S. AutoForce brand U.S. Oil also operates about a dozen warehouses in Illinois Minnesota Missouri Nebraska Iowa South Dakota and Wisconsin offering auto parts (for brakes exhausts and suspensions) and tires. U.S. Venture operates 12 refined products terminals across the Midwest (with a total storage capacity of about 127 million gallons at its bulk fuel storage tanks) including the Cheboygan 164000 barrels facility. It also stores and wholesales biofuels.

The company has grown its geographic presence through acquisitions of complementary companies. In a move to expand its MidContinent petroleum products distribution business in 2010 the company acquired Houston-based refined products marketing and trading company Saracen Energy Partners.

Growing is presence in North Central Wisconsin and the Upper Peninsula of Michigan in 2012 the bought Draeger Oil Company's branded dealer division. Under the terms of the deal U.S. Oil provides fuel supply to more than 50 retail gas stations while Draeger retains the transportation portion.

U.S. Ventures (U.S. Oil) also expanded its petroleum products distribution presence in Indiana in 2012 through the purchase of Farmersburg-based Trueblood Oil's branded wholesale fuel supply business.

U.S. Oil was established in the 1950s as Schmidt Oil by the sons of local fuel distributor Albert Schmidt who landed his first job in the oil business in 1923. The company changed its name to U.S. Venture in 2010 to reflect the company's increasingly diverse portfolio of entrepreneurial businesses.

EXECUTIVES

Chairman, Thomas A. (Tom) Schmidt
CFO, Paul Bachman
General Counsel, Marjorie Young
President and CEO, John Schmidt
Director Safety and Risk Management, Tom Titzkowski
Director Human Resources, Lori Hoersch
CIO, Mark Duening

LOCATIONS

HQ: U.S. Venture Inc.
425 Better Way, Appleton WI 54915
Phone: 920-739-6101 **Fax:** 920-788-0531
Web: www.usventure.com

PRODUCTS/OPERATIONS

Selected Operations

Custom Manufacturing (tube bending and fabrication)
Design Air (heating and air conditioning equipment)
Express Convenience Centers (gas stations and car washes)
Petroleum Equipment (petroleum-related equipment installation)
U.S. AutoForce (exhaust pipe manufacturing and autoparts distribution)
U.S. Lubricants (motor oil and related products)
U.S. Oil (gasoline fuel oil and natural gas)

COMPETITORS

7-Eleven	Quality State Oil
Apex Oil	Company
Marathon Oil	QuikTrip
Motiva Enterprises	Sunoco

HISTORICAL FINANCIALS

Company Type: Private

Income Statement

FYE: July 31

	REVENUE ($ mil.)	NET INCOME ($ mil.)	NET PROFIT MARGIN	EMPLOYEES
07/12	5,906	60	1.0%	1,000
07/11	4,847	27	0.6%	0
07/10	1,940	38	2.0%	0
07/09	1,707	39	2.3%	0
Annual Growth	51.2%	15.1%	—	—

2012 Year-End Financials

Debt ratio: ——
Return on equity: 1.00%
Cash ($ mil.): 31
Current ratio: 0.50
Long-term debt ($ mil.): —

Dividends
Yield: —
Payout: —
Market value ($ mil.): —

UC HEALTH

UC Health is Cincinnati's scholarly health care provider. The medical provider is a partnership between the University of Cincinnati the 480-bed University of Cincinnati Medical Center and the University of Cincinnati Physicians organization. Additionally UC Health is home to the 160-bed West Chester Hospital (a full-service community hospital) the Drake Center long-term acute care (rehabilitation) hospital the UC Health Surgical Hospital and the Lindner Center of HOPE (mental health services). Specialized services include cancer cardiovascular neuroscience and metabolic disease treatment. The not-for-profit UC Health was formed in 1994.

Operations

After a major reorganization in 2010 the surviving UC Health organization core operations are comprised of University Medical Center West Chester Medical Center and its primary and specialty care centers. Through its affiliation with the University of Cincinnati the medical organization conducts educational and research programs.

Strategy

UC Health is working to expand its network through acquisitions. For instance it added a new women's health practice to its provider network in 2012 to widen its specialty service offerings.

UC Health acquired full control of the Drake Center from former partner (and former network member) Jewish Hospital in 2011. It also added the Lindner Center of HOPE to its network that year.

Company Background

Formerly known as The Health Alliance of Greater Cincinnati the company changed its name to UC Health in 2010 after a number of its hospital members left the system and the University of Cincinnati took control of the remaining operations. Rumors of dissolution had swirled around the organization since its members began jumping ship starting in 2007.

Four of the organization's founding hospitals ultimately left the system: The 175-bed Fort Hamilton Hospital (now part of Kettering Health Network) and the 210-bed Jewish Hospital (now part of Catholic Healthcare Partners) departed in 2010. Two other hospitals (St. Luke's and Christ Hospital) broke off from the alliance after a long legal struggle in 2007.

EXECUTIVES

SVP External Affairs, Karen Bankston
VP Organizational Effectiveness, Andrea Stewart
CIO, Jay Brown
Director Human Resources, Bob Griffith
Director Plant Operations West Chester Medical Center, Mike Kuechenmeister
Co-CEO, Rick Hinds
VP Government and Public Relations, Tony Condia
Co-CEO, Dorman Fawley
SVP and Chief Human Resources Officer, Debbe Endres
SVP Strategic Planning and Business Development, Gayla Harvey
VP Patient Care Services and Chief Nursing Officer West Chester Medical Center, Cyndi Traficant

LOCATIONS

HQ: UC Health
3200 Burnet Ave., Cincinnati OH 45229
Phone: 513-585-6000 **Fax:** 619-238-1562
Web: www.neil-dymott.com

PRODUCTS/OPERATIONS

Selected Ohio Facilities

Drake Center (Cincinnati)
Linder Center of HOPE (Mason)

UC Health Surgical Hospital (West Chester)
University of Cincinnati Physicians (Cincinnati)
University of Cincinnati Medical Center (Cincinnati)
West Chester Hospital (West Chester)

COMPETITORS

Catholic Health	Kettering Health
Initiatives	Network
Christ Hospital	Premier Health
Cincinnati Children' s	Partners
Hospital	St. Elizabeth
Greene Memorial	Healthcare
Hospital	

HISTORICAL FINANCIALS
Company Type: Private - Not-for-Profit

Income Statement
FYE: June 30

	REVENUE ($ mil.)	NET INCOME ($ mil.)	NET PROFIT MARGIN	EMPLOYEES
06/11	146	14	9.9%	13,000
06/10	138	(81)	—	0
06/09	102	0	—	0
06/08	205	59	29.2%	0
Annual Growth	(10.7%)	(37.8%)	—	—

2011 Year-End Financials
Debt ratio: ——
Return on equity: 9.90%
Cash ($ mil.): 20
Current ratio: 0.10
Long-term debt ($ mil.): ——

Dividends
Yield: —
Payout: —
Market value ($ mil.): —

UMASS MEMORIAL HEALTH CARE INC

LOCATIONS
HQ: UMASS MEMORIAL HEALTH CARE INC
365 PLANTATION ST STE 300, WORCESTER, MA
01605-2397
Phone: 508-334-1000
Web: www.minimalaccess.com

HISTORICAL FINANCIALS
Company Type: Private

Income Statement
FYE: June 30

	REVENUE ($ mil.)	NET INCOME ($ mil.)	NET PROFIT MARGIN	EMPLOYEES
06/12*	1,671	25	1.5%	10,000
09/11	2,290	(36)	—	0
09/10	2,276	55	2.4%	0
09/09	2,128	460	21.6%	0
Annual Growth	(7.7%)	(61.9%)	—	—

*Fiscal year change

2012 Year-End Financials
Debt ratio: ——
Return on equity: 1.50%
Cash ($ mil.): 114
Current ratio: 1.10
Long-term debt ($ mil.): ——

Dividends
Yield: —
Payout: —
Market value ($ mil.): —

UMASS MEMORIAL HOSPITALS INC.

LOCATIONS
HQ: UMASS MEMORIAL HOSPITALS INC.
119 BELMONT ST, WORCESTER, MA 01605-2903
Phone: 508-334-1000
Web: www.umassmemorial.org

HISTORICAL FINANCIALS
Company Type: Private

Income Statement
FYE: September 30

	REVENUE ($ mil.)	NET INCOME ($ mil.)	NET PROFIT MARGIN	EMPLOYEES
09/11	379	7	1.9%	10,000
09/08	332	9	2.9%	0
09/07	302	15	5.1%	0
09/06	1,982	0	—	0
Annual Growth	—	2637.8%	—	—

2011 Year-End Financials
Debt ratio: ——
Return on equity: 1.90%
Cash ($ mil.): 37
Current ratio: 1.60
Long-term debt ($ mil.): ——

Dividends
Yield: —
Payout: —
Market value ($ mil.): —

UMASS MEMORIAL MEDICAL CENTER INC.

LOCATIONS
HQ: UMASS MEMORIAL MEDICAL CENTER INC.
119 BELMONT ST, WORCESTER, MA 01605-2903
Phone: 508-334-1000
Web: www.umassmemorialmedicalcenter.com

HISTORICAL FINANCIALS
Company Type: Private

Income Statement
FYE: September 30

	REVENUE ($ mil.)	NET INCOME ($ mil.)	NET PROFIT MARGIN	EMPLOYEES
09/11	1,366	(34)	—	0
09/09	1,316	119	9.0%	0
09/08	1,234	3	0.3%	0
09/07	1,107	(26)	—	0
Annual Growth	7.3%	—	—	—

2011 Year-End Financials
Debt ratio: ——
Return on equity: (-2.50)%
Cash ($ mil.): 123
Current ratio: 1.40
Long-term debt ($ mil.): ——

Dividends
Yield: —
Payout: —
Market value ($ mil.): —

UNIFIED GROCERS INC.

This company's unity of purpose helps put groceries on the shelves. Unified Grocers is a leading wholesale cooperative grocery distributor that serves about 3000 independent grocers cash and carry outlets and major grocery chains mostly in the western US. The cooperative operates about a dozen distribution centers that supply its members and nonmember stores with more than 100000 items including meat dairy goods fresh produce and general merchandise. It offers many national brands as well as private labels including Cottage Hearth Golden Creme and Western Family. Unified Grocers boasts about 450 members with about 3000 stores. The cooperative was formed in 1922 as Certified Grocers of California.

Unified Grocers' wholesale distribution provides products and services to member and non-members through its cooperative division which sells products like dry grocery frozen food meat eggs general merchandise and health and beauty care items. The division covers Southern California Northern California and the Pacific Northwest. Its Southern California Dairy division processes pasteurizes and bottles milk from its processing plant in Los Angeles. The plant also bottles water and a variety of fruit punch drinks. The Pacific Northwest Dairy division sells dairy products manufactured by third-party vendors. The diary products are then distributed by the Milwaukie Oregon and Seattle facilities to customers in the Pacific Northwest. Its Market Centre subsidiary sells ethnic gourmet natural organic and specialty foods. Unified International a sales subsidiary sells products and ships to non-member customers.

The cooperative has also an insurance business which is comprised of two subsidiaries: Springfield Insurance Company and Springfield Insurance Company Limited. The businesses provide insurance and insurance-related products to the cooperative along to its member and non-member customers. Insurance products include workers' compensation and liability insurance policies (around 80% and 20% respectively of 2011 revenues). In addition to its core wholesale distribution business Unified Grocers offers its customers such services as liability insurance financing and other support services. It also owns more than 20% of Western Family Foods a distributor of private-label goods sold under the Western Family and Shurfine brands.

The cooperatives' net sales accounted for $3.8 billion in 2011 vs. $3.9 billion in 2010 a decrease of $73.3 million. The cooperative cited the loss of members and store closures affected overall net sales in 2011 by $62.8 million and $71.7 million respectively. The cooperatives' wholesale distribution segment accounted for 99% of net sales. The cooperatives' 100000 national and regional branded products accounted for some 88% of net sales within its wholesale distribution segment. The cooperatives' insurance segment which primarily included premium revenues and investment income accounted for the remaining 1% of net sales. The co-op's largest customer cash and carry warehouse operator Smart & Final accounted for 12% of sales in 2011.

Like other wholesale distributors Unified Grocers focuses on keeping its operating expenses in check so that it can supply its customers at the lowest possible cost. The cooperative's efforts to improve efficiencies throughout its supply chain in part have involved investments in information technology. It competes with national distribution giants such as C & S Wholesale and Nash-Finch as well as other regional co-ops such as Associated Food Stores and URM Stores.

HISTORY

Certified Grocers of California evolved from a group of 15 independent Southern California grocers that formed a purchasing cooperative in 1922 to compete against large grocery chains. Certified Grocers of California incorporated in 1925 and issued stock to 50 members.

The co-op merged with a small retailer-owned wholesale company called Co-operative Grocers in 1928. It acquired Walker Brothers Grocery in 1929 and nearly tripled the previous year's sales. By 1938 the co-op had grown to 310 members and 380 stores and sales passed $10 million.

Certified launched a line of private-label products under the Springfield name in 1947. In the early 1950s it added nonfood items and began processing its own private-label coffee and bean products. The co-op added delicatessen items in 1956. During the 1960s and 1970s Certified added a meat center a frozen food and deli warehouse a produce distribution center a creamery a central bakery and a specialty foods warehouse.

In 1989 the co-op opened several membership warehouse stores called Convenience Clubs. The Save Mart and Boys Markets chains left the fold in 1991. The co-op lost about 30% of its business during the next two years including the Bel Air and Williams Bros. chains. After disappointing returns in 1992 Certified sold its warehouse stores cut staff and consolidated warehouses.

CFO (and former Atlantic Richfield executive) Al Plamann was appointed CEO in 1994 succeeding Everett Dingwell. In 1996 the co-op began to convert its customers' older retail stores to Apple Markets in Southern California. Revenues began to dip in 1997 as the result of reduced purchases from some supermarkets and the sale the previous year of one of its subsidiaries Hawaiian Grocery Stores.

Member chain Stumps converted to the Apple Markets banner in 1998. Faced with a declining customer base in 1999 Certified merged with United Grocers of Oregon to form Unified Western Grocers.

Dr. R. Norton F. L. Freeburg and A. C. Brinckerhoff founded United Grocers of Oregon in 1915 as a way for grocers in Portland to cooperate in purchasing merchandise. By the next year the co-op had 35 members. In the 1950s United formed a trucking department and established a general merchandise division. It also grew rapidly in the 1950s through acquisitions buying Northwest Grocery Company and the Fridegar Grocery Company. In 1963 United formed its frozen food department when it purchased Raven Creamery.

By 1975 the company's Northwest Grocery Company subsidiary had 14 Cash and Carry warehouses that sold goods to small grocers and restaurants. In 1995 United bought California food distributor Market Wholesale. Three years later the company sold its Cash and Carry warehouse-style stores to Smart & Final.

Upon completion of the merger in 1999 Certified's president and CEO Plamann was named to head the new organization. Soon after Unified consolidated warehouse operations eliminated duplicate personnel and combined its private labels. Also in 1999 the company acquired California-based Gourmet Specialties.

The next year it bought the specialty foods business of J. Sosnick and Son another California company and Central Sales of Washington State. The

company attributed net losses during 2001 to delays in moving the source for northern California specialty merchandise from southern to northern California and to the costs of entering the Washington marketplace among other factors.

In 2002 Unified closed seven retail stores in Northern California and Oregon (under the Apple Markets and SavMax Foods banners) that accounted for sales of about $140 million as part of its plan to reduce debt and focus on wholesaling. In 2003 the co-op sold or closed all 12 of its company-owned SavMax Foods stores as part of its plan to exit its unprofitable retail business and focus on its wholesale division (99% of total sales).

As part of an expansion effort Unified acquired Associated Grocers a Seattle-based wholesale cooperative for about $40 million. It later changed its name to Unified Grocers.

EXECUTIVES

President, Robert M. Ling Jr., age 55, $463,654 total compensation
EVP Finance and Administration and CFO, Richard J. (Rich) Martin, age 66, $393,173 total compensation
CEO, Alfred A. (Al) Plamann, age 69, $781,250 total compensation
EVP and Chief Marketing and Procurement Officer, Philip S. (Phil) Smith, age 61, $367,692 total compensation
First Vice Chairman, Louis A. (Lou) Amen, age 82
VP Insurance, Joseph A. (Joe) Ney, age 64
SVP Operations, Rodney L. (Rod) VanBebber, age 57
SVP Perishables and Retail Services, Daniel J. (Dan) Murphy, age 65, $307,923 total compensation
VP Information Services and CIO, Gary S. Herman
VP Human Resources, Donald E. (Don) Gilpin
SVP Finance and Treasurer, Christine E. Neal, age 59
VP Marketing, Dirk T. Davis
VP Procurement, Robert (Bob) Lutz
SVP Sales, Joseph L. (Joe) Falvey, age 52
SVP Accounting and International Sales, Randall G. (Randy) Scoville, age 52
VP Manufacturing, John C. Bedrosian
VP Credit, Carolyn S. Fox
VP Real Estate, Gary C. Hammett
Second Vice Chairman, John Najjar, age 55
Chairman, Richard E. (Dick) Goodspeed, age 75
Director, Thomas S. (Tom) Sayles, age 61
First Vice Chairman, Louis A. (Lou) Amen, age 82
Director, Mark Kidd, age 61
Director, Michael A. (Mike) Provenzano Jr., age 69
Director, John Berberian, age 60
Director, Darioush A. Khaledi, age 65
Director, Jay T. McCormack, age 61
Director, Douglas A. (Doug) Nidiffer, age 62
Director, Mimi R. Song, age 53
Director, Robert E. Stiles, age 72
Director, Kenneth R. (Ken) Tucker, age 64
Director, Richard L. (Dick) Wright, age 74
Director, John D. Lang, age 58
Second Vice Chairman, John Najjar, age 55
Director, Oscar Gonzalez, age 41
Director, Terry H. Halverson, age 61
Director, Paul Kapioski, age 54
Director, Michael S. (Mike) Trask, age 57
Auditors: Deloitte&ToucheLLP

LOCATIONS

HQ: Unified Grocers Inc.
5200 Sheila St., Commerce CA 90040
Phone: 323-264-5200   **Fax:** 323-265-4006
Web: www.unifiedgrocers.com

PRODUCTS/OPERATIONS

2011 Sales

	$ mil.	% of total
% of total		
Wholesale		99
Insurance &		1
Total		**100**

COMPETITORS

Associated Food	Safeway
C&S Wholesale	SUPERVALU
Kroger	URM Stores
McLane	Wal-Mart
Nash-Finch	

HISTORICAL FINANCIALS

Company Type: Private - Cooperative

Income Statement

FYE: September 29

	REVENUE ($ mil.)	NET INCOME ($ mil.)	NET PROFIT MARGIN	EMPLOYEES
09/12*	3,796	1	0.1%	2,950
10/11	3,847	7	0.2%	0
10/10	3,921	10	0.3%	0
10/09	4,050	14	0.4%	0
Annual Growth	(2.1%)	(49.0%)	—	—

*Fiscal year change

2012 Year-End Financials

Debt ratio: —
Return on equity: 0.10%
Cash ($ mil.): 11
Current ratio: 0.70
Long-term debt ($ mil.): —

Dividends
Yield: —
Payout: —
Market value ($ mil.): —

UNION COLLEGE

LOCATIONS

HQ: UNION COLLEGE
807 UNION ST, SCHENECTADY, NY 12308-3107
Phone: 518-388-6000
Web: www.union.edu

HISTORICAL FINANCIALS

Company Type: Private

Income Statement

FYE: June 30

	REVENUE ($ mil.)	NET INCOME ($ mil.)	NET PROFIT MARGIN	EMPLOYEES
06/11	114	39	34.7%	1
Annual Growth	—	—	—	—

2011 Year-End Financials

Debt ratio: —
Return on equity: 34.70%
Cash ($ mil.): 21
Current ratio: —
Long-term debt ($ mil.): —

Dividends
Yield: —
Payout: —
Market value ($ mil.): —

UNION HEALTH SERVICE INC

Union Health Service brings together doctors and patients in the Chicago area. The company is a not-for-profit health care services provider which supplies health insurance to its members through HMO (health maintenance organization) and medical prepayment plans. Union Health Service also provides primary health care as well as vision laboratory radiology and pharmacy services to its members through about 20 group practice clinics in Aurora Chicago Norridge Oak Park and other area communities. The company was established in 1955.

EXECUTIVES

Executive Director, Joe Garrett
Medical Director, Angelo P. Creticos
Director Operations, Ramesh Joshi
Director Health Services, Carol DeMarco

LOCATIONS

HQ: Union Health Service Inc.
1634 W. Polk St., Chicago IL 60612
Phone: 312-423-4200   **Fax:** 212-697-0910
Web: www.kcsa.com

COMPETITORS

Advocate Health Care	Humana
Aetna	Kaiser Foundation
Carle Physician Group	Health Plan
CIGNA	Provena Health
Coventry Health Care	SSM Health Care
Harmony Health Plan	UnitedHealth Group
HCSC	WellPoint
Health Net	

HISTORICAL FINANCIALS

Company Type: Private - Not-for-Profit

Income Statement

FYE: December 31

	REVENUE ($ mil.)	NET INCOME ($ mil.)	NET PROFIT MARGIN	EMPLOYEES
12/11	58	2	3.7%	302
12/09	54	1	3.3%	0
12/05	40	0	0.2%	0
12/04	38	0	1.9%	0
Annual Growth	14.9%	43.0%	—	—

2011 Year-End Financials

Debt ratio: ——
Return on equity: 3.70%
Cash ($ mil.): 8
Current ratio: 0.90
Long-term debt ($ mil.): —

Dividends
Yield: —
Payout: —
Market value ($ mil.): —

UNION HOSPITAL INC.

Union Hospital is the flagship facility of the Union Hospital Health Group a health care system that serves communities in western Indiana and eastern Illinois. The not-for-profit hospital has about 350 beds boasts an equal number of physicians and provides general medical and surgical care as well as specialty services in areas such as women's health cancer cardiovascular disease and sports medicine. It also offers occupational health and physical rehabilitation as well as medical training programs. Other facilities that comprise the Union system include Union Hospital Clinton physician practices specialty clinics and a home health agency. Union Hospital's roots go back to 1892.

Geographic Reach
The teaching hospital serves those who reside in west-central Indiana and eastern Illinois.

Operations
Besides the main Union Hospital which averages some 17000 patient admissions each year the hospital operates Union Hospital Clinton specialty clinics a home health agency and physician practices.

Strategy
Union Hospital's main campus underwent a nearly $180 million expansion project in recent years. The patient tower provides for private rooms instead of six- to eight-bed wards.

As part of a strategic focus to extend the reach of its operations Union Hospital partners with AP&S Clinic a multi -specialty physician group practice to expand the two entities' services. Operating as Union Health System the collaboration looks to increase coordination of care between physician specialists.

EXECUTIVES

President and CEO, David (Dave) Doerr
SVP Finance and CFO, Wayne Hutson
VP Information Systems, Kym Pfrank
VP and Administrator Union Hospital Clinton, Terri Hill
VP Patient Care Services, Carol Roesch
Manager Public Relations, Kristi Roshel
Director Public Relations, Lorrie Heber
EVP and COO, Scott Teffeteller
Assistant VP Human Resources, Sally Zuel
Medical Director, Ronald Leach

LOCATIONS

HQ: Union Hospital Inc.
1606 N. 7th St., Terre Haute IN 47804
Phone: 812-238-7000   **Fax:** 812-238-7151
Web: www.uhhg.org/

PRODUCTS/OPERATIONS

Selected Services

Acupuncture
Advanced Medical Technology
Asthma
Behavioral Healthcare
Breast Care
Cancer Care Services
Cardiovascular Testing
Clara Fairbanks Center for Women
Clay City Center for Family Medicine
Cork Medical Center
Family Medicine Center
Infections - MRSA
Joint Replacement Center
Landsbaum Center
Lugar Center for Rural Health
Medical Rehabilitation Center
Neonatal Intensive Care Unit (NICU)
Pediatrics
Pulmonary and Lung Health
Wound Healing Center
Union Hospital Terre Haute
Union Hospital Clinton
Union Hospital Foundation

COMPETITORS

Ascension Health	IU Health Bloomington
Carle Hospital	Hospital
Franciscan Alliance	Kosciusko Community
HCA	Hospital
IU Health	Provena Health

HISTORICAL FINANCIALS

Company Type: Private - Not-for-Profit

Income Statement

FYE: August 31

	REVENUE ($ mil.)	NET INCOME ($ mil.)	NET PROFIT MARGIN	EMPLOYEES
08/11	420	(0)	—	1,960
08/10	400	(3)	—	0
08/09	408	18	4.5%	0
08/08	373	14	4.0%	0
Annual Growth	4.0%	—	—	—

2011 Year-End Financials

Debt ratio: ——
Return on equity: —
Cash ($ mil.): 28
Current ratio: 1.70
Long-term debt ($ mil.): —

Dividends
Yield: —
Payout: —
Market value ($ mil.): —

UNIPRO FOODSERVICE INC

UniPro Foodservice knows there's strength in numbers. As the largest US foodservice cooperative its members include more than 650 independent member companies that provide food and food-related products to more than 800000 foodservice customers including health care and educational institutions military installations and restaurants. UniPro provides training collective purchasing and marketing materials to all distributors. Its products —which include dry groceries and frozen and refrigerated foods —are sold under the brand names CODE ComSource Nifda and Nugget. Suppliers include Kraft Foods Reynolds Food Packaging Solo Cup Tyson Foods and Unilever Foodsolutions.

The cooperative's Multi-Unit Group (MUG) formed in 1985 to service multi-unit foodservice operators include some of the largest member distributors in the UniPro network. MUG members are like a one-stop shop for multi-unit operators offering fresh produce paper products and small wares from a single source in an effort to improve efficiency.

Progressive Group Alliance a business unit distributes and supplies partners with sales marketing and advice to customers. Brands include Alliance Pro (non-food) Coral Princess (seafood) GourMates (condiments) Harvest Gold (cheese butter and dairy-related products) and Premium Recipe (prepared entrees salsas and sauces).

While privately-owned Unipro Foodservice doesn't report its financial results collectively the cooperatives ring up an estimated $60 billion in sales annually.

EXECUTIVES

President and CEO, Roger Toomey
CIO, R. C. Alexander III

SVP Logistics/Redistribution, John L. Burke
SVP Procurement, Ray Goldman
CFO, David Joss
Director Human Resources, Charlotte N. Phillips
SVP Sales East, Don Gilligan
SVP Sales West, Scott Strull
Departmental VP Financial Planning, Jonathan
  Adams
Chairman, Jim Kite
SVP Sales East, Keith Durnell

LOCATIONS

HQ: UniPro Foodservice Inc.
  2500 Cumberland Pkwy. Ste. 600, Atlanta GA 30339
Phone: 770-952-0871　　**Fax:** 770-952-0872
Web: www.uniprofoodservice.com

PRODUCTS/OPERATIONS

Selected Suppliers
Cargill Foodservice
Durable Packaging International
Handgards Inc.
Kraft Foods
Reynolds Foodservice Packaging
Solo Cup Company
Unilever Foodsolutions

COMPETITORS

Ben E. Keith
Foodbuy
Golden State Foods
Keystone Foods
MAINES
Martin-Brower
McLane Foodservice
Meadowbrook Meat
  Company
Nash-Finch
Performance Food
Services Group of
  America
Sysco
US Foods

HISTORICAL FINANCIALS
Company Type: Private - Cooperative

Income Statement
FYE: December 31

	REVENUE ($ mil.)	NET INCOME ($ mil.)	NET PROFIT MARGIN	EMPLOYEES
12/11	881	0	—	140
12/10	657	0	—	0
12/09	631	(0)	—	0
12/08	627	13	2.1%	0
Annual Growth	12.0%	—	—	—

2011 Year-End Financials
Debt ratio: ——
Return on equity: —
Cash ($ mil.): 9
Current ratio: 1.00
Long-term debt ($ mil.): —
Dividends
  Yield: —
  Payout: —
Market value ($ mil.): —

UNIQUE STAFF LEASING I LTD.

LOCATIONS

HQ: UNIQUE STAFF LEASING I LTD.
  4646 CORONA DR STE 100, CORPUS CHRISTI, TX
  78411-4383
Phone: 361-852-6392

HISTORICAL FINANCIALS
Company Type: Private

Income Statement
FYE: December 31

	REVENUE ($ mil.)	NET INCOME ($ mil.)	NET PROFIT MARGIN	EMPLOYEES
12/11	80	0	0.9%	3,400
12/10	14	1	9.9%	0
12/09	12	1	8.3%	0
12/08	104	0	0.9%	0
Annual Growth	(8.3%)	(10.1%)	—	—

2011 Year-End Financials
Debt ratio: ——
Return on equity: 0.90%
Cash ($ mil.): 2
Current ratio: 1.90
Long-term debt ($ mil.): —
Dividends
  Yield: —
  Payout: —
Market value ($ mil.): —

UNITED CEREBRAL PALSY ASSOCIATIONS OF NEW YORK STATE INC.

Cerebral Palsy Associations of New York State (CP of NYS) provides health care services for people suffering with cerebral palsy and other developmental disabilities. The organization includes 24 associations that provide day treatment programs community dwelling access and at-home residential support as well as early childhood mental health and transportation services. Serving more than 100000 patients throughout the state it also acts as an advocate for its patients through legislative involvement. CP of NYS was founded in 1946 by parents seeking health and advocacy services for their children. The organization provides services directly to patients.

EXECUTIVES

**VP Financial Management and Support Affiliate
  Services Office,** Thomas J. Hamel, age 53
President and CEO, Susan Constantino
Administrative Assistant Affiliate Services Office,
  Cheryl Bradway
**VP Government Relations Affiliate Services
  Office,** Barbara Crosier
**VP Policy and Program Services Affiliate Services
  Office,** Judi Gerson

VP Communications Affiliate Services Office,
  Alan Shibley
Secretary and Director, Cora Baliff
Chairwoman, Idajean Windell
EVP COO Metro Services, Duane Schielke
EVP Affiliate Services Office, Michael Alvaro
EVP CFO and Chief Administratve Officer,
  Thomas Mandelkow
General Counsel, Steven H. Mosenson
VP Human Resources, Janis Pshena
**VP Reimbursement and Regulatory Compliance
  Affiliate Services Office,** Deb Williams
Vice Chairman, Jack M. Weinstein
Assistant to the President and CEO, Heidi
  McManus
Executive Assistant, Mary Bourne
Administrative Assistant, Hedwig Dooley
EVP and COO, Joseph M. Pancari
Executive Assistant, Loretta Orelien
Executive Secretary Affiliate Services Office,
  Marie Colbert
**VP Regulatory Affairs and Policy Development
  Affiliate Services Office,** Susan Hornbeck
Executive Assistant, Tracy Johnson
Director, Robert C. Miller
Secretary and Director, Cora Baliff
Director, Thomas J. Caserta Jr.
Director, John R. Horvath
Director, Marvin S. Reed
Director, Ernest E. Southworth
Director Emeritus, Beatrice S. Wellens
Vice Chairman, Jack M. Weinstein
Director, David Eichenauer
Director, Andrew C. Koenig
Director, Stephen C. Lipinski
Director, Ann B. LeMark
Director, Barbara N. Scherr
Director, Joseph P. Dutkowsky

LOCATIONS

HQ: Cerebral Palsy Associations of New York State
  330 W. 34th St. 15th Fl., New York NY 10001-2488
Phone: 212-947-5770　　**Fax:** 212-290-8475
Web: www.cpofnys.org

PRODUCTS/OPERATIONS

Selected Affiliates and Locations
Able2
Aspire of Western New York
Center for Disability Services
Cerebral Palsy of the North Country
Cerebral Palsy of Ulster County
Cerebral Palsy of Westchester
CP of NYS Affiliate Services Office
CP Rochester
E. John Gavras Center
Enable
Franziska Racker Centers
Handicapped Childrens Association of Southern New
  York
Happiness House
Hudson Valley Cerebral Palsy Association
Inspire of Orange County
Jawonio
Metro Services CP of NYS
Niagara Cerebral Palsy
Prospect Child & Family Center
Queens Centers for Progress
The Center for Discovery
UCP of NYC
United Cerebral Palsy Association of Nassau County Inc.
United Cerebral Palsy of Suffolk
Upstate Cerebral Palsy

HISTORICAL FINANCIALS

Company Type: Private - Not-for-Profit

Income Statement

FYE: June 30

	REVENUE ($ mil.)	NET INCOME ($ mil.)	NET PROFIT MARGIN	EMPLOYEES
06/11	110	1	1.6%	1,700
06/10	109	2	2.5%	0
06/09	105	2	1.9%	0
06/06	95	3	3.6%	0
Annual Growth	5.0%	(20.0%)	—	—

2011 Year-End Financials

Debt ratio: ——
Return on equity: 1.60%
Cash ($ mil.): 3
Current ratio: 0.60
Long-term debt ($ mil.): ——
Dividends
Yield: —
Payout: —
Market value ($ mil.): —

UNITED CEREBRAL PALSY OF NEW YORK CITY INC

LOCATIONS

HQ: UNITED CEREBRAL PALSY OF NEW YORK CITY INC
80 MAIDEN LN FL 8, NEW YORK, NY 10038-4837
Phone: 212-683-6700
Web: www.manhattanchildrenscenter.org

HISTORICAL FINANCIALS

Company Type: Private

Income Statement

FYE: June 30

	REVENUE ($ mil.)	NET INCOME ($ mil.)	NET PROFIT MARGIN	EMPLOYEES
06/11	107	7	7.2%	1,400
06/10	104	1	1.2%	0
06/09	96	(8)	—	0
06/08	94	2	2.2%	0
Annual Growth	4.7%	55.5%	—	—

2011 Year-End Financials

Debt ratio: ——
Return on equity: 7.20%
Cash ($ mil.): 17
Current ratio: 0.60
Long-term debt ($ mil.): ——
Dividends
Yield: —
Payout: —
Market value ($ mil.): —

UNITED FARMERS COOPERATIVE

United Farmers Cooperative has it all altogether. The agricultural cooperative supplies products and services to its members through 17 locations in eight rural communities across Minnesota. The farmer-owned co-op offers farm supplies such as energy feed seed fertilizer grain milling and blending and farm machinery as well as construction finance insurance and repair services. Originally known as the Cooperative Creamery Association United Farmers Cooperative (UFC) has been helping farmers in central Minnesota since 1915 (the creamery division was sold to Mid America Dairies in 1969).

EXECUTIVES

CEO and General Manager, Jeff Nielsen
CFO, Lorie Reinarts
Manager Agronomy Department, Butch Altmann
Manager Grain Department, Jim Johnson
Manager Feed Department, Steve LeBrun
Manager Farm and Consumer Supply Department, Leon Portner
Manager Energy Department, Darv Turbes
Board President, Kevin Lauwagie
Board VP, Todd Nelson
Board Secretary, David Braun
Director Marketing and Communications, Teresa Wenninger
Manager Human Resources, Cheri LeBrun
Assistant General Manager and COO, Clif Gipp
Controller, Carol Steffl
Risk Management, Marc (Pete) Peterson
Information Systems Coordinator, Ryan Altmann
Credit Manager, Shelley Quast
Board VP, Todd Nelson
Board Secretary, David Braun

LOCATIONS

HQ: United Farmers Cooperative
705 E. 4th St., Winthrop MN 55396
Phone: 507-647-6600   **Fax:** 507-647-6620
Web: www.ufcmn.com

COMPETITORS

ADM
CHS
Frontier Agriculture
Land O' Lakes Purina Feed
Minn-Dak Co-op
SMBSC
Watonwan Farm Service

HISTORICAL FINANCIALS

Company Type: Private - Cooperative

Income Statement

FYE: August 31

	REVENUE ($ mil.)	NET INCOME ($ mil.)	NET PROFIT MARGIN	EMPLOYEES
08/11	233	4	2.1%	230
08/07	127	2	1.9%	0
08/06	93	1	1.5%	0
08/05	72	2	3.0%	0
Annual Growth	47.9%	29.8%	—	—

2011 Year-End Financials

Debt ratio: ——
Return on equity: 2.10%
Cash ($ mil.): 0
Current ratio: 0.20
Long-term debt ($ mil.): ——
Dividends
Yield: —
Payout: —
Market value ($ mil.): —

UNITED FASHIONS HOLDING INC

LOCATIONS

HQ: UNITED FASHIONS HOLDING INC
4629 MACRO, SAN ANTONIO, TX 78218-5420
Phone: 210-662-7140

HISTORICAL FINANCIALS

Company Type: Private

Income Statement

FYE: July 29

	REVENUE ($ mil.)	NET INCOME ($ mil.)	NET PROFIT MARGIN	EMPLOYEES
07/12	124	3	2.9%	1,200
07/11*	118	2	2.4%	0
08/04	72	27	38.5%	0
Annual Growth	31.3%	(64.0%)	—	—

*Fiscal year change

2012 Year-End Financials

Debt ratio: ——
Return on equity: 2.90%
Cash ($ mil.): 3
Current ratio: 0.20
Long-term debt ($ mil.): ——
Dividends
Yield: —
Payout: —
Market value ($ mil.): —

UNITED FASHIONS OF TEXAS LTD

LOCATIONS

HQ: UNITED FASHIONS OF TEXAS LTD
4629 MACRO, SAN ANTONIO, TX 78218-5420
Phone: 210-662-7140

HISTORICAL FINANCIALS

Company Type: Private

Income Statement

FYE: July 29

	REVENUE ($ mil.)	NET INCOME ($ mil.)	NET PROFIT MARGIN	EMPLOYEES
07/12*	124	3	2.9%	1,500
08/09	88	1	1.2%	0
08/08	97	4	4.2%	0
07/07	81	0	—	0
Annual Growth	—	3835.6%	—	—

*Fiscal year change

2012 Year-End Financials

Debt ratio: ——
Return on equity: 2.90%
Cash ($ mil.): 3
Current ratio: 0.20
Long-term debt ($ mil.): ——
Dividends
Yield: —
Payout: —
Market value ($ mil.): —

UNITED HARDWARE DISTRIBUTING CO

United Hardware Distributing builds relationships. The member-owned distributor delivers hammers nails and all the other hardware necessities to dealers in more than 18 states in the central US. The company is not a franchiser but it does provide retail support education buying markets and consultants to its members. In addition to the hardware of hardware retailing United provides expertise in accounting store design pricing marketing purchasing and merchandising. Member stores include Hardware Hank Trust Worthy Golden Rule Lumber Ranch & Pet Supply and other independent retailers.

United's membership in Distribution America a buying group with more than $2 billion in buying power lets it offer members the lowest price on merchandise. The company's South Dakota distribution center stocks over 55000 items.

EXECUTIVES

President and CEO, David Heider
Treasurer and Controller, Lori Long
VP Sales, Robert (Bob) Branton

LOCATIONS

HQ: United Hardware Distributing Company
5005 Nathan Lane North, Plymouth MN 55442
Phone: 763-559-1800   **Fax:** 763-559-5031
Web: unitedhardware.com/Default.aspx

COMPETITORS

84 Lumber	Northern Tool
Ace Hardware	Sears
Do it Best	Sherwin-Williams
Home Depot	True Value
Lowe's	Wal-Mart

HISTORICAL FINANCIALS
Company Type: Private

Income Statement
FYE: November 30

	REVENUE ($ mil.)	NET INCOME ($ mil.)	NET PROFIT MARGIN	EMPLOYEES
11/11	189	5	3.1%	330
11/10	178	3	2.2%	0
11/09	180	3	2.2%	0
11/08	185	4	2.2%	0
Annual Growth	0.8%	12.9%	—	—

2011 Year-End Financials
Debt ratio: ——
Return on equity: 3.10%
Cash ($ mil.): 6
Current ratio: 0.80
Long-term debt ($ mil.): —

Dividends
Yield: —
Payout: —
Market value ($ mil.): —

UNITED HEALTH SERVICES HOSPITAL INC.

United Health Services Hospitals (UHS Hospitals) can service injuries from a slip in the snow or a slipped disc to health that's just plain slipping. The organization operates Binghamton General Hospital (about 200 beds) Wilson Medical Center (some 280 beds) and a group of primary and specialty care clinics in upstate New York. Specialty services include cardiology dialysis neurology rehabilitation pediatrics and psychiatry. The Wilson Medical Center serves as a teaching hospital offering residency and fellowship programs. UHS Hospitals is a subsidiary of United Health Services which operates a network of affiliated hospitals clinics long-term care centers and home health agencies in the region.

Geographic Reach

Binghamton General is located in Binghamton New York while Wilson Medical Center is located in Johnson City New York both within the boundaries of Broome County. UHS Hospitals also operates primary and specialty care clinics in Broome Chenango Delaware and Tioga counties in upstate New York.

Strategy

United Health Services Hospitals is investing in equipment upgrades and facility improvements at Binghamton General to help the facility remain at the forefront of medical technology and services. Wilson Medical Center which acts as a regional referral center in areas including emergency medicine newborn care neurology and heart surgery has also been the subject of enhancement measures. The hospital recently completed construction of the new Decker Center for Advanced Medical Treatment which offers high-tech diagnostic and acute care services.

EXECUTIVES

CFO, Robert Gomulka
President and CEO; 2nd Vice Chair, Matthew J. Salanger
President and CEO Delaware Valley Hospital, David Polge
Chairman, Diana Bendz
Secretary, Susan Mistretta
VP Strategy and Business Development, Robin Kinslow-Evans
President Chenango Memorial Hospital, Drake M. Lamen
President and CEO; 2nd Vice Chair, Matthew J. Salanger
1st Vice Chair, Bruce Bowling
Director, Barbara Chaffee
Director, William Craine
Director, Alex DePersis
Director, Garabed Fattal
Director, Sara Gueldner
Director, Frank Kelley
Director, Carol Miller
Director, David Niermeyer
Director, Judith C. Peckham
Director, Jay Riccardi
Director, Teresa Webb
Auditors: PricewaterhouseCoopersLLP

LOCATIONS

HQ: United Health Services Hospitals
10-42 Mitchell Ave., Binghamton NY 13903-1617
Phone: 607-762-2200   **Fax:** 607-762-3874
Web: www.uhs.net/ourhospitals

COMPETITORS

Albany Medical Center
Guthrie Healthcare
Kaleida Health
Lifetime Health
Oneida Healthcare Center
St. Joseph's Hospital Health Center
SUNY Upstate Medical University
Unity Health System
Upstate University Hospital at Community General

HISTORICAL FINANCIALS
Company Type: Subsidiary

Income Statement
FYE: December 31

	REVENUE ($ mil.)	NET INCOME ($ mil.)	NET PROFIT MARGIN	EMPLOYEES
12/11	455	18	4.0%	5,000
12/10	442	22	5.1%	0
12/09	412	14	3.5%	0
12/08	382	(28)	—	0
Annual Growth	6.0%	—	—	—

2011 Year-End Financials
Debt ratio: ——
Return on equity: 4.00%
Cash ($ mil.): 16
Current ratio: 0.80
Long-term debt ($ mil.): —

Dividends
Yield: —
Payout: —
Market value ($ mil.): —

UNITED HOSPITAL CENTER INC.

LOCATIONS

HQ: UNITED HOSPITAL CENTER INC.
327 MEDICAL PARK DR, BRIDGEPORT, WV 26330-9006
Phone: 681-342-1000
Web: www.uhcwv.org

HISTORICAL FINANCIALS
Company Type: Private

Income Statement
FYE: December 31

	REVENUE ($ mil.)	NET INCOME ($ mil.)	NET PROFIT MARGIN	EMPLOYEES
12/11	239	(9)	—	2,000
12/09	214	30	14.1%	0
12/07	185	19	10.5%	0
12/06	313	11	3.7%	0
Annual Growth	(8.6%)	—	—	—

2011 Year-End Financials
Debt ratio: ——
Return on equity: (-4.00)%
Cash ($ mil.): 7
Current ratio: 1.50
Long-term debt ($ mil.): —

Dividends
Yield: —
Payout: —
Market value ($ mil.): —

UNITED HOSPITAL SYSTEM INC.

LOCATIONS

HQ: UNITED HOSPITAL SYSTEM INC.
6308 8TH AVE, KENOSHA, WI 53143-5031
Phone: 262-656-2011
Web: www.unitedhospitalsystem.org

HISTORICAL FINANCIALS

Company Type: Private

Income Statement				FYE: June 30
	REVENUE ($ mil.)	NET INCOME ($ mil.)	NET PROFIT MARGIN	EMPLOYEES
06/11	288	21	7.4%	1,500
06/10	277	26	9.6%	0
06/09	266	20	7.9%	0
06/08	244	37	15.6%	0
Annual Growth	5.7%	(17.5%)	—	—

2011 Year-End Financials

Debt ratio: —
Return on equity: 7.40%
Cash ($ mil.): 20
Current ratio: 0.70
Long-term debt ($ mil.): —
Dividends
Yield: —
Payout: —
Market value ($ mil.): —

UNITED NATIONS FOUNDATION INC.

LOCATIONS

HQ: UNITED NATIONS FOUNDATION INC.
1800 MASS AVE NW STE 400, WASHINGTON, DC
20036-1218
Phone: 202-887-9040
Web: www.endpolionow.com

HISTORICAL FINANCIALS

Company Type: Private

Income Statement				FYE: December 31
	REVENUE ($ mil.)	NET INCOME ($ mil.)	NET PROFIT MARGIN	EMPLOYEES
12/11*	136	60	44.5%	102
10/09	114	(25)	—	0
12/00	51	(40)	—	0
12/99	1,823	0	—	0
Annual Growth	—	1446.7%	—	—

*Fiscal year change

2011 Year-End Financials

Debt ratio: —
Return on equity: 44.50%
Cash ($ mil.): 20
Current ratio: 3.50
Long-term debt ($ mil.): —
Dividends
Yield: —
Payout: —
Market value ($ mil.): —

UNITED SEATING & MOBILITY LLC

LOCATIONS

HQ: UNITED SEATING & MOBILITY LLC
975 HORNET DR, HAZELWOOD, MO 63042-2309
Phone: 314-447-7500

HISTORICAL FINANCIALS

Company Type: Private

Income Statement				FYE: December 31
	REVENUE ($ mil.)	NET INCOME ($ mil.)	NET PROFIT MARGIN	EMPLOYEES
12/11	123	5	4.8%	844
12/10	90	4	4.8%	0
12/06	43	0	1.6%	0
Annual Growth	67.9%	194.1%	—	—

2011 Year-End Financials

Debt ratio: —
Return on equity: 4.80%
Cash ($ mil.): 1
Current ratio: 1.60
Long-term debt ($ mil.): —
Dividends
Yield: —
Payout: —
Market value ($ mil.): —

UNITED SERVICES ASSOCIATION INC.

LOCATIONS

HQ: UNITED SERVICES ASSOCIATION INC.
11280 AURORA AVE, DES MOINES, IA 50322-7905
Phone: 515-276-6763
Web: www.unitedservicesassociation.com

HISTORICAL FINANCIALS

Company Type: Private

Income Statement				FYE: June 30
	REVENUE ($ mil.)	NET INCOME ($ mil.)	NET PROFIT MARGIN	EMPLOYEES
06/12	116	0	0.3%	16
06/11	103	0	0.7%	0
06/10	56	0	0.7%	0
06/09	75	0	0.9%	0
Annual Growth	15.6%	(19.1%)	—	—

2012 Year-End Financials

Debt ratio: —
Return on equity: 0.30%
Cash ($ mil.): 4
Current ratio: 0.80
Long-term debt ($ mil.): —
Dividends
Yield: —
Payout: —
Market value ($ mil.): —

UNITED STATES GOLF ASSOCIATION

Making sure golf stays clear of the rough is par for the course at this organization. The United States Golf Association is the governing body for golf in the US its territories and Mexico. The not-for-profit group writes and interprets the rules of the game provides handicap information offers turf consulting and funds equipment and course maintenance research and testing. It also holds several national championship events including the US Open the US Women's Open and the US Senior Open. The group generates most of its revenue from the sale of broadcast rights to championship tournaments and other matches as well as through membership fees. The USGA was founded in 1894.

EXECUTIVES

Treasurer Executive Committee, Irving Fish
Secretary Executive Committee, James T. (Jim) Bunch
Chairman Women's Committee, Barbara Douglas
President Executive Committee, James B. Hyler Jr.
President Executive Committee, James F. Vernon
Director Communications and USGA Museum, Rand Jerris
Managing Director Digital Media, Alex Withers
Senior Director Hadicaping Regional Affairs Information Systems and Golf Handicaping and Information Network., Kevin O'Connor
VP Executive Committee, Cameron J. Rains
General Counsel Executive Committee, Joseph Anthony
Treasurer Executive Committee, John Kim
VP and Member Executive Committee, Glen D. Nager
Secretary and Member Executive Committee, Thomas J. O'Toole Jr.
Senior Director Finance, Pamela Martin
Controller, Suzanne Colon
Director Broadcasting, Mark Carlson
Manager Broadcast Operations, Kristin Xippolitos
Chief Business Officer, Peter Bevacqua
Manager Business Operations, Zack Lang
Manager Web Developmant, Karen Keller
Senior Web Developer and Chief Systems Officer, Scott Kinne
Editor USGA Website, Kenneth Klavon
Coordinator Digital Media, Jason Koblin
Manager Internet Services, William Lacey
Senior Web Developer, Matthew Schwenderman
Product Manager Digital Media, Ellen Mullin
Executive Director, David Fay
Director Facilities Management, Felix Sorge
Director Golf Handicap and Information Network, Kevin Hartigan
Manager Technical Support Golf Handicap and Information Network, Brian Bennicas
Coordinator Information Technology Support Golf Handicap and Information Network, Joseph Cavallo
Software Engineer Golf Handicap and Information Network, Lisa Christie
Senior Software Engineer and Application Architect Golf Handicap and Information Network, Anthony Cornetto
Assistant Director Regional Association Services and Software Development Golf Handicap and Information Network, Steven Edmondson
Coordinator Web Services Beta Testing and Help Desk Golf Handicap and Information Network, Lisa Gooley

Programmer Golf Handicap and Information Network Mainframe, Kevin Jorgensen
Assistant Manager Technical Support Golf Handicap and Information Network, John Stern
Senior Director Human Resources, Jane Swiggett
Managing Director Information Technologies, Jessica Carroll
Chief Legal Officer, John Redpath
Chief Marketing Officer, Barry Hyde
Manager Corporate Marketing, Amy Engel
Technical Support and Training Specialist II, Theresa Albert
Technical Support Specialist I, Vincent Capone
Programmer and Analyst, Patricia Carhart
Assistant Manager Technical Support and Training, Nate Engel
Manager Technical Support and Training, Carol Englehardt
Database Analyst, Mauyra Eska
Supervisor Data Entry, Nancy Fitzpatrick
Manager Network Administration, George Griesler
Senior Computer Operator Application Support Analyst and Tester, Victoria Irizarry
Network Administrator I, Erik Keller
Network Administrator II, Paul Klein
Programmer and Analyst, Thomas Laudati
Administratve Assistant Information Technologies, Susan Maziarski
Director Application Development and Database Administration, Michael Overhiser
Technical Support and Training Specialist II, Oscar Parada
Programmer and Analyst, Ken Roxbury
Manager Application Development, Eric Wolf
Director Members Program, Fiona Dolan
Director Licensing and U.S. Open Merchandising, Mary Lopuszynski
Senior Director Rules and Competitions, Michael Davis
Member Executive Committee, Christopher A. Liedel
Treasurer Executive Committee, Irving Fish
Secretary Executive Committee, James T. (Jim) Bunch
President Executive Committee, James F. Vernon
VP Executive Committee, Cameron J. Rains
Member Executive Committee, Christie Austin
Member Executive Committee, Pat Kaufman
Treasurer Executive Committee, John Kim
Member Executive Committee, Gene McClure
VP and Member Executive Committee, Glen D. Nager
Secretary and Member Executive Committee, Thomas J. O'Toole Jr.
Member Executive Committee, Brigid Shanley Lamb
Member Executive Committee, Steve Smyers
Member Executive Committee, Geoffrey Y. Yang

LOCATIONS

HQ: United States Golf Association
Golf House 77 Liberty Corner Rd., Far Hills NJ 07931-0708
Phone: 908-234-2300   **Fax:** 908-234-9687
Web: www.usga.org

PRODUCTS/OPERATIONS

US Open Champions

Willie Anderson	(1901	1,903
Tommy Armour (1927)		
Laurence Auchterlonie (1902)		
James M. Barnes (1921)		
Tommy Bolt (1958)		
Julius Boros	(1952	1,963
Billy Burke (1931)		
Angel Cabrera (2007)		
Michael Campbell (2005)		
Bill Casper Jr.	(1959	1,966
Olin Dutra (1934)		
Ernie Els	(1994	1,997
Charles Evans Jr. (1916)		
Johnny Farrell (1928)		
Jack Fleck (1955)		
Raymond Floyd (1986)		
James Foulis (1896)		
Ed Furgol (1954)		
Jim Furyk (2003)		
Lucas Glover (2009)		
John Goodman (1933)		
Retief Goosen	(2001	2,004
David Graham (1981)		
Lou Graham (1975)		
Hubert Green (1977)		
Ralph Guldahl (1937-38)		
Walter Hagen	(1914	1,919
Fred Herd (1898)		
Ben Hogan	(1948	1,950	1,953
Hale Irwin (1974)	1,979	1,990
Tony Jacklin (1970)		
Lee Janzen	(1993	1,998
Robert T. Jones Jr. (1923	1,926	1,929
Steve Jones (1996)		
Tom Kite (1992)		
Lawson Little (1940)		
Gene Littler (1961)		
Joe Lloyd (1897)		
William Macfarlane (1925)		
Tony Manero (1936)		
Lloyd Mangrum (1946)		
Dick Mayer (1957)		
John J. McDermott (1911-12)		
Rory McIlroy (2010)		
Fred McLeod (1908)		
Cary Middlecoff	(1949	1,956
John Miller (1973)		
Orville Moody (1969)		
Byron Nelson (1939)		
Larry Nelson (1983)		
Jack Nicklaus (1962 1967	1,972	1,980
Andy North	(1978	1,985
Geoff Ogilvy (2006)		
Francis Ouimet (1913)		
Arnold Palmer (1960)		
Sam Parks Jr. (1935)		
Jerry Pate (1976)		
Corey Pavin (1995)		
Gary Player (1965)		
Horace Rawlins (1895)		
Edward Ray (1920)		
Alex Ross (1907)		
Gene Sarazen	(1922	1,932
George Sargent (1909)		
Scott Simpson (1986)		
Alex Smith	(1906	1,910
Willie Smith (1899)		
Payne Stewart	(1991	1,999
Curtis Strange (1988-89)		
Jerome D. Travers (1915)		
Lee Trevino	(1968	1,971
Harry Vardon (1900)		
Ken Venturi (1964)		
Cyril Walker (1924)		
Tom Watson (1982)		
Craig Wood (1941)		
Tiger Woods (2000)	2,002	2,008
Lew Worsham (1947)		
Fuzzy Zoeller (1984)		

COMPETITORS

Augusta National	Professional Bowlers
Major League Baseball	Association
NBA	The R&A
NFL	USA Track & Field
NHL	USSF
PGA	USTA
PGA TOUR	

HISTORICAL FINANCIALS

Company Type: Private - Association

Income Statement

FYE: November 30

	REVENUE ($ mil.)	NET INCOME ($ mil.)	NET PROFIT MARGIN	EMPLOYEES
11/11	155	33	21.5%	340
11/10	131	29	22.5%	0
11/09	152	0	—	0
11/08	185	(38)	—	0
Annual Growth	(5.8%)	—	—	—

2011 Year-End Financials

Debt ratio: ——	
Return on equity: 21.50%	Dividends
Cash ($ mil.): 16	Yield: —
Current ratio: 0.50	Payout: —
Long-term debt ($ mil.): —	Market value ($ mil.): —

UNIVERSAL WILDE INC.

Sometimes the world of direct-mail marketing can seem like a jungle but W.A. Wilde can serve as your guide. The company provides tools and services for direct marketing campaigns such as fulfillment mailing print management statement processing and telemarketing. Its offerings can be purchased as a package or a la carte. The company operate through three main units: Wilde Agency a full-service direct-marketing provider; Wilde Interactive which specializes in online campaigns; and L.W. Robbins Associates an agency catering to nonprofit organizations. Family-owned W.A. Wilde traces its roots back to 1868 when William A. Wilde began publishing books.

LOCATIONS

HQ: UNIVERSAL WILDE INC.
26 DARTMOUTH ST STE 1, WESTWOOD, MA 02090-2332
Phone: 781-251-2700
Web: www.mgraphics.net

HISTORICAL FINANCIALS

Company Type: Private

Income Statement

FYE: December 31

	REVENUE ($ mil.)	NET INCOME ($ mil.)	NET PROFIT MARGIN	EMPLOYEES
12/11	104	(0)	—	560
Annual Growth	—	—	—	—

2011 Year-End Financials

Debt ratio: ——	
Return on equity: (-0.10)%	Dividends
Cash ($ mil.): 0	Yield: —
Current ratio: 1.50	Payout: —
Long-term debt ($ mil.): —	Market value ($ mil.): —

UNIVERSITY ENTERPRISES INC.

LOCATIONS

HQ: UNIVERSITY ENTERPRISES INC.
6000 J ST, SACRAMENTO, CA 95819-2605
Phone: 916-278-6672
Web: www.hornetsports.com

HISTORICAL FINANCIALS

Company Type: Private

Income Statement

FYE: June 30

	REVENUE ($ mil.)	NET INCOME ($ mil.)	NET PROFIT MARGIN	EMPLOYEES
06/11	88	3	3.9%	1,856
06/10	79	3	3.9%	0
06/09	69	0	—	0
06/08	75	5	7.9%	0
Annual Growth	5.7%	(16.5%)	—	—

2011 Year-End Financials

Debt ratio: ——
Return on equity: 3.90%
Cash ($ mil.): 7
Current ratio: 0.20
Long-term debt ($ mil.): —

Dividends
Yield: —
Payout: —
Market value ($ mil.): —

UNIVERSITY HEALTH SYSTEMS OF EASTERN CAROLINA INC.

University Health Systems of Eastern Carolina is an integrated not-for-profit health system that serves more than 1 million residents in 29 counties in eastern North Carolina. Doing business as Vidant Health it operates 10 hospitals including nine community hospitals and its tertiary care center Vidant Medical Center with 850 beds and academic affiliation with the Brody School of Medicine at East Carolina University. Vidant Health also operates centers for surgery home health hospice and wellness and engages in community health programs. Its physician group has more than 300 primary and specialty care providers who operate from more than 50 locations.

University Health Systems rebranded itself in 2012 in its effort to reflect its vibrant and vital position within the region as it advances its transformation to patient- and family-centered care.

The health system experienced a positive fiscal year in 2011 mainly due to greater inpatient demand and improvements in quality of care combined with gains in clinical efficiency and keeping costs low. The system which is the largest employer in eastern North Carolina was able to add 270 new positions due to patient demand that year.

Because the system operates as a not-for-profit enterprise it reinvests its earnings in capital improvements equipment and new services. In 2011

these included investing more than $76 million in equipment and infrastructure the Beaufort and Duplin hospitals the initial phase of the James and Connie Maynard Children's Hospital and pediatric emergency department at Vidant Medical Center and in expanding and integrating cancer services with the Brody School of Medicine.

Other facilities that have been constructed in recent years include the East Carolina Heart Institute a $150 million heart specialty hospital with 120 beds (2009) and a wound healing center.

EXECUTIVES

President and COO, David C. Herman
CIO, Stuart M. James
CEO, David C. (Dave) McRae
CFO, Jack W. Holsten
General Counsel, Nancy B. Aycock
President East Carolina Health and HealthAccess, Roger Robertson
President Pitt County Memorial Hospital, Stephen J. Lawler
Public Relations Coordinator, Barbara D. Dunn
Chief Human Resources Officer, Tyree Walker
Assistant VP Financial Services, Valerie J. Dixon
VP Supply Chain Management and Finance Support Services, Preston N. Comeaux III
Senior Projects Officer, Linda Roberson
President Heritage Hospital, Wendell (Wick) Baker
Chief External Affairs Officer and President UHS/PMH Foundations, Joel K. Butler
VP Information Technology and Chief Medical Information Officer, David Michael
Chief Audit and Compliance Officer, John C. Falcetano
President Roanoke-Chowan Hospital, Susan S. Lassiter
Government Relations Officer, J. Craig Quick
President Bertie Memorial Hospital and Chowan Hospital, Jeffrey N. Sackrison
VP Corporate Accreditation and Regulatory Compliance, Carmen R. Vincent
Chief Design and Construction Officer, Timothy J. McDonnell
Media Specialist, Beth Anne Atkins
VP Service and Patient Family Experience, Sue Collier
Chief Strategic Development and Marketing Officer, Anissa B. Davenport
VP Financial Services East Carolina Health, Lynn Lanier
Chief Administrative Officer, Janet Mullaney
Executive Director University Health Systems of Eastern Carolina Foundation and Pitt Memorial Hospital Foundation, Kenneth M. Turpen
Chief Quality and Patient Safety Officer, Joan D. Wynn
President Duplin General Hospital, William H. Case
President The Outer Banks Hospital, Van Smith
Chief Growth and Development Officer, Kathy G. Barger
VP Community Benefit and Government Relations, Michelle Brooks
VP UHS Physician Services, Travis Douglass
Executive Director UHS Foundation, N. Kinney Hart
President Albemarle Hospital, Sharon Tanner
Chief Human Resources Officer, Jeff Chambers
SVP Financial Services Vidant Health, David Hughes

LOCATIONS

HQ: University Health Systems of Eastern Carolina Inc.
2100 Stantonsburg Rd., Greenville NC 27835-6028
Phone: 252-847-4100   **Fax:** 303-295-8261
Web: www.hollandhart.com

PRODUCTS/OPERATIONS

2011 Revenues

	$ mil.	% of total
Patient revenues	1,252	96
Other operating revenues	52	4
Total	**1,304**	**100**

Selected Hospitals

Albemarle Health (managed hospital Elizabeth City)
Beaufort Hospital dba Vidant Beaufort Hospital (Washington)
Bertie Memorial Hospital dba Vidant Bertie Hospital (Windsor)
Chowan Hospital dba Vidant Chowan Hospital (Edenton)
Duplin General Hospital dba Vidant Duplin Hospital (Kenansville)
Heritage Hospital dba Vidant Edgecombe Hospital (Tarboro)
The Outer Banks Hospital (jointly owned with Chesapeake Regional Medical Center Nags Head)
Pitt County Memorial Hospital dba Vidant Medical Center (affiliated with the Brody School of Medicine at East Carolina University Greenville)
Pungo Hospital. dba Vidant Pungo Hospital (Belhaven)
Roanoke-Chowan Hospital dba Vidant Roanoke-Chowan Hospital (Ahoskie)

Selected Services

Air and ground critical care transport
Asthma program (pediatric)
Audiology
Behavioral and mental health
Cancer care
Child life
Children's Hospital
Children's care
Community health programs
Diagnostic imaging
Emergency
Endoscopy
Gamma knife
Heart and vascular care
Heartburn treatment clinic
Home health
Hospice care
Hyperbaric oxygen therapy
Injury prevention
Mammography
Medical weight loss (OPTIFAST)
Mental health
MRI (Magnetic Resonance Imaging)
Neurosciences
Neurosurgery
Open MRI
Orthopedics
Pain management
Pediatric cardiology
Pediatric
Pediatric weight loss
Psychiatry
Radiology
Rehabilitation Center
Rehabilitation
Senior
Sleep
Specialty
Speech pathology
Spine surgery
Sports medicine
Stroke care
Surgical
Transplant
Trauma
Vascular surgery
Weight loss
Wellness and prevention
Women's services
Wound healing

COMPETITORS

Alamance Regional Medical Center
Carolinas HealthCare System
Grace Hospital
Novant Health
Rex Healthcare
Rowan Regional Medical

Cumberland County Hospital System
Duke University Health System
Center
UNC Hospitals
WakeMed

HISTORICAL FINANCIALS
Company Type: Private - Not-for-Profit

Income Statement
FYE: September 30

	REVENUE ($ mil.)	NET INCOME ($ mil.)	NET PROFIT MARGIN	EMPLOYEES
09/11*	1,304	68	5.2%	8,373
12/10	318	30	9.5%	0
09/09	0	0	—	0
Annual Growth	—	—	—	—

*Fiscal year change

2011 Year-End Financials

Debt ratio: —
Return on equity: 5.20%
Cash ($ mil.): 101
Current ratio: 1.50
Long-term debt ($ mil.): —
Dividends
Yield: —
Payout: —
Market value ($ mil.): —

UNIVERSITY HEALTHSYSTEM CONSORTIUM

LOCATIONS

HQ: UNIVERSITY HEALTHSYSTEM CONSORTIUM
155 N WACKER DR STE 4000, CHICAGO, IL 60606-1720
Phone: 312-775-4100

HISTORICAL FINANCIALS
Company Type: Private

Income Statement
FYE: December 31

	REVENUE ($ mil.)	NET INCOME ($ mil.)	NET PROFIT MARGIN	EMPLOYEES
12/11	223	127	57.2%	250
12/10	207	131	63.5%	0
Annual Growth	7.6%	(3.2%)	—	—

2011 Year-End Financials

Debt ratio: —
Return on equity: 57.20%
Cash ($ mil.): 12
Current ratio: 0.70
Long-term debt ($ mil.): —
Dividends
Yield: —
Payout: —
Market value ($ mil.): —

UNIVERSITY MEDICAL CENTER INC

LOCATIONS

HQ: UNIVERSITY MEDICAL CENTER INC
530 S JACKSON ST, LOUISVILLE, KY 40202-1675
Phone: 502-562-3000
Web: www.drloyd.yourmd.com

HISTORICAL FINANCIALS
Company Type: Private

Income Statement
FYE: December 31

	REVENUE ($ mil.)	NET INCOME ($ mil.)	NET PROFIT MARGIN	EMPLOYEES
12/11	450	(7)	—	2,000
12/10	448	13	3.0%	0
12/09	415	5	1.4%	0
12/08	402	8	2.0%	0
Annual Growth	3.9%	—	—	—

2011 Year-End Financials

Debt ratio: —
Return on equity: (-1.70)%
Cash ($ mil.): 32
Current ratio: 1.10
Long-term debt ($ mil.): —
Dividends
Yield: —
Payout: —
Market value ($ mil.): —

UNIVERSITY OF FLORIDA FOUNDATION INC

LOCATIONS

HQ: UNIVERSITY OF FLORIDA FOUNDATION INC
2012 W UNIVERSITY AVE, GAINESVILLE, FL 32603-1734
Phone: 352-392-1691
Web: www.gatorclub.com

HISTORICAL FINANCIALS
Company Type: Private

Income Statement
FYE: June 30

	REVENUE ($ mil.)	NET INCOME ($ mil.)	NET PROFIT MARGIN	EMPLOYEES
06/11	153	32	21.4%	450
06/10	132	7	5.9%	0
06/09	0	(0)	—	0
06/08	190	71	37.7%	0
Annual Growth	(7.1%)	(23.1%)	—	—

2011 Year-End Financials

Debt ratio: —
Return on equity: 21.40%
Cash ($ mil.): 35
Current ratio: 1.50
Long-term debt ($ mil.): —
Dividends
Yield: —
Payout: —
Market value ($ mil.): —

UNIVERSITY OF GEORGIA

Located in the quintessential college town of Athens The University of Georgia (UGA) offers a wide range of degree programs to nearly 35000 students. Forest resources veterinary medicine and law are a few of the school's academic programs. UGA which also runs 170-plus study-abroad and exchange programs administers the prestigious Peabody Awards which honors media achievements and boasts one of the nation's largest map collections. Famous alumni include former US Senator Phil Gramm TV journalist Deborah Norville and former PBS president Pat Mitchell. The University of Georgia was chartered by the State of Georgia in 1785 and graduated its first class in 1804.

Operations

As part of its business UGA offers nearly two dozen bachelor's degrees in about 140 fields and roughly 35 master's degrees in nearly 140 fields. Its doctorate or professional degrees cover a broad spectrum of disciplines such as law pharmacy veterinary medicine and 90 other areas. The university has a student-teacher ratio of about 12:1.

Strategy

Despite its annual endowment of more than $50 million UGA has logged decreases in state appropriations in recent years due to overall declines in Georgia's budget. The result spurred UGA to cut its budget increase undergraduate tuition fees institute a "Special Institutional" mandatory fee of $200 per semester reduce employer health insurance contributions and increase energy conservation measures. Going forward UGA has also not ruled out the possibility of hiking tuition further citing that an increase of up to 30% would help to replace all of the state funding the university has lost due to the recession.

Sales and Marketing

The university sources 80% of its students from the Peach State. Since 1851 25 Georgia governors have graduated from UGA. The institution also boasts nine Pulitzer Prize recipients 17 presidents or provosts of US colleges and universities and four members of the National Academy of Sciences.

EXECUTIVES

President, Michael F. Adams
VP Student Affairs and Dean Students, Rodney D. Bennett
SVP Finance and Administration, Tim Burgess
VP Research, David C. Lee
VP Public Affairs, Tom Jackson
SVP External Affairs, Tom S. Landrum
SVP Academic Affairs and Provost, Jere W. Morehead

LOCATIONS

HQ: The University of Georgia
456 E. Broad St., Athens GA 30601
Phone: 706-542-3000   Fax: 706-425-3255
Web: www.uga.edu

PRODUCTS/OPERATIONS

Selected Schools and Colleges
Agricultural and Environmental Sciences
Arts and Sciences Business
Ecology

Education
Environment and Design
Family and Consumer Sciences
Forest Resources
Graduate School
Journalism and Mass Communication
Law
Pharmacy
Public Health
Public and International Affairs
Social Work
Veterinary Medicine
The GHSU/UGA Medical Partnership
Engineering

HISTORICAL FINANCIALS

Company Type: School

Income Statement

FYE: June 30

	REVENUE ($ mil.)	NET INCOME ($ mil.)	NET PROFIT MARGIN	EMPLOYEES
06/11	691	(12)	—	17,800
06/10	636	134	21.2%	0
06/09	627	63	10.0%	0
06/08	600	93	15.6%	0
Annual Growth	4.8%	—	—	—

2011 Year-End Financials

Debt ratio: —
Return on equity: (-1.80)%
Cash ($ mil.): 272
Current ratio: 2.50
Long-term debt ($ mil.): —
Dividends
Yield: —
Payout: —
Market value ($ mil.): —

UNIVERSITY OF GEORGIA ATHLETIC ASSOCIATION INC.

LOCATIONS

HQ: UNIVERSITY OF GEORGIA ATHLETIC
ASSOCIATION INC.
1 SELIG CIR B, ATHENS, GA 30602-1501
Phone: 706-542-1306

HISTORICAL FINANCIALS

Company Type: Private

Income Statement

FYE: June 30

	REVENUE ($ mil.)	NET INCOME ($ mil.)	NET PROFIT MARGIN	EMPLOYEES
06/11	90	11	13.1%	400
06/10	86	9	10.8%	0
06/09	80	7	9.3%	0
06/08	81	14	18.3%	0
Annual Growth	3.6%	(7.2%)	—	—

2011 Year-End Financials

Debt ratio: —
Return on equity: 13.10%
Cash ($ mil.): 99
Current ratio: 0.80
Long-term debt ($ mil.): —
Dividends
Yield: —
Payout: —
Market value ($ mil.): —

UNIVERSITY OF KANSAS CENTER FOR RESEARCH INC.

LOCATIONS

HQ: UNIVERSITY OF KANSAS CENTER FOR
RESEARCH INC.
2385 IRVING HILL RD, LAWRENCE, KS 66045-7563
Phone: 785-864-3441
Web: www.navub.org

HISTORICAL FINANCIALS

Company Type: Private

Income Statement

FYE: June 30

	REVENUE ($ mil.)	NET INCOME ($ mil.)	NET PROFIT MARGIN	EMPLOYEES
06/11	160	16	10.5%	2
06/10	151	11	7.8%	0
06/09	130	0	—	0
06/08	132	7	5.3%	0
Annual Growth	6.6%	33.6%	—	—

2011 Year-End Financials

Debt ratio: —
Return on equity: 10.50%
Cash ($ mil.): 11
Current ratio: 1.20
Long-term debt ($ mil.): —
Dividends
Yield: —
Payout: —
Market value ($ mil.): —

UNIVERSITY OF KENTUCKY HOSPITAL AUXILIARY INC.

For the times when there's a physical reason to be carried "back to my old Kentucky home" being lugged to University of Kentucky Chandler Hospital (UK Chandler Hospital) might be a better option. The 500-bed academic hospital is operated by the University of Kentucky Auxiliary. It is located within the University of Kentucky Medical Center complex which includes the specialized medical colleges of the University of Kentucky and their affiliated clinical treatment facilities (organized under the UK HealthCare umbrella). UK Chandler Hospital's services include oncology pediatrics cardiology orthopedics and women's health and it operates eastern Kentucky's only Level I trauma and Level III neonatal ICU units.

In addition to overseeing the UK Chandler Hospital UK HealthCare operates the Kentucky Children's Hospital (located within the Chandler Hospital building) the Markey Cancer Center and other outpatient clinics located within the UK Medical Center complex. UK HealthCare also manages the 300-bed UK Good Samaritan Hospital which is located nearby and numerous regional primary and specialty care clinics.

The Lexington campus also houses six UK health-related colleges: medicine nursing dentistry pharmacy health science and public health. UK Chandler Hospital conducts a variety of training and residency programs in partnership with the schools.

UK HealthCare completed the first phase of the new UK Chandler Hospital pavilion in 2011 adding new emergency trauma and inpatient bed facilities. The new pavilion is gradually being expanded and will eventually (in six to 10 years) take over as the primary building for the UK Chandler Hospital replacing the current facilities (which date back to 1962).

The UK Chandler Hospital was organized in 1957 on the university's Lexington campus and was named after former Kentucky governor Albert B. "Happy" Chandler.

EXECUTIVES

VP Medical Center Operations, Frank A. Butler
Associate VP Clinical Network Development,
  Joseph O. (Joe) Claypool
Associate VP Information Technology, Zed Day
Associate VP Medical Center Operations, Murray B.
  Clark Jr.
EVP Health Affairs, Michael Karpf
Director Strategic Marketing, Bill Gombeski
VP Clinical Affairs; Dean College of Medicine The
  University of Kentucky, Jay Perman
CFO, Sergio Melgar
Chief Medical Officer, Richard (Rick) Lofgrenn
Chief of Staff, Courtney Higdon
Auditors: Deloitte&ToucheLLP

LOCATIONS

HQ: University of Kentucky Hospital Auxiliary Inc.
  800 Rose St., Lexington KY 40536-0293
Phone: 859-323-5000   **Fax:** 859-323-1918
Web: www.mc.uky.edu

COMPETITORS

Appalachian Regional Healthcare
Baptist Health
Bon Secours Health
Catholic Health Initiatives
Community Health Systems
Highlands Health
Jewish Hospital & St. Mary' s HealthCare
Norton Healthcare
Pikeville Medical Center
SunBridge Healthcare Corporation

HISTORICAL FINANCIALS

Company Type: Subsidiary

Income Statement

FYE: June 30

	REVENUE ($ mil.)	NET INCOME ($ mil.)	NET PROFIT MARGIN	EMPLOYEES
06/12	912	13	1.4%	2,879
06/11	797	41	5.2%	0
06/10	785	39	5.0%	0
06/09	704	(47)	—	0
Annual Growth	9.0%	—	—	—

2012 Year-End Financials

Debt ratio: —
Return on equity: 1.40%
Cash ($ mil.): 12
Current ratio: 0.70
Long-term debt ($ mil.): —
Dividends
Yield: —
Payout: —
Market value ($ mil.): —

UNIVERSITY OF LOUISIANA AT LAFAYETTE

LOCATIONS

HQ: UNIVERSITY OF LOUISIANA AT LAFAYETTE
104 UNIVERSITY CIR, LAFAYETTE, LA 70503
Phone: 337-482-1000
Web: www.louisiana.edu

HISTORICAL FINANCIALS
Company Type: Private

Income Statement
FYE: June 30

	REVENUE ($ mil.)	NET INCOME ($ mil.)	NET PROFIT MARGIN	EMPLOYEES
06/12	145	(11)	—	1,942
06/11	145	46	32.3%	0
06/10	140	(2)	—	0
06/09	111	(16)	—	0
Annual Growth	9.3%	—	—	—

2012 Year-End Financials

Debt ratio: —
Return on equity: (-8.10)%
Cash ($ mil.): 64
Current ratio: 3.10
Long-term debt ($ mil.): —

Dividends
  Yield: —
  Payout: —
Market value ($ mil.): —

UNIVERSITY OF MINNESOTA PHYSICIANS

LOCATIONS

HQ: UNIVERSITY OF MINNESOTA PHYSICIANS
720 WASHINGTON AVE SE # 200, MINNEAPOLIS, MN 55414-2924
Phone: 612-884-0600
Web: www.umphysicians.org

HISTORICAL FINANCIALS
Company Type: Private

Income Statement
FYE: June 30

	REVENUE ($ mil.)	NET INCOME ($ mil.)	NET PROFIT MARGIN	EMPLOYEES
06/11	373	3	1.1%	200
06/10	368	4	1.2%	0
06/09	0	0	—	0
06/08	289	6	2.2%	0
Annual Growth	8.8%	(14.4%)	—	—

2011 Year-End Financials

Debt ratio: —
Return on equity: 1.10%
Cash ($ mil.): 27
Current ratio: 0.80
Long-term debt ($ mil.): —

Dividends
  Yield: —
  Payout: —
Market value ($ mil.): —

UNIVERSITY OF MOBILE INC.

The University of Mobile touts a "distinctively Christian" environment as it offers bachelor's degrees associate's degrees and pre-professional programs in more than 40 areas of study across six schools: the College of Arts and Sciences the School of Business the School of Education the School of Leadership Development the School of Nursing and the School of Christian Studies. It also offers master's programs in Business Administration Nursing Education and Religious Studies. Affiliated with the Southern Baptist Convention the university was founded in 1961. It has an enrollment of approximately 2000 students.

EXECUTIVES

VP Campus Operations, Leon M. Pirkle
President, Mark R. Foley
VP Academic Affairs, Audrey Eubanks
VP Business Affairs, J. Stephen Lee
Director Human Resources, Diane S. Black
Chancellor, William K. Weaver Jr.
Dean Academic Services and Registrar, Donald K. Berry
Director Center for Performing Arts, J. Roger Breland
Director Library Services, Jeffrey D. Calametti
Director Public Relations, Kathy P. Dean
Director Planned Giving and Stewardship, Marlena M. Himes
Director Marketing, Lesa G. Moore
Director Financial Aid, Marie Thomas
Executive Director of Development, Marty Vignes
Director Institutional Operations, Vicki Burgin
Executive Director InformationTechnology Services and Director Center for Academic Technology, Michael Davis
Director of Leadership & Cultural Studies, Svetlana Khokhlova

LOCATIONS

HQ: University of Mobile
5735 College Pkwy., Mobile AL 36613
Phone: 251-442-2273   **Fax:** 303-322-3019
Web: www.ilona.com/

COMPETITORS

Auburn University
Birmingham-Southern College
Troy University
University of Alabama
University of Alabama at Birmingham
University of South Alabama

HISTORICAL FINANCIALS
Company Type: School

Income Statement
FYE: June 30

	REVENUE ($ mil.)	NET INCOME ($ mil.)	NET PROFIT MARGIN	EMPLOYEES
06/11	33	2	6.2%	251
06/10	30	(1)	—	0
06/09	27	0	—	0
06/08	27	(0)	—	0
Annual Growth	7.2%	—	—	—

2011 Year-End Financials

Debt ratio: —
Return on equity: 6.20%
Cash ($ mil.): 1
Current ratio: —
Long-term debt ($ mil.): —

Dividends
  Yield: —
  Payout: —
Market value ($ mil.): —

UNIVERSITY OF MONTANA

LOCATIONS

HQ: UNIVERSITY OF MONTANA
32 CAMPUS DR, MISSOULA, MT 59812-0004
Phone: 406-243-5082
Web: www.umt.edu

HISTORICAL FINANCIALS
Company Type: Private

Income Statement
FYE: June 30

	REVENUE ($ mil.)	NET INCOME ($ mil.)	NET PROFIT MARGIN	EMPLOYEES
06/11	267	21	7.9%	0
Annual Growth	—	—	—	—

2011 Year-End Financials

Debt ratio: —
Return on equity: 7.90%
Cash ($ mil.): 73
Current ratio: 1.20
Long-term debt ($ mil.): —

Dividends
  Yield: —
  Payout: —
Market value ($ mil.): —

UNIVERSITY OF NORTH DAKOTA

Way up in the Upper Midwest is the University of North Dakota (UND) the largest and oldest institution of higher learning in the state with an enrollment of approximately 15000 students. It offers undergraduate and graduate programs in close to 300 fields through nine colleges and schools (aerospace sciences arts and sciences business and public administration education and human development engineering and mines law medical and health sciences nursing and a graduate school). The university also has nearly 20 doctoral programs as well as certificate degree programs distance degree programs and a continuing education division. UND was founded in 1883 six years before North Dakota achieved statehood.

UND's medical school offers residencies in family and community medicine internal medicine psychiatry surgery and transitional medicine. The transitional medicine program allows medical students to rotate through five medical specialties before choosing the final specialty on which they plan to base their career.

In 2011 UND awarded more than 2600 degrees. The majority of those were undergraduate degrees (1689) followed by master's (565) certificates (128) doctoral (103) law (81) and medicine (56). Enrollment at UND has been steadily growing over the past few years; in 2006 enrollment was at about 12800 it dropped slightly in 2007 to 12700 but then went right back up in 2008 to 12750. Enrollment grew to 13170 in 2009 and was up to roughly 14200 in 2010.

UND has an international reputation for research; most notably in the health sciences nutrition energy and environmental protection aerospace and engineering. In fiscal year 2010 the university received about $144 million from various sources to perform research projects in areas that include neuroscience Unmanned Aerial Systems vaccines advanced electronics nanotechnology high-tech coatings and alternative fuels.

Along with its nine colleges and schools 290 academic fields of study including undergraduate graduate law and medicine UND offers its students online and long-distance learning. Long-distance learners can achieve their bachelor's master's and doctoral degrees in a manner that fits in with any adult's busy lifestyle.

EXECUTIVES

Director Human Resources, Diane Nelson
VP Student and Outreach Services, Robert Boyd
President, Robert O. Kelley
VP Finance and Operations, Alice Brekke
VP Academic Affairs and Provost, Paul LeBel
VP Health Affairs and Dean School of Medicine and Health Sciences, H. David Wilson
SEVP Health Affairs and Executive Dean School of Medicine and Health Science, Joshua Wynne
VP Research and Economic Development, Barry Milavetz
CIO, Joshua Riedy
University Registrar, Suzanne Anderson
Executive Associate VP University Relations, Peter Johnson
General Counsel, Julie Evans
EVP University of North Dakota Alumni Association and Foundation, Tim O'Keefe
Director Campus Safety and Security and Risk Manager, Jason Uhlir
Director Student Financial Aid, Robin Holden
Associate VP Enrollment Management, Alice Hoffert
Director Career Services, Mark Thompson

LOCATIONS

HQ: University of North Dakota
Twamley Hall Centennial Drive, Grand Forks ND 58202
Phone: 701-777-2011   **Fax:** 701-777-3866
Web: www.und.edu

PRODUCTS/OPERATIONS

Selected Schools and Colleges

John D. Odegard School of Aerospace Sciences

College of Arts and Sciences
College of Business and Public Administration
College of Education and Human Development
School of Engineering and Mines
The Graduate School
School of Law
School of Medicine and Health Sciences
College of Nursing
Online and Distance Programs
Career and Personal Development

HISTORICAL FINANCIALS

Company Type: School

Income Statement

FYE: June 30

	REVENUE ($ mil.)	NET INCOME ($ mil.)	NET PROFIT MARGIN	EMPLOYEES
06/11	278	27	9.8%	2,756
06/09	637	(40)	—	0
06/08	616	31	5.1%	0
06/06	1,972,371	0	0.0%	0
Annual Growth	**(94.8%)**	**382.4%**	—	—

2011 Year-End Financials

Debt ratio: —
Return on equity: 9.80%
Cash ($ mil.): 16
Current ratio: 0.70
Long-term debt ($ mil.): —
Dividends
Yield: —
Payout: —
Market value ($ mil.): —

UNIVERSITY OF NORTH TEXAS HEALTH SCIENCE CENTER AT FORT WORTH

LOCATIONS

HQ: UNIVERSITY OF NORTH TEXAS HEALTH SCIENCE CENTER AT FORT WORTH
3500 CAMP BOWIE BLVD, FORT WORTH, TX 76107-2644
Phone: 817-735-2000
Web: www.txphtrainingcenter.org

HISTORICAL FINANCIALS

Company Type: Private

Income Statement

FYE: August 31

	REVENUE ($ mil.)	NET INCOME ($ mil.)	NET PROFIT MARGIN	EMPLOYEES
08/11	143	14	10.0%	1,710
08/08	119	8	6.9%	0
08/07	110	18	16.8%	0
08/06	1,423	0	0.0%	0
Annual Growth	**(53.5%)**	**3448.3%**	—	—

2011 Year-End Financials

Debt ratio: —
Return on equity: 10.00%
Cash ($ mil.): 90
Current ratio: 2.10
Long-term debt ($ mil.): —
Dividends
Yield: —
Payout: —
Market value ($ mil.): —

UNIVERSITY OF OKLAHOMA FOUNDATION INC

LOCATIONS

HQ: UNIVERSITY OF OKLAHOMA FOUNDATION INC
100 W TIMBERDELL RD RM 1, NORMAN, OK 73019-5016
Phone: 405-321-1174
Web: www.oufoundation.org

HISTORICAL FINANCIALS

Company Type: Private

Income Statement

FYE: June 30

	ASSETS ($ mil.)	NET INCOME ($ mil.)	INCOME AS % OF ASSETS	EMPLOYEES
06/11	1,041	108	10.4%	20
06/10	805	40	5.0%	0
06/09	776	0	—	0
06/08	1,016	147	14.5%	0
Annual Growth	**0.8%**	**(9.7%)**	—	—

2011 Year-End Financials

Debt ratio: —
Return on equity: 51.90%
Cash ($ mil.): 36
Current ratio: —
Long-term debt ($ mil.): —
Dividends
Yield: —
Payout: —
Market value ($ mil.): —

UNIVERSITY OF PENNSYLVANIA

LOCATIONS

HQ: UNIVERSITY OF PENNSYLVANIA
3451 WALNUT ST RM 100, PHILADELPHIA, PA 19104-6243
Phone: 215-898-5000

HISTORICAL FINANCIALS

Company Type: Private

Income Statement

FYE: June 30

	REVENUE ($ mil.)	NET INCOME ($ mil.)	NET PROFIT MARGIN	EMPLOYEES
06/11	6,036	1,600	26.5%	70
Annual Growth	—	—	—	—

2011 Year-End Financials

Debt ratio: —
Return on equity: 26.50%
Cash ($ mil.): 965
Current ratio: —
Long-term debt ($ mil.): —
Dividends
Yield: —
Payout: —
Market value ($ mil.): —

UNIVERSITY OF REDLANDS

University of Redlands is a private liberal arts and sciences university. Its College of Arts and Sciences and School of Education are located in Southern California's City of Redlands; its School of Business is located on campus and in regional centers throughout Southern California. The university offers more than 40 undergraduate majors about a dozen master's degree programs a doctorate in leadership for educational justice and professional credential and certificate programs. It has an enrollment of approximately 2400 students. University of Redlands was founded in 1907 on land donated by banker and Baptist layman Karl C. Wells and maintains an informal relationship with the American Baptist church.

EXECUTIVES

Chancellor, James R. (Jim) Appleton, age 75
President, Stuart B. Dorsey
CFO and Treasurer, Cory Nomura
VP University Relations, Neil Macready
Director Human Resources, Roberta Dellhime
Assistant VP Information Technology and CIO, Hamid Etesamnia
VP and Dean Student Life, Char Burgess
EVP Operations and Planning, Phil Doolittle
VP Marketing and Strategic Communications, Gail Guge
VP Academic Affairs, David Fite
Director Financial Operations and Controller, Pat Caudle
Director Admissions College of Arts and Sciences, Paul Driscoll
Registrar, Teresa Area
Director Alumni Relations, Paul Granillo
Director Development, Randy Possinger
Interim Director Financial Aid, Bethann Corey

LOCATIONS

HQ: University of Redlands
1200 E. Colton Ave., Redlands CA 92374-3755
Phone: 909-793-2121   **Fax:** 909-793-2029
Web: www.redlands.edu

HISTORICAL FINANCIALS
Company Type: School

Income Statement
FYE: June 30

	REVENUE ($ mil.)	NET INCOME ($ mil.)	NET PROFIT MARGIN	EMPLOYEES
06/11	148	(1)	—	1,017
06/10	141	(4)	—	0
06/08	136	0	0.2%	0
06/07	89	16	18.6%	0
Annual Growth	**18.4%**	—	—	—

2011 Year-End Financials

Debt ratio: —
Return on equity: (-0.80)%
Cash ($ mil.): 10
Current ratio: —
Long-term debt ($ mil.): —

Dividends
Yield: —
Payout: —
Market value ($ mil.): —

UNIVERSITY OF RHODE ISLAND

The University of Rhode Island (URI) offers more than 100 bachelor's degrees (nursing is the most popular) as well as master's doctoral and professional degrees from nine colleges at four campuses across the state. Its main campus is in Kingston while the W. Alton Jones Campus in West Greenwich offers environmental education. URI's Graduate School of Oceanography is located on Narragansett Bay; and Providence is home to the university's Alan Shawn Feinstein College of Continuing Education. URI has an enrollment of more than 16000 students. The university was chartered as the state's agricultural school in 1888.

EXECUTIVES

President, Robert L. Carothers
Assistant VP Human Resources Administration, Anne Marie Coleman
Assistant VP Public Affairs, Andrea M. Hopkins
VP University Advancement, Robert M. Beagle
VP Student Affairs, Thomas R. Dougan
VP Administration, Robert A. Weygand
Associate VP Development, Paul H. Witham
Assistant VP Business Services, J. Vernon Wyman
Assistant VP Student Affairs, Lester K. Yensan
VP Academic Affairs and Provost, Donald H. Dehayes
Director Budget and Financial Planning, Linda Barrett
Vice Provost Information Technology Services, Garry Bozylinsky
Director Security, Robert F. Drapeau
Director Enrollment Services, Horace J. Amaral Jr.
VP Research and Economic Development, Peter Alfonso
Director Purchasing and University Stores, Elizabeth A. Gil

LOCATIONS

HQ: University of Rhode Island
35 Campus Ave., Kingston RI 02881
Phone: 401-874-1000   **Fax:** 401-874-5272
Web: www.uri.edu

PRODUCTS/OPERATIONS

Selected Schools and Colleges
College of Arts and Sciences
College of Business Administration
College of Continuing Education
College of Engineering
College of Environment and Life Sciences
College of Human Science and Services
College of Nursing
College of Pharmacy
Graduate School of Oceanography
University College

HISTORICAL FINANCIALS
Company Type: School

Income Statement
FYE: June 30

	REVENUE ($ mil.)	NET INCOME ($ mil.)	NET PROFIT MARGIN	EMPLOYEES
06/11	392	58	14.9%	2,500
06/08	319	49	15.5%	0
06/07	290	43	15.1%	0
06/06	258	0	—	0
Annual Growth	**14.9%**	—	—	—

2011 Year-End Financials

Debt ratio: —
Return on equity: 14.90%
Cash ($ mil.): 96
Current ratio: 2.40
Long-term debt ($ mil.): —

Dividends
Yield: —
Payout: —
Market value ($ mil.): —

UNIVERSITY OF RICHMOND

Suffering from arachnophobia? You may not want to mail that application to University of Richmond (UR) where more than 4000 "Spiders" attend classes. UR consists of five schools: Jepson School of Leadership Studies Richmond School of Law Robins School of Business School of Arts and Sciences and School of Continuing Studies. The university offers some 60 undergraduate majors as well as graduate and master's programs in business accounting and law. UR also offers some 75 study-abroad programs in which more than half of its students participate. Founded in 1830 by Virginia Baptists as a seminary for men the school became Richmond College in 1840.

EXECUTIVES

VP Information Services, Kathryn J. (Kathy) Monday
Associate VP Human Resources, Carl Sorensen
VP Student Development, Steve Bisese
Registrar, Susan D. Breeden
Director Media and Public Relations, Brian Eckert
Assistant VP Alumni Relations, Kristin Woods
Director Career Development Center, Leslie Williams Stevenson
University Librarian, Jim Rettig
President, Edward L. Ayers
VP Business and Finance, Hossein Sadid
Assistant VP Communications, Lisa Van Riper
Administrative Coordinator Communications, Debbie Hardy
Associate Director Marketing Communications, Jan Hatchette
Assistant Director Media and Public Relations, Linda Evans
Media and Public Relations Officer, Holly Rodriguez
Head Library Systems, Nancy Woodall
Provost and VP Academic Affairs, Steve Allred
Auditors: KPMGLLP

LOCATIONS

HQ: University of Richmond
28 Westhampton Way, Richmond VA 23173
Phone: 804-289-8000   **Fax:** 804-287-6003
Web: www.richmond.edu

HISTORICAL FINANCIALS
Company Type: School

Income Statement
FYE: June 30

	REVENUE ($ mil.)	NET INCOME ($ mil.)	NET PROFIT MARGIN	EMPLOYEES
06/11	219	270	122.9%	1,400
06/10	210	83	39.7%	0
06/09	197	(314)	—	0
06/08	187	76	40.7%	0
Annual Growth	5.5%	52.6%	—	—

2011 Year-End Financials
Debt ratio: —
Return on equity: 122.90%
Cash ($ mil.): 115
Current ratio: —
Long-term debt ($ mil.): —

Dividends
Yield: —
Payout: —
Market value ($ mil.): —

UNIVERSITY OF SAN FRANCISCO INC

Known for their devotion to education as well as their investment portfolio the Jesuits are evident to all who visit the University of San Francisco (USF). One of 28 Jesuit Catholic colleges and universities in the US the main USF campus sits on 55 acres near Golden Gate Park in San Francisco. The school which was formed in 1855 as St. Ignatius Academy enrolls more than 10000 students. It operates five schools and colleges including the schools of business and management education law and nursing and the colleges of arts and sciences. In addition to its main campus the university operates five satellite sites in Northern and Southern California.

Operations

USF operates a handful of schools and colleges including schools of management education law nursing and the colleges of arts and sciences. More than 400 full-time faculty members offer 100-plus undergraduate and degree programs. With a student-faculty ratio of 16:1 USF's 10000-plus student enrollment includes 6250 undergraduates 2950 graduates 670 law students and 150 non-degree students.

The independent private not-for-profit university is one of the nation's most ethnically diverse schools. Some 43% of its students are Asian African-American Latino Native Hawaiian/Pacific Islander or multi-ethnic.

Strategy

To keep up with growth USF in 2011 acquired the Folger Building located at 101 Howard Street in downtown San Francisco. The university also changed the name of its school of nursing to the School of Nursing and Health Professions to reflect the institution's commitment and expansion of its master of public health degree.

Financial Performance

USF logged a 10% decrease in revenue in 2012 as compared to 2011 due to contribution declines and a net realized and unrealized loss on investments in 2012 over a gain in 2011. Meanwhile net income dropped 85% during the same reporting period. Dips in revenue and rises in total expenses both attributed to increases in auxiliary enterprises

scholarships and fellowships and institutional support expenses.

EXECUTIVES
President, Rev Stephen A. Privett, age 69
VP Accounting and Business Services, Charles E. (Charlie) Cross
Chancellor, Rev John Lo Schiavo
Executive Assistant to the President and Secretary of the Board, Jaci Neesam
VP Communications and Marketing, David F. MacMillan
VP International Relations, Stanley D. Nel
General Counsel, Donna J. Davis
Dean College of Arts and Sciences, Jennifer E. Turpin
Dean School of Education, Walter H. Gmelch
Dean School of Law, Jeffrey S. Brand
Dean University Library, Tyrone H. Cannon
Vice Provost Academic and Enrollment Services, Elizabeth J. Johnson
Director Budget, Michael Harrington
Director Institutional Research, Alan Ziajka
Director Recreation Sports, Charlies B. White Jr.
Associate VP Accounting and Business Services, Kim Kvaal
Manager University Bookstore, Robert Gibson
Associate VP University Advancement and Director Corporate/Foundation Relations, Sally Dalton
Assistant VP University Advancement and Director Planned Giving, David Cunningham
Director Alumni Relations, Annette Anton
Assistant VP Public Affairs and University Communications, Gary McDonald
Assistant Dean Academic Programs, Sue Stavn
University Librarian, Joseph Garity
Head Special Collections University Library, John Hawk
Head of Collection Reference and Research Services Library, Locke J. Morrisey
Reference Librarian Law Library, Lee Ryan
Head Acquisitions University Library, Kathy Woo
Director Priscilla A. Scotlan Career Services Center, James Catiggay
Vice Provost Planning Budget and Review and Professor of Accounting, Salvador Aceves
Senior Associate VP Advancement, Nancy Sackson
Vice Provost Academic Affairs and Professor of Psychology, Gerardo Marin
Dean School of Nursing, Judith F. Karshmer
Director Center for Global Education, Sharon Li
Director Sponsored Projects, Pamela Miller
Director Institutional Assessment, William Murry
Associate Dean Student Development, Linda L. Thomas
Assistant Dean Multicultural Student Services, Mary Grace Almandrez
Assistant Dean Students, Julie E. Orio
Vice Chair, Charles H. Smith
Provost and Academic Vice President, Jennifer E. Turpin
VP Information Technology, Stephen J. Gallagher
Chairman, Thomas E. Malloy
Vice Chair, Charles H. Smith
Trustee, Alfonso T. Yuchengco
Trustee, David Agger
Trustee, Richard L. Bechelli
Trustees, Joseph J. Bonocore
Trustee, Teresa J. Win
Trustee, Patrick McNicholas
Trustee, Susan G. Marineau
Trustee, Rev Philip L. Boroughs
Trustee, Rev J. Dean Brackley
Trustee, Francis J. Butler
Trustee, Rev Gregory Chisholm

Trustee, Rt. Hon. Martin J. Jenkins
Trustee, Rev Thomas J. Scirghi
Trustee, Alfred S. Chuang
Trustee, Rev Jon D. Fuller
Trustee, Suzanne Troxel
Trustee, J. Malcolm Visbal
Trustee, James Holub
Trustee, Arthur A. Ciocca
Trustee, Rt. Hon. Maria P. Rivera
Trustee, Jeanne M. Cunicelli, age 45
Trustee, Ricky J. Curotto
Trustee, Steven M. Read
Trustee, Charles M. Geschke
Trustee, Suzanne M. Giraudo
Trustee, Rose Guilbault
Trustee, Wayne E. Jerves
Trustee, Lawrence R. O'Connor
Trustee, Oliver T. Johnson
Trustee, Rev William R. Stoeger
Trustee, Peter K. Maier
Trustee, Antoinette M. Malveaux
Trustee, Rev Michael J. Sheeran
Trustee, Putra Masagung
Trustee, Rev Mark Ravizza
Trustee, Rev Mario J. Prietto
Trustee, Rev John J. O'Callaghan
Trustee, Joan M. McGrath
Trustee, John F. Nicolai
Trustee, Rev Patrick B. O'Leary
Auditors: Deloitte&ToucheLLP

LOCATIONS
HQ: University of San Francisco
2130 Fulton St., San Francisco CA 94117-1080
Phone: 415-422-5555   **Fax:** 317-692-7854
Web: www.infarmbureau.org

PRODUCTS/OPERATIONS

Selected Schools and Colleges
College of Arts
College of Sciences
School of Education
School of Law
School of Management
School of Nursing

HISTORICAL FINANCIALS
Company Type: School

Income Statement
FYE: May 31

	REVENUE ($ mil.)	NET INCOME ($ mil.)	NET PROFIT MARGIN	EMPLOYEES
05/11	380	55	14.5%	1,200
05/10	334	25	7.7%	0
05/09	299	0	—	0
05/05	247	0	—	0
Annual Growth	15.4%	—	—	—

2011 Year-End Financials
Debt ratio: —
Return on equity: 14.50%
Cash ($ mil.): 112
Current ratio: —
Long-term debt ($ mil.): —

Dividends
Yield: —
Payout: —
Market value ($ mil.): —

UNIVERSITY OF SOUTH FLORIDA

The University of South Florida (USF) is bullishly educational. The school has some 47000 students at three campuses in Tampa St. Petersburg and Sarasota/Manatee as well as a satellite office in Lakeland. It offers some 230 undergraduate graduate specialty and doctoral degree programs through more than a dozen colleges including Arts and Sciences Business Education Engineering Marine Science Pharmacy and Public Health. USF also offers graduate certificates continuing education courses and teacher certifications. The university has some 2000 teaching faculty members and maintains a 27-to-1 student-faculty ratio. USF was founded in 1960; its mascot is the bull.

Geographic Reach

USF has increased enrollment of international students by about 90% between 2007 and 2012. It has a total of more than 2100 international students or about 4% of the total student population. USF also supports study abroad programs. The university's campuses in Florida encompass some 1600 acres.

Operations

The university has an extensive health sciences program including medical nursing pharmacy and public health colleges grouped under the USF Health banner. The health organization also includes patient care facilities such as family care practices emergency clinics and Alzheimer's centers. USF Health also hosts medical research programs in areas such as neurological conditions cardiovascular care pediatrics infectious disease and biotechnology.

Strategy

In the face of rising competition in Florida's health care market USF is looking to further its medical training capabilities by forming partnerships with hospital systems in the eastern US. It completed construction of a $30 million high-tech surgical training facility in Tampa in 2012. In addition USF Health formed a partnership with Florida Hospital (part of Adventist Health System) to conduct research programs and provide collaborative care in the region.

Another area of growth for USF has been music: The university completed construction of a new School of Music facility in 2011. The $38 million project includes new concert halls classroom and studios and practice rooms. The building is part of a larger university capital improvement plan that started in 1982.

EXECUTIVES

President and Corporate Secretary, Judy L. Genshaft
SVP USF Health and Dean USF Morsani College of Medicine, Stephen K. Klasko
Vice Provost Human Resources Management and Space Planning, Kofi Glover
VP Administrative Services, Sandy Lovins
Associate VP Information Technologies, George W. Ellis
Regional Chancellor USF Sarasota-Manatee Campus, Arthur M. Guilford
VP Information Technology, Michael A. Pearce
EVP and Provost, Ralph Wilcox
VP International Affairs Center, Karen A. Holbrook
General Counsel, Steven D. Prevaux
Director Financial Aid, Billie Jo Hamilton
Director Registrar Office, Angela DeBose

Associate VP Decision Support, Michael Moore
Director Career Center, Drema Howard
COO, John W. Long
Senior Vice Provost, Dwayne Smith
Vice Provost Strategic and Budget Planning, Graham Tobin
Vice Provost Student Success, Paul Dosal
Treasurer, Fe;; Stubbs
Regional Chancellor USF St. Petersburg Campus, Margaret Sullivan
Interim Regional Chancellor and Campus Executive Officer USF Polytechnic, David M. Touchton

LOCATIONS

HQ: University of South Florida
   4202 E. Fowler Ave., Tampa FL 33620
Phone: 813-974-2011   **Fax:** 813-974-5530
Web: www.usf.edu

PRODUCTS/OPERATIONS

Selected Colleges

The Arts
Arts & Sciences
Behavioral & Community Sciences
Business
Education
Engineering
Global Sustainability
Honors College
Marine Science
Medicine
Nursing
Pharmacy
Public Health
University College (graduate school)

COMPETITORS

Florida Atlantic University	University of Central Florida
Florida International University	University of Florida
Florida State University	University of Miami
	University of North Florida

HISTORICAL FINANCIALS

Company Type: School

Income Statement

FYE: June 30

	REVENUE ($ mil.)	NET INCOME ($ mil.)	NET PROFIT MARGIN	EMPLOYEES
06/11	1,013	94	9.3%	16,165
06/09	892	42	4.7%	0
06/07	533	148	27.8%	0
06/06	480	35	7.4%	0
Annual Growth	**28.3%**	**38.9%**	—	—

2011 Year-End Financials

Debt ratio: ——
Return on equity: 9.30%
Cash ($ mil.): 116
Current ratio: 0.90
Long-term debt ($ mil.): ——

Dividends
   Yield: ——
   Payout: ——
Market value ($ mil.): ——

UNIVERSITY OF ST. THOMAS

Far from any Bahamian beaches or Caribbean hot spots sits The University of St. Thomas (UST). The school is a Catholic university with campuses in Minneapolis and St. Paul Minnesota. It offers about 90 undergraduate and 60 graduate programs in seven academic divisions: education and philosophy arts and sciences business engineering divinity law and social work. The school has an enrollment of about 11000 undergraduate and graduate students with a student-to-teacher ratio of 14:1. UST along with military prep school St. Thomas Academy grew out of St. Thomas Aquinas Seminary which was founded in 1885 by Archbishop John Ireland.

Geographic Reach

UST has campuses in Minneapolis and St. Paul as well as the Daniel C. Gainey Conference Center in Owatonna Minnesota and the Bernardi Campus in Rome Italy.

Financial Performance

UST reported revenues of some $239 million in 2012 up slightly (about 1%) from the previous year's results. The university's revenues come from a mix of student tuition and fees sales and service enterprises grants gifts and contracts. Meanwhile its net income for 2012 dropped 96% to some $3 million. The university has an annual operating budget of about $195 million and its tuition runs around $33000 per student. UST has an endowment of some $400 million.

EXECUTIVES

President and Trustee, Father Dennis Dease
VP Information Resources and Technologies, Samuel (Sam) Levy
VP Business Affairs and CFO, Mark D. Vangsgard
EVP and Chief Academic Officer, Thomas R. Rochon
EVP and Chief Administrative Officer, Mark Dienhart
Associate VP Enrollment Services, Marla Friederichs
VP Mission, Gene Scapanski
VP University and Government Relations, Doug Hennes
Executive Director Development, Steve Hoeppner
Executive Director Alumni and Constituent Relations, Rachel Wobschall
Executive Director Institutional Advancement, Kristine M. Aasheim
VP Student Affairs, Jane Canney
Director Alumni Association, Greg Hendricks
Associate VP Human Resources, Edna R. Comedy
Director News Service, Jim Winterer
Executive Director Marketing Communications, William V. Kirchgessner
Director Neighborhood Relations, John Hershey
Associate VP Academic Affairs, Angeline Barretta-Herman
University Regsitrar, Paul M. Simmons
Director International Education, Sarah A. Stevenson
Associate VP Academic Affairs, Joseph L. Kreitzer
Director International Studies Program, Robert J. Riley
Director Faculty Grants, David F. Steele
Associate VP Administration, Linda Halverson
Director University Libraries and Information Technology, Dan R. Gjelten

Director Web and Media Services, Elizabeth J. Houle
Director Telecommunication and Network, Dave L. Naugle
Director Athletics and Recreation, Steven J. Fritz
Associate VP and Controller, Gary L. Thyen
Associate VP Auxiliary Services, Bruce Van den Berghe
Chief Investment Officer, Michael F. Sullivan
VP Mission and Trustee, Rev John M. Malone
VP St. Paul Seminary School of Divinity and Rector, Aloysius Callaghan
Director Purchasing Services, Karen M. Harthorn
Director Information Security, Christopher S. Gregg
EVP and Chief Academic Officer, Susan Huber
Chief Treasury and Investment Officer, Carol Peterfeso
General Counsel and Chief Human Resources Officer, Sara Gross Methner
Trustee, George W. Buckley, age 65
Trustee, Gail J. Dorn
Trustee, Richard M. (Dick) Schulze, age 71
Trustee, Robert J. (Bob) Ulrich, age 68
Trustee, Stephen J. (Steve) Hemsley, age 59
Trustee, John M. Morrison, age 75
Trustee, Mark A. Zesbaugh, age 47
Trustee, Timothy P. (Tim) Flynn, age 55
Trustee, Ann L. Winblad
Trustee, Lee R. Anderson Sr.
Trustee, Gerald A. (Gerry) Rauenhorst
Trustee, Michael V. Ciresi, age 66
Trustee, Stanley S. Hubbard
Trustee, Stephen P. Nachtsheim
Trustee, Maureen A. Fay, age 77
Trustee, Timothy P. Flynn, age 61
Trustee, Rodney P. Burwell, age 73
Trustee, Michael E. Dougherty, age 71
Trustee, Kathleen J. (Kathy) Higgins Victor, age 55
President and Trustee, Father Dennis Dease
Trustee, Rev Edward A. Malloy, age 71
Trustee, John Bannigan Jr.
Trustee, Burton Cohen
Trustee, John J. (Hap) Fauth
Trustee, Father Harry J. Flynn
Trustee, Eugene U. Frey
Trustee, Antoine M. Garibaldi
Trustee, Pierson M. Grieve
Trustee, Laurence E. LeJeune
Trustee, Rev Kevin McDonough
Trustee, Harry G. McNeely Jr.
Trustee, Diana E. Murphy
Trustee, John F. O'Shaughnessy Jr.
Trustee, Frank Sunberg
Trustee, Frank B. Wilderson
Trustee, Geoffrey C. Gage
Trustee, Amy R. Goldman
Trustee, Daniel J. Haggerty
Trustee, Patricia Jaffray
Trustee, Sister Carol Keehan
VP Mission and Trustee, Rev John M. Malone
Trustee, Mary G. Marso
Trustee, Alvin E. McQuinn

LOCATIONS

HQ: University of St. Thomas
2115 Summit Ave., St. Paul MN 55105
Phone: 651-962-5000   **Fax:** 651-962-6110
Web: www.stthomas.edu

PRODUCTS/OPERATIONS

Academic Divisions
College of Arts and Sciences (Bachelor's and Master&apo
College of Education Leadership and Counseling Education (Bachelor's Master's Specialist Doctorate) and Professional Psychology (Master's and Doctorate)
Opus College of Business (Bachelor's and Master&apo
Saint Paul Seminary School of Divinity (Master&ap

School of Engineering (Bachelor's and Master&apo
School of Law (Juris Doctor)
School of Social Work (Bachelor's and Master&apo

HISTORICAL FINANCIALS

Company Type: School

Income Statement

FYE: June 30

	REVENUE ($ mil.)	NET INCOME ($ mil.)	NET PROFIT MARGIN	EMPLOYEES
06/11	56	17	31.6%	1,900
06/10	234	46	19.8%	0
06/09	223	(75)	—	0
06/08	223	9	4.3%	0
Annual Growth	(36.8%)	23.0%	—	—

2011 Year-End Financials

Debt ratio: ——
Return on equity: 31.60%
Cash ($ mil.): 10
Current ratio: —
Long-term debt ($ mil.): —

Dividends
Yield: —
Payout: —
Market value ($ mil.): —

UNIVERSITY OF THE PACIFIC

Situated next to the largest body of water on earth is a pretty big body of knowledge: the University of the Pacific. The school offers 80 majors and academic programs in such fields as art Asian languages and studies biology business computer science engineering history and music. It offers undergraduate graduate and professional degree programs in nine colleges and enrolls nearly 6700 students at its main campus in Stockton California the McGeorge School of Law in Sacramento and the Arthur A. Dugoni School of Dentistry in San Francisco. California's first chartered institution of higher education the university was founded in 1851.

EXECUTIVES

VP Business and Finance, Patrick D. Cavanaugh
Dean Arthur A. Dugoni School of Dentistry, Patrick J. Ferrillo Jr., age 60
Provost, Philip N. Gilbertson
Associate Provost and CIO, Larry Frederick
Univeristy Registrar, Cecilia M. Rodriguez
Associate VP and Chief Investment Officer, Larry G. Brehm
Executive Director Pacific Alumni Association, Bill Coen
Assistant VP Diversity and Community Engagement, John Carvana
Dean McGeorge School of Law, Elizabeth Rindskopf Parker
VP Student Life, Elizabeth Griego
President and Regent, Pamela A. (Pam) Eibeck
Chair, Tom Zuckerman
VP University Advancement, Ted Leland
Executive Director Marketing and University Communications, Richard Rojo
Director International Programs and Services, David Schmidt
Dean Library, C. Brigid Welch
Director Institutional Research, Mike Rogers
Director Admission, Richard Toledo
Director Financial Aid, S. Lynn Fox

Director Human Resources, Kara Bell
Assistant VP and Controller, Deborah Denney
Dean Eberhardt School of Business, Richard Flaherty
Dean Students, Joanna Royce-Davis
Dean College of the Pacific, Thomas Krise
Dean Conservatory of Music, Giulio Maria Ongaro
Dean Gladys L. Benerd School of Education, Lynn G. Beck
Dean School of Engineering and Computer Science, Ravi K. Jain
Dean School of International Studies and Associate Provost International Initiatives, Margee Ensign
Dean Thomas J. Long School of Pharmacy and Health Sciences, Phillip Oppenheimer
Dean Graduate Studies and Associate Provost Research and Collaborative Programs, Jin Gong
Manager Purchasing, Ronda Marr
Director Public Safety, Mike Belcher
Regent, Steven F. Leer, age 59
Regent, Walter E. Robb IV, age 59
Regent, Diane D. Miller, age 59
President and Regent, Pamela A. (Pam) Eibeck
Regent, Janice R. Brown
Regent, Sigmund H. Abelson
Regent, D. Kirkwood Bowman
Regent, Connie M. Callahan
Regent, Tony Chan
Regent, Ronald D. (Ron) Cordes
Regent, Robert J. Corkern
Regent, Morrison C. England Jr.
Regent, Steven J. Goulart, age 53
Regent, Jose M. Hernandez
Regent, Kathleen Lagorio Janssen
Regent, Howard M. Koff
Regent, Larry Leasure
Regent, Russell E. Leatherby
Regent, Jim Mair
Regent, Hayne R. Moyer
Regent, Fredric C. Nelson
Regent, Dianne Philibosian
Regent, Jeannette Powell
Regent, Ronald Redmond
Regent, Barry L. Ruhl
Regent, Elizabeth A. (Betsy) Sanders
Regent, Lori Best Sawdon
Regent, Naka (Nick) Ushijima
Auditors: KPMGLLP

LOCATIONS

HQ: UNIVERSITY OF THE PACIFIC
3601 PACIFIC AVE, STOCKTON, CA 95211-0197
Phone: 209-946-2401
Web: www.pacifictigers.cstv.com

PRODUCTS/OPERATIONS

Selected Schools and Colleges

Arthur A. Dugoni School of Dentistry
Benerd School of Education
College of the Pacific (Arts and Sciences)
Conservatory of Music
Eberhardt School of Business
McGeorge School of Law
School of Engineering and Computer Science
School of International Studies
Thomas J. Long School of Pharmacy and Health Sciences

HISTORICAL FINANCIALS
Company Type: School

Income Statement
FYE: June 30

	REVENUE ($ mil.)	NET INCOME ($ mil.)	NET PROFIT MARGIN	EMPLOYEES
06/12	330	20	6.3%	1,500
06/11	317	43	13.8%	0
06/10	354	11	3.2%	0
06/09	309	0	—	0
Annual Growth	2.2%	—	—	—

2012 Year-End Financials
Debt ratio: ——
Return on equity: 6.30%
Cash ($ mil.): 5
Current ratio: —
Long-term debt ($ mil.): —

Dividends
Yield: —
Payout: —
Market value ($ mil.): —

UNIVERSITY OF THE SCIENCES IN PHILADELPHIA

LOCATIONS
HQ: UNIVERSITY OF THE SCIENCES IN PHILADELPHIA
600 S 43RD ST, PHILADELPHIA, PA 19104-4418
Phone: 215-596-8800
Web: www.usp.edu

HISTORICAL FINANCIALS
Company Type: Private

Income Statement
FYE: June 30

	REVENUE ($ mil.)	NET INCOME ($ mil.)	NET PROFIT MARGIN	EMPLOYEES
06/11	89	21	24.2%	500
06/10	89	16	18.9%	0
06/09	87	(27)	—	0
06/08	84	(9)	—	0
Annual Growth	2.1%	—	—	—

2011 Year-End Financials
Debt ratio: ——
Return on equity: 24.20%
Cash ($ mil.): 9
Current ratio: —
Long-term debt ($ mil.): —

Dividends
Yield: —
Payout: —
Market value ($ mil.): —

UNIVERSITY OF WEST GEORGIA

Go West young men and women and join the approximately 11600 students who attend University of West Georgia (UWG). UWG students major in some 110 areas through the university's schools and colleges (Arts and Sciences Business Education and the Graduate School). UWG also allows select high school students to earn both college and high school credits simultaneously. UWG also offers a full program of distance education via the Internet through its eCore program. The school was founded in 1906 as the Fourth District Agricultural and Mechanical School in Carrollton Georgia. The school became State University of West Georgia in 1996; it dropped "State" from its name in 2005.

Geographic Reach

UWG serves those who reside in and around Georgia including more than 40 states and nearly 70 countries. The university sits in the foothills of the Appalachian Mountains.

Operations

The educational institution with a 19:1 student/faculty ratio boasts more than 1100 full-time faculty and staff members. It provides programs of study at the bachelor's level (55 programs) master's and specialist levels (36) doctoral level (3) and certificate level (12).

Strategy

In 2013 UWG began to concentrate on property purchases. It's working to acquire property on the site of the historic Newnan Hospital facility to offer improved access to education for the area's traditional and non-traditional students.

Sales and Marketing

Students across the UWG campus come from 44 states and another 69 nations. It sources its overseas students primarily from Nigeria China Canada Germany and the Republic of Korea. Outside Georgia the university receives out of state students from Alabama Florida Tennessee New York and California.

EXECUTIVES
President, Beheruz N. Sethna
Director Human Resources, Stephanie Rooks
VP Academic Affairs and Provost, Thomas J. Hynes Jr.
VP Student Affairs and Enrollment Management and Dean Students, Melaine McClellan
Assistant VP University Communications and Marketing, Lisa Ledbetter
CIO, Kathy Kral
Information Security Officer, Mardel Shumake
Associate VP Enrollment Management, Scot Lingrell
Director Financial Aid, Kimberly Jordan
Manager Purchasing Services, Kim Henderson
Director Career Services, Wanda Rainey McGukin
University Controller, Richard Sears
VP Business and Finance, James Sutherland
Registrar, Bonnie B. Stevens

LOCATIONS
HQ: University of West Georgia
1601 Maple St., Carrollton GA 30118
Phone: 678-839-5000   **Fax:** 678-839-4747
Web: www.westga.edu

PRODUCTS/OPERATIONS

Selected Colleges and Schools
College of Arts and Humanities
College of Science and Mathematics
College of Social Studies
College of Education
Richards College of Business
School of Nursing
Honors College and Extended Degree Programs
Graduate Studies
UWG - Newnan

HISTORICAL FINANCIALS
Company Type: School

Income Statement
FYE: June 30

	REVENUE ($ mil.)	NET INCOME ($ mil.)	NET PROFIT MARGIN	EMPLOYEES
06/11	82	9	11.6%	993
06/10	93	25	27.1%	0
06/09	79	32	40.6%	0
06/06	81	0	—	0
Annual Growth	0.3%	—	—	—

2011 Year-End Financials
Debt ratio: ——
Return on equity: 11.60%
Cash ($ mil.): 41
Current ratio: 2.90
Long-term debt ($ mil.): —

Dividends
Yield: —
Payout: —
Market value ($ mil.): —

UNIVERSITY OF WISCONSIN MEDICAL FOUNDATION INC.

UW Medical Foundation provides administrative services to more than 900 faculty physicians at the University of Wisconsin School of Medicine and Public Health. The foundation a not-for-profit organization works in cooperation with the UW Hospital and Clinics and more than 60 other clinical group practices throughout the Badger State. The foundation coordinates clinical sites and provides technical and professional staffing services as well as administrative function such legal marketing information technology and logistics. UW Medical Foundation merged with Physicians Plus Medical Group in 1998 and with the University Community Clinics in 2003.

EXECUTIVES
President CEO and Director, Jeffrey Grossman
EVP and COO, Peter Christman
VP Finance and CFO, Robert W. Flannery
VP Marketing, Elizabeth Zaher
VP Patient Business Services, Connie Kinsella
Medical Director Ambulatory Clinic Operations, Richard Welnick
Medical Director Care Management, Lawrence Fleming
VP Legal Services and Compliance, Claudia Sanders
VP Human Resources, William Schrum
VP Operations, Steven Sibley
VP Public Affairs, Ronald Gilmore
VP Care and Quality Innovations, Sue Ertl
VP Leadership and Strategy Development, Roger A. Formisano
Medical Director Care and Quality Innovations, Sally Kraft
VP Information Services, Sandy Clark
Director, Patricia Lipton
President CEO and Director, Jeffrey Grossman
Director, Robert Golden
Director, James E. Burgess
Director, Caroline Fribance
Director, Roger Hauck
Director, Byron J. Marquez

Director, Dennis P. Lund
Director, Frederick Wenzel
Director, Eliot Williams
Director, Christopher Green
Director, Thomas M. Grist
Director, K. Craig Kent
Director, Stephen Y. Nakada
Director, Richard Page
Director, Rodney A. Welch
Auditors: Ernst&YoungLLP

LOCATIONS

HQ: University of Wisconsin Medical Foundation Inc.
7974 UW Health Court, Middleton WI 53562-5531
Phone: 608-821-4223   **Fax:** -5031
Web: www.nisshin-steel-hd.co.jp/en/

COMPETITORS

Ascension Health
Beaver Dam Community
  Hospitals
Beloit Memorial
  Hospital
Catholic Health
  Initiatives
Dean Health Systems
  Inc.
Hospital Sisters
  Health System

Marian Health System
Meriter Health
  Services
ProHealth Care
SSM Health Care
Stoughton Hospital
ThedaCare Inc.
Tomah Memorial
  Hospital

HISTORICAL FINANCIALS

Company Type: Private - Foundation

Income Statement

FYE: June 30

	REVENUE ($ mil.)	NET INCOME ($ mil.)	NET PROFIT MARGIN	EMPLOYEES
06/11	604	10	1.8%	3,200
06/10	571	22	4.0%	0
06/09	518	(8)	—	0
06/08	503	13	2.6%	0
Annual Growth	6.3%	(6.9%)	—	—

2011 Year-End Financials

Debt ratio: ——
Return on equity: 1.80%
Cash ($ mil.): 107
Current ratio: ——
Long-term debt ($ mil.): ——
Dividends
  Yield: —
  Payout: —
  Market value ($ mil.): —

UPPER CUMBERLAND ELECTRIC MEMBERSHIP CORPORATION

LOCATIONS

HQ: UPPER CUMBERLAND ELECTRIC MEMBERSHIP
CORPORATION
138 GORDONSVILLE HWY, CARTHAGE, TN
37030-1810
Phone: 615-735-2940
Web: www.ucemc.com

HISTORICAL FINANCIALS

Company Type: Private

Income Statement

FYE: June 30

	REVENUE ($ mil.)	NET INCOME ($ mil.)	NET PROFIT MARGIN	EMPLOYEES
06/12	103	2	2.7%	139
06/11	108	7	7.0%	0
06/10	96	3	3.6%	0
06/09	104	5	4.9%	0
Annual Growth	(0.5%)	(18.5%)	—	—

2012 Year-End Financials

Debt ratio: ——
Return on equity: 2.70%
Cash ($ mil.): 29
Current ratio: 1.80
Long-term debt ($ mil.): ——
Dividends
  Yield: —
  Payout: —
  Market value ($ mil.): —

UPSON COUNTY HOSPITAL INC.

Upson Regional Medical Center is a 115-bed hospital that serves the communities in and around Thomaston Georgia. In addition to general surgery and acute care the hospital offers specialty services including occupational therapy rehabilitation pediatrics and emergency care. Upson Regional also houses a neonatal special care unit a sleep disorders center and a wound healing center. The medical center has expanded its footprint with new medical offices and dining facilities.

EXECUTIVES

CFO, John Williams
Director Quality and Risk Management, Lyn Ray
CEO, David Castleberry
Chief Nursing Officer, Josee Gill
Director Human Resources, Rich Williams

LOCATIONS

HQ: Upson Regional Medical Center
801 W. Gordon St., Thomaston GA 30286
Phone: 706-647-8111   **Fax:** 706-646-3310
Web: www.urmc.org

COMPETITORS

Piedmont Fayette
  Hospital

Tenet Healthcare

HISTORICAL FINANCIALS

Company Type: Private

Income Statement

FYE: December 31

	REVENUE ($ mil.)	NET INCOME ($ mil.)	NET PROFIT MARGIN	EMPLOYEES
12/11	86	10	12.4%	560
12/10	94	14	15.3%	0
12/09	91	14	15.7%	0
12/08	88	2	2.4%	0
Annual Growth	(0.5%)	73.1%	—	—

2011 Year-End Financials

Debt ratio: ——
Return on equity: 12.40%
Cash ($ mil.): 16
Current ratio: 3.00
Long-term debt ($ mil.): ——
Dividends
  Yield: —
  Payout: —
  Market value ($ mil.): —

US FLOUR CORP

LOCATIONS

HQ: US FLOUR CORP
1 HUNTINGTON QUAD 2S14, MELVILLE, NY
11747-4401
Phone: 631-393-6950

HISTORICAL FINANCIALS

Company Type: Private

Income Statement

FYE: March 31

	REVENUE ($ mil.)	NET INCOME ($ mil.)	NET PROFIT MARGIN	EMPLOYEES
03/11	97	0	0.2%	8
Annual Growth	—	—	—	—

2011 Year-End Financials

Debt ratio: ——
Return on equity: 0.20%
Cash ($ mil.): 0
Current ratio: 1.10
Long-term debt ($ mil.): ——
Dividends
  Yield: —
  Payout: —
  Market value ($ mil.): —

USA COMPRESSION PARTNERS LP

LOCATIONS

HQ: USA COMPRESSION PARTNERS LP
100 CONGRESS AVE STE 1550, AUSTIN, TX
78701-2744
Phone: 512-473-2662
Web: www.usacompression.com

HISTORICAL FINANCIALS

Company Type: Private

Income Statement

FYE: December 31

	REVENUE ($ mil.)	NET INCOME ($ mil.)	NET PROFIT MARGIN	EMPLOYEES
12/11	98	0	0.1%	222
Annual Growth	—	—	—	—

2011 Year-End Financials

Debt ratio: ——
Return on equity: 0.10%
Cash ($ mil.): 0
Current ratio: 0.40
Long-term debt ($ mil.): ——
Dividends
  Yield: —
  Payout: —
  Market value ($ mil.): —

USA HOCKEY INC.

Whenever a puck is dropped boards banged or empty nets scored on USA Hockey is there. The group serves as the governing body for amateur hockey and works to promote the sport with more than 585000 members (ice and in-line hockey players coaches and officials). An official representative to the United States Olympic Committee and the International Ice Hockey Federation the organization supports development of hockey through its affiliation with more than 30 amateur leagues. It trains Olympians and works with the National Hockey League and the National Collegiate Athletic Association as well as publishing American Hockey Magazine. In-line skaters were included in 1994; the group formed in 1936.

EXECUTIVES

President, Ron DeGregorio
Chairman, Walter L. Bush Jr.
International Department Consultant, Art Berglund
Senior Director of Corporate Affairs and Fundraising, Mike Bertsch
Director of Media and Public Relations, Dave Fischer
Corporate Marketing and Consumer Products Manager, Gretchen Hursh
Senior Director of Hockey Operations, Jim Johannson
Director of Corporate Marketing and Consumer Products, Lee Meyer
Director of Internet Communications, Lauren Pasquale
Senior Director of Finance and Administration, Bob Weldon
Director USA Hockey InLine, Gary Del Vecchio
Executive Director, David (Dave) Ogrean

LOCATIONS

HQ: USA Hockey Inc.
1775 Bob Johnson Dr., Colorado Springs CO 80906
Phone: 719-576-8724   **Fax:** 719-538-1160
Web: www.usahockey.com

HISTORICAL FINANCIALS

Company Type: Private

Income Statement

	REVENUE ($ mil.)	NET INCOME ($ mil.)	NET PROFIT MARGIN	EMPLOYEES
				FYE: August 31
08/11	34	(0)	—	38
08/10	33	0	0.1%	0
08/09	30	1	3.5%	0
08/08	26	(0)	—	0
Annual Growth	8.8%	—	—	—

2011 Year-End Financials

Debt ratio: —
Return on equity: (-1.10)%
Cash ($ mil.): 5
Current ratio: 2.70
Long-term debt ($ mil.): —
Dividends
  Yield: —
  Payout: —
Market value ($ mil.): —

USC CARE MEDICAL GROUP INC.

LOCATIONS

HQ: USC CARE MEDICAL GROUP INC.
1510 SAN PABLO ST STE 649, LOS ANGELES, CA 90033-5404
Phone: 626-457-4029

HISTORICAL FINANCIALS

Company Type: Private

Income Statement

	REVENUE ($ mil.)	NET INCOME ($ mil.)	NET PROFIT MARGIN	EMPLOYEES
				FYE: June 30
06/11	182	(10)	—	80
06/10	178	(3)	—	0
06/09	38	0	—	0
Annual Growth	118.8%	—	—	—

2011 Year-End Financials

Debt ratio: —
Return on equity: (-5.60)%
Cash ($ mil.): 0
Current ratio: 0.80
Long-term debt ($ mil.): —
Dividends
  Yield: —
  Payout: —
Market value ($ mil.): —

USES CORP.

LOCATIONS

HQ: USES CORP.
15109 HETHRW FRST PKWY # 150, HOUSTON, TX 77032-3887
Phone: 504-279-9930
Web: www.usesgroup.com

HISTORICAL FINANCIALS

Company Type: Private

Income Statement

	REVENUE ($ mil.)	NET INCOME ($ mil.)	NET PROFIT MARGIN	EMPLOYEES
				FYE: December 31
12/11	226	29	13.1%	0
Annual Growth	—	—	—	—

2011 Year-End Financials

Debt ratio: —
Return on equity: 13.10%
Cash ($ mil.): 31
Current ratio: 1.30
Long-term debt ($ mil.): —
Dividends
  Yield: —
  Payout: —
Market value ($ mil.): —

UT MEDICAL GROUP INC.

UT Medical Group knows that a little practice can go a long way. The organization is the private physician practice affiliated with the University of Tennessee Health Science Center. The not-for-profit physician group consists of more than 350 doctors serving the greater Memphis Tennessee area. Specialized practices include emergency medicine pediatrics surgery ophthalmology and cardiology. The company was founded in 1974 as the Faculty Medical Practice Corporation; one decade later its name was changed to reflect its association with University of Tennessee.

In 2009 UTMG expanded its services to nearby Mud Island when it purchased Harbor Health a primary care office and clinic. The facility sees more than 8400 patients a year.

EXECUTIVES

President and CEO, Steven H. Burkett
CFO, Brenda H. Jeter
COO, Richard O. Baer
VP Marketing and Managed Care, C. Denise Bollheimer
EVP Chief Medical Officer and Director, J. Lacey Smith
Chairman, Steve J. Schwab
VP and CIO, Jill Truitt
VP Child Health Services, Lexanne Horton
Manager Public Relations and Publications, Joy Sutherland
VP Adult Multispecialty Services, Shannon Tacker
EVP Chief Medical Officer and Director, J. Lacey Smith
Director, Robert B. Canada
Director, Raza A. Dilawari
Director, Timothy Fabian
Director, James C. Fleming
Director, Edith Kelly-Green
Director, David L. Maness
Director, Herman Morris Jr.
Director, Elizabeth Pritchard
Director, Guy Reed
Director, Ronald D. Reddin
Director, Dennis Stokes
Director, John Zenella Jr.

LOCATIONS

HQ: UT Medical Group Inc.
66 N. Pauline, Memphis TN 38105
Phone: 901-448-6610   **Fax:** 901-448-7692
Web: www.utmedicalgroup.com

COMPETITORS

Baptist Memorial Health Care
Shelby County Health Care
Tenet Healthcare

HISTORICAL FINANCIALS
Company Type: Private

Income Statement
FYE: June 30

	REVENUE ($ mil.)	NET INCOME ($ mil.)	NET PROFIT MARGIN	EMPLOYEES
06/11	127	2	1.8%	1,207
06/10	135	1	0.8%	0
Annual Growth	(6.3%)	115.6%	—	—

2011 Year-End Financials
Debt ratio: —
Return on equity: 1.80%
Cash ($ mil.): 20
Current ratio: 1.10
Long-term debt ($ mil.): —

Dividends
Yield: —
Payout: —
Market value ($ mil.): —

HISTORICAL FINANCIALS
Company Type: Private

Income Statement
FYE: June 30

	REVENUE ($ mil.)	NET INCOME ($ mil.)	NET PROFIT MARGIN	EMPLOYEES
06/11	122	24	19.6%	2,200
06/10	112	22	20.2%	0
06/09	104	(108)	—	0
06/08	11	6	56.9%	0
Annual Growth	120.5%	54.6%	—	—

2011 Year-End Financials
Debt ratio: —
Return on equity: 19.60%
Cash ($ mil.): 102
Current ratio: 4.20
Long-term debt ($ mil.): —

Dividends
Yield: —
Payout: —
Market value ($ mil.): —

HISTORICAL FINANCIALS
Company Type: School

Income Statement
FYE: May 31

	REVENUE ($ mil.)	NET INCOME ($ mil.)	NET PROFIT MARGIN	EMPLOYEES
05/12	67	2	4.4%	646
05/11	62	4	7.9%	0
05/10	57	1	2.1%	0
05/09	54	(1)	—	0
Annual Growth	7.7%	—	—	—

2012 Year-End Financials
Debt ratio: —
Return on equity: 4.40%
Cash ($ mil.): 12
Current ratio: 1.20
Long-term debt ($ mil.): —

Dividends
Yield: —
Payout: —
Market value ($ mil.): —

UTAH HOUSING CORPORATION

LOCATIONS

HQ: UTAH HOUSING CORPORATION
2479 S LAKE PARK BLVD, WEST VALLEY CITY, UT 84120-8217
Phone: 801-902-8200
Web: www.utahhousingcorp.org

HISTORICAL FINANCIALS
Company Type: Private

Income Statement
FYE: June 30

	ASSETS ($ mil.)	NET INCOME ($ mil.)	INCOME AS % OF ASSETS	EMPLOYEES
06/12	1,668	(0)	—	64
06/11	2,060	0	0.0%	0
06/10	2,132	0	0.0%	0
06/09	1,985	3	0.2%	0
Annual Growth	(5.6%)	—	—	—

2012 Year-End Financials
Debt ratio: —
Return on equity: (-0.60)%
Cash ($ mil.): 100
Current ratio: 0.80
Long-term debt ($ mil.): —

Dividends
Yield: —
Payout: —
Market value ($ mil.): —

UTAH VALLEY UNIVERSITY

LOCATIONS

HQ: UTAH VALLEY UNIVERSITY
800 W UNIVERSITY PKWY, OREM, UT 84058-6703
Phone: 801-863-8000
Web: www.uvu.edu

UTICA COLLEGE

Utica College is a liberal arts college with an enrollment of approximately 2500 full- and part-time students. The private school was founded in 1946 by Syracuse University and became an independent institution in 1995. Utica College offers about 30 undergraduate majors and 15 graduate programs. Its students earn Syracuse baccalaureate degrees for undergrads and Utica College master's and doctorate degrees.

EXECUTIVES

Vice Chair, David A. Caputo
Secretary, Frances D. Fergusson, age 67
President, Todd S. Hutton
Chair, Lisa Marsh Ryerson
Treasurer, Father Charles J. Beirne
Director Business Operations, Ed Lewandrowski
VP Institutional Advancement, Laura Casamento
Director Development, Anthony Villanti
Director Annual Giving, Susan Risler
Director Facilities Management, Donald Harter
Director Human Resources, Ramona B. (Mona) Rice
VP Academic Affairs and Dean of the Faculty, Judith A. Kirkpatrick
VP Student Affairs and Dean of Students, Kenneth E. Kelly
VP Financial Affairs and Treasurer, R. Barry White
VP Enrollment Management, Patrick A. Quinn
Director Physical Education and Athletics, James A. Spartano
Director Library, Beverly J. Marcoline

LOCATIONS

HQ: Utica College
1600 Burrstone Rd., Utica NY 13502
Phone: 315-792-3006   **Fax:** 315-792-3003
Web: www.utica.edu

VALDOSTA STATE UNIVERSITY

Valdosta State University (VSU) nurtures higher education students as they blossom into professionals. The school a regional university of the University System of Georgia is located in the southern Georgia town of Valdosta which is known for its flower gardens and trails. The school has two campuses less than a mile apart that house six colleges and offer about 60 undergraduate and 40 graduate degree programs as well as doctorates in education and public administration. VSU was founded in 1906 as South Georgia State Normal College. Originally a girls' school the institution became co-educational in 1950. It has some 650 faculty members and a student body of about 12500.

Geographic Reach

About 90% of VSU's students come from Georgia with the remaining 10% coming from across the US and 60 international countries.

Financial Performance

VSU has reported revenue growth over the last five years with the exception of 2009. Revenues in 2011 increased 10% to $101.5 million up from $92 million in 2010. Most of VSU's revenues come from tuition education and general funds and state appropriations.

Strategy

Enrollment at VSU has increased by more than 80% over the last decade. To accommodate its increased campus population the university is expanding its facilities and its curriculum. It opened a new literacy center formed a new Center for Applied Social Sciences and launched several new online degree programs (a master's in literature and language and a bachelor's in organization leadership) during 2011.

EXECUTIVES

VP Academic Affairs, Louis H. Levy
VP Student Affairs, Kurt J. Keppler
Director Information Technology, Joseph A. (Joe) Newton
President, Patrick J. Schloss
Director Business Services, Bill Filtz
Director Environmental and Occupational Safety, Robert DeLong

Director Human Resources and Employee
 Development, Denise Bogart

Director University Police, Scott Doner
Director Financial Aid, Douglas Tanner
Dean Students, Russ Mast
Director Career Services, Winifred V. Collins
Director University Marketing and Community
 Relations, Mary Gooding
Director Alumni, John Trombetta
Interim Registrar, Stanley Jones
Interim VP Finance and Administration, Traycee
 Martin

LOCATIONS

HQ: Valdosta State University
 1500 N. Patterson St., Valdosta GA 31698
Phone: 229-333-5800   Fax: 229-245-3891
Web: www.valdosta.edu

PRODUCTS/OPERATIONS

Selected Services

College of Arts and Sciences
College of the Arts
College of Nursing
Dewar College of Education
Honors College
Langdale College of Business Administration

HISTORICAL FINANCIALS

Company Type: School

Income Statement   FYE: June 30

	REVENUE ($ mil.)	NET INCOME ($ mil.)	NET PROFIT MARGIN	EMPLOYEES
06/11	101	9	8.9%	1,956
06/10	92	13	14.8%	0
06/08	80	3	4.5%	0
06/07	739	0	—	0
Annual Growth	—	3312.4%	—	—

2011 Year-End Financials

Debt ratio: ——
Return on equity: 8.90%   Dividends
Cash ($ mil.): 25   Yield: —
Current ratio: 2.30   Payout: —
Long-term debt ($ mil.): —   Market value ($ mil.): —

VALLEY CO-OPS INC.

LOCATIONS

HQ: VALLEY CO-OPS INC.
 1833 S LINCOLN AVE, JEROME, ID 83338-6138
Phone: 208-324-8000
Web: www.shoshonecity.com

HISTORICAL FINANCIALS

Company Type: Private

Income Statement   FYE: August 31

	REVENUE ($ mil.)	NET INCOME ($ mil.)	NET PROFIT MARGIN	EMPLOYEES
08/12	109	3	3.6%	83
08/11	98	2	3.0%	0
08/10	79	1	1.5%	0
08/09	70	2	2.9%	0
Annual Growth	15.8%	23.7%		

2012 Year-End Financials

Debt ratio: ——
Return on equity: 3.60%   Dividends
Cash ($ mil.): 1   Yield: —
Current ratio: 1.00   Payout: —
Long-term debt ($ mil.): —   Market value ($ mil.): —

VAN ARPIN LINES INC

From the fairway to the highway and home again Arpin Van Lines provides a wide range of moving services for residential business and government customers which have included the LPGA. The company formerly known as Paul Arpin Van Lines operates through a network of independent agents throughout North America. (The agents handle local moves within assigned geographic territories; Arpin Van Lines coordinates interstate moves.) Arpin Van Lines' fleet includes some 700 trucks. The company which is run by members of the founding Arpin family is a division of Arpin Group which also includes Arpin International Group and Arpin Moving Systems (Canada). The original Arpin moving company was founded in 1900.

Arpin Group scored big in May 2010 when it acquired Affiliated Transportation Systems (ATSI) along with eight related companies. ATSI which is based in Oklahoma is a household goods transportation service provider serving military personnel primarily; it will continue as a stand-alone subsidiary of Arpin Group. Arpin Van Lines will pack and move the shipments that are booked by ATSI.

EXECUTIVES

President and CEO, David Arpin
VP Agency Development, David Henderson
VP Operations, David Vieira
Chairman, Paul Arpin
CFO, Edward Braks
VP GSA Division, Matt Shea
SVP Commercial and Business Development,
 Robert Sullivan

LOCATIONS

HQ: Arpin Van Lines Inc.
 99 James P. Murphy Hwy., West Warwick RI 02893
Phone: 401-828-8111   Fax: 401-823-5714
Web: www.arpin.com

COMPETITORS

AMERCO	Ryder System
Atlas World Group	SIRVA
Bekins	Suddath
Graebel	UniGroup
National Van Lines	

HISTORICAL FINANCIALS

Company Type: Private

Income Statement   FYE: December 31

	REVENUE ($ mil.)	NET INCOME ($ mil.)	NET PROFIT MARGIN	EMPLOYEES
12/11	102	(1)	—	275
12/10	105	0	0.3%	0
12/09	105	1	1.0%	0
12/07	113	0	0.5%	0
Annual Growth	(3.5%)	—	—	—

2011 Year-End Financials

Debt ratio: ——
Return on equity: (-1.50)%   Dividends
Cash ($ mil.): 0   Yield: —
Current ratio: ——   Payout: —
Long-term debt ($ mil.): —   Market value ($ mil.): —

VAN BUDD LINES INC

No hothouse flower Budd Van Lines aims to be a hardy perennial of the corporate relocation business. From coast to coast the independent van line company moves the household goods of employees who are relocating at the behest of their employers about 6500 annually. It offers packing and moving services to all 48 contiguous states from branch offices in New Jersey California Wisconsin Georgia Ohio and Texas. Companies that have called upon Budd Van Lines to help employees move include Bristol-Myers Squibb Merck & Co. and PricewaterhouseCoopers. Budd Van Lines was founded in 1975.

Once an agent of other moving companies Budd Van Lines declared its independence in 1984. The company works to distinguish itself from rivals by minimizing the number of contact points for families that are being moved.

Budd Van Lines assigns teams of drivers to each move that also handle packing and unpacking for customers. Moving companies that operate through networks of agents might instead have different people responsible for loading driving and unloading.

EXECUTIVES

Chairman and CEO, David Budd Sr.
SVP, Kim Budd
President and COO, Ray Gunst
VP Finance and CFO, William Soltesz
VP National Services, Cathy Trementozzi
VP National Sales, Gary Grund
VP IST, Douglas Soltesz

LOCATIONS

HQ: Budd Van Lines Inc.
 24 Schoolhouse Rd., Somerset NJ 08873
Phone: 732-627-0600   Fax: 281-558-5255
Web: www.shipcomwireless.com

COMPETITORS

Atlas World Group	UniGroup
SIRVA	

HISTORICAL FINANCIALS
Company Type: Private

Income Statement
FYE: December 31

	REVENUE ($ mil.)	NET INCOME ($ mil.)	NET PROFIT MARGIN	EMPLOYEES
12/11	50	1	2.6%	155
12/10	47	1	2.2%	0
12/08	47	0	0.7%	0
12/07	47	0	1.6%	0
Annual Growth	2.0%	18.5%	—	—

2011 Year-End Financials
Debt ratio: ——
Return on equity: 2.60%
Cash ($ mil.): 0
Current ratio: 1.50
Long-term debt ($ mil.): —

Dividends
Yield: —
Payout: —
Market value ($ mil.): —

VAN HORN METZ & CO. INC.

Van Horn Metz & Co. (or Van Horn Metz) distributes chemical ingredients such as pigments dyes extenders additives resins lubricants and base stocks. The company's customers include makers of plastic and rubber products inks adhesives and sealants and paints and coatings. Founded in 1950 by Harold Van Horn and Donald Metz the company serves customers throughout the eastern half of the US. Van Horn Metz operates 12 warehouses and six sales offices.

EXECUTIVES
President, H. Morgan Smith
EVP, Barrett C. Fisher III
Controller, Anthony Crisafulli
Inside Sales, Shannon Warner

LOCATIONS
HQ: Van Horn Metz & Co. Inc.
201 E. Elm St., Conshohocken PA 19428
Phone: 610-828-4500   **Fax:** 610-828-0936
Web: www.vanhornmetz.com

COMPETITORS
Aceto
Brenntag North America
Univar

HISTORICAL FINANCIALS
Company Type: Private

Income Statement
FYE: December 31

	REVENUE ($ mil.)	NET INCOME ($ mil.)	NET PROFIT MARGIN	EMPLOYEES
12/11	39	0	—	24
12/10	39	0	—	0
12/09	35	0	—	0
12/08	45	0	—	0
Annual Growth	(5.0%)	—	—	—

2011 Year-End Financials
Debt ratio: ——
Return on equity: —
Cash ($ mil.): 0
Current ratio: 0.60
Long-term debt ($ mil.): —

Dividends
Yield: —
Payout: —
Market value ($ mil.): —

VANASSE HANGEN BRUSTLIN INC.

LOCATIONS
HQ: VANASSE HANGEN BRUSTLIN INC.
101 WALNUT ST, WATERTOWN, MA 02472-4026
Phone: 617-924-1770
Web: www.infrastructure2000.com

HISTORICAL FINANCIALS
Company Type: Private

Income Statement
FYE: December 31

	REVENUE ($ mil.)	NET INCOME ($ mil.)	NET PROFIT MARGIN	EMPLOYEES
12/11	114	1	1.1%	1,079
12/10	113	2	2.6%	0
12/09	107	2	2.7%	0
12/08	146	1	1.4%	0
Annual Growth	(7.8%)	(15.2%)	—	—

2011 Year-End Financials
Debt ratio: ——
Return on equity: 1.10%
Cash ($ mil.): 0
Current ratio: 1.00
Long-term debt ($ mil.): —

Dividends
Yield: —
Payout: —
Market value ($ mil.): —

VERDE VALLEY MEDICAL CENTER

LOCATIONS
HQ: VERDE VALLEY MEDICAL CENTER
269 S CANDY LN, COTTONWOOD, AZ 86326-4170
Phone: 928-634-2251
Web: www.verdevalleymedicalcenter.com

HISTORICAL FINANCIALS
Company Type: Private

Income Statement
FYE: June 30

	REVENUE ($ mil.)	NET INCOME ($ mil.)	NET PROFIT MARGIN	EMPLOYEES
06/11	148	9	6.3%	500
06/10	160	17	10.9%	0
06/09	154	0	—	0
06/08	152	21	14.0%	0
Annual Growth	(0.8%)	(24.1%)	—	—

2011 Year-End Financials
Debt ratio: ——
Return on equity: 6.30%
Cash ($ mil.): 18
Current ratio: 0.50
Long-term debt ($ mil.): —

Dividends
Yield: —
Payout: —
Market value ($ mil.): —

VERST GROUP LOGISTICS INC.

Verst wants to be first when it comes to storing its customers' items. A warehousing and distribution specialist Verst Group Logistics maintains over 5 million sq. ft. of warehouse space. The company operates from facilities in the Cincinnati metropolitan area and in northern Kentucky. Verst Group Logistics uses its own trucking fleet to provide freight transportation services through subsidiary Zenith Logistics and a network of carriers to arrange long-distance transportation of customers' freight. It serves customers residing in the food and beverage retail and consumer products paper and automotive industries. William Verst the father of president and CEO Paul Verst founded the company in 1968.

EXECUTIVES
President and CEO, Paul T. Verst
COO, Robert P. (Bob) Jackson
CFO, James W. (Jim) Stadtmiller
Chairman, William G. Verst
Director Human Resources, Lynne Shank

LOCATIONS
HQ: Verst Group Logistics Inc.
300 Shorland Dr., Walton KY 41094-9328
Phone: 859-485-1212   **Fax:** 859-485-1428
Web: www.verstgroup.com

COMPETITORS
DSC Logistics
GENCO Distribution System
Kenco Logistics Services
Ozburn-Hessey Logistics

HISTORICAL FINANCIALS
Company Type: Private

Income Statement
FYE: December 31

	REVENUE ($ mil.)	NET INCOME ($ mil.)	NET PROFIT MARGIN	EMPLOYEES
12/11	143	0	—	1,200
12/10	140	0	—	0
12/09	122	0	—	0
12/08	137	0	—	0
Annual Growth	1.5%	—	—	—

2011 Year-End Financials
Debt ratio: ——
Return on equity: —
Cash ($ mil.): 4
Current ratio: 1.40
Long-term debt ($ mil.): —

Dividends
Yield: —
Payout: —
Market value ($ mil.): —

VILLANOVA UNIVERSITY IN THE STATE OF PENNSYLVANIA

Founded in 1842 by the friars of the Order of St. Augustine and named for St. Thomas of Villanova Villanova University retains its Catholic identity to this day. The oldest and largest Catholic institution of higher learning in Pennsylvania the university offers more than 60 academic undergraduate programs at its four main colleges: Business Engineering Liberal Arts and Science and Nursing. It also has a School of Law and it offers graduate programs in most of its disciplines. Villanova University has an enrollment of more than 10000 undergraduate and graduate students and has a student-to-faculty ratio of 11:1.

Strategy

While it is focused on providing a well-rounded Catholic-based liberal arts education to its students Villanova University also strives to participate in the community of Philadelphia through outreach and service efforts. In addition the university has launched a long-term plan to upgrade the university's campus facilities.

As part of the campus master plan in 2011 Villanova launched a $22.5 million project to enhance its landscape including adding aesthetic mobility and pedestrian solutions with the ultimate goal of making the campus vehicle-free. The university also plans to add more residence halls a performing arts center and retail and parking facilities.

EXECUTIVES

VP Academic Affairs, John R. Johannes
VP Administration and Finance, Kenneth G. (Ken) Valosky
Chair, Herbert F. (Herb) Aspbury, age 66
VP and General Counsel, Dorothy A. Malloy
VP Student Life, Rev John P. Stack
VP Technology and CIO, Stephen W. Fugale
Director Athletics, Vincent Nicastro
Director University Shop, Frank L. Henninger
Associate VP Alumni Relations; Executive Director and Board Member University Alumni Association, Gary R. Olsen
Director Career Services, Nancy J. Dudak
Dean Students, Paul F. Pugh
President and Trustee, Rev Peter M. Donohue, age 59
VP Mission and Ministry, Barbara E. Wall
Executive Director Office of Planning Training and Institutional Research, John M. Kelley
VP University Advancement, Michael J. (Mike) O'Neill
VP University Communication, Ann E. Diebold
Director Creative Services, Bernadette Dierkes
Director Media Relations, Jonathan Gust
Director Marketing, Peter Bickel
Director Enterprise Operations and Academic Computing, Robin Allen
Director Web Services and Technologies, Marybeth Avioli
CTO, Timothy Ay
Director Instructional Technologies, Joan Lesovitz
Director Network and Communications, Robert Mays
Director Strategic Planning and Consulting, Daniel McGee
Director Technology Support Services, Matthew Morrissey

Director University Information Systems, Cletus Rickert
Acting Dean and Professor Law School, Doris DelTosto Brogan
Associate Director Human Resources, Lisa Hutcherson
Associate Director Human Resources, Raymond Duffy
Associate Director Human Resources, Bev Das
Director Procurement, John Durham
Chairman, Terence M. O'Toole
Secretary, Rev James D. Paradis
Vice Chair, Catherine M. Keating
VP Academic Affairs, Rev Kail C. Ellis
Associate VP and Affirmative Action Officer, Ellen Ryan Krutz
Interim Dean Villanova School of Business, Kevin D. Clark
Dean Liberal Arts & Sciences, Jean Ann Linney
Dean College of Nursing, M. Louise Fitzpatrick
Dean Engineering, Gary A. Gabriele
Dean School of Law, John Y. Gotanda
President and Trustee, Rev Peter M. Donohue, age 59
Vice Chair, Terence M. O'Toole
Trustee, Richard P. Brennan
Trustee, Kimble A. Byrd
Trustee, Tara S. Cortes
Trustee, James C. Curvey
Trustee, James D. Danella
Trustee, James C. Davis
Trustee, Denise L. Devine
Trustee, Nance K. Dicciani
Trustee, Rev Raymond F. Dlugos
Trustee, Darryl J. Ford
Trustee, Rev Paul W. Galetto
Trustee, William M. Gibson
Trustee, Patricia H. Imbesi
Trustee, John P. Jones III
Vice Chair, Catherine M. Keating
Trustee, Leonard J. LoBiondo
Trustee, Rev Gary N. McCloskey
Trustee, Anne Welsh McNulty
Trustee, Thomas M. Mulroy
Trustee, Mary D. Naylor
Trustee, James V. O?Donnell
Trustee, James F. Orr III
Trustee, Rev Donald F. Reilly
Trustee, Rev Bernard C. Scianna
Trustee, Robert Thornton
Trustee, Joseph V. Topper Jr., age 56
Trustee, Paul A. Tufano
Trustee, Rev Luis A. Vera
Auditors: PricewaterhouseCoopersLLP

LOCATIONS

HQ: Villanova University
800 E. Lancaster Ave., Villanova PA 19085-1603
Phone: 610-519-6000 **Fax:** 610-519-6450
Web: www.villanova.edu

PRODUCTS/OPERATIONS

Selected Schools and Programs
Undergraduate
  College of Arts & Sciences
  College of Engineering
  College of Nursing
  Villanova School of Business
Graduate Studies
  Engineering
  Liberal Arts and Sciences
  Nursing
  School of Law
  Villanova School of Business
Other Offerings
  Continuing Studies

Part-Time Studies

HISTORICAL FINANCIALS
Company Type: School

Income Statement
FYE: May 31

	REVENUE ($ mil.)	NET INCOME ($ mil.)	NET PROFIT MARGIN	EMPLOYEES
05/12	385	(4)	—	2,022
05/11	378	89	23.7%	0
05/10*	368	56	15.4%	0
06/09	0	(0)	—	0
Annual Growth	1294.6%	—	—	—

*Fiscal year change

2012 Year-End Financials
Debt ratio: —
Return on equity: (-1.20)%
Cash ($ mil.): 150
Current ratio: —
Long-term debt ($ mil.): —

Dividends
  Yield: —
  Payout: —
Market value ($ mil.): —

VIRGINIA BEACH PUBLIC SCHOOL SYSTEM

LOCATIONS

HQ: VIRGINIA BEACH PUBLIC SCHOOL SYSTEM
2512 GEORGE MASON DR, VIRGINIA BEACH, VA 23456-9105
Phone: 757-263-1100
Web: www.oceanlakeshs.vbschools.com

HISTORICAL FINANCIALS
Company Type: Private

Income Statement
FYE: June 30

	REVENUE ($ mil.)	NET INCOME ($ mil.)	NET PROFIT MARGIN	EMPLOYEES
06/11	788	(21)	—	10,576
06/09	0	(0)	—	0
06/07	826	7	0.9%	0
06/06	0	0	63.5%	0
Annual Growth	1165.2%	—	—	—

VIRGINIA WEST UNIVERSITY FOUNDATION INC

The West Virginia University Foundation provides fund raising services and manages the assets of West Virginia University. The Foundation seeks support for faculty programs services equipment and facilities that the state of West Virginia might not be able to fund. The university founded the organization in 1954 as an independent non-profit corporation.

EXECUTIVES

VP Development, D. Lyn Dotson
President and CEO, R. Wayne King
Director Human Resources, Erin Pardue
Director Communications, Bill Nevin
VP Finance and CFO, Patricia Robertson
VP Investments and Chief Investment Officer, Dale Marie Hunt
VP Technology and Facilities, Mark Cottrill
Auditors: Ernst&YoungLLP

LOCATIONS

HQ: West Virginia University Foundation Inc.
1 Waterfront Place 7th Fl., Morgantown WV 26507
Phone: 304-284-4000　　**Fax:** 304-284-4001
Web: www.wvuf.wvnet.edu

HISTORICAL FINANCIALS

Company Type: Private - Foundation

Income Statement

FYE: June 30

	REVENUE ($ mil.)	NET INCOME ($ mil.)	NET PROFIT MARGIN	EMPLOYEES
06/11	155	89	57.4%	70
06/10	66	16	24.4%	0
06/09	66	10	16.1%	0
06/08	73	13	18.6%	0
Annual Growth	28.2%	86.8%	—	—

2011 Year-End Financials

Debt ratio: ——
Return on equity: 57.40%
Cash ($ mil.): 11
Current ratio: —
Long-term debt ($ mil.): —
Dividends
　Yield: —
　Payout: —
Market value ($ mil.): —

VIRGINIA WEST UNIVERSITY MEDICAL CORPORATION

LOCATIONS

HQ: VIRGINIA WEST UNIVERSITY MEDICAL CORPORATION
255 SCOTT AVE, MORGANTOWN, WV 26508-8803
Phone: 304-285-7122

HISTORICAL FINANCIALS

Company Type: Private

Income Statement

FYE: December 31

	REVENUE ($ mil.)	NET INCOME ($ mil.)	NET PROFIT MARGIN	EMPLOYEES
12/11*	116	5	4.7%	1,185
06/11	214	4	2.3%	0
06/10	209	9	4.3%	0
06/09	194	0	0.3%	0
Annual Growth	(15.7%)	117.7%	—	—

*Fiscal year change

2011 Year-End Financials

Debt ratio: ——
Return on equity: 4.70%
Cash ($ mil.): 6
Current ratio: 0.90
Long-term debt ($ mil.): —
Dividends
　Yield: —
　Payout: —
Market value ($ mil.): —

VISION INFORMATION TECHNOLOGIES INC.

LOCATIONS

HQ: VISION INFORMATION TECHNOLOGIES INC.
3031 W GRAND BLVD STE 600, DETROIT, MI 48202-3014
Phone: 313-420-2000
Web: www.mapconline.com

HISTORICAL FINANCIALS

Company Type: Private

Income Statement

FYE: December 31

	REVENUE ($ mil.)	NET INCOME ($ mil.)	NET PROFIT MARGIN	EMPLOYEES
12/11	238	2	0.9%	880
12/08	101	3	3.0%	0
12/07	107	4	4.2%	0
12/06	376	0	—	0
Annual Growth	—	404.1%	—	—

2011 Year-End Financials

Debt ratio: ——
Return on equity: 0.90%
Cash ($ mil.): 1
Current ratio: 1.60
Long-term debt ($ mil.): —
Dividends
　Yield: —
　Payout: —
Market value ($ mil.): —

VOLUNTEER ENERGY COOPERATIVE

In the strong tradition of volunteering in Tennessee Volunteer Energy Cooperative is voluntarily cooperating with its members to serve their energy needs. The distribution utility serves more than 109000 customers (who also own the cooperative) in 17 central and eastern Tennessee counties. It operates more than 9000 miles of power lines. Volunteer Energy purchases its power supply from the Tennessee Valley Authority. The company also provides metered natural gas and propane service and offers telecommunications (Internet access and long-distance phone) services. In addition Volunteer Energy offers its customer surge protection and security equipment.

The cooperative grows its customer base by about 2000 new accounts per year. It plans to add a number of electrical substations to keep pace with growing demand.

Volunteer Energy is governed by a board of 12 members who represent the 17 counties in its service area.

Higher rates and increased demand lifted the company's revenue and net income in 2011 despite the extra costs incurred by infrastructure damage caused by six tornados that ripped through the cooperative's service area in April 2011.

Volunteer Energy was formed as Meigs County Electric Membership Cooperative in 1935 largely at the prompting of Tennessee Agricultural Extension Agent for Meigs County Willis Shadow.

EXECUTIVES

Executive Assistant, Alesia McNelley
VP Operations, Clyde Jolley
VP Marketing and Economic Development, Patty Hurley
VP Accounting and Finance, Mark Verstynen
President and CEO, Rody Blevins
Chairman, Gene Carmichael
Vice Chairman, Laney Colvard
Secretary Treasurer and Director, Sammy Norton
Assistant Secretary Assistant Treasurer and Director, Larry Storie
VP IT, Karen Davis
Director, William J. Campbell
Director, Keith Phillips
Director, Randy Bond
Director, Charles Fitch
Vice Chairman, Laney Colvard
Director, Jerry Henley
Director, Scott Humberd
Secretary Treasurer and Director, Sammy Norton
Director, Aubie Smith
Director, Marvin Stinnett
Assistant Secretary Assistant Treasurer and Director, Larry Storie

LOCATIONS

HQ: VOLUNTEER ENERGY COOPERATIVE
18359 HWY 58 N, DECATUR, TN 37322
Phone: 423-334-1020
Web: www.vec.org

PRODUCTS/OPERATIONS

2011 Sales

	$ mil.	% of total
% of total		
Electric energy		
Residential		65
Industrial		22
Commercial		9
Street lighting & Other		2
Other		2
Total		100

COMPETITORS

AGL Resources　　　　Inergy
CenturyLink

HISTORICAL FINANCIALS

Company Type: Private - Cooperative

Income Statement
FYE: June 30

	REVENUE ($ mil.)	NET INCOME ($ mil.)	NET PROFIT MARGIN	EMPLOYEES
06/11	235	13	5.5%	175
06/10	206	10	5.1%	0
06/09	220	12	5.8%	0
06/08	192	12	6.7%	0
Annual Growth	6.9%	0.1%	—	—

2011 Year-End Financials

Debt ratio: ——
Return on equity: 5.50%
Cash ($ mil.): 13
Current ratio: 0.40
Long-term debt ($ mil.): —

Dividends
Yield: —
Payout: —
Market value ($ mil.): —

VSC FIRE & SECURITY INC.

LOCATIONS

HQ: VSC FIRE & SECURITY INC.
10343B KINGS ACRES RD, ASHLAND, VA 23005-8059
Phone: 804-459-2220
Web: www.vasc.com

HISTORICAL FINANCIALS

Company Type: Private

Income Statement
FYE: December 31

	REVENUE ($ mil.)	NET INCOME ($ mil.)	NET PROFIT MARGIN	EMPLOYEES
12/11	113	0	—	926
12/10	113	0	—	0
12/09	0	0	—	0
12/08	113	0	—	0
Annual Growth	(0.0%)	—	—	—

2011 Year-End Financials

Debt ratio: ——
Return on equity: —
Cash ($ mil.): 9
Current ratio: 2.20
Long-term debt ($ mil.): —

Dividends
Yield: —
Payout: —
Market value ($ mil.): —

VT MILCOM INC.

LOCATIONS

HQ: VT MILCOM INC.
532 VIKING DR, VIRGINIA BEACH, VA 23452-7316
Phone: 757-463-2800
Web: www.vtmilcom.com

HISTORICAL FINANCIALS

Company Type: Private

Income Statement
FYE: March 31

	REVENUE ($ mil.)	NET INCOME ($ mil.)	NET PROFIT MARGIN	EMPLOYEES
03/12	141	3	2.3%	950
03/11	154	4	2.8%	0
03/10	177	5	2.8%	0
03/09	153	4	3.2%	0
Annual Growth	(2.7%)	(13.5%)	—	—

2012 Year-End Financials

Debt ratio: ——
Return on equity: 2.30%
Cash ($ mil.): 10
Current ratio: 0.50
Long-term debt ($ mil.): —

Dividends
Yield: —
Payout: —
Market value ($ mil.): —

W. DOUGLASS DISTRIBUTING LTD.

LOCATIONS

HQ: W. DOUGLASS DISTRIBUTING LTD.
325 E FOREST AVE, SHERMAN, TX 75090-8832
Phone: 903-893-1181
Web: www.douglassdist.com

HISTORICAL FINANCIALS

Company Type: Private

Income Statement
FYE: December 31

	REVENUE ($ mil.)	NET INCOME ($ mil.)	NET PROFIT MARGIN	EMPLOYEES
12/11	368	1	0.4%	130
12/10	275	0	0.2%	0
12/09	204	0	0.2%	0
12/08	313	1	0.6%	0
Annual Growth	5.6%	(5.9%)	—	—

2011 Year-End Financials

Debt ratio: ——
Return on equity: 0.40%
Cash ($ mil.): 1
Current ratio: 0.90
Long-term debt ($ mil.): —

Dividends
Yield: —
Payout: —
Market value ($ mil.): —

W. E. AUBUCHON CO. INC.

Old houses in New England get a facelift with assistance from W.E. Aubuchon. The company operates more than 125 hardware stores throughout New England and New York as well as at HardwareStore.com. Stores stock about 50000 products including appliances plumbing camping gear hardware housewares paint and tools. W.E. Aubuchon carries such name brands as Delta Faucet

Honeywell Stanley and Weber. Store services include rug cleaner rentals propane tank filling free assembling and delivery and key cutting among other services. Founded in 1908 by William Aubuchon a French-Canadian immigrant the company is still owned by the Aubuchon family.

Geographic Reach
W.E. Aubuchon serves those who reside in New York and the New England states. It also caters to customers across the US through its e-commerce site HardwareStore.com.

Strategy
To compete against the onslaught of big-box retailers Home Depot and Lowe's Aubuchon relies on convenient in-town locations customer service and its HardwareStore.com website which allows it to sell merchandise nationwide.

Company Ownership
W.E. Aubuchon is owned by the Aubuchon family.

EXECUTIVES

CEO, William E. Aubuchon III
President and Treasurer, M. Marcus Moran Jr.

LOCATIONS

HQ: W. E. AUBUCHON CO. INC.
95 AUBUCHON DR, WESTMINSTER, MA 01473-1470
Phone: 978-874-0521
Web: www.aubuchon.com

PRODUCTS/OPERATIONS

Selected Services

Cut Glass & Plexiglasss
Knife & Sharpening Services
Lamp Repair
Lock Servives & Key Duplication
Pipe Cutting
Propane Filling and/or Exchange Tanks
Window Screen Repair
Window Shade Cutting

Selected Products

Electrical
Farm & Pet
Fasteners
Hand Tools
Hardware
Heating and Cooling
Housewares
Lawn and Garden
Outdoor Living
Paint and Supplies
Plumbing
Power Tools

COMPETITORS

84 Lumber	OfficeMax
Ace Hardware	Sears
Do it Best	Staples
Home Depot	Stock Building Supply
Kmart	Target Corporation
Lowe' s	True Value
Northern Tool	Wal-Mart
Office Depot	

HISTORICAL FINANCIALS
Company Type: Private

Income Statement
FYE: December 31

	REVENUE ($ mil.)	NET INCOME ($ mil.)	NET PROFIT MARGIN	EMPLOYEES
12/11	140	1	1.0%	1,113
12/10	133	0	0.4%	0
12/09	133	1	1.3%	0
12/08	139	1	1.2%	0
Annual Growth	0.3%	(6.3%)	—	—

2011 Year-End Financials

Debt ratio: —
Return on equity: 1.00%
Cash ($ mil.): 0
Current ratio: 0.10
Long-term debt ($ mil.): —

Dividends
  Yield: —
  Payout: —
  Market value ($ mil.): —

W. T. BYLER CO. INC.

LOCATIONS

HQ: W. T. BYLER CO. INC.
  15203 LILLJA RD, HOUSTON, TX 77060-5299
Phone: 281-445-2070
Web: www.wtbyler.com

HISTORICAL FINANCIALS
Company Type: Private

Income Statement
FYE: December 31

	REVENUE ($ mil.)	NET INCOME ($ mil.)	NET PROFIT MARGIN	EMPLOYEES
12/11	124	15	12.7%	500
Annual Growth	—	—	—	—

2011 Year-End Financials

Debt ratio: —
Return on equity: 12.70%
Cash ($ mil.): 6
Current ratio: 1.60
Long-term debt ($ mil.): —

Dividends
  Yield: —
  Payout: —
  Market value ($ mil.): —

W.J. BRADLEY MORTGAGE CAPITAL LLC

LOCATIONS

HQ: W.J. BRADLEY MORTGAGE CAPITAL LLC
  6465 GREENWOOD PLAZA BLVD # 500,
  CENTENNIAL, CO 80111-5056
Phone: 303-825-5670
Web: www.morasch.com

HISTORICAL FINANCIALS
Company Type: Private

Income Statement
FYE: December 31

	ASSETS ($ mil.)	NET INCOME ($ mil.)	INCOME AS % OF ASSETS	EMPLOYEES
12/11	225	3	1.3%	705
12/09	42	0	0.1%	0
Annual Growth	428.1%	4775.5%	—	—

2011 Year-End Financials

Debt ratio: —
Return on equity: 3.50%
Cash ($ mil.): 3
Current ratio: —
Long-term debt ($ mil.): —

Dividends
  Yield: —
  Payout: —
  Market value ($ mil.): —

W.S. BADCOCK CORPORATION

W.S. Badcock furnishes homes down in Dixie and beyond. As one of the largest privately-owned furniture retailers in the US the company sells furniture for every room in the house. It sells its furniture and accessories through more than 300 stores that operate under the banner names Badcock Home Furnishing Centers and Badcock &more. Aside from its e-commerce site Badcock's stores network extends to nearly 10 southeastern states. Stores also carry appliances lawn equipment electronics mattresses rugs bedding lighting wall art and other decorative accessories. The company was founded by Henry S. Badcock in 1904 as a general mercantile store. Today it is in its fourth generation of family management.

Geographic Reach

Headquartered in Mulberry Florida with more than 1200 corporate employees W.S. Badcock operates primarily in the southeastern US. Its operations span the states of Georgia Alabama Mississippi Tennessee and the Carolinas expanding into Virginia West Virginia and Kentucky.

Strategy

Through the company's dealer business model more than 80% of Badcock's stores are individually owned. As part of the model the company does not require a franchise fee but instead consigns merchandise to the dealers. As opposed to the typical franchise system startup this consignment method aims to allow for a quicker startup along with the benefits of business ownership.

Already established in half a dozen states Badcock has been expanding its store network in Virginia Kentucky and West Virginia. Despite a slowdown in its expansion plans amid the recession and downturn in furniture retailing the company aims to grow its stores network again throughout the Southeast.

EXECUTIVES

SVP Corporate Administration and Property, Robert (Rob) Burnette
CEO, Michael J. (Mike) Price, age 52
Chairman and EVP Product Development, Ben M. Badcock, age 51
EVP Government and Public Affairs, Wogan S. (Wogie) Badcock III, age 53

EVP Marketing, William T. (Bill) Daughtrey
VP Merchandising Buyer, Gary Wiggs
VP Merchandising Buyer, Cathy Allen
VP Collections, Albert Chattelle
EVP Strategic Planning, Henry C. Badcock, age 53
EVP Retail Operations, William K. (Bill) Pou Jr.
VP Warehouse Operations and Logistics, Randy Wilkerson
VP and General Counsel, Phil Bayt
VP Merchandising Buyer, Tim Birge
VP Merchandising Buyer, Mike Estridge
VP Merchandising Buyer, Terry Johnson
SVP and CFO, Michael Ray
VP and Controller, Steve Bargamin
VP and CIO, Bill Trimble
VP Administration, Charles A. (Charlie) Bowden
Director Dealer Development, Mike Whitten
Director Purchasing, Rick Meyer
Director Training and Development, Anthony Koch
VP Supply Chain, Greg Brinkman
SVP Supply Chain, Chuck Sajeski
VP Human Resources, Lori Walsh

LOCATIONS

HQ: W.S. Badcock Corporation
  200 N. Phosphate Blvd., Mulberry FL 33860
Phone: 863-425-4921   **Fax:** 863-425-7513
Web: www.badcock.com

PRODUCTS/OPERATIONS

Selected Products
Accessories
Appliances
Electronics
Furniture
Mattresses

COMPETITORS

Aaron's Inc.	Ethan Allen
Ashley Furniture	Havertys
Baer's Furniture	Klaussner Furniture
Bassett Furniture	La-Z-Boy
City Furniture	Rooms To Go
El Dorado Furniture	Sealy

HISTORICAL FINANCIALS
Company Type: Private

Income Statement
FYE: June 30

	REVENUE ($ mil.)	NET INCOME ($ mil.)	NET PROFIT MARGIN	EMPLOYEES
06/12	455	12	2.6%	1,000
06/11	431	6	1.6%	0
06/10	446	8	1.9%	0
06/08	519	12	2.4%	0
Annual Growth	(4.3%)	(1.7%)	—	—

2012 Year-End Financials

Debt ratio: —
Return on equity: 2.60%
Cash ($ mil.): 0
Current ratio: 2.80
Long-term debt ($ mil.): —

Dividends
  Yield: —
  Payout: —
  Market value ($ mil.): —

WABASH COLLEGE

If co-educational higher learning turns out to just be a fad then Wabash College will be ahead of the curve once things change back. Wabash College is a private all-male liberal arts school that confers Bachelor of Arts digress in 21 majors. Engineering and law programs are offered in conjunction with Washington University in St. Louis and Columbia University. Wabash College has an enrollment of about 850 students and a student-faculty ratio of approximately 10-to-1. Supported by an endowment of more than $400 million the independent and non-sectarian college was founded in 1832 by Presbyterian ministers and is patterned after the conservative liberal arts colleges of New England.

EXECUTIVES

Director Athletics, Thomas E. (Tom) Bambrey
Dean Admissions and Financial Aid, Steven J. (Steve) Klein
Director Alumni and Parent Relations, Tom Runge
Director Purchasing and Bookstore, Thomas E. Keedy
CFO and Treasurer, Larry B. Griffith
Dean College, Gary A. Phillips
President, Patrick E. White
Director Public Affairs and Marketing and Secretary, James L. Amidon
Director Financial Aid, R. Clint Gasaway
Registrar, Julie A. Olsen

LOCATIONS

HQ: Wabash College
301 W. Wabash Ave., Crawfordsville IN 47933
Phone: 765-361-6100 **Fax:** 765-361-6070
Web: www.wabash.edu

HISTORICAL FINANCIALS
Company Type: School

Income Statement
FYE: June 30

	REVENUE ($ mil.)	NET INCOME ($ mil.)	NET PROFIT MARGIN	EMPLOYEES
06/11	77	18	23.7%	225
06/10	68	6	9.5%	0
06/09	60	(94)	—	0
06/08	45	(56)	—	0
Annual Growth	19.1%	—	—	—

2011 Year-End Financials
Debt ratio: ——
Return on equity: 23.70%
Cash ($ mil.): 14
Current ratio: ——
Long-term debt ($ mil.): ——
Dividends
Yield: —
Payout: —
Market value ($ mil.): —

WACCAMAW COMMUNITY HOSPITAL

LOCATIONS

HQ: WACCAMAW COMMUNITY HOSPITAL
4070 HIGHWAY 17, MURRELLS INLET, SC 29576-5033
Phone: 843-652-1000
Web: www.georgetownhospitalsystem.org

HISTORICAL FINANCIALS
Company Type: Private

Income Statement
FYE: September 30

	REVENUE ($ mil.)	NET INCOME ($ mil.)	NET PROFIT MARGIN	EMPLOYEES
09/11	146	10	7.2%	500
09/09	135	7	5.8%	0
09/08	113	3	3.4%	0
09/07	103	3	3.5%	0
Annual Growth	12.4%	42.6%	—	—

2011 Year-End Financials
Debt ratio: ——
Return on equity: 7.20%
Cash ($ mil.): 2
Current ratio: 1.70
Long-term debt ($ mil.): ——
Dividends
Yield: —
Payout: —
Market value ($ mil.): —

WACHTER INC.

LOCATIONS

HQ: WACHTER INC.
16001 W 99TH ST, LENEXA, KS 66219-1293
Phone: 913-541-2500
Web: www.wachter.com

HISTORICAL FINANCIALS
Company Type: Private

Income Statement
FYE: December 31

	REVENUE ($ mil.)	NET INCOME ($ mil.)	NET PROFIT MARGIN	EMPLOYEES
12/11	157	0	0.4%	1,000
12/10	160	12	7.8%	0
12/09	98	0	0.1%	0
12/08	125	2	2.4%	0
Annual Growth	8.0%	(38.6%)	—	—

2011 Year-End Financials
Debt ratio: ——
Return on equity: 0.40%
Cash ($ mil.): 2
Current ratio: 0.10
Long-term debt ($ mil.): ——
Dividends
Yield: —
Payout: —
Market value ($ mil.): —

WADA FARMS MARKETING GROUP LLC

The Wada folks have heard absolutely all the Mr. Potato Head jokes known to mankind; still they press resolutely on growing packing and supplying Idaho potatoes all of us meat-and-potatoes folks. And in addition to everyone's favorite starchy tuber Wada Farms Potatoes does the same with sweet potatoes and onions. It also offers value-added items such as Easy-Bakers and Easy-Steamers —potatoes packaged in special plastic that can be cooked right in their packaging. The Idaho company cultivates more than 30000 acres of farmland

and operates a 140000-sq.-ft. processing facility. Wada's customers include retail food food wholesaler and foodservice companies throughout the US.

Through its Wada Farms Marketing Group the company has an exclusive marketing agreement for all potatoes (white and sweet) and onions sold under the Dole label in the US. It has been a Wal-Mart supplier for more than 15 years.

Wada formed a relationship with the Shoshone Bannock Tribe and in 2009 the company began growing more than 13000 acres of grain and potatoes on the Shoshone Bannock Tribe Reservation near Blackfoot Idaho.

EXECUTIVES

VP Marketing, Kevin Stanger
COO, Bryan Wada
Sales Manager, Joe Esta
Transportation Coordinator, Terry Hansen
CEO, Bob Meek
VMI Team Leader, Tom Barnes
Sales and Packaging, Cindy Morgan
Sales and Production Coordinator, Kirk Yellowhair
Systems Administrator, Jay Stowell
Accounting Manager, Jill Edgley

LOCATIONS

HQ: Wada Farms Potatoes Inc.
326 S. 1400 West, Pingree ID 83262
Phone: 208-684-9801 **Fax:** 208-684-4157
Web: www.wadafarms.com

PRODUCTS/OPERATIONS

Selected Produce
Onions
Red
Sweet
White
Yellow
Potatoes
Fingerling
Idaho
Red
Red skin yellow flesh
Russets
Sweet
White
Yellow

COMPETITORS

Agrow Fresh Produce	Jones Produce
Appleton Produce	JR Simplot
Chiquita Brands	Larsen Farms
Fresh Del Monte Produce	MountainKing Potatoes
Idaho Fresh-Pak	Nonpareil Corporation
Idaho Supreme Potatoes	O' Leary Potato

HISTORICAL FINANCIALS
Company Type: Private

Income Statement
FYE: December 31

	REVENUE ($ mil.)	NET INCOME ($ mil.)	NET PROFIT MARGIN	EMPLOYEES
12/11	201	2	1.0%	30
12/10	150	1	1.0%	0
12/09	160	2	1.3%	0
12/08	188	1	0.7%	0
Annual Growth	2.4%	16.0%	—	—

WAGSTAFF INC.

LOCATIONS

HQ: WAGSTAFF INC.
3910 N FLORA RD, SPOKANE VALLEY, WA
99216-1720
Phone: 509-922-1404
Web: www.wagstaff.com

HISTORICAL FINANCIALS

Company Type: Private

Income Statement

FYE: December 31

	REVENUE ($ mil.)	NET INCOME ($ mil.)	NET PROFIT MARGIN	EMPLOYEES
12/11	82	10	12.5%	300
12/10	66	3	4.7%	0
12/09	89	7	8.5%	0
12/06	69	9	13.5%	0
Annual Growth	**5.6%**	**2.8%**	—	—

2011 Year-End Financials

Debt ratio: ——
Return on equity: 12.50%
Cash ($ mil.): 34
Current ratio: 1.40
Long-term debt ($ mil.): ——

Dividends
Yield: ——
Payout: ——
Market value ($ mil.): ——

WAKEFERN FOOD CORP.

Some might say you aren't shopping right if you don't get your groceries from stores supplied by this company. Wakefern Food is the largest member-owned wholesale distribution cooperative in the US supplying groceries and other merchandise to a chain of more than 220 ShopRite supermarkets in eight eastern states including parts of New Jersey New York Connecticut Delaware Maryland Massachusetts Rhode Island and Pennsylvania. The company supplies both national brands and private-label products (ShopRite and PriceRite) to its member stores; Wakefern also offers advertising merchandising and other business support services. The co-op which boasts more than 45 members was founded by seven grocers in 1946.

PriceRite a subsidiary of Wakefern Food and its more than 40 supermarkets offer over 500 grocery items at discounted prices such as fresh fruits and vegetables breads pre-packaged meat and seafood kosher products and national brands. Stores average about 35000 square feet in size which are smaller than traditional supermarkets. ShopRite another subsidiary stores sell over 3000 private label brands and serves over 5 million customers

weekly. The majority of ShopRite stores are family-owned.

The company also supplies grocery stores like Saker ShopRite (New Jersey) Village Super Market (New Jersey and Pennsylvania) and Inserra Supermarkets (New York and New Jersey).

Even though the private-cooperative doesn't report its financial results the cooperative reported an estimated $12.8 billion in sales in fiscal 2011 (ends October).

Like other wholesale distributors Wakefern Food's success depends on its ability to distribute goods at the lowest possible cost to its customers meaning the company focuses on keeping expenses low and improving efficiencies throughout its supply operation. But as a member-owned cooperative the company differs from other wholesalers such as Nash-Finch in that its primary focus is on its member stores. Wakefern Food also has the added responsibility of promoting its ShopRight retail chain and helping its member retailers expand the chain's footprint.

The ShopRite chain boasts a loyal following in its core markets but the supermarkets have been feeling the pinch from rivals in the price-competitive grocery business. The company is especially feeling pressure from non-supermarket chains such as Wal-Mart CVS/Caremark and Wawa. To help boost customer loyalty Wakefern has turned to new technology in the form of mobile applications (developed in partnership with technology firm MyWebGrocer) for the Apple iPhone that allow users to get alerts about weekly store specials in their area. The company also rolled out an online pharmacy where customers can place orders through the Internet.

Wakefern Food announced in 2012 it was supplying New York-based Food Bazaar stores which has supermarkets in New York New Jersey and Connecticut. Wakefern will supply ShopRite private label brands along with non-private labels such as dairy frozen food grocery nonfoods and specialty products.

HISTORY

Wakefern Food was founded in 1946 by seven New York- and New Jersey-based grocers: Louis Weiss Sam and Al Aidekman Abe Kesselman Dave Fern Sam Garb and Albert Goldberg. The company got its name by taking the first letters of the last names of five of the original founders (Weiss Sam and Al Aidekman Kesselman and Fern). Like many cooperatives the association sought to lower costs by increasing its buying power as a group.

They each put in $1000 and began operating a 5000-sq.-ft. warehouse often putting in double time to keep both their stores and the warehouse running. The shopkeepers' collective buying power proved valuable enabling the grocers to stock many items at the same prices as their larger competitors.

In 1951 Wakefern members began pooling their resources to buy advertising space. A common store name —ShopRite —was chosen and each week co-op members met to decide which items would be sale priced. Within a year membership had grown to over 50. Expansion became a priority and in the mid-1950s co-op members united in small groups to take over failed supermarkets. One such group called the Supermarkets Operating Co. (SOC) was formed in 1956. Within 10 years it had acquired a number of failed stores remodeled them and given them the ShopRite name.

During the late 1950s sales at ShopRite stores slumped after Wakefern decided to buck the supermarket trend of offering trading stamps (which

could then be exchanged for gifts) figuring that offering the stamps would ultimately lead to higher food prices. The move initially drove away customers but Wakefern cut grocery prices across the board and sales returned. The company did embrace another supermarket trend: stocking stores with nonfood items.

The co-op was severely shaken in 1966 when SOC merged with General Supermarkets a similar small group within Wakefern becoming Supermarkets General Corp. (SGC). SGC was a powerful entity with 71 supermarkets 10 drugstores six gas stations a wholesale bakery and a discount department store. Many Wakefern members opposed the merger and attempted to block the action with a court order. By 1968 SGC had beefed up its operations to include department store chains as well as its grocery stores. In a move that threatened to break Wakefern SGC broke away from the co-op and its stores were renamed Pathmark.

Wakefern not only weathered the storm it grew under the direction of chairman and CEO Thomas Infusino elected shortly after the split. The co-op focused on asserting its position as a seller of low-priced products. Wakefern developed private-label brands including the ShopRite brand. In the 1980s members began operating larger stores and adding more nonfood items to the ShopRite product mix. With its number of superstores on the rise and facing increased competition from club stores in 1992 Wakefern opened a centralized nonfood distribution center in New Jersey.

In 1995 30-year Wakefern veteran Dean Janeway was elected president of the co-op. The company debuted its ShopRite MasterCard co-branded with New Jersey's Valley National Bank in 1996. The following year the co-op purchased two of its customers' stores in Pennsylvania then threatened to close them when contract talks with the local union deteriorated. In 1998 Wakefern settled the dispute then sold the stores.

The company partnered with Internet bidding site priceline.com in 1999 offering customers an opportunity to bid on groceries and then pick them up at ShopRite stores. Big V Wakefern's biggest customer filed for Chapter 11 bankruptcy protection in 2000 and said it was ending its distribution agreement with the co-op. In July 2002 however Wakefern's ShopRite Supermarkets subsidiary acquired all of Big V's assets for approximately $185 million in cash and assumed liabilities.

Infusino retired in May 2005 after 35 years with Wakefern Food. He was succeeded by former vice chairman Joseph Colalillo. The cooperative added to its footprint in 2007 when it acquired about 10 underperforming retail locations from Stop & Shop. The stores located mostly in South Jersey were rebranded under the ShopRite banner.

EXECUTIVES

President and COO, Dean Janeway
President and COO, Joseph Sheridan
SVP, Natan Tabak
CFO, Douglas (Doug) Wille
SVP, Frank Rostan
VP Consumer and Corporate Communications, Karen Meleta
VP Strategic Development and Member Relations, William (Bill) Crombie
VP E-Commerce, Cheryl Williams
Chairman and CEO, Joseph S. (Joe) Colalillo, age 51
VP Logistics, Peter (Pete) Rolandelli
VP Information Services Division, Alan Aront
SVP Marketing, Jeff Reagan
SVP Perishables, Bill Mayo
VP Human Resources, Ann Marie Burke

SVP Non-Perishables, Chris Lane
Corporate Communications and Media Relations
 Specialist, Jeannette Castaneda
VP Quality Assurance, Mike Ambrosio
President PriceRite, Neil Duffy
President ShopRite Supermarkets Inc., David
 Figurelli

LOCATIONS

HQ: Wakefern Food Corp.
 5000 Riverside Dr., Keasbey NJ 08832
Phone: 908-527-3300   Fax: 908-527-3397
Web: www.wakefern.com

COMPETITORS

A&P	Krasdale Foods
Acme Markets	Nash-Finch
Associated Wholesalers	Pathmark Stores
Bozzuto' s	Stop & Shop
C&S Wholesale	SUPERVALU
CVS Caremark	Wal-Mart
Hannaford Bros.	Wawa Inc.
IGA	White Rose

HISTORICAL FINANCIALS
Company Type: Private - Cooperative

Income Statement
FYE: October 1

	REVENUE ($ mil.)	NET INCOME ($ mil.)	NET PROFIT MARGIN	EMPLOYEES
10/11*	10,325	5	0.0%	3,500
09/08	8,396	6	0.1%	0
09/07	7,846	5	0.1%	0
09/06	1,340,014	0	—	0
Annual Growth	—	146.2%	—	—

*Fiscal year change

2011 Year-End Financials
Debt ratio: ——
Return on equity: —
Cash ($ mil.): 124
Current ratio: 0.40
Long-term debt ($ mil.): —

Dividends
 Yield: —
 Payout: —
 Market value ($ mil.): —

WALKER COUNTY BOARD OF EDUCATION

LOCATIONS

HQ: WALKER COUNTY BOARD OF EDUCATION
 201 S DUKE ST, LA FAYETTE, GA 30728-3518
Phone: 706-638-1240
Web: www.lafayettehigh.org

WALSH CONSTRUCTION COMPANY

LOCATIONS

HQ: WALSH CONSTRUCTION COMPANY
 929 W ADAMS ST, CHICAGO, IL 60607-3037
Phone: 312-563-5400
Web: www.walshgroup.com

HISTORICAL FINANCIALS
Company Type: Private

Income Statement
FYE: December 31

	REVENUE ($ mil.)	NET INCOME ($ mil.)	NET PROFIT MARGIN	EMPLOYEES
12/11	1,697	28	1.7%	3,000
12/10	1,627	35	2.2%	0
12/09	1,711	56	3.3%	0
12/08	1,847	68	3.7%	0
Annual Growth	(2.8%)	(25.2%)	—	—

2011 Year-End Financials
Debt ratio: ——
Return on equity: 1.70%
Cash ($ mil.): 42
Current ratio: 0.90
Long-term debt ($ mil.): —

Dividends
 Yield: —
 Payout: —
 Market value ($ mil.): —

WALTERS WHOLESALE ELECTRIC CO.

Walters Wholesale Electric keeps its customers calm cool and connected. The family-owned company distributes a variety of products including electrical ballasts and transformers wire and cable conduit and fans and heaters. As part of its business it also distributes lamps lighting systems sensors and AC/DC motors. Founded in 1953 by Lester Walter (father of CEO John Walter) the

namesake company serves the construction industry from some 25 strategically located offices across Southern California. Walters Wholesale Electric also runs a distribution center in Brea California. It serves customers in a timely manner thanks to its fleet of about 60 trucks.

Geographic Reach

From its headquarters in Signal Hill California Walters Wholesale Electric operates more than 25 locations throughout Southern California. To support its business the company boasts a 170000-sq.-ft. central distribution center and Commercial Lighting Division in Brea California.

Operations

Specialty divisions operating under the Walters Wholesale Electric umbrella sell low voltage industrial automation and energy efficient products for use in residential construction and roadway and street lighting projects. Each of the company's branches benefits from Walters Wholesale Electric's central billing and warehouse so that customers can pick up products closest to their job site.

EXECUTIVES

President of the company, John Walter
President, Bill Durkee
EVP Purchasing, Jimmy Johnson
VP Sales, Dick Benbow
VP Credit, Denis Evert
CFO, Roland Wood
Director IT, Kirk Woloshyn
Human Resources, Irene Iannitti
Director Purchasing Central Distribution Center,
 Jay Melfi
Manager Cerritos CA, Garen Jahn
Manager Compton CA, Gene Grabast
Manager Costa Mesa CA, Andy Salz
Manager Fullerton CA, Dave Frommelt
Manager Los Angeles, Lee Kornegay
Manager Lake Forest CA, Chris Peters
Manager Long Beach CA, Van Van Doren
Manager Pasadena CA, Bill Brock
Manager Rancho Cucamonga CA, Cookie Chagolla
Manager Riverside CA, Bob Hicks
Manager San Dimas CA, Tom Enochs
Manager Santa Ana CA, Phil Bradley
Manager Santa Fe Springs CA, Brian Guley
Manager Torrance CA, Bruce Flint
Manager Victorville CA, Don Reeder
Manager Westminster CA, Tom Kimmerle
Manager Industrial Energy Automation Group
 and Manager Vernon CA, Glenn Kriske
Manager Residential Housing Products, Ron Czar
General Manager Telecomm and Security, Tom
 Baldwin
Sales Manager Low Voltage Division, Israel Lopez
Manager Housing Construction Division, Steve
 Davis
Manager Roadway and Street Lighting Division,
 Ryan Thibault
Manager Sun Valley CA, Kevin Cox
Manager Vista CA, Jeff Sims
Operations Manager Central Distribution Center,
 Ron Byrd
Marketing Manager Low Voltage Division, Tom
 Fessler
Manager Corona CA, Eric Peters
Manager San Diego, John Jordan
General Manager Low Voltage Division, Wayne
 Brushett
Manager Anaheim CA, Kevin Evert
Manager Canoga Park CA, Vince Lopez
Manager Culver City CA, Russell Lawrence

HISTORICAL FINANCIALS
Company Type: Private

Income Statement
FYE: June 30

	REVENUE ($ mil.)	NET INCOME ($ mil.)	NET PROFIT MARGIN	EMPLOYEES
06/11	97	0	0.1%	1,500
06/10	39	7	19.6%	0
06/09	39	7	19.6%	0
06/08	94	(1)	—	0
Annual Growth	0.9%	—	—	—

2011 Year-End Financials
Debt ratio: ——
Return on equity: 0.10%
Cash ($ mil.): 33
Current ratio: —
Long-term debt ($ mil.): —

Dividends
 Yield: —
 Payout: —
 Market value ($ mil.): —

LOCATIONS

HQ: Walters Wholesale Electric Co.
2825 Temple Ave., Signal Hill CA 90755
Phone: 562-988-3100 **Fax:** 562-988-3150
Web: www.walterswholesale.com

PRODUCTS/OPERATIONS

Selected Products

Energy management
Industrial automation
Lighting and controls
Low voltage
Residential/commercial lighting
Roadway and street lighting
Tools division

COMPETITORS

Bay City Electric Works	Consolidated Electrical
Beacon Electric Supply	Independent Electric Supply
Central Wholesale Electrical	OneSource Distributors

HISTORICAL FINANCIALS

Company Type: Private

Income Statement

FYE: March 31

	REVENUE ($ mil.)	NET INCOME ($ mil.)	NET PROFIT MARGIN	EMPLOYEES
03/11	246	0	—	475
03/10	0	0	—	0
03/09	0	0	—	0
03/08	0	0	—	0
Annual Growth	—	—	—	—

2011 Year-End Financials

Debt ratio: ——
Return on equity: —
Cash ($ mil.): 8
Current ratio: 1.60
Long-term debt ($ mil.): —

Dividends
Yield: —
Payout: —
Market value ($ mil.): —

WALTHALL OIL COMPANY

LOCATIONS

HQ: WALTHALL OIL COMPANY
2510 ALLEN RD, MACON, GA 31216-6397
Phone: 478-781-1234
Web: www.walthall-oil.com

HISTORICAL FINANCIALS

Company Type: Private

Income Statement

FYE: September 30

	REVENUE ($ mil.)	NET INCOME ($ mil.)	NET PROFIT MARGIN	EMPLOYEES
09/11	177	0	0.3%	130
09/10	141	0	0.3%	0
09/09	117	0	0.5%	0
09/08	199	0	0.1%	0
Annual Growth	(3.9%)	43.9%	—	—

2011 Year-End Financials

Debt ratio: ——
Return on equity: 0.30%
Cash ($ mil.): 0
Current ratio: 0.10
Long-term debt ($ mil.): —

Dividends
Yield: —
Payout: —
Market value ($ mil.): —

WALTON & POST INC.

Walton & Post is a wholesale distributor of food and related products that serves retail and whole-sale customers. The company supplies such products as canned and packaged goods fresh fruit and produce and ethnic food items as well as candies chocolates health and beauty products and paper goods. It primarily serves customers in the southeastern US. Part of Miami-based Garrido Group Walton & Post is one of several distribution businesses owned by the Garrido family.

EXECUTIVES

Chairman, Jose A. Garrido Sr.
President and CEO, Jose A. Garrido Jr.
VP Sales, Carlos J. Diaz
President, Alfredo Cuadrado
President, Jose Filipe Cos
Senior Accountant, Esteban Falero
Manager Information Systems and Operations, Luis M. Perez
Manager Purchasing, Enrique Cos

LOCATIONS

HQ: Walton & Post Inc.
8105 NW 77th St., Miami FL 33166
Phone: 305-591-1111 **Fax:** 305-593-7070
Web: www.waltonpost.com

COMPETITORS

Alex Lee	GSC Enterprises
C&S Wholesale	SUPERVALU

HISTORICAL FINANCIALS

Company Type: Private

Income Statement

FYE: December 31

	REVENUE ($ mil.)	NET INCOME ($ mil.)	NET PROFIT MARGIN	EMPLOYEES
12/11	51	1	2.0%	75
12/10	39	1	2.5%	0
12/09	38	0	0.4%	0
12/08	36	0	1.0%	0
Annual Growth	12.5%	39.8%	—	—

2011 Year-End Financials

Debt ratio: ——
Return on equity: 2.00%
Cash ($ mil.): 1
Current ratio: 0.60
Long-term debt ($ mil.): —

Dividends
Yield: —
Payout: —
Market value ($ mil.): —

WARD TRANSPORT & LOGISTICS CORP.

LOCATIONS

HQ: WARD TRANSPORT & LOGISTICS CORP.
1436 WARD TRUCKING DR, ALTOONA, PA 16602-7110
Phone: 814-944-0803

HISTORICAL FINANCIALS

Company Type: Private

Income Statement

FYE: December 31

	REVENUE ($ mil.)	NET INCOME ($ mil.)	NET PROFIT MARGIN	EMPLOYEES
12/11	150	10	7.2%	2
12/10	137	0	0.7%	0
12/09	125	1	0.8%	0
Annual Growth	9.6%	228.0%	—	—

2011 Year-End Financials

Debt ratio: ——
Return on equity: 7.20%
Cash ($ mil.): 10
Current ratio: 1.10
Long-term debt ($ mil.): —

Dividends
Yield: —
Payout: —
Market value ($ mil.): —

WARD TRUCKING LLC

Less-than-truckload (LTL) carrier Ward Trucking operates primarily in the northeastern and mid-Atlantic US. (LTL carriers consolidate freight from multiple shippers into a single truckload.) In addition to its LTL business the company offers full truckload and logistics services through the Ward Transport & Logistics brand name. Ward Trucking operates a fleet of about 450 tractors 60 trucks and 1180 trailers from a network of terminals stretching from New York to Illinois. William W. Ward founded the company in 1931 to haul freight from central Pennsylvania to New York City. Ward Trucking is run by members of the Ward family.

EXECUTIVES

Chairman, G. William Ward
EVP CFO and General Counsel, Glynn Stewart
Director Management Information Systems, Michael (Mike) Zupon
President and CEO, Bill T. Ward
President Truckload Express, Tim Ward
Director Sales West Region LTL, Tom Reger
Director Sales East Region LTL, Jeff Heiselmeyer
Manager Service Center Scranton and Newburgh, George Abraham
Regional Sales Manager National Accounts Baltimore, Joe Bontz
Manager Customer Service, Maggie McCulloch
Director Pricing, Joe Colapietro
Director Risk Management, Dan Dillen
VP Asset Management, Gregory (Greg) Confer
VP LTL, Rick Fleischer
Manager Service Center Altoona, Mike Euker
Personnel Coordinator, Christine Beck
Manager Operations Allentown, Ken Humma

Dispatcher Allentown, John Billiard
National Accounts Allentown, Kevin Ryczak
Territory Sales Manager Altoona, Kevin Roesch
Manager Service Center Erie and Youngstown,
Ken Hollen
Territory Sales Manager Erie and Youngstown,
Dick Morelli
Territory Sales Manager Erie and Youngstown,
Tony M. Liberatore
Manager Operations Harrisburg, Jim Savard
Dispatcher Harrisburg, Paul Kamarer
Territory Sales Manager Harrisburg, Joe Dominick
Territory Sales Manager Harrisburg, Bill Swingler
Territory Sales Manager Harrisburg, Janet
Leinbach
Manager Service Center Milton, Tim Diehl
Territory Sales Manager Milton, Dave Sabotchick
Territory Sales Manager Philadelphia, Ed R. Gaudio
Territory Sales Manager Philadelphia, Mike
Johnson
Territory Sales Manager Philadelphia, Brian
Kratzer
Manager Service Center Pittsburgh, Ed Slater
Territory Sales Manager Pittsburgh, John
Strenkowski
Territory Sales Manager Pittsburgh, Greg Hrebinko
Territory Sales Manager Pittsburgh, Ray Passieu
Territory Sales Manager Scranton, Bob M. Wolfel
Operations Supervisor Cincinnati, Tim Dunn
Territory Sales Manager Cincinnati, Barbara Gilbert
Territory Sales Manager Cleveland, Bob Kane
Manager Service Center Cleveland, Rick Kraft
Dispatcher Cleveland, Jeff Gosser
Territory Sales Manager Cleveland, Charlie Harris
Territory Sales Manager Cleveland, Debbie Wright
Territory Sales Manager Columbus, Jason E. Leeds
Director Financial Administration, Mark Fusco
Director Human Resources, Bob Casti
Director Operations East Region LTL, John Bates
Regional Operations Manager Baltimore and
Director Operations Southern Region LTL, Mike
Aljets
Director National Accounts LTL, Jeff Shurock
VP Logistics, Dan Schultz
Territory Sales Manager Allentown, Michael Aiello
Territory Sales Manager Philadelphia, Joe Latch
Territory Sales Manager Allentown, Mike
Finnerman
Territory Sales Manager Baltimore, Cathy OKane
Territory Sales Manager Baltimore, Carroll
Cauthorn
Manager Service Center Charlotte, Doug Newton
Dispatcher Charlotte, Ken Ramseur
Territory Sales Manager Charlotte, Lori Adam
Operations Supervisor Raleigh/Durham, Calvin
Slaughter
Territory Sales Manager Richmond, Steve Oates
Manager Service Center Allentown, Peter Zekas
Territory Sales Manager Allentown, Greg McNichol
Manager Service Center Harrisburg, Charles
Dunlap
Manager Operations Scranton, Brian Windwalker
Territory Sales Manager Scranton, Kim Phillips
Territory Sales Manager Cincinnati, Nathan Deaton
Territory Sales Manager Columbus, Jacob
Hardbarger
Manager Service Center Buffalo, Pete Chenier
Territory Sales Manager Buffalo, Jerry Norcia
Territory Sales Manager Buffalo, Mike Pandolfi
Manager Operations Newburgh, Chris Kane
Territory Sales Manager Newburgh, Brian Socci
Territory Sales Manager Newburgh, Joseph Fagan
Territory Sales Manager Charlotte, Laurie
Carpenter
Manager Service Center and Territory Sales
Manager Raleigh/Durham, Bryan Horvath
Manager Service Center Winchester, Chip Sirbaugh

Territory Sales Manager Winchester, Ray Martin
SVP Sales and Marketing, Jeff Groenke
Manager Safety, Jeffrey Kovacik

LOCATIONS
HQ: Ward Trucking LLC
1436 Ward Trucking Dr. Ward Tower, Altoona PA
16603
Phone: 814-944-0803   **Fax:** 814-944-5470
Web: www.wardtrucking.com

COMPETITORS

Con-way Freight   Pitt Ohio Express
Estes Express   Schneider National
J.B. Hunt   UPS Freight
NEMF   YRC Worldwide
Old Dominion Freight

HISTORICAL FINANCIALS
Company Type: Private

Income Statement

	REVENUE ($ mil.)	NET INCOME ($ mil.)	NET PROFIT MARGIN	EMPLOYEES
12/11	150	10	7.2%	1,057
12/10	137	0	0.7%	0
12/09	125	1	0.8%	0
12/08	166	(4)	—	0
Annual Growth	(3.4%)	—	—	—

FYE: December 31

2011 Year-End Financials

Debt ratio: —
Return on equity: 7.20%   Dividends
Cash ($ mil.): 10   Yield: —
Current ratio: 1.10   Payout: —
Long-term debt ($ mil.): —   Market value ($ mil.): —

WARING OIL COMPANY LLC

LOCATIONS
HQ: WARING OIL COMPANY LLC
431 PORT TERMINAL CIR, VICKSBURG, MS
39183-9070
Phone: 601-636-1065
Web: www.waringoil.com

HISTORICAL FINANCIALS
Company Type: Private

Income Statement

	REVENUE ($ mil.)	NET INCOME ($ mil.)	NET PROFIT MARGIN	EMPLOYEES
12/11	250	3	1.3%	46
12/02	167	1	1.1%	0
12/01	162	1	0.7%	0
12/00	167	1	0.6%	0
Annual Growth	14.4%	43.9%	—	—

FYE: December 31

2011 Year-End Financials

Debt ratio: —
Return on equity: 1.30%   Dividends
Cash ($ mil.): 2   Yield: —
Current ratio: 1.30   Payout: —
Long-term debt ($ mil.): —   Market value ($ mil.): —

WARREN DISTRIBUTION INC.

LOCATIONS
HQ: WARREN DISTRIBUTION INC.
727 S 13TH ST, OMAHA, NE 68102-3204
Phone: 402-341-9397
Web: www.wd-wpp.com

HISTORICAL FINANCIALS
Company Type: Private

Income Statement

	REVENUE ($ mil.)	NET INCOME ($ mil.)	NET PROFIT MARGIN	EMPLOYEES
02/12	470	5	1.1%	300
02/11	378	11	3.1%	0
02/10	315	13	4.2%	0
02/09	309	3	1.0%	0
Annual Growth	15.0%	21.4%	—	—

FYE: February 25

2012 Year-End Financials

Debt ratio: —
Return on equity: 1.10%   Dividends
Cash ($ mil.): 0   Yield: —
Current ratio: 1.40   Payout: —
Long-term debt ($ mil.): —   Market value ($ mil.): —

WASHINGTON & JEFFERSON COLLEGE

LOCATIONS
HQ: WASHINGTON & JEFFERSON COLLEGE
60 S LINCOLN ST, WASHINGTON, PA 15301-4812
Phone: 724-222-4400
Web: www.washjeff.edu

HISTORICAL FINANCIALS
Company Type: Private

Income Statement

	REVENUE ($ mil.)	NET INCOME ($ mil.)	NET PROFIT MARGIN	EMPLOYEES
06/11	87	15	17.2%	300
06/10	72	2	3.6%	0
06/09	73	0	—	0
06/08	71	8	12.5%	0
Annual Growth	6.9%	19.0%	—	—

FYE: June 30

WASHINGTON COLLEGE

LOCATIONS

HQ: WASHINGTON COLLEGE
300 WASHINGTON AVE, CHESTERTOWN, MD
21620-1197
Phone: 410-778-2800
Web: www.lax-camps.com

HISTORICAL FINANCIALS

Company Type: Private

Income Statement

FYE: June 30

	REVENUE ($ mil.)	NET INCOME ($ mil.)	NET PROFIT MARGIN	EMPLOYEES
06/11	82	6	7.8%	450
06/10	79	10	13.0%	0
06/09	63	0	—	0
06/08	62	9	15.6%	0
Annual Growth	9.7%	(13.1%)	—	—

2011 Year-End Financials

Debt ratio: ——
Return on equity: 7.80%
Cash ($ mil.): 23
Current ratio: ——
Long-term debt ($ mil.): ——

Dividends
Yield: —
Payout: —
Market value ($ mil.): —

WASHINGTON HEALTHCARE MARY

Health care is Mary Washington Healthcare's realm in the Old Dominion State. The medical provider offers a comprehensive range of health services to residents of Fredericksburg and surrounding communities in central Virginia through its not-for-profit regional system of two hospitals and 28 healthcare facilities. The hub of this system is Mary Washington Hospital a 400-bed acute care medical center that provides services including emergency/trauma care and surgical procedures. The health system also includes outpatient care programs and facilities providing primary care and specialty care services for women seniors and children.

Operations

Other facilities provide hospice care and behavioral health services that include inpatient psychiatric care. Its Homecare America segment is a full-service unit providing home health care products and training. Mary Washington Healthcare also owns 14 specialty practices.

Geographic Reach

The company serves patients in Fredericksburg and surrounding communities in central Virginia.

Strategy

Expanding its network to meet growing demand in 2013 Mary Washington Healthcare purchased Reese Medical Associates (its third primary care practice). The company also owns Ladysmith Medical Center and the Medical Center of Stafford on Garrisonville Road.

Company Background

In an attempt to reduce overcrowding at its Mary Washington Hospital the health system opened a 100-bed full service hospital in 2009 called Stafford Hospital Center. The hospital features all private inpatient rooms a full service emergency department a dedicated birthing unit inpatient and outpatient surgery and a comprehensive range of advanced diagnostic capabilities including MRI and CT scan.

EXECUTIVES

President CEO and Director, Fred M. Rankin III
EVP and COO, Walter J. Kiwall
VP Information Services, Stephen S. Cooley
EVP and Chief Medical Officer, Tom Ryan
Director Marketing and Public Relations, Kathleen Allenbaugh
EVP Human Resources and Organizational Development, Kathy Wall
EVP and CFO, Sean Barden
Chairman, Joseph R. Wilson
Vice Chairman, Homer L. Hite
Secretary/Treasurer and Director, Donald H. Newlin
SVP and Chief Nursing Officer, Barbara A. Kane
Director Corporate and Community Services, Edd Houck
Administrator and SVP Operations Mary Washington Hospital, Kevin Van Renan
VP Nursing, Eileen Dohmann
VP Support Services, Sam Miller
VP Financial Operations and General Accounting, Ravi Mathur
VP Quality and Patient Safety, Amy Adome
VP Regulatory Affairs and Risk Management, Jina Haikey
VP Properties and Ambulatory Services, Marie Frederick
VP Clinical Support, Marianna Bedway
VP Medical Affairs, Jamie Gerbosky
EVP Community Affairs; President MWH Foundation, Xavier Richardson
Administrator Stafford Hospital Center, Cathy Yablonski
Director, John M. (Jack) Albertine, age 67
President CEO and Director, Fred M. Rankin III
Director, Patrick McManus
Director, James A. Lewis
Director, Jane R. Ingalls
Vice Chairman, Homer L. Hite
Director, Rev Allen H. Fisher Jr.
Director, John F. Fick III
Director, Peter O. Carey
Director, John D. Burrow
Director, Daniel M. Hoffman
Director, Michael P. McDermott
Secretary/Treasurer and Director, Donald H. Newlin
Director, Raymond L. Slaughter
Director, Jonathan D. Wallace
Director, Cindy S. Marrow
Director, Richard C. Earnhardt

LOCATIONS

HQ: Mary Washington Healthcare Incorporated
2300 Fall Hill Ave. Ste. 308, Fredericksburg VA 22401
Phone: 540-741-1100   **Fax:** 317-803-4251
Web: www.aprimo.com

PRODUCTS/OPERATIONS

Selected Operations

Cancer Center of Virginia
Carriage Hill Rehabilitation and Nursing Center
Diabetes Management - MWH
The Family Health Center at North Stafford
Fredericksburg Ambulatory Surgery Center Inc. (FASC)
Homecare America
Imaging Center for Women
Kids' Station
Ladysmith Medical Center
Mary Washington Hospice
Mary Washington Hospital
Mary Washington Hospital Foundation
Mary Washington Hospital Home Health
Mary Washington Thrift Shoppe to benefit Mary Washington Hospital
MediCorp Medical Center
MWH Auxiliary Regional Mobile Health Clinic
MWH Community Services Fund
MWH Outreach Laboratories
Medical Arts Pharmacy
Medical Center of Stafford
Medical Imaging of Fredericksburg
Medical Imaging at Lee's Hill
MediCorp Health Link
Mobile Mammography
Psychiatric Associates
Rappahannock Wound Healing Center
Rehabilitation Services of Fredericksburg
Rehabilitation Services of Lee's Hill
Rehabilitation Services of North Stafford
School of Radiologic Technology
Senior Care Services
Sleep Disorders Center
Snowden Academy (mental health)
Snowden at Fredericksburg (mental health)
Stafford Hospital

COMPETITORS

Bon Secours Health	Inova
Centra Health Inc.	Martha Jefferson
Civista Health	Hospital
Dimensions Healthcare	MedStar Health
Fauquier Hospital	Prince William Health
Georgetown University	System
Hospital	University of Virginia
HCA Capital Division	Health System

HISTORICAL FINANCIALS

Company Type: Private - Not-for-Profit

Income Statement

FYE: September 30

	REVENUE ($ mil.)	NET INCOME ($ mil.)	NET PROFIT MARGIN	EMPLOYEES
09/12*	435	(2)	—	4,000
03/12	154	6	4.5%	0
03/11	174	6	3.8%	0
12/10	712	16	2.3%	0
Annual Growth	(15.1%)	—	—	—

*Fiscal year change

2012 Year-End Financials

Debt ratio: ——
Return on equity: (-0.70)%
Cash ($ mil.): 49
Current ratio: 2.40
Long-term debt ($ mil.): ——

Dividends
Yield: —
Payout: —
Market value ($ mil.): —

WASHTENAW INTERMEDIATE SCHOOL DISTRICT

LOCATIONS

HQ: WASHTENAW INTERMEDIATE SCHOOL DISTRICT
1819 S WAGNER RD, ANN ARBOR, MI 48103-9715
Phone: 734-994-8100

HISTORICAL FINANCIALS
Company Type: Private

Income Statement
FYE: June 30

	REVENUE ($ mil.)	NET INCOME ($ mil.)	NET PROFIT MARGIN	EMPLOYEES
06/12	98	(3)	—	200
06/11	95	(0)	—	0
06/10	88	(4)	—	0
06/09	87	0	0.7%	0
Annual Growth	4.1%	—	—	—

2012 Year-End Financials
Debt ratio: ——
Return on equity: (-3.10)%
Cash ($ mil.): 39
Current ratio: —
Long-term debt ($ mil.): —

Dividends
Yield: —
Payout: —
Market value ($ mil.): —

WATERTOWN COOPERATIVE ELEVATOR ASSOCIATION

LOCATIONS

HQ: WATERTOWN COOPERATIVE ELEVATOR ASSOCIATION
811 BURLINGTON NORTHERN D, WATERTOWN, SD 57201-4159
Phone: 605-886-3039
Web: www.watertowncoop.com

HISTORICAL FINANCIALS
Company Type: Private

Income Statement
FYE: December 31

	REVENUE ($ mil.)	NET INCOME ($ mil.)	NET PROFIT MARGIN	EMPLOYEES
12/11	134	3	2.7%	45
12/10	88	3	4.2%	0
12/09	85	3	4.7%	0
12/07	54	0	1.4%	0
Annual Growth	35.5%	67.8%	—	—

2011 Year-End Financials
Debt ratio: ——
Return on equity: 2.70%
Cash ($ mil.): 0
Current ratio: 0.10
Long-term debt ($ mil.): —

Dividends
Yield: —
Payout: —
Market value ($ mil.): —

WATONWAN FARM SERVICE INC

Watonwan Farm Service which does business as WFS helps out its south central Minnesota and north central Iowa member-farmers with complete farm-management services and products. Offering marketing opportunities financial services and farming supplies such as chemicals fertilizers livestock feed petroleum products and seed the agricultural cooperative serves more than 4000 producers from its 22 locations. The primary crops of its members include corn soybean and specialty canning crops; most of its livestock farmers raise hogs and cattle. The co-op was called the Consumers Cooperative Oil Company of St. James when it was founded in 1937.

EXECUTIVES
CFO, Bill Day
Manager Energy Division, Randy Cole
Manager Feed Division, Jerry Svoboda
Agronomy and Grain Operations Manager, Mike Minnehan
Director Human Resources, Dawn Abel
Vice Chairman, Doug Kuhlman
CEO, Todd Ludwig
Director Marketing and Communications, Jo Anne Gumto
Manager Grain Division, Craig Kilian
Chairman, Ken Klug
Director, Harold Wolle Jr.
Director, Tom Blackstad
Director, Jim Fisher
Vice Chairman, Doug Kuhlman
Director, Neil Schlaak
Director, Danny Rynearson
Director, Tom Winch

LOCATIONS
HQ: Watonwan Farm Service Co.
233 W. Ciro St., Truman MN 56088
Phone: 507-776-2831   **Fax:** 507-776-2871
Web: www.wfsag.com

COMPETITORS
ADM	Gold-Eagle Cooperative
Ag Processing Inc.	Heartland Co-op
Cargill	Minn-Dak Co-op
CHS	NEW Cooperative
Farm Service Cooperative	United Farmers Cooperative
Farmers Cooperative Society	

HISTORICAL FINANCIALS
Company Type: Private - Cooperative

Income Statement
FYE: July 31

	REVENUE ($ mil.)	NET INCOME ($ mil.)	NET PROFIT MARGIN	EMPLOYEES
07/12	592	6	1.1%	255
07/11	534	7	1.3%	0
07/10	366	9	2.5%	0
07/09	484	11	2.4%	0
Annual Growth	7.0%	(17.2%)	—	—

2012 Year-End Financials
Debt ratio: ——
Return on equity: 1.10%
Cash ($ mil.): 3
Current ratio: 0.10
Long-term debt ($ mil.): —

Dividends
Yield: —
Payout: —
Market value ($ mil.): —

WATTS PETROLEUM CORPORATION

LOCATIONS

HQ: WATTS PETROLEUM CORPORATION
1505 RUTHERFORD ST, LYNCHBURG, VA 24501-3826
Phone: 434-846-6509

HISTORICAL FINANCIALS
Company Type: Private

Income Statement
FYE: December 31

	REVENUE ($ mil.)	NET INCOME ($ mil.)	NET PROFIT MARGIN	EMPLOYEES
12/11	84	0	0.4%	38
12/10	68	0	1.0%	0
12/09	58	0	1.4%	0
12/07	66	(0)	—	0
Annual Growth	8.6%	—	—	—

2011 Year-End Financials
Debt ratio: ——
Return on equity: 0.40%
Cash ($ mil.): 0
Current ratio: 1.00
Long-term debt ($ mil.): —

Dividends
Yield: —
Payout: —
Market value ($ mil.): —

WAUKESHA SCHOOL DISTRICT

LOCATIONS

HQ: WAUKESHA SCHOOL DISTRICT
222 MAPLE AVE, WAUKESHA, WI 53186-4725
Phone: 262-970-1038
Web: www.roseglenelementary.com

HISTORICAL FINANCIALS

Company Type: Private

Income Statement

FYE: June 30

	REVENUE ($ mil.)	NET INCOME ($ mil.)	NET PROFIT MARGIN	EMPLOYEES
06/11	167	(0)	—	1,500
06/10	134	(1)	—	0
06/08	153	3	2.5%	0
06/07	148	0	0.3%	0
Annual Growth	4.3%	—	—	—

2011 Year-End Financials

Debt ratio: —
Return on equity: (-0.10)%
Cash ($ mil.): 33
Current ratio: 0.80
Long-term debt ($ mil.): —

Dividends
Yield: —
Payout: —
Market value ($ mil.): —

WAUKESHA-PEARCE INDUSTRIES INC.

Waukesha-Pearce Industries (WPI) wants its customers to start their engines. Through its Engine Division the company designs and packages engine-driven equipment such as power generators pumps blowers control panels and switchgear. WPI also offers a slate of heavy construction and mining products including earth movers and demolition equipment made by such OEMs as Komatsu and Gradall Industries through its Construction Machinery Division. As part of its business the company sells used equipment and leases heavy earth-moving equipment. Founded as Portable Rotary Rig Co. in 1924 by Louis M. Pearce Sr. the company is owned and run by the Pearce family.

Geographic Reach

From its headquarters in Houston WPI serves customers through more than a dozen locations in Texas and another dozen across Louisiana Oklahoma New Mexico Arkansas Alabama Kansas California and Pennsylvania. The company's training facility is located in Sugar Land Texas outside Houston.

Operations

WPI's engine equipment lineup includes its own Enginator used in field gas compression and power generation. Its Engine Division further supports WPI's performance by offering less economy-driven services such as certified remanufactured engines and revamping.

WPI's Construction Machinery arm benefits from a broad products portfolio paired with distributor affiliations. Such alliances include Bomag (compaction equipment) Allied/Rammer (demolition equipment) Esco Crushing (wearparts) Sennebogen (material handling) and Valmet (cranes). Like the Engine Division it is able to mitigate the recession's impact on capital equipment sales by providing repair and onsite maintenance services along with a multi-million-dollar inventory of used and rental equipment and parts.

Strategy

WPI in 2011 extended the reach of its territory from seven to 30 states through its affiliation with behemoth GE. When GE acquired Dresser that year GE reviewed the North American distributors for the Waukesha line of gas compression engines

and subsequently named WPI one of two distributors in North America and significantly boosting its sales territory.

Sales and Marketing

Core markets for WPI include land clearing highway and heavy construction site development mining scrap petrochemical energy exploration and utility construction as well as a number of government agencies.

Company Ownership

WPI is owned and operated by the founding Pearce family.

EXECUTIVES

CEO Pearce Industries Inc., Gary M. Pearce
Secretary and Treasurer, Richard E. Bean, age 68
President, Louis M. Pearce III
Chairman Pearce Industries Inc., Louis M. Pearce Jr.
VP Operations Engine Division, Robert Lyde
VP Operations Construction Machinery Division, Michael (Mike) Green
Director Sales Construction Machine Division, David Stange
Director Human Resources, Scott McKenzie
Director Product Support Branch Operations Engine Division, Ronnie Patterson
CFO, Albert H. Bentley
Director Information Systems, Louis T. Holden

LOCATIONS

HQ: Waukesha-Pearce Industries Inc.
12320 S. Main St., Houston TX 77235-5068
Phone: 713-723-1050 **Fax:** 713-551-0454
Web: www.wpi.com

PRODUCTS/OPERATIONS

Selected Services

Earth moving
Gas compression
Mining
Power generation
Recycling
Service and replacement parts
Small engine and lawn

Selected Products

Engines
  Arrow VR engines
  BOB-CAT mowers
  Dresser Waukesha
  Generac Industrial
  Generac Residential
  HIPOWER generating sets
  Kohler engines
  Little Wonder products
  Mantis yard & garden products
  Powerhouse catalytic converters
  Remanufactured engines
  Revamp services
  Ryan turf renovation products
  WPI brand
Construction Machinery
  Allied/Rammer
  Bomag
  Bucyrus Blades
  Cummins Engines
  Dressta
  Esco
  Fleetguard Filters
  Gradall
  Hensley
  JRB
  Komatsu
  LaBounty
  Sennebogen
  Valmet

COMPETITORS

AGCO	Deere
Berry Companies	Dewey Electronics
Caterpillar	Emerson Electric
CNH Global	Kubota
Connell Company	
Cummins Power Generation	

HISTORICAL FINANCIALS

Company Type: Private

Income Statement

FYE: March 31

	REVENUE ($ mil.)	NET INCOME ($ mil.)	NET PROFIT MARGIN	EMPLOYEES
03/11	248	4	1.9%	600
03/10	197	1	0.8%	0
03/03	183	(2)	—	0
03/02	187	0	—	0
Annual Growth	9.9%	—	—	—

2011 Year-End Financials

Debt ratio: —
Return on equity: 1.90%
Cash ($ mil.): 0
Current ratio: —
Long-term debt ($ mil.): —

Dividends
Yield: —
Payout: —
Market value ($ mil.): —

WAUWATOSA SCHOOL DISTRICT

LOCATIONS

HQ: WAUWATOSA SCHOOL DISTRICT
12121 W NORTH AVE, WAUWATOSA, WI 53226-2096
Phone: 414-773-1050
Web: www.wauwatosaschools.com

HISTORICAL FINANCIALS

Company Type: Private

Income Statement

FYE: June 30

	REVENUE ($ mil.)	NET INCOME ($ mil.)	NET PROFIT MARGIN	EMPLOYEES
06/12	82	2	3.2%	830
06/11	88	1	2.0%	0
06/10*	83	1	1.3%	0
07/09	0	0	6.0%	0
Annual Growth	1345.0%	1074.9%	—	—

*Fiscal year change

WAYLAND BAPTIST UNIVERSITY INC

You gotta have faith to attend Wayland Baptist University. The private co-educational Baptist institution offers more than 40 undergraduate majors about a dozen pre-professional programs and graduate programs in fields such as business administration Christian ministry counseling education management public administration religion and science. It has an enrollment of approximately 7000 students at some 15 campuses in Alaska Arizona Hawaii New Mexico Oklahoma and Texas as well as Kenya. The university was founded in 1906 by Dr. and Mrs. Henry Wayland and the Staked Plains Baptist Association.

EXECUTIVES

President, Paul W. Armes
CFO, James Smith
Director Human Resources, Ron Appling
VP Enrollment Management, Claude Lusk
VP Academic and Graduate Services and Provost, Bobby L. Hall
Executive Director Institutional Advancement, Martha Cross
Director Alumni Development, Danny Andrews
University Registrar, Julie Bowen
Director Financial Aid, Karen LaQuey
Director Information Technology, Katrina Smith
Executive Director Student Services and Dean Students, Emmitt R. Tipton
Director Communications and Public Relations, Teresa Young

LOCATIONS

HQ: Wayland Baptist University
1900 W. 7th St., Plainview TX 79072
Phone: 806-291-1000   **Fax:** 806-291-1955
Web: www.wbu.edu

HISTORICAL FINANCIALS

Company Type: School

Income Statement

FYE: June 30

	REVENUE ($ mil.)	NET INCOME ($ mil.)	NET PROFIT MARGIN	EMPLOYEES
06/12	66	7	11.3%	281
06/11	61	7	12.5%	0
06/10	51	0	0.9%	0
06/09	55	7	14.1%	0
Annual Growth	6.1%	(1.3%)	—	—

2012 Year-End Financials

Debt ratio: —
Return on equity: 11.30%
Cash ($ mil.): 7
Current ratio: —
Long-term debt ($ mil.): —
Dividends
Yield: —
Payout: —
Market value ($ mil.): —

WAYNE BOARD OF EDUCATION

LOCATIONS

HQ: WAYNE BOARD OF EDUCATION
50 NELLIS DR, WAYNE, NJ 07470-3576
Phone: 973-633-3000
Web: www.wayneschools.com

HISTORICAL FINANCIALS

Company Type: Private

Income Statement

FYE: June 30

	REVENUE ($ mil.)	NET INCOME ($ mil.)	NET PROFIT MARGIN	EMPLOYEES
06/11*	144	1	0.7%	2,000
12/05	0	0	—	0
06/99	79	(2)	—	0
06/98	73	0	0.6%	0
Annual Growth	25.5%	33.4%		
*Fiscal year change

2011 Year-End Financials

Debt ratio: —
Return on equity: 0.70%
Cash ($ mil.): 3
Current ratio: —
Long-term debt ($ mil.): —
Dividends
Yield: —
Payout: —
Market value ($ mil.): —

WEBCO HAWAII INC

LOCATIONS

HQ: WEBCO HAWAII INC
2840 MOKUMOA ST, HONOLULU, HI 96819-4499
Phone: 808-839-4551
Web: www.awdhi.com

HISTORICAL FINANCIALS

Company Type: Private

Income Statement

FYE: March 31

	REVENUE ($ mil.)	NET INCOME ($ mil.)	NET PROFIT MARGIN	EMPLOYEES
03/12	113	0	0.6%	260
03/11	98	0	0.9%	0
03/10	83	0	0.8%	0
03/09	86	1	1.2%	0
Annual Growth	9.7%	(15.6%)	—	—

2012 Year-End Financials

Debt ratio: —
Return on equity: 0.60%
Cash ($ mil.): 3
Current ratio: 0.50
Long-term debt ($ mil.): —
Dividends
Yield: —
Payout: —
Market value ($ mil.): —

WEBSTER UNIVERSITY

They have more than dictionaries at Webster. Webster University is a private school that serves about 21000 undergraduate and graduate students through an international network of more than 100 campuses. Its main campus in St. Louis Missouri has an enrollment of more than 8000 students and around 700 faculty and staff members. Other locations span the US and are also present in Europe and Australasia; many campuses are on military bases. Alumni include former shuttle commander Eileen Collins actress Marsha Mason and Indonesia's first democratically elected president Susilo Bambang Yudhoyono. Webster

University was founded as a small Catholic women's college in 1915.

EXECUTIVES

Chairman, George H. Walker III
VP Finance and Administration and Treasurer, David Garafola
Associate VP Human Resources, Betsy Schmutz
President, Neil George
Dean Student Affairs Office, Ted F. Hoef
Director Professional Development, Larry Mabrey
Benefits Representative, Gloria Barbre
Head of Reference Services Library, Ellen Eliceiri
Acquisitions Library, Maya Grach
Dean University Library, Laura Rein
Director Advancement Services, Ryan Elliott
Director Alumni Programs, Jennifer Jezek-Taussig
Director Global MBA Program, Trevor Barker
Director Career Services, Tamara Gegg-LaPlume
Director Operations, Caprice Moore
Associate Chair, Alyce Herndon
Secretary, Kristi Evans
Compensation Chair, Terri Jones
Membership Chair, Bethany Keller
Special Events Chair, DeLyle Bowen
VP Academic Affairs, James Staley
VP Development and Alumni Programs, Faith D. Maddy
VP Executive Assistant to President and Secretary, Karen M. Luebbert
Vice Chairman, Laurance L. Browning Jr.
Trustee, James D. Weddle
Trustee, A. Bayard Clark III, age 66
Trustee, George F. Scherer
Trustee, Michael A. (Mike) DeHaven
Trustee, Richard A. (Dick) Liddy, age 76
Trustee, Michael F. Neidorff, age 69
Trustee, Brenda D. Newberry, age 58
Trustee, Thomas G. Cornwell
Trustee, P. Joseph (Joe) McKee III
Trustee, Susan M. (Sue) Neumann, age 58
Trustee, Donna M. Vandiver
Trustee, Michael Staenberg, age 58
Trustee, Mark E. Burkhart
Trustee, George C. Roman
Trustee, Randy Adams
Trustee, Sheila Baxter
Trustee, Amelia Bond
Trustee, Dale Cammon
Trustee, Donna K. Martin
Trustee, Jerry E. Ritter
Vice Chairman, Laurance L. Browning Jr.
Trustee, Steven O. Swyers
Trustee, Elizabeth T. Robb
Trustee, Paul Lee
Trustee, John R. Capps
Trustee, David Steward
Trustee, John R. Roberts
Trustee, Donald M. Suggs
Trustee, Robert Q. Costas
Trustee, Julie Reese
Trustee, James D. Weddle
Trustee, Joseph J. Mokwa
Trustee, Margaret Bush Wilson
Trustee, Jane B. Hart
Trustee, Mary Alice Dwyer-Dobbin
Trustee, Ronald J. Kruszewski
Trustee, Tom Irwin
Trustee, Douglas E. Hill
Trustee, Edward L. Glotzbach
Trustee, Steven L. Finerty

HQ: Webster University
470 E. Lockwood Ave., St. Louis MO 63119
Phone: 314-968-6900 **Fax:** 314-968-7112
Web: www.westeruniv.edu

HISTORICAL FINANCIALS
Company Type: School

Income Statement
FYE: May 31

	REVENUE ($ mil.)	NET INCOME ($ mil.)	NET PROFIT MARGIN	EMPLOYEES
05/12	213	7	3.4%	4,500
05/11	202	21	10.4%	0
05/10	199	21	10.8%	0
05/09	193	4	2.2%	0
Annual Growth	3.4%	20.3%	—	—

2012 Year-End Financials

Debt ratio: ——
Return on equity: 3.40%
Cash ($ mil.): 21
Current ratio: 1.40
Long-term debt ($ mil.): —

Dividends
Yield: —
Payout: —
Market value ($ mil.): —

WEIRTON MEDICAL CENTER INC.

There's nothing weird about Weirton Medical Center. The 240-bed not-for-profit hospital provides a wide range of health services to the tri-state region of West Virginia Ohio and Pennsylvania. Inpatient services include pediatrics obstetrics and other acute care services. Founded in 1953 the hospital also offers clinical and diagnostic care services such as emergency medicine home health care rehabilitation and occupational therapy. Weirton Medical Center has seen a steady decrease in patient volumes in recent years forcing the hospital to enact a number of cost-saving measures including cutting back on some services and laying off employees.

In early 2009 the hospital reduced its workforce by about 4% due to the decrease in patient volume which it blamed on a faltering economy and lost income on investments.

Several months later Weirton Medical announced a plan to close its 18-bed inpatient psychiatric center (outpatient psychiatric services will continue) and stop contributing to its employees' pension plans by the end of the year. The hospital expects to save about $7 million as a result of the changes. The hospital is evaluating other services including the continued operation of its pediatric wing.

EXECUTIVES

President and CEO, Joseph Endrich
Director Human Resources, Jennifer Anderson
VP Finance and CFO, Michael Miller

LOCATIONS

HQ: Weirton Medical Center Inc.
601 Colliers Way, Weirton WV 26062-5091
Phone: 304-797-6000 **Fax:** 304-797-6176
Web: www.weirtonmedical.com

COMPETITORS

Allegheny General Hospital
Butler Health System
Heritage Valley Health
Jefferson Regional Medical Center of Arkansas
Ohio Valley Medical Center
St. Clair Health
The Western Pennsylvania Hospital
Trinity Health System
UPMC
UPMC Mercy
West Penn Allegheny Health System

HISTORICAL FINANCIALS
Company Type: Private - Not-for-Profit

Income Statement
FYE: June 30

	REVENUE ($ mil.)	NET INCOME ($ mil.)	NET PROFIT MARGIN	EMPLOYEES
06/11	95	(1)	—	1,000
06/10	95	(3)	—	0
06/09	96	(13)	—	0
06/08	100	(2)	—	0
Annual Growth	(1.4%)	—	—	—

2011 Year-End Financials

Debt ratio: ——
Return on equity: (-1.30)%
Cash ($ mil.): 3
Current ratio: 0.40
Long-term debt ($ mil.): —

Dividends
Yield: —
Payout: —
Market value ($ mil.): —

WEITSMAN SHREDDING LLC

LOCATIONS

HQ: WEITSMAN SHREDDING LLC
1 RECYCLE DR, OWEGO, NY 13827-3213
Phone: 607-687-7777

HISTORICAL FINANCIALS
Company Type: Private

Income Statement
FYE: September 30

	REVENUE ($ mil.)	NET INCOME ($ mil.)	NET PROFIT MARGIN	EMPLOYEES
09/12*	182	7	4.4%	200
12/11	233	14	6.4%	0
Annual Growth	(21.9%)	(46.3%)	—	—
*Fiscal year change

2012 Year-End Financials

Debt ratio: ——
Return on equity: 4.40%
Cash ($ mil.): 0
Current ratio: 0.60
Long-term debt ($ mil.): —

Dividends
Yield: —
Payout: —
Market value ($ mil.): —

WELCH FOODS INC

Welch Foods has a taste for the grape. An operating subsidiary of the 1090-farmer owner National Grape Cooperative Welch produces the Welch's brand grape and white grape juices and jellies. Its beverage line includes refrigerated and sparkling juices and cocktails frozen and shelf-stable concentrates and single-serve drinks. Welch supplies fresh grapes as well as preserved offerings (jams and spreads) which are also sold under the BAMA label. The co-op licenses the Welch's name to other manufactures of frozen fruit confections dried fruit and carbonated beverages among many. Its 400-plus products are purchased by grocery retailers and foodservice operators in the US and nearly 50 other countries.

Despite Welch's iconic status on the store shelf the economic recession has dented earnings as cash-strapped consumers look for less expensive alternatives. The company responded to pricing pressures by expanding its product portfolio to 50% and 10% juice value-offerings which helped to buoy sales volumes. Concurrently it focused on streamlining operations to cut expenses and offset the headwinds of higher commodity costs. The effort included reducing corporate headcount by more than 15% in 2010 and initiating modest layoffs along with a consolidation of its manufacturing and distribution activities in 2011.

EXECUTIVES

VP International, William C. Hewins
Chairman; President National Grape Cooperative Association, Joseph C. Falcone
VP Legal General Counsel and Secretary, Vivian S. Y. Tseng
President CEO and Director, Bradley C. (Brad) Irwin, age 53
VP Corporate Planning, Judy B. Carr
VP Operations and Technology, David F. Engelkemeyer, age 57
VP Human Resources, Lisa Delisle Flynn
VP Sales and International, Damon G. Hart
VP Marketing, Christopher D. (Chris) Heye
VP and CFO, Michael J. Perda
Media Contact, Teleia Farrell
Chief Marketing Officer, Matthew Wohl
Director, Stephen B. Morris
President CEO and Director, Bradley C. (Brad) Irwin, age 53
Director, Douglas R. Forraht
Director, Jerry A. Czebotar
Director, Timothy E. Grow
Director, Joseph J. (Joe) Schena, age 54
Director, Stephen H. Warhover
Director, James T. Winton
Director, Robert T. DeMartini, age 51
Director, Thomas G. Wilkinson
Auditors: KPMGLLP

LOCATIONS

HQ: Welch Foods Inc. A Cooperative
3 Concord Farms 575 Virginia Rd., Concord MA 01742-9101
Phone: 978-371-1000 **Fax:** 978-371-3879
Web: www.welchs.com

PRODUCTS/OPERATIONS

Selected Brands and Products
BAMA
Jams jellies and preserves
Peanut butter

Welch
  Bottled and canned juices
  Dried fruit
  Fresh table grapes
  Frozen juices
  Fruit juice bars
  Jams jellies and preserves
  Pourable concentrated juices
  Refrigerated juices
  Single-serve juices

COMPETITORS

Chiquita Brands	Old Orchard
Coca-Cola	Silver Springs
Coloma Frozen Foods	Smucker
Dole Food	Snapple
Florida' s Natural	South Beach Beverage
Fresh Del Monte	Stapleton-Spence
Produce	Packing
Great Western Juice	Sun-Maid
Lion Raisins	Sunny Delight
Monster Beverage	Sunview Vineyards
Mott' s	Tree Top
Naked Juice	Tropicana
National Raisin	Unilever NV
Ocean Spray	Wet Planet Beverages
Odwalla	

HISTORICAL FINANCIALS

Company Type: Subsidiary

Income Statement

	REVENUE ($ mil.)	NET INCOME ($ mil.)	NET PROFIT MARGIN	EMPLOYEES
08/12	649	74	11.5%	1,300
08/11*	640	74	11.6%	0
05/10	487	63	13.0%	0
08/07	653	59	9.1%	0
Annual Growth	(0.2%)	7.7%	—	—

*Fiscal year change

FYE: August 31

2012 Year-End Financials

Debt ratio: ——
Return on equity: 11.50%
Cash ($ mil.): 4
Current ratio: 0.70
Long-term debt ($ mil.): —

Dividends
  Yield: —
  Payout: —
Market value ($ mil.): —

WELDED CONSTRUCTION LP

LOCATIONS

HQ: WELDED CONSTRUCTION LP
  26933 ECKEL RD, PERRYSBURG, OH 43551-1215
Phone: 419-874-3548
Web: www.welded-construction.com

HISTORICAL FINANCIALS

Company Type: Private

Income Statement

FYE: December 31

	REVENUE ($ mil.)	NET INCOME ($ mil.)	NET PROFIT MARGIN	EMPLOYEES
12/11	83	(18)	—	40
12/10	49	0	0.7%	0
12/09	252	54	21.7%	0
12/08	559	105	18.9%	0
Annual Growth	(46.9%)	—	—	—

2011 Year-End Financials

Debt ratio: ——
Return on equity: (-22.70)%
Cash ($ mil.): 13
Current ratio: 3.10
Long-term debt ($ mil.): —

Dividends
  Yield: —
  Payout: —
Market value ($ mil.): —

WELLMONT HEALTH SYSTEM

At Wellmont Health System wellness is paramount. Wellmont Health System provides general and advanced medical-surgical care to residents of northeastern Tennessee and southwestern Virginia. The health system consists of about a dozen owned and affiliated hospitals that collectively have more than 1000 licensed beds. One of its facilities is a rehabilitation hospital operated in partnership with HealthSouth. Wellmont also operates numerous ancillary facilities including an assisted living center a mental health clinic home health care and hospice agencies and outpatient centers. The health system was founded in 1996.

Wellmont has grown over the years primarily through acquisitions including Lee Regional Medical Center Mountain View Regional Medical Center and the Takoma Regional Hospital in Tennessee (through a partnership with Adventist Health).

Today Wellmont is one of the region's largest employers with a staff of more than 6500 medical professionals. Nearly 600 physicians deliver care at Wellmont's facilities that include eight hospitals in Tennessee and Virginia. Other facilities include an outpatient surgery center a child development center hospice a cancer center urgent care centers and a health network of physicians that include occupational health providers.

The hospital also offers nearly immediate transport for its most urgent patient cases with its Wellmont One Air Transport.

EXECUTIVES

Chairman, Roger K. Mowen Jr., age 67
President and CEO, Margaret (Denny) DeNarvaez, age 56
CFO, Elizabeth S. (Beth) Ward, age 51
SVP Business Development and Rural Strategy, David L. Brash
System Director Marketing Communications, Amy D. Stevens
SVP Human Resources, Hamlin Wilson
President Bristol Regional Medical Center, Bart Hove

President Hawkins County Memorial Hospital and Hancock County Hospital, Fred Pelle
President and CEO, Michael D. (Mike) Snow, age 57
SVP Marketing Communications, Patrick Kane
SVP Legal Affairs, Gary Miller
President Holston Valley Medical Center, Blaine Douglas
Executive Director Wellmont Foundation, Todd Norris
COO, Tracey Moffatt
President Lee Regional Medical Center, Ron Prewitt
CIO, Bill Moran
President Jenkins Community Hospital, Sherrie Newcomb
Media Relations Coordinator, Brad Lifford
President and CEO Takoma Regional Hospital, Daniel Wolcott
Vice Chairman, David Crockett
Secretary, Jeff Byrd
Treasurer, E. Wayne Kirk
Chief Medical Officer, Dale Sargent
CFO, Alice Pope
Director, David Crockett Sr.
Director, John Williams
Director, Peter Gale
Director, David Thompson
Director, T.C. Greene
Director, Thomas Pugh
Director, Ravan Krickbaum
Director, Glen (Skip) Skinner
Director, Spencer Quesenberry
Director, Fielding Rolston
Director, T. Arthur (Buddy) Scott
Auditors: KPMGLLP

LOCATIONS

HQ: Wellmont Health System
  1905 American Way, Kingsport TN 37660
Phone: 423-230-8200   **Fax:** 423-230-8225
Web: www.wellmont.org

PRODUCTS/OPERATIONS

Selected Facilities

Bristol Regional Medical Center (Bristol Tennessee)
Hancock County Hospital (Sneedville Tennessee)
Hawkins County Memorial Hospital (Rogersville Tennessee)
HealthSouth Rehabilitation Hospital of Kingsport (HealthSouth partnership; Kingsport Tennessee)

Lee Regional Medical Center (Pennington Gap Virginia)
Lonesome Pine Hospital (Big Stone Gap Virginia)
Mountain View Regional Medical Center (Norton Virginia)
Takoma Regional Hospital (Adventist Health partnership; Greeneville Tennessee)

COMPETITORS

Ascension Health	Kindred Healthcare
Baptist Memorial	LifePoint Hospitals
Health Care	Mountain States Health
Community Health	Tenet Healthcare
Systems	
Cookeville Regional	
Medical Center	

HISTORICAL FINANCIALS
Company Type: Private - Not-for-Profit

Income Statement
FYE: June 30

	REVENUE ($ mil.)	NET INCOME ($ mil.)	NET PROFIT MARGIN	EMPLOYEES
06/11	673	30	4.6%	6,114
06/10	622	33	5.5%	0
06/09	2	0	—	0
06/08	5	2	45.9%	0
Annual Growth	397.6%	130.5%		

2011 Year-End Financials
Debt ratio: —
Return on equity: 4.60%
Cash ($ mil.): 29
Current ratio: 0.20
Long-term debt ($ mil.): —
Dividends
Yield: —
Payout: —
Market value ($ mil.): —

WELLSPAN MEDICAL GROUP (INC)

LOCATIONS
HQ: WELLSPAN MEDICAL GROUP (INC)
140 N DUKE ST, YORK, PA 17401-1170
Phone: 717-851-6515

HISTORICAL FINANCIALS
Company Type: Private

Income Statement
FYE: June 30

	REVENUE ($ mil.)	NET INCOME ($ mil.)	NET PROFIT MARGIN	EMPLOYEES
06/11	192	(19)	—	709
06/10	172	(19)	—	0
06/09	144	(19)	—	0
06/08	138	3	2.3%	0
Annual Growth	11.7%	—	—	—

2011 Year-End Financials
Debt ratio: —
Return on equity: (-10.20)%
Cash ($ mil.): 0
Current ratio: 0.80
Long-term debt ($ mil.): —
Dividends
Yield: —
Payout: —
Market value ($ mil.): —

WELSPUN TUBULAR LLC

LOCATIONS
HQ: WELSPUN TUBULAR LLC
9301 FRAZIER PIKE, LITTLE ROCK, AR 72206-9280
Phone: 501-301-8800
Web: www.welspunpipes.us.com

HISTORICAL FINANCIALS
Company Type: Private

Income Statement
FYE: March 31

	REVENUE ($ mil.)	NET INCOME ($ mil.)	NET PROFIT MARGIN	EMPLOYEES
03/12	354	46	13.0%	5
Annual Growth	—	—	—	—

2012 Year-End Financials
Debt ratio: —
Return on equity: 13.00%
Cash ($ mil.): 26
Current ratio: 0.40
Long-term debt ($ mil.): —
Dividends
Yield: —
Payout: —
Market value ($ mil.): —

WENTWORTH INSTITUTE OF TECHNOLOGY INC.

LOCATIONS
HQ: WENTWORTH INSTITUTE OF TECHNOLOGY INC.
550 HUNTINGTON AVE, BOSTON, MA 02115-5998
Phone: 617-989-4590
Web: www.wit.edu

HISTORICAL FINANCIALS
Company Type: Private

Income Statement
FYE: June 30

	REVENUE ($ mil.)	NET INCOME ($ mil.)	NET PROFIT MARGIN	EMPLOYEES
06/11	113	6	6.1%	450
06/10	105	3	3.5%	0
06/09	96	0	—	0
06/08	81	(8)	—	0
Annual Growth	11.8%	—	—	—

2011 Year-End Financials
Debt ratio: —
Return on equity: 6.10%
Cash ($ mil.): 33
Current ratio: —
Long-term debt ($ mil.): —
Dividends
Yield: —
Payout: —
Market value ($ mil.): —

WESLEYAN UNIVERSITY

Wesleyan University is a private institution offering liberal arts and sciences education from its 360-acre campus in Middleton Connecticut. Some 3500 undergraduate and graduate students attend the university which has programs in academic areas including American studies film studies and psychology. Notable alumni include television producer Joss Whedon and educational writer Ted Fiske. Founded in 1831 Wesleyan was the first of several US colleges and universities to be named after John Wesley founder of the Methodist church; it ended its formal affiliation with the church in 1937.

EXECUTIVES
VP Finance and Administration, John Meerts
VP University Relations, Barbara-Jan Wilson
Director Human Resources, Julia Hicks
Associate VP Information Technology Services, Ganesan Ravishanker
VP Academic Affairs and Provost, Joseph Bruno
Registrar, Anna van der Burg
President, Michael S. Roth

LOCATIONS
HQ: Wesleyan University
Wesleyan Station 186 College St., Middletown CT 06459
Phone: 860-685-3700   Fax: 909-621-8360
Web: www.hmc.edu

HISTORICAL FINANCIALS
Company Type: School

Income Statement
FYE: June 30

	REVENUE ($ mil.)	NET INCOME ($ mil.)	NET PROFIT MARGIN	EMPLOYEES
06/11	194	67	34.6%	900
06/07	179	90	50.3%	0
06/06	172	95	55.2%	0
06/05	163	23	14.2%	0
Annual Growth	6.0%	42.5%	—	—

2011 Year-End Financials
Debt ratio: —
Return on equity: 34.60%
Cash ($ mil.): 15
Current ratio: —
Long-term debt ($ mil.): —
Dividends
Yield: —
Payout: —
Market value ($ mil.): —

WEST COAST NOVELTY CORPORATION

West Coast Novelty Corp. founded in the 1920s doesn't make concessions as one of the largest suppliers of licensed sports merchandise in the US. The firm has grown from its beginnings as a souvenir and concession operator to a nationwide distributor of licensed items such as jerseys T-shirts and headwear. West Coast Novelty boasts a vast portfolio of team licenses based on its agreements with the NFL MLB NBA WWF and the Collegiate Licensing Company. To extend its reach into the Eastern and Southern US the company operates a distribution center in Memphis Tennessee to supplement operations at its Alameda California facility.

EXECUTIVES
VP Distribution, John Bragg
CEO, Brian T. McCroden
President, John Allenberg
CFO, Lance Littlejohn

LOCATIONS
HQ: West Coast Novelty Corp.
2401 Monarch St., Alameda CA 94501
Phone: 800-347-7678   Fax: 510-748-4478
Web: www.westcoastnovelty.com

HISTORICAL FINANCIALS

Company Type: Private

Income Statement

FYE: August 31

	REVENUE ($ mil.)	NET INCOME ($ mil.)	NET PROFIT MARGIN	EMPLOYEES
08/11	52	0	0.8%	80
08/10	37	(0)	—	0
08/09	45	(0)	—	0
08/08	60	1	1.9%	0
Annual Growth	(4.2%)	(29.5%)	—	—

2011 Year-End Financials

Debt ratio: ——
Return on equity: 0.80%
Cash ($ mil.): 0
Current ratio: 0.40
Long-term debt ($ mil.): —

Dividends
Yield: —
Payout: —
Market value ($ mil.): —

WEST FARGO SCHOOL DISTRICT 6

LOCATIONS

HQ: WEST FARGO SCHOOL DISTRICT 6
207 MAIN AVE W, WEST FARGO, ND 58078-1725
Phone: 701-356-2000
Web: www.west-fargo.k12.nd.us

HISTORICAL FINANCIALS

Company Type: Private

Income Statement

FYE: June 30

	REVENUE ($ mil.)	NET INCOME ($ mil.)	NET PROFIT MARGIN	EMPLOYEES
06/11	89	12	14.4%	700
06/08	62	1	3.1%	0
06/07	57	(15)	—	0
06/06	51	(5)	—	0
Annual Growth	20.0%	—	—	—

WEST SIDE UNLIMITED CORPORATION

LOCATIONS

HQ: WEST SIDE UNLIMITED CORPORATION
4201 16TH AVE SW, CEDAR RAPIDS, IA 52404-1207
Phone: 319-390-4466
Web: www.westsideunlimited.com

HISTORICAL FINANCIALS

Company Type: Private

Income Statement

FYE: December 31

	REVENUE ($ mil.)	NET INCOME ($ mil.)	NET PROFIT MARGIN	EMPLOYEES
12/11	126	4	3.6%	550
12/08	117	5	4.6%	0
12/06	97	5	6.1%	0
12/05	2,112	0	0.0%	0
Annual Growth	(60.9%)	2200.7%	—	—

2011 Year-End Financials

Debt ratio: ——
Return on equity: 3.60%
Cash ($ mil.): 2
Current ratio: 0.40
Long-term debt ($ mil.): —

Dividends
Yield: —
Payout: —
Market value ($ mil.): —

WEST WINDSOR-PLAINSBORO REGIONAL BOARD OF EDUCATION

LOCATIONS

HQ: WEST WINDSOR-PLAINSBORO REGIONAL BOARD OF EDUCATION
505 VILLAGE RD W, PRINCETON JUNCTION, NJ 08550-2034
Phone: 609-716-5000

HISTORICAL FINANCIALS

Company Type: Private

Income Statement

FYE: June 30

	REVENUE ($ mil.)	NET INCOME ($ mil.)	NET PROFIT MARGIN	EMPLOYEES
06/12	172	8	5.1%	1,100
06/11	162	6	4.2%	0
06/08	156	(1)	—	0
06/07	152	15	10.0%	0
Annual Growth	4.2%	(16.9%)	—	—

2012 Year-End Financials

Debt ratio: ——
Return on equity: 5.10%
Cash ($ mil.): 34
Current ratio: —
Long-term debt ($ mil.): —

Dividends
Yield: —
Payout: —
Market value ($ mil.): —

WESTECH ENGINEERING INC.

LOCATIONS

HQ: WESTECH ENGINEERING INC.
3665 S WEST TEMPLE, SALT LAKE CITY, UT 84115-4409
Phone: 801-265-1000
Web: www.westech-inc.com

HISTORICAL FINANCIALS

Company Type: Private

Income Statement

FYE: June 30

	REVENUE ($ mil.)	NET INCOME ($ mil.)	NET PROFIT MARGIN	EMPLOYEES
06/12	143	2	2.1%	380
06/11	127	2	1.8%	0
06/10	107	4	4.2%	0
06/09	121	6	5.6%	0
Annual Growth	5.8%	(24.2%)	—	—

2012 Year-End Financials

Debt ratio: ——
Return on equity: 2.10%
Cash ($ mil.): 3
Current ratio: 1.10
Long-term debt ($ mil.): —

Dividends
Yield: —
Payout: —
Market value ($ mil.): —

WESTED

LOCATIONS

HQ: WESTED
730 HARRISON ST STE 500, SAN FRANCISCO, CA 94107-1242
Phone: 415-565-3000
Web: www.edgateway.net

HISTORICAL FINANCIALS

Company Type: Private

Income Statement

FYE: November 30

	REVENUE ($ mil.)	NET INCOME ($ mil.)	NET PROFIT MARGIN	EMPLOYEES
11/11	123	3	3.2%	645
11/10	108	2	2.0%	0
11/08	109	3	3.5%	0
11/07	98	9	9.4%	0
Annual Growth	8.0%	(24.5%)	—	—

2011 Year-End Financials

Debt ratio: ——
Return on equity: 3.20%
Cash ($ mil.): 24
Current ratio: 2.40
Long-term debt ($ mil.): —

Dividends
Yield: —
Payout: —
Market value ($ mil.): —

WESTERN FARMERS ELECTRIC COOPERATIVE

Who would guess that those Oklahoma sodbusters and claim-jumpers would need so much power? The Western Farmers Electric Cooperative. Led by its coal- and natural gas-fueled generating plants –three in Anadarko one in Mooreland and one in Hugo (all in Oklahoma) –the generation and transmission co-op produces more than 1700 MW of capacity. It pipes power over 3650 miles of transmission lines to two-thirds of rural Oklahoma and parts of New Mexico. It also operates 271 substations and 57 switch stations. Western Farmers Electric Cooperative which is owned by its member distribution cooperatives supplies 23 distribution co-ops and Altus Air Force base which serve a total of a half million members.

Responding to growing demand for power in 2009 the power co-op completed an expansion project at its gas-fueled Anadarko plant adding some 145 MW of power generating capacity.

Western Farmers Electric Cooperative has diversified its fuel mix to meet green energy regulations and boasts one of the state's largest renewable energy portfolios (wind energy and hydro power accounted for 19% of its 2010 fuel mix).

Increased demand (thanks to a hotter-than-usual summer) and higher wholesale prices helped to lift the co-op's revenues and net income in 2010.

Growing its geographic coverage in late 2010 Western Farmers Electric Cooperative added four New Mexico-based cooperatives (Farmers' Central Valley Lea County and Roosevelt County with a total of 400 MW of load) to its membership.

Western Farmers Electric Cooperative was organized in 1941 by western Oklahoma rural electric distribution cooperatives in order to secure power generation and distribution at an affordable rate. The co-op began generating power in 1950.

EXECUTIVES

CEO, Gary R. Roulet
Treasurer and Financial Risk Officer, Ron Cunningham
General Manager Legal and Administration, Brian Hobbs
CFO, Jane Lafferty
General Manager Power Resources, Bob Orme
General Manager Marketing and Communications, Jim O'Neill
General Manager Power Production, Gary Gilleland
Director Marketing, Mark Faulkenberry
Commercial and Industrial Marketing Manager and Legislative Coordinator, Scott Williams
VP, Bob Thomasson
President, Bob Allen
Secretary and Treasurer, Ray Smith
Assistant Secretary-Treasurer, Rusty Grissom
Marketing Coordinator, Nikki Gordon
Information Specialist, Maria Crowder
Executive VP CEO, Randy Ethridge
Chief Executive Officer, Brent Hartin
Vice President, Charles Hickey
Chief Executive Officer, Dale Nye
Senior Manager of Planning, Dan Fleming
Executive V.P. CEO, Jim Jackson
Senior Manager of Market Planning, Roy Klusmeyer
Executive V.P. CEO, Gary Hurse
Auditors: KPMGLLP

LOCATIONS

HQ: Western Farmers Electric Cooperative
701 NE 7th St., Anadarko OK 73005
Phone: 405-247-3351　　**Fax:** 405-247-4451
Web: www.wfec.com

PRODUCTS/OPERATIONS

2010 Fuel Mix

% of total	
Coal	35
Natural	22
Purchased	20
Hydropower	10
Wind	9
Other	4
Total	**100**

2010 Sales

	$ mil.	% of total
Members & cities	418	92
Other	37	8
Total	**455**	**100**

COMPETITORS

Empire District Electric	OGE Energy
Entergy	ONEOK
Grand River Dam Authority	PG&E Corporation

HISTORICAL FINANCIALS

Company Type: Private - Cooperative

Income Statement
FYE: December 31

	REVENUE ($ mil.)	NET INCOME ($ mil.)	NET PROFIT MARGIN	EMPLOYEES
12/11	462	10	2.3%	378
12/10	455	23	5.3%	0
12/09	360	13	3.8%	0
12/08	457	21	4.6%	0
Annual Growth	0.4%	(20.9%)	—	—

2011 Year-End Financials

Debt ratio: ——
Return on equity: 2.30%　　Dividends
Cash ($ mil.): 2　　Yield: —
Current ratio: 0.60　　Payout: —
Long-term debt ($ mil.): —　　Market value ($ mil.): —

WESTERN GOVERNORS UNIVERSITY

LOCATIONS

HQ: WESTERN GOVERNORS UNIVERSITY
4001 S 700 E STE 700, SALT LAKE CITY, UT 84107-2533
Phone: 801-274-3280
Web: www.wgu.edu

HISTORICAL FINANCIALS

Company Type: Private

Income Statement
FYE: June 30

	REVENUE ($ mil.)	NET INCOME ($ mil.)	NET PROFIT MARGIN	EMPLOYEES
06/11	148	8	5.4%	208
06/10	114	10	9.0%	0
06/09	79	0	—	0
06/08	61	3	6.3%	0
Annual Growth	34.2%	27.3%	—	—

2011 Year-End Financials

Debt ratio: ——
Return on equity: 5.40%　　Dividends
Cash ($ mil.): 9　　Yield: —
Current ratio: 1.20　　Payout: —
Long-term debt ($ mil.): —　　Market value ($ mil.): —

WESTERN NEW ENGLAND UNIVERSITY

LOCATIONS

HQ: WESTERN NEW ENGLAND UNIVERSITY
1215 WILBRAHAM RD, SPRINGFIELD, MA 01119-2612
Phone: 413-782-1219
Web: www.wne.edu

HISTORICAL FINANCIALS

Company Type: Private

Income Statement
FYE: June 30

	REVENUE ($ mil.)	NET INCOME ($ mil.)	NET PROFIT MARGIN	EMPLOYEES
06/12	93	(5)	—	800
06/11	93	7	8.2%	0
06/10	92	9	10.4%	0
06/09	113	0	—	0
Annual Growth	(6.1%)	—	—	—

2012 Year-End Financials

Debt ratio: ——
Return on equity: (-5.80)%　　Dividends
Cash ($ mil.): 18　　Yield: —
Current ratio: ——　　Payout: —
Long-term debt ($ mil.): —　　Market value ($ mil.): —

WESTERN STATES FIRE PROTECTION COMPANY INC

Western States Fire Protection (WSFP) is sprinkling its own brand of safety west of the Mississippi. The company a division of APi Group installs water-based fire sprinklers and other fire suppression systems for the commercial residential and industrial markets primarily in the western US. It designs installs and maintains fire protection systems at defense gaming high-tech institutional medical processing and sports facilities. Specific projects include installing systems at the Colorado Convention Center and Microsoft's data storage facility in Washington. WSFP also manufactures fire sprinklers at its own fabrication workshops. The company was founded in 1985.

In addition to its water-based fire sprinklers WSFP serves hazardous facilities with FM-200 and carbon dioxide systems. FM-200 is a dry chemical that extinguishes fire through a combination of chemically-based inhibition and cooling. These systems are used in facilities where water damage must be avoided such as art galleries historical libraries and record and storage facilities.

EXECUTIVES

Chairman, Lee R. Anderson Sr.
Treasurer, Sandra Barker
President, Gene Postma
VP, Rick Charles

LOCATIONS

HQ: WESTERN STATES FIRE PROTECTION COMPANY INC
7026 S TUCSON WAY, CENTENNIAL, CO 80112-3921
Phone: 303-792-0022
Web: www.statewidefire.com

COMPETITORS

China Fire
COSCO Fire Protection
Sharpfibre
Siemens Building
 Technologies
SimplexGrinnell
Tyco Fire &
 Security
UTC Climate Controls
 & Security

HISTORICAL FINANCIALS

Company Type: Subsidiary

Income Statement — FYE: December 31

	REVENUE ($ mil.)	NET INCOME ($ mil.)	NET PROFIT MARGIN	EMPLOYEES
12/11	165	12	7.3%	1,400
12/10	150	11	7.5%	0
12/09	185	13	7.4%	0
12/08	230	18	8.0%	0
Annual Growth	(10.4%)	(12.9%)	—	—

2011 Year-End Financials

Debt ratio: ——
Return on equity: 7.30%
Cash ($ mil.): 0
Current ratio: 0.70
Long-term debt ($ mil.): —
Dividends
Yield: —
Payout: —
Market value ($ mil.): —

WESTERN TEAMSTERS WELFARE TRUST

LOCATIONS

HQ: WESTERN TEAMSTERS WELFARE TRUST
2323 EASTLAKE AVE E, SEATTLE, WA 98102-3305
Phone: 206-329-4900

HISTORICAL FINANCIALS

Company Type: Private

Income Statement — FYE: August 31

	REVENUE ($ mil.)	NET INCOME ($ mil.)	NET PROFIT MARGIN	EMPLOYEES
08/11	107	(1)	—	3
08/10	106	(6)	—	0
Annual Growth	1.1%	—	—	—

2011 Year-End Financials

Debt ratio: ——
Return on equity: (-1.00)%
Cash ($ mil.): 102
Current ratio: 5.60
Long-term debt ($ mil.): —
Dividends
Yield: —
Payout: —
Market value ($ mil.): —

WESTERN UNIVERSITY OF HEALTH SCIENCES

LOCATIONS

HQ: WESTERN UNIVERSITY OF HEALTH SCIENCES
309 E 2ND ST, POMONA, CA 91766-1854
Phone: 909-623-6116
Web: www.banweb.westernu.edu

HISTORICAL FINANCIALS

Company Type: Private

Income Statement — FYE: June 30

	REVENUE ($ mil.)	NET INCOME ($ mil.)	NET PROFIT MARGIN	EMPLOYEES
06/11	126	1	1.1%	824
06/10	110	1	1.0%	0
06/09	101	10	10.0%	0
06/08	92	7	8.1%	0
Annual Growth	11.0%	(42.6%)	—	—

2011 Year-End Financials

Debt ratio: ——
Return on equity: 1.10%
Cash ($ mil.): 1
Current ratio: —
Long-term debt ($ mil.): —
Dividends
Yield: —
Payout: —
Market value ($ mil.): —

WESTLAKE DISTRIBUTORS INC.

LOCATIONS

HQ: WESTLAKE DISTRIBUTORS INC.
1320 E OLYMPIC BLVD # 208, LOS ANGELES, CA 90021-1946
Phone: 213-624-8676

HISTORICAL FINANCIALS

Company Type: Private

Income Statement — FYE: December 31

	REVENUE ($ mil.)	NET INCOME ($ mil.)	NET PROFIT MARGIN	EMPLOYEES
12/11	126	1	1.4%	42
12/07	129	7	5.8%	0
12/05*	46	3	8.2%	0
06/05	1,669	0	—	0
Annual Growth	(57.7%)	6915.2%	—	—

*Fiscal year change

2011 Year-End Financials

Debt ratio: ——
Return on equity: 1.40%
Cash ($ mil.): 0
Current ratio: 0.80
Long-term debt ($ mil.): —
Dividends
Yield: —
Payout: —
Market value ($ mil.): —

WESTLIE MOTOR COMPANY

LOCATIONS

HQ: WESTLIE MOTOR COMPANY
500 S BROADWAY, MINOT, ND 58701-4451
Phone: 701-852-1354
Web: www.westlietruckcenter.com

HISTORICAL FINANCIALS

Company Type: Private

Income Statement — FYE: December 31

	REVENUE ($ mil.)	NET INCOME ($ mil.)	NET PROFIT MARGIN	EMPLOYEES
12/11	104	4	4.3%	120
Annual Growth	—	—	—	—

2011 Year-End Financials

Debt ratio: ——
Return on equity: 4.30%
Cash ($ mil.): 0
Current ratio: 0.30
Long-term debt ($ mil.): —
Dividends
Yield: —
Payout: —
Market value ($ mil.): —

WESTLINK TRADING LLC

LOCATIONS

HQ: WESTLINK TRADING LLC
 9001 FREY RD STE A, HOUSTON, TX 77034-3556
Phone: 832-476-5495

HISTORICAL FINANCIALS

Company Type: Private

Income Statement

FYE: August 31

	REVENUE ($ mil.)	NET INCOME ($ mil.)	NET PROFIT MARGIN	EMPLOYEES
08/12*	149	0	0.2%	6
12/11	78	0	0.3%	0
12/10	65	0	0.3%	0
12/09	60	0	0.3%	0
Annual Growth	**34.9%**	**26.7%**	—	—

*Fiscal year change

2012 Year-End Financials

Debt ratio: ——
Return on equity: 0.20%
Cash ($ mil.): 0
Current ratio: 1.50
Long-term debt ($ mil.): —

Dividends
 Yield: —
 Payout: —
Market value ($ mil.): —

WESTMINSTER COLLEGE

Westminster College is a private liberal arts school that offers nearly 40 undergraduate majors conferring bachelor of arts and bachelor of science degrees as well as a half dozen graduate degrees. Its academic programs are offered through four schools devoted to arts and sciences business education and nursing and health sciences. The school has an enrollment of approximately 2000 undergraduate students and 600 graduate students and has nearly 300 full- and part-time faculty members. Westminster College was founded in 1875 as a preparatory school called the Salt Lake Collegiate Institute. It first offered college classes in 1897 (as Sheldon Jackson College) and adopted its current name in 1902.

EXECUTIVES

President, Michael B. Bassis
VP Institutional Advancement, Steve Morgan
VP Information Technology and Associate Provost, Sheryl Phillips
Dean School of Education, Mark Ankeny
VP Enrollment Services, Joel Bauman
Dean Students, Mark Ferne
Associate Provost Student Development, Susan Heath
Interim Dean Gore School of Business, Aric Krause
VP Institutional Advancement and Alumni Relations, Nancy Michalko
VP Academic Affairs and Provost, James (Cid) Seidelman
Director Development, Kris Jensen
Director Research, Marilyn Campbell
Manager Advancement Services, Angela Hill
Director Alumni and Parent Relations, Dana Tumpowsky

Assistant VP and Director Campaign Gifts, Phyllis Hockett
VP Principal Gifts, Janet A. Glaeser
Director Corporate Giving, Angela Wilcox
Director Foundation Relations, Laurie J. Staton
Director Gift Planning, Lisa Actor
VP Finance and Administration, Curtis Ryan
Director Accounting Services, Jennifer Medrano
Manager Accounts Receivable, Natalee Nelson
Payroll Coordinator, Vickie Reese
Director Budget, Sydney Tervort
Director Patrol and Safety, Saeed Rezai
Director Conferences and Summer Programs, Jeff Brown
Director Mail Room and Copy Center, Tracy Fowler
Custodial Manager, Arnoldo Castillo
Director Sodexho Food Service, Emily Bolding
Director Plant Operations, Richard Brockmyer
Director Facilities, Claudia Marques
Maintenance Supervisor, Walter Kortkamp
Manager Grounds, Dale Bianucci
Director Purchasing, Al Johansen
Director Risk Management, Kelly Hill
Director Athletics, Tommy Connor
Director Sport Information, JD Gustin
Director Career Resource Center, Bev Christy
Director Residential Life, Cullen Green
Director Annual Giving, Jane Campbell
Graphic Designer, Tom Cronin
Director of Student International Services, Sara Demko
Assistant Director of Communications, Robin Boon
Director of Diversity Student Affairs and Support, Luciano Marzulli
Associate Director of Communications, Krista DeAngelis
Director of Communications, Jeremy Pugh
Assistant Director of Residence Life, Aimee Frost
Assistant Director Student Involvement & Orientation, Karnell Black
Director of Residence Life, Nicola Miller
Trustee, David E. Simmons
Trustee, Susan Glasmann
Trustee, Jack Behnken
Trustee, Gretchen Anderson
Trustee, Jesselie B. Anderson
Trustee, Martha Felt Barton
Trustee, Peter Behrens
Trustee, Judith Billings
Trustee, James R. Clark
Trustee, Curt P. Crowther
Trustee, E. R. (Zeke) Dumke III
Trustee, Thomas A. Ellison
Trustee, Robert J. Frankenberg
Trustee, Thomas Fey
Trustee, P. Michael Gibbons
Trustee, Alan E. Guskin
Trustee, George M. Haley
Trustee, W. Eugene (Gene) Hansen
Trustee, Thomas G. Nycum
Trustee, William Orchow
Trustee, D. N. (Nick) Rose
Trustee, Noreen Rouillard
Trustee, Byron Russell
Trustee, Andrew J. Schilly
Trustee, R. Anthony Sweet
Trustee, Verl R. Topham
Trustee, Alonzo W. Watson Jr.
Trustee, Robert A. (Bob) Garda

LOCATIONS

HQ: Westminster College
 1840 S. 1300 East, Salt Lake City UT 84105
Phone: 801-484-7651   **Fax:** 801-832-3101
Web: www.westminstercollege.edu

HISTORICAL FINANCIALS

Company Type: School

Income Statement

FYE: June 30

	REVENUE ($ mil.)	NET INCOME ($ mil.)	NET PROFIT MARGIN	EMPLOYEES
06/11	95	9	10.3%	500
06/10	69	13	18.8%	0
06/09	38	(15)	—	0
06/08	56	5	9.1%	0
Annual Growth	**19.4%**	**24.3%**	—	—

2011 Year-End Financials

Debt ratio: —
Return on equity: 10.30%
Cash ($ mil.): 16
Current ratio: —
Long-term debt ($ mil.): —

Dividends
 Yield: —
 Payout: —
Market value ($ mil.): —

WESTMINSTER COLLEGE

Westminster College is a private liberal arts school that offers nearly 40 undergraduate majors conferring bachelor of arts and bachelor of science degrees as well as a half dozen graduate degrees. Its academic programs are offered through four schools devoted to arts and sciences business education and nursing and health sciences. The school has an enrollment of approximately 2000 undergraduate students and 600 graduate students and has nearly 300 full- and part-time faculty members. Westminster College was founded in 1875 as a preparatory school called the Salt Lake Collegiate Institute. It first offered college classes in 1897 (as Sheldon Jackson College) and adopted its current name in 1902.

EXECUTIVES

President, Michael B. Bassis
VP Institutional Advancement, Steve Morgan
VP Information Technology and Associate Provost, Sheryl Phillips
Dean School of Education, Mark Ankeny
VP Enrollment Services, Joel Bauman
Dean Students, Mark Ferne
Associate Provost Student Development, Susan Heath
Interim Dean Gore School of Business, Aric Krause
VP Institutional Advancement and Alumni Relations, Nancy Michalko
VP Academic Affairs and Provost, James (Cid) Seidelman
Director Development, Kris Jensen
Director Research, Marilyn Campbell
Manager Advancement Services, Angela Hill
Director Alumni and Parent Relations, Dana Tumpowsky
Assistant VP and Director Campaign Gifts, Phyllis Hockett
VP Principal Gifts, Janet A. Glaeser
Director Corporate Giving, Angela Wilcox
Director Foundation Relations, Laurie J. Staton
Director Gift Planning, Lisa Actor
VP Finance and Administration, Curtis Ryan
Director Accounting Services, Jennifer Medrano
Manager Accounts Receivable, Natalee Nelson
Payroll Coordinator, Vickie Reese
Director Budget, Sydney Tervort
Director Patrol and Safety, Saeed Rezai

Director Conferences and Summer Programs, Jeff Brown
Director Mail Room and Copy Center, Tracy Fowler
Custodial Manager, Arnoldo Castillo
Director Sodexho Food Service, Emily Bolding
Director Plant Operations, Richard Brockmyer
Director Facilities, Claudia Marques
Maintenance Supervisor, Walter Kortkamp
Manager Grounds, Dale Bianucci
Director Purchasing, Al Johansen
Director Risk Management, Kelly Hill
Director Athletics, Tommy Connor
Director Sport Information, JD Gustin
Director Career Resource Center, Bev Christy
Director Residential Life, Cullen Green
Director Annual Giving, Jane Campbell
Graphic Designer, Tom Cronin
Director of Student International Services, Sara Demko
Assistant Director of Communications, Robin Boon
Director of Diversity Student Affairs and Support, Luciano Marzulli
Associate Director of Communications, Krista DeAngelis
Director of Communications, Jeremy Pugh
Assistant Director of Residence Life, Aimee Frost
Assistant Director Student Involvement & Orientation, Karnell Black
Director of Residence Life, Nicola Miller
Trustee, David E. Simmons
Trustee, Susan Glasmann
Trustee, Jack Behnken
Trustee, Gretchen Anderson
Trustee, Jesselie B. Anderson
Trustee, Martha Felt Barton
Trustee, Peter Behrens
Trustee, Judith Billings
Trustee, James R. Clark
Trustee, Curt P. Crowther
Trustee, E. R. (Zeke) Dumke III
Trustee, Thomas A. Ellison
Trustee, Robert J. Frankenberg
Trustee, Thomas Fey
Trustee, P. Michael Gibbons
Trustee, Alan E. Guskin
Trustee, George M. Haley
Trustee, W. Eugene (Gene) Hansen
Trustee, Thomas G. Nycum
Trustee, William Orchow
Trustee, D. N. (Nick) Rose
Trustee, Noreen Rouillard
Trustee, Byron Russell
Trustee, Andrew J. Schilly
Trustee, R. Anthony Sweet
Trustee, Verl R. Topham
Trustee, Alonzo W. Watson Jr.
Trustee, Robert A. (Bob) Garda

LOCATIONS

HQ: Westminster College
1840 S. 1300 East, Salt Lake City UT 84105
Phone: 801-484-7651   **Fax:** 801-832-3101
Web: www.westminstercollege.edu

HISTORICAL FINANCIALS

Company Type: School

Income Statement

FYE: June 30

	REVENUE ($ mil.)	NET INCOME ($ mil.)	NET PROFIT MARGIN	EMPLOYEES
06/12	38	(1)	—	350
06/11	54	17	31.5%	0
06/10	44	8	19.0%	0
06/09	15	(21)	—	0
Annual Growth	34.7%	—	—	—

2012 Year-End Financials

Debt ratio: —
Return on equity: (-3.80)%
Cash ($ mil.): 12
Current ratio: —
Long-term debt ($ mil.): —

Dividends
  Yield: —
  Payout: —
Market value ($ mil.): —

WESTMONT COLLEGE

LOCATIONS

HQ: WESTMONT COLLEGE
955 LA PAZ RD, SANTA BARBARA, CA 93108-1099
Phone: 805-565-6000
Web: www.westmont.edu

HISTORICAL FINANCIALS

Company Type: Private

Income Statement

FYE: June 30

	REVENUE ($ mil.)	NET INCOME ($ mil.)	NET PROFIT MARGIN	EMPLOYEES
06/11	85	12	14.4%	300
06/10	72	9	13.5%	0
06/09	47	(59)	—	0
06/08	57	7	13.1%	0
Annual Growth	14.1%	18.0%	—	—

2011 Year-End Financials

Debt ratio: —
Return on equity: 14.40%
Cash ($ mil.): 17
Current ratio: —
Long-term debt ($ mil.): —

Dividends
  Yield: —
  Payout: —
Market value ($ mil.): —

WHEATON COLLEGE

Wheaton College (not to be confused with a school of the same name in Illinois) is a four-year private liberal arts college that enrolls about 1600 undergraduates for study in more than 40 major fields as well as 60 minors. The college boasts a student-faculty radio of 11:1. The most popular courses of study include biology economics English history psychology and sociology. The Wheaton College campus is located 35 miles south of Boston and 15 miles north of Providence. Founded as a seminary for women in 1834 it was chartered as a women's liberal arts college in 1912. Wheaton became coeducational in 1987.

EXECUTIVES

VP College Advancement, Mary M. Casey
President, Ronald A. Crutcher
VP Enrollment and Marketing, Gail Berson
VP Finance and Operations and Treasurer, Roderick G. Wallick
College Librarian and Associate VP Technology and Information Services, Terry Metz
Assistant VP Communications, Michael (Mike) Graca
Assistant VP and Director Human Resources, Barbara Lema
Associate Director Human Resources, Remle Gordon
Provost, Linda Eisenmann
VP Student Affairs and Dean of Students, Lee B. Williams
Chair Board of Trustees, Deborah H. Dluhy
Assistant to the President and Secretary, Trishia S. Lichauco
Director Events, Monica E. Key
Administrative Associate, Loretta C. Baldwin
Administrative Assistant, Susan C. Hayes
Executive Director Athletics, Chad Yowell
Registrar and Dean Academic Systems, Patricia B. Santilli
Director Institutional Research and Assessment, Audrey Adam

LOCATIONS

HQ: Wheaton College (Massachusetts)
26 E. Main St., Norton MA 02766-2322
Phone: 508-286-8200   **Fax:** 508-286-3539
Web: www.wheatonma.edu

HISTORICAL FINANCIALS

Company Type: School

Income Statement

FYE: June 30

	REVENUE ($ mil.)	NET INCOME ($ mil.)	NET PROFIT MARGIN	EMPLOYEES
06/12	70	(8)	—	545
06/08	102	11	10.8%	0
06/06	69	18	26.9%	0
06/05	62	15	24.3%	0
Annual Growth	4.4%	—	—	—

2012 Year-End Financials

Debt ratio: —
Return on equity: (-11.60)%
Cash ($ mil.): 9
Current ratio: —
Long-term debt ($ mil.): —

Dividends
  Yield: —
  Payout: —
Market value ($ mil.): —

WHEATON FRANCISCAN SERVICES INC.

Wheaton Franciscan Services (WFSI) is the parent company for more than 100 health care housing and social service organizations in Colorado Illinois Iowa and Wisconsin. Also known as Wheaton Franciscan Healthcare WFSI operates more than 15 hospitals including Affinity Health System Rush Oak Park Hospital and United Hospital System. WFSI also includes long-term care centers home health agencies and physician offices. Its Franciscan Ministries division provides affordable housing units including assisted-living facilities and low-income dwellings. The not-for-profit health system is sponsored by The Franciscan Sisters Daughters of the Sacred Hearts of Jesus and Mary.

Many of WFSI's hospitals are operated in partnership with other area providers. For instance the Affinity Health System in Wisconsin is jointly sponsored by Wheaton Franciscan Sisters and Ministry Health Care while the Rush Oak Park Hospital in Illinois is operated through a partnership between WFSI and the Rush System for Health.

The health care system occasionally expands its network both by forming new partnerships and through acquisitions. In 2009 WFSI opened the Midwest Orthopedic Specialty Hospital in partnership with a group of independent orthopedic doctors. The new orthopedic center is part of the Franklin Hospital; WFSI completed construction on the new $90 million acute care facility in Franklin Wisconsin in 2008. The Franklin Hospital provides emergency surgery imaging and primary and specialty care.

The health system also partnered with the YMCA of Milwaukee to try to address chronic health concerns of area residents. The two organizations converted a local YMCA campus into the YMCA Healthy Lifestyle Village which opened in 2009. The center offers health screenings health education outpatient therapy and fitness services. WFSI and the YMCA have more Healthy Lifestyle Village campuses planned for other locations within their service areas.

In addition to increase the scope of specialty health care services it can provide to the community WFSI continues to recruit new physicians and specialists to the Wheaton Franciscan Medical Group. The system is also working to improve communication among its physicians and facilities by adding electronic health record (EHR) systems.

The Franciscan Sisters Daughters of the Sacred Hearts of Jesus and Mary (also known as the Wheaton Franciscan Sisters) founded WSFI in 1983 as a holding company for their ministry operations. The health system traces its roots back to the founding of the St. Mary's Hospital in Racine Wisconsin in 1882.

EXECUTIVES

Chairperson, Joseph W. Lewis, age 77
President South Market Southeast Wisconsin, Kenneth R. (Ken) Buser
President and CEO Affinity Health System, Daniel E. (Dan) Neufelder
President CEO and Director, John D. Oliverio
SVP and CIO, Gregory A. (Greg) Smith
SVP and Chief Administrative Officer, Jon L. Wachs
SVP and Chief Administrative Officer, Michael Lepore
SVP Strategy and Corporate Affairs, Richard J. Canter
VP Strategic Planning, Abigail L. Navti
SVP and COO Wheaton Franciscan and All Saints, Susan E. Boland
President and CEO Wheaton Franciscan Medical Group, Loren M. Meyer
SVP Mission Services, Therese M. (Terri) Rocole
VP Payer Contracting and Relations, Coreen Dicus-Johnson
President and CEO Wheaton Franciscan Healthcare Iowa, Jack Dusenbery
President and CEO United Hospital System, Richard O. Schmidt Jr.
President and CEO Marianjoy, Kathleen C. Yosko

VP Communications and Public Relations, Anne Ballentine
SVP Organizational Change and Leadership Development, Brenda J. Bowers
SVP and Chief Medical Officer, Stephen Cardamone
SVP and COO Wheaton Franciscan Medical Group, Robert De Vita
SVP Human Resources, Wayne Frangesch
President Wheaton Franciscan Continuing Care and Allied Services, James (Jim) Gresham
SVP and General Counsel, Sarah Herzog
VP Operations Central Market Southeast Wisconsin, Roberta Johnson
President Central Market Southeast Wisconsin, Dan Mattes
SVP Operations North Market Southeast Wisconsin, Norma McCutcheon
SVP Operations Iowa, Dave Olejniczak
SVP Finance Operations, Jon Sohn
President North Market Southeast Wisconsin, Debra K. Standridge
Chief Nursing Officer Iowa, Nancy Weber
CFO, Jon W. Sohn
Interim Chief Medical Officer and Chief Medical Information Officer, Rita Hanson
Director, Michael J. Murry, age 63
President CEO and Director, John D. Oliverio
Director, Michael Lepore
Director, Sister Mary Beth Glueckstein
Director, James Concannon
Director, Stephen Evans
Director, Carolyn Hodge-West
Director, Jack O. Lanier
Director, Michael Mack
Director, Robert O. Walker
Director, Parke Behn

LOCATIONS

HQ: Wheaton Franciscan Services Inc.
26 W. 171 Roosevelt Rd., Wheaton IL 60189-0667
Phone: 630-909-6900   **Fax:** 630-909-8001
Web: www.wfhealthcare.org

PRODUCTS/OPERATIONS

Selected Operations

Franciscan Ministries Inc. (housing in Colorado Illinois Iowa and Wisconsin)
Illinois
    Marianjoy Rehabilitation Hospital (Wheaton)
    Rush Oak Park Hospital (affiliate Oak Park)
Iowa (Wheaton Franciscan Healthcare of Iowa)
    Covenant Medical Center (Waterloo)
    Mercy Hospital (Oelwein)
    Sartori Memorial Hospital (Cedar Falls)
Wisconsin
    Affinity Health System (partnership with Minstry Health Care)
        Calumet Medical Center (Chilton)
        Mercy Medical Center (Oshkosh)
        St. Elizabeth Hospital (Appleton)
    Wheaton Franciscan Healthcare of Southeast Wisconsin
        All Saints Hospital (two campuses in Racine)
        Elmbrook Memorial Hospital (Brookfield)
        Franklin Hospital (Franklin)
        St. Francis Hospital (Milwaukee)
        St. Joseph Hospital (Milwaukee)
        Wisconsin Heart Hospital (Wauwatosa)
    United Hospital System Inc. (affiliated system)
        Kenosha Medical Center (Kenosha)
        St. Catherine's Medical Center (Pleasant Prairie)

COMPETITORS

Advocate Health Care
Alden Management
  Services
Children' s Hospital

Loyola University
  Health System
Ministry Health Care
Morris Hospital

and Health System
Columbia St. Mary' s
Elmhurst Memorial
  Healthcare
FHN
Froedtert Hospital
Hospital Sisters
  Health System
KishHealth

NorthShore University
  HealthSystem
OSF Healthcare System
ProHealth Care
Resurrection Health
  Care
Rockford Health System
SwedishAmerican Health
  System

HISTORICAL FINANCIALS

Company Type: Private - Not-for-Profit

Income Statement   FYE: June 30

	REVENUE ($ mil.)	NET INCOME ($ mil.)	NET PROFIT MARGIN	EMPLOYEES
06/12	1,723	(112)	—	18,000
06/11	1,710	173	10.2%	0
06/10	1,850	56	3.1%	0
06/09	1,876	(127)	—	0
Annual Growth	(2.8%)	—	—	—

2012 Year-End Financials

Debt ratio: ——
Return on equity: (-6.50)%   Dividends
Cash ($ mil.): 59   Yield: —
Current ratio: 0.80   Payout: —
Long-term debt ($ mil.): —   Market value ($ mil.): —

WHEELING-NISSHIN INC.

Wheeling-Nisshin a subsidiary of Nisshin Steel produces a variety of hot-dip coated steels such as stainless steel. The company's output includes 400000 tons produced at its aluminizing and galvanizing line facility and 300000 tons produced at its continuous galvanizing line facility. Both of the facilities are located at the company's headquarters site in West Virginia. Its primary customers are in the automotive appliance and construction industries. Wheeling-Nisshin was founded in 1986. It had been a joint venture between Nisshin and US steel producer Wheeling Pitt (now operating as Severstal Wheeling) until the Japanese steel company bought out its partner in early 2008.

EXECUTIVES

COO, Richard Carter
General Manager Sales, Kenichi (Ken) Hoshi
Customer Service, Matthew (Matt) Bonar
EVP and General Manager Commercial, Ricky Onishi
Manager Information Systems, Greg Lauri
Manager Quality Assurance and Customer Service, Art Bertol
General Manager Operations, Pat Pendleton
Manager Operations, Frank Mollica
CEO, Noboru Onishi

LOCATIONS

HQ: Wheeling-Nisshin Inc.
400 Penn St., Follansbee WV 26037
Phone: 304-527-2800   **Fax:** 304-527-0985
Web: www.wheeling-nisshin.com

COMPETITORS

Dofasco
ThyssenKrupp Stainless

United States Steel

HISTORICAL FINANCIALS
Company Type: Subsidiary

Income Statement
FYE: December 31

	REVENUE ($ mil.)	NET INCOME ($ mil.)	NET PROFIT MARGIN	EMPLOYEES
12/11	489	9	2.0%	175
12/10	434	10	2.4%	0
12/09	271	2	1.1%	0
12/08	576	13	2.3%	0
Annual Growth	(5.3%)	(9.3%)	—	—

2011 Year-End Financials
Debt ratio: —
Return on equity: 2.00%
Cash ($ mil.): 54
Current ratio: 2.80
Long-term debt ($ mil.): —
Dividends
Yield: —
Payout: —
Market value ($ mil.): —

WHITE RIVER COOPERATIVE INC.

LOCATIONS
HQ: WHITE RIVER COOPERATIVE INC.
610 CHURCH ST, LOOGOOTEE, IN 47553-1311
Phone: 812-295-4835

HISTORICAL FINANCIALS
Company Type: Private

Income Statement
FYE: December 31

	REVENUE ($ mil.)	NET INCOME ($ mil.)	NET PROFIT MARGIN	EMPLOYEES
12/11	142	2	1.8%	103
12/10	105	1	1.8%	0
12/08	116	0	0.2%	0
12/06	65	1	2.5%	0
Annual Growth	29.6%	17.4%	—	—

2011 Year-End Financials
Debt ratio: —
Return on equity: 1.80%
Cash ($ mil.): 4
Current ratio: 0.40
Long-term debt ($ mil.): —
Dividends
Yield: —
Payout: —
Market value ($ mil.): —

WHITEHEAD INSTITUTE FOR BIO-MEDICAL RESEARCH

The Whitehead Institute for Biomedical Research blazes new trails in bioscience. The organization funded by both the public and private sectors investigates such diseases as Parkinson's and cancer and dives into the depths of biology genomics and genetics to gain new understanding about disease and health. The Whitehead Institute contributed to the international effort to map the human genome and is actively researching stem cells. Other achievements include discovering a system for multiplying adult stem cells and creating the first genetically defined human cancer cell. The enterprise draws researchers from nearby MIT (with which it is affiliated in its teaching activities) and from all over the world.

Operations

The Whitehead Institute serves as a major resource for the pharmaceutical and biotechnology industry with more than 100 licensing agreements on technologies. Research at the institute is conducted by up to 19 principal investigators (members and fellows) and more than 200 visiting scientists postdoctoral fellows graduate students and undergraduate students from all over the world.

Financial Performance

The Whitehead Institute reported revenues of $78 million in 2011.It gets its revenues from Federal Research Grants Whitehead Support Gifts and from corporations and foundations.

Strategy

Institute scientists have focused on human genetics cancer heart disease immunology and developmental biology. The Whitehead Institute was the core institution for one of the six original National Cooperative Vaccine Development Groups for AIDS (established by the National Institutes of Health to speed the development of an AIDS vaccine).

Company Background

The institute was founded in 1982 by philanthropist Edwin "Jack" Whitehead with the help of MIT biology professor and Nobel Laureate David Baltimore.

EXECUTIVES
Chairman, Charles D. Ellis
President and Board Member, David C. Page
Secretary and Board Member, Arthur W. Brill
Vice Chair, Susan E. Whitehead
Director Physical Plant, Steve Clark
Director Finance and Treasurer, John Travia
VP, Martin Mullins
Associate VP and Director Human Resources, Marianne Howard
Director Bioinformatics and Research Computing, Fran Lewitter
Director Communications and Public Affairs and Interim Director Development, Matt Fearer
Director Environmental Health and Safety, Elizabeth Gross
Director Information Technology, Roger Roach
Director Intellectual Property and Sponsored Programs, Carla D. DeMaria
Director Procurement, Marcia S. Glatt
Director Research Finance, Seamus Boshell
Board Member, Jonathan M. Goldstein
Board Member, Phillip A. Sharp, age 67
Board Member, Robert S. (Bob) Langer Jr., age 63
Board Member, John J. Whitehead, age 67
President and Board Member, David C. Page
Secretary and Board Member, Arthur W. Brill
Vice Chair, Susan E. Whitehead
Board Member Emeritus, Abraham J. Siegel
Board Member, Peter J. Whitehead
Board Member, London T. Clay
Board Member, Barbara Imperiali
Board Member, Brit J. d'Arbeloff
Board Member, Peter M. Hecht
Board Member Emeritus, Paul L. Joskow
Board Member, Peter S. Kim
Board Member, David H. Koch
Board Member, Marc C. Lapman

LOCATIONS
HQ: Whitehead Institute for Biomedical Research
9 Cambridge Center, Cambridge MA 02142-1479
Phone: 617-258-5000 **Fax:** 617-258-5121
Web: www.wi.mit.edu

COMPETITORS
Celera
Howard Hughes Medical Institute
Jackson Laboratory
Sandford Burnham Institute
Wellcome Trust

HISTORICAL FINANCIALS
Company Type: Private - Not-for-Profit

Income Statement
FYE: June 30

	REVENUE ($ mil.)	NET INCOME ($ mil.)	NET PROFIT MARGIN	EMPLOYEES
06/11	65	(3)	—	550
06/10	67	(9)	—	0
06/09	0	0	—	0
06/08	32	(43)	—	0
Annual Growth	26.1%	—	—	—

2011 Year-End Financials
Debt ratio: —
Return on equity: (-5.30)%
Cash ($ mil.): 5
Current ratio: 0.20
Long-term debt ($ mil.): —
Dividends
Yield: —
Payout: —
Market value ($ mil.): —

WHITMAN COLLEGE

Students attending this Walla Walla school hope to get more Bing Bang for their educational buck. Whitman College located in Walla Walla Washington is an independent co-educational non-sectarian undergraduate school. It offers bachelor's degrees in more than 40 liberal arts and sciences areas including education environmental studies biology English music mathematics and religion. It has about 1400 students and a 10 to 1 student-faculty ratio. Whitman College was founded in 1882 in honor of Marcus and Narcissa Whitman who established a medical mission and a school to serve the Cayuse Indians and immigrants on the Oregon Trail.

EXECUTIVES
Director Institutional Research and Registrar, Ronald F. Urban
CFO and Treasurer, Peter W. Harvey
Controller, Walter Froese
Associate Dean of the Faculty, Thomas A. Callister Jr.
Director Penrose Library, Dalia L. Hagan
Director International Programs, Susan Holme Brick
Dean of Admission and Financial Aid, J. Antonio Cabasco
Director Financial Aid Services, Varga Fox
Dean of Students, Charles E. (Chuck) Cleveland
Associate Dean of Students and Campus Center Director, Barbara A. Maxwell
VP Development and College Relations and Secretary, John W. Bogley
Associate VP Development, Lynn B. Lunden
Director Alumni Relations, Polly C. Schmitz

LOCATIONS

HQ: Whitman College
345 Boyer Ave., Walla Walla WA 99362
Phone: 509-527-5111   **Fax:** 509-527-4967
Web: www.whitman.edu

HISTORICAL FINANCIALS

Company Type: School

Income Statement

	REVENUE ($ mil.)	NET INCOME ($ mil.)	NET PROFIT MARGIN	EMPLOYEES
06/12	55	(10)	—	399
06/11	68	68	100.9%	0
06/10	64	43	68.7%	0
06/09	61	(99)	—	0
Annual Growth	(3.8%)	—	—	—

2012 Year-End Financials

Debt ratio: —	
Return on equity: (-19.80)%	Dividends
Cash ($ mil.): 15	Yield: —
Current ratio: —	Payout: —
Long-term debt ($ mil.): —	Market value ($ mil.): —

WHITNEY MUSEUM OF AMERICAN ART

The Whitney Museum of American Art houses some 12000 works of 20th- and 21st-century American art including paintings sculptures drawings photographs and prints by about 2000 artists. It contains the entirety of Edward Hopper's artistic estate as well as pieces by artists such as Georgia O'Keefe Kiki Smith Louise Nevelson and Andy Warhol. The museum also offers public programs including lectures seminars and performances. The museum is housed in a large granite building at the corner of Madison Avenue and 75th Street de-signed by the Hungarian-born Bauhaus-trained architect Marcel Breuer. Whitney Museum of American Art was founded in 1930 by sculptor and art patron Gertrude Vanderbilt Whitney.

Originally housed on 8th Street the Whitney relocated in 1954 to West 54th Street and in 1966 moved to its present home on Madison Avenue.

A second location for the Whitney is planned for downtown New York City. The new six-storey 185000-square-foot building will be located in the Meatpacking District on Gansevoort Street and is to be designed by the Italian architect Renzo Piano. The museum has launched a $680 million fundraising campaign to cover the construction costs and to bolster its own endowment.

EXECUTIVES

LOCATIONS

HQ: Whitney Museum of American Art
945 Madison Ave., New York NY 10021
Phone: 212-570-3676   **Fax:** 212-570-4169
Web: www.whitney.org

HISTORICAL FINANCIALS

Company Type: Private

Income Statement

FYE: June 30

	REVENUE ($ mil.)	NET INCOME ($ mil.)	NET PROFIT MARGIN	EMPLOYEES
06/11	147	107	73.0%	167
06/10	33	(8)	—	0
06/09	28	0	—	0
06/08	206	170	82.4%	0
Annual Growth	(10.6%)	(14.1%)	—	—

2011 Year-End Financials

Debt ratio: —	
Return on equity: 73.00%	Dividends
Cash ($ mil.): 24	Yield: —
Current ratio: —	Payout: —
Long-term debt ($ mil.): —	Market value ($ mil.): —

WHOLESALE FUELS INC.

LOCATIONS

HQ: WHOLESALE FUELS INC.
2200 E BRUNDAGE LN, BAKERSFIELD, CA 93307-3066
Phone: 661-327-4900
Web: www.wholesalefuels.com

HISTORICAL FINANCIALS

Company Type: Private

Income Statement

FYE: December 31

	REVENUE ($ mil.)	NET INCOME ($ mil.)	NET PROFIT MARGIN	EMPLOYEES
12/11	134	0	0.4%	54
Annual Growth	—	—	—	—

2011 Year-End Financials

Debt ratio: —	
Return on equity: 0.40%	Dividends
Cash ($ mil.): 1	Yield: —
Current ratio: 2.00	Payout: —
Long-term debt ($ mil.): —	Market value ($ mil.): —

WHOLESALE SUPPLY GROUP INC.

Wholesale Supply Group is a wholesale and retail supplier of electrical HVAC and plumbing products to customers in Alabama Georgia Kentucky

North Carolina Tennessee and Virginia. The company carries new and discontinued products under the American Water Heaters Aqua Glass Kohler Delta Moen GE Appliances Progress Lighting Square D Lithonia and Luxaire brands. Its customers include home owners local contractors electricians and plumbers in commercial residential and industrial markets. The enterprise which began as a concrete block-making business founded by Roy Higgins and Gene Davis in 1942 operates from more than 30 branches.

EXECUTIVES

Chairman and President, Lloyd D. Rogers
VP Operations, Ronny Guthrie
VP Administration and Finance, Reggie Bishop
VP Inventory Control, Gary Millaway
Secretary, Steve Rapier
Director Purchasing, Ben Ammons
Assistant Secretary, Lisa Sullivan

LOCATIONS

HQ: Wholesale Supply Group Inc.
885 Keith St. NW, Cleveland TN 37320
Phone: 423-479-5997 **Fax:** 423-479-2644
Web: www.wsginc.com

PRODUCTS/OPERATIONS

Appliances
Electrical controls and devices
HVAC
Plumbing fixtures and hardware
Tools

COMPETITORS

ABC Appliance	Ferguson Enterprises
Anixter International	Mayer Electric
Electrical Equipment Company	Snap-on

HISTORICAL FINANCIALS
Company Type: Private

Income Statement
FYE: July 31

	REVENUE ($ mil.)	NET INCOME ($ mil.)	NET PROFIT MARGIN	EMPLOYEES
07/12	44	(0)	—	335
07/11	42	(0)	—	0
07/10	44	(0)	—	0
07/09	48	(0)	—	0
Annual Growth	(2.7%)	—	—	—

2012 Year-End Financials

Debt ratio: —
Return on equity: (-0.50)%
Cash ($ mil.): 0
Current ratio: 1.20
Long-term debt ($ mil.): —
Dividends
Yield: —
Payout: —
Market value ($ mil.): —

WHOLESOME SWEETENERS INCORPORATED

LOCATIONS

HQ: WHOLESOME SWEETENERS INCORPORATED
8016 HIGHWAY 90A, SUGAR LAND, TX 77478-2961
Phone: 281-275-3199
Web: www.wholesomesweeteners.com

HISTORICAL FINANCIALS
Company Type: Private

Income Statement
FYE: September 2

	REVENUE ($ mil.)	NET INCOME ($ mil.)	NET PROFIT MARGIN	EMPLOYEES
09/11	117	11	9.6%	41
Annual Growth	—	—	—	—

2011 Year-End Financials

Debt ratio: —
Return on equity: 9.60%
Cash ($ mil.): 1
Current ratio: 0.30
Long-term debt ($ mil.): —
Dividends
Yield: —
Payout: —
Market value ($ mil.): —

WIDENER UNIVERSITY

You probably won't find any narrow-minded students at Widener. A private co-educational liberal arts college Widener University offers a curriculum that emphasizes social awareness and civic engagement. It has an enrollment of some 6500 students and a student-to-faculty ratio of 12:1. The university grants undergraduate and graduate degrees in about 60 different fields; its programs are divided into eight schools and colleges that cover areas including arts and sciences business engineering law hospitality human services and nursing. Widener University has had its current name since 1979 but its roots reach back to a group of 19th century boys' military academies.

Geographic Reach

In addition to its main 110-acre campus located about 20 miles outside of Philadelphia in Chester Pennsylvania Widener operates three auxiliary campuses in Pennsylvania (Harrisburg and Exton) and Delaware (Wilmington) including the University College campus geared towards part-time adult undergraduates. The university's students come from more than 20 states and 25 countries. About 35% of its student base participates in study abroad programs.

Financial Performance

Widener reported a 2% increase in revenues in fiscal 2011 to some $155 million. Operating income was also up $5 to nearly $7 million.

Strategy

Widener has enhanced its attractiveness to students and faculty alike in recent years by expanding and upgrading facilities including the completion of a new nursing school building. In 2012 it

opened a new international study center to help non-US students acclimate.

As part of its civic engagement curriculum Widener encourages students to participate in community service activities volunteer programs and internships. To help facilitate such activities as well as to enhance community relations in 2012 Widener opened a new science learning center wing on its Widener Partnership Charter School (a partnership with Chester Pennsylvania) and it established an early career and college partnership with the Sussex Technical School District.

EXECUTIVES

President, James T. Harris III
SVP Administration and Finance, Joseph J. Baker
SVP and Provost, Jo Allen
VP University Advancement, Linda S. Durant
Associate VP Administration, George E. Hassel
Assistant VP University Relations, LouAnne Bulik
Associate VP Enrollment Management, Lawrence T. Lesick
Associate VP and Controller, Catherine McGeehan
Director Operations, Carl G. Pierce
CIO, Peter Shoudy
Director Corporate and Foundation Relations, Michael Bivens
Director Career Advising and Planning Services, Barbara Buckley
Associate Provost and Dean Students, Deborrah Hebert
Director Government and External Relations, Robert Skomorucha
Director Campus Safety, Patrick Sullivan
Director Student Financial Services, Thomas K. Malloy
Auditors: KPMGLLP

LOCATIONS

HQ: Widener University
1 University Place, Chester PA 19013
Phone: 610-499-4000 **Fax:** 610-499-1231
Web: www.widener.edu

PRODUCTS/OPERATIONS

Selected Colleges and Schools
College of Arts and Sciences
School of Business Administration
School of Engineering
School of Hospitality Management
School of Human Service Professions
School of Law
School of Nursing
University College

HISTORICAL FINANCIALS
Company Type: School

Income Statement
FYE: June 30

	REVENUE ($ mil.)	NET INCOME ($ mil.)	NET PROFIT MARGIN	EMPLOYEES
06/11	200	9	4.9%	1,021
06/10	188	5	2.7%	0
06/09	184	9	5.2%	0
06/08	172	4	2.4%	0
Annual Growth	5.1%	33.8%	—	—

2011 Year-End Financials

Debt ratio: —
Return on equity: 4.90%
Cash ($ mil.): 40
Current ratio: —
Long-term debt ($ mil.): —
Dividends
Yield: —
Payout: —
Market value ($ mil.): —

WILBUR-ELLIS COMPANY

Seed 'em weed 'em and feed 'em could be the motto of San Francisco's Wilbur-Ellis Co. (aka WECO). Through its agribusiness division WECO sells fertilizer herbicides insecticides seed and farm machinery in North America. The Connell Bros. unit exports and distributes food ingredients and specialty chemicals throughout the Pacific Rim. Its feed division serves international customers in the livestock pet food and aquaculture industries. Additionally WECO provides consulting pesticide application and other agriculture-related services. Beyond North America WECO has operations in about 15 countries in the Asia-Pacific Region. WECO was founded in 1921 by Brayton Wilbur Sr. and Floyd Ellis.

Operations

WECO's Agribusiness division is one of the top marketers and distributors of agricultural products in the US with sales of $1.8 billion. Connell Bros. is the largest marketer and distributor of specialty chemicals and ingredients with about three dozen offices across the Asia Pacific region and annual sales of about $815 million. The $500-million-in-sales Feed division supplies value-added feed ingredients and markets for customers' by-products.

Geographic Reach

The San Francisco-based company has agribusiness operations in the West Southwest and Midwest regions on the US. Connell Bros. has offices in 16 countries across the Asia-Pacific Region including Australia China and Vietnam. The Feed unit has operations in North America and in Australia and New Zealand.

Strategy

WECO employs a strategy of acquiring successful businesses and integrating them into its existing operations. Geography is no barrier when it comes to buying companies. Indeed WECO has acquired operations in such faraway places as Malaysia Taiwan the Philippines China Australia and New Zealand. With more than $3 billion in sales WECO continues to expand both through acquisitions and organically across its three divisions. Its Connell Bros. division expanded its food formulation services in Australia and New Zealand with the opening in 2012 of a food formulation facility in Sydney. Other infrastructure and facility investments made by Connell Bros. in 2012 include the construction of a 20000 square-foot warehouse in Mumbai India and a coatings lab in Bangkok. WECO's Feed division was also active overseas through the purchase in 2011 of the assets of New Zealand and Australian Pet Food Ingredients (NZAPFI) including deboning facilities in New Zealand. Closer to home the Agribusiness division acquired the assets of Smith Air LLC an aerial application business that applies crop protection and fertility products to alfalfa dry beans potatoes and other crops in Eastern Washington. The purchase added to WECO's Agribusiness unit's aerial operations in California Texas and several other agricultural states.

Ownership

Family-owned WECO is transitioning to the fourth generation of family ownership. CEO and president John Thacher is the grandson of founder Brayton Wilbur Sr.

EXECUTIVES

VP and General Counsel, William R. Sawyers, age 43
VP Operations Northern Plains, Mike Thomas
Chairman, Herbert B. Tully

Manager Northwest Feed Division, Ron Salter
VP Treasurer and CFO, James D. Crawford
EVP Agribusiness Division, Daniel R. (Dan) Vradenburg
President and CEO, John P. Thacher
VP Operations Arizona California New Mexico and Texas, Steven J. Dietze
President Connell Bros., Theodore L. (Ted) Eliot III
Controller, Charles Crume
Vice Chairman, Carter P. Thacher, age 86
CIO, Jerry Coupe
Director Credit, Robert Syron
Assistant Treasurer, Alison Amonette
President and Business Unit Manager John Taylor Fertilizers Rio Linda California, Jeff Taylor
Manager Connell Bros Perth Australia, David Raw
Managing Director Connell Bros Hong Kong, Mark Curtis
Manager Connell Bros Beijing China, Alex Niu
Manager Connell Bros Chongqing China, David Lee
Manager Connell Bros Guangzhou China, Bill Ho
General Manager Connell Bros Shanghai China, Lawrence Chan
General Manager Connell Bros India, Yogesh Mathur
Manager Connell Bros Indonesia, Yosef Herwanto
General Manager Connell Bros Naha Japan, K. Kohoma
Manager Connell Bros Osaka Japan, Harry Sueyoshi
President Connell Bros Japan, Ken Kanai
President Connell Bros Korea, M.H. Oh
General Manager Connell Bros Malaysia and Singapore, Scott Graddy
General Manager Connell Bros Express Chemical Supplies Malaysia, David MacDonald
Managing Director Connell Bros Myanmar, U. Htein Win
General Manager Connell Bros Philippines, Silverio Ambrosio
General Manager Connell Bros Thailand, Michael Wilbur
Manager Connell Bros Vietnam, David Hagerman
General Manager Canadian Feed Division Lethbridge; Manager Hay Division LethbridgeAlberta Hay Plant, Brent Quintin
General Manager Canadian Feed Division North Vancouver and Saskatoon, Rob Fullerton
General Manager Canadian Feed Division Tecumseh, Bill Standeven
General Manager Northwest Feed Division Knox McDaniel Company, Jeff McDaniel
General Manager Northwest Feed Division INMAN, Dennis McDermott
General Manager Western Feed Supplements Yakima, Steve Jones
Manager Fresno Feed Division, Tim Cockburn
Manager Mowe's Scientific Nutritional Service, Job Mowe
Director Human Resources, Tim McMullen
Export Manager Connell Brothers, Tejas Parekh
Import Manager, Carl Martin
Director Human Resources, Anne E. Cleary
National Director Seed, Troy W. Johnson
VP National Marketing and Supplier Relations, James M. (Jim) Loar
VP Feed Division, Ronald G Salter
VP General Counsel, David P Granoff
Vice Chairman, Carter P. Thacher, age 86
Director, Bruce L. Beretta
Director, Judith Wilbur
Auditors: Hood&Strong

LOCATIONS

HQ: WILBUR-ELLIS COMPANY
345 CALIFORNIA ST FL 27, SAN FRANCISCO, CA 94104-2644
Phone: 415-772-4000
Web: www.wilburellis.com

PRODUCTS/OPERATIONS

Selected Products and Services

Agribusiness Division
  Agricultural chemicals
  Fertilizers
  Fungicides
  Herbicides
  Insecticides
  Machinery
  Pesticides
  Seed protectants
  Seed treatments
  Sprayers
  Supply-chain management
Connell Bros. Division
  Industrial chemicals
Feed Division
  Aquaculture products
  Feed ingredients
  Food oils
  Forage products
  Pet food
Professional Products
  Forestry
    Fungicides
    Herbicides
  Golf
    Fungicides
  Landscape
    Fungicides
  Nursery/Greenhouse
    Fungicides
  Vegetation Management

Selective and nonselective growth regulators

COMPETITORS

ADM	DuPont Agriculture
Ag Processing Inc.	Frontier Agriculture
AGRI Industries	Goulding Chemicals
Agrium	GROWMARK
Andersons	Ingredion
BASF SE	JR Simplot
Bayer CropScience	Land O' Lakes Purina
Cargill	Feed
CF Industries	Monsanto Company
CHS	Southern States
Dow AgroSciences	

HISTORICAL FINANCIALS

Company Type: Private

Income Statement   FYE: December 31

	REVENUE ($ mil.)	NET INCOME ($ mil.)	NET PROFIT MARGIN	EMPLOYEES
12/11	2,812	0	—	3,200
12/10	2,342	0	—	0
12/09	0	0	—	0
12/00	1,100	0	—	0
Annual Growth	**36.7%**	**—**	**—**	**—**

WILDE AUTOS INC.

LOCATIONS

HQ: WILDE AUTOS INC.
1710A HWY 164 S, WAUKESHA, WI 53186-3937
Phone: 262-970-5900

HISTORICAL FINANCIALS

Company Type: Private

Income Statement

FYE: December 31

	REVENUE ($ mil.)	NET INCOME ($ mil.)	NET PROFIT MARGIN	EMPLOYEES
12/11	114	4	3.7%	145
12/10	109	3	3.5%	0
12/09	85	2	2.9%	0
12/08	90	2	2.6%	0
Annual Growth	8.0%	21.9%	—	—

2011 Year-End Financials

Debt ratio: ——
Return on equity: 3.70%
Cash ($ mil.): 3
Current ratio: 0.90
Long-term debt ($ mil.): ——

Dividends
Yield: —
Payout: —
Market value ($ mil.): —

WILDE OF WEST ALLIS INC.

LOCATIONS

HQ: WILDE OF WEST ALLIS INC.
3225 S 108TH ST, MILWAUKEE, WI 53227-4021
Phone: 414-545-8010
Web: www.wildetoyota.com

HISTORICAL FINANCIALS

Company Type: Private

Income Statement

FYE: December 31

	REVENUE ($ mil.)	NET INCOME ($ mil.)	NET PROFIT MARGIN	EMPLOYEES
12/11	139	3	2.4%	210
12/10	145	4	2.8%	0
12/09	163	5	3.2%	0
12/08	160	3	2.3%	0
Annual Growth	(4.4%)	(2.8%)	—	—

2011 Year-End Financials

Debt ratio: ——
Return on equity: 2.40%
Cash ($ mil.): 1
Current ratio: 0.20
Long-term debt ($ mil.): ——

Dividends
Yield: —
Payout: —
Market value ($ mil.): —

WILDLIFE CONSERVATION SOCIETY

From Congo gorillas to humpback whales off the coast of Gabon all life is worth conserving to the Wildlife Conservation Society (WCS). The group founded in 1895 works to protect wildlife and lands throughout the world and to instill in humans a concern about nature. The not-for-profit organization operates New York City's Bronx Zoo New York Aquarium Central Park Zoo Prospect Park Zoo and the Queens Zoo. The society's environmental education programs are used in schools throughout the US and in other nations. It has ongoing efforts in more than 60 countries to protect endangered species and ecosystems. About a quarter of the funding for the society's work comes from visitors at its handful of parks.

Despite the nation's economic woes WCS logged a record attendance of about 4.5 million visitors among its parks in 2010. As more New Yorkers and other Americans chose to vacation closer to home due to tightened discretionary spending WCS benefitted. With those visitors came a noteworthy boost in income from gate admissions exhibits and contributions from visitor services such as food merchandising and parking. All told attendance-driven revenues in 2010 reached a record $52.8 million.

The conservation group points to its operational diversity for being able to keep its head above water when funding from the state and other entities it had relied on had slimmed.

To stay true to its mission and remain a viable wildlife supporter WCS was forced to make some cuts. It opted in 2010 to close the doors on its namesake magazine Wildlife Conservation which had cost WCS $1.4 million to produce in 2009. Besides also eliminating personnel WCS cut its capital expenditures from $33.8 million in 2009 to $13.9 million in 2010 by putting off many planned improvements at its parks. One project it kept on the front burner is the renovation and expansion of the New York Aquarium Conservation Hall which began in 2010 and was completed in the spring of 2011.

WCS hopes to ramp up its construction in 2011. The group's revised Master Plan includes enhancements at the Bronx Zoo's C.V. Starr Science Campus with the Special Care Unit and LaMattina Wildlife Ambassador Center the Queens Zoo's jaguar exhibit and the Ocean Wonders exhibit.

During the past decade WCS has spent $243 million to fund physical plant improvements on its five campuses. They were financed through grants from New York City and the federal government private gifts and the proceeds from WCS's Series 2004 tax-exempt bond issue.

EXECUTIVES

EVP Conservation and Science, John G. Robinson
Chairman Emeritus, David T. Schiff
SVP General Counsel and Deputy Secretary, W.B. McKeown
EVP Administration and CFO, Patricia Calabrese
EVP Public Affairs, John Calvelli
VP and CTO, Paula L. Simon
President and CEO, Steven E. Sanderson
SVP Business Services, Robert A. Moskovitz
VP and Comptroller, Robert Calamo
Secretary and Trustee, Andrew H. Tisch
Treasurer and Trustee, Brian J. Heidtke
Vice Chair, Gordon B. Pattee

VP Human Resources, Laura Stolzenthaler
VP Conservation Strategy, Kent H. Redford
VP Policy and Government Relations, Linda Krueger
VP and Director New York Aquarium, Jon Forrest Dohlin
VP Communications and Public Affairs, Mary A. Dixon
VP Planning and Design and Chief Architect, Susan A. Chin
VP Species Conservation, Elizabeth L. Bennett
SVP and General Counsel, Joshua R. Ginsberg
SVP Living Institutions; Director Bronx Zoo, James J. Breheny
EVP and General Director Living Institutions, Robert A. Cook
EVP Global Resources, Bertina Ceccarelli
Trustee, Judith H. Hamilton, age 67
SVP General Counsel and Deputy Secretary, W.B. McKeown
Trustee, Eleanor Briggs
Trustee, Gilbert Butler
Trustee, Edith McBean
Trustee, Barbara Hrbek Zucker
Trustee, Frederick W. Beinecke
Trustee, C. Diane Christensen
Trustee, Ward W. Woods
Trustee, Paul A. Gould
Trustee, Jonathan L. Cohen
Trustee, Katharina Otto-Bernstein
Secretary and Trustee, Andrew H. Tisch
Trustee, Katherine L. Dolan
Trustee, Bradley L. Goldberg
Trustee, Jonathan D. Green
Treasurer and Trustee, Brian J. Heidtke
Trustee, Caroline N. Sidnam
Trustee, Walter C. Sedgwick
Trustee, Warren L. Schwerin
Trustee, David T. Schiff
Trustee, John N. Irwin III
Trustee, Anita L. Keefe
Trustee, H. Merritt Paulson III
Vice Chair, Gordon B. Pattee
Trustee, Ambrose K. Monell

LOCATIONS

HQ: Wildlife Conservation Society
2300 Southern Blvd., Bronx NY 10460
Phone: 718-220-5100   **Fax:** 718-220-2685
Web: www.wcs.org

PRODUCTS/OPERATIONS

2010 Revenues

	$ mil.	% of total
Contributed	44	22
Federal agencies	29	15
Gate & exhibit admissions	28	14
City of New York	24	12
Visitor services	24	12
Investment income	18	9
Non-governmental organization grants	12	6
Membership dues	10	5
New York State	3	2
Education programs	1	1
Sponsorship licensing & royalties	1	1
Other	1	1
Total	**201**	**100**

Selected Areas of Focus

Climate change
Natural resource exploitation
Sustainable development of human livelihoods

HISTORICAL FINANCIALS
Company Type: Private - Not-for-Profit

Income Statement
FYE: June 30

	REVENUE ($ mil.)	NET INCOME ($ mil.)	NET PROFIT MARGIN	EMPLOYEES
06/11	206	0	0.0%	4,000
06/10	228	9	4.1%	0
06/09	197	0	—	0
06/06	227	52	22.9%	0
Annual Growth	(3.2%)	(89.7%)	—	—

2011 Year-End Financials
Debt ratio: —
Return on equity: —
Cash ($ mil.): 65
Current ratio: 0.60
Long-term debt ($ mil.): —

Dividends
Yield: —
Payout: —
Market value ($ mil.): —

WILKES UNIVERSITY

LOCATIONS
HQ: WILKES UNIVERSITY
84 W SOUTH ST, WILKES BARRE, PA 18766-0003
Phone: 570-408-4200

HISTORICAL FINANCIALS
Company Type: Private

Income Statement
FYE: May 31

	REVENUE ($ mil.)	NET INCOME ($ mil.)	NET PROFIT MARGIN	EMPLOYEES
05/11	105	2	2.3%	370
05/05	73	4	6.0%	0
05/04	52	10	19.7%	0
05/03	45	0	1.4%	0
Annual Growth	32.1%	56.9%	—	—

2011 Year-End Financials
Debt ratio: —
Return on equity: 2.30%
Cash ($ mil.): 18
Current ratio: —
Long-term debt ($ mil.): —

Dividends
Yield: —
Payout: —
Market value ($ mil.): —

WILKINSON-COOPER PRODUCE INC

Wilkinson-Cooper Produce is a fresh vegetable wholesaler. Its products include corn cucumbers endives green beans parsley peppers radishes squash watercress and zucchinis. It ships wholesale mixed vegetables from Florida between November and May and from Georgia in June and July. The Florida-based company has been shipping vegetables across the continental US as well as Canada and Europe since 1965.

EXECUTIVES
President, Charles D. (Randy) Wilkinson Jr.
Salesman, Gibson C. Wilkinson
Salesman, Lamar Groves
VP, Margaret Wilkinson

LOCATIONS
HQ: Wilkinson-Cooper Produce Inc.
701 NW 12th St., Belle Glade FL 33430
Phone: 561-996-6537 **Fax:** 561-996-6588
Web: www.wilkinson-cooper.com

HISTORICAL FINANCIALS
Company Type: Private

Income Statement
FYE: July 31

	REVENUE ($ mil.)	NET INCOME ($ mil.)	NET PROFIT MARGIN	EMPLOYEES
07/12	41	(0)	—	15
07/11	37	0	0.0%	0
07/10	31	0	0.3%	0
07/07	30	0	0.2%	0
Annual Growth	11.2%	—	—	—

2012 Year-End Financials
Debt ratio: —
Return on equity: (-0.20)%
Cash ($ mil.): 0
Current ratio: 1.40
Long-term debt ($ mil.): —

Dividends
Yield: —
Payout: —
Market value ($ mil.): —

WILLAMETTE UNIVERSITY

According to itself Willamette University is the first university in the West. Nearly 3000 students are enrolled in the private co-educational liberal arts school that offers undergraduate and graduate degrees. Undergraduate degrees encompass nearly 50 fields (politics biology English psychology and economics are among the most pursued majors) and graduate degrees in business law and education. The university has a student to faculty ratio of 10 to 1. Founded in the early days of the Oregon Territory by missionary Jason Lee as a school for Native American children Willamette University was established in 1842.

The school has an operating budget of nearly $125 million and an endowment of roughly $230 million. Its sponsored research expenditures were $1.1 million during the 2011/2012 school year.

Willamette University offers study abroad programs nearly worldwide in countries that include Bulgaria China Estonia Finland South Africa Sweden and many others. Students are sent to learn the language and culture of the country in which they are studying. Students may enroll directly through the school through co-study centers in the country of destination or through a hybrid program in which they study courses from both Willamette and the destination University.

EXECUTIVES
President, M. Lee Pelton, age 61
Interim VP Financial Affairs Treasurer and Controller, Robert N. (Bob) Olson

VP Administrative Services, James R. (Jim) Bauer
Associate VP Communications, Janis J. Nichols
VP University Relations, Ronald J. Korvas
Executive Director Integrated Technology Services, John Balling
Director Human Resources, Keith A. Grimm

LOCATIONS
HQ: Willamette University
900 State St., Salem OR 97301-3930
Phone: 503-370-6300 **Fax:** 503-375-5466
Web: www.willamette.edu

PRODUCTS/OPERATIONS

Selected schools
College of Liberal Arts
College of Law
Graduate School of Education
Willamette MBA (Atkinson School)
Mark O. Hatfield Library
J. W. Long Law Library
Hallie Ford Museum of Art

HISTORICAL FINANCIALS
Company Type: School

Income Statement
FYE: May 31

	REVENUE ($ mil.)	NET INCOME ($ mil.)	NET PROFIT MARGIN	EMPLOYEES
05/12	102	(21)	—	700
05/11	93	25	26.7%	0
05/10*	90	8	9.4%	0
06/09	0	(0)	—	0
Annual Growth	976.4%	—	—	—

*Fiscal year change

2012 Year-End Financials
Debt ratio: —
Return on equity: (-21.10)%
Cash ($ mil.): 23
Current ratio: —
Long-term debt ($ mil.): —

Dividends
Yield: —
Payout: —
Market value ($ mil.): —

WILLIAM H. PORTER INC.

LOCATIONS
HQ: WILLIAM H. PORTER INC.
414 E CLEVELAND AVE, NEWARK, DE 19711-3715
Phone: 302-453-6800
Web: www.porterauto.com

HISTORICAL FINANCIALS
Company Type: Private

Income Statement
FYE: December 31

	REVENUE ($ mil.)	NET INCOME ($ mil.)	NET PROFIT MARGIN	EMPLOYEES
12/11	92	3	3.8%	140
12/10	76	2	3.5%	0
12/09	65	2	3.2%	0
12/02	97	0	—	0
Annual Growth	(1.6%)	—	—	—

2011 Year-End Financials

Debt ratio: —
Return on equity: 3.80%
Cash ($ mil.): 1
Current ratio: 0.10
Long-term debt ($ mil.): —

Dividends
Yield: —
Payout: —
Market value ($ mil.): —

WILLIAM MARSH RICE UNIVERSITY INC

You have to be as wise as an owl to attend Rice University and have really good SAT scores. Often referred to as the "Ivy League of the South" Rice — with mascot "Sammy the Owl" —consistently appears at the top of college academic rankings including those published by U.S. News & World Report. The private university has an enrollment of more than 6000 and about 1100 full-time part-time and adjunct faculty members (giving it a student-teacher ratio of about 6:1). Rice offers programs through eight schools in areas such as engineering computer science economics music and architecture. The university opened in 1912 with funds from the estate of William Marsh Rice.

Operations Rice's research programs span a dizzying array of disciplines that include energy health and tax policy science and technology conflict resolution and border policy. About 80% of Rice students are from the US including about 45% from Texas. Strategy The school is in the process of increasing the number of its undergraduates to 3800 students while still maintaining its very low student-faculty ratio. The change which began in 2008 and will take place over 10 years could involve building two new residential colleges the expansion of existing colleges and a possible Rice-affiliated off-campus facility to house both undergraduate and graduate students.

EXECUTIVES

President, David W. (Dave) Leebron, age 57
VP Finance, Kathy Collins
Provost, George McLendon
Vice Provost Information Technology, Kamran Khan
Vice Provost and University Librarian, Sara Lowman
VP International and Interdisciplinary Initiatives, Carol Quillen
Vice Provost Research, James Coleman
VP Administration, Kevin E. Kirby
VP Enrollment, Chris Mu?oz
VP Public Affairs, Linda L. Thrane
VP Resource Development, Darrow Zeidenstein
General Counsel, Richard A. Zansitis

LOCATIONS

HQ: Rice University
6100 Main, Houston TX 77005-1827
Phone: 713-348-0000   **Fax:** 713-348-5479
Web: www.rice.edu

PRODUCTS/OPERATIONS

Selected Departments and Interdisciplinary Programs

Air Force Science
Ancient Mediterranean Civilizations
Anthropology
Applied Physics Graduate Program
Architecture
Art History
Asian Studies
Bioengineering
Biosciences
Center for Digital Learning and Scholarship
Center for the Study of Languages
Chemical Engineering
Chemistry
Civil and Environmental Engineering
Classical Studies
Cognitive Sciences
Computational and Applied Mathematics
Computer Science
Earth Science
Economics
Education
Education Certification
Electrical and Computer Engineering
English
Environmental Analysis and Decision Making
Environmental Studies
French Studies
German and Slavic Studies
Hispanic Studies
History
Kinesiology
Leadership Rice
Lifetime Physical Activity Program
Linguistics
Management and Accounting
Managerial Studies
Master of Liberal Studies
Mathematics
Mechanical Engineering and Materials Science
Medieval Studies
Military Science
Music
Nanoscale Physics
Naval Science
Neurosciences
Philosophy
Physics and Astronomy
Policy Studies
Political Science
Psychology
Religious Studies
Sociology
Statistics
Subsurface Geoscience
The Program for the Study of Women and Gender

HISTORICAL FINANCIALS

Company Type: School

Income Statement
FYE: June 30

	REVENUE ($ mil.)	NET INCOME ($ mil.)	NET PROFIT MARGIN	EMPLOYEES
06/12	551	(33)	—	2,600
06/11	550	695	126.2%	0
06/10	519	189	36.5%	0
06/09	467	(1,026)	—	0
Annual Growth	5.6%	—	—	—

2012 Year-End Financials

Debt ratio: —
Return on equity: (-6.20)%
Cash ($ mil.): 9
Current ratio: —
Long-term debt ($ mil.): —

Dividends
Yield: —
Payout: —
Market value ($ mil.): —

WILLIAM PENN SCHOOL DISTRICT INC.

LOCATIONS

HQ: WILLIAM PENN SCHOOL DISTRICT INC.
100 GREEN AVE, LANSDOWNE, PA 19050-1449
Phone: 610-284-8000
Web: www.wpsd.k12.pa.us

HISTORICAL FINANCIALS

Company Type: Private

Income Statement
FYE: June 30

	REVENUE ($ mil.)	NET INCOME ($ mil.)	NET PROFIT MARGIN	EMPLOYEES
06/11	88	14	17.0%	495
06/09	78	1	1.4%	0
06/08	77	0	0.1%	0
06/07	75	(0)	—	0
Annual Growth	5.4%	—	—	—

2011 Year-End Financials

Debt ratio: —
Return on equity: 17.00%
Cash ($ mil.): 6
Current ratio: —
Long-term debt ($ mil.): —

Dividends
Yield: —
Payout: —
Market value ($ mil.): —

WILLIS-KNIGHTON MEDICAL CENTER

LOCATIONS

HQ: WILLIS-KNIGHTON MEDICAL CENTER
2600 GREENWOOD RD, SHREVEPORT, LA 71103-3908
Phone: 318-212-4000
Web: www.drclaudelockhart.yourmd.com

HISTORICAL FINANCIALS

Company Type: Private

Income Statement
FYE: September 30

	REVENUE ($ mil.)	NET INCOME ($ mil.)	NET PROFIT MARGIN	EMPLOYEES
09/11	807	76	9.4%	3,089
09/10	818	47	5.8%	0
09/09	768	46	6.0%	0
09/08	734	34	4.7%	0
Annual Growth	3.2%	30.5%	—	—

2011 Year-End Financials

Debt ratio: —
Return on equity: 9.40%
Cash ($ mil.): 121
Current ratio: 0.60
Long-term debt ($ mil.): —

Dividends
Yield: —
Payout: —
Market value ($ mil.): —

WILLOUGHBY EASTLAKE CITY SCHOOL DISTRICT

LOCATIONS

HQ: WILLOUGHBY EASTLAKE CITY SCHOOL
DISTRICT
37047 RIDGE RD, WILLOUGHBY, OH 44094-4130
Phone: 440-946-5000
Web: www.weschools.org

HISTORICAL FINANCIALS
Company Type: Private

Income Statement
FYE: June 30

	REVENUE ($ mil.)	NET INCOME ($ mil.)	NET PROFIT MARGIN	EMPLOYEES
06/11	101	19	19.6%	1,100
06/10	95	(3)	—	0
06/01	0	0	—	0
06/00	65	1	2.6%	0
Annual Growth	15.6%	126.3%	—	—

WILMINGTON UNIVERSITY INC.

LOCATIONS

HQ: WILMINGTON UNIVERSITY INC.
320 N DUPONT HWY, NEW CASTLE, DE 19720-6491
Phone: 302-356-6824
Web: www.wilmu.edu

HISTORICAL FINANCIALS
Company Type: Private

Income Statement
FYE: June 30

	REVENUE ($ mil.)	NET INCOME ($ mil.)	NET PROFIT MARGIN	EMPLOYEES
06/12	90	10	11.9%	1,200
06/11	82	14	17.1%	0
06/10	73	8	11.5%	0
06/09	65	1	1.8%	0
Annual Growth	11.6%	107.5%	—	—

2012 Year-End Financials

Debt ratio: ——
Return on equity: 11.90%
Cash ($ mil.): 29
Current ratio: 1.90
Long-term debt ($ mil.): ——
Dividends
Yield: —
Payout: —
Market value ($ mil.): —

WINDOW TO THE WORLD COMMUNICATIONS INC.

Window To The World Communications (WTTW) broadcasts arts children's current events humanities and science programming via its Chicago television station (WTTW Channel 11 with the nation's largest viewer base) and radio station (98.7 WFMT). The company's programming focuses on events and issues that effect the Chicago metropolitan area and special emphasis is given to cultural and educational topics. WTTW is a nonprofit governed by about 50 trustees representing the greater Chicago community. It is licensed by the FCC as a public TV station and is funded and governed by the community it serves. The station started by Inland Steel chairman Edward Ryerson began broadcasting in 1955.

In addition to local programming including Check Please! (restaurant reviews) Chicago Stories and Arts Across Illinois WTTW also produces Retirement Revolution Sound Stage Handy Ma'am with Beverly DeJulio and Grannies on Safari for national audiences.

In 2007 the company added Spanish language channel V-me to its lineup and launched an international classical music stream online bringing its digital channel total to three. It also produced local programming to go with the PBS program The War: A Ken Burns Film and opened a new operations center.

Major supporters and underwriters include American Airlines Blue Man Group Adler Planetarium Fox Searchlight Pictures Entenmann's Bakeries and Illinois Lottery.

EXECUTIVES

President CEO and Trustee, Daniel J. (Dan) Schmidt
EVP and CFO, Reese P. Marcusson
SVP; Executive in Charge WTTW National Productions, Parke Richeson
SVP Production and Community Partnerships, V. J. McAleer
SVP Corporate Communications and Direct Marketing, Joanie Bayhack
EVP Radio and Project Development, Steve Robinson
SVP Marketing and Interactive, Anne Gleason, age 39
General Sales Manager WFMT, Paul Ansell
Vice Chairman, Deborah L. (Deb) DeHaas
Secretary and Trustee, James H. Wooten Jr., age 63
Vice Chairman, Renee Crown
General Sales Manager WTTW, Howard Fisher
VP Development, Chip Fry
EVP and Chief Development Officer, Greg Cameron
SVP and Chief Television Content Officer, Daniel Soles
Chairman, Norman R. Bobins
Treasurer and Trustee, John L. Brennan
Vice Chairman, David C. Blowers
Trustee, Robert S. Hamada, age 74
Trustee, Roger L. Plummer, age 70
President CEO and Trustee, Daniel J. (Dan) Schmidt
Trustee, Sandra P. (Sandy) Guthman, age 68
Trustee, Robert S. Silver
Vice Chairman, Deborah L. (Deb) DeHaas
Trustee, Marvin S. Goldsmith
Trustee, Richard Gray
Secretary and Trustee, James H. Wooten Jr., age 63
Vice Chairman, Renee Crown
Treasurer and Trustee, John L. Brennan
Vice Chairman, David C. Blowers

Trustee, John W. Ballantine
Trustee, Alan A. Brown
Trustee, William G. Brown
Trustee, Adela Cepeda
Trustee, Alison Chung
Trustee, Robert Clifford
Trustee, Richard W. Colburn
Trustee, Michelle L. Collins
Trustee, Thomas R. Donovan
Trustee, Maxine P. Farrell
Trustee, James D. Firth
Trustee, Marshall B. Front
Trustee, Michael W. Gonzalez
Trustee, Chester A. Gougis
Trustee, John P. Hesselmann
Trustee, Mark A. Hoppe
Trustee, Daniel J. Hyman
Trustee, D. Carroll Joynes
Trustee, Kevin N. Knight
Trustee, Daniel E. Levin
Trustee, James W. Mabie
Trustee, Michael B. McCaskey
Trustee, Cary D. McMillan
Trustee, Peter B. McNitt
Trustee, Alexandra C. Nichols
Trustee, Carlos M. Pineiro
Trustee, Mark Pinsky
Trustee, Barbara Gardner Proctor
Trustee, George A. Ranney Jr.
Trustee, Shirley Welsh Ryan
Trustee, Gene R. Scaffold
Trustee, Gordon Segal
Trustee, Scott P. Serota
Trustee, Joan E. Steel
Trustee, Susan A. Stone
Trustee, Harlan Teller
Trustee, Howard A. Tullman
Trustee, Joan H. Walker
Trustee, Roxanne Ward
Trustee, Robert J. Washlow
Trustee, David E. Zyer

LOCATIONS

HQ: Window To The World Communications Inc.
5400 N. St. Louis Ave., Chicago IL 60625-4698
Phone: 773-583-5000   **Fax:** 773-583-3046
Web: www.wttw.com

HISTORICAL FINANCIALS
Company Type: Private - Not-for-Profit

Income Statement
FYE: June 30

	REVENUE ($ mil.)	NET INCOME ($ mil.)	NET PROFIT MARGIN	EMPLOYEES
06/11	41	3	9.0%	192
06/10	45	(7)	—	0
06/09	49	0	—	0
06/08	62	6	10.7%	0
Annual Growth	(12.6%)	(17.6%)	—	—

2011 Year-End Financials

Debt ratio: ——
Return on equity: 9.00%
Cash ($ mil.): 0
Current ratio: 0.50
Long-term debt ($ mil.): ——
Dividends
Yield: —
Payout: —
Market value ($ mil.): —

WINSTON-SALEM/FORSYTH COUNTY SCHOOLS

LOCATIONS
HQ: WINSTON-SALEM/FORSYTH COUNTY SCHOOLS
4801 BETHANIA STATION RD, WINSTON SALEM, NC
27105-1202
Phone: 336-727-2816
Web: www.westforsythfootball.net

HISTORICAL FINANCIALS
Company Type: Private

Income Statement
FYE: June 30

	REVENUE ($ mil.)	NET INCOME ($ mil.)	NET PROFIT MARGIN	EMPLOYEES
06/11	528	(4)	—	6,841
06/08	484	0	0.1%	0
06/07	451	0	—	0
06/06	145	28	19.9%	0
Annual Growth	53.8%	—	—	—

2011 Year-End Financials
Debt ratio: —
Return on equity: (-0.90)%
Cash ($ mil.): 17
Current ratio: 1.30
Long-term debt ($ mil.): —
Dividends
  Yield: —
  Payout: —
  Market value ($ mil.): —

WISCONSIN ENERGY CONSERVATION CORPORATION

LOCATIONS
HQ: WISCONSIN ENERGY CONSERVATION
CORPORATION
431 CHARMANY DR STE 102, MADISON, WI
53719-1234
Phone: 608-249-9322
Web: www.weccusa.org

HISTORICAL FINANCIALS
Company Type: Private

Income Statement
FYE: June 30

	REVENUE ($ mil.)	NET INCOME ($ mil.)	NET PROFIT MARGIN	EMPLOYEES
06/12	86	1	1.7%	170
06/11	144	1	1.1%	0
06/10	158	1	1.1%	0
06/09	106	0	0.9%	0
Annual Growth	(6.7%)	15.8%	—	—

WISS JANNEY ELSTNER ASSOCIATES INC.

LOCATIONS
HQ: WISS JANNEY ELSTNER ASSOCIATES INC.
330 PFINGSTEN RD, NORTHBROOK, IL 60062-2003
Phone: 847-272-7400
Web: www.wje.com

HISTORICAL FINANCIALS
Company Type: Private

Income Statement
FYE: December 31

	REVENUE ($ mil.)	NET INCOME ($ mil.)	NET PROFIT MARGIN	EMPLOYEES
12/11	90	0	0.4%	500
12/10	90	0	0.4%	0
12/09	106	0	0.2%	0
12/08	87	(0)	—	0
Annual Growth	1.2%	—	—	—

2011 Year-End Financials
Debt ratio: —
Return on equity: 0.40%
Cash ($ mil.): 14
Current ratio: 1.70
Long-term debt ($ mil.): —
Dividends
  Yield: —
  Payout: —
  Market value ($ mil.): —

WISSAHICKON SCHOOL DISTRICT

LOCATIONS
HQ: WISSAHICKON SCHOOL DISTRICT
601 KNIGHT RD, AMBLER, PA 19002-3413
Phone: 215-619-8000
Web: www.wsdweb.org

HISTORICAL FINANCIALS
Company Type: Private

Income Statement
FYE: June 30

	REVENUE ($ mil.)	NET INCOME ($ mil.)	NET PROFIT MARGIN	EMPLOYEES
06/12	82	(2)	—	630
06/11	83	(0)	—	0
06/10	82	(2)	—	0
06/09	83	(2)	—	0
Annual Growth	(0.4%)	—	—	—

WITHAM MEMORIAL HOSPITAL

LOCATIONS
HQ: WITHAM MEMORIAL HOSPITAL
2605 N LEBANON ST, LEBANON, IN 46052-1476
Phone: 765-485-8000
Web: www.witham.org

HISTORICAL FINANCIALS
Company Type: Private

Income Statement
FYE: December 31

	REVENUE ($ mil.)	NET INCOME ($ mil.)	NET PROFIT MARGIN	EMPLOYEES
12/11	120	6	5.7%	630
12/10	80	0	0.9%	0
12/09	76	4	6.5%	0
12/08	0	(0)	—	0
Annual Growth	633.3%	—	—	—

2011 Year-End Financials
Debt ratio: —
Return on equity: 5.70%
Cash ($ mil.): 14
Current ratio: 1.10
Long-term debt ($ mil.): —
Dividends
  Yield: —
  Payout: —
  Market value ($ mil.): —

WOLFINGTON BODY COMPANY INC

LOCATIONS
HQ: WOLFINGTON BODY COMPANY INC
RR 100 BOX N, EXTON, PA 19341
Phone: 610-458-8501
Web: www.wolfington.com

HISTORICAL FINANCIALS
Company Type: Private

Income Statement
FYE: December 31

	REVENUE ($ mil.)	NET INCOME ($ mil.)	NET PROFIT MARGIN	EMPLOYEES
12/11	90	0	0.1%	109
12/10	79	0	0.1%	0
12/09	80	0	0.1%	0
12/08	71	0	0.1%	0
Annual Growth	8.2%	(5.2%)	—	—

2012 Year-End Financials (WISS JANNEY ELSTNER ASSOCIATES INC.)
Debt ratio: —
Return on equity: 1.70%
Cash ($ mil.): 1
Current ratio: 1.30
Long-term debt ($ mil.): —
Dividends
  Yield: —
  Payout: —
  Market value ($ mil.): —

2012 Year-End Financials (WITHAM MEMORIAL HOSPITAL)
Debt ratio: —
Return on equity: (-3.20)%
Cash ($ mil.): 7
Current ratio: —
Long-term debt ($ mil.): —
Dividends
  Yield: —
  Payout: —
  Market value ($ mil.): —

LOCATIONS

HQ: Wolverine Power Supply Cooperative Inc.
10125 W. Watergate Rd., Cadillac MI 49601
Phone: 231-775-5700   **Fax:** 231-775-2077
Web: www.wpsci.com

COMPETITORS

ITC Holdings Corp.
Lansing Board of Water
  and Light
Midland Cogeneration
  Venture

WOLVERINE POWER SUPPLY COOPERATIVE INC.

Named after a voracious carnivore Wolverine Power Supply Cooperative makes sure that that voracious consumer of electricity –the American public –gets the power its needs. The non-profit company is an electric generation and transmission utility that provides services to five member distribution cooperatives in Michigan. Wolverine Power Supply Cooperative monitors and operates 1600 miles of bulk transmission lines and owns five power plants that generate 200 megawatts of capacity. It also maintains about 130 distribution substations and 36 transmission stations as well as purchases power (including windpower energy) from other utilities and marketers to distribute to its customers.

Wolverine Power Supply Cooperative's five members are Cherryland Electric Cooperative Great Lakes Energy Home Works Tri-County Electric Cooperative Presque Isle Electric & Gas Co-op and Wolverine Power Marketing Cooperative.

The cooperative is developing a coal-fired power plant near Rogers City Michigan and plans to build two 300W units and a wind turbine farm. It also expanded in late 2009 with an agreement to buy a generation facility in Michigan from FirstEnergy.

EXECUTIVES

VP Engineering and Operations, Danny R. Janway
President and CEO, Eric D. Baker
EVP, Craig A. Borr
VP Human Resources, Craig S. Borton
Staff Attorney, Brian E. Valice
VP Finance Accounting and Risk Management, Richard R. Kehl
VP Generation, Daniel H. (Dan) DeCoeur
VP Rates and Administrative Services, Kimberly B. Molitor
VP Power Supply and Energy Control, Michael P. (Peter) Chase
Executive Assistant, Dawn Coon
Chairman, Frederick F. Vermeersch
Vice Chairman, Jerry Akers
CFO, Janet L. Kass
Director, John Olson
Director, Glen Alsobrooks
Director, Dave Williamson
Director, Laverne Hansen
Director, Allen Bruder
Director, Wayne Swiler
Vice Chairman, Jerry Akers
Director, Jack Pope
Director, Dale Farrier
Director, Mike McDonald

HISTORICAL FINANCIALS

Company Type: Private - Cooperative

Income Statement

FYE: December 31

	REVENUE ($ mil.)	NET INCOME ($ mil.)	NET PROFIT MARGIN	EMPLOYEES
12/11	346	12	3.6%	110
12/10	294	(16)	——	0
12/09	256	13	5.2%	0
12/07	239	15	6.6%	0
Annual Growth	13.1%	(8.0%)	——	——

2011 Year-End Financials

Debt ratio: ——
Return on equity: 3.60%
Cash ($ mil.): 3
Current ratio: 0.60
Long-term debt ($ mil.): ——

Dividends
  Yield: ——
  Payout: ——
  Market value ($ mil.): ——

WOOD COUNTY HOSPITAL ASSOCIATION

LOCATIONS

HQ: WOOD COUNTY HOSPITAL ASSOCIATION
950 W WOOSTER ST, BOWLING GREEN, OH 43402-2699
Phone: 419-354-8900
Web: www.woodcountyhospital.org

HISTORICAL FINANCIALS

Company Type: Private

Income Statement

FYE: June 30

	REVENUE ($ mil.)	NET INCOME ($ mil.)	NET PROFIT MARGIN	EMPLOYEES
06/12	90	(8)	——	548
06/11	90	17	19.1%	0
06/10	83	1	2.0%	0
06/09	82	(14)	——	0
Annual Growth	3.4%	——	——	——

2012 Year-End Financials

Debt ratio: ——
Return on equity: (-9.90)%
Cash ($ mil.): 18
Current ratio: 0.70
Long-term debt ($ mil.): ——

Dividends
  Yield: ——
  Payout: ——
  Market value ($ mil.): ——

WOODS SERVICES INC.

LOCATIONS

HQ: WOODS SERVICES INC.
40 MARTIN GROSS DR, LANGHORNE, PA 19047-1616
Phone: 215-750-4000
Web: www.woods.org

HISTORICAL FINANCIALS

Company Type: Private

Income Statement

FYE: June 30

	REVENUE ($ mil.)	NET INCOME ($ mil.)	NET PROFIT MARGIN	EMPLOYEES
06/11	135	15	11.8%	2,300
06/10*	113	3	2.9%	0
05/10	126	13	10.8%	0
06/08	5	4	87.5%	0
Annual Growth	195.9%	51.7%	——	——

*Fiscal year change

2011 Year-End Financials

Debt ratio: ——
Return on equity: 11.80%
Cash ($ mil.): 20
Current ratio: 2.30
Long-term debt ($ mil.): ——

Dividends
  Yield: ——
  Payout: ——
  Market value ($ mil.): ——

WORCESTER POLYTECHNIC INSTITUTE

LOCATIONS

HQ: WORCESTER POLYTECHNIC INSTITUTE
100 INSTITUTE RD, WORCESTER, MA 01609-2280
Phone: 508-831-5000
Web: www.richfalco.com

HISTORICAL FINANCIALS

Company Type: Private

Income Statement

FYE: June 30

	REVENUE ($ mil.)	NET INCOME ($ mil.)	NET PROFIT MARGIN	EMPLOYEES
06/12	182	(5)	——	873
06/11	174	76	44.0%	0
06/10	164	31	19.3%	0
06/09	155	(92)	——	0
Annual Growth	5.4%	——	——	——

2012 Year-End Financials

Debt ratio: ——
Return on equity: (-3.00)%
Cash ($ mil.): 37
Current ratio: ——
Long-term debt ($ mil.): ——

Dividends
  Yield: ——
  Payout: ——
  Market value ($ mil.): ——

WORKMAN OIL COMPANY

LOCATIONS

HQ: WORKMAN OIL COMPANY
14680 FOREST RD, FOREST, VA 24551-4468
Phone: 434-525-1615

HISTORICAL FINANCIALS

Company Type: Private

Income Statement

FYE: March 31

	REVENUE ($ mil.)	NET INCOME ($ mil.)	NET PROFIT MARGIN	EMPLOYEES
03/12	255	0	0.2%	385
03/11	223	1	0.6%	0
03/10	196	0	0.4%	0
Annual Growth	13.9%	(15.4%)	—	—

2012 Year-End Financials

Debt ratio: ——
Return on equity: 0.20%
Cash ($ mil.): 2
Current ratio: 0.40
Long-term debt ($ mil.): —

Dividends
Yield: —
Payout: —
Market value ($ mil.): —

WORLD LEARNING INC.

LOCATIONS

HQ: WORLD LEARNING INC.
165 KIPLING RD, BRATTLEBORO, VT 05301
Phone: 802-257-7751
Web: www.worldlearning.org

HISTORICAL FINANCIALS

Company Type: Private

Income Statement

FYE: June 30

	REVENUE ($ mil.)	NET INCOME ($ mil.)	NET PROFIT MARGIN	EMPLOYEES
06/12	132	(3)	—	450
06/11	133	2	1.6%	0
06/10	119	1	1.3%	0
06/09	107	(10)	—	0
Annual Growth	7.3%	—	—	—

2012 Year-End Financials

Debt ratio: ——
Return on equity: (-2.80)%
Cash ($ mil.): 3
Current ratio: —
Long-term debt ($ mil.): —

Dividends
Yield: —
Payout: —
Market value ($ mil.): —

WOROCO MANAGEMENT LLC

LOCATIONS

HQ: WOROCO MANAGEMENT LLC
40 WOODBRIDGE AVE STE 3, SEWAREN, NJ
07077-1335
Phone: 732-855-7720

HISTORICAL FINANCIALS

Company Type: Private

Income Statement

FYE: December 31

	REVENUE ($ mil.)	NET INCOME ($ mil.)	NET PROFIT MARGIN	EMPLOYEES
12/11	267	1	0.6%	14
12/10	169	1	0.6%	0
12/09	110	(0)	—	0
12/08	218	2	1.3%	0
Annual Growth	6.9%	(17.1%)	—	—

2011 Year-End Financials

Debt ratio: ——
Return on equity: 0.60%
Cash ($ mil.): 4
Current ratio: 0.80
Long-term debt ($ mil.): —

Dividends
Yield: —
Payout: —
Market value ($ mil.): —

WRIGHT STATE UNIVERSITY

Wright State University named after aviation pioneers the Wright Brothers has an enrollment of some 20000 students and offers more than 100 undergraduate degrees and about 90 graduate and professional degrees. It consists of eight colleges (including education and human services business engineering and computer science liberal arts nursing and health and science and mathematics) and three schools (graduate studies medicine professional psychology). Wright State has about 900 faculty members. Originally a branch campus of Ohio State University and Miami University Wright State became an independent university in 1967.

Geographic Reach

Along with its main campus in Dayton Ohio Wright State also offers classes at its smaller Lake Campus in Celina Ohio.

Financial Performance

Wright State University reported a 2% increase in revenues to $263 million in fiscal 2012 due to increased student tuition and fees for the third year running. Increased earnings in 2012 were partly offset by lower government appropriations (state and federal) grants and contracts and auxiliary revenues. Net income dropped to a loss of $9 million (down from profits of $40 million in 2011) due to lower appropriations and higher expenses in areas including salaries benefits instruction research and academic support.

Tuition runs at over $8000 per year for Ohio residents and $16000 for out-of-state students. The university has increased tuition in recent years to replace lower state appropriation levels (resulting from harsh economic conditions).

Strategy

In 2012 Wright State issued $55 million in bonds to pay for construction and renovation efforts on academic and administrative buildings both on new and existing facilities. It is also upgrading campus infrastructures and student recreation and athletic facilities.

In addition the university is adopting a new budgeting model that it hopes will provide more transparency while allowing academic units to strategically identify new revenue sources. The system also aims to help divisions identify programs that are not adding academic or financial value.

EXECUTIVES

Chair, Robert C. Nevin, age 65
VP Business and Fiscal Affairs, Mark Polatajko
President, David R. Hopkins
Assistant VP Finance and Controller, Jeff Ulliman
VP Student Affairs, Dan Abrahamowicz
Assistant VP Human Resources, Allan Boggs
SVP Business and Fiscal Affairs, Matthew V. Filipic
General Counsel, Gwen M. Mattison
Director Career Services, Cheryl Krueger
Director Student Support Services, Katie Deedrick
Provost, Steven R. Angle
EVP Planning, Robert J. Sweeney
SVP Curriculum and Instruction, Lillie Howard
VP Research and Grad Studies, Robert E. Fyffe
Vice Chairman, Nina Joshi
Chairman, Larry R. Klaben
Secretary, John C. Kunesh
Vice Chair, Vishal Soin
Associate VP Facilities Planning and Development, Vicky Davidson
Executive Director Alumni Association, Susan Smith
VP University Advancement and President WSU Foundation, Bryan Rowland
Director Financial Aid, Willie Boyd
University Librarian and Associate VP International Affairs, Stephen P. Foster
Head Information Delivery Services University Libraries, Susan Wehmeyer
Dean Raj Soin College of Business, Berkwood M. Farmer
Interim Provost, Thomas Sudkamp
Trustee, Don R. Graber, age 68
Trustee and Board Secretary, J. Thomas Young
Trustee, Katie L. Bullinger
Trustee, Nina Joshi
Trustee, Larry R. Klaben
Trustee, John C. Kunesh
Trustee, Timothy R. (Tim) McEwen
Vice Chair, Vishal Soin
Auditors: PricewaterhouseCoopersLLP

LOCATIONS

HQ: Wright State University
3640 Colonel Glenn Hwy., Dayton OH 45435
Phone: 937-775-3333   **Fax:** 937-775-3663
Web: www.wright.edu

PRODUCTS/OPERATIONS

Selected Schools and Colleges

Colleges
Education and Human Services
Engineering and Computer Science
Liberal Arts
Nursing and Health
Raj Soin College of Business
Professional Psychology
Science and Mathematics

University College
WSU-Lake Campus
Schools
  Boonshoft School of Medicine
  Graduate Studies
  Professional Psychology

HISTORICAL FINANCIALS

Company Type: School

Income Statement

FYE: June 30

	REVENUE ($ mil.)	NET INCOME ($ mil.)	NET PROFIT MARGIN	EMPLOYEES
06/11	263	53	20.4%	2,748
06/10	253	24	9.7%	0
06/09	237	(25)	—	0
06/08	238	(10)	—	0
Annual Growth	3.5%	—	—	—

2011 Year-End Financials

Debt ratio: ——
Return on equity: 20.40%
Cash ($ mil.): 32
Current ratio: 0.60
Long-term debt ($ mil.): —

Dividends
  Yield: —
  Payout: —
Market value ($ mil.): —

WYNRIGHT CORPORATION

LOCATIONS

HQ: WYNRIGHT CORPORATION
2500 YORK RD, ELK GROVE VILLAGE, IL 60007-6319
Phone: 847-595-9400
Web: www.wynright.net

HISTORICAL FINANCIALS

Company Type: Private

Income Statement

FYE: December 31

	REVENUE ($ mil.)	NET INCOME ($ mil.)	NET PROFIT MARGIN	EMPLOYEES
12/11	164	0	—	350
12/10	134	0	—	0
12/08*	0	0	—	0
01/03	45	1	3.6%	0
Annual Growth	53.3%	—	—	—

*Fiscal year change

2011 Year-End Financials

Debt ratio: ——
Return on equity: —
Cash ($ mil.): 4
Current ratio: 0.80
Long-term debt ($ mil.): —

Dividends
  Yield: —
  Payout: —
Market value ($ mil.): —

WYOMING MEDICAL CENTER INC.

Wyoming Medical Center is The Cowboy State's largest medical facility. The hospital founded in 1911 offers those who live in and around Wyoming's Natrona County more than 50 medical specialties thanks to its 150 physicians. The health care services provider boasts nearly 1300 skilled staff members and more than 190 beds. It offers services such as an emergency air transport system trauma care diagnostic services diabetes care center nephrology and surgical care. The facility is a community-owned not-for-profit hospital.that also operates the Heart Center of Wyoming the Wyoming Neuroscience and Spine Institute and a network of about a dozen community clinics throughout Wyoming.

Geographic Reach

The health care provider serves the Wyoming communities of Natrona County and its surrounding counties.

EXECUTIVES

VP Human Resources and Legal Services, Dick Williams
VP Information Management and CIO, Don Claunch
President and CEO, Vickie Diamond
Chairman, Diane Payne
CFO, Nancy Brandt
Marketing and Public Relations Representative, Shauna VanderLinden
Chief Business Development Officer, Chris Lorenzen
Chief Planning Officer, Mary Lynne Shickich
Chief Medical Officer, Gene Ogrod
SVP Patient Care and Chief Nursing Officer, Julie Cann-Taylor
Chief of Staff and Director, David Wheeler
Vice Chair, Mary MacGuire
Secretary, Eugene Duquette
Director, John Baily
Director, Susie McMurry
Director, James Anderson
Director, Linda Young
Director, Mark Dowell
Director, Steve Sasser
Chief of Staff and Director, David Wheeler
Director, John Masterson
Director, Ruth Moran
Director, Jon Campbell
Vice Chair, Mary MacGuire

LOCATIONS

HQ: Wyoming Medical Center
1233 E. 2nd St., Casper WY 82601
Phone: 307-577-7201   Fax: 307-237-1703
Web: www.wmcnet.org

PRODUCTS/OPERATIONS

Selected Services

AHA Training
Casper Pulmonary
da Vinci System
Diabetes Care Center
Heart Center of Wyoming
Hometown Specialty Clinics
Professional Lab Services
Sage Primary Care
Weight Management Program
Wyoming Brain & Spine Associates
Wyoming Life Flight
Wyoming Nephrology
Wyoming Relay Health

COMPETITORS

Banner Health
Billings Clinic
Evanston
LifePoint Hospitals
North Colorado Medical Center
Poudre Valley Health System
Universal Health Services

HISTORICAL FINANCIALS

Company Type: Private - Not-for-Profit

Income Statement

FYE: June 30

	REVENUE ($ mil.)	NET INCOME ($ mil.)	NET PROFIT MARGIN	EMPLOYEES
06/11	227	14	6.3%	1,033
06/10	236	8	3.7%	0
06/09	204	(24)	—	0
06/08	206	11	5.5%	0
Annual Growth	3.3%	8.1%	—	—

2011 Year-End Financials

Debt ratio: ——
Return on equity: 6.30%
Cash ($ mil.): 41
Current ratio: 1.70
Long-term debt ($ mil.): —

Dividends
  Yield: —
  Payout: —
Market value ($ mil.): —

XAVIER UNIVERSITY

Xavier University is a not-for-profit Jesuit Catholic institution that operates from a single campus located in Cincinnati Ohio. The private school which has recently grown its enrollment numbers to about 7000 students offers nearly 90 undergraduate programs and about 20 graduate programs. Xavier University's programs range from arts and sciences to social sciences and business. Boasting small class sizes the university's student-to-faculty ratio is a noteworthy 12:1. Known among sports circles as having a highly respected men's basketball program Xavier University also manages to graduate every member of its men's Musketeers group. Xavier University was founded in 1831.

Geographic Reach

The university serves about 7000 students from its 190-acre campus located in Cincinnati Ohio.

Operations

The university is the nation's sixth-oldest Catholic university as compared to 27 other Jesuit colleges in the US. Xavier University's enrollment of about 7000 students includes 4540 undergraduates. Across its three colleges the university offers 87 undergraduate majors 55 minors and 19 graduate programs.

Sales and Marketing

Xavier University is the top school in the Midwest for graduation and approximately 77% of its student population is accepted to medical school. Across the university's sports disciplines it has 16 Division I teams.

Financial Performance

For the reporting period of 2012 vs. 2011 Xavier University posted flat revenue due to an increase in tuition and fees and auxiliary enterprise revenue. This was offset however by a decrease in government grants as well as a decline in contracts private gifts grants and endowment income. Net income for 2012 as compared to 2011 declined by 199% thanks to contributions and change in contributions receivable for non-operating purpose and investment return net of amounts in operations.

EXECUTIVES

Chairman Board of Trustees, Robert J. (Bob) Kohlhepp, age 68
President, Rev Michael J. Graham
Assistant VP Human Resources, Kathleen Riga
Academic VP and Provost, Roger A. Fortin
Administrative VP, John F. Kucia
VP University Relations, Gary R. Massa
Associate Provost Student Life and Leadership, Kathleen E. Simons
VP Student Enrollment, Terry Richards
VP Information and CIO, David Dodd
Interim VP Mission and Identity, Rev Eugene (Gene) Charmichael
Vice Provost Diversity, Cheryl L. Nu?ez
University Registrar, Allen Cole
Director Career Services Center, Sheila Spisak
VP Financial Administration, Maribeth Amyot
Associate Provost Academic Affairs, Kandi Stinson
Director Public Relations, Debora Del Valle
Auditors: Ernst&YoungLLP

LOCATIONS

HQ: Xavier University
3800 Victory Pkwy., Cincinnati OH 45207
Phone: 513-745-3000 **Fax:** 513-745-4223
Web: www.xavier.edu

PRODUCTS/OPERATIONS

Selected Colleges
College of Arts& Sciences
College of Social Sciences Health & Education
Williams College of Business

HISTORICAL FINANCIALS

Company Type: School

Income Statement   FYE: June 30

	REVENUE ($ mil.)	NET INCOME ($ mil.)	NET PROFIT MARGIN	EMPLOYEES
06/12	166	(22)	—	940
06/11*	167	22	13.5%	0
05/10	154	24	15.7%	0
05/09	144	(29)	—	0
Annual Growth	5.0%	—	—	—

*Fiscal year change

2012 Year-End Financials

Debt ratio: ——
Return on equity: (-13.50)%
Cash ($ mil.): 19
Current ratio: ——
Long-term debt ($ mil.): ——
Dividends
Yield: —
Payout: —
Market value ($ mil.): —

XORIANT CORPORATION

Xoriant provides outsourced application development engineering and consulting services to technology startups such as software developers as well as banks telecommuncations companies and health care providers among other businesses. The company specializes in implementing technology to enable cloud Web social networking media and mobile applications and services. Other services included testing and technical support. The company has international offices development facilities and support operations in the UK and India. Xoriant's customers have included TIBCO Software. The company was founded in 1990 by CEO Girish Gaitonde.

EXECUTIVES

VP India Operations, R. (Bala) Balachandran
CEO, Girish Gaitonde
CFO, Mahesh Nalavade
VP Business Development High Technology Practice, Shirish Gosavi

LOCATIONS

HQ: Xoriant Corporation
1248 Reamwood Ave., Sunnyvale CA 94089
Phone: 408-743-4400 **Fax:** 408-743-4490
Web: www.xoriant.com

COMPETITORS

Accenture	HP Enterprise Services
CIBER	IBM Global Services
Cognizant Tech Solutions	Indus Consultancy
Computer Sciences Corp.	Infosys
	Keane
Global Software Resources	Logica
	Patni Computer Systems
HCL Technologies	Tata Consultancy
HiSoft	Wipro

HISTORICAL FINANCIALS

Company Type: Private

Income Statement   FYE: December 31

	REVENUE ($ mil.)	NET INCOME ($ mil.)	NET PROFIT MARGIN	EMPLOYEES
12/11	55	1	3.5%	134
12/10	40	0	1.7%	0
12/09	25	1	5.5%	0
12/08	24	1	6.6%	0
Annual Growth	30.9%	6.7%		

2011 Year-End Financials

Debt ratio: ——
Return on equity: 3.50%
Cash ($ mil.): 0
Current ratio: 1.80
Long-term debt ($ mil.): ——
Dividends
Yield: —
Payout: —
Market value ($ mil.): —

YALE-NEW HAVEN HOSPITAL INC.

Yale-New Haven supports its community and the brainiacs at Yale. Yale-New Haven Hospital (YNHH) is the flagship member of the Yale New Haven Health System. It provides tertiary care in more than 100 medical specialties to residents of southwestern Connecticut. The hospital has more than 1500 beds on two campuses. Its main location includes the Yale-New Haven Children's Hospital and the Yale-New Haven Psychiatric Hospital. Smilow Cancer Hospital with 170 beds is also a part of the hospital complex. YNHH provides cardiac and cancer care performs organ transplants and offers a variety of outpatient clinics. The medical center serves as the primary teaching hospital for Yale University's medical school.

With expansion as a key component of its growth strategy YNHH acquired the Saint Raphael Healthcare System and the Hospital of Saint Raphael (HSR) in 2012. The company then moved to merge the entities to create one hospital on two campuses with the Hospital of Saint Raphael operating as YNHH-Saint Raphael Campus.

The hospital also operates the 170-bed Smilow Cancer Hospital and it conducts cancer research in partnership with the Yale Cancer Center. Together YNHH and Yale University also operate the Center for Outcomes Research and Evaluation (CORE) research center which selectively works on projects to assess health care quality and evaluate clinical decision-making and the comparative effectiveness of specific health care interventions.

Also in 2012 YNHH continued with its plans to develop an outpatient center in North Haven. The center which is expected to open in 2013 will be a walk-in/primary care center providing comprehensive medical services including cancer and inflammatory disease care and imaging and laboratory services; in addition some of YNHH's information technology offices in New Haven will be consolidated and moved to the North Haven site.

In fiscal 2011 revenue from patient services contributed 97% of the hospital's total operating revenue which grew by about 8% from the previous year.

EXECUTIVES

CEO and Trustee, Marna P. Borgstrom
SVP Technology and Information Systems, Mark L. Andersen
SVP Finance and CFO, James M. Staten
Vice Chair, Julia M. McNamara, age 70
SVP Medical Affairs Chief of Staff and Trustee, Peter N. Herbert
VP Facilities Planning and Management, Patrick M. Luddy
SVP Patient Services and Chief Nursing Officer, Patricia Sue Fitzsimons
SVP Public Affairs, Vincent P. (Vin) Petrini
SVP Administration, Norman G. Roth
Media Coordinator, Mark D'Antonio
Chair, Joseph R. Crespo
Secretary and Trustee, Robert A. Haversat
VP Development, Kevin F. Walsh
Chief Orthopedics, Gary E. Friedlaender, age 66
President and COO, Richard D'Aquila
VP Surgical Services, Marjorie Guglin
SVP Human Resources, Kevin A. Myatt
Chief Neurology, David A. Hafler
CIO, Daniel Barchi
VP Performance Management and Associate Chief of Staff, Thomas J. Balczak
Administrative Director, Victor A. Morris
Chief Anesthesiology, Roberta L. Hines
Chief Child Psychiatry, Fred R. Volkmar
Chief Dentistry, Suher Baker
Chief Dermatology, Richard L. Edelson
Chief Diagnostic Radiology, James Brink
Chief Emergency Medicine, Gail D'Onofrio
Chief Internal Medicine, Jack A. Elias
Chief Laboratory Medicine, Brian R. Smith
Chief Neurosurgery, Dennis D. Spencer

Chief Obstetrics and Gynecology, Charles J.
  Lockwood
Chief Ophthalmology, James C. Tsai
Chief Pathology, Jon S. Morrow
Chief Pediatrics, Margaret Hostetter
Chief Psychiatry, John H. Krystal
Chief Surgery, Robert Udelsman
Chief Therapeutic Radiology, Peter M. Glazer
Director Yale Cancer Center and Physician-in-
  Chief Smilow Cancer Hospital, Thomas J. Lynch
SVP and Chief Medical Officer Children's Hospital
  of Philadelphia, Michael Apkon
VP Legal Services and General Counsel, William J.
  Aseltyne
VP Yale New Haven Health System, Richard
  Lisitano
VP and Executive Director Smilow Cancer
  Hospital, Abe Lopman
VP Administration, Thomas Leary
VP Administration, Stephen Merz
Vice President Patient Services and Associate
  Chief Nursing Officer, Diane Vorio
VP Ambulatory Services Division, Richard S. Stahl
VP Yale New Haven Health System, John Skelly
VP Human Resources, Paul N. Patton
Trustee, Peyton R. Patterson, age 55
Trustee, Linda Koch Lorimer, age 60
Trustee, Richard C. Levin, age 64
Trustee, Carlton L. Highsmith, age 59
Trustee, John L. Lahey, age 65
CEO and Trustee, Marna P. Borgstrom
Vice Chair, Julia M. McNamara, age 70
SVP Medical Affairs Chief of Staff and Trustee,
  Peter N. Herbert
Trustee, Susan Whetstone
Trustee, Marvin K. Lender
Secretary and Trustee, Robert A. Haversat
Trustee, Theodore L. Brooks
Trustee, Michael H. Flynn
Trustee, Betty Ruth Hollander
Trustee, Robert J. Alpern, age 61
Trustee, Thomas M. Hanson
Trustee, Thomas B. Ketchum
Trustee, Thanasis M. Molokotos
Trustee, Rt. Hon. Barrington D Parker Jr.
Trustee, Diane F. Petra
Trustee, William W. Ginsberg

LOCATIONS

HQ: Yale-New Haven Hospital Inc.
  20 York St., New Haven CT 06510-3202
Phone: 203-688-4242   Fax: 203-688-6937
Web: www.ynhh.org

PRODUCTS/OPERATIONS

2011 Revenue

	$ mil.	% of total
Patient services	1,442	97
Other	46	3
Total	1,488	100

Selected Services

Ambulatory (outpatient) services
Bariatric surgery
Blood draw stations
Dental center
Diabetes and endocrinology
Diagnostic radiology
Ear nose and throat
Emergency services
Endocrine surgery
Gastroenterology
Geriatrics
Kidney disease
Maternity
Psychiatry
Pulmonology

Urology

COMPETITORS

Bristol Hospital	New Milford Hospital
Connecticut Children's	St. Raphael Healthcare
Medical Center	St. Vincent's Health
Griffin Hospital	Services
Hartford Health Care	Waterbury Hospital
MidState Medical	Western Connecticut
Center	Healthcare

HISTORICAL FINANCIALS
Company Type: Subsidiary

Income Statement   FYE: September 30

	REVENUE ($ mil.)	NET INCOME ($ mil.)	NET PROFIT MARGIN	EMPLOYEES
09/11	1,488	31	2.1%	6,000
09/09	1,237	52	4.3%	0
09/04	727	35	4.9%	0
09/03	664	645	97.1%	0
Annual Growth	30.9%	(63.3%)	—	—

2011 Year-End Financials

Debt ratio: ——
Return on equity: 2.10%
Cash ($ mil.): 65
Current ratio: 1.00
Long-term debt ($ mil.): ——

Dividends
  Yield: —
  Payout: —
  Market value ($ mil.): —

YOCO INC.

LOCATIONS

HQ: YOCO INC.
  1314 OLD HIGHWAY 601, MOUNT AIRY, NC
  27030-7211
Phone: 336-789-5561

HISTORICAL FINANCIALS
Company Type: Private

Income Statement   FYE: September 30

	REVENUE ($ mil.)	NET INCOME ($ mil.)	NET PROFIT MARGIN	EMPLOYEES
09/11	107	0	0.2%	30
09/10	96	0	0.1%	0
09/09	84	0	0.8%	0
09/08	119	0	0.3%	0
Annual Growth	(3.6%)	(15.0%)	—	—

2011 Year-End Financials

Debt ratio: ——
Return on equity: 0.20%
Cash ($ mil.): 0
Current ratio: 1.80
Long-term debt ($ mil.): ——

Dividends
  Yield: —
  Payout: —
  Market value ($ mil.): —

YORK ELECTRIC COOPERATIVE INC

LOCATIONS

HQ: YORK ELECTRIC COOPERATIVE INC
  1385 E ALEXANDER LOVE HWY, YORK, SC
  29745-7705
Phone: 803-684-4247
Web: www.yorkelectric.net

HISTORICAL FINANCIALS
Company Type: Private

Income Statement   FYE: December 31

	REVENUE ($ mil.)	NET INCOME ($ mil.)	NET PROFIT MARGIN	EMPLOYEES
12/11	90	0	—	93
12/10	91	3	3.5%	0
12/09	84	2	3.5%	0
12/08	77	0	—	0
Annual Growth	5.3%	—	—	—

2011 Year-End Financials

Debt ratio: ——
Return on equity: —
Cash ($ mil.): 8
Current ratio: 0.10
Long-term debt ($ mil.): ——

Dividends
  Yield: —
  Payout: —
  Market value ($ mil.): —

YORK HOSPITAL

York Hospital takes its name from the community whose health it seeks to preserve. Part of
WellSpan Health York Hospital has nearly 575
beds and serves a population of 520000 in York
and the surrounding area of south-central Pennsylvania. It is a regional leader in cardiovascular
and orthopedic care and has programs in other
specialty areas including oncology behavioral
health and geriatrics. Additionally the hospital operates a Level 1 trauma center offers outpatient
surgery emergency home health and diagnostic
imaging services. It is also has teaching and research programs. The hospital also known as
WellSpan York Hospital was founded in 1880.

EXECUTIVES

President, Richard L. Seim
VP Medical Affairs, Peter H. Hartmann
VP Marketing and Public Relations, Maria Royce
VP Patient Care Services, Valerie S. Hardy-Sprinkle
VP Operations, Raymond Rosen

LOCATIONS

HQ: YORK HOSPITAL
  1001 S GEORGE ST, YORK, PA 17403-3645
Phone: 717-851-3055

COMPETITORS

Ascension Health	Hanover Healthcare
Catholic Health	Hershey Medical Center
Initiatives	Holy Spirit
Geisinger Health	Lancaster General

System | Memorial Hospital (PA)
Guthrie Healthcare | PinnacleHealth System

HISTORICAL FINANCIALS
Company Type: Subsidiary

Income Statement
FYE: June 30

	REVENUE ($ mil.)	NET INCOME ($ mil.)	NET PROFIT MARGIN	EMPLOYEES
06/11	807	90	11.2%	6,200
06/10	755	73	9.8%	0
06/09	708	(65)	—	0
06/08	657	(7)	—	0
Annual Growth	7.1%	—	—	—

2011 Year-End Financials
Debt ratio: —
Return on equity: 11.20%
Cash ($ mil.): 30
Current ratio: 2.00
Long-term debt ($ mil.): —

Dividends
Yield: —
Payout: —
Market value ($ mil.): —

HISTORICAL FINANCIALS
Company Type: Subsidiary

Income Statement
FYE: June 30

	REVENUE ($ mil.)	NET INCOME ($ mil.)	NET PROFIT MARGIN	EMPLOYEES
06/11	156	3	2.5%	535
06/10	148	5	3.6%	0
06/09	141	0	—	0
06/08	242	(1)	—	0
Annual Growth	(13.5%)	—	—	—

2011 Year-End Financials
Debt ratio: —
Return on equity: 2.50%
Cash ($ mil.): 8
Current ratio: 1.80
Long-term debt ($ mil.): —

Dividends
Yield: —
Payout: —
Market value ($ mil.): —

YORK HOSPITAL

York Hospital takes its name from the community whose health it seeks to preserve. Part of WellSpan Health York Hospital has nearly 575 beds and serves a population of 520000 in York and the surrounding area of south-central Pennsylvania. It is a regional leader in cardiovascular and orthopedic care and has programs in other specialty areas including oncology behavioral health and geriatrics. Additionally the hospital operates a Level 1 trauma center offers outpatient surgery emergency home health and diagnostic imaging services. It is also has teaching and research programs. The hospital also known as WellSpan York Hospital was founded in 1880.

EXECUTIVES

President, Richard L. Seim
VP Medical Affairs, Peter H. Hartmann
VP Marketing and Public Relations, Maria Royce
VP Patient Care Services, Valerie S. Hardy-Sprinkle
VP Operations, Raymond Rosen

LOCATIONS

HQ: YORK HOSPITAL
15 HOSPITAL DR, YORK, ME 03909-1099
Phone: 207-363-4321
Web: www.yorkhospital.com

COMPETITORS

Ascension Health
Catholic Health Initiatives
Geisinger Health System
Guthrie Healthcare

Hanover Healthcare
Hershey Medical Center
Holy Spirit
Lancaster General
Memorial Hospital (PA)
PinnacleHealth System

YORK PENNSYLVANIA HOSPITAL COMPANY LLC

Memorial Hospital serves the York County region of southeastern Pennsylvania in the midst of Amish country. The hospital offers emergency critical care diagnostic surgery and rehabilitation services as well as specialty cardiovascular orthopedic and obstetric services. In addition to the 100-bed acute care facility Memorial Hospital operates Greenbriar Medical Center (a diagnostic imaging and rehabilitation center) the Surgical Center of York (outpatient surgery facility) home health and hospice agencies and primary and specialist care clinics. Memorial Hospital is part of the Community Health Systems (CHS) network.

Operations

Memorial Hospital serves as a teaching facility for a number of area universities including John Hopkins University Temple University and the University of Pittsburgh. It offers internship residency and rotation programs with a focus on fields including emergency family practice internal medicine general surgery orthopedics and obstetrics and gynecology (OB/GYN).

Strategy

To expand and improve services in the region which is experiencing population growth CHS has committed to building a replacement facility for Memorial Hospital (within five years of Memorial Hospital's acquisition by CHS in 2012).

As part of CHS Memorial Hospital is also part of CHS' efforts to recruit high quality physicians and share hospital best practices among its facilities. CHS intends to keep active associates charity care policies and residency training programs in place at Memorial Hospital.

Ownership

CHS acquired Memorial Hospital and its parent company Memorial Health Systems in 2012. The transaction resulted in Memorial Hospital becoming a tax-paying entity. Proceeds from the deal were used to form a not-for-profit foundation to benefit wellness and health initiatives in the York community. The hospital continues to be overseen by a board of trustees made up of staff and community representatives.

EXECUTIVES

VP Quality and Strategy Development, Flavius Lilly
President and Director, Sally J. Dixon
Secretary and Treasurer, Jody Keller
CFO, Richard Imbimbo
VP Business Development, Michael Hady
VP Community Relations and Development, John DeHaas
Chairperson, Chloe R. Eichelberger
President Medical Staff and Director, Carol L. St. George
Manager Human Resources, Corey Hudak
CIO, Jim Mahoney
Director, Jack R. Kay
President and Director, Sally J. Dixon
Vice Chair, Randall A. Gross
Director, Scott E. Hartman
Director, Hugh E. Palmer
Director, Richard D. Poole
Director, Luther Sowers
Director, Delaine Toerper
Director, James R. Zarfoss Jr.
Director, Harry Zimmerman
President Medical Staff and Director, Carol L. St. George
Director, Terry N. York
Director, David Freeman
Auditors: PricewaterhouseCoopersLLP

LOCATIONS

HQ: Memorial Hospital
325 S. Belmont St., York PA 17405
Phone: 717-843-8623 **Fax:** 717-849-5489
Web: www.mhyork.org

PRODUCTS/OPERATIONS

Selected Services
Cardiology Services
Emergency Care
Family Birth Center
Family Medicine
Greenbriar Medical Center
Home Health Services
Imaging Services
Laboratory Services
Occupational Health
Other Patient Care Services
Outpatient Clinic
Outpatient Surgery Center
Patient Care
Robotic Surgery
Surgical Services
Women's Health

Selected Educational Affiliates
Bloomsburg School of Public Health
Des Moines University College of Osteopathic Medicine
Duquesne University
Harrisburg Area Community College
John Hopkins University
Kirksville College of Osteopathic Medicine
Lake Erie College of Osteopathic Medicine
Lancaster General College
New England College of Osteopathic Medicine
Philadelphia College of Osteopathic Medicine
Temple University
Touro University College of Osteopathic Medicine
University of Osteopathic Medicine & Health Sciences College of Osteopathic Medicine & Surgery
University of Pittsburgh
University of Scranton
West Virginia School of Osteopathic Medicine
York College of Pennsylvania
York County School of Technology

COMPETITORS

Community Health Systems

St. Luke's University Health Network

Hanover Healthcare
Jefferson Health System
Pennsylvania Hospital
Tenet Healthcare
WellSpan Health
York Hospital

HISTORICAL FINANCIALS
Company Type: Private - Not-for-Profit

Income Statement
FYE: June 30

	REVENUE ($ mil.)	NET INCOME ($ mil.)	NET PROFIT MARGIN	EMPLOYEES
06/11	106	0	0.4%	900
06/10	100	2	2.1%	0
06/09	100	0	—	0
06/08	98	(0)	—	0
Annual Growth	2.9%	—	—	—

2011 Year-End Financials

Debt ratio: ——
Return on equity: 0.40%
Cash ($ mil.): 4
Current ratio: 1.90
Long-term debt ($ mil.): ——

Dividends
Yield: —
Payout: —
Market value ($ mil.): —

YOSEMITE FARM CREDIT ACA

LOCATIONS

HQ: YOSEMITE FARM CREDIT ACA
800 W MONTE VISTA AVE, TURLOCK, CA 95382-7242
Phone: 209-667-2366
Web: www.yosemitefarmcredit.com

HISTORICAL FINANCIALS
Company Type: Private

Income Statement
FYE: December 31

	ASSETS ($ mil.)	NET INCOME ($ mil.)	INCOME AS % OF ASSETS	EMPLOYEES
12/11	1,676	54	3.2%	100
12/10	1,609	32	2.0%	0
12/09	1,582	25	1.6%	0
12/08	1,410	17	1.2%	0
Annual Growth	5.9%	46.6%	—	—

2011 Year-End Financials

Debt ratio: ——
Return on equity: 56.30%
Cash ($ mil.): 2
Current ratio: ——
Long-term debt ($ mil.): ——

Dividends
Yield: —
Payout: —
Market value ($ mil.): —

YOUNG ADULT INSTITUTE INC.

LOCATIONS

HQ: YOUNG ADULT INSTITUTE INC.
460 W 34TH ST FL 11, NEW YORK, NY 10001-2382
Phone: 212-563-7474
Web: www.yai.org

HISTORICAL FINANCIALS
Company Type: Private

Income Statement
FYE: June 30

	REVENUE ($ mil.)	NET INCOME ($ mil.)	NET PROFIT MARGIN	EMPLOYEES
06/11	201	5	3.0%	5,000
06/10	168	(12)	—	0
06/09	173	0	—	0
06/08	164	0	0.5%	0
Annual Growth	6.9%	90.7%	—	—

2011 Year-End Financials

Debt ratio: ——
Return on equity: 3.00%
Cash ($ mil.): 21
Current ratio: ——
Long-term debt ($ mil.): ——

Dividends
Yield: —
Payout: —
Market value ($ mil.): —

YOUNG LIFE INC.

Young Life is focused on promoting Christianity among teenagers in the US and in more than 50 other countries. Founded in 1941 the not-for-profit organization provides activities and support for junior high middle school and high school students located in rural and urban communities. Young Life also operates week-long summer camp programs at about 20 locations throughout North America as well as retreats held throughout the year. The group has grown throughout the years from a single club in Texas to about 600 international Young Life ministries dotting the globe. The organization boasts about 3000 staffers and more than 27000 volunteers.

EXECUTIVES

CFO, Jeff Stedman
President, Dennis (Denny) Rydberg
SVP Western Division, Ty Saltzgiver
Chair, John Bradford
SVP International South Division, Marty Caldwell
SVP International North Division, Lee Corder
VP Field Ministries Eastern Division, Jim Dyson
SVP Northern Division, Gail Ebersole
VP Field Ministries Southern Division, Bebe Hobson
VP and Special Assistant to the President, Bill Paige
VP Field Ministries Northern Division, Wiley Scott
SVP Southern Division, John Vicary
SVP Eastern Division, John Wagner
Auditors: BKDLLP

LOCATIONS

HQ: Young Life
420 N. Cascade Ave., Colorado Springs CO 80903-3325
Phone: 719-381-1800 **Fax:** 719-381-1755
Web: www.younglife.org

HISTORICAL FINANCIALS
Company Type: Private - Not-for-Profit

Income Statement
FYE: September 30

	REVENUE ($ mil.)	NET INCOME ($ mil.)	NET PROFIT MARGIN	EMPLOYEES
09/11	245	19	7.8%	3,100
09/10*	222	6	2.9%	0
12/09	236	14	6.3%	0
09/09	236	14	6.3%	0
Annual Growth	1.2%	8.8%	—	—

*Fiscal year change

2011 Year-End Financials

Debt ratio: ——
Return on equity: 7.80%
Cash ($ mil.): 42
Current ratio: 2.10
Long-term debt ($ mil.): ——

Dividends
Yield: —
Payout: —
Market value ($ mil.): —

YOUNG MEN'S CHRISTIAN ASSOCIATION OF GREATER NEW YORK

LOCATIONS

HQ: YOUNG MEN' S CHRISTIAN ASSOCIATION OF GREATER NEW YORK
5 W 63RD ST FL 6, NEW YORK, NY 10023-7162
Phone: 212-630-9600

HISTORICAL FINANCIALS
Company Type: Private

Income Statement
FYE: December 31

	REVENUE ($ mil.)	NET INCOME ($ mil.)	NET PROFIT MARGIN	EMPLOYEES
12/11	154	(0)	—	4,500
12/09	141	(3)	—	0
12/04	111	0	0.6%	0
12/03	108	18	16.9%	0
Annual Growth	12.4%	—	—	—

2011 Year-End Financials

Debt ratio: ——
Return on equity: (-0.50)%
Cash ($ mil.): 17
Current ratio: 0.20
Long-term debt ($ mil.): ——

Dividends
Yield: —
Payout: —
Market value ($ mil.): —

YOUNG WOMEN'S CHRISTIAN ASSOCIATION OF GREATER PITTSBURGH

LOCATIONS

HQ: YOUNG WOMEN' S CHRISTIAN ASSOCIATION OF GREATER PITTSBURGH
305 WOOD ST, PITTSBURGH, PA 15222-1914
Phone: 412-391-5100
Web: www.ywcapgh.org

HISTORICAL FINANCIALS
Company Type: Private

Income Statement
FYE: June 30

	REVENUE ($ mil.)	NET INCOME ($ mil.)	NET PROFIT MARGIN	EMPLOYEES
06/11	88	(0)	—	210
06/10	86	(0)	—	0
06/09	92	(0)	—	0
06/08	89	(4)	—	0
Annual Growth	(0.5%)	—	—	—

2011 Year-End Financials

Debt ratio: ——
Return on equity: (-0.10)%
Cash ($ mil.): 10
Current ratio: 1.20
Long-term debt ($ mil.): —

Dividends
Yield: —
Payout: —
Market value ($ mil.): —

YUMA REGIONAL MEDICAL CENTER INC

Yuma Regional Medical Center (YRMC) is an acute care hospital that provides medical services for Yuma Arizona and its surrounding communities. The hospital which has about 370 beds offers a cardiac catheterization lab children's health services outpatient and inpatient surgical services a sleep disorder diagnostic lab a cancer treatment center and a variety of other medical services. YRMC also offers home health care school health care medical equipment rentals (through First Health Medical Supply) and cardiac and pulmonary rehabilitation services off-site.

YRMC is a not-for-profit corporation governed by a 12-member volunteer board. The hospital is funded by the Foundation of Yuma Regional Medical Center which raises money through various means including donations bequests and special events.

Being a somewhat regional hospital YRMC works hard to recruit physicians who might rather practice are larger teaching hospitals with more advanced technological equipment and complex medical cases. YRMC especially has a hard time recruiting specialists to the region in areas such as cardiac surgery endocrinology pathology and pe-

diatrics among others. In order to lure in such specialists the hospital offers extended medical education career weekends and a number of specialized centers in which physicians can perform procedures solely in their specialty. For example some centers include a neo-natal ICU and a pediatric sub-specialty unit.

YRMC also offers a free program called Silver Care in which patients who are 55 and older are encouraged to live active and healthy lives by being offered a number of benefits such as discounts at local stores specially reduced rates on selected lab tests including cholesterol and blood glucose screenings. Additionally Silver Care members are eligible for free membership in the Fit for Life cardiac wellness program to monitor their cardiac health.

EXECUTIVES

VP Human Resources, Sharon Gardner
VP Medical Affairs and Chief Medical Officer, Stewart Hamilton
VP Professional and Support Services, Jim Hall
VP Patient Care Services and Chief Nursing Officer, Karen Jensen
Director Materials Management, Robin Finn
Director Community Relations, Machele Headington
Interim CFO, Tony Struck
President and CEO, Pat Walz
VP Planning and Business Development, Mark Parston
VP Information Technology and CIO, Gene Shaw
Administrative Director Women's and Children's Services, Pam Dallabetta
Director Medical Staff Services, Sandra Cady
Director Diagnostic Imaging, Eldon Dyer
Vice Chairperson, Tom Tyree
Chairman, Joann Linville
Director ICU, Karen Hardy
Director Contracts, Todd Hirte
Director Care Coordination, Jill Labossiere
Director Community Services, Pam Miller
Director Patient Access, Lori Mitchell
Director 2 West Medical, Marla Moore
Director Recruitment and Educational Services, Teri Norris
Director Foundation of Yuma Regional Medical Center, Debbie Stahl
Director Plant Operations, Roger Neifert
Director MedWest, Claudette Rodstrom
Director Tower 2, Lynn Smith
Director 3 West, Randy K. Fike
Director OR Materials Management, Tim Brooks
Director Clinical Education, Leslie Dalton
Director Patient Accounts, Sheri Hanson
Director Quality Services and Patient Safety, Mark Hutsell
Director Surgical Services, Julie Lubecki
Director Children and Women, Jennifer Stanton
Director Risk Management, Ann Totsch
Director Pharmacy, Tom Van Hassel
Director Employee Benefits, Alex Wade
Director Health Records, Deborah Foxford
Chief of Staff, Lou Miller
Officer of Physician Relations, Clarence Clark
Vice Chief of Staff, Divesh Anireddy
Administrative Director Adult Acute Care, Deborah Carver
Corporate Compliance Officer, Linda Johnson
Director Information Systems, Fred Peet
Director Nutrition Services, Sharyl Strongman
Corporate Communications Specialist, Michele Cohen
Director, James K. Paquin
Director, Roberto Garcia
Director, Woodrow (Woody) Martin

Vice Chairperson, Tom Tyree
Director, Kathy Watson
Director, Louie Hirth
Director, Victor Smith
Director, Ian Watkinson
Director, Russ Clark
Director, Mario Jauregui
Director, Phillip Richemont

LOCATIONS

HQ: Yuma Regional Medical Center
2400 S. Ave. A, Yuma AZ 85364
Phone: 928-344-2000   **Fax:** 928-336-7308
Web: www.yumaregional.org

PRODUCTS/OPERATIONS

Selected Services
Bronchoscopy services
Children's health services
Critical care
Diagnostic imaging
Emergency department
Endoscopy services
Medical services
Pharmacy
Respiratory care
Surgical services
Women's services

COMPETITORS

Banner Health
Community Health Systems
Dignity Health
HCA
Iasis Healthcare
Inova
John C. Lincoln Health Network
Northern Arizona Healthcare

Phoenix Children' s Hospital
Poudre Valley Health System
Providence Health & Services
Scottsdale Healthcare
St. Joseph Health System
University Medical Center

HISTORICAL FINANCIALS
Company Type: Private - Not-for-Profit

Income Statement
FYE: September 30

	REVENUE ($ mil.)	NET INCOME ($ mil.)	NET PROFIT MARGIN	EMPLOYEES
09/11	330	4	1.2%	1,600
09/10	317	21	6.7%	0
09/09	328	10	3.1%	0
09/08	315	6	2.2%	0
Annual Growth	1.6%	(15.8%)	—	—

2011 Year-End Financials

Debt ratio: ——
Return on equity: 1.20%
Cash ($ mil.): 77
Current ratio: 4.80
Long-term debt ($ mil.): —

Dividends
Yield: —
Payout: —
Market value ($ mil.): —

ZAHM & MATSON INC.

LOCATIONS

HQ: ZAHM & MATSON INC.
1756 LINDQUIST DR, FALCONER, NY 14733-9720
Phone: 716-665-3110
Web: www.zahmandmatson.com

HISTORICAL FINANCIALS

Company Type: Private

Income Statement

FYE: December 31

	REVENUE ($ mil.)	NET INCOME ($ mil.)	NET PROFIT MARGIN	EMPLOYEES
12/11	80	1	1.4%	135
12/10	68	1	2.4%	0
12/09	62	0	0.9%	0
12/08	63	0	0.7%	0
Annual Growth	8.4%	40.0%	—	—

2011 Year-End Financials

Debt ratio: —
Return on equity: 1.40%
Cash ($ mil.): 1
Current ratio: 0.10
Long-term debt ($ mil.): —

Dividends
Yield: —
Payout: —
Market value ($ mil.): —

ZEN-NOH GRAIN CORPORATION

LOCATIONS

HQ: ZEN-NOH GRAIN CORPORATION
1127 HWY 190 E SERVICE RD, COVINGTON, LA
70433-4929
Phone: 985-867-3500
Web: www.cgb.com

HISTORICAL FINANCIALS

Company Type: Private

Income Statement

FYE: May 31

	REVENUE ($ mil.)	NET INCOME ($ mil.)	NET PROFIT MARGIN	EMPLOYEES
05/11	6,217	66	1.1%	213
05/10	5,988	55	0.9%	0
05/09	5,454	37	0.7%	0
05/08	5,719	47	0.8%	0
Annual Growth	2.8%	12.3%	—	—

2011 Year-End Financials

Debt ratio: —
Return on equity: 1.10%
Cash ($ mil.): 35
Current ratio: 1.00
Long-term debt ($ mil.): —

Dividends
Yield: —
Payout: —
Market value ($ mil.): —

ZEOLYST INTERNATIONAL

LOCATIONS

HQ: ZEOLYST INTERNATIONAL
300 LINDENWOOD DR, MALVERN, PA 19355-1740
Phone: 610-651-4200
Web: www.zeolyst.com

HISTORICAL FINANCIALS

Company Type: Private

Income Statement

FYE: December 31

	REVENUE ($ mil.)	NET INCOME ($ mil.)	NET PROFIT MARGIN	EMPLOYEES
12/11	198	45	23.1%	115
12/09	126	30	24.2%	0
Annual Growth	56.7%	49.9%	—	—

2011 Year-End Financials

Debt ratio: —
Return on equity: 23.10%
Cash ($ mil.): 0
Current ratio: 1.30
Long-term debt ($ mil.): —

Dividends
Yield: —
Payout: —
Market value ($ mil.): —

ZOOLOGICAL SOCIETY OF SAN DIEGO

Talk about animal magnetism! The Zoological Society of San Diego is a not-for-profit organization that operates the 100-acre San Diego Zoo which cares for more than 4000 individual animals as well as a collection of some 6500 species of plants. The Zoological Society also manages the 1800-acre San Diego Zoo's Wild Animal Park and the center for Conservation and Research for Endangered Species. The zoo entertains all with its daily shows in-park restaurants guided tours and special events. The society also supports conservation education and efforts such as planned travel adventure-tours to exotic destinations such as Mexico or Africa. It was founded by Dr. Harry Wegeforth in 1916.

EXECUTIVES

President and Trustee, Berit N. Durler
Treasurer and Trustee, Frank C. Alexander
VP and Trustee, Frederick A. Frye
Secretary and Trustee, Rick Gulley
Executive Director, Douglas G. Myers
Treasurer and Trustee, Frank C. Alexander
VP and Trustee, Frederick A. Frye
Secretary and Trustee, Rick Gulley
Trustee, David S. Woodruff
Trustee, Thompson Fetter
Trustee, Weldon Donaldson
Trustee, George L. Gildred
Trustee, Judith A. Wheatley
Trustee, Nan Katona
Trustee, Sandra Brue
Trustee, William H. May

LOCATIONS

HQ: Zoological Society of San Diego
2920 Zoo Dr., San Diego CA 92101
Phone: 619-231-1515   **Fax:** 619-557-3937
Web: www.sandiegozoo.org

HISTORICAL FINANCIALS

Company Type: Private - Not-for-Profit

Income Statement

FYE: January 1

	REVENUE ($ mil.)	NET INCOME ($ mil.)	NET PROFIT MARGIN	EMPLOYEES
01/12*	227	6	2.9%	2,300
12/10	193	(6)	—	0
12/09	173	(15)	—	0
01/06	173	17	10.0%	0
Annual Growth	9.5%	(27.8%)	—	—

*Fiscal year change

2012 Year-End Financials

Debt ratio: —
Return on equity: 2.90%
Cash ($ mil.): 40
Current ratio: 0.30
Long-term debt ($ mil.): —

Dividends
Yield: —
Payout: —
Market value ($ mil.): —

Index of Executives

Avery, Larry 396
Aveson, Jill 518
Avila, Mike 114
Avioli, Marybeth 589
Avis, Anne 281
Avis, Anne 281
Aviv, Diana 526
Avramidis, Manny 28
Axelrod, Susan F. 194
Axelrod, Neal 539
Axene, David 52
Axtman, Bryan David 125
Axworthy, Lloyd 247
Ay, Timothy 589
Ayala, Gladys M. 352
Aycock, Nancy B. 574
Ayers, Frank 176
Ayers, Tom 278
Ayers, William L. (Bill) 408
Ayers, Edward L. 579
Ayers-Miller, Patricia A. (Trisha) 121
Ayotte, Kelly A. 53
Ayotte, Conrad L. 309
Ayoub, Walid 247
Ayres, Kathleen (Kathy) 315
Azari, Farang 295
Azarian-McCullough, Barbara 474
Azavedo, Sarah 185
Azima, Ali 548
Azuah, Unoma 286

B

Baak, Marinus W. 440
Babashanian, Mark 168
Babbin, Laura Papa 334
Babbio, Lawrence T. (Larry) 488
Babbitt, Katrina 104
Babcock, Jean 5
Babe, Gregory S. (Greg) 164
Babington, Catherine V. 540
Babish, Brendan 114
Baccante, Richard 27
Bachelder, Cheryl A. 559
Bacheldor, H. Lee 420
Bachman, Paul 565
Bachmann, John W. 544
Bachraty, James J. 146
Bachwich, Dale 412
Backlund, Mary 54
Bacon, Marilyn 131
Bacon, Scott 175
Baczko, Joseph R. 380
Badavas, Robert P. (Bob) 63
Badcock, Ben M. 592
Badcock, Wogan S. (Wogie) 592
Badcock, Henry C. 592
Baden, Marvin (Butch) 401
Baehr, Marie 120
Baensch, Robert E. 133
Baer, Robert (Rob) 77
Baer, David A. 77
Baer, Bob 99
Baer, Douglas M. (Doug) 212
Baer, David E. 273
Baer, Candace 417
Baer, Richard O. 585
Baeza, Mario L. 546
Baggett, Billie 486
Bagley, Elizabeth 9
Bagley, Karen 401
Bagley, Patrick 516
Bagley, Patrick 516
Bagnall, Jonathan 287
Bahke, Torsten 30
Bahls, Steven C. 47
Baig, Khadar 113
Baile, Charles C. 42
Bailey, Larry D. 8
Bailey, Larry D. 8
Bailey, Edward N. 21
Bailey, Vicky A. 57
Bailey, Mike 99
Bailey, Veronica 151

Bailey, Colin 205
Bailey, Bruce P. 214
Bailey, Larry 254
Bailey, Rich 307
Bailey, Rich 307
Bailey, David 338
Bailey, D. Russell 404
Bailey, Ann Marie 463
Bailey, Sue 492
Baily, John 622
Bailye, John E. 185
Bainbridge, Craig 261
Bainecke, Frances G. 345
Baines, Sidney 175
Bair, Ryan 77
Bair, Paul 295
Bair, Margaret E. Jones 538
Baity, Dawn 126
Bakas, James (Jim) 349
Baker, Marilyn L. 30
Baker, Sally A. 121
Baker, Barry G. 154
Baker, Deb 175
Baker, Karen 234
Baker, Karen 234
Baker, Shawn K. 235
Baker, David 251
Baker, Newell A. 264
Baker, Donna 290
Baker, Greg 298
Baker, Rudy 312
Baker, Peter H. 314
Baker, Jim 332
Baker, Jay H. 347
Baker, Vicki 401
Baker, Glen 409
Baker, William F. 457
Baker, Shirley K. 543
Baker, Jane 560
Baker, Wendell (Wick) 574
Baker, Joseph J. 613
Baker, Eric D. 620
Baker, Suher 623
Baky, John 288
Balachandran, Indra 12
Balachandran, R. (Bala) 623
Baladassari, Bob 402
Balcezak, Thomas J. 623
Baldassari, Bob 402
Baldino, Frank 506
Baldock, Elisabeth 105
Baldovin, John F. 184
Baldwin, Charlene 100
Baldwin, Richard 146
Baldwin, Clive 247
Baldwin, Dwight 258
Baldwin, Mark 261
Baldwin, Wendy 520
Baldwin, Tom 595
Baldwin, Loretta C. 609
Bale, John 38
Baliff, Cora 569
Baliff, Cora 569
Ball, Gregory 101
Ball, Margaret T. 199
Ball, Wilmot C. 524
Ball, Wilmot C. 524
Ball, Kim 537
Ballantine, John W. 618
Ballantyne, Trina 488
Ballard, William W. 68
Ballard, Diane 254
Ballentine, Anne 610
Ballhaus, William F. 515
Balling, John 616
Ballots, Joan H. 506
Ballou-Watts, Rt. Hon. Vicki 223
Balmer, Stephanie S. 9
Balmer, Stephanie 157
Balog, John A. 266
Balsano, Tony 202
Balzano, Shery 431
Balzer, Brenda 489
Bambrey, Thomas E. (Tom) 593
Bamwine, Patrick 286

Banas, Les C. 508
Banco, Leonard 131
Bando, Patricia 560
Bane, Irvin 181
Baney, Mary Ellen 164
Banford, David 224
Bangel, Edward 146
Bangledorf, Debbie 524
Baniewicz, Phil 62
Bankston, Mary G. 9
Bankston, Tony 251
Bankston, Karen 565
Bannigan, John 582
Bantivoglio, Barbara 546
Bantz, Don 181
Baranco, Juanita Powell 44
Baratian, Jacqueline (Jackie) 316
Barazzone, Esther L. 101
Barbakoff, Richard 314
Barber, Dennis 137
Barbour, Emily 416
Barbre, Gloria 601
Barchi, Robert L. (Bob) 547
Barchi, Daniel 623
Barclay, C. Duane 152
Barden, Leslie A. 326
Barden, Sean 598
Barefoot, Glenn 491
Barfuss, Mike 139
Bargamin, Steve 592
Barge, Gayle 509
Barger, David 103
Barger, Kathy G. 574
Barghols, Brad 340
Barhight, G. Scott 321
Bariyanga, James 8
Bariyanga, Joseph 286
Barker, Doug 319
Barker, William G. (Bill) 343
Barker, John 491
Barker, Marvin 507
Barker, Marvin 507
Barker, Trevor 601
Barker, Sandra 607
Barkmeier, Wayne W. 142
Barksdale, Kenneth P. 222
Barlaam, Maria 311
Barletta, Frank 533
Barna, Julie 180
Barnaby, Paul 514
Barnds, Kent 47
Barnes, Thomas O. 131
Barnes, Laura 167
Barnes, Rick 362
Barnes, Tom 593
Barnett, Kara M. 295
Barnett, J. Bruce 413
Barnett, Gary L. 442
Barnett, Trevor 563
Barnette, Brian 198
Barnhardt, Phyllis 74
Baroni, Greg 28
Baroody, Fadi N. 118
Baroudi, George 299
Barr, James D. 61
Barr, Bret 134
Barr, Rosemarie 402
Barr, Anne 499
Barr, Jim 516
Barrack, Leonard 506
Barranco, Yolairis 54
Barrath, Paul 116
Barrett, Carol 182
Barrett, Carolyn A. 266
Barrett, Linda 579
Barretta-Herman, Angeline 581
Barrick, Martha A. 180
Barrick, Martha A. 180
Barris, Julie 434
Barron, Risa 419
Barron, Kathleen 505
Barrood, James 185
Barros, A. Richard 153
Barrow, Henry 115
Barrow-Klein, Vickie J. 136

Barry, Rev Edward M. 87
Barry, Timothy J. 367
Barry, Timothy J. 367
Barry, Edward W. 369
Barry, John F. 403
Barry, John F. 403
Barry-Ipema, Cathy 272
Barshay, Stanley F. 299
Barshefsky, Charlene 138
Barth, Joel 173
Barth, Carin 509
Barthel, Paul 462
Bartholomew, Chris 249
Bartini, Grace 314
Bartle, James 61
Barto, Jack 349
Bartol, Michelle M. 275
Barton, Richard J. 28
Barton, Joyce 30
Barton, Timothy A. (Tim) 204
Barton, Rick 255
Barton, Karey W. 428
Barton, Delores K. 470
Barton, Lt. Col. Pamela 517
Barton, Martha Felt 608
Barton, Martha Felt 609
Bartsch, Don 361
Baruch, Ralph M. 546
Barulich, Steve 66
Barulich, William (Bill) 66
Basandra, Sangeeta 400
Baseler, Mark 445
Basom, Jean W. 430
Basore, Neff 135
Bass, Norma 311
Bass, Robert M. 535
Bassett, Robert 100
Bassett, Dorothy 164
Bassett, Michael (Mike) 446
Bassett, Kathleen (Kathy) 446
Bassis, Michael B. 608
Bassis, Michael B. 608
Basso, Marty 492
Basu, Sam 545
Bata, Thomas G. 344
Bateman, Bradley 154
Bateman, Shane 182
Bateman, Maureen 311
Bateman, Mark T. 430
Bates, David 26
Bates, Jonathan R. (Jon) 38
Bates, Jonathan R. (Jon) 38
Bates, Paul 167
Bates, Scott D. 290
Bates, Timothy D. 290
Bates, Shirley 303
Bates, J. Dan 468
Bates, J. Dan 468
Bates, Wesley C. 483
Bates, Steve 505
Bates, Jennifer 535
Bates, John 597
Batkins, Dale 179
Batkins, Sara 179
Batson, Rebecca E. 153
Battey, Colden R. 461
Battle, Lynwood 105
Battle, Michael 166
Battle, Darlene 300
Baucum, Carlton E. 530
Baucum, Carlton E. 530
Baudanza, Anthony J. 408
Bauer, Virginia S. 139
Bauer, August A. 242
Bauer, August A. 242
Bauer, Paul 273
Bauer, John H. 431
Bauer, John H. 432
Bauer, Wayne 484
Bauer, George P. 544
Bauer, Daniel (Dan) 544
Bauer, Jennifer 545
Bauer, James R. (Jim) 616
Bauermann, Charles L. 524

Evans, Kristi 601
Evans, Stephen 610
Evans, Nancy Bell 612
Everding, Gerry 544
Everett, Daryl 344
Everitt, Pamela A. 461
Everson, Russ 361
Everson, Lori 361
Evert, Denis 595
Evert, Kevin 595
Evnin, Anthony B. (Tony) 535
Ewald, Kurt 135
Ewald, Elizabeth 278
Ewald, Glen S. 318
Ewer, Galen 108
Ewing, A. Hugh 105
Ewing, Jim 364
Exler, Michael J. 162

F

Fabares, Shelley 20
Fabian, Timothy 585
Fabritius, Stephanie L. 99
Facciani, Jennifer 304
Faerber, Craig 226
Faga, Martin C. 531
Fagan, Kathleen 199
Fagan, Mary 410
Fagan, Sha 442
Fagan, Joseph 597
Fagerlie, Stephen R. (Steve) 504
Fagerstrom, Rick 535
Faherty, Robert L. 513
Fahey, Thomas J. 87
Fahrenkopf, Frank J. 521
Fahrenkopf, Frank J. 521
Fain, Margaret A. 118
Fainstein, Victor 530
Fair, Kenneth 447
Fairbanks, Karen 258
Fairbanks, Ren L. 495
Fairweather, Rev Newton 197
Faja, Garry C. 556
Falade, Ukeme 8
Falaguerra, Robert J. 433
Falardeau, George E. 40
Falcetano, John C. 574
Falcone, Elena 133
Falcone, Joseph C. 343
Falcone, Anthony J. 343
Falcone, Joseph C. 343
Falcone, Anthony J. 343
Falcone, Arthur J. 364
Falcone, Carmine 534
Falcone, Joseph C. 602
Falero, Esteban 596
Falk, Sigo 101
Falletta, Gaye 371
Fallgatter, Doug 7
Fallia, Rick 235
Falls, Dee 483
Falls, Keffus S. 509
Falvey, Joseph L. (Joe) 567
Fan, Lori W. 77
Fan, Peter 545
Fanfera, Paul 440
Fannin, James 483
Fanning, Mark S. 27
Fanning, Timothy W. 545
Fannon, Brian W. 98
Fanto, Stephen M. 61
Farah, Roger N. 344
Farber, Scott 408
Farber, David J. 489
Farber, Jack 547
Farberman, Rhea K. 29
Fare, Bridget 164
Farias, Pablo J. 523
Farina, Leah 320
Farkas, Terese 23
Farley, Rod 139
Farley, Katherine G. 295
Farmer, Bradley D. 75

Farmer, Bradley D. 76
Farmer, Ronald 100
Farmer, Michelle 254
Farmer, Jim 362
Farmer, Kent D. 413
Farmer, Patricia J.B. 473
Farmer, Berkwood M. 621
Farr, Ron 49
Farrell, Marty 30
Farrell, Michael K. 105
Farrell, Maggie 369
Farrell, Terence 465
Farrell, Jef 500
Farrell, Teleia 602
Farrell, Maxine P. 618
Farrier, Dale 620
Farris, John C. 42
Farris, Jerome 337
Farrow, Jeff 339
Farstad, Jeff 470
Farvardin, Nariman 489
Fasbender, Bob 550
Fascitelli, Michael D. 535
Faskianos, Irina A. 138
Fasserzke, Mike 484
Fassler, Michael S. 65
Fastert, Henry 454
Fathi, David 247
Fattahi, Nooraldin 286
Fattal, Garabed 571
Faul, Mark 544
Faulkenberry, Mark 606
Faulkner, Matthew (Matt) 313
Faulkner, Dave 491
Faunce, Kerry 336
Fauth, John J. (Hap) 582
Faux, Maureen 301
Favello, Helen 290
Fawaz, Rami A. 149
Fawley, Dorman 565
Fax, Gene E. 513
Fay, Steven J. 124
Fay, Matt 302
Fay, Ron 393
Fay, David 572
Fay, Maureen A. 582
Feagans, Brian 136
Fearer, Matt 611
Feasel, Jeffrey 176
Feather, Jeffrey P. (Jeff) 292
Featheringill, William W. 467
Feathers, Robert 339
Fecik, George 164
Feck, Maureen 559
Federico, Ed 547
Fedorkowicz, Paul D. 102
Feekes, Stan 188
Feeley, Elizabeth 185
Feeney, James 191
Feeney, James 191
Feeney, Tara 288
Feese, Suzanne C. 9
Fegley, Walter J. (Walt) 415
Fehlau, Fred 40
Feickert, Peter 473
Feigenbaum, Adam 249
Feiner, Edward 519
Feiner, Barbara A. 544
Feinerman, Leon 241
Feintech, Irving 94
Feldblum, Miriam 394
Felder, William D. (Bill) 373
Feldman, Brant 46
Feldman, Larry 159
Feldman, Eric 322
Feldman, Harriet R. 380
Feldman, Amy E. 526
Felgar, Alvin D. (Al) 206
Felgoise, Judith A. 506
Felitto, Brent W. 126
Felitto, Donald 290
Felitto, Donald 290
Feller, Mimi A. 142
Feller, Nancy P. 523
Felmlee, Cheryl 365

Feltes, Carol A. 535
Felton, Stephen 43
Felton, Barbara 97
Felton, Jon 497
Feltz, Ross 434
Feng, Yi 114
Fenske, David E. 162
Fenstermacher, Robert L. (Bob) 22
Fenwick, Charles C. 222
Fenwick, Leslie T. 246
Feola, Dorothy 545
Ferchland-Parella, Joanne 364
Ferdinand, Norma J. 285
Ferencz, Steve 97
Ferguson, Patricia H. 18
Ferguson, David B. 23
Ferguson, L. Joe 174
Ferguson, Lisa 202
Ferguson, Alfred L. 334
Ferguson, Robert 345
Ferguson, Irene 364
Ferguson, Anthony (Tony) 369
Ferguson, Richard C. 408
Ferguson, John J. 474
Ferguson, Keith 527
Fergusson, Frances D. 586
Ferland, Bernie 104
Fern, Kathy 411
Fernandes, Manuel D. 474
Fernandez, Gerald A. 270
Fernandez, Luis G. 557
Fernandi, Jack S. 468
Ferne, Mark 608
Ferne, Mark 608
Ferrara, Thomas G. 87
Ferrara, V. Raymond 170
Ferrara, Hania 185
Ferrari, Elva B. 156
Ferrari, Pierre 235
Ferrari, Dan 493
Ferrari, Mauro 530
Ferre, Francois 19
Ferreira, Sean 312
Ferreira, Robert 404
Ferrell, Jim 265
Ferrell, John R. 428
Ferren, Alison L. 3
Ferrentino, Andy 249
Ferrer, Fernando A. 131
Ferreri, Michael F. 527
Ferrey, Patricia A. 15
Ferrillo, Patrick J. 582
Ferris, Robert A. 199
Ferris, Colleen 405
Ferrucci, Gabriel 408
Fertman, Don 159
Fessenden, Elizabeth A. 367
Fessenden, Elizabeth A. 367
Fessler, Tom 595
Fetsch, Brent 362
Fett, Neil 428
Fetter, Thompson 628
Fettig, Sister Jeanette 430
Feustle, Judith 539
Fey, Thomas 608
Fey, Thomas 609
Fialkowski, Mary 272
Ficalora, Joseph R. 191
Ficalora, Joseph R. 191
Fick, Edmund J. 524
Fick, John F. 598
Fico, Dayna 77
Fieckert, Peter D. 473
Fiege, Dan 463
Field, Meredith Paige 82
Fielding, James D. (Jim) 310
Fields, Mark 151
Fields, Jerry 302
Fields, Mary 401
Fienman, Barbara 417
Fierens, Louis J. (Lou) 556
Fiet, Rachel 269
Fifield, Rod 258
Figueroa, Hector 153
Figurelli, David 595

Fike, Randy K. 627
Filaski, William 27
Filby, Robert 202
Filipiak, John A. 159
Filipic, Matthew V. 621
Filippi, Carolyn R. 473
Filizetti, Gary 155
Fillhaber, Mitchell J. (Mitch) 453
Fillmore, Mark 85
Filmeck, Frank 83
Filter, Phillip 495
Filtz, Bill 586
Finan, Richard H. 540
Findlay, Steve 133
Fine, Stuart H. 221
Finerty, Steven L. 601
Finger, Jeff A. 62
Finger, Mary C. 151
Fingerhut, Eric D. 57
Finley, Joseph C. 227
Finley, Delvecchio 499
Finn, MJ Knoll 177
Finn, Louise 301
Finn, Michael 314
Finn, Barry C. 426
Finn, Robin 627
Finnegan, Robert 27
Finnegan, Sister Rosemary T. 54
Finnegan, Paul F. 353
Finnerman, Mike 597
Finnerty, Alice Ann 539
Finney, Joe 85
Finney, Richard 286
Finney, Ebben D. 539
Finney, Ebben D. 539
Fiore, Frank 414
Firman, Julie 465
Firth, James D. 618
Fisch, Michael G. 247
Fischer, Alexander R. 57
Fischer, Rob 288
Fischer, Gary 397
Fischer, Ita 538
Fischer, William 540
Fischer, Dave 585
Fish, David J. 200
Fish, Jon 510
Fish, Irving 572
Fish, Irving 573
Fisher, John 98
Fisher, Michael 105
Fisher, Richard (Rick) 173
Fisher, Scott 179
Fisher, Scott 185
Fisher, Rowland 265
Fisher, Peter E. 292
Fisher, Robert J. (Bob) 345
Fisher, A. Kent 405
Fisher, Weston 514
Fisher, Tom 536
Fisher, Jay 541
Fisher, Jerome 562
Fisher, Barrett C. 588
Fisher, Rev Allen H. 598
Fisher, Jim 599
Fisher, Howard 618
Fishman, Jay S. 562
Fisk, Kellee J. 68
Fisk, Francine 542
Fitch, Barbara 105
Fitch, Charles 590
Fite, David 100
Fite, David 579
Fitten, Daniel Lee 287
Fitts, Michael A. 561
Fitz, James F. 540
Fitz, Rev James F. 540
Fitzer, Christina 371
Fitzgerald, William A. 142
Fitzgerald, Lisa R. 171
Fitzgerald, Paul J. 184
Fitzgerald, Celie 295
Fitzgerald, Al 454
FitzGerald, James P. (Jim) 517
Fitzgerald, David P. 540

Houfek, James T. (Jim) 369
Hough, Mike 10
Hough, Claudia Keenan 168
Houghtaling, Doug 135
Houghton, Ellen 255
Houle, Elizabeth J. 582
Houlihan, Robert C. 334
Houpt, Julia Beyer 154
House, Robin 113
House, Vanesa 286
House-Browning, Virnette 77
Houston, Ramona 45
Hout, Thys Van 159
Houweling, Douglas E. Van 18
Houze, Philippe 344
Hove, Bart 603
Hoverman, Isabel V. 272
Hoverman, Isabel V. 272
Hovland, Richard 20
Howald, Judy 278
Howard, Rev Lloyd E. 23
Howard, Derrick 112
Howard, Derrick 112
Howard, Randy S. 300
Howard, Troy 303
Howard, Mark 319
Howard, Douglas W. 319
Howard, Phillip 337
Howard, Keith 337
Howard, Denise 537
Howard, Drema 581
Howard, Marianne 611
Howard, Lillie 621
Howe, Peter W. 199
Howe, Louise M. 408
Howe, Kenneth F. 466
Howe, Jim 484
Howe, Denise 527
Howell, Eleanor V. 142
Howell, James 235
Howell, Arthur 337
Howell, R. Rodney 340
Howell, R. Rodney 340
Howerton, Mary Teresa 432
Howery, David 234
Howland, N. Lyle 53
Howland, N. Lyle 53
Howland, Carol 150
Hoy, Thomas L. 22
Hoy, David 519
Hoying, Cheryl 105
Hoyle, Nigel 428
Hoyt, Jim 181
Hrabowski, Freeman A. 542
Hrebinko, Greg 597
Hricak, Judy L. 196
Hu, Gary A. 451
Hu-DeHart, Evelyn 122
Huang, Minsiu 5
Hubbard, William (Bill) 23
Hubbard, Marilyn French 98
Hubbard, Marilyn French 98
Hubbard, Stanley S. 582
Hubble, Don W. 270
Hubbuch, Ann 294
Huber, Mark D. 142
Huber, Maureen E. 146
Huber, Shawn 425
Huber, Susan 582
Hubert, Barbara 100
Hubert, Michael F. 263
Hubert, Jeffrey 309
Hudak, Corey 625
Huddie, Patrick 245
Huddleston, Richard F. 417
Hudec, Susan 473
Hudson, Lea Ann Grimes 9
Hudson, Lea Ann Grimes 9
Hudson, Wallace E. 61
Hudson, Joseph R. 61
Hudson, Carol 136
Hudson, Frederick M. (Fred) 223
Hudson, Sterling 337
Hudson, Jane 451
Hudson, J. Clifford (Cliff) 523

Hudson, R. Burton 537
Hueners, Craig 415
Huennekens, Gregg 35
Huennekens, Chad 35
Huerta, Guillermo 141
Huether, Douglas 223
Hufendick, Keith 181
Huff, Stan 258
Huff, Joe 511
Huffman, Anne M. 208
Huffman, Jerry 448
Huffman, Stephen D. 531
Huffman, Virginia 535
Huffmon, George (Van) 349
Hufford, Bob 44
Huftalin, Deneece 438
Huggins, Lance 205
Hughes, Emily 11
Hughes, William L. 34
Hughes, Jan Mowder 138
Hughes, Craig 146
Hughes, Joseph 162
Hughes, Christine 177
Hughes, Brenda 246
Hughes, Elizabeth J. 251
Hughes, Barbara (Barb) 274
Hughes, Peter N. 461
Hughes, Colleen 518
Hughes, David 574
Hugo, Paul 399
Huie, Janice Riggle 530
Huizenga, H. Wayne 364
Hulings, Jonin 485
Hull, Brian 184
Hull, Judy 507
Hull, Judy 507
Hulse, Russell A. 57
Hulstein, Kevin 188
Humberd, Scott 590
Hume, John Griffith 432
Humeston, Howard D. 54
Humma, Ken 596
Hummel, Robert J. 111
Hummel, Jeffrey C. 180
Hummel, Lauren C. 552
Humphrey, Marion 38
Humphrey, Karen 65
Humphrey, Mike 161
Humphrey, L'Argent 251
Hund, Kristi 490
Hungerford, Constance Cain 500
Hunt, Torrence M. 90
Hunt, Robert 224
Hunt, Thomas 250
Hunt, Andrea S. 310
Hunt, Tamara 336
Hunt, David 417
Hunt, James W. 469
Hunt, Peter 473
Hunt, Peter F. 473
Hunt, Gordon C. 497
Hunt, Lacy H. 506
Hunt, William J. 529
Hunt, William J. 529
Hunt, Dale Marie 590
Hunter, Jim 125
Hunter, Reuben 197
Hunter, Meredith Pierce 240
Hunter, Edith 241
Hunter, Rod 258
Hunter, Bettye 286
Hunter, R. Alan 290
Hunter, Jack 332
Hunter, Jill S. 518
Hunter, Richard E. 612
Hunter-Pillion, Melody 416
Huntress, Catherine N. 266
Hupp, William T. (Billy) 179
Hupp, Stephen E. 179
Hurd, John D. 98
Hurd, Timothy M. 553
Hurley, Shamus 51
Hurley, George 161
Hurley, John 181
Hurley, Patty 590

Hurse, Gary 606
Hursh, Gretchen 585
Hurshe, Joseph (Joe) 95
Hurst, Ronald D. (Ron) 390
Hurst, Victor 459
Hurst, Robert J. (Bob) 612
Huson, Jennifer 146
Hussey, Timothy B. 121
Hussey, Sylvia M. 561
Husson, Jim 560
Huston, Paul J. 184
Hutchenrider, E. Kenneth 326
Hutcherson, Lisa 589
Hutcheson, Sumner 197
Hutchins, Ann B. 53
Hutchins, Tracie 182
Hutchins, J. Mark 507
Hutchins, J. Mark 507
Hutchinson, Matt 48
Hutchinson, Tom 238
Hutchinson, Thomas A. 292
Hutchison, Heather 20
Hutchison, J. Robert (Rob) 273
Huth, F. Robert 399
Hutsell, Mark 627
Hutson, Blake 133
Hutson, Wayne 568
Hutt, Dana 40
Hutt, Louis G. 245
Hutt, Louis G. 544
Hutton, Kim 55
Hutton, Dave 340
Hutton, Todd S. 586
Hwang, Bill Sung-Kook 208
Hyatt, Joel Z. 337
Hybl, William J. 67
Hyde, Mark 462
Hyde, Michael E. 525
Hyde, Barry 573
Hyder, S. Shiraz 475
Hyfler, Robert 526
Hyland, John 289
Hyler, James B. 572
Hyman, Craig 134
Hyman, Elizabeth 518
Hyman, Robert 526
Hyman, Gail 526
Hyman, Daniel J. 618
Hynek, Adrienne 488
Hynes, Thomas J. 583

I

Iannitti, Irene 595
Iannuzzi, Salvatore (Sal) 299
Ibarguen, Alberto 138
Ichimura, Lance 451
Ide, R. William (Bill) 45
Ieyoub, Kalil P. 317
Iffert, John 298
Ilseng, Rodney 493
Imbert, Anabel Anderson 499
Imbesi, Patricia H. 589
Imbimbo, Richard 625
Imgrund, Stephen 130
Imgrund, Stephen 130
Imhoff, Michael A. 48
Imhoff, Kathleen R. T. 369
Imhoff, Maren E. 535
Imholz, Elizabeth (Betsy) 133
Imm, Robert (Bob) 534
Imperiali, Barbara 611
Inanli, Oz 286
Incarnati, Philip A. 58
Incarnati, Philip A. 168
Indyk, Martin 513
Ingalls, Jane R. 598
Inglis, I. Martin 57
Ingoldsby, Tim 27
Ingraham, Jim 174
Ingram, Lawrence P. (Larry) 389
Ingram, Mark 396
Ings, Margaret Ann 177
Inman, Emma 450

Innella, Michael (Mike) 30
Inouye, Irene Y. Hirano 523
Inouye, Irene Y. Hirano 523
Introne, James E. 87
Inzana, Lou 290
Ireland, Jay W. 473
Irish, Mark 380
Irish, Charles A. (Chuck) 544
Irizarry, Victoria 573
Irvin, Zoe 245
Irvin, William K. 432
Irvine, Laura 326
Irving, Lewis 256
Irwin, Joe 100
Irwin, Robert 359
Irwin, Robert G. 422
Irwin, Tom 601
Irwin, Bradley C. (Brad) 602
Irwin, Bradley C. (Brad) 602
Irwin, John N. 615
Isaacs, Linda 499
Isaacson, Jon F. 99
Isbey, Caroline 272
Isely, Charles Christian 8
Isenberg, Walter L. 270
Isenburg, Mark 5
Isgur, David (Dave) 541
Ishida, Franklin 235
Isip, Michael 281
Ismail, Geilan 504
Ismail, Geilan 504
Isom, Candace 254
Isom, Ellisha Dawn 432
Ispir, Sheri L. 270
Isquith, Irwin 185
Isquith, Susan 191
Isquith, Susan 191
Israel, Dan 508
Israel, Edouard 514
Isyk, Ronald J. (Ron) 349
IV, J. Douglass Cates 102
IV, Franklin W. (Fritz) Hobbs 205
IV, John E. Laird 284
IV, Hollis Gentry 380
IV, Henry D. Felton 490
IV, John Joseph Hoey 536
IV, Walter E. Robb 582
IV, Paul C. (Chip) Schorr 612
Ivers, Jim 307
Iversen, Rick 527
Iverson, Douglas J. (Doug) 190
Ivory, Clark D. 258
Iwanowicz, Susan (Sue) 12
Izumi, Carol 133

J

Jabaji, George J. 321
Jablonski, Sue 371
Jabs, Jacob (Jake) 26
Jackle, Jerry C. 242
Jackson, Joanne 32
Jackson, Dorsey 38
Jackson, John 53
Jackson, Brian 67
Jackson, Brian 67
Jackson, Don 126
Jackson, Don 126
Jackson, Shirley Ann 138
Jackson, Joe 152
Jackson, Jorinne 161
Jackson, Alexa 177
Jackson, Brenda 185
Jackson, Athena 197
Jackson, Michael 286
Jackson, Ron 314
Jackson, Wes 335
Jackson, Ches 335
Jackson, Margaret 336
Jackson, Weldon 337
Jackson, Doug 392
Jackson, Lorne W. 423
Jackson, Michael J. 441
Jackson, Lauren 451

Michael, David 574
Michaels, Julie B. 23
Michaels, Andrea 560
Michaelson, John C. 519
Michalkiewicz, Barbara 447
Michalko, Jim 369
Michalko, Nancy 608
Michalko, Nancy 608
Michaud, Paul 413
Michel, John W. H. (Doc) 409
Michel, J. V. (Mike) 409
Michel, J. V. (Beau) 409
Micheletti, Kristen 430
Michelli, Thomas J. 334
Michener, Jill 426
Miciak, Alan 164
Mickel, Christine 288
Mickens, Walt 478
Middlebrooks, David 265
Middleton, Sara 113
Middleton, Sara 113
Middleton, Jackie 326
Midei, Ron 364
Mieras, Barbara A. 149
Migliori, Barbara 488
Mikell, Frank 244
Miki, Nobuyuki 282
Mikulecky, Donna 108
Milam, Milton 44
Milam, Ebony 286
Milam, Hughes 359
Milan, Jesse 18
Milan, Diane S. 139
Milano, Frank 508
Milavetz, Barry 578
Milby, Kevin 99
Miles, John C. 175
Miles, John C. 175
Miles, David 185
Miles, Todd 205
Miles, Vernon 303
Miles, Ray 328
Miles, Arletha 380
Milford, Susan 95
Millard, Robert B. 520
Millard, Frank 563
Millard, Suzanne Turtle 563
Millard, Jayne 563
Millaway, Gary 613
Millen, Robert P. (Bob) 371
Miller, Michael C. 22
Miller, Kimberly 40
Miller, Michael M. (Mike) 42
Miller, Kristine T. 48
Miller, Richard K. 53
Miller, Kurt 58
Miller, Kim 59
Miller, Kim 59
Miller, Nathan R. 63
Miller, Silvana 86
Miller, Flortina 96
Miller, Scott 113
Miller, George E. 113
Miller, Cheryl 132
Miller, Richard 141
Miller, Jane E. 142
Miller, John 150
Miller, David 151
Miller, James 164
Miller, Kendall 181
Miller, Milton J. 190
Miller, Kenneth C. 192
Miller, Kenneth C. 192
Miller, Fred 209
Miller, Jane E. 211
Miller, Jeffrey S. (Jeff) 239
Miller, Don 255
Miller, Robert (Bob) 256
Miller, James R. (Jim) 264
Miller, Kristine 272
Miller, Mike 273
Miller, Melissa 286
Miller, John 287
Miller, William L. 292
Miller, James H. (Jim) 292

Miller, Sean 302
Miller, Roy 309
Miller, Lisa 334
Miller, H. Gilbert 357
Miller, Don 407
Miller, Larry F. 423
Miller, Jonathan 424
Miller, Jonathan 424
Miller, Kenneth 424
Miller, Sister Amata 432
Miller, Jo 433
Miller, Sandra 450
Miller, Rudy 455
Miller, Byron D. 461
Miller, Gary P. 475
Miller, Nancy 475
Miller, Nancy 492
Miller, Dionne 499
Miller, Randy 501
Miller, Ed 514
Miller, Steve 514
Miller, Franklin C. (Frank) 515
Miller, Mary John 542
Miller, Nancy J. 554
Miller, Paul F. 562
Miller, Robert C. 569
Miller, Carol 571
Miller, Pamela 580
Miller, Diane D. 582
Miller, Sam 598
Miller, Michael 602
Miller, Gary 603
Miller, Nicola 608
Miller, Nicola 609
Miller, Pam 627
Miller, Lou 627
Millerick, Timothy P. (Tim) 48
Millett, April 317
Milligan, Michael D. (Mike) 51
Milligan, Gary 289
Milligan, Susan 373
Millikan, J. Scott 68
Millikan, J. Scott 68
Millikan, Grant C. 207
Milliren, Carmen 195
Millis, Jack 114
Millner, F. Ann 258
Mills, Jack 58
Mills, Alice 185
Mills, Jeffery N. 334
Mills, Terry L. 337
Mills, Tony G. 428
Mills, J. William 506
Mills, Christopher 520
Mills, Jim 530
Millsaps, Joseph R. 364
Millstead, Bart 465
Millstone, I. E. 544
Milne, Roy 289
Milne, George M. 515
Milrany, Cindy P. 204
Milstein, Howard P. 351
Milton, Kerry 436
Mindich, Eric 612
Mindich, Eric 612
Minehan, Cathy E. 531
Mineo, Michael C. 199
Miner, Lenny 43
Miner, James D. 527
Mines, Timothy F. 123
Minetti, Robert H. (Bob) 63
Mingle, Regina 285
Miniaci, Albert J. 364
Minick, Thomas 49
Minnehan, Mike 599
Minnis, Stephen D. 62
Minor, Hassan 246
Minor, David M. 419
Minter, Leigh 152
Minter, Penny 286
Minton, Dwight C. 337
Mintz, Eric 45
Miotke, Katherine E. (Kathy) 564
Mirabal, Morella 451
Miramontes, Victor 432

Miranda, Mark 334
Miranda, Jim 378
Miranto, Mike 147
Mirmirani, Maj 176
Miscik, Jami 138
Mish, Margie 2
Mishra, Sanjeeb 113
Miskey, Mary B. 285
Miskin, Russell 21
Mismash, Mike 500
Mistretta, Susan 571
Misuraca, Tammi 533
Mitchell, Tony 26
Mitchell, Ken 68
Mitchell, Judson C. 77
Mitchell, Brian Christopher 82
Mitchell, Van T. 113
Mitchell, Marjo 129
Mitchell, Jonathan (Jon) 136
Mitchell, Edward 175
Mitchell, Patricia J. 222
Mitchell, Patricia J. 223
Mitchell, Pat 247
Mitchell, Sandie 263
Mitchell, Ernest 286
Mitchell, Phyllis K. 293
Mitchell, Elizabeth 309
Mitchell, Shelly 344
Mitchell, Thomas W. (Tom) 388
Mitchell, Paul F. 433
Mitchell, Jodi 448
Mitchell, Steve 497
Mitchell, Thomas 505
Mitchell, Sue E. 517
Mitchell, M. Cameron 521
Mitchell, M. Cameron 521
Mitchell, William B. 531
Mitchell, Robert (Rob) 544
Mitchell, Joann 561
Mitchell, Andrea 562
Mitchell, Marshall H. 562
Mitchell, Lori 627
Mitnick, Eric J. 547
Mitola, Joseph (Joe) 488
Mitra, Sanjukta 95
Mitry, Norman F. 237
Mitry, Norman F. 237
Mitsunaga, Jean 40
Mladenovic, Jeanette 374
Mnick, Jeffrey J. (Jeff) 224
Mnuchin, Steven T. (Steve) 612
Mobley, Judith L. 57
Mobley, Archie L. 197
Mobley, Stacey J. 246
Mocadlo, Larry 257
Mock, John F. 554
Modell, Mitchell B. (Mitch) 236
Modell, Mitchell B. 344
Moderow, Joseph R. (Joe) 453
Modesto, Becky 393
Modica, Charles R. 55
Modisher, Christine 507
Moe, Richard 523
Moeller, Oskar 504
Moffat, Anne J.M. 370
Moffatt, Tracey 603
Moffett, Kevin 389
Mogahed, Dalia 211
Moglia, Joseph H. (Joe) 142
Mohandas, Sunil U. 190
Mohideen, Feizal 87
Mohr, Todd M. 7
Mohr, Joan Isaac 408
Mohr, Julian B. 453
Mokwa, Joseph J. 601
Molitor, Kimberly B. 620
Moliver, Donald M. 334
Moll, Jonathan 53
Mollica, Prof Louis 294
Mollica, Frank 610
Mollison, Sister Mary 556
Mollison, Mary 556
Molloy, Mark 179
Molloy, Chris 254
Molnar, Attila 90

Molokotos, Thanasis M. 624
Moloney, Thomas E. 366
Molony, Leslie 441
Molseed, Richard 49
Monaghan, Thomas S. 49
Monaghan, Thomas S. 49
Monahan, Susan 163
Monahan, Michael J. 351
Monan, J. Donald 560
Monarch, Ed 66
Mondanaro, Don 536
Monday, Kathryn J. (Kathy) 579
Mondello, Judith 213
Mondora, Stephen A. (Steve) 235
Monedero, Ann Francis 432
Monell, Ambrose K. 615
Monette, Victor 432
Monforte, Joe 19
Mongan, Maria 93
Monge, Eduardo A. 101
Monk, Anne T. 118
Monk, Wade 198
Monkmeyer, Jim 85
Monkolchayut, Mikki 546
Monson, Mark 59
Monson, Kevin 313
Montagnese, Rob 294
Montagnese, Rob 294
Montague, Dennis 137
Montalvo, Darrin 478
Montecalvo, Frank 434
Montelaro, Daniel D. 377
Montes, Luis 352
Montgomery, John 10
Montgomery, Charlene 66
Montgomery, Bernard 185
Montgomery, Dale A. 233
Montgoris, William J. 121
Montoro, John B. 102
Montoy, Hilda C. 430
Montoya, Ron 500
Montoya, Ron 501
Montplaisir, Daniel (Dan) 176
Monts, Lester P. 122
Moody, Jeff 159
Moody, John 256
Moon, Marilyn 27
Moon, Deborah 90
Moon, Marvin 300
Moon, Vicki 459
Mooney, Thelma 245
Mooney, James L. 302
Mooney, John E. 432
Mooney, Kim M. 473
Mooney, Paul 529
Moore, Jeffrey G. (Jeff) 18
Moore, Alan 19
Moore, Brad 35
Moore, Barbara 38
Moore, Jennifer 52
Moore, Gerald W. 55
Moore, Robert H. 61
Moore, Barbara C. 62
Moore, Rob 67
Moore, Cory 68
Moore, Thomas 98
Moore, Arthur L. 99
Moore, David 101
Moore, John 112
Moore, Monika 114
Moore, Evelyn 120
Moore, Robert 124
Moore, Robin 130
Moore, Rob 145
Moore, Garret 154
Moore, Linda 177
Moore, Eleanor 182
Moore, William M. 185
Moore, Dan L. 190
Moore, Sue M. 215
Moore, Greg 218
Moore, Cornell Leverette 246
Moore, Mark E. 254
Moore, Charley 281
Moore, Teri 286

Zimmerman, Gina Val 272
Zimmerman, Christine 473
Zimmerman, Joel 496
Zimmerman, Sheldon 526
Zimmerman, Harry 625
Zineddin, Abdulilah Z. 196
Zink, Janis I. 541
Zionts, Paul 151
Zivkovich, John 97
Zix, Theresa 40
Zokan, Mary 426
Zoldos, Gary M. 193
Zolkos, Timm M. 123
Zore, Edward J. 206
Zore, Edward J. 206
Zorger, Charles R. (Charlie) 19
zovko, Robert 97
Zub, Patty 376
Zube, Duff 154
Zucker, Barbara Hrbek 615
Zuckerman, Gary W. 19
Zuckerman, Tom 582
Zuel, Sally 568
Zumaran, Pat 311
Zumwalt, Rosemary Levy 9
Zungolo, Eileen 163
Zupon, Michael (Mike) 596
Zuschlag, Richard 4
Zweifler, Richard M. 450
Zweng, Bill 420
Zwerling, Gary 53
Zychlin, Claus P. von 556
Zychowski, Ron 170
Zyer, David E. 618
Zylman, Carole J. 38
Zylstra, Gina 156

WRITING COACH

Online

INTERACTIVE
WHITEBOARD
READY!

To preview Writing Coach Online, follow these easy steps:

1. Go to www.phwritingcoach.com

2. Click on "Preview Writing Coach Online."

3. Register for a free demo account and explore.

Access online demonstrations of the following student resources:

 Interactive Writing Coach™ for paragraph and essay scoring

 Online Journal for writing notes, ideas, and drafts

 Interactive Graphic Organizers for help planning your writing

 Videos on effective writing strategies

 Interactive Models of Mentor Texts and Student Models with audio

 Resources for additional support and information

- Student Edition eText   - Grammar Tutorials   - Grammar Practice

DIMENSION L™  Powered By PEARSON

Video game to help you master grammar

www.phwritingcoach.com/DimensionL

Writing COACH

Writing and Grammar for the 21st Century

Upper Saddle River, New Jersey
Boston, Massachusetts
Chandler, Arizona
Glenview, Illinois

WRITING COACH

PEARSON

0-13-253141-0

978-0-13-253141-2

3 4 5 6 7 8 9 10 V052 14 13 12 11

WELCOME TO Writing COACH

Seven Great Reasons to Learn to Write Well

1 Writing is hard, but hard is **rewarding**.

2 Writing helps you **sort things out**.

3 Writing helps you **persuade** others.

4 Writing makes you a **better reader**.

5 Writing makes you **smarter**.

6 Writing helps you get into and through **college**.

7 Writing **prepares you** for the world of work.

AUTHORS

The contributing authors guided the direction and philosophy of *Prentice Hall Writing Coach*. Working with the development team, they helped to build the pedagogical integrity of the program and to ensure its relevance for today's teachers and students.

Program Authors

Jeff Anderson

Jeff Anderson has worked with struggling writers and readers for almost 20 years. His works integrate grammar and editing instruction into the processes of reading and writing. Anderson has written articles in NCTE's **Voices from the Middle, English Journal**, and **Educational Leadership.** Anderson won the NCTE Paul and Kate Farmer Award for his **English Journal** article on teaching grammar in context. He has published two books, **Mechanically Inclined: Building Grammar, Usage, and Style into Writer's Workshop** and **Everyday Editing: Inviting Students to Develop Skill and Craft in Writer's Workshop** as well as a DVD, **The Craft of Grammar.**

Grammar gives me a powerful lens through which to look at my writing. It gives me the freedom to say things exactly the way I want to say them.

Kelly Gallagher

Kelly Gallagher is a full-time English teacher at Magnolia High School in Anaheim, California. He is the former co-director of the South Basin Writing Project at California State University, Long Beach. Gallagher is the author of **Reading Reasons: Motivational Mini-Lessons for the Middle and High School, Deeper Reading: Comprehending Challenging Texts 4–12, Teaching Adolescent Writers,** and **Readicide.** He is also featured in the video series, **Building Adolescent Readers.** With a focus on adolescent literacy, Gallagher provides training to educators on a local, national and international level. Gallagher was awarded the Secondary Award of Classroom Excellence from the California Association of Teachers of English—the state's top English teacher honor.

The best swimmers swim the most; the best writers write the most. There's only one way to become a good writer: write!

Contributing Authors

Evelyn Arroyo

Evelyn Arroyo is the author of **A+RISE,** Research-based Instructional Strategies for ELLs (English Language Learners). Her work focuses on closing the achievement gap for minority students and English language learners. Through her publications and presentations, Arroyo provides advice, encouragement, and practical success strategies to help teachers reach their ELL students.

> *Your rich, colorful cultural life experiences are unique and can easily be painted through words. These experiences define who you are today, and writing is one way to begin capturing your history. Become a risk-taker and fall in love with yourself through your own words.*

> *When you're learning a new language, writing in that language takes effort. The effort pays off big time, though. Writing helps us generate ideas, solve problems, figure out how the language works, and, above all, allows us to express ourselves.*

Jim Cummins, Ph.D.

Jim Cummins is a Professor in the Modern Language Centre at the University of Toronto. A well-known educator, lecturer, and author, Cummins focuses his research on bilingual education and the academic achievement of culturally diverse students. He is the author of numerous publications, including **Negotiating Identities: Education for Empowerment in a Diverse Society.**

Grant Wiggins, Ed.D.

Grant Wiggins is the President of Authentic Education. He earned his Ed.D. from Harvard University. Grant consults with schools, districts, and state education departments; organizes conferences and workshops; and develops resources on curricular change. He is the co-author, with Jay McTighe, of **Understanding By Design,** the award-winning text published by ASCD.

> *I hated writing as a student—and my grades showed it. I grew up to be a writer, though. What changed? I began to think I had something to say. That's ultimately why you write: to find out what you are really thinking, really feeling, really believing.*

> *Concepts of grammar can sharpen your reading, communication, and even your reasoning, so I have championed its practice in my classes and in my businesses. Even adults are quick to recognize that a refresher in grammar makes them keener—and more marketable.*

Gary Forlini

Gary Forlini is managing partner of the School Growth initiative **Brinkman—Forlini—Williams,** which trains school administrators and teachers in Classroom Instruction and Management. His recent works include the book **Help Teachers Engage Students** and the data system **ObserverTab** for district administrators, **Class Acts: Every Teacher's Guide To Activate Learning**, and the initiative's workshop **Grammar for Teachers**.

CONTENTS IN BRIEF

WRITING

Writing without grammar only goes so far. Grammar and writing work together. To write well, grammar skills give me great tools.

CORE WRITING CHAPTERS

GRAMMAR

GRAMMAR GAME PLAN

  **20** **Major Grammatical Errors and How to Fix Them**

> *Grammar without writing is only a collection of rules, but when these rules are put into action as I write, the puzzle comes together.*

CORE GRAMMAR CHAPTERS

STUDENT RESOURCES

Handbooks

Glossaries

Writing COACH

How to Use This Program

This program is organized into two distinct sections: one for WRITING and one for GRAMMAR.

In the **WRITING** section, you'll learn strategies, traits, and skills that will help you become a better writer.

In the **GRAMMAR** section, you'll learn the rules and conventions of grammar, usage, and mechanics.

What DIGITAL writing and grammar resources are available?

The Writing Coach Online boxes will indicate opportunities to use online tools.

In **Writing,** use the **Interactive Writing Coach™** in two ways to get personalized guidance and support for your writing.
- Paragraph Feedback and
- Essay Scorer

WRITING COACH
Online
www.phwritingcoach.com

👍 **Interactive Writing Coach™**
- Choosing from the Topic Bank gives you access to the Interactive Writing Coach™.
- Submit your writing and receive instant personalized feedback and guidance as you draft, revise, and edit your writing.

WRITING COACH
Online
www.phwritingcoach.com

Grammar Tutorials
Brush up on your grammar skills with these animated videos.

Grammar Practice
Practice your grammar skills with Writing Coach Online.

Grammar Games
Test your knowledge of grammar in this fast-paced interactive video game.

In **Grammar,** view grammar tutorials, practice your grammar skills, and play grammar video games.

What will you find in the WRITING section?

Writing Genre

Each chapter introduces a different **writing genre.**

Learn about the key characteristics of the **genre** before you start writing.

Focus on a single form of the genre with the **Feature Assignment**.

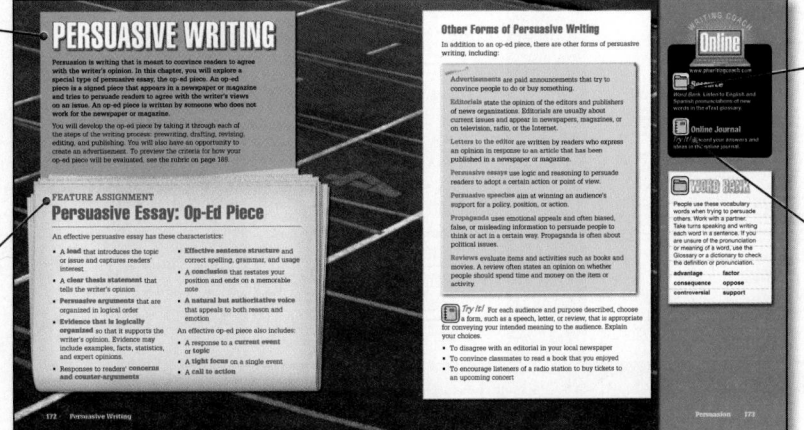

Writing Coach Online

- View the **Word Bank** words in the eText glossary, and hear them pronounced in both English and Spanish.

- Use your **Online Journal** to record your answers and ideas as you respond to *Try It!* activities.

Mentor Text and Student Model

The **Mentor Text** and **Student Model** provide examples of the genre featured in each chapter.

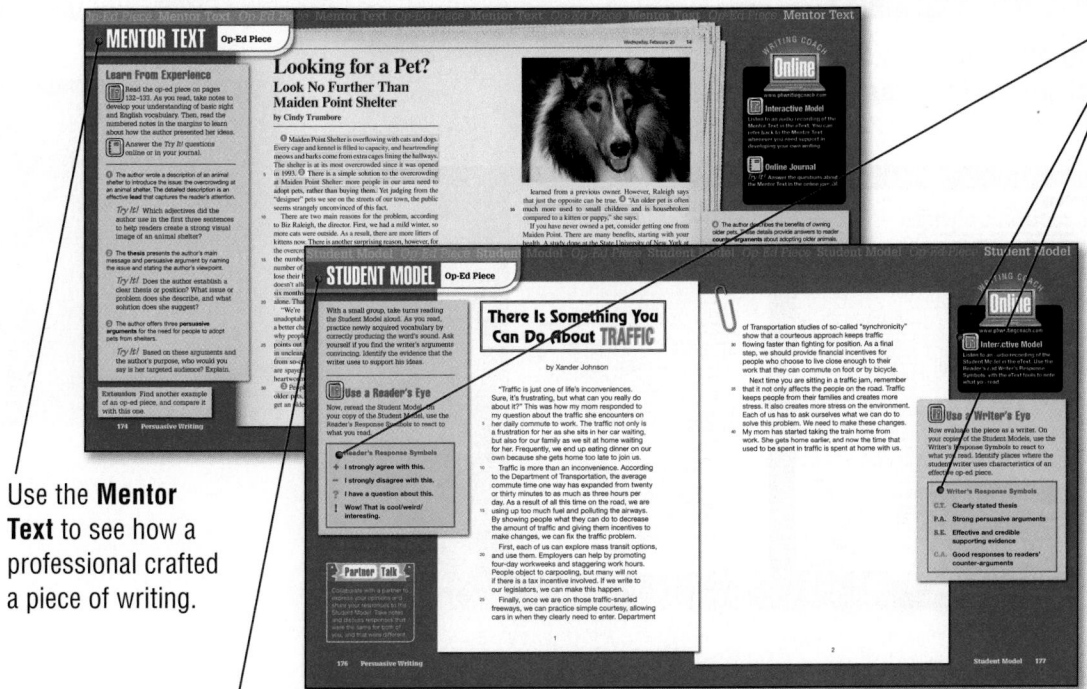

Writing Coach Online

- Use the **Interactive Model** to mark the text with Reader's and Writer's Response Symbols.

- Listen to an audio recording of the **Mentor Text** or **Student Model**.

Use the **Mentor Text** to see how a professional crafted a piece of writing.

Review the **Student Model** as a guide for composing your own piece.

The **Topic Bank** provides prompts for the **Feature Assignment.**

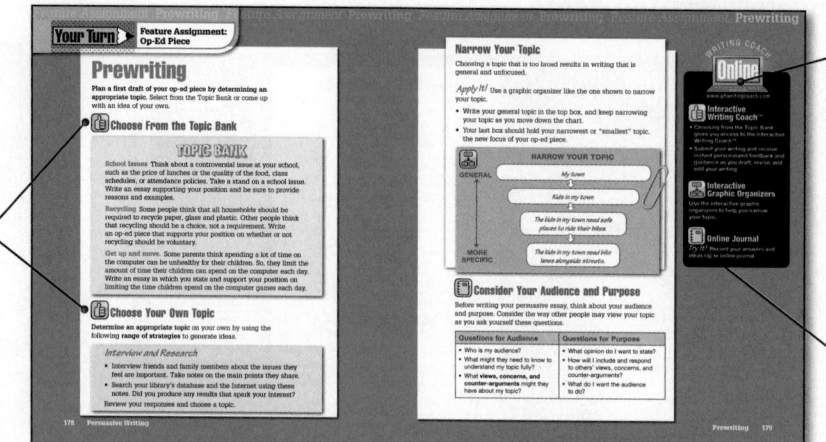

Choose from a bank of topics, or follow steps to find an idea of your own.

Writing Coach Online

- As you narrow your topic, get the right type of support! You'll find three different forms of graphic organizers— one model, one with step-by-step guidance, and one that is blank for you to complete.

- Use **Try It!** ideas to practice new skills. Use **Apply It!** activities as you work on your own writing.

Whether you are working on your essay drafts online or with a pen and paper, an **Outline for Success** can get you started.

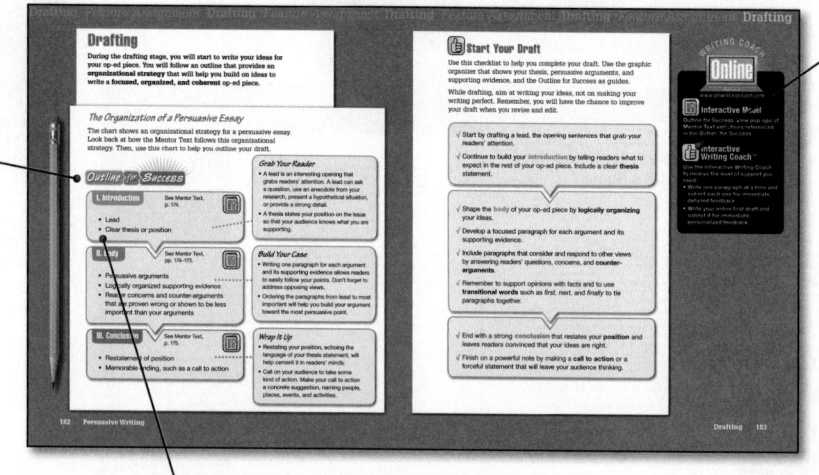

Consult this **outline** for a quick visual specific to the writing task assigned in each chapter.

Follow the bulleted suggestions for each part of your draft, and you'll be on your way to success.

Writing Coach Online

- Start with just a paragraph and build up to your essay draft, or if you are ready, go straight to submitting your essay. The choice is yours!

You can use the **Revision RADaR** strategy as a guide
for making changes to improve your draft.

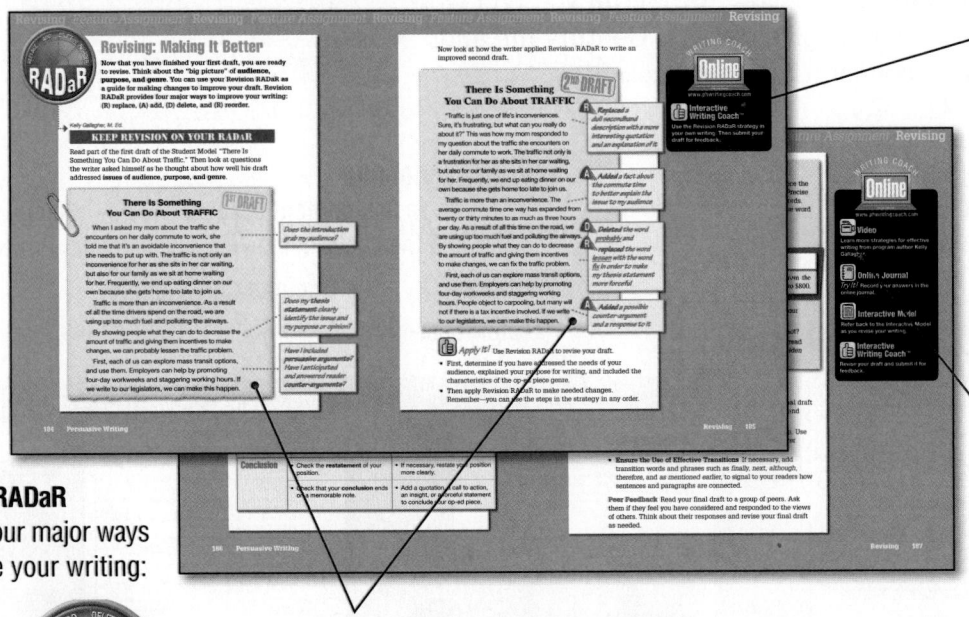

Revision RADaR
provides four major ways
to improve your writing:
- **R**eplace
- **A**dd
- **D**elete
- **R**eorder

Check out these example drafts to
see how to apply **Revision RADaR.**

Writing Coach Online

- With **Interactive Writing Coach™**, submit your paragraphs and essays multiple times. View your progress in your online writing portfolio. Feel confident that your work is ready to be shared in peer review or teacher conferencing.

- View **videos** with strategies for writing from program author **Kelly Gallagher.**

In the editing stage, **What Do You Notice?** and
Mentor Text help you zoom in on powerful sentences.

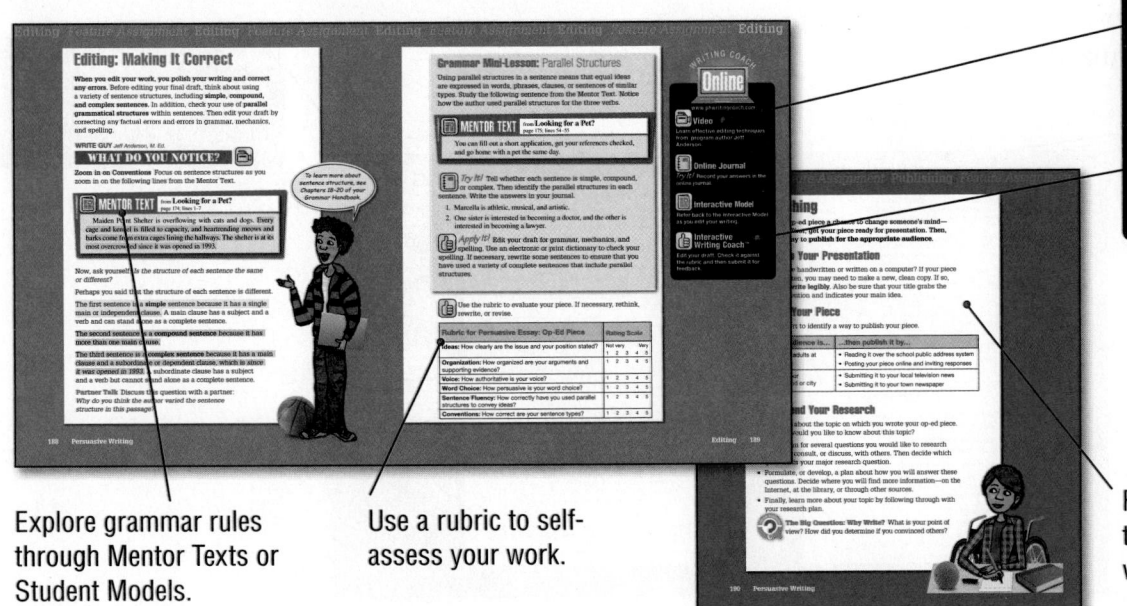

Writing Coach Online

- View **videos** with strategies for writing from program author **Jeff Anderson.**

- Submit your essay for feedback and a score.

Explore grammar rules
through Mentor Texts or
Student Models.

Use a rubric to self-
assess your work.

Find the best way
to share your writing
with others.

How do end-of-chapter features help you apply what you've learned?

21st Century Learning

In **Make Your Writing Count** and **Writing for Media** you will work on innovative assignments that involve the 21st Century life and career skills you'll need for communicating successfully.

Make Your Writing Count

Work collaboratively on project-based assignments and share what you have learned with others. Projects include:

- Debates
- TV Talk Shows
- News Reports

Writing for Media

Complete an assignment on your own by exploring media forms, and then developing your own content. Projects include:

- Blogs
- Storyboards
- Documentary Scripts
- Multimedia Presentations

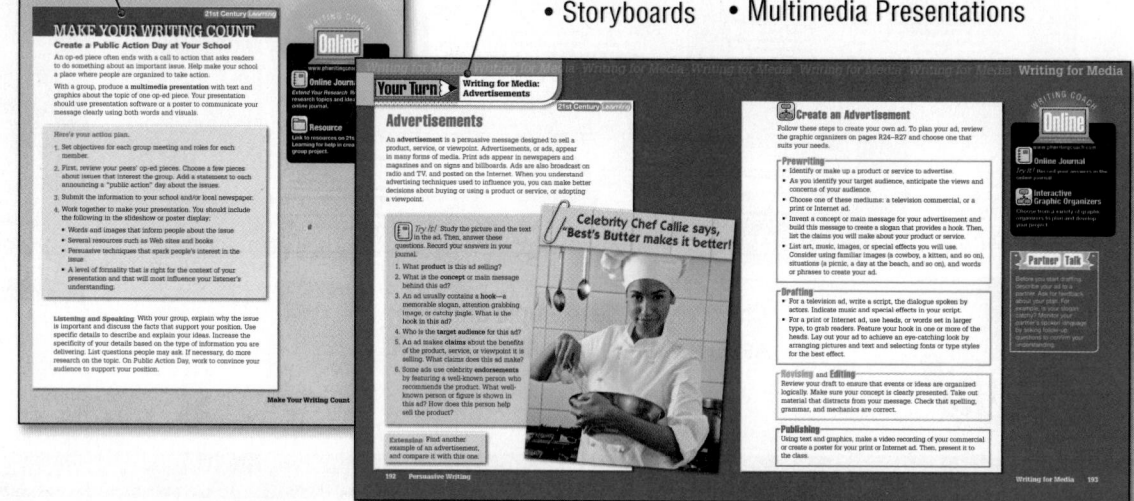

Test Prep

The **Writing for Assessment** pages help you prepare for important standardized tests.

 Notice these icons that emphasize the types of writing you'll find on high-stakes tests.

Use **The ABCDs of On-Demand Writing** for a quick, memorable strategy for success.

Writing Coach Online
Submit your essay for feedback and a score.

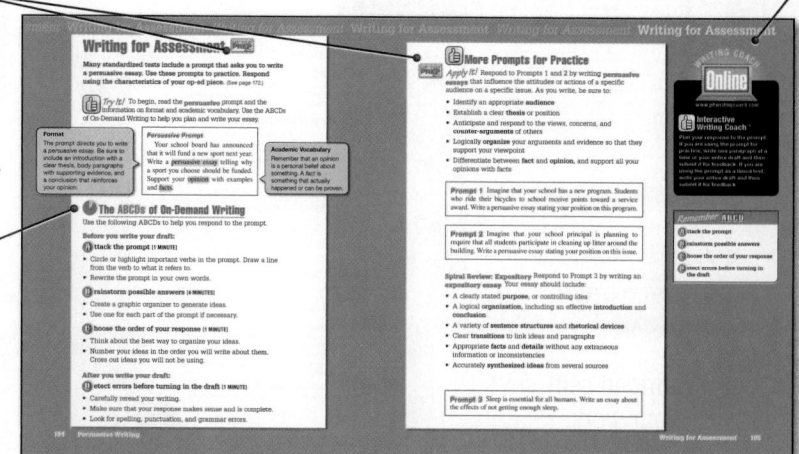

What will you find in the GRAMMAR section?

The **Find It/Fix It** reference guide helps you fix the **20** most common errors in student writing.

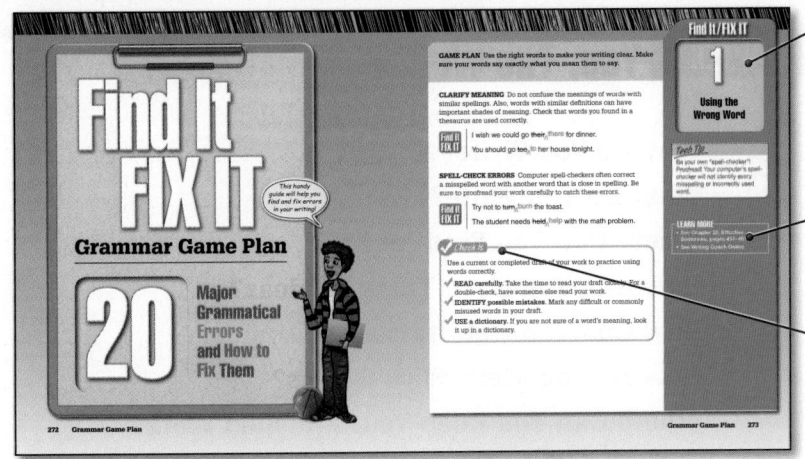

Study each of the 20 common errors and their corrections, which are clearly explained on each page.

Follow cross-references to more instruction in the grammar chapters.

Review the **Check It** features for strategies to help you avoid these errors.

Each grammar chapter begins with a **What Do You Notice?** feature and **Mentor Text.**

Use the **Mentor Text** to help you zoom in on powerful sentences. It showcases the correct use of written language conventions.

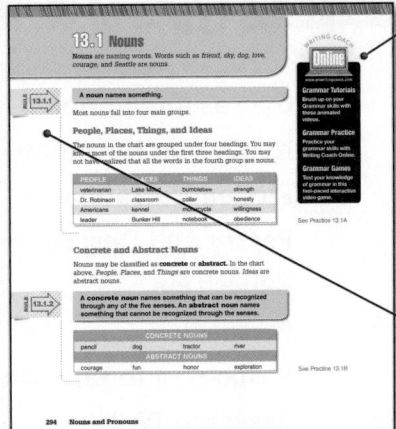

Writing Coach Online
The **Writing Coach Online** digital experience for Grammar helps you focus on just the lessons and practice you need.

Use the grammar section as a quick reference handbook. Each **grammar rule** is highlighted and numbered.

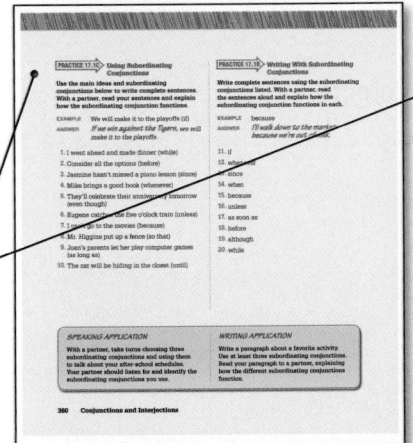

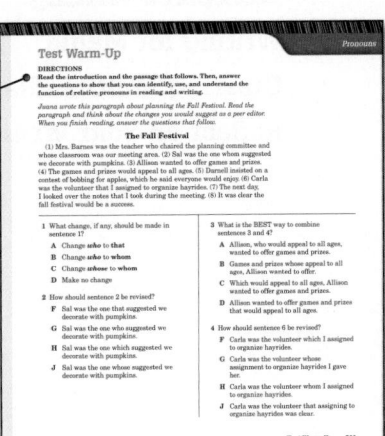

Try **Practice** pages and **Test Warm-Ups** to help you check your progress.

CONTENTS

WRITING

WRITING GAME PLAN

WRITING COACH
Online
www.phwritingcoach.com

All content available online

- Interactive Writing Coach™
- Interactive Graphic Organizer
- Interactive Models
- Online Journal
- Resources
- Video

WRITING

CHAPTER 5 Nonfiction Narration

64

Connect to the Big Questions

- **What do you think?**
  What do our accomplishments say about us?

- **Why write?**
  What should we put in and leave out to be accurate and honest?

Connect to the Big Questions

- **What do you think?**
  How do challenges help us grow?

- **Why write?**
  What can fiction do better than nonfiction?

www.phwritingcoach.com

All content available online
- Interactive Writing Coach™
- Interactive Graphic Organizer
- Interactive Models
- Online Journal
- Resources
- Video

WRITING

CHAPTER 7 Poetry and Description   118

Connect to the Big Questions

- **What do you think?**
  When is a picture better than words?

- **Why write?**
  How does one best convey feelings through words on a page?

WRITING

Connect to the Big Questions

- **What do you think?**
Which do you think is more important and why—the community's right to ensure that students are not distracted by cell phones or the individual student's right to use a cell phone?

- **Why write?**
What is your point of view? How will you know if you've convinced others?

Connect to the Big Questions

- **What do you think?**
  What do readers bring to a text that writers may not?

- **Why write?**
  What should you write about to make others interested in a text?

WRITING COACH

Online

www.phwritingcoach.com

All content available online

- Interactive Writing Coach™
- Interactive Graphic Organizer
- Interactive Models
- Online Journal
- Resources
- Video

WRITING

CHAPTER 11 Research Writing 222

Connect to the Big Questions

- **What do you think?**
  What kinds of scientific discoveries affect our lives the most?

- **Why write?**
  Do you understand your subject well enough to write about it? How will you find out what all the facts are?

Connect to the Big Questions

- **What do you think?**
  What is the best way to share information?

- **Why write?**
  What do daily workplace communications require of format, content, and style?

WRITING COACH
Online
www.phwritingcoach.com

All content available online
- Interactive Writing Coach™
- Interactive Graphic Organizer
- Interactive Models
- Online Journal
- Resources
- Video

GRAMMAR

WRITING COACH

Online

www.phwritingcoach.com

All content available online

- Grammar Tutorials
- Grammar Practice
- Grammar Games

GRAMMAR

WRITING COACH

Online

www.phwritingcoach.com

All content available online

- Grammar Tutorials
- Grammar Practice
- Grammar Games

GRAMMAR
USAGE

MECHANICS

WRITING COACH

Online

www.phwritingcoach.com

All content available online

- Grammar Tutorials
- Grammar Practice
- Grammar Games

GRAMMAR

WRITING COACH

Online

www.phwritingcoach.com

All content available online
- Grammar Tutorials
- Grammar Practice
- Grammar Games

STUDENT RESOURCES

NONFICTION NARRATION *Personal Narrative* FICTION NARRATION *Sci*
EXPOSITION *Compare-and-Contrast Essay* PERSUASION *Op-Ed Piece* RESP
WORKPLACE WRITING *Friendly Letter, Letter of Opinion, Letter of Request* NO
Short Story POETRY and DESCRIPTION *Free Verse Poem and Lyric Poem* E
TERATURE *Review of a Short Story* RESEARCH *Informational Research Repor*
TION NARRATION *Personal Narrative* FICTION NARRATION *Science Ficti*
TION *Compare-and-Contrast Essay* PERSUASION *Op-Ed Piece* RESPONSE T
LACE WRITING *Friendly Letter, Letter of Opinion, Letter of Request* NONFICT
ory POETRY and DESCRIPTION *Free Verse Poem and Lyric Poem* EXPOS

Writing

YOU, THE WRITER

Why Do You Write?

Writing well is one of the most important life skills you can develop. Being a good writer can help you achieve success in school and beyond. Most likely, you write for many reasons. You write:

To Share

You probably often write to **share** your experiences with others. Writing can be an easy way to **reach out** to people and connect with them.

To Persuade People

Writing can also be an effective way to **persuade** people to consider your opinions. For example, you may find it's easier to convince someone of your point of view when you've effectively organized your thoughts in an essay or a letter.

To Inform

Another reason to write is to **inform.** Perhaps you want to tell an audience how you built your computer network or how you finally got your e-mail to function properly.

To Enjoy

Personal fullfillment is another important motivation for writing, since writing enables you **to express** your thoughts and feelings. In addition, writing can also help you recall an event, or let you escape from everyday life.

Fortunately, writing well is a skill you can learn and one that you can continue to improve and polish. This program will help you improve your writing skills and give you useful information about the many types of writing.

What Do You Write?

Writing is already an important part of your everyday life. Each day is full of opportunities to write, allowing you to capture, express, think through and share your thoughts and feelings, and demonstrate what you know. Here are some ways you might write.

- Recording thoughts in a journal
- Texting friends or posting on social networking sites
- E-mailing thank-you notes to relatives
- Creating lists of things to do or things you like
- Writing research reports, nonfiction accounts, fiction stories, and essays in school

How Can You Find Ideas?

The good news is that ideas are all around you. You just need to be aware of the rich resources that are available.

By Observing

Observing is a good way to start to find ideas. Did you see anything interesting on your way to school? Was there something unusual about the video game you played last night?

By Reading

Reading is another useful option— look through newspaper articles and editorials, magazines, blogs, and Web sites. Perhaps you read something that surprised you or really made you feel concerned. Those are exactly the subjects that can lead to the ideas you want to write about.

By Watching

Watching is another way to get ideas— watch online videos or television programs, for example.

❝ Writer to Writer ❞

I write when I want to be heard or connect. Writing lets me be a vital part of my community and reach outside it as well. All the while, I get to be me—my unique self.

—Jeff Anderson

How Can You Keep Track of Ideas?

You may sometimes think of great writing ideas in the middle of the night or on the way to math class. These strategies can help you remember those ideas.

Start an Idea Notebook or a Digital Idea File

Reserving a small **notebook** to record ideas can be very valuable. Just writing the essence of an idea, as it comes to you, can later help you develop a topic or essay. A **digital idea file** is exactly the same thing—but it's recorded on your computer, cell phone, or other electronic device.

Keep a Personal Journal

Many people find that keeping a **journal** of their thoughts is helpful. Then, when it's time to select an idea, they can flip through their journal and pick up on the best gems they wrote— sometimes from long ago.

Maintain a Learning Log

A **learning log** is just what it sounds like—a place to record information you have learned, which could be anything from methods of solving equations to computer shortcuts. Writing about something in a learning log might later inspire you to conduct further research on the same topic.

Free Write

Some individuals find that if they just let go and write whatever comes to mind, they eventually produce excellent ideas. **Free writing** requires being relaxed and unstructured. This kind of writing does not require complete sentences, correct spelling, or proper grammar. Whatever ends up on the paper or on the computer screen is fine. Later, the writer can go back and tease out the best ideas.

How Can You Get Started?

Every writer is different, so it makes sense that all writers should try out techniques that might work well for them. Regardless of your writing style, these suggestions should help you get started.

Get Comfortable

It's important to find and create an environment that encourages your writing process. Choose a spot where you'll find it easy to concentrate. Some writers prefer quiet. Others prefer to work in a room with music playing softly.

Have Your Materials Ready

Before starting to write, gather all the background materials you need to get started, including your notes, free writing, reader's journal, and portfolio. Make sure you also have writing tools, such as a pen and paper or a computer.

Spend Time Wisely

Budgeting your available writing time is a wise strategy. Depending on your writing goal, you may want to sketch out your time on a calendar, estimating how long to devote to each stage of the writing process. Then, you can assign deadlines to each part. If you find a particular stage takes longer than you estimated, simply adjust your schedule to ensure that you finish on time.

◄ October ►						
SUNDAY	MONDAY	TUESDAY	WEDNESDAY	THURSDAY	FRIDAY	SATURDAY
		1 Start Research	2 Finish Research	3 Write Outline	4	5
6	7	8 Finish First Draft	9 Finish Revising	10 Finish Proof-reading	11	12
13	14 DUE DATE	15	16	17	18	19
20	21	22	23	24	25	26
27	28	29	30	31		

How Do You Work With Others?

If you think of writing as a solitary activity, think again. Working with others can be a key part of the writing process.

Brainstorming

Brainstorming works when everyone in a group feels free to suggest ideas, whether they seem commonplace or brilliant.

Cooperative Writing

Cooperative writing is a process in which each member of a group concentrates on a different part of an assignment. Then, the group members come together to discuss their ideas and write drafts.

Peer Feedback

Peer feedback comes from classmates who have read your writing and offered suggestions for improvements. When commenting, it's important to provide constructive, or helpful, criticism.

21st Century Learning

Collaborate and Discuss

In **collaborative writing,** each group member takes a role on a writing project. The goal is to work and rework the writing until all members feel they have produced the best result.

Possible Roles in a Collaborative Writing Project

LEADER	**FACILITATOR**	**COMPROMISER**	**LISTENER**
Initiates the discussion by clearly expressing group goals and moderates discussions	Works to move the discussion forward and clarify ideas	Works to find practical solutions to differences of opinion	Actively listens and serves to recall details that were discussed

Using Technology

Technology allows collaboration to occur in ways that were previously unthinkable.

- By working together on the Internet, students around the world have infinite opportunities to collaborate online on a wide range of projects.

- Collaboration can range from projects that foster community cooperation, such as how to improve debates during local elections, to those that increase global awareness, such as focusing on how to encourage more recycling.

- Being able to log in and to contribute to media, such as journals, blogs, and social networks, allows you to connect globally, express your views in writing, and join a world-wide conversation.

Where Can You Keep Your Finished Work?

A **portfolio,** or growing collection of your work, is valuable for many reasons. It can serve as a research bank of ideas and as a record of how your writing is improving. You can create a portfolio on a computer or in a folder or notebook. You'll learn more about managing a portfolio in chapter 3.

A **Reader's Journal,** in which you record quotes and ideas from your reading, can also be used to store original ideas. Your journal can be housed on a computer or in a notebook.

Reflect on Your Writing

Analyzing, making inferences, and drawing conclusions about how you find ideas can help you become a better, more effective writer. Find out more about how you write by asking yourself questions like these:

- Which strategies have I found most effective for finding good ideas for writing?

- What pieces of writing represent my best work and my weakest work? What do the pieces in each group have in common?

Partner Talk

With a partner, talk about your collaborative writing experiences. Be sure to share your responses to such questions as these: What project did you work on as a collaborative effort? What did you learn that you might not have discovered if you were developing a writing project by yourself?

CHAPTER 2

TYPES *of* WRITING

Genres and Forms

Genres are types, or categories, of writing.

- Each genre has a specific **purpose,** or goal. For example, the purpose of persuasive writing is to convince readers to agree with the writer's point of view.

- Each genre has specific **characteristics.** Short stories, for example, have characters, a setting, and a plot.

In this chapter, you will be introduced to several genres: nonfiction narratives, fiction narratives, poetry and descriptive writing, expository writing, persuasive writing, responses to literature, and workplace writing.

Forms are subcategories of genres that contain all the characteristics of the genre plus some unique characteristics of their own. For example, a mystery is a form of short story. In addition to plot, characters, and setting, it has a mystery to be solved.

Selecting Genres

In some writing situations, you may need to select the correct genre for conveying your intended meaning.

- To **entertain,** you may choose to write a short story or a humorous essay.

- To **describe** an emotion, writing a poem may be best.

- To **persuade** someone to your point of view, you may want to write a persuasive essay or editorial.

Each genre has unique strengths and weaknesses, and your specific goals will help you decide which is best.

Nonfiction Narration

Nonfiction narratives are any kind of literary text that tells a story about real people, events, and ideas. This genre of writing can take a number of different forms but includes well-developed conflict and resolution, interesting and believable characters, and a range of literary strategies, such as dialogue and suspense. Examples include Jean Fritz's "mk" and Annie Dillard's "An American Childhood."

WRITING COACH

Online

www.phwritingcoach.com

Online Journal

Try It! Record your notes, answers, and ideas in the online journal. You can also record and save your answers and ideas on pop-up sticky notes in the eText.

Personal Narratives

Personal narratives tell true stories about events in a writer's life. These types of writing are also called **autobiographical essays.** The stories may tell about an experience or relationship that is important to the writer, who is the main character. They have a clearly defined focus and communicate the reasons for actions and consequences.

Biographical Narratives

In a **biographical narrative,** the writer shares facts about someone else's life. The writer may describe an important period, experience, or relationship in that other person's life, but presents the information from his or her own perspective.

Blogs

Blogs are online journals that may include autobiographical narratives, reflections, opinions, and other types of comments. They may also reflect genres other than nonfiction such as expository writing, and they may include other media, such as photos, music, or video.

Diary and Journal Entries

Writers record their personal thoughts, feelings, and experiences in **diaries** or **journals.** Writers sometimes keep diaries and journals for many years and then analyze how they reacted to various events over time.

Eyewitness Accounts

Eyewitness accounts are nonfiction writing that focus on historical or other important events. The writer is the narrator and shares his or her thoughts about the event. However, the writer is not the main focus of the writing.

Memoirs

Memoirs usually focus on meaningful scenes from writers' lives. These scenes often reflect on moments of a significant decision or personal discovery. For example, many modern U.S. presidents have written memoirs after they have left office. These memoirs help the public gain a better understanding of the decisions they made while in office.

Reflective Essays

Reflective essays present personal experiences, either events that happened to the writers themselves or that they learned about from others. They generally focus on sharing observations and insights they had while thinking about those experiences. Reflective essays often appear as features in magazines and newspapers.

Try It! With a small group, discuss which of the narrative nonfiction forms would be the best choice for each of these purposes. For each, identify two ideas you would expect the writing to address. Discuss your ideas and report your decisions.

- To tell about seeing a championship kite-flying tournament
- To write about one of the first astronauts to walk in space
- To record personal thoughts about a favorite teacher

Fiction Narration

Fiction narratives are literary texts that tell a story about imagined people, events, and ideas. They contain elements such as characters, a setting, a sequence of events, and often, a theme. As with nonfiction narratives, this genre can take many different forms, but most forms include well-developed **conflict** and **resolution.** They also include **interesting and believable elements** and a range of **literary strategies,** such as dialogue and suspense. Examples include Cynthia Rylant's "Papa's Parrot" and Lucille Clifton's "The Luckiest Time of All."

Realistic Fiction

Realistic fiction portrays invented characters and events in everyday situations. Because the focus is on everyday life, realistic fiction often presents problems that many people face and solutions they devise to solve them.

Fantasy Stories

Fantasy stories stretch the imagination and take readers to unreal worlds. Animals may talk, people may fly, or characters may have superhuman powers. Good fantasy stories manage to keep the fantastic elements believable.

Historical Fiction

Historical fiction is about imaginary people living in real places and times in history. Usually, the main characters are fictional people who know and interact with famous people and participate in important historical events.

Mystery Stories

Mystery stories present unexplained or strange events that characters try to solve. These stories are often packed full of suspense and surprises. Some characters in mystery stories, such as Sherlock Holmes, have become so famous that many people think of them as real people.

Myths and Legends

Myths and **legends** are traditional stories, told in cultures around the world. They were created to explain natural events that people could not otherwise explain or understand. They may, for example, tell about the origin of fire or thunder. Many myths and legends include gods, goddesses, and heroes who perform superhuman actions.

Science Fiction

Science fiction stories tell about real and imagined developments in science and technology and their effects on the way people think and live. Space travel, robots, and life in the future are popular topics in science fiction.

Tall Tales

You can tell a **tall tale** from other story types because it tells about larger-than-life characters in realistic settings. These characters can perform amazing acts of strength and bravery. One very famous hero of tall tales is Pecos Bill, who could ride just about anything—even a tornado!

Try It! Think about what you've read about narrative fiction and narrative nonfiction genres. Then, discuss in a group which **genre** would be best if you were planning a first draft and had these purposes in mind. Select the correct genre for conveying your intended meaning to your audiences. Then, identify two or three ideas that you would expect to include in a first draft. Be sure to explain your choices.

- To tell about a Texas rancher who can lasso lightning
- To share a true story about a famous person
- To tell the story of your most exciting day at school

Poetry and Description

Poetry and other kinds of descriptive literature express ideas and feelings about real or imagined people, events, and ideas. They use rhythm, rhyme, precise language, and sensory details—words that appeal to the senses—to create vivid images. In addition, they use figurative language—writing that means something beyond what the words actually say—to express ideas in new, fresh, and interesting ways.

Structural elements, such as line length and stanzas, also help the poet express ideas and set a mood. Some examples of poetry include Naomi Shihab Nye's "The Rider" and Nikki Giovanni's "Winter."

Ballad

A **ballad** is a form of lyric poetry that expresses the poet's emotions toward someone or something. Ballads rhyme, and some have refrains that repeat after each stanza, which makes them easy to translate into songs.

In many places, traditional folk ballads were passed down as oral poems or songs and then later written. Some ballads tell about cultural heroes. Other ballads tell sad stories or make fun of certain events.

Free Verse

Free verse is poetry that has no regular rhyme, rhythm, or form. Instead, a free verse poem captures the patterns of natural speech. The poet writes in whatever form seems to fit the ideas best. A free verse poem can have almost anything as its subject.

Partner Talk

Think about an example of fiction that you've especially enjoyed reading. Then, choose a partner and report your choices to each other. Be sure to explain what made the fiction piece so enjoyable, interesting, or exciting.

Prose Poem

A **prose poem** shares many of the features of other poetry, but it takes the form of prose, or non-verse writing. Therefore, a prose poem may look like a short story on a page.

Sonnet

The **sonnet** is a form of rhyming lyric poetry with set rules. It is 14 lines long and usually follows a rhythm scheme called iambic pentameter. Each line has ten syllables and every other syllable is accented.

Haiku

Haiku is a form of non-rhyming poetry that was first developed in Japan hundreds of years ago. Typically, the first line has seven syllables, the second line has five syllables, and the third line has seven syllables. Haiku poets often write about nature and use vivid visual images.

Other Descriptive Writing

Descriptive writing includes descriptive essays, travel writing, and definition essays.

- **Descriptive essays** often use words that involve the senses to create a clear picture of a subject.
- A **travel essay** uses sensory words to describe a place.
- A **definition essay** can draw on a writer's emotional experience to describe something abstract, like friendship or happiness.

  Description can be used in other types of writing. For example, a short story may include strong description.

Try It! Now that you've learned more about poetry and description, discuss which specific **genre** would be best for each of these purposes. Select the correct genre for conveying your intended meaning to your audiences. Then, identify two or three types of information that you would want to include in a first draft. Be ready to explain your thinking.

- To tell about a trip to a beach in Mexico
- To describe a drop of rain
- To tell the story of a character who lives in the wilderness

Exposition

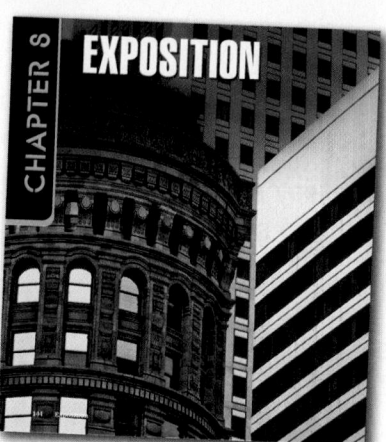

Exposition is writing that seeks to communicate ideas and information. It relies on facts to inform or explain.

- Effective expository writing includes effective introductory paragraphs, body paragraphs, and concluding paragraphs.
- In addition, good expository writing uses a variety of sentence structures and rhetorical devices—deliberate uses of language for specific effects.

Examples of expository writing include Ruwanthi Vigilant's "Houston's Chinatown" and Larry Lunxer's "Mongoose on the Loose."

Analytical Essay

An **analytical essay** explores a topic by supplying relevant information in the form of facts, examples, reasons, and valid inferences to support the writer's claims.

- An **introductory paragraph** presents a thesis statement, the main point to be developed.
- The **body of the essay** provides facts about the topic, using a variety of sentence structures and transitions.
- The **concluding paragraph** sums up ideas.

Compare-and-Contrast Essay

A **compare-and-contrast** essay explores similarities and differences between two or more things for a specific purpose. As with other expository essays, the compare-and-contrast essay offers clear, factual details about the subject.

Cause-and-Effect Essay

A **cause-and-effect essay** traces the results of an event or describes the reasons an event happened. It is clearly organized and gives precise examples that support the relationship between the cause and effect.

Partner **Talk**

Choose a different partner this time. Discuss a poem that you've read in class. Share your thoughts about the poem and describe what made the piece successful.

Classification Essay

In a **classification essay,** a writer organizes a subject into categories and explains the category into which an item falls.

- An effective classification essay **sorts** its subjects—things or ideas—into several categories.

- It then offers **examples** that fall into each category. For example, a classification essay about video games might discuss three types of video games—action, adventure, and arcade.

- The essay might conclude with a statement about how the items classified are different or about how they are similar.

Problem-Solution Essay

A **problem-solution essay** presents a problem and then offers solutions to that problem. This type of essay may contain opinions, like a persuasive essay, but it is meant to explain rather than persuade.

- An effective problem-solution essay presents a clear statement of the problem, including a summary of its causes and effects.

- Then, it proposes at least one realistic solution and uses facts, statistics, or expert testimony to support the solution.

- The essay should be clearly organized, so that the relationship between the problem and the solution is obvious.

Pro-Con Essay

A **pro-con essay** examines arguments for and against an idea or topic.

- It has a topic that has two sides or points of view. For example, you might choose the following as a topic: Is it right to keep animals in zoos?

- Then, you would develop an essay that tells why it's good to keep animals in zoos, as well as why it's harmful to keep animals in zoos.

- It's important to be sure to give a clear analysis of the topic.

Newspaper and Magazine Articles

Newspaper and **magazine articles** offer information about news and events. They are typically factual and do not include the writer's opinions. They often provide an analysis of events and give readers background information on a topic. Some articles may also reflect genres other than the analytical essay, such as an editorial that aims to persuade.

Internet Articles

Articles on the **Internet** can supply relevant information about a topic.

- They are often like newspaper or magazine articles but may include shorter sentences and paragraphs. In addition, they include more visuals, such as charts and bulleted lists. They may also reflect genres other than analytical essays.

- It's always wise to consider the source when reading Internet articles because only the most reputable sources should be trusted to present correct facts.

On-Demand Writing

Because essay questions often appear on school tests, knowing how to write to **test prompts**, especially under time limits, is an important skill.

Test prompts provide a clear topic with directions about what should be addressed. The effective response to an essay demonstrates not only an understanding of academic content but also good writing skills.

 *Try It!* Think about what you've learned about expository writing and consider the other genres you've discussed. Then, discuss in a group which **genre** would be best if you were planning a first draft with these purposes in mind. Select the correct genre for conveying your intended meaning to your audiences. Then, identify two or three key ideas that you would want to include in a first draft. Be sure to explain your choices.

- To weigh the benefits of two kinds of pets
- To imagine what life would be like on the moon

Persuasion

Persuasive writing aims to influence the attitudes or actions of a specific audience on specific issues. A strong persuasive text is logically organized and clearly describes the issue. It also provides precise and relevant evidence that supports a clear thesis statement. Persuasive writing may contain diagrams, graphs, or charts. These visuals can help to convince the reader. Examples include Barbara Jordan's "All Together Now" and Louis L'Amour's "The Eternal Frontier."

Persuasive Essays or Argumentative Essays

A **persuasive essay** or **argumentative essay** uses logic and reasoning to persuade readers to adopt a certain point of view or to take action. A strong persuasive essay starts with a clear thesis statement and provides supporting arguments based on evidence. It also anticipates readers' counter-arguments and responds to them as well.

Persuasive Speeches

Persuasive speeches are presented aloud and aim to win an audience's support for a policy, position, or action. These speeches often appeal to emotion and reason to convince an audience. Speakers sometimes change their script in order to address each specific audience's concerns.

Editorials

Editorials state the opinion of the editors and publishers of news organizations. Editorials usually present an opinion about a current issue, starting with a clear thesis statement and then offering strong supporting evidence.

Op-Ed Pieces

An **op-ed, or opposite-editorial, piece** is an essay that tries to convince readers to agree with the writer's views on an issue. The writer may not work for the publication and is often an expert on the issue or has an interesting point of view.

Letters to the Editor

Readers write **letters to editors** at print and Internet publications to express opinions in response to previously published articles. A good letter to the editor gives an accurate and honest representation of the writer's views.

Reviews

Reviews evaluate items and activities, such as books, movies, plays, and music, from the writer's point of view. A review often states opinions on the quality of an item or activity and supports those opinions with examples, facts, and other evidence.

Advertisements

Advertisements in all media—from print to online sites to highway billboards—are paid announcements that try to convince people to buy something or do something. Good advertisements use a hook to grab your attention and support their claims. They contain vivid, persuasive language and multimedia techniques, such as music, to appeal to a specific audience.

Propaganda

Propaganda uses emotional appeals and often biased, false, or misleading information to persuade people to think or act in a certain way. Propaganda may tap into people's strongest emotions by generating fear or attacking their ideas of loyalty or patriotism. Because propaganda appears to be objective, it is wise to be aware of the ways it can manipulate people's opinions and actions.

Partner Talk

Share your experiences with various types of persuasive texts with a partner. Talk about the types of persuasive text that you think are most effective, honest, and fair. Be sure to explain your thinking.

Try It! Think about what you have learned about exposition, description, and persuasion. Form a group to discuss and draw conclusions about which **genres** would be best if you were planning a first draft with each of these intentions in mind. Select the correct genre for conveying your intended meaning to your audiences. Then, identify two or three types of information that you would want to include in a first draft.

- To explain how an event happened
- To describe a beautiful landscape
- To encourage teens to buy teeth-whitening toothpaste

Responses to Literature

Responses to literature analyze and interpret an author's work. They use clear **thesis statements** and **evidence from the text using embedded quotations to support the writer's ideas.** They also evaluate how well authors have accomplished their goals. Effective responses to literature extend beyond literal analysis to evaluate and discuss how and why the text is effective or not effective.

Critical Reviews

Critical reviews evaluate books, plays, poetry, and other literary works. Reviews present the writer's opinions and support them with specific examples. The responses may analyze the aesthetic effects of an author's use of language in addition to responding to the content of the writing.

Compare-and-Contrast Essays

Compare-and-contrast essays explore similarities and differences between two or more works of literature. These essays provide relevant evidence to support the writer's opinions.

Letters to Authors

Readers write **letters to authors** to share their feelings and thoughts about a work of literature directly.

Blog Comments

Blog comments on an author's Web site or book retailer pages let readers share their ideas about a work. Readers express their opinions and give interpretations of what an author's work means.

Try It! As a group, decide which **genre** would be most appropriate if you were planning a first draft for each of these purposes. Select the correct genre for conveying your intended meaning to your audiences. Then, identify two or three key questions that you would want to answer in a first draft.

- To tell an author why you think her book is excellent
- To write an opinion about a newspaper article
- To imagine how a certain landform came to be

> ### Partner Talk
>
> Interview your partner about his or her experiences writing interpretative responses. Be sure to ask questions such as these:
>
> - How did you support your opinion of the author's work?
> - How did you choose evidence, such as quotes, to support your analysis or opinion?

Research Writing

Research writing is based on factual information from outside sources. Research reports organize and present ideas and information. They present evidence in support of a clear thesis statement.

Research Reports and Documented Essays

Research reports and **documented essays** present information and analysis about a topic that the writer has studied. Start with a clear thesis statement. Research reports often include graphics and illustrations. Documented essays are less formal research writing that show the source of every fact, quote, or borrowed idea in parentheses.

Experiment Journals and Lab Reports

Experiment journals and **lab reports** focus on the purposes, procedures, and results of a lab experiment. They often follow a strict format that includes dates and specific observation notes.

Statistical Analysis Reports

A **statistical analysis report** presents numerical data. Writers of this type of report must explain how they gathered their information, analyze their data, tell what significance the findings may have, and explain how these findings support their thesis.

Annotated Bibliographies

An **annotated bibliography** lists the research sources a writer used. It includes the title, author, publication date, publisher, and brief notes that describe and evaluate the source.

Try It! Discuss which kinds of reports you might write if you were planning a first draft for these purposes. **Select the correct form** for conveying your intended meaning to your audiences. Then, identify two or three key questions that you would want to answer in a first draft. Explain your choices.

- To accompany a project you plan to enter in a science fair
- To write about a poll taken to predict the results of an election

Partner Talk

Share with a partner the kinds of research writing you've done in school. Explain which projects you've enjoyed and why.

Workplace Writing

Workplace writing is writing done on the job or as part of a job, often in an office setting. It usually communicates details about a particular job or work project. This type of writing features organized and accurately conveyed information and should include reader-friendly formatting techniques, such as clearly defined sections and enough blank space for easy reading.

Business Letters and Friendly Letters

A **business letter** is a formal letter written to, from, or within a business. It can be written to make requests or to express concerns or approval. For example, you might write to a company to ask about job opportunities. Business letters follow a specific format that includes an address, date, formal greeting, and closing.

In contrast, a **friendly letter** is a form of correspondence written to communicate between family, friends, or acquaintances. For example, you might write a thank-you note for a gift.

Memos

Memos are short documents usually written from one member of an organization to another or to a group. They are an important means of communicating information within an organization.

E-mails

E-mail is an abbreviation for "electronic mail" and is a form of electronic memo. Because it can be transmitted quickly allowing for instant long-distance communication, e-mail is a very common form of communication that uses a computer and software to send messages.

Forms

Forms are types of workplace writing that ask for specific information to be completed in a particular format. Examples include applications, emergency contact information forms, and tax forms.

Instructions

Instructions are used to explain how to complete a task or procedure. They provide clear, step-by-step guidelines. For example, recipes and user manuals are forms of instructions.

Project Plans

Project plans are short documents usually written from one member of an organization to another. They outline a project's goals and objectives and may include specific details about how certain steps of a project should be achieved.

Résumés

A **résumé** is an overview of a person's experience and qualifications for a job. This document lists a person's job skills and work history. Résumés can also feature information about a person's education.

College Applications

College applications are documents that ask for personal information and details about someone's educational background. College administrators use this information to decide whether or not to accept a student.

Job Applications

Job applications are similar to résumés in that they require a person to list work experience and educational background. Most employers will require a completed job application as part of the hiring process.

Try It! As a group, discuss which form of workplace writing would be best for each of these purposes. Select the correct form for conveying your intended meaning to your audiences. Identify two or three types of information you would expect to include in a first draft.

- To inform the company that made your cell phone that it does not work properly
- To prepare information about your qualifications for a job search
- To create a plan for your group assignment in science class

Partner Talk

Share with a partner your experience with workplace and procedural writing. For example, have you ever written instructions, created a résumé, or completed a job application? What do you find are particular challenges with this type of writing?

Writing for Media

The world of communication has changed significantly in recent years. In addition to writing for print media such as magazines and books, writers also write for a variety of other **media**, in forms such as:

- Scripts for screenplays, video games, and documentaries
- Storyboards for graphic novels and advertisements
- Packaging for every kind of product
- Web sites and blogs

Scripts

Scripts are written for various media, such as documentaries, theater productions, speeches, and audio programs. Movies, television shows, and video games also have scripts.

- A good script focuses on a clearly expressed or implied **theme** and has a specific **purpose**.
- It also contains interesting details, which contribute to a definite **mood or tone**.
- A good script also includes a clear **setting**, **dialogue**, and well-developed **action**.

Blogs

Blogs address just about every purpose and interest. For example, there are blogs about local issues, pets, or food.

Advertisements

Advertisements are designed to persuade someone to buy a product or service. Advertisements use images, words, and music to support their message. Writers write the content of advertisements. In addition, they may help create music and design the sound and the images in the ad.

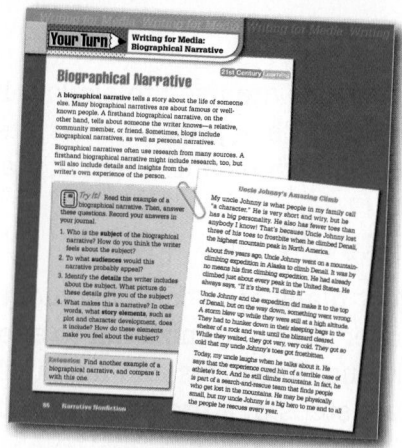

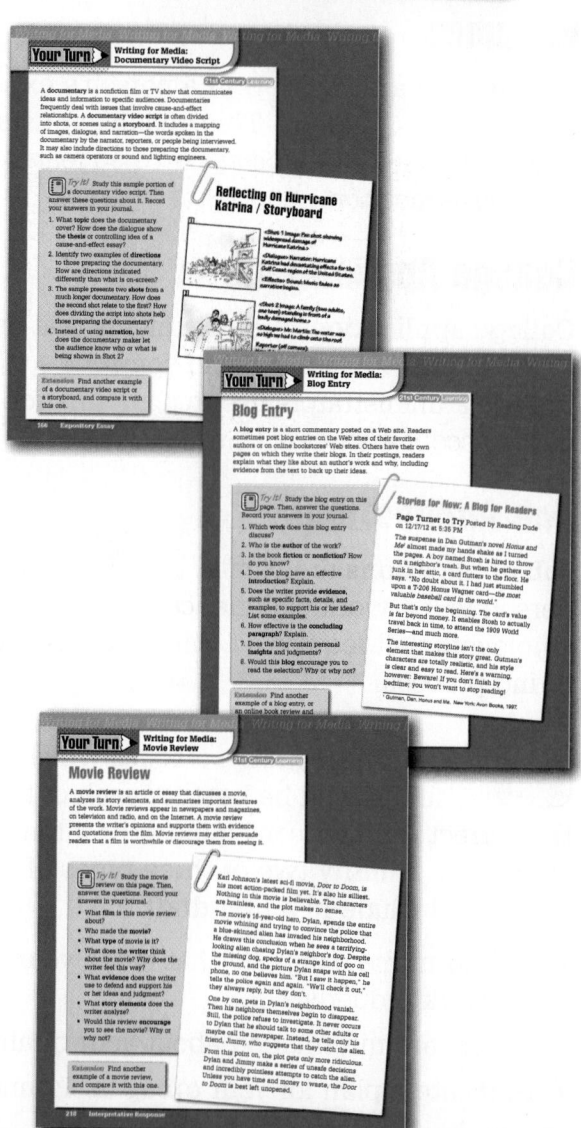

Creating Multimedia Projects

A **multimedia project** or presentation uses sound, video, and other media to convey a point or entertain an audience. No matter what type of project you choose as your own multimedia project, it is important to follow these steps:

- Decide on the project's **purpose** and your target **audience.**

- Choose **media** that will effectively convey your **message.**

- **Plan** your presentation. Will you work alone or with a partner or group? If you work with others, how you will assign the tasks?

- What **equipment** will you need? Will you produce artwork, record audio, and take photographs? Should you produce a storyboard to show the sequence of details in your presentation? Be sure to allow enough time to produce the text and all the other elements in your project.

- Keep the **writing process** in mind. There should be working and reworking along the way.

- **Assess** the progress of the project as you work. Ask questions, such as: Does my project incorporate appropriate writing genres? Will the presentation interest my audience? Have I kept my purpose in mind?

- **Rehearse!** Before presenting your project, be sure to do several "practice runs" to weed out and correct any errors.

- Keep an electronic record of your presentation for future reference.

- After your presentation, have others assess the project. Their critique will help you to do an even better job next time!

Reflect on Your Writing

Learning more about the different types of writing can help you focus on the characteristics of each type so you can keep improving your own writing. Think about what you've learned in Chapter 2 as you answer these questions:

- What type of writing most interests you?

- What type of writing do you think is most useful? Why?

Partner Talk

Share with a partner your experience with writing for media or multimedia projects. Have you created a Web site or contributed to one? Have you had to complete multimedia projects for a class assignment or for a personal project on which you worked? Talk about how writing for media presents different challenges from more traditional writing and how you have dealt with those challenges.

CHAPTER 3

THE WRITING PROCESS

Writing Traits

Good writing has specific qualities, or traits. In this chapter you will learn about these traits and how to use rubrics to evaluate them. You will also learn how to apply traits during the stages of the writing process.

Ideas

Good writing sends a strong message or presents a clear "angle" or point of view on a subject. It is also informative. The ideas are well developed, or explained with examples and other details.

Organization

A well-organized paper has an obvious plan. You will want to make sure that your ideas move from sentence to sentence and paragraph to paragraph in a logical way. For example, events in a story often appear in the order in which they occurred.

Voice

Voice is the combination of word choice and personal writing style that makes your writing unique. Voice connects a reader to the writer. It can show your personality or "take" on a story.

Word Choice

Your choice of words can help you achieve your purpose. Precise word choice means choosing the word that says exactly what you mean to say. Vivid word choice involves choosing words that create pictures for readers, describing how a subject looks, sounds, smells, and so on.

Sentence Fluency

Good writing is like a song—it has fluency, or a rhythm and a flow. By varying sentence patterns, writers ensure that the rhythm of their writing stays interesting.

Conventions

By following the rules of spelling, capitalization, punctuation, grammar, and usage, you help readers understand your ideas.

Overview of Writing Traits	
Ideas	• Significant ideas and informative details • Thorough development of ideas • Unique perspective or strong message
Organization	• Obvious plan • Clear sequence • Strong transitions
Voice	• Effective word choice • Attention to style
Word Choice	• Precise, not vague, words • Vivid, not dull, words • Word choices suited to audience and purpose
Sentence Fluency	• Varied sentence beginnings, lengths, and structures • Smooth sentence rhythms
Conventions	• Proper spelling and capitalization • Correct punctuation, grammar, usage, and sentence structure

Rubrics and How To Use Them

You can use rubrics to evaluate the traits of your writing. A rubric allows you to score your writing on a scale in different categories. You will use a six-point rubric like this to help evaluate your writing in chapters 5–12.

Writing Traits	Rating Scale					
	Not very				Very	
Ideas: How interesting, significant, or original are the ideas you present? How well do you develop ideas?	1	2	3	4	5	6
Organization: How logically is your piece organized? Do your transitions, or movements from idea to idea, make sense?	1	2	3	4	5	6
Voice: How authentic and original is your voice?	1	2	3	4	5	6
Word Choice: How precise and vivid are the words you use? To what extent does your word choice help achieve your purpose?	1	2	3	4	5	6
Sentence Fluency: How well do your sentences flow? How strong and varied is the rhythm they create?	1	2	3	4	5	6
Conventions: How correct is your punctuation? Your capitalization? Your spelling?	1	2	3	4	5	6

Each trait appears in the first column. The rating scale appears in the second column. The higher your score for a trait, the better your writing exhibits that trait.

Using a Rubric on Your Own

A rubric can be a big help in assessing your writing while it is still in process. Imagine you've just started writing a piece of narrative fiction. You know that narrative fiction should have characters, a setting, and a conflict and resolution. You can check the rubric as you write to make sure you are on track. For example, you may use the rubric and decide that you have not developed the conflict well. You can revise to improve your writing and get a better score.

Narrative Fiction Elements	Rating Scale					
	Not very				Very	
Interesting characters	1	2	3	4	5	6
Believable setting	1	2	3	4	5	6
Literary strategies	1	2	3	4	5	6
Well-developed conflict	1	2	3	4	5	6
Well-developed resolution	1	2	3	4	5	6

 Try It! If you checked your story against the rubric and rated yourself mostly 1s and 2s, what actions might you want to take next?

Using a Rubric With a Partner

In some cases, building your own rubric can help you ensure that your writing will meet your expectations. For example, if your class has an assignment to write a poem, you and a partner might decide to construct a rubric to check one another's work. A rubric like the one shown here can help point out whether you should make any changes. Extra lines allow room for you to add other criteria.

Poetry Elements	Rating Scale					
	Not very				Very	
Good sensory details	1	2	3	4	5	6
Colorful adjectives	1	2	3	4	5	6
	1	2	3	4	5	6
	1	2	3	4	5	6
	1	2	3	4	5	6

 Try It! What other elements might you add to the rubric?

Using a Rubric in a Group

It is also helpful to use a rubric in a group. That way you can get input on your writing from many people at the same time. If the group members' ratings of your piece are similar, you will probably have an easy time deciding whether to make changes. If the responses vary significantly, you might want to discuss the results with the group. Then, analyze what led to the differing opinions and make careful judgments about what changes you will make.

WRITING COACH

Online

www.phwritingcoach.com

Online Journal

Try It! Record your answers and ideas in the online journal. You can also record and save your answers and ideas on pop-up sticky notes in the eText.

What Is the Writing Process?

The five steps in the writing process are prewriting, drafting, revising, editing, and publishing. Writing is a process because your idea goes through a series of changes or stages before the product is finished.

Study the diagram to see how moving through the writing process can work. Remember, you can go back to a stage in the process. It does not always have to occur in order.

Prewriting

In prewriting, you will:
- Explore ideas
- Choose a purpose and an audience
- Gather details
- Sequence ideas

Drafting

In drafting, you will:
- Put ideas down
- Develop a thesis or controlling idea
- Structure ideas in a sustained way

In publishing, you will:
- Produce a final polished copy of your writing
- Share your writing

Publishing

In the editing phase, you will:
- Check the accuracy of facts
- Correct errors in spelling, grammar, usage, and mechanics

In revising, you will:
- Re-read draft to see what works and what does not
- Use a rubric to evaluate
- Analyze what you want to change or improve
- Make changes

Revising

Editing

Why Use the Writing Process?

Writing involves careful thinking, which means you will make changes as you write. Even professional writers don't just write their thoughts and call it a finished work of art. They use a process. For example, some writers keep going back to the revising stage many times, while others feel they can do the revision in just one step. It is up to each writer to develop the style that works best to produce the best results.

You might find that the writing process works best for you when you keep these tips in mind:

- Remember that the five steps in the writing process are equally important.
- Think about your audience as you plan your paper and develop your writing.
- Make sure you remember your topic and stick to your specific purpose as you write.
- Give your writing some time to "rest." Sometimes it can be good to work on a piece, walk away, and look at it later, with a fresh eye and mind.

The following pages will describe in more detail how to use each stage of the writing process to improve your writing.

" Writer to Writer "

Writing process gives us the freedom to write like mad, tinker like an engineer, evaluate like a judge—playing different roles at different stages. Most importantly it gives us the freedom to get our words out of our heads and into the world.

—Jeff Anderson

Prewriting

Prewriting
Drafting
Revising
Editing
Publishing

No matter what kind of writing you do, planning during the prewriting stage is crucial. During prewriting, you determine the topic of your writing, its purpose, and its specific audience. Then, you narrow the topic and gather details.

Determining the Purpose and Audience

What Is Your Purpose?

To be sure your writing communicates your ideas clearly, it is important to clarify why you are writing. Consider what you want your audience to take away from your writing. You may want to entertain them, or you may want to warn them about something. Even when you write an entry in a private journal, you're writing for an audience—you!

Who Is Your Audience?

Think about the people who will read your work and consider what they may already know about your topic. Being able to identify this group and their needs will let you be sure you are providing the right level of information.

Choosing a Topic

Here are just a few of the many techniques you can use to determine an appropriate topic.

- **Brainstorm**

  You can brainstorm by yourself, with a partner, or with a group. Just jot down ideas as they arise, and don't rule out anything. When brainstorming in a group, one person's idea often "piggybacks" on another.

- **Make a Mind Map**

  A mind map is a quick drawing you sketch as ideas come to you. The mind map can take any form. The important thing is to write quick notes as they come to you and then to draw lines to connect relationships among the ideas.

- **Interview**

  A fun way to find a writing topic is to conduct an interview. You might start by writing interview questions for yourself or someone else. Questions that start with *what, when, why, how,* and *who* are most effective. For example, you might ask, "When was the last time you laughed really hard?" "What made you laugh?" Then, conduct the interview and discover the answers.

- **Review Resources and Discuss Ideas**

  You can review resources, such as books, magazines, newspapers, and digital articles, to get ideas. Discussing your initial ideas with a partner can spark even more ideas.

Narrowing Your Topic

Once you have settled on a topic idea you really like, it may seem too broad to tackle. How can you narrow your topic?

- **Use Graphic Organizers**

  A graphic organizer can help narrow a topic that's too broad. For example, you might choose "Animals" as a topic. You might make your topics smaller and smaller until you narrow the topic to "The Habitat of Emperor Penguins."

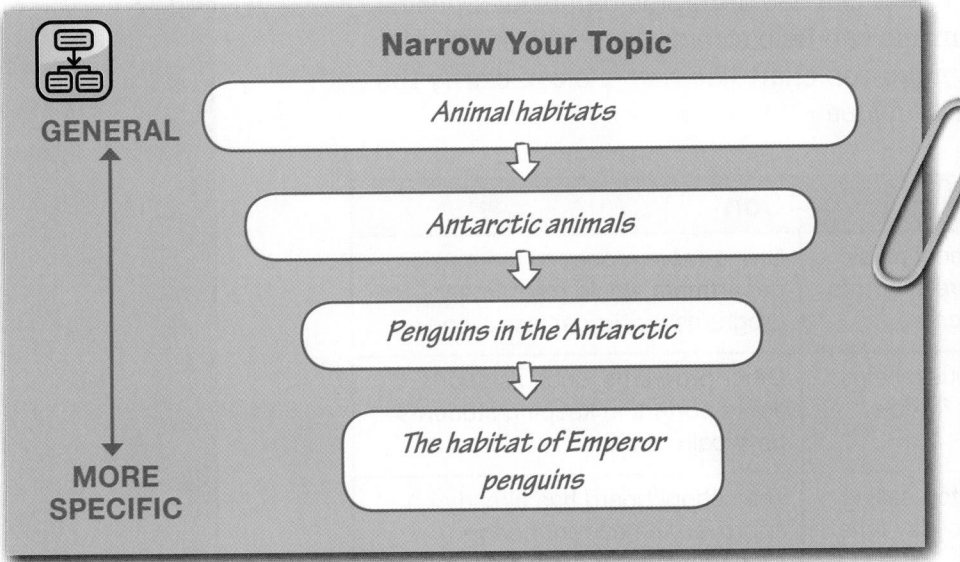

Narrow Your Topic

GENERAL

Animal habitats

↓

Antarctic animals

↓

Penguins in the Antarctic

↓

The habitat of Emperor penguins

MORE SPECIFIC

WRITING COACH

Online

www.phwritingcoach.com

Online Journal

Try It! Record your answers and ideas in the online journal. You can also record and save your answers and ideas on pop-up sticky notes in the eText.

❝ Writer to Writer ❞

Put something down. Anything. Then, magic will happen.

—Jeff Anderson

Prewriting (continued)

Prewriting

Drafting

Revising

Editing

Publishing

- **Use Resource Materials**
  The resource materials you use to find information can also help you narrow a broad topic. Look up your subject online in an encyclopedia or newspaper archive. Scan the resources as you look for specific subtopics to pursue.

Gather Details

After you decide on a topic, you will want to explore and develop your ideas. You might start by looking through online resources again, talking with people who are knowledgeable about your topic, and writing everything you already know about the topic. It will be helpful to gather a variety of details. Look at these types:

- Facts
- Statistics
- Personal observations
- Expert opinions
- Examples
- Descriptions
- Quotations
- Opposing viewpoints

After you have narrowed your topic and gathered details, you will begin to plan your piece. During this part of prewriting, you will develop your essay's thesis or controlling idea—its main point.

As you plan your piece, you can use a graphic organizer. Specific kinds of graphic organizers can help structure specific kinds of writing. For example, a pro-con chart like this one can clarify the reasons for and against an idea.

Pro	Con
Adding funds to the school music budget would allow more students to learn to play instruments.	Giving more money to the music department would mean other programs would get less money.
Research shows that music helps the brain become more flexible.	Other programs, such as sports, are important in keeping students physically healthy.
Band members could stop selling gift-wrap materials at holiday time.	The school board has already approved the current budget allocations.

Drafting

In the drafting stage, you get your ideas down. You may consult an outline or your prewriting notes as you build your first draft.

Prewriting

Drafting

Revising

Editing

Publishing

WRITING COACH

Online

www.phwritingcoach.com

Online Journal

Try It! Record your answers and ideas in the online journal. You can also record and save your answers and ideas on pop-up sticky notes in the eText.

The Introduction

Most genres should have a strong introduction that immediately grabs the reader's attention and includes the thesis. Even stories and poems need a "hook" to grab interest.

 *Try It!* Which of these first sentences are strong openers? Read these examples of first sentences. Decide which ones are most interesting to you. Explain why they grab your attention. Then, explain why the others are weak.

- Have you ever wondered what it would be like to wake up one morning to find you're someone else?
- There are many ways to paint a room.
- Autumn is a beautiful season.
- On Sunday, we went to the store.
- When I woke up that morning, I had no idea that it would be the best day of my life.

The Body

The body of a paper develops the main idea and details that elaborate on and support the thesis. These details may include interesting facts, examples, statistics, anecdotes or stories, quotations, personal feelings, and sensory descriptions.

The Conclusion

The conclusion typically restates the thesis and summarizes the most important concepts of a paper.

Revising: Making It Better

Prewriting

Drafting

Revising

Editing

Publishing

No one gets every single thing right in a first draft. In fact, most people require more than two drafts to achieve their best writing and thinking. When you have finished your first draft, you're ready to revise.

Revising means "re-seeing." In revising, you look again to see if you can find ways to improve style, word choice, figurative language, sentence variety, and subtlety of meaning. As always, check how well you've addressed the issues of purpose, audience, and genre. Carefully analyze what you'd want to change and then go ahead and do it. Here are some helpful hints on starting the revision stage of the writing process.

Take a Break

Do not begin to revise immediately after you finish a draft. Take some time away from your paper. Get a glass of water, take a walk, or listen to some music. You may even want to wait a day to look at what you've written. When you come back, you will be better able to assess the strengths and weaknesses of your work.

Put Yourself in the Place of the Reader

Take off your writer's hat and put on your reader's hat. Do your best to pretend that you're reading someone else's work and see how it looks to that other person. Look for ideas that might be confusing and consider the questions that a reader might have. By reading the piece with an objective eye, you may find items you'd want to fix and improve.

Read Aloud to Yourself

It may feel strange to read aloud to yourself, but it can be an effective technique. It allows you to hear the flow of words, find errors, and hear where you might improve the work by smoothing out transitions between paragraphs or sections. Of course, if you're more comfortable reading your work aloud to someone else, that works, too.

Share Your Work to Get Feedback

Your friends or family members can help you by reading and reacting to your writing. Ask them whether you've clearly expressed your ideas. Encourage them to tell you which parts were most and least interesting and why. Try to find out if they have any questions about your topic that were not answered. Then, evaluate their input and decide what will make your writing better.

Use a Rubric

A rubric might be just what you need to pinpoint weaknesses in your work. You may want to think about the core parts of the work and rate them on a scale. If you come up short, you'll have a better idea about the kinds of things to improve. You might also use a rubric to invite peer review and input.

21st Century Learning

Collaborate and Discuss

When presenting and sharing drafts in the revision stage with a small group, it may be wise to set some ground rules. That way, the group is more likely to help each other analyze their work and make thoughtful changes that result in true improvements.

Here are some suggestions for reviewing drafts as a group:

- Cover the names on papers the group will review to keep the work anonymous.
- Print out copies for everyone in the group.
- Show respect for all group members and their writing.
- Be sure all critiques include positive comments.
- While it is fine to suggest ways to improve the work, present comments in a positive, helpful way. No insults are allowed!
- Plan for a second reading with additional input after the writer has followed selected suggestions.

WRITING COACH

Online

www.phwritingcoach.com

Online Journal

Try It! Record your answers and ideas in the online journal. You can also record and save your answers and ideas on pop-up sticky notes in the eText.

Partner Talk

After a group revision session, talk with a partner to analyze each other's feelings on how the session went. Discuss such issues as these: Did the group adhere to the ground rules? What suggestions could you and your partner make to improve the next session?

Revision RADaR

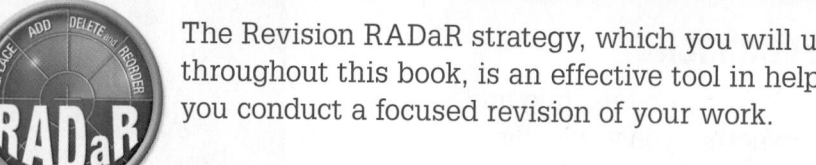

Prewriting

Drafting

Revising

Editing

Publishing

The Revision RADaR strategy, which you will use throughout this book, is an effective tool in helping you conduct a focused revision of your work.

You can use your Revision RADaR to revise your writing. The letters **R**, **A**, **D**, and **R** will help you remember to **r**eplace, **a**dd, **d**elete, and **r**eorder.

To understand more about the Revision RADaR strategy, study the following chart.

R	**A**	**D** and	**R**
Replace . . .	**Add . . .**	**Delete . . .**	**Reorder . . .**
• Words that are not specific • Words that are overused • Sentences that are unclear	• New information • Descriptive adjectives and adverbs • Rhetorical or literary devices	• Unrelated ideas • Sentences that sound good, but do not make sense • Repeated words or phrases • Unnecessary details	• So most important points are last • To make better sense or to flow better • So details support main ideas

R Replace

You can strengthen a text by replacing words that are not specific, words that are overused, and sentences that are unclear. Take a look at this before and after model.

BEFORE
I kicked the soccer ball hard into the goal.

AFTER
With amazing power, I slammed the soccer ball into the goal.

Apply It! How did the writer replace the overused word *kicked*? What other replacement do you see? How did it improve the text?

A Add

You can add new information, descriptive adjectives and adverbs, and rhetorical or literary devices to make your piece more powerful. Study this before and after model.

BEFORE
I was happy when I won the award.

AFTER
I was beyond thrilled when I won the Science Fair award.

Apply It! How did the second sentence make you feel, compared with the first? Explain. What information was added to the second sentence?

D Delete

Sometimes taking words out of a text can improve clarity. Analyze this before and after model.

BEFORE
I knew the test would be difficult, so I should have studied harder for the test before the test day.

AFTER
I knew the test would be difficult, so I should have studied harder for it.

Apply It! Describe the revision you see. How did taking out unnecessary repetition of the word *test* help the sentences flow more naturally?

R Reorder

When you reorder, you can make sentences flow more logically.

BEFORE
Today, I have band practice, but yesterday I didn't.

AFTER
I didn't have band practice yesterday, but today I do.

Apply It! Which of the models flows more logically? Why?

WRITING COACH

Online

www.phwritingcoach.com

Online Journal

Try It! Record your answers and ideas in the online journal. You can also record and save your answers and ideas on pop-up sticky notes in the eText.

USING TECHNOLOGY

Most word processing programs have a built-in thesaurus tool. You can use the thesaurus to find descriptive words that can often substitute for weaker, overused words.

Revision RADaR (continued)

Prewriting

Drafting

Revising

Editing

Publishing

Read the first draft of the Student Model—a review of the novel *End Game.* Think about how you might use your Revision RADaR to improve the text in a second draft.

Kelly Gallagher, M. Ed.

KEEP REVISION ON YOUR RADaR

End Game Fails to Thrill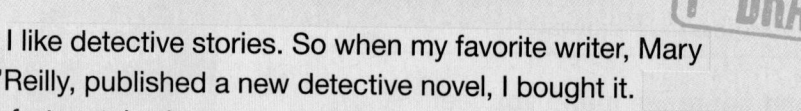

I like detective stories. So when my favorite writer, Mary O'Reilly, published a new detective novel, I bought it. Unfortunately, the novel, *End Game,* was incredibly disappointing.

In the story, an online video gamer disappears. A detective, Katherine, tries to track down the missing man through gaming Web sites. But here's where O'Reilly really messed up. It's clear that she didn't research the technology involved in online gaming. For example: "Katherine waited while her dial-up modem connected her to the virtual world."

The cheesy and ridiculous dialogue made my reading experience even worse. The errors in the book were bad enough! For example, the suspect says to Katherine, "I'm gonna get you, copper!" Now, this is the year 2010. A modern-day criminal would never use such outdated, silly lines. Instead of making the story exciting, the dialogue made it laughably bad.

O'Reilly has written many great books. My favorites were *On the High Seas* and *Danger in Denver.* They were great. I loved them! But I think it's time for O'Reilly to put down her pen. She clearly doesn't have what it takes any more to be a great writer. And as for *End Game*…don't waste your money!

Is my introduction interesting? Does it grab my readers' attention?

Have I fully analyzed and explained my examples from the text?

Is my information logically ordered?

Is my information relevant to the thesis? Have I included only necessary information?

After writing a draft, the student asked questions like these:

- What could I **replace**?
- What could I **add**?
- What words might I **delete**?
- Should I **reorder** anything?

The student writer created this second draft.

End Game Fails to Thrill

The suspense and high-paced action in detective stories are so thrilling! I simply can't get enough of these books. So when my favorite writer, Mary O'Reilly, published a new detective novel, I ran to the store to buy my copy. Unfortunately, the novel, *End Game,* was incredibly disappointing.

> **R** *Replaced dull first line with a more engaging opening.*

In the story, an online video gamer disappears. A detective, Katherine, tries to track down the missing man through gaming Web sites. But here's where O'Reilly really messed up. It's clear that she didn't research the technology involved in online gaming. For example: "Katherine waited while her dial-up modem connected her to the virtual world." Dial-up modems aren't fast enough to do serious online gaming!

> **A** *Added a sentence to better explain to my audience why the information from the text was incorrect.*

Although the errors in the book were bad enough, the cheesy and ridiculous dialogue made my reading experience even worse. For example, the suspect says to Katherine, "I'm gonna get you, copper!" Now, this is the year 2010. A modern-day criminal would never use such outdated, silly lines. Instead of making the story exciting, the dialogue made it laughably bad.

> **R** *Reordered text so that the information about the errors connected the ideas in the second and third paragraphs.*

I think it's time for O'Reilly to put down her pen. She clearly doesn't have what it takes any more to be a great writer. And as for *End Game*…don't waste your money!

> **D** *Deleted unnecessary information.*

Try It! What other words did the writer replace? Add? Delete? Reorder?

Partner Talk

Work with a partner to come up with a list of words that describe detective stories. For example, you might use "high-paced action" or "thrilling." Then discuss the value of using more specific words in your writing.

Editing: Making It Correct

Prewriting

Drafting

Revising

Editing

Publishing

Editing is the process of checking the accuracy of facts and correcting errors in spelling, grammar, usage, and mechanics. Using a checklist like the one shown here can help ensure you've done a thorough job of editing.

Editing Checklist

Task	Ask Yourself
Check your facts and spelling	❑ Have I checked that my facts are correct? ❑ Have I used spell check or a dictionary to check any words I'm not sure are spelled correctly?
Check your grammar	❑ Have I written any run-on sentences? ❑ Have I used the correct verbs and verb tenses? ❑ Do my pronouns match their antecedents, or nouns they replace?
Check your usage	❑ Have I used the correct form of irregular verbs? ❑ Have I used object pronouns, such as *me, him, her, us,* and *them* only after verbs or prepositions? ❑ Have I used subject pronouns, such as *I, he, she, we,* and *they* correctly—usually as subjects?
Check for proper use of mechanics	❑ Have I used correct punctuation? ❑ Does each sentence have the correct end mark? ❑ Have I used apostrophes in nouns but not in pronouns to show possession? ❑ Have I used quotation marks around words from another source? ❑ Have I used correct capitalization? ❑ Does each sentence begin with a capital letter? ❑ Do the names of specific people and places begin with a capital letter?

Using Proofreading Marks

Professional editors use a set of proofreading marks to indicate changes in a text. Here is a chart of some of the more common proofreading marks.

Proofreader's Marks

Mark	Meaning
(b.f.)	boldface
⌐	break text|start new line
(caps)	capital letter
⌒	clos e up
e	deletes
a/	insert ∧ word
﹀/	insert∧comma
=/	insert∧hyphen
+/	insert let∧er
⊙/	insert period∧
(ital)	italic type
(Stet)	let stand as is
(l.f.)	**lightface**
(l.c.)	Lower case letter
⌐	⌐move left
⌐	⌐move right
¶	new paragraph
(rom)	roman type
	run ⌐text up
(sp)	spell out whole word
	transpo(es)

www.phwritingcoach.com

 Online Journal

Try It! Record your answers and ideas in the online journal. You can also record and save your answers and ideas on pop-up sticky notes in the eText.

USING TECHNOLOGY

Many word processing programs have automatic spelling and grammar checks. While these tools can be helpful, be sure to pay attention to any suggestions they offer. That's because sometimes inappropriate substitutes are inserted automatically!

Editing: Making It Correct (continued)

Prewriting

Drafting

Revising

Editing ›

Publishing

WRITE GUY *Jeff Anderson, M. Ed.*

WHAT DO YOU NOTICE?

Using an editing checklist is a great way to check for correct grammar. However, using a checklist is not enough to make your writing grammatically correct. A checklist tells you what to look for, but not how to correct mistakes you find. To do that, you need to develop and apply your knowledge of grammar.

Looking closely at good writing is one way to expand your grammar know-how. The *What Do You Notice?* feature that appears throughout this book will help you zoom in on passages that use grammar correctly and effectively.

As you read this passage, from "Jobs for Kids," zoom in on the sentences in the passage.

I have a paper route. After school, I deliver newspapers on my bike to my neighbors. I love this job because I get exercise, and I get to be outside.

Now, ask yourself: *What do you notice about the sentences in this passage?*

Maybe you noticed that the writer uses sentences of varying lengths and with different structures.

After asking a question that draws your attention to the grammar in the passage, the *What Do You Notice?* feature provides information on a particular grammar topic. For example, following the passage and question, you might read about simple and complex sentences, which are both used in the passage.

The *What Do You Notice?* feature will show you how grammar works in actual writing. It will help you learn how to make your writing correct.

WRITING COACH

Online

www.phwritingcoach.com

Online Journal

Try It! Record your answers and ideas in the online journal. You can also record and save your answers and ideas on pop-up sticky notes in the eText.

Jobs for Kids

I like having my own money. That way, I can buy things I want and can also save money for my future. But here's the problem: How can we, as kids, make money? There are many types of jobs for kids, but each job has pluses and minuses.

I have a paper route. After school, I deliver newspapers on my bike to my neighbors. I love this job because I get exercise, and I get to be outside. This job isn't for everyone, though. Some kids have a lot of after-school activities, so they don't go straight home. Because papers have to be delivered on time, this can be challenging.

A friend of mine babysits because she has fun with and loves taking care of children. To be a babysitter, you have to find out if your state has a law about how old you have to be before you can babysit. You also have to be a patient, responsible person who is good with children. Finally, it helps to know first-aid, just in case a child gets injured.

My brother does yard work for neighbors. He rakes leaves, weeds gardens, and mows lawns. He loves to be outside and doesn't mind getting dirty. However, there are certain safety issues involved. For example, you have to know how to handle a lawnmower properly and wear protective gear.

What type of job is right for you? What are your interests? Get creative, and start making some money!

"Writer to Writer"

If I wonder how to write any kind of writing, I look at models—well-written examples of the kind of writing I want to do. Models are the greatest how-to lesson I have ever discovered.

—Jeff Anderson

Try It! Read "Jobs for Kids." Then, zoom in on two more passages. Write a response to each question in your journal.

1. What do you notice about the pronouns (*you, he*) in the fourth paragraph?

2. How does the writer use transitions, such as the word *finally*, to connect ideas in the third paragraph?

Publishing

Prewriting

Drafting

Revising

Editing

Publishing

When you publish, you produce a final copy of your work and present it to an audience. When publishing you'll need to decide which form will best reach your audience, exhibit your ideas, show your creativity, and accomplish your main purpose.

To start assessing the optimal way to publish your work, you might ask yourself these questions:

- What do I hope to accomplish by sharing my work with others?
- Should I publish in print form? Give an oral presentation? Publish in print form and give an oral presentation?
- Should I publish online, in traditional print, or both?
- What specific forms are available to choose from?

The answers to most of these questions will most likely link to your purpose for writing and your audience. Some choices seem obvious. For example, if you've written a piece to contribute to a blog, you'll definitely want to send it electronically.

Each publishing form will present different challenges and opportunities and each will demand different forms of preparation. For example, you may need to prepare presentation slides for a speech, or you may want to select music and images if you will be posting a video podcast online.

Ways to Publish

There are many ways to publish your writing. This chart shows some of several opportunities you can pursue to publish your work.

Genre	Publishing Opportunities	
Narration: Nonfiction	• Blogs • Book manuscript • Audio recording	• Private diary or journal entries • Electronic slide show
Narration: Fiction	• Book manuscript • Film	• Audio recording • Oral reading to a group
Poetry and Description	• Bound collection • Visual display	• Audio recording • Oral reading to a group
Exposition and Persuasion	• Print or online article • Web site • Slide show • Visual display	• Film • Audio recording • Oral reading or speech
Response to Literature	• Print or online letters • Visual displays	• Blogs • Slide show
Research Writing	• Traditional paper • Print and online experiment journals	• Multimedia presentation

Reflect on Your Writing

Think about what you learned in Chapter 3 as you answer these questions:

- What did you learn about the writing process?
- What steps in the writing process do you already use in your writing?
- Which stage do you think is the most fun? Which one may be most challenging for you? Explain.

WRITING COACH

Online

www.phwritingcoach.com

Online Journal

Try It! Record your answers and ideas in the online journal. You can also record and save your answers and ideas on pop-up sticky notes in the eText.

Partner Talk

Discuss the chart on this page with a partner. If there are ways to publish that neither of you has ever tried, talk about how you might go about experimenting with those forms.

SENTENCES, PARAGRAPHS, *and* COMPOSITIONS

Good writers know that strong sentences and paragraphs help to construct effective compositions. Chapter 4 will help you use these building blocks to structure and style excellent writing. It will also present ways to use rhetorical and literary devices and online tools to strengthen your writing.

The Building Blocks: Sentences and Paragraphs

A **sentence** is a group of words with two main parts: a subject and a predicate. Together, these parts express a complete thought.

A **paragraph** is built from a group of sentences that share a common idea and work together to express that idea clearly. The start of a new paragraph has visual clues—either an indent of several spaces in the first line or an extra line of space above it.

In a good piece of writing, each paragraph supports, develops, or explains the main idea of the whole work. Of course, the traits of effective writing—ideas, organization, voice, word choice, sentence fluency, and conventions—appear in each paragraph as well.

Writing Strong Sentences

To write strong paragraphs, you need strong sentences. While it may be your habit to write using a single style of sentences, adding variety will help make your writing more interesting. Combining sentences, using compound elements, forming compound sentences, and using subordination all may help you make your sentences stronger, clearer, or more varied.

Combine Sentences

Putting information from one sentence into another can make a more powerful sentence.

BEFORE	Basketball is a fun game. It takes a lot of skill and practice.
AFTER	Basketball, which takes a lot of skill and practice, is a fun game.

Use Compound Elements

You can form compound subjects, verbs, or objects to help the flow.

BEFORE	Students enjoy many different hobbies. Some play sports. Some write poetry. Some paint.
AFTER	Students enjoy many different hobbies, such as playing sports, writing poetry, and painting.

Form Compound Sentences

You can combine two sentences into a compound sentence.

BEFORE	Some people enjoy skateboarding. It can be a dangerous hobby.
AFTER	Some people enjoy skateboarding, but it can be a dangerous hobby.

Use Subordination

Combine two related sentences by rewriting the less important one as a subordinate clause.

BEFORE	Horseback riding allows you to be outside in the fresh air. That is good for you.
AFTER	Horseback riding allows you be outside in the fresh air, which is good for you.

WRITING COACH
Online
www.phwritingcoach.com

Online Journal
Try It! Record your answers and ideas in the online journal. You can also record and save your answers on pop-up sticky notes in the eText.

LEARN MORE
For more on sentence combining see Chapter 20.

Writing Strong Paragraphs

If all the sentences in a paragraph reflect the main idea and work together to express that idea clearly, the result will be a strong paragraph.

Express Your Main Idea With a Clear Topic Sentence

A **topic sentence** summarizes the main idea of a paragraph. It may appear at the beginning, middle, or end of a paragraph. It may even be unstated. When the topic sentence comes at the beginning of a paragraph, it introduces the main idea and leads the reader naturally to the sentences that follow it. When it appears at the end of a paragraph, it can draw a conclusion or summarize what came before it. If the topic sentence is unstated, the rest of the paragraph must be very clearly developed, so the reader can understand the main idea from the other sentences.

Think about the topic sentence as you read this paragraph.

There is no question that computer skills are necessary to have today. Without these skills, it will be difficult to get a college degree and find a good job. Most assignments in college must be done on a computer. Much research in college is done on the Internet, and many libraries have switched from a paper card catalog to a digital catalog. In addition, many companies won't hire someone who has no computer skills. After all, if you can't send e-mails and create important documents in word processing programs, how will you be able to properly do many jobs?

 Try It! Look back at the sample paragraph to answer these questions.

1. What is the topic sentence?
2. Does the topic sentence introduce the main idea or draw a final conclusion? Explain.
3. What makes this topic sentence strong?

Write Effective Supporting Sentences

A clear topic sentence is a good start, but it needs to be accompanied by good details that support the paragraph's main idea. Your supporting sentences might tell interesting facts, describe events, or give examples. In addition, the supporting sentences should also provide a smooth transition, so that the paragraph reads clearly and logically.

Think about the topic sentences and supporting details as you read this paragraph.

Owning a dog can be hard work, but it is well worth it! A dog owner must be very responsible and take good care of her pet. She has to feed and walk the dog every day and bathe it regularly. Every dog also needs a lot of play time with its owner! All of this takes a great deal of time and energy. However, a dog can be your best friend. It will love you and protect you, and sometimes make you laugh! Plus, what could be better than snuggling up with a sweet, loving dog?

WRITING COACH

Online

www.phwritingcoach.com

Online Journal

Try It! Record your answers and ideas in the online journal. You can also record and save your answers on pop-up sticky notes in the eText.

 Try It! Look at the paragraph and answer these questions.

1. What is the topic sentence of the paragraph?

2. Do you think it's an effective topic sentence? Why or why not?

3. What supporting details does the writer provide?

4. If you were the writer, what other supporting details might you add to strengthen the paragraph?

Include a Variety of Sentence Lengths, Structures, and Beginnings

To be interesting, a paragraph should include sentences of different lengths, types, and beginnings. Similarly, if every sentence has the same structure—for example, article, adjective, noun, verb—the paragraph may sound boring or dry.

Collaborate and Discuss

With a group, study this writing sample.

> On the night of the school concert, I didn't think I'd survive my stage fright. My hands felt cold and clammy, and a lump was stuck in my throat. A trickle of sweat slipped between my shoulder blades and down my back. I was so nervous! As the band began playing the opening notes of the first song and I stepped up to the microphone, the glare of the bright lights blinded me. I closed my eyes, took a deep breath, and belted out the song without even thinking. When the song was over, the audience responded with deafening applause. I had done it!

Discuss these questions about the paragraph.

1. What is the topic sentence? How does it draw in the reader?
2. What details support the topic sentence in each paragraph?
3. Point out some examples of varying sentence lengths and beginnings.
4. What examples can you find of sentences with a variety of sentence structures?

Partner Talk

Work with a partner to take another look at the writing sample on this page. Talk about what you think the writer did well. Then, discuss what might make the paragraph even stronger.

USING TECHNOLOGY

It's often better to use the tab key, rather than the space bar, to indent a paragraph. Using the tab key helps to ensure that the indents in all paragraphs will be uniform.

Composing Your Piece

You've learned that the building blocks of writing are strong sentences and paragraphs. Now it's time to use those building blocks to construct a composition. While the types of writing vary, most types have a definite structure with clearly defined parts.

The Parts of a Composition

Writers put together and arrange sentences and paragraphs to develop ideas in the clearest way possible in a composition. Some types of writing, such as poetry and advertisements, follow unique rules and may not have sentences and paragraphs that follow a standard structure. However, as you learned in Chapter 3, most compositions have three main sections: an introduction, a body, and a conclusion.

I. Introduction

The introduction of a composition introduces the focus of the composition, usually in a thesis statement. The introduction should engage the reader's interest, with such elements as a question, an unusual fact, or a surprising scene.

II. Body

Just as supporting statements develop the ideas of a topic sentence, the body of a composition develops the thesis statement and main idea. It provides details that help expand on the thesis statement. The paragraphs in the body are arranged in a logical order.

III. Conclusion

As the word implies, the conclusion of a composition concludes or ends a piece of writing. A good way to ensure the reader will remember your thesis statement is to restate it or summarize it in the conclusion. When restating the thesis, it's usually most effective to recast it in other words. Quotations and recommendations are other ways to conclude a composition with memorable impact. The conclusion should provide a parting insight or reinforce the importance of the main idea.

" Writer to Writer "

Strong, varied sentences and unified paragraphs are the building blocks of effective writing.

—Kelly Gallagher

Rhetorical and Literary Devices

Like any builders, good writers have a set of tools, or devices, at their fingertips to make their writing interesting, engaging, and effective. Writers can use the rhetorical devices of language and their effects to strengthen the power of their style. This section presents some tools you can store in your own writing toolbox to develop effective compositions.

Sound Devices

Sound devices, which create a musical or emotional effect, are most often used in poetry. The most common sound devices include these:

- **Alliteration** is the repetition of consonant sounds at the beginning of words that are close to one another.

  Example: The sweet sound of singing swam in the breeze.

- **Assonance** is the repetition of vowel sounds in words that are close to one another.

  Example: We see shells on the beach, by the sea.

- **Consonance** is the repetition of consonants within or at the end of words.

  Example: The doctor checked the sick patient at three o'clock.

Structural Devices

Structural devices determine the way a piece of writing is organized. Rhyme and meter are most often used to structure poetry, as are stanzas and many other structural devices.

- **Rhyme** is the repetition of sounds at the ends of words. Certain poetry forms have specific rhyme schemes.
- **Meter** is the rhythmical pattern of a poem, determined by the stressed syllables in a line.
- **Visual elements**, such as stanzas, line breaks, line length, fonts, readability, and white space, help determine how a piece of writing is read and interpreted. These elements can also affect the emotional response to a piece.

Other Major Devices

You can use these devices in many forms of writing. They help writers express ideas clearly and engage their readers.

Device	Example
Figurative language is writing that means something beyond what the words actually say. Common forms of figurative language include these: • A **simile** compares two things using the words *like* or *as*. • A **metaphor** compares two things by mentioning one thing as if it is something else. It does not use *like* or *as*. • **Personification** gives human characteristics to a non-human object.	*His voice sounded like nails on a chalkboard.* *The trapeze artist was a bird in flight.* *The sun smiled down on us.*
Hyperbole is exaggeration used for effect.	*I felt stronger than a superhero!*
Irony is a contradiction between what happens and what is expected.	In a famous story, a wife cuts her hair to buy her husband a watch fob, and he sells his watch to buy her a brush.
Paradox is a statement that contains elements that seem contradictory, but could be true.	Mother Teresa said, "…if you love until it hurts, there can be no more hurt, only more love."
An **oxymoron** is word or phrase that seems to contradict itself.	The movie was seriously funny!
Symbolism is an object that stands for something else.	The American flag is often considered a symbol of freedom.
An **allegory** is a narrative that has a meaning other than what literally appears.	Some say the story of the sinking ship is an allegory for the effects of pride.
Repetition (or tautology) occurs when content is repeated—sometimes needlessly—for effect.	The band's song was loud, loud and far too long.

WRITING COACH

Online

www.phwritingcoach.com

Online Journal

Try It! Record your answers and ideas in the online journal. You can also record and save your answers on pop-up sticky notes in the eText.

USING TECHNOLOGY

Most word processing programs have a built-in thesaurus tool. You can use the thesaurus to find descriptive words that can often substitute for weaker, overused words.

Partner Talk

There are many online tools that can help you strengthen your writing. For example, you can search for examples of figurative language and sound devices. Then you can model your own writing after the samples. Just be sure that you don't plagiarize or copy the written work of others.

Using Writing Traits to Develop an Effective Composition

You read about rubrics and traits in Chapter 3. Now it's time to look at how they function in good writing.

Ideas

A good writer clearly presents and develops important information, a strong message, and original ideas.

As you read the sample, think about the ideas it presents.

Achoo!

Achoo! The common cold can be a major downer. Who wants to be home with a runny nose and sore throat? It happens more often than you might think, though. According to the Mayo Clinic, students can get as many as six to ten colds a year! If you understand the causes of the common cold and take precautions, you can successfully avoid catching a cold.

A common cold is caused by a virus. Many different viruses could be responsible for your runny nose, but all of them have one thing in common: they're very contagious. A common-cold virus can spread in the air when a sick person coughs, sneezes, or even talks.

Once you know how colds spread, you can see that avoiding a cold is fairly easy, if you follow some simple rules. Wash your hands often. Keep doorknobs and countertops clean. Don't share drinking glasses or silverware. Most importantly, avoid being around sick people. If you do happen to catch a cold, sneeze or cough into your elbow to help keep your cold from spreading to others. No one likes to be sick!

Try It! Think about ideas in the writing sample as you answer this question.

What is the writer's message? List three details that clearly convey or give support for this message.

Interactive Writing Coach and the Writing Process

You can begin to use Essay Scorer during the drafting section of the writing process. It is best to complete a full draft of your essay before submitting to Essay Scorer. (While you are drafting individual paragraphs, you may want to use Paragraph Feedback.) Keep in mind, however, that your draft does not need to be perfect or polished before you submit to Essay Scorer. You will be able to use feedback from Essay Scorer to revise your draft many times. This chart shows how you might use the Interactive Writing Coach and incorporate Essay Scorer into your writing process.

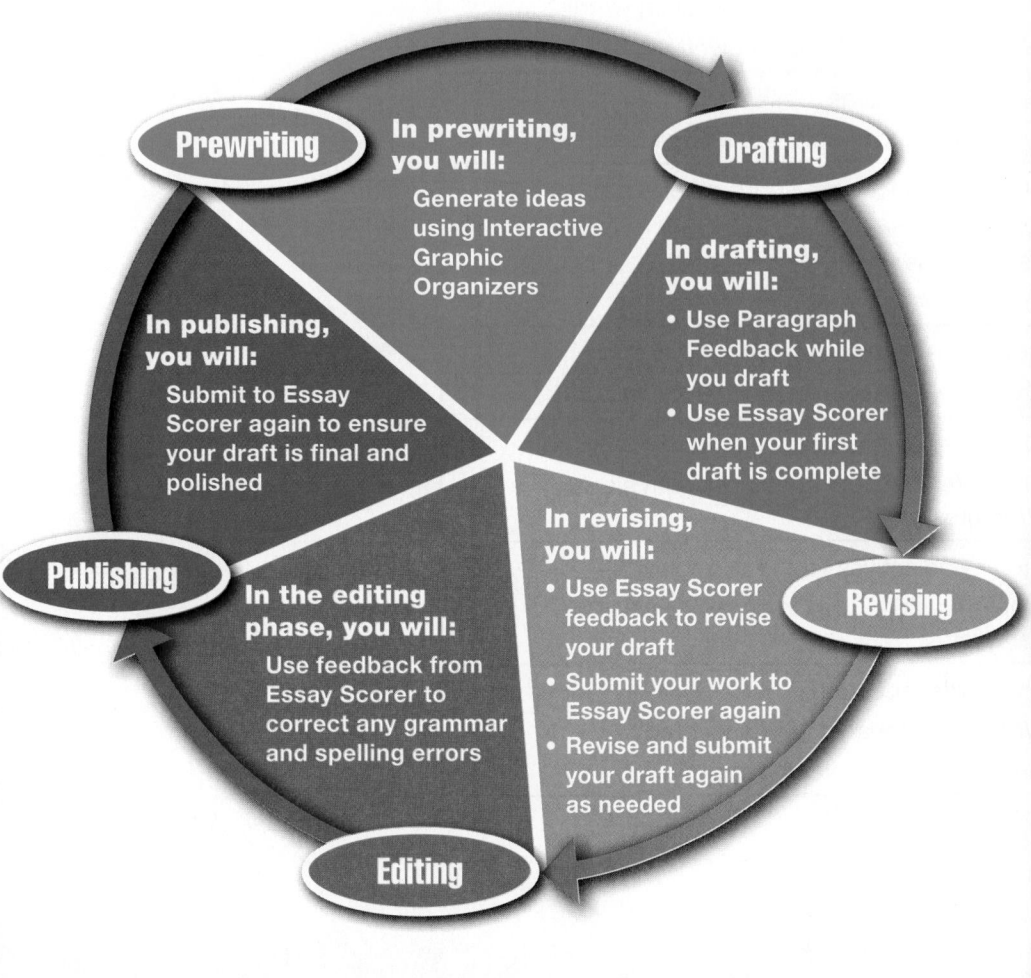

Prewriting

In prewriting, you will:

Generate ideas using Interactive Graphic Organizers

Drafting

In drafting, you will:

• Use Paragraph Feedback while you draft
• Use Essay Scorer when your first draft is complete

In publishing, you will:

Submit to Essay Scorer again to ensure your draft is final and polished

In revising, you will:

• Use Essay Scorer feedback to revise your draft
• Submit your work to Essay Scorer again
• Revise and submit your draft again as needed

Revising

Publishing

In the editing phase, you will:

Use feedback from Essay Scorer to correct any grammar and spelling errors

Editing

Paragraph Feedback With Interactive Writing Coach

Paragraph Feedback assesses the ideas and topic support for each paragraph you write. You can enter your work into Paragraph Feedback one paragraph at a time. This makes it easy to work on individual paragraphs and get new feedback as you revise each one. Here are some things that Paragraph Feedback will be able to tell you.

Overall Paragraph Support	• Does the paragraph support the main idea? • Which sentences do not support the main idea?
Transitions	• Which sentences contain transition words? • Which words are transition words?
Ideas	• How well are ideas presented? • Which sentences have too many ideas?
Sentence Length and Variety	• Which sentences are short, medium, and long? • Which sentences could be longer or shorter for better sense or variety? • Are sentences varied?
Sentence Beginnings	• How do sentences begin? • Are sentence beginnings varied?
Sentence Structure	• Are sentence structures varied? • Are there too many sentences with similar structures?
Vague Adjectives	• Are any adjectives vague or unclear? • Where are adjectives in sentences and paragraphs?
Language Variety	• Are words repeated? • Where are repeated words located? • How can word choice be improved?

Essay Scoring With Interactive Writing Coach

Essay Scorer assesses your essay. It looks at the essay as a whole, and it also evaluates individual paragraphs, sentences, and words. Essay Scorer will help you evaluate the following traits.

www.phwritingcoach.com

Interactive Writing Coach™

Interactive Writing Coach provides support and guidance to help you improve your writing skills.
- Select a topic to write about from the Topic Bank.
- Use the interactive graphic organizers to narrow your topic.
- Go to Writing Coach Online and submit your work, paragraph by paragraph or as a complete draft.
- Receive immediate, personalized feedback as you write, revise, and edit your work.

Ideas	• Are the ideas significant or original? Is a clear message or unique perspective presented? • Is the main idea clearly stated? • Is the main idea supported by informative details?
Organization	• Is the organization logical? • Is the introduction clear? Is the conclusion clear? • What transitions are used, and are they effective?
Voice	• Does the writing have a unique, individual "sound" showing the personality or perspective of the writer? • Does the tone match the audience and purpose?
Word Choice	• Are precise words used? • Are vivid words used? • Do the word choices suit the purpose and audience?
Sentence Fluency	• Are sentence beginnings, lengths, and structures varied? • Do the sentences flow smoothly?
Conventions	• Is spelling correct? • Is capitalization used properly? • Is all punctuation (ending, internal, apostrophes) accurate? • Do subjects and verbs agree? • Are pronouns used correctly? • Are adjectives and adverbs used correctly? • Are plurals formed correctly? • Are commonly confused words used correctly?

Whenever you see the Interactive Writing Coach icon, you can go to Writing Coach Online and submit your writing, either paragraph by paragraph or as a complete draft, for personalized feedback and scoring.

CHAPTER 5

NONFICTION NARRATION

What Do You Remember?

Why are accomplishments important? What might make accomplishments interesting to other people?

To tell a story about an accomplishment, you will need to remember details of the experience. Using vivid details to describe an accomplishment will make the story more interesting to others.

Try It! Think about a recent accomplishment. Consider these questions as you participate in an extended discussion with a partner. Take turns expressing your ideas and feelings.

- What led up to the accomplishment?
- What challenges did you face?
- What did you see, smell, touch, feel, and hear during the experience?

Review the list you made, and then think about how you would include these details when telling someone about your accomplishment.

What's Ahead

In this chapter, you will review two strong examples of a personal narrative: a Mentor Text and a Student Model. Then, using the examples as guidance, you will write a personal narrative of your own.

 **Connect to the Big Questions**

Discuss these questions with your partner:

1 What do you think? What do our accomplishments say about us?

2 Why write? What should we put in and leave out to be accurate and honest?

NARRATIVE NONFICTION

In this chapter, you will explore a special type of narrative nonfiction: the personal narrative. A personal narrative is a true story in which YOU are the leading character. By writing personal narratives, you can tell readers about yourself and your life. You can entertain them—and maybe make them think, too!

You will develop your personal narrative by taking it through each of the steps of the writing process: prewriting, drafting, revising, editing, and publishing. You will also have an opportunity to create a letter or e-mail about a personal event. To preview the criteria for how your personal narrative will be evaluated, see the rubric on page 83.

FEATURE ASSIGNMENT

Narrative Nonfiction: Personal Narrative

An effective narrative nonfiction essay has these characteristics:

- A **clearly defined focus** that shows why this narrative is worth sharing

- A **sequence of events in chronological, or time, order**

- Details that **communicate the importance of or reason for actions and/or consequences**

- A **plot line with a conflict and resolution**, or a clear problem and its solution, to make the narrative complete and interesting

- **Specific details and quotations**, or dialogue, to help readers imagine characters' actions, gestures, and expressions

- Effective sentence structure and correct **spelling, grammar, and usage**

A personal narrative also includes:

- A focus on yourself, the writer, as the main character

- Vivid images and feelings to help readers experience the setting, characters, and action as you did

Other Forms of Narrative Nonfiction

In addition to a personal narrative, there are other forms of narrative nonfiction, including:

Biographical narratives are stories that share facts about someone else's life.

Blogs are comments that writers share in online forums. They may include personal narratives, opinions, and other types of comments. Blogs often invite other writers to respond online, too. They usually are not thought of as "permanent" writing.

Diary entries, which are highly personal, include experiences, thoughts, and feelings. The audience, however, is private, unless writers choose to share the diary entries.

Narrative essays use personal narratives to illustrate or support a main idea.

Memoirs focus on an important person or event from the writer's own life. Book-length memoirs by famous people are often quite popular.

Reflective essays present personal experiences—events that happened to the writers or that the writers learned about from others. Reflective essays stand out because they do more than tell a story: They also share the writers' thoughts about those experiences. Reflective essays often appear as features in magazines and newspapers.

Try It! For each audience and purpose described, choose a form, such as a blog, diary entry, or reflective essay, that is appropriate for conveying your intended meaning to the audience. Explain your choices.

- To tell online friends a funny story about yourself
- To remind yourself, for the future, about what happened today at your grandmother's birthday party
- To tell and share your feelings about a storm

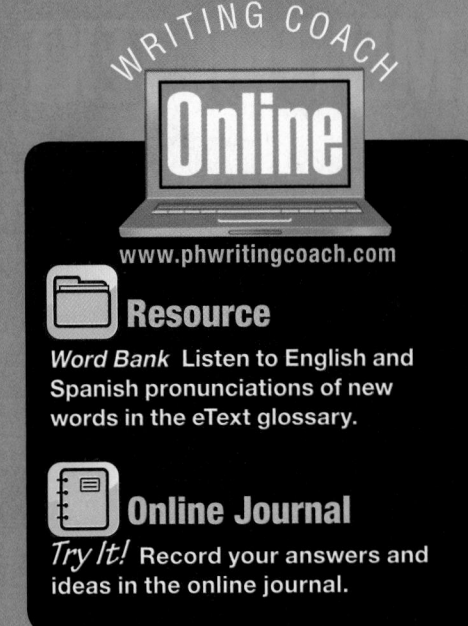

WRITING COACH

Online

www.phwritingcoach.com

Resource

Word Bank Listen to English and Spanish pronunciations of new words in the eText glossary.

Online Journal

Try It! Record your answers and ideas in the online journal.

WORD BANK

People often use these basic and content-based vocabulary words when they talk about narrative nonfiction writing. Work with a partner. Take turns writing each word in a sentence. If you are unsure of the meaning of a word, use the Glossary or a dictionary to check the definition.

conflict	image
consequences	personal
focus	resolution

MENTOR TEXT

Personal Narrative

Learn From Experience

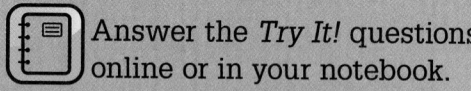 Read the personal narrative on pages 68–69. As you read, take notes to develop your understanding of basic sight and English vocabulary. Then, read the numbered notes in the margins to learn about how the author presented his ideas.

Answer the *Try It!* questions online or in your notebook.

---

1 The **focus** is clearly defined from the start. A clear focus helps readers anticipate what the narrative will be about and builds interest in reading it.

Try It! What is the focus of the narrative? Write a sentence telling what you think.

2 The author describes the events that led up to the **conflict,** or trouble, that he experienced.

Try It! What is the conflict? What reason does the author give for not handing over the paddle?

3 The author gives **details** to describe how the conflict came to a head.

Try It! Which adjectives and verbs in this section help you picture the high point of the conflict?

Extension Find an example of a personal narrative to compare with this one. What insights about life does each offer?

From
The Pigman & Me

by Paul Zindel

1 When trouble came to me, it didn't involve anybody I thought it would. It involved the nice, normal, smart boy by the name of John Quinn. Life does that to us a lot. Just when we think something awful's going to happen one way,
5 it throws you a curve and the something awful happens another way. This happened on the first Friday, during gym period, when we were allowed to play games in the school yard. **2** A boy by the name of Richard Cahill, who lived near an old linoleum factory, asked me if I'd like to play
10 paddle ball with him, and I said, "Yes." Some of the kids played softball, some played warball, and there were a few other games where you could sign out equipment and do what you wanted. What I didn't know was that you were allowed to sign out the paddles for only fifteen minutes per
15 period so more kids could get a chance to use them. I just didn't happen to know that little rule, and Richard Cahill didn't think to tell me about it. Richard was getting a drink from the water fountain when John Quinn came up to me and told me I had to give him my paddle.
20   "No," I said, being a little paranoid about being the new kid and thinking everyone was going to try to take advantage of me.
   "Look, you have to give it to me," John Quinn insisted.
   3 That was when I did something berserk. I was so
25 wound up and frightened that I didn't think, and I struck out at him with my right fist. I had forgotten I was holding the paddle, and it smacked into his face, giving him an instant black eye. John was shocked. I was shocked. Richard Cahill came running back and he was shocked.

WRITING COACH

Online

www.phwritingcoach.com

Interactive Model

Listen to an audio recording of the Mentor Text in the eText. You can refer back to the Mentor Text whenever you need support in developing your own writing.

Online Journal

Try It! Answer the questions about the Mentor Text in the online journal.

30   ④ "What's going on here?" Mr. Trellis, the gym teacher, growled.

"He hit me with the paddle," John moaned, holding his eye. He was red as a beet, as Little Frankfurter, Conehead, Moose, and lots of the others gathered around.

35   "He tried to take the paddle away from me!" I complained.

"His time was up," John said.

Mr. Trellis set me wise to the rules as he took John over to a supply locker and pulled out a first-aid kit.

"I'm sorry," I said, over and over again.

40   ⑤ Then the bell rang, and all John Quinn whispered to me was that he was going to get even. He didn't say it like a nasty rotten kid, just more like an all-American boy who knew he'd have to regain his dignity about having to walk around school with a black eye. Before the end of school,

45   Jennifer came running up to me in the halls and told me John Quinn had announced to everyone he was going to exact revenge on me after school on Monday. That was the note of disaster my first week at school ended on, and I was terrified because I didn't know how to fight. I had

50   never even been in a fight. What had happened was all an accident. It really was.

④ The author uses dialogue to explain the **resolution,** or outcome, of the conflict here.

Try It! What is the effect of using dialogue to describe the resolution? What insights into the characters does the dialogue give you?

⑤ The author finishes describing the **resolution** here.

Try It! What are the consequences, or results, of the author hitting John Quinn with a paddle?

STUDENT MODEL | Personal Narrative

With a small group, take turns reading the Student Model aloud. Look for techniques the writer uses to draw you, the reader, into the story. Also look for evidence that supports your ideas.

 Use a Reader's Eye

Now, reread the Student Model. On your copy of the Student Model, use the Reader's Response Symbols to react to what you read.

Reader's Response Symbols

+ **I like where this is going.**

– **This isn't clear to me.**

? **What will happen next?**

! **Wow! That is really cool/weird/ interesting!**

 **Partner Talk**

Participate in an extended discussion with a partner. Express your opinions and share your responses to the Student Model. Discuss what you each thought was the main point of the narrative and why.

Alone in the SPOTLIGHT

by Mark Walker Williams

Have you ever had that nightmare—the one where everyone is staring at you? That nightmare came true for me!

I was in third grade. My school was preparing
5 a show for Independence Day, and my class was going to sing "This Is My Country." Mr. Lee, the music teacher, helped us learn the song. When I sang it at home, my parents were impressed.

"Wonderful!" cried Mom.

10 Dad added, "I can't wait to hear you sing on Friday afternoon."

"You won't be able to hear just me," I said, "but my class sounds great."

For the rest of that week, my class rehearsed
15 our song in the auditorium. We practiced marching onto the risers without tripping. And we practiced standing still without fainting. Then we practiced marching off the stage while singing the chorus two final times. A color guard was going to carry
20 flags onto the stage while we did that. If we could keep from crashing into each other, it would look good. Otherwise, it would be a disaster.

We made mistakes at first, and we joked about each one. Even when we got better, though,
25 I scowled. Someone still might mess up!

The big day came. I sat with my class, but I turned and waved at Mom, Dad, Aunt Miriam,

1

and Grandpa just before the program began. Grandpa grinned and gave me a "thumbs
30 up." I needed that because I was nervous!

The first- and second-graders did a good job. Then it was our turn.

As we sang, my nervousness disappeared. I was inspired—so inspired that I didn't notice
35 my classmates marching off the stage, and I didn't notice the color guard marching onto the stage. I didn't notice the end of the music, either. I just stood there and kept singing!

Finally, Mr. Lee came onto the stage and got my
40 attention. When I walked off with him, I felt like a complete fool.

Afterward, my family met me at my classroom. Before I could apologize, Grandpa exclaimed, "Mark, you were terrific!" Mom, Dad, and Aunt
45 Miriam agreed. They completely ignored my mistake!

"Come on," said Mom as she helped me put on my jacket. "Let's all sing that song while we walk to the bus stop." And we did!

2

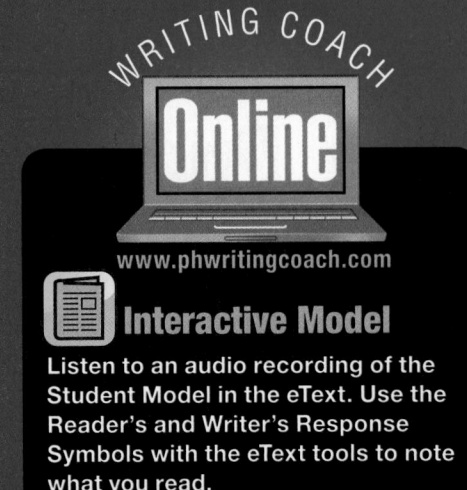

WRITING COACH

Online
www.phwritingcoach.com

Interactive Model

Listen to an audio recording of the Student Model in the eText. Use the Reader's and Writer's Response Symbols with the eText tools to note what you read.

Use a Writer's Eye

Now evaluate the narrative as a writer. On your copy of the Student Model, use the Writer's Response Symbols to react to what you read. Identify places where the student writer uses characteristics of an effective personal narrative.

Writer's Response Symbols	
E.S.	**Engaging story**
C.R.	**Clear, well-developed conflict and resolution**
B.C.	**Believable characters**
S.D.	**Specific and vivid details**

Your Turn

Prewriting

Plan a first draft of your personal narrative by choosing a topic based on your experience. You may select from the Topic Bank or come up with an idea of your own.

 ## Choose From the Topic Bank

TOPIC BANK

I Was There! Think of a memorable event you have attended. It might be a sporting event, a concert, a field trip, a theatrical performance, or even a family reunion. Write a personal narrative in which you describe the event and explain why it was so special.

It's a Group Thing Think about a group you belong to. It could be an informal group of friends or a more formal group, like a sports team or a school club. Write a personal narrative that describes your group and tells about an event that involved you and your group.

First Contact Think of a friend and how you two met. Write a personal narrative that describes how you and your friend met and explains why you became friends.

 ## Choose Your Own Topic

Determine an appropriate topic on your own by using the following **range of strategies** to generate ideas.

Question and Remember

- List some questions that people might ask about you. Which questions could you answer in a personal narrative?

- Ask family members what they remember about your early childhood. Look for story ideas in their answers.

- Remember something that you have done—something that made you happy. How could you show why you took that action and what the results were?

Review your responses and choose a topic.

Narrow Your Topic

If your topic is too broad, readers might not understand why you are writing. Choose a topic that gives your personal narrative a clearly defined focus.

Apply It! Use a graphic organizer like the one shown to narrow your topic.

- Write the main topic of your story in the top box. Move down the chart, row by row, narrowing your topic.
- Your last box should hold the main focus of your plot.

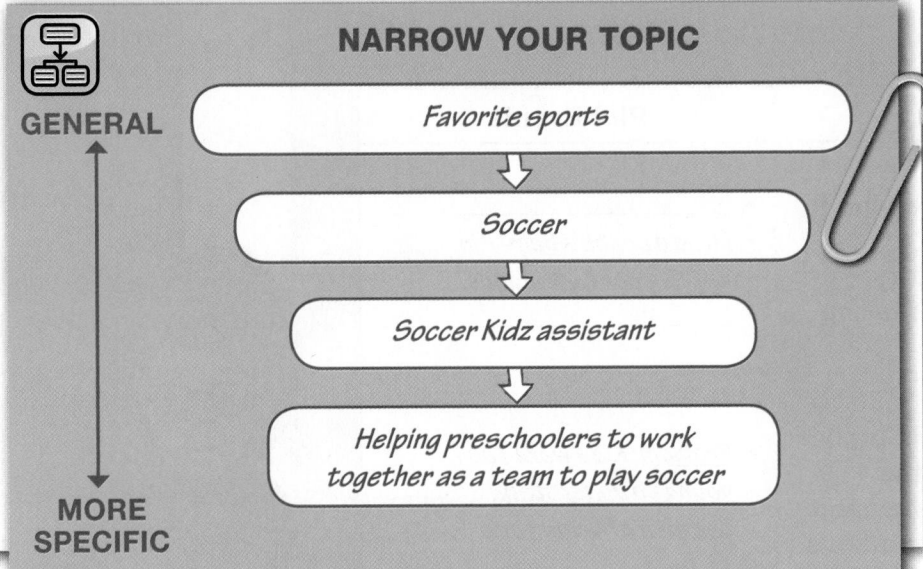

NARROW YOUR TOPIC

GENERAL

Favorite sports

⬇

Soccer

⬇

Soccer Kidz assistant

⬇

Helping preschoolers to work together as a team to play soccer

MORE SPECIFIC

 Consider Your Audience

Before writing, think about your audience and purpose. Consider how your writing conveys the intended meaning to this audience. Consider the views of the other as you ask these questions.

Questions for Audience	Questions for Purpose
• Who are the people in my audience? What should I tell them about myself? • What background information will my audience need?	• Why am I writing this personal narrative? What do I want to show, explain, or teach? • What point will this story make?

Record your answers in your writing journal.

WRITING COACH

Online

www.phwritingcoach.com

 **Interactive Writing Coach™**

- Choosing from the Topic Bank gives you access to the Interactive Writing Coach™.
- Submit your writing and receive instant personalized feedback and guidance as you draft, revise, and edit your writing.

 **Interactive Graphic Organizers**

Use the interactive graphic organizers to help you narrow your topic.

 **Online Journal**

Try It! Record your answers and ideas in the online journal.

Plan Your Piece

You will use a graphic organizer like the one shown to define your focus, gather details, and plan your piece. When it is complete, you will be ready to write your first draft.

Define Your Focus Your narrative should have **a clearly defined focus**. Complete a chart that uses chronological order to show a conflict and resolution. Include details that show the **importance of or reason for actions** in the narrative, as well as their **consequences**.

Develop Your Personal Narrative

Part of Story	Plot Events
BEGINNING • A few details about who I am • The topic of the story • Hint about why I'm telling the story	• _____ • *I was a coach's helper in the Soccer Kidz league.* • _____
MIDDLE • Action revealing the problem (conflict) and the reason(s) that it happened • Specific details/quotations about how the problem got worse and why it needed to be solved	• *Problem: Kids were too young to understand the idea of teamwork.* • _____ • _____
END • Action that ended the problem (resolution) • The consequences of that action	• *Solution: Had kids think of the game as if acting out a story.* • _____
SETTING: Soccer field at Lincoln Park	
CHARACTERS: Me, Coach Tyler, Julia, Enrique, _____ , _____	

Gather Details

To bring their personal narratives to life, writers usually focus on these literary elements.

- **Characters:** *"Josh," Coach Tyler said, "I want you to be my helper for my Soccer Kidz team this summer. Can you handle preschoolers?" "You bet!" I shouted. "I'll be great with them!"*

- **Setting:** *The sun warmed the green field as the kids arrived on Saturday morning. When I waved, they ran across the grass to me.*

- **Plot:** *Despite my instructions, the kids swarmed all over the field. Everyone tried to kick the ball at once. How could we win a game, or even score a goal, if I couldn't get them to understand teamwork?*

Good writers are careful to present **a clearly defined focus**. They also use specific details and vivid images to bring their narratives to life.

Try It! Read the Student Model excerpt. Which details help readers understand some of the characters in this personal narrative?

 **STUDENT MODEL** from **Alone in the Spotlight**
pages 70–71; lines 26–30

> The big day came. I sat with my class, but I turned and waved at Mom, Dad, Aunt Miriam, and Grandpa just before the program began. Grandpa grinned and gave me a "thumbs up." I needed that because I was nervous!

 Apply It! Review the elements that narrative writers often use. Decide how your planned story details will make those elements clear.

- Choose details that will help readers zero in on your focus and communicate your purpose for writing.
- Select details that show why events happen, why they are important, and what their outcomes are.
- Add each detail to the correct part of your graphic organizer.

 WRITING COACH
Online
www.phwritingcoach.com

 Interactive Graphic Organizers

Use the interactive graphic organizers to help you create a plan for your writing.

Interactive Model

Refer back to the Interactive Model in the eText as you plan your writing.

Drafting

During the drafting stage, you will start to write your ideas for your personal narrative. You will follow an outline that provides an **organizational strategy**, or plan, that will help you build on ideas to write a **focused, organized, and coherent** personal narrative—one in which all the ideas work together.

The Organization of a Nonfiction Narrative

The chart shows an organizational strategy for a nonfiction narrative. Look back at how the Mentor Text follows this organizational strategy. Then, use this chart to help you outline your draft.

Outline for Success

I. Beginning

See Mentor Text, p. 68.

- Clearly defined focus
- Details about the writer

Grab Your Reader

- A personal narrative should focus on a specific series of events.
- Personal details help focus the topic, establish the setting, and set the scene for the conflict to come.

II. Middle

See Mentor Text, pp. 68–69.

- Plot line with a conflict
- Importance of or reasons for actions
- Specific details about characters' movement, expressions, and gestures

Develop Your Plot

- The plot line is usually in chronological order.
- The conflict, or problem, is what gets readers interested in your narrative. It may affect one, some, or all of the characters.
- Specific details about the characters, setting, and action help readers feel as though they are part of the story.

III. End

See Mentor Text, p. 69.

- Resolution
- Consequences of actions

Wrap It Up

- The resolution of a story tells how the problem was solved or events ended it.
- Ending your narrative with a quotation or detail that makes the resolution clear helps sum up the story for the reader.

 # Start Your Draft

Use this checklist to help you complete your draft. Use the graphic organizer that shows the beginning, middle, and end of your narrative, and the Outline for Success as guides.

While drafting, aim at writing your ideas, not on making your writing perfect. Remember, you will have the chance to improve your draft when you revise and edit.

√ Start by drafting an attention-getting **opening** sentence.

√ Continue your **beginning** by focusing on the topic and connecting with readers in a way that makes them want to keep reading. Make sure your narrative has a clearly defined **focus**.

√ Use chronological order to develop the **middle** of your personal narrative. Present a series of plot events that show **reasons for actions and** the consequences of those actions.

√ Keep the narrative interesting by including vivid images and specific **details** about the characters, setting, and action.

√ At the **end** of your narrative, show the **resolution**—how the conflict worked out.

√ Finish in a way that shows the importance of actions and their **consequences** in the narrative.

WRITING COACH

Online

www.phwritingcoach.com

 Interactive Model

Outline for Success View pop-ups of Mentor Text selections referenced in the Outline for Success.

 **Interactive Writing Coach**™

Use the Interactive Writing Coach to receive the level of support you need:
- Write one paragraph at a time and submit each one for immediate, detailed feedback.
- Write your entire first draft and submit it for immediate, personalized feedback.

Revising: Making It Better

Now that you have finished your first draft, you are ready to revise. Think about the "big picture" of **audience**, **purpose**, and **genre**. You can use the Revision RADaR strategy as a guide for making changes to improve your draft. Revision RADaR provides four major ways to improve your writing: (R) replace, (A) add, (D) delete, and (R) reorder.

Kelly Gallagher, M. Ed.

KEEP REVISION ON YOUR RADaR

Read part of the first draft of the Student Model "Alone in the Spotlight." Then, look at questions the writer asked himself as he thought about how well his draft **addressed issues of audience, purpose, and genre**.

Alone in the Spotlight

We made mistakes at first, and we joked about each one. Even when we got better, though, I scowled.

The big day came. I sat with my class, but I turned and waved at Mom, Dad, Aunt Miriam, and Grandpa. The first- and second-graders did a good job. Then it was our turn. Grandpa grinned and gave me a "thumbs up." I needed that because I was nervous!

As we sang, my nervousness disappeared. I felt fabulous! I was inspired—so inspired that I didn't notice my classmates marching off the stage, and I didn't notice the color guard.

Finally, Mr. Lee came onto the stage and got my attention. When I walked off with him, I felt like a complete fool.

Afterward, my family met me at my classroom. Before I could apologize, Grandpa exclaimed, "Mark, you were terrific!" Mom, Dad, and Aunt Miriam agreed. They actually sounded happy!

A narrative should show reasons for actions. Will readers know why I scowled?

These details aren't quite the way I remember them. Will the sequence be clear to my audience?

Does "I felt fabulous" help my purpose, or do readers already understand that? Also, my purpose here is to be funny. Do I have enough funny details?

A resolution is an important part of writing in this genre. Does my resolution tell about the outcome?

Create an Event Letter

Follow these steps to create your own event letter. To plan your event letter, review the graphic organizers on R24–R27 and choose one that suits your needs.

Prewriting

- Identify your target audience. Think about who will read your letter. Will they understand your story?
- Select a topic that you want to share. You might want to share a funny story, or an experience that was out of the ordinary.
- Think about what you want to tell your audience, and make sure that you focus on a single event.
- List or map out the plot of the narrative—its beginning, middle, and end.
- Fill in the details; for example, note things that you or other characters said and how you felt as the action was happening.

Drafting

- Use chronological order to recount the event.
- Write a narrative that tells your personal story and includes details that explain the reasons for actions. You may also want to hint at their importance. Don't forget to reveal consequences.
- Remember to connect to the person who will read the event letter. Think of details or comments that your audience will appreciate.

Revising and Editing

- Review your draft to ensure that your narrative is complete and interesting. Look for specific words and vivid images.
- Review the tone of the letter. If necessary, make changes to give it a more friendly tone.
- Check that spelling, grammar, and mechanics are correct.

Publishing

If you are mailing the letter, create a clean copy and then mail it. If you are sending it as an e-mail, make sure that the recipient's address is correct before you hit SEND. You also may want to attach a photo related to the event.

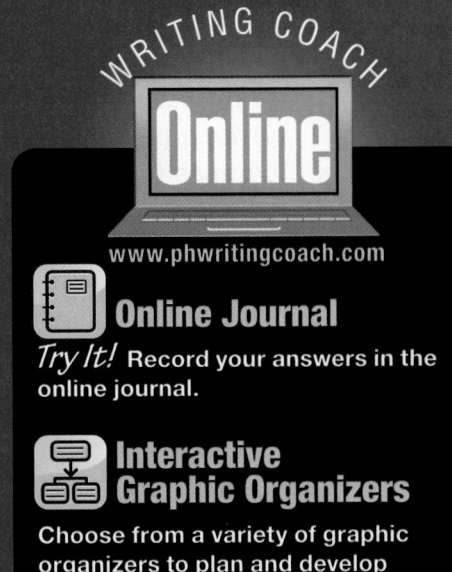

WRITING COACH

Online

www.phwritingcoach.com

Online Journal

Try It! Record your answers in the online journal.

 **Interactive Graphic Organizers**

Choose from a variety of graphic organizers to plan and develop your project.

Partner Talk

Before you start drafting, explain your event letter to a partner. Ask for feedback about your plan. For example, are you telling the story completely? In a friendly way?

Writing for Assessment

Many standardized tests include a prompt that asks you to write a personal narrative. Use these prompts to practice. Your compositions should have the same characteristics as your personal narrative. (See page 66.)

 Try It! Read the prompt and the information on format and academic vocabulary. Then, write a **personal narrative** using the ABCDs of On-Demand Writing.

Format

The prompt directs you to write a *personal narrative*. Make sure that you keep a clearly defined focus through your narrative's beginning, middle, and end.

Narrative Prompt

What is the best trip you ever took? Think about what made that trip "best" and then write a personal narrative to share the story. Be sure to include a beginning, a middle, and an end.

Academic Vocabulary

Remember that the *beginning*, *middle*, and *end* make a story. Be sure to include all three parts in your personal narrative.

The ABCDs of On-Demand Writing

Use the following ABCDs to help you respond to the prompt.

Before you write your draft:

A ttack the prompt [1 MINUTE]

- Circle or highlight important verbs in the prompt. Draw a line from the verb to what it refers to.
- Rewrite the prompt in your own words.

B rainstorm possible answers [4 MINUTES]

- Create a graphic organizer to generate ideas.
- Use one for each part of the prompt if necessary.

C hoose the order of your response [1 MINUTE]

- Think about the best way to organize your ideas.
- Number your ideas in the order you will write about them. Cross out ideas you will not be using.

After you write your draft:

D etect errors before turning in the draft [1 MINUTE]

- Carefully reread your writing.
- Make sure that your response makes sense and is complete.
- Look for spelling, punctuation, and grammar errors.

 **More Prompts for Practice**

Apply It! Respond to Prompts 1 and 2 by writing **personal narratives** with **a clearly defined focus**. As you write, be sure to:

- Identify an appropriate audience for your intended purpose
- Use a graphic organizer, such as a beginning-middle-end organizer, to organize and structure your ideas
- Explain **the importance of or reason for your actions and their consequences**

> **Prompt 1** How far back can you remember? Think about your earliest childhood memory. Then, write a personal narrative to tell the story of what happened to you at that memorable moment.

> **Prompt 2** Recall a time when you gave a very special gift to someone. In a personal narrative, recount that event. Show why you chose that gift and how the person who received the gift reacted to it.

More Strategies for Writing for Assessment

- Consider several possible topics and quickly list details that you might use in your response. Then, choose the topic for which you have the strongest ideas.
- If you do not understand any words in the prompt, use context clues to determine the meaning of the unknown words.
- Be sure to follow the ABCDs for writing to a prompt. Planning is an important part of writing. Don't just start writing right away.
- Make sure to reread your piece after you have completed it. This will give you time to find and correct errors. If you are in a timed situation, be sure to leave enough time for this step.

WRITING COACH

www.phwritingcoach.com

Interactive Writing Coach™

Plan your response to the prompt. If you are using the prompt for practice, write one paragraph at a time or your entire draft and then submit it for feedback. If you are using the prompt as a timed test, write your entire draft and then submit it for feedback.

Remember **ABCD**

Attack the prompt

Brainstorm possible answers

Choose the order of your response

Detect errors before turning in the draft

CHAPTER 6

FICTION NARRATION

What's the Story?

What is happening in the photograph? What story can you tell about what happened shortly before this photograph was taken?

Many stories have realistic settings. Believable details about setting, such as a mountain bike trail in a forest, help get the reader interested and add to the story. Conflict is also important. Conflict is a challenge or problem the main character faces.

Try It! Think about what might have happened in the moments before the photograph was taken. Write notes about what the biker was doing.

Consider these questions as you participate in an extended discussion with a partner. Take turns expressing your ideas and feelings.

- Why is this person riding through the forest?
- What is this person's challenge?
- How do you think this person feels?

Review your notes. Use your notes to tell a story about the biker. Be sure to use details to make your story believable.

What's Ahead

In this chapter, you will review two strong examples of a fiction story: a Mentor Text and a Student Model. Then, using the examples as guidance, you will write a fiction story of your own.

 **Connect to the Big Questions**

Discuss these questions with your partner:

1 What do you think? How do challenges help us grow?

2 Why write? What can fiction do better than non-fiction?

SHORT STORY

In this chapter, you will write a short story, or a series of events that have a beginning, middle, and end. You will also explore a special type of literary text called science fiction. A science fiction short story focuses on real or imagined developments in science and technology and their effects on the way people think and live. Space travel, robots, and life in the future are popular topics for science fiction.

You will develop a science fiction story by taking it through each of the steps of the writing process: prewriting, drafting, revising, editing, and publishing. You will also have an opportunity to write a dramatic scene. To preview the criteria for how your science fiction story will be evaluated, see the rubric on page 111.

FEATURE ASSIGNMENT

Short Story: Science Fiction

An effective imaginative short story has these characteristics:

- **A specific, believable setting** created through the use of **sensory details**

- **An engaging plot**, or storyline, with **well-paced action** that **holds reader interest**

- One or more **well-developed, interesting characters**

- A **range of literary strategies and devices**, such as flashback and foreshadowing, to enhance the **style** and **tone**, or attitude

- **Effective sentence structure** and correct spelling, grammar, and usage

A science fiction story also includes:

- A **setting** with more advanced technology than existed when the story was written

- An action-packed **plot** with a **conflict**, or problem, between people's needs and technology, or between people from Earth and aliens

- A **theme** about the relationship between humans and science

Other Forms of Short Stories

In addition to science fiction, there are other forms of short stories, including:

Fantasy stories stretch the imagination and take readers to unreal worlds. Animals may talk, people may fly, or characters may have superhuman powers.

Historical fiction tells about imaginary people living in real places and times in history. Usually, the main characters are fictional people who know and interact with famous people in history and participate in important historical events.

Mystery stories focus on unexplained or strange events that one of the characters tries to solve. These stories are often full of suspense and surprises.

Myths and legends are traditional stories that different cultures have told to explain natural events, human nature, or the origins of things. They often include gods and goddesses from ancient times and heroes who do superhuman things.

Realistic fiction portrays invented characters and events in everyday life that most readers would find familiar.

Tall tales are about larger-than-life characters in realistic settings. The main character typically solves a problem or reaches a goal by doing something wild and fantastic that normal people could never do.

Try It! For each audience and purpose described, choose a story form, such as a fantasy story, mystery, or realistic fiction, that is appropriate for conveying your intended meaning to the audience. Explain your choices.

- To describe how a mystery was solved
- To show how a fictional teen deals with a problem
- To catch the imagination of young children

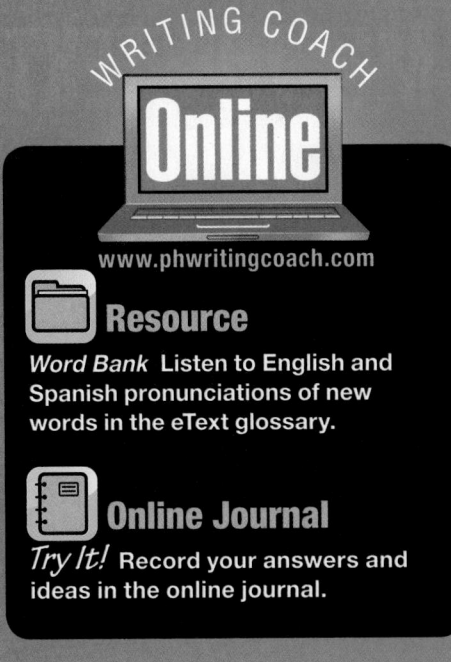

WRITING COACH
Online
www.phwritingcoach.com

Resource
Word Bank Listen to English and Spanish pronunciations of new words in the eText glossary.

Online Journal
Try It! Record your answers and ideas in the online journal.

WORD BANK

People often use these words when talking about short stories. Work with a partner. Take turns saying each word aloud. If you are unsure of the meaning of a word, use the Glossary or a dictionary to check the definition. Then, write a sentence using each word.

develop	style
imagery	theme
sensory	tone

MENTOR TEXT
Science Fiction

Learn From Experience

 Read the science fiction story on pages 94–97. As you read, take notes to develop your understanding of basic sight and English vocabulary. Then, read the numbered notes in the margins to learn about how the author presented her ideas.

Answer the *Try It!* questions online or in your notebook.

---

❶ The introduction identifies the main **character** and creates a believable **setting.**

Try It! Who is the main character in this story? What details does the author use to set the scene of the story?

❷ Words such as *chatter, rustling, sighing,* and *sharp calls* are all **sensory details.**

Try It! To which of the five senses do these details appeal? Why might the author be stressing this particular sense in the story?

❸ Here, and throughout the story, the author uses a consistent **point of view.**

Try It! From which point of view is the story told: first person or third person? How can you tell?

Extension Find another science fiction story, and compare it with this one. How is the language similar? How is it different?

Traveler
by Barbara Davis

❶ "Here!" Luis shouted. "We can camp here. It's perfect!" His three friends trudged into the forest clearing. Luis had found a beautiful, grassy area ringed with tall pines and oaks. The boys could see the sun shining off the
5 surface of a small lake not too far from where they stood. After carrying heavy backpacks through miles and miles of forest trails, they relished the idea of a swim in cool water.

Joel groaned as he swung his backpack off his shoulders. He dropped down on the grass and wiped the sweat from
10 his face with the bottom of his T-shirt. "Looks great to me. Plenty of dry wood to start a fire, rocks for a fire ring, a place to swim—I vote we set up camp."

Soon, the four were busy setting up tents and hanging their food in trees to discourage bears. "How about you guys
15 finish up here, and I'll go collect firewood?" Luis suggested. Since finding firewood meant even more walking around in the forest, the other boys readily agreed.

❷ As Luis headed into the forest, the boys' campsite chatter faded from his hearing. Instead, Luis heard the
20 light breeze rustling the leaves in the trees. The tall pines sounded like they were sighing. Every once in awhile, he heard the sharp calls of unseen crows. The bushes rustled with the passage of some kind of small animal. At least Luis *hoped* it was a small animal and not a bear.

25 ❸ Listening to all the forest sounds, Luis lost track of time. Eventually, the increasing weight of the firewood sack he had tied around his shoulder let him know it was time to start making his way back to camp. He had gone much farther into the forest than he had intended. He
30 wasn't worried, though. There wasn't a trail yet that Luis couldn't follow. Shifting the weight of the firewood to a more comfortable position, Luis started to take a step back along the way he had come. Suddenly, a voice said, "Not that way!"

35 Luis was so surprised, he almost dropped the firewood. He whipped his head around to see who had spoken. No one was there. He carefully scanned the area around him. Nothing. Luis wasn't the type of kid to imagine voices but, obviously, he had imagined this one. Shrugging off the
40 mystery, he once again started down the trail.

④ "You *really* don't want to go that way." Same voice. This time Luis was sure it wasn't just his imagination.

His heart beating just a little bit faster, Luis asked, "Who are you? Where are you?" At first, there was no response.
45 Then, Luis heard the tree leaves just above his head start to rustle. He peered closely into the tree, but still couldn't see anything. He focused his eyes even harder. There! He saw something. It looked like a really skinny kid straddling the lowest branch.

50 The kid seemed to be wearing some type of camouflage clothing that allowed him to blend in with the surrounding leaves. If Luis took his eyes off the kid for even a second, the kid blended right back into the tree. ④ "Ah! You can finally see me. Took you long enough."

55 Now that Luis could see that it was just a kid, he felt foolish for having been slightly scared. "Yeah, I can see you. Why are you telling me not to go this way? This is the way back to my campsite."

The kid in the tree just smiled. He said, "Maybe. But you
60 still don't want to go that way."

The bundle of wood was getting heavier by the minute, and Luis didn't feel like playing a game of riddles. Part of him wanted to know who the kid was and what he was doing there in the middle of the forest. The other part of
65 him wanted to get back to the campsite. The second part won out. Luis said, "Yeah, okay. Whatever." With that, he turned and continued down the path. When he looked over his shoulder, all he could see were the leaves of the tree. No kid. Luis shook his head and kept going.

70 ⑤ He wasn't sure when he noticed that the forest had grown still. No breeze, no birds, no sounds at all. It was as if the forest was holding its breath. The sun was still shining in streaks along the path, causing the air to shimmer. In the

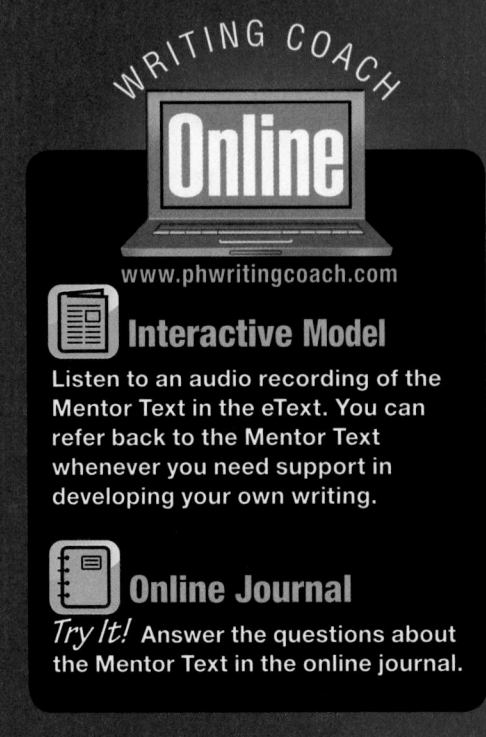

WRITING COACH

Online

www.phwritingcoach.com

Interactive Model

Listen to an audio recording of the Mentor Text in the eText. You can refer back to the Mentor Text whenever you need support in developing your own writing.

Online Journal

Try It! Answer the questions about the Mentor Text in the online journal.

④ **Dialogue** helps develop the story and reveal the characters' motivations.

Try It! How does the dialogue help to move the story forward? What do Luis's lines tell you about him?

⑤ Here, the author uses **suspense,** which adds interest to the story.

Try It! How does suspense keep readers engaged in a story?

6 The author again uses **sensory details** to describe the scene's setting.

Try It! To which of the five senses do these details appeal? Which details in this passage help you to feel as if you are there, witnessing the action?

7 **Descriptive details** about a character can be a subtle way of saying something about the character's personality.

Try It! What do you think the author is trying to convey about the creature in describing its small, sharp teeth?

8 Further **dialogue** gives more information about the characters and their motives.

Try It! What does the dialogue reveal about the two main characters in this story? What does their conversation reveal about the differences in the times and cultures in which they live?

9 **Action words** can move a story along by changing the pace. In this paragraph, the author uses words such as *burst, panting,* and *skidded* to create a feeling of urgency.

Try It! What other words in the story convey a strong sense of action?

75   time it took Luis to wonder at how odd the shafts of light looked, he had passed through one of them. When he did, the first thing he realized was that the forest was no longer silent.

It took a moment for him to recognize the sound of water crashing down on rocks. A waterfall? That was impossible. Luis knew for a fact that there were no waterfalls in
80   the forest he and his friends had hiked through. After a few more steps, though, it was clear that he was wrong. **6** There, in all its rushing power was the highest waterfall Luis had ever seen. Even more amazing were the things flying in the air, diving into and out of the frothing water
85   and laughing with the fun of it all. Skinny kids with bat-like wings? Luis's mouth hung open in disbelief. As if that weren't enough, he heard the now-familiar voice: "I told you not to go that way."

This time it was much easier to see the kid because he
90   was standing right next to Luis. Except Luis could now see that it wasn't really a kid at all. With his pointy nose and chin, he almost looked like a cross between a human and a fox. He didn't have fur, though, and his arms and legs were as skinny as twigs. He also had that bizarre quality of
95   looking as if he was constantly blending into and out of his surroundings. Although Luis had a million questions in his brain, none of them were making it to his mouth. For once, "cool as a cucumber in a crisis" Luis was speechless.

7 The creature smiled at Luis. Up close, those teeth
100   were small and sharp. **8** "You're not dreaming. You haven't fallen and conked your head on a stone or anything like that. What you *have* done is pass through one of our portals."

"Portals?" Luis whispered.
105   "Doorways. Places where we can step between worlds. I'm a Traveler. I travel to other times and other worlds. In Earth years, I'm from about 500 years in the future, and I like this time in your world quite a bit. It's similar to my world. Lots of trees, water. Many of the other places I visit are quite
110   different. Fire, extreme heat, dust. Not so much fun."

The creature smiled again, but it wasn't a pleasant smile. "The thing is, though, we really don't like visitors to *our* world." Luis didn't see what came next, but he felt it—a

hard shove against his chest. The next thing he knew, he
115 was sitting on the forest trail looking up at the sunlight. In
seconds, he dumped his load of wood and ran as fast as he
could back to the campsite.

⑨ He burst out of the forest, wide-eyed and panting.
Brad, Tran, and Joel were still pitching the tents and looked
120 up in surprise. Luis skidded into the clearing ready to sputter
about what he'd just seen, but he stopped himself. What was
he going to say to his friends? They would think he was
crazy. His reputation as a practical, not-easily-fooled kind
of guy would be ruined. Luis shook his head. He wasn't
125 going to say a word.

"Hey, Luis! What's up? Why are you running? Where's the
wood?" Brad and Tran's questions tumbled over each other.

"Nothing. It's nothing. I just thought I heard a bear and
got a little spooked." Luis replied. "I must have dropped the
130 load of wood. I'll go back and get it."

⑩ Joel hadn't said anything at all. He gave Luis an odd
look and said, "I'll go back with you and give you a hand."
Luis was too shaken to protest so he just nodded his head.
As the two friends walked back into the forest, Joel said,
135 "So, you met a Traveler, huh?"

WRITING COACH

Online

www.phwritingcoach.com

Interactive Model

Listen to an audio recording of the
Mentor Text in the eText. You can
refer back to the Mentor Text
whenever you need support in
developing your own writing.

Online Journal

Try It! Answer the questions about
the Mentor Text in the online journal.

⑩ The story's **resolution** contains a device
called a **teaser.** Teasers are sometimes used to
suggest there is more to the story than what is
specifically written.

Try It! What teaser does the author
use? How does it make the story more
interesting?

STUDENT MODEL Science Fiction

With a small group, take turns reading this Student Model aloud. As you read, practice newly acquired vocabulary by correctly producing the word's sound. Also watch for the ways the characters interact with technology. Think about how the culture the characters live in influences that interaction.

 Use a Reader's Eye

Now, reread the Student Model. On your copy of the Student Model, use the Reader's Response Symbols to react to what you read.

Reader's Response Symbols

+ This is a good description.

− This isn't clear to me.

! This is really cool/weird/ interesting!

? What will happen next?

Express your ideas and feelings about the Student Model with a partner. Discuss what you thought did and didn't work in the story.

Be Careful Where You Wish For

by Linda Radner

Sandy's IDP/D woke her up on time, of course. She carefully checked the top of her earlobe. Yes! It was there! Now she was one of the first to have the latest application for her Internal Daily Planner/
5   Doer (IDP/D). Her IDP/D made sure she was always where she was supposed to be on time. This new app would take her wherever she wished to go!

Sandy found her brother Joe in the kitchen, stirring steamy oatmeal. He was kind of an anti-
10   techno-geek who liked to do things on his own.

"Hey Sis, how's that new app working for you?" Joe asked a little meanly. "Is it living up to the commercials' promises?"

"Haven't tried it yet," Sandy yawned. "But
15   wait: I'd like to have breakfast in the yard." Nothing happened. Then Sandy remembered the new app's default check. She tapped her forehead to confirm her wish.

FLASH! Sandy was freezing in the yard
20   in a storm. Icy rain ran down her neck. She thought about her toasty warm kitchen, tapped her forehead, and FLASH! She was immediately back at the kitchen table.

Joe was laughing. "What happens if
25   you're whisked away in the middle of a class like a crumb off a table?"

"Don't be ridiculous! This app is foolproof. All the commercials say so." Sandy's first class was math. She was already chilled from her soaking

1

30 breakfast. As class started, Sandy looked out the window, wishing she was someplace sunny and warm. But she knew she had to be in school. So she leaned her forehead on her fist and tried to listen.

FLASH! She dropped into a desert of bright
35 sun and hot sand. Dripping with sweat, Sandy thought about the cool lake where they swam each summer. As she wiped the sweat off her face, FLASH! and SPLASH! she landed in the middle of the freezing lake. Shivering and out of breath,
40 Sandy wished herself back in her warm kitchen.

Nothing. The app had failed. Her IDP/D took over and dropped her, like a soaked sponge, back in school where she was supposed to be. There she stayed, cold and dripping, until the last bell.

45 After school she walked to the accessories store and had the new app removed. Back at home, Joe had already heard all about her adventure. "So, how did the new toy work out?" he teased.

"Just fine!" Sandy answered. "But I'm
50 going to wait for the new and improved version before I try it again!"

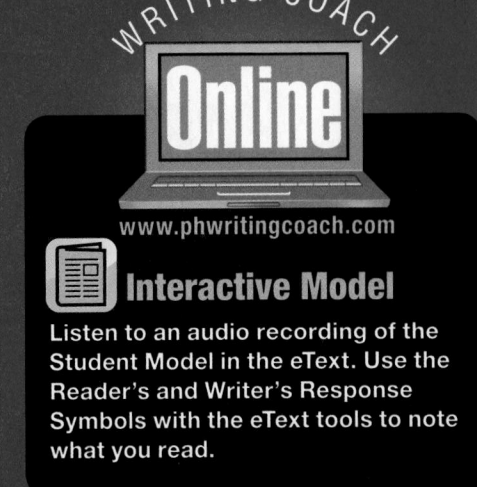

www.phwritingcoach.com

Interactive Model

Listen to an audio recording of the Student Model in the eText. Use the Reader's and Writer's Response Symbols with the eText tools to note what you read.

Use a Writer's Eye

Now, evaluate the piece as a writer. On your copy of the Student Model, use the Writer's Response Symbols to react to what you read.

Writer's Response Symbols

R.D. Realistic and believable dialogue

S.D. Vivid sensory details that create imagery and suggest mood

W.C. Well-developed, interesting characters

E.S. Engaging story

2

Prewriting

Plan a first draft of your science fiction story by determining an appropriate topic. You can select from the Topic Bank or come up with an idea of your own.

Choose From the Topic Bank

TOPIC BANK

Living on the Moon Imagine living with other Earthlings in a colony on the moon. Where would you live? What would you eat? Write a science fiction story about your experiences.

New Technology Imagine an amazing technological breakthrough. Write a story about the invention and its effects on a group of characters.

The Alien and the Earthling Two characters—one human and one alien—become friends. Write a short story that explains how they meet and how their friendship grows.

Choose Your Own Topic

Determine an appropriate topic on your own by using the following **range of strategies** to generate ideas.

Research and Discuss

- Skim books or Web sites about the universe to find topics that spark your interest. Take notes on the topics that interest you.
- Research some technology you know well. What's ahead for this technology? How might people use it in the future?
- With a group, discuss some ways science could help, or harm, the world. Brainstorm for a list of possibilities. Monitor spoken language by asking follow-up questions to confirm your understanding.

Review your responses and choose a topic.

Narrow Your Topic

Narrowing the topic of your story will help you focus your thinking to write a compelling story.

Apply It! Use a graphic organizer like the one shown to narrow your topic.

- Write the main topic of your story in the top box. Move down the chart, narrowing your topic.
- Your last box should hold the main focus of your plot.

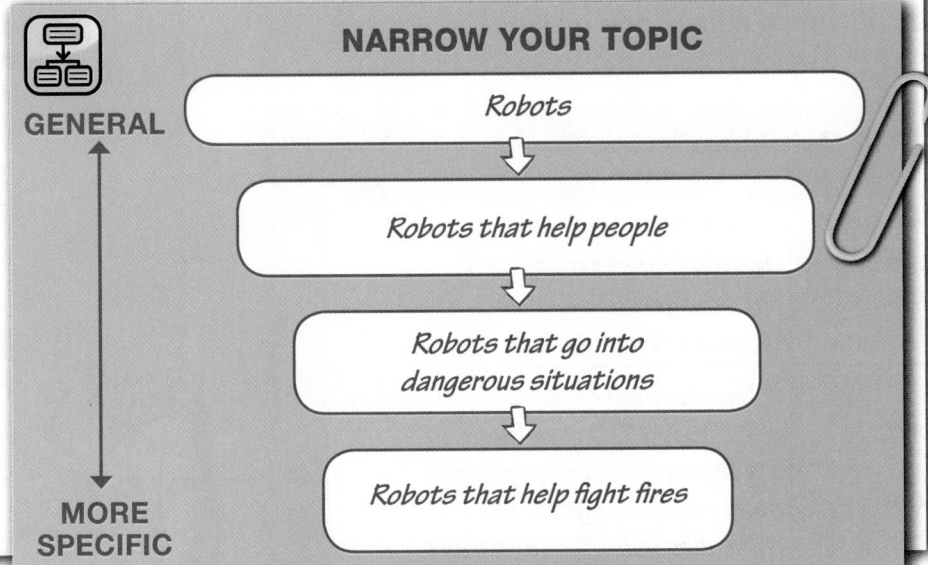

NARROW YOUR TOPIC

GENERAL

Robots

Robots that help people

Robots that go into dangerous situations

Robots that help fight fires

MORE SPECIFIC

Interactive Graphic Organizers

Use the interactive graphic organizers to help you narrow your topic.

Online Journal

Try It! Record your answers and ideas in the online journal.

Consider Your Audience and Purpose

Before writing, think about your audience and purpose. Consider how the form you selected conveys the intended meaning to this audience. Consider the views of others as you ask these questions.

Questions for Audience	Questions for Purpose
<ul><li>Who is my audience?</li><li>What kinds of story lines will my audience find interesting?</li><li>What will my audience need to know about science or technology to understand my science fiction story?</li></ul>	<ul><li>Why am I writing the story? Do I want to entertain readers, make them think, or scare them?</li><li>What literary strategies and devices can I use to enhance the style and tone?</li></ul>

Record your answers in your writing journal.

Plan Your Piece

You will use the graphic organizer to identify your central idea and main character, plan a plot, and identify details. When it is complete, you will be ready to write your first draft.

Develop an Engaging Story Line Use sensory details to create **a specific, believable setting, and interesting characters** as part of a story line that engages your audience.

Organize Your Science Fiction Story Use a graphic organizer to plan **a plot with well-paced action** that sustains, or holds, readers' interest by building toward a climax and includes a beginning, middle, and end.

Develop Your Science Fiction Story	
Main character and the way he/she/it reflects future technology or scientific knowledge	*Robot FF172 is a robot designed to help firefighters by going into dangerous situations to protect human lives.*
Beginning • **A specific, believable setting** • **Interesting characters** • **A conflict, problem, or goal**	• *The story takes place in a small city.* • *Robot FF172 is the leader of a team of robots specifically developed to fight fires.* • *The human firefighters aren't sure they can trust FF172 or the other robots.*
Middle • **Events that build suspense about the conflict** • **Characters' thoughts and actions** • **The climax, the point of highest tension in the main conflict**	
End • **How the conflict is resolved** • **Wrap-up the theme, showing something about the relationship between humans and technological innovations**	• *After FF172 saves a human firefighter's life, the other humans begin to trust the robots.*

Gather Details

To make the audience want to keep reading, develop interesting characters and a believable setting through the use of **sensory details**. Use details that appeal to the senses of:

- **Sight:** *Snow-white foam blanketed the fire.*
- **Sound:** *The clanging fire alarm rang in our ears.*
- **Taste:** *I craved the fresh, crisp taste of an apple.*
- **Smell:** *The pungent smell of smoke stuck to her clothes.*
- **Touch:** *Water splashed against his skin, cooling his face.*

Writers also use a **range of literary strategies and devices to enhance the style and tone** of a story.

- **Flashback:** *The chief remembered the time before they had robots: Every firefighter at the station went into the danger zone.*
- **Foreshadowing:** *Tran laughed, "You mean someday you might save my life? Right."*
- **Suspense:** *The beam crashed down and blocked the doorway.*

Try It! Read the Student Model excerpt and identify which kinds of details and devices the author uses.

STUDENT MODEL

from **Be Careful Where You Wish For** page 98; lines 19–26

FLASH! Sandy was freezing in the yard in a storm. Icy rain ran down her neck. She thought about her toasty warm kitchen, tapped her forehead, and FLASH! She was immediately back at the kitchen table.

Joe was laughing. "What happens if you're whisked away in the middle of a class like a crumb off a table?"

 Apply It! Review the types of details and literary strategies a short story writer can use. Then, include at least one sensory detail and literary strategy or device for each story section.

- Plan to include flashback and foreshadowing **to enhance the style and tone of your story**.
- Be sure to **use sensory details that help create a realistic setting** or help build suspense.

 Interactive Graphic Organizers

Use the interactive graphic organizers to help you create a plan for your writing.

Interactive Model

Refer back to the Interactive Model in the eText as you plan your writing.

Drafting

During the drafting stage, you will start to write your ideas for your science fiction story. You will follow an outline that provides an **organizational strategy** that will help you build on ideas to write a **focused, organized, and coherent** science fiction story.

The Organization of a Short Story

The chart shows an organizational strategy for an imaginative short story. Look back at how the Mentor Text follows this organizational strategy. Then, use this chart to help you outline your draft.

Outline for Success

Beginning

See Mentor Text, p. 94.

- Setting and characters
- Conflict or problem introduced

Middle

See Mentor Text, pp. 94-97.

- Plot with well-paced action, foreshadowing, and flashbacks
- Events that develop the conflict and theme
- Climax

End

See Mentor Text, p. 97.

- Resolution
- Summary of theme

Set the Scene

- The setting of a story is the place and time that it happens. Settings and characters come alive with the use of sensory details.
- The conflict of a story is a problem or struggle. This struggle can be between outside forces, such as humans and technology, or between conflicting emotions within a character.

Build Suspense

- Plots gain momentum as each event intensifies the conflict. Foreshadowing hints at what will happen later. Flashbacks interrupt the sequence of events to show something that happened earlier.
- The theme of a story is its central idea.
- The climax of a story is the point at which the conflict reaches a crisis and suspense is at its highest.

Wrap It Up

- The resolution of a story tells how the conflict was resolved.
- The summary of theme can be shown with character dialogue, an action, or a general statement.

Start Your Draft

Use this checklist to help you complete your draft. Use the graphic organizer that shows the beginning, middle, and end, as well as the Outline for Success as guides.

While drafting, aim at writing your ideas, not on making your writing perfect. Remember, you will have the chance to improve your draft when you revise and edit.

WRITING COACH

Online

www.phwritingcoach.com

Interactive Model

Outline for Success Refer back to Mentor Text in the eText as you write your draft.

√ Start by drafting the opening of your imaginative story. Describe the setting and characters. Include specific details that will **sustain reader interest.**

√ Set up the **conflict,** or problem, to come.

√ Create a specific, **believable setting** and an engaging story line by building curiosity or suspense. Use vivid words and **sensory details** to help readers experience what the characters experience.

√ Create and develop **interesting characters** who respond to each situation based on their individual personalities.

√ Keep the action moving at a good **pace** and focused on the conflict. Describe events in time order, building to the climax.

√ Try to use a **range of literary strategies** and devices, such as foreshadowing and flashbacks, to enhance the style and tone of your writing.

√ Finish by describing how the conflict is resolved or the problem is **solved** and by showing how the character's ideas or feelings have changed as a result of the story events.

Revising: Making It Better

Now that you have finished your first draft, you are ready to revise. Think about the "big picture" of **audience, purpose, and genre.** You can use the Revision RADaR strategy as a guide for making changes to improve your draft. Revision RADaR provides four major ways to improve your writing: (R) replace, (A) add, (D) delete, and (R) reorder.

Kelly Gallagher, M. Ed.

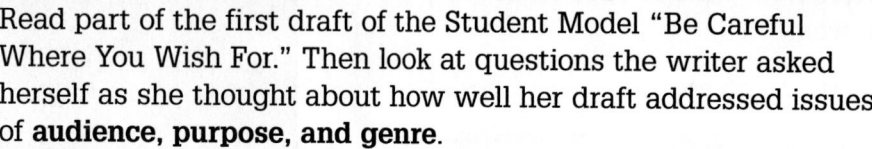

Read part of the first draft of the Student Model "Be Careful Where You Wish For." Then look at questions the writer asked herself as she thought about how well her draft addressed issues of **audience, purpose, and genre**.

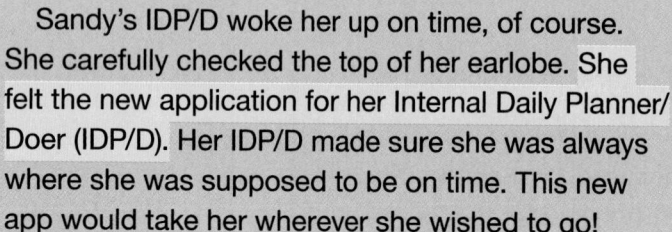

Be Careful Where You Wish For

Sandy's IDP/D woke her up on time, of course. She carefully checked the top of her earlobe. She felt the new application for her Internal Daily Planner/Doer (IDP/D). Her IDP/D made sure she was always where she was supposed to be on time. This new app would take her wherever she wished to go!

Sandy found her brother Joe in the kitchen, stirring steamy oatmeal. He was kind of an anti-techno-geek who liked to do things on his own.

"Good morning, Sandy," Joe said. "How is your new IDP/D application? Is it as great as you hoped?"

"Haven't tried it yet," Sandy yawned. "I'm still too sleepy to think. But wait: I'd like to have breakfast in the yard." Nothing happened. Then Sandy tapped her forehead.

FLASH! Sandy was freezing in the yard in a storm. She had remembered the new app's default check. She had to tap her forehead to confirm her wish.

Does my opening introduce an interesting main character?

*Does my **dialogue** help develop the story and enhance the tone?*

Are my events arranged in chronological order?

Now look at how the writer applied Revision RADaR to write an improved second draft.

Be Careful Where You Wish For

2ND DRAFT

Sandy's IDP/D woke her up on time, of course. She carefully checked the top of her earlobe. Yes! It was there! Now she was one of the first to have latest application for her Internal Daily Planner/ Doer (IDP/D). Her IDP/D made sure she was always where she was supposed to be on time. This new app would take her wherever she wished to go!

Sandy found her brother Joe in the kitchen, stirring steamy oatmeal. He was kind of an anti-techno-geek who liked to do things on his own.

"Hey Sis, how's that new app working for you?" Joe asked a little meanly. "Is it living up to the commercials' promises?"

"Haven't tried it yet," Sandy yawned. "But wait: I'd like to have breakfast in the yard." Nothing happened. Then Sandy remembered the new app's default check. She tapped her forehead to confirm her wish.

FLASH! Sandy was freezing in the yard in a storm.

A *Added details describing Sandy's attitude toward her new app to better develop her character*

R *Replaced boring dialogue with realistic dialogue that reflects characters' attitudes and tone*

D *Deleted the unnecessary words I'm still too sleepy to think*

R *Reordered sentences to keep events in chronological order*

Apply It! Use your Revision RADaR to revise your draft.

- First, determine if you have engaged your audience, created a specific setting, developed interesting characters, and made the conflict or problem clear.
- Then apply the Revision RADaR strategy to make needed changes. Remember—you can use the steps in the strategy in any order.

Look at the Big Picture

Use the chart and your analytical skills to evaluate how well each section of your short story addresses **purpose**, **audience**, and **genre**. When necessary, use the suggestions in the chart to revise your story.

Section	Evaluate	Revise
Beginning	• Check the **opening**. Does it introduce an engaging story line? Will it grab readers' attention and make them want to read more?	• Include details about a character, the setting, or the culture that lets readers know this is science fiction. Use precise word choice and vivid images.
	• Make sure that the **conflict** or problem has been introduced.	• Include dialogue, action, and characters' thoughts to help set up the conflict.
	• Check that the **setting** is specific and believable and the characters are realistic and interesting.	• Use sensory and other details to specifically and believably describe the characters, their surroundings, and the technology they use.
Middle	• Check that the **action** is well-paced and the **plot** coherent.	• Present events in time order leading up to the climax.
	• Number in order the **events** that build suspense. Make sure they all build to the **climax**.	• Reorder details as necessary to better build suspense. Take out or replace details that don't contribute to building the story.
	• Use **literary strategies** and **devices** to reinforce the **style** and **tone** of your story.	• Add elements like foreshadowing and flashback to help create suspense.
Conclusion	• Check that **loose ends** of the story are tied up.	• Add details that answer questions such as *What happened then? How did the characters think or act after the climax?*
	• Make sure you sum up the **theme**.	• Add dialogue, events, or a character's thoughts to show how the story illustrates the theme.

Focus on Craft: Internal and External Coherence

Coherence in a piece of writing means that all the parts fit together, support the central idea, and make sense. In a paragraph with **internal coherence**, the sentences follow one another in logical order and all support the central idea of that paragraph. In a composition with **external coherence**, the paragraphs all fit together logically and support the central idea of the story as a whole.

Think about internal and external coherence as you read the excerpt from the Student Model.

 **STUDENT MODEL** | from **Be Careful Where You Wish For** page 99; lines 34–40

> FLASH! She dropped into a desert of bright sun and hot sand. Dripping with sweat, Sandy thought about the cool lake where they swam each summer. As she wiped the sweat off her face, FLASH! and SPLASH! she landed in the middle of the freezing lake. Shivering and out of breath, Sandy wished herself back in her warm kitchen.

 Try It! Now, ask yourself these questions. Record your answers in your journal.

- What is the topic—or central idea—of this paragraph?
- How does each sentence support the central idea? Explain.

Fine-Tune Your Draft

Apply It! Use the revision suggestions to prepare your final draft.

- **Ensure Internal and External Coherence** Make sure that ideas, sentences, and paragraphs are organized in a logical sequence and that they flow easily.
- **Ensure Vivid Images** Substitute vivid images for vague or boring words and phrases. For example, change *waited nervously* to *drummed her fingers nervously on the table.*
- **Ensure Consistent Point of View** Make sure that the same person, or voice, tells the whole story.

Peer Feedback Read your final draft to a group of peers. Ask if you have **sustained their interest**. Think about their responses and revise your final draft as needed.

WRITING COACH

Online

www.phwritingcoach.com

Online Journal

Try It! Record your answers in the online journal.

Interactive Model

Refer back to the Interactive Model as you revise your writing.

Editing: Making It Correct

Editing your draft means polishing your work and correcting errors. You may want to read through your work several times, looking for different errors and issues each time.

Before editing your draft, review any pronouns you have used in your writing. Each pronoun must have a clear antecedent, or a clearly stated person, place, or thing that the pronoun later replaces. For example, look at these sentences: *Karen and Walter missed the bus. They were late for school.* The pronoun *they* clearly refers to Karen and Walter. Now look at these sentences: *I am going away for the weekend with my family. It should be fun!* The antecedent for *it* is unclear. The second sentence could be corrected this way: *The trip should be fun!*

WRITE GUY *Jeff Anderson, M. Ed.*

WHAT DO YOU NOTICE?

Zoom in on Conventions Focus on the use of pronouns as you read these sentences from the Student Model.

 **STUDENT MODEL** from **Be Careful Where You Wish For** page 99; lines 34–37

> She dropped into a desert of bright sun and hot sand. Dripping with sweat, Sandy thought about the cool lake where they swam each summer.

To learn more about pronouns, see Chapter 23 of your Grammar Handbook.

Now, ask yourself: Which sentence contains a vague pronoun reference?

Perhaps you chose the second sentence, which contains a vague pronoun reference. It is unclear as to whom the pronoun *they* is referring. To correct this vague pronoun reference, the sentence would read: *Dripping with sweat, Sandy thought about the cool lake where she and her family swam each summer.* In this sentence, the antecedent *she* is clear and the vague pronoun *they* is replaced by the specific noun *family*.

It is important to make the antecedents of your pronouns clear when you write. If you have vague pronoun references in your writing, your readers may be confused. Because of this, they will be less likely to want to continue reading your work.

Grammar Mini-Lesson: Antecedents

To learn more, see Chapter 13.

A **pronoun** is a word that stands for or replaces a noun or another pronoun. The noun that is being replaced is called the **antecedent**. Often, the antecedent appears in a sentence before the pronoun does. Notice how the use of pronouns and antecedents in the Student Model helps keep the writing coherent.

 **STUDENT MODEL** from **Be Careful Where You Wish For** page 98; lines 1–7

> Sandy's IDP/D woke her up on time, of course. She carefully checked the top of her earlobe…. This new app would take her wherever she wished to go!

Try It! Underline each pronoun and identify its antecedent. If the antecedent is unclear, rewrite to clarify the pronoun-antecedent relationship. Write the answers in your journal.

1. Lorenzo gave Rob his book, and then he studied Chapter 3. *(compound sentence)*

2. Rob turned in the report that he completed the night before. *(complex sentence)*

Apply It! Edit your draft for **grammar, mechanics, capitalization, and spelling.** If necessary, rewrite sentences to make sure you have used **pronouns** with clear **antecedents**.

WRITING COACH

Online

www.phwritingcoach.com

 Video

Learn effective editing techniques from program author Jeff Anderson.

 Online Journal

Try It! Record your answers in the online journal.

 Interactive Model

Refer back to the Interactive Model as you edit your writing.

Use the rubric to evaluate your piece. If necessary, rethink, rewrite, or revise.

Rubric for Short Story: Science Fiction	Rating Scale					
Ideas: How well have you developed your characters and plot?	Not very 1	2	3	4	5	Very 6
Organization: How clearly organized is the sequence of events in your story?	1	2	3	4	5	6
Voice: How well does your style engage the reader?	1	2	3	4	5	6
Word Choice: How effective is your word choice in creating setting and characters?	1	2	3	4	5	6
Sentence Fluency: How well have you developed coherence in your writing?	1	2	3	4	5	6
Conventions: How correct are your pronouns and antecedents?	1	2	3	4	5	6

Publishing

Get your science fiction story ready to present. Then choose a way to **publish your work for an appropriate audience**.

Wrap Up Your Presentation

Is your story handwritten or written on a computer? If you use a computer, be sure to choose a readable font. The purpose of publishing is to share your writing with readers, which means you must choose a plain, easy-to-read font.

Publish Your Piece

Use this chart to identify a way to publish your written work.

If your audience is...	...then publish it by...
A group of science fiction book or movie fans	• Reading it aloud, then holding a question-answer session about the technology in your story's "world" • Posting the story online and inviting comments
Other students in your class	• Submitting it to a class anthology or Web site of science fiction • Producing it as a graphic novel

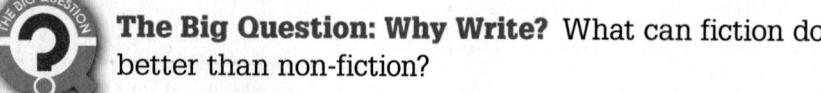 Reflect on Your Writing

Now that you are done with your science fiction story, read it over and use your writing journal to answer these questions. Use specific details to describe and explain your reflections. Increase the specificity of your details based on the type of information requested.

- What did you enjoy about writing the story? Why?
- Are there any parts of the story with which you struggled? If so, what did you learn from the process?
- Do you think you will try writing fiction again? Explain.

 **The Big Question: Why Write?** What can fiction do better than non-fiction?

Manage Your Portfolio You may wish to include your published science fiction story in your writing portfolio. If so, consider what this piece reveals about your writing and your growth as a writer.

MAKE YOUR WRITING COUNT

Make a Sci-Fi Film Trailer

Science fiction writing has long been a favorite genre for movie producers. Create a **trailer**—a film advertisement shown in movie theaters—for an imaginary film based on your science fiction story.

With a group, produce your trailer as a **multimedia presentation,** blending text, graphics, sound, and other media. As you work, be open and responsive to all of your group members' opinions and perspectives. Present your trailer in a live performance, or video-record it.

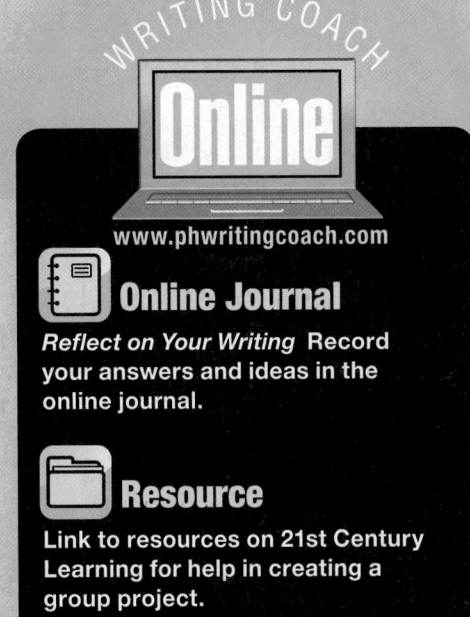

WRITING COACH

Online

www.phwritingcoach.com

Online Journal

Reflect on Your Writing Record your answers and ideas in the online journal.

Resource

Link to resources on 21st Century Learning for help in creating a group project.

Here's your action plan.

1. Choose roles, such as writer, artist, actor, narrator, and director.

2. Review your group's sci-fi stories. Choose one with great action.

3. Find examples of trailers online. Note what elements are especially strong.

4. Create a storyboard, or a series of sketches showing the visual elements of each scene. Your storyboard should:

   - Introduce the main characters and setting
   - Hint at the main conflict without giving away the ending
   - Build excitement about the movie, perhaps through energetic music or rapidly paced shots
   - Show the title of the movie

5. Rehearse and then present the trailer for your class. Record your efforts on video using available technology, if possible.

Listening and Speaking Work as a team to improvise any dialogue or voice-over narration required in the storyboard. Then, use the storyboard to rehearse the dialogue and action. Give each other feedback during and after rehearsal. Present your trailer in a live performance, or video-record it, keeping the feedback in mind.

Your Turn **Writing for Media:
Dramatic Scene**

Dramatic Scene

A **dramatic scene** is a story written to be performed by actors on stage or on film. The purpose of a dramatic scene is generally to entertain, but some contain a message, or theme, the writer wants to convey. Dramatic scenes are written as scripts, with lines for each character and stage directions telling actors how to speak and move. Like other stories, they have a setting, characters, plot, and well-paced action.

Try It! Study the example of a dramatic scene. Then, answer these questions. Record your answers in your journal.

1. At what **audience** is this scene most likely aimed?

2. Is the **story line** of "Power Label" engaging? Explain why or why not.

3. What is the **purpose** of "Power Label"?

4. How would you describe the **pace of events**?

5. Which **character** is most interesting to you? Why?

Extension Find another example of a dramatic scene, and compare it with this one.

Power Label

[Two friends standing in a kitchen. Friend 1 is holding a large box, like a cereal box, reading its label and looking dreamy.]

FRIEND 1. [reads excitedly from box label] "Crunchy golden goodness. Power packed in every bite!"

FRIEND 2. [slouching in a chair] Yeah, sounds good.

FRIEND 1. [continues reading, getting more excited] "All the fuel a body needs for a healthy day."

FRIEND 2. [sits up straighter, leans toward Friend 1] Yeah, that could help some, but…

FRIEND 1. [interrupts Friend 2] We have to try this now! Just think how good we'd feel! How strong we'd be! [starts wildly tearing the box to open it, but has trouble getting it open]

FRIEND 2. [stands, walks over to Friend 1] Here, give it to me. Cool down!

FRIEND 1. [hands over the box, but bounces up and down excitedly] Hurry, hurry. I'm so anxious to try it!

FRIEND 2. [gently pushes Friend 1 into a chair; shakes his head] Dude, no food. We're droids, remember? Solar packs, no stomachs? Chill!

FRIEND 1. [head in hands, sadly] But it looks so good.…

Create a Dramatic Scene

Follow these steps to create your own dramatic scene. Review the graphic organizers on pages R24–R27 and choose one that suits your needs.

Prewriting

- Identify and narrow a topic, then identify the target audience for your scene. Determine the purpose for writing to this specific audience.
- Create characters and a setting for your scene. When those are in place, outline the story line: the beginning, middle, and end of your scene.

Drafting

- Use a script form to draft your scene. Write an opening that grabs your audience.
- Introduce the characters and create a specific, believable setting.
- Develop an engaging story line with well-paced action through the beginning, middle, and end.
- Write dialogue that gives each of your characters a unique "voice," or way of talking, that characterizes him, her, or it.

Revising and Editing

- Review your draft to make sure events are organized logically. Make sure the conflict, or problem, is clear.
- Use the Revision RADaR strategy to improve your draft.
- Check that spelling, grammar, and mechanics are correct.

Publishing

- Read through your scene with classmates, and then rehearse the scene and perform it for the class with actors and a narrator.
- You may want to record your performance using video. You can also use available technology, such as multimedia software, to add text, graphics, and sound to create a short film from the recording.

WRITING COACH

www.phwritingcoach.com

 **Online Journal**

Try It! Record your answers in the online journal.

Interactive Graphic Organizers

Choose from a variety of graphic organizers to plan and develop your project.

Partner Talk

Before you start drafting, explain your dramatic scene to a partner. Use specific details to describe and explain your ideas. Increase the specificity of your details based on the type of information you are delivering. Ask questions about your ideas and plan. For example, will your story hold readers' interest?

Writing for Assessment

Some prompts ask you to write an imaginative work. Use these prompts to practice. Respond using the characteristics of your science fiction story. (See page 92.)

Try It! To begin, read the **short story** prompt and the information on format and academic vocabulary. Then use the ABCDs of On-Demand Writing to help you plan and write your short story.

Format

The prompt asks you to write a *short story*. Be sure to start with a beginning that grabs readers' attention and introduces the characters and conflict.

Short Story Prompt

Write a short story about a spaceship crash. Be sure to develop an engaging story line. Use dialogue, foreshadowing and other literary devices in your story.

Academic Vocabulary

Remember, *dialogue* is the conversation between two or more characters in a work of literature. *Foreshadowing* is an author's use of clues about something that will happen later in the story.

The ABCDs of On-Demand Writing

Use the following ABCDs to help you respond to the prompt.

Before you write your draft:

Attack the prompt [1 MINUTE]

- Circle or highlight important verbs in the prompt. Draw a line from the verb to what it refers to.
- Rewrite the prompt in your own words.

Brainstorm possible answers [4 MINUTES]

- Create a graphic organizer to generate ideas.
- Use one for each part of the prompt if necessary.

Choose the order of your response [1 MINUTE]

- Think about the best way to organize your ideas.
- Number your ideas in the order you will write about them. Cross out ideas you will not be using.

After you write your draft:

Detect errors before turning in the draft [1 MINUTE]

- Carefully reread your writing.
- Make sure that your response makes sense and is complete.
- Look for spelling, punctuation, and grammar errors.

More Prompts for Practice

Apply It! Respond to Prompts 1 and 2 by writing **imaginative short stories** with **engaging story lines** that **sustain the reader's interest**.

- Identify an appropriate audience
- Establish a clear plot focus
- Develop logical and well-paced action
- Create a specific, believable setting through the use of sensory details
- Use **literary strategies and devices** to enhance your **style and tone**

Prompt 1 Write a short story about a character who has an unusual job in the year 2500. Develop an engaging story with a cohesive plot through beginning, middle, and end. Include a believable setting and interesting characters.

Prompt 2 Write a short story about a group of aliens who come to Earth to try and save our planet from an asteroid that is hurtling toward Earth. Develop a story line that retains readers' interest throughout the story.

Spiral Review: Narrative Respond to Prompt 3 by writing a **personal narrative**. Make sure your narrative reflects all of the characteristics described on page 66, including **a clearly defined focus** and **explanations of the importance of or reasons for actions and their consquences.**

Prompt 3 Think about a time when you succeeded in doing something that was difficult. Write an appealing narrative that describes what you tried to do and how you succeeded in that attempt. Tell how you felt about your success and describe any other results of your actions.

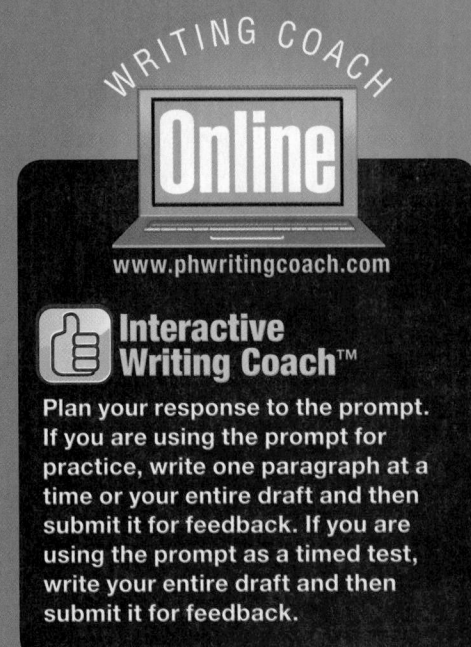

WRITING COACH

www.phwritingcoach.com

Interactive Writing Coach™

Plan your response to the prompt. If you are using the prompt for practice, write one paragraph at a time or your entire draft and then submit it for feedback. If you are using the prompt as a timed test, write your entire draft and then submit it for feedback.

Remember **ABCD**

- **A**ttack the prompt
- **B**rainstorm possible answers
- **C**hoose the order of your response
- **D**etect errors before turning in the draft

POETRY *and* DESCRIPTION

What Do You See?

People see different things when they look at something. Some people may look at this photograph and see a group of horses. Others may look at it and see strength or beauty.

People also use different words to describe what they see. Words can be a powerful way to capture a moment or feeling.

Try It! Take a few minutes to list what you see in the photograph. Remember, you might describe the actual image or you might describe how it makes you feel.

Consider these questions as you participate in an extended discussion with a partner. Take turns expressing your ideas and feelings.

- What details do you see in the photograph?
- What emotions does this photograph make you feel?
- What might you feel if you saw these horses?
- What do the horses mean to you?

Review the list you made. Use your list to describe to a partner what you see in this photograph.

What's Ahead

In this chapter, you will review some strong examples of poems: Mentor Texts and Student Models. Then, using the examples as guidance, you will write a poem of your own.

 **Connect to the Big Questions**

Discuss these questions with your partner:

1 What do you think? When is a picture better than words?

2 Why write? How does one best convey feeling through words on a page?

POETRY AND DESCRIPTION

In this chapter, you will focus on writing a poem. Poetry uses imaginative language, rhythm, and sometimes rhyme to express ideas and feelings in a few strokes. Every single word in a poem has meaning. Therefore, poets look for words that are exact, colorful, and striking to hear. Graphic elements, such as the placement of words and line breaks, are also important in poetry. Description is central to poetry, as it is to most other kinds of writing. Sensory details and vivid language help readers see, hear, smell, taste, or feel something through words.

You will develop a free verse or lyric poem by taking it through each stage of the writing process: prewriting, drafting, revising, editing, and publishing. To preview the criteria for how your poem will be evaluated, see the rubric on page 137. You will also have an opportunity to use your descriptive skills to create an entry describing your hometown for an online travel site.

FEATURE ASSIGNMENT

Poem

An effective poem includes these characteristics and **poetic techniques:**

- A clear **topic, theme,** or **controlling idea**

- **Structural elements,** such as rhyme and meter

- **Figurative language,** such as comparisons that convey mood by pointing out similarities between things that do not seem the same

- **Sensory details** and **imagery** that allow the reader to see, smell, hear, taste, and feel what the poet describes

- **Sound devices** that create a musical or emotional effect

A lyric poem also has these characteristics:

- A strong focus on the poet's feelings about a person, place, thing, or event

- No specific form. Lyric poems can use rhyme and meter or can be free verse.

A free verse poem also has these characteristics:

- Language meant to reflect the patterns of natural speech

- No specific rhyme pattern or meter

- No specific length

Forms of Poetry and Description

There are many forms of poetry and description, including:

Ballads are poems that tell a story and are often meant to be sung. Ballads have a regular rhyme pattern and meter, or "beat." Most ballads repeat words or phrases.

Descriptive essays use precise images and details to help readers imagine a person, place, thing, or event. Like all essays, they include an introduction, body, and conclusion.

Free verse is poetry that imitates the rhythms of everyday speech. Freed of set rhythm and rhyme patterns, free verse uses figurative language and sound devices to convey ideas and feelings.

Haiku are three-line poems first developed in Japan. The first and last lines have five syllables, and the middle line has seven syllables. Haiku are usually about nature.

Lyric poems are poems expressing the speaker's feelings about a certain person, place, thing, or event. Lyric poems can use rhyme and meter or can be free verse.

Prose poems look like prose, or regular text you might find in a story or essay, but use poetic techniques to create a memorable description of a person, place, thing, or event.

Sonnets are 14-line poems with a regular meter and rhyme. One type, the English sonnet, is made up of three four-line stanzas and a final couplet, or two rhyming lines. In each stanza, alternating lines rhyme.

Try It! For each audience and purpose described, choose a form, such as a ballad, lyric poem, or prose poem, that is appropriate for conveying your intended meaning to the audience. Explain your choices.

- To tell classmates about the adventures of your elderly great-uncle, a former test pilot
- To share your feelings with the general public about the first leaves in spring
- To honor your school team's championship with a song

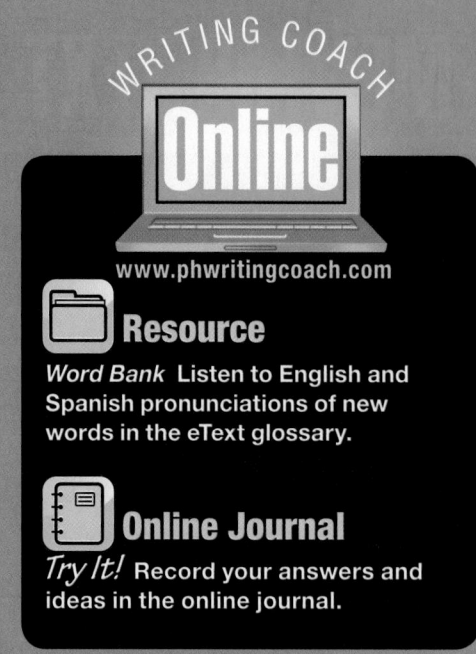

WORD BANK

People often use these basic and content-based vocabulary words when they talk about poetry. Work with a partner. Take turns saying each word aloud. Then, write one sentence using each word. If you are unsure of the meaning of a word, use the Glossary or a dictionary to check the definition.

emotion	stanza
line	symbol
meter	verse

MENTOR TEXT

Free Verse and Lyric Poems

Learn From Experience

 After reading the free verse and lyric poems on pages 122–123, read the numbered notes in the margins to learn about how the poets presented their ideas.

Answer the *Try It!* questions online or in your notebook.

---

❶ The poem is written in free verse divided into two-line stanzas. This **graphic element** helps characterize the speaker in the poem.

> *Try It!* How do you think the speaker sounds? How do the short stanzas help characterize the speaker as an alien from outer space?

❷ The poet uses **figurative language** to convey the alien's interpretation of what it sees.

> *Try It!* What two things are being compared? What does the alien think it sees? What does it actually see?

❸ The last stanza helps reveal the alien's **feelings** about what it sees.

> *Try It!* How does the alien feel about the "people" it sees? How can you tell?

Extension Find other examples of poems to compare with these. Evalute the ways that literal and figurative language affect readers' perceptions.

Southbound on the Freeway

by May Swenson

❶ A tourist came in from Orbitville,
parked in the air, and said:

The creatures of this star
are made of metal and glass.

5 Through the transparent parts
you can see their guts.

Their feet are round and roll
on diagrams or long

measuring tapes, dark
10 with white lines.

They have four eyes.
The two in back are red.

❷ Sometimes you can see a five-eyed
one, with a red eye turning

15 on the top of his head.
He must be special—

The others respect him
and go slow

when he passes, winding
20 among them from behind.

They all hiss as they glide,
like inches, down the marked

❸ tapes. Those soft shapes,
shadowy inside

25 the hard bodies—are they
their guts or their brains?

December Leaves

by Kaye Starbird

The fallen leaves are cornflakes
4 That fill the lawn's wide dish,
And night and noon
The wind's a spoon
5   That stirs them with a swish.

5 The sky's a silver sifter,
A-sifting white and slow,
That gently shakes
On crisp brown flakes
10   The sugar known as snow.

WRITING COACH

Online

www.phwritingcoach.com

Interactive Model

Listen to an audio recording of the Mentor Text in the eText. You can refer back to the Mentor Text whenever you need support in developing your own writing.

Online Journal

Try It! Answer the questions about the Mentor Text in the online journal.

4 This lyric poem has a set **rhyme scheme** and a regular "beat," or **meter.** Read the stanza aloud to hear the rhymes and the beat.

Try It! Read the second stanza. Is the rhyme scheme the same as that in the first stanza? Explain.

5 Like the first stanza, the second stanza contains **figurative language.** The metaphor in the stanza compares snow falling to a sifter sifting sugar.

Try It! What are the "crisp brown flakes" in the second stanza?

STUDENT MODEL
Free Verse and Lyric Poems

With a small group, take turns reading the Student Models aloud. As you read, note the structures and elements of poetry. You may want to take a look at the Poet's Toolbox on page 129. Ask yourself how the poetic language informs and shapes your understanding of the poems.

 Use a Reader's Eye

Now, reread the Student Models. On your copies of the Student Models, use the Reader's Response Symbols to react to what you read.

Reader's Response Symbols

+ **I can picture this.**

– **This image could be stronger.**

? **I wonder what this means.**

! **This is cool!**

Participate in an extended discussion with a partner. Express your opinions and share your responses to the Student Model. On what do you agree? How do your feelings about the poems differ?

Grandma's Cupboard

A Free Verse Poem by Jonathan Williamson

Some of Grandma's furniture
lives at our house now.

My favorite is a tall wooden cupboard.
It is golden oak, soft and worn,
5   and it is very,
very old.

It takes me back to Grandma's.
I open its glass doors,
and it smells like her living room
10 a thousand miles away,
with someone else living in it now.

Now, at my own house, in my own living room,
I open the old cupboard doors,
I take a deep breath,
15 and WHOOSH!
I am back in Grandma's house once more.
The cupboard says,
"Welcome back! Good to see you!"

1

Sweet Harmony

A Lyric Poem by Clara Montgomery

It's hard to be sad when you sing,
(It might be a deep-breathing thing),
You open your mouth,
And your rib cage goes south,
5 And your heart feels as grand as a king.

The best is to sing with a friend
And melt your tones to a blend.
It's not "you"—it's not "me"—
It's a glorious "WE!"
10 Such sweet harmony never should end!

2

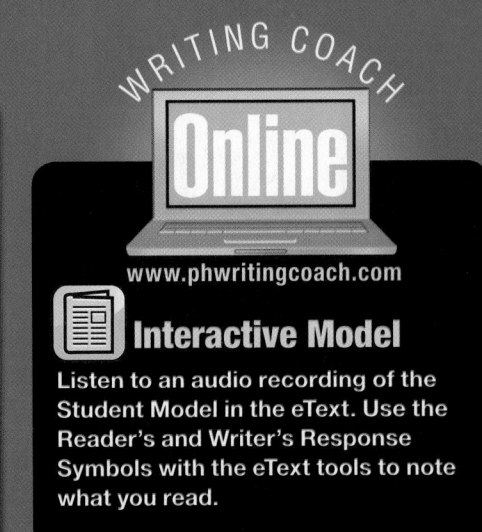

www.phwritingcoach.com

Interactive Model

Listen to an audio recording of the Student Model in the eText. Use the Reader's and Writer's Response Symbols with the eText tools to note what you read.

Use a Writer's Eye

Now, evaluate the poems as a writer. On your copies of the Student Models, use the Writer's Response Symbols to react to what you read. Identify places where the student writers use characteristics of an effective poem.

Writer's Response Symbols	
R.R.	**Rhythm or rhyme fits poem's form**
S.D.	**Effective use of sound devices**
F.L.	**Figurative language conveys a mood**
I.D.	**Images and details appeal to senses**

Prewriting

Plan a first draft of your poem by deciding which form of poem you want to write—a free verse, lyric, or other type of poem— and then **determining an appropriate topic.** Select a topic from the Topic Bank or come up with an idea of your own.

Choose From the Topic Bank

TOPIC BANK

Amazing Place Write a poem to describe the most exciting, most enjoyable, or weirdest place you have ever visited.

Favorite Thing Write a poem about your most prized possession. Describe the object and tell why it is so important to you.

My Hero Write a poem about a person you consider to be a hero. Describe that person and explain why you admire him or her. Be detailed and specific.

Choose Your Own Topic

Determine an **appropriate topic** on your own by using the following **range of strategies** to generate ideas.

Brainstorm, List, and Read

- Work with a partner to brainstorm for categories of places, things, and people to write about, such as historical sites, electronic gadgets, famous people, and so on.

- List specific places, things, and people matching those categories. Circle the topics that interest you most.

- Look through a literature book or poetry collection from American, European, and world literature to get ideas from topics published poets chose.

Review your responses and choose a topic.

Create a Travel Blog

Follow these steps to create your own blog entry describing your hometown for an online travel site. To plan your blog entry, review the graphic organizers on pages R24–R27 and choose one that suits your purpose.

Prewriting

- Identify the place to be described, your town.
- Identify a specific audience and consider its needs and interests. Plan questions about the place that will appeal to your readers.
- Write notes on the details you want to include in your travel writing. Answer these questions as you think about details to include: What are the main attractions of the place? Who in your audience would be most likely to visit it? What does your audience need to know in order to plan a visit?

Drafting

- Format the travel writing as a blog entry.
- First, write a title identifying your town. Then, present your travel information, with interesting and helpful details and strong images. Keep your information clear, specific, and accurate.
- As you write, aim for a lively, colorful style to appeal to your audience. Use a conversational tone and humor appropriate to blog writing.
- Select pictures to include with your blog entry.

Revising and Editing

- Review your draft to ensure that the description is logically organized and the details and images are specific.
- Take out details that do not serve your purpose or that might confuse the reader.
- Check that spelling, grammar, and mechanics are correct.

Publishing

Use the information from your travel blog as the basis for a multimedia presentation. Use some of the text from your writing, as well as photos and other graphics you can find or create. Then, present it to the class.

WRITING COACH

Online

www.phwritingcoach.com

Online Journal

Try It! Record your answers in the online journal.

Interactive Graphic Organizers

Choose from a variety of graphic organizers to plan and develop your project.

Partner Talk

Before you start drafting, describe the place to a partner or small group as your blog writer would. Make sure your description is specific and detailed, and ask for feedback about it. For example, does it sound appealing?

Writing for Assessment

Writing a good poem can take a lot of practice. You can use these prompts to do just that—practice writing poems. Your responses should include the characteristics on page 120.

Try It! To begin, read the prompt and the information on format and academic vocabulary. Use the ABCDs of On-Demand Writing to help you plan and write your **poem**.

Format
The prompt directs you to write a *poem*. Develop your topic by choosing details that convey your main idea.

Poetry Prompt
Think about a tree you have often seen—perhaps one near your home or school. Write a poem describing that tree and your feelings about it. Choose a poetic form and use poetic techniques.

Academic Vocabulary
Remember that *poetic techniques* are the tools poets use to convey their ideas. Each poem has a specific *poetic form*, such as the lyric or free verse poem.

 ## The ABCDs of On-Demand Writing

Use the following ABCDs to help you respond to the prompt.

Before you write your draft:

Attack the prompt [1 MINUTE]

- Circle or highlight important verbs in the prompt. Draw a line from the verb to what it refers to.
- Rewrite the prompt in your own words.

Brainstorm possible answers [4 MINUTES]

- Create a graphic organizer to generate ideas.
- Use one for each part of the prompt if necessary.

Choose the order of your response [1 MINUTE]

- Think about the best way to organize your ideas.
- Number your ideas in the order you will write about them. Cross out ideas you will not be using.

After you write your draft:

Detect errors before turning in the draft [1 MINUTE]

- Carefully reread your writing.
- Make sure that your response makes sense and is complete.
- Look for spelling, punctuation, and grammar errors.

More Prompts for Practice

Apply It! Respond to Prompt 1 by writing a **poem** that uses poetic techniques, figurative language, and graphic elements. Be sure to:

- Identify your audience and choose from a variety of **poetic forms** and use **graphic elements,** such as line breaks and stanzas appropriate to your chosen form
- Establish a clear topic, theme, or **controlling idea**
- Use **poetic techniques** and **figurative language** to develop ideas

> **Prompt 1** Poets often get inspiration from their surroundings. Look outside your window right now and think about what you see. Write a poem about something you notice outside your window.

Spiral Review: Narrative If you choose to write a **personal narrative** in response to Prompt 2, make sure your story reflects the characteristics described on page 66.

> **Prompt 2** Write a personal narrative about something funny or interesting that happened when you took a trip somewhere. The place could be another state or country, or somewhere close to home.

Spiral Review: Imaginative Short Story If you choose to write a **short story** in response to Prompt 3, be sure that your story reflects the characteristics described on page 92. Your writing should express your ideas and feelings about the real or imagined people, events, and ideas that you describe. In addition, be sure to:

- Sustain **reader interest**
- Develop an **engaging story line** with **interesting characters, well-paced action** and a well-developed conflict that is resolved
- Use **sensory details** to present a specific, believable **setting**
- Use a range of **literary strategies** and **devices** to enhance the **style** and **tone** of the story

> **Prompt 3** Write a serious or humorous short story about a misunderstanding between friends. Make the misunderstanding the main conflict, and be sure that plot events center around it.

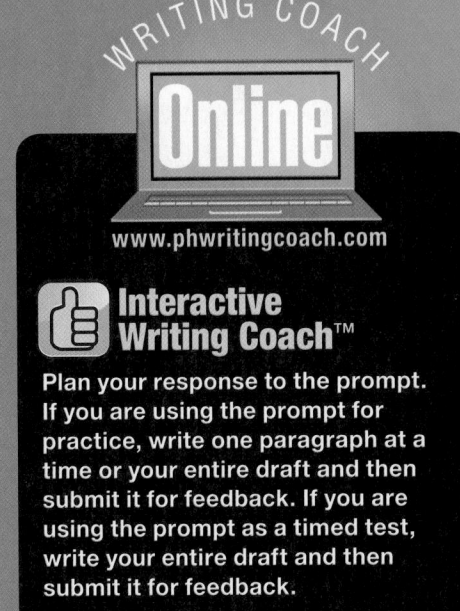

WRITING COACH

Online

www.phwritingcoach.com

Interactive Writing Coach™

Plan your response to the prompt. If you are using the prompt for practice, write one paragraph at a time or your entire draft and then submit it for feedback. If you are using the prompt as a timed test, write your entire draft and then submit it for feedback.

Remember **ABCD**

Attack the prompt

Brainstorm possible answers

Choose the order of your response

Detect errors before turning in the draft

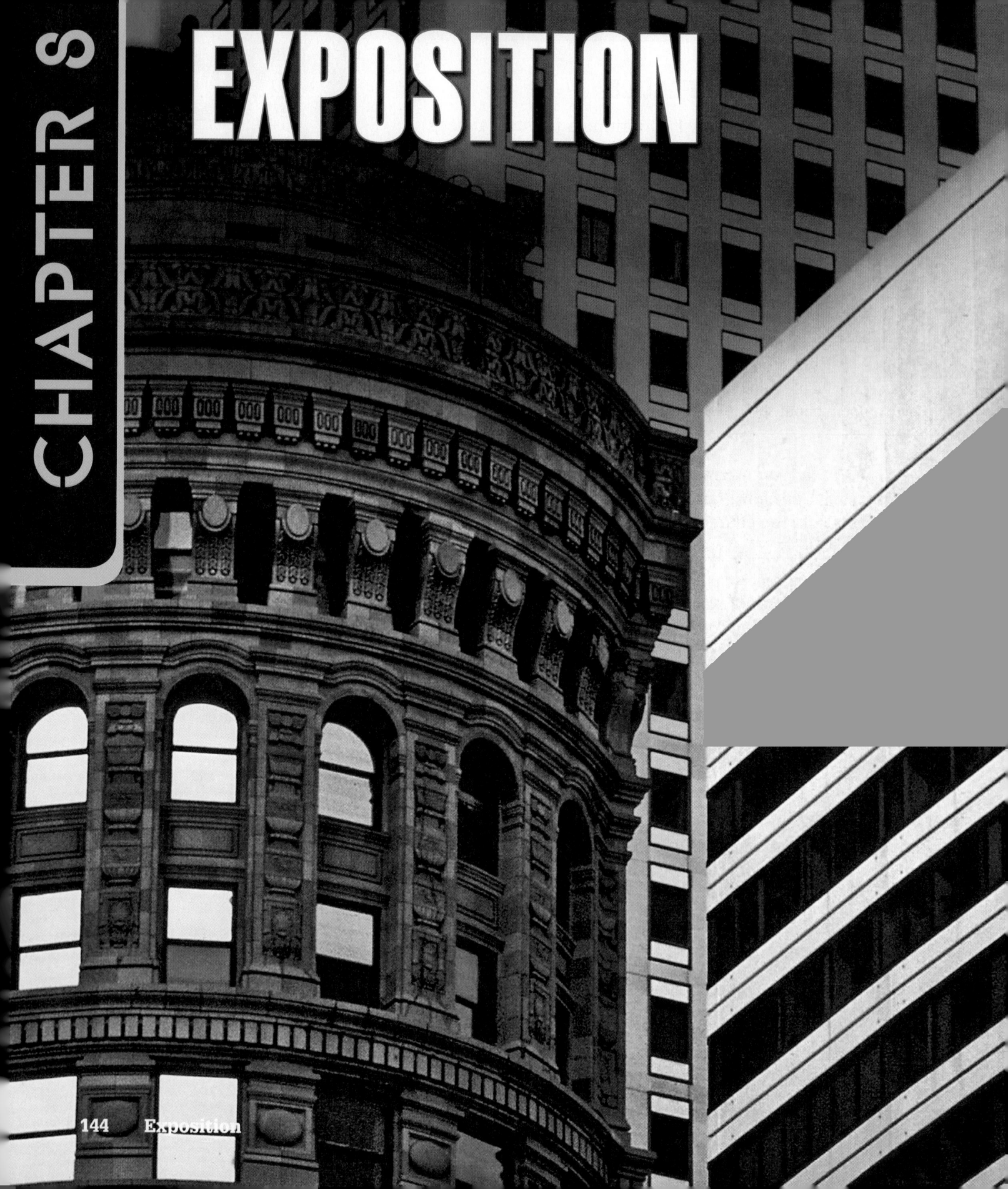

CHAPTER 8

EXPOSITION

How Can You Explain This?

What do you know about old and new buildings? What ideas and information about buildings could you share with others?

Information can be presented in many ways. For example, you can compare two things, you can discuss causes and effects, or you can present a problem and a solution.

Try It! How could you compare these two buildings? Take notes as you consider these questions. Then participate in an extended discussion with a partner. Review the ideas you wrote. Then, discuss your comparison. Take turns expressing your ideas and feelings.

- How are these two buildings similar?
- How are these two buildings different?
- What details would you use to describe the buildings?

What's Ahead

In this chapter, you will review two strong examples of an analytical essay: a Mentor Text and a Student Model. Then, using the examples as guides, you will write an expository essay in the compare and contrast form.

WRITING COACH

Online

www.phwritingcoach.com

Online Journal

Try It! Record your answers and ideas in the online journal.

You can also record and save your answers and ideas on pop-up sticky notes in the eText.

Connect to the Big Questions

Discuss these questions with your partner:

1 What do you think? Is newer always better?

2 Why write? What should we tell and what should we describe to make information clear?

EXPOSITORY ESSAY

An expository essay explains a topic by providing facts, quotations, and other details about it. In this chapter, you will learn to write a type of expository essay known as a compare-and-contrast essay. A compare-and-contrast essay provides details about similarities and differences between two or more aspects of a broader topic. For instance, it may examine the similarities and differences between two or more historical events or two or more aspects of nature. It may show how two or more people, places, objects, or experiences are alike or how they are different.

You will develop your compare-and-contrast essay by taking it through each of the steps of the writing process: prewriting, drafting, revising, editing, and publishing. You will also have an opportunity to write a technical newsletter. To preview the criteria for how your compare-and-contrast essay will be evaluated, see the rubric on page 163.

FEATURE ASSIGNMENT

Expository Essay: Compare-and-Contrast Essay

An effective expository essay has these characteristics:

- A **specific topic** about which the essay conveys information

- An **effective introduction** and **conclusion**

- A **clearly stated purpose** and **controlling idea,** or **thesis**

- **Clear, logical organization** that supports the controlling idea or thesis

- A **variety of transitions** to link details, ideas, and paragraphs

- A **variety of sentence structures** and **rhetorical devices**, such as analogies and rhetorical questions, that help express ideas clearly

- **Facts, quotations**, and **other details** that support the explanations

- **No** unnecessary or **extraneous information** or **inconsistencies**, or facts that do not match

- Ideas that are **accurately synthesized** from **several sources**

A compare-and-contrast essay also includes:

- A **thesis** about **two or more aspects of a broader topic**

- An examination of the **similarities** and **differences** between the two aspects

Other Forms of Expository Essays

In addition to a compare-and-contrast essay, there are other forms of expository essays, including:

Cause-and-effect essays trace the results of an event or the reasons an event happened.

Classification essays organize a subject into categories or explain the category into which an item falls.

Newspaper and magazine articles in print or published on the Internet supply relevant information about a particular topic by analyzing the topic's elements. They may also reflect genres other than expository essays (for example, persuasive writing or narrative nonfiction writing).

Pro-con essays examine the arguments for and against a particular action or decision.

Problem-solution essays identify a problem and explain one or more ways to solve it.

Try It! For each audience and purpose described, choose a form, such as a pro-con essay or a problem-solution essay, that is appropriate for conveying your intended meaning to your audience. Explain your choices.

- To describe the results of a volcanic eruption to students in your science class
- To explain to a friend who is interested in nutrition the categories in which different foods are grouped
- To provide shoppers with an idea of the benefits and drawbacks of a particular product

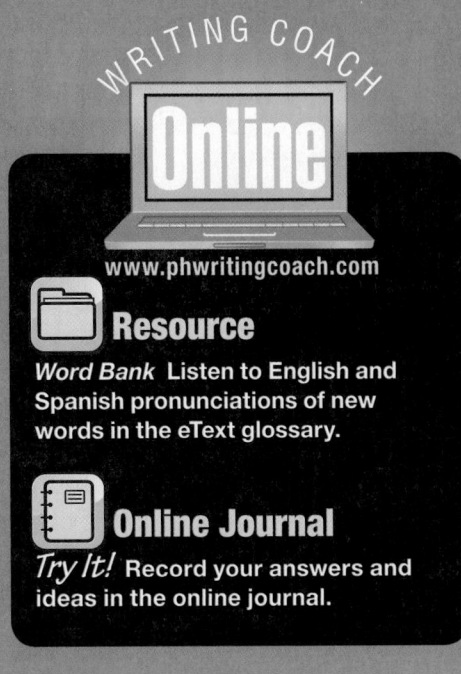

WRITING COACH

Online

www.phwritingcoach.com

Resource

Word Bank Listen to English and Spanish pronunciations of new words in the eText glossary.

Online Journal

Try It! Record your answers and ideas in the online journal.

WORD BANK

People often use these vocabulary words when they talk about expository writing. Work with a partner. Take turns writing each word in a sentence. If you are unsure of the meaning of a word, use the Glossary or a dictionary to check the definition.

analyze	information
comparison	logical
contradict	synthesize

MENTOR TEXT

Expository Essay

Learn From Experience

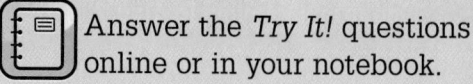
After reading the expository essay on pages 148–149, read the numbered notes in the margins to learn about how the author presented her ideas. Later you will read a Student Model, which shares these characteristics and also has the characteristics of a compare-and-contrast essay.

Answer the *Try It!* questions online or in your notebook.

---

1 The introduction has a clearly stated **controlling idea.** The introduction also **grabs readers' interest** by suggesting a comparison between bees and humans.

Try It! What is the **controlling idea** of this essay? What comparison is the author suggesting between bees and humans?

2 A **quotation** from an expert **supports** the controlling idea and sets up the explanations to come.

Try It! How do you know Shaowu Zhang is an expert in bee behavior? What does quoting an expert add to the essay?

3 The author uses a **variety of sentence structures** to explain effectively what Zhang and his team trained the honeybees to do.

Try It! Rewrite this paragraph using only simple sentences. How easy is your version to follow? What other differences do you notice when comparing the two versions?

Brainy Bees Know Two from Three

by Liz Savage

1 One, two, three. . . That's how high you could count if you were a bee. A new study found that honeybees can recognize a pattern based only on the number of elements in it.

5 If the bees learn to recognize three blue dots, then later they can find three yellow stars, three yellow lemons or three purple blobs. For such tiny creatures, that's a big deal.

Many animals—pigeons, raccoons, dolphins, even salamanders—have shown off their numerical abilities in 10 research experiments. But few studies have ever examined invertebrates, like honeybees.

Honeybees are pretty clever. They can tell which items are similar to each other and which are different. They can even count the landmarks they pass on the way to get their 15 food. **2** "I have been studying honeybees since 1980, and I am often surprised by our experimental results. The bee is smart," says Shaowu Zhang at the Australian National University in Canberra.

3 Zhang and his team trained about 20 honeybees 20 to fly through a tunnel and into a hole that was marked with either two or three blue dots. On the other side, bees found a chamber with two exits. Each exit was marked with a pattern, either two or three blue dots. If the bees remembered the first pattern and picked the matching 25 hole, the one with the right number of dots, they received a sugary treat. By repeating this training, the bees learned that if they matched the pattern, they would get a reward.

The honeybees may not think about counting "one, two, three" the same way we do. But the bees got their sugar 30 snack about 70 percent of the time. This confirmed for the

WRITING COACH

Online

www.phwritingcoach.com

Interactive Model

Listen to an audio recording of the Mentor Text in the eText. You can refer back to the Mentor Text whenever you need support in developing your own writing.

Online Journal

Try It! Answer the questions about the Mentor Text in the online journal.

researchers that the bees were able to detect "sameness," which earlier studies had suggested.

❹ Then the tests got harder. The scientists wanted to see whether the bees could apply that matching rule to new
35 patterns. The bees might have to match two blue dots to two yellow lemons and later on, three green leaves to three yellow stars. Even in these more difficult tests, the bees could tell the difference between two objects and three.

❹ When they were trained to learn a pattern with
40 three items, the bees could distinguish between three and four items, but couldn't do the reverse. Given a four-item pattern, the bees could not tell the difference between four and three. Four was too much to keep track of.

❺ Before you decide bees are dumb, you should know
45 that memory studies have suggested that the number of items a person can consciously remember at any one time is around—four.

❹ The author uses **transitions** to link the sentences in **logical order.**

Try It! How do the transitions help you understand the order in which the events occurred?

❺ The author concludes by **synthesizing information** from other studies to show an unexpected **similarity** between bees and humans.

Try It! What is the similarity between bees and humans? How does this concluding information affect the way you think about bees?

Extension Find another example of an expository essay, and compare it with this one.

STUDENT MODEL | Compare-and-Contrast Essay

With a small group, take turns reading this Student Model aloud. Identify the different characteristics that are being compared or contrasted, and decide if the comparisons and contrasts are clear.

 ## Use a Reader's Eye

Now, reread the Student Model. On your copy of the Student Model, use the Reader's Response Symbols to react to what you read.

Reader's Response Symbols

+ **Aha! That makes sense to me.**

− **This isn't clear to me.**

? **I have a question about this.**

! **Wow! That is cool/weird/ interesting.**

Canines in the WILD

by Eliot Rayburn

Last summer, my family visited Yellowstone National Park. One morning we saw some animals in the distance. "Look, coyotes!" my sister exclaimed. But a forest ranger told us they weren't coyotes—they were wolves.

5   My sister's mistake was a common one. Coyotes and wolves have many similarities, even though they are different animals.

Both coyotes and wolves are members of the canine, or dog, family. Their faces are both doglike
10   in appearance and triangular in shape. They are also similar in coloring. Usually their fur is grayish brown, though it can also be rusty, yellowish, white, or black. Wolves have thicker fur than coyotes do, and a coyote's nose and ears are pointier than a
15   wolf's. Still, these differences are rather small.

The biggest difference in appearance is one of size. A full-grown coyote is only about 20 inches tall; a wolf can be nearly twice that tall. A wolf weighs more, too. Some wolves can weigh as much as 80 pounds. In contrast,
20   most coyotes weigh from 20 to 30 pounds. Nevertheless, the size difference won't always help you tell the difference between wolves and coyotes. As the forest ranger at Yellowstone explained, "It's easy to confuse a full-grown coyote with a younger, smaller wolf."

25   In terms of behavior, wolves and coyotes have many differences. Wolves usually hunt in packs, while coyotes hunt in pairs. Wolves often hunt large animals, like deer and elk. Since coyotes are smaller, they usually go after smaller animals, like mice and

1

30 rabbits. And coyotes aren't fussy eaters—they will also eat insects, fruits, vegetables, and even garbage!

Wolves have trouble surviving in places where a lot of people live. In the United States, wolves are a protected species, which means they are in danger
35 of becoming extinct. Coyotes, on the other hand, have an incredible talent for adapting. There are coyotes living right in the middle of Los Angeles! Coyotes can be found in the East, too. They began traveling east on the interstate highway system when
40 it was completed in the 1950s. Now they are fairly common in places like rural New England, where wolves once roamed but are no longer found.

Thus, while coyotes and wolves look alike, their behaviors and situations are different.
45 Wolves are growing rarer and rarer. Coyotes, on the other hand, are thriving.

Wolf

Coyote

WRITING COACH

Online

www.phwritingcoach.com

Interactive Model

Listen to an audio recording of the Student Model in the eText. Use the Reader's and Writer's Response Symbols with the eText tools to note what you read.

Use a Writer's Eye

Now evaluate the Student Model as a writer. On your copy of the Student Model, use the Writer's Response Symbols to react to what you read. Identify places where the student writer uses the characteristics of an effective compare-and-contrast essay.

Writer's Response Symbols	
C.T.	**Clearly stated thesis**
I.C.	**Effective introduction and conclusion**
R.D.	**Good use of rhetorical devices**
S.E.	**Effective supporting evidence**

 **Feature Assignment:**
Compare-and-Contrast Essay

Prewriting

Plan a first draft of your compare-and-contrast essay. Select from the Topic Bank or come up with an idea of your own.

Choose From the Topic Bank

TOPIC BANK

Film Adaptations It's fascinating to think about how screenwriters make a movie from a book. Think of a book that has been made into a movie. Write a compare-and-contrast essay that explains what is similar and what is different about the two. Be sure to discuss which one you enjoyed more and why.

Methods of Communication People communicate with each other in different ways. Some people just talk to each other face-to-face. Others use "snail mail," e-mail, the telephone, books and magazines, radio, and TV to communicate. Write an essay in which you compare and contrast two ways that people communicate with each other.

Subjects Think about the subjects you are learning in school. You probably have a favorite subject and a subject that you don't like as well or that is more difficult for you. Write an essay in which you compare and contrast your favorite class or subject with another class or subject.

Choose Your Own Topic

Determine a topic on your own by using these ideas.

Associate and Synthesize

- With a partner, play a game of word association in which one of you names something and the other names something that is either the opposite or closely related. After listing your associations, choose one pair to explore in a compare-and-contrast essay.

- List a broad category, such as sports or music. Then, list your favorite type in that category—for example, your favorite type of music might be jazz. Brainstorm for other types in the same category to compare.

Review your responses and choose a topic.

Narrow Your Topic

Some topics are too broad to cover in a compare-and-contrast essay. By narrowing your topic, you can focus on specific similarities and differences.

Apply It! Use a graphic organizer like the one shown to narrow your topic to a manageable size.

- Write your general topic in the top box, and keep narrowing your topic as you move down the chart.
- Your last box should hold your narrowest topic, which will be the new focus of your compare-and-contrast essay.

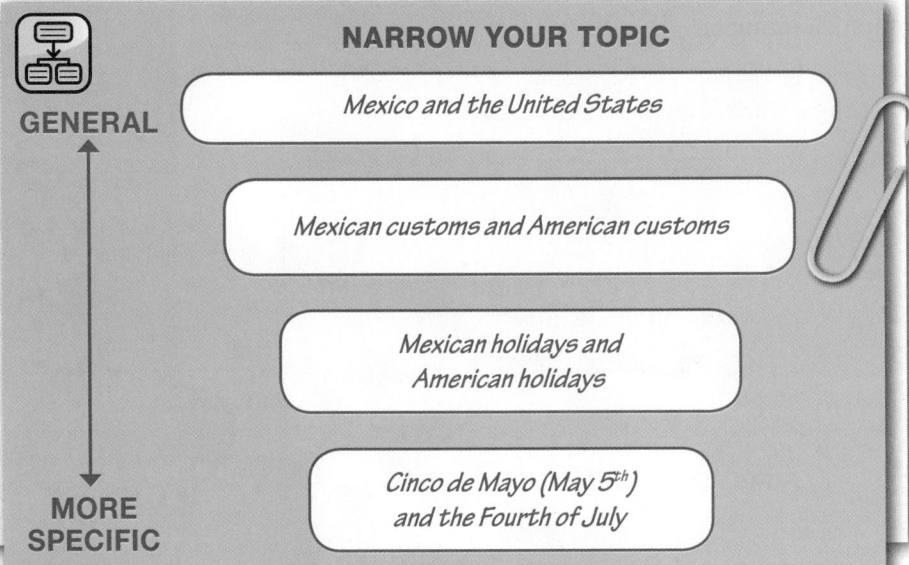

NARROW YOUR TOPIC

GENERAL

Mexico and the United States

Mexican customs and American customs

Mexican holidays and American holidays

Cinco de Mayo (May 5th) and the Fourth of July

MORE SPECIFIC

Consider Your Audience and Purpose

Before writing, think about your audience and purpose. Consider how the form you selected conveys the intended meaning to this audience. Consider the views of others as you ask these questions.

Questions for Audience	Questions for Purpose
• Who is my audience? • Is my audience familiar with my topic? • What questions might my audience have about my topic?	• How might I make the comparisons and contrasts clear to my audience? • What main point about all my comparisons and contrasts do I want to make in my thesis?

Record your answers in your writing journal.

Plan Your Essay

You will use the graphic organizer to state your thesis and identify details that show how your topics are alike and different. When it is complete, you will be ready to write your first draft.

Develop a Clear Thesis Look over your ideas to help you develop a clear thesis, or controlling idea. Your thesis should make a general statement about the similarities and differences in your essay. List it at the top of a graphic organizer like this one.

Logically Organize Your Details Ask yourself how the two aspects of your topic are alike and how they are different. Synthesize the information by listing the details, similarities, and differences in the appropriate sections of the graphic organizer.

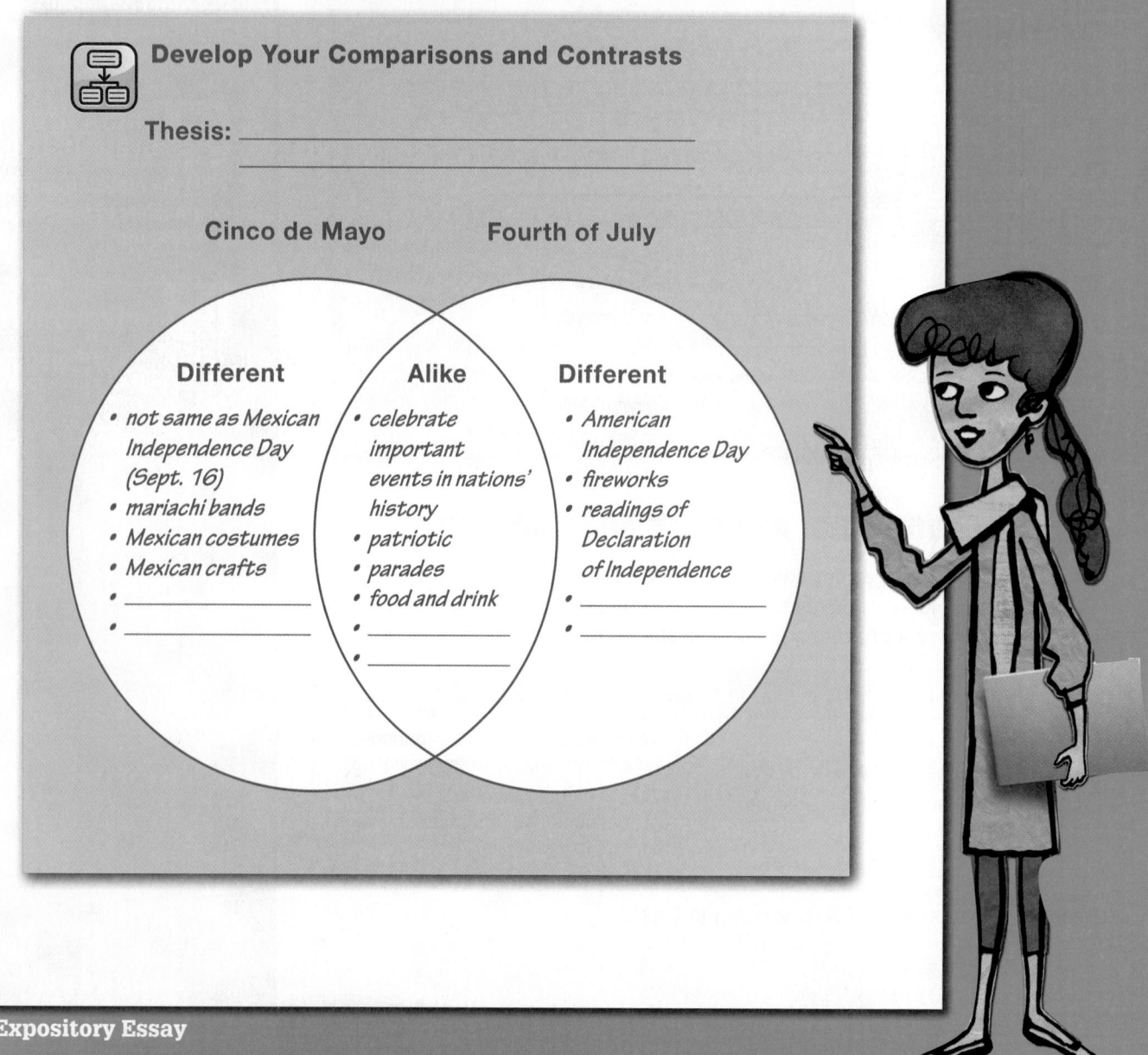

Develop Your Comparisons and Contrasts

Thesis: _____
_____

Cinco de Mayo   **Fourth of July**

Different
- not same as Mexican Independence Day (Sept. 16)
- mariachi bands
- Mexican costumes
- Mexican crafts
- _____
- _____

Alike
- celebrate important events in nations' history
- patriotic
- parades
- food and drink
- _____
- _____

Different
- American Independence Day
- fireworks
- readings of Declaration of Independence
- _____
- _____

Gather Details

When explaining similarities and differences, writers use some or all of these categories of details. Look at these examples.

- **Facts:** *Cinco de Mayo commemorates a Mexican victory against the French in the Battle of Puebla in 1862.*

- **Quotations:** *"Our annual Cinco de Mayo Festival celebrates the Mexican cultural heritage of many area residents."—Sonia Verdugo, Chairwoman, Cinco de Mayo Festival of Martina, Colorado*

- **Examples:** *Tacos are among the Mexican foods served at Cinco de Mayo celebrations.*

- **Personal Experiences:** *In the Cinco de Mayo parade I saw last year, most people on the floats wore traditional Mexican clothing.*

Try It! Read this Student Model excerpt. Then, identify and take notes about which kinds of details the author used to support his ideas.

STUDENT MODEL from **Canines in the Wild**
page 150; lines 19–24

In contrast, most coyotes weigh from 20 to 30 pounds. Nevertheless, the size difference won't always help you tell the difference between wolves and coyotes. As the forest ranger at Yellowstone explained, "It's easy to confuse a full-grown coyote with a younger, smaller wolf."

 *Apply It!* Review the types of support an expository essay can use. Think about the different types you might use in discussing the similarities and differences that support your thesis. Also consider which details might be useful for an **effective introduction or conclusion** to your essay.

- Decide which details best support your purpose as stated in your thesis. Eliminate details that do not seem tightly related or relevant, or change your thesis to take them into account.

- Review your notes to find similarities. Then, **synthesize** your information and identify any **inconsistencies.** Do more research, if necessary, to clear up the inconsistencies.

- Identify one or two details that could help make your **introduction or conclusion more effective.** Sometimes a quotation or a personal experience can help capture reader attention in your introduction or make your conclusion more memorable.

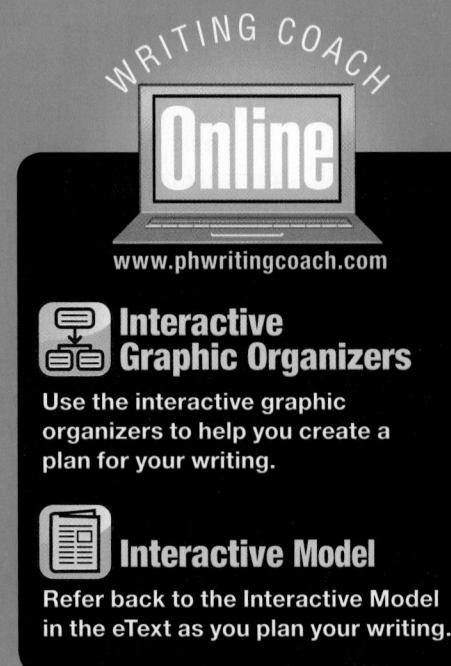

WRITING COACH

Online

www.phwritingcoach.com

Interactive Graphic Organizers

Use the interactive graphic organizers to help you create a plan for your writing.

Interactive Model

Refer back to the Interactive Model in the eText as you plan your writing.

Drafting

During the drafting stage, you will start to write your ideas for your essay. You will follow an outline that provides an appropriate **organizational strategy** that will help you build on ideas to write a **focused**, **organized**, and **coherent** compare-and-contrast essay.

The Organization of a Compare-and-Contrast Essay

The chart provides an organizing structure for a compare-and-contrast essay. As you adapt it for your particular compare-and-contrast essay, be sure to keep in mind your audience and purpose.

Outline for Success

I. Introduction

See Mentor Text, p. 148.

- Attention-grabbing opening
- Thesis that states what you are comparing and contrasting

Grab Your Reader

- An interesting opening captures the reader's attention with a quotation, a personal experience, or another strong detail.
- A thesis is a general statement about the two or more aspects that you are comparing and contrasting.

II. Body

See Mentor Text, pp. 148–149.

- **Points of comparison and contrast**

Point-by-Point
- Point 1: Topic A and B
- Point 2: Topic A and B
- Point 3: Topic A and B

- **Logical organization of points**

Block Organization
- Topic A: Points 1, 2, and 3
- Topic B: Points 1, 2, and 3

Compare and Contrast

- Each point of comparison and contrast is supported with evidence that explains your points and informs your reader.
- A clear organizational structure helps readers follow your ideas easily. A point-by-point or block organization structure is a good way to structure your ideas. Block organization works best if you have only one or two points of comparison. Point-by-point is used when you have several points of comparison.

III. Conclusion

See Mentor Text, p. 149.

- Restatement of thesis
- Memorable ending

Wrap It Up

- A strong conclusion restates the thesis and briefly summarizes your points of comparison and contrast.
- Analogies or rhetorical questions— questions that make the reader think or emphasize a point—help make your ideas memorable.

Start Your Draft

Use this checklist to help you complete your draft. Use the graphic organizer that shows your comparisons and contrasts, and the Outline for Success as guides.

While drafting, aim at writing your ideas, not on making your writing perfect. Remember, you will have the chance to improve your draft when you revise and edit.

√ Start with **opening** sentences that capture your reader's interest and introduce the topic for comparison and contrast.

√ Continue building an **effective introduction** by including a thesis that states your controlling idea about the similarities and differences you will be discussing.

√ Develop the **body** of your compare-and-contrast essay by providing similarities and differences that support your **thesis.**

√ **Synthesize,** or blend together, ideas and information from several sources.

√ Logically organize your essay by including specific facts and details that support your main idea. Make sure to avoid **extraneous,** or unnecessary, information and inconsistencies.

√ Be sure to use **transitions** to link sentences and paragraphs and to make your comparisons and contrasts clear.

√ Use an appropriate **organizing structure** such as point-by-point organization, discussing each similarity and difference one at a time, or block organization, discussing all the qualities of one thing before moving on to the other.

√ Use a variety of different **sentence structures,** such as short or long and simple or complex to keep your writing lively and interesting.

√ End with an effective **conclusion** that restates your thesis in an interesting way and uses a variety of **rhetorical devices** to help your audience see the importance of your topic.

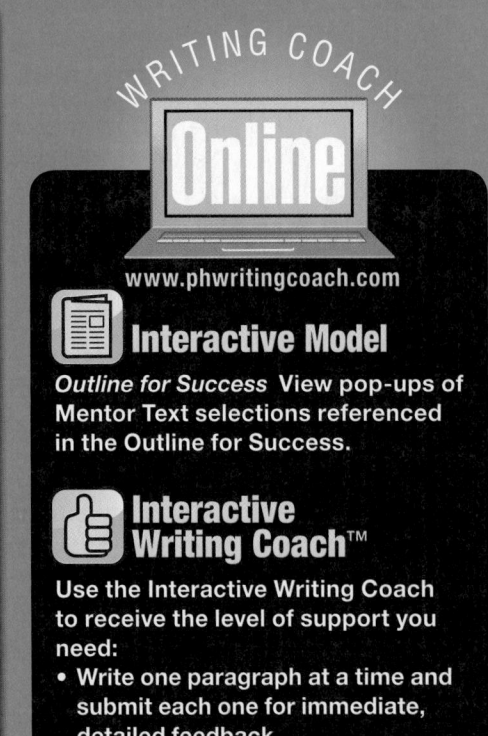

WRITING COACH

Online
www.phwritingcoach.com

Interactive Model
Outline for Success View pop-ups of Mentor Text selections referenced in the Outline for Success.

Interactive Writing Coach™

Use the Interactive Writing Coach to receive the level of support you need:
• Write one paragraph at a time and submit each one for immediate, detailed feedback.
• Write your entire first draft and submit it for immediate, personalized feedback.

Revising: Making It Better

Now that you have finished your first draft, you are ready to revise. Think about the "big picture" of **audience, purpose,** and **genre.** You can use the Revision RADaR strategy as a guide for making changes to improve your draft. Revision RADaR provides four major ways to improve your writing: (R) replace, (A) add, (D) delete, and (R) reorder.

Kelly Gallagher, M. Ed.

KEEP REVISION ON YOUR RADaR

Read part of the first draft of the Student Model "Canines in the Wild." Then, look at questions the writer asked himself as he thought about how well his draft **addressed issues of audience, purpose, and genre.**

Canines in the Wild

It's easy to mix up wolves and coyotes. Lots of people can't tell the difference, especially from a distance. My sister mixed them up last summer. Her mistake is a common one.

Both coyotes and wolves are members of the canine, or dog, family. The word *coyote* comes from a Native American word. The two animals' faces have a similar dog-like appearance and triangular shape. They are also similar in coloring. Usually their fur is grayish brown. It can be rusty or yellowish. It can also be white or black. Wolves have thicker fur than coyotes do. And a coyote's nose and ears are pointier than a wolf's. Still, these differences are rather small.

The biggest difference in appearance is one of size. A full-grown coyote is only about 20 inches tall; a wolf can be nearly twice that tall. A wolf weighs more, too. Some wolves can weigh as much as 80 pounds.

Does the introduction grab my audience and clearly state my thesis?

*Is this detail **relevant** to the comparisons and contrasts, or is it **extraneous information?***

How can I vary sentence structures to avoid so many short, choppy sentences?

Now look at how the writer applied Revision RADaR to write an improved second draft.

Canines in the WILD

Last summer, my family visited Yellowstone National Park. One morning we saw some animals in the distance. "Look, coyotes!" my sister exclaimed. But a forest ranger told us they weren't coyotes—they were wolves.

My sister's mistake was a common one. Coyotes and wolves have many similarities, even though they are different animals.

Both coyotes and wolves are members of the canine, or dog, family. Their faces are both doglike in appearance and triangular in shape. They are also similar in coloring. Usually their fur is grayish brown, though it can also be rusty, yellowish, white, or black. Wolves have thicker fur than coyotes do, and a coyote's nose and ears are pointier than a wolf's. Still, these differences are rather small.

The biggest difference in appearance is one of size. A full-grown coyote is only about 20 inches tall; a wolf can be nearly twice that tall. A wolf weighs more, too. Some wolves can weigh as much as 80 pounds.

R *Replaced a more personal anecdote to make the introduction more effective, and*
A *added a thesis that makes a clear statement about my topic*

D *Deleted extraneous information not relevant to the comparisons and contrasts I am making*

R *Reordered sentences by combining them to vary sentence structures*

 Apply It! Use your Revision RADaR to revise your draft.

- Include all the appropriate characteristics of the expository essay genre.
- Keep your audience and purpose in mind. Make sure that your introduction is effective, interesting, and presents a clearly stated thesis.
- Exchange drafts with a partner. Listen as your partner provides direction for how to improve your work.
- Then, apply the Revision RADaR strategy to make needed changes. Remember—you can use the steps in the strategy in any order.

REPLACE ADD DELETE and REORDER

RADaR

Look at the Big Picture

Use the chart and your analytical skills to evaluate how well each section of your compare-and-contrast essay addresses **purpose**, **audience**, and **genre**. When necessary, use the suggestions in the chart to revise your essay.

Section	Evaluate	Revise
Introduction	• Make sure your **opening** grabs readers' attention.	• Use a quotation, a question, or another strong detail to make your introduction effective.
	• Be sure your **thesis** clearly states the two or more aspects of your topic that you are comparing and contrasting.	• Complete and answer these questions to help form a thesis: In general, *how are _____ and _____ (or _____, _____, and _____) alike, and how are they different? Why does it matter?*
Body	• Check that you clearly identify **comparisons** and contrasts.	• Add transitions such as *similarly* and *in contrast* to make your ideas clear.
	• Check that your source information is **synthesized** from several sources.	• Combine similar ideas from separate sources to avoid repetition.
	• Check that you have **organized** your comparisons and contrasts in a logical and coherent way.	• Discuss each similarity or difference one at a time, or discuss all the qualities of first one thing and then the other.
	• Check that your **facts** and details are appropriate. Avoid extraneous information or inconsistencies that do not support your thesis.	• Delete details that are not relevant to your thesis or explanations. Confirm that your information is correct and remove any errors or inconsistencies.
	• Check that you have used a variety of **sentence structures.**	• Break or combine sentences to vary their structures.
Conclusion	• Check that you have restated your thesis and summed up **main ideas.**	• Rewrite to sum up all your main points and only your main points.
	• Make sure that your essay ends on a **memorable** note.	• Add rhetorical devices, such as analogies, comparisons, or rhetorical questions, to make your conclusion more effective. Help your audience see why your subject is meaningful.

Focus on Craft: Effective Transitions

Your writing will be smoother if you use clear **transitions**, words and phrases that show the connections between ideas. Transitions that indicate a comparison include *similarly*, *likewise*, *in the same way*, and *once again*. Transitions that indicate a contrast include *although*, *in contrast*, *on the other hand*, and *however*.

Look for a transition as you read these sentences from the Student Model.

 **STUDENT MODEL** from **Canines in the Wild**
page 151; lines 33–36

> In the United States, wolves are a protected species, which means they are in danger of becoming extinct. Coyotes, on the other hand, have an incredible talent for adapting.

 Try It! Now, ask yourself these questions. Record your answers in your journal.

- What relationship does the transition *on the other hand* signal?
- Would the relationship between ideas in these sentences be different if the transition *similarly* replaced the current transition? Why or why not?

 **Fine-Tune Your Draft**

Apply It! Use these revision suggestions to prepare your final draft after rethinking how well questions of purpose, audience, and genre have been addressed.

- **Choose Effective Transitions to Convey Meaning** To ensure your ideas flow logically, use transitions between sentences and between paragraphs. Use transitions to clarify relationships between points and to be certain that you have a consistent point of view.

- **Ensure Internal and External Coherence** To present a cohesive essay within each section and as a whole, make sure that ideas, sentences, and paragraphs are organized in a logical sequence and that they flow easily.

- **Check Consistent Point of View** Make sure that the entire essay uses the same person, or voice, consistently. For example, avoid switching from first-person "I" to third-person "she."

Teacher Feedback After submitting your final draft for teacher review, **revise it in response to feedback from your teacher.**

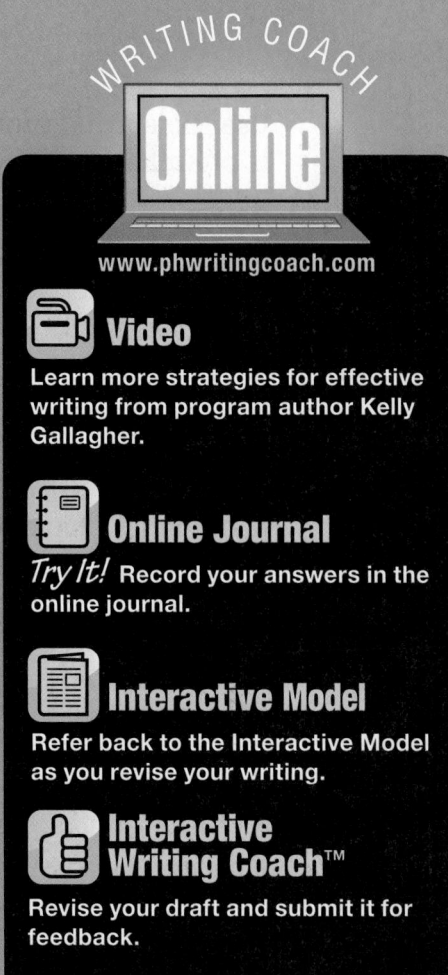

WRITING COACH

Online

www.phwritingcoach.com

Video
Learn more strategies for effective writing from program author Kelly Gallagher.

Online Journal
Try It! Record your answers in the online journal.

Interactive Model
Refer back to the Interactive Model as you revise your writing.

Interactive Writing Coach™
Revise your draft and submit it for feedback.

Editing: Making It Correct

Use the editing process to polish your work and correct errors. It is often helpful to work with a partner when editing your drafts.

As you edit, think about whether or not you have used **transitions** effectively. A transition is a word or phrase that creates a clear relationship between ideas. Then, edit your final draft for any factual errors and errors in **grammar, mechanics, and spelling**.

WRITE GUY *Jeff Anderson, M. Ed.*

WHAT DO YOU NOTICE?

Zoom in on Conventions Focus on transitions as you zoom in on these sentences from the Student Model.

> 📰 **STUDENT MODEL** from **Canines in the Wild**
> page 151; lines 33–36, 43–44
>
> In the United States, wolves are a protected species, which means they are in danger of becoming extinct. Coyotes, on the other hand, have an incredible talent for adapting....
>
> Thus, while coyotes and wolves look alike, their behaviors and situations are different.

Now, ask yourself: *Which words and phrases create a relationship between ideas?*

Perhaps you identified the transition *on the other hand,* which makes clear the relationship of contrast between the first two sentences in the passage.

The transition *Thus* makes clear the cause-and-effect relationship between the last paragraph and the paragraphs that came before it.

Partner Talk Discuss this question with a partner: *What other transitions could the Student Model author have used to express the same relationships?*

> To learn more about phrases and clauses, see Chapter 19 of your Grammar Handbook.

Grammar Mini-Lesson: Commas With Transitions

To learn more, see Chapter 25.

Most **transitions** should be set off from the rest of the sentence by **commas.** The comma may be omitted after a short introductory transition if the sentence is clear without it. Notice how commas set off transitions in the Student Model.

 STUDENT MODEL from **Canines in the Wild** page 150; lines 19–22

In contrast, most coyotes weigh from 20 to 30 pounds. Nevertheless, the size difference won't always help you tell the difference between wolves and coyotes.

 Try It! Identify two transitions in this passage. Also indicate if any commas need to be added.

The Fourth of July celebrates American independence. In contrast Cinco de Mayo commemorates a Mexican victory in a battle. Accordingly it is a celebration of Mexican culture.

 Apply It! **Edit your draft for grammar, punctuation, capitalization, and spelling errors.** Capitalize appropriate words correctly and use an electronic or print dictionary or other resource to check your spelling. Make sure to use transitions for **coherence** between sentences and paragraphs. Use commas correctly.

 Video
Learn effective editing techniques from program author Jeff Anderson.

 Online Journal
Try It! Record your answers in the online journal.

Interactive Model
Refer back to the Interactive Model as you edit your writing.

 **Interactive Writing Coach™**
Edit your draft. Check it against the rubric and then submit it for feedback.

 Use the rubric to evaluate your essay. If necessary, rethink, rewrite, or revise.

Rubric for Expository Writing: Compare-and-Contrast Essay	Rating Scale
Ideas: How well do you explain the similarities and differences of your topics?	Not very Very 1 2 3 4 5 6
Organization: How well do you organize the similarities and differences of your topic?	1 2 3 4 5 6
Voice: How well do you engage the reader?	1 2 3 4 5 6
Word Choice: How clearly do your words convey your specific ideas?	1 2 3 4 5 6
Sentence Fluency: How effectively do you use transitions?	1 2 3 4 5 6
Conventions: How correct is your usage of commas with transitions?	1 2 3 4 5 6

WRITING COACH
Online
www.phwritingcoach.com

Publishing

Get your compare-and-contrast essay ready for presentation so you can share what you learned with others. Then, choose a way to **publish it for the appropriate audience**.

Wrap Up Your Presentation

To get your essay ready, you may need to make a new, clean copy. Be sure to add images of the items you're comparing to help readers see the similarities and differences. Finally, make sure that your title grabs the reader's attention and indicates your essay's topic.

Publish Your Essay

Use the chart to identify a way to publish your essay.

If your audience is...	...then publish it by...
Classmates and others at your school	• Submitting it to a school newspaper or magazine • Creating a podcast for classmates to hear
Your local community	• Submitting it to a local print or online newspaper • Reading and discussing it on local public-access TV
The larger community	• Posting it online and inviting responses • Entering it in a regional or national essay contest

 Extend Your Research

Think more about the topic on which you wrote your compare-and-contrast essay. What else would you like to know about this topic? As you write your ideas, use specific details to describe and explain. Increase the specificity of your details based on the type of information you are recording.

- Brainstorm for several questions you would like to research and then consult, or discuss, with others.

- Formulate, or develop, a plan about how you will answer these questions. Decide where you will find more information—on the Internet, at the library, or through other sources.

- Finally, learn more about your topic by following through with your research plan.

 **The Big Question: Why Write?** What should we tell and what should we describe to make information clear?

21st Century Learning

MAKE YOUR WRITING COUNT

Entertain Audiences With a Humorous Skit

Compare-and-contrast essays identify similarities and differences between two people, things, or issues. In another context, points of contrast can be emphasized for humor. In fact, comedians often use differences as the basis for skits. Use humor to communicate the message of one of your compare-and-contrast essays.

Produce a **humorous skit** inspired by the differences explored in a compare-and-contrast essay. Develop interesting characters representing the two people, items, or issues analyzed in one of your peers' essays. Perform the skit live or video-record it.

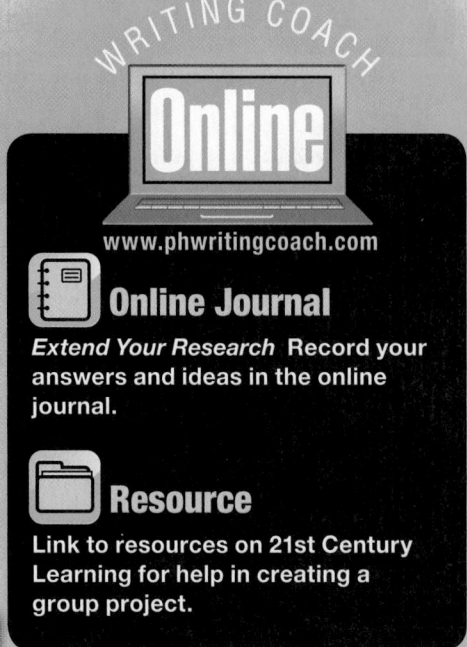

WRITING COACH

Online

www.phwritingcoach.com

Online Journal
Extend Your Research Record your answers and ideas in the online journal.

Resource
Link to resources on 21st Century Learning for help in creating a group project.

Here's your action plan.

1. Choose roles, including writer, director, performer, and prop master.

2. With your group, evaluate your peers' compare-and-contrast essays. Choose one that compares items or ideas that are easily represented—and that might lend themselves to comedy.

3. View comical skits online. Then, write a skit that portrays each item or idea as a character.

   - Write funny dialogue for each character.
   - Make sure that similarities and differences are clear. Exaggeration may help enhance the humor.
   - Assign two group members to play the parts.
   - Work as a team to rehearse the skit, using costumes and props.
   - If possible, perform and record the skit using a video camera.

4. Present the skit to the class or school either live or as a video. Consider posting the video online.

Listening and Speaking Listen actively as your group writes the skit together. Take turns making suggestions for adding humor during the planning and rehearsal stages. During the performance, keep your peers' feedback in mind. Work as a team to entertain and inform your audience. Listen for feedback.

Your Turn ▶ **Writing for Media: Technical Newsletter**

Technical Newsletter

A **technical newsletter** gives information about the latest advances in electronics or other technologies. It often compares and contrasts new developments or products to help readers make informed decisions. Newsletters are often e-mailed or sent as direct-mail, or mail sent to a specific target audience. Many technical newsletters are geared to audiences of subscribers who are already familiar with the technical field. Others are aimed at more general audiences who need to make a purchase or research new developments in the field.

 *Try It!* Study this sample technical newsletter. Then, answer the five questions about it. Record your answers in your journal.

1. What topic does the newsletter address? Restate the **controlling idea** in your own words.

2. Describe the newsletter's **audience**—are they general readers ready to buy, or "techies" familiar with the topic? Cite details to explain your answer.

3. List the main **similarities** and **differences** that the newsletter points out.

4. Does the newsletter **use point-by-point** or **block organization?** Does the organization help make the similarities and differences clear to you? Why or why not?

5. What **transitions** help make the similarities and differences clearer?

Extension Find another example of a technical newsletter, and compare it with this one.

TECHNO-TIPS

MP3 Players

An MP3 player is a pocket-sized electronic device that stores and plays back music or other audio files. There are two basic kinds: hard-drive-based MP3 players and flash-based MP3 players. Each has its benefits and drawbacks.

Hard-drive-based MP3 players, sometimes called hard-disk players, have the most gigabytes. This means they have more storage space for your music collection. In fact, some hard-drive-based players can store as many as 40,000 songs. In terms of cost, you get the most storage space for your money with one of these players. However, you also get the largest and heaviest MP3 player. Micro-version, but they also have less storage space. They also do not solve the biggest problem of all hard-drive-based players: Sudden movements cause them to skip. Thus, hard-drive-based players are impractical to use while jogging, running, or working out.

Flash-based MP3 players, sometimes called flash-memory players, are the original MP3 design. They are smaller and lighter than other players, and they do not skip. Their storage space, however, is fairly small. Depending on the model, it ranges from as few as 10 to as many as 8,000 songs. Also, per unit of storage space, flash-based players cost more than their hard-drive-based cousins. Moreover, they can be harder to operate, especially if they have lots of special features.

Create a Technical Newsletter

Follow these steps to create a technical newsletter for a specific audience. To plan your newsletter, review the graphic organizers on pages R24–R27 and choose one that suits your needs.

Prewriting

- Choose a technology that you might like to research. For example, you might choose video games, cell phones, or cameras.
- Determine your audience and purpose. Will you be updating an already informed audience or teaching a more general audience?
- After doing research, decide on two aspects of the topic that you will compare and contrast.
- List the similarities and differences that you would like to discuss.
- Develop a controlling idea that makes a general statement about the similarities and differences.

Drafting

- Begin with a paragraph that identifies your topic. Include a thesis about the two aspects of the topic you will discuss.
- Discuss similarities and differences using block or point-by-point organization. Include graphic elements, such as subheadings or boldfaced text, to help organize your ideas.
- Use correct terminology in discussing the topic. If your audience is new to the topic, include definitions or explanations of unfamiliar terms.
- Use clear transitions to show comparisons, contrasts, and other relationships.
- Give your newsletter a catchy title that identifies its content.

Revising and Editing

- Check that your information is accurate and uses correct terminology.
- Make sure that your information is logically organized and will be clear to your particular audience.
- Remove any details that are not relevant to your purpose.

Publishing

Create your own technical Web site and post your newsletter as a multimedia presentation. Use available technology to add text and graphics to the Web site and your newsletter.

WRITING COACH

Online

www.phwritingcoach.com

Online Journal

Try It! Record your answers in the online journal.

Interactive Graphic Organizers

Choose from a variety of graphic organizers to plan and develop your project.

Partner Talk

Discuss your topic with a partner. Ask what questions or concerns he or she might have on the topic of your newsletter, and take notes about his or her responses. Consider your partner's responses in deciding on the information to include in your newsletter.

Writing for Assessment

Many standardized tests include a prompt that asks you to write an expository essay. You can use the prompts on these pages to practice. Your responses should include most of the same characteristics as your compare-and-contrast essay. (See page 146.)

 Try It! To begin, read the **expository** prompt and the information on format and academic vocabulary. Then write an essay by following the instructions shown in the ABCDs of On-Demand Writing.

Format
The prompt directs you to write a compare-and-contrast *expository essay*. Include an introduction, body paragraphs with similarities and differences, and a conclusion.

Expository Prompt
Write an expository essay that compares and contrasts two different kinds of household pets. Discuss similarities and differences of owning each pet and the work involved in caring for each.

Academic Vocabulary
Remember that *similarities* are elements that are alike; *differences* are elements that are not alike.

The ABCDs of On-Demand Writing

Use the following ABCDs to help you respond to the prompt.

Before you write your draft:

A ttack the prompt [1 MINUTE]

- Circle or highlight important verbs in the prompt. Draw a line from the verb to what it refers to.
- Rewrite the prompt in your own words.

B rainstorm possible answers [4 MINUTES]

- Create a graphic organizer to generate ideas.
- Use one for each part of the prompt if necessary.

C hoose the order of your response [1 MINUTE]

- Think about the best way to organize your ideas.
- Number your ideas in the order you will write about them. Cross out ideas you will not be using.

After you write your draft:

D etect errors before turning in the draft [1 MINUTE]

- Carefully reread your writing.
- Make sure that your response makes sense and is complete.
- Look for spelling, punctuation, and grammar errors.

 More Prompts for Practice

Apply It! Respond to Prompts 1 and 2 by writing **expository essays**. As you write, be sure to:

- Grab readers' attention with an **effective introductory paragraph** that states a **clear purpose** and end with a memorable **concluding paragraph**

- Use a **variety of sentence structures, rhetorical devices, and transitions** to help make your writing cohesive and interesting

- Use a variety of examples and details to support your ideas. Accurately **synthesize ideas** into a cohesive whole

- For your body, choose a logical **organizing structure appropriate to your facts and details**

- Include **relevant information** with **no inconsistencies**. Remove any extraneous information

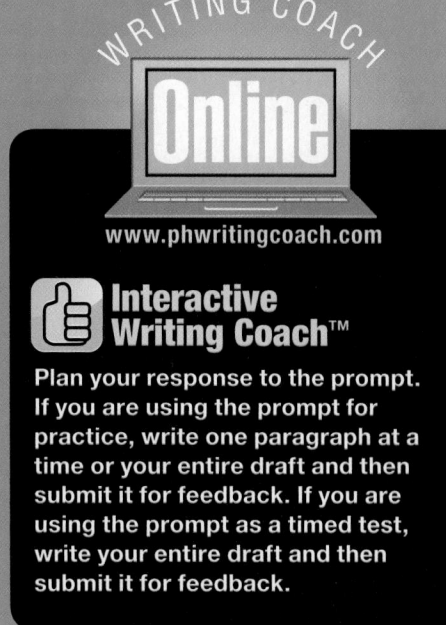

WRITING COACH

Online
www.phwritingcoach.com

Interactive Writing Coach™

Plan your response to the prompt. If you are using the prompt for practice, write one paragraph at a time or your entire draft and then submit it for feedback. If you are using the prompt as a timed test, write your entire draft and then submit it for feedback.

Remember **ABCD**

Attack the prompt

Brainstorm possible answers

Choose the order of your response

Detect errors before turning in the draft

Prompt 1 Soccer vs. football? Swimming vs. track? Choose two sports, and write an essay comparing and contrasting them. Be sure that you explain the similarities and differences in a way that would be clear to someone unfamiliar with the sport.

Prompt 2 Write a compare-and-contrast essay in which you discuss the similarities and differences between two foods you enjoy. Focus on their nutritional benefits as well as their taste. You might also consider other qualities, such as the cost or ease of preparation.

Spiral Review: Poetry Respond to Prompt 3 by writing a **poem**. Make sure your poem reflects all of the characteristics described on page 120, including:

- **Poetic techniques**
- **Figurative language**
- **Graphic elements**

Prompt 3 Think about your school. What are your favorite things about your school? What are the best things that have happened there? Write a poem expressing your ideas and feelings about your school.

CHAPTER 9

PERSUASION

What Do You Think?

Should students be allowed to use cell phones in school? This is an issue that people debate. Some schools forbid students to carry and use cell phones; other schools allow cell phones.

Maybe you already have an opinion on student cell phone use. Or perhaps you want to learn more about the issue before taking a position. In either case, one day you might want to convince someone to share your opinion. When you use words to convince people to think or act in a certain way, you are using persuasion.

Try It! Take a few minutes to list reasons why students should and should not be allowed to use cell phones in school.

Consider these questions as you work on your list.

- What do students use their cell phones for in school?
- What useful purposes could cell phones serve in the classroom?
- How could cell phone use in school affect learning?
- Is having a cell phone in school a safety issue? Why?

Review the list you made, and then choose a position on the issue. **Plan a draft by developing a clear thesis or controlling idea** that states your position. Then find a partner, and take turns expressing your thesis ideas to one another.

What's Ahead

In this chapter, you will review two strong examples of a persuasive essay: a Mentor Text and a Student Model. Then, using the examples as guidance, you will write a persuasive essay of your own.

WRITING COACH

Online

www.phwritingcoach.com

Online Journal

Try It! Record your answers and ideas in the online journal.

You can also record and save your answers and ideas on pop-up sticky notes in the eText.

Connect to the Big Questions

Discuss these questions with your partner:

1 What do you think? Which do you think is more important and why—the community's right to ensure that students are not distracted by cell phones or the individual student's right to use a cell phone?

2 Why write? What is your point of view? How will you know if you have convinced others?

PERSUASIVE WRITING

Persuasion is writing that is meant to convince readers to agree with the writer's opinion. In this chapter, you will explore a special type of persuasive essay, the op-ed piece. An op-ed piece is a signed piece that appears in a newspaper or magazine and tries to persuade readers to agree with the writer's views on an issue. An op-ed piece is written by someone who does not work for the newspaper or magazine.

You will develop the op-ed piece by taking it through each of the steps of the writing process: prewriting, drafting, revising, editing, and publishing. You will also have an opportunity to create an advertisement. To preview the criteria for how your op-ed piece will be evaluated, see the rubric on page 189.

FEATURE ASSIGNMENT

Persuasive Essay: Op-Ed Piece

An effective persuasive essay has these characteristics:

- A **lead** that introduces the topic or issue and captures readers' interest

- A **clear thesis statement** that tells the writer's opinion

- **Persuasive arguments** that are organized in logical order

- **Evidence that is logically organized** so that it supports the writer's opinion. Evidence may include examples, facts, statistics, and expert opinions.

- Responses to readers' **concerns and counter-arguments**

- **Effective sentence structure** and correct spelling, grammar, and usage

- A **conclusion** that restates your position and ends on a memorable note

- **A natural but authoritative voice** that appeals to both reason and emotion

An effective op-ed piece also includes:

- A response to a **current event** or **topic**

- A **tight focus** on a single event

- A **call to action**

Other Forms of Persuasive Writing

In addition to an op-ed piece, there are other forms of persuasive writing, including:

Advertisements are paid announcements that try to convince people to do or buy something.

Editorials state the opinion of the editors and publishers of news organizations. Editorials are usually about current issues and appear in newspapers, magazines, or on television, radio, or the Internet.

Letters to the editor are written by readers who express an opinion in response to an article that has been published in a newspaper or magazine.

Persuasive essays use logic and reasoning to persuade readers to adopt a certain action or point of view.

Persuasive speeches aim at winning an audience's support for a policy, position, or action.

Propaganda uses emotional appeals and often biased, false, or misleading information to persuade people to think or act in a certain way. Propaganda is often about political issues.

Reviews evaluate items and activities such as books and movies. A review often states an opinion on whether people should spend time and money on the item or activity.

Try It! For each audience and purpose described, choose a form, such as a speech, letter, or review, that is appropriate for conveying your intended meaning to the audience. Explain your choices.

- To disagree with an editorial in your local newspaper
- To convince classmates to read a book that you enjoyed
- To encourage listeners of a radio station to buy tickets to an upcoming concert

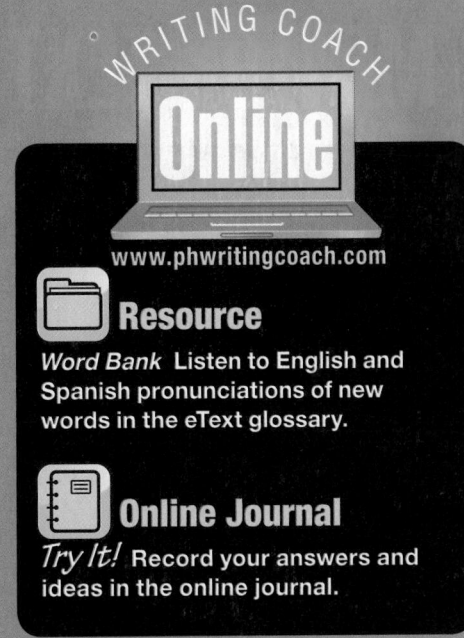

WORD BANK

People use these vocabulary words when trying to persuade others. Work with a partner. Take turns speaking and writing each word in a sentence. If you are unsure of the pronunciation or meaning of a word, use the Glossary or a dictionary to check the definition or pronunciation.

advantage	factor
consequence	oppose
controversial	support

MENTOR TEXT — Op-Ed Piece

Learn From Experience

Read the op-ed piece on pages 174–175. As you read, take notes to develop your understanding of basic sight and English vocabulary. Then, read the numbered notes in the margins to learn about how the author presented her ideas.

Answer the *Try It!* questions online or in your journal.

---

1 The author wrote a description of an animal shelter to introduce the issue: the overcrowding at an animal shelter. The detailed description is an effective **lead** that captures the reader's attention.

Try It! Which adjectives did the author use in the first three sentences to help readers create a strong visual image of an animal shelter?

2 The **thesis** presents the author's main message and persuasive argument by naming the issue and stating the author's viewpoint.

Try It! Does the author establish a clear thesis or position? What issue or problem does she describe, and what solution does she suggest?

3 The author offers three **persuasive arguments** for the need for people to adopt pets from shelters.

Try It! Based on these arguments and the author's purpose, who would you say is her targeted audience? Explain.

Extension Find another example of an op-ed piece, and compare it with this one.

Looking for a Pet?
Look No Further Than Maiden Point Shelter

by Cindy Trumbore

1 Maiden Point Shelter is overflowing with cats and dogs. Every cage and kennel is filled to capacity, and heartrending meows and barks come from extra cages lining the hallways. The shelter is at its most overcrowded since it was opened in 1993. **2** There is a simple solution to the overcrowding at Maiden Point Shelter: more people in our area need to adopt pets, rather than buying them. Yet judging from the "designer" pets we see on the streets of our town, the public seems strangely unconvinced of this fact.

There are two main reasons for the problem, according to Biz Raleigh, the director. First, we had a mild winter, so more cats were outside. As a result, there are more litters of kittens now. There is another surprising reason, however, for the overcrowding. Raleigh has noticed a direct link between the number of mortgage foreclosures in our area, and the number of pets that get brought to the shelter. When people lose their homes, they are often forced to find housing that doesn't allow pets. **3** In fact, Raleigh says that in the past six months, Maiden Point received nearly 200 cats and dogs alone. That's a 100% increase over the previous six months.

"We're at the point where we'll have to start putting unadoptable animals down to make room for the ones with a better chance," Raleigh says, sighing. "I really don't know why people looking for a pet don't come here first." **3** She points out that pets from pet stores have often been raised in unclean, unhealthy, crowded conditions, especially dogs from so-called "puppy mills." In contrast, the shelter pets are spayed and neutered, and treated for problems such as heartworm and fleas, before they are adopted out.

3 People especially need to open their minds to adopting older pets, she says. Some people assume that when they get an older pet, they will have to "undo" the bad habits it

learned from a previous owner. However, Raleigh says that just the opposite can be true. ❹ "An older pet is often

35   much more used to small children and is housebroken compared to a kitten or puppy," she says.

If you have never owned a pet, consider getting one from Maiden Point. There are many benefits, starting with your health. A study done at the State University of New York at

40   Buffalo in 2001 found that dog and cat owners with high blood pressure who were in stressful job situations had lower increases in pressure than people without pets.

There is a very practical reason to consider adopting from the Maiden Shelter. A "designer" dog or cat can easily

45   cost $500 to $800. At Maiden Point, says Raleigh, for a mere $100 you can get a cat or dog that is already spayed or neutered, a month's supply of pet food, a safety collar or flea collar, and a free check-up with a veterinarian. In case you have your heart set on a certain breed, Raleigh says that

50   many popular breeds, such as labs, beagles, and Siamese cats, occasionally turn up at the shelter.

❺ So if you're pet-shopping, make Maiden Point Shelter (555-555-2000 or www.maidenpointshelter.org) your first stop. You can fill out a short application, get your references

55   checked, and go home with a pet the same day. The shelter is open weekdays from 9:00 to 5:30 p.m. and Saturdays from 10:00 a.m. through 3:00. The pet you save will reward you with many years of love, gratitude, and good health.

❹ The author describes the benefits of owning older pets. These details provide answers to reader **counter-arguments** about adopting older animals.

Try It! The author uses a quotation to address reader counter-arguments. Do you think stating someone's exact words might help to convince the reader? Why or why not?

❺ In her **conclusion,** the author includes a clear call to action by inviting readers to help solve the problem.

Try It! Why do you think the author included a telephone number and Web site in her call to action?

STUDENT MODEL Op-Ed Piece

With a small group, take turns reading the Student Model aloud. As you read, practice newly acquired vocabulary by correctly producing the word's sound. Ask yourself if you find the writer's arguments convincing. Identify the evidence that the writer uses to support his ideas.

 ## Use a Reader's Eye

Now, reread the Student Model. On your copy of the Student Model, use the Reader's Response Symbols to react to what you read.

Reader's Response Symbols

+ I strongly agree with this.

− I strongly disagree with this.

? I have a question about this.

! Wow! That is cool/weird/interesting.

Collaborate with a partner to express your opinions and share your responses to the Student Model. Take notes and discuss responses that were the same for both of you, and that were different.

There Is Something You Can Do About TRAFFIC

by Xander Johnson

"Traffic is just one of life's inconveniences. Sure, it's frustrating, but what can you really do about it?" This was how my mom responded to my question about the traffic she encounters on

5 her daily commute to work. The traffic not only is a frustration for her as she sits in her car waiting, but also for our family as we sit at home waiting for her. Frequently, we end up eating dinner on our own because she gets home too late to join us.

10 Traffic is more than an inconvenience. According to the Department of Transportation, the average commute time one way has expanded from twenty or thirty minutes to as much as three hours per day. As a result of all this time on the road, we are

15 using up too much fuel and polluting the airways. By showing people what they can do to decrease the amount of traffic and giving them incentives to make changes, we can fix the traffic problem.

First, each of us can explore mass transit options,

20 and use them. Employers can help by promoting four-day workweeks and staggering work hours. People object to carpooling, but many will not if there is a tax incentive involved. If we write to our legislators, we can make this happen.

25 Finally, once we are on those traffic-snarled freeways, we can practice simple courtesy, allowing cars in when they clearly need to enter. Department

1

More Prompts for Practice

Apply It! Respond to Prompts 1 and 2 by writing **persuasive essays** that influence the attitudes or actions of a specific audience on a specific issue. As you write, be sure to:

- Identify an appropriate **audience**
- Establish a clear **thesis** or position
- Anticipate and respond to the views, concerns, and **counter-arguments** of others
- Logically **organize** your arguments and evidence so that they support your viewpoint
- Differentiate between **fact** and **opinion**, and support all your opinions with facts

> **Prompt 1** Imagine that your school has a new program. Students who ride their bicycles to school receive points toward a service award. Write a persuasive essay stating your position on this program.

> **Prompt 2** Imagine that your school principal is planning to require that all students participate in cleaning up litter around the building. Write a persuasive essay stating your position on this issue.

Spiral Review: Expository Respond to Prompt 3 by writing an **expository essay**. Your essay should include:

- A clearly stated **purpose**, or controlling idea
- A logical **organization**, including an effective **introduction** and **conclusion**
- A variety of **sentence structures** and **rhetorical devices**
- Clear **transitions** to link ideas and paragraphs
- Appropriate **facts** and **details** without any extraneous information or inconsistencies
- Accurately **synthesized ideas** from several sources

> **Prompt 3** Sleep is essential for all humans. Write an essay about the effects of not getting enough sleep.

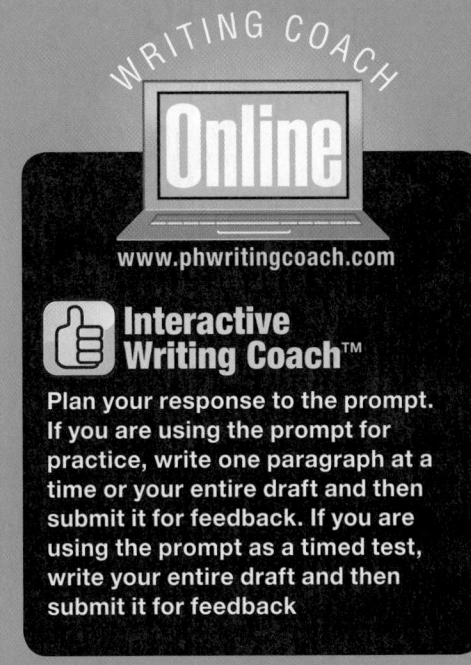

WRITING COACH

Online

www.phwritingcoach.com

Interactive Writing Coach™

Plan your response to the prompt. If you are using the prompt for practice, write one paragraph at a time or your entire draft and then submit it for feedback. If you are using the prompt as a timed test, write your entire draft and then submit it for feedback

Remember **ABCD**

- **A**ttack the prompt
- **B**rainstorm possible answers
- **C**hoose the order of your response
- **D**etect errors before turning in the draft

CHAPTER 10

RESPONSE *to* LITERATURE

What Do You Think?

Authors have purposes for writing. Some authors write to inform. Some write to entertain. Others write to persuade.

Part of being an active reader is analyzing the author's purpose. You think about the author's purpose and find details that show how the author achieves that purpose.

Try It! Think about your favorite book. What do you think the author was trying to communicate by writing this book?

Consider these questions as you participate in an extended discussion with a partner. Take turns expressing your ideas and feelings.

- How did you feel when reading this book?
- How did the author achieve his or her purpose?
- Do you think the author did a good job achieving his or her purpose? Why or why not?
- What details support your answer?

What's Ahead

In this chapter, you will review two strong examples of an interpretative response essay: a Mentor Text and a Student Model. Then, using the examples as guides, you will write an interpretative response essay of your own.

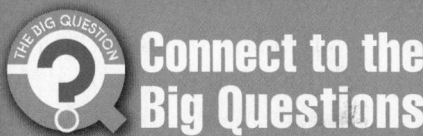
THE BIG QUESTION

Connect to the Big Questions

Discuss these questions with your partner:

1 What do you think? What do readers bring to a text that writers may not?

2 Why write? What should you write about to make others interested in a text?

INTERPRETATIVE RESPONSE

In this chapter, you will explore a special kind of interpretative response, the review of a short story. An interpretative response analyzes an author's work. It often examines story elements, such as theme and plot, as well as features, such as imagery and mood. It discusses what the work communicates to the reader. The reader states his or her opinions about the work and supports those opinions with details from the text.

You will develop your review of a short story by taking it through each of the steps of the writing process: prewriting, drafting, revising, editing, and publishing. You will also have an opportunity to write a movie review. To preview the criteria for how your review of a short story will be evaluated, see the rubric on page 215.

FEATURE ASSIGNMENT

Interpretative Response: Review of a Short Story

An effective interpretative response has these characteristics:

- A strong, interesting **focus or thesis statement**

- **Details** that are focused, organized, and coherent

- A **summary of important features** of the author's work

- **Sustained evidence,** such as examples and quotations from the text to defend and support ideas

- **Ideas and arguments** that demonstrate personal insights, judgments, and understanding of the text

- **Effective sentence structure** and correct spelling, grammar, and usage

A review of a short story also includes:

- an **analysis of story elements,** such as character, plot, setting, and theme

- details about the imagery and mood the author created

- summary of the author's message and overall opinion of the story

Other Forms of Interpretative Response

In addition to a review of a short story, there are other forms of interpretative response, including:

Blog comments on an author's Web site share readers' ideas about an author's work. Readers express their opinions and discuss their understanding of what an author's work means.

Comparison essays explore similarities and differences between two or more works of literature. For example, a comparison essay may compare how main characters in two stories handle a similar problem.

Letters to authors analyze an author's work and explain the reader's response to it. The reader shares with the author of the work his or her thoughts and feelings about the content of the work and about the author's writing style.

Response to literature essays analyze and interpret an author's work. These kinds of essays examine what an author states directly and indirectly and what those statements mean. Response to literature essays also judge how well an author has accomplished what he or she has set out to do.

Try It! For each audience and purpose described, choose a form, such as a letter to an author or a comparison essay, that is appropriate for conveying your intended meaning to the audience. Explain your choices.

- To show a teacher how two novels are alike
- To tell an author how much her poetry meant to you
- To persuade classmates to read a particular book

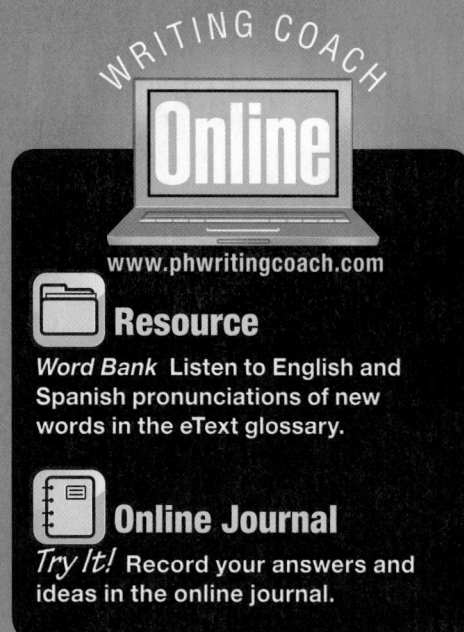

WRITING COACH

Online

www.phwritingcoach.com

Resource

Word Bank Listen to English and Spanish pronunciations of new words in the eText glossary.

Online Journal

Try It! Record your answers and ideas in the online journal.

WORD BANK

Affixes are word parts used to change the meaning of a root word. For example, the word *write* becomes *prewriting* when the prefix *pre-* and the suffix *-ing* are added to the root word *write*. Work with a partner. Take turns using each word in a sentence. If you are unsure of the meaning of a word, identify any roots or affixes that might help you infer its meaning. If you are still unsure, use the Glossary or a dictionary to check the definition.

analysis	plausible
consider	profound
offensive	reflect

MENTOR TEXT

Review of a Short Story

Learn From Experience

 After reading the review on pages 200–201, read the numbered notes in the margins to learn how the author presented her ideas.

Answer the *Try It!* questions online or in your notebook.

---

1 The **introduction** provides background about Sandra Cisneros.

Try It! What does the reviewer mean when she says that Cisneros grew up "straddling two countries"?

2 The reviewer **summarizes** an **important feature** of *The House on Mango Street,* supporting it with a **quotation** from Sandra Cisneros.

Try It! How is each story like a pearl? How is the book as a whole like a necklace?

3 The **thesis statement** provides a strong focus for the review.

Try It! What does the thesis statement reveal about the plot of *The House on Mango Street*?

Extension Find another example of a review of short story, and compare it with this one.

From Sandra Cisneros: Latina Writer and Activist

by Caryn Mirriam-Goldberg

1 Sandra Cisneros was born in Chicago, Illinois, but she was actually born into the traditions, histories, and languages of two countries: the United States and Mexico. Her father was Mexican, and her mother was Mexican American. Her family spoke two languages and frequently journeyed to Mexico for long visits with her father's family. Cisneros grew up straddling two countries, each with its own challenges and gifts, each with its own way of defining Mexicans, Americans, and Mexican Americans. . . .

Each of the pieces [in Sandra Cisneros's *The House on Mango Street*] tells of the bittersweet life in a Chicago barrio. **2** While each chapter works as a story on its own, each is also part of the larger story. This structure, according to Cisneros, was not an accident. She wanted to write a book that a reader could pick up, open to any chapter, and find a story that made its own sense. "You would understand each story like a little pearl, or you could look at the whole thing like a necklace," says Cisneros. "That's what I always knew from the day that I wrote the first one. I said, "I'm going to do a whole series of these, and it's going to be like this, and it's all connected."

3 She succeeded in creating both pearls and a necklace linking them, but she did more than that. She told a story of a girl similar to herself, named Esperanza, who found herself becoming an artist to escape "the trap of the barrio." Cisneros wanted to show people what life in the barrio was like as well as what it was not like. The book stood in sharp contrast to "those people who want to make our barrios look like Sesame Street or some place really warm and beautiful," Cisneros says. At a time when homes like the one she grew up in were either portrayed as "warm and beautiful" or ignored, Cisneros portrayed how poverty weighs people down, and how people may triumph anyway. . . .

35   Esperanza, a girl who believes in and hopes for a better life in *The House on Mango Street*, lives the everyday challenges of being poor and Mexican. **4** But through her name, she helps readers see the hope buried under the trash and danger: "In English my name means hope,"
40 Esperanza says. "In Spanish it means too many letters. It means sadness, it means waiting. It is like the number nine. A muddy color. It is the Mexican records my father plays on Sunday mornings when he is shaving, songs like sobbing." Esperanza leads readers through the barrio,
45 always dreaming of a real house, one with stairs, several bathrooms, and a big yard full of trees and grass. She hopes, just like Cisneros hoped, for a house so that "we don't have to pay rent to anybody, or share the yard with the people downstairs, or be careful not to make too much noise, and
50 there isn't a landlord banging on the ceiling with a broom."
    5 Eventually both the fictional Esperanza and the real Cisneros find a home in their own hearts. And they make a promise to return and speak for the family and friends in the barrio they left behind.

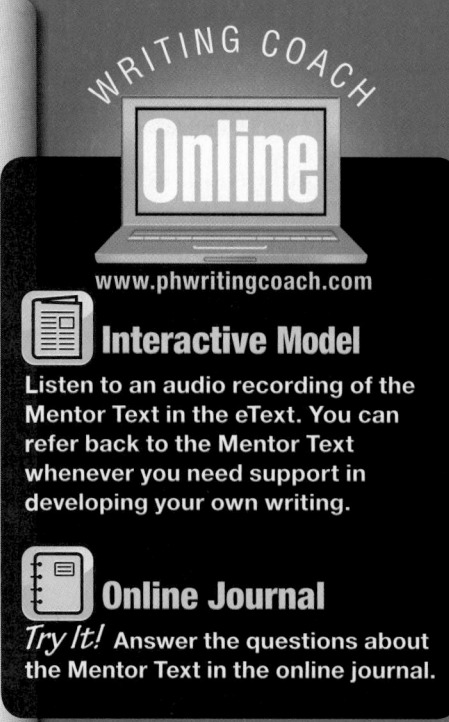

WRITING COACH

Online

www.phwritingcoach.com

Interactive Model
Listen to an audio recording of the Mentor Text in the eText. You can refer back to the Mentor Text whenever you need support in developing your own writing.

Online Journal
Try It! Answer the questions about the Mentor Text in the online journal.

4 The author provides **relevant evidence** from the book, including a **quotation**.

    Try It! How does the evidence support the thesis of the review?

5 The **conclusion** reveals how Esperanza resolves her conflict.

    Try It! Why is an examination of the book's resolution a logical way to end the review?

STUDENT MODEL

Review of a Short Story

With a small group, take turns reading this Student Model aloud. As you read, practice newly acquired vocabulary by correctly producing the word's sound. Look for evidence in the text that supports your understanding of the review.

 ## Use a Reader's Eye

Now, reread the Student Model. On your copy of the Student Model, use the Reader's Response Symbols to react to what you read.

Reader's Response Symbols

+   **I agree with this point.**

−   **This isn't clear to me.**

?   **I have a question about this.**

!   **Well said!**

Express your opinions, ideas, and feelings about the Student Model to a partner. Take notes on your partner's thoughts and discuss responses that were the same for both of you, as well as responses that were different.

Gary Soto's "Seventh Grade": Something We Can All Relate To

by Stephanie Chang

Have you ever liked someone so much that you tried too hard to get that person's attention? I have, and I bet you have, too. That's exactly what happens in Gary Soto's short story "Seventh
5 Grade." You'll laugh as you read about the things Victor does to get a girl named Teresa to notice him. This story is about what happens when you pretend to be something you are not. The characters in this story sound like people you know.

10 The story takes place on the first day of seventh grade. Victor and his friend Michael are thinking about silly ways, such as making faces, to get girls' attention. Victor has a major crush on Teresa and wants to get her attention.

15 Victor is like other kids our age. He is not sure how to act or what to say. When Teresa first greets him, saying, "Hi, Victor," his cheeks turn red as he says, "Yeah, that's me." He's embarrassed that he said something so silly and
20 gets frustrated. He wonders why he couldn't just say "something nice." This has happened to me too.

Later that day, in French class, the teacher asks if anyone knows French. Victor sees a chance to show off in front of the girl of his dreams. He raises
25 his hand, even though he doesn't know French. Unfortunately for him, the teacher asks him a

1

question in French. The author helps the reader imagine Victor's reaction when he writes: "Great rosebushes of red bloomed on Victor's cheeks."

30   Victor is lucky that Teresa doesn't know French, so he ends up impressing her. The reader knows Victor is thrilled because the "rosebushes" of shame on his cheeks become "bouquets of love"! His cheeks are still red but for another reason.

35   We've all been embarrassed at one time or another, and the author does a great job of showing how that happens. Not all of our embarrassments end on a happy note, but the happy ending of "Seventh Grade" makes you smile. At the same
40 time, you'll clearly see the author's point: you can save yourself a lot of worry and embarrassment if you just be yourself. You'll enjoy this story because it's easy to understand how the characters feel.

2

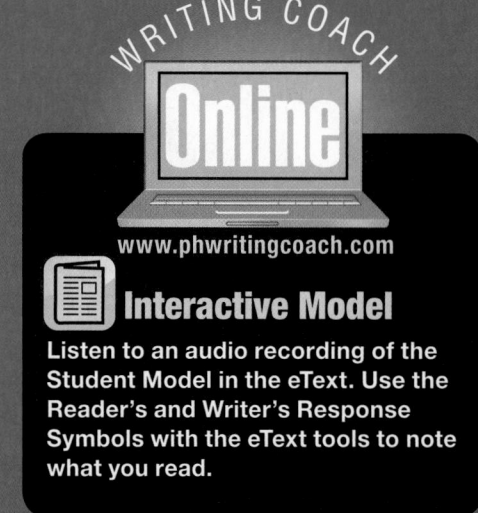

WRITING COACH

Online

www.phwritingcoach.com

Interactive Model

Listen to an audio recording of the Student Model in the eText. Use the Reader's and Writer's Response Symbols with the eText tools to note what you read.

Use a Writer's Eye

Now, evaluate the piece as a writer. On your copy of the Student Model, use the Writer's Response Symbols to react to what you read. Identify places where the student writer uses characteristics of an effective review of a short story.

Writer's Response Symbols	
C.T.	**Clearly stated thesis**
I.A.	**In-depth analysis**
S.E.	**Effective supporting evidence**
E.Q.	**Effective quotations**

Your Turn

**Feature Assignment:
Review of a Short Story**

Prewriting

Plan a first draft of your review of a short story **by determining an appropriate topic.** You can select from the Topic Bank or come up with an idea of your own.

 Choose From the Topic Bank

TOPIC BANK

Response to Amy Tan's "Two Kinds" Choose one of the memorable characters in "Two Kinds" by Amy Tan. Write a review of the story in which you discuss the traits that make this character stand out.

Response to Plot Think about a story you've read that you enjoyed reading. Write a review of the story in which you summarize the plot and explain why you enjoyed the story.

Response to a Mentor Text Read the excerpt from *The Pigman & Me* by Paul Zindel on page 68. Write a review of the story in which you summarize the conflict between the two characters and discuss the characters' responses.

 Choose Your Own Topic

Determine an appropriate topic on your own by using the following **range of strategies** to generate ideas.

Thought and Discussion

- Discuss a favorite story with friends. Take notes about their ideas and feelings. How are their reactions alike? How do they differ?
- Think about a story that surprised you in some way. Consider the reasons why you were surprised. Compare your reaction with that of another student.

Review your responses and choose a topic.

Narrow Your Topic

If you choose a topic that is too broad, your writing will not have a clear focus.

Apply It! Use a graphic organizer like the one shown to narrow your topic.

- Write your general topic in the first box, and narrow your topic as you move down the chart.
- Your last box should hold your narrowest or "smallest" topic, the new focus of your review of a short story.

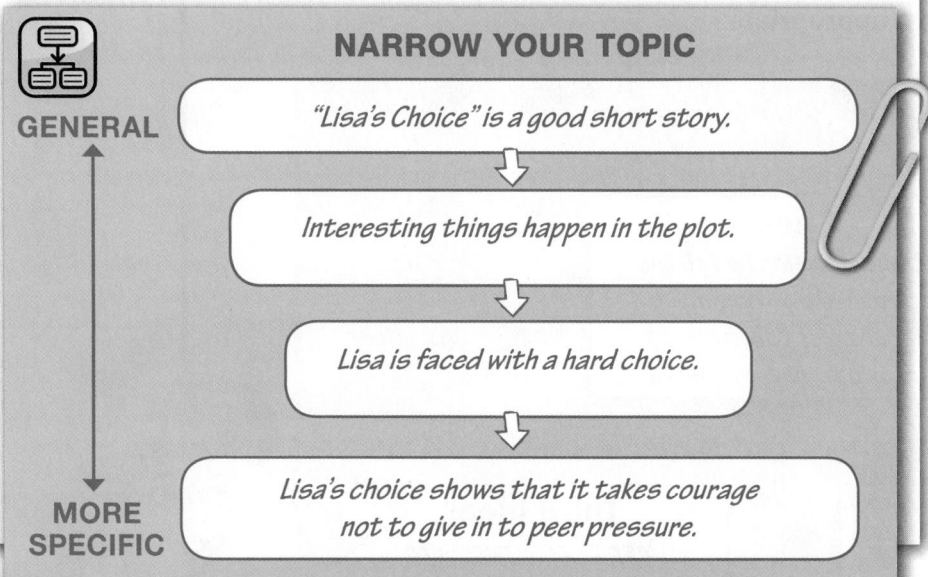

NARROW YOUR TOPIC

GENERAL

"Lisa's Choice" is a good short story.

Interesting things happen in the plot.

Lisa is faced with a hard choice.

MORE SPECIFIC

Lisa's choice shows that it takes courage not to give in to peer pressure.

Consider Your Audience and Purpose

Before writing, think about your audience and purpose. Consider the views of others as you ask yourself these questions.

Questions for Audience	Questions for Purpose
• Who will read my review? My teacher? My classmates?	• What do I want my readers to know about the story?
• What will my audience need to know to understand my opinions?	• What ideas and feelings do I want to convey in my review?
• Is my audience familiar with the selection I will discuss?	• What approches should I use to show I understand the writer's audience and purpose?

Record your answers in your writing journal.

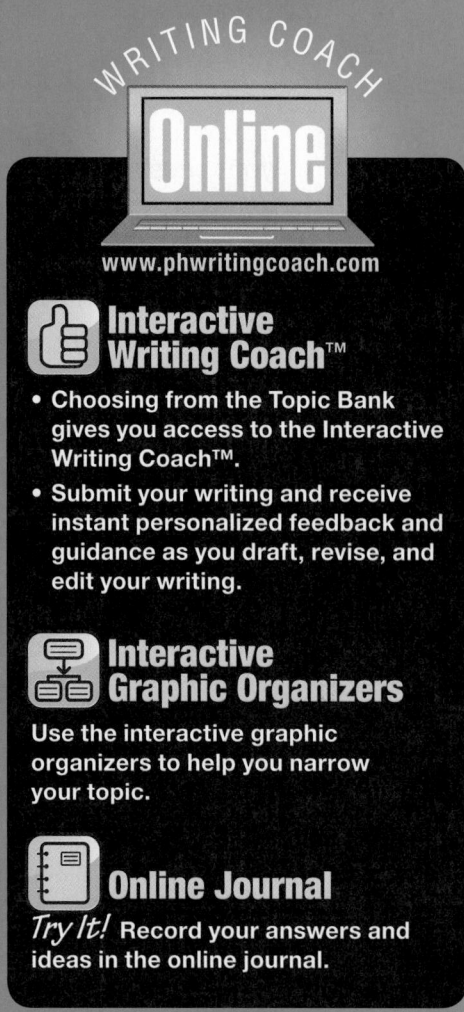

WRITING COACH

Online

www.phwritingcoach.com

Interactive Writing Coach™

- Choosing from the Topic Bank gives you access to the Interactive Writing Coach™.
- Submit your writing and receive instant personalized feedback and guidance as you draft, revise, and edit your writing.

Interactive Graphic Organizers

Use the interactive graphic organizers to help you narrow your topic.

Online Journal

Try It! Record your answers and ideas in the online journal.

Plan Your Piece

You will use a graphic organizer like the one shown to state your thesis, organize your ideas, and identify details. When it is complete, you will be ready to write your first draft.

Develop Your Thesis Think about your reaction to the short story. State your feelings and thoughts in a **clear thesis**. Add your thesis statement to the graphic organizer.

Logically Organize Your Supporting Evidence Use a graphic organizer to help you organize **sustained evidence from the text, including quotations when appropriate.**

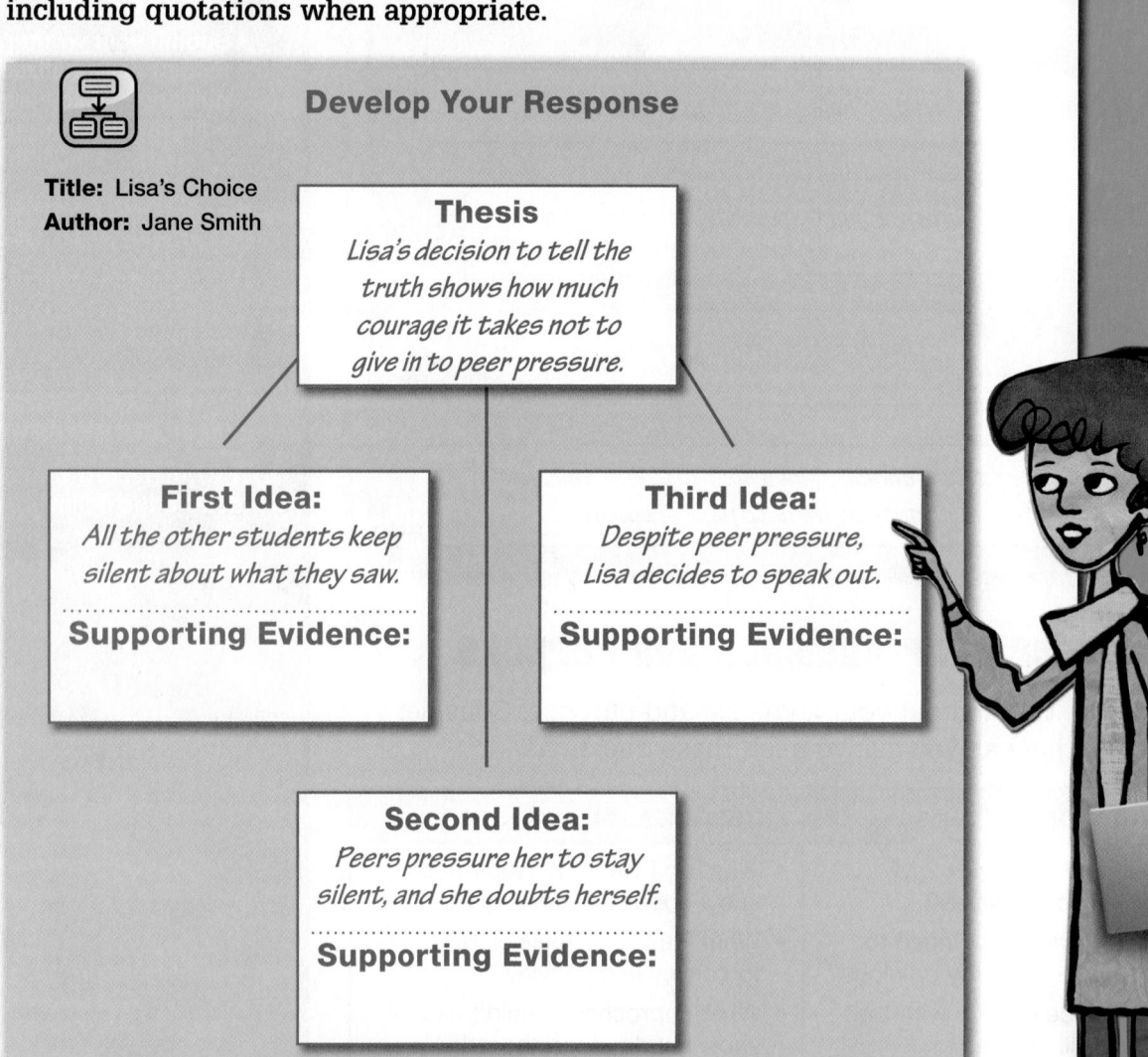

Develop Your Response

Title: Lisa's Choice
Author: Jane Smith

Thesis
Lisa's decision to tell the truth shows how much courage it takes not to give in to peer pressure.

First Idea:
All the other students keep silent about what they saw.

Supporting Evidence:

Third Idea:
Despite peer pressure, Lisa decides to speak out.

Supporting Evidence:

Second Idea:
Peers pressure her to stay silent, and she doubts herself.

Supporting Evidence:

Gather Details

To support their ideas, writers **provide sustained evidence** from the text such as the types of details in these examples:

- **Quotations:** *"I have to do what's right," Lisa said.*
- **Details:** *The classroom was suddenly as silent as a graveyard, and the teacher's eyes followed Lisa like a spotlight.*
- **Examples:** *Jason tried to make a joke, but the other kids were too frightened to laugh.*
- **Relevant Information and Judgments:** *Lisa wasn't trying to be a hero. She didn't even like the accused girl.*
- **Personal Insights:** *The situation described could happen to anyone, in school or out of school.*

Try It! Read the Student Model excerpt and identify the evidence that the author uses to support her ideas.

STUDENT MODEL

from **Gary Soto's "Seventh Grade":
Something We Can All Relate To**
page 203; lines 27–34

The author helps the reader imagine Victor's reaction when he writes: "Great rosebushes of red bloomed on Victor's cheeks."

Victor is lucky that Teresa doesn't know French, so he ends up impressing her. The reader knows Victor is thrilled because the "rosebushes" of shame on his cheeks become "bouquets of love"! His cheeks are still red but for another reason.

Apply It! Review the types of supporting evidence that can be used in a review of a short story. Then identify and write one piece of relevant evidence of each type.

- Review your evidence to make sure it supports your ideas. Be sure to include one or more pieces of each kind of sustained evidence from the text.
- Add your ideas and supporting evidence to your graphic organizer. Remember that your goal is to write a review that is logically organized with appropriate details.
- Be sure to make clear how your evidence supports your thesis.

Drafting

During the drafting stage, you will start to write your ideas for your review of a short story. You will follow an outline that provides an **organizational strategy** that will help you **build on ideas to write a focused, organized, and coherent** review of a short story.

The Organization of an Interpretative Response

The chart shows an organizational strategy for an interpretative response. Look back at how the Mentor Text follows this organizational strategy. Then, use this chart to help you outline your draft.

Outline for Success

I. Introduction

See Mentor Text, p. 200.

- Strong opening paragraph
- Name of the work and the author
- Clear thesis statement

Grab Your Reader

- An interesting opening can make a strong statement, ask a question, or refer to a character or event in the author's work.
- Both the work about which you are writing and its author should be identified.
- The thesis statement focuses on your overall ideas about the text. The rest of your response will support your thesis.

II. Body

See Mentor Text, pp. 200–201.

- Introduction to and summary of the work
- Evidence from the text
- Analysis of elements
- Personal insights

Develop Your Ideas

- The important features of the work should be briefly summarized.
- Evidence from the text, including quotations and other examples, should support your ideas about the text.
- An analysis of story elements includes your thoughts of character, plot, setting, and theme.
- Your ideas and arguments should show your personal insights and judgments.

III. Conclusion

See Mentor Text, p. 201.

- Restatement of thesis in concluding paragraph
- Explanation of the significance of main points

Wrap It Up

- Briefly restating your thesis in slightly different wording reinforces your point.
- An explanation of the significance of your thesis or main points will leave readers with a clear understanding of your ideas and feelings.

 **Start Your Draft**

Use this checklist to help you complete your draft. Use the graphic organizer that shows your thesis and supporting evidence, and the Outline for Success as guides.

While drafting, aim at writing your ideas, not on making your writing perfect. Remember, you will have the chance to improve your draft when you revise and edit.

√ Start with a strong **opening** that will grab your reader's interest.

√ Your **introduction** should **identify** the story, poem, or other work about which you're writing, as well as the author of the work.

√ Present your thesis statement.

√ The **body** of your review should demonstrate the writing skills for multi-paragraph essays by presenting your **ideas and opinions** in a logical way.

√ Be sure to also include a brief summary of key features of the work.

√ Your ideas and opinions should show your understanding of the text and be supported with **sustained evidence** from the text, including quotations.

√ Include an **analysis** of story elements that relate to your ideas, such as themes or specific plot events.

√ In your **conclusion**, restate or paraphrase your **thesis.**

√ End with a strong **final statement** that clearly expresses your thoughts and feelings about the work.

WRITING COACH

Online

www.phwritingcoach.com

 **Interactive Model**

Outline for Success View pop-ups of Mentor Text referenced in the Outline for Success.

Interactive Writing Coach™

Use the Interactive Writing Coach to receive the level of support you need:
• Write one paragraph at a time and submit each one for immediate, detailed feedback.
• Write your entire first draft and submit it for immediate, personalized feedback.

Revising: Making It Better

Now that you have finished your first draft, you are ready to revise. Think about the "big picture" of **audience, purpose, and genre.** You can use the Revision RADaR strategy as a guide for making changes to improve your draft. Revision RADaR provides four ways to improve your writing: (R) replace, (A) add, (D) delete, and (R) reorder.

Kelly Gallagher, M. Ed.

KEEP REVISION ON YOUR RADaR

Read part of the first draft of the Student Model, "Gary Soto's 'Seventh Grade': Something We Can All Relate To." Then look at the questions the writer asked herself as she thought about how well her draft **addressed issues of audience, purpose, and genre.**

Gary Soto's "Seventh Grade": Something We Can All Relate To

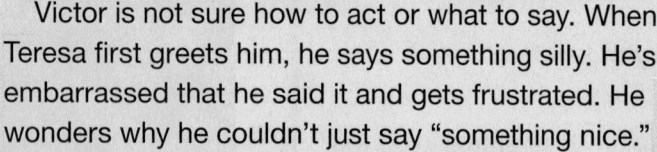

Victor is not sure how to act or what to say. When Teresa first greets him, he says something silly. He's embarrassed that he said it and gets frustrated. He wonders why he couldn't just say "something nice."

In French class, the teacher asks if anyone knows French. Victor sees a chance to show off in front of the girl of his dreams. He raises his hand, even though he doesn't know French. Unfortunately for him, the teacher asks him a question in French.

The author shows Victor's embarrassment in this moment by using great imagery. Victor does his best to bluff his way out of the situation, but he fears he has made a fool of himself in front of Teresa. Victor is thrilled. Luckily, Teresa doesn't know French, so she actually *is* impressed.

Have I used supporting details, including quotations from the text? Do my ideas demonstrate insights and understanding of the text?

Have I included transitions to link paragraphs?

Have I used supporting details, such as examples from the text? Are my ideas presented in a logical order?

Now look at how the writer applied Revision RADaR to write an improved second draft.

Gary Soto's "Seventh Grade": Something We Can All Relate To

 **2ND DRAFT**

Like most people our age, though, Victor is not sure how to act or what to say. When Teresa first greets him, saying, "Hi, Victor," he blushes and says, "Yeah, that's me." He's embarrassed that he said something so silly and gets frustrated. He wonders why he couldn't just say "something nice." I know that this has happened to me and my friends many times!

A *Added information to show my understanding of the text*

R *Replaced vague language with quotations from the text*

Later that day, in French class, the teacher asks if anyone knows French. Victor sees a chance to impress the girl of his dreams. He raises his hand, even though he doesn't know French. Unfortunately for him, the teacher asks him a question in French.

A *Added a transition to show that time has gone by and to link the ideas in the two paragraphs*

The author helps the reader imagine Victor's reaction when he writes: "Great rosebushes of red bloomed on Victor's cheeks."

R *Reordered sentences to present information more clearly*

Victor is lucky that Teresa doesn't know French, so he ends up impressing her. The reader knows Victor is thrilled because the "rosebushes" of shame on his cheeks become "bouquets of love"! His cheeks are still red but for another reason.

Apply It! Use your Revision RADaR to revise your draft.

- First, ask yourself: Have I addressed the needs of my audience, made clear my purpose for writing, and included the characteristics of the interpretative response genre?
- Then, apply the Revision RADaR strategy to make needed changes. Remember—you can use the strategy steps in any order.

Look at the Big Picture

Use the chart and your analytical skills to evaluate how well each section of your review of a short story addresses **purpose, audience, and genre.** When necessary, use the suggestions in the chart to revise your piece.

Section	Evaluate	Revise
Introduction	• Check the **opening.** It should grab readers' interest and make them want to read on.	• Make your opening more interesting by writing a strong first sentence or asking a rhetorical question.
	• Make sure the **thesis** clearly expresses the main idea of your response.	• Does your thesis reflect your thoughts about the story and the controlling idea of your review? If not, rewrite it so that it does.
Body	• Make sure that you have included **sustained evidence** from the text to defend and support ideas.	• Add more supporting evidence as needed. Look for key quotations that support your ideas.
	• Check that you've included ideas and arguments that show personal insights, judgments, and **understanding** of the text.	• Think about the meaning of the story. Add sentences that convey your understanding to readers, if necessary.
	• Make sure you have included an **analysis** of story elements, such as character, plot, setting, and theme.	• Add specific information about story elements to develop and support your main ideas.
	• Check that you have **logically organized** your ideas and supporting evidence. Make sure that you have not included any unnecessary information.	• Reorder text so that sentences and paragraphs are logically organized. Delete information that does not relate to the controlling idea.
Conclusion	• Check the **restatement** of your thesis.	• If necessary, discuss your restatement with a classmate and ask for suggestions.
	• Check that your **conclusion** leaves readers with a clear understanding of your thoughts.	• Add a final statement that sums up how you feel about the work or why it is meaningful to you.

Focus on Craft: Consistent Point of View

Your audience will be confused if you don't have a **consistent point of view** in your review of a short story. Many reviews are written in the first-person point of view, using words such as *I* and *we*. Other reviews are written in the second-person point of view, using *you* and *your*, or in third-person point of view, using *he*, *she*, and *it*.

Think about point of view as you read the following example from the Student Model.

 **STUDENT MODEL** | from **Gary Soto's "Seventh Grade": Something We Can All Relate To** | page 202; lines 5–8

> You'll laugh as you read about the things Victor does to get a girl named Teresa to notice him. This story is about what happens when you pretend to be something you are not.

 Try It! Now, ask yourself these questions:

- What point of view does the author of the Student Model use? Why might that be a good choice for a review of a short story?

- Why might a change in point of view confuse the reader?

 Fine-Tune Your Draft

Apply It! Use the revision suggestions to prepare your final draft **after rethinking how well questions of purpose, audience, and genre have been addressed.**

- **Use Consistent Point of View** Avoid changing point of view within paragraphs or from one paragraph to the next.

- **Improve Sentence Structure** Break or combine sentences to achieve a variety of sentence structures such as simple, compound, and complex.

Peer Feedback Show your final draft to a group of your peers and ask if your evidence supports your main idea. Listen carefully to their ideas and make revisions as needed.

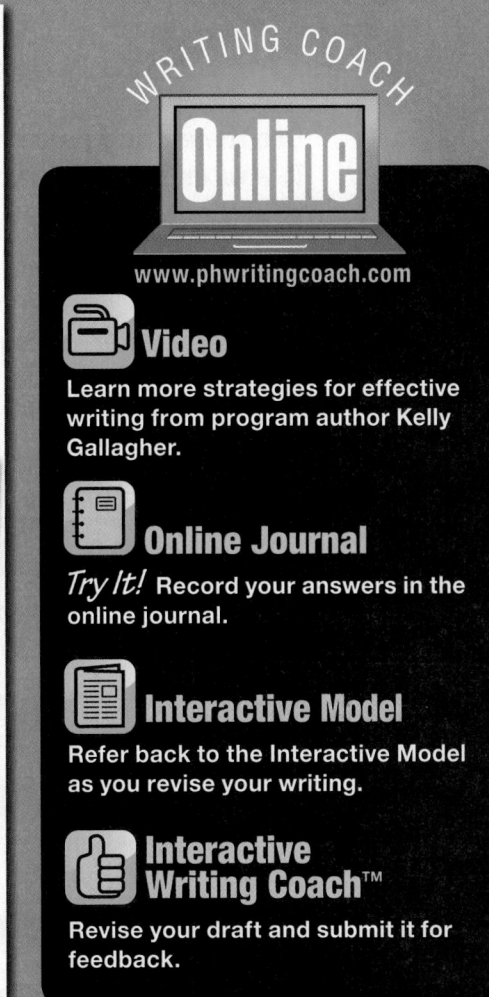

WRITING COACH

Online

www.phwritingcoach.com

Video
Learn more strategies for effective writing from program author Kelly Gallagher.

Online Journal
Try It! Record your answers in the online journal.

Interactive Model
Refer back to the Interactive Model as you revise your writing.

Interactive Writing Coach™
Revise your draft and submit it for feedback.

Editing: Making It Correct

Use the editing process to polish your work and correct errors. It is often helpful to work with a partner when editing your drafts.

Before editing, think about how **prepositions and prepositional phrases** may **influence subject-verb agreement**. Also think about the importance of using **consistent tenses** so that readers can follow the order, or sequence, of events. Then, edit your draft by correcting factual errors and errors in **grammar, mechanics, and spelling.** Use a dictionary to check your spelling.

 WRITE GUY *Jeff Anderson, M. Ed.*

WHAT DO YOU NOTICE?

Zoom in on Conventions Focus on subject-verb agreement as you zoom in on this sentence from the Student Model.

 **STUDENT MODEL** from **Gary Soto's "Seventh Grade": Something We Can All Relate To** page 203; lines 32–33

> The "rosebushes" of shame on his cheeks become "bouquets of love"!

Now, ask yourself: *What role does the word "rosebushes" play in the sentence?*

Perhaps you said that "rosebushes" is the subject of the sentence. The verb is *become.* Two prepositional phrases separate the subject and verb: *of shame* and *on his cheeks.*

A prepositional phrase is a group of words that begins with a preposition and contains a noun or pronoun that is the object of the preposition. Subjects and verbs must agree even when they are separated by prepositional phrases, as in the Student Model.

The subject of a sentence is never part of a prepositional phrase. So, neither *shame* nor *cheeks* can be the subject. The plural subject *rosebushes* agrees with the plural verb *become.* A singular subject agrees with a singular verb, for example: *The rosebush of shame on his cheek becomes "a bouquet of love"!*

Partner Talk Discuss this question with a partner: *How do perpositions and prepositional phrases affect subject-verb agreement?*

> To learn more about subject-verb agreement, see Chapter 23 of your Grammar Handbook.

Grammar Mini-Lesson: Consistent Tenses

To learn more, see page 284.

Tenses are verb forms that tell if an action takes place in the past, present, or future. It is important to **use tenses consistently** so readers can follow your writing. Sometimes, though, tenses must vary to show sequence, or the order of events. For example: *Last year, he* studied *Spanish, but this year he* studies *French.* Notice how the Student Model author uses present tense verbs consistently to help readers follow the order of events.

 **STUDENT MODEL** | from **Gary Soto's "Seventh Grade": Something We Can All Relate To** pages 202–203; lines 23–27

> Victor sees a chance to show off in front of the girl of his dreams. He raises his hand, even though he doesn't know French. Unfortunately for him, the teacher asks him a question in French.

 Try It! Complete each sentence using a consistent verb tense. Write the answers in your journal.

1. A box of candies (sat) on the table, and I (know) they are delicious.
2. After we watched the game, we (drive) into town and (eat) dinner.

 Apply It! **Edit your draft for grammar, mechanics, and spelling**. Make sure you have used a **variety of complete sentences** that includes consistent tenses. Make sure that **prepositional phrases** do not interrupt **subject-verb agreement**.

 Use the rubric to evaluate your piece. If necessary, rethink, rewrite, or revise.

Rubric for Interpretative Response: Review of a Short Story	Rating Scale					
Ideas: How well does your response present a focused statement about the work?	Not very 1	2	3	4	5	Very 6
Organization: How clearly organized is your analysis?	1	2	3	4	5	6
Voice: How well have you engaged the reader and sustained his or her interest?	1	2	3	4	5	6
Word Choice: How clearly do your words state your views?	1	2	3	4	5	6
Sentence Fluency: How well have you used a consistent point of view in your writing?	1	2	3	4	5	6
Conventions: How correct is your use of consistent verb tenses?	1	2	3	4	5	6

WRITING COACH

Online

www.phwritingcoach.com

 Video

Learn effective editing techniques from program author Jeff Anderson.

 Online Journal

Try It! Record your answers in the online journal.

 Interactive Model

Refer back to the Interactive Model as you edit your writing.

 Interactive Writing Coach™

Edit your draft. Check it against the rubric and then submit it for feedback.

Publishing

Share the ideas expressed in your review—publish it! First, get your review ready for presentation. Then, choose a way to **publish it for the appropriate audience.**

Wrap Up Your Presentation

Now that you have finished your draft, add the final details. Include page numbers on each page of your final draft.

Publish Your Review

Use the chart to identify a way to publish your review.

If your audience is...	...then publish it by...
People in your community	• Submitting it to a local newspaper • Creating a multimedia presentation for kids at your local library
Students at school	• Reading it aloud in English class • Posting it online and inviting comments

Extend Your Research

Think more about the topic of the story on which you wrote your review. What else would you like to know about this topic?

- Brainstorm for several questions you would like to research and then consult, or discuss, with others. Then, decide which question is your major research question.

- Formulate, or develop, a plan about how you will answer the question. Decide where you will find more information—on the Internet, at the library, or through other sources.

- Finally, learn more about your topic by following through with your research plan.

 **The Big Question: Why Write?** What should you write about to make others interested in a text?

Manage Your Portfolio You may wish to include your published review of a short story in your writing portfolio. If so, consider what this review reveals about your writing and your growth as a writer.

21st Century Learning

MAKE YOUR WRITING COUNT

Build an Advertisement for a Story of Your Choice

Reviews tell readers whether a story is worth reading. An advertisement for a story encourages readers to want to read it. Catch the attention of potential readers by creating an **advertisement for a story**.

In a group, choose one story review to turn into a **multimedia presentation** of an advertisement. The text of your ad should include the story's title, author, selling points, reviewer comment, and an excerpt. The ad should also include graphics. Create your ad in print or by using available technology.

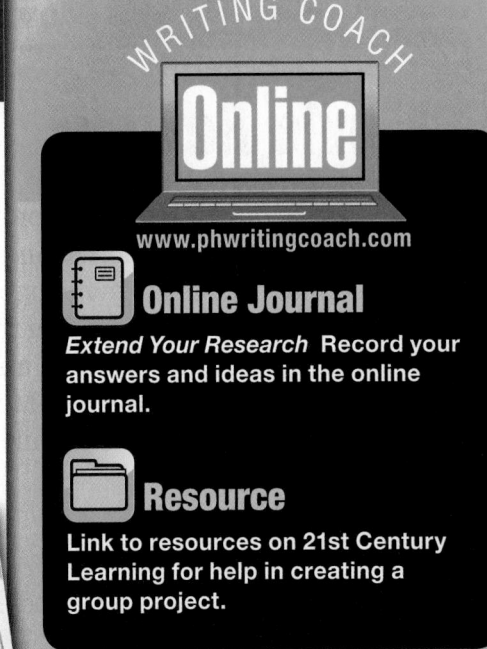

Here's your action plan.

1. Analyze book ads in newspapers, magazines, or online.

2. With your group, choose a story review to turn into an advertisement. Take notes to refer to as you create the ad.

3. Use catchy phrases, an excerpt, and an image in your ad.

   - Highlight the selling points of the story, including a comment from the review.
   - Choose a short excerpt from the story to attract potential readers.
   - Display the title and author of the story.

4. Create a "cover" for the story (or the book it appears in) to include in the ad.

5. Present your advertisement to the class. If possible, post it on the class Web site.

Listening and Speaking Rehearse the presentation of your advertisement. Although your ad is based on text and graphics, try to bring these elements to life by speaking and gesturing expressively. Listen actively during the presentations of other groups so that you can analyze their ads and give positive feedback.

WRITING COACH

Online

www.phwritingcoach.com

Online Journal

Extend Your Research Record your answers and ideas in the online journal.

Resource

Link to resources on 21st Century Learning for help in creating a group project.

Your Turn

**Writing for Media:
Movie Review**

Movie Review

A **movie review** is an article or essay that discusses a movie, analyzes its story elements, and summarizes important features of the work. Movie reviews appear in newspapers and magazines, on television and radio, and on the Internet. A movie review presents the writer's opinions and supports them with evidence and quotations from the film. Movie reviews may either persuade readers that a film is worthwhile or discourage them from seeing it.

Try It! Study the movie review on this page. Then, answer the questions. Record your answers in your journal.

- What **film** is this movie review about?
- Who made the **movie?**
- What **type** of movie is it?
- What does the **writer** think about the movie? Why does the writer feel this way?
- What **evidence** does the writer use to defend and support his or her ideas and judgment?
- What **story elements** does the writer analyze?
- Would this review **encourage** you to see the movie? Why or why not?

Extension Find another example of a movie review, and compare it with this one.

Karl Johnson's latest sci-fi movie, *Door to Doom*, is his most action-packed film yet. It's also his silliest. Nothing in this movie is believable. The characters are brainless, and the plot makes no sense.

The movie's 16-year-old hero, Dylan, spends the entire movie whining and trying to convince the police that a blue-skinned alien has invaded his neighborhood. He draws this conclusion when he sees a terrifying-looking alien chasing Dylan's neighbor's dog. Despite the missing dog, specks of a strange kind of goo on the ground, and the picture Dylan snaps with his cell phone, no one believes him. "But I saw it happen," he tells the police again and again. "We'll check it out," they always reply, but they don't.

One by one, pets in Dylan's neighborhood vanish. Then his neighbors themselves begin to disappear. Still, the police refuse to investigate. It never occurs to Dylan that he should talk to some other adults or maybe call the newspaper. Instead, he tells only his friend, Jimmy, who suggests that they catch the alien.

From this point on, the plot gets only more ridiculous. Dylan and Jimmy make a series of unsafe decisions and incredibly pointless attempts to catch the alien. Unless you have time and money to waste, the *Door to Doom* is best left unopened.

Write a Movie Review

Follow these steps to write your own movie review. To plan your movie review, review the graphic organizers on pages R24–R27 and choose one that best suits your needs.

Prewriting

- Choose a movie you have recently seen and have strong feelings about—positive *or* negative. Consider why you feel as you do.
- Think about the kind of movie it is, such as a comedy or an adventure film.
- Identify the audience for the movie. Consider not only which people are sure to go see it but also which people *might* see it.
- Think about how to persuade people to see or avoid the movie.
- Consider what evidence from the movie you will use to support your opinion.

Drafting

- Begin with a strong opening. It should grab your readers' interest and express your main idea.
- Write a brief summary. Include an analysis of story elements, such as character and plot. Analyze how the film may have been influenced by myths or literature from a variety of world cultures.
- Defend and support your ideas and opinions with sustained evidence. Include quotations when appropriate.
- End with a strong statement that sums up your feelings.

Revising and Editing

Make sure that your ideas are logically organized and that you support them with details and examples. Be sure you present evidence in a clear and persuasive way. Also be sure to check that spelling, grammar, and mechanics are correct.

Publishing

Post your movie review on a school Web site, and invite classmates to share their opinions. You might also create a multimedia presentation for your class that combines your review with quotes and images from the film.

WRITING COACH

Online

www.phwritingcoach.com

 Online Journal

Try It! Record your answers in the online journal.

 **Interactive Graphic Organizers**

Choose from a variety of graphic organizers to plan and develop your project.

Partner Talk

Before you start drafting, summarize the movie you are reviewing. Then describe and explain your planned movie review to a partner and ask for feedback. For example, you might ask whether you've chosen convincing evidence to support your opinion. Monitor your partner's spoken language by asking follow up questions to confirm your understanding.

Writing for Assessment

You may be asked to write to an **interpretative response** prompt. Use the prompts on these pages to practice. Your responses should include the same characteristics as your review of a short story. (See page 198.)

 Try It! To begin, read the prompt and the information on format and academic vocabulary. Use the ABCDs of On-Demand Writing to help you write your essay.

Format

The prompt directs you to write an *interpretative response* to a story, book, or poem. Make sure to create a fully developed introduction, body, and conclusion.

Interpretative Response Prompt

Write a critical review interpretative response of a short story, book, or poem you have read. Analyze and evaluate the work. Support your analysis and judgment with specific details, such as examples and quotations from the work.

Academic Vocabulary

Remember that an *analysis* of a story, book, or poem is a study of its elements and parts. Your *judgment* about the work is your opinion of it. Be sure to use key points from the text to support your analysis and opinion.

The ABCDs of On-Demand Writing

Use the following ABCDs to help you respond to the prompt.

Before you write your draft:

Attack the prompt [1 MINUTE]

- Circle or highlight important verbs in the prompt. Draw a line from the verb to what it refers to.
- Rewrite the prompt in your own words.

Brainstorm possible answers [4 MINUTES]

- Create a graphic organizer to generate ideas.
- Use one for each part of the prompt if necessary.

Choose the order of your response [1 MINUTE]

- Think about the best way to organize your ideas.
- Number your ideas in the order you will write about them. Cross out ideas you will not be using.

After you write your draft:

Detect errors before turning in the draft [1 MINUTE]

- Carefully reread your writing.
- Make sure that your response makes sense and is complete.
- Look for spelling, punctuation, and grammar errors.

 **More Prompts for Practice**

Apply It! Respond to Prompts 1 and 2 by writing **interpretative responses** that use supporting **evidence from the text.** Be sure to:

- Express the main idea of your response in a clear **thesis statement**
- Summarize **important features of the work**
- Include **sustained evidence from the text to support ideas**
- Use **quotations from the text** when appropriate
- Analyze **story elements,** such as character, plot, and theme

> **Prompt 1** Many stories have memorable characters. Write an essay that compares and contrasts two characters from two different stories. Support your ideas with details from the texts.

> **Prompt 2** Most literary works express a theme. For instance, the theme for a work might be "forgiveness is the key to happiness." In an essay, interpret a theme in a short story, book, or poem you have read.

SAT/PSAT PREP ACT **Spiral Review: Persuasive** Respond to Prompt 3 by writing a **persuasive essay** with a **clearly stated thesis or position.** Make sure your persuasive essay has all of the characteristics described on page 172, including:

- A goal to **influence** the attitudes or actions of a specific **audience** about the specific **issue**
- Anticipation of and response to the **concerns, views,** and **counter-arguments** of others
- Logically **organized** arguments and evidence that support a viewpoint
- Distinctions between **fact** and **opinion**

> **Prompt 3** Write a persuasive essay to convince someone that a particular season of the year is the best. Include types of weather and seasonal activities in your supporting evidence.

www.phwritingcoach.com

 **Interactive Writing Coach™**

Plan your response to the prompt. If you are using the prompt for practice, write one paragraph at a time or your entire draft and then submit it for feedback. If you are using the prompt as a timed test, write your entire draft and then submit it for feedback.

Remember **ABCD**

Attack the prompt

Brainstorm possible answers

Choose the order of your response

Detect errors before turning in the draft

CHAPTER 11

RESEARCH WRITING

What Do You Want To Know?

How do people find out more information about interesting topics? They do research to gather, organize, and present information.

One of the first steps of research writing is to identify a topic that interests you and then formulate open-ended research questions. Open-ended research questions ask what you want to find out about the topic. For example, if you want to find out more about the scientist in the photograph, you would first decide what you want to know.

Try It! Take a few minutes to brainstorm for some things you want to know about the scientist. Write them in a list.

Consider these questions as you work on your list.

- What do you want to know about the scientist?
- What do you want to know about the protective gear the scientist is wearing?
- What do you want to know about the machine the scientist is using?

Review your list of questions with a partner. Compare lists to determine if any questions overlap or if you can build off each other's ideas. Then, discuss where you would go to research answers to your questions.

What's Ahead

In this chapter, you will review a strong example of an informational research report. Then, using the example as guidance, you will develop your own research plan and write your own informational research report.

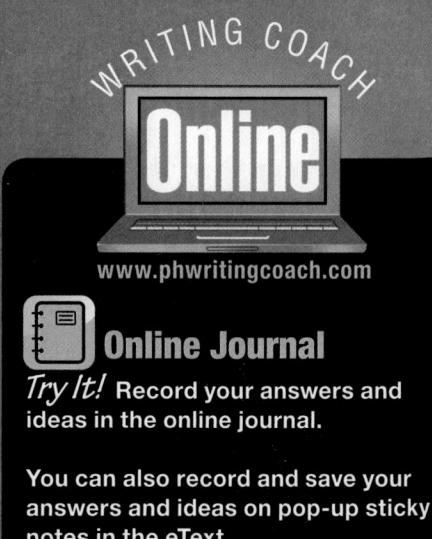

THE BIG QUESTION

Connect to the Big Questions

Discuss these questions with your partner:

1 What do you think? What kinds of scientific discoveries affect our lives the most?

2 Why write? Do you understand your subject well enough to write about it? How will you find out what all the facts are?

RESEARCH WRITING

Research writing is a way to gather information, and then synthesize, or combine, that information into a report for others to read. In this chapter, you will write an informational research report. Your report will provide information about a topic that interests you. Before you write, you will search for information about your topic in different kinds of sources. You will decide which facts and details to use in your report, and organize your ideas clearly for your audience.

You will develop your informational research report by taking it through each of the steps of the writing process: prewriting, drafting, revising, editing, and publishing. You will also have an opportunity to use your informational research report in an oral report or multimedia presentation involving text and graphics that uses technology available to you. To preview the criteria for how your research report will be evaluated, see the rubric on page 247.

FEATURE ASSIGNMENT

Research Writing: Informational Research Report

An effective informational research report has these characteristics:

- **A clear thesis statement** that explains the **conclusions** of the research and how those conclusions will be supported with evidence

- **Quotations** from—as well as **summaries** or **paraphrases** of—research findings, based on reliable and accurate **primary and secondary sources**

- **Clearly organized evidence,** in the form of relevant facts and details, that explains the topic and the writer's conclusions

- **Graphics,** such as charts, maps, or illustrations, that help explain the research

- Proper **documentation** of sources to show where the writer found information

- Effective sentence structure and **correct spelling, grammar, and usage**

Other Forms of Research Writing

In addition to an informational research report, there are other forms of research writing, including these:

Biographical profiles give specific details about the life and work of a real person. The person may be living or dead, someone famous, or someone familiar to the writer.

Documentaries are filmed reports that focus on a specific topic or issue. These multimedia presentations use spoken and written text as well as photographs, videos, music, and other sound effects.

Historical reports give in-depth information about a past event or situation. These kinds of reports focus on a narrow topic and may discuss causes and effects.

Health reports analyze information and data about new research in health and wellness. A health report might explain new findings about the links between nutrition and health, or the latest news on disease research.

I-Search reports blend informational and personal writing. In an I-search report, you tell the story of your research and investigations, including the dead-ends and small victories, in addition to presenting the results of your research.

Lab reports describe scientific experiments, including observations and conclusions.

Try It! For each research report described, brainstorm for possible topics with others. Then, consult with others to decide on and write a major research question for each topic. As you write, keep your audience and purpose in mind.

- A biographical profile of someone in the news
- A health report about school lunches
- A documentary about a family member for a special occasion

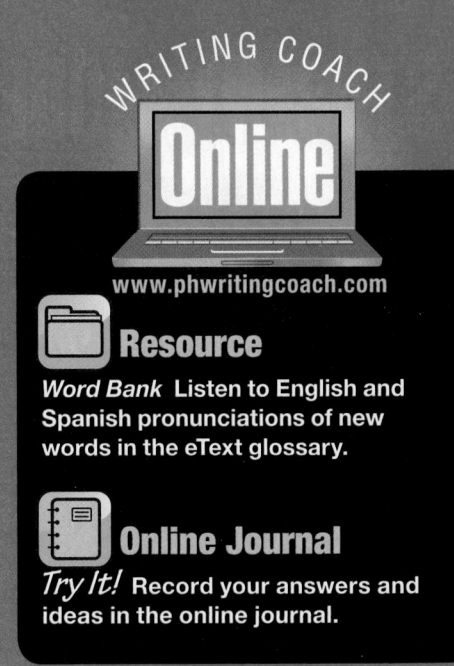

WRITING COACH

Online

www.phwritingcoach.com

Resource

Word Bank Listen to English and Spanish pronunciations of new words in the eText glossary.

Online Journal

Try It! Record your answers and ideas in the online journal.

WORD BANK

People use these basic and content-based words when they talk about writing that reports information. Work with a partner. Take turns saying and writing each word in a sentence. If you are unsure of the meaning of a word, use the Glossary or a dictionary to check the definition.

authority	research
information	subject
note	support

STUDENT MODEL

Informational Research Report

❶ Emma Alvarez
Mrs. Davidson
History 7A
13 December 2009

❶ **The Cowboy: Myth Versus Reality**

Everyone can spot a cowboy a mile away. He is a tall, strong man wearing a big hat, high boots, and bandana. He roams the West on horseback, like a knight of old. He spends most of his time alone except for his

5 best friend—his horse. He is brave, self-reliant, and, above all, free. To many, he represents America itself (Savage 6). ❷ How does this image relate to the real cowboys? The popular image has its roots in the real men who herded cattle for a few decades after the Civil War. However,

10 advertising and popular media reshaped the cowboys' image and smoothed away the less appealing parts of their lives (Savage 9). ❷ This report will show that the popular image of the cowboy is more myth than reality.

The era of the real—that is, working—American cowboy

15 lasted only about twenty-five years, from around 1865 to 1890. It began with the first railroads, which connected the large eastern cities with a few western centers like Chicago, Omaha, and Abilene. At this time, the railroads did not go into Texas cattle country. Cattlemen needed to get their herds to eastern

20 markets, where they would earn much higher prices. So the ranchers hired young men—cowboys—to herd the cattle over hundreds of miles to the nearest railhead. There the animals were loaded onto freight trains going east.

As time passed, however, cowboys were less essential

25 to the cattle industry. Railroads had expanded, so that rail depots were much closer to the cattle ranches. Therefore, long cattle drives every spring and fall were no longer needed. Although some cowboys continued to tend cattle on ranches, by the late 1880s, the era of the working cowboy had wound

30 down (Utley 245). At that point, the cowboy myth began to take over.

Use a Reader's Eye

Read the Student Model on pages 226–229. On your copy of the Student Model, use the Reader's Response Symbols to react to what you read.

Reader's Response Symbols

√ **OK. I understand this. It's very clearly explained.**

? **I don't follow what the writer is saying here.**

+ **I think the writer needs more details here.**

− **This information doesn't seem relevant.**

! **Wow! That is cool/weird/interesting.**

Learn From Experience

Read the numbered notes as you reread the Student Model to learn about how the writer presented her ideas.

Answer the *Try It!* questions online or in your notebook.

❶ The writer uses **proper formatting** for the first page and pagination of research report.

❷ The writer reveals the **research question;** then she reveals her conclusion about it in the **thesis statement.**

Try It! Read the thesis statement. What is the main idea? What research question does it answer? What is the author's purpose?

Alvarez 2

Before the cowboy myth was created, the cowboy had not been a very popular figure. One person who had seen "real cowboys" remarked that a cowboy is "just a plain bowlegged
35 human who smelled very horsey at times" (Burns). The public saw cowboys as dirty, unruly men—and they often were just that (figure 1). ❸ In 1875, a Wyoming newspaper described a group of "real" cowboys as "rough men with shaggy hair and wild staring eyes in butternut trousers stuffed into great rough
40 boots" (Schultz and Tishler).

In 1884, William F. Cody (known as "Buffalo Bill") began to shine up the cowboy's image:

> ❹ Cody took a six-foot, five-inch Texas cowpuncher
> named William Levi Taylor and in 1884 introduced
45 > him to the audiences of Buffalo Bill's Wild West as
> Buck Taylor, 'the King of the Cowboys.' Buck Taylor
> thus became the first bona fide cowboy hero. . . .
> Cody's careful management of Taylor's career as an
> entertainer did much to alter the public's perception
50 > of cowboys. He portrayed the young Texan as a
> wistful soul who seemed to be longing to return to
> the bucolic environs of the Great Plains. Promotional
> literature assured the public that Taylor, despite his
> size, was a gentle fellow who liked children (Savage).

55 ❺ In other words, Cody's publicity campaign romanticized and softened the image of the cowboy in order to make his Wild West show more popular. The campaign worked, and the myth

Figure 1. Typical cowboy. Photo taken by D.C.H. Grabill in *Sturgis Dakota Territory* (Washington, DC: Library of Congress; ppmscs 02638; print).

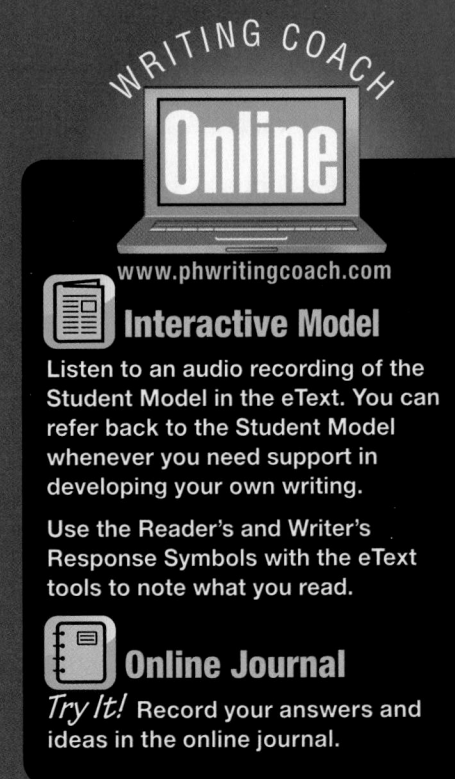

WRITING COACH

Online

www.phwritingcoach.com

Interactive Model

Listen to an audio recording of the Student Model in the eText. You can refer back to the Student Model whenever you need support in developing your own writing.

Use the Reader's and Writer's Response Symbols with the eText tools to note what you read.

Online Journal

Try It! Record your answers and ideas in the online journal.

❸ This **quotation** gives a firsthand view of nineteenth-century cowboys, **relevant details** provided by an eyewitness who lived among them.

❹ Extended quotations of four lines or more are set off from the text, indented, and not set in quotation marks.

❺ **Evidence** is provided to support the conclusion that the cowboy image was a carefully created myth.

Try It! How does the evidence about Buck Taylor support the writer's thesis statement?

Alvarez 3

6 **Relevant facts,** in the form of statistics, back up the idea that the cowboys came from varied backgrounds.

Try It! What new ideas about cowboys do these statistics help to support?

7 Here and elsewhere, the writer **summarizes** information she found during her research.

Try It! Do you think this summary helps support the contrast between the cowboy myth and reality? Why or why not?

8 The final paragraph restates the writer's **reason for her conclusion** about the cowboy image, and adds a new thought.

Try It! What new thought does the conclusion add to the report? How does this new thought change your ideas of cowboys?

9 The Works Cited list provides proper **documentation** by listing publication information for each source used to write the report. The **formatting** of the list follows the MLA (Modern Language Association) style manual.

Try It! Study the Works Cited list on page 229. Why is it helpful to readers to list sources in alphabetical order? Why might readers want to know what types of resources—print, Web, and so on—were used?

Extension Review the text features and graphics in this report. How do they help you form an overview and locate information?

of the cowboy was born. The myth soon grew, fed by novels in the nineteenth century. In the twentieth century, the myth was greatly enlarged by movies and television programs (Savage 9–10).

The real cowboy was different in many ways from his myth, beginning with his stature and background. The mythical cowboy is tall. In contrast, Schultz and Tishler say, most actual cowboys were short and slight (though wiry), so as not to weigh down their horses. Like the "King of the Cowboys," the mythical cowboy is Caucasian and a Westerner. **6** However, of the 35,000 men who worked as cowboys between 1865 and 1885, about 25% were African-American; about 12% were Hispanic (Schultz and Tishler).

Many cowboys were not Westerners. They were former Confederate soldiers or sons of Southern families whose properties had been lost in the Civil War. They were also young men from Eastern cities and even Europeans who came west (Burns).

The typical cowboy took up cowpunching in his late teens and left it by the time he turned 30. The salary was relatively low: $30–$40 a month ("Cowboy"). Due to inflation, $40 per month in 1880 would be equal to about $870 in today's money (Officer and Williamson).

The mythical cowboy did not earn much money either, but was seen as a romantic loner who bravely faced down gunslingers. **7** In contrast, the real cowboy led a hard and very boring life, riding for 14 hours a day. He needed his large hat to protect his neck and eyes from the blistering sun and wore a kerchief so that he could breathe during dust storms. Far from being a romantic loner, his life depended on teaming up with his fellow cowboys (figure 2). They had to keep watchful eyes on the cattle, which would often wander away, or, worse, stampede and kill their herders. The cattle, terrain, and weather were all greater threats to real cowboys than gunslingers were. While the cowboy myth celebrates freedom, the actual cowboy was far from

Alvarez 4

Figure 2. Cowboys worked together to herd cattle hundreds of miles. Taken by D.C.H. Grabill in *Sturgis Dakota Territory* (Washington, DC: Library of Congress ppmscs 02628; print).

free. He was a hired hand who worked day and night for a
95 rich cattle rancher, and almost every moment of his day was bound over to the animals he herded (Schultz and Tishler).

Like any legendary figure, the mythical cowboy was more heroic and exciting than the reality. ❽ So the cowboy myth, eventually repeated by powerful media like movies
100 and television, blotted out the real cowboy in people's minds. However, this is not to say that the working cowboy vanished completely from the American West. Real cowboys (and cowgirls) tend cattle on ranches to this day, much as their nineteenth-century counterparts did. We just have to look
105 behind the towering myth to see them.

❾ Works Cited

Burns, Ken. "Episode 5: 'Cowboys'." *The West*. WETA. 2001. Web. 2 Nov. 2009.

"Cowboy." *The New Encyclopedia of the American West*. Ed. Howard R. Lamar. New Haven: Yale UP, 1998. Print.

Officer, Lawrence H. and Samuel H. Williamson. "Six Ways to Compute the Relative Value of a U.S. Dollar Amount, 1774 to Present." *Measuring Worth*. MeasuringWorth, 2009. Web. 2 Nov. 2009.

Savage, William W., Jr. *Cowboy Life: Reconstructing an American Myth*. Norman, Oklahoma: U of Oklahoma P, 1975. Print.

Schultz, Stanley K. and William P. Tishler. "Which 'Old West' and Whose?" *American History 102, Lecture 3*. State Historical Society of Wisconsin, 1997. Web. 2 Nov. 2009.

Utley, Robert M., ed. *The Story of the West*. New York: DK Publishing, Inc., 2003. Print.

WRITING COACH

Online

www.phwritingcoach.com

Interactive Model

Listen to an audio recording of the Student Model in the eText. You can refer back to the Student Model whenever you need support in developing your own writing. Use the Reader's and Writer's Response Symbols with the eText tools to note what you read.

Use a Writer's Eye

Now go back to the beginning of the Student Model and evaluate the piece as a writer. On your copy of the Student Model, use the Writer's Response Symbols to react to what you read. Identify places where the student writer uses characteristics of an effective informational research report.

Writer's Response Symbols

T.S.   **Thesis statement**

S.E.   **Supporting evidence**

R.G.   **Relevant graphic**

D.S.   **Proper documentation of sources**

Feature Assignment:
Informational Research Report

Prewriting

Begin to plan a first draft by choosing an appropriate topic. You can select from the Topic Bank or come up with one of your own.

Choose From the Topic Bank

Balls, Courts, and Hoops People in other times played many games that share traits with today's sports. Learn about a sport developed by Native Americans or another civilization from the Middle Ages to the twentieth century. What were its origins? How was it played?

Making the Headlines Certain dates in history have special meaning to various localities. What date means a great deal to your community or state? What makes the date important?

What's Living in My Backyard? Our communities host many life forms, from microscopic to human size. Research an ecosystem or microhabitat near your home. Describe this habitat and its organisms. How do these organisms co-exist with human beings?

Choose Your Own Topic

Determine an appropriate topic of your own by using the following range of strategies to generate ideas.

Brainstorm and Browse

- **Consult** with a partner to **brainstorm** for and decide upon a list of topics that interest you.
- **Ask research questions** about your topics. Circle key words and phrases in your questions. Use your key words and phrases to browse your library's reference works and other resources.
- Search the Internet, using the same key words. Work with your partner to help you **decide which topics to research.**
- Review your work and choose a topic.

Formulate Your Research Question

A broad, general topic is almost impossible to research well and cover thoroughly. Plan to do some preliminary research in order to narrow your topic and then formulate a major research question.

Apply It! Use a printed or online graphic organizer like the one shown to narrow your topic.

- Write your general topic in the top box, and keep narrowing your topic with research questions as you move down the chart.

- Your last box should hold your narrowest or "smallest" research question. This will be the focus of your informational research report.

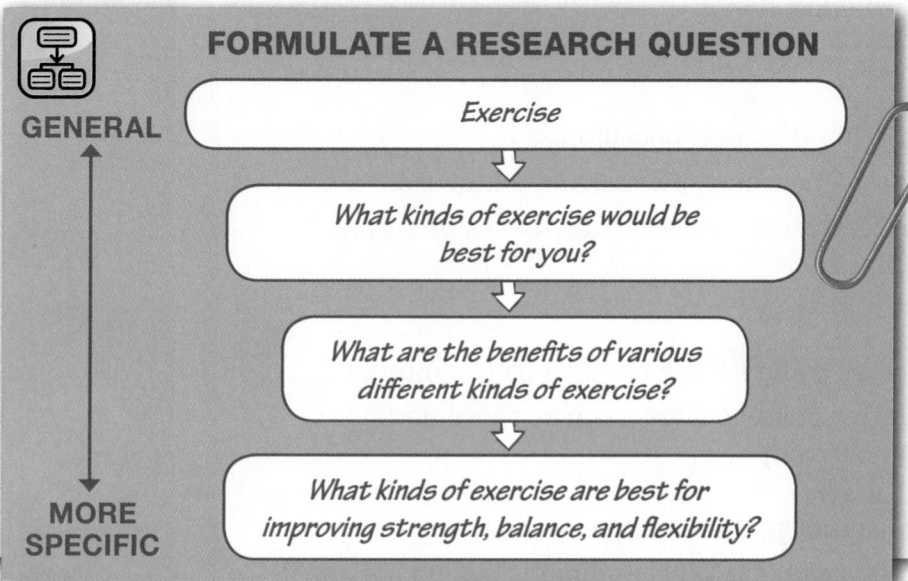

FORMULATE A RESEARCH QUESTION

GENERAL

Exercise

What kinds of exercise would be best for you?

What are the benefits of various different kinds of exercise?

MORE SPECIFIC

What kinds of exercise are best for improving strength, balance, and flexibility?

Consider Your Audiences and Purposes

Before you start researching, think about audiences and purposes. Consider the views of others as you ask yourself these questions.

Questions About Audiences	Questions About Purposes
• Who are my audiences: My teacher? My classmates? Someone else?	• Why am I writing the report: To inform? To make my audiences want to learn more about the topic?
• What do my audiences need and want to know about the topic for my research report?	• How do I want my audiences to react to my report as they read it?
• What technical terms will I need to explain to my audiences?	• What is my point of view, or attitude, toward my topic?

Record your answers in your writing journal.

WRITING COACH

Online

www.phwritingcoach.com

 **Interactive Writing Coach™**

- **Choosing from the Topic Bank gives you access to the Interactive Writing Coach™.**
- **Submit your writing paragraph by paragraph and receive detailed feedback and guidance as you draft, revise, and edit your writing.**

 Interactive Graphic Organizers

Use the interactive graphic organizers to help you narrow your topic.

 Online Journal

Record your answers and ideas in the online journal.

Make a Research Plan

Once you have your research question, you are ready to make a research plan. As part of your plan, you will create a time line for finishing your report. You also will find and evaluate sources of information.

Find Authoritative, Objective Sources For your report, you will need to **compile data,** or gather information, from a variety of sources. Make sure the sources you plan to use are **relevant**— they should be related to the topic you are researching and not out of date. Use a variety of **advanced search strategies** including electronic databases, card catalogues, and search engines to locate your resources. For most topics, there are different resources from which to choose. Look at these tips:

Print Resources

- Find print resources in libraries and bookstores.
- Use encyclopedias, magazines, newspapers, and textbooks.
- Search for print resources using electronic databases or with help from the reference librarian.

Electronic Resources

- Find electronic resources using search engines on the Internet.
- Choose only authoritative, reliable sites, such as those ending in:
  .edu (educational institution)
  .gov (government group)
  .org (not-for-profit organization; these may be biased)
- If you are not sure that a site is reliable and unbiased, do not use it.

Interviews with Experts

- Ask questions of an expert on your topic.
- Set up a short in-person, e-mail, or telephone interview.
- Record the interview and take good notes.

Multimedia Resources

- Watch film or TV documentaries about your topic.
- Listen to podcasts related to the topic.
- Search for relevant photos, diagrams, charts, and graphs.

Evaluate Your Sources Do not assume that all sources of information on your topic are useful, good, or trustworthy. Use the checklist on page 233 to evaluate sources of information you find. The more questions that you can answer with a yes, the more likely you should use the source.

Checklist for Evaluating Sources

Does the source of information:

❏ Contain **relevant** information that answers your research questions?

❏ Provide **facts** and not just unsupported **subjective** opinions?

❏ Give facts and details at a level you can understand?

❏ Tell all sides of a story, so that it is **unbiased**?

❏ Provide **authoritative and accurate** information written or compiled by experts?

❏ Have a recent **publication date**, indicating it is up-to-date?

WRITING COACH

Online

www.phwritingcoach.com

Online Journal

Record your answers and ideas in the online journal.

Distinguish Between Types of Sources As you research, you will discover two kinds of sources: primary sources and secondary sources. Your teacher may require that you use both.

- A **primary source** is an original document you use for a firsthand account or investigation of your topic. For example, population data collected by the parks department is a primary source. Letters, diaries, and speeches are other examples.

- A **secondary source** is research that someone else has conducted and published. For example, a book called *The Birds of Central Texas* is a secondary source. When you use a secondary source, you are using another researcher's point of view on a topic.

Partner Talk

Review your sources with a partner. Discuss why one source is more useful than another.

Apply It! Create a written **research plan** and timeline with steps you can apply to obtain and evaluate information and to finish your report. After you have done some research in reference works and completed some additional text searches, create and follow a written research plan. List at least four relevant sources, including print and electronic resources, of information that you plan to use.

- Work with your teacher to set deadlines for finishing each step: research, thesis statement, drafting, and final report.

- For each source you plan to use, record full **bibliographic** information in a **standard format**. (See page 236.)

- Use the Checklist for Evaluating Sources to explain whether each of your sources is **reliable and valid**.

- Note whether each source is primary or secondary.

Modify Your Plan After you begin to research and investigate a topic, you may need to **narrow, or broaden, your research question**. If you cannot find answers to a research question, you may decide to refocus, or change the emphasis of, your topic.

Collect and Organize Your Data

As you follow your research plan for your informational research report, you will need to use **multiple sources** of information. Notes will help you remember and keep track of your sources and information. Different forms of notes include handwritten notes on note cards, typed notes in an electronic document, and a learning log summarizing what you know and still need to know about your topic.

Keep Track of Multiple Sources You can create a card for each source, and give each its own number. **Note the full bibliographic information,** or publishing details for the source, including the author, title, city of publication, publisher, and copyright date. The example shown is from the Student Model. It matches MLA style used in the Works Cited on page 229.

Take Notes When you take notes from a relevant print or electronic source, follow these guidelines.

- Note only **relevant** information—facts and details that get at your research question.

- Look for longer thematic patterns or constructs in the information you investigate. **Categorize** the notes using headings that sum up the **theme** or main idea of each group of notes.

- Be very careful to use your own words. It's all right to use abbreviations and incomplete sentences in your notes.

- If you want to quote someone, enclose the exact words in large quotation marks. If you are taking notes on a computer, you might also boldface the whole quotation. These techniques will remind you that the words are someone else's and not your own.

Apply It! Create numbered source cards for all of your sources. Take notes from each source, creating a different note card for each category of information. Organizing notes by **categories or themes** can help you to make connections between data and to see big ideas. Paraphrase or summarize the information in your own words. If you want to include a direct quotation, carefully copy the original and enclose the quotation in quotation marks.

Source 3

Utley, Robert M., ed. _The Story of the West._ New York: DK Publishing, Inc., 2003. Print.

Notes From Source 3

Cowboys and railroads

- *Till about 1880, rr lines were far from cattle ranches, so cowboys had to drive cattle to railheads.*

- *As rr lines came West, long cattle drives no longer needed.*

Avoid Plagiarism

Plagiarism is presenting someone else's words or ideas as your own, without documenting, or identifying, the source of the information. Plagiarism is a serious error with severe consequences. Do not plagiarize.

Careful Note-taking Matters You can plagiarize without meaning to do so. The student who wrote this note card made mistakes. She followed the original source too closely. Also, she didn't include a source number that would link the note card to its source's full publication information.

www.phwritingcoach.com

Online Journal
Record your answers and ideas in the online journal.

> The cradle of the range-cattle industry was post-Civil-War Texas, and there livestock dominated the economy, despite depressed conditions of local markets. Little else was available to returning Confederate veterans who sought employment, or to the adolescent sons of men killed in the war.

Original Source

Post-Civil War

Post-Civil War Texas was the cradle of the cattle industry. Livestock dominated the Texas economy, even though local markets were sometimes depressed. Returning Confederate veterans had little employment available to them. This was also true of sons of men killed in the war.

from Cowboy Life: Reconstructing an American Myth by William W. Savage, Jr.

Plagiarized Notes

Partner Talk

Review taking notes with a partner. Explain why each of these is important:

- Citing valid and reliable sources
- Using your own words to summarize ideas
- Making large quotation marks for direct quotations

Monitor your partner's spoken language by asking follow-up questions.

Use these strategies to avoid plagiarism.

- **Paraphrase** When you paraphrase information from a source, restate the writer's idea using your own words. Read a passage, and think about what it means. Then, write it as you might explain it to someone else.

- **Summarize** When you summarize a long passage from a source, briefly state its most important ideas in your own words.

- **Direct Quote** If you use a direct quotation, enclose the writer's exact words in quotation marks, and identify who said it.

Try It! Look at the plagiarized notes in the example. Highlight the parts to differentiate the lines that are plagiarizing rather than paraphrasing the original. Now, write a new note based on the original source. Do not plagiarize.

Document Your Sources

When you write a research report, you need to cite all **researched information** that is not common knowledge, and cite it **according to a standard format.**

Works Cited On the Works Cited page at the end of your report, list all the sources that you used. Do not include sources you looked into but did not use. Follow the format shown in a standard style manual, such as that of the Modern Language Association (MLA) or American Psychological Association (APA). Your teacher will tell you which standard format style to use.

Look at the example citations. Use these and the MLA Style for Listing Sources on page R16 as a guide for writing your citations. Pay attention to formatting, including italics, abbreviations, and punctuation.

Book

Author's last name, author's first name followed by the author's middle name or initial (if given). *Full title of book.* City where book was published: Name of publisher, year of publication. Medium of publication.

Slatta, Richard W. *Cowboy: The Illustrated History.* New York: Sterling, 2006. Print.

Magazine Article

Author's last name, author's first name followed by the author's middle name or initial (if given). "Title of article." *Title of magazine* Full date of magazine issue: page numbers or plus sign (+) if the article appears on nonconsecutive pages. Medium of publication.

Draper, Robert. "21st Century Cowboys: Why the Spirit Endures." *National Geographic* Dec. 2007: 114+. Print.

Web Page

Author's last name, author's first name followed by author's middle name or initial (if given) OR compiler, or editor (if given). "Name of page." *Name of Web site.* Name of publisher, institution, or sponsor OR N.p if none given, date of posting OR n.d. if none given. Medium of publication. Date on which you accessed the page.

Officer, Lawrence H. and Samuel H. Williamson. "Six Ways to Compute the Relative Value of a U.S. Dollar Amount, 1774 to Present." *Measuring Worth.* Measuring Worth, 2009. Web. 2 Nov 2009.

Parenthetical Citations A parenthetical citation refers to a source listed on the Works Cited page. It helps you to **avoid plagiarizing by integrating,** or including, **source information** right in your report. Because a parenthetical citation gives just the author or title and page number, it does not interrupt **the flow ideas.** Here is a parenthetical citation from the Student Model.

 **STUDENT MODEL** from **"The Cowboy: Myth Versus Reality"** page 227; lines 33–35

> One person who had seen "real cowboys" remarked that a cowboy is "just a plain bowlegged human who smelled very horsey at times" (Burns).

If the name of the author is mentioned in the sentence, only the page number is given in parentheses.

> In contrast, Schultz and Tishler say, most actual cowboys were short and slight (though wiry), so as not to weigh down their horses (2).

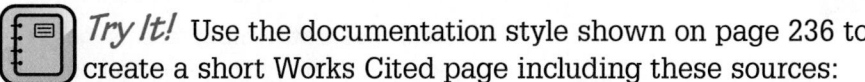 *Try It!* Use the documentation style shown on page 236 to create a short Works Cited page including these sources:

- A Web page called "Rawhide Rodeo Company." The Web site is called rawhiderodeo.com. No information about the author, publisher, or date is available. The writer looked at the page on December 20, 2009.

- An article titled "Calling All Cowboys" by Suzanne Bopp in *National Geographic TRAVELER* magazine. It was published in September 2008 on pages 60–64.

Critique Your Research Process

At every step in the research process, be prepared to adjust or change your research plan. If you can't find enough information, **try broadening your research question.** If you have too much information, you might need to **narrow your question.** In either case, it's important to stick to your **timetable.** If you've found answers to your research question, you're ready to start drafting.

 *Apply It!* Write an entry on your Works Cited page for every source you used for information in your report. To format your sources correctly, use MLA style or the style your teacher has directed you to use. Confirm that you have researched enough information to begin writing your draft.

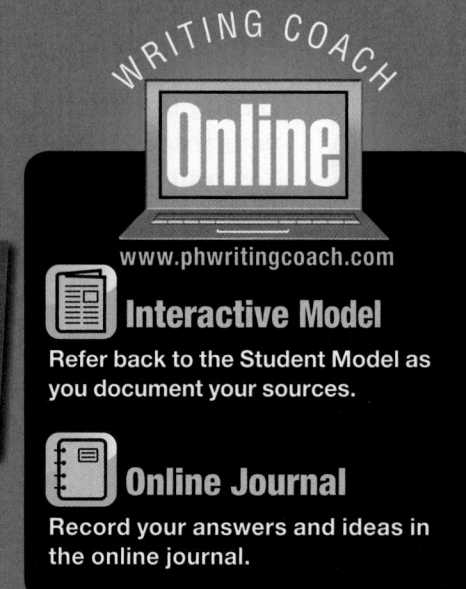

WRITING COACH

Online

www.phwritingcoach.com

Interactive Model

Refer back to the Student Model as you document your sources.

Online Journal

Record your answers and ideas in the online journal.

Partner Talk

Get together with a partner to discuss research sources. Where have you looked for information on your topic? What sources are reliable? How have you been keeping track of the sources you have used? As you speak, practice newly acquired vocabulary by correctly producing the word's sound.

Drafting

During the drafting stage, you will start to write your ideas for your research report. You will write a **clear thesis statement**. You will follow an outline that provides an **organizational strategy** to help you write a **focused, organized, and coherent** research report. As you write your draft or prepare your notes for an oral report, remember to keep your audience in mind.

The Organization of an Informational Research Report

The chart shows an organizational strategy for a research report. Look back at how the Student Model follows this same strategy. Then, create a detailed outline for your research report. Use the template on page R26 to develop your outline. Refer to your Outline for Success as you work.

Outline for Success

I. Introduction
See Student Model, p. 226.

- Lively opening
- Clear thesis statement

II. Body
See Student Model, pp. 226–228.

- Synthesis of information from multiple sources
- Systematic organization of research findings
- Evidence that supports the thesis statement
- Graphics and illustrations to explain concepts

III. Conclusion
See Student Model, p. 229.

- Restatement of thesis
- Memorable ending with a final thought or conclusion

Introduce Your Thesis Statement

- A quotation, story, question, or interesting fact will grab the reader's attention.
- A **clear thesis statement** reflects the major conclusion you have drawn from your research.

Support Your Thesis Statement

- The body of your report synthesizes, or brings together, information to support your **thesis statement**.
- You've grouped your note cards by category, and these categories become major headings in your outline.
- Each paragraph states a major idea and supports it with **evidence,** such as facts, statistics, and examples.
- Photos, charts, diagrams, or other visuals help convey complicated information.

Add a Final Thought

- Your **conclusion** about your topic is restated in the final paragraph.
- You may suggest a new idea or follow-up to the report. In the Student Model, for example, the writer suggests that the reader view a video about contemporary cowboys.

Start Your Draft

To complete your draft, use the checklist. Use your specific thesis statement; your detailed outline that shows your topic sentence and supporting evidence, and your plan for the logical organization of the main ideas; and the Outline for Success as guides.

While drafting, aim at writing your ideas, not on making your writing perfect. Remember, you will have the chance to improve your draft when you revise and edit.

√ Begin your **introduction** with several sentences that catch your reader's attention.

√ End with a clearly worded **thesis statement** based on the **conclusion** you've drawn about your research question.

√ Present your findings in a meaningful format. Develop the **body** of the report one paragraph at a time. Choose only the strongest **supporting evidence** for each **idea**.

√ For each paragraph, draft a **topic sentence** stating the main idea. Each main idea should support your thesis.

√ Marshal the evidence you have collected and organized, then synthesize it to support and explain your topic.

√ Include conclusions you draw from your research. Summarize or paraphrase your research findings in a systematic way that readers can understand. Remember to give relevant, logical reasons for your conclusions.

√ Draft a **concluding paragraph** that restates your thesis. Try to add a final thought to make the ending more memorable or interesting.

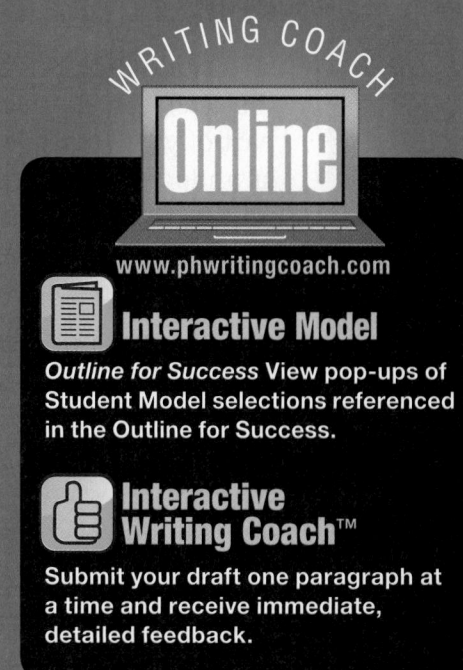

WRITING COACH

Online

www.phwritingcoach.com

Interactive Model

Outline for Success View pop-ups of Student Model selections referenced in the Outline for Success.

Interactive Writing Coach™

Submit your draft one paragraph at a time and receive immediate, detailed feedback.

Provide and Document Evidence

While you are drafting, you will provide **evidence** to support your thesis statement and related claims. Your **claims** are an important part of your **analysis** of your topic. They are your **point of view** or understanding of information connected to you. Be careful to differentiate between your opinions and ideas and those of other people. To do so, **document** the words and ideas of other people when you provide evidence.

Give Facts and Statistics Facts are convincing evidence because they can be proven true. Statistics, or facts stated in numbers, are also convincing when they come from authoritative and up-to-date sources. Document facts and statistics that are not common knowledge or that could not be found in most sources about a topic.

Give Examples Use concrete examples to make abstract or complicated ideas easier to understand. You must identify the source of examples that you found in your research, but you do not need to document examples from your personal experience or observations.

Quote Authorities Direct quotations can be convincing evidence. However, you should not use a quotation when **summarizing** or **paraphrasing** would be just as clear. Weave quotations and citations into the flow of your ideas as shown in this example from the Student Model.

 **STUDENT MODEL** from **"The Cowboy: Myth Versus Reality"** page 227; lines 37–40

> In 1875, a Wyoming newspaper described a group of "real" cowboys as "rough men with shaggy hair and wild staring eyes in butternut trousers stuffed into great rough boots" (Schultz and Tishler).

Remember these guidelines:

- Use your own words to identify the expert, integrating quotations and citations into your text to maintain the flow of ideas.
- Separate and inset a quote of four lines or more.
- Use correct punctuation and an accepted format. (See pages 246–247.)
- Follow quotes with a proper parenthetical citation.

Apply It! Draft a paragraph for your research report. Your paragraph should include facts, examples, a quotation, and citation. Remember to correctly format your quotations and citations to avoid interrupting the flow of your ideas.

Use Graphics and Illustrations

Your report can present evidence in graphics and visuals as well as words. For a report on a scientific topic, diagrams, charts, and other types of graphics can help your audience understand your ideas. In other reports, photographs, maps, and other graphics can add valuable concrete detail. Be sure to refer to the graphic (usually called a "figure") in your text. Then, label your visual with a figure or table number, caption, and source citations for the data. Use caution when copying an existing graphic because you will need permission from the copyright holder if you publish your work for use outside school.

- **Photographs** Use a photograph to help your audience picture how something looks. If you insert a photograph in your report, include a caption, or brief sentence explaining what the photo shows.

- **Maps** By providing geographic information visually, maps give your reader a better idea of locations you mention in your report. Always include a legend and a compass rose.

- **Charts, Tables, and Graphs** Create a chart, table, or graph to provide information in a more visual or organized way. Give each a title that tells what it shows. If you include more than one, number them in numerical order. Include a citation for the source of information you used to create the chart, table, or graph.

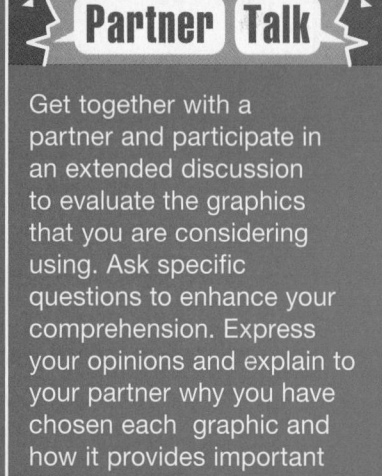

Ethnicity of Cowboys in the Old West

- **25%** African-American Cowboys
- **63%** Anglo and other (including Native American) Cowboys
- **12%** Mexican and other Hispanic Cowboys

Source: Based on data from Schultz and Tishler

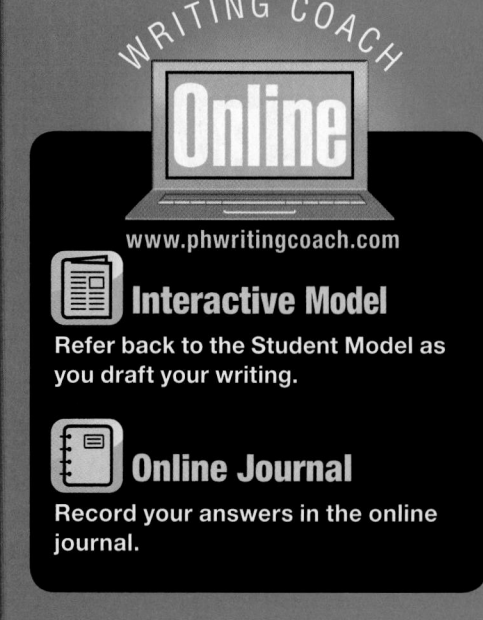

Partner Talk

Get together with a partner and participate in an extended discussion to evaluate the graphics that you are considering using. Ask specific questions to enhance your comprehension. Express your opinions and explain to your partner why you have chosen each graphic and how it provides important information for your report.

Apply It! Brainstorm for two graphics that you might use to present information in your informational research report in the most meaningful format.

- Be sure to identify the type of information each graphic would explain, find or create the two graphics, and integrate them into your report.

- Remember to give your graphics titles.

- Use a style manual to format graphics and to document your sources.

- Use peer, teacher, or family feedback to check that the quality of your created and researched visuals is appropriate for your report.

Revising: Making It Better

Now that you have finished your draft, you are ready to revise. Think about the "big picture" of **audience, purpose, and genre**. You can use the Revision RADaR strategy as a guide for making changes to improve your draft. Revision RADaR provides four major ways to improve your writing: (R) replace, (A) add, (D) delete, and (R) reorder.

Kelly Gallagher, M. Ed.

KEEP REVISION ON YOUR RADAR

Read part of the first draft of the Student Model "The Cowboy: Myth Versus Reality." Then, look at the writer's questions about how well her draft addressed issues of audience, purpose, and genre.

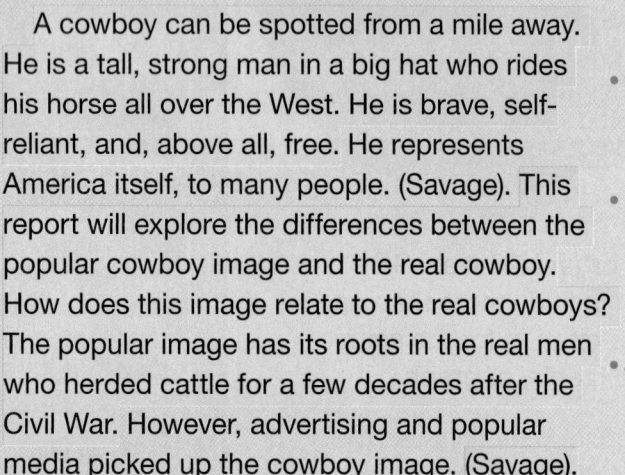

The Cowboy: Myth Versus Reality

1ST DRAFT

A cowboy can be spotted from a mile away. He is a tall, strong man in a big hat who rides his horse all over the West. He is brave, self-reliant, and, above all, free. He represents America itself, to many people. (Savage). This report will explore the differences between the popular cowboy image and the real cowboy. How does this image relate to the real cowboys? The popular image has its roots in the real men who herded cattle for a few decades after the Civil War. However, advertising and popular media picked up the cowboy image. (Savage).

*Have I created a lively **opening** that grabs my reader's attention?*

*Is this the best statement of what I plan to do? Should this **thesis statement** come later in the paragraph?*

*Have I used the **appropriate format** to credit my source?*

*Is this **evidence** relevant? Does it support my thesis?*

Now look at how the writer applied Revision RADaR to write an improved second draft.

The Cowboy: Myth Versus Reality

Everyone can spot a cowboy a mile away. He is a tall, strong man wearing a big hat, high boots, and bandana. He roams the West on horseback, like a knight of old. He spends most of his time alone except for his best friend—his horse. He is brave, self-reliant, and, above all, free. To many, he represents America itself. (Savage 6). How does this image relate to the real cowboys? The popular image has its roots in the real men who herded cattle for a few decades after the Civil War. However, advertising and popular media reshaped the cowboys' image and smoothed away the less appealing parts of their lives (Savage 9). This report will show that the popular image of the cowboy is more myth than reality.

D *Added the sentences to make the beginning livelier*

A *Added the page number to make the citation complete*

R *Replaced vague information about the media and popular culture with specific information, paraphrased from a source*

R *Reordered the thesis statement, placing it at the end of the introductory paragraph*

Video

Learn more strategies for effective writing from program author Kelly Gallagher.

Interactive Writing Coach™

Use the Revision RADaR Strategy in your own writing. Then, submit your draft paragraph by paragraph for feedback.

 Apply It! Use your Revision RADaR to revise your draft.

- First, determine whether you have addressed the needs of your audience, stated your thesis, and included the characteristics of an effective research report. Then, check that your ideas make sense within each paragraph and sentence, to track whether your text has **internal coherence.** Also check for **external coherence** by making sure the entire report flows logically.

- Then, apply Revision RADaR to make needed changes. Remember—you can use the steps in the strategy in any order.

REPLACE ADD DELETE and REORDER

RADaR

Look at the Big Picture

Use the chart and your analytical skills to evaluate how well each section of your research report addresses **purpose, audience, and genre.** When necessary, use the suggestions in the chart to revise your piece.

Section	Evaluate	Revise
Introduction	• Check that the **opening paragraphs** grab readers' attention and make them want to learn more about your topic.	• Add a quotation, anecdote (brief story), or question to make your introduction lively.
	• Make sure you have a **clear thesis statement** that sets forth the major ideas your report will develop.	• Clarify your thesis statement to be sure it identifies the conclusions you have drawn about the topic.
Body	• Make sure each body paragraph develops one main idea and uses **marshalled evidence** to explain the topic.	• Add a topic sentence to each paragraph. Add evidence to support weakly developed paragraphs.
	• Evaluate the **relevance** of the reasons and evidence you use to support your conclusions.	• Take out any details that are not clearly tied to your purposes.
	• Check that information and major ideas are summarized, paraphrased, and organized in a **systematic way**.	• Compare paragraphs to your original outline to make sure similar ideas are categorized by theme or subtopic.
	• Make sure that you have used graphics when a visual can best illustrate the data.	• Convert data into graphics or pick up existing graphics to present your findings in the most meaningful format.
	• Make sure quotations and facts that are not common knowledge are **documented** and **formatted** and do not interrupt the flow of ideas.	• Review your note cards and source cards to confirm the source of each quotation. Add **parenthetical citations** in the correct format and style.
Conclusion	• Check that your final paragraph **restates your thesis**.	• If needed, revise the introduction and conclusion to ensure they agree.
	• Make sure your research report ends with a new **insight.**	• Add a quotation or fact that brings your report to a definite end.
Works Cited/ Bibliography	• Complete your **source list** using the style specified by your teacher.	• Add all documented sources you used in your paper to the Works Cited page.

Focus on Craft: Sentence Variety

Sentences can have different lengths and structures. Some are short and punchy, while others can flow on, connecting several ideas. Sentences can begin in different ways: with a pronoun or noun, with a series of adjectives, or with a prepositional or participial phrase. When you write a research report, try to vary the lengths, structures, and beginnings of your sentences. If you do, your writing will be more interesting to read and will flow more effectively. Look at these sentences from the Student Model.

 **STUDENT MODEL** from **"The Cowboy: Myth Versus Reality"** page 226; lines 1–7

Everyone can spot a cowboy a mile away. He is a tall, strong man wearing a big hat, high boots, and bandana. He roams the West on horseback, like a knight of old. He spends most of his time alone except for his best friend—his horse. He is brave, self-reliant, and, above all, free. To many, he represents America itself (Savage 6).

 Try It! Now, ask yourself these questions. Record your answers in your journal.

1. Compare the first and second drafts (pages 242–243). Why does the student writer change the structure of the first sentence?

2. Do any sentences in this paragraph begin in the same way? Would you advise the writer to change more sentence beginnings, or is repetition effective here?

Fine-Tune Your Draft

Apply It! Use the revision suggestions to prepare your final draft. Make sure you keep your audience and purpose in mind.

- **Focus on Sentence Variety** Ensure a mix of shorter and longer sentences. Follow a simple sentence with a compound or complex sentence.

- **Use Effective Transitions** Use transitional words and phrases such as *also* and *as a result* to link ideas and connect sentences and paragraphs. Because of the length of your work, you may need transitional sentences or paragraphs to help readers follow your thinking.

Teacher and Family Feedback Share your draft with your teacher or a family member. Carefully review the comments you receive and revise your final draft as needed.

Editing: Making It Correct

Before editing your final draft, you need to make sure you have accurately **paraphrased, summarized, quoted,** and **cited** all researched information. Edit your draft to correctly document sources and format the source material, including quotations. Your teacher can provide guidance on which standard format to follow. Finally, edit your final draft for errors in grammar, mechanics, and spelling.

WRITE GUY *Jeff Anderson, M. Ed.*

WHAT DO YOU NOTICE?

Zoom in on Conventions Focus on quotations as you zoom in on these lines from the Student Model.

 **STUDENT MODEL** from **"The Cowboy: Myth Versus Reality"**
page 227; lines 37–40

> In 1875, a Wyoming newspaper described a group of "real" cowboys as "rough men with shaggy hair and wild staring eyes in butternut trousers stuffed into great rough boots" (Schultz and Tishler).

To learn more about integrating quotations, see Grammar Game Plan Error 18, page 290.

Now, ask yourself this question: *How well has the writer integrated the quotation into her paragraph?*

Perhaps you noted that the writer used these helpful techniques to surround the quotation:

- Provided an introductory phrase that tells when the quotation occurred
- Indicated where the quotation originally appeared and what its purpose was
- Told where the quotation was found, using the standard format for parenthetical citations

Partner Talk Discuss this question with a partner: *How easy or hard is it to figure out which words from the Student Model are the student's and which words are not the student's?*

Grammar Mini-Lesson: Punctuation

Punctuating Quotations With Citations Quotations follow some specific rules for punctuation. Study the sentence from the Student Model. Notice how the writer punctuated the quotation with a citation. Notice the period comes after the citation in parentheses.

> *To learn more, see Chapter 25.*

 **STUDENT MODEL** from **"The Cowboy: Myth Versus Reality"**
page 227; lines 33–35

One person who had seen "real cowboys" remarked that a cowboy is "just a plain bowlegged human who smelled very horsey at times" (Burns).

 *Try It!* Which of these sentences uses correct punctuation for the quotation and for the citation in the parentheses? Write the answers in your journal.

1. Ken Burns and Stephen Ives, the filmmakers, have said "America without the West is unthinkable now." (Episode 5.)

2. Ken Burns and Stephen Ives, the filmmakers, have said, "America without the West is unthinkable now" (Episode 5).

 Apply It! Edit your draft for grammar, mechanics, and spelling. If necessary, rewrite sentences to integrate quotations more smoothly into your text to maintain the flow of ideas. Punctuate and cite quotations correctly.

 Use the rubric to evaluate your piece. If necessary, rethink, rewrite, or revise.

WRITING COACH **Online**

www.phwritingcoach.com

Video
Learn effective editing techniques from program author Jeff Anderson.

Online Journal
Try It! Record your answers in the online journal.

Interactive Model
Refer back to the Student Model as you edit your writing.

Interactive Writing Coach™
Edit your draft and check it against the rubric. Submit it paragraph by paragraph for feedback.

Rubric for Informational Research Writing	Rating Scale					
Ideas: How focused and clearly supported is your thesis statement?	Not very 1	2	3	4	5	Very 6
Organization: How logical is the progression of your ideas?	1	2	3	4	5	6
Voice: How clearly is your point of view expressed?	1	2	3	4	5	6
Word Choice: How effectively does your word choice develop and support your thesis statement?	1	2	3	4	5	6
Sentence Fluency: How well have you varied the sentence types in your report?	1	2	3	4	5	6
Conventions: How correctly are your sources formatted?	1	2	3	4	5	6

Publishing

It is time to share your research report. When you've finished your final draft, publish it for an appropriate audience.

Wrap Up Your Presentation

You teacher may require you to turn in a typed report. Follow the guidelines provided. Create a cover sheet, table of contents, and Works Cited list. Also be sure to add a lively title that indicates the topic of the report.

Publish Your Piece

Use a chart to brainstorm for ways to publish your research report to an appropriate audience. You may decide to circulate or post a written report or share an oral report or multimedia presentation.

If your audience is...	...then publish it by...
Students or teachers at school	• Displaying your report in the library, media center, or other public place • Posting your report on a Web site dedicated to student work
A club with a special interest like science, music, or history	• Giving a talk or doing a multimedia presentation at one of the club's meetings • Submitting your report to the club's newsletter or Web site

 ## Reflect on Your Writing

Now that you are done with your informational research report, read it over and use your writing journal to answer these questions.

- Which parts of your research report please you the most? Which parts could be improved?
- What will you do differently for your next research report?
- What useful things have you learned about doing research?

 **The Big Question: Why Write?** Did you understand your subject well enough to write about it? How did you find out what all the facts were?

Manage Your Portfolio You may include your published informational research report in your writing portfolio. If so, consider what this piece reveals about your writing and your growth as a writer.

MAKE YOUR WRITING COUNT

Write a Press Conference Script

Research reports often reveal surprising answers to the questions they pose. Inform your schoolmates about a surprising research report by preparing a **script for a press conference.**

In a press conference, someone with information to share with the press invites journalists to hear that announcement and ask questions. With a group, write a script for a mock press conference about information from a research report. Then, produce a **multimedia presentation.** Your presentation should use text and graphics. Act out your script for classmates, or record it and present it as a podcast.

WRITING COACH

Online

www.phwritingcoach.com

Online Journal

Reflect on Your Writing Record your answers and ideas in the online journal.

Resource

Link to resources on 21st Century Learning for help in creating a group project.

Here's your action plan.

1. With your group, choose roles such as moderator, one or more experts, and reporters.

2. Select a report from your group that reveals surprising information. Create text, such as a bulleted list of key points, and a supporting graphic to share the news.

3. View a press conference online. Notice how reporters and speakers interact. Pay attention to text and graphics.

4. Plan and write your script.

   - The moderator introduces the experts and topic.
   - The experts give a statement and answer questions, referring to supporting text and graphics.
   - The reporters ask questions and dig for the truth.

5. Practice your presentation. Act out your script for classmates.

6. If presenting a podcast, video-record your press conference and play it for the class.

Listening and Speaking As a group, discuss how to present your script. Memorize the text of the script, and practice your presentation using the graphics. Ask listeners to give feedback on the position and evidence given. Presenters should adjust their content, volume, and pacing accordingly. During the presentation, work to act like participants in a real press conference.

Your Turn

Writing For Media:
Online Consumer Report

Online Consumer Report

21st Century Learning

What kinds of applications do various cell phones have? Do some work better than others? Which airlines are the most economical and give the best service? Which commercial dog foods have received the highest recommendations? You can find answers to all your consumer questions by searching the Internet.

In this assignment, you will create your own **online consumer report** about a product or service. You'll follow a research plan as you gather information from multiple sources. Then, you'll put it all together to tell your audience about the pros and cons of various competing products or services. You may provide links from parenthetical citations to a separate Works Cited page.

Try It! Study the excerpt from the online consumer report shown. Then, answer these questions. Record your answers in your journal.

1. What **consumer** product or service is the writer describing?

2. What do you think is the writer's **purpose?** Who do you think is the intended audience?

3. An online consumer report gives **essential information** about a specific product or service, often including statistics about its quality. What information is shown here?

4. Is the writing **subjective,** presenting the writer's opinion, or **objective,** presenting only factual information? How can you tell?

5. What effect does the **photograph** have? What other kinds of visuals would be helpful in this report?

Off to a Flying Start

Airline passengers can sometimes feel like excess baggage. They trudge through long lines at airports. They hover for hours at the gates before they are allowed onto a late-arriving plane. After they squeeze into their seats, they often sit for an hour or more on the tarmac waiting for the plane to take off. The good news is that a relatively new airline, Jet Plane Air, has paid more-than-usual attention to being flyer-friendly.

Jet Plane started flying in 2007, and so far, its "on-time arrival" rate is 82%, which places it near the top among airlines and well above the average of 77%. So far, the airline's in-flight service has received high marks from consumers. Coach passengers have 7% more seating room and legroom than average. *(Jet Plane Air Annual Report, 2009)* Also, passengers in coach receive free meals and free in-flight movies.

Jet Plane Air is not perfect, of course. It schedules fewer flights than larger airlines, although it does fly to most large cities in the U.S. and Canada. It also has no overseas flights. Because it is a new airline, we do not know if Jet Plane Air will maintain its high consumer ratings and excellent flight record. For now, this new airline is off to a flying start. For the latest information, visit the Department of Transportation's Aviation Consumer Protection Division Web site *(Air Consumer on the Web)*.

Create an Online Consumer Report

Follow these steps to create your own **online consumer report**. To plan your online consumer report, review the graphic organizers on pages R24–R27 and choose one that suits your needs.

Prewriting

- Consult with others and brainstorm for a list of products and services that you or your family might want to purchase or use in the home or outside the home. When you've finished, circle the topic you have chosen.

- Be sure to identify the target **audience** for your online report. Are you writing to **inform** an audience of teenagers? Families? Parents?

- It's important to create a **research plan** to identify what specific **research question** you will try to answer. You'll need to **gather information** from **a wide variety of sources**. Include steps in your plan for **obtaining and evaluating** information.

- After some preliminary research in reference works and additional texts, create a **written plan** for more specific resources, including print and electronic sources.

- **Evaluate** every source you consider using. Decide whether a source is **reliable** and **valid.** The Internet has the most up-to-date reviews of products and services, but be careful to evaluate review sites for bias.

- **Categorize** your notes to help you see broader patterns. You may need to **broaden or narrow** your research question in order to produce better results. Refine your plan as needed.

- As you take notes, **paraphrase** or **summarize** information. If you use a **direct quotation,** enclose it in big quotation marks to avoid plagiarism. Categorize your notes according to themes or subtopics in order to make connections and see big ideas.

- Find **graphics** and **illustrations** to add to your report. Be sure to record source information for any graphics you intend to use.

- Document your **sources** by making a source card for each source you use. For all notes, record bibliographic information according to a standard format.

WRITING COACH

www.phwritingcoach.com

Online Journal

Try It! **Record your answers in the online journal.**

Interactive Graphic Organizers

Choose from a variety of graphic organizers to plan and develop your project.

Partner Talk

Work with a partner to critique your research plan and research. Discuss:
- The difference between plagiarism and paraphrasing
- The importance of citing valid and reliable sources
- The reasons that one source is more useful than another

Your Turn ▶ **Online Consumer Report** (*continued*)

Drafting

- **Categorize** your notes by subject heading, such as Product Description, Strong Points, Weak Points, or Overall Recommendation. Create an outline based on your subject headings. Then, start writing sentences and paragraphs.

- Present your findings in a **systematic way,** based on your outline and using summarizing or paraphrasing to share your findings. Lively **subheadings** will organize your report and help readers understand the conclusions you have drawn.

- Do not plagiarize. Use your own words, and enclose any direct quotations in quotation marks.

- A good consumer report anticipates the reader's needs and questions about the product or service. Begin with a lively opening that leads up to a **thesis statement** and clearly reveals the **conclusion** you've drawn from your research.

- Marshal the evidence you have collected and organized to **describe** the product or service. Use **graphics** and **illustrations** to present your findings in a meaningful format. Give readers logical and **relevant reasons** for your conclusions.

- Acknowledge your **sources** as needed in context or in a credits section. Avoid interrupting the flow of the report. Use accepted formats for integrating quotations and citations.

Revising

Use Revision RADaR techniques as you review your draft carefully.

- **Replace** general terms with vivid details and unclear explanations with precise ideas.

- **Add** specific details or missing information to support your argument.

- **Delete** information that does not support your thesis or develop your argument.

- **Reorder** sentences and paragraphs to present ideas clearly and logically.

Read aloud your online report to make sure it reads smoothly. Vary sentence lengths. Tie ideas together with transition words.

Editing

Now take the time to check your Online Consumer Report carefully before you post it online. Focus on each sentence and then on each word. Look for these common kinds of errors:

- Errors in subject-verb agreement
- Errors in pronoun usage
- Run-on sentences and sentence fragments
- Spelling and capitalization mistakes
- Omitted punctuation marks
- Improper citations and punctuation of quotations

Publishing

- If your school newspaper has an online version, submit your online consumer report to the editor.
- Search for online forums specializing in the type of product or service that you are writing about, and submit your report as a comment. Some sites specialize in communication technology products, while others provide more general consumer information sites.
- Post your consumer report as a blog entry. Search for one of the Web sites that allow users to create a free blog.
- With your classmates, compile your consumer reports into a Student Consumer Guide. Organize the guide by type of product or service. Print it for classroom display or for your school library.

Extension Find another example of an Online Consumer Report, and compare it with the one you are writing.

WRITING COACH
Online
www.phwritingcoach.com

Interactive Graphic Organizers

Choose from a variety of graphic organizers to plan and develop your project.

Partner Talk

Exchange drafts with a partner, and give each other feedback. Ask specific questions to help present an effective product. Is your report logically organized and clearly written? Does it give enough information? Consider your partner's suggestions as you revise your draft.

Writing for Assessment

Some tests include a prompt that asks you to critique a research plan. Use these prompts to practice. In your response, use the characteristics of your informational research report. (See page 224.)

 *Try It!* Read the prompt carefully, and then create a detailed **research plan.** Use the ABCDs of On-Demand Writing to help you plan and write your research plan.

Format

Write your *research plan* in the form of an outline. List everything you would do in the order you would do it. Use a main heading, such as *Topic,* and subheadings, for example, *Primary Sources.*

Research Plan Prompt

Write a research plan about a person or event related to an American president. Your plan should include a research topic and question, a list of possible sources, the audience, and the steps you'll take following a timeline. [30 minutes]

Academic Vocabulary

A research plan tells what your major research subject is and what *sources* you will use. It also includes a timeline for researching, drafting, and finalizing your report. One of the most important steps is narrowing your research question for a brief research report.

The ABCDs of On-Demand Writing

Use the following ABCDs to help you respond to the prompt.

Before you write your draft:

Attack the prompt [1 MINUTE]

- Circle or highlight important verbs in the prompt. Draw a line from the verb to what it refers to.
- Rewrite the prompt in your own words.

Brainstorm possible answers [4 MINUTES]

- Create a graphic organizer to generate ideas.
- Use one for each part of the prompt if necessary.

Choose the order of your response [1 MINUTE]

- Think about the best way to organize your ideas.
- Number your ideas in the order you will write about them. Cross out ideas you will not be using.

After you write your draft:

Detect errors before turning in the draft [1 MINUTE]

- Carefully reread your writing.
- Look for spelling, punctuation, and grammar errors.
- Make sure that your response makes sense and is complete.

More Prompts for Practice

Apply It! **Critique the research plan** in Prompt 1. In a written response, report on your ideas and make specific suggestions to improve the research plan.

- Does the writer need to broaden or narrow the **research question**? Is it appropriate for the audience and purpose?
- Is the writer planning to find enough sources? Are they varied?
- Does the writer plan to include graphics?
- Does the research plan say anything about evaluating sources?

> **Prompt 1** Cheryl wrote this research plan. Evaluate her plan to determine what she did well and what needs improvement.
>
> *My Topic:* I'm going to research the beginning of World War II. My question is, what started the war?
>
> *My Research:* I'll look for books and old newspaper articles about what triggered the conflict. I'll also search the Internet.
>
> *My Writing:* Once I have my notes, I can copy them into a draft and then revise it.

Spiral Review: Narrative If you choose to respond to Prompt 2, write a **personal narrative**. Make sure your story reflects the characteristics described on page 66.

> **Prompt 2** Write about a person who has had a major impact on you. This person could be a friend, family member, teacher, or community member. Tell about a significant experience you shared with this person and how it affected you. Use specific details and dialogue.

Spiral Review: Response to Literature If you choose to respond to Prompt 3, write a response to literature. Make sure your response to literature reflects the characteristics on page 198 and includes:

- The writing skills for a **multi-paragraph essay** (See page 146.)
- **Evidence** from the text, including **quotations**
- An analysis of the effects of the author's style or use of literary devices

> **Prompt 3** Choose an expository or literary text that you feel has an interesting conflict. Write an interpretative response about how the writer created that conflict. Include information about the problem and how it was solved, as well as an analysis of why the conflict was important.

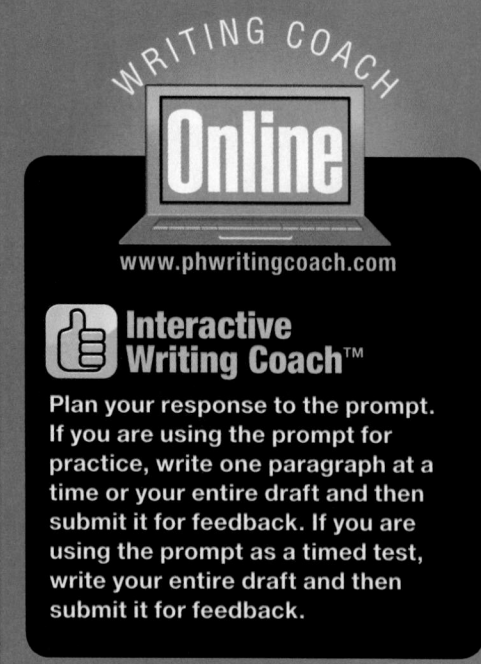

WRITING COACH

Online

www.phwritingcoach.com

Interactive Writing Coach™

Plan your response to the prompt. If you are using the prompt for practice, write one paragraph at a time or your entire draft and then submit it for feedback. If you are using the prompt as a timed test, write your entire draft and then submit it for feedback.

Remember **ABCD**

Attack the prompt

Brainstorm possible answers

Choose the order of your response

Detect errors before turning in the draft

CHAPTER 12

WORKPLACE WRITING

What's Ahead

In this chapter, you will learn how you can write workplace and practical documents, including business letters and instructions. All of these functional documents should present organized information that is accurately conveyed, or written, and presented in a reader-friendly format.

Characteristics of Writing

Effective workplace and practical writing has these characteristics:

- **Information** that is clear, concise, and focused
- A clear **purpose** and intended **audience**
- **Formal, polite** language
- **Reader-friendly formatting techniques,** such as sufficient white or blank space and clearly defined sections
- Correct **grammar, punctuation,** and **spelling** appropriate to the form of writing

Forms of Writing

Forms of workplace writing include:

Instructions are used to explain how to complete a task or procedure. They are written in a step-by-step format.

Letters of opinion are formal correspondence written to a newspaper, magazine, or other publication. They are written to express an opinion. Letters to the editor are one example of letters of opinion.

Letters of request are formal correspondence written to a business or outside organization. They are written to request information.

Memos are short documents usually written from one member of a group or organization to another or to another group. They assume some background on the topic.

Other forms of practical writing include:

Friendly letters are informal correspondence written to a friend or acquaintance. They can be written for various reasons, including to ask how someone is doing or just to say hello.

 *Try It!* For each audience and purpose described, select the appropriate form, such as a letter of request, a friendly letter, instructions, or a letter of opinion. Explain your choices.

- To ask for a class schedule from a community center
- To respond to an article in a newspaper

Connect to the Big Questions

Discuss these questions:

1 What do you think? What is the best way to share information?

2 Why write? What do daily workplace communications require of format, content, and style?

 WORD BANK

These vocabulary words are often used with workplace writing. Use the Glossary or a dictionary to check the definitions.

connection	opinion
introduce	quality

STUDENT MODEL | Friendly Letter

Learn From Experience

 After reading the friendly letter on this page, read the numbered notes in the margin to learn about how the writer presented her ideas. As you read, take notes to develop your understanding of basic sight and English vocabulary.

Try It! Record your answers and ideas in the online journal.

① The friendly letter includes a **date line** and **salutation**. Notice that a comma is placed after the salutation.

② The writer **clearly explains the reason for writing.**

③ The writer anticipates questions the reader may have and addresses them.

④ The letter ends with an appropriate **closing.** Notice that when a writer sends a friendly letter on paper, he or she signs it.

Try It!

- What is the purpose of this letter? Who is the intended audience?

- Why is it helpful to state a letter's purpose early in the letter?

- How does the writer of the Student Model create a friendly tone?

- What other appropriate closings might the writer have used to end her letter?

---

① May 18, 2010

Dear Isabel,

I'm excited to hear that you are coming to stay with your aunt this summer. Last year we had so much fun! Will you be staying for the whole month of July like last year?

② I'm wondering if you want to practice with our local swim team while you're here. Remember what a great time we had at the pool? I've joined the swim team, and I thought you might want to participate in summer practices with me.

③ My mom has already talked to Coach Buckley, and she said it would be fine for you to practice with the team.

Think about it and let me know. We have plenty of time, and whatever you decide I know we will have lots of fun this summer. I can't wait to see you!

④ Your friend,

Janine

 **Feature Assignment: Friendly Letter**

Prewriting

- Plan a first draft of your **friendly letter.** You can select from the Topic Bank or come up with an idea of your own.

TOPIC BANK

Reach Out Suppose you have a pen pal who lives in a faraway place. Write a friendly letter to your pen pal, asking what life is like in his or her part of the world.

Good Times Write a friendly letter to a relative, expressing your opinion about a family event you both attended. Include details about the time, place, and purpose of the event.

- Brainstorm for a list of ideas you would like to include in your letter. Consider what **requests for information** you might make.
- Use a telephone directory or online resource to find the accurate contact information for the letter's recipient.

 Drafting

- Use reader-friendly formatting techniques, including all the features of an informal letter.
- Use a salutation that matches your relationship with the recipient.
- **Organize the information** so that your purpose is clearly stated.
- Accurately convey information by double-checking your ideas.

Revising and Editing

Before you revise, review your draft to ensure that information is presented accurately and concisely. Ask yourself if the purpose for your letter is clearly identified and addressed.

Publishing

- Print the letter or write it neatly on paper or stationery suitable for the recipient.
- If you plan to e-mail the letter, confirm the correct e-mail address and attach your letter to a message as a Portable Document Format (PDF).

STUDENT MODEL

Letter of Opinion

Learn From Experience

 After reading the letter of opinion on this page, read the numbered notes in the margin to learn how the writer presented his ideas.

Try It! Record your answers and ideas in the online journal.

---

❶ The writer uses conventional business letter formatting, including:

- Writer's address with street, town, state, and zip code
- Date showing day, month, and year
- Recipient's address with full name
- Formal greeting and closing

❷ Notice that a colon is placed after the **salutation** of a business letter.

❸ The writer states his **opinion** in this **clear thesis statement.**

❹ **Facts and details support the point** that the writer is not the only one who thinks kids should have a voice.

❺ The writer includes a closing signature along with his typed name, following proper business formatting.

Try It!

- What is the purpose of the letter?
- In your opinion, does the letter fulfill its purpose? Why or why not?

Extension Use the letter's tone to help you distinguish fact from opinion. Write a response that summarizes the issue and responds to the writer's inferred attitude.

---

❶ Eddie Gates
4307 Windy Circle
Palm Beach Gardens, FL 33418

September 9, 2010

Mr. Maxwell Cooper, Editor
The Downtown Daily
2437 Winston Road
Palm Beach, FL 33480

❷ Dear Mr. Cooper:

❸ I am very unhappy that the Kids' Review section is being dropped from your newspaper. My parents subscribe to *The Downtown Daily,* and the Kids' Review is the first section I turn to when the newspaper arrives.

The reviews of books, movies, and video games written by kids are interesting to read and give useful information. I think it is important for kids to have a voice in their community, and I know that I am not alone.

❹ For example, *Today's News,* in Palm Beach, has a kid's editorial column where young people can give their opinions.

Please do not let kids in our community down. Keep the Kids' Review in *The Downtown Daily.*

Sincerely yours,

❺ Eddie Gates

Eddie Gates

 **Feature Assignment: Letter of Opinion**

Prewriting

- Plan a first draft of your **letter of opinion.** You can select from the Topic Bank or come up with an idea of your own.

> ### TOPIC BANK
>
> **Read All About It!** Many students opt to spend their free time playing video games or watching television rather than reading a book for enjoyment. Write a letter to the president of your town's school board about getting students more interested in reading. Offer ideas on how to get students to choose reading over other types of entertainment.
>
> **School Days** Write a letter to the editor of your school paper, either supporting or opposing its coverage of a school sports team or club.

- Brainstorm for a list of things that your letter's recipient will need to know about you and your purpose for writing the letter.
- Find the accurate contact information for the letter's recipient in a telephone directory or online resource.

 Drafting

- Use a formal salutation that matches your relationship with the recipient.
- Include organized information that clearly states your opinion.
- Accurately convey information by double-checking your facts.

Revising and Editing

- Review your draft to ensure **precise word choices**. Check to see if you have clearly expressed your opinion or **registered a complaint** in a business context.

Publishing

- If you plan to mail the letter, print the letter on paper suitable for business correspondence.
- If you plan to e-mail the letter, confirm the correct e-mail address and attach your letter to a message as a PDF.

WRITING COACH

Online

www.phwritingcoach.com

 Interactive Model
Listen to an audio recording of the Student Model.

 Online Journal
Try It! Record your answers and ideas in the online journal.

 Interactive Writing Coach™
Submit your writing and receive personalized feedback and support as you draft, revise, and edit.

 Video
Learn strategies for effective revising and editing from program authors Jeff Anderson and Kelly Gallagher.

 **Partner Talk**

Work with a partner to revise your letter. Ask for feedback on the content and organization of the information. Is your opinion clear? Is it well-supported?

STUDENT MODEL Letter of Request

Learn From Experience

 After reading the letter of request on this page, read the numbered notes in the margin to learn about how the writer presented her ideas.

Try It! Record your answers and ideas in the online journal.

---

❶ The writer uses conventional **business letter format,** including writer's address, date, recipient's address, formal salutation, and closing.

❷ The letter begins with a **clear introduction** that expresses the purpose of the letter.

❸ This **request for information** is **clear and focused**. Writers are more likely to get the results they want when their request is clear.

❹ In **formal, polite language,** the writer gives a reasonable deadline for receiving the information.

Try It!

- What impression do you think the writer makes on the reader by using proper business letter format?

- Did the writer include all the information the reader would need to fulfill her request? Explain.

- In your opinion, does the letter fulfill its purpose? Why or why not?

---

❶ Amy Parkland
539 Sunset Road
Western Springs, IL 60558

❶ March 1, 2010

❶ David Nixon, Director
Camp Shady Lanes
2400 Old Oak Lane
Hayward, WI 54843

❶ Dear Mr. Nixon,

❷ I am writing to ask about Camp Shady Lanes' programs for kids ages thirteen and up. My eight-year-old sister attended the camp last summer, and she had a great time. I think I might like to attend the camp this summer if it has programs for older kids like me.

❸ Would you please send me a brochure and any other information about the programs at Camp Shady Lanes? I am in the seventh grade, and I am looking for a camp with a lot of outdoor activities. I especially enjoy swimming and horseback riding. Does the camp offer these?

❹ It would be helpful if I could receive the information by April 15. That way, I can make a decision before the April 30 registration deadline. Thank you for your help!

❶ Sincerely,

Amy Parkland

Amy Parkland

 **Feature Assignment:
Letter of Request**

www.phwritingcoach.com

Prewriting

- Plan a first draft of your **letter of request.** You can select from the Topic Bank or come up with an idea of your own.

TOPIC BANK

How It Works Imagine that you have just gotten a new video game or electronic device, but it didn't come with any instructions. Write a letter of request to the company asking it to send you the missing instructions.

Money Back You have purchased an item and now you have changed your mind. Write a letter requesting a refund from the company. Include details about what the item is and why you no longer want it.

- Brainstorm for a list of things that your letter's recipient will need to know about you and your purpose for writing the letter.

- Find the accurate contact information for the letter's recipient in a telephone directory or online resource.

 **Drafting**

- Use reader-friendly formatting techniques, including all of the features of a business letter.

- Organize the information so that the purpose and the request are clearly stated in the letter. Use formal, business language.

- Accurately convey information by double-checking your facts.

 Revising and **Editing**

Review your draft to ensure that information is presented accurately and concisely. Ask yourself if your letter fulfills the purpose: **to request information in a business context.**

Publishing

- If you plan to mail the letter, print the letter on suitable paper.

- If you plan to e-mail the letter, confirm the correct e-mail address and attach your letter to a message as a PDF.

 **Interactive Model**

Listen to an audio recording of the Student Model.

 **Online Journal**

Try It! Record your answers and ideas in the online journal.

 **Interactive Writing Coach™**

Submit your writing and receive personalized feedback and support as you draft, revise, and edit.

 **Video**

Learn strategies for effective revising and editing from program authors Jeff Anderson and Kelly Gallagher.

Partner Talk

Read your final draft to a partner. Ask him or her if your request is clearly stated. Monitor your partner's spoken language by asking follow-up questions to confirm your understanding.

21st Century **Learning**

MAKE YOUR WRITING COUNT

Present a Research Report on Activities for Kids

Letters help people communicate important information to specific audiences. These workplace documents may involve the seeds for activities or ideas that will help classmates learn more. Make a **research report** and presentation to share with your classmates.

With a group, **brainstorm** for several topics from among your work in this chapter. Have a discussion with others and **decide on a topic** that will be helpful to someone thinking about fun activities for kids in and out of school. Work together to **formulate an open-ended research question** that will help you to produce a research report about the topic. Consider topics like joining sports teams, volunteering at local organizations, or planning a family event. Conduct some **preliminary research** in reference works and by searching additional texts to make sure that your question is a good one.

Group members should **consult** one another and **critique the process** as you work, and be prepared to adjust and clarify the research question and process as needed. Remember that a research report should:

- State a specific thesis
- Meet the needs of audience and purpose
- Express a clear point of view
- Provide supporting evidence
- Present ideas in a logical way
- Document sources using correct formatting

Organize a Kids' Fun Day to present your research results to students in your school. Share the information you have gathered in a **multimedia presentation** that uses text and graphics. You may use posters and other displays or an electronic slide show that uses presentation software.

Here's your action plan.

1. Research takes time. In a group, make a plan for several group meetings. Set objectives and choose roles for each member.

2. Work together to develop a **written research plan** that includes:

   - Obtaining and evaluating a variety of sources, including a range of **print and electronic sources** as well as data and **quotations from experts**

   - **Categorizing notes by theme** or sub-topic to big ideas

   - Using a standard format to record **bibliographic information** for all notes and sources

   - Checking elements such as publication date and point of view to ensure that your sources are **reliable and valid**

3. Discuss your findings. **Evaluate the sources,** discussing the importance of citing valid and reliable sources. Reject sources that are biased or dated and explain why they aren't useful. Work together to create a **clear thesis statement**.

4. Outline the report. Assign sections of the outline to each group member. You may need to **narrow or broaden your research question** and research further before you draft.

5. Work together to write a draft by **compiling** collected data and using the **marshalled**—collected and organized—evidence to explain the topic. As a group, discuss the difference between **plagiarism** and **paraphrasing.** Use the proper style for acknowledging sources and for **integrating quotations and citations** without interrupting the flow of ideas.

6. Revise and edit to ensure that the thesis statement is **supported by evidence.** Be sure your report **states relevant reasons for conclusions** and **summarizes** your findings in a systematic way.

7. Finally, add appropriate audio and visuals that help explain the topic and present your findings in a **meaningful format.**

8. Present your report to students, counselors, and teachers.

Listening and Speaking Practice the presentation in front of another group or each other. Listen to questions or comments from the audience to help you make improvements. On Kids' Fun Day, speak clearly and confidently to your audience.

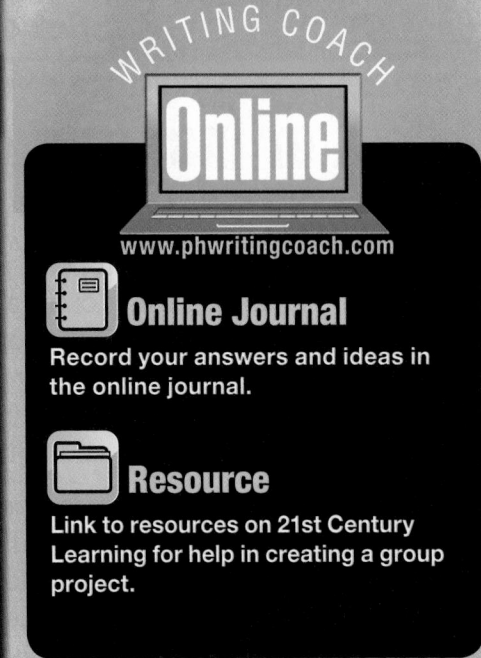

WRITING COACH

Online

www.phwritingcoach.com

Online Journal

Record your answers and ideas in the online journal.

Resource

Link to resources on 21st Century Learning for help in creating a group project.

**Writing for Media:
Set of Instructions**

21st Century Learning

Set of Instructions

Multimedia presentations are frequently used in schools, in the workplace, at conferences, and online. They are an effective way to present information to a wide audience. Multimedia presentations use a combination of text, images, music, charts, graphics, and animation. They allow people to share information on a variety of topics. A slide show allows the presenter to share only key points in text while giving an oral presentation.

A multimedia presentation is a good way to share a set of instructions. The presenter can provide information to the audience one point at a time, helping the audience to focus. Often, printed versions of the presentation are also given to the audience for reference.

Try It! Study the slides on this page. Then, answer the questions. Record your answers in your journal.

1. How does the **title slide** communicate the purpose of the multimedia presentation?

2. How do the **photos and maps** help the reader follow along?

3. Is the amount of **text** per slide reader-friendly? Explain.

4. What do you think the **presenter** should say as each slide is shown?

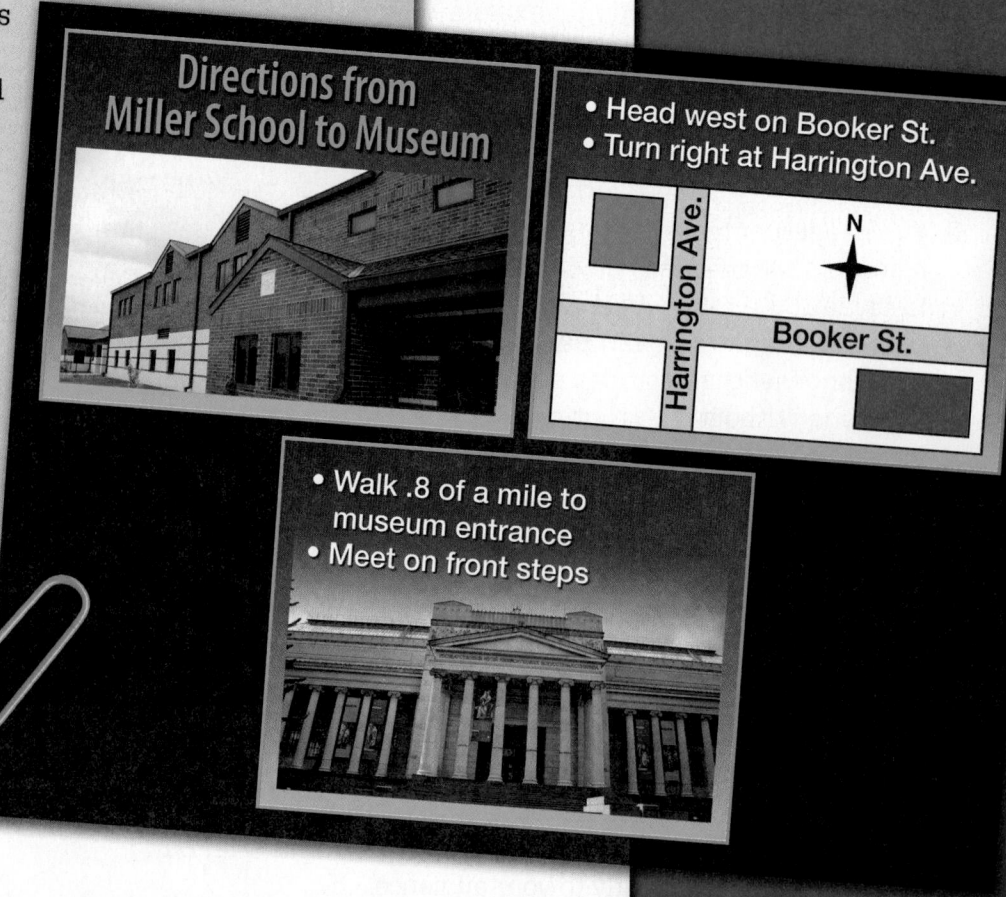

Extension Find another example of a multimedia presentation, and compare it with this one.

Create a Set of Instructions

Follow these steps to create your own multimedia slide show that features a **set of instructions.** Review the graphic organizers on R24–R27 and choose one that suits your needs.

Prewriting

- Brainstorm for a list of places to which you could provide directions using a slide show.
- Choose the one place you think is best.
- Make a list of the steps involved in the directions.
- Consider the needs of your specific audience. What does the audience already know? What do they need to know?

Drafting

- Divide your directions into slides. Each slide should contain only a small amount of text. This will allow your audience to focus on your **multimedia presentation.**
- Number the steps and order them according to what is done first, second, next, and so on. Include simple maps to show landmarks and stops along the way.
- Write a script for the oral presentation. Organize the information to support the content of each slide.
- Choose colors, backgrounds, **text fonts, and graphics** that will make it easy for your audience to read each slide.

Revising and Editing

- As you revise, review each slide to be sure that its content correctly matches each section of your oral presentation.
- Be sure the design of your slides makes them easy to read.
- Double-check the accuracy of information on your slides.
- Check spelling and grammar.

Publishing

- Present your slide show to your class or another audience. If you use the slide show for multiple presentations, you may need to adjust it for different **audiences and purposes.**
- Speak clearly and allow time for audience questions.

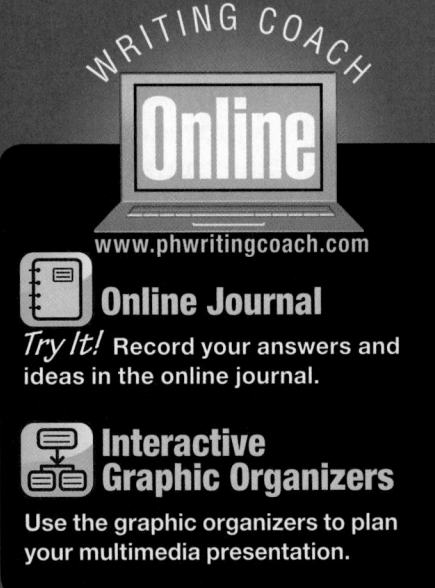

WRITING COACH

Online

www.phwritingcoach.com

Online Journal

Try It! Record your answers and ideas in the online journal.

Interactive Graphic Organizers

Use the graphic organizers to plan your multimedia presentation.

 **Partner Talk**

Before publishing, practice your presentation with a partner. Practice newly acquired vocabulary by correctly producing the word's sound.

Writing for Assessment

Many standardized tests include a prompt that asks you to write a procedural text. Use these prompts to practice. Respond using the characteristics of a procedural text. (See pages 266–267.)

 Try It! Read the **procedural text prompt** and the information on the format and academic vocabulary. Use the ABCDs of On-Demand Writing to help you plan and write your procedural text.

Format

The prompt directs you to write a *procedural text*. Describe the purpose of the text in the first section. Be sure to include steps with organized information such as a numbered list or materials list.

Procedural Text Prompt

Your new science lab partner wants to know how to set up for an experiment. He wants written instructions to help him. Write a procedural text that includes stepped-out instructions on how to set up your lab table. [30 minutes]

Academic Vocabulary

A procedural text is a kind of text that tells somebody how to perform a task. *Stepped-out instructions* have numbered lists that provide details in the order they are used.

The ABCDs of On-Demand Writing

Use the following ABCDs to help you respond to the prompt.

Before you write your draft:

A ttack the prompt [1 MINUTE]

- Circle or highlight important verbs in the prompt. Draw a line from the verb to what it refers to.
- Rewrite the prompt in your own words.

B rainstorm possible answers [4 MINUTES]

- Create a graphic organizer to generate ideas.
- Use one for each part of the prompt if necessary.

C hoose the order of your response [1 MINUTE]

- Think about the best way to organize your ideas.
- Number your ideas in the order you will write about them. Cross out ideas you will not be using.

After you write your draft:

D etect errors before turning in the draft [1 MINUTE]

- Carefully reread your writing.
- Make sure that your response makes sense and is complete.
- Look for spelling, punctuation, and grammar errors.

More Prompts for Practice

 Apply It! Respond to Prompt 1 by writing a **procedural text.** As you write, be sure to:

- Consider what your **audience** knows and needs to know
- **Organize** information into steps or paragraphs
- **Define** any terms that your audience may not know

> **Prompt 1** Your mom needs directions from your house to your friend's house. Write a procedural text that includes stepped-out instructions she can follow when she comes to pick you up.

Spiral Review: Expository If you choose to respond to Prompt 2, write a compare-and-contrast **expository essay**. Make sure your essay reflects the characteristics described on page 146.

> **Prompt 2** Protecting the environment is an important global concern. However, people have different opinions about what must be done on an everyday basis. Write an expository essay that compares and contrasts two different ways you could choose to help protect the environment in your daily life.

Spiral Review: Research Plan If you choose to respond to Prompt 3, write a **critique of the research plan**. Make sure your critique evaluates all of the characteristics described on page 224. Your critique should determine if the research plan:

- Contains a **narrowed topic** and is appropriate for the **audience**
- Includes enough **primary** and **secondary sources,** and says something about **evaluating** sources

> **Prompt 3** Henri wrote this research plan. Explain what he did well and what needs improvement.
> *My Topic:* I'm interested in comparing real cowboys to cowboys in stories.
> *My Research:* I'm going to search the Internet, talk to the reference librarian, and look for print sources. I know that William H. Cody was a real cowboy, so I'll look for and read books and articles about him.
> *My Drafting:* After a month of research, I will copy my notes to write my draft.

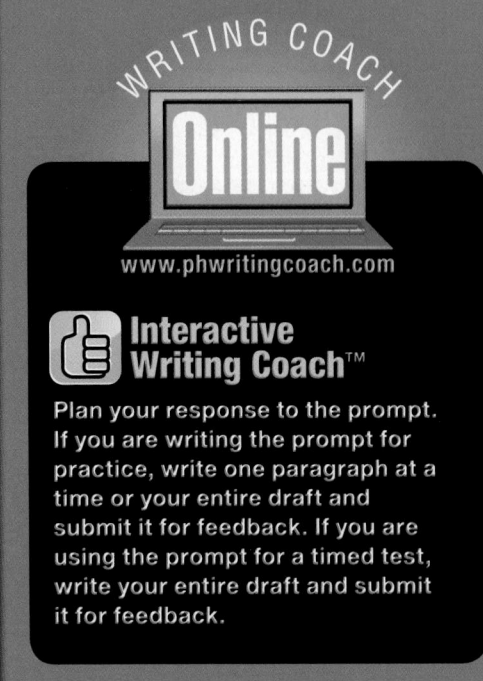

WRITING COACH

Online

www.phwritingcoach.com

Interactive Writing Coach™

Plan your response to the prompt. If you are writing the prompt for practice, write one paragraph at a time or your entire draft and submit it for feedback. If you are using the prompt for a timed test, write your entire draft and submit it for feedback.

Remember **ABCD**

Attack the prompt

Brainstorm possible answers

Choose the order of your response

Detect errors before turning in the draft

ADJECTIVES AND ADVERBS *Interrogative Adjectives* PREPOSITIONS *Prep*
BASIC SENTENCE PARTS *Subjects and Predicates* PHRASES AND CLAUSES
ON NOUNS AND PRONOUNS *Concrete and Abstract Nouns* VERBS *Transi*
position or Adverb? CONJUNCTIONS AND INTERJECTIONS *Subordinating*
SES *tive Phrases* EFFECTIVE SENTENCES *Combining Sentence Parts*
Transitive *ives* PRE
ing Conjunctions *PHRA*
Parts *Abstract Nou*
REPO *ositions* *INTERJECTIO*

Grammar

Find It FIX IT

Grammar Game Plan

This handy guide will help you find and fix errors in your writing!

20 Major Grammatical Errors and How to Fix Them

GAME PLAN Use the right words to make your writing clear. Make sure your words say exactly what you mean them to say.

CLARIFY MEANING Do not confuse the meanings of words with similar spellings. Also, words with similar definitions can have important shades of meaning. Check that words you found in a thesaurus are used correctly.

I wish we could go ~~their~~ ₍ₐ₎ there for dinner.

You should go ~~too~~ ₍ₐ₎ to her house tonight.

Tech Tip

Be your own "spell-checker"! Proofread! Your computer's spell-checker will not identify every misspelling or incorrectly used word.

SPELL-CHECK ERRORS Computer spell-checkers often correct a misspelling with a different, similarly spelled word. Be sure to proofread your work carefully to catch these errors. In each of the following examples, the word with a strikethrough represents an inappropriate spell-checker correction.

Try not to ~~turn~~ ₍ₐ₎ burn the toast.

The student needs ~~held~~ ₍ₐ₎ help with the math problem.

—LEARN MORE—
- See Chapter 20, Effective Sentences, pages 457–461
- See Writing Coach Online

✔ Check It

Use a current or completed draft of your work to practice using words correctly.

✔ **READ carefully.** Take the time to read your draft closely. For a double-check, have someone else read your work.

✔ **IDENTIFY possible mistakes.** Mark any difficult or commonly misused words in your draft.

✔ **USE a dictionary.** If you are not sure of a word's meaning, look it up in a dictionary.

2

Missing Comma After Introductory Element

Tech Tip

Remember to add commas to introductory elements that you cut and paste from different parts of a sentence or paragraph.

LEARN MORE
- See Chapter 25, Punctuation, pages 561, 564
- See Writing Coach Online

GAME PLAN Place a comma after the following introductory elements in your work.

WORDS Place a comma after introductory words.

Hello,ᴧ I'm here for the party.

Well,ᴧ it's good to have you.

PHRASES Place a comma after introductory prepositional phrases. If the prepositional phrase has only two words, a comma is not necessary.

Before dinner at 5:00,ᴧ you can wash the tomatoes.

In the evening,ᴧ please remember to take out the trash.

After dinner you should wash the dishes.

CLAUSES Introductory adverbial clauses should be followed by a comma.

When the audience clapped,ᴧ the orchestra stood up to take a bow.

✔ Check It

Use a current or completed draft of your work to practice placing commas after introductory clauses.

✔ **SCAN your draft.** Look for introductory words, phrases, and clauses.

✔ **IDENTIFY missing commas.** Mark sentence starters that might need a comma.

✔ **USE your textbook.** Check the grammar section of your textbook if you are not sure whether or not to use a comma.

GAME PLAN Provide complete citations for borrowed words and ideas. Use the citation style (such as MLA) that your teacher recommends.

MISSING CITATIONS Cite sources of direct quotes and statistics. Remember–when in doubt, cite the source.

The doctor stated, "This is the most interesting case I've seen"ᴧ(Roberts 12).

Dr. Jones reported that 1 in 10 patients have the disorderᴧ(Jones 18).

INCOMPLETE CITATIONS Make sure your citations include complete source information. This information will vary depending on the source and the citation style. It often includes the author's name, the source's title, and the page numbers. You may use the shortened version you see here if your paper includes a bibliography where the reader can get the title of the source and the author's first name.

The book has been called "a beautifully written piece" (ᴧLynn 8).

An 18 percent increase in sales was reported (Appletonᴧ72).

> ### Tech Tip
>
> When researching for an assignment on the Internet, be sure to use only reputable sources that cite their information. Then, use the correct citation style for Internet sources, which often includes the Web site URL and date visited.

> **LEARN MORE**
> - See Chapter 11, Research Writing, pages 234–237
> - See Writing Coach Online

✔ Check It

Use a current or completed draft of your work to practice documenting your sources.

✔ **REVIEW your notes.** Look for introductory words, phrases, and clauses.

✔ **USE a style guide.** Check the correct format for your citations in the style guide your teacher recommends.

4

Vague Pronoun Reference

LEARN MORE

- See Chapter 6, Fiction Narration, pages 110–111
- See Writing Coach Online

GAME PLAN Create clear pronoun-antecedent relationships to make your writing more accurate and powerful.

VAGUE IDEA Pronouns such as *which*, *this*, *that*, and *these* should refer to a specific idea. To avoid a vague reference, try changing a pronoun to an adjective that modifies a specific noun.

Abigail bought her younger brother a baseball and a basketball. That ∧basketball is the one he has been asking for.

UNCLEAR USE OF *IT, THEY,* AND *YOU* Be sure that the pronouns *it*, *they*, and *you* have a clearly stated antecedent. Replacing the personal pronoun with a specific noun can make a sentence clearer.

My teacher has taught us about World War I and World War II. I̶t̶ ∧World War II will be on the test next week.

The team members asked the coaches i̶f̶ ̶t̶h̶e̶y̶ ̶c̶o̶u̶l̶d̶ ∧to practice the play again.

To make the basketball team, y̶o̶u̶ ∧potential team members must attend every tryout.

✔ Check It

Use a current or completed draft of your work to practice identifying vague pronoun references.

✔ **READ** carefully. Read your draft slowly to locate pronouns.

✔ **IDENTIFY** possible errors. Mark any vague pronoun references.

✔ **REVISE** your draft. Rewrite sentences with vague pronoun-antecedent relationships.

PRACTICE 13.2C > Recognizing Personal Pronouns

Read the sentences. Then, write the personal pronouns in each sentence.

EXAMPLE   I would like to tell you about my experience.

ANSWER   *I, you, my*

1. He did not hear what I said.

2. Alicia said that she is trying out for the swim team.

3. After you complete this form, give it to the instructor.

4. She practices the piano every day.

5. We thought they wanted to go with us.

6. After Mike helped us, we thanked him.

7. Sarah's mother drove them to the skating rink.

8. Did you remember to tell her what time to come?

9. He doesn't speak to me anymore.

10. They could not find my street, but someone gave them directions from their house to mine.

PRACTICE 13.2D > Supplying Reflexive and Intensive Pronouns

Read the sentences. Write the reflexive or intensive pronoun that completes each sentence.

EXAMPLE   The principal made the announcement _____.

ANSWER   *herself*

11. Will you and Jim do all the work _____?

12. I bought _____ a new jacket.

13. She wondered whether she could lift the huge bundle _____.

14. You should be able to complete this project _____.

15. We did not care for the location, but the house _____ was lovely.

16. The students _____ made all the posters.

17. Jason promised _____ he would exercise more often.

18. We planned the entire event _____.

19. Liz sometimes gives _____ pep talks.

20. We _____ were not interested in seeing that exhibit.

SPEAKING APPLICATION

Tell a partner about something you and a friend did recently. Your partner will listen for and name four personal pronouns you use.

WRITING APPLICATION

Write three sentences, using sentences 12, 14, and 16 as models. Replace the nouns and pronouns in those sentences with your own.

Demonstrative Pronouns

Demonstrative pronouns point to people, places, and things, much as you point to them with your finger.

> A **demonstrative pronoun** points to a specific person, place, or thing.

There are two singular and two plural demonstrative pronouns.

DEMONSTRATIVE PRONOUNS			
SINGULAR		**PLURAL**	
this	that	these	those

This and *these* point to what is near the speaker or writer. *That* and *those* point to what is more distant.

NEAR

This is where I sleep.

These are my favorite movies of the year.

FAR

Is **that** the library across the street?

Those are my books.

See Practice 13.2E

Using Relative Pronouns

Relative pronouns are connecting words.

> A **relative pronoun** begins a subordinate clause and connects it to another idea in the same sentence.

There are five relative pronouns.

RELATIVE PRONOUNS				
that	which	who	whom	whose

The chart on the next page gives examples of relative pronouns connecting subordinate clauses to independent clauses. (See Chapter 19 to find out more about relative pronouns and clauses.)

INDEPENDENT CLAUSES	SUBORDINATE CLAUSES
Here is the earring	that Tara lost.
Felix bought our old car,	which needs to be repaired.
She is a painter	who has an unusual talent.
Is this the woman	whom you saw earlier?
She is the one	whose house has a new alarm.
That is the book	that was critiqued yesterday.
Scamper chased the ball	that was under the bed.

See Practice 13.2F
See Practice 13.2G
See Practice 13.2H

Interrogative Pronouns

To interrogate means "to ask questions."

> An **interrogative pronoun** is used to begin a question.

13.2.8 RULE

All five interrogative pronouns begin with *w*.

INTERROGATIVE PRONOUNS				
what	which	who	whom	whose

Most interrogative pronouns do not have antecedents.

EXAMPLES **What** did the teacher say?

Which is the best tutoring center?

Who wants to run a mile with me?

From **whom** will you receive the loan?

Whose was the best story?

See Practice 13.2I

Indefinite Pronouns

RULE 13.2.9

An **indefinite pronoun** refers to a person, place, thing, or idea that is not specifically named.

EXAMPLES   **Everything** is ready for our trip to Florida.

Everyone wants to see the Harry Potter park.

Anyone can learn to play an instrument.

Something fell out of the closet when I opened the door.

An indefinite pronoun can function either as an adjective or as the subject of a sentence. If it functions as an adjective, it is called an indefinite adjective.

ADJECTIVE   **Both** children want to be writers.

SUBJECT   **Both** want to be writers.

A few indefinite pronouns can be either singular or plural, depending on their use in the sentence.

INDEFINITE PRONOUNS			
SINGULAR		PLURAL	SINGULAR OR PLURAL
another	much	both	all
anybody	neither	few	any
anyone	nobody	many	more
anything	no one	others	most
each	nothing	several	none
either	one		some
everybody	other		
everyone	somebody		
everything	someone		
little	something		

See Practice 13.2J

PRACTICE 13.2E > **Identifying Demonstrative Pronouns**

Read the sentences. Then, write the demonstrative pronoun and the noun to which it refers.

EXAMPLE   This is the latest version of the computer.

ANSWER   *this, computer*

1. These are the most comfortable shoes I have ever worn.

2. Of all the pictures, I like those best.

3. This is a new book, and that is an old one.

4. Is that your brother over there?

5. Those are confident students.

6. Is this your final answer?

7. That seems to be the best way to get to the city.

8. Those were the good old days!

9. This is the camera I would like to have.

10. That may be a difficult choice.

PRACTICE 13.2F > **Supplying Relative Pronouns**

Read the sentences. Then, write the correct relative pronoun (e.g., *whose, that, which*) for each sentence.

EXAMPLE   I know the person _____ lives here.

ANSWER   *who*

11. She planted flowers _____ bloom every spring.

12. It's a popular place _____ kids love.

13. The person _____ answered my questions was very polite.

14. Sondra's outburst, _____ surprised everyone, stopped all conversation.

15. I don't know _____ you're referring to.

16. It was a decision _____ he did not regret.

17. Lee, _____ is very friendly, was the first to greet the new student.

18. We visited the Metropolitan Museum of Art, _____ is on Fifth Avenue in New York.

19. These are the guidelines _____ you must follow.

20. Colin, _____ brother is a star athlete, prefers a quiet life.

SPEAKING APPLICATION

With a partner, take turns identifying and describing items in the classroom. Use relative pronouns (e.g., *whose, that, which*) in your sentences.

WRITING APPLICATION

Write three sentences, and include one of the following relative pronouns in each: *whose, that, which*. Read your sentences aloud to a partner. Have your partner identify each relative pronoun. Then change roles.

PRACTICE 13.2G > Using Relative Pronouns

For each independent clause, supply a subordinate clause using a relative pronoun. Write the new sentence. Then, read your sentences aloud and have your partner identify the relative pronoun.

EXAMPLE   He is the chemist

ANSWER   *He is the chemist who won the Nobel Prize.*

1. Liz gathered the ingredients
2. The dentist looked at the tooth
3. There is the bike
4. Raphael took the picture
5. Those are the pants
6. Is he the captain
7. Here are the essay topics
8. Bob is the one
9. Wynn wrote the book
10. Tomorrow is the day

PRACTICE 13.2H > Writing With Relative Pronouns

For each subordinate clause, supply an independent clause to create a complete sentence. Write the new sentence. With a partner, take turns reading your best sentences and discussing why you wrote what you did.

EXAMPLE   which she will bring to the party

ANSWER   *Jenna made a casserole,* which she will bring to the party.

11. who taught me how to swim
12. which needed to be washed
13. that Scott borrowed
14. that Mr. Pizzo bought
15. whom you want on your team
16. whose painting took first prize
17. which has all the latest fashions
18. who trained his dog to dance
19. whom I helped in math class
20. that he buried in the yard

SPEAKING APPLICATION

With a partner, take turns talking about your favorite sports, hobbies, or other interests. Use relative pronouns in your questions and answers and identify them.

WRITING APPLICATION

Write three sentences about an interesting person you know or admire. Use a relative pronoun in each sentence.

Test Warm-Up

DIRECTIONS
Read the introduction and the passage that follows. Then, answer the questions to show that you can identify, use, and understand the function of relative pronouns in reading and writing.

Juana wrote this paragraph about planning the Fall Festival. Read the paragraph and think about the changes you would suggest as a peer editor. When you finish reading, answer the questions that follow.

The Fall Festival

(1) Mrs. Barnes was the teacher who chaired the planning committee and whose classroom was our meeting area. (2) Sal was the one whom suggested we decorate with pumpkins. (3) Allison wanted to offer games and prizes. (4) The games and prizes would appeal to all ages. (5) Darnell insisted on a contest of bobbing for apples, which he said everyone would enjoy. (6) Carla was the volunteer that I assigned to organize hayrides. (7) The next day, I looked over the notes that I took during the meeting. (8) It was clear the fall festival would be a success.

1 What change, if any, should be made in sentence 1?

A Change *who* to **that**

B Change *who* to **whom**

C Change *whose* to **whom**

D Make no change

2 How should sentence 2 be revised?

F Sal was the one that suggested we decorate with pumpkins.

G Sal was the one who suggested we decorate with pumpkins.

H Sal was the one which suggested we decorate with pumpkins.

J Sal was the one whose suggested we decorate with pumpkins.

3 What is the BEST way to combine sentences 3 and 4?

A Allison, who would appeal to all ages, wanted to offer games and prizes.

B Games and prizes whose appeal to all ages, Allison wanted to offer.

C Which would appeal to all ages, Allison wanted to offer games and prizes.

D Allison wanted to offer games and prizes that would appeal to all ages.

4 How should sentence 6 be revised?

F Carla was the volunteer which I assigned to organize hayrides.

G Carla was the volunteer whose assignment to organize hayrides I gave her.

H Carla was the volunteer whom I assigned to organize hayrides.

J Carla was the volunteer that assigning to organize hayrides was clear.

PRACTICE 13.2I ▷ Identifying Interrogative Pronouns

Read the sentences. Then, write the interrogative pronoun in each sentence.

EXAMPLE   What is your favorite television show?

ANSWER   *What*

1. Who are those people on the stage?
2. What should I do about my lost wallet?
3. Which is the best route to Tulsa?
4. Whose is the nicest outfit?
5. What is her occupation?
6. Who lives in that big house?
7. With whom are you going to the dance?
8. What will happen if I don't follow the directions exactly?
9. Which is worse: being late or not doing your homework?
10. What should we do when we reach the next intersection?

PRACTICE 13.2J ▷ Supplying Indefinite Pronouns

Read the sentences. Then, write an appropriate indefinite pronoun for each sentence.

EXAMPLE   _____ was asking about you.

ANSWER   *Someone*

11. _____ likes pizza!
12. _____ of the clerks could help me find what I wanted.
13. _____ of these questions have more than one answer.
14. _____ of my friends are conscientious students.
15. _____ of the vocabulary words are familiar to me.
16. I don't know _____ who would say such a thing.
17. _____ of the monuments will be decorated for the holidays.
18. _____ find the reward worth the risk of the investment.
19. _____ of the bystanders watched the rescue, and _____ tried to help.
20. _____ must be put away before you leave.

SPEAKING APPLICATION

Interview a partner, asking five questions that begin with interrogative pronouns. Your partner should name the interrogative pronouns.

WRITING APPLICATION

Write a brief paragraph describing an incident you observed. Use at least three relative pronouns and indefinite pronouns in your paragraph. You may use the sentences in Practice 13.2J as models.

CHAPTER 14

VERBS

To bring your writing to life, use verbs that describe actions that can be seen and those that cannot be seen.

WRITE GUY *Jeff Anderson, M.Ed.*

WHAT DO YOU NOTICE?

Pinpoint the action verbs as you zoom in on these sentences from the story "The Bear Boy" by Joseph Bruchac.

MENTOR TEXT

> The trackers crept close, hoping to grab the boy and run. But as soon as the mother bear caught their scent, she growled and pushed her cubs and the boy back into the cave.

Now, ask yourself the following questions:

- Which verbs describe actions that you could see or hear?
- How do the verbs *hoping* and *caught* describe a different kind of action?

The verbs *crept*, *grab*, *run*, *growled*, and *pushed* describe actions that could be seen or heard. However, the verbs *hoping* and *caught* describe actions that could not be seen or heard. You could not see the trackers *hoping* because it is something they are feeling. You could not see that the mother bear *caught* the trackers' scent because that action involves her senses.

Grammar for Writers Writers must remember that action is more than just what you do; it is also what you think, feel, and experience. Use verbs to capture every kind of action in your writing.

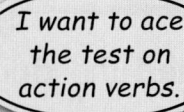

I want to ace the test on action verbs.

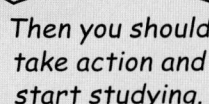

Then you should take action and start studying.

14.1 Action Verbs

Verbs such as *walk, sailed, played, migrate, raced, crossed, learn,* and *arrive* all show some kind of action.

RULE 14.1.1

An **action verb** tells what action someone or something is performing.

EXAMPLES   Mother **carries** the platter.

The train **chugged** into the station.

I **believe** it will rain today.

Heather **remembered** to bring her book.

The verb *carries* explains what Mother did with the platter. The verb *chugged* tells what the train did. The verb *believe* explains my action about the weather. The verb *remembered* explains Heather's action with the book.

Some actions, such as *carries* or *chugged,* can be seen. Some actions, such as *believe* or *remembered,* cannot be seen.

See Practice 14.1A

Using Transitive Verbs

RULE 14.1.2

An action verb is **transitive** if the receiver of the action is named in the sentence. The receiver of the action is called the **object** of the verb.

EXAMPLES   Mrs. Brown **opened** the **door** with great difficulty.
            verb   object

The bus suddenly **hit** a nearby **tree**.
                  verb   object

In the first example, *opened* is transitive because the object of the verb—*door*—names what Mrs. Brown opened. In the second example, *hit* is transitive because the object of the verb—*tree*—tells what the bus hit.

Using Intransitive Verbs

> An action verb is **intransitive** if there is no receiver of the action named in the sentence. An intransitive verb does not have an object.

14.1.3 RULE

EXAMPLES

The class **began**.

The dog **raced** through the new gate.

The employees **gathered** in the conference room.

The fire alarm **rang** at 1:00 P.M.

Some action verbs can be transitive or intransitive. You need to determine if the verb has an object or not.

TRANSITIVE VERB   Kodia **raced** **Terrence** yesterday.

INTRANSITIVE VERB   Kodia **raced** across the finish line.

TRANSITIVE VERB   The pilot **flew** the **plane**.

INTRANSITIVE VERB   The plane **flew** to Cancun, Mexico.

TRANSITIVE VERB   The guests **rang** the **doorbell**.

See Practice 14.1B   INTRANSITIVE VERB   The doorbell **rang** and the dog barked.

PRACTICE 14.1A **Finding Action Verbs**

Read the sentences. Then, write each action verb.

EXAMPLE   The airplane landed on the ground.

ANSWER   *landed*

1. Alex and a friend hiked up the mountain trail.
2. Hannah played the harp in the talent contest.
3. Kaylee thought she knew the answer.
4. Max expressed his concern to the principal.
5. A tornado rolled across the prairie last week.
6. Devon worries about the future.
7. The chef poured the dressing onto the salad.
8. The crowd cheered wildly when the team scored.
9. My grades in science top those in math.
10. Claire stomped out and slammed the door.

PRACTICE 14.1B **Identifying Transitive and Intransitive Verbs**

Read the sentences. Write each verb and label it *transitive* or *intransitive*.

EXAMPLE   Tina wants a summer job.

ANSWER   *wants* — transitive

11. The cruise ship leaves tomorrow.
12. A fierce blizzard hit the Northeast.
13. The work crew never arrives on time.
14. Clouds gathered before the storm.
15. My glasses fell and broke.
16. Some people smile all the time.
17. My mother grows vegetables and flowers in her garden.
18. Good jobs usually require a high school diploma.
19. No one likes people who complain all the time.
20. Advanced math courses provide a challenge for some.

SPEAKING APPLICATION

Tell a partner about a movie you saw recently. Your partner should listen for and name three action verbs.

WRITING APPLICATION

Write two sentences with transitive verbs and two sentences with intransitive verbs.

14.2 Linking Verbs

Some widely used verbs do not show action. They are called **linking verbs**.

A **linking verb** is a verb that connects a subject with a word that describes or identifies it.

RULE 14.2.1

EXAMPLES

IDENTIFIES

Kevin **was** a Navy **SEAL**.
subject · linking verb · predicate nominative

IDENTIFIES

The **winners** **were** **Tara and I**.
subject · linking verb · predicate nominative

DESCRIBES

We **felt** extremely **tired** after our long flight.
subject · linking verb · predicate adjective

Recognizing Forms of *Be*

In English, the most common linking verb is *be.* This verb has many forms.

FORMS OF *BE*		
am	can be	has been
are	could be	have been
is	may be	had been
was	might be	could have been
were	must be	may have been
am being	shall be	might have been
are being	should be	must have been
is being	will be	shall have been
was being	would be	should have been
were being		will have been
		would have been

Using Other Linking Verbs

Several other verbs also function as linking verbs. They connect the parts of a sentence in the same way as the forms of *be*. In the sentence below, *shocked* describes *teacher*.

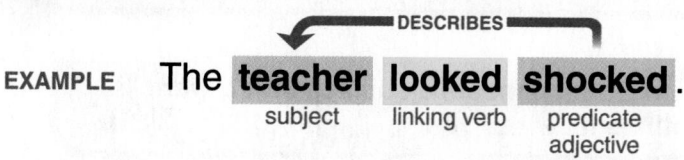

EXAMPLE   The **teacher** **looked** **shocked**.
subject   linking verb   predicate adjective

OTHER LINKING VERBS		
appear	look	sound
become	remain	stay
feel	seem	taste
grow	smell	turn

Action Verb or Linking Verb?

Some verbs can be used either as linking verbs or action verbs.

LINKING   The glass **looked** dirty.
(*Looked* links *glass* and *dirty*.)

ACTION   The host **looked** at the glass.
(The host performed an action.)

LINKING   The crowd **grew** impatient.
(*Grew* links *crowd* and *impatient*.)

ACTION   The farmer **grew** strawberries.
(The farmer performed an action.)

To test whether a verb is a linking verb or an action verb, replace the verb with *is, am,* or *are.* If the sentence still makes sense, then the verb is a linking verb.

EXAMPLE   The crowd **is** impatient.
linking verb

See Practice 14.2A
See Practice 14.2B
See Practice 14.2C
See Practice 14.2D

PRACTICE 14.2A > **Identifying Action Verbs and Linking Verbs**

Read the sentences. Write the verb in each sentence, and label it either *action* or *linking*.

EXAMPLE   We are optimistic about the outcome.

ANSWER   *are* — linking

1. The couple attended the opening night of the play.
2. Matt Perez will be the captain of the team.
3. I love Van Gogh's painting *Starry Night*.
4. Your idea seems like a good one.
5. Those two women have been friends for years.
6. Robbie chopped wood for the campfire.
7. May I ask you a question?
8. This chili tastes bland.
9. The bell rang at the end of class.
10. The sky became cloudy very quickly.

PRACTICE 14.2B > **Using *Be* and Other Linking Verbs**

Read the pairs of words below. For each pair of words, write a sentence that uses a linking verb to connect them.

EXAMPLE   trip   adventure

ANSWER   *A trip to Alaska could be an adventure.*

11. soccer   popular
12. contestants   confident
13. Emma   hungry
14. Corey   energetic
15. Louis Sachar   author
16. cellphone   lost
17. Yvonne   president
18. hurricanes   dangerous
19. Oscar   handsome
20. You   winner

SPEAKING APPLICATION

With a partner, take turns describing someone you admire. Use at least two linking and two action verbs. Your partner should identify and label the verbs.

WRITING APPLICATION

Write a short paragraph about some aspect of the weather. In your paragraph, use three different linking verbs.

PRACTICE 14.2C > **Identifying Action Verbs and Linking Verbs**

Read the sentences. Then, write the verb or verbs in each sentence, and label them either *action* or *linking*.

EXAMPLE   Oliver grew uneasy as he climbed the front steps of the deserted house.

ANSWER   *grew*— linking; *climbed*— action

1. The factory coughed puffs of steam out of its smokestacks.

2. Harry seemed excited for the chance to play goalie.

3. When a cat is nearby, the neighborhood birds sound the alarm.

4. With Eleanor at the wheel, a drive to school seems terrifying.

5. Maura appeared out of nowhere, and she startled us.

6. When she answered the phone, Maria sounded sleepy.

7. The car must have been towed because today is street cleaning day.

8. Mom tasted the soup; then, she poured it into bowls.

9. Sean threw the ball, and it swooshed into the basket.

10. The spectators became amazed at the elephant's tricks.

PRACTICE 14.2D > **Writing With Action and Linking Verbs**

Read the verbs below. For each verb, write a sentence using a form of the verb as indicated below.

EXAMPLE   turned — linking

ANSWER   *At forty years old, his hair turned gray.*

11. be — linking

12. feel — linking

13. smell — linking

14. grow — action

15. sound — action

16. look — action

17. turn — action

18. seem — linking

19. appear — action

20. become — linking

SPEAKING APPLICATION

With a partner, take turns reading the sentences you wrote in Practice 14.2D. Discuss how your sentences are similar and how they are different.

WRITING APPLICATION

Imagine you are exploring another planet. Write a brief paragraph describing this experience. Use four action verbs and four linking verbs in your paragraph.

Test Warm-Up

DIRECTIONS
Read the introduction and the passage that follows. Then, answer the questions to show that you can use and understand the function of linking verbs and action verbs in reading and writing.

Denzel wrote this paragraph describing a dream in which he was a famous lion tamer. Read the paragraph and think about the changes you would suggest as a peer editor. When you finish reading, answer the questions that follow.

The Amazing Denzel

(1) I felt a cold breeze as I approached the lion's cage and unlocked it. (2) The lion sounded asleep, but that was about to change. (3) When the door clanged, he opened one golden eye. (4) As he slowly got to his feet, I seemed increasingly nervous. (5) He might have been able to sense my fear. (6) Fortunately, my pockets contained raw meat. (7) As the lion came toward me, I asked him if he wouldn't mind performing a backflip. (8) He was looking like he was hesitant. (9) I think he was about to do the flip when my alarm went off.

---

1 The meaning of sentence 2 can be clarified by changing the word ***sounded*** to —

   A became

   B was

   C grew

   D turned

2 The meaning of sentence 4 can be clarified by changing the word ***seemed*** to —

   F appeared

   G stayed

   H looked

   J became

3 What is the BEST way to rewrite sentence 5?

   A He was seeming to sense my fear.

   B He sensed my fear.

   C He had to have been sensing my fear.

   D He seemed to sense my fear.

4 What is the BEST way to rewrite sentence 8?

   F He felt hesitant.

   G He turned hesitant.

   H He sounded hesitant.

   J He seemed hesitant.

14.3 Helping Verbs

Sometimes, a verb in a sentence is just one word. Often, however, a verb will be made up of several words. This type of verb is called a **verb phrase**.

WRITING COACH

Online

www.phwritingcoach.com

Grammar Practice

Practice your grammar skills with Writing Coach Online.

Grammar Games

Test your knowledge of grammar in this fast-paced interactive video game.

RULE 14.3.1

Helping verbs are added before another verb to make a **verb phrase.**

Notice how these helping verbs change the meaning of the verb *open.*

EXAMPLES   open   **might have** opened

                    had opened   **should have** opened

                    will have opened   **will be** opened

Recognizing Helping Verbs

Forms of *Be* Forms of *be* are often used as helping verbs.

SOME FORMS OF *BE* USED AS HELPING VERBS	
HELPING VERBS	**MAIN VERBS**
am	growing
has been	warned
was being	told
will be	reminded
will have been	waiting
is	opening
was being	trained
should be	written
had been	sent
might have been	played

See Practice 14.3A

Other Helping Verbs Many different verb phrases can be formed using one or more of these helping verbs. The chart below shows just a few.

HELPING VERBS	MAIN VERBS	VERB PHRASES
do	remember	do remember
has	written	has written
would	hope	would hope
shall	see	shall see
can	believe	can believe
could	finish	could finish
may	attempt	may attempt
must have	thought	must have thought
should have	grown	should have grown
might	win	might win
will	jump	will jump
have	planned	have planned
does	want	does want

Sometimes the words in a verb phrase are separated by other words, such as *not* or *certainly*. The parts of the verb phrase in certain types of questions may also be separated.

WORDS SEPARATED

She **could** certainly **have thought** that was hers.

This **has** not **changed** how we feel.

Jeffrey **has** certainly **hit** the most home runs.

The dentist **had** carefully **examined** my teeth.

Did you ever **expect** to be so scared?

When **may** we **open** the envelope?

Did you ever **expect** to see that kind of experiment?

Sophia **must** not **have taken** the car.

Would you ever **want** to go fishing?

See Practice 14.3B

Helping Verbs   323

PRACTICE 14.3A Identifying Helping and Main Verbs

Read the sentences. Write *main verb* if the underlined verb is a main verb. Write *helping verb* if it is a helping verb.

EXAMPLE   Luanne is <u>having</u> a party.

ANSWER   *main verb*

1. The city has <u>built</u> a new basketball court in the park.

2. I <u>will be</u> going right home after school.

3. Has your brother <u>returned</u> yet?

4. The puppy <u>has been</u> barking for an hour.

5. I could have <u>done</u> better if I had tried harder.

6. <u>May</u> I be excused now?

7. The group <u>had been</u> in the gym for a long time.

8. <u>Am</u> I bothering you?

9. We <u>had</u> expected a better performance from the group.

10. The witnesses were being <u>questioned</u> by the police.

PRACTICE 14.3B Using Verb Phrases

Read the verb phrases. Use each verb phrase in an original sentence.

EXAMPLE   have heard

ANSWER   I *have heard* the good news.

11. has been going

12. have been

13. did get

14. could remember

15. has learned

16. might want

17. is known

18. will have graduated

19. had been produced

20. should be completed

SPEAKING APPLICATION

With a partner, take turns telling about something that didn't go exactly as planned. Your partner should listen for and identify two verb phrases and name the main and helping verbs in the phrases.

WRITING APPLICATION

Write three sentences with verb phrases. Underline the verb phrases in your sentences.

CHAPTER 15

ADJECTIVES *and* ADVERBS

Enrich your descriptions of people, places, and events by using adjectives and adverbs in your writing.

WRITE GUY *Jeff Anderson, M.Ed.*

WHAT DO YOU NOTICE?

Spot the adjectives and adverbs as you zoom in on these sentences from the story "Zoo" by Edward Hoch.

MENTOR TEXT

> The citizens of Earth clustered around as Professor Hugo's crew quickly collected the waiting dollars, and soon the good Professor himself made an appearance, wearing his many-colored rainbow cape and top hat.

Now, ask yourself the following questions:

- Which adverb modifies the verb *collected*?
- Which adjectives does the author use to describe the cape?

The adverb *quickly* modifies the verb *collected,* creating an image of the speed at which the crew gathered the money. The author uses the adjective *rainbow* to modify the noun *cape.* Words such as *rainbow*, which are usually used as nouns, can also be used as adjectives. Because the word *many-colored* modifies the adjective *rainbow*, *many-colored* is an adverb.

Grammar for Writers Use adjectives and adverbs to enrich your writing, but vary how you use them. For example, if you place several adjectives in a row before a noun in one sentence, use fewer or no adjectives in the next sentence.

Which adjective would you use to describe my bike? Speedy or quick?

I would go with flat. Look at your tires!

15.1 Adjectives

Adjectives are words that make language come alive by adding description or information.

Adjectives help make nouns more specific. For example, *car* is a general word, but a *red two-door car* is more specific. Adjectives such as *red* and *two-door* make nouns and pronouns clearer and more vivid.

> An **adjective** is a word that describes a noun or pronoun.

Adjectives are often called *modifiers*, because they modify, or change, the meaning of a noun or pronoun. You can use more than one adjective to modify a noun or pronoun. Notice how *shoes* is modified by each set of adjectives below.

EXAMPLES   **old-fashioned** shoes

           new **red** shoes

           children's **dress** shoes

           old **brown** shoes

Adjectives answer several questions about nouns and pronouns. They tell *What kind? Which one? How many?* or *How much?* Numeral adjectives, such as *eleven*, tell exactly how many. In the chart below, notice how adjectives answer these questions.

WHAT KIND?	WHICH ONE?	HOW MANY?	HOW MUCH?
stone house	this judge	two tulips	no time
white paper	each answer	several roses	enough apples
serious argument	those sisters	both brothers	many hobbies
colorful shirts	that student	one car	some birds

Adjective Position An adjective usually comes before the noun it modifies, as do all the adjectives in the chart on the previous page. Sometimes, however, adjectives come after the nouns they modify.

EXAMPLES

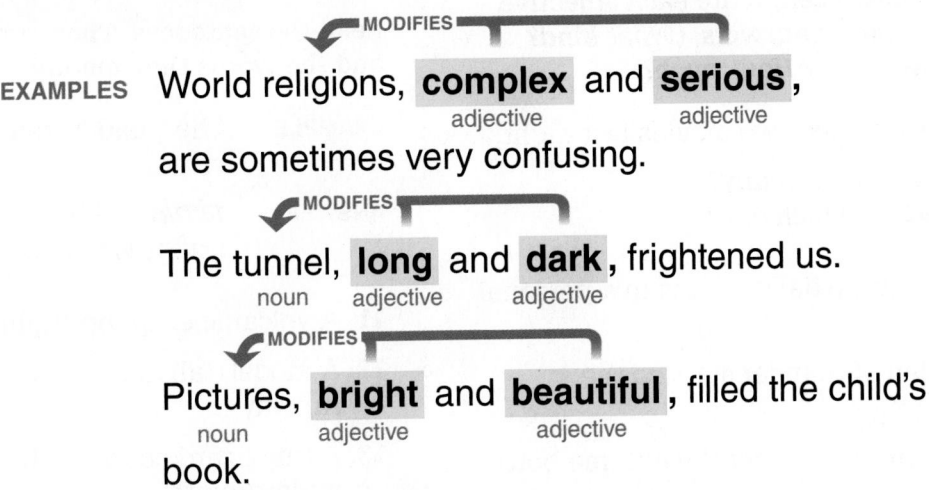

World religions, **complex** and **serious**, are sometimes very confusing.

The tunnel, **long** and **dark**, frightened us.

Pictures, **bright** and **beautiful**, filled the child's book.

Adjectives that modify pronouns usually come after linking verbs. Sometimes, however, adjectives may come before the pronoun.

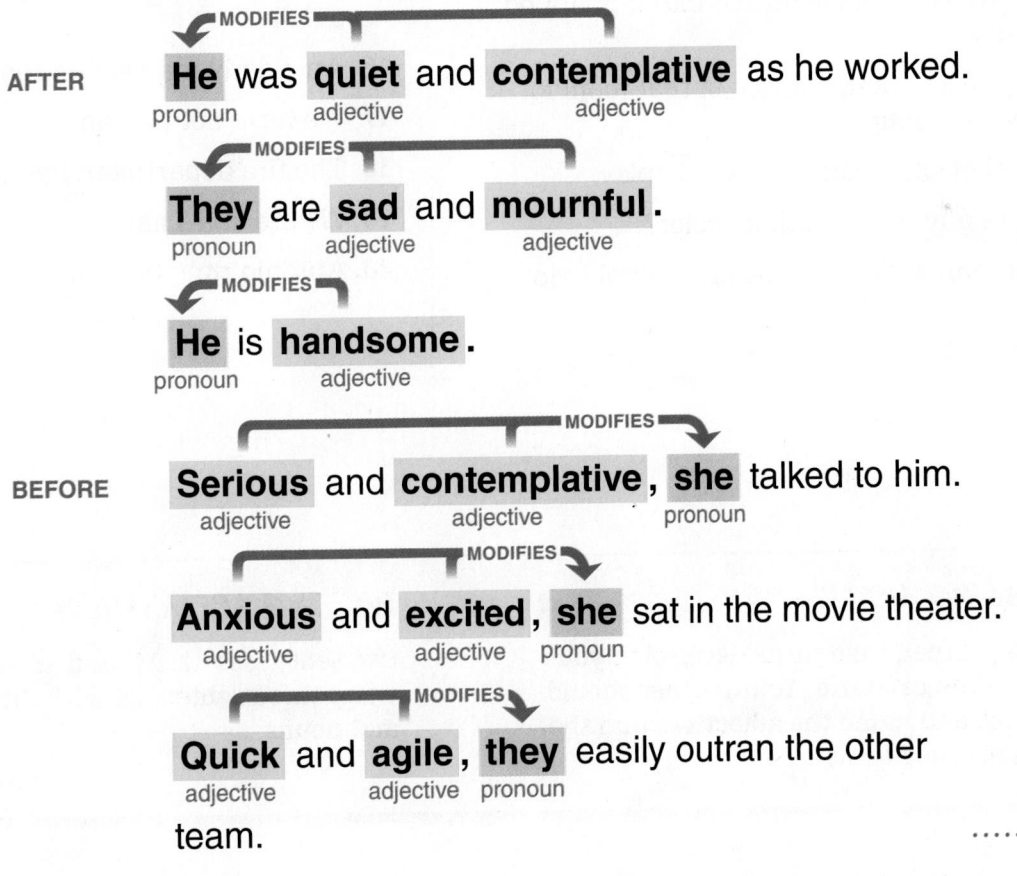

AFTER

He was **quiet** and **contemplative** as he worked.

They are **sad** and **mournful**.

He is **handsome**.

BEFORE

Serious and **contemplative**, she talked to him.

Anxious and **excited**, she sat in the movie theater.

Quick and **agile**, they easily outran the other team.

See Practice 15.1A
See Practice 15.1B

PRACTICE 15.1A Identifying Adjectives

Read the sentences. Then, write each adjective and list the question it answers. (*What kind? Which one? How many? How much?*)

EXAMPLE   We watched two movies last night.

ANSWER   *two*— How many?
          last— Which one?

1. Some people write daily entries in a personal journal.

2. A sudden clap of thunder startled the sleeping dogs.

3. I'll give you five dollars for the antique bottle.

4. Regular exercise contributes to good health.

5. This assignment will take more time.

6. The two explorers ventured into unmapped territory.

7. There is not enough space in that room for the whole group.

8. Several electric cars were on display.

9. Is there any water in that cooler?

10. This organization provides free legal help.

PRACTICE 15.1B Identifying Adjectives and Words They Modify

Read the sentences. Then, write the adjectives and the words they modify.

EXAMPLE   The timid kitten hid from the noisy visitors.

ANSWER   *timid, kitten*
          noisy, visitors

11. A volcanic eruption frightened the islanders.

12. A model, tall and elegant, strode along the runway.

13. A tiny lizard scurried through the thick undergrowth.

14. These books are heavy!

15. I don't have much change, but I can give you a dollar.

16. An elderly man sat on the shady porch.

17. We have not had any rain for two weeks.

18. The fire department has a new ladder truck.

19. We ate at a Thai restaurant for the first time.

20. Antonio runs two miles every day.

SPEAKING APPLICATION

With a partner, take turns describing your lunch in the cafeteria. Your partner should listen for and name the adjectives and the questions they answer.

WRITING APPLICATION

Use sentences 12, 14, and 19 as models, and write three sentences with different adjectives and nouns.

Articles

Three frequently used adjectives are the words *a*, *an*, and *the*. They are called **articles.** Articles can be **definite** or **indefinite.** Both types indicate that a noun will soon follow.

> ***The*** is a **definite article.** It points to a specific person, place, thing, or idea. ***A*** and ***an*** are **indefinite articles.** They point to any member of a group of similar people, places, things, or ideas.

15.1.2 RULE

DEFINITE   Dr. Kashkin is **the** one to call. (a specific person)

Go into **the** restaurant. (a specific place)

I want to learn **the** song. (a specific thing)

INDEFINITE   I want to see **a** movie. (any movie)

Please take **an** application. (any application)

You should ask **a** coach for advice. (any coach)

A is used before consonant sounds. *An* is used before vowel sounds. You choose between *a* and *an* based on sound. Some letters are tricky. The letter *h*, a consonant, may sound like either a consonant or a vowel. The letters *o* and *u* are vowels, but they may sometimes sound like consonants.

USING *A* AND *AN*	
A WITH CONSONANT SOUNDS	**AN WITH VOWEL SOUNDS**
a pink dress	an endangered lion
a happy memory (*h* sound)	an honest president (no *h* sound)
a one-person chair (*w* sound)	an old book (*o* sound)
a union worker (*y* sound)	an uncle (*u* sound)
a truck	an odd shoe
a banana	an apple
a unicorn (*y* sound)	an opponent

See Practice 15.1C

PRACTICE 15.1C > **Identifying Definite and Indefinite Articles**

Read the sentences. Then, write the articles and label them *definite* or *indefinite*.

EXAMPLE   The travelers boarded a plane to Madrid.

ANSWER   *the*— definite
a— indefinite

1. I can't wait to meet the new director.
2. A minute can sometimes seem like an hour.
3. Do you have the time?
4. Mr. Chu was elected to the city council.
5. The students dutifully read the novel.
6. There is an old, rundown car in the driveway.
7. We can spend the afternoon at the beach.
8. A mysterious stranger appeared on the scene.
9. This is an interesting dilemma.
10. The storm caused a huge traffic jam.

SPEAKING APPLICATION

With a partner, take turns describing an item without naming it. Your partner should guess what the item is and name at least five definite and indefinite articles you use.

WRITING APPLICATION

Use sentences 2, 8, and 10 as models, and write three sentences in which you use definite and indefinite articles. Circle the articles and label them *definite* or *indefinite*.

Using Proper Adjectives

A **proper adjective** begins with a capital letter. There are two types of proper adjectives.

> A **proper adjective** is (1) a proper noun used as an adjective or (2) an adjective formed from a proper noun.

15.1.3 RULE

A proper noun used as an adjective does *not* change its form. It is merely placed in front of another noun.

PROPER NOUNS	USED AS PROPER ADJECTIVES
Truman	the Truman Library (*Which* library?)
Florida	Florida wetlands (*Which* wetlands?)
December	December weather (*What kind* of weather?)

When an adjective is formed from a proper noun, the proper noun will change its form. Notice that endings such as *-n, -ian,* or *-ese* have been added to the proper nouns in the chart below or the spelling has been changed.

PROPER NOUNS	PROPER ADJECTIVES FORMED FROM PROPER NOUNS
America	American history (*Which kind* of history?)
Japan	Japanese cities (*Which* cities?)
Norway	Norwegian legends (*Which* legends?)
Inca	Incan empire (*Which* empire?)
Florida	Floridian sunset (*Which* sunset?)

See Practice 15.1D

Using Nouns as Adjectives

Nouns can sometimes be used as adjectives. A noun used as an adjective usually comes directly before another noun and answers the question *What kind?* or *Which one?*

NOUNS	USED AS ADJECTIVES
shoe	a shoe salesperson (*What kind* of salesperson?)
waterfowl	the waterfowl refuge (*Which* refuge?)
court	a court date (*What kind* of date?)
morning	a morning appointment (*What kind* of appointment?)

Using Compound Adjectives

Adjectives, like nouns, can be compound.

RULE 15.1.4

> A **compound adjective** is made up of more than one word.

Most **compound adjectives** are written as hyphenated words. Some are written as combined words, as in "a *runaway* horse." If you are unsure about how to write a compound adjective, look up the word in a dictionary.

HYPHENATED	COMBINED
a well-known actress	a featherweight boxer
a full-time job	a freshwater lake
snow-covered mountains	a sideways glance
one-sided opinions	heartbreaking news
so-called experts	a nearsighted witness

See Practice 15.1E

PRACTICE 15.1D ▷ Using Proper Adjectives

Read the sentences. Then, rewrite each sentence to include a proper adjective before the underlined noun.

EXAMPLE   My favorite subject is <u>history</u>.

ANSWER   *My favorite subject is American history.*

1. Camels are used for travel in the <u>desert</u>.

2. Ana is interested in <u>geography</u>.

3. Rob really enjoys <u>food</u>.

4. The <u>language</u> is easy to learn.

5. We will wear traditional <u>clothing</u> for the play.

6. Bruce wants to study <u>architecture</u>.

7. The Martins visited the <u>ruins</u> on their trip.

8. Ashley dresses in <u>style</u>.

9. When does your <u>class</u> meet?

10. Trina has a <u>pen pal</u>.

PRACTICE 15.1E ▷ Recognizing Nouns Used as Adjectives

Read the sentences. Write the noun, proper noun, or compound noun used as an adjective. Then, write the noun that the adjective modifies.

EXAMPLE   Do you like my new gym clothes?

ANSWER   *gym, clothes*

11. Did you get my text message?

12. Elena doesn't like the July heat.

13. Mr. Preston is an expert on shore birds.

14. You may carry the baseball bats.

15. Spencer would like to be an airplane mechanic.

16. Tomorrow, we will follow our usual Friday schedule.

17. I would like to know what the weekend weather will be.

18. Scott spends his free time playing video games.

19. I'll meet you at the tennis court at 3:00.

20. Will you be going to the Valentine's Day dance?

SPEAKING APPLICATION

With a partner, take turns describing a trip you'd like to take. Your partner should listen for and name the nouns used as adjectives and proper adjectives you use.

WRITING APPLICATION

Write three sentences and include one of the following in each: a noun used as an adjective, a proper noun used as an adjective, or a proper adjective.

Using Pronouns as Adjectives

Pronouns, like nouns, can sometimes be used as adjectives.

> **A pronoun becomes an adjective if it modifies a noun.**

EXAMPLES   We see the new puppies on **this** side of the porch.

Which puppies are the females?

In the first example, the demonstrative pronoun *this* modifies *side*, and in the second example, the interrogative pronoun *which* modifies *puppies*.

Using Possessive Nouns and Pronouns as Adjectives

The following personal pronouns are often **possessive adjectives:** *my, your, her, his, its, our,* and *their*. They are adjectives because they come before nouns and answer the question *Which one?* They are pronouns because they have antecedents.

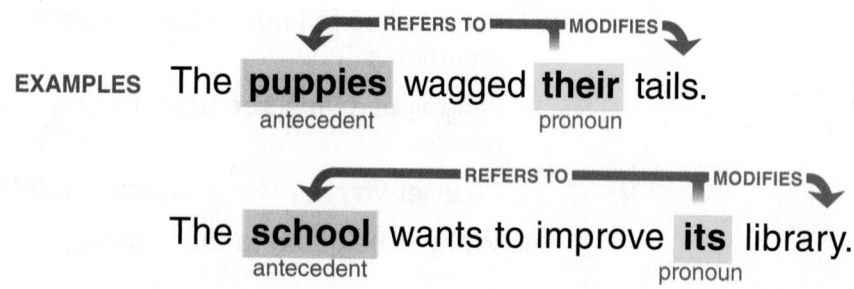

EXAMPLES   The **puppies** wagged **their** tails.
              antecedent   pronoun

The **school** wants to improve **its** library.
          antecedent   pronoun

In the first example, *their* is an adjective because it modifies *tails*. At the same time, it is a pronoun because it refers to the antecedent *puppies*.

In the second example, *its* is an adjective because it modifies *library*. The word *its* is also a pronoun because it refers to the antecedent *school*.

Note About Possessive Nouns Possessive nouns function as adjectives when they modify a noun.

EXAMPLES   The field is on the **Wongs'** property.

My **dog's** tail wags when I come home.

See Practice 15.1F

See Practice 15.1G

Using Demonstrative Adjectives

This, that, these, and *those*—the four demonstrative pronouns—can also be **demonstrative adjectives.**

PRONOUN   We heard that .

ADJECTIVE   That hive is home to many bees.

PRONOUN   Why do you want these ?

ADJECTIVE   These puppies are searching for a chew toy.

Using Interrogative Adjectives

Which, what, and *whose*—three of the interrogative pronouns—can be **interrogative adjectives.**

PRONOUN   Which do you think she will like?

ADJECTIVE   Which puppy do you think he will buy?

PRONOUN   Whose is that?

ADJECTIVE   Whose cat can that be?

Using Indefinite Adjectives

A number of indefinite pronouns—*both, few, many, each, most,* and *all,* among others—can also be used as **indefinite adjectives.**

PRONOUN   I made one of each .

ADJECTIVE   Each member has a vote.

PRONOUN   I don't have any .

ADJECTIVE   Wasn't there any soup left?

See Practice 15.1H
See Practice 15.1I

PRACTICE 15.1F ▷ Recognizing Possessive Nouns and Pronouns Used as Adjectives

Read the sentences. Then, write the possessive noun or pronoun used as an adjective in each sentence. Some sentences have more than one answer.

EXAMPLE   Ted's canoe almost tipped over.

ANSWER   *Ted's*

1. Chelsea would like a piece of your cake.
2. The doctor's waiting room was crowded.
3. Sasha accidentally stepped on her cat's tail.
4. Our class has its own Web page.
5. The bicycle's tires need air.
6. Harry removed his boots when he came inside.
7. The children came in right away when their mother called them.
8. The team's trophies are in the display case.
9. We had our pictures taken for the yearbook.
10. Mrs. Palumbo buys fresh bread at Maria's bakery.

PRACTICE 15.1G ▷ Using Possessive Nouns and Pronouns Used as Adjectives

Read the sentences. Then, rewrite each sentence, completing it with a possessive noun or pronoun used as an adjective.

EXAMPLE   John's dog has a mind of _____ own.

ANSWER   *its*

11. Marco's hard work resulted in _____ success.
12. _____ dress has flowers around its hem.
13. The team's new black and gold uniforms were _____ pride and joy.
14. Ben's grandparents offered to pay for _____ education.
15. After dinner, I took _____ leftovers back to my house.
16. Mrs. Schaffer's computer is _____ link to the rest of the world.
17. My neighbors spend every Saturday in _____ garden.
18. Serena's concentration was broken by _____ bad music.
19. The city's aquarium feeds _____ fish only once a day.
20. On _____ trip, Luis bought a keychain for his brother.

SPEAKING APPLICATION

With a partner, take turns describing something that belongs to another person. Your partner should identify at least one possessive noun and one possessive pronoun used as an adjective.

WRITING APPLICATION

Write a paragraph in which you compare and contrast yourself with a real or imagined brother. Use possessive nouns and pronouns as adjectives to discuss your different tastes and hobbies.

PRACTICE 15.1H > **Supplying Demonstrative, Interrogative, and Indefinite Adjectives**

Read the sentences. Then, write whether the underlined adjective is demonstrative, interrogative, or indefinite.

EXAMPLE   <u>Whose</u> hamster is that running around the yard?

ANSWER   *interrogative*

1. <u>Which</u> hamster belongs to the Garcia family?

2. <u>These</u> apples are my favorite.

3. <u>Which</u> apples do you prefer?

4. <u>Some</u> baseball players are switch hitters.

5. <u>What</u> kind of music do you like to listen to?

6. I like <u>most</u> types of music.

7. I didn't have <u>any</u> money left after I bought the book.

8. Is <u>this</u> book the best one in the series?

9. Casey and Samantha are friends with <u>those</u> girls.

10. <u>Whose</u> car should we take to the game?

PRACTICE 15.1I > **Identifying Demonstrative, Interrogative, and Indefinite Adjectives**

Read the sentences. Then, write the adjective in each sentence and label it *demonstrative*, *interrogative*, or *indefinite*.

EXAMPLE   Whose keys are these?

ANSWER   *Whose*— interrogative

11. Several students lingered after the game.

12. What difference will five more minutes make?

13. I will turn fourteen this month.

14. Which movie are you going to see?

15. Here are some magazines for you to read.

16. That building is more than two hundred years old.

17. Most children have a natural curiosity.

18. Do you want that CD?

19. These chairs are so comfortable.

20. Whose umbrella did you borrow?

SPEAKING APPLICATION

With a partner, take turns asking each other questions about your favorite movie, television show, and song. The person asking the questions should use interrogative adjectives.

WRITING APPLICATION

Use sentences 11, 12, and 18 in Practice 15.1I as models, and write three sentences in which you use demonstrative, interrogative, and indefinite adjectives. Circle and label the adjectives.

Test Warm-Up

DIRECTIONS

Read the introduction and the passage that follows. Then, answer the questions to show that you can use and understand the function of adjectives in reading and writing.

Jada wrote this paragraph about the school bake sale. Read the paragraph and think about the changes you would suggest as a peer editor. When you finish reading, answer the questions that follow.

The Bake Sale

(1) Our school's bake sale took place last Saturday. (2) These sales raise money for their activities—and they're fun. (3) In this case, the money was going to the art department's supplies. (4) Each student who came had a great time. (5) Students, whose contributions to Saturday sale included pies, cakes, and brownies, showed their enthusiasm for art. (6) There were so many donations; I wasn't sure that student brought what. (7) At the end of the sale, there weren't no items left. (8) That sale was our most successful to date.

---

1 What change should be made in sentence 2?

  A Change *These* to **Which**

  B Change *their* to **our**

  C Change *their* to **my**

  D Change *These* to **That**

2 What change should be made in sentence 5?

  F Change *Saturday* to **Saturday's**

  G Change *whose* to **which**

  H Change *Students* to **Students'**

  J Change *their* to **her**

3 The meaning of sentence 6 can be clarified by changing the word *that* to —

  A what

  B whose

  C why

  D which

4 How should sentence 7 be revised?

  F At the end of the sale, there weren't each items left.

  G At the end of the sale, there weren't these items left.

  H At the end of the sale, there weren't any items left.

  J At the end of the sale, there weren't much items left.

15.2 Adverbs

Adverbs can modify three different parts of speech. They make the meaning of verbs, adjectives, or other adverbs more precise.

> **An adverb** modifies a verb, an adjective, or another adverb.

RULE 15.2.1

Although adverbs may modify adjectives and other adverbs, they generally modify verbs.

Using Adverbs That Modify Verbs

Adverbs that modify verbs will answer one of these four questions: *Where? When? In what way? To what extent?* These adverbs are also known as *adverbs of place, adverbs of time, adverbs of manner,* and *adverbs of degree.*

ADVERBS THAT MODIFY VERBS			
WHERE?	**WHEN?**	**IN WHAT WAY?**	**TO WHAT EXTENT?**
push upward	will leave soon	works carefully	hardly ate
fell there	comes daily	speaks well	really surprised
stay nearby	swims often	chews noisily	almost cried
go outside	exhibits yearly	acted willingly	partly finished
is here	report later	walk quietly	nearly won
jump away	come tomorrow	smiled happily	fully agree
drove down	went yesterday	moved gracefully	totally oppose

Negative adverbs, such as *not, never,* and *nowhere,* also modify verbs.

EXAMPLES Mark **never** **arrived** at the meeting.
adverb   verb

She **could** **not** **understand** the essay.
verb   adverb   verb

The line of questioning **led** **nowhere** .
verb   adverb

See Practice 15.2A

Using Adverbs That Modify Adjectives

An adverb modifying an adjective answers only one question: *To what extent?*

> When adverbs modify adjectives or adverbs, they answer the question *To what extent?*

ADVERBS THAT MODIFY ADJECTIVES	
very upset	extremely tall
definitely wrong	not hungry

EXAMPLE Beaches can be **very** **beautiful**.

The adverb *very* modifies the adjective *beautiful.*

EXAMPLE The speaker is **extremely** **tall**.

The adverb *extremely* modifies the adjective *tall.*

Adverbs Modifying Other Adverbs

When adverbs modify other adverbs, they again answer the question *To what extent?*

ADVERBS MODIFYING ADVERBS	
traveled less slowly	move very cautiously
lost too easily	lived almost happily

EXAMPLE Polar bears are **hardly** **ever** seen in this part of the park.

The adverb *hardly* modifies the adverb *ever.*

EXAMPLE When driving, I tire **too** **quickly**.

The adverb *too* modifies the adverb *quickly.*

See Practice 15.2B

PRACTICE 15.2A > **Identifying How Adverbs Modify Verbs**

Read the sentences. Write the adverb in each sentence and list the question it answers. (*When? Where? In what way? To what extent?*)

EXAMPLE Danielle will leave tonight.

ANSWER *tonight* — When?

1. We have had good success lately.
2. Jared climbed the rock wall slowly and carefully.
3. We hardly noticed the storm brewing.
4. An unhappy customer complained loudly.
5. The coach almost tripped over the equipment on the floor.
6. Tiffany never thought it could happen to her.
7. I need your help now.
8. Ike quietly walked away from the disturbance.
9. Sophia was completely surprised by the remark.
10. Sherwin pulled ahead in the last lap.

PRACTICE 15.2B > **Recognizing Adverbs and Words They Modify**

Read the sentences. Write the word that each underlined adverb modifies. Then, write whether that word is a *verb*, an *adjective*, or an *adverb*.

EXAMPLE The students moved <u>very</u> quickly out of the building during the fire drill.

ANSWER *quickly* — adverb

11. Ashley looks <u>extremely</u> serious.
12. Dad <u>usually</u> naps after working <u>so</u> hard.
13. Because of the weather, the traffic was moving <u>very</u> slowly.
14. I <u>often</u> walk in the park to think.
15. The mail should be coming <u>soon</u>.
16. Many students thought the assignment was <u>too</u> difficult.
17. Alex slept <u>soundly</u> before the exam.
18. Adam does <u>not</u> want to join our study group.
19. She spoke <u>rather</u> inappropriately.
20. Carson got an <u>exceptionally</u> high grade on his project.

SPEAKING APPLICATION

With a partner, take turns telling about your morning routine of preparing for school. Your partner should listen for and identify at least three adverbs and state how they modify the verbs.

WRITING APPLICATION

Write a brief paragraph in which you praise or criticize a book you've read. Use at least four adverbs. Underline each adverb and draw an arrow to the word it modifies.

Practice **341**

Finding Adverbs in Sentences

Adverbs can be found in different places in sentences. The chart below shows examples of possible locations for adverbs. Arrows point to the words that the adverbs modify.

LOCATION OF ADVERBS IN SENTENCES	
LOCATION	EXAMPLE
At the beginning of a sentence	Silently, she approached the baby.
At the end of a sentence	She approached the baby silently.
Before a verb	She silently approached the baby.
After a verb	She tiptoed silently toward the baby.
Between parts of a verb phrase	She had silently approached the baby.
Before an adjective	The baby was always quiet.
Before another adverb	The baby cried rather quietly.

Conjunctive adverbs **Conjunctive adverbs** are adverbs that join independent clauses. (See Chapter 17 for more about conjunctive adverbs.)

EXAMPLES   Her car broke down; **therefore**, she missed her
                                     conjunctive adverb
class.

Mike was worried that he would fail; **however**,
                                                conjunctive adverb
he passed with flying colors.

See Practice 15.2C

Adverb or Adjective?

Some words can function as adverbs or as adjectives, depending on their use in a sentence.

> If a noun or pronoun is modified by a word, that modifying word is an **adjective.** If a verb, adjective, or adverb is modified by a word, that modifying word is an **adverb.**

15.2.3 RULE

An adjective will modify a noun or pronoun and will answer one of the questions *What kind? Which one? How many?* or *How much?*

An adverb will modify a verb, an adjective, or another adverb and will answer one of the questions *Where? When? In what way?* or *To what extent?*

ADVERB MODIFYING VERB	Shopkeepers **work** **hard**. verb adverb
	When we came to the intersection, we **turned** **left**. verb adverb
ADJECTIVE MODIFYING NOUN	Shopkeepers accomplish **hard** **tasks**. adjective noun
	This is the **right** **format** to read the adjective noun finished manuscript.

While most words ending in *-ly* are adverbs, some are not. Several adjectives also end in *-ly*. These adjectives are formed by adding *-ly* to nouns.

ADJECTIVES WITH -LY ENDINGS	a **weekly** show
	a **cuddly** puppy
EXAMPLES	I like movies, but I prefer a **weekly** show.
	Kodie is different because he's such a **cuddly** puppy.

See Practice 15.2D

PRACTICE 15.2C > **Locating Adverbs**

Read the sentences. Then, write each adverb and the word or words it modifies.

EXAMPLE   His excuse was quite unbelievable.

ANSWER   *quite, unbelievable*

1. Unhappily, the losing team left the field.

2. Camille takes a multivitamin daily.

3. Please move over, so we can all sit comfortably.

4. I have never been so upset as I was then.

5. The student actors performed brilliantly.

6. Most students were thoroughly happy with their report cards.

7. Suddenly, the room went dark!

8. Elisa did not perform well yesterday because she had a headache.

9. You must aim high to achieve success.

10. Karen always greets everyone cheerfully.

PRACTICE 15.2D > **Recognizing Adverbs and Adjectives**

Read the sentences. Then, write whether each underlined word is an *adjective* or an *adverb*.

EXAMPLE   It's been a <u>long</u> time since I've seen him.

ANSWER   *adjective*

11. I arrived at school <u>early</u> this morning.

12. Dad caught the <u>early</u> train to work today.

13. Lianna speaks <u>first</u> in the debate.

14. The player easily scored his <u>first</u> goal.

15. Anna brushed her <u>straight</u> hair.

16. Stand up <u>straight</u>!

17. We had trouble planting vegetables in the <u>hard</u> ground.

18. Hassan and James worked <u>hard</u> on their project.

19. Keep your eyes <u>wide</u> open.

20. The parade route includes all of the <u>wide</u> streets in town.

SPEAKING APPLICATION

With a partner, take turns telling about an exciting event. Use at least three adverbs in different sentence locations. Your partner should identify the adverbs.

WRITING APPLICATION

Use sentences 13 and 14 as models, and write one sentence in which *first* is used as an adjective and one sentence in which *first* is used as an adverb.

PREPOSITIONS

Use prepositions in your writing to illustrate how words are related to each other.

CHAPTER 16

WRITE GUY *Jeff Anderson, M.Ed.*

WHAT DO YOU NOTICE?

Seek out prepositions as you zoom in on this sentence from the essay "Volar: To Fly" by Judith Ortiz Cofer.

MENTOR TEXT

> From up there, over the rooftops, I could see everything, even beyond the few blocks of our barrio; with my X-ray vision I could look inside the homes of people who interested me.

Now, ask yourself the following questions:

- Which prepositions help show the author's physical location as she describes what she sees?
- Which noun is part of the prepositional phrase beginning with *beyond*?

The author uses the prepositions *up* and *over* to convey her location as she observes her surroundings. The preposition *beyond* begins the prepositional phrase *beyond the few blocks*, and the noun included is *blocks*. The phrase that follows, *of the barrio*, is a separate prepositional phrase that begins with *of* and ends with the noun *barrio*.

Grammar for Writers Writers can use prepositions like markers on a map to show where events in a story take place. Prepositions also help show the timing of events.

My list of prepositions was just on my desk. Where did it go?

Let's see ... inside, outside, behind, underneath....

16.1 Prepositions

Prepositions function as connectors, relating one word to another within a sentence.

They allow a speaker or writer to express the link between separate items. **Prepositions** can convey information about location, time, or direction or provide details.

RULE 16.1.1

> A **preposition** relates the noun or pronoun following it to another word in the sentence.

EXAMPLES

RELATES   RELATES

The panda sat **on** the branch **of** the tree.

preposition   noun preposition   noun

RELATES

The child ran **across** the room and

preposition   noun

RELATES

hid **underneath** the bed.

preposition   noun

In the first example, the panda sat where? (on the branch) It was on what? (the tree). In the second example, the child ran where? (across the room) The child hid where? (underneath the bed)

FIFTY COMMON PREPOSITIONS				
about	behind	during	off	to
above	below	except	on	toward
across	beneath	for	onto	under
after	beside	from	opposite	underneath
against	besides	in	out	until
along	between	inside	outside	up
among	beyond	into	over	upon
around	but	like	past	with
at	by	near	since	within
before	down	of	through	without

See Practice 16.1A

Compound Prepositions Prepositions consisting of more than one word are called **compound prepositions.** Some of them are listed in the chart below:

COMPOUND PREPOSITIONS		
according to	by means of	instead of
ahead of	in addition to	in view of
apart from	in back of	next to
aside from	in front of	on account of
as of	in place of	on top of
because of	in spite of	out of

Because prepositions have different meanings, using a particular preposition will affect the way other words in a sentence relate to one another. In the first sentence, for example, notice how each preposition changes the relationship between *parade* and *City Hall.*

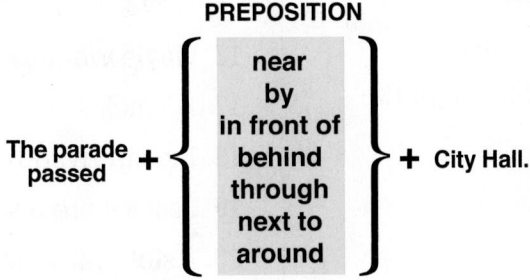

In this sentence, the preposition changes the relationship between *girls* and *gym.*

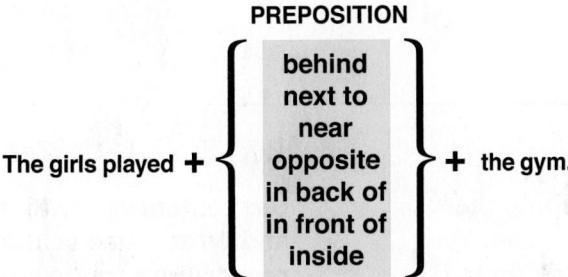

See Practice 16.1B

PRACTICE 16.1A ▷ Identifying Prepositions

Read the sentences. Then, write the preposition in each sentence.

EXAMPLE   I will give you an answer by tomorrow.

ANSWER   *by*

1. The price of the leather jacket was reduced.
2. In the mountains, the air is cooler.
3. Josh left his muddy boots outside the door.
4. Lia saw Julie between classes.
5. It appears that the train is on schedule.
6. I found a dollar near the bus stop.
7. Serena felt nervous before the concert.
8. Who is that standing beside Mike?
9. I like stories from Greek mythology.
10. Little Red Riding Hood walked through the forest.

PRACTICE 16.1B ▷ Identifying Compound Prepositions

Read the sentences. Then, write the compound preposition in each sentence.

EXAMPLE   In spite of his good intentions, Rob was late.

ANSWER   *In spite of*

11. School started late on account of the snow.
12. You must turn in your notes in addition to your essay.
13. According to the weather forecast, it will be sunny this week.
14. The principal wants to speak to Sam because of the incident.
15. Your dinner is staying warm on top of the stove.
16. Gayle went to the mall instead of the library.
17. A truck stopped in front of the house.
18. Ike survived by means of his wits.
19. Jessica ate a sandwich in place of a salad.
20. As of today, no one has responded to the ad.

SPEAKING APPLICATION

With a partner, take turns describing the location of another person in the room. Your partner should listen for and name three prepositions that you use.

WRITING APPLICATION

Use sentences 13, 16, and 19 as models, and write three sentences. Use the same prepositions, but change the other words.

Prepositions Used in Sentences

A preposition is never used by itself in a sentence. Instead, it appears as part of a phrase containing one or more other words.

> **A preposition** in a sentence always introduces a **prepositional phrase.**

Prepositional Phrases

A **prepositional phrase** is a group of words that begins with a preposition and ends with a noun or pronoun. The noun or pronoun following the preposition is the **object of the preposition.**

Some prepositional phrases contain just two words—the preposition and its object. Others are longer because they contain modifiers.

EXAMPLES   **in** **soil**
preposition object

from the rain **forest**
preposition   object

in place of the older, cracked **phone**
   preposition   object

inside the large, comfortable **car**
preposition   object

with **you**
preposition object

according to the new **principal**
    preposition   object

See Practice 16.1C
See Practice 16.1D
See Practice 16.1F

Prepositional phrases convey information about location, time, or direction or provide details. (See Chapter 23 to learn about prepositional phrases and their influence on subject–verb agreement.)

Preposition or Adverb?

Some words can be used either as prepositions or as adverbs. The following chart lists some examples. When the word is used as a preposition, it begins a prepositional phrase and is followed by the object of the preposition. If the word has no object, it is probably being used as an adverb.

PREPOSITION OR ADVERB		
above	inside	outside
after	nearby	past
around	opposite	underneath
before	out	within

PREPOSITION   The broken shutter was **outside** the house.

ADVERB   The man saw the broken shutter **outside**.

PREPOSITION   He appeared **before** the class.

ADVERB   He had not heard that **before**.

PREPOSITION   The man drove **past** the food store.

ADVERB   The car drove **past** quickly.

PREPOSITION   He sat **inside** the restaurant.

ADVERB   Please go **inside** now.

PREPOSITION   The beautician stood **behind** her client.

ADVERB   Ann waited **behind**.

PREPOSITION   The children waited **nearby** the playground.

ADVERB   I like that the stores are **nearby**.

See Practice 16.1E

See Practice 16.1G

See Practice 16.1H

PRACTICE 16.1C **Recognizing Prepositional Phrases**

Read the sentences. Write the prepositional phrase in each sentence, and underline the object of the preposition.

EXAMPLE   This old trunk is covered with dust.

ANSWER   *with dust*

1. The woman in the black coat dropped her purse.
2. Not many people stayed until the end.
3. The golfer hit a ball into the pond.
4. Everyone except Ashley brought lunch.
5. Birds start singing at daybreak.
6. Mrs. Dominguez received a basket of fruit.
7. Keep your papers inside your notebook.
8. He handed the ball to me.
9. We sat around the table discussing the book.
10. That's my brother leaning against the wall.

PRACTICE 16.1D **Distinguishing Prepositions and Prepositional Phrases**

Read the sentences. Write the prepositional phrases. Then, underline the preposition in each phrase.

EXAMPLE   Scrabble is among my favorite games.

ANSWER   *among my favorite games*

11. Two ferries go across that river.
12. There is a fascinating world beneath the ocean.
13. The guests are playing croquet on the lawn.
14. There was a long line outside the theater.
15. The new student is from Alabama.
16. I have a gift for you.
17. You can come through the front door.
18. Your phone fell out of your pocket.
19. Please do not stand in front of the window.
20. We can talk about the schedule later.

SPEAKING APPLICATION

With a partner, take turns describing the location of an object in the room. Use at least two prepositional phrases. Your partner should listen for and identify the prepositional phrases and the objects of each preposition.

WRITING APPLICATION

Write directions to your home from school. Underline the prepositional phrases in your directions.

PRACTICE 16.1E **Distinguishing Prepositions and Adverbs**

Read the sentences. Label each underlined word *preposition* or *adverb*.

EXAMPLE   Evan left his bicycle <u>outside</u>.

ANSWER   *adverb*

1. Let's go <u>in</u> now.

2. I have not seen Dave <u>around</u> lately.

3. The noise <u>outside</u> the apartment was distracting.

4. I've been to that deli <u>before</u>.

5. My notebook fell <u>behind</u> the desk.

6. We will have to go <u>around</u> the construction site.

7. Set your bundles <u>down</u> onto the table.

8. Dad needs to repair the hole <u>in</u> the fence.

9. We need to be home <u>before</u> 9:00 P.M.

10. Del lives just <u>down</u> the street from me.

PRACTICE 16.1F **Supplying Prepositions and Prepositional Phrases**

Read the sentences. Then, expand each sentence by adding a prepositional phrase that begins with the preposition in parentheses.

EXAMPLE   You may do your research. (on)

ANSWER   *You may do your research on the Internet.*

11. The tree will be cut down. (by)

12. The ball sailed. (over)

13. Our game was postponed. (with)

14. Malika baked banana bread. (for)

15. Everyone listened intently. (during)

16. Construction will begin soon. (of)

17. The child was crying. (in)

18. I can't go. (without)

19. Why don't you use this pen? (instead of)

20. You need to make up your mind. (prior to)

SPEAKING APPLICATION

With a partner, say a sentence using one of these words: *below, inside.* Your partner should identify whether you used the word as an adverb or a preposition.

WRITING APPLICATION

Write this sentence three times, expanding it with two different prepositional phrases each time: *A student dropped a book.*

PRACTICE 16.1G **Distinguishing Prepositions and Adverbs**

Read the sentences. Then, label each underlined word *preposition* or *adverb*.

EXAMPLE   The dog chased the squirrel <u>around</u> the yard.

ANSWER   *preposition*

1. Did you remember to put the garbage <u>out</u>?

2. We went <u>out</u> the door quickly.

3. The school is <u>nearby</u> the library.

4. My best friend lives in a house <u>nearby</u>.

5. I had never seen that movie <u>before</u>.

6. We bought our tickets <u>before</u> the movie started.

7. Melinda went <u>inside</u> the house to get her books.

8. Melinda forgot her books <u>inside</u>.

9. I waited for her <u>outside</u> the school.

10. The rain was soaking the flowers <u>outside</u>.

PRACTICE 16.1H **Supplying Prepositions and Adverbs**

For each word below, write two sentences. In the first sentence, use the word as a preposition. In the second sentence, use the word as an adverb.

EXAMPLE   above

ANSWER   *I placed my suitcase in the bin above my seat.* [preposition]

Look at the helicopter hovering above. [adverb]

11. after

12. around

13. before

14. inside

15. nearby

16. out

17. outside

18. past

19. underneath

20. within

SPEAKING APPLICATION

Take turns with a partner. Choose five of the words in Practice 16.1H. For each word, read aloud one of the sentences you wrote. Your partner should identify whether you used the word as an adverb or as a preposition.

WRITING APPLICATION

Write a paragraph that describes your home or your neighborhood. Use at least three of the following words: *nearby, past, before, after, inside, outside.* Then, underline the word and above it write (p) for preposition or (a) for adverb.

Test Warm-Up

DIRECTIONS
Read the introduction and the passage that follows. Then, answer the questions to show that you can use and understand the function of prepositions and prepositions used as adverbs in reading and writing.

The following paragraph gives directions for making peppermint pull candy. Read the paragraph and think about the changes you would suggest as a peer editor. When you finish reading, answer the questions that follow.

Peppermint Pull Candy

(1) When correctly made, peppermint pull candy will melt. (2) Rub a piece of marble with unsalted butter. (3) Put three drops of peppermint oil on. (4) Boil a mixture of sugar and water on the stove. (5) Use a candy thermometer so you know when the sugar reaches the correct temperature. (6) Once the sugar is ready, pour it over. (7) Let it sit for a few minutes to cool. (8) Then, with both hands, pull the candy. (9) Dip it in food coloring and keep pulling. (10) Finally, stretch it and cut it with scissors.

---

1 What change should be made in sentence 1?

A Add the adverb **inside** after *made*

B Add the prepositional phrase **in the comfort of home** after *made*

C Add the prepositional phrase **in your mouth** after *melt*

D Add the adverb **before** after *melt*

2 What is the BEST way to rewrite the ideas in sentence 3?

F Put on three drops of peppermint oil on.

G Put three drops of peppermint oil.

H Put three drops of peppermint oil around on.

J Put three drops of peppermint oil on the marble.

3 What change should be made in sentence 6?

A Replace the adverb **over** with the prepositional phrase **over the marble**

B Replace the adverb **over** with the adverb **outside**

C Replace the adverb **over** with the prepositional phrase **over the floor**

D Replace the adverb **over** with the adverb **within**

4 The meaning of sentence 10 can be clarified by inserting the adverb **out** —

F After *stretch*

G Before *with*

H Before *stretch*

J After *it*

CHAPTER 17

CONJUNCTIONS and INTERJECTIONS

Use conjunctions when you want to compare and contrast words or ideas in your writing; use interjections to add bursts of emotion.

WRITE GUY *Jeff Anderson, M.Ed.*

WHAT DO YOU NOTICE?

Check for conjunctions as you zoom in on these sentences from the essay "Life Without Gravity" by Robert Zimmerman.

MENTOR TEXT

> Some meals on the space station are eaten with forks and knives, but scooping food with a spoon doesn't work. If the food isn't gooey enough to stick to the spoon, it will float away.

Now, ask yourself the following questions:

- In the first sentence, which conjunction does the author use to show how two things can be used in a similar way?
- In the second sentence, which conjunction introduces a dependent idea?

The coordinating conjunction *and* links the words *forks* and *knives* to show that both tools can be used for eating meals on the space station. The conjunction *but* introduces the contrasting idea that spoons do not work well. In the second sentence, the subordinating conjunction *if* introduces the dependant idea *the food isn't gooey enough to stick to the spoon*. The main idea is *it will float away*.

Grammar for Writers You can use conjunctions to connect two words of the same part of speech or to connect complete sentences to form a new idea.

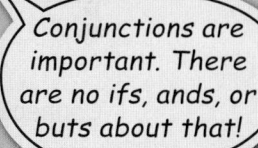

> Conjunctions are important. There are no ifs, ands, or buts about that!

17.1 Conjunctions

Conjunctions are like links in a chain: They help you join words and ideas.

RULE 17.1.1

> A **conjunction** connects words or groups of words.

Conjunctions fall into three groups: **Coordinating conjunctions, correlative conjunctions,** and **subordinating conjunctions.**

Coordinating Conjunctions

RULE 17.1.2

> **Coordinating conjunctions** connect words of the same kind, such as two or more nouns or verbs. They can also connect larger groups of words, such as prepositional phrases or even complete sentences.

COORDINATING CONJUNCTIONS						
and	but	for	nor	or	so	yet

In the following examples, notice the coordinating conjunctions that connect the highlighted words.

Connecting Nouns	My sister and her friend went to dinner last night to celebrate.
Connecting Verbs	They left for a picnic but forgot the basket.
Connecting Prepositional Phrases	Put the groceries onto the counter or into the refrigerator.
Connecting Two Sentences	The traffic was light, yet we were still late for the meeting.

See Practice 17.1A

Correlative Conjunctions

Correlative conjunctions are *pairs* of words that connect similar kinds of words or groups of words.

CORRELATIVE CONJUNCTIONS		
both . . . and	neither . . . nor	whether . . . or
either . . . or	not only . . . but also	

Notice the correlative conjunctions in the following examples.

Connecting Nouns	Either the train or the bus will take us there.
Connecting Pronouns	Neither they nor I are at fault.
Connecting Verbs	Every night, she both works out and reads.
Connecting Prepositional Phrases	They'll be here—whether on time or late, I can't say.
Connecting Two Clauses	Not only does he cook, but also he cleans!

See Practice 17.1B

Subordinating Conjunctions

Subordinating conjunctions connect two ideas by making one idea dependent on the other.

17.1.3 RULE

FREQUENTLY USED SUBORDINATING CONJUNCTIONS				
after	as soon as	if	though	whenever
although	as though	in order that	till	where
as	because	since	unless	wherever
as if	before	so that	until	while
as long as	even though	than	when	

The Dependent Idea The subordinating conjunction always introduces the dependent idea. The subordinating conjunction connects the dependent idea to the main idea.

EXAMPLES   I started dinner **after** **she called**.

When **I heard the phone ring**, I jumped.

The examples show that the main idea can come at the beginning or at the end of the sentence. When the dependent idea comes first, it must be separated from the main idea with a comma. If the dependent idea comes second, no comma is necessary.

See Practice 17.1C
See Practice 17.1D

Conjunctive Adverbs

Conjunctive adverbs are used as conjunctions to connect complete ideas. They are often used as transitions, connecting different ideas by showing comparisons, contrasts, or results.
Transitions are used in writing to improve the coherence from sentence to sentence and paragraph to paragraph and make your writing smoother.

CONJUNCTIVE ADVERBS			
accordingly	consequently	indeed	otherwise
again	finally	instead	then
also	furthermore	moreover	therefore
besides	however	nevertheless	thus

Notice the punctuation that is used before and after the conjunctive adverb in the following example. (See Chapter 25 for more about punctuation with conjunctive adverbs.)

EXAMPLE   That movie was great; **however**, I still prefer the book.

See Practice 17.1E
See Practice 17.1F

PRACTICE 17.1A > **Supplying Coordinating Conjunctions**

Read the sentences. Then, write each sentence, replacing the blank with a coordinating conjunction that makes sense in the sentence.

EXAMPLE   Cats _____ dogs are the most popular house pets.

ANSWER   *Cats and dogs are the most popular house pets.*

1. My sister _____ I do chores after school.

2. The lunch choices are pizza, soup, _____ sandwiches.

3. Billy swept _____ washed the floor.

4. I like science, _____ I prefer math.

5. Chris is inexperienced _____ eager to learn.

6. Mel did not do the assignment, _____ did he come to class.

7. He was late for the bus, _____ he started to run.

8. This tennis racket is light _____ sturdy.

9. We should hurry, _____ the show is about to begin.

10. Laurie has several extracurricular activities, _____ she keeps up her grades.

PRACTICE 17.1B > **Writing Sentences With Correlative Conjunctions**

Write ten sentences, using each of the correlative conjunctions below.

EXAMPLE   whether . . . or

ANSWER   *Ellie could not decide whether to go to the movies or to the mall.*

The game will be played whether it rains or not.

11. both . . . and

12. either . . . or

13. neither . . . nor

14. whether . . . or

15. not only . . . but also

16. both . . . and

17. either . . . or

18. neither . . . nor

19. whether . . . or

20. not only . . . but also

SPEAKING APPLICATION

With a partner, take turns telling about something you saw yesterday or today. Use two coordinating conjunctions in your sentences. Your partner should listen for and name the conjunctions.

WRITING APPLICATION

Write a brief paragraph using two of the correlative conjunction pairs listed above.

Use the main ideas and subordinating conjunctions below to write complete sentences. With a partner, read your sentences and explain how the subordinating conjunction functions.

EXAMPLE   We will make it to the playoffs (if)

ANSWER   *If we win against the Tigers,* we will make it to the playoffs.

1. I went ahead and made dinner (while)

2. Consider all the options (before)

3. Jasmine hasn't missed a piano lesson (since)

4. Mike brings a good book (whenever)

5. They'll celebrate their anniversary tomorrow (even though)

6. Eugene catches the five o'clock train (unless)

7. I can't go to the movies (because)

8. Mr. Higgins put up a fence (so that)

9. Joan's parents let her play computer games (as long as)

10. The cat will be hiding in the closet (until)

Write complete sentences using the subordinating conjunctions listed. With a partner, read the sentences aloud and explain how the subordinating conjunction functions in each.

EXAMPLE   because

ANSWER   *I'll walk down to the market because we're out of milk.*

11. if

12. whenever

13. since

14. when

15. because

16. unless

17. as soon as

18. before

19. although

20. while

SPEAKING APPLICATION

With a partner, take turns choosing three subordinating conjunctions and using them to talk about your after-school schedules. Your partner should listen for and identify the subordinating conjunctions you use.

WRITING APPLICATION

Write a paragraph about a favorite activity. Use at least three subordinating conjunctions. Read your paragraph to a partner, explaining how the different subordinating conjunctions function.

PRACTICE 17.1E › Using Conjunctive Adverbs in Sentences

Read the sentences. Then, rewrite each sentence, filling in the blank with a conjunctive adverb. Read each sentence to a partner and explain the function of the conjunctive adverb.

EXAMPLE I started reading that book; _____, I soon lost interest.

ANSWER *I started reading that book;* **however***, I soon lost interest.*

1. Doctors want people to exercise; _____, many people jog or play sports.

2. Jennifer scored the winning goal in the game; _____, the coach praised her ability.

3. We wanted to play outside after school; _____, it was warm and sunny.

4. I don't want to see that movie; _____, you already saw it last week.

5. Donnie must find his textbook before the test; _____, he will not be prepared.

6. My dad reminds me to turn off the lights; _____, I still forget to do it.

7. Cory thought his jacket was in the car; _____, we did not find it there.

8. Jane ran; _____, she boarded the bus in time.

9. My mom's speech took her all day to write; _____, she worked on it at night.

10. Joaquin likes to write stories; _____, he shares them.

PRACTICE 17.1F › Using and Writing Conjunctive Adverbs and Transitions

Read the pairs of sentences. Then, use conjunctive adverbs and transitions to write one new sentence. Read each new sentence to a partner and explain the function of the conjunctive adverbs and the transitions.

EXAMPLE I have to remind Betsy. She might forget to pick me up.

ANSWER *I have to remind Betsy;* **otherwise***, she might forget to pick me up.*

11. I studied hard. I got an A this semester.

12. Maria babysat five times. She has enough money to buy her mom a present.

13. I enjoyed the first book. I bought the second book.

14. There is a new girl in our lab group. I am no longer the only one.

15. Houston is usually hot in the summer. You should pack light clothing.

16. I practiced basketball a lot. I made the team.

17. We were excited to go to the concert. We were going to see our favorite band.

18. The traffic on the way to the airport was heavy. We missed our flight.

19. Three players on the team were injured in the game. We lost the championship.

20. The play begins in 10 minutes. We ran to our seats.

SPEAKING APPLICATION

With a partner, take turns talking about a book you are reading. Use at least two conjunctive adverbs and one transition. Have your partner identify which ones you used.

WRITING APPLICATION

Write a paragraph about what you did last weekend. Use subordinating conjunctions, conjunctive adverbs, and transitions. Explain to a partner the function of each conjunction.

Test Warm-Up

DIRECTIONS

Read the passage that follows. Then, answer the questions to show that you can identify, use, and understand the function of subordinating conjunctions, conjunctive adverbs, and transitions in reading and writing.

One of Those Days

(1) When I woke up last Tuesday I had a funny feeling it was going to be a bad day. (2) I overslept by 40 minutes. (3) I had to rush to get ready for school. (4) I jumped in the shower, then, I discovered there was no hot water. (5) I put two pieces of bread in the toaster. (6) After that, I went back to my room to make my bed. (7) Suddenly, the smoke detectors in the entire house were going off, my toast had burned. (8) I grabbed a granola bar and ran for the bus. (9) I was five minutes late; however, the bus had just arrived. (10) The driver said, "I'm sorry I'm late. It's one of those days." (11) I answered, "I know what you mean."

---

1 What change, if any, should be made in sentence 1?

  A Add a comma after *feeling*

  B Add a semicolon after *feeling*

  C Add a comma after *Tuesday*

  D Make no change

2 What is the BEST way to combine sentences 2 and 3?

  F I overslept by 40 minutes; otherwise, I had to rush to get ready for school.

  G I overslept by 40 minutes; nevertheless, I had to rush to get ready for school.

  H I overslept by 40 minutes; therefore, I had to rush to get ready for school.

  J I had to rush to get ready for school; because I overslept by 40 minutes.

3 What change, if any, should be made in sentence 4?

  A Delete the comma after *shower*

  B Change the comma after *shower* to a semicolon

  C Delete the comma after *then*

  D Make no change

4 What is the BEST way to revise sentence 7?

  F Suddenly, the smoke detectors in the entire house were going off because my toast had burned.

  G Suddenly, the smoke detectors in the entire house were going off; consequently, my toast had burned.

  H Suddenly, the smoke detectors in the entire house were going off before my toast had burned.

  J Suddenly, the smoke detectors in the entire house were going off; however, my toast had burned.

17.2 Interjections

The **interjection** is the part of speech that is used the least. Its only use is to express feelings or emotions.

> An **interjection** expresses feeling or emotion and functions independently from the rest of a sentence.

RULE 17.2.1

An interjection has no grammatical relationship to any other word in a sentence. It is, therefore, set off from the rest of the sentence with a comma or an exclamation mark.

Interjections can express different feelings or emotions.

JOY	**Wow!** I can't believe you paid so little.
SURPRISE	**Oh**, I just made plans before you called.
PAIN	**Ouch!** That curling iron is hot.
IMPATIENCE	**Hey!** When are we leaving?
HESITATION	I, **uh**, thought you already knew.

Interjections are used more in speech than in writing. They are informal, rather than formal, expressions. When you do see them in writing, they are often included in dialogue. The following chart lists words often used as interjections.

See Practice 17.2A
See Practice 17.2B

INTERJECTIONS			
ah	gosh	nonsense	ugh
aha	great	oh	uh
alas	heavens	oops	um
boy	hey	ouch	well
darn	huh	psst	what
eureka	hurray	shh	whew
fine	my	terrible	wonderful
golly	never	terrific	wow

PRACTICE 17.2A Identifying Interjections

Read the sentences. Write the interjection in each sentence. Then, write what emotion the interjection conveys.

EXAMPLE   Wow! Did you see that catch?

ANSWER   *Wow!*— surprise

1. Gosh, I didn't know that.

2. Whew! That was a long walk.

3. Hey! Why did you do that?

4. Oh, no! I can't find my key.

5. Ouch! I stubbed my toe!

6. I, uh, don't really know the answer.

7. Oh, brother, here were go again.

8. Hurray! I knew we would win.

9. Oops! I dropped it again.

10. Terrific! That's great news.

PRACTICE 17.2B Supplying Interjections

Read the sentences. Rewrite each sentence, using an appropriate interjection in place of the feeling shown in parentheses. Use a comma or an exclamation mark after each interjection.

EXAMPLE   I forgot my umbrella.
           (disappointment)

ANSWER   *Darn,* I forgot my umbrella.

11. I just don't believe that. (surprise)

12. She is always late. (impatience)

13. A bee stung me! (pain)

14. I'm so glad you're home safe. (joy)

15. That is a great poster. (surprise)

16. I thought we would never finish. (impatience)

17. Is that all you brought? (impatience)

18. I beg your pardon. (surprise)

19. When did you think it was due? (impatience)

20. I have never seen such ugly colors. (disappointment)

SPEAKING APPLICATION

With a partner, take turns role-playing someone who has just received some news, good or bad. Say your response to the news using an interjection. Your partner should listen for and identify the interjection.

WRITING APPLICATION

Write three sentences, each containing a different interjection. Use a comma or an exclamation mark after each interjection.

PRACTICE 1 > Writing Sentences With Nouns

Write five sentences, each using one of the following kinds of nouns. Circle those nouns, and underline any other nouns you use.

1. a common noun that names a place
2. a proper noun that names a person
3. a concrete noun
4. a hyphenated compound noun
5. a non-count noun

PRACTICE 2 > Identifying Pronouns

Read the sentences. Then, write the pronouns that each sentence contains. Label each pronoun *personal*, *reflexive*, *intensive*, *demonstrative*, *relative*, *interrogative*, or *indefinite*.

1. Tony, who carves wood, made me a spoon.
2. Whose is that?
3. The lifeguard himself said that the pool is open.
4. Everybody enjoyed your fruit salad.
5. Her cat can take care of itself.
6. Has anyone seen this before?
7. Who knows anything about nutrition?
8. Toby, who studied hard, deserved his *A*.
9. My mom sometimes goes to the movies by herself.
10. I myself could never stay up so late.

PRACTICE 3 > Using Action and Linking Verbs

Write two sentences for each word below. In the first sentence, use the word as an action verb; in the second sentence, use it as a linking verb.

1. smell
2. look
3. taste
4. feel
5. turn

PRACTICE 4 > Identifying Helping Verbs and Main Verbs in Verb Phrases

Read the sentences. Write the complete verb phrase in each sentence. Then, label the parts of each verb phrase *helping* or *main*.

1. The boys have completed all their chores.
2. Betsy's flight will leave at noon.
3. I do not like some of those vegetables.
4. The extra study time has helped me.
5. The task must be finished in one hour.
6. No one can ever remember those song lyrics.
7. I will never again make that mistake.
8. The party has been over since ten o'clock.
9. Did you go to the playground on Monday?
10. She should have dressed in warmer clothing.

Continued on next page ▶

Cumulative Review Chapters 13–17

 **PRACTICE 5** Revising Sentences With Adjectives and Adverbs

Read the sentences. Then, rewrite each sentence by adding at least one adjective to modify a noun or a pronoun or one adverb to modify a verb, an adjective, or another adverb.

1. Wendy found her sweater.
2. The girl takes a bus to school.
3. Grandfather snores loudly.
4. A lovely butterfly landed on the flower.
5. The weather was nasty all day.
6. The boat raced through the water.
7. Cows sat in the meadow.
8. She shouted to me from the hallway.
9. The silk shimmered like a rainbow.
10. Have you read a detective story?

 **PRACTICE 6** Writing Sentences With Prepositions and Adverbs

Write ten sentences describing different scenes. In your first five sentences, use the prepositional phrases in items 1–5. In your next five sentences, use the words in items 6–10 as adverbs.

1. under the tree branch
2. outside the house
3. before sunrise
4. behind the fence
5. down the chimney
6. under
7. outside
8. before
9. behind
10. down

PRACTICE 7 Identifying Conjunctions

Read the sentences. Then, identify each underlined word or pair of words as a *coordinating conjunction*, a *subordinating conjunction*, *correlative conjunctions*, or a *conjunctive adverb*.

1. It rained a lot, <u>but</u> we still enjoyed the trip.
2. I laughed <u>because</u> the clown looked so silly.
3. <u>Neither</u> Joshua <u>nor</u> Eric is going to the party.
4. I skipped lunch; <u>nevertheless</u>, I'm not hungry.
5. Alicia <u>and</u> Ellie have joined the Girl Scouts.

PRACTICE 8 Revising to Include Interjections

Rewrite the following dialogue, adding interjections to help show the speakers' emotions. Use either a comma or an exclamation mark after each interjection.

ELIOT: Did you see the eclipse yesterday?

JANA: I guess I missed it because I had to study.

ELIOT: My brother let me observe the sky through his telescope. It was pretty fantastic.

JANA: I wish I had seen it. I've never seen an eclipse.

ELIOT: I think it will be a long time before there is another eclipse.

JANA: I am so disappointed.

ELIOT: I know. We can research when the next eclipse is expected.

JANA: What a great idea.

CHAPTER 18

BASIC SENTENCE PARTS

Form well-crafted sentences in your writing by pairing carefully chosen subjects and verbs.

WRITE GUY *Jeff Anderson, M.Ed.*

WHAT DO YOU NOTICE?

Zero in on subjects and verbs as you zoom in on these sentences from the essay "The Eternal Frontier" by Louis L'Amour.

MENTOR TEXT

The question I am most often asked is, "Where is the frontier now?" The answer should be obvious. Our frontier lies in outer space.

Now, ask yourself the following questions:

- In the second and third sentences, what are the simple subjects and simple predicates?
- What are the complete subjects and complete predicates in the second and third sentences?

The simple subject in the second sentence is *answer,* and the simple predicate is *should be.* In the third sentence, the simple subject is *frontier,* and the simple predicate is *lies.* The complete subject in the second sentence is *the answer,* and the complete predicate is *should be obvious.* In the third sentence, the complete subject is *our frontier,* and the complete predicate is *lies in outer space.*

Grammar for Writers Make your sentences shorter or longer by working with your subjects and predicates. Think of your simple subject and simple predicate as the starting points of your sentences and build from there.

In the sentence "History is my favorite subject," history is the simple subject.

Well, it might be simple for you, but it's complex for me!

18.1 The Basic Sentence

There are many kinds of sentences. Some are short; others are long. Some are simple, and others are more complex. In order to be considered complete, a sentence must have two things: a subject and a verb.

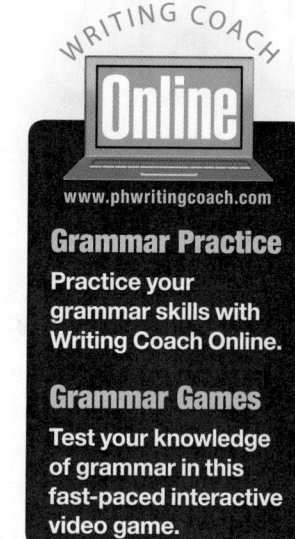

The Two Basic Parts of a Sentence

Every sentence, regardless of its length, must have a subject and a verb.

RULE 18.1.1 ▷ A complete **sentence** contains a subject and a verb and expresses a complete thought.

The Subject

A sentence must have a **subject.** Most subjects are nouns or pronouns. The subject is usually, but not always, found near the beginning of the sentence.

RULE 18.1.2 ▷ The **subject** of a sentence is the word or group of words that names the person, place, thing, or idea that performs the action or is described. It answers the question *Who?* or *What?* before the verb.

EXAMPLES   The **keys** are lost.

Mr. Levy lost his keys.

He has lost his keys before.

The **keys** are in his pockets.

The noun *keys* is the subject in the first sentence. It tells *what* is lost. In the next sentence, the proper noun *Mr. Levy* tells *who* lost his keys. The pronoun *he* in the third sentence tells *who* lost his keys before.

The Verb

As one of the basic parts of a sentence, the **verb** tells something about the subject.

RULE 18.1.3

> The **verb** in a sentence tells what the subject does, what is done to the subject, or what the condition of the subject is.

EXAMPLES

My dog **won** first place.

The ribbon **was given** at a ceremony.

He **seems** sleepy now.

See Practice 18.1A

Won tells what *my dog* did. *Was given* explains what was done with *the ribbon*. *Seems*, a linking verb, tells something about the condition of *he* by linking the subject to *sleepy*.

Using Subjects and Verbs to Express Complete Thoughts

Every basic sentence must express a complete thought.

RULE 18.1.4

> A sentence is a group of words with a subject and a verb that expresses a complete thought and can stand by itself and still make sense.

INCOMPLETE THOUGHT

in the closet in the hall

(This group of words cannot stand by itself as a sentence.)

This incomplete thought contains two prepositional phrases. The phrases can become a sentence only after *both* a subject and a verb are added to them.

COMPLETE THOUGHT

The **towels** **are** in the closet in the hall.
       subject   verb

(This group of words can stand by itself as a sentence.)

See Practice 18.1B

In grammar, incomplete thoughts are often called **fragments.**

PRACTICE 18.1A ▷ **Finding Subject and Verb**

Read the sentences. Write the subject and verb of each sentence.

EXAMPLE   The passengers boarded the plane.

ANSWER   *passengers, boarded*

1. We enjoyed a picnic in the park.
2. Winston has two paintings in the exhibit.
3. A skunk wandered through the yard.
4. Huge trucks haul goods across the country.
5. Jane knows who left the note.
6. Kendra has not done her homework yet.
7. The door banged shut behind him.
8. I miss my old neighborhood and school.
9. Where did you get that hat?
10. Marcus fixed the flat tire.

PRACTICE 18.1B ▷ **Recognizing Complete Sentences**

Read the following groups of words. If a group of words expresses a complete thought, write *complete*. If a group of words expresses an incomplete thought, write *incomplete*.

EXAMPLE   The new store in the mall.

ANSWER   *incomplete*

11. Along a bumpy road.
12. Gloria asked them to be quiet.
13. My new MP3 player on the table.
14. Chloe has never been to Chicago.
15. Destroyed in a wildfire.
16. Randall sings in a band.
17. Finally arrived an hour late.
18. You look happy today.
19. Since I last saw you.
20. Please turn out the lights.

SPEAKING APPLICATION

With a partner, take turns talking about today's weather. Your partner should listen for and name three subjects and three verbs in your sentences.

WRITING APPLICATION

Choose three of the incomplete sentences in Practice 18.1B and write them as complete sentences.

18.2 Complete Subjects and Predicates

Have you ever seen tiles laid on a floor? First, a line is drawn in the center of the room. One tile is placed to the left of the line, and another is placed to the right. Then, more tiles are added in the same way: one to the left and one to the right.

WRITING COACH

Online

www.phwritingcoach.com

Grammar Tutorials

Brush up on your Grammar skills with these animated videos.

Grammar Practice

Practice your grammar skills with Writing Coach Online.

Grammar Games

Test your knowledge of grammar in this fast-paced interactive video game.

Imagine that the first tile on the left is a subject and the first tile on the right is a verb. You would then have a subject and a verb separated by a vertical line, as shown in the example.

EXAMPLE   **Water** | **flowed** .

Now, in the same way that you would add a few more tiles if you were tiling a floor, add a few more words.

EXAMPLE   Cold **water** | **flowed** into the sink.

At this point, you could add still more words.

EXAMPLE   Icy cold **water** | **flowed** into the old metal sink in a steady stream.

The centerline is important in laying tiles. It is just as important in dividing these sentences into two parts. All the words to the left of the line in the preceding examples are part of the **complete subject.** The main noun in the complete subject, *water*, is often called the **simple subject.**

> The **complete subject** of a sentence consists of the subject and any words related to it.

RULE
18.2.1

As in the examples above, the complete subject may be just one word—*water*—or several words—*icy cold water.*

Look at the example sentences again, plus one with new words added.

EXAMPLES Cold **water** | **flowed** into the sink.

The icy cold **water** | **flowed** into the old metal sink.

Icy cold **water** | **had flowed** into the old metal sink in a steady stream.

All the words to the right of the line in the preceding examples are part of the **complete predicate.** The verb *flowed,* or a verb phrase such as *had flowed,* on the other hand, is often called the **simple predicate.**

See Practice 18.2A

RULE
18.2.2

> The **complete predicate** of a sentence consists of the verb and any words related to it.

As the examples show, a complete predicate may be just the verb itself or the verb and several other words.

Many sentences do not divide so neatly into subject and predicate. Look at the subjects and predicates in the following sentences.

EXAMPLES **After the game** , our **family** **went out to eat** .

With the snow falling , the **ski team** **began to practice** .

In these sentences, part of the predicate comes *before* the subject, and the rest of the predicate follows the subject.

As you have seen, a complete simple sentence contains a simple subject and a simple predicate. In addition, a complete simple sentence expresses a complete thought.

See Practice 18.2B

PRACTICE 18.2A **Identifying Complete Subjects and Predicates**

Read the sentences. Rewrite each sentence, and draw a vertical line between the complete subject and the complete predicate. Then, underline the subject once and the verb twice.

EXAMPLE   The Larsons took a train to Washington, D.C.

ANSWER   The <u>Larsons</u> | <u><u>took</u></u> a train to Washington, D.C.

1. Our new television has a very clear picture.

2. Coyotes roam this area at night.

3. The children enjoyed the skateboard ramp in the park.

4. Aidan delivers newspapers every day.

5. Laurie Halse Anderson wrote the novel *Speak*.

6. Reggie is looking for a job after school.

7. Nat and Roseanne did not hear about the changed schedule.

8. The hockey players usually practice early in the morning.

9. My aunt from New York has been visiting us this week.

10. Summer vacation will be here soon.

PRACTICE 18.2B **Writing Complete Sentences**

Read the items. Each item contains either a complete subject or a complete predicate. Rewrite each item along with the missing part to create complete sentences.

EXAMPLE   _____ are coming with us.

ANSWER   *My cousins from California are coming with us.*

11. _____ spread through the forest.

12. The governor of our state _____.

13. Skills in computer science _____.

14. _____ rolled off the counter and broke.

15. Three teenage athletes _____.

16. _____ toppled over.

17. _____ can be prevented.

18. A beautiful rainbow _____.

19. That car with the dent in its fender _____.

20. _____ occurs in the summer.

SPEAKING APPLICATION

With a partner, take turns describing one of your hobbies or pastimes using simple sentences. Your partner should listen for and identify the complete subject and predicate in your sentences.

WRITING APPLICATION

Write three sentences about any kind of animal. Draw a vertical line between the complete subject and complete predicate of each sentence.

18.3 Compound Subjects and Compound Verbs

Some sentences have more than one subject. Some have more than one verb.

WRITING COACH

Online

www.phwritingcoach.com

Grammar Tutorials
Brush up on your Grammar skills with these animated videos.

Grammar Practice
Practice your grammar skills with Writing Coach Online.

Grammar Games
Test your knowledge of grammar in this fast-paced interactive video game.

Recognizing Compound Subjects

A sentence containing more than one subject is said to have a **compound subject.**

RULE 18.3.1

> A **compound subject** is two or more subjects that have the same verb and are joined by a conjunction such as *and* or *or*.

EXAMPLES

Isabella and Michael **are** popular baby names.
compound subject   verb

Birds, rabbits, and other animals **will make**
compound subject   verb

nests to live in.

Recognizing Compound Verbs

A sentence with two or more verbs is said to have a **compound verb.**

RULE 18.3.2

> A **compound verb** is two or more verbs that have the same subject and are joined by a conjunction such as *and* or *or*.

EXAMPLES

The **team** **may win or lose**.
      subject   compound verb

She **reads, edits, and writes** her books.
subject   compound verb

Sometimes a sentence will have both a compound subject and a compound verb.

EXAMPLE

Liz and Josh **sang and danced** in
compound subject   compound verb

the play.

See Practice 18.3A
See Practice 18.3B

374 **Basic Sentence Parts**

PRACTICE 18.3A Recognizing Compound Subjects and
Compound Verbs

**Read the sentences. Write the compound subject and/or the
compound verb in each sentence.**

EXAMPLE   Brad and Tony work for the Recreation Department.

ANSWER   *Brad and Tony*

1. Yolanda designs and sews her own clothes.

2. Oranges, grapefruits, and lemons are citrus fruits.

3. Nina sat in the shade and sipped a cool drink.

4. Either Ollie or Oscar left his sweatshirt here.

5. Nikki wrote a story and posted it on her Web site.

6. Canada, the United States, and Mexico are countries in
   North America.

7. You may climb the stairs or ride the escalator.

8. Several people in the room coughed and sneezed.

9. We looked for wild strawberries but didn't find any.

10. My friends and I sometimes go to the track and run
    several laps.

SPEAKING APPLICATION

With a partner, take turns
describing a crowd that
you saw somewhere. Your
partner should listen for
and identify at least one
compound subject and one
compound verb in your
description.

WRITING APPLICATION

Use sentences 4, 7, and
10 as models, and write
three sentences that have
compound subjects and/or
compound verbs.

PRACTICE 18.3B > **Combining Sentences With Compound Subjects and Compound Verbs**

Read the sentences. Combine each pair of sentences by using compound subjects or compound verbs.

EXAMPLE   Sylvia aimed the ball carefully. She made a basket.

ANSWER   *Sylvia aimed the ball carefully and made a basket.*

1. This street needs repair. The sidewalk does, too.

2. Jonathan tried out for the team. He made it.

3. I drank a glass of juice. Then, I ran for the school bus.

4. Oil paintings were on sale at the craft fair. Pottery was also on sale.

5. Renee wrote a long letter. She sent it to the editor of the newspaper.

6. Nick mowed the grass. He raked the lawn.

7. The teacher was happy about the test scores. The students were, too.

8. Wind is a renewable energy source. Water is as well.

9. A police officer examined the accident site. She questioned all the witnesses.

10. Tulips grew along the path. Daffodils grew there also.

SPEAKING APPLICATION

With a partner, take turns describing something in your schoolyard. Use a compound subject or a compound verb in one of your sentences. Your partner should listen for and identify the compound.

WRITING APPLICATION

Write two short sentences about what you like to do after school. Then, combine the two short sentences into one longer sentence that has a compound subject and/or compound verb.

18.4 Hard-to-Find Subjects

It can be difficult to identify simple subjects in certain sentences. These sentences do not follow **normal word order** in which the subject comes before the verb. Sometimes the subject will follow the verb or part of a verb phrase. This is called **inverted word order**. Questions are often presented in inverted word order.

NORMAL WORD ORDER

The **meeting** **will begin** at 9:00 A.M. sharp!
        subject   verb

INVERTED WORD ORDER

When **will** the **meeting** **begin**?
       verb   subject   verb

Sometimes the subject will not actually be stated in the sentence. It will be understood to be the pronoun *you*. This is often true in sentences that express commands or requests.

The Subject of a Command or Request

When a sentence commands or requests someone to do something, the subject is often unstated.

> The subject of a command or request is understood to be the pronoun *you*.

RULE **18.4.1**

COMMANDS OR REQUESTS	HOW THE SENTENCES ARE UNDERSTOOD
Go!	You go!
Start at once.	You start at once.
Please get up.	You get up.
Heather, write it down.	Heather, you write it down.
Tara, get the confirmation number.	Tara, you get the confirmation number.

See Practice 18.4A

Even though a command or request may begin with the name of the person spoken to, the subject is still understood to be *you*.

Finding Subjects in Questions

Questions are often presented in inverted word order. You will usually find the subject in the middle of the sentence.

> **In questions, the subject often follows the verb.**

Some questions in inverted word order begin with the words *what, whom, when, where, why,* and *how.* Others begin with the verb itself or with a helping verb.

EXAMPLES   How **are** the **muffins** today?

Did you make them fresh this morning?

Have you found a basket for them yet?

If you ever have trouble finding the subject in a question, use this trick: Change the question into a statement. The subject will then appear in normal word order before the verb.

QUESTIONS	REWORDED AS STATEMENTS
How **are you** feeling today?	**You are** feeling how today.
What **did** the **nurse say**?	The **nurse did say** what.
Were the **newspapers** delivered?	The **newspapers were** delivered.
Did she bring the newspaper with her?	**She did bring** the newspaper with her.

Not every question is in inverted word order. Some are in normal word order, with the subject before the verb. Questions beginning with *who, whose,* or *which* often follow normal word order.

EXAMPLES   **Who has** the new car?

Whose new **car was** right here?

Which **driver should look** at the car?

See Practice 18.4B

PRACTICE 18.4A Identifying Subjects in Commands or Requests

Read the sentences. Write the subject of each sentence.

EXAMPLE   Please bring your own lunch.

ANSWER   *you*

1. Open your books now.
2. Reese, please show me your photos.
3. Pass the ball to Lonnie.
4. Hand me that towel, please.
5. Take the first left after the stoplight.
6. Recharge the battery when it runs down.
7. Do not leave yet.
8. Lou, work with Robert today.
9. Please call me when you get home.
10. Do not forget your gloves.

PRACTICE 18.4B Identifying Subjects in Questions

Read the questions. Write the subject of each question. If you have trouble finding the subject in a question, change the question into a statement.

EXAMPLE   Have you seen Jack today?

ANSWER   *You*

11. Is the report due tomorrow?
12. Did Rosemary enjoy the show?
13. Do you know what prize you won?
14. Does Kerri have an extra pen?
15. Did you bring water for everyone?
16. Would you like me to arrange these chairs?
17. Did Sarah put my folder on my desk?
18. Will we take a field trip?
19. Is she worried about her father?
20. Has everyone had a chance to respond?

SPEAKING APPLICATION

With a partner, take turns explaining how to do a simple task. Your partner should identify the subjects of your sentences.

WRITING APPLICATION

Use sentences 15, 16, and 20 as models and write three sentences of your own. Circle the subjects in your sentences.

Finding the Subject in Sentences Beginning With *There* or *Here*

Sentences beginning with *there* or *here* are usually in inverted word order.

> **There** or **here** is never the subject of a sentence.

There can be used to start a sentence.

SENTENCE
STARTER
There are two professors from Harvard teaching today.

There and *here* can be used as adverbs at the beginning of sentences. As adverbs, these two words point out *where* and modify the verbs.

ADVERB
There goes the town mayor.

Here are the cards from the ceremony.

Be alert to sentences beginning with *there* and *here*. They are probably in inverted word order, with the verb appearing before the subject. If you cannot find the subject, reword the sentence in normal word order. If *there* is just a sentence starter, you can drop it from your reworded sentence.

SENTENCES BEGINNING WITH *THERE* OR *HERE*	REWORDED WITH SUBJECT BEFORE VERB
There is a mistake on the dinner order.	A mistake is on the dinner order.
Here is the correct list of orders.	The correct list of orders is here.

See Practice 18.4C

Finding the Subject in Sentences Inverted for Emphasis

Sometimes a subject is intentionally put after its verb to draw attention to the subject.

> **In some sentences, the subject follows the verb in order to emphasize the subject, or make it stand out.**

18.4.4 RULE

In the following examples, notice how the order of the words builds suspense by leading up to the subject.

EXAMPLES   In the midst of the crowd outside the restaurant

stood my **parents**.
       verb   subject

Flying above the yard **was** a large red-tailed
  verb   verb
hawk.
 subject

Hiding under the warm blanket **was** my little
  verb   verb
black **puppy**.
        subject

You can reword sentences such as these in normal word order to make it easier to find the subject.

INVERTED WORD ORDER	REWORDED WITH SUBJECT BEFORE VERB
In the midst of the crowd outside the restaurant stood my parents.	My parents stood in the midst of the crowd outside the restaurant.
Flying above the yard was a large red-tailed hawk.	A large red-tailed hawk was flying above the yard.
Hiding under the warm blanket was my little black puppy.	My little black puppy was hiding under the blanket.

See Practice 18.4D

PRACTICE 18.4C ▷ Identifying Subjects in Sentences Beginning With *Here* or *There*

Read the sentences. Write the subject of each sentence.

EXAMPLE   Here are the materials you need.

ANSWER   *materials*

1. There are two unread messages in my e-mail.
2. Here comes the coach now.
3. There stood a solitary tree in the field.
4. There goes the last bus without us.
5. Here are a few more players.
6. There is only one right answer.
7. There had been dairy farms in this area.
8. Here lives a famous writer.
9. There are only a few stars out tonight.
10. Here is a map you can follow.

PRACTICE 18.4D ▷ Identifying Subjects in Sentences Inverted for Emphasis

Read the sentences. Write the subject of each sentence.

EXAMPLE   Overhead flew a flock of geese.

ANSWER   *flock*

11. In the middle of the hall hung Grandfather's portrait.
12. Into the office stormed an angry parent.
13. Nowhere will you find better merchandise.
14. Under the porch were two stray kittens.
15. Two blocks from here is the ice cream shop.
16. His good looks he got from his father.
17. All over the yard were broken branches.
18. On these shores landed the first settlers.
19. Down the drain swirled the muddy water.
20. Under no circumstances are you to disturb me!

SPEAKING APPLICATION

With a partner, take turns pointing out two or three things in your classroom using sentences that begin with *Here* or *There*. Your partner should identify the subjects of your sentences.

WRITING APPLICATION

Use sentences 11, 13, and 20 as models, and write three sentences with inverted order of subjects and verbs. Circle the subjects.

18.5 Complements

Often, a subject and verb alone can express a complete thought. For example, *Birds fly* can stand by itself as a sentence, even though it contains only two words, a subject and a verb. Other times, however, the thought begun by a subject and its verb must be completed with other words. For example, *Jacob bought, The waiter told, Our waiter was, Isabella felt,* and *Carolyn won* all contain a subject and verb, but none expresses a complete thought. All these ideas need **complements**.

> A **complement** is a word or group of words that completes the meaning of a sentence.

RULE 18.5.1

Complements are usually nouns, pronouns, or adjectives. They are located right after or very close to the verb. The complements are shown below in blue. The complements answer questions about the subject or verb in order to complete the sentence.

DIFFERENT KINDS OF COMPLEMENTS

Jacob **bought** **dinner**.
subject · verb · complement

The **waiter** **told** **us** the **specials**.
subject · verb · complements

Our **waiter** **was** **impatient**.
subject · verb · complement

Isabella **felt** **happy**.
subject · verb · complement

Carolyn **won** the **game**.
subject · verb · complement

This section will describe three types of complements: **direct objects, indirect objects,** and **subject complements.** All complements add information about the subjects or verbs in the sentence. They paint a clearer picture that helps the reader understand the writer's thoughts.

Recognizing Direct Objects

Direct objects follow action verbs.

> A **direct object** is a noun or pronoun that receives the action of a verb.

You can find a direct object by asking *What?* or *Whom?* after an action verb.

EXAMPLES   My younger **sister** **found** the hidden **presents**.
                                subject   verb   direct object

                  I **called** **Christina** later that day.
               subject   verb   direct object

                  My dog **Tinker** **likes** a long **run**
                         subject   verb   direct object
                  in the yard.

Presents, Christina, and *run* are the direct objects of the verbs in the examples. In the first sentence, *presents* answers the question *Found what?* In the second sentence, *Christina* answers the question *Called whom?* In the third sentence, *run* answers the question *Likes what?*

Compound Direct Objects

Like subjects and verbs, direct objects can be compound. That is, one verb can have two or more direct objects.

EXAMPLES   The **baby** **eats** **peas** and other **food**.
                           subject   verb   direct object   direct object

                  The **PTA** **chose** **Mrs. Dorf**,
                    subject   verb   direct object

                  Mrs. Malia, and **Mrs. Niles** to plan the
                  direct object   direct object
                  next formal.

See Practice 18.5A

See Practice 18.5B

PRACTICE 18.5A > Recognizing Direct Objects

Read the sentences. Write the direct object or the compound direct object in each sentence.

EXAMPLE   Walter Dean Myers has won many awards for his books.

ANSWER   *awards*

1. I usually buy my lunch in the cafeteria.

2. The troop hiked ten miles last week.

3. The rain soaked my jacket.

4. Our teacher showed a film in class.

5. Samantha washed the pots and pans after dinner.

6. Come see the view from here.

7. Tammy saved her money for six months.

8. We brought grapes and apples for snacks.

9. Carole plays both the piano and the flute.

10. Ben asked Joel and me for help.

PRACTICE 18.5B > Adding Complements

Read the sentences. Rewrite the sentences, and fill in the blanks with appropriate direct objects. Use both nouns and pronouns.

EXAMPLE   We are reading _____ in English class.

ANSWER   We are reading *Where the Red Fern Grows* in English class.

11. Nadia saved _____ to buy a camera.

12. My family will visit _____ this summer.

13. I asked _____ for a ride home.

14. Our teacher instructed _____ and _____ to hand out the books.

15. We saw _____ , _____ , and a _____ at the fair.

16. Dan met _____ that day.

17. On a clear night, he watches the _____ .

18. Nick designs _____ for a living.

19. I've seen that _____ , but I don't know _____ .

20. Brian put the _____ into the trash can.

SPEAKING APPLICATION

With a partner, take turns telling how a particular sport is played. Your partner should listen for and name at least two direct objects.

WRITING APPLICATION

Use sentences 14 and 15 as models, and write two more sentences with direct objects.

Practice   385

Distinguishing Between Direct Objects, Adverbs, and Objects of Prepositions

Not all action verbs have direct objects. Be careful not to confuse a direct object with an adverb or with the object of a preposition. If you are unsure if a word or phrase is a direct object, ask yourself who or what is receiving the action of the verb.

RULE 18.5.3

> **A direct object is never an adverb or the noun or pronoun at the end of a prepositional phrase.**

Compare the following examples. Notice that the action verb *rode* has a direct object in only the first sentence.

EXAMPLES

Dan **rode** his **bike** .
subject   verb   direct object

Dan **rode** **quickly** .
subject   verb   adverb

Dan **rode** **through town** .
subject   verb   prepositional phrase

Each example shows a very common sentence type. The first consists of a subject, a verb, and a direct object. The noun *bike* is the direct object of the verb *rode*.

The second example consists of a subject, a verb, and an adverb. Nothing after the verb in the sentence answers the question *What?* so there is no direct object. *Quickly* modifies the verb and tells *how* Dan rode.

The third example consists of a subject, a verb, and a prepositional phrase. Again, no noun or pronoun answers the question *What?* after the verb. The prepositional phrase tells *where* Dan rode.

Notice also that a single sentence can contain more than one of these three parts.

EXAMPLE

Dan rode his **bike** **quickly**
         direct object   adverb
through town .
prepositional phrase

See Practice 18.5C

Finding Direct Objects in Questions

In normal word order, a direct object follows a verb. In questions that are in inverted word order, however, the direct object often appears before the verb and subject.

> **A direct object in a question will sometimes be found before the verb.**

18.5.4 RULE

In the following chart, questions are paired with sentences reworded in normal word order. Direct objects are highlighted in pink, subjects are highlighted in yellow, and verbs are highlighted in orange. Compare the positions of the direct objects in each.

QUESTIONS	REWORDED IN NORMAL WORD ORDER
What recipes does your grandmother make?	Your grandmother does make what recipes.
What does the baby eat?	The baby does eat what.
Which shoes do you like, the cute flat ones or the fancy boots?	You do like which shoes, the cute flat ones or the fancy boots.
Whom did you meet at the nursery?	You did meet whom at the nursery.

In each of the five questions, the direct object appears before, rather than after, the verb. To locate the direct object in a question, put the sentence into normal word order with the subject appearing before the verb. Then, the direct object will be found in its usual position after the verb.

See Practice 18.5D

PRACTICE 18.5C ▷ **Distinguishing Direct Object, Adverb, and Object of a Preposition**

Read the sentences. Label each underlined word *DO* for direct object, *ADV* for adverb, and *OP* for object of a preposition.

EXAMPLE   Melissa keeps a parrot in a <u>cage</u>.

ANSWER   *OP*

1. Brad noticed two eggs in the bird's <u>nest</u>.
2. The firefighters responded <u>immediately</u> to the alarm.
3. The art students learned the <u>basics</u> of oil painting.
4. Morgan made a mistake on her math <u>problem</u>.
5. The students sat <u>quietly</u> through the assembly.
6. Phoebe will take Spanish <u>next</u>.
7. Daniel revised and edited his <u>essay</u>.
8. A skater glided smoothly across the <u>ice</u>.
9. Workers removed <u>litter</u> from the roadside.
10. From the top of that hill, you can see for <u>miles</u>.

PRACTICE 18.5D ▷ **Finding Direct Objects in Questions**

Read the questions. Write the direct object in each question.

EXAMPLE   Which bus do you take?

ANSWER   *bus*

11. What answer did you give to Lucy?
12. How many points did Kevin score?
13. Whom did the team choose as captain?
14. What program should we watch tonight?
15. Whose phone did you borrow?
16. Which shoes do you prefer?
17. What sources did you use for your project?
18. How many books did Tim read?
19. What will you do about your missing keys?
20. Whom did you see there?

SPEAKING APPLICATION

With a partner, take turns talking about something you did yesterday. Your partner should listen for and identify at least one direct object, one adverb, and one object of a preposition.

WRITING APPLICATION

Use sentences 13, 16, and 19 as models, and write three questions. Underline the direct object in each question.

Recognizing Indirect Objects

Sentences with a direct object may also contain another kind of complement, called an **indirect object.** A sentence cannot have an indirect object unless it has a direct object.

> An **indirect object** is a noun or pronoun that comes after an action verb and before a direct object. It names the person or thing to which something is given or for which something is done.

RULE 18.5.5

An indirect object answers the questions *To* or *for whom?* or *To* or *for what?* after an action verb. To find an indirect object, find the direct object first. Then, ask the appropriate question.

EXAMPLE   Tovah's **dad told us** the **story** .
                                    indirect object   direct object

(Told *what?* [*story*])
(Told the story *to whom?* [*us*])

Keep in mind the following pattern: *Subject + Verb + Indirect Object + Direct Object*. An indirect object will almost always come between the verb and the direct object in a sentence.

Compound Indirect Objects

Like a subject, verb, or direct object, an indirect object can be compound.

EXAMPLES   **Joe gave** each **flower and bush** a
                 subject   verb   compound indirect object

trim .
direct object

(Gave *what?* [*trim*])
(Gave a trim *to what?* [*each flower and bush*])

Dad offered Hannah and me
subject   verb   compound indirect object

dinner and a movie .
        compound direct object

(Offered *what?* [*dinner and a movie*])
(Offered dinner and a movie *to whom?* [*Hannah and me*])

See Practice 18.5E

Distinguishing Between Indirect Objects and Objects of Prepositions

Do not confuse an indirect object with the object of a preposition.

> **An indirect object never follows the preposition *to* or *for* in a sentence.**

Compare the following examples.

EXAMPLES   Grandpa bought **her** a **television**.
                              indirect   direct object
                              object

Grandpa bought a **television** for **her**.
                  direct object   object of
                                       preposition

In the first example above, *her* is an indirect object. It comes after the verb *bought* and before the direct object *television*. In the second example, *her* is the object of the preposition *for* and follows the direct object *television*.

EXAMPLES   Heather gave **Tara** a **book**.
                           indirect   direct
                           object   object

Heather gave a **book** to **Tara**.
                 direct   object of
                 object   preposition

To find the indirect object in the first example above, you must first find the direct object. Ask yourself what Heather gave. She gave a book, so *book* is the direct object. Then, ask yourself to whom Heather gave the book. She gave it to *Tara*, so *Tara* is the indirect object.

Use the same questions in the second example. Again, *book* is the direct object of *gave*; however, *Tara* is no longer the indirect object. Instead, it is the object of the preposition *to*.

See Practice 18.5F

PRACTICE 18.5E > **Recognizing Indirect Objects**

Read the sentences. Write the indirect object in each sentence.

EXAMPLE   The principal asked Tad some questions.

ANSWER   *Tad*

1. I've already sent her two messages.
2. Carrie fed her cats tuna.
3. Seth made his mother a solemn promise.
4. Please show me your new video game.
5. The boys gave each other a high-five.
6. The baby sitter told the children bedtime stories.
7. Will you lend him a pencil?
8. The business gave the school a donation for new equipment.
9. Our class wrote the author a letter.
10. Many people gave the hurricane victims food and shelter.

PRACTICE 18.5F > **Distinguishing Indirect Object and Object of a Preposition**

Read the sentences. Write whether the underlined word is an *indirect object* or an *object of a preposition*.

EXAMPLE   Mr. Murphy teaches <u>us</u> social studies.

ANSWER   *indirect object*

11. Phil told <u>Mario</u> the answer.
12. Vanessa wrote her <u>aunt</u> a thank-you note.
13. Do you have any news for <u>us</u>?
14. Let's make <u>ourselves</u> a snack.
15. The teacher explained the assignment to <u>Veronica</u>.
16. Ivy did her research in the <u>library</u>.
17. David passed <u>Brett</u> the ball.
18. Cecilia wanted time for <u>herself</u>.
19. The Chamber of Commerce gives one worthy <u>student</u> a scholarship.
20. Tara whispered a secret to <u>Jocelyn</u>.

SPEAKING APPLICATION

With a partner, tell about a birthday or holiday celebration. Your partner should listen for and name two indirect objects that you use.

WRITING APPLICATION

Rewrite sentences 11, 14, and 19 to include a prepositional phrase.

Subject Complements

Both direct objects and indirect objects are complements used with action verbs. Linking verbs, however, have a different kind of complement called a **subject complement.** Like direct and indirect objects, subject complements add information to a sentence. However, subject complements give readers more information about the subject of the sentence, not the verb.

RULE 18.5.7

> A **subject complement** is a noun, pronoun, or adjective that follows a linking verb and provides important details about the subject.

Predicate Nouns and Pronouns

Both nouns and pronouns are sometimes used as subject complements after linking verbs.

RULE 18.5.8

> A **predicate noun** or **predicate pronoun** follows a linking verb and renames or identifies the subject of the sentence.

It is easy to recognize predicate nouns and predicate pronouns. The linking verb acts much like an equal sign between the subject and the noun or pronoun that follows the verb. Both the subject and the predicate noun or pronoun refer to the same person or thing.

EXAMPLES

Bonnie **will be** the **head** of our committee.
   subject   verb   predicate noun

(The predicate noun *head* renames the subject *Bonnie.*)

My first **car** **was** a white **convertible**.
     subject verb   predicate noun

(The predicate noun *convertible* identifies the subject *car.*)

The two **winners** **are** **we**.
       subject   verb predicate pronoun

(The predicate pronoun *we* identifies the subject *winners.*)

See Practice 18.5G

Predicate Adjectives

A linking verb can also be followed by a **predicate adjective.**

> **A predicate adjective** follows a linking verb and describes the subject of the sentence.

RULE 18.5.9

A predicate adjective is considered part of the complete predicate of a sentence because it comes after a linking verb. In spite of this, a predicate adjective does not modify the words in the predicate. Instead, it describes the noun or pronoun that serves as the subject of the linking verb.

EXAMPLES

The **flight** to Mexico **was** **long**.
　　subject　　　　　　　verb　predicate adjective

(The predicate adjective *long* describes the subject *flight.*)

The **teacher** **seemed** very **sensitive**
　　subject　　　verb　　　　　predicate adjective
to the needs of her students.

(The predicate adjective *sensitive* describes the subject *teacher*.)

Compound Subject Complements

Like other sentence parts, subject complements can be compound.

> **A compound subject complement** consists of two or more predicate nouns, pronouns, or adjectives joined by a conjunction such as *and* or *or*.

RULE 18.5.10

EXAMPLES

My two best **subjects** **are** **English and history**.
　　　　　　subject　　verb　　compound predicate noun

The **grass** **felt** **warm and wet**.
　　subject　　verb　compound predicate adjective

See Practice 18.5H
See Practice 18.5I
See Practice 18.5J

The **dessert** **was** **ice cream and fruit**.
　　subject　　verb　　compound predicate adjective

PRACTICE 18.5G Identifying Predicate Nouns and Predicate Pronouns

Read the sentences. Write the predicate noun and/or the predicate pronoun in each sentence.

EXAMPLE   Whales are the largest mammals.

ANSWER   *mammals*

1. Gabe's favorite sport is lacrosse.
2. Regina is becoming a good painter.
3. The capital of Texas is Austin.
4. Mr. Hughes has been the director for years.
5. The group leaders are Isabel and she.
6. The best part of camp was the swimming.
7. Jordan will be our representative in the debate.
8. Shakespeare is probably the most famous playwright ever.
9. Amy remains my friend even though she moved away.
10. Your new car should be a hybrid.

PRACTICE 18.5H Identifying Predicate Adjectives

Read the sentences. Write the predicate adjective or adjectives in each sentence.

EXAMPLE   Robin appears confident about her chances.

ANSWER   *confident*

11. That antique table seems valuable.
12. As the storm continued, the roads became slippery.
13. The character in the black shirt looks suspicious.
14. Thanksgiving dinner was delicious and filling.
15. Laura sounded joyful about the news.
16. You should be thankful for your good health.
17. These plants grow taller every day.
18. This soup tastes so good.
19. The weather for our outing was breezy and warm.
20. Stefan felt better after a break.

SPEAKING APPLICATION

With a partner, make a statement about someone or something. Use a predicate noun or predicate adjective in your statement. Your partner should listen for and name the predicate noun or predicate adjective.

WRITING APPLICATION

Write a short paragraph describing someone or something. Use at least one predicate adjective and one predicate noun or predicate pronoun, and underline them in your paragraph.

PRACTICE 18.5I ▷ **Writing With Predicate Nouns, Predicate Pronouns, and Predicate Adjectives**

Read the sentence starters. Then, as indicated in parentheses, write a complete sentence using a predicate noun, predicate pronoun, or predicate adjective.

EXAMPLE   (predicate noun) Mr. Sloan might become

ANSWER   *Mr. Sloan might become the basketball coach.*

1. (predicate noun) The O'Reillys are our

2. (predicate adjective) Sunning themselves on the beach, my parents seemed

3. (predicate noun) Ms. Long could be the best

4. (predicate pronoun) The last person on the bus was

5. (predicate adjective) After dance class, she looked

6. (predicate noun) Last September, Kali became

7. (predicate pronoun) The big winner was

8. (predicate adjective) This chili tastes

9. (predicate adjective) The student council members are

10. (predicate adjective) After the game the team seemed

PRACTICE 18.5J ▷ **Writing With Compound Subject Complements**

Read the sentence starters. Then, add a compound subject complement to create a complete sentence.

EXAMPLE   Ice cream, when left out too long, becomes

ANSWER   *Ice cream, when left out too long, becomes **warm and runny**.*

11. Your speech sounded

12. My grandfather was a

13. To his friends, José seemed

14. Just how I like it, the sandwich is

15. The last two contestants were

16. Her best friend from kindergarten is now

17. After a day of exercising, Darnell is

18. The water looks

19. My two favorite foods are

20. His flight delayed again, Ted grew

SPEAKING APPLICATION

With a partner, take turns discussing sports. Use at least one predicate noun, one predicate pronoun, and one predicate adjective. Your partner should listen for and name the types of subject complements you used.

WRITING APPLICATION

Write a letter recommending a friend for a babysitting job. Use predicate nouns, predicate pronouns, and predicate adjectives. Include at least one compound subject complement.

Test Warm-Up

DIRECTIONS
**Read the introduction and the passage that follows. Then,
answer the questions to show that you can use and understand
the function of subject complements in reading and writing.**

*Sasha wrote this paragraph about a school event called Battle of the
Bands. Read the paragraph and think about the changes you would
suggest as a peer editor. When you finish reading, answer the questions
that follow.*

Battle of the Bands

(1) The Battle of the Bands competition were hosted by my school.
(2) It is my favorite school event. (3) This year, the four bands were
Union Bay Band, Tim and Cat, Sushi Rocks, and Candyband.
(4) Union Bay Band was amazing. (5) Union Bay Band was the best.
(6) The members were very talented and energetic. (7) Candyband was
the runner-up. (8) I thought their second song was much better than
their first. (9) My favorites were Union Bay Band and Sushi Rocks.
(10) Overall, it was a great show.

---

1 What change, if any, should be made in
sentence 1?

  A Change *were* to **is**

  B Add a comma after *competition*

  C Add an apostrophe after the *d* in *Bands*

  D Make no change

2 What is the BEST way to combine
sentences 4 and 5 to create a compound
subject complement?

  F Union Bay Band was amazing.

  G Union Bay Band was the best.

  H Union Bay Band was amazing and the
best.

  J Union Bay Band was the best, and Union
Bay Band was amazing.

3 What change, if any, should be made in
sentence 6?

  A Change *were* to **was**

  B Change *and* to **or**

  C Add a comma after *were*

  D Make no change

4 What change, if any, should be made to
sentence 9?

  F Change *favorites* to **favorite**

  G Change *were* to **was**

  H Change *favorites were* to **favorite is**

  J Make no change

CHAPTER 19

PHRASES *and* CLAUSES

Knowing how to construct phrases and clauses will help you add information to your sentences and make them more interesting.

WRITE GUY *Jeff Anderson, M.Ed.*

WHAT DO YOU NOTICE?

Search for phrases and clauses as you zoom in on lines from the poem "The Rider" by Naomi Shihab Nye.

MENTOR TEXT

> A boy told me
> if he rollerskated fast enough
> his loneliness couldn't catch up to him,
>
> the best reason I ever heard
> for trying to be a champion.

Now, ask yourself the following questions:

- What makes the entire second line a clause?
- In the third line, what makes the words *to him* a phrase?

The second line is a clause because it is a group of words that has its own subject and verb. The subject is *he* and the verb is *rollerskated*. In the third line, *to him* is a phrase because a phrase is a group of words that does not contain a subject and verb. Phrases are used to add more information to a sentence.

Grammar for Writers Phrases and clauses are an important part of a writer's toolbox. Use them to create complex sentences and to tell more about the main nouns and verbs in your sentences.

You added some interesting information to your sentences.

It must be a phrase I'm going through.

19.1 Phrases

Sentences are usually built with more than just a subject and a predicate. **Phrases** play an important role in sentences by adding more information.

RULE
19.1.1

A **phrase** is a group of words that functions in a sentence as a single part of speech. Phrases do not contain a subject and a verb.

Prepositional Phrases

A **prepositional phrase** has at least two parts, a preposition and a noun or pronoun that is the object of the preposition.

EXAMPLES   near **beaches**
           prep   object

               around **palm trees**
               prep   object

The object of the preposition may be modified by one or more adjectives.

EXAMPLES   near warm sandy **beaches**
           prep adj   adj   object

               around beautiful tall **palm trees**
               prep   adj   adj   object

The object may also be a compound, consisting of two or more objects connected by a conjunction such as *and* or *nor*.

EXAMPLES   near warm sandy **beaches** and **lakes**
           prep adj   adj   object   object

               around beautiful tall **palm trees** and **cacti**
               prep   adj   adj   object   object

In a sentence, some prepositional phrases can act as adjectives that modify a noun or pronoun. Other prepositional phrases can act as adverbs that modify a verb, adjective, or adverb.

See Practice 19.1A

Using Prepositional Phrases That Act as Adjectives

A prepositional phrase that acts as an adjective in a sentence is called an **adjective phrase** or **adjectival phrase.**

> An **adjective phrase** or **adjectival phrase** is a prepositional phrase that modifies a noun or pronoun by telling *what kind* or *which one.*

19.1.2 **RULE**

Unlike one-word adjectives, which usually come before the nouns or pronouns they modify, adjectival phrases usually come after the nouns or pronouns they modify.

ONE-WORD ADJECTIVES	ADJECTIVAL PHRASES
The sandy beach began there.	The beach with two lighthouses began there.
The anxious lifeguard stopped us.	The lifeguard with the anxious face stopped us.

Adjectival phrases answer the same questions as one-word adjectives do. *What kind* of beach began there? *Which* lifeguard stopped us?

USES OF ADJECTIVAL PHRASES	
Modifying a Subject	The sound of the rain scared us.
Modifying a Direct Object	It beat against the windows in the house.

When two adjectival phrases appear in a row, the second phrase may modify the object of the preposition in the first phrase or both phrases may modify the same noun or pronoun.

See Practice 19.1B
See Practice 19.1C

ADJECTIVAL PHRASES IN A ROW	
Modifying the Object of a Preposition	The gutters on the house in the field filled rapidly.
Modifying the Same Noun	There was a smell of roses in the house.

Using Prepositional Phrases That Act as Adverbs

A prepositional phrase that acts as an adverb modifies the same parts of speech as a one-word adverb does.

> An **adverbial phrase** or **adverb phrase** is a prepositional phrase that modifies a verb, an adjective, or an adverb. Adverbial phrases point out *where, when, in what way,* or *to what extent.*

Adverbial phrases are used in the same way as one-word adverbs, but they sometimes provide more precise details.

ONE-WORD ADVERBS	ADVERBIAL PHRASES
Bring your shoes here .	Bring your shoes into the garage .
The concert began early .	The concert began at exactly 6:00 P.M .

Adverbial phrases can modify verbs, adjectives, and adverbs.

USES OF ADVERBIAL PHRASES	
Modifying a Verb	Snow fell in heavy clumps . (Fell *in what way?*)
Modifying an Adjective	The day was cold for May . (Cold *in what way?*)
Modifying an Adverb	The snow fell heavily for that time of year . (Heavily *in what way?*)

See Practice 19.1D
See Practice 19.1E
See Practice 19.1F

Adverbial phrases, unlike adjectival phrases, are not always located near the words they modify in a sentence.

EXAMPLE   **During the storm**, people closed up their shops.

Two or more adverbial phrases can also be located in different parts of the sentence and still modify the same word.

EXAMPLE   **During the night**, the cold was felt **throughout the house**.

PRACTICE 19.1A ▷ Identifying Prepositional Phrases

Read the sentences. Then, write the prepositional phrase in each sentence, and underline the object of the preposition.

EXAMPLE   That story about wolves was fascinating.

ANSWER   *about wolves*

1. The sound of a harp is very soothing.

2. Please take your feet off the chair.

3. Were you able to find Quentin and Stewart in the crowd?

4. Justin likes to browse through magazines.

5. Rebecca will finish her project by Monday.

6. Elizabeth II is the queen of England.

7. Everyone reads the notices on the board.

8. The train to Chicago was late.

9. Valentina likes all vegetables except eggplant.

10. I do not watch television during the week.

PRACTICE 19.1B ▷ Identifying Adjectival Phrases

Read the sentences. Then, write the adjectival phrase in each sentence. One sentence has two adjectival phrases.

EXAMPLE   The leaves on the trees are turning brown.

ANSWER   *on the trees*

11. The head of the committee read the report.

12. The plant near the window is a bamboo.

13. The singer with the deep voice stole the show.

14. Ramona delivered an excellent presentation on colonial cooking.

15. Brandon is wearing a shirt with a school logo.

16. Do you have the solution to this problem?

17. The trail up the mountain is well marked.

18. The photo in the newspaper was not very clear.

19. The girl beside Carla is her sister.

20. The first room on the left in that corridor is the nurse's office.

SPEAKING APPLICATION

With a partner, tell about your neighborhood. Your partner should listen for and name at least one adjectival phrase, one prepositional phrase, and the object of the preposition.

WRITING APPLICATION

Write this sentence twice, adding two different adjectival phrases each time: *Two girls walked into the store.* Explain to a partner how the phrase functions in the sentence.

Practice   401

Read each sentence. Rewrite each sentence adding one or more adjectival phrases. Then, read the sentences to a partner who identifies the adjectival phrase.

EXAMPLE   The book was dusty.

ANSWER   The book *on the top shelf* was dusty.

1. The fountain is a good place to make wishes.
2. Cindy bought the sparkling earrings.
3. The waiter has arrived.
4. The audience fell silent.
5. Arkee sensed something wrong.
6. The get-well-soon cards piled up.
7. My family is planning a vacation.
8. The flowers look thirsty.
9. Lin's broken collarbone healed.
10. The first bite tasted delicious.

Read the sentences. Then, write the adverbial phrase in each sentence. One sentence has two adverbial phrases.

EXAMPLE   A hawk dived from the tree.

ANSWER   *from the tree*

11. I can help you in a minute.
12. Oliver is very good at chess.
13. Franklin was bored during the recital.
14. Olivia included two graphs in her report.
15. That car parked by the hydrant was ticketed.
16. The winner stepped onto the platform.
17. The kayaker moved steadily across the lake.
18. Lily fastened the necklace around her neck.
19. The dog woke up from his nap with a start.
20. Let's go without further delay.

SPEAKING APPLICATION

With a partner, take turns talking about your favorite pastimes. Use three adjectival and three adverbial phrases. Have your partner listen for and identify the phrases you used.

WRITING APPLICATION

Write a brief description of a movie you have seen or would like to see. Use three adjectival and three adverbial phrases. Read your description to a partner, and discuss the function of each phrase.

PRACTICE 19.1E **Writing Adverbial Phrases**

Read the sentences. Then, rewrite the sentences adding an adverbial phrase. Read your new sentences to a partner, who should identify the adverbial phrase.

EXAMPLE   The janitor locked the door.

ANSWER   *The janitor locked the door **at night**.*

1. Hernando read ten novels.
2. The executives presented the proposal.
3. Mr. Trigg checks the mail.
4. I have to write a two-page essay.
5. The tiger waited to pounce.
6. The marching band played.
7. Violet must finish cleaning her room.
8. Principal Caprio inspires trust.
9. The heat penetrated the car.
10. Tony brought donuts.

PRACTICE 19.1F **Writing Adjectival and Adverbial Phrases**

Read the sentences. Then, rewrite the sentences by adding adjectival or adverbial phrases, as directed in parentheses.

EXAMPLE   I found your book. (adverbial phrase)

ANSWER   *I found your book **under the desk**.*

11. A lifeguard dived. (adverbial phrase)
12. The cat yawned and walked away. (adjectival phrase)
13. The statue attracts many visitors. (adjectival phrase)
14. Scientists study the moon. (adverbial phrase)
15. Everyone admired Jana's new haircut. (adjectival phrase)
16. The jacket was extremely uncomfortable. (adjectival phrase)
17. We waited. (adverbial phrase)
18. She gave me a bowl. (adjectival phrase)
19. You will find everything you need. (adverbial phrase)
20. Four men moved furniture. (adjectival phrase, adverbial phrase)

SPEAKING APPLICATION

With a partner, take turns describing the location of something. Your partner should listen for and identify at least three adverbial phrases. Together, discuss the function, or purpose, of these phrases in the sentences.

WRITING APPLICATION

Write a paragraph about a television program. Use at least one adjectival and one adverbial phrase. Underline the prepositional phrases, and label them *adjectival* or *adverbial*. Then, explain the purpose of these phrases in your writing.

Test Warm-Up

DIRECTIONS
Read the introduction and the passage that follows. Then, answer the questions to show that you can use and understand the function of adjectival phrases and adverbial phrases in reading and writing.

Sonya wrote the following paragraph about a jazz band called the Hot Five. Read the paragraph and think about the changes you would suggest as a peer editor. When you finish reading, answer the questions that follow.

The Hot Five

(1) My dad took me to see his favorite jazz band, the Hot Five, on Friday night. (2) The small club was packed. (3) The band started with *Nights in Tunisia*. (4) The rhythm seemed to guide the rest of the group. (5) The bass set the rhythm. (6) While his solo, the piano player rearranged the melody to delight. (7) When the trumpet played by itself, the room was quiet. (8) At the break, there was a sense. (9) No one could wait to hear what they would play next.

---

1 How should sentence 2 be revised?

  A The small was packed.

  B The small club was packed with eager listeners.

  C The small in the club was packed.

  D The small club was with the packed.

2 What is the BEST way to combine sentences 4 and 5?

  F The rhythm seemed to guide the rest of the group and the bass.

  G The rhythm, seemed to guide the rest of the group.

  H The rhythm seemed to guide the bass.

  J The rhythm of the bass seemed to guide the rest of the group.

3 What is the BEST way to rewrite the ideas in sentence 6?

  A On his solo, the piano player rearranged the melody to delight.

  B During his solo, the piano player rearranged the melody to the delight of everyone.

  C His solo rearranged the melody to delight.

  D After his solo, the piano player rearranged the melody to delight me.

4 What is the BEST way to revise sentence 8?

  F At the break, there was a sense of excitement in the room.

  G At the break, there was a sense the night was over.

  H At the break, there was a sense of finality.

  J At the break, there was a sense to hear more.

Using Appositives and Appositive Phrases

Appositives, like adjectival phrases, give information about nouns or pronouns.

> An **appositive** is a noun or pronoun placed after another noun or pronoun to identify, rename, or explain the preceding word.

Appositives are very useful in writing because they give additional information without using many words.

┌─ MODIFIES ─┐

EXAMPLES   The tour guide **Mr. Torres** led an exciting tour of the London Tower.

┌─ MODIFIES ─┐

I admire the artist **Vincent Van Gogh**.

An appositive with its own modifiers creates an **appositive phrase.**

> An **appositive phrase** is a noun or pronoun with modifiers. It is placed next to a noun or pronoun and adds information or details.

See Practice 19.1G
See Practice 19.1H

The modifiers in an appositive phrase can be adjectives or adjectival phrases.

EXAMPLES   Aunt Kelly, my **favorite** **aunt**, writes novels.
                        adjective   noun

It is a photograph, a **portrait** **in black and white**.
                        noun   adj phrase

Appositives and appositive phrases can also be a compound.

EXAMPLE   Athletes, **men** and **women**, played together.
                      compound noun

PRACTICE 19.1G Identifying Appositives and Appositive Phrases

Read the sentences. Then, write the appositive or appositive phrase in each sentence. Explain which word the phrase modifies.

EXAMPLE My science teacher, Mr. Rodriguez, directed our lab experiments.

ANSWER *Mr. Rodriguez*

1. We are reading a novel, *Holes* by Louis Sachar, for English class.

2. My brother John has been accepted by the state college.

3. She and Molly, the first ones to arrive, organized the activities.

4. Owen, a sports fan, won tickets to the game.

5. Bianca Wilson, my best friend, is in most of my classes.

6. The magnificent sight, a panoramic view of the valley, took our breath away.

7. Barack Obama, the first African American president, took office on January 20, 2009.

8. The Notables, a local singing group, will perform at the assembly.

9. A member of the audience threw a bouquet, yellow and white roses, to the singer.

10. Janelle, the group's photographer, took pictures everywhere they went.

PRACTICE 19.1H Combining Sentences With Appositive Phrases

Read the sentences. Combine each pair of sentences by using an appositive phrase.

EXAMPLE Mrs. Reedy took the band to a competition. She is the director.

ANSWER *Mrs. Reedy, the director, took the band to a competition.*

11. Isabel finished her assignment early. Her assignment was a report on animal behavior.

12. A car was wrecked. It was a white sedan.

13. Harry's brothers went with him to play basketball. Ron and Sam are his brothers.

14. Vivian enjoys her favorite pastime. Her favorite pastime is solving puzzles.

15. Warren Wilkes is a reporter for *The Daily Times.* He wrote a story on the trial.

16. Elvis Presley was the king of rock-and-roll. He lived in a mansion in Memphis.

17. The child had no fear of the dog. The child was a four-year-old boy.

18. I read a good article in this magazine. The article was "Eating Well for Health."

19. Consuela Carter presented a talk on ecology. She is a professor of earth science.

20. Give your job application to Mr. Haynes. He is the hiring manager.

SPEAKING APPLICATION

In a small group, take turns introducing one another, using one sentence with an appositive phrase in it. The group members should listen for and identify the appositive phrase. As a group, discuss the function or purpose of these appositive phrases.

WRITING APPLICATION

Use your combined sentences 13 and 20 as models, and write two new sentences with appositive phrases. Then, read each sentence aloud and explain the function, or purpose, of these appositive phrases.

Using Verbals and Verbal Phrases

A **verbal** is any verb form that is used in a sentence not as a verb but as another part of speech.

Like verbs, verbals can be modified by an adverb or adverbial phrase. They can also be followed by a complement. A verbal used with a modifier or a complement is called a **verbal phrase.**

Participles

Participles are verb forms with two basic uses. When they are used with helping verbs, they are verbs. When they are used alone to modify nouns or pronouns, they become adjectives.

> A **participle** is a form of a verb that is often used as an adjective.

There are two kinds of participles, **present participles** and **past participles.** Each kind can be recognized by its ending.

All present participles end in *-ing*.

EXAMPLES talking   doing   eating   wanting

See Practice 19.1I
See Practice 19.1J

Most past participles end either in *-ed* or in *-d*.

EXAMPLES opened   jumped   played   moved

Other past participles end in *-n*, *-t*, *-en*, or another irregular ending.

EXAMPLES grown   felt   bought   eaten   held

Both present and past participles can be used in sentences as adjectives. They tell *what kind* or *which one*.

PRESENT PARTICIPLES	PAST PARTICIPLES
She led a walking tour.	Chilled fruit juice is refreshing.
Speaking slowly, he gave us directions.	She was, by then, a grown woman.

Participle or Verb?

Sometimes, verb phrases (verbs with helping verbs) are confused with participles. A verb phrase always begins with a helping verb. A participle used as an adjective stands by itself and modifies a noun or pronoun.

VERB PHRASES	PARTICIPLES
The bicyclist was racing around the corner.	The racing bicyclist crashed into the tree.
Explorers may have traveled down this road.	The traveled road led to the finish line.

Participial Phrases

A participle can be expanded into a participial phrase by adding a complement or modifier.

RULE 19.1.7

> A **participial phrase** is a present or past participle and its modifiers. The entire phrase acts as an adjective in a sentence.

Participial phrases can be formed by adding an adverb, an adverbial phrase, or a complement to a participle.

EXAMPLES   The teacher, **speaking slowly**, explained the essay requirements.

The well-known instructor, **honored by the award**, began his speech.

The first participial phrase contains the adverb *slowly* added to the participle *speaking*. The second includes the adverbial phrase *by the award* added to the participle *honored*.

A participial phrase can also be placed at the beginning of a sentence. The phrase is usually followed by a comma.

EXAMPLE   **Honored by the award**, the well-known instructor began his speech.

See Practice 19.1K
See Practice 19.1L

PRACTICE 19.1I ▷ **Identifying Present and Past Participles**

Read the sentences. Then, write the participle in each sentence, and label it *present participle* or *past participle*.

EXAMPLE   We just watched an exciting match.

ANSWER   *exciting* — *present participle*

1. Mel separated the good pieces of furniture from the damaged ones.

2. Sherlock Holmes solved many baffling mysteries.

3. Lucy put a frozen dinner into the microwave.

4. The gathering clouds made the picnickers finish quickly and leave.

5. Elroy made a running dive for the football.

6. A hushed audience waited for the curtain to rise.

7. The campers ate toasted sandwiches around the fire.

8. A soldier knelt by his fallen comrade.

9. Keep in mind the intended audience for your essay.

10. The rising noise level indicated that everyone was having a good time.

PRACTICE 19.1J ▷ **Distinguishing Verbs and Participles**

Read the sentences. Then, write *verb* or *participle* for the underlined word in each sentence. Explain how each participle or verb functions in the sentence.

EXAMPLE   No one noticed him <u>walking</u> away.

ANSWER   *participle*

11. We had not <u>expected</u> such a large turnout.

12. <u>Coming</u> closer, Fiona grabbed my hand.

13. An unhappy customer was <u>muttering</u> to himself.

14. We avoided the dogs <u>snarling</u> behind the fence.

15. Determined to get a good grade, Jane has been <u>studying</u> hard every night.

16. Has anyone ever <u>stolen</u> your lunch?

17. <u>Stunned</u> by the headlights, the deer just stood in the road.

18. Let's review the vocabulary we <u>studied</u> last week.

19. The river is <u>rising</u> from all the rain.

20. I must have <u>broken</u> it unintentionally.

SPEAKING APPLICATION

With a partner, take turns making up two sentences using these words as participles: *swinging* and *broken*. Take turns telling your sentences to your partner, who should identify what the words modify.

WRITING APPLICATION

Write two sentences using both of these words in each sentence: *dangling* and *crowded*. Use each word once as a participle and once as a verb. Read your sentences aloud to a partner. Have your partner identify which word is a participle and which is a verb.

PRACTICE 19.1K ▷ **Identifying Participial Phrases**

Read the sentences. Then, write the participial phrase in each sentence. Underline the participle.

EXAMPLE   Everyone was out enjoying the lovely day.

ANSWER   *enjoying the lovely day*

1. Jeffrey sat there, wondering what to do.

2. Cramming her papers into her notebook, Vicki hurried out of the room.

3. The shop, closed for the day, was dark and quiet.

4. Smiling sweetly, the little ballerina danced her part.

5. You can see an osprey sitting on its nest in the bird sanctuary.

6. Waving his arms and shouting, Clay ran after the bus.

7. Pedro, tired after the game, relaxed on the couch.

8. *The Adventures of Huckleberry Finn,* written by Mark Twain, is a classic American novel.

9. Lola rehearsed her oral report, reading it aloud several times.

10. The glove found on the sidewalk was muddy and torn.

PRACTICE 19.1L ▷ **Combining Sentences Using Participial Phrases**

Read the sentences. Combine each pair of sentences by using a participial phrase. Read the new sentences to a partner. Discuss how the participles function in each sentence.

EXAMPLE   Felicia did not hear the teacher's question. She was lost in a daydream.

ANSWER   *Lost in a daydream, Felicia did not hear the teacher's question.*

11. Mia was speaking very softly. She explained what happened.

12. The gymnasts performed like ballet dancers. They were trained by professionals.

13. The children were squealing excitedly. They played games in the yard.

14. The dog was restrained on a leash. It was unable to chase other dogs.

15. A fire truck sped down the street. Its siren was blasting.

16. Pam was thrilled by her victory. She jumped up and down.

17. Kent finally found his homework paper. It was tucked between the pages of his book.

18. The old letter was difficult to read. It was creased at its folds.

19. Jed was startled by the noise. He sat upright.

20. Eli went over to speak to the girl. The girl was smiling at him.

SPEAKING APPLICATION

With a partner, use one of the sentences in Practice 19.1K as a model, and describe an item. Use at least one participial phrase. Your partner should listen for and identify the participial phrase.

WRITING APPLICATION

Use your combined sentences 12, 15, and 20 as models, and write two new sentences with participial phrases. Read your sentences to a partner. Have your partner identify each participle and explain how it is used in the sentence.

Gerunds

Like present participles, **gerunds** end in *-ing.* While present participles are used as adjectives, gerunds can be used as subjects, direct objects, predicate nouns, and objects of prepositions.

> A **gerund** is a form of a verb that acts as a noun.

USE OF GERUNDS IN SENTENCES	
Subject	Rebuilding houses for charity was a good idea.
Direct Object	Amy enjoys drawing .
Predicate Noun	Her favorite activity is running .
Object of a Preposition	Kate never gets tired of reading .

Gerund Phrases

Gerunds can also be part of a phrase.

> A **gerund phrase** is a gerund with modifiers or a complement, all acting together as a noun.

This chart shows how gerunds are expanded to form gerund phrases.

FORMING GERUND PHRASES	
Gerund With Adjectives	The loud, piercing ringing went on all afternoon.
Gerund With Direct Object	Reading historical fiction has inspired many playwrights.
Gerund With Prepositional Phrase	Her favorite activity is running through the forest .
Gerund With Adverb and Prepositional Phrases	The painter amazed the spectators by painting skillfully with brushes on the window .

See Practice 19.1M
See Practice 19.1N

Infinitives

Infinitives are verb forms that are used as nouns, adjectives, and adverbs. Like participles and gerunds, they can be combined with other words to form phrases.

RULE 19.1.10

An **infinitive** is a verb form that can be used as a noun, an adjective, or an adverb. The word *to* usually appears before the verb.

EXAMPLES It is important **to speak**.

He is the one **to see**.

To be serious can be difficult sometimes.

Infinitive Phrases

RULE 19.1.11

An **infinitive phrase** is an infinitive with modifiers or a complement, all acting together as a single part of speech.

EXAMPLES It is important **to speak quietly**.

It is not polite **to speak loudly in class**.

They want **to tell you a secret**.

An **infinitive phrase** can be used in a sentence as a noun, an adjective, or an adverb. As a noun, an infinitive phrase can function as a subject, an object, or an appositive.

USES OF INFINITIVES	
Used as a Subject	To remain calm is important.
Used as an Object	She tried to remain calm.
Used as an Appositive	The officer's suggestion, to remain calm, had worked.
Used as an Adjective	It was her intention to remain calm.
Used as an Adverb	It isn't always easy to remain calm when you're upset.

See Practice 19.1O
See Practice 19.1P

PRACTICE 19.1M Identifying Gerund Phrases

Read the sentences. Then, write the gerund phrase from each sentence, and underline the gerund. Remember to include all modifiers with the phrase.

EXAMPLE   Listening to music relaxes me.

ANSWER   <u>Listening</u> to music

1. Naomi likes reading historical novels.

2. Forecasting the weather can be a challenge.

3. You might be able to gain an advantage by using strategy.

4. Silas recently tried skateboarding on a ramp.

5. The first step in the assignment is locating appropriate sources.

6. Veronica could not stop laughing at the joke.

7. Annabel and Diana were exhausted from working all afternoon.

8. Winning the match is not everything.

9. The mayor opposed raising the speed limit through town.

10. Playing the drums is Neil's only interest.

PRACTICE 19.1N Writing Gerunds and Gerund Phrases

Read the sentences. Then, rewrite each sentence, completing it with a gerund or gerund phrase.

EXAMPLE   The team celebrated by _____.

ANSWER   *The team celebrated by singing the school song.*

11. _____ motivates Zelda to earn money after school.

12. Eva's family enjoyed _____ last summer.

13. Duncan sends text messages while _____.

14. Henry Ford is famous for _____.

15. _____ is the way Selena memorizes her lines for the play.

16. A fox escaped its pursuer by _____.

17. _____ builds strength and flexibility.

18. Jason thought he might give _____ a try.

19. _____ was easier than Amy expected.

20. Alonzo's job is _____.

SPEAKING APPLICATION

With a partner, take turns telling about something you like to do. Your partner should listen for and identify a gerund or gerund phrase that you use.

WRITING APPLICATION

Use sentences 12, 13, and 19 as models, and write three sentences with gerunds or gerund phrases.

PRACTICE 19.10 ▶ Identifying Infinitives and Infinitive Phrases

Read the sentences. Then, write the infinitive phrase from each sentence, and underline the infinitive. Also write *noun*, *adjective*, or *adverb* to describe each infinitive phrase.

EXAMPLE　We stopped by the roadside to admire the view.

ANSWER　<u>*to admire*</u> *the view* — adverb

1. Wade likes to swim in the lake.
2. Mrs. Manning planned to visit the museum.
3. To break that record will be a challenge.
4. That is the best place to go fishing.
5. This poem is easy to understand.
6. The child tried to hide in the closet.
7. It's time to leave for school now.
8. The Wilsons plan to sell their house.
9. The driver swerved to avoid the puddle.
10. Justin's goal is to be a singer in a band.

PRACTICE 19.1P ▶ Writing Infinitives and Infinitive Phrases

Read the sentences. Then, rewrite each sentence, completing it with an infinitive or an infinitive phrase.

EXAMPLE　Kirk still has plenty of work _____.

ANSWER　*Kirk still has plenty of work* **to finish by tomorrow.**

11. The teacher raised her hands _____.
12. _____ is Martha's plan for this year.
13. Your next book _____ is *Dragonwings*.
14. Judy's role is _____.
15. An assembly _____ will start at 9:00 o'clock.
16. _____ may not be wise.
17. The best way _____ is _____.
18. I think it is best _____.
19. The first person _____ will win a ticket.
20. Ariana got into position _____.

SPEAKING APPLICATION

In a small group, take turns "selling" each other a simple item, such as a pencil or paper clip. The group members should listen for and identify the infinitive phrases you use.

WRITING APPLICATION

Write a short paragraph explaining the purpose of the item you "sold" in the Speaking Application. Use at least two infinitive phrases and underline them.

19.2 Clauses

Clauses are the basic structural unit of a sentence.

A clause is a group of words with its own subject and verb.

RULE 19.2.1

There are two basic kinds of clauses, **main** or **independent clauses** and **subordinate clauses.**

A main or independent clause has a subject and a verb and can stand by itself as a complete sentence.

RULE 19.2.2

As you can see in the examples below, a main clause can be long or short. All main clauses express a complete thought and can stand by themselves as complete sentences.

EXAMPLES

The **girl** **skipped**.
      subject   verb

Later that night, **he** **began** reading his book.
                  subject verb

A subordinate clause, also known as a dependent clause, has a subject and a verb but cannot stand by itself as a complete sentence. It is only part of a sentence.

RULE 19.2.3

SUBORDINATE CLAUSES

after **she** **presented** her paper
      subject verb

while the **group** **studied**
          subject   verb

After reading a subordinate clause, you will still need more information to have a complete sentence.

Subordinate clauses begin with subordinating conjunctions or relative pronouns.

Some subordinate clauses begin with **subordinating conjunctions,** such as *if, since, when, although, after, because,* and *while.* Others begin with **relative pronouns,** such as *who, which,* or *that.* These words are clues that the clause may not be able to stand alone. Notice how the addition of subordinating words changes the meaning of the main clauses in the examples below.

COMPARING TWO KINDS OF CLAUSES	
MAIN	**SUBORDINATE**
She speaks this afternoon.	*when* she speaks this afternoon
The garden has green tomatoes.	*because* the garden has green tomatoes
I planted the cucumbers.	the cucumbers *that* I planted

In order to form a complete thought, a subordinate clause must be combined with a main clause.

EXAMPLES **After she presented her paper** , Rachael felt
                subordinate clause   main clause

relaxed.

The board applauded **after Rachael presented**
       main clause   subordinate clause

her paper .

It was Rachael **who was asked to present last** .
   main clause   subordinate clause

When they arrive tonight , the Woods will eat.
       subordinate clause   main clause

See Practice 19.2A
See Practice 19.2B

PRACTICE 19.2A ▷ **Identifying Main and Subordinate Clauses**

Read the sentences. Then, write the main and subordinate clauses in each sentence, and label them *main clause* or *subordinate clause*.

EXAMPLE   After you left, Maria opened her presents.

ANSWER   *After you left* — subordinate clause
Maria opened her presents — main clause

1. Although they do not always agree, Jake and Chris are best friends.

2. Dino thought about baseball practice as he walked home.

3. Please take out the garbage before you leave.

4. Because my dog is afraid of thunder, he hides under the bed during storms.

5. If you want to come with me, make sure you bring an umbrella.

6. Let's wait here until Stephen arrives.

7. We eat outside when the weather is nice.

8. Let's discuss the plans as we'll be traveling together.

9. Ethan and Grace are ready to leave as soon as the bus arrives.

10. The painting that you bought is hanging in the hallway.

PRACTICE 19.2B ▷ **Identifying and Using Main and Subordinate Clauses**

Read the clauses. Write *main clause* or *subordinate clause* for each clause. Then, expand each subordinate clause into a complete complex sentence by adding a main clause.

EXAMPLE   Unless we find the shovel.

ANSWER   *subordinate clause*
We cannot clear away the snow unless we find the shovel.

11. Here is a picture of my cousin.

12. That my mother bought for me.

13. Robots are used in many factories.

14. Although my brother is a talented musician.

15. Our show did not make a profit.

16. When you make up your mind.

17. Two other people waited in the office.

18. As soon as Elizabeth gets home.

19. I just can't decide.

20. Who found Hal's wallet.

SPEAKING APPLICATION

With a partner, take turns selecting two subordinate clauses from the sentences in Practice 19.2A. Add a main clause to each, and then say the sentence.

WRITING APPLICATION

Write two complex sentences that contain both main and subordinate clauses. Underline the subordinate clauses. Explain to a partner how the main and subordinate clauses function in the sentence together.

Adjectival Clauses

A subordinate clause will sometimes act as an adjective in a sentence. An adjectival clause or adjective clause is a dependent clause and cannot stand on its own.

> An **adjectival clause** or **adjective clause** is a subordinate clause that modifies a noun or a pronoun.

Like one-word adjectives and adjectival phrases, **adjectival clauses** tell *what kind* or *which one*.

WHAT KIND?

EXAMPLES stars **that are bright and glowing**

WHICH ONE?

the country **where I was born**

Recognizing Adjectival Clauses

Most adjectival clauses begin with the words *that, which, who, whom,* and *whose*. Sometimes an adjectival clause begins with a subordinating conjunction, such as *since, where,* or *when*. In the chart below, the adjectival clauses are hightlighted in pink.

ADJECTIVAL CLAUSES
The professor whom I had asked for help met with me before class. (*Which* professor?)
The charity auction, which was advertised in the local paper, is Friday. (*Which* charity auction?)
In the months since she started working, Anne has become an accomplished teacher. (*Which* months?)
I hid my jewelry box in the hall closet on which there is a lock. (*Which* closet?)
We visited the theme park that honors cultures around the world. (*Which* park?)
The theme park whose rides include teacups is located in Florida. (*Which* park?)

See Practice 19.2C

Combining Sentences With Adjectival Clauses

Two sentences can be combined into one sentence by changing one of them into an adjectival clause. Sometimes you will need to add a relative pronoun or subordinating conjunction to make the sentence read correctly. In the sentences below, the adjectival clauses are highlighted in pink.

TWO SENTENCES	COMBINED WITH AN ADJECTIVAL CLAUSE
My English professor has written novels based on fictional stories. My professor is a famous author.	My English professor, who has written novels based on fictional stories, is a famous author.
We visited the Air and Space Museum. The Air and Space Museum is my favorite museum.	We visited the Air and Space Museum, which is my favorite.
We decided to shop at the outlet mall. We usually get the best deals there.	We decided to shop at the outlet mall where we usually get the best deals.
Emma visited her grandparents. Emma's grandparents live in an apartment in New York.	Emma visited her grandparents, who live in an apartment in New York.
Carolyn goes to dance class. Her class is in a ballet studio.	Carolyn goes to dance class that is in a ballet studio.

See Practice 19.2C
See Practice 19.2D

PRACTICE 19.2C > **Identifying Adjectival Clauses**

Read the sentences. Then, write the adjectival clause in each sentence.

EXAMPLE   This is a movie that I will never forget.

ANSWER   *that I will never forget*

1. The men who came in a jeep are repairing the fence now.

2. This is the time of year when people take vacations.

3. Follow these directions, which will take you right to the campground.

4. Thomas Jefferson is the president who is responsible for the Louisiana Purchase.

5. I have a pearl necklace that belonged to my grandmother.

6. The road came to an end, where we had to turn around.

7. Hollywood, which is part of Los Angeles, is a tourist destination.

8. The manager needs someone who will stock the shelves.

9. Christa, whom you met earlier, will also be on the committee.

10. This is the house that my uncle fixed up.

PRACTICE 19.2D > **Combining Sentences Using Adjectival Clauses**

Read the sentences. Combine the pairs of sentences by changing one of them into an adjectival clause. Read the new sentences and discuss how the adjectival clause functions.

EXAMPLE   The runner is being congratulated. She won the race.

ANSWER   *The runner who won the race is being congratulated.*

11. The rain fell for two days. It kept the farmers from planting their crops.

12. I need to write two more sentences. These sentences will support my topic sentence.

13. Many adventurers have climbed Mt. Everest. Mt. Everest is the highest peak in the world.

14. The train leaves at 7:00. It arrives in Washington, D.C., at 11:30.

15. I like to look up information on the Internet. You can find everything there.

16. The woman was upset. Her purse was lost.

17. Here are some sponges. You can use these to wash the car.

18. A mechanic tuned up the car. It had not been running well.

19. David told a story. It made everyone laugh.

20. Alexa is my friend. She made this playlist for me.

SPEAKING APPLICATION

With a partner, summarize a mystery story that you have read or seen on television. Use at least one sentence with an adjectival clause. Your partner should listen for and identify the adjectival clause. Together, discuss the function, or purpose, of the adjectival clause.

WRITING APPLICATION

Use your combined sentences 11, 16, and 19 as models, and write three new sentences with adjectival clauses. Read the sentences and explain how the adjectival clauses function in the sentences.

Adverbial Clauses

Subordinate clauses can also be used as adverbs. Adverbial clauses or adverb clauses are dependent clauses.

> An **adverbial clause** or **adverb clause** is a subordinate clause that modifies a verb, an adjective, or an adverb.

Adverbial clauses can answer any of the following questions about the words they modify: *Where? When? In what manner? To what extent? Under what conditions?* or *Why?*

ADVERBIAL CLAUSES	
Modifying Verbs	Put the luggage wherever you find an empty closet . (Put *where?*)
	The game will begin after we sing the National Anthem . (Will begin *when?*)
	Amy spoke as if she were very serious . (Spoke *in what manner?*)
	I will go to Greece if you do too . (Will go *under what conditions?*)
Modifying an Adjective	I am tired because I have been working all day . (Tired *why?*)
Modifying an Adverb	She knows more than other teachers do . (More *to what extent?*)

Recognizing Adverbial Clauses

> A **subordinating conjunction** introduces an adverbial clause.

A **subordinating conjunction** always introduces an adverbial clause. In a sentence, the conjunction will usually appear in one of two places—either at the beginning, when the adverbial clause begins the sentence, or in the middle, connecting the independent clause to the subordinate clause. In the examples on the next page, the subordinating conjunctions are highlighted in purple.

Because you slept late, I will prepare breakfast.

I will prepare breakfast **because** you slept late.

Whenever you have a test, I expect you to study.

I expect you to study **whenever** you have a test.

Common Subordinating Conjunctions

Here are the most common subordinating conjunctions. Knowing them can help you recognize adverbial clauses.

COMMON SUBORDINATING CONJUNCTIONS		
after	even though	unless
although	if	until
as	in order that	when
as if	since	whenever
as long as	so that	where
because	than	wherever
before	though	while

Elliptical Adverbial Clauses

In certain adverbial clauses, words are left out. These clauses are said to be elliptical.

RULE 19.2.8

> In an **elliptical adverbial clause,** the verb or the subject and verb are understood rather than stated.

Many elliptical adverbial clauses are introduced by one of two subordinating conjunctions, *as* or *than*. In the following examples, the understood words have been added in parentheses. The first elliptical adverbial clause is missing a verb; the second is missing a subject and a verb.

EXAMPLES   My sister can eat as much **as I** (can eat).

I like this movie more **than** (I liked) **that one**.

See Practice 19.2E

See Practice 19.2F

PRACTICE 19.2E **Identifying Adverbial Clauses and Recognizing Elliptical Adverbial Clauses**

Read the sentences. Then, write the adverbial clauses. For any of the adverbial clauses that are elliptical, add the understood words in parentheses.

EXAMPLE   Isabel likes reading mysteries more than biographies.

ANSWER   *than (she likes reading) biographies*

1. After we took a walk, we stopped for ice cream.

2. Kurt did not give his oral report today because he has laryngitis.

3. Although Maria is not especially tall, she plans to try out for basketball.

4. Driving can be unpleasant when there is a lot of traffic.

5. Brett waited while Alan collected his equipment.

6. You have grown since we last saw you.

7. We can leave as long as you are ready.

8. If you are really interested, talk to Miss Knox.

9. This computer is older than that one.

10. I am not allowed to watch television unless my homework is finished.

PRACTICE 19.2F **Combining Sentences With Adverbial Clauses**

Read the sentences. Combine each pair of sentences by changing one of them into an adverbial clause. Use an appropriate subordinating conjunction, and drop or change words as necessary.

EXAMPLE   Gabe stayed in the car. I ran into the store.

ANSWER   *Gabe stayed in the car while I ran into the store.*

11. Veronica took notes. We made our plans.

12. Jude was not nervous. He stepped onstage.

13. Laura did very well on her science test. She had studied.

14. I will tell you. You must keep it a secret.

15. Robin will rehearse carefully. She will give her presentation.

16. Keith feels much more energetic. He has started jogging.

17. Volunteers put sandbags on the banks. The river overflowed its banks.

18. The garden will dry up. It rains.

19. We worked hard all week. We wanted to have the weekend free.

20. I will call you. I need help.

SPEAKING APPLICATION

With a partner, make up an excuse for being late or for not doing something, using two adverbial clauses. Your partner should listen for and identify the adverbial clauses.

WRITING APPLICATION

Write a few sentences about something you learned in your social studies class. Use at least two adverbial clauses and appropriate subordinating conjunctions. Read your sentences to a partner. Discuss how the adverbial clause and subordinating conjunction function in each sentence.

19.3 Classifying Sentences by Structure

All sentences can be classified according to the number and kinds of clauses they contain.

WRITING COACH

Online

www.phwritingcoach.com

Grammar Tutorials

Brush up on your Grammar skills with these animated videos.

Grammar Practice

Practice your grammar skills with Writing Coach Online.

Grammar Games

Test your knowledge of grammar in this fast-paced interactive video game.

The Simple Sentence

The **simple sentence** is the most common type of sentence structure.

RULE 19.3.1

> A **simple sentence** consists of a single independent clause.

Simple sentences vary in length. Some are quite short; others can be several lines long. All simple sentences, however, contain just one subject and one verb. They may also contain adjectives, adverbs, complements, and phrases in different combinations.

Simple sentences can also have various compound parts. They can have a compound subject, a compound verb, or both. Sometimes, they will also have other compound elements, such as a compound direct object or a compound phrase.

All of the following sentences are simple sentences.

TYPES OF SIMPLE SENTENCES	
With One Subject and Verb	The snow fell.
With a Compound Subject	Snow and ice are common.
With a Compound Verb	The window squeaked and shook.
With a Compound Subject and Compound Verb	My brother and sister brought bagels and made coffee for brunch.
With a Compound Direct Object	She opened the flower box and the card. direct object direct object
With a Compound Prepositional Phrase	You can drive from the east coast or from the west. prep phrase prep phrase

A simple sentence never has a subordinate clause, and it never has more than one main or independent clause.

The Compound Sentence

A **compound sentence** is made up of more than one simple sentence.

> **A compound sentence** consists of two or more main or independent clauses.

In most compound sentences, the main or independent clauses are joined by a comma and a coordinating conjunction (*and, but, for, nor, or, so,* or *yet*). They may also be connected with a semicolon (;) or a colon (:).

EXAMPLES   **Jamie ran** a two-day athletic clinic **, and** four professional **athletes donated** their time.

All of the athletes **spoke** on the first day **; one was missing** the second day.

See Practice 19.3A
See Practice 19.3B

Notice in both of the preceding examples that there are two separate and complete main clauses, each with its own subject and verb. Like simple sentences, compound sentences never contain subordinate clauses.

The Complex Sentence

Complex sentences contain subordinate clauses, which can be either adjectival clauses or adverbial clauses.

> **A complex sentence** consists of one main or independent clause and one or more subordinate clauses.

In a complex sentence, the independent clause is often called the **main clause.** The main clause has its own subject and verb, as does each subordinate clause.

In a complex sentence, the main clause can stand alone as a simple sentence. The subordinate clause cannot stand alone as a sentence.

EXAMPLES   **May 14, 1948, is the day** **that Israel became**
              main clause   subordinate clause

           a state .

           Because this day is so important, **celebrations**
                   subordinate clause

           of all kinds take place .
                   main clause

In some complex sentences, the main clause is split by a subordinate clause that acts as an adjective.

EXAMPLE   **Citizens** , **who have the day off** , **participate in**

           exciting activities .

The two parts of the main clause form one main clause: *Citizens participate in exciting activities.*

See Practice 19.3C
See Practice 19.3D
See Practice 19.3E
See Practice 19.3F

The Compound-Complex Sentence

A **compound-complex sentence,** as the name indicates, contains the elements of both a compound sentence and a complex sentence.

RULE
19.3.4

> A **compound-complex sentence** consists of two or more
> main or independent clauses and one or more subordinate
> clauses.

EXAMPLE   **As he was leaving for work** ,
                   subordinate clause

           Andy remembered to take his glasses , but
                           main clause

           he forgot the presentation **that he had worked**
                   main clause   subordinate clause

           on the night before .

426   **Phrases and Clauses**

 **PRACTICE 19.3A** **Distinguishing Simple and Compound Sentences**

Read the sentences. Then, write *simple* or *compound* for each sentence.

EXAMPLE   Many people now drive fuel-efficient cars.

ANSWER   *simple*

1. Laurel discovered a box of old photos in the back of the closet.

2. Marissa watered the plants and fertilized them.

3. Calcium and vitamin D are important for strong bones, so I drink milk.

4. Evan sent a text message to his girlfriend.

5. Please follow the ushers to your seat, for the show will start soon.

6. This may be your lucky day.

7. Tourists throw coins into the fountain for good luck.

8. George thanked the presenters and sat down.

9. Martin tried to share his ideas with Eugene, but Eugene was not listening.

10. The library hired a new assistant, but I have not met him yet.

PRACTICE 19.3B **Combining Simple Sentences to Form Compound Sentences**

Read the sentences. Combine the pairs of simple sentences to form compound sentences.

EXAMPLE   The newspaper was delivered this morning. I have not read it yet.

ANSWER   *The newspaper was delivered this morning, but I have not read it yet.*

11. The lilacs will bloom in May. The roses and lilies bloom later.

12. No one answered the phone. I left a voice message.

13. The rain had left puddles. The children splashed through them.

14. A tornado roared through the edge of town. No one was injured.

15. Celeste stepped inside. The room became quiet.

16. Some people have good fortune. Others always struggle with hardships.

17. Martha lowered her head. Tears fell from her eyes.

18. We should hurry. The show will start soon.

19. Bea had a headache. She did not complain.

20. Rosa forgot to turn off the lights. They stayed on all night.

SPEAKING APPLICATION

With a partner, take turns describing an action. Use only simple sentences.

WRITING APPLICATION

Use your compound sentences 11, 12, and 15 as models, and write three new compound sentences.

Read the sentences. Then, label each sentence *complex* or *not complex*.

EXAMPLE   A wave destroyed the sand castle, so the children were sad.

ANSWER   *not complex*

1. If you give me the seeds, I will plant them.

2. National park rangers lead natural history tours through the parks.

3. Emily tore the paper in half and gave half to Sue.

4. Our dog was waiting as we pulled into the driveway.

5. Wendy, who has been taking art lessons, showed us a pencil sketch.

6. After she spoke with a counselor, Amber changed her mind.

7. Only the finest musicians play in the symphony orchestra.

8. On a clear night, you can see satellites moving through the sky.

9. Mimi was wearing pants that were too long.

10. The crowd roared when the designated hitter struck out.

Read the sentences. Combine each pair of sentences by changing one of them into a subordinating clause. Add or drop words and punctuation as necessary.

EXAMPLE   I will cook dinner. Buy some vegetables at the store.

ANSWER   *I will cook dinner if you buy some vegetables at the store.*

11. We should pick up Kayla at her house. It is on the left side of the street.

12. My grandparents live in Austin. It is 350 miles away.

13. The car stopped suddenly. It ran out of gas.

14. On Saturday, the temperature reached 102 degrees. It was the third day of the heat wave.

15. I finished the math test before everyone else. It was so easy.

16. Pedro walks his dog three times a day. Pedro is fond of animals.

17. The volleyball players were exhausted. They practiced for four hours.

18. The car accident caused the traffic to come to a complete stop. It started to move again soon.

19. I might vote for Carla. Carla is both smart and fair.

20. I cannot seem to finish this book. This book is long and complicated.

SPEAKING APPLICATION

With a partner, take turns telling about a program you watch on television. Your partner should listen for and identify at least one complex sentence.

WRITING APPLICATION

Write three complex sentences about your favorite holiday. Share your sentences with a partner, and have your partner label the main and subordinate clauses.

PRACTICE 19.3E ▷ **Writing Complex Sentences**

Read each subordinate clause. Then, write a main clause and unite the main and subordinate clauses into a complex sentence.

EXAMPLE   because his birthday is in July

ANSWER   *Because his birthday is in July, Diego will have his party at a water park.*

1. if you can leave a little earlier

2. who learn a second language at an early age

3. although pet fish need feeding only once a day

4. when my alarm went off

5. that the librarian recommended

6. unless the temperature drops below 50 degrees

7. which will probably win an award

8. while Toby was away at summer camp

9. whose jewelry designs are popular

10. before she left for school

PRACTICE 19.3F ▷ **Distinguishing Compound and Complex Sentences**

Read the sentences. Then, label each sentence *compound* or *complex*.

EXAMPLE   When Tanya lost her phone, she was very upset.

ANSWER   *complex*

11. The hikers, who had not yet had lunch, were getting hungry.

12. The fog rolled in, and everyone felt cold.

13. Summer will be here before you know it.

14. William likes horror stories, so he has been reading Edgar Allan Poe's short stories.

15. Dorie read about the discovery in the newspaper, where there was a full-page article.

16. Seals and dolphins are sometimes stranded on beaches when the tide goes out.

17. Arlo is very well-informed, so I trust his judgment.

18. Even after we stopped shouting, we could hear the echoes in the mountains.

19. Naomi has agreed to participate, but Luanne is still thinking about it.

20. Nick is so good at chess that no one can beat him.

SPEAKING APPLICATION

With a partner, take turns explaining a process. The process could be directions for how to make something. Your partner should listen for and identify at least two complex sentences. Together discuss the function of the main clause and the subordinate clause in each sentence.

WRITING APPLICATION

Write one compound and one complex sentence. Use these words as the subject and verb in one of the clauses in each sentence: *James rode.*

Test Warm-Up

DIRECTIONS
Read the introduction and the passage that follows.
Then, answer the questions to show that you can write complex sentences and differentiate between main versus subordinate clauses in reading and writing.

Hernando wrote this paragraph about his favorite side dish, mashed potatoes. Read the paragraph and think about the changes you would suggest as a peer editor. When you finish reading, answer the questions that follow.

The Best Mashed Potatoes

(1) I love my mom's mashed potatoes. (2) My mom makes the best mashed potatoes I have ever tasted. (3) First, take four large red potatoes that are easy to find in the supermarket. (4) Peel the potatoes. (5) Cut the potatoes, they are already peeled. (6) Place the potatoes in boiling water for 8 minutes. (7) Strain them and add them to a large bowl. (8) Place ¼ cup of lowfat milk and two tablespoons of butter in the large bowl first. (9) Mix the potatoes, milk, and butter with a hand mixer until smooth. (10) Add salt as needed and serve immediately.

1 What is the BEST way to combine sentences 1 and 2?

 A I love my mom's mashed potatoes, she makes the best mashed potatoes I have ever tasted.

 B I love my mom's mashed potatoes, which are the best I have ever tasted.

 C The best mashed potatoes are my mom's, which I have ever tasted.

 D The best mashed potatoes which I love are my mom's.

2 What change, if any, should be made in sentence 3?

 F Delete the comma after *First*

 G Change *that* to **which**

 H Change *that* to **which** and add a comma before **which**

 J Make no change

3 What is the BEST way to revise sentence 5?

 A Peel the potatoes, which have already been cut.

 B Cut the potatoes that are peeled.

 C Peel the cut potatoes.

 D Cut the potatoes, already.

4 What is the BEST way to combine sentences 7 and 8?

 F Strain them and add them to a large bowl, which should contain ¼ cup of lowfat milk and two tablespoons of butter.

 G Strain them and add them first to a large bowl of ¼ cup of lowfat milk and two tablespoons of butter.

 H Strain them and place ¼ cup of lowfat milk and two tablespoons of butter.

 J Strain them and add them to a large bowl, place ¼ cup of lowfat milk and two tablespoons of butter in the large bowl first.

CHAPTER 20

EFFECTIVE SENTENCES

Knowing how different types of sentences function will help you construct clear, meaningful ideas in your writing.

WRITE GUY *Jeff Anderson, M.Ed.*

WHAT DO YOU NOTICE?

Keep an eye out for different types of sentences as you zoom in on these sentences from the screenplay *The Monsters Are Due on Maple Street* by Rod Serling.

MENTOR TEXT

> So I've got a car that starts by itself—well, that's a freak thing, I admit it. But does that make me some kind of a criminal or something? I don't know why the car works—it just does!

Now, ask yourself the following questions:

- Which sentence is interrogative? How can you tell?
- What does the end punctuation tell you about the last sentence?

The second sentence is interrogative because it asks a question. You can tell the second sentence is interrogative because there is a question mark at the end of it. The exclamation mark at the end of the last sentence tells you that it is exclamatory. The purpose of an exclamatory sentence is to convey strong emotion.

Grammar for Writers Using a variety of sentences allows writers to make their writing sound lively. Think carefully about which end punctuation mark is most appropriate in each of your sentences. Try not to overuse exclamation marks or they will lose their effect.

How can I tell if a sentence is imperative?

When it's a command. Now, raise your hand before asking a question.

431

20.1 Classifying the Four Functions of a Sentence

Sentences can be classified according to what they do. Some sentences present facts or information in a direct way, while others pose questions to the reader or listener. Still others present orders or directions. A fourth type of sentence expresses strong emotion.

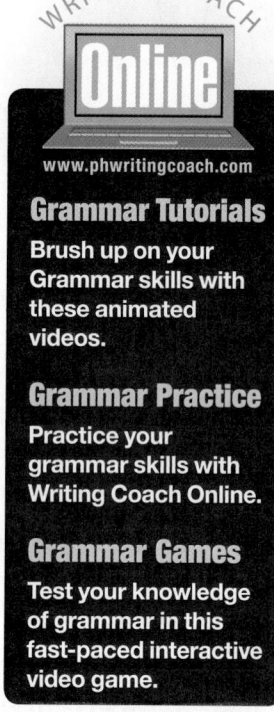

These four types of sentences are called **declarative, interrogative, imperative,** and **exclamatory.** As well as having a different purpose, each type of sentence is constructed in a different way.

The type of sentence you are writing determines the punctuation mark you use to end the sentence. The three end marks are the **period (.),** the **question mark (?),** and the **exclamation mark (!).**

The **declarative sentence** is the most common type of sentence. It is used to state, or "declare," facts.

RULE 20.1.1

> A **declarative sentence** states, or declares, an idea and ends with a period.

DECLARATIVE
: The cellphone rang.

  Cellphones help us keep in touch with our friends and family.

  Although cellphones are useful in emergencies, used too often, they can lead people to waste a lot of time.

Interrogative means "asking." An **interrogative sentence** is a question. Interrogative sentences often begin with *who, what, when, why, how,* or *how many.* They end with a question mark.

> **An interrogative sentence** asks a question and ends with a question mark.

20.1.2 RULE

INTERROGATIVE   When is band practice going to start?

Where will the concert be held?

What songs are we going to play?

> **An imperative sentence** gives an order, or command, or a direction and ends with either a period or an exclamation mark.

20.1.3 RULE

The word *imperative* comes from the Latin word that means "commanding." **Imperative sentences** are commands or directions. Most imperative sentences start with a verb. In this type of sentence, the subject is understood to be *you.*

IMPERATIVE   Take the stairs, not the elevator.

Walk, don't run!

Notice the punctuation at the end of these examples. In the first sentence, the period suggests that a mild command is being given in an ordinary tone of voice. The exclamation mark at the end of the second sentence suggests a strong command, one given in a loud voice.

> **An exclamatory sentence** conveys strong emotion and ends with an exclamation mark.

20.1.4 RULE

See Practice 20.1A
See Practice 20.1B
See Practice 20.1C
See Practice 20.1D

Exclaim means "to shout out." **Exclamatory sentences** are used to "shout out" emotions such as happiness, fear, delight, or anger.

EXCLAMATORY   He isn't watching where he's going!

The glass is going to tip over!

Read the sentences. Then, identify each type of sentence by writing *declarative*, *interrogative*, *imperative*, or *exclamatory*.

EXAMPLE   Read the instructions before you begin.

ANSWER   *imperative*

1. Who brought those delicious cookies?

2. Both generals signed the treaty.

3. Ted, take your feet off the chair.

4. We all had such a good time!

5. Do you know where Erin is?

6. Ricardo is interested in entomology, the study of insects.

7. Presidents' Day celebrates the birthdays of Presidents Washington and Lincoln.

8. I forgot my money!

9. Please leave now.

10. Why are you laughing?

Read the sentences. Then, rewrite each sentence, adding the correct end punctuation.

EXAMPLE   What time does practice start

ANSWER   *What time does practice start?*

11. My subscription to this magazine is about to expire

12. Explain how you arrived at that solution

13. What are you studying in social studies

14. Who is that lurking in the hall

15. Come quickly

16. Cynthia Rylant is a writer whose books I enjoy

17. You look so happy

18. Tell us about your trip

19. What movie did you see last weekend

20. I can't find my notes

SPEAKING APPLICATION

With a small group, carry on a brief dialogue. One person will begin with a question. Each person in the group will continue with a different type of sentence until you have used all types of sentences at least once.

WRITING APPLICATION

Write a brief paragraph in which you use all four types of sentences at least once.

PRACTICE 20.1C > **Writing Four Types of Sentences**

Read the topics. For each topic, write the type of sentence specified in parentheses. Be sure to use the appropriate end punctuation.

EXAMPLE this door (interrogative)

ANSWER *Why is this door locked?*

1. the bicycle trail (declarative)
2. the comedian (exclamatory)
3. you (interrogative)
4. you (imperative)
5. the kitchen in our apartment (declarative)
6. a dump truck (declarative)
7. Sam (interrogative)
8. Selena (exclamatory)
9. you (imperative)
10. who (interrogative)

PRACTICE 20.1D > **Revising Four Types of Sentences**

Read the sentences. Rewrite each sentence, changing it to the type of sentence specified in parentheses. Be sure to use the appropriate end punctuation.

EXAMPLE The rain stopped late in the day. (exclamatory)

ANSWER *The rain finally stopped!*

11. Audrey is a very talented musician. (exclamatory)
12. Spencer had to wait for two hours. (interrogative)
13. Where will the meeting be held? (declarative)
14. Is Fiona planning to swim today? (declarative)
15. This water is cold. (exclamatory)
16. Will you take this list to the office? (imperative)
17. The fire was started by a careless camper. (interrogative)
18. What has Lisa broken? (declarative)
19. She will walk the dog. (interrogative)
20. I would like you to pay attention. (imperative)

SPEAKING APPLICATION

With a partner, name a type of sentence. Your partner will say that type of sentence and then name a different type for you to say.

WRITING APPLICATION

Write a short conversation between two people. Use each type of sentence at least once in the conversation.

20.2 Combining Sentences

Good writing should include sentences of varying lengths and complexity to create a flow of ideas. One way to achieve sentence variety is to combine sentences to express two or more related ideas or pieces of information in a single sentence.

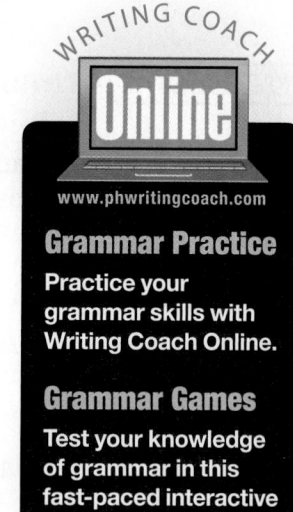

WRITING COACH
Online
www.phwritingcoach.com

Grammar Practice
Practice your grammar skills with Writing Coach Online.

Grammar Games
Test your knowledge of grammar in this fast-paced interactive video game.

Look at the example below. Then, look at how the ideas are combined in different ways.

EXAMPLE	I went to the movies. I saw an adventure film.
COMBINED	I went to the movies and saw an adventure film.
	I saw an adventure film when I went to the movies.

Combining Sentence Parts

RULE 20.2.1

Sentences can be combined by using a **compound subject**, a **compound verb**, or a **compound object**.

EXAMPLE	Anne Marie enjoys watching mysteries.
	Susan enjoys watching mysteries.
COMPOUND SUBJECT	**Anne Marie** and **Susan** enjoy watching mysteries.
EXAMPLE	Ken sells movie tickets in the evening.
	Ken sweeps the theater after the last show.
COMPOUND VERB	Ken **sells** movie tickets in the evening and **sweeps** the theater after the last show.
EXAMPLE	Marta loves romantic comedies.
	Marta loves adventure films.
COMPOUND OBJECT	Marta loves romantic **comedies** and adventure **films** .

See Practice 20.2A

436   **Effective Sentences**

Joining Clauses

A **compound sentence** consists of two or more main or independent clauses. (See Chapter 19 for more information about clauses.) Use a compound sentence when combining related ideas of equal weight.

To create a compound sentence, join two main clauses with a comma and a coordinating conjunction. Common conjunctions include *and, but, nor, for, so, or,* and *yet.* You can also link the two sentences with a semicolon (;) if they are closely related.

> Sentences can be combined by joining two main clauses to create a **compound sentence.**

20.2.2

RULE

EXAMPLE	Janice went to a dance recital.
	She saw several different styles of dance.
COMPOUND SENTENCE	Janice went to a dance recital, and she saw several different styles of dance.
EXAMPLE	Janice enjoyed watching jazz and tap dancing.
	She particularly liked watching ballet.
COMPOUND SENTENCE	Janice enjoyed watching jazz and tap dancing, but she particularly liked watching ballet.
EXAMPLE	Janice thought she would like to learn to dance.
	She asked the teacher if she could take lessons.
COMPOUND SENTENCE	Janice thought she would like to learn to dance, so she asked the teacher if she could take lessons.
EXAMPLE	Janice goes to dance class.
	She loves the way dancing makes her feel.
COMPOUND SENTENCE	Janice goes to dance class; she loves the way dancing makes her feel.

See Practice 20.2B

RULE

20.2.3

Sentences can be combined by changing one of them into a subordinate clause.

A **complex sentence** consists of one **main** or **independent clause** and one or more **subordinate clauses.** (See Chapter 19 for more information about clauses.) Combine sentences into a complex sentence to emphasize that one of the ideas in the sentence depends on the other. A subordinating conjunction will help readers understand the relationship. Common subordinating conjunctions are *after*, *although*, *because*, *before*, *since*, and *unless*. Generally no punctuation is required when a main and a subordinate clause are combined. When the subordinate clause comes first, a comma is needed. (See Chapter 25 for more information on punctuation.)

EXAMPLE   The sky grew dark. The storm clouds blew in.

COMBINED   The sky grew dark because the storm clouds

blew in.

See Practice 20.2C

RULE

20.2.4

Sentences can be combined by changing one of them into a phrase.

When combining sentences in which one of the sentences simply adds details, change one of the sentences into a **phrase.**

EXAMPLE   The Capitol Building is interesting to visit.

It is in Washington, D.C.

COMBINED   The Capitol Building in Washington, D.C. is

interesting to visit.

EXAMPLE   The White House is in Washington, D.C.

The president and his family live there.

COMBINED   The White House, where the president and his

family live, is in Washington, D.C.

See Practice 20.2D

PRACTICE 20.2A **Combining Sentences Using Compound Subjects, Verbs, and Objects**

Read the sentences. Combine the sentences in each group into a single sentence. Identify each combination as *compound subject, compound verb,* or *compound object.*

EXAMPLE   Leo opened the box. He took out the contents.

ANSWER   *Leo opened the box and took out the contents.* — compound verb

1. Cars filled the lot. Pickup trucks were there.

2. Lia vacuumed the floor. She dusted furniture.

3. The rescue squad was at the accident site in a few minutes. Firefighters were there, too.

4. Quentin delivered two pizzas. He also delivered a large salad.

5. We often see a movie on the weekend. We often go to the mall on the weekend.

6. Hannah found some old letters in the attic. She also found some documents.

7. Mr. Pierce studied law. He also studied math.

8. Lee participated in the swim meet. I did, too.

9. The audience applauded. The audience cheered wildly.

10. We donated blankets to the shelter. We also donated food.

PRACTICE 20.2B **Combining Sentences Using Main Clauses**

Read the sentences. Combine each pair into a compound sentence, using the coordinating conjunction in parentheses. Be sure to use the correct punctuation for compound sentences.

EXAMPLE   I spent an hour on the crossword puzzle. I did not finish it. (but)

ANSWER   *I spent an hour on the crossword puzzle, but I did not finish it.*

11. José likes to cook. He prepares meals. (so)

12. Becky stopped searching. She no longer expected to find her lost bracelet. (for)

13. You could borrow the book from the library. You could buy it. (or)

14. Emily takes piano lessons. She practices an hour a day. (and)

15. Henry VIII was Queen Elizabeth's father. Her mother was Anne Boleyn. (;)

16. Soccer used to be Ryan's favorite sport. Now he prefers basketball. (but)

17. Patrick did not come to the meeting. He did not send in his report. (and)

18. Nelson had hoped to be the first in line for tickets. He did not arrive in time. (but)

19. Miners found gold in California in 1848. Fortune seekers soon flocked there. (and)

20. You can visit Abby in the hospital. You can wait until she comes home. (or)

SPEAKING APPLICATION

With a partner, tell about two people who did something and two things that they did. Use a compound subject and a compound verb. Your partner should listen for and identify them.

WRITING APPLICATION

Use the sentences you wrote for 11, 13, and 18 as models, and write three new compound sentences with the connectors shown in parentheses.

PRACTICE 20.2C > **Combining Sentences Using Subordinate Clauses**

Read the sentences. Combine each pair by changing one sentence into a subordinate clause, using the subordinating conjunction in parentheses. Be sure to use the correct punctuation for complex sentences.

EXAMPLE Dave paced back and forth. He rehearsed his speech. (as)

ANSWER *Dave paced back and forth as he rehearsed his speech.*

1. The fog clears. The plane will take off. (when)

2. Caleb did his chores early in the day. It would be too hot to work later. (because)

3. Lara cannot play field hockey. Her fracture is healed. (until)

4. Our team has better guards. Central has some good players. (although)

5. Morgan entered the room. The lights went out. (as)

6. Dennis cast his fishing line into the stream. He has caught five fish. (since)

7. You must leave now. I'll walk with you. (if)

8. He worked hard. He did not succeed. (though)

9. The driver pulled to the side of the road. The tire blew out. (when)

10. People do not believe everything Dawn says. Dawn always exaggerates. (because)

PRACTICE 20.2D > **Combining Sentences Using Phrases**

Read the sentences. Combine each pair of sentences by changing one into a phrase.

EXAMPLE Olivia sells pottery. She attends craft fairs.

ANSWER *Olivia sells pottery at craft fairs.*

11. You can take the subway. It goes from Central to South Station.

12. The book sold out quickly. It was an exciting thriller.

13. Children splashed in the fountain. It was in the park.

14. The rock was very smooth. It had been tossed around by the waves.

15. The watchdog snarled and barked. It barked at the intruder.

16. I found this article. It is about the new school.

17. Alan walked through a dark room. He tripped over some shoes on the floor.

18. People celebrate Thanksgiving. They eat turkey.

19. In some countries, people use camels. Camels are their transportation.

20. Many ponds and valleys were formed. They were formed by glaciers.

SPEAKING APPLICATION

With a partner, take turns talking about something you agree or disagree with. Use subordinating conjunctions. Your partner should listen for and name the conjunctions.

WRITING APPLICATION

Use the sentences you wrote for 11, 12, and 14 as models, and write three new combined sentences. Include phrases in different locations in the sentences.

20.3 Varying Sentences

When you vary the length and form of the sentences you write, you are able to create a rhythm, achieve an effect, or emphasize the connections between ideas.

There are several ways you can introduce variety into the sentences you write.

> Varying the length of sentences makes writing lively and interesting to read.

Varying Sentence Length

Reading too many long sentences in a row can be just as uninteresting as reading too many short sentences in a row. When you want to emphasize a point or surprise a reader, insert a short, direct sentence to interrupt the flow of several long sentences.

EXAMPLE   Veteran's Day is a holiday that is observed in the United States to honor all of those who served in the armed forces in times of war. The holiday has not always been called Veteran's Day. **It was first called Armistice Day.** It is celebrated in most states on November 11.

You can also break some longer sentences into shorter sentences. If the longer sentence contains two or more ideas, you can break up the ideas into separate sentences. However, if a longer sentence contains only one main idea, you should not break it apart.

LONGER SENTENCE   Veteran's Day was proclaimed in 1919 by President Wilson to commemorate the ending of World War I.

TWO SENTENCES   Veteran's Day was proclaimed in 1919 by President Wilson. It commemorated the ending of World War I.

See Practice 20.3A

Varying Sentence Beginnings

Another way to create variety is by changing from the usual subject–verb order in a sentence.

> **RULE 20.3.2**
>
> Sentence beginnings can also be varied by reversing the traditional subject–verb order or starting the sentence with an adverb or a phrase.

EXAMPLES

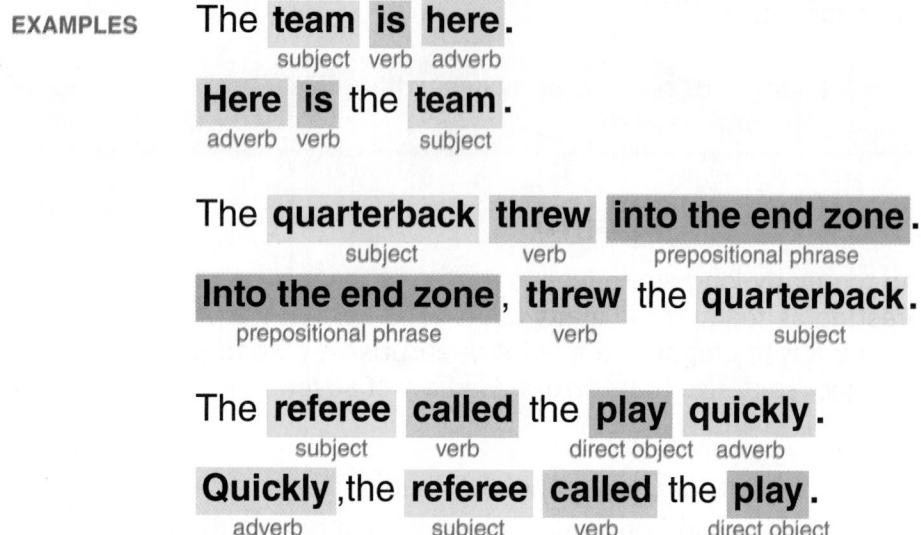

The **team** **is** **here**.
     subject verb adverb

Here **is** the **team**.
adverb verb   subject

The **quarterback** **threw** **into the end zone**.
    subject   verb   prepositional phrase

Into the end zone, **threw** the **quarterback**.
prepositional phrase   verb   subject

The **referee** **called** the **play** **quickly**.
    subject   verb   direct object adverb

Quickly, the **referee** **called** the **play**.
adverb   subject   verb   direct object

Another way to vary your sentences is to begin them in different ways. For instance, you can start sentences with different parts of speech.

See Practice 20.3B

WAYS TO VARY SENTENCE BEGINNINGS	
Start with a noun.	Sweaters, surprisingly, are not difficult to knit.
Start with an adverb.	Surprisingly, sweaters are not difficult to knit.
Start with an infinitive.	To knit sweaters is, surprisingly, not difficult.
Start with a gerund.	Knitting sweaters is, surprisingly, not difficult.
Start with a prepositional phrase.	For a person who likes to knit, sweaters are not difficult to make.

PRACTICE 20.3A ▷ Varying Sentence Length

Read the sentences. Rewrite each long compound sentence as two or more shorter sentences.

EXAMPLE   Ivan thought he should do the yard work he had agreed to do or his homework, but instead he decided to spend his Saturday morning riding his bike.

ANSWER   *Ivan thought he should do the yard work he had agreed to do or his homework. Instead, he decided to spend his Saturday morning riding his bike.*

1. If you want to take really good photographs, you could practice a lot or you could take a course or you could learn how to fix up your pictures using a computer program.

2. The doorbell rang, and Erin ran to answer it, and the dog slipped out the open door, so she ran after him.

3. Canada is a very large country with a relatively small population and only a few big cities, but these cities are close to the United States, so American tourists often visit them.

4. It was drizzling, but it was a warm rain, so people were not uncomfortable standing under big umbrellas watching a track meet.

5. Mimi had gone with her mother to an appointment, and then she went shopping with her, but she really wanted to stay home and read her book.

PRACTICE 20.3B ▷ Varying Sentence Beginnings

Read the sentences. Rewrite each sentence, changing the beginning as specified in parentheses. If there are two sentences, combine them, using one of the sentences to help you create the specified beginning.

EXAMPLE   We stopped to get sandwiches on our way home. (Begin with a prepositional phrase.)

ANSWER   *On our way home,* we stopped to get sandwiches.

6. Wendy smiled to herself, remembering the good time she had. (Begin with a participial phrase.)

7. The ice melted slowly. (Begin with an adverb.)

8. The chorus came next onto the stage. (Reverse the subject-verb order.)

9. Rob dropped his notes. It was in the middle of his speech. (Begin with a prepositional phrase.)

10. Mrs. Kane is a bird-watcher. She travels around the country to see different birds. (Begin with an appositive phrase.)

SPEAKING APPLICATION

With a partner, discuss your reasons for dividing one of the long compound sentences in Practice 20.3A into shorter sentences.

WRITING APPLICATION

Use your revised sentences 6–10 as models and write five sentences with varied beginnings.

20.4 Avoiding Sentence Problems

Recognizing problems with sentences will help you avoid and fix any problems in your writing.

Correcting Fragments

Some groups of words—even though they have a capital letter at the beginning and a period at the end—are not complete sentences. They are **fragments.**

RULE 20.4.1

> A **fragment** is a group of words that does not express a complete thought.

A fragment can be a group of words that includes a possible subject but no verb. A fragment could also be a group of words that includes a possible verb but no subject. It can even be a group of words that contains no subject and no verb. Fragments can be turned into complete sentences by adding a subject, a verb, or both.

FRAGMENTS	COMPLETE SENTENCES
was ready for bed	**I** was ready for bed. (A subject is added.)
the clock on the wall	The clock on the wall **needs** to be reset. (A verb is added.)
in my room	My **jeans** **are** in my room. (A subject and verb are added.)

See Practice 20.4A

Correcting Phrase Fragments A **phrase fragment** cannot stand alone because it does not have both a subject and a verb.

RULE 20.4.2

> A **phrase fragment** should not be capitalized and punctuated as if it were a sentence.

A phrase fragment can be corrected in one of two ways: (1) by adding it to a nearby sentence or (2) by adding whatever is needed to make it a complete sentence.

PHRASE FRAGMENT	The circus will begin at 8:00 on Sunday. **in the arena**
ADDED TO OTHER SENTENCE	The circus will begin at 8:00 on Sunday **in the arena** .
PHRASE FRAGMENT	There will be lions and elephants. **and tightrope walkers**
COMPLETE SENTENCES	There will be lions and elephants. There will also be **tightrope walkers** .

CHANGING PHRASE FRAGMENTS INTO SENTENCES	
PHRASE FRAGMENT	**COMPLETE SENTENCE**
into the center ring	The horses galloped **into the center ring** .
cheering the acrobats	The crowd was **cheering the acrobats** .
to see the clowns	The children waited **to see the clowns** .

See Practice 20.4B

Correcting Clause Fragments

All clauses have subjects and verbs, but some cannot stand alone as sentences.

> **A subordinate clause** should not be capitalized and punctuated as if it were a sentence.

Subordinate clauses do not express complete thoughts. Although a subordinate adjective or adverb clause has a subject and a verb, it cannot stand by itself as a sentence. (See Chapter 19 for more information about subordinate clauses and the words that begin them.)

Like phrase fragments, **clause fragments** can usually be corrected in either of two ways: (1) by attaching the fragment to a nearby sentence or (2) by adding whatever words are needed to turn the fragment into a sentence.

CLAUSE FRAGMENT	I saw the show. **that you described in your last letter**
COMPLETE SENTENCE	I saw the show **that you described in your last letter** .
CLAUSE FRAGMENT	I bought tickets as soon as they went on sale. **because I wanted good seats**
COMPLETE SENTENCE	I bought tickets as soon as they went on sale **because I wanted good seats** .
CLAUSE FRAGMENT	I wanted to sit in the first row. **so I could see everything**
COMPLETE SENTENCE	I wanted to sit in the first row **so I could see everything** .

To change a clause fragment into a sentence by the second method, you must add an independent clause to the fragment.

CHANGING CLAUSE FRAGMENTS INTO SENTENCES	
CLAUSE FRAGMENT	**COMPLETE SENTENCE**
that was ringing	Everyone heard the bell **that was ringing** . The bell **that was ringing** was heard by everyone.
when we got home	Dinner was ready **when we got home** . **When we got home** , dinner was ready.
what we were seeing	I could not believe **what we were seeing** .

See Practice 20.4C

See Practice 20.4D

PRACTICE 20.4A **Recognizing Fragments**

Read the groups of words. Then, write whether each group of words is a *sentence* or a *fragment*.

EXAMPLE   Searching for a lost ship.

ANSWER   *fragment*

1. When Rodney went to Curtis Middle School.

2. Today will be a very important day.

3. Under extreme pressure.

4. Which is a very good deal.

5. A television news reporter on the scene.

6. Walking on an icy pavement can be dangerous.

7. Torn at the edges.

8. By today at noon.

9. Val was not able to take notes because the speaker talked too fast.

10. He did.

PRACTICE 20.4B **Changing Phrase Fragments Into Sentences**

Read the phrase fragments. Then, use each fragment in a sentence.

EXAMPLE   during the week

ANSWER   *Danielle sometimes babysits during the week.*

11. on the computer for two hours

12. aside from that

13. walking by the shore

14. a children's doctor

15. hidden from sight

16. in the waiting room of the hospital

17. the guidance counselor

18. to answer all the questions on the test

19. not on weekends

20. in the sunshine by the window

SPEAKING APPLICATION

With a partner, take turns turning three of the fragments in Practice 20.4A into sentences.

WRITING APPLICATION

Choose two of the fragments in Practice 20.4B, and write two more sentences for each of them.

PRACTICE 20.4C Changing Clause Fragments Into Sentences

Read the clause fragments. Then, use each fragment in a sentence.

EXAMPLE   after the book was published

ANSWER   *After the book was published, the author was famous.*

1. until you told me
2. as if it had been trampled
3. when the nurse left the room
4. wherever you go
5. because the race ended in a tie
6. as the clock struck midnight
7. before the bell rings
8. as you probably know
9. though the motor was running
10. since we last met

PRACTICE 20.4D Changing Fragments Into Sentences

Read the groups of words. If a group of words is a fragment, use it in a sentence. If a group of words is already a sentence, write *sentence*.

EXAMPLE   As Olivia waited.

ANSWER   *As Olivia waited, she thought about what she would say.*

11. On the top shelf in the closet.
12. Before it's too late.
13. Who did all the artwork.
14. An e-mail message came with five attachments.
15. Diving from the rocks.
16. Born on Valentine's Day.
17. Meet me in front of the entrance.
18. Thinking about the problem.
19. His favorite author, Walter Dean Myers.
20. Although it was very cold out.

SPEAKING APPLICATION

With a partner, choose one of the fragments in Practice 20.4C, and use it again in two new sentences. Take turns saying these sentences.

WRITING APPLICATION

Write two more sentences for two fragments in Practice 20.4D.

Run-on Sentences

A fragment is an incomplete sentence. A **run-on,** on the other hand, is two or more complete sentences that are punctuated as though they were one sentence.

> A **run-on** is two or more complete sentences that are not properly joined or separated.

Find It/ FIX IT
15
Grammar Game Plan

20.4.4

Find It/ FIX IT
16
Grammar Game Plan

Run-ons are usually the result of carelessness. Check your sentences carefully to see where one sentence ends and the next one begins.

Two Kinds of Run-ons

There are two kinds of run-ons. The first one is made up of two sentences that are run together without any punctuation between them. This is called a **fused sentence.**

The second type of run-on consists of two or more sentences separated by only a comma. This type of run-on is called a **comma splice.**

FUSED SENTENCES	I go to the fair every year I like the crafts.
	Jake practices hard he wants to make the team.
COMMA SPLICE	There will be fireworks on July 4, I like the parade, too.
	Keisha is a great dancer, I love it when she shows me new steps.

See Practice 20.4E

A good way to distinguish between a run-on and a sentence is to read the words aloud. Your ear will tell you whether you have one or two complete thoughts and whether you need to make a complete break between the thoughts.

Three Ways to Correct Run-ons

There are three ways to correct run-on sentences. You can use end marks, commas and coordinating conjunctions, or semicolons.

Using End Marks

Periods, question marks, and exclamation marks are useful to fix run-on sentences.

> **Use an end mark to separate a run-on sentence into two sentences.**

Sometimes the best way to correct a run-on is to use an end mark to split the run-on into two shorter but complete sentences. End marks help your reader pause and group your ideas more effectively.

RUN-ON	I have to babysit on the weekends, my brother goes to practice.
CORRECTED	I have to babysit on the weekends. My brother goes to practice.
RUN-ON	Watch out the ball is coming toward you.
CORRECTED	Watch out! The ball is coming toward you.
RUN-ON	Have you bought your tickets I have mine.
CORRECTED	Have you bought your tickets? I have mine.
RUN-ON	What's going on, I can't figure out where I'm supposed to stand.
CORRECTED	What's going on? I can't figure out where I'm supposed to stand.

Using Commas and Coordinating Conjunctions

Sometimes the two parts of a run-on are related and should be combined into a compound sentence.

> **Use a comma and a coordinating conjunction to combine two independent clauses into a compound sentence.**

To separate the clauses properly, use both a comma and a coordinating conjunction. The most common coordinating conjunctions are *and, but, or, for, nor,* and *yet.* Before you separate a sentence into parts, though, be sure each part expresses a complete thought.

RUN-ON	May went to the store, she forgot her shopping list.
CORRECTED	May went to the store, but she forgot her shopping list.
RUN-ON	She remembered most of the things she needed, she bought a few extra things.
CORRECTED	She remembered most of the things she needed, and she bought a few extra things.

Using Semicolons

You can sometimes use a semicolon to connect the two parts of a run-on into a correct sentence.

> **Use a semicolon to connect two closely related ideas into one sentence.**

Use a semicolon only when the ideas in both parts of the sentence are closely related.

RUN-ON	My first class next year starts at 8:00, my last class ends at 3:00.
CORRECTED	My first class next year starts at 8:00; my last class ends at 3:00.

See Practice 20.4F

PRACTICE 20.4E > **Recognizing Run-ons**

Read the groups of words. Then, write whether each group is a *sentence* or a *run-on*.

EXAMPLE   The movie was a fast-paced thriller, Kirk likes thrillers.

ANSWER   *run-on*

1. My cousin from San Diego visited me, and we talked until midnight.

2. Callie writes children's stories, she reads them during the library story hour.

3. Mark picked up the newspaper and read the headlines, then he scanned the sports section.

4. In some areas, trees are being destroyed by insects.

5. He wanted to graduate from high school he did.

6. Warren, a careful person, is serious about whatever he does.

7. Benjamin Franklin was a printer, an inventor, a diplomat, and a convention delegate.

8. Some people like to play sports, others prefer to be spectators.

9. Roy waved at me from the stands, I waved back.

10. Abby sent Troy a text message he did not reply.

PRACTICE 20.4F > **Correcting Run-ons**

Read the sentences. Rewrite each run-on sentence to correct the problem.

EXAMPLE   Computers have changed drastically in fifty years, they have become faster and smaller.

ANSWER   *Computers have changed drastically in fifty years. They have become faster and smaller.*

11. The sun dropped behind the horizon over the lake, we watched the spectacular sunset.

12. The lobby was filled with teenagers, they wanted to buy tickets to the concert.

13. Caleb likes to read limericks he read some in Edward Lear's *A Book of Nonsense*.

14. Lola graduated from college then she took a job in New York.

15. Firefighters quickly arrived they were able to bring the fire under control.

16. Rock climbing can be exciting but dangerous, rock climbers need to be cautious.

17. First, boil the water then add the rice.

18. Ethan did not like the movie Erica enjoyed it very much.

19. Alec had a good game, he scored two runs and made two outs.

20. Mark Twain created two famous characters these characters are Tom Sawyer and Huckleberry Finn.

SPEAKING APPLICATION

With a partner, identify one sentence and one run-on in Practice 20.4E. Explain why the sentence is correct and the run-on is not.

WRITING APPLICATION

Use sentences 17 and 18 as models, and write a new sentence for each in the same way you corrected them.

Properly Placing Modifiers

If a phrase or clause acting as an adjective or adverb is not placed near the word it modifies, it may seem to modify a different word. Then the sentence may seem unclear or odd.

> **A modifier should be placed as close as possible to the word it describes.**

20.4.8 RULE

A modifier placed too far away from the word it describes is called a **misplaced modifier.**

MISPLACED MODIFIER

Mark went scuba diving in the lake **with his flippers**.

The misplaced phrase *with his flippers* makes it seem as though the lake has flippers.

See Practice 20.4G

See Practice 20.4H

PROPERLY PLACED MODIFIER

Mark went scuba diving **with his flippers** in the lake.

Below is a different type of misplaced modifier that is sometimes called a **dangling modifier.** A dangling modifier at the beginning of a sentence causes the sentence to be unclear.

DANGLING MODIFIER

Sitting on the boat, the sun felt hot.

In this sentence, *sitting on the boat* should modify a person or people. Instead, it incorrectly modifies *sun*.

CORRECTED

Sitting on the boat, we felt the hot sun.

PRACTICE 20.4G ▶ **Revising to Correct Misplaced Modifiers**

Read the sentences. Then, rewrite each sentence to correct the underlined misplaced modifier.

EXAMPLE   Simon found a twenty-dollar bill underline{walking home from school}.

ANSWER   *Walking home from school, Simon found a twenty-dollar bill.*

1. Hillary has a cat named Tiger with stripes.

2. Glen searched for the hidden clues with a GPS system.

3. Working on my computer, the power went out.

4. We watched seals diving for fish standing on the shore.

5. Victoria reviewed the speech that she would give sitting in the backyard.

6. I watched the squirrels and pigeons eating my lunch in the park.

7. Accompanied by the First Lady, the crowd cheered as the president arrived.

8. Listening to my MP3 player, the work gets done quickly.

9. A black jacket was found by a student with red sleeves.

10. Please summarize what you just read with your book closed.

PRACTICE 20.4H ▶ **Recognizing and Correcting Misplaced Modifiers**

Read the sentences. If a sentence has a misplaced modifier, rewrite the sentence so the modifier is properly placed. If a sentence is correct, write *correct*.

EXAMPLE   With her tail twitching, Audra watched her cat stalk a squirrel.

ANSWER   *Audra watched her cat twitching its tail and stalking a squirrel.*

11. Evan got up early and turned on the television still in his pajamas.

12. Rosa waited for the bus with her friends.

13. Putting on her best clothes, Kate prepared for an interview.

14. A man jumped into the pond to rescue the dog with all his clothes on.

15. Remembering his promise, Luis left early.

16. Because of the rain, Claire walked her dog with an umbrella.

17. On her way home, Victoria stopped at the library.

18. I saw a red-tailed hawk looking through my binoculars.

19. Gil stomped out, slamming the door.

20. I saw my friend Pedro talking to his brother in the hall.

SPEAKING APPLICATION

With a partner, take turns describing your favorite season of the year. Be sure to use a combination of simple, compound, and complex sentences with modifiers. Your partner should identify the modifiers and correct any misplaced modifiers.

WRITING APPLICATION

Write a brief description of one of your favorite meals. Include one simple sentence, one compound sentence, and one complex sentence. Then, discuss your sentences with a partner. Your partner should identify the modifiers and correct any misplaced modifiers.

Avoiding Double Negatives

Negative words, such as *nothing* and *not*, are used to deny or to say *no*. Some people mistakenly use **double negatives**—two negative words—when only one is needed.

> **Avoid writing sentences that contain double negatives.**

20.4.9 RULE

In the following examples, negative words are highlighted. The first sentence in each example contains double negatives. The corrected sentences show two ways to correct each double-negative sentence.

DOUBLE NEGATIVES	Maggie **didn't** invite **nobody**.
CORRECTED SENTENCES	Maggie **didn't** invite anybody.
	Maggie invited **nobody**.
DOUBLE NEGATIVES	I **haven't no** more money.
CORRECTED SENTENCES	I have **no** more money.
	I **haven't** any more money.
DOUBLE NEGATIVES	Jack and Phil **didn't** go **nowhere**.
CORRECTED SENTENCES	Jack and Phil **didn't** go anywhere.
	Jack and Phil went **nowhere**.
DOUBLE NEGATIVES	It seems the sun **doesn't** shine **no** more.
CORRECTED SENTENCES	It seems the sun **doesn't** shine any more.
	It seems the sun shines **no** more.
DOUBLE NEGATIVES	A few rainy days **didn't** bother **no one**.
CORRECTED SENTENCES	A few rainy days **didn't** bother anyone.
	A few rainy days bothered **no one**.

See Practice 20.4I
See Practice 20.4J

| PRACTICE 20.4I | Using Negatives Correctly |

Read the sentences. Then, write the word in parentheses that makes each sentence negative without creating a double negative.

EXAMPLE The teacher didn't hear (no one, anyone) answer.

ANSWER *anyone*

1. Sue doesn't go (anywhere, nowhere) without her phone.

2. Christa said she didn't want (any, no) bread.

3. Jon didn't bring (any, no) money with him.

4. Ollie (can, can't) never remember his locker combination.

5. Nadine didn't bring (anything, nothing) to the party.

6. He never has (no, any) time to help me.

7. Claudia couldn't find her ring (anywhere, nowhere).

8. Tabitha doesn't know (anyone, no one) in that class.

9. By the time we were ready for dessert, there wasn't (any, none) left.

10. Zach claims he didn't do (anything, nothing).

| PRACTICE 20.4J | Revising to Correct Double Negatives |

Read the sentences. Then, rewrite each sentence to correct the double negative.

EXAMPLE He didn't want no help with the cleanup.

ANSWER *He didn't want any help with the cleanup.*

11. There wasn't nowhere to hang up the coats.

12. I didn't get no text message from Liz.

13. Isn't there no one here who can give me directions?

14. The sweatshirt didn't have no hood.

15. I can't find nothing in this closet.

16. That old house hasn't had no paint for years.

17. There isn't no one at the ticket window.

18. Tony didn't remember nothing about the accident.

19. Amber never said nothing to no one.

20. Tonia didn't see nothing in the store that she liked.

SPEAKING APPLICATION

With a partner or small group, take turns telling each other a very brief narrative in which you use the words *no one, nothing,* and *nowhere.* Be sure not to use double negatives.

WRITING APPLICATION

Write three sentences in which you use three of these negative words without creating a double negative: *never, no,* and *none.*

Avoiding Common Usage Problems

Find It/ FIX IT

1

Grammar
Game Plan

Find It/ FIX IT

5

Grammar
Game Plan

This section contains fifteen common usage problems in alphabetical order. Some are expressions that you should avoid in both your speaking and your writing. Others are words that are often confused because of similar spellings or meanings.

(1) accept, except   Do not confuse the spelling of these words. *Accept*, a verb, means "to take what is offered" or "to agree to." *Except*, a preposition, means "leaving out" or "other than."

VERB   Meg **accepted** her award.

PREPOSITION   Everyone was given a raise **except** me.

(2) advice, advise   Do not confuse the spelling of these related words. *Advice*, a noun, means "an opinion." *Advise*, a verb, means "to give an opinion."

NOUN   What **advice** can you give me about studying?

VERB   I **advise** you to study every night.

(3) affect, effect   *Affect*, a verb, means "to influence" or "to cause a change in." *Effect*, usually a noun, means "result."

VERB   The hurricane **affected** the dunes on the beach.
NOUN   The **effects** of hurricanes may be seen for years.

(4) at   Do not use *at* after *where*.

INCORRECT   Does your mother know **where** you're **at**?
CORRECT   Does your mother know **where** you are?

(5) because   Do not use *because* after *the reason*. Eliminate one or the other.

INCORRECT   **The reason** I'm happy is **because** I won the race.
CORRECT   I'm happy **because** I won the race.
             The **reason** I'm happy is **that** I won the race.

(6) beside, besides   These two prepositions have different meanings and cannot be interchanged. *Beside* means "at the side of" or "close to." *Besides* means "in addition to."

My classroom is **beside** hers on this floor.

No one **besides** us is here in the afternoon.

(7) different from, different than   *Different from* is preferred over *different than*.

The new buses are **different from** last year's buses.

(8) farther, further   *Farther* is used to refer to distance. *Further* means "additional" or "to a greater degree or extent."

His house was **farther** than mine.
I will have no **further** communication with you.

(9) in, into   *In* refers to position. *Into* suggests motion.

My books are **in** my backpack.
I put my backpack **into** my locker.

(10) kind of, sort of   Do not use *kind of* or *sort of* to mean "rather" or "somewhat."

I'm **sort of** good at swimming.
I'm **rather** good at swimming.

(11) like   *Like*, a preposition, means "similar to" or "in the same way as." It should be followed by an object. Do not use *like* before a subject and a verb. Use *as* or *that* instead.

My sister looks **like** our dad.
This apple doesn't taste **like** it should.
This apple doesn't taste **as** it should.

(12) that, which, who   *That* and *which* refer to things. *Who* refers only to people.

THINGS	People liked the music **that** I played.
PEOPLE	The man **who** played the trumpet is my dad.

(13) their, there, they're   Do not confuse the spelling of these three words. *Their*, a possessive adjective, always modifies a noun. *There* is usually used as a sentence starter or as an adverb. *They're* is a contraction of *they are*.

POSSESSIVE ADJECTIVE	The students lined up for **their** buses.
SENTENCE STARTER	**There** is the Broadway bus.
ADVERB	The bus stop is over **there** .
CONTRACTION	**They're** waiting in the rain.

(14) to, too, two   Do not confuse the spelling of these words. *To* plus a noun creates a prepositional phrase. *To* plus a verb creates an infinitive. *Too* is an adverb and modifies verbs, adjectives, and other adverbs. *Two* is a number.

PREPOSITION	**to** the store	**to** Texas
INFINITIVE	**to** stand	**to** run
ADVERB	**too** cloudy	**too** badly
NUMBER	**two** shoes	**two** shirts

(15) when, where, why   Do not use *when, where,* or *why* directly after a linking verb such as *is*. Reword the sentence.

INCORRECT	To explore the ruins is **why** we went to Mexico.
CORRECT	We went to Mexico to explore the ruins.
INCORRECT	In the evening is **when** I do my homework.
CORRECT	I do my homework in the evening.

See Practice 20.4K
See Practice 20.4L
See Practice 20.4M
See Practice 20.4N

Read the sentences. Then, write the word in parentheses that best completes each sentence.

EXAMPLE   The hikers went (farther, further) than they had planned.

ANSWER   *farther*

1. The judges have made (there, their) decision.

2. Toby took his equipment (in, into) the locker room.

3. The (affects, effects) of the hurricane are still evident.

4. Everyone has had a turn (accept, except) Lindsay.

5. I could use some (advice, advise) on how to run this machine.

6. Steve introduced his grandfather (that, who) had been a general in the army.

7. Abe's brother wanted (to, too) much money for the bike.

8. Laura needed (farther, further) encouragement to audition for the play.

9. You can place your backpack (beside, besides) the others.

10. Julian is different (from, than) his brother.

Read the sentences. If the underlined word is used correctly, write *correct*. If the word is incorrect, write the correct word.

EXAMPLE   Rick is standing <u>besides</u> Cassie in the picture.

ANSWER   *beside*

11. Poor nutrition can <u>affect</u> your ability in school.

12. Grace is a person <u>that</u> is always willing to help.

13. Jeff walked <u>in</u> the classroom.

14. Eve and Tara worked on <u>they're</u> project after school.

15. I have no <u>further</u> information for you at this time.

16. Gwen's idea is different <u>than</u> Rebecca's.

17. The students <u>who</u> made the banner are seventh graders.

18. Jocelyn offers <u>advise</u>, even if you don't want it.

19. Mark was honored to <u>except</u> the award.

20. Brian wants a game <u>like</u> Leo's.

SPEAKING APPLICATION

With a partner, use the words *advice* and *effect* to tell an observation you have made about people in general. Your partner should check that you have used the words correctly.

WRITING APPLICATION

Write two or three related sentences using all of these words correctly: *accept, advice, their,* and *too*.

PRACTICE 20.4M **Recognizing and Correcting Usage Problems**

Read the sentences. Then, if a sentence has a usage problem, rewrite it to correct the problem. If a sentence is correct, write *correct*.

EXAMPLE   Robin wondered where the meeting was at.

ANSWER   *Robin wondered where the meeting was.*

1. The person who can help you is not here today.

2. A late paper could effect your grade.

3. Luke's goals are different from mine.

4. The Mancinos took there dog with them on vacation.

5. The reason I am late is because the bus broke down.

6. The best time is when everyone else has left and it's quiet.

7. We sat besides the Owens family.

8. People that want respect should give respect.

9. I don't know why you always say that.

10. Archie refused to accept payment for helping Mrs. Holden shovel her walk.

PRACTICE 20.4N **Avoiding Usage Problems**

Read the pairs of words. For each pair of words, write two sentences that are related in meaning.

EXAMPLE   accept, except

ANSWER   *The teacher accepted the papers early. Everyone except Crystal had finished.*

11. besides, beside

12. into, in

13. as, like

14. who, that

15. too, to

16. advice, advise

17. farther, further

18. their, there

19. except, accept

20. effect, affect

SPEAKING APPLICATION

With a partner, choose two of the incorrect sentences in Practice 20.4M, and explain why the usage is incorrect.

WRITING APPLICATION

Write a short paragraph in which you use all of these words correctly: *beside, affect, except,* and *there.*

Using Parallel Structures

Good writers try to present a series of ideas in similar grammatical structures. This way, the ideas read smoothly. If one element in a series is not parallel with the others, the result may be confusing. Parallel structures are important in simple, compound, and complex sentences.

Recognizing the Correct Use of Parallelism

To present a series of ideas of equal importance, you should use parallel grammatical structures.

> **Parallelism** involves presenting equal ideas in words, phrases, clauses, or sentences of similar types.

PARALLEL WORDS	The lost dog looked **scared, dirty,** and **hungry**.
PARALLEL PHRASES	I wanted more than anything to **take him home, give him a bath,** and **feed him**.
PARALLEL CLAUSES	The dog **that you found** and **that you want to bring home** belongs to someone else.
PARALLEL SENTENCES	**We have to find his owner. We have to do the right thing.**

Correcting Faulty Parallelism

Faulty parallelism occurs when a writer uses unequal grammatical structures to express related ideas. This can cause sentences to sound unbalanced.

> Correct a sentence with faulty parallelism by rewriting it so that each parallel idea is expressed in the same grammatical structure.

Faulty parallelism can involve words, phrases, and clauses in a series or in comparisons.

Nonparallel Words, Phrases, and Clauses in a Series
Always check for parallelism when your writing contains items in a series.

Correcting Faulty Parallelism in a Series

NONPARALLEL STRUCTURES	Three steps in the writing process are **drafting**, **revision**, and **editing**.
	gerund noun gerund
CORRECTION	Three steps in the writing process are **drafting**, **revising**, and **editing**.
	gerund gerund gerund

Nonparallel Words, Phrases, and Clauses in Comparison
In writing comparisons, you generally should compare a phrase with the same type of phrase. Similarly, you should compare a clause with the same type of clause.

Correcting Faulty Parallelism in Comparisons

NONPARALLEL STRUCTURES	I think **that drafting is the easiest step**, but
	noun clause
	the most patience is required for revising.
	independent clause
CORRECTION	I think **that drafting is the easiest step** but
	noun clause
	that revising requires the most patience.
	noun clause
NONPARALLEL STRUCTURES	**Jocelyn** prefers swimming **in cold water** while
	subject prepositional phrase
	the warm **water** delights her **friends**.
	subject direct object
CORRECTION	**Jocelyn** prefers swimming **in cold water** while
	subject prepositional phrase
	her **friends** prefer swimming **in warm water**.
	subject prepositional phrase

See Practice 20.4O
See Practice 20.4P

PRACTICE 20.4O Using Parallel Structures With Items in a Series

Read each sentence. Then, rewrite the sentences to correct the faulty parallelism. If the item is correct, then write *correct*. Read your new sentences to a partner. Your partner should identify the parallelism.

EXAMPLE   My mother is an excellent dentist, a great cook, and plays the piano well.

ANSWER   *My mother is an excellent dentist, a great cook, and **a good pianist.***

1. I bought two bags of potatoes, three tomatoes that were ripe, and one head of lettuce.

2. I could not wait to use my new surfboard, and visiting my friend, Kelly.

3. The teacher assigned one book report and is giving us a test tomorrow.

4. My hobbies are going to the movies and chess.

5. For your birthday, we can go bowling but no swimming is allowed.

6. Some of my friends think that ping pong is not a sport, and that it shouldn't be in the Olympics.

7. Pat likes diving, swimming, and to surf.

8. We will miss the bus and be late for the play.

9. I like to paint, sketch and drawing.

10. My best subject is English, and I am not bad at math and science.

PRACTICE 20.4P Using Parallel Structures in Comparisons

Read each sentence. Then, rewrite the sentences to correct the faulty parallelism in comparisons. Read your new sentences to a partner. Your partner should identify the parallel structures.

EXAMPLE   I left school at 4:30 P.M. rather than going home at 3:00 P.M.

ANSWER   *I left school at 4:30 P.M. **rather than at 3:00 P.M.***

11. Most people work during the day not night.

12. Shane did the dishes while Joanna cooks.

13. I enjoyed my meal more than Christopher.

14. I am as fond of dogs as much as I like cats.

15. Pia is as good a softball player as basketball is Shania's strength.

16. Because of traffic, my mother arrived at 7:00 P.M. instead of coming home at 5:30 P.M.

17. Juan enjoyed the nonfiction book as much as the science fiction story is his brother's favorite.

18. I prefer waking up late while my sister is an early riser.

19. My sister prefers apples to eating oranges.

20. Geraldo enjoys playing the clarinet as much as guitar appeals to his brother.

SPEAKING APPLICATION

With a partner, take turns talking about your favorite foods. Include at least one simple sentence, one compound sentence, and one complex sentence and use parallel structures. You partner should identify where you have used parallel structures.

WRITING APPLICATION

Write a paragraph about your school subjects. Include one simple, one compound, and one complex sentence. Show parallel structures in a series and in comparison. Read your paragraph. Your partner should identify where you have used parallel structures.

Test Warm-Up

DIRECTIONS

Read the introduction and the passage that follows. Then, answer the questions to show that you can use a variety of complete sentences (e.g., simple, compound, complex) that include parallel structures in reading and writing.

Fiona wrote this paragraph about her summer vacation. Read the paragraph and think about the changes you would suggest as a peer editor. When you finish reading, answer the questions that follow.

Summer Fun

(1) This summer, I did many different things and went to lots of places. (2) The first two weeks of the summer break, I went to the swim club, my grandma's house, and the mall was somewhere I spent time, as well. (3) The last two weeks in July, I went away to camp. (4) My favorite camp activities were tennis, arts and crafts, and of course, going to swim. (5) The last Saturday at camp is visiting day, which means that parents come to visit. (6) Friends can also come.

---

1 What change, if any, should be made in sentence 1?

A Change *did* to **went**

B Change *went* to **did**

C Change *lots of* to **many different**

D Make no change

2 What would be the BEST way to rewrite the ideas in sentence 2?

F The first two weeks of the summer break, I went to the swim club, my grandma's house, and the mall was somewhere I spent time.

G The first two weeks of the summer break, I went to the swim club, to my grandma's house, and to the mall.

H The first two weeks of the summer break, the swim club, my grandma's house, and the mall were somewhere I spent time.

J I went to the swim club and my grandma's house, as well as the mall the first two weeks of summer.

3 What change, if any, should be made in sentence 4?

A Change *going to swim* to **swimming**

B Insert **playing** after *were*

C Insert **making** before *arts*

D Make no change

4 What is the BEST way to combine sentences 5 and 6?

F The last Saturday at camp is visiting day, which means that parents come to visit and that friends can also come.

G The last Saturday at camp is visiting day, which means that parents and friends can come to visit.

H The last Saturday at camp is visiting day, which means that parents come and friends also come to visit.

J The last Saturday at camp, parents and friends come to visit on visiting day.

Using Consistent Tenses

Verbs have a number of different tenses that tell when actions happen. For example, past tense is used for actions that happened in the past. Present tense shows actions that happen in the present or that happen regularly. Future tense is used to show actions that will take place in the future. Switching from one tense to another can be confusing in any type of sentence: simple, compound, and complex.

RULE **20.4.12**

> **Use consistent verb tenses to show actions that occur during the same period of time.**

INCONSISTENT TENSES

I **went** to the movies, and
past

I **see** my friend waiting for me.
present

CONSISTENT TENSES

I **went** to the movies, and
past

I **saw** my friend waiting for me.
past

The verb *went* sets the action in the past. The other action also occurred in the past.

Using Inconsistent Tenses Correctly

Sometimes, actions take place at different times. In these instances, you may switch from one tense to another. Sometimes you may use a time word or phrase to explain the switch in tense.

EXAMPLE

I **stayed** up really late last night, so now
past

I **am** very sleepy.
present

See Practice 20.4Q
See Practice 20.4R

PRACTICE 20.4Q > Writing Sentences With Consistent Verb Tenses

Read each sentence. Then, rewrite the sentences to correct inconsistent verb tenses. Read your new sentences to a partner. Your partner should identify the consistent verb tenses.

EXAMPLE   Helene goes to the mall and bought a new pair of shoes.

ANSWER   Helene *went* to the mall and bought a new pair of shoes.

1. After I finished my homework, I go outside to shoot baskets with Jamie.
2. Every morning, my mom drops me off at school and then went to work.
3. Ms. Jones taught us about the scientific method and then gives a pop quiz.
4. Even though she apologized before, I was still mad at Kaitlin now.
5. Yesterday, I woke up early so that I have time to finish my report.
6. Did you go to the football game or did you went straight home?
7. The bus driver gets mad when we screamed.
8. I like when my dad came home early and plays baseball with me.
9. I am a good chess player but I was even better at checkers.
10. Lydia was mad at Amy for the mean things Amy says about Mia.

PRACTICE 20.4R > Writing Sentences With Consistent Verb Tenses

Read the verb pairs. Then, write a sentence using each pair in the present, past, or future tense. Read your sentences to a partner. Your partner should identify the consistent tenses.

EXAMPLE   leave, wait

ANSWER   *Because I left my house before my sister, I waited for her on the corner.*

11. study, take
12. remember, be
13. work, play
14. cook, clean
15. enjoy, dislike
16. tell, laugh
17. win, celebrate
18. arrive, depart
19. become, dream
20. sleep, forget

SPEAKING APPLICATION

With a partner, take turns discussing your favorite weekend activities. Include at least one simple sentence, one compound sentence, and one complex sentence. Use consistent tenses in your sentences. Your partner should identify the consistent tenses.

WRITING APPLICATION

Write a paragraph about a recent event in sports, at school, or in your community. Include at least one simple, one compound, and one complex sentence. Use consistent tenses. Read your paragraph to a partner, who should identify the tenses.

Cumulative Review  Chapters 18–20

PRACTICE 1 ▷ Using Complete Subjects and Predicates

Each item below contains only a complete subject or a complete predicate. Rewrite each item, making a sentence by adding the missing part indicated in parentheses.

1. The supermarket cashier (add a predicate).
2. (add a subject) enjoyed the performance.
3. The television weather forecaster (add a predicate).
4. Was (add a subject) difficult to do?
5. The roller coaster (add a predicate).
6. (add a subject) raced across the room.
7. The new community center (add a predicate).
8. (add a subject) made a huge hole.
9. The boy and his parents (add a predicate).
10. (add a subject) entered another contest.

PRACTICE 2 ▷ Using Direct Objects

Rewrite each incomplete sentence, supplying a direct object where indicated in parentheses. You may also include the article *a*, *an*, or *the* or another modifier along with the direct object.

1. Dogs need (direct object).
2. The children are making (direct object).
3. In the school office, I saw (direct object).
4. Janice paints (direct object) for a living.
5. Barry left (direct object) on the table.
6. He asked (direct object) for change for a dollar.
7. I enjoyed (direct object) at the parade.
8. Last week, Diane met (direct object) in the park.
9. The pilot showed us (direct object).
10. What caused (direct object) on the moon?

PRACTICE 3 ▷ Identifying Indirect Objects

Read the sentences. Then, write the indirect object in each sentence. If there is no indirect object, write *none*.

1. The nurse gave the patient an injection.
2. Eddie told us a very funny joke.
3. My mom bought herself a lovely silk blouse.
4. Craig clips coupons for supermarket savings.
5. Don't hand her the scissors the wrong way.
6. The rodeo performer showed us a rope trick.
7. Amy offered her seat to a lady with a baby.
8. We wish you a happy holiday.
9. The police officer asked the driver for her license.
10. Who will give the dog a bath?

PRACTICE 4 ▷ Identifying Subject Complements

Read the sentences. Then, write the subject complement in each sentence. Also indicate whether it is a *predicate noun*, *predicate pronoun*, or *predicate adjective*.

1. The student with the best grades is you.
2. Jack London was a popular adventure writer.
3. The cousins looked happy to see each other.
4. Trina will be the next class president.
5. The drive to Springfield seemed very scenic.
6. Lucia has been the manager for ten years.
7. Of all the skaters, the most graceful one is you.
8. Please do not be late to the concert.
9. That magic show was really something.
10. Are we being careful enough?

PRACTICE 5 > Using Prepositional Phrases

Read the sentences. Then, rewrite each sentence, supplying the type of prepositional phrase indicated in parentheses.

1. Paco joined the club. (Add an adjectival phrase.)

2. Lillian tossed a Frisbee. (Add an adverbial phrase.)

3. The noise was loud. (Add an adjectival phrase.)

4. Dad grilled chicken. (Add an adverbial phrase.)

5. Dina rang the bell. (Add an adjectival phrase.)

PRACTICE 6 > Identifying Appositive, Participial, Gerund, and Infinitive Phrases

Read the sentences. Then, write whether the underlined phrase in each sentence is an *appositive phrase*, a *participial phrase*, a *gerund phrase*, or an *infinitive phrase*.

1. We need to buy light bulbs.

2. Alex plans on running the marathon.

3. Scared by the cat, the mouse scampered off.

4. We looked through binoculars to see the spotted owl.

5. The thesaurus, a book of synonyms, is also available online.

6. The figure dashing through the trees seemed like an owl in the fog.

7. An enthusiastic fisherman, Ernest Hemingway lived for a time in Key West.

8. Knitting woolen sweaters is one of my sister's special skills.

9. Packing her suitcase, Audra broke a fingernail.

10. Max plans to become a skiing instructor.

PRACTICE 7 > Recognizing Main and Subordinate Clauses

Read the sentences. Then, write and label the *main clause* and the *subordinate clause* in each sentence.

1. The school bus was late because the traffic on Manning Boulevard was terrible.

2. When the bus neared his stop, Martin rang the bell at the rear door.

3. The state senator, who was first elected more than ten years ago, is running for office again.

4. We will visit Montana in two weeks unless a blizzard prevents the trip.

5. I watched the first episode, which I had seen before.

PRACTICE 8 > Combining Sentences With Subordinate Clauses

Read the sentences. Combine each pair of sentences by turning one into a subordinate clause. Then, underline the subordinate clause, and indicate whether it is an *adjectival clause* or an *adverbial clause*.

1. My cousin is wearing a cast. She broke her leg skating on the ice last week.

2. My brother will be applying to several colleges. He is a junior in high school.

3. I hunted in every closet. I finally found that old family photo album.

4. The department store will open earlier than usual. It has a big sale today.

5. We walked nearly five miles today. My feet are very sore.

Continued on next page ▶

Cumulative Review Chapters 18–20

 **PRACTICE 9** Writing Sentences

For each item, write the indicated type of sentence, using the words provided.

1. Write a compound sentence using *the inventor* as one of the subjects.

2. Write a declarative sentence using *the elevator* as the subject.

3. Write a complex sentence using *is running* as one of the verbs.

4. Write an exclamatory sentence using the word *marvelous*.

5. Write an imperative sentence using *unlock* as the verb.

 **PRACTICE 10** Combining Sentences

Read the sentences. Combine each pair of sentences by using compound structures. Indicate whether your sentence contains a *compound subject*, a *compound verb*, or a *compound object*, or whether it is a *compound sentence*.

1. Geraldo waited in the ticket line. Frederica waited there, too.

2. Jacques ordered a turkey sandwich for lunch. He also ordered a salad.

3. The designer selected the fabrics carefully. She also matched them carefully.

4. Fern may have left her keys on the kitchen counter. She may have left her scarf in the car.

5. They were hoping for an experienced baker. The person they finally hired has little experience.

PRACTICE 11 Revising to Correct Fragments and Run-ons

Read each group of words. If it is a fragment, use it in a sentence. If it is a run-on, correct the run-on. If a sentence needs no correction, write *correct*.

1. The groom waiting at the altar.

2. The child was riding on the merry-go-round.

3. I was reading in bed my eyes were closing.

4. When you arrive for the picnic.

5. The movie was awful, I sat through it anyway.

PRACTICE 12 Revising to Correct Common Usage Problems

Read the sentences. Then, rewrite each sentence to correct misplaced modifiers, double negatives, and other usage problems.

1. What does the financial planner advice your family to do?

2. Lack of sufficient daylight during the short winter days effects the mood of some people.

3. Coughing so much, she could speak no farther.

4. Wearing a warm coat, the cold weather did not bother me.

5. I like every vegetable accept cabbage.

6. Madeline didn't see none of her friends at the block party.

7. The reason I left is because I have another appointment.

8. The girls were to tired to do they're homework.

9. Phyllis wore new boots that were apparently too big on her feet.

10. Meteorology is where you study the weather.

CHAPTER 21

USING VERBS

Understanding the different tenses of regular and irregular verbs will help you clearly convey actions in your writing.

WRITE GUY *Jeff Anderson, M.Ed.*

WHAT DO YOU NOTICE?

Lock onto the verbs as you zoom in on these sentences from "Two Kinds," an excerpt from *The Joy Luck Club* by Amy Tan.

MENTOR TEXT

> "No!" I said, and I now felt stronger, as if my true self had finally emerged. So this was what had been inside me all along.

Now, ask yourself the following questions:

- What principal part of the verb *emerge* is used in the first sentence?
- What forms of irregular verbs are used in both sentences?

In the first sentence, the principal part of the verb *emerge* is the past participle *had emerged*. The verb phrase is formed by combining the past tense *emerged* with the helping verb *had*. The forms of irregular verbs used in these sentences are *said, felt, was,* and *been*, which are past forms of *say, feel,* and *be*. They are irregular because their principal parts do not follow a pattern, such as adding *-ed* or *-d* to the present form to create the past tense.

Grammar for Writers Knowing how to use the principal parts of a verb correctly allows writers to communicate a time of action or state of being. Watch out for irregular verbs, and be prepared to check that you are using the correct tenses.

How do you keep from getting stuck in the past?

That's easy. Stop using the past tense!

21.1 The Four Principal Parts of Verbs

Verbs have different tenses to express time. The tense of the verb *walk* in the sentence "They *walk* very fast" expresses action in the present. In "They *walked* too far from home," the tense of the verb shows that the action happened in the past. In "They *will walk* home from school," the verb expresses action in the future. These forms of verbs are known as **tenses.**

A verb's **tense** shows the time of the action or state of being that is being described. To use the tenses of a verb correctly, you must know the **principal parts** of the verb.

RULE 21.1.1

> A verb has four **principal parts: the present, the present participle, the past,** and the **past participle.**

THE FOUR PRINCIPAL PARTS OF *VISIT*			
PRESENT	PRESENT PARTICIPLE	PAST	PAST PARTICIPLE
visit	(am) visiting	visited	(have) visited

The first principal part, called the present, is the form of a verb that is listed in a dictionary. The present participle and the past participle must be combined with helping verbs before they can be used as verbs in sentences. The result will always be a verb phrase.

EXAMPLES   He **visits** the library every day.

Jake **was visiting** the library yesterday.

They **visited** the library.

We **have visited** the library in the last three weeks.

The way the past and past participle of a verb are formed shows whether the verb is **regular** or **irregular.**

Using Regular Verbs

Most verbs are **regular,** which means that their past and past participle forms follow a standard, predictable pattern.

> **The past and past participle of a regular verb** are formed by adding **-ed** or **-d** to the present form.

To form the past and past participle of a regular verb such as *chirp* or *hover*, you simply add *-ed* to the present. With regular verbs that already end in *e*—verbs such as *move* and *charge*—you simply add *-d* to the present.

PRINCIPAL PARTS OF REGULAR VERBS			
PRESENT	PRESENT PARTICIPLE	PAST	PAST PARTICIPLE
call	(am) calling	called	(have) called
change	(am) changing	changed	(have) changed
charge	(am) charging	charged	(have) charged
chirp	(am) chirping	chirped	(have) chirped
contain	(am) containing	contained	(have) contained
describe	(am) describing	described	(have) described
fix	(am) fixing	fixed	(have) fixed
hover	(am) hovering	hovered	(have) hovered
jump	(am) jumping	jumped	(have) jumped
lift	(am) lifting	lifted	(have) lifted
look	(am) looking	looked	(have) looked
move	(am) moving	moved	(have) moved
play	(am) playing	played	(have) played
save	(am) saving	saved	(have) saved
serve	(am) serving	served	(have) served
ski	(am) skiing	skied	(have) skied
talk	(am) talking	talked	(have) talked
type	(am) typing	typed	(have) typed
visit	(am) visiting	visited	(have) visited
walk	(am) walking	walked	(have) walked

See Practice 21.1A
See Practice 21.1B

PRACTICE 21.1A Identifying Principal Parts of Regular Verbs

Read the sentences. Then, label each underlined verb *present*, *present participle*, *past*, or *past participle*.

EXAMPLE   Angie <u>has invited</u> twenty people to her party.

ANSWER   *past participle*

1. The boss <u>ordered</u> all work to stop at once.

2. We <u>missed</u> you at the group meeting today.

3. I <u>presume</u> this is the right place.

4. Alicia <u>was laughing</u> at Joel's joke.

5. No one <u>had noticed</u> that Del was not there.

6. Hugo <u>has attended</u> every rehearsal.

7. Kim <u>is wondering</u> why you said that.

8. Alex <u>did</u> not <u>continue</u> his speech.

9. Tamara <u>has</u> not <u>submitted</u> her report yet.

10. It <u>was raining</u>, but the soccer team <u>practiced</u> anyway.

PRACTICE 21.1B Supplying the Principal Parts of Regular Verbs

Read the verbs. Then, write and label the four principal parts of each verb. Use a form of the helping verb *be* with the present participle and a form of the helping verb *have* with the past participle.

EXAMPLE   talk

ANSWER   *talk* — present
is talking — present participle
talked — past
has talked — past participle

11. watch

12. burn

13. complete

14. suggest

15. ski

16. carry

17. work

18. try

19. stop

20. continue

SPEAKING APPLICATION

With a partner, take turns making a statement in which you use two principal parts of one of the verbs in Practice 21.1B. Your partner should identify which principal parts you use.

WRITING APPLICATION

Write several sentences or a brief paragraph in which you use three principal parts of one of these verbs: *disappear*, *return*, and *discuss*.

Using Irregular Verbs

While most verbs are regular, many very common verbs are **irregular**—their past and past participle forms do not follow a predictable pattern.

> The past and past participle of an **irregular verb** are not formed by adding *-ed* or *-d* to the present tense form.

21.1.3 RULE

IRREGULAR VERBS WITH THE SAME PAST AND PAST PARTICIPLE			
PRESENT	**PRESENT PARTICIPLE**	**PAST**	**PAST PARTICIPLE**
bring	(am) bringing	brought	(have) brought
build	(am) building	built	(have) built
buy	(am) buying	bought	(have) bought
catch	(am) catching	caught	(have) caught
fight	(am) fighting	fought	(have) fought
find	(am) finding	found	(have) found
get	(am) getting	got	(have) got *or* (have) gotten
hold	(am) holding	held	(have) held
lay	(am) laying	laid	(have) laid
lead	(am) leading	led	(have) led
lose	(am) losing	lost	(have) lost
pay	(am) paying	paid	(have) paid
say	(am) saying	said	(have) said
sit	(am) sitting	sat	(have) sat
sleep	(am) sleeping	slept	(have) slept
spin	(am) spinning	spun	(have) spun
stand	(am) standing	stood	(have) stood
stick	(am) sticking	stuck	(have) stuck
swing	(am) swinging	swung	(have) swung
teach	(am) teaching	taught	(have) taught
win	(am) winning	won	(have) won

Check a dictionary whenever you are in doubt about the correct form of an irregular verb.

IRREGULAR VERBS WITH THE SAME PRESENT, PAST, AND PAST PARTICIPLE

PRESENT	PRESENT PARTICIPLE	PAST	PAST PARTICIPLE
bid	(am) bidding	bid	(have) bid
burst	(am) bursting	burst	(have) burst
cost	(am) costing	cost	(have) cost
hurt	(am) hurting	hurt	(have) hurt
put	(am) putting	put	(have) put
set	(am) setting	set	(have) set

IRREGULAR VERBS THAT CHANGE IN OTHER WAYS

PRESENT	PRESENT PARTICIPLE	PAST	PAST PARTICIPLE
arise	(am) arising	arose	(have) arisen
be	(am) being	was	(have) been
bear	(am) bearing	bore	(have) borne
beat	(am) beating	beat	(have) beaten
begin	(am) beginning	began	(have) begun
blow	(am) blowing	blew	(have) blown
break	(am) breaking	broke	(have) broken
choose	(am) choosing	chose	(have) chosen
come	(am) coming	came	(have) come
do	(am) doing	did	(have) done
draw	(am) drawing	drew	(have) drawn
drink	(am) drinking	drank	(have) drunk
drive	(am) driving	drove	(have) driven
eat	(am) eating	ate	(have) eaten
fall	(am) falling	fell	(have) fallen
fly	(am) flying	flew	(have) flown
forget	(am) forgetting	forgot	(have) forgotten
freeze	(am) freezing	froze	(have) frozen

IRREGULAR VERBS THAT CHANGE IN OTHER WAYS (CONTINUED)			
PRESENT	**PRESENT PARTICIPLE**	**PAST**	**PAST PARTICIPLE**
give	(am) giving	gave	(have) given
go	(am) going	went	(have) gone
grow	(am) growing	grew	(have) grown
know	(am) knowing	knew	(have) known
lie	(am) lying	lay	(have) lain
ride	(am) riding	rode	(have) ridden
ring	(am) ringing	rang	(have) rung
rise	(am) rising	rose	(have) risen
run	(am) running	ran	(have) run
see	(am) seeing	saw	(have) seen
shake	(am) shaking	shook	(have) shaken
sing	(am) singing	sang	(have) sung
sink	(am) sinking	sank	(have) sunk
speak	(am) speaking	spoke	(have) spoken
spring	(am) springing	sprang	(have) sprung
strive	(am) striving	strove	(have) striven
swear	(am) swearing	swore	(have) sworn
swim	(am) swimming	swam	(have) swum
take	(am) taking	took	(have) taken
tear	(am) tearing	tore	(have) torn
throw	(am) throwing	threw	(have) thrown
wear	(am) wearing	wore	(have) worn
weave	(am) weaving	wove	(have) woven
write	(am) writing	wrote	(have) written

See Practice 21.1C
See Practice 21.1D
See Practice 21.1E
See Practice 21.1F

As you can see, there are many irregular verbs. For most of these verbs, you should memorize the different forms. Whenever you are not sure of which form of an irregular verb to use, check a dictionary.

Supplying the Principal Parts of Irregular Verbs

Read the verbs. Then, write and label the four principal parts of each verb. Use a form of the helping verb *be* with the present participle, and a form of the helping verb *have* with the past participle.

EXAMPLE   fly

ANSWER   *fly* — *present*

is flying — *present participle*

flew — *past*

has flown — *past participle*

1. go
2. ride
3. tear
4. ring
5. choose
6. draw
7. eat
8. arise
9. hurt
10. wear

Choosing the Correct Form of Irregular Verbs

Read the sentences. Then, choose and write the form of the verb in parentheses that correctly completes each sentence.

EXAMPLE   We had (drove, driven) all day.

ANSWER   *driven*

11. The balloon (burst, bursted).
12. Aunt Lucy (bring, brought) us a gift.
13. My grandfather (shook, shaked) the apples off the tree.
14. Some of those trees in the back have (grew, grown) too tall.
15. Diana has (took, taken) piano lessons.
16. The wind (blowed, blew) fiercely all night.
17. The construction workers have already (builded, built) the foundation.
18. Ken (caught, catched) three fish during his fishing expedition.
19. Have you (wrote, written) a thank-you note to your grandmother?
20. Rhondella has (led, leaded) her team to victory.

SPEAKING APPLICATION

With a partner, take turns making a statement in which you use two principal parts of one of the verbs listed in Practice 21.1C. Your partner should identify which principal parts you use.

WRITING APPLICATION

Write three sentences, using different principal parts of these verbs: *know*, *choose*, and *tell*. You may use any of the sentences in Practice 21.1D as models.

PRACTICE 21.1E ▷ Using Irregular Verbs

Read the sentences. Rewrite each sentence, using the form of the verb in parentheses that correctly completes the sentence.

EXAMPLE   Daniel (sing) the lead in last year's musical.

ANSWER   *Daniel sang the lead in last year's musical.*

1. Marty has not (speak) to anyone about her plan.
2. Alexa has (choose) a new ring tone for her phone.
3. The little child has (put) his shoes on the wrong feet.
4. Curtis (pay) the bill for our meal.
5. Who (see) the shooting stars last night?
6. In the 1770s and 1780s, American colonists (fight) for independence.
7. Marya (stand) staring at her feet, trying to think of an answer.
8. The chorus (rise) together when the director (give) the signal.
9. Gary's socks (shrink) in the wash.
10. Ryan (bring) some video games for us to play.

PRACTICE 21.1F ▷ Revising for Irregular Verbs

Read the sentences. Then, if the underlined verb is in the correct form, write *correct*. If it is not, rewrite the sentence with the correct verb form.

EXAMPLE   The water in the birdbath had <u>froze</u>.

ANSWER   *The water in the birdbath had frozen.*

11. Abby <u>blowed</u> out the candle before she left the room.
12. Anthony's uncle <u>taught</u> him to play the banjo.
13. Maggie and Jennifer <u>brung</u> sandwiches for the group.
14. We have <u>sat</u> here too long.
15. Colin <u>drank</u> the water.
16. The *Titanic* <u>sunk</u> after hitting an iceberg.
17. That window has been <u>broken</u> twice this year.
18. The boots <u>costed</u> too much, so I did not buy them.
19. Sophie <u>swum</u> across the pond and back today.
20. I <u>seen</u> that movie before.

SPEAKING APPLICATION

With a partner, take turns telling about an event you have observed. Use the past and past participle forms of three of these verbs: *come, see, stand,* and *speak.*

WRITING APPLICATION

Write three sentences using the past or past participle forms of these verbs: *begin, drive,* and *write.* You may use the sentences in Practices 21.1E and 21.1F as models.

21.2 The Six Tenses of Verbs

In English, verbs have six **tenses**: the **present**, the **past**, the **future**, the **present perfect**, the **past perfect**, and the **future perfect**.

RULE
21.2.1

The **tense** of a verb shows the time of the action or state of being.

Every tense has both **basic** forms and **progressive** forms.

Identifying the Basic Forms of the Six Tenses

The chart below shows the **basic** forms of the six tenses, using *speak* as an example. The first column gives the name of each tense. The second column gives the basic form of *speak* in all six tenses. The third column gives the principal part needed to form each tense. Only three of the four principal parts are used in the basic forms: the present, the past, and the past participle.

BASIC FORMS OF THE SIX TENSES OF *SPEAK*		
TENSE	BASIC FORM	PRINCIPAL PART USED
Present	I speak.	Present
Past	I spoke.	Past
Future	I will speak.	Present
Present Perfect	I have spoken.	Past Participle
Past Perfect	I had spoken.	Past Participle
Future Perfect	I will have spoken.	Past Participle

Study the chart carefully. First, learn the names of the tenses. Then, learn the principal parts needed to form them. Notice also that the last four tenses need helping verbs.

As you have already learned, some verbs form their tenses in a regular, predictable pattern. Other verbs use an irregular pattern. *Speak* is an example of an irregular verb.

See Practice 21.2A

Conjugating the Basic Forms of Verbs

A helpful way to become familiar with all the forms of a verb is by **conjugating** it.

> **A conjugation** is a list of the singular and plural forms of a verb in a particular tense.

Each tense in a conjugation has six forms that fit with first-, second-, and third-person forms of the personal pronouns. These forms may change for each personal pronoun, and they may change for each tense.

To conjugate any verb, begin by listing its principal parts. For example, the principal parts of the verb *go* are *go, going, went,* and *gone.* The following chart shows the conjugation of all the basic forms of *go* in all six tenses. The forms of the helping verbs may also change for each personal pronoun and tense.

See Practice 21.2B

CONJUGATION OF THE BASIC FORMS OF GO		
TENSE	**SINGULAR**	**PLURAL**
Present	I go. You go. He, she, or it goes.	We go. You go. They go.
Past	I went. You went. He, she, or it went.	We went. You went. They went.
Future	I will go. You will go. He, she, or it will go.	We will go. You will go. They will go.
Present Perfect	I have gone. You have gone. He, she, or it has gone.	We have gone. You have gone. They have gone.
Past Perfect	I had gone. You had gone. He, she, or it had gone.	We had gone. You had gone. They had gone.
Future Perfect	I will have gone. You will have gone. He, she, or it will have gone.	We will have gone. You will have gone. They will have gone.

Conjugating *Be*

The verb *be* is an important verb to know how to conjugate. It is both the most common and the most irregular verb in the English language. You have already seen how to use forms of *be* with the perfect tenses. You will also use the basic forms of *be* when you conjugate the progressive forms of verbs later in this section.

PRINCIPAL PARTS OF *BE*			
PRESENT	PRESENT PARTICIPLE	PAST	PAST PARTICIPLE
be	being	was	been

Once you know the principal parts of *be*, you can conjugate all of the basic forms of *be*.

CONJUGATION OF THE BASIC FORMS OF *BE*		
TENSE	SINGULAR	PLURAL
Present	I am. You are. He, she, or it is.	We are. You are. They are.
Past	I was. You were. He, she, or it was.	We were. You were. They were.
Future	I will be. You will be. He, she, or it will be.	We will be. You will be. They will be.
Present Perfect	I have been. You have been. He, she, or it has been.	We have been. You have been. They have been.
Past Perfect	I had been. You had been. He, she, or it had been.	We had been. You had been. They had been.
Future Perfect	I will have been. You will have been. He, she, or it will have been.	We will have been. You will have been. They will have been.

See Practice 21.2C
See Practice 21.2D
See Practice 21.2E
See Practice 21.2F

PRACTICE 21.2A **Identifying Present, Past, and Future Tenses of Verbs**

Read the sentences. Then, label each underlined verb *present*, *past*, or *future*.

EXAMPLE   I <u>will give</u> you an answer later.

ANSWER   *future*

1. <u>May</u> I <u>interrupt</u> you for a moment?

2. Judith <u>squeezed</u> the lemon into her tea.

3. You <u>will enjoy</u> the performance tomorrow.

4. Betsy <u>saves</u> the bottles to recycle.

5. We <u>will remember</u> this day forever.

6. Shyly, Neal <u>smiled</u> at Lizzie.

7. The team <u>hopes</u> for a victory tonight.

8. Kirsten <u>attended</u> a different school last year.

9. Felicia quickly <u>brushed</u> her teeth and <u>left</u> for school.

10. After you read the chapter, you <u>will discuss</u> it in groups.

PRACTICE 21.2B **Identifying Perfect Tenses of Verbs**

Read the sentences. Then, write the verb in each sentence, and label it *present perfect*, *past perfect*, or *future perfect*.

EXAMPLE   The group has chosen James as its spokesperson.

ANSWER   *has chosen — present perfect*

11. Everyone had left the cafeteria by 1:00 P.M.

12. I have not seen Will since yesterday.

13. By December, the birds will have migrated south for the winter.

14. Brandon had left his book in the gym after practice.

15. The rain has delayed the opening of the game.

16. By this time tomorrow, I will have completed my research project.

17. Mandy has seen three of the five home games.

18. I have worn my favorite red sweatshirt many times.

19. Beth had thoughtfully marked her draft for revision.

20. How long have you known her?

SPEAKING APPLICATION

With a partner, use the verbs in sentences 4, 5, and 6 to make three statements in which you use present, past, and future tenses. Your partner should identify the verb tense in each statement.

WRITING APPLICATION

Use the perfect verb tenses in sentences 11, 16, and 18, and write three sentences with other verbs in the perfect tense.

Writing Sentences Using the Perfect Tenses of Verbs

Read each present tense verb. Then, write a sentence using the perfect tense indicated in parentheses. Read your sentences to a partner, who should listen for and name the perfect tense verbs.

EXAMPLE   leave (past perfect)

ANSWER   *I had left the house when I realized that I forgot my backpack.*

1. be (present perfect)
2. give (future perfect)
3. allow (past perfect)
4. remember (present perfect)
5. score (future perfect)
6. speak (past perfect)
7. forget (present perfect)
8. go (future perfect)
9. skate (past perfect)
10. cook (present perfect)

Writing Sentences Using the Perfect Tenses of Verbs

Read the sentences. Then, use the subjects and verbs provided to write new sentences using the perfect tense indicated in parentheses. Read your sentences to a partner, who should listen for and name the perfect tense verbs.

EXAMPLE   I am. (present perfect)

ANSWER   *I have been to Sharon's house many times.*

11. She runs. (future perfect)
12. My mother goes. (past perfect)
13. The dog sleeps. (present perfect)
14. The cat plays. (future perfect)
15. I study. (past perfect)
16. Juana forgets. (present perfect)
17. Michael remembers. (future perfect)
18. My father arrives. (past perfect)
19. I enjoy. (present perfect)
20. I prefer. (past perfect)

SPEAKING APPLICATION

With a partner, take turns talking about the actions of a dog or cat. Use perfect tense verbs in at least three sentences. Your partner should listen for and name the perfect tense verbs.

WRITING APPLICATION

Write six sentences about a topic of your choice. In each sentence, use a perfect tense verb. Then, underline and identify the perfect tense verb in each sentence.

PRACTICE 21.2E **Forming Verb Tenses**

Read the sentences, which are all in the present tense. Then, rewrite each sentence, changing it to the tense indicated in parentheses.

EXAMPLE   The teacher repeats the directions. (future)

ANSWER   The teacher *will repeat* the directions.

1. Tina confides her plan to Rhonda. (past)
2. Ashley hints about a party. (present perfect)
3. Dom insists on paying for my lunch. (past)
4. By 9:00 P.M., the store closes. (future perfect)
5. Karen proposes a solution to the dilemma. (past perfect)
6. No one believes your excuse. (future)
7. Nick works on his project in the library. (past)
8. Hailey sketches the scene on her drawing pad. (future)
9. Noah thinks about the consequences. (past perfect)
10. Amanda performs in the talent show. (present perfect)

PRACTICE 21.2F **Using Verb Tenses Correctly**

Read the sentences. Then, write the verb in parentheses that correctly completes each sentence.

EXAMPLE   Starting next week, stores (are, will be) open later for the holidays.

ANSWER   *will be*

11. Joanna (eats, ate) salmon for dinner yesterday.
12. Tony never (imagined, will imagine) that he could win the spelling bee.
13. By next week, the play (has completed, will have completed) its run.
14. I (will meet, have met) you at 5:00 P.M.
15. David (shouts, shouted) with glee when he heard the news.
16. The committee (will discuss, has discussed) your proposal when it meets later this week.
17. Did you get the message I (sent, have sent) this morning?
18. I (will give, have given) you my answer already.
19. Until today, Mark (has, had) perfect attendance.
20. The ticket office (is, was) closed when we went to buy tickets.

SPEAKING APPLICATION

With a partner, take turns talking about jobs or careers that might interest you. In your sentences, use at least three perfect tense verbs. Your partner should listen for and name the perfect tense verbs.

WRITING APPLICATION

Write a paragraph about how you spent your time last summer. Use at least three perfect tense verbs. Read your paragraph to a partner. Your partner should listen for and name the perfect tense verbs.

Test Warm-Up

DIRECTIONS
Read the introduction and the passage that follows. Then, answer the questions to show that you can use and understand the function of perfect tense verbs in reading and writing.

Nate wrote this paragraph about his dog, Jake. Read the paragraph and think about the changes you would suggest as a peer editor. When you finish reading, answer the questions that follow.

Where Had Jake Gone?

(1) My dog, Jake, had ate breakfast and wanted to go out. (2) I had opened the back door before breakfast because I had know he was going to scratch at the door. (3) I had left the room to make my bed. (4) He must have slipped out. (5) I heard my sister shouting, "Jake, where are you? Come, boy!" (6) Where had Jake gone? (7) After we had searching for 20 minutes, my mom said that we had to go to school, and that she would find him. (8) We reluctantly opened the front door, and there was Jake, wagging his little tail. (9) He had run around the yard to the front door!

---

1 What change, if any, should be made in sentence 1?

A Change *had ate* to **had eaten**

B Change *had ate* to **has eaten**

C Change *wanted* to **has want**

D Make no change

2 What change, if any, should be made in sentence 2?

F Change *had opened* to **have opened**

G Change *had know* to **had known**

H Change *had know* to **have known**

J Make no change

3 What is the BEST way to combine sentences 3 and 4?

A I had left the room to make my bed; he must have slipped out.

B He must have slipped out; I had left the room to make my bed.

C Before I leave the room to make my bed, he must slip out.

D He must have slipped out after I had left the room to make my bed.

4 The meaning of sentence 7 can be clarified by changing the word *searching* to —

F search

G searched

H looking

J look

Recognizing the Progressive Tense of Verbs

The six tenses of *go* and *be* in their basic forms were shown in the charts earlier in this section. Each of these tenses also has a progressive tense or form. The progressive form describes an event that is in progress. In contrast, the basic forms of a verb describe events that have a definite beginning and end.

> The **progressive tense,** or form, of a verb shows an action or condition that is ongoing.

21.2.3 RULE

All six of the progressive tenses of a verb are made using just one principal part: the present participle. This is the principal part that ends in *-ing*. Then, the correct form of *be* is added to create the progressive tense or form.

Progressive Tenses of *Write*

PROGRESSIVE TENSE = be + present participle

PRESENT I **am writing** in the class.
    be present participle

PAST I **was writing** in class all day.
    be present participle

FUTURE I **will be writing** in class this week.
    be present participle

PRESENT PERFECT I **have been writing** since I was young.
    be present participle

PAST PERFECT I **had been writing** only in class, but now
    be present participle
I also write at home.

FUTURE PERFECT I **will have been writing** in class for twelve
    be present participle
years by the time I graduate high school.

Conjugating Progressive Tenses

To create the progressive tenses or forms of a verb, you must know the basic forms of *be*.

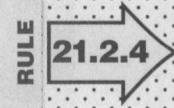

RULE 21.2.4

> **To conjugate the progressive forms of a verb, add the present participle of the verb to a conjugation of the basic forms of *be*.**

A conjugation of the basic forms of *be* is shown earlier in this section. Compare that conjugation with the following conjugation of the progressive forms of *see*. Notice that, even though the present participle form of the verb does not change, the form of the helping verb does change. It is the form of *be* that tells you whether the action or condition is taking place in the past, present, or future.

CONJUGATION OF THE PROGRESSIVE FORMS OF *SEE*		
TENSE	**SINGULAR**	**PLURAL**
Present Progressive	I am seeing. You are seeing. He, she, or it is seeing.	We are seeing. You are seeing. They are seeing.
Past Progressive	I was seeing. You were seeing. He, she, or it was seeing.	We were seeing. You were seeing. They were seeing.
Future Progressive	I will be seeing. You will be seeing. He, she, or it will be seeing.	We will be seeing. You will be seeing. They will be seeing.
Present Perfect Progressive	I have been seeing. You have been seeing. He, she, or it has been seeing.	We have been seeing. You have been seeing. They have been seeing.
Past Perfect Progressive	I had been seeing. You had been seeing. He, she, or it had been seeing.	We had been seeing. You had been seeing. They had been seeing.
Future Perfect Progressive	I will have been seeing. You will have been seeing. He, she, or it will have been seeing.	We will have been seeing. You will have been seeing. They will have been seeing.

See Practice 21.2G

See Practice 21.2H

PRACTICE 21.2G > **Identifying the Progressive Tenses of Verbs**

Read the sentences. Then, write whether the underlined verb tense in each sentence is *present progressive, past progressive, future progressive, present perfect progressive, past perfect progressive,* or *future perfect progressive.*

EXAMPLE The group <u>was singing</u> on the bus.

ANSWER *past progressive*

1. Lisa <u>is sitting</u> next to Michael.
2. I <u>had been planning</u> to clean my room today.
3. We <u>have been hoping</u> to see the exhibit at the library.
4. Our guests <u>will be arriving</u> any minute now.
5. By the time we finish, we <u>will have been painting</u> the porch for two days.
6. He <u>was nodding</u> his head in agreement.
7. I <u>had been thinking</u> about you before you called.
8. They <u>are preparing</u> to leave now.
9. Our science class <u>will be studying</u> the solar system soon.
10. I <u>have been spending</u> my money foolishly.

PRACTICE 21.2H > **Using Progressive Tenses of Verbs**

Read the sentences. Then, rewrite each sentence using the tense of the verb in parentheses.

EXAMPLE Eric _____ for a summer job. (*look*, present progressive)

ANSWER *Eric is looking for a summer job.*

11. I _____ to ask you something. (*mean*, present perfect progressive)
12. The leaves _____ faster than we could rake them. (*fall*, past perfect progressive)
13. I _____ for two hours. (*study*, present perfect progressive)
14. Will you _____ the drama club? (*join*, future progressive)
15. Carson _____ to go to the Grand Canyon. (*plan*, present perfect progressive)
16. Lou and Tom _____ at Todd's silly pun. (*laugh*, past progressive)
17. The track team _____ every day after school. (*run*, present perfect progressive)
18. Your flight _____ soon. (*depart*, future progressive)
19. We _____ to rehearse for the play. (*continue*, present progressive)
20. Vanessa _____ to use the computer. (*wait*, past progressive)

SPEAKING APPLICATION

With a partner, take turns talking about school events. Your partner should listen for and identify two verbs you use in a progressive tense.

WRITING APPLICATION

Write a paragraph about a current event. Use a variety of sentences with progressive tense verbs. Then, exchange papers with a partner. Read your sentences aloud and discuss the purpose of the progressive tense verbs.

Identifying Active and Passive Voice

Just as verbs change tense to show time, they may also change form to show whether or not the subject of the verb is performing an action.

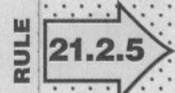

RULE 21.2.5

> The **voice** of a verb shows whether or not the subject is performing the action.

In English, most verbs have two **voices: active,** to show that the subject is performing an action, and **passive,** to show that the subject is having an action performed on it.

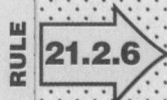

RULE 21.2.6

> A verb is in the **active voice** when its subject performs the action.

ACTIVE
VOICE

Mike **plays** the guitar.

Sandra **sang** the song.

In each example above, the subject performs the action, so the verb is said to be in the active voice.

RULE 21.2.7

> A verb is in the **passive voice** when its subject does not perform the action.

PASSIVE
VOICE

The guitar **is being played** by Mike.

The song **was sung** by Sandra.

In each example above, the person doing the action becomes the object of the preposition *by* and is no longer the subject. Both subjects—*guitar* and *song*—are receivers rather than performers of the action. When the subject is acted upon, the verb is said to be in the passive voice.

See Practice 21.2I

Forming the Tenses of Passive Verbs

A passive verb always has two parts.

> **A passive verb** is always a verb phrase made from a form of *be* plus a past participle.

The following chart shows a conjugation of the passive forms of the verb *present* with the pronoun *it*.

CONJUGATION OF THE PASSIVE FORMS OF *PRESENT*	
TENSE	PASSIVE FORM
Present	It is presented.
Past	It was presented.
Future	It will be presented.
Present Perfect	It has been presented.
Past Perfect	It had been presented.
Future Perfect	It will have been presented.

While there are uses for the passive voice, most writing is more lively when it is in the active voice. Think about how to change each sentence below to the active voice. Follow the pattern in the first two examples.

PASSIVE   It **is marked** on the board.

ACTIVE   We **have marked** it on the board.

PASSIVE   It **was marked** on the board.

ACTIVE   We **marked** it on the board.

PASSIVE   It **will be marked** on the board for the class.

It **has been marked** on the board.

It **had been marked** on the board.

It **will have been marked** on the board.

Using Active and Passive Voices

Each of the two voices has its proper use in English.

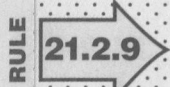

> Use the **active voice** whenever possible.

Sentences with active verbs are less wordy and more forceful than those with passive verbs. Compare, for example, the following sentences. Notice the different number of words each sentence needs to report the same information.

ACTIVE	Students **studied** an exam guide.
PASSIVE	An exam guide **was studied** by students.

Although you should aim to use the active voice in most of your writing, there will be times when you will need to use the passive voice.

> Use the **passive voice** to emphasize the receiver of an action rather than the performer of an action.

In the following example, the receiver of the action is the subject *coach*. It is the *team* (the direct object) that is actually performing the action.

EMPHASIS ON RECEIVER	The coach **was supported** by the team.

The passive voice should also be used when there is no performer of the action.

> Use the **passive voice** to point out the receiver of an action when the performer is unknown or not named in the sentence.

PERFORMER UNKNOWN	The new book **was written** sometime last year.

See Practice 21.2J

Distinguishing Active and Passive Voice

Read the sentences. Then, write *AV* if the underlined verb is in active voice or *PV* if the verb is in passive voice.

EXAMPLE   The injured player <u>was carried</u> off the field.

ANSWER   *PV*

1. A new delegate <u>was appointed</u> by the governor.

2. A meter maid <u>ticketed</u> the illegally parked car.

3. The principal <u>brought</u> the matter to our attention.

4. The halls of the building <u>had been swept</u> during the night.

5. The new city hall <u>was designed</u> by a local architect.

6. Undoubtedly, the audience <u>will be persuaded</u> by your speech.

7. Deer <u>have eaten</u> the bark on these trees.

8. The contract <u>had been signed</u> by both parties.

9. The chef <u>presented</u> an appetizing meal.

10. The fence <u>had been painted</u> white.

PRACTICE 21.2J **Revising to Use Active Voice**

Read the sentences. Then, rewrite each sentence that is in passive voice so that it is in active voice. If the sentence is already in active voice, write *active*.

EXAMPLE   The fallen tree has been removed by the landscaper.

ANSWER   *The landscaper removed the fallen tree.*

11. The clerk is wrapping the package.

12. After the performance, the tents were taken down by the circus crew.

13. The principal has not yet told the students about the early dismissal.

14. The dog was walked by Thalia.

15. The coaches are planning next year's schedules.

16. These flowers were arranged by the garden committee.

17. New computers have been purchased by the school.

18. Anne has given an excellent oral report.

19. My seat was taken by someone during intermission.

20. We have been assigned two chapters by Miss Romero.

SPEAKING APPLICATION

With a partner, choose a sentence from Practice 21.2I or 21.2J and say it aloud. If the sentence is in active voice, say it again in passive voice. If it is passive, change it to active. Your partner should do the same for another sentence.

WRITING APPLICATION

Write three sentences about a performance you have seen. Use only active voice.

Moods of Verbs

Verbs in English also use **mood** to describe the status of an action.

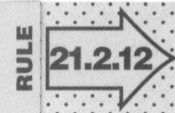
RULE 21.2.12

> There are three moods for English verbs: the **indicative mood,** the **subjunctive mood**, and the **imperative mood.**

The **indicative mood** indicates, or states, something. It is also used to ask questions. The **subjunctive mood** describes a wish or a condition that may be contrary to fact.

INDICATIVE MOOD	SUBJUNCTIVE MOOD
Tim **is** on my team.	I wish Bill **were** on my team too.
Kate **has** a new DVD.	If Susan **had brought** the DVD over, we could have watched it together.
I **would** like to be captain of the team.	If I **were** captain of the hockey team, I would be fair to everyone.

The subjunctive mood can be used to describe situations that are unlikely to happen or not possible. It is often used in clauses that begin with *if* or *that.* In these cases, use the plural form of the verb.

EXAMPLES   If I **were** you, I would run to the store before the snow.
(I am not you, so the situation is not possible.)

John wished that he **were going** to the game this week.
(He is not going until next month, so the situation is not possible.)

The **imperative** mood states a request or command and always uses the present tense. A mild imperative is followed by a period; a strong imperative is followed by an exclamation point.

EXAMPLES   **Call** me when you get home.
Watch out!

See Practice 21.2K
See Practice 21.2L

Notice that the subject, *you,* is understood but omitted.

PRACTICE 21.2K Identifying Moods of Verbs

Read the sentences. Then, write *indicative, subjunctive,* or *imperative* for the mood of the underlined verb in each sentence.

EXAMPLE If John <u>were</u> here now, what would he think?

ANSWER *subjunctive*

1. <u>Tell</u> your mother where you are going.
2. Ben <u>went</u> to the soccer game.
3. <u>Listen</u> to this lovely music!
4. I wish I <u>had heard</u> about this earlier.
5. Wade <u>sat</u> next to me at the play.
6. If I <u>were</u> you, I'd study for the quiz.
7. Please <u>stay</u> here for a little while.
8. We <u>went</u> out for a pizza last night.
9. If Jaime <u>were</u> captain, he would be fair.
10. Katherine <u>has</u> an appointment with her orthodontist today.

PRACTICE 21.2L Writing Sentences to Express Mood

Read the verbs. Write sentences using the different moods of verbs as indicated below.

EXAMPLE were (subjunctive)

ANSWER *If I were a contestant, I'd win the prize.*

11. turn (imperative)
12. disturbs (indicative)
13. had finished (subjunctive)
14. wanted (indicative)
15. answer (imperative)
16. had been (subjunctive)
17. stop (imperative)
18. were (subjunctive)
19. delivers (indicative)
20. take (imperative)

SPEAKING APPLICATION

Use sentences 1, 5, and 6 as models, and make up sentences of your own using the same moods. Take turns saying your sentences to a partner, who will identify the mood of each sentence.

WRITING APPLICATION

Use sentences 2, 3, and 9 as models, and write three sentences in which you use the same mood as in the model sentences.

21.3 Troublesome Verbs

The following verbs cause problems for many speakers and writers of English. Some of the problems involve using the principal parts of certain verbs. Others involve learning to distinguish between the meanings of certain confusing pairs of verbs.

(1) ain't   *Ain't* is not considered standard English. Avoid using it in speaking and in writing.

INCORRECT	He **ain't** the first to reach the mountain top.
CORRECT	He **isn't** the first to reach the mountain top.

(2) did, done   Remember that *done* is a past participle and can be used as a verb only with a helping verb such as *have* or *has*. Instead of using *done* without a helping verb, use *did*.

INCORRECT	I already **done** my English homework.
CORRECT	I already **did** my English homework.
	I **have** already **done** my English homework.

See Practice 21.3A

(3) dragged, drug   *Drag* is a regular verb. Its principal parts are *drag, dragging, dragged,* and *dragged. Drug* is never correct as the past or past participle of *drag*.

INCORRECT	The dog **drug** the ball across the yard.
CORRECT	The dog **dragged** the ball across the yard.

(4) gone, went   *Gone* is the past participle of *go* and can be used as a verb only with a helping verb such as *have* or *has. Went* is the past of *go* and is never used with a helping verb.

INCORRECT	James and Alice **gone** to the beach.
	We **should have went** along with them.
CORRECT	James and Alice **went** (or **have gone**) to the beach.
	We **should have gone** along with them.

(5) *have, of* The words *have* and *of* often sound very similar. Be careful not to write *of* when you mean the helping verb *have* or its contraction *'ve*.

INCORRECT	We should **of** waited for Tim.
CORRECT	We should **have** (or **should've**) waited for Tim.

(6) *lay, lie* These verbs look and sound almost alike and have similar meanings. The first step in distinguishing between *lay* and *lie* is to memorize the principal parts of both verbs.

PRINCIPAL PARTS	lay	laying	laid	laid
	lie	lying	lay	lain

Lay usually means "to put (something) down" or "to place (something)." It is almost always followed by a direct object. *Lie* means "to rest in a reclining position" or "to be situated." This verb is used to show the position of a person, place, or thing. *Lie* is never followed by a direct object.

EXAMPLES	The teacher **lays** her chalk on the desk.
	The doctor must **lie** down to rest.

Pay special attention to the past tense of *lay* and *lie*. *Lay* is the past tense of *lie*. The past tense of *lay* is *laid*.

PRESENT TENSE OF *LAY*	I **lay** the mug on the counter.
PAST TENSE OF *LAY*	The painter **laid** his brush on the easel.
PAST TENSE OF *LIE*	The dog **lay** down in his bed.

See Practice 21.3B

(7) *leave, let* *Leave* means "to allow to remain." *Let* means "to permit." Do not reverse the meanings.

INCORRECT	**Leave** me to review the exam.
	Let the answer sheet alone.
CORRECT	**Let** me review the exam.
	Leave the answer sheet alone.

(8) raise, rise *Raise* can mean "to lift (something) upward," "to build (something)," or "to increase (something)." It is usually followed by a direct object. *Rise* is not usually followed by a direct object. This verb means "to get up," "to go up," or "to be increased."

EXAMPLES   **Raise** the blinds so we can see the sun.

The runners must **rise** early to train.

(9) saw, seen *Seen* is a past participle and can be used as a verb only with a helping verb such as *have* or *has*.

INCORRECT   I **seen** the painting last month.

CORRECT   I **saw** the painting last month.

(10) says, said A common mistake in reporting what someone said is to use *says* (present tense) rather than *said* (past tense).

INCORRECT   The doctor **says**, "It is urgent."

CORRECT   The doctor **said**, "It is urgent."

(11) set, sit The first step in learning to distinguish between *set* and *sit* is to become thoroughly familiar with their principal parts.

PRINCIPAL PARTS			
set	setting	set	set
sit	sitting	sat	sat

Set means "to put (something) in a certain place or position." It is usually followed by a direct object. *Sit* usually means "to be seated" or "to rest." It is usually not followed by a direct object.

EXAMPLES   She **set** the plate on the table.

We **have set** the china safely in the cabinet.

Tyler **sat** in the reclining chair.

The eagle **has sat** on the branch since morning.

See Practice 21.3C
See Practice 21.3D

PRACTICE 21.3A ▷ **Using *Did* and *Done***

Read the sentences. Then, for each sentence, if *did* or *done* is used correctly, write *correct*. If it is not, write *incorrect*.

EXAMPLE   We done a group activity in class today.

ANSWER   *incorrect*

1. Jeremy has done an excellent job on his science fair project.
2. We did our work quietly in study hall.
3. I done everything you asked.
4. The artist did a sketch before he began to paint.
5. We done a good job.
6. Rolanda did her homework every day.
7. Charles has done his share of the work already.
8. That red car done a U-turn in the middle of the road.
9. Lynn did ten laps in the pool today.
10. Jane and Judie have already done the grocery shopping.

PRACTICE 21.3B ▷ **Using *Lay* and *Lie***

Read the sentences. Then, choose and write the correct form of the verb from the pair in parentheses.

EXAMPLE   The note (lay, lie) unread on the table.

ANSWER   *lay*

11. I would like to (lie, lay) down for a nap.
12. Those magazines have been (lying, laying) on the floor for a week.
13. Isabella was so tired that she (laid, lay) down right after dinner.
14. The cat has (laid, lain) in the sun all afternoon.
15. Mia (laid, lie) out two place settings at the table.
16. Natalie and Kelly (lay, lie) down in the snow and made snow angels.
17. The workers had (laid, lain) the foundation before starting on the wall.
18. (Lay, Lie) out all your notecards on your desk so you can rearrange them.
19. Earlier today, the children (laid, lay) the blocks in a circle.
20. Hal likes to (lie, lay) on the floor and read.

SPEAKING APPLICATION

With a partner, take turns using *did* and *done* in sentences.

WRITING APPLICATION

Write three sentences in which you correctly use different forms of *lay* and *lie*. You may use sentences from Practice 21.3B as models.

PRACTICE 21.3C > Using *Set* and *Sit*

Read the sentences. Then, choose and write the correct form of the verb from the pair in parentheses.

EXAMPLE   Please (sit, set) your bags on the table.

ANSWER   *set*

1. Rebecca (set, sat) the money on her dresser.

2. We had (set, sat) in the waiting room for almost an hour.

3. Sasha (sat, set) all the chairs in rows.

4. Will you stay and (sit, set) with me for a while?

5. Ray (set, sat) his GPS device on the table.

6. Grandfather (set, sat) his feet on a stool.

7. You can read a book while you're (sitting, setting) on the train.

8. Please (set, sit) down over there.

9. When you put the cookies in the oven, (set, sit) the timer for 10 minutes.

10. Let's (sit, set) in the shade under those trees.

PRACTICE 21.3D > Using Troublesome Verbs

Read the sentences. If the underlined verb is used correctly, write *correct*. If it is not, rewrite the sentence using the correct verb.

EXAMPLE   The girls have <u>went</u> for a walk.

ANSWER   *The girls have gone for a walk.*

11. <u>Let</u> your jacket on the bench while you mow the lawn.

12. Alicia <u>went</u> to basketball camp for a week.

13. I <u>seen</u> Rich at the baseball field yesterday.

14. We probably should <u>of</u> asked for directions.

15. In some yoga positions, you <u>raise</u> your arms above your head.

16. I saw Joey in the hall, and he <u>says</u>, "Help me make a spreadsheet."

17. Kelsey <u>dragged</u> the cursor down the menu to choose the file she wanted.

18. Wyatt <u>isn't</u> here yet.

19. <u>Let</u> the soup cool before you eat it.

20. The temperature <u>raised</u> 10 degrees in the last hour.

SPEAKING APPLICATION

With a partner, take turns describing a favorite activity. Use at least two of the troublesome verbs in Practices 21.3C and 21.3D. Your partner should confirm that you are using the verbs correctly.

WRITING APPLICATION

Write three sentences in which you use these verbs correctly: *raise, seen,* and *should have.*

USING PRONOUNS

CHAPTER 22

Make your writing easy for readers to follow by using pronouns correctly.

WRITE GUY *Jeff Anderson, M.Ed.*

WHAT DO YOU NOTICE?

Focus on the pronouns as you zoom in on these sentences from the book *Angela's Ashes* by Frank McCourt.

MENTOR TEXT

Patricia says she has two books by her bed. One is a poetry book and that's the one she loves.

Now, ask yourself the following questions:

- In the first sentence, which pronoun shows possession?
- What purpose does the pronoun *she* serve in these sentences?

In the first sentence, the pronoun *her* is possessive because it shows that the bed belongs to Patricia. The pronoun *she*, used in both sentences, refers to *Patricia*. Using *she* helps the author avoid repeating Patricia's name.

Grammar for Writers A writer can use pronouns to create sentences that flow smoothly. Keep an eye out for areas of your writing that could benefit from replacing nouns with pronouns.

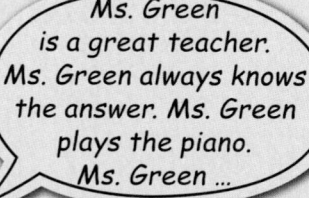

Ms. Green is a great teacher. Ms. Green always knows the answer. Ms. Green plays the piano. Ms. Green ...

I get the idea. She can do anything.

22.1 Recognizing Cases of Personal Pronouns

In Chapter 13, you learned that personal pronouns can be arranged in three groups: first person, second person, and third person. Pronouns can also be grouped by their **cases**.

RULE 22.1.1

English has three cases: nominative, objective, and possessive.

The chart below shows the personal pronouns grouped according to the three cases. The case shows whether a pronoun is being used as a subject, an object, or a possessive.

THE THREE CASES OF PERSONAL PRONOUNS	
NOMINATIVE CASE	**USE IN A SENTENCE**
I, we, you, he, she, it, they	subject of a verb predicate pronoun
OBJECTIVE CASE	**USE IN A SENTENCE**
me, us, you, him, her, it, them	indirect object object of a preposition direct object
POSSESSIVE CASE	**USE IN A SENTENCE**
my, mine, our, ours, your, yours, his, her, hers, its, their, theirs	to show ownership

SUBJECT OF A VERB	**We** wanted badly to see the movie.
PREDICATE PRONOUN	The oldest is **she**.
INDIRECT OBJECT	Please give **me** the notebook.
OBJECT OF A PREPOSITION	Please show the diploma to **me**.
DIRECT OBJECT	A soccer ball hit **her** on the head.
TO SHOW OWNERSHIP	That is **my** sweater, not **yours**.

See Practice 22.1A
See Practice 22.1B

PRACTICE 22.1A > **Identifying Cases of Personal Pronouns**

Read the sentences. Then, identify the case of each underlined personal pronoun by writing *nominative*, *objective*, or *possessive*.

EXAMPLE   They used to live on this street.

ANSWER   *nominative*

1. A reporter asked <u>him</u> some questions.
2. Do you know <u>her</u>?
3. <u>She</u> and <u>I</u> are best friends.
4. <u>We</u> try hard to be on time.
5. That sweatshirt on the floor is <u>his</u>.
6. Kerrie watched <u>them</u> through the window.
7. <u>He</u> and Glen are in the computer lab.
8. The manager thanked <u>us</u> for <u>our</u> help.
9. That seat is <u>yours</u>.
10. Kara brought <u>it</u> for <u>me</u>.

PRACTICE 22.1B > **Identifying Pronoun Cases and Uses**

Read the sentences. Write the case of each underlined pronoun. Then, label it *subject of a verb*, *predicate pronoun*, *direct object*, *indirect object*, or *object of a preposition*.

EXAMPLE   She and Tonia led the march.

ANSWER   *nominative, subject of a verb*

11. Please come to the pool with <u>me</u>.
12. <u>They</u> held a bake sale to raise money.
13. Selena waved to <u>them</u> from the window.
14. <u>She</u> did not answer my message.
15. Can you give <u>us</u> some information?
16. The first person to sign up was <u>he</u>.
17. Jay dribbled the ball and passed <u>it</u> to Boyd.
18. <u>We</u> went to the airport in a taxi.
19. Can you lend <u>her</u> your bicycle helmet?
20. The winner was <u>I</u>.

SPEAKING APPLICATION

With a partner, take turns describing one of your friends and telling something about him or her. Your partner should listen for and name the personal pronouns you use.

WRITING APPLICATION

Write a short paragraph about an event in which you participated. Underline your pronouns and identify the case of each.

The Nominative Case

Personal pronouns in the nominative case have two uses.

RULE
22.1.2

> **Use the nominative case for (1) the subject of a verb and (2) a predicate pronoun.**

Note that predicate pronouns follow linking verbs. Pronouns that follow linking verbs should be in the nominative case. The linking verbs are highlighted in orange in the examples below.

SUBJECTS	**She** hopes to be in the chorus.
	Excitedly, **they** prepared for the show.
PREDICATE PRONOUNS	It **was** **I** who suggested a hike.
	The best players **are** **she** and Frank.

Checking for Errors in the Nominative Case

People seldom forget to use the nominative case for a pronoun that is used by itself as a subject. Problems sometimes arise, however, when the pronoun is part of a compound subject.

INCORRECT	Chris and **me** played chess.
CORRECT	Chris and **I** played chess.

To make sure you are using the correct case of the pronoun in a compound subject, isolate the pronoun and the verb in the sentence. *Me played chess* is obviously wrong, so the nominative case *I* should be used instead.

If the sentence is in verb–subject order, rearrange it into subject–verb order, and then isolate the pronoun and verb.

INCORRECT	Are you and **her** going to the park?
REARRANGED	You and **?** are going to the park.
CORRECT	Are you and **she** going to the park?

See Practice 22.1.C
See Practice 22.1.D

The Objective Case

Personal pronouns in the objective case have three uses.

> Use the **objective** case for (1) a direct object, (2) an indirect object, and (3) the object of a preposition.

22.1.3 | RULE

DIRECT OBJECT	Joe's comment on the play upset **me**.
	The coach lectured **her**.
INDIRECT OBJECT	Tell **her** the plan.
	My friend gave **me** instructions to follow.
OBJECT OF PREPOSITION	Our class president voted for **him**.
	The bees swarmed around **me**.

Checking for Errors in the Objective Case

As with the nominative case, people seldom forget to use the objective case for a pronoun that is used by itself as a direct object, indirect object, or object of a preposition. Problems may arise, however, when the pronoun is part of a compound object.

INCORRECT	The bees swarmed around Patty and **I**.
CORRECT	The bees swarmed around Patty and **me**.

To make sure you are using the correct case of the pronoun in a compound object, use only the pronoun with the rest of the sentence. *The bees swarmed around I* is obviously wrong, so the objective case *me* should be used instead.

If the sentence is in verb–subject order, rearrange it into subject–verb order.

INCORRECT	Did my mother give Alice and **she** an apple?
REARRANGED	My mother gave Alice and **?** an apple.
CORRECT	Did my mother give Alice and **her** an apple?

See Practice 22.1E
See Practice 22.1F

The Possessive Case

Personal pronouns in the possessive case show ownership of one sort or another.

> Use the **possessive** case of personal pronouns before nouns to show possession. In addition, certain personal pronouns may also be used by themselves to indicate possession.

BEFORE NOUNS

The team won **its** race.

Chris held **my** baseball.

BY THEMSELVES

Is this ruler **yours** or **mine**?

Hers was the best essay.

Checking for Errors in the Possessive Case

Personal pronouns in the possessive case are never written with an apostrophe because they already show ownership. Keep this in mind, especially with possessive pronouns that end in *s*.

INCORRECT

This table is **our's**, not **their's**.

CORRECT

This table is **ours**, not **theirs**.

When the pronoun *it* is followed by an apostrophe and an *s*, the word becomes *it's*, which is a contraction of *it is*. The possessive pronoun *its* does not have an apostrophe.

CONTRACTION

It's going to snow today.

POSSESSIVE PRONOUN

The team loves **its** stadium.

To check if you need the contraction *it's* or the possessive pronoun *its*, substitute *it is* and reread the sentence.

INCORRECT

My jacket has lost **it's** button.

CORRECT

My jacket has lost **its** button.

See Practice 22.1G
See Practice 22.1H

PRACTICE 22.1C > **Identifying Nominative Case Pronouns**

Read the sentences. Write the correct pronoun from the choices in parentheses. Then, label the pronoun *subject of a verb* or *predicate pronoun*.

EXAMPLE   (She, Her) and I went together.

ANSWER   *She* — subject of a verb

1. (They, Them) and the others left early.

2. Have you and (she, her) finished your project?

3. You and (me, I) should start a band.

4. (He, Him) and (me, I) both read the same book.

5. The second- and third-place winners were Ramon and (he, him).

6. The last person to leave was (she, her).

7. (She, Her) and Hugh offered to decorate the gym for the dance.

8. The Bulldogs and (we, us) made it to the finals.

9. The person who called you was (he, him).

10. The culprits in the case were (they, them).

PRACTICE 22.1D > **Writing Sentences Using Nominative Case Pronouns**

Read the sentences. Then, rewrite each sentence, filling in the blank with a nominative case pronoun. Label the pronoun *subject of a verb* or *predicate pronoun*.

EXAMPLE   It was _____ who called Kelly last night.

ANSWER   *It was I who called Kelly last night.* — predicate pronoun

11. Max and _____ are the stars of the play.

12. _____ kids want to see them perform.

13. She and _____ are going to the dress rehearsal.

14. The best character in the play is _____.

15. Do you and _____ want to come with us tonight?

16. It is _____ who has to take care of the younger kids.

17. _____ and Veronica are well behaved.

18. He and _____ also go to bed very early.

19. It was _____ who wanted me to eat dinner at their house.

20. You and _____ have much in common.

SPEAKING APPLICATION

Tell a partner about something you and a friend did. Your partner should identify two pronouns in the nominative case.

WRITING APPLICATION

Write three sentences about a type of physical exercise you enjoy. Include a nominative case pronoun in each sentence. Then, underline each nominative case pronoun.

Read the sentences. Write an objective case pronoun to complete each sentence. Then, label each pronoun *direct object, indirect object*, or *object of a preposition*.

EXAMPLE   I asked _____ for directions.

ANSWER   *him* — direct object

1. Wayne told _____ his latest joke.

2. Between you and _____, I'd rather not go.

3. You can probably find _____ on the tennis court.

4. Meredith made dinner for Julian and _____.

5. Go with Colleen and _____ to the show.

6. I have some good news for you and _____.

7. Give _____ a turn at bat.

8. A puppy followed _____ to the bus stop.

9. The coach gave Manny and _____ some extra pointers.

10. There was a disagreement between Traci and _____.

Read each objective case pronoun. Then, write a complete sentence using the objective case pronoun. The pronoun should function as a direct object, an indirect object, or an object of a preposition, as indicated in parentheses.

EXAMPLE   Her (object of a preposition)

ANSWER   Her mother spoke to *her* about her behavior.

11. me (direct object)

12. her (indirect object)

13. him and her (object of a preposition)

14. him and me (object of a preposition)

15. them (indirect object)

16. him (direct object)

17. them (direct object)

18. me (indirect object)

19. him (object of a preposition)

20. her and me (object of a preposition)

SPEAKING APPLICATION

With a partner, take turns describing a recent gathering with family or friends. Use at least three objective case pronouns. Your partner should identify and check for correct usage of the objective case pronouns in your statements.

WRITING APPLICATION

Write a brief paragraph about pets. Use at least three objective case pronouns in your paragraph. Then, underline the objective case pronouns and label them *direct object, indirect object,* or *object of a preposition*.

PRACTICE 22.1G **Using Possessive Case
Pronouns**

Read the sentences. Write the correct pronoun
from the choices in parentheses.

EXAMPLE   That equipment is (their's, theirs).

ANSWER   *theirs*

1. (My, Mine) is the green bag.

2. Caleb's notebook is on the table with
   (your, yours).

3. The choice will be (hers, her's) alone.

4. My shirt is missing one of (its, it's) buttons.

5. If this is Gillian's sweater, then that one is
   (yours, your's).

6. (Ours, Our's) is the best float in the parade.

7. This car has had (its, it's) problems.

8. Dr. Swenson is (their, theirs) dentist.

9. The large sculpture on the corner table is
   (her, hers).

10. Here is (my, mine) mother now.

PRACTICE 22.1H **Supplying Possessive Case
Pronouns**

Read each possessive case pronoun. Then, write
a complete sentence using the possessive case
pronoun.

EXAMPLE   its

ANSWER   *The dog chewed on its toy bone.*

11. our

12. my

13. her

14. its

15. their

16. our

17. your

18. their

19. his

20. yours

SPEAKING APPLICATION

With a partner, take turns making statements
about the ownership of items in your
classroom. Your partner should identify the
possessive case pronouns in your statements
and make sure that they were used correctly.

WRITING APPLICATION

Write a brief paragraph about your most
prized possession, such as a piece of jewelry or
clothing, a book, or a photograph of someone
special. Describe the object, using at least
three possessive case pronouns.

Test Warm-Up

DIRECTIONS

Read the introduction and the passage that follows. Then, answer the questions to show that you can use and understand the function of nominative, objective, and possessive case pronouns in reading and writing.

Chloe wrote this paragraph about her younger brothers, who are twins. Read the paragraph and think about the changes you would suggest as a peer editor. When you finish reading, answer the questions that follow.

Seeing Double

(1) My younger brothers are identical twins. (2) There names are Zach and Jack. (3) Them and I get along just fine. (4) However, sometimes they work together or alone to play tricks on people. (5) One day, Zach, wearing a blue shirt, asked our uncle for money. (6) He gave Zach a dollar, and Zach walked out. (7) Five minutes later, a boy in a red shirt came in and asked for money. (8) Assuming it was Jack, our uncle handed he a dollar as well. (9) Just then, the real Jack walked into the room. (10) "Hey, I must be seeing double, Zach, give us one dollar back!" exclaimed our uncle.

1 What change, if any, should be made in sentence 2?

A Change *There* to **Their**

B Change *are* to **were**

C Change *and* to **or**

D Make no change

2 What change, if any, should be made in sentence 3?

F Change *I* to **me**

G Change *Them* to **They**

H Change *Them and I* to **Us all**

J Make no change

3 What is the BEST way to revise sentence 8?

A Assuming it was Jack, our uncle handed him a dollar as well.

B Assuming it was Jack, our uncle handed Jack a dollar as well.

C Assuming it was him, our uncle handed Jack a dollar as well.

D Assuming it was him, our uncle handed him a dollar as well.

4 The meaning of sentence 10 can be clarified by changing the word *us* to —

F my

G our

H him

J me

Cases of *Who* and *Whom* The pronouns *who* and *whom* are often confused. *Who* is a nominative case pronoun, and *whom* is an objective case pronoun. *Who* and *whom* have two common uses in sentences: They can be used in questions or to begin subordinate clauses in complex sentences.

> **Use *who* for the subject of a verb. Use *whom* for (1) the direct object of a verb and (2) the object of a preposition.**

22.1.5 RULE

You will often find *who* used as the subject of a question. *Who* may also be used as the subject of a subordinate clause in a complex sentence.

SUBJECT OF A QUESTION	**Who** scored the most goals?
SUBJECT OF A SUBORDINATE CLAUSE	I admire the player **who** scored the most goals.

The following examples show *whom* used in questions.

DIRECT OBJECT	**Whom** did you see at the dinner?
OBJECT OF PREPOSITION	From **whom** is he getting a new puppy?

Questions that include *whom* are generally in inverted word order, with the verb appearing before the subject. If you reword the first example in subject–verb word order, you will see that *whom* is the direct object of the verb *did see: You did see whom?* In the second example, *whom* is the object of the preposition *from: He is getting the new puppy from whom?*

Subordinate clauses that begin with *whom* can be rearranged to show that the pronoun is a direct object.

EXAMPLE	The substitute teacher was not **whom** I expected.
REARRANGED SUBORDINATE CLAUSE	I expected **whom**?

See Practice 22.1I
See Practice 22.1J

PRACTICE 22.1I ▷ **Using *Who* and *Whom***

Read the sentences. Write the pronoun in parentheses that correctly completes each sentence.

EXAMPLE   (Who, Whom) did you tell first?

ANSWER   *Whom*

1. We wanted to know (who, whom) was there.

2. (Whom, Who) taught you to play a guitar?

3. (Who, Whom) do you think we should nominate?

4. To (whom, who) should I address the letter?

5. (Who, Whom) could possibly want that old thing?

6. I do not know (whom, who) you're referring to.

7. The one (who, whom) gave me this locket is my Aunt Cecile.

8. I don't know (who, whom) I can ask for advice.

9. (Whom, Who) did you hear that from?

10. (Who, Whom) did he pick for the team?

PRACTICE 22.1J ▷ **Revising to Correct *Who* and *Whom***

Read the sentences. Then, if a sentence uses *who* or *whom* incorrectly, rewrite the sentence with the correct pronoun form. If a sentence has no pronoun error, write *correct*.

EXAMPLE   Who did you vote for?

ANSWER   *Whom did you vote for?*

11. Do you know whom is the fastest runner on the team?

12. Portia goes to Dr. Shah, who is an orthodontist.

13. Whom did you sit with at the game?

14. This is my friend Madelyn, who I told you about.

15. Did you see who that was?

16. Who are you looking for?

17. Who forgot to put the lid back onto the jar?

18. Luther is someone who you can always count on.

19. Who is that gift for?

20. Please see whom is at the door.

SPEAKING APPLICATION

With a partner, take turns asking two questions: one beginning with *who* and one beginning with *whom*. Your partner should identify how these pronouns are used in your sentences.

WRITING APPLICATION

Use sentences 2 and 3 as models, and write two questions using *who* and *whom* correctly.

Singular and Plural Verbs

Like nouns, verbs have singular and plural forms. Problems involving number in verbs normally involve the third-person forms in the present tense (*she wants, they want*) and certain forms of the verb *be* (*I am, he is* or *was, we are* or *were*).

The chart shows all the basic forms of several different verbs in the present tense.

SINGULAR AND PLURAL VERBS IN THE PRESENT TENSE		
SINGULAR		PLURAL
First and Second Person	**Third Person**	**First, Second, and Third Person**
(I, you) send	(he, she, it) sends	(we, you, they) send
(I, you) go	(he, she, it) goes	(we, you, they) go
(I, you) look	(he, she, it) looks	(we, you, they) look
(I, you) dance	(he, she, it) dances	(we, you, they) dance
(I, you) visit	(he, she, it) visits	(we, you, they) visit
(I, you) work	(he, she, it) works	(we, you, they) work
(I, you) run	(he, she, it) runs	(we, you, they) run
(I, you) discuss	(he, she, it) discusses	(we, you, they) discuss
(I, you) vote	(he, she, it) votes	(we, you, they) vote
(I, you) choose	(he, she, it) chooses	(we, you, they) choose
(I, you) learn	(he, she, it) learns	(we, you, they) learn

Notice that the form of the verb changes only in the third-person singular, when an *-s* or *-es* is added to the verb. Unlike nouns, which usually become plural when *-s* or *-es* is added, verbs with *-s* or *-es* added to them are singular.

The helping verb *be* may also indicate whether a verb is singular or plural. The following chart shows only those forms of the verb *be* that are always singular.

FORMS OF THE HELPING VERB *BE* THAT ARE ALWAYS SINGULAR			
am	is	was	has been

Making Verbs Agree With Singular and Plural Subjects

To check subject–verb agreement, determine the number of the subject. Then, make sure the verb has the same number.

SINGULAR
SUBJECT
AND VERB

Jeff **enjoys** swimming.

She **was** at the park earlier today.

PLURAL
SUBJECT
AND VERB

They **enjoy** swimming.

Joggers **were** at the park earlier today.

A prepositional phrase that comes between a subject and its verb does not affect subject–verb agreement.

Often, a subject is separated from its verb by a prepositional phrase. In these cases, it is important to remember that the object of a preposition is never the subject of a sentence.

INCORRECT   The **arrival** of the fire trucks **have caused** much excitement at the parade.

CORRECT   The **arrival** of the fire trucks **has caused** much excitement at the parade.

See Practice 23.1A
See Practice 23.1B

INCORRECT   The **cheers** of the crowd **was heard** outside.

CORRECT   The **cheers** of the crowd **were heard** outside.

In the first example, the subject is *arrival*, not *fire trucks* which is the object of the preposition *of*. Because *arrival* is singular, the singular verb *has caused* must be used. In the second example, the subject is the plural *cheers*, not *crowd*; therefore, it takes the plural verb *were heard*.

PRACTICE 23.1A > **Making Subjects and Verbs Agree**

Read the sentences. Write the verb in parentheses that agrees with the subject. Then, label the subject *singular*, *plural* or *both*. Be sure to think about prepositional phrases and their influence on subject-verb agreement.

EXAMPLE   Usually, ducks (swim, swims) in this pond.

ANSWER   *swim — plural*

1. You (was, were) early today!

2. Lisa (recognize, recognizes) the backpack as her own.

3. The computers in the lab (is, are) available for use.

4. Where (is, are) my keys?

5. One of these machines (is, are) not working.

6. My teeth (chatter, chatters) in the cold.

7. These boots (cost, costs) too much.

8. Some word problems in math (is, are) challenging.

9. There (is, are) twenty-five students in this room.

10. That bag of pretzels (is, are) not enough.

PRACTICE 23.1B > **Revising for Subject-Verb Agreement**

Read the sentences. Then, if a sentence has an error in subject-verb agreement, rewrite the sentence correctly. Read your corrected sentences to your partner and have your partner confirm that the subject-verb agreement is correct. If a sentence has no error, write *correct*.

EXAMPLE   Craters on the moon is visible through telescopes.

ANSWER   *Craters on the moon are visible through telescopes.*

11. The pictures hanging on the wall is dusty.

12. Was you able to find what you needed?

13. Members of the committee are wearing nametags.

14. There's already five people waiting for the door to open.

15. The benches in the garden are wet.

16. The list of winners are posted on the bulletin board.

17. The decision of the judges is final.

18. Here is the groceries you wanted.

19. Where was the playoffs held?

20. One of the guides are able to help you.

SPEAKING APPLICATION

With a partner, take turns summarizing a story or book you read, using the present tense of the verbs and making sure the verbs agree with your subjects. Include a prepositional phrase in at least one of your sentences, and have your partner identify the phrase.

WRITING APPLICATION

Use sentences 4 and 5 as models, and write two sentences, making sure the verbs agree with the subjects. Be sure to think about prepositional phrases and their influence on subject-verb agreement.

Making Verbs Agree With Collective Nouns

Collective nouns—such as *assembly, audience, class, club,* and *committee*—name groups of people or things. Collective nouns are challenging as subjects because they can take either singular or plural verbs. The number of the verb depends on the meaning of the collective noun in the sentence.

Use a singular verb with a collective noun acting as a single unit. Use a plural verb when the individual members of the group are acting individually.

SINGULAR The **committee** **votes** on the topics.

PLURAL The **committee** **have split** the responsibilities.

SINGULAR The dance **class** **plans** a recital.

PLURAL The dance **class** **were pleased** with their performances.

SINGULAR The garden **club** **grows** vegetables and flowers.

PLURAL The garden **club** **have chosen** to plant vegetables and flowers.

SINGULAR The scout **troop** **marches** on Main Street.

PLURAL The scout **troop** **have prepared** different sandwiches for lunch.

SINGULAR The **team** **cheers** after the game.

PLURAL The **team** **scatter** across the playing field.

See Practice 23.1C
See Practice 23.1D

PRACTICE 23.1C > Making Verbs Agree With Collective Nouns

Read the sentences. Then, write the verb in parentheses that agrees with the subject.

EXAMPLE   The audience (is, are) waiting for the concert to begin.

ANSWER   *is*

1. The team (arrive, arrives) separately before the game.

2. Our family (try, tries) to eat dinner together every evening.

3. A flock of geese (land, lands) near the river every day.

4. The jury (find, finds) the defendant guilty.

5. The board of directors (don't, doesn't) always agree among themselves.

6. The computer club (discuss, discusses) new applications.

7. A group of older kids (hang, hangs) out in the pizza parlor.

8. The army (need, needs) more volunteers.

9. The flight crew (is, are) attentive to the passengers.

10. The choir (sing, sings) every Sunday.

PRACTICE 23.1D > Revising for Agreement Between Verbs and Collective Nouns

Read the sentences. Then, if a sentence has an error in subject-verb agreement, rewrite the sentence correctly. If a sentence has no error, write *correct*.

EXAMPLE   The orchestra give a free concert every year.

ANSWER   *The orchestra gives a free concert every year.*

11. The herd are waiting to be fed.

12. This bunch of radishes look wilted.

13. The navy sail around the world.

14. The faculty has a meeting at 2:30 P.M.

15. The band are rehearsing in separate rooms.

16. The crowd are eager for the candidate to appear.

17. At summer camp, the scout troop learns survival skills.

18. The staff at the fitness center are very helpful.

19. The committee don't always follow the agenda at meetings.

20. The cheerleading squad practices twice a week.

SPEAKING APPLICATION

With a partner, tell about the activities of a group you belong to or know about. Use at least two collective nouns, such as *group*, *team*, and *club*, as subjects in your sentences, and be sure your verbs agree.

WRITING APPLICATION

Write three sentences in the present tense, using these collective nouns as subjects: *crew*, *band*, and *crowd*.

Making Verbs Agree With Compound Subjects

A **compound subject** refers to two or more subjects that share a verb. Compound subjects are connected by conjunctions such as *and, or,* or *nor.*

EXAMPLES
The **museums** and **historical sites** in New York
            compound subject
City **attract** many visitors.
      plural verb

Either **Jamal** or **Catherine** **knows** the way to the
            compound subject   singular
                                          verb
train station.

Neither the **Statue of Liberty** nor **Ellis Island**
                        compound subject
disappoints tourists.
  singular
  verb

A number of rules can help you choose the right verb to use with a compound subject.

Compound Subjects Joined by *And*

RULE 23.1.4

> When a compound subject is connected by *and,* the verb that follows is usually plural.

EXAMPLE
Dallas and **Houston** **are** my favorite Texas cities.
compound subject   plural verb

There is an exception to this rule: If the parts of a compound subject are thought of as one person or thing, the subject is singular and takes a singular verb.

EXAMPLES
Bacon and eggs **is** my favorite breakfast.
compound subject   singular
                    verb

Cream and sugar **is** in the kitchen.
compound subject   singular
                    verb

Compound Subjects Joined by *Or* or *Nor*

> When two singular subjects are joined by *or* or *nor,* use a singular verb. When two plural subjects are joined by *or* or *nor,* use a plural verb.

RULE 23.1.5

SINGULAR A **bus** or a **subway** **provides** good
compound subject   singular verb
transportation to the city.

PLURAL Neither **children** nor **adults** **like** to be told what
compound subject   plural verb
to do.

In the first example, *or* joins two singular subjects. Although two vehicles make up the compound subject, the subject does not take a plural verb. Either a bus or a subway provides good transportation, not both of them.

> When a compound subject is made up of one singular and one plural subject joined by *or* or *nor,* the verb agrees with the subject closer to it.

RULE 23.1.6

EXAMPLES Either the **monuments** or the **White House**
plural subject   singular subject

is closed to visitors today.
singular verb

Either the **White House** or the **monuments**
singular subject   plural subject

are closed to visitors today.
plural verb

See Practice 23.1E

Agreement in Inverted Sentences

In most sentences, the subject comes before the verb. Sometimes, however, this order is turned around, or **inverted.** In other sentences, the helping verb comes before the subject even though the main verb follows the subject.

When a subject comes after the verb, the subject and verb still must agree with each other in number.

EXAMPLE

Do the historical **sites** in Philadelphia sound
plural verb   plural subject

exciting to you?

Sentences Beginning With a Prepositional Phrase

In sentences that begin with a prepositional phrase, the object of the preposition may look like a subject, even though it is not.

EXAMPLE

Along the shore **were** many gray **seagulls**.
plural verb   plural subject

In this example, the plural verb *were* agrees with the plural subject *seagulls.* The singular noun *shore* is the object of the preposition *along.*

Sentences Beginning With *There* or *Here*

Sentences beginning with *there* or *here* are almost always in inverted word order.

EXAMPLES

There **were** several **books** about the economy.
plural verb   plural subject

Here **is** the latest **book** about the economy.
singular verb   singular subject

The contractions *there's* and *here's* both contain the singular verb *is: there is* and *here is.* Do not use these contractions as plural subjects.

INCORRECT   Here**'s** the **books** for the library.

CORRECT   Here **are** the **books** for the library.

Questions With Inverted Word Order

Many questions are also written in inverted word order.

EXAMPLE

Where **are** the **books** for the library?
plural verb   plural subject

See Practice 23.1F

PRACTICE 23.1E **Making Verbs Agree With Compound Subjects**

Read the sentences. Then, write the verb in parentheses that agrees with the subject.

EXAMPLE   A book and an apple (is, are) lying on the table.

ANSWER   *are*

1. Either Dad or Mom (make, makes) breakfast every morning.

2. English and math (is, are) my favorite subjects.

3. Neither the baseball bats nor the gloves (was, were) put away.

4. Sarah or her sister (take, takes) the dog for a walk every day.

5. The book and papers (stay, stays) in the locker.

6. Neither the jacket nor the shoes (fit, fits) well.

7. Carrie, Gillian, or Hugh (write, writes) the blog each day.

8. Mrs. Carter and her daughters often (dress, dresses) alike.

9. The chairs and the table (has, have) not been moved in yet.

10. E-mail and text messaging (make, makes) communication almost instantaneous.

PRACTICE 23.1F **Revising for Agreement Between Verbs and Compound Subjects**

Read the sentences. Then, if a sentence has an error in subject-verb agreement, rewrite the sentence correctly. If a sentence has no error, write *correct*.

EXAMPLE   Neither Billy nor John have arrived yet.

ANSWER   *Neither Billy nor John has arrived yet.*

11. Joe and Ted always comes early.

12. Either Jake or Sophia collects the papers today.

13. Jeff or the dog have tracked mud onto the floor.

14. Milk or lemon is used with tea.

15. Either my watch or that clock are fast.

16. In the center of the park is a playground and a basketball court.

17. Either Regina or Zoe own that scarf.

18. Neither the plumber nor the electrician is here.

19. Eva's positive outlook and her willingness to help wins her many friends.

20. That old barn and farmhouse seems deserted.

SPEAKING APPLICATION

With a partner, take turns discussing things in the classroom, using sentence 3 as a model. Your partner should check for subject-verb agreement in your sentences.

WRITING APPLICATION

Use sentences 17, 18, and 19 as models, and write three sentences with correct subject-verb agreement.

Verb Agreement With Indefinite Pronouns

Indefinite pronouns refer to people, places, or things in a general way.

> When an **indefinite pronoun** is the subject of a sentence, the verb must agree in number with the pronoun.

INDEFINITE PRONOUNS				
SINGULAR			**PLURAL**	**SINGULAR OR PLURAL**
anybody	everyone	nothing	both	all
anyone	everything	one	few	any
anything	much	other	many	more
each	neither	somebody	several	most
either	nobody	someone	others	none
everybody	no one	something		some

Indefinite Pronouns That Are Always Singular

Indefinite pronouns that are always singular take singular verbs. Do not be misled by a prepositional phrase that follows an indefinite pronoun. The singular verb agrees with the indefinite pronoun, not with the object of the preposition.

EXAMPLES   **Each** of the soccer team uniforms **is** red
            singular subject   singular verb
            and gold.

            Either of the sweaters on the bed **is** warm.
            singular subject   singular verb

            Everyone in the theater **was** delighted
            singular subject   singular verb
            by the play.

            Each of the boys **takes** guitar lessons.
            singular subject   singular verb

Indefinite Pronouns That Are Always Plural

Indefinite pronouns that are always plural are used with plural verbs.

EXAMPLE **Both** of my sisters **are going** to the concert.
plural subject   plural verb

Many of my friends **are coming** to cheer for me at
plural subject   plural verb

my first track meet.

Several **have started** to research their reports.
plural subject   plural verb

Few **are happy** with the new uniforms.
plural subject   plural verb

Indefinite Pronouns That May Be Either Singular or Plural

Many indefinite pronouns can take either a singular or a plural verb.

> **The number of the indefinite pronoun is the same as the number of its referent, or the noun to which it refers.**

The indefinite pronoun is singular if the referent is singular. If the referent is plural, the indefinite pronoun is plural.

SINGULAR   **Some** of the **juice** **is** frozen.

PLURAL   **Some** of the **oranges** **are** frozen, too.

In the examples above, *some* is singular when it refers to *juice*, but plural when it refers to *oranges*.

SINGULAR   **All** of my **spaghetti** **is** gone.

PLURAL   **All** of these **meatballs** **are** for you.

See Practice 23.1G
See Practice 23.1H

In these examples, *all* is singular when it refers to *spaghetti*, but plural when it refers to *meatballs*.

PRACTICE 23.1G > **Making Verbs Agree With Indefinite Pronouns**

Read the sentences. Then, write the verb in parentheses that agrees with the subject.

EXAMPLE   Each of the students (was, were) eager to begin.

ANSWER   *was*

1. Nobody (want, wants) to take responsibility.

2. Some of these sandwiches (is, are) vegetarian.

3. Both of my sisters (sing, sings) in the chorus.

4. Everyone in the class (is, are) present today.

5. Anyone (is, are) able to solve that problem.

6. All of the computers (is, are) being used right now.

7. Many of the contestants (has, have) excellent qualifications.

8. If someone (answer, answers) the ad, let me know.

9. Most of the money (has, have) been spent.

10. Neither of the jobs (require, requires) much experience.

PRACTICE 23.1H > **Revising for Agreement Between Verbs and Indefinite Pronouns**

Read the sentences. Then, if a sentence has an error in subject-verb agreement, rewrite the sentence correctly. If a sentence has no error, write *correct*.

EXAMPLE   Neither were willing to concede defeat.

ANSWER   *Neither was willing to concede defeat.*

11. Several of the batteries has to be replaced.

12. Nobody like to be on the losing side.

13. Either are a good title for your story.

14. Many of these used books are in good condition.

15. Some of these poems are pretty good.

16. All of the grapes has been eaten.

17. A few of my friends goes to a different school.

18. Most of the jewelry on display were quite expensive.

19. None of these games are much fun.

20. Any of your drawings are good enough to be exhibited.

SPEAKING APPLICATION

With a partner, tell about something in your class, using sentence 4 as a model. Your partner should listen for and confirm that your verb agrees with your subject.

WRITING APPLICATION

Use sentences 10, 13, and 19 as models, and write three sentences of your own with correct subject-verb agreement.

23.2 Agreement Between Pronouns and Antecedents

Find It/ FIX IT

17

Grammar
Game Plan

An **antecedent** is the word or words for which a pronoun stands. A pronoun's antecedent may be a noun, a group of words acting as a noun, or even another pronoun. As with subjects and verbs, pronouns should agree with their antecedents.

WRITING COACH

Online

www.phwritingcoach.com

Grammar Practice
Practice your grammar skills with Writing Coach Online.

Grammar Games
Test your knowledge of grammar in this fast-paced interactive video game.

Making Personal Pronouns and Antecedents Agree

Person tells whether a pronoun refers to the person speaking (first person), the person spoken to (second person), or the person, place, or thing spoken about (third person). **Number** tells whether the pronoun is singular or plural. **Gender** tells whether a third-person-singular antecedent is masculine or feminine.

> **A personal pronoun must agree with its antecedent in person, number, and gender.**

23.2.1

RULE

EXAMPLE   I told **Betsy** to bring a sweater with **her**.

In this example, the pronoun *her* is third person and singular. It agrees with its feminine antecedent, *Betsy.*

Avoiding Shifts in Person
A personal pronoun must have the same person as its antecedent. Otherwise, the meaning of the sentence is unclear.

INCORRECT   The **drivers** know **we** must check the speed limit on local streets.
(Who must check the speed limit? *We* must.)

CORRECT   The **drivers** know **they** must check the speed limit on local streets.
(Who must check the speed limit? *The drivers* must.)

As you can see, a shift in the person of the personal pronoun can make it unclear who is going to check the speed limit.

Avoiding Problems With Number and Gender

Making pronouns and antecedents agree in number and gender can be difficult. Problems may arise when the antecedent is a collective noun, when the antecedent is a compound joined by *or* or *nor,* or when the gender of the antecedent is not known.

Making Pronouns Agree in Number With Collective Nouns
Collective nouns are challenging because they can take either singular or plural pronouns. The number of the pronoun depends on the meaning of the collective noun in the sentence.

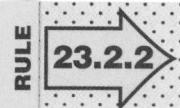

> Use a singular pronoun to refer to a collective noun that names a group that is acting as a single unit. Use a plural pronoun to refer to a collective noun when the members or parts of a group are acting individually.

SINGULAR   The **class** **showed** **its** appreciation with applause.

PLURAL   The **class** **voted** for **their** favorite books.

In the first example above, the class is acting as a single unit when it applauds, so the singular pronoun, *its,* refers to *class.* In the second example, each member of the class is voting individually, so the plural pronoun, *their,* refers to *class.*

Making Pronouns Agree in Number With Compound Nouns

> Use a singular personal pronoun to refer to two or more singular antecedents joined by *or* or *nor.* Use a plural pronoun with two or more singular antecedents joined by *and.*

Two or more singular antecedents joined by *or* or *nor* must have a singular pronoun, just as they must have a singular verb.

INCORRECT   **Andrew** or **Jeff** will take **their** basketball.

CORRECT   **Andrew** or **Jeff** will take **his** basketball.

CORRECT   **Andrew** and **Jeff** will take **their** basketballs.

Avoiding Problems With Gender

When the gender of a third-person-singular antecedent is not known, you can make the pronoun agree with its antecedent in one of three ways:

(1) Use *he or she, him or her,* or *his or hers.*

(2) Rewrite the sentence so that the antecedent and pronoun are both plural.

(3) Rewrite the sentence to eliminate the pronoun.

Traditionally, the masculine pronouns *he* and *his* have been used to stand for both males and females. Today, using *he or she* and *him or her* is preferred. If any of these corrections seem awkward to you, rewrite the sentence.

Making Personal Pronouns and Indefinite Pronouns Agree

Indefinite pronouns are words such as *each, everybody, either,* and *one.* Pay special attention to the number of a personal pronoun when the antecedent is a singular indefinite pronoun.

> **Use a singular personal pronoun when its antecedent is a singular indefinite pronoun.**

23.2.4 RULE

Do not be misled by a prepositional phrase that follows an indefinite pronoun. The personal pronoun agrees with the indefinite pronoun, not with the object of the preposition.

INCORRECT **One** of the dogs has lost **their** bone.

CORRECT **One** of the dogs has lost **its** bone.

INCORRECT **Everyone** in the history class wanted to tell about **their** idea.

CORRECT **Everyone** in the history class wanted to tell about **his or her** idea.

See Practice 23.2A
See Practice 23.2B
See Practice 23.2C
See Practice 23.2D

CORRECT **All** of the students in the history class told about **their** ideas.

Using Correct Antecedents

Read these simple, compound, and complex sentences. Then, rewrite the sentences to correct pronoun-antecedent agreement. Circle the pronoun and underline the antecedent.

EXAMPLE   When we went to the beach, she lent me our sunscreen.

ANSWER   *When we went to the beach, she lent me her sunscreen.*

1. Alex lent us their car that was about to run out of gas.

2. Erin wanted us to meet their friend, who is about to enter our class.

3. After the movie ended, everyone told their impressions.

4. No one wanted to give up their Saturday, so we rescheduled the meeting.

5. The kitten curled up their little body and slept in front of the fire.

6. I lost its CD, so I had to buy her a replacement.

7. Since it stopped raining, we can ride its bikes.

8. Laslo offered to help, but the team preferred to work on their own.

9. Did you forget to bring me our scarf?

10. The students know they must study, and they form our own study groups.

Writing Sentences With Pronoun-Antecedent Agreement

Write complete sentences with pronoun-antecedent agreement. Use each subject provided and add the correct pronoun. Write the type of sentence that is indicated in parentheses.

EXAMPLE   Everyone (compound sentence)

ANSWER   *Everyone offered his or her suggestion, and we decided to vote.*

11. The teachers (simple sentence)

12. Each (simple sentence)

13. The musicians (compound sentence)

14. Billy (complex sentence)

15. Everyone (compound sentence)

16. The dog (complex sentence)

17. One (complex sentence)

18. Lisa and Margot (complex sentence)

19. All (compound sentence)

20. The orchestra (simple sentence)

SPEAKING APPLICATION

Use the sentences on this page as models. With a partner, make up one simple, one compound, and one complex sentence. Your partner should check that your pronouns and antecedents agree and then tell you a sentence.

WRITING APPLICATION

Write one simple, one compound, and one complex sentence about your favorite type of music. Read your sentences aloud to a partner. Work with your partner to correct any sentences that have incorrectly identified antecedents.

PRACTICE 23.2C ▶ **Revising for Pronoun-Antecedent Agreement**

Read the sentences. Rewrite each sentence choosing the correct pronoun in parentheses. Circle the pronoun and underline the antecedent.

EXAMPLE Neither Janie nor Maria has returned (their, her) books to the library.

ANSWER *Neither Janie nor Maria has returned (her) books to the library.*

1. Each boy paid for (their, his) own lunch, and each boy bought a sandwich.

2. If a person asks for directions, please try to help (them, him or her).

3. Everyone should fasten (their, his or her) seat belt.

4. All students choose (their, our) classes.

5. Has Marco or Dina given (their, his or her) oral report yet?

6. If there is time, some of the students may read (their, our) poems aloud.

7. Both Andrew and Arnold were wearing (their, his) new team caps.

8. None of these pencils have (their, his) erasers, and all of them are red.

9. Everyone should cast (his or her, their) vote.

10. Each student has (his or her, their) own goals.

PRACTICE 23.2D ▶ **Writing Sentences With Pronoun-Antecedent Agreement**

Write complete sentences with pronoun-antecedent agreement. Use each subject provided and add the correct pronoun. Write the type of sentence that is indicated in parentheses.

EXAMPLE The class (complex sentence)

ANSWER *While the class wrote their reports, the teacher graded test papers.*

11. The group (simple sentence)

12. All (compound sentence)

13. Each (complex sentence)

14. Esther or Briana (simple sentence)

15. Tanya and Victor (complex sentence)

16. Everyone (complex sentence)

17. The community (simple sentence)

18. The voters (compound sentence)

19. The police department (complex sentence)

20. The police officers (simple sentence)

SPEAKING APPLICATION

With a partner, take turns discussing advantages and disadvantages of pets. Using correct pronoun-antecedent agreement, speak in a variety of simple, compound, and complex sentences. Your partner should listen for pronoun-antecedent agreement.

WRITING APPLICATION

Write one simple, one compound, and one complex sentence about a person or group you admire. Be sure to use correct pronoun-antecedent agreement. Have a partner read your sentences aloud and check for agreement.

Test Warm-Up

DIRECTIONS

Read the introduction and the passage that follows. Then, answer the questions to show that you can use a variety of complete sentences (e.g., simple, compound, complex) that include correctly identified antecedents in reading and writing.

Mario wrote this paragraph about his favorite teacher. Read the paragraph and think about the changes you would suggest as a peer editor. When you finish reading, answer the questions that follow.

Teacher of the Year

(1) This year, the school will vote for their Teacher of the Year. (2) Everyone in the school is allowed to give their opinion. (3) Most of us believe that Mr. Fernandez, who teaches Spanish and Latin, is the best because he is patient and fun. (4) For example, when the new words in a chapter is hard, Mr. Fernandez draws pictures to help us remember it. (5) Those strategies really work, and they make learning fun. (6) We hope Mr. Fernandez wins the award. (7) Our class agrees that Mr. Fernandez is its Teacher of the Year.

---

1 What change, if any, should be made in sentence 1?

A Change *their* to **his or her**

B Change *their* to **its**

C Change *their* to **your**

D Make no change

2 What change, if any, should be made in sentence 2?

F Change *their* to **his or her**

G Change *their* to **its**

H Change *their* to **your**

J Make no change

3 What is the BEST way to revise sentence 4?

A For example, when the new words in a chapter are hard, Mr. Fernandez draws pictures to help us remember it.

B For example, when the new words in a chapter is hard, Mr. Fernandez draws pictures to help us remember them.

C For example, when the new words in a chapter are hard, Mr. Fernandez draws pictures to help us remember them.

D For example, when the new words in a chapter is hard, Mr. Fernandez draws a picture to help us remember him.

4 The meaning of sentence 7 can be clarified by changing the word *its* to —

F his or her

G their

H our

J your

USING MODIFIERS

Using adjectives and adverbs to make comparisons will help you create strong images in your writing.

WRITE GUY *Jeff Anderson, M.Ed.*

WHAT DO YOU NOTICE?

Search for modifiers as you zoom in on these sentences from the story "Ribbons" by Laurence Yep.

MENTOR TEXT

> Suddenly I felt as if there were an invisible ribbon binding us, tougher than silk and satin, stronger even than steel; and it joined her to Mom and Mom to me.

Now, ask yourself the following questions:

- Which adjective modifies the noun *ribbon*?
- Why does the author add the ending *-er* to the words *tough* and *strong*?

The adjective *invisible* modifies the noun *ribbon*. The author uses the ending *-er* to make the comparative form of the adjectives *tough* and *strong*. *Tougher* compares the ribbon to silk and then to satin, and *stronger* compares the ribbon to steel.

Grammar for Writers Writers use the forms of comparison to create more precise descriptions. Use the different forms of adjectives to paint vivid images for readers.

This is the longest quiz I've ever taken.

Wait until you see tomorrow's quiz! It's even longer.

24.1 Comparisons Using Adjectives and Adverbs

You may recall that adjectives and adverbs are **modifiers**. Adjectives can modify nouns or pronouns. Adverbs can modify verbs, adjectives, or other adverbs. You can use modifiers to make comparisons.

Three Forms of Comparison

Modifiers change their form when they show comparison. These different forms are called **forms,** or **degrees, of comparison.**

RULE 24.1.1

> Most adjectives and adverbs have three forms, or degrees, of comparison: **positive, comparative,** and **superlative.**

The **positive degree** is used when no comparison is being made. This is the form of a word that is listed in a dictionary. The **comparative degree** is used when two items are being compared. The **superlative degree** is used when three or more items are being compared. When the superlative degree is used, the article *the* is often added.

DEGREE	ADJECTIVE	ADVERB
Positive	The family moved into a large home.	Tom swam fast.
Comparative	Soon, they will need a larger home.	Tom swam faster than Joe.
Superlative	The family is living in the largest home on the street.	Of the three swimmers, Tom is the fastest.

Like verbs, adjectives and adverbs change forms in different ways. Some adjectives and adverbs change in regular ways, or according to predictable patterns. As you can see in the chart above, *large* and *fast* form their comparative and superlative degrees regularly, by adding *-er* and *-est* to their positive form.

Regular Modifiers With One or Two Syllables

Most modifiers are **regular**—their degrees of comparison are formed in predictable ways.

> **Use *-er* or *more* to form the comparative degree and use *-est* or *most* to form the superlative degree of most one- and two-syllable modifiers.**

COMPARATIVE AND SUPERLATIVE DEGREES FORMED WITH *-ER* AND *-EST*		
POSITIVE	COMPARATIVE	SUPERLATIVE
deep	deeper	deepest
fast	faster	fastest
friendly	friendlier	friendliest
narrow	narrower	narrowest
sunny	sunnier	sunniest

Use *more* to form a modifier's comparative degree when adding *-er* sounds awkward. Use *most* to form a modifier's superlative degree when adding *-est* sounds awkward.

COMPARATIVE AND SUPERLATIVE DEGREES FORMED WITH *MORE* AND *MOST*		
POSITIVE	COMPARATIVE	SUPERLATIVE
careful	more careful	most careful
complete	more complete	most complete
handsome	more handsome	most handsome
often	more often	most often
quietly	more quietly	most quietly

More and *most* should not be used when the result sounds awkward, however. If you are not sure which form to use, check a dictionary. Most dictionaries list modifiers formed with *-er* and *-est*.

See Practice 24.1A

Regular Modifiers With Three or More Syllables

Modifiers for words with three or more syllables follow the same rules.

RULE 24.1.3

Use *more* and *most* to form the comparative and superlative degrees of all modifiers of three or more syllables. Do not use *-er* or *-est* with modifiers of more than two syllables.

DEGREES OF MODIFIERS WITH THREE OR MORE SYLLABLES		
POSTIVE	COMPARATIVE	SUPERLATIVE
expensive	more expensive	most expensive
flexible	more flexible	most flexible

Adverbs Ending in *-ly*

To modify most adverbs ending in *-ly*, use *more* or *most*.

RULE 24.1.4

Use *more* to form the comparative degree and *most* to form the superlative degree of most adverbs ending in *-ly*.

EXAMPLES   slowly, more slowly, most slowly

quietly, more quietly, most quietly

Using *Less* and *Least*

Less and *least* can show decreasing comparisons.

RULE 24.1.5

Use *less* with a modifier to form the decreasing comparative degree and *least* to form the decreasing superlative degree.

EXAMPLES   friendly, less friendly, least friendly

quickly, less quickly, least quickly

See Practice 24.1B

PRACTICE 24.1A ▸ **Forming Comparatives and Superlatives of One- and Two-Syllable Modifiers**

Read the modifiers. Write the comparative and superlative forms of each modifier.

EXAMPLE   quiet

ANSWER   *quieter, quietest*

1. slim
2. rich
3. happy
4. shy
5. helpful
6. soon
7. polite
8. late
9. evenly
10. dirty

PRACTICE 24.1B ▸ **Using Forms of Modifiers**

Read the sentences. Then, write each sentence, using the form of the modifier in parentheses.

EXAMPLE   Today is the _____ day of the year! (*hot*, superlative)

ANSWER   *Today is the hottest day of the year!*

11. Damian's _____ brother is starting college in the fall. (*old*, superlative)

12. I thought this book was _____ than the other one I read. (*funny*, comparative)

13. Celia is the _____ of the two skaters. (*graceful*, comparative)

14. Curtis felt _____ after his snack than before. (*energetic*, comparative)

15. Morgan is the _____ reader in our class. (*fast*, superlative)

16. Of all the speakers, Kara gave the _____ presentation. (*thorough*, superlative)

17. The play was _____ than we had expected. (*exciting*, comparative)

18. The sidewalk is _____ on this side of the street. (*safe*, comparative)

19. January and February are usually the _____ months. (*cold*, superlative)

20. This cereal is _____ than I like. (*sweet*, comparative)

SPEAKING APPLICATION

Tell a partner about a trait or quality of several people you know. Use a comparative and a superlative form of an adjective in this structure: Jack is taller than Kim. Dane is the tallest of all my friends.

WRITING APPLICATION

Write a paragraph comparing different versions of a game or song or several episodes of a television program. Use at least one comparative form and one superlative form of each modifier.

Irregular Adjectives and Adverbs

A few adjectives and adverbs are irregular.

RULE 24.1.6

Memorize the comparative and superlative forms of adjectives and adverbs that have irregular spellings.

The chart lists the most common irregular modifiers.

DEGREES OF IRREGULAR ADJECTIVES AND ADVERBS		
POSITIVE	COMPARATIVE	SUPERLATIVE
bad (adjective)	worse	worst
badly (adverb)	worse	worst
far (distance)	farther	farthest
far (extent)	further	furthest
good (adjective)	better	best
well (adverb)	better	best
many	more	most
much	more	most

When you are unsure about how a modifier forms its degrees of comparison, check a dictionary.

See Practice 24.1C

Using Comparative and Superlative Degrees

Keep these rules in mind when you use the comparative and superlative degrees.

RULE 24.1.7

Use the comparative degree to compare *two* people, places, or things. Use the superlative degree to compare *three or more* people, places, or things.

Usually, you do not need to mention specific numbers when you are making a comparison. Other words in the sentence should help make the meaning clear whether you are comparing two items or three or more items.

EXAMPLES   The coach felt **better** once all the swimmers were in the locker room on time.

The swim team competed the practice session in their **best** time this week.

Pay particular attention to the modifiers you use when you are comparing just two items. Do not use the superlative degree with fewer than three items.

INCORRECT   Of their two relay races, that one was the **best**.

CORRECT   Of their two relay races, that one was **better**.

INCORRECT   Mark's car was the **fastest** of the two cars.

CORRECT   Mark's car was the **faster** of the two cars.

> **Do not make double comparisons.** Do not use both *-er* and *more* to form the comparative degree or both *-est* and *most* to form the superlative degree. Also, be sure not to use *-er, more,* and *most* with an irregular modifier.

24.1.8 RULE

INCORRECT   She read the story the **most fastest**.

CORRECT   She read the story the **fastest**.

INCORRECT   The snowstorm was **more worse** than any they had seen in years.

CORRECT   The snowstorm was **worse** than any they had seen in years.

See Practice 24.1D

PRACTICE 24.1C Forming Comparatives and Superlatives of Irregular Adjectives and Adverbs

Read the modifiers. Write the comparative and superlative forms of each modifier.

EXAMPLE   well (adverb)

ANSWER   *better, best*

1. far (extent)

2. badly (adverb)

3. much

4. bad (adjective)

5. far (distance)

6. good (adjective)

7. many

PRACTICE 24.1D Using Comparatives and Superlatives of Irregular Adjectives and Adverbs

Read the sentences. Then, write each sentence, using the form of the modifier in parentheses.

EXAMPLE   That was the _____ meal I have ever eaten. (*bad*, superlative)

ANSWER   *That was the worst meal I have ever eaten.*

8. This book is _____ than the author's previous one. (*good*, comparative)

9. This is the _____ fun I have had all week! (*much*, superlative)

10. Peter and Matthew had to travel _____ to get here. (*far*, superlative)

11. The storm was _____ than expected. (*bad*, comparative)

12. I have no _____ interest in this subject. (*far*, comparative)

13. Quentin usually does _____ on tests than I do. (*well*, comparative)

14. Who is the _____ artist in the class? (*good*, superlative)

15. Marcus has _____ songs on his playlist than Nelson does. (*many*, comparative)

16. Are you feeling _____ today? (*well*, comparative)

17. The comic performed _____ than the singer. (*good*, comparative)

SPEAKING APPLICATION

Tell a partner about an event. You may exaggerate the details. Use comparative and superlative forms of any of the modifiers above.

WRITING APPLICATION

Write a short paragraph comparing several versions or brands of an item. Use at least one comparative form and one superlative form.

Making Logical Comparisons

In most situations, you will have no problem forming the degrees of modifiers and using them correctly in sentences. Sometimes, however, you may find that the way you have phrased a sentence makes your comparison unclear. You will then need to think about the words you have chosen and revise your sentence, making sure that your comparison is logical.

> **When you make a comparison, be sure you are comparing things that have clear similarities.**

Balanced Comparisons

Most comparisons make a statement or ask a question about the way in which similar things are either alike or different.

EXAMPLE   Is the **Atlantic Ocean** **deeper** than the **Pacific Ocean**?

(Both bodies of water have depths that can be measured and compared.)

Because the sentence compares depth to depth, the comparison is balanced. Problems can occur, however, when a sentence compares dissimilar things. For example, it would be illogical to compare the depth of one ocean to the shape of another ocean. Depth and shape are not similar things and cannot be compared meaningfully.

ILLOGICAL   The stories in my book are longer than your book.

(*Stories* and *book* cannot be logically compared.)

LOGICAL   The stories in my book are longer than the stories in your book.

(Two sets of stories can be logically compared.)

> **Make sure that your sentences compare only similar items.**

An unbalanced comparison is usually the result of carelessness. The writer may have simply left something out. Read the following incorrect sentences carefully.

INCORRECT	**Planting grass** is **easier** than a **garden**. The **number of inlets** on the East Coast is **larger** than the **West Coast**.

In the first sentence, planting grass is mistakenly compared to a garden. In the second sentence, the number of inlets are compared to the West Coast. Both sentences can easily be corrected to make the comparisons balanced.

CORRECT	**Planting grass** is **easier** than **planting a garden**. The **number of inlets** on the East Coast is **larger** than the **number** on the West Coast.

See Practice 24.1E

Other and *Else* in Comparisons

Another common error in writing comparisons is to compare something to itself.

RULE 24.1.11

> **When comparing one of a group to the rest of the group, make sure your sentence contains the word *other* or *else*.**

Adding *other* or *else* can make a comparison clear. For example, in the second sentence below, because *Edward* is himself a student, he cannot logically be compared to *all students*. He must be compared to *all other students*.

PROBLEM SENTENCES	CORRECTED SENTENCES
At the track meet, my brother sprinted to the finish line before anyone.	At the track meet, my brother sprinted to the finish line before anyone else.
Edward collected more kinds of shells than any student did.	Edward collected more kinds of shells than any other student did.

See Practice 24.1F

PRACTICE 24.1E > Making Balanced Comparisons

Read the sentences. Rewrite each sentence, correcting the unbalanced comparison.

EXAMPLE   My grade on the second test was better than the first.

ANSWER   *My grade on the second test was better than my grade on the first.*

1. The information on this Web site is more detailed than that one.

2. Ben's scoring record is better than Jason.

3. I like the details in this painting better than Vanessa's.

4. The weather here is as cold as Alaska.

5. There are fewer berries in my basket than yours.

6. The service at Mario's Restaurant is better than Lucky's.

7. I think the articles in this magazine are more interesting than that magazine.

8. Josie's dog is not as obedient as Ingrid.

9. Eddie's video game has better features than Manny.

10. The toddler got more food on the floor than his mouth.

PRACTICE 24.1F > Using *Other* and *Else* to Make Comparisons

Read the sentences. Rewrite each sentence, adding *other* or *else* to make the comparisons logical.

EXAMPLE   Gabby is faster than anyone on the team.

ANSWER   *Gabby is faster than anyone else on the team.*

11. Dion plays his drum louder than anyone in the band.

12. Jan's outfit is more colorful than anyone's.

13. Tom uses better strategy than any player.

14. Our school has a better debate team than any school in the league.

15. Greg sings better than anyone in the group.

16. Joanne helps out as much as anyone in her family.

17. Maddie's argument is more logical than anyone's.

18. That movie was more exciting than any I have seen lately.

19. Ollie gave a better demonstration than anyone.

20. Alison was more tired than anyone in the group after the long practice.

SPEAKING APPLICATION

With a partner, use your corrected sentence 1 as a model, and make a logical comparison between two items. Your partner should check that your comparison is correct.

WRITING APPLICATION

Use sentences 12, 13, and 14 as models, and write three new sentences making logical comparisons.

24.2 Troublesome Adjectives and Adverbs

The common adjectives and adverbs listed below often cause problems in both speaking and writing.

WRITING COACH
Online
www.phwritingcoach.com

Grammar Practice
Practice your grammar skills with Writing Coach Online.

Grammar Games
Test your knowledge of grammar in this fast-paced interactive video game.

(1) bad and badly   *Bad* is an adjective. Use it after linking verbs, such as *are, appear, feel, look,* and *sound. Badly* is an adverb. Use it after action verbs, such as *act, behave, do,* and *perform.*

INCORRECT	Marco looked **badly** after the game.
CORRECT	Marco looked **bad** after the game.

INCORRECT	My sister did **bad** on the test.
CORRECT	My sister did **badly** on the test.

(2) good and well   *Good* is an adjective. *Well* can be either an adjective or an adverb, depending on its meaning. A common mistake is the use of *good* after an action verb. Use the adverb *well* instead.

INCORRECT	The puppy behaved **good** all day.
	The book is **well**.
CORRECT	The puppy behaved **well** all day.
	The book is **good**.

As adjectives, *good* and *well* have slightly different meanings, which are often confused. *Well* usually refers simply to health.

EXAMPLES	Charlie felt **good** after hockey practice.
	The spaghetti smells **good**.
	That kitten is not **well**.

(3) ***fewer and less*** Use the adjective *fewer* to answer the question, "How many?" Use the adjective *less* to answer the question, "How much?"

HOW MANY	**fewer** dollars	**fewer** children
HOW MUCH	**less** money	**less** water

(4) ***just*** When used as an adverb, *just* often means "no more than." When *just* has this meaning, place it right before the word it logically modifies.

INCORRECT   Does he **just** want **one bottle of water**?

CORRECT   Does he want **just** **one bottle of water**?

(5) ***only*** The position of *only* in a sentence sometimes affects the sentence's entire meaning. Consider the meaning of these sentences.

EXAMPLES   **Only** he went to the baseball game.
(Nobody else went to the game.)

He **only** went to the baseball game.
(He did nothing else except go to the game.)

He went **only** to the baseball game.
(He went to the baseball game and nowhere else.)

Mistakes involving *only* usually occur when its placement in a sentence makes the meaning unclear.

UNCLEAR   **Only** follow directions from me.

BETTER   Follow directions **only** from me.
(not from anyone else)

See Practice 24.2A
See Practice 24.2B
See Practice 24.2C
See Practice 24.2D

Follow **only** directions from me.
(nothing but directions)

PRACTICE 24.2A > Using *Bad* and *Badly*, *Good* and *Well*

Read the sentences. Write the word in parentheses that correctly completes each sentence.

EXAMPLE   My little brother behaves (bad, badly) when he is upset.

ANSWER   *badly*

1. Marissa is a (good, well) swimmer.

2. Lee's new job is working out (good, well).

3. Unfortunately, the repair work was done (bad, badly).

4. Casey did (good, well) on his project.

5. This old car is running (bad, badly).

6. Charlotte looks (good, well) in her prom dress.

7. Walt looked (bad, badly) after the race.

8. The weather is looking (good, well) for the picnic.

9. Rosemary is feeling (bad, badly) today.

10. It seemed like a (good, well) idea, but it did not turn out (good, well).

PRACTICE 24.2B > Revising for Troublesome Modifiers

Read the sentences. Rewrite the sentences that contain errors in the use of modifiers. If a sentence has no error, write *correct*.

EXAMPLE   Jorge feels well about his decision.

ANSWER   *Jorge feels good about his decision.*

11. The patient is feeling good today.

12. The plants looked badly because they had not been watered.

13. Chloe felt bad about her mistake.

14. We all look good in those pictures.

15. Nicole and Arianna danced good in the show.

16. Olivia and Sue work well together.

17. That flutist plays good.

18. Because the event was badly planned, it was not successful.

19. Joshua draws really good.

20. Rachel's intentions were good, but she did not follow through.

SPEAKING APPLICATION

Tell a partner two sentences using *bad* and *badly*. Your partner should say two sentences using *good* and *well*.

WRITING APPLICATION

Write a short paragraph evaluating a movie or television show you have recently seen. Use *bad*, *badly*, *good*, and *well* to describe the plot, the characters, or any other details of the movie or show.

PRACTICE 24.2C > Writing Sentences Using *Fewer* or *Less*

Read the sentences. If the underlined word in the sentence is incorrect, rewrite the sentence correctly. If the underlined word in the sentence is correct, write *correct*.

EXAMPLE   I have <u>less</u> quarters than dimes.

ANSWER   *I have **fewer** quarters than dimes.*

1. Do you have <u>less</u> money than you had last week?

2. There are <u>less</u> students in my math class than in my science class.

3. We have <u>fewer</u> time left to spend at the pool than I thought.

4. My mother thought the recipe called for <u>fewer</u> eggs than four.

5. The car had <u>less</u> gallons of gas than we needed to get there.

6. The car had <u>less</u> gas than we needed to get there.

7. Is 90 greater than or <u>less</u> than 900?

8. There are <u>less</u> grapes in this bowl than in that one.

9. I bought a small popcorn instead of a large because I wanted <u>fewer</u> popcorn.

10. It is healthier to eat <u>less</u> salty snacks and more fruit each day.

PRACTICE 24.2D > Writing Sentences Using *Just* and *Only*

Read the sentences below. For each one, write a new sentence using the word *just* or *only* to match the meaning of the sentence given.

EXAMPLE   We are going to this specific movie tonight. (only)

ANSWER   *We are going to **only** this movie tonight.*

11. We have the exact amount of milk needed for the recipe. (just)

12. The person from our school at the skating rink was Brian. (only)

13. The teacher said, "Follow instructions from nobody else but me."(only)

14. Zach wants a sandwich for lunch and nothing else. (just)

15. Arlene is the one person who brought a present. (just)

16. Cindy bought oatmeal at the store and nothing else. (only)

17. Cindy was the one person who bought oatmeal at the store. (only)

18. The parents gave the babysitter their cell phone number and no other information. (just)

19. The babysitter was the one person who had the parents' cell phone number. (just)

20. Remember to do the odd-numbered math problems, not the even-numbered ones. (just)

SPEAKING APPLICATION

With a partner, take turns discussing homework or other school projects. Use *fewer, less, just,* and *only* at least once. Your partner should listen for proper use of the words and correct any errors.

WRITING APPLICATION

Write a brief paragraph about a shopping trip you plan to take. Use *fewer, less, just,* and *only* at least once. Exchange paragraphs with a partner. Check for and correct any errors in the paragraph.

Test Warm-Up

DIRECTIONS

Read the introduction and the passage that follows. Then, answer the questions to show that you can use troublesome adjectives and adverbs (e.g., *bad/badly*; *good/well*; *fewer/less*; *just/only*) correctly in reading and writing.

Shanequa wrote this paragraph about her first job as a babysitter. Read the paragraph and think about the changes you would suggest as a peer editor. When you finish reading, answer the questions that follow.

Fewer Than Five

(1) I just completed a course in babysitting, and I think I did pretty good. (2) So, when my neighbor asked me to watch her five children on Friday, I agreed. (3) My neighbor said that she needed only me from 4:00 P.M. until 7:00 P.M. (4) She also said that if she finished her errands in less time, she'd be home earlier. (5) I wish I could say that my first babysitting experience went well, but it went bad. (6) The five kids fought the entire time. (7) I think next time I'll babysit for a family with less children.

---

1 What change, if any, should be made in sentence 1?

A Change *good* to **bad**

B Change *good* to **well**

C Delete *pretty*

D Make no change

2 How should sentence 3 be revised?

F Only my neighbor said that she needed me from 4:00 P.M. until 7:00 P.M.

G My neighbor said only that she needed only me from 4:00 P.M. until 7:00 P.M.

H My neighbor said that she needed me only from 4:00 P.M. until 7:00 P.M.

J My only neighbor said that she needed me from 4:00 P.M. until 7:00 P.M.

3 What change, if any, should be made in sentence 5?

A Change *well* to **good**

B Change *well* to **better**

C Change *bad* to **badly**

D Make no change

4 What change, if any, should be made in sentence 7?

F Change *less* to **lesser**

G Change *less* to **fewer**

H Change *less* to **just**

J Make no change

Cumulative Review Chapters 21–24

PRACTICE 1 ▷ Identifying Verb Tenses

Read the sentences. For each sentence, write whether the verb tense is *present*, *past*, *future*, *present perfect*, *past perfect*, or *future perfect*. Also indicate if the verb is *progressive*.

1. Ms. Paloma has worked at the bank for years.

2. My mother is preparing a huge meal for the holidays.

3. The committee will meet tomorrow morning.

4. On June 1, Troy will have been living in San Antonio for exactly five years.

5. Penelope has been designing her own clothing for some time.

6. Restaurants generally throw away their leftovers.

7. My father studied to be a chemical engineer.

8. The standardized test for seventh graders will be starting in half an hour.

9. A dozen swans were floating in the pond.

10. No one else had ever grown anything like Mr. Marshall's hybrid lily.

PRACTICE 2 ▷ Revising to Use Active Voice

Read the sentences. Then, rewrite each passive voice sentence so that it is in active voice. If a sentence is already in active voice, write *active*.

1. The story was written by Shirley Jackson.

2. The best guacamole is prepared by Suzie.

3. The treehouse is in the maple tree by the creek.

4. Mr. Levinson's generous gift to the town was accepted by the mayor in a special ceremony.

5. Anita is flying to Minneapolis tomorrow.

PRACTICE 3 ▷ Using Verbs Correctly

Read the sentences. Then, rewrite the sentences to correct any incorrect verb forms. If a sentence has no errors, write *correct*.

1. Last evening, I drunk a mug of cocoa.

2. I have never flew on that airline.

3. Yesterday morning, Portia lay this funny mouse pad in front of my computer.

4. You should not set in the sun for so many hours.

5. Yesterday at the movies, Peggy says to me, "Popcorn is low in calories."

6. Dad finally done his tax return.

7. The voters have chose a new person to become our state's governor.

8. I seen my cousins from the Philippines for the first time last August.

9. The bucket has apparently sprang a leak.

10. This past winter, the pipes in the old house froze and burst.

PRACTICE 4 ▷ Identifying Pronoun Cases and Uses

Read the sentences. Write whether each underlined pronoun is in the *nominative*, *objective*, or *possessive* case. Then, write whether it is used as a *subject*, a *predicate pronoun*, a *direct object*, an *indirect object*, or the *object of a preposition*.

1. The babysitter sang to <u>her</u> until she fell asleep.

2. The driving instructor gave <u>him</u> a lesson.

3. <u>Hers</u> is the bright blue coat.

4. The quiet music calmed <u>me</u>.

5. The best athletes on the team were Jasper and <u>I</u>.

Continued on next page ▶

Cumulative Review Chapters 21–24

PRACTICE 5 > **Using Pronouns Correctly**

Read the sentences. Then, rewrite the sentences to correct any incorrect pronouns. If a sentence has no errors, write *correct*.

1. Claudia and him exchanged papers.
2. The coyote howled it's long and lonesome cry.
3. Whom did the artist portray in the painting?
4. The best swimmers are Drew and me.
5. The bus driver gave Bridget and I change.
6. Share the dessert between you and he.
7. Viv is the one who the class chose as president.
8. Their's is the last truck on the left.
9. Don't discourage Sonny and she.
10. I have no idea whom that politician is.

PRACTICE 6 > **Revising for Subject–Verb Agreement**

Read the sentences. Then, rewrite the sentences to correct any errors in subject–verb agreement. If a sentence has no errors, write *correct*.

1. Each of the pianists practice for hours.
2. Neither Abe nor he see many movies.
3. A box of mints always sit atop her dresser.
4. The committee quarrels about choosing new members.
5. None of those golfers ride in the cart.
6. Deirdre and Lex enjoy line dancing.
7. Ham and eggs are my favorite breakfast.
8. The lawyer or her associates argues in court.
9. Do the mayor or the governor know the facts?
10. The class has been dismissed for the day.

PRACTICE 7 > **Revising for Pronoun–Antecedent Agreement**

Read the sentences. Then, rewrite the sentences to correct any errors in pronoun–antecedent agreement. If a sentence has no errors, write *correct*.

1. None of the computers lost its memory.
2. Either the cat or the dog lost its collar.
3. Each of the chairs had their upholstery replaced.
4. Natasha has a job at which you input data.
5. In the past, everyone kept their hats in hatboxes.
6. Amelia and Leah wore ribbons in her hair.
7. Neither George nor Pete did their chores.
8. Several of the birds had damage to its wings.
9. Some of the beauticians did his or her own hair.
10. Did everybody know his or her state senator?

PRACTICE 8 > **Using Modifiers Correctly**

Read the sentences. Then, rewrite the sentences to correct any errors involving modifiers. If a sentence has no errors, write *correct*.

1. The stagnant pond smells really badly.
2. I can do nothing farther for you.
3. I am feeling more well than I felt before.
4. Less customers shop here on weekends.
5. Of their three bad songs, this is the baddest.
6. The tour boats only sail in the summer.
7. Tammy is kinder than I am.
8. Beau performed good on the test.
9. In my opinion, robins are prettier than any bird.
10. Is there a guitarist more good than he is?

Using Commas With Addresses and in Letters

Commas are also used in addresses, salutations of friendly letters, and closings of friendly or business letters.

> **Use a comma after each item in an address made up of two or more parts.**

RULE 25.2.15

In the following example, commas are placed after the name, street, and city. There is no comma between the state and the ZIP Code.

EXAMPLE   He is writing to John Keen, 137 Adams Street, Reno, Nevada 89509.

Fewer commas are needed when an address is written in a letter or on an envelope.

EXAMPLE   Greg Harrison
92 Essex Avenue
Roselle, New Jersey 07203

> **Use a comma after the salutation in a personal letter and after the closing in all letters.**

RULE 25.2.16

See Practice 25.2K
See Practice 25.2L

SALUTATION   Dear Bill,   CLOSING   Yours truly,

Using Commas With Direct Quotations

Commas are also used to separate **direct quotations** from other phrases in a sentence.

> **Use commas to set off a direct quotation from the rest of a sentence.**

RULE 25.2.17

EXAMPLES   Naomi said, "Please wait for me."

"I will," Rosa answered, "if you walk faster."

PRACTICE 25.2K ▸ Using Commas in Addresses and Letters

Read the items. Rewrite each item, adding commas where needed. If no commas are needed, write *correct*.

EXAMPLE   Very truly yours

ANSWER   *Very truly yours,*

1. Longview TX 75603
2. Dear Mr. Knox
3. 2662 Steele Road
4. With best regards
5. 5109 Greenway Boulevard
6. 25 Prospect Street, Apt. 3
7. Yours sincerely
8. Molly's address is 442 Ocean Avenue 3rd floor Tallahassee Florida 32306.
9. Dear Grandma
10. The Holloways
    16 Sunset Avenue
    Scottsdale AZ 85250

PRACTICE 25.2L ▸ Revising a Letter by Adding Commas

Read the letter. Rewrite the letter, adding commas where necessary.

EXAMPLE   Dear Mrs. Juarez

ANSWER   *Dear Mrs. Juarez,*

1421 Mountain Drive
Madison WI 53716

April 21 2010

Dear Aunt Glenda

Thank you very much for the sweater you sent for my birthday. It fits perfectly and you know I love blue! I've already worn it to school and I received three compliments on it. You are so thoughtful to remember me.

Much love
Emily

WRITING APPLICATION

Write this sentence, completing it with your own address: *I live at _____.*

WRITING APPLICATION

Write a letter or note to a relative or friend. Use correct letter form, and use commas as needed.

25.3 Semicolons and Colons

The **semicolon (;)** joins related **independent clauses** and signals a longer pause than a comma. The **colon (:)** is used to introduce lists of items and in other special situations.

Using Semicolons to Join Independent Clauses

Sometimes two **independent clauses** are so closely connected in meaning that they make up a single sentence, rather than two separate sentences.

> Use a **semicolon** to join related **independent clauses** that are not joined by the conjunctions *and, or, nor, for, but, so,* or *yet.*

25.3.1 RULE

| INDEPENDENT CLAUSES | Bill enjoys exploring jungle areas. |
| | His sister is more interested in deserts. |

CLAUSES JOINED BY SEMICOLONS Bill enjoys exploring jungle areas**;** his sister is more interested in deserts.

A semicolon should be used only when there is a close relationship between the two independent clauses. If the clauses are not very closely related, they should be written as separate sentences with a period or another end mark to separate them or joined with a coordinating conjunction.

Note that when a sentence contains three or more related independent clauses, they may still be separated with semicolons.

EXAMPLES Dark clouds rolled in**;** the ocean became rough**;** the sand began to blow.

Bea wrote about insects**;** Nat wrote about spiders**;** Frank wrote about insects and spiders.

Semicolons and Colons   571

Using Semicolons to Join Clauses Separated by Conjunctive
Adverbs or Transitional Expressions

Semicolons help writers show how their ideas connect.

RULE 25.3.2

> **Use a semicolon to join independent clauses separated by either a conjunctive adverb or a transitional expression.**

CONJUNCTIVE ADVERBS	*also, besides, consequently, first, furthermore, however, indeed, instead, moreover, nevertheless, otherwise, second, then, therefore, thus*
TRANSITIONAL EXPRESSIONS	*as a result, at this time, for instance, in fact, on the other hand, that is*
EXAMPLE	We met Tomas at the concession stand ; **otherwise** , we would never have found him at the theater.

Remember to place a comma after the conjunctive adverb or transitional expression. The comma sets off the conjunctive adverb or transitional expression, which acts as an introductory expression to the second clause.

Using Semicolons to Avoid Confusion

Sometimes, to avoid confusion, semicolons are used to separate items in a series.

RULE 25.3.3

> **Consider the use of semicolons to avoid confusion when items in a series already contain commas.**

See Practice 25.3A
See Practice 25.3B

Place a semicolon after all but the last complete item in a series.

EXAMPLES	The dark , country road ; the still , silent forest ; and the sky , black and moonless , encouraged them to head toward home.
	Three important dates for my family are January 1 , 2001 ; April 5 , 2003 ; and May 28 , 2000.

Using Colons

The **colon (:)** is used to introduce lists of items and in certain special situations.

> **Use a colon after an independent clause to introduce a list of items.**

The independent clause that comes before the colon often includes the words *the following, as follows, these,* or *those.*

EXAMPLE   Manny's family is planning to visit the following cities : Dallas , Fort Worth , and Austin.

Remember to use commas to separate three or more items in a series.

> **In most cases, do not use a colon after a verb, and never use a colon after a preposition.**

INCORRECT   I like to play : football , baseball , and soccer.

CORRECT   I like to play football , baseball , and soccer.

> **Use a colon to introduce a long or formal quotation.**

EXAMPLE   The sign clearly states the law : "No motor vehicles allowed beyond this point at any time."

See Practice 25.3C
See Practice 25.3D

SOME ADDITIONAL USES OF THE COLON	
To Separate Hours and Minutes	8 : 45 A.M. 10 : 05 P.M.
After the Salutation in a Business Letter	Dear Sir or Madam : Dear Ms. Langly :
On Warnings and Labels	Notice : Shop is closed for repairs. Note : Please turn off cellphones.

Read the sentences. Rewrite each sentence, adding any necessary semicolons.

EXAMPLE   I opened the shades sunlight poured into the room.

ANSWER   *I opened the shades; sunlight poured into the room.*

1. I'll prepare dinner meanwhile, you set the table.

2. Suzanne likes crossword puzzles Kevin prefers chess.

3. Mammals have hair birds have feathers amphibians have neither.

4. The weather forecast was for rain instead, we had sleet.

5. Andrew's alarm did not go off consequently, he was late for school.

6. Please turn on the fan we need some air.

7. Some people are very confident at least, they act that way.

8. In some stores, you can get newspapers and magazines household supplies, such as batteries and cleaners and sandwiches and soups to go.

9. The sky was gray the wind blew the waves crashed on the rocks.

10. Peter can give you some tips he is an excellent tennis player.

Read the sentences below. Then, write new sentences by adding a related independent clause to each sentence provided. Use semicolons correctly in your new sentences.

EXAMPLE   The class was going to end in four minutes.

ANSWER   *The class was going to end in four minutes; therefore, we had only enough time to finish one problem.*

11. I wish I could go to camp this summer.

12. Charlie found a part-time job mowing lawns.

13. We have to hurry if we are going to catch the bus.

14. I prefer pears to apples.

15. Emily brought an umbrella to school today.

16. We should make stir-fry for dinner tonight.

17. Put the laundry in the dresser.

18. The election was very close.

19. My mother said that I could go to your house.

20. We have to walk three more blocks.

WRITING APPLICATION

Work with a partner. Use sentences 2, 3, and 5 in Practice 25.3A as models. Write three sentences of your own. Then, read your sentences to your partner and explain the purpose of each semicolon.

WRITING APPLICATION

Work with a partner. Write one sentence using semicolons in a series. Write one sentence using a semicolon to separate two independent clauses. Have your partner read your sentences aloud, checking for the correct use of semicolons.

PRACTICE 25.3C > Using Colons

Read the sentences. Rewrite each sentence, adding any necessary colons. If no colon is needed, write *correct*.

EXAMPLE   Your appointment is at 915 A.M.

ANSWER   *Your appointment is at 9:15 A.M.*

1. This is what you should do apologize and give her flowers.
2. You must be ready by 6:30 P.M.
3. Warning Hard hats required at this site.
4. Microchips are found in hundreds of common devices telephones, GPS systems, and MP3 players, for example.
5. Margo packed only three things pajamas, a toothbrush, and a change of clothes.
6. So far, I have found only one good source for my report: the author's official Web site.
7. This evening's program is as follows opening remarks at 700, presentations from 715 to 800, closing remarks at 815.
8. Caution Bridge is slippery when wet.
9. Dear Sir or Madam:
10. Put the following ingredients into your salad lettuce, spinach, sliced apples, and dried cranberries.

PRACTICE 25.3D > Writing Sentences Using Colons

Read the rules for using colons below. Write a sentence using a colon for each rule. Then, have a partner read your sentences aloud to check for the correct use of colons.

EXAMPLE   to introduce a list of items

ANSWER   *You will need the following supplies for the camping trip: a sleeping bag, a water bottle, a flashlight, and a warm jacket.*

11. to introduce a long or formal quotation
12. to separate hours and minutes
13. after the salutation in a business letter
14. on a warning
15. to introduce a list of items
16. to introduce a long or formal quotation
17. to separate hours and minutes
18. after the salutation in a business letter
19. on a label
20. to introduce a list of items

SPEAKING APPLICATION

With a partner, take turns reading aloud the sentences created in Practice 25.3D. Read the word *colon* whenever there is a colon. Then, discuss which usages of colons are most common.

WRITING APPLICATION

Write three sentences about school. In your sentences, use colons in three different ways. Exchange papers with your partner. Your partner should read your sentences aloud and explain the use of each colon.

Test Warm-Up

DIRECTIONS
Read the introduction and the passage that follows. Then, answer the questions to show that you can use correct punctuation, including semicolons and colons, in reading and writing.

Vince wrote this business letter to a potential employer, the owner of a convenience store. Read the letter and think about the changes you would suggest as a peer editor. When you finish reading, answer the questions that follow.

(1) Dear Mrs. Gonzalez;

(2) I am writing to express my interest in working in your store: I would like to own a convenience store some day myself. (3) I work well with others, I am friendly, helpful, and good at working with money. (4) I am also responsible; in fact, people say I'm mature for my age. (5) Please note that I can be flexible about my hours. (6) I will look forward to hearing from you.

(7) Sincerely,
(8) Vince Bradford

---

1 What change, if any, should be made in sentence 1?

  A Change the semicolon to a colon

  B Delete the semicolon

  C Change the semicolon to a comma

  D Make no change

2 What change, if any, should be made in sentence 2?

  F Change the colon to a comma

  G Change the colon to a semicolon

  H Change the period to an exclamation point

  J Make no change

3 What change, if any, should be made in sentence 3?

  A Delete the comma after *others*

  B Change the comma after *others* to a semicolon

  C Change the comma after *others* to a colon

  D Make no change

4 What change, if any, should be made in sentence 4?

  F Change the semicolon to a comma

  G Change the semicolon to a colon

  H Delete the semicolon

  J Make no change

25.4 Quotation Marks, Underlining, and Italics

Quotation marks (" ") set off direct quotations, dialogue, and certain types of titles. Other types of titles may be **underlined** or set in *italics,* a slanted type style.

Using Quotation Marks With Quotations

Quotation marks identify the spoken or written words of others. A **direct quotation** represents a person's exact speech or thoughts. An **indirect quotation** reports the general meaning of what a person said or thought.

Both types of quotations are acceptable when you write. Direct quotations, however, generally result in a livelier writing style.

Direct quotations should be enclosed in quotation marks.

RULE 25.4.1

EXAMPLE   Janine said, "Tomorrow we are going hiking."

"Does anyone know the way?" asked Ted.

Indirect quotations do not require quotation marks.

RULE 25.4.2

EXAMPLES   John said that he would feed the fish.

Scott wondered why the coach hadn't called him about rescheduling the game.

Using Direct Quotations With Introductory, Concluding, and Interrupting Expressions

Commas help you set off introductory information so that your reader understands who is speaking. Writers usually identify a speaker by using words such as *he asked* or *she said* with a quotation. These expressions can introduce, conclude, or interrupt a quotation.

Direct Quotations With Introductory Expressions

Commas are also used to indicate where **introductory expressions** end.

RULE 25.4.3

> When an **introductory expression** precedes a direct quotation, place a comma after the introductory expression, and write the quotation as a full sentence.

EXAMPLES

Barney asked the tour guide, "Is it difficult to identify artifacts?"

Dorothy wondered, "What play will the drama club choose to present this year?"

If an introductory expression is very long, set it off with a colon instead of a comma.

EXAMPLE

At the end of the practice, Miguel outlined his goals for the future: "I would like to increase my speed by the end of the year."

Direct Quotations With Concluding Expressions

Direct quotations may sometimes end with **concluding expressions.**

RULE 25.4.4

> When a **concluding expression** follows a direct quotation, write the quotation as a full sentence ending with a comma, question mark, or exclamation mark inside the quotation mark. Then, write the concluding expression. Be sure to use end punctuation to close the sentence.

Concluding expressions are not complete sentences; therefore, they do not begin with capital letters. Notice also that the closing quotation marks are always placed outside the punctuation at the end of direct quotations.

EXAMPLE

"I think you would have fun at our camp!" said Timothy excitedly.

Direct Quotations With Interrupting Expressions

You may use an interrupting expression in a direct quotation, which is also called a **divided quotation.** Interrupting expressions help writers clarify who is speaking and can also break up a long quotation.

> When the direct quotation of one sentence is interrupted, end the first part of the direct quotation with a comma and a quotation mark. Place a comma after the **interrupting expression,** and then use a new set of quotation marks to enclose the rest of the quotation.

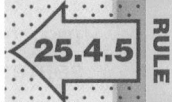

RULE 25.4.5

EXAMPLES   "Because the camp is located on a lake," explained Ginnie, "we can go swimming and boating."

"Do you think," interrupted Juana, "that I could learn to water ski?"

Do not capitalize the first word of the second part of the sentence.

> When two sentences in a direct quotation are separated by an **interrupting expression,** end the first quoted sentence with a comma, question mark, or exclamation mark and a quotation mark. Place a period after the interrupter, and then write the second quoted sentence as a full quotation.

RULE 25.4.6

EXAMPLES   "We came face to face with a grizzly bear on one of our hikes," said Juan. "It was scary."

"That must have been amazing!" exclaimed Jenna. "How close did you get to the bear?"

See Practice 25.4A
See Practice 25.4B

PRACTICE 25.4A **Using Quotation Marks With Direct Quotations**

Read the sentences. If the sentence contains a direct quotation, write *D*. If it contains an indirect quotation, write *I*. Then, rewrite each sentence that contains a direct quotation, adding the quotation marks where needed.

EXAMPLE   Jenna reported that no one was injured during the game.

ANSWER   *I*

1. When you come home from school, Mother said, please do your laundry.

2. Martha wanted to know what I did yesterday.

3. I wonder, mused Catherine, whatever happened to our former neighbors.

4. Jamie announced, I feel confident about this test.

5. Abby thought that something was wrong.

6. When is this project due? Jordan asked.

7. Brian told us that he joined the drama club.

8. May I see your tickets? the usher asked.

9. Wendy said that she would join us later.

10. No, Clayton replied, I don't think that's a good idea.

PRACTICE 25.4B **Punctuating With Expressions**

Read the sentences. Rewrite each sentence, adding commas and quotation marks where needed.

EXAMPLE   Where should we begin? Kristen asked.

ANSWER   *"Where should we begin?" Kristen asked.*

11. Please let me see that magazine said Dane.

12. Gregory said I will teach you how to play this game.

13. Juan groaned I think I've misplaced my phone.

14. I would be happy to be your partner! Elisa exclaimed.

15. Let's call Randall Mac suggested. He always has some good ideas.

16. I'm not sure Rick said hesitantly where to go from here.

17. We can park here for an hour Carl noted. Then we'll have to add more money to the parking meter.

18. I want you to notice Steven declared that I have arrived on time today!

19. Maya's text message read See you at lunch.

20. I have just printed my final draft Vinny declared. After I proofread it, I'll hand it in.

SPEAKING APPLICATION

With a partner, take turns reporting direct and indirect conversational remarks. Your partner should tell whether each remark is a direct or an indirect quotation. You may use the examples in Practice 25.4A as models.

WRITING APPLICATION

Write three statements reporting something that you have said or that you have heard someone else say in the last few days. Use expressions (for example, *she said*), and put the speaker's words in quotation marks.

Using Quotation Marks With Other Punctuation Marks

You have seen that a comma or period used with a direct quotation goes inside the final quotation mark. In some cases, however, end marks should be placed outside of quotation marks.

Find It/ FIX IT

6

Grammar
Game Plan

> **Always place a comma or a period inside the final quotation mark.**

RULE 25.4.7

EXAMPLES   "Our class trip is this Tuesday," said Janet.

Matthew added, "We are leaving the school very early by bus."

> **Place a question mark or an exclamation mark inside the final quotation mark if the end mark is part of the quotation. Do not use an additional end mark outside the quotation marks.**

RULE 25.4.8

EXAMPLES   Joe asked, "What animal eats the most leaves?"

Peter said to Andy, "Help me get this raccoon out of my car!"

> **Place a question mark or exclamation mark outside the final quotation mark if the end mark is part of the entire sentence, not part of the quotation.**

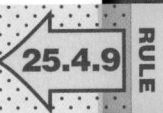

RULE 25.4.9

EXAMPLES   Don't say, "I doubt that will work"!

What famous person said, "We have nothing to fear but fear itself"?

See Practice 25.4C

Using Single Quotation Marks for Quotations Within Quotations

Double quotation marks are used to enclose the main quotation. The rules for using commas and end marks with **single quotation marks (' ')** are the same as they are with double quotation marks.

Single quotation marks are used to separate a quote that appears inside of another quotation.

RULE 25.4.10

Use **single quotation marks** to set off a quotation within a quotation.

EXAMPLES   "I thought I heard him say, 'I lost my wallet!' as he ran off," said Neil.

Nate said, "Someone yelled, 'Fire!' right before we smelled the smoke."

Punctuating Explanatory Material Within Quotes

Sometimes it is necessary to add information to a quotation that explains the quote more fully. In that case, brackets tell your reader which information came from the original speaker and which came from someone else. (See Section 25.7 for more information on brackets.)

RULE 25.4.11

Use brackets to enclose an explanation located within a quotation to show that the explanation is not part of the original quotation.

EXAMPLE   The mayor said, "The new park is the result of two communities [New City and Hillsdale] working together."

"We [the citizens of Brookfield] dedicate the new community center to our senior citizens." See Practice 25.4D

PRACTICE 25.4C > **Using Quotation Marks With Other Punctuation Marks**

Read the sentences. Decide whether the missing punctuation goes inside or outside the quotation marks. Then, rewrite the sentences, adding the proper punctuation for quotations.

EXAMPLE   Who wrote, "Hold fast to dreams"

ANSWER   *Who wrote, "Hold fast to dreams"?*

1. Did I hear someone say, "Let's have ice cream"

2. "Who gave permission to leave" asked the assistant principal.

3. Someone shouted, "Time out"

4. Did she answer, "Not right now, thank you"

5. A new student asked, "Can you direct me to the nurse's office"

6. Did your mother really say, "I'll give you the money if you need it"

7. Milton asked, "Is it too late to apply"

8. "I knew you could do it" my dad exclaimed.

9. Dee wondered, "Where did everyone go"

10. The boating instructor shouted, "Put on your lifejackets"

PRACTICE 25.4D > **Punctuating Quotations Within Quotations and Explanatory Material**

Read the sentences. Rewrite each sentence, adding single quotation marks or brackets where needed.

EXAMPLE   Jon said, "I enjoyed reading The Treasure of Lemon Brown."

ANSWER   *Jon said, "I enjoyed reading 'The Treasure of Lemon Brown.'"*

11. "For tomorrow," Mrs. May said, "please read the story Amigo Brothers."

12. Jan asked, "Did he say, I'll help?"

13. Paula asked, "Can anyone recite the poem Sarah Cynthia Sylvia Stout?"

14. "Did she say, I lost my hat?" Mom asked.

15. Lori wondered, "What does Longfellow mean by Each burning deed and thought?"

16. Mr. Metzger said, "I will now recite the poem Casey at the Bat."

17. "Did you hear him say, I've had it?" asked Liz.

18. The music director announced, "Miss Amory will sing Greensleeves, an old folk song."

19. Ron said, "When did you ever hear him Mr. Shah say, I don't want pizza?"

20. Sheila asked, "Does anyone know the words to the second verse of America?"

WRITING APPLICATION

Write three sentences in which you correctly use punctuation inside and outside quotation marks.

WRITING APPLICATION

Write two sentences with quotations within quotations. In your sentences, use single and double quotation marks correctly.

Using Quotation Marks for Dialogue

A conversation between two or more people is called a **dialogue.**
Adding dialogue makes your writing lively because it brings
different points of view into your work. It makes your work sound
like speech, so dialogue makes your reader feel involved in the
scene you describe.

RULE

25.4.12

> When you are writing a **dialogue,** indent to begin a new
> paragraph with each change of speaker. Also be sure to add
> quotation marks around a speaker's words. When a new
> speaker is quoted, be sure to indicate the change to your reader
> by adding information that identifies the new speaker.

EXAMPLE

"Will you be going with us on the family trip
again this summer ? " Noreen asked her cousin .

Gwen hesitated before answering . "I'm afraid
so . My parents think I enjoy the experience of
traveling with our whole family . "

"You fooled me , too , " Noreen replied .
"Maybe the trip will be better this year . I think
we're going to places that have large parks . If
we're lucky , we might even be able to go on a
few rides . "

"Well , at least it can't be any worse , " sighed
Gwen . "On the last trip , we waited in line for one
hour at three different historic homes in one day ! "

"I remember those lines , " said Noreen .
"Didn't you get sunburned while we were
waiting? "

Notice that each sentence is punctuated according to the rules
discussed earlier in this section.

See Practice 25.4E

See Practice 25.4F

584   Punctuation

PRACTICE 25.4E > **Using Quotation Marks in Dialogue**

Read the dialogue. Then, rewrite the dialogue. Use proper spacing for quotations and create additional paragraphs where needed. Be sure to use quotation marks and other punctuation correctly.

EXAMPLE   Can I ask you something? Matt asked Angelo. Sure Angelo answered. What?

ANSWER   *"Can I ask you something?" Matt asked Angelo.*

            "Sure," Angelo answered. "What?"

I would like to learn about forensic science Rose commented. You've been watching too many crime shows laughed Tim. Really Rose said it's fascinating, and I would even consider it as a career. Well there are many colleges that offer courses, but I think they're tough courses. There's a lot of science involved, Tim said. That's all right, I like science Rose replied. You could probably look online to find the requirements and places that offer courses Tim suggested. That's what I'll do Rose concluded.

PRACTICE 25.4F > **Revising Dialogue for Punctuation and Paragraphs**

Read the dialogue. Then, rewrite the dialogue. Add quotation marks and other punctuation, and begin new paragraphs where needed.

EXAMPLE   Hello, my name is Gwendolyn, the new girl said. What's your name? I'm Elizabeth. Nice to meet you.

ANSWER   *"Hello, my name is Gwendolyn," the new girl said. "What's your name?"*

            "I'm Elizabeth. Nice to meet you."

Justin and Marina walked into the sandwich shop for lunch. When they were seated at a table, a waiter came to take their order. What can I get you the waiter asked. I'll have the tuna salad sandwich with pickles Justin said. I'll have the vegetarian special Marina added. What would you like to drink with that asked the waiter. We'll both have water Marina responded. The waiter said Thank you. I'll bring your orders shortly. Then, he walked away.

SPEAKING APPLICATION

Read the dialogue in Practice 25.4E with a partner, each of you taking the part of one speaker. Read it again after you have revised it. Discuss why the original dialogue is confusing to read and your revised dialogue is easy to read.

WRITING APPLICATION

Write a dialogue in which you have participated, or you can make up a conversation. Use expressions (for example, *he said, she replied*), quotation marks, and correct paragraphing.

Using Quotation Marks in Titles

Quotation marks are generally used to set off the titles of shorter works.

RULE
25.4.13

> **Use quotation marks** to enclose the titles of short written works and around the title of a work that is mentioned as part of a collection.

WRITTEN WORKS THAT USE QUOTATION MARKS	
Title of a Short Story	"The Gift of the Magi"
Chapter From a Book	"The Test Is in the Tasting" from *No-Work Garden Book*
Title of a Short Poem	"Lucy"
Title of an Article	"How to Build a Birdhouse"
Title Mentioned as Part of a Collection	"Uncle Vanya" in *Eight Great Comedies*

RULE
25.4.14

> **Use quotation marks** around the titles of episodes in a television or radio series, songs, and parts of a long musical composition.

ARTISTIC WORKS THAT USE QUOTATION MARKS	
Title of an Episode	"The Nile" from *Cousteau Odyssey*
Title of a Song	"The Best Things in Life Are Free"
Title of a Part of a Long Musical Work	"The Storm" from the *William Tell Overture*

Using Underlining and Italics in Titles

Underlining and **italics** help make titles and other special words and names stand out in your writing. Underlining is used only in handwritten or typewritten material. In printed material, italic (slanted) print is used instead of underlining.

UNDERLINING   <u>The Secret Garden</u>   ITALICS   *The Secret Garden*

Underline or **italicize** the titles of long written works and publications that are published as a single work.

25.4.15 RULE

WRITTEN WORKS THAT ARE UNDERLINED OR ITALICIZED	
Title of a Book or Play	*The Giver; West Side Story*
Title of a Long Poem	*The Song of Hiawatha*
Title of a Magazine or Newspaper	*Time; The Washington Post*

Underline or **italicize** the titles of movies, television and radio series, long works of music, and art.

25.4.16 RULE

ARTISTIC WORKS THAT ARE UNDERLINED OR ITALICIZED	
Title of a Movie	*Schindler's List*
Title of a Television Series	*Lost*
Title of a Long Work of Music	*The Four Seasons*
Title of a Music Album	*Abbey Road*
Title of a Painting	*Starry Night*
Title of a Sculpture	*Venus de Milo*

Underline or **italicize** the names of individual air, sea, and spacecraft.

25.4.17 RULE

EXAMPLES   *Apollo 13*   the USS *Intrepid*

Underline or **italicize** words and letters used as names for themselves and foreign words.

25.4.18 RULE

EXAMPLES   How do you spell *Mississippi?*

My family uses the toast *santé,* which means

"good health" in French.

See Practice 25.4G
See Practice 25.4H

Quotation Marks, Underlining, and Italics

PRACTICE 25.4G Underlining Titles, Names and Words

Read the sentences. Rewrite each sentence, underlining titles, names, and words where needed. You can use italics if you are typing your answers.

EXAMPLE   I loved Stuart Little when I was younger.

ANSWER   I loved <u>Stuart Little</u> when I was younger.

1. Our class performed The Phantom Tollbooth.

2. Caroline knows all the songs from The Sound of Music.

3. Suzie read Goodnight Moon to the children she was babysitting.

4. Amanda was uncertain of the meaning of amorphous, so she looked it up in Webster's New World Dictionary.

5. My mom reads The Houston Chronicle.

6. We plan to see High School Musical at the theater next month.

7. Chloe really enjoyed the RMS Titanic exhibition at the children's museum.

8. For his biography report, Jethro read Walter Dean Myers's memoir Bad Boy.

9. I can't wait to see The Lion King again.

10. You can see the famous painting George Washington Crossing the Delaware at the Metropolitan Museum of Art.

PRACTICE 25.4H Using Underlining and Quotation Marks

Read the sentences. Rewrite each sentence, enclosing the titles in quotation marks or underlining them. You can use italics if you are typing your answers.

EXAMPLE   The choir sang Oh Shenandoah.

ANSWER   The choir sang "Oh Shenandoah."

11. My mom liked to read Pat the Bunny to me when I was very young.

12. I read an article in Now magazine titled How to Survive a Computer Crash.

13. The concert will end with America the Beautiful.

14. In honor of Black History Month, LaVerne will sing Lift Every Voice and Sing.

15. My little brother's favorite television program is Krazy Kats Cartoons.

16. My friend Jim, who likes technology, reads Future magazine.

17. One of Rodin's famous statues is The Thinker.

18. The Apollo 13 astronauts faced life-threatening challenges in space.

19. Our assignment for tomorrow is to read Laurence Yep's story Ribbons.

20. David memorized and recited The Raven by Edgar Allan Poe.

WRITING APPLICATION

Write several sentences in which you refer to a movie you have seen, a television program you watch, and a book you have read recently. Underline the titles.

WRITING APPLICATION

Make a list of the following: a song that you like, a poem that you have read in language arts, and a magazine with which you are familiar. Punctuate the titles correctly.

25.5 Hyphens

Hyphens (-) are used to combine words and to show a connection between the syllables of words that are broken at the ends of lines.

Find It / FIX IT

19
Grammar
Game Plan

Using Hyphens in Numbers

Hyphens are used to join compound numbers and fractions.

> Use a **hyphen** when you write two-word numbers from twenty-one through ninety-nine.

EXAMPLES	twenty-four	fifty-one

> Use a **hyphen** when you use a fraction as an adjective but not when you use a fraction as a noun.

ADJECTIVE   The class is three-fourths full.

NOUN   Two thirds of the students attended.

Using Hyphens for Prefixes and Suffixes

Many words with common prefixes are no longer hyphenated. The following prefixes are often used before proper nouns: *ante-*, *anti-*, *post-*, *pre-*, *pro-*, and *un-*. Check a dictionary when you are unsure about using a hyphen.

> Use a **hyphen** after a prefix that is followed by a proper noun or adjective.

EXAMPLES	post-Revolutionary	mid-April

> Use a **hyphen** in words with the prefixes *all-*, *ex-*, and *self-* and the suffix *-elect*.

EXAMPLES	all-powerful	ex-leader

Using Hyphens in Compound Words

Compound words are two or more words that must be read together to create a single idea.

Use a **hyphen** to connect two or more nouns that are used as one compound word, unless a dictionary gives a different spelling.

EXAMPLES   son-in-law   great-grandmother

Using Hyphens With Compound Modifiers

Hyphens help your reader group information properly.

Use a hyphen to connect a **compound modifier** that comes before a noun. Do not use a hyphen with a compound modifier that includes a word ending in *-ly* or in a compound proper adjective.

EXAMPLE   The team used a full-court press.

INCORRECT   poorly-written text   South-Asian tourist

CORRECT   poorly written text   South Asian tourist

A hyphen is not necessary when a compound modifier follows the noun it describes.

See Practice 25.5A
See Practice 25.5B

MODIFIER
BEFORE NOUN   The storm moved in an east-to-west direction.

MODIFIER
AFTER NOUN   The storm moved in the direction east to west.

However, if a dictionary spells a word with a hyphen, the word must always be hyphenated, even when it follows a noun.

EXAMPLE   The goalie is happy-go-lucky.

PRACTICE 25.5A > **Using Hyphens in Numbers and Words**

Read the following items. Write each item, adding hyphens where needed. If an item is already correct, write *correct*.

EXAMPLE   a world famous star

ANSWER   *a world-famous star*

1. mid January temperature
2. sixty six pencils
3. a bench that is well built
4. self respect
5. one third of a cup
6. one hundred people
7. two thirds of the students
8. well known actor
9. post Civil War
10. president elect

PRACTICE 25.5B > **Proofreading for Hyphens**

Read the sentences. Rewrite each sentence, adding hyphens where needed.

EXAMPLE   At the half, our team was ahead by twenty two points.

ANSWER   *At the half, our team was ahead by* ***twenty-two*** *points.*

11. Success builds self confidence.
12. Red hot embers glowed in the fireplace.
13. The recipe calls for one half teaspoon of cinnamon.
14. In London, we rode on the top level of a double decker bus.
15. My brother in law took me to the movies yesterday.
16. Sometimes, Beau's friends are annoyed by his all knowing attitude.
17. Rubble from a torn down building was strewn over the lot.
18. The ex governor stood on the platform beside the governor elect.
19. Fifty five people attended the fund raiser last night.
20. The adventurers will need an off road vehicle to get to that remote campsite.

SPEAKING APPLICATION

With a partner, brainstorm and list five terms that you use or have seen that are written with a hyphen. Take turns using these terms in phrases or sentences.

WRITING APPLICATION

Write two sentences in which you use words with *self-* or *ex-* as prefixes.

Using Hyphens at the Ends of Lines

Hyphens serve a useful purpose when they are used to divide words at the ends of lines. They should not, however, be used more often than is necessary because they can make reading feel choppy.

Avoid dividing words at the end of a line whenever possible. If a word must be divided, always divide it between syllables.

EXAMPLE   Marcia seems to have taken my advice most seriously and is doing better.

Check a dictionary if you are unsure how a word is divided into syllables. Looking up the word *seriously*, for example, you would find that its syllables are *se-ri-ous-ly*.

A hyphen used to divide a word should never be placed at the beginning of the second line. It must be placed at the end of the first line.

INCORRECT   Julio has taken many photo
-graphs of animals.

CORRECT   Julio has taken many photographs of animals.

Using Hyphens Correctly to Divide Words

One-syllable words cannot be divided.

Do *not* divide one-syllable words even if they seem long or sound like words with two syllables.

INCORRECT   fif-th   brow-se   stra-ight

CORRECT   fifth   browse   straight

25.5.10 RULE

Do *not* divide a word so that a single letter stands alone.

INCORRECT	i-dle	a-lone	ink-y
CORRECT	idle	alone	inky

Also avoid placing *-ed* at the beginning of a new line.

INCORRECT   Our last soccer game of the year was interrupted by lightning.

CORRECT   Our last soccer game of the year was
interrupted by lightning.

25.5.11 RULE

Avoid dividing proper nouns or proper adjectives.

INCORRECT	Dal-las	Don-ald
CORRECT	Dallas	Donald

See Practice 25.5C
See Practice 25.5D

25.5.12 RULE

Divide a hyphenated word only immediately following the existing hyphen.

INCORRECT   Students are taking an ever-in-
creasing interest in the environment.

CORRECT   Students are taking an ever-
increasing interest in the environment.

PRACTICE 25.5C > **Using Hyphens to Divide Words**

Read the following words. Rewrite each word. Then, draw vertical lines between syllables that can be divided at the end of a line. Do nothing to words that cannot be divided.

EXAMPLE   vocabulary

ANSWER   *vo|cab|u|lar|y*

1. tornado

2. warned

3. sacrifice

4. special

5. prediction

6. question

7. readjust

8. investigate

9. forgetful

10. collapse

PRACTICE 25.5D > **Using Hyphens in Words in Sentences**

Read the sentences. If a word has been divided correctly, write *correct*. If not, rewrite the sentence, dividing the word correctly or writing it as one word if it cannot be divided.

EXAMPLE   Many of my friends are interested in learning Spanish.

ANSWER   *correct*

11. The water was blue and the sunlight sparkled on the waves.

12. The university students participated in a rally.

13. We strolled the streets of our neighborhood after dinner.

14. Please tell me if the plumber has called about our broken sink.

15. My mother will be driving us to the concert.

16. A mid-April snowstorm took everyone by surprise.

17. Next week, the school-wide tournament will begin.

18. I believe Stephen was the only player who missed the game.

19. Do you have any specific questions about the quiz instructions?

20. Mrs. Marquez asked us to circle the correct answer.

WRITING APPLICATION

Look at a draft of a piece of writing you have done. Select three words and write them in syllables, showing how you would break them at the end of a line using a hyphen.

WRITING APPLICATION

Use three sentences from Practice 25.5D as models, and write sentences with hyphenated words.

25.6 Apostrophes

The **apostrophe** (') is used to show possession or ownership. It is also used in shortened forms of words called contractions. In a contraction, the apostrophe marks the place where letters have been omitted.

Using Apostrophes With Possessive Nouns

Apostrophes are used with nouns to show ownership or possession.

> **Add an apostrophe and -s to show the possessive case of most singular nouns and plural nouns that do not end in -s or -es.**

25.6.1 RULE

EXAMPLES   The doctor**'**s advice included plenty of rest.

The men**'**s store in town is having a huge sale.

Even when a singular noun already ends in *-s*, you can usually add an apostrophe and *-s* to show possession.

EXAMPLE   It was her boss**'**s idea to work longer hours.

In classical or ancient names that end in *-s*, it is common to omit the final *-s* to make pronunciation easier.

EXAMPLE   Ulysses**'** wisdom was well known.

> **Add an apostrophe to show the possessive case of plural nouns ending in -s or -es. Do not add an -s.**

25.6.2 RULE

EXAMPLE   The bees**'** buzzing was all I could hear.

Apostrophes   595

Add an apostrophe and -*s* (or just an apostrophe if the word is a plural ending in -*s*) to the last word of a compound noun to form the possessive.

EXAMPLES   the Boy Scouts**'** camping trip

my grandfather**'**s house

See Practice 25.6A

Using Apostrophes With Pronouns

Both indefinite and personal pronouns can show possession.

Use an apostrophe and -*s* with indefinite pronouns to show possession.

EXAMPLES   anyone**'**s seat   everyone else**'**s name

 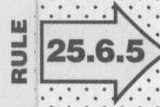
Do not use an apostrophe with possessive personal pronouns.

POSSESSIVE PERSONAL PRONOUNS		
	SINGULAR	PLURAL
First Person	I, me, my, mine	we, us, our, ours
Second Person	you, your, yours	you, your, yours
Third Person	he, him, his; she, her, hers; it, its	they, them; their, theirs

Some of these pronouns act as adjectives.

EXAMPLES   The dog carried a ball in its mouth.

Their house is for sale.

Others act as subjects, objects, and subject complements.

EXAMPLES   Mine is the blue jacket.

The red jacket is hers.

See Practice 25.6B

Using Apostrophes With Contractions

Contractions are used in informal speech and writing, especially in dialogue because they create the sound of speech.

> Use an **apostrophe** in a **contraction** to show where one or more letters have been omitted.

RULE 25.6.6

COMMON CONTRACTIONS		
Verb + *not*	is not = isn'␣t	cannot = can'␣t
Noun or Pronoun + *will*	I will = I'␣ll	we will = we'␣ll
Noun or Pronoun + *be*	you are = you'␣re	Andy is = Andy'␣s
Noun or Pronoun + *would*	she would = she'␣d	who would = who'␣d

> Avoid using contractions in formal speech and writing.

RULE 25.6.7

Contractions may be used in dialogue and in informal speech and writing, but they should be avoided in formal usage.

INFORMAL WRITING   What'␣s the latest news?

FORMAL WRITING   What is the latest news?

Using Apostrophes to Create Plurals

Do not use an apostrophe to form plurals, except in specific instances.

> Use an **apostrophe** and *-s* to create the plural form of a letter, numeral, or a word used as a name for itself.

RULE 25.6.8

See Practice 25.6C
See Practice 25.6D

EXAMPLES   Remember your *thank you*'␣s.

Your *b*'␣s and *d*'␣s look alike.

Read each phrase. Write the possessive form of each item.

EXAMPLE   clothing store for men

ANSWER   *men's clothing store*

1. work of the painter

2. hat belonging to Nina

3. apartment where the Maldonados live

4. eyes of a cat

5. the strength of Atlas

6. pizzeria owned by Mario

7. a vacation for a week

8. the soccer team for girls

9. the mitt belonging to the catcher

10. an idea from the brother of Ollie

Read the sentences. If all pronouns in a sentence are used correctly, write *correct*. If one or more pronouns are used incorrectly, rewrite the sentence correctly.

EXAMPLE   Her's is the best drawing.

ANSWER   *Hers is the best drawing.*

11. This is someone elses scarf, not mine.

12. We found everyone else's folder but not his.

13. No ones ideas will be ignored.

14. The dog was favoring its left front paw.

15. Everyones support is necessary.

16. The seats in the first row are our's.

17. Someones equipment was left in the gym.

18. The choice will be your's alone.

19. After you read your poem aloud, Julie will read hers.

20. Our writing group shared papers with another group; we read their's and they read ours.

WRITING APPLICATION

Look around the classroom. List five items or characteristics that you see and the possessor of each.

WRITING APPLICATION

Write two or three sentences in which you use *our, ours,* and the possessive form of *someone.*

25.8 Ellipses and Dashes

An **ellipsis** (. . .) shows where words have been omitted from a quoted passage. It can also mark a pause in dialogue. A **dash** (—) shows a strong, sudden break in thought or speech.

Using the Ellipsis

An **ellipsis** consists of three evenly spaced periods, or ellipsis points, in a row. There is a space before the first ellipsis point, between ellipsis points, and after the last ellipsis point. The plural form of the word *ellipsis* is *ellipses.*

> Use an **ellipsis** to show where words have been omitted from a quoted passage. Including an ellipsis shows the reader that the writer has chosen to omit some information.

RULE 25.8.1

QUOTED PASSAGE

"Four score and seven years ago our fathers brought forth on this continent a new nation conceived in liberty and dedicated to the proposition that all men are created equal." –Abraham Lincoln, *The Gettysburg Address,* November 19, 1863

QUOTED PASSAGE WITH WORDS OMITTED

"Fourscore and seven years ago our fathers brought forth . . . a new nation . . . dedicated to the proposition that all men are created equal."

Ellipses in Advertising

Ellipses are commonly used in ads for movies and other media. When you see an ellipsis in an ad, think about what might have been omitted. You might want to find the original review because the ad might be giving a different impression from what the reviewer intended.

ORIGINAL REVIEW

"I am amazed that anyone would think this movie is exciting or even worth seeing."

AD WORDING

" . . . exciting . . . worth seeing"

RULE 25.8.2 > Use an **ellipsis** to mark a pause in a dialogue or speech.

EXAMPLE   "But, in a larger sense, we can not dedicate ... we can not consecrate ... we can not hallow ... this ground."

RULE 25.8.3 > It is not necessary to use an **ellipsis** to show an omission at the beginning of material you are quoting. However, if you choose to omit any words *within* material you quote, you must use an ellipsis to show where information has been omitted.

UNNECESSARY   " ... Now we are engaged in a great civil war, testing whether that nation, or any nation, so conceived and so dedicated, can long endure."

CORRECT   "Now we are engaged in a great civil war, testing whether that nation, or any nation so conceived and so dedicated, can long endure."

RULE 25.8.4 > Use an **ellipsis** to show an omission, pause, or interruption in the middle of a sentence.

EXAMPLE   "But, in a larger sense, we cannot dedicate ... this ground."

RULE 25.8.5 > Use an **ellipsis** and an end mark to show an omission or a pause at the end of a sentence.

EXAMPLE   "I don't know how we are going to get this mess cleaned up. Maybe we could ... ."

If you omit words from a source you are quoting, omit the punctuation that accompanies the words unless it is correct in your sentence.

See Practice 25.8A

604   Punctuation

Dashes

Like commas and parentheses, **dashes** separate certain words, phrases, or clauses from the rest of the sentence or paragraph. Dashes, however, signal a stronger, more sudden interruption in thought or speech than commas or parentheses. A dash may also take the place of certain words before an explanation.

> **Use a dash to show a strong, sudden break in thought or speech.**

25.8.6 RULE

EXAMPLE   I can't believe how quickly we arrived—hey, where are you going?

If the interrupting expression is in the middle of the sentence, use a dash on either side of it to set it off from the rest of the sentence.

EXAMPLE   I read a book—it's in the library—about dinosaurs that have been newly discovered.

> **Use a dash in place of *in other words, namely,* or *that is* before an explanation.**

25.8.7 RULE

EXAMPLES   Dario reads books for one purpose—to learn.

To come in first in the relay race—this was the team's hope.

Dashes can also be used to set off nonessential appositives or modifiers.

EXAMPLE   A team player—someone who will make sacrifices for the good of the team—is what we need.

See Practice 25.8B

PRACTICE 25.8A > **Using Ellipses**

Read the sentences. For each sentence, tell whether ellipses (or ellipsis points) are used to indicate a *pause* or an *omission*.

EXAMPLE   "Well . . . I'm not sure about this," said Luis.

ANSWER   *pause*

1. Wow . . . I don't know how to thank you.

2. In her review, Kate wrote, "This exciting movie kept me on the edge of my seat . . . I can't wait to see it again."

3. Of course, we could always . . . uh . . . try a different tactic.

4. John F. Kennedy said, "Ask not what your country can do for you . . . ."

5. Mom . . . are you sure I can't go to Max's house after I finish my homework?

6. The Preamble to the Constitution reads, "We the people of the United States . . . do ordain and establish this Constitution for the United States of America."

7. Well . . . um . . . let me think about it.

8. The words of Dr. Martin Luther King Jr., "Let freedom ring . . . From every mountainside, let freedom ring," still move us today.

9. Keena . . . are you still there . . . or did you hang up?

10. The last line of "All Summer in a Day" reads, "They unlocked the door . . . and let Margot out."

PRACTICE 25.8B > **Using Dashes**

Read the sentences. Rewrite each sentence, adding dashes where they are needed.

EXAMPLE   Bernard plays several instruments guitar, banjo, and drums.

ANSWER   *Bernard plays several instruments —guitar, banjo, and drums.*

11. There's only one thing I still need to pack for my trip sunscreen.

12. All of the preparations for the dance including the decorations have been made.

13. I would like to present the winner Hector Rodriguez.

14. I already have all of the ingredients for this recipe even the walnuts.

15. Head east on the trail wait, you forgot the map!

16. The money thirty dollars is on the table.

17. The committee announced what they need to get the job done more money, more time, more people.

18. Jonah had only one goal to be the fastest sprinter on the team.

19. My favorite restaurant The Corner Diner is closed for renovations.

20. An Academy Award an Oscar recognizes outstanding work in a motion picture.

SPEAKING APPLICATION

With a partner, read aloud Sentences 7 and 9. Then, together, write a sentence that uses ellipsis points for the same purpose.

WRITING APPLICATION

Copy a passage from a selection in your literature textbook. Leave out a part of the passage, either in the middle or at the end, and use ellipses to show where the omission occurs.

CHAPTER 26

CAPITALIZATION

Understanding the rules of capitalization will help you to craft clear sentences.

WRITE GUY *Jeff Anderson, M.Ed.*

WHAT DO YOU NOTICE?

Locate capital letters as you zoom in on sentences from the folktale "Sun and Moon in a Box," retold by Alfonso Ortiz and Richard Erdoes.

MENTOR TEXT

> "Let us steal the box," said Coyote.
> "No, that would be wrong," said Eagle. "Let us just borrow it."
> When the Kachinas were not looking, Eagle grabbed the box and flew off. Coyote ran after him on the ground.

Now, ask yourself the following questions:

- Why are the words *eagle* and *coyote* capitalized?
- In Eagle's quotation, why are the words *no* and *let* capitalized?

The words *eagle* and *coyote* are usually common nouns, but here they are the names of characters, so they are capitalized as proper nouns. Because Eagle's quotation includes two complete sentences, the first word of each sentence begins with a capital letter.

Grammar for Writers A capital letter not only signals the start of a sentence, but it can also show the beginning of a quotation. When writing dialogue, be sure to follow capitalization rules, so readers can hear your character's words clearly.

What word should be capitalized in this sentence?

What? The word what!

26.1 Using Capitalization

Capital letters are used for the first words in all sentences and in many quotations. They are also used for the word *I*, whatever its position in a sentence.

The Word *I*

RULE 26.1.1

The pronoun *I* is always capitalized.

EXAMPLE **I** worked for two years as an assistant before **I** received a promotion.

Sentences

One of the most common uses of a capital letter is to signal the beginning of a sentence. The first word in a sentence must begin with a capital letter.

RULE 26.1.2

Capitalize the first word in **declarative, interrogative, imperative,** and **exclamatory** sentences.

DECLARATIVE **S**trong gusts of wind made it very difficult to golf on the course.

INTERROGATIVE **W**ho found the answer to that very difficult question?

IMPERATIVE **T**hink carefully before you answer.

EXCLAMATORY **W**hat an amazing situation this is!

See Practice 26.1A

Sometimes only part of a sentence is written. The rest of the sentence is understood. In these cases, a capital is still needed for the first word.

EXAMPLES **W**here? **W**ho said? **S**urely!

See Practice 26.1B

Quotations

A capital letter also signals the first word in a **direct quotation,** a person's exact words.

> Capitalize the first word in a quotation if the quotation is a complete sentence.

RULE 26.1.3

EXAMPLES   Several people shouted, "**S**top the car!"

"**S**he really wants to see that play," Helen confided.

Randy asked, "**H**as anyone seen my dog?"

> When a quotation consists of one complete sentence in two parts, only capitalize the first part of the quotation.

RULE 26.1.4

EXAMPLES   "**H**ow much longer," asked Bob, "**w**ill this game continue?"

"**P**enguins seem to have no special fear of humans," she said, "**a**nd have approached groups of explorers without hesitation."

> If a quotation contains more than one sentence, the first word of each sentence begins with a capital.

RULE 26.1.5

EXAMPLES   "**P**lease distribute these menus to everyone," said the waiter. "**T**hey show the specials of the day."

See Practice 26.1C
See Practice 26.1D

"**R**emember to bring your project," said my friend. "**Y**ou will need it for class tomorrow."

Writing Sentences Using Capitalization

Read the sentences. Rewrite each sentence, adding the missing capitalization.

EXAMPLE   i went back to the school to get the book i needed for homework.

ANSWER   *I* went back to the school to get the book *I* needed for homework.

1. My mother said i could buy the shoes that i saw in the magazine.

2. i want to read another book by that author i like.

3. Because i am the youngest, i often get chores no one else wants.

4. i know that i am my dog's favorite person in the family.

5. i thought i told you that i was going to be late.

6. i played football after i finished my homework.

7. i have to practice the piano every day if i want to improve.

8. i tried out for the school play, and i was chosen for a part.

9. i cannot decide what i want to be when i grow up.

10. i didn't think i would be good at golf, but i am.

Writing Sentences Using Capitalization

Read the sentences. Rewrite each sentence, adding the missing capitals. Then, write if the sentence is declarative, interrogative, imperative, or exclamatory.

EXAMPLE   did you really get the highest grade in the class?

ANSWER   *Did* you really get the highest grade in the class? — interrogative

11. i can't believe it either!

12. ask me the next time you borrow my sweater.

13. it is time to go home now.

14. why can't we stay a little longer?

15. do your homework after dinner.

16. todd wasn't able to fix the computer.

17. i miss you, too!

18. when are you going on your fishing trip?

19. i love your new shoes!

20. aren't they great?

WRITING APPLICATION

Write four sentences using the word *I*. Remember to capitalize each sentence correctly. Exchange sentences with a partner. Check each other's work for correct capitalization.

WRITING APPLICATION

Write a paragraph about your favorite holiday. Use at least one declarative, one interrogative, one imperative, and one exclamatory sentence in your paragraph. Exchange paragraphs with a partner and check for correct capitalization.

PRACTICE 26.1C > **Supplying Capitalization**

Read the sentences. Rewrite each sentence, adding the missing capitals.

EXAMPLE   she and i became good friends.

ANSWER   *She and I became good friends.*

1. my teacher thinks i have a good chance to get the role i want in the play.

2. spencer asked, "where did you get that hat?"

3. what should we do first?

4. will you come with us? why not?

5. who said, "i have but one life to give for my country"?

6. "my favorite color," said kerrie, "is blue."

7. are you going to the rodeo? when?

8. what a great idea that is!

9. "start your research in the library," our teacher told us. "the media specialist will help you find sources."

10. jen asked, "do you have a pencil i may borrow?"

PRACTICE 26.1D > **Proofreading for Capitalization**

Read the sentences. Rewrite each sentence, correcting any capitalization errors.

EXAMPLE   Which book should i read for my report?

ANSWER   *Which book should I read for my report?*

11. I don't know what i'll wear to the dance.

12. Gail called and said, "i need some help with my math homework. Will you come over soon?"

13. "where," wondered Mrs. Getz, "is my measuring cup?"

14. let me see your artwork.

15. Perry quoted this line from *Hamlet*: "to be, or not to be: that is the question."

16. did you ask Jackie to distribute some of these flyers?

17. "I'll be finished by six o'clock," Dorie said. She added, "may I meet you then?"

18. if you wait a minute, i'll walk with you.

19. Wow! did you see that home run?

20. wait for the signal before you begin.

WRITING APPLICATION

Using sentences 6 and 9 in Practice 26.1C as models, write two new sentences with correct capitalization in quotations.

WRITING APPLICATION

Write a short conversation you had with someone yesterday or today. Check that you have used correct capitalization.

Test Warm-Up

DIRECTIONS
Read the introduction and the passage that follows. Then, answer the questions to show that you can use and understand the function of conventions of capitalization in reading and writing.

Carmen wrote this paragraph about a weekend trip to her cousin's house. Read the paragraph and think about the changes you would suggest as a peer editor. When you finish reading, answer the questions that follow.

My Cousin Robyn

(1) My cousin robyn and i are close, but we live many miles apart. (2) Robyn lives in Austin, and I live in Houston. (3) I was excited to visit her over a long weekend. (4) "It's hard to believe, Robyn exclaimed when she saw me, "How tall you've gotten." (5) She was right; I have grown over four inches this year. (6) We enjoyed our time together, shopping and eating at a fabulous mexican restaurant. (7) It was sad saying goodbye. (8) "Do you promise," Robyn asked, "to e-mail me the pictures you took?" (9) I sent Robyn the pictures the next day!

1 What change, if any, should be made in sentence 1?

  A Change *cousin* to **Cousin**

  B Change *are* to **is**

  C Change *robyn and i* to **Robyn and I**

  D Make no change

2 What is the BEST way to edit sentence 4?

  F "It's hard to believe, Robyn exclaimed when she saw me, "how tall you've gotten."

  G "It's hard to believe," Robyn exclaimed when she saw me, "How tall you've gotten!"

  H "It's hard to believe," Robyn exclaimed when she saw me, "how tall you've gotten!"

  J "It's hard to believe, Robyn exclaimed when she saw me, "how tall you've gotten?"

3 What change, if any, should be made in sentence 6?

  A Change *restaurant* to **Restaurant**

  B Change *mexican* to **Mexican**

  C Change *shopping* to **Shopping**

  D Make no change

4 What change, if any, should be made in sentence 8?

  F Change *to* to **To**

  G Delete the comma after asked

  H Change the question mark to an exclamation mark

  J Make no change

Using Capitalization for Proper Nouns

An important use of capital letters is to show that a word is a **proper noun.** Proper nouns name specific people, places, or things.

> **Capitalize all proper nouns.**

RULE
26.1.6

EXAMPLES   **J**ack **K**ennedy
Devils **T**ower **N**ational **M**onument
George **W**ashington **B**ridge
Sears **T**ower

Names of People

> **Capitalize each part of a person's full name, including initials.**

RULE
26.1.7

EXAMPLES   **M**ary **L**ynn **S**wanson
Eric **J**. **T**. **W**atson
L. **T**. **A**lworth

When a last name has two parts and the first part is *Mac, Mc, O',* or *St.*, the second part of the last name must also be capitalized.

EXAMPLES   **M**ac**D**onald
Mc**L**aughlin
O'Gill
St. **P**eter

For two-part last names that do not begin with *Mac, Mc, O',* or *St.*, the capitalization varies. Check a reliable source, such as a biographical dictionary, for the correct spelling.

See Practice 26.1E

Geographical Places

Any specific geographical location listed on a map should be capitalized.

26.1.8

Capitalize geographical names.

GEOGRAPHICAL NAMES	
Streets	Warren Street, Carlton Avenue, Interstate 10
Cities	Baltimore, London, Memphis, Tokyo
States	Arizona, Florida, Hawaii, Idaho
Nations	Italy, Canada, Kenya, France, Peru, South Korea
Continents	North America, Asia, Africa, Antarctica
Deserts	Sahara, Negev, Mojave
Mountains	Mount Everest, Rocky Mountains
Regions	Great Plains, Appalachian Highlands, Northwest
Islands	Canary Islands, Fiji Islands
Rivers	Mississippi River, Amazon River
Lakes	Lake Michigan, Great Salt Lake, Lake Erie
Bays	Hudson Bay, Baffin Bay, Biscayne Bay
Seas	Black Sea, Mediterranean Sea, North Sea
Oceans	Atlantic Ocean, Arctic Ocean

Regions and Map Directions

Names of regions, such as the South and the Northeast, are capitalized because they refer to a specific geographical location. Map directions that do not refer to a specific geographical location are not capitalized.

26.1.9

Do not capitalize compass points, such as north, southwest, or east, when they simply refer to direction.

REGION — My uncle lives in the **S**outheast.

DIRECTION — Our car headed **s**outh on River Street.

Specific Events and Time Periods

> **Capitalize the names of specific events, periods of time, and documents.**

The following chart contains examples of events, periods of time, and documents that require capitalization.

SPECIFIC EVENTS AND TIMES	
Historical Periods	Age of Enlightenment, Middle Ages, the Renaissance
Historical Events	World War II, Boston Tea Party, Battle of Lexington
Documents	Bill of Rights, Treaty of Paris, Declaration of Independence
Days	Wednesday, Saturday
Months	December, October
Holidays	Thanksgiving, Labor Day
Religious Days	Christmas, Passover, Ramadan
Special Events	Fiddlers' Convention, Boston Marathon, Super Bowl

Names of Seasons

The names of the seasons are an exception to this rule. Even though they name a specific period of time, the seasons of the year are not capitalized unless they are part of a title or an event name.

SEASONS   A popular activity this **w**inter is skiing.

The students traveled in the **f**all.

TITLE   During a hot **s**pring, I read *The Long Winter.*

EVENT   It was so hot at the **S**pring Festival it felt

like **s**ummer.

See Practice 26.1F

PRACTICE 26.1E **Using Capitalization for Names of People**

Read the sentences. Write each name, adding the missing capitals.

EXAMPLE   ina and ivy are twins.

ANSWER   *Ina, Ivy*

1. The mcmullens live next door to us.

2. Our class read a story by edgar allan poe.

3. t. j. gonzales will be the speaker at the assembly.

4. gina deangelo and paul o'connor are both in my social studies class.

5. pete named his dog scottie.

6. May I have a piece of cake, mom?

7. louis l'amour wrote stories and essays about the West.

8. susan b. anthony was an American civil rights leader.

9. Today is grandma's birthday.

10. My full name is julianna claire maria lugo, but my friends call me juli.

PRACTICE 26.1F **Using Capitalization for Geographical Places, Specific Events, and Time Periods**

Read the sentences. Write the name of each geographical place, specific event, and time period, adding the missing capitals.

EXAMPLE   The colorado river flows through the grand canyon.

ANSWER   *Colorado River, Grand Canyon*

11. My brother lives in tokyo, japan.

12. The panama canal links the caribbean sea with the pacific ocean.

13. Last july, my family visited warsaw, poland.

14. Huck Finn and Jim floated down the mississippi river on a raft.

15. World leaders are trying to resolve the conflicts in the middle east.

16. The Morrisons gave a slide show of their safari in kenya.

17. We visited three new england states: maine, new hampshire, and vermont.

18. My cousin plans to run in the new york city marathon next year.

19. During the middle ages in europe, many towns and cities grew as trade developed.

20. My grandparents sold their house in pennsylvania and moved south.

WRITING APPLICATION

Write your full name and the names of your siblings if you have any. Then, write the names of your teachers and your principal.

WRITING APPLICATION

Write your address, including your city and state. Then, list any bodies of water or mountains in your region.

Specific Groups

Proper nouns that name specific groups also require capitalization.

> Capitalize the names of various organizations, government bodies, political parties, and nationalities, as well as the languages spoken by different groups.

26.1.11 RULE

EXAMPLES   We made a very generous donation to the **R**ed **C**ross.

My friend Shirley, who speaks **C**hinese fluently, works as a translator.

The **D**epartment of **T**ransportation often issues travel alerts.

The proper nouns shown in the chart are groups with which many people are familiar. All specific groups, however, must be capitalized, even if they are not well known.

SPECIFIC GROUPS	
Clubs	Kiwanis Club Rotary Club
Organizations	National Governors Association National Organization for Women
Institutions	Massachusetts Institute of Technology Smithsonian Institution
Businesses	Simon Chemical Corporation Fido's Favorite Pet Foods
Government Bodies	United States Congress Supreme Court
Political Parties	Democrats Republican Party
Nationalities	Chinese, German Nigerian, Iranian
Languages	English, Spanish Korean, Swahili

See Practice 26.1G

Religious References

Use capitals for the names of the religions of the world and certain other words related to religion.

RULE **26.1.12**

Capitalize references to religions, deities, and religious scriptures.

The following chart presents words related to five of the world's major religions. Next to each religion are examples of some of the related religious words that must be capitalized. Note that the name of each religion is also capitalized.

RELIGIOUS REFERENCES	
Christianity	God, Lord, Father, Holy Spirit, Bible, books of the Bible (Genesis, Deuteronomy, Psalms, and so on)
Judaism	Lord, Father, Prophets, Torah, Talmud, Midrash
Islam	Allah, Prophet, Mohammed, Qur'an
Hinduism	Brahma, Bhagavad Gita, Vedas
Buddhism	Buddha, Mahayana, Hinayana

Note in the following examples, however, that the words *god* and *goddess* in references to mythology are not capitalized. A god's or goddess's name, however, is capitalized.

EXAMPLES   In Greek mythology, the supreme god was Zeus.

The goddess Hera was the wife of Zeus and was the goddess of women.

Specific Places and Items

Monuments, memorials, buildings, celestial bodies, awards, the names of specific vehicles, and trademarked products should be capitalized.

> **Capitalize the names of specific places and items.**

OTHER SPECIAL PLACES AND ITEMS	
Monuments	Statue of Liberty Washington Monument
Memorials	Winston Churchill Memorial Vietnam Veterans Memorial
Buildings	Houston Museum of Fine Arts Empire State Building the Capitol Building (in Washington, D.C.)
Celestial Bodies (except the moon and sun)	Earth, Milky Way Jupiter, Aries
Awards	Newbery Medal Nobel Peace Prize
Air, Sea, and Space Craft	*Spirit of St. Louis* *Monitor* *Voyager 2* *Metroliner*
Trademarked Brands	Krazy Korn Eco-Friendly Cleanser
Names	Zenox Kermit the Frog the Great Houdini

> **Capitalize the names of awards.**

Notice that *the* is not capitalized in these examples.

EXAMPLES   the Emmy Awards

the Rhodes Scholarship

the Most Valuable Player Award

the Purple Heart

See Practice 26.1H

PRACTICE 26.1G **Using Capitalization for Groups and Organizations**

Read the sentences. Write each group or organization, adding the missing capitals.

EXAMPLE   My little brother just joined the cub scouts.

ANSWER   *Cub Scouts*

1. The green valley cyclers go on biking trips every weekend.

2. The international red cross provides local assistance after disasters.

3. The college board sponsors college entrance exams.

4. That case went all the way to the supreme court.

5. Our superintendent graduated from howard university.

6. The girl scouts sell cookies every year.

7. I found local information at the chamber of commerce.

8. You can get new running shoes at sammy's sporting goods.

9. The city council meets every Wednesday.

10. You can take some interesting and unusual courses at northern community college.

PRACTICE 26.1H **Using Capitalization for Religious References and Specific Items and Places**

Read the sentences. Write each term that should be capitalized, adding the missing capitals.

EXAMPLE   Author Toni Morrison won a nobel prize in literature.

ANSWER   *Nobel Prize in Literature*

11. The planet mars has always fascinated scientists.

12. The Goldbergs host a seder dinner during passover.

13. In Washington, D.C., we visited the vietnam veterans memorial and the capitol.

14. Many muslims make an annual pilgrimage to Mecca, called the hajj.

15. The president travels on *air force one*.

16. I enjoy watching the oscars ceremony.

17. My father took the *acela* train from Providence to New York.

18. yogi's yogurt yummies are my new favorite snack.

19. The bible, the torah, and the qur'an are three major religious texts.

20. The USS *john f. kennedy* aircraft carrier is no longer in operation.

WRITING APPLICATION

Write the names of five organizations or groups in your school and community. Capitalize the names correctly.

WRITING APPLICATION

Write the names of the following:

- a religious event or holiday
- a planet
- your favorite cereal
- a building in your town or city

Using Capitalization for Proper Adjectives

When a proper noun or a form of a proper noun is used to describe another noun, it is called a **proper adjective.** Proper adjectives usually need a capital letter.

> Capitalize most **proper adjectives.**

In the following examples, notice that both proper nouns and proper adjectives are capitalized. Common nouns that are modified by proper adjectives, however, are not capitalized.

PROPER NOUNS

W orld **W** ar II

M exico

PROPER ADJECTIVES

a **W** orld **W** ar II **b** attleship

a **M** exican **h** at

The names of some countries and states must be modified to be used as proper adjectives. For example, something from Kenya is Kenyan, someone from Texas is Texan, a chair from Spain is a Spanish chair, and a building in France is a French building.

Brand Names as Adjectives

Trademarked brand names are considered to be proper nouns. If you use a brand name to describe a common noun, the brand name becomes a proper adjective. In this case, capitalize only the proper adjective and not the common noun.

> Capitalize brand names used as adjectives.

PROPER NOUN

F ruit **G** rains

PROPER ADJECTIVE

F ruit **G** rains **c** ereal

Notice that only the proper adjective *Fruit Grains* is capitalized. The word *cereal* is not capitalized because it is a common noun; it is not part of the trademarked name.

See Practice 26.1I

Using Capitalization for Titles of People

A person's title shows his or her or relationship to other people. Whether a title is capitalized often depends on how it is used in a sentence.

Social and Professional Titles

Social and professional titles may be written before a person's name or used alone in place of a person's name.

RULE 26.1.17

> **Capitalize the title of a person when the title is followed by the person's name or when it is used in place of a person's name in direct address.**

BEFORE A NAME   Reverend O'Connor and Doctor Brennan have arrived.

IN DIRECT ADDRESS   Look, Lieutenant, here is the missing clue!

TITLES OF PEOPLE	
Social	Mister, Madam or Madame, Miss, Ms., Sir
Business	Doctor, Professor, Superintendent, Attorney
Religious	Reverend, Father, Rabbi, Bishop, Sister
Military	Private, Ensign, Captain, General, Admiral
Government	President, Senator, Representative, Governor, Mayor, Prince, Queen, King

In most cases, do not capitalize titles that are used alone or that follow a person's name—especially if the title is preceded by the articles *a, an,* or *the.*

EXAMPLES   Roger Simmons, the detective assigned to the case, will call you.

Tell your **state representative** how you feel about the issue.

My brother George, who is a private in the army, will be home on leave soon.

Government Officials

> Capitalize the titles of government officials when they immediately precede the name of specific officials. If no person is named, these titles should be written in lower case.

EXAMPLES

Vice **P**resident **B**iden will preside at the meeting.

The club **v**ice **p**resident will preside at the meeting.

Superintendent **W**aller will speak to the students about the quality of education.

The **s**uperintendent of **s**chools is responsible for the quality of education.

Note: Certain honorary titles are always capitalized, even if the title is not used with a proper name or direct address. These titles include the First Lady of the United States, Speaker of the House of Representatives, Queen Mother of England, and the Prince of Wales.

Titles for Family Relationships

> Capitalize titles showing family relationships when the title is used with the person's name or as the person's name—except when the title comes after a possessive noun or pronoun.

BEFORE A NAME

We respect **A**unt Betsy's opinion.

IN PLACE OF A NAME

Is **G**randfather going?

AFTER POSSESSIVES

Jeff's **f**ather is the team doctor.

See Practice 26.1J

Notice that the family title *father* used in the last example is not capitalized because it is used after the possessive word *Jeff's.*

PRACTICE 26.1I ▷ **Using Capitalization for Proper Adjectives**

Read the sentences. Write the proper adjectives, adding the correct capitalization.

EXAMPLE   The canadian winters can be quite severe.

ANSWER   *Canadian*

1. The egyptian pyramids are one of the wonders of the world.

2. I saw an exhibit of japanese woodblock prints at the museum.

3. Mary Shelley wrote *Frankenstein*, an early gothic novel.

4. My mother enjoys irish breakfast tea.

5. Ivan was interested in the german sports cars at the auto show.

6. We went to a restaurant for thai food.

7. Bill and Cindy Duquette are dreaming about a caribbean vacation.

8. In 1776, american colonists declared independence from their english rulers.

9. We drink florida orange juice every day.

10. Will you help me study for the spanish test?

PRACTICE 26.1J ▷ **Using Capitalization for Titles of People**

Read the sentences. If the title in each sentence is correctly capitalized, write *correct*. If it is not, rewrite the title correctly.

EXAMPLE   My mother took me to doctor Perez when I had the flu.

ANSWER   *Doctor*

11. In the opening ceremony, Mayor Massey will cut the ribbon and give a speech.

12. All in the court rose as judge Saris entered.

13. The evening news featured an interview with governor Chase.

14. An army recruiter, lieutenant Carson, will be here next week.

15. The ceremony was performed by Reverend Walker.

16. I went on a camping trip with uncle Stan.

17. Perhaps you should write a letter to senator Olson.

18. General Colin Powell later became Secretary of State.

19. My grandma Ginny loves to cook.

20. The library will present a lecture by professor Watkins on green energy.

WRITING APPLICATION

Write three proper adjectives and the nouns they modify. You may use the proper adjectives in the sentences above as models. Capitalize the proper adjectives.

WRITING APPLICATION

Write the title and name of one of your town or city officials, the governor of your state, and one senator and representative from your state.

Using Capitalization for Titles of Works

Capital letters are used for the titles of things such as written works, pieces of art, and school courses.

> **Capitalize the first word and all other key words in the titles of books, newspapers, magazines, short stories, poems, plays, movies, songs, and artworks.**

RULE 26.1.20

Do not capitalize articles (*a, an, the*), prepositions (*of, to*), and conjunctions (*and, but*) that are fewer than four letters long unless they begin a title. Verbs and personal pronouns, no matter how short, are always capitalized in titles.

EXAMPLE   "**I**n **E**xile" by Anton Chekhov

> **Capitalize the title of a school course when it is followed by a course number or when it refers to a language. Otherwise, do not capitalize school subjects.**

RULE 26.1.21

EXAMPLES   **G**erman   **L**iterature 130   **S**cience II

I have **s**cience this morning.

Using Capitalization in Letters

Several parts of friendly and business letters are capitalized.

> **In the heading, capitalize the street, city, state, and month.**

RULE 26.1.22

EXAMPLES   **F**irst **S**treet   **B**oonton   **M**aryland   **J**une

> **In the salutation, capitalize the first word, any title, and the name of the person or group mentioned. In the closing, capitalize the first word.**

RULE 26.1.23

See Practice 26.1K

See Practice 26.1L

SALUTATIONS   **M**y **d**ear **J**ustin,   **D**ear **A**unt **S**ally,

CLOSINGS   **Y**our **n**eighbor,   **B**est **w**ishes,   **L**ove,

| PRACTICE 26.1K | **Using Capitalization for Titles of Things** |

Read the sentences. Write the titles, adding the correct capitalization.

EXAMPLE   *star wars* has become a classic movie.

ANSWER   *Star Wars*

1. Our teacher gave a dramatic reading of the poem "the highwayman" by Alfred Noyes.

2. Do you know how Tom got people to whitewash the fence in *the adventures of tom sawyer?*

3. Everyone stood when "the star-spangled banner" was played.

4. My dad reads *the wall street journal.*

5. The book *charlie and the chocolate factory* was made into a film.

6. I would like to see the *mona lisa* in the Louvre Museum in Paris.

7. The children in nursery school sang "twinkle, twinkle, little star."

8. Andy used *newsweek* magazine as one of his sources for his report.

9. The poem "a noiseless patient spider" by Walt Whitman is one of my favorites.

10. In 1620, the Pilgrims crossed the Atlantic on the *mayflower.*

| PRACTICE 26.1L | **Using Capitalization for Titles of Things** |

Read the sentences. Rewrite each sentence, adding the missing capitals.

EXAMPLE   I am taking first-year spanish.

ANSWER   *I am taking first-year Spanish.*

11. Today in language arts class, we discussed "all summer in a day."

12. Allie has seen *the lion king* six times.

13. Our class enjoyed Gary Soto's story "seventh grade."

14. Estelle read *kira-kira* for her independent reading report.

15. Laura has been learning to play J. S. Bach's "minuet in g."

16. Vincent Van Gogh's painting *starry night* has inspired many people.

17. Caitlin has done well in algebra I, so next year she'll take algebra II.

18. Jeff faithfully reads *sports illustrated.*

19. My sister is taking chemistry 101 at her college.

20. One of Shakespeare's most popular plays is *the tragedy of romeo and juliet.*

WRITING APPLICATION

Write titles of the following, with correct capitalization:

- a short story you have read
- a book you like
- your favorite movie
- a television program

WRITING APPLICATION

Write statements in which you make an evaluation of each of the following:

- a book or article you have read recently
- a movie or program you have viewed recently

Capitalize titles correctly.

Using Capitalization in Abbreviations, Acronyms, and Initials

An **abbreviation** is a shortened form of a word or phrase. An **acronym** is an abbreviation of a phrase that takes one or more letters from each word in the phrase being abbreviated.

> In general, capitalize **abbreviations, acronyms,** and **initials** if the words or names they stand for are capitalized.

RULE 26.1.24

INITIALS	**A . C .** Black
TITLES	**D** r. Samuel Green **S** r.
ACADEMIC DEGREES	Samuel Green, **M.D.** , Ben Queen, **Ph.D.**
ACRONYMS	**UNICEF** , **ROTC**

Abbreviations for most units of measurement are not capitalized.

EXAMPLES	**i** n. (inches) **t** bsp. (tablespoon)

> Capitalize **abbreviations** that appear in addresses.

RULE 26.1.25

Use a two-letter state abbreviation without periods when the abbreviation is followed by a ZIP code in an address. Capitalize both letters of the state abbreviation.

EXAMPLE	Trenton, **NJ** 08629

> Capitalize **acronyms** that stand for proper nouns, such as businesses, government bodies, and organizations.

RULE 26.1.26

Spell out the name of an organization and include its acronym in parentheses the first time you use it. Use only the acronym in later references.

EXAMPLE	Have you heard of the Food and Drug Administration (**FDA**)? The **FDA** is responsible for protecting the public health.

See Practice 26.1M
See Practice 26.1N

PRACTICE 26.1M > Using Capitalization for Abbreviations

Read the items. Rewrite each item, adding capitals as needed. If the item is already correct, write *correct*.

EXAMPLE   Columbia rd.

ANSWER   Columbia *Rd.*

1. Gov. Brown
2. dr. Suarez
3. Atlanta, ga 30301
4. uss *Constitution*
5. Richard Smith jr.
6. one tsp. salt
7. Sixth Ave.
8. maj. Armstrong
9. 146 lake st.
10. 5 ft 2 in.

PRACTICE 26.1N > Using Capitalization for Initials and Acronyms

Read the sentences. Write the initials and acronyms, adding capitals as needed. If the sentence is correct, write *correct*.

EXAMPLE   Have you read *The Lord of the Rings* trilogy by j.r.r. Tolkien?

ANSWER   *J.R.R.*

11. We visited nasa's Johnson Space Center when we were in Houston.
12. Arthur Kelly, d.v.m., works at the veterinary hospital where we take our dog.
13. The John F. Kennedy Presidential Library and Museum in Boston opened in 1979.
14. Check the SPF before you buy that sunscreen.
15. The ncaa basketball tournament is a popular event every spring.
16. The speed limit on this street is 25 mph.
17. The naacp played an active role in the civil rights movement in the 1960s.
18. My brother's name is Christopher John, but he likes to be called cj.
19. Because she loves animals, Heather volunteers for the aspca.
20. We flew into t. f. Green Airport in Providence, r.i.

SPEAKING APPLICATION

Make up an acronym and use it in a sentence. Share your sentence with a partner, who will guess what the acronym stands for. Explain the acronym if necessary.

WRITING APPLICATION

Address a letter envelope to a relative or acquaintance. Use the person's title and full name, including middle initial. Use abbreviations for the street and state.

 **PRACTICE 1** Using Periods, Question Marks, and Exclamation Marks

Read the sentences. Then, rewrite the sentences, adding periods, question marks, and exclamation marks where needed.

1. Ana lives on St Charles Ave in New Orleans
2. Is he coming to the picnic
3. She asked if she left her umbrella here
4. Please set the table for dinner
5. What a brilliant student he is
6. Watch out for the monster
7. On what street is the office located
8. Yikes Did I forget your birthday
9. The stranger knocked on every door Why
10. How excited I am about the concert

PRACTICE 2 Using Commas Correctly

Read the sentences. Then, rewrite the sentences, adding commas where needed. If a sentence is correct as is, write *correct.*

1. To get enough calcium drink plenty of milk.
2. A pencil would work but a pen would be better.
3. The gerbil a small rodent resembles a hamster.
4. Josie said "So Agnes where are you going?"
5. His scarred rugged face showed character.
6. The news is in the paper on television and online.
7. They got those two black dogs in May 2008.
8. We served precisely 1211 meals on July 4 2009.
9. "You did well on the test of course" said Lee.
10. It's at 77 East Adams Street Chicago Illinois 60603.

PRACTICE 3 Using Colons, Semicolons, and Quotation Marks

Read the sentences. Then, rewrite the sentences, using colons, semicolons, and quotation marks where needed. If a sentence is correct as is, write *correct.*

1. Dad likes tennis, however, he likes golf more.
2. Please buy the following milk, eggs, and bread.
3. Who said, Whatever you are, be a good one?
4. Yes, said Mrs. Ross, the class ends at 330.
5. The artist has a new exhibit, I love her work.
6. Caution Do not walk between the subway cars.
7. Marla asked, Did you see my hat anywhere?
8. How I enjoyed the poem The Highwayman!
9. Tomas asked that we turn off our cellphones.
10. Originating in Africa are okra, a plant, gumbo, a stew, and the banjo, a musical instrument.

PRACTICE 4 Using Apostrophes Correctly

Read the sentences. Then, rewrite the sentences, adding or removing apostrophes as needed. If a sentence is correct as is, write *correct.*

1. This is clearly Lucas's work and nobody elses.
2. Jans not here and cant help with Als homework.
3. The dog gnaws on it's bone when its hungry.
4. Most students' grades are A's or B's.
5. The Greek myth described Zeus's anger.
6. My sister Sarahs photo is in the yearbook.
7. I'm shocked that you dont tell her shes right.
8. Hers is the nicest shop on Main Street.
9. Randy would'nt go anywhere on Friday's.
10. Please indicate whats theirs and whats yours.

Continued on next page ▶

Cumulative Review Chapters 25–26

 **PRACTICE 5** Using Underlining (or Italics), Hyphens, Dashes, Parentheses, Brackets, and Ellipses

Read the sentences. Then, rewrite the sentences, adding underlining (or italics if you type your answers on the computer), hyphens, dashes, brackets, parentheses, and ellipses. If a sentence is correct as is, write *correct.*

1. My brother in law is a self taught tennis player.

2. Who wrote the novel To Kill a Mockingbird?

3. The book is set during World War I 1914–1918.

4. We invited Gretchen she is a new student to come to the tryouts for the school play.

5. The paper published her nicely written letter.

6. In her speech, the mayor said, "He Mr. Rodriguez did a great service for our city."

7. Our founders accepted as "unalienable rights . . . Life, Liberty, and the Pursuit of Happiness."

8. The legislature voted on the bill. See page 3 for a list of members' votes column 1.

9. The ship on which Columbus himself sailed was the Santa Maria.

10. Sandra's goal an Olympic medal seemed as distant as ever.

PRACTICE 6 Using Correct Capitalization

Read the sentences. Then, rewrite each sentence, using capital letters where needed.

1. the american revolution formally ended with the signing of the treaty of paris.

2. t. s. eliot, a british author born in america, wrote the poem "the love song of j. alfred prufrock."

3. each spring, grandpa buys good guys fertilizer.

4. author toni morrison has won the nobel prize in literature.

5. visiting the northwest, we saw mount hood.

6. the planet venus is named for the roman goddess venus, whom the greeks called aphrodite.

7. "the last time doctor abis left the usa for a vacation," ingrid said, "was in june of 2007."

8. the high museum of art is just east of interstate 85 at 1280 peachtree street in atlanta, georgia.

9. metro networks monitors traffic conditions in the new york area from atop the empire state building.

10. the current president of the united states belongs to the democratic party.

11. is aunt margie a member of the aarp?

12. We spoke with reverend graves last sunday.

13. "i met ms. lee," said ian, "last summer in iowa."

14. my cousin takes biology 101 at duke university.

15. the vedas are sacred scriptures of hinduism.

 **PRACTICE 7** Writing Sentences With Correct Capitalization

Read the following items. Then, write a sentence about each item. Be sure to use correct capitalization.

1. a local politician

2. a famous or local zoo

3. your favorite beach or park

4. your favorite movie

5. a novel that you really liked or really disliked

RESOURCES FOR Writing COACH

WRITING IN THE
Content Areas

Writing in the content areas—math, social studies, science, the arts, and various career and technical studies—is an important tool for learning. The following pages give examples of content area writing along with strategies.

FORMS OF MATH WRITING

Written Estimate An estimate, or informed idea, of the size, cost, time, or other measure of a thing, based on given information.

Analysis of a Problem A description of a problem, such as figuring out how long a trip will take, along with an explanation of the mathematical formulas or equations you can use to solve the problem.

Response to an Open-Ended Math Prompt A response to a question or writing assignment involving math, such as a word problem or a question about a graph or a mathematical concept.

Writing in Math

Prewriting

- **Choosing a Topic** If you have a choice of topics, review your textbook and class notes for ideas, and choose one that interests you.

- **Responding to a Prompt** If you are responding to a prompt, read and then reread the instructions, ensuring that you understand all of the requirements of the assignment.

Drafting

- **State Problems Clearly** Be clear, complete, and accurate in your description of the problem you are analyzing or reporting on. Make sure that you have used technical terms, such as *ratio*, *area*, and *factor*, accurately.

- **Explain Your Solution** Tell readers exactly which mathematical rules or formulas you use in your analysis and why they apply. Clearly spell out each step you take in your reasoning.

- **Use Graphics** By presenting quantitative information in a graph, table, or chart, you make it easier for readers to absorb information. Choose the format appropriate to the material, as follows:
  - ✔ **Line Graphs** Use a line graph to show the relationship between two variables, such as time and speed in a problem about a moving object. Clearly label the x- and y-axis with the variable each represents and with the units you are using. Choose units appropriately to make the graph manageable. For example, do not try to represent time in years if you are plotting changes for an entire century; instead, use units of ten years each.
  - ✔ **Other Graphs** Use a pie chart to analyze facts about a group, such as the percentage of students who walk to school, the percentage who drive, and the percentage who take the bus. Use a bar graph to compare two or more things at different times or in different categories. Assign a single color to each thing, and use that color consistently for all the bars representing data about that thing.
  - ✔ **Tables** Use a table to help readers look up specific values quickly, such as the time the sun sets in each month of the year. Label each column and row with terms that clearly identify the data you are presenting, including the units you are using.

Revising

- **Ensure Accuracy** For accuracy, double-check the formulas you use and the calculations you make.

- **Revise for Traits of Good Writing** Ask yourself the following questions: *How well have I applied mathematical ideas? Does my organizational plan help readers follow my reasoning? Is my voice suitable to my audience and purpose? Have I chosen precise words and used mathematical terms accurately? Are my sentences well constructed and varied? Have I made any errors in grammar, usage, mechanics, and spelling?* Use your answers to help you revise and edit your work.

Writing in Science

Prewriting

- **Choosing a Topic** If you have a choice of topics, look through class notes and your textbook, or conduct a "media flip-through," browsing online articles, or watching television news and documentaries to find a science-related topic.

- **Responding to a Prompt** If you are responding to a prompt, read the instructions carefully, analyzing the requirements and parts of the assignment. Identify key direction words in the prompt or assignment, such as *explain* and *predict*.

- **Gathering Details**
    ✔ If your assignment requires you to conduct research, search for credible and current sources. Examples of strong sources may include articles in recent issues of science magazines or recently published books. Confirm key facts in more than one source.

    ✔ If your assignment requires you to conduct an experiment, make sure you follow the guidelines for the experiment accurately. Carefully record the steps you take and the observations you make, and date your notes. Repeat the experiment to confirm results.

Drafting

- **Focus and Elaborate** In your introduction, clearly state your topic. Make sure you tell readers why your topic matters. As you draft, give sufficient details, including background, facts, and examples, to help your readers understand your topic. Summarize your findings and insights in your conclusion.

- **Organize** As you draft, follow a suitable organizational pattern. If you are telling the story of an important scientific breakthrough, consider telling events in chronological order. If you are explaining a natural process, consider discussing causes and the effects that follow from them. If you are defending a solution to a problem, you might give pros and cons, answering each counterargument in turn.

- **Present Data Visually** Consider presenting quantitative information, such as statistics or measurements, in a graph, table, or chart. Choose the format appropriate to the material. (Consult the guidance on visual displays of data under "Use Graphics" on page R2.)

Revising

- **Meet Your Audience's Needs** Identify places in your draft where your audience may need more information, such as additional background, more explanation, or the definition of a technical term. Add the information required.

- **Revise for Traits of Good Writing** Ask yourself the following questions: *How clearly have I presented scientific ideas? Will my organization help a reader see the connections I am making? Is my voice suitable to my audience and purpose? Have I chosen precise words and used technical terms accurately? Are my sentences well constructed and varied? Have I made any errors in grammar, usage, mechanics, and spelling?* Use your answers to revise and edit your work.

FORMS OF SCIENCE WRITING

Lab Report A firsthand report of a scientific experiment, following an appropriate format. A standard lab report includes a statement of the hypothesis, or prediction, that the experiment is designed to test; a list of the materials used; an account of the steps performed; a report of the results observed; and the experimenter's conclusions.

Cause-and-Effect Essay A scientific explanation of the causes and effects involved in natural or technical phenomena, such as solar flares, the digestion of food, or the response of metal to stress.

Technical Procedure Document A step-by-step guide to performing a scientific experiment or performing a technical task involving science. A well-written technical procedure document presents the steps of the procedure in clear order. It breaks steps into substeps and prepares readers by explaining what materials they will need and the time they can expect each step to take.

Response to an Open-Ended Science Prompt A response to a question or writing assignment about science.

Summary of a Science-Related Article A retelling of the main ideas in an article that concerns science or technology, such as an article on a new medical procedure.

Writing in Social Studies

FORMS OF SOCIAL STUDIES WRITING

Social Studies Research Report An informative paper, based on research, about a historical period or event or about a specific place or culture. A well-written research report draws on a variety of sources to develop and support a thoughtful point of view on the topic. It cites those sources accurately, following an accepted format.

Biographical Essay An overview of the life of a historically important person. A well-written biographical essay reports the life of its subject accurately and clearly explains the importance of his or her contributions.

Historical Overview A survey, or general picture, of a historical period or development, such as the struggle for women's right to vote. A successful historical overview presents the "big picture," covering major events and important aspects of the topic without getting lost in details.

Historical Cause-and-Effect Essay An analysis of the causes and effects of a historical event. A well-written historical explanation makes clear connections between events to help readers follow the explanation.

Prewriting

- **Choosing a Topic** If you have a choice of topics, find a suitable topic by looking through class notes and your textbook. Make a quick list of topics in history, politics, or geography that interest you and choose a topic based on your list.

- **Responding to a Prompt** If you are responding to a prompt, read the instructions carefully, analyzing the requirements and parts of the assignment. Identify key direction words in the prompt or assignment, such as *compare*, *describe*, and *argue*.

- **Gathering Details** If your assignment requires you to conduct research, consult a variety of credible sources. For in-depth research, review both primary sources (documents from the time you are investigating) and secondary sources (accounts by those who analyze or report on the information). If you find contradictions, evaluate the likely reasons for the differences.

Drafting

- **Establish a Thesis or Theme** If you are writing a research report or other informative piece, state your main point about your topic in a thesis statement. Include your thesis statement in your introduction. If you are writing a creative piece, such as a historical skit or short story, identify the theme, or main message, you wish to convey.

- **Support Your Thesis or Theme** Organize your work around your main idea.

  ✔ In a research report, support and develop your thesis with well-chosen, relevant details. First, provide background information your readers will need, and then discuss different subtopics in different sections of the body of your report. Clearly connect each subtopic to your main thesis.

  ✔ In a creative work, develop your theme through the conflict between characters. For example, a conflict between two brothers during the Civil War over which side to fight on might dramatize the theme of divided loyalties. Organize events to build to a climax, or point of greatest excitement, that clearly conveys your message.

Revising

- **Sharpen Your Focus** Review your draft for sections that do not clearly support your thesis or theme, and consider eliminating them. Revise unnecessary repetition of ideas. Ensure that the sequence of ideas or events will help reader comprehension.

- **Revise for Traits of Good Writing** Ask yourself the following questions: *How clearly have I developed my thesis or my theme? Will my organization help a reader follow my development of my thesis or theme? Is my voice suitable to my audience and purpose? Have I chosen precise and vivid words, accurately using terms from the period or place about which I am writing? Are my sentences well constructed and varied? Have I made any errors in grammar, usage, mechanics, and spelling?* Use your answers to revise and edit your work.

Writing About the Arts

Prewriting

Experience the Work Take notes on the subject of each work you will discuss. Consider its mood, or general feeling, and its theme, or insight into life.

✔ For visual arts, consider the use of color, light, line (sharp or smooth, smudged or definite), mass (heavy or light), and composition (the arrangement and balance of forms).

✔ For music, consider the use of melody, rhythm, harmony, and instrumentation. Also, consider the performers' interpretation of the work.

Drafting

Develop Your Ideas As you draft, support your main ideas, including your insights into or feelings about a work, with relevant details.

Revising

Revise for Traits of Good Writing Ask yourself the following questions: *How clearly do I present my ideas? Will my organization help a reader follow my points? Is my voice suitable to my audience and purpose? Have I chosen precise and vivid words, to describe the works? Are my sentences varied? Have I made any errors in grammar, usage, and mechanics?* Use your answers to revise and edit your work.

Writing in Career and Technical Studies

Prewriting

Choosing a Topic If you have a choice of topics, find a suitable one by looking through class notes and your textbook or by listing your own related projects or experiences.

Drafting

Organize Information As you draft, follow a logical organization. If you are explaining a procedure, list steps in the order that your readers should follow. If they need information about the materials and preparation required, provide that information first. Use formatting (such as headings, numbered steps, and bullet points), graphics (such as diagrams), and transitional words and phrases (such as *first*, *next*, and *if… then*).

Revising

Revise for Traits of Good Writing Ask yourself the following questions: *Have I given readers all the information they will need? Will my organization help a reader follow my points? Is my voice suitable to my audience and purpose? Have I chosen precise words, using technical terms accurately? Are my sentences well constructed? Have I made errors in grammar, usage, and mechanics?* Use your answers to revise and edit your work.

FORMS OF WRITING ABOUT THE ARTS

Research Report on a Trend or Style in Art An informative paper, based on research, about a specific group of artists or trend in the arts.

Biographical Essay An overview of the life of an artist or performer.

Analysis of a Work A detailed description of a work offering insights into its meaning and importance.

Review of a Performance or Exhibit An evaluation of an artistic performance or exhibit.

FORMS OF CAREER AND TECHNICAL WRITING

Technical Procedure Document A step-by-step guide to performing a specialized task, such as wiring a circuit or providing first aid.

Response to an Open-Ended Practical Studies Prompt A response to a question or writing assignment about a task or concept in a specialized field.

Technical Research Report An informative paper, based on research, about a specific topic in a practical field, such as a report on balanced diet in the field of health.

Analysis of a Career An informative paper explaining the requirements for a particular job, along with the responsibilities, salary, benefits, and job opportunities.

WRITING FOR
Media

New technology has created many new ways to communicate. Today, it is easy to contribute information to the Internet and send a variety of messages to friends far and near. You can also share your ideas through photos, illustrations, video, and sound recordings.

Writing for Media gives you an overview of some ways you can use today's technology to create, share, and find information. **Here are the topics you will find in this section:**

- **Blogs**
- **Social Networking**
- **Widgets and Feeds**
- **Multimedia Elements**
- **Podcasts**
- **Wikis**

Blogs

A **blog** is a common form of online writing. The word *blog* is a contraction of *Web log*. Most blogs include a series of entries known as posts. The posts appear in a single column and are displayed in reverse chronological order. That means that the most recent post is at the top of the page. As you scroll down, you will find earlier posts.

Blogs have become increasingly popular. Researchers estimate that 75,000 new blogs are launched every day. Blog authors are often called bloggers. They can use their personal sites to share ideas, songs, videos, photos, and other media. People who read blogs can often post their responses with a comments feature found in each new post.

Because blogs are designed so that they are easy to update, bloggers can post new messages as often as they like, often daily. For some people blogs become a public journal or diary in which they share their thoughts about daily events.

Types of Blogs

Not all blogs are the same. Many blogs have a single author, but others are group projects. These are some common types of blog:

- **Personal blogs** often have a general focus. Bloggers post their thoughts on any topic they find interesting in their daily lives.

- **Topical blogs** focus on a specific theme, such as movie reviews, political news, class assignments, or health-care opportunities.

WEB SAFETY Using the Internet safely means keeping personal information personal. Never include your address (e-mail or physical), last name, or telephone numbers. Avoid mentioning places you go to often.

Never give out passwords you use to access other Web sites and do not respond to e-mails from people you do not know.

Anatomy of a Blog

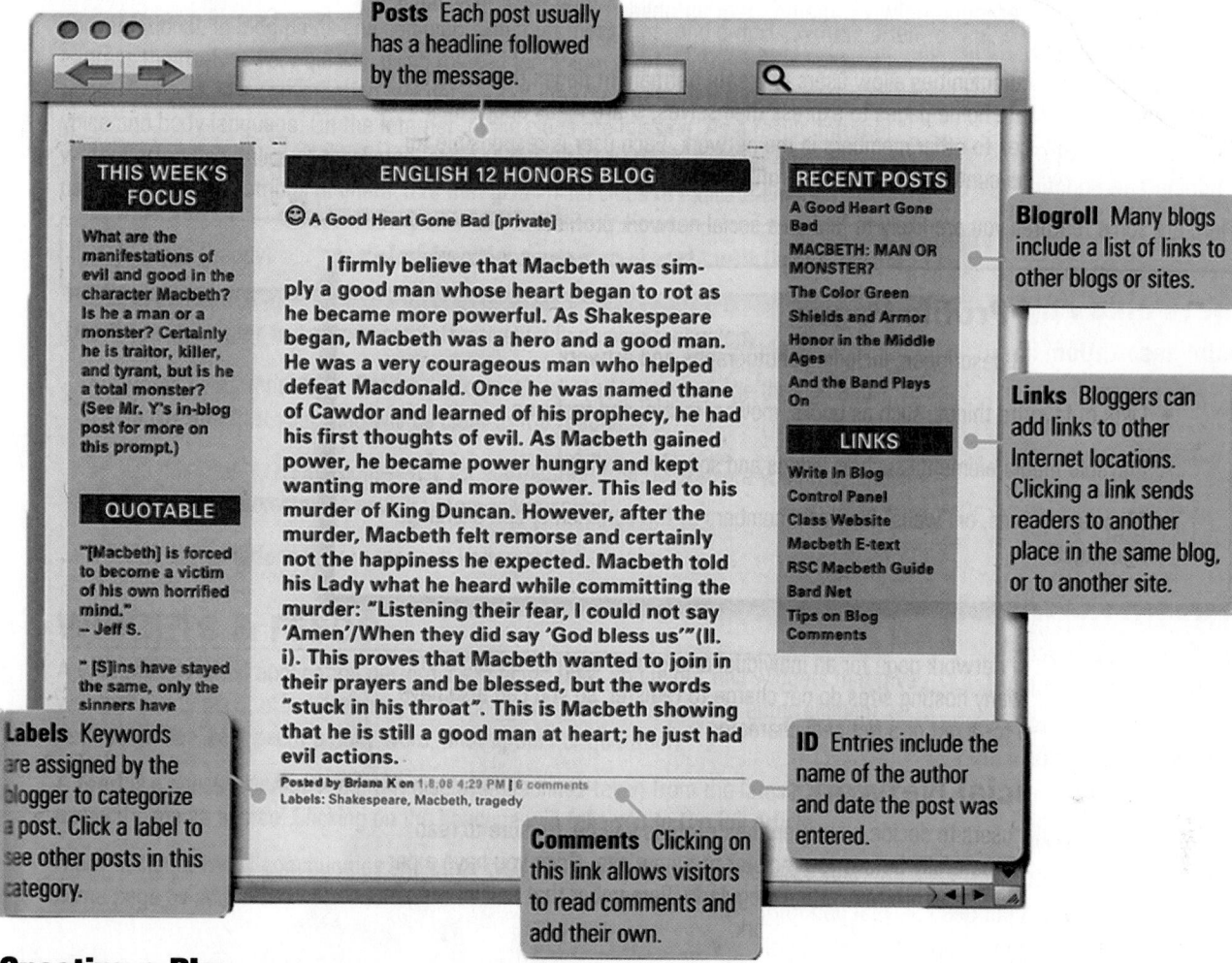

Posts Each post usually has a headline followed by the message.

THIS WEEK'S FOCUS

What are the manifestations of evil and good in the character Macbeth? Is he a man or a monster? Certainly he is traitor, killer, and tyrant, but is he a total monster? (See Mr. Y's in-blog post for more on this prompt.)

QUOTABLE

"[Macbeth] is forced to become a victim of his own horrified mind."
— Jeff S.

" [S]ins have stayed the same, only the sinners have

Labels Keywords are assigned by the blogger to categorize a post. Click a label to see other posts in this category.

ENGLISH 12 HONORS BLOG

☺ A Good Heart Gone Bad [private]

I firmly believe that Macbeth was simply a good man whose heart began to rot as he became more powerful. As Shakespeare began, Macbeth was a hero and a good man. He was a very courageous man who helped defeat Macdonald. Once he was named thane of Cawdor and learned of his prophecy, he had his first thoughts of evil. As Macbeth gained power, he became power hungry and kept wanting more and more power. This led to his murder of King Duncan. However, after the murder, Macbeth felt remorse and certainly not the happiness he expected. Macbeth told his Lady what he heard while committing the murder: "Listening their fear, I could not say 'Amen'/When they did say 'God bless us'" (II. i). This proves that Macbeth wanted to join in their prayers and be blessed, but the words "stuck in his throat". This is Macbeth showing that he is still a good man at heart; he just had evil actions.

Posted by Briana K on 1.8.08 4:29 PM | 6 comments
Labels: Shakespeare, Macbeth, tragedy

RECENT POSTS

A Good Heart Gone Bad
MACBETH: MAN OR MONSTER?
The Color Green
Shields and Armor
Honor in the Middle Ages
And the Band Plays On

LINKS

Write in Blog
Control Panel
Class Website
Macbeth E-text
RSC Macbeth Guide
Bard Net
Tips on Blog Comments

Blogroll Many blogs include a list of links to other blogs or sites.

Links Bloggers can add links to other Internet locations. Clicking a link sends readers to another place in the same blog, or to another site.

ID Entries include the name of the author and date the post was entered.

Comments Clicking on this link allows visitors to read comments and add their own.

Creating a Blog

Keep these hints and strategies in mind to help you create an interesting and fair blog:

- Focus each blog entry on a single topic.

- Vary the length of your posts. Sometimes, all you need is a line or two to share a quick thought. Other posts will be much longer.

- Choose font colors and styles that can be read easily.

- Many people scan blogs rather than read them closely. You can make your main ideas pop out by using clear or clever headlines and boldfacing key terms.

- Give credit to other people's work and ideas. State the names of people whose ideas you are quoting or add a link to take readers to that person's blog or site.

- If you post comments, try to make them brief and polite.

Social Networking

Social networking means any interaction between members of an online community. People can exchange many different kinds of information, from text and voice messages to video images. Many social network communities allow users to create permanent pages that describe themselves. Users create home pages to express themselves, share ideas about their lives, and post messages to other members in the network. Each user is responsible for adding and updating the content on his or her profile page.

Here are some features you are likely to find on a social network profile:

Features of Profile Pages

- A **biographical description**, including photographs and artwork

- **Lists of favorite things**, such as books, movies, music, and fashions

- **Playable media** elements such as videos and sound recordings

- **Message boards**, or "walls," on which members of the community can exchange messages

Privacy in Social Networks

Social networks allow users to decide how open their profiles will be. Be sure to read introductory information carefully before you register at a new site. Once you have a personal profile page, monitor your privacy settings regularly. Remember that any information you post will be available to anyone in your network.

Users often post messages anonymously or using false names, or pseudonyms. People can also post using someone else's name. Judge all information on the net critically. Do not assume that you know who posted some information simply because you recognize the name of the post author. The rapid speed of communication on the Internet can make it easy to jump to conclusions—be careful to avoid this trap.

You can create a social network page for an individual or a group, such as a school or special interest club. Many hosting sites do not charge to register, so you can also have fun by creating a page for a pet or a fictional character.

Writing Friendly Letters

Friendly letters are less formal than business letters. You can use this form to write to a friend, a family member, or anyone with whom you'd like to communicate in a personal, friendly way. Like business letters, friendly letters have the following parts: heading, inside address, salutation, body, closing, and signature. The purpose of a friendly letter might be:

- to share news and feelings
- to send or answer an invitation
- to express thanks

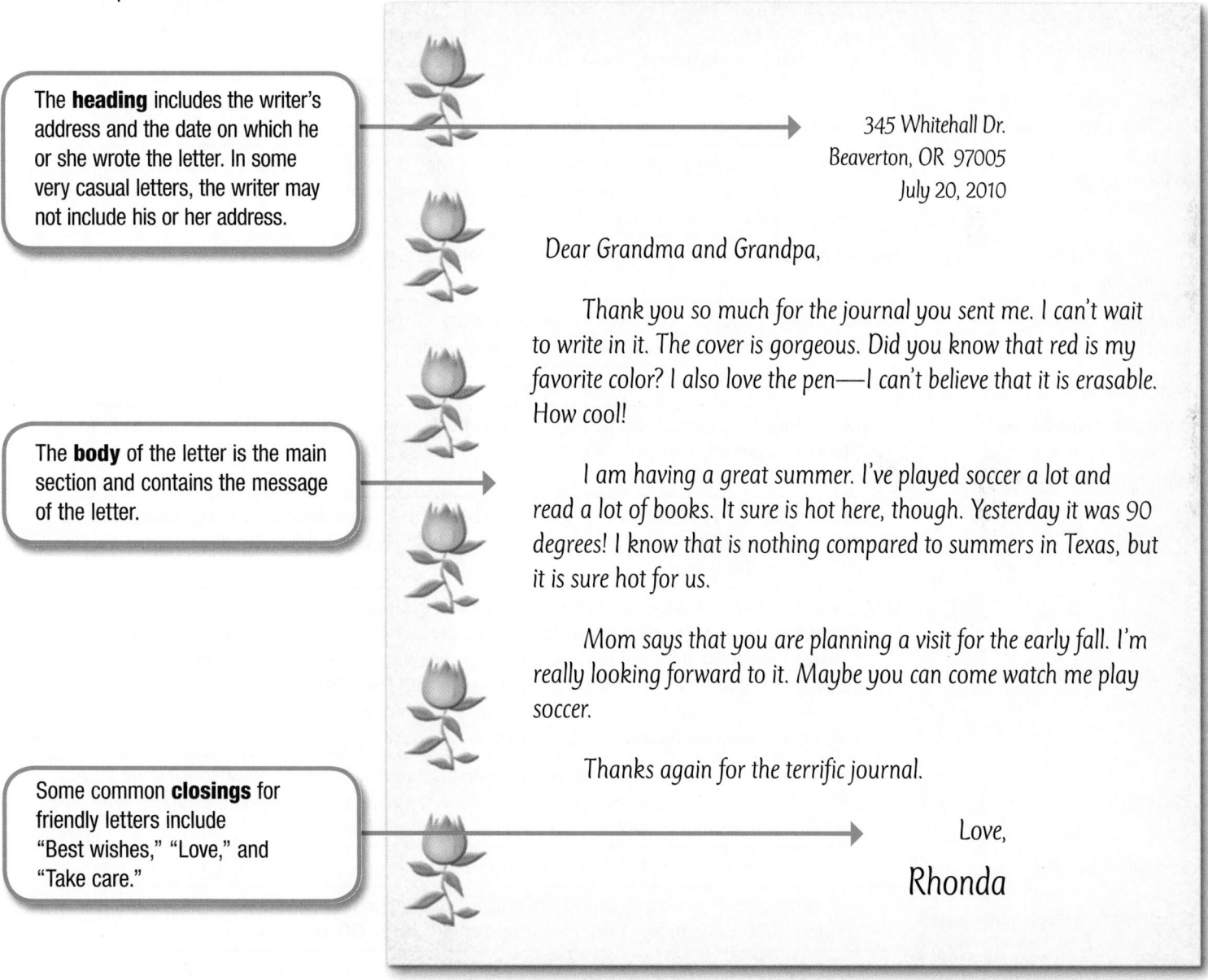

The **heading** includes the writer's address and the date on which he or she wrote the letter. In some very casual letters, the writer may not include his or her address.

The **body** of the letter is the main section and contains the message of the letter.

Some common **closings** for friendly letters include "Best wishes," "Love," and "Take care."

345 Whitehall Dr.
Beaverton, OR 97005
July 20, 2010

Dear Grandma and Grandpa,

Thank you so much for the journal you sent me. I can't wait to write in it. The cover is gorgeous. Did you know that red is my favorite color? I also love the pen—I can't believe that it is erasable. How cool!

I am having a great summer. I've played soccer a lot and read a lot of books. It sure is hot here, though. Yesterday it was 90 degrees! I know that is nothing compared to summers in Texas, but it is sure hot for us.

Mom says that you are planning a visit for the early fall. I'm really looking forward to it. Maybe you can come watch me play soccer.

Thanks again for the terrific journal.

Love,

Rhonda

MLA Style for Listing Sources

Book with one author	London, Jack. *White Fang.* Clayton, DE: Prestwick House, 2007. Print.
Book with two or three authors	Veit, Richard, and Christopher Gould. *Writing, Reading, and Research.* 8th ed. Boston: Wadsworth Cengage, 2009. Print.
Book prepared by an editor	Twain, Mark. *The Complete Essays of Mark Twain.* Ed. Charles Neider. New York: Da Capo, 2000. Print.
Book with more than three authors or editors	Donald, Robert B., et al. *Writing Clear Essays.* 3rd ed. Upper Saddle River, NJ: Prentice Hall, Inc., 1996. Print.
A single work from an anthology	Poe, Edgar Allan. "The Fall of the House of Usher." *American Literature: A Chronological Approach.* Ed. Edgar H. Schuster, Anthony Tovatt, and Patricia O. Tovatt. New York City, NY: McGraw-Hill, 1985. 233–247. Print. [Indicate pages for the entire selection.]
Introduction, foreward, preface, or afterward in a book	Vidal, Gore. Introduction. *Abraham Lincoln: Selected Speeches and Writings.* By Abraham Lincoln. New York: Vintage, 1992. xxi–xxvii. Print.
Signed article in a weekly magazine	Walsh, Brian. "Greening This Old House." *Time* 4 May 2009: 45–47. Print. [For a multi-page article that does not appear on consecutive pages, write only the first page number on which it appears, followed by a plus sign.]
Signed article in a monthly magazine	Fischman, Josh. "A Better Life with Bionics." *National Geographic* Jan. 2010: 34–53. Print.
Unsigned editorial or story	"Wind Power." Editorial. *New York Times* 9 January 2010: A18. Print. [If the editorial or story is signed, begin with the author's name.]
Signed pamphlet	[Treat the pamphlet as though it were a book.]
Audiovisual media, such as films, slide programs, videocassettes, DVDs	*Where the Red Fern Grows.* Dir. Norman Toker. Perf. James Whitmore, Beverly Garland, and Stewart Peterson. 1974. Sterling Entertainment, 1997. DVD.
Radio or TV broadcast transcript	"Texas High School Football Titans Ready for Clash." *Weekend Edition Sunday.* Host Melissa Block. Guests Mike Pesca and Tom Goldman. Natl. Public Radio. KUHF, Houston, 18 Dec. 2009. Print. Transcript.
A single page on a Web site	U.S. Census Bureau: Customer Liaison and Marketing Services Office. "State Facts for Students: Texas." *U.S. Census Bureau.* U.S. Census Bureau, 15 October 2009. Web. 1 November 2009. [Indicate the date of last update if known or use n.d. if not known. After the medium of publication, include the date you accessed the information. You do not need the URL unless it is the only way to find the page. If needed, include it in angled brackets at the end, i.e. <http://www.census.gov/schools/facts/texas.html >.]
Newspaper	Yardley, Jim. "Hurricane Sweeps into Rural Texas; Cities Are Spared." *New York Times* 23 Aug. 1999: A1. Print. [For a multipage article that does not appear on consecutive pages, write only the first page number on which it appears, followed by a plus sign.]
Personal interview	Jones, Robert. Personal interview. 4 Sept. 2006.
Audio with multiple publishers	Simms, James, ed. *Romeo and Juliet.* By William Shakespeare. Oxford: Attica Cybernetics; London: BBC Education; London: HarperCollins, 1995. CD-ROM.
Signed article from an encyclopedia	Askeland, Donald R. "Welding." *World Book Encyclopedia.* 1991 ed. Print. [For a well-known reference, you do not need to include the publisher information, only the edition and year, followed by the medium used.]

Commonly Misspelled Words

The list on this page presents words that cause problems for many people. Some of these words are spelled according to set rules, but others follow no specific rules. As you review this list, check to see how many of the words give you trouble in your own writing.

absence	benefit	conscience	excellent	library	prejudice
absolutely	bicycle	conscientious	exercise	license	previous
accidentally	bought	conscious	experience	lightning	probably
accurate	brief	continuous	explanation	likable	procedure
achievement	brilliant	convenience	extension	literature	proceed
affect	bulletin	coolly	extraordinary	mathematics	pronunciation
agreeable	bury	cooperate	familiar	maximum	realize
aisle	buses	correspondence	fascinating	minimum	really
all right	business	courageous	February	misspell	receipt
allowance	cafeteria	courteous	fiery	naturally	receive
analysis	calendar	criticism	financial	necessary	recognize
analyze	campaign	curiosity	foreign	neighbor	recommend
ancient	canceled	deceive	fourth	niece	rehearse
anniversary	candidate	decision	generally	ninety	repetition
answer	capital	defendant	genuine	noticeable	restaurant
anticipate	capitol	definitely	government	occasion	rhythm
anxiety	career	dependent	grammar	occasionally	sandwich
apologize	cashier	description	guidance	occur	schedule
appearance	category	desert	height	occurred	scissors
appreciate	ceiling	dessert	humorous	occurrence	theater
appropriate	certain	dining	immediately	opinion	truly
argument	changeable	disappointed	immigrant	opportunity	usage
athletic	characteristic	distinguish	independence	parallel	valuable
attendance	clothes	effect	independent	particularly	various
awkward	colonel	eighth	individual	personally	vegetable
bargain	column	embarrass	intelligence	persuade	weight
battery	commercial	enthusiastic	judgment	physician	weird
beautiful	commitment	envelope	knowledge	possibility	whale
beginning	condemn	environment	lawyer	precede	yield
believe	congratulate	especially	legible	preferable	

A

action (ak´shən) *n.* in a story or play, the events which are part of the plot

advantage (ad vant´ij) *n.* something that puts a person in a better position than others; a way in which one thing is better than another

analysis (ə nal´ə sis) *n.* the process of looking at something closely to understand its meaning, structure, or parts

analyze (an´ə līz) *v.* to look at something carefully to understand its meaning or structure

anticipate (an tis´ə pāt´) *v.* to expect or predict; to foresee and then be ready to deal with

argument (är´gyü mənt) *n.* a discussion (written or spoken) which aims to persuade; a set of statements putting forward and backing up an idea or position

audience (ô´dē əns) *n.* the readers of a book or other piece of writing; a group of listeners or viewers

authority (ə thôr´ə tē) *n.* a person or written work that is accepted as a source of reliable or expert information

C

cause (kôz) *n.* a person, object, or event that makes something happen

character (kar´ik tər) *n.* a person (or animal) who plays a part in the action of a story, play, or movie

chronological (krän´ə läj´i kəl) *adj.* described or arranged in the order of time, starting with what happened first

coherence (kō hir´ənts) *n.* the state of having ideas that are clear and logical

coherent (kō hir´ənt) *adj.* well-planned, clear, logical; holding together well

compare (kəm par´) *v.* to examine the differences and similarities between things

comparison (kəm par´ə sən) *n.* the act of comparing, examining the differences and similarities between two or more things

conclusions (kən klü´zhənz) *n.* opinions and ideas formed about something after careful study or thought

conflict (kän´flikt´) *n.* the struggle between people or opposing forces which creates the dramatic action in a play or story

connection (kə nek´shən) *n.* an event or thing that brings together people or ideas; a relationship between people and/or ideas

consequence (kän´si kwens´) *n.* the result, or outcome, of a previous action

consider (kən sid´ər) *v.* to take into account; to think about with care

contradict (kän´trə dikt´) *v.* to say something is wrong or not true

contrast (kən trast´) *v.* to compare in a way that shows differences

controversial (kän´trə vur´shəl) *adj.* something which is likely to stir up strong disagreement

convey (kən vā´) *v.* to make something (for example, an idea or a feeling) known to someone; to communicate

counter-argument (kount´ər är´gyü mənt) *n.* a reason against the original argument

D

demonstrate (dem´ən strāt´) *v.* to make a fact clear by giving proof or evidence

detail (dē´tāl´) *n.* a specific fact or piece of information about something

develop (di vel´əp) *v.* to explain or build an idea or example bit by bit

device (di vīs´) *n.* the use of words to gain a particular effect in a piece of writing

dialogue (dī´ə lôg´) *n.* a conversation between two or more people in a book, play, or movie

differentiate (dif´ər en´shē āt´) *v.* to notice differences in information

documentation (däk´yü mən tā´shən) *n.* the noting of sources to back up an idea or opinion

E

effect (e fekt´) *n.* the way that something changes because of a separate action

effective (e fekt´iv) *adj.* successful in getting the desired results

emotion (ē mō´shən) *n.* a feeling, such as love or joy; feelings and automatic responses, as opposed to logical thoughts and conclusions

evidence (ev´ə dəns) *n.* anything that gives proof or shows something to be true

external (ek stūr´nəl) *adj.* on the outside

extraneous (ek strā´nē əs) *adj.* not relevant, unnecessary; unrelated to the subject being discussed

F

factor (fak´tər) *n.* something that is one of the reasons for a particular result or outcome

fact (fakt) *n.* a piece of information that can be shown to be true

focus (fō´kəs) *n.* the main topic or most important point; the center of attention

formal (fôr´məl) *adj.* reflecting language that is traditional and correct, not casual

formatting (fôr´mat´ing) *adj.* related to the arrangement of text, images, and graphics on a page

G

genre (zhän´rə) *n.* a type of writing that contains certain features

H

hyperbole (hī pur´bə lē) *n.* over-the-top exaggeration

I

idiom (id´ē əm) *n.* an expression, made up of a group of words, where the meaning as a whole is different from what the words mean individually

image (im´ij) *n.* a word or phrase in a poem or other kind of writing which appeals to one or more of the five senses

imagery (im´ij rē) *n.* descriptive language that paints pictures in the mind or appeals to the senses

inconsistencies (in´kən sis´tən sēz) *n.* things that contradict each other

information (in´fər mā´shən) *n.* facts about a subject or topic

insight (in´sīt´) *n.* a useful, important, and deep understanding about a topic

internal (in tūr´nəl) *adj.* on the inside

introduce (in´trə düs) *v.* to present a person or information to another for the first time

introduction (in´trə duk´shən) *n.* the part at the beginning of a piece of writing which often tells what the rest will be about

J

judgment (juj´mənt) *n.* an opinion or conclusion formed after careful thought and evaluation

L

letter (let´ər) *n.* a written or printed message

line (līn) *n.* the direction of the action in a plot or story ("plot line" and "story line"); one row of words in a poem; one set of words spoken by an actor in a play or movie

literary (lit´ər ar ē) *adj.* of or relating to books or other written material

logical (läj´i kəl) *adj.* clear and reasonable; based on logic

M

meter (mēt´ər) *n.* a poem's rhythmic pattern, made by the number of beats in each line

N

narrative (nar´ə tiv) *n.* a story, either fiction or nonfiction

note (nōt) *v.* to observe and/or mention

O

offensive (ə fens´iv) *adj.* upsetting, embarrassing, rude, hurtful or angering; aggressive, attacking

opinion (ə pin´yən) *n.* a belief or view that is not necessarily based on facts

oppose (ə pōz´) *v.* go against, disagree

organized (ôr´gə nīzd´) *adj.* the state of being in order

P

paraphrase (par´ə frāz´) *v.* to reword information into one's own words

personal (pūr´sən əl) *adj.* individual, relating to a particular person

personification (pər sän´ə fə kā´shən) *n.* a type of figurative language where animals or other non-humans are given human characteristics

plausible (plô´zə bəl) *adj.* likely to be true or valid

point of view (point uv vyü) *n.* the perspective from which a story is told; an attitude, position, standpoint, or way of looking at a situation; an opinion

position (pə zish´ən) *n.* a point of view or attitude toward something

profound (prō found´) *adj.* very deep, intense, or strong; full of insight

Q

quality (kwôl´ə tē) *n.* the degree of excellence of something

quotation (kwō tā´shən) *n.* a group of words copied exactly from a speech or piece of writing

R

reader-friendly (rēd´ər frend´lē) *adj.* easy for an audience to read and understand

research (rē´surch´) *v.* to carefully study information on a topic; *n.* the careful study of information on a topic

reasoning (rē´zən ing) *n.* the process of reaching a conclusion by looking at the facts

reflect (ri flekt´) *v.* to show, make apparent

resolution (rez´ə lü´shən) *n.* what happens to resolve the conflict in the plot of a story

rhetorical devices (ri tôr´i kəl di vī´səz) *n.* strategies and techniques, for example metaphor and hyperbole, used by writers to draw in or persuade readers

S

scheme (skēm) *n.* (for a poem) a design or ordered structure

sensory (sen´sər ē) *adj.* of or relating to the five senses

sequence (sē´kwəns) *n.* when the items in a group follow each other in a particular order

setting (set´ing) *n.* the time and place of the action in a story or other piece of writing

stanza (stan´zə) *n.* a group of lines of poetry, usually with a similar length and pattern, separated from other lines with spaces

strategy (strat´ə jē) *n.* in a piece of writing, a literary tactic or method (such as flashback or foreshadowing) used by the writer to achieve a certain goal or effect

structure (struk´chər) *n.* the way something is organized and put together; *v.* to put together according to a pattern or plan

style (stīl) *n.* a way of doing something; a way of writing

subject (sub´jekt) *n.* something that is discussed or studied; a topic

support (sə pôrt´) *v.* to hold up, to back

suspense (sə spens´) *n.* a feeling of anxiety and uncertainty about what will happen in a story or other piece of writing

sustain (sə stān´) *v.* to keep up, hold up; to affirm or support as true

symbol (sim´bəl) *n.* anything that stands for or represents something else

synthesize (sin´thə sīz´) *v.* to combine, to bring different parts together into a whole

T

technique (tek nēk´) *n.* a special way of doing something

theme (thēm) *n.* a central message, concern, or purpose in a literary work

thesis (thē´sis) *n.* an idea or theory that is stated and then discussed in a logical way

tone (tōn) *n.* a writer's attitude toward his or her subject

topic (täp´ik) *n.* a subject that is written about or discussed

transition (tran zish´ən) *n.* the change from one part, place, or idea to another; in writing, the change between sentences, paragraphs, and ideas

V

verse (vūrs) *n.* a group of lines that make a unit in a poem, a stanza; writing, such as poetry, that has a meter

viewpoint (vyü´point´) *n.* an attitude, position, standpoint, or way of looking at a situation

Spanish Glossary

A

action / acción *s.* en una historia u obra de teatro, los eventos que son parte del argumento

advantage / ventaja *s.* algo que le pone a alguien en una mejor posición que a otros; la forma en la que una cosa es mejor que otra

analysis / análisis *s.* el proceso de examinar algo detenidamente para entender su significado, su estructura o sus partes

analyze / analizar *v.* examinar algo detenidamente para entender su significado o estructura

anticipate / anticipar *v.* esperar o predecir; prever y estar preparado para tratar con algo

argument / argumento *s.* razonamiento (escrito o hablado) con el fin de persuadir; una serie de declaraciones que proponen o apoyan una idea o postura

audience / audiencia, público *s.* los lectores de un libro u otra obra escrita; un grupo de oyentes o espectadores

authority / autoridad *s.* una persona u obra escrita que es aceptada como una fuente de información fiable o experta

C

cause / causa *s.* una persona, objeto, o evento que hace que ocurra algo

character / personaje *s.* un individuo (humano o animal) que tiene un papel en la acción de un cuento, una obra de teatro o una película

chronological / cronológico *adj.* descrito o arreglado en el orden temporal, empezando con el evento que ocurrió primero

coherence / coherencia *s.* el estado de tener ideas claras y lógicas

coherent / coherente *adj.* bien planeado, claro, lógico; congruente

compare / comparar *v.* examinar las diferencias y semejanzas entre cosas

comparison / comparación *s.* el acto de comparar, examinar las diferencias y semejanzas entre dos más cosas

conclusions / conclusiónes *s.* opiniones o ideas sobre una materia o deducción a que se ha llegado tras su estudio o análisis

conflict / conflicto *s.* la lucha entre personas o fuerzas opuestas que crea la acción dramática en una obra de teatro o un cuento

connection / conexión *s.* un evento o una cosa que une a las personas o ideas; una relación entre personas y/o ideas

consequence / consecuencia *s.* el resultado de una acción previa

consider / considerar *v.* tomar en cuenta; meditar sobre algo

contradict / contradecir *v.* decir algo que no es correcto o que no es verdad

contrast / contrastar *v.* comparar dos o más cosas para señalar las diferencias entre ellas

controversial / controvertido *adj.* algo que tiende a levantar diferencias de opiniones

convey / expresar *v.* darse a entender algo a alguien (por ejemplo una idea o sentimiento); comunicar

counter-argument / contraargumento *s.* una razón contra el argumento original

D

demonstrate / demostrar *v.* aclarar un hecho por dar pruebas o evidencia

detail / detalle *s.* un dato específico o información específica de algo

develop / desarrollar *v.* explicar o exponer poco a poco una idea o ejemplo

device / técnica (literaria) *s.* el uso de palabras para tener un efecto específico en una obra escrita

dialogue / diálogo *s.* una conversación entre dos personajes o más en un libro, obra de teatro o película

differentiate / diferenciar *v.* notar las diferencias

documentation / documentación *s.* la anotación de fuentes para apoyar una idea u opinión

E

effect / efecto *s.* la manera en la que algo cambia a causa de una acción separada

effective / efectivo, eficaz *adj.* exitoso en producir los resultados deseados

emotion / sentimiento *s.* una sensación emotiva como el amor o la alegría; sensaciones y respuestas automáticas, en contraste a los pensamientos y conclusiones lógicos

evidence / pruebas *s.* cualquier cosa que demuestre o indique que algo es cierto

external / externo *adj.* afuera de

extraneous / superfluo *adj.* irrelevante, innecesario, no relacionado al tema tratado

F

factor / factor *s.* algo que es una de las razones de un resultado determinado

fact / hecho *s.* un dato que se puede verificar

focus / foco, idea central *s.* el tema principal o la idea más importante; el centro de atención

formal / formal *adj.* que refleja lenguaje tradicional y correcto, no informal

formatting / formateo *s.* la colocación de texto, imágenes y gráficos en una página

G

genre / género *s.* una clase de escritura que tiene características específicas

H

hyperbole / hipérbole *s.* exageración excesiva

I

idiom / modismo *s.* una expresión compuesta de un grupo de palabras cuyo significado en conjunto es diferente de lo que significan las palabras individuales

image / imagen *s.* una palabra o frase en un poema u otra clase de escritura que atrae uno o más de los cinco sentidos

imagery / imágenes *s.* lenguaje descriptivo que crea dibujos en la mente o que atrae los sentidos

inconsistencies / inconsecuencias *s.* cosas que se contradicen

information / información *s.* datos sobre un asunto o tema

insight / perspicacia *s.* el profundo entendimiento útil e importante de un tema

internal / interno *adj.* dentro de

introduce / presentar *v.* dar a conocer a una persona o información por primera vez

introduction / introducción *s.* la parte inicial de una obra escrita que muchas veces cuenta de qué se trata el resto de la obra

J

judgment / juicio *s.* una opinión o conclusión formada después de una consideración y evaluación cuidadosa

L

letter /carta *s.* un mensaje escrito o impreso

line / línea, verso *s.* la dirección de la acción en un argumento o historia (por ejemplo, "plot line" y "story line" en inglés); una línea de palabras en un poema; un grupo de palabras habladas por un actor en una obra de teatro o película

literary / literario *adj.* perteneciente o relativo a los libros u otra materia escrita

logical / lógico *adj.* claro y razonable; basado en la lógica

M

meter / métrica *s.* el patrón rítmico de un poema, marcado por el tiempo y ritmo de cada verso

N

narrative / narrativa *s.* un cuento de ficción o no ficción

note / notar *v.* observar y/o mencionar

O

offensive / ofensivo *adj.* que provoca disgusto, vergüenza, daño o enfado; grosero, agresivo, combativo

opinion / opinión *s.* una creencia o perspectiva que no es necesariamente basada en los hechos

oppose / oponerse *v.* estar en contra, no estar de acuerdo

organized / organizado *adj.* que está ordenado

P

paraphrase / parafrasear *v.* formular información utilizando sus propias palabras

personal / personal *adj.* individual, relativo a una persona particular

personification / personificación *n.* un tipo de lenguaje figurado en el que los animales u otros seres no humanos tienen características humanas

plausible / creíble *adj.* con buena probabilidad de ser verdadero o válido

point of view / punto de vista *n.* la perspectiva de la cual se cuenta una historia; una actitud, postura, o manera de ver una situación; una opinión

position / postura *n.* el punto de vista o la actitud hacia algo

profound / profundo *adj.* muy intenso o fuerte; lleno de perspicacia

Q

quality / calidad *s.* el grado de excelencia de algo

quotation / cita *s.* un grupo de palabras copiadas exactamente de un discurso o texto

R

reasoning / razonamiento *s.* el proceso de llegar a una conclusión por examinar los hechos

reflect / reflejar *v.* mostrar, hacer aparente

research / investigar *v.* estudiar cuidadosamente la información sobre un tema; investigación s. el estudio cuidadoso de la información sobre un tema

resolution / resolución *s.* lo que ocurre para resolver el conflicto en el argumento de una historia

rhetorical devices / técnicas retóricas *s.* estrategias y técnicas, por ejemplo la metáfora y la hipérbole, utilizadas por los escritores para atraer o persuadir a los lectores

S

scheme / esquema *s.* (para un poema) un diseño o estructura ordenada

sensory / sensorial *adj.* perteneciente o relativo a los cinco sentidos

sequence / secuencia *s.* cuando una serie de eventos ocurre en un orden determinado

setting / escenario *s.* el lugar y el momento de la acción en un cuento u otra obra escrita

stanza / estrofa *s.* un grupo de líneas de poesía, normalmente con un patrón y extensión similar, separado por espacios de otras líneas

strategy / estrategia *s.* en un texto, una táctica o método literario (como el flashback o el presagio) empleado por el autor para lograr un objetivo o efecto específico

structure / estructura *s.* la manera en la que algo está organizado o compuesto; estructurar v. organizar o componer según un patrón o plan

style / estilo *s.* una manera de hacer algo; una forma de escribir

subject / tema *s.* algo de que se habla o que se estudia; un tema

support / apoyar *v.* sostener, respaldar

suspense / suspenso *s.* una sensación de ansiedad e incertidumbre sobre lo que va a pasar en una historia u otra obra escrita

sustain / sostener *v.* mantener, apoyar; afirmar o confirmar como verdadero

symbol / símbolo *s.* algo que representa o significa otra cosa

synthesize / sintetizar *v.* combinar, unir diferentes partes para formar una totalidad

T

technique / técnica *s.* una manera especial de hacer algo

theme / tema *s.* una idea, asunto, o propósito principal de una obra literaria

thesis / tesis *s.* una idea o teoría que se expone y que se discute de una manera lógica

tone / tono *s.* la actitud del autor hacia su tema o materia

topic / tema *s.* una idea de la cual se escribe y que se discute

transition / transición *s.* el cambio entre partes, lugares y conceptos; en la escritura, el cambio entre oraciones, párrafos e ideas

V

verse / verso *s.* un grupo de líneas que componen una unidad en un poema, una estrofa; texto, como la poesía, que tiene una métrica

viewpoint / punto de vista *s.* una actitud, postura, o manera de interpretar una situación

Meeting Agenda

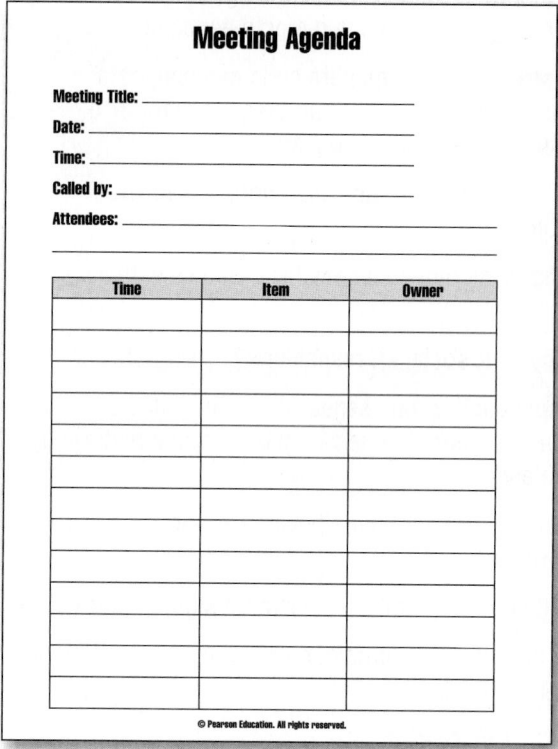

Cause and Effect Chart

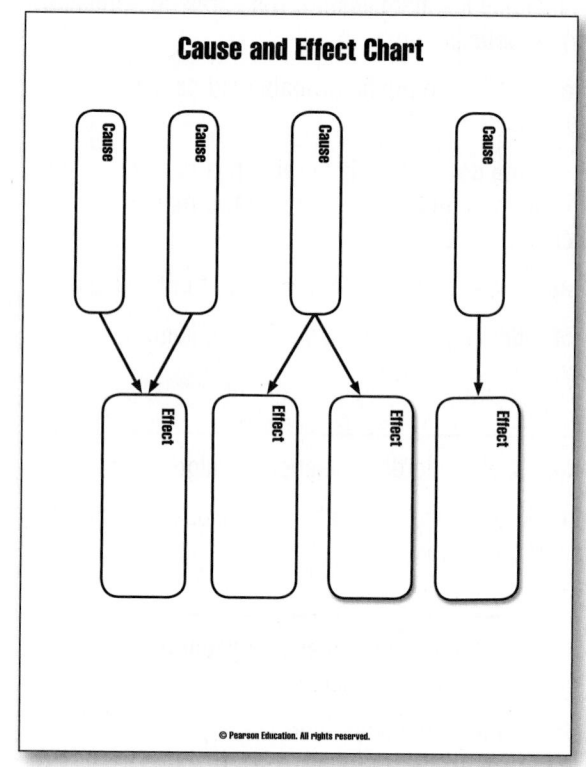

Cluster Diagram

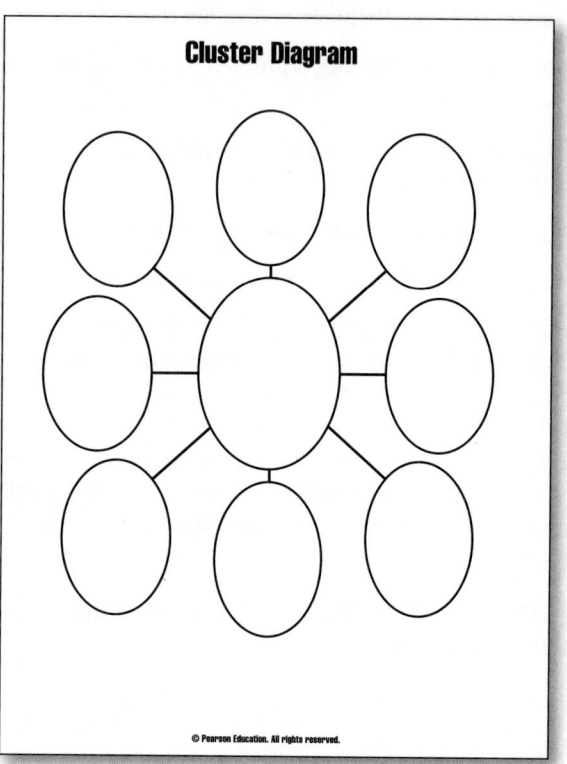

Five Ws Chart

Use these questions as you read, and write important details. Remember, you may not need to answer every question.

Who?
What?
When?
Where?
Why?

KWL Chart

Topic:

What I Know	What I Want to Know	What I Learned

Main Idea and Details Web

Use these questions as you read, and write important details. Remember, you may not need to answer every question.

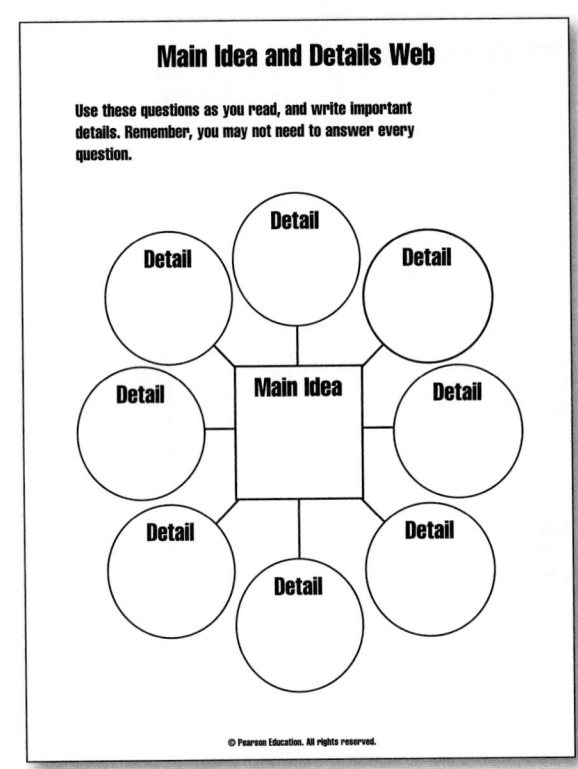

Meeting Notes

Topic

Decisions

Next Steps

Note Card

Topic:

Source:
-
-
-

Topic:

Source:
-
-
-

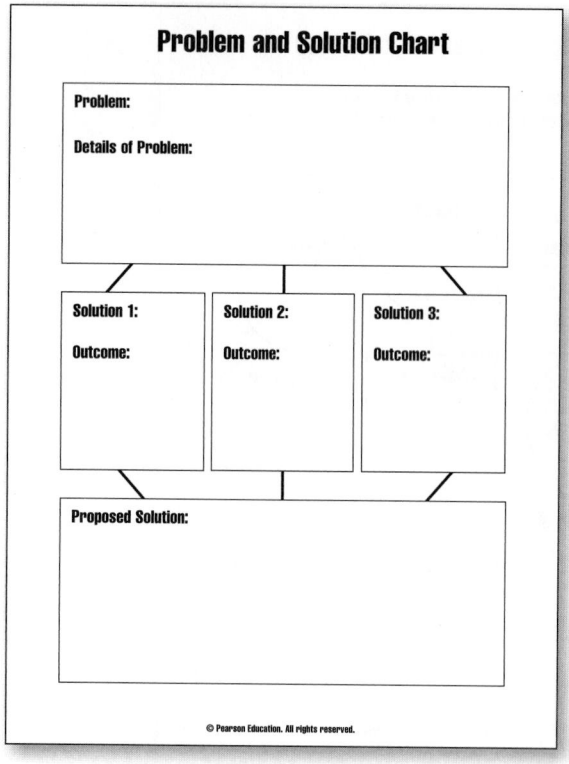

Problem and Solution Chart

Problem:

Details of Problem:

Solution 1:

Outcome:

Solution 2:

Outcome:

Solution 3:

Outcome:

Proposed Solution:

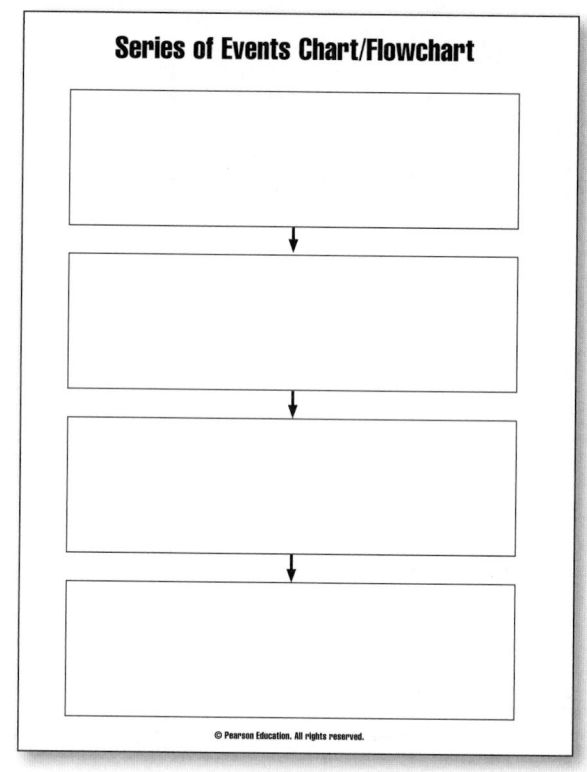

Series of Events Chart/Flowchart

Source Card

Source Number: _____

Source Name: _____

Kind of Source: _____

Author(s): _____

Editor (when applicable): _____

Publisher: _____

Publication Date: _____

Publication Location: _____

Other Information _____

Source Number: _____

Source Name: _____

Kind of Source: _____

Author(s): _____

Editor (when applicable): _____

Publisher: _____

Publication Date: _____

Publication Location: _____

Other Information _____

Outline

Topic   I. _____

  Subtopic   A. _____

    Supporting details

    1. _____
    2. _____
    3. _____
    4. _____

  Subtopic   B. _____

    Supporting details

    1. _____
    2. _____
    3. _____
    4. _____

Topic   II. _____

  Subtopic   A. _____

    Supporting details

    1. _____
    2. _____
    3. _____
    4. _____

  Subtopic   B. _____

    Supporting details

    1. _____
    2. _____
    3. _____
    4. _____

Steps in a Process Chart

Steps	Details
Step 1:	
Step 2:	
Step 3:	
Step 4:	
Step 5:	

Storyboard

Timeline

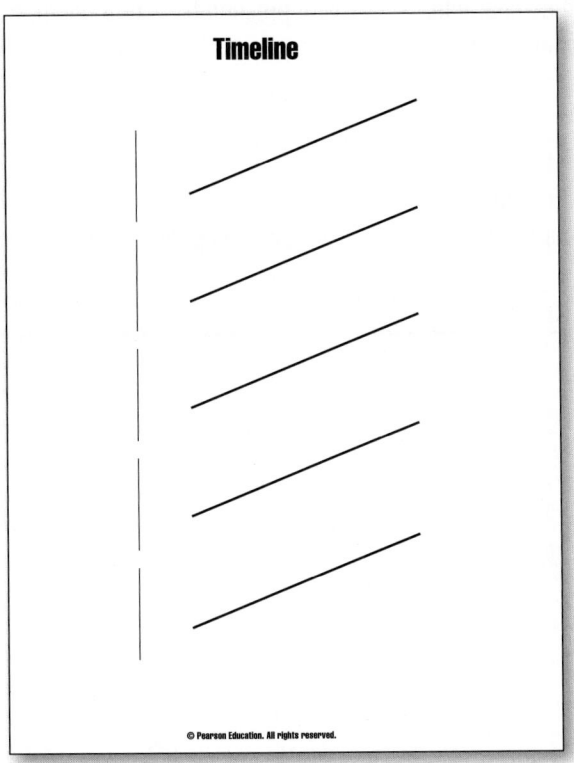

Venn Diagram

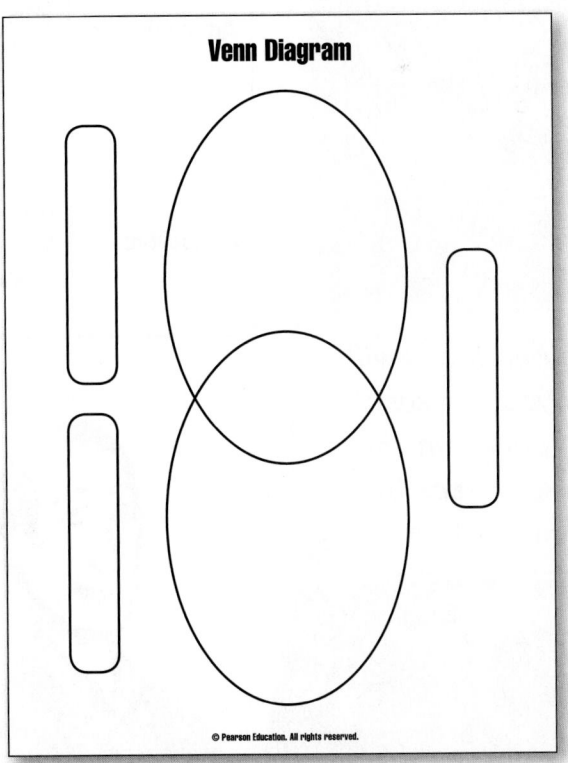

Listening and Speaking Handbook

Communication travels between people in many forms. You receive information by listening to others, and you convey information through speaking. The more developed these skills are, the more you will be able to communicate your ideas, as well as to comprehend the ideas of others.

If you improve your listening skills, it will become easier to focus your attention on classroom discussions and to identify important information more accurately. If you develop good speaking skills, you will be better prepared to contribute effectively in group discussions, to give formal presentations with more confidence, and to communicate your feelings and ideas to others more easily.

Listening

Different situations call for different types of listening. Learn more about the four main types of listening—critical, empathic, appreciative, and reflective—in the chart below.

Types of Listening		
Type	**How to Listen**	**Situations**
Critical	Listen for facts and supporting details to understand and evaluate the speaker's message.	Informative or persuasive speeches, class discussions, announcements
Empathic	Imagine yourself in the other person's position, and try to understand what he or she is thinking.	Conversations with friends or family
Appreciative	Identify and analyze aesthetic or artistic elements, such as character development, rhyme, imagery, and descriptive language.	Oral presentations of a poem, dramatic performances
Reflective	Ask questions to get information, and use the speaker's responses to form new questions.	Class or group discussions

This handbook will help you increase your ability in these two key areas of communication.

Using Different Types of Questions

A speaker's ideas may not always be clear to you. You may need to ask questions to clarify your understanding. If you understand the different types of questions, you will be able to get the information you need.

- An **open-ended question** does not lead to a single, specific response. Use this question to open up a discussion: "What did you think of the piano recital?"

- A **closed question** leads to a specific response and must be answered with a yes or no: "Did you play a piece by Chopin at your recital?"

- A **factual question** is aimed at getting a particular piece of information and must be answered with facts: "How many years have you been playing the piano?"

Participating in a Group Discussion

In a group discussion, you openly discuss ideas and topics in an informal setting. The group discussions in which you participate will involve, for the most part, your classmates and focus on the subjects you are studying. To get the most out of a group discussion, you need to participate in it.

Use group discussions to express and to listen to ideas in an informal setting.

Communicate Effectively Think about the points you want to make, the order in which you want to make them, the words you will use to express them, and the examples that will support these points before you speak.

Ask Questions Asking questions can help you improve your comprehension of another speaker's ideas. It may also call attention to possible errors in another speaker's points.

Make Relevant Contributions Stay focused on the topic being discussed. Relate comments to your own experience and knowledge, and clearly connect them to your topic. It is important to listen to the points others make so you can build off their ideas. Work to share the connections you see. For example, say whether you agree or disagree, or tell the goup how your ideas connect.

Speaking

Giving a presentation or speech before an audience is generally recognized as public speaking. Effective speakers are well prepared and deliver speeches smoothly and with confidence.

Recognizing Different Kinds of Speeches

There are four main kinds of speeches: informative speeches, persuasive speeches, entertaining speeches, and extemporaneous speeches.

Consider the purpose and audience of your speech before deciding what kind of speech you will give.

- Give an **informative speech** to explain an idea, a process, an object, or an event.

- Give a **persuasive speech** to get your listeners to agree with your position or to take some action. Use formal English when speaking.

- Give an **entertaining speech** to offer your listeners something to enjoy or to amuse them. Use both informal and formal language.

- Give an **extemporaneous speech** when an impromptu occasion arises. It is an informal speech because you do not have a prepared manuscript.

Preparing and Presenting a Speech

If you are asked to deliver a speech, begin choosing a topic that you like or know well. Then, prepare your speech for your audience.

To prepare your speech, research your topic. Make an outline, and use numbered note cards.

Gather Information Use the library and other resources to gather reliable information and to find examples to support your ideas.

Organizing Information Organize your information by writing an outline of main ideas and major details. Then, when you deliver your speech, write the main ideas, major details, quotations, and facts on note cards.

When presenting your speech, use rhetorical forms of language and verbal and nonverbal strategies.

Use Rhetorical Language Repeat key words and phrases to identify your key points. Use active verbs and colorful adjectives to keep your speech interesting. Use parallel phrases to insert a sense of rhythm.

Use Verbal and Nonverbal Strategies Vary the pitch and tone of your voice, and the rate at which you speak. Speak loudly and emphasize key words or phrases. Avoid consistently reading your speech from your notes. Work to maintain eye contact with the audience. As you speak, connect with the audience by using gestures and facial expressions to emphasize key points.

Evaluating a Speech

Evaluating a speech gives you the chance to judge another speaker's skills. It also gives you the opportunity to review and improve your own methods for preparing and presenting a speech.

When you evaluate a speech, you help the speaker and yourself to learn from experience. Listed below are some questions you might ask yourself while evaluating another person's speech or one of your own speeches.

- Did the speaker introduce the topic clearly, develop it well, and conclude it effectively?

- Did the speaker support each main idea with appropriate details?

- Did the speaker approach the platform confidently and establish eye contact with the audience?

- Did the speaker's facial expressions, gestures, and movements appropriately reinforce the words spoken?

- Did the speaker vary the pitch of his or her voice and the rate of his or her speaking?

- Did the speaker enunciate all words clearly?

Listening Critically to a Speech

Hearing happens naturally as sounds reach your ears. Listening, or critical listening, requires that you understand and interpret these sounds.

Critical listening requires preparation, active involvement, and self-evaluation from the listener.

Learning the Listening Process Listening is interactive; the more you involve yourself in the listening process, the more you will understand.

Focus Your Attention Focus your attention on the speaker and block out all distractions—people, noises, and objects. Find out more about the subject that will be discussed beforehand.

Interpret the Information To interpret a speaker's message successfully, you need to identify and understand important information. You might consider listening for repeated words or phrases, pausing momentarily to memorize and/or write key statements, watching non-verbal signals, and combining this new information with what you already know.

Respond to the Speaker's Message Respond to the information you have heard by identifying the larger message of the speech, its most useful points, and your position on the topic.

Index

classification, 16, 147
comparison, 199
definition, 14
descriptive, 14, 121
documented, 21
narrative, 67
problem-solution, 16, 147
pro-con, 16, 147
reflective, 10, 67
travel, 14
See also Compare-and-contrast
essays; Expository essays;
Persuasive essays

Event letter, 86–87

Event names, 615

Evidence
embedded quotations as, 20
in persuasive essays, 172, 181, 186
in research reports, 224, 227, 239,
240, 265
in review of short stories, 201,
206–207

Examples
in classification essays, 16
in expository essays, 155
in research reports, 240
in review of short stories, 210

Exclamation mark, 554, *555*
interjections set off by, 363
in quotations, 578, 579, 581, *583*
sentence function and, 432, 433, *434,*
435
to separate run-ons, 450

Exclamatory sentences, 433, *434–435,*
610

Experiment journals, 21

Explanatory material
within parentheses, 600–601, 602
within quotes, 582, *583*
using dash before, 605

Exposition, 15–17, 144–169, 146
See also Compare-and-contrast
essays

Expository essays, 144–169, 146
characteristics of, 146
forms of, 147
organization of, 156
quotations in, 148, 155
writing to prompt, *168–169, 195, 269*

Expressions
essential/nonessential, 562–563, 565
introductory/concluding/interrupting,
577–579, 580, 581, 605
parenthetical, 562, 565
transitional, 572

Extemporaneous speeches, R30

External coherence, 109, 161, 243

F

Facilitator, in collaborative group, 6

Facts, 181, 194
checking, 42
as details, 155
opinions versus, 181, 233
in research reports, 228, 240

Family relationship titles, 623

Fantasy stories, 11, 93

Feedback
benefits of, 37, 135, 139, 241, 245
peer, 6, 85, 109, 187, 213
teacher, 81, 161, 135, 245

Feeds, R9

Feelings. *See* Emotions/feelings

Fiction narration, 11–12, 90–117
forms of, 11–12

rubric for, 28–29
writing to prompt, 116–117
See also Science fiction; Stories

Figurative language, 55
metaphor, 55, 129
personification, 55, 129
in poetry, 120, 122–123, 129, 131,
134
simile, 55, 129

Film trailer, sci-fi, 113

Five Ws chart, R24

Flashbacks, 103, 104

Fluency, sentence, 27, 28, 58, 63
in compare-and-contrast essays, 163
in op-ed pieces, 189
in personal narratives, 83
in poetry, 137
in research reports, 247
in reviews of short stories, 215
in science fiction, 111

Focus
clearly defined, in personal narratives,
66, 68, 74–75, 77, 80, 81
of event letter, 86

Fonts, 54, 112

Foreign words, 587, 617

Foreshadowing, 103, 104, 116

Formatting
reader-friendly, 22, 257
of research report, 226, 228, 244

Forms, 8
of expository essays, 147
of fiction narration, 11–12
of interpretative response, 199
of nonfiction narration, 9–10, 67
of persuasion, 18–19, 173
of poetry, 13–14, 121, 131, 142

Multimedia projects, 25
advertisement for story, 217
instructions, 266–267
poetry, 139
press conference script, 249
public action day, 191
research report, 264
sci-fi film trailer, 113

Multimedia resources, 232

Music, sharing, R10

Music titles. *See* Titles

Mystery stories, 11, 93

Myths, 12, 93

quotations in, 66
revising, 78–81
rubric for, 83
script for, 85
setting for, 74–75
spelling, grammar and usage in, 66,
82–83
teacher feedback with, 81
topics for, 72–73
writing to prompt, *88–89, 117, 143,
255*

Personal observations, 181

Personal pronouns, 303, *305*
apostrophe with, 596
by case, 502, *503*, 504–506, *507–
510*, 511, *512*
by person, 303–304, *305*
in pronoun-antecedent agreement,
289, 527–529

Personification, 55, 129

Persuasion, 2, 18, 170–195
forms of, 18–19, 173
genres for, 8

Persuasive essays, 18, 173
arguments in, 172, 174, 180
call to action in, 183, 191
characteristics of, 172
counter-arguments and concerns in,
172, 175, 180
evidence in, 172, 181, 186
lead in, 172, 174, 183
organization of, 182, 189
thesis/thesis statements in, 172, 183
voice in, 172, 189
writing to prompt, *194–195, 221*
See also Op-ed pieces

Persuasive speeches, 18, R30

Photographs, 91, 119, 241, 250, R10
See also Slide show, multimedia

Phrase fragments
correcting, 292, 444–445, *447*
expressing incomplete thought, 369,
370

Phrases, 397, 398
adjectival, 137, 399, *401–404*
adverbial, 137, 400, *401–404*
appositival, 405, *406*, 563
combining sentences using, 438, *440*
commas and, 556, 561, 562–563, *564*
gerund, 411, *413*
that ask a question, 553
See also Specific types

Plagiarism, 235

Planning, 25
See also Organization; Prewriting

Plot
with conflict and resolution, in
personal narratives, 66, 68–69,
74–77, 80
for event letter, 86
See also Story line

Plural words, 514
apostrophe to create, 286, 595, 597
possessive case of (apostrophe),
595–596
in pronoun-antecedent agreement,
528–529
in subject-verb agreement, 514–516,
518, 520–521, 525

Podcasts, R11

Poetry, 13, 118–143
audience for, 121, 127, 132, 134, 138
ballads, 13, 121
characteristics and techniques for,
120, 134–135, 142
description and, 13–14, 120–121
drafting, 130–131
editing, 136–137
emotions/feeling and, 122

figurative language in, 120, 122–123,
129, 131, 134
forms of, 13–14, 121, 142
free verse, 13, 120, 121, 122–138
graphic elements in, 129, 131, 134,
135
haiku, 14, 121
images in, 120, 132, 135, 139
lyric, 13, 14, 120, 121, 122–138
organization of, 130, 137
Partner Talk, 15, 124, 136
prewriting, 126–129
prose poem, 14, 121
publishing, 138
purpose for, 121, 127, 132, 134
revising, 132–135
rhetorical and literary devices for, 54,
129
rubric for, 29, 137
sensory details in, 120, 128, 131, 134
sonnet, 14, 121
sound devices in, 120, 129, 134
structural elements of, 13, 120, 123,
129, 134
symbols in, 129
topics for, 120, 126–128, 131, 134
writing to prompt, *142–143, 169*

Poet's Toolbox, 129

Point of view
consistent, 161, 213
evidence/claims as, 240
in science fiction, 94, 109

Political parties, names of, 617

Portfolio, 7
managing, 84, 112, 138, 216, 248

Positive forms, 534
of irregular modifiers, 538–539, *540*
of regular modifiers, 535–536, *537*

Possessive adjectives, 334, 336

Proofreading marks, 43

Propaganda, 19, 173

Proper adjectives, 331, *333*
capitalization, 331, 621, *624*
hyphens not dividing, 593
no hyphen with compound, 291, 590

Proper nouns, 298, *299*
as adjective, 331
capitalization of, 280, 298, 613–615, 616, 617–619, *620*
hyphenating, 589, 593

Prose poem, 14, 121

Public action day, at school, 191

Publications. *See* Titles

Publishing, 30, 46–47
advertisements, 193
compare-and-contrast essays, 164
dramatic scene, 115
event letter, 87
instructions, 267
letters, 259, 261, 263
movie review, 219
online consumer report, 253
op-ed pieces, 190
personal narratives, 84
poetry, 138
research reports, 248
review of short stories, 216
science fiction, 112
technical newsletter, 167
travel blog, 141
ways to publish, 47, 84, 112, 138, 164, 190, 216, 248

Punctuation
error with quotations, 278
in good writing, 551

Purpose
of dramatic scene, 114

of event letter, 86
of multimedia project, 25

Q

Question marks, 553, 555
quotations and, 578–579, 581, *583*
sentence function and, 433, 434
to separate run-ons, 450

Questions
direct object in, 387, 388
finding subject in, 378, 379
period to end indirect, 552
types of, R29
who and *whom* in, 511
See also Interrogative sentences; Research questions

Quotation marks, 577–580
dialogue and, 584, 585
with other punctuation marks, 278, 581, 583
in quotation with expressions, 577–579, 580
titles and, 586, 588
using single, 582, 583

Quotations
capitalization and, 579, 608–609
colon to introduce long/formal, 573
comma to set off, 569, 570
in conclusion, 53
direct, 251, 278, 569, *570*, 577
divided, 579, 580
embedded, as evidence, 20
explanatory material within (brackets), 582, 583, 601
in expository essay, 148, 155
indenting extended, 227
indirect, 278, 577
with other expressions, 577–579, 580
other quotations within, 582, 583

in personal narrative, 66
poorly integrated, 290
punctuating, with citations, 247
punctuation error with, 278
quotation marks to enclose, 577, 580
in research reports, 224, 227, 234, 235, 240, 246
in review of short stories, 200, 201, 207, 210
to show omission in (passage), 603

R

Radio series titles. *See* Titles

Readability, 55, 112

Reader's Journal, 7

Reading
aloud, revising and, 36
finding ideas for writing by, 3

Realistic fiction, 11, 93

Recommendations, in conclusion, 53

Reflective essays, 10, 67

Reflexive pronouns, 304, 305

Regions, 614

Relative pronouns, 111, 306–307, 309, *310–312*, 416

Religious references/titles, 618, 620, 622

Reorder. *See* Revision RADaR

Repetition, 55

Replace. *See* Revision RADaR

compound, 374, 375–376
indefinite pronouns as, 308–309
in questions, 378, 379
singular/plural, 514
unstated, 422, 494
of verbs
nominative case for, 502, 504, *510*, 511
in sentences, 368–369, 370
word order and finding, 377–378, 379, 380–381, *382*

Subject-verb agreement, 513, 526
collective nouns and, 518, 519
compound subjects and, 520–521, 523
indefinite pronouns and, 524–525, 526
in inverted sentences, 521–522, 523
in number, 514–516, 517
prepositions, prepositional phrases and, 214

Subjunctive mood, 494

Subordinate clauses, 415–416, 417
adjectival clauses as, 418
adverbial clauses as, 421
commas and, 556
forming sentences using, 49, 292, 425–426, 438, *440*
as fragments, 292, 415–416, *417*, 445–446
main versus, *428–430*
relative pronouns and, 306–307, 309, *310*
who and *whom* beginning, 511

Subordinating conjunctions, 357, *360–362*
in adverbial clauses, 421, 423
common, listed, 422
in complex sentences, 438
in subordinate clauses, 416

Suffixes, hyphens for, 589

Summaries, 224, 228, 234, 235, 240

Superlative forms, 534
of irregular modifiers, 538–539, 540
of regular modifiers, 535–536, 537
rules for using, 538–539, 540

Suspense, 103, 104

Syllables
hyphens dividing, 592–593, 594
modifiers with one or two, 535, 540
modifiers with three or more, 535, 540

Symbolism, 55

Symbols, in poetry, 129

Synthesizing information, 149, 155

T

Tables, 241

Tall tales, 12, 93

Taste, as sensory detail, 103

Technical newsletter, 166–167

Technology, 7, 39, 43, 52, 55
See also Media, writing for

Television series titles. *See* Titles

Tense, 472, 480
See also Verbs

Theme
in notes, 234, 265
in science fiction, 92, 102, 104, 108
for scripts, 24
See also Topics

Thesaurus, 39, 55, 273

Thesis/thesis statements
developing, 34, 53, 154
in persuasive essays, 172, 183
in research reports, 224, 226, 238–239, 244, 265
in responses to literature, 20
restating, 35, 53
for review of short stories, 200, 206
supporting, 35

Things. *See* Nouns

Thoughts, complete/incomplete
to show sudden break in, 605
using clauses, 415–416, 417
|using complements, 383–384, 385
using subjects/verbs, 292, 369, 370
See also Expressions; Fragments

Time (hours of day), *573*

Time management
research process and, 237
revising and, 36
writing process and, 5

Time periods, 615

Timeline, R27

Titles
of people, capitalization of, 622–623, *624*
of works
capitalization of, 280, 625
quotation marks in, 586, 588
underlining/italics in, 586–587, 588

Tone, 24, 103, 117
See also Moods

in sentences, 369, 370
singular/plural, 515
subjects after
    agreement in, 521–522, 523
    for emphasis, 381, 382
    in questions, 378, 379
    for variety, 442, 443
substitutions for verb *walk*, 41
tenses, 471
    conjugating, 481–482, 485, 488, 489
    identifying, 480, 483, 487, *489*
    perfect, 82–83, *484–486*
    progressive, 82–83, 487, 488, *489*
    switching between, 284, 466
    using consistent, 82–83, 214–215, 284, 466, *467*
transitive, 314, 316
troublesome, 496–498, 499–500
unstated, in elliptical adverbial clause, 422
See also Action verbs; Compound verbs; Helping verbs; Linking verbs

Video, R10

Visual elements, 54

Vivid images, 81, 109, 135

Voice, 26–28, 57, 63
    active, 490, 492, *493*
    adding, to Web page, R10
    in compare-and-contrast essays, 163
    passive, 490, 491–492, 493
    in personal narratives, 83
    in persuasive essays, 172, 189
    in poetry, 137
    in research reports, 247
    in review of short stories, 215
    in science fiction, 111

Vowel sound, 329

Watching, finding ideas by, 3

Web page
    adding voice to, R10
    citation of, 236

Web safety, R6

White space, 54

Widgets, R9

Wikis, R11

Word choice, 27, 28, 58, 63
    in compare-and-contrast essays, 163
    in personal narratives, 83
    in persuasive essays, 187, 189
    in poetry, 137
    in research reports, 247
    in reviews of short stories, 215
    in science fiction, 111
    wrong, 273

Word order
    agreement in inverted, 521–522, 523
    normal/inverted, 377–378, 379
    reversing, for variety, 442, 443
    rewording inverted
        to identify pronoun case, 511, 512
        to identify subject, 378–381, *382*

Words
    commonly misspelled, R17
    feelings through, 119
    missing, 281
    single, commas separating, 285
    student's, 246
    See also Specific types

Workplace writing, 22–23, 256–269
    characteristics of, 257
    forms of, 22, 257

Works Cited list, 228, 234, 236–237, 244

Writing
    collaborative writing, **6,** 7
    cooperative, 6
    free, 4
    to inform, 2, 251
    objective versus subjective, 250
    online tools for strengthening, 55
    for persuasion, 2, 18–19
    portfolio for, 7
    Reader's Journal for, 7
    reasons/purposes for, 2, 65, 197, 258
    reflecting on, 7, 25, 47, 84, 112, 138, 248
    types of, 3, 8–25, 53
    See also Research writing; Workplace writing; specific forms and genres

Writing process, 26–47
    comfortable environment for, 5
    five steps in, 30
    materials for, 5
    for multimedia projects, 25
    reasons for using, 31
    rubrics in, 28–29
    time management and, 5
    working with others in, 6–7
    See also Drafting; Editing; Organization; Planning; Prewriting; Publishing; Revising

Writing traits, 26–27, 48, 63
    for developing composition, 56–59
    See also Conventions; Fluency, sentence; Ideas; Organization; Voice; Word choice

Index of Authors and Titles

Acknowledgments